Glencoe World History

Features and Benefits

Dynamic Instructional Strategies	**. . . present a clear and comprehensive coverage of world history.** • Each engaging section introduction includes Big Ideas, Content and Academic Vocabulary, People and Events, a Reading Strategy, and reading focus prompts. • The Chapter Visual Summary offers a concise outline of important chapter topics and can be used to preview, review, or summarize chapter content.
A Strong Reading Strand	**. . . encourages active reading and learning for students of all reading levels.** • The Primary Source and World Literature Library asks students to analyze excerpts from literature and primary sources tied to unit topics. • Reading Checks help students assess their reading comprehension. • Main Idea and History & You at the beginning of each main heading give students a focus and a reason for reading.
Differentiated Instruction	**. . . makes *Glencoe World History* accessible to students of all learning levels.** • Differentiated Instruction activities and strategies can be found in the Teacher Wraparound Edition, the Unit Resource Booklets, the Differentiated Instruction Activities ancillary, and online. • *World History in Graphic Novel* is one motivating tool among many for differentiating instruction and engaging learners in history.
Standardized Test Preparation	**. . . gives students the opportunity to practice for state and national exams.** • Chapter Assessments are now in standardized test format to provide truly useful standardized test practice. • Prescriptive prompts on each chapter assessment page guide students to where they can revisit the material.
A Variety of History Activities and Features	**. . . are essential for student success and get students excited about history.** • Connecting to the United States features align the period under study to more familiar topics within the United States, helping students see the cyclical nature of history. • Turning Point features highlight those moments in history that had a huge impact on what came after. • National Geographic's Geography and History helps students understand the impact of geography on events.
Teacher Resources	**. . . provide convenient strategies to help new and experienced teachers.** • The Teacher Wraparound Edition contains the "Brackets and Letters" system identifying Reading, Differentiated Instruction, Writing Support, Critical Thinking, and Skill Practice activities at *exact* point of use. • Unit Resource Fast Files™ contain a wide variety of reproducible masters organized by unit to save you time.
Technology	**. . . provides time-saving software products to help you creatively engage your students and reduce your prep time.** • *TeacherWorks Plus*™ DVD contains the Interactive Teacher Edition, all ancillaries and transparencies, *editable* blackline masters, and the most powerful and easy-to-use lesson planner. • Presentation Plus! with MindJogger Checkpoint DVD contains a PowerPoint™ presentation of the textbook, all program transparencies, and the interactive MindJogger quiz game. • History Online provides lesson plans, updates, economics activities, and links to other resources at **glencoe.com**

Improving Active Reading and Study Skills

Dinah Zike's FOLDABLES™

Foldables are easy-to-make, three-dimensional, interactive graphic organizers that students create out of simple sheets of paper. The Teacher Classroom Resources include *Dinah Zike's High School World History Reading and Study Skills*. This booklet provides you with step-by-step instructions for using Foldables in your classroom. Each Foldable is designed to be used as a study guide for the main ideas and key points presented in a chapter. Foldables can also be used for a more in-depth investigation of a concept, idea, opinion, or event, or people or places studied in a chapter. These unique hands-on tools for study and review were created exclusively for Glencoe by education specialist Dinah Zike.

Why Use Foldables in Social Studies?

Because they:

- organize, display, and arrange information, making it easier for students to grasp social studies concepts, theories, facts, opinions, questions, research, and ideas.
- are student-made study guides that students themselves create as they listen for main ideas, read their textbook, or conduct research.
- provide a multitude of creative formats in which students can present projects, research, interviews, and inquiry-based reports.
- replace teacher-generated writing or photocopied sheets with student-generated print.
- incorporate the use of such skills as comparing and contrasting, recognizing cause-and-effect relationships, and understanding similarities and differences.
- reinforce previously learned vocabulary, concepts, information, generalizations, ideas, and theories, providing students with a strong foundation that they can build upon with new observations, concepts, and knowledge.
- can be used by students or teachers to easily communicate data through graphs, tables, charts, models, and diagrams, including Venn diagrams.
- allow students to make their own journals for recording observations, information, primary and secondary source data, surveys, and so on.
- can be used as alternative assessment tools by teachers to evaluate student progress or by students to evaluate their own progress.
- integrate language arts, the sciences, and mathematics into the study of social studies.
- provide a sense of student ownership or investment in the social studies curriculum.

Teacher Wraparound Edition

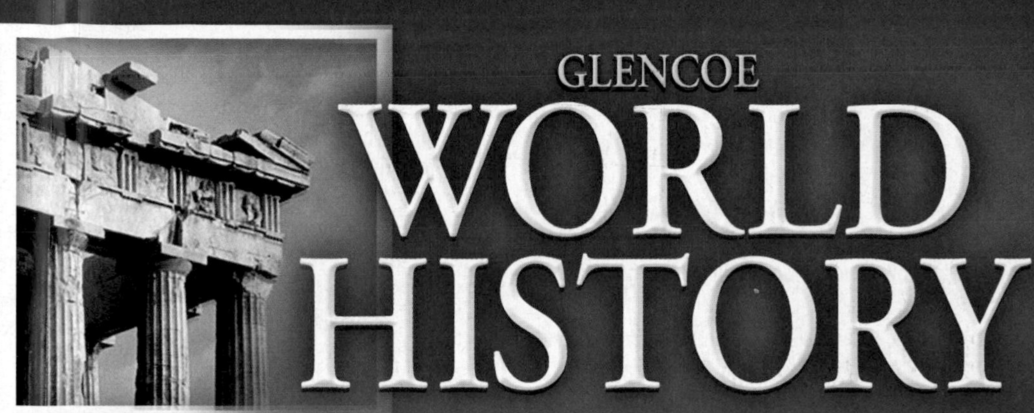

JACKSON J. SPIELVOGEL, PH.D.

NATIONAL GEOGRAPHIC

New York, New York Columbus, Ohio Chicago, Illinois Woodland Hills, California

AUTHORS

JACKSON J. SPIELVOGEL

Jackson J. Spielvogel is associate professor emeritus of history at The Pennsylvania State University. He received his Ph.D. from The Ohio State University, where he specialized in Reformation history under Harold J. Grimm. His articles and reviews have appeared in such journals as *Moreana, Journal of General Education, Archiv für Reformationsgeschichte,* and *American Historical Review.* He has also contributed chapters or articles to *The Social History of the Reformation, The Holy Roman Empire: A Dictionary Handbook, Simon Wiesenthal Center Annual of Holocaust Studies,* and *Utopian Studies.* His book *Hitler and Nazi Germany* was published in 1987 (fifth edition, 2005). His book *Western Civilization* was published in 1991 (sixth edition, 2006). He is the co-author (with William Duiker) of *World History,* published in 1994 (fifth edition, 2007). Professor Spielvogel has won five major university-wide teaching awards, and in 1997, he became the first winner of the Schreyer Institute's Student Choice Award for innovative and inspiring teaching.

The National Geographic Society, founded in 1888 for the increase and diffusion of geographic knowledge, is the world's largest nonprofit scientific and educational organization. Since its earliest days, the Society has used sophisticated communication technologies, from color photography to holography, to convey geographic knowledge to a worldwide membership. The School Publishing Division supports the Society's mission by developing innovative educational programs—ranging from traditional print materials to multimedia programs including CD-ROMs, videos, and software.

CONTRIBUTING AUTHOR

Dinah Zike, M.Ed., is an award-winning author, educator, and inventor known for designing three-dimensional hands-on manipulatives and graphic organizers known as Foldables™. Foldables are used nationally and internationally by teachers, parents, and educational publishing companies. Dinah has developed over 150 supplemental educational books and materials. She is the author of *The Big Book of Books and Activities,* which was awarded Learning Magazine's Teachers' Choice Award. In 2004 Dinah was honored with the CESI Science Advocacy Award. Dinah received her M.Ed. from Texas A&M, College Station, Texas.

ABOUT THE COVER

Main image: Parthenon on the Acropolis in Greece
Top images (left to right): Nelson Mandela; bust of Nefertiti; terra-cotta warrior from Xi'an, China; painting of Simón Bolívar; Indira Gandhi.

The *McGraw·Hill* Companies

Glencoe

Send all inquiries to:
Glencoe/McGraw-Hill
8787 Orion Place
Columbus, OH 43240-4027

ISBN: 978-0-07-874526-3
MHID: 0-07-874526-8

Printed in the United States of America.

2 3 4 5 6 7 8 9 10 071/055 12 11 10 09 08 07

Consultants & Reviewers

Academic Consultants

Jeremy Baskes, Ph.D.
Associate Professor
Department of History
Ohio Wesleyan University
Delaware, Ohio

David Berger, Ph.D.
Broeklundian Professor of History
Brooklyn College and the Graduate Center
City University of New York
Brooklyn, New York

Stephen F. Dale, Ph.D.
Professor
Department of History
The Ohio State University
Columbus, Ohio

Steven Gish, Ph.D.
Distinguished Research Professor
Department of History
Auburn University Montgomery
Montgomery, Alabama

Richard Golden, Ph.D.
Professor of History and Director, Jewish Studies Program
University of North Texas
Denton, Texas

Lyman Johnson, Ph.D.
Professor
Department of History
The University of North Carolina at Charlotte
Charlotte, North Carolina

Lisa Lindsay, Ph.D.
Associate Professor
Department of History
The University of North Carolina at Chapel Hill
Chapel Hill, North Carolina

Farid Mahdavi, Ph.D.
Lecturer
Department of History
San Diego State University
San Diego, California

Guy Welbon, Ph.D.
Emeritus Associate Professor
Department of South Asia Studies
University of Pennsylvania
Philadelphia, Pennsylvania

Teacher Reviewers

Maggie Favretti
Scarsdale High School
Scarsdale, New York

Jane McGrigor Forde
Needham B. Broughton High School
Raleigh, North Carolina

Carl Hansen
Hilton High School
Hilton, New York

Lee Holder
North Lenoir High School
LaGrange, North Carolina

Thomas J. Lawson
McCluer High School
Florissant, Missouri

Laura Delmore Lay
James River High School
Midlothian, Virginia

Christopher M. Lee
West Memphis High School
West Memphis, Arkansas

Rosanne Lichatin
West Morris Central High School
Chester, New Jersey

Donald V. Morabito
Great Valley High School
Malvern, Pennsylvania

Donald Perreault
Valley Regional High School
Deep River, Connecticut

Richard J. Shaw
Cleveland High School
Cleveland, Tennessee

Christina M. Smith
Algonquin Regional High School
Northborough, Massachusetts

Kathleen H. Stokes
Cherokee High School
Marlton, New Jersey

Denise Tanner
Friendswood High School
Friendswood, Texas

Michele Roussel Wasson
North Little Rock High School, East Campus
North Little Rock, Arkansas

CONTENTS

◀ **Phaestos Disc, Minoan writing (see page 18)**

◀ Bronze figure of a bard from Crete (see page 110)

◀ Muslim high school student wearing hijrab, United States (see page 494)

Ci Xi, unofficial ruler of China ▶ for 47 years (see page 728)

◀ President Jimmy Carter at UN in 1977 (see page 970)

TOWARD A GLOBAL CIVILIZATION, *1945–Present* 896

REFERENCE SECTION

FEATURES

ANALYZING PRIMARY SOURCES

PEOPLE in HISTORY

NATIONAL GEOGRAPHIC GEOGRAPHY & HISTORY

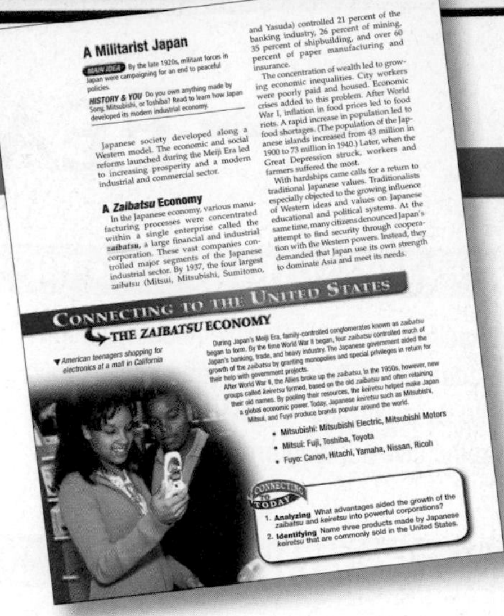

A Militarist Japan

MAIN IDEA By the late 1920s, militant forces in Japan were campaigning for an end to peaceful policies.

HISTORY & YOU Do you own anything made by Sony, Mitsubishi, or Toshiba? Read to learn how Japan developed its modern industrial economy.

Japanese society developed along a Western model. The economic and social reforms launched during the Meiji Era led to increasing prosperity and a modern industrial and commercial sector.

A *Zaibatsu* Economy

In the Japanese economy, various manufacturing processes were concentrated within a single enterprise called the **zaibatsu**, a large financial and industrial corporation. These vast companies controlled major segments of the Japanese industrial sector. By 1937, the four largest *zaibatsu* (Mitsui, Mitsubishi, Sumitomo, and Yasuda) controlled 21 percent of the banking industry, 26 percent of mining, 35 percent of shipbuilding, and over 60 percent of paper manufacturing and insurance.

The concentration of wealth led to growing economic inequalities. City workers were poorly paid and housed. Economic crises added to this problem. After World War I, inflation in food prices led to food riots. A rapid increase in population led to food shortages. (The population of the Japanese islands increased from 43 million in 1900 to 73 million in 1940.) Later, when the Great Depression struck, workers and farmers suffered the most.

With hardships came calls for a return to traditional Japanese values. Traditionalists especially objected to the growing influence of Western ideas and values on Japanese educational and political systems. At the same time, many citizens denounced Japan's attempt to find security through cooperation with the Western powers. Instead, they demanded that Japan use its own strength to dominate Asia and meet its needs.

CONNECTING TO THE UNITED STATES

THE ZAIBATSU ECONOMY

▼ *American teenagers shopping for electronics at a mall in California*

During Japan's Meiji Era, family-controlled conglomerates known as *zaibatsu* began to form. By the time World War II began, four *zaibatsu* controlled much of Japan's banking, trade, and heavy industry. The Japanese government aided the growth of the *zaibatsu* by granting monopolies and special privileges in return for their help with government projects.

After World War II, the Allies broke up the *zaibatsu*. In the 1950s, however, new groups called *keiretsu* formed, based on the old *zaibatsu* and often retaining their old names. By pooling their resources, the *keiretsu* helped make Japan a global economic power. Today, Japanese *keiretsu* such as Mitsubishi, Mitsui, and Fuyo produce brands popular around the world.

- Mitsubishi: Mitsubishi Electric, Mitsubishi Motors
- Mitsui: Fuji, Toshiba, Toyota
- Fuyo: Canon, Hitachi, Yamaha, Nissan, Ricoh

CONNECTING TO TODAY

1. **Analyzing** What advantages aided the growth of the *zaibatsu* and *keiretsu* into powerful corporations?
2. **Identifying** Name three products made by Japanese *keiretsu* that are commonly sold in the United States.

CONNECTING TO THE UNITED STATES

SCIENCE, TECHNOLOGY, & SOCIETY

POLITICAL CARTOONS — PRIMARY SOURCE

◀ **Stevenson's *Rocket*, English steam engine, 1829 (see page 618)**

TIME LINE

HISTORY & ARTS PRIMARY SOURCE

PRIMARY SOURCE HISTORY & ARTS

Kinship with Ancestors in African Societies

Many peoples placed mother-and-child figures in shrines near graves.

Face masks worn during initiation and funerary rites also linked the living to ancestors. Ancestors were consulted for advice and aid before a significant event or undertaking.

DOCUMENT-BASED QUESTIONS

In many African societies, the spirits of ancestors were believed to participate in family and community life. They also were invoked and honored during regular celebrations, such as a harvest festival, and during rites that marked birth, adulthood, marriage, and death.

1. **Making Inferences** Why were ancestors held in such high esteem in African societies?
2. **Drawing Conclusions** Why might mother-and-child figures have had significance in African societies?

Family and Lineage

Few Africans, of course, ever had an audience with their kings. Most people lived in small villages in the countryside. Their sense of identity was determined by their membership in an extended family and a lineage group.

At the basic level was the extended family, made up of parents, children, grandparents, and other family dependents. They lived in small, round dwellings made of packed mud, with a thatch roof of plant material such as straw. These extended family units were in turn combined into larger communities known as **lineage groups.**

Lineage groups served as the basic building blocks of African society. All members of a lineage group could claim to be descended from a real or legendary common ancestor. As in China, the elders—the leading members of the lineage group—had much power over the others in the group. A lineage group provided mutual support for all its members. Members of extended families and lineage groups were expected to take care of one another.

The Role of Women

Women were usually subordinate to men in Africa, as they were in most early societies around the world. In some cases, they were valued for the work they could do or for their role in having children and thus increasing the size of the lineage group. Women often worked in the fields while the men of the village tended the cattle or hunted. In some communities, women were merchants.

There were some key differences between the role of women in Africa and elsewhere.

CHAPTER 7 Early African Civilizations 251

TURNING POINT

TIME NOTEBOOK

Social History

INFOGRAPHICS

Muslim women protest outside French Embassy, 2004 **(see page 942)**

Primary Source Quotes

Unit 1
The First Civilizations and Empires

Chapter 1 *The First Humans*

Chapter 2 *Western Asia and Egypt*

Chapter 3 *India and China*

Chapter 4 *Ancient Greece*

Chapter 5 *Rome and the Rise of Christianity*

Unit 2
New Patterns of Civilization

Chapter 6 *The World of Islam*

Chapter 7 *Early African Civilizations*

Chapter 8 *The Asian World*

Bronze helmet ▶ and breastplate from era of Peloponnesian War (see page 122)

◀ **Akbar, ruler, of Mogul Empire, 1556–1605 (see page 500)**

Chapter 18 *The French Revolution and Napoleon*

UNIT 4
An Era of European Imperialism

Chapter 19 *Industrialization and Nationalism*

Chapter 20 *Mass Society and Democracy*

Chapter 21 *The Height of Imperialism*

Chapter 22 *East Asia Under Challenge*

Jomo Kenyatta, first president of Kenya, 1963 (see page 988) ▶

Women protesting unequal pay, 1971 (see page 948)

UNIT 5
The Twentieth-Century Crisis

Chapter 23 *War and Revolution*

Chapter 24, *The West Between the Wars*

Chapter 25 *Nationalism Around the World*

Chapter 26 *World War II*

UNIT 6
Toward a Global Civilization

Chapter 27 *Cold War and Postwar Changes*

Chapter 28 *The Contemporary Western World*

Chapter 29 *Latin America*

Chapter 30 *Africa and the Middle East*

Chapter 31 *Asia and the Pacific*

Chapter 32 *Challenges and Hopes*

PRIMARY SOURCE LIBRARY

◀ Former UN Secretary-General Kofi Annan speaking about the Millenium Development Goals **(see page 1052)**

CHARTS, GRAPHS, & TABLES

MAPS

NATIONAL GEOGRAPHIC

REFERENCE ATLAS

UNIT 1

UNIT 2

UNIT 3

UNIT 4

UNIT 5

UNIT 6

Maps In MOtion See *StudentWorks™ Plus* or glencoe.com.

Maps labeled with the In Motion icon have been specially enhanced on the StudentWorks™ Plus DVD and on glencoe.com. These In Motion maps allow you to interact with layers of displayed data and to listen to audio components.

Entries in **blue** indicate In Motion maps.

UNDERSTANDING THE BIG IDEAS

World history is the story of the human community—how people lived on a daily basis, how they shared ideas, how they ruled and were ruled, and how they fought. As you read, you will see a number of "big ideas" or broad themes behind world history events. These big ideas are described below.

▶ Order and Security

Throughout history, people and governments have tried to resolve conflicts and establish order and security.

People have sought ways to protect themselves from danger and uncertainty. To provide for their security, people have created communities, nations, and organizations. To help provide order, people have created laws and economic systems.

▶ Ideas, Beliefs, and Values

Ideas, beliefs, and values have resulted in distinct societies and political systems.

Throughout history, people have sought to find a deeper meaning to human life. Religion, cultural values, and codes of ethics have always influenced social customs, laws, and forms of government.

▶ Physical Geography

Physical geography influences the development of culture and trade.

People and societies have been affected by the physical world in which they exist. In turn, human activities have had a profound impact on the world.

▶ Self-Determination

The quest for national self-determination is universal.

Free will is the cornerstone of humanity. People unite as a nation because they believe that independence is essential to freedom—and that freedom is essential to leading a full life.

▶ Struggle for Rights
Throughout history, people have struggled for rights.
The struggle for rights has been reflected in struggles for the vote, for economic freedom, for personal liberties, and for national independence. There are few nations in the world whose history has not been marked by a struggle for rights among its people.

▶ New Technologies
New technologies bring changes that can be both positive and negative for societies.
For thousands of years, people have made scientific discoveries and technological innovations that have changed the world. New discoveries can bring benefits, or pose new dangers, to the world.

▶ Devastation of War
War causes immeasurable devastation.
Wars have always meant destruction and disruption to some level. In the modern period, wars usually have brought greater devastation than in earlier epochs. Genocide and ethnic cleansing have also characterized the wars of the twentieth century. Recovering from such losses is costly, and the desire for revenge or triumph can color the attitudes of an entire generation.

▶ Competition Among Countries
Countries compete for natural resources and strategic advantages over other countries.
Competition among nations has led to the development of stable economies in some cases, but also to the depletion of economies in others. Strong economies tend to mean stronger governments, and this provides a sense of safety for citizens.

▶ Human Rights
A totalitarian system violates human rights in pursuit of power.
By definition, the totalitarian state smothers the individuality of its citizens. This system seeks to control political, economic, social, intellectual, and cultural areas of life and does so through propaganda and through force.

Using the BIG IDEAS

You will find BIG IDEAS listed at the beginning of each section in the text. Use these clues to help you preview the material you are about to read. You can also use the BIG IDEAS to compare and contrast how different peoples and societies dealt with similar issues.

SCAVENGER HUNT

Glencoe World History contains a wealth of information. The trick is to know where to look to access all the information in the book. If you run through this scavenger hunt exercise with your teachers or parents, you will see how the textbook is organized, and how to get the most out of your reading and study time. Let's get started!

1. How many chapters and how many units are in the book? ***32 chapters; 6 units***
2. What time period does Unit 2 cover? ***400–1500***
3. On what pages is the time line for Chapter 24? ***788–789***
4. In what two places can you find the Content Vocabulary for Section 2 of Chapter 6? ***Guide to Reading and Section Review***
5. Where can you find a map on imperialism in Africa? ***page 693***
6. How are the Academic Vocabulary words for Section 3 of Chapter 12 indicated in the narrative? ***boldface type***
7. The Web site has six activities for each chapter. The first previews the chapter. The second has activities. The third has quizzes. What do the others do? ***Puzzles, Flashcards, Interactive Maps***
8. Where do you look if you want to quickly find all the maps in the book? ***Table of Contents***
9. Most sections of a chapter include primary sources from the time in the narrative. Where else can you find extended primary sources in the textbook? ***With visuals in the chapter and in the Primary Source and Literature Library***
10. Where can you learn the definition of a physical map, a political map, and a thematic map? ***Geography Skills Handbook***

Correlation of *Glencoe World History* to the NCSS Ten Thematic Strands

	Theme and Performance Expectations	Student Pages
	I. Culture **The study of culture helps students understand similarities and differences within groups of people. By studying a culture's beliefs, values, and traditions, students begin to gain a perspective that helps them relate to different groups. In high school, students can understand and use complex cultural concepts such as adaptation, assimilation, and acculturation to explain how culture and cultural systems function.**	
A.	Analyze and explain ways groups, societies, and cultures address human needs and concerns.	8, 12–13, 19, 31, 36, 75, 92, 169, 617, 623, 636, 667, 753, 811, 881, 889, 920
B.	Predict how data and experiences may be interpreted by people from diverse cultural perspectives and frames of references.	10, 91, 139, 173
C.	Apply an understanding of culture as an integrated whole that explains the functions and interactions of language, literature, the arts, traditions, beliefs and values, and behavioral patterns.	19, 28, 31, 36, 42, 43, 48, 51, 58–59, 69, 73, 75, 80, 81, 83, 87, 93, 95, 110, 111, 116, 125, 128, 131, 133, 138, 159, 163, 169, 172, 173, 190, 191, 207, 254, 255, 268, 269, 274, 275, 281, 282, 287, 288, 289, 293, 295, 305, 306, 324, 327, 337, 347, 349, 350, 351, 373, 376, 387, 416, 420, 421, 437, 439, 459, 473, 474, 475, 487, 489, 494, 502, 503, 518, 519, 525, 527, 531, 553, 562, 563, 565, 577, 578, 585, 623, 664, 706, 736, 849, 920, 923, 965, 979, 995, 1027, 1031
D.	Compare and analyze societal patterns for preserving and transmitting culture while adapting to environment or social change.	19, 28, 42, 43, 45, 50, 64, 90, 93, 257, 403, 408, 411, 434, 524, 551, 552, 553, 736, 814, 843, 1031
E.	Demonstrate the value of cultural diversity, as well as cohesion, within and across groups.	40, 99, 183, 206, 207, 238, 248, 275, 285, 294, 295, 325, 422, 423, 434, 459, 528, 529, 541, 558, 742, 747, 843, 920
F.	Interpret patterns of behavior reflecting values and attitudes that contribute or pose obstacles to cross-cultural understanding.	11, 40, 41, 71, 75, 93, 122, 123, 157, 165, 202, 203, 251, 252, 254, 255, 268, 269, 295, 307, 311, 338, 378, 410, 414, 475, 494, 514, 518, 525, 547, 549, 577, 578, 617, 623, 640, 656, 707, 948
G.	Construct reasoned judgments about specific cultural responses to persistent human issues.	18, 167, 416, 877, 878, 822
H.	Explain and apply ideas, theories, and modes of inquiry drawn from anthropology and sociology in the examination of persistent issues and social problems.	5, 6, 9, 11, 32, 33, 73, 95, 99, 108, 111, 249, 251, 255, 361, 609
	II. Time, Continuity, and Change **Understanding time, continuity, and change involves being knowledgeable about what things were like in the past and how things change and develop over time. Knowing how to read and reconstruct the past helps students gain a historical perspective. In high school, students examine the past's relationship with the present while extrapolating into the future. They also integrate individual stories about people, events, and situations to form a more complete conception, in which continuity and change persist in time and across cultures. Students will use their knowledge of history to make informed choices and decisions in the present.**	
A.	Demonstrate that historical knowledge and the concept of time are socially influenced constructions that lead historians to be selective in the questions they seek to answer and the evidence they use.	2–3, 24–25, 64–65, 104–105, 144–145, 186–187, 234–235, 262–263, 300–301, 332–333, 366–367, 396–397, 428–429, 452–453, 482–483, 508–509, 536–537, 574–575, 612–613, 650–651, 684–685, 722–723, 756–757, 788–789, 820–821, 854–855, 898–899, 928–929, 958–959, 984–985, 1010–1011, 1036–1037
B.	Apply key concepts such as time, chronology, causality, change, conflict and complexity to explain, analyze, and show connections among patterns of historical change and continuity.	4, 14, 15, 16, 17, 18, 19, 20, 32, 33, 43, 71, 91, 111, 117, 120, 124–131, 137–139, 172, 174–177, 195, 236, 243, 246, 249, 270, 280, 316, 318, 322, 334–335, 341, 352–359, 361, 412, 418–423, 434–436, 437, 440, 447, 456, 460, 463, 491, 494, 502, 514, 542, 551–553, 590–591, 600, 611, 617, 618, 621, 652, 672, 673, 677, 697–699, 702, 703, 715, 744, 758–761, 766, 769, 772–777, 782–783, 793, 796–803, 814, 826, 833, 838, 849, 859, 861, 864, 885, 895, 904, 919, 933, 942, 944, 965, 968, 970, 971, 972, 991, 993, 1012, 1022, 1038, 1043, R14

Theme and Performance Expectations	Student Pages
C. Identify and describe significant historical periods and patterns of change within and across cultures, such as the development of ancient cultures and civilizations, the rise of nation-states, and social, economic, and political revolutions.	13, 15, 16, 17, 18, 26, 27, 28, 29, 30, 31, 32, 33, 34, 35, 36, 37, 38, 39, 40, 41, 42, 43, 54–55, 66–75, 76–81, 84–93, 94–99, 120, 172, 195, 201, 245, 246, 280, 318, 354, 436, 456, 458–463, 491, 502, 514, 542, 566–569, 574, 576–583, 586–593, 596–603, 609, 610, 611, 617, 624–629, 630–637, 673, 677, 686–691, 692–699, 700–701, 702–707, 708–715, 724–731, 738–745, 772, 773, 774, 775, 776, 777, 793, 833, 836–841, 844–849, 885, 904, 933, 970, 991, 986–993, 1022
D. Systematically employ processes of critical historical inquiry to reconstruct and reinterpret the past, such as using a variety of sources and checking their credibility, validating and weighing evidence for claims, and searching for causality.	3, 10, 11, 19, 31, 36, 48, 51, 55, 58–59, 81, 93, 97, 99, 110, 116, 125, 127, 151, 163, 164, 173, 207, 282, 318, 323, 349, 358, 370, 371, 386–387, 423, 446, 489, 513, 519, 569, 594–595, 622–623, 673, 679, 691, 699, 731, 737, 760, 766, 795, 796, 805, 808, 809, 813, 835, 841, 849, 859, 861, 862–863, 870, 903, 906, 916, 919, 935, 939, 951, 993, 1004–1005, 1029, 1052, 1053, R31, R21, R32–R45
E. Investigate, interpret, and analyze multiple historical and contemporary viewpoints within and across cultures relating to important events, recurring dilemmas, and persistent issues, while employing empathy, skepticism, and critical judgment.	198, 207, 386–387, 541, 621, 698, 766, 862–863, 1004–1005
F. Apply ideas, theories, and modes of historical inquiry to analyze historical and contemporary developments, and to inform and evaluate actions concerning public policy issues.	463, 580–583, 594–595, 598–599, 622–623, 661, 662–665, 679, 768, 769, 808, 809, 822–827, 833, 918–921, 948, 951, 986–991, 993, 1023
III. People, Places, and Environments **The study of people, places, and environments will help students as they create their spatial views and geographic perspectives of the world. Students begin to make informed and critical decisions about the relationship between humans and their environment. In high school, geographic concepts become central to student's comprehension of global connections as they expand their knowledge of diverse cultures, both historical and contemporary.**	
A. Refine mental maps of locales, regions, and the world that demonstrate understanding of relative locations, direction, size, and shape.	GH9, 17, 27, 107, 113, 119, 135, 147, 193, 237, 265, 291, 353, 369, 383, 413, 431, 901
B. Create, interpret, use, and synthesize information from various representations of the earth, such as maps, globes, and photographs.	GH3, GH5, GH6, GH7, GH8, GH12, 5, 17, 27, 35, 47, 52, 53, 67, 68, 75, 77, 78, 85, 86, 97, 98, 107, 115, 119, 135, 147, 150, 158, 171, 175, 176, 189, 193, 195, 197, 200, 237, 238, 239, 245, 246, 248, 249, 253, 265, 271, 279, 280, 291, 303, 309, 317, 320, 326, 339, 353, 357, 369, 374, 383, 399, 413, 417, 419, 431, 441, 445, 455, 456, 460, 467, 468, 485, 490, 491, 493, 499, 511, 513, 521, 527, 539, 547, 555, 559, 567, 600, 602, 610, 615, 625, 628, 631, 646, 653, 659, 669, 687, 691, 693, 694, 700–701, 705, 709, 725, 733, 739, 759, 761, 763, 773, 779, 791, 797, 801, 823, 829, 837, 845, 857, 860, 865, 866, 868, 875, 886, 901, 903, 908, 931, 937, 941, 950, 961, 963, 964, 965, 967, 970, 973, 987, 997, 998, 1013, 1016, 1019, 1022, 1023, 1025, 1041, 1049, 1053, R18, R27
C. Use appropriate resources, data sources, and geographic tools such as aerial photographs, satellite images, geographic information systems (GIS), map projections, and cartography to generate, manipulate, and interpret information such as atlases, data bases, grid systems, charts, graphs, and maps.	GH3, GH5, GH6, GH7, GH8, GH12, 4, 5, 14, 15, 17, 26, 27, 33, 34, 35, 47, 51, 52, 53, 57, 67, 68, 75, 76, 77, 78, 85, 86, 97, 98, 99, 107, 115, 119, 120, 125, 135, 147, 149, 150, 158, 171, 175, 176, 189, 193, 195, 197, 200, 237, 238, 239, 245, 246, 248, 249, 253, 265, 271, 279, 280, 291, 293, 303, 305, 306, 307, 309, 317, 320, 323, 326, 334, 337, 339, 342, 348, 353, 354, 357, 368, 369, 371, 372, 374, 379, 383, 399, 406, 411, 413, 417, 419, 422, 430, 431, 441, 443, 445, 447, 454, 455, 456, 458, 460, 463, 464, 467, 468, 469, 472, 484, 485, 489, 490, 491, 493, 495, 498, 499, 503, 511, 513, 515, 517, 521, 522, 526, 527, 529, 538, 539, 542, 544, 547, 554, 555, 559, 560, 563, 566, 567, 569, 592, 600, 602, 610, 615, 621, 624, 625, 628, 629, 631, 643, 646, 653, 657, 658, 659, 669, 674, 679, 686, 687, 689, 691, 692, 693, 694, 699, 700–701, 702, 703, 705, 707, 709, 715, 724, 725, 732, 733, 739, 759, 761, 763, 772, 773, 777, 778, 779, 783, 791, 793, 797, 801, 804, 815, 823, 829, 837, 844, 845, 846, 856, 857, 860, 861, 864, 865, 866, 868, 871, 875, 880, 881, 886, 887, 901, 903, 904, 908, 911, 913, 915, 930, 931, 935, 936, 937, 939, 941, 945, 946, 948, 950, 951, 961, 963, 964, 965, 967, 970, 973, 977, 986, 987, 997, 998, 1003, 1012, 1013, 1016, 1017, 1019, 1022, 1023, 1025, 1041, 1049, 1053, R6, R18, R27, R28, R29
D. Calculate distance, scale, area, and density, and distinguish spatial distribution patterns.	GH1, GH8, GH9, GH10, GH11, 265, 317, 353, 456, 653, 1013, 1019, 1041

Theme and Performance Expectations	Student Pages
E. Describe, differentiate, and explain the relationships among various regional and global patterns of geographic phenomena such as landforms, soils, climate, vegetation, natural resources, and population.	11, 12, 13, 14–19, 34–35, 66–67, 84–85, 106–107, 234–235, 236–237, 290, 291, 334–341, 368–371, 430–437, 526–529, 598, 700–701, 706, 713, 910, 970, 990, 998–999, 1042, 1043, 1051
F. Use knowledge of physical system changes such as seasons, climate and weather, and the water cycle to explain geographic phenomena.	66–67, 278, 992, 1044
G. Describe and compare how people create places that reflect culture, human needs, government policies, and current values and ideals as they design and build specialized buildings, neighborhoods, shopping centers, urban centers, industrial parks, and the like.	36, 45, 64, 65, 82–83, 113, 125, 126, 189, 325, 339, 348–351, 452, 501, 502, 508, 519, 608, 651, 658–665, 684, 713
H. Examine, interpret, and analyze physical and cultural patterns and their interactions, such as land use, settlement patterns, cultural transmission of customs and ideas, and ecosystem change.	14–19, 26, 36, 45, 66–68, 82–83, 144–145, 234–235, 236–237, 246, 247, 276–277, 278, 290, 600, 679, 693–694
I. Describe and assess ways that historical events have been influenced by, and have influenced, physical and human geographic factors in local, regional, national, and global settings.	11, 119, 122, 135, 171, 172, 271, 280, 431, 436, 440–443, 526–529, 602–603, 673, 679, 693–694, 713, 826, 827, 885, 996, 997, 998, 1022
J. Analyze and evaluate social and economic effects of environmental changes and crises resulting from phenomena such as floods, storms, and drought.	34, 278, 989, 992, 1044
K. Propose, compare, and evaluate alternative policies for the use of land and other resources in communities, regions, nations, and the world.	795, 947, 1041, 1042, 1043, 1044
IV. Individual Development and Identity **People and culture influence a person's identity. Examining the different forms of human behavior improves one's understanding of social relationships and the development of personal identity. The study of human behavior helps students become aware of how social processes influence a person's identity. In high school, students use methods from the behavioral sciences to examine individuals, societies, and cultures.**	
A. Articulate personal connections to time, place, and social/cultural system.	538–545, 546–553, 554–563, 832, 833, 938, 939, 973, 974
B. Identify, describe, and express appreciation for the influence of various historical and contemporary cultures on an individual's daily life.	554–563, 922–923, 942, 949, 951, 1030–1031, 1044
C. Describe the ways family, religion, gender, ethnicity, nationality, socioeconomic status, and other groups and cultural influences contribute to the development of a sense of self.	19, 27, 41, 50, 51, 70, 71, 72–75, 121, 122, 334–338, 406–411, 658, 660, 661, 662, 663, 826, 828–830, 833, 849
D. Apply concepts, methods, and theories about the study of human growth and development, such as physical endowment, learning, motivation, behavior, perception, and personality.	6, 7, 8–11, 14–19, 31, 33, 42, 43, 89, 118–123, 398–403, 406–411, 412–417, 538–545, 546–553, 554–563, 658, 674–679
E. Examine the interaction of ethnic, national, or cultural influences in specific situations or events.	832, 833, 874–879, 882, 900–907, 919, 948, 951, 986–990, 991, 1019, 1020, 1023
F. Analyze the role of perceptions, attitudes, values, and beliefs in the development of personal identity.	27, 41, 50, 51, 72–75, 86–93, 121, 122, 334–338, 406–411, 661, 662, 826
G. Compare and evaluate the impact of stereotyping, conformity, acts of altruism, and other behaviors on individuals and groups.	832, 833, 874–879, 882, 919, 948, 951, 986–990, 991, 1019, 1020, 1023
H. Work independently and cooperatively within groups and institutions to accomplish goals.	11, 19, 33, 43, 51, 57, 75, 81, 93, 99, 111, 117, 123, 131, 139, 151, 159, 165, 173, 177, 191, 199, 203, 207, 239, 249, 255, 269, 275, 283, 289, 295, 307, 313, 321, 327, 341, 347, 351, 359, 371, 379, 385, 403, 411, 417, 423, 437, 443, 447, 457, 463, 469, 477, 489, 495, 503, 515, 519, 525, 529, 545, 553, 563, 569, 583, 593, 603, 621, 629, 637, 643, 657, 665, 673, 679, 691, 699, 707, 715, 731, 737, 745, 761, 769, 777, 783, 795, 803, 809, 815, 827, 835, 841, 849, 861, 871, 879, 887, 907, 913, 921, 935, 939, 945, 951, 965, 971, 977, 993, 1003, 1017, 1023, 1029, 1047, 1053
I. Examine factors that contribute to and damage one's mental health and analyze issues related to mental health and behavioral disorders in contemporary society.	677, 944–945, 1046

Theme and Performance Expectations		Student Pages
	V. Individuals, Groups, and Institutions **Institutions, such as schools, governments, and churches, influence people and often reflect a society's values. Because of the vital role that institutions play in people's lives, it is important that students know how institutions develop, what controls and influences them, and how humans react to them. High school students must understand the traditions and theories that support social and political traditions.**	
A.	Apply concepts such as role, status and social class in describing the connections and interactions of individuals, groups, and institutions in society.	19, 70–71, 75, 89, 122, 162, 163, 164, 202–203, 251, 252, 267, 280, 311, 336–338, 340–341, 378–379, 384, 402–403, 440–443, 444–447, 501, 522, 523, 551, 576–578, 609, 616, 617, 620–621, 636, 637, 655, 658–665, 671, 742, 745, 875, 918, 919, 920, 1019
B.	Analyze group and institutional influences on people, events, and elements of culture in both historical and contemporary settings.	398–403, 406–411, 412–417, 804–809, 810–811, 813, 839–841, 842–843, 856–859, 1044
C.	Describe the various forms institutions take, and explain how they develop and change over time.	49–51, 168–173, 176–177, 307, 308–313, 412–417, 652–657, 658–665, 708–715
D.	Identify and analyze examples of tensions between expressions of individuality and efforts used to promote social conformity by groups and institutions.	412–417, 432, 433, 541, 832, 833, 849, 882, 918, 919, 951, 1015
E.	Describe and examine belief systems basic to specific traditions and laws in contemporary and historical movements.	49, 50, 51, 58–59, 72, 73, 74, 75, 76–77, 80, 81, 89, 90–93, 98, 168–169, 170–173, 189–190, 191, 247, 253, 254, 256–257, 273, 275, 282, 283, 284–289, 295, 304–306, 342–347, 412–414, 415, 416, 417, 418–423, 487, 976, 1019
F.	Evaluate the role of institutions in furthering both continuity and change.	49–51, 168–173, 176–177, 307, 308–313, 412–417, 652–657, 658–665, 708–715, 1044
G.	Analyze the extent in which groups and institutions meet individual needs and promote the common good in contemporary and historical settings.	32–33, 317–318, 323, 544–545, 546–548, 551, 566–569, 1044
H.	Explain and apply ideas and modes of inquiry drawn from behavioral science and social theory in the examination of persistent issues and social changes.	12–13, 44–45, 82–83, 132–133, 166–167, 208–209, 256–257, 276–277, 314–315, 360–361, 380–381, 404–405, 438–439, 470–471, 496–497, 530–531, 564–565, 584–585, 644–645, 666–667, 716–717, 746–747, 770–771, 810–811, 842–843, 888–889, 922–923, 952–953, 978–979, 994–995, 1030–1031
	VI. Power, Authority, and Governance **Studying structures of power, authority, and governance and their functions in the United States and around the world is important for developing a notion of civic responsibility. Students will identify the purpose and characteristics of various types of government and how people try to resolve conflicts. Students will also examine the relationship between individual rights and responsibilities. High school students study the various systems that have been developed over time to allocate and employ power and authority in the governing process.**	
A.	Examine persistent issues involving the rights, roles, and status of the individual in relation to the general welfare.	112–113, 120, 121, 122, 148, 149, 150, 152–159, 340, 463, 476, 477, 576–583, 588, 593, 594–595, 598, 599, 626, 627–628, 635, 662, 663, 665, 668, 669, 671, 708–715, 743, 769, 832, 918, 919, 948, 986–987, 988, 991, 993, 1016, 1023, 1024, 1025, 1026
B.	Explain the purpose of government and analyze how its powers are acquired, used, and justified.	149–150, 174–176, 317–318, 323, 461, 463, 476–477, 546, 548, 550, 581
C.	Analyze and explain ideas and mechanisms to meet needs and wants of citizens, regulate territory, manage conflict, establish order and security, and balance competing conceptions of a just society.	33, 37, 149–150, 250, 317–318, 323, 378, 461, 463, 476–477, 546, 548, 549, 550, 568, 581, 594–595, 948, 991
D.	Compare and analyze the ways nations and organizations respond to conflicts between forces of unity and forces of diversity.	672, 673, 758–761, 762–769, 778–783, 856–861, 862–863, 864–871, 874–879, 880–887, 888–889, 900–907, 910–913, 914–923, 930–935, 936–939, 1012–1017, 1018–1023, 1024–1029
E.	Compare different political systems (their ideologies, structure, institutions, processes, and political processes) with that of the United States, and identify representative political leaders from selected historical and contemporary settings.	92, 112, 120, 175, 323, 476

Theme and Performance Expectations	Student Pages
F. Analyze and evaluate conditions, actions, and motivations that contribute to conflict and cooperation within and among nations.	54–57, 135–136, 195, 322–327, 356–357, 436, 440–443, 454–457, 503, 558–561, 598, 673, 790, 886, 887, 970, 999, 1000, 1048–1049, 1052–1053
G. Evaluate the role of technology in communications, transportation, information-processing, weapons development, or other areas as it contributes to or helps resolve conflicts.	238, 402, 538–545, 693–694, 764, 765, 770–771, 871, 884, 885, 946, 1038–1040
H. Explain and apply ideas, theories, and modes of inquiry drawn from political science to the examination of persistent ideas and social problems.	417, 461–463, 546–553, 582, 810–811, 823, 824, 833
I. Evaluate the extent in which governments achieve their stated ideals and policies at home and abroad.	115–117, 444–447, 476–477, 502, 528–529, 671, 686–691, 692–699, 702–707, 781, 782, 807, 996
J. Prepare a public policy paper and present and defend it before an appropriate forum in school or community.	33, 51, 57, 81, 159, 177, 199, 307, 385, 469, 507, 553, 673, 721, 787, 803, 841, 861, 871, 977
VII. Production, Distribution, and Consumption **Societies try to meet people's needs and wants by trying to answer the basic economic questions: What is to be produced? How should goods be produced? How should goods and services be distributed? How should land, labor, capital, and management be allocated? By studying how needs and wants are met, students learn how trade and government economic policies develop. In high school students develop economic perspectives and a deeper understanding of key economic concepts and processes.**	
A. Explain how the scarcity of productive resources (human, capital, technological, and natural) requires the development of economic systems to make decisions about how goods and services are to be produced and distributed.	516, 902, 903, 1041
B. Analyze the role that supply and demand, process, incentives, and profits play in determining what is produced and distributed in a competitive market system.	338, 440, 441, 446, 447, 458, 523, 614, 618, 652–655, 808, 911, 989, 1044
C. Consider the costs and benefits to society of allocating goods and services through private and public sectors.	654, 741, 799, 800, 801, 930–931, 960, 966, 972, 975
D. Describe the relationships among the various economic institutions that comprise economic systems such as households, business firms, banks, government agencies, labor unions, and corporations.	338, 341, 496–497, 618, 655, 834, 974, 1026, 1051
E. Analyze the role of specialization and exchange in economic processes.	48, 82–83, 158, 159, 197, 200, 201, 238, 239, 240–241, 242–249, 338–341, 435, 436, 526, 945, 976, 1052
F. Compare how values and beliefs influence economic decisions in different societies.	69, 446, 621, 667, 704, 741, 834, 988, 1012–1013, 1026
G. Compare basic economic systems according to how rules and procedures deal with demand, supply, prices, the role of government, banks, labor and labor unions, savings and investments, and capital.	294, 338, 340, 436, 440, 516, 621, 767, 911, 1026
H. Apply economic concepts and reasoning when evaluating historical and contemporary social developments and issues.	29, 159, 340, 353, 447, 549, 550, 614, 662
I. Distinguish between the domestic and global economic systems, and explain how the two interact.	961, 1051, 1052
J. Apply knowledge of production, distribution, and consumption in the analysis of a public issue such as the allocation of health care or the consumption of energy, and devise an economic plan for accomplishing a socially desirable outcome related to that issue.	353, 657, 665, 843, 882
K. Distinguish between economics as a field of inquiry and the economy.	549, 550

Theme and Performance Expectations	Student Pages
VIII. Science, Technology, and Society **The study of science, technology, and society is ever changing. It raises questions about who will benefit from it and how fundamental values and beliefs can be preserved in a technology-driven society. In high school students will confront issues that balance the benefits of science and technology against the accompanying social consequences.**	
A. Identify and describe both current and historical examples of the interaction and interdependence of science, technology, and society in a variety of cultural settings.	14, 15, 99, 205, 246, 274, 334, 433, 538, 539, 615, 616, 618, 619, 652–657, 693, 694, 699, 770–771, 946, 947, 1038–1042
B. Make judgments about how science and technology have transformed the physical world and human society and our understanding of time, space, place, and human-environment interactions.	9, 31, 43, 208–209, 274, 402, 544, 622–623, 770–771
C. Analyze how society and technology influence the core values, beliefs, and attitudes of society, and how core values, beliefs, and attitudes of society change scientific and technological change.	334, 349, 402, 538, 540, 541, 542, 544, 617, 619, 641, 652–657, 699, 840
D. Evaluate various policies that have been proposed as ways of dealing with social changes resulting from new technologies, such as genetically engineered plants and animals.	617, 947, 1040, 1041, 1042
E. Recognize and interpret varied perspectives about human societies and the physical world using scientific knowledge, ethical standards, and technologies from diverse world cultures.	9, 81, 138, 205, 208–209, 617, 621, 764–765, 946, 947, 951, 1041, 1042, 1047
F. Formulate strategies and develop policies for influencing public discussions associated with technology-society issues, such as the greenhouse effect.	622–623, 1047
IX. Global Connections **As countries grow more interdependent, understanding global connections among world societies becomes important. Students will analyze global issues in many different fields. They will also investigate relationships among the different cultures of the world. High school students will address critical issues such as peace, human rights, trade, and global ecology.**	
A. Explain how language, art, music, belief systems, and other cultural elements can facilitate global understanding or cause misunderstanding.	19, 28, 31, 36, 42, 43, 48, 49, 50, 51, 58–59, 69, 72, 73, 74, 75, 76–77, 80, 81, 83, 87, 89, 90–93, 95, 98, 101, 110, 111, 116, 125, 128, 131, 133, 138, 159, 163, 168–169, 170–173, 189–190, 191, 207, 247, 253, 254, 255, 268, 269, 273, 274, 275, 281, 282, 283, 284–289, 293, 295, 304–306, 324, 327, 337, 342–347, 349, 350, 351, 373, 376, 387, 412–414, 415, 416, 417, 418–423, 437, 439, 459, 473, 474, 475, 487, 489, 494, 502, 503, 518, 519, 525, 527, 531, 553, 562, 563, 565, 577, 578, 585, 623, 664, 706, 736, 849, 920, 923, 949, 965, 976, 979, 995, 1019, 1027, 1031
B. Explain conditions and motivations that contribute to conflict, cooperation, and interdependence among groups, societies, and nations.	54–57, 135–136, 195, 322–327, 356–357, 436, 440–443, 454–457, 503, 558–561, 598, 673, 781, 782, 790, 886, 887, 905, 906, 907, 917, 945, 962, 967, 970, 999, 1000, 1039, 1042, 1048–1049, 1050–1053
C. Analyze and evaluate the effects of changing technologies on the global community.	99, 655, 814, 946, 947, 949, 1038–1040, 1049, 1051, 1052, 1053
D. Analyze the causes, consequences, and possible solutions to persistent, contemporary, and emerging global issues, such as health, security, resource allocation, economic development, and environmental quality.	934, 935, 940, 944, 945, 946, 947, 989, 993, 999, 1001, 1002, 1003, 1007, 1038–1047, 1048–1053
E. Analyze the relationships and tensions between national sovereignty and global interests, in such matters as territory, economic development, nuclear and other weapons, use of natural resources, and human rights concerns.	827, 829, 856, 857, 858, 859, 874, 885, 901, 903–907, 933, 938, 939, 946, 947, 951, 969, 970, 996–1003, 1022, 1040, 1041, 1042, 1045, 1046, 1047, 1048–1053
F. Analyze or formulate policy statements demonstrating an understanding of concerns, standards, issues, and conflicts related to universal human rights.	878, 882, 919, 991, 1045, 1047
G. Describe and evaluate the role of international and multinational organizations in the global arena.	781, 790–795, 826, 860, 863, 878, 939, 996, 999, 1028, 1045, 1048, 1049
H. Illustrate how individual behaviors and decisions connect with global systems.	832, 833, 876–878, 882, 905, 906, 918, 919, 931, 944, 945, 1000, 1001, 1002, 1020

	Theme and Performance Expectations	Student Pages
	X. Civic Ideals and Practices **Understanding civic ideals and practices is crucial to complete participation in society and is the main purpose of social studies. Students will learn about civic participation and the role of the citizen within his or her community, country, and world. High school students learn, through experience, to identify social needs, setting directions for public policy, and working to support both individual dignity and the common good.**	
A.	Explain the origin and interpret the continuing influence of key ideals of the democratic republican form of government, such as individual human dignity, liberty, justice, equality, and the rule of law.	32–33, 112, 113, 114, 117, 120, 149, 317, 318, 323, 476, 477, 551, 553, 568, 569, 573
B.	Identify, analyze, interpret, and evaluate sources and examples of citizens' rights and responsibilities.	112–113, 120, 121, 122, 148, 149, 150, 152–159, 340, 463, 476, 477, 576–583, 588, 593, 594–595, 598, 599, 626, 627–628, 635, 662, 663, 665, 668, 669, 671, 708–715, 743, 769, 832, 918, 919, 948, 986–987, 988, 991, 993, 1016, 1023, 1024, 1025, 1026
C.	Locate, access, analyze, organize, synthesize, evaluate, and apply information about selected public issues-identifying, describing, and evaluating multiple points of view.	51, 139, 361, 434, 439, 443, 494, 541, 568, 583, 594–595, 621, 622–623, 661, 665, 787, 861, 862–863, 983, 1005, 1023, 1047
D.	Practice forms of civic discussion and participation consistent with the ideals of citizens in a democratic republic.	139, 921, 1003
E.	Analyze and evaluate the influence of various forms of citizen action on public policy.	130, 919, 920, 921, 951, 974, 990, 991, 993, 1015
F.	Analyze a variety of public policies and issues from the perspective of formal and informal political actors.	416, 427, 541, 542, 582, 833, 835, 871, 887, 919, 939, 1000, 1020, 1053
G.	Evaluate the effectiveness of public opinion in influencing and shaping public policy developments and decision-making.	130, 918, 919, 920, 921, 974, 990, 1041, 1042
H.	Evaluate the degree to which public policies and citizen behaviors reflect or foster the stated ideals of a democratic republican form of government.	130, 568, 594–595, 833, 948, 974, 991, 993, 1015, 1046, 1047
I.	Construct a policy statement and an action plan to achieve one or more goals related to an issue of public concern.	623, 1035
J.	Participate in activities to strengthen the "common good," based upon careful evaluation of possible options for citizen action.	130, 921, 1046

Using the Teacher Wraparound Edition

To Teachers:

Welcome to the the Teacher Wraparound Edition of *Glencoe World History.* We have created this teacher edition based on input from experienced teachers and educational consultants. Our goal is to provide you with teaching strategies and activities, which are labeled for you at point of use. The following pages will show the structure of the Teacher Wraparound Edition.

Student-Based Instruction

Point-of-Use
- Strategies and activities apply directly to student content.

Differentiated Instruction
- Leveled activities and options for differentiated instruction help meet the needs of all your students, including English language learners.

Review and Reinforcement
- Reading and critical thinking skills are reinforced throughout the lesson.

Assessment and Intervention
- Chapter Assessments provide standardized test practice.
- Assessments gauge student mastery of content.
- Additional resources provide intervention options.

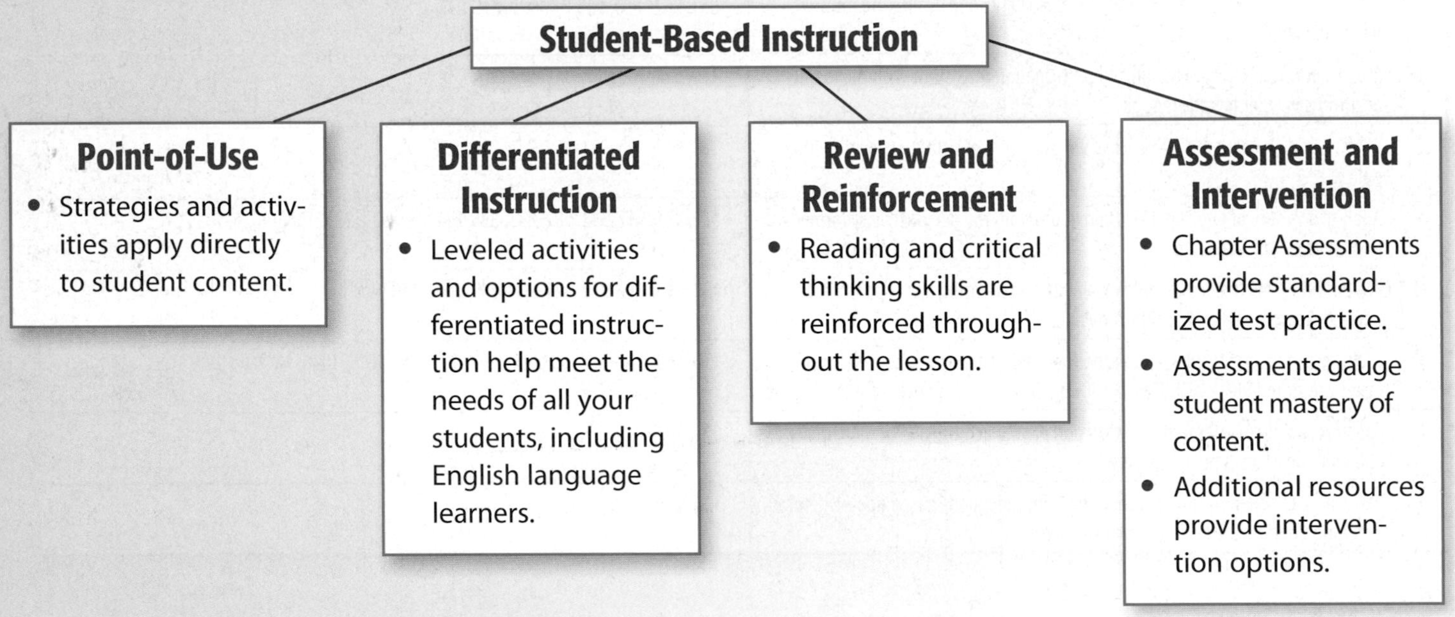

Planning and Teaching the Unit

Planning pages appear at the beginning of each unit.

Pacing Chart

Provides time management suggestions for teaching the unit

Author Note

Highlights author's ideas for teaching the time period

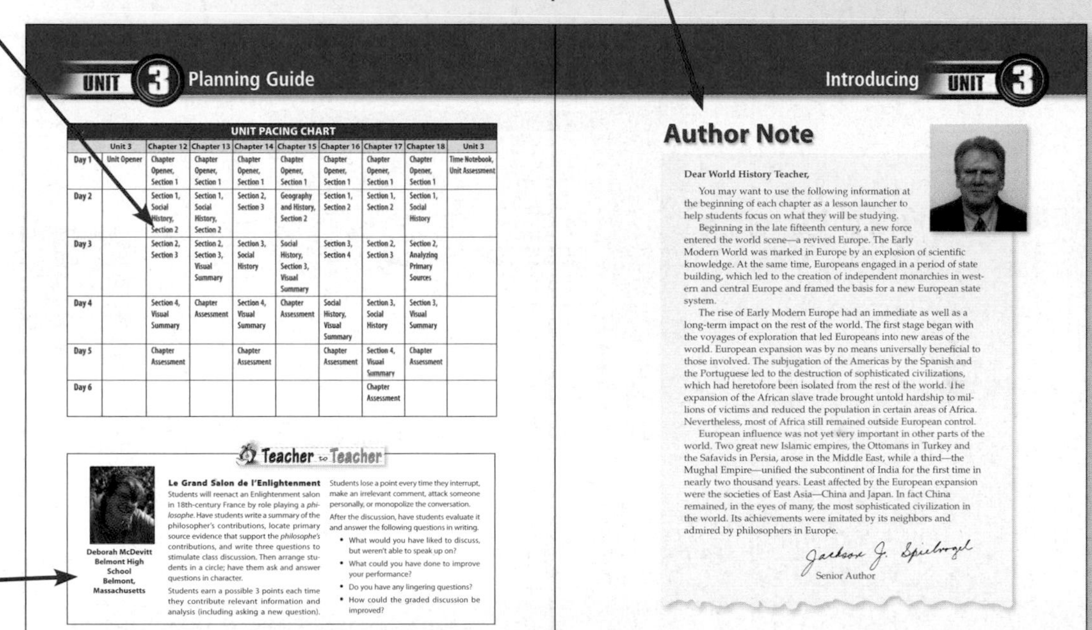

UNIT 3 Planning Guide

UNIT PACING CHART

	Unit 3	Chapter 12	Chapter 13	Chapter 14	Chapter 15	Chapter 16	Chapter 17	Chapter 18	Unit 3
Day 1	Unit Opener	Chapter Opener, Section 1	Chapter Opener, Section 1	Chapter Opener, Section 1	Chapter Opener, Section 1	Chapter Opener, Section 1	Chapter Opener, Section 1	Chapter Opener, Section 1	Time Notebook, Unit Assessment
Day 2		Section 1, Social History, Section 2	Section 1, Social History, Section 2	Section 2, Section 3	Geography and History, Section 2	Section 1, Section 2	Section 1, Section 2	Section 1, Social History	
Day 3		Section 2, Section 3	Section 2, Section 3, Visual Summary	Section 3, Social History	Social History, Section 3, Visual Summary	Section 3, Section 4	Section 2, Section 3	Section 2, Analyzing Primary Sources	
Day 4		Section 4, Visual Summary	Chapter Assessment	Section 4, Visual Summary	Chapter Assessment	Social History, Visual Summary	Section 3, Social History	Section 3, Visual Summary	
Day 5		Chapter Assessment		Chapter Assessment		Chapter Assessment	Section 4, Visual Summary	Chapter Assessment	
Day 6							Chapter Assessment		

Teacher to Teacher

Deborah McDevitt
Belmont High School
Belmont, Massachusetts

Le Grand Salon de l'Enlightenment Students will reenact an Enlightenment salon in 18th-century France by role playing a *philosophe*. Have students write a summary of the philosopher's contributions, locate primary source evidence that support the *philosophe's* contributions, and write three questions to stimulate class discussion. Then arrange students in a circle; have them ask and answer questions in character.

Students earn a possible 3 points each time they contribute relevant information and analysis (including asking a new question). Students lose a point every time they interrupt, make an irrelevant comment, attack someone personally, or monopolize the conversation.

After the discussion, have students evaluate it and answer the following questions in writing.

- What would you have liked to discuss, but weren't able to speak up on?
- What could you have done to improve your performance?
- Do you have any lingering questions?
- How could the graded discussion be improved?

394A

Introducing UNIT 3

Author Note

Dear World History Teacher,

You may want to use the following information at the beginning of each chapter as a lesson launcher to help students focus on what they will be studying.

Beginning in the late fifteenth century, a new force entered the world scene—a revived Europe. The Early Modern World was marked in Europe by an explosion of scientific knowledge. At the same time, Europeans engaged in a period of state building, which led to the creation of independent monarchies in western and central Europe and framed the basis for a new European state system.

The rise of Early Modern Europe had an immediate as well as a long-term impact on the rest of the world. The first stage began with the voyages of exploration that led Europeans into new areas of the world. European expansion was by no means universally beneficial to those involved. The subjugation of the Americas by the Spanish and the Portuguese led to the destruction of sophisticated civilizations, which had heretofore been isolated from the rest of the world. The expansion of the African slave trade brought untold hardship to millions of victims and reduced the population in certain areas of Africa. Nevertheless, most of Africa still remained outside European control.

European influence was not yet very important in other parts of the world. Two great new Islamic empires, the Ottomans in Turkey and the Safavids in Persia, arose in the Middle East, while a third—the Mughal Empire—unified the subcontinent of India for the first time in nearly two thousand years. Least affected by the European expansion were the societies of East Asia—China and Japan. In fact China remained, in the eyes of many, the most sophisticated civilization in the world. Its achievements were imitated by its neighbors and admired by philosophers in Europe.

Jackson J. Spielvogel
Senior Author

394B

Teacher to Teacher

Includes activities from the classrooms of successful teachers

Why It Matters

Provides an activity to help students discover why the events they will study are important

Skill Practice

Point-of-use skill-based activities help students practice historical analysis and geography skills

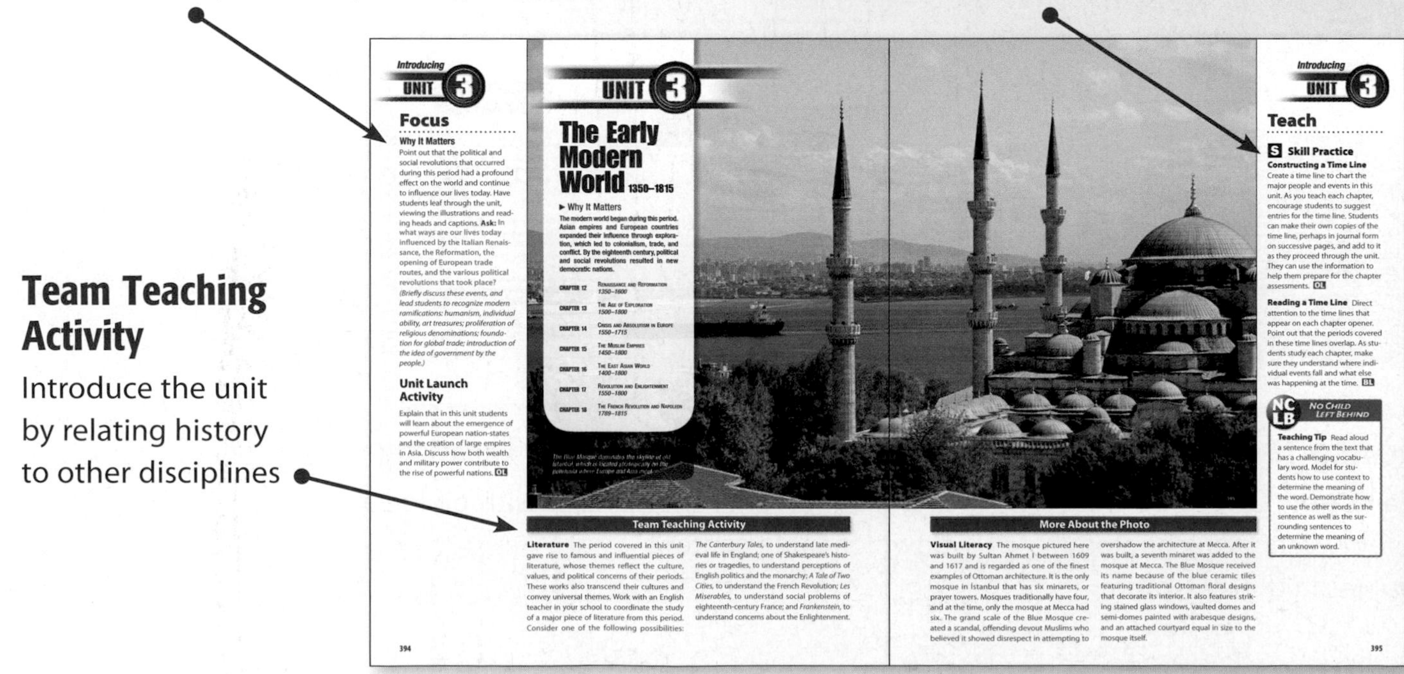

Introducing UNIT 3

Focus

Why It Matters
Point out that the political and social revolutions that occurred during this period had a profound effect on the world and continue to influence our lives today. Have students leaf through the unit, viewing the illustrations and reading heads and captions. **Ask:** In what ways are our lives today influenced by the Italian Renaissance, the Reformation, the opening of European trade routes, and the various political revolutions that took place? *(Briefly discuss these events, and lead students to recognize modern ramifications: humanism, individual ability, art treasures; proliferation of religious denominations; foundation for global trade; introduction of the idea of government by the people.)*

Unit Launch Activity
Explain that in this unit students will learn about the emergence of powerful European nation-states and the creation of large empires in Asia. Discuss how both wealth and military power contribute to the rise of powerful nations. OL

UNIT 3

The Early Modern World 1350–1815

► Why It Matters
The modern world began during this period. Asian empires and European countries expanded their influence through exploration, which led to colonialism, trade, and conflict. By the eighteenth century, political and social revolutions resulted in new democratic nations.

CHAPTER 12 Renaissance and Reformation 1350–1600
CHAPTER 13 The Age of Exploration 1500–1800
CHAPTER 14 Crisis and Absolutism in Europe 1550–1715
CHAPTER 15 The Muslim Empires 1450–1800
CHAPTER 16 The East Asian World 1400–1800
CHAPTER 17 Revolution and Enlightenment 1550–1800
CHAPTER 18 The French Revolution and Napoleon 1789–1815

Team Teaching Activity

Literature The period covered in this unit gave rise to famous and influential pieces of literature, whose themes reflect the culture, values, and political concerns of their periods. These works also transcend their cultures and convey universal themes. Work with an English teacher in your school to coordinate the study of a major piece of literature from this period. Consider one of the following possibilities: *The Canterbury Tales*, to understand late medieval life in England; one of Shakespeare's histories or tragedies, to understand perceptions of English politics and the monarchy; *A Tale of Two Cities*, to understand the French Revolution; *Les Miserables*, to understand social problems of eighteenth-century France; and *Frankenstein*, to understand concerns about the Enlightenment.

394

More About the Photo

Visual Literacy The mosque pictured here was built by Sultan Ahmet I between 1609 and 1617 and is regarded as one of the finest examples of Ottoman architecture. It is the only mosque in İstanbul that has six minarets, or prayer towers. Mosques traditionally have four, and at the time, only the mosque at Mecca had six. The grand scale of the Blue Mosque created a scandal, offending devout Muslims who believed it showed disrespect in attempting to overshadow the architecture at Mecca. After it was built, a seventh minaret was added to the mosque at Mecca. The Blue Mosque received its name because of the blue ceramic tiles featuring traditional Ottoman floral designs that decorate its interior. It also features striking stained glass windows, vaulted domes and semi-domes painted with arabesque designs, and an attached courtyard equal in size to the mosque itself.

Introducing UNIT 3

Teach

S Skill Practice
Constructing a Time Line
Create a time line to chart the major people and events in this unit. As you teach each chapter, encourage students to suggest entries for the time line. Students can make their own copies of the time line, perhaps in journal form on successive pages, and add to it as they proceed through the unit. They can use the information to help them prepare for the chapter assessments. OL

Reading a Time Line Direct attention to the time lines that appear on each chapter opener. Point out that the periods covered in these time lines overlap. As students study each chapter, make sure they understand where individual events fall and what else was happening at the time. BL

NCLB No Child Left Behind

Teaching Tip Read aloud a sentence from the text that has a challenging vocabulary word. Model for students how to use context to determine the meaning of the word. Demonstrate how to use the other words in the sentence as well as the surrounding sentences to determine the meaning of an unknown word.

395

Team Teaching Activity

Introduce the unit by relating history to other disciplines

Planning the Chapter

Chapter Planning Guides provide a snapshot of the scope of resources available to enhance and extend learning in each chapter.

Incorporating Resources

Utilizes a structured lesson plan to incorporate additional resources

Leveled Activities

Organizes resources by appropriate ability levels

*Spanish Resources

Provides resources for English language learners

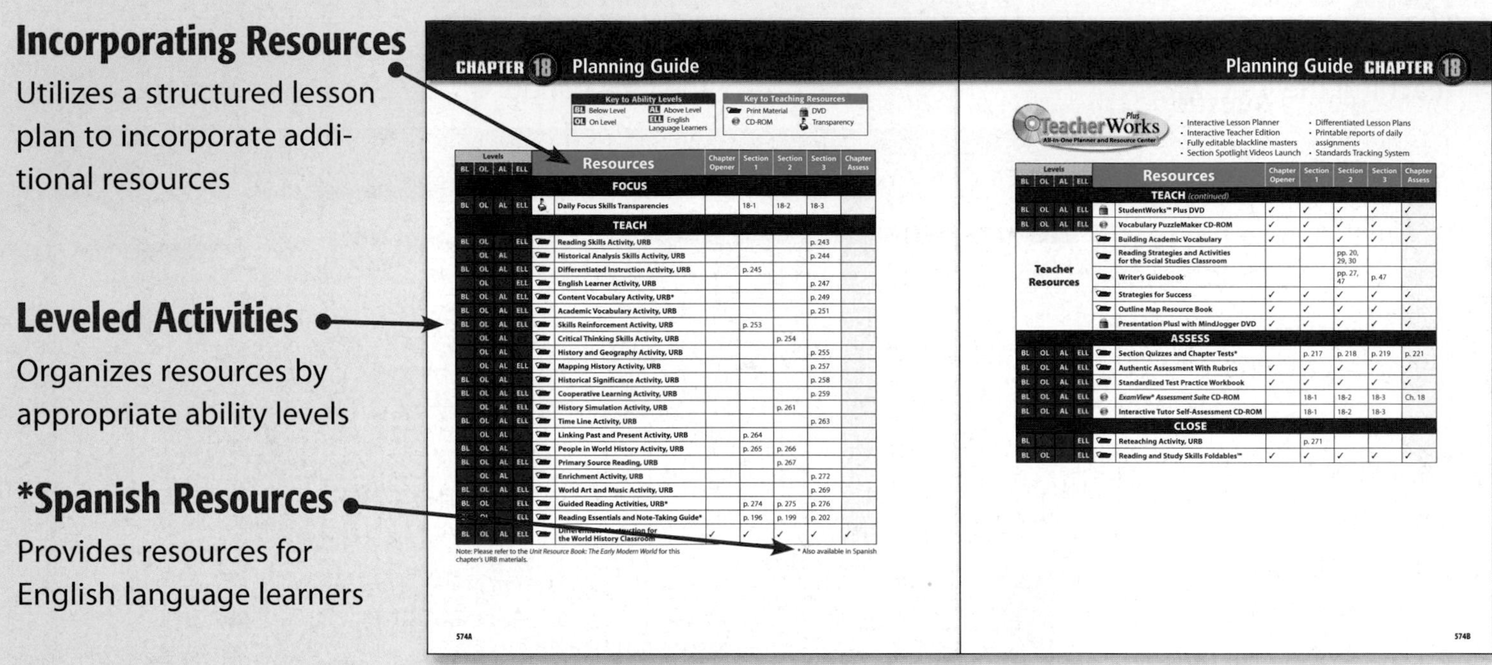

CHAPTER 18 Planning Guide

Key to Ability Levels	
BL Below Level	AL Above Level
OL On Level	ELL English Language Learners

Key to Teaching Resources	
Print Material	DVD
CD-ROM	Transparency

BL	OL	AL	ELL	Resources	Chapter Opener	Section 1	Section 2	Section 3	Chapter Assess
				FOCUS					
BL	OL	AL	ELL	Daily Focus Skills Transparencies		18-1	18-2	18-3	
				TEACH					
BL	OL		ELL	Reading Skills Activity, URB				p. 243	
	OL	AL		Historical Analysis Skills Activity, URB				p. 244	
BL	OL	AL	ELL	Differentiated Instruction Activity, URB		p. 245			
	OL		ELL	English Learner Activity, URB				p. 247	
BL	OL	AL	ELL	Content Vocabulary Activity, URB*				p. 249	
BL	OL	AL	ELL	Academic Vocabulary Activity, URB				p. 251	
BL	OL	AL	ELL	Skills Reinforcement Activity, URB		p. 253			
	OL	AL		Critical Thinking Skills Activity, URB			p. 254		
	OL	AL		History and Geography Activity, URB				p. 255	
	OL	AL	ELL	Mapping History Activity, URB				p. 257	
BL	OL	AL		Historical Significance Activity, URB				p. 258	
BL	OL	AL	ELL	Cooperative Learning Activity, URB				p. 259	
	OL	AL	ELL	History Simulation Activity, URB			p. 261		
BL	OL	AL	ELL	Time Line Activity, URB				p. 263	
	OL	AL		Linking Past and Present Activity, URB		p. 264			
BL	OL	AL		People in World History Activity, URB		p. 265	p. 266		
BL	OL	AL	ELL	Primary Source Reading, URB			p. 267		
	OL	AL		Enrichment Activity, URB				p. 272	
BL	OL	AL	ELL	World Art and Music Activity, URB				p. 269	
BL	OL		ELL	Guided Reading Activities, URB*		p. 274	p. 275	p. 276	
[illegible]	[illegible]		ELL	Reading Essentials and Note-Taking Guide*		p. 196	p. 199	p. 202	
BL	OL	AL	ELL	Differentiated Instruction for the World History Classroom	✓	✓	✓	✓	✓

Note: Please refer to the *Unit Resource Book: The Early Modern World* for this chapter's URB materials.

* Also available in Spanish

574A

Planning Guide CHAPTER 18

TeacherWorks Plus All-In-One Planner and Resource Center

- Interactive Lesson Planner
- Interactive Teacher Edition
- Fully editable blackline masters
- Section Spotlight Videos Launch
- Differentiated Lesson Plans
- Printable reports of daily assignments
- Standards Tracking System

BL	OL	AL	ELL	Resources	Chapter Opener	Section 1	Section 2	Section 3	Chapter Assess
				TEACH *(continued)*					
BL	OL	AL	ELL	StudentWorks™ Plus DVD	✓	✓	✓	✓	✓
BL	OL	AL	ELL	Vocabulary PuzzleMaker CD-ROM	✓	✓	✓	✓	✓
Teacher Resources				Building Academic Vocabulary	✓	✓	✓	✓	✓
				Reading Strategies and Activities for the Social Studies Classroom			pp. 20, 29, 30		
				Writer's Guidebook			pp. 27, 47	p. 47	
				Strategies for Success	✓	✓	✓	✓	✓
				Outline Map Resource Book	✓	✓	✓	✓	✓
				Presentation Plus! with MindJogger DVD	✓	✓	✓	✓	✓
				ASSESS					
BL	OL	AL	ELL	Section Quizzes and Chapter Tests*		p. 217	p. 218	p. 219	p. 221
BL	OL	AL	ELL	Authentic Assessment With Rubrics	✓	✓	✓	✓	✓
BL	OL	AL	ELL	Standardized Test Practice Workbook	✓	✓	✓	✓	✓
BL	OL	AL	ELL	*ExamView® Assessment Suite* CD-ROM		18-1	18-2	18-3	Ch. 18
BL	OL	AL	ELL	Interactive Tutor Self-Assessment CD-ROM		18-1	18-2	18-3	
				CLOSE					
BL			ELL	Reteaching Activity, URB		p. 271			
BL	OL		ELL	Reading and Study Skills Foldables™	✓	✓	✓	✓	✓

574B

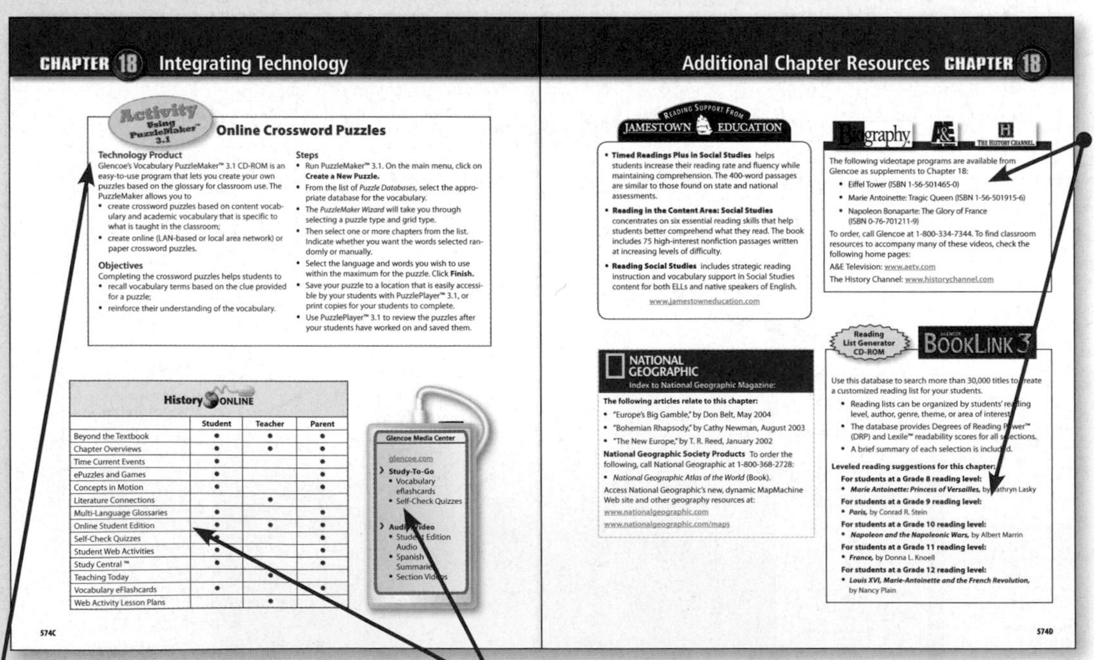

CHAPTER 18 Integrating Technology

Activity Using PuzzleMaker™ 3.1

Online Crossword Puzzles

Technology Product

Glencoe's Vocabulary PuzzleMaker™ 3.1 CD-ROM is an easy-to-use program that lets you create your own puzzles based on the glossary for classroom use. The PuzzleMaker allows you to

- create crossword puzzles based on content vocabulary and academic vocabulary that is specific to what is taught in the classroom;
- create online (LAN-based or local area network) or paper crossword puzzles.

Objectives

Completing the crossword puzzles helps students to

- recall vocabulary terms based on the clue provided for a puzzle;
- reinforce their understanding of the vocabulary.

Steps

- Run PuzzleMaker™ 3.1. On the main menu, click on **Create a New Puzzle.**
- From the list of *Puzzle Databases*, select the appropriate database for the vocabulary.
- The *PuzzleMaker Wizard* will take you through selecting a puzzle type and grid type.
- Then select one or more chapters from the list. Indicate whether you want the words selected randomly or manually.
- Select the language and words you wish to use within the maximum for the puzzle. Click **Finish.**
- Save your puzzle to a location that is easily accessible by your students with PuzzlePlayer™ 3.1, or print copies for your students to complete.
- Use PuzzlePlayer™ 3.1 to review the puzzles after your students have worked on and saved them.

History ONLINE

	Student	Teacher	Parent
Beyond the Textbook	•	•	•
Chapter Overviews	•	•	•
Time Current Events	•		•
ePuzzles and Games	•		•
Concepts in Motion	•		•
Literature Connections		•	
Multi-Language Glossaries	•		•
Online Student Edition	•	•	•
Self-Check Quizzes	•		•
Student Web Activities	•		•
Study Central ™	•		•
Teaching Today		•	
Vocabulary eFlashcards	•		•
Web Activity Lesson Plans		•	

Glencoe Media Center

glencoe.com

› Study-To-Go
- Vocabulary eflashcards
- Self-Check Quizzes

› Audio/Video
- Student Edition Audio
- Spanish Summaries
- Section Videos

574C

Additional Chapter Resources CHAPTER 18

Reading Support From JAMESTOWN EDUCATION

- **Timed Readings Plus in Social Studies** helps students increase their reading rate and fluency while maintaining comprehension. The 400-word passages are similar to those found on state and national assessments.
- **Reading in the Content Area: Social Studies** concentrates on six essential reading skills that help students better comprehend what they read. The book includes 75 high-interest nonfiction passages written at increasing levels of difficulty.
- **Reading Social Studies** includes strategic reading instruction and vocabulary support in Social Studies content for both ELLs and native speakers of English.

www.jamestowneducation.com

Biography. A&E THE HISTORY CHANNEL

The following videotape programs are available from Glencoe as supplements to Chapter 18:

- Eiffel Tower (ISBN 1-56-501465-0)
- Marie Antoinette: Tragic Queen (ISBN 1-56-501915-6)
- Napoleon Bonaparte: The Glory of France (ISBN 0-76-701211-9)

To order, call Glencoe at 1-800-334-7344. To find classroom resources to accompany many of these videos, check the following home pages:

A&E Television: www.aetv.com

The History Channel: www.historychannel.com

NATIONAL GEOGRAPHIC

Index to National Geographic Magazine:

The following articles relate to this chapter:

- "Europe's Big Gamble," by Don Belt, May 2004
- "Bohemian Rhapsody," by Cathy Newman, August 2003
- "The New Europe," by T. R. Reed, January 2002

National Geographic Society Products To order the following, call National Geographic at 1-800-368-2728:

- *National Geographic Atlas of the World* (Book).

Access National Geographic's new, dynamic MapMachine Web site and other geography resources at:

www.nationalgeographic.com

www.nationalgeographic.com/maps

Reading List Generator CD-ROM

Glencoe BOOKLINK 3

Use this database to search more than 30,000 titles to create a customized reading list for your students.

- Reading lists can be organized by students' reading level, author, genre, theme, or area of interest.
- The database provides Degrees of Reading Power™ (DRP) and Lexile™ readability scores for all selections.
- A brief summary of each selection is included.

Leveled reading suggestions for this chapter:

For students at a Grade 8 reading level:
- ***Marie Antoinette: Princess of Versailles,*** by Kathryn Lasky

For students at a Grade 9 reading level:
- ***Paris,*** by Conrad R. Stein

For students at a Grade 10 reading level:
- ***Napoleon and the Napoleonic Wars,*** by Albert Marrin

For students at a Grade 11 reading level:
- ***France,*** by Donna L. Knoell

For students at a Grade 12 reading level:
- ***Louis XVI, Marie-Antoinette and the French Revolution,*** by Nancy Plain

574D

Additional Resources

Identifies resources for supplementing the chapter

Teaching Technology

Explains how to incorporate different Glencoe technology resources in the classroom

Online and Downloadable Learning

Engages students and parents with online and downloadable content

Teaching the Chapter

The Big Ideas and Essential Question at the beginning of the chapter help you teach the most important chapter contents.

Making Connections

Introductory questions lead to an exploration of big ideas. These questions activate students' prior knowledge and lead students to see not only the "big picture," but also the relevancy of what they are learning. These lesson launcher activities compel students to consider the Big Idea of the chapter.

The Big Ideas

Big Ideas are themes, issues, concepts, questions, or ideas tied to the main concepts of the chapter and of each section. The Essential Question leads to an understanding of Big Ideas. These questions are broad and have no right or wrong answers. Essential Questions are thought-provoking, challenge old assumptions, and stimulate discussion. Student activities throughout the chapter will refer back to the Essential Question, leading to a greater comprehension of chapter themes.

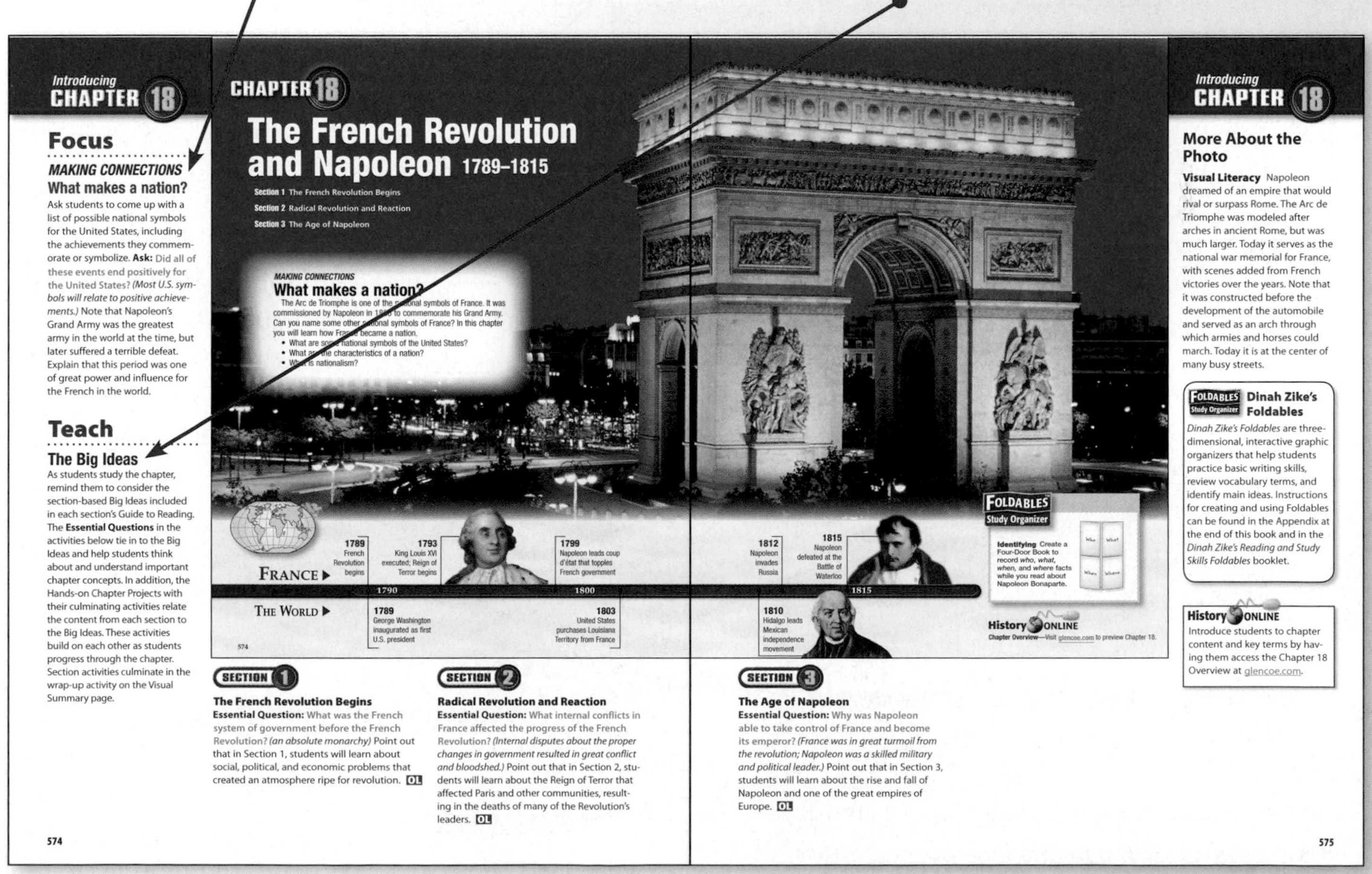

Introducing CHAPTER 18

Focus

MAKING CONNECTIONS
What makes a nation?
Ask students to come up with a list of possible national symbols for the United States, including the achievements they commemorate or symbolize. **Ask:** Did all of these events end positively for the United States? *(Most U.S. symbols will relate to positive achievements.)* Note that Napoleon's Grand Army was the greatest army in the world at the time, but later suffered a terrible defeat. Explain that this period was one of great power and influence for the French in the world.

Teach

The Big Ideas
As students study the chapter, remind them to consider the section-based Big Ideas included in each section's Guide to Reading. The **Essential Questions** in the activities below tie in to the Big Ideas and help students think about and understand important chapter concepts. In addition, the Hands-on Chapter Projects with their culminating activities relate the content from each section to the Big Ideas. These activities build on each other as students progress through the chapter. Section activities culminate in the wrap-up activity on the Visual Summary page.

CHAPTER 18

The French Revolution and Napoleon 1789–1815

Section 1 The French Revolution Begins
Section 2 Radical Revolution and Reaction
Section 3 The Age of Napoleon

MAKING CONNECTIONS
What makes a nation?
The Arc de Triomphe is one of the national symbols of France. It was commissioned by Napoleon in 18[illegible] to commemorate his Grand Army. Can you name some other national symbols of France? In this chapter you will learn how France became a nation.
- What are some national symbols of the United States?
- What are the characteristics of a nation?
- What is nationalism?

FRANCE ▶
1789 French Revolution begins
1793 King Louis XVI executed; Reign of Terror begins
1799 Napoleon leads coup d'état that topples French government
1812 Napoleon invades Russia
1815 Napoleon defeated at the Battle of Waterloo

1790 — 1800 — 1815

THE WORLD ▶
1789 George Washington inaugurated as first U.S. president
1803 United States purchases Louisiana Territory from France
1810 Hidalgo leads Mexican independence movement

574

FOLDABLES Study Organizer
Identifying Create a Four-Door Book to record *who, what, when,* and *where* facts while you read about Napoleon Bonaparte.
Who / What / When / Where

History ONLINE
Chapter Overview—Visit glencoe.com to preview Chapter 18.

SECTION 1
The French Revolution Begins
Essential Question: What was the French system of government before the French Revolution? *(an absolute monarchy)* Point out that in Section 1, students will learn about social, political, and economic problems that created an atmosphere ripe for revolution. OL

SECTION 2
Radical Revolution and Reaction
Essential Question: What internal conflicts in France affected the progress of the French Revolution? *(Internal disputes about the proper changes in government resulted in great conflict and bloodshed.)* Point out that in Section 2, students will learn about the Reign of Terror that affected Paris and other communities, resulting in the deaths of many of the Revolution's leaders. OL

SECTION 3
The Age of Napoleon
Essential Question: Why was Napoleon able to take control of France and become its emperor? *(France was in great turmoil from the revolution; Napoleon was a skilled military and political leader.)* Point out that in Section 3, students will learn about the rise and fall of Napoleon and one of the great empires of Europe. OL

Introducing CHAPTER 18

More About the Photo

Visual Literacy Napoleon dreamed of an empire that would rival or surpass Rome. The Arc de Triomphe was modeled after arches in ancient Rome, but was much larger. Today it serves as the national war memorial for France, with scenes added from French victories over the years. Note that it was constructed before the development of the automobile and served as an arch through which armies and horses could march. Today it is at the center of many busy streets.

FOLDABLES Study Organizer **Dinah Zike's Foldables**
Dinah Zike's Foldables are three-dimensional, interactive graphic organizers that help students practice basic writing skills, review vocabulary terms, and identify main ideas. Instructions for creating and using Foldables can be found in the Appendix at the end of this book and in the *Dinah Zike's Reading and Study Skills Foldables* booklet.

History ONLINE
Introduce students to chapter content and key terms by having them access the Chapter 18 Overview at glencoe.com.

574 575

Lesson Structure

Each lesson in *Glencoe World History* is presented in a structured lesson plan: Focus, Teach, Assess, and Close.

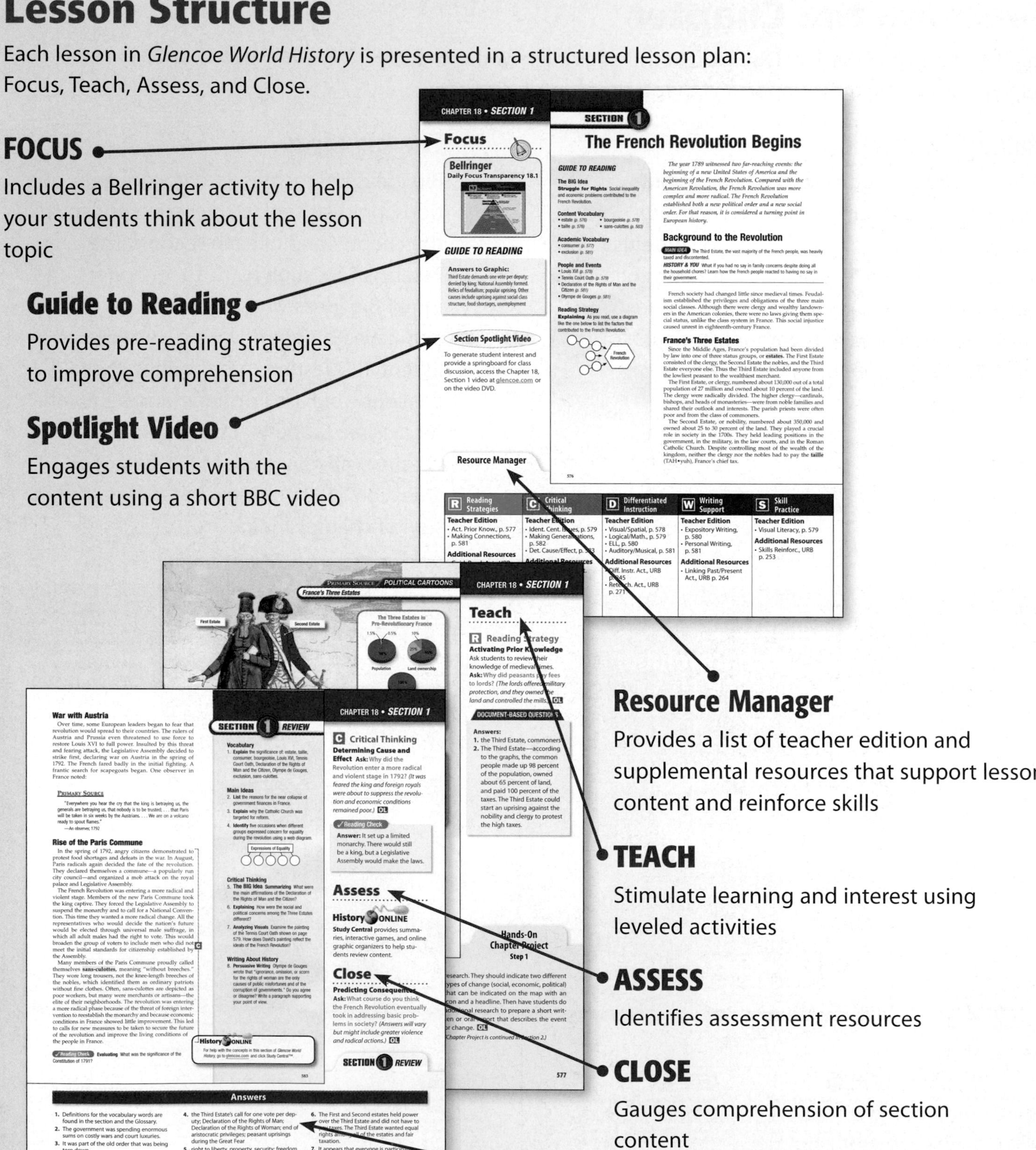

FOCUS

Includes a Bellringer activity to help your students think about the lesson topic

Guide to Reading

Provides pre-reading strategies to improve comprehension

Spotlight Video

Engages students with the content using a short BBC video

Resource Manager

Provides a list of teacher edition and supplemental resources that support lesson content and reinforce skills

TEACH

Stimulate learning and interest using leveled activities

ASSESS

Identifies assessment resources

CLOSE

Gauges comprehension of section content

Answers

Lists the answers to Student Edition questions

Understanding the Brackets and Letters

Brackets

Brackets on the reduced Student Edition page correspond to teaching strategies and activities in the Teacher Wraparound Edition. As you teach the section, the brackets show you exactly where to teach these strategies and activities.

Letters*

The letters on the reduced Student Edition page identify the type of strategy or activity. See the key below to learn about the different types of strategies and activities.

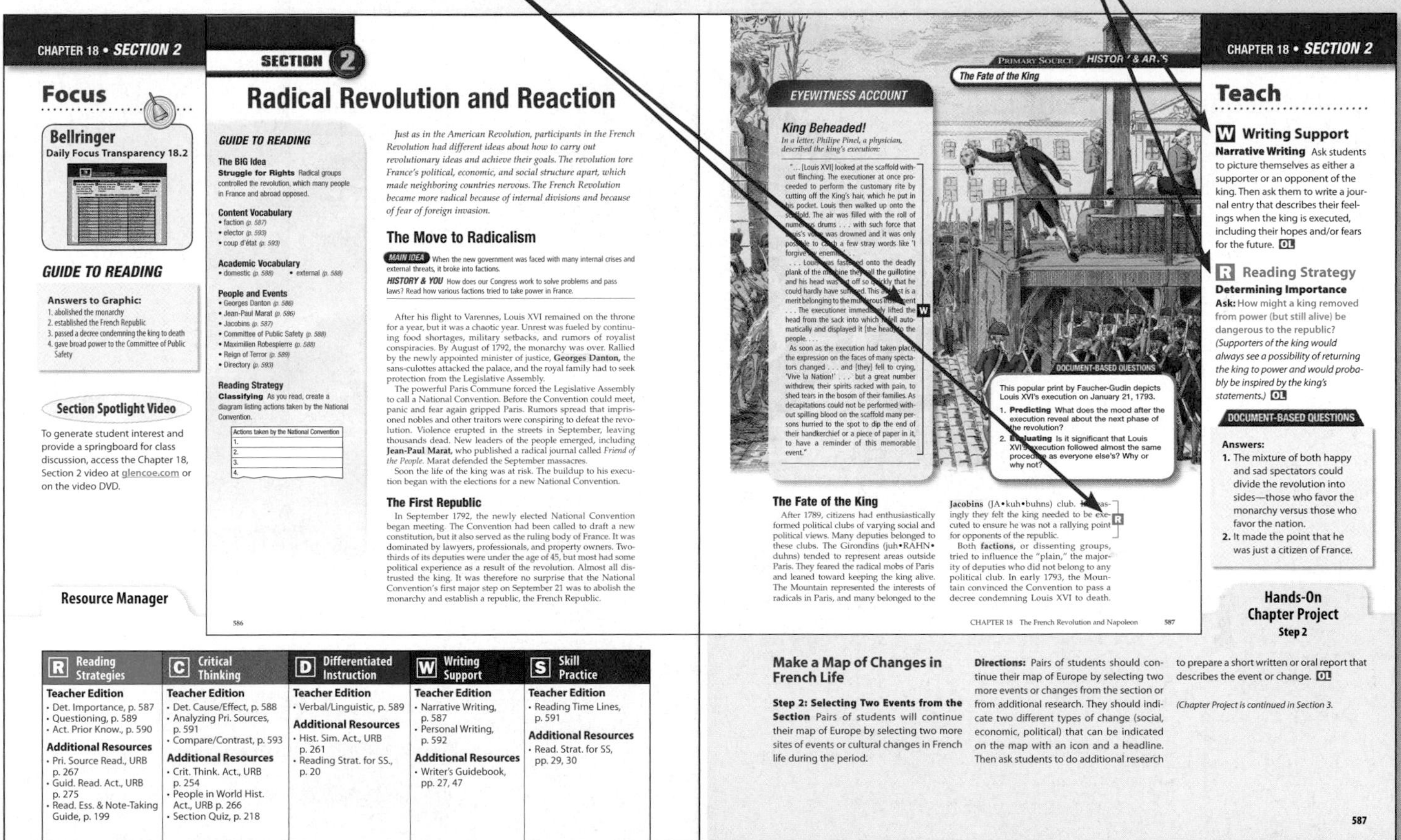

CHAPTER 18 • SECTION 2

Focus

Bellringer
Daily Focus Transparency 18.2

GUIDE TO READING

Answers to Graphic:
1. abolished the monarchy
2. established the French Republic
3. passed a decree condemning the king to death
4. gave broad power to the Committee of Public Safety

Section Spotlight Video

To generate student interest and provide a springboard for class discussion, access the Chapter 18, Section 2 video at glencoe.com or on the video DVD.

Resource Manager

SECTION 2

Radical Revolution and Reaction

GUIDE TO READING

The BIG Idea
Struggle for Rights Radical groups controlled the revolution, which many people in France and abroad opposed.

Content Vocabulary
- faction (p. 587)
- elector (p. 593)
- coup d'état (p. 593)

Academic Vocabulary
- domestic (p. 588)
- external (p. 588)

People and Events
- Georges Danton (p. 586)
- Jean-Paul Marat (p. 586)
- Jacobins (p. 587)
- Committee of Public Safety (p. 588)
- Maximilien Robespierre (p. 588)
- Reign of Terror (p. 589)
- Directory (p. 593)

Reading Strategy
Classifying As you read, create a diagram listing actions taken by the National Convention.

Actions taken by the National Convention
1.
2.
3.
4.

Just as in the American Revolution, participants in the French Revolution had different ideas about how to carry out revolutionary ideas and achieve their goals. The revolution tore France's political, economic, and social structure apart, which made neighboring countries nervous. The French Revolution became more radical because of internal divisions and because of fear of foreign invasion.

The Move to Radicalism

MAIN IDEA When the new government was faced with many internal crises and external threats, it broke into factions.

HISTORY & YOU How does our Congress work to solve problems and pass laws? Read how various factions tried to take power in France.

After his flight to Varennes, Louis XVI remained on the throne for a year, but it was a chaotic year. Unrest was fueled by continuing food shortages, military setbacks, and rumors of royalist conspiracies. By August of 1792, the monarchy was over. Rallied by the newly appointed minister of justice, **Georges Danton,** the sans-culottes attacked the palace, and the royal family had to seek protection from the Legislative Assembly.

The powerful Paris Commune forced the Legislative Assembly to call a National Convention. Before the Convention could meet, panic and fear again gripped Paris. Rumors spread that imprisoned nobles and other traitors were conspiring to defeat the revolution. Violence erupted in the streets in September, leaving thousands dead. New leaders of the people emerged, including **Jean-Paul Marat,** who published a radical journal called *Friend of the People.* Marat defended the September massacres.

Soon the life of the king was at risk. The buildup to his execution began with the elections for a new National Convention.

The First Republic

In September 1792, the newly elected National Convention began meeting. The Convention had been called to draft a new constitution, but it also served as the ruling body of France. It was dominated by lawyers, professionals, and property owners. Two-thirds of its deputies were under the age of 45, but most had some political experience as a result of the revolution. Almost all distrusted the king. It was therefore no surprise that the National Convention's first major step on September 21 was to abolish the monarchy and establish a republic, the French Republic.

586

PRIMARY SOURCE / HISTORY & ARTS

The Fate of the King

EYEWITNESS ACCOUNT

King Beheaded!
In a letter, Philipe Pinel, a physician, described the king's execution:

"… [Louis XVI] looked at the scaffold without flinching. The executioner at once proceeded to perform the customary rite by cutting off the King's hair, which he put in his pocket. Louis then walked up onto the scaffold. The air was filled with the roll of numerous drums … with such force that Louis's voice was drowned and it was only possible to catch a few stray words like 'I forgive my enemies'…

… Louis was fastened onto the deadly plank of the machine they call the guillotine and his head was cut off so quickly that he could hardly have suffered. This at least is a merit belonging to the murderous instrument … The executioner immediately lifted the head from the sack into which it fell automatically and displayed it [the head] to the people. … W

As soon as the execution had taken place, the expression on the faces of many spectators changed … and [they] fell to crying, 'Vive la Nation!' … but a great number withdrew, their spirits racked with pain, to shed tears in the bosom of their families. As decapitations could not be performed without spilling blood on the scaffold many persons hurried to the spot to dip the end of their handkerchief or a piece of paper in it, to have a reminder of this memorable event."

DOCUMENT-BASED QUESTIONS

This popular print by Faucher-Gudin depicts Louis XVI's execution on January 21, 1793.

1. **Predicting** What does the mood after the execution reveal about the next phase of the revolution?
2. **Evaluating** Is it significant that Louis XVI's execution followed almost the same procedure as everyone else's? Why or why not?

The Fate of the King

After 1789, citizens had enthusiastically formed political clubs of varying social and political views. Many deputies belonged to these clubs. The Girondins (juh•RAHN•duhns) tended to represent areas outside Paris. They feared the radical mobs of Paris and leaned toward keeping the king alive. The Mountain represented the interests of radicals in Paris, and many belonged to the **Jacobins** (JA•kuh•buhns) club. Increasingly they felt the king needed to be executed to ensure he was not a rallying point for opponents of the republic. R

Both **factions,** or dissenting groups, tried to influence the "plain," the majority of deputies who did not belong to any political club. In early 1793, the Mountain convinced the Convention to pass a decree condemning Louis XVI to death.

CHAPTER 18 The French Revolution and Napoleon 587

CHAPTER 18 • SECTION 2

Teach

W Writing Support
Narrative Writing Ask students to picture themselves as either a supporter or an opponent of the king. Then ask them to write a journal entry that describes their feelings when the king is executed, including their hopes and/or fears for the future. OL

R Reading Strategy
Determining Importance
Ask: How might a king removed from power (but still alive) be dangerous to the republic? *(Supporters of the king would always see a possibility of returning the king to power and would probably be inspired by the king's statements.)* OL

DOCUMENT-BASED QUESTIONS

Answers:
1. The mixture of both happy and sad spectators could divide the revolution into sides—those who favor the monarchy versus those who favor the nation.
2. It made the point that he was just a citizen of France.

Hands-On Chapter Project
Step 2

Make a Map of Changes in French Life

Step 2: Selecting Two Events from the Section Pairs of students will continue their map of Europe by selecting two more sites of events or cultural changes in French life during the period.

Directions: Pairs of students should continue their map of Europe by selecting two more events or changes from the section or from additional research. They should indicate two different types of change (social, economic, political) that can be indicated on the map with an icon and a headline. Then ask students to do additional research to prepare a short written or oral report that describes the event or change. OL

(Chapter Project is continued in Section 3.

R Reading Strategies	C Critical Thinking	D Differentiated Instruction	W Writing Support	S Skill Practice
Teacher Edition • Det. Importance, p. 587 • Questioning, p. 589 • Act. Prior Know., p. 590 **Additional Resources** • Pri. Source Read., URB p. 267 • Guid. Read. Act., URB p. 275 • Read. Ess. & Note-Taking Guide, p. 199	**Teacher Edition** • Det. Cause/Effect, p. 588 • Analyzing Pri. Sources, p. 591 • Compare/Contrast, p. 593 **Additional Resources** • Crit. Think. Act., URB p. 254 • People in World Hist. Act., URB p. 266 • Section Quiz, p. 218	**Teacher Edition** • Verbal/Linguistic, p. 589 **Additional Resources** • Hist. Sim. Act., URB p. 261 • Reading Strat. for SS., p. 20	**Teacher Edition** • Narrative Writing, p. 587 • Personal Writing, p. 592 **Additional Resources** • Writer's Guidebook, pp. 27, 47	**Teacher Edition** • Reading Time Lines, p. 591 **Additional Resources** • Read. Strat. for SS, pp. 29, 30

587

KEY for Using the Teacher Wraparound Edition

R **Reading Strategies** activities help you teach reading skills and vocabulary.

C **Critical Thinking** strategies help students apply and extend what they have learned.

D **Differentiated Instruction** activities provide differentiated instruction for students learning to speak English, along with suggestions for teaching various types of learners.

S **Skill Practice** strategies help students practice historical analysis and geography skills.

W **Writing Support** activities provide writing opportunities to help students comprehend the text.

* Letters are followed by a number when there is more than one of the same type of strategy or activity on the page.

Hands-On Chapter Projects

Extend student learning with unique interactive projects in each chapter. The Hands-On Chapter Projects allow students to take concepts and put them to practical use. Activities are progressive and require teamwork. Students conceptualize, plan, and execute their vision in a hands-on approach that makes history come alive.

Steps

Each lesson includes a self-contained activity, with one lesson building on knowledge gained from previous lessons.

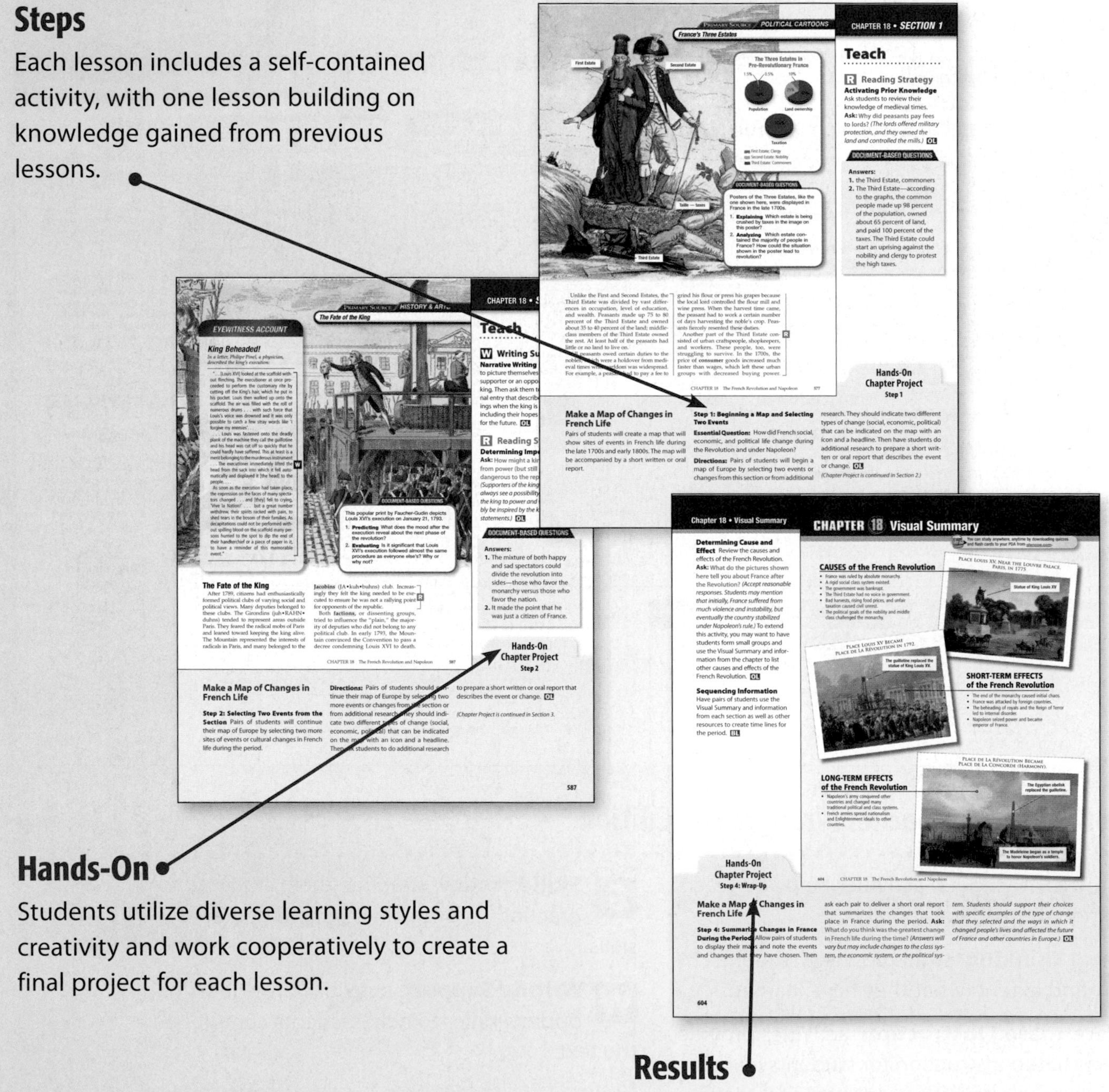

Hands-On

Students utilize diverse learning styles and creativity and work cooperatively to create a final project for each lesson.

Results

The Hands-On project culminates in a summary activity that ties the other activities in the chapter together.

Differentiated Instruction

Each section of the Teacher Wraparound Edition of *Glencoe World History* provides differentiated instruction activities to meet the diverse needs of every student.

Differentiated Instruction

Innovative ideas meet each student's interests and learning styles through point-of-use activities.

Additional Resources

Provides suggestions for incorporating additional resources based on students' different learning abilities

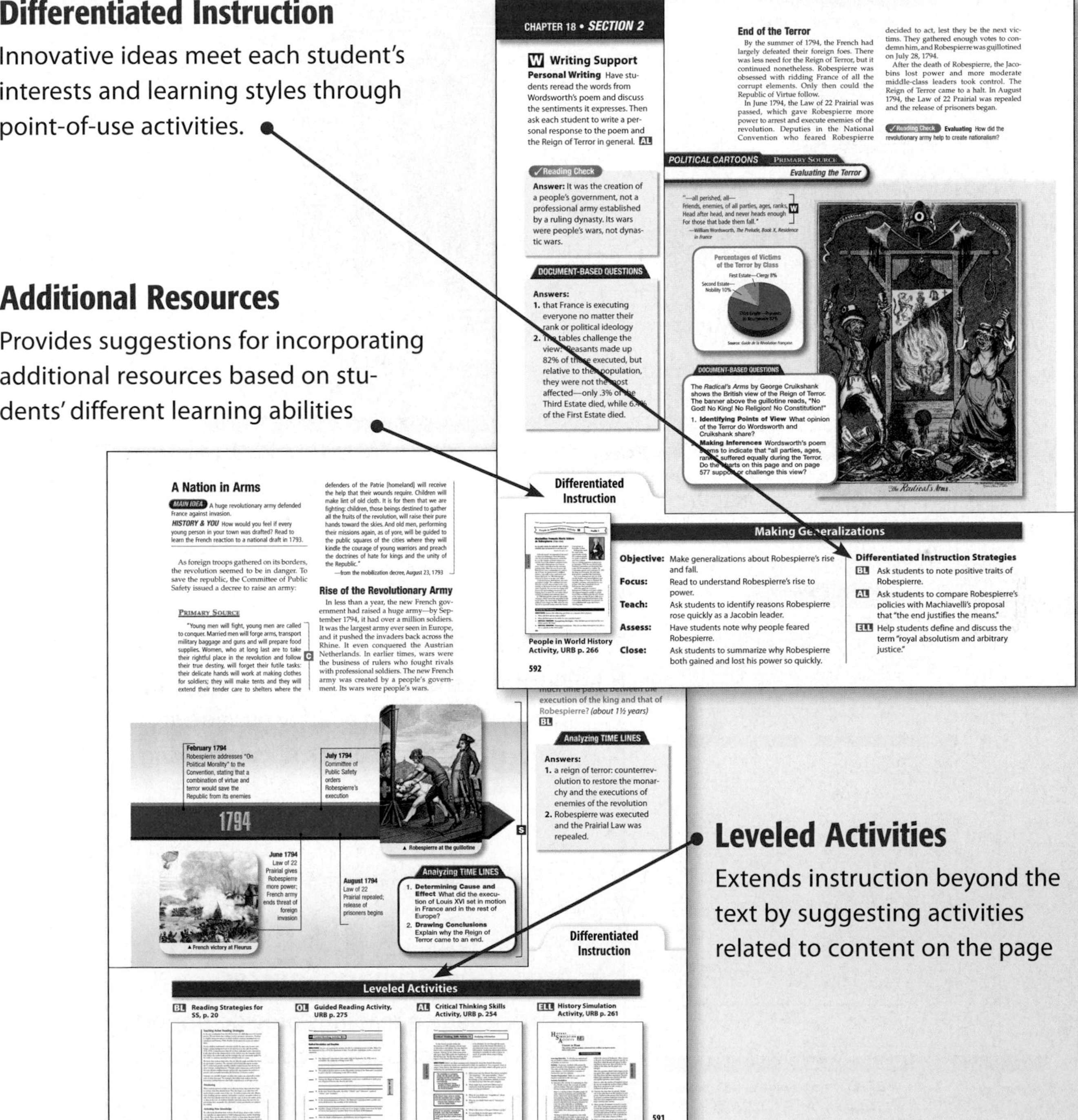

Leveled Activities

Extends instruction beyond the text by suggesting activities related to content on the page

Dynamic Features

Use the creative features in the textbook to dig deep into the fascinating issues and people covered in the text.

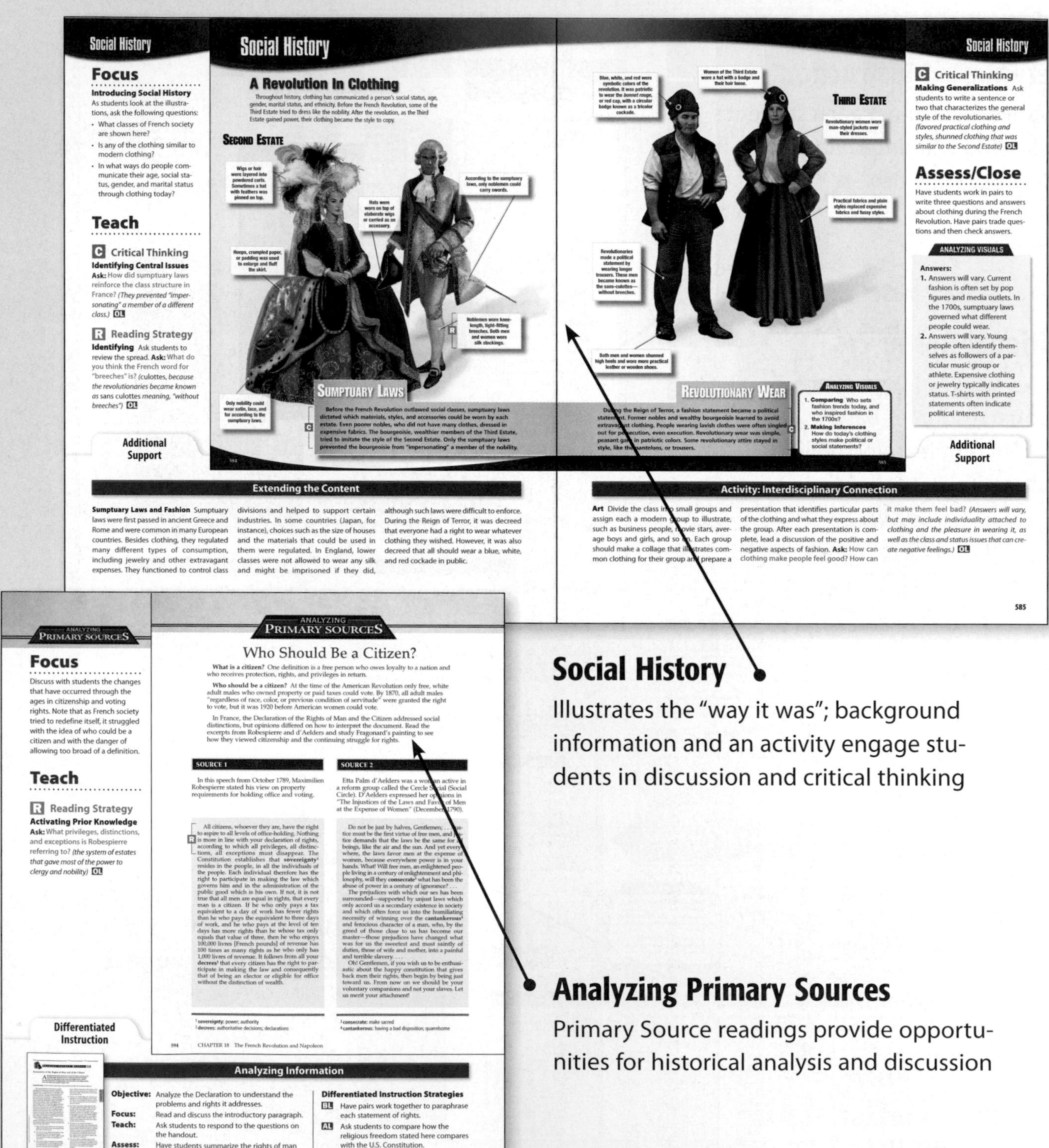

Social History

Illustrates the "way it was"; background information and an activity engage students in discussion and critical thinking

Analyzing Primary Sources

Primary Source readings provide opportunities for historical analysis and discussion

Chapter Summary and Assessment

Visual Summary

Summary activities help students to synthesize major chapter themes.

Standardized Test Practice

Answers incorporate analysis and identify potential student pitfalls, challenges, distracters, and test-taking strategies.

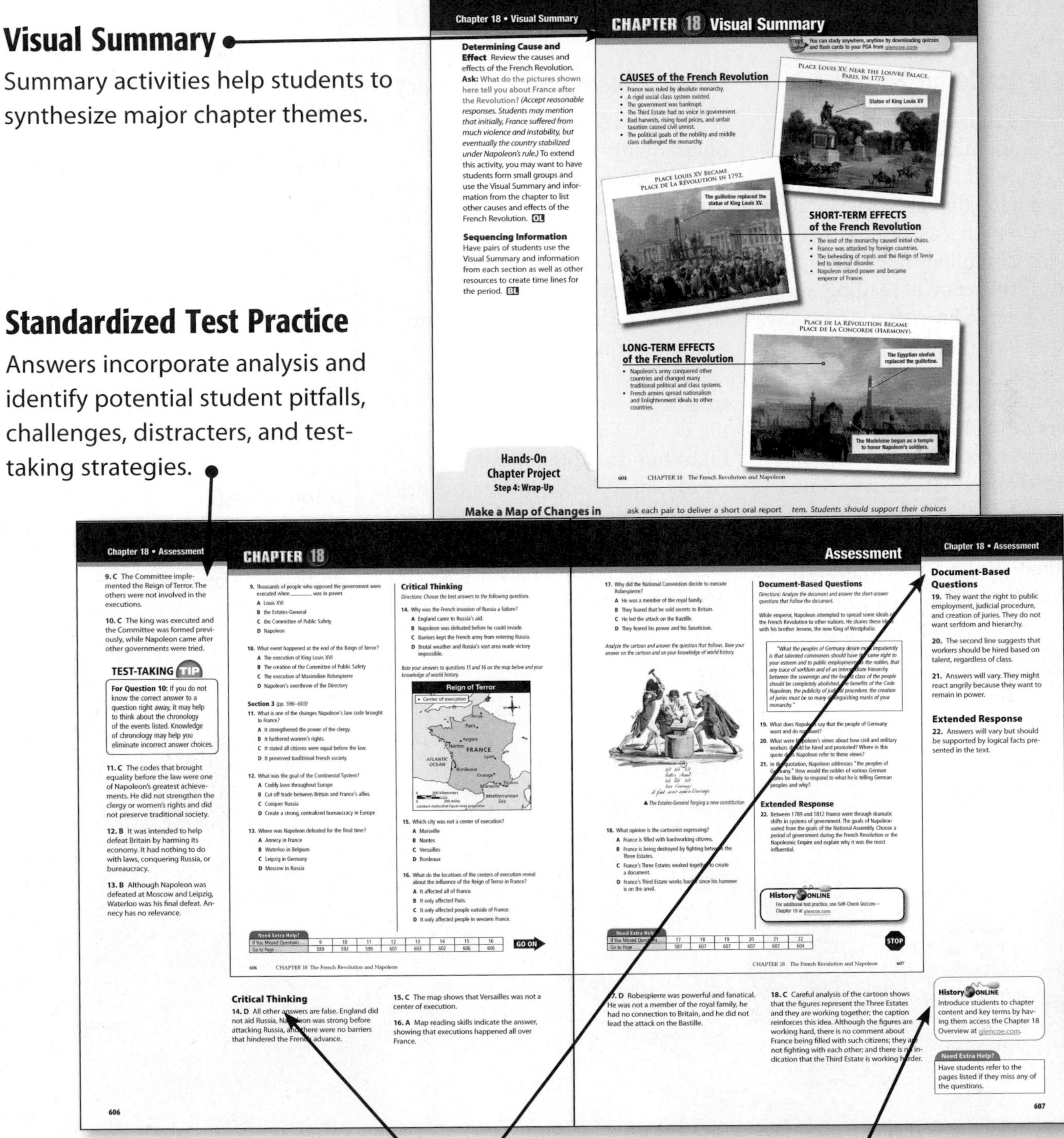

Chapter 18 • Visual Summary

Determining Cause and Effect Review the causes and effects of the French Revolution. **Ask:** What do the pictures shown here tell you about France after the Revolution? *(Accept reasonable responses. Students may mention that initially, France suffered from much violence and instability, but eventually the country stabilized under Napoleon's rule.)* To extend this activity, you may want to have students form small groups and use the Visual Summary and information from the chapter to list other causes and effects of the French Revolution. OL

Sequencing Information Have pairs of students use the Visual Summary and information from each section as well as other resources to create time lines for the period. BL

CHAPTER 18 Visual Summary

CAUSES of the French Revolution
- France was ruled by absolute monarchy.
- A rigid social class system existed.
- The government was bankrupt.
- The Third Estate had no voice in government.
- Bad harvests, rising food prices, and unfair taxation caused civil unrest.
- The political goals of the nobility and middle class challenged the monarchy.

Place Louis XV near the Louvre Palace, Paris, in 1775

Statue of King Louis XV

Place Louis XV became Place de la Révolution in 1792.

The guillotine replaced the statue of King Louis XV.

SHORT-TERM EFFECTS of the French Revolution
- The end of the monarchy caused initial chaos.
- France was attacked by foreign countries.
- The beheading of royals and the Reign of Terror led to internal disorder.
- Napoleon seized power and became emperor of France.

Place de la Révolution became Place de la Concorde (Harmony).

LONG-TERM EFFECTS of the French Revolution
- Napoleon's army conquered other countries and changed many traditional political and class systems.
- French armies spread nationalism and Enlightenment ideals to other countries.

The Egyptian obelisk replaced the guillotine.

The Madeleine began as a temple to honor Napoleon's soldiers.

604 CHAPTER 18 The French Revolution and Napoleon

Hands-On Chapter Project Step 4: Wrap-Up

Make a Map of Changes in

Chapter 18 • Assessment

9. C The Committee implemented the Reign of Terror. The others were not involved in the executions.

10. C The king was executed and the Committee was formed previously, while Napoleon came after other governments were tried.

TEST-TAKING TIP

For Question 10: If you do not know the correct answer to a question right away, it may help to think about the chronology of the events listed. Knowledge of chronology may help you eliminate incorrect answer choices.

11. C The codes that brought equality before the law were one of Napoleon's greatest achievements. He did not strengthen the clergy or women's rights and did not preserve traditional society.

12. B It was intended to help defeat Britain by harming its economy. It had nothing to do with laws, conquering Russia, or bureaucracy.

13. B Although Napoleon was defeated at Moscow and Leipzig, Waterloo was his final defeat. Annecy has no relevance.

CHAPTER 18 Assessment

Critical Thinking

Reign of Terror

Document-Based Questions

Extended Response

606 CHAPTER 18 The French Revolution and Napoleon

CHAPTER 18 The French Revolution and Napoleon 607

Critical Thinking

14. D All other answers are false. England did not aid Russia, Napoleon was strong before attacking Russia, and there were no barriers that hindered the French advance.

15. C The map shows that Versailles was not a center of execution.

16. A Map reading skills indicate the answer, showing that executions happened all over France.

17. D Robespierre was powerful and fanatical. He was not a member of the royal family, he had no connection to Britain, and he did not lead the attack on the Bastille.

18. C Careful analysis of the cartoon shows that the figures represent the Three Estates and they are working together; the caption reinforces this idea. Although the figures are working hard, there is no comment about France being filled with such citizens; they are not fighting with each other; and there is no indication that the Third Estate is working harder.

Chapter 18 • Assessment

Document-Based Questions

19. They want the right to public employment, judicial procedure, and creation of juries. They do not want serfdom and hierarchy.

20. The second line suggests that workers should be hired based on talent, regardless of class.

21. Answers will vary. They might react angrily because they want to remain in power.

Extended Response

22. Answers will vary but should be supported by logical facts presented in the text.

History ONLINE

Introduce students to chapter content and key terms by having them access the Chapter 18 Overview at glencoe.com.

Need Extra Help?

Have students refer to the pages listed if they miss any of the questions.

606

607

Critical Thinking and Document-Based Questions

Extends answers and analysis through document and graphic assessment

History Online

Provides additional assessment opportunities.

Classroom Solutions

Academic Vocabulary

How Can I Help My Students Learn Academic Vocabulary?

What Is Academic English?

Academic English is the language used in academics, business, and courts of law. It is the type of English used in textbooks, and contains linguistic features associated with academic disciplines like social studies. Proficiency in reading and using academic English is especially related to long-term success in all parts of life.

By reinforcing academic English, teachers can help learners to access authentic, academic texts—not simplified texts that dummy down the content. In this way, they can provide information that will help build their students' background knowledge rapidly.

What Is Academic Vocabulary?

Academic vocabulary is based on academic English. By the time children have completed elementary school, they must have acquired the knowledge needed to understand academic vocabulary. How many words should they acquire to be able to access their textbooks? A basic 2,000-word vocabulary of high-frequency words makes up 87% of the vocabulary of academic texts. Eight hundred other academic words comprise an additional 8% of the words. Three percent of the remaining words are technical words. The remaining 2% are low-frequency words. There may be as many as 123,000 low-frequency words in academic texts.

Why Should Students Learn Academic Vocabulary?

English learners who have a basic 2,000-word vocabulary are ready to acquire most general words found in their texts.

Knowledge of academic words and general words can significantly boost a student's comprehension level of academic texts. Students who learn and practice these words before they graduate from high school are likely to master academic material with more confidence and speed. They waste less time and effort in guessing words or

consulting dictionaries than those who only know the basic 2,000 words that characterize general conversation.

How Do I Include Academic Vocabulary and Academic English in My Teaching?

Teachers can provide students with academic vocabulary and help students understand the academic English of their text.

To develop academic English, learners must have already acquired basic proficiency in the grammar of everyday English.

Academic English should be taught within contexts that make sense. In terms of instruction, teaching academic English includes providing students with access to core curriculum—in this case social studies.

Academic English arises in part from social practices in which academic English is used. The acquisition of academic vocabulary and grammar is necessary to advance the development of academic English.

Tips for Teaching Academic Vocabulary:

✔ **Expose Students to Academic Vocabulary** You do not need to call attention to words students are learning because they will acquire them subconsciously.

✔ **Do Not Correct Students' Mistakes When Using the Vocabulary Words** All vocabulary understanding and spelling errors will disappear once the student reads more.

✔ **Help Students Decode the Words Themselves** Once they learn the alphabet, they should be able to decode words. Decoding each word they don't recognize will help them more than trying to focus on sentence structure. Once they can recognize the words, they can read "authentic" texts.

✔ **Do Not Ignore the English Learner in This Process** They can learn academic vocabulary before they are completely fluent in oral English.

✔ **Helping Students Build Academic Vocabulary Leads to Broader Learning** Students who have mastered the basic academic vocabulary are ready to continue acquiring words from the rest of the groups. To help determine which words are in the 2,000-word basic group, refer to *West's General Service List of English Words*, 1953. The list is designed to serve as a guide for teachers and as a checklist and goal list for students. For additional information about the list, visit: http://www.vuw.ac.nz/lals/research/awl.

Guidelines for Teaching Academic Vocabulary

1. Direct and planned instruction	4. Practice
2. Models—that have increasingly difficult language	5. Motivation
3. Attention to form—pointing out linguistic features of words	6. Instructional feedback
	7. Assessment—on a regular basis

Classroom Activity

Writing About Modern America

Give students a brief writing assignment. Ask them to write a short essay about one of the topics listed below in the left column. Have students use as many of the academic vocabulary words in the right column as they can in their essay. When completed, ask student volunteers to share their writing. Note what academic vocabulary words they use.

Topic	Academic Vocabulary
The challenges of reducing poverty in America	sufficient
	minimum
	medical
	income
Recent technological advances	innovate
	technology
	media
	potential
	data
	transmit

Classroom Solutions

Meeting the Diverse Needs of Our Students

by Douglas Fisher, Ph.D.

Today's classroom contains students from a variety of backgrounds with a variety of learning styles, strengths, and challenges. As teachers we are facing the challenge of helping students reach their educational potential. With careful planning, you can address the needs of all students in the social studies classroom. The basis for this planning is universal access. When classrooms are planned with universal access in mind, fewer students require specific accommodations.

What Is a Universal Access Design for Learning?

Universal design was first conceived in architectural studies when businesspeople, engineers, and architects began making considerations for physical access to buildings. The idea was to plan the environment in advance to ensure that everyone had access. As a result, the environment would not have to be changed later for people with physical disabilities, people pushing strollers, workers who had injuries, or others for whom the environment would be difficult to negotiate. The Center for Universal Design at www.design.ncsu.edu/cud defines Universal Design as:

The design of products and environments to be usable by all people, to the greatest extent possible, without the need for adaptation or specialized design.

Universal Design and Access in Education

Researchers, teachers, and parents in education have expanded the development of built-in adaptations and inclusive accommodations from architectural space to the educational experience, especially in the area of curriculum.

In 1998, the National Center to Improve the Tools of Educators (NCITE), with the partnership of the Center for Applied Special Technology (CAST), proposed an expanded definition of universal design focused on education:

In terms of learning, universal design means the design of instructional materials and activities that allows the learning goals to be achievable by individuals with wide differences in their abilities to see, hear, speak, move, read, write, understand English, attend, organize, engage, and remember.

How Does Universal Design Work in Education?

Universal design and access, as they apply to education and schooling, suggest the following:

✔ **Inclusive Classroom Participation** Curriculum should be designed with all students and their needs in mind. The Glencoe/McGraw-Hill social studies texts and materials were designed with a wide range of students in mind. For example, understanding that English learners and students who struggle with reading would be using this textbook, vocabulary is specifically taught and reinforced. Similarly, the teacher-support materials provide multiple instructional points to be used depending on the needs of the students in the class. Further, the text is written such that main ideas are identified for all learners. Activating prior knowledge is also taken into consideration by the text. Connections between what students know and think about are made within the text.

- ✔ **Maximum Text Readability** In universally designed classrooms that provide access for all students, texts use direct language, clear noun-verb agreements, and clear construct-based wording. In addition to these factors, the Glencoe Social Studies text uses embedded definitions for difficult terms, provides for specific instruction in reading skills, uses a number of visual representations, and includes note-taking guides.
- ✔ **Adaptable and Accommodating** The content in this textbook can be easily translated, read aloud, or otherwise changed to meet the needs of students in the classroom. The section and end-of-chapter assessments provide students with multiple ways of demonstrating their content knowledge while also ensuring that they have practice with thinking in terms of multiple-choice questions. Critical thinking and analysis skills are also practiced.

How Is Differentiated Instruction the Key to Universal Access?

To differentiate instruction, teachers must acknowledge student differences in background knowledge and current reading, writing, and English language skills. They must also consider student learning styles and preferences, interests, and needs, and react accordingly. There are a number of general guidelines for differentiating instruction in the classroom to reach all students, including:

- ✔ **Link Assessment With Instruction** Assessments should occur before, during, and after instruction to ensure that the curriculum is aligned with what students do and do not know. Using assessments in this way allows you to plan instruction for whole groups, small groups, and individual students. Backward planning, where you establish the assessment before you begin instruction, is also important.
- ✔ **Clarify Key Concepts and Generalizations** Students need to know what is essential and how this information can be used in their future learning. In addition, students need to develop a sense of the **Big Ideas**—ideas that transcend time and place.
- ✔ **Emphasize Critical and Creative Thinking** The content, process, and products used or assigned in the classroom should require that students think about what they are learning. While some students may require support, additional motivation, varied tasks, materials, or equipment, the overall focus on critical and creative thinking allows for all students to participate in the lesson.
- ✔ **Include Teacher- and Student-Selected Tasks** A differentiated classroom includes both teacher- and student-selected activities and tasks. At some points in the lesson or day, the teacher must provide instruction and assign learning activities. In other parts of the lesson, students should be provided choices in how they engage with the content. This balance increases motivation, engagement, and learning.

How Do I Support Individual Students?

The vast majority of students will thrive in a classroom based on universal access and differentiated instruction. However, wise teachers recognize that no single option will work for all students and that there may be students who require unique systems of support to be successful.

Classroom Activity

Display a map of imperialism in Africa around 1914. Discuss with students the map's general information and have them list each country under the European power that controlled it.

To differentiate this activity:

- Have students imagine they are living in the early 1900s. Have them write a letter to a British newspaper about colonial rule in Africa.
- Have students record the number of African countries under European rule. Have them take the data and create a bar graph that shows which European powers were the most active colonizers at the time.
- Have students compose a song or poem about European rule in Africa, from an African's point of view.
- Have students chose a country of modern Africa to research. Have them write a three-page paper discussing how that country was affected by colonialism and how it has changed since the days of European rule.

Tips For Instruction

The following tips for instruction can support your efforts to help all students reach their maximum potential.

- ✔ Survey students to discover their individual differences. Use interest inventories of their unique talents so you can encourage contributions in the classroom.
- ✔ Be a model for respecting others. Adolescents crave social acceptance. The student with learning differences is especially sensitive to correction and criticism, particularly when it comes from a teacher. Your behavior will set the tone for how students treat one another.
- ✔ Expand opportunities for success. Provide a variety of instructional activities that reinforce skills and concepts.
- ✔ Establish measurable objectives and decide how you can best help students meet them.
- ✔ Celebrate successes and make note of and praise "work in progress."
- ✔ Keep it simple. Point out problem areas if doing so can help a student effect change. Avoid overwhelming students with too many goals at one time.
- ✔ Assign cooperative group projects that challenge all students to contribute to solving a problem or creating a product.

How Do I Reach Students With Learning Disabilities?

- ✔ Provide support and structure. Clearly specify rules, assignments, and responsibilities.
- ✔ Practice skills frequently. Use games and drills to help maintain student interest.
- ✔ Incorporate many modalities into the learning process. Provide opportunities to say, hear, write, read, and act out important concepts and information.
- ✔ Link new skills and concepts to those already mastered.
- ✔ If possible, allow students to record answers on audiotape.
- ✔ Allow extra time to complete assessments and assignments.
- ✔ Let students demonstrate proficiency with alternative presentations, including oral reports, role plays, art projects, and musical presentations.
- ✔ Provide outlines, notes, or tape recordings of lecture material.
- ✔ Pair students with peer helpers, and provide class time for pair interaction.

How Do I Reach Students With Behavioral Challenges?

- ✔ Provide a structured environment with clear-cut schedules, rules, seat assignments, and safety procedures.
- ✔ Reinforce appropriate behavior and model it for students.
- ✔ Cue distracted students back to the task through verbal signals and teacher proximity.
- ✔ Set goals that can be achieved in the short term. Work for long-term improvement in the big areas.

How Do I Reach Students With Physical Challenges?

- ✔ Openly discuss with the student any uncertainties you have about when to offer aid.
- ✔ Ask parents or therapists and students what special devices or procedures are needed and whether any special safety precautions need to be taken.
- ✔ Welcome students with physical challenges into all activities, including field trips, special events, and projects.
- ✔ Provide information to assist class members and adults in their understanding of support needed.

How Do I Reach Students with Visual Impairments?

- ✔ Facilitate independence. Modify assignments as needed.
- ✔ Teach classmates how and when to serve as visual guides.
- ✔ Limit unnecessary noise in the classroom if it distracts the student with visual impairments.
- ✔ Provide tactile models whenever possible.
- ✔ Foster a spirit of inclusion. Describe people and events as they occur in the classroom. Remind classmates that the student with visual impairments cannot interpret gestures and other forms of nonverbal communication.
- ✔ Provide taped lectures and reading assignments for use outside the classroom.
- ✔ Team the student with a sighted peer for written work.

How Do I Reach Students With Hearing Impairments?

- ✔ Seat students where they can see your lip movements easily and where they can avoid any visual distractions.
- ✔ Avoid standing with your back to the window or light source.
- ✔ Use an overhead projector so you can maintain eye contact while writing information for students.
- ✔ Seat students where they can see speakers.
- ✔ Write all assignments on the board, or hand out written instructions.
- ✔ If the student has a manual interpreter, allow both student and interpreter to select the most favorable seating arrangements.
- ✔ Teach students to look directly at each other when they speak.

How Do I Reach English Learners?

- ✔ Remember, students' ability to speak English does not reflect their academic abilities.
- ✔ Try to incorporate the students' cultural experience into your instruction. The help of a bilingual aide may be effective.
- ✔ Avoid any references in your instruction that could be construed as cultural stereotypes.
- ✔ Preteach important vocabulary and concepts.
- ✔ Encourage students to preview text before they begin reading, noting headings.
- ✔ Remind students not to ignore graphic organizers, photographs, and maps since there is much information in these visuals.
- ✔ Use memorabilia and photographs whenever possible to build background knowledge and understanding. An example of this would be coins in a foreign currency or a raw cotton ball to reinforce its importance in history.

How Do I Reach Gifted Students?

- ✔ Make arrangements for students to take selected subjects early and to work on independent projects.
- ✔ Ask "what if" questions to develop high-level thinking skills. Establish an environment safe for risk taking in your classroom.
- ✔ Emphasize concepts, theories, ideas, relationships, and generalizations about the content.
- ✔ Promote interest in the past by inviting students to make connections to the present.
- ✔ Let students express themselves in alternate ways such as creative writing, acting, debates, simulations, drawing, or music.
- ✔ Provide students with a catalog of helpful resources, listing such things as agencies that provide free and inexpensive materials, appropriate community services and programs, and community experts who might be called upon to speak to your students.
- ✔ Assign extension projects that allow students to solve real-life problems related to their communities.

Douglas Fisher is a professor at San Diego State University, San Diego, CA.

Classroom Activity

Students respond eagerly to a subject when they can relate it to their own experiences. With the growing number of students who come from other world regions, explaining geography through a global theme (such as volcanoes) can give them a worldwide as well as a regional perspective. To develop this awareness, display a large world map. Have students use the library or the Internet to research the latitude and longitude of 15 major volcanoes around the world. Ask them to mark these locations on the map and answer the following questions:

- What patterns do you see in volcanic activity?
- What causes volcanic activity?
- Where in the world are volcanoes most active?

As a follow-up, suggest students go to http://volcano.und.nodak.edu/vwdocs/kids/legends.html to find legends about the origins of some of the world's volcanoes. Encourage students to share what they find with the class.

Teaching Maps, Graphs, and Charts

How Can I Use Visuals to Improve Students' Reading Comprehension?

Maps, graphs, and charts are visual tools. By using images rather than words, these tools present complex information in an easy-to-understand format. Teach students the following generalized viewing strategies, and encourage them to apply these strategies as they study each chapter.

- ✔ **Asking Questions** Students should start by looking over the graphic and asking themselves questions, such as "What is my purpose for looking at this image?" Then students can identify questions they hope to answer, such as "What is being compared?" or "What are the most important features?"
- ✔ **Finding Answers** Next, students should use the graphic's features, such as the title, labels, colors, and symbols, to help them find answers to their questions. If the source of the graphic is available, students should also determine its reliability.
- ✔ **Drawing Conclusions** After studying the visual, students should summarize its main points and draw conclusions.
- ✔ **Connecting** Students also should relate what they learned from the visual with what they gained from reading the text selection. Students can examine how the visual supports or extends the meaning of the text.

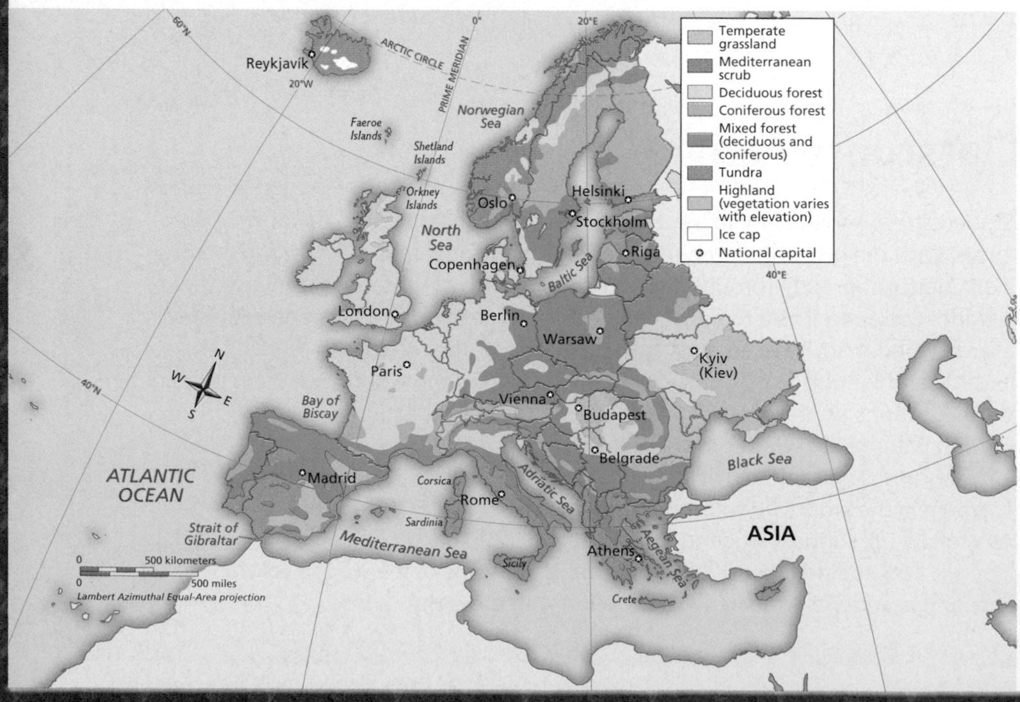

Maps

Maps show the relative size and location of specific geographic areas. Two of the most common general purpose maps are political maps and physical maps.

Parts of Maps

All maps contain parts that assist in interpreting the information. Help students learn to identify the following map parts.

- ✔ **Title** The map title identifies the area shown on the visual. The title can also identify a map's special focus.
- ✔ **Map Key** The map key, or legend, explains the symbols presented on the map, thus unlocking the map's information.
- ✔ **Compass Rose** A compass rose is a direction marker. It is a symbol that points out where the cardinal directions—north, south, east, and west—are positioned.
- ✔ **Scale** A measuring line, often called a scale bar, indicates the relationship between the distances on the map and the actual distances on Earth.
- ✔ **Latitude and Longitude** Mapmakers use lines of latitude and longitude to pinpoint exact locations on maps and globes. The imaginary horizontal lines that circle the globe from east to west are lines of latitude, also called parallels. The imaginary vertical lines are lines of longitude, also called meridians. Both parallels and meridians are measured in degrees.

Graphs

Graphs are a way of showing numbers or statistics in a clear, easy-to-read way. Because graphs summarize and present information visually, readers have an easier time understanding the data and drawing conclusions. The most common types of graphs are bar graphs, line graphs, circle graphs, and pictographs.

- ✔ **Bar Graphs** A bar graph shows how two or more subjects or statistics compare. It provides information along two sides or axes. The horizontal axis is the line across the bottom of the graph. The vertical axis is the line along the side. The bars may be either vertical or horizontal. In most cases the labels on one axis show quantity, while the labels on the opposite axis show the categories of data being compared.
- ✔ **Line Graphs** A line graph shows change over time. Like a bar graph, it organizes information along the horizontal and vertical axes. The horizontal axis usually shows passing time, such as months, years, or decades. The vertical axis usually shows quantity or amount. Sometimes more than one set of data is shown in a line graph. A double-line graph, for instance, plots data for two related quantities, which may be represented in different colors or patterns.
- ✔ **Circle Graphs** A circle graph, also called a pie graph, shows how each part or percentage relates to the whole. A circle graph enables a viewer to make comparisons between parts and to analyze the relationship of each part to the whole.
- ✔ **Pictograph** A pictograph uses rows of small symbols or pictures, each representing a particular amount. Like a bar graph, a pictograph is useful for making comparisons.

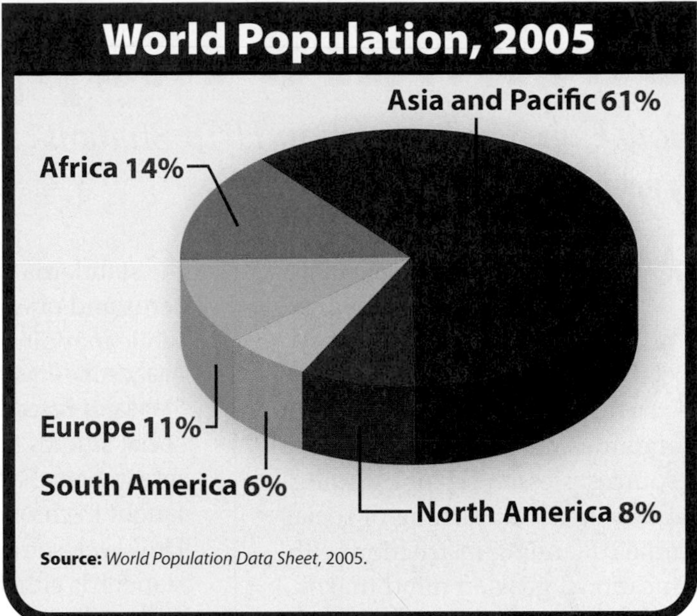

Source: *World Population Data Sheet*, 2005.

Charts

While all charts present information or data in a visual way, the type of chart is often dictated by the nature of the information and by the chart-maker's purposes.

- ✔ **Tables** Tables show information, including numerical data, in columns and rows. This organized arrangement facilitates comparisons between categories of information. Labels are usually located at the top of each column and on the left-hand side of the table.
- ✔ **Diagrams** Diagrams are specialized drawings. They can show steps in a process; point out parts of an object, organization, or idea; or explain how something works. Arrows or lines may join parts of a figure and can show relationships between parts or the flow of steps.

Classroom Activity

Create a Graph

Graphs can be difficult to interpret and understand. Help students by having them create their own graphs. First, separate students into small groups. Then have each group take a survey of classmates and make a graph to show their results. Suggest that students select a bar graph, line graph, circle graph, or pictograph to show their data. To prompt students' thinking, ask the following questions.

- *Do you play on a sports team? Which sport(s)?*
- *What do you plan to do after high school?*
- *About how much time do you spend watching TV each day? About how much time did you spend on TV when you were 10 years old? When you were five years old?*

After students have these graphs completed, invite each group to share its work. Discuss the types of graphs students made and their reasons for choosing them. Each group should then take the graph done by another group and transfer the information to another type of graph.

Backward Mapping

How Can My Instruction Help Students Succeed in a Standards-Based System?

by Emily M. Schell, Ed.D.

Content standards articulate what students should know and be able to do in every social studies classroom. Effective instructional planning based in the standards and maximizing available resources is essential for meaningful teaching and learning of social studies. Planning instruction with educational goals in mind makes for the most effective teaching.

How Do I Map My Curriculum?

Mapping the curriculum from beginning to end, and from the end to the beginning—backward mapping—makes for solid instruction. Mapping out the curriculum allows teachers to achieve several goals. These goals include a better understanding of the standards and content-specific objectives, organization and pacing of the curriculum, and focused assessment related to specific goals and objectives.

- ✔ **Begin the Process of Curriculum Mapping** To begin, teachers analyze the body of content standards for one grade level. They then compare and contrast these standards to additional sources of information that support effective teaching and learning at that grade level and in that subject area. This process works best with same-grade colleagues who bring varying perspectives and expertise to teaching this subject. As a result of this collaboration, strengths and weaknesses of the standards become apparent. Teachers will have a better understanding of the standards and identify concerns and questions for follow-up while mapping.
- ✔ **Analyze the Organization of the Standards-Based Content** Most social studies teachers agree with researchers that history is best taught in chronological order. However, some grade-level standards either do not or cannot present the content in chronological order. Rich discussions about themes and concepts tend to emerge, and teachers identify meaningful methods for presenting complex and overlapping information. In this way students will see the connections that transcend chronology.
- ✔ **Identify the Content and Order of Teaching** A plan is developed to present certain content first, then second, then third and so on. Folding in content that is either missing from the standards or essential in building background knowledge with students enters the curriculum map as well. Outside resources brought into the classroom are good supplements.
- ✔ **Separate Overlapping Units** Identify areas of instruction for the topics, themes, big ideas, or concepts. It is at this stage that backward planning is introduced for the development of instructional units, which will support the grade-level curriculum map. The instruction must support the planned assessment.
- ✔ **Map Curriculum at Each Grade Level** Curriculum planning should be shared among grade levels. Teachers will have a better understanding of what knowledge and skills students bring to their coursework if they take into consideration what has been learned previously.

How Do I Use Backward Mapping?

After a year-long course of study is mapped out, each unit must be further developed through backward mapping. You will start with the end in mind—knowing your curricular goals and objectives at the outset, which are often found in the content standards and articulated in the curriculum maps.

Once goals have been determined, teachers develop assessments that will show progress toward those goals and objectives. In the final step of this backward mapping process, teachers determine meaningful teaching and learning strategies and identify useful resources that support the assessment.

To use backward mapping in developing your units of instruction, consider the following steps:

Step One: Know Your Targets

First, identify exactly what students must know and do in this unit. Analyze content standards and any other resources that support curricular goals and objectives for this unit. As you plan, ask yourself:

- ✔ What do I want my students to know as a result of this unit?
- ✔ What skills will students develop during the course of this unit?
- ✔ How do I describe these goals clearly and concisely to my students so they understand where we should be at the end of this unit?
- ✔ What essential knowledge will students need to access to make sense of this information?
- ✔ Do my instructional goals align with strategies identified in the curriculum map?
- ✔ Have I introduced any Big Ideas that are pertinent to this content?

Step Two: Identify and Develop Assessments

- ✔ Second, consider the multiple forms of formal and informal assessments that will help you determine to what degree each student has achieved the stated goals and objectives seen in Step One. Some assessments are embedded throughout the instructional unit, while others come at the end of the unit. Some assessments are performance-based, while others are not. Some are authentic applications of information and skills, while others require the formal recall of information. Ask yourself:
- ✔ What do I want to know and see from each student?
- ✔ What are the best methods for students to demonstrate what they know and can do based on the goals and objectives?
- ✔ How many assessments do I need to determine what students know and can do?
- ✔ How will I balance informal and formal assessments?
- ✔ How will I assess students with diverse learning styles, skills, and abilities?
- ✔ How can I prepare and support students?
- ✔ How will these assessments promote student progress in social studies?
- ✔ At what time(s) during the unit will I administer these assessments?

Step Three: Develop Meaningful Instruction

After the assessments for the unit have been determined, consider the meaningful and effective teaching strategies that will support learning and student achievement on assessments. While developing lesson plans for instruction, ask yourself:

- ✔ How will students learn what they are expected to know?
- ✔ How will I engage students in the studies of this unit?
- ✔ In what ways might students relate or connect to this information?
- ✔ Which research-based strategies will be most effective with my students and in these studies?
- ✔ How will I differentiate my instruction to meet the diverse needs of my students?
- ✔ How will I scaffold or provide access to the curriculum for my English learners?
- ✔ What vocabulary requires attention in this unit?
- ✔ How much time will I have to effectively teach this unit?
- ✔ How will I use the textbook and other resources to support the goals and objectives for this unit?
- ✔ What lessons will I develop?
- ✔ In what sequence will I teach these lessons during this unit?
- ✔ How will these lessons support the assessments from Step Two?

Step Four: Locate and Manage Resources

Effective teaching and learning of social studies requires the use of multiple forms of text and varied resources. Consider what you have available in your classroom, including your textbook, and identify resources you will add in order to teach this unit successfully. Ask yourself:

- ✔ What parts of the textbook are required for the lessons determined in Step Three?
- ✔ What ancillary materials are needed for the lessons in this unit?
- ✔ What Web sites will I recommend to students to support these lessons?
- ✔ Do I need to contact guest speakers or obtain outside resources?
- ✔ What literature resources are available to support this unit?

Emily Schell is Visiting Professor, San Diego State University, and Social Studies Education Director, SDSU City Heights Educational Collaborative, San Diego, CA.

Primary Source Strategies

How Do I Use Primary Sources in My Classroom?

A primary source is an oral or written account obtained from actual participants in an event. Examples of primary sources include the following:

- ✔ official documents (records, statistics)
- ✔ political declarations, laws, and rules for governance
- ✔ speeches and interviews
- ✔ diaries, memoirs, and oral histories
- ✔ autobiographies
- ✔ recipes and cookbooks
- ✔ advertisements and posters
- ✔ letters
- ✔ Physical objects, such as tools, dishes, fine art, photographs, maps, films, and videotapes
- ✔ songs and audio recordings

Why Use Primary Sources in Your Classroom?

Using primary sources transforms the study of social studies from a passive process to an active one. Students become investigators—finding clues, formulating hypotheses and drawing inferences, making judgments, and reaching conclusions. Using primary sources, students can think critically about events, issues, and concepts rather than just memorizing dates, names, and generalizations. Thinking critically then becomes a habit that can help students become good citizens.

How Do I Introduce Students to Primary Sources?

Carefully explain the nature of primary sources to students. Alert students to the fact that primary sources contain biases and prejudices and must be approached with caution. Every primary source reflects the creator's point of view. Students must consider the authorship and why the primary source was written.

Choosing Primary Sources

Expose students to a variety of sources, including historic photographs, folk or popular music, financial records as well as letters, journals, and historic documents.

When choosing print sources, consider the interests and reading levels of your students. Many texts contain challenging vocabulary and unfamiliar sentence structure. You may need to create a reader's guide that defines key vocabulary and paraphrases the main points of the reading.

Some documents may be too long. Decide whether using an excerpt will provide enough information for students to draw conclusions. You also may need to provide different primary sources to expose students to a variety of perspectives.

Decide how students will access the primary sources: through the Internet, the library, a museum, or other print resources. Consider the possibility of an Internet virtual field trip for students. Students can visit museum sites and other Web pages to view artifacts, interpret data, and read journals, letters, and official documents.

Interpreting a Primary Source

Before students interpret a primary source, they need to know the source's context. Then they can use guidelines, such as those below, to help them analyze and interpret the primary source.

Interpreting a Primary Source

Print Sources

- Who created the source, and what was the purpose for doing so?
- Did the writer personally experience or witness the event(s)?
- Who was the intended audience?
- Was the writer trying to record facts, express an opinion, or persuade others to take action?
- What bias does it reflect?
- What information about the topic can you gather from this document?
- Compare this document with what you know about the topic. Does it confirm those ideas or introduce a new perspective?
- How might other accounts about this topic support or modify the message this source delivers?

Visual Sources

- Who created the source, and what was the purpose for doing so?
- What does the image show?
- Who or what dominates the image or catches your eye?
- How does the view impact the message?
- What is excluded from view?
- What bias does the visual reflect?
- What information about the topic can you gather from this visual?
- How might other visuals about this topic support or modify the message this one delivers?

Audio Sources

- Who created the source? What was the purpose for creating this source?
- What is the main idea of the audio?
- What bias does the audio text reflect?
- What information about the topic can you gather from this audio source?
- Compare the information in this source with what you already know about the topic. Does it confirm those ideas or introduce a new perspective?
- How might other sources about this topic support or modify the message that this one delivers?

Exploring Information

Provide a variety of primary sources related to a topic or time period. Have students compare and contrast the items, analyzing the information, making inferences, and drawing conclusions about the period.

Evaluation Activities

Have students evaluate a primary source and tell how it supports or refutes what they learned in the textbook, or have students read a primary source document that provides one perspective on a topic and have students write their own account, presenting another perspective or opinion.

Prereading Activities

Present a primary source for students to study at the beginning of a new chapter or topic. Have students analyze the source, using the questions and guidelines presented above. Then have students make predictions about what they might learn in the upcoming lessons.

Classroom Activity

Use this activity to explore the use of primary sources. This activity is especially beneficial when a less-proficient reader is paired with a more-proficient reader.

1. Before class make a list of student reading partners. Make sure one of the two is a good reader.
2. Have students read a primary source document, taking turns as they go. They should "mark" any words that they do not understand.
3. After each paragraph, the student pair should stop and restate what it says in their own words.
4. Students should look up unfamiliar words they've marked and create an illustrated dictionary entry for each term.
5. Ask student pairs to present their paraphrased primary source to the rest of the class.

Test-Taking Strategies

How Can I Help My Students Succeed on Tests?

It's not enough for students to learn social studies facts and concepts—they must be able to show what they know in a variety of test-taking situations.

How Can I Help My Students Do Well on Objective Tests?

Objective tests may include multiple choice, true/false, and matching questions. Applying the following strategies can help students do their best on objective tests.

How Can I Help My Students Do Well on Essay Tests?

Essay tests require students to provide well-organized written responses, in addition to telling what they know. Help students use the following strategies on essay tests.

- ✔ **Analyze** To analyze means to systematically and critically examine all parts of an issue or event.
- ✔ **Classify or Categorize** To classify or categorize means to put people, things, or ideas into groups, based on a common set of characteristics.
- ✔ **Compare and Contrast** To compare is to show how things are similar, or alike. To contrast is to show how things are different.
- ✔ **Describe** To describe means to present a sketch or impression. Rich details, especially details that appeal to the senses, flesh out a description.
- ✔ **Discuss** To discuss means to systematically write about all sides of an issue or event.
- ✔ **Evaluate** To evaluate means to make a judgment and support it with evidence.
- ✔ **Explain** To explain means to clarify or make plain.
- ✔ **Illustrate** To illustrate means to provide examples or to show with a picture or other graphic.
- ✔ **Infer** To infer means to read between the lines or to use knowledge and experience to draw conclusions.
- ✔ **Justify** To justify means to prove or to support a position with specific facts and reasons.
- ✔ **Predict** To predict means to tell what will happen in the future, based on an understanding of prior events and behaviors.
- ✔ **State** To state means to briefly and concisely present information.
- ✔ **Summarize** To summarize means to give a brief overview of the main points of an issue or event.
- ✔ **Trace** To trace means to present the steps in sequential order.

Objective Texts

Multiple-Choice Questions

- Students should read the directions carefully to learn what answer the test requires—the best answer or the right answer. This is especially important when answer choices include "all of the above" or "none of the above."
- Advise students to watch for negative words in the questions, such as not, except, unless, never, and so forth. If the question contains a negative, the correct answer choice is the one that does not fit.
- Students should try to mentally answer the question before reading the answer choices.
- Students should read all the answer choices and cross out those that are obviously wrong. Then they should choose an answer from those that remain.

True/False Questions

- It is important that students read the entire question before answering. For an answer to be true, the entire statement must be true. If one part of a statement is false, the answer should be marked False.
- Remind students to watch for words like all, never, every, and always. Statements containing these words are often false.

Matching Questions

- Students should read through both lists before they mark any answers.
- Unless an answer can be used more than once, students should cross out each choice as they use it.
- Using what they know about grammar can help students find the right answer. For instance, when matching a word with its definition, the definition is often the same part of speech (noun, verb, adjective, and so forth) as the word.

Read the Question

The key to writing successful essay responses lies in reading and interpreting questions correctly. Teach students to identify and underline key words in the questions, and to use these words to guide them in understanding what the question asks. Help students understand the meaning of some of the most common key words, listed in the chart on the previous page.

Plan and Write the Essay

After students understand the question, they should follow the writing process to develop their answer. Encourage students to follow the steps below to plan and write their essays.

1. **Map out an answer.** Make lists, webs, or an outline to plan the response.
2. **Decide on an order** in which to present the main points.
3. **Write an opening statement** that directly responds to the essay question.
4. **Write the essay.** Expand on the opening statement. Support key points with specific facts, details, and reasons.
5. **Write a closing statement** that brings the main points together.
6. **Proofread** to check for spelling, grammar, and punctuation.

How Can I Help My Students Prepare for Standardized Tests?

Students can follow the steps below to prepare for standardized assessments they are required to take.

- ✔ **Read About the Test** Students can familiarize themselves with the format of the test, the types of questions that will be asked, and the amount of time they will have to complete the test. Emphasize that it is very important for students to budget their time during test-taking.
- ✔ **Review the Content** Consistent study throughout the school year will help students build social studies knowledge and understanding. If there are specific objectives or standards that are tested on the exam, help students review these facts or skills to be sure they are proficient.
- ✔ **Practice** Provide practice, ideally with real released tests, to build students' familiarity with the content, format, and timing of the real exam. Students should practice all the types of questions they will encounter on the test.
- ✔ **Pace** Students should pace themselves differently depending on how the test is administered. If the test is timed, students should not allow themselves to become stuck on any one question. If the test is untimed, students should work slowly and carefully. If students have trouble with an item, they should mark it and come back to it later.
- ✔ **Analyze Practice Results** Help students improve test-taking performance by analyzing their test-taking strengths and weaknesses.

Spend time discussing students' completed practice tests. Help students identify what kinds of questions they had the most difficulty with. Look for patterns in errors and then tailor instruction to review appropriate skills or content.

Classroom Activity

Below is an example of an assessment review activity. Reviewing graded tests is a great way for students to assess their test-taking skills. It also helps teachers teach test-taking strategies and review content. As the class rereads each test question, guide students to think logically about their answer choices. Show students how to:

1. Read each question carefully to determine its meaning.
2. Look for key words in the question to support their answers.
3. Recognize synonyms in the answer choices that may match phrases in the question.
4. Narrow down answer choices by eliminating ones that don't make sense.
5. Anticipate the answer before looking at the answer choices.
6. Circle questions of which they are unsure and go back to them later. Sometimes a clue will be found in another question on the test.

Classroom Solutions

Project CRISS

How Can I Teach My Students How to Learn Social Studies?

by Carol M. Santa, Ph.D.

We all know that teaching social studies involves far more than teaching just course content. We understand that students need to become engaged, confident learners. Achieving that goal means helping them to understand, organize, and retain information.

Teaching Both Content and Skills

In other words, we want our students to have the skills and confidence to be lifelong learners. With its rich content, social studies offers an ideal arena for teaching both content and skills.

- **A Dual Responsibility** Let's take a moment to consider why the dual responsibility of teaching both content and skills is so important. Think back to your own middle and high school years. What do you remember about the content you learned? If I recall my experiences, I find I remember remarkably little content. What did I learn in biology or history? What did my textbooks look like? As the years go by, I don't even remember the names of most of my teachers.
- **An Inspiring Teacher** Yet I have vivid memories of my eighth-grade social studies teacher, who came out of retirement to fill in for a history teacher who left on maternity leave. I remember how fascinated I became with ancient history; I recall giving oral reports and how she helped me become comfortable speaking before a group. In fact, I remember more from her class than any other I took during high school.
- **Teach How to Learn** More important, I now understand that she taught me how to learn to learn. She showed me how to underline, how to organize information using different note-taking formats, and how to write coherent answers on essay tests. She taught me the need to test myself on what I knew. And during that vulnerable, adolescent year, I went from being a mediocre student to being an excellent one.

This inspirational teacher did something else for me. At some point during that eighth-grade year, I decided to become a teacher. Later I realized that she had launched me on my professional mission—to spread her wisdom to others. Eventually this led to Project CRISS.

What Is CRISS?

CRISS stands for CReating Independence through Student-owned Strategies. It is a staff development program that I created in collaboration with middle and high school teachers in Kalispell, Montana.

- **Origin of CRISS** CRISS had its start 20 years ago in a lunchtime conversation in a teachers' lounge. One of the social studies teachers said, "My students aren't doing a good job of answering chapter questions. In fact, I don't think they even read my assignments. My reading assignments are becoming a waste of time!" His words struck a chord. "My students don't have a clue about how to study, and they don't write very well either," another teacher lamented.
- **Evolving Strategies** Supported by a state grant, we started working together to find practical ways to help students read, write, and learn content. We met in teams, read professional literature, and designed studies to test classroom strategies. From these efforts, we evolved a project to help students become better readers, writers, and learners. Once the project took shape, we shared our discoveries with other teachers by offering a two- or three-day CRISS workshop to schools and districts in the state.
- **Constant Growth** Over the last two decades, Project CRISS has spread from teacher to teacher across this country, into Canada, and to several European countries. The project seems to sell itself. Teachers who use CRISS principles and strategies find that their students attain a deeper understanding of course content and become better readers, writers, and learners at the same time. In fact, data from numerous quantitative studies shows that using CRISS strategies improves student learning. (For the most recent data and for information on CRISS workshops, see www.projectcriss.com.)

CRISS Strategies in the Teacher Edition

When the editors of Glencoe/McGraw-Hill asked me and my colleagues to help them integrate CRISS strategies into their social studies texts, we welcomed the opportunity. In this teacher wraparound edition, we offer many references to CRISS strategies. We have packed the pages with strategies that help students gain a deeper understanding of specific content.

CRISS Training

We have one word of caution, however: the integration of CRISS strategies within this teacher wraparound edition does not take the place of a Project CRISS workshop, which provides an in-depth knowledge of CRISS. So, if you haven't yet participated in a CRISS workshop, we encourage you to do so. During a workshop, CRISS trainers take you step-by-step through the philosophy and instructional strategies. Participants are actively involved in all aspects of the program—practicing, adapting, and applying strategies to meet teaching needs.

Long-lasting change occurs when teachers and administrators work together to share, extend ideas, and problem solve. The most effective implementations occur when the initial workshop is supported by follow-up sessions, including a specific follow-up day. At this session, teachers bring examples of strategies they have used since the initial training. Part of this time may be spent in review and in learning new strategies. The rest of the time is for sharing applications. Additional ongoing support can occur in teacher planning periods.

In any case, for those of you unfamiliar with Project CRISS, let's begin with a little background knowledge. In this way you will have some context for the various activities suggested throughout the teacher wraparound edition.

The CRISS Philosophy

The first thing to know is that Project CRISS is more than a collection of learning strategies. Its underlying power rests not on the individual strategies but on the teaching philosophy behind them. This philosophy integrates work from cognitive psychology, social learning theory, and neurological research about how the brain learns. It includes these overlapping principles:

- ✔ background knowledge and purposeful reading
- ✔ author's craft
- ✔ active involvement
- ✔ discussion
- ✔ organization
- ✔ writing
- ✔ teacher modeling

Let's look at each of these principles in more detail, along with examples of instructional strategies that illustrate them.

Background knowledge and purposeful reading are powerful determinants of reading comprehension.

Teachers involved in Project CRISS often talk about the importance of background knowledge. Readers are far more likely to learn new information when they have some previous knowledge and have a purpose in mind before they read or listen.

✔ **More Than Simply Reading** We warn students not to simply begin reading. We ask them, "What might you already know about the topic? What questions do you have about the topic?" We also remind them to preview the assignment and think about their goals for reading. We often have to be very explicit about the goals. For example, we might tell students, "After reading this selection, you should be able to . . . ," or, "After viewing the video, you should be able to identify . . ."

✔ **KWLH** In the teaching strategies included for each chapter in this book, we offer ideas for helping students tap into their background knowledge. For example, we suggest that students preview their reading assignment and consider what they already know about a topic. Or, we might develop a whole-class KWLH chart (Know, Want to learn, Learned, How to learn more), where students work on this task together. They can generate questions about what they want to learn, and then, after completing the assignment, they can list the new information they have learned and how they can learn more.

K	W	L	H
What I **Know**	What I **Want** to Find Out	What I **Learned**	**How** I Can Learn More

✔ **Reading Goals** We also suggest ways to make sure your students have clear goals for their reading. Each section opener lists reading strategies and main ideas that outline reading goals. Most students will skip over this material and simply start reading. Teachers need to help students understand that the reading goals are important tools for understanding. We tell students, *"Don't ignore your purposes for reading. Take time to think about them before delving into your reading."* Project CRISS also provides hints about how to get students to use these purpose statements to evaluate whether they have understood their reading.

Reading social studies materials has its own special considerations. CRISS specialist Malla S. Kolhoff shares this advice:

"As educators, it is our responsibility to set a purpose for historical reading. Students often must struggle to connect history with their own lives. To compare and contrast, establish cause and effect, and sequence events in chronological order presents a challenge for even the best reader. CRISS strategies allow students to move beyond words to the real significance for their society. With CRISS, my students are able to become engaged in the learning process through:

a. background knowledge
b. active reading, listening, and learning
c. discussion
d. metacognition
e. writing
f. organization
g. understanding

I have found that these strategies help my students attain a higher level of historical thinking and understanding."

Good readers have an intuitive understanding of the author's craft.

When students know how authors craft their writing, they can more readily understand and remember what they read.

- ✔ **Pay Attention** Good readers and writers know that paying attention to how text is organized—its headings and paragraphs, for example—makes it easier to comprehend its content. Good readers will analyze the author's style of presentation as they read. They might ask themselves, "What is this author doing to help me learn key concepts? How does the writer lead me from one idea to the next?" When students become aware of what the author is doing to impart content, they have a clearer idea of what the author is saying.
- ✔ **The Walk-Through** Walk students through the first lesson of the text. Point out the parts of the lesson to help students discover the author's style of presentation. Point out the surface structure (headings, bold print, color coding of topical headings, italicized words), but also point out main ideas in sample paragraphs to analyze how the author elaborates on key topics.

Effective learners are actively involved when they listen and read.

We learn best when we act on the information presented. We can do this by using a variety of organizing activities that require us to write, talk, and transform the information we are absorbing. None of us learns much from reading alone—it's far too passive.

CRISS strategies encourage active engagement in learning. We might ask students to read a section and describe what they are learning to a partner, or we might be more elaborate and have students develop concept maps or write summaries.

Students need many opportunities to talk with one another about what they are learning.

Discussion is critical to learning. The discussions we advocate are different from those in which the teacher remains the authority figure, with students simply reciting answers to questions. If discussion becomes mere recitation and there is little interaction among students, little learning occurs. Thus we focus on how to get students to lead their own discussions about a topic. We want them to understand that it is their discussing, their oral grappling with meaning—not ours—that leads to deeper understanding.

Competent readers know several ways to organize information for learning.

Learning depends on organization. We show students different ways to organize information. They can take notes, underline selectively, develop concept maps, and summarize ideas in charts. Once we have taught students these techniques, we tell them, "You have to do more than just read this assignment. How are you going to organize the information from this assignment? You have to change it, to transform it so that it becomes your own."

For each chapter of this text, we offer ideas for assisting students in organizing information. Once students have learned a variety of organizing systems, we suggest ways to help them apply these structures independently.

Students deserve opportunities to write about what they are learning.

Writing is an integral part of the CRISS project. Writing lets us figure out what we know and what we still need to know. We cannot write about something we do not understand. While we teach students how to write expository papers and essay exams, we also encourage students to write more informally by questioning, speculating, and writing explanations in learning logs. We make sure that students are writing continually about what they are learning.

For each chapter of this text, we offer ideas for assisting students in organizing information. Once students have learned a variety of organizing systems, we suggest ways to help them apply these structures independently.

Teaching involves explanation and modeling.

Our final principle has to do with our own teaching. Students learn to think strategically when we use these processes as part of our instruction. Our demonstrations are especially critical for struggling readers. Most have never been taught how to learn. We have to show them how.

✔ **Take Center Stage** When you introduce a new strategy, you should take the center stage: showing, telling, modeling, demonstrating, and explaining not only the content but the process of active reading. As students learn, gradually release responsibility to them. Strategy instruction involves two overlapping steps. First, we explain what the strategy is and why students should use it. If students do not know why they are performing an activity, they will rarely use the activity on their own. Next, we demonstrate and talk about procedures for carrying out the strategy. We discuss, demonstrate, and think aloud while modeling. Then, students practice under our guidance and feedback.

✔ **A Systematic Approach** Project CRISS is a valuable basis for instruction. It provides a systematic approach for using what we now know about teaching and learning. The following chart lists questions we need to continually ask ourselves while we are teaching. Use this chart to monitor your efforts to incorporate CRISS principles into your teaching.

CRISS Principles	The CRISS Philosophy	Yes	No	Somewhat
Background Knowledge:	Did I assist students in thinking about what they already knew about the topic before beginning the unit? Did I develop necessary concepts before students read?			
Purpose/ Setting:	Did my students have a clear purpose about what they were going to learn before beginning the lesson?			
Author's Craft:	Can my students use the author's style of presentation to facilitate their understanding?			
Active Involvement:	Were my students engaged in the topic? Did I help students become actively involved in their learning?			
Discussion:	Did my students have opportunities to talk about what they were learning?			
Organization:	Did my students organize information in a variety of ways?			
Writing:	Did my students write about what they were learning?			
Teacher Modeling:	Did I do enough teacher modeling of learning strategies so that students could begin doing them on their own?			

Reference Atlas

NATIONAL GEOGRAPHIC

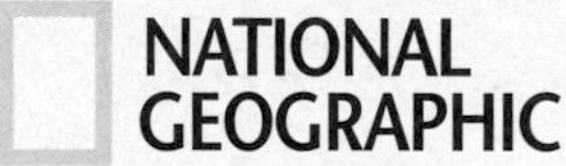

ATLAS KEY

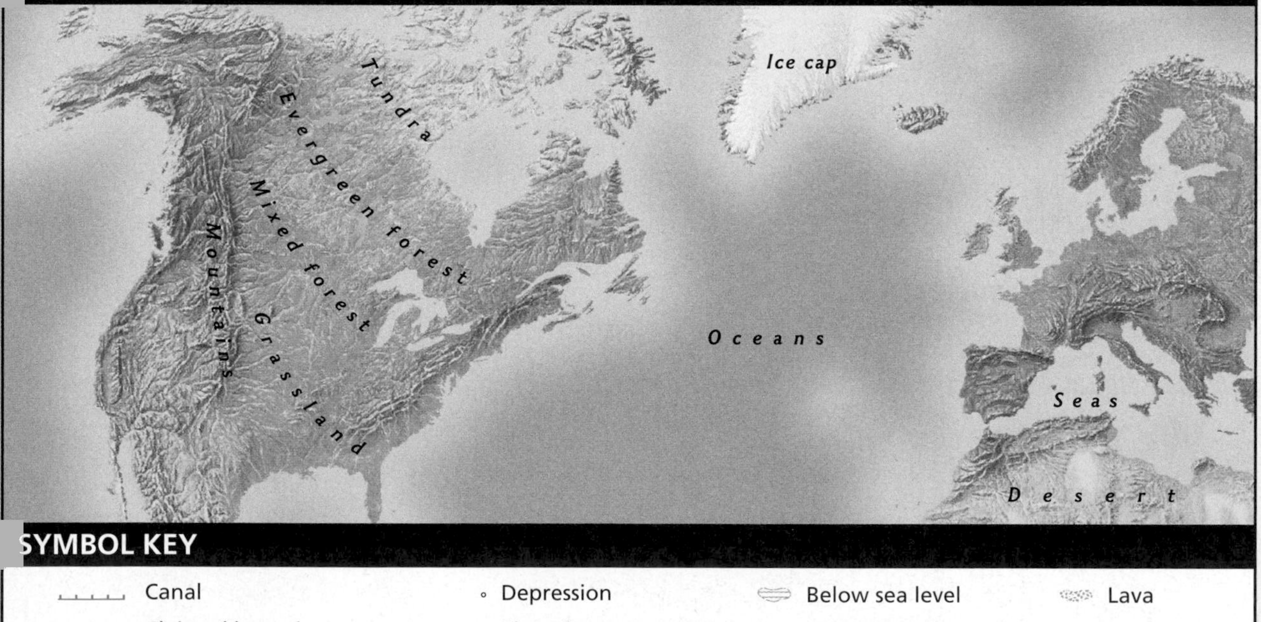

Tundra
Evergreen forest
Mixed forest
Mountains
Grassland
Ice cap
Oceans
Seas
Desert

SYMBOL KEY

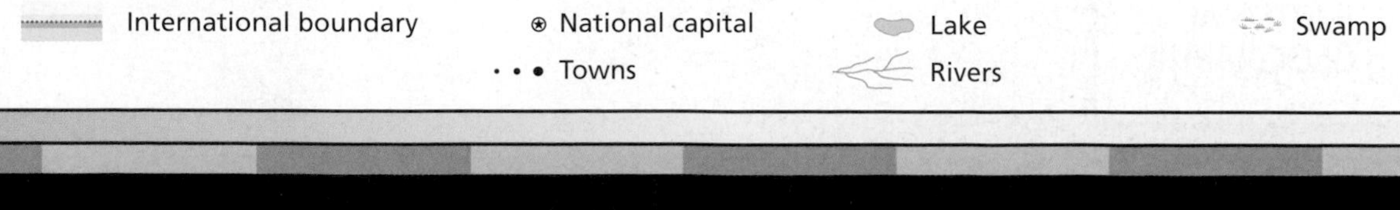

Canal
Claimed boundary
International boundary
Depression
Elevation
National capital
Towns
Below sea level
Dry salt lake
Lake
Rivers
Lava
Sand
Swamp

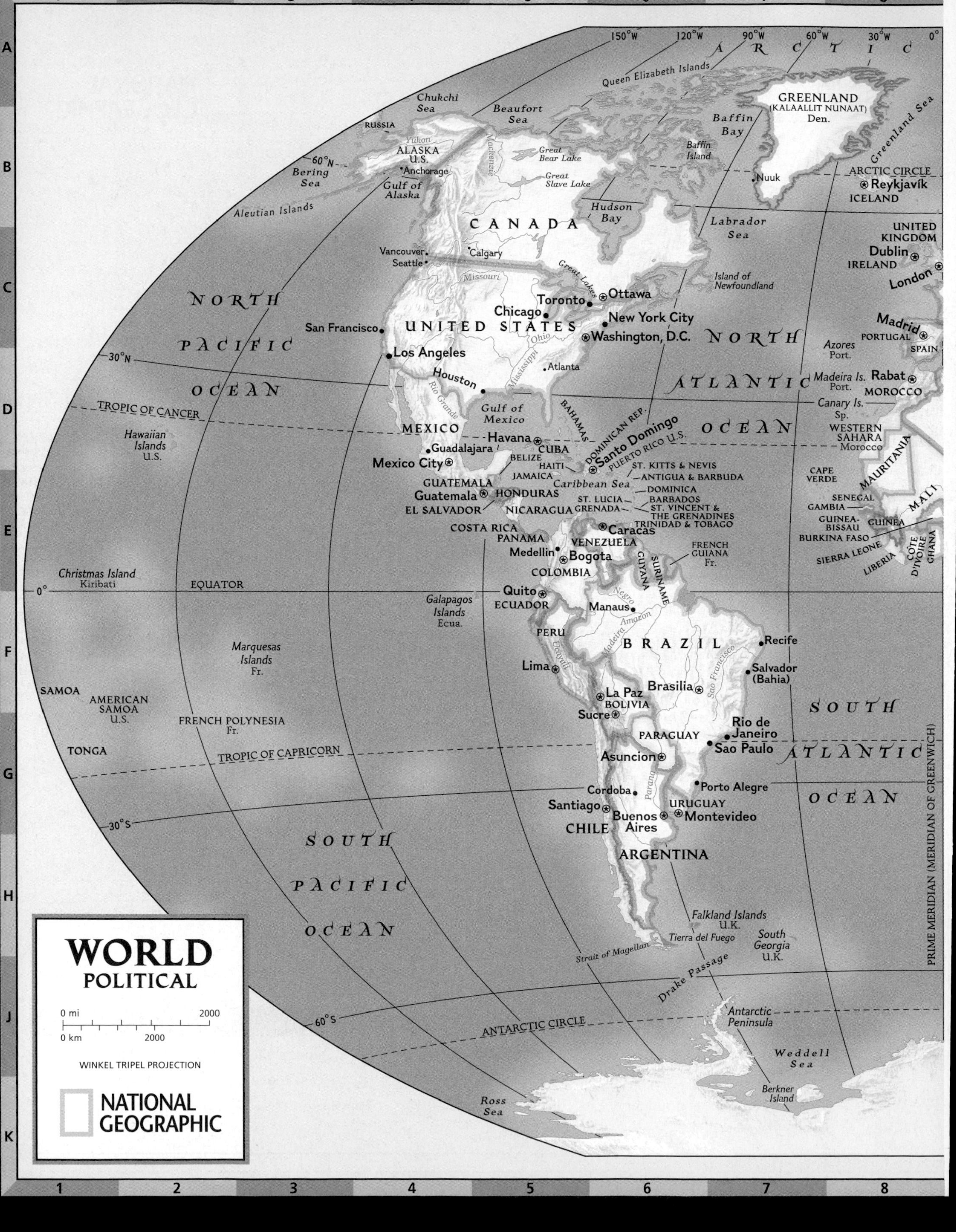
WORLD
POLITICAL
0 mi 2000
0 km 2000
WINKEL TRIPEL PROJECTION
NATIONAL GEOGRAPHIC
NORTH PACIFIC OCEAN
NORTH ATLANTIC OCEAN
SOUTH PACIFIC OCEAN
SOUTH ATLANTIC OCEAN
ARCTIC
CANADA
UNITED STATES
MEXICO
BRAZIL
ARGENTINA
CHILE
GREENLAND (KALAALLIT NUNAAT) Den.
ALASKA U.S.
RUSSIA
ICELAND
UNITED KINGDOM
IRELAND
PORTUGAL
SPAIN
MOROCCO
WESTERN SAHARA Morocco
MAURITANIA
MALI
SENEGAL
GAMBIA
GUINEA-BISSAU
GUINEA
SIERRA LEONE
LIBERIA
COTE D'IVOIRE
GHANA
BURKINA FASO
CAPE VERDE
CUBA
BELIZE
HAITI
JAMAICA
DOMINICAN REP.
PUERTO RICO U.S.
BAHAMAS
GUATEMALA
HONDURAS
EL SALVADOR
NICARAGUA
COSTA RICA
PANAMA
ST. KITTS & NEVIS
ANTIGUA & BARBUDA
DOMINICA
BARBADOS
ST. LUCIA
ST. VINCENT & THE GRENADINES
GRENADA
TRINIDAD & TOBAGO
VENEZUELA
COLOMBIA
GUYANA
SURINAME
FRENCH GUIANA Fr.
ECUADOR
PERU
BOLIVIA
PARAGUAY
URUGUAY
SAMOA
AMERICAN SAMOA U.S.
TONGA
FRENCH POLYNESIA Fr.
Anchorage
Vancouver
Seattle
Calgary
San Francisco
Los Angeles
Chicago
Toronto
Ottawa
New York City
Washington, D.C.
Atlanta
Houston
Havana
Guadalajara
Mexico City
Guatemala
Santo Domingo
Caracas
Medellin
Bogota
Quito
Manaus
Lima
La Paz
Sucre
Brasilia
Recife
Salvador (Bahia)
Rio de Janeiro
Sao Paulo
Asuncion
Porto Alegre
Cordoba
Santiago
Buenos Aires
Montevideo
Nuuk
Reykjavík
Dublin
London
Madrid
Rabat
Chukchi Sea
Beaufort Sea
Bering Sea
Gulf of Alaska
Queen Elizabeth Islands
Baffin Bay
Baffin Island
Greenland Sea
Great Bear Lake
Great Slave Lake
Hudson Bay
Labrador Sea
Island of Newfoundland
Great Lakes
Aleutian Islands
Yukon
Mackenzie
Missouri
Ohio
Mississippi
Rio Grande
Gulf of Mexico
Caribbean Sea
Hawaiian Islands U.S.
Azores Port.
Madeira Is. Port.
Canary Is. Sp.
Christmas Island Kiribati
Galapagos Islands Ecua.
Marquesas Islands Fr.
Negro
Amazon
Madeira
Ucayali
Sao Francisco
Parana
Falkland Islands U.K.
South Georgia U.K.
Tierra del Fuego
Strait of Magellan
Drake Passage
Antarctic Peninsula
Weddell Sea
Berkner Island
Ross Sea
ARCTIC CIRCLE
TROPIC OF CANCER
EQUATOR
TROPIC OF CAPRICORN
ANTARCTIC CIRCLE
PRIME MERIDIAN (MERIDIAN OF GREENWICH)
150°W
120°W
90°W
60°W
30°W
0°
60°N
30°N
0°
30°S
60°S

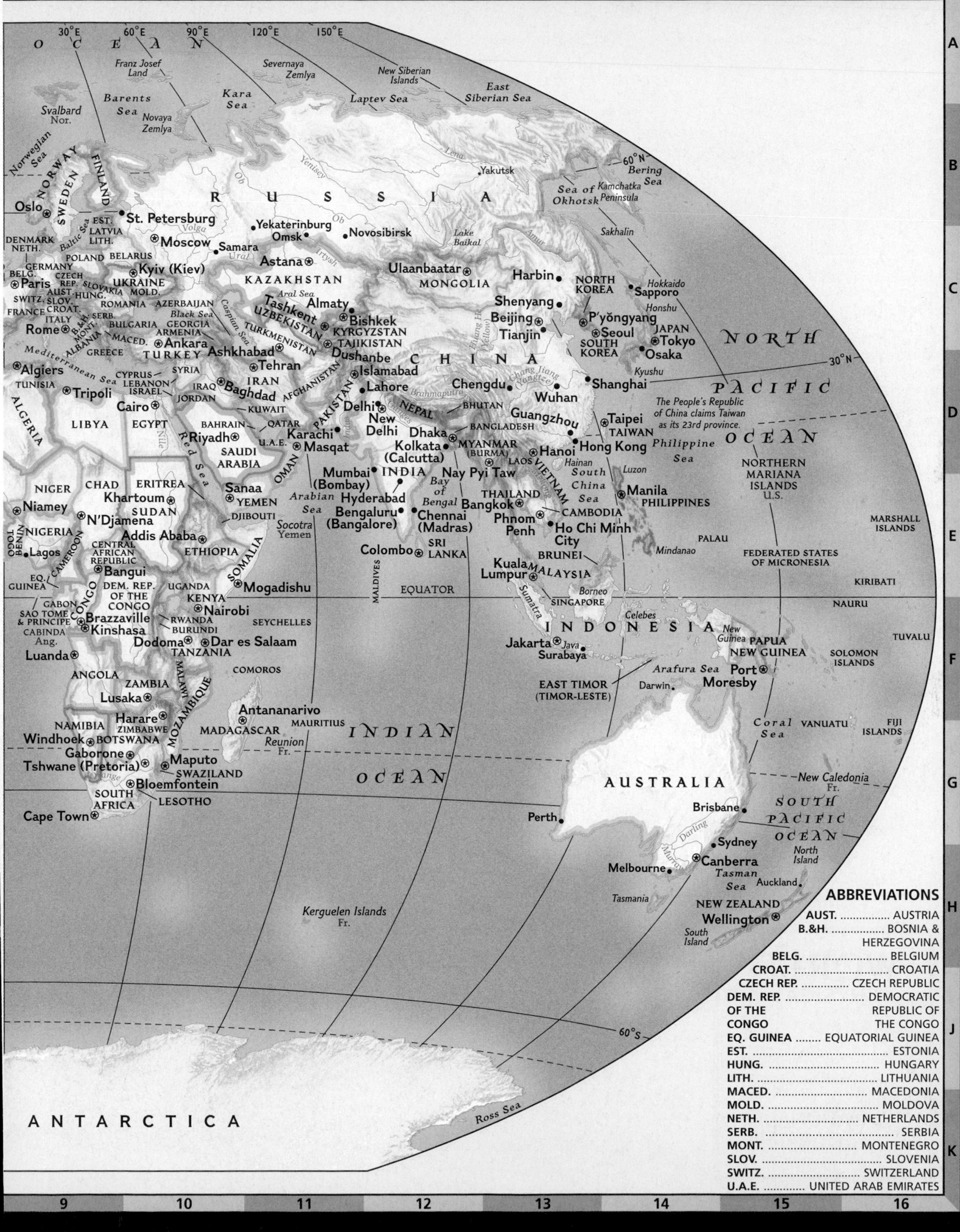

9
10
11
12
13
14
15
16
A
B
C
D
E
F
G
H
J
K
30°E
60°E
90°E
120°E
150°E
OCEAN
Franz Josef Land
Severnaya Zemlya
New Siberian Islands
East Siberian Sea
Laptev Sea
Kara Sea
Barents Sea
Svalbard Nor.
Novaya Zemlya
Norwegian Sea
NORWAY
SWEDEN
FINLAND
Lena
Yenisey
Ob
60°N
Bering Sea
Yakutsk
Sea of Okhotsk
Kamchatka Peninsula
RUSSIA
Oslo
St. Petersburg
Volga
EST.
LATVIA
LITH.
Baltic Sea
Moscow
Yekaterinburg
Ob
Omsk
Novosibirsk
Lake Baikal
Amur
Sakhalin
DENMARK
NETH.
Samara
Ural
POLAND
BELARUS
Astana
Irtysh
GERMANY
BELG.
CZECH REP.
Kyiv (Kiev)
Ulaanbaatar
Harbin
NORTH KOREA
Hokkaido
Sapporo
Paris
SLOVAKIA
UKRAINE
KAZAKHSTAN
MONGOLIA
AUST.
HUNG.
MOLD.
Aral Sea
SWITZ.
SLOV.
CROAT.
ROMANIA
AZERBAIJAN
Tashkent
Almaty
Shenyang
Honshu
FRANCE
ITALY
B.&H.
SERB.
Black Sea
Caspian Sea
UZBEKISTAN
Bishkek
Beijing
P'yŏngyang
MONT.
BULGARIA
GEORGIA
ARMENIA
KYRGYZSTAN
Huang He (Yellow)
JAPAN
Rome
ALBANIA
MACED.
Ankara
TURKMENISTAN
TAJIKISTAN
Tianjin
Seoul
Tokyo
NORTH
GREECE
TURKEY
Ashkhabad
Dushanbe
CHINA
SOUTH KOREA
Osaka
Mediterranean Sea
Tehran
Islamabad
Kyushu
30°N
Algiers
CYPRUS
SYRIA
IRAN
AFGHANISTAN
Lahore
Chang Jiang (Yangtze)
Shanghai
TUNISIA
Tripoli
LEBANON
ISRAEL
IRAQ
Baghdad
Brahmaputra
Chengdu
Wuhan
PACIFIC
JORDAN
KUWAIT
PAKISTAN
Delhi
NEPAL
BHUTAN
The People's Republic of China claims Taiwan as its 23rd province.
ALGERIA
Cairo
LIBYA
EGYPT
BAHRAIN
QATAR
New Delhi
Ganges
Indus
Guangzhou
Taipei
Nile
Riyadh
U.A.E.
Karachi
Dhaka
BANGLADESH
TAIWAN
Red Sea
SAUDI ARABIA
Masqat
Kolkata (Calcutta)
MYANMAR (BURMA)
Hanoi
Hong Kong
Philippine Sea
OCEAN
OMAN
Mumbai (Bombay)
INDIA
Nay Pyi Taw
LAOS
Hainan
South China Sea
Luzon
NORTHERN MARIANA ISLANDS U.S.
NIGER
CHAD
ERITREA
Bay of Bengal
VIETNAM
Mekong
Khartoum
SUDAN
Sanaa
YEMEN
Arabian Sea
Hyderabad
THAILAND
Manila
Niamey
Bangkok
PHILIPPINES
N'Djamena
DJIBOUTI
Bengaluru (Bangalore)
Chennai (Madras)
CAMBODIA
Phnom Penh
MARSHALL ISLANDS
TOGO
BENIN
NIGERIA
Addis Ababa
Socotra Yemen
Ho Chi Minh City
PALAU
Lagos
CAMEROON
CENTRAL AFRICAN REPUBLIC
ETHIOPIA
SOMALIA
Colombo
SRI LANKA
BRUNEI
Mindanao
FEDERATED STATES OF MICRONESIA
Bangui
MALDIVES
Kuala Lumpur
MALAYSIA
EQ. GUINEA
DEM. REP. OF THE CONGO
CONGO
UGANDA
Mogadishu
KIRIBATI
EQUATOR
Borneo
GABON
KENYA
SINGAPORE
NAURU
SAO TOME & PRINCIPE
Brazzaville
RWANDA
Nairobi
Sumatra
CABINDA Ang.
Kinshasa
BURUNDI
SEYCHELLES
Celebes
INDONESIA
New Guinea
PAPUA NEW GUINEA
TUVALU
Dodoma
Dar es Salaam
Jakarta
Java
Surabaya
Luanda
TANZANIA
SOLOMON ISLANDS
COMOROS
Arafura Sea
Port Moresby
ANGOLA
MALAWI
EAST TIMOR (TIMOR-LESTE)
Darwin
ZAMBIA
Lusaka
MOZAMBIQUE
Antananarivo
NAMIBIA
Harare
ZIMBABWE
MAURITIUS
MADAGASCAR
INDIAN
Coral Sea
VANUATU
FIJI ISLANDS
Windhoek
BOTSWANA
Reunion Fr.
Gaborone
Tshwane (Pretoria)
Maputo
SWAZILAND
OCEAN
New Caledonia Fr.
Orange
Bloemfontein
AUSTRALIA
SOUTH AFRICA
LESOTHO
SOUTH PACIFIC OCEAN
Cape Town
Perth
Brisbane
Darling
Sydney
North Island
Murray
Melbourne
Canberra
Tasman Sea
Auckland
Tasmania
NEW ZEALAND
Kerguelen Islands Fr.
Wellington
South Island
60°S
Ross Sea
ANTARCTICA
ABBREVIATIONS
AUST. .... AUSTRIA
B.&H. .... BOSNIA & HERZEGOVINA
BELG. .... BELGIUM
CROAT. .... CROATIA
CZECH REP. .... CZECH REPUBLIC
DEM. REP. OF THE CONGO .... DEMOCRATIC REPUBLIC OF THE CONGO
EQ. GUINEA .... EQUATORIAL GUINEA
EST. .... ESTONIA
HUNG. .... HUNGARY
LITH. .... LITHUANIA
MACED. .... MACEDONIA
MOLD. .... MOLDOVA
NETH. .... NETHERLANDS
SERB. .... SERBIA
MONT. .... MONTENEGRO
SLOV. .... SLOVENIA
SWITZ. .... SWITZERLAND
U.A.E. .... UNITED ARAB EMIRATES

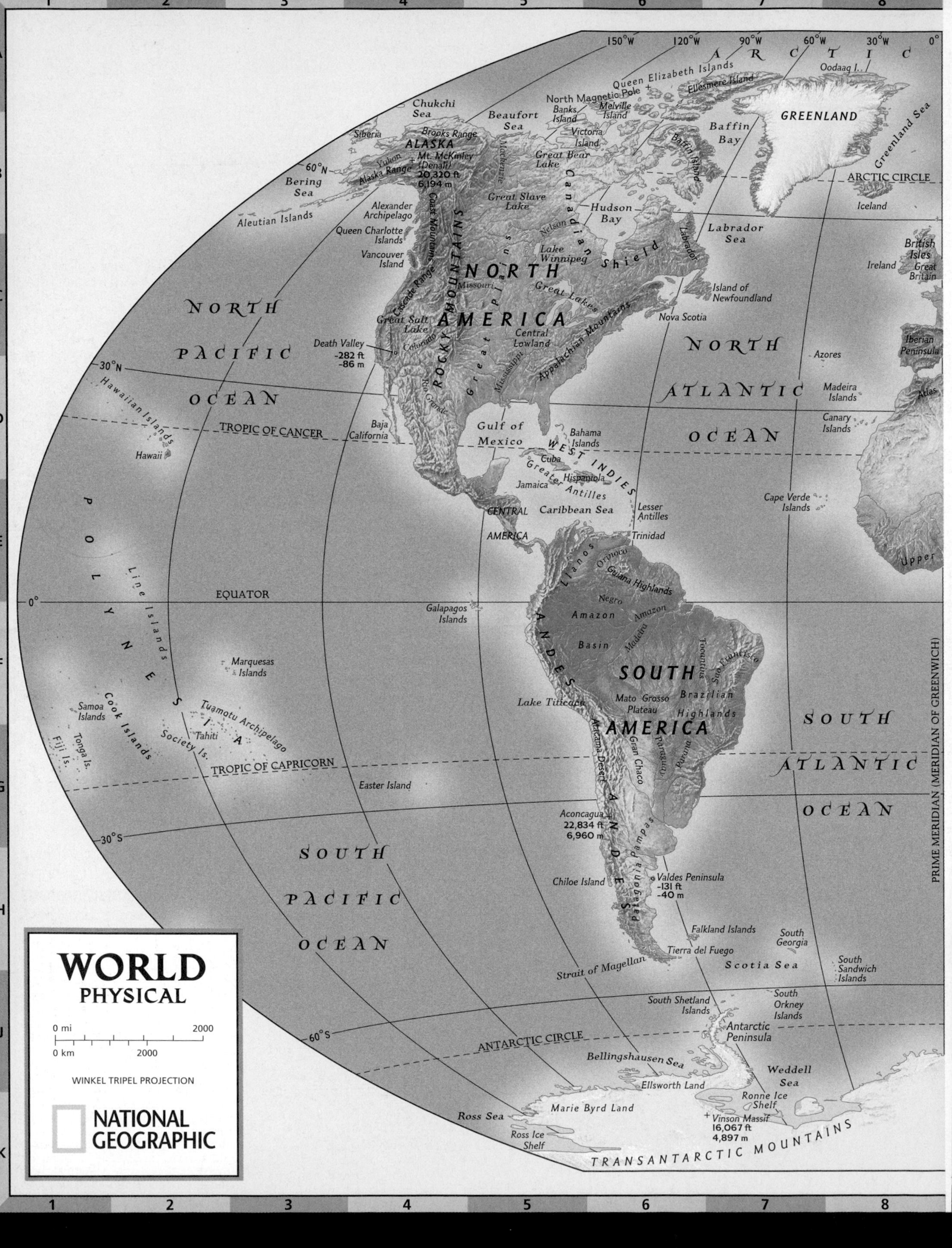
WORLD
PHYSICAL
0 mi 2000
0 km 2000
WINKEL TRIPEL PROJECTION
NATIONAL GEOGRAPHIC
ARCTIC
NORTH AMERICA
SOUTH AMERICA
NORTH PACIFIC OCEAN
SOUTH PACIFIC OCEAN
NORTH ATLANTIC OCEAN
SOUTH ATLANTIC OCEAN
GREENLAND
ALASKA
Mt. McKinley (Denali) 20,320 ft 6,194 m
Death Valley -282 ft -86 m
Aconcagua 22,834 ft 6,960 m
Valdes Peninsula -131 ft -40 m
Vinson Massif 16,067 ft 4,897 m
ROCKY MOUNTAINS
Canadian Shield
Great Plains
Appalachian Mountains
Central Lowland
Great Lakes
Hudson Bay
Gulf of Mexico
Caribbean Sea
WEST INDIES
Greater Antilles
Lesser Antilles
CENTRAL AMERICA
Amazon Basin
Brazilian Highlands
Mato Grosso Plateau
Guiana Highlands
ANDES
Gran Chaco
Pampas
Patagonia
Atacama Desert
Lake Titicaca
Strait of Magellan
Tierra del Fuego
Falkland Islands
Scotia Sea
Weddell Sea
Bellingshausen Sea
Ross Sea
Ross Ice Shelf
Ronne Ice Shelf
Marie Byrd Land
Ellsworth Land
Antarctic Peninsula
TRANSANTARCTIC MOUNTAINS
EQUATOR
TROPIC OF CANCER
TROPIC OF CAPRICORN
ARCTIC CIRCLE
ANTARCTIC CIRCLE
PRIME MERIDIAN (MERIDIAN OF GREENWICH)
POLYNESIA
Hawaiian Islands
Hawaii
Line Islands
Marquesas Islands
Tuamotu Archipelago
Tahiti
Society Is.
Samoa Islands
Cook Islands
Tonga Is.
Fiji Is.
Easter Island
Galapagos Islands
Aleutian Islands
Bering Sea
Chukchi Sea
Beaufort Sea
Baffin Bay
Labrador Sea
Greenland Sea
Iceland
British Isles
Ireland
Great Britain
Iberian Peninsula
Azores
Madeira Islands
Canary Islands
Cape Verde Islands
Bahama Islands
Cuba
Hispaniola
Jamaica
Trinidad
Baja California
Island of Newfoundland
Nova Scotia
Queen Elizabeth Islands
Ellesmere Island
Oodaaq I.
North Magnetic Pole
Banks Island
Melville Island
Victoria Island
Baffin Island
Great Bear Lake
Great Slave Lake
Lake Winnipeg
Great Salt Lake
Alexander Archipelago
Queen Charlotte Islands
Vancouver Island
Coast Mountains
Cascade Range
Brooks Range
Alaska Range
Siberia
South Georgia
South Sandwich Islands
South Shetland Islands
South Orkney Islands
Chiloe Island
Atlas
Upper

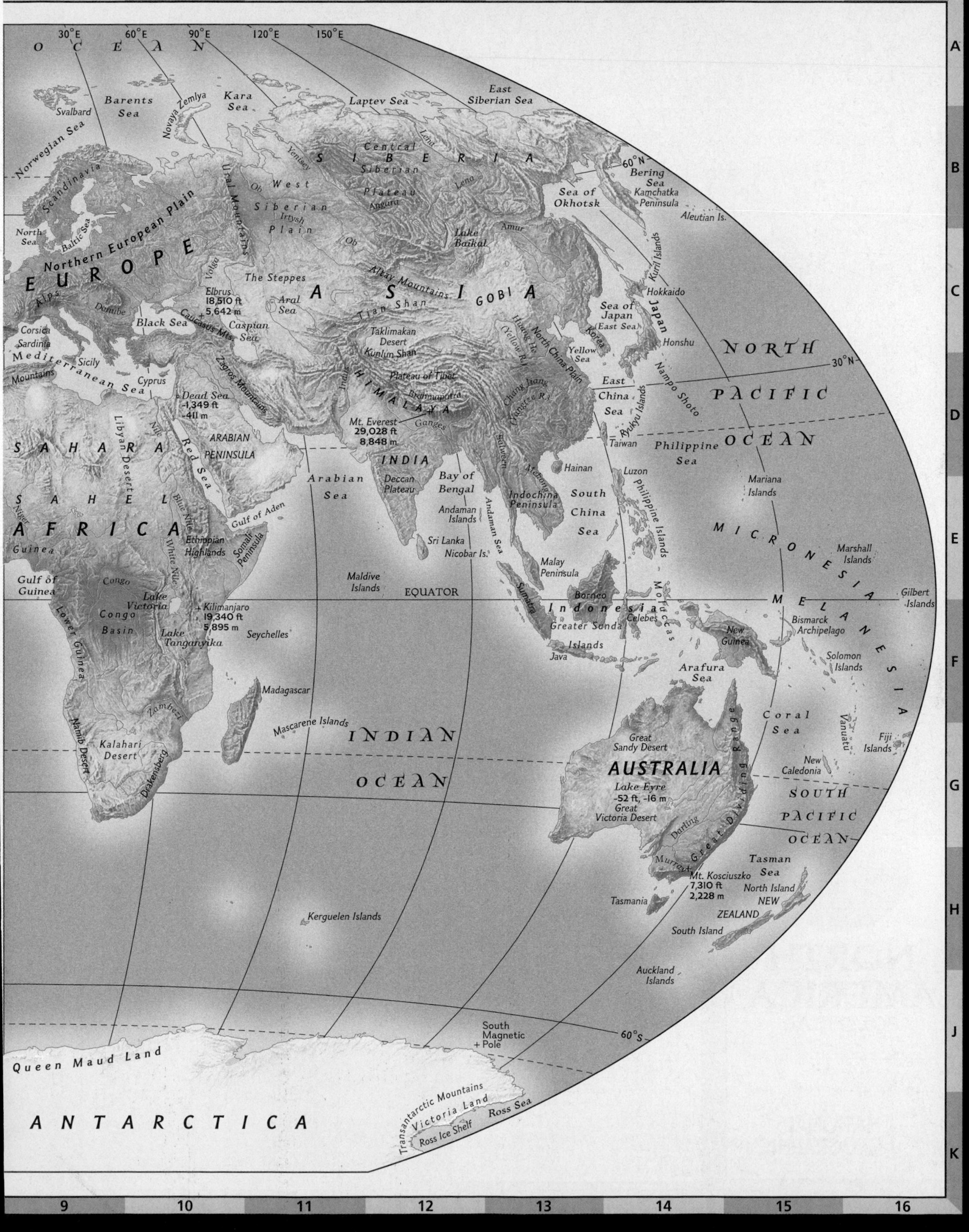

EUROPE
ASIA
AFRICA
AUSTRALIA
ANTARCTICA
INDIAN OCEAN
NORTH PACIFIC OCEAN
SOUTH PACIFIC OCEAN
Barents Sea
Kara Sea
Laptev Sea
East Siberian Sea
Norwegian Sea
Svalbard
Novaya Zemlya
Scandinavia
North Sea
Baltic Sea
Northern European Plain
Ural Mountains
West Siberian Plain
Central Siberian Plateau
SIBERIA
Bering Sea
Kamchatka Peninsula
Aleutian Is.
Sea of Okhotsk
Lake Baikal
Kuril Islands
Hokkaido
Japan
Honshu
Sea of Japan (East Sea)
Korea
Yellow Sea
East China Sea
Ryukyu Islands
Nampo Shoto
Taiwan
Philippine Sea
Luzon
Philippine Islands
Mariana Islands
MICRONESIA
MELANESIA
Marshall Islands
Gilbert Islands
Alps
Danube
Black Sea
Caucasus Mts.
Caspian Sea
Elbrus 18,510 ft 5,642 m
Aral Sea
The Steppes
Altay Mountains
GOBI
Tian Shan
Taklimakan Desert
Kunlun Shan
Plateau of Tibet
HIMALAYA
Mt. Everest 29,028 ft 8,848 m
North China Plain
Corsica
Sardinia
Sicily
Mediterranean Sea
Cyprus
Zagros Mountains
Dead Sea -1,349 ft -411 m
ARABIAN PENINSULA
Red Sea
SAHARA
Libyan Desert
SAHEL
Gulf of Aden
Ethiopian Highlands
Somali Peninsula
Arabian Sea
INDIA
Deccan Plateau
Bay of Bengal
Andaman Islands
Andaman Sea
Sri Lanka
Nicobar Is.
Indochina Peninsula
Hainan
South China Sea
Malay Peninsula
Sumatra
Borneo
Indonesia
Celebes
Moluccas
Greater Sunda Islands
Java
New Guinea
Bismarck Archipelago
Solomon Islands
Arafura Sea
Coral Sea
Vanuatu
Fiji Islands
New Caledonia
Guinea
Gulf of Guinea
Congo
Congo Basin
Lake Victoria
Kilimanjaro 19,340 ft 5,895 m
Lake Tanganyika
Seychelles
Maldive Islands
EQUATOR
Madagascar
Mascarene Islands
Zambezi
Kalahari Desert
Namib Desert
Drakensberg
Great Sandy Desert
Lake Eyre -52 ft, -16 m
Great Victoria Desert
Great Dividing Range
Darling
Murray
Mt. Kosciuszko 7,310 ft 2,228 m
Tasmania
Tasman Sea
North Island
NEW ZEALAND
South Island
Auckland Islands
Kerguelen Islands
South Magnetic Pole
60°S
60°N
30°N
Queen Maud Land
Transantarctic Mountains
Victoria Land
Ross Ice Shelf
Ross Sea

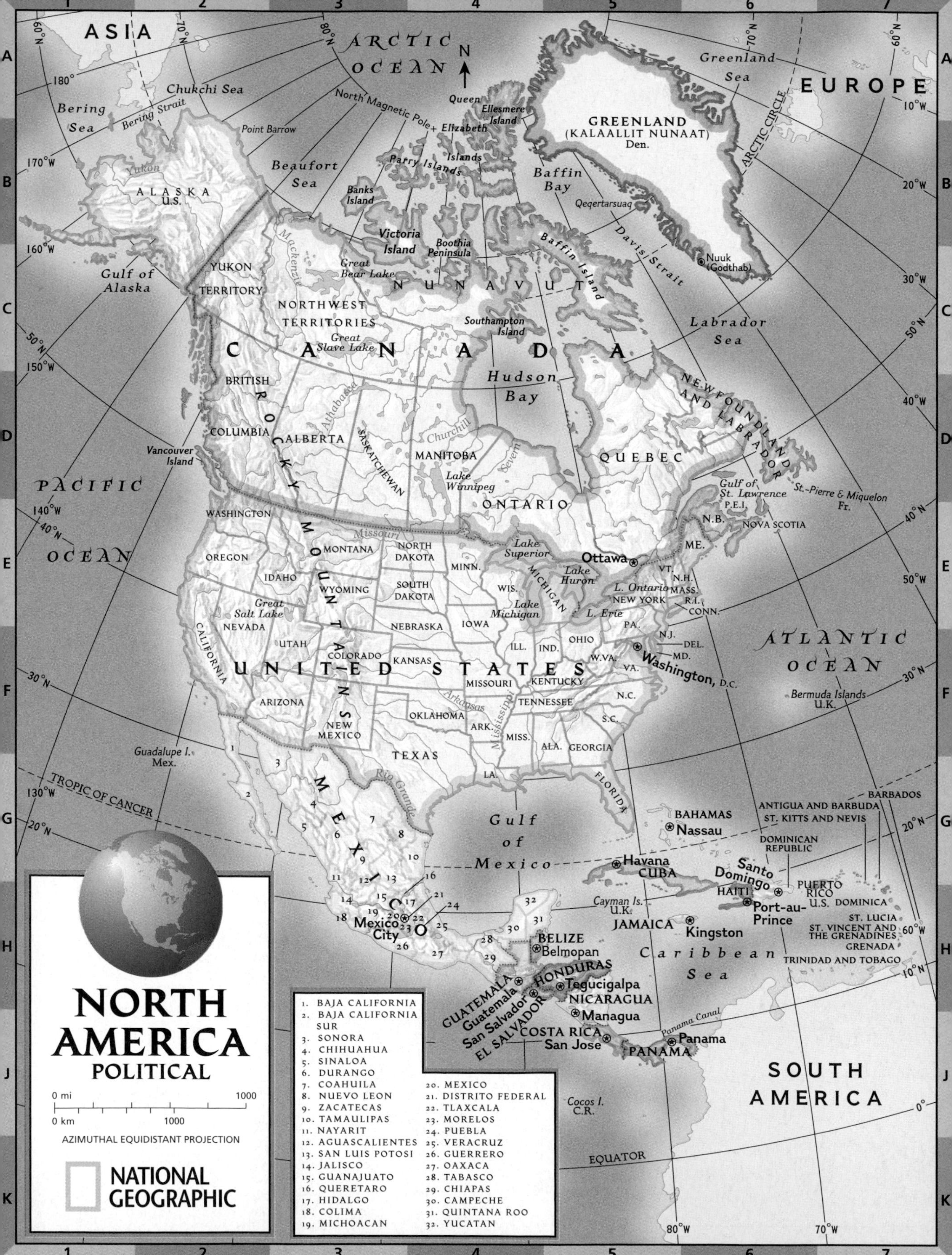
NORTH
AMERICA
POLITICAL
0 mi 1000
0 km 1000
AZIMUTHAL EQUIDISTANT PROJECTION
NATIONAL GEOGRAPHIC
1. BAJA CALIFORNIA
2. BAJA CALIFORNIA SUR
3. SONORA
4. CHIHUAHUA
5. SINALOA
6. DURANGO
7. COAHUILA
8. NUEVO LEON
9. ZACATECAS
10. TAMAULIPAS
11. NAYARIT
12. AGUASCALIENTES
13. SAN LUIS POTOSI
14. JALISCO
15. GUANAJUATO
16. QUERETARO
17. HIDALGO
18. COLIMA
19. MICHOACAN
20. MEXICO
21. DISTRITO FEDERAL
22. TLAXCALA
23. MORELOS
24. PUEBLA
25. VERACRUZ
26. GUERRERO
27. OAXACA
28. TABASCO
29. CHIAPAS
30. CAMPECHE
31. QUINTANA ROO
32. YUCATAN
ASIA
ARCTIC OCEAN
N
EUROPE
Greenland Sea
GREENLAND
(KALAALLIT NUNAAT)
Den.
Chukchi Sea
Bering Sea
Bering Strait
Point Barrow
North Magnetic Pole
Queen Elizabeth Islands
Ellesmere Island
Parry Islands
Beaufort Sea
Banks Island
Victoria Island
Boothia Peninsula
Baffin Bay
Qeqertarsuaq
Baffin Island
Davis Strait
Nuuk (Godthab)
ARCTIC CIRCLE
ALASKA U.S.
Yukon
Gulf of Alaska
YUKON TERRITORY
Mackenzie
Great Bear Lake
NUNAVUT
NORTHWEST TERRITORIES
Great Slave Lake
Southampton Island
Labrador Sea
CANADA
Hudson Bay
NEWFOUNDLAND AND LABRADOR
BRITISH COLUMBIA
ROCKY MOUNTAINS
Athabasca
ALBERTA
SASKATCHEWAN
Churchill
MANITOBA
Severn
Lake Winnipeg
QUEBEC
Vancouver Island
PACIFIC OCEAN
ONTARIO
Gulf of St. Lawrence
P.E.I.
St.-Pierre & Miquelon Fr.
N.B.
NOVA SCOTIA
WASHINGTON
Missouri
MONTANA
NORTH DAKOTA
MINN.
Lake Superior
Ottawa
ME.
VT.
N.H.
MASS.
R.I.
CONN.
OREGON
IDAHO
WYOMING
SOUTH DAKOTA
WIS.
MICHIGAN
Lake Huron
L. Ontario
NEW YORK
Great Salt Lake
NEVADA
Lake Michigan
L. Erie
PA.
NEBRASKA
IOWA
N.J.
CALIFORNIA
UTAH
COLORADO
KANSAS
ILL.
IND.
OHIO
DEL.
MD.
W.VA.
VA.
Washington, D.C.
ATLANTIC OCEAN
UNITED STATES
MISSOURI
KENTUCKY
Arkansas
ARIZONA
OKLAHOMA
TENNESSEE
N.C.
Bermuda Islands U.K.
NEW MEXICO
ARK.
Mississippi
S.C.
MISS.
ALA.
GEORGIA
Guadalupe I. Mex.
TEXAS
LA.
Rio Grande
FLORIDA
TROPIC OF CANCER
MEXICO
Gulf of Mexico
BAHAMAS
Nassau
ANTIGUA AND BARBUDA
BARBADOS
ST. KITTS AND NEVIS
DOMINICAN REPUBLIC
Havana
CUBA
Santo Domingo
HAITI
PUERTO RICO U.S.
DOMINICA
Mexico City
Cayman Is. U.K.
Port-au-Prince
ST. LUCIA
JAMAICA
Kingston
ST. VINCENT AND THE GRENADINES
GRENADA
BELIZE
Belmopan
Caribbean Sea
TRINIDAD AND TOBAGO
HONDURAS
Tegucigalpa
GUATEMALA
Guatemala
San Salvador
EL SALVADOR
NICARAGUA
Managua
Panama Canal
COSTA RICA
San Jose
Panama
PANAMA
SOUTH AMERICA
Cocos I. C.R.
EQUATOR
180°
170°W
160°W
150°W
140°W
130°W
60°N
70°N
80°N
50°N
40°N
30°N
20°N
10°N
0°
10°W
20°W
30°W
40°W
50°W
60°W
80°W
70°W
1 2 3 4 5 6 7
A B C D E F G H J K

NORTH AMERICA
PHYSICAL
0 mi 1000
0 km 1000
AZIMUTHAL EQUIDISTANT PROJECTION
NATIONAL GEOGRAPHIC
ASIA
EUROPE
SOUTH AMERICA
ARCTIC OCEAN
PACIFIC OCEAN
ATLANTIC OCEAN
CANADA
UNITED STATES
MEXICO
GREENLAND
ALASKA
CENTRAL AMERICA
Chukchi Sea
Bering Sea
Beaufort Sea
Lincoln Sea
Greenland Sea
Baffin Bay
Labrador Sea
Hudson Bay
Gulf of Alaska
Gulf of Mexico
Caribbean Sea
Oodaaq Island
Queen Elizabeth Islands
Ellesmere Island
Hayes Peninsula
Gunnbjorn 12,139 ft 3,700 m
ARCTIC CIRCLE
Point Barrow
North Magnetic Pole
Seward Peninsula
St. Lawrence Island
Nunivak Island
North Slope
Brooks Range
Yukon
Kuskokwim
Mt. McKinley (Denali) 20,320 ft 6,194 m
Bristol Bay
Aleutian Range
Alaska Range
Kenai Peninsula
Kodiak I.
Banks Island
Melville Island
Devon I.
Somerset I.
Prince of Wales I.
Victoria Island
Boothia Peninsula
Melville Peninsula
Baffin Island
Davis Strait
Nuuk (Godthab)
Cape Farewell
Mackenzie Mts.
Mackenzie
Great Bear Lake
Foxe Basin
Southampton Island
Hudson Strait
Ungava Bay
Yukon Plateau
19,551 ft 5,959 m Mt. Logan
Great Slave Lake
Slave
Peace
Lake Athabasca
Athabasca
Churchill
Nelson
Alexander Archipelago
Queen Charlotte Islands
Coast Mountains
ROCKY MOUNTAINS
Fraser Plateau
Columbia Mts.
CANADIAN SHIELD
Belcher Islands
James Bay
LABRADOR
Island of Newfoundland
Avalon Peninsula
Laurentian Mountains
Gaspe Pen.
Gulf of St. Lawrence
Cape Breton Island
Prince Edward Island
Nova Scotia
Bay of Fundy
Gulf of Maine
Cape Cod
Long Island
Vancouver Island
Olympic Peninsula
Cascade Range
Coast Ranges
Saskatchewan
Lake Winnipeg
GREAT PLAINS
Missouri
Lake Superior
Ottawa
St. Lawrence
Lake Michigan
Lake Huron
L. Ontario
L. Erie
Columbia Plateau
Snake
Cape Mendocino
Sierra Nevada
Great Basin
Great Salt Lake
Mt. Whitney 14,494 ft 4,418 m
Death Valley -282 ft -86 m
Colorado Plateau
Grand Canyon
Platte
High Plains
CENTRAL LOWLAND
Ohio
APPALACHIAN MOUNTAINS
Washington
Chesapeake Bay
Cape Hatteras
Bermuda Islands
Ozark Plateau
Arkansas
Red
Mississippi
COASTAL PLAIN
Florida
Channel Islands
Colorado
Sonoran Desert
Baja California
Gulf of California
Rio Grande
TROPIC OF CANCER
Sierra Madre Occidental
Sierra Madre Oriental
BAHAMAS
Florida Keys
Havana
CUBA
WEST INDIES
Virgin Islands
Puerto Rico
Hispaniola
HAITI
DOMINICAN REPUBLIC
Guadeloupe
Martinique
Lesser Antilles
Greater Antilles
Cayman Islands
JAMAICA
Kingston
Trinidad
Orizaba 18,855 ft 5,747 m
Mexico City
Yucatan Peninsula
Cozumel Island
Isthmus of Tehuantepec
Gulf of Tehuantepec
BELIZE
Belmopan
HONDURAS
Tegucigalpa
GUATEMALA
Guatemala
San Salvador
EL SALVADOR
NICARAGUA
Managua
Lake Nicaragua
COSTA RICA
San José
Isthmus of Panama
Panama
PANAMA
EQUATOR

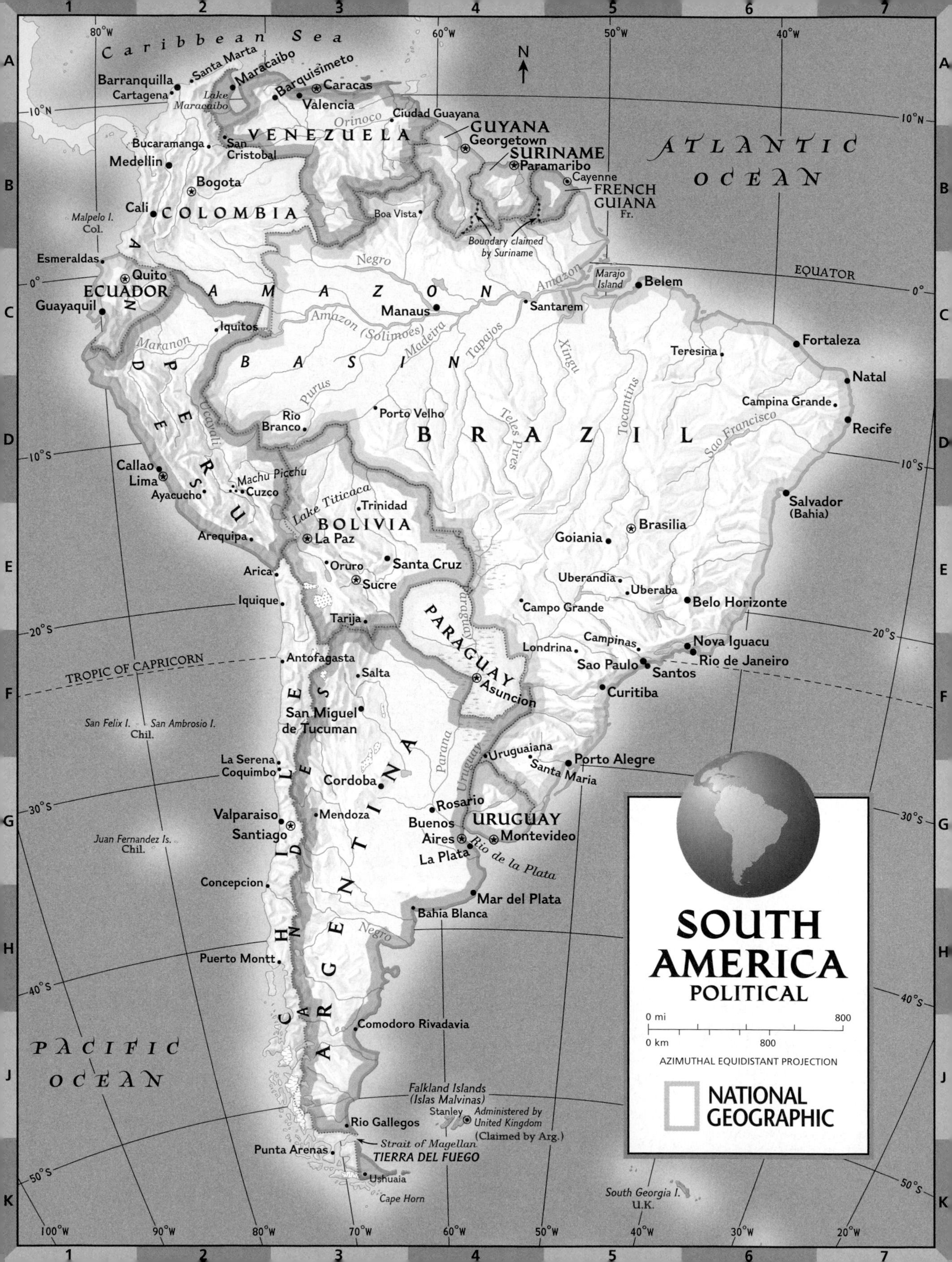
SOUTH AMERICA
POLITICAL
0 mi 800
0 km 800
AZIMUTHAL EQUIDISTANT PROJECTION
NATIONAL GEOGRAPHIC
N
Caribbean Sea
ATLANTIC OCEAN
PACIFIC OCEAN
Barranquilla
Cartagena
Santa Marta
Lake Maracaibo
Maracaibo
Barquisimeto
Caracas
Valencia
Orinoco
Ciudad Guayana
VENEZUELA
GUYANA
Georgetown
SURINAME
Paramaribo
Cayenne
FRENCH GUIANA Fr.
Boundary claimed by Suriname
Bucaramanga
San Cristobal
Medellin
Bogota
Cali
COLOMBIA
Malpelo I. Col.
Boa Vista
Esmeraldas
Quito
ECUADOR
Guayaquil
Negro
AMAZON BASIN
Amazon
Marajo Island
Belem
EQUATOR
Manaus
Santarem
Amazon (Solimoes)
Iquitos
Maranon
Madeira
Tapajos
Xingu
Fortaleza
Teresina
Natal
Campina Grande
Recife
Tocantins
Teles Pires
Purus
Rio Branco
Porto Velho
BRAZIL
Sao Francisco
ANDES
PERU
Ucayali
Callao
Lima
Machu Picchu
Cuzco
Ayacucho
Lake Titicaca
Trinidad
BOLIVIA
La Paz
Arequipa
Salvador (Bahia)
Brasilia
Goiania
Arica
Oruro
Santa Cruz
Sucre
Uberandia
Uberaba
Belo Horizonte
Campo Grande
Iquique
Tarija
PARAGUAY
Paraguay
Londrina
Campinas
Nova Iguacu
Rio de Janeiro
Sao Paulo
Santos
TROPIC OF CAPRICORN
Antofagasta
Salta
Asuncion
Curitiba
San Felix I.
San Ambrosio I.
Chil.
San Miguel de Tucuman
Parana
Uruguay
Uruguaiana
Santa Maria
Porto Alegre
La Serena
Coquimbo
Cordoba
Rosario
URUGUAY
Valparaiso
Mendoza
Santiago
Buenos Aires
Montevideo
Juan Fernandez Is. Chil.
La Plata
Rio de la Plata
Concepcion
Mar del Plata
Bahia Blanca
Negro
CHILE
ARGENTINA
Puerto Montt
Comodoro Rivadavia
Falkland Islands (Islas Malvinas)
Stanley
Administered by United Kingdom
(Claimed by Arg.)
Rio Gallegos
Punta Arenas
Strait of Magellan
TIERRA DEL FUEGO
Ushuaia
Cape Horn
South Georgia I. U.K.
80°W
60°W
50°W
40°W
10°N
0°
10°S
20°S
30°S
40°S
50°S
100°W
90°W
70°W
30°W
20°W
1 2 3 4 5 6 7
A B C D E F G H J K

SOUTH AMERICA
PHYSICAL
0 mi 800
0 km 800
AZIMUTHAL EQUIDISTANT PROJECTION
NATIONAL GEOGRAPHIC
Caribbean Sea
ATLANTIC OCEAN
PACIFIC OCEAN
Lake Maracaibo
Caracas
Orinoco
VENEZUELA
LLANOS
Angel Falls
Total drop= 3,212 ft 979 m
GUYANA
Georgetown
SURINAME
Paramaribo
Cayenne
FRENCH GUIANA
GUIANA HIGHLANDS
Boundary claimed by Suriname
Bogota
COLOMBIA
Malpelo I.
Quito
ECUADOR
Negro
Amazon
Marajo Island
EQUATOR
AMAZON
Selvas
BASIN
Madeira
Tapajos
Xingu
Purus
Ucayali
Teles Pires
Tocantins
Sao Francisco
BRAZIL
ANDES
PERU
Lima
Machu Picchu
Lake Titicaca
BOLIVIA
La Paz
Altiplano
Sucre
Salar de Uyuni
MATO GROSSO
PLATEAU
Brasilia
BRAZILIAN
HIGHLANDS
Paraguay
PARAGUAY
Asuncion
Iguazu Falls
TROPIC OF CAPRICORN
GRAN CHACO
San Felix I.
San Ambrosio I.
Parana
Uruguay
ARGENTINA
PAMPAS
Aconcagua 22,834 ft 6,960 m
Santiago
Juan Fernandez Is.
Buenos Aires
URUGUAY
Montevideo
Rio de la Plata
Negro
Chiloe Island
-131 ft -40 m
Valdes Peninsula
PATAGONIA
Gulf of San Jorge
Taitao Peninsula
Wellington I.
Falkland Islands (Islas Malvinas)
Stanley
Strait of Magellan
Tierra del Fuego
Cape Horn
South Georgia I.
80°W
60°W
50°W
40°W
10°N
0°
10°S
20°S
30°S
40°S
50°S
100°W
90°W
70°W
30°W
20°W
N

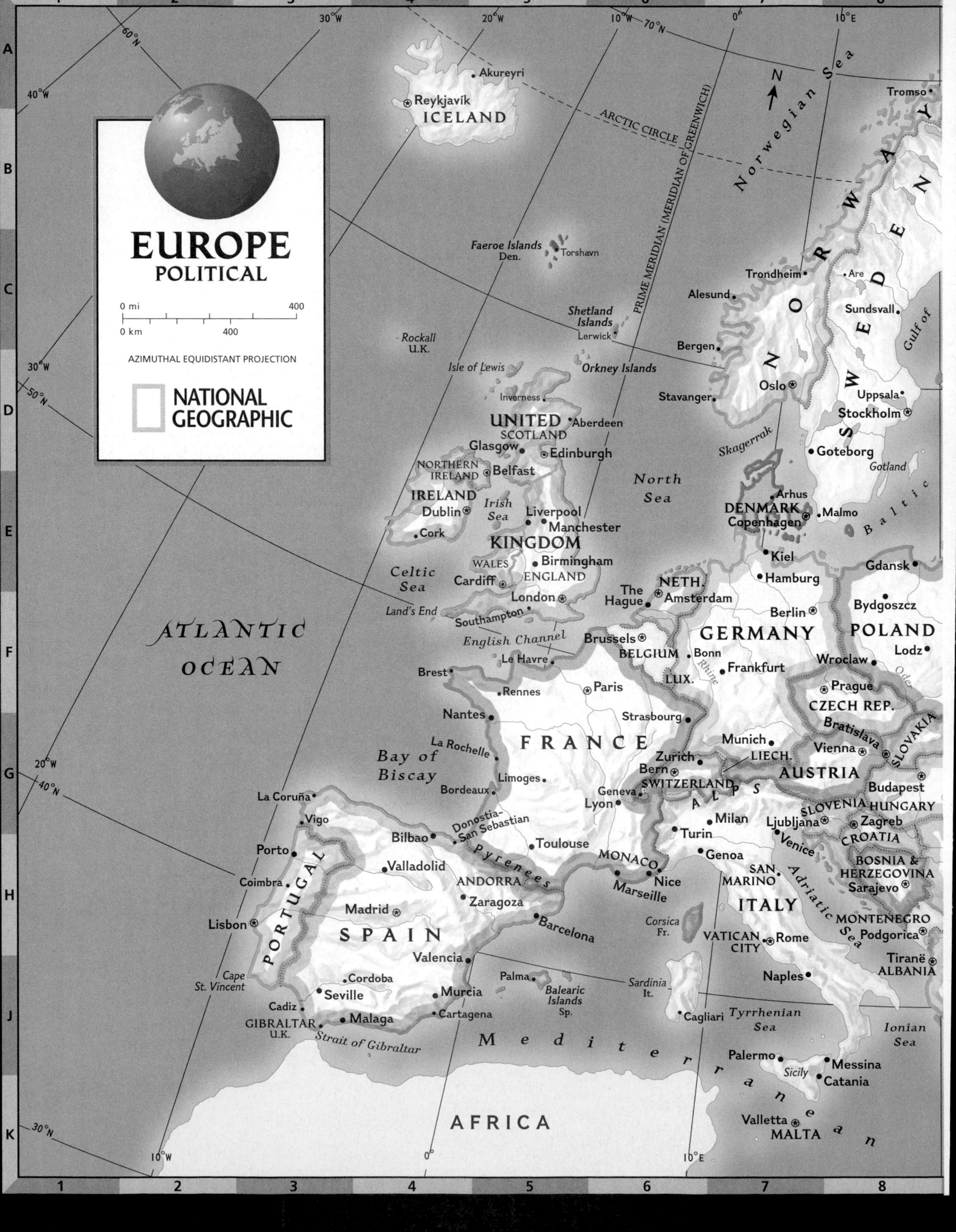
EUROPE
POLITICAL
AZIMUTHAL EQUIDISTANT PROJECTION
NATIONAL GEOGRAPHIC
ATLANTIC OCEAN
ICELAND
Reykjavík
Akureyri
Faeroe Islands Den.
Torshavn
Shetland Islands
Lerwick
Orkney Islands
Rockall U.K.
Isle of Lewis
UNITED KINGDOM
SCOTLAND
NORTHERN IRELAND
WALES
ENGLAND
IRELAND
Dublin
Cork
Belfast
Glasgow
Edinburgh
Inverness
Aberdeen
Liverpool
Manchester
Birmingham
Cardiff
London
Southampton
Land's End
Celtic Sea
Irish Sea
North Sea
Norwegian Sea
ARCTIC CIRCLE
PRIME MERIDIAN (MERIDIAN OF GREENWICH)
NORWAY
SWEDEN
Tromso
Trondheim
Are
Alesund
Bergen
Stavanger
Oslo
Sundsvall
Uppsala
Stockholm
Goteborg
Gotland
Skagerrak
Gulf of
Baltic
DENMARK
Arhus
Copenhagen
Malmo
Kiel
Hamburg
Gdansk
Bydgoszcz
POLAND
Lodz
Wroclaw
Oder
GERMANY
Berlin
Bonn
Rhine
Frankfurt
Munich
NETH.
The Hague
Amsterdam
BELGIUM
Brussels
LUX.
English Channel
Le Havre
Brest
Rennes
Paris
Strasbourg
Nantes
La Rochelle
FRANCE
Limoges
Bordeaux
Lyon
Geneva
Toulouse
Marseille
Nice
MONACO
Bay of Biscay
CZECH REP.
Prague
SLOVAKIA
Bratislava
Vienna
AUSTRIA
LIECH.
SWITZERLAND
Zurich
Bern
ALPS
HUNGARY
Budapest
SLOVENIA
Ljubljana
Zagreb
CROATIA
BOSNIA & HERZEGOVINA
Sarajevo
MONTENEGRO
Podgorica
ALBANIA
Tiranë
Milan
Turin
Genoa
Venice
SAN MARINO
ITALY
VATICAN CITY
Rome
Naples
Adriatic Sea
Corsica Fr.
Sardinia It.
Cagliari
Tyrrhenian Sea
Ionian Sea
Palermo
Sicily
Messina
Catania
Valletta
MALTA
SPAIN
PORTUGAL
La Coruña
Vigo
Porto
Coimbra
Lisbon
Bilbao
Donostia-San Sebastian
Valladolid
ANDORRA
Pyrenees
Zaragoza
Madrid
Barcelona
Valencia
Palma
Balearic Islands Sp.
Cordoba
Seville
Murcia
Cartagena
Cadiz
Malaga
GIBRALTAR U.K.
Strait of Gibraltar
Cape St. Vincent
Mediterranean Sea
AFRICA

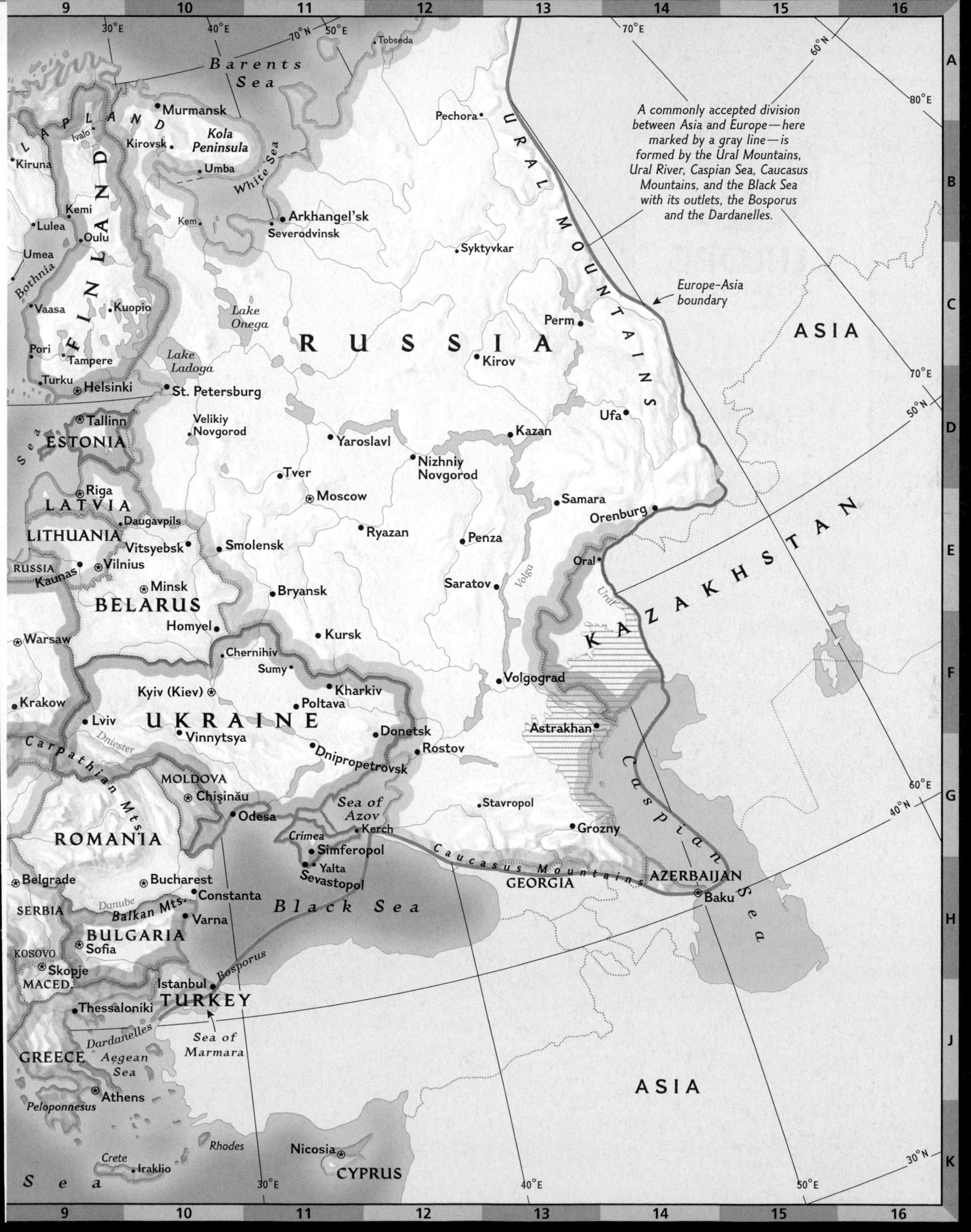
A commonly accepted division between Asia and Europe—here marked by a gray line—is formed by the Ural Mountains, Ural River, Caspian Sea, Caucasus Mountains, and the Black Sea with its outlets, the Bosporus and the Dardanelles.
Europe-Asia boundary
RUSSIA
ASIA
KAZAKHSTAN
FINLAND
ESTONIA
LATVIA
LITHUANIA
BELARUS
UKRAINE
MOLDOVA
ROMANIA
SERBIA
BULGARIA
KOSOVO
MACED.
GREECE
TURKEY
GEORGIA
AZERBAIJAN
CYPRUS
Barents Sea
White Sea
Black Sea
Sea of Azov
Caspian Sea
Aegean Sea
Sea of Marmara
Ural Mountains
Caucasus Mountains
Carpathian Mts.
Balkan Mts.
Moscow
St. Petersburg
Kyiv (Kiev)
Minsk
Helsinki
Istanbul
Athens
Baku
Reference Atlas A11

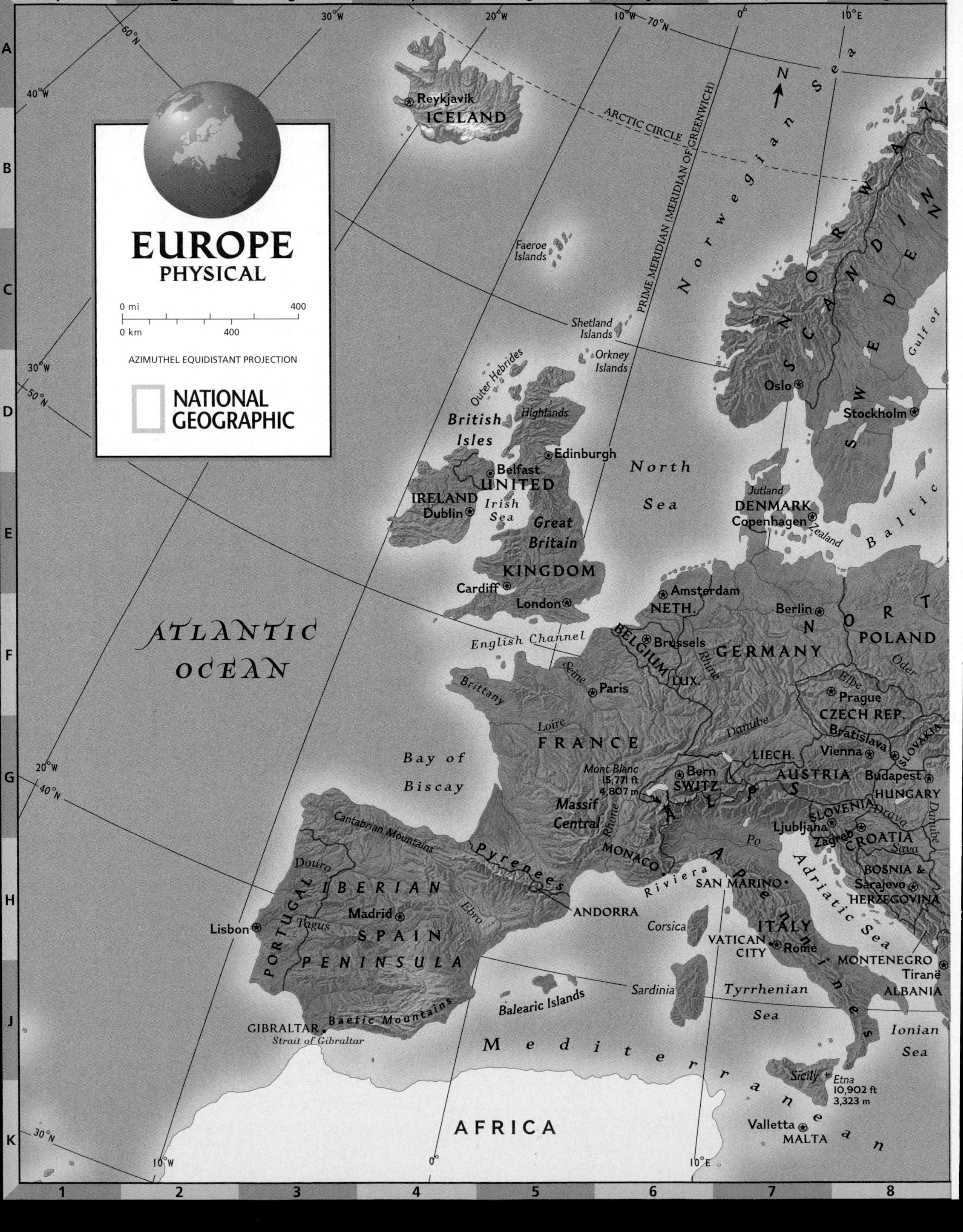
EUROPE
PHYSICAL
0 mi 400
0 km 400
AZIMUTHEL EQUIDISTANT PROJECTION
NATIONAL GEOGRAPHIC
ATLANTIC OCEAN
Reykjavik
ICELAND
ARCTIC CIRCLE
PRIME MERIDIAN (MERIDIAN OF GREENWICH)
Norwegian Sea
Faeroe Islands
Shetland Islands
Orkney Islands
Outer Hebrides
Highlands
British Isles
Edinburgh
Belfast
UNITED KINGDOM
IRELAND
Dublin
Irish Sea
Great Britain
Cardiff
London
North Sea
NORWAY
SWEDEN
SCANDINAVIA
Oslo
Stockholm
Gulf of
Jutland
DENMARK
Copenhagen
Zealand
Baltic
Amsterdam
NETH.
Berlin
NORT
POLAND
Oder
BELGIUM
Brussels
GERMANY
Rhine
LUX.
English Channel
Brittany
Seine
Paris
Elbe
Prague
CZECH REP.
Danube
Bratislava
SLOVAKIA
Vienna
Loire
FRANCE
LIECH.
Bay of Biscay
Mont Blanc 15,771 ft 4,807 m
Bern
SWITZ.
AUSTRIA
Budapest
HUNGARY
Massif Central
Rhone
ALPS
SLOVENIA
Drava
Ljubljana
Zagreb
CROATIA
Sava
Po
Cantabrian Mountains
Pyrenees
MONACO
Riviera
SAN MARINO
Adriatic Sea
BOSNIA & HERZEGOVINA
Sarajevo
Douro
PORTUGAL
IBERIAN PENINSULA
Madrid
SPAIN
Ebro
Tagus
Lisbon
ANDORRA
Corsica
ITALY
Apennines
VATICAN CITY
Rome
MONTENEGRO
Tiranë
ALBANIA
Sardinia
Tyrrhenian Sea
Balearic Islands
Baetic Mountains
GIBRALTAR
Strait of Gibraltar
Ionian Sea
Mediterranean
Sicily
Etna 10,902 ft 3,323 m
Valletta
MALTA
AFRICA

Barents Sea
North Cape
Kola Peninsula
White Sea
Pechora
URAL MOUNTAINS
FINLAND
Bothnia
Lake Region
Lake Onega
Lake Ladoga
Northern Dvina
EUROPEAN PLAIN
RUSSIA
Europe-Asia boundary
ASIA
Helsinki
Gulf of Finland
Tallinn
ESTONIA
Kama
Ural
Volga
Riga
LATVIA
Moscow
LITHUANIA
Oka
Vilnius
RUSSIA
CENTRAL RUSSIAN UPLAND
Minsk
BELARUS
Dnieper
Don
Warsaw
KAZAKHSTAN
Caspian Depression
Vistula
Kyiv (Kiev)
UKRAINE
Dniester
Carpathian Mountains
MOLDOVA
Chişinău
Sea of Azov
Caspian Sea
Crimea
Elbrus 18,510 ft 5,642 m
ROMANIA
Caucasus Mountains
Belgrade
Bucharest
AZERBAIJAN
GEORGIA
Baku
BALKAN PENINSULA
Danube
Black Sea
SERBIA
BULGARIA
Balkan Mountains
Sofia
Skopje
MACED.
Bosporus
TURKEY
GREECE
Dardanelles
Sea of Marmara
Aegean Sea
Athens
Peloponnesus
ASIA
Rhodes
Nicosia
Crete
CYPRUS
Sea

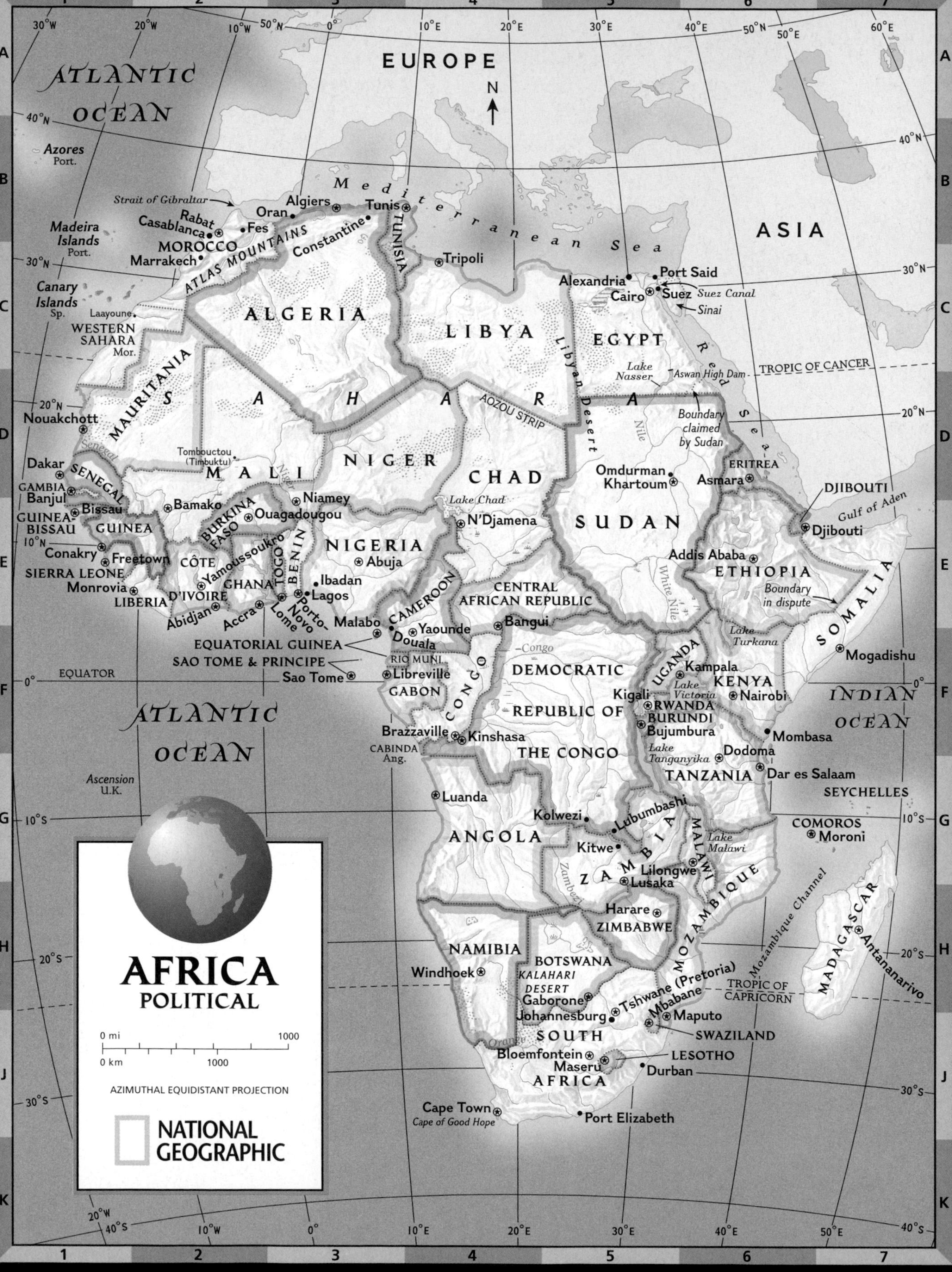

AFRICA
POLITICAL
EUROPE
ASIA
ATLANTIC OCEAN
INDIAN OCEAN
Mediterranean Sea
Red Sea
Gulf of Aden
Mozambique Channel
MOROCCO
ALGERIA
TUNISIA
LIBYA
EGYPT
WESTERN SAHARA Mor.
MAURITANIA
MALI
NIGER
CHAD
SUDAN
ERITREA
DJIBOUTI
ETHIOPIA
SOMALIA
SENEGAL
GAMBIA
GUINEA-BISSAU
GUINEA
SIERRA LEONE
LIBERIA
CÔTE D'IVOIRE
BURKINA FASO
GHANA
TOGO
BENIN
NIGERIA
CAMEROON
CENTRAL AFRICAN REPUBLIC
EQUATORIAL GUINEA
SAO TOME & PRINCIPE
RIO MUNI
GABON
CONGO
DEMOCRATIC REPUBLIC OF THE CONGO
UGANDA
KENYA
RWANDA
BURUNDI
TANZANIA
ANGOLA
ZAMBIA
MALAWI
MOZAMBIQUE
ZIMBABWE
NAMIBIA
BOTSWANA
SOUTH AFRICA
SWAZILAND
LESOTHO
MADAGASCAR
SEYCHELLES
COMOROS
Azores Port.
Madeira Islands Port.
Canary Islands Sp.
Ascension U.K.
CABINDA Ang.
SAHARA
ATLAS MOUNTAINS
Libyan Desert
AOZOU STRIP
KALAHARI DESERT
Strait of Gibraltar
Suez Canal
Sinai
Lake Nasser
Aswan High Dam
Boundary claimed by Sudan
Boundary in dispute
TROPIC OF CANCER
TROPIC OF CAPRICORN
EQUATOR
Lake Chad
Lake Turkana
Lake Victoria
Lake Tanganyika
Lake Malawi
Nile
White Nile
Niger
Senegal
Congo
Zambezi
Orange
Cape of Good Hope
Rabat
Casablanca
Fes
Marrakech
Oran
Algiers
Constantine
Tunis
Tripoli
Alexandria
Port Said
Cairo
Suez
Laayoune
Nouakchott
Tombouctou (Timbuktu)
Dakar
Banjul
Bissau
Bamako
Niamey
Ouagadougou
Conakry
Freetown
Monrovia
Yamoussoukro
Abidjan
Accra
Lome
Porto-Novo
Lagos
Ibadan
Abuja
N'Djamena
Omdurman
Khartoum
Asmara
Djibouti
Addis Ababa
Mogadishu
Malabo
Douala
Yaounde
Bangui
Sao Tome
Libreville
Brazzaville
Kinshasa
Kampala
Nairobi
Kigali
Bujumbura
Mombasa
Dodoma
Dar es Salaam
Luanda
Kolwezi
Lubumbashi
Kitwe
Lilongwe
Lusaka
Moroni
Harare
Antananarivo
Windhoek
Gaborone
Tshwane (Pretoria)
Mbabane
Maputo
Johannesburg
Bloemfontein
Maseru
Durban
Cape Town
Port Elizabeth
N
0 mi 1000
0 km 1000
AZIMUTHAL EQUIDISTANT PROJECTION
NATIONAL GEOGRAPHIC

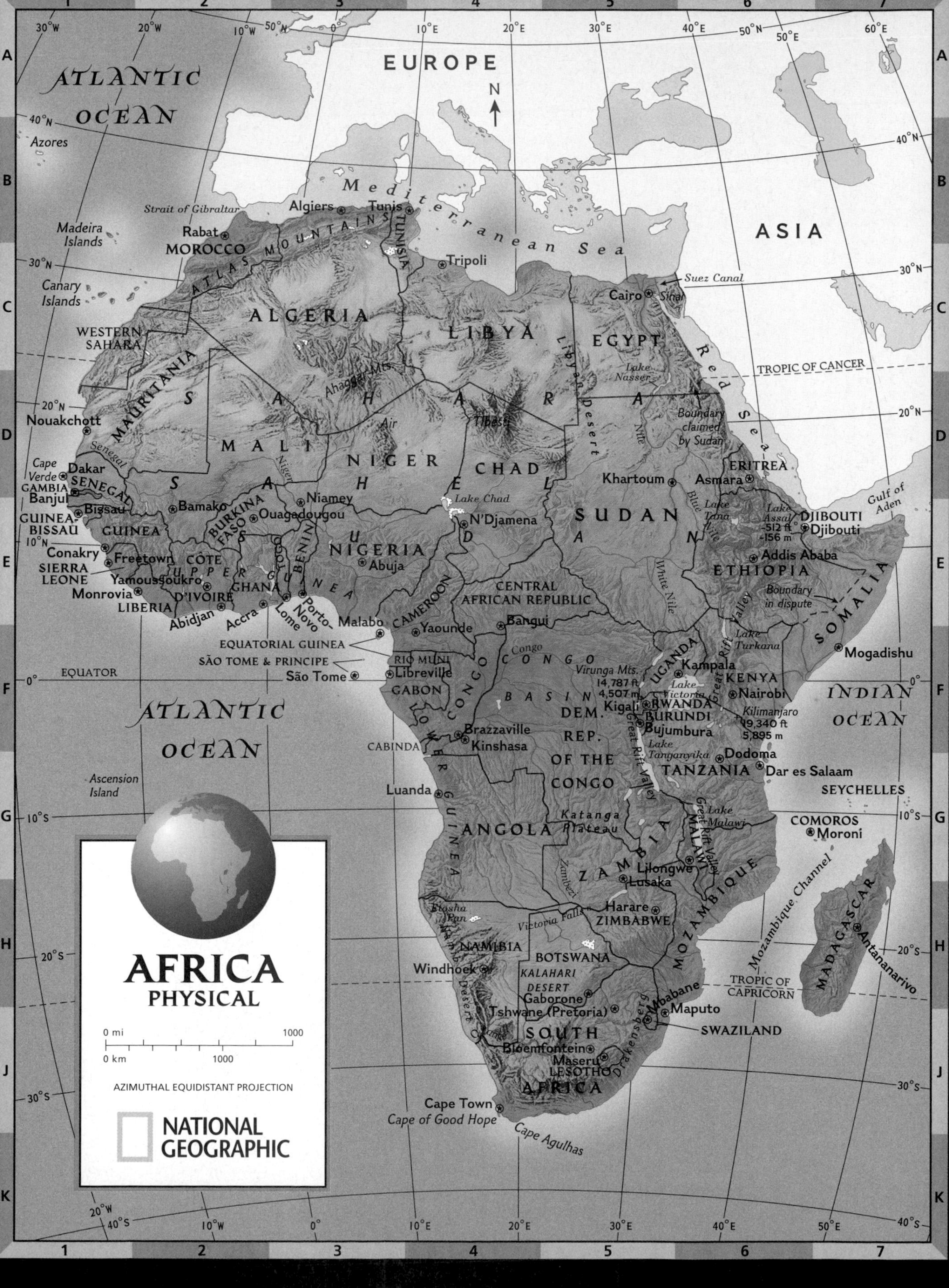
AFRICA
PHYSICAL
0 mi
1000
0 km
1000
AZIMUTHAL EQUIDISTANT PROJECTION
NATIONAL GEOGRAPHIC
EUROPE
ASIA
ATLANTIC OCEAN
ATLANTIC OCEAN
INDIAN OCEAN
Mediterranean Sea
Red Sea
Gulf of Aden
Mozambique Channel
Azores
Madeira Islands
Canary Islands
Cape Verde
Ascension Island
Strait of Gibraltar
Suez Canal
Sinai
ATLAS MOUNTAINS
Ahaggar Mts.
Air
Tibesti
Libyan Desert
Lake Nasser
Boundary claimed by Sudan
TROPIC OF CANCER
EQUATOR
TROPIC OF CAPRICORN
S A H A R A
S A H E L
U P P E R G U I N E A
L O W E R G U I N E A
CONGO BASIN
Lake Chad
Niger
Senegal
Nile
Blue Nile
White Nile
Congo
Zambezi
Lake Tana
Lake Assal -512 ft -156 m
Lake Turkana
Lake Victoria
Lake Tanganyika
Lake Malawi
Great Rift Valley
Virunga Mts. 14,787 ft 4,507 m
Kilimanjaro 19,340 ft 5,895 m
Boundary in dispute
Katanga Plateau
Victoria Falls
Etosha Pan
Namib Desert
KALAHARI DESERT
Drakensberg
Cape of Good Hope
Cape Agulhas
MOROCCO
Rabat
Algiers
Tunis
TUNISIA
ALGERIA
LIBYA
Tripoli
EGYPT
Cairo
WESTERN SAHARA
MAURITANIA
Nouakchott
MALI
NIGER
CHAD
SUDAN
Khartoum
ERITREA
Asmara
DJIBOUTI
Djibouti
ETHIOPIA
Addis Ababa
SOMALIA
Mogadishu
SENEGAL
Dakar
GAMBIA
Banjul
GUINEA-BISSAU
Bissau
GUINEA
Conakry
SIERRA LEONE
Freetown
LIBERIA
Monrovia
CÔTE D'IVOIRE
Yamoussoukro
Abidjan
Bamako
BURKINA FASO
Ouagadougou
Niamey
GHANA
Accra
TOGO
Lome
BENIN
Porto-Novo
NIGERIA
Abuja
N'Djamena
CAMEROON
Yaounde
Malabo
EQUATORIAL GUINEA
SÃO TOME & PRINCIPE
São Tome
RIO MUNI
Libreville
GABON
CONGO
Brazzaville
CENTRAL AFRICAN REPUBLIC
Bangui
DEM. REP. OF THE CONGO
Kinshasa
CABINDA
UGANDA
Kampala
KENYA
Nairobi
RWANDA
Kigali
BURUNDI
Bujumbura
TANZANIA
Dodoma
Dar es Salaam
SEYCHELLES
COMOROS
Moroni
ANGOLA
Luanda
ZAMBIA
Lusaka
MALAWI
Lilongwe
MOZAMBIQUE
Maputo
ZIMBABWE
Harare
NAMIBIA
Windhoek
BOTSWANA
Gaborone
SOUTH AFRICA
Tshwane (Pretoria)
Bloemfontein
Cape Town
LESOTHO
Maseru
SWAZILAND
Mbabane
MADAGASCAR
Antananarivo

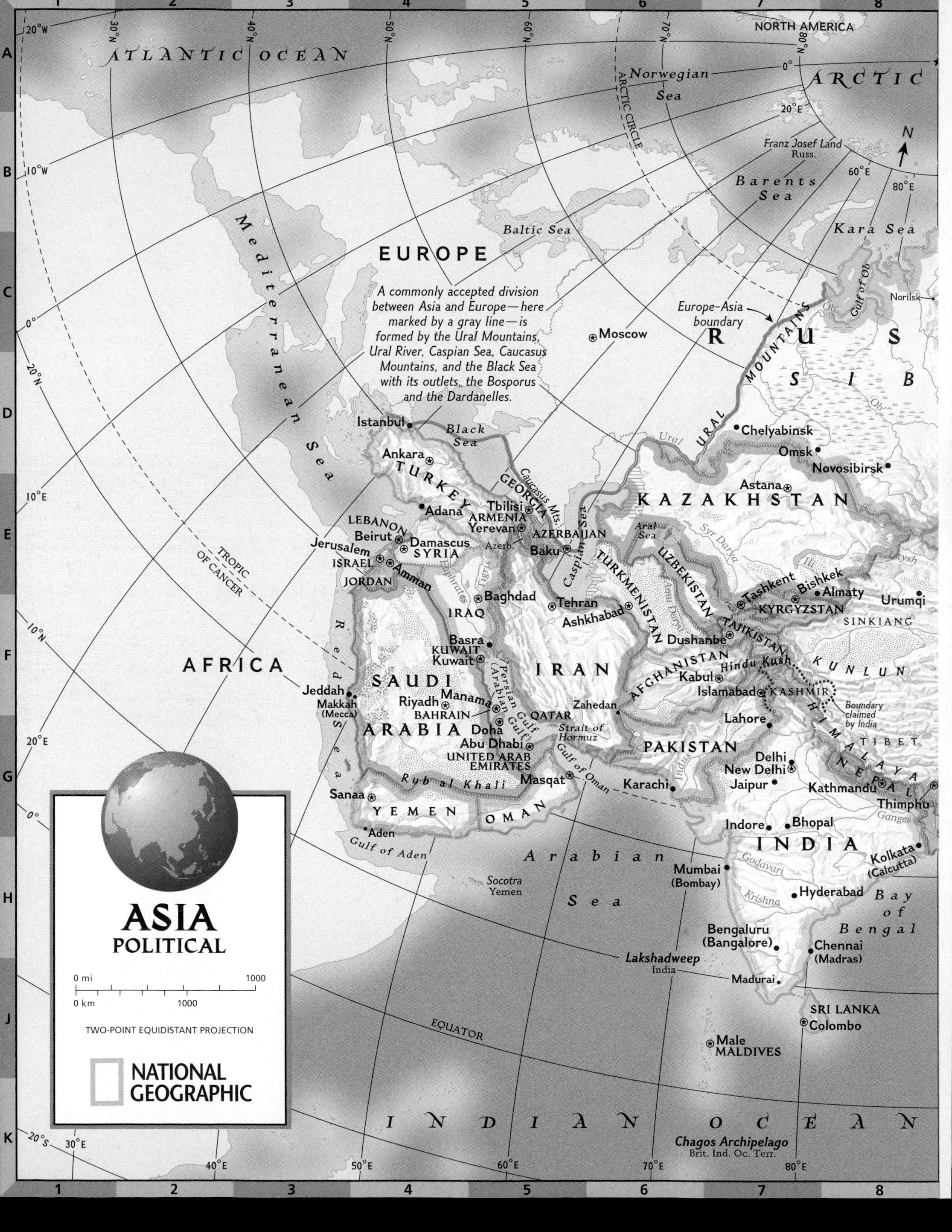
ASIA
POLITICAL
0 mi 1000
0 km 1000
TWO-POINT EQUIDISTANT PROJECTION
NATIONAL GEOGRAPHIC
ATLANTIC OCEAN
NORTH AMERICA
ARCTIC
Norwegian Sea
ARCTIC CIRCLE
Franz Josef Land Russ.
Barents Sea
Kara Sea
Baltic Sea
EUROPE
Mediterranean Sea
A commonly accepted division between Asia and Europe—here marked by a gray line—is formed by the Ural Mountains, Ural River, Caspian Sea, Caucasus Mountains, and the Black Sea with its outlets, the Bosporus and the Dardanelles.
Europe-Asia boundary
Moscow
RUSS
SIB
URAL MOUNTAINS
Gulf of Ob
Ob'
Norilsk
Ural
Chelyabinsk
Omsk
Novosibirsk
Astana
KAZAKHSTAN
Istanbul
Black Sea
Ankara
TURKEY
GEORGIA
Caucasus Mts.
Tbilisi
ARMENIA
Yerevan
AZERBAIJAN
Azerb.
Baku
Caspian Sea
Adana
LEBANON
Beirut
Damascus
SYRIA
Jerusalem
ISRAEL
Amman
JORDAN
TROPIC OF CANCER
Aral Sea
Syr Darya
UZBEKISTAN
TURKMENISTAN
Amu Darya
Tashkent
Bishkek
Almaty
KYRGYZSTAN
Urumqi
SINKIANG
Euphrates
Tigris
Baghdad
IRAQ
Tehran
Ashkhabad
Dushanbe
TAJIKISTAN
Basra
KUWAIT
Kuwait
Red Sea
AFRICA
IRAN
AFGHANISTAN
Kabul
Hindu Kush
Islamabad
KASHMIR
Boundary claimed by India
KUNLUN
Jeddah
Makkah (Mecca)
SAUDI ARABIA
Riyadh
Manama
BAHRAIN
Persian Gulf (Arabian Gulf)
QATAR
Doha
Zahedan
Strait of Hormuz
Lahore
HIMALAYA
TIBET
Abu Dhabi
UNITED ARAB EMIRATES
PAKISTAN
Indus
Delhi
New Delhi
Jaipur
NEPAL
Kathmandu
Thimphu
Ganges
Gulf of Oman
Masqat
Karachi
Rub al Khali
Sanaa
YEMEN
OMAN
Aden
Gulf of Aden
Indore
Bhopal
INDIA
Kolkata (Calcutta)
Arabian Sea
Mumbai (Bombay)
Godavari
Socotra Yemen
Krishna
Hyderabad
Bay of Bengal
Bengaluru (Bangalore)
Chennai (Madras)
Lakshadweep India
Madurai
SRI LANKA
Colombo
EQUATOR
Male
MALDIVES
INDIAN OCEAN
Chagos Archipelago Brit. Ind. Oc. Terr.
20°W
10°W
0°
20°N
10°E
10°N
20°E
0°
20°S
30°E
40°E
50°E
60°E
70°E
80°E
30°N
40°N
50°N
60°N
70°N
80°N
0°
20°E
60°E
80°E
1 2 3 4 5 6 7 8
A B C D E F G H J K

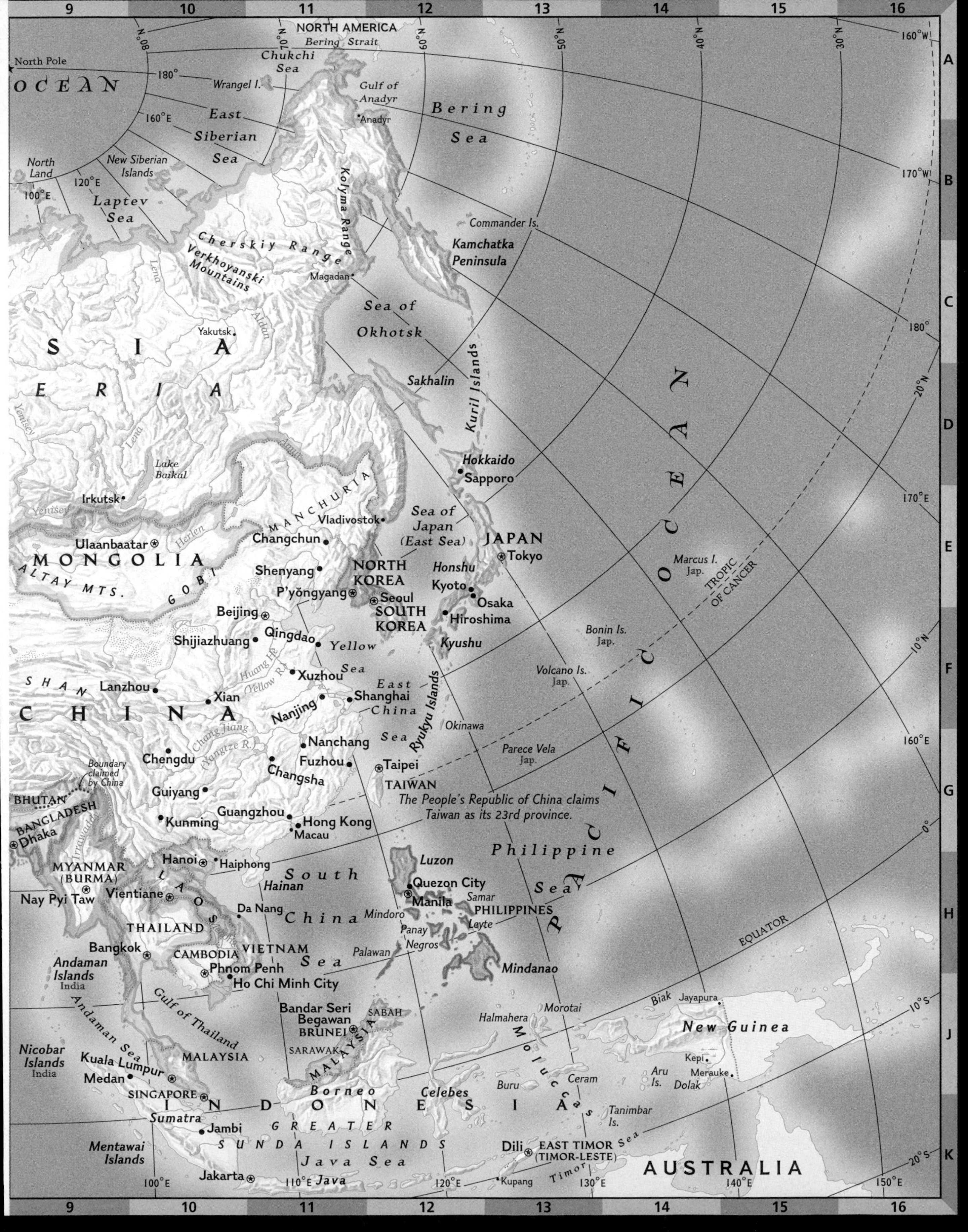
NORTH AMERICA
Bering Strait
North Pole
Chukchi Sea
Wrangel I.
OCEAN
Gulf of Anadyr
Anadyr
Bering Sea
East Siberian Sea
New Siberian Islands
North Land
Laptev Sea
Kolyma Range
Commander Is.
Kamchatka Peninsula
Cherskiy Range
Verkhoyanski Mountains
Magadan
Lena
Sea of Okhotsk
Yakutsk
Aldan
SIA
ERIA
Sakhalin
Kuril Islands
PACIFIC OCEAN
Yenisey
Amur
Lake Baikal
Hokkaido
Sapporo
Irkutsk
MANCHURIA
Vladivostok
Sea of Japan (East Sea)
JAPAN
Tokyo
Ulaanbaatar
Herlen
Changchun
MONGOLIA
ALTAY MTS.
GOBI
Shenyang
NORTH KOREA
Honshu
Marcus I. Jap.
TROPIC OF CANCER
P'yŏngyang
Seoul
SOUTH KOREA
Kyoto
Osaka
Hiroshima
Beijing
Qingdao
Yellow Sea
Kyushu
Bonin Is. Jap.
Shijiazhuang
Huang He (Yellow R.)
Xuzhou
East China Sea
Volcano Is. Jap.
SHAN
Lanzhou
Xian
CHINA
Nanjing
Shanghai
Ryukyu Islands
Okinawa
Chang Jiang (Yangtze R.)
Nanchang
Chengdu
Fuzhou
Taipei
Parece Vela Jap.
Boundary claimed by China
Changsha
TAIWAN
Guiyang
BHUTAN
The People's Republic of China claims Taiwan as its 23rd province.
BANGLADESH
Dhaka
Kunming
Guangzhou
Hong Kong
Macau
Irrawaddy
Hanoi
Haiphong
Luzon
Philippine Sea
MYANMAR (BURMA)
LAOS
South China Sea
Hainan
Quezon City
Nay Pyi Taw
Vientiane
Manila
Samar
PHILIPPINES
Da Nang
Mindoro
Leyte
THAILAND
Panay
Negros
EQUATOR
Bangkok
CAMBODIA
VIETNAM
Palawan
Mekong
Andaman Islands India
Phnom Penh
Ho Chi Minh City
Mindanao
Gulf of Thailand
Andaman Sea
Bandar Seri Begawan
BRUNEI
SABAH
Morotai
Biak
Jayapura
Halmahera
New Guinea
Nicobar Islands India
MALAYSIA
SARAWAK
Moluccas
Kuala Lumpur
Kepi
Medan
Aru Is.
Merauke
Dolak
Buru
Ceram
SINGAPORE
Borneo
Celebes
INDONESIA
Sumatra
Tanimbar Is.
Jambi
GREATER SUNDA ISLANDS
Mentawai Islands
Dili
EAST TIMOR (TIMOR-LESTE)
Timor Sea
Java Sea
AUSTRALIA
Jakarta
Java
Kupang
80°N
70°N
60°N
50°N
40°N
30°N
20°N
10°N
0°
10°S
20°S
180°
160°E
120°E
100°E
160°W
170°W
170°E
110°E
130°E
140°E
150°E
9
10
11
12
13
14
15
16
A
B
C
D
E
F
G
H
J
K

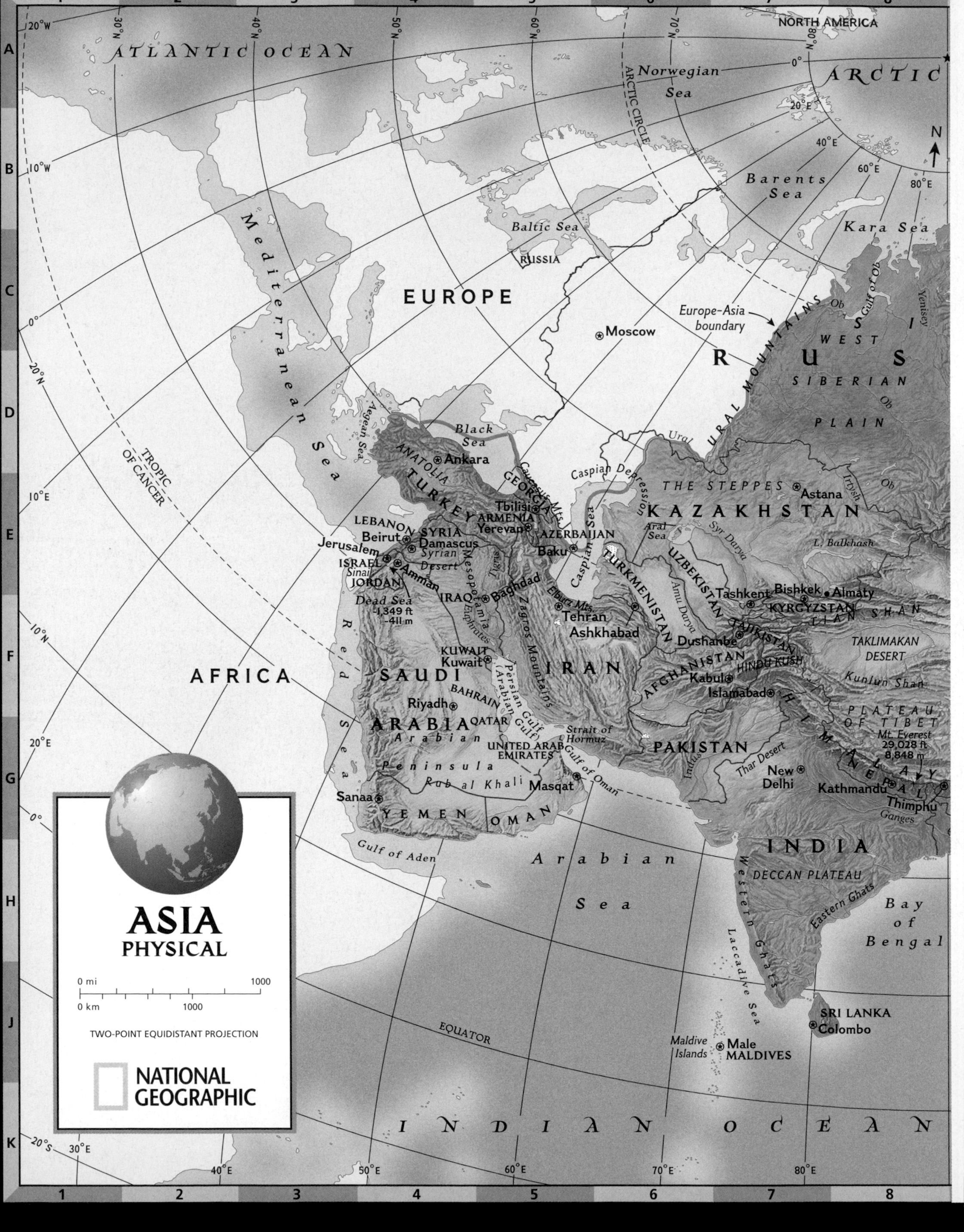
ASIA
PHYSICAL
0 mi 1000
0 km 1000
TWO-POINT EQUIDISTANT PROJECTION
NATIONAL GEOGRAPHIC
ATLANTIC OCEAN
ARCTIC
NORTH AMERICA
Norwegian Sea
Barents Sea
Kara Sea
Baltic Sea
RUSSIA
EUROPE
Moscow
Europe-Asia boundary
URAL MOUNTAINS
WEST SIBERIAN PLAIN
Mediterranean Sea
Aegean Sea
Black Sea
ANATOLIA
Ankara
TURKEY
GEORGIA
Caucasus Mts.
Tbilisi
ARMENIA
Yerevan
AZERBAIJAN
Baku
Caspian Depression
Caspian Sea
THE STEPPES
Astana
KAZAKHSTAN
Aral Sea
Syr Darya
L. Balkhash
UZBEKISTAN
TURKMENISTAN
Amu Darya
Tashkent
Bishkek
Almaty
KYRGYZSTAN
TIAN SHAN
TAJIKISTAN
Dushanbe
TAKLIMAKAN DESERT
LEBANON
Beirut
SYRIA
Damascus
Syrian Desert
Jerusalem
ISRAEL
Sinai
JORDAN
Amman
Dead Sea -1,349 ft -411 m
IRAQ
Baghdad
Mesopotamia
Euphrates
Tigris
Zagros Mountains
Elburz Mts.
Tehran
Ashkhabad
IRAN
AFGHANISTAN
Kabul
HINDU KUSH
Islamabad
Kunlun Shan
PLATEAU OF TIBET
Mt. Everest 29,028 ft 8,848 m
HIMALAYA
KUWAIT
Kuwait
SAUDI ARABIA
BAHRAIN
Riyadh
QATAR
Persian Gulf (Arabian Gulf)
Strait of Hormuz
UNITED ARAB EMIRATES
Arabian Peninsula
Rub al Khali
Masqat
Gulf of Oman
OMAN
YEMEN
Sanaa
Gulf of Aden
AFRICA
Red Sea
PAKISTAN
Indus
Thar Desert
New Delhi
Kathmandu
NEPAL
Thimphu
Ganges
INDIA
DECCAN PLATEAU
Western Ghats
Eastern Ghats
Bay of Bengal
Arabian Sea
Laccadive Sea
SRI LANKA
Colombo
Maldive Islands
Male
MALDIVES
INDIAN OCEAN
EQUATOR
TROPIC OF CANCER
ARCTIC CIRCLE
Ural
Ob
Irtysh
Yenisey
Gulf of Ob

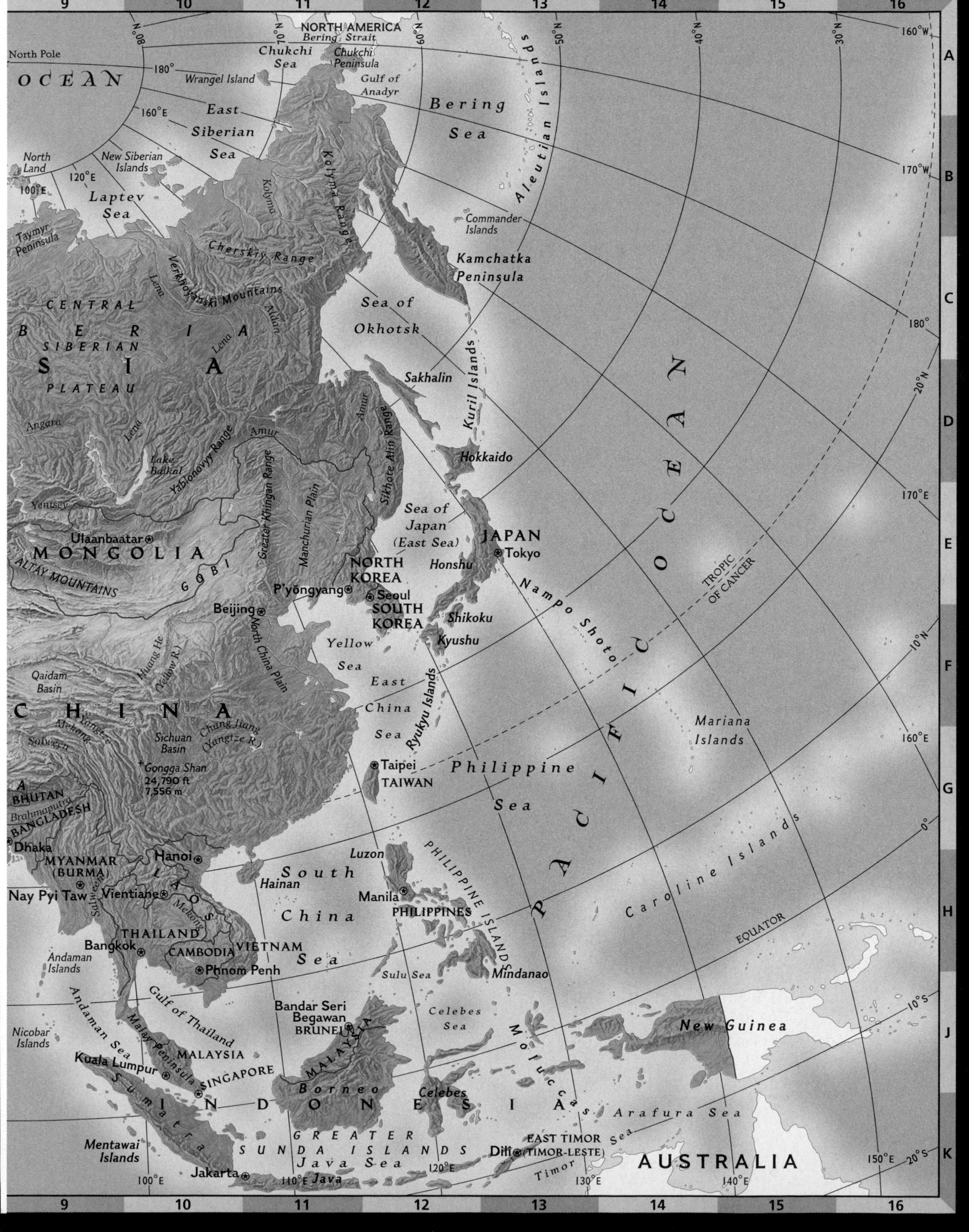
NORTH AMERICA
Bering Strait
Chukchi Sea
Chukchi Peninsula
North Pole
OCEAN
Wrangel Island
Gulf of Anadyr
East Siberian Sea
Bering Sea
Aleutian Islands
North Land
New Siberian Islands
Laptev Sea
Taymyr Peninsula
Kolyma
Kolyma Range
Commander Islands
Cherskiy Range
Kamchatka Peninsula
Verkhoyanski Mountains
Lena
Aldan
CENTRAL SIBERIAN PLATEAU
SIBERIA
ASIA
Sea of Okhotsk
Sakhalin
Kuril Islands
PACIFIC OCEAN
Angara
Amur
Sikhote Alin Range
Lake Baikal
Yablonovyy Range
Hokkaido
Yenisey
Greater Khingan Range
Manchurian Plain
Sea of Japan (East Sea)
JAPAN
Tokyo
Ulaanbaatar
MONGOLIA
GOBI
ALTAY MOUNTAINS
NORTH KOREA
Honshu
P'yŏngyang
Seoul
SOUTH KOREA
Beijing
North China Plain
Shikoku
Kyushu
Nampo Shoto
TROPIC OF CANCER
Yellow Sea
Huang He (Yellow R.)
Qaidam Basin
East China Sea
Ryukyu Islands
CHINA
Yangtze
Mekong
Salween
Chang Jiang (Yangtze R.)
Sichuan Basin
Mariana Islands
Gongga Shan 24,790 ft 7,556 m
Taipei
TAIWAN
Philippine Sea
BHUTAN
Brahmaputra
BANGLADESH
Dhaka
Caroline Islands
MYANMAR (BURMA)
Hanoi
LAOS
Luzon
PHILIPPINE ISLANDS
South China Sea
Hainan
Nay Pyi Taw
Vientiane
Manila
PHILIPPINES
THAILAND
Bangkok
CAMBODIA
VIETNAM
Phnom Penh
Andaman Islands
Sulu Sea
Mindanao
EQUATOR
Andaman Sea
Gulf of Thailand
Malay Peninsula
MALAYSIA
Bandar Seri Begawan
BRUNEI
Celebes Sea
Moluccas
New Guinea
Nicobar Islands
Kuala Lumpur
SINGAPORE
Borneo
Celebes
Sumatra
INDONESIA
Arafura Sea
GREATER SUNDA ISLANDS
EAST TIMOR (TIMOR-LESTE)
Dili
Mentawai Islands
Java Sea
Java
Jakarta
Timor Sea
AUSTRALIA
80°N 70°N 60°N 50°N 40°N 30°N 20°N 10°N 0° 10°S 20°S
180° 160°E 120°E 100°E 160°W 170°W 170°E 160°E 150°E 140°E 130°E 120°E 110°E 100°E
9 10 11 12 13 14 15 16
A B C D E F G H J K

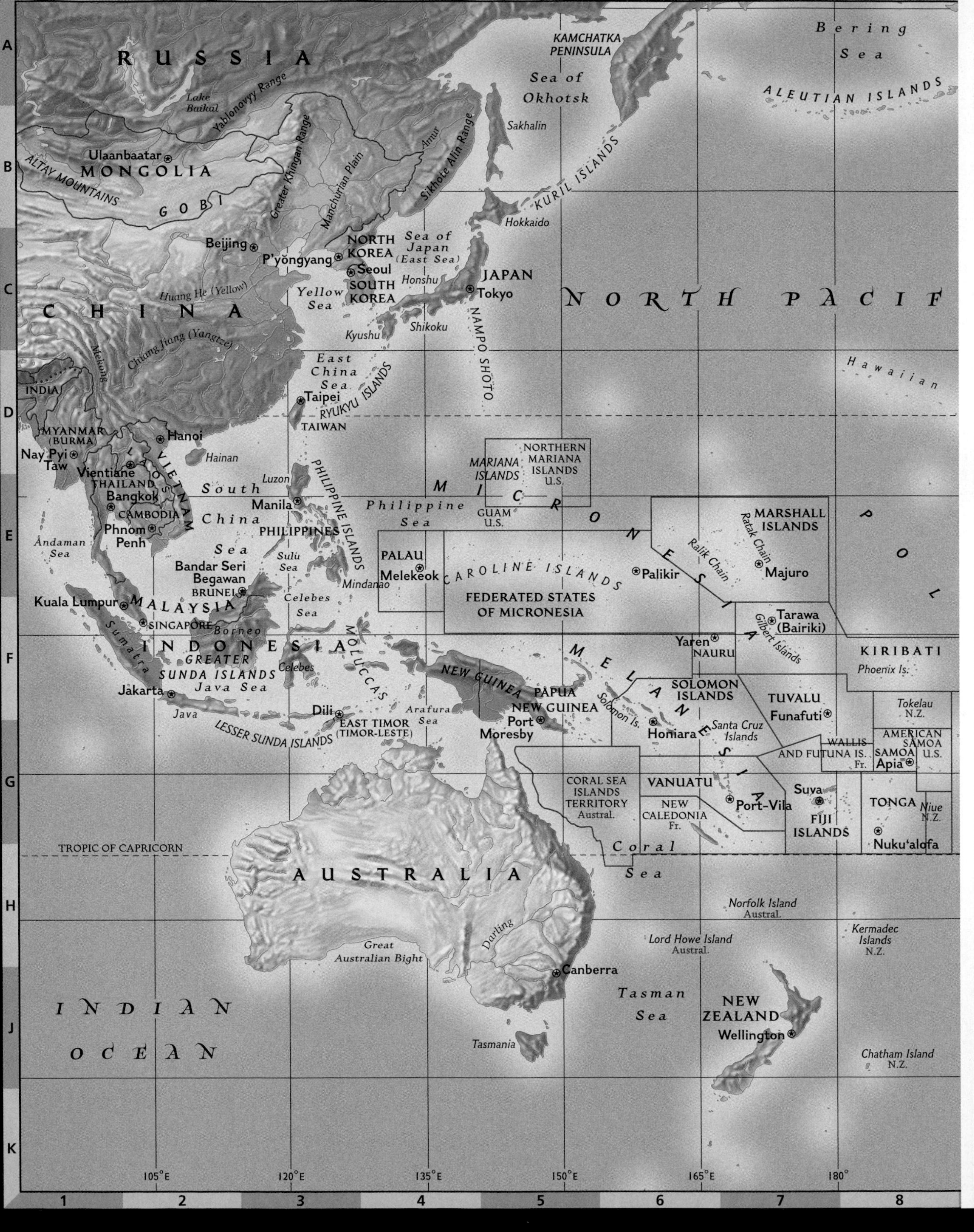
RUSSIA
KAMCHATKA PENINSULA
Bering Sea
Sea of Okhotsk
ALEUTIAN ISLANDS
Lake Baikal
Yablonovyy Range
Sakhalin
Ulaanbaatar
MONGOLIA
ALTAY MOUNTAINS
GOBI
Greater Khingan Range
Manchurian Plain
Amur
Sikhote Alin Range
KURIL ISLANDS
Hokkaido
Beijing
P'yŏngyang
NORTH KOREA
Sea of Japan (East Sea)
Seoul
SOUTH KOREA
Honshu
JAPAN
Tokyo
NORTH PACIF
Huang He (Yellow)
Yellow Sea
CHINA
Chang Jiang (Yangtze)
Kyushu
Shikoku
NAMPO SHOTO
Mekong
East China Sea
RYUKYU ISLANDS
Hawaiian
INDIA
Taipei
TAIWAN
MYANMAR (BURMA)
Hanoi
Nay Pyi Taw
LAOS
VIETNAM
Hainan
Vientiane
THAILAND
Luzon
PHILIPPINE ISLANDS
NORTHERN MARIANA ISLANDS U.S.
MARIANA ISLANDS
South China Sea
Bangkok
CAMBODIA
Manila
Philippine Sea
MICRONESIA
GUAM U.S.
MARSHALL ISLANDS
Ratak Chain
Ralik Chain
POLYNESIA
Andaman Sea
Phnom Penh
PHILIPPINES
PALAU
Melekeok
CAROLINE ISLANDS
Palikir
Majuro
Bandar Seri Begawan
Sulu Sea
BRUNEI
Mindanao
FEDERATED STATES OF MICRONESIA
Kuala Lumpur
MALAYSIA
Celebes Sea
SINGAPORE
Borneo
Tarawa (Bairiki)
Gilbert Islands
Sumatra
INDONESIA
MOLUCCAS
Yaren
NAURU
KIRIBATI
Phoenix Is.
GREATER SUNDA ISLANDS
Celebes
NEW GUINEA
MELANESIA
Java Sea
PAPUA NEW GUINEA
SOLOMON ISLANDS
TUVALU
Tokelau N.Z.
Jakarta
Solomon Is.
Funafuti
Java
Dili
EAST TIMOR (TIMOR-LESTE)
Arafura Sea
Port Moresby
Honiara
Santa Cruz Islands
AMERICAN SAMOA U.S.
LESSER SUNDA ISLANDS
WALLIS AND FUTUNA IS. Fr.
SAMOA
Apia
CORAL SEA ISLANDS TERRITORY Austral.
VANUATU
Suva
Port-Vila
TONGA
NEW CALEDONIA Fr.
FIJI ISLANDS
Niue N.Z.
TROPIC OF CAPRICORN
Coral Sea
Nuku'alofa
AUSTRALIA
Norfolk Island Austral.
Darling
Kermadec Islands N.Z.
Great Australian Bight
Lord Howe Island Austral.
Canberra
Tasman Sea
NEW ZEALAND
INDIAN OCEAN
Wellington
Tasmania
Chatham Island N.Z.
105°E
120°E
135°E
150°E
165°E
180°
1
2
3
4
5
6
7
8
A
B
C
D
E
F
G
H
J
K

PACIFIC RIM
PHYSICAL/POLITICAL
0 mi
1500
0 km
1500
MILLER CYLINDRICAL PROJECTION
NATIONAL GEOGRAPHIC
Gulf of Alaska
Kodiak I.
Alexander Archipelago
Queen Charlotte Islands
Vancouver Island
Coast Mountains
ROCKY MOUNTAINS
Cascade Range
GREAT PLAINS
CANADA
CANADIAN SHIELD
Hudson Bay
Ottawa
Great Lakes
Missouri
Mississippi
CENTRAL LOWLAND
APPALACHIAN MTS.
Washington, D.C.
UNITED STATES
COASTAL PLAIN
ATLANTIC OCEAN
PACIFIC OCEAN
Baja California
Gulf of California
Sierra Madre Occidental
Sierra Madre Oriental
MEXICO
Gulf of Mexico
Mexico City
TROPIC OF CANCER
Nassau
BAHAMAS
Havana
CUBA
JAMAICA
HAITI
DOMINICAN REPUBLIC
Santo Domingo
BELIZE
HONDURAS
Tegucigalpa
GUATEMALA
Guatemala
San Salvador
EL SALVADOR
NICARAGUA
Managua
San Jose
COSTA RICA
Panama
PANAMA
Caribbean Sea
Caracas
LLANOS
VENEZ.
Bogota
COLOMBIA
Quito
ECUADOR
Galapagos Islands Ecua.
EQUATOR
AMAZON BASIN
BRAZIL
ANDES
PERU
Lima
La Paz
BOLIVIA
Santiago
CHILE
ARGENTINA
PATAGONIA
Chiloe Island
Hawaiian Islands
HAWAII U.S.
Kiritimati
Line Islands
POLYNESIA
Marquesas Is.
Tuamotu Archipelago
Society Is.
COOK ISLANDS N.Z.
FRENCH POLYNESIA Fr.
Austral Is.
Pitcairn Island U.K.
SOUTH PACIFIC OCEAN
45°N
30°N
15°N
0°
15°S
30°S
45°S
165°W
150°W
135°W
120°W
105°W
90°W
75°W

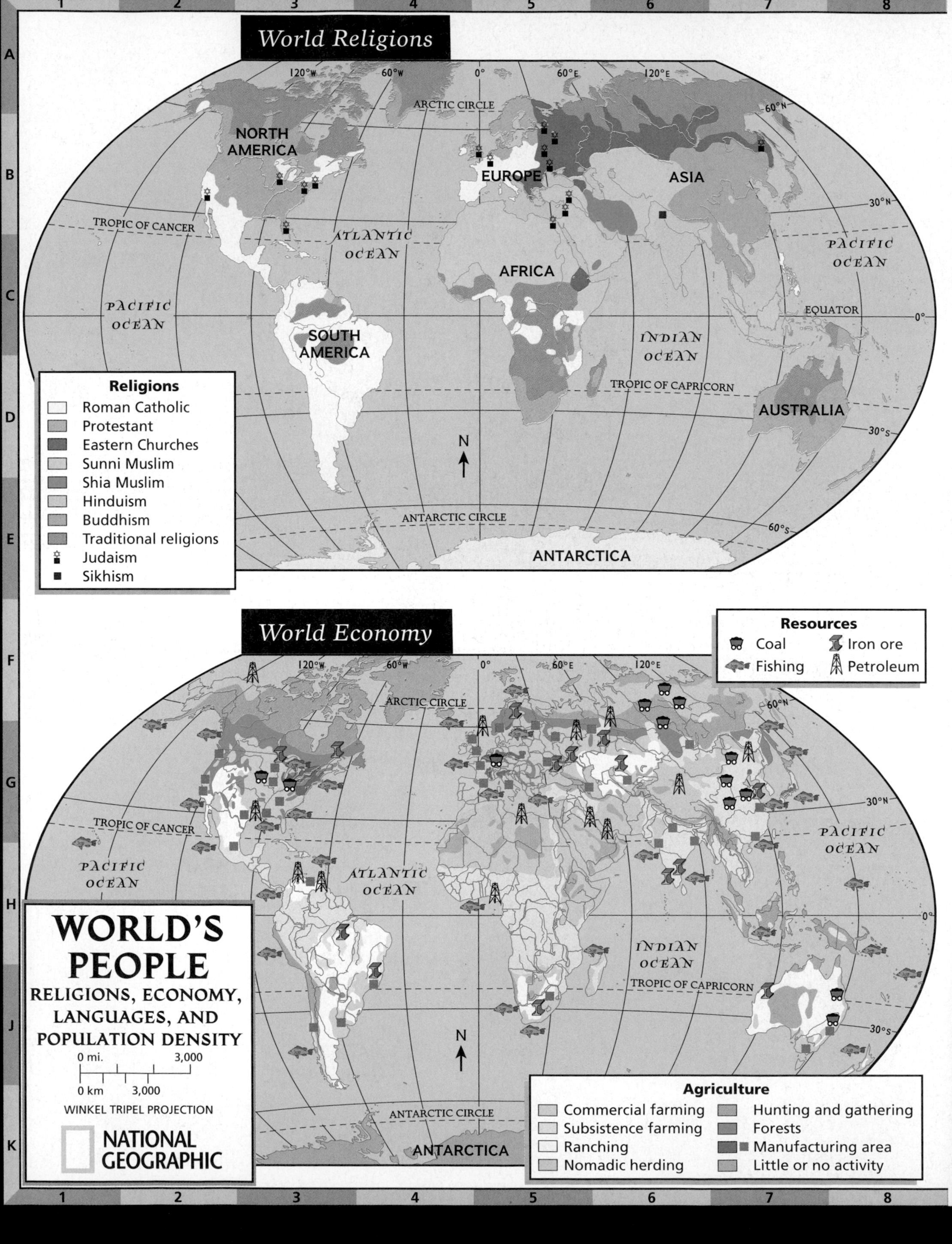
World Religions
NORTH AMERICA
SOUTH AMERICA
EUROPE
ASIA
AFRICA
AUSTRALIA
ANTARCTICA
ARCTIC CIRCLE
TROPIC OF CANCER
EQUATOR
TROPIC OF CAPRICORN
ANTARCTIC CIRCLE
ATLANTIC OCEAN
PACIFIC OCEAN
INDIAN OCEAN
Religions
Roman Catholic
Protestant
Eastern Churches
Sunni Muslim
Shia Muslim
Hinduism
Buddhism
Traditional religions
Judaism
Sikhism
World Economy
Resources
Coal
Iron ore
Fishing
Petroleum
Agriculture
Commercial farming
Subsistence farming
Ranching
Nomadic herding
Hunting and gathering
Forests
Manufacturing area
Little or no activity
WORLD'S PEOPLE
RELIGIONS, ECONOMY, LANGUAGES, AND POPULATION DENSITY
0 mi. 3,000
0 km 3,000
WINKEL TRIPEL PROJECTION
NATIONAL GEOGRAPHIC

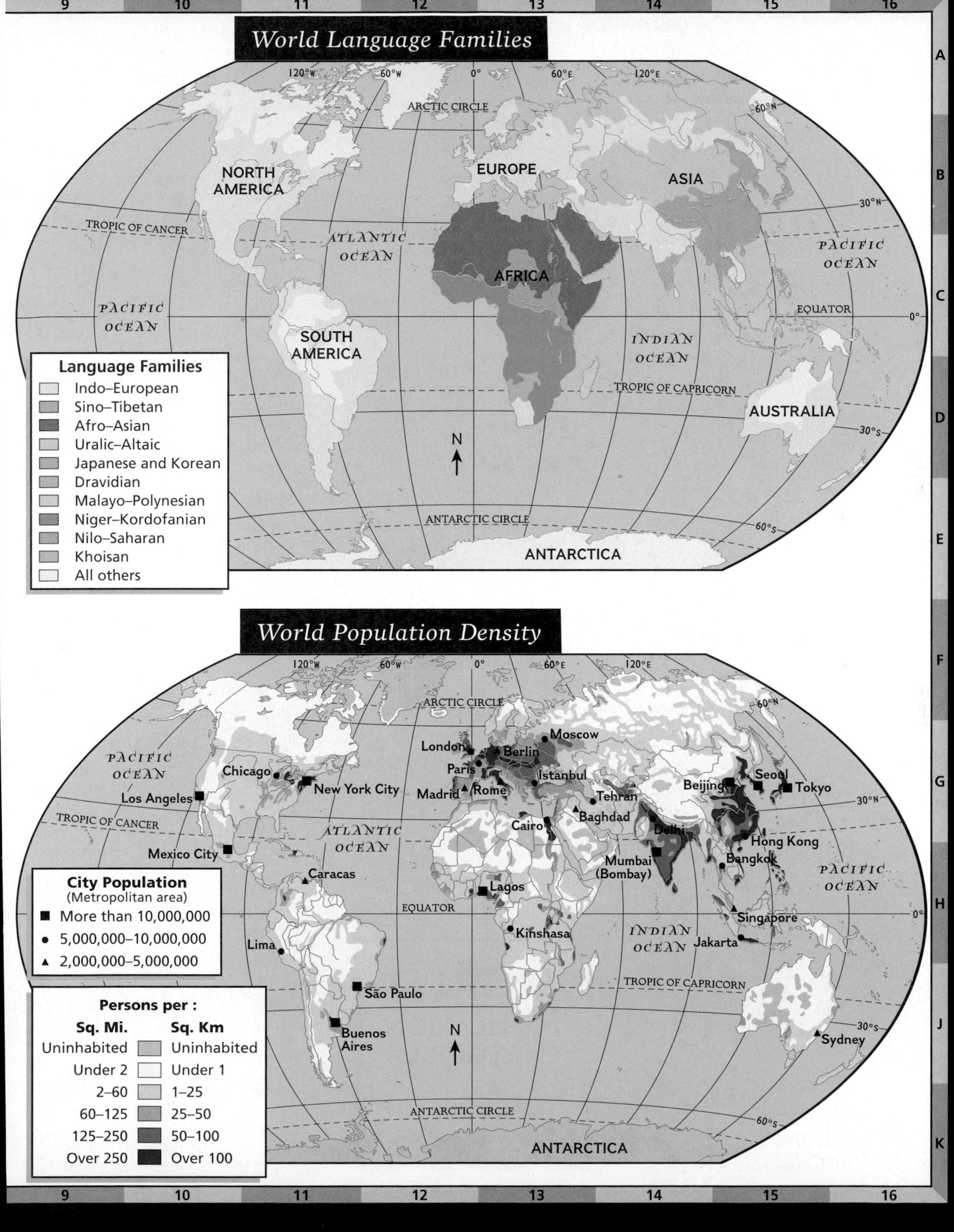
World Language Families
NORTH AMERICA
EUROPE
ASIA
AFRICA
SOUTH AMERICA
AUSTRALIA
ANTARCTICA
ATLANTIC OCEAN
PACIFIC OCEAN
INDIAN OCEAN
ARCTIC CIRCLE
TROPIC OF CANCER
EQUATOR
TROPIC OF CAPRICORN
ANTARCTIC CIRCLE
120°W
60°W
0°
60°E
120°E
60°N
30°N
0°
30°S
60°S
N
Language Families
Indo–European
Sino–Tibetan
Afro–Asian
Uralic–Altaic
Japanese and Korean
Dravidian
Malayo–Polynesian
Niger–Kordofanian
Nilo–Saharan
Khoisan
All others
World Population Density
PACIFIC OCEAN
ATLANTIC OCEAN
INDIAN OCEAN
ANTARCTICA
ARCTIC CIRCLE
TROPIC OF CANCER
EQUATOR
TROPIC OF CAPRICORN
ANTARCTIC CIRCLE
Chicago
New York City
Los Angeles
Mexico City
Caracas
Lima
São Paulo
Buenos Aires
London
Berlin
Moscow
Paris
Madrid
Rome
Istanbul
Tehran
Baghdad
Cairo
Lagos
Kinshasa
Delhi
Mumbai (Bombay)
Beijing
Seoul
Tokyo
Hong Kong
Bangkok
Singapore
Jakarta
Sydney
City Population
(Metropolitan area)
More than 10,000,000
5,000,000–10,000,000
2,000,000–5,000,000
Persons per :
Sq. Mi.
Sq. Km
Uninhabited
Uninhabited
Under 2
Under 1
2–60
1–25
60–125
25–50
125–250
50–100
Over 250
Over 100
9 10 11 12 13 14 15 16
A B C D E F G H J K

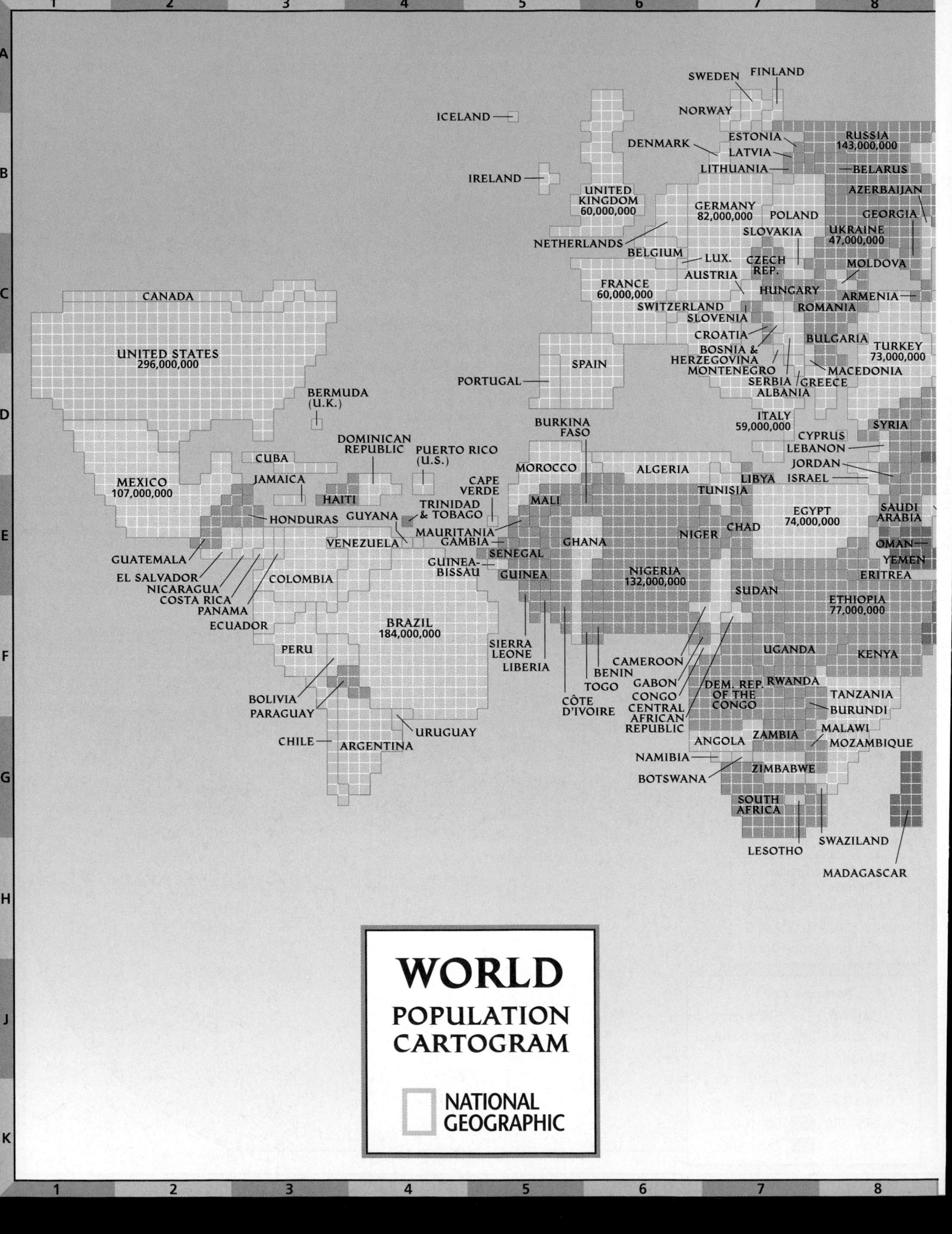
WORLD
POPULATION
CARTOGRAM
NATIONAL
GEOGRAPHIC
ICELAND
SWEDEN
FINLAND
NORWAY
RUSSIA
143,000,000
DENMARK
ESTONIA
LATVIA
LITHUANIA
BELARUS
IRELAND
UNITED
KINGDOM
60,000,000
AZERBAIJAN
GERMANY
82,000,000
POLAND
GEORGIA
UKRAINE
47,000,000
SLOVAKIA
NETHERLANDS
BELGIUM
LUX.
CZECH
REP.
MOLDOVA
AUSTRIA
FRANCE
60,000,000
HUNGARY
ARMENIA
CANADA
SWITZERLAND
ROMANIA
SLOVENIA
CROATIA
BULGARIA
BOSNIA &
HERZEGOVINA
TURKEY
73,000,000
UNITED STATES
296,000,000
SPAIN
MONTENEGRO
MACEDONIA
PORTUGAL
SERBIA
GREECE
ALBANIA
BERMUDA
(U.K.)
ITALY
59,000,000
BURKINA
FASO
SYRIA
CYPRUS
DOMINICAN
REPUBLIC
PUERTO RICO
(U.S.)
LEBANON
CUBA
MOROCCO
ALGERIA
JORDAN
LIBYA
ISRAEL
MEXICO
107,000,000
JAMAICA
CAPE
VERDE
TUNISIA
HAITI
MALI
EGYPT
74,000,000
SAUDI
ARABIA
TRINIDAD
& TOBAGO
HONDURAS
GUYANA
CHAD
MAURITANIA
NIGER
GAMBIA
GHANA
OMAN
VENEZUELA
GUATEMALA
SENEGAL
YEMEN
GUINEA-
BISSAU
NIGERIA
132,000,000
ERITREA
EL SALVADOR
GUINEA
COLOMBIA
NICARAGUA
SUDAN
COSTA RICA
ETHIOPIA
77,000,000
PANAMA
BRAZIL
184,000,000
ECUADOR
PERU
SIERRA
LEONE
UGANDA
KENYA
CAMEROON
LIBERIA
BENIN
RWANDA
GABON
TOGO
DEM. REP.
OF THE
CONGO
TANZANIA
BOLIVIA
CONGO
CÔTE
D'IVOIRE
BURUNDI
PARAGUAY
CENTRAL
AFRICAN
REPUBLIC
URUGUAY
MALAWI
ZAMBIA
CHILE
ARGENTINA
ANGOLA
MOZAMBIQUE
NAMIBIA
ZIMBABWE
BOTSWANA
SOUTH
AFRICA
SWAZILAND
LESOTHO
MADAGASCAR

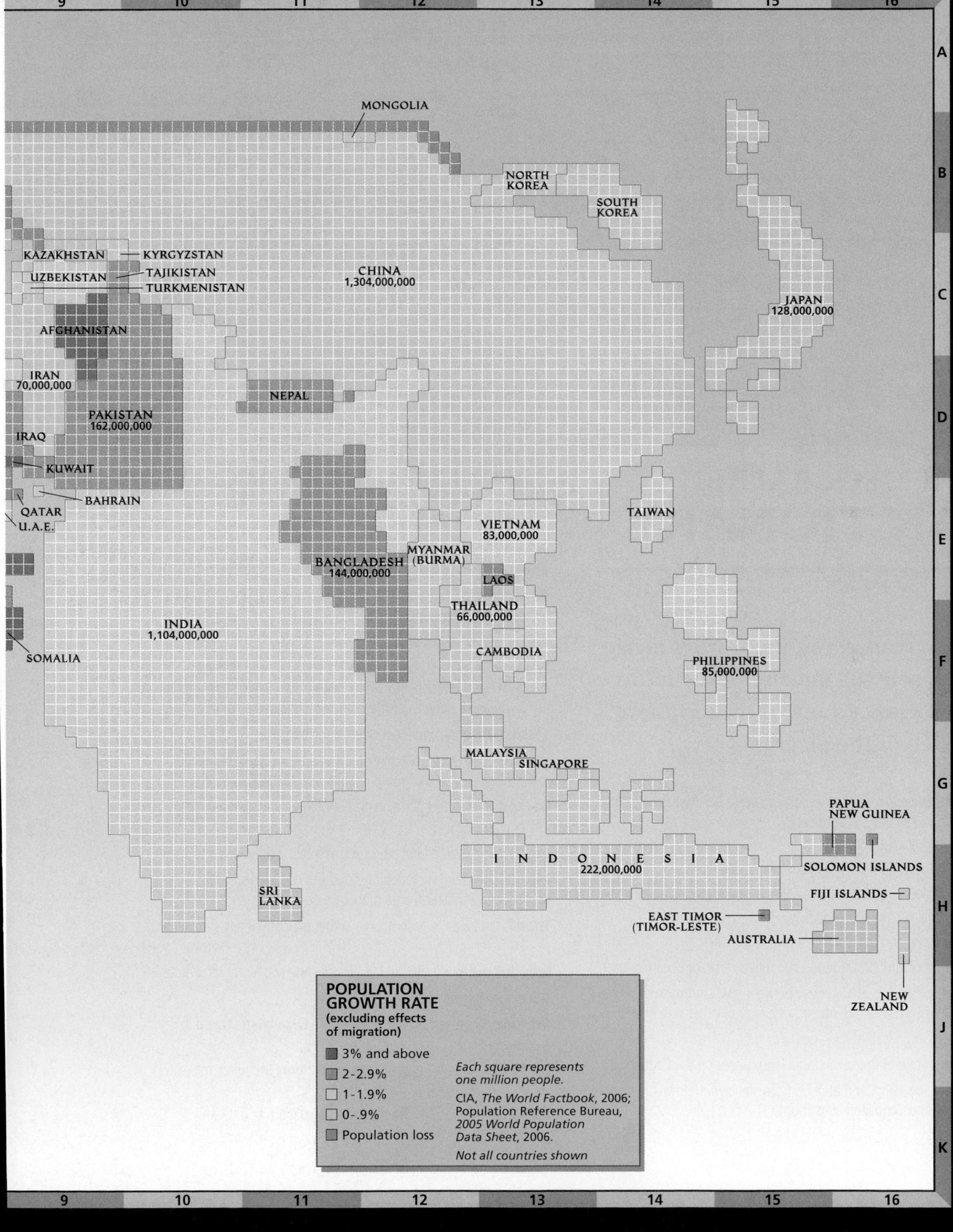

MONGOLIA
NORTH KOREA
SOUTH KOREA
KAZAKHSTAN
KYRGYZSTAN
TAJIKISTAN
UZBEKISTAN
TURKMENISTAN
CHINA 1,304,000,000
JAPAN 128,000,000
AFGHANISTAN
IRAN 70,000,000
NEPAL
PAKISTAN 162,000,000
IRAQ
KUWAIT
BAHRAIN
QATAR
U.A.E.
TAIWAN
VIETNAM 83,000,000
MYANMAR (BURMA)
BANGLADESH 144,000,000
LAOS
THAILAND 66,000,000
INDIA 1,104,000,000
SOMALIA
CAMBODIA
PHILIPPINES 85,000,000
MALAYSIA
SINGAPORE
PAPUA NEW GUINEA
INDONESIA 222,000,000
SOLOMON ISLANDS
SRI LANKA
FIJI ISLANDS
EAST TIMOR (TIMOR-LESTE)
AUSTRALIA
NEW ZEALAND
POPULATION GROWTH RATE
(excluding effects of migration)
3% and above
2-2.9%
1-1.9%
0-.9%
Population loss
Each square represents one million people.
CIA, The World Factbook, 2006; Population Reference Bureau, 2005 World Population Data Sheet, 2006.
Not all countries shown

GEOGRAPHIC DICTIONARY

As you read about the world's geography, you will encounter the terms listed below. Many of the terms are pictured in the diagram.

absolute location exact location of a place on the Earth described by global coordinates

basin area of land drained by a given river and its branches; area of land surrounded by lands of higher elevations

bay part of a large body of water that extends into a shoreline, generally smaller than a gulf

canyon deep and narrow valley with steep walls

cape point of land that extends into a river, lake, or ocean

channel wide strait or waterway between two landmasses that lie close to each other; deep part of a river or other waterway

cliff steep, high wall of rock, earth, or ice

continent one of the seven large landmasses on the Earth

delta flat, low-lying land built up from soil carried downstream by a river and deposited at its mouth

divide stretch of high land that separates river systems

downstream direction in which a river or stream flows from its source to its mouth

elevation height of land above sea level

Equator imaginary line that runs around the Earth halfway between the North and South Poles; used as the starting point to measure degrees of north and south latitude

glacier large, thick body of slowly moving ice

gulf part of a large body of water that extends into a shoreline, generally larger and more deeply indented than a bay

harbor a sheltered place along a shoreline where ships can anchor safely

highland elevated land area such as a hill, mountain, or plateau

hill elevated land with sloping sides and rounded summit; generally smaller than a mountain

island land area, smaller than a continent, completely surrounded by water

isthmus narrow stretch of land connecting two larger land areas

lake a sizable inland body of water

latitude distance north or south of the Equator, measured in degrees

longitude distance east or west of the Prime Meridian, measured in degrees

lowland land, usually level, at a low elevation

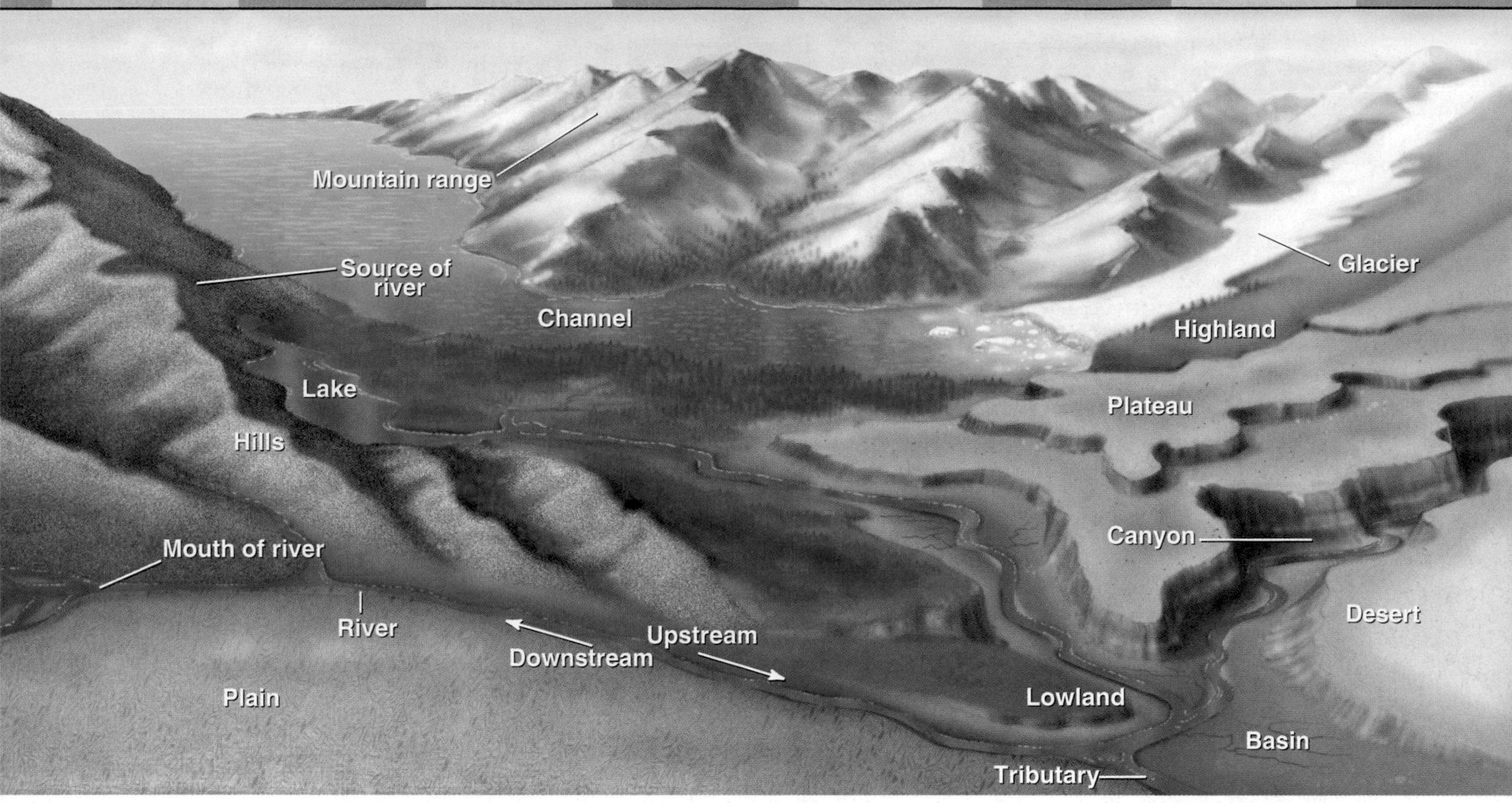

map drawing of the Earth shown on a flat surface

meridian one of many lines on the global grid running from the North Pole to the South Pole; used to measure degrees of longitude

mesa broad, flat-topped landform with steep sides; smaller than a plateau

mountain land with steep sides that rises sharply (1,000 feet or more) from surrounding land; generally larger and more rugged than a hill

mountain peak pointed top of a mountain

mountain range a series of connected mountains

mouth (of a river) place where a stream or river flows into a larger body of water

ocean one of the four major bodies of salt water that surround the continents

ocean current stream of either cold or warm water that moves in a definite direction through an ocean

parallel one of many lines on the global grid that circles the Earth north or south of the Equator; used to measure degrees of latitude

peninsula body of land jutting into a lake or ocean, surrounded on three sides by water

physical feature characteristic of a place occurring naturally, such as a landform, body of water, climate pattern, or resource

plain area of level land, usually at low elevation and often covered with grasses

plateau area of flat or rolling land at a high elevation, about 300 to 3,000 feet (90 to 900 m) high

Prime Meridian line of the global grid running from the North Pole to the South Pole at Greenwich, England; starting point for measuring degrees of east and west longitude

relief changes in elevation over a given area of land

river large natural stream of water that runs through the land

sea large body of water completely or partly surrounded by land

seacoast land lying next to a sea or an ocean

sound broad inland body of water, often between a coastline and one or more islands off the coast

source (of a river) place where a river or stream begins, often in highlands

strait narrow stretch of water joining two larger bodies of water

tributary small river or stream that flows into a large river or stream; a branch of the river

upstream direction opposite the flow of a river; toward the source of a river or stream

valley area of low land usually between hills or mountains

volcano mountain or hill created as liquid rock and ash erupt from inside the Earth

—Essential Elements—

How Do I Study Geography?

Geographers have tried to understand the best way to teach and learn about geography, so they created the *Five Themes of Geography.* The themes acted as a guide for teaching the basic ideas about geography to students. However, many thought that the Five Themes were too broad. In 1994, geographers created 18 national geography standards. These standards were more detailed about what should be taught and learned. The Six Essential Elements act as a bridge connecting the Five Themes with the standards.

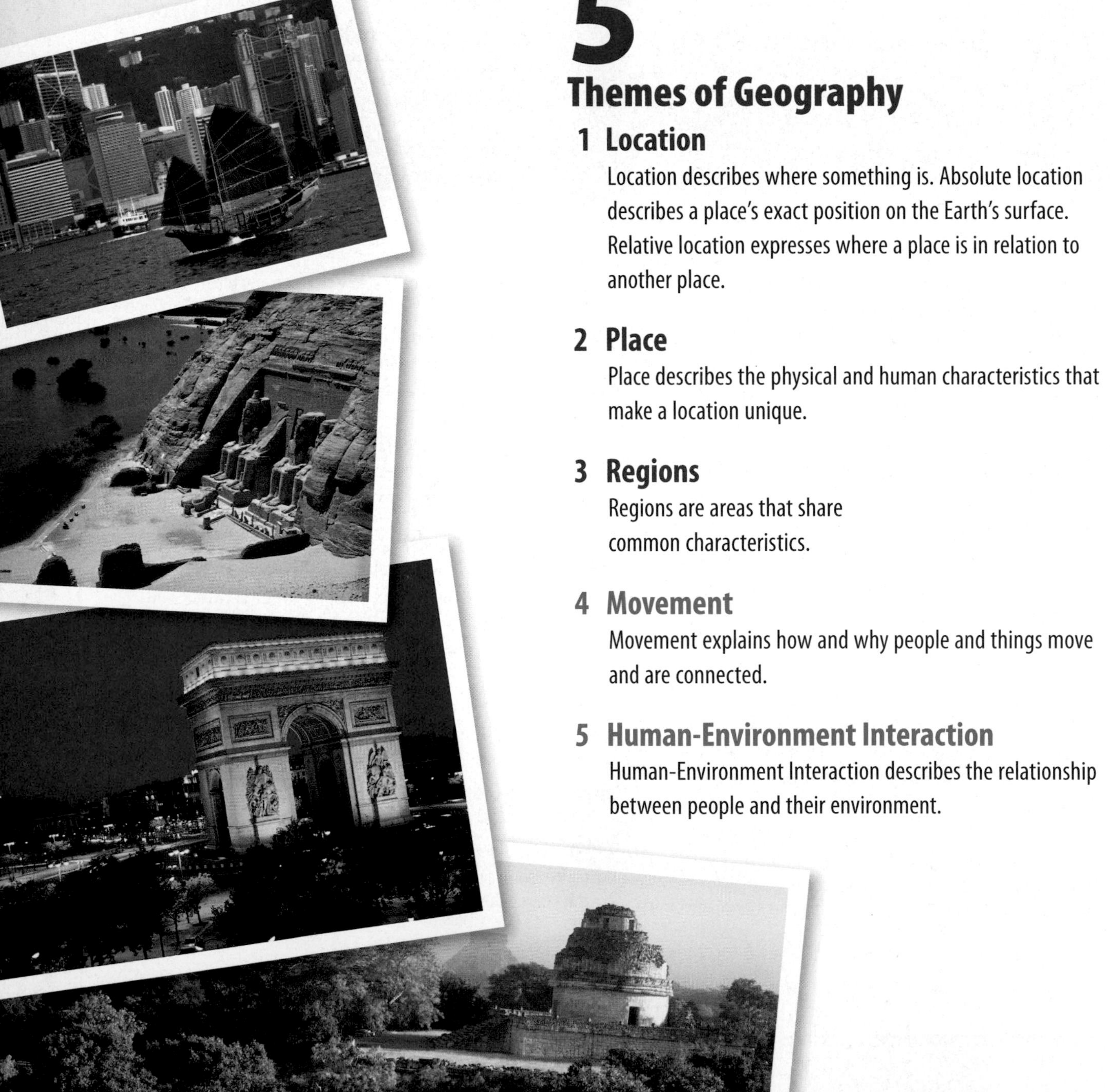

5 Themes of Geography

1 Location

Location describes where something is. Absolute location describes a place's exact position on the Earth's surface. Relative location expresses where a place is in relation to another place.

2 Place

Place describes the physical and human characteristics that make a location unique.

3 Regions

Regions are areas that share common characteristics.

4 Movement

Movement explains how and why people and things move and are connected.

5 Human-Environment Interaction

Human-Environment Interaction describes the relationship between people and their environment.

6 Essential Elements

18 Geography Standards

I. The World in Spatial Terms
Geographers look to see where a place is located. Location acts as a starting point to answer "Where Is It?" The location of a place helps you orient yourself as to where you are.

1 How to use maps and other tools
2 How to use mental maps to organize information
3 How to analyze the spatial organization of people, places, and environments

II. Places and Regions
Place describes physical characteristics such as landforms, climate, and plant or animal life. It might also describe human characteristics, including language and way of life. Places can also be organized into regions. **Regions** are places united by one or more characteristics.

4 The physical and human characteristics of places
5 How people create regions to interpret Earth's complexity
6 How culture and experience influence people's perceptions of places and regions

III. Physical Systems
Geographers study how physical systems, such as hurricanes, volcanoes, and glaciers, shape the surface of the Earth. They also look at how plants and animals depend upon one another and their surroundings for their survival.

7 The physical processes that shape Earth's surface
8 The distribution of ecosystems on Earth's surface

IV. Human Systems
People shape the world in which they live. They settle in certain places but not in others. An ongoing theme in geography is the movement of people, ideas, and goods.

9 The characteristics, distribution, and migration of human populations
10 The complexity of Earth's cultural mosaics
11 The patterns and networks of economic interdependence
12 The patterns of human settlement
13 The forces of cooperation and conflict

V. Environment and Society
How does the relationship between people and their natural surroundings influence the way people live? Geographers study how people use the environment and how their actions affect the environment.

14 How human actions modify the physical environment
15 How physical systems affect human systems
16 The meaning, use, and distribution of resources

VI. The Uses of Geography
Knowledge of geography helps us understand the relationships among people, places, and environments over time. Applying geographic skills helps you understand the past and prepare for the future.

17 How to apply geography to interpret the past
18 How to apply geography to interpret the present and plan for the future

Geography Skills Handbook

Throughout this text, you will discover how geography has shaped the course of events in world history. Landforms, waterways, climate, and natural resources all have helped or hindered human activities. Usually people have learned either to adapt to their environments or to transform it to meet their needs. The resources in this Geography Skills Handbook will help you get the most out of your textbook—and provide you with skills you will use for the rest of your life.

Geographers use a wide array of tools to collect and analyze information to help them understand the Earth. The study of geography is more than knowing a lot of facts about places. Rather, it has more to do with asking questions about the Earth, pursuing their answers, and solving problems. Thus, one of the most important geographic tools is inside your head: the ability to think geographically.

Globes and Maps

A **globe** is a scale model of the Earth. Because Earth is round, a globe presents the most accurate depiction of geographic information such as area, distance, and direction. However, globes show little close-up detail. A printed **map** is a symbolic representation of all or part of the planet. Unlike globes, maps can show small areas in great detail.

From 3-D to 2-D

Think about the surface of the Earth as the peel of an orange. To flatten the peel, you have to cut it like the globe shown here. To create maps that are not interrupted, mapmakers, or **cartographers,** use mathematical formulas to transfer information from the three-dimensional globe to the two-dimensional map. However, when the curves of a globe become straight lines on a map, distortion of size, shape, distance, or area occurs. **D**

Great Circle Routes

A straight line of true direction—one that runs directly from west to east, for example—is not always the shortest distance between two points. This is due to the curvature of the Earth. To find the shortest distance, stretch a piece of string around a globe from one point to the other. The string will form part of a *great circle,* an imaginary line that follows the curve of the Earth. Ship captains and airline pilots use these **great circle routes** to reduce travel time and conserve fuel. **C**

The idea of a great circle route is an important difference between globes and maps. A round globe accurately shows a great circle route, as indicated on the top right map. However, the flat map below it shows the great circle distance (dotted line) between Tokyo and Los Angeles to be far longer than the true direction distance (solid line). In fact, the great circle distance is 345 miles (555 km) shorter.

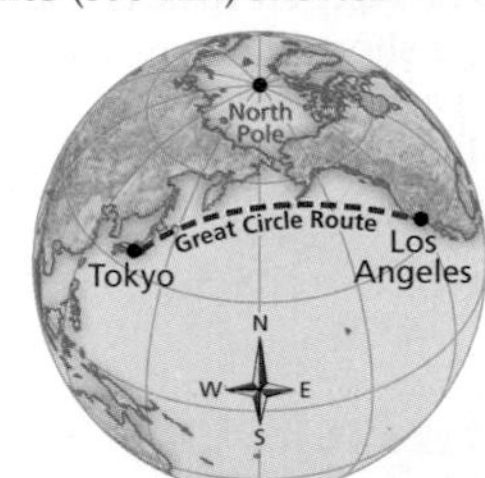

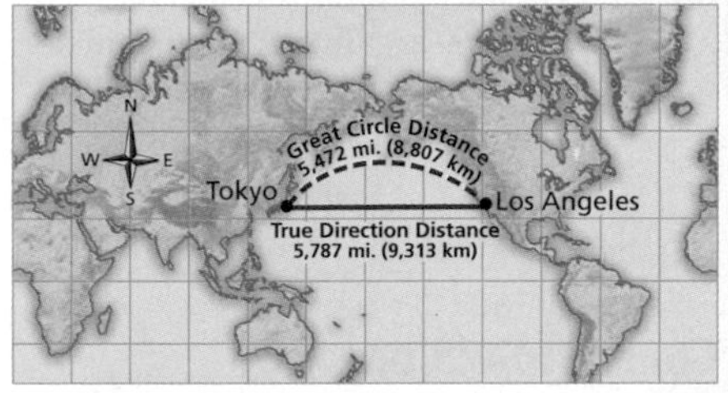

PRACTICING THE SKILL

1. **Explain** the significance of: globe, map, cartographer, great circle route.
2. **Describe** the problems that arise when the curves of a globe become straight lines on a map.
3. **Use** a Venn diagram like the one below to identify the similarities and differences between globes and maps.

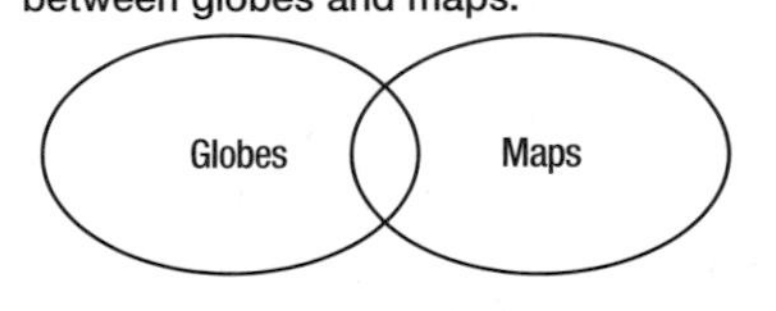

GEOGRAPHY SKILLS HANDBOOK

Teach

D Differentiated Instruction

Visual/Spatial Use an orange to illustrate the challenges of transferring measurements from a three-dimensional to a two-dimensional form. Sketch an outline of the continents and two or three lines of longitude and latitude onto an orange. Then carefully remove the peel (in one piece, if possible) and gently flatten it. Allow students to examine the peel, and point out how lines and shapes are distorted when the curved peel is flattened. **OL**

C Critical Thinking

Making Inferences Have students use a piece of string and a globe to find the shortest route from New York to Hong Kong. *(over the top of the globe)* **OL**

Practicing the Skill: Answers

1. globe: scale model of the Earth; map: symbolic representation of all or part of the planet; cartographer: mapmakers; great circle route: routes that follow the great circle along the curve of the Earth
2. Size, shape, distance, or area becomes distorted.
3. Globes present the most accurate depiction of geographic information such as area, distance, and direction, but they do not show close-up detail. Maps are symbolic representations of all or part of the planet and can show areas in great detail. Both show information about places on the Earth.

C Critical Thinking

Identifying Central Issues

Ask: Why do mapmakers use projections? *(Projections help in transferring information from a three-dimensional surface to a two-dimensional surface.)* **OL**

D Differentiated Instruction

Kinesthetic If students are struggling with the concept of projection, give them a large sheet of paper or poster board and a globe. Have students place the paper and the globe in the same physical relationships shown in the illustrations. Check to make sure students can visualize how each projection offers a different approximation of the sphere. **BL**

Differentiated Instruction

Projections

To create maps, cartographers project the round Earth onto a flat surface—making a **map projection.** Distance, shape, direction, or size may be distorted by a projection. As a result, the purpose of the map usually dictates which projection is used. There are many kinds of map projections, some with general names and some named for the cartographers who developed them. Three basic categories of map projections are shown here: **planar, cylindrical,** and **conic.**

Planar Projection

A planar projection shows the Earth centered in such a way that a straight line coming from the center to any other point represents the shortest distance. Also known as an azimuthal projection, it is most accurate at its center. As a result, it is often used for maps of the Poles.

Cylindrical Projection

A cylindrical projection is based on the projection of the globe onto a cylinder. This projection is most accurate near the Equator, but shapes and distances are distorted near the Poles.

Conic Projection

A conic projection comes from placing a cone over part of a globe. Conic projections are best suited for showing limited east-west areas that are not too far from the Equator. For these uses, a conic projection can indicate distances and directions fairly accurately.

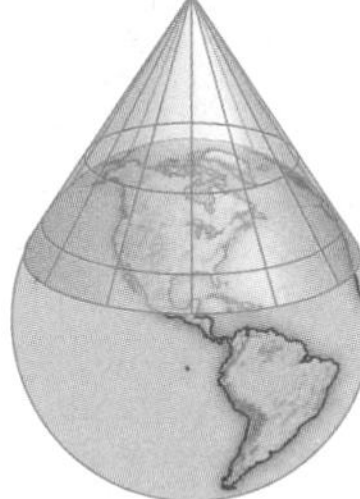

Activity: Creating a Graphic Organizer

Visual/Spatial To help students remember the several different categories and examples of maps discussed in this section, guide them in creating a graphic organizer entitled "Types of Maps." Branching from this main head should be three boxes labeled "Political," "Physical," and "Special-Purpose." Have students complete the organizer by taking notes on each of the different types of maps. **OL**

GEOGRAPHY SKILLS HANDBOOK

Common Map Projections

Each type of map projection has advantages and some degree of inaccuracy. Four of the most common projections are shown here.

Winkel Tripel Projection

Most general reference world maps are the Winkel Tripel projection. It provides a good balance between the size and shape of land areas as they are shown on the map. Even the polar areas are depicted with little distortion of size and shape.

Robinson Projection

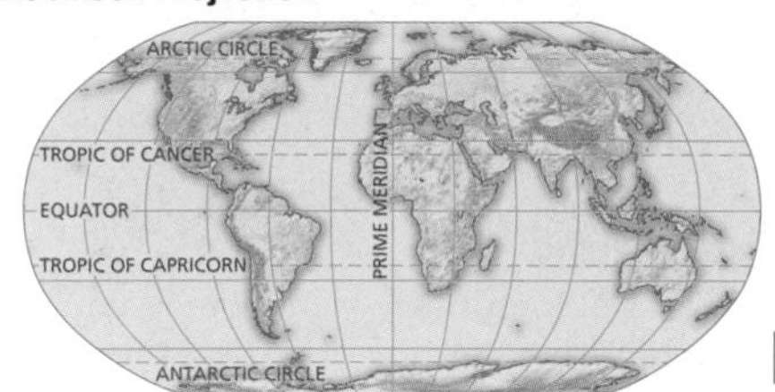

The Robinson projection has minor distortions. The sizes and shapes near the eastern and western edges of the map are accurate, and outlines of the continents appear much as they do on the globe. However, the polar areas are flattened.

Goode's Interrupted Equal-Area Projection

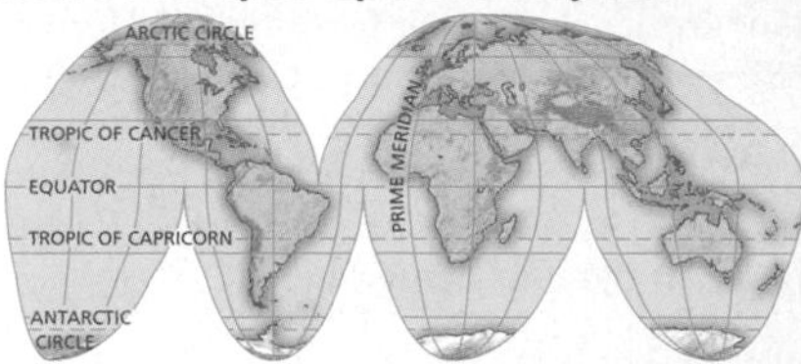

C

An **interrupted projection** looks something like a globe that has been cut apart and laid flat. Goode's Interrupted Equal-Area projection shows the true size and shape of Earth's landmasses, but distances are generally distorted.

Mercator Projection

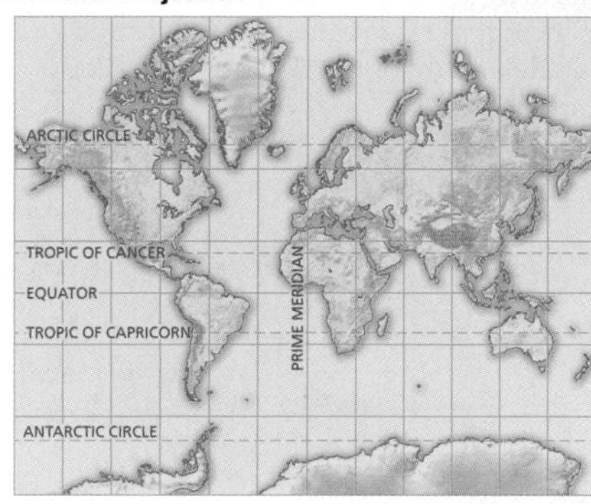

R

The Mercator projection increasingly distorts size and distance as it moves away from the Equator. However, Mercator projections do accurately show true directions and the shapes of landmasses, making these maps useful for sea travel.

PRACTICING THE SKILL

1. **Explain** the significance of: map projection, planar, cylindrical, conic, interrupted projection.
2. **How** does a cartographer determine which map projection to use?
3. **How** is Goode's Interrupted Equal-Area projection different from the Mercator projection?
4. **Which** of the four common projections described above is the best one to use when showing the entire world? Why?
5. **Use** a Venn diagram like the one below to identify the similarities and differences between the Winkel Tripel and Mercator projections.

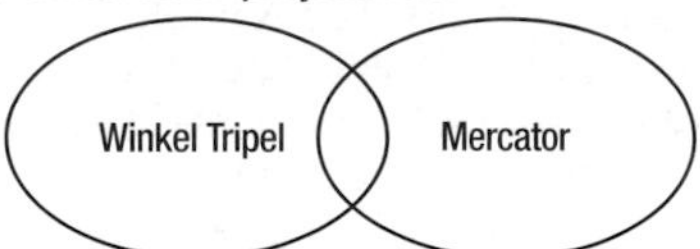

C Critical Thinking

Comparing and Contrasting

Ask students to cover the text and look at the selected projections. **Ask:** What is one similarity and one difference between the Winkle Tripel Projection and the Goode's Interrupted Equal-Area Projection? *(Similarity: both show all of the continents; difference: Goode's projection splits Antarctica into four pieces, while the Winkel Tripel projection does not.)* **BL**

R Reading Strategy

Analyzing Text Structure

Have students read the selected captions. **Ask:** How is the information structured in these captions? *(Both captions propose a benefit of the projection, followed by a drawback.)* **OL**

Practicing the Skill: Answers

1. map projection: projecting image of Earth onto a flat surface to make a map, different projections have their advantages/disadvantages. planar: shows shortest distance between points, most often used for maps of the Poles; cylindrical: most accurate near the Equator; conic: best for limited east-west areas not too far from the Equator; interrupted projection: shows true size and shape of Earth but distorts distances
2. by deciding what it will be used for to determine the least distortion
3. Goode distorts distances while showing the true size and shape. Mercator distorts size and distances but shows true directions.
4. Winkel Tripel, because it distorts the size and shape of landmasses the least
5. Both show all continents with little to no distortion of shape. Mercator shows true direction but distorts land size and distance. Winkel Tripel shows little size distortion.

S Skill Practice

Visual Literacy Have students study the selected figures. **Ask:** What are two differences between longitude and latitude? *(Lines of latitude run horizontally and are parallel. Lines of longitude run vertically and intersect at the Poles.)* **OL**

D Differentiated Instruction

Logical/Mathematical Have students use the Internet or library resources to determine their exact absolute location. If you have access to GPS equipment, you may wish to let students use it to check their work. **OL**

Determining Location

Geography is often said to begin with the question: *Where?* The basic tool for answering the question is **location.** Lines on globes and maps provide information that can help you locate places. These lines cross one another forming a pattern called a **grid system,** which helps you find exact places on the Earth's surface.

A **hemisphere** is one of the halves into which the Earth is divided. Geographers divide the Earth into hemispheres to help them classify and describe places on Earth. Most places are located in two of the four hemispheres.

Latitude

Lines of **latitude,** or parallels, circle the Earth parallel to the Equator and measure the distance north or south of the Equator in degrees. The Equator is measured at 0° latitude, while the Poles lie at latitudes 90°N (north) and 90°S (south). Parallels north of the Equator are called north latitude. Parallels south of the Equator are called south latitude.

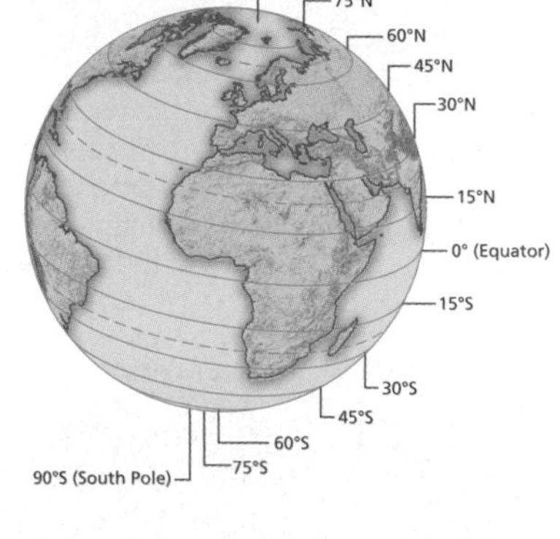

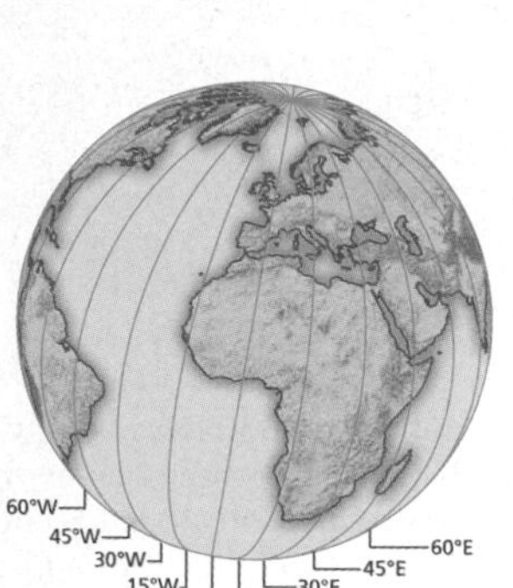

Longitude

Lines of **longitude,** or meridians, circle the Earth from Pole to Pole. These lines measure distance east or west of the **Prime Meridian** at 0° longitude. Meridians east of the Prime Meridian are known as east longitude. Meridians west of the Prime Meridian are known as west longitude. The 180° meridian on the opposite side of the Earth is called the International Date Line.

The Global Grid

Every place has a global address, or **absolute location.** You can identify the absolute location of a place by naming the latitude and longitude lines that cross exactly at that place. For example, Tokyo, Japan, is located at 36°N latitude and 140°E longitude. For more precise readings, each degree is further divided into 60 units called minutes.

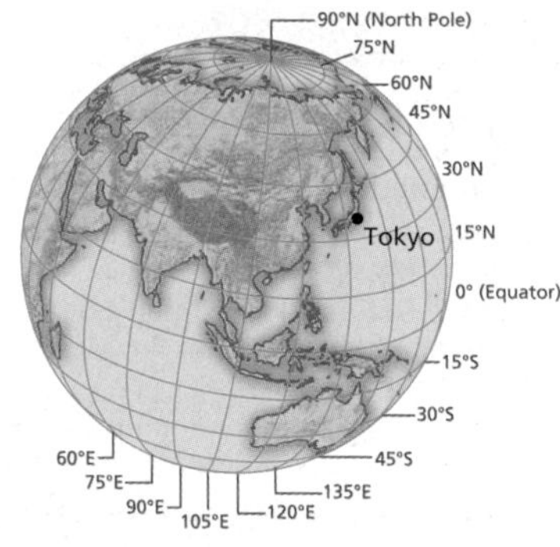

Hands-On Chapter Project

Creating a Global Treasure Hunt

Directions Organize students into teams and have each team choose 10 places on Earth to research and study. Students may choose places that are well-known or unfamiliar. However, all places should be on land and located at least 50 miles (80 km) from each other. Tell students to make a list of 8–10 interesting facts about each place.

Putting It Together Tell students to "bury" their treasure in each of the locations. Then have students use the facts they learned about the place to create clues for a Treasure Atlas. Clues will be locations that, when followed, will lead to the buried treasure. The correct response to each clue will be a place name and coordinates that can be easily looked up. Clues should be written on index cards. Students should list all the clues with their answers on a separate sheet of paper. Each correct answer earns another clue to a new location, eventually leading to the buried treasure, so remind students to make sure their clues follow a logical route. **OL**

GEOGRAPHY SKILLS HANDBOOK

Northern and Southern Hemispheres

The diagram below shows that the Equator divides the Earth into the Northern and Southern Hemispheres. Everything north of the Equator is in the **Northern Hemisphere.** Everything south of the Equator is in the **Southern Hemisphere.**

Northern Hemisphere

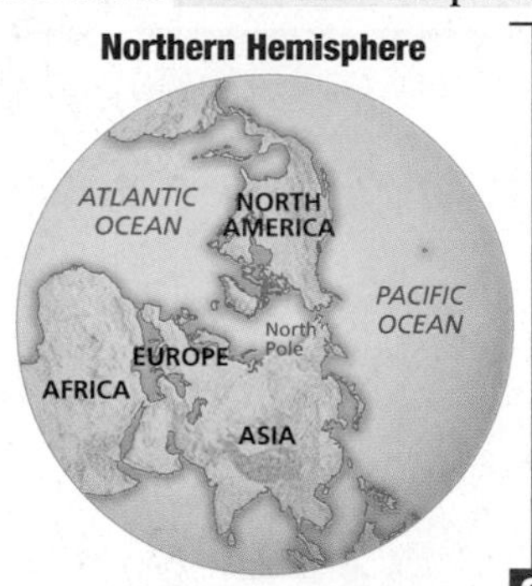

Southern Hemisphere

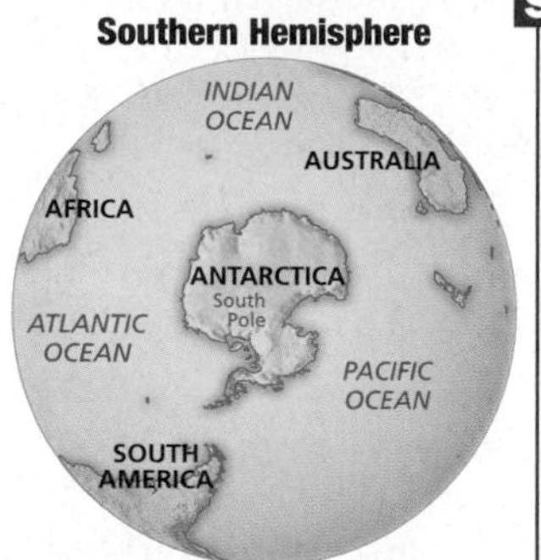

S

Eastern and Western Hemispheres

The Prime Meridian and the International Date Line divide the Earth into the Eastern and Western Hemispheres. Everything east of the Prime Meridian for 180° is in the **Eastern Hemisphere.** Everything west of the Prime Meridian for 180° is in the **Western Hemisphere.**

Eastern Hemisphere

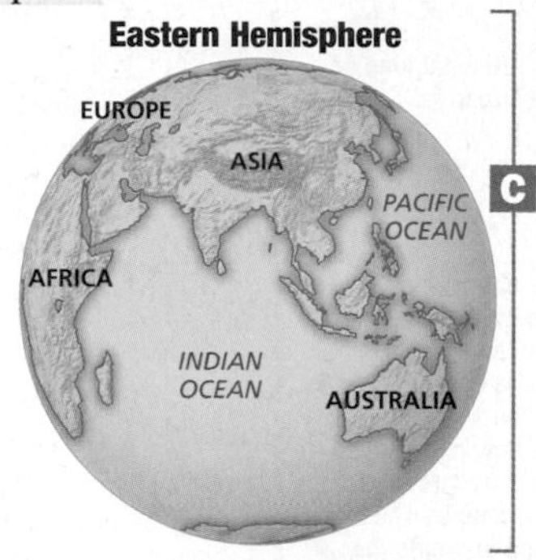

C

Western Hemisphere

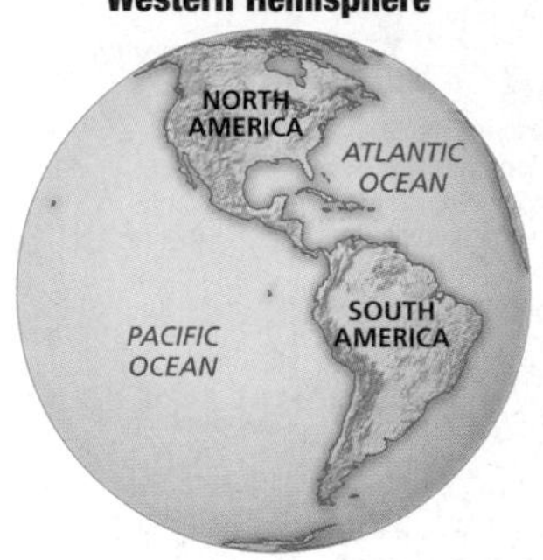

PRACTICING THE SKILL

1. **Explain** the significance of: location, grid system, hemisphere, Northern Hemisphere, Southern Hemisphere, Eastern Hemisphere, Western Hemisphere, latitude, longitude, Prime Meridian, absolute location.
2. **Why** do all maps label the Equator 0° latitude and the Prime Meridian 0° longitude?
3. **Which** lines of latitude and longitude divide the Earth into hemispheres?
4. **Using** the Reference Atlas maps, fill in a chart like the one below by writing the latitude and longitude of three world cities. Have a partner try to identify the cities.
5. **Use** a chart like the one below to identify the continents in each hemisphere. Some may be in more than one hemisphere.

Hemisphere	Continents
Northern	
Southern	
Eastern	
Western	

S Skill Practice

Visual Literacy Point out that most people probably are not used to seeing the globe from these angles. **Ask:** What view do these illustrations show? *(the globe viewed from the top and the bottom)* **Ask:** How do you generally view the globe? *(from the side, along the Equator)* If students still struggle to understand the difference between these views, use an actual globe to show them the view reflected in the illustration. **BL**

C Critical Thinking

Detecting Bias Ask: Since planet Earth has no true top or bottom, why do globes show Europe on the top half of Earth? *(Early mapmakers and explorers were from Europe.)* **AL**

Practicing the Skill: Answers

1. location: a specific place on Earth; grid system: pattern formed as the lines of latitude and longitude cross one another; hemisphere: half of a sphere or globe; Northern Hemisphere: everything north of the Equator; Southern Hemisphere: everything south of the Equator; Eastern Hemisphere: everything east of the Prime Meridian for 180°; Western Hemisphere: everything west of the Prime Meridian for 180°
2. They are where the divisions between north/south (N/S) and east/west (E/W) occur, respectively.
3. Equator and Prime Meridian
4. Answers will vary according to cities chosen.
5. Northern: North America, Asia, Europe, Africa; Eastern: Asia, Europe, Africa, Australia; Southern: Antarctica, Australia, South America, Africa; Western: North America, South America

Reading a Map

In addition to latitude and longitude, maps feature other important tools to help you interpret the information they contain. Learning to use these map tools will help you read the symbolic language of maps more easily.

Key
The key lists and explains the symbols, colors, and lines used on the map. The key is sometimes called a legend.

Title
The title tells you what kind of information the map is showing.

Scale Bar **S**
The scale bar shows the relationship between map measurements and actual distances on the Earth. By laying a ruler along the scale bar, you can calculate how many miles or kilometers are represented per inch or centimeter. The map projection used to create the map is often listed near the scale bar.

Compass Rose
The compass rose indicates directions. The four cardinal directions—north, south, east, and west—are usually indicated with arrows or the points of a star. The intermediate directions—northeast, northwest, southeast, and southwest—may also be shown.

Cities
Cities are represented by a dot. Sometimes the relative sizes of cities are shown using dots of different sizes.

Capitals
National capitals are often represented by a star within a circle.

Boundary Lines
On political maps of large areas, boundary lines highlight the borders between different countries or states.

S Skill Practice

Using Geography Skills Have students use the scale bar on the map to calculate the distance in kilometers between Paris and Stockholm. First, have students use a ruler to measure the distance between the cities on the map in centimeters. *(4.5 cm)* Then, have students measure the map's scale in centimeters. (600 km = 1.7 cm) **Ask:** How can you use this to find the distance between Paris and Stockholm? *(set up a proportion:*

$$\frac{600\ km}{1.7\ cm} = \frac{x}{4\ cm}$$

$$x = \frac{600\ km \times 4\ cm}{1.7\ cm}$$

x = 1,412 km) **OL**

R Reading Strategy

Reading Maps **Ask:** According to the map, what is the capital of Russia? *(St. Petersburg)* **Ask:** What major city is located southeast of Vienna? *(Budapest)* **OL**

Additional Support

Activity: Technology Connection

Contrasting Have students use an Internet mapping Web site to help them understand scale. Tell students to find a particular location, such as their school or home address. Then have them use the map's zoom function to help visualize the benefits of increasing and decreasing scale when viewing a location. **Ask:** To find the nearest lake, would you use a distant or a close view? *(distant view)* **Ask:** What view would show the names of neighboring streets? *(closer view)* Point out that a distant view corresponds to an increase in scale: it allows you to view a wider area but you cannot see much detail. Conversely, a close view corresponds to a decrease in scale: detail is increased, but the size of the area is diminished. **OL**

GEOGRAPHY SKILLS HANDBOOK

Using Scale

All maps are drawn to a certain scale. **Scale** is a consistent, proportional relationship between the measurements shown on the map and the measurement of the Earth's surface.

Small-Scale Maps A small-scale map, like this political map of France, can show a large area but little detail. Note that the scale bar on this map indicates that about 1 inch is equal to 200 miles.

Large-Scale Maps A large-scale map, like this map of Paris, can show a small area with a great amount of detail. Study the scale bar. Note that the map measurements correspond to much smaller distances than on the map of France.

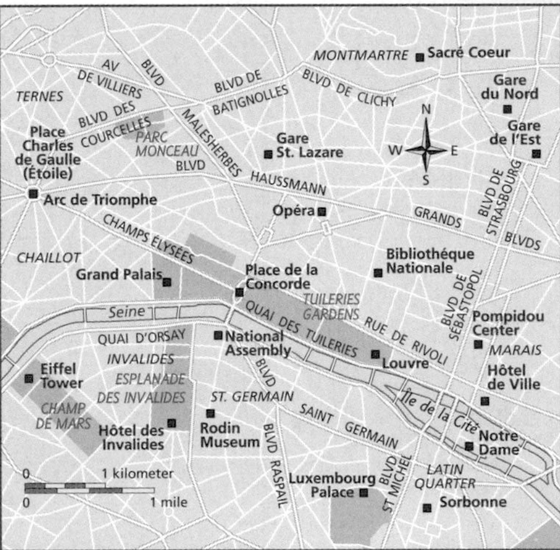

Absolute and Relative Location

As you learned on page GH6, absolute location is the exact point where a line of latitude crosses a line of longitude. Another way to indicate location is by **relative location,** or the location of one place in relation to another. To find relative location, find a reference point—a location you already know—on a map. Then look in the appropriate direction for the new location. For example, locate Paris (your reference point) on the map of France above. The relative location of Lyon can be described as southeast of Paris.

PRACTICING THE SKILL

1. **Explain** the significance of: key, compass rose, cardinal directions, intermediate directions, scale bar, scale, relative location.
2. **Describe** the elements of a map that help you interpret the information displayed on the map.
3. **How** does the scale bar help you determine distances on the Earth's surface?
4. **Describe** the relative location of your school in two different ways.
5. **Use** a Venn diagram to identify the similarities and differences of small-scale maps and large-scale maps.

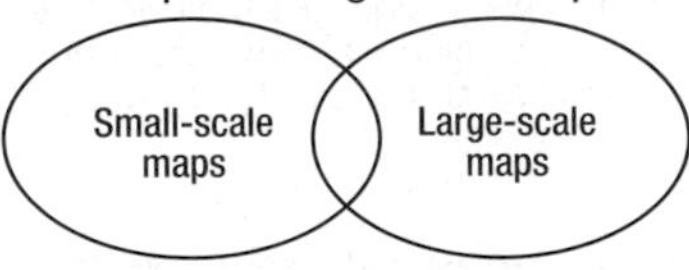

W Writing Support

Expository Writing To give students practice thinking about scale, have them write about two imaginary experiences. First, have students imagine they are an ant beginning to climb a tree. Next, have them imagine they are giants bending down to look at a nest in the top of the same tree. **OL**

D Differentiated Instruction

Kinesthetic Have two students stand side-by-side, but 10 feet (3 m) apart. **Ask:** What is the relative position of each student to the other? *(One is 10 feet (3 m) to the left. The other is 10 feet (3 m) to the right.)* **BL**

Practicing the Skill: Answers

1. key: lists and explains symbols, colors, and lines on map; compass rose: indicates direction; cardinal directions: north, south, east, and west; intermediate directions: northeast, northwest, southeast, and southwest; scale bar: shows relationship between map measurements and actual distances on Earth; scale: consistent, proportional relationship between measurements shown on map and measurement of Earth's surface; relative location: location of one place in relation to another
2. title tells kind of information shown on map; key lists and explains symbols, colors, and lines used on map; scale bar shows relationship between map measurements and actual distances on Earth; compass rose indicates direction
3. shows the relationship between map measurements and actual distances
4. Answers will vary according to school.
5. Small scale shows large areas but little detail. Large scale shows small area with great detail. Both show location.

W Writing Support

Narrative Writing Have interested students research and write a story about a physical feature that affected history. Students can explore how mountain ranges and cliffs have served as protection, how frozen lakes and straits allowed for travel, or even how the construction of a canal changed transportation. **AL**

C Critical Thinking

Making Generalizations

Ask: What can relief and elevation tell you about rivers? *(Both features give a sense of direction: water flows downhill so rivers flow from high elevation to lower elevation.)* **OL**

Physical Maps

A **physical map** shows the location and the **topography,** or shape of the Earth's physical features. A study of a country's physical features often helps to explain the historical development of the country. For example, mountains may be barriers to transportation, and rivers and streams can provide access into the interior of a country.

Relief
Physical maps use shading and texture to show general relief—the differences in elevation, or height, of landforms.

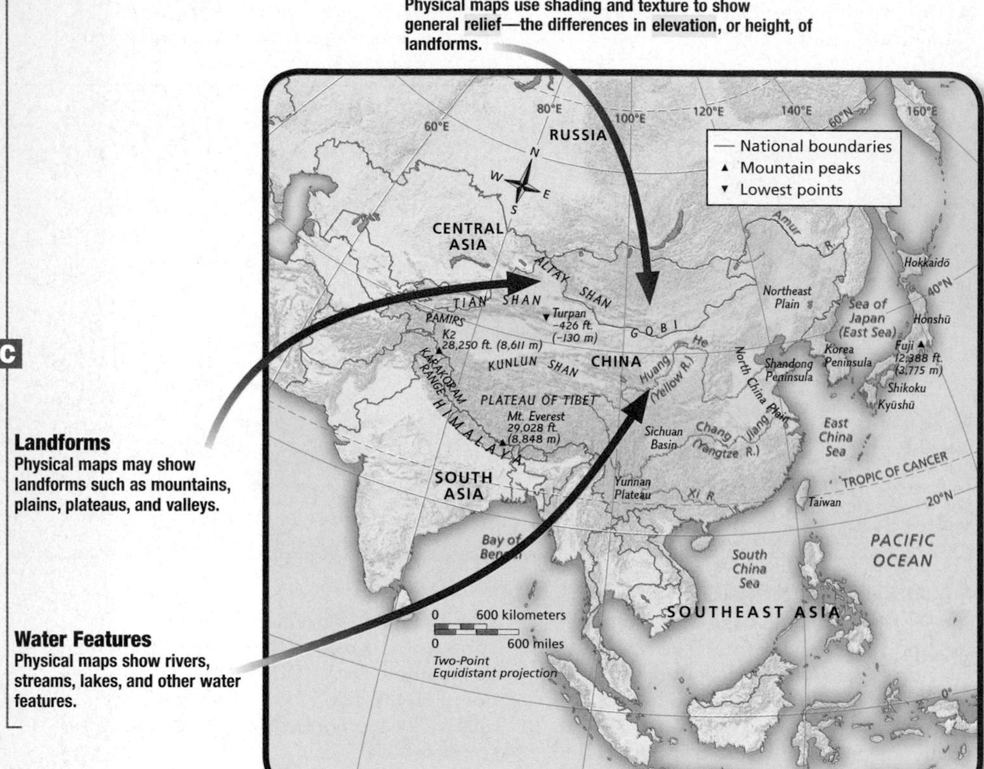

Landforms
Physical maps may show landforms such as mountains, plains, plateaus, and valleys.

Water Features
Physical maps show rivers, streams, lakes, and other water features.

PRACTICING THE SKILL

1. **Explain** the significance of: physical map, topography, relief, elevation.
2. **Complete** a table like the one to the right to explain what you can learn from the map about each of the physical features listed.

Physical Feature	What You Can Learn From the Map
Tian Shan	
Chang Jiang	
Northeast Plain	

Practicing the Skill: Answers

1. physical map: shows location and topography of Earth's physical features; topography: shape of Earth's physical features; relief: difference in elevation of landforms; elevation: height
2. Tian Shan: elevation, length; Chang Jiang: length, route; Northeast Plain: elevation, length

GEOGRAPHY SKILLS HANDBOOK

Political Maps

A **political map** shows the boundaries and locations of political units such as countries, states, counties, cities, and towns. Many features depicted on a political map are **human-made,** or determined by humans rather than by nature. Political maps can show the networks and links that exist within and between political units. **D**

Human-Made Features
Political maps show human-made features such as boundaries, capitals, cities, roads, highways, and railroads. **C**

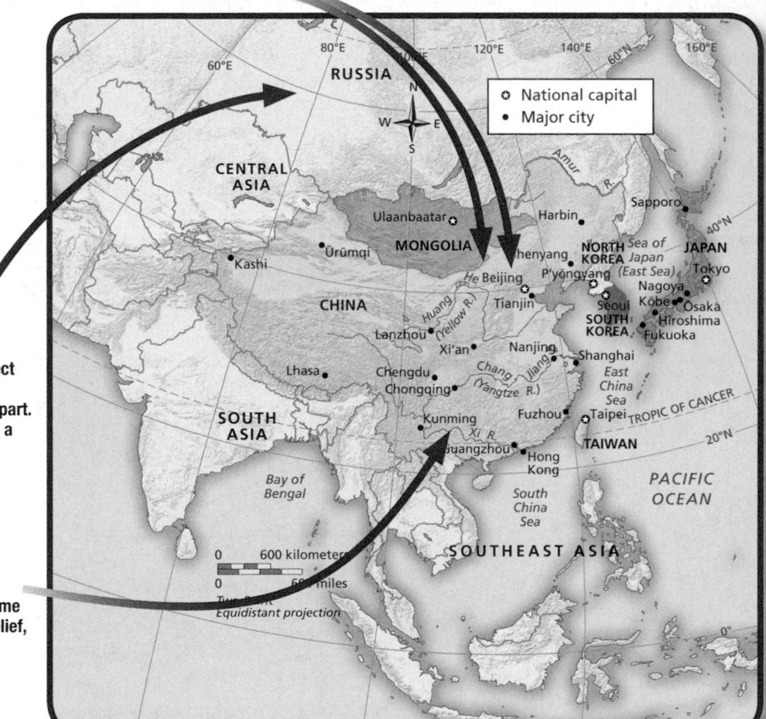

Nonsubject Area
Areas surrounding the subject area of a map are usually a different color to set them apart. They are labeled to give you a context for the area you are studying.

Physical Features
Political maps may show some physical features such as relief, rivers, and mountains.

PRACTICING THE SKILL

1. **Explain** the significance of: political map, human-made.
2. **What** types of information would you find on a political map that would not appear on a physical map?
3. **Complete** a table like the one to the right to explain what you can learn from the map about each of the human-made features listed.

Human-Made Feature	What You Can Learn From the Map
Seoul	
Tokyo	
North Korea/South Korea boundary	

Practicing the Skill: Answers

1. political map: shows boundaries and locations of political units such as countries, states, counties, cities, and towns; human-made: determined by humans rather than nature
2. capitals, cities, roads, highways, railroads
3. Seoul: location, that it is the capital city of South Korea; Tokyo: location, that it is the capital city of Japan; North Korea/South Korea boundary: what country borders North Korea, what body of water forms South Korea's southern border

D Differentiated Instruction

Gifted and Talented Political maps change more rapidly than physical maps. Have interested students select an area and research how political maps of this area have changed over time. Students may be interested to learn how their own state or region has changed politically, or they may wish to study another area. Have students create a presentation of their findings. **AL**

C Critical Thinking

Comparing and Contrasting

Ask: When you fly in an airplane and look down at the ground, what human-made features can you see? *(roads, buildings, farms, dams, some lakes, railroads)* **Ask:** What human-made features can you not see? *(boundaries, capital designation)* **BL**

S Skill Practice

Visual Literacy Have students study the "Europe: Slavic Migrations" map. **Ask:** What do the arrows on this map represent? *(the main routes of migration taken by Slavic peoples in A.D. 700)* **Ask:** How is color used to present information in this map? *(It distinguishes the three major groups of Slavs by their place of origin.)* **Ask:** How would you explain the forks that appear in several arrows? *(These indicate places where immigrants from the same area of origin diverged into two groups.)* **OL**

Thematic Maps

Maps that emphasize a single idea or a particular kind of information about an area are called **thematic maps.** There are many kinds of thematic maps, each designed to serve a different need. This textbook includes thematic maps that show ancient civilizations, the spread of religious ideas, exploration and trade, and war and political conflicts.

Qualitative Maps

Maps that use colors, symbols, lines, or dots to show information related to a specific idea are called **qualitative maps.** Such maps are often used to depict historical information. For example, the qualitative map below shows the primary exports of Latin America.

Flow-Line Maps

Maps that illustrate the movement of people, animals, goods, and ideas, as well as physical processes like hurricanes and glaciers, are called **flow-line maps.** Arrows are usually used to represent the flow and direction of movement. The flow-line map below shows the movement of Slavic peoples throughout Europe.

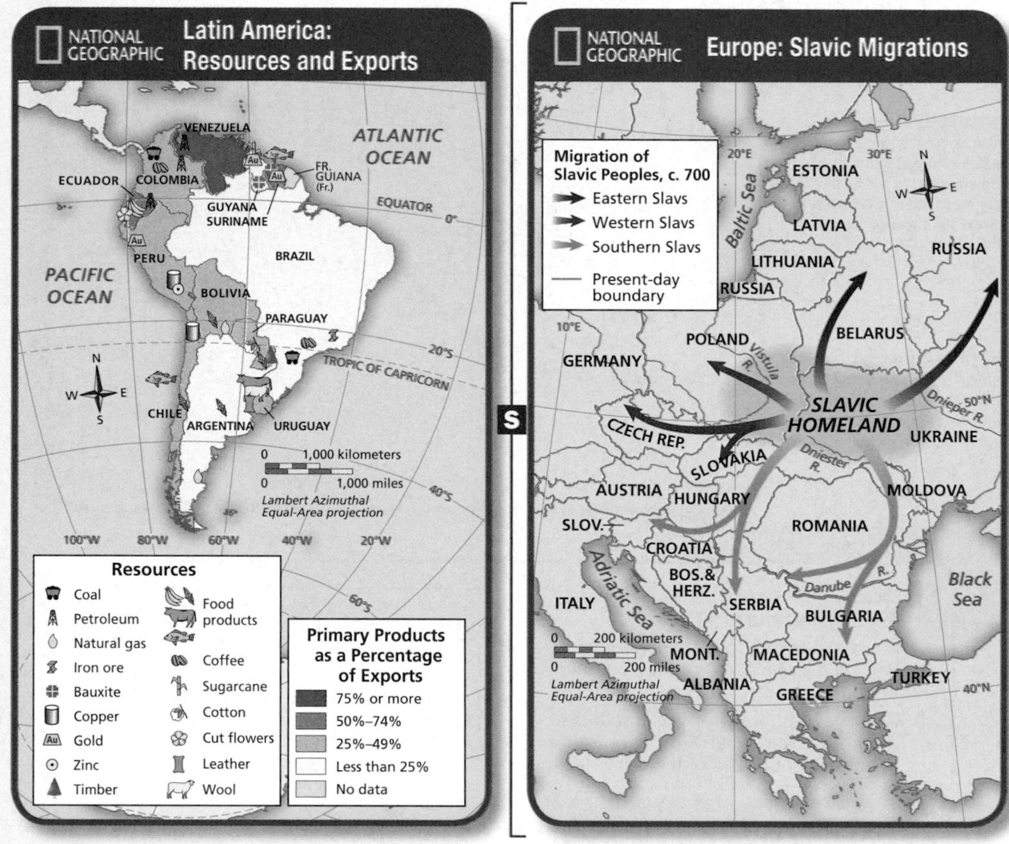

Additional Support

Teacher Tip

Collaborative Learning

Ask students if they have difficulty distinguishing one color from another on this map. If so, these students may benefit from other resources, such as maps that make distinctions using shading or symbols rather than color.

Activity: Collaborative Learning

Making Thematic Maps Divide the class into several groups. Each group will research a theme that interests them and create a thematic map to present to the class. Themes may be national (for example, a U.S. map showing the location of roller coasters or professional football stadiums) or local (for example, a city map displaying the location of public libraries or city parks). After groups choose their themes, each group should designate tasks (research, drawing maps, creating the presentation) among themselves so that each group member participates. Schedule a period for all the groups to present their maps to the class. **OL**

Geographic Information Systems

Modern technology has changed the way maps are made. Most cartographers use computers with software programs called **geographic information systems (GIS).** A GIS is designed to accept data from different sources—maps, satellite images, printed text, and statistics. The GIS converts the data into a digital code, which arranges it in a database. Cartographers then program the GIS to process the data and produce maps. With GIS, each kind of information on a map is saved as a separate electronic layer.

The first layer of information in a GIS pinpoints the area of interest. This allows the user to see, in detail, the area he or she needs to study. In this case, the area of study is a 5-mile (8-km) radius around Christ Hospital in Jersey City, New Jersey.

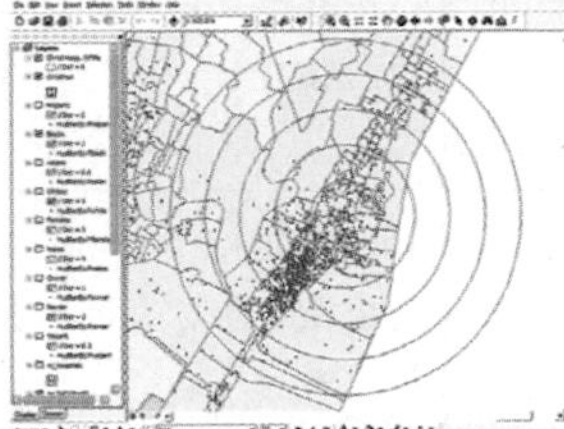

Additional layers of information are added based on the problem or issue being studied. In this case, hospital administrators want to find out about the population living in neighborhoods near the hospital so they can offer the community what it needs. A second layer showing African Americans who live within the 5-mile (8-km) radius has been added to the GIS.

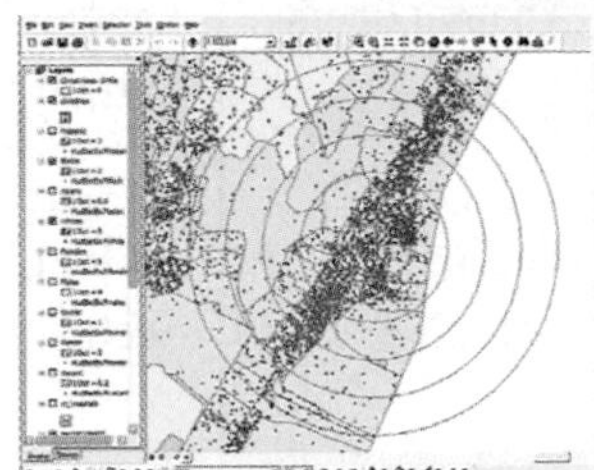

Complex information can be presented using more than one layer. For example, the hospital's surrounding neighborhoods include other groups in addition to African Americans. A third layer showing whites who live within the 5-mile (8-km) radius has been added to the GIS. Administrators can now use this information to help them make decisions about staffing and services associated with the hospital.

S

PRACTICING THE SKILL

1. **Explain** the significance of: thematic maps, qualitative maps, flow-line maps.
2. **Which** type of thematic map would best show the spread of Islam during Muhammad's time?
3. **Which** type of thematic map would best show average income per capita in the United States?
4. **How** does GIS allow cartographers to create maps and make changes to maps quickly and easily?
5. **Complete** a chart like the one below by identifying three examples of each type of thematic map found in this textbook. Note the page numbers of each.

Qualitative Maps	Flow-Line Maps

S Skill Practice

Visual Literacy **Ask:** How could you make GIS maps without a computer? *(You could draw the data on transparencies and layer the transparencies.)* **OL**

Assess

Summarizing Have students work in pairs to make study cards for the Geography Handbook. Students can use main headings and subheadings to organize the section material. When the cards are finished, have students take turns testing each other on what they have learned. **OL**

Close

Identifying **Ask:** What are the four main types of maps? *(physical, political, qualitative, and flow-line)*

Practicing the Skill: Answers

1. thematic map: emphasizes a single idea or particular kind of information about an area; qualitative map: uses colors, symbols, lines, or dots to show information related to a specific idea; flow-line maps: illustrate movement of people, animals, goods, and ideas, as well as physical processes like hurricanes and glaciers
2. qualitative
3. flow-line
4. by allowing information to be printed on separate electronic layers
5. Answers will vary. Note that most maps in the text are qualitative maps; most climate maps are qualitative and flow-line.

UNIT 1 Planning Guide

UNIT PACING CHART							
	Unit 1	Chapter 1	Chapter 2	Chapter 3	Chapter 4	Chapter 5	Unit 1
Day 1	Unit Opener	Chapter Opener, Section 1	Chapter Opener, Section 1	Chapter Opener, Section 1	Chapter Opener, Section 1	Chapter Opener, Section 1	Time Notebook, Unit Assessment
Day 2		Section 1, Social History	Section 1, Section 2	Section 1, Section 2	Section 1, Section 2	Section 2, Section 3	
Day 3		Section 2, Visual Summary	Section 2	Section 2, Social History	Section 2, Section 3	Section 3, Social History	
Day 4		Chapter Assessment	Social History, Section 3	Section 3, Section 4	Section 3, Section 4	Section 4, Section 5	
Day 5			Geography and History, Section 4	Section 4, Visual Summary	Section 4, Social History	Section 5, Visual Summary	
Day 6			Analyzing Primary Sources, Visual Summary	Chapter Assessment	Section 5, Visual Summary	Chapter Assessment	
Day 7			Chapter Assessment		Chapter Assessment		

Teacher to Teacher

Ray Barron
Heritage High School
Littleton, Colorado

Comparing Pericles' *Funeral Oration* and Lincoln's *Gettysburg Address* The purpose of this activity is to enable students to see the similarities among all civil wars and to make connections between the American Civil War and that of the ancient Greeks.

Have students read both Pericles' *Funeral Oration* and Abraham Lincoln's *Gettysburg Address*. Have them use a Venn diagram to list the qualities of individuals, government, and war that are mentioned, including qualities that are mentioned in both orations. Organize students into groups and have each group reach a consensus as to which qualities are essential in both orations and why this is so.

Have students write a paragraph explaining why these two speeches were made to the people of Greece and the United States, respectively, and summarize what we can learn about civil war from the speeches.

Author Note

Dear World History Teacher,

As you begin to teach this unit, a number of important concepts stand out. For hundreds of thousands of years, human beings lived in small communities, seeking to survive by hunting, fishing, and gathering food and supplies in an often hostile environment. Then, in the space of a few thousand years, there was an abrupt change of direction. Human beings in a few widely scattered areas of the globe began to master the art of growing food crops. As more food was produced, the population in these areas grew, and people began to live in larger communities. Governments were formed to protect the people and provide other needed services. Cities appeared and became centers for cultural and religious development. Historians call this process the beginnings of civilization. It occurred at about the same time in four different areas of the world—Western Asia, Egypt, India, and China.

From the beginnings of the first civilizations around 3000 B.C., there was an ongoing movement toward the creation of larger states with more sophisticated systems of control. This process reached a high point in the first millennium B.C. Between 1000 B.C. and 500 B.C., the Assyrians and Persians created empires that included either large areas or all of the ancient Middle East. The conquests of Alexander the Great in the fourth century B.C. created an even larger, if short-lived, empire that soon divided into four kingdoms. Later, the western portion of these kingdoms, as well as the Mediterranean world and much of western Europe, fell subject to the mighty empire of the Romans. At the same time, much of India became part of the Mauryan Empire. Finally, in the last few centuries B.C., the rulers of China created a unified Chinese Empire.

Jackson J. Spielvogel

Senior Author

Focus

Why It Matters

Explain that the civilizations discussed in this unit laid the groundwork for our legal system, democratic form of government, many of the world's major religions, and important inventions such as the alphabet. **Ask:** **How do we know about the earliest humans, and how did they become a stepping stone for the great civilizations that were to follow?** *(Briefly discuss the role archaeologists play in gathering information about how early humans lived. Then discuss how the rise of the ancient civilizations was dependent on the agricultural techniques invented by the first humans.)*

Unit Launch Activity

Have students compare modern and ancient civilizations. For example, point out that farming is essential to both modern and ancient civilizations. Ask students to brainstorm other similarities. **OL**

UNIT 1

The First Civilizations and Empires

Prehistory–A.D. 500

▶ Why It Matters

For hundreds of thousands of years, human beings survived by hunting, fishing, and gathering food and supplies in an often hostile environment. In the space of a few thousand years, human beings began to master the art of growing food crops. As more food was produced, the population grew, and people began to live in cities, form governments, and develop writing and art. Historians call this process the beginning of civilization.

The "Maiden Porch" of the Erechtheum, overlooking the city of Athens, Greece, is an example of Greek architecture from the fifth century B.C.

Team Teaching Activity

Science What we know about the lives of early humans comes from ongoing excavations and scientific explorations in various archaeological sites around the world. Work with a science teacher to coordinate a study of recent findings of both human and animal life. For example, in 2001, researchers in Kenya found an almost complete skull of a new human species dating from 3.5 million years ago. In China, new dinosaur remains are being unearthed. Explore with students how these remains are located and identified, and how dating is done.

Teach

S Skill Practice

Using Geography Skills Tell students that the word *acropolis* refers to a high spot on a hill. Usually an acropolis has a number of buildings on it. **Ask:** Why do you think the people of ancient Athens chose to build their temples on an acropolis? *(Answers may include that being on a hilltop makes it easier to defend against attacks. Also, temples on a hill would be awe-inspiring.)* **OL**

Visual Literacy Direct students' attention to the photo of the Erechtheum temple. Ask them to suppose that they are standing near the monument and to describe what they see. How would they describe the terrain? **BL**

No Child Left Behind

Teaching Tip Incorporate into daily lesson plans opportunities for students to see how technology can expand their awareness of history by using Internet resources.

More About the Photo

Visual Literacy The Erechtheum was built during the Greek Classical period, 450–330 B.C. Like many structures on the Acropolis, the Erechtheum pays tribute to Athena—the patron goddess and protector of Athens. According to Greek mythology, Athena won the honor by defeating Poseidon, the sea god, in a competition proposed by King Cecrops. Each was required to give the city a gift. Poseidon plunged his spear into the Acropolis and created a well, but the water was salty, like the sea. Athena touched the ground and a fig tree appeared, and she won the contest. Consequently the city was named after her. The Erechtheum is named after Erechtheus, a mythical king who Athena is said to have raised. Inside the temple are sections devoted to Athena, Poseidon, and Erechtheus. The photograph shows the Porch of the Caryatids. Caryatids are statues that function as pillars or columns.

CHAPTER 1 Planning Guide

Key to Ability Levels	
BL Below Level	AL Above Level
OL On Level	ELL English Language Learners

Key to Teaching Resources	
Print Material	DVD
CD-ROM	Transparency

BL	OL	AL	ELL	Resources		Chapter Opener	Section 1	Section 2	Chapter Assess
				FOCUS					
BL	OL	AL	ELL	Transparency	**Daily Focus Skills Transparencies**		1-1	1-2	
				TEACH					
BL	OL	AL	ELL	Print Material	**Charting and Graphing Activity, URB**			✓	
	OL	AL		Print Material	**Economics and History Activity, URB**			✓	
BL	OL		ELL	Print Material	**Reading Skills Activity, URB**		p. 17		
	OL	AL		Print Material	**Historical Analysis Skills Activity, URB**			p. 18	
BL	OL	AL	ELL	Print Material	**Differentiated Instruction Activity, URB**		p. 19		
	OL		ELL	Print Material	**English Learner Activity, URB**			p. 21	
BL	OL	AL	ELL	Print Material	**Content Vocabulary Activity, URB***			p. 23	
BL	OL	AL	ELL	Print Material	**Academic Vocabulary Activity, URB**			p. 25	
BL	OL	AL	ELL	Print Material	**Skills Reinforcement Activity, URB**		p. 27		
	OL	AL		Print Material	**Critical Thinking Skills Activity, URB**			p. 28	
	OL	AL		Print Material	**History and Geography Activity, URB**			p. 29	
	OL	AL	ELL	Print Material	**Mapping History Activity, URB**		p. 31		
BL	OL	AL		Print Material	**Historical Significance Activity, URB**		p. 32		
BL	OL	AL	ELL	Print Material	**Cooperative Learning Activity, URB**		p. 33		
	OL	AL	ELL	Print Material	**History Simulation Activity, URB**		p. 35		
BL	OL	AL	ELL	Print Material	**Time Line Activity, URB**			p. 37	
	OL	AL		Print Material	**Linking Past and Present Activity, URB**		p. 38		
BL	OL	AL		Print Material	**People in World History Activity, URB**		pp. 39, 40		
BL	OL	AL	ELL	Print Material	**Primary Source Reading, URB**		p. 41		
	OL	AL		Print Material	**Enrichment Activity, URB**			p. 46	
BL	OL	AL	ELL	Print Material	**World Art and Music Activity, URB**		p. 43		
BL	OL		ELL	Print Material	**Guided Reading Activities, URB***		p. 48	p. 49	
BL	OL		ELL	Print Material	**Reading Essentials and Note-Taking Guide***		p. 1	p. 4	
BL	OL	AL	ELL	Print Material	**Differentiated Instruction for the World History Classroom**	✓	✓	✓	✓

Note: Please refer to the *Unit Resource Book: The First Civilizations and Empires* for this chapter's URB materials.

* Also available in Spanish

- Interactive Lesson Planner
- Interactive Teacher Edition
- Fully editable blackline masters
- Section Spotlight Videos Launch
- Differentiated Lesson Plans
- Printable reports of daily assignments
- Standards Tracking System

Levels				Resources		Chapter Opener	Section 1	Section 2	Chapter Assess
BL	OL	AL	ELL						
TEACH *(continued)*									
BL	OL	AL	ELL		**StudentWorks™ Plus DVD**	✓	✓	✓	✓
BL	OL	AL	ELL		**Vocabulary PuzzleMaker CD-ROM**	✓	✓	✓	✓
Teacher Resources					**Building Academic Vocabulary**	✓	✓	✓	✓
					Writer's Guidebook		p. 43		
					Strategies for Success	✓	✓	✓	✓
					Outline Map Resource Book	✓	✓	✓	✓
					Presentation Plus! with MindJogger DVD	✓	✓	✓	✓
ASSESS									
BL	OL	AL	ELL		**Section Quizzes and Chapter Tests***		p. 1	p. 2	pp. 3–10
BL	OL	AL	ELL		**Authentic Assessment With Rubrics**	✓	✓	✓	✓
BL	OL	AL	ELL		**Standardized Test Practice Workbook**	✓	✓	✓	✓
BL	OL	AL	ELL		***ExamView® Assessment Suite* CD-ROM**		1-1	1-2	Ch. 1
BL	OL	AL	ELL		**Interactive Tutor Self-Assessment CD-ROM**		1-1	1-2	
CLOSE									
BL			ELL		**Reteaching Activity, URB**			p. 45	
BL	OL		ELL		**Reading and Study Skills Foldables™**	✓	✓	✓	✓

Read and Listen Simultaneously

Technology Product

Glencoe's *StudentWorks*™ *Plus* contains everything your students need, including the complete Student Edition, text in audio, access to all student workbooks, and links to online activities and resources.

- Students can read chapters with Adobe Acrobat Reader software, which is opened automatically by the *StudentWorks*™ *Plus* program.
- The complete textbook is available with audio via the *StudentWorks*™ *Plus*.
- Students can read and listen simultaneously with page-by-page audio, which can improve content comprehension for all your students.
- Use this component with struggling readers or to emphasize an important concept.

Objectives

Using *StudentWorks*™ *Plus* will help your students

- practice their reading skills;
- improve their listening comprehension.

Steps

Provide students with the following information:

- Launch *StudentWorks*™ *Plus*.
- Select the **Student Edition with Audio** from the launch screen.
- Use the bookmarks along the left side to navigate to the desired chapter or use the **Page Navigator** link in the bookmarks to link to the exact page number in the Student Edition.
- Click on the audio icon located on each page in the upper left corner to launch the audio.
- Read along with the audio.

History ONLINE

	Student	Teacher	Parent
Beyond the Textbook	●	●	●
Chapter Overviews	●	●	●
Time Current Events	●		●
ePuzzles and Games	●		●
Concepts in Motion	●		●
Literature Connections		●	
Multi-Language Glossaries	●		●
Online Student Edition	●	●	●
Self-Check Quizzes	●		●
Student Web Activities	●		●
Study Central ™	●		●
Teaching Today		●	
Vocabulary eFlashcards	●		●
Web Activity Lesson Plans		●	

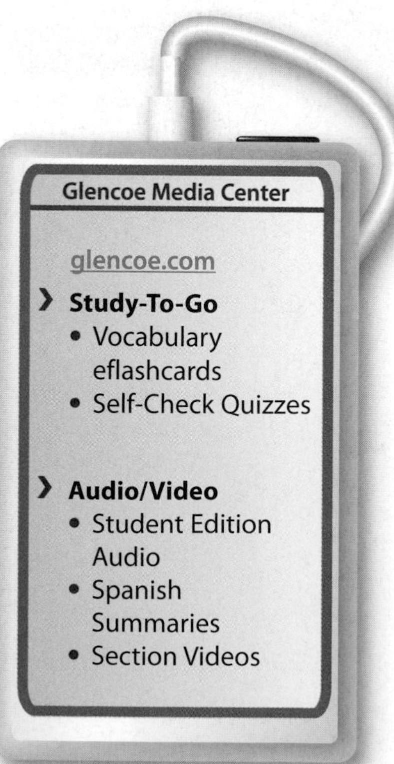

- **Timed Readings Plus in Social Studies** helps students increase their reading rate and fluency while maintaining comprehension. The 400-word passages are similar to those found on state and national assessments.
- **Reading in the Content Area: Social Studies** concentrates on six essential reading skills that help students better comprehend what they read. The book includes 75 high-interest nonfiction passages written at increasing levels of difficulty.
- **Reading Social Studies** includes strategic reading instruction and vocabulary support in Social Studies content for both ELLs and native speakers of English.

www.jamestowneducation.com

Biography  

The following videotape program is available from Glencoe as a supplement to Chapter 1:

- Seven Wonders of the Ancient World (ISBN: 0-07-700401-9)

To order, call Glencoe at 1-800-334-7344. To find classroom resources to accompany many of these videos, check the following home pages:

A&E Television: www.aetv.com

The History Channel: www.historychannel.com

NATIONAL GEOGRAPHIC

Index to National Geographic Magazine:

The following articles relate to this chapter:

- "The Origin of Childhood," by Christopher P. Sloan, November 2006
- "Guardian of a Ghost World," by David Roberts, August 2006
- "Hands Across Time," by Luc-Henri Fage, August 2005

National Geographic Society Products To order the following, call National Geographic at 1-800-368-2728:

- *National Geographic Atlas of the World* (Book).

Access National Geographic's new, dynamic MapMachine Web site and other geography resources at:
www.nationalgeographic.com
www.nationalgeographic.com/maps

GLENCOE BOOKLINK 3

Use this database to search more than 30,000 titles to create a customized reading list for your students.

- Reading lists can be organized by students' reading level, author, genre, theme, or area of interest.
- The database provides Degrees of Reading Power™ (DRP) and Lexile™ readability scores for all selections.
- A brief summary of each selection is included.

Leveled reading suggestions for this chapter:

For students at a Grade 8 reading level:

- ***Ancient Mesopotamia,*** by Cynthia Klingel and Robert B. Noyed

For students at a Grade 9 reading level:

- ***The Story of the Ice Age*** by Rose Wyler and Gerald Ames

For students at a Grade 10 reading level:

- ***Painters of the Caves,*** by Patricia Lauber

For students at a Grade 11 reading level:

- ***In the Land of Ur: The Discovery of Ancient Mesopotamia,*** by Hans Baumann

For students at a Grade 12 reading level:

- ***Ancient Agriculture: From Foraging to Farming*** by Michael Woods and Mary Woods

Introducing **CHAPTER 1**

Focus

MAKING CONNECTIONS
What is civilization?

Activate students' prior knowledge by having them brainstorm what they know about early humans. Responses may include that before the establishment of civilizations, early humans traveled from place to place, looking for food. Then discuss how the development of agriculture allowed early humans to settle into one area. Wrap up the discussion by having students give examples of how agriculture continues to be an important aspect of society, politics, and economics today.

Teach

The Big Ideas

As students study the chapter, remind them to consider the section-based Big Ideas presented in each section's Guide to Reading. The **Essential Questions** in the activities below tie in to the Big Ideas and help students think about and understand important chapter concepts. In addition, the Hands-On Chapter Projects with their culminating activities relate the content from each section to the Big Ideas. These activities build on each other as students progress through the chapter. Section activities culminate in the wrap-up activity on the Visual Summary page.

CHAPTER 1

The First Humans

Prehistory–3500 B.C.

Section 1 Early Humans

Section 2 The Neolithic Revolution

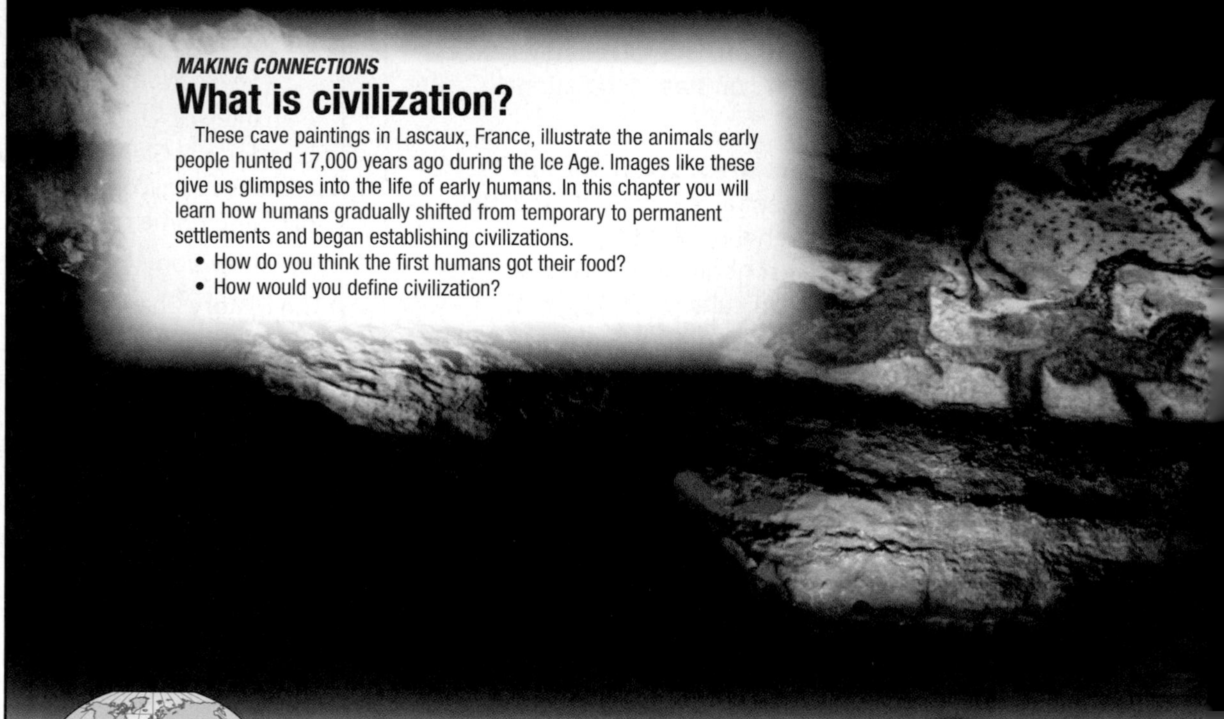

MAKING CONNECTIONS

What is civilization?

These cave paintings in Lascaux, France, illustrate the animals early people hunted 17,000 years ago during the Ice Age. Images like these give us glimpses into the life of early humans. In this chapter you will learn how humans gradually shifted from temporary to permanent settlements and began establishing civilizations.

- How do you think the first humans got their food?
- How would you define civilization?

THE WORLD ▶

3,500,000 B.C. | 2,000,000 B.C. | 200,000 B.C.

c. 3,000,000 B.C. Australopithecines flourish in Africa

c. 2,500,000 B.C. Paleolithic humans carve with stone tools

c. 1,500,000 B.C. *Homo erectus* appears

c. 250,000 B.C. *Homo sapiens* species develops

2

Early Humans

Essential Question: What important developments took place in the Paleolithic Age? *(Early humans began using tools and fire. As they hunted and gathered food, they also moved from placed to place to survive.)* Point out that in Section 1 students will learn about the history of early humans as shown through the research of various archaeologists in Africa and other areas of the world. **OL**

The Neolithic Revolution

Essential Question: How does agriculture affect our society? *(Agriculture is a foundation of our society because it provides food for populations. Without agriculture, people would need to spend most of their time trying to hunt and gather enough food to survive.)* Point out that in Section 2 students will learn how systematic agriculture engendered changes in the economy, politics, and society of early humans. **OL**

Introducing
CHAPTER 1

More About the Photo

Visual Literacy This modern photograph was taken at Lascaux in southwestern France. Teenagers discovered the cave in 1940. These paintings of bulls and other animals were done more than 17,000 years ago. After World War II, the cave entrance was made larger so that people could see the paintings. However, all the people coming to the cave also caused the paintings to start deteriorating. The cause of the problem was the carbon dioxide that people visiting the cave exhaled. In order to preserve the paintings, the cave was closed to the public in 1963, but a replica was created of two galleries so that tourists can experience looking at cave paintings.

c. 100,000 B.C. Neanderthals living in Germany

c. 8000 B.C. Systematic agriculture develops

150,000 B.C. — 10,000 B.C. — 3500 B.C.

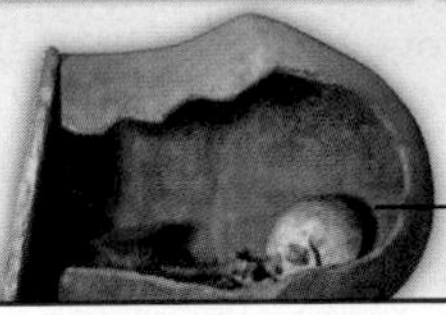

c. 8000 B.C. Neolithic humans practice burial rituals

3000 B.C. Bronze Age begins

FOLDABLES Study Organizer

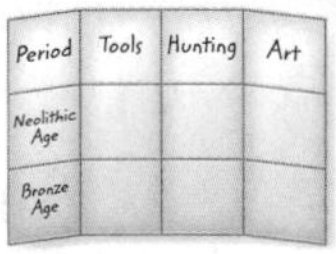

Describing Create a Three-Tab Book to record aspects of tools, hunting, and art that occurred during the Neolithic Age and the Bronze Age. Conduct additional research to add facts, illustrations, or maps to your Foldable.

Period	Tools	Hunting	Art
Neolithic Age			
Bronze Age			

History ONLINE
Chapter Overview—Visit glencoe.com to preview Chapter 1.

Dinah Zike's Foldables

Dinah Zike's Foldables are three-dimensional, interactive graphic organizers that help students practice basic writing skills, review vocabulary terms, and identify main ideas. Instructions for creating and using Foldables can be found in the Appendix at the end of this book and in the *Dinah Zike's Reading and Study Skills Foldables* booklet.

History ONLINE
Introduce students to chapter content and key terms by having them access the Chapter 1 Overview at glencoe.com.

Focus

Bellringer

Daily Focus Transparency 1.1

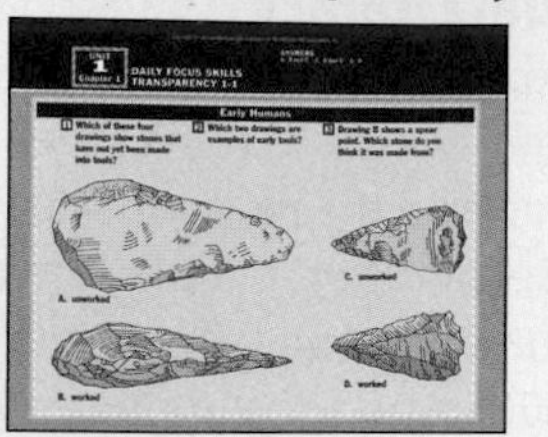

GUIDE TO READING

Answers to Graphic:

Tool	Effect
bone harpoon and fishhook	increased the catch of fish
sharp-edged tools	made it easier to cut and dig
scraping tools	made it easier to clean animal hides

Section Spotlight Video

To generate student interest and provide a springboard for class discussion, access the Chapter 1, Section 1 video at glencoe.com or on the video DVD.

SECTION 1

Early Humans

GUIDE TO READING

The BIG Idea

Physical Geography Human life developed in different stages over millions of years and by 10,000 B.C., *Homo sapiens sapiens* had spread throughout the world.

Content Vocabulary

- prehistory *(p. 4)*
- archaeology *(p. 4)*
- artifact *(p. 4)*
- anthropology *(p. 4)*
- fossil *(p. 4)*
- hominid *(p. 6)*
- *Australopithecus (p. 7)*
- *Homo sapiens sapiens (p. 7)*
- "out-of-Africa" theory *(p. 7)*

Academic Vocabulary

- theory *(p. 4)*
- survive *(p. 8)*

People and Places

- Olduvai Gorge *(p. 6)*
- Paleolithic Age *(p. 8)*

Reading Strategy

Summarizing Information As you read, create a chart like the one below showing the effects of three tools on the lifestyle of early humankind.

Tool	Effect

Where did early humans live? How did they live, and what happened to them? To answer these questions, scientists study the evidence left by prehistoric people. Although researchers have new and better ways of studying the past, there is much we still do not know.

Before History

MAIN IDEA Scientists use fossils and artifacts as clues to how early humans lived.

HISTORY & YOU What would people in the future think of American culture based on what we leave behind?

Historians rely mostly on documents, or written records, to create their pictures of the past. However, no written records exist for the prehistory of humankind. In fact, **prehistory** means the time before writing was developed. The story of prehistoric humans depends on archaeological and, more recently, biological evidence. Archaeologists and anthropologists use this information to create **theories** about our early past.

Archaeology and Anthropology

Archaeology is the study of past societies through analysis of what people left behind. Archaeologists dig up and examine **artifacts**—objects made by humans. Artifacts may be tools, weapons, art, and even buildings made by early humans.

Anthropology is the study of human life and culture. Culture includes what people wear, how they organize their society, and what they value. Anthropologists use artifacts and human **fossils** to create a picture of people's everyday lives. Fossils are rocklike remains of biological organisms—a leaf imprint or a skeleton.

Archaeologists and anthropologists have developed scientific methods to carry out their work. They excavate, or dig up land, at sites around the globe to uncover fossil remains of early humans, ancient cities, burial grounds, and other objects. The examination and analysis of these remains give archaeologists a better understanding of ancient societies. By examining artifacts such as pottery, tools, and weapons, for example, these scientists learn about the social and military structures of a society. By analyzing bones, skins, and plant seeds, they are able to piece together the diet and activities of early people. One of the most important and difficult jobs of both archaeologists and anthropologists is dating their finds.

Resource Manager

R Reading Strategies	C Critical Thinking	D Differentiated Instruction	W Writing Support	S Skill Practice
Teacher Edition • Organizing, p. 7 • Previewing, p. 8 • Summarizing, p. 10 **Additional Resources** • Read. Skills Act., URB p. 17 • Cont. Vocab. Act., URB p. 23 • Guid. Read. Act., URB p. 48 • Read. Ess. & Note-Taking Guide, p. 1	**Teacher Edition** • Drawing Con., p. 6 • Compare/Contrast, p. 8 • Making Inferences, p. 9 **Additional Resources** • Hist. Sim. Act., URB p. 35 • Linking Past/Present Act., URB p. 38 • People in World Hist. Act., URB pp. 39, 40 • Section Quiz, p. 1	**Teacher Edition** • ELL, p. 5 • Visual/Spatial, p. 6 **Additional Resources** • Diff. Instr. Act., URB p. 19 • Coop. Learn. Act., URB p. 33 • World Art & Music Act., URB p. 43	**Teacher Edition** • Descriptive Writing, p. 9 **Additional Resources** • Hist. Sig. Act., URB p. 32 • Writer's Guidebook, p. 43	**Teacher Edition** • Analyzing a Theory, p. 7 • Visual Literacy, p. 11 **Additional Resources** • Skills Reinforc. Act., URB p. 27 • Mapping Hist. Act., URB p. 31

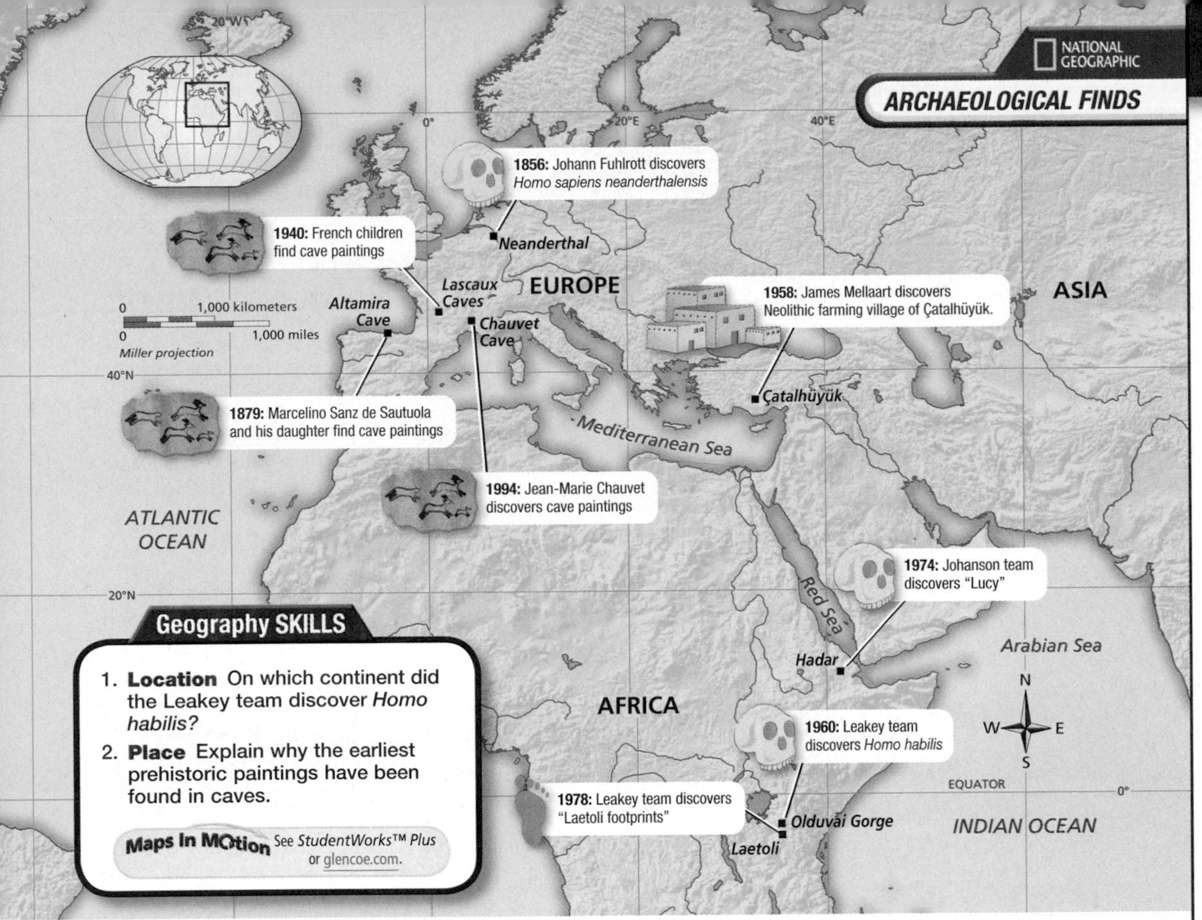

Geography SKILLS

1. **Location** On which continent did the Leakey team discover *Homo habilis?*
2. **Place** Explain why the earliest prehistoric paintings have been found in caves.

Maps In MOtion See StudentWorks™ Plus or glencoe.com.

Dating Artifacts and Fossils

Dating human fossils and artifacts helps scientists understand when and where the first humans lived.

One method used to determine age is radiocarbon dating. All living things absorb a small amount of radioactive carbon, or C-14, from the atmosphere. After a living thing dies, it slowly loses C-14. By measuring the amount left in an object, a scientist can figure its age. This method is accurate for objects no more than about 50,000 years old.

For objects dating back to 200,000 years ago, scientists can make relatively precise measurements using thermo-luminescence. This measures the light given off by electrons trapped in the soil surrounding fossils and artifacts. **D**

Microscopic and biological analyses of organic remains—such as blood, hairs, and plant tissues left on tools and weapons—give scientists still more information. Such analyses have shown that blood molecules may survive millions of years. This recent scientific discovery is especially useful in telling us more about humans, their use of tools, and the animals they killed. Ancient deoxyribonucleic acid (DNA) is providing new information on human evolution. The analysis of plant remains on stone tools yields evidence on the history of farming. All of these techniques give us insight into the lives of early peoples.

✓Reading Check **Describing** How do archaeologists and anthropologists determine the ages of fossils and artifacts?

Teach

D Differentiated Instruction

English Language Learners
As a group, decide how the context clue "measures the light given off by electrons" helps the reader determine the meaning of *thermoluminescence*. Point out that the Latin word part *lumin* or *lumen*, meaning "an opening or light," also shows that the word is related to light. **OL**

✓Reading Check

Answer: Archaeologists and anthropologists determine the ages of fossils and artifacts using radiocarbon dating, thermoluminescence dating, and by studying DNA (deoxyribonucleic acid).

Geography SKILLS

Answers:
Have students answer these questions after reading Section 1.
1. Africa
2. caves provided some protections for the paints that allowed them to survive

Additional Support

Activity: Technology Connection

Finding Dating Methods Remind students that radiocarbon dating and thermoluminescence are two methods of dating artifacts. Tell students that there are other methods that archaeologists use to help them date artifacts. **Ask:** **What other methods might archaeologists use to help them date human fossils and artifacts?** *(Discuss that there are probably several different methods that archaeologists use now and have used in the past to date objects. Note that all the methods have some error.)* Have small groups of students use the Internet to research dating methods used currently and historically. Each group should choose one method to research. The groups should use at least three Internet resources in their research, but they may also use other resources. Each group should create a presentation explaining the dating method they investigated. Their presentations should include a description of the way the dating is done and should also include information about a time that the dating method was used. If students are investigating a historical dating method, they may also want to contrast dates found using their method with dates found using more modern dating.

Early Development

MAIN IDEA Using remains and technology, scientists identify important stages in human development.

HISTORY & YOU How did humans change? Read about the early stages of human development.

In recent decades, modern science has produced a clearer picture of how early humans developed. Pieces of the puzzle are still missing, however. When a new skull or skeleton is unearthed, scientists may find that they have to revise their ideas about prehistoric human life.

Hominids to *Homo Sapiens*

What is a **hominid**? A hominid was a humanlike creature that walked upright. The earliest hominids lived in Africa four million years ago. They existed for millions of years, slowly changing over time.

Louis and Mary Leakey spent most of their lives searching for clues about early human life. They made a dramatic discovery of a skeleton at **Olduvai Gorge** in East Africa. According to their son:

C

PRIMARY SOURCE

"My father was ill that morning, so my mother set out alone . . . but found very little until just before noon, when she noticed a scrap of enormously thick bone protruding from beneath the surface. She instantly realized that it was part of a hominid skull—and that two teeth were embedded in the rock just above it. Elated, she drove back to camp to tell my father Louis. As he remembered it, she rushed in crying, 'I've got him! I've got him! I've got him!'"

—Richard Leakey, *TIME*, July 17, 1959

Leakey's discovery of a hominid in 1959 was the oldest at that time—about 1.8 million years old.

PEOPLE *in* HISTORY

Louis Leakey 1903–1972

Mary Leakey 1913–1996 Paleoanthropologists

Paleoanthropologists study early human society. For three generations, beginning with the husband and wife team of Louis and Mary, the Leakeys have searched for early human remains in Africa.

Born in Kenya, Louis discovered some stone tools and an interest in prehistory. In the 1930's, Louis and Mary began looking for evidence of early humans at Olduvai Gorge. Mary is credited with discovering *Proconsul africanus* in 1948, *Australopithecus boisei* in 1959, *Homo habilis* in 1960, and an 89-foot-long trail of early human footprints called the "Laetoli footprints" in 1979. **What do the Leakeys' finds illustrate about where early human life began?**

D

Richard Leakey 1942–present

Louise Leakey 1972–present

Meave Leakey 1942–present Paleoanthropologists

Richard, a son of Louis and Mary, found his first fossil at age six. Meave, a zoologist, joined Richard's expedition in 1969. Richard and Meave focused their search at Koobi Fora, near Lake Turkana in Kenya. Over a thirty-year period, this Leakey team made 200 significant fossil finds.

Meave and Louise Leakey were named National Geographic Society's explorers-in-residence in 2002. The Leakey mother and daughter paleontologists found a 3.5-million-year-old skull near Turkana. **Why were the Leakeys' fossil finds significant?**

C Critical Thinking

Drawing Conclusions Ask: Why was this find so exciting to the Leakeys? *(The Leakeys had spent much time searching for the skeleton of an early human in East Africa. The bones found in 1959 proved to be the oldest at that time.)* **OL**

D Differentiated Instruction

Visual/Spatial Ask small groups of students to research one of the finds that the Leakeys made in Africa. Ask them to learn more about the find and how it pertains to the work of paleoanthropologists. Encourage students to create drawings and maps, or to use photographs with captions to explain what they have learned. **AL**

PEOPLE *in* HISTORY

Answers:

Louis Leakey, Mary Leakey—The Leakeys' finds show that early human life most likely began in Africa; **Richard Leakey, Louise Leakey, Meave Leakey**—The Leakeys' fossil finds were significant because they contributed new knowledge to our understanding of early human development.

Additional Support

Extending the Content

Studying Early Humans The Leakeys spent much of their lives putting together evidence for early human existence. Louis Leakey began his work at the Olduvai Gorge in 1931. Finds such as the ones the Leakeys made in the Olduvai Gorge do not give a complete history and they leave many questions unanswered. The remains must be interpreted. Determining the age of the remains, essential to constructing a chronology of human development, is also challenging. Dating methods are constantly being refined. Remind students that information changes frequently as new discoveries are made. Hypotheses are reevaluated as scientists interpret and reinterpret the information. **Ask:** What is the value of scientific inquiry and how does science contribute to human knowledge? *(Students' discussion should include facts to support their opinions.)* **AL**

For decades, scientists assumed these earliest of upright creatures must also have used tools. In 1974, Donald Johanson challenged this theory when his team found a new skeleton in Ethiopia. Johanson nicknamed the female skeleton "Lucy" and suggested that she was the common ancestor for several types of early human life. Scientists called this type of hominid ***Australopithecus*** (aw•STRAY•loh•PIH•thuh•kuhs), or "southern ape." It flourished in eastern and southern Africa.

In a 1991 interview, Johanson explained why "Lucy" changed the ideas of many scientists about hominids that walked upright:

PRIMARY SOURCE

> "People felt that there were a number of evolutionary changes, which all went together. That our ancestors stood up to free their hands so that they could make and use stone tools. In order to make and use stone tools, they had to have large brains . . . Here comes Lucy, about 3.5 million years old . . . very small brain, . . . and we have never found any stone tool, stone artifacts, associated with her species. Yet she is walking upright. So it appears that . . . walking on two legs, precedes by perhaps as much as a million and a half years, the manufacture of stone tools and the expansion of the brain."
>
> —Donald Johanson, 1991 interview

S

From 2.5 to 1.6 million years ago, a more advanced hominid developed with a somewhat larger brain. This hominid was named *Homo habilis*, meaning "handy human." *Homo habilis* may have used stone tools. The earliest remains of this hominid were discovered near Olduvai Gorge. Another hominid, *Homo erectus*, "upright human," existed from 1.8 million to 100,000 years ago. Although other hominids walked on two legs, *Homo erectus* had arms and legs in modern human proportion. Remains in Asia show that *Homo erectus* was probably the first hominid to leave Africa.

Around 200,000 years ago, *Homo sapiens* emerged. *Homo sapiens*, "wise human," showed rapid brain growth and mastered fire. Two kinds of early humans descended from *Homo sapiens:* Neanderthals and *Homo sapiens sapiens*. In the Neanderthal, a valley in Germany, the earliest remains of Neanderthals, or Neandertals, were found. They probably lived between 100,000 B.C. and 30,000 B.C. Other Neanderthal remains have been found in Europe and Turkey. Besides using many kinds of stone tools, European Neanderthals made their clothes from animal skins. Neanderthals seem to be the first early people to bury their dead. According to some scholars, burying the dead indicates a belief in an afterlife.

Homo Sapiens Sapiens

The second group descended from *Homo sapiens* is ***Homo sapiens sapiens***, meaning "wise, wise human." These are the first to have an anatomy similar to people today. Physical evidence suggests that *Homo sapiens sapiens* appeared in Africa between 150,000 and 200,000 years ago. They probably spread out of Africa to other parts of the world about 100,000 years ago, replacing populations of earlier hominids in Europe and Asia. This is referred to as the **"out-of-Africa" theory** (or replacement theory).

Another theory, the multiregional model, states that the development from earlier hominids to anatomically modern humans occurred in different locations in Africa, Asia, and Europe. The timing and reasons for early human migrations are still debated among scholars. R

By 30,000 B.C., *Homo sapiens sapiens* had replaced the Neanderthals. The Neanderthals died out, possibly as a result of conflicts with *Homo sapiens sapiens*. The spread of these first modern humans was a slow process. Over many thousands of years, *Homo sapiens sapiens* spread over the globe as they searched for food and new hunting grounds. In a whole generation, they may have moved only two to three miles. Over hundreds of thousands of years, this was enough to populate the world. Today, all humans, whether they are Europeans, Australian Aborigines (A•buh•RIHJ•NEES), or Africans, belong to the same subgroup of human beings.

✓Reading Check **Summarizing** Identify and describe all the important stages in early human development.

S Skill Practice

Analyzing a Theory **Ask:** How did the work of Donald Johanson change a theory that scientists had about hominids' use of tools? *(Johanson and others found a new skeleton that provided new information to the scientific community. It challenged the view that hominids began standing up so they could use tools.)* **OL**

R Reading Strategy

Organizing Have students create a three-column chart titled "Early Human Development." In the left column, students should list the types of hominids mentioned in the text. The middle column should list the approximate dates that each type of hominid was prevalent. In the right column, students should write a characteristic of each type of hominid. **OL**

✓Reading Check

Answer: Students' responses should include stages of development such as *Australopithecus, Homo habilis, Homo erectus,* Neanderthals, and *Homo sapiens.*

Differentiated Instruction

Leveled Activities

BL **Content Vocabulary Activity, URB p. 23**

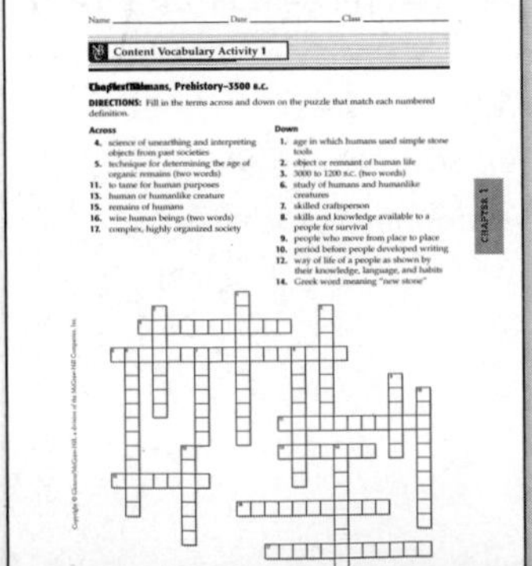

OL **Guided Reading Activity, URB p. 48**

AL **Historical Significance Activity, URB p. 32**

ELL **Differentiated Instruction Activity, URB p. 19**

R Reading Strategy

Previewing Have students preview the Paleolithic Age by writing the heads on this page in a spider graphic organizer. Ask students to write notes about the topics for each head as they read the page. BL

C Critical Thinking

Comparing and Contrasting Have students compare and contrast the specific roles of women, children, and families in early civilization with these same roles in the United States today. OL

The Paleolithic Age

MAIN IDEA Early humans used fire, made tools, and adapted to survive.

HISTORY & YOU Could you live in the wild with only tools you made? Read how early humans managed to survive.

R

One of the basic distinguishing features of the human species is the ability to make tools. The term **Paleolithic Age** is used to designate the early period of human history (approximately 2,500,000 B.C. to 10,000 B.C.) in which humans used simple stone tools. Paleolithic is Greek for "old stone," and the Paleolithic Age is sometimes called the Old Stone Age.

Hunting and Gathering

For hundreds of thousands of years, humans relied on hunting and gathering for their daily food. Paleolithic peoples had a close relationship with their environment. They came to know what animals to hunt and what plants to eat. They gathered wild nuts, berries, fruits, wild grains, and green plants. Around the world, they hunted and ate various animals, including buffalo, horses, bison, and reindeer. In coastal areas, fish and shellfish provided a rich source of food.

The Paleolithic Way of Life

Early humans were able to sustain themselves through the use of stone tools. To make such tools, early people used very hard stones, such as flint. They used one stone to chip away parts of another, creating an edge. Hand axes of various kinds—pointed tools with one or more cutting edges—were the most common. Hand axes eventually were set in wooden handles, making them easier to use. By attaching wooden poles to spear points and hardening the tips in fire, humans created spears to kill large animals.

Over the years, Paleolithic hunters developed better tools. The invention of the spear, and later the bow and arrow, made hunting much easier. Harpoons and fishhooks made of bone increased the catch of fish.

Early humans used sharp-edged tools to cut up plants, dig up roots, and cut branches to build simple shelters. Scraping tools were used to clean animal hides for clothing and shelter. By the end of the Paleolithic period, there is evidence of such refined tools as bone needles. These needles could be used for making nets and baskets and even sewing hides together for clothing.

Because Paleolithic people were hunters and gatherers, they had to follow animal migrations and vegetation cycles. Paleolithic humans were nomads—people who move from place to place to **survive.** Archaeologists and anthropologists think these nomads probably lived in small groups of twenty or thirty. Hunting depended on careful observation of animal behavior patterns and demanded group cooperation for success.

The Roles of Men and Women

The main job of Paleolithic peoples was finding enough to eat. Both men and women were responsible for finding the food needed for survival. Paleolithic parents passed on their practices, skills, and tools to their children to ensure the survival of later generations.

Since women bore and raised children, they probably stayed closer to camp. They played an important role in acquiring food by gathering berries, nuts, roots, and grains. Women taught the children C which foods were edible. They trapped small animals and kept the camp safe.

In the constant search for food, men had to travel far from camp to hunt herds of large animals. What the women caught and gathered had to feed the group if there was no game. Because both men and women were responsible for finding and acquiring the food needed to sustain life, many scientists believe there was equality between them. It is likely that both men and women made decisions that affected the activities of the Paleolithic group.

Adapting to Survive

Groups of Paleolithic people, especially those groups who lived in cold climates, found shelter in natural caves. Over a

Hands-On Chapter Project Step 1

Creating a Poster of Peoples' Lives

Pairs of students will start a poster showing types of artifacts from the early history of humans.

Step 1: Starting the Poster

Essential Question: What artifacts are typical of human life and culture in different ages?

Directions: As a class, discuss what artifacts archaeologists and anthropologists use in their study of societies and human life and culture. Write the term *artifacts* on the chalkboard and ask students to brainstorm examples—tools, weapons, art, or buildings. Then have pairs of students review the text and consult reference sources to plan which artifacts they would like to use to represent early humans. Encourage students to use old magazine photographs, illustrations, and other visuals to depict the artifacts. Some students may want to experiment with creating their own cave paintings as a background. Remind students to write captions for the visual information and to keep a bibliography of their sources. OL

(Chapter Project is continued in Section 2.)

period of time, people created new types of shelter as well. Perhaps most common was a simple structure made of wood poles or sticks covered with animal hides. In places where wood was scarce, they might use the large bones of mammoths to build frames that were then covered by animal hides. The systematic use of fire made it possible to provide a source of both light and heat within both the caves and the handmade structures in which they lived.

Use of Fire

Another important result from the migration of early hominids was the use of fire. As early hominids moved from the tropics into colder regions, they needed to adjust to new climate conditions. In response, *Homo erectus* first learned to make fires. Archaeologists have discovered the piled remains of ashes in caves that prove that Paleolithic people used fire systematically as long ago as 500,000 years. C W

C Critical Thinking

Making Inferences Ask: What is one thing that scientists needed to do in order to use the piled remains of ashes as proof that Paleolithic people used fire? *(Scientists needed to date the ashes in order to determine that they were created by Paleolithic people.)* OL

W Writing Support

Descriptive Writing Have students write a paragraph that uses descriptive words about fire. Suggest that students write about a time that they experienced a fire in a hearth or a campfire. OL

SCIENCE, TECHNOLOGY, & SOCIETY

Field Archaeology: How We Learn about the Spread of Early Humans

Archaeologists use scientific methods to learn more about prehistory. The techniques and materials used on a "dig" combine older tools and modern technology.

First archaeologists search computer databases, maps, aerial photos, and satellite images to find a promising site. At the site, the team will record the exact location with a global positioning device. Then using survey equipment, they map the area and set up a grid to pinpoint the location and depths of the finds. Workers still use trowels and brushes to unearth artifacts.

Once an object is found, archaeologists record it in their field notes. Then they clean, label, photograph, and enter the find on a database. A rough "dating" is made using stratigraphy, indicating age by the soil layer it was found in. Other tests—radiocarbon dating, potassium-argon dating, DNA, thermoluminescence, and dendrochronology—are done in a lab.

▲ Laptops make recording and analyzing information from the dig easier.

▲ Hand-held GPS (Global Positioning System)

◄ At an excavation of an Inca cemetery near Lima, Peru, a man brushes dirt from a skull with hair still intact.

CRITICAL THINKING SKILLS

1. **Explaining** Why does it take archaeologists many years to excavate a site?
2. **Drawing Conclusions** Why do archaeologists record the locations of where objects are found in such detail?

CRITICAL THINKING

Answers:

1. Excavating is time-consuming because scientists must proceed slowly and carefully so they can preserve all potential evidence.
2. detailed information about where items were found is important for dating the artifacts and finding patterns in the artifacts

Additional Support

Activity: Interdisciplinary Connection

Geography Tell students that archaeological sites are sometimes difficult to find. Recently scientists have used high-resolution commercial satellite images and data from NASA's Airborne Synthetic Aperture Radar (AIRSAR) to find Maya sites in Guatemala. These technologies showed that the jungle vegetation at Maya sites was discolored when compared to the rest of an area. This fact helped scientists to pinpoint the sites.

Have students work in small groups. Spark discussion by asking students where in the local area a good archaeological site might exist. Have each group confirm their predictions by researching local archaeological sites. Encourage students to use the Internet and also to call local colleges and universities or local historical societies to gather information. OL

R Reading Strategy

Summarizing Have students summarize in one or two sentences what they have learned about how Paleolithic peoples used fire. OL

Did You Know?

Chauvet Cave was discovered in 1994 by Jean-Marie Chauvet and his friends Éliette Brunel and Christian Hillaire. In 1995, the cave was made a Historic Monument. In order to protect the cave, the state took ownership of it in 1997. Only a few people are authorized to visit the cave each year.

DOCUMENT-BASED QUESTIONS

Answers:

1. The "Panel of Horses" depicts horses, mammoths, rhinos, cave bears, and cave lions.
2. Possible answer: The animals in the cave art look much the same as their modern counterparts.

Differentiated Instruction

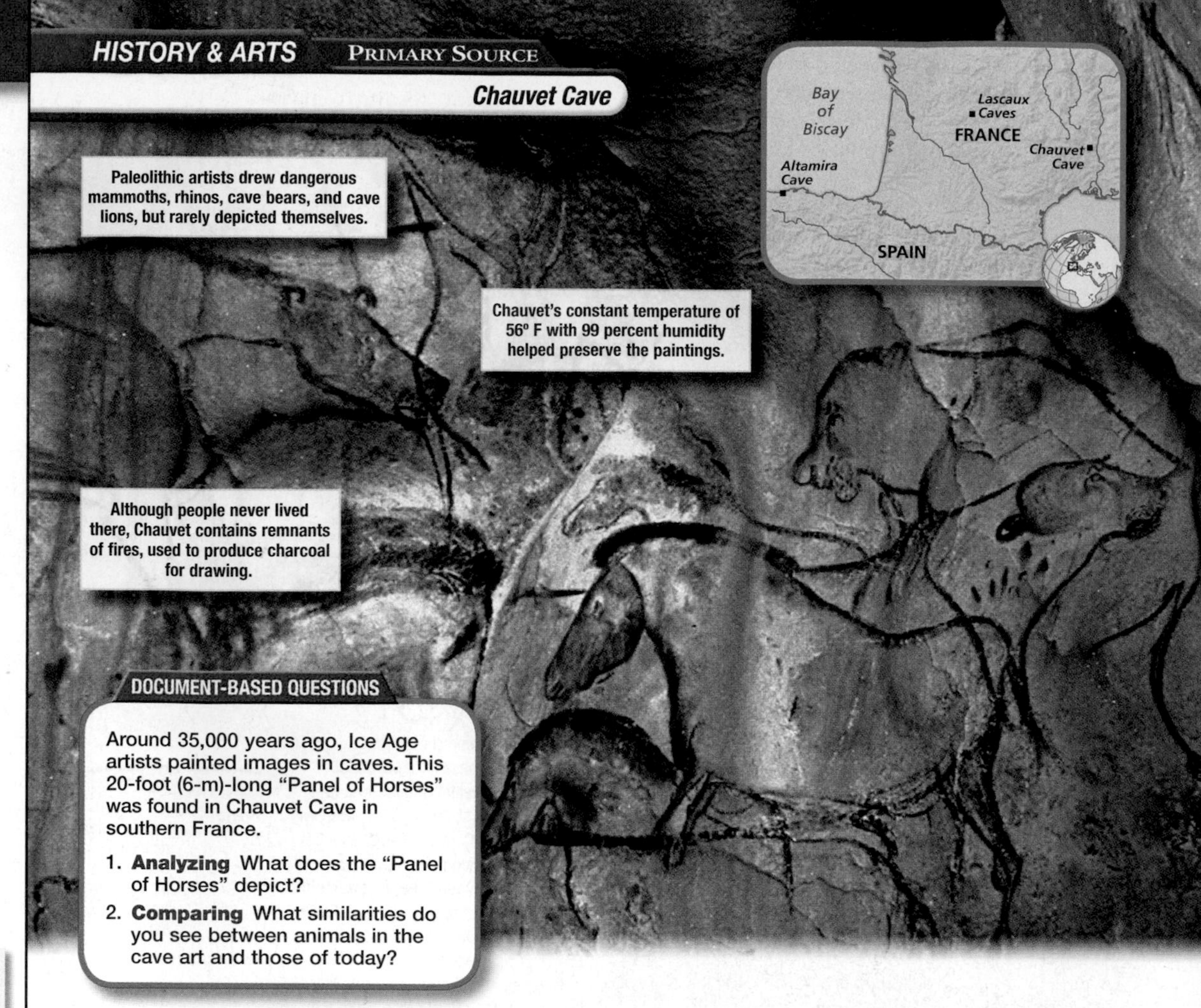

At a *Homo erectus* site in northern China, remnants of hearths, ashes, charcoal, and charred bones have been dated to 400,000 years ago.

Fire not only gave warmth, but kept wild animals away from the campsite. Armed with spears, hunters used fire to flush out wild pigs for the kill. People gathered around the fire to trade stories and to cook. R Cooked food tasted better, lasted longer, and was easier to chew and digest (in the case of some plants, such as wild grains), so it seems likely that nutrition improved.

Scholars believe that the discovery of a means for starting fires occurred independently throughout the world, in different places at different times. Archaeologists lack concrete evidence on how early peoples started fires. They have been able to examine the methods used by traditional peoples. On that basis, archaeologists deduce that the earliest humans used friction to start fires.

Eventually, some Paleolithic peoples developed sturdy, drill-like wooden devices to start fires. Other early humans discovered that a certain stone, iron pyrites, gave off a spark when struck against a rock and that spark could ignite dry grass or leaves.

Mapping History Activity, URB p. 31

Analyzing Information

Objective: Understand how *Homo sapiens* migrated throughout the world, eventually developing agriculture.

Focus: Have students use the map to answer the questions.

Teach: Discuss the relationship between migration and agriculture.

Assess: Ask students to describe the general pattern of the migratory routes.

Close: Draw conclusions about the changes in society brought about by changes in food procurement.

Differentiated Instruction Strategies

BL Have pairs or small groups create a three-column chart of *Homo sapiens* sites based on dates shown in map key.

AL Have students research the kinds of foods grown in a selected region and ask them to compare the first foods grown in that region to foods grown today.

ELL Have students work with English-proficient partners to complete the questions.

The Ice Ages

Having fire to create a source of heat was especially important when Ice Age conditions descended on the Paleolithic world. The most recent Ice Age began about 100,000 B.C. and ended about 8000 B.C. During this time, sheets of thick ice covered large parts of Europe, Asia, and North America. As sea levels went down, people migrated across land bridges that had not existed before.

Ice Age conditions posed a serious threat to human life, and the ability to adapt was crucial to human survival. The use of fire, for example, reminds us that early humans sometimes adapted not by changing themselves to better fit their environment but by changing the environment.

Creating Art

The importance of art to human life is basic. Art existed even in prehistory among the hunters and gatherers of the Paleolithic Age. In 1940, a bad storm near Lascaux (la•SKOH) in southern France uprooted a large tree, revealing a cave. French children playing nearby soon found the cave and the paintings inside. Many of these paintings had deteriorated, but scientists used special tools to determine what is being depicted, such as horses, bulls, and stags.

Another famous discovery was made in Spain in 1879 when a little girl wandered into a cave on her grandfather's farm near Altamira. Like many other caves covered with Paleolithic art, the cave near Altamira shows evidence that the paintings may have been created over a span of time, not all at once. Scientists can date the art based on pigments from the paintings. **S**

In 1994, Jean-Marie Chauvet and his friends discovered paintings in southern France. Carbon dating showed works at Chauvet Cave were nearly twice as old as those at Lascaux and Altamira, but the drawings were more advanced. Scholars had assumed the opposite—that the earliest art would be crude and gradually would become more detailed.

Using stone lamps filled with animal fat to light the caves, early artists painted with fingers and twigs and even blew paint through hollow reeds. They mixed mineral ores with animal fat to make red, yellow, and black paint. A variety of realistically painted animals cover the caves. Few humans appear in these paintings, and when they do appear, they are drawn as sticklike figures. This has led some scholars to think the work was done for a magical or religious ritual to bring success in hunting. Others believe the paintings were made simply to please the eye. Recent discoveries of art by early humans show that prehistoric art existed in other areas of the world.

✓Reading Check **Identifying** What are two important innovations of Paleolithic peoples?

SECTION 1 REVIEW

Vocabulary

1. **Explain** the significance of: prehistory, archaeology, artifact, anthropology, fossil, hominid, Olduvai Gorge, *Australopithecus, Homo sapiens sapiens*, "out-of-Africa" theory, Paleolithic Age.

Main Ideas

2. **Discuss** what kinds of materials archaeologists use to study prehistory.
3. **Explain** what the caves of Lascaux suggest about early human society.
4. **Create** a diagram like the one shown below to compare and contrast australopithecus and Neanderthal.

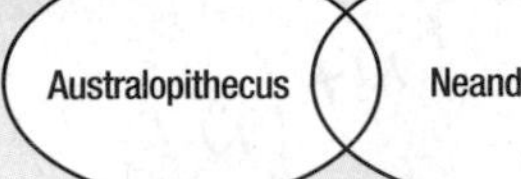

Critical Thinking

5. **The BIG Idea Explaining** Explain the difference between the "out-of-Africa" and multiregional theories.
6. **Comparing** Discuss the difference between the roles of Paleolithic men and women.
7. **Analyzing Visuals** Examine the cave paintings shown on page 10. What do they tell you about human/animal interactions during the Paleolithic Age?

Writing About History

8. **Descriptive Writing** Imagine you are part of an archaeological team at a recently discovered site, keeping a daily journal. Describe the conditions of the site, the sorts of artifacts you are finding, and what you hope to find based on the evidence so far. Read magazine articles or books in a library or on the Web to help you with this project.

History ONLINE
For help with the concepts in this section of *Glencoe World History*, go to glencoe.com and click Study Central™.

11

S Skill Practice

Visual Literacy Invite students to create their own "cave" paintings that represent animals in their daily lives, such as dogs, cats, birds, and squirrels. Encourage them to try to capture the spirit of the animals they are depicting. **BL**

✓Reading Check

Answer: the making of tools and the use of fire

Assess

History ONLINE

Study Central™ provides summaries, interactive games, and online graphic organizers to help students review content.

Close

Summarizing Ask: What key human characteristic is shown in the actions of the Paleolithic peoples? *(Human beings find ways to adapt to their environment or to change the environment to suit their needs.)*

Answers

1. Definitions for the vocabulary words are found in the section and the Glossary.
2. radiocarbon dating, thermoluminescence, microscopic and biological analyses, DNA analysis, databases, maps, aerial photos, satellite images, trowels, brushes
3. The caves suggest that art is basic to human life.
4. **Australopithecines:** 3–4 million years ago in eastern-southern Africa; **Neanderthals:** Between 100,000 and 30,000 B.C. in Europe and Southwest Asia, buried their dead; **Both:** Walked upright, used tools
5. "Out-of-Africa" supporters think humans spread from Africa replacing hominids; others think that the development of modern humans occurred in different locations.
6. Women gathered berries, nuts, and grains; men hunted. People had to find food for survival.
7. Humans were hunting animals for food.
8. Students' writing should describe location, site conditions, artifacts, and dig goals. Writing should show that students have done research to describe a site realistically.

Focus

Introducing Social History

Lead a preview of this feature for students. As students look at the illustrations, ask questions such as the following:

- What kinds of houses are shown here?
- How are they the same or different from houses in your neighborhood?

Remind students that when they read this kind of feature they may want to look at the pictures and read the text several times so they can use the information to answer the questions.

Teach

D Differentiated Instruction

Visual/Spatial Have students do additional research about the types of houses constructed around the world. Suggest that students narrow their research to a specific region. Ask students to prepare a short visual presentation to explain their research. OL

Additional Support

Early Housing

What a house looks like has much to do with where it is located, when it was built, and what materials were available. Zhoukoudianzhen Cave, in China, shows evidence of use from around 700,000 to around 200,000 years ago. Pincevent, in modern-day France, shows how early humans lived in northern Europe at the end of the Ice Age, around 13,000 years ago. And Çatalhüyük, in modern-day Turkey, was an early farming village from 6700 B.C. to 5700 B.C. D

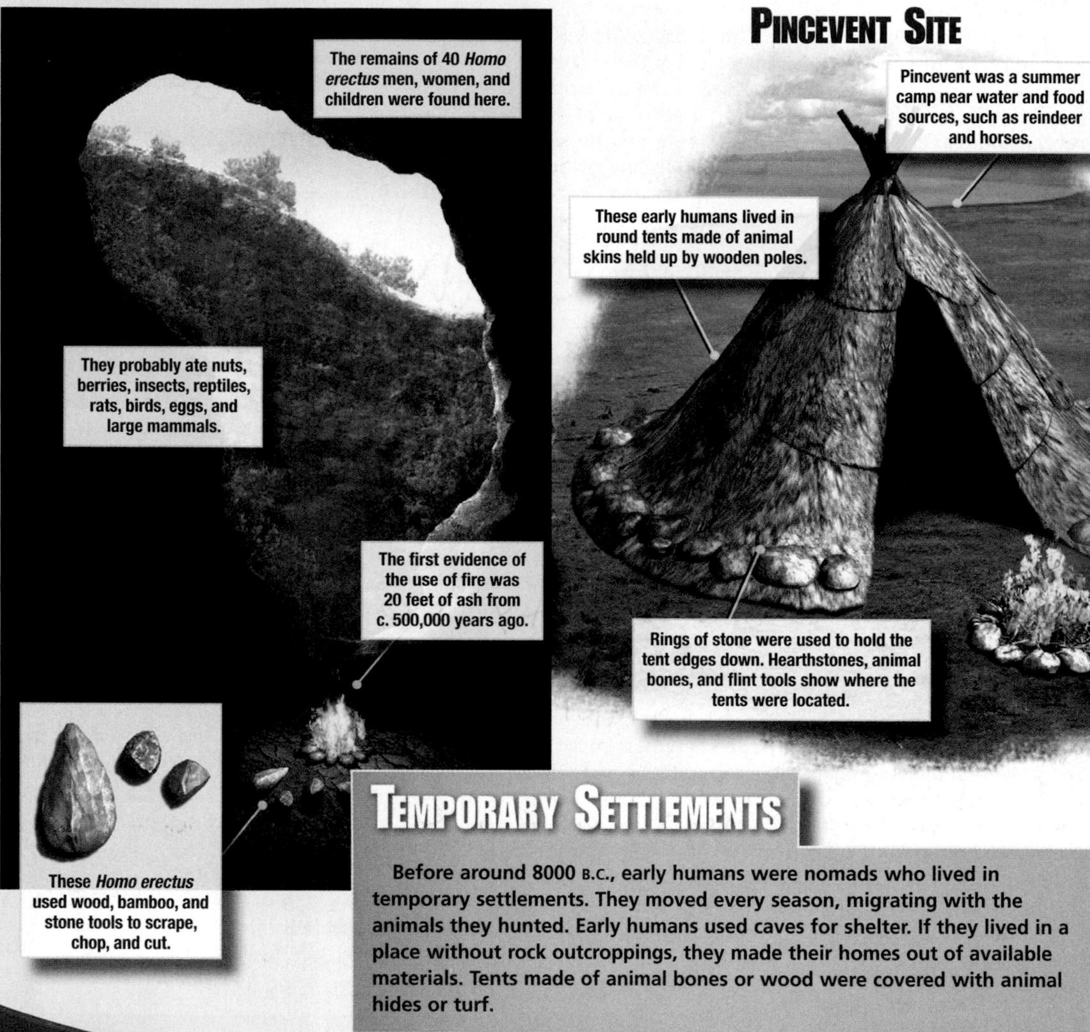

Temporary Settlements

Before around 8000 B.C., early humans were nomads who lived in temporary settlements. They moved every season, migrating with the animals they hunted. Early humans used caves for shelter. If they lived in a place without rock outcroppings, they made their homes out of available materials. Tents made of animal bones or wood were covered with animal hides or turf.

12

Extending the Content

Life in Early Housing Scientists look for evidence at sites that shows how humans lived and developed. From this page, students have learned that Zhoukoudianzhen Cave was occupied by *Homo erectus*. This site has been studied since the early 1900s. In 1929, the first skullcap was found. It helped scientists confirm that *Homo erectus* was a distinct stage in human development. The examination of the human fossils is one aspect of the work at Zhoukoudianzhen Cave. Another aspect is the examination of the mammal fossils, artifacts, and ashes found at the site. Study of the artifacts showed that the humans in this early housing used vein quartz, quartz crystals, flint, and sandstone to make tools. It was evident that over time the toolmakers discovered techniques to make smaller and better quality tools. **Ask:** What do you think was learned from examining the mammal fossils? *(Answers may include that mammal fossils showed what the people ate and how they hunted.)* The fossil record shows that the cave was occupied by *Homo erectus* for approximately 260,000 years.

ÇATALHÜYÜK

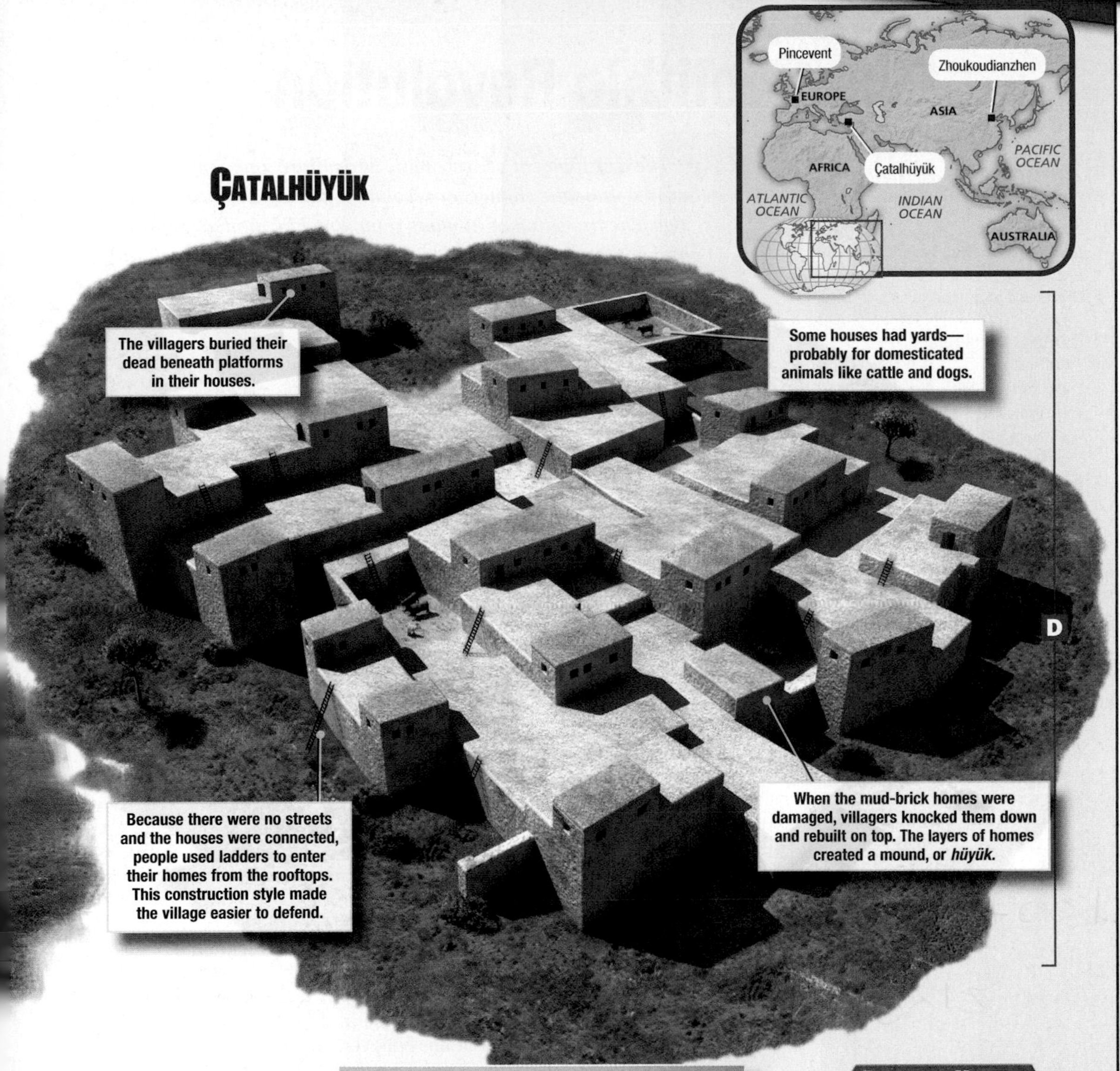

Pincevent
Zhoukoudianzhen
EUROPE
ASIA
AFRICA
Çatalhüyük
PACIFIC OCEAN
ATLANTIC OCEAN
INDIAN OCEAN
AUSTRALIA

The villagers buried their dead beneath platforms in their houses.

Some houses had yards—probably for domesticated animals like cattle and dogs.

Because there were no streets and the houses were connected, people used ladders to enter their homes from the rooftops. This construction style made the village easier to defend.

When the mud-brick homes were damaged, villagers knocked them down and rebuilt on top. The layers of homes created a mound, or *hüyük.*

D

PERMANENT SETTLEMENTS

After 8000 B.C., people began settling in one place, planting crops and raising livestock. These farming settlements began in river valleys in the Fertile Crescent and in Turkey. Rivers provided water for irrigation and transportation. Permanent walls provided protection from the weather, as well as from other humans—many of whom were still nomads—and animals.

ANALYZING VISUALS

1. **Comparing** Why are there similarities between the homes despite the differences in era and location?
2. **Analyzing** What are three major differences between temporary and permanent settlements?

D Differentiated Instruction

Logical/Mathematical Have students discuss how the lack of streets at Çatalhüyük made the village easier to defend. Point out that the picture shows many flat walls on the outside of the buildings. There are also small, high windows. **Ask:** How would this type of construction style make it difficult for people to attack the village? *(Possible answer: It would be more difficult to get into the buildings to try to hurt the people or steal livestock.)* **BL**

Assess/Close

Have student pairs write three questions and answers about early housing. Have pairs trade questions and then check answers.

ANALYZING VISUALS

Answers:

1. Humans have similar housing needs so dwellings have some similarities even if they are built with different building materials or in different eras.
2. Differences include the types of materials used, the size, and the location.

Identifying Central Issues

Objective: Understand Paleolithic life and use of natural resources.

Focus: Have students read the Background paragraph and the Group Directions.

Teach: Have groups brainstorm a list of critical needs.

Assess: Ask students to explain the reasons for the decisions they have made.

Close: Compare Paleolithic use of resources to resource use today.

Differentiated Instruction Strategies

BL Have students make a list of five ways the mammoth could be used.

AL Research the animals that Paleolithic people hunted. Draw a map showing in which parts of the world Paleolithic people are thought to have hunted certain animals.

ELL Give students an article about mammoths. Read the article as a group.

Differentiated Instruction

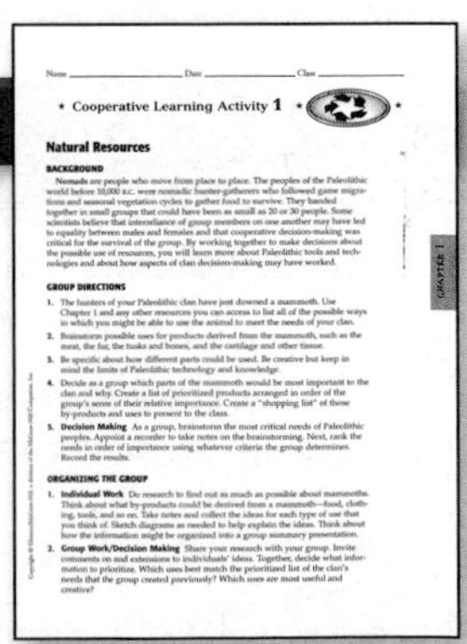
Cooperative Learning Activity 1

Natural Resources

Cooperative Learning Activity, URB p. 33

Focus

Bellringer

Daily Focus Transparency 1.2

GUIDE TO READING

Answers to Graphic:

1. cities	4. social structure
2. government	5. writing
3. religion	6. art

Section Spotlight Video

To generate student interest and provide a springboard for class discussion, access the Chapter 1, Section 2 video at glencoe.com or on the video DVD.

SECTION 2

The Neolithic Revolution

GUIDE TO READING

The BIG Idea
Ideas, Beliefs, and Values
Systematic agriculture brought huge economic, political, and social changes for early humans.

Content Vocabulary
- systematic agriculture *(p. 14)*
- domestication *(p. 14)*
- artisan *(p. 16)*
- culture *(p. 18)*
- civilization *(p. 18)*
- monarch *(p. 18)*
- priest *(p. 19)*

Academic Vocabulary
- revolution *(p. 14)*
- role *(p. 16)*

People and Places
- Neolithic Revolution *(p. 14)*
- Mesoamericans *(p. 15)*
- Çatalhüyük *(p. 16)*
- Bronze Age *(p. 16)*
- Iron Age *(p. 16)*

Reading Strategy
Comparing and Contrasting As you read, create a chart like the one below listing the six major characteristics of a civilization.

Civilization	
1.	4.
2.	5.
3.	6.

The development of systematic agriculture and civilization were a dramatic change, or revolution, during the Neolithic Age. The transition of humans from nomadic hunters to farmers and herders is part of the Neolithic Revolution. This revolution led to the development of traditional economies based on agriculture with limited trade.

The Neolithic Revolution

MAIN IDEA Civilization developed from the agricultural revolution of the Neolithic Age.

HISTORY & YOU How did early American pioneers meet their basic needs? Read how the Neolithic farmers affected human progress.

The end of the last Ice Age, around 8000 B.C., was followed by what is called the **Neolithic Revolution**—that is, the **revolution** that occurred in the Neolithic Age, the period of human history from 8000 B.C. to 4000 B.C. The word *Neolithic* is Greek for "new stone." The name *New Stone Age,* however, is somewhat misleading. The real change in the Neolithic Revolution was the shift from the hunting of animals and the gathering of food to the keeping of animals and the growing of food on a regular basis—what we call **systematic agriculture**.

Early humans had to move from place to place, following the herds and finding plants. During the Neolithic Age, humans began planting crops, providing a regular food source. **Domestication** of animals, adapting them for human use, added a reliable source of meat, milk, and wool. Animals could also be used to do work. Growing crops and taming food-producing animals caused an agricultural revolution. Because there was enough food, humans had more control over their lives. It also meant they could give up their nomadic ways of life and begin to live in settled communities. Some historians believe this revolution was the single most important development in human history.

This shift to food producing from hunting and gathering was not as sudden as was once believed. During the Mesolithic Age ("Middle Stone Age," about 10,000 B.C. to 7000 B.C.) there was a gradual shift from the old food-gathering and hunting economy to a food-producing one. There was also a gradual taming of animals. Moreover, throughout the Neolithic period, hunting and gathering remained a way of life for many people around the world.

Resource Manager

R Reading Strategies	C Critical Thinking	D Differentiated Instruction	W Writing Support	S Skill Practice
Teacher Edition • Academic Vocab., p. 16 **Additional Resources** • Cont. Vocab. Act., URB p. 23 • Academic Vocab. Act., URB p. 25 • Guid. Read. Act., URB p. 49 • Read. Ess. & Note-Taking Guide, p. 4	**Teacher Edition** • Making Inferences, p. 17 • Analyzing Info., p. 19 **Additional Resources** • Econ. & Hist. Act., URB p. 6 • Hist. Analysis Skills Act., URB p. 18 • Section Quiz, p. 2 • Chapter Test, p. 7	**Teacher Edition** • Visual/Spatial, p. 15 **Additional Resources** • English Learner Act., URB p. 21 • Crit. Think. Act., URB p. 28 • Reteach. Act., URB p. 45	**Teacher Edition** • Narrative Writing, p. 16 • Expository Writing, p. 18 **Additional Resources** • Enrich. Act., URB p. 46	**Teacher Edition** • Using Geo Skills, p. 16 **Additional Resources** • Chart. & Graph. Act., URB p. 3 • Hist. & Geo. Act., URB p. 29 • Time Line Act., URB p. 37

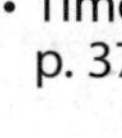

Connecting to the United States

Today's Agricultural Revolution

The Neolithic Agricultural Revolution made the first cities possible. In the United States and other developed countries, the agricultural revolution continues. American farmers produce more food than ever before to support most Americans, who live in cities or suburbs. Cities continue to spread as farmland shrinks. Until now, most Americans have never raised their own food or faced food shortages.

- Productivity means high crop yields produced on less land by fewer people.
- High productivity creates surpluses, which may be stored or traded.
- The United States exports billions of dollars worth of agricultural products annually.

Large crops are harvested more quickly due to modern machinery. ▼

Number of Farms in the U.S., 1940–2004

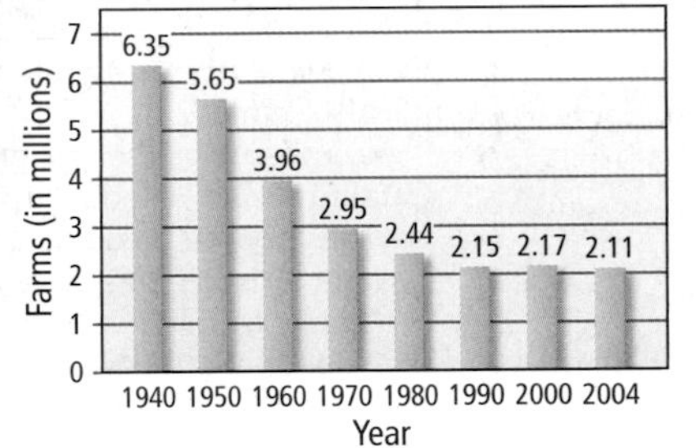

Source: *National Agricultural Statistics Service, U.S. Dept. of Agriculture; The World Almanac and Book of Facts 2006.*

Connecting to Today

1. **Examining** Which period shows the largest decrease in farms?
2. **Drawing Conclusions** What is the impact of urbanization on farming?

The Growing of Crops

Between 8000 B.C. and 5000 B.C., systematic agriculture developed in various parts of the world. In Southwest Asia, people began growing wheat and barley and domesticating pigs, cows, goats, and sheep by 8000 B.C. From there, farming spread into Southeastern Europe. By 4000 B.C., farming was **D** well established in central Europe and the coastal regions of the Mediterranean Sea.

By 6000 B.C., the cultivation of wheat and barley had spread into the Nile Valley of Egypt. These crops soon spread up the Nile to other areas of Africa—Sudan and Ethiopia. In central Africa, a separate farming system emerged. There, people grew root crops called tubers, such as yams, and tree crops, such as bananas. Farming wheat and barley also moved eastward into India between 7000 B.C. and 5000 B.C.

By 5000 B.C., farmers in Southeast Asia were growing rice. From there, rice farming spread into southern China. By 6000 B.C., farming millet and domesticating dogs and pigs seem to have been established in northern China. In the Western Hemisphere, **Mesoamericans**—inhabitants of present-day Mexico and Central America—grew beans, squash, and maize. They also domesticated dogs and fowl in this period between 7000 B.C. and 5000 B.C.

Teach

D Differentiated Instruction

Visual/Spatial Distribute an outline map of the world. Have students label the events related to systematic agriculture on the map as they read. Students should label each region described in the text, then create a map key with symbols for the plants and animals and add each symbol to the map with the corresponding date. **AL**

Did You Know?

Many diseases are the result of humans living in close proximity to animals. Influenza is known to originate from pigs and ducks. Cattle are responsible for anthrax, smallpox, and tuberculosis.

Answers:

1. 1950–1960
2. More crops must be harvested on less land.

Additional Support

Extending the Content

Connecting to the United States Discuss how the relationship between humans and the environment changed as people began to raise crops and domesticate animals. **Ask:** How does the relationship between humans and the environment during the Neolithic Revolution compare with Americans' attitudes toward agriculture and the environment today? *(People continue to change the natural environment more drastically. They rely less on nature and more on technology and globalization.)* Point out to students that technological advances and population growth fueled both movements.

Have students work in small groups to compare and contrast the effects of the Neolithic Agricultural Revolution and the agricultural revolution in the United States today. *(Both led to the growth of settlements, but the effects today are on a much larger scale, as high productivity allows for increased urbanization to the point where little farmland remains.)* When students have finished, ask each group to comment on the consequences of today's agricultural revolution and suggest possible solutions. **OL**

S **Skill Practice**

Using Geography Skills Point out the location of Çatalhüyük on the map on page 5. **Ask:** **In what areas do you think the people of Çatalhüyük practiced trade? Explain.** *(areas along the Mediterranean, because it served as a transportation route)* **AL**

R **Reading Strategy**

Academic Vocabulary Point out the uses of the term *role* on this page. Help students use context clues to define the term. Then have them use the term in a sentence that describes other changing roles during the Neolithic Revolution. **ELL**

W **Writing Support**

Narrative Writing Have students find out more about a tool that was used in the Neolithic Age, the Bronze Age, or the Iron Age. Then have them write a brief narrative from the point of view of an artisan who made the tool or a laborer who will use the tool. **OL**

✓**Reading Check**

Answer: It led to different occupations in society.

Neolithic Farming Villages

Growing crops on a regular basis gave rise to more permanent settlements called Neolithic farming villages. These villages appeared in Europe, India, Egypt, China, and Mesoamerica. The oldest and biggest of these, however, were located in Southwest Asia. Jericho near the Dead Sea, was in existence by 8000 B.C.

S **Çatalhüyük** (chah•TAHL hoo•YOOK) in modern Turkey was an even larger community covering 32 acres. Between 6700 B.C. and 5700 B.C., the city probably had about 6,000 inhabitants. Their simple mud brick houses were built so close together that there were few streets. People walked on the roofs and entered their homes through holes in the rooftops.

Archaeologists have found a dozen products that were grown outside the city walls, including fruits, nuts, and three kinds of wheat. Domesticated animals provided meat, milk, and hides. Scenes on the walls of the city's ruins show that the people also hunted.

As a result of the steady food supply, Çatalhüyük had a food surplus. This meant not all people needed to farm. Some became **artisans**, or skilled workers, making goods to trade with neighboring people. Goods were bartered, or exchanged, not sold. This was the beginning of a traditional economy based on agriculture and limited trade.

Besides homes, Çatalhüyük had special buildings that were shrines containing figures of gods and goddesses. Statues of women giving birth or nursing a child have also been found there. Both the shrines and the statues point to the growing **role** of religion in the lives of Neolithic peoples.

Neolithic Revolution—Effects

The Neolithic agricultural revolution caused dramatic changes that affected how people would live to the present day. Once people began settling in villages or towns, they saw the need to build walls for protection and storehouses for goods. Storing surplus products encouraged trade. Trading encouraged more people to learn crafts. This led to the division of labor.

As artisans became more skilled, they made more refined tools. Flint blades were used to make sickles and hoes for farming. Eventually, many of the food plants still in use today began to be cultivated. Some plants, such as flax and cotton, were used to make yarn and cloth.

The change to systematic agriculture also had consequences for how men and women related to one another. Men became more active in farming and herding animals, jobs that took them away from the settlement. Instead of the whole family moving as in earlier times, women remained behind. **R** They cared for children, wove cloth for clothes, and did other tasks that kept them in one place. As men took on more and more responsibility for obtaining food and protecting the settlement, they began to play a more dominant role in society.

The End of the Neolithic Age

Between 4000 B.C. and 3000 B.C., new develop-ments began to affect some Neolithic towns. Even before 4000 B.C., craftspeople discovered that by heating metal-bearing rocks they could turn the metal to liquid. The liquid metal could then be poured into molds, or casts, to make tools and weapons. The use of metals marked a new level of control over the environment.

W Copper was the first metal to be used in making tools. After 4000 B.C., artisans in western Asia discovered that combining copper and tin created bronze—a metal harder and more durable than copper.

The widespread use of bronze led to the **Bronze Age** from around 3000 B.C. to 1200 B.C. After about 1000 B.C., the use of iron tools and weapons became common, an era known as the **Iron Age.**

The Neolithic Age set the stage for major changes to come. As people mastered farming, some villages developed more complex and wealthier societies. To protect their wealth they built armies and city walls. By the beginning of the Bronze Age, large numbers of people were concentrated in the river valleys of Mesopotamia, Egypt, India, and China. These farming villages led to the development of cities.

✓**Reading Check** **Identifying** What was the result of systematic agriculture?

Additional Support

Teacher Tip

Collaborative Learning This activity allows students with different levels of academic skills and intelligences to work together. As you form groups, consider the needed skills and choose students accordingly.

Activity: Collaborative Learning

Presenting a Visual Summary Ask: **What characterized the beginning and the end of the Neolithic Age?** *(systematic agriculture; the emergence of civilization)* Assign small groups one of the three sections of text on this page. Have students read and discuss the text. Then have them prepare a "visual summary" to teach their assigned topic to the rest of the class. Suggest various types of visuals and graphic organizers to students, such as maps, time lines, outlines, or tables. Tell students to consider what types of visuals might be most effective in their presentations. Students can conduct additional research as questions arise or to provide more background information or examples. After each presentation, allow time for a question-and-answer period and a student critique. **OL**

TURNING POINT — NEOLITHIC REVOLUTION

The Neolithic Revolution was the beginning of systematic agriculture. This revolution was marked by the establishment and growth of farming villages such as Jericho. Located near a spring, which made the land especially fertile, Jericho was established by 8000 B.C. It was one of the largest Neolithic farming villages, with an estimated population over 1,000.

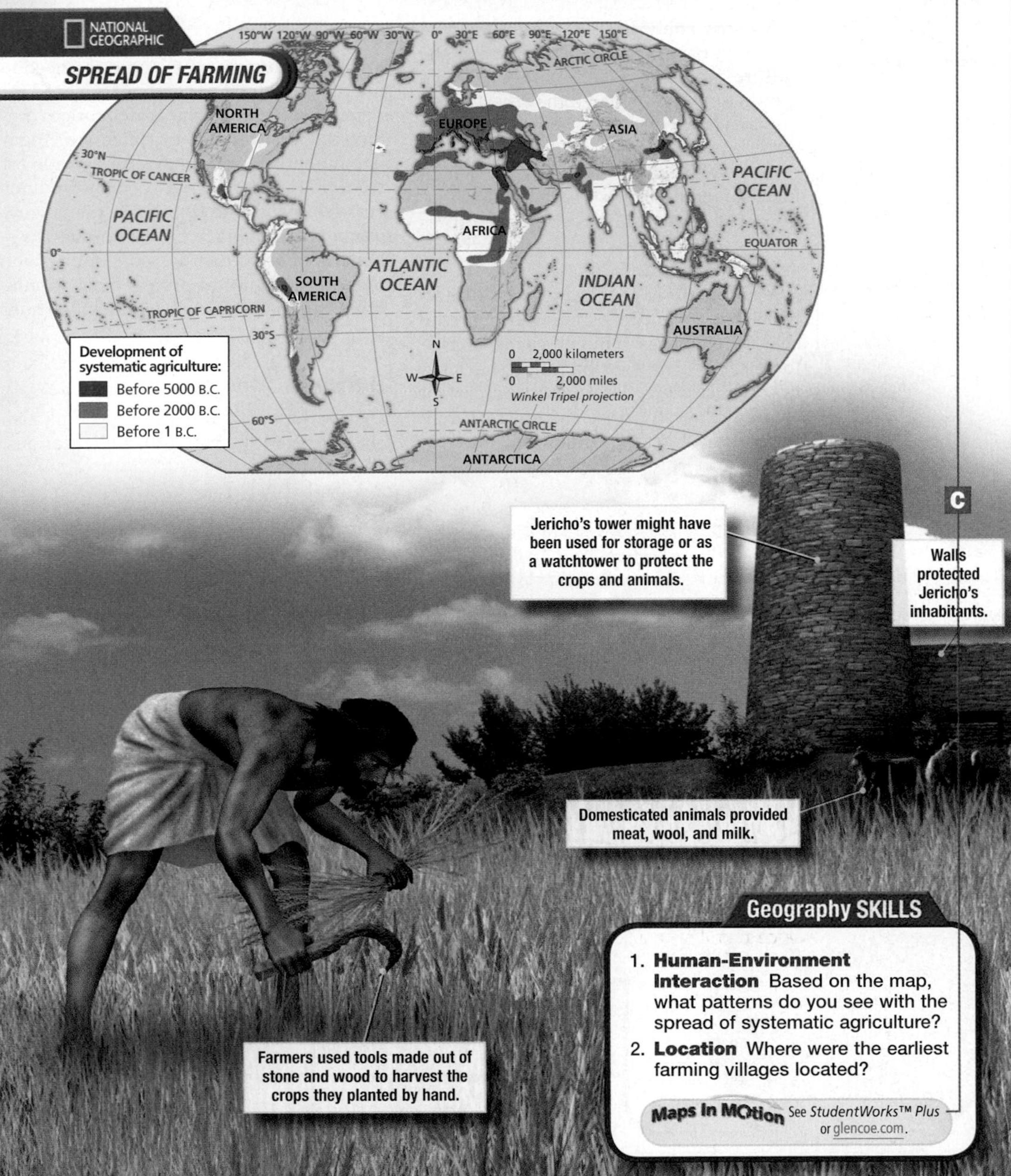

Geography SKILLS

1. **Human-Environment Interaction** Based on the map, what patterns do you see with the spread of systematic agriculture?
2. **Location** Where were the earliest farming villages located?

Maps In MOtion See StudentWorks™ Plus or glencoe.com.

C Critical Thinking

Making Inferences Located in the Jordan Valley, Jericho is believed to be the oldest continuously inhabited settlement in the world. The settlement was surrounded by 12-foot stone walls and a circular tower that was more than 26 feet high. **Ask:** Why do you think Jericho was so heavily fortified? *(to protect their inhabitants and wealth)* **OL**

Geography SKILLS

Answers:

1. Systematic agriculture mainly began in river valleys and areas along the Mediterranean and slowly spread to wider areas over time.
2. northeastern Africa, southwestern Asia, northern Mediterranean coast, northwestern India, northeastern China, middle Central America, and middle South America

Hands-On Chapter Project Step 2

Creating a Poster of Peoples' Lives

Step 2: Mapping the Poster Student pairs will continue adding illustrations of artifacts to the poster started in Section 1. They will also create a map to locate important archaeological sites.

Directions: Write the Big Idea on the board. Have students collect illustrations of artifacts related to the Neolithic Revolution and the emergence of civilization for their posters. Then have them trace the map on this page. Allow students to use the Internet and an atlas to indicate the locations of early settlements. Students should find and label the location of Jericho, as well as other sites that have been investigated by archaeologists and anthropologists, such as Pincevent and Zhoukoudianzhen. Have students arrange their illustrations and the map before attaching them to their posters. **OL**

(Chapter Project is continued on the Visual Summary Page.)

W Writing Support

Expository Writing Have students write a brief essay to explain how the Catalhüyük community described on page 16 exhibited the basic characteristics of civilization. OL

DOCUMENT-BASED QUESTIONS

Answers:

1. People had the time and desire to develop skills and create artwork. It may have been produced for pleasure, profit, or religious purposes.
2. possibly to bring into the afterlife and offer as gifts to the gods

Civilization Emerges

MAIN IDEA Some villages grew into cities and became early civilizations.

HISTORY & YOU What characteristics make our society a civilization? Learn which features defined early civilizations.

History ONLINE
Student Web Activity—
Visit glencoe.com and complete the activity about early peoples.

Whether analyzing societies of the past or present, anthropologists describe the **culture**—the way of life—of a people in a certain time and place. From earliest times, humans lived in small nomadic groups with simple cultures that helped them survive. When humans settled in permanent villages, their cultures became more complex. Gradually, more complex cultures developed into a new form of human society called civilization.

W A **civilization** is a complex culture in which large numbers of human beings who share a number of common elements. Historians have identified the basic characteristics of civilizations. Six of the most important characteristics are cities, government, religion, social structure, writing, and art.

Cities

The first civilizations developed in river valleys where people could carry on the large-scale farming that was needed to feed a large population. As farming became abundant, more people would live in the city. New patterns of living soon emerged.

Government

Growing numbers of people, the need to maintain the food supply, and the need for defense soon led to the growth of governments. Governments organize and regulate human activity. They also provide for smooth interaction between individuals and groups. In the first civilizations, governments usually were led by **monarchs**—kings or queens who rule a kingdom—who organized armies to protect their populations and made laws to regulate their subjects' lives.

Religion

Important religious developments also characterized the new urban civilizations.

HISTORY & ARTS PRIMARY SOURCE

Bronze Age Artifacts

Although these three artifacts were made during the same period, the Bronze Age, each is unique. They are different in origin, material, and subject. Each reveals valuable information about the civilization that created it.

The Phaestos Disc, from around 1600 B.C., probably came from the Minoan civilization on Crete. The terra-cotta disc proves the existence of a written Minoan language, but no one has been able to translate the hieroglyphs.

This terra-cotta jug, from around 1800 B.C., was in a tomb near the settlement of Jericho. Shaped like a bird, the jug is both functional and decorative.

During China's Shang dynasty, rulers had a monopoly on bronze work. This gilded bronze head could be the image of a king or a god. Created about 1200 B.C., the head was found in a pit with more than 50 similar artifacts.

DOCUMENT-BASED QUESTIONS

1. **Concluding** What does the presence of artwork say about a culture?
2. **Theorizing** Why might the jug and bronze head have been buried in tombs or pits?

Differentiated Instruction

Critical Thinking Activity, URB p. 28

Determining Cause and Effect

Objective: Understand the emergence of civilizations as a series of causes and effects.

Focus Have students read and discuss the introductory paragraph.

Teach: Have students read the directions and complete the flowchart.

Assess: Ask students to share and compare their charts explaining how the events are connected.

Close: Discuss the economic, political, and social issues related to each event on the flowchart.

Differentiated Instruction Strategies

- BL Have pairs of students work together on their charts.
- AL Ask students to research and report on the emergence of the Minoan civilization, citing examples of causes and effects.
- ELL As they work on the activity, remind students to use context clues to help them define unfamiliar terms.

All of them developed religions to explain the forces of nature and their roles in the world.

They believed that gods and goddesses were important to the community's success. To win their favor, **priests** supervised rituals aimed at pleasing them. This gave the priests special power and made them very important people. Rulers also claimed that their power was based on divine approval, and some rulers claimed to be divine.

Social Structure

A new social structure based on economic power also arose. Rulers and an upper class of priests, government officials, and warriors dominated society. Below this class was a large group of free people—farmers, artisans, and craftspeople. At the bottom was a slave class.

The demand of the upper class for luxury items, such as jewelry and pottery, encouraged artisans and craftspeople to create new products. As urban populations exported finished goods to neighboring populations in exchange for raw materials, organized trade began to grow. Because trade brought new civilizations into contact with one another, it often led to the transfer of new technology, such as metals for tools and new farming techniques, from one region to another.

By and large, however, the early river valley civilizations developed independently. Each one was based on developments connected to the agricultural revolution of the Neolithic Age and the cities that this revolution helped to produce. Taken together, the civilizations of Mesopotamia, Egypt, India, and China constituted nothing less than a revolutionary stage in the growth of human society. C

Writing

Writing was an important feature in the life of these new civilizations. Above all, rulers, priests, merchants, and artisans used writing to keep accurate records. Of course, not all civilizations depended on writing to keep records. The Inca in Peru (see Chapter 11), for example, relied on well-trained memory experts to keep track of their important matters. Eventually, the earliest civilizations used writing for creative expression as well as for record keeping. This produced the world's first works of literature.

Art

Significant artistic activity was another feature of the new civilizations. Architects built temples and pyramids as places for worship or sacrifice, or for the burial of kings and other important people. Painters and sculptors portrayed stories of nature. They also provided depictions of the rulers and gods they worshiped.

✓Reading Check **Describing** Describe the new social structure that arose in Neolithic cities.

SECTION 2 REVIEW

Vocabulary

1. **Explain** the significance of: Neolithic Revolution, systematic agriculture, domestication, Mesoamericans, Çatalhüyük, artisan, Bronze Age, Iron Age, culture, civilization, monarch, priest.

Main Ideas

2. **Identify** what are three of the six institutions or customs that people can share in a distinct culture.
3. **Label** in geographic terms where the earliest civilizations developed.
4. **Create** a diagram like the one below to show how changes during the Neolithic Revolution led to the emergence of civilization.

Critical Thinking

5. **The BIG Idea** **Explaining** Why did systematic farming make it possible for cities to develop?
6. **Describing** What was the relationship between artistic activities, religion, and government during the rise of civilization?
7. **Analyzing Visuals** Look at the Phaestos Disc on page 18. What does this piece of art reveal about the Minoan writing?

Writing About History

8. **Expository Writing** Conduct research on Çatalhüyük or another early site of the Neolithic period. Then write a short essay explaining how people may have lived in that city in its early history. You should include a description of the daily lives of different groups in the city—adults and children, farmers and artisans, leaders and ordinary people.

History ONLINE

For help with the concepts in this section of *Glencoe World History*, go to glencoe.com and click Study Central™.

C Critical Thinking

Analyzing Information Ask: How did religion affect the social structure of early civilizations? *(Since people believed gods and goddesses were important to the community, religion and priests were very important.)* OL

✓Reading Check

Answer: Rulers and an upper class of priests, government officials, and warriors dominated society. The middle class included free farmers, artisans, and craftspeople. Enslaved people made up the lowest class.

Assess

History ONLINE

Study Central provides summaries, interactive games, and online graphic organizers to help students review content.

Close

Summarizing Have students list and discuss the main factors that led to the Neolithic Revolution and the development of early civilizations. OL

Answers

1. Definitions for the vocabulary words are found in the section and the Glossary.
2. Students should list three of the following: cities, government, religion, social structure, writing, or art.
3. See the map on page 17. Responses should connect the existence of systematic farming to earliest civilizations.
4. acquiring a regular food source; establishing permanent settlements; trading of goods; the division of labor
5. People no longer had to move from place to place in search of food.
6. Rulers claimed that their power came from divine approval. Architects built temples and pyramids for religious services or to honor dead rulers. Painters and sculptors portrayed rulers and gods.
7. Minoan writing uses pictures or symbols, the symbols seem organized together to form words or sentences
8. Essays should describe the daily lives of various groups of people in Çatalhüyük or another early site.

Questioning Have students read through the causes and effects in the Visual Summary. Point out that the Visual Summary is an outline of important information from the chapter. Ask students to look at the effect statements and to identify pages in the chapter where the text discusses the points made. Then tell students that they can use this Visual Summary as a study tool. Suggest that students use the Visual Summary to create questions out of the statements that they can use to help them study and remember the information in the chapter.

Have students work in small groups to write questions and answers for each section of the Visual Summary. Encourage students to turn back to the text to verify their answers.

As a class, discuss students' questions and answers, as well as the importance of asking questions while reading and studying. **OL**

Cause and Effect Ask students to go back into the text and write at least one effect for each cause statement in the Visual Summary. **BL**

CHAPTER 1 Visual Summary

STUDY TO GO You can study anywhere, anytime by downloading quizzes and flash cards to your PDA from glencoe.com.

CAUSE

Early humans learn to make tools and fire.

EFFECTS

- Tools make hunting easier.
- Early humans become more efficient hunters.
- Cooking food over fire improves nutrition.
- Fire keeps humans warm in cooler climates.

CAUSE

After the Ice Age ends, temperatures rise and humans begin to practice systematic agriculture—the keeping of animals and the growing of food on a regular basis.

EFFECTS

- A steady food supply leads humans to settle in farming villages.
- Surplus food is stored.
- The villagers and food supply must be protected.

CAUSE

Civilizations begin to develop in river valleys in Mesopotamia, Egypt, India, and China.

EFFECTS

- Governments develop to organize and protect the cities.
- Not all villagers are needed for farming, so some become artisans, government workers, priests, artists, and scribes.
- Division of labor leads to a social structure.
- Surplus food and products are traded with other settlements.

Hands-On Chapter Project
Step 3: Wrap Up

Creating a Poster of Peoples' Lives

Step 3: Present the Poster Student pairs will present their posters to the class or in small groups.

Directions: Write the Essential Question on the board. Ask students to discuss their work in general. Were they able to find interesting artifacts to represent early humans and the Neolithic Age? What conclusions can they draw about the work of archaeologists and anthropologists who use artifacts to inform their work?

Then ask each pair of students to present their work to the class or in small breakout groups. Have them discuss each part of their poster and add details about the origin and age of the artifacts. If students illustrated parts of their poster themselves, ask them to identify what they based their work on. Encourage students to talk about the process they followed to find and organize the images they gathered or illustrated. **OL**

STANDARDIZED TEST PRACTICE

TEST-TAKING TIP

Make sure to read the entire question and each possible answer before deciding on the correct answer.

Reviewing Vocabulary

Directions: Choose the word or words that best complete the sentence.

1. Archaeologists study ________, or objects made by humans.
A rivers
B animals
C artifacts
D oceans

2. Donald Johanson and his team found an example of a/an ________ in Ethiopia.
A *Homo habilis*
B *Australopithecus*
C *Homo erectus*
D Neanderthal

3. The keeping of animals and the growing of food on a regular basis is known as ________.
A systematic agriculture
B domesticated agriculture
C Neolithic agriculture
D Paleolithic agriculture

4. ________ were skilled workers who made products such as weapons and jewelry.
A Farmers
B Anthropologists
C Artisans
D Priests

Reviewing Main Ideas

Directions: Choose the best answers to the following questions.

Section 1 *(pp. 4–11)*

5. Which type of scientist uses fossils and artifacts to study early humans?
A Chemists
B Physicists
C Anthropologists
D Geologists

6. Which hominids do scientists believe were probably the first to leave Africa?
A *Homo erectus*
B *Australopithecus*
C *Homo sapiens sapiens*
D Neaderthals

7. How did early humans adapt in order to survive?
A Following animal migrations
B Painting cave art
C Living in isolation
D Keeping records

8. Which invention made hunting easier for early humans?
A Cave art
B Fire
C The spear
D Farming

Need Extra Help?

If You Missed Questions . . .	1	2	3	4	5	6	7	8
Go to Page . . .	4	7	14	16	4	7	7	8

Answers and Analyses

Reviewing Vocabulary

1. C Students should realize that rivers, animals, and oceans do not represent objects made by humans, so *artifacts* is the correct answer.

2. B Remind students that Donald Johanson discovered "Lucy" in Ethiopia. Tell students that when they are working with choices and they are not certain of the answer, they should try to eliminate choices that are obviously wrong.

3. A Students can eliminate *Paleolithic agriculture* because the section discusses the Neolithic Age. The context clue "on a regular basis" should point them to the term *systematic* in answer A, helping them to eliminate the other options.

4. C Point out the context clue, "made products such as weapons and jewelry." The word *art* is part of the word *artisans*. This helps to eliminate *farmers, priests,* and *anthropologists*.

Reviewing Main Ideas

5. C Anthropologists study human life and culture by examining artifacts and human fossils. Chemists, physicists, and geologists all provide support for anthropologists' work.

6. A Remains in Asia show that *Homo erectus* was probably the first hominid to leave Africa.

7. A In order to survive, early humans followed migrating animals because they provided a source of food.

8. C Spears made it easier for humans to hunt larger animals. The other choices can be eliminated because they are not related to hunting.

9. C Some choices can be eliminated because students should know that the Paleolithic and Ice Ages occurred before agriculture and civilization, whereas the use of Bronze came after the agricultural revolution began.

10. D Choices A, B, and C are all things that were happening before the beginning of civilization, while the domestication of animals was a key change that led to life in settled communities.

11. B Students should infer that river valleys provided water and good soil for systematic agriculture. Deserts, forests, and mountain valleys did not have terrain as advantageous to human life and agriculture.

12. A Governments were needed to organize and regulate human activity. Monarchs led governments by organizing armies to protect the people and making laws to regulate people's lives.

13. B Mesoamericans is correct. Students can eliminate Mesopotamians, Egyptians, and Chinese because they were not farming in the Western Hemisphere.

Critical Thinking

14. C Students should recall that Paleolithic peoples were more concerned with the procurement of food than with fleeing or fighting enemies or with finding a more habitable climate.

CHAPTER 1

Section 2 *(pp. 14–19)*

9. During which age did the agricultural revolution lead to the development of civilization?
   - A Paleolithic
   - B Ice
   - C Neolithic
   - D Bronze

10. What was one indicator of early farming villages?
    - A Eating cooked food
    - B Hunting
    - C Creating paintings in caves
    - D Domestication of animals

11. Where did many early civilizations develop?
    - A Deserts
    - B River valleys
    - C Mountain valleys
    - D Forests

12. Who led governments in early civilizations?
    - A Monarchs
    - B Priests
    - C Warriors
    - D Artisans

13. Who was farming in the Western Hemisphere by 7000 B.C.?
    - A Mesopotamians
    - B Mesoamericans
    - C Egyptians
    - D The Chinese

Critical Thinking

Directions: Choose the best answers to the following questions.

14. Why were Paleolithic peoples nomads?
    - A Fear of enemies kept them moving.
    - B Rival groups drove each other out of settled areas.
    - C They had to follow animal migrations.
    - D They had to look for more habitable climates.

Base your answer to questions 15 and 16 on the map below.

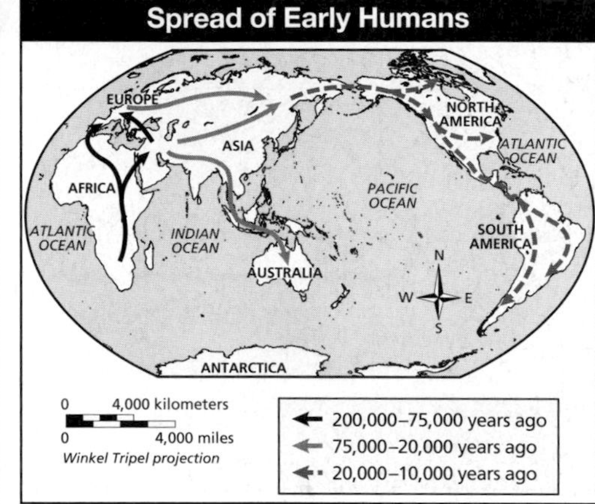

15. In which areas of Africa did human life begin?
    - A Eastern and southern
    - B Eastern and northern
    - C Western and southern
    - D Western and northern

16. Into which areas did early humans spread most recently?
    - A Asia
    - B Europe
    - C Australia
    - D North and South America

Need Extra Help?								
If You Missed Questions . . .	9	10	11	12	13	14	15	16
Go to Page . . .	14	14	18	18	15	14	22	22

GO ON

15. A It is important to read the question carefully to determine that the answer refers to the origins of the arrows that represent earliest dates, 200,000 to 75,000 years ago.

16. D The most recent spread of humans is shown with a dashed line on the map.

TEST-TAKING TIP

For Question 15: Remind students that a careful examination of the map key as well as the map itself will point to the correct answer.

17. Why was writing important to many early governments?

- **A** To describe court life
- **B** To express individual beliefs
- **C** To keep records
- **D** To write songs

Analyze the chart and answer the question that follows. Base your answer on the chart and on your knowledge of world history.

Before great civilizations could develop, early humans had to go through many cultural changes, movements, and technological innovations.

Changes, Prehistory–3500 B.C.

Event	Cultural Change	Movement	Technological Innovation
• Early humans migrate to warmer climates during the Ice Ages.		X	
• Early humans learn how to control fire and make tools.	X		X
• Caves are painted with religious and decorative art.	X		
• Neanderthals inhabit Europe and Asia.		X	
• Neolithic people domesticate animals.	X		X

18. What technological innovations were made by early humans?

- **A** Neolithic peoples migrate to warmer climates and control fire.
- **B** Neolithic peoples create cave paintings and domesticate animals.
- **C** Neolithic peoples control fire, make tools, and domesticate animals.
- **D** Neolithic peoples are first to bury their dead.

Document-Based Questions

Directions: Analyze the document and answer the short-answer questions that follow the document.

The anthropologist Donald Johanson, along with his team, found a new type of hominid in Ethiopia. Johanson discusses how this *Australopithecus*, or Lucy, as she was nicknamed, presented a new view about the development of hominids:

> *"People felt that there were a number of evolutionary changes, which all went together. That our ancestors stood up to free their hands so that they could make and use stone tools. In order to make and use stone tools, they had to have large brains . . . Here comes Lucy, about 3.5 million years old . . . very small brain, . . . and we have never found any stone tool, stone artifacts, associated with her species. Yet she is walking upright. So it appears that . . . walking on two legs, precedes by perhaps as much as a million and a half years, the manufacture of stone tools and the expansion of the brain."*

19. According to Johanson, what did scientists believe about early hominids before the discovery of Lucy?

20. What does the discovery of Lucy reveal to anthropologists?

21. What is the time frame Johanson discusses? What does this reveal about the development of hominids?

Extended Response

22. Early humans went through many stages before civilizations developed. Explain how the Neolithic revolution influenced the shift from a nomadic existence to life in a village and ultimately to a civilization. Be sure to explore the six basic characteristics of civilization.

History ONLINE

For additional test practice, use Self-Check Quizzes—Chapter 1 at glencoe.com.

Need Extra Help?

If You Missed Questions . . .	17	18	19	20	21	22
Go to Page . . .	19	23	23	23	23	14

STOP

Document-Based Questions

19. Answers should include that scientists believed that early humans stood up in order to free their hands to use tools.

20. The discovery of Lucy meant that early humans were standing upright long before they started to use tools.

21. Answers will vary but should be supported by logical arguments. Students may write that the time frame that Johanson discusses is about a million and a half years, revealing that the development of hominids was very slow.

Extended Response

22. Students' answers should explain how systematic agriculture led people to settle in villages. This in turn led to more agriculture and also led to cities, governments, religion, a new social structure, and writing. Students should explore the basic characteristics of civilization with examples from the text.

17. C In order to answer this question, students need to think about what might have been most important to early governments. Writing songs, describing court life, and expressing individual beliefs are not things that a government would find essential.

18. C Remind students that the question refers specifically to the technological innovations of early humans. The chart has a column with the heading Technological Innovations. Based on the chart, Neolithic people learned how to control fire, make tools, and domesticate animals.

History ONLINE

Introduce students to chapter content and key terms by having them access the Chapter 1 Overview at glencoe.com.

Need Extra Help?

Have students refer to the pages listed if they miss any of the questions.

CHAPTER 2 Planning Guide

Key to Ability Levels	
BL Below Level	AL Above Level
OL On Level	ELL English Language Learners

Key to Teaching Resources	
Print Material	DVD
CD-ROM	Transparency

BL	OL	AL	ELL	Resources	Chapter Opener	Section 1	Section 2	Section 3	Section 4	Chapter Assess
				FOCUS						
BL	OL	AL	ELL	Daily Focus Skills Transparencies		2-1	2-2	2-3	2-4	
				TEACH						
BL	OL	AL	ELL	Charting and Graphing Activity, URB					✓	
	OL	AL		Economics and History Activity, URB		✓				
BL	OL		ELL	Reading Skills Activity, URB				p. 53		
	OL	AL		Historical Analysis Skills Activity, URB					p. 54	
BL	OL	AL	ELL	Differentiated Instruction Activity, URB		p. 55				
	OL		ELL	English Learner Activity, URB		p. 57				
BL	OL	AL	ELL	Content Vocabulary Activity, URB*					p. 59	
BL	OL	AL	ELL	Academic Vocabulary Activity, URB					p. 61	
BL	OL	AL	ELL	Skills Reinforcement Activity, URB		p. 63				
	OL	AL		Critical Thinking Skills Activity, URB			p. 64			
	OL	AL		History and Geography Activity, URB		p. 65				
	OL	AL	ELL	Mapping History Activity, URB		p. 67				
BL	OL	AL		Historical Significance Activity, URB		p. 68				
BL	OL	AL	ELL	Cooperative Learning Activity, URB			p. 69			
	OL	AL	ELL	History Simulation Activity, URB					p. 71	
BL	OL	AL	ELL	Time Line Activity, URB			p. 73			
	OL	AL		Linking Past and Present Activity, URB		p. 74				
BL	OL	AL		People in World History Activity, URB			p. 75	p. 76		
BL	OL	AL	ELL	Primary Source Reading, URB			p. 77			
	OL	AL		Enrichment Activity, URB			p. 82			
BL	OL	AL	ELL	World Art and Music Activity, URB			p. 79			
BL	OL		ELL	Guided Reading Activities, URB*		p. 84	p. 85	p. 86	p. 87	
BL	OL		ELL	Reading Essentials and Note-Taking Guide*		p. 7	p. 10	p. 13	p. 16	
BL	OL	AL	ELL	Differentiated Instruction for the World History Classroom	✓	✓	✓	✓	✓	✓

Note: Please refer to the *Unit Resource Book: The First Civilizations and Empires* for this chapter's URB materials.

* Also available in Spanish

- Interactive Lesson Planner
- Interactive Teacher Edition
- Fully editable blackline masters
- Section Spotlight Videos Launch
- Differentiated Lesson Plans
- Printable reports of daily assignments
- Standards Tracking System

Levels BL	OL	AL	ELL		Resources	Chapter Opener	Section 1	Section 2	Section 3	Section 4	Chapter Assess
TEACH *(continued)*											
BL	OL	AL	ELL		StudentWorks™ Plus DVD	✓	✓	✓	✓	✓	✓
BL	OL	AL	ELL		Vocabulary PuzzleMaker CD-ROM	✓	✓	✓	✓	✓	✓
Teacher Resources					Building Academic Vocabulary	✓	✓	✓	✓	✓	✓
					Reading Strategies and Activities for the Social Studies Classroom				p. 50	p. 86	
					Writer's Guidebook			p. 23	p. 31		
					Strategies for Success	✓	✓	✓	✓	✓	✓
					Outline Map Resource Book	✓	✓	✓	✓	✓	✓
					Presentation Plus! with MindJogger DVD	✓	✓	✓	✓	✓	✓
ASSESS											
BL	OL	AL	ELL		Section Quizzes and Chapter Tests*		p. 11	p. 12	p. 13	p. 14	p. 15
BL	OL	AL	ELL		Authentic Assessment With Rubrics	✓	✓	✓	✓	✓	✓
BL	OL	AL	ELL		Standardized Test Practice Workbook	✓	✓	✓	✓	✓	✓
BL	OL	AL	ELL		*ExamView® Assessment Suite* CD-ROM		2-1	2-2	2-3	2-4	Ch. 2
BL	OL	AL	ELL		Interactive Tutor Self-Assessment CD-ROM		2-1	2-2	2-3	2-4	
CLOSE											
BL			ELL		Reteaching Activity, URB			p. 81			
BL	OL		ELL		Reading and Study Skills Foldables™	✓	✓	✓	✓	✓	✓

Daily Assignments and Grade Logs

Technology Project

Glencoe's *StudentWorks*™ *Plus* contains everything your students need, including the complete Student Edition and access to all student workbooks. *StudentWorks*™ *Plus* also includes a Daily Assignment and Activity Log that allows students to

- record and track progress on their daily assignments and responsibilities;
- log results achieved, including their grades;
- sort assignments alphabetically or by category;
- view and print the assignment and grade log in a table or calendar format.

Objectives

Using *StudentWorks*™ *Plus* will help your students

- take responsibility for their individual tasks;
- improve independent study skills.

Steps

Provide students with the following information:

- Launch *StudentWorks*™ *Plus*.
- Select the **Daily Assignments and Grade Log** button at the bottom of the launch screen.
- Create a new file or open an existing one. The log is organized as a table, with a row of information for each assignment.
- Add information for each assignment, including the date of the assignment, the name, additional comments, the due date, and the grade.
- Edit rows as assignment information is provided or changed. Add a new row to the log for each new assignment.

History ONLINE

	Student	Teacher	Parent
Beyond the Textbook	●	●	●
Chapter Overviews	●	●	●
Time Current Events	●		●
ePuzzles and Games	●		●
Concepts in Motion	●		●
Literature Connections		●	
Multi-Language Glossaries	●		●
Online Student Edition	●	●	●
Self-Check Quizzes	●		●
Student Web Activities	●		●
Study Central ™	●		●
Teaching Today		●	
Vocabulary eFlashcards	●		●
Web Activity Lesson Plans		●	

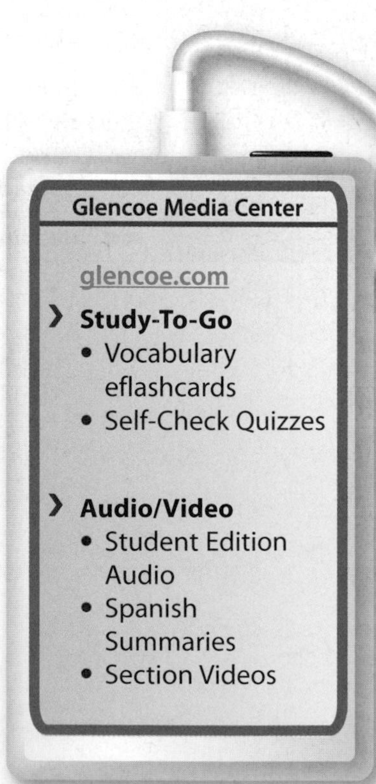

- **Timed Readings Plus in Social Studies** helps students increase their reading rate and fluency while maintaining comprehension. The 400-word passages are similar to those found on state and national assessments.
- **Reading in the Content Area: Social Studies** concentrates on six essential reading skills that help students better comprehend what they read. The book includes 75 high-interest nonfiction passages written at increasing levels of difficulty.
- **Reading Social Studies** includes strategic reading instruction and vocabulary support in Social Studies content for both ELLs and native speakers of English.

www.jamestowneducation.com

The following videotape programs are available from Glencoe as supplements to Chapter 2:

- The Great Pharaohs of Egypt (4 pack) (ISBN 0-76-700273-3)
- Cleopatra: Destiny's Queen (ISBN 1-56-501454-5)
- Ramses the Great (ISBN 0-76-700665-8)
- Great Pyramids of Giza and Other Pyramids (ISBN 0-76-700207-5)
- Mummies and the Wonders of Ancient Egypt (4 pack) (ISBN 1-56-501773-0)
- Tomb of the Gods: The Great Pyramid (ISBN 0-76-700081-1)

To order, call Glencoe at 1-800-334-7344. To find classroom resources to accompany many of these videos, check the following home pages:

A&E Television: www.aetv.com

The History Channel: www.historychannel.com

Index to National Geographic Magazine:

The following articles relate to this chapter:

- "King Tut Revealed," by A. R. Williams, June 2005
- "Who Were the Phoenicians?" by Rick Gore, October 2004
- "Beyond the Looting," by Andrew Lawler, October 2003
- "Egypt's Hidden Tombs Revealed," by Zahi Hawass, September 2001

National Geographic Society Products To order the following, call National Geographic at 1-800-368-2728:

- *National Geographic Atlas of the World* (Book)
- *The Fertile Crescent* (PicturePak)

Access National Geographic's new, dynamic MapMachine Web site and other geography resources at:
www.nationalgeographic.com
www.nationalgeographic.com/maps

GLENCOE BOOKLINK 3

Use this database to search more than 30,000 titles to create a customized reading list for your students.

- Reading lists can be organized by students' reading level, author, genre, theme, or area of interest.
- The database provides Degrees of Reading Power™ (DRP) and Lexile™ readability scores for all selections.
- A brief summary of each selection is included.

Leveled reading suggestions for this chapter:

For students at a Grade 8 reading level:
- ***Next Year in Jerusalem: 3000 Years of Jewish Stories,*** by Howard Schwartz

For students at a Grade 9 reading level:
- ***Mummies and the Secrets of Ancient Egypt,*** by John Malam

For students at a Grade 10 reading level:
- ***Cleopatra: The Queen of Kings,*** by Fiona MacDonald

For students at a Grade 11 reading level:
- ***The Pharaohs of Ancient Egypt,*** by Elizabeth Payne

For students at a Grade 12 reading level:
- ***Ancient Mesopotamia,*** by Don Nardo

Introducing CHAPTER 2

Focus

MAKING CONNECTIONS

How does progress affect history?

Ask students to brainstorm examples that they think reflect progress in their community, such as a new store, mall, or park. Then discuss the pros and cons of one or two examples. For example, a new mall may add new jobs, but it may also mean a loss of farmland. Point out that a community has to evaluate whether the pros outweigh the cons in deciding whether to go forward with a new project. This process can divide communities, because people may hold differing viewpoints on the project. Close the discussion by asking students to discuss this question: Can progress go forward and still preserve history?

Teach

The Big Ideas

As students study the chapter, remind them to consider the section-based Big Ideas included in each section's Guide to Reading. The **Essential Questions** in the activities below tie in to the Big Ideas and help students think about and understand important chapter concepts. In addition, the Hands-on Chapter Projects with their culminating activities relate the content from each section to the Big Ideas. These activities build on each other as students progress through the chapter. Section activities culminate in the wrap-up activity on the Visual Summary page.

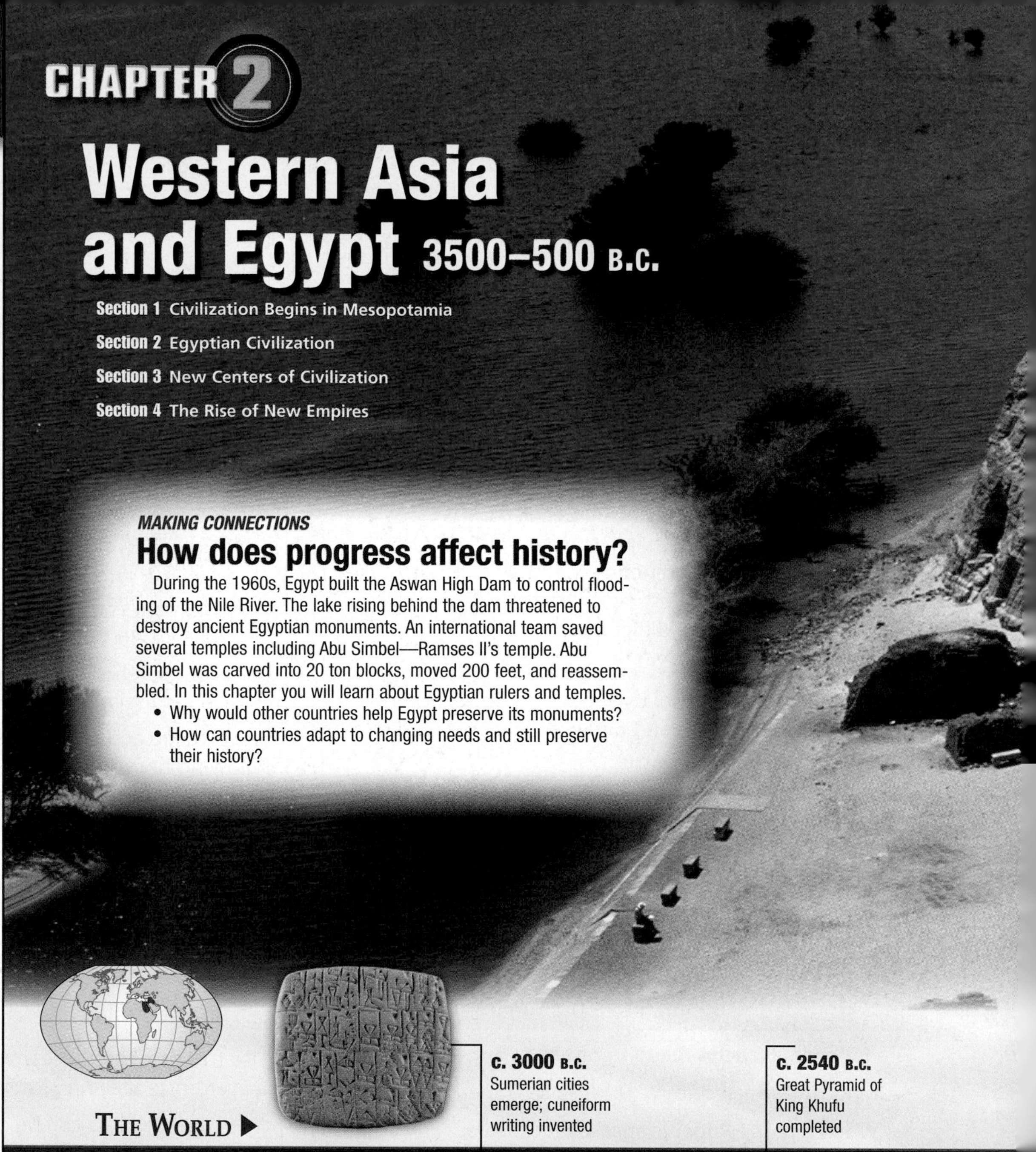

CHAPTER 2

Western Asia and Egypt 3500–500 B.C.

Section 1 Civilization Begins in Mesopotamia

Section 2 Egyptian Civilization

Section 3 New Centers of Civilization

Section 4 The Rise of New Empires

MAKING CONNECTIONS

How does progress affect history?

During the 1960s, Egypt built the Aswan High Dam to control flooding of the Nile River. The lake rising behind the dam threatened to destroy ancient Egyptian monuments. An international team saved several temples including Abu Simbel—Ramses II's temple. Abu Simbel was carved into 20 ton blocks, moved 200 feet, and reassembled. In this chapter you will learn about Egyptian rulers and temples.

- Why would other countries help Egypt preserve its monuments?
- How can countries adapt to changing needs and still preserve their history?

THE WORLD ▶

C. 3000 B.C. Sumerian cities emerge; cuneiform writing invented

C. 2540 B.C. Great Pyramid of King Khufu completed

3500 B.C. — 2500 B.C.

C. 2700 B.C. Egypt's Old Kingdom begins

24

SECTION 1

Civilization Begins in Mesopotamia

Remind students that agriculture was the foundation for societies that became the first civilizations. **Essential Question:** Why were the first farming societies located along rivers? *(The rivers flooded, leaving fertile soil. Irrigation systems could be built using the river's water.)* After students have discussed the question, tell them that in Section 1, they will learn more about the civilizations in the Fertile Crescent. **OL**

SECTION 2

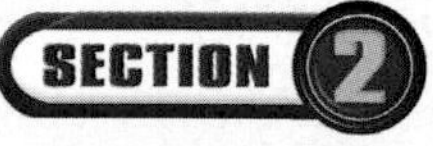

Egyptian Civilization

Essential Question: What factors contribute to a stable and lasting civilization? *(Answers will vary, but students may say that prosperity, efficient government, a unifying set of beliefs or values, a series of wise and strong leaders, and contentment of the people all help to create stability.)* Tell students that in Section 2, they will learn about the achievements of the ancient Egyptians and their influence on later societies. **OL**

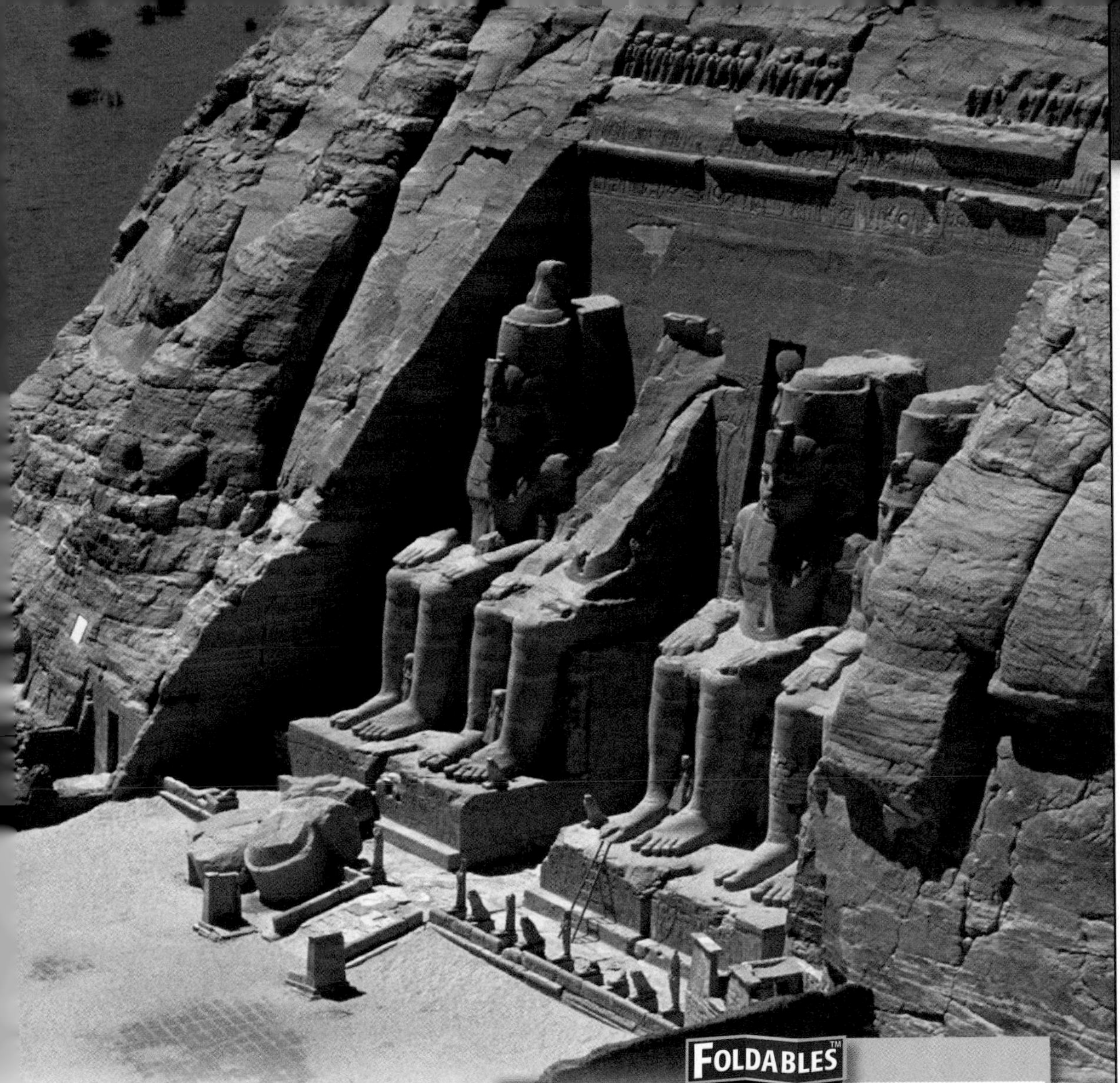

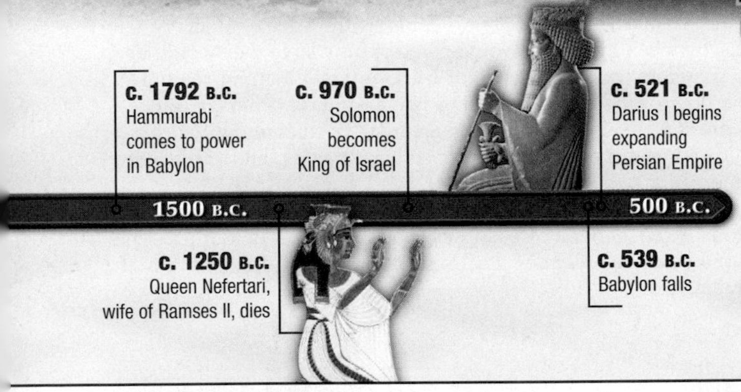

c. 1792 B.C.
Hammurabi comes to power in Babylon
c. 970 B.C.
Solomon becomes King of Israel
c. 521 B.C.
Darius I begins expanding Persian Empire
1500 B.C.
500 B.C.
c. 1250 B.C.
Queen Nefertari, wife of Ramses II, dies
c. 539 B.C.
Babylon falls

FOLDABLES™ Study Organizer

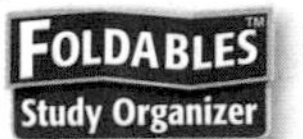

Summarizing
Create a Layered-Look Book with four layers to review the history of ancient Egypt. Summarize the important facts about each era in each layer.

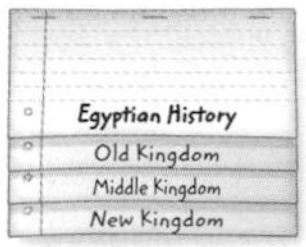

Egyptian History
Old Kingdom
Middle Kingdom
New Kingdom

History ONLINE
Chapter Overview—Visit glencoe.com to preview Chapter 2.

SECTION 3

New Centers of Civilization

Discuss with students why some ideas change the course of humankind. **Essential Question:** How did the monotheism of the Israelites differ from religious beliefs of previous cultures? *(Many ancient civilizations were polytheistic. Judaism recognized one God, who created and ruled the world, and gave humans laws to follow.)* After students have discussed the question, tell them that they will learn how the Jewish religion influenced Western civilization. **OL**

SECTION 4

The Rise of New Empires

Have students identify empires with which they are familiar. **Essential Question:** What did lasting empires have in common? *(They had efficient means of communication, linking the parts of the empire together; they organized government to include local officials.)* After students have discussed the question, tell them that in Section 4, they will learn more about the Assyrian and Persian Empires. **OL**

Introducing **CHAPTER 2**

More About the Photo

Visual Literacy Abu Simbel was built on the west bank of the Nile, in what was then Nubia. The four giant statues are of Ramses II, which were damaged by earthquakes of ancient times. The temple has a series of inner halls and rooms that extend over 180 feet back from the entrance. At the rear interior wall of the temple are four statues: one of Ramses II and three of Egypt's state gods at the time (Ra-Harakhte of Heliopolis, Ptah of Memphis, and Amun-Ra of Thebes). The temple was oriented so that the sun would shine directly into the entrance and onto this rear wall just two days of the year: once in October and once in February—on Ramses II's birthday.

FOLDABLES™ Study Organizer **Dinah Zike's Foldables**

Dinah Zike's Foldables are three-dimensional, interactive graphic organizers that help students practice basic writing skills, review vocabulary terms, and identify main ideas. Instructions for creating and using Foldables can be found in the Appendix at the end of this book and in the *Dinah Zike's Reading and Study Skills Foldables* booklet.

History ONLINE

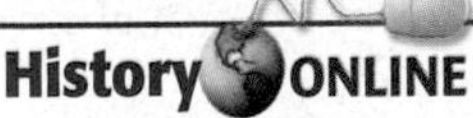

Introduce students to chapter content and key terms by having them access the Chapter 2 Overview at glencoe.com.

Focus

Bellringer

Daily Focus Transparency 2.1

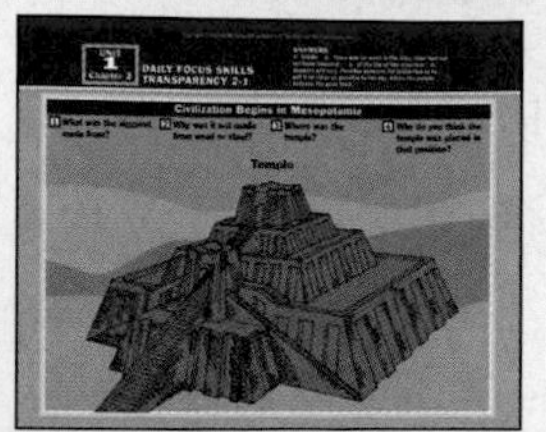

GUIDE TO READING

Answers to Graphic:

Political Life	Cultural Life	Inventions
organized government	religion	writing
law code	architecture	wagon wheel
	literature	arch
		bronze
		sundial
		number system

Section Spotlight Video

To generate student interest and provide a springboard for class discussion, access the Chapter 2, Section 1 video at glencoe.com or on the video DVD.

Resource Manager

SECTION 1

Civilization Begins in Mesopotamia

GUIDE TO READING

The BIG Idea

Physical Geography Fertile soil between the Tigris and Euphrates Rivers allowed an early civilization to flourish in Mesopotamia.

Content Vocabulary

- polytheistic *(p. 27)*
- city-state *(p. 28)*
- ziggurat *(p. 29)*
- theocracy *(p. 29)*
- cuneiform *(p. 30)*
- empire *(p. 32)*
- patriarchal *(p. 33)*

Academic Vocabulary

- transport *(p. 29)*
- innovations *(p. 30)*

People and Places

- Tigris River *(p. 26)*
- Euphrates River *(p. 26)*
- Mesopotamia *(p. 26)*
- Fertile Crescent *(p. 26)*
- Sumerians *(p. 26)*
- Uruk *(p. 28)*
- Akkadians *(p. 32)*
- Sargon *(p. 32)*
- Babylon *(p. 33)*
- Hammurabi *(p. 33)*

Reading Strategy

Categorizing Information As you read, complete a chart like the one below to explain the Sumerians' contributions to civilization.

Political Life	Cultural Life	Inventions

Mesopotamia, located in what is now southern Iraq, was one area where civilization began. Its people developed complex economic, political, and social structures. Such inventions as written language improved the quality of their lives. As different groups fought for power, they set up the world's first empires and codified their laws.

Geography and Religion

MAIN IDEA The physical environment of Mesopotamia supported the development of civilization and influenced people's religious beliefs.

HISTORY & YOU Is your town located near a river? Read about how the fertile soil of a river valley supported the transition from a nomadic lifestyle to agriculture and the birth of civilization.

Civilization depends on large permanent settlements. Fertile river valleys that can support a large population are ideal locations for such settlements. Highly organized societies then evolved in these regions.

The Fertile Crescent

The ancient Greeks spoke of the valley between the **Tigris** and **Euphrates Rivers** as **Mesopotamia,** the land "between the rivers." Mesopotamia was at the eastern end of the **Fertile Crescent,** an arc of land from the Mediterranean Sea to the Persian Gulf. Rich soil and abundant crops allowed the land to sustain an early civilization.

Mesopotamia had little rain, but over the years its soil had been enriched by layers of silt—material deposited by the two rivers. In late spring, the Tigris and Euphrates often overflowed their banks and deposited their fertile silt. This flooding, however, was unpredictable. It depended on the melting of snows in the upland mountains where the rivers began. People in the valley could not tell exactly when the floods would come or how large they would be.

Therefore, people in ancient Mesopotamia learned to control the flow of the rivers. By using irrigation and drainage ditches, farmers were able to grow crops regularly. An abundance of food allowed many people to live together in cities, and civilization emerged.

Mesopotamian civilization refers to the achievements of people from three general areas: Assyria, Akkad, and Sumer. The **Sumerians** were the creators of the first Mesopotamian civilization.

R Reading Strategies

Teacher Edition
- Read. Pri. Sources, p. 27
- Det. Importance, p. 28
- Identifying, p. 29

Additional Resources
- Guid. Read. Act., URB p. 84
- Read. Ess. & Note-Taking Guide, p. 7

C Critical Thinking

Teacher Edition
- Making Inferences, p. 28
- Analyzing Pri. Sources, p. 29
- Drawing Con., pp. 30, 31
- Analyzing Info., p. 32

Additional Resources
- Skills Reinforc. Act., URB p. 63
- Section Quiz, p. 11

D Differentiated Instruction

Teacher Edition
- Visual/Spatial, p. 29
- Adv. Learners, p. 30

Additional Resources
- Diff. Instr. Act., URB p. 55
- English Learner Act., URB p. 57

W Writing Support

Teacher Edition
- Descriptive Writing, p. 30

Additional Resources
- Hist. Sig. Act., URB p. 68
- Linking Past/Present Act., URB p. 74

S Skill Practice

Teacher Edition
- Using Geo. Skills, p. 27

Additional Resources
- Econ. & Hist. Act., URB p. 5
- Hist. & Geo. Act., URB p. 65
- Mapping Hist. Act., URB p. 67

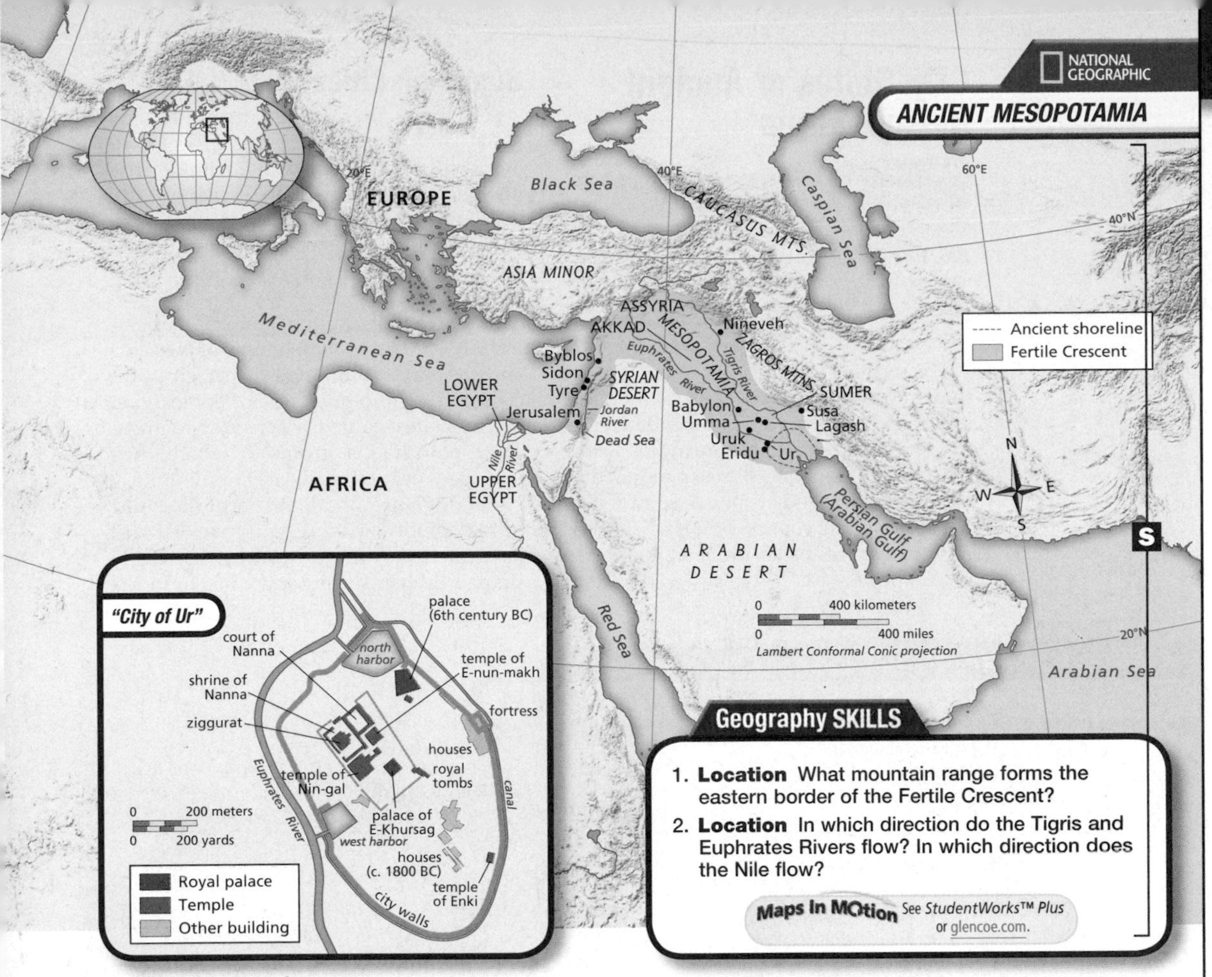

Geography SKILLS

1. **Location** What mountain range forms the eastern border of the Fertile Crescent?
2. **Location** In which direction do the Tigris and Euphrates Rivers flow? In which direction does the Nile flow?

Maps In MOtion See *StudentWorks™ Plus* or glencoe.com.

The Growth of Religion

The physical environment affected the way Mesopotamians viewed the world. A harsh climate and frequent famines convinced them that unreliable supernatural forces controlled this world. In the presence of nature, Mesopotamians could easily feel helpless, as this poem relates:

PRIMARY SOURCE

"The rampant flood which no man can oppose,
Which shakes the heavens and causes earth to tremble,
In an appalling blanket folds mother and child,
And drowns the harvest in its time of ripeness."

—in "Mesopotamia," from *Before Philosophy*, Henri Frankfort et al.

R

In Mesopotamia, people looked to religion to answer their questions about life. To them, powerful spiritual beings—gods and goddesses—permeated all aspects of the universe. The Mesopotamians identified nearly three thousand gods and goddesses. Their religion was **polytheistic** because of this belief in many gods. According to the beliefs of the Mesopotamians, humans were supposed to obey and serve the gods. By their nature, humans were inferior to the gods and could never be sure what the gods might do to or for them.

✓Reading Check **Explaining** What role did geography play in the development of Mesopotamian civilization?

S Skill Practice

Using Geography Skills Have students compare this map with a modern one of the region. **Ask:** In which modern nation is Babylon located? Tyre? Jerusalem? *(Iraq; Syria; Israel)* **OL**

For additional practice on this skill, see the **Skills Handbook**.

R Reading Strategy

Reading Primary Sources
Ask: According to the poem, when did the rivers become a menace rather than a source of life-giving water? *(The last line suggests that the flooding of the rivers at the wrong time of year could wipe out an entire harvest.)* **OL**

Geography SKILLS

Answers:
1. Zagros Mountains
2. Southeast; North

✓Reading Check

Answer: The land between the two rivers was filled with silt, making the soil rich enough for systematic agriculture.

Additional Support

Extending the Content

Did You Know?

Anu (or An) was the highest god in the Sumerian religion. He was the sky god and the father of all of the gods, as well as of their counterparts, evil spirits and demons. Two other major gods, Enki and Enlil, figure more prominently in myths, however.

- Enki was the god of water. According to some myths, he created man to serve the gods. He is also credited with assigning each god his or her role and establishing civilization.
- Enlil, the third god in the triad, was the god of wind, both harsh and gentle, and of agriculture. In one myth, it is related how he broke apart heaven and earth to form fields for seeds to grow. When he invented the hoe and used it to break open the earth, men sprang forth. His interactions with his wife Ninlil explain the growing cycle.

These gods were omnipotent and capricious, demanding that the Sumerians work hard to keep them happy.

R Reading Strategy

Determining Importance **Ask:** How were city-states important in the development of government in Mesopotamia? *(City-states were the basic units of Sumerian civilization. As they expanded, they gained control over the surrounding countryside.)* **OL**

C Critical Thinking

Making Inferences **Ask:** Why did Sumerians build walls around their cities? *(Walls gave them protection from attacks by other city-states or nomadic groups.)* **BL**

DOCUMENT-BASED QUESTIONS

Answers:

1. Answers will vary, but students might suggest that priests were considered the most holy and needed to enter to carry out rituals and ceremonies.
2. Sumerians believed in the idea that gods resided in the heavens above the Earth. The idea of worshipping in a temple atop a ziggurat brings a person closer to his/her god.

City-States of Ancient Mesopotamia

MAIN IDEA Religion played a powerful role in the economic, political, and social structure of Mesopotamian city-states.

HISTORY & YOU How are state and local government related in your community? Read about the connection in Mesopotamia.

The origins of the Sumerian people remain a mystery. By 3000 B.C., they had established a number of independent cities in southern Mesopotamia, including Eridu, **R** Ur, and **Uruk.** As the cities expanded, they gained political and economic control over the surrounding countryside. They formed **city-states,** the basic units of Sumerian civilization.

Sumerian Cities

Sumerian cities were surrounded by walls. Uruk, for example, was encircled by a wall six miles (10 km) long, with defense **C** towers located every 30 to 35 feet (9 to 10 m) along the wall. It is estimated that Uruk had a population of around 50,000 people by 2700 B.C., making it one of the largest city-states.

City dwellings, built of sun-dried bricks, included both the small houses of peasants and the larger buildings of the city officials, priests, and priestesses. People living in city-states gained a sense of identity. They now had a group to which they belonged, beyond the basic family unit.

Although Mesopotamia had little stone or wood for building purposes, it did have plenty of mud. Mud bricks, easily shaped by hand, were left to bake in the

HISTORY & ARCHITECTURE — PRIMARY SOURCE

Ziggurat at Ur, c. 2100 B.C.

The ziggurat at Ur was constructed during the reign of Ur-Nammu around 2100 B.C. It stands approximately 70 feet (21 m) high. The temple is believed to have been for the moon god, Nanna.

Ziggurats ceased to be built after Mesopotamia was conquered by the Persians in the 500s B.C.

Only priests were allowed to climb to the temple. One theory suggests the steps represented a stairway to heaven, bringing the priests closer to the gods.

DOCUMENT-BASED QUESTIONS

1. **Making Inferences** Why do you think priests were the only people permitted to enter the temples?
2. **Drawing Conclusions** Why do you suppose Sumerians built temples on top of ziggurats?

Differentiated Instruction

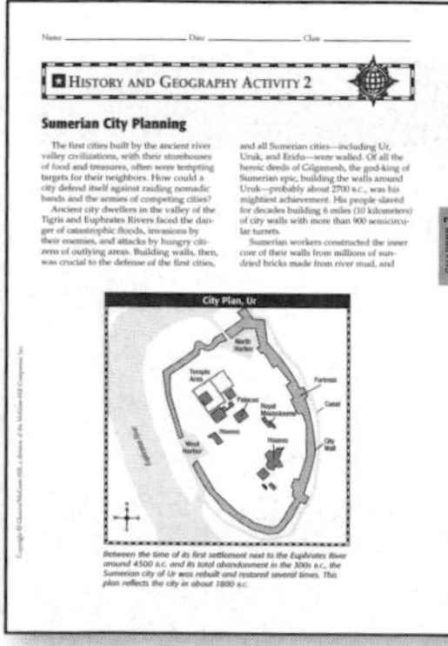
History and Geography Activity 2

Sumerian City Planning

City Plan, Ur

History and Geography Activity, URB p. 65

Comparing and Contrasting

Objective: Learn about the walled city-states of Sumer.

Focus: Read the description of Sumerian city planning.

Teach: As a class, discuss characteristics of a Sumerian city.

Assess: Have students draw a plan of their own city to compare to the Sumerian plan.

Close: Have students use a chart to compare and contrast Sumerian and modern American cities.

Differentiated Instruction Strategies

BL Have students create a model of the Sumerian walled city-state and label its features.

AL Have students research the excavation of Sumerian city-states and organize a display of their findings.

ELL Have students create a labeled plan of their "ideal" city.

hot sun until they were hard enough to use for building. People in Mesopotamia were remarkably creative with mud bricks. They invented the arch and the dome, and they built some of the largest brick buildings in the world. Mud bricks are still used in rural areas of Southwest Asia today.

Religion and Rulers

The most prominent building in a Sumerian city was the temple dedicated to the chief god or goddess of the city. This temple was often built atop a massive stepped tower called a **ziggurat.** The Sumerians believed that gods and goddesses owned the cities. The people devoted much of their wealth to building temples and elaborate houses for the priests and priestesses who served the gods. The temples and related buildings served as the center of the city physically, economically, and even politically. Surplus food and crafts were stored in the temples, which could then be distributed or traded. R

The priests and priestesses who supervised the temples held a great deal of power. In fact, historians believe that in the early stages of the city-states, priests and priestesses played an important role in ruling. The Sumerians believed that the gods ruled the cities, making the state a **theocracy**—a government by divine authority.

Even when power passed into the hands of kings, Sumerians believed that these rulers derived their power from the gods and were the agents of the gods. As one person said in a petition to his king:

PRIMARY SOURCE

> "You in your judgement, you are the son of Anu [god of the sky]. Your commands, like the work of a god, cannot be reversed. Your words, like rain pouring down from heaven, are without number."
>
> —anonymous Sumerian petitioner

C

Regardless of their origins, kings held great power. They led armies, supervised the building of public works, and organized workers for the irrigation projects on which farming depended. The army, the government, and the priests and priestesses all aided the kings in their rule. As befitted their power, Sumerian kings, their wives, and their children lived in large palaces.

Economy and Society

Although the Sumerian city-states had a traditional economy based chiefly on farming, trade and industry became important as well. The peoples of Mesopotamia made woolen textiles and pottery, but they were particularly well known for their metalwork.

Copper, gold, and silver were already being used for jewelry and some tools. The Sumerians discovered that when tin is added to copper, it makes bronze. Bronze has a lower melting point, which makes it easier to cast than copper. Bronze is also a harder metal than copper and corrodes less. It could also be melted down and remade when it wore out.

The Sumerians imported copper, tin, and timber in exchange for dried fish, wool, barley, wheat, and metal goods. Traders traveled by land to the eastern Mediterranean in the west and by sea to India in the east. The invention of the wheel, around 3000 B.C., led to wheeled carts, which made the **transport** of goods much easier.

Sumerian city-states contained three major social groups: nobles, commoners, and slaves. Nobles included royal and priestly officials and their families. Commoners worked for palace and temple estates and as farmers, merchants, fishers, and craftspeople. Probably 90 percent or more of the people were farmers. Slaves belonged to palace officials, who used them mostly in building projects. Temple officials most often used female slaves to weave cloth and grind grain. Rich landowners also used slaves to farm their lands. D

✓Reading Check **Explaining** Why were the early Mesopotamian city-states considered to be theocracies?

R Reading Strategy

Identifying Ask: What does the position and function of the ziggurat tell us about the relationship of religion to the city-states? *(Religion, government, and the economy were all interconnected.)* **OL**

C Critical Thinking

Analyzing Primary Sources
Ask: What does this quotation suggest about the authority of the king in Sumerian society? *(His authority was absolute; his wisdom undisputed.)* **OL**

D Differentiated Instruction

Visual/Spatial Have students work in pairs to graphically represent the three social groups in Sumerian society. **Ask:** What was the primary occupation of the Sumerians? *(farming)* **OL**

✓Reading Check

Answer: City-states were theocracies because those holding power were either priests and priestesses or else kings who were seen as gods' agents.

Hands-On Chapter Project
Step 1

Publishing a Coffee Table Book

Small groups create a coffee table book on ancient civilizations.

Step 1: Writing the First Chapter

Essential Question: What debt does modern society owe to the early civilizations of western Asia and Egypt?

Directions: Write the Big Idea on the board. Tell students that they will use the facts in this section to present information on the civilizations of the Fertile Crescent. Suggest that they examine the government, economy, religion, achievements, and people of Sumer and later kingdoms.

Because it is a coffee table book, they should use bold graphics and an interesting format to present the most important ideas. Tell students that each chapter of their book should include a foldout illustration. For this chapter, they should create a colorfully illustrated, labeled map of Mesopotamia.

Summarizing: Have students share what they learned about the Big Idea while writing their chapter. **OL**

(Chapter Project is continued in Section 2.)

C Critical Thinking

Drawing Conclusions Discuss the importance of writing in the development of civilization. **Ask:** Why were the scribes different from the rest of the population, and why did they receive important government positions? *(The scribes were from the wealthy class and the only ones who knew how to read and write cuneiform. This made them indispensable to the government.)* OL

W Writing Support

Descriptive Writing Have students discuss the primary source describing Sumerian schools. Ask them to write short descriptions that convey the modern duties of teachers and students. As a class, compare descriptions with the primary source. AL

D Differentiated Instruction

Advanced Learners Ask: What can be learned about a society from studying its epic poetry? *(Epic poetry gives us information about its values, traditions, and religious beliefs. It may also be useful as a record of actual historical events.)* AL

Additional Support

The Creativity of the Sumerians

MAIN IDEA The Sumerians invented writing and several new technologies that made life easier.

HISTORY & YOU What are some examples of how writing makes your life better? Read about Sumerian writing innovations.

The Sumerians created many inventions that still affect our lives today. Probably their greatest invention was their writing. In addition, historians credit them with many technological **innovations.**

Writing and Literature

Around 3000 B.C., the Sumerians created a **cuneiform** ("wedge-shaped") system of writing. Using a reed stylus (a tool for writing), they made wedge-shaped impressions on clay tablets, which were then baked or dried in the sun. Once dried, these tablets lasted a very long time. Several hundred thousand tablets have been found. They have been a valuable source of information for modern scholars.

Mesopotamian peoples used writing primarily for record keeping. Cuneiform texts, however, were also used in schools to train scribes, members of the learned class who served as copyists, teachers, and jurists.

For boys of the upper class in Mesopotamia, becoming a scribe was the key to a successful career. Men who began their careers as scribes became the leaders of their cities, temples, and armies. Scribes came to hold the most important positions in Sumerian society.

To become scribes, boys from wealthy families, many of them the sons of scribes, attended the new schools that were in operation by 2500 B.C. Young boys seeking to become scribes began school when they were small children and trained until they were young men. School days began at sunrise and ended at sunset. Discipline was harsh. The following essay, written by a teacher as a copying exercise for pupils, shows that punishments—being caned or beaten with a stick—were frequent:

PRIMARY SOURCE

"In the tablet-house, the monitor said to me:
'Why are you late?' I was afraid, my heart beat fast. I entered before my teacher, took my place.
My 'school-father' read my tablet to me,
said, 'The word is cut off,' caned me.
He who was in charge of drawing said 'Why when I was not here did you stand up?' caned me.
He who was in charge of the gate said 'Why when I was not here did you go out?' caned me.
My teacher said 'Your hand is not good,' caned me."

—James B. Pritchard, *Ancient Near Eastern Texts*

Scribal students spent most of their school days following the same routine. They copied and recopied standard works on clay tablets and then recited from them. Although boring, this was probably the scribe's only way of learning how to form the cuneiform writing signs neatly and correctly.

PRIMARY SOURCE

"'What did you do in school?'
'I read my tablet, wrote it, finished
it; then my prepared lines were
prepared for me and in the
afternoon, my hand copies were
prepared for me.'"

—James B. Pritchard, *Ancient Near Eastern Texts*

Writing was important because it allowed a society to keep records and to pass along knowledge from person to person and from generation to generation. Writing also made it possible for people to communicate ideas in new ways. This is especially evident in *The Epic of Gilgamesh.*

Gilgamesh is an epic poem that records the exploits of a legendary king named Gilgamesh. Gilgamesh is wise, strong, and perfect in body. He is part man and part god. Gilgamesh befriends a hairy beast named Enkidu. Together, they set off to do great deeds. When Enkidu dies, Gilgamesh feels the pain of death and begins a search for the secret of immortality. His efforts fail, and Gilgamesh remains mortal. This Mesopotamian epic makes clear that "everlasting life" is only for the gods.

Activity: Interdisciplinary Connection

Literature Tell students that *The Epic of Gilgamesh* has been reconstructed from 12 tablets found at Nineveh. In the epic, Gilgamesh and Enkidu battle enemies, such as the guardian of a cedar forest and the divine bull. After Enkidu's death, Gilgamesh seeks out the survivors of the Babylonian flood, who have the secret of eternal life. Discuss with students how epics reveal the values and belief system of the society from which they originate.

Then have small groups of students find and read excerpts from tablets III, IX, X, or XI. Have them use these questions to analyze the significance of their excerpt:

- Who is the speaker? What happens?
- What does the excerpt show about the relationship between the gods and humans?
- What picture of Gilgamesh emerges from the excerpt?
- What appears to be important to the Mesopotamian culture based on the qualities shown by the characters?

Have students present their analyses. AL

The Standard of Ur

The Standard of Ur was found in a grave in the Royal Cemetery at Ur. The Standard has two main panels titled "War" and "Peace." The "War" panel, shown here, depicts a Sumerian army. It should be read from the bottom up, and left to right.

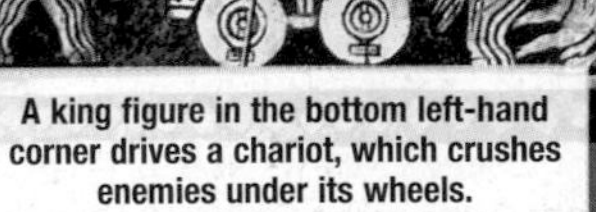

The top panel shows the king receiving prisoners and other spoils of war.

Sumerian soldiers use spears to drive their prisoners forward, in the middle panel.

It is believed that the middle panel depicts men carrying tribute to their conquerors.

A king figure in the bottom left-hand corner drives a chariot, which crushes enemies under its wheels.

DOCUMENT-BASED QUESTIONS

1. **Describing** What events are depicted in these panels?
2. **Interpreting** What does the "War" panel reveal about Sumerian society?

Technology

The Sumerians invented several tools and devices that made daily life easier and more productive. They developed the wagon wheel, for example, to help transport people and goods from place to place. The potter's wheel to shape containers, the sundial to keep time, and the arch used in construction are other examples of Sumerian technology. The Sumerians were the first to make bronze out of copper and tin, creating finely crafted metalwork. The Sumerians also made outstanding achievements in mathematics and astronomy. In math, they devised a number system based on 60. They used geometry to measure fields and to erect buildings. In astronomy, the Sumerians charted the heavenly constellations. A quick glance at your watch and its division of an hour into 60 minutes should remind you of our debt to the Sumerians. **C**

✓Reading Check **Identifying** Name two major inventions of the Sumerians, and tell how those inventions affect our lives today.

C Critical Thinking

Drawing Conclusions

Discuss the achievements of the Sumerians. **Ask:** What words might be used to describe the Sumerian civilization between 3000 B.C. and 2500 B.C.? *(The Sumerians were advanced and ingenious. They were problem-solvers.)* **OL**

DOCUMENT-BASED QUESTIONS

Answers:

1. war scenes, such as prisoners of war, tribute being brought to the victorious, and chariots crushing enemies
2. Answers may vary: The Sumerians were conquerors; they were artistic; they had a monarchy.

✓Reading Check

Answer: Answers may include the following: writing—we still use writing as a major means of communication; the wagon wheel—much of our transportation is still dependent upon vehicles with wheels; a number system based on 60—we still use this system for minutes and seconds.

Differentiated Instruction

Leveled Activities

BL Differentiated Instruction Activity, URB p. 55

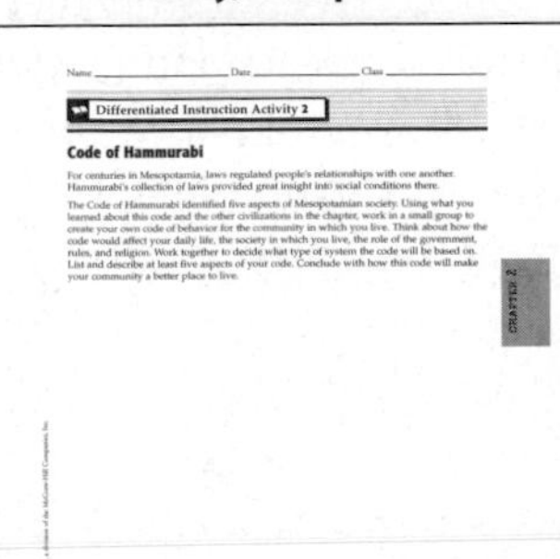

OL Skills Reinforcement Activity, URB p. 63

AL Linking Past & Present Activity, URB p. 74

ELL English Learner Activity, URB p. 57

C Critical Thinking

Analyzing Information

Ask: Why was the Code of Hammurabi carved on a stela? *(Hammurabi wanted everyone to know the laws, so they could not be ignored. Universal knowledge of the laws would ensure greater justice and impartiality.)* **AL**

For additional practice on this skill, see the **Skills Handbook**.

DOCUMENT-BASED QUESTIONS

Answers:

1. Students should make a connection between Hammurabi's code and the laws that are found in these religious texts. Answers will vary, but should show an understanding of the concept that laws are needed to keep order and to establish a culture of morals and values.
2. Answers may vary, but students may suggest that the image of Hammurabi conveys his power and the importance of following the law.

Empires in Ancient Mesopotamia

MAIN IDEA Strong leaders established empires and codified the laws of Mesopotamia.

HISTORY & YOU How might a written code of laws change the system of justice in a country? Read about the law code Hammurabi developed.

As the number of Sumerian city-states grew and the city-states expanded, new conflicts arose. City-states fought for control of land and water. Located on flat land, the Sumerian city-states were also open to invasion by other groups.

Akkadian and Babylonian Empires

To the north of the Sumerian city-states were the **Akkadians** (uh•KAY•dee•uhnz). They spoke a Semitic language. Around 2340 B.C., **Sargon,** leader of the Akkadians, overran the Sumerian city-states and set up the first empire in world history. An **empire** is a large political unit or state,

TURNING POINT — HAMMURABI'S CODE

Although there were earlier Mesopotamian law codes, the Code of Hammurabi is the most complete. It influenced law codes in later civilizations. The code's influence is also apparent in the precepts of the major world religions including Judaism, Christianity, and Islam though there are significant differences.

	THE INFLUENCE OF HAMMURABI'S CODE
1	If anyone commits a robbery and is caught, then he shall be put to death.—Hammurabi's code Thou shalt not steal.—Bible (Old Testament)
2	If a man wishes to separate from a woman who has borne him children, or from his wife who has borne him children, then he shall give that wife her dowry, and a part of the usufruct [right of use] of field, garden, and property, so that she can rear her children.—Hammurabi's code Those who die and leave wives, a will shall provide their wives with support for a year, provided they stay within the same household.—Quran
3	If a man put out the eye of another man, his eye shall be put out.—Hammurabi's code If any harm follows, then you shall give life for life, eye for eye, tooth for tooth, hand for hand, foot for foot, burn for burn, wound for wound, stripe for stripe.—Bible (Old Testament)

DOCUMENT-BASED QUESTIONS

1. **Comparing** What similarities do you see between Hammurabi's code and the Bible and the Quran?
2. **Speculating** Why do you think the images were included at the top of the stela with Hammurabi's code?

C

Hammurabi's code was written on a 7-foot (2-m) monument called a stela.

The upper section of the stela shows Hammurabi standing in front of a seated sun god.

In some ways the laws of Hammurabi's code were harsher than earlier Sumerian laws. The laws were also more progressive in the areas of family law and women's rights.

Additional Support

Teacher Tip

Collaborative Learning This activity allows students with different levels of academic skills and intelligences to work together. As you form groups, consider the needed skills and choose students accordingly.

Activity: Collaborative Learning

Identifying Central Issues Distribute the Historical Significance Activity found in the Unit 1 Unit Resources Book on page 66, entitled "The Code of Hammurabi." Have students read the selection. **Ask:** Why was the Code of Hammurabi a turning point for civilization? *(It provided the first consistent rule of law; established a social order based on individual rights; removed justice from the hands of the individual.)* Have students then work in small groups to locate and review several provisions of Hammurabi's code. Have groups create and share examples of the applications of each law in modern society. **OL**

usually under a single leader, that controls many peoples or territories. Empires are often easy to create, but they can be difficult to maintain. The rise and fall of empires is an important part of history.

Attacks from neighbors caused the Akkadian Empire to fall by 2100 B.C. After that, the system of warring city-states lasted until 1792 B.C. In **Babylon,** a city-state south of Akkad, **Hammurabi** (HA•muh•RAH•bee) came to power. He gained control of Sumer and Akkad, thus creating a new Mesopotamian kingdom. After his death in 1750 B.C., however, a series of weak kings was unable to keep the empire united, and it finally fell to new invaders.

The Code of Hammurabi

For centuries in Mesopotamia, laws had regulated people's relationships with one another. Hammurabi's collection of laws provides great insight into social conditions there. The Code of Hammurabi was based on a system of strict justice. Penalties for criminal offenses were severe, and they varied according to the social class of the victim. A crime against a noble by a commoner was punished more severely than the same offense against a member of the lower class. Moreover, the principle of retaliation ("an eye for an eye, a tooth for a tooth") was a fundamental part of this system of justice.

Hammurabi's code took seriously the duties of public officials. Officials who failed to solve crimes had to make personal restitution to the victims or their families. Judges could be penalized for ruling incorrectly on a case.

The law code also included what we would call consumer-protection laws. Builders were held responsible for the buildings they constructed. If a house collapsed and caused the owner to die, the builder was put to death.

The largest category of laws in the Code of Hammurabi focused on marriage and the family. Parents arranged marriages for their children. After marriage, the two parties signed a marriage contract, which made the marriage legal.

Mesopotamian society was **patriarchal**—that is, men dominated the society. Hammurabi's code shows that women had far fewer rights in marriage than did men.

A woman's place was definitely in the home. A husband could divorce his wife if she failed to fulfill her duties, was unable to bear children, or tried to leave home to engage in business. Even harsher, a wife who neglected her home or humiliated her husband could be drowned.

Fathers ruled their children as well. Obedience was expected: "If a son has struck his father, he shall cut off his hand." If a son committed a serious enough offense, his father could disinherit him. Hammurabi's laws clearly covered almost every aspect of people's lives.

✓Reading Check **Identifying** Identify five aspects of Mesopotamian society as revealed by the Code of Hammurabi.

SECTION 1 REVIEW

Vocabulary

1. **Explain** the significance of: Tigris River, Euphrates River, Mesopotamia, Fertile Crescent, Sumerians, polytheistic, Uruk, city-state, ziggurat, theocracy, transport, innovations, cuneiform, Akkadians, Sargon, empire, Babylon, Hammurabi, patriarchal.

Main Ideas

2. **Explain** how the physical environment affected the way Mesopotamians viewed the world.
3. **Describe** how temples served as the center of Mesopotamian cities.
4. **Create** a chart like the one shown below to list Sumerian achievements and the effects of these achievements on our lives today.

Achievements	Effects on our lives today

Critical Thinking

5. **BIG Idea** **Analyzing** How did the Tigris and Euphrates Rivers support a strong economy in Mesopotamia?
6. **Evaluating** Which type of government—separate city-states or an empire—would have been most advantageous to the people of Mesopotamia?
7. **Analyzing Visuals** Examine the image on page 31. What does it reveal about life in Sumer?

Writing About History

8. **Expository Writing** Explain why Hammurabi's code was a significant development. Develop a set of laws based on the Code of Hammurabi that would apply to your community today. Explain why your code differs from that developed by Hammurabi or why it is similar.

For help with the concepts in this section of *Glencoe World History,* go to glencoe.com and click Study Central™.

33

✓Reading Check

Answer: severe penalties for criminal offenses; different social classes not treated the same; officials held strictly accountable for enforcing laws; consumers protected against shoddy workmanship; regulated marriage; patriarchal society; women had few rights and privileges

Assess

Study Central provides summaries, interactive games, and online graphic organizers to help students review content.

Close

Determining Cause and Effect Ask: Why were the Sumerian city-states unable to keep out the Akkadian invaders? *(Their location on flat land offered no protection. Their internal conflicts meant that they were not united for fighting off a common enemy.)* OL

Answers

1. Definitions for the vocabulary words are found in the section and the Glossary.
2. The harsh environment made them believe that unreliable supernatural beings controlled the world.
3. They were the most prominent buildings and the centers of political and economic life.
4. **Achievement:** writing; **Effect:** still the basis for communication; **Achievement:** wheel; **Effect:** Cars, trucks, and trains still use wheels.
5. The rivers created fertile soil that promoted agriculture and supported cities where trade and industry could thrive.
6. City-states are easier to govern, but they are relatively defenseless against invaders. Empires have size, diversity, and power but tend to be unstable.
7. War was a part of life and was commemorated.
8. Students should develop a law code that is based on the Code of Hammurabi and is relevant to their community today.

Focus

Bellringer

Daily Focus Transparency 2.2

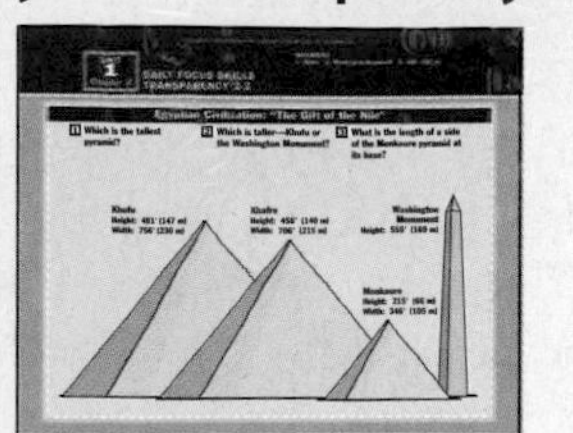

GUIDE TO READING

Answers to Graphic:

Old Kingdom	Middle Kingdom	New Kingdom
divine kings built pyramids	pharaohs as shepherds	militaristic
	period of expansion	massive wealth
		religious revolution

Section Spotlight Video

To generate student interest and provide a springboard for class discussion, access the Chapter 2, Section 2 video at glencoe.com or on the video DVD.

SECTION 2

Egyptian Civilization

GUIDE TO READING

The BIG Idea

Order and Security Continuity and stability were characteristics of Egyptian civilization for thousands of years.

Content Vocabulary

- dynasty *(p. 36)*
- pharaoh *(p. 37)*
- bureaucracy *(p. 37)*
- vizier *(p. 37)*
- mummification *(p. 37)*
- hieroglyphics *(p. 42)*
- hieratic script *(p. 43)*

Academic Vocabulary

- major *(p. 34)*
- identifying *(p. 36)*
- physical *(p. 37)*

People and Places

- Nile River *(p. 34)*
- Lower Egypt *(p. 34)*
- Upper Egypt *(p. 34)*
- Menes *(p. 36)*
- Giza *(p. 37)*
- Hyksos *(p. 39)*
- Hatshepsut *(p. 40)*
- Akhenaten *(p. 40)*
- Tutankhamen *(p. 40)*
- Ramses II *(p. 40)*
- Cleopatra VII *(p. 40)*

Reading Strategy

Identifying As you read, complete a chart like the one below listing characteristics of three major periods in Egyptian history.

The Old Kingdom	The Middle Kingdom	The New Kingdom

Egypt, like Mesopotamia, was one of the first river-valley civilizations. Egyptian history includes three long periods of stability and achievement interspersed with shorter periods of political disorder. Egyptian society was organized in layers, but most people worked the land.

Geography and Religion

MAIN IDEA The Nile was fundamental to the development of Egyptian civilization.

HISTORY & YOU How does the geography of your region affect your outlook on life? Learn how the Egyptians in the Nile Valley used their geography.

The Nile River played an important role in Egyptian civilization. Egyptians wrote of their reliance on the great river in "Hymn to the Nile," praising it as the "creator of all good" in its ability to bring them food and other riches. Like their religious beliefs, the Nile provided a sense of well-being and comfort to the Egyptians.

The Nile

The **Nile River** begins in the heart of Africa and courses northward for more than 4,000 miles (6,436 km). It is the longest river in the world. Before it empties into the Mediterranean, the Nile splits into two **major** branches. This split forms a triangular territory called a delta. The Nile Delta is called **Lower Egypt;** the land upstream, to the south, is called **Upper Egypt.** Egypt's important cities developed at the tip of the delta, the point at which the Nile divides.

The ancient Egyptians referred to the river's yearly flooding as the "miracle" of the Nile. The river rose in the summer from heavy rains in central Africa, reached its highest point in Egypt in early autumn, and left a deposit of mud that created an area of rich soil several miles wide on both sides of the river. The Egyptians called this dark-colored, fertile land the "Black Land." Beyond it lay the deserts, the "Red Land."

Farmers in the Nile Valley grew a surplus of food, which made Egypt prosperous. The river also served as a unifying factor in Egyptian history. In ancient times, the Nile was the fastest way to travel through the land, making both transportation and communication easier. North winds pushed sailboats south, and the Nile's current carried them north.

Unlike Mesopotamia, which was subject to constant invasion, Egypt was blessed by natural barriers that gave it protection from

Resource Manager

R Reading Strategies	C Critical Thinking	D Differentiated Instruction	W Writing Support	S Skill Practice
Teacher Edition • Questioning, p. 37 • Making Connections, p. 37 • Summarizing, pp. 39, 41 • Inferring, p. 42 **Additional Resources** • Guid. Read. Act., URB p. 85 • Read. Ess. & Note-Taking Guide, p. 10	**Teacher Edition** • Compare/Contrast, p. 36 • Drawing Con., p. 37 • Making Inferences, p. 38 • Det. Cause/Effect, pp. 39, 40 **Additional Resources** • Crit. Think. Act., URB p. 64 • World Art & Music Act., URB p. 79 • Section Quiz, p. 12	**Teacher Edition** • ELL, p. 38 **Additional Resources** • Reteach. Act., URB p. 81 • Enrich. Act., URB p. 82	**Teacher Edition** • Expository Writing, p. 41 **Additional Resources** • Pri. Source Read., URB p. 77 • Writer's Guidebook, p. 23	**Teacher Edition** • Using Geo. Skills, p. 35 **Additional Resources** • Coop. Learn. Act., URB p. 69 • Time Line Act., URB p. 72 • People in World Hist. Act., URB p. 75

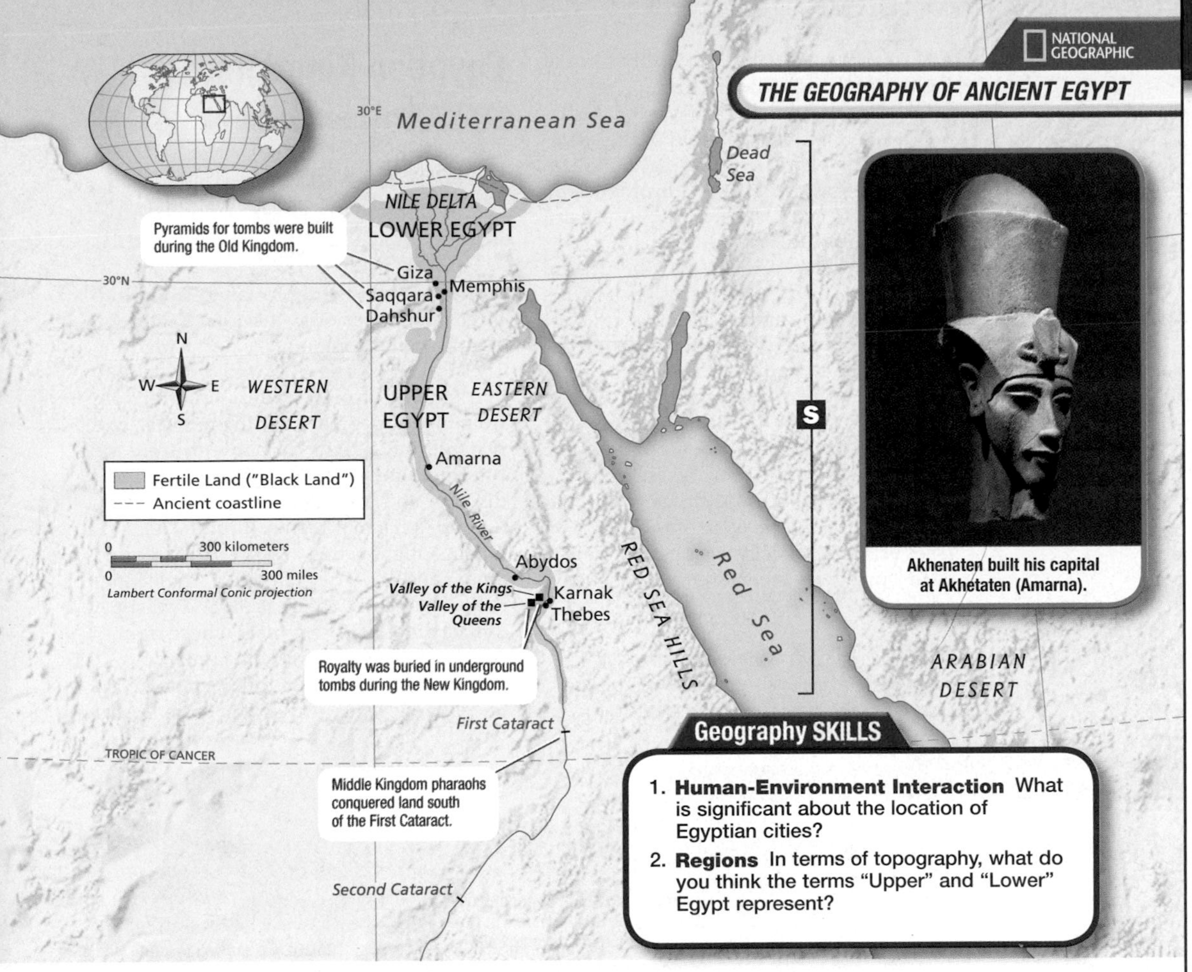

Akhenaten built his capital at Akhetaten (Amarna).

invasion and a sense of security. These barriers included the deserts to the west and east; the Red Sea to the east; the cataracts, or rapids, on the southern part of the Nile, which made defense relatively easy; and the Mediterranean Sea to the north.

The regularity of the Nile floods and the relative isolation of the Egyptians created a feeling of security and changelessness. To the ancient Egyptians, when the Nile flooded each year, "the fields laugh and people's faces light up." Unlike people in Mesopotamia, Egyptians faced life with a spirit of confidence in the stability of things. Ancient Egyptian civilization was marked by a remarkable degree of continuity over thousands of years.

The Growth of Religion

Religion, too, provided the Egyptians with a sense of security and timelessness. They had no word for religion. For them, religious ideas represented an inseparable part of the entire world order. The Egyptians were polytheistic. They had a number of gods associated with heavenly bodies and natural forces. Two groups, sun gods and land gods (including river gods), came to have special significance in view of the importance of the sun and the fertile land along the Nile to Egypt's well-being.

The sun, the source of life, was worthy of worship. The sun god took on different forms and names based on his role. The Egyptian ruler took the title "Son of Re."

S Skill Practice

Using Geography Skills Ask: Using the scale, what is the distance between the first and second cataracts? *(about 450 miles)* **OL**

Did You Know?

The Nile Delta covers 9,650 square miles. It received its name because ancient geographers saw that its shape resembled the Greek letter *delta*. Changes in irrigation resulting from the construction of the Aswan Dam in 1971 and the creation of Lake Nasser mean that modern Egyptian farmers in this area now have two or three growing seasons instead of just one.

Geography SKILLS

Answers:

1. They are all located along the Nile.
2. Upper Egypt has a higher altitude than Lower Egypt.

Hands-On Chapter Project
Step 2

Publishing a Coffee Table Book

Students create the next chapter of their book.

Step 2: Writing the Second Chapter

Directions: Write the Big Idea on the board. Have groups use the facts in this section to compose the next chapter of their coffee table book. Remind them to keep their focus on the most significant ideas about ancient Egypt. For this chapter's foldout page, suggest that they create a pictorial summary of the process of mummification practiced by the Egyptians.

Summarizing: Have groups share what they learned about the Big Idea while writing their second chapter. **OL**

(Chapter Project is continued in Section 3.)

C Critical Thinking

Comparing and Contrasting

Ask: How were Egyptian rulers different from Sumerian kings? *(Sumerian rulers were the agents of the gods; pharaohs were seen as gods themselves.)* **OL**

For additional practice on this skill, see the **Skills Handbook**.

✓Reading Check

Answer: Flooding patterns were regular in Egypt, leading to a feeling of stability. The flooding in Mesopotamia was unpredictable, leading to a belief that the world was at the mercy of harsh and unreliable gods.

DOCUMENT-BASED QUESTIONS

Answers:

1. Pyramids contained items needed for the afterlife; pharaohs thought they might need them.
2. It is smaller, but has more elaborate surrounding structures and statues such as the Great Sphinx.

C The rulers were seen as an earthly form of Re, one of the sun god's names.

River and land gods included Osiris and Isis. A famous myth told of the struggle between Osiris, who brought civilization to Egypt, and his evil brother Seth. When Seth cut Osiris into pieces and tossed them into the Nile, Isis, Osiris's wife, found the pieces. With help from other gods, she brought Osiris back to life. Osiris became a symbol of resurrection, or rebirth. By **identifying** with Osiris, Egyptians hoped to gain new life after death. The dead were placed in tombs (in the case of kings, in pyramid tombs) and through rituals would become Osiris. Like Osiris, they would then be reborn. The flooding of the Nile and the new life that it brought to Egypt were symbolized by Isis's bringing all of Osiris's parts together each spring in the festival of the new land.

✓Reading Check **Contrasting** How did the flooding patterns of rivers in Egypt and Mesopotamia cause the two civilizations to develop differently?

Egyptian Kingdoms

MAIN IDEA Egyptian history is divided into three major periods, called kingdoms.

HISTORY & YOU Why might periods of political stability also be times of cultural achievement? Learn about Egypt's accomplishments.

Scholars divide Egyptian history into three major periods: the Old Kingdom, Middle Kingdom, and New Kingdom. These were periods of long-term stability marked by strong leadership, freedom from invasion, great building projects, and rich cultural activity. In between were the Intermediate periods, times of political disorder and invasion.

Egypt's history begins around 3100 B.C., when King **Menes** (MEE•NEEZ) united Upper and Lower Egypt into a single kingdom and created the first royal dynasty. A **dynasty** is a family of rulers whose right to rule is passed on within the family.

From then on, the Egyptian ruler would be called "King of Upper and Lower

HISTORY & ARTS PRIMARY SOURCE

Pyramids at Giza

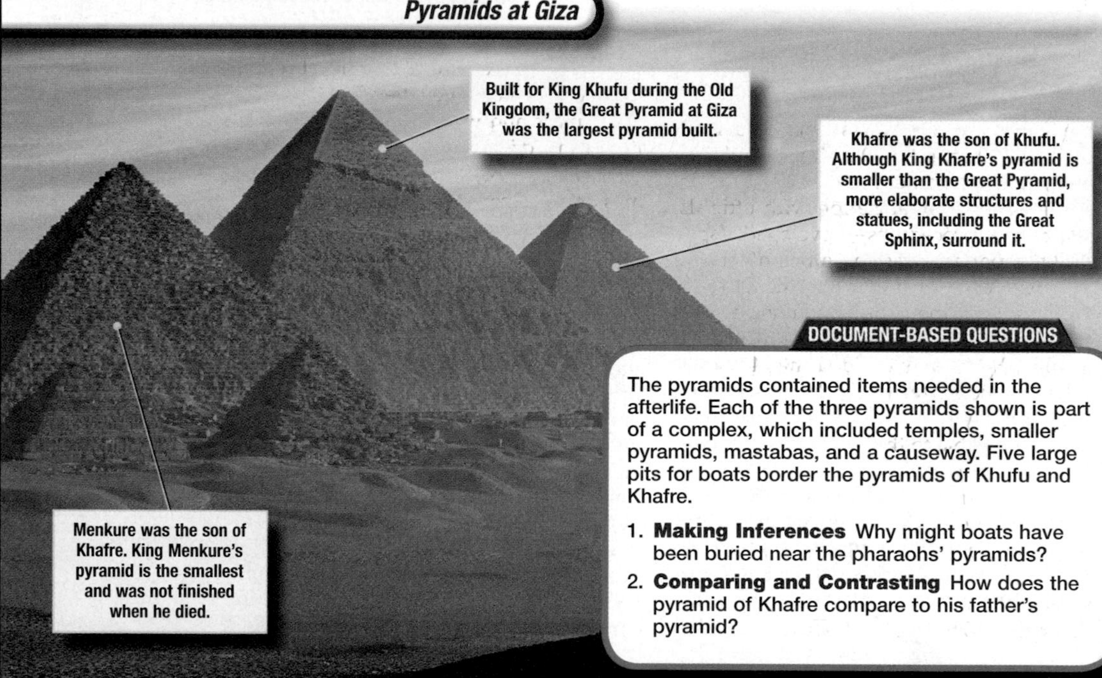

DOCUMENT-BASED QUESTIONS

The pyramids contained items needed in the afterlife. Each of the three pyramids shown is part of a complex, which included temples, smaller pyramids, mastabas, and a causeway. Five large pits for boats border the pyramids of Khufu and Khafre.

1. **Making Inferences** Why might boats have been buried near the pharaohs' pyramids?
2. **Comparing and Contrasting** How does the pyramid of Khafre compare to his father's pyramid?

Additional Support

Teacher Tip

Collaborative Learning This activity allows students with different levels of academic skills and intelligences to work together. As you form groups, consider the needed skills and choose students accordingly.

Activity: Collaborative Learning

Creating Encyclopedia Entries Tell students that there were many Egyptian gods and goddesses, each fulfilling a specific role. Have small groups work together to find out more about the Egyptian deities, such as the following: Amun, Anubis, Bastet, Horus, Isis, Nephthys, Nun, Osiris, Re, Sekhmet, and Seth. Then have groups create illustrated encyclopedia entries for an assigned god or gods. Students should place their entries in a binder for use as a classroom reference. **Ask:** Which gods were most closely tied to everyday life of the Egyptians? *(Answers will vary, but students may name Horus, Isis, Osiris, and Re.)* **OL**

Egypt." The crown was a double crown, indicating the unity of all Egypt. Just as the Nile served to unite Upper Egypt and Lower Egypt physically, kingship united them politically.

The Old Kingdom

The Old Kingdom, which lasted from around 2700 B.C. to 2200 B.C., was an age of prosperity and splendor. Like the kings of the Sumerian city-states, the monarchs of the Old Kingdom were powerful rulers over a unified state. Among the various titles of Egyptian monarchs, that of **pharaoh**—originally meaning "great house" or "palace"—eventually became the most common.

Kingship was a divine institution in ancient Egypt and formed part of a universal cosmic order: "What is the king of Upper and Lower Egypt? He is a god by whose dealings one lives, the father and mother of all men, alone by himself, without an equal." In obeying their pharaoh, subjects believed that they were helping to maintain a stable world order. A breakdown in royal power could only mean that citizens were offending the gods and weakening that order.

Egyptian pharaohs possessed absolute power—that is, they had complete, unlimited power to rule their people. Nevertheless, they had help in ruling. At first, members of the pharaoh's family provided this help. During the Old Kingdom, however, a government **bureaucracy**—an administrative organization with officials and regular procedures—developed. Especially important was the office of **vizier**, the steward of the whole land. Directly responsible to the pharaoh, the vizier was in charge of the government bureaucracy. In time, Egypt was divided into 42 provinces, which were run by governors appointed by the pharaoh. Each governor was responsible to the pharaoh and vizier. R1

An example of the splendor of the Old Kingdom—and one of the great achievements of Egyptian civilization—is the building of pyramids. Pyramids were built as part of a larger complex of buildings dedicated to the dead—in effect, a city of the dead. The area included several structures: a large pyramid for the pharaoh's burial; smaller pyramids for his family; and several mastabas, rectangular structures with flat roofs used as tombs for the pharaoh's officials.

The tombs were well prepared for their residents. They contained rooms stocked with supplies, including chairs, boats, chests, weapons, games, dishes, and a variety of foods. The Egyptians believed that human beings had two bodies—a **physical** one and a spiritual one, which they called the *ka*. If the physical body was properly preserved and the tomb furnished with all the various objects of regular life, the *ka* could return. Surrounded by the earthly comforts, the spiritual *ka* could then continue its life despite the death of the physical body. R2

To preserve the physical body after death, the Egyptians practiced **mummification**, a process of slowly drying a dead body to prevent it from rotting. This process took place in workshops run by priests, primarily for the wealthy families who could afford it. Workers first removed the liver, lungs, stomach, and intestines and placed them in four special jars that were put in the tomb with the mummy. The priests also removed the brain by extracting it through the nose. They then covered the corpse with a natural salt that absorbed the body's water. Later, they filled the body with spices and wrapped it with layers of linen soaked in resin. At the end of the process, which took about 70 days, a lifelike mask was placed over the head and shoulders of the mummy. The mummy was then sealed in a case and placed in its tomb. C

Pyramids were tombs for the mummified bodies of pharaohs. The largest and most magnificent of all the pyramids was built under King Khufu (KOO•FOO). Constructed at **Giza** around 2540 B.C., the famous Great Pyramid of King Khufu covers 13 acres (5.3 ha), measures 756 feet (230 m) at each side of its base, and stands 481 feet (147 m) high.

The building of the Great Pyramid was an enormous construction project. The Greek historian Herodotus reported the traditional story that it took 100,000 Egyptians 20 years to build the Great Pyramid.

R1 Reading Strategy

Questioning Ask: What circumstances prompted the formation of a bureaucracy? *(As Egypt grew, the pharaohs needed an organized system of government to help them rule.)* **OL**

R2 Reading Strategy

Making Connections Discuss the preparations made by the Egyptians for the afterlife. **Ask:** In what ways are modern burials different from or similar to Egyptian traditions? *(Students' responses will vary. They should supply specific examples.)* **OL**

C Critical Thinking

Drawing Conclusions Ask: What conclusion might be drawn about the Egyptians' knowledge of the human body, based on their process of mummification? *(They knew a lot about internal organs and ways to preserve and protect the body.)* **OL**

Differentiated Instruction

Questioning

Objective: Discover more about the Egyptian pyramids.
Focus: Formulate effective questions.
Teach: Have students take turns reading the passage aloud.
Assess: Have students write down five research questions that they would like to find answers to after reading the article.
Close: Have teams research their questions and report on the answers.

Differentiated Instruction Strategies

BL Have students use a KWL chart to help them ask questions and find answers.

AL Have students use their research to hypothesize how the pyramids were built.

ELL Have students draw or build model pyramids and describe the process they used.

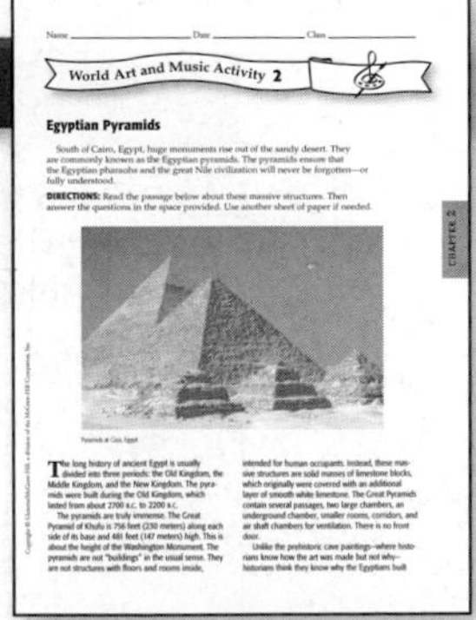

World Art and Music Activity, URB p. 79

C Critical Thinking

Making Inferences **Ask:** How did the pyramids symbolize the power of the pharaohs? *(The pyramids required many workers and held vast treasures. In addition, the pyramids reflected the advances of Egyptian civilization.)* **AL**

D Differentiated Instruction

English Language Learners
Point out the metaphorical phrase "golden age." Ask students to think of qualities or values that they associate with gold. *(precious, beautiful)* Have students use these associations to define a "golden age." Ask them what kinds of accomplishments might characterize such an age. **ELL**

Did You Know?

Nubia, in what is now northern Sudan, was the site of many precious minerals and a rival of Egypt. At different times, Egypt ruled Nubia, and Nubia controlled Egypt, resulting in the mixing of African and Egyptian cultures.

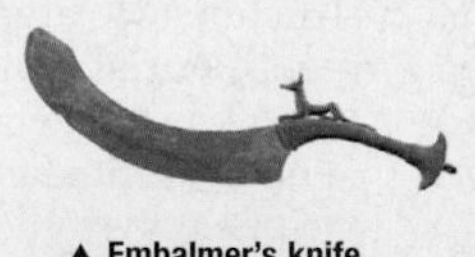

▲ Embalmer's knife

c. 3100 B.C. King Menes unites the villages of Upper and Lower Egypt

c. 2540 B.C. The building of the Great Pyramid of King Khufu at Giza

c. 2055 B.C. Middle Kingdom begins—a golden age of stability and expansion into Africa and western Asia

3200 — 2500 — 2000

c. 2700 B.C. Old Kingdom begins—a time of strong leadership and a unified Egypt

▲ Double crown of unified Egypt

c. 2180 B.C. First Intermediate Period begins, consisting of nearly 150 years without centralized leadership

Herodotus wrote two thousand years after the event, however, and speculation still surrounds the building of the Great Pyramid. Especially puzzling is how the builders achieved their amazing level of precision. The stone slabs on the outside of the Great Pyramid, for example, fit so tightly side by side that even a hair cannot be pushed into the joints between them.

Guarding the Great Pyramid at Giza is a huge figure carved from rock, known as the Great Sphinx. This colossal statue is 240 feet (73 m) long and 66 feet (20 m) high. It has the body of a lion and a human head. The head is believed by many to be a likeness of Khufu's son Khafre, who ordered the statue's construction. Historians do not agree on the purpose of the Great Sphinx. Many Egyptians, however, believed that the mythical sphinx was an important guardian of sacred sites.

C The Great Pyramid still stands as a visible symbol of the power of the Egyptian pharaohs of the Old Kingdom. No pyramid built later matched its size or splendor. The pyramid was not only the pharaoh's tomb but also an important symbol of royal power. It could be seen for miles and served to remind people of the glory, might, and wealth of the ruler who was a living god on Earth.

The Middle Kingdom

The Old Kingdom eventually collapsed, followed by a period of disorder that lasted about 150 years. Finally, a new dynasty gained control of all Egypt and began the Middle Kingdom, a period of stability lasting from about 2055 B.C. to 1650 B.C. **D** Egyptians later portrayed the Middle Kingdom as a golden age of stability.

As evidence of its newfound strength, Egypt began a period of expansion. Nubia, which was located south of Egypt, was conquered. Fortresses were built to protect the new frontier. Egypt sent armies into Palestine and Syria although they did not

Differentiated Instruction

Leveled Activities

BL Guided Reading Activity, URB p. 85

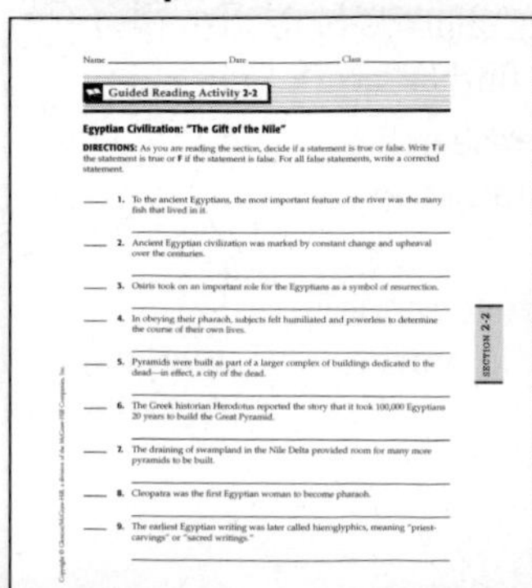

OL Critical Thinking Skills Activity, URB p. 64

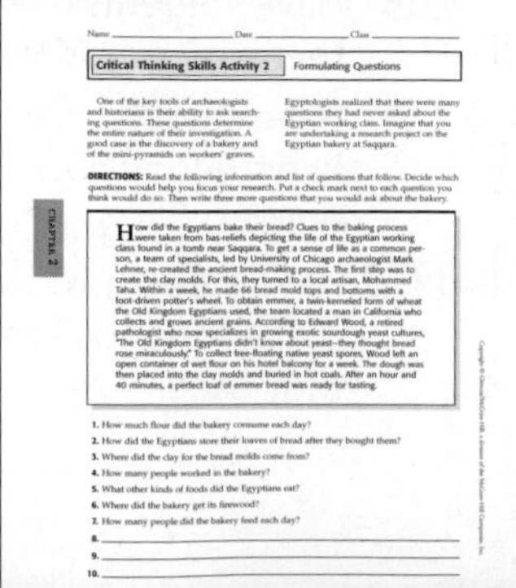

AL Cooperative Learning Activity, URB p. 69

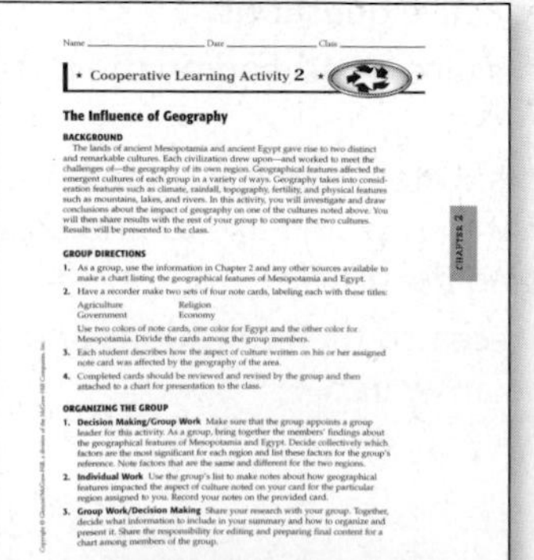

ELL Time Line Activity, URB p. 73

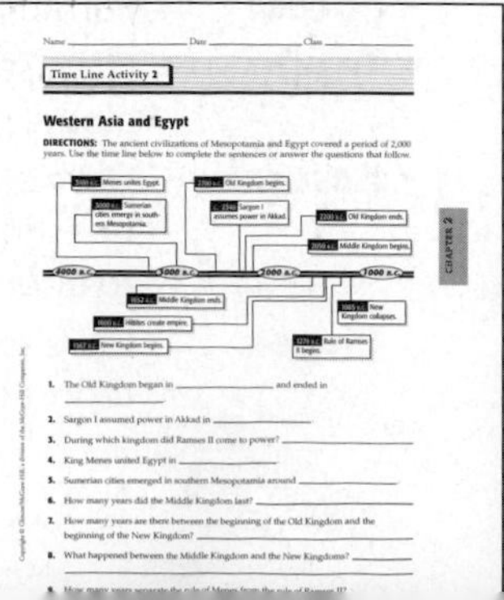

c. 1550 B.C. New Kingdom begins—through military campaigns Egypt becomes the most powerful empire in Southwest Asia

c. 1470 B.C. Hatshepsut dies and Thutmose III becomes pharaoh

c. 1364 B.C. Akhenaten (Amenhotep IV) takes the throne and establishes a monotheistic cult; religious disputes cause unrest

c. 1347 B.C. Tutankhamen's reign begins; he restores the old gods

c. 1279 B.C. The reign of Ramses II begins; he fights to regain control of lands in Africa and western Asia

c. 1070 B.C. Post-empire Egypt begins

1500

1000

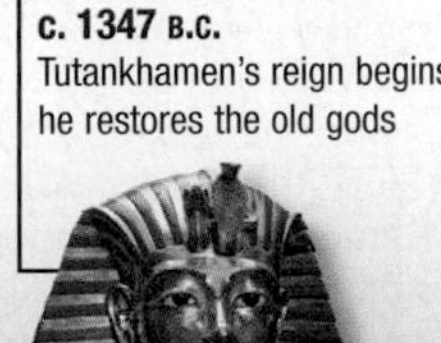

◂ Tutankhamen

Analyzing TIME LINES

1. **Differentiating** Which event shows how powerful the leadership was during the Old Kingdom?
2. **Making Inferences** What was the response to Akhenaten's religious reforms?

remain there. Pharaohs also sent traders to Kush, Syria, Mesopotamia, and Crete.

One feature of the Middle Kingdom was a new concern of the pharaohs for the people. In the Old Kingdom, the pharaoh had been seen as a god-king far removed from his people. Now he was portrayed as the shepherd of his people and expected to build public works and provide for the public welfare. Pharaohs of the Middle Kingdom undertook a number of helpful projects. The draining of swampland in the Nile Delta provided thousands of acres of new farmland. The digging of a canal to connect the Nile River to the Red Sea aided trade and transportation. R

The New Kingdom

The Middle Kingdom came to an end around 1650 B.C. with the invasion of Egypt by a group of people from western Asia known as the **Hyksos** (HIHK•SAHS). The Hyksos used horse-drawn war chariots to overwhelm the Egyptian soldiers, who fought from donkey carts.

For almost a hundred years, the Hyksos ruled much of Egypt. The conquered Egyptians learned a great deal from their conquerors. From the Hyksos, the Egyptians learned to use bronze in the making of their farming tools and their weapons. The Egyptians also mastered many of the military skills of the Hyksos, especially the use of horse-drawn war chariots. C

Eventually, a new dynasty of pharaohs used the new weapons to drive out the Hyksos and reunite Egypt. The New Kingdom was established and lasted approximately from 1550 B.C. to 1070 B.C. This reunification launched the Egyptians along a new militaristic path. During the period of the New Kingdom, Egypt created an empire and became the most powerful state in Southwest Asia.

Massive wealth boosted the power of the New Kingdom pharaohs. They showed their wealth by building new temples.

R Reading Strategy

Summarizing Ask: How did the pharaohs of the Middle Kingdom improve life for the common people? *(They drained swampland to create new farmland; they improved trade and transportation by digging a canal from the Nile River to the Red Sea.)* OL

C Critical Thinking

Determining Cause and Effect Ask: How did the invasion by the Hyksos change Egyptian history? *(Egyptians learned to use bronze, creating new farming tools and weapons. They improved their military skills, learning to use chariots. These advancements helped them drive out the Hyksos and establish their own empire.)* OL

Analyzing TIME LINES

Answers:
1. the building of the Great Pyramid of King Khufu at Giza in 2540 B.C.
2. Answers will vary, but should note that the reforms were likely not accepted since Tutankhamen restored the old gods about 20 years later.

Additional Support

Activity: Technology Connection

Analyzing Information Tell students that Tutankhamen is one of the most famous pharaohs of Egypt because of the discovery of his tomb, which appeared to have been untouched for 3,000 years when it was found by Howard Carter in 1922. Have students work in small groups to find out more about this landmark excavation, using Internet resources. Suggest that different groups focus on one or more of these topics: Howard Carter, King Tutankhamen and his reign, steps leading to the discovery of the tomb, the stages of the excavation, significant articles found in the tomb, the "King Tut" exhibition. Have students create a display to convey what they have learned and show why the information is important. **Ask:** Why was this such an amazing discovery? What conclusions about the ancient Egyptians might you draw from this discovery? OL

C Critical Thinking

Determining Cause and Effect **Ask:** What were the long-term effects of Akhenaton's reign? *(The removal of the old gods led to discontent with Akhenaton's rule. This weakened Egypt internally, which led to the loss of territory and an inability to fight off later invaders.)* **OL**

For additional practice on this skill, see the **Skills Handbook**.

✓Reading Check

Answer: Old: divine kings built pyramids; **Middle:** pharaohs as shepherds, period of expansion; **New:** militaristic, massive wealth, religious revolution

PEOPLE *in* HISTORY

Answers: Ramses II—No, because the terms of the treaty were favorable to the Hittites; **Hatshepsut**—Men were more respected as rulers; to show her power; so people would see her as strong.

Hatshepsut—one of the first women to become pharaoh—built a great temple at Deir el-Bahri, near Thebes. Hatshepsut was succeeded by her nephew Thutmose (thoot•MOH•suh) III. He led 17 military campaigns into Syria and Palestine and even reached as far east as the Euphrates River. His forces occupied Palestine and Syria and moved westward into Libya. Magnificent new buildings and temples were constructed to show the greatness of the empire.

The New Kingdom was not without troubles, however. The pharaoh Amenhotep IV introduced the worship of Aten, god of the sun disk, as the sole god. Amenhotep changed his own name to **Akhenaten,** "It is well with Aten," and closed the temples of other gods. In a society that had always been tolerant of many gods, Akhenaten's actions in destroying the old gods meant to many Egyptians the destruction of Egypt itself. Akhenaten's changes were soon undone after his death by the boy-pharaoh **Tutankhamen,** who restored the old gods.

C The upheavals associated with Amenhotep's religious revolution led to a loss of Egypt's empire. Under **Ramses II,** who reigned from c. 1279 B.C. to 1213 B.C., the Egyptians went back on the offensive. They regained control of Palestine but were unable to reestablish the borders of their earlier empire. New invasions in the 1200s B.C. by the "Sea Peoples," as the Egyptians called them, drove the Egyptians back within their old frontiers and ended the Egyptian Empire. The New Kingdom itself collapsed in 1070 B.C.

For the next thousand years, Egypt was dominated periodically by Libyans, Nubians, Persians, and, finally, Macedonians after the conquest of Alexander the Great. In the first century B.C., the pharaoh **Cleopatra VII** tried to reestablish Egypt's independence. Her involvement with Rome led to her defeat and suicide, and Egypt became a province in Rome's empire.

✓Reading Check **Contrasting** What were the major differences among the Old Kingdom, the Middle Kingdom, and the New Kingdom?

PEOPLE *in* HISTORY

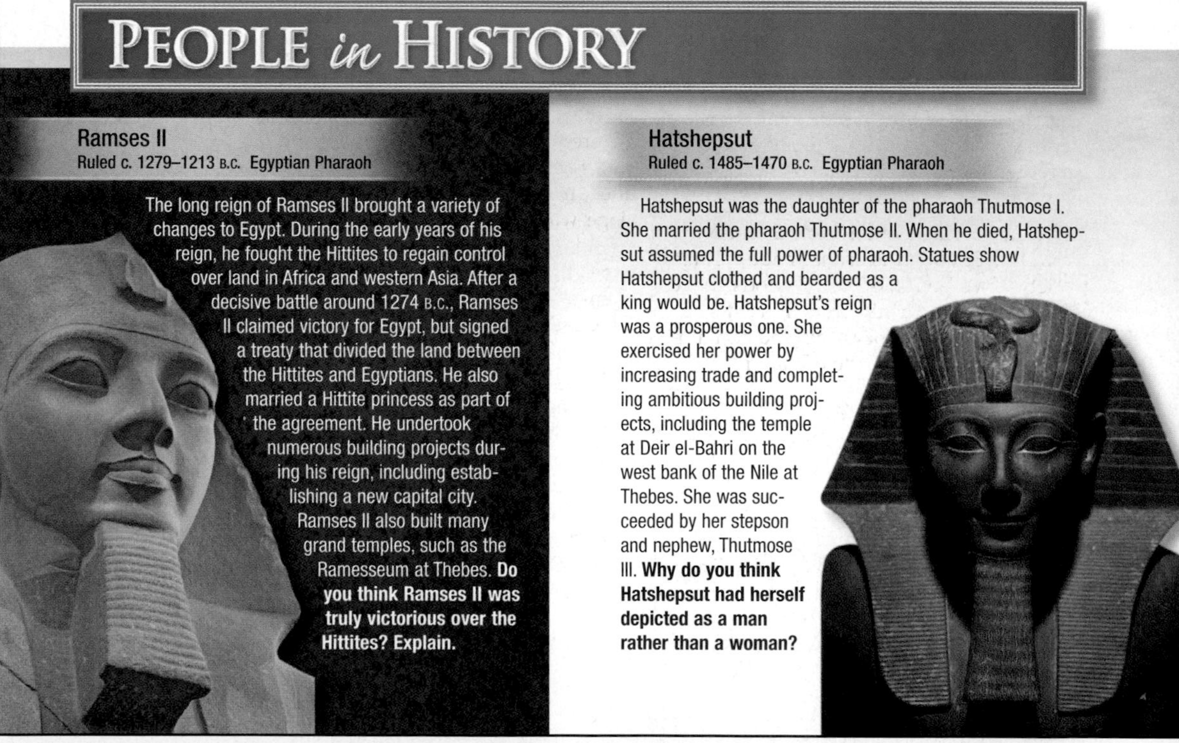

Ramses II
Ruled c. 1279–1213 B.C. Egyptian Pharaoh

The long reign of Ramses II brought a variety of changes to Egypt. During the early years of his reign, he fought the Hittites to regain control over land in Africa and western Asia. After a decisive battle around 1274 B.C., Ramses II claimed victory for Egypt, but signed a treaty that divided the land between the Hittites and Egyptians. He also married a Hittite princess as part of the agreement. He undertook numerous building projects during his reign, including establishing a new capital city. Ramses II also built many grand temples, such as the Ramesseum at Thebes. **Do you think Ramses II was truly victorious over the Hittites? Explain.**

Hatshepsut
Ruled c. 1485–1470 B.C. Egyptian Pharaoh

Hatshepsut was the daughter of the pharaoh Thutmose I. She married the pharaoh Thutmose II. When he died, Hatshepsut assumed the full power of pharaoh. Statues show Hatshepsut clothed and bearded as a king would be. Hatshepsut's reign was a prosperous one. She exercised her power by increasing trade and completing ambitious building projects, including the temple at Deir el-Bahri on the west bank of the Nile at Thebes. She was succeeded by her stepson and nephew, Thutmose III. **Why do you think Hatshepsut had herself depicted as a man rather than a woman?**

Additional Support

Extending the Content

Ramses II Some modern historians debate whether Ramses II deserves the epithet "the Great." Certainly in his lifetime, his people perceived him as such, and nine later pharaohs named themselves after him. Plus, Egypt maintained its imperial strength throughout his reign. But, he also excelled at "marketing" himself through monuments and records that proclaimed his greatness. **Ask:** Why did later pharaohs take his name? *(They wanted to associate themselves with his qualities and greatness.)* **OL**

Hatshepsut After her death, Hatshepsut's stepson Thutmose III ensured that she received a state funeral. A few years later, however, many of her monuments, bearing the record of her reign, were destroyed. Thutmose may have wanted to erase her memory out of revenge. A stronger possibility is that he wanted her reign to fade into obscurity so as not to detract from his. **Ask:** Why would Thutmose have wanted to draw attention away from Hatshepsut? *(Her reign was remarkable, not just because she was a woman.)* **OL**

Life in Ancient Egypt

MAIN IDEA Egyptian society was organized into classes.

HISTORY & YOU How does wealth or social status affect lifestyle? Learn how various classes of Egyptians lived.

Egyptian society was highly structured. The existence of a large lower class of peasants allowed a small upper class of the pharaoh and nobles to live in splendor and to build elaborate temples and pyramids. Class was important in determining individual rights.

Egyptian Society

Over a period of thousands of years, Egyptian society maintained a simple structure. It was organized like a pyramid, with the god-king at the top. The pharaoh was surrounded by an upper class of nobles and priests, who joined in the elaborate rituals of the pharaoh's life. The members of this ruling class ran the government and managed their own landed estates, which provided much of their wealth.

Below the upper class were merchants, artisans, scribes, and tax collectors. Middle-class homes, mostly in the city, were comfortable but not elegant. Merchants carried on an active trade up and down the Nile, as well as in local markets. Some merchants also engaged in international **W** trade. They were sent by the pharaoh to Crete and Syria to obtain wood and other products. Egyptian artisans made a huge variety of well-built, beautiful goods: stone dishes; wooden furniture; painted boxes; gold, silver, and copper tools and containers; paper and rope made of papyrus; and linen clothing.

By far, the largest number of people in Egypt simply worked the land. In theory, the pharaoh owned all the land but granted portions of it to his subjects. Large sections of land were held by nobles and by the priests who supervised the numerous temples. Most of the lower classes were peasants who farmed the land of these estates. They paid taxes in the form of crops to the pharaoh, nobles, and priests; lived in small villages; and provided military service and forced labor for building projects.

Daily Life in Ancient Egypt

Ancient Egyptians had a positive attitude toward daily life on Earth. They married young (girls at 12 and boys at 14) and established homes and families. Monogamy (marriage to one person) was the general rule, but a husband could have additional wives if his first wife was childless.

The husband was master in the house, but wives were very well respected. Wives were in charge of the household and the education of the children. From a book of wise sayings came this advice:

See page R34 to read excerpts from Vizier Ptah-hotep's *An Egyptian Father's Advice to His Son* in the **Primary Sources and Literature Library.**

PRIMARY SOURCE

> "If you are a man of standing, you should love your wife at home as is fitting. Fill her belly; clothe her back. . . . Make her heart glad as long as you live."
>
> —B.G. Trigger et al., *Ancient Egypt: A Social History*

R

Women's property and inheritance stayed in their hands, even in marriage. Most careers and public offices were closed to women, but some women did operate businesses. Peasant women worked long hours in the fields and in the home. Upper-class women could become priestesses, and four queens became pharaohs.

Parents arranged marriages for their children. Their chief concerns were family and property. The main purpose of marriage was to produce children, especially sons. Only sons could carry on the family name. Daughters were not ignored, however, and numerous tomb paintings show the close and affectionate relationship parents had with both sons and daughters. Although marriages were arranged, the surviving love poems from ancient Egypt suggest that some marriages included an element of romance. Marriages could and did end in divorce, which included compensation for the wife.

✓Reading Check **Summarizing** List the social classes of ancient Egypt and identify the contributions each class made to society.

W Writing Support

Expository Writing Have students write an essay in which they compare and contrast aspects of Mesopotamian and Egyptian society. Encourage them to cite specific examples to support their comparisons. They might wish to focus on social structure, religion, government, economy, and culture. **AL**

R Reading Strategy

Summarizing Ask: What were the primary responsibilities of a wife in an Egyptian home? *(Wives were in charge of the household and children's education.)* **OL**

✓Reading Check

Answer: At the top was the ruling class of pharaohs, nobles, and priests. This class ran the government and managed their own landed estates. Below this class was a middle class of merchants, artisans, scribes, and tax collectors. These people obtained wealth through trade or created goods. At the bottom was a large peasant class. They farmed the land and provided military service and forced labor for building projects.

Additional Support

Activity: Economics Connection

Taking Notes Ask: Is bartering still used in the modern economy? Discuss with students when they have bartered or seen examples of bartering. For example, have they ever offered to help a classmate in math in return for help in another class? Tell students that the ancient Egyptians bartered. Then ask students to work in pairs to find out more about bartering in ancient Egypt, such as:

- How were the values of goods or services decided?
- How were wages and taxes paid?
- What kinds of goods were most frequently bartered?

Have students take notes on the information they find, including specific examples of exchanges of goods and services. Have them develop a short oral presentation or role play, which takes place in an ancient Egyptian marketplace, to illustrate the principles of bartering. **AL**

R **Reading Strategy**

Inferring Ask: Why did the Egyptians have a different form of writing for everyday purposes? *(A faster method of writing was preferable for daily business and communication purposes.)* **OL**

DOCUMENT-BASED QUESTIONS

Answers:

1. Scribes were well respected, since writing required skill and recording the lives of the pharaohs was an important job.
2. Merchants could write lists of items to buy or sell, debts and inventories could be recorded, and agreements could be signed.

Additional Support

Egyptian Accomplishments

MAIN IDEA Egyptians developed complex writing and made advances in the arts and sciences.

HISTORY & YOU How would society be affected if girls and boys were educated differently? Read about Egyptian education.

R Although hieroglyphics is the best-known form of Egyptian writing, it was not the form people most commonly used. Writing for everyday purposes, including business, was less likely to be preserved than writing in temples and tombs. Only boys from the upper or middle classes would receive formal education in any system of writing.

Writing and Education

One system of writing in Egypt emerged around 3000 B.C. The Greeks later called this earliest Egyptian writing **hieroglyphics,** meaning "priest-carvings" or "sacred writings."

HISTORY & ARTS PRIMARY SOURCE

Hieroglyphics

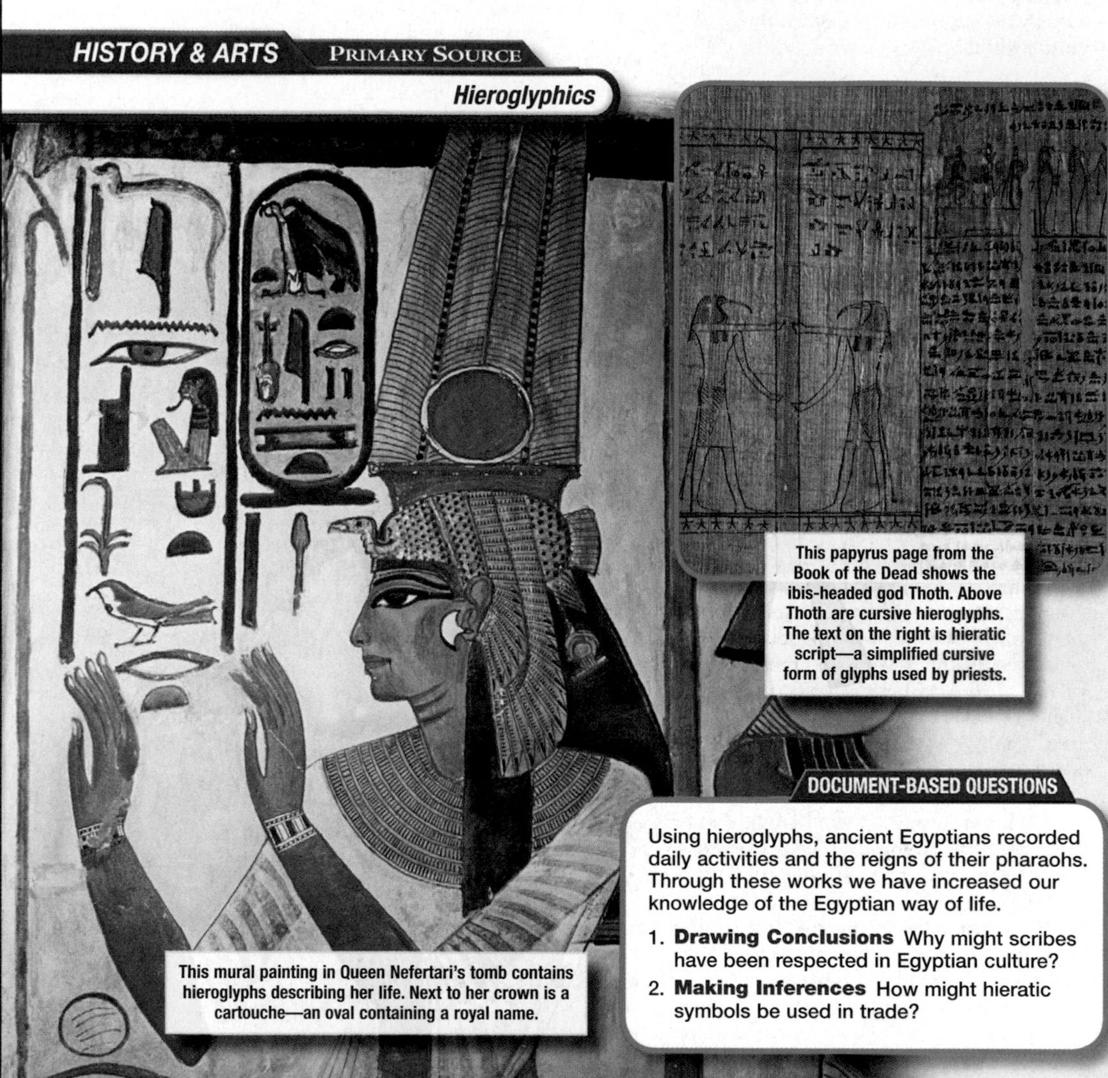

This mural painting in Queen Nefertari's tomb contains hieroglyphs describing her life. Next to her crown is a cartouche—an oval containing a royal name.

This papyrus page from the Book of the Dead shows the ibis-headed god Thoth. Above Thoth are cursive hieroglyphs. The text on the right is hieratic script—a simplified cursive form of glyphs used by priests.

DOCUMENT-BASED QUESTIONS

Using hieroglyphs, ancient Egyptians recorded daily activities and the reigns of their pharaohs. Through these works we have increased our knowledge of the Egyptian way of life.

1. **Drawing Conclusions** Why might scribes have been respected in Egyptian culture?
2. **Making Inferences** How might hieratic symbols be used in trade?

Extending the Content

Did You Know? Egyptian hieroglyphs were used from about 3300 B.C. to about A.D. 300. At that time, the Coptic language, which was composed of the Greek alphabet and just a few hieroglyphs, developed. Over the years, Coptic replaced hieroglyphics, and knowledge of the older script was lost. This meant that ancient documents and monuments could not be translated. In 1799, however, part of a stela was found by soldiers digging the foundation for a fort near Rosetta in the Nile Delta. This stone had hieroglyphs as well as text in ancient Greek—and both seemed to be translations of the same inscription. Scholars Thomas Young and Jean-François Champollion were able to work from the ancient Greek to decipher the meaning of the hieroglyphs, thus cracking the code of the lost language of the ancient Egyptians. Today, the Rosetta Stone can be found in the British Museum.

The hieroglyphic system of writing, which used both pictures and more abstract forms, was complex. Learning and practicing it took much time and skill. Hieroglyphic script was used for writing on temple walls and in tombs. A highly simplified version of hieroglyphics, known as **hieratic script**, came into being. It used the same principles as hieroglyphic writing, but the drawings were simplified by using dashes, strokes, and curves to represent them. Hieratic script was used for business transactions, record keeping, and the general needs of daily life.

Egyptian hieroglyphs were at first carved in stone. Later, hieratic script was written on papyrus, a paper made from the papyrus reed that grew along the Nile. Most of the ancient Egyptian literature that has come down to us was written on rolls of papyrus.

The Egyptian scribes were masters of the art of writing and also its teachers. At the age of 10, boys of the upper classes went to schools run by scribes. Training to be a scribe took many years. Students learned to read and write by copying texts. Discipline was strict, as is evident from the following Egyptian saying: "A boy's ears are on his back. He listens only when he is beaten." Girls remained at home and learned housekeeping skills from their mothers.

Art and Science

Pyramids, temples, and other monuments bear witness to the architectural and artistic achievements of the ancient Egyptians. Artists and sculptors were expected to follow particular formulas in style. This gave Egyptian art a distinctive look for many thousands of years. For example, the human body was often portrayed as a combination of profile, semi-profile, and frontal view to accurately represent each part.

Egyptians also made advances in mathematics. Mathematics helped them in building their massive monuments. Egyptians were able to calculate area and volume and used geometry to survey flooded land.

The Egyptians developed an accurate 365-day calendar by basing their year not only on the movements of the moon, but also the bright star Sirius. Sirius rises in the sky just before the annual flooding of the Nile River, providing a standard date from which to calculate.

The practice of embalming (preserving a dead body to protect it from decay) led to medical expertise in human anatomy. Archaeologists have recovered directions from doctors for using splints, bandages, and compresses for treating fractures, wounds, and disease. Other ancient civilizations acquired medical knowledge from the Egyptians.

✓Reading Check **Describing** What was distinctive about Egyptian art?

SECTION 2 REVIEW

Vocabulary
1. **Explain** the significance of: Nile River, major, Lower Egypt, Upper Egypt, identifying, Menes, dynasty, pharaoh, bureaucracy, vizier, physical, mummification, Giza, Hyksos, Hatshepsut, Akhenaten, Tutankhamen, Ramses II, Cleopatra VII, hieroglyphics, hieratic script.

Main Ideas
2. **Explain** why Egyptians saw the Middle Kingdom as a golden age.
3. **Describe** some of the rights Egyptian women had.
4. **Create** a diagram like the one shown below to describe the impact the Nile had on life in ancient Egypt.

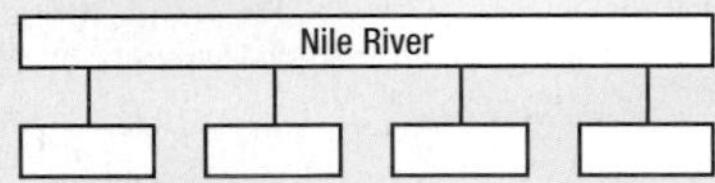

Critical Thinking
5. **BIG Idea Determining Cause and Effect** How did the Hyksos both threaten and improve Egypt's security?
6. **Drawing Conclusions** What is the significance of the famous Egyptian myth of the struggle between Osiris and his evil brother Seth? Why did Osiris take on an important role for the Egyptians?
7. **Analyzing Visuals** Examine the image on page 42. How did ancient Egyptians paint the human form?

Writing About History
8. **Descriptive Writing** Assume you are a tour guide leading a tour of the Great Pyramid. Explain to your group why the pyramids were built and what historians believe is their significance. Create an advertising brochure to promote and sell your tour.

History ONLINE
For help with the concepts in this section of *Glencoe World History*, go to glencoe.com and click Study Central™.

43

✓Reading Check

Answer: Egyptian artists and sculptors followed stylistic formulas. For example, the human body was often painted in profile, semi-profile, and frontal views.

Assess

History ONLINE

Study Central provides summaries, interactive games, and online graphic organizers to help students review content.

Close

Summarizing Ask: What were the major accomplishments of the Egyptian civilization? *(The pyramids showed the Egyptians' engineering and architectural expertise; other civilizations drew upon their medical knowledge; they made mathematical advances and developed an accurate 365-day calendar.)* **OL**

Answers

1. Definitions for the vocabulary words are found in the section and the Glossary.
2. Egypt expanded during this period of stability. Pharaohs took better care of their people.
3. They could own property and run some businesses. They received compensation if divorced.
4. **Impact of Nile:** provided fertile farmland, facilitated travel, cataracts aided protection, regular flooding influenced religion
5. They conquered Egypt, but from them Egyptians learned new technologies and better ways to defend themselves.
6. By resurrecting Osiris, Isis created the idea of life after death. The myth also symbolized the flooding of the Nile and the new life it brought each year.
7. The head, arms, and legs were shown in profile, but the body faced forward. The eye is enlarged. The hands and feet are not opposite, but duplicated.
8. Students should explain that the pyramid is a tomb and that it symbolizes the power of the pharaohs and a belief in an afterlife.

Focus

Introducing Social History
Before students examine the images and text, draw upon their previous knowledge by asking them to identify the functions of the ancient Egyptian tombs. List their ideas on the board and return to them after discussing the feature. Then have students take turns reading the text aloud.

Teach

C1 Critical Thinking

Making Generalizations
Ask: How did the ancient Egyptians most likely feel about death? *(For those who believed they led a good life, death was not something to be feared. In fact, death was something to be anticipated with pleasure.)* OL

C2 Critical Thinking

Drawing Conclusions **Ask:** What does this *ka* statue suggest about the Egyptians' impression of their role in the afterlife? *(They would occupy similar positions after their death as they did during their life.)* OL

Additional Support

Preparing for the Afterlife

C1 Every culture must deal with death. Death for Egyptians was a gateway to an eternal afterlife. The Egyptians believed the god Osiris judged the dead and that those who led a good life would enjoy an eternity of the most pleasant activities they enjoyed on earth.

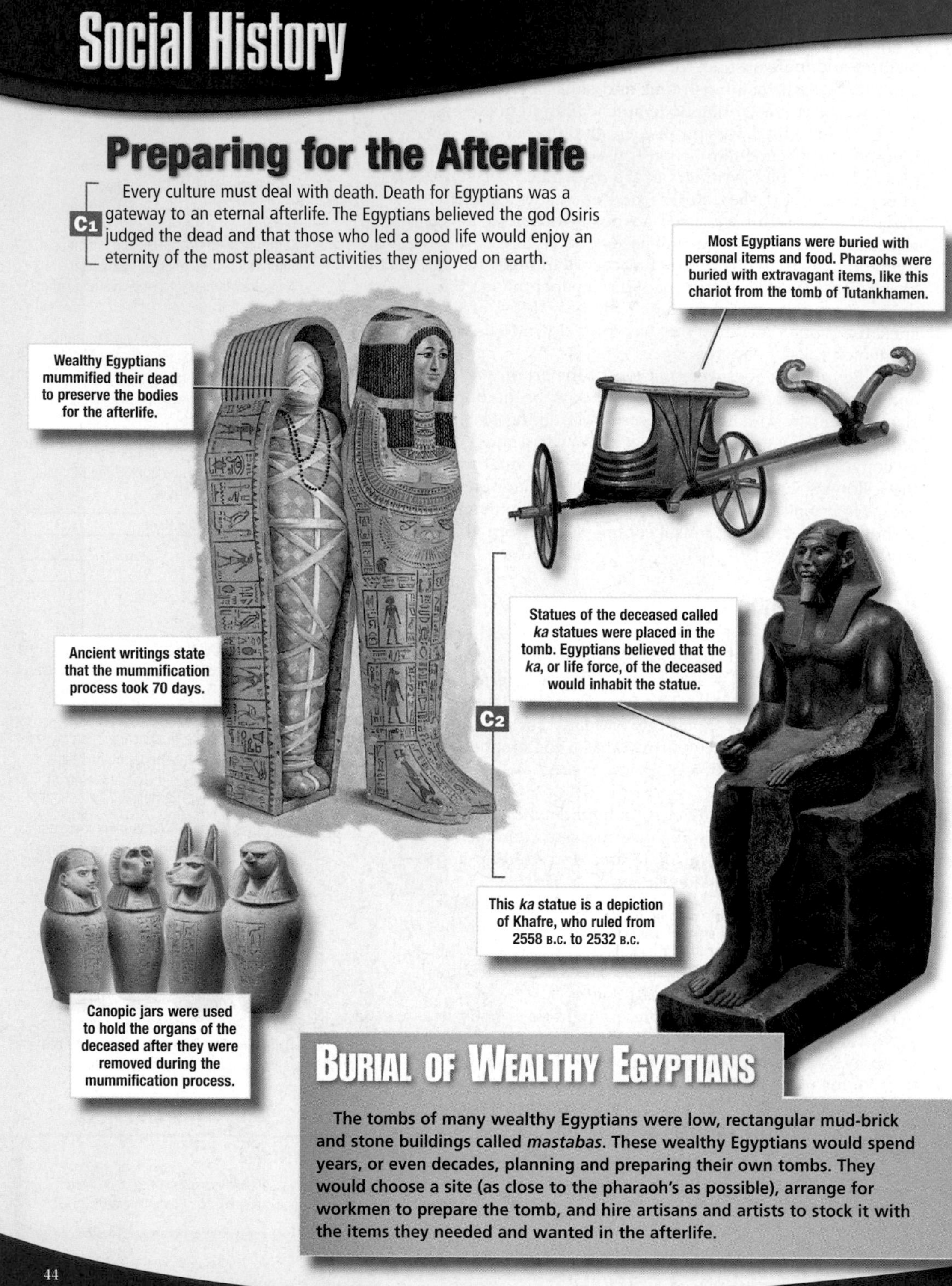

Most Egyptians were buried with personal items and food. Pharaohs were buried with extravagant items, like this chariot from the tomb of Tutankhamen.

Wealthy Egyptians mummified their dead to preserve the bodies for the afterlife.

Ancient writings state that the mummification process took 70 days.

C2 Statues of the deceased called *ka* statues were placed in the tomb. Egyptians believed that the *ka*, or life force, of the deceased would inhabit the statue.

This *ka* statue is a depiction of Khafre, who ruled from 2558 B.C. to 2532 B.C.

Canopic jars were used to hold the organs of the deceased after they were removed during the mummification process.

Burial of Wealthy Egyptians

The tombs of many wealthy Egyptians were low, rectangular mud-brick and stone buildings called *mastabas*. These wealthy Egyptians would spend years, or even decades, planning and preparing their own tombs. They would choose a site (as close to the pharaoh's as possible), arrange for workmen to prepare the tomb, and hire artisans and artists to stock it with the items they needed and wanted in the afterlife.

Background

Valley of the Kings The transition to pyramids may have occurred after a ruler placed several *mastabas* on top of each other, forming a kind of step pyramid. Eventually step pyramids evolved into the smooth-sided ones favored by the pharaohs of the Old Kingdom. Later rulers, however, realized that pyramids were an invitation to grave robbers. They returned to the earlier practice of tunneling through rock to locate their burial sites. Most pharaohs of the New Kingdom placed their tombs in the Valley of the Kings, an area west of the Nile River in Upper Egypt known as Thebes. Although each tomb was different, they had some similarities. Generally, they had long hallways that descended into the mountain with several shafts and the main chamber at the end. Since the 19th century, the Valley of the Kings has been extensively excavated. In fact, many archaeologists believed that Howard Carter had found the last unexplored tomb in 1922, when he unearthed King Tutankhamen's burial site. But, the discovery of a new tomb in 2006 revealed that there is much left to learn from the Valley of the Kings.

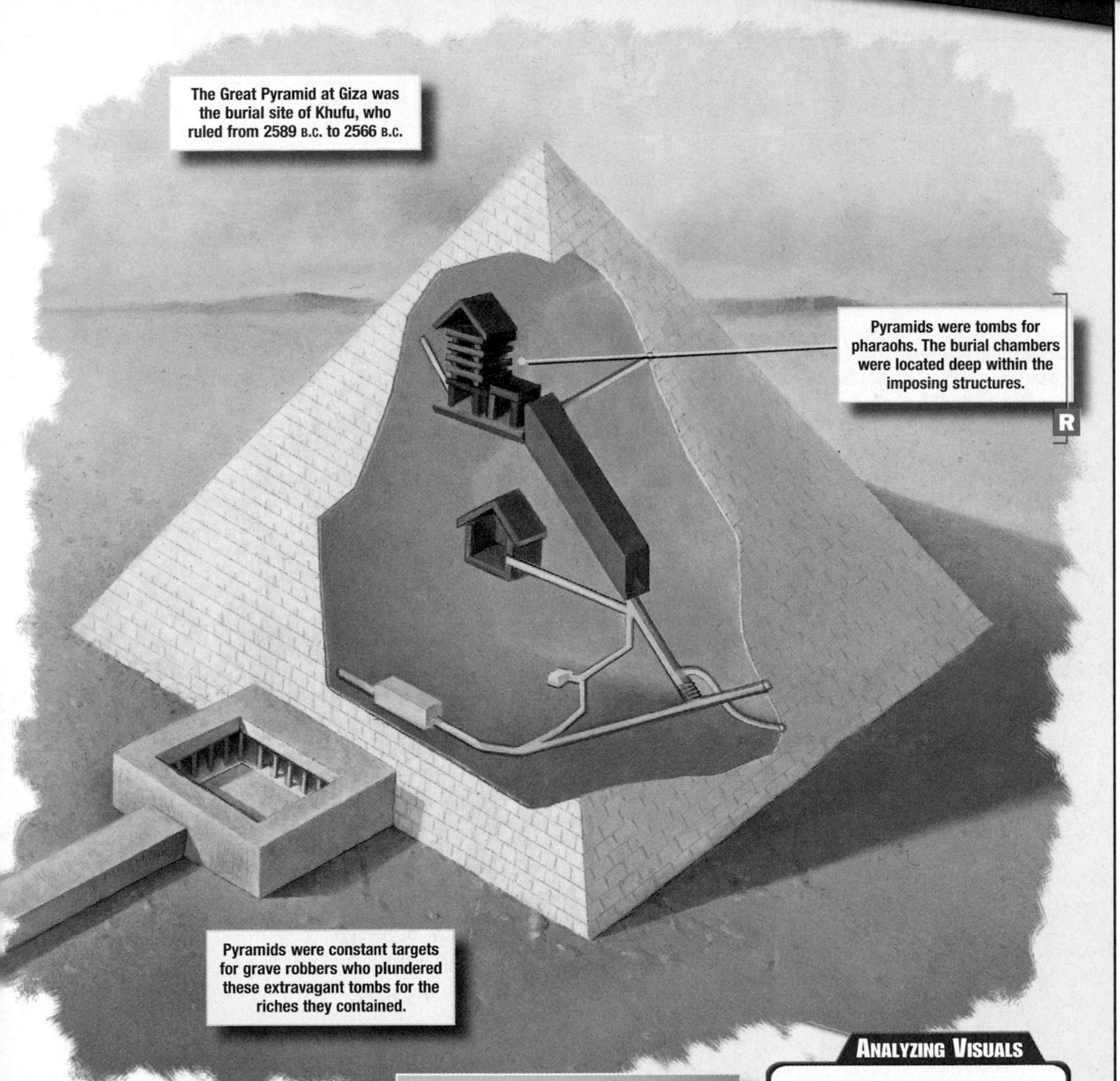

BURIAL OF PEASANTS

The majority of Egyptians could not afford the elaborate funerals of the upper class. Most—including farmworkers and laborers—were merely wrapped in cloth and placed in individual or communal graves. The afterlife was of great importance to Egyptians at all levels of society, so relatives might leave some food or simple objects with them. That way, the dead would be comforted by familiar things.

ANALYZING VISUALS

1. **Making Inferences** How was the class structure of ancient Egyptian society reflected in its funerary practices?
2. **Comparing** How was the ancient Egyptian view of death similar to and different from views of death today?

45

R Reading Strategy

Inferring Ask: What is the purpose of the burial chamber's location within the pyramid? *(It is placed deep within the structure to protect it from intruders.)* **OL**

Assess/Close

Summarizing Have students explain what the burial practices reveal about the Egyptian culture.

ANALYZING VISUALS

Answers:

1. Peasants were buried in communal graves. They were simply wrapped in cloth, although objects or food usually accompanied them. The wealthy, however, had elaborate tombs or *mastabas* built and stocked with the goods they would want and need in the afterlife.
2. Various religious groups still believe in an afterlife as the Egyptians did. Most people today do not stock tombs with food or treasured items, however, since their idea of an afterlife involves their soul or spirit rather than their body.

Activity: Interdisciplinary Connection

Art Divide students into small groups. Tell them that they will be creating a model of a royal Egyptian tomb. To do this, they will first need to research facts about actual tombs using the Internet. Once they have acquired information about the art, contents, and structure of burial chambers, they should begin by constructing a tomb, using a cardboard box or other materials. Then they should decorate the interior with appropriate scenes and furnish their tomb with several items, including a sarcophagus and other artifacts such as those that have been recovered at Egyptian burial sites. After students have built their models, have them display and present them to the class.

Ask: Which items would be found in most tombs? *(Answers may include items such as the sarcophagus, funeral mask, canopic jars, and jars of food.)* **OL**

Suggestions for rubrics may be found in the Authentic Assessment Activities and Rubrics booklet.

Focus

Bellringer

Daily Focus Transparency 2.3

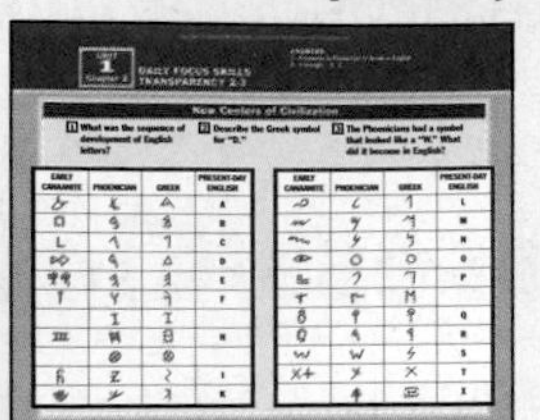

GUIDE TO READING

Answers to Graphic:

Phoenicians: improved ships; developed sea trade; charted new sea routes; created colonies in the western Mediterranean; exported alphabet

Section Spotlight Video

To generate student interest and provide a springboard for class discussion, access the Chapter 2, Section 3 video at glencoe.com or on the video DVD.

Resource Manager

SECTION 3

New Centers of Civilization

GUIDE TO READING

The BIG Idea

Ideas, Beliefs, and Values The Israelites' belief in one God resulted in a distinct society.

Content Vocabulary

- pastoral nomad *(p. 46)*
- monotheistic *(p. 50)*

Academic Vocabulary

- created *(p. 46)*
- technology *(p. 46)*
- domesticated *(p. 46)*

People and Places

- Indo-Europeans *(p. 46)*
- Hittites *(p. 47)*
- Phoenicians *(p. 48)*
- Israelites *(p. 49)*
- King Solomon *(p. 49)*
- Jerusalem *(p. 49)*

Reading Strategy

Summarizing Information As you read, complete a diagram like the one below to show how the Phoenicians affected development of civilization in Southwest Asia.

Phoenicians

Nomadic peoples played an important role in the spread of civilization in western and central Asia. After about 1200 B.C., there was no dominant power in the region. The Phoenicians emerged as the most important trading kingdom in the Mediterranean area. The Israelites did not create an empire, but they left a world religion, Judaism, that influenced the later religions of Christianity and Islam.

The Role of Nomadic Peoples

MAIN IDEA Nomadic peoples, especially the Indo-Europeans, served an important function for civilized societies by spreading goods and new technology.

HISTORY & YOU Why are residents of a community sometimes suspicious of or hostile to strangers? Learn how civilizations related to nomads.

Our story of civilization so far has focused on Mesopotamia and Egypt. Recent evidence suggests that another civilization flourished in central Asia (in what are now the republics of Turkmenistan and Uzbekistan) around 4,000 years ago. These people built mud-brick buildings, raised sheep and goats, had bronze tools, and used irrigation to grow wheat and barley. Recently discovered inscriptions show that these early people may have had writing.

On the fringes of these civilizations lived nomadic peoples who depended on hunting and gathering, herding, and sometimes farming for their survival. Most important were the **pastoral nomads** who on occasion overran settled communities and then **created** their own empires. Pastoral nomads **domesticated** animals for food and clothing. They followed regular migratory routes to provide food for their animals.

People who lived in settled communities often viewed nomads as hostile and barbaric. The groups did interact, however. Nomads traded animals and animal products for grains and vegetables they were unable to grow. Pastoral nomads also carried products between civilized centers. In this way nomads often passed on new **technology,** such as the use of bronze and iron, that helped strengthen civilizations. When overpopulation or drought disrupted the pastoral nomads' normal patterns, however, they often attacked the civilized communities to obtain relief.

The **Indo-Europeans** were one of the most important nomadic peoples. The term *Indo-European* refers to a particular group of people who spoke a language derived from a single parent tongue. Indo-European languages include Greek, Latin, Persian, Sanskrit, and the Germanic languages. The original Indo-Europeans were

R Reading Strategies	C Critical Thinking	D Differentiated Instruction	W Writing Support	S Skill Practice
Teacher Edition • Det. Importance, p. 48 • Sequencing Info., p. 49 **Additional Resources** • Guid. Read. Act., URB p. 86 • Read. Ess. & Note-Taking Guide, p. 13	**Teacher Edition** • Det. Cause/Effect, p. 48 • Ident. Cent. Issues, p. 51 **Additional Resources** • People in World Hist. Act., URB p. 76 • Section Quiz, p. 13	**Teacher Edition** • Kinesthetic, p. 49 **Additional Resources** • Read. Skills Act., URB p. 53	**Teacher Edition** • Expository Writing, p. 50 **Additional Resources** • Writer's Guidebook, p. 31	**Teacher Edition** • Using Geo. Skills, p. 47 **Additional Resources** • Read. Strat. for SS, p. 50

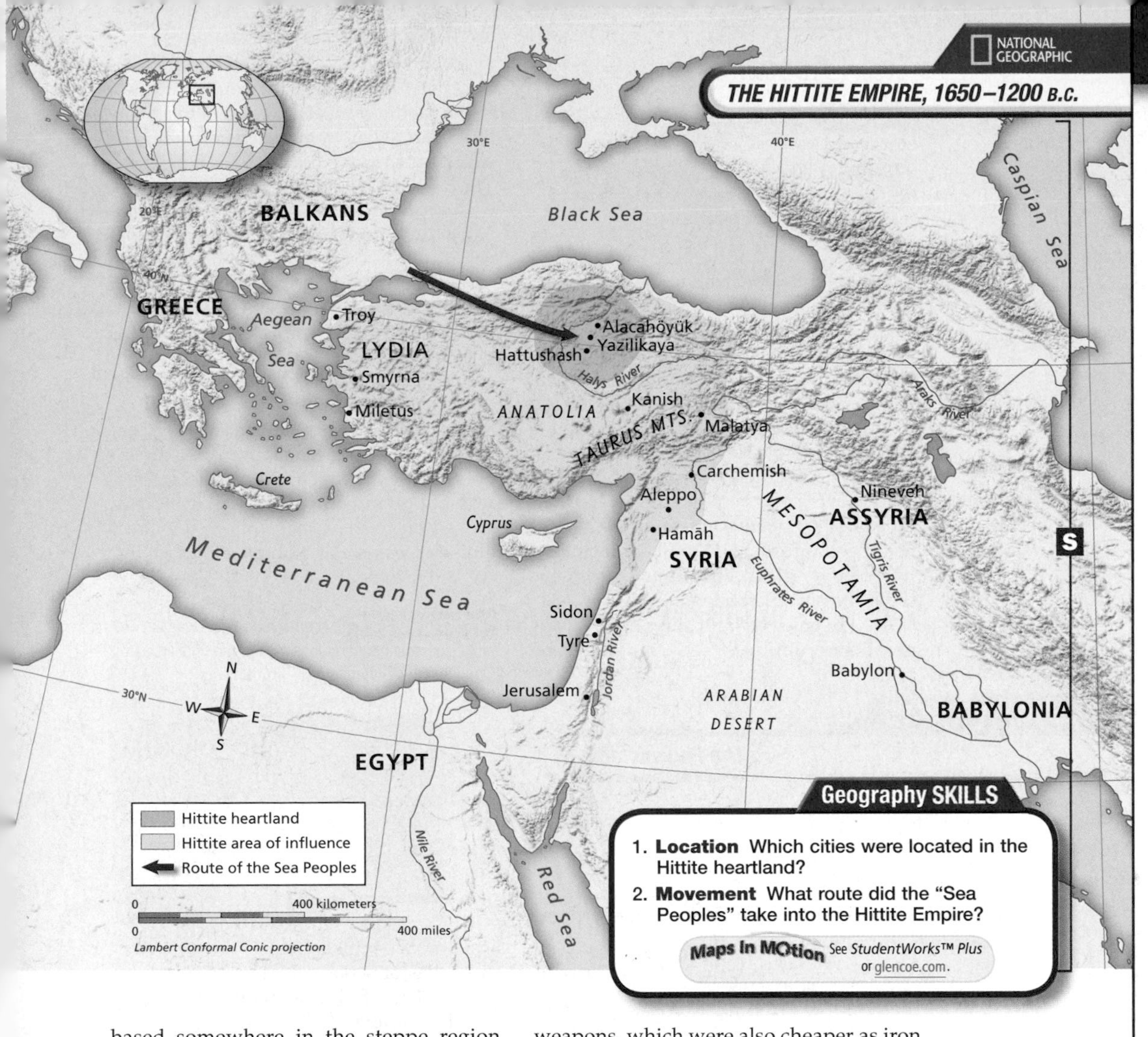

Geography SKILLS

1. **Location** Which cities were located in the Hittite heartland?
2. **Movement** What route did the "Sea Peoples" take into the Hittite Empire?

Maps In MOtion See *StudentWorks™ Plus* or glencoe.com.

based somewhere in the steppe region north of the Black Sea or in Southwest Asia. Around 2000 B.C. they began to move into Europe, India, and western Asia. One group moved into Asia Minor and Anatolia around 1750 B.C. With the native peoples, they formed the Hittite kingdom with its capital at Hattushash (Bogazköy in modern Turkey).

Between 1600 B.C. and 1200 B.C., the **Hittites** created an empire in western Asia and threatened the power of the Egyptians. The Hittites were the first Indo-Europeans to use iron. Iron made stronger weapons, which were also cheaper as iron ore was abundant. New invaders, the "Sea Peoples," destroyed the Hittite Empire.

The end of the Hittite kingdom and the weakening of Egypt around 1200 B.C. temporarily left no dominant powers in western Asia. As a result, several small kingdoms and city-states emerged, notably around Syria and Palestine. The Phoenicians were one of these peoples.

✓Reading Check **Identifying** Who were the first Indo-Europeans to use iron?

Teach

S Skill Practice

Using Geography Skills

Discuss the geographical location of the Hittite Empire on the Anatolian peninsula. Point out that a series of waterways connects the Mediterranean Sea and the Black Sea. Tell students that this peninsula will be of great strategic value to other empires they will read about later. **Ask:** **Why was Egypt vulnerable to attack from the Hittites?** *(The Hittites could attack Egypt by sea.)* **OL**

For additional practice on this skill, see the **Skills Handbook**.

Geography SKILLS

Answers:

1. Hattushash, the capital; Alacahöyük; and Yazilikaya
2. They approached from the Mediterranean Sea.

✓Reading Check

Answer: the Hittites

Hands-On Chapter Project
Step 3

Publishing a Coffee Table Book

Students create the next chapter of their book.

Step 3: Writing the Third Chapter

Directions: Write the Big Idea on the board. Tell students that in this chapter of their book, they will examine the contributions of the Indo-European and Semitic language speakers to western civilization, focusing on the Hittites, Phoenicians, and Israelites. Remind students to present their information in an appealing format. For their foldout page, they might wish to create a collage that highlights key ideas connected to each group, such as the use of iron by the Hittites or the construction of the First Temple by Solomon.

Summarizing: Have groups discuss what they have learned about the Big Idea through their work on this chapter. **OL**

(Chapter Project is continued in Section 4.)

C Critical Thinking

Determining Cause and Effect Ask: How did the location of the Phoenicians influence the growth of their civilization? *(Their natural resources and proximity to the sea benefited trade. Through trade, they grew prosperous, spread their culture, and assimilated ideas from other societies.)* **OL**

R Reading Strategy

Determining Importance
Ask: How would an alphabet make writing more efficient? *(An alphabet would make writing more accessible and versatile.)* **OL**

✓Reading Check

Answer: the alphabet

DOCUMENT-BASED QUESTIONS

Answers:

1. From it derived the Greek alphabet and from the Greek, the Roman, or Latin.
2. They show communication between trading powers; they show the importance of international communication.

Additional Support

The Phoenicians

MAIN IDEA The Phoenicians created an international trade empire and invented an alphabet.

HISTORY & YOU Why would using an alphabet make writing easier than using picture symbols? Learn about the Phoenician alphabet.

The **Phoenicians** lived in the area of Palestine along the Mediterranean coast on a narrow band of land 120 miles (193 km) long. After the downfall of the Hittites and the Egyptians, the newfound political independence of the Phoenicians helped them expand their trade. Trade had long been the basis of their prosperity. The chief cities of Phoenicia—Byblos, Tyre, and Sidon—were ports on the eastern Mediterranean. The Phoenicians produced a number of goods for foreign markets, including purple dye, glass, and lumber from the cedar forests of Lebanon.

The Phoenicians built ships and became great international sea traders. They eventually created a trade empire. The Phoenicians charted new routes not only in the Mediterranean but also in the Atlantic Ocean, where they reached Britain and sailed south along the west coast of Africa. They set up a number of colonies in the western Mediterranean. Carthage, on the North African coast, was their most famous colony.

Phoenician culture is best known for its alphabet. The Phoenicians, who spoke a Semitic language, simplified their writing by using 22 different signs to represent the sounds of their speech. These 22 characters, or letters, could be used to spell out all the words in the Phoenician language. Although the Phoenicians were not the only people to invent an alphabet, theirs was important because it was eventually passed on to the Greeks. From the Greek alphabet came the Roman alphabet that we still use today.

✓Reading Check **Identifying** What was the most significant cultural invention of the Phoenicians?

HISTORY & ARTS

The Phoenicians

It is hard to separate the Phoenicians' cultural accomplishments from their economic accomplishments. Their sophisticated ships took them to far-off lands, spreading their alphabet, as well as their trade goods, throughout the Mediterranean.

Hebrew, Phoenician, and Latin Alphabets

Hebrew

א ב ג ד ה ו ז ח ט י כ ל מ נ ס ע פ צ ק ר ש ת

Phoenician

𐤀𐤁𐤂𐤃𐤄𐤅𐤆𐤇𐤈𐤉𐤊𐤋𐤌𐤍𐤎𐤏𐤐𐤑𐤒𐤓𐤔𐤕

Imperial Latin

A B C D E F G H I K L M N O P Q R S T V X Y Z

Imperial Latin did not distinguish between I and J or between V and U. There was no W. Y and Z were introduced after 100 B.C. for foreign words only.

The Phoenician alphabet influenced the Greek alphabet, which was the basis for the Latin, or Roman, alphabet.

Marker with Greek and Phoenician—bilingual—inscription on Malta

DOCUMENT-BASED QUESTIONS

1. **Making Inferences** Why is the Phoenician alphabet important to our society?
2. **Explaining** Why would there have been ancient bilingual documents and markers?

Activity: Interdisciplinary Connection

Comparing and Contrasting Have students look at the Phoenician, Greek, and English alphabets. **Ask:** Which characters are similar in each? *(Students may say A, K, O, M.)* Remind students that an alphabet is based on sounds. Discuss with students why some alphabets may have more or fewer characters. *(There may be more or fewer sounds in the language.)* Then ask students to work together to find examples of other written alphabets, using the dictionary or the Internet. As a class, create a language tree that shows the various branches of each family of languages. Place students' alphabets in the appropriate location on the tree, and then discuss similarities and differences among them. **OL**

The Israelites

MAIN IDEA The Israelites had lasting influence through their religious beliefs rather than from military power.

HISTORY & YOU How might religious beliefs affect the ways in which people interact? Read to learn about the interaction between religions in the eastern Mediterranean.

To the south of the Phoenicians lived another group of Semitic-speaking people known as the **Israelites.** They were a minor factor in the politics of the region. However, their religion—known today as Judaism—flourished and later influenced the religions of Christianity and Islam.

Much of the Israelites' history and religious beliefs was eventually written down in the Hebrew Bible, which is known to Christians as the Old Testament. According to Israelite traditions, they are descendants of the patriarch Abraham. Their ancestors migrated from Mesopotamia to Canaan. Their lifestyle was based on grazing animals rather than on farming. Then, because of drought, the Israelites moved to Egypt, where they were enslaved until Moses led them out of Egypt. They wandered for many years in the desert until they returned to Canaan.

Some interpretations of recent archaeological evidence contradict the details of the biblical account. It is generally agreed, however, that between 1200 B.C. and 1000 B.C., the Israelites organized in tribes and established a united kingdom known as Israel.

The United Kingdom

Under King David, who ruled from about 1010 B.C. to 970 B.C., the Israelites had established control over all the land that came to be called Israel and made **Jerusalem** into its capital. David's son **King Solomon** expanded the government and army and encouraged trade. Solomon is best known for building a temple in the city of Jerusalem. The Israelites viewed the temple as the symbolic center of their religion and of the Israelite kingdom itself. Under King Solomon, ancient Israel reached the height of its power.

King Solomon was also known for his wisdom. Once, two women brought a child before him, each claiming that she was the child's mother. Solomon ordered his servant to cut the child in half, giving one half to each woman. The first woman objected: "Please, my lord, give her the living baby! Don't kill him!" The second woman replied, "Neither I nor you shall have him. Cut him in two!" Then Solomon said: "Give the baby to the first woman. Do not kill him; she is his mother." According to the biblical account, "When all Israel heard the verdict the king had given, they held the king in awe, because they saw that he had wisdom from God to administer justice." **D**

The Divided Kingdom

After Solomon's death, tension among the tribes within Israel led to the creation of two separate kingdoms. The Kingdom of Israel was composed of the ten northern tribes and had its capital at Samaria. To the south, the Kingdom of Judah consisted of two tribes and had its capital at Jerusalem. **R**

In 722 or 721 B.C., the Assyrians overran the Kingdom of Israel and sent many Israelites to other parts of the Assyrian Empire. Most of these scattered Israelites (the "ten lost tribes") merged with neighboring peoples and gradually lost their identity.

The Kingdom of Judah managed to retain its independence for a while, but a new enemy soon appeared on the horizon. The Chaldeans (kal•DEE•uhnz) defeated Assyria, conquered the Kingdom of Judah, and completely destroyed Jerusalem in 586 B.C. Many people of Judah were sent as captives to Babylonia. Only the poorest remained. The words of Psalm 137 evoke the memory of their exile:

PRIMARY SOURCE

> "By the rivers of Babylon, we sat and wept when we remembered Zion. . . . How can we sing the songs of the Lord while in a foreign land? If I forget you, O Jerusalem, may my right hand forget its skill. May my tongue cling to the roof of my mouth if I do not remember you, if I do not consider Jerusalem my highest joy."
>
> —Psalms 137: 1, 4–6

Did You Know?

The Ark of the Covenant was the chest in which the tablets containing the Ten Commandments were kept. Solomon's temple, also known as the First Temple, was built to house the ark and provide a place for the Israelites to meet.

D Differentiated Instruction

Kinesthetic Invite groups of students to dramatize this story associated with Solomon. Have each group present its version to the class. **BL**

R Reading Strategy

Sequencing Information Have students work together to create a time line charting the events after the death of Solomon. **Ask:** What happened to the Israelites and people of Judah by 586 B.C.? *(Israelites were scattered throughout the peninsula. Judah was conquered, Jerusalem destroyed, and many of its people taken as captives into Babylonia.)* **OL**

Differentiated Instruction

People in World History Activity, URB p. 76

Summarizing

Objective: Learn more about David, king of Israel.

Focus: Read the biography of David.

Teach: Discuss the ways in which David was a strong and accomplished leader.

Assess: Have students create a character sketch of David.

Close: Have pairs of students role-play an interview with David that reveals his traits and achievements.

Differentiated Instruction Strategies

- **BL** Have students tell the story of David in their own words.
- **AL** Ask students to locate the psalms attributed to David and summarize significant themes and images.
- **ELL** Have students summarize the story of David's life in words and pictures.

W Writing Support

Expository Writing Have students write an essay in which they summarize the major Jewish beliefs. **OL**

Answers:

1. Students may argue that displaying religious text in a courthouse demonstrates a bias toward members of the religion in the legal system.
2. Students should point out both similarities and differences between U.S. laws and the Ten Commandments

The Babylonian captivity did not last. New conquerors, the Persians, allowed the people of Judah to return to Jerusalem and rebuild their city and temple. The revived province of Judah was controlled by Persia until the conquests of Alexander the Great in the 300s B.C. The people of Judah survived, eventually becoming known as the Jews and giving their name to Judaism.

Judaism

The Jews were **monotheistic;** they believed in one God called Yahweh (YAH•WAY), the Creator of the world and everything in it. In the Jews' view, God ruled the world; all peoples were his servants, whether they knew it or not. God had created nature but was not in nature. The sun, the wind, and other natural phenomena were not gods, but God's creations to be admired but not worshiped.

This powerful creator was not removed from the life he had created. God was just and good, and he expected goodness from his people. If they did not obey his will, they would be punished. However, he was also "compassionate, slow to anger, and rich in love." Each person could have a personal relationship with this being.

The covenant, law, and prophets were three aspects of the Jewish religious tradition. The Jews believed that during the exodus from Egypt, when Moses led his people out of bondage, God made a covenant, or contract, with them. Yahweh promised to guide them if they obeyed the laws of God as expressed most prominently in the Ten Commandments. According to the Bible, Yahweh gave these laws to Moses on Mount Sinai. The Jews believed God sent certain religious teachers, or prophets, to serve as his voice to his people.

Connecting to the United States

The Ten Commandments

The Ten Commandments

1. I am the Lord thy God. . . . Thou shalt have no other gods before me.
2. Thou shalt not make unto thee any graven image. . . .
3. Thou shalt not take the name of the Lord thy God in vain. . . .
4. Remember the Sabbath day, to keep it holy.
5. Honor thy father and thy mother. . . .
6. Thou shalt not kill.
7. Thou shalt not commit adultery.
8. Thou shalt not steal.
9. Thou shalt not bear false witness against thy neighbor.
10. Thou shalt not covet . . . anything that is thy neighbor's.

Source: Exodus 20: 1–17

According to Jewish beliefs, Yahweh (God) gave his laws, the Ten Commandments, to Moses. These laws are not only fundamental to Judaism but to Christianity as well. In the United States, the Ten Commandments have been posted in classrooms and carved on courthouse monuments. However, displaying the Ten Commandments in public facilities—schools, parks, and government offices—has sparked debate.

Although other countries have had a state, or official, religion, the United States does not. James Madison, drafter of the First Amendment and later president, believed the government should not tax its citizens to support religious activities or beliefs and that all religions should be treated equally and fairly. The First Amendment to the U.S. Constitution states, "Congress shall make no law respecting an establishment of religion . . ."

The debate continues. Does displaying the Ten Commandments promote law-abiding behavior or does it indicate a bias toward particular religious groups?

- The Ten Commandments are the fundamental laws of Judaism.
- The Commandments are part of a shared Judeo-Christian heritage.

1. **Identifying Points of View** Why would some people think that posting the Ten Commandments in a courthouse shows bias?
2. **Making Connections** How do the Ten Commandments relate to the laws in the United States?

Additional Support

Extending the Content

Connecting to the United States There have been several waves of Jewish immigrants to the United States since the colonial times. The first Jewish community in the late 18th century was quite small, but was supplemented in the mid-19th century by an influx of Central European Jews. These new immigrants opened Jewish community centers and generally renewed Judaism in America. Many joined the westward movement, carrying the Jewish faith throughout the continental United States. Another large wave of immigration occurred between 1881 and 1914 as Jews from Eastern Europe, including many rabbis, made their way to the United States. According to census reports, there are presently about 6 million people who practice Judaism in the United States, many of whom reside in states along the East Coast, including New York, New Jersey, Maryland, and Massachusetts. **Ask: What might have prompted large numbers of Jews to come to the United States at the turn of the 20th century?** *(persecution in their homelands)* **AL**

The age of prophecy lasted from the 1000s B.C. to the 400s B.C., a time when the people were threatened or conquered by powerful neighbors. The prophets declared that faithlessness to God would bring catastrophe, but that turning from evil would bring God's mercy. The prophets introduced concepts that enriched the Jewish tradition. Later prophets embraced a concern for all humanity. All nations would come to the God of Israel and find peace.

Primary Source

"They will beat their swords into plowshares and their spears into pruning hooks. Nation will not take up sword against nation, nor will they train for war anymore."

—Isaiah 2:4

The prophets also cried out against social injustice. They condemned the rich for causing the poor to suffer. They denounced luxuries, and they threatened Israel with prophecies of dire punishments for these sins. They said that God's command was to live justly, share with others, and care for the poor and the unfortunate. These words became a source for ideals of social justice.

The following selection makes clear the prophets' belief that unjust actions would bring God's punishment.

Primary Source

"The Lord enters into judgment against the elders and leaders of his people: 'It is you who have ruined my vineyard; the plunder from the poor is in your houses. What do you mean by crushing my people and grinding the faces of the poor?' . . . Your men will fall by the sword, your warriors in battle. The gates of Zion will lament and mourn. . . .'"

—Isaiah 3:14–17, 24–26

The religion of Israel was unique among the religions of western Asia and Egypt. The biggest difference was its belief in only one God (monotheism). In other ancient religions, only priests (and some rulers) had access to the gods. In the Jewish tradition, God's wishes, though communicated to the people through prophets, had been written down. No leader of Israel could claim that he alone knew God's will. This knowledge was available to anyone who could read the Hebrew Bible. C

Although the prophets developed a concern for all humanity, the demands of Judaism—the need to obey God—encouraged a separation between Jews and their non-Jewish neighbors. Unlike most other peoples of Southwest Asia, Jews would not accept the gods of their conquerors or neighbors and could consequently not be integrated into another community.

✓Reading Check **Identifying** Which aspect of Israelite culture had the greatest impact on Western civilization?

SECTION 3 REVIEW

Vocabulary

1. **Explain** the significance of: pastoral nomads, created, domesticated, technology, Indo-Europeans, Hittites, Phoenicians, Israelites, King Solomon, Jerusalem, monotheistic.

Main Ideas

2. **Describe** how the Hittites used new technology to gain power.
3. **List** the areas reached by Phoenician traders. Also list the areas that were colonized by the Phoenicians.
4. **Create** a chart like the one below to show the significance of three major events in the history of the Israelites.

Event	Significance
1.	
2.	
3.	

Critical Thinking

5. **BIG Idea** **Contrasting** How did the Jews' religious beliefs make them different from other peoples of their time and place?
6. **Evaluating** How did nomadic peoples both contribute to and slow down the development of civilization?
7. **Analyzing Visuals** Examine the image on page 48. What similarities do you see between the three alphabets?

Writing About History

8. **Informative Writing** Using the Internet, news magazines, and newspapers, research the current conflicts in the Middle East. Prepare a brief research report summarizing what you have learned about current events and movements toward peace in the region.

History ONLINE

For help with the concepts in this section of *Glencoe World History*, go to glencoe.com and click Study Central™.

51

C Critical Thinking

Identifying Central Issues

Ask: What was the main difference between Judaism and other religions of the time? *(their belief in only one god, or monotheism)* OL

✓Reading Check

Answer: their religion, Judaism

Assess

History ONLINE

Study Central provides summaries, interactive games, and online graphic organizers to help students review content.

Close

Summarizing **Ask:** What role did nomadic peoples play in world history? *(They spread civilization and developed a world religion, Judaism, that influenced later world religions, Christianity and Islam.)* OL

Answers

1. Definitions for the vocabulary words are found in the section and the Glossary.
2. They made weapons from iron that were stronger than those used by other peoples in the region.
3. Britain, the west coast of Africa, the western Mediterranean, Carthage
4. **Event:** reign of Solomon; **Significance:** Israel at height of its power; **Event:** Israel overrun by Assyrians; **Significance:** scattered the Israelites throughout the empire; **Event:** Judah conquered; **Significance:** destruction of Jerusalem
5. The Jewish people believed in one God and did not worship the forces of nature. They would not take on beliefs of other people or obey rulers who threatened their beliefs.
6. They spread their languages and new technologies, such as iron; they also overran and destroyed established civilizations.
7. Answers will vary: H, L, M are similar in all three; A, D, E, K, O, T are similar in Phoenician and Latin; 22 letters in Hebrew and Phoenician.
8. Answers will vary, depending on current events.

NATIONAL GEOGRAPHIC
GEOGRAPHY & HISTORY

Focus

Phoenicia, mainly situated in what is now Lebanon, never built an empire based on military might, as did Assyria and Persia. Instead, the Phoenicians established what we might today consider a commercial empire. With numerous colonies spread across the Mediterranean region—and with contacts extending well beyond the region—the Phoenicians were able to trade effectively as well as spread their culture.

Teach

Relatively little is known of Phoenician art and literature, even though their alphabet is generally considered their most significant contribution to humanity. Discuss with students why little is known about Phoenician art and literature. *(They may have emphasized commercial matters more than artistic or literary ones. Also, because of their location, they were often conquered by other peoples, who may have destroyed these aspects of Phoenician culture.)*

Additional Support

NATIONAL GEOGRAPHIC GEOGRAPHY & HISTORY

Trade goods, like this flask used for storing oils, helped Phoenicia build strong trade ties throughout the Mediterranean, 969 B.C.

Phoenician merchant ships transport cedar wood from Tyre in this Assyrian bas-relief. In the 900s B.C. and 800s B.C., Tyre became the leading Phoenician city.

Activity: Economics Connection

Commercial Empires: Past and Present Discuss other commercial empires students have prior knowledge of, such as the British Empire in the 1700s and 1800s. Have students brainstorm how a commercial empire is built and maintained. Then ask them to define a *commercial empire.* Next talk about whether the United States today could be considered a commercial empire. You may also want to discuss whether multinational corporations could also be considered modern commercial empires. Then ask if their definition needs to be revised. To extend this activity, have pairs of students choose a commercial empire to research and report on. Ask students to answer this question: What were/are the pros and cons of this commercial empire? **OL**

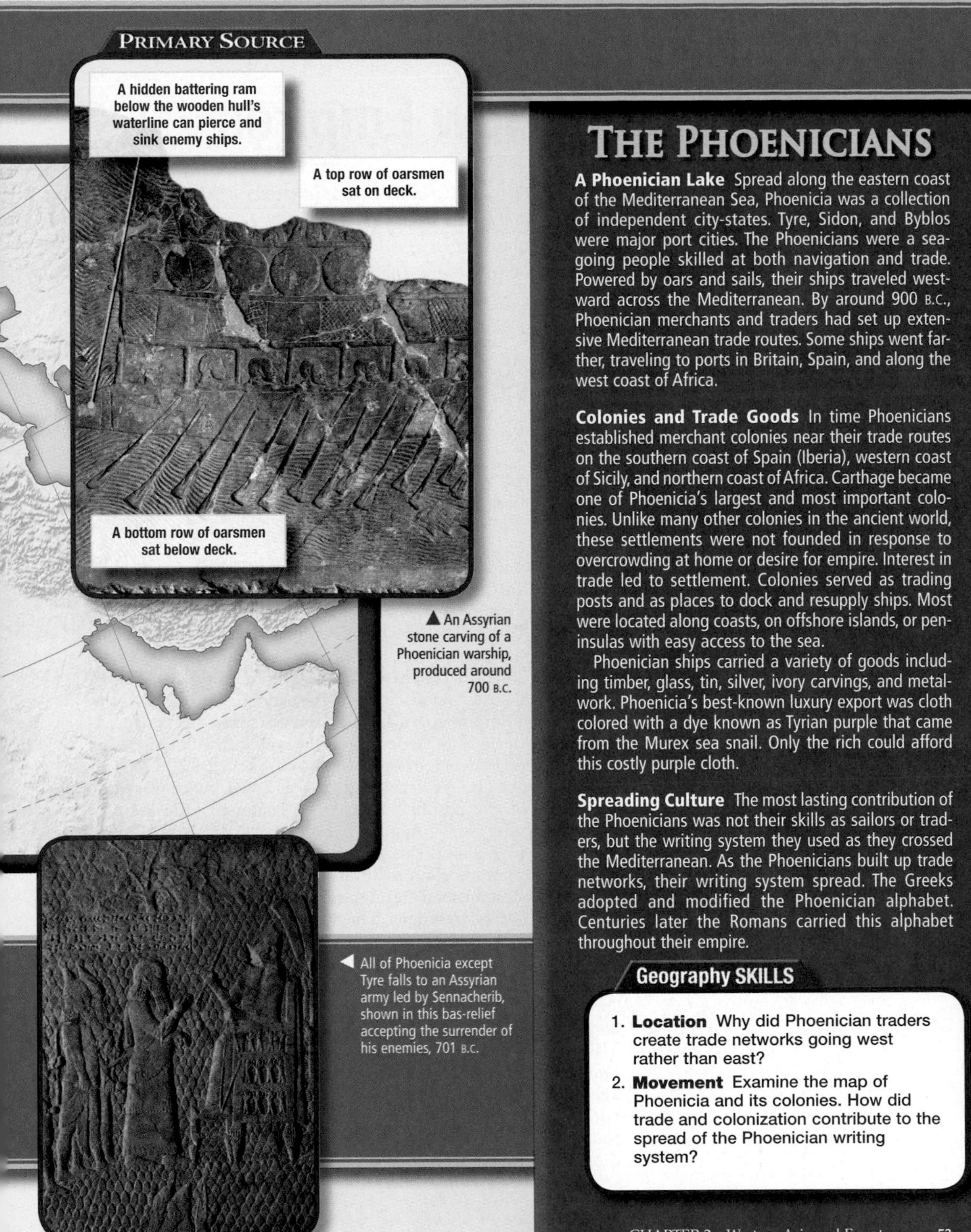

▲ An Assyrian stone carving of a Phoenician warship, produced around 700 B.C.

◀ All of Phoenicia except Tyre falls to an Assyrian army led by Sennacherib, shown in this bas-relief accepting the surrender of his enemies, 701 B.C.

THE PHOENICIANS

A Phoenician Lake Spread along the eastern coast of the Mediterranean Sea, Phoenicia was a collection of independent city-states. Tyre, Sidon, and Byblos were major port cities. The Phoenicians were a seagoing people skilled at both navigation and trade. Powered by oars and sails, their ships traveled westward across the Mediterranean. By around 900 B.C., Phoenician merchants and traders had set up extensive Mediterranean trade routes. Some ships went farther, traveling to ports in Britain, Spain, and along the west coast of Africa.

Colonies and Trade Goods In time Phoenicians established merchant colonies near their trade routes on the southern coast of Spain (Iberia), western coast of Sicily, and northern coast of Africa. Carthage became one of Phoenicia's largest and most important colonies. Unlike many other colonies in the ancient world, these settlements were not founded in response to overcrowding at home or desire for empire. Interest in trade led to settlement. Colonies served as trading posts and as places to dock and resupply ships. Most were located along coasts, on offshore islands, or peninsulas with easy access to the sea.

Phoenician ships carried a variety of goods including timber, glass, tin, silver, ivory carvings, and metalwork. Phoenicia's best-known luxury export was cloth colored with a dye known as Tyrian purple that came from the Murex sea snail. Only the rich could afford this costly purple cloth.

Spreading Culture The most lasting contribution of the Phoenicians was not their skills as sailors or traders, but the writing system they used as they crossed the Mediterranean. As the Phoenicians built up trade networks, their writing system spread. The Greeks adopted and modified the Phoenician alphabet. Centuries later the Romans carried this alphabet throughout their empire.

Geography SKILLS

1. **Location** Why did Phoenician traders create trade networks going west rather than east?
2. **Movement** Examine the map of Phoenicia and its colonies. How did trade and colonization contribute to the spread of the Phoenician writing system?

NATIONAL GEOGRAPHIC GEOGRAPHY & HISTORY

Assess/Close

Tell students that the Phoenicians—in spite of their success as traders—were for much of their history ruled over by many of the empires of the ancient world, including the Egyptians, Greeks, and Romans. **Ask:** Why would Phoenicia be desired by other people? *(Answers may include the Phoenicians' wealth and natural resources as well as their colonies and trading contacts.)* **OL**

Geography SKILLS

Answers:

1. Answers may include that as skilled shipbuilders and sailors they could more efficiently create a sea-based trade network going west, rather than a land-based one going east.
2. Trade and colonization likely depended on a system of written communication, which spread as trade and colonization expanded.

Additional Support

Extending the Content

Phoenician Ships and Shipbuilding One key advantage that the Phoenicians had over their maritime rivals was in natural resources. They had plenty of cedar trees that were tall and hard—and perfect for building ships. Phoenician shipbuilders crafted merchant ships that could travel long distances at sea. They also built some of the ancient world's most effective fighting ships, called biremes (two banks of oars) and triremes (three banks of oars). Because these ships were so well-built, some historians think that it was possible that the Phoenicians may have sailed to the Americas long before Columbus did. A key feature of Phoenician merchant ships was their ability to carry great loads of cargo. To make the best use of their cargo space, the Phoenicians often used ceramic amphoras—such as the one shown on the opposite page—to store wine and oils. These uniform containers—the forerunners of modern packaging—also made the actual trading of goods much more efficient.

Focus

Bellringer
Daily Focus Transparency 2.4

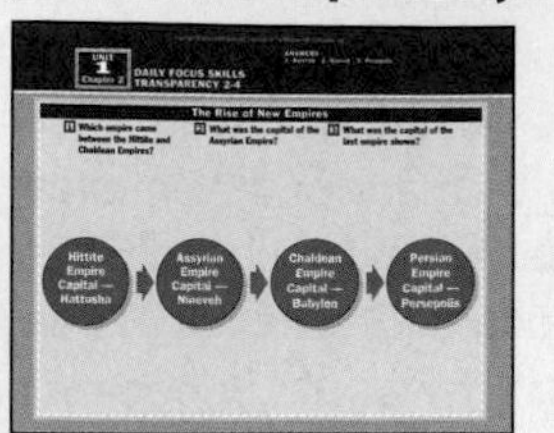

GUIDE TO READING

Answers to Graphic:
Assyrian Empire: destroyed enemy land; treated captives poorly; **Persian Empire:** respected conquered peoples; showed mercy for captives; developed strong government; **Both:** had large efficient armies; had effective communication systems; kings had absolute power

Section Spotlight Video

To generate student interest and provide a springboard for class discussion, access the Chapter 2, Section 4 video at glencoe.com or on the video DVD.

SECTION 4

The Rise of New Empires

GUIDE TO READING

The BIG Idea
Competition Among Countries The Assyrians and the Persians established vast empires in the ancient world.

Content Vocabulary
- satrapy *(p. 57)*
- satrap *(p. 57)*
- monarchy *(p. 57)*

Academic Vocabulary
- restraint *(p. 56)*
- sought *(p. 56)*
- sustained *(p. 57)*

People and Places
- Assyrians *(p. 54)*
- Nebuchadnezzar *(p. 56)*
- Persians *(p. 56)*
- Cyrus *(p. 56)*
- Darius *(p. 56)*
- Royal Road *(p. 57)*
- Immortals *(p. 57)*
- Zoroaster *(p. 57)*

Reading Strategy
Compare and Contrast As you read, complete a Venn diagram like the one below identifying similarities and differences between the Assyrian Empire and Persian Empire.

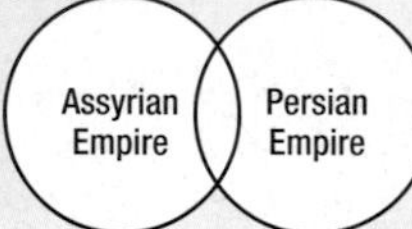

After 700 B.C., new empires arose in western Asia that covered vast stretches of the ancient world. The Assyrians were better at conquest than at ruling, and their empire lasted less than one hundred years. The Persian Empire brought many years of peace to Southwest Asia, increasing trade and the general well-being of its people.

The Assyrian Empire

MAIN IDEA The Assyrians ruled with harsh tactics that brought about the fall of their empire.

HISTORY & YOU Why do you think a country that is good at fighting might not be as good at ruling? Read how the Assyrians built and lost an empire.

The first of the new empires was formed in Assyria, located on the upper Tigris River. The **Assyrians** were a Semitic-speaking people who exploited the use of iron weapons to establish an empire by 700 B.C. The Assyrian Empire included Mesopotamia, parts of the Plateau of Iran, sections of Asia Minor, Syria, Israel, and Egypt down to Thebes. In less than a hundred years, however, internal strife and resentment of Assyrian rule began to tear the Assyrian Empire apart. In 612 B.C., the empire fell to a coalition of Chaldeans and Medes (people who lived in the east), and it was divided between those powers.

At its height, the Assyrian Empire was ruled by kings whose power was seen as absolute. Under their leadership, the Assyrian Empire became well organized. Local officials were directly responsible to the king. The Assyrians also developed an efficient system of communication to administer their empire. A network of posts was established throughout the empire that used relays of horses to carry messages. The system was so effective that a governor anywhere in the empire could send a question and receive an answer from the king within a week. One of the last Assyrian kings, Ashurbanipal, established one of the world's first libraries at Nineveh. This library has provided abundant information concerning ancient Southwest Asian civilizations.

The Assyrians were good at conquering others. Through many years of practice they developed effective military leaders and fighters. The Assyrian army was large, well organized, and disciplined. A force of infantrymen was its core, joined by cavalrymen and horse-drawn war chariots that were used as platforms for shooting arrows. Moreover, the Assyrians had the first large armies equipped with iron weapons.

Resource Manager

R Reading Strategies	C Critical Thinking	D Differentiated Instruction	W Writing Support	S Skill Practice
Teacher Edition • Read. Pri. Sources, p. 55 **Additional Resources** • Cont. Vocab. Act., URB p. 59 • Guid. Read. Act., URB p. 87 • Read. Ess. & Note-Taking Guide, p. 16	**Teacher Edition** • Det. Cause/Effect, p. 55 • Drawing Con., p. 56 **Additional Resources** • Hist. Analysis Skills Act., URB p. 54 • Section Quiz, p. 14 • Chapter Test, p. 15	**Teacher Edition** • Adv. Learners, p. 57 **Additional Resources** • Hist. Sim. Act., URB p. 71	**Teacher Edition** • Descriptive Writing, p. 56 **Additional Resources** • Academic Vocab. Act., URB p. 61 • Writer's Guidebook, p. 43	**Teacher Edition** • Using Geo. Skills, p. 56 **Additional Resources** • Chart. Graph. Act., URB p. 3 • Read. Strat. for SS, p. 86

PRIMARY SOURCE / HISTORY & ARTS

Panel of Ashurbanipal, c. 650 B.C.

This relief of Ashurbanipal hunting lions is from his palace at Nineveh. It depicts a ceremonial hunt where King Ashurbanipal, aided by servants, hunts lions who are released from cages into a closed arena. Many reliefs depicting stories were used to decorate the king's palace.

The depiction of the king is idealized. He is muscular and attractive to signify his strength and importance.

Servants are shown protecting the king from the lions attempting to attack the king from behind.

The lions are realistically represented. They are depicted as strong and noble, which adds significance to the king's victory.

DOCUMENT-BASED QUESTIONS

1. **Making Inferences** Where does the hunt take place? Why might this be significant?
2. **Analyzing Visuals** Why do you think Ashurbanipal hunted lions rather than some other type of animal?

Another factor in the army's success was its ability to use different military tactics. The Assyrians could wage guerrilla warfare in the mountains, set battles on open ground, and lay siege to cities. They used battering rams and siege towers to hammer at the city's walls. Then they would tunnel under them, making them collapse.

The Assyrians used terror as an instrument of warfare. They regularly laid waste to the land in which they were fighting. They smashed dams; looted and destroyed **C** towns; set crops on fire; and cut down trees, particularly fruit trees. The Assyrians were especially known for committing atrocities on their captives. King Ashurbanipal recorded this account of his treatment of prisoners:

PRIMARY SOURCE

"3,000 of their combat troops I felled with weapons. . . . Many I took alive; from some of these I cut off their hands to the wrist, from others I cut off their noses, ears, and fingers; I put out the eyes of many of the soldiers. . . . I burned their young men and women to death." **R**

—H.W.F. Saggs, *The Might That Was Assyria*

✓Reading Check **Summarizing** Why were the Assyrians so successful at conquering others?

Teach

C Critical Thinking

Determining Cause and Effect **Ask:** Why did the Assyrians raze the lands of their enemies? *(It terrorized their enemies and destroyed their culture.)* AL

R Reading Strategy

Reading Primary Sources

Ask: How would this treatment of captives both help and harm the Assyrian's empire-building? *(Fear of the Assyrians would encourage cities to surrender, but this cruelty would inspire no loyalty.)* OL

DOCUMENT-BASED QUESTIONS

Answers:

1. in an arena, not in the wild; it shows the king's power
2. Lions are king of the animal world, so Ashurbanipal, as king, might hunt them to show his power.

✓Reading Check

Answer: They had developed iron weapons, which were harder than bronze weapons.

Hands-On Chapter Project

Step 4

Publishing a Coffee Table Book

Students add the last chapter to their coffee table book.

Step 4: Writing the Fourth Chapter

Directions: Write the Big Idea on the board. Tell students that they will use the facts in this section to develop a chapter on the Assyrian and Persian Empires. Remind students to plan what they want to include before they begin to write and to keep their text brief and accurate. For their foldout, suggest that groups create an annotated time line that shows the sequential relationship of the empires to each other.

Putting It Together: Have students collate their chapters and design a simple cover with a title for their book. Ask groups to exchange, read, and discuss each other's books. Then have them share insights on the Big Idea. OL

(Chapter Project is completed on Visual Summary page.)

S Skill Practice

Using Geography Skills Ask: What was the distance a message traveled between Sardis and Susa? *(about 1600 miles)* **OL**

W Writing Support

Descriptive Writing Have students find out more about the legendary "hanging gardens of Babylon" and write a short poem describing them. **AL**

C Critical Thinking

Drawing Conclusions Ask: How did Cyrus's style of governing unify his empire? *(Groups under his rule accepted him as their leader and did not rebel.)* **OL**

For additional practice on this skill, see the **Skills Handbook**.

Geography SKILLS

Answers:

1. Answers should include that Susa was the capital. The road may have moved west toward the population centers near the sea.
2. Maps will vary, but divisions should be based on logical conclusions.

The Persian Empire

MAIN IDEA Strong Persian leaders conquered and ruled a vast empire for more than 200 years.

HISTORY & YOU What qualities do you think make a great leader? Read to learn why Cyrus was considered a great leader.

After the collapse of the Assyrian Empire, the Chaldean king **Nebuchadnezzar** (NEH•byuh•kuhd•NEH•zuhr) II made Babylonia the leading state in western Asia. He rebuilt Babylon as the center of his empire and gave it a reputation as one of the great cities of the ancient world, but Babylon fell to the Persians in 539 B.C.

The Rise of the Persian Empire

The **Persians** were Indo-Europeans who lived in what is today southwestern Iran. Primarily nomadic, the Persians were eventually unified by one family. One member of this family, **Cyrus,** created a powerful Persian state that stretched from Asia Minor to India. Cyrus ruled from 559 B.C. to 530 B.C. In 539 B.C., he captured Babylon. His treatment of Babylonia showed remarkable **restraint** and wisdom. He also allowed the Jews who had been held there as captives to return to Israel.

The people of his time called Cyrus "the Great." He demonstrated wisdom and compassion in the conquest and organization of his empire. Unlike the Assyrian rulers, Cyrus had a reputation for mercy. Medes, Babylonians, and Jews all accepted him as their ruler. Cyrus had a genuine respect for other civilizations. For example, he used Assyrian, Babylonian, and Egyptian designs for building his palaces.

Cyrus's successors **sought** to extend the territory of the Persian Empire. His son Cambyses (kam•BY•SEEZ) successfully invaded Egypt.

Darius, who ruled from 521 B.C. to 486 B.C., added a new Persian province in

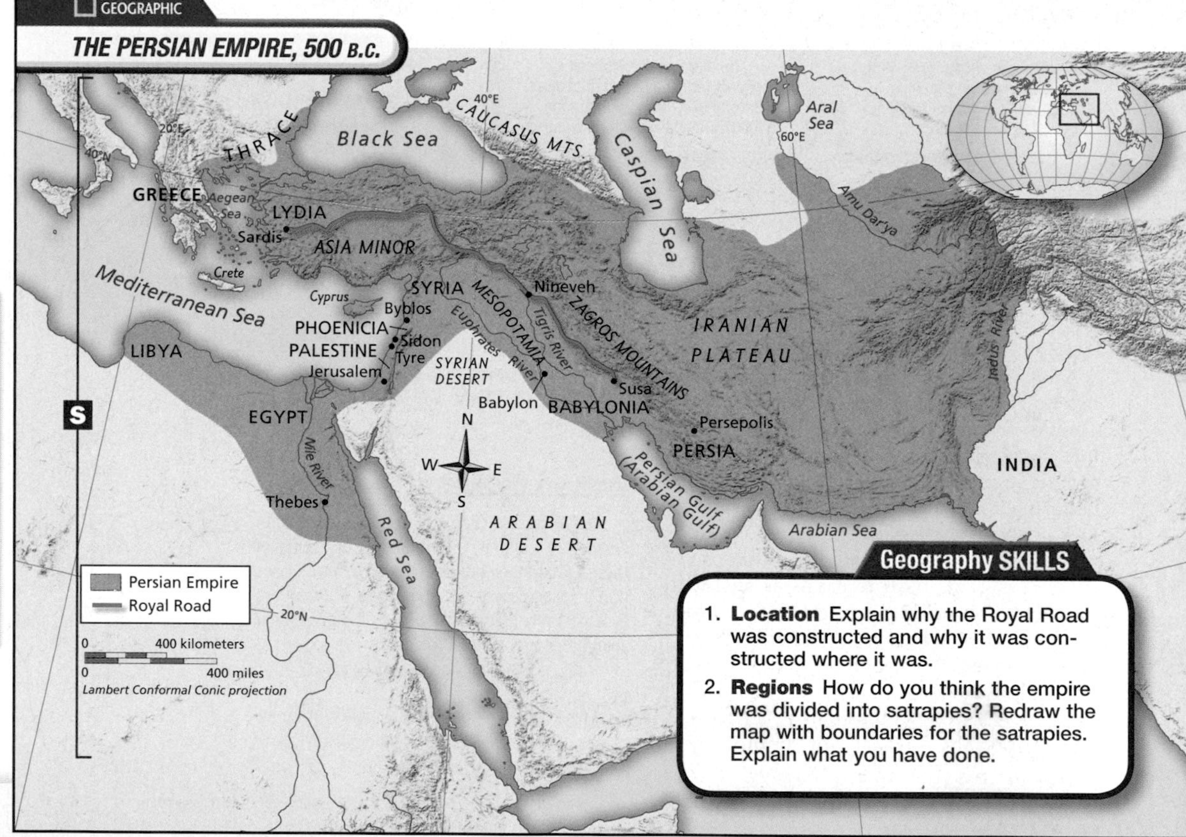

Geography SKILLS

1. **Location** Explain why the Royal Road was constructed and why it was constructed where it was.
2. **Regions** How do you think the empire was divided into satrapies? Redraw the map with boundaries for the satrapies. Explain what you have done.

Differentiated Instruction

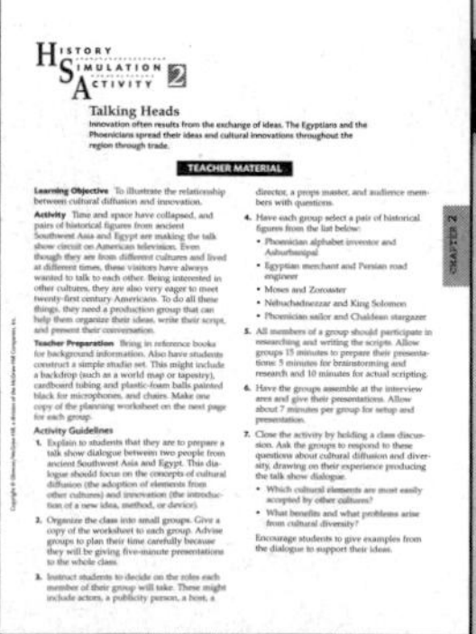

History Simulation Activity, URB p. 71

Making Inferences

Objective: Describe the relationship between cultural diffusion and innovation.

Focus: Have students create a dialogue between people from ancient Southwest Asia and Egypt.

Teach: Guide students in completing the activity.

Assess: Have students present their dialogues.

Close: Discuss the questions in step 7.

Differentiated Instruction Strategies

BL Provide students with information on historical figures from this time period and region.

AL Have students present their dialogue as a video recording.

ELL Assign roles to ensure an even balance in terms of English-speaking abilities.

western India. He then conquered Thrace in Europe, creating the world's largest empire to that time. Contact with Greece led Darius to invade the Greek mainland.

Darius strengthened the Persian government. He divided the empire into 20 provinces, called **satrapies** (SAY•truh•pees). A governor, or **satrap,** literally a "protector of the kingdom", ruled each province. Each satrap collected taxes, provided justice, and recruited soldiers.

An efficient communication system **sustained** the Persian Empire. Officials easily traveled through the empire on well-maintained roads dotted with way stations that provided food, shelter, and fresh horses. The **Royal Road** stretched from Lydia to Susa, the empire's chief capital.

In this system, the Persian king—the "Great King"—held an exalted position. He had the power of life and death.

Much of the empire's power depended on the military. By the time of Darius, Persian kings had created a standing army of professional soldiers from all over the empire. At its core were a cavalry force and an elite infantry force. They were known as the **Immortals** because whenever a member was killed, he was immediately replaced.

The Fall of the Persian Empire

After Darius, the Persian kings became isolated at their courts, surrounded by luxuries. As the kings increased taxes, loyalty to the empire declined. Struggles over the throne weakened the **monarchy** (rule by a king or queen).

Persian kings had many wives and children. The sons had little real power and many engaged in plots to gain the throne. This bloody struggle for the throne weakened the empire and led to its conquest by the Greek ruler Alexander the Great during the 330s B.C.

Persian Religion

Zoroastrianism (ZOHR•uh•WAS•tree•uh•NIH•zuhm), the Persians' religion, was their most original cultural contribution. According to tradition, **Zoroaster,** revered as a prophet of the "true religion," was born in 660 B.C. His teachings were recorded in the *Zend Avesta*, the sacred book of Zoroastrianism.

Like the Jews, Zoroastrians were monotheistic. To Zoroaster, Ahuramazda (the "Wise Lord") was a supreme god **D** who created all things. Ahuramazda was supreme, but he was not unopposed. At the beginning of the world, the evil spirit Ahriman opposed him. Humans played a role in the struggle between good and evil. Ahuramazda gave humans the freedom to choose between right and wrong. The good person chooses the way of Ahuramazda, who would eventually triumph.

✓Reading Check **Examining** What caused the Persian Empire to decline after the death of Darius?

SECTION 4 REVIEW

Vocabulary
1. **Explain** the significance of: Assyrians, Nebuchadnezzar, Persians, Cyrus, restraint, sought, Darius, satrapy, satrap, sustained, Royal Road, Immortals, monarchy, Zoroaster.

Main Ideas
2. **Describe** some of the harsh tactics used by the Assyrians.
3. **List** the duties of the satraps of the Persian government.
4. **Create** a chart like the one shown below to identify the differences between a religious system based on monotheism and one based on polytheism.

Monotheism	Polytheism

Critical Thinking
5. **BIG Idea** **Making Inferences** Why was a strong army so important in maintaining the Persian Empire's power?
6. **Contrasting** How were the Assyrian and Persian systems of government different?
7. **Analyzing Visuals** Examine the relief of Ashurbanipal on page 55. Describe what you see in this image. Why do you think images such as this were made of Persian rulers?

Writing About History
8. **Persuasive Writing** Suppose that you are Cyrus ruling the Babylonians, a people you have just conquered. Explain to your government officials why you believe that mercy and tolerance are better policies than harshness.

For help with the concepts in this section of *Glencoe World History*, go to glencoe.com and click Study Central™.

57

D Differentiated Instruction

Advanced Learners Have students research Zoroastrianism and report on its primary beliefs and significance today. **AL**

Answer: After Darius, kings became isolated and raised taxes. The king's many sons also fought over who should succeed to the throne.

Assess

Study Central provides summaries, interactive games, and online graphic organizers to help students review content.

Close

Summarizing Have students draw a labeled diagram of the organization of the Persian government under Darius. **OL**

SECTION 4 REVIEW

Answers

1. Definitions for the vocabulary words are found in the section and the Glossary.
2. They destroyed the lands where they fought, treated captives brutally, and sought to destroy the captured people's culture.
3. They collected taxes, provided justice and security, and recruited soldiers.
4. **Monotheism:** one god, beyond nature; **Polytheism:** many gods, part of nature
5. It allowed the Persians to conquer other countries and to deter those countries from rebelling against Persian rule.
6. Assyrians used terror as a part of warfare, laid waste to the land, and committed atrocities to gain and hold onto power. Persians built and expanded their empire by respecting conquered civilizations and showing the people mercy, and by creating a well-organized government and professional standing army.
7. Answers may include that such images signified the power and strength of Persian rulers.
8. Answers will vary, but students should cite specific details and use logic to support their conclusions.

ANALYZING
PRIMARY SOURCES

Focus

Tell students that creation accounts are distinguished by their explanations of how the universe began. No matter how each culture views the origin of the universe, however, all stories include the creation of human beings by a supernatural or divine force.

Teach

C Critical Thinking

Making Inferences **Ask:** What impression of Marduk is created by his actions? *(He is strong and decisive. He is also creative and humble enough to confer with his father, the god of wisdom.)* **OL**

S Skill Practice

Making Connections **Ask:** In what way is the Hebrew perception of creation different from the Babylonian? *(The process of creation in Genesis involves less violence than in the Babylonian account. Also God views his work with satisfaction. In the Babylonian story, there is no sense of Marduk's feelings about his creation.)* **OL**

ANALYZING
PRIMARY SOURCES

What Did Ancient Societies Believe About Creation?

How were ancient creation stories similar and different? The ancient peoples of Mesopotamia, Egypt, and Israel formulated different stories about the creation of the world. The various accounts, however, contain several similarities.

What do creation stories reveal about ancient religious beliefs? Religion played a central role in the lives of ancient peoples. Creation stories describe the gods they worshipped and help explain how ancient societies interpreted the world around them.

Creation accounts provide insights into the cultures of the people who developed them. Read the excerpts and study the painting to find out what the Babylonians, Hebrews, and Egyptians believed about the creation of the world.

SOURCE 1

The Babylonian story of creation is part of an epic poem titled *Enûma elish.*

C

The lord **[Marduk[1]]** trod upon the hinder part of **Tiâmat[2],**
And with his unsparing club he split her skull. . . .
He split her open like a mussel into two parts;
Half of her he set in place and formed the sky therewith as a roof. . . .
He fixed the crossbar and posted guards;
He commanded them not to let her waters escape. . . .
The lord measured the dimensions of the ***Apsû[3]***,
And a great structure, its counterpart, he established, namely, **Esharra[4]**,
The great structure Esharra which he made as a canopy. . . .
As Marduk hears the words of the gods,
His heart prompts him to create ingenious things.
He conveys his idea to **Ea[5]**,
Imparting the plan which he had conceived in his heart:
"Blood will I form and cause bone to be;
Then will I set up ***lullû[6]***, 'Man' shall be his name!
Yes, I will create *lullû:* Man!
Upon him shall the services of the gods be imposed that they may be at rest."

SOURCE 2

The book of Genesis contains an account of the Hebrew story of creation.

S

In the beginning God created the heavens and the earth. . . .

And God said, "Let there be light," and there was light. God saw that the light was good, and he separated the light from the darkness. God called the light "day," and the darkness he called "night." And there was evening and there was morning—the first day.

And God said, "Let there be an expanse between the waters to separate water from water." So God made the expanse and separated the water under the expanse from the water above it. And it was so. God called the expanse "sky." And there was evening, and there was morning—the second day.

And God said, "Let the water under the sky be gathered to one place, and let dry ground appear." And it was so. God called the dry ground "land," and the gathered waters he called "seas." And God saw that it was good. . . .

Then God said, "Let us make man in our image, in our likeness, and let them rule over the fish of the sea and the birds of the air, over the livestock, over all the earth, and over all the creatures that move along the ground."

So God created man in his own image, in the image of God he created him; male and female he created them.

1 **Marduk:** ruler of the gods in Babylonian mythology
2 **Tiâmat:** monster goddess; the earliest salt water
3 **Apsû:** husband of Tiâmat; the earliest freshwater
4 **Esharra:** a poetic name for the Earth

Differentiated Instruction

Name ____ Date ____ Class ____
PRIMARY SOURCE READING 2
Finding Tutankhamen's Tomb

Primary Source Reading, URB p. 77

Analyzing Primary Sources

Objective: Analyze the primary source account of Carter's discovery.

Focus: Learn what Carter found in Tutankhamen's tomb.

Teach: Have volunteers read the passage aloud.

Assess: Have students explain the implications of the wealth of objects found in the antechamber.

Close: Have students create a web diagram illustrating the significance of Carter's discovery.

Differentiated Instruction Strategies

BL Have pairs of students illustrate the most important ideas in the passage.

AL Have students find and interpret other significant passages from Carter's account.

ELL Read the passage aloud to students, modeling how to determine the significance of the information included.

▲ The sun god, Re, makes his night journey in this drawing and relief from the tomb of Horemheb in Egypt, c. 1300 B.C.

C

SOURCE 3

The ancient Egyptians had several creation myths. In one account, Re, the sun god, emerged from an egg that appeared on the surface of the ocean. Re later produced gods of air, earth, and heaven. Afterward, Re made humans and all other beings and objects on Earth. In the above painting, Re, the ram-headed figure, crosses through the underworld in his boat, carrying the spirits of Egyptians who have died. When Re reappears above the horizon at the beginning of each new day, the souls of the dead are reborn into new lives with him.

Egyptians spent every day surrounded by symbols of their religion. They saw gods in the natural world, they had gods important to their hometowns, and they believed in gods of trade, justice, and prosperity. They expected the gods to care for them in the afterlife.

[5] **Ea:** god of wisdom and magic; father of Marduk
[6] **lullû:** humans

DOCUMENT-BASED QUESTIONS

1. **Explaining** Why did the Babylonian god Marduk create humans?
2. **Clarifying** In the Hebrew account, what was the expanse that separated water from water?
3. **Analyzing** How does the Egyptian god Re represent the sun?
4. **Contrasting** How is the depiction of the Hebrew deity different from those in the other two creation stories?
5. **Comparing** What similar event is found in all three creation accounts?
6. **Drawing Conclusions** What is the role of humans in each of the three creation stories?
7. **Synthesizing** How would you describe the beliefs that ancient societies held about the creation of the world?

C Critical Thinking

Analyzing Primary Sources
Ask: How did the ancient Egyptians picture Re? *(has body of man but head of ram; larger, more imposing than human spirits; conveys impression of power, strength)* **OL**

Assess/Close

Comparing and Contrasting
Have students use a chart to compare and contrast elements of each creation story. **OL**

DOCUMENT-BASED QUESTIONS

Answers:
1. to serve the gods
2. the sky
3. goes underground at night; reappears each morning
4. In the Hebrew account, there is only one god.
5. The gods create humans.
6. **Babylonian:** serve the gods to make their lives easier; **Hebrew:** take care of the land and all creatures on it; **Egyptian:** to be reborn with the gods
7. Answers should have analysis from all three accounts.

Additional Support

Activity: Interdisciplinary Connection

Literature Ask: Why do so many cultures have accounts of creation? *(Having an explanation for the existence of the world helped early people to feel less fearful about the mystery of creation and gave them a set of beliefs to help structure and organize their lives.)* Have students form small groups. Ask each group member to find a creation story from a different culture. They might choose from among the following: Hopi, Norse, Maori, Cherokee, Japanese, Chinese, ancient Greek, Aztec, Hindu. Have students share their stories with their groups. Then have groups organize a poster display that summarizes the important elements of each story and compares and contrasts them. Encourage groups to include illustrations and graphic organizers on their poster and to present the information in a way that is easy to understand. As a class, discuss similarities and differences between the stories in the text and those that students have presented. **OL**

Categorizing Information
Tell students that there are many ways to organize facts and details. Point out that this Visual Summary groups ideas under the headings Ancient Environments, Ancient Religions, and Ancient Innovations. Have volunteers read aloud the bullet points under each heading. **Ask:** What is another way in which these same details might be organized? *(Answers will vary, but students might say that the names of the cultures identified could be the headings: Mesopotamian, Egyptian, Phoenician, Persian, Israelite.)* Display a chart on the board, such as an expanded version of the one below, that incorporates sets of headings. Have students complete their charts. **BL**

	Persian	Egyptian
environment		
religion		
innovation		

Summarizing Have students use their charts to summarize what they have learned about each culture in their own words. **OL**

CHAPTER 2 Visual Summary

You can study anywhere, anytime by downloading quizzes and flash cards to your PDA from glencoe.com.

TOMB AT SAQQARA, EGYPT

Egyptian farmers drive cattle across a river.

ANCIENT ENVIRONMENTS

- The Egyptians received fertile soil from the floodwaters of the Nile for farming.
- The Phoenicians set up a trading empire and colonies on the Mediterranean.
- The Mesopotamians created irrigation and flood control systems.

ANCIENT RELIGIONS

- The Mesopotamians and the Egyptians, who both were polytheistic, believed their rulers derived their power from the gods.
- The Israelites were monotheistic and believed God communicated through prophets.
- The Persians followed Zoroastrianism, a monotheistic religion.

TEMPLE AT URUK, MESOPOTAMIA

The ancient Sumerian city of Uruk was one of the first cities in the world.

ACCOUNTING TABLET, MESOPOTAMIA

Sumerians used cuneiform to keep accounts, like this tablet account of donkeys harnessed for ploughing.

ANCIENT INNOVATIONS

- The Mesopotamians established a collection of laws, along with inventing the arch, dome, wheel, and a system of writing.
- The Phoenicians invented the alphabet.
- The Persians created the concept of a standing army.

Hands-On Chapter Project
Step 5: Wrap-Up

Publishing a Coffee Table Book

Students will synthesize what they have learned in Steps 1–4.

Step 5: Complete the Book

Directions: Display a Spider Map on the board. Add enough legs so that each can be labeled with the name of one of the civilizations discussed in this chapter. Have students review their coffee table books as well as the text to identify ways in which each civilization was noteworthy. Their details might include innovations in architecture, government, communication, science, or transportation as well as turning points in culture, religion, or language. Return to the Essential Question. Tell students that their answer to this question will form the introduction to their book. Have groups review the Spider Map and their own material before writing their introductions. Have students share their introductions and revise them as necessary before inserting them into their completed books. **OL**

Assessment

STANDARDIZED TEST PRACTICE

TEST-TAKING TIP

When a question asks for an answer related to a specific topic, such as geography, eliminate any choices that do not mention anything about that topic. Then choose the best answer from the choices that remain.

Reviewing Vocabulary

Directions: Choose the word or words that best complete the sentence.

1. Another word for province is ________.
- **A** city-state
- **B** empire
- **C** satrap
- **D** vizier

2. A ________ is a Sumerian stepped tower.
- **A** ziggurat
- **B** pyramid
- **C** stylus
- **D** papyrus

3. ________ is belief in one god rather than many gods.
- **A** Polytheism
- **B** Monotheism
- **C** Theocracy
- **D** Monarchy

4. In a ________, ruling power is passed from one generation to the next.
- **A** theocracy
- **B** bureaucracy
- **C** dynasty
- **D** patriarchy

Reviewing Main Ideas

Directions: Choose the best answers to the following questions.

Section 1 *(pp. 26–33)*

5. Who created the first Mesopotamian civilization?
- **A** Akkadians
- **B** Assyrians
- **C** Babylonians
- **D** Sumerians

6. Which ruler set up the first empire in world history?
- **A** Darius
- **B** Hammurabi
- **C** Sargon
- **D** Solomon

7. What was the most important Sumerian invention?
- **A** Alphabet
- **B** Writing
- **C** Bronze
- **D** Number system

Section 2 *(pp. 34–43)*

8. What god symbolized the new life brought to Egypt by the Nile?
- **A** Akhenaten
- **B** Osiris
- **C** Re
- **D** Seth

Need Extra Help?

If You Missed Questions . . .	1	2	3	4	5	6	7	8
Go to Page . . .	57	29	50	36	26	32	30	36

GO ON

Answers and Analyses

Reviewing Vocabulary

1. C Students should make sure they understand the meaning of *province* first. A province is a territory that is governed as part of a political unit. Since a vizier is a steward, or official, D can be eliminated. Both a city-state and an empire are political units in themselves, eliminating both A and B. A satrapy, which is a division of the Persian Empire, is equivalent to a province, making it the correct choice.

2. A Remind students to eliminate choices that they know are incorrect. A stylus is a writing implement, and papyrus is a type of material used to write on. Therefore, only ziggurat and pyramid remain. Although both are structures that rise into the sky, a pyramid is smoothly sloped.

TEST-TAKING TIP

For Question 2: The key word in the question for students to focus on is *Sumerian*. The only answer choice that is associated with Sumerian culture is ziggurat. The other three choices are associated with Egyptian culture.

3. B Tell students to use word parts to help them figure out the meanings of the choices. *Poly-* means "many," *mono-* means "one," and *theo* refers to "god." The only word that combines both *mono* and *theo* is *monotheism*.

4. C Again, tell students to examine the words themselves carefully for clues to their meaning. A theocracy is rule by divine authority. A bureaucracy is government by departments or bureaus. A patriarchy is a system in which males or a father has control. Therefore, dynasty is the correct answer.

Reviewing Main Ideas

5. D Sumer was the first civilization in this region. Their innovations and culture were expanded upon by later civilizations such as the Akkadians, Babylonians, and Assyrians.

6. C Remind students that an empire is a large political unit, made up of many territories or groups of people. Sargon, leader of the Akkadians, was the first to conquer surrounding city-states and merge them into one unit.

7. B All of these choices contributed to the advancement of civilization. However, the alphabet is associated with the Phoenicians. Bronze and the number system, both inventions of the Sumerians, were not as revolutionary.

8. B Remind students of the myth of Osiris, in which he is killed by Seth and tossed into the Nile, then brought back to life by his wife Isis.

9. A This question might be challenging because all of the choices name pharaohs. However, the Old Kingdom was the time during which most pyramid construction took place. Khufu is the only Old Kingdom pharaoh named.

10. C Indo-Europeans spoke several different languages, but they were all derived from the same origin. C is the best choice because it was common to all Indo-Europeans.

11. D Students should remember from their reading that Phoenicians invented the set of characters known as the first alphabet. Hittites were perhaps best known for their use of iron; Chaldeans for their defeat of Assyria and of Judah; and Israelites for their religion.

12. C Remind students that the Assyrians were brutal and harsh conquerors who displaced the people in the territories they overran and plundered the countryside before them. Therefore, A and B are incorrect. D is also incorrect, because the Persian Empire was the largest.

13. B Ashurbanipal was an Assyrian king; therefore, he would not be noted for his compassion, leaving two Persian kings and the king of Babylonia. Of these choices, Cyrus is correct, since his treatment of conquered peoples won him their respect and enabled his empire to grow through generations.

Critical Thinking

14. B Although the Code of Hammurabi removed personal vengeance from the system of justice, the punishments were often equivalent to the crime.

CHAPTER 2

9. During whose reign was the Great Pyramid at Giza built?

A Khufu
B Hatshepsut
C Ramses II
D Tutankhamen

Section 3 *(pp. 46–51)*

10. What was the common characteristic of Indo-Europeans?

A Their weapons
B Their crops
C Their language
D Their religion

11. Who invented the alphabet that influenced the Greeks and Romans?

A Chaldeans
B Hittites
C Israelites
D Phoenicians

Section 4 *(pp. 54–57)*

12. Which statement best describes the Assyrians?

A They respected other civilizations.
B They were admired by their captives.
C They were good at conquering others.
D They had the world's largest empire.

13. Which Persian ruler was known for his wisdom and compassion?

A Ashurbanipal
B Cyrus
C Darius
D Nebuchadnezzar

Critical Thinking

Directions: Choose the best answers to the following questions.

14. Which statement best reflects the principles in the Code of Hammurabi?

A Women and men are equal.
B Demand an eye for an eye.
C Let the buyer beware.
D Judges are above the law.

15. Why were the pharaohs of the Middle Kingdom different from those of earlier periods?

A They felt more responsible for taking care of their people.
B They believed in the sun god as the most important god.
C They engaged in the practice of mummification.
D They defeated the Hyksos and created an empire.

Base your answer to question 16 on the chart below and your knowledge of world history.

Comparing Life in Mesopotamia and Egypt

	Mesopotamia	Egypt
Landforms	Flat plains	Deserts, seas, cataracts
Government	City-states ruled by divinely selected kings	Rural villages ruled by dynastic god-kings
Social Structure	Nobles; commoners; slaves	Nobles and priests; merchants, scribes, artisans and tax collectors; farmers

16. How was life in Mesopotamia and Egypt similar?

A They were both extremely hierarchical.
B They both were made up of rural villages.
C Egypt's kings were treated as gods, while Mesopotamia's kings were men who were divinely selected.
D Commoners had no rights in either society.

Need Extra Help?

If You Missed Questions . . .	9	10	11	12	13	14	15	16
Go to Page . . .	37	46	48	54	56	33	38	26

GO ON

TEST-TAKING TIP

For Question 14: Remind students that questions such as these that ask them to recall main ideas from the text require a careful reading of their textbooks. From their reading, students should be able to identify one of the main principles of these laws: the emphasis on the principle of retribution.

15. A Remind students that pharaohs of the Middle Kingdom were known as shepherds, who took care of their flock, or people.

16. A Remind students to evaluate each statement based on the chart information and what the question is asking. Since Mesopotamia was made up of city-states, B can be eliminated. Although C is an accurate statement, it states a difference between the societies. D cannot be judged based on the chart. A is correct since both societies have different levels of social classes.

Assessment

17. Which of the following shows the correct chronological order of empires in the ancient world?

A Akkadian, Assyrian, Egyptian, Persian
B Akkadian, Egyptian, Assyrian, Persian
C Egyptian, Akkadian, Assyrian, Persian
D Assyrian, Persian, Akkadian, Egyptian

Analyze the map and answer the question that follows. Base your answer on the map.

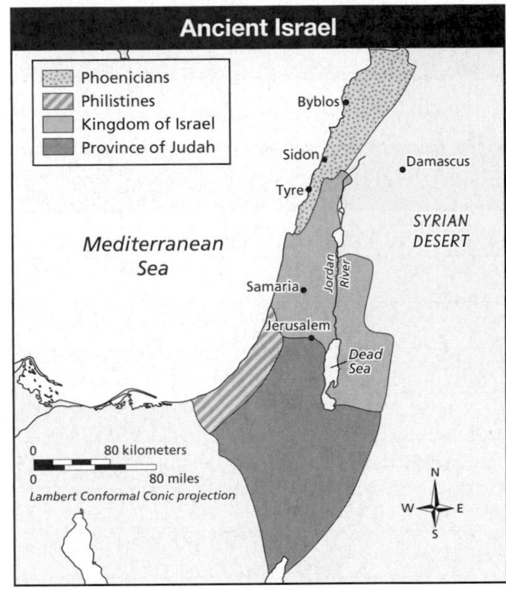

18. Based on the map, how did the Phoenicians probably trade with other civilizations?

A Along the Mediterranean Sea
B Across the Syrian Desert
C Trade was likely unimportant.
D Trade went through Samaria.

Document-Based Questions

Directions: Analyze the document and answer the short answer questions that follow the document.

Read the following Mesopotamian poem.

> *"The rampant flood which no man can oppose,*
> *Which shakes the heavens and causes earth to tremble,*
> *In an appalling blanket folds mother and child,*
> *And drowns the harvest in its time of ripeness."*

19. How does this poem represent the Mesopotamians' attitude toward nature?

20. Explain the meaning of the line: "Which shakes the heavens and causes earth to tremble."

Extended Response

21. Literature often reflects a people's worldview. How does this poem represent the importance of the physical environment and religion in the lives of the Mesopotamians?

History ONLINE
For additional test practice, use Self-Check Quizzes—Chapter 2 at glencoe.com.

Need Extra Help?

If You Missed Questions . . .	17	18	19	20	21
Go to Page . . .	32	26	63	63	63

STOP

Document-Based Questions

19. It shows how the power of nature made them feel helpless, since they were dependent on this unpredictable force.

20. It refers to powerful storms related to the floods and to possible earthquakes or strong thunder, which can cause the ground to shudder.

Extended Response

21. Answers will vary, but may include these ideas: Mesopotamians depended on the rivers, but the floods were unpredictable and caused great hardship. They had to control the rivers to grow crops well. Their experience of nature caused them to have a harsh view of the world and to see the gods as unpredictable and often harmful.

TEST-TAKING

For extended response questions, remind students of the importance of organizing their answers to ensure a well-thought-out response and of budgeting their time to allow them a chance to revise and proofread their essays.

17. B Remind students to use the facts that they know to help them determine the correct sequence. The Akkadian Empire was the first in world history, so C and D can be eliminated. The Persian Empire followed the Assyrian. Therefore, B is correct.

18. A Have students check the choices against the map. Since the Phoenicians were a seafaring people, they would most likely trade along the coast, so students can eliminate B and D. Trade was very important to the Phoenicians, so C can also be eliminated.

History ONLINE
Introduce students to chapter content and key terms by having them access the Chapter 2 Overview at glencoe.com.

Need Extra Help?
Have students refer to the pages listed if they miss any of the questions.

CHAPTER 3 Planning Guide

Key to Ability Levels

BL Below Level
OL On Level
AL Above Level
ELL English Language Learners

Key to Teaching Resources

Print Material
CD-ROM
DVD
Transparency

Levels				Resources	Chapter Opener	Section 1	Section 2	Section 3	Section 4	Chapter Assess
BL	OL	AL	ELL							
				FOCUS						
BL	OL	AL	ELL	**Daily Focus Skills Transparencies**		3-1	3-2	3-3	3-4	
				TEACH						
BL	OL	AL	ELL	**Charting and Graphing Activity, URB**					✓	
	OL	AL		**Economics and History Activity, URB**					✓	
BL	OL		ELL	**Reading Skills Activity, URB**		p. 91				
	OL	AL		**Historical Analysis Skills Activity, URB**		p. 92				
BL	OL	AL	ELL	**Differentiated Instruction Activity, URB**		p. 93				
	OL		ELL	**English Learner Activity, URB**			p. 95			
BL	OL	AL	ELL	**Content Vocabulary Activity, URB***		p. 97				
BL	OL	AL	ELL	**Academic Vocabulary Activity, URB**		p. 99				
BL	OL	AL	ELL	**Skills Reinforcement Activity, URB**				p. 101		
	OL	AL		**Critical Thinking Skills Activity, URB**		p. 102				
	OL	AL		**History and Geography Activity, URB**			p. 103			
	OL	AL	ELL	**Mapping History Activity, URB**			p. 105			
BL	OL	AL		**Historical Significance Activity, URB**				p. 106		
BL	OL	AL	ELL	**Cooperative Learning Activity, URB**		p. 107				
	OL	AL	ELL	**History Simulation Activity, URB**					p. 109	
BL	OL	AL	ELL	**Time Line Activity, URB**					p. 111	
	OL	AL		**Linking Past and Present Activity, URB**			p. 112			
BL	OL	AL		**People in World History Activity, URB**			p. 113		p. 114	
BL	OL	AL	ELL	**Primary Source Reading, URB**					p. 115	
	OL	AL		**Enrichment Activity, URB**				p. 120		
BL	OL	AL	ELL	**World Art and Music Activity, URB**					p. 117	
BL	OL		ELL	**Guided Reading Activities, URB***		p. 122	p. 123	p. 124	p. 125	
BL	OL		ELL	**Reading Essentials and Note-Taking Guide***		p. 19	p. 22	p. 25	p. 28	
BL	OL	AL	ELL	**Differentiated Instruction for the World History Classroom**	✓	✓	✓	✓	✓	✓

Note: Please refer to the *Unit Resource Book: The First Civilizations and Empires* for this chapter's URB materials.

* Also available in Spanish

- Interactive Lesson Planner
- Interactive Teacher Edition
- Fully editable blackline masters
- Section Spotlight Videos Launch
- Differentiated Lesson Plans
- Printable reports of daily assignments
- Standards Tracking System

Levels BL	OL	AL	ELL		Resources	Chapter Opener	Section 1	Section 2	Section 3	Section 4	Chapter Assess
					TEACH *(continued)*						
BL	OL	AL	ELL		StudentWorks™ Plus DVD	✓	✓	✓	✓	✓	✓
BL	OL	AL	ELL		Vocabulary PuzzleMaker CD-ROM	✓	✓	✓	✓	✓	✓
Teacher Resources					Building Academic Vocabulary	✓	✓	✓	✓	✓	✓
					Reading Strategies and Activities for the Social Studies Classroom				pp. 26, 29, 30		
					Writer's Guidebook		pp. 27, 43	pp. 43, 47			
					Foods Around the World				pp. 26, 29, 30		
					Strategies for Success	✓	✓	✓	✓	✓	✓
					Outline Map Resource Book	✓	✓	✓	✓	✓	✓
					Presentation Plus! with MindJogger DVD	✓	✓	✓	✓	✓	✓
					ASSESS						
BL	OL	AL	ELL		Section Quizzes and Chapter Tests*		p. 23	p. 24	p. 25	p. 26	p. 27
BL	OL	AL	ELL		Authentic Assessment With Rubrics	✓	✓	✓	✓	✓	✓
BL	OL	AL	ELL		Standardized Test Practice Workbook	✓	✓	✓	✓	✓	✓
BL	OL	AL	ELL		*ExamView® Assessment Suite* CD-ROM		3-1	3-2	3-3	3-4	Ch. 3
BL	OL	AL	ELL		Interactive Tutor Self-Assessment CD-ROM		3-1	3-2	3-3	3-4	
					CLOSE						
BL			ELL		Reteaching Activity, URB					p. 119	
BL	OL		ELL		Reading and Study Skills Foldables™	✓	✓	✓	✓	✓	✓

Using the Glencoe Web Site

Chapter Overviews

Technology Product

The Glencoe Web site offers in-depth overviews that summarize the content of each chapter. The overviews consist of brief chapter summaries and separate overviews for each section. The chapter overviews

- summarize and reinforce chapter content;
- provide discussion points to use in class.

Objectives

The overviews help students

- prepare for better understanding chapter content;
- practice reading and comprehension skills.

Steps

Provide students with the following steps to complete the activities:

- Locate the Web page for the textbook being studied on the Glencoe Web site glencoe.com.
- Click on **Student Center** under the textbook title.
- Once you are in the Student Center, select a unit from the Unit Resources menu and a chapter from the Chapter Activities menu using the drop-down arrows.
- Click on the **Chapter Overviews** link.
- Have students read the chapter overview in preparation for a reading assignment or activity.

History ONLINE

	Student	Teacher	Parent
Beyond the Textbook	●	●	●
Chapter Overviews	●	●	●
Time Current Events	●		●
ePuzzles and Games	●		●
Concepts in Motion	●		●
Literature Connections		●	
Multi-Language Glossaries	●		●
Online Student Edition	●	●	●
Self-Check Quizzes	●		●
Student Web Activities	●		●
Study Central ™	●		●
Teaching Today		●	
Vocabulary eFlashcards	●		●
Web Activity Lesson Plans		●	

- **Timed Readings Plus in Social Studies** helps students increase their reading rate and fluency while maintaining comprehension. The 400-word passages are similar to those found on state and national assessments.
- **Reading in the Content Area: Social Studies** concentrates on six essential reading skills that help students better comprehend what they read. The book includes 75 high-interest nonfiction passages written at increasing levels of difficulty.
- **Reading Social Studies** includes strategic reading instruction and vocabulary support in Social Studies content for both ELLs and native speakers of English.

www.jamestowneducation.com

Biography  

The following videotape programs are available from Glencoe as supplements to Chapter 3:

- Confucius: World of Wisdom (0-76-700407-8)
- The Great Wall of China (0-76-700361-6)

To order, call Glencoe at 1-800-334-7344. To find classroom resources to accompany many of these videos, check the following home pages:

A&E Television: www.aetv.com

The History Channel: www.historychannel.com

Index to National Geographic Magazine:

The following articles relate to this chapter:

- "Buddha Rising," by Perry Garfinkel, December 2005
- "Jewels in the Ash," by Cliff Tarpy, August 2005
- "The Han Dynasty," by Mike Edwards, February 2004

National Geographic Society Products To order the following, call National Geographic at 1-800-368-2728:

- *Ancient China* (PicturePack)
- *Ancient India* (PicturePack)
- *National Geographic Atlas of the World* (Book).

Access National Geographic's new, dynamic MapMachine Web site and other geography resources at:

www.nationalgeographic.com

www.nationalgeographic.com/maps

GLENCOE BOOKLINK 3

Use this database to search more than 30,000 titles to create a customized reading list for your students.

- Reading lists can be organized by students' reading level, author, genre, theme, or area of interest.
- The database provides Degrees of Reading Power™ (DRP) and Lexile™ readability scores for all selections.
- A brief summary of each selection is included.

Leveled reading suggestions for this chapter:

For students at a Grade 8 reading level:
- ***Qin Shi Huangdi,*** by Peggy Pancella

For students at a Grade 9 reading level:
- ***India,*** by Amanda Barker

For students at a Grade 10 reading level:
- ***The Emperor's Silent Army: Terracotta Warrior,*** by Jane O'Connor

For students at a Grade 11 reading level:
- ***Confucius: The Golden Rule,*** by Russell Freedman

For students at a Grade 12 reading level:
- ***Life in the Ancient Indus River Valley,*** by Hazel Richardson

Introducing
CHAPTER 3

Focus

MAKING CONNECTIONS
How can location protect historical artifacts?

Activate students' prior knowledge by asking them to recall important archaeological discoveries that they read about in Chapters 1 and 2. *(Answers may include fossils discovered by the Leakeys, cave paintings in southwestern France and northern Spain, walled cities and villages of the Neolithic Age, and temples and tombs of Egypt and Mesopotamia.)* Discuss how well artifacts were preserved in the different types of locations.

Teach

The Big Ideas

As students study the chapter, remind them to consider the section-based Big Ideas included in each section's Guide to Reading. The **Essential Questions** in the activities below tie in to the Big Ideas and help students think about and understand important chapter concepts. In addition, the Hands-on Chapter Projects with their culminating activities relate the content from each section to the Big Ideas. These activities build on each other as students progress through the chapter. Section activities culminate in the wrap-up activity on the Visual Summary page.

CHAPTER 3

India and China 3000 B.C.–A.D. 500

MAKING CONNECTIONS

How can location protect historical artifacts?

In 1819 a hunting party stumbled upon the hidden caves of Ajanta. From about 200 B.C. to A.D. 650, Buddhist monks excavated 32 caves and carved stairs, columns, and sculptures into the cliffs. By oil lamp, they painted the life of the Buddha as well as scenes from nature and daily life. In this chapter you will learn about ancient India and China.

- How would the caves' isolation have helped preserve them?
- Why are buildings abandoned in your area? What happens to them?

THE WORLD ▶

c. 3000 B.C. Cities built in Indus River valley

c. 1500 B.C. Aryans enter India

3500 B.C. | 2500 B.C. | 1500 B.C.

c. 1750 B.C. Shang dynasty begins

64

Early Civilizations in India
Essential Question: What geographic factors do you think influenced the development of Indian civilizations? *(climate, land, water access)* Point out that in Section 1, students will learn about the geography of India and its early civilizations. **OL**

New Empires in India
Essential Question: What do you think helped bring about early empires in India? *(defeat of enemy invaders, growth of trade)* Point out that in Section 2, students will learn about the early empires of India, including their leaders. **OL**

Introducing
CHAPTER 3

More About the Photo

Visual Literacy India's Ajanta Caves were discovered in 1819 by British army officers who were on a tiger hunt. These caves were retreats for Buddhist monks as far back as the 2nd century B.C. Later, during the Gupta period of the 5th and 6th centuries A.D., a number of beautifully decorated caves were added. The paintings and sculptures that are located in the caves are seen as masterpieces of Buddhist religious art and continue to influence the art world today.

Dinah Zike's Foldables

Dinah Zike's Foldables are three-dimensional, interactive graphic organizers that help students practice basic writing skills, review vocabulary terms, and identify main ideas. Instructions for creating and using Foldables can be found in the Appendix at the end of this book and in the *Dinah Zike's Reading and Study Skills Foldables* booklet.

History ONLINE

Introduce students to chapter content and key terms by having them access the Chapter 3 Overview at glencoe.com.

c. 563 B.C. Birth of the Buddha, Siddhārtha Gautama

c. 200 B.C. Travel on the Silk Road begins

500 B.C. — 500 A.D.

c. 551 B.C. Birth of Confucius

c. A.D. 200 Han dynasty famous for bronze sculptures

FOLDABLES Study Organizer

Organizing Create a Four-Tab Book to record What, Where, When, and Why/How facts while you read about the Great Wall of China or the Silk Road.

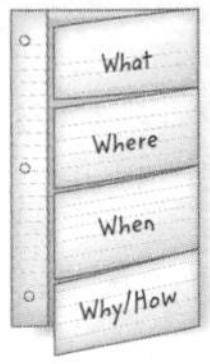

What / Where / When / Why/How

History ONLINE

Chapter Overview—Visit glencoe.com to preview Chapter 3.

SECTION 3

Early Chinese Civilizations

Essential Question: Why did Chinese civilizations develop in river valleys? *(Water from the rivers could be used to grow crops.)* Point out that in Section 3, students will learn how the geography of China influenced the development of its early civilizations. **OL**

SECTION 4

Rise and Fall of Chinese Empires

Essential Question: Why were government and social structure important to early Chinese dynasties? *(They helped bring stability to the empires.)* Point out that in Section 4, students will learn about the achievements of the Qin and Han dynasties. **OL**

Focus

Bellringer

Daily Focus Transparency 3.1

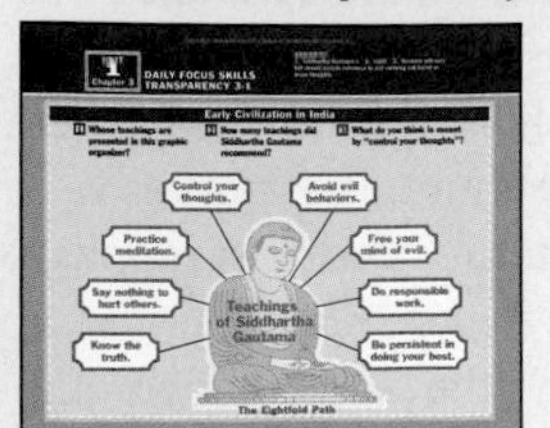

GUIDE TO READING

Answers to Graphic:

life of privilege; awareness of suffering; self-denial; intense meditation; enlightenment

Section Spotlight Video

To generate student interest and provide a springboard for class discussion, access the Chapter 3, Section 1 video at glencoe.com or on the video DVD.

Early Civilizations in India

GUIDE TO READING

The BIG Idea

Physical Geography Changes to the physical environment and the migration of the Aryans led to major changes in India's culture beginning around 1800 B.C.

Content Vocabulary

- monsoon *(p. 66)*
- Sanskrit *(p. 70)*
- *varnas* *(p. 70)*
- caste *(p. 71)*
- Hinduism *(p. 72)*
- yoga *(p. 72)*
- reincarnation *(p. 73)*
- karma *(p. 73)*
- dharma *(p. 73)*
- Buddhism *(p. 73)*
- nirvana *(p. 74)*

Academic Vocabulary

- via *(p. 69)*
- reveal *(p. 70)*

People and Places

- Himalaya *(p. 66)*
- Indus River *(p. 66)*
- Harappa *(p. 68)*
- Mohenjo Daro *(p. 68)*
- Aryans *(p. 69)*
- Siddhārtha Gautama *(p. 73)*

Reading Strategy

Sequencing Information As you read, use a diagram like the one below to illustrate the process that led Siddhārtha Gautama to enlightenment.

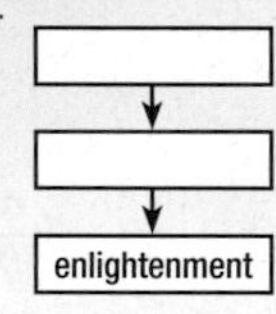

The Indus River valley was the largest of the early river valley civilizations. An extensive river system supported agriculture, the development of cities, and widespread trade. Climate also was important to India's agriculture and development.

The Impact of Geography

MAIN IDEA India's mountains and location have played an important part in the development of the Indian subcontinent. Monsoons coming from the north and the south bring moisture to the farmers who live there.

HISTORY & YOU What is the climate like in your region? How does the climate affect your clothing, activities, and architecture? Learn about the effects of monsoons on India's climate.

India is a land of diversity. Today, about 110 languages and more than 1,000 dialects—varieties of language—are spoken in India. Diversity is also apparent in India's geography. The Indian subcontinent, shaped like a triangle hanging from the southern ridge of Asia, is composed of a number of core regions, including mountain ranges, river valleys, a dry interior plateau, and fertile coastal plains.

Mountains, Rivers, and Plains

In the far north are the **Himalaya,** the highest mountains in the world. Directly south of the Himalaya is the rich valley of the Ganges (GAN•jeez) River, one of the chief regions of Indian culture. To the west is the **Indus River** valley, a relatively dry plateau that forms the backbone of the modern state of Pakistan. In ancient times, the Indus Valley enjoyed a more moderate climate and served as the cradle of Indian civilization.

South of India's two major river valleys—the valleys of the Ganges and the Indus—lies the Deccan Plateau, which extends from the Ganges Valley to the southern tip of India. The interior of the plateau is relatively hilly and dry. India's eastern and western coasts are lush plains. These plains have historically been among the most densely populated regions of India.

Monsoons

The primary feature of India's climate is the **monsoon,** a seasonal wind pattern in southern Asia. During the months of June through September, monsoon winds from the south and southwest blow across the Arabian Sea, part of the Indian Ocean. These summer monsoons carrying moisture-laden air cause heavy rainfall across

Resource Manager

R Reading Strategies	C Critical Thinking	D Differentiated Instruction	W Writing Support	S Skill Practice
Teacher Edition • Inferring, p. 70 • Academic Vocab., p. 72 • Identifying, p. 72 **Additional Resources** • Read. Skills Act., URB p. 91 • Cont. Vocab. Act., URB p. 97 • Read. Ess. & Note-Taking Guide, p. 19	**Teacher Edition** • Making Inferences, pp. 68, 73 • Analyzing Info., p. 70 • Drawing Con., p. 73 • Compare/Contrast, p. 74 • Det. Cause/Effect, p. 74 **Additional Resources** • Crit. Think. Act., URB p. 102 • Section Quiz, p. 23	**Teacher Edition** • Adv. Learners, p. 68 • Visual/Spatial, p. 69 **Additional Resources** • Diff. Instr. Act., URB p. 93 • Coop. Learn. Act., URB p. 107 • Guid. Read. Act., URB p. 122	**Teacher Edition** • Descriptive Writing, p. 69 • Expository Writing, p. 71 **Additional Resources** • Writer's Guidebook, pp. 27, 43	**Teacher Edition** • Interpreting Graphs, p. 67 **Additional Resources** • Hist. Analysis Skills Act., URB p. 92 • Academic Vocab. Act., URB p. 99

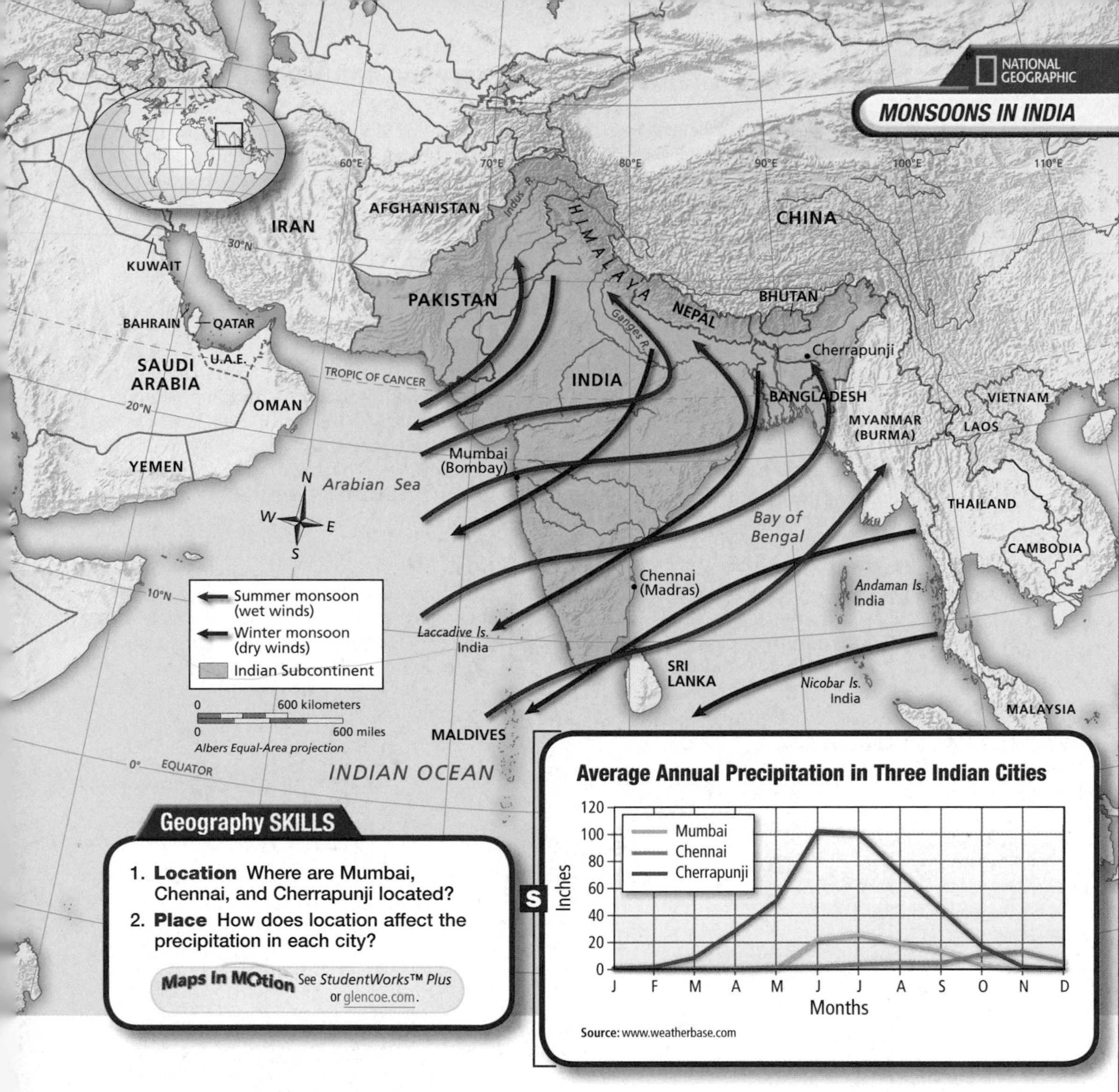

Geography SKILLS

1. **Location** Where are Mumbai, Chennai, and Cherrapunji located?
2. **Place** How does location affect the precipitation in each city?

Maps In MOtion See StudentWorks™ Plus or glencoe.com.

the subcontinent, especially on the west coast near Mumbai, once called Bombay.

During the cooler season, from October through February, the wind pattern reverses direction and blows from the north and northeast. Although this air is cooler and drier than the summer monsoons, the winter monsoons bring significant rainfall to the east coast of India.

The wettest place on earth is in the mountains of northeast India. Winds blow over the plains below, rise up the mountainside, cool, and release rain.

Throughout history, Indian farmers have depended on the heavy rains brought by the southwest monsoons. If the rains come early or late, or too much or too little rain falls, crops are destroyed and thousands starve.

✓Reading Check **Describing** How does the monsoon affect Indian farmers?

Teach

S Skill Practice

Interpreting Graphs Ask: Which city receives the most precipitation annually? *(Cherrapunji)* **BL**

For additional practice on this skill, see the **Skills Handbook**.

Geography SKILLS

Answers:

1. **Mumbai**: on the west coast of India; **Chennai:** on the east coast; **Cherrapunji:** in the mountains
2. Summer monsoons create extensive precipitation in Mumbai, winter monsoons affect Chennai, but both monsoons affect Cherrapunji, which is the wettest place on earth.

✓Reading Check

Answer: They depend on it for growing their crops. Too much rain or too little can wipe out the crops.

Hands-On Chapter Project Step 1

Creating a Poster of Early India and China

Students will design a poster depicting early civilizations of India and China.

Step 1: Gathering Information

Essential Question: What was life like in early India and China?

Directions: Tell students that they will work independently to design a poster depicting early India and China. As they study Section 1, they can begin gathering information for the poster. Write the Section 1 Big Idea on the board and tell students to use it as a guide for selecting material. Tell them to look for social, political, and economic events or movements to include. Items can be written on note cards to be used later for creating text and captions for the poster.

Summarizing: Allow time for students to share what they learned about the Section 1 Big Idea while searching for poster material. Students will continue to gather information as they study Section 2. In addition, they will plan a format for their poster. **OL**

(Chapter Project is continued in Section 2.)

C Critical Thinking

Making Inferences Ask: Why do you think the Harappan people built walls around their neighborhoods? *(They probably needed the walls to safeguard their possessions or for protection against enemies or invasions.)* OL

For additional practice on this skill, see the **Skills Handbook**.

D Differentiated Instruction

Advanced Learners Students who are artistically inclined might enjoy drawing a scene depicting some aspect of Harappan life. Possibilities include a walled neighborhood, a typical house, or cutaways of the trash or drainage systems. Tell students to base their drawings on the descriptions provided in the text. OL

Additional Support

Indus Valley Civilization

MAIN IDEA The cities of the Indus Valley civilization were well planned and very advanced.

HISTORY & YOU What kinds of public services does your city provide? Find out about the Indus Valley cities.

As in Mesopotamia and Egypt, early civilizations in India and China emerged in river valleys. Between 3000 B.C. and 1500 B.C., the valleys of the Indus River supported a flourishing civilization that extended hundreds of miles from the Himalaya to the coast of the Arabian Sea. Archaeologists have found the remains of more than a thousand settlements in this region. Two of the ruins, about 400 miles (644 km) apart, were sites of the cities of **Harappa** (huh•RA•puh) and **Mohenjo Daro** (moh•hehn•joh DAHR•oh). An advanced civilization flourished in these cities for hundreds of years. Historians call it the Harappan or Indus civilization.

Harappa and Mohenjo Daro

At its height, Harappa had 35,000 inhabitants, and Mohenjo Daro about 35,000 to 40,000. Both cities were carefully planned. The broad main streets ran in a north-south direction and were crossed by smaller east-west roads. Both cities were divided into large walled neighborhoods, with narrow lanes separating the rows of houses. Houses varied in size, some as high as three stories, but all followed the same plan of a square courtyard surrounded by rooms.

Most buildings were constructed of oven-baked mud bricks and were square, forming a grid pattern. Public wells provided a regular supply of water for all the inhabitants. Bathrooms featured an advanced drainage system. Wastewater flowed out to drains located under the streets and then was carried to sewage pits beyond the city walls. A system of chutes took household trash from houses to street-level garbage bins. Only a well-organized government could have maintained such carefully structured cities.

NATIONAL GEOGRAPHIC

INDUS CIVILIZATION AND TRADE

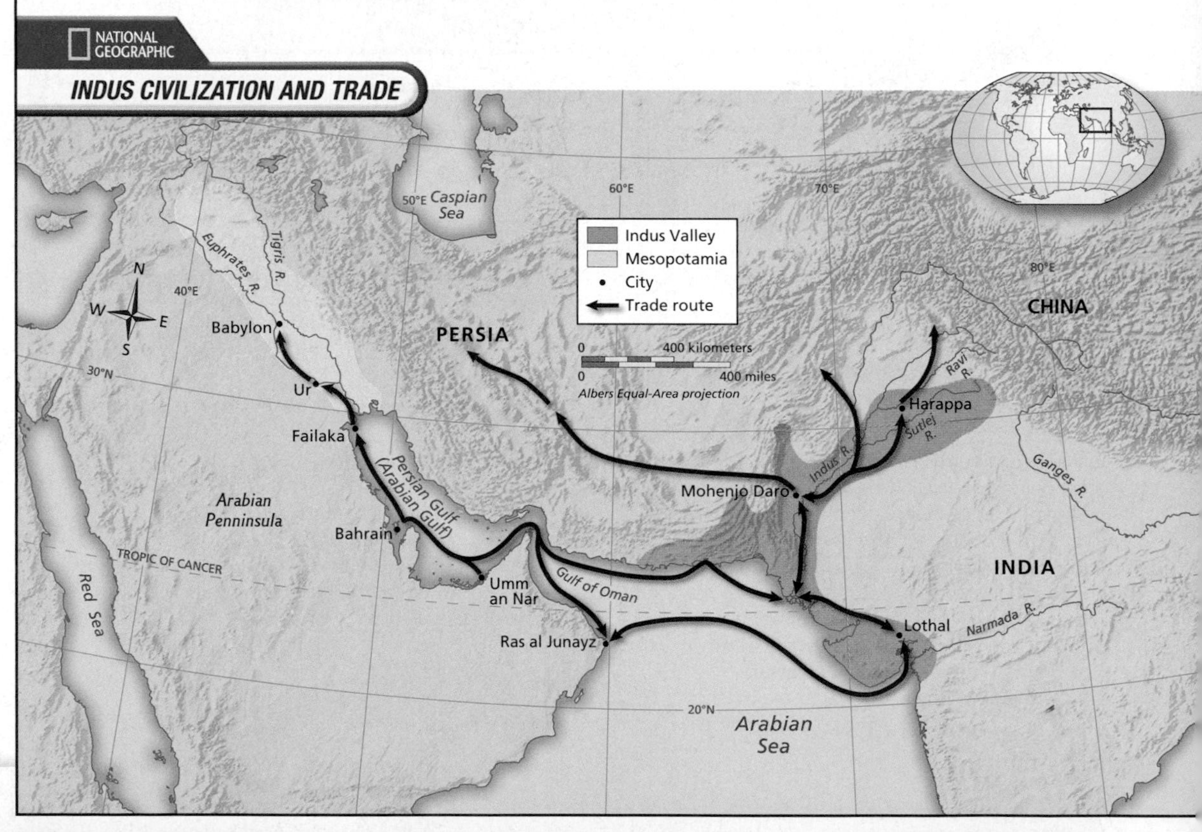

Extending the Content

Harappan Language Historians believe that the Harappan language may have been Dravidian in origin; the writing probably included between 250 and 500 characters. The seals were made from steatite (a soft stone). In addition to the fantastical creature shown on page 69, seals depicted a variety of real animals, as well as beasts that were a combination of animals. Some seals also depicted human figures. Archaeologists have also found examples of small stone sculptures that depict humans and gods. Though much about the end of Harappan civilization is still debated, archaeological evidence strongly indicates that Mohenjo Daro was severely damaged by a series of floods and that its destruction was probably hastened by the arrival of the Aryans.

Rulers and the Economy

As in Egypt and Mesopotamia, Harappan rulers based their power on a belief in divine assistance. Religion and political power were closely linked. That the royal palace and the holy temple were combined in the citadel, or fortress, at Harappa shows this close connection. Priests probably prayed to a fertility deity to guarantee the annual harvest.

The Harappan economy was based on farming. The Indus River flooded every year, providing rich soil to grow wheat, barley, and peas. The Indus Valley civilization also carried on trade as far away as Mesopotamia. Sumerian textiles and food were traded for Indus Valley copper, lumber, precious stones, cotton, and various luxury goods. Although some trade goods were carried overland, most goods went on ships **via** the Persian Gulf. **W**

✓Reading Check **Explaining** What evidence indicates that there were well-organized governments in Harappa and Mohenjo Daro?

Seals pressed into wet clay identified the owner of the goods. Unicorns were the most common animals on seals.

Geography SKILLS

1. **Place** What were the dominant physical characteristics of the Indus Valley civilization?
2. **Human-Environment Interaction** How did the Indus people use their environment for trade?

Migration and Interaction

MAIN IDEA Around 1500 B.C., India's culture changed, and the Indus Valley cities were abandoned.

HISTORY & YOU Have you seen news stories about floods and other natural disasters? Read how climate changes may have changed India's culture.

How the Indus Valley civilization came to an end continues to be a mystery. Archaeologists have discovered signs of gradual decay in Indus Valley cities beginning around 1800 B.C. Floods, an earthquake, changes in climate, and even a change in the course of the Indus River weakened the once-flourishing civilization in the Indus River valley. The final blow to the cities may have been an influx of new people. While other theories about the end of the Indus Valley civilization abound, all agree that about 1500 B.C. there was a major shift in India's culture. Many historians explain this shift as the result of a foreign migration.

Arrival of the Aryans

Around 2000 B.C. a group of Indo-European-speaking nomadic peoples began to move out of the steppes of central Asia. Indo-Europeans all spoke similar languages. Some migrated west to Europe. Others moved south to Iran and later to the Indus Valley. One group, known as the **Aryans,** moved south across the Hindu Kush mountain range into the plains of northern India. Historians know little about the origins and early culture of the Aryans. The Aryans lived in tribal groups and had a strong warrior tradition. As they settled in northern India, the nomads came into contact with the Indus Valley civilization. **D**

From around 1500 B.C. to 1000 B.C., the Aryan peoples gradually advanced eastward from the Indus Valley, across the fertile plain of the Ganges, and later southward into the Deccan Plateau. Eventually they extended their political control throughout all of India. The ongoing migrations and interaction between the Aryans and the Dravidians—descendants of the Indus Valley people—eventually resulted in a new and unique culture.

W Writing Support

Descriptive Writing Have students write a paragraph summarizing the information that describes what is known about Harappan civilization. **OL**

D Differentiated Instruction

Visual/Spatial Students who learn better visually may benefit from seeing the Aryan migration route. Use the physical map of Asia in the Atlas to help students trace the route across the Hindu Kush, down into the Indus Valley, then east across the Ganges, and south into the Deccan Plateau. **BL**

Geography SKILLS

Answers:

1. mountains to north, river systems, surrounded by seas
2. used the river system and seas for shipping

✓Reading Check

Answer: There were accommodations for public drinking water, sewer, drainage, and trash.

Activity: Collaborative Learning

Creating a Display of Harappan Life

Ask: How do you imagine Harappan life? Divide the class into small groups. Have each group create a display of Harappan civilization based on information in this section. If you have assigned the Writing Support activity provided on this page, suggest that students consult their paragraphs for ideas to include in the display. Encourage groups to exercise creativity in formatting their displays. Formats can include a chart with categories for various aspects of Harappan life, models or other visuals with explanatory captions, or a combination of these and other elements. Have each group select a member to present and explain the display to the class. **OL**

Teacher Tip

Collaborative Learning This activity allows students with different levels of academic skills and intelligences to work together. As you form groups, consider the needed skills and choose students accordingly.

R1 **Reading Strategy**

Academic Vocabulary Explain to students that the word *ultimate* can mean either "greatest possible" or "final." **Ask:** How might both of these definitions apply to the concept of Brahman? *(Possible answers: Meditation can lead to the highest state or greatest possible reality; uniting with Brahman after death is the final reality.)* **OL**

R2 **Reading Strategy**

Identifying **Ask:** What purpose do the human-like gods and goddesses serve for Hindu believers? *(They provide concrete images that ordinary people can relate to in terms of heavenly salvation.)* **OL**

Religions of India

MAIN IDEA Hinduism and Buddhism share some common beliefs.

HISTORY & YOU How has religion influenced your society? Learn how Hinduism and Buddhism were crucial in shaping the civilization of India.

Two of the world's great religions, Hinduism and Buddhism, began in India. Both were crucial in shaping civilization in India. Aryan beliefs blended with the religious practices of the Dravidians to form Hinduism. In the sixth century B.C., a new religion, known as Buddhism, emerged to rival Hinduism.

Hinduism

Hinduism had its origins in the religious beliefs of the Aryan peoples who settled in India. Evidence about the religious beliefs of the Aryan peoples comes from the Vedas, collections of hymns and religious ceremonies that were passed down orally by Aryan priests and then eventually written down.

R1 Early Hindus believed in the existence of a single force in the universe, a form of ultimate reality or god, called *Brahman*. It was the duty of the individual self—called the *atman*—to seek to know this ultimate reality. By doing so, the self would merge with Brahman after death.

How does one achieve oneness with god? Hindus developed the practice of **yoga**, a method of training designed to lead to such union. The goal of yoga, which means "union," is to leave behind earthly life and join Brahman in a kind of dreamless sleep. One Hindu text states, "When all the senses are stilled, when the mind is at rest, that, say the wise, is the highest state."

R2 Most ordinary Indians, however, could not easily relate to this ideal and needed a more concrete form of heavenly salvation. It was probably for this reason that Hinduism came to have a number of human-like gods and goddesses. The three chief gods are Brahma the Creator, Vishnu the Preserver, and Shiva (SIH•vuh) the Destroyer. Many Hindus regard these gods as simply

HISTORY & ARTS PRIMARY SOURCE

Hindu Gods in Art

In Hindu art, the three main human forms are Brahma, Vishnu, and Shiva. Each may have other forms, with its own symbols and adherents. Artists have painted and sculpted Hindu gods for thousands of years, so the representations vary greatly.

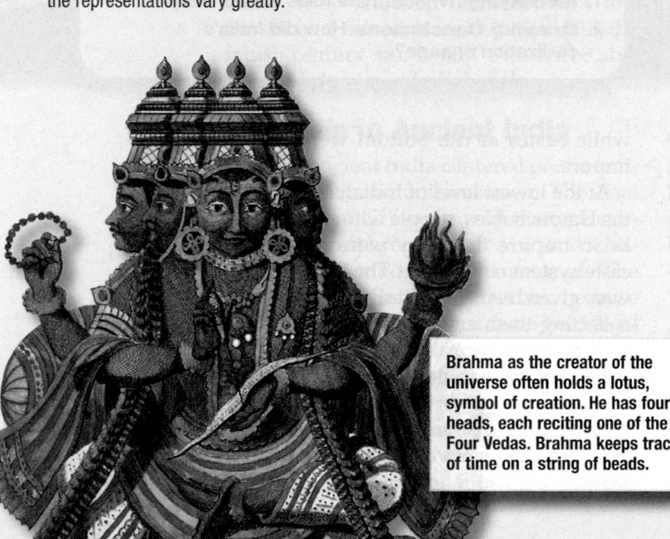

Brahma as the creator of the universe often holds a lotus, symbol of creation. He has four heads, each reciting one of the Four Vedas. Brahma keeps track of time on a string of beads.

Shiva was first portrayed as Nataraja—the King of Dance—around A.D. 1000. The ring of flames represents the universe, and his drum symbolizes the sound of creation. Shiva's foot stamps out ignorance, portrayed as a little man.

Additional Support

Extending the Content

Hindu Gods in Art Of the three chief gods, Vishnu and Shiva are the most popular among Hindu believers. Like the many other gods of Hinduism, they have their origin in the *Vedas*. **Ask:** What are the origins of the *Vedas*? Beginning about the time of Christ, Vishnu and Shiva began to grow in importance among Hindu believers. Over a period of time, sects devoted to the worship of Vishnu (Vaishnavism) or to Shiva (Saivism) developed throughout the Hindu world. Today, Vaishnavism and Saivism are the two dominant forms of Hinduism. In a sense, Vishnu and Shiva represent opposite expressions of the same idea. Vishnu (the Sustainer or Preserver) is perceived by Hindus as beneficent—a loving god who works to improve the well-being of humanity. Shiva (the Destroyer) is often seen as an intimidating presence—stern, meditative, removed from human endeavors—yet he is viewed as a compassionate god, one who destroys the world from time to time in order to re-create it. **OL**

different expressions of the one ultimate reality, Brahman. However, the various gods and goddesses give ordinary Indians a way to express their religious feelings. Through devotion at a Hindu temple, they seek not only salvation but also a means of gaining the ordinary things they need in life. Hinduism is still the religion of the majority of the Indian people.

Principles of Hinduism

By the sixth century B.C., the idea of **reincarnation** had appeared in Hinduism. Reincarnation is the belief that the individual soul is reborn in a different form after death. As the Bhagavad Gita, India's great religious poem, says, "Worn-out garments are shed by the body/Worn-out bodies are shed by the dweller [the soul]." After a number of existences in the earthly world, the soul reaches its final goal in a union with Brahman. According to Hinduism, all living beings seek to achieve this goal.

Important to this process is the idea of **karma,** the force generated by a person's actions that determines how the person will be reborn in the next life. According to this idea, what people do in their current lives determines what they will be in their next lives. In the same way, a person's current status is not simply an accident. It is a result of the person's actions in a past existence. C1

The concept of karma is ruled by the **dharma,** or the divine law. The law requires all people to do their duty. People's duties vary, depending on their status in society. More is expected of those high on the social scale, such as the Brahmins, than of the lower castes. One story from the Bhagavad Gita illustrates the importance of duty. As he prepared for battle, Arjuna, a warrior, appealed to the god Krishna. Many of Arjuna's friends were in the opposing army.

PRIMARY SOURCE

> "O Krishna, when I see my own people . . . eager for battle, my limbs shudder, my mouth is dry, my body shivers, and my hair stands on end. I can see no good in killing my own kinsmen." Krishna replied, "Do not despair of your duty. If you do not fight this just battle, you will fail in your own law and in your honor."
>
> —Bhagavad Gita

Arjuna understood that he must do his duty regardless of the consequences.

The system of reincarnation provided a religious basis for the rigid class divisions in Indian society. It justified the privileges of those on the higher end of the scale. After all, they would not have these privileges if they did not deserve them. At the same time, the concept of reincarnation gave hope to those lower on the ladder of life. The poor, for example, could hope that if they behaved properly in this life, they would improve their condition in the next. C2

Vishnu appeared in ten different avatars (forms), one the color of the clouds. The spinning disc, or *chakra*, is a weapon but also symbolizes enlightenment. Vishnu's throne is a deity in snake form, related to immortality.

DOCUMENT-BASED QUESTIONS

1. **Identifying** What are the symbols for the Creation in Hindu art?
2. **Drawing Conclusions** Why is it easier to study contemporary artifacts rather than ancient?

Buddhism

In the sixth century B.C., a new doctrine, called **Buddhism,** appeared in northern India and soon became a rival of Hinduism. The founder of Buddhism was **Siddhārtha Gautama** (sih•DAHR•tuh GOW•tuh•muh), known as the Buddha, or "Enlightened One."

Siddhārtha Gautama came from a small kingdom in the foothills of the Himalaya (in what is today part of southern Nepal).

History ONLINE
Student Web Activity—
Visit glencoe.com and complete the activity on Buddhism.

C1 Critical Thinking

Making Inferences Ask: Under what circumstances might individuals be reincarnated in a form lower than their previous existence? *(if they neglected their duties and/or behaved improperly)* **OL**

C2 Critical Thinking

Drawing Conclusions Ask: If Hindu believers faithfully execute their duties and conduct their lives in accordance with Hindu teachings, members of which social caste are most likely to achieve final union with Brahman first? *(the highest caste—Brahmin)* **OL**

DOCUMENT-BASED QUESTIONS

Answers:
1. lotus, sound
2. They are more familiar and there is more information available on them.

Differentiated Instruction

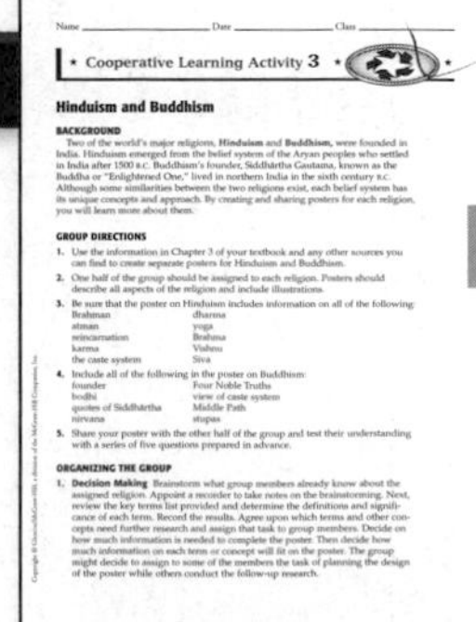

Cooperative Learning Activity, URB p. 107

Comparing and Contrasting

Objective: Compare and contrast Hinduism and Buddhism.

Focus: Ask students to list unique and similar aspects of Hinduism and Buddhism.

Teach: Have students work together to create posters based on research.

Assess: Have students present their posters and discuss their thoughts about working together on the project.

Close: Ask students how Hinduism and Buddhism still affect India today.

Differentiated Instruction Strategies

BL Have students list similarities and differences between Hinduism and Buddhism.

AL Ask students to write a report that compares Hinduism and Buddhism to other religions.

ELL Help students with pronunciations of difficult words shown on the posters.

C1 Critical Thinking

Determining Cause and Effect Ask students to identify some of the factors that caused Siddhārtha to advocate a path of moderation called the Middle Way. *(He almost died practicing extreme self-denial and found enlightenment through meditation.)* OL

C2 Critical Thinking

Comparing and Contrasting
Ask: What similarities exist between Hinduism and Buddhism? *(Both stress abandoning material or earthly concerns; both employ meditation techniques to seek peace and enlightenment; both seek the goal of achieving a state of ultimate reality.)* OL

PEOPLE in HISTORY

Answer: Refer to the quote at the beginning of this feature, which implies that the physical is not as important as the spiritual.

See page R39 to read excerpts from the Buddha's sermon in the **Primary Sources and Literature Library.**

Born around 563 B.C., he was the son of a ruling family. The young and very handsome Siddhārtha was raised in the lap of luxury and lived a sheltered life. At the age of 16, he married a neighboring princess and began to raise a family.

Siddhārtha appeared to have everything: wealth, a good appearance, a model wife, a child, and a throne that he would someday inherit. In his late twenties, however, Siddhārtha became aware of the pain of illness, the sorrow of death, and the effects of old age on ordinary people.

He exclaimed, "Would that sickness, age, and death might be forever bound!" He decided to spend his life seeking the cure for human suffering. He gave up his royal clothes, shaved his head, abandoned his family, and set off to find the true meaning of life.

At first he followed the example of the ascetics, people who practiced self-denial to achieve an understanding of ultimate reality. The abuse of his physical body, however, only led to a close brush with death from not eating. He abandoned asceticism and turned instead to an intense period of meditation. In Hinduism, this was a way to find oneness with god. One evening, while sitting in meditation under a tree, Siddhārtha reached enlightenment as to the meaning of life. He spent the rest of his life preaching what he had discovered. His teachings became the basic principles of Buddhism.

It is not certain that Siddhārtha Gautama ever intended to create a new religion or doctrine. In some ways, his ideas could be seen as an attempt to reform Hinduism. In his day, Hinduism had become complex and dependent on the Brahmins as keepers of religious secrets. Siddhārtha advised, "Do not go by what is handed down, nor by the authority of your traditional teachings. When you know of yourselves, 'These teachings are good or not good,' only then accept or reject them."

In his lifetime, the Buddha gained thousands of devoted followers. People would come to him seeking to know more about him, asking, "Are you a god?"

"No," he answered.

"Are you an angel?"

"No."

"Are you a saint?"

"No."

"Then what are you?"

The Buddha replied, "I am awake."

The religion of Buddhism began with a man who claimed that he had awakened and seen the world in a new way.

PEOPLE in HISTORY

Siddhārtha Gautama
563–483 B.C.

"All that we are is the result of what we have thought," said Siddhārtha Gautama. Through meditation, Gautama Buddha discovered the Middle Way—a path of moderation with worldwide appeal. Emperor Aśoka first spread the Buddha's teachings throughout India. As Buddhism spread, each region developed its own artistic vision of the Buddha. For centuries, he was represented as an icon, not as a human, so all representations of the Buddha are symbolic. Often he appears seated in meditation or reclining and is shown with signs of his enlightenment. In images of the Buddha, a bump on the top of his head symbolizes his intelligence, and long earlobes portray his perception and spirituality.
Why does it not matter how Siddhārtha Gautama looked?

C2 Principles of Buddhism

Siddhārtha denied the reality of the material world. The physical surroundings of humans, he believed, were simply illusions. The pain, poverty, and sorrow that afflict human beings are caused by their attachment to things of this world. Once people let go of their worldly cares, pain C1 and sorrow can be forgotten. Then comes *bodhi*, or wisdom. The word *bodhi* is the root of the word *Buddhism* and of Siddhārtha's usual name—Gautama Buddha. Achieving wisdom is a key step to achieving **nirvana,** or ultimate reality—the end of the self and a reunion with the Great World Soul.

Additional Support

Teacher Tip

Collaborative Learning In this activity, students prepare a list of questions for a class quiz. Tell students to make sure they write enough questions so that each student has a chance to answer at least one question.

Activity: Collaborative Learning

Conducting a Class Quiz on Buddhism
Ask: What is the Middle Way? Divide the class into two groups. Assign each group the task of preparing a list of questions about the principles of Buddhism. Bring the class together and position the groups facing one another across the room. Conduct a quiz, using the questions each group has prepared. Have a member of one group pose one of the prepared questions to a member of the other group. Then have a member of the second group ask the next question. Repeat, alternating between the two groups, until all questions have been answered. OL

Siddhārtha preached this message in a sermon to his followers in the Deer Park at Sarnath, outside India's holy city of Varanasi. It is a simple message based on the Four Noble Truths:

FOUR NOBLE TRUTHS
1. Ordinary life is full of suffering.
2. This suffering is caused by our desire to satisfy ourselves.
3. The way to end suffering is to end desire for selfish goals and to see others as extensions of ourselves.
4. The way to end desire is to follow the Middle Path.

This Middle Path is also known as the Eightfold Path, because it consists of eight steps:

THE EIGHTFOLD PATH
1. *Right view* We need to know the Four Noble Truths.
2. *Right intention* We need to decide what we really want.
3. *Right speech* We must seek to speak truth and to speak well of others.
4. *Right action* The Buddha gave five precepts: "Do not kill. Do not steal. Do not lie. Do not be unchaste. Do not take drugs or drink alcohol."
5. *Right livelihood* We must do work that uplifts our being.
6. *Right effort* The Buddha said, "Those who follow the Way might well follow the example of an ox that arches through the deep mud carrying a heavy load. He is tired, but his steady, forward-looking gaze will not relax until he comes out of the mud."
7. *Right mindfulness* We must keep our minds in control of our senses: "All we are is the result of what we have thought."
8. *Right concentration* We must meditate to see the world in a new way.

Siddhārtha accepted the idea of reincarnation, but he rejected the Hindu division of human beings into rigidly defined castes based on previous reincarnations. He taught instead that all human beings could reach nirvana as a result of their behavior in this life. This made Buddhism appealing to the downtrodden peoples at the lower end of the social scale.

Buddhism also differed from Hinduism in its simplicity. Siddhārtha rejected the multitude of gods that had become identified with Hinduism. He forbade his followers to worship either his person or his image after his death. For that reason, many Buddhists see Buddhism as a philosophy rather than as a religion.

Siddhārtha Gautama died in 480 B.C. at the age of 80 in what is today Nepal. After his death, his followers traveled throughout India, spreading his message. Temples sprang up throughout the countryside. Buddhist monasteries were established to promote his teaching and provide housing and training for monks dedicated to the simple life and the pursuit of wisdom.

✓Reading Check **Contrasting** How does Buddhism differ from Hinduism?

SECTION 1 REVIEW

Vocabulary

1. **Explain** the significance of: Himalaya, Indus River, monsoon, Harappa, Mohenjo Daro, via, Aryans, Sanskrit, reveal, *varnas*, caste, Hinduism, yoga, reincarnation, karma, dharma, Buddhism, Siddhārtha Gautama, nirvana.

Main Ideas

2. **Locate** the Indian subcontinent, Himalaya, Indus River, and Deccan Plateau on a map.
3. **List** the Four Noble Truths.
4. **Describe** the relationship between karma, dharma, and reincarnation.

Critical Thinking

5. **The BIG Idea** **Finding the Main Idea** What major changes occurred in Indian civilization around 1500 B.C.?
6. **Evaluating** How did Arjuna's decision to fight illustrate the importance of dharma in Indian life?
7. **Comparing and Contrasting** Prepare a Venn diagram like the one shown below to show the similarities and differences between Hinduism and Buddhism.

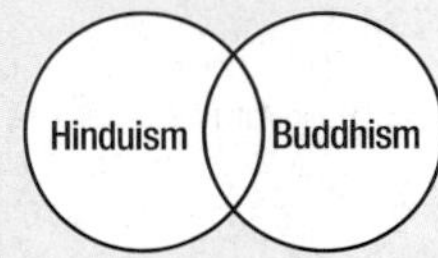

8. **Analyzing Visuals** Examine the chart on page 71. Explain how the diagram of the body represents the caste system in India.

Writing About History

9. **Expository Writing** Most untouchables did not convert to other religions or emigrate to other countries to escape their lot in life. What social pressures might prevent a person from renouncing his or her culture?

History ONLINE
For help with the concepts in this section of *Glencoe World History*, go to glencoe.com and click Study Central™.

✓Reading Check

Answer: The Buddha rejected the Hindu gods and the caste system, and taught that all could achieve nirvana.

Assess

History ONLINE

Study Central provides summaries, interactive games, and online graphic organizers to help students review content.

Close

Sequencing Information

Have volunteers identify and describe, in chronological order, early Indian cultures, beginning with the Indus Valley settlements and ending with the spread of Buddhism. *(Students' answers should include descriptions of Harappan civilization in the Indus Valley, the arrival of nomadic Aryans and their spread east and south across India, the development and characteristics of the caste system and Hinduism, and the founding and characteristics of Buddhism.)* OL

Answers

1. Definitions for the vocabulary words are found in the section and the Glossary.
2. Refer to the map on page 67.
3. Life is filled with suffering caused by the desire to satisfy ourselves. The way to end suffering is to stop our selfish desires and to follow the Middle Path.
4. Dharma requires a person to do his or her duty. This divine law rules the concept of kharma, which is the force generated by a person's actions. A person's kharma determines how he or she will be reincarnated in the next life.
5. shift to farming, settlement into pastoral villages, development of the caste system, use of new farming tools, establishment of Hinduism as the dominant religion, use of Sanskrit as a written language
6. The law of dharma states that all people must do their duty. Arjuna decided to fight because he knew he had to do his duty despite the consequences.
7. **Hinduism:** no single founder, caste system, multiple gods, poor cannot achieve ultimate reality; **Buddhism:** founded by Siddhārtha Gautama, rejected multiple gods, stressed the Four Noble Truths and the Middle Way, all believers can achieve ultimate reality; **Both:** rejection of material concerns, use of meditation, reincarnation, seeking achievement of ultimate reality
8. Each caste has a role to play in society like the parts of a body.
9. Students should support their opinions with examples.

Focus

Bellringer

Daily Focus Transparency 3.2

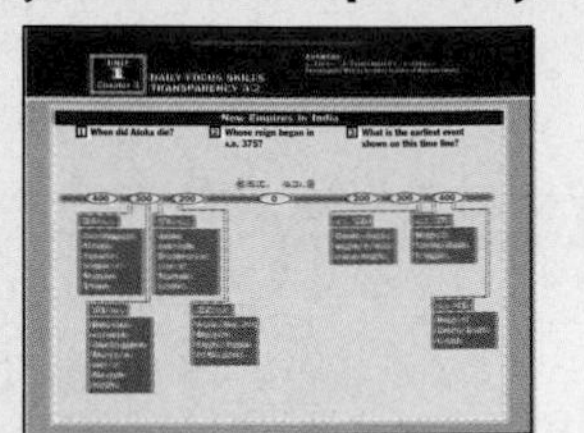

GUIDE TO READING

Answers to Graphic:
Mauryan Empire—Dates: 324–301 B.C.; **Government:** kings, centralized government, provinces ruled by governors; **Economy:** expanded regional trade, major crossroads of vast commercial network; **Gupta Empire—Dates:** A.D. 320–late fifth century; **Government:** kings; **Economy:** prosperous trade with China, Southeast Asia, Mediterranean Sea region

Section Spotlight Video

To generate student interest and provide a springboard for class discussion, access the Chapter 3, Section 2 video at glencoe.com or on the video DVD.

SECTION 2

New Empires in India

GUIDE TO READING

The BIG Idea
Ideas, Beliefs, and Values New Indian empires grew rich through trade and left a lasting legacy of accomplishments.

Content Vocabulary
- Silk Road *(p. 78)*
- pilgrims *(p. 79)*
- Vedas *(p. 80)*
- Bhagavad Gita *(p. 80)*

Academic Vocabulary
- conversion *(p. 76)*
- welfare *(p. 76)*

People
- Aśoka *(p. 76)*
- Faxian *(p. 79)*
- Kālidāsa *(p. 81)*
- Āryabhata *(p. 81)*

Reading Strategy
Categorizing Information As you read this section, complete a chart identifying the indicated characteristics of the Mauryan and Gupta Empires.

	Mauryan Empire	Gupta Empire
Dates		
Government		
Economy		

While two religions—Hinduism and Buddhism—spread through India, there was little political unity. Between 1500 B.C. and 400 B.C., warring kingdoms and shifting alliances prevented a lasting peace.

Three New Empires

MAIN IDEA Warring kingdoms united to force out invaders, which led to three Indian empires.

HISTORY & YOU Is it better to be loved or feared? Learn how some famous rulers held their kingdoms together.

After 400 B.C., India faced threats from invaders. First came Persia, which extended its empire into western India. Then came the Greeks and Macedonians. Alexander the Great had heard of the riches of India. After conquering Persia, he swept into India in 327 B.C., but his soldiers refused to continue fighting. His army departed almost as quickly as it came. Alexander's conquests in western India, however, gave rise to the first Indian Empire.

The Mauryan Empire

The new Indian state was founded by Candragupta Maurya (KUHN•druh•GUP•tuh MAH•oor•yuh), who ruled from 324 B.C. to 301 B.C. He drove out the foreign forces and established the capital of his new Mauryan Empire in northern India at Pataliputra, modern Patna, in the Ganges Valley.

This first Indian Empire was highly centralized. According to the *Arthasastra,* a political text written by a Mauryan court official, "It is power and power alone which, only when exercised by the king with impartiality, . . . maintains both this world and the next."

The king divided his empire into provinces, ruled by governors he appointed. According to Megasthenes, the Greek ambassador to the Mauryan court, Candragupta Maurya was always afraid of assassination despite having a large army and a secret police. All food was tasted in his presence, and he made a practice of never sleeping two nights in a row in the same bed in his large palace.

The Mauryan Empire flourished during the reign of **Aśoka** (uh•SHOH•kuh), the grandson of Candragupta Maurya. Aśoka is generally considered to be the greatest ruler in the history of India. After his **conversion** to Buddhism, Aśoka used Buddhist ideals to guide his rule. He set up hospitals for the **welfare** of both people and animals. He ordered that trees and shelters be placed along the road to provide shade and rest for weary travelers.

Resource Manager

R Reading Strategies	C Critical Thinking	D Differentiated Instruction	W Writing Support	S Skill Practice
Teacher Edition • Act. Prior Know., p. 80 **Additional Resources** • Guid. Read. Act., URB p. 123 • Read. Ess. & Note-Taking Guide, p. 22	**Teacher Edition** • Drawing Con., p. 78 **Additional Resources** • Linking Past/Present Act., URB p. 112 • People in World Hist. Act., URB p. 113 • Section Quiz, p. 24	**Teacher Edition** • ELL, p. 77 • Visual/Spatial, p. 78 **Additional Resources** • English Learner Act., URB p. 95 • Mapping Hist. Act., URB p. 105	**Teacher Edition** • Expository Writing, p. 79 • Persuasive Writing, p. 80 **Additional Resources** • Writer's Guidebook, pp. 43, 47	**Teacher Edition** • Using Geo. Skills, p. 79 **Additional Resources** • Hist. & Geo. Act., URB p. 103

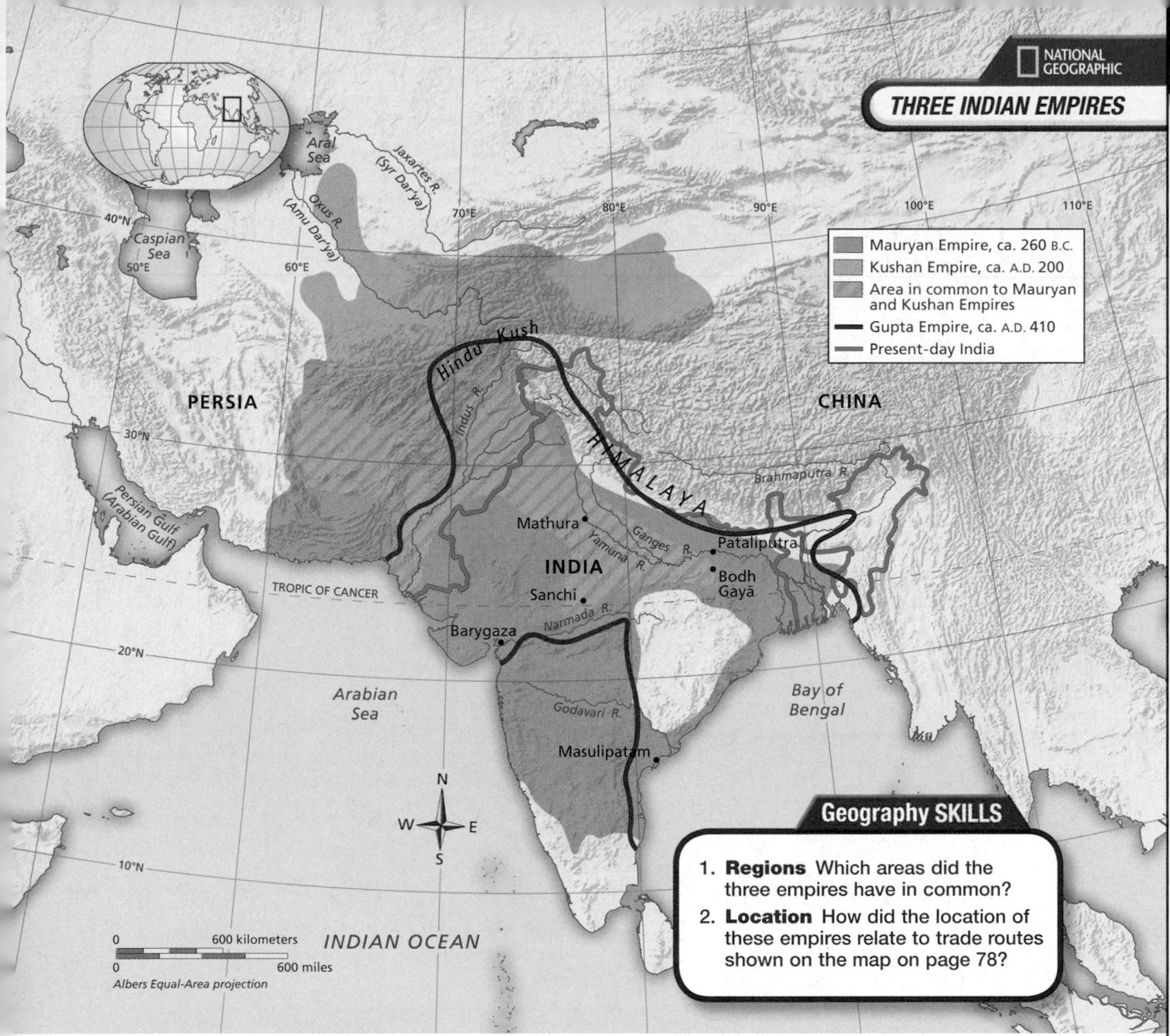

NATIONAL GEOGRAPHIC

THREE INDIAN EMPIRES

- Mauryan Empire, ca. 260 B.C.
- Kushan Empire, ca. A.D. 200
- Area in common to Mauryan and Kushan Empires
- Gupta Empire, ca. A.D. 410
- Present-day India

Aral Sea, Jaxartes R. (Syr Darya), Oxus R. (Amu Darya), Caspian Sea, PERSIA, Persian Gulf (Arabian Gulf), Hindu Kush, Indus R., HIMALAYA, Brahmaputra R., CHINA, Mathura, Ganges R., Yamuna R., Pataliputra, Bodh Gayā, INDIA, Sanchi, Narmada R., Barygaza, TROPIC OF CANCER, Arabian Sea, Bay of Bengal, Godavari R., Masulipatam, INDIAN OCEAN, 40°N, 30°N, 20°N, 10°N, 50°E, 60°E, 70°E, 80°E, 90°E, 100°E, 110°E

0 — 600 kilometers; 0 — 600 miles

Albers Equal-Area projection

Geography SKILLS

1. **Regions** Which areas did the three empires have in common?
2. **Location** How did the location of these empires relate to trade routes shown on the map on page 78?

One of the decrees of Aśoka read:

PRIMARY SOURCE

"By order of the Beloved of the Gods [Aśoka] to the officers in charge: Let us win the affection of all people. All people are my children, and as I wish all welfare and happiness in this world and the rest for my own children, so do I wish it for all men. . . . For that purpose many officials are employed among the people to instruct them in righteousness and to explain it to them."

—*Aśoka Maurya,* B. G. Gokhale, 1966

Aśoka was more than a kind ruler. His kingdom prospered as India's role in regional commerce expanded. India became a major crossroads in a trade network that extended from the rim of the Pacific to Southwest Asia and the Mediterranean Sea. After Aśoka's death in 232 B.C., the Mauryan Empire began to decline. In 183 B.C., the last Mauryan ruler was killed by one of his military leaders, and India fell into disunity. **D**

✓**Reading Check** **Evaluating** Why was Aśoka considered a great ruler?

Teach

D Differentiated Instruction

English Language Learners

Explain that *crossroads* means "place where two roads intersect or cross." It is used figuratively to indicate that India was a major intersecting point for traders going east and west on the route linking the Roman Empire and China. **ELL**

Geography SKILLS

Answers:

1. northwest India, part of the Ganges, foothills of the Hindu Kush
2. The empires controlled the main east-west route south of the Himalaya and one or more of the north-south routes.

✓**Reading Check**

Answer: He built hospitals, was concerned for the welfare of his people, and expanded trade, which led to prosperity.

Differentiated Instruction

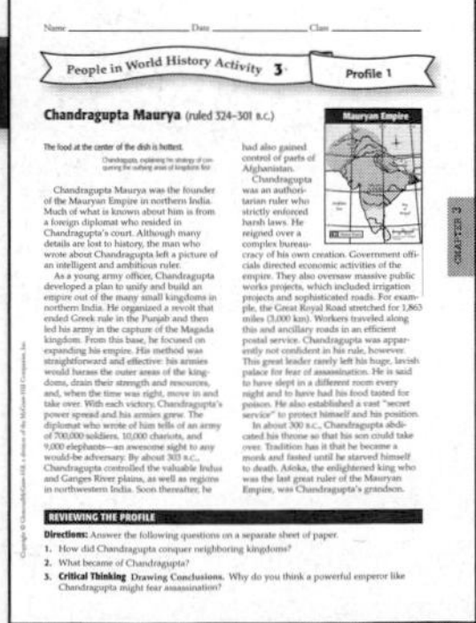

People in World History Activity, URB p. 113

Analyzing Information

Objective: Analyze information about the life of Candragupta Maurya.

Focus: Review the extent of the Mauryan Empire.

Teach: Have students read the selection and answer the questions.

Assess: Ask students to identify Candragupta's achievements, views, and life after leaving power.

Close: Discuss the effectiveness of Candragupta's rule.

Differentiated Instruction Strategies

BL Ask students to identify what they think is the most important part of Candragupta's rule.

AL Have students research and report on other leaders of the Mauryan Empire.

ELL Ask students to explain the significance of the Great Royal Road.

C Critical Thinking

Drawing Conclusions **Ask:** What economic consideration is implied in the statement that only luxury goods were traded because of the dangers and expense involved? *(The potential profits to be gained from the demand for luxury goods would have justified the risks.)* **OL**

D Differentiated Instruction

Visual/Spatial For students who are strong visual learners, locate Bactria on the Trade Routes map and point out its relationship to the nearby Hindu Kush mountains and the section of trade route that crosses over the Hindu Kush. Use the political map of Asia in the Reference Atlas to help students see the relationship between India and present-day Afghanistan, noting that today they are separated by Pakistan. **OL**

Geography SKILLS

Answers:

1. Gobi desert, Himalaya, Hindu Kush
2. They had different destination points.

The Kushān Empire

After the collapse of the Mauryan Empire, a number of new kingdoms arose along the edges of India in Bactria, known today as Afghanistan. In the first century A.D., nomadic warriors seized power and established the new Kushān kingdom. For the next two centuries, the Kushāns spread over northern India as far as the central Ganges Valley. In the rest of India, other kingdoms fought for control.

The Kushāns prospered from the trade that passed through their empire between the Mediterranean countries and the countries bordering the Pacific Ocean. Most of that trade was between the Roman Empire and China. It was shipped along the route known as the **Silk Road,** so called because silk was China's most valuable product. One section of the Silk Road passed through the mountains northwest of India.

The Silk Road, which had arisen between 200 B.C. and A.D. 100, reached from the city of Changan in China across central Asia to Mesopotamia. The route covered a distance of about 4,000 miles (6,436 km) and wound through mountains and deserts, ending at Antioch in Syria, a port city on the Mediterranean Sea. At Antioch, luxury goods from the West were traded for luxury goods from the East, which were then shipped across the Mediterranean to Greece and Rome. Only luxury goods were carried on the Silk Road because camel caravans were difficult, dangerous, and thus expensive.

Chinese merchants made large fortunes by trading luxury goods, such as silk, spices, teas, and porcelain. Indian merchants sent ivory, textiles, precious stones, and pepper. These were exchanged for woolen and linen clothes, glass, and precious stones from the Roman Empire.

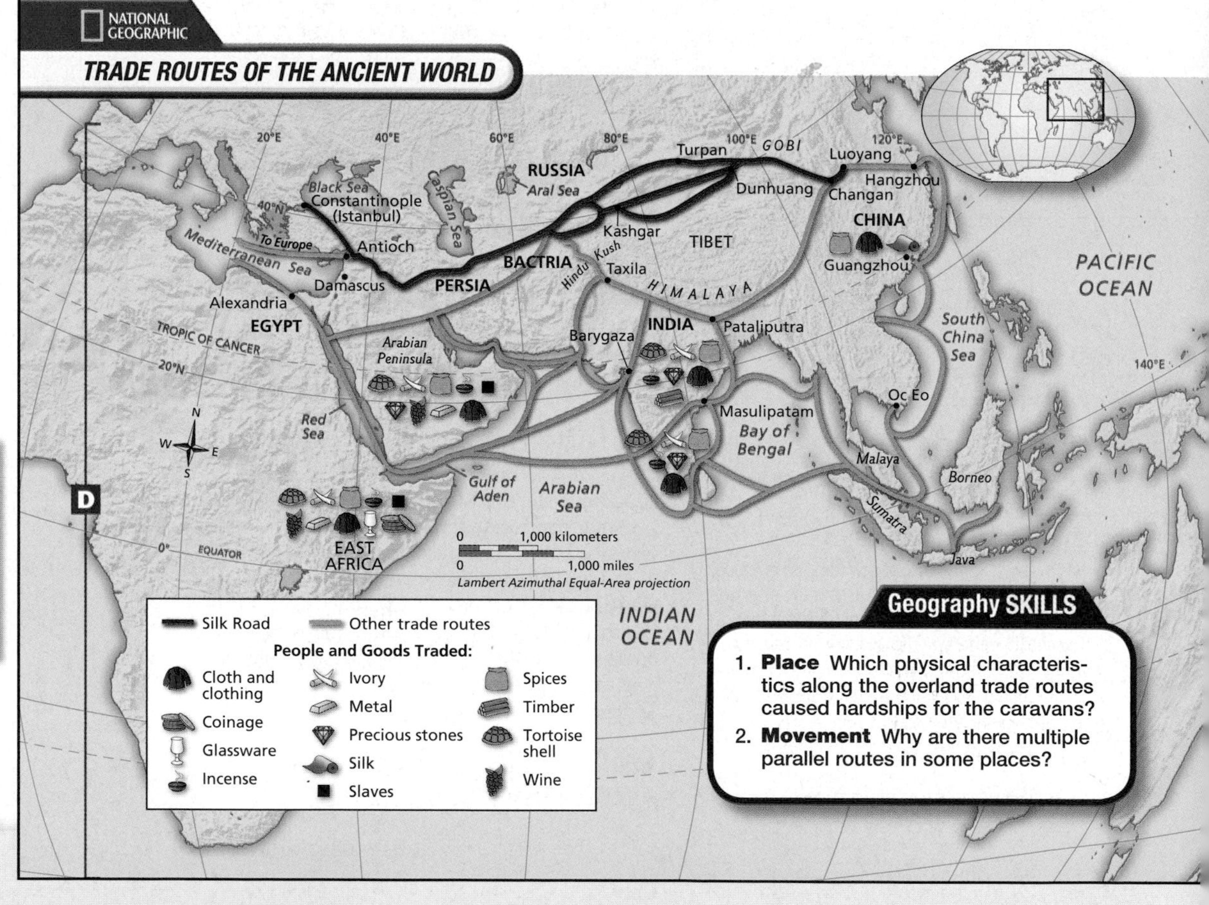

Geography SKILLS

1. **Place** Which physical characteristics along the overland trade routes caused hardships for the caravans?
2. **Movement** Why are there multiple parallel routes in some places?

Hands-On Chapter Project
Step 2

Creating a Poster of Early India and China

Step 2: Formatting the Poster Students will decide what visual elements to include on the posters they began in Section 1.

Directions: Tell students to use the Section 2 Big Idea as a guide for continuing to gather information for the poster. Instruct them to decide on a format. Encourage them to review Section 1 and to preview material in the remaining sections to determine what design elements to include. Point out that formats should take into account an even distribution of information for both countries.

Summarizing: Allow time for pairs to share what they learned about the Section 2 Big Idea while searching for poster material. Remind them that they will continue to search for material when they study Section 3 and they will also begin preparing entries for the poster. **OL**

(Chapter Project is continued in Section 3.)

Silk was especially desired by the Romans, who considered it worth its weight in gold. In fact, the Romans knew China as *Serica*, which means "Land of Silk."

The Empire of the Guptas

The Kushān kingdom came to an end in the third century A.D., when invaders from Persia overran it. In 320, a new state was created in the central Ganges Valley by a local prince named Candra Gupta—no relation to the earlier Candragupta Maurya. He located his capital at Pataliputra, the site of the decaying palace of the Mauryas. **S**

His successor, his son Samudra Gupta, expanded the empire into surrounding areas. A court official wrote of Samudra Gupta that:

PRIMARY SOURCE

"[He] was skillful in waging hundreds of battles with only the strength of his arms. The beauty of his charming body was enhanced by the number of wounds, caused by the blows of battle axes, arrows, spears, pikes, barbed darts, swords, lances, javelins, iron arrows, and many other weapons."

—court official

Eventually the Gupta kingdom became the dominant political force in northern India. It also established loose control over central India, thus becoming the greatest state in India since the Mauryan Empire.

Under a series of efficient monarchs—especially Candra Gupta II, who reigned from 375 to 415—the Guptas created a golden age of Indian culture shown in the flowering of Hindu and Buddhist arts.

The Gupta Empire actively engaged in trade with China, Southeast Asia, and the Mediterranean and also encouraged domestic trade in cloth, salt, and iron. Cities famous for their temples as well as for their prosperity rose along the main trade routes throughout India.

Much of the trade in the Gupta Empire was managed by the Gupta rulers, who owned silver and gold mines and vast lands. They earned large profits from their dealings. They lived in luxury, awakening to the sound of music and spending much time in dining with followers and guests. It was said that "the king and his companions drank wine out of ruby cups while lutes were strummed."

Much of their wealth came from religious trade as **pilgrims** (people who travel to religious places) from across India and as far away as China came to visit the major religious centers. Not surprisingly, many new Hindu and Buddhist temples and shrines were built during the Gupta era.

A Buddhist monk from China, **Faxian** (FAY•SYEN), visited India in search of documents about the teachings of the Buddha. Faxian's writings from the fifth century describe the Gupta rulers, their respect for Buddhism, and the prosperity of the empire.

PRIMARY SOURCE

"Beyond the deserts are the territories of western India. The kings of these territories are all firm believers in the law of [the] Buddha. They remove their caps of state when they make offerings to the priests. The members of the royal household and the chief ministers personally direct the food giving. When the distribution of food is over, they spread a carpet on the ground and sit down before it. . . .

Southward from this is the so-called middle-country. . . . The people are very well off, without poll-tax or official restrictions. Only those who farm the royal lands return a portion of profit of the land [to the king]. If they desire to go, they go; if they like to stop, they stop. The kings govern without corporal punishment; criminals are fined, according to circumstances, lightly or heavily. Even in cases of repeated rebellion they only cut off the right hand. . . . In this country they do not keep swine nor fowls, and do not deal in cattle; they have no shambles or wine-shops in their market-places." **W**

—Faxian, *Describing Life under the Guptas*

The good fortunes of the Guptas did not last. Beginning in the late fifth century A.D., invasions by nomadic Huns from the northwest gradually reduced the power of the empire. A military commander briefly revived the empire in the middle of the seventh century, but after his death, the empire collapsed. North India would not be reunited for hundreds of years.

✓Reading Check **Examining** What characteristics made the Gupta Empire great?

S Skill Practice

Using Geography Skills
Refer students to the Three Indian Empires map on page 77. **Ask:** How large was the Gupta Empire? *(It covered the entire northern half of India.)* **BL**

W Writing Support

Expository Writing Have students write a paragraph in which they summarize Faxian's observations on the Gupta Empire. Tell them to focus on aspects of the Empire that impressed Faxian. **OL**

✓Reading Check

Answer: Gupta rulers were fair and tolerant and the empire was prosperous.

Additional Support

Extending the Content

Pepper and the Indian Economy One of the primary exports of southern India was pepper. In the ancient world, spices, especially peppercorns, were an important commodity because of the difficulty in preserving food. Pepper was often used to cover the flavor of meat that had become rancid. Once ancient Europeans discovered this flavor enhancer, they were willing to pay its weight in gold. Indians received so many gold coins from the Roman Empire that emperor Nero banned the importation of peppercorns in order to stop the drain on the Roman economy. This same condiment would later play a role in history as the enticement for European traders and explorers of the fifteenth and sixteenth centuries.

R Reading Strategy

Activating Prior Knowledge Have students recall the quotation from the Bhagavad Gita on page 73 of Section 1. **Ask:** What other concern, besides success or failure, should an individual ignore in the course of performing a moral duty? *(the consequences)* OL

W Writing Support

Persuasive Writing Have students think about the dilemma confronting the warrior in the Bhagavad Gita. Then ask them to write a paragraph in which they offer their own opinion on this question: Do you agree that an individual should always perform his or her moral duty regardless of success, failure, or consequences? Why or why not? OL

CRITICAL THINKING SKILLS

Answers:

1. pagoda, shrine, or temple
2. As Buddhism spread to other countries, the stupa took on local names and architecture styles.

Additional Support

Indian Accomplishments

MAIN IDEA India produced great works in almost all cultural fields, including literature, architecture, and science.

HISTORY & YOU Have you studied algebra or geography? Learn about India's contributions to the arts and sciences.

Literature

Few cultures are as rich and varied as India. Its literature reflects that. The earliest known Indian literature are the **Vedas**, which contain religious chants and stories. Originally passed down orally from generation to generation, the Vedas were recorded in Sanskrit after the development of writing. India's great epics, the *Mahabharata* (muh•HAH•BAH•ruh•tuh) and the *Ramayana,* were also put into written form about 100 B.C. Both of these works tell of the legendary deeds of great warriors.

The *Mahabharata,* consisting of over 90,000 stanzas, or lines of poetry, is the longest poem in any written language. Taking place around 1000 B.C., it describes a war between cousins for control of the kingdom. **R** The most famous section of the book, called the **Bhagavad Gita** (BAH•guh•VAHD GEE•tuh), is a sermon by the god Krishna on the eve of a major battle. In this sermon, he sets forth one of the key points **W** of Indian society: In taking action, one must not worry about success or failure. One should only be aware of the moral rightness of the act itself.

The *Ramayana,* written at about the same time, is much shorter than the *Mahabharata.* It is an account of the fictional ruler Rama. As a result of a palace plot, Rama is banished from the kingdom and forced to live in the forest. Later, he fights the demon-king of Ceylon, who had kidnapped his beloved wife Sita.

Like the *Mahabharata* and most works of the ancient world, the *Ramayana* is strongly imbued with religious and moral lessons.

INFOGRAPHICS

Stupas Show Spread of Buddhism

Evolution of Buddhist Architecture
a. third to first century B.C. Indian stupa
b. second century A.D. Indian stupa
c. fifth to seventh century A.D. Chinese pagoda
d. seventh century A.D. Japanese pagoda

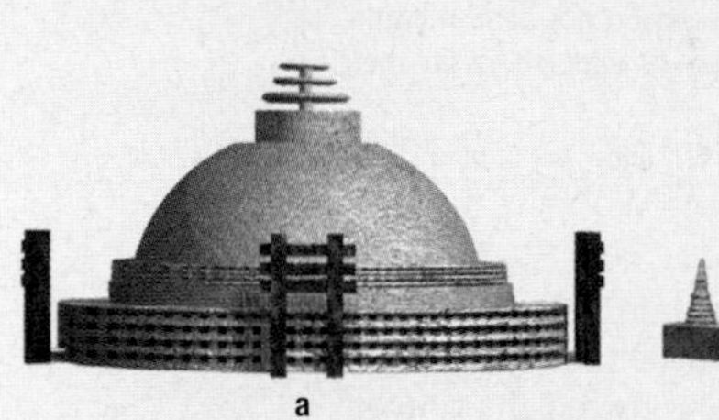

a

b

c

d

According to legend, the Buddha told his followers to place his relics at four sites: at his birthplace, at the bodhi tree, at the place where he preached his first sermon, and at the place where he died. Then he folded his robe into a cube and placed his begging bowl upside down on top to indicate the shape of the monuments. Over centuries in different countries, stupas changed, but five basic components remained: a square base, a dome, a spire, a crescent moon, and a circular disc; symbolizing earth, water, fire, air, and space.

CRITICAL THINKING SKILLS

1. **Identifying** What is another name for a Buddhist stupa?
2. **Drawing Conclusions** Why did the shape and name for stupas change?

Activity: Interdisciplinary Connection

Literature Mention to students that the Bhagavad Gita, in addition to being the most famous section of the *Mahabharata,* is also one of the most revered sacred texts of Hinduism. In it, the god Vishnu assumes the avatar of Krishna, who presents himself in human form as a friend of the warrior hero Arjuna. Explain to students that the immense popularity of the *Ramayana* can be attributed to its thrilling plot, its poetic language, and its inspiring moral and spiritual message. In it, Vishnu appears in human form as the hero Rama, who represents the epitome of Hindu manhood. He is courageous, handsome, and steadfast in his devotion to his wife. Ask volunteers to read independently a brief portion of the Bhagavad Gita or the *Ramayana.* Tell them to prepare an oral report describing the content and their response to it. **Ask:** Why are these epics still popular today? *(Encourage students to use details from the texts to support their opinions.)* OL

Rama is seen as the ideal hero, a perfect ruler, and ideal son. Sita projects the supreme duty of wifely loyalty to her husband. To this day, the *Mahabharata* and *Ramayana* continue to inspire the people of India.

One of ancient India's most famous authors from the Gupta era was **Kālidāsa.** His poem, *The Cloud Messenger,* remains one of the most popular Sanskrit poems. In the poem, an exiled male earth spirit shares his grief and longing for his wife.

Architecture

Some of the earliest examples of Indian architecture stem from the time of Aśoka, when Buddhism became the state religion. The desire to spread the ideas of Gautama Buddha inspired the great architecture of the Mauryan dynasty and the period that followed.

The three main types of structures, all serving religious purposes, were the pillar, the stupa, and the rock chamber. During Aśoka's reign, many stone pillars were erected along roads to mark sites of events in the Buddha's life. The polished sandstone pillars weighed up to 50 tons (45.4 t) each and rose as high as 50 feet (15 m). Each was topped with a carved lion, uttering the Buddha's message.

A stupa was originally meant to house a relic of the Buddha, such as a lock of his hair. These structures were built in the form of burial mounds. Eventually, the stupa became a place for devotion and the most familiar form of Buddhist architecture. Each stupa rose to considerable heights and was surmounted by a spire. According to legend, Aśoka ordered the construction of 84,000 stupas throughout India.

The final development in early Indian architecture was the rock chamber, carved out of rock cliffs. This structure was developed by Aśoka to provide a series of rooms to house monks and to serve as a hall for religious ceremonies.

Science and Mathematics

Ancient Indians possessed an impressive amount of scientific knowledge, particularly in astronomy. They charted the movements of the stars and recognized that Earth was a sphere that rotated on its axis and revolved around the sun. Their most important contribution was in the field of mathematics. **Aryabhata,** the most famous mathematician of the Gupta Empire, was one of the first scientists known to have used algebra. Indian mathematicians also introduced the concept of zero and used a symbol (0) for it.

After Arabs conquered parts of India in the eighth century A.D., Arab scholars adopted the Indian system. In turn, European traders borrowed it from the Arabs, and it spread through Europe in the 1200s. Today it is called the Indian-Arabic numerical system.

✓Reading Check **Evaluating** How have Indian advances in science and mathematics influenced our world today?

SECTION 2 REVIEW

Vocabulary

1. **Explain** the significance of: Aśoka, conversion, welfare, Silk Road, pilgrim, Faxian, Vedas, Bhagavad Gita, Kālidāsa, Aryabhata.

Main Ideas

2. **Use** a table like the one below to show the parts of India the three empires controlled.

Region/Empire	Mauryan	Kushān	Gupta
Rivers			
Plains			
Coasts			

3. **Explain** what types of goods were carried on the Silk Road and why.
4. **List** three kinds of early Indian architecture and their uses.

Critical Thinking

5. **The Big Idea** **Making Inferences** How did prosperity lead to contributions in the arts and sciences?
6. **Analyzing** How do the historic epics *Mahabharata* and *Ramayana* reflect the values of early India?
7. **Analyzing Primary Sources** What are the similarities between Aśoka's decrees and Faxian's observations of the Gupta Empire?
8. **Analyzing Visuals** Examine the diagram on page 80, and use it to explain why the shape of stupas changed.

Writing About History

9. **Persuasive Writing** Write a short essay about whether a ruler should be loved or feared or both. Use examples from the Mauryan and Gupta Empires.

History ONLINE

For help with the concepts in this section of *Glencoe World History,* go to glencoe.com and click Study Central™.

✓Reading Check

Answer: Students study the rotation of Earth on its axis, learn algebra, and use zero in mathematics.

Assess

History ONLINE

Study Central provides summaries, interactive games, and online graphic organizers to help students review content.

Close

Summarizing Divide the class into four groups. Assign one topic to each: *Mauryan Empire, Kushān Empire, Gupta Empire, Arts and Science.* Tell groups to prepare summaries of the accomplishments achieved in the category assigned. Have groups present the summaries. OL

SECTION 2 REVIEW

Answers

1. Definitions for the vocabulary words are found in the section and the Glossary.
2. **Mauryan—rivers:** Ganges, Indus; **plains:** Deccan; **coasts:** east and west; **Kushān—rivers:** Ganges, Indus; **coasts:** a little on west coast; **Gupta—rivers:** Ganges, Indus; **plains:** Deccan; **coasts:** mostly west coast
3. Luxury goods such as silk and cotton textiles, pepper and spices, teas, porcelains, ivory, and gems were carried because they were the most profitable.
4. Pillars mark sites of events in Buddha's life. Stupas housed relics of Buddha or became memorials. Rock chambers housed monks and served as halls for religious ceremonies.
5. It allowed people to pursue learning instead of just surviving. Trade encouraged the spread of ideas as well as goods.
6. They emphasized duty, bravery, loyalty, and doing things for the right reasons.
7. Both show a concern for the welfare of the people, fairness, impartiality of treatment, and benevolence or mercy.
8. Stupas began as simple structures but eventually became places of devotion. In China and Japan, stupas took on the shape of traditional local architecture.
9. Students should support their opinions with examples from the section.

Focus

Introducing Social History Ask a volunteer to read the introduction aloud to the class. Draw attention to the illustrations of the silk-making process and the "Silk in History" information side bar. Explain that students will study the origins and process of silk making and a brief history of the incredible demand for it.

Teach

D Differentiated Instruction

Visual/Spatial Use a ball of string or twine to illustrate the structure of a silkworm's cocoon. An egg-shaped package of crinkle tie (available in the gift wrap section of stores) would provide an ideal model. Explain that silkworms secrete a single, continuous filament to spin the cocoon and that an average cocoon yields a strand of filament more than 2,000 feet long. OL

Additional Support

The Silk Road: Famous Fabric

As early as 1000 B.C., caravans carried luxury goods from China to Persia. Finally in the nineteenth century, the ancient trade route was dubbed the Silk Road in honor of China's most famous export. According to legend, the wife of an early emperor discovered how to spin the fiber from the silkworm's cocoon. For centuries, the process of making silk was a well-kept secret, known only in China. China maintained its monopoly on silk production for several hundred years.

D Silk moth eggs hatch and become caterpillars or worms. The worms eat mulberry leaves for six weeks and then spin their cocoons.

Silk in History

- Farm women in ancient China raised silkworms and produced silk as part of their household duties.
- Ancient Persians unraveled Chinese silk cloth and rewove it into Persian designs.
- When Alexander the Great conquered Persia, he demanded enormous quantities of silk as spoils.
- Roman statesman Julius Caesar limited silk to his exclusive use.
- About A.D. 550, Christian monks smuggled mulberry seeds and silkworm eggs out of China, ending the silk monopoly.

Background

The Discovery of Silk According to Chinese legend, around 2700 B.C. Xilingshi, the wife of Emperor Huangdi, discovered silk by accident. Supposedly, when her husband asked her to check his damaged mulberry trees, Xilinghsi saw worms eating the leaves, and, by mistake, she dropped a cocoon into hot water and watched it gradually unravel into a single, tangled thread. Xilinghsi convinced her husband to provide her with a garden of mulberry trees where she could cultivate more silkworms and the cocoons they produced. Whether or not there is any truth to the legend, historians agree that silk was first produced in China. The Chinese were so determined to keep their discovery a secret that they made it known that persons guilty of revealing the origin of silk to anyone outside of China would be subject to public humiliation and even death. After the secret was discovered, silk making spread to other parts of Asia, the Middle East, and Europe. Today, Japan, South Korea, Thailand, Brazil, and India are important producers of silk, but China still leads the world both in the production of raw silk and in the manufacturing of silk products.

ANALYZING VISUALS

1. **Drawing Conclusions** What motivated merchants to undertake the long and dangerous journey along the Silk Road?
2. **Analyzing** What made silk such a valuable commodity?

83

C Critical Thinking

Analyzing Information Have students do some independent research to learn more about the silk trade. Encourage them to uncover an interesting or little-known fact about an aspect of the trade not covered in their textbook. Tell them to prepare a brief, oral report for the class, explaining what they found. **AL**

Assess/Close

Drawing Conclusions Point out this statement in the introduction: "Culture was also traded on the Silk Road." Discuss the kinds of social/cultural changes that would have occurred in the ancient world as a result of the silk trade. **OL**

ANALYZING VISUALS

Answers:
1. Luxury goods were very profitable.
2. Silk was rare; it conferred status because it was worn by royalty; it was comfortable and soft.

Activity: Collaborative Learning

Demonstrating the Silk-Making Process
Ask: How were the Chinese able to keep the silk-making process a secret for so long? Select a small group of students to demonstrate the stages of the silk-making process. Provide the group with one or more articles from standard reference sources. Allow the group the options of demonstrating a modern process or one they imagine the ancient Chinese would have used. The group can choose from a variety of formats for their demonstration: orally explaining each step, creating storyboards to illustrate the steps, acting out the steps, or a combination of these. Encourage the group not to be afraid to use creativity in interpreting how to demonstrate each step. Explain that the demonstration's purpose is to reinforce understanding of the basic steps involved, not to duplicate exact techniques. Steps should include raising silkworms, harvesting cocoons, reeling, dyeing, and weaving. **OL**

Focus

Bellringer

Daily Focus Transparency 3.3

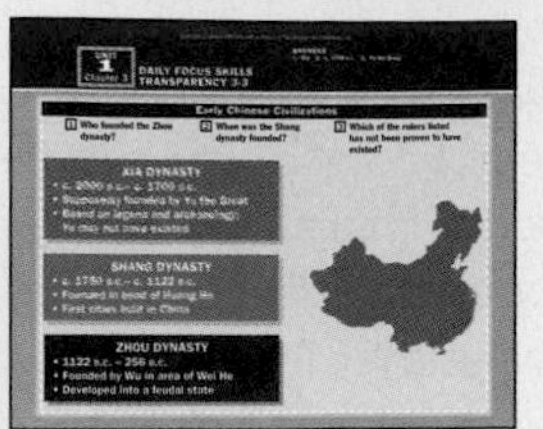

GUIDE TO READING

Answers to Graphic:
The top box is filled in for students. Moving clockwise, the next box should read: Dynasty rules successfully for many years, then begins to decline. The bottom box should read: Central government begins to collapse; rebellions and invasions begin. The left box should read: The dynasty collapses.

Section Spotlight Video

To generate student interest and provide a springboard for class discussion, access the Chapter 3, Section 3 video at glencoe.com or on the video DVD.

Resource Manager

SECTION 3

Early Chinese Civilizations

GUIDE TO READING

The BIG Idea
Ideas, Beliefs, and Values China developed unique philosophies, political theories, and products.

Content Vocabulary
- aristocracy *(p. 86)*
- Mandate of Heaven *(p. 87)*
- Dao *(p. 87)*
- filial piety *(p. 89)*
- pictographs *(p. 90)*
- ideographs *(p. 90)*
- Confucianism *(p. 90)*
- Daoism *(p. 92)*
- Legalism *(p. 93)*

Academic Vocabulary
- cycle *(p. 88)*
- philosophy *(p. 90)*
- ethical *(p. 90)*

People and Places
- Huang He *(p. 84)*
- Chang Jiang *(p. 84)*
- Confucius *(p. 90)*
- Laozi *(p. 92)*

Reading Strategy
Classifying Information As you read this section, create a diagram like the one below that illustrates the dynastic cycle.

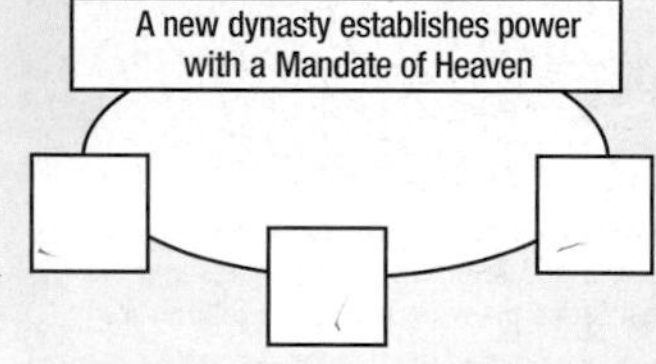

As in Mesopotamia, Egypt, and the Indus Valley, China's early civilizations followed the spread of agriculture along the river valleys. Most of the rivers in China flow east to the Pacific Ocean, which meant China's civilizations developed near the east coast. The mountains to the west and the deserts to the north further isolated China from outside influences.

The Impact of Geography

MAIN IDEA China's physical geography influenced the location of its early civilizations.

HISTORY & YOU Would you rather live near the ocean or the mountains? Learn how China's geography shaped its development.

Dating back more than six thousand years, China has one of the world's oldest cultures. China also has the largest population of any nation and is made up of more than 50 ethnic groups, speaking several languages and many dialects. The diversity of its people reflects the diversity of its land and climate.

Rivers and Mountains

The **Huang He** (HWAHNG•HUH), or Yellow River, stretches across China for more than 2,900 miles (4,666 km), carrying its rich yellow silt all the way from Mongolia to the Pacific Ocean. The **Chang Jiang** (CHAHNG•JYAHNG), or Yangtze River, is even longer, flowing for about 3,400 miles (5,470 km) across central China before emptying into the Yellow Sea. The densely cultivated valleys of these two rivers began to emerge as one of the great food-producing areas of the ancient world.

China, however, is not just a land of fertile fields. In fact, only 10 percent of the total land area is suitable for farming, compared with 19 percent of the United States. Much of the rest of the land in China consists of mountains and deserts that ring the country on its northern and western frontiers.

This forbidding landscape is a dominant feature of Chinese life and has played an important role in Chinese history. Geographical barriers—mountains and deserts—isolated the Chinese people from peoples in other parts of Asia. In the frontier regions created by these barriers lived peoples of Mongolian, Indo-European, and Turkish backgrounds. The contacts of these groups with the Chinese were often marked by conflict. The northern frontier of China became one of the areas of conflict in Asia as Chinese armies tried to protect their precious farmlands.

R Reading Strategies	C Critical Thinking	D Differentiated Instruction	W Writing Support	S Skill Practice
Teacher Edition • Act. Prior Know., pp. 85, 92 • Using Context Clues, p. 87 • Making Connections, p. 90 **Additional Resources** • Guid. Read. Act., URB p. 124 • Read. Ess. & Note-Taking Guide, p. 25	**Teacher Edition** • Making Inferences, pp. 86, 89 • Compare/Contrast, p. 87 • Det. Cause/Effect, p. 88 • Analyzing Info., pp. 89, 91 **Additional Resources** • Section Quiz, p. 25	**Teacher Edition** • ELL, p. 89 • Adv. Learners, p. 90 **Additional Resources** • Enrich. Act., URB p. 120	**Teacher Edition** • Expository Writing, p. 88 • Persuasive Writing, p. 91 **Additional Resources** • Hist. Sig. Act., URB p. 106	**Teacher Edition** • Using Geo. Skills, pp. 85, 86 **Additional Resources** • Read. Strat. for SS, pp. 26, 29, 30

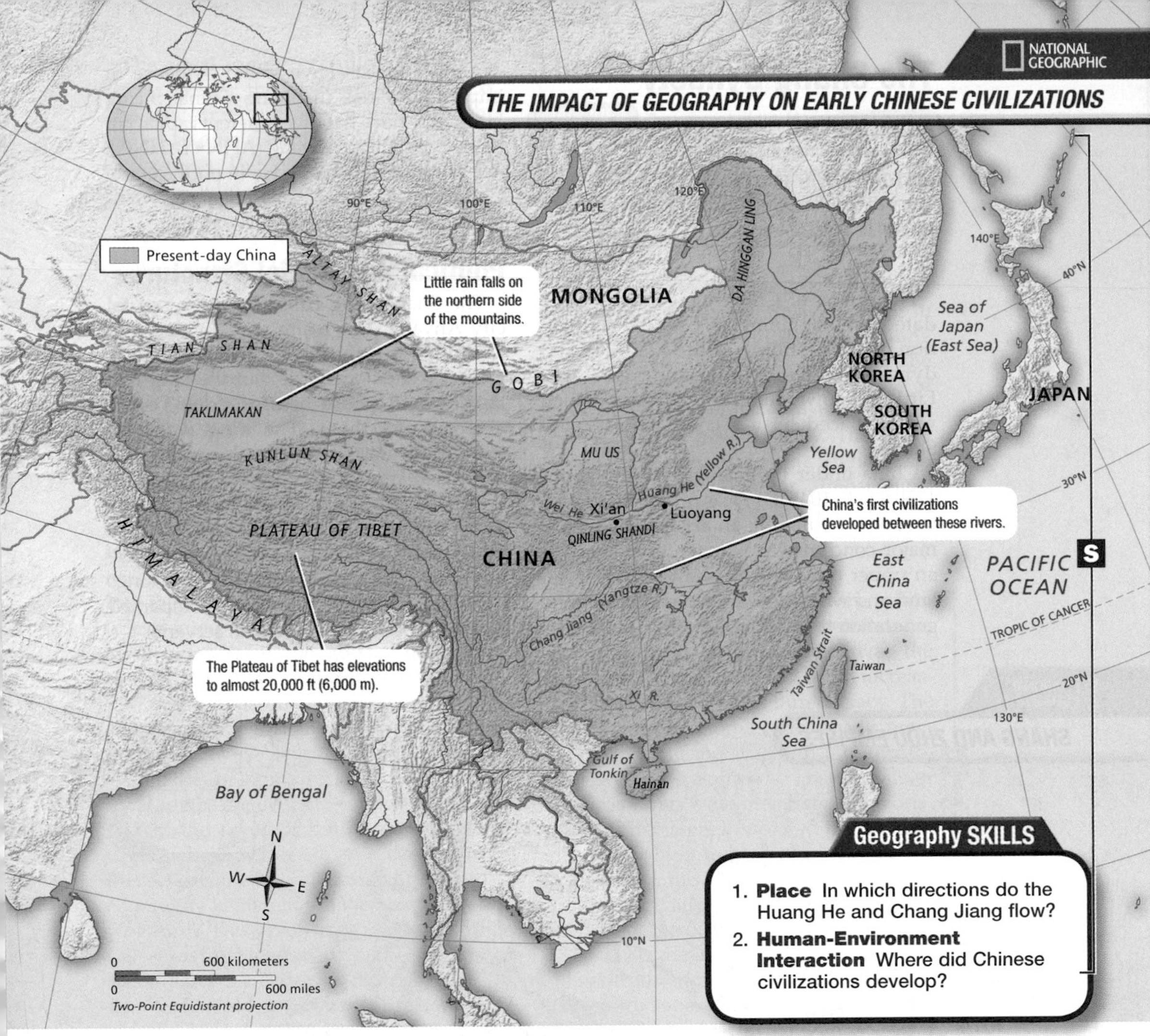

Geography SKILLS

1. **Place** In which directions do the Huang He and Chang Jiang flow?
2. **Human-Environment Interaction** Where did Chinese civilizations develop?

Climate

China's climates vary from region to region based on the elevation and the monsoons. In winter, monsoons blowing from the mountainous regions are cold and dry. In summer, the monsoons blow from the south across the seas, bringing rain.

The dry season alternating with wet monsoons creates significant temperature differences in winter and summer. The Chang Jiang serves as a dividing line between the northern region and the southern region of the country.

In the north, winters are long and cold, but the short summers are sunny and hot. In the center of the country, along the Chang Jiang, there are four seasons, including hot summers and cold winters. The warmest temperatures year round are in the south, which has a subtropical climate with hot summers and mild winters.

✓Reading Check **Describing** What isolated the Chinese people from peoples in other parts of Asia?

Teach

S Skill Practice

Using Geography Skills Ask: Based on the map, what areas of China do you think would be the least populated? *(mountain areas in the west and desert areas in the north)* OL

R Reading Strategy

Activating Prior Knowledge Ask: Although monsoons helped bring water to crops, under what circumstances would the summer monsoons be considered problematic? *(If they bring too much rain, crops could be ruined.)* OL

Geography SKILLS

Answers:

1. from west to east
2. in the river valleys of the Huang He and Chang Jiang

✓Reading Check

Answer: mountains and deserts

Hands-On Chapter Project Step 3

Creating a Poster of Early India and China

Step 3: Preparing the Content In addition to gathering information, students will begin preparing the content of the posters they worked on in Sections 1 and 2.

Directions: Tell students to use the Section 3 Big Idea as a guide for continuing to gather information for the poster. Instruct them to begin preparing entries based on the design elements planned for the poster.

Summarizing: Allow time for students to share what they learned about the Section 3 Big Idea while working on their posters. Remind them that they will complete their search for material and preparation of entries when they study Section 4. They will also assemble their posters at that time. OL

(Chapter Project is continued in Section 4.)

C Critical Thinking

Determining Cause and Effect **Ask:** **In theory, under what circumstances did a king's subjects have a right to revolt?** *(if a king was corrupt or did not rule effectively)* **BL**

For additional practice on this skill, see the **Skills Handbook**.

W Writing Support

Expository Writing Ask students to write a paragraph in which they explain how the statement "He who wins is the king; he who loses is the rebel" applies to Chinese dynastic cycles. **OL**

ANALYZING VISUALS

Answers:

1. It justified overthrowing ineffective rulers and the Shang dynasty.
2. Their accomplishments were followed by a period of decline and revolution.

Additional Support

This would protect the people from natural disaster or a bad harvest. If the king failed to rule effectively, he could be overthrown and replaced by a new ruler. **C**

This theory has political side effects. It sets forth a "right of revolution" to overthrow a corrupt ruler. It also makes clear that the king, though serving as a representative of Heaven, is not a divine being himself. In practice, each founder of a new dynasty would say he had earned the Mandate of Heaven. Who could disprove it except by overthrowing the king? The saying, "He who wins is the king; he who loses is the rebel," sums up this view. **W**

The Mandate of Heaven was closely tied to the pattern of dynastic **cycles.** From the beginning of Chinese history to A.D. 1912, China was ruled by a series of dynasties, which all went through a cycle of change. A new dynasty established its power, ruled successfully for many years, and then began to decline. The government lost power, giving rise to rebellions or invasion. When a new dynasty took over, the cycle began again.

The Fall of the Zhou Dynasty

After almost eight hundred years, the Zhou dynasty collapsed. For centuries, the dynasty ruled wisely and efficiently, but later Zhou rule declined intellectually and morally. The Zhou kingdom had been divided into several small territories, some of which evolved into powerful states that challenged

INFOGRAPHICS
Dynastic Cycles and the Mandate of Heaven

When the Zhou overthrew the Shang dynasty, they explained their right to rule as a Mandate of Heaven. Dynasties that abused their power lost the Mandate of Heaven. The Mandate passed to another family who overthrew the old dynasty and established a new one.

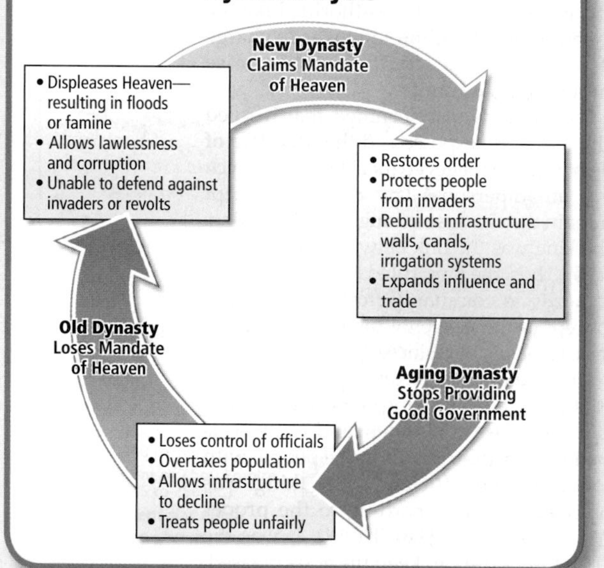

Dynastic Cycle

New Dynasty Claims Mandate of Heaven
- Restores order
- Protects people from invaders
- Rebuilds infrastructure—walls, canals, irrigation systems
- Expands influence and trade

Aging Dynasty Stops Providing Good Government
- Loses control of officials
- Overtaxes population
- Allows infrastructure to decline
- Treats people unfairly

Old Dynasty Loses Mandate of Heaven
- Displeases Heaven—resulting in floods or famine
- Allows lawlessness and corruption
- Unable to defend against invaders or revolts

Early Dynasties of China

DYNASTY	DATES	ACCOMPLISHMENTS
Shang	1750–1045 B.C.	First dynasty, writing, ancestor worship, bronze
Zhou	1045–256 B.C.	Classical arts, silk discovered, Daoism and Confucianism
Qin	221–206 B.C.	China united, measurements and writing standardized
Han	202 B.C.–A.D. 220	Silk Road, civil service, paper invented, Buddhism

Analyzing VISUALS

1. **Recognizing Bias** Why did the Zhou dynasty develop the concept of the Mandate of Heaven?
2. **Theorizing** Why do you think each of the dynasties came to an end?

Activity: Interdisciplinary Connection

Civics The political philosophy of the Mandate of Heaven provided an ethical foundation for the right to rule: a ruler was selected by Heaven to rule for the benefit of his people. If he did not rule properly, a would-be ruler could overthrow him. During the Zhou dynasty, no other civilization in the world had a more advanced ethical foundation. More than two thousand years later, Niccolò Machiavelli (see p. 401) proposed a different ethic: morality plays no role in governing; if it works, do it. Have students apply these differing philosophies to contemporary world politics.

Ask: **Are a majority of governments today guided by Machiavelli's ideas, by ethical ideas similar to those of the Zhou, or by a combination of these philosophies?** *(Encourage students to support their opinions with examples taken from current events.)* **OL**

the Zhou ruler. In 403 B.C., civil war broke out, beginning an age known in Chinese history as the Period of the Warring States.

By this time, warfare had also changed in China. Iron weapons, more powerful than bronze weapons, came into use. Foot soldiers, or infantry, and soldiers on horseback, or cavalry, made their appearance. The cavalry was armed with the powerful crossbow, a Chinese invention of the seventh century B.C. Eventually, one of the warring states—the Qin (CHIHN)—took control. The Qin created a new dynasty in 221 B.C.

Social Structure

During the Zhou dynasty, the basic features of Chinese economic and social life began to take shape. The Zhou continued the pattern of land ownership that had existed under the Shang. The peasants worked on lands owned by their lord. Each peasant family farmed an outer plot for its own use and then joined with other families to work the inner one for their lord.

A class of artisans and merchants lived in walled towns under the direct control of the local lord. Merchants did not operate freely but were considered the property of the local lord. There was also a slave class.

Trade in this period involved the exchange of local products that were used on an everyday basis. Eventually, trade increased to include goods brought in from distant regions. Among these goods were salt, iron, cloth, and various luxury items.

Few social institutions have been as closely identified with China as the family. As in most agricultural societies, in ancient China the family served as the basic economic and social unit. However, the family there took on an almost sacred quality as a symbol of the entire social order.

What explains the importance of the family in ancient China? Certainly, the need to work together on the land was a significant factor. In ancient times, farming required the work of many people. This was especially true in growing rice, which had become the chief crop in the region of the Chang Jiang and the provinces to the south.

Growing rice requires hard work to plant, grow, and harvest. An irrigation network bringing water to the fields must also be kept in operation. Children were essential to the family because they worked in the fields. Later, sons were expected to take over the physical labor on the family plots and provide for their parents.

At the heart of the concept of family in China was the idea of **filial piety.** *Filial* refers to a son or daughter. *Filial piety*, then, refers to the duty of members of the family to subordinate their needs and desires to those of the male head of the family. More broadly, the term describes a system in which every family member had his or her place. This concept is important in Confucianism, covered later in this section. **D**

Male supremacy was a key element in the social system of China, as it was in the other civilizations of the time. The male was responsible for providing food for his family. In ancient China, men worked the fields and were the warriors, scholars, and government ministers. Women raised the children and worked in the home. **C1**

Although women did not hold positions of authority, some did influence politics. This was especially true at the royal court, where female members of the royal family played a part in court affairs. These activities were clearly looked down upon by males, as this Chinese poem indicates:

PRIMARY SOURCE **C2**

> "A clever man builds a city,
> A clever woman lays one low;
> With all her qualifications, that clever woman
> is but an ill-omened bird."
>
> —Herbert A. Giles, *A History of Chinese Literature*

Zhou Accomplishments

The period from the sixth to the third centuries B.C. was an age of significant economic growth and technological change, especially in farming. For thousands of years, farmers had depended on rainfall to water crops such as rice and millet. By the sixth century B.C., irrigation was in wide use. Large-scale water projects were set in motion to control the flow of rivers and spread water evenly to the fields.

C1 Critical Thinking

Analyzing Information Ask: Why is the family considered a symbol of the entire Chinese social order? *(It reflects male supremacy and a system in which people subordinate their personal needs to the wishes of the head of the family or state.)* **AL**

D Differentiated Instruction

English Language Learners Have students use word structure to guess the meaning of *subordinate*—"to make lower in importance." (*The prefix* sub- *means "under" or "below." From this students can guess that, in context, the word means placing needs below those of fathers.)* **OL**

C2 Critical Thinking

Making Inferences Ask: Is women's influence on politics viewed favorably or unfavorably in this poem? How do you know? *(unfavorably—The narrator implies women are a disruptive, undermining influence in political endeavors.)* **OL**

Activity: Collaborative Learning

Debating Views on Zhou Society Review the information about the Zhou political and social structure. Then divide the class into two groups. **Ask:** Did the Zhou social order, in which all individuals knew their place in society and performed the duties expected of them, benefit all members of society? Have each group defend opposing views in a class debate. Allow time for groups to meet and prepare their arguments. Tell them to appoint one member to present an opening argument, another to rebut the opposition's opening, and a third to make a concluding statement. After the debate, discuss the strengths and weaknesses of each side's arguments. **OL**

R Reading Strategy

Activating Prior Knowledge

Point out that the quotation "Do not do unto others what you would not wish done to yourself" is an example of an aphorism: a short statement that offers practical wisdom. **Ask:** What other short, wise sayings can you think of that are commonly heard in society today? *(Provide students with examples to stimulate thinking—"the early bird gets the worm," "a fool and his money are soon parted," and so on.)* As students offer examples, write the sayings on the board. Have students copy them to use with the Interdisciplinary Activity suggested at the bottom of this page. OL

Answers:

1. Confucius and others made merit a cultural value; it took an assassination for it to become important in the United States.
2. The patronage system, appointing political supporters to federal jobs, was a well-established way for politicians to pay back their supporters.

Additional Support

As Confucius stated, "If there is righteousness in the heart, there will be beauty in the character. If there is beauty in the character, there will be harmony in the home. If there be harmony in the home, there will be order in the nation. If there be order in the nation, there will be peace in the world."

Above all, the ruler must set a good example. If the king followed the path of goodness, then subjects would respect him, and society would prosper. Confucius said, "Let the ruler be filial and kind to all people; then they will be faithful to him. Let him advance the good and teach the incompetent; then they will eagerly seek to be virtuous."

The second key element in the Confucian view of the Dao is humanity—compassion and empathy for others. Confucius said, "Do not do unto others what you would not wish done to yourself." Confucius urged people to "measure the feelings of others by one's own," for "within the four seas all men are brothers." After his death in 479 B.C., his message spread widely throughout China.

Confucius was a harsh critic of his own times. He stressed a return to the values of the Golden Age of the early Zhou dynasty. Confucius saw it as an age of perfection. "When the Great Way was practiced, the world was shared by all alike."

Confucius, however, was not just living in the past. Many of his key ideas looked forward. Perhaps his most significant political idea was that the government service should not be limited to those of noble birth but should be open to all men of superior talent. This concept of rule by merit was not popular with the aristocrats who held political offices based on their noble birth. Although Confucius's ideas did not have much effect in his lifetime, they opened the door to a new idea of statecraft that would later be put into widespread use.

Daoism

Daoism was a system of ideas based on the teachings of **Laozi** (LOW•DZUH). According to tradition, Laozi, or the Old Master, lived around the same time period as Confucius.

Connecting to the United States

CIVIL SERVICE REFORM

By 1881, the number of people who wanted presidential appointments to jobs had gotten out of hand. That year a disappointed office seeker shot President Garfield. Public anger over Garfield's assassination led to the passage of the Civil Service Act of 1883. Civil service reform made competitive examination, not politics, the basis for filling federal jobs. In 1978, President James Carter established the U.S. Office of Personnel Management, which administers a nationwide merit system for federal employees including recruitment, examination, and training programs.

Assassination attempt on President James Garfield

1. **Contrasting** What is the difference between the Chinese and the American reasons for adopting civil service examinations?
2. **Making Inferences** Why was it difficult to pass civil service reform laws?

Activity: Interdisciplinary Connection

Language Arts Tell students that proverbs, epigrams, and paradoxes are closely related to aphorisms in that they also are sayings that express a truth or offer practical wisdom. Proverbs are sayings used by many people over a long period of time that express commonly held truths: "Wealth is not his who has it but his who enjoys it." Epigrams emphasize wit and can include satire: "He knows the cost of everything and the value of nothing." Paradoxes are statements that appear to contradict fact, common sense, or themselves: "All generalizations are false, including this one." **Ask:** Which one of these types of sayings most closely resembles an aphorism? *(proverb)* Have students do either or both of the following activities:

1. Consult books of quotations to find other examples of sayings attributed to Confucius. Think about what practical wisdom these examples offer. Report what you learn to the class.
2. Research the sayings generated in class to determine their type and origin. Report what you learn about the ones you find. OL

Scholars do not know if Laozi actually existed. Nevertheless, the ideas people associate with him became popular in the fifth and fourth centuries B.C.

The chief ideas of Daoism are discussed in a short work known as *Tao Te Ching*, or *The Way of the Dao*. Scholars have argued for centuries over its meaning. Nevertheless, the basic ideas of Daoism, as interpreted by its followers, are straightforward. Daoism, like Confucianism, does not concern itself with the meaning of the universe. Rather, it sets forth proper forms of human behavior.

Daoism is also quite different from Confucianism. Followers of Confucius believe that it is the duty of human beings to work hard to improve life here on Earth. Daoists believe that the way to follow the will of Heaven is not through action but inaction:

PRIMARY SOURCE

> "Without going outside, you may know the whole world.
> Without looking through the window, you may see the ways of heaven.
> The farther you go, the less you know.
> Thus the sage [wise man] knows without traveling;
> He sees without looking;
> He works without doing."

The best way to act in harmony with the universal order is not to interfere with the natural order.

PRIMARY SOURCE

> "The universe is sacred.
> You cannot improve it.
> If you try to change it, you will ruin it.
> If you try to hold it, you will lose it."
> —Lao Tsu, *Tao Te Ching*

Legalism

A third philosophy that became popular was **Legalism.** Unlike Confucianism or Daoism, Legalism proposed that human beings were evil by nature. Legalists were referred to as the "School of Law" because they rejected the Confucian view that government by "superior men" could solve society's problems. Instead, they argued for a system of impersonal laws.

The Legalists believed that a strong ruler was required to create an orderly society. Confucius had said, "Lead the people by virtue and restrain them by the rules of good taste, and the people will have a sense of shame, and moreover will become good." The Legalists believed that only harsh laws and stiff punishments would cause the common people to serve the interests of the ruler. To them, people were not capable of being good. The ruler did not have to show compassion for the people.

✓Reading Check **Summarizing** What three philosophies became popular in early China?

SECTION 3 REVIEW

Vocabulary

1. **Explain** the significance of: Huang He, Chang Jiang, aristocracy, Mandate of Heaven, Dao, filial piety, pictographs, ideographs, Confucius, Confucianism, Daoism, Laozi, Legalism.

Main Ideas

2. **Describe** the relationship between China's geography—including the Huang He, Chang Jiang, and the mountains—and its climate.
3. **Summarize** the relationship between the dynastic cycle and the Mandate of Heaven.
4. **Explain** the importance of filial piety to the Chinese. How does the concept of filial piety relate to the Confucian view of how society should function?
5. **List** some of the agricultural advances developed in ancient China and explain how they increased food production.

Critical Thinking

6. **The BIG Idea** **Drawing Conclusions** How would writing with pictographs be more complex than using an alphabet?
7. **Diagramming** Create a diagram showing the Five Constant Relationships and the duty of each.

Relationship	Duty	Duty
Parent and child		

8. **Contrasting** How do Chinese philosophies differ from Buddhism and Hinduism?

Writing About History

9. **Expository Writing** Write a paper about the philosophical traditions of Confucianism, Daoism, and Legalism. Research to find examples of how these three philosophies influenced historic and contemporary world events.

History ONLINE

For help with the concepts in this section of *Glencoe World History*, go to glencoe.com and click Study Central™.

✓Reading Check

Answer: Confucianism, Daoism, and Legalism

Assess

History ONLINE

Study Central provides summaries, interactive games, and online graphic organizers to help students review content.

Close

Comparing and Contrasting

Ask: In what ways did Confucianism, Daoism, and Legalism differ from one another? *(Confucianism emphasized working hard to improve life. Daoism advocated inaction, not interfering with the natural order of things. Legalism rejected the Confucian principle of leading by virtue, believing instead that harsh laws and stiff punishments were needed to preserve order.)* OL

Answers

1. Definitions for the vocabulary words are found in the section and the Glossary.
2. When the monsoons blow toward the mountains, the air rises and cools, and rain falls on the mountainside.
3. A dynasty comes to power, claiming the Mandate of Heaven. After a period of effective rule, corruption sets in and the dynasty declines. A rebel leader claims the old dynasty has lost the Mandate of Heaven and takes over, establishing a new dynasty with its Mandate of Heaven.
4. central concept of the family; basis for Confucianism
5. Irrigation spread water evenly and reduced flooding; iron plowshares increased viable farmlands.
6. An alphabet represents a limited number of speech sounds. There are thousands of words so there would have to be pictographs for each. It is easier to learn 26 symbols than thousands.
7. **parent and child:** parent, loving; child, revering of parents; **husband and wife:** husbands, fulfill duties; wives, be obedient; **elder sibling and younger sibling:** elder, kind; younger, respectful; **older friend and younger friend:** older, considerate; younger, deferential; **ruler and subjects:** ruler, benevolent; subjects, loyal
8. Chinese philosophies do not attempt to explain the meaning of the universe, they guide human behavior.
9. Essays should reflect accurate information.

SECTION 4

Rise and Fall of Chinese Empires

Focus

Bellringer

Daily Focus Transparency 3.4

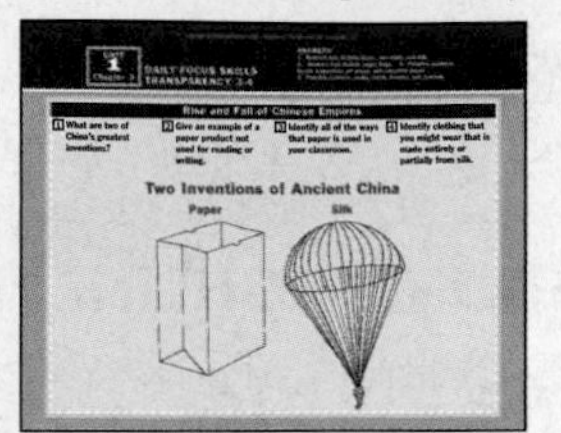

GUIDE TO READING

Answers to Graphic:

Qin dynasty: Legalism, single monetary system, system of roads, Great Wall, life-size terra-cotta sculptures; **Han dynasty:** Confucianism, civil service exam, new technology (water mills, iron casting, steel, paper, rudder, fore-and-aft rigging), major expansion of trade; **Both:** division of central government into three ministries, government officials appointed by emperor, expanded empire

Section Spotlight Video

To generate student interest and provide a springboard for class discussion, access the Chapter 3, Section 4 video at glencoe.com or on the video DVD.

GUIDE TO READING

The BIG Idea

Order and Security The Qin and Han dynasties established strong central governments that were the basis for future dynasties.

Content Vocabulary

- regime *(p. 96)*
- censorate *(p. 96)*

Academic Vocabulary

- individuality *(p. 95)*
- instituted *(p. 96)*
- ideology *(p. 96)*

People and Places

- Qin Shihuangdi *(p. 94)*
- Gobi *(p. 95)*
- Xiongnu *(p. 95)*
- Liu Pang *(p. 98)*
- Han Wudi *(p. 98)*
- South China Sea *(p. 98)*

Reading Strategy

Compare and Contrast As you read this section, compare and contrast the Qin and Han dynasties using a Venn diagram.

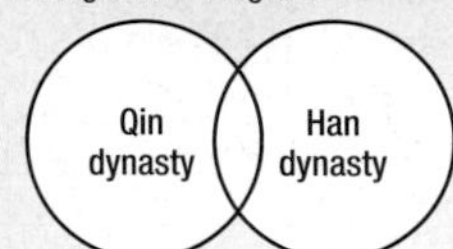

The First Qin Emperor unified the Chinese world, though his dynasty was short-lived. The Han dynasty that followed, however, lasted more than four hundred years. These dynasties made contributions to literature, art, and technology that have endured to the present.

The Qin Dynasty

MAIN IDEA Qin Shihuangdi unified the Chinese world using force against invaders and harsh treatment of his subjects.

HISTORY & YOU What makes you want to obey rules? Learn how the Chinese responded to repression.

As we have seen, from about 400 B.C. to 200 B.C., China experienced bloody civil war. Powerful states fought one another and ignored the authority of the Zhou kings. One state—that of Qin—gradually defeated its chief rivals. In 221 B.C., the Qin ruler declared the creation of a new dynasty.

Qin Shihuangdi

The ruler of the Qin dynasty was **Qin Shihuangdi** (CHIHN SHUH•HWAHNG•DEE), meaning "the First Qin Emperor." An ambitious person, he came to the throne in 246 B.C. at the age of 13. In 221 B.C., he defeated the last of his rivals and founded a new dynasty, with himself as emperor. The famous Chinese historian Sima Qian described Qin Shihuangdi as having "the chest of a bird of prey, the voice of a jackal, and the heart of a tiger." Those were just the qualities Qin Shihuangdi used to unite China. He created a single monetary system and ordered the building of a system of roads throughout the entire empire. Many of these roads led out from his capital city of Xianyang (SHYEN•YAHNG), just north of modern-day Xi'an (SHEE•AHN).

Qin Shihuangdi was equally aggressive in foreign affairs. His armies advanced to the south, extending the border of China to the edge of the Yuan (YOO•AHN) River, or Red River, in modern-day Vietnam. To supply his armies, he had a canal dug from the Chang Jiang in central China to what is now the modern city of Guangzhou (GWAHNG•JOH).

The Emperor's Army

Surprisingly, the emperor left behind a remarkable artistic legacy too. In 1974, farmers digging a well about 35 miles (56 km) east of Xi'an discovered an underground pit near the burial mound

Resource Manager

R Reading Strategies	C Critical Thinking	D Differentiated Instruction	W Writing Support	S Skill Practice
Teacher Edition • Act. Prior Know., p. 96 • Making Connections, p. 98 **Additional Resources** • Cont. Vocab. Act., URB p. 97 • Guid. Read. Act., URB p. 125 • Read. Ess. & Note-Taking Guide, p. 28	**Teacher Edition** • Making Inferences, p. 97 **Additional Resources** • Econ. & Hist. Act., URB p. 5 • People in World Hist. Act., URB p. 114 • Section Quiz, p. 26 • Chapter Test, p. 27	**Teacher Edition** • ELL, p. 95 • Visual/Spatial, p. 98 **Additional Resources** • Hist. Sim. Act., URB p. 109 • World Art & Music Act., URB p. 117 • Reteach Act., URB p. 119	**Teacher Edition** • Persuasive Writing, p. 96 • Expository Writing, p. 97 **Additional Resources** • Pri. Source Read., URB p. 115	**Teacher Edition** • Visual Literacy, p. 95 **Additional Resources** • Chart. Graph. Act., URB p. 3 • Time Line Act., URB p. 111

PRIMARY SOURCE / HISTORY & ARTS

The Emperor's Army

Outside Xi'an is the emperor Qin Shihuangdi's tomb complex. In the emperor's tomb, archaeologists have found sculptures, buildings, and cemeteries.

East of the tomb, a museum houses the emperor's army. The infantry is lined up in one large pit. Another pit contains cavalry and chariots. A third pit holds army headquarters.

The soldiers stand between 5 feet 8 inches and 6 feet 2 inches tall; their commanders are taller. The figures are weighted—the lower half of the ceramic bodies are solid, the upper half hollow. Traces of color show the statues were once vividly painted.

S

DOCUMENT-BASED QUESTIONS

1. **Analyzing** What about the soldiers is individualized?
2. **Theorizing** Why would the lower bodies be solid and the upper hollow?

of the First Qin Emperor. The pit contained a vast army made of terra-cotta, or hardened clay. Chinese archaeologists believe that it was a re-creation of Qin Shihuangdi's imperial guard, meant to be with the emperor on his journey to the next world.

Archaeologists estimate that there are more than six thousand figures in the first pit alone, along with horses, wooden chariots, and seven thousand bronze weapons. The figures are slightly larger than life-size. They were molded, fired, and painted in brilliant colors and then dressed in uniforms. To achieve **individuality** in the faces of the soldiers, ten different head shapes were used, which were finished by hand. Besides preparing for the next world, the Qin emperor was busy keeping out invaders.

D

The Great Wall

The Qin emperor's major foreign concern was in the north. In the vicinity of the **Gobi,** there resided a nomadic people known to the Chinese as the **Xiongnu** (SHYUNG•NOO). Mounted on horses, they ranged far and wide in search of pastures.

Teach

S Skill Practice

Visual Literacy Have students study the faces of the soldiers in the photo. **Ask:** What do you think their expressions were intended to convey regarding their attitude toward and purpose for being in the tomb? *(possibly their determination to defend or protect the king from an enemy attack)* **OL**

D Differentiated Instruction

English Language Learners Students with limited knowledge of English may be confused by the term *fired*. Explain that *firing* is the process of baking clay to harden it. Ceramic pottery, after being molded into a particular shape, is baked in furnaces called kilns. The clay soldiers were made in a similar manner. **ELL**

DOCUMENT-BASED QUESTIONS

Answers:

1. their height, faces
2. to help keep them upright

Additional Support

Extending the Content

Terra-Cotta Soldiers The terra-cotta soldiers in the tomb compound—archers, infantrymen, charioteers, and rear guard—are arranged according to customary battle formations of the time. They face east, which was the direction from which Qin's enemies had launched attacks. The entire compound covers about 20 square miles. The emperor's tomb is located about three-quarters of a mile from where the soldiers stand on guard. Supposedly, hundreds of thousands of workers labored nearly 40 years to construct the tomb's interior. Ssu-ma Chien, a historian of the time, described their efforts this way: "[The labourers] built models of palaces, pavilions, and offices and filled the tomb with fine vessels, precious stones, and rarities. Artisans [installed] mechanically triggered crossbows set to shoot any intruder. With quicksilver the various waterways of the empire . . . and even the great ocean itself were created and made to flow and circulate mechanically. With shining pearls the heavenly constellations were depicted above, and with figures of birds in gold and silver and of pine trees carved of jade the earth was laid out below."

R Reading Strategy

Activating Prior Knowledge

Ask: What assumption did Legalism make about human beings? *(They are evil by nature, incapable of being good.)* OL

W Writing Support

Persuasive Writing Have students write a paragraph expressing their opinion on this question: Why did Qin Shihuangdi fail in his goal to establish a dynasty for ten thousand generations? OL

✓Reading Check

Answer: civil division, military division, censorate

The Xiongnu were organized loosely into tribes, and moved with the seasons from one pasture to another with their flocks of cattle, sheep, or goats. The Xiongnu had mastered the art of fighting on horseback. The historian Sima Qian remarked:

PRIMARY SOURCE

> "[T]he little boys start out by learning to ride sheep and shoot birds and rats with a bow and arrow, and when they get a little older they shoot foxes and rabbits, which are used for food. Thus all the young men are able to use a bow and act as armed cavalry in time of war."
>
> —Sima Qian

When the Xiongnu challenged Chinese communities near the northern frontier, a number of states constructed walls to keep the nomads out. Qin Shihuangdi's answer to the problem was to strengthen the existing system of walls and link them together to create The Wall of Ten Thousand *Li*—a *li* is about a third of a mile, or half a kilometer. Today we know Qin Shihuangdi's project as the Great Wall of China. However, the wall that we know from films and photographs was not built until 1,500 years later. Some of the walls built by Shihuangdi do remain, but most of them were built of loose stone, sand, or piled rubble and disappeared long ago.

This is not to say, of course, that the wall was not a massive project. It required the efforts of thousands of laborers. Many of them died while working there and, according to legend, are now buried within the wall. With his wall, the First Qin Emperor had some success in fighting off the nomads, but the victory was only temporary. Over the next two thousand years, China's northern frontier became one of the great areas of conflict in Asia.

Political Changes

See page R35 to read a passage from Li Su, a chief minister of the First Qin Emperor, in the **Primary Sources and Literature Library.**

The Qin dynasty dramatically changed Chinese politics. Legalism was adopted as the **regime's**—the government in power—official **ideology**. Books presenting ideas opposed to the official views were publicly burned. Those who opposed the policies of the new regime were punished or executed.

The Qin dynasty made a number of important administrative and political changes, which served as models for future dynasties. Unlike the Zhou dynasty, the Qin dynasty ruled a highly centralized state. The central bureaucracy was divided into three parts: the civil division, the military division, and the **censorate.** The censorate had inspectors who checked on government officials to make sure they were doing their jobs. This became standard for future Chinese dynasties.

Below the central government were two levels of administration: provinces and counties. Unlike under the Zhou, these officials did not inherit their positions but were appointed and dismissed by the emperor. The censors also watched over these officials, and those found guilty of wrongdoing were executed. Qin Shihuangdi also reduced the powers of the landed aristocrats by dividing their estates among the peasants, who were now taxed directly by the state. In doing so, he eliminated possible rivals and gained tax revenues for the central government.

Fall of the Qin Dynasty

By ruthlessly controlling the empire, Qin Shihuangdi hoped to establish a rule that "would be enjoyed by his sons for ten thousand generations." In fact, Shihuangdi was to be his dynasty's only ruler. Landed aristocrats and Confucian intellectuals, as well as the common people, groaned under the censorship of speech, harsh taxes, and forced labor projects **instituted** by the ruler. Sima Qian said of Qin Shihuangdi:

PRIMARY SOURCE

> "He killed men as though he thought he could never finish, he punished men as though he were afraid he would never get around to them all, and the whole world revolted against him."
>
> —Sima Qian

The emperor died in 210 B.C., and his dynasty was overthrown four years later. The fall of the Qin dynasty was followed by a period of civil war, but it did not last long. A new dynasty soon arose.

✓Reading Check **Identifying** What three parts of the central bureaucracy were developed by the Qin dynasty?

Hands-On Chapter Project Step 4

Creating a Poster of Early India and China

Step 4: Assembling the Poster In addition to gathering information and preparing entries, students will assemble the posters they worked on in sections 1–3.

Directions: Tell students to use the Section 4 Big Idea as a guide for completing their search for poster information. After they have finished preparing entries, students should assemble the various elements on the poster, making sure they proofread any captions and text.

Summarizing: Allow time for students to share what they learned about the Section 4 Big Idea while completing their search for poster material. OL

(Chapter Project is continued on the Visual Summary page.)

INFOGRAPHICS PRIMARY SOURCE

The Great Wall of China: In History and Legend

The Great Wall winds across China's landscape and through its history. Over 2,000 years, piled stone gave way to elaborate watchtowers and forts. In the seventeenth century, visiting Europeans mistakenly assumed the wall was one continuous structure and called it "The Great Wall of China." Besides guarding trade routes, the wall became the source of legends. **W**

The Legend of Meng Jiangnu Whose Wails Split the Wall

Near Shanhaiguan Pass is a temple to Meng Jiangnu. Fan, Meng's husband, was one of thousands forced to work on the wall. With winter coming, Meng carried warm clothes to Fan. When Meng reached the place where her husband had been working, she learned that Fan had died from overwork and been buried in the wall. Hearing this awful news, Meng wept so loudly that miles of wall collapsed, exposing the bodies of laborers. **C**

NATIONAL GEOGRAPHIC

BUILDING THE GREAT WALL

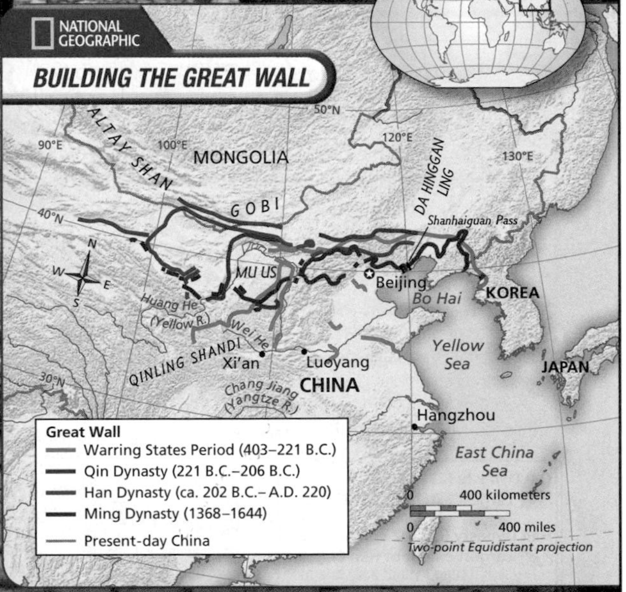

ALTAY SHAN, MONGOLIA, GOBI, DA HINGGAN LING, Shanhaiguan Pass, MU US, Beijing, Bo Hai, KOREA, Huang He (Yellow R.), Wei He, QINLING SHANDI, Xi'an, Luoyang, CHINA, Chang Jiang (Yangtze R.), Yellow Sea, JAPAN, Hangzhou, East China Sea; 90°E, 100°E, 120°E, 130°E, 50°N, 40°N, 30°N

Great Wall
- Warring States Period (403–221 B.C.)
- Qin Dynasty (221 B.C.–206 B.C.)
- Han Dynasty (ca. 202 B.C.–A.D. 220)
- Ming Dynasty (1368–1644)
- Present-day China

0 400 kilometers; 0 400 miles; Two-point Equidistant projection

Geography SKILLS

1. **Location** Which border of the empires was the wall supposed to protect?
2. **Human-Environment Interaction** What physical features of the environment made it difficult to build the Great Wall?

Maps In MOtion See *StudentWorks™ Plus* or glencoe.com.

W Writing Support

Expository Writing Have students write a research report on a subject related to the Great Wall. Topics might include legends about the wall, its physical characteristics, a comparison of the present wall to the one built during the Qin dynasty, and so on. **OL**

C Critical Thinking

Making Inferences Tell students that legends are often born out of a need to explain some phenomenon in nature or society. **Ask:** What might have prompted the development of the legend of Meng Jiangnu? *(Possible answers: as a response to harsh conditions during construction or cruelty to workers; to explain erosion or damaged areas of the wall; to dramatize the sacrifices of workers' families)* **OL**

Geography SKILLS

Answers:

1. Part of the Silk Road and the other trade routes run next to the Great Wall.
2. There are numerous mountains and deserts that would make working on the wall hazardous.

Differentiated Instruction

Analyzing Information

Objective: Analyze information related to the Great Wall of China.

Focus: Ask students to identify the historic importance of the Great Wall.

Teach: Have students read the passage and answer the questions.

Assess: Ask students to explain the purpose of the Great Wall and why it is considered a work of art.

Close: Ask students what other cities or regions still have protective walls.

Differentiated Instruction Strategies

BL Have students create a drawing of the Great Wall.

AL Have students research the Great Wall and prepare a report explaining one aspect of its history.

ELL Help students make the connection between the words "wall" and "fortress."

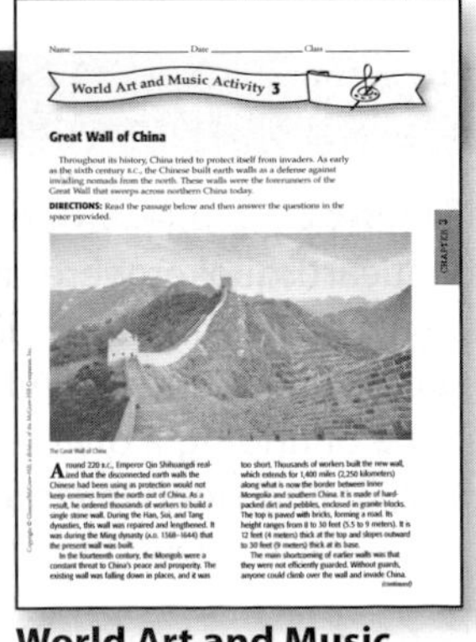

World Art and Music Activity, URB p. 117

Comparing and Contrasting **Ask:** Where did civilizations develop in India and China? *(**India:** Indus River Valley, Deccan Plateau; **China:** along river routes of Huang He and Chang Jiang)* **OL**

Summarizing Have students summarize the achievements of one Indian empire and one Chinese dynasty. **OL**

Synthesizing **Ask:** How are dynastic cycles and Mandate of Heaven related? *(Cycles included the rise of dynasty, efficient rule, decline, and takeover by another. The Mandate of Heaven gave dynasties an ethical justification for overthrowing an existing dynasty.)* **OL**

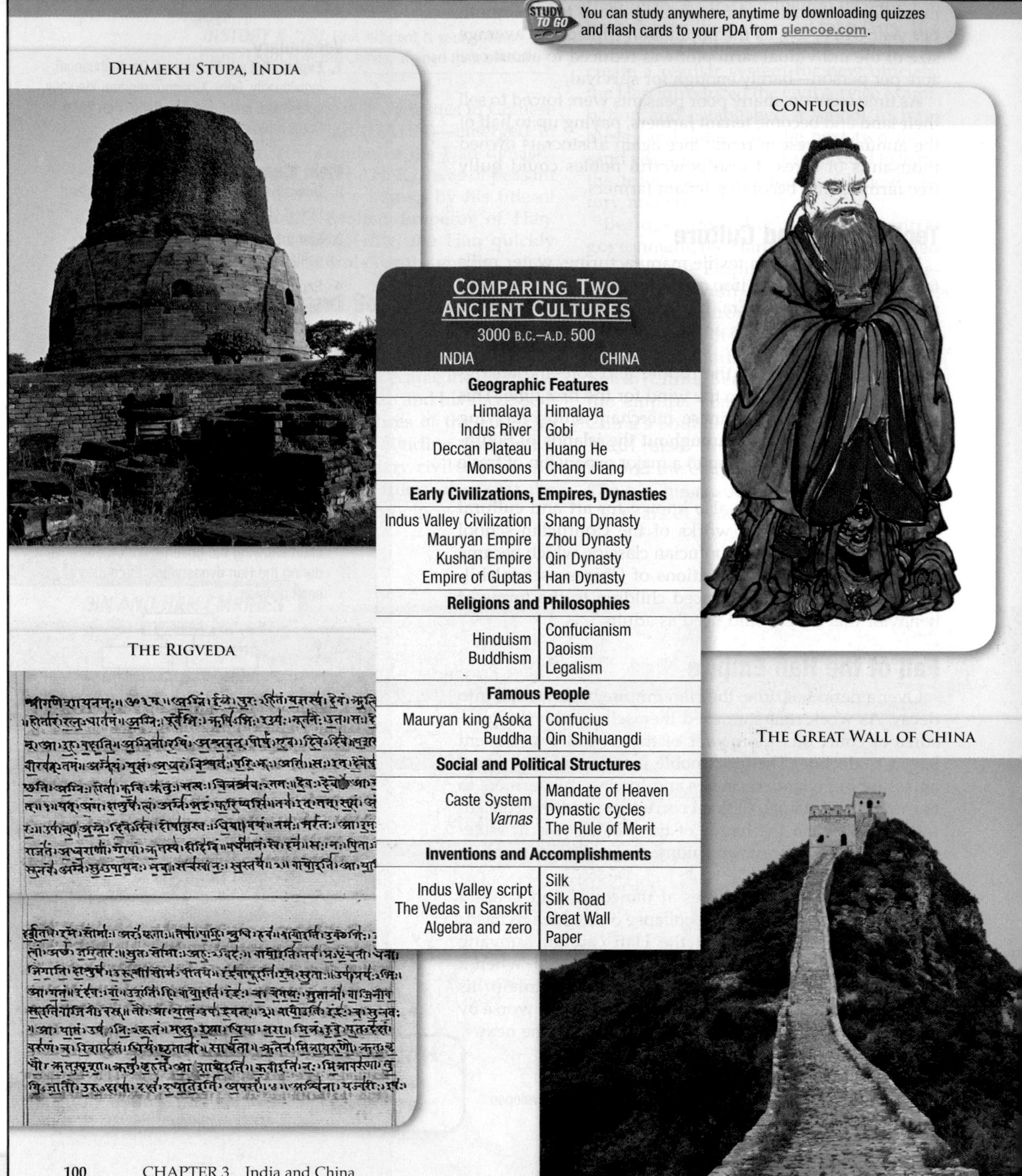

COMPARING TWO ANCIENT CULTURES
3000 B.C.–A.D. 500

INDIA	CHINA
Geographic Features	
Himalaya Indus River Deccan Plateau Monsoons	Himalaya Gobi Huang He Chang Jiang
Early Civilizations, Empires, Dynasties	
Indus Valley Civilization Mauryan Empire Kushan Empire Empire of Guptas	Shang Dynasty Zhou Dynasty Qin Dynasty Han Dynasty
Religions and Philosophies	
Hinduism Buddhism	Confucianism Daoism Legalism
Famous People	
Mauryan king Aśoka Buddha	Confucius Qin Shihuangdi
Social and Political Structures	
Caste System *Varnas*	Mandate of Heaven Dynastic Cycles The Rule of Merit
Inventions and Accomplishments	
Indus Valley script The Vedas in Sanskrit Algebra and zero	Silk Silk Road Great Wall Paper

Hands-On Chapter Project
Step 5: Wrap-Up

Creating a Poster of Early India and China

Step 5: Presenting the Poster Students will synthesize what they learned in Steps 1–4.

Directions: Write the Essential Question on the board. Under it, write the Big Ideas from each section of the chapter. Conduct a class discussion to connect the important ideas in the Essential Question and the Big Ideas to specific examples in the chapter. Have students use their posters to point out important ideas. Conclude by directing attention to the Visual Summary on this page. Have students discuss the items listed in it and compare them to the information they have included in their posters. Display the posters around the room for students to review and compare. **OL**

STANDARDIZED TEST PRACTICE

TEST-TAKING TIP

Even if you don't know the correct answer, you still may know which answer choices are *wrong*. Eliminate the answer choices you know are wrong. Then choose the best answer from the choices that remain.

Reviewing Vocabulary

Directions: Choose the word or words that best complete the sentence.

1. Monsoons are seasonal ________ in China and the Indian subcontinent.

A winds
B thunderstorms
C floods
D cyclones

2. According to Confucius, the key to proper behavior was to behave in accordance with the ________ (Way).

A Yoga
B Dao
C Dharma
D Censorate

3. In Buddhism, reaching ________, or ultimate reality, is the end of the self and a reunion with the Great World Soul.

A reincarnation
B karma
C nirvana
D ascetic

4. The English word for the social divisions in India based on occupation and family is ________.

A caste
B untouchables
C raja
D reincarnation

Reviewing Main Ideas

Directions: Choose the best answers to the following questions.

Section 1 *(pp. 66–75)*

5. Which of the following is not a characteristic of the Indus Valley civilization?

A Well-planned cities
B Large in size
C Easily understood writing
D Widespread trade

6. Out of what did the caste system grow?

A Rajas
B Aryans
C Vedas
D *Varnas*

7. What do the majority of India's people practice?

A Hinduism
B Suttee
C Buddhism
D Asceticism

8. Which of the following is a true statement about Buddhists?

A They are the majority in India.
B They try to follow the Middle Path.
C They believe in a rigid caste system.
D They worship the Buddha as a god.

Need Extra Help?

If You Missed Questions . . .	1	2	3	4	5	6	7	8
Go to Page . . .	64	88	71	68	66	68	70	71

Answers and Analyses

Reviewing Vocabulary

1. A Students can eliminate D since it is not mentioned in the text. They may have difficulty eliminating either B or C. Point out that both are results of the monsoon winds.

2. B Choices A and C relate to Hinduism, and D is one of the divisions of the Qin and Han dynasties.

3. C Nirvana is the ultimate reality. A and D are obviously wrong. Some students may be tempted to choose B but this refers to a concept in Hinduism.

4. A Choices C and D are obviously wrong. Point out that B is one category of Indian social class and is not considered a part of the caste system.

Reviewing Main Ideas

5. C Choice C is the only possible answer. All the other choices were characteristic of the Indus Valley civilization.

6. D Rajas were rulers. Members of all castes were Aryans. The Vedas were Hindu religious books.

7. A Choice A is correct. Choices B and D were or are practiced by some of India's people. Buddhism is practiced by a minority.

8. B Choice B is the only possible answer. The other choices are clearly false. Hindus are the majority in India. The Buddha rejected the caste system and forbade his followers from worshiping him.

CHAPTER 4 Planning Guide

Key to Ability Levels

- **BL** Below Level
- **OL** On Level
- **AL** Above Level
- **ELL** English Language Learners

Key to Teaching Resources

- Print Material
- CD-ROM
- DVD
- Transparency

Levels					Resources	Chapter Opener	Sect. 1	Sect. 2	Sect. 3	Sect. 4	Sect. 5	Chapter Assess
BL	OL	AL	ELL									
					FOCUS							
BL	OL	AL	ELL	Transparency	Daily Focus Skills Transparencies		4-1	4-2	4-3	4-4	4-5	
					TEACH							
BL	OL	AL	ELL	Print Material	Charting and Graphing Activity, URB						✓	
	OL	AL		Print Material	Economics and History Activity, URB		✓					
		AL		Print Material	World Literature Reading, URB					✓		
BL	OL		ELL	Print Material	Reading Skills Activity, URB		p. 129					
	OL	AL		Print Material	Historical Analysis Skills Activity, URB				p. 130			
BL	OL	AL	ELL	Print Material	Differentiated Instruction Activity, URB		p. 131					
	OL		ELL	Print Material	English Learner Activity, URB		p. 133					
BL	OL	AL	ELL	Print Material	Content Vocabulary Activity, URB*		p. 135					
BL	OL	AL	ELL	Print Material	Academic Vocabulary Activity, URB			p. 137				
BL	OL	AL	ELL	Print Material	Skills Reinforcement Activity, URB					p. 139		
	OL	AL		Print Material	Critical Thinking Skills Activity, URB				p. 140			
	OL	AL		Print Material	History and Geography Activity, URB						p. 141	
	OL	AL	ELL	Print Material	Mapping History Activity, URB		p. 143					
BL	OL	AL		Print Material	Historical Significance Activity, URB				p. 144			
BL	OL	AL	ELL	Print Material	Cooperative Learning Activity, URB					p. 145		
	OL	AL	ELL	Print Material	History Simulation Activity, URB					p. 147		
BL	OL	AL	ELL	Print Material	Time Line Activity, URB						p. 149	
	OL	AL		Print Material	Linking Past and Present Activity, URB			p. 150				
BL	OL	AL		Print Material	People in World History Activity, URB		p. 151	p. 152				
BL	OL	AL	ELL	Print Material	Primary Source Reading, URB				p. 153			
	OL	AL		Print Material	Enrichment Activity, URB					p. 158		
BL	OL	AL	ELL	Print Material	World Art and Music Activity, URB					p. 155		
BL	OL		ELL	Print Material	Guided Reading Activities, URB*		p. 160	p. 161	p. 162	p. 163	p. 164	
BL	OL		ELL	Print Material	Reading Essentials and Note-Taking Guide*		p. 31	p. 34	p. 37	p. 40	p. 43	
BL	OL	AL	ELL	Print Material	Differentiated Instruction for the World History Classroom	✓	✓	✓	✓	✓	✓	✓

Note: Please refer to the *Unit Resource Book: The First Civilizations and Empires* for this chapter's URB materials.

* Also available in Spanish

- Interactive Lesson Planner
- Interactive Teacher Edition
- Fully editable blackline masters
- Section Spotlight Videos Launch
- Differentiated Lesson Plans
- Printable reports of daily assignments
- Standards Tracking System

Levels BL	OL	AL	ELL	Resources	Chapter Opener	Sect. 1	Sect. 2	Sect. 3	Sect. 4	Sect. 5	Chapter Assess
TEACH *(continued)*											
BL	OL	AL	ELL	StudentWorks™ Plus DVD	✓	✓	✓	✓	✓	✓	✓
BL	OL	AL	ELL	Vocabulary PuzzleMaker CD-ROM	✓	✓	✓	✓	✓	✓	✓
Teacher Resources				Building Academic Vocabulary	✓	✓	✓	✓	✓	✓	✓
				Reading Strategies and Activities for the Social Studies Classroom				p. 59			
				Writer's Guidebook		p. 47				p. 47	
				Strategies for Success	✓	✓	✓	✓	✓	✓	✓
				Outline Map Resource Book	✓	✓	✓	✓	✓	✓	✓
				Presentation Plus! with MindJogger DVD	✓	✓	✓	✓	✓	✓	✓
ASSESS											
BL	OL	AL	ELL	Section Quizzes and Chapter Tests*		p. 35	p. 36	p. 37	p. 38	p. 39	p. 41
BL	OL	AL	ELL	Authentic Assessment With Rubrics	✓	✓	✓	✓	✓	✓	✓
BL	OL	AL	ELL	Standardized Test Practice Workbook	✓	✓	✓	✓	✓	✓	✓
BL	OL	AL	ELL	*ExamView® Assessment Suite* CD-ROM		4-1	4-2	4-3	4-4	4-5	Ch. 4
BL	OL	AL	ELL	Interactive Tutor Self-Assessment CD-ROM		4-1	4-2	4-3	4-4	4-5	
CLOSE											
BL			ELL	Reteaching Activity, URB						p. 157	
BL	OL		ELL	Reading and Study Skills Foldables™	✓	✓	✓	✓	✓	✓	✓

Using Puzzlemaker™ 3.1

Online Word Search Puzzles

Technology Product

Glencoe's Vocabulary PuzzleMaker™ 3.1 CD-ROM is an easy-to-use program that lets you create your own puzzles based on the glossary for classroom use. The PuzzleMaker allows you to

- create word search puzzles based on content vocabulary and academic vocabulary that is specific to what is taught in the classroom;
- create online (LAN-based or local area network) or paper word search puzzles.

Objectives

After students complete the word search puzzles, they will be able to

- recall academic vocabulary terms based on the clues provided for a puzzle;
- reinforce their understanding of the vocabulary.

Steps

- Run PuzzleMaker™ 3.1. On the main menu, click on **Create a New Puzzle.**
- Select the *Puzzle Database* for the vocabulary.
- The *PuzzleMaker Wizard* will take you through selecting a puzzle type and grid type.
- Then select one or more chapters from the list. Indicate whether you want the words selected randomly or manually.
- Select the language and words you wish to use within the maximum for the puzzle. Click **Finish.**
- Save your word search puzzle to a location that is easily accessible by your students with PuzzlePlayer™ 3.1, or print copies for your students to complete.
- Use PuzzlePlayer™ 3.1 to review the puzzles after your students have worked on and saved them.

History ONLINE

	Student	Teacher	Parent
Beyond the Textbook	●	●	●
Chapter Overviews	●	●	●
Time Current Events	●		●
ePuzzles and Games	●		●
Concepts in Motion	●		●
Literature Connections		●	
Multi-Language Glossaries	●		●
Online Student Edition	●	●	●
Self-Check Quizzes	●		●
Student Web Activities	●		●
Study Central ™	●		●
Teaching Today		●	
Vocabulary eFlashcards	●		●
Web Activity Lesson Plans		●	

- **Timed Readings Plus in Social Studies** helps students increase their reading rate and fluency while maintaining comprehension. The 400-word passages are similar to those found on state and national assessments.
- **Reading in the Content Area: Social Studies** concentrates on six essential reading skills that help students better comprehend what they read. The book includes 75 high-interest nonfiction passages written at increasing levels of difficulty.
- **Reading Social Studies** includes strategic reading instruction and vocabulary support in Social Studies content for both ELLs and native speakers of English.

www.jamestowneducation.com

Biography A&E Home Video THE HISTORY CHANNEL.

The following videotape programs are available from Glencoe as supplements to Chapter 4:

- Mystical Monuments of Ancient Greece (ISBN 0-76-700012-9)
- Powerful Gods of Mt. Olympus (ISBN 1-56-501927-X)
- The Trojan City (ISBN 0-76-700647-X)

To order, call Glencoe at 1-800-334-7344. To find classroom resources to accompany many of these videos, check the following home pages:

A&E Television: www.aetv.com

The History Channel: www.historychannel.com

Index to National Geographic Magazine:

The following articles relate to this chapter:

- "Golden Age Treasures," by George F. Bass, March 2002
- "Ancient Greece," by Caroline Alexander, December 1999, February 2000, March 2000

National Geographic Society Products To order the following, call National Geographic at 1-800-368-2728:

- *Ancient Greece* (PicturePack)
- *Ancient Civilizations: Greece & Rome* (CD-ROM)

Access National Geographic's new, dynamic MapMachine Web site and other geography resources at:

www.nationalgeographic.com

www.nationalgeographic.com/maps

GLENCOE BOOKLINK 3

Use this database to search more than 30,000 titles to create a customized reading list for your students.

- Reading lists can be organized by students' reading level, author, genre, theme, or area of interest.
- The database provides Degrees of Reading Power™ (DRP) and Lexile™ readability scores for all selections.
- A brief summary of each selection is included.

Leveled reading suggestions for this chapter:

For students at a Grade 8 reading level:

- ***You Are in Ancient Greece,*** by Ivan Minnis

For students at a Grade 9 reading level:

- ***Pandora of Athens: 399 B.C.,*** by Barry Denenberg

For students at a Grade 10 reading level:

- ***Aristotle Leads the Way,*** by Joy Hakim

For students at a Grade 11 reading level:

- ***The Iliad of Homer,*** by Homer

For students at a Grade 12 reading level:

- ***Living in Ancient Greece,*** by Don Nardo

Introducing
CHAPTER 4

Focus

MAKING CONNECTIONS
How did the Greeks shape our culture?

Activate students' prior knowledge by asking them to identify major achievements of the ancient Greeks. *(Answers may include examples of achievements in literature, art, government, philosophy, science, athletics, mathematics, drama, and architecture.)* Then discuss specific examples of Greek influences in modern society, such as the democratic process, architectural influences, the theater, or sporting events.

Teach

The Big Ideas

As students study the chapter, remind them to consider the section-based Big Ideas included in each section's Guide to Reading. The **Essential Questions** in the activities below tie in to the Big Ideas and help students think about and understand important chapter concepts. In addition, the Hands-on Chapter Projects with their culminating activities relate the content from each section to the Big Ideas. These activities build on each other as students progress through the chapter. Section activities culminate in the wrap-up activity on the Visual Summary page.

CHAPTER 4

Ancient Greece 1900–133 B.C.

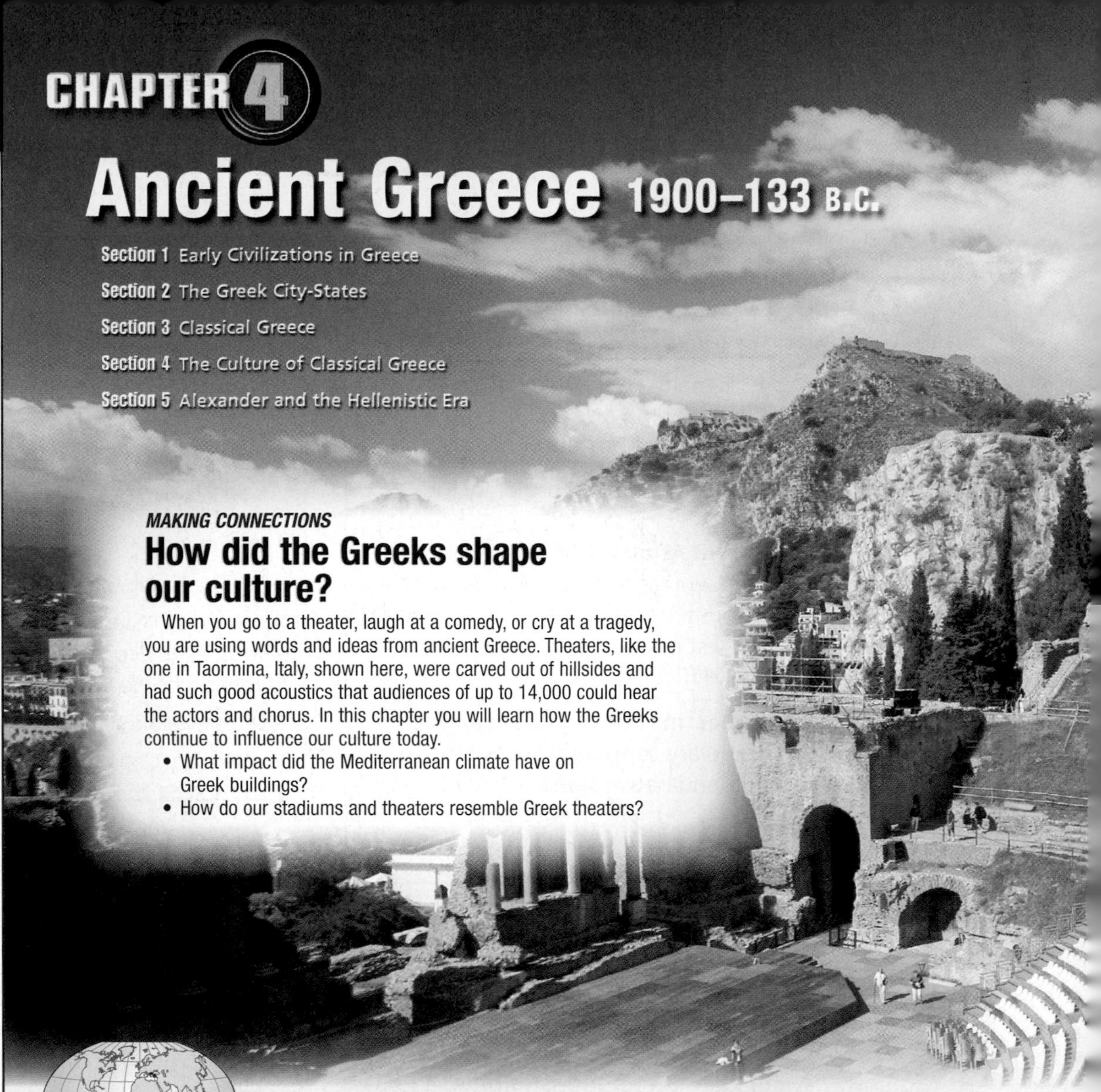

MAKING CONNECTIONS

How did the Greeks shape our culture?

When you go to a theater, laugh at a comedy, or cry at a tragedy, you are using words and ideas from ancient Greece. Theaters, like the one in Taormina, Italy, shown here, were carved out of hillsides and had such good acoustics that audiences of up to 14,000 could hear the actors and chorus. In this chapter you will learn how the Greeks continue to influence our culture today.

- What impact did the Mediterranean climate have on Greek buildings?
- How do our stadiums and theaters resemble Greek theaters?

THE WORLD ▶

1900 B.C. — 1500 B.C. — 1000 B.C.

c. 1900 B.C. Peak of Minoan civilization

776 B.C. First Olympic Games held

c. 1500 B.C. King Agamemnon ruled Mycenae

104

Early Civilizations in Greece

Discuss with students the influence of geography on a region's economy and customs. **Essential Question:** In what ways did proximity to the sea influence the development of early Greek civilizations? *(The ancient Greeks became seafarers, developing trade networks and using the resources of the sea.)* Tell students that in Section 1, they will learn about the Minoan and Mycenaean societies of Ancient Greece. **OL**

The Greek City-States

Discuss how Sparta and Athens exemplify different political systems. **Essential Question:** Why do some political ideas live on, while others are discarded? *(Accept all reasonable responses.)* Tell students that in Section 2, they will learn about the relationship between Sparta and Athens and the beginnings of democracy. **OL**

499–479 B.C.
Persian Wars

323 B.C.
Death of Alexander the Great

133 B.C.

500 B.C.
Height of Classical Greece

431–404 B.C.
Spartans fought Athenians in the Peloponnesian War

FOLDABLES Study Organizer

Organizing Review the text for information about the Hellenistic Era and then create a Shutter Fold to organize facts about the era and Alexander the Great.

WHO? WHAT? Alexander the Great / The Hellenistic Era

History ONLINE
Chapter Overview—Visit glencoe.com to preview Chapter 4.

Introducing
CHAPTER 4

More About the Photo

Visual Literacy This photograph shows an ancient Greek theater in Taormina, a town in eastern Sicily. Taormina flourished under the Greeks in the third century B.C. The outdoor theater was an important part of ancient Greek life. Today Taormina is a popular tourist destination, and the theater itself still serves as an arts venue.

FOLDABLES Study Organizer Dinah Zike's Foldables

Dinah Zike's Foldables are three-dimensional, interactive graphic organizers that help students practice basic writing skills, review vocabulary terms, and identify main ideas. Instructions for creating and using Foldables can be found in the Appendix at the end of this book and in the *Dinah Zike's Reading and Study Skills Foldables* booklet.

History ONLINE

Introduce students to chapter content and key terms by having them access the Chapter 4 Overview at glencoe.com.

SECTION 3

Classical Greece

Essential Question: What leads to rivalry between nations? *(Answers may include that fundamental ideological differences and desire for power or property may create conflict.)* Tell students that in Section 3, they will learn about the causes of the Great Peloponnesian War. OL

SECTION 4

The Culture of Classical Greece

Essential Question: How has classical Greece influenced Western civilization? *(Answers may include examples of Greek influence on Western art, architecture, literature, and philosophy.)* Tell students that in Section 4, they will trace the legacy of classical Greece. OL

SECTION 5

Alexander and the Hellenistic Era

Essential Question: What makes a great leader? *(Accept all reasonable responses.)* Tell students that in Section 5, they will learn about Alexander the Great and the empire that he forged. OL

Focus

Bellringer
Daily Focus Transparency 4.1

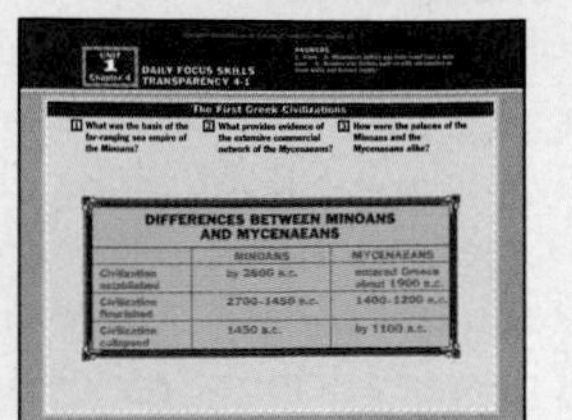

GUIDE TO READING

Answers to Graphic:
Minoan: island culture, bronze weapons, sea trade with Greece and Egypt, paintings show sporting and nature scenes; **Mycenaean:** Indo-European, fortified palaces, warrior people, murals show war and hunting scenes; **Both:** monarchies, extensive trade with other civilizations, created paintings that reflected values

Section Spotlight Video

To generate student interest and provide a springboard for class discussion, access the Chapter 4, Section 1 video at glencoe.com or on the video DVD.

SECTION 1

Early Civilizations in Greece

GUIDE TO READING

The BIG Idea
Physical Geography The earliest Greek civilizations that appeared in the second millennium B.C. were influenced by their physical environment.

Content Vocabulary
- epic poem *(p. 111)*
- arete *(p. 111)*

Academic Vocabulary
- participate *(p. 106)*
- debated *(p. 109)*

People, Places, and Events
- Aegean Sea *(p. 107)*
- Black Sea *(p. 107)*
- Bronze Age *(p. 108)*
- Crete *(p. 108)*
- Minoan *(p. 108)*
- Mycenaean *(p. 109)*
- Homer *(p. 109)*
- Ionia *(p. 110)*

Reading Strategy
Compare and Contrast As you read, create a diagram like the one below to help you study the Minoan and Mycenaean civilizations.

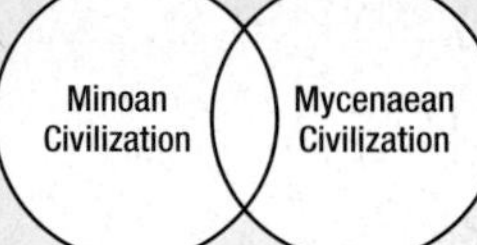

During the third millennium B.C., the island of Crete was home to the most advanced civilization in Europe. Although Minoan Crete was not Greek, it did have some influence on the first Greek state. The story of ancient Greek civilization begins when a group of Greek-speaking Indo-European people moved into Greece around 1900 B.C. The Mycenaeans provided the inspiration for Homer's epics and paved the way for the political and cultural developments of Greece in the first millennium B.C.

The Impact of Geography

MAIN IDEA The mountains that divided Greece led to cultural and political divisions between Greeks. However, the seas linked Greece to the rest of the world.

HISTORY & YOU How does the physical geography of your town influence life in your community? What physical features affect your everyday life? Read about the effects of geography on development of Greek civilization.

Geography played an important role in the development of Greek civilization. Compared with the landmasses of Mesopotamia and Egypt, Greece occupies a small area. It consists of a mountainous peninsula and numerous islands that encompass about 50,000 square miles (about 129,500 square km) of territory—about the size of the state of Louisiana. The mountains and the sea played especially significant roles in the development of Greek history.

Mountains

Two peninsulas make up much of the Greek landmass. The Isthmus of Corinth connects the Peloponnese peninsula to the mainland. About 80 percent of Greece is mountainous. Olympus is the highest peak in the Pindus Mountains, which divide the mainland. Much of Greece consists of small plains and river valleys surrounded by high mountain ranges from 8,000 to 10,000 feet (2,438 to 3,048 m) high. These mountains isolated Greeks from one another, causing different Greek communities to develop their own ways of life.

Over a period of time, these communities became fiercely independent. It is probable that the small size of these independent communities encouraged people to **participate** in political affairs. On the other hand, the rivalry between the communities led to warfare that devastated Greek society.

Resource Manager

R Reading Strategies	C Critical Thinking	D Differentiated Instruction	W Writing Support	S Skill Practice
Teacher Edition • Summarizing, p. 109 • Identifying, p. 110 • Inferring, p. 111 **Additional Resources** • Cont. Vocab. Act., URB p. 135 • Guid. Read. Act., URB p. 160 • Read. Ess. & Note-Taking Guide, p. 31	**Teacher Edition** • Compare/Contrast p. 109 **Additional Resources** • Econ. & Hist. Act., URB p. 5 • People in World Hist. Act., URB p. 151 • Section Quiz, p. 35	**Teacher Edition** • Verbal/Linguistic, p. 108 • ELL, p. 110 **Additional Resources** • Diff. Instr. Act., URB p. 131 • English Learner Act., URB p. 133	**Teacher Edition** • Expository Writing, p. 109 **Additional Resources** • Writer's Guidebook, p. 47	**Teacher Edition** • Using Geo. Skills, p. 107 **Additional Resources** • Read. Skills Act., URB p. 129 • Mapping Hist. Act., URB p. 143

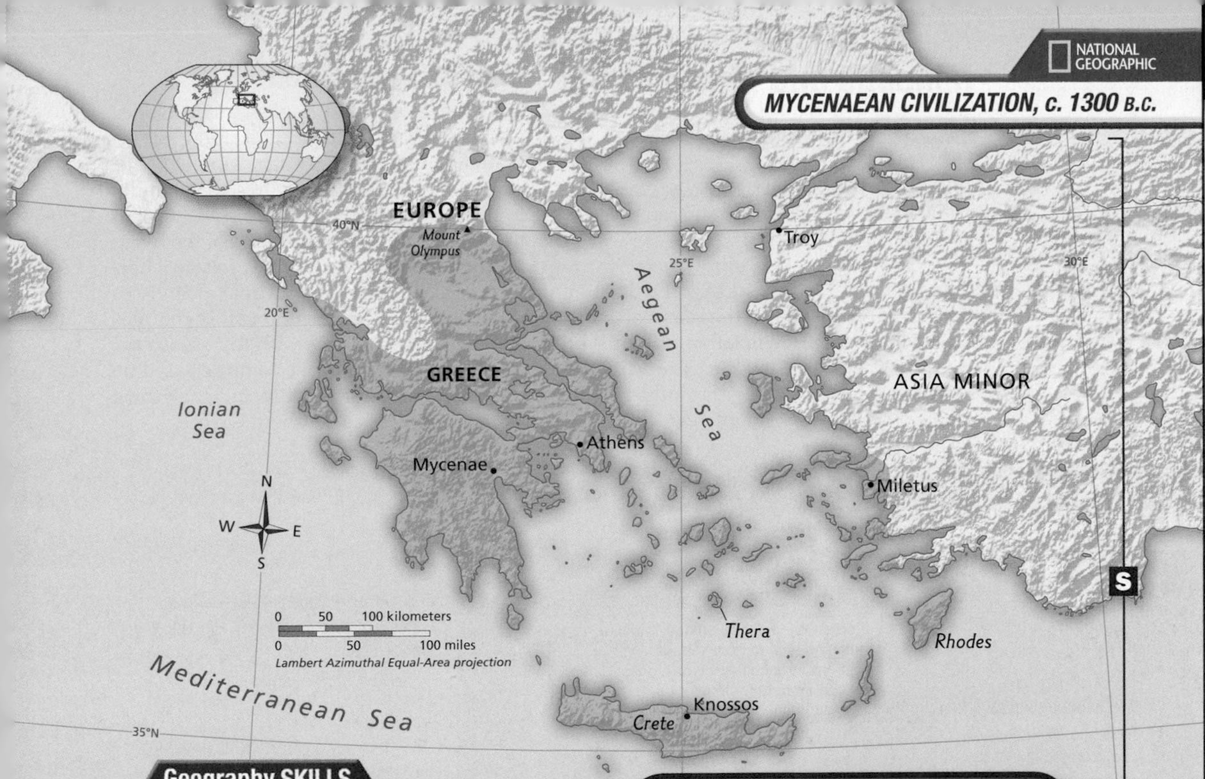

NATIONAL GEOGRAPHIC

MYCENAEAN CIVILIZATION, c. 1300 B.C.

Geography SKILLS

The physical geography of Greece had a major impact on the development of civilizations in Greece.

1. **Human-Environment Interaction** How has Greece's geography affected settlement patterns?
2. **Regions** Using the map, discuss what might account for differences in the cultures of Mycenae and Troy.

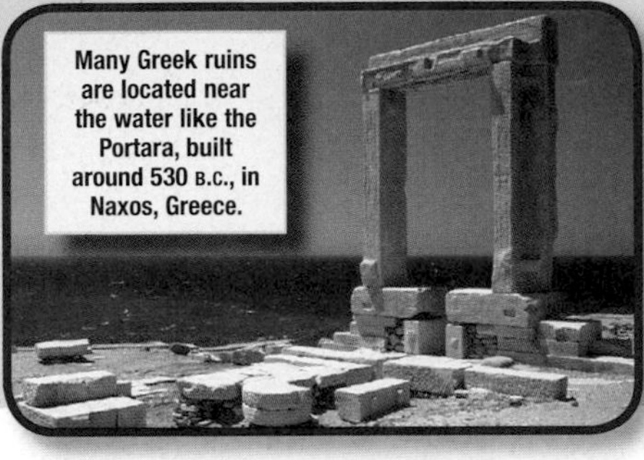

Many Greek ruins are located near the water like the Portara, built around 530 B.C., in Naxos, Greece.

Seas

The sea also influenced the evolution of Greek society. The **Aegean,** Mediterranean, and Ionian Seas make up the eastern, southern, and western borders of Greece. Its location on a peninsula gives Greece a long seacoast dotted by bays and inlets that provided many harbors. Although Greece is small, it has an 8,500-mile (13,700-km) coastline. In fact, no part of the Greek mainland is more than 60 miles (100 km) from a body of water. The ancient Greeks also lived on a number of islands to the west, south, and east of the Greek mainland. Surrounded by water, it was no accident that the Greeks became seafarers. They sailed out into the Aegean Sea, the Mediterranean Sea, and the **Black Sea,** making contact with the outside world. Later they established several colonies that spread Greek civilization throughout the Mediterranean world.

✓Reading Check **Explaining** What role did the mountains and the sea play in the development of Greek history?

Teach

S Skill Practice

Using Geography Skills Ask: What trade advantages did Troy possess? *(It could control the passage of ships between the Aegean and Black Seas.)* **OL**

Geography SKILLS

Answers:

1. High mountain ranges isolated Greek communities from one another. The many islands and harbors encouraged Greeks to migrate across the Aegean Sea, and eventually the Mediterranean Sea.
2. Troy is located on the outskirts of the Greek civilization, meaning that it is likely influenced by cultures from Asia Minor. Mycenae is at the heart of Greece, muting the effect of outside influences.

✓Reading Check

Answer: Very high mountains isolated Greeks from one another; a number of bays and inlets provided harbors, which encouraged them to become seafarers and, eventually, traders.

Differentiated Instruction

Leveled Activities

BL Guided Reading Activity, URB p. 160

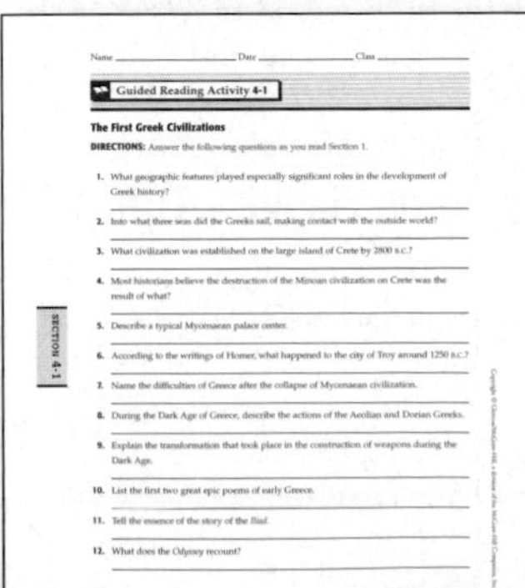

OL People in World History Activity, URB p. 151

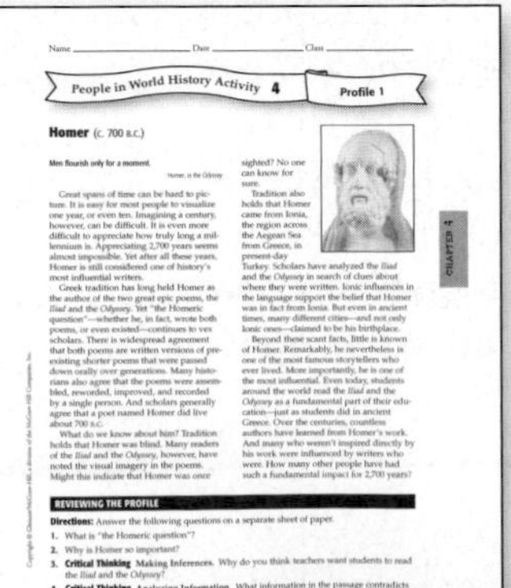

AL Economics and History Activity, URB p. 5

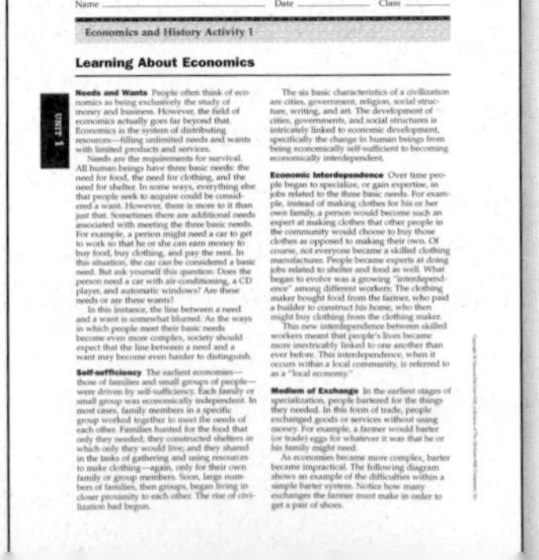

ELL English Learner Activity, URB p. 133

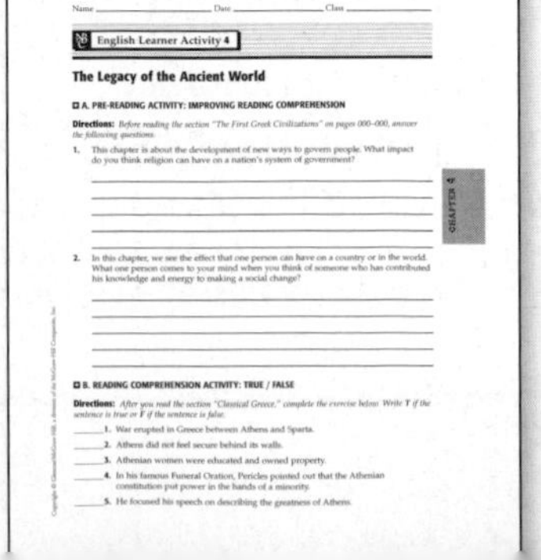

D Differentiated Instruction

Verbal/Linguistic Have students locate the Greek myth that tells the story of Theseus and the Minotaur. Ask students to prepare an original retelling of the tale. Encourage them to use voice expression to convey emotion and meaning. Discuss how the tale relates to the location and remains of Knossos. AL

Did You Know?

Arthur Evans first became interested in ancient Crete when he encountered some stone seals in his work as curator at the Ashmolean Museum in Oxford. Once Crete became independent from Turkey, Evans was able to buy the site of Knossos and begin excavations.

DOCUMENT-BASED QUESTIONS

Answers:

1. home for many people, warehouse, art workshops
2. The civilization in Crete used a writing system.

Minoans and Mycenaeans

MAIN IDEA The Mycenaeans created the first Greek civilization.

HISTORY & YOU What do buildings say about society? Read about the Minoan and Mycenaean cultures.

By 2800 B.C., a **Bronze Age** civilization had been established on the island of **Crete.** Called the **Minoan** civilization, it flourished from 2700 B.C. to 1450 B.C. The Minoans were not Greek, but they did influence the peoples of the Greek mainland.

Minoan Civilization

Arthur Evans, the English archaeologist who first discovered the civilization, named it after Minos, the legendary king of Crete, because some of its structures were similar to the labyrinth that King Minos was said to have built. At the beginning of the twentieth century, Evans discovered an enormous palace complex on Crete at Knossos (NAH•suhs). The remains of this complex revealed a rich culture, with Knossos as the center of a far-ranging sea empire based on trade. The ships of the Minoans took them to Egypt as well as southern Greece.

INFOGRAPHICS PRIMARY SOURCE

The Palace at Knossos

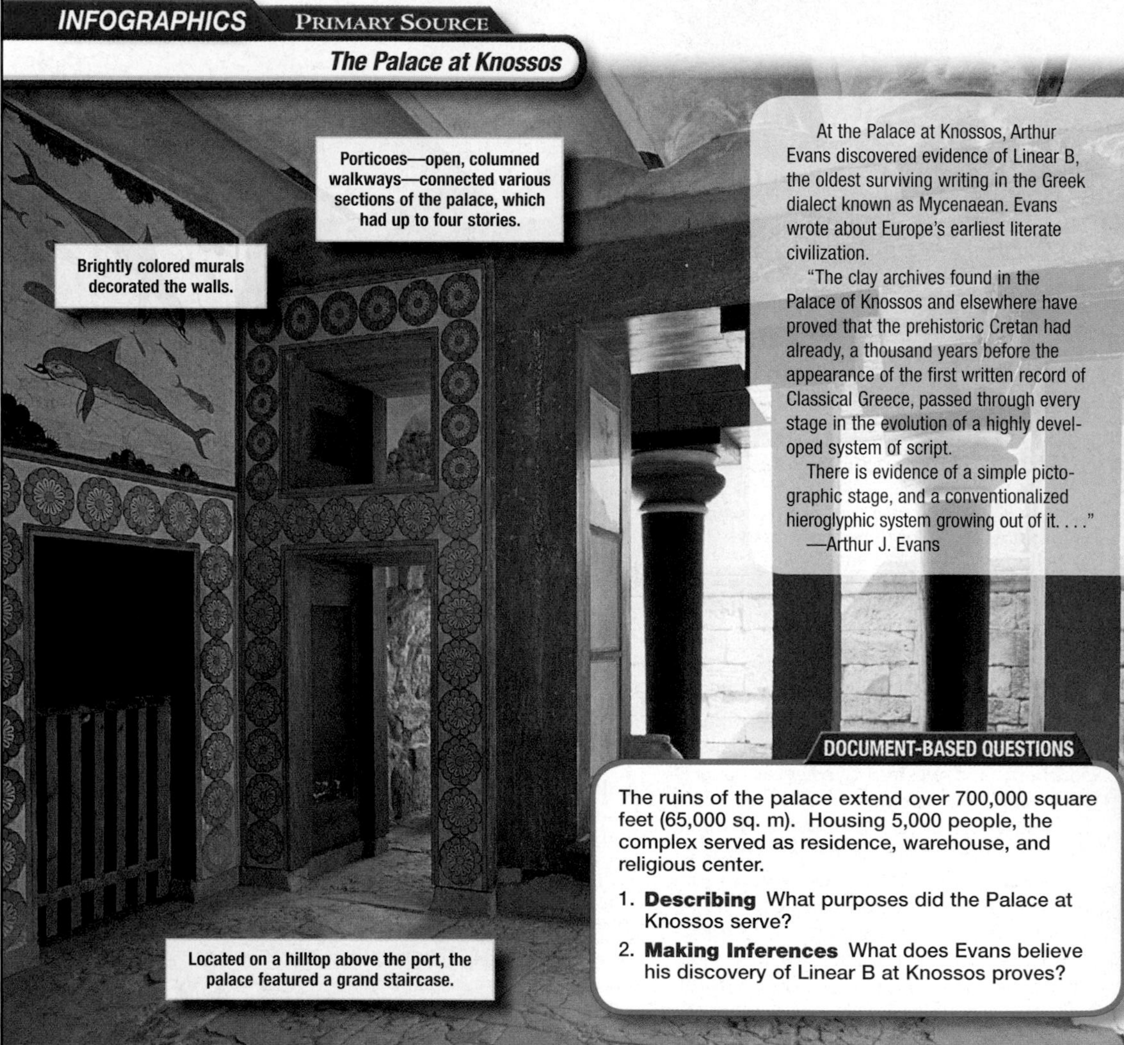

Porticoes—open, columned walkways—connected various sections of the palace, which had up to four stories.

Brightly colored murals decorated the walls.

Located on a hilltop above the port, the palace featured a grand staircase.

At the Palace at Knossos, Arthur Evans discovered evidence of Linear B, the oldest surviving writing in the Greek dialect known as Mycenaean. Evans wrote about Europe's earliest literate civilization.

"The clay archives found in the Palace of Knossos and elsewhere have proved that the prehistoric Cretan had already, a thousand years before the appearance of the first written record of Classical Greece, passed through every stage in the evolution of a highly developed system of script.

There is evidence of a simple pictographic stage, and a conventionalized hieroglyphic system growing out of it. . . ."

—Arthur J. Evans

DOCUMENT-BASED QUESTIONS

The ruins of the palace extend over 700,000 square feet (65,000 sq. m). Housing 5,000 people, the complex served as residence, warehouse, and religious center.

1. **Describing** What purposes did the Palace at Knossos serve?
2. **Making Inferences** What does Evans believe his discovery of Linear B at Knossos proves?

Hands-On Chapter Project Step 1

Keeping a Travel Journal

Small groups of students will create an illustrated journal recording highlights of a trip to ancient Greece.

Step 1: Mapping Itinerary

Essential Question: Should ancient Greece be called the birthplace of Western civilization?

Directions: Write the Big Idea on the board. Tell students that the first page of their journal should be a map of ancient Greece. On this map they will keep track of the locations they visit. Then have students use the information in this section to write their observations of Knossos and Mycenae from the perspective of a tourist. Ask them to include drawings or photographs of what they see as well as descriptions of sights, sounds, smells, and even the food they eat. They should note conversations they have with residents of both places and list the souvenirs they buy.

Summarizing: After completing their first journal entry, students should share what they learned about the Big Idea. OL

(Chapter Project is continued in Section 2.)

There, they traded finely crafted pottery and gold and silver jewelry from Crete for other goods. Trade also helped the Minoans improve the goods they produced: they drew inspiration from techniques and designs from objects from other lands. Although the Minoans built palaces on several sites in Crete, the palace at Knossos was the royal seat of the kings. This elaborate building included numerous private living rooms for the royal family and workshops for making decorated vases, ivory figurines, and jewelry. Even bathrooms, **R** with elaborate drains, formed part of the complex. Rooms were decorated with brightly colored paintings showing sporting events and nature scenes. Storerooms held gigantic jars of oil, wine, and grain that were paid as taxes to the king.

The centers of Minoan civilization on Crete suffered a sudden and catastrophic collapse around 1450 B.C. Some historians believe that a tidal wave triggered by a powerful volcanic eruption on the island **W** of Thera (THIHR•uh) was responsible for the devastation. Most historians, however, believe that the destruction was the result of invasion by mainland Greeks known as the Mycenaeans (my•suh•NEE•uhnz).

Mycenae: The First Greek State

The term **Mycenaean** comes from Mycenae (my•SEE•nee), a fortified site on the Greek mainland that was first discovered by the German archaeologist Heinrich Schliemann. Mycenae was one center in a Mycenaean Greek civilization that flourished between 1600 B.C. and 1100 B.C.

The Mycenaean Greeks were part of the Indo-European family of peoples who spread into Europe and Asia. One of these groups entered Greece around 1900 B.C. and gradually gained control of the Greek mainland. Mycenaean civilization, which reached its high point between 1400 B.C. and 1200 B.C., was made up of powerful monarchies. Each resided in a fortified palace center. Like Mycenae, these centers were built on hills and surrounded by gigantic stone walls. The monarchies in these various centers of power probably formed a loose alliance of independent states. While the royal families lived within the walls of these complexes, the civilian populations lived scattered outside the walls. Among the noticeable features of these Mycenaean centers were the tombs where members of the royal families were buried. Known as *tholos* tombs, they were built into hillsides. An entryway led into a circular tomb chamber constructed of cut stone blocks in a domed shape that resembled a beehive.

The Mycenaeans were, above all, a warrior people who prided themselves on their heroic deeds in battle. Mycenaean wall murals often show war and hunting scenes, the natural occupations of a warrior aristocracy.

Archaeological evidence also indicates that the Mycenaean monarchies developed an extensive commercial network. Mycenaean pottery has been found throughout the Mediterranean area, in Syria and Egypt to the east and Sicily and southern Italy to the west. However, some historians believe that the Mycenaeans, led by Mycenae itself, also spread outward militarily, conquering Crete and making it part of the Mycenaean **C** world. Some of the Aegean islands also fell subject to Mycenaean control.

The most famous of all their supposed military adventures is recounted in the poetry of **Homer.** According to Homer, Mycenaean Greeks, led by Agamemnon, king of Mycenae, sacked (plundered) the city of Troy on the northwestern coast of Asia Minor around 1250 B.C.

Did this event really occur? Ever since the excavations of Schliemann, begun in 1870, scholars have **debated** this question. (See discussion of archaeological methods featured in Chapter 1.) Many believe that Homer's account of the attack on Troy does have a basis in fact.

By the late thirteenth century B.C., Mycenaean Greece was showing signs of serious trouble. Mycenaean states fought one another, and major earthquakes caused widespread damage. In the twelfth century B.C., new waves of Greek-speaking invaders moved into Greece from the north. By 1100 B.C., Mycenaean civilization had collapsed.

✓Reading Check **Explaining** How was the Mycenaean government organized?

R Reading Strategy

Summarizing Ask: Why is it said that the Minoan civilization was advanced? *(The palace at Knossos had many elaborate rooms, workshops for making vases, jewelry, and ivory figurines, and bathrooms with drains.)* **OL**

W Writing Support

Expository Writing Have students research the collapse of the Minoan civilization and write a paragraph explaining their opinion about what might have happened. **AL**

C Critical Thinking

Comparing and Contrasting Ask: In what ways were the Mycenaean and Minoan civilizations similar? *(Both had an extensive trading network and show evidence of an advanced culture.)* **BL**

✓Reading Check

Answer: It was made up of powerful monarchies that formed a loose alliance of independent states.

Additional Support

Activity: Collaborative Learning

Analyzing Artifacts Tell students that archaeologists draw conclusions about ancient cultures by examining the art, artifacts, and architecture that they excavate. Divide students into groups. Have them find illustrations or photographs of objects discovered in Mycenae, including seals, fragments of script, frescoes, pottery, and art objects. Ask them to create a display that includes a caption with dates and other relevant information for each image. Then have students examine each display. **Ask:** What conclusions might be drawn about the skills of the artists and craftsmen in the Mycenaean civilization? What can you learn about daily life and traditions from examining the artifacts of ancient Mycenae? *(Have students discuss the answers to these questions.)* **OL**

Teacher Tip

Collaborative Learning This activity allows students with different levels of academic skills and intelligences to work together. As you form groups, consider the needed skills and choose students accordingly.

R Reading Strategy

Identifying **Ask:** In what ways did women contribute to Sparta's military society? *(They ran the households so that the men could live in barracks and perform their military duties. They brought their sons up to believe in the military ideal, encouraging them to be courageous in war.)* **OL**

D Differentiated Instruction

Visual/Spatial Have students graphically represent the organization of Sparta's government and the functions of each of its levels. Have them display their diagrams and discuss the pros and cons of this type of government. **OL**

They could live at home, but they stayed in the army until the age of 60.

While their husbands lived in the barracks, Spartan women lived at home. Because of this separation, Spartan women had greater freedom of movement and greater power in the household than was common elsewhere in Greece. **R** Spartan women were expected to remain fit to bear and raise healthy children.

Many Spartan women upheld the strict Spartan values, expecting their husbands and sons to be brave in war. The story is told of a Spartan mother who, as she handed her son his shield, told him to come back carrying his shield or being carried on it. In other words, he was not to drop his shield in retreat, but to be victorious or to die bravely.

The Spartan government was an oligarchy headed by two kings, who led the Spartan army on its campaigns. A group of five men, known as the **ephors** (EH•fuhrs), **D** were elected each year and were responsible for the education of youth and the conduct of all citizens. A council of elders, composed of the two kings and 28 citizens over the age of 60, decided on the issues that would be

HISTORY & ARTS — PRIMARY SOURCE

Everyday Art in Athens

The Greeks made pottery for every possible use. The best Greek pottery came from Athens because the clay found there was easy to bake in a kiln. At first, the pottery was decorated with geometric shapes. Later scenes from everyday life, stories of the gods, wars, and Olympic events decorated the pottery. Before 500 B.C., the pottery was red with figures that appeared black after they were baked. After 500 B.C., craftsmen discovered how to create red figures on a black background.

The *kylix* was a type of two-handled drinking cup. Potters decorated the inside and outside of the *kylix*.

The krater was a wide-mouthed mixing bowl used to mix water with wine—the most popular beverage with meals. A special krater on a stand was part of the wedding ceremony. This red-figured krater depicts the winner of a music contest.

The amphora, a jar to store wine, oil, and grain, came in all sizes. Winners of athletic contests in Athens won an amphora filled with olive oil. This black-figured amphora shows people gathering olives.

DOCUMENT-BASED QUESTIONS

1. **Making Inferences** Based on the information provided, which pot was most likely produced after 500 B.C.? Explain.
2. **Drawing Conclusions** What conclusions can you draw about Greek life from the scenes depicted on the pottery?

DOCUMENT-BASED QUESTIONS

Answers:

1. the krater; Craftsmen discovered how to create red figures on a black background after this time.
2. Answers may include that the arts, music, agriculture, and animals were an important part of life.

Differentiated Instruction

Linking Past and Present Activity 4

The Legacy of Athenian Democracy

Linking Past and Present Activity, URB p. 150

Analyzing Information

Objective: Analyze the legacy of Athenian democracy.

Focus: Have students read the passage and answer the questions.

Teach: Discuss features of both Athenian and American democracy.

Assess: Have students identify the responsibilities of citizens in a democracy.

Close: Have students argue for or against direct democracy in the United States.

Differentiated Instruction Strategies

BL Have students diagram the structure of the Athenian government.

AL Have students analyze key events in U.S. history that led to universal suffrage.

ELL Have students explain the structure of the government in their countries of origin.

presented to an assembly made up of male citizens. This assembly did not debate; it only voted on the issues.

To make their new military state secure, the Spartans turned their backs on the outside world. Foreigners, who might have brought in new ideas, were discouraged from visiting. Except for military reasons, Spartans were not allowed to travel abroad, where they might encounter ideas dangerous to the stability of the state. Likewise, Spartan citizens were discouraged from studying philosophy, literature, or the arts. The art of war was the Spartan ideal. All other arts were frowned upon.

Athens

By 700 B.C., **Athens** had become a unified polis on the peninsula of Attica. Early Athens was ruled by a king. By the seventh century B.C., however, Athens had become an oligarchy under the control of its aristocrats. These aristocrats owned the best land and controlled political life. The assembly of all the citizens had few powers.

Near the end of the seventh century B.C., Athens faced political turmoil because of serious economic problems. Many Athenian farmers were sold into slavery when they were unable to repay their debts to their aristocratic neighbors. Over and over, there were cries to cancel the debts and give land to the poor. Civil war seemed likely.

The ruling Athenian aristocrats reacted to this crisis in 594 B.C. by giving full power to **Solon,** a reform-minded aristocrat. Solon canceled all land debts and freed people who had fallen into slavery for debts. He refused, however, to take land from the rich and give it to the poor. Despite Solon's reforms aristocrats were still powerful and poor peasants could not obtain land. Internal strife finally led to the very thing Solon had hoped to avoid—tyranny.

Peisistratus (pih•SIHS•truh•tuhs), an aristocrat, seized power in 560 B.C. He then aided Athenian trade as a way of pleasing the merchants. He also gave aristocrats' land to the peasants in order to gain the favor of the poor.

The Athenians rebelled against Peisistratus's son, who had succeeded him, and ended the tyranny in 510 B.C. Two years later, with the backing of the Athenian people, **Cleisthenes** (KLYS•thuh•NEEZ), another reformer, gained the upper hand.

Cleisthenes created a council of 500 that supervised foreign affairs, oversaw the treasury, and proposed laws. The Athenian assembly, composed of male citizens, was given final authority to pass laws after free and open debate. Because the assembly now had the central political role, the reforms of Cleisthenes created the foundations for Athenian democracy.

✓Reading Check **Contrasting** How was a Spartan man's life different from an Athenian man's?

SECTION 2 REVIEW

Vocabulary

1. **Explain** the significance of: polis, acropolis, agora, assemble, hoplite, phalanx, Hellespont, Bosporus, Byzantium, implies, tyrant, democracy, oligarchy, Sparta, helot, ephor, Athens, Solon, Cleisthenes.

Main Ideas

2. **Summarize** how the city-states' military system had changed by 700 B.C.
3. **Sequence** the causes and effects of Greek colonization, trade, and industry. Create a cause-and-effect sequence chart like the one below to record your answer.

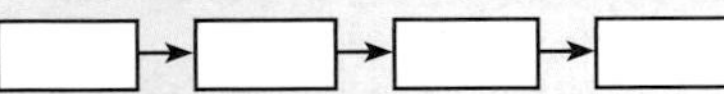

4. **Explain** the different political systems in Athens and Sparta.

Critical Thinking

5. **Big Idea Making Generalizations** Discuss the ideas, beliefs, and values that are implied in forms of government that the Spartans and Athenians adopted.
6. **Comparing and Contrasting** In what way(s) is Athenian democracy similar to American democracy? In what way(s) is it different?
7. **Analyzing Visuals** Examine the photograph of the Acropolis on page 113 of your text. Why do you think the Athenians decided to place their important buildings on top of a hill?

Writing About History

8. **Descriptive Writing** Imagine that you are a 25-year-old male living in Sparta in 700 B.C. Create a diary in which you record your activities for one week. Write one diary page for each day.

History ONLINE
For help with the concepts in this section of *Glencoe World History*, go to glencoe.com and click Study Central™.

117

W Writing Support

Persuasive Writing Have students write a short essay arguing whether new ideas can have value to a warrior. OL

✓Reading Check

Answer: Spartan men: tightly controlled, couldn't vote until age 30, served in military until age 60; Athenian men: fewer restrictions, key role in government under Cleisthenes for males who were citizens

Assess

History ONLINE

Study Central provides summaries, interactive games, and online graphic organizers to help students review content.

Close

Comparing and Contrasting
Ask: How did the political process differ in Sparta and in Athens under Cleisthenes? *(Sparta: assembly restricted to voting only; Athens: assembly could vote, pass laws)* OL

Answers

1. Definitions for the vocabulary words are found in the section and the Glossary.
2. The military system, which was once dominated by aristocratic cavalry soldiers, now depended on hoplites, heavily armed infantry soldiers.
3. lack of farmland; securing control of waterways; increased wealth; tyranny
4. **Athens:** king → oligarchy of aristocrats → tyranny → democracy; **Sparta:** oligarchy with two kings
5. Answers may include: The Spartans' government showed a focus on security and stability. It did not seem to value individual freedoms. Athenian government continually moved toward increasing individuals' power in government, even at the expense of the society's stability.
6. **Athenian:** Assembly passed laws; male citizens participated. **American:** Representatives pass laws; all adult citizens can vote. **Both:** Citizens participate.
7. easy to defend; There were steps to the top of the Acropolis and a door; attackers would be exposed to spears and rocks thrown from above.
8. Students' diaries should be consistent with section content.

Focus

Introducing Social History Have students recall what they know about Greek culture and religion. **Ask:** Why did the Greeks name their major religious center Olympia? *(because they believed the gods lived on Mount Olympus)* **OL**

Teach

D Differentiated Instruction

Logical/Mathematical Draw a time line with 776 B.C. on one end and A.D. 393 on the other. **Ask:** How long were the ancient Olympics held? *(1,169 years; 776 + 393)* How many times were the games likely held in that time? *(293; 1,169 ÷ 4 +1 for the first games)* **BL**

W Writing Support

Descriptive Writing Have students research the events of the ancient pentathlon and write an article describing the competition. **AL**

Additional Support

Social History

The Olympics: Festival and Games in Ancient Greece

The Olympic Games of ancient Greece began in 776 B.C. and were held between the city-states every four years until they were banned in A.D. 393 by the Roman emperor Theodosius. The Greeks honored both their athletes and **D** Greek gods at the games. A special truce was declared throughout the land as a matter of religious respect and as a practical step to allow people to travel to the games safely. In their heyday, the games lasted for five days and included standard events.

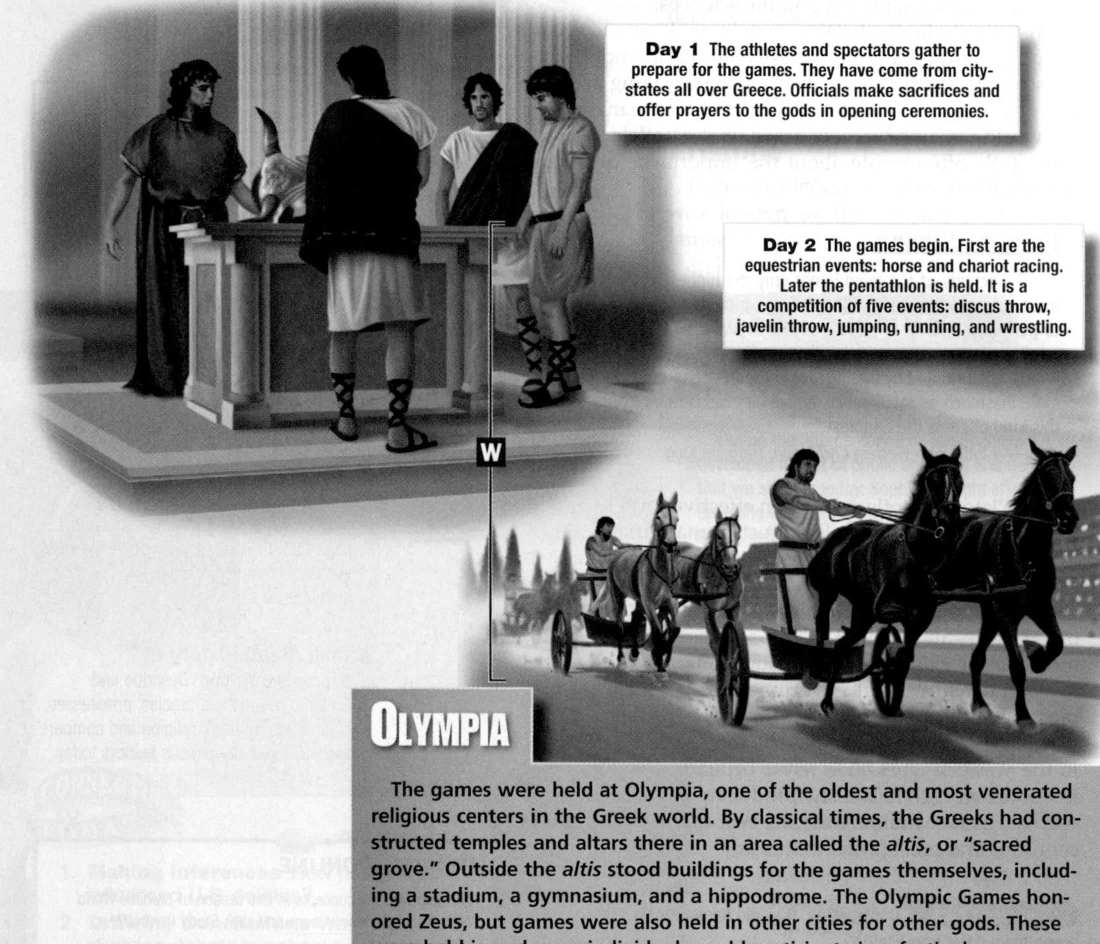

Day 1 The athletes and spectators gather to prepare for the games. They have come from city-states all over Greece. Officials make sacrifices and offer prayers to the gods in opening ceremonies.

Day 2 The games begin. First are the equestrian events: horse and chariot racing. Later the pentathlon is held. It is a competition of five events: discus throw, javelin throw, jumping, running, and wrestling. **W**

Olympia

The games were held at Olympia, one of the oldest and most venerated religious centers in the Greek world. By classical times, the Greeks had constructed temples and altars there in an area called the *altis*, or "sacred grove." Outside the *altis* stood buildings for the games themselves, including a stadium, a gymnasium, and a hippodrome. The Olympic Games honored Zeus, but games were also held in other cities for other gods. These were held in cycles, so individuals could participate in a festival every year.

Background

The Greek Olympic Games At first, the Olympic Games consisted only of footraces. Later, wrestling, boxing, javelin and discus throwing, long jumping, and chariot racing were added. Competitions were always between individuals, not groups. Only young men took part until contests for boys were added by 632 B.C. Beginning in 472 B.C., the games were held over a five-day period. The long-held belief that athletes in the Olympic Games were amateurs is simply not true. City-states supported both athletes and their trainers. This practice freed them to train for long periods of time in the hope that they would bring back victories—and glory—to their communities. Larger city-states even bribed winners from other city-states to move to their communities and compete for them in the next games. The first modern Olympic Games were held in Athens, Greece, in 1896.

Superstars of the Ancient World

A victor in the games was awarded a crown of olive leaves pulled from a sacred tree and permission to have a statue of himself placed at Olympia. But winning athletes often received much more from their home city-states, grateful for the glory, fame, and heightened reputation the community gained by producing an Olympic winner. Like modern sports stars, these athletes were rewarded with celebrity and a wide variety of gifts.

Analyzing Visuals

1. **Making Inferences** Why do you think religious practices were such a large part of the ancient Greek Olympics?
2. **Comparing** How were the ancient Greek Olympic Games similar to the modern Olympics?

133

C Critical Thinking

Making Inferences **Ask:** Why would it be a special honor for a winner to have a statue of himself placed at Olympia? *(There were also statues of Greek gods there.)* OL

R Reading Strategy

Making Connections Discuss with students how modern sports stars compare to early Olympic athletes. OL

Assess/Close

Have small groups of students discuss the roles of sports in ancient Greece and in the world today. OL

Analyzing Visuals

Answers:

1. Religion touched every aspect of Greek life; the games were held to honor Zeus and other gods.
2. sports competitions; included some of the same events; athletes from many places

Activity: Interdisciplinary Connection

Daily Life The first modern marathon—named after the battle that led to the famous run of Pheidippides—was held at the Olympic Games in Athens in 1896. The length of the marathon varied until 1924, when it was officially set at 26 miles, 385 yards (42.19 kilometers). In 1908 the Olympics were held in London, and the marathon was run from Windsor Castle to the royal family's viewing box in London. The distance between those locations became the official distance. **Ask:** How has the marathon spread beyond the Olympics? Have students research and report on famous marathons of today, such as those of Boston; New York City; Los Angeles; Portland, Oregon; and Dublin, Ireland. If there is a marathon in your community or state, students may also research that. Students' reports should include the history of the event, the time and place in which it is staged, the average number of runners, the names of important recent winners, and the time it took these people to run the race. They may want to compare this information to the latest marathon held at the Olympics. OL

Focus

Bellringer

Daily Focus Transparency 4.5

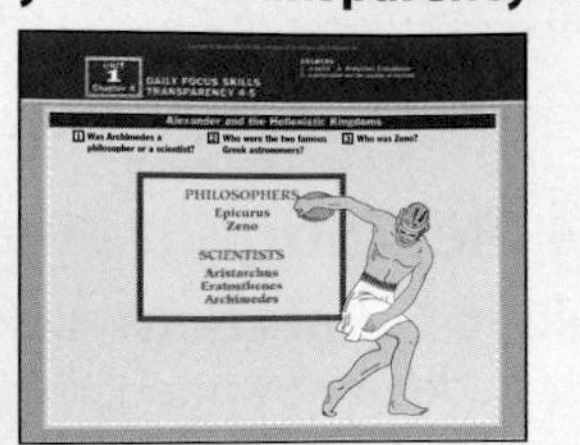

GUIDE TO READING

Answers to Graphic:
Classical Age of Greece: development of drama and history, finest examples of Greek architecture, sculpture depicted idealized male figures; **Hellenistic:** great wealth, expansion of Greek culture and language, sculpture more realistic, advances in science and mathematics; **Both:** technical skill in sculpture, Athens center for philosophy

Section Spotlight Video

To generate student interest and provide a springboard for class discussion, access the Chapter 4, Section 5 video at glencoe.com or on the video DVD.

SECTION 5

Alexander and the Hellenistic Era

GUIDE TO READING

The BIG Idea
Ideas, Beliefs and Values Greek culture spread to new lands.

Content Vocabulary
- Hellenistic Era *(p. 137)*
- Stoicism *(p. 139)*
- Epicureanism *(p. 139)*

Academic Vocabulary
- subsidizing *(p. 138)*
- founder *(p. 139)*

People and Places
- Macedonia *(p. 134)*
- Philip II *(p. 134)*
- Alexander the Great *(p. 134)*
- Alexandria *(p. 135)*
- Pergamum *(p. 137)*
- Eratosthenes *(p. 138)*
- Euclid *(p. 138)*
- Archimedes *(p. 139)*

Reading Strategy
Compare and Contrast As you read, create a diagram like the one below to help you study. Compare and contrast the characteristics of the classical and Hellenistic periods.

Under the leadership of Alexander the Great, Macedonians and Greeks united to invade and conquer the Persian Empire. In the conquered lands, Greeks and non-Greeks formed a new society in what is known as the Hellenistic Era.

Macedonians Invade Greece

MAIN IDEA Under Alexander the Great, Macedonians and Greeks conquered the Persian Empire.

HISTORY & YOU Who are some of the military leaders you know about in American history? Read about how Alexander the Great led his army to create an empire.

The Greeks viewed their northern neighbors, the Macedonians, as barbarians. They were a rural people of farmers and agricultural laborers, organized into groups, not in city-states like the Greeks. They were probably not Greek, and they had not been involved in the rivalries of Greek city-states—their leaders focused mostly on defending their northern borders. By the end of the fifth century B.C., however, **Macedonia** emerged as a powerful kingdom.

Philip and Alexander

In 359 B.C., **Philip II** came to the throne. He built a powerful army and turned Macedonia into the chief power of the Greek world. Philip was soon drawn into Greek affairs. A great admirer of Greek culture, he longed to unite all of Greece under Macedonia.

Fearing Philip, the Athenians allied with a number of other Greek states and fought the Macedonians at the Battle of Chaeronea (KEHR•uh•NEE•uh), near Thebes, in 338 B.C. The Macedonian army crushed the Greeks.

Philip quickly gained control of all Greece, bringing an end to the freedom of the Greek city-states. He insisted that the Greek states form a league and then cooperate with him in a war against Persia. Before Philip could undertake his invasion of Asia, however, he was assassinated, leaving the task to his son Alexander.

Alexander the Great was only 20 when he became king of Macedonia. Philip had carefully prepared his son for kingship. By taking Alexander along with him on military campaigns, Philip taught Alexander the basics of military leadership. After his father's death, Alexander moved quickly to fulfill his father's dream—the invasion of the Persian Empire. He was motivated by the desire for glory and empire but also by the desire to avenge the Persian burning of Athens in 480 B.C.

Resource Manager

R Reading Strategies	C Critical Thinking	D Differentiated Instruction	W Writing Support	S Skill Practice
Teacher Edition • Read. Pri. Sources, p. 136 • Inferring, p. 137 • Identifying, p. 137 • Act. Prior Know., p. 138 **Additional Resources** • Guid. Read. Act., URB p. 164 • Read. Ess. & Note-Taking Guide, p. 43	**Teacher Edition** • Pred. Consequences, p. 137 • Drawing Con., p. 138 • Compare/Contrast, p. 139 **Additional Resources** • Hist. & Geo. Act., URB p. 141 • Section Quiz, p. 39 • Chapter Test, p. 41	**Teacher Edition** • ELL, p. 135 **Additional Resources** • Cont. Vocab. Act., URB p. 135 • Reteach. Act., URB p. 157	**Teacher Edition** • Expository Writing, p. 136 **Additional Resources** • Writer's Guidebook, p. 47	**Teacher Edition** • Using Geo. Skills, p. 135 **Additional Resources** • Chart. Graph. Act., URB p. 3 • Time Line Act., URB p. 149

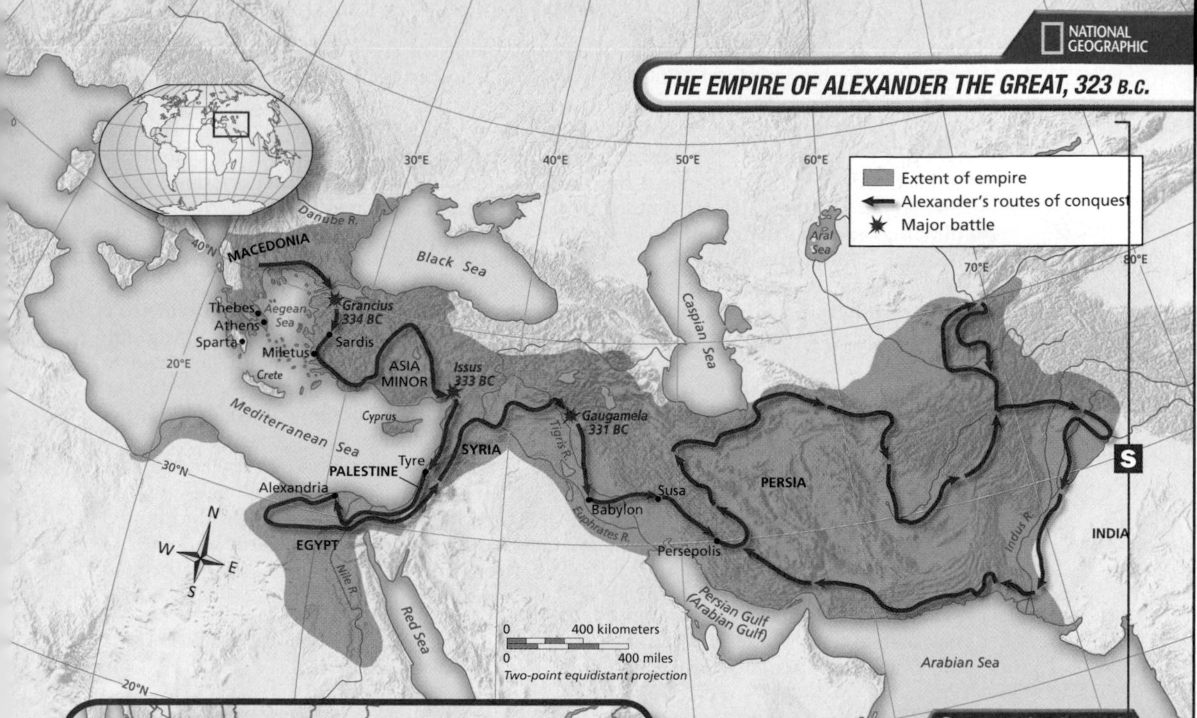

NATIONAL GEOGRAPHIC

THE EMPIRE OF ALEXANDER THE GREAT, 323 B.C.

Extent of empire
Alexander's routes of conquest
Major battle

0 400 kilometers
0 400 miles
Two-point equidistant projection

Modern-day borders

Geography SKILLS

The empire of Alexander the Great stretched across three continents and over 200,000 miles. The inset map shows the present-day equivalent of Alexander's empire.

1. **Human-Environment Interaction** Does it appear that physical boundaries limited the extent of Alexander's empire? Explain.
2. **Place** Compare the inset map to the large map. What modern states correspond to Alexander's empire?

Alexander's Conquests

Alexander was taking a chance in attacking the Persian Empire. Although weakened, it was still a strong state in the spring of 334 B.C. when Alexander entered Asia Minor with an army of some 37,000 men, both Macedonians and Greeks. The cavalry, which would play an important role as a striking force, numbered about 5,000.

By the next year, Alexander had freed the Ionian Greek cities of western Asia Minor from the Persians and defeated a large Persian army at Issus. He then turned south. By the winter of 332 B.C., Alexander had Syria, Palestine, and Egypt under his control. He built **Alexandria** as the Greek capital of Egypt. It became and remains today one of the most important cities in both Egypt and the Mediterranean world. It was also the first of a series of cities named after him.

In 331 B.C., Alexander turned east and fought the decisive battle with the Persians at Gaugamela, not far from Babylon. Soon after, Alexander controlled the rest of the Persian Empire. Over the next three years, Alexander moved as far as modern Pakistan.

Teach

S Skill Practice

Using Geography Skills Have students note the locations of Alexander's major battles. **Ask:** Based on the map, what conclusions might be drawn about Alexander's conquest of Egypt and central Persia? *(He took control of Egypt and Persia without a great deal of resistance.)* **OL**

D Differentiated Instruction

English Language Learners Have students create an annotated time line of Alexander's conquests of the Persian Empire. Remind them to use the dates within the paragraphs to order the events. **ELL**

Geography SKILLS

Answers:

1. Answers may include that it was limited by desert but not mountains or waterways.
2. Greece, Turkey, Syria, Iraq, Iran, Egypt, Afghanistan, Pakistan, Lebanon, Israel, and parts of other countries

Differentiated Instruction

Leveled Activities

BL Reteaching Activity, URB p. 157

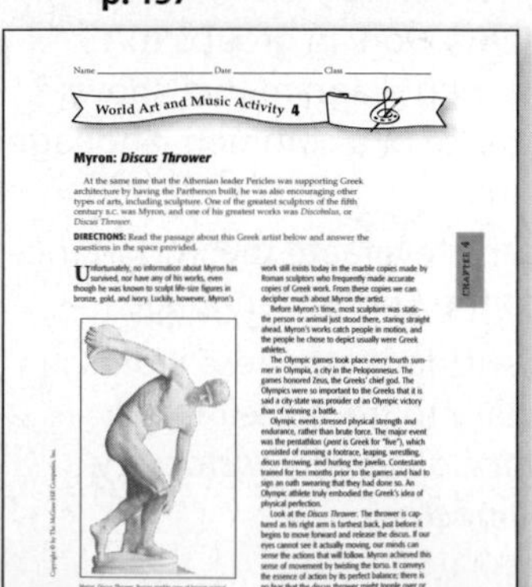

OL Guided Reading Activity, URB p. 164

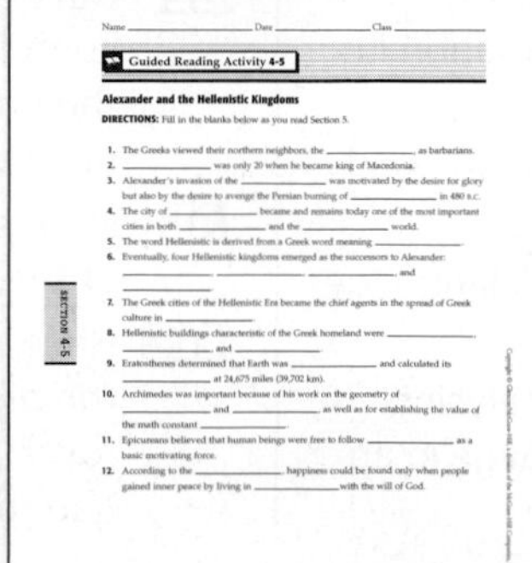

AL Differentiated Instruction Activity, URB p. 131

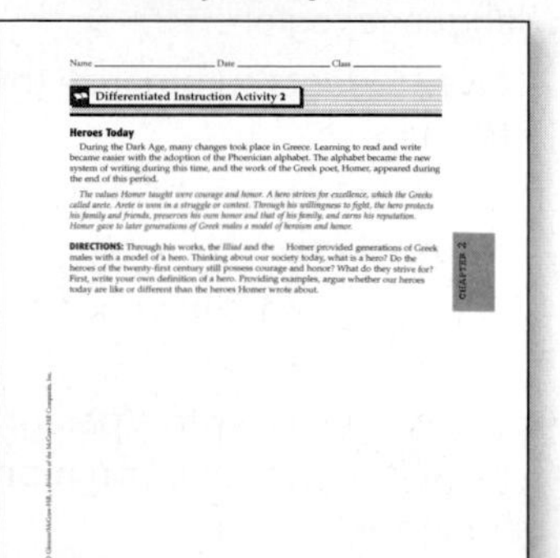

ELL Time Line Activity, URB p. 149

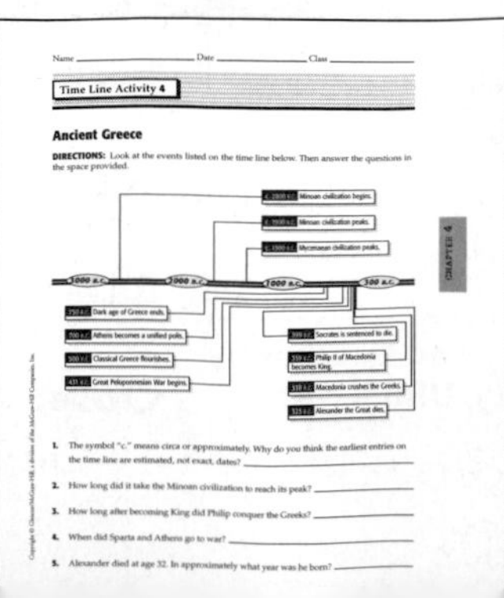

R **Reading Strategy**

Reading Primary Sources
Ask: Based on the excerpt, why did Alexander pour the water on the ground? *(He was showing that he considered himself one with his men. If everyone else could not drink, he would not.)* **OL**

W **Writing Support**

Expository Writing Have students write a eulogy for Alexander's funeral. **AL**

✓Reading Check

Answer: They brought an end to the freedom of Greek city-states; stimulated the Greek economy; spread Greek language, architecture, literature, and art; and exposed Greeks to aspects of Eastern culture.

DOCUMENT-BASED QUESTIONS

Answers:
1. Answers may include less protected, more courageous, and younger.
2. by wearing protective armor made of bronze

History ONLINE
Student Web Activity—
Visit glencoe.com and complete the activity about Alexander the Great and his conquests.

In 326 B.C., Alexander reached India, where the campaigning was hard. When his soldiers refused to go farther, he agreed to go home. He led his troops across the desert of today's southern Iran. Many were dying of heat and thirst. At one point, some soldier found a little water and offered it to him. According to an ancient Greek writer, Alexander poured it on the ground: "So extraordinary was the effect of this action that the water wasted by Alexander was as good as a drink for every man in the army."

Alexander returned to Babylon, planning more conquests. But in 323 B.C., exhausted from wounds, fever, and too much alcohol, he died. He was 32 years old.

Alexander's Legacy

Alexander's extraordinary success is explained by his leadership and military skills. He was a master of strategy and tactics, able to fight in all terrains and against all kinds of opponents. Brave and even reckless, he risked his own life, an example that inspired his soldiers to follow him. Alexander sought to imitate Achilles, the hero of Homer's *Iliad*. He kept a copy of the *Iliad*—and a dagger—under his pillow.

Alexander created an enormous legacy. He extended Greek and Macedonian rule over a vast area, which brought large quantities of gold and silver into their economies.

Alexander's successors tried to imitate him, using force and claims of divine rule to create military monarchies. Although mainland Greeks remained committed to the ideals of the city-state, the creation of the monarchies became part of Alexander's political legacy.

Alexander also left a cultural legacy. Due to his conquests, Greek language, architecture, literature, and art spread throughout Southwest Asia, Central Asia, and parts of North Africa. The Greeks also absorbed aspects of Eastern culture.

✓Reading Check **Identifying** How did Philip II and Alexander change Greece?

HISTORY & ARTS PRIMARY SOURCE

Alexander's Army

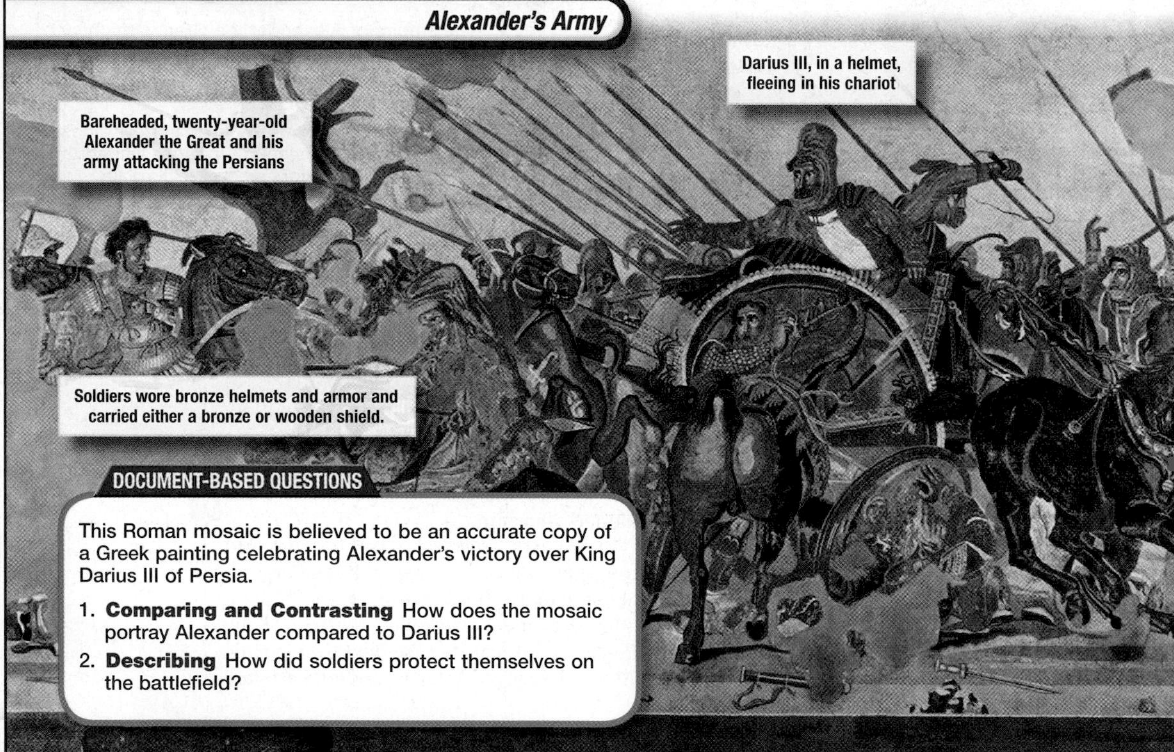

DOCUMENT-BASED QUESTIONS

This Roman mosaic is believed to be an accurate copy of a Greek painting celebrating Alexander's victory over King Darius III of Persia.

1. **Comparing and Contrasting** How does the mosaic portray Alexander compared to Darius III?
2. **Describing** How did soldiers protect themselves on the battlefield?

Differentiated Instruction

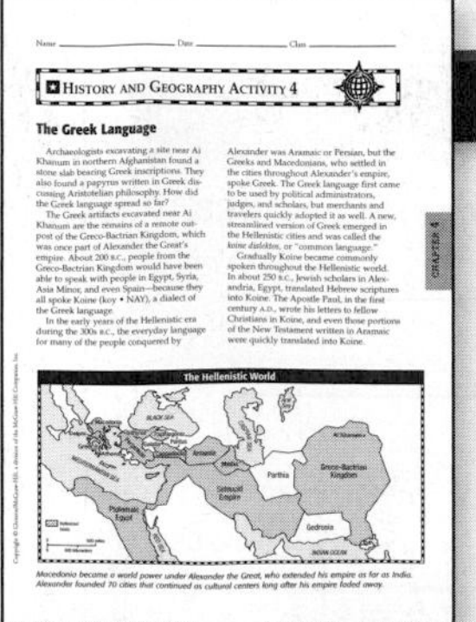

History and Geography Activity, URB p. 141

Analyzing Information

Objective: Analyze information related to the Greek language region.

Focus: Have students summarize the information in the map.

Teach: Have students read the passage and answer the questions.

Assess: Discuss the ways in which the Greek language spread.

Close: Have students write a paragraph analyzing the importance of a common language in an empire.

Differentiated Instruction Strategies

BL Have students work in groups to complete a web diagram that shows the importance of a common language in an empire.

AL Have students evaluate the importance of Greek to the English language.

ELL Have students look up these words in the dictionary to trace their Greek roots: *politics, oligarchy, aristocracy, tyranny, democracy.*

The Hellenistic Era

MAIN IDEA As a result of Alexander's conquests, Hellenistic cities became centers for the spread of Greek language, art, architecture, and literature.

HISTORY & YOU How many different cultures do you encounter in your daily life? Read about the Hellenistic world.

Alexander created a new age, the **Hellenistic Era.** The word *Hellenistic* comes from a Greek word meaning "to imitate Greeks." It is an appropriate way to describe an age that saw the expansion of the Greek language and ideas to the non-Greek world of Southwest Asia and beyond.

Hellenistic Kingdoms

The united empire that Alexander created by his conquests fell apart soon after his death as the most important Macedonian generals engaged in a struggle for power. By 300 B.C., any hope of unity was dead. Eventually, four Hellenistic kingdoms emerged as the successors to Alexander: Macedonia, Syria in the east, the **C** kingdom of **Pergamum** in western Asia Minor, and Egypt. All were eventually conquered by the Romans.

Alexander the Great had planned to fuse Macedonians, Greeks, and Persians in his new empire by using Persians as officials and encouraging his soldiers to marry native women. The Hellenistic monarchs who succeeded him, however, relied only on Greeks and Macedonians to form the new ruling class. Even those from eastern regions who did advance to important government posts had learned Greek, for all government business was transacted in Greek. The Greek ruling class was determined to maintain its position.

In his conquests, Alexander had created a series of new cities and military settlements. Hellenistic kings did likewise. These new population centers varied in size from military settlements of only a few hundred men to cities with thousands of people. Alexandria, which Alexander had founded in Egypt, was the largest city in the Mediterranean region by the first century B.C.

Hellenistic rulers encouraged a spread of Greek colonists to Southwest Asia. Greeks (and Macedonians) provided not only new recruits for the army but also a pool of civilian administrators and workers. Architects, engineers, dramatists, and actors were all in demand in the new Greek cities. The Greek cities of the Hellenistic Era spread Greek culture to Southwest and Central Asia—as far, in fact, as modern Afghanistan and India.

Hellenistic Arts and Literature

The Hellenistic Era was a period of considerable cultural accomplishment in many areas, especially science and philosophy. These achievements occurred throughout the Hellenistic world. Certain centers, however—especially the great Hellenistic city of Alexandria—stood out. Alexandria became home to poets, writers, philosophers, and scientists—scholars of all kinds.

The library in Alexandria became the **R1** largest in ancient times, with more than 500,000 scrolls. The library encouraged the careful study of literature and language. There was also a museum that welcomed scholarly research.

Pergamum, the most important city in Asia Minor, also became a leading cultural center. As a result, Pergamum also attracted both scholars and artists. The library at Pergamum was second only to Alexandria's library.

The founding of new cities and the rebuilding of old ones presented many opportunities for Greek architects and sculptors. Hellenistic kings were very willing to spend their money to beautify the cities within their states. The buildings characteristic of the Greek homeland—baths, theaters, and temples—lined the streets of these cities.

Both Hellenistic kings and rich citizens patronized sculptors. Thousands of statues were erected in towns and cities all over the Hellenistic world. Hellenistic sculptors maintained the technical skill of the classical period, but they moved away from the **R2** idealism of earlier classicism to a more emotional and realistic art. This is especially evident in the numerous statues of old women and little children.

C Critical Thinking

Predicting Consequences
Have students examine Alexander's plan for his empire. **Ask:** What did he hope to achieve through these measures? *(Alexander wanted to blend cultures as well as erase any resentment from the people he conquered. He wanted to set the foundation of a harmonious empire.)* **OL**

For additional practice on this skill, see the **Skills Handbook**.

R1 Reading Strategy

Inferring Ask: What does the character of Alexandria suggest about Alexander's values? *(He valued knowledge.)* **AL**

R2 Reading Strategy

Identifying Ask: Why did Hellenistic artists strive for realism? *(They found more scope for their artistic vision in the variety of people around them.)* **OL**

Hands-On Chapter Project Step 5

Keeping a Travel Journal

Step 5: Recording the Last Entry In this step, groups add the last entry to the travel journals they worked on in Sections 1–4.

Directions: Write the Big Idea on the board. Tell students that in this section of their travel journals they will describe their observations of Alexander's empire. Remind students to plot their stops on their journal map. They may choose just to focus on a visit to Alexandria or also include details from the perspective of an observer embedded in Alexander's army. Have students use the details in this section to create a vivid description of what they see, hear, and experience during this portion of their trip. Remind students to incorporate illustrations into their entries as well.

Putting It Together: Have students review their entries, making sure they are complete. Have them share their thoughts about the Big Idea based on their last journal entry. **OL**

(Chapter Project is completed on the Visual Summary page.)

R Reading Strategy

Activating Prior Knowledge Remind students that Aristophanes was a well-known dramatist in classical Greece. One of his comedies satirized Socrates, and, in fact, was instrumental in turning public opinion against the philosopher. **Ask:** How did Hellenistic comedies differ from those of classical Greece? *(They avoided controversial subjects, such as politics or social issues.)* **OL**

C Critical Thinking

Drawing Conclusions Ask: Why was astronomy an important field of study for Hellenistic scholars? *(Alexandria was a port; therefore, scholars were aware of the need to increase the accuracy of navigation through improved knowledge of astronomy.)* **AL**

DOCUMENT-BASED QUESTIONS

Answers:

1. Jason and Medea enter a grove, are threatened by a serpent, charm it, and Jason is able to obtain the Golden Fleece.
2. Stories of heroic accomplishment could be inspirational during this period of militaristic and cultural expansion.

Additional Support

HISTORY & ARTS — PRIMARY SOURCE

Jason and the Golden Fleece

Apollonius of Rhodes told the story of Jason and the Golden Fleece, around the third century B.C., in the epic poem *Argonautica.* Jason is a hero who must complete impossible tasks to take his place in society. In this particular task, Jason must capture the Golden Fleece, which is guarded by a serpent in a garden, so that he can become king. He accomplishes this with the help of Medea, as Apollonius describes:

"And they two by the pathway came to the sacred grove, seeking the huge oak tree on which was hung the fleece, like to a cloud that blushes red with the fiery beams of the rising sun. But right in front the serpent with his keen sleepless eyes saw them coming, and stretched out his long neck and hissed in awful wise. . . . And as he writhed, the maiden came before his eyes, with sweet voice calling to her aid sleep, highest of gods, to charm the monster . . . so at that time did Jason uplift the mighty fleece in his hands. . . . And he strode on now with the fleece covering his left shoulder from the height of his neck to his feet, and now again he gathered it up in his hands; for he feared exceedingly, lest some god or man should meet him and deprive him thereof."

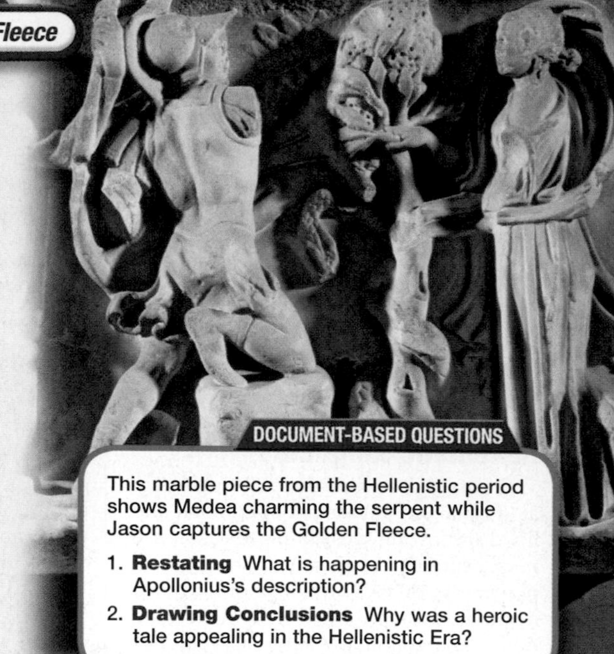

DOCUMENT-BASED QUESTIONS

This marble piece from the Hellenistic period shows Medea charming the serpent while Jason captures the Golden Fleece.

1. **Restating** What is happening in Apollonius's description?
2. **Drawing Conclusions** Why was a heroic tale appealing in the Hellenistic Era?

The Hellenistic Age also produced a great quantity of literature. Writing talent was held in high esteem, especially by Hellenistic leaders, who spent large amounts of money **subsidizing** writers. Unfortunately, very little of this literature has survived.

Apollonius of Rhodes wrote the epic poem *Argonautica,* which tells the story of Jason's search for the Golden Fleece. Theocritus wrote short poems that expressed a love of nature and an appreciation of its beauty. Unlike Apollonius, Theocritus believed that it was best not to attempt epic poems, for which Homer had established a standard that many scholars felt could not be matched.

Athens remained the center of Greek theatre. A new type of comedy developed that sought only to entertain and amuse and avoided political commentary. Menander was perhaps the most successful of these new playwrights.

Science and Philosophy

The Hellenistic Age witnessed considerable advances in the sciences. Astronomy and mathematics were two areas of progress. One astronomer, Aristarchus (AR•uh•STAHR•kuhs) of Samos, developed the theory that the sun is at the center of the universe while the Earth rotates around the sun in a circular orbit. The prevailing view, in contrast, held that Earth was at the center of the universe. The new theory was not widely accepted at the time.

Eratosthenes (EHR•uh•TAHS•thuh•NEEZ) was another important astronomer. He determined that Earth was round and calculated Earth's circumference at 24,675 miles (39,702 km), an estimate that was within 185 miles (298 km) of the actual figure. The mathematician **Euclid** wrote the *Elements,* a textbook on plane geometry. This work has been used up to modern times.

Activity: Interdisciplinary Connection

Mathematics Tell students that although the practical inventions of Archimedes appear to have made an enormous impression upon his contemporaries, in fact, he did not deem them worthy enough even to write about. Instead, the body of work that he did leave is mostly concerned with his theories of mathematics. Later mathematicians expanded upon some of these ideas, although some of his work was lost for centuries, by which time others had made similar discoveries. Assign small groups of students to research one of Archimedes' inventions or his mathematical theories, such as his screw, Archimedes' principle, his discovery of the relation between the surface and volume of a sphere and cylinder, his calculation of pi, or his system of base notation. Ask students to create an informational poster to present to the class. **Ask:** How did Archimedes advance scientific and mathematical knowledge? (*Encourage students to consider modern applications of his principles.)* **AL**

The most famous scientist of the Hellenistic Era was **Archimedes** (AHR•kuh•MEE•deez) of Syracuse. He worked on the geometry of spheres and cylinders and also established the value of the mathematical constant pi. A practical inventor, too, he may have devised the "Archimedes' screw," a machine used to pump water out of mines and to lift irrigation water.

Archimedes' achievements inspired a number of stories. Supposedly, he discovered specific gravity by observing the water he displaced in his bath. He then became so excited by his realization that he jumped out of the water and ran home naked, shouting, "Eureka!" ("I have found it!"). He is said to have emphasized the importance of levers by proclaiming to the king of Syracuse, "Give me a lever and a place to stand on and I will move the earth." The king encouraged Archimedes to lower his sights and build defensive weapons instead.

Athens remained the chief center for philosophy in the Hellenistic Era, attracting famous thinkers from all over who established schools there. The development of two new systems of thought, Epicureanism and Stoicism, strengthened Athens's reputation as a philosophical center.

Epicurus, the **founder** of **Epicureanism**, began a school in Athens at the end of the fourth century B.C. He believed that human beings were free to follow their own self-interest and make happiness their goal. The means to happiness was the pursuit of pleasure, the only true good.

Epicurus did not speak of the pursuit of pleasure in a physical sense (which is what our word *epicurean* has come to mean). Instead, pleasure was freedom from emotional turmoil and worry. To achieve this, people had to free themselves from public activity. However, they were not to give up all social life. To Epicurus, a life could only be complete when it was centered on the ideal of friendship.

Another school of thought was **Stoicism.** It became the most popular philosophy of the Hellenistic world and later flourished in the Roman Empire as well. Stoicism was the product of a teacher named Zeno. A Syrian who came to Athens as a merchant, Zeno lost his possessions on the sea voyage. A philosopher in Athens consoled Zeno **C** by teaching him that material possessions were not necessary in order to be happy. After learning from other philosophers in Athens, Zeno began to teach in a building known as the Painted Portico (the *Stoa Poikile*—hence, the word *Stoicism*).

Like Epicureans, Stoics wanted to find happiness, but they thought it could be found only by living in harmony with the will of God. Then they could bear whatever life offered (hence, our word *stoic*). Unlike Epicureans, Stoics did not want to separate themselves from the world. Public service was regarded as noble. The real Stoic was a good citizen.

✓Reading Check **Summarizing** In which fields did Hellenistic scholars make advancements?

SECTION 5 REVIEW

Vocabulary

1. **Explain** the significance of: Macedonia, Philip II, Alexander the Great, Alexandria, Hellenistic Era, Pergamum, subsidizing, Eratosthenes, Euclid, Archimedes, founder, Epicureanism, Stoicism.

Main Ideas

2. **Describe** the defining characteristics of the Hellenistic period.
3. **List** the three most famous scientists of the Hellenistic Age and describe their contributions.
4. **Organize** information using a cluster diagram to show Alexander's goals for his empire.

Critical Thinking

5. **BIG Idea** **Defending** What was the most important effect of Macedonia's conquest of Greece? Explain your answer.
6. **Evaluating** Why is Alexander called "the Great"? Do you think the title is justified? Why or why not?
7. **Analyzing Visuals** View the image on page 136 of Alexander the Great. What does this tell you about the style of warfare during his conquests?

Writing About History

8. **Persuasive Writing** Choose an Epicurean or Stoic perspective and argue whether an individual should participate in government and civic affairs.

History ONLINE
For help with the concepts in this section of *Glencoe World History*, go to glencoe.com and click Study Central™.

139

C Critical Thinking

Comparing and Contrasting
Ask: What was the main concern of both the Stoic and Epicurean schools of philosophy? *(Both philosophies were concerned with the way people lived their lives and attained happiness.)* **OL**

Answer: literature, mathematics, philosophy, science, war

Assess

History ONLINE

Study Central provides summaries, interactive games, and online graphic organizers to help students review content.

Close

Summarizing **Ask:** What were the major accomplishments of the Hellenistic world in science? *(developed theories of a helio-centered universe; calculated circumference of Earth; organized principles of geometry; established the value of pi)* **OL**

Answers

1. Definitions for the vocabulary words are found in the section and the Glossary.
2. spread of Greek culture; creation of new urban centers; advances in science
3. **Aristarchus:** Earth rotates around the sun; **Eratosthenes:** calculated Earth's circumference; **Archimedes:** established value of pi
4. defeat Persian Empire; gain personal glory; spread Greek language and ideas; fuse Macedonians, Greeks, and Persians into a single empire
5. Answers may include: The mixing of cultures was the most important effect because it changed the way many people lived and thought.
6. In his brief life he created a huge empire through which Greek culture and language were spread. Students should give examples to support their opinions.
7. There was hand-to-hand battle and confusion on the battlefield; rulers fought alongside their armies.
8. Arguments should either represent the Epicurean perspective that individuals should not participate or the Stoic view that public service is noble.

Taking Notes Have volunteers read the Visual Summary aloud. **Ask:** What are the elements of a summary? *(A summary includes the main ideas and most important supporting details of a portion of text.)* Point out that because this summary encompasses an entire chapter, it consists only of main idea statements inferred from the supporting details in the textbook. Tell students that ideally both main ideas and significant details should be included in their notes. Display a two-column chart with the headings "Main Ideas" and "Supporting Details." Have groups of students each take a statement from the first section of the summary and identify its supporting details from the text. Complete the chart together and have students copy it into their notebooks. Repeat the process for the second and third sections of the Visual Summary. **BL**

Organizing Have students weave each set of main idea statements into a paragraph, using appropriate transitions and inserting significant details where necessary. They should develop the heading of each section of the Visual Summary into a topic sentence for their paragraphs. **OL**

CHAPTER 4 Visual Summary

STUDY TO GO You can study anywhere, anytime by downloading quizzes and flash cards to your PDA from glencoe.com.

EARLY GREECE AND THE POLIS

- Greek civilization emerged with the Mycenaeans, who reflected aristocratic and warrior values; later these were celebrated in Homer's epics.
- A difficult Dark Age dispersed Greeks in colonies around the Mediterranean.
- The polis, or city-state, became the central unit of Greek political and social life.
- Sparta and Athens, the leading city-states, followed very different ideals; in Athens democracy emerged.

MYCENAEAN KING AGAMEMNON

Agamemnon led the attack on Troy in Homer's *Iliad.*

DETAIL FROM THE NORTH FRIEZE OF THE PARTHENON

These water carriers are a clear example of Greek classical principles in the arts.

CLASSICAL GREECE

- To defend their lands, the Greeks fought and defeated the Persians.
- Under Pericles, Athens embraced democracy at home, but not in the empire.
- Sparta destroyed Athenian domination, ending the classical age.
- Greek drama probed eternal questions while Greek philosophy pioneered rational thought.
- Greeks wrote the first analytical history, while balance and harmony guided their art and architecture.

THE HELLENISTIC AGE

- Alexander the Great unified Greece, then spread its culture as he conquered other lands.
- Hellenistic kingdoms in Egypt, Persia, and elsewhere absorbed Greek language and culture.

HELLENISTIC MASTERPIECE

Nike of Samothrace embodies the artistic movement of Hellenistic Greece.

Hands-On Chapter Project
Step 6: Wrap-Up

Keeping a Travel Journal

Step 6: Reviewing Journal Entries Students will synthesize what they have learned in Steps 1–5.

Directions: Write the Essential Question on the board. Then display a tree diagram with the phrase "Ancient Greece" in the top box and three large boxes on the second level, labeled "Knossos and Mycenae," "Classical Greece," and "Alexander's Empire." Have groups share their journal entries with each other and identify highlights of each culture. Students can include political, artistic, technological, literary, or even military achievements. Record groups' ideas in the boxes to complete the tree diagram. Then hold an informal class debate in which students formulate a response to the Essential Question and argue whether ancient Greece can truly be called the "birthplace of Western civilization." Students should incorporate specific examples to support their argument. **OL**

STANDARDIZED TEST PRACTICE

TEST-TAKING TIP

Look for key words such as *best, always,* and *never* in questions and answer choices.

Reviewing Vocabulary

Directions: Choose the word or words that best complete the sentence.

1. Heavily armed infantrymen or foot soldiers are known as ________.
   - **A** phalanx
   - **B** Spartans
   - **C** cavalry
   - **D** hoplites

2. Athenians devised the practice of ________ to protect themselves against overly ambitious politicians.
   - **A** tyranny
   - **B** ostracism
   - **C** democracy
   - **D** warfare

3. In order to know the will of the gods, the Greeks consulted a(n) ________.
   - **A** oracle
   - **B** Delphi
   - **C** festival
   - **D** temple

4. ________ comes from the Greek word that means "love of wisdom."
   - **A** Literature
   - **B** Theatre
   - **C** Philosophy
   - **D** Mathematics

Reviewing Main Ideas

Directions: Choose the best answers to the following questions.

Section 1 *(pp. 106–111)*

5. How did the physical geography of Greece affect the Greeks?
   - **A** It helped to make their city-states fiercely independent.
   - **B** It encouraged them to focus on truth and beauty.
   - **C** It was one of the factors that made them fierce, skilled warriors.
   - **D** It prevented contact with other civilizations.

Section 2 *(pp. 112–117)*

6. Which of the following best describes Sparta?
   - **A** A city-state that valued alliances with other cultures
   - **B** A Macedonian democracy
   - **C** A strict society run by helots
   - **D** A military state focused on the art of war

7. How did Cleisthenes create the foundation for democracy in Athens?
   - **A** By declaring war on Sparta
   - **B** By giving the Athenian assembly a central political role
   - **C** By giving aristocrats' land to the poor
   - **D** By discouraging the study of the arts

Section 3 *(pp. 118–123)*

8. What brought Sparta and Athens together as allies?
   - **A** Their common values, beliefs, and culture
   - **B** The movement of the Delian League to Athens
   - **C** The threat of the Persian Empire
   - **D** The Great Peloponnesian War

Need Extra Help?

If You Missed Questions . . .	1	2	3	4	5	6	7	8
Go to Page . . .	113	121	124	128	106	115	117	118

Answers and Analyses

Reviewing Vocabulary

1. D *Phalanx, cavalry,* and *hoplites* are all military terms, making this question somewhat challenging. Students might recall, however, that a phalanx is a formation of foot soldiers, or hoplites. Cavalry can be eliminated if students remember that these are soldiers on horseback.

2. B Democracy in Athens grew from the reforms of Cleisthenes, not in reaction to corrupt politicians. Tyranny refers to taking control by force, certainly not a security measure against ambitious leaders. Therefore, ostracism, employed by the citizens themselves, is the logical choice.

TEST-TAKING TIP

For Question 2: Remind students to eliminate choices that they know are incorrect, such as warfare. Then students can evaluate the remaining possibilities.

3. A The only possible answer is oracle. Delphi is a place, a festival is an event, and a temple is a building.

4. C Encourage students to look at word parts. *Philo-* means "loving" or "love of."

Reviewing Main Ideas

5. A Remind students that Greece's extensive coastline and good harbors encouraged trading with other civilizations, and that its mountainous terrain separated city-states from each other.

6. D During the Persian Wars, Sparta did form alliances, but they were temporary and served a specific purpose. Sparta was neither in Macedonia nor a democracy. The helots were the slaves, kept strictly under control by the citizens of Sparta.

7. B Only the right to assemble and participate in the governing process would lead to democracy. Giving land to the poor would help their economic welfare, but would not guarantee political rights.

8. C A common enemy is often the catalyst for unification. When Persia threatened the Greek mainland, Sparta and Athens formed an alliance.

9. A If the city-states were preoccupied with each other, an outsider would benefit. Therefore, Philip II of Macedonia is the logical choice.

10. C Students should identify Aristotle as a philosopher, in which case he would be associated with logic.

11. C Remind students that Aeschylus is the author of the *Oresteia,* a trilogy about the fate of Agamemnon, and Sophocles wrote *Oedipus Rex.*

12. B Have students evaluate each statement in light of what they know. Alexander was a Macedonian and therefore unlikely as a young boy to have lived in Athens or to have been a Spartan soldier. He was tutored by Aristotle, not Socrates, who lived before this time.

13. B Have students think carefully about the meaning of the phrase *cultural legacy.* Language, architecture, literature, and art comprise elements of culture.

Critical Thinking

14. D The four civilizations did not exist at the same time, but Sparta, a later civilization, did have its location and values in common with the Mycenaeans.

TEST-TAKING 

For Question 14: Remind students to prove or disprove each statement based on the data presented in the chart. For example, there are no common entries for Sparta and Athens.

CHAPTER 4

9. Who benefited from the power struggles of Athens, Sparta, and Thebes?
- **A** Philip II of Macedonia
- **B** The Delian League
- **C** Women in all three societies
- **D** Pericles of Athens

Section 4 *(pp. 124–131)*

10. Which of the following is true of Aristotle?
- **A** He developed the Pythagorean theorem.
- **B** He designed the Parthenon, the greatest example of the classical Greek temple.
- **C** He defined the subject of logic.
- **D** He is considered the greatest historian of the ancient world.

11. What do Aeschylus and Sophocles have in common?
- **A** They developed mathematical proofs.
- **B** They studied under Plato.
- **C** They wrote tragedies.
- **D** They were gifted historians.

Section 5 *(pp. 134–139)*

12. How did Alexander's father prepare him for kingship?
- **A** By having him brought up in Athens
- **B** By bringing him on military campaigns
- **C** By enlisting him in the Spartan army
- **D** By sending for Socrates to tutor him

13. What was Alexander's cultural legacy?
- **A** The gold and silver that his conquests brought to Greece and Macedonia
- **B** The spread of Greek language, architecture, literature, and art
- **C** The possession of the entire Persian Empire
- **D** His strong skills as a military leader

Critical Thinking

Directions: Choose the best answers to the following questions.

Use the following information to answer question 14.

Ancient Civilizations of Greece

	Minoans	Mycenaeans	Spartans	Athenians
Location	Crete	Peloponnese	Peloponnese	Attica
Values	sports, nature	heroic deeds	discipline, military arts	philosophy, art
Trade	sea trading empire	pottery	trade discouraged	pottery

14. Which of the following statements is supported by the information in the table?
- **A** The Spartans and the Athenians had many common interests.
- **B** The Minoans and the Mycenaeans were allies.
- **C** All four civilizations existed at the same time.
- **D** The Spartans had more in common with the Mycenaeans than with the other civilizations.

15. A Greek dramatist would most likely be a citizen of which of the following?
- **A** The Minoan civilization
- **B** The Mycenaean civilization
- **C** Sparta
- **D** Athens

16. How did the formation of the Delian League give proof to the saying that strength lies in unity?
- **A** After the collapse of the Delian League, the Greeks were conquered.
- **B** When the Macedonians and Greeks worked together, they ended the Persian Empire.
- **C** The Delian League led to the spread of Greek language in modern-day Pakistan.
- **D** The Delian League provided a democratic forum for all Greek city-states.

Need Extra Help?

If You Missed Questions . . .	9	10	11	12	13	14	15	16
Go to Page . . .	123	131	126	134	136	142	126	121

GO ON

15. D Being a strictly military society, Sparta discouraged interest in the arts, whereas Athens encouraged learning and artistic endeavors, such as the performance of drama.

16. A The Delian League was a defensive alliance of Greek city-states against the Persian Empire. When the alliance broke down and the city-states began to fight each other, Macedonia was able to conquer Greece.

17. What event blinded the major Greek states to the threat from Macedonia?
   - **A** The Age of Pericles
   - **B** The establishment of Sparta
   - **C** The Great Peloponnesian War
   - **D** The end of the Persian Empire

Analyze the map and answer the question that follows. Base your answer on the map.

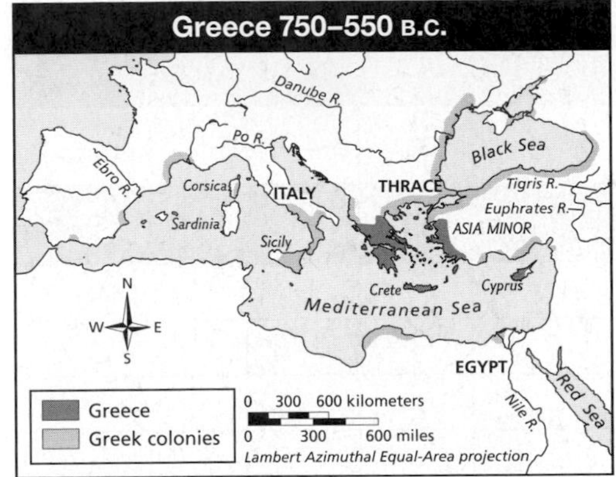

18. Based on the map, which of the following is most likely true?
   - **A** The Greeks relied heavily on their navy.
   - **B** The Greeks planned to conquer all of Western Europe.
   - **C** The Greeks had little interest in colonization.
   - **D** Greece was the largest colony in the empire.

Document-Based Questions

Directions: Analyze the document and answer the short-answer questions that follow the document. Base your answers on the document and on your knowledge of world history.

While Athens was at war with Sparta, Pericles spoke at a public funeral to honor those who had died in combat. He spoke of the greatness of Athens and the strength of its political system. Read the following excerpt.

> *"Our Constitution is called a democracy because the power is in the hands not of a minority but of the whole people. When it is a question of settling private disputes, everyone is equal before the law. Just as our political life is free and open, so is our day-to-day life in our relations with each other. . . . Here each individual is interested not only in his own affairs but in the affairs of the state as well."*
>
> —Pericles

19. According to Pericles, what is the relationship between the individual and the state in a democracy?

20. What is the historical significance of this speech in Pericles' own day and now?

Extended Response

21. Some classicists translate Sophocles' work on Oedipus as "Oedipus Tyrannus," or "Oedipus the Tyrant." Using what you know about Greek history, explain why some people might want to talk about Oedipus as a tyrant rather than a king.

History ONLINE
For additional test practice, use Self-Check Quizzes—Chapter 4 at glencoe.com.

Need Extra Help?

If You Missed Questions . . .	17	18	19	20	21
Go to Page . . .	123	143	143	121	114

STOP

Document-Based Questions

19. Each individual takes an interest in the affairs of the state.

20. In Pericles's day, such ideas would have been revolutionary. Other nations were monarchies, oligarchies, aristocracies, or theocracies, ruled over by an elite few. Only in Athens did all citizens have an equal share in government and equality before the law. These values support today's democracies.

Extended Response

21. The word *tyrant* had a different meaning in Greek times. It was a person who seized power by force. In killing his father, Oedipus acts as a tyrant—although, as it turns out, he is fulfilling the prophecy and is actually the legitimate heir.

17. C The Peloponnesian War preoccupied the city-states for many decades, making them unaware of the growing power of Macedonia.

18. A The map contains no information about Greek plans, so students should be able to easily eliminate B. Since the map shows Greek colonies, students can infer that the Greeks were interested in colonization, so C can be eliminated. Greece was the ruler of the empire, not a subject, or colony, eliminating D.

Introduce students to chapter content and key terms by having them access the Chapter 4 Overview at glencoe.com.

Need Extra Help?

Have students refer to the pages listed if they miss any of the questions.

CHAPTER 5 Planning Guide

Key to Ability Levels	
BL Below Level	**AL** Above Level
OL On Level	**ELL** English Language Learners

Key to Teaching Resources	
Print Material	DVD
CD-ROM	Transparency

Levels				Resources	Chapter Opener	Sect. 1	Sect. 2	Sect. 3	Sect. 4	Sect. 5	Chapter Assess
BL	OL	AL	ELL								
				FOCUS							
BL	OL	AL	ELL	**Daily Focus Skills Transparencies**		5-1	5-2	5-3	5-4	5-5	
				TEACH							
BL	OL	AL	ELL	**Charting and Graphing Activity, URB**			✓				
	OL	AL		**Economics and History Activity, URB**			✓				
BL	OL		ELL	**Reading Skills Activity, URB**		p. 167					
	OL	AL		**Historical Analysis Skills Activity, URB**				p. 168			
BL	OL	AL	ELL	**Differentiated Instruction Activity, URB**			p. 169				
	OL		ELL	**English Learner Activity, URB**		p. 171					
BL	OL	AL	ELL	**Content Vocabulary Activity, URB***		p. 173				p. 173	
BL	OL	AL	ELL	**Academic Vocabulary Activity, URB**				p. 175			
BL	OL	AL	ELL	**Skills Reinforcement Activity, URB**						p. 177	
	OL	AL		**Critical Thinking Skills Activity, URB**			p. 178				
	OL	AL		**History and Geography Activity, URB**						p. 179	
	OL	AL	ELL	**Mapping History Activity, URB**						p. 181	
BL	OL	AL		**Historical Significance Activity, URB**		p. 182					
BL	OL	AL	ELL	**Cooperative Learning Activity, URB**					p. 183		
	OL	AL	ELL	**History Simulation Activity, URB**				p. 185			
BL	OL	AL	ELL	**Time Line Activity, URB**					p. 187		
	OL	AL		**Linking Past and Present Activity, URB**		p. 188					
BL	OL	AL		**People in World History Activity, URB**					pp. 189, 190		
BL	OL	AL	ELL	**Primary Source Reading, URB**				p. 191			
	OL	AL		**Enrichment Activity, URB**		p. 196					
BL	OL	AL	ELL	**World Art and Music Activity, URB**				p. 193			
BL	OL		ELL	**Guided Reading Activities, URB***		p. 198	p. 199	p. 200	p. 201	p. 202	
BL	OL		ELL	**Reading Essentials and Note-Taking Guide***		p. 46	p. 49	p. 52	p. 55	p. 58	
BL	OL	AL	ELL	**Differentiated Instruction for the World History Classroom**	✓	✓	✓	✓	✓	✓	✓

Note: Please refer to the *Unit Resource Book: The First Civilizations and Empires* for this chapter's URB materials.

* Also available in Spanish

- Interactive Lesson Planner
- Interactive Teacher Edition
- Fully editable blackline masters
- Section Spotlight Videos Launch
- Differentiated Lesson Plans
- Printable reports of daily assignments
- Standards Tracking System

BL	OL	AL	ELL	Resources	Chapter Opener	Sect. 1	Sect. 2	Sect. 3	Sect. 4	Sect. 5	Chapter Assess
				TEACH *(continued)*							
BL	OL	AL	ELL	StudentWorks™ Plus DVD	✓	✓	✓	✓	✓	✓	✓
BL	OL	AL	ELL	Vocabulary PuzzleMaker CD-ROM	✓	✓	✓	✓	✓	✓	✓
Teacher Resources				Building Academic Vocabulary	✓	✓	✓	✓	✓	✓	✓
				Reading Strategies and Activities for the Social Studies Classroom		p. 50	p. 56				
				Writer's Guidebook			p. 12			p. 47	
				World Art and Architecture Transparencies					p. 17		
				Strategies for Success	✓	✓	✓	✓	✓	✓	✓
				Outline Map Resource Book	✓	✓	✓	✓	✓	✓	✓
				Presentation Plus! with MindJogger DVD	✓	✓	✓	✓	✓	✓	✓
				ASSESS							
BL	OL	AL	ELL	Section Quizzes and Chapter Tests*		p. 49	p. 50	p. 51	p. 52	p. 53	p. 55
BL	OL	AL	ELL	Authentic Assessment With Rubrics	✓	✓	✓	✓	✓	✓	✓
BL	OL	AL	ELL	Standardized Test Practice Workbook	✓	✓	✓	✓	✓	✓	✓
BL	OL	AL	ELL	*ExamView® Assessment Suite* CD-ROM		5-1	5-2	5-3	5-4	5-5	Ch. 5
BL	OL	AL	ELL	Interactive Tutor Self-Assessment CD-ROM		5-1	5-2	5-3	5-4	5-5	
				CLOSE							
BL			ELL	Reteaching Activity, URB						p. 195	
BL	OL		ELL	Reading and Study Skills Foldables™	✓	✓	✓	✓	✓	✓	✓

Using the McGraw-Hill Learning Network

Presentation Builder

Technology Product

Presentation Builder is a convenient and dynamic McGraw-Hill Learning Network tool to create online presentations. Use the Presentation Builder to

- create your own presentation slides;
- insert graphics from your Glencoe textbook;
- distribute presentations to students using **Assignments** from the *Classroom Tools.*

Steps

- On the McGraw-Hill Learning Network home page (www.mhln.com), log in as a member.
- Choose **Presentation Builder** under **Resources**.
- Click the **New Presentation** button.
- Enter a title in the **Presentation Title** box, then follow the prompts to select colors and fonts.
- Click the **Next** button and select a slide. Follow the prompts to insert information and complete the slide. The text boxes automatically adjust in size to accommodate the length of each question.
- Click the **Add Slide** button if you have additional presentation information and follow the prompts.
- Click **Review Presentation** when you are done.
- Click **View Presentation** to review the presentation in a pop-up window.
- Click on an underlined slide title to edit slides; use the drop-down keys to change the order of the slides; push the **Delete** button to delete a slide; and press **Insert Slide** to add a slide.
- Click the **Save** button when you are satisfied with your presentation. The presentation is saved to your **File Cabinet** and can be distributed to students through **Assignments**.

History ONLINE

	Student	Teacher	Parent
Beyond the Textbook	●	●	●
Chapter Overviews	●	●	●
Time Current Events	●		●
ePuzzles and Games	●		●
Concepts in Motion	●		●
Literature Connections		●	
Multi-Language Glossaries	●		●
Online Student Edition	●	●	●
Self-Check Quizzes	●		●
Student Web Activities	●		●
Study Central ™	●		●
Teaching Today		●	
Vocabulary eFlashcards	●		●
Web Activity Lesson Plans		●	

- **Timed Readings Plus in Social Studies** helps students increase their reading rate and fluency while maintaining comprehension. The 400-word passages are similar to those found on state and national assessments.
- **Reading in the Content Area: Social Studies** concentrates on six essential reading skills that help students better comprehend what they read. The book includes 75 high-interest nonfiction passages written at increasing levels of difficulty.
- **Reading Social Studies** includes strategic reading instruction and vocabulary support in Social Studies content for both ELLs and native speakers of English.

www.jamestowneducation.com

Index to National Geographic Magazine:

The following articles relate to this chapter:

- The World According to Rome," by T. R. Reid, August 1997
- "Brindisi Bronzes," by O. Louis Mazzatenta, April 1995
- "The Eternal Etruscans," by Rick Gore, June 1988

National Geographic Society Products To order the following, call National Geographic at 1-800-368-2728:

- *National Geographic Atlas of the World* (Book)
- *Ancient Rome* (PicturePack)

Access National Geographic's new, dynamic MapMachine Web site and other geography resources at:

www.nationalgeographic.com

www.nationalgeographic.com/maps

Biography

The following videotape programs are available from Glencoe as supplements to Chapter 5:

- Ancient Rome (ISBN 0-76-701263-1)
- Julius Caesar: Master of the Roman World (ISBN 0-76-700572-4)

To order, call Glencoe at 1-800-334-7344. To find classroom resources to accompany many of these videos, check the following home pages:

A&E Television: www.aetv.com

The History Channel: www.historychannel.com

GLENCOE BOOKLINK 3

Use this database to search more than 30,000 titles to create a customized reading list for your students.

- Reading lists can be organized by students' reading level, author, genre, theme, or area of interest.
- The database provides Degrees of Reading Power™ (DRP) and Lexile™ readability scores for all selections.
- A brief summary of each selection is included.

Leveled reading suggestions for this chapter:

For students at a Grade 8 reading level:
- ***Ancient Rome,*** by Peter Connolly

For students at a Grade 9 reading level:
- ***Women in Ancient Rome,*** by Fiona Macdonald

For students at a Grade 10 reading level:
- ***In Ancient Rome: Food and Feasts,*** by Philip Steele

For students at a Grade 11 reading level:
- ***Ancient Rome,*** by Simon James

For students at a Grade 12 reading level:
- ***Imperial Rome,*** by H. E. L. Mellersh

Introducing CHAPTER 5

Focus

MAKING CONNECTIONS

What did we learn about city planning from the Romans?

Activate students' prior knowledge by asking them to identify Roman influences in modern cities. *(Responses may include the use of concrete; domes, columns, and arches; amphitheaters; irrigation systems, etc.)* Discuss how architects and engineers have improved Roman innovations over time.

Teach

The Big Ideas

As students study the chapter, remind them to consider the section-based Big Ideas included in each section's Guide to Reading. The **Essential Questions** in the activities below tie in to the Big Ideas and help students think about and understand important chapter concepts. In addition, the Hands-on Chapter Projects with their culminating activities relate the content from each section to the Big Ideas. These activities build on each other as students progress through the chapter. Section activities culminate in the wrap-up activity on the Visual Summary page.

CHAPTER 5

Rome and the Rise of Christianity 600 B.C.–A.D. 500

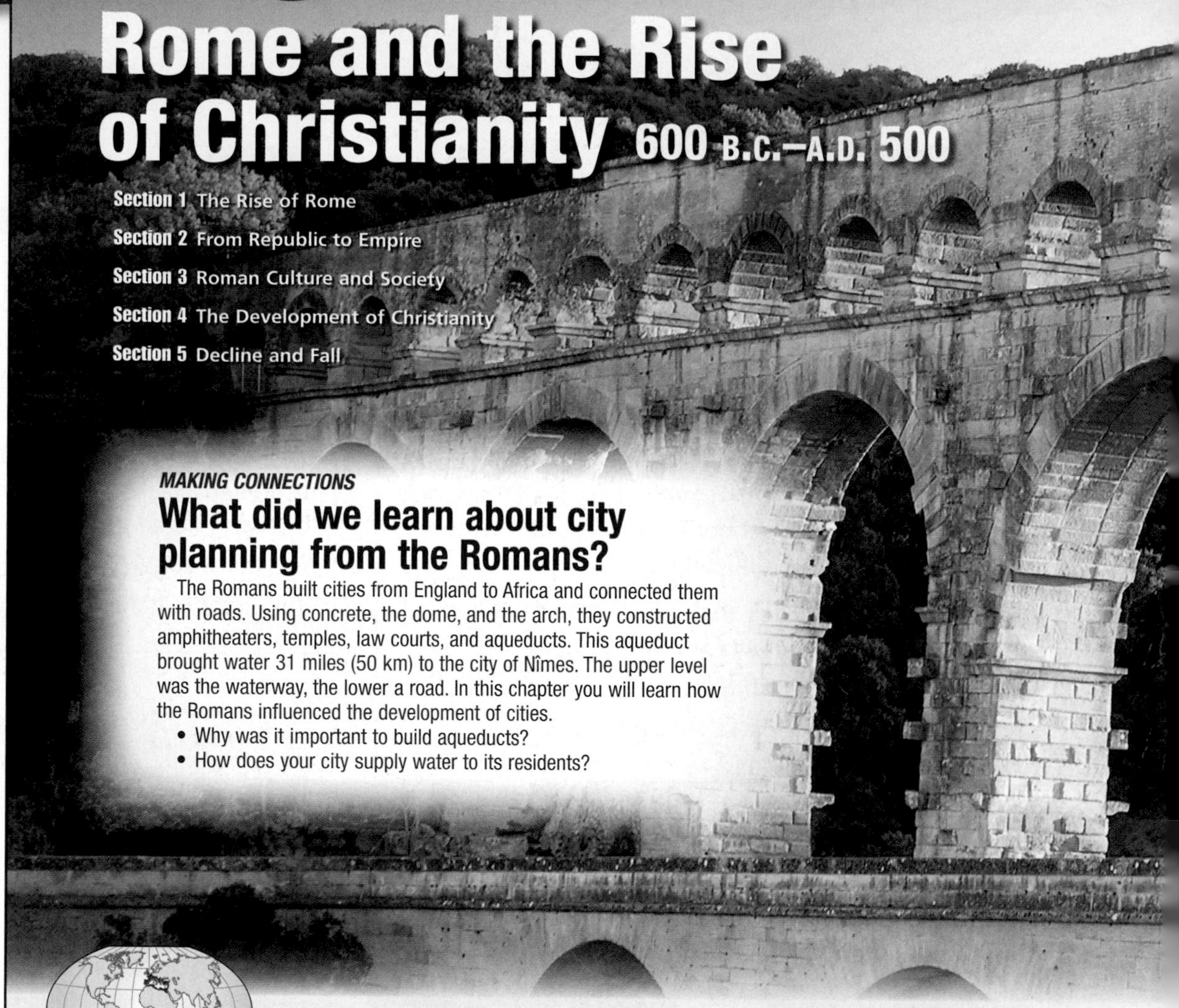

MAKING CONNECTIONS

What did we learn about city planning from the Romans?

The Romans built cities from England to Africa and connected them with roads. Using concrete, the dome, and the arch, they constructed amphitheaters, temples, law courts, and aqueducts. This aqueduct brought water 31 miles (50 km) to the city of Nîmes. The upper level was the waterway, the lower a road. In this chapter you will learn how the Romans influenced the development of cities.

- Why was it important to build aqueducts?
- How does your city supply water to its residents?

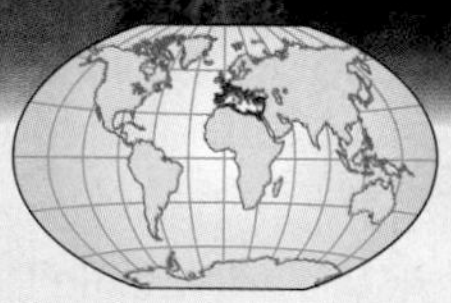

THE WORLD ▶

650 B.C. Etruscans rule Rome

600 B.C.

509 B.C. Start of Roman Republic

300 B.C.

264–146 B.C. The Punic Wars

27 B.C. Augustus becomes Roman emperor

A.D. 1

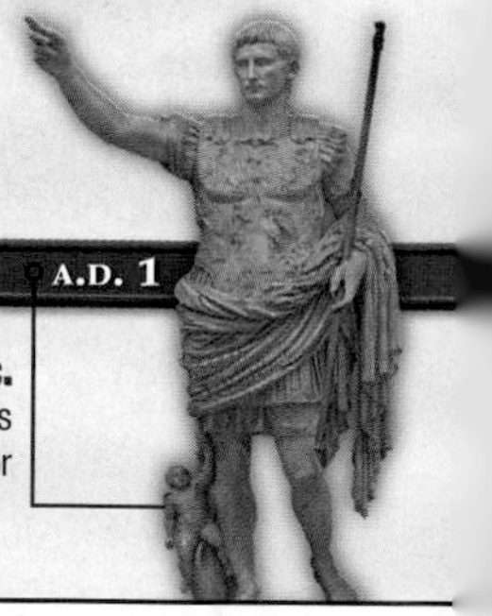

SECTION 1

The Rise of Rome

Remind students that history has recorded the rise of many groups through conquest. **Essential Question:** **What supported Rome in conquering the Mediterranean?** *(military and political skills of leaders)* After students have discussed the question, tell them that in Section 1, they will learn more about how the Roman system led to success. **OL**

From Republic to Empire

Tell students that governments and cultures change over time with the changing needs of the populace. **Essential Question:** **What factors contributed to the destabilization of the Roman Republic?** *(political and social unrest; new military system)* Tell students that in Section 2, they will learn about the end of the Roman Republic and the beginning of the Roman Empire. **OL**

Roman Culture and Society

Discuss Roman art and culture with students. **Essential Question:** **How widespread was the influence of Greek and Roman culture?** *(It spread throughout the empire.)* Tell students that in Section 3, they will learn more about arts and society in Ancient Rome. **OL**

A.D. 33
Death of Jesus in Jerusalem
A.D. 313
Constantine legalizes Christianity
A.D. 300
A.D. 500
A.D. 79
Volcano destroys Pompeii
A.D. 476
Fall of the Western Roman Empire
FOLDABLES™
Study Organizer
Analyzing Create a Four-Door Book to analyze the impact of geography on the rise of Rome. On the inside of the book, write descriptive phrases explaining the geographic importance of Rome, Sicily, Carthage and the Alps to Rome's rise.
Rome
Sicily
Carthage
Alps
History ONLINE
Chapter Overview—Visit glencoe.com to preview Chapter 5.

Introducing
CHAPTER 5

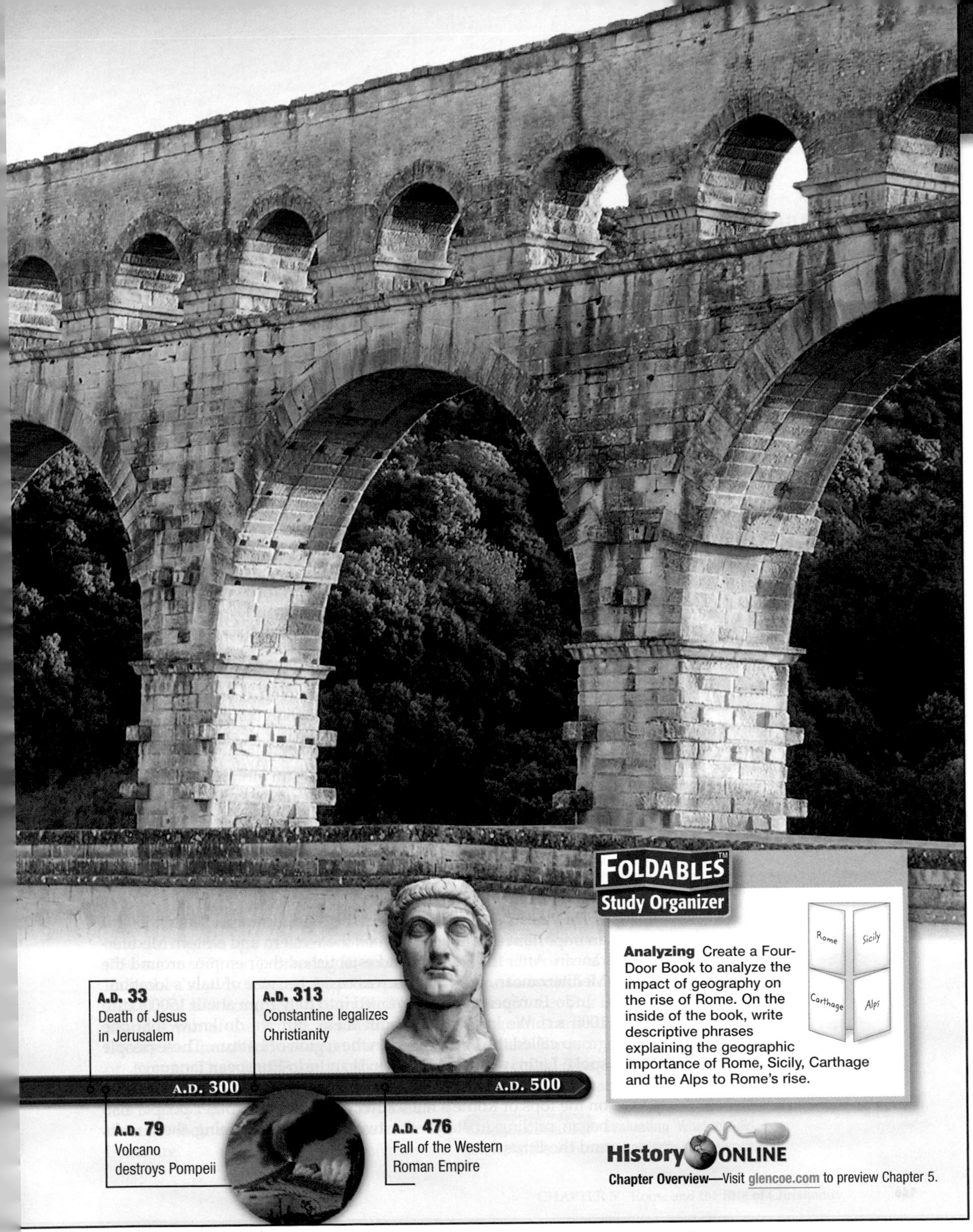

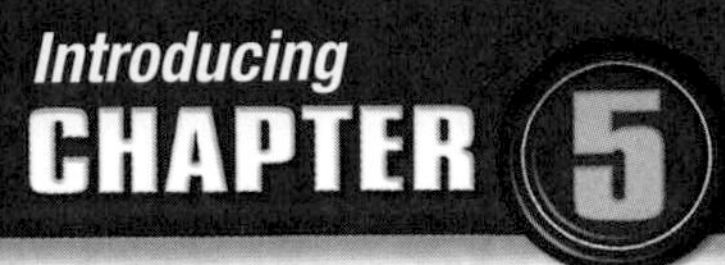

More About the Photo

Visual Literacy The Pont du Gard is an ancient Roman aqueduct that spans a broad valley in Nîmes, a city in southern France. Aqueducts are structure or bridges built to carry water across great distances. Constructed in the early first century A.D., the Pont du Gard contains a series of arched openings framed by columns built using concrete faced with stone. This method of construction was used in other Roman edifices such as the Colosseum in Rome. The Pont du Gard exhibits the high quality of Roman engineering.

FOLDABLES™ Study Organizer Dinah Zike's Foldables

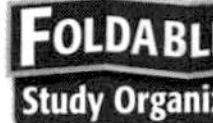

Dinah Zike's Foldables are three-dimensional, interactive graphic organizers that help students practice basic writing skills, review vocabulary terms, and identify main ideas. Instructions for creating and using Foldables can be found in the Appendix at the end of this book and in the *Dinah Zike's Reading and Study Skills Foldables* booklet.

History ONLINE

Introduce students to chapter content and key terms by having them access the Chapter 5 Overview at glencoe.com.

SECTION 4

The Development of Christianity

Essential Question: How did Christianity change the Roman Empire? *(Christianity eventually became the state religion of Rome.)* After students have discussed the question, tell them that in Section 4, they will learn more about the development of Christianity. **OL**

SECTION 5

Decline and Fall

Discuss the fall of Rome. **Essential Question:** What led to the eventual end of the Roman Empire? *(Invaders from Asia and Germany brought the Empire to an end despite strong emperors who tried to revive it.)* Tell students that they will learn more about the end of the Roman Empire in Section 5. **OL**

C Critical Thinking

Predicting Consequences
Ask: What do you think will happen in Rome as a result of Sulla's legacy? *(Possible response: His success at using the army to seize power may lead others to attempt the same, resulting in more instability.)* **AL**

For additional practice on this skill, see the **Skills Handbook**.

D Differentiated Instruction

Auditory/Musical Have students read this quote aloud. Then ask them to summarize what Sallust is saying in their own words. **OL**

R Reading Strategy

Summarizing Review the flow chart format and then have students use a flow chart to trace the steps that led Caesar to become dictator of Rome. **ELL**

Sulla won and seized Rome itself in 82 B.C., conducting a reign of terror to wipe out all opposition. Then Sulla restored power to the hands of the Senate and eliminated most of the powers of the popular assemblies.

C Sulla hoped that he had created a firm foundation to restore a traditional Roman republic governed by a powerful Senate. His real legacy was quite different from what he had intended, however. His example of using an army to seize power would prove most attractive to ambitious men.

The First Triumvirate

For the next 50 years (82–31 B.C.), Roman history was characterized by civil wars as many individuals competed for power. As the Roman historian Sallust observed:

PRIMARY SOURCE

D "But when our country had grown great through toil, when great kings had been vanquished in war, when Carthage, the rival of Rome's sway, had perished root and branch, then Fortune began to grow cruel. . . . Hence the lust for power first, then for money, grew upon them; these were, I may say, the root of all evils. For greed destroyed honor, integrity, and all other noble qualities. Ambition drove many men to become false; to have one thought locked in the breast, another ready on the tongue; to value friendships and enmities not on their merits but by the standard of self-interest."

—*Sallust*, J. C. Rolfe, trans., 1921

Three men—Crassus, Pompey, and Julius Caesar—emerged as victors of the civil wars. **Crassus** was known as the richest man in Rome. **Pompey** had returned from a successful command in Spain as a military hero. **Julius Caesar** also had a military command in Spain. The combined wealth and power of these three men was enormous and enabled them to dominate the **R** political scene and achieve their basic aims.

In 60 B.C., Caesar joined with Crassus and Pompey to form the First Triumvirate. A **triumvirate** is a government by three people with equal power.

Pompey received a command in Spain, Crassus was given a command in Syria, and Caesar was granted a special military command in Gaul—modern France—where he achieved success and distinction as a military leader. When Crassus was killed in battle in 53 B.C., only two powerful men were left. Fearing Caesar's popularity, leading senators decided that rule by Pompey alone would be to their benefit. They voted for Caesar to lay down his command.

Caesar refused to obey the Senate. While serving in Gaul, he had gained military experience, as well as an army of loyal veterans. He chose to keep his army and to enter Italy by illegally crossing the **Rubicon,** the river that formed the southern boundary of his province. The phrase "crossing the Rubicon" means to take a decisive action that cannot be taken back. Disobeying the Senate was serious. As Judas Maccabees, a Jewish military leader, said of Romans a century earlier:

PRIMARY SOURCE

"They had defeated Antiochus the Great, king of Asia. . . . Yet for all this not one of the Romans has put on a crown, but they have built for themselves a senate chamber, and every day three hundred senators constantly deliberate concerning the people, to govern them well."

—Margaret L. King, *Western Civilization*, 2000

Caesar's march on Rome started a civil war between his forces and those of Pompey and his allies. Pompey's defeat left Caesar in complete control of the Roman government.

Caesar was officially made **dictator,** or absolute ruler, in 45 B.C. This position was usually temporary, only used in emergencies. Realizing the need for reforms, Caesar gave land to the poor and increased the Senate to 900 members. By filling it with many of his supporters and increasing the number of members, he weakened the power of the Senate. He granted citizenship to his supporters in the provinces and introduced the solar calendar. Caesar had plans for building projects and military campaigns to the east. Many Senators thought that he had plans to continue as dictator. That is why in 44 B.C., a group of leading senators assassinated him.

Hands-On Chapter Project Step 2

Creating a Visual Presentation About Rome

Step 2: Illustrating the Roman Empire Small groups of students will continue to create the visual presentation they began in Section 1 on page 148.

Directions: Write the Big Idea on the board. Tell students that as they read this section, they should jot down key events and images they think would help tell the story of the fall of the Roman Republic and the rise of the Roman Empire in poster form. Groups can then come together to decide what to include and how to present the information in their second visual panel. Encourage students to think creatively about how to present important information from the section. Some groups may want to do additional research to add depth to their presentation.

Summarizing: Allow time for groups to discuss why they decided to include the events and images they did for this panel. They will complete another panel in Section 3. **OL**

(Chapter Project is continued in Section 3.)

The Second Triumvirate

A new power struggle followed the death of Caesar. Three men—**Octavian,** Caesar's heir and grandnephew; **Antony,** Caesar's ally and assistant; and Lepidus, who had been commander of Caesar's cavalry—joined forces to form the Second Triumvirate. Within a few years after Caesar's death, however, only two men divided the Roman world between them. Octavian took the west; Antony, the east.

The empire of the Romans, large as it was, was still too small for two masters. Octavian and Antony soon came into conflict. Antony allied himself with the Egyptian queen Cleopatra VII. At the Battle of **C** Actium in Greece in 31 B.C., Octavian's forces smashed the army and the navy of Antony and Cleopatra. Both fled to Egypt, where they committed suicide a year later. The Roman historian Florus, writing 40 years later, described the scene.

PRIMARY SOURCE

> "Antony was the first to commit suicide, by the sword. Cleopatra threw herself at Octavian's feet . . . It was not her life she was after . . . but a portion of her kingdom. When she realized this was hopeless . . . she took advantage of her guard's carelessness to get herself into the royal tomb. Once there, she put on the royal robes . . . lay down in a richly perfumed coffin beside her Antony. Then she applied poisonous snakes to her veins and passed into death as though into a sleep."
>
> —Florus, *Epitome of Roman History*

D

Octavian, at the age of 32, stood supreme over the Roman world. The civil wars had ended. So had the republic. The period beginning in 31 B.C. and lasting until A.D. 14 came to be known as the Age of Augustus.

✓Reading Check **Summarizing** How did Caesar weaken the power of the Senate?

PEOPLE *in* HISTORY

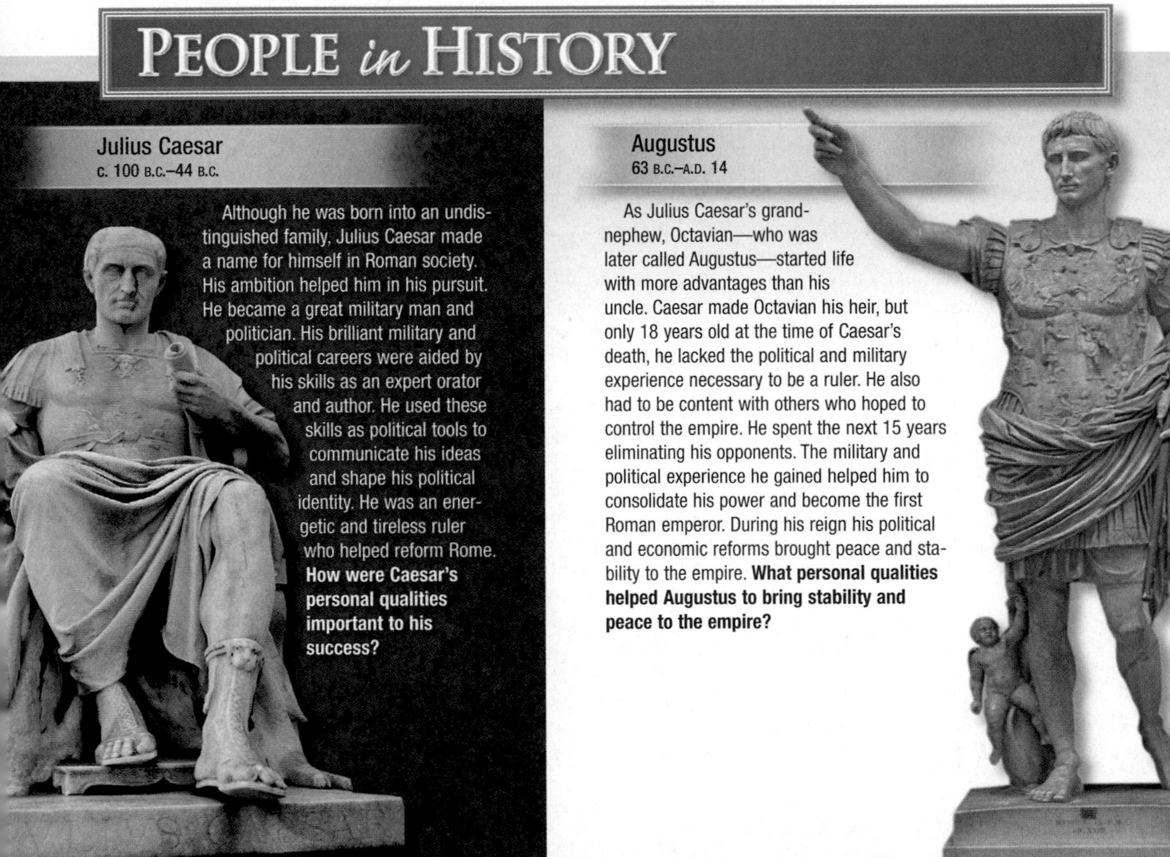

Julius Caesar
c. 100 B.C.–44 B.C.

Although he was born into an undistinguished family, Julius Caesar made a name for himself in Roman society. His ambition helped him in his pursuit. He became a great military man and politician. His brilliant military and political careers were aided by his skills as an expert orator and author. He used these skills as political tools to communicate his ideas and shape his political identity. He was an energetic and tireless ruler who helped reform Rome. **How were Caesar's personal qualities important to his success?**

Augustus
63 B.C.–A.D. 14

As Julius Caesar's grandnephew, Octavian—who was later called Augustus—started life with more advantages than his uncle. Caesar made Octavian his heir, but only 18 years old at the time of Caesar's death, he lacked the political and military experience necessary to be a ruler. He also had to be content with others who hoped to control the empire. He spent the next 15 years eliminating his opponents. The military and political experience he gained helped him to consolidate his power and become the first Roman emperor. During his reign his political and economic reforms brought peace and stability to the empire. **What personal qualities helped Augustus to bring stability and peace to the empire?**

C Critical Thinking

Determining Cause and Effect Ask: What impact did the Battle of Actium have on the Roman Republic? *(Octavian gained control. The republic soon became the Roman Empire.)* **OL**

D Differentiated Instruction

Advanced Learners Tell students that Shakespeare wrote about Antony and Cleopatra. Have them read the play and a critical essay about it, and then write a brief essay on why they think Shakespeare chose to dramatize the tale. **AL**

✓Reading Check

Answer: by increasing membership and appointing his supporters

PEOPLE *in* HISTORY

Answers: Caesar—His ambition and skill helped him achieve greatness; **Augustus**—His persistence and political strength helped him stabilize the empire.

Additional Support

Extending the Content

Julius Caesar Julius Caesar's name is known throughout the Western world. The name Caesar has come to signify a powerful ruler—such as *Kaiser* in German and *tsar* in Slavic languages. In addition, while Caesar was still alive, the Roman month Quintilus was renamed "July" after Julius Caesar.

Augustus Octavian's mother was the daughter of Julius Caesar's sister. His father was a Roman Senator. When Julius Caesar was assassinated, Octavian was studying in what is now Albania. Upon Caesar's death, he learned that his great uncle had named him heir. Although he was only 18, and his father advised against it, Octavian decided to go to Rome to claim his inheritance.

C1 Critical Thinking

Comparing and Contrasting Octavian was awarded many titles during his reign. He became *Augustus*, the revered one; *imperator*, commander-in-chief; *princeps*, first citizen; and *pontifex maximus*, chief pontiff, or head of the official state religion. Ask students whether they think it's unusual for a leader to have so many titles. Then point out that the president of the United States also has several titles: chief executive, commander-in-chief, head of state. Have students discuss differences and similarities in the titles. **OL**

For additional practice on this skill, see the **Skills Handbook**.

C2 Critical Thinking

Predicting Consequences **Ask:** How might European history have been different if the Romans had defeated the German warriors? *(Answers may include that all of Europe might have become Roman territory, with Latin replacing local languages and Roman law providing a unified legal code.)* **OL**

Additional Support

The Beginning of the Roman Empire

MAIN IDEA Octavian, titled Caesar Augustus, created a new order that began the Roman Empire.

HISTORY & YOU What makes a good government? Learn how the Roman Empire expanded and grew prosperous.

In 27 B.C., Octavian proclaimed the "restoration of the Republic." He knew that only traditional republican forms would satisfy the Senate. At the same time, he was aware that the republic could not be fully restored. Although he gave some power to the Senate, Octavian in fact became the first Roman emperor.

The Age of Augustus

C1 In 27 B.C., the Senate awarded Octavian the title of **Augustus**—the revered one, a fitting title in view of his power. Augustus proved to be highly popular. No doubt people were glad the civil wars had ended, but his continuing control of the army was the chief source of his power. The Senate gave Augustus the title **imperator,** or commander in chief. The English word *emperor* comes from *imperator*.

Augustus maintained a standing army of 28 legions, or about 151,000 men. A legion was a military unit of about 5,000 troops. Only Roman citizens could be legionnaires—members of a legion. Subject peoples could serve as auxiliary forces, which numbered around 130,000 under Augustus. Augustus also instituted a praetorian guard of roughly 9,000 men who had the important task of guarding the emperor.

While claiming to have restored the republic, Augustus began a new system for governing the provinces. Under the Roman Republic, the Senate had appointed the governors of the provinces. Now, the emperor controlled certain provinces and appointed deputies to govern them.

C2 Augustus stabilized the frontiers of the Roman Empire, conquering many new areas. His attempt to conquer Germany failed, however, when three Roman legions led by the Roman general Varus were massacred by German warriors. These defeats in Germany taught Augustus that Rome's power was not unlimited. This knowledge devastated him. For months, he would beat his head on a door, shouting, "Varus, give me back my legions!"

After the death of Augustus in A.D. 14, a series of new emperors ruled Rome. This period, ending in A.D. 180, is called the Early Empire.

Emperors and the Early Empire

Augustus's new political system allowed the emperor to select his successor from his natural or adopted family. The first four emperors after Augustus came from his family. They were Tiberius, Caligula, Claudius, and Nero. During their reigns, these emperors took over more and more of the responsibilities that Augustus had given to the Senate. As the emperors grew more powerful, many became more corrupt.

Wherever the Romans went, they built baths. This one in Bath, England, has the original Roman lead pipes.

Activity: Interdisciplinary Connection

Language Arts The Romans helped define rules of rhetoric, the art of using words persuasively. Cicero was one of Rome's most famous orators. Ask students to research the life of Cicero, listing his contributions to public speaking and some of his most famous speeches. Each student should bring one of Cicero's speeches to class and extract the words that are used for persuasion during a class discussion. **Ask:** How are persuasive words used in modern life? *(political campaigns, advertising, sales, personal and public causes)* Have students bring a copy of a modern-day politician's speech to class, and compare it to the Cicero speech they found. Discuss similarities and differences in the persuasive techniques used. Ask students to evaluate which speech is more effective. **AL**

Nero, for example, had people killed if he wanted them out of the way, including his own mother. Without troops, the senators were unable to oppose his excesses, but the Roman legions finally revolted. Nero, abandoned by his guards, committed suicide after allegedly uttering these final words: "What an artist the world is losing in me."

After Nero's death, a civil war broke out in A.D. 69. It soon became obvious that the Roman Empire had a major flaw. Without a system for selecting a new emperor, emperors could be made and deposed by the Roman legions.

At the beginning of the second century, a series of five so-called good emperors came to power. They were Nerva, Trajan, Hadrian, Antoninus Pius, and Marcus Aurelius. These emperors concluded a period of peace and prosperity known as the **Pax Romana**—the Roman Peace. The Pax Romana lasted for almost 200 years (27 B.C.–A.D. 180). These rulers treated the ruling classes with respect, ended arbitrary executions, maintained peace in the empire, and supported domestic policies generally helpful to the empire. Although they were absolute rulers, they were known for their tolerance. By adopting capable men as their sons and successors, the first four good emperors reduced the chances of succession problems.

W Under the five good emperors, the powers of the emperor continued to expand at the expense of the Senate's powers. Officials appointed and directed by the emperor took over the running of the government. The good emperors also created new social programs. Trajan, for example, provided state funds to assist poor parents in the raising and educating of their children. The good emperors were widely praised for their building programs. Trajan and Hadrian were especially active in building public works—aqueducts, bridges, roads, and harbor facilities—throughout the provinces and in Rome.

INFOGRAPHICS

Hadrian's Wall

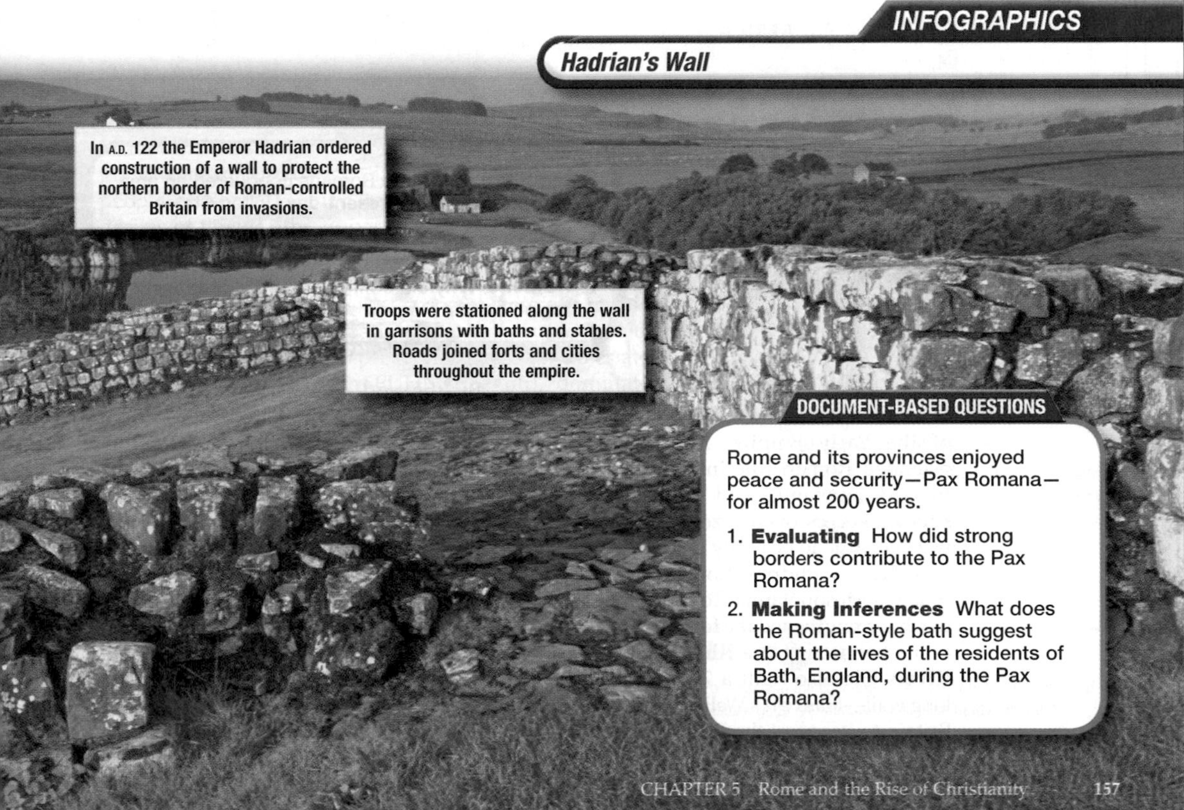

In A.D. 122 the Emperor Hadrian ordered construction of a wall to protect the northern border of Roman-controlled Britain from invasions.

Troops were stationed along the wall in garrisons with baths and stables. Roads joined forts and cities throughout the empire.

DOCUMENT-BASED QUESTIONS

Rome and its provinces enjoyed peace and security—Pax Romana—for almost 200 years.

1. **Evaluating** How did strong borders contribute to the Pax Romana?
2. **Making Inferences** What does the Roman-style bath suggest about the lives of the residents of Bath, England, during the Pax Romana?

W Writing Support

Expository Writing Have students write an essay in which they identify the similarities to and differences between the way the five good emperors ruled and the way Nero ruled. AL

DOCUMENT-BASED QUESTIONS

Answers:

1. They kept the provinces peaceful and secure, allowing them to thrive economically and politically.
2. Possible response: It shows that Roman culture had a great influence upon the province. Building such a luxury suggests that at least some of the residents had wealth and leisure time. Some students may also say that the building of the baths indicates that the city wanted to attract others (Romans) to Bath.

Differentiated Instruction

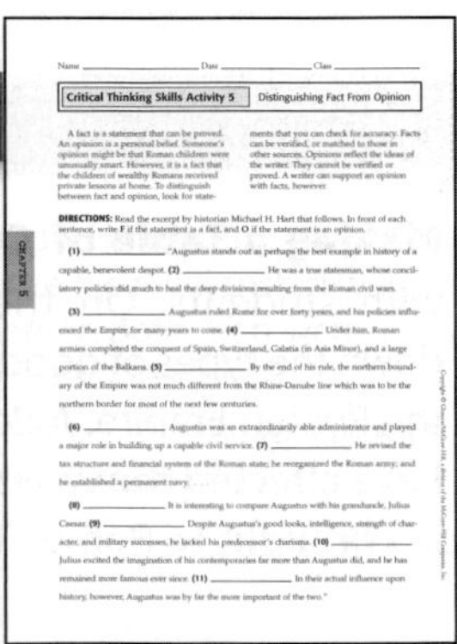

Critical Thinking Skills Activity, URB p. 178

Analyzing Information

Objective: Practice identifying fact and opinion.

Focus: Decide if statements are fact or opinion.

Teach: Ask students to skim the selection and underline words and phrases that might indicate opinions.

Assess: Have volunteers explain how they made their decisions about the statements.

Close: Review how authors indicate fact and opinion. Discuss when the use of opinion is appropriate.

Differentiated Instruction Strategies

BL Model answering the first three statements. Have students work with a partner to complete the page.

AL Analyze the use of fact and opinion in a newspaper. Have students present their conclusions to the class.

ELL Have partners read statements aloud to aid comprehension before completing the activity.

Focus

Bellringer

Daily Focus Transparency 5.3

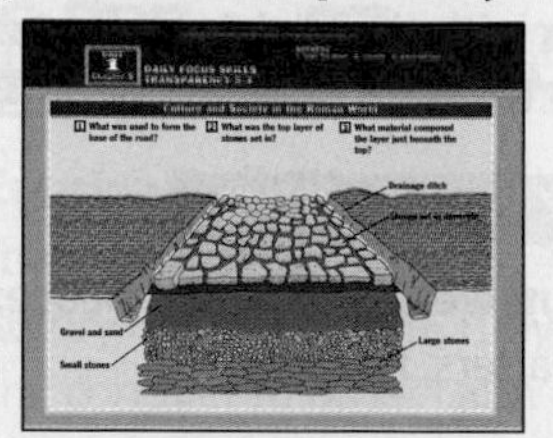

GUIDE TO READING

Answers to Graphic:
Wealthy Patrician: comfortable villas, women had more rights and privileges, owned slaves, educated, many luxuries; **Poor Citizen:** lived in crowded apartments, given food by emperor; **Both:** citizenship, women barred from politics

Section Spotlight Video

To generate student interest and provide a springboard for class discussion, access the Chapter 5, Section 3 video at glencoe.com or on the video DVD.

Resource Manager

SECTION 3

Roman Culture and Society

GUIDE TO READING

The BIG Idea
Ideas, Beliefs, and Values The Romans spread both Greek and Roman contributions to art, architecture, and literature throughout the empire.

Content Vocabulary
- paterfamilias *(p. 162)*
- *insulae (p. 165)*

Academic Vocabulary
- primary *(p. 162)*
- contractor *(p. 164)*

People and Places
- Virgil *(p. 161)*
- Livy *(p. 162)*
- Horace *(p. 161)*
- Spartacus *(p. 164)*

Reading Strategy
Compare and Contrast As you read this section, create a Venn diagram like the one shown below comparing and contrasting the lifestyle of a wealthy Roman with that of a poor citizen.

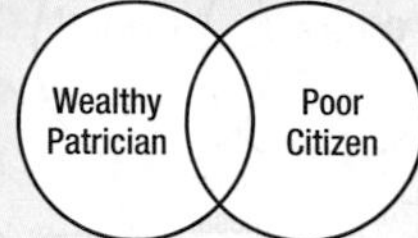

After they conquered Greece, the Romans adopted many aspects of Greek culture and society. As the Roman poet Horace said, "Captive Greece took captive her rude conqueror."

Roman Arts and Literature

MAIN IDEA The Romans spread Greco-Roman arts and culture throughout the empire.

HISTORY & YOU Have you ever borrowed a style from someone you admire? Learn how Rome borrowed from Greece.

As part of their plunder, Roman military commanders shipped Greek manuscripts and artworks back to Rome. By adapting Greek styles, the Romans spread Greco-Roman civilization throughout their empire.

Art and Architecture

During the third and second centuries B.C., the Romans adopted many features of the Greek style of art. They developed a taste for Greek statues, which they placed in public buildings and in their houses. Reproductions of Greek statues became popular once the supply of original works ran low. While Greek sculptors aimed for an ideal appearance in their figures, Roman sculptors produced more realistic works that included even unattractive physical details. They painted portraits and landscapes on the walls of villas.

The Romans excelled in architecture, a highly practical art. Although they continued to use Greek styles such as colonnades and rectangular buildings, the Romans also used curved forms: the arch, the vault, and the dome. The Romans were the first people in antiquity to use concrete on a massive scale. Using concrete along with the new architectural forms made it possible for the Romans to construct huge buildings undreamed of by the Greeks.

The Romans were superb builders. Their remarkable engineering skills were put to use constructing roads, bridges, and aqueducts. The Romans built a network of some 50,000 miles (80,450 km) of roads throughout the empire. In Rome, almost a dozen aqueducts kept a population of one million supplied with water.

Literature

Although there were many talented writers, the high point of Latin literature was reached in the Age of Augustus. Indeed, the

R Reading Strategies	C Critical Thinking	D Differentiated Instruction	W Writing Support	S Skill Practice
Teacher Edition • Making Connections, pp. 162, 164, 165 **Additional Resources** • Guid. Read. Act., URB p. 200 • Read. Ess. & Note-Taking Guide, p. 52	**Teacher Edition** • Analyzing Info., p. 162 • Compare/Contrast, p. 164 **Additional Resources** • Hist. Analysis Skills Act., URB p. 168 • Hist. Sim. Act., URB p. 185 • Section Quiz, p. 51	**Teacher Edition** • Visual/Spatial p. 161 • Adv. Learners, p. 161 **Additional Resources** • World Art & Music Act., URB p. 193	**Teacher Edition** • Narrative Writing, p. 163 **Additional Resources** • Pri. Source Read., URB p. 191	**Teacher Edition** • Visual Literacy, p. 163 **Additional Resources** • Academic Vocab. Act., URB p. 175

Connecting to the United States

Washington, D.C.

When Pierre Charles L'Enfant developed the plan for Washington, D.C., he based it on Roman city planning. Streets were laid out in a grid and government buildings arranged around an open area—The Mall. Many of the capital's buildings are also based on Roman models. Unlike Greek temples, Roman buildings were raised on a podium with steps at the front leading to a columned porch. In addition to these features, the United States Capitol also has a dome, which is based on the Roman Pantheon.

- Roman building styles influenced much of the architecture in Washington, D.C.
- The layout of the city also reflects the influence of Roman city planning.

1. **Identifying** Name three other buildings in Washington, D.C., that may have been based on Roman architecture.
2. **Evaluating** Based on what you know about Rome, why do you think the architects of Washington, D.C., based much of its design on Rome and its buildings?

D1

Augustan Age has been called the golden age of Latin literature.

The most distinguished poet of the Augustan Age was **Virgil.** The son of a small landholder in northern Italy near Mantua, he welcomed the rule of Augustus and wrote his masterpiece, the *Aeneid* (ih•NEE•uhd), in honor of Rome. Virgil's epic poem was meant to rival the work of Homer. The character Aeneas is the ideal Roman whose virtues are duty, piety, and faithfulness. Aeneas fulfilled his purpose by establishing the Romans in Italy and starting Rome on its mission to rule the world. The poem was also meant to express that Rome's gift was the art of ruling.

PRIMARY SOURCE

"Let others fashion from bronze more lifelike, breathing images—For so they shall—and evoke living faces from marble; Others excel as orators, others track with their instruments the planets circling in heaven and predict when stars will appear. But, Romans, never forget that government is your medium! Be this your art: to practise men in the habit of peace, generosity to the conquered, and firmness against aggressors."

—*Aeneid*, C. Day Lewis, trans., 1952

D2

Another prominent Augustan poet was **Horace,** a friend of Virgil's. He was a sophisticated writer who enjoyed pointing out some of the "follies and vices of his age."

Teach

D1 Differentiated Instruction

Visual/Spatial Take students on a virtual tour of the public buildings of Washington, D.C. Use photos in books, slides, videos, or a DVD. Point out Roman influences on the architecture. OL

D2 Differentiated Instruction

Advanced Learners Provide students with longer excerpts from Virgil's *Aeneid*. Have them take turns reading parts of the poem aloud. AL

Answers:

1. Possible answers: Treasury, Lincoln Memorial, National Gallery of Art
2. Answers should mention the power and longevity of Rome as a capital city.

Making Generalizations

Objective: Learn about frescoes and think about bias.

Focus: Examine the fresco example and read the text.

Teach: As students read the text, have them stop periodically and discuss how the frescoes are painted and what they depict.

Assess: In small groups, have students discuss their answers.

Close: Decide as a group why people who are describing types of art may do so with some bias.

Differentiated Instruction Strategies

- **BL** Read the passage with the students. Ask whether frescoes would survive in their local climate.
- **AL** Have students find more examples of frescoes from Pompeii. Discuss what they depict about daily life of the era.
- **ELL** Have partners read the text and write answers. Remind them to use words from the text to express their ideas.

Differentiated Instruction

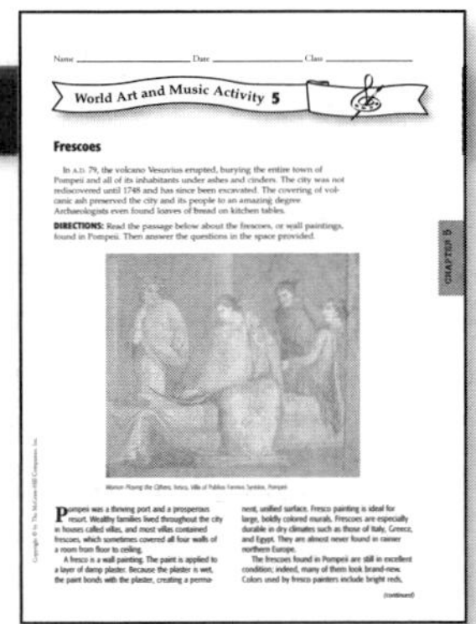

World Art and Music Activity, URB p. 193

9. D America had no contact with the Roman world, so A can be eliminated. The Etruscans had other influences in Rome, but Roman art and architecture were influenced by the Greeks.

10. C Explain that Virgil and Horace were poets, and Plato was a Greek philosopher. Livy is the only historian.

11. B Students should be able to eliminate A, C, and D when they think about whether these aspects of the Roman Empire are still in place today. The Christian church is the one contribution listed here that remains.

TEST-TAKING TIP

For Question 11: Remind students that when they read a test item, they should read the item carefully to determine what is being asked. For example, in this item, the word *lasting* is a clue to the fact that the answer will apply to a contribution that is still in effect.

12. A Students can look at the way the question is asked for clues. The phrase "do for the Roman Empire" implies that the reforms had a positive effect. Therefore, B, C, and D can be eliminated, making A the only logical choice.

13. A Again, the clue can be found in the phrasing of the question. The final event before the fall of the Empire was migration of Germanic tribes.

CHAPTER 5

Section 3 *(pp. 160–165)*

9. What culture influenced Roman art and architecture?
 - A American
 - B Persian
 - C Egyptian
 - D Greek

10. Who wrote *The Early History of Rome*?
 - A Virgil
 - B Horace
 - C Livy
 - D Plato

Section 4 *(pp. 168–173)*

11. What was one lasting contribution of the Roman Empire?
 - A The idea of the Triumvirate
 - B The Christian church
 - C The gladiatorial shows
 - D Pax Romana

Section 5 *(pp. 174–177)*

12. What did the reforms of Diocletian and Constantine do for the Roman Empire?
 - A Revived the Roman Empire
 - B Caused a decline in trade
 - C Brought on additional civil wars and invasions
 - D Placed the empire in a state of political unrest

13. What finally caused the fall of the Roman Empire?
 - A Migration of Germanic tribes
 - B An increase in taxes
 - C The rise of the Christian religion
 - D Death of Constantine

Critical Thinking

Directions: Choose the best answers to the following questions.

Use the following map to answer questions 14 and 15.

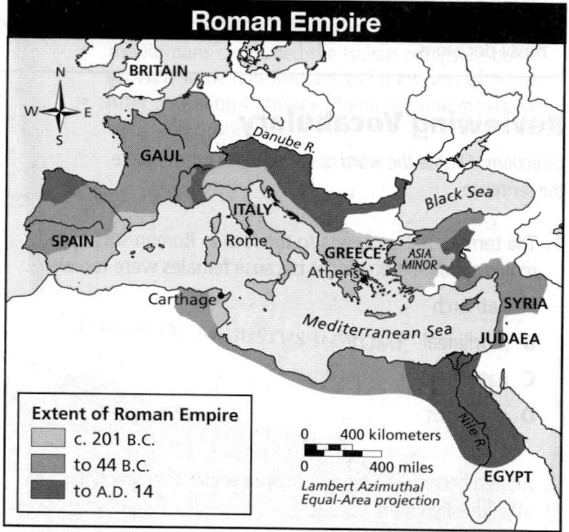

14. Around what body of water did the Roman Empire expand?
 - A Danube River
 - B Mediterranean Sea
 - C Black Sea
 - D Nile River

15. What region was added to the Roman Empire from 44 B.C. to A.D. 14?
 - A Egypt
 - B Italy
 - C Britain
 - D Gaul

Need Extra Help?

If You Missed Questions . . .	9	10	11	12	13	14	15
Go to Page . . .	160	162	173	174	176	180	180

GO ON

Critical Thinking

14. B Although the empire reached all bodies of water listed as answer choices, it expanded *around* the Mediterranean Sea.

15. A Remind students to look at the map key to help them answer this question. Egypt was the only region listed that was added during this time period.

Use the following time line to answer question 16.

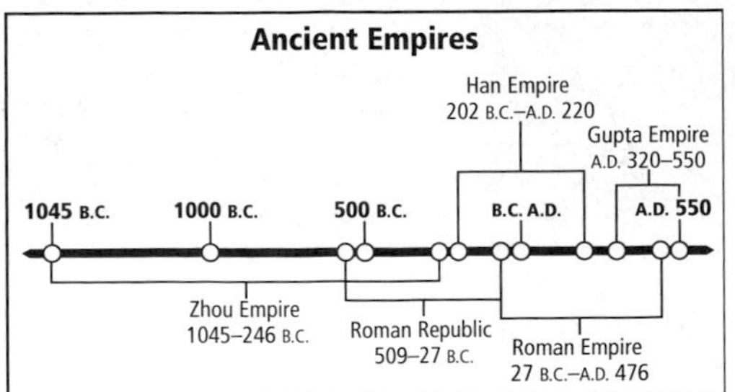

16. How long did the Roman civilization last?

A Almost 1,000 years
B 2,000 years
C 50 years
D About 500 years

17. On which group of people were Romans dependent for manual labor on farms and to help build roads and buildings?

A Women
B Greeks
C Slaves
D Children

18. Which Roman emperor helped spread Christianity?

A Crassus
B Constantine
C Antony
D Octavian

Document-Based Questions

Directions: Analyze the document and answer the questions that follow the document. Base your answers on the document and on your knowledge of world history.

Read the following poem by Virgil, and answer the questions.

> *Let others fashion from bronze more lifelike, breathing images—*
> *For so they shall—and evoke living faces from marble;*
> *Others excel as orators, others track with their instruments*
> *The planet circling in heaven and predict when stars will appear.*
> *But, Romans, never forget that government is your medium!*
> *Be this your art: to practise men in the habit of peace,*
> *Generosity to the conquered, and firmness against aggressors."*

19. What did the poet feel was Rome's gift? Who are the "others" mentioned in the poem?

20. How does this poem summarize the fundamental ideas of Western civilization that originated in Rome?

Extended Response

21. Find a picture of Roman architecture. Discuss how it demonstrates Roman culture, including potential influence from other cultures. In what ways do archaeologists and anthropologists analyze Roman culture, based on the limited remains of architecture and artifacts? Justify your answer with outside research.

History ONLINE
For additional test practice, use Self-Check Quizzes—Chapter 5 at glencoe.com.

Need Extra Help?

If You Missed Questions . . .	16	17	18	19	20	21
Go to Page . . .	181	164	172	181	181	161

STOP

Document-Based Questions

19. its ability to rule; the Greeks

20. The role of government is to promote peace and to defend its people.

Extended Response

21. Answers will vary. Encourage students to use their research to determine the processes that archaeologists and anthropologists use to gather information and draw conclusions about the culture they are studying.

16. A The Roman civilization began around 509 B.C. and the Empire fell in A.D. 476, making A the correct answer. Students need to read the question carefully to focus on the key word *civilization.* This tells them that both the Republic and the Empire are included.

17. C Students may think Greeks were slaves, but they were mostly employed as tutors, doctors, musicians, and artists. Women and children are less likely choices for manual labor.

18. B Crassus and Antony were not emperors, and Octavian died before Christianity began. Constantine is the only logical choice.

Introduce students to chapter content and key terms by having them access the Chapter 5 Overview at glencoe.com.

Need Extra Help?

Have students refer to the pages listed if they miss any of the questions.

CHAPTER 6 Planning Guide

Key to Ability Levels
- **BL** Below Level
- **OL** On Level
- **AL** Above Level
- **ELL** English Language Learners

Key to Teaching Resources
- Print Material
- CD-ROM
- DVD
- Transparency

Levels				Resources	Chapter Opener	Section 1	Section 2	Section 3	Section 4	Chapter Assess
BL	OL	AL	ELL							
FOCUS										
BL	OL	AL	ELL	Daily Focus Skills Transparencies		6-1	6-2	6-3	6-4	
TEACH										
		AL		World Literature Reading, URB					✓	
BL	OL		ELL	Reading Skills Activity, URB			p. 17			
	OL	AL		Historical Analysis Skills Activity, URB					p. 18	
BL	OL	AL	ELL	Differentiated Instruction Activity, URB					p. 19	
	OL		ELL	English Learner Activity, URB		p. 21				
BL	OL	AL	ELL	Content Vocabulary Activity, URB*		p. 23				
BL	OL	AL	ELL	Academic Vocabulary Activity, URB					p. 25	
BL	OL	AL	ELL	Skills Reinforcement Activity, URB					p. 27	
	OL	AL		Critical Thinking Skills Activity, URB				p. 28		
	OL	AL		History and Geography Activity, URB		p. 29				
	OL	AL	ELL	Mapping History Activity, URB			p. 31			
BL	OL	AL		Historical Significance Activity, URB					p. 32	
BL	OL	AL	ELL	Cooperative Learning Activity, URB			p. 33			
	OL	AL	ELL	History Simulation Activity, URB					p. 35	
BL	OL	AL	ELL	Time Line Activity, URB				p. 37		
	OL	AL		Linking Past and Present Activity, URB			p. 38			
BL	OL	AL		People in World History Activity, URB			p. 39		p. 40	
BL	OL	AL	ELL	Primary Source Reading, URB		p. 41				
	OL	AL		Enrichment Activity, URB		p. 46				
BL	OL	AL	ELL	World Art and Music Activity, URB				p. 43		
BL	OL		ELL	Guided Reading Activities, URB*		p. 48	p. 49	p. 50	p. 51	
BL	OL		ELL	Reading Essentials and Note-Taking Guide*		p. 61	p. 64	p. 67	p. 70	
BL	OL	AL	ELL	Differentiated Instruction for the World History Classroom	✓	✓	✓	✓	✓	✓

Note: Please refer to the *Unit Resource Book: New Patterns of Civilization* for this chapter's URB materials.

* Also available in Spanish

- Interactive Lesson Planner
- Interactive Teacher Edition
- Fully editable blackline masters
- Section Spotlight Videos Launch
- Differentiated Lesson Plans
- Printable reports of daily assignments
- Standards Tracking System

Levels					Resources	Chapter Opener	Section 1	Section 2	Section 3	Section 4	Chapter Assess
BL	OL	AL	ELL								
					TEACH *(continued)*						
BL	OL	AL	ELL		**StudentWorks™ Plus DVD**	✓	✓	✓	✓	✓	✓
BL	OL	AL	ELL		**Vocabulary PuzzleMaker CD-ROM**	✓	✓	✓	✓	✓	✓
Teacher Resources					**Building Academic Vocabulary**	✓	✓	✓	✓	✓	✓
					Reading Strategies and Activities for the Social Studies Classroom		p. 26		p. 26		
					Writer's Guidebook		p. 54	p. 47	p. 47		
					Strategies for Success	✓	✓	✓	✓	✓	✓
					Outline Map Resource Book	✓	✓	✓	✓	✓	✓
					Presentation Plus! with MindJogger DVD	✓	✓	✓	✓	✓	✓
					ASSESS						
BL	OL	AL	ELL		**Section Quizzes and Chapter Tests***		p. 67	p. 68	p. 69	p. 70	p. 71
BL	OL	AL	ELL		**Authentic Assessment With Rubrics**	✓	✓	✓	✓	✓	✓
BL	OL	AL	ELL		**Standardized Test Practice Workbook**	✓	✓	✓	✓	✓	✓
BL	OL	AL	ELL		***ExamView® Assessment Suite* CD-ROM**		6-1	6-2	6-3	6-4	Ch. 6
BL	OL	AL	ELL		**Interactive Tutor Self-Assessment CD-ROM**		6-1	6-2	6-3	6-4	
					CLOSE						
BL			ELL		**Reteaching Activity, URB**					p. 45	
BL	OL		ELL		**Reading and Study Skills Foldables™**	✓	✓	✓	✓	✓	✓

Using the Glencoe Web Site

Student Web Activities

Technology Product

The Glencoe Web site provides Web activities to students that reinforce and enrich chapter content. The Student Web Activities

- introduce *topics* relevant to chapter content, along with *links* to Web sites that provide information about the topics;
- prompt students to complete tasks specific to the activity;
- assess student comprehension of the material.

Objectives

The Student Web Activities help students

- learn online research and study skills;
- practice reading and comprehension skills.

Steps

Provide students with the following steps to complete the activities:

- Locate the Web page for the textbook being studied on the Glencoe Web site glencoe.com.
- Click on **Student Center** under the textbook title.
- In the Student Center, select a unit from the Unit Resources menu and a chapter from the Chapter Activities menu using the drop-down arrows.
- Click on the **Student Web Activities** link.
- Have students complete the activity on the page, clicking on the featured Web link for the chapter selected and answering the activity questions.

Provide students with an e-mail address to submit their answers for grading.

History ONLINE

	Student	Teacher	Parent
Beyond the Textbook	•	•	•
Chapter Overviews	•	•	•
Time Current Events	•		•
ePuzzles and Games	•		•
Concepts in Motion	•		•
Literature Connections		•	
Multi-Language Glossaries	•		•
Online Student Edition	•	•	•
Self-Check Quizzes	•		•
Student Web Activities	•		•
Study Central ™	•		•
Teaching Today		•	
Vocabulary eFlashcards	•		•
Web Activity Lesson Plans		•	

- **Timed Readings Plus in Social Studies** helps students increase their reading rate and fluency while maintaining comprehension. The 400-word passages are similar to those found on state and national assessments.
- **Reading in the Content Area: Social Studies** concentrates on six essential reading skills that help students better comprehend what they read. The book includes 75 high-interest nonfiction passages written at increasing levels of difficulty.
- **Reading Social Studies** includes strategic reading instruction and vocabulary support in Social Studies content for both ELLs and native speakers of English.

www.jamestowneducation.com

Index to National Geographic Magazine:

The following articles relate to this chapter:

- "Empty Quarter," by Donovan Webster, February 2005
- "Reaching for Power," by Janine Di Giovanni, June 2004
- "Beyond the Looting," by Andrew Lawler, October 2003
- "World of Islam," by Don Belt, January 2002

National Geographic Society Products To order the following, call National Geographic at 1-800-368-2728:

- *National Geographic Atlas of the World* (Book).
- *Ancient Civilizations: Egypt & Fertile Crescent* (CD-ROM).

Access National Geographic's new, dynamic MapMachine Web site and other geography resources at:

www.nationalgeographic.com

www.nationalgeographic.com/maps

Biography

The following videotape programs are available from Glencoe as supplements to Chapter 6:

- The Crusades (ISBN 1-56-501505-3)
- Legends of the Arabian Nights (ISBN 0-76-700232-6)

To order, call Glencoe at 1-800-334-7344. To find classroom resources to accompany many of these videos, check the following home pages:

A&E Television: www.aetv.com

The History Channel: www.historychannel.com

Reading List Generator CD-ROM

GLENCOE BOOKLINK 3

Use this database to search more than 30,000 titles to create a customized reading list for your students.

- Reading lists can be organized by students' reading level, author, genre, theme, or area of interest.
- The database provides Degrees of Reading Power™ (DRP) and Lexile™ readability scores for all selections.
- A brief summary of each selection is included.

Leveled reading suggestions for this chapter:

For students at a Grade 8 reading level:
- ***Turkey: A Question and Answer Book,*** by Mary Englar

For students at a Grade 9 reading level:
- ***Aladdin and Other Tales from the Arabian Nights,*** by Rosalind Kerven

For students at a Grade 10 reading level:
- ***Saladin: Noble Prince of Islam,*** by Diane Stanley

For students at a Grade 11 reading level:
- ***The Bedouin of the Middle East,*** by Elizabeth Losleben

For students at a Grade 12 reading level:
- ***Crusades: The Struggle for the Holy Lands,*** by Christopher Rice and Melanie Rice

Introducing
CHAPTER 6

Focus

MAKING CONNECTIONS

How can cities survive for thousands of years?

Activate students' prior knowledge by asking them to identify some of the world's oldest cities. *(Answers may include Athens, Beirut, Byblos, Delhi, Harappa, Jericho, Jerusalem, and Mohenjo-daro.)* Discuss similarities and differences in the history and geography of each city.

Teach

The Big Ideas

As students study the chapter, remind them to consider the section-based Big Ideas included in each section's Guide to Reading. The **Essential Questions** in the activities below tie in to the Big Ideas and help students think about and understand important chapter concepts. In addition, the Hands-on Chapter Projects with their culminating activities relate the content from each section to the Big Ideas. These activities build on each other as students progress through the chapter. Section activities culminate in the wrap-up activity on the Visual Summary page.

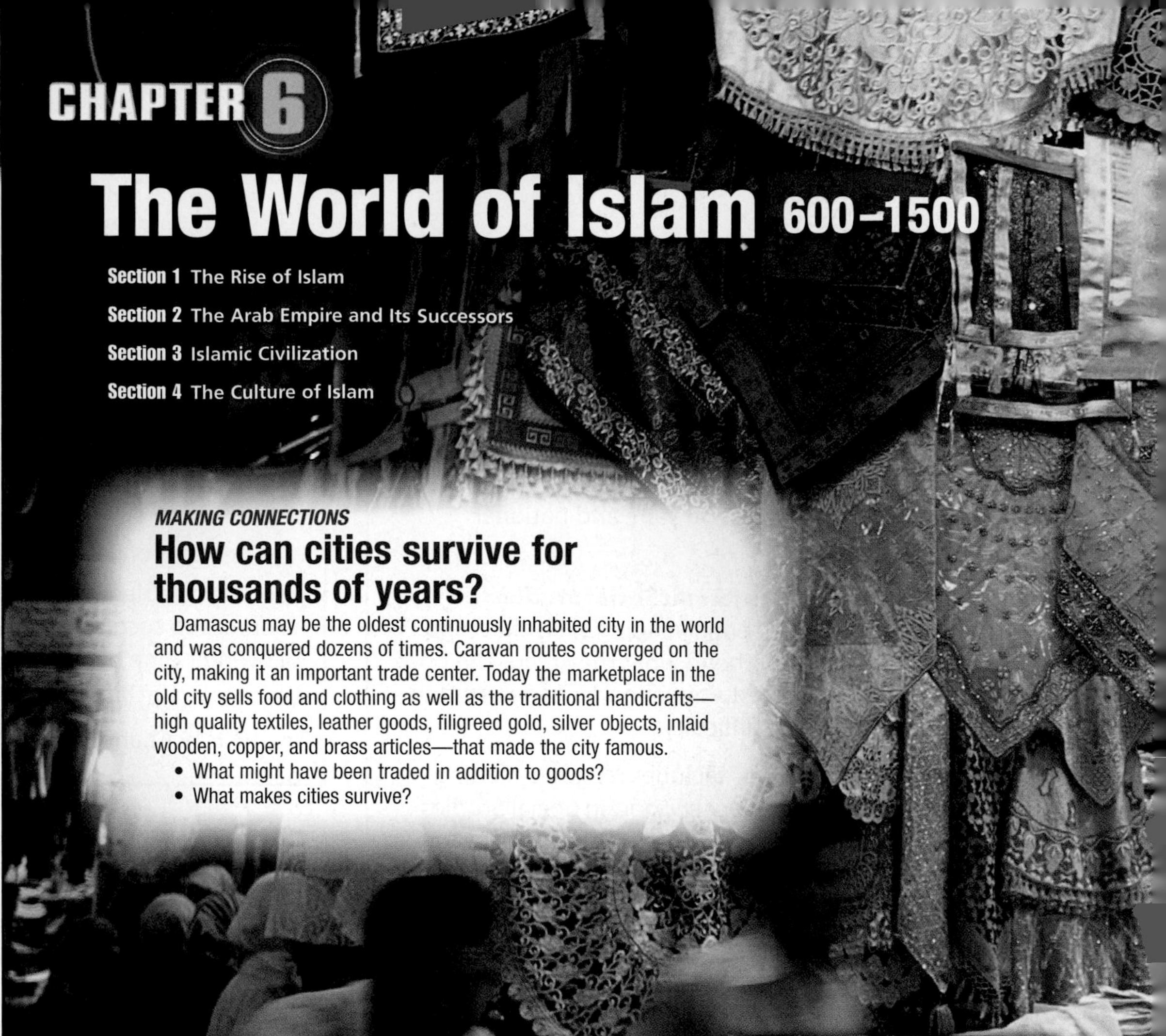

CHAPTER 6

The World of Islam 600–1500

MAKING CONNECTIONS

How can cities survive for thousands of years?

Damascus may be the oldest continuously inhabited city in the world and was conquered dozens of times. Caravan routes converged on the city, making it an important trade center. Today the marketplace in the old city sells food and clothing as well as the traditional handicrafts—high quality textiles, leather goods, filigreed gold, silver objects, inlaid wooden, copper, and brass articles—that made the city famous.

- What might have been traded in addition to goods?
- What makes cities survive?

ISLAMIC WORLD ▶

- **630** Muhammad returns to Makkah
- **732** Charles Martel defeats Arab forces at Battle of Tours
- **852** Great Mosque of Sāmarrā' finished

600 — 700 — 800 — 900

THE WORLD ▶

- **618** Tang dynasty begins in China
- **c. 800** Civilization at Teotihuacán collapses

186

The Rise of Islam

Essential Question: What are dominant religions in the world today? *(Students will probably answer Christianity, Islam, Judaism, Buddhism, and Hinduism.)* After students have discussed the question, tell them that in Section 1, they will learn about the origins and importance of Islam. **OL**

The Arab Empire and Its Successors

Tell students that within a few centuries of Islam's founding, Muslims had built an extensive empire. **Essential Question:** Why do people convert to a different faith? *(Answers may include that people are attracted by its message, they admire its leaders, or they want to fit in with those around them.)* Point out that in Section 2, students will learn how Muslims extended their rule over Southwestern Asia, parts of Africa, and into Europe. **OL**

Introducing
CHAPTER 6

More About the Photo

Visual Literacy Damascus, the capital of Syria, is thought to be one of the oldest continuously inhabited cities in the world. It is both modern and old, with the historic central core consisting of several bazaars, or covered streets that contain cafes and shops. Some streets or sections of the Old City sell specific merchandise, such as slippers or spices. Much of the jewelry, glassware, copperware, and cloth sold in the Old City is still traditionally handcrafted.

FOLDABLES Study Organizer **Dinah Zike's Foldables**

Dinah Zike's Foldables are three-dimensional, interactive graphic organizers that help students practice basic writing skills, review vocabulary terms, and identify main ideas. Instructions for creating and using Foldables can be found in the Appendix at the end of this book and in the *Dinah Zike's Reading and Study Skills Foldables* booklet.

History ONLINE

Introduce students to chapter content and key terms by having them access the Chapter 6 Overview at glencoe.com.

1187 Saladin's army invades Jerusalem

1382 Ibn-Khaldūn teaches at university in Cairo

1000 — 1200 — 1500

1347 Plague spreads to Italy and France

FOLDABLES Study Organizer

Analyzing Create a Folded Chart to record the advancements made by Muslims in philosophy, mathematics, science, medicine, art, and architecture. Names, places, and dates should be included on the chart.

History ONLINE
Chapter Overview—Visit glencoe.com to preview Chapter 6.

SECTION 3

Islamic Civilization

Tell students that despite the insistence of the Quran on equality, there was a distinct class system in Islamic society. **Essential Question:** **What factors may have influenced social status in the Islamic Empire?** *(Students may mention wealth, education, political power, and conversion to Islam.)* Point out that in Section 3, students will learn more about the economy, social structure, and daily lives of Muslims during the height of the empire. **OL**

SECTION 4

The Culture of Islam

Discuss with students how the Muslims of the early Middle Ages formed a bridge between the ancient civilizations and medieval Europe. **Essential Question:** **How do the achievements of one culture help to foster growth of another?** *(Cultures build on the accomplishments of earlier civilizations and extend their knowledge.)* Tell students that in Section 4, they will learn about the invaluable contributions of Muslims to Western civilization. **OL**

R Reading Strategy

Identifying Ask: What are the characteristics of Confucian society? *(It is hierarchical and ordered. Lower classes show respect to those higher in rank; those of elevated status take care of lower classes.)* OL

C Critical Thinking

Drawing Conclusions Ask: What does the symbol of the yin-yang reveal about the Confucian view of life's hardships? *(Possible answer: Dark and difficult events that cause sadness are as much a part of life as bright, happy times. The symbol shows that both are necessary for a complete and balanced life.)* OL

Confucianism

Confucianism began more than 2,500 years ago in China. Although considered a religion, it is actually a philosophy. It is based upon the teachings of Confucius, which are grounded in ethical behavior and good government.

The teachings of Confucius focused on three areas: social philosophy, political philosophy, and education. Confucius taught that relationships are based on rank. Persons of higher rank are responsible for caring for those of lower rank. Those of lower rank should respect and obey those of higher rank. Eventually his teachings spread from China to other East Asian societies.

Students studying Confucianism, Chunghak-dong, South Korea

The Analects

Sacred Text Confucius was famous for his sayings and proverbs. These teachings were gathered into a book called the *Analects* after Confucius's death. Below is an example of Confucius's teachings.

Confucius said:

> *"To learn and to practice what is learned time and again is pleasure, is it not? To have friends come from afar is happiness, is it not? To be unperturbed when not appreciated by others is gentlemanly, is it not?"*
>
> —*The* Analects

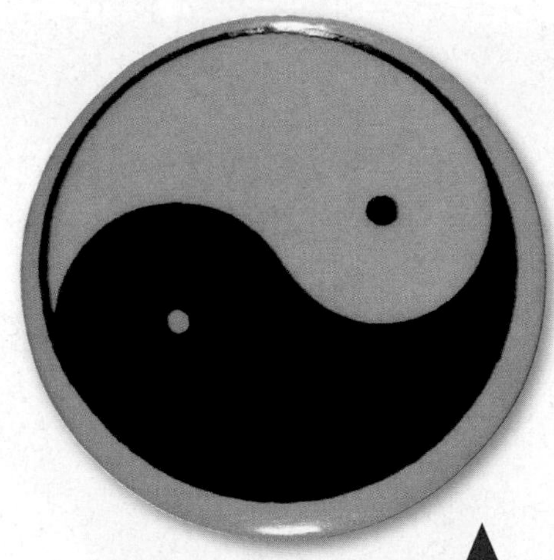

Sacred Symbol The symbol of Confucianism, yin-yang, symbolizes the harmony the philosophy offers. The white is *yin*, the light, bright, cheerful, playful aspect of life. The black is *yang*, the dark, mysterious, serious part of life. The two act together to balance one another.

Additional Support

Activity: Interdisciplinary Connection

Literature Tell students that through his teaching, Confucius both affirmed traditional values and illuminated new truths. Although Confucianism fell out of favor under the Communist regime in China, in recent years, his teachings have been viewed more favorably. To help students better understand the wisdom of Confucius, have them locate copies of the *Analects*, either in the library or on the Internet. Ask students to choose ten or more quotations that they find meaningful. Have students copy the quotations, explain them in their own words, and give examples of how they might be applied today. Have students share their interpretations. **Ask:** Why might societies and governments still find meaning in the words of Confucius? *(Answers may include that wisdom endures through all ages. Confucius conveys truths, not just about contemporary situations, but about the human condition.)* AL

Sacred Site The temple at Qufu is a group of buildings dedicated to Confucius. It is located on Confucius's ancestral land. It is one of the largest ancient architectural complexes in China. Every year followers gather at Qufu to celebrate the birthday of Confucius.

Worship and Celebration Confucianism does not have a god or clergy, but there are temples dedicated to Confucius, the spiritual leader. Those who follow his teachings see Confucianism as a way of life and a guide to ethical behavior and good government. C

C Critical Thinking

Comparing and Contrasting Have students review what they have learned about Buddhism and Christianity. **Ask:** How is Confucianism similar to and different from Christianity and Buddhism? (***Similarities:*** *All three religions advocate trying to live a virtuous life and one that has meaning; in all three, there is an individual who is the source of wisdom and the model for followers; all three have sites of worship or places to gather.* ***Differences:*** *Confucianism does not concern itself with an afterlife. Confucianism grew out of secular concerns.)* OL

Differentiated Instruction

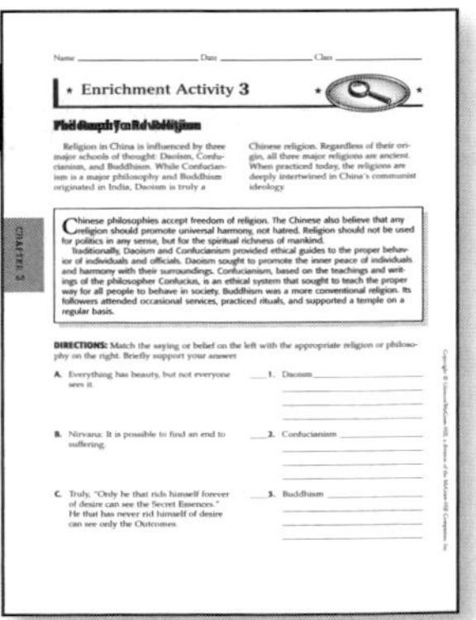

Enrichment Activity, URB (Unit 1) p. 118

Comparing and Contrasting

Objective: Compare and contrast China's religious traditions.

Focus: Discuss the origins of Confucianism, Daoism, and Buddhism.

Teach: Assign teams of students to research one of the three religions.

Assess: Have teams create charts illustrating important ideas.

Close: Discuss significant differences and similarities among the religions.

Differentiated Instruction Strategies

BL Have teams research one religion and volunteer what they learn. Record their ideas in a three-column chart.

AL Have students research and compare the influence of each religion on modern Chinese life.

ELL Read the passage aloud before recording differences and similarities in a three-way Venn diagram.

Introducing CHAPTER 8

Focus

MAKING CONNECTIONS

How does architecture record history?

Discuss public buildings in your community, such as schools and libraries, and private ones, such as banks and office towers. Ask students how the building's architecture reflects the time it was built and its current use. You may want to note the example of factories built in the 1800s and early 1900s. These buildings fell into disrepair as jobs moved south or overseas. In recent times, many of these buildings—with their distinctive wood floors and brick walls—have been converted into new uses, such as for offices, restaurants, retail shops, and condominiums. To close the discussion, have students choose a building in your community and write about what they think it will look like and be used for 50 years from now.

Teach

The Big Ideas

As students study the chapter, remind them to consider the section-based Big Ideas included in each section's Guide to Reading. The **Essential Questions** in the activities below tie in to the Big Ideas and help students think about and understand important chapter concepts. In addition, the Hands-on Chapter Projects with their culminating activities relate the content from each section to the Big Ideas. These activities build on each other as students progress through the chapter. Section activities culminate in the wrap-up activity on the Visual Summary page.

CHAPTER 8

The Asian World 400–1500

MAKING CONNECTIONS

How does architecture record history?

Angkor Wat is a symbol of Cambodia and appears on its flag. First built by the Khmer as a Hindu temple, it has served as a Buddhist shrine since the fourteenth century. Although most of the walls have carvings of Hindu stories, there are images of the Buddha. In this chapter you will learn about the changes in the Asian world.

- How does the architecture in your city or state relate to its history?
- Which structures have been changed based on their use?

ASIA ▶

- **c. 600** Silk Road trade flourishes during Tang dynasty
- **802** Jayavarman II unites Khmer of Angkor
- **c. 1000** Chinese invent movable type

500 — 700 — 900

THE WORLD ▶

- **565** Roman Emperor Justinian dies
- **c. 800** Maya civilization declines

262

China Reunified

Essential Question: What was the result of the collapse of the Han Dynasty? *(China suffered three hundred years of chaos and disorder.)* Point out that in Section 1 students will learn about the dynasties that once again unified China and brought a long period of progress and prosperity. **OL**

The Mongols and China

Essential Question: What do you think were strengths of the Mongolian military? *(As a pastoral people, they were skilled horsemen and used this expertise in military attacks.)* Point out that in Section 2 students will learn how the Mongols conquered China, bringing order and prosperity, while keeping apart from Chinese society. **OL**

Introducing
CHAPTER 8

More About the Photo

Visual Literacy Have students try to imagine how such a magnificent complex as Angkor Wat could have been largely ignored for centuries. During this time, it was overgrown by the jungle, eroded by weathering, looted, then severely damaged by the Khmer Rouge in the 1970s and 1980s. Although Angkor Wat is now a protected World Heritage Site, looting still occurs. Nearly one million tourists visit each year, also threatening its preservation.

Dinah Zike's Foldables

Dinah Zike's Foldables are three-dimensional, interactive graphic organizers that help students practice basic writing skills, review vocabulary terms, and identify main ideas. Instructions for creating and using Foldables can be found in the Appendix at the end of this book and in the *Dinah Zike's Reading and Study Skills Foldables* booklet.

History ONLINE

Introduce students to chapter content and key terms by having them access the Chapter 8 Overview at glencoe.com.

1192 Minamoto Yoritomo establishes Kamakura shogunate

1206 Mongols elect Temüjin Genghis Khan

1100 — 1300 — 1500

1325 Mansa Mūsā begins Timbuktu mosque

FOLDABLES™ Study Organizer

Identifying Create a Four-Tab Book to record Who, What, When, and Where facts while you read about Kublai Khan or Genghis Khan.

Who / What / When / Where

History ONLINE
Chapter Overview—Visit glencoe.com to preview Chapter 8.

Early Japan and Korea

Essential Question: How did Japan's geography affect its development? *(It helped Japan keep out invaders, but also enabled Japan to isolate itself.)* Point out that in Section 3 students will learn how Japan developed and interacted with other cultures. OL

India After the Guptas

Essential Question: Which religions had a major impact in Indian society? *(Buddhism, Hinduism, Islam)* Point out that in Section 4 students will learn how different religions influenced culture in India. OL

Civilization in Southeast Asia

Essential Question: Which civilizations most influenced Southeast Asia? *(China, India)* Point out that in Section 5 students will learn how India and China affected the development of Southeast Asia. OL

SECTION 1

China Reunified

Focus

Bellringer

Daily Focus Transparency 8.1

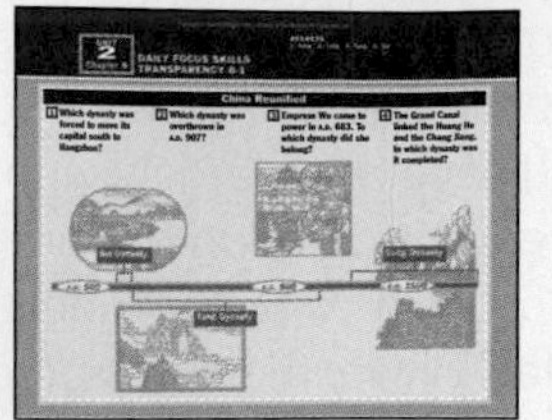

GUIDE TO READING

Answers to Graphic:
Sui: 581–618, Sui Yangdi, high taxes, extravagant and luxurious lifestyle, and military failures, caused a rebellion; **Tang:** 618–907, Tang Xuanzang, corruption and rebellion; **Song:** 960–1279, conquered by Mongols

Section Spotlight Video

To generate student interest and provide a springboard for class discussion, access the Chapter 8, Section 1 video at glencoe.com or on the video DVD.

Resource Manager

GUIDE TO READING

The BIG Idea
Order and Security After centuries of chaos and civil war, three dynasties unified China, bringing peace, stability, and technological progress.

Content Vocabulary
- scholar-gentry *(p. 269)*
- dowry *(p. 269)*

Academic Vocabulary
- period *(p. 266)*
- complexity *(p. 267)*

People and Places
- Sui Yangdi *(p. 264)*
- Tibet *(p. 265)*
- Tang Xuanzang *(p. 265)*
- Uighurs *(p. 266)*
- Hangzhou *(p. 266)*
- Changan *(p. 268)*
- Marco Polo *(p. 269)*
- Wu Zhao *(p. 269)*

Reading Strategy
Summarizing Information As you read, create three charts like the one shown below to help you study. Summarize the time periods, the most important rulers, and the reasons for decline of the Sui, Tang, and Song dynasties.

In 581 the Sui dynasty succeeded in unifying China for the first time in hundreds of years. Over the next several centuries, with only a brief period of disorder in the 900s, a series of three dynasties would bring progress and stability to China. During this period, China would invent block printing and gunpowder, participate in increased foreign trade, and reinstitute a merit-based system of civil service.

Three Dynasties

MAIN IDEA The Sui, Tang, and Song dynasties restored peace to China in between periods of chaos and disorder.

HISTORY & YOU Do you know what tests are required to qualify for government jobs in the United States? Learn about merit-based civil service in early China.

The Han dynasty is considered to have set the standard for the Chinese dynasties that followed. In fact, the Chinese word for someone who is Chinese means "a man of Han."

The Sui Dynasty

The Han dynasty came to an end in 220, and China fell into chaos. For the next three hundred years, the Chinese suffered through disorder and civil war. Then, in 581, a new Chinese empire was set up under a dynasty known as the Sui (SWAY). The Sui dynasty (581–618) did not last long, but it managed to unify China once again under the emperor's authority.

Sui Yangdi, the second emperor of the dynasty, completed the Grand Canal, built to link the two great rivers of China, the Huang He (Yellow River) and the Chang Jiang (Yangtze River). Both rivers flowed from west to east. The new canal linked north and south, making it easier to ship rice from the south to the north.

Sui Yangdi was a cruel ruler. He used forced labor to build the Grand Canal, which he used to keep an eye on his empire. This practice, together with high taxes, his extravagant and luxurious lifestyle, and military failures, caused a rebellion. The emperor was murdered, and his dynasty came to an end.

The Tang Dynasty

A new dynasty, the Tang (TAHNG), soon emerged. It would last for nearly three hundred years, from 618 until 907. The early Tang rulers began their reigns by instituting reforms, as rulers often did in the early days of new dynasties. They tried to create a more

R Reading Strategies	C Critical Thinking	D Differentiated Instruction	W Writing Support	S Skill Practice
Teacher Edition • Making Connections, p. 265 • Summarizing, p. 269 **Additional Resources** • Econ. & Hist. Act., URB p. 5 • Guid. Read. Act., URB p. 122 • Read. Ess. & Note-Taking Guide, p. 82	**Teacher Edition** • Making Inferences, p. 267 • Pred. Consequences, p. 267 **Additional Resources** • Hist. Analysis Skills Act., URB p. 92 • People in World Hist. Act., URB p. 113 • Section Quiz, p. 91	**Teacher Edition** • Adv. Learners, p. 266 **Additional Resources** • Diff. Instr. Act., URB p. 93 • English Learner Act., URB p. 95 • Read. Strat. for SS, p. 47	**Teacher Edition** • Narrative Writing, p. 266 • Personal Writing, p. 268 **Additional Resources** • Linking Past/Present Act., URB p. 112 • Writer's Guidebook, p. 12	**Teacher Edition** • Using Geo. Skills, p. 265 **Additional Resources** • Chart. Graph. Act., URB p. 3 • Coop. Learn. Act., URB p. 107 • Read. Strat. for SS, p. 62

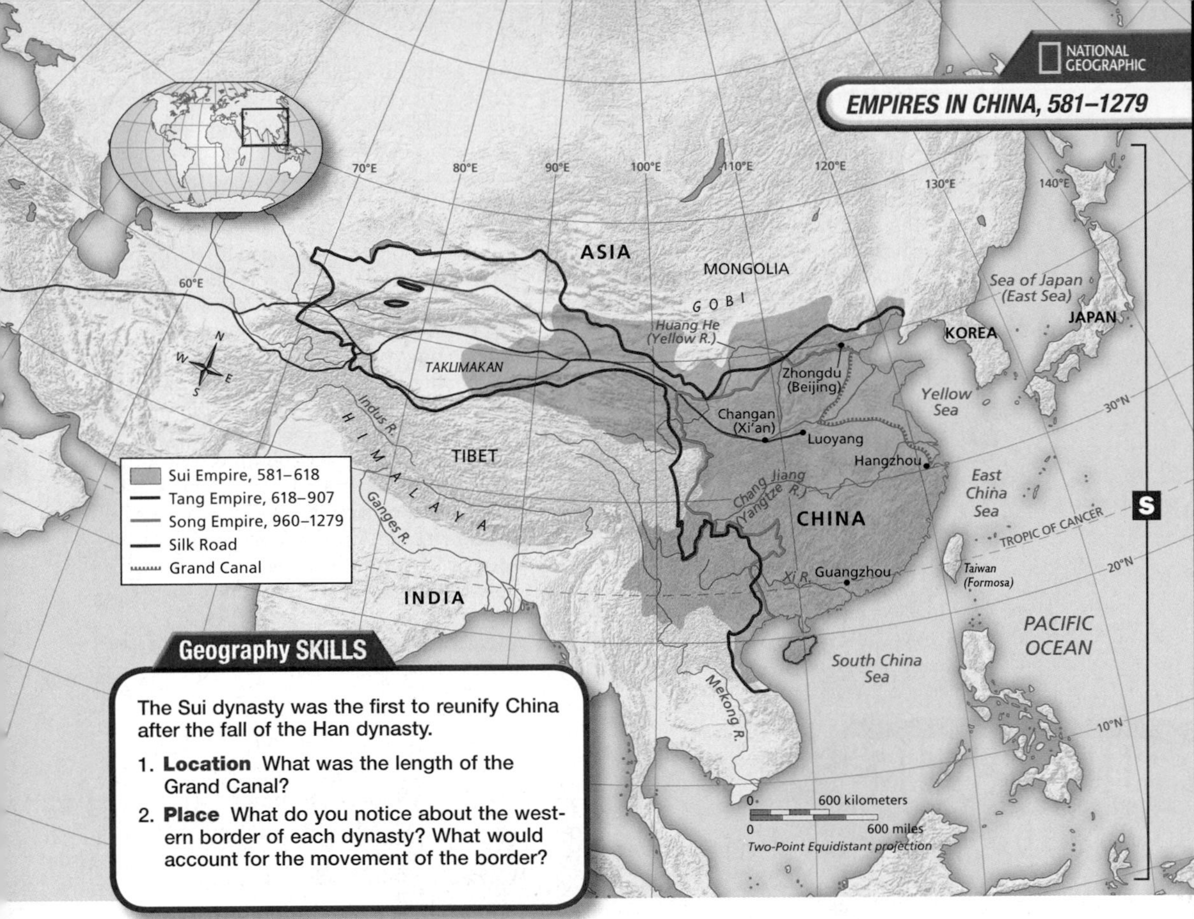

Geography SKILLS

The Sui dynasty was the first to reunify China after the fall of the Han dynasty.

1. **Location** What was the length of the Grand Canal?
2. **Place** What do you notice about the western border of each dynasty? What would account for the movement of the border?

stable economy by giving land to the peasants and breaking up the power of the owners of the large estates. They also restored the civil service examination from earlier times to serve as the chief method of recruiting officials for the civilian bureaucracy.

The civil service examination tested a student's grasp of Confucian principles. Young men who were preparing to take the examination memorized all of the Confucian classics. During their studies, they had little free time for recreation and were forbidden to take part in any strenuous physical activities. They were taught never to use their hands except for painting or writing. Even after many years of education, only about one in five students managed to pass the examination and receive a position in the civil service.

Tang rulers worked hard to restore the power of China in East Asia. They brought peace to northwestern China and expanded their control to the borders of **Tibet,** an area north of the Himalaya. China claimed to be the greatest power in East Asia. Neighboring states, including Korea, offered tribute to China. The Chinese imperial court also set up trade and diplomatic relations with the states of Southeast Asia.

Like the Han, however, the Tang sowed the seeds of their own destruction. Tang rulers were unable to prevent plotting and government corruption. One emperor was especially unfortunate.

Emperor **Tang Xuanzang** (SHWAHN• DZAHNG) is remembered for his devotion to a commoner's daughter, Yang Guifei. To entertain her, he kept hundreds of dancers and musicians at court.

Teach

S Skill Practice

Using Geography Skills Ask: Why do you think the Silk Road takes several different routes in western Asia? *(Answers may include: to connect to more trading centers; to avoid mountains.)* **BL**

For additional practice on this skill, see the **Skills Handbook**.

R Reading Strategy

Making Connections Have students discuss the Tang dynasty's civil service test. **Ask:** How does this process compare to college "prep" testing today? *(Like today, the test was very important for people's futures, and rigorous preparation was required.)* **OL**

Geography SKILLS

Answers:

1. about 1,100 miles (1,171 km), or the equivalent of about half the length of China running north/south
2. Border changes reflect each dynasty's relationship with Tibet and other states.

Hands-On Chapter Project
Step 1

Planning a Web Site for Early Asian History

Pairs of students will begin to plan a Web site on important developments in early Asian history.

Step 1: Developments in Early China

Essential Question: What were the key historical developments in early Asia?

Directions: Student pairs begin to plan a Web site on early Asian developments that includes one Web page for each section of the chapter, plus a home page. (Depending on availability, Web pages can be created using computer resources; otherwise, they can be created on paper.) For each section's Web page, students should find or create one image and write text that explains the background and significance of their selected development. For Section 1, students will choose one key aspect of early China, such as reforms under the Tang dynasty.

Summarizing: Allow time for groups to discuss what they learned about the Big Idea during this activity. **OL**

(Chapter Project is continued in Section 2.)

W Writing Support

Narrative Writing Ask students to review the story of Tang Xuanzang. Then have them do additional research and write a narrative of the story in their own words. OL

D Differentiated Instruction

Advanced Learners Discuss the concept of mercenaries as illustrated by the hiring of Uighurs during the Tang dynasty. Then ask students to research and report on other uses of mercenaries in history. AL

✓Reading Check

Answer: In contrast to the Sui rulers, the Tang rulers reinstituted civil service exams, gave land to peasants, broke up the power of the large landowners, and brought peace to northern China.

He also ordered riders to travel thousands of miles to bring her fresh fruit.

Finally, the emperor's favorite general led a bloody revolt. The army demanded that someone be held accountable for the W war and strife in the country. For this reason the emperor invited his true love to hang herself from a nearby tree, although it is said that for the rest of his life, the emperor "washed his face everyday with a fountain of tears."

During the eighth century, the Tang dynasty weakened and became prey to rebellions. Tang rulers hired **Uighurs** D (WEE•GURZ), a northern tribal group of Turkic-speaking people, to fight for the dynasty. Continued unrest, however, led to the collapse of Tang rule in 907.

The Song Dynasty

In 960 a new dynasty known as the Song (SUNG) rose to power. The Song ruled during a **period** of economic prosperity and cultural achievement, from 960 to 1279. From the start, however, the Song also experienced problems, especially from northern neighbors. These groups crossed into northern China and occupied large parts of Chinese territory. Because of this threat, Song rulers were forced to move the imperial court farther south to **Hangzhou** (HAHNG•JOH), on the coast just south of the Chang Jiang river delta. The Song also lost control over Tibet.

The Song dynasty could never overcome the challenge from the north. During the 1200s, the Mongols—a nomadic people from the Gobi—carried out wars of conquest and built a vast empire. Within 70 years, they controlled all of China. The Song had formed a defensive alliance with the Mongols. As we shall see, however, the Mongols overthrew the Song and created a new Mongol dynasty in China.

✓Reading Check **Contrasting** How did the Tang and Sui rulers differ?

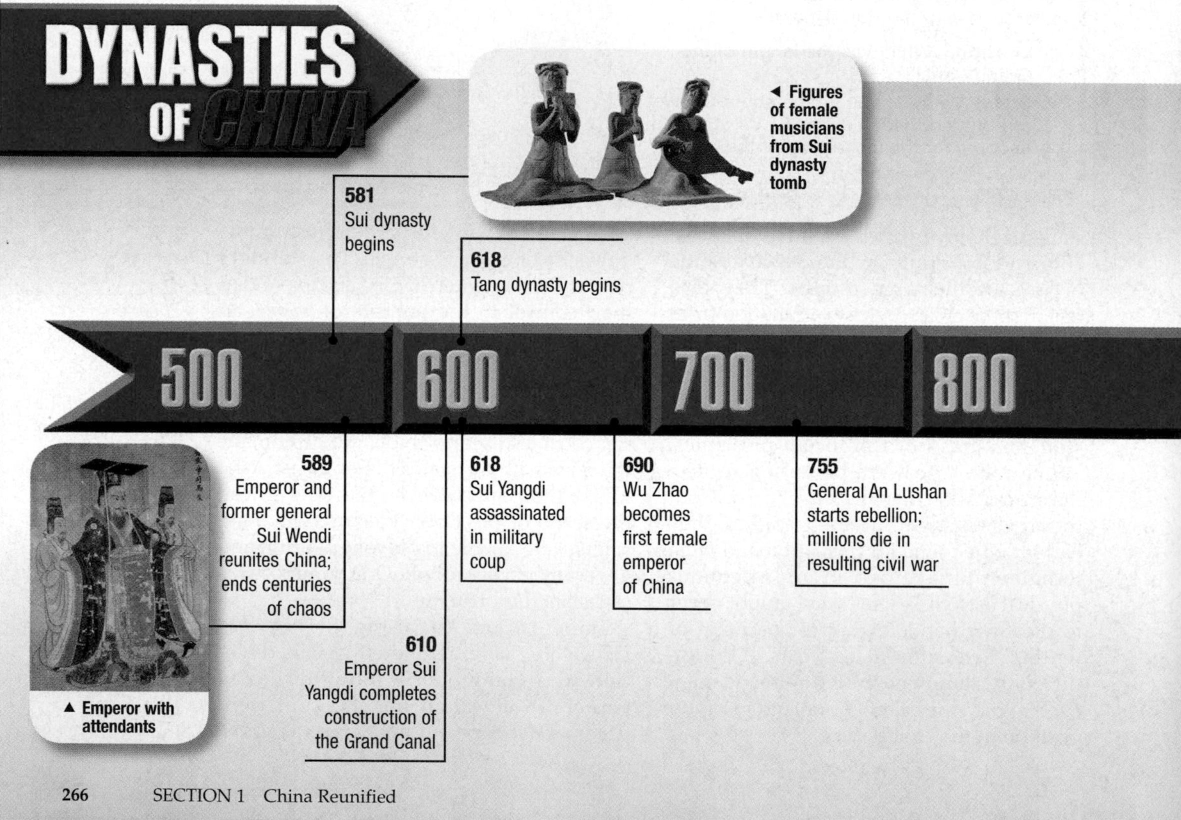

◄ Figures of female musicians from Sui dynasty tomb

▲ Emperor with attendants

Additional Support

Activity: Collaborative Learning

Expanding the Dynasties of China Time Line Review the time line with students. Discuss the span of time covered and the types of information highlighted by the entries. Point out the layout of the illustrations and the lines used to organize the time line. Then form small groups and assign each one a ruler from the time line on this page. Have each group research the ruler and create a time line of his or her life. (Group time lines should also list the related dynasty dates from the time line on this page.) Then have each group post their completed time line on a classroom wall or bulletin board to form an expanded time line of the Dynasties of China. **Ask:** **By expanding the time line, what more does it tell us about this time period in China's history?** *(Answers will vary, but should be based on logical conclusions.)* OL

Government and Economy

MAIN IDEA For 700 years, the Chinese economy grew in size and sophistication.

HISTORY & YOU Would you be able to survive as a farmer? Learn about the lives of peasants during the Tang dynasty and the Song dynasty.

The era from the beginning of the Sui dynasty to the end of the Song dynasty lasted nearly 700 years. During that period, a mature political system based on principles first put into practice during the Qin and Han dynasties gradually emerged in China. As in the Han era, China was a monarchy that employed a relatively large bureaucracy. Confucian ideals were still the cement that held the system together.

During the long period between the Sui and Song dynasties, the Chinese economy grew in size and **complexity.** Agriculture flourished, and manufacturing and trade grew dramatically.

China was still primarily a farming society. In the long period of civil war, aristocratic families had taken control of most of the land, and the majority of peasants had become serfs or slaves. The Song government, however, worked to weaken the power of the large landholders and help poor peasants obtain their own land. These reform efforts and improved farming techniques led to an abundance of food. C1

In Chinese cities, technological developments added new products and stimulated trade. During the Tang dynasty, for example, the Chinese began to make steel by mixing cast iron and wrought iron in a blast furnace, which was heated by the burning of coal. The steel was then used to make swords and sickles. The introduction of cotton made it possible to make new kinds of clothes.

Another Chinese innovation, gunpowder, was created during the Tang dynasty. C2

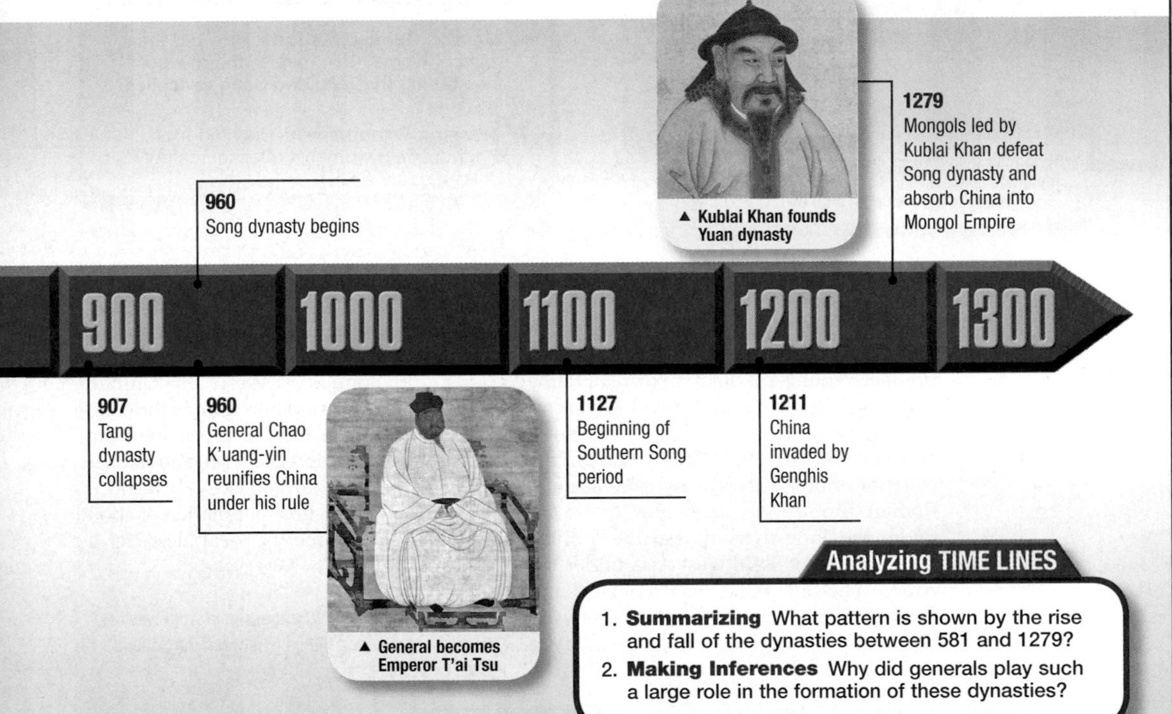

Analyzing TIME LINES

1. **Summarizing** What pattern is shown by the rise and fall of the dynasties between 581 and 1279?
2. **Making Inferences** Why did generals play such a large role in the formation of these dynasties?

C1 Critical Thinking

Making Inferences Ask: Why do you think Chinese agriculture, manufacturing, and trade flourished during this period? *(It was a period of relative stability with a strong government and local control.)* **OL**

C2 Critical Thinking

Predicting Consequences
Ask: What do you think the result of the invention of gunpowder will be? *(It was an initial military advantage for the Chinese, but later spread to other cultures and led to the invention of more deadly weapons.)* **OL**

Analyzing TIME LINES

Answers:

1. Possible answers: Long periods of relative unity were interrupted by shorter periods of division; new emperors were often generals; unrest often took place in the north.
2. Generals have military might at their command, so they have the ability to unite and control large areas of land.

Activity: Interdisciplinary Connection

Science Ask students to research the differences in iron and steel. Note that steel was produced by accident at first. Small groups can prepare a short report and possibly a diagram or display which illustrates the differences in the two as well as their relative strengths. After the reports are given, discuss their findings. **Ask:** What advantages does a society that can produce steel have over one that can only produce iron? *(stronger tools and military weapons)* **OL**

Teacher Tip

Researching Before students begin their research, review your expectations concerning plagiarism and sources. Discuss how you want students to record information about their sources and if you want actual copies. Remind students that diagrams and illustrations they use or adapt should also have source information.

W Writing Support

Personal Writing Ask students to write about the issue of social expectations and the possible repercussions from not meeting them. Suggest to students that they reread the information about foot binding. **Ask:** Are there things that you are expected to do? *(Answers may include dressing a certain way, addressing older people a certain way.)* **AL**

✓Reading Check

Answer: The Silk Road was revived; trade with regions near China increased.

DOCUMENT-BASED QUESTIONS

Answers:

1. Although some women were educated and had some freedoms, women were still treated as social inferiors to men.
2. Foot binding kept women from being physically active or self-sufficient, which limited their independence.

INFOGRAPHICS

The Role of Women in the Tang and Song Dynasties

During the Tang dynasty, Wu Zhao began as the emperor's concubine and became Empress Wu, ruling in her own right after 690.

One of the most famous women of the Tang dynasty is Empress Wu. Born Wu Zhao, she became mistress to the emperor in 649. She so longed for power that she accused the empress of a crime. The emperor deposed his wife and chose Wu Zhao as his new empress. After his death she gained supreme power.

Known for her ruthlessness, she was also a strong leader. She was the first ruler to give graduates of the civil service examinations the highest government positions. She also formed an alliance with Korea and lowered taxes.

Most women, however, had few rights and privileges during the Tang dynasty. Women were allowed to join in sports such as horseback riding and polo, and activities such as dancing and playing music. Most marriages were arranged, and a woman was permitted to marry only once in her lifetime.

W During the Song dynasty, the practice of foot binding became popular among upper-class women. Foot binding, which made feet unnaturally small, permanently deformed women's feet, caused great pain, and often made women unable to stand or walk without assistance. A woman's willingness to bind her feet was considered a sign of her virtue. On the other hand, two-thirds of aristocratic women in the Song dynasty were literate and well-educated. Some women benefited from new inheritance rights. If there was no male heir, the estate could pass to a woman in the family.

DOCUMENT-BASED QUESTIONS

1. **Making Generalizations** How did the roles of women compare to the roles of men during the Tang and Song dynasties in China?
2. **Drawing Conclusions** How did foot binding affect women's roles in society?

It was used to make explosives and a primitive flamethrower called a fire-lance. The fire-lance could spit out a mixture of flame and projectiles that could travel 40 yards.

Long-distance trade had declined between the 300s and 500s as a result of the collapse of both the Han dynasty and the Roman Empire. Trade began to revive under the Tang dynasty and the unification of much of Southwest Asia under the Arabs. The Silk Road was renewed and thrived as caravans carried goods between China and the regions of Southwest Asia and South Asia.

Trade with regions near China, such as Japan and Korea, also increased during the Tang and Song dynasties. The Chinese exported tea, silk, and porcelain to the countries beyond the South China Sea. In return, they received exotic woods, precious stones, and various tropical goods. As a result of trade, **Changan**, with a population of about two million, became the wealthiest city in the world.

✓Reading Check **Comparing** In what ways did trade improve during the time between the Sui and Song dynasties?

Differentiated Instruction

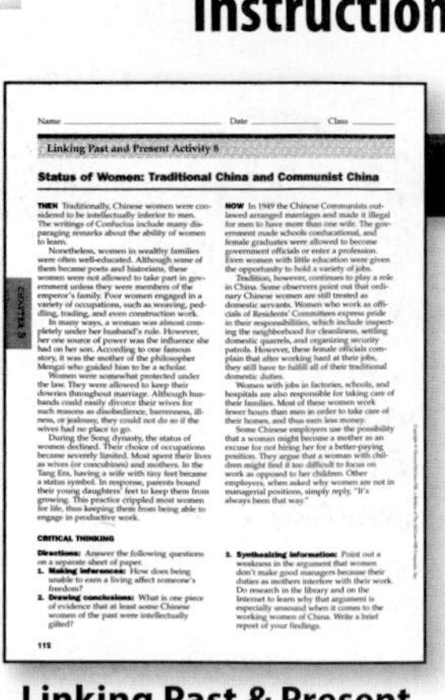

Linking Past and Present Activity 8

Status of Women: Traditional China and Communist China

Linking Past & Present Activity, URB p. 112

Comparing and Contrasting

Objective: Compare and contrast women's status in China then and now.

Focus: Synthesize information about women's roles in China.

Teach: Ask students to identify changes in women's status in China today.

Assess: Have students discuss their answers to questions 1 and 2.

Close: Discuss whether Chinese women have more influence today or in the past.

Differentiated Instruction Strategies

BL Ask students to suggest ways a parent can influence a son or daughter.

AL Ask students to research foot-binding and report on its influence today.

ELL Discuss the sentence "It's always that way" in the final paragraph. Talk about other traditions that continue for the same reason.

Chinese Society

MAIN IDEA The political stability established by the three dynasties allowed Chinese society to grow in complexity.

HISTORY & YOU How does the status of women today compare with the status of women in early China? Read about Chinese society and the status of women.

Economic changes had an impact on Chinese society. For wealthier city dwellers, the Tang and Song eras were an age of prosperity. There was probably no better example than the Song capital of Hangzhou. In the late 1200s, the Italian merchant **Marco Polo** described the city to European readers as one of the largest and wealthiest cities on Earth. "So many pleasures may be found," he said, "that one fancies himself to be in Paradise."

For rich Chinese during this period, life offered many pleasures. There were new forms of entertainment, such as playing cards and chess (brought from India). The paddle-wheel boat and horseback riding (made possible by the introduction of the stirrup) made travel easier. The invention of block printing in the eighth century provided new ways to communicate.

The vast majority of the Chinese people still lived off the land in villages. Most peasants never left their villages except for an occasional visit to a nearby market town. Changes were taking place in the countryside, however. Before, there had been a great gulf between wealthy landowners and poor peasants. A more complex mixture of landowners, free peasants, sharecroppers, and landless laborers now emerged.

Most significant was the rise of the landed gentry. This R group controlled much of the land and at the same time produced most of the candidates for the civil service. The **scholar-gentry,** as this class was known, replaced the old landed aristocracy as the political and economic elite of Chinese society.

Few Chinese women had any power. An exception was **Wu Zhao** (WOO JOW), known as Empress Wu. The concubine of the second Tang emperor, she then became empress of China and ruled for half a century.

As in other parts of the world, female children were considered less desirable than male children. In times of famine, female infants might be killed if there was not enough food to feed the whole family. When a girl married, she became part of her husband's family. In addition, a girl's parents were expected to provide a **dowry**—money, goods, or property—to her husband when she married. Poor families often sold their daughters to wealthy villagers.

✓Reading Check **Identifying** Which group in Chinese society replaced the landed aristocracy?

Vocabulary

1. **Explain** the significance of: Sui Yangdi, Tibet, Tang Xuanzang, Uighurs, period, Hangzhou, complexity, Changan, Marco Polo, scholar-gentry, Wu Zhao, dowry

Main Ideas

2. **Describe** the process of studying for the civil service examination during the Tang and Song dynasties.
3. **List** China's main exports and imports during the Tang and Song dynasties.
4. **Create** a diagram like the one shown below to compare and contrast the status of women in early China with the status of women in the United States today.

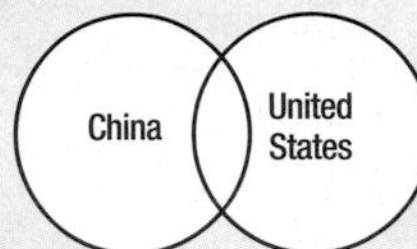

Critical Thinking

5. **The BIG Idea** **Hypothesizing** If China had never been unified by the dynasties, how might society in China have been different during this period?
6. **Assessing** The Chinese form of government was adopted by many other countries. Describe the basis for the Chinese form of government and evaluate its effectiveness.
7. **Analyzing Visuals** Examine the painting of Wu Zhao on page 268. What indicates her status in Chinese society?

Writing About History

8. **Expository Writing** Suppose that you have just heard about one of the Tang dynasty innovations, perhaps the process of making steel, but you do not understand it. Write a letter of inquiry to the Tang emperor asking for more information.

History ONLINE

For help with the concepts in this section of *Glencoe World History*, go to glencoe.com and click Study Central™.

R Reading Strategy

Summarizing Have students summarize the most important change to China's countryside. *(Possible answer: More social classes emerged.)* OL

Answer: scholar-gentry, because they controlled much of the land and produced most of the candidates for civil service

Assess

History ONLINE

Study Central provides summaries, interactive games, and online graphic organizers to help students review content.

Close

Making Generalizations

Ask: What areas of Chinese society grew stronger during this period? *(the economy, government, science and technology, culture in cities)* OL

Answers

1. Definitions for the vocabulary words are found in the section and the Glossary.
2. memorized Confucian classics, learned to paint and write, did not participate in physical activities
3. **Exports:** tea, silk, porcelain; **Imports:** exotic woods, precious stones, tropical goods
4. **China:** few had power, undesirable as children, arranged marriage, inferior to men, some could read and write; **United States:** women have power, can read and write, equal to men, choose own husband
5. Disorder and civil war might have continued.
6. China was a monarchy with a large bureaucracy; country divided into provinces, districts, villages; used civil service exams to select civil servants by merit; competent bureaucrats were very effective.
7. Her fine jewelry and clothing indicate her high status.
8. Letters should be consistent with material presented in the section.

Focus

Bellringer

Daily Focus Transparency 8.2

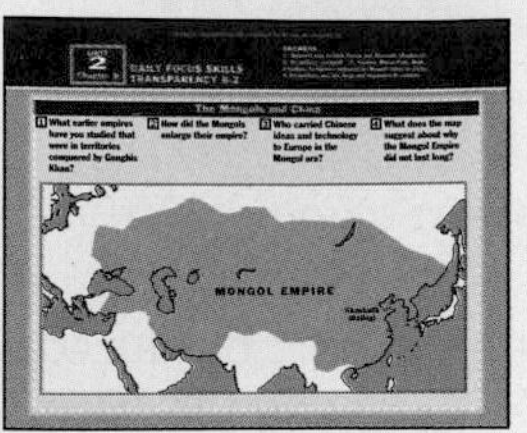

GUIDE TO READING

Answers to Graphic:

Causes: Temüjin unifies the Mongols; Temüjin elected Genghis Khan; Genghis Khan devotes himself to conquest; Mongols attack China, encountering gunpowder and the firelance; firelance evolves into more effective handgun and cannon.

Section Spotlight Video

To generate student interest and provide a springboard for class discussion, access the Chapter 8, Section 2 video at glencoe.com or on the video DVD.

SECTION 2

The Mongols and China

GUIDE TO READING

The BIG Idea

Ideas, Beliefs, and Values Shifts in religious belief caused major changes in the organization of Chinese society, which were intensified when the Mongol Empire conquered China.

Content Vocabulary

- khanate *(p. 270)*
- porcelain *(p. 275)*
- neo-Confucianism *(p. 273)*

Academic Vocabulary

- acquired *(p. 273)*
- vision *(p. 275)*
- available *(p. 274)*

People and Places

- Mongolia *(p. 270)*
- Beijing *(p. 271)*
- Genghis Khan *(p. 270)*
- Li Bo *(p. 274)*
- Gobi *(p. 270)*
- Du Fu *(p. 274)*
- Kublai Khan *(p. 271)*

Reading Strategy

Cause and Effect As you read, use a chart like the one below to help you study how the Mongols acquired the world's largest land empire.

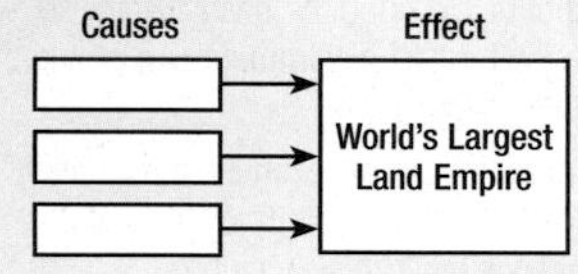

At the time of the Mongol invasion, art and literature in China were in the middle of a golden age, spurred, in part, by the invention of porcelain and the printing press. Also, religious attitudes were changing in favor of a revived Confucianism, which would remain the basis of Chinese government for centuries.

The Mongols

MAIN IDEA The Mongols created the world's largest land empire by conquering all of China.

HISTORY & YOU What do you think drove rulers to expand their empires? How would the lives of the citizens of these conquered lands have to change?

Due in large part to their military prowess, the Mongols rose to power in Asia with stunning speed. The Mongols were a pastoral people from the region of modern-day **Mongolia** who were organized loosely into clans. Temüjin (TEHM•yuh•juhn), born during the 1160s, gradually unified the Mongols. In 1206 he was elected **Genghis Khan**—strong ruler—at a massive meeting somewhere in the **Gobi.** From that time on, he devoted himself to conquest. The military tactics of the Mongols were devastatingly effective. John of Plano Carpini, a Franciscan friar, wrote:

PRIMARY SOURCE

> "As soon as they discover the enemy they charge and each unleashes three or four arrows. If they see they cannot break him, they retreat in order to entice the enemy to pursue, thus luring him into an ambush prepared in advance. If they conclude that the enemy army is stronger, they retire for a day or two and ravage neighboring areas. Or they [set up] camp in a well chosen position, and when the enemy army begins to pass by, they appear unexpectedly."
>
> —John of Plano Carpini, in *L'Empire des Steppes,* Rene Grousset, 1939

The Mongols brought much of the Eurasian landmass under a single rule, creating the largest land empire in history. To rule the new Mongol Empire, Genghis Khan set up a capital city at Karakorum. Mongol armies traveled both to the west and to the east. Some went as far as central Europe.

After the death of Genghis Khan in 1227, the empire began to change. Following Mongol custom, upon the death of the ruling khan, his heirs divided the territory. The once-united empire of Genghis Khan was split into several separate territories called **khanates,** each under the rule of one of his sons. It may be that

Resource Manager

R Reading Strategies	C Critical Thinking	D Differentiated Instruction	W Writing Support	S Skill Practice
Teacher Edition • Making Connections, p. 274 • Read. Pri. Sources, p. 275 **Additional Resources** • Guid. Read. Act., URB p. 123 • Read. Ess. & Note-Taking Guide, p. 85	**Teacher Edition** • Det. Cause/Effect, p. 271 • Analyzing Pri. Sources, p. 272 **Additional Resources** • Section Quiz, p. 92	**Teacher Edition** • ELL, p. 272 • Visual/Spatial, p. 274 **Additional Resources** • World Art & Music Act., URB p. 117 • Enrich. Act., URB p. 120	**Teacher Edition** • Expository Writing, p. 273 **Additional Resources** • Writer's Guidebook, p. 27	**Teacher Edition** • Using Geo. Skills, p. 271 **Additional Resources** • Chart. Graph. Act., URB p. 3 • Reteach. Act., URB p. 119

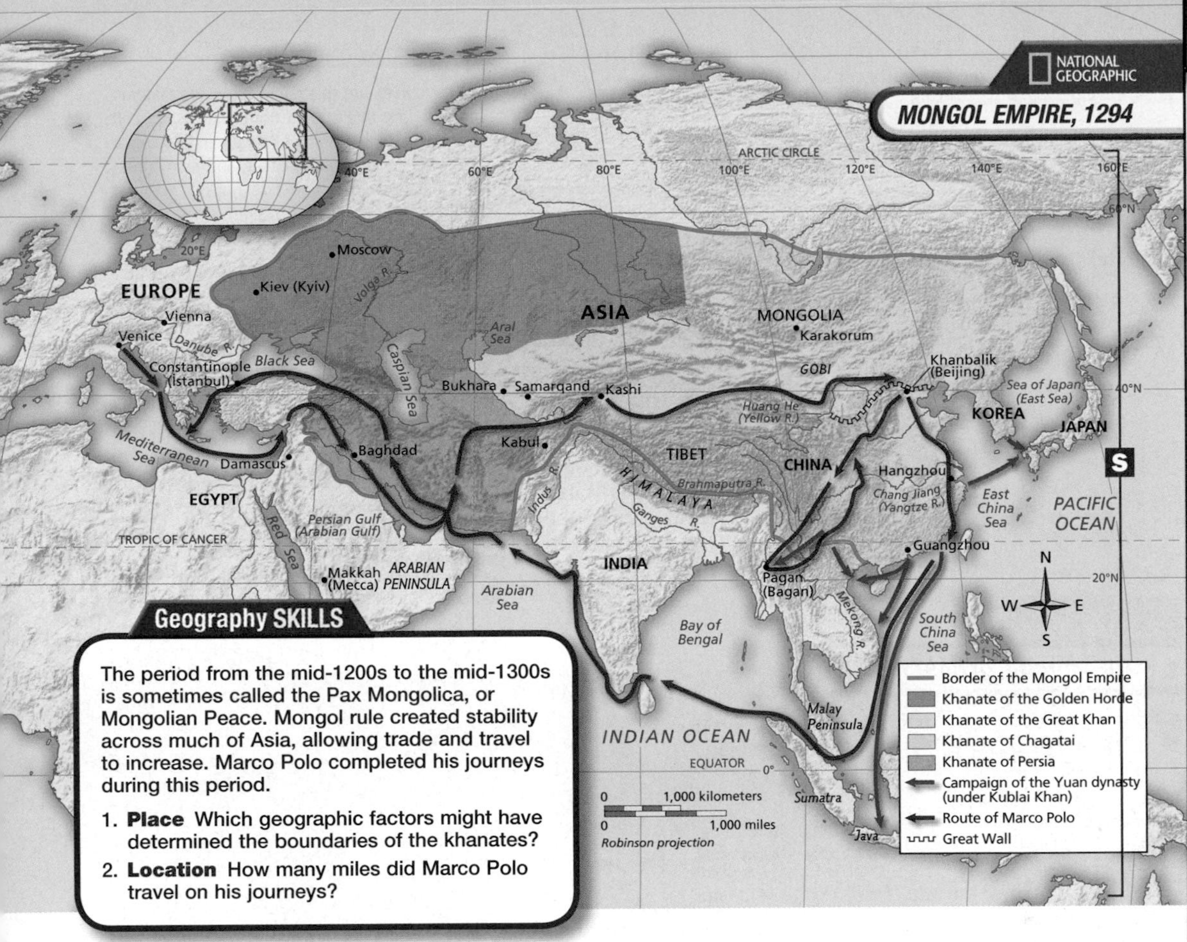

Geography SKILLS

The period from the mid-1200s to the mid-1300s is sometimes called the Pax Mongolica, or Mongolian Peace. Mongol rule created stability across much of Asia, allowing trade and travel to increase. Marco Polo completed his journeys during this period.

1. **Place** Which geographic factors might have determined the boundaries of the khanates?
2. **Location** How many miles did Marco Polo travel on his journeys?

only the death of Genghis Khan kept the Mongols from attacking western Europe. In 1231 the Mongols attacked Persia and then defeated the Abbasids at Baghdad in 1258. Mongol forces attacked the Song dynasty in China in the 1260s.

C In their attack on the Chinese, the Mongols encountered the use of gunpowder and the fire-lance. By the end of the thirteenth century, the fire-lance had evolved into the much more effective gun and cannon. By the early fourteenth century, foreigners employed by the Mongol rulers of China had introduced the use of gunpowder and firearms into Europe.

In 1279 one of Genghis Khan's grandsons, named **Kublai Khan** (KOO•bluh KAHN), completed the conquest of the Song and established a new Chinese dynasty, the Yuan (YWAHN). Kublai Khan, who ruled China until his death in 1294, established his capital at Khanbalik—the city of the Khan—later known by the Chinese name **Beijing.**

Under the leadership of the talented Kublai Khan, the Yuan, or Mongol, dynasty continued to expand the empire. Mongol armies advanced into Vietnam, and Mongol fleets were launched against Java and Sumatra and twice against the islands of Japan. Only Vietnam was conquered, however, and then only for a while. The other campaigns failed. The Mongols used tactics such as cavalry charges and siege warfare.

History ONLINE
Student Web Activity—
Visit glencoe.com and complete the activity about the Mongol dynasty.

Teach

S Skill Practice

Using Geography Skills Ask: What city was the farthest west in the Mongol Empire? *(Kiev)* OL

C Critical Thinking

Determining Cause and Effect Ask: How might the death of Genghis Khan have prevented the Mongols from attacking Western Europe? *(Because the khanate was split among his heirs, the empire was no longer united and much weaker.)* OL

For additional practice on this skill, see the **Skills Handbook**.

Geography SKILLS

Answers:

1. Some seem to follow bodies of water (e.g., between khanate of Chagatai and khanate of Persia), and the southern end of the khanate of the Great Khan seems to be drawn by the Himalayas.
2. over 18,000

Hands-On Chapter Project Step 2

Planning a Web Site for Early Asian History

Step 2: Developments during the Mongol Empire Pairs of students will continue designing their Web site on important developments in early Asian history.

Directions: Pairs of students will select one important development in the military, government, religion, the arts, or another area in early China under the Mongols from this section to cover. Have students review the chapter for possible ideas, such as the building of what is now Beijing and the high point of landscape painting. Students should find or create an image to include and write text that explains the background and significance of their selected development. OL

(Chapter Project is continued in Section 3.)

D Differentiated Instruction

English Language Learners
Ask students to brainstorm synonyms for the adjective *magnificent. (Possible answers may include* astounding *and* spectacular.*)* List these on the board and have students use them in sentences. **BL**

C Critical Thinking

Analyzing Primary Sources
Ask: Why do you think Europeans had a hard time believing descriptions such as Marco Polo's? *(They probably could not believe that the Mongol Empire was as advanced—or even more so—as European cultures.)* **AL**

✓Reading Check
Answer: Mongol rulers adapted to the Chinese political system and made use of Chinese bureaucrats.

These were not very effective in tropical and hilly regions.

The Mongols had more success in ruling China. Mongol rulers adapted to the Chinese political system and made use of Chinese bureaucrats. Culturally the Mongols were quite different from the Chinese and became a separate class with their own laws. The highest positions in the bureaucracy were usually staffed by Mongols. **C**

Over time, the Mongol dynasty won the support of many Chinese people. Some came to respect the stability and economic prosperity that the Mongols at first brought to China. The capital at Khanbalik reflected Mongol prosperity. It was a magnificent city, and foreign visitors were impressed by its splendor. One such visitor was Marco Polo, who lived in Khanbalik during the reign of Kublai Khan. Polo's stories of the glories of China seemed unbelievable to the Europeans. **D**

PRIMARY SOURCE

"The streets are so straight and wide that you can see right along them from end to end and from one gate to the other. And up and down the city there are beautiful palaces, and many great and fine hostelries, and fine houses in great numbers."

—Marco Polo, Italian traveler

The Mongol dynasty eventually fell victim to the same problems that had plagued other dynasties: too much spending on foreign conquests, corruption at court, and growing internal instability. In 1368 Zhu Yuanzhang (JOO YWAHN•JAHNG), the son of a peasant, put together an army, ended the Mongol dynasty, and set up a new dynasty, the Ming.

✓Reading Check **Summarizing** Why were the Mongols so successful in ruling China?

NATIONAL GEOGRAPHIC

THE MONGOL DYNASTY IN CHINA

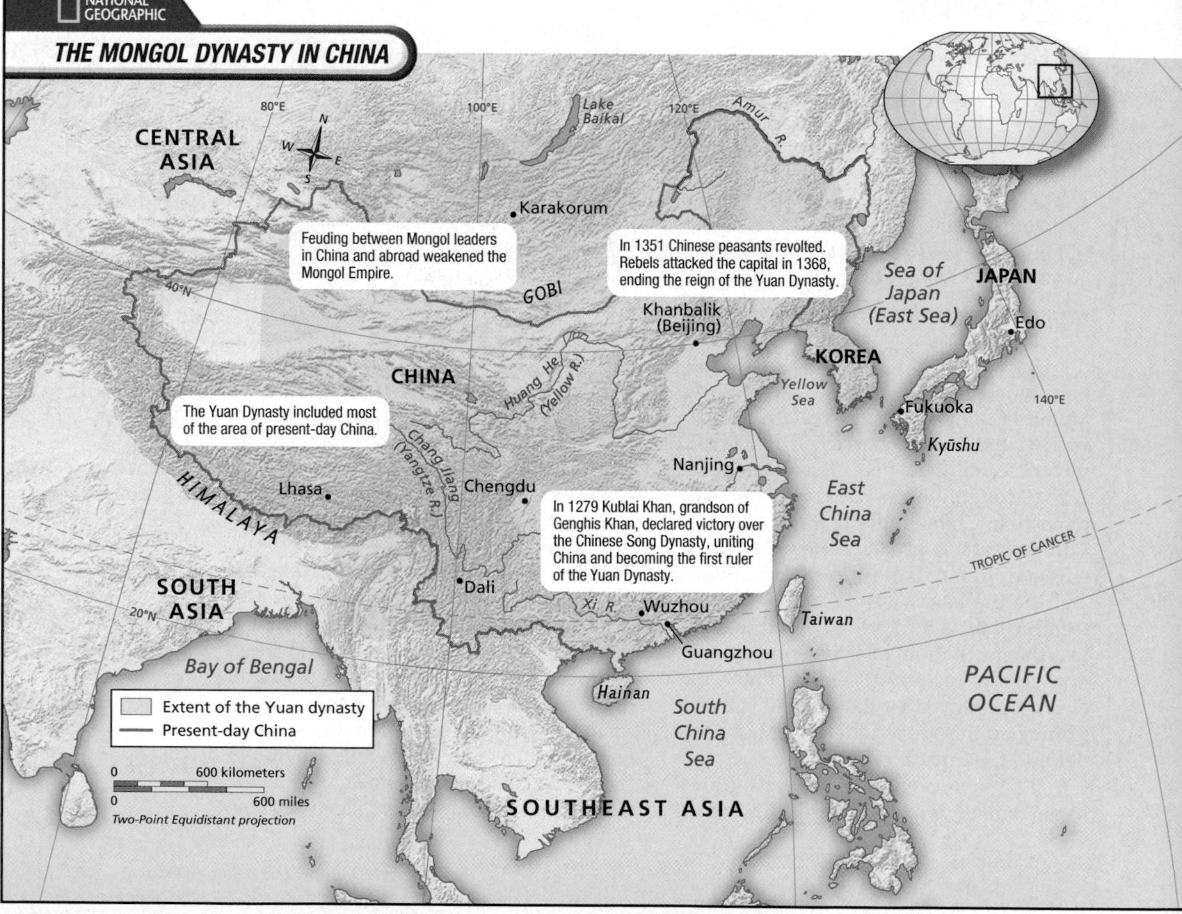

Additional Support

Activity: Economics Connection

Analyzing the Purpose of a Capital A new capital city is a sign of wealth and power. Kublai Khan selected a site near the Yellow River (Huang He) and connected the new city to the river by canal. On what is now the site of Beijing, he used Muslim architects and Central Asian craftworkers to design and create a magnificent new city which was a wonder to European merchant visitors. The streets were straight and broad enough to allow nine military horseriders to gallop side-by-side. The streets were laid out in squares, north-south and east-west, so that a guard at one of the four gates could see all the way across the city to the opposite gate. **Ask:** How does a new capital signify wealth and power? *(Construction requires vast materials and labor, and a new design shows the skill and knowledge of the rulers.)* **OL**

Religion and Government

MAIN IDEA Between the Han and Yuan dynasties, religion's role in Chinese government changed.

HISTORY & YOU Throughout history, all religions have tried to answer some basic questions. What do you think some of these questions are?

Confucian principles became the basis for Chinese government during the Han dynasty. By the time of the Sui and Tang dynasties, Buddhism and Daoism rivaled the influence of Confucianism.

Buddhism and Daoism

Buddhism was brought to China in the first century A.D. by merchants and missionaries from India. At first, only merchants and intellectuals were intrigued by the new ideas. However, as a result of the insecurity that prevailed after the collapse of the Han dynasty, both Buddhism and Daoism became more attractive to many people. Both philosophies gained support among the ruling classes.

See page R39 to read excerpts from The Buddha's Sermon in the **Primary Sources and Literature Library.**

The growing popularity of Buddhism continued into the early years of the Tang dynasty. Early Tang rulers lent their support to Buddhist monasteries that were set up throughout the country. Buddhists even became advisers at the imperial court but ultimately lost favor.

Buddhism was criticized for being a foreign religion. Like Christian monasteries in Europe during the Middle Ages, Buddhist monasteries had **acquired** thousands of acres of land and serfs. With land came corruption. The government reacted strongly. During the later Tang period, it destroyed countless Buddhist temples and monasteries and forced more than 260,000 monks and nuns to leave the monasteries and return to secular life.

Buddhists taught that the material world was not real, but an illusion. By teaching this, Buddhism was denying the very essence of Confucian teachings—the need for devotion to family and hard work. These were virtues that the Chinese state had reason to support.

Neo-Confucianism

From the Song dynasty to the end of the dynastic system in the twentieth century, official support went to a revived Confucianism, which became the heart of the state government. This new doctrine, called **neo-Confucianism,** served as a Confucian response to Buddhism and Daoism. It teaches that the world is real, not an illusion, and that fulfillment comes from participation in the world. **W**

Neo-Confucianists divide the world into a material world and a spiritual world. Humans live in the material world but are also linked with the Supreme Ultimate. The goal is to move beyond the material world to reach union with the Supreme Ultimate. Humans do this through a careful examination of the moral principles that rule the universe.

✓**Reading Check** **Explaining** What caused Buddhism to lose favor with the Chinese government?

Genghis Khan built a powerful empire.

Geography SKILLS

1. **Hypothesizing** How might Mongol rulers have prevented the decline of the empire?
2. **Describing** What tactics did the Mongols use to expand their empire?

W Writing Support

Expository Writing Ask students to research the basic tenets of Confucianism. Then have them write a short essay that explains the differences in Confucianism and neo-Confucianism, and speculates on why neo- Confucianism worked well for China for so long. **AL**

✓**Reading Check**

Answer: It was a foreign religion; the Buddhists gained land and became corrupt.

Geography SKILLS

Answers:

1. by permitting the native Chinese a greater voice in the government; by reducing or sharing the burden of their building projects and invasions
2. brutal force, scare tactics, massacres, lowering the status of those conquered

Activity: Collaborative Learning

Creating Biographies Genghis Khan and his grandson were both warriors, but both also had many other achievements. For example, Genghis Khan worked to fuse many tribes into a single people and imposed uniform laws. Kublai Khan completed the unification of China, promoted economic prosperity, and fostered Chinese scholarship and arts. Divide students into small groups, assigning Genghis Khan to half and Kublai Khan to the other half. Ask students to research the life and accomplishments of their assigned figure and to work together on a class presentation that includes visuals (posters, time lines, transparencies, and so on) and oral reports. **OL**

Teacher Tip

Presentation This activity requires students to research and present. Discuss with students the elements of a successful presentation including interesting visuals, organized presentations, and good tone and volume. Remind students that a polished presentation requires practice and perhaps revision.

R Reading Strategy

Making Connections Have students discuss poetry, including musical lyrics, in the United States today. **Ask:** What poems have been read by American children for many years? *(Answers may include some nursery rhymes and patriotic songs.)* **OL**

D Differentiated Instruction

Visual/Spatial Ask students to make a working sample of either block printing or movable type and demonstrate it for the class. Then have students compare the ease of printing today with the challenges of printing in the past. **OL**

CRITICAL THINKING SKILLS

Answers:

1. Materials would be printed faster, more cheaply, and in greater quantities. As a result, more people would be able to learn to read.
2. Single characters could be replaced fairly easily. When carving a woodblock, one mistake would mean ruining the whole block.

See page R40 to read five poems by Li Bo in the **Primary Sources and Literature Library.**

A Golden Age in Literature and Art

MAIN IDEA With the invention of printing, a golden age of literature and art emerged in China.

HISTORY & YOU In what way does the creation of the Internet compare to the invention of printing? Read about the impact of printing on Chinese art and literature.

The period between the Tang and Ming dynasties was in many ways the great age of Chinese literature. The invention of printing during the Tang dynasty helped to make literature more readily **available** and more popular. Art, especially landscape painting and ceramics, flourished during this period.

Poetry

It was in poetry, above all, that the Chinese of this time best expressed their literary talents. The Tang dynasty is viewed as the great age of poetry in China. At least 48,000 poems were written by some 2,200 authors. Chinese poems celebrated the beauty of nature, the changes of the seasons, and the joys of friendship. They **R** expressed sadness at the shortness of life and the necessity of parting.

Li Bo (LEE BWAW) and **Du Fu** (DOO FOO) were two of the most popular poets during the Tang era. Li Bo was a free spirit whose writing often centered on nature. Probably the best-known poem in China, "Quiet Night Thoughts" has been memorized by schoolchildren for centuries.

SCIENCE, TECHNOLOGY, & SOCIETY

The Development of Printing in China

Pi Sheng invented movable type in the eleventh century.

Woodblock printing began in the seventh century A.D., during the Tang dynasty. Each page of a text required its own wooden block, with each character carefully carved in reverse into it. The wooden block was then inked and a piece of paper applied. The printer rubbed the sheet of paper with a brush to transfer inked text. **D** Each block could be reused to make thousands of copies.

Woodblock printing was a major advancement in printing, but no changes could be made to a page once it was carved. In the eleventh century, Pi Sheng solved this problem by inventing movable type. With movable type, the printer arranged individual characters to compose a page, making changes easier.

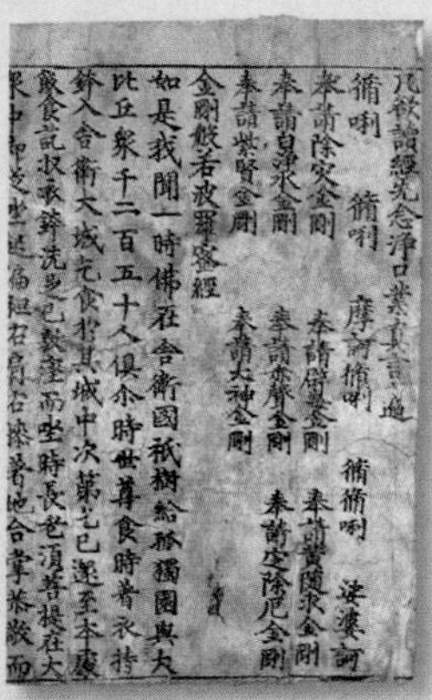

The earliest known printed book is a Chinese translation of the Diamond Sutra, a Buddhist text from A.D. 868.

CRITICAL THINKING SKILLS

1. **Drawing Inferences** What effect would the invention of movable type have upon the availability of books? How would societies be affected?
2. **Explaining** Explain why movable type was an improvement over woodblocks.

Differentiated Instruction

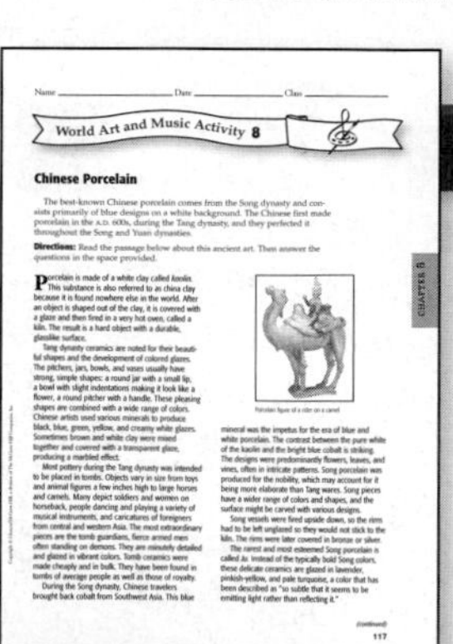

World Art and Music Activity 8

Chinese Porcelain

World Art and Music Activity, URB p. 117

Drawing Conclusions

Objective: Draw conclusions about porcelain objects in China during the period.

Focus: Have students read and discuss the passage.

Teach: Have students complete questions 1–3.

Assess: Have students review and revise their answers with a partner.

Close: Ask students to draw conclusions about the styles of porcelain from each dynasty.

Differentiated Instruction Strategies

- **BL** Ask students to explain why porcelain of the Song dynasty was so valued.
- **AL** Ask students to research and report on porcelain of the Ming dynasty.
- **ELL** Help students find images of Song dynasty porcelain and describe them in their own words.

Primary Source

"Beside my bed the bright moonbeams bound
Almost as if there were frost on the ground.
Raising up, I gaze at the Mountain moon;
Lying back, I think of my old home town."
—Li Bo

Where Li Bo was carefree, Du Fu was a serious Confucian. In "Spring Prospect," the poet has returned to his home in the capital after a rebellion has left the city in ruins.

Primary Source

"The capital is taken. The hills and streams are left,
And with spring in the city the grass and trees grown dense.
Mourning the times, the flowers trickle their tears;
Saddened with parting, the birds make my heart flutter.
The army beacons have flamed for three months;
A letter from home would be worth ten thousand in gold.
My white hairs have I anxiously scratched ever shorter;
But such disarray! Even hairpins will do no good."
—Du Fu

Painting and Ceramics

During the Song and Mongol dynasties, landscape painting reached its high point. Influenced by Daoism, artists went into the mountains to find the Dao, or Way, in nature. The word *landscape* in Chinese means "mountain-water" and reflects the Daoist search for balance between the earth and water. Chinese artists tried to reveal the hidden forms of the landscape. Rather than depicting the realistic shape of a specific mountain, for example, they tried to portray the idea of "mountain." Empty spaces were left in the paintings because in the Daoist **vision,** one cannot know the whole truth. Daoism also influenced the portrayal of humans as insignificant in the midst of nature. Chinese artists painted people as tiny figures fishing in small boats or wandering up a hillside trail, living in but not dominating nature.

Tang artisans perfected the making of **porcelain**—a ceramic made of fine clay baked at very high temperatures. Porcelain-making techniques did not reach Europe until the eighteenth century. An Arab traveler in 851 described Chinese porcelain:

Primary Source

"There is in China a very fine clay from which are made vases having the transparency of glass bottles; water in these vases is visible through them, and yet they are made of clay."

✓Reading Check **Summarizing** What invention helped make literature both more available and more popular?

SECTION 2 REVIEW

Vocabulary

1. **Explain** the significance of: Mongolia, Genghis Khan, Gobi, khanate, Kublai Khan, Beijing, acquired, neo-Confucianism, available, Li Bo, Du Fu, vision, porcelain.

Main Ideas

2. **Explain** how neo-Confucianism differs from Confucianism.
3. **List** the ways in which Daoism is represented in Chinese art of the Song and Yuan dynasties.
4. **Create** a time line like the one shown below that illustrates the Mongols' rise to power.

Mongols' Rise to Power

Critical Thinking

5. **The BIG Idea** **Contrasting** What is the difference between the Buddhist and neo-Confucian philosophies? What impact might these two philosophies have had on early Chinese society?
6. **Evaluating** During the Yuan dynasty, how did the Mongols and Chinese affect each other's cultures?
7. **Analyzing Visuals** Examine the illustration of Genghis Khan on page 273. Compare and contrast it with the illustration of the Empress Wu on page 268. How do their expressions differ? What is similar about the portraits?

Writing About History

8. **Persuasive Writing** Write a letter to Marco Polo. Tell him why he should hire you for his next expedition to China. Include the reasons you want to go as well as how you would be a helpful member of his crew.

History ONLINE
For help with the concepts in this section of *Glencoe World History,* go to glencoe.com and click Study Central™.

R Reading Strategy

Reading Primary Sources
Ask students to compare the themes of each poet. **Ask:** Which type of poetry do you prefer? Why? *(Answers will vary, but should be supported by logical conclusions.)* **OL**

✓Reading Check
Answer: movable type printing

Assess

History ONLINE
Study Central provides summaries, interactive games, and online graphic organizers to help students review content.

Close

Drawing Conclusions **Ask:** How successful were the Mongols in conquering and governing China? *(They were very successful in China, creating an empire with a strong economy and organized government.)* **OL**

Answers

1. Definitions for the vocabulary words are found in the section and the Glossary.
2. **Confucianism:** primarily a system of social ethics and political ideals; **neo-Confucianism:** encourages speculation on the nature of the universe and humanity's place in it
3. empty spaces left in paintings; humans insignificant in the midst of nature
4. **1160s:** Temüjin born; **1206:** Temüjin elected Genghis Khan; **1231:** Mongols attack Persia; **1258:** Mongols defeat Abbasids; **1260s:** Mongols attack Song dynasty; **1279:** Kublai Khan conquers Song.
5. **Buddhism:** material world not real; **neo-Confucianism:** world real, fulfillment comes from participation in the world; action over contemplation; **Impact:** Both would have affected all levels of society.
6. Mongols invaded China, adopted Chinese political system and bureaucrats, but remained culturally separated.
7. **Similar:** Both images suggest leadership qualities; **Different:** His expression seems fiercer and strict while hers suggests more openness.
8. Letters will vary, but should show an understanding of travel and trade during this time period.

Focus

Mongolians today view Genghis Khan as the father of their country. Even as a young man, Genghis Khan was known for leadership—and for vengeance. Was he a great leader? Or was he a merciless killer and looter? Many modern historians say he was both.

Teach

C Critical Thinking

Drawing Conclusions Tell students that during Genghis Khan's long treks, horses also provided sustenance to his troops. It is said that mare's milk and blood drawn from a cut in a horse's side helped his troops survive long journeys across harsh environments such as the Gobi Desert. **Ask:** Why were horses so important to Khan's troops? *(His troops depended on them for transportation, for quick maneuvering in battle, and in some instances for food.)* OL

Additional Support

Background

More About Mongolian Cavalry Equipment Discuss with students the differences in equipment between the Mongolian cavalry and the knights of Europe during the Middle Ages. In general, Mongolian cavalry wore much lighter leather armor than European knights in their heavy chain mail. As a result, Mongolian riders were better able to maneuver on horseback. They also used special stirrups that helped them to stay in control during battle—and fire arrows forward or backward. Mongolian cavalry also wore loose robes over tightly-woven tunics to help block enemy arrows.

The Mongolian People Today The Mongolian people are sometimes stereotyped as having a simplistic or unfriendly culture, as would seem to fit any ancestors of Genghis Khan. However, living in a harsh environment (as the Mongolians have for centuries) fosters cooperation and hospitality—and Mongolians are well-known for these two characteristics. You may want to discuss with students why cooperation and hospitality are necessary for survival in harsh environments.

W

Mongol Meals

"An army," Napoleon Bonaparte was believed to have said, "marches on its stomach." Genghis Khan knew as much 500 years earlier. Not surprisingly, meat and dairy products formed the basis of the marching Mongols' diet. They cooked mutton and lamb over rocks heated by dung fires. Milk tea and fermented mare's milk were common drinks.

Analyzing Visuals

1. **Evaluating** What do you think the *tumen's* main strengths were? Its greatest weaknesses?
2. **Comparing and Contrasting** How was life for Mongol children similar to and different from the life of children in other cultures you have read about?

277

W Writing Support

Descriptive Writing Brainstorm adjectives to describe the visual and list them on the board as you do. Then have students use these adjectives to write a paragraph about life in Genghis Khan's army. **ELL**

Assess/Close

Tell students that many great cities of central Asia—Samarqand, Bukhara, Urgench, Balkh, Merv, Nishapur, Heart, and Ghaznī—fell quickly to Genghis Khan's highly-mobile army. In just five years, his troops were able to conquer China. Later conquests took Genghis Khan and his troops through northern India and into Europe.

Analyzing Visuals

Answers:

1. **Strengths:** mobile, well-trained, well-skilled fighters; **Weaknesses:** only had basic weapons, supplies could be difficult to obtain when away from home.
2. **Similar:** had chores, roles based on gender; **Differences:** traveled with troops, rather than stayed at home.

Activity: Interdisciplinary Connection

Geography The Gobi Desert makes up about 30 percent of Mongolia. Summer temperatures often reach 104° F, and winter temperatures can drop as low as –40° F. The Gobi is home to wild horses, whose ancestors Genghis Khan used. It is also home to snow leopards, wild camels, and other animals. Have students work in pairs to research one aspect of the Gobi Desert environment, such as plant life, animal life, fossil finds, and influence on daily life in Mongolia today. Then have students present their findings to the class. Encourage students to include visuals that they make or find with their presentation. **Ask:** **How would you summarize the influences of the Gobi Desert on plants, animals, and humans?** *(Students' summaries will vary, but should be based on reasonable conclusions.)* **OL**

Focus

Bellringer
Daily Focus Transparency 8.3

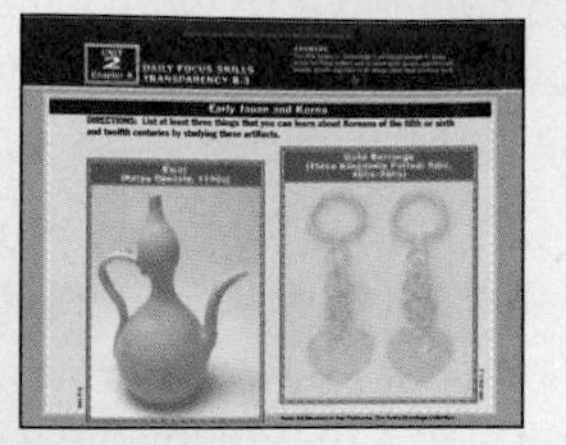

GUIDE TO READING

Answers to Graphic:
Japan: centralized government under a supreme ruler; divided country into administrative districts, with rural villages as the basic unit of government;
Korea: Koryo dynasty adopted Chinese political institutions.

Section Spotlight Video

To generate student interest and provide a springboard for class discussion, access the Chapter 8, Section 3 video at glencoe.com or on the video DVD.

SECTION 3

Early Japan and Korea

GUIDE TO READING

The BIG Idea
Physical Geography The geography of Japan, a string of islands, and of Korea, a peninsula bordering China, have had a huge impact on their respective histories.

Content Vocabulary
- samurai *(p. 280)*
- Bushido *(p. 280)*
- shogun *(p. 281)*
- daimyo *(p. 281)*
- Shinto *(p. 282)*
- Zen *(p. 282)*

Academic Vocabulary
- revenue *(p. 279)*
- code *(p. 280)*

People and Places
- Ōsaka *(p. 278)*
- Kyōto *(p. 278)*
- Shōtoku Taishi *(p. 279)*
- Minamoto Yoritomo *(p. 281)*
- Murasaki Shikibu *(p. 282)*
- Yi Sŏng-gye *(p. 283)*

Reading Strategy
Categorizing Information As you read, create a chart like the one below to help you study which elements of Chinese culture were adopted by Korea and Japan.

Chinese Culture in . . .

Japan	Korea

Early Japan was unified by a noble family that gave rise to a line of emperors. Over time, power passed from the hands of the emperor to powerful aristocratic families, then to military leaders called shoguns. Finally, centralized power disappeared altogether. Korea's history during this period is one of a struggle for independence against the neighboring Chinese.

Early Japan

MAIN IDEA Japan's history has been marked by power struggles between rulers and independent families.

HISTORY & YOU How has geography played an important role in the growth of your area? Read about geography's role in the development of Japan.

The ancestors of present-day Japanese settled in the Yamato Plain near the location of the modern cities of **Ōsaka** and **Kyōto** in the first centuries A.D. Their society was made up of clans. The people were divided between a small aristocratic class (the rulers) and a large population of rice farmers, artisans, and household servants. The local ruler of each clan protected the population in return for a share of the annual harvest.

Eventually, one ruler of the Yamato clan achieved supremacy over the others and became, in effect, ruler of Japan.

The Impact of Geography

Chinese and Japanese societies have historically been very different. One of the reasons for these differences is geography. Whereas China is located on a vast continent, Japan is a chain of many islands. The population is concentrated on four main islands: Hokkaidō, the main island of Honshū, and the two smaller islands of Kyūshū and Shikoku. Japan's total land area is approximately 146,000 square miles (378,000 sq. km)—about the size of the state of Montana.

Like China, much of Japan is mountainous. Only about 11 percent of the total land area can be farmed. The mountains are volcanic in origin. Volcanic soils are very fertile, which has helped Japanese farming. The area, however, is prone to earthquakes. In 1923 an earthquake nearly destroyed the entire city of Tokyo.

The fact that Japan is an island nation has also affected its history. Because of their geographical isolation, the Japanese developed a number of unique qualities. These qualities contributed to the Japanese belief that they had a destiny separate from that of the peoples on the continent.

Resource Manager

R Reading Strategies	C Critical Thinking	D Differentiated Instruction	W Writing Support	S Skill Practice
Teacher Edition • Summarizing, p. 280 • Inferring, p. 281 **Additional Resources** • Guid. Read. Act., URB p. 124 • Read. Ess. & Notetaking Guide, p. 88	**Teacher Edition** • Making Inferences, pp. 281, 283 **Additional Resources** • Section Quiz, p. 93	**Teacher Edition** • Adv. Learners, p. 280 • Visual/Spatial, p. 282 **Additional Resources** • Read. Strat. for SS., p. 80	**Teacher Edition** • Personal Writing, p. 279 **Additional Resources** • Writer's Guidebook, p. 54	**Teacher Edition** • Using Geo. Skills, p. 279 **Additional Resources** • Chart. Graph. Act., URB p. 3 • Skills Reinforc. Act., URB p. 101

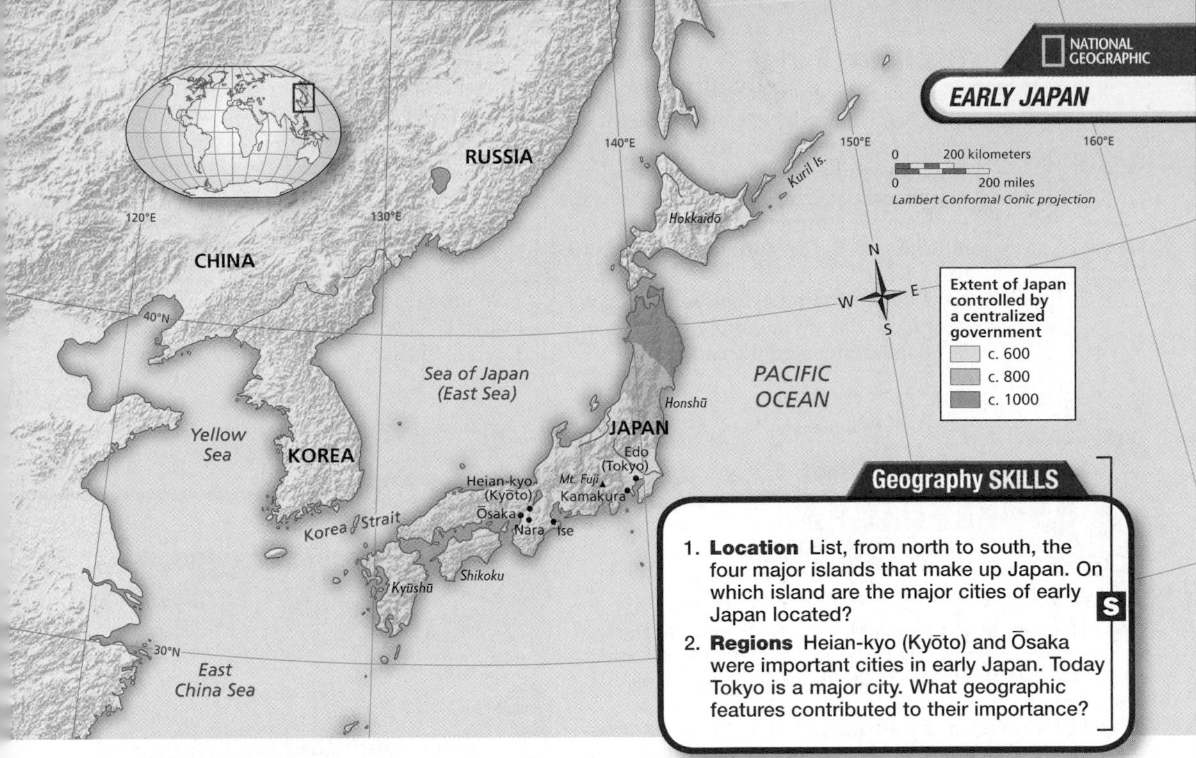

Geography SKILLS

1. **Location** List, from north to south, the four major islands that make up Japan. On which island are the major cities of early Japan located? **S**
2. **Regions** Heian-kyo (Kyōto) and Ōsaka were important cities in early Japan. Today Tokyo is a major city. What geographic features contributed to their importance?

Chinese Influences

In the early seventh century, **Shōtoku Taishi,** a Yamato prince, tried to unify the various clans so that the Japanese could more effectively resist an invasion by the Chinese. To do this, Prince Shōtoku sent representatives to the Tang capital of China to learn how the Chinese organized their government. He then began to create a new centralized system of government in Japan, **W** based roughly on the Chinese model.

Prince Shōtoku wanted a centralized government under a supreme ruler. His objective was to limit the powers of the aristocrats and enhance the Yamato ruler's (his own) authority. As a result, the ruler was portrayed as a divine figure and the symbol of the Japanese nation.

Shōtoku Taishi's successors continued to make reforms based on the Chinese model. The territory of Japan was divided into administrative districts, and the senior official of each district was selected from among the local nobles. As in China, the rural village was the basic unit of government. A new tax system was set up. Now all farmland technically belonged to the state. All taxes were to be paid directly to the central government rather than to local aristocrats.

The Nara Period

After Shōtoku Taishi's death in 622, political power fell into the hands of the Fujiwara clan. A Yamato ruler was still emperor. He was, however, strongly influenced by the Fujiwara family. In 710 a new capital was established at Nara. The emperor began to use the official title "Son of Heaven."

Though the reforms begun by Prince Shōtoku continued during this period, Japan's central government could not overcome the power of the aristocrats. These powerful families were able to keep the taxes from the lands for themselves. Unable to gain tax **revenues,** the central government steadily lost power and influence.

Teach

S Skill Practice

Using Geography Skills Ask: What bodies of water separate Japan from Korea? What is the distance between Japan and Korea? *(Korea Strait and Sea of Japan; about 75 miles)* **BL**

W Writing Support

Personal Writing Discuss the actions of Shōtoku Taishi. Note that although he feared a Chinese invasion, he was willing to learn and use Chinese methods of governing. Then ask students to write a paragraph about one thing they have learned from others and how this helps them in their everyday life. **OL**

Geography SKILLS

Answers:

1. Hokkaidō, Honshū, Shikoku, Kyūshū, Honshū
2. large flat plain, protected by a peninsula, located on a bay

Differentiated Instruction

Identifying Central Issues

Objective: Identify the views of Prince Shōtoku on government and society.

Focus: Have students read the passage by Prince Shōtoku.

Teach: Ask students to answer questions 1–3.

Assess: Have students write a paragraph that summarizes Prince Shōtoku's views.

Close: Ask volunteers to share their work. Identify common themes as a class.

Differentiated Instruction Strategies

BL Ask pairs of students to summarize Section III.

AL Ask students to write a paragraph, explaining the sentence, "Few men are utterly bad," in Section II.

ELL Have volunteers read each section aloud. Discuss any difficult words and ask students to use them in sentences.

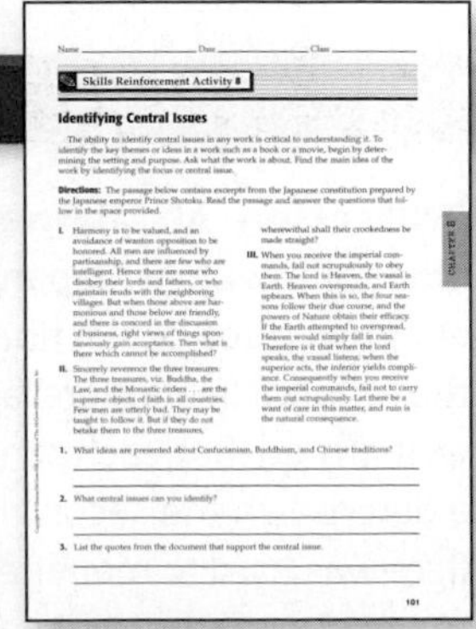

Skills Reinforcement Activity, URB p. 101

R Reading Strategy

Summarizing Ask students to write a summary of the changes in Japan during the Heian period. *(Powerful landowners regained control and hired military forces—the samurai—to protect them.)* **OL**

D Differentiated Instruction

Advanced Learners Ask students to research and present a report on Japanese samurai and Bushido. They should address what effect this system had on Japanese culture during a specific time period. **AL**

DOCUMENT-BASED QUESTIONS

Answers:

1. It gave the Japanese a sense of invincibility and led them to avoid foreign contact.
2. Isolationism helped Japan to prosper and reinforced national pride. It also held the country back technologically.

Additional Support

The Heian Period

R In 794 the emperor moved the capital from Nara to nearby Heian-kyo, on the site of present-day Kyōto. At Heian-kyo, the emperor continued to rule in name, but actual power remained in the hands of the Fujiwara clan. In fact, the government was returning to the decentralized system that had existed before the time of Shōtoku Taishi. Powerful families whose wealth was based on the ownership of tax-exempt farmland dominated the rural areas.

With the decline of central power, local aristocrats took justice into their own hands. They turned to military force, and a new class of military servants emerged whose purpose was to protect the security and property of their employers. Called the **samurai** ("those who serve"), these warriors fought on horseback, clad in helmet D and armor, and carried a sword and a bow. Like knights, the samurai were supposed to live by a strict warrior **code**, known in Japan as **Bushido** ("the way of the warrior").

TURNING POINT — JAPANESE ISOLATION

Mongol emperor Kublai Khan expected an easy victory when he attacked Japan in 1272. Strengthened with Korean and Chinese troops, the Mongols seized the beach at Hakata when a huge storm sank 200 of his ships, drowning about 13,000 men.

In 1281, Kublai Khan attacked with a larger fleet, but most of the ships were destroyed by a typhoon. The Japanese called the storms *kamikaze*, or "divine wind." They took this as a sign that they were invincible because they were protected by divine powers. After defeating the Mongol invaders, Japan isolated itself from foreign influence until 1945.

Japanese samurai attacking a Mongol ship

NATIONAL GEOGRAPHIC

MONGOL CAMPAIGNS, 1200s

- Mongol dynasty in 1260
- Mongol acquisitions by 1279
- Mongol campaigns
- Present-day China

DOCUMENT-BASED QUESTIONS

1. **Determining Cause and Effect** How did the Mongol attacks change Japan?
2. **Evaluating** How did Japan's policy of isolation help the country? How was it detrimental to the country?

Extending the Content

Protection of Divine Wind In both Mongol invasions, Japanese religious leaders prayed for protection. It was clear that the Mongol fleets were large and the armies well-armed. But each time, nature provided a defense. In the second invasion, the huge fleet was hard to manage and so was forced to anchor off the Japanese coast for about six weeks. Ships had been chained together to keep them near each other, and when the great typhoon hit, they had no chance of escaping to deep water. The legendary name of the typhoon that saved Japan in 1281, *kamikaze,* was later applied to Japanese pilots who flew suicide missions in World War II. These pilots crashed planes filled with explosives into U.S. warships in a final attempt at defense. The kamikaze pilots managed to sink 34 ships and damage hundreds of others. Their success was a factor in the U.S. decision to use atomic weapons.

The Kamakura Shogunate

By the end of the twelfth century, rivalries among Japanese aristocratic families had led to almost constant civil war. Finally, a powerful noble named **Minamoto Yoritomo** defeated several rivals and set up his power near the modern city of Tokyo.

C To strengthen the state, he created a more centralized government under a military leader known as the **shogun** (general). In this new system—called the shogunate—the emperor remained ruler in name only, and the shogun exercised the actual power. The Kamakura shogunate, founded by Yoritomo, lasted from 1192 to 1333.

At first the system worked well. The Japanese were fortunate that it did, because the government soon faced a serious challenge from the Mongols. In 1281 Kublai Khan invaded Japan with an army nearly 150,000 strong. Fortunately for the Japanese, almost the entire fleet was destroyed by a massive typhoon (violent storm).

Fighting the Mongols put a strain on the political system. In 1333 the Kamakura shogunate was overthrown by a group of powerful families led by the Ashikaga family.

Collapse of Central Rule

The power of the local aristocrats grew during the fourteenth and fifteenth centuries. Heads of noble families, now called **daimyo** (DY•mee•OH), "great names," controlled vast landed estates that owed no taxes to the government. As family rivalries continued, the daimyo relied on the samurai for protection, and political power came into the hands of a loose coalition of noble families.

By 1500, Japan was close to chaos. A disastrous civil war known as the Onin War, which lasted from 1467 to 1477, led to the virtual destruction of the capital city of Kyōto. Central authority disappeared. Powerful aristocrats in rural areas seized control over large territories, which they ruled as independent lords. Their rivalries caused almost constant warfare.

✓Reading Check **Summarizing** What were the effects of the Onin War?

Life in Early Japan

MAIN IDEA Japan's small size and relative isolation have had a major effect on the development of its economy, religion, and culture.

HISTORY & YOU Have you read any books categorized as "women's literature"? Read about female authors in early Japan.

Early Japan was mostly a farming society. Its people took advantage of the limited amount of farmland and abundant rainfall to grow wet rice (rice grown in flooded fields). Trade in Japan was slow to develop. Barter, rather than money, was used until the twelfth century.

Manufacturing began to develop during the Kamakura period. Markets appeared in the larger towns, and industries such as the making of paper and porcelain and iron casting emerged. R Trade between regions also grew. Goods were carried in carts, on boats, or on human backs. Foreign trade, mainly with Korea and China, began during the eleventh century. Japan shipped raw materials, paintings, swords, and other manufactured items in return for silk, porcelain, books, and copper coins.

The Role of Women

In early Japan, women may have had a certain level of equality with men. An eighth-century law code, for example, guaranteed the inheritance rights of women. Wives who were abandoned could divorce and remarry. Later practices, however, show women were considered subordinate to men. A husband could divorce his wife if she did not produce a son or if she committed adultery, talked too much, was jealous, or had a serious illness.

Although women did not possess the full legal and social rights of men, they played an active role at various levels of society. Aristocratic women were prominent at court. Some became known for their artistic or literary talents.

Women often appear in the paintings of the period along with men. The women are doing the spring planting, threshing and hulling rice, and acting as salespersons and entertainers.

C Critical Thinking

Making Inferences Ask: Why do you think it was important for the Japanese people to continue to have an emperor even though he had no real power? *(The emperor was connected to religious beliefs and was an important symbol for the Japanese people.)* **OL**

For additional practice on this skill, see the **Skills Handbook**.

R Reading Strategy

Inferring Ask: Why did most of Japan's imports come from China and Korea? *(Answers may include that China and Korea were closest to Japan geographically and culturally.)* **OL**

✓Reading Check

Answer: The capital city of Kyōto was virtually destroyed; central authority disappeared; aristocrats ruled vast territories as independent lords; rivalries between lords caused almost constant warfare.

Hands-On Chapter Project
Step 3

Planning a Web Site for Early Asian History

Step 3: Developments in Early Japan and Korea Pairs of students will continue designing their Web site on important developments in early Asian history.

Directions: Pairs of students will select one important development in the military, government, religion, the arts, or another area in early Japan or in early Korea.

Have students review the chapter for possible ideas, such as the samurai in Japan or the Yi dynasty in Korea. Students should find or create an image to include and write text that explains the background and significance of their selected development. **OL**

(Chapter Project is continued in Section 4.)

D Differentiated Instruction

Visual/Spatial Discuss the concept of landscape to the Japanese. Then show (or have students research) images that display this concept of harmony between grounds and building. Finally, ask students to illustrate their own example of this concept. OL

DOCUMENT-BASED QUESTIONS

Answers:

1. She served in the court of the empress, so she had first-hand experience with the nobility.
2. The aristocracy valued physical beauty and the arts, such as dance. Also, ritual seemed to play a large part in their lives.

✓Reading Check

Answer: Answers may include the following. **Social:** It was mostly a farming society; women had some rights in the early period. **Religious:** Japanese spirit worship developed into a religion called Shinto. **Cultural:** women were the most productive writers of prose fiction in Japan.

Additional Support

HISTORY & ARTS — PRIMARY SOURCE

Murasaki Shikibu and The Tale of Genji

The Tale of Genji covers four generations of a fictitious imperial family and reveals much about the culture of the aristocracy in Heian-era Japan. Most of the book focuses on the nobleman Genji's life, his many love affairs, and the consequences of these relationships upon his career as a government official. An excerpt from *The Tale of Genji*, translated by Suyematz Kenchio, describes the young Genji:

> "The young Prince, whom we now style Genji (the Gen), was still with the Emperor. . . . When he attained the age of twelve the ceremony of Gembuk (or crowning) took place. . . .
>
> About ten o'clock in the forenoon Genji appeared on the scene. The boyish style of his hair and dress excellently became his features; and it almost seemed matter for regret that it should be altered. The Okura-Kiô-Kurahito, whose office it was to rearrange the hair of Genji, faltered as he did so. . . . After he had been crowned the Prince withdrew to a dressing-room, where he attired himself in the full robes of manhood. Then descending to the Court-yard he performed a measured dance in grateful acknowledgment. This he did with so much grace and skill that all present were filled with admiration; and his beauty, which some feared might be lessened, seemed only more remarkable from the change."

Three-part woodblock illustration from *The Tale of Genji*

DOCUMENT-BASED QUESTIONS

Little is known about the life of Lady Murasaki Shikibu, the author of *The Tale of Genji*—even her real name is unknown. It is believed that she began writing *Genji* around the time of her husband's death in 1001. In 1006, she was called to serve in the court of the empress and probably completed writing *The Tale of Genji* a few years later.

1. **Analyzing** How did the circumstances of Shikibu's life help her write *Genji*?
2. **Making Inferences** What does the excerpt tell us about the aristocracy of Heian-era Japan?

Religion in Early Japan

Early Japanese people worshiped spirits, called *kami,* whom they believed resided in trees, rivers, streams, and mountains. The Japanese also believed that the spirits of their ancestors were present in the air around them. In Japan, these beliefs evolved into a religion called **Shinto** ("the Sacred Way" or "the Way of the Gods"), which is still practiced today. Over time, Shinto became a state doctrine linked to a belief in the divinity of the emperor and the sacredness of the Japanese nation.

Shinto, however, did not satisfy the spiritual needs of all the Japanese people. Some turned to Buddhism, which Buddhist monks from China brought to Japan during the sixth century A.D. Among the aristocrats in Japan, one sect, known as **Zen,** became the most popular. Zen beliefs became part of the samurai warrior's code of behavior. Zen Buddhism teaches that enlightenment comes through strong self-discipline and a long process of meditation.

Culture in Early Japan

During much of the history of early Japan, aristocratic men believed that prose fiction was merely "vulgar gossip" and was thus beneath them. Consequently, from the ninth to the twelfth centuries, women were the most productive writers of prose fiction in Japanese. From this tradition appeared one of the world's great novels, *The Tale of Genji,* written by court author **Murasaki Shikibu.** Her novel traces the life of nobleman Genji as he moves from youthful adventures to a life of compassion in his later years.

D In Japanese art and architecture, landscape serves as an important means of expression. The landscape surrounding the Golden Pavilion in Kyōto displays a harmony of garden, water, and architecture that makes it one of the treasures of the world.

✓Reading Check **Summarizing** Give one example of each of these aspects of life in Japan: social, religious, and cultural.

Activity: Interdisciplinary Connection

Language Arts Discuss the meaning of the last sentence in the section on religion: "Zen Buddhism teaches that enlightenment comes through strong self-discipline...." **Ask:** What are some examples of self-discipline? (*Answers may include taking care of one's health and working hard in school.*) Remind students that a parable is a short story that is intended to teach a religious or moral lesson. Relate this idea to Zen koans. Koans are riddles that are intended to help Zen Buddhists meditate and gain knowledge. Koans often contain paradoxes, or statements that seem to be contradictory, but may actually be true. Direct students to Zen koans you have collected or to ones that are available on a Web site you have reviewed. Then ask pairs of students to select one Zen koan and read it to the class. Ask each pair what a possible response might be to the posed question. Discuss how the Zen koans are alike and how they differ. OL

The Emergence of Korea

MAIN IDEA The early history of Korea was marked by the presence of dominating neighbors.

HISTORY & YOU Recall the Chinese response to the Mongol invasion. As you read, compare it with the Korean response.

The Korea Peninsula, only slightly larger than the state of Minnesota, is relatively mountainous. Its closeness to both China and Japan has greatly affected its history. Indeed, no society in East Asia was more strongly influenced by the Chinese model than Korea.

In 109 B.C., the northern part of the Korea Peninsula came under the control of the Chinese. The Koreans, however, drove them out in the A.D. 200s. Eventually, three separate kingdoms emerged: Koguryo in the north, Paekche (PAK•chuh) in the southwest, and Silla in the southeast. Each of the kingdoms was governed by the combination of a hereditary monarch and powerful aristocratic families. From the fourth to the seventh centuries, the three kingdoms were bitter rivals. This period also saw the introduction of Buddhism to Korea, which quickly became the state religion of each of the kingdoms. After 527 Silla kings adopted Buddhist names and sponsored the building of many Buddhist temples. One was a nine-story wooden pagoda, which was perhaps the tallest in East Asia. As the Silla kingdom became more allied with the Chinese, the monarchy turned to Confucian ideals to run the country.

Gradually, with the support of the Tang dynasty of China, the kingdom of Silla gained control of the peninsula. After the king of Silla was assassinated, however, Korea sank into civil war. Finally, in the early tenth century, a new dynasty called Koryo (the root of the modern word *Korea*) arose in the north. This kingdom adopted Chinese political institutions in order to unify its territory and remained in power for four hundred years. **C**

In the thirteenth century, the Mongols seized the northern part of Korea. By accepting Mongol authority, the Koryo dynasty managed to remain in power. Mongol rule led to much suffering for the Korean people, especially the thousands of peasants and artisans who were forced to build ships for Kublai Khan's invasion of Japan.

After the collapse of the Mongol dynasty in China, the Koryo dynasty broke down. In 1392 **Yi Sŏng-gye,** a military commander, seized power and founded the Yi dynasty, which would rule Korea for over five hundred years. The Korean people were once again in charge of their own destiny.

✓Reading Check **Identifying** Which Asian country had the greatest influence on Korean political institutions?

SECTION 3 REVIEW

Vocabulary
1. **Explain** the significance of: Ōsaka, Kyōto, Shōtoku Taishi, revenue, samurai, code, Bushido, Minamoto Yoritomo, shogun, daimyo, Shinto, Zen, Murasaki Shikibu, Yi Sŏng-gye.

Main Ideas
2. **List** the reforms in government made by Shōtoku Taishi and his successors.
3. **Create** a cluster diagram like the one below that clarifies the role of women in early Japan.

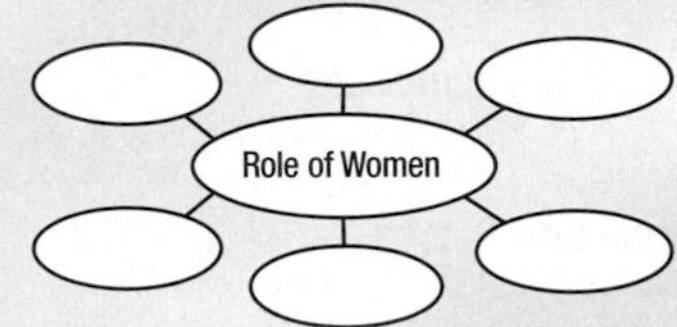

4. **Explain** why China had such a large role in Korea's history.

Critical Thinking
5. **The BIG Idea** **Hypothesizing** If Korea had been an island instead of a peninsula, how might its history have been different?
6. **Assessing** How did the samurai and shogun affect the government of early Japan?
7. **Analyzing Visuals** Examine the color woodblock on page 282. What does the illustration tell us about the clothing, customs, and living conditions among the nobility in Heian-era Japan?

Writing About History
8. **Descriptive Writing** Imagine you are a samurai living in Japan during the fourteenth century. Explain why you became a samurai and describe your duties.

History ONLINE
For help with the concepts in this section of *Glencoe World History*, go to glencoe.com and click Study Central™.

283

C Critical Thinking

Making Inferences Ask: How do you think the Tang Dynasty supported the kingdom of Silla in gaining control of Korea? *(possibly with military or economic support)* **OL**

✓Reading Check

Answer: China

Assess

History ONLINE

Study Central provides summaries, interactive games, and online graphic organizers to help students review content.

Close

Drawing Conclusions Ask: How did isolation affect Japan? *(Japan developed many unique cultural elements, but did not develop as rapidly in technology because of its limited contact with other cultures.)* **OL**

Answers

1. Definitions for the vocabulary words are found in the section and the Glossary.
2. portrayed ruler as a divine figure; divided territory into administrative districts; taxes paid directly to central government
3. had inheritance rights; abandoned wives could divorce; husbands could divorce wives for many reasons; played active role in society; women became artists and writers; women shared work
4. The northern part of Korea was at one point under control of China; Korea adopted Chinese political institutions.
5. Answers will vary, but should discuss Korea's connection to China.
6. **samurai:** kept Japan from developing strong central government; **shogun:** aristocrat who effectively ruled Japan
7. Answers may include that the clothing and customs appear to be very elaborate while the living conditions appear to be simple.
8. Answers will vary, but should be consistent with the material presented.

Focus

Bellringer

Daily Focus Transparency 8.4

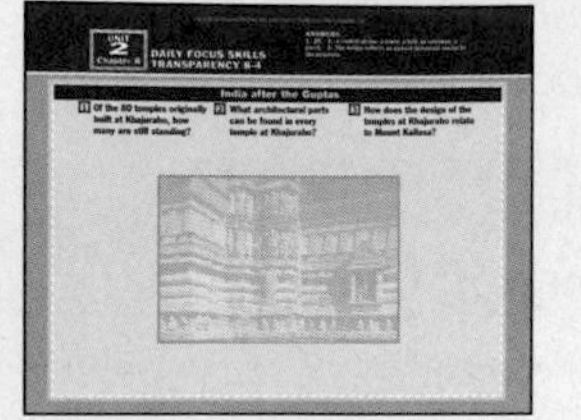

GUIDE TO READING

Answers to Graphic:
Theravada: Buddhism a philosophy; Buddha a wise man, not divine; nirvana achieved through understanding of self; no belief in salvation or afterlife; **Mahayana:** Buddhism a religion; the Buddha a divine figure; nirvana achieved through devotion to the Buddha; belief in the possibility of salvation and an afterlife

Section Spotlight Video

To generate student interest and provide a springboard for class discussion, access the Chapter 8, Section 4 video at glencoe.com or on the video DVD.

India After the Guptas

GUIDE TO READING

The BIG Idea
Ideas, Beliefs, and Values When Islamic peoples conquered much of India, tension arose between the Muslim rulers and the majority Hindu population.

Content Vocabulary
- Theravada *(p. 284)*
- Mahayana *(p. 284)*

Academic Vocabulary
- retained *(p. 284)*
- traditional *(p. 289)*

People and Places
- Ghazna (Ghaznī) *(p. 286)*
- Maḥmūd of Ghazna *(p. 286)*
- Rajputs *(p. 286)*
- sultanate of Delhi *(p. 286)*
- Timur Lenk *(p. 286)*
- Samarqand *(p. 286)*
- Moguls *(p. 286)*
- Daṇḍin *(p. 289)*

Reading Strategy
Contrasting As you read, use a chart like the one below to help you study the main differences between Theravada and Mahayana Buddhism.

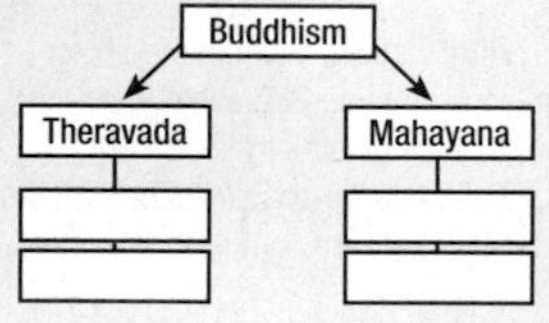

After the Gupta Empire collapsed, Muslim conquerors moved into India, eventually taking control of nearly all of the subcontinent. The majority of the population in India remained Hindu, which often led to tension and open conflict.

The Impact of Religion

MAIN IDEA Buddhism, Hinduism, and Islam all influenced the development of India.

HISTORY & YOU How have patterns of religious belief changed in your own state or region? Read about the patterns of religion in India.

For hundreds of years, Buddhism had **retained** widespread acceptance among the Indian people. The teachings of the Buddha came to be interpreted in different ways, however. People did not always agree on the meaning of the Buddha's teachings. As a result, a split developed among the followers of Buddhism in India.

One group believed that they were following the original teachings of the Buddha. They called themselves the school of **Theravada,** "the teachings of the elders." Followers of Theravada see Buddhism as a way of life, not a religion that is centered on individual salvation. They continue to insist that an understanding of oneself is the chief way to gain nirvana, or release from the "wheel of life."

Another view of Buddhist doctrine was emerging in northwest India. This school, known as **Mahayana** Buddhism, said that Theravada teachings were too strict for ordinary people. To Mahayana Buddhists, Buddhism is a religion, not a philosophy. The Buddha is not just a wise man, but also a divine figure. Nirvana is not just a release from the wheel of life, but a true heaven. Through devotion to the Buddha, people can achieve salvation in this heaven after death.

The Decline of Buddhism

In the end, neither the Mahayana nor the Theravada sect of Buddhism remained popular in Indian society. By the 600s, Theravada had declined rapidly. Mahayana was absorbed by a revived Hinduism and later by a new arrival, Islam. Despite their decline in India, though, both schools of Buddhism found success abroad. Carried by monks to China, Korea, Southeast Asia, and Japan, the practice of Buddhism has remained active in all four areas to the present.

Resource Manager

R Reading Strategies	C Critical Thinking	D Differentiated Instruction	W Writing Support	S Skill Practice
Teacher Edition • Det. Importance., p. 287 • Outlining, p. 289 **Additional Resources** • Read. Skills Act., URB p. 91 • Hist. Sig. Act., URB p. 106 • Guid. Read. Act., URB p. 125 • Read. Ess. & Note-Taking Guide, p. 91	**Teacher Edition** • Making Inferences, p. 285 • Analyzing Pri. Sources, p. 285 **Additional Resources** • Hist. & Geo. Act., URB p. 103 • Section Quiz, p. 94	**Teacher Edition** • ELL, p. 287 • Kinesthetic, p. 288 **Additional Resources** • Read. Strat. for SS., p. 68 • Foods Around the World, p. 30	**Teacher Edition** • Descriptive Writing, p. 286 **Additional Resources** • People in World Hist. Act., URB p. 114 • Writer's Guidebook, p. 43	**Teacher Edition** • Visual Literacy, p. 288 **Additional Resources** • Pri. Source Read., URB p. 115

INFOGRAPHICS

Buddhism, Hinduism, and Islam in India

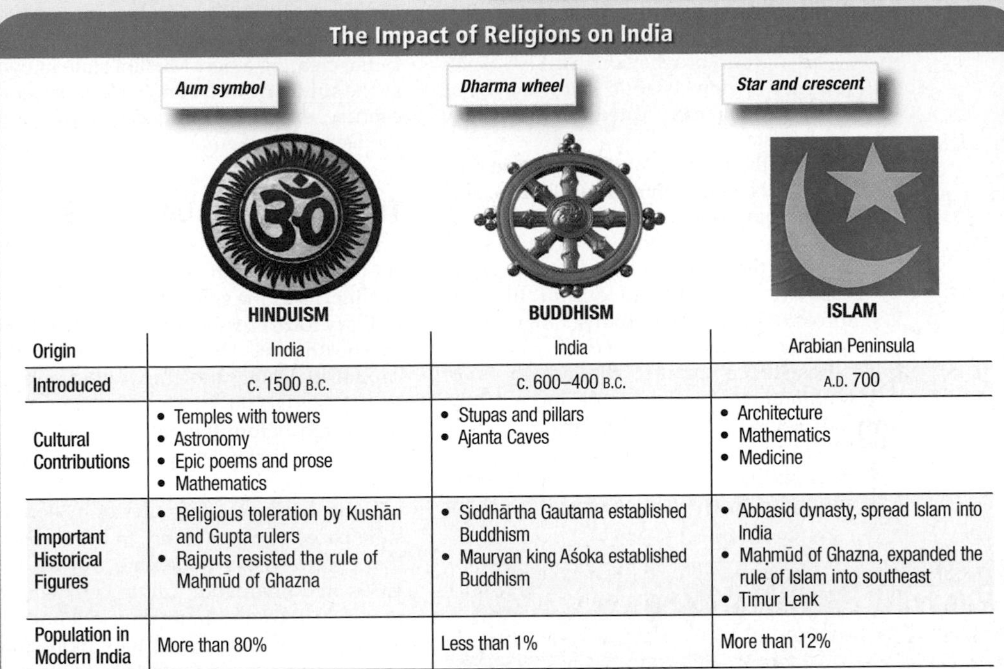

The Impact of Religions on India

	HINDUISM (Aum symbol)	BUDDHISM (Dharma wheel)	ISLAM (Star and crescent)
Origin	India	India	Arabian Peninsula
Introduced	c. 1500 B.C.	c. 600–400 B.C.	A.D. 700
Cultural Contributions	• Temples with towers • Astronomy • Epic poems and prose • Mathematics	• Stupas and pillars • Ajanta Caves	• Architecture • Mathematics • Medicine
Important Historical Figures	• Religious toleration by Kushān and Gupta rulers • Rajputs resisted the rule of Maḥmūd of Ghazna	• Siddhārtha Gautama established Buddhism • Mauryan king Aśoka established Buddhism	• Abbasid dynasty, spread Islam into India • Maḥmūd of Ghazna, expanded the rule of Islam into southeast • Timur Lenk
Population in Modern India	More than 80%	Less than 1%	More than 12%

Chart SKILLS

1. **Analyzing** Why would Buddhism and Hinduism share many similarities?
2. **Making Inferences** Why might it be difficult to trace the religious history of India?

The Eastward Expansion of Islam

In the early eighth century, Islam became popular in the northwestern part of the Indian subcontinent and had a major impact on Indian civilization. This impact is still evident today in the division of the subcontinent into mostly Hindu India and two Islamic states, Bangladesh and Pakistan. One reason for Islam's success was the state of political disunity in India when it arrived. The Gupta Empire had collapsed, and no central authority had **C1** replaced it. India was divided into about 70 states, which fought constantly. During this time, warriors were held in very high esteem. One Indian poet wrote:

PRIMARY SOURCE

> "When you see a fight, rush to the front, divide your enemy's forces, stand before them, and get your body scarred by the deep cuts of their swords; thus your fame is pleasant to the ear, not your body to the eye. As for your enemies, when they see you, they turn their backs, and with bodies whole and unscarred, they are pleasant to the eye, not so their shame to the ear." **C2**

Teach

C1 Critical Thinking

Making Inferences Ask: How do you think political disunity helped Islam succeed in South Asia? *(Because of upheaval and conflict, old religions might have been seen as ineffective; people might have been looking for a new religious belief system.)* **OL**

C2 Critical Thinking

Analyzing Primary Sources Ask students to re-read the quotation carefully. **Ask:** Which does the poet think is better for a warrior—having an unscarred or a scarred body? *(scarred, because fame for being brave in battle is better than remaining unscarred and retreating in battle)* **OL**

Chart SKILLS

Answers:

1. Answers may include that both were ancient religions that originated in India.
2. Possible answer: because of the many changes that took place in India over the centuries

Hands-On Chapter Project Step 4

Planning a Web Site for Early Asian History

Step 4: Developments in India After the Guptas Pairs of students will continue designing their Web site on important developments in early Asian history.

Directions: Pairs of students will select one important development in the military, government, religion, the arts, or another area in India during the time period studied.

Have students review the chapter for possible ideas, such as the spread of Islam in northwest India or the impact of Timur Lenk.

Students should find or create an image to include and write text that explains the background and significance of the selected development. **OL**

(Chapter Project is continued in Section 5.)

W Writing Support

Descriptive Writing Ask students to discuss the military tactics of using infantry backed by elephants and those using mounted cavalry. Students might want to do additional research. Then have them write two descriptive paragraphs that describe an actual or imagined battle between these types of troops. **AL**

PEOPLE in HISTORY

Answers: He built an empire; his cruelty toward others was striking.

✓Reading Check

Answer: Islam was a unifying force, and today Bangladesh and Pakistan are primarily Islamic states.

When the Arab armies reached India in the early eighth century, they did little more than move into the frontier regions. At the end of the tenth century, however, a new phase of Islamic expansion took place when a group of rebellious Turkish slaves founded a new Islamic state known as **Ghazna (Ghaznī),** located in what is now Afghanistan.

When the founder of the new state died in 997, his son, **Maḥmūd of Ghazna,** succeeded him. Maḥmūd, an ambitious man, began to attack neighboring Hindu kingdoms to the southeast. Before his death in 1030, he was able to extend his rule throughout the upper Indus Valley and as far south as the Indian Ocean.

W Resistance against the advances of Maḥmūd and his successors into northern India was led by the **Rajputs,** who were Hindu warriors. They fought bravely, but their military tactics, based on infantry supported by elephants, were no match for the cavalry of the invaders. Maḥmūd's cavalry was able to strike with great speed. Maḥmūd's successors continued their advances. By 1200, Muslim power had reached over the entire plain of northern India, creating a new Muslim state known as the **sultanate of Delhi.** In the fourteenth century, this state extended its power into the Deccan Plateau.

PEOPLE in HISTORY

Timur Lenk
Turkic Conqueror 1336–1405

Timur Lenk was a shrewd warrior who built an empire that stretched from modern-day Iraq to India, and from the Arabian Sea to modern-day Kazakhstan. His initial rise to power involved first rebelling against the khan to whom he had vowed allegiance, then turning on the brother-in-law who had helped him overthrow the khan. His cruelty toward his enemies and the people he conquered was legendary. For example, when conquered Persians tried to rebel against Timur's forces in 1395, the residents of entire cities were killed and towers built of the victims' skulls. **Why might Timur's life have been the subject of legends?**

The Impact of Timur Lenk

During the latter half of the fourteenth century, the sultanate of Delhi began to decline. Near the end of the century, a new military force crossed the Indus River from the northwest. The invaders raided the capital of Delhi, and then withdrew. As many as 100,000 Hindu prisoners were massacred before the gates of the city. It was India's first meeting with **Timur Lenk** (Tamerlane).

Timur Lenk was the ruler of a Mongol state based in **Samarqand,** to the north of the Pamirs. Born sometime during the 1330s in Samarqand, Timur Lenk seized power in 1369 and immediately launched a program of conquest. It took more than a century for the city of Delhi to recover from the destruction caused by the invasion.

During the 1380s, Timur Lenk placed the entire region east of the Caspian Sea under his authority and then occupied Mesopotamia. After his brief foray into northern India, he turned to the west. He died in 1405 in the midst of a military campaign.

The death of Timur Lenk removed a major menace from the various states of the Indian subcontinent, but the calm did not last long. By the early sixteenth century, two new challenges had appeared from beyond the horizon. One came from the north in the form of the **Moguls,** a newly emerging nomadic power. The other came from Europe, from Portuguese traders arriving by sea in search of gold and spices. Both the Moguls and the Portuguese would exert a major impact on the later course of Indian civilization.

✓Reading Check **Evaluating** What was the impact of the introduction of Islam in India?

Differentiated Instruction

Historical Significance Activity, URB p. 106

Analyzing Information

Objective: Make connections between Islam and economics.

Focus: Have students explain the passage's central metaphor (the circulatory system).

Teach: Discuss how the Quran serves as a "manual for businessmen."

Assess: Have students identify ways Islam has guided economic activities.

Close: Ask students to summarize the connections between Islam and economics.

Differentiated Instruction Strategies

- **BL** Have students illustrate the passage's central metaphor and label it.
- **AL** Have students report on the connection of another religion to economics and then compare both approaches.
- **ELL** Help students interpret "sluggishness," "blood clots," and "capillaries" within the central metaphor.

Indian Society and Culture

MAIN IDEA The ruling class of India was made up of Muslims, but some members of the Hindu population also prospered. The rich culture of India was reflected in its art, literature, architecture, and technological advances.

HISTORY & YOU Recall the interaction between Aryans and Dravidians. Read to compare with the interaction between Hindus and Muslims.

The imposition of Islamic rule by Maḥmūd of Ghazna and his successors created a level of general tension in Indian society. The life of the typical Indian, however, remained about the same as it had been for the past several hundred years.

Islam and Indian Society

The Muslim rulers in India viewed themselves as foreign conquerors. They tried to maintain a strict separation between the Muslim ruling class and the Hindu population.

Like rulers elsewhere at this time, many Muslim rulers in India were intolerant of other faiths. They generally used peaceful means, however, to encourage people to convert to Islam. Still, some could be fierce when their religious zeal was aroused. Said one,

PRIMARY SOURCE

> "I forbade the infliction of any severe punishment on the Hindus in general, but I destroyed their idol temples and raised mosques in their place."
>
> —a Muslim ruler

Most Muslim rulers realized that there were simply too many Hindus to convert them all. They reluctantly accepted the need to tolerate religious differences. Nevertheless, Muslim rulers did impose many Islamic customs on Hindu society. Overall, **R** the relationship between Muslims and Hindus was that of conqueror and conquered, a relationship marked by suspicion and dislike rather than friendship and understanding.

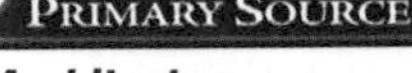

PRIMARY SOURCE — HISTORY & ARTS

Islamic Architecture

Adhai-Din-Ka Jhonpra was built by the Jains, a minority religious group in India with similarities to both Hinduism and Buddhism. The building may have been a temple and college for teaching Sanskrit. In 1198, the sultan of Delhi turned it into a mosque and built a seven-arched wall inscribed with verses in Arabic. The wall and minarets may have been built with mortar from Hindu and Jain temples that the Sultan destroyed. The interior of the Jhonpra resembles a Hindu temple more than a mosque. The pointed arches and minarets are characteristic of Islamic architecture. **D**

DOCUMENT-BASED QUESTIONS

1. **Drawing Conclusions** Why did the sultan of Delhi destroy Hindu and Jain temples?
2. **Describing** How does this mosque represent Indo-Islamic architecture?

R Reading Strategy

Determining Importance

Ask: What was the most important factor in Muslim rulers' decisions to generally tolerate the Hindu religion? *(There were too many Hindus to be able to force them to convert to Islam, so they allowed them to continue practicing Hindu beliefs.)* **BL**

D Differentiated Instruction

English Language Learners

Ask a volunteer to read aloud the text for the Islamic Architecture feature. Then write on the board: *arch, minaret, mortar.* In their notebooks, have students define these terms and use each in a complete sentence. To extend the activity, have students do the same for other terms related to Islamic architecture. **ELL**

DOCUMENT-BASED QUESTIONS

Answers:

1. Possible answer: The sultan may have wanted only Islam to be followed.
2. It combines Hindu elements (the interior) with Islamic elements (the exterior).

Leveled Activities

BL Guided Reading Activity, URB p. 125

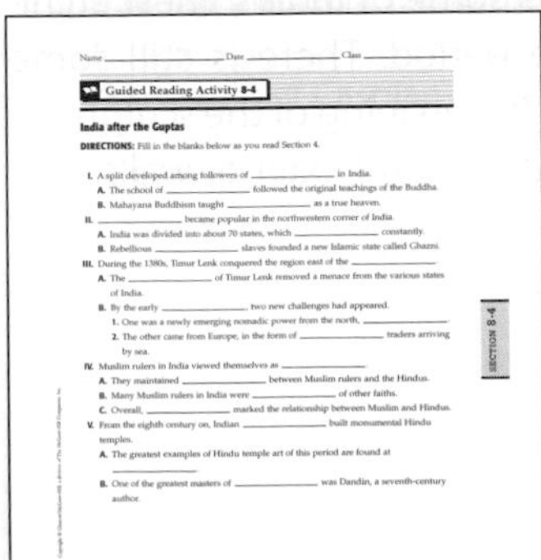

OL History & Geography Activity, URB p. 103

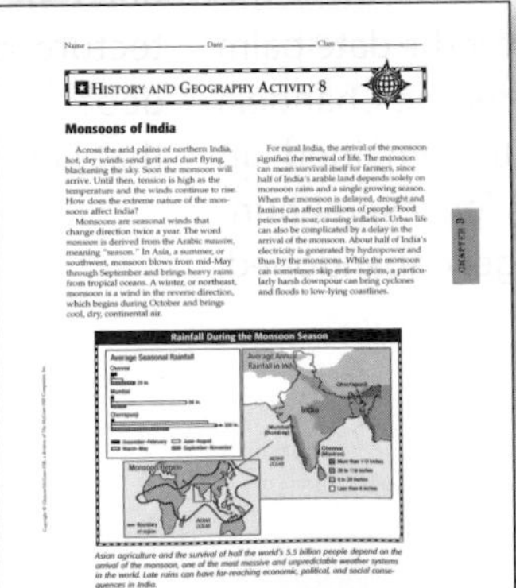

AL Primary Source Reading, URB p. 115

ELL Reading Strategies for Social Studies, p. 68

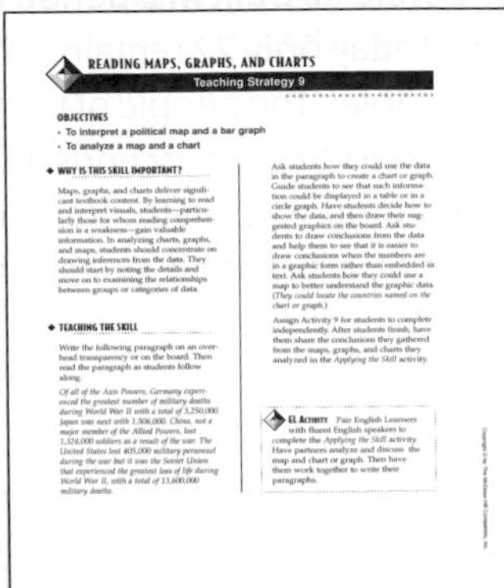

Focus

Bellringer

Daily Focus Transparency 8.5

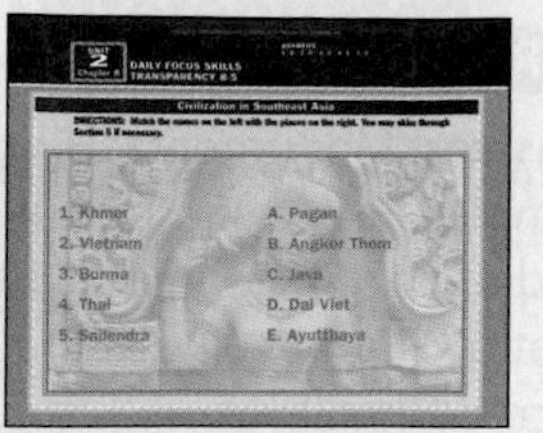

GUIDE TO READING

Answers to Graphic:
Vietnam: based on Chinese model; agricultural; Chinese-Confucianism; **Angkor:** based on Indian model; agricultural; Indian; **Thailand:** based on Indian model, agricultural; Indian-Buddhist; **Burma:** based on Indian model; agricultural, sea trade; Indian-Buddhist; **Malay:** kingdoms based on Indian model, sultanates based on Islamic model; trade, agricultural; Indian, Islamic

Section Spotlight Video

To generate student interest and provide a springboard for class discussion, access the Chapter 8, Section 5 video at glencoe.com or on the video DVD.

Civilization in Southeast Asia

GUIDE TO READING

The BIG Idea
Physical Geography The mountains, river valleys, and islands of Southeast Asia had a major effect on its political, cultural, and economic development.

Content Vocabulary
- archipelago *(p. 290)*
- agricultural society *(p. 294)*
- trading society *(p. 294)*

Academic Vocabulary
- region *(p. 290)*
- area *(p. 290)*

People and Places
- Malay Peninsula *(p. 290)*
- Vietnam *(p. 291)*
- Angkor *(p. 292)*
- Jayavarman *(p. 292)*
- Pagan *(p. 292)*
- Thai *(p. 292)*
- Thailand *(p. 292)*
- Strait of Malacca *(p. 293)*
- Melaka *(p. 294)*

Reading Strategy
Categorizing Information As you read, create a chart like the one below to help you study characteristics of the states in Southeast Asia.

	Government	Economy	Culture
Vietnam			
Angkor			
Thailand			
Burma			
Malay			

Unlike most of the other regions of Asia, Southeast Asia was never unified under a single government, largely due to its formidable geographic barriers. Therefore, the history of the area tells of the competition and interaction between several small states.

The Formation of States

MAIN IDEA The geography of Southeast Asia led to the development of distinct cultures throughout the region.

HISTORY & YOU Millions of people have visited the monuments in Southeast Asia. Which structures would you be most interested in seeing?

Between 500 and 1500, a number of organized states developed throughout Southeast Asia. When the peoples of the region began to form states, they used models from China and India. At the same time, they adapted these models to their own needs and created their own unique states.

The Impact of Geography

Between China and India lies the **region** that today is called Southeast Asia. It has two major parts. One is the mainland region, extending southward from the Chinese border down to the tip of the **Malay Peninsula.** The other is an extensive **archipelago,** or chain of islands, most of which is part of present-day Indonesia and the Philippines.

Ancient mariners called the **area** the "golden region" or "golden islands." Located between India and China—two highly advanced and densely populated regions—Southeast Asia contains a vast mixture of races, cultures, and religions.

Mainland Southeast Asia consists of several north-south mountain ranges. Between these ranges are fertile river valleys that run in a southerly or southeasterly direction. The mountains are densely forested and often infested with malaria-bearing mosquitoes. Thus, the people living in the river valleys were often cut off from one another and had only limited contact with the people living in the mountains.

These geographical barriers may help explain why Southeast Asia is one of the few regions in Asia that was never unified under a single government. The geographical barriers encouraged the development of separate, distinctive cultures within Southeast Asia, with diverse cultural practices, such as different religions and languages.

Resource Manager

R Reading Strategies

Teacher Edition
- Act. Prior Know., p. 292
- Det. Importance., p. 293

Additional Resources
- Cont. Vocab. Act., URB p. 97
- Guid. Read. Act., URB p. 126
- Read. Ess. & Note-Taking Guide, p. 94

C Critical Thinking

Teacher Edition
- Analyzing Pri. Sources, p. 291
- Det. Cause/Effect, p. 292
- Ident. Cent. Issues, p. 294

Additional Resources
- Crit. Think. Act., URB p. 102
- Section Quiz, p. 95
- Chapter Test, p. 97

D Differentiated Instruction

Teacher Edition
- Visual/Spatial, p. 293
- ELL, p. 295

Additional Resources
- Hist. Sim. Act., URB p. 109
- Read. Strat. for SS., p. 89

W Writing Support

Teacher Edition
- Descriptive Writing, p. 294

Additional Resources
- Academic Vocab. Act., URB p. 99
- Writer's Guidebook, p. 57

S Skill Practice

Teacher Edition
- Using Geo. Skills, p. 291

Additional Resources
- Mapping Hist. Act., URB p. 105
- Time Line Act., URB p. 111

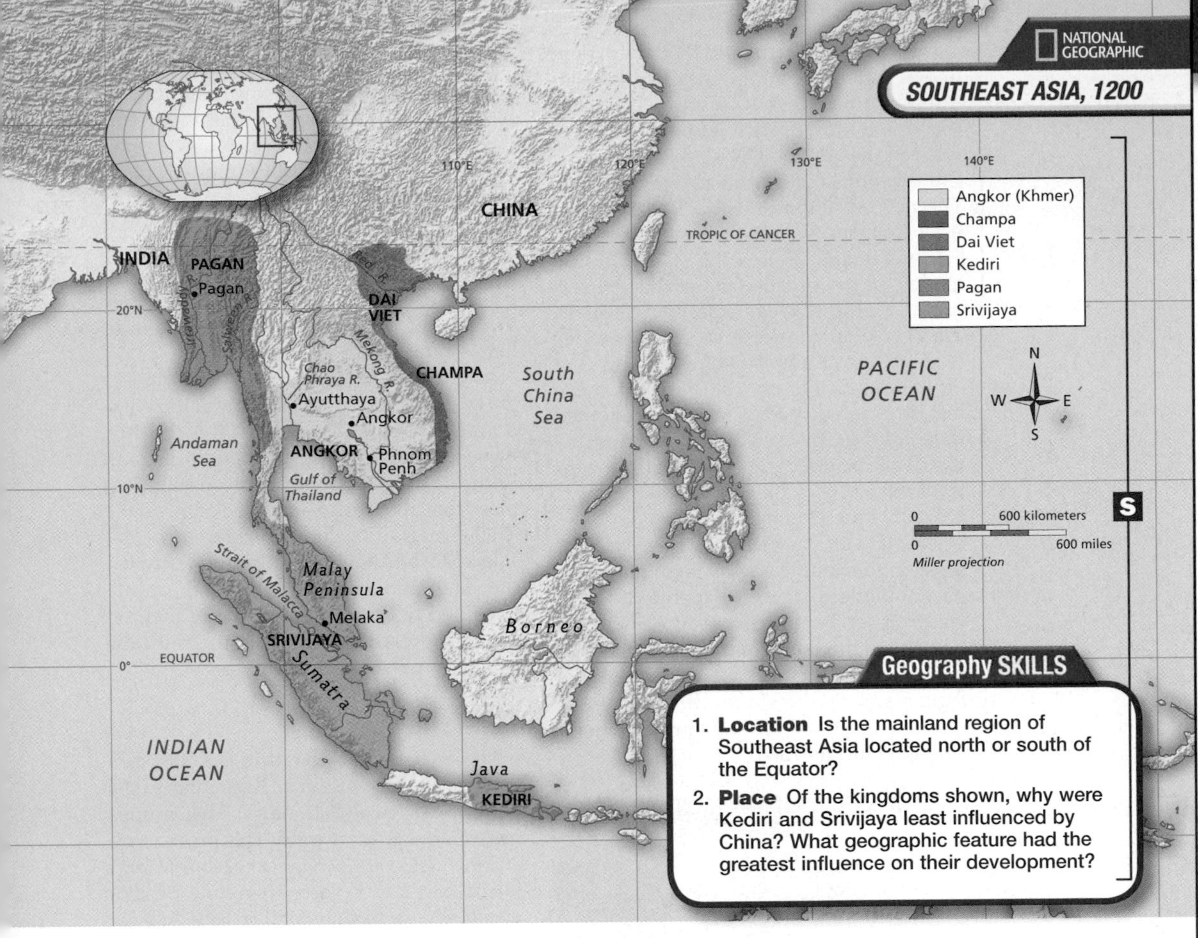

Geography SKILLS

1. **Location** Is the mainland region of Southeast Asia located north or south of the Equator?
2. **Place** Of the kingdoms shown, why were Kediri and Srivijaya least influenced by China? What geographic feature had the greatest influence on their development?

Vietnam

The Vietnamese were one of the first peoples in Southeast Asia to develop their own state and their own culture. This strong sense of cultural identity caused difficulties for would-be conquerors. China, larger and more powerful than Vietnam, first attempted an invasion in the 200s B.C., but quickly ran into problems:

PRIMARY SOURCE

"The Viet people fled into the depths of the mountains and forests, and it was not possible to fight them. The soldiers were kept in garrisons to watch over abandoned territories. This went on for a long time, and the soldiers grew weary. Then the Viet came out and attacked; the Chinese soldiers suffered a great defeat; the dead and wounded were many. After this, the emperor deported convicts to hold the garrisons against the Viet people."

— Keith W. Taylor, *The Birth of Vietnam*

After over a hundred years of warfare, the Chinese finally conquered **Vietnam** in 111 B.C. They tried for centuries to make Vietnam part of China; however, Chinese officials were often frustrated by the Vietnamese. As one official said,

PRIMARY SOURCE

"The people are like birds and beasts; they wear their hair tied up and go barefoot, while for clothing they simply cut a hole in a piece of cloth for their head or they fasten their garments on the left side. It is useless to try to change them."

— Keith W. Taylor, *The Birth of Vietnam*

Teach

S Skill Practice

Using Geography Skills

Ask: Why do you think much of Borneo did not develop as quickly as other areas? *(Mountains presented geographical barriers.)* **BL**

C Critical Thinking

Analyzing Primary Sources

Discuss how Chinese culture might have differed from that of Vietnam at the time. **Ask:** How do you think the people of Vietnam would have described their Chinese conquerors? *(Answers will vary, but should show an understanding of how different cultures frequently misunderstand each other.)* **AL**

Geography SKILLS

Answers:

1. north
2. They were located farther from China; the fact that they were on an island and/or peninsula.

Hands-On Chapter Project
Step 5

Planning a Web Site for Early Asian History

Step 5: Developments in Southeast Asia Pairs of students will continue designing their Web site on important developments in early Asian history.

Directions: Pairs of students will select one important development in the military, government, religion, the arts, or another area in Southeast Asia during the time period studied.

Have students review the chapter for possible ideas, such as the development of the Vietnamese state, called Dai Viet, or the development of Melaka on the Malay Peninsula. Students should find or create an image to include and write text that explains the background and significance of the selected development. Students should also begin planning a home page for their Web site. **OL**

(Chapter Project is completed on the Visual Summary page.)

R Reading Strategy

Activating Prior Knowledge
Review how Japan's rulers related to Chinese influence at the time.
Ask: How were the reactions of Japan's rulers to Chinese culture similar to those of Vietnam's rulers? *(Both resisted Chinese invasions and control, yet adopted a Chinese model of government.)* **OL**

C Critical Thinking

Determining Cause and Effect **Ask:** How did Angkor's location affect its ability to defend itself? *(Because Angkor was surrounded by enemies, it was very hard to protect its people and culture.)* **OL**

For additional practice on this skill, see the **Skills Handbook**.

People in History

Answer: He was likely a Khmer, and his *devaraja* cult incorporated local religious traditions.

Differentiated Instruction

The Vietnamese clung to their own identity. In the tenth century, they finally overthrew Chinese rule. Chinese influence remained, however. Vietnamese rulers realized the advantages of taking over the Chinese model of centralized government. The new Vietnamese state, which called itself Dai Viet—Great Viet—adopted state Confucianism. Following the Chinese model, the rulers called themselves emperors and adopted Chinese court rituals. They also introduced the civil service examination as a means of recruiting government officials on the basis of merit instead of heredity. The Vietnamese adopted much of the Chinese administrative structure. This included the village at the lowest level, which, like its Chinese model, was basically independent.

The state of Dai Viet became a dynamic force on the Southeast Asian mainland. As its population grew, it expanded southward. Several centuries of bitter warfare with its southern neighbor, Champa, ended in Vietnamese victory by 1500. Continuing their march to the south, the Vietnamese reached the Gulf of Thailand (formerly Gulf of Siam) by 1600.

People in History

Jayavarman II
c. 770–850 Founder of Khmer Empire

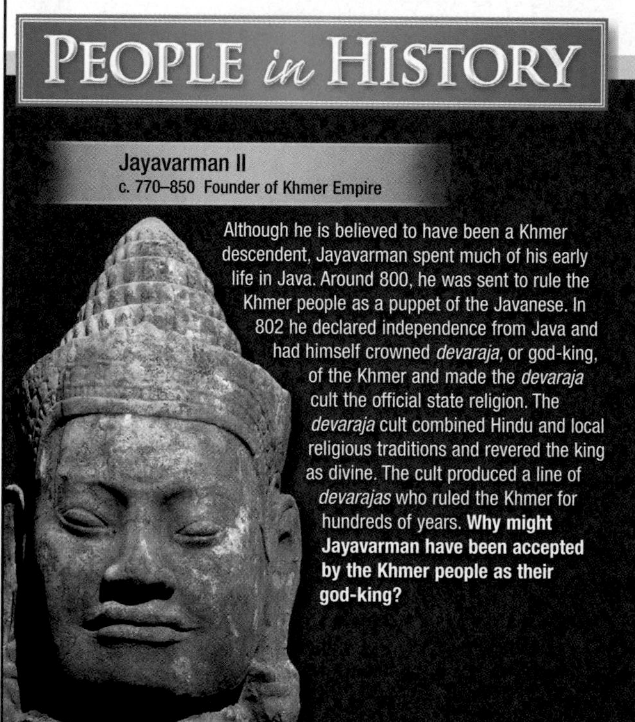

Although he is believed to have been a Khmer descendent, Jayavarman spent much of his early life in Java. Around 800, he was sent to rule the Khmer people as a puppet of the Javanese. In 802 he declared independence from Java and had himself crowned *devaraja*, or god-king, of the Khmer and made the *devaraja* cult the official state religion. The *devaraja* cult combined Hindu and local religious traditions and revered the king as divine. The cult produced a line of *devarajas* who ruled the Khmer for hundreds of years. **Why might Jayavarman have been accepted by the Khmer people as their god-king?**

Angkor

In the ninth century, the kingdom of **Angkor** arose in the region that is present-day Cambodia. The kingdom was formed when a powerful figure named **Jayavarman** united the Khmer (kuh•MEHR) people and established a capital at Angkor Thom. In 802 Jayavarman was crowned as god-king of his people. For several hundred years, Angkor—or the Khmer Empire—was the most powerful state in mainland Southeast Asia.

Angkor faced enemies on all sides. To the east were the Vietnamese and the kingdom of Champa. To the west was the Burmese kingdom of **Pagan** (modern Bagan). With the arrival in the 1300s of new peoples from the north—known today as the **Thai**—Angkor began to decline.

In 1432 the Thai from the north destroyed the Angkor capital. The Angkor ruling class fled to the southeast, where they set up a new capital near Phnom Penh, the capital of present-day Cambodia.

Thailand

The Thai first appeared in the 500s as a frontier people in China. Beginning in the eleventh or twelfth century, Thai groups began moving southward. This process was encouraged by the Mongol invasion of China in the mid-1200s. These migrating peoples eventually came into conflict with Angkor, destroying the Angkor capital in 1432.

The Thai set up their own capital at Ayutthaya (AH•yoo•TY•uh) on the Chao Phraya River, where they remained as a major force in the region for the next 400 years. Although many converted to Buddhism, the Thai were also influenced by Hindu religion and Indian culture in their political practices, dance, and literature. This unique blend eventually became the modern-day culture of **Thailand.**

Burma

The Thai were also threatened from the west by the Burmese peoples, who had formed their society along the Salween and Irrawaddy Rivers. The Burmese had migrated from Tibet beginning in the 600s, probably to escape Chinese armies.

Leveled Activities

BL Guided Reading Activity, URB p. 126

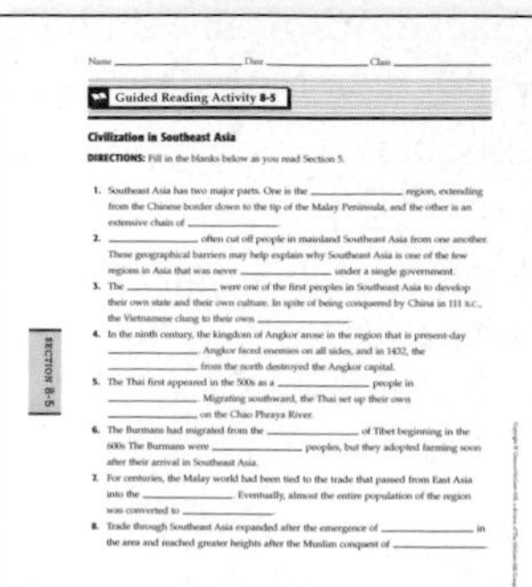

OL Critical Thinking Skills Activity, URB p. 102

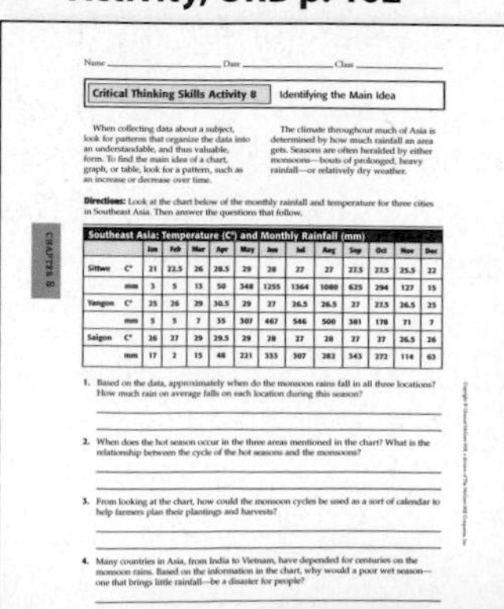

AL Mapping History Activity, URB p. 105

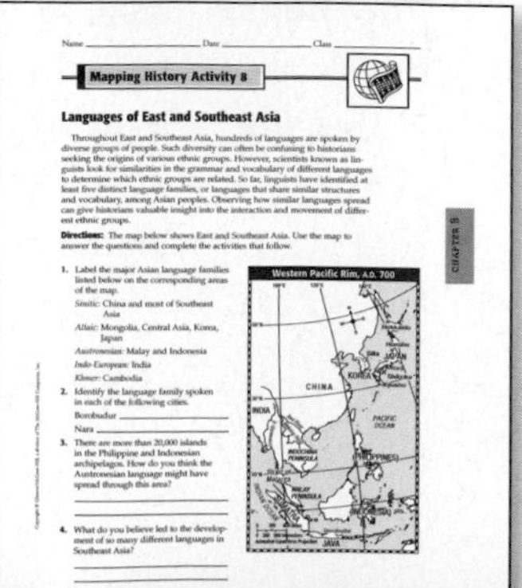

ELL History Simulation Activity, URB p. 109

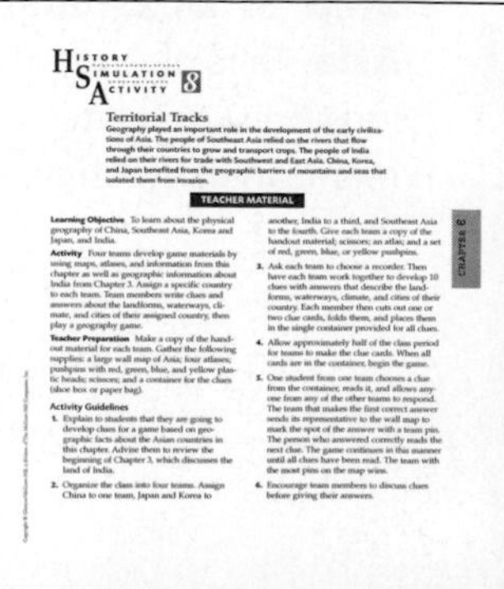

States of Southeast Asia, 111 B.C.–A.D. 1600

STATE	ERA	CULTURAL INFLUENCE(S)	ECONOMIC BASE
Mainland			
Vietnam	Conquered by China in 111 B.C.; independent in A.D. 939	China, Confucianism	Agriculture
Angkor	Arose in 9th century; destroyed by Thailand in 1432	India	Agriculture
Thailand	Thai people first appeared in 6th century, settling in area of present-day Thailand in 15th century	India, Buddhism	Agriculture
Burma (Pagan)	11th–13th centuries	India, Buddhism	Agriculture, sea trade
Malay Peninsula and Indonesian Archipelago			
Srivijaya	8th century	India	Sea trade
Sailendra	8th century	India	Agriculture
Majapahit	13th–15th centuries	Islam	Trade, agriculture
Melaka	15th century	Islam	Sea trade

D

Chart SKILLS

1. **Summarizing** What religions influenced these states?
2. **Analyzing** Explain why Majapahit and Melaka do not appear on the map on page 291.

The Burmese were pastoral peoples, but they adopted farming soon after their arrival in Southeast Asia. In the eleventh century, they founded the first great Burmese state, the kingdom of Pagan. Like the Thai, they converted to Buddhism and adopted Indian political institutions and culture.

R During the next two hundred years, Pagan became a major force in the western part of Southeast Asia. The capital city was at the center of a network of highways, which allowed it to exert power over large distances. It also played an active role in sea trade throughout the region. Attacks by the Mongols in the late 1200s, however, weakened Pagan, causing it to decline.

The Malay World

In the Malay Peninsula and the Indonesian archipelago, a different pattern emerged. For centuries, this area had been tied to the trade that passed from East Asia into the Indian Ocean. The area had never been united under a single state, however. The vast majority of the people of the region were of Malay background, but the peoples were divided into numerous separate communities.

Two organized states eventually emerged in the region. In the eighth century, the state of Srivijaya (SREE•wih•JAW•yuh) came to dominate the trade route passing through the **Strait of Malacca.**

At the same time, the kingdom of Sailendra emerged in eastern Java. Both states were influenced by Indian culture. Whereas Srivijaya depended on trade, the wealth of Sailendra was based primarily on farming.

In the late 1200s, the new kingdom of Majapahit (MAH•jah•PAH•hiht) was founded. It became the greatest empire the region had yet seen. In the mid-fourteenth century, Majapahit incorporated most of the archipelago and perhaps even parts of the mainland under a single rule. Majapahit did not have long to enjoy its status, however. By the 1400s, a new state was beginning to emerge in the region.

D Differentiated Instruction

Visual/Spatial To help students who have trouble analyzing charts, ask basic comprehension questions. **Ask:** When did the Thai people first appear? *(6th century)* **Ask:** Which states did Buddhism influence? *(Thailand, Burma [Pagan])* **BL**

R Reading Strategy

Determining Importance

Ask: How vital was transportation to the kingdom of Pagan? *(A system of roads allowed Pagan to control large areas and influence sea trade throughout the region.)* **OL**

Chart SKILLS

Answers:

1. Islam, Confucianism, Hinduism, Buddhism
2. Majapahit and Melaka do not appear on the map because the map represents Southeast Asia in 1200, which was before these states began.

Additional Support

Activity: Interdisciplinary Connection

Geography Have students draw their own maps of Southeast Asia and its various states. Have them pay special attention to topographical features and then evaluate which states would be more suited for agricultural societies and which would be more suited for maritime ones. In addition, ask students to analyze their maps and draw inferences about why Southeast Asia did not form a single civilization and why it was so prone to attack from abroad. Students should see that both Southeast Asia and India were prone to attack from abroad. **Ask:** Were these two areas prone to attack for the same reason? Why or why not? *(Answers may vary, but should be supported with logical conclusions.)* **OL**

C Critical Thinking

Identifying Central Issues

Ask: How were Islam and economic issues related in the growth of Melaka? *(Muslim traders expanded trade there, which allowed Islam to spread.)* **OL**

W Writing Support

Descriptive Writing Ask students to visualize trade in Southeast Asia. Then have them write a paragraph that describes what they might have seen at the time, such as a ship loaded with spices. **BL**

DOCUMENT-BASED QUESTIONS

Answers:

1. It includes bas-reliefs of ancient Indian stories; mimics the traditional Hindu model of the universe; was a place of worship for Hindus and Buddhists.
2. Answers will vary, but may include helping keep out overgrowth by the jungle.

✓Reading Check

Answer: geographic barriers, distinct cultures, diverse languages and religions

Additional Support

After the Muslim conquest of northern India, Muslim merchants—either Arabs or Indian converts—settled in port cities in the region and began to convert the local population. Around 1400, an Islamic state began to form in **Melaka,** a small town on the western coast of the Malay Peninsula. Traders found it a natural place to replenish their supplies of food and water. Melaka soon became the major trading port in the region and a chief rival to Majapahit. From Melaka, Muslim traders and the Muslim faith moved into the interior of the peninsula. Eventually, almost the entire population of the region was converted to Islam and became part of the sultanate of Melaka.

✓Reading Check **Examining** Why was Southeast Asia never unified under a single government?

Life in Southeast Asia

MAIN IDEA The growth of the states of Southeast Asia depended largely on trade and agriculture.

HISTORY & YOU What is the most impressive building in the United States? Read about the temple of Angkor Wat in Southeast Asia.

The states of Southeast Asia can be divided into two groups: **agricultural societies,** whose economies were largely based on farming, and **trading societies,** which depended primarily on trade for income. States such as Vietnam, Angkor, Pagan, and Sailendra drew most of their wealth from the land. Others, such as Srivijaya and the sultanate of Melaka, supported themselves chiefly through trade.

HISTORY & ARTS PRIMARY SOURCE

Angkor Wat

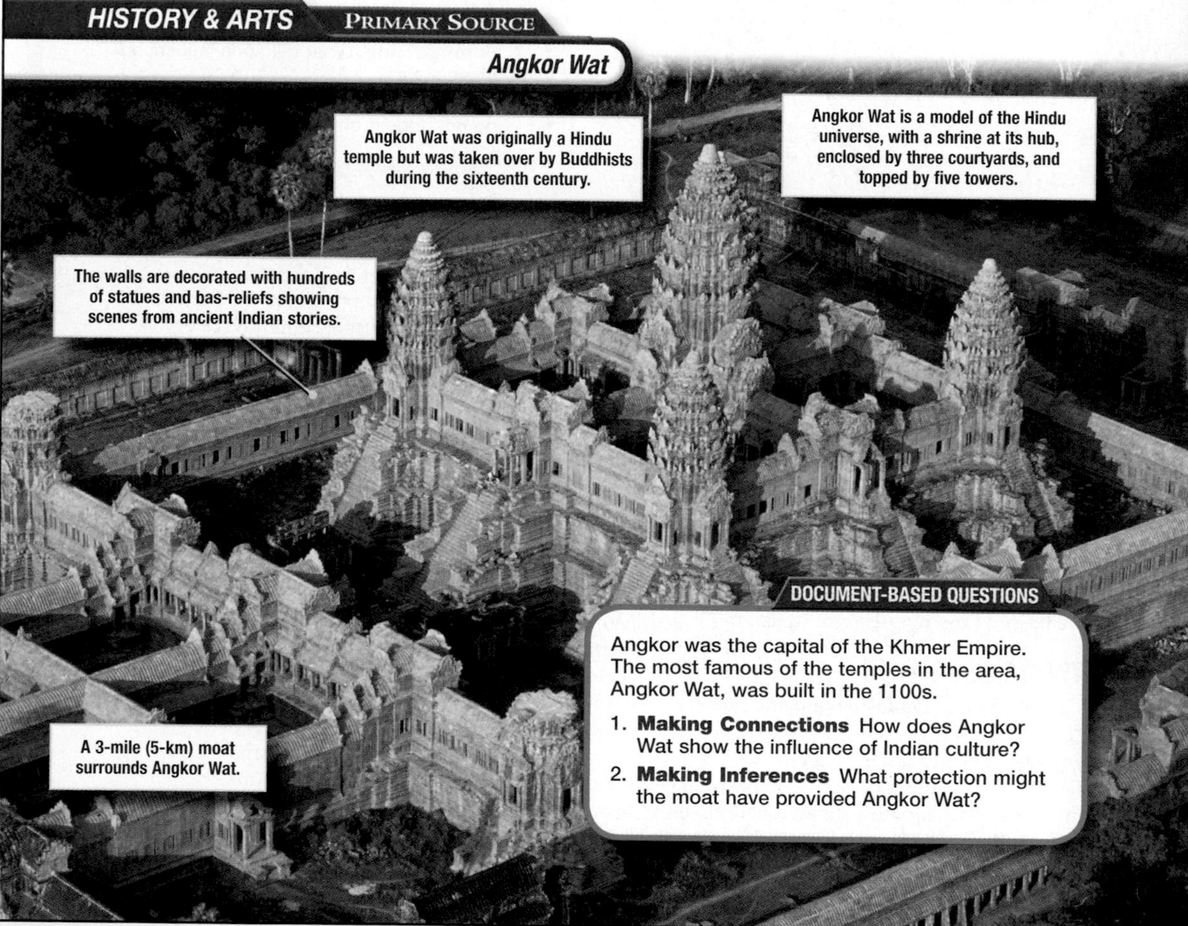

DOCUMENT-BASED QUESTIONS

Angkor was the capital of the Khmer Empire. The most famous of the temples in the area, Angkor Wat, was built in the 1100s.

1. **Making Connections** How does Angkor Wat show the influence of Indian culture?
2. **Making Inferences** What protection might the moat have provided Angkor Wat?

Extending the Content

Spice Trade Spices became very valuable trading commodities in early civilizations because they naturally grew only in certain areas. For example, both cloves and nutmeg are native to islands of what is now Indonesia, which Europeans had named the Spice Islands. At one point, Italian traders from Venice dominated the spice trade using overland routes, but their prices were very high. Ships from Portugal and Spain began to take long voyages of discovery beginning in the 1400s to find sea routes to the Spice Islands. One reason for Columbus' voyage in 1492 was to discover a quicker route for the Asian spice trade.

Trade through Southeast Asia expanded after the emergence of states in the area and reached even greater heights after the Muslim conquest of northern India. The rise in demand for spices also added to the growing volume of trade. As the wealth of Europe and Southeast Asia increased, demand grew for the products of East Asia.

At the top of the social ladder in most Southeast Asian societies were the hereditary aristocrats. They held both political power and economic wealth. Most aristocrats lived in the major cities. Angkor Thom, for example, was a city with royal palaces and parks, a massive parade ground, reservoirs, and numerous temples. **D**

Beyond the major cities lived the rest of the population, which consisted of farmers, fishers, artisans, and merchants. In most Southeast Asian societies, the majority of people were probably rice farmers who lived at a bare level of subsistence and paid heavy rents or taxes to a landlord or local ruler.

Most of the societies in Southeast Asia gave greater rights to women than did their counterparts in China and India. Women worked side by side with men in the fields and often played an active role in trading activities.

Chinese culture made an impact on Vietnam. In many other areas of Southeast Asia, Indian cultural influence prevailed. The most visible example of this influence was in architecture. Of all the existing structures at Angkor Thom, the temple of Angkor Wat is the most famous and most beautiful. It combines Indian architectural techniques with native inspiration in a structure of impressive grace. Surrounded by walls measuring 1,700 by 1,500 feet (518 by 457 m), Angkor Wat rises like a 200-foot-high (61-m-high) mountain in a series of three great terraces. The construction of Angkor Wat, which took 40 years to complete, required an enormous quantity of stone—as much as it took to build Egypt's Great Pyramid.

Hindu and Buddhist ideas began to move into Southeast Asia in the first millennium A.D. However, the new religions did not entirely replace existing beliefs. In all Southeast Asian societies, as in China and Japan, old beliefs were blended with those of the new faiths. In this process, the king played a central role. The ruler of Angkor, for example, was seen as a living link between the people and the gods.

Buddhism also spread to Southeast Asia. It made little impact, however, until the introduction of Theravada Buddhism in the eleventh century. From Burma, Theravada spread rapidly to other areas of Southeast Asia.

Eventually, Theravada Buddhism became the religion of the masses in much of Southeast Asia. Why did it have such appeal? For one thing, it teaches that people can seek nirvana through their own efforts; they do not need priests or rulers. Moreover, it tolerated local gods and posed no threat to established faith.

✓Reading Check **Identifying** Which countries most influenced the cultural development of Southeast Asia?

SECTION 5 REVIEW

Vocabulary

1. **Explain** the significance of: region, Malay Peninsula, archipelago, area, Vietnam, Angkor, Jayavarman, Pagan, Thai, Thailand, Strait of Malacca, Melaka, agricultural society, trading society.

Main Ideas

2. **Explain** the importance of Islam in the development of Melaka.
3. **Create** a diagram like the one shown below to represent the social hierarchy in most Southeast Asian societies discussed in this section.

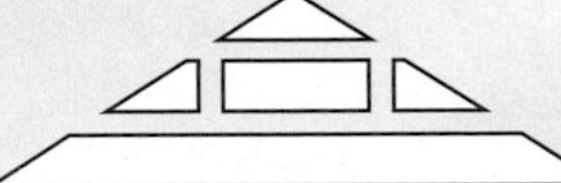

Critical Thinking

4. **The Big Idea Contrasting** How did the development of the Malay Peninsula and the Indonesian archipelago differ from the development of Southeast Asia?
5. **Considering** How would an increase in trade and exporting cause a region to develop more complex forms of political and social organization? Use examples from the text to support your answer.
6. **Analyzing Visuals** Compare the temple on page 288 with Angkor Wat on page 294. What features do they have in common?

Writing About History

7. **Descriptive Writing** When Vietnam was conquered by China, the people clung to their own identity. Write a paragraph describing the aspects of conquered peoples that conquerors would want to change and why.

History ONLINE
For help with the concepts in this section of *Glencoe World History*, go to glencoe.com and click Study Central™.

D Differentiated Instruction

English Language Learners
Review the meaning of *hereditary*. Ask students to discuss the pros and cons of living in a country where most power is inherited. **ELL**

✓Reading Check

Answer: China and India

Assess

History ONLINE

Study Central provides summaries, interactive games, and online graphic organizers to help students review content.

Close

Drawing Conclusions Ask: Why was Southeast Asia's spice trade so valued? *(It was vital to many countries' economies and a source of products not found elsewhere.)* **OL**

Answers

1. Definitions for the vocabulary words are found in the section and the Glossary.
2. Muslim merchants settled in port cities, leading to the formation of an Islamic state.
3. **Top:** aristocrats; **Middle:** farmers, fishers, artisans, merchants; **Bottom:** subsistence farmers
4. The independence of countries of Southeast Asia was a result of different languages and religions, as well as geographic barriers.
5. Cities grow; new classes, (merchants, artisans) evolve; to maintain control, more sophisticated forms of political organization are needed.
6. They have many features in common, such as bas relief sculptures, statues, and towers.
7. Answers will vary, but should be based on supporting details and sound conclusions.

Comparing and Contrasting Review the Visual Summary as a class. Ask a few volunteers to identify either one similarity or one difference between two countries or regions, such as religion in China and Japan. Then have students work individually to write comparison and contrast statements, being sure to include each country or region in at least one statement. **Ask:** What role did geography play in the Asian world at this time? *(Encourage students to use the information in the Visual Summary to help them answer this question. Answers may include that geography played a key role in every aspect of development in the Asian world, including religion, government, and economics.)* OL

Auditory/Musical Play a recording of traditional music from Asia (check your local or school library, or ask students to bring in appropriate recordings). Then discuss what the music can tell us about a particular culture and how it connects to the relevant section of the Visual Summary. OL

CHAPTER 8 Visual Summary

STUDY TO GO You can study anywhere, anytime by downloading quizzes and flash cards to your PDA from glencoe.com.

CHINA'S DYNASTIES

- The Tang dynasty, stable for 300 years, renewed trade in silk and porcelain over the Silk Road.
- The Song dynasty took over in the 900s and vastly increased crop yields and trade.
- In the 800s, the scholar-gentry class emerged, an influential group down to 1911, while a revived, practical Confucianism was dominant in religion.
- Northern invaders, always a threat, finally triumphed with the Mongol Invasion in 1270.
- Chinese poetry and ceramics were inspired by nature and Confucian philosophy.

THE SONG DYNASTY

Silk played an important role in China's economy and society.

THE KAMAKURA PERIOD

This Japanese battle scene reflects the frequent civil chaos of the 1200s.

JAPAN AND KOREA

- The islands of Japan are isolated and mountainous.
- The heads of Japanese noble families, daimyos, competed for power with fighting samurai, which led to frequent civil wars.
- The religion of Shinto contributed to emperor worship, while Buddhism's spirituality appealed to other Japanese.
- Korea, dominated by nearby China, and borrowing many cultural elements, finally gained its independence in the 900s.

BUDDHISM IN SOUTHEAST ASIA

Wat Arun, in Bangkok, is one of the thousands of Buddhist temples in Thailand.

SOUTH AND SOUTHEAST ASIA

- India fragmented into many states in the medieval period; later rulers from the north introduced Islam, but Hinduism remained the religion of most Indians.
- In Southeast Asia, new states were influenced by the Chinese and Indian examples in both government and religion.
- The trade in spices was profitable for several southeastern Asian states.

Hands-On Chapter Project
Step 6: Wrap-Up

Planning a Web Site for Early Asian History

Step 6: Presenting the Web Sites Student pairs will complete their Web sites and present them to the class.

Directions: Remind students that their completed home pages should provide "links" to their other Web pages. Have student pairs present their Web site to the class, either as a computer display or as an oral presentation. Students should be prepared to answer questions while viewers should be prepared to offer constructive feedback. Afterward, have students write a paragraph that answers the Essential Question: What were the key historical developments in early Asia?

Ask: What aspects of early Asian development do you think have had the longest lasting effects? *(Answers may include religious and other cultural developments, trade, printing, and gunpowder.)* OL

STANDARDIZED TEST PRACTICE

TEST-TAKING 

If you do not immediately know the right answer to a question, look at each answer choice carefully. Try to recall the context in which these events were discussed in class. Remembering this context may help you eliminate incorrect answer choices.

Reviewing Vocabulary

Directions: Choose the word or words that best complete the sentence.

1. ________ is a type of translucent ceramic made from very fine clay.

A Dowry

B Archipelago

C Porcelain

D Daimyo

2. The heirs of Genghis Khan divided up his empire into ________.

A khanates

B samurais

C dowries

D trading societies

3. ________ was the name for the strict code of behavior followed by the warrior class of early Japan.

A Bushido

B Shogunate

C Daimyo

D Mahayana

4. In early Chinese society, ________ produced most of the candidates for civil service.

A artisans

B farmers

C scholar-gentry

D traders

Reviewing Main Ideas

Directions: Choose the best answers to the following questions.

Section 1 *(pp. 264–269)*

5. What emperor used forced labor to build the Grand Canal?

A Wu Zhao

B Sui Yangdi

C Tang Xuanzang

D Kublai Khan

6. When a girl in early China married, how would her life change?

A She became part of her husband's family.

B She remained with her parents.

C She was able to participate in business and trade.

D She was able to take the civil service examination.

Section 2 *(pp. 270–275)*

7. Which of the following best describes the Mongol Empire?

A Militarily powerful, but poor

B The largest land empire in history

C The last government to control China

D An Islamic state

8. Which of these was most often the philosophical basis of Chinese government?

A Buddhism

B Daoism

C Islam

D Confucianism

Need Extra Help?

If You Missed Questions . . .	1	2	3	4	5	6	7	8
Go to Page . . .	275	270	280	269	264	269	270	273

Answers and Analyses

Reviewing Vocabulary

1. C All the other choices are not relevant. *Dowry* is a marriage custom; *archipelago* is a geography term; and *daimyo* is a Japanese term for head of a ruling family.

TEST-TAKING 

For Question 1: Remind students to use the process of elimination to figure out the answer to questions such as this one. By eliminating answers they know are incorrect, they can narrow their choices to better determine the correct answer.

2. A The word *Khan* helps indicate the correct answer. *Samurais* relate to Japan, *dowries* relate to marriage, and *trading societies* is a general term which isn't applicable in this case.

3. A Knowledge of the content is essential because all choices are foreign terms not in common usage. *Shogunate* and *daimyo* also relate to Japan, but are not a code of behavior, while *Mahayana* relates to Buddhism.

4. C Knowledge of the changes in Chinese society is required to answer this question correctly. The scholar-gentry group gained more political power while the other groups did not.

Reviewing Main Ideas

5. B Knowledge of the content is essential because all the choices are Chinese rulers. The Grand Canal was considered one of Sui Yangdi's greatest achievements.

6. A General knowledge of Chinese society at the time helps to indicate the correct answer. Few women had power or opportunities in early China.

7. B The process of elimination indicates the correct answer. The Mongol Empire was powerful militarily, but it was not poor. It was not the last government to control China; and it was not Islamic.

8. D Knowledge of the chapter content about Chinese culture is essential. All of the religions listed have had effects on different societies, although Daoism and Islam were not central in China's early history.

9. D Knowledge of the chapter content about Japanese culture is essential. Taishi and Yoritomo were important figures in Japan's history, but neither was the author of the work. Sŏng-gye was connected to Korea.

10. A Students can eliminate choice D because Kamakura is related to Japan. Based on the chapter content, students should know that Paekche and Koguryo were defeated by Silla.

11. B Students will need to distinguish between the various types of Buddhism to answer the question correctly. Daoism is not related to concepts of the Buddha.

12. D None of the other answer choices makes sense. Moguls later attacked India from the north, samurai are related to Japan, and Uighurs fought in early China.

13. A Students should recall that Dai Viet is connected with Vietnam, Timur Lenk conquered much of India, and Daṇḍin was an Indian author.

Critical Thinking

14. B Skills for analyzing text will indicate the correct answer. Riding ability, an initiation ritual, and hatred of the sea are not central to the code of the samurai.

TEST-TAKING 

For Question 14: Remind students to consider whether an answer makes sense. For example, answer D doesn't make sense since a hatred for the sea is not logically connected to the code of the samurai.

CHAPTER 8

Section 3 *(pp. 278–283)*

9. Who was the author of *The Tale of Genji,* one of the finest achievements of world literature?

A Yi Sŏng-gye
B Minamoto Yoritomo
C Shōtoku Taishi
D Murasaki Shikibu

10. After a long struggle, which kingdom gained control over the Korean peninsula?

A Silla
B Paekche
C Koguryo
D Kamakura

Section 4 *(pp. 284–289)*

11. Which of these introduced the idea that the Buddha was not just a wise man, but a divine figure?

A Theravada Buddhism
B Mahayana Buddhism
C Zen Buddhism
D Daoism

12. Who were the Hindu warriors who led the resistance against the advances of Maḥmūd and his successors into northern India?

A Moguls
B Samurai
C Uighurs
D Rajputs

Section 5 *(pp. 290–295)*

13. Who founded the kingdom of Angkor?

A Jayavarman
B Dai Viet
C Timur Lenk
D Daṇḍin

Critical Thinking

Directions: Choose the best answers to the following questions.

Use the following quote about the Japanese Samurai to answer question 14.

> *"I spurred my horse on, careless of death in the face of the foe.*
> *I braved the dangers of wind and wave, not reckoning that my body*
> *might sink to the bottom of the sea, and be devoured by monsters of the deep."*

14. How does this quote reflect the code of the samurai?

A It describes the riding ability of the samurai.
B It shows the importance placed on honor and loyalty, above all other concerns.
C It portrays the most common initiation ritual of the samurai.
D It displays the samurai's hatred of the sea.

15. Which of the following religions did not play a major role in the history of Southeast Asia?

A Islam
B Theravada Buddhism
C Mahayana Buddhism
D Hinduism

16. In early Japan, why was prose fiction written primarily by women?

A All men were samurai and therefore had little time for artistic pursuits.
B Women were better educated than men.
C Men believed prose fiction was beneath them.
D The Shinto religion forbade the writing of fiction by men.

17. What was a major cause of the expansion of trade throughout Southeast Asia?

A The construction of stronger vessels
B The blessings of important religious figures
C The growing demand for spices
D The construction of beautiful temples

Need Extra Help?

If You Missed Questions . . .	9	10	11	12	13	14	15	16	17
Go to Page . . .	282	283	284	286	292	298	295	282	294

GO ON

15. C Knowledge of the content is essential to determine the correct answer. Mahayana Buddhism was centered in northwest India and did not have a strong effect in Southeast Asia.

16. C Knowledge of the chapter content about Japanese culture is essential. Prose fiction was considered "vulgar gossip" and an undignified pursuit for men.

17. C Economic demand is often a strong spur for trade. Although A is a plausible answer, it was not a major cause of the expansion of trade. Religious blessings and beautiful temples have little relevance to trade expansion.

18. Which of the following images would you most likely see in an early Chinese painting?
   A A small figure in the midst of a nature scene
   B An aristocrat at home with his family
   C Warriors in battle
   D People worshiping at a temple

Analyze the map and answer the question that follows. Base your answer on the map.

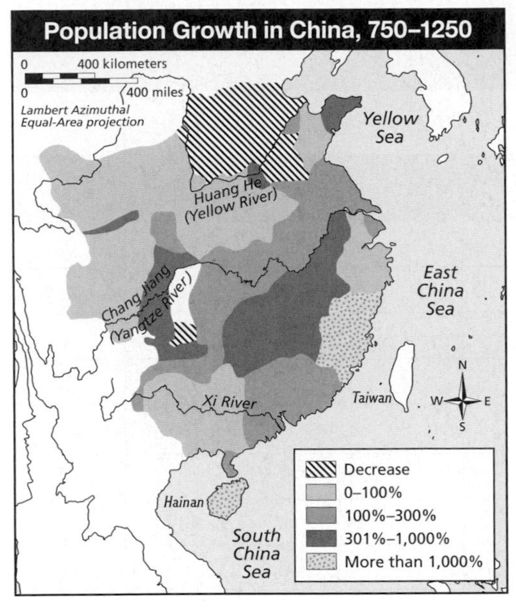

19. In what geographic direction did the population shift during this period?
   A To the northeast
   B To the northwest
   C To the southeast
   D To the southwest

Document-Based Questions

Directions: Analyze the document and answer the short-answer questions that follow the document. Base your answers on the document and on your knowledge of world history.

Chang Tsai, a neo-Confucian philospher, wrote the following in the eleventh century:

> *"Heaven is my father and Earth is my mother, and even such a small being as I finds a central abode in their midst. Therefore that which fills the universe I regard as my body and that which directs the universe I consider as my nature. All people are my brothers and sisters, and all things are my companions."*
>
> —Chang Tsai

20. Can you detect any echoes of Daoism in this excerpt? What are they?

21. How do the ideas in this quotation conflict with the basic ideas of Buddhism?

Extended Response

22. Imagine that you are a Korean person who is traveling through the states of Southeast Asia during the fifteenth century. Which states will seem most familiar to you? Which will seem most foreign? Why?

History ONLINE
For additional test practice, use Self-Check Quizzes—Chapter 8 at glencoe.com.

Need Extra Help?					
If You Missed Questions . . .	18	19	20	21	22
Go to Page . . .	275	299	299	299	290

STOP

Document-Based Questions

20. The unity of all creation is evoked in the last sentence. Also, the phrase "that which directs the universe I consider as my nature" echoes the concept of the Dao.

21. The quotation treats the world and the individual self as being of great importance, while Buddhism teaches that the world and the self are both illusory.

Extended Response

22. Answers will vary. Vietnam would likely be the most familiar state, because of its shared Chinese influence (and its shared resistance against Chinese invasion). Thailand would be less familiar, because of its greater Indian influence. Majapahit and Melaka might seem very alien, because of their Islamic beliefs and almost total isolation from any significant Chinese influences. Note that Pagan, Angkor, Srivijaya, and Sailendra no longer existed during the fifteenth century.

18. A Although answer choices B, C, and D are plausible because they are common in certain styles of painting, early Chinese painting styles are best known for their scenes of nature.

19. C Map reading skills, especially an understanding of direction and a careful reading of the legend, will help students determine the correct answer.

History ONLINE
Introduce students to chapter content and key terms by having them access the Chapter 8 Overview at glencoe.com.

Need Extra Help?
Have students refer to the pages listed if they miss any of the questions.

CHAPTER 9 Planning Guide

Key to Ability Levels

- **BL** Below Level
- **OL** On Level
- **AL** Above Level
- **ELL** English Language Learners

Key to Teaching Resources

- Print Material
- CD-ROM
- DVD
- Transparency

Levels				Resources	Chapter Opener	Section 1	Section 2	Section 3	Section 4	Chapter Assess
BL	OL	AL	ELL							
				FOCUS						
BL	OL	AL	ELL	**Daily Focus Skills Transparencies**		9-1	9-2	9-3	9-4	
				TEACH						
BL	OL		ELL	**Reading Skills Activity, URB**					p. 129	
	OL	AL		**Historical Analysis Skills Activity, URB**				p. 130		
BL	OL	AL	ELL	**Differentiated Instruction Activity, URB**					p. 131	
	OL		ELL	**English Learner Activity, URB**					p. 133	
BL	OL	AL	ELL	**Content Vocabulary Activity, URB***		p. 135			p. 135	
BL	OL	AL	ELL	**Academic Vocabulary Activity, URB**				p. 137		
BL	OL	AL	ELL	**Skills Reinforcement Activity, URB**					p. 139	
	OL	AL		**Critical Thinking Skills Activity, URB**				p. 140		
	OL	AL		**History and Geography Activity, URB**			p. 141			
	OL	AL	ELL	**Mapping History Activity, URB**					p. 143	
BL	OL	AL		**Historical Significance Activity, URB**					p. 144	
BL	OL	AL	ELL	**Cooperative Learning Activity, URB**					p. 145	
	OL	AL	ELL	**History Simulation Activity, URB**					p. 147	
BL	OL	AL	ELL	**Time Line Activity, URB**					p. 149	
	OL	AL		**Linking Past and Present Activity, URB**				p. 150		
BL	OL	AL		**People in World History Activity, URB**				p. 152	p. 151	
BL	OL	AL	ELL	**Primary Source Reading, URB**					p. 153	
	OL	AL		**Enrichment Activity, URB**					p. 158	
BL	OL	AL	ELL	**World Art and Music Activity, URB**					p. 155	
BL	OL		ELL	**Guided Reading Activities, URB***		p. 160	p. 161	p. 162	p. 163	
BL	OL		ELL	**Reading Essentials and Note-Taking Guide***		p. 97	p. 100	p. 103	p. 106	
BL	OL	AL	ELL	**Differentiated Instruction for the World History Classroom**	✓	✓	✓	✓	✓	✓

Note: Please refer to the *Unit Resource Book: New Patterns of Civilization* for this chapter's URB materials.

* Also available in Spanish

- Interactive Lesson Planner
- Interactive Teacher Edition
- Fully editable blackline masters
- Section Spotlight Videos Launch
- Differentiated Lesson Plans
- Printable reports of daily assignments
- Standards Tracking System

Levels				Resources	Chapter Opener	Section 1	Section 2	Section 3	Section 4	Chapter Assess
BL	OL	AL	ELL							
				TEACH *(continued)*						
BL	OL	AL	ELL	**StudentWorks™ Plus DVD**	✓	✓	✓	✓	✓	✓
BL	OL	AL	ELL	**Vocabulary PuzzleMaker CD-ROM**	✓	✓	✓	✓	✓	✓
Teacher Resources				**Building Academic Vocabulary**	✓	✓	✓	✓	✓	✓
				Reading Strategies and Activities for the Social Studies Classroom		pp. 21, 44	p. 22	p. 17		
				Writer's Guidebook		p. 17	p. 51			
				Strategies for Success	✓	✓	✓	✓	✓	✓
				Outline Map Resource Book	✓	✓	✓	✓	✓	✓
				Presentation Plus! with MindJogger DVD	✓	✓	✓	✓	✓	✓
				ASSESS						
BL	OL	AL	ELL	**Section Quizzes and Chapter Tests***		p. 105	p. 106	p. 107	p. 108	p. 109
BL	OL	AL	ELL	**Authentic Assessment With Rubrics**	✓	✓	✓	✓	✓	✓
BL	OL	AL	ELL	**Standardized Test Practice Workbook**	✓	✓	✓	✓	✓	✓
BL	OL	AL	ELL	***ExamView® Assessment Suite* CD-ROM**		9-1	9-2	9-3	9-4	Ch. 9
BL	OL	AL	ELL	**Interactive Tutor Self-Assessment CD-ROM**		9-1	9-2	9-3	9-4	
				CLOSE						
BL			ELL	**Reteaching Activity, URB**					p. 157	
BL	OL		ELL	**Reading and Study Skills Foldables™**	✓	✓	✓	✓	✓	✓

Using the McGraw-Hill Learning Network

Researching World Book™ Select

Technology Product

World Book Select offers thousands of detailed articles chosen from the *World Book Encyclopedia* and covers all curricular areas. World Book Select allows students to research national and international topics and issues in economics and other curriculum areas.

Objectives

After students learn to use World Book Select, they will be able to

- develop and expand research and study skills;
- practice reading and writing skills.

Steps

Give students the following directions to use World Book Select:

- From the McGraw-Hill Learning Network home page (www.mhln.com), click on **For Students.**
- Choose **World Book Select** below **Homework Help.**
- Click the letter for the encyclopedia volume you want to use.
- On the search page for the volume selected:
  -click the title of a featured article on the right side of the page; or
  -click on a topic from the list on the left side of the page; then click on the title of an article of interest on the right.
- Read the article and take notes.

History ONLINE

	Student	Teacher	Parent
Beyond the Textbook	●	●	●
Chapter Overviews	●	●	●
Time Current Events	●		●
ePuzzles and Games	●		●
Concepts in Motion	●		●
Literature Connections		●	
Multi-Language Glossaries	●		●
Online Student Edition	●	●	●
Self-Check Quizzes	●		●
Student Web Activities	●		●
Study Central ™	●		●
Teaching Today		●	
Vocabulary eFlashcards	●		●
Web Activity Lesson Plans		●	

- **Timed Readings Plus in Social Studies** helps students increase their reading rate and fluency while maintaining comprehension. The 400-word passages are similar to those found on state and national assessments.
- **Reading in the Content Area: Social Studies** concentrates on six essential reading skills that help students better comprehend what they read. The book includes 75 high-interest nonfiction passages written at increasing levels of difficulty.
- **Reading Social Studies** includes strategic reading instruction and vocabulary support in Social Studies content for both ELLs and native speakers of English.

www.jamestowneducation.com

The following videotape programs are available from Glencoe as supplements to Chapter 9:

- Knights and Armour (ISBN 1-56-501443-X)
- Justinian: The Last of the Romans (ISBN 0-76-700579-1)
- Richard the Lionheart (ISBN 1-56-501916-4)

To order, call Glencoe at 1-800-334-7344. To find classroom resources to accompany many of these videos, check the following home pages:

A&E Television: www.aetv.com

The History Channel: www.historychannel.com

Index to National Geographic Magazine:

The following articles relate to this chapter:

- "In Search of Vikings," by Priit J. Vesiland, May 2000

National Geographic Society Products To order the following, call National Geographic at 1-800-368-2728:

- *National Geographic Atlas of the World* (Book).
- *Ancient Rome* (PicturePack).
- *The Middle Ages* (CD-ROM).

Access National Geographic's new, dynamic MapMachine Web site and other geography resources at:
www.nationalgeographic.com
www.nationalgeographic.com/maps

GLENCOE BOOKLINK 3

Use this database to search more than 30,000 titles to create a customized reading list for your students.

- Reading lists can be organized by students' reading level, author, genre, theme, or area of interest.
- The database provides Degrees of Reading Power™ (DRP) and Lexile™ readability scores for all selections.
- A brief summary of each selection is included.

Leveled reading suggestions for this chapter:

For students at a Grade 8 reading level:
- ***If You Lived in the Days of the Knights,*** by Ann McGovern

For students at a Grade 9 reading level:
- ***King Arthur and the Knights of the Round Table (Adapted),*** by Howard Pyle

For students at a Grade 10 reading level:
- ***The Real Vikings: Craftsmen, Traders, and Fearsome Raiders,*** by Melvin and Gilda Berger

For students at a Grade 11 reading level:
- ***King Richard the Lionhearted and the Crusades in World History,*** by Katherine M. and Craig A. Doherty

For students at a Grade 12 reading level:
- ***The Byzantine Empire,*** by Elsa Marston

Introducing CHAPTER 9

Focus

MAKING CONNECTIONS
How important is the location of a city?

Activate students' prior knowledge by having them discuss the location of the first cities of the ancient world, such as those in Mesopotamia. *(In general, they were along rivers.)* Then talk abut how and why the location of cities changed over time. *(Responses may include that they were built along trading routes such as port cities or along land routes such as the Silk Road.)* Close the discussion by having students summarize the role location played in the development of cities.

Teach

The Big Ideas

As students study the chapter, remind them to consider the section-based Big Ideas included in each section's Guide to Reading. The **Essential Questions** in the activities below tie in to the Big Ideas and help students think about and understand important chapter concepts. In addition, the Hands-on Chapter Projects with their culminating activities relate the content from each section to the Big Ideas. These activities build on each other as students progress through the chapter. Section activities culminate in the wrap-up activity on the Visual Summary page.

CHAPTER 9

Emerging Europe and the Byzantine Empire 400–1300

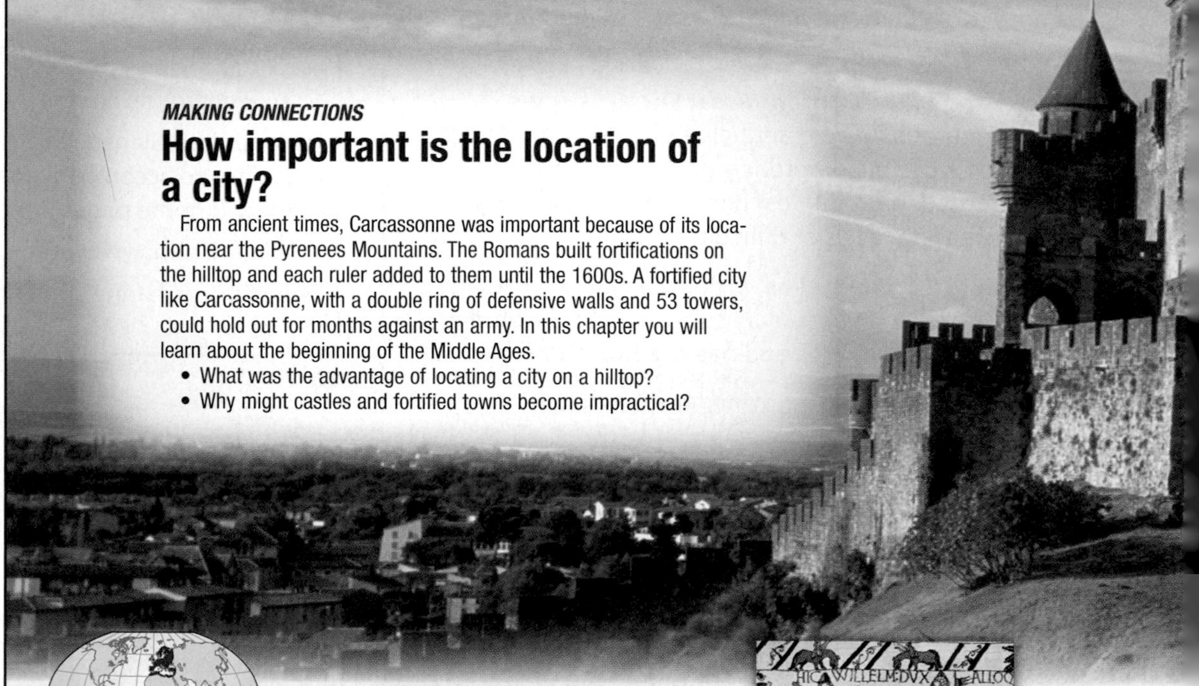

MAKING CONNECTIONS

How important is the location of a city?

From ancient times, Carcassonne was important because of its location near the Pyrenees Mountains. The Romans built fortifications on the hilltop and each ruler added to them until the 1600s. A fortified city like Carcassonne, with a double ring of defensive walls and 53 towers, could hold out for months against an army. In this chapter you will learn about the beginning of the Middle Ages.

- What was the advantage of locating a city on a hilltop?
- Why might castles and fortified towns become impractical?

EUROPE ▶

400 / 700 ... 1000

800 Charlemagne crowned Roman emperor

1066 William of Normandy invades England

THE WORLD ▶

762 Abbasids build capital at Baghdad

960 Song dynasty comes to power in China

300

Transforming the Roman World

Essential Question: Why was Rome the center of the Christian world at the beginning of the period? *(The Roman Empire had become Christian. As the empire broke apart, Rome continued to be a center for Christianity.)* Point out that in Section 1 students will learn about Europe uniting under a strong leader and how it experienced a renaissance. **OL**

Feudalism

Essential Question: What purposes does a strong central government serve? *(It establishes relationships and provides a social order.)* Point out that in Section 2 students will learn about how Europeans reacted to the fall of the Carolingian Empire and developed a system of social, economic, and political relationships called feudalism. **OL**

Introducing
CHAPTER 9

More About the Photo

Visual Literacy Today, Carcassonne, France, is like two cities in one. There's Lower Carcassonne (known as the "new" part of town since it was built in A.D. 1247) and La Cité Médiévale, also known as the ancient city (since it was acquired as early as 600 B.C.). Its double ring of walls is about two miles in length. Its eastern gate, the Narbonne gate, includes two tall towers. Two sites of interest within the walled city include the town's oldest wells, built during Roman times, and the Inquisition House, used to try people for heresy. Because Carcassonne is Europe's oldest city to survive from the Middle Ages, it attracts over three million tourists each year.

1096 Crusades begin

1215 King John signs Magna Carta

1100 — 1300

1187 Saladin's army invades Jerusalem

c. 1300 Yorubas produce metal and terra-cotta sculptures

FOLDABLES Study Organizer

Identifying Create a Layered-Look Book to identify important people, events, and government institutions of England, France, the Holy Roman Empire, Central and Eastern Europe, and Russia.

History ONLINE
Chapter Overview—Visit glencoe.com to preview Chapter 9.

FOLDABLES Study Organizer Dinah Zike's Foldables

Dinah Zike's Foldables are three-dimensional, interactive graphic organizers that help students practice basic writing skills, review vocabulary terms, and identify main ideas. Instructions for creating and using Foldables can be found in the Appendix at the end of this book and in the *Dinah Zike's Reading and Study Skills Foldables* booklet.

SECTION 3

The Growth of European Kingdoms

Essential Question: How do you think the Magna Carta affected the development of the U.S. government? *(Many of its principles served as the ideals for later governments, including the U.S. government.)* Point out that in Section 3 students will learn how England and France established stable central governments. **OL**

SECTION 4

Byzantine Empire and Crusades

Essential Question: What was the purpose of the Crusades? *(to retake Christian holy lands from the Muslims)* Point out that in Section 4 students will learn how the Eastern Roman Empire experienced a period of power and prosperity and how the Crusades affected Europeans and the Middle East. **OL**

History ONLINE

Introduce students to chapter content and key terms by having them access the Chapter 9 Overview at glencoe.com.

Focus

Bellringer

Daily Focus Transparency 9.1

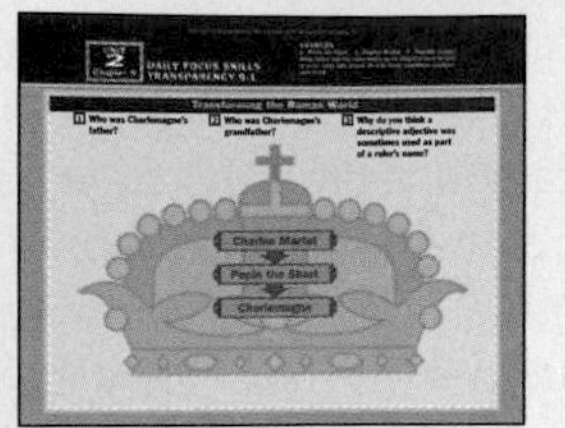

GUIDE TO READING

Answers to Graphic:

The Importance of Monasticism: monastic movement was used to convert the pagan peoples of Germanic Europe; monks' dedication to God became the highest ideal of Christian life; monks provided schools, hospitality, and hospitals; monks copied Latin works, passing the legacy of the ancient world to the new European civilization

Section Spotlight Video

To generate student interest and provide a springboard for class discussion, access the Chapter 9, Section 1 video at glencoe.com or on the video DVD.

SECTION 1

Transforming the Roman World

GUIDE TO READING

The BIG Idea

Ideas, Beliefs, and Values The new European civilization combined Germanic, Roman, and Christian elements.

Content Vocabulary

- wergild *(p. 304)*
- ordeal *(p. 304)*
- bishopric *(p. 304)*
- pope *(p. 304)*
- monk *(p. 305)*
- monasticism *(p. 305)*
- missionary *(p. 306)*
- nun *(p. 306)*
- abbess *(p. 306)*

Academic Vocabulary

- excluded *(p. 302)*
- ensure *(p. 307)*

People and Places

- Clovis *(p. 302)*
- Gregory I *(p. 304)*
- Saint Benedict *(p. 305)*
- Pépin *(p. 306)*
- Charlemagne *(p. 306)*
- Carolingian Empire *(p. 307)*

Reading Strategy

Summarizing Information Create a diagram like the one below to list the reasons why monasticism was an important factor in the development of European civilization.

Germanic tribes became the dominant political force in Europe during the Early Middle Ages, while Christianity became the dominant religion. Rome became the center of the Catholic Church's power. Ultimately a new empire emerged that was linked to the idea of a lasting Roman Empire.

The New Germanic Kingdoms

MAIN IDEA The Frankish kingdom was the strongest of the early German states and developed new laws based on the importance of family in Germanic society.

HISTORY & YOU How might laws be different if they were based on settling personal feuds rather than on protecting society as a whole? Read about Germanic laws and wergild.

The Germanic peoples had begun to move into the lands of the Roman Empire by the third century. The Visigoths occupied Spain and Italy until the Ostrogoths, another Germanic tribe, took control of Italy in the fifth century. By 500, the Western Roman Empire had been replaced by a number of states ruled by German kings. The merging of Romans and Germans took different forms in the various Germanic kingdoms.

Both the kingdom of the Ostrogoths in Italy and the kingdom of the Visigoths in Spain retained the Roman structure of government. However, a group of Germanic warriors came to dominate the considerably larger native populations and eventually **excluded** Romans from holding power.

Roman influence was even weaker in Britain. When the Roman armies abandoned Britain at the beginning of the fifth century, the Angles and Saxons, Germanic tribes from Denmark and northern Germany, moved in and settled there. Eventually, these peoples became the Anglo-Saxons.

The Kingdom of the Franks

Only one of the German states on the European continent proved long lasting—the kingdom of the Franks. The Frankish kingdom was established by **Clovis,** a strong military leader who around 500 became the first Germanic ruler to convert to Christianity. At first, Clovis had refused the pleas of his Christian wife to adopt Christianity as his religion. According to Gregory of Tours, a sixth-century historian, Clovis had remarked to his wife, "Your God can do nothing."

During a battle with another Germanic tribe, however, Clovis's army faced certain destruction. Clovis was reported to have cried

Resource Manager

R Reading Strategies	C Critical Thinking	D Differentiated Instruction	W Writing Support	S Skill Practice
Teacher Edition • Questioning, p. 303 **Additional Resources** • Cont. Vocab. Act., URB p. 135 • Guid. Read. Act., URB p. 160 • Read. Ess. & Note-Taking Guide, p. 97	**Teacher Edition** • Compare/Contrast, pp. 304, 306 • Drawing Con., p. 305 **Additional Resources** • Section Quiz, p. 105	**Teacher Edition** • Verbal/Linguistic, p. 305 • Auditory/Musical, p. 307 **Additional Resources** • Read. Strat. for SS, p. 21	**Teacher Edition** • Descriptive Writing, p. 304 **Additional Resources** • Writer's Guidebook, p. 17	**Teacher Edition** • Using Geo. Skills, p. 303 **Additional Resources** • Read. Strat. for SS, p. 44

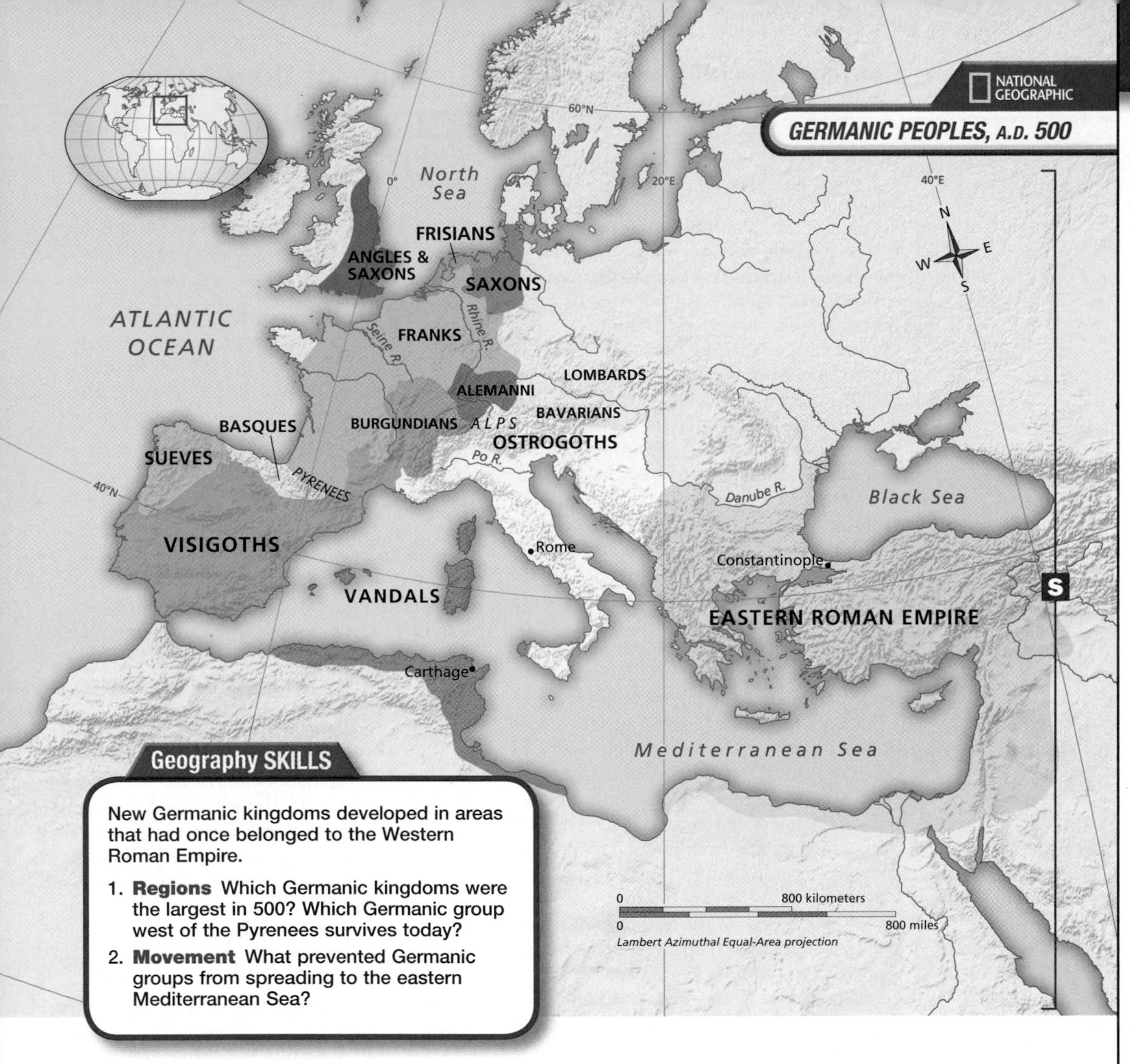

Geography SKILLS

New Germanic kingdoms developed in areas that had once belonged to the Western Roman Empire.

1. **Regions** Which Germanic kingdoms were the largest in 500? Which Germanic group west of the Pyrenees survives today?
2. **Movement** What prevented Germanic groups from spreading to the eastern Mediterranean Sea?

out, "Jesus Christ, if you shall grant me victory over these enemies, I will believe in you and be baptized." After he uttered these words, the enemy began to flee, and Clovis soon became a Christian.

Clovis found that his conversion to Christianity won him the support of the Roman Catholic Church, as the Christian church in Rome was now known. Not surprisingly, the Catholic Church was eager to gain the friendship of a major ruler in the Germanic states.

By 510, Clovis had established a powerful new Frankish kingdom that stretched from the Pyrenees in the southwest to German lands in the east—modern-day France and western Germany. He defeated the many Germanic tribes surrounding him and unified the Franks as a people. After Clovis's death his sons followed Frankish custom and divided his newly created kingdom among themselves. The once-united Frankish kingdom came to be divided into three major areas.

Teach

R Reading Strategy

Questioning Discuss the creation of legends and myths.
Ask: Is it important to determine whether the story of Clovis's conversion to Christianity is literally true? *(Answers may include: The fact of his conversion and the resulting changes it caused are more important than his exact words or circumstances.)* **OL**

S Skill Practice

Using Geography Skills
Ask: Which Germanic kingdom was located partially in Africa? *(kingdom of the Vandals)* **Ask:** Who controlled most of what is now Spain? *(Visigoths)* **BL**

For additional practice on this skill, see the **Skills Handbook**.

Geography SKILLS

Answers:
1. The kingdoms of the Franks, Ostrogoths, and Visigoths; the Basques
2. the Eastern Roman Empire and the Alps

Hands-On Chapter Project
Step 1

Creating a TV Documentary

Small groups of students create short documentaries for each section on emerging Europe and the Byzantine Empire.

Step 1: Documentary on the Transformation of the Roman World

Essential Question: What was daily life like during this time period?

Directions: Divide students into small groups. Each group will prepare a TV documentary set in emerging Europe and the Byzantine Empire. Groups will use information from the section and their own research to create a documentary about life during this period. Remind students that their documentary can take several forms. They may want to consider using a narrator to explain scenes or skits that illustrate life at the time. Students may want to dress in period costume and give their TV station a name.

Summarizing: Allow time for groups to share what they learned about the Big Idea while preparing information for their documentary. **OL**

(Chapter Project is continued in Section 2.)

W Writing Support

Descriptive Writing Have students do additional research to discover facts about Germanic society. Ask students to write a paragraph about what life must have been like for families that worked the land together. AL

C Critical Thinking

Comparing and Contrasting Ask students to write a sentence that identifies the key difference between the Roman and Germanic system of justice. *(Crimes were considered to be against society in the Roman system, but against the family in the German system.)* OL

For additional practice on this skill, see the **Skills Handbook**.

✓Reading Check

Answer: Clovis's conversion gained him the support of the Roman Catholic Church.

Germanic Society

Over time, Germans and Romans intermarried and began to create a new society. As they did, some of the social customs of the Germanic people came to play an important role.

The crucial social bond among the Germanic peoples was the family, especially the extended family of husbands, wives, children, brothers, sisters, cousins, and W grandparents. This extended family worked the land together and passed it down to future generations. The family also provided protection, which was much needed in the violent atmosphere of the time.

The German concept of family affected the way Germanic law treated the problem of crime and punishment. In the Roman system, as in our own, a crime such as murder was considered an offense against C society or the state. Thus, a court would hear evidence and arrive at a decision. Germanic law, on the other hand, was personal. An injury by one person against another could mean a blood feud, and the feud could lead to savage acts of revenge.

To avoid bloodshed, a new system developed, based on a fine called **wergild** (WUHR•gihld). Wergild was the amount paid by a wrongdoer to the family of the person he or she had injured or killed. Wergild, which means "money for a man," was the value of a person in money. The value varied according to social status. An offense against a member of the nobility, for example, cost considerably more than an offense against an ordinary person or a slave. Germanic laws were now established by custom, not at the whim of a king or codified like Roman law.

One means of determining guilt in Germanic law was the ordeal. The **ordeal** was based on the idea of divine intervention. All ordeals involved a physical trial of some sort, such as holding a red-hot iron. It was believed that divine forces would not allow an innocent person to be harmed. If the accused person was unharmed after a physical trial, or ordeal, he or she was presumed innocent.

✓Reading Check **Analyzing** What was the significance of Clovis's conversion to Christianity?

The Role of the Church

MAIN IDEA The Bishop of Rome became the leader of the Christian Church.

HISTORY & YOU How does someone take over the leadership of an organization? Read how the Bishop of Rome claimed to be the leader of the Christian Church.

By the end of the fourth century, Christianity had become the supreme religion of the Roman Empire. As the official Roman state fell apart, the Church played an increasingly important role in the growth of the new European civilization.

Organization of the Church

By the fourth century, the Christian Church had developed a system of organization. Priests led local Christian communities called parishes. A group of parishes was headed by a bishop, whose area of authority was called a **bishopric,** or diocese. The bishoprics were joined together under an archbishop.

Over time, one bishop—the Bishop of Rome—began to claim that he was the leader of what had become the Roman Catholic Church. Catholics believed that Jesus gave the keys to the kingdom of Heaven to Peter, who was considered the chief apostle and the first bishop of Rome. Later bishops of Rome were viewed as Peter's successors. They came to be known as **popes** (from the Latin word *papa,* "father") of the Catholic Church.

Western Christians came to accept the bishop of Rome—the pope—as head of the Church, but they did not agree on how much power he should have. In the sixth century, a strong pope, **Gregory I,** known as Gregory the Great, strengthened the power of the papacy (office of the pope) and the Church.

Gregory I, pope from 590 to 604, was also leader of the city of Rome and its surrounding territories (later called the Papal States), thus giving the papacy a source of political power. Gregory I increased his spiritual authority over the Church in the West. He was especially active in converting non-Christian peoples of Germanic

Additional Support

Activity: Collaborative Learning

Dramatizing the Germanic Justice System Ask students to review the section content on wergilds and ordeals. Then ask small groups of students to dramatize a meeting between two families in which one has wronged another. For example, a member of one family may have unintentionally damaged the crops of the other family. Note that they will need to know the social status of the injured person to help argue for a payment of wergild. Each person should be assigned a role in the meeting. **Ask:** Do you think the Germanic system promoted justice? *(Students may think not because strong emotions were involved; varying payments for different social classes does not fit the modern sense of justice; an ordeal is not a reasonable method of determining guilt.)* OL

Europe to Christianity. He did this through the monastic movement.

Monks and Monasteries

A **monk** is a man who separates himself from ordinary society to dedicate himself to God. The practice of living the life of a monk is known as **monasticism**. At first, Christian monasticism was based on the hermit who led an isolated spiritual life. In the sixth century, however, **Saint Benedict** wrote a set of rules to guide a community of monks he founded. This community became the model for monasticism in the Catholic Church, and the Benedictine rule came to be used by other monastic groups.

Benedict's rule divided each day into a series of activities, with primary emphasis on prayer and manual labor. Physical work was required of all monks for several hours a day, because idleness was "the enemy of the soul." **D** At the very heart of community practice was prayer, the proper "Work of God." Although prayer included private meditation and reading, all monks gathered together seven times during the day for common prayer and the chanting of Psalms—sacred songs. A Benedictine life was a communal one. Monks ate, worked, slept, and worshiped together.

Each Benedictine monastery was led by an abbot or "father," whom the monks were expected to obey. The abbot had complete authority over the monks. Each monastery owned lands that enabled it to be self-sustaining and isolated from the world. In the monastery, monks were to fulfill their vow of poverty.

Monks became the new Christian heroes, an important force in the new European civilization. The monastic community set the highest ideal of Christian life and provided a moral example to all. Monks were the social workers of their communities, **C** providing schools for the young, hospitality for travelers, and hospitals for the sick. They also taught peasants carpentry and weaving and made agricultural improvements that they passed on to others.

INFOGRAPHICS

Monastic Life

A Monk's Daily Timetable

MORNING		AFTERNOON		EVENING	
2:00	Church service	12:00	Meal	5:45	Meal
3:30	Sleep	1:00	Reading or private prayer	6:00	Church service
4:00	Church service	1:45	Sleep	7:15	Reading or private prayer
5:00	Reading or private prayer	3:00	Work	7:45	Church service
6:00	Church service, breakfast			8:00	Sleep
7:00	Work				
8:00	Church service				
9:15	Work				
11:45	Church service				

Monks were men who devoted their lives to the Church. They took vows of poverty, chastity, and obedience. They also took a vow of stability, swearing to remain in the monastery until death, closed off from the rest of the world.

St. Benedict established a daily timetable for monks. Along with Church service and prayer, monks worked. They did manual labor along with intellectual work, creating illuminated manuscripts and transcribing religious works.

CRITICAL THINKING SKILLS

1. **Making Inferences** How much time did the monks spend working each day? What kinds of work might those living at the monastery do?
2. **Drawing Conclusions** Why might structure like the monk's timetable be important to monastic life?

D Differentiated Instruction

Verbal/Linguistic Discuss possible meanings for the idea that idleness was "the enemy of the soul." Then ask students to write a paragraph in support or disagreement of this idea, including their reasons. **AL**

C Critical Thinking

Drawing Conclusions Ask: Why were monks the "new Christian heroes?" *(They were examples of an ideal society, set a moral example, helped people in the community, and improved agriculture.)* **OL**

CRITICAL THINKING SKILLS

Answers:

1. Approximately 6 hours and 15 minutes. Answers may include manual labor (cooking, tending animals, farming, milling grain), working in the infirmary, and so on.
2. It probably helped economically sustain the monastery, maintain order, and made sure monks followed Benedict's rules regarding physical work and prayer.

Activity: Interdisciplinary Connection

Music A Gregorian chant is made up of a single melodic line that is sung in unison without a set rhythm. The timelessness of this music was demonstrated in the early 1990s when a recording of Church hymns by the Benedictine monks of Santo Domingo de Silos became a best-seller. Ask interested students to bring in recordings of Gregorian chants (available in most public libraries). For example, students might wish to look into the discography of Hildegard of Bingen (1098–1179), a German nun who wrote beautiful chants that have become quite popular in recent years. **Ask:** What have you learned about the history, form, and rhythm of Gregorian chants? *(Discuss the answer with examples of the music.)* **OL**

C Critical Thinking

Comparing and Contrasting

Ask: How were the lives of nuns similar to those of monks? *(They lived as a group, removed from the world; education and learning was an important part of their lives.)* **OL**

✓Reading Check

Answer: Through its monasteries, the Catholic Church converted the pagans, preserved learning, and provided social services. Monks became the new heroes of Christian civilization.

DOCUMENT-BASED QUESTIONS

Answers:

1. They include expanding the empire, retaining local laws, using inspectors to keep him informed about how his provinces were run, strengthening the military, and promoting learning.
2. promoting learning

Monasteries became centers of learning. The monks worked to spread Christianity to all of Europe. English and Irish monks were very enthusiastic **missionaries**—people sent out to carry a religious message—who undertook the conversion of non-Christian peoples, especially in German lands. By 1050 most western Europeans had become Catholics.

C Although the first monks were men, women, called **nuns,** also began to withdraw from the world to dedicate themselves to God. These women played an important role in the monastic movement. Nuns lived in convents headed by **abbesses.** Many of the abbesses belonged to royal houses, especially in Anglo-Saxon England. In the kingdom of Northumbria, for example, Hilda founded the monastery of Whitby in 657. As abbess, she was responsible for giving learning an important role in the life of the monastery and helped educate five future bishops.

✓Reading Check **Describing** How did the Catholic Church affect the new European civilization?

The Carolingian Empire

MAIN IDEA Charlemagne expanded the Frankish kingdom and created the Carolingian Empire.

HISTORY & YOU Who provides your education? Read how Charlemagne promoted learning.

During the 600s and 700s, the Frankish kings gradually lost their power to the mayors of the palace, chief officers of the king's household. One of them, **Pépin,** finally took the logical step of assuming the kingship for himself and his family. Pépin was the son of Charles Martel, the leader who defeated the Muslims at the Battle of Tours in 732. Upon Pépin's death in 768, his son became the new Frankish king. This powerful ruler is known to history as Charles the Great, or **Charlemagne.** He was a determined and decisive man who was highly intelligent and curious. Charlemagne was a fierce warrior, a strong statesman, and a pious Christian. Although possibly unable to write, he was a wise patron—supporter—of learning.

INFOGRAPHICS

The Carolingian Empire

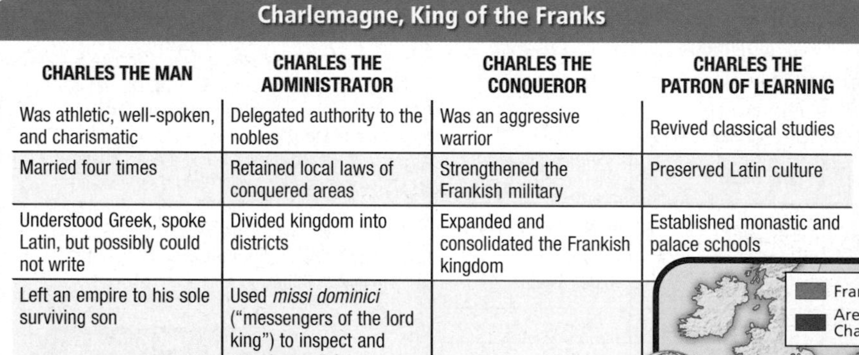

Charlemagne, King of the Franks

CHARLES THE MAN	CHARLES THE ADMINISTRATOR	CHARLES THE CONQUEROR	CHARLES THE PATRON OF LEARNING
Was athletic, well-spoken, and charismatic	Delegated authority to the nobles	Was an aggressive warrior	Revived classical studies
Married four times	Retained local laws of conquered areas	Strengthened the Frankish military	Preserved Latin culture
Understood Greek, spoke Latin, but possibly could not write	Divided kingdom into districts	Expanded and consolidated the Frankish kingdom	Established monastic and palace schools
Left an empire to his sole surviving son	Used *missi dominici* ("messengers of the lord king") to inspect and report on provinces		

DOCUMENT-BASED QUESTIONS

1. **Evaluating** Which of Charlemagne's actions helped strengthen his empire?
2. **Drawing Conclusions** Which of Charlemagne's actions continue to affect civilization today?

Differentiated Instruction

Guided Reading Activity, URB p. 160

Identifying Central Issues

Objective: Identify central issues of the transforming of the Roman world.

Focus: Review the section content.

Teach: Have students answer questions 1–11.

Assess: Have students trade papers with a partner and correct each other's answers.

Close: Ask students to summarize how and why the Roman world was transformed.

Differentiated Instruction Strategies

BL Have students work in pairs to answer the questions.

AL Ask students to research the Carolingian Renaissance and report on its importance.

ELL Discuss how Roman, Germanic, and Christian cultures blended and how cultures blend today in the United States.

During his long rule from 768 to 814, Charlemagne greatly expanded the Frankish kingdom and created what came to be known as the **Carolingian** (KAR•uh•LIN•jee•uhn) **Empire.** At its height, this empire covered much of western and central Europe. Not until Napoleon Bonaparte's time in the nineteenth century would an empire its size be seen again in Europe.

The administration of the empire depended both on Charlemagne's household staff and on counts (German nobles) who acted as the king's chief local representatives. In order to limit the counts' powers, Charlemagne set up the *missi dominici* (messengers of the lord king)—two men sent out to local districts to **ensure** that the counts carried out the king's wishes. **D**

Charlemagne as Roman Emperor

As Charlemagne's power grew, so too did his prestige as the most powerful Christian ruler. One monk even described Charlemagne's empire as the "kingdom of Europe." In 800, Charlemagne acquired a new title—emperor of the Romans.

Charlemagne's coronation as Roman emperor showed the strength of the idea of an enduring Roman Empire. After all, his coronation took place 300 years after the collapse of the Western Roman Empire.

The coronation also symbolized the joining of Roman, Christian, and Germanic elements. A Germanic king had been crowned emperor of the Romans by the pope, the spiritual leader of Western Christendom. A new civilization had emerged.

Carolingian Renaissance

Charlemagne had a strong desire to promote learning in his kingdom. This desire stemmed from his own intellectual curiosity and from the need to educate Catholic clergy and government officials. His efforts led to an intellectual revival sometimes called the Carolingian Renaissance, or rebirth. This revival involved renewed interest in Latin culture and classical works—the works of the Greeks and Romans.

The monasteries, many of which had been founded by Irish and English missionaries, played a central role in this cultural renewal. By the 800s, the work asked of Benedictine monks included copying manuscripts. Monasteries established scriptoria, or writing rooms, where monks copied not only the works of early Christianity, such as the Bible, but also the works of classical Latin authors. Their work was a crucial factor in the preservation of the ancient legacy. Most of the ancient Roman works we have today exist because they were copied by Carolingian monks.

✓Reading Check **Explaining** What was the importance of the *missi dominici*?

SECTION 1 REVIEW

Vocabulary

1. **Explain** the significance of: excluded, Clovis, wergild, ordeal, bishopric, pope, Gregory I, monk, monasticism, Saint Benedict, missionary, nun, abbess, Pépin, Charlemagne, Carolingian Empire, ensure.

Main Ideas

2. **Explain** how the *missi dominici* helped Charlemagne establish a strong empire.
3. **Summarize** the crucial social bond among the Germanic peoples, along with one area of its application.
4. **List** the daily activities undertaken by the Benedictine monks.

Daily Activities of a Monk

Critical Thinking

5. **The BIG Idea** **Explaining** What significance did Charlemagne's coronation as Roman emperor have to the development of European civilization?
6. **Summarizing Information** Identify the rulers discussed in the chapter and explain how they were significant in both religious and political realms.
7. **Analyzing Visuals** Analyze the chart on page 306. Which of Charlemagne's accomplishments is the most significant? Why?

Writing About History

8. **Persuasive Writing** You have been asked to apply Germanic law to modern society. List at least five common crimes that occur today and argue what wergild you think should be established for each crime. Be sure to explain why.

History ONLINE

For help with the concepts in this section of *Glencoe World History*, go to glencoe.com and click Study Central™.

D Differentiated Instruction

Auditory/Musical Ask groups of four students to ad-lib dialogue between two students who are *missi dominici* and two who are counts who have not fulfilled their duties. **OL**

Answer: These messengers of the king (or lord) ensured that the counts carried out the king's orders. They helped centralize administration and kept the counts in check.

Assess

History ONLINE

Study Central provides summaries, interactive games, and online graphic organizers to help students review content.

Close

Ask: What was the result of Charlemagne's strength as a ruler? (*He ensured a period of stability that included an emphasis on learning.*) **OL**

SECTION 1 REVIEW

Answers

1. Definitions for the vocabulary words are found in the section and the Glossary.
2. They traveled to local districts to make sure counts followed the king's wishes.
3. The family was the central bond; it affected the concept of crime and punishment.
4. attending church service; private prayer; meals; manual labor
5. His coronation symbolized the union of Roman, Christian, and Germanic elements.
6. **Clovis:** converted to Christianity; expanded Frankish kingdom; **Gregory I:** extended papal authority; controlled Rome; **Charlemagne:** crowned by pope; created Carolingian Empire.
7. Possible answer: Established schools; because monks learned how to write and copy texts, information about the past has been handed down to us.
8. Students' responses will vary, but should be consistent with the section content about wergild.

Focus

Bellringer

Daily Focus Transparency 9.2

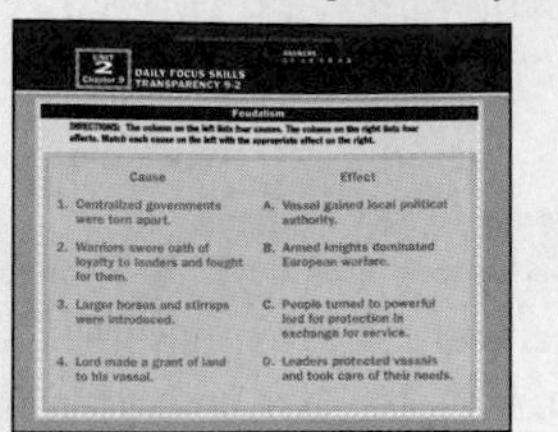

GUIDE TO READING

Answers to Graphic:
Rulers: Clovis; Gregory I; Charlemagne
Religious Realm: conversion; extended papal authority; crowned by pope
Political Realm: Frankish Kingdom; controlled Rome; Carolingian Empire

Section Spotlight Video

To generate student interest and provide a springboard for class discussion, access the Chapter 9, Section 2 video at glencoe.com or on the video DVD.

SECTION 2

Feudalism

GUIDE TO READING

The BIG Idea
Order and Security The collapse of central authority in Europe led to a new political order known as feudalism.

Content Vocabulary
- feudalism *(p. 310)*
- vassal *(p. 310)*
- knight *(p. 310)*
- fief *(p. 310)*
- feudal contract *(p. 311)*
- tournament *(p. 312)*
- chivalry *(p. 313)*

Academic Vocabulary
- enabled *(p. 309)*
- contract *(p. 311)*

People and Places
- Magyars *(p. 308)*
- Hungary *(p. 308)*
- Vikings *(p. 308)*
- Normandy *(p. 309)*
- Eleanor of Aquitaine *(p. 313)*

Reading Strategy
Identifying Information Use a diagram like the one below to show the system of loyalties created under feudalism.

Rulers	Religious Realm	Political Realm

The Carolingian Empire was weakened from within by division after Charlemagne's death and from outside by enemy attacks. Local nobles became more important as people turned to them for the protection that the empire could no longer provide. The result was feudalism, a new political and social order in Europe.

The End of the Carolingian Empire

MAIN IDEA Vikings, Magyars, and Muslims invaded Europe during the ninth and tenth centuries.

HISTORY & YOU Why might the death of a strong leader make a country vulnerable to attack? Read how the death of Charlemagne left his kingdom vulnerable.

Charlemagne held his empire together with his personal power and prestige as a leader and the strong administrative system he established. His death created a vacuum of leadership that left the empire vulnerable. The Frankish tradition of dividing an estate among the surviving heirs also weakened the empire. As the Germanic tribes had moved into the Roman Empire and helped create a new European civilization, new invaders entered Europe and influenced its culture.

Invaders

The Carolingian Empire began to fall apart soon after Charlemagne's death in 814. Less than 30 years later, it was divided among his grandsons into three major sections: the west Frankish lands, the eastern Frankish lands, and the Middle Kingdom. Local nobles gained power while the Carolingian rulers fought each other. Invasions in different parts of the old Carolingian world added to the process of disintegration.

In the ninth and tenth centuries, western Europe was beset by a wave of invasions. The Muslims attacked the southern coasts of Europe and sent raiding parties into southern France. The **Magyars,** a people from western Asia, moved into central Europe at the end of the ninth century, settled on the plains of **Hungary,** and invaded western Europe.

The most far-reaching attacks of the time, however, came from the Norsemen or Northmen of Scandinavia, also called the **Vikings.** The Vikings were a Germanic people. Their great love of adventure and their search for spoils of war and new avenues of trade may have been what led them to invade other areas of Europe.

Resource Manager

R Reading Strategies	C Critical Thinking	D Differentiated Instruction	W Writing Support	S Skill Practice
Teacher Edition • Read. Pri. Sources, p. 310 **Additional Resources** • Guid. Read. Act., URB p. 161 • Read. Ess. & Note-Taking Guide, p. 100	**Teacher Edition** • Pred. Consequences, p. 309 • Det. Cause/Effect, p. 310 • Making Inferences, p. 312 • Compare/Contrast, p. 313 **Additional Resources** • Section Quiz, p. 106	**Teacher Edition** • ELL, p. 311 **Additional Resources** • Read. Strat. for SS, p. 22	**Teacher Edition** • Expository Writing, p. 312 **Additional Resources** • Writer's Guidebook, p. 51	**Teacher Edition** • Using Geo. Skills, p. 309 **Additional Resources** • Hist. & Geo. Act., URB p. 141

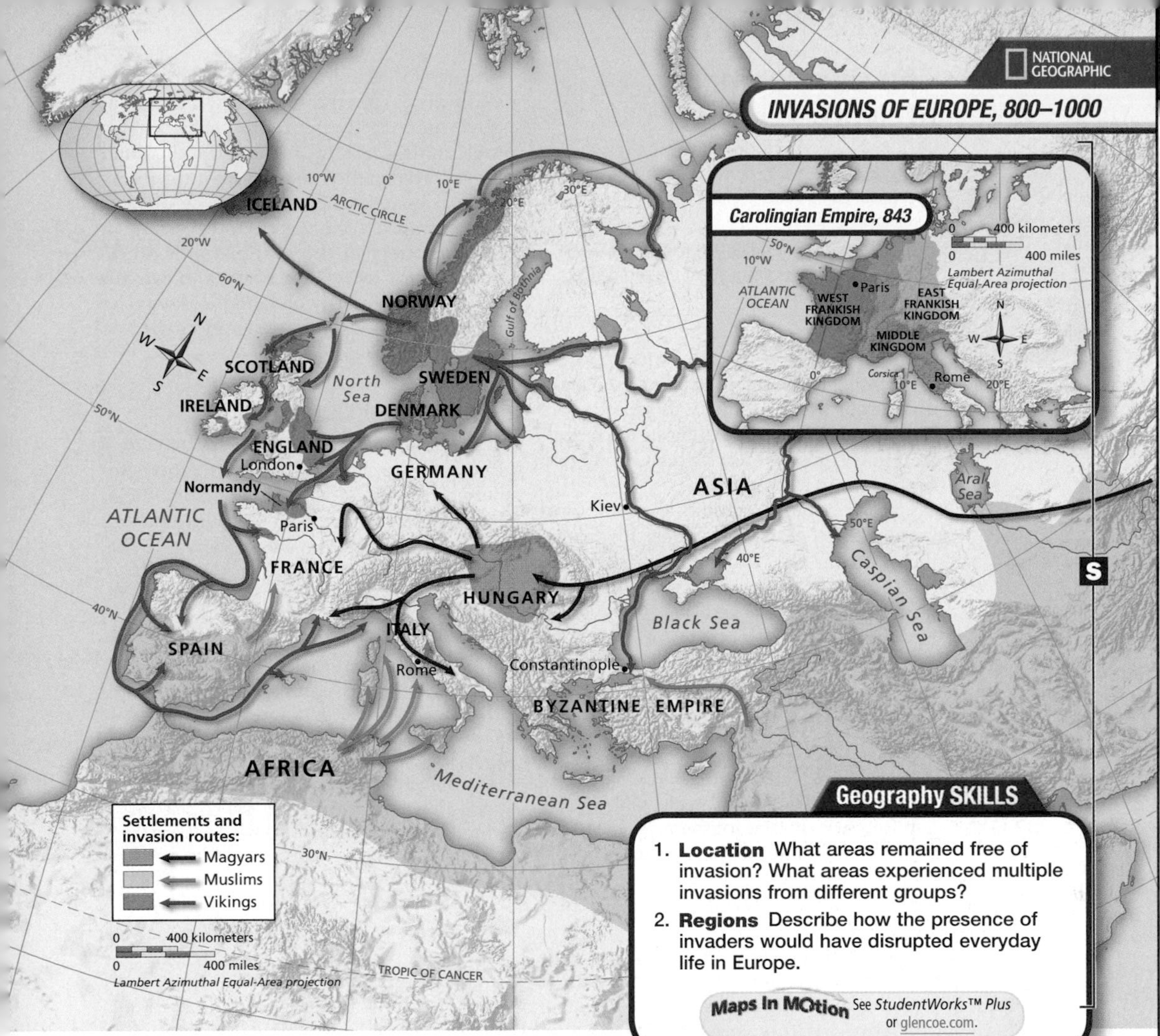

NATIONAL GEOGRAPHIC

INVASIONS OF EUROPE, 800–1000

Carolingian Empire, 843

Settlements and invasion routes:
- Magyars
- Muslims
- Vikings

Geography SKILLS

1. **Location** What areas remained free of invasion? What areas experienced multiple invasions from different groups?
2. **Regions** Describe how the presence of invaders would have disrupted everyday life in Europe.

Maps In MOtion See StudentWorks™ Plus or glencoe.com.

In the ninth century, Vikings sacked villages and towns, destroyed churches, and easily defeated small local armies. The Vikings were warriors, and they were superb shipbuilders and sailors. Their ships were the best of the period. Long and narrow with beautifully carved, arched prows, the Viking dragon ships carried about 50 men. The construction of the ships **enabled** them to sail up European rivers and attack places far inland. By the mid-ninth century, the Vikings had begun to build various European settlements.

Beginning in 911, the ruler of the west Frankish lands gave one band of Vikings land at the mouth of the Seine River, forming a section of France that came to be known as **Normandy.** The Frankish policy of settling the Vikings and converting them to Christianity was a deliberate one. As a result of their conversion to Christianity, the Vikings were soon made a part of European civilization.

✓Reading Check **Evaluating** What factors helped the Vikings invade Europe successfully?

Teach

S Skill Practice

Using Geography Skills

Ask: What island that the Vikings invaded is located near the Arctic Circle? *(Iceland)* BL

C Critical Thinking

Predicting Consequences

Ask: What do you think the effect of giving the Vikings more land might have been? *(It might have discouraged further Viking invasions, allowed Christianity to influence them, and made them a part of European society.)* OL

✓Reading Check

Answer: The Vikings were warriors and superb shipbuilders and sailors.

Geography SKILLS

Answers:

1. Scandinavia remained free; England, France, and central Europe experienced multiple invasions.
2. fear, loss of property, interruption of daily life to prepare for attacks and defend villages

Drawing Conclusions

Objective: Draw conclusions about the Vikings.

Focus: Have students analyze the map and text about the Vikings.

Teach: Have students answer questions 1–4.

Assess: Organize a debate as in item 5.

Close: Ask students to make a general statement about the historical significance of the Vikings.

Differentiated Instruction Strategies

- **BL** Have students review the section content on the Vikings before completing this activity.
- **AL** Ask students to report on a specific Viking settlement or cultural aspect.
- **ELL** Have students work in pairs to complete the questions.

Differentiated Instruction

History and Geography Activity, URB p. 141

C Critical Thinking

Determining Cause and Effect **Ask:** What were some reasons that knights rose in military importance during this period? *(Larger horses could carry knights in heavy suits of armor; the invention of stirrups helped riders to stay in the saddle when they attacked. People began turning to local aristocrats for protection.)* **OL**

For additional practice on this skill, see the **Skills Handbook**.

R Reading Strategy

Reading Primary Sources Ask students to look up the definition of *homage*. Then ask them to reread the primary source and explain how the ceremony fits the definition. **OL**

The Development of Feudalism

History ONLINE
Student Web Activity— Visit glencoe.com and complete the activity about medieval Europe.

MAIN IDEA A system of lords and vassals spread throughout Europe after the collapse of the Carolingian Empire.

HISTORY & YOU What do you think of when you hear the term *knight*? Learn about the social order of feudalism.

The Vikings and other invaders posed a large threat to the safety of people throughout Europe. Rulers found it more and more difficult to defend their subjects as centralized governments such as the Carolingian Empire were torn apart.

Thus, people began to turn to local landed aristocrats, or nobles, to protect them. To survive, it became important to find a powerful lord who could offer protection in return for service. This led to a new political and social order known as **feudalism.**

Knights and Vassals

At the heart of feudalism was the idea of vassalage. In Germanic society, warriors swore an oath of loyalty to their leaders and fought in battles for them. The leaders, in turn, took care of the warriors' needs. By the eighth century, a man who served a lord in a military capacity was known as a **vassal.**

The Frankish army had originally consisted of foot soldiers dressed in coats of mail (armor made of metal links or plates) and armed with swords. Horsemen had been throwers of spears. In the eighth century, however, larger horses and the stirrup were introduced. Now, horsemen were armored in coats of mail (the larger horses **C** could carry the weight). They wielded long lances that enabled them to act as battering rams (the stirrups kept them on their horses). For almost five hundred years, warfare in Europe was dominated by heavily armored cavalry, or **knights,** as they came to be called. The knights had great social prestige and formed the backbone of the European aristocracy.

It was expensive to have a horse, armor, and weapons. It also took more time and practice to learn to use these instruments skillfully. With the breakdown of royal governments, the more powerful nobles took control of large areas of land. When these lords wanted men to fight for them, they granted each vassal a piece of land that supported the vassal and his family. In the society of the Early Middle Ages, where there was little trade and wealth was based primarily on land, land was the most important gift a lord could give to a vassal.

The Feudal Contract

In feudal society, having loyalty to one's lord was the chief virtue. The relationship between lord and vassal was made official by a public ceremony. To become a vassal, a man performed an act of homage to his lord:

PRIMARY SOURCE

"The man should put his hands together as a sign of humility, and place them between the two hands of his lord as a token that he vows everything to him and promises faith to him; and the lord should receive him and promise to keep **R** faith with him. Then the man should say: 'Sir, I enter your homage and faith and become your man by mouth and hands [that is, by taking the oath and placing his hands between those of the lord], and I swear and promise to keep faith and loyalty to you against all others.'"

—*A Source Book for Medieval History*

By the ninth century, the grant of land made to a vassal had become known as a **fief** (FEEF). Vassals who held fiefs came to hold political authority within them. As the Carolingian world fell apart, the number of separate, powerful lords and vassals increased. Instead of a single government, many different people were responsible for keeping order.

Feudalism became increasingly complicated. The vassals of a king, who were great lords, might also have vassals who would owe them military service in return for a grant of land taken from their estates. Those vassals, in turn, might likewise have vassals. At that level, the vassals would be simple knights with barely enough land to provide income for their equipment.

Hands-On Chapter Project Step 2

Creating a TV Documentary

Step 2: Documentary on Feudalism Students plan a section of their documentary set during the feudal era in Europe.

Directions: Each group does research to write a script that describes life during this period of time. Encourage students to focus their research. They may want to narrow their research to describe the life of any of the following: a king, great lord, knight, vassal, an ordinary woman, or an aristocratic woman. Their main goal for this step is to complete their script for this portion of their documentary. Remind students to divide roles and to think about the Essential Question.

Summarizing: Allow time for groups to share what they learned about the Big Idea while preparing their scripts. **OL**

(Chapter Project is continued in Section 3.)

The lord-vassal relationship bound together greater and lesser landowners. It was an honorable relationship between free men and implied no sense of servitude. Feudalism came to be characterized by a set of unwritten rules—known as the **feudal contract**—that determined the relationship between a lord and his vassal. The major obligation of a vassal to his lord was to perform military service, usually about 40 days a year.

When summoned, a vassal had to appear at his lord's court to give advice. Vassals were responsible for making payments to the lord on certain occasions, for example, the knighting of the lord's eldest son or marriage of his eldest daughter.

Under the feudal **contract**, the lord also had responsibilities to his vassals. Of course, he supported a vassal by granting him land but he also had to protect his vassal by defending him militarily or by taking his side in a dispute. D

✓Reading Check **Explaining** Why was land the most important gift a lord could give a vassal?

Feudal Society

MAIN IDEA Men and women of the nobility were guided by a code of ethical behavior and society's expectations of their roles.

HISTORY & YOU How do sports provide people with an outlet? Read how tournaments provided an outlet for knights.

Feudal society was built around a culture of warfare as vassals prepared to fight for their lords when called upon. However, such a society also needed to find ways to prevent conflicts and violence from tearing the society apart.

Nobility and Chivalry

In the Middle Ages, European society, like Japanese society during the same period, was dominated by men whose chief concern was warfare. Like the Japanese samurai, many European nobles loved war. As one nobleman wrote in a poem on the subject:

INFOGRAPHICS

Feudalism

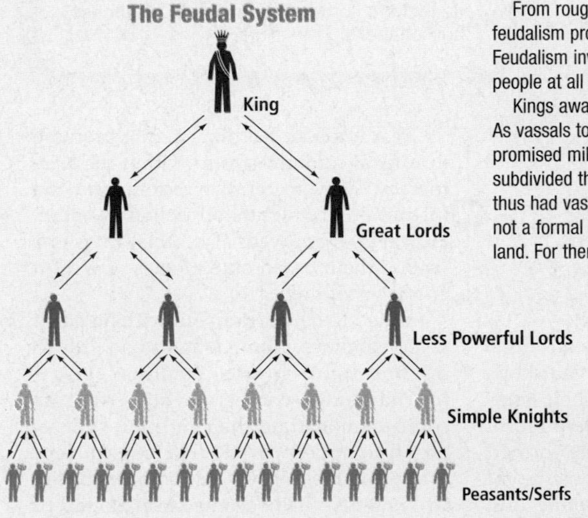

From roughly 800 to 1500, the social system of feudalism provided security for most of Europe. Feudalism involved a complex web of obligations for people at all levels of society.

Kings awarded tracts of land, called fiefs, to nobles. As vassals to the king, nobles pledged their loyalty and promised military services as a knight. Wealthier nobles subdivided their land into fiefs for lesser nobles and thus had vassals of their own. Peasants and serfs were not a formal part of feudalism. They were tied to the land. For them, the feudal order meant security.

CRITICAL THINKING SKILLS

1. **Comparing and Contrasting** How did the obligations of the serfs differ from those of lords and knights?
2. **Evaluating** What does the chart reveal about feudal values?

D Differentiated Instruction

English Language Learners
Discuss the concept of a feudal "contract" with students. Next, discuss modern contracts the students may be familiar with such as a business contract to provide certain services. **ELL**

✓Reading Check

Answer: because wealth was based primarily on land, which could be used to maintain the expense of being a knight

CRITICAL THINKING SKILLS

Answers:
1. Serfs were not part of feudalism but worked the land; lords and knights were bound by mutual oaths related to land grants and military service.
2. Feudal society was dominated by landholders and a culture of warfare. The majority of people who worked the land had little power.

Additional Support

Activity: Interdisciplinary Connection

Daily Life Discuss the organization of feudal society as a way to provide security and order within medieval society. Then discuss ways that modern American society provides security and order. Create a chart that lists different levels of people (king, vassals, knights, peasants) and their duties. Then create a second chart alongside which lists how similar levels and duties are structured today. For example, the king received taxes and provided protection while today, local, state, and federal governments collect taxes and provide protection. **Ask:** Would a feudal system work in modern society? *(Students may think not, since society is much more complex, not all people are attached to the land, and modern warfare can't rely on privately trained warriors.)* **OL**

C Critical Thinking

Making Inferences Ask: How did a moat help protect a castle from attack? *(Men and horses couldn't cross the moat to attack the walls; even if they swam across, there was no land to stand on.)* **BL**

For additional practice on this skill, see the **Skills Handbook**.

W Writing Support

Expository Writing Ask students to review the section content and to do additional research as necessary to gain a fuller understanding of "knighthood." Then ask them to write a short essay that explains how knighthood could unite as well as divide great lords and ordinary knights. **AL**

ANALYZING VISUALS

Answers:

1. barbican, portcullis, moat, drawbridge
2. A castle needed to be self-sufficient to withstand a siege.

Additional Support

INFOGRAPHICS

Medieval Castle

Analyzing VISUALS

By the end of the twelfth century, a castle's keep was the strongest part of the castle, but people lived, entertained, worshiped, and conducted business in smaller buildings on the bailey.

1. **Making Inferences** Which structures in a late medieval castle helped to protect the castle from invaders?
2. **Drawing Conclusions** Why might a castle include its own offices, stables, kitchen, and chapel?

PRIMARY SOURCE

"And well I like to hear the call of
'Help' and see the wounded fall,
Loudly for mercy praying,
And see the dead, both great and small,
Pierced by sharp spearheads one and all."

—*Sources of the Western Tradition, vol. 1*

The nobles were the kings, dukes, counts, barons, and even bishops and archbishops who had large landed estates. Their landholdings gave them considerable political power in medieval society. They formed an aristocracy, or nobility, that consisted of people who held political, economic, and social power.

W Great lords and ordinary knights came to form a common group within the aristocracy. They were all warriors, and the institution of knighthood united them all. However, there were also social divisions among them based on extremes of wealth and landholdings.

Trained to be warriors but with no adult responsibilities, young knights had little to do but fight. In the twelfth century, **tournaments**—contests where knights could demonstrate their fighting skills—began to appear. By the late twelfth century, the joust—individual combat between two knights—had become the main part of the tournament.

Extending the Content

Jousting and Tournaments Tournaments allowed knights to maintain their fighting skills while providing entertainment for people. In some tournaments, groups of knights would battle on a field; in others the combat would be limited to two knights. There were also practice jousts where knights attempted to spear rings on their lances. In some cases, knights battled to the death, but this practice was soon opposed by the Church and by kings. Rules were established around 1300, which limited the risk of death. Changes in warfare, such as improved longbows and, later, gunpowder, eventually made mounted knights obsolete. Jousting still remains popular, with "tournaments" at many medieval fairs today. It's even the official state sport of Maryland!

Knights saw tournaments as an excellent way to train for war. One knight expressed it in these words: "A knight cannot distinguish himself in war if he has not trained for it in tourneys."

In the eleventh and twelfth centuries, under the influence of the Catholic Church, there gradually evolved among the nobility an ideal of civilized behavior, called **chivalry.** Chivalry was a code of ethics that knights were supposed to uphold. In addition to their oath to defend the Church and defenseless people, knights were expected to treat captives as honored guests instead of putting them in dungeons. In terms of the treatment of women, chivalry put the aristocratic woman on a pedestal. A knight was to treat her with tenderness and respect. C

Chivalry also implied that knights should fight only for glory and not for material rewards. Of course, this ideal was not always followed.

Aristocratic Women's Roles

Although women could legally hold property, most remained under the control of men—of their fathers until they married and of their husbands after they married. Still, aristocratic women had many opportunities to play important roles.

Because the lord was often away at war or court, the lady of the castle had to manage the estate. Households could include large numbers of officials and servants, so this was no small responsibility. Care of the financial accounts alone took considerable knowledge. The lady of the castle was also responsible for overseeing the food supply and maintaining all the other supplies needed for the smooth operation of the household.

Women were expected to be subservient to their husbands, but there were many strong women who advised, and even dominated, their husbands. Perhaps the most famous of these was **Eleanor of Aquitaine.** Eleanor was one of the most remarkable personalities of twelfth-century Europe. Heiress to the duchy of Aquitaine in southwestern France, she was married at the age of 15 to King Louis VII of France. The marriage was not a happy one, and Louis had their marriage annulled. Eleanor married again, only eight weeks later, to Duke Henry of Normandy, who soon became King Henry II of England.

Henry II and Eleanor had a stormy relationship. She spent much time abroad in her native Aquitaine, where she created a brilliant court dedicated to cultural activities. She and Henry had eight children (five were sons). Two of her sons—Richard and John—became kings of England.

As Eleanor aged, she continued to travel to arrange royal and noble weddings and to manage her estates. She lived until her eighties, dying in 1204 in an abbey.

✓Reading Check **Summarizing** List three features of chivalry.

SECTION 2 REVIEW

Vocabulary
1. **Explain** the significance of: Magyars, Hungary, Vikings, enabled, Normandy, feudalism, vassal, knight, fief, feudal contract, contract, tournament, chivalry, Eleanor of Aquitaine.

Main Ideas
2. **Explain** how Frankish traditions weakened the Carolingian Empire following Charlemagne's death.
3. **Describe** the benefits granted a vassal under feudalism. What was a vassal's primary obligation to his lord?
4. **List** the invasions that besieged the Carolingian Empire throughout the ninth and tenth centuries.

Critical Thinking
5. **The BIG Idea Summarize** What factors helped feudalism develop in western Europe throughout the ninth and tenth centuries?
6. **Contrasting Information** Use a table like the one below to list the differences between the social order of feudalism and empires.

Feudalism	Empires

7. **Analyzing Visuals** Analyze the castle on page 312. What does its structure reveal about medieval life?

Writing About History
8. **Descriptive Writing** Describe a twelfth-century tournament, using details to create vivid images. Use your local library or the Internet to supplement the text information. What questions would you ask about tournaments, knights, and jousting?

History ONLINE
For help with the concepts in this section of *Glencoe World History,* go to glencoe.com and click Study Central™.

313

C Critical Thinking

Comparing and Contrasting
Ask: How do you think the code of chivalry compares to expectations of modern soldiers? *(Answers may include treating captives as guests are not expectations of modern soldiers but defending the defenseless could be comparable.)* OL

Answer: Knights were to defend the Church and the defenseless, treat captives as honored guests, and fight only for glory.

Assess

History ONLINE
Study Central provides summaries, interactive games, and online graphic organizers to help students review content.

Close

Making Generalizations
Ask: What purposes did feudalism serve in Europe? *(It provided a social, political, and economic system.)*

Answers

1. Definitions for the vocabulary words are found in the section and the Glossary.
2. The tradition of dividing an estate among the heirs weakened the empire.
3. The benefits included land and protection. A vassal's primary obligation to his lord was military service.
4. The empire was invaded by Muslims, Magyars, and Vikings.
5. The key factors were the collapse of central authority and invasions by Muslims, Magyars, and Vikings.
6. **Feudalism:** local; voluntary relationship based on feudal contract; many people responsible for keeping order; **Empires:** large political unit; control usually obtained through military conquest; control is usually centralized.
7. Answers will vary but should note how the castle's features emphasize the need for physical security in medieval society.
8. Students' responses will vary, but should be logical and consistent with the section content about tournaments, knights, and jousting.

Focus

Introducing Social History Have students recall what they know about feudalism. **Ask:** Why might a group of young men dedicated to warfare need a code of conduct? *(Answers may include to ensure they used their skills for the right purposes.)* OL

Teach

W Writing Support

Personal Writing Have students write a short essay exploring how the four values of chivalry might be reflected in their own lives. OL

D Differentiated Instruction

Verbal/Linguistic Explain that several words derive from the Latin word *caballarius* meaning "horseman." In French it is *chevalier*, in Italian *cavaliere*, in Spanish *cabaliero*, and in English *cavalier*. However, the word *knight* is more commonly used in English. AL

The Code of Chivalry

Beginning in the eleventh and twelfth centuries, the idea of chivalry developed. This was an idealized set of rules and behaviors that knights were called on to follow. These rules varied according to time and place, but generally the ideal heroic knight was influenced by courtesy, fairness, piety, and devotion to an honorable idea. W

D The word "chivalry" comes from *cheval*, the French word for horse.

In the feudal system, a knight swore his oath of loyalty to his liege lord. This oath helped form a basis for the ideals of chivalry.

The code of chivalry was reserved for wealthy and noble horse soldiers, called knights.

More Romance than Reality

Chivalry existed to a certain degree, but it hardly controlled the way knights behaved or courts were run. It was first a literary movement—troubadours and bards spread romantic tales of noble, usually fictitious knights. The stories were also based on the ideas of "courtly love," in which courtesy toward women was considered the most important quality. It began in the "courts of love" in southern France and then spread, but was never adopted by any large numbers of the nobility. It was a romanticized idea, but, as one historian states, chivalry was "more playacting than real."

Additional Support

Background

Knights and Chivalry The term *chivalry* originally referred to knights themselves and later came to mean the code of conduct expected of knights. It then came to have the broader meaning of "courtesy." Boys might begin training for knighthood as early as age 7 and would go through several stages of education and responsibility. Before he could be knighted, a young man had to demonstrate his skill in fighting and be able to pay for his own horse and armor. The practice of chivalry was perhaps closest to reality during and just after the Crusades. During that period, European knights were united in fighting for a religious cause. They also sought to help pilgrims who came to the newly reclaimed Holy Land.

A Chivalrous Knight Pledged Loyalty and Service...

To the Church
The Roman Catholic Church was a major influence on life in the Middle Ages. Rigorous observance of Church doctrine was expected, although Church practices varied across the continent.

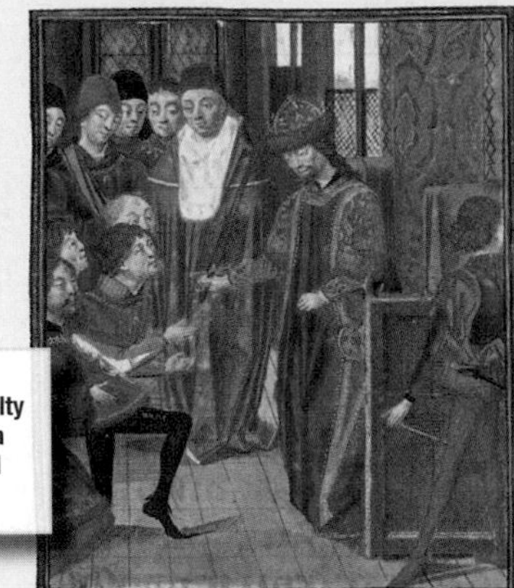

To His Lord
The knight was a soldier. Loyalty to his lord was essential in a feudal society, and a central element of chivalry.

To Women
Knights were expected to be honorable in their dealing with noblewomen. In time, a romantic idea developed: a knight was supposed to pledge his devotion and service to a noble lady, who might be married to someone else.

To the Weak
Ideally, a knight would be expected to use his military skill and social standing to protect the most vulnerable people in society.

Periods of Chivalry

R The history of chivalry is sometimes viewed in four periods. The first was during the Crusades, when knights pledged themselves to their holy task. The second was in the Crusades' aftermath, when military orders, like the Knights Templar, were formed, and member knights took chivalric oaths. The third was during the Hundred Years' War, when the concepts of honor in battle and with women dominated chivalric ideals. The fourth period was during the 1400s, when chivalry was carried out in ceremonies in royal courts.

Analyzing Visuals

1. **Evaluate** How important do you think chivalry was in the history of Europe? Explain your answer.
2. **Comparing** Are there any modern equivalents of chivalry? Give some examples.

R Reading Strategy

Sequencing Events Help students understand the sequence by giving them the dates for the Crusades (1096–1204, see pages 325–327) and the Hundred Years' War (1337–1453, see pages 356–357). Make sure they understand the meaning of *aftermath*. **BL**

Assess/Close

Have students answer the Analyzing Visuals questions and share their responses with a partner. Have students compare the different periods of chivalry. **OL**

Analyzing Visuals

Answers:

1. Answers may include that it was mainly an ideal important to cultural and literary history.
2. Students may suggest rules of sportsmanship, or academic honor codes.

Activity: Collaborative Learning

Dramatizing Chivalry The stories of chivalry began with the French troubadours, and they included stories of Britain's King Arthur and his Knights of the Round Table. Discuss with students what they know about the Arthurian legend from books or movies. **Ask:** How do these stories exemplify the values of chivalry? *(Students may mention that Arthur and the knights were dedicated to maintaining peace, went on religious quests for the Holy Grail, and practiced the ideal of courtly love).* Organize students into groups and instruct them to choose a short example from an Arthurian story to use as the basis for a skit that demonstrates the ideals of chivalry. Tell students to make sure that all members of their group have a role in creating and acting in the skit. Some may write the script and others make or find simple props. Invite each group to present its skit and discuss how it reflects the code of chivalry. **OL**

R **Reading Strategy**

Summarizing Ask students to reread the paragraph at the top of page 318 and write a summary of it. *(The Magna Carta made it clear that the monarch's powers were limited; Parliament passed laws, levied taxes, and included representatives of common people and nobles.)* **OL**

D **Differentiated Instruction**

Advanced Learners Have students read a copy of the original Magna Carta. Then ask them to rewrite a section of it, using standard modern English. **AL**

✓**Reading Check**

Answer: It's the date of William of Normandy's victory over the Anglo-Saxons, and heralded major changes in English government, language, and culture.

DOCUMENT-BASED QUESTIONS

Answers:

1. so the king could not fight the nobles
2. The Magna Carta put limits on the power of the monarchy.

Additional Support

It was called the **Magna Carta,** or the Great Charter. Feudal custom had recognized that the relationship between king and vassals was based on mutual rights and obligations. The Magna Carta gave written recognition to that fact and was used in later years to strengthen the idea that a monarch's power was limited, not absolute.

R In the thirteenth century, during the reign of Edward I, an important institution in the development of representative government—the English **Parliament**—also emerged. It was composed of two knights from every county, two people from every town, and all of the nobles and bishops throughout England. Eventually, nobles and church lords formed the House of Lords; knights and townspeople, the House of Commons. The Parliaments of Edward I granted taxes, discussed politics, and passed laws.

✓**Reading Check** **Analyzing** Why was 1066 a turning point in history?

TURNING POINT — THE MAGNA CARTA

In the Magna Carta's 63 clauses, King John vowed that the church would remain free, listed rights due to landholders, said he would dismiss his mercenaries from foreign countries, and gave a council of 25 barons the right to go to war with him if he did not honor the Magna Carta. John was not the first king to make promises to his barons. However, previous monarchs had made general promises and granted them freely, while King John's barons demanded the very specific promises from him. By recognizing the rights of nobles, the Magna Carta limited the power of English monarchs.

39. No freeman shall be . . . imprisoned . . . except by the lawful judgment of his peers or by the law of the land.
40. To no one will we sell, to no one will we refuse or delay, right or justice.
51. As soon as peace is restored, we will banish from the kingdom all foreign-born knights, cross-bowmen, serjeants, and mercenary soldiers . . .
52. If anyone has been dispossessed or removed by us, without the legal judgment of his peers, from his lands, castles, franchises, or from his right, we will immediately restore them to him . . .
55. All fines made with us unjustly and against the law of the land, and all amercements[1] imposed unjustly and against the law of the land, shall be entirely remitted . . .

—from the *Magna Carta*

[1] **amercements:** punishments by fine

D

▲ *A depiction of John of England signing the Magna Carta from* Cassell's History of England—Century Edition

DOCUMENT-BASED QUESTIONS

1. **Making Inferences** Why might the nobles have insisted that King John send away his foreign army?
2. **Summarizing** What permanent effects did the Magna Carta have on the English monarchy?

Activity: Interdisciplinary Connection

Civics Have students review the articles of the Magna Carta listed in the Turning Point feature. Then ask students to imagine living under a government that did not have these limits. **Ask:** What might happen to you if your government did not have these limits? *(A person could be arrested and imprisoned without a trial; punishment of crimes could be avoided through payment; people could be held for unreasonable amounts of time without trial; mercenaries from other countries might be hired as police; property could be taken without reason; unjust fines could be levied.)* **OL**

France in the Middle Ages

MAIN IDEA One section of Charlemagne's empire became France.

HISTORY & YOU Which states were originally French territory? Read about the development of the French monarchy.

In 843, the Carolingian Empire was divided into three sections. One of them, the west Frankish lands, formed the core of the kingdom of France. In 987, after the last Carolingian king died, the west Frankish nobles made Hugh Capet their king, establishing the Capetian (kuh•PEE•shuhn) dynasty of French kings.

Although they were called kings, the Capetians had little real power. The royal domain, or lands they controlled, included only the area around **Paris,** known as the Ile-de-France. Formally, they were above the great dukes of France, but many of the dukes were actually more powerful.

The reign of **Philip II Augustus,** who reigned from 1180 to 1223, was a turning point in the French monarchy, expanding its income and power. Philip fought wars against the English to take control of the French territories of Normandy, Maine, Anjou, and Aquitaine. Philip's successors continued to add lands to the royal domain.

Much of the thirteenth century was dominated by the reign of Louis IX. Deeply religious, he was later made a saint by the Catholic Church. Louis was known for trying to bring justice to his people by hearing their complaints in person. Philip IV, called Philip the Fair, ruled from 1285 to 1314. He made the monarchy stronger by expanding the royal bureaucracy. Indeed by 1300, France was the largest and best-governed monarchy in Europe. Philip IV also created a French parliament by meeting with members of the three **estates,** or classes—the clergy (first estate), the nobles (second estate), and the townspeople and peasants (third estate). The meeting, in 1302, began the Estates-General, the first French parliament. **W**

✓**Reading Check** **Evaluating** Why was the reign of King Philip II Augustus important to the growth of the French monarchy?

The Holy Roman Empire

MAIN IDEA Unlike England and France, the lands of Germany and Italy did not become united during the Middle Ages.

HISTORY & YOU What characteristics would make one group unite with another? Read how the Holy Roman Emperors failed.

In the tenth century, the powerful dukes of the Saxons became kings of the eastern Frankish kingdom, which came to be known as Germany. The best-known Saxon king of Germany was **Otto I.** Otto was a patron of German culture and brought the Church under his control. In return for protecting the pope, Otto I was crowned emperor of the Romans in 962. The title had not been used since the time of Charlemagne. Otto's creation of a new Roman Empire in the hands of the Germans had long-range consequences.

Struggles in Italy

As leaders of a new Roman Empire, the German kings attempted to rule both German and Italian lands. Many a German king lost armies in Italy in pursuit of the dream of an empire. The two most famous members of one particular German dynasty prove this. **C**

Frederick I and Frederick II, instead of building a strong German kingdom, tried to create a new kind of empire. Frederick I planned to get his chief revenues from Italy. He considered Italy the center of a "holy empire," as he called it—hence the name Holy Roman Empire.

Frederick's attempt to conquer northern Italy led to severe problems. The pope opposed him, fearing that he wanted to include Rome and the Papal States as part of his empire. The cities of northern Italy, which had become used to their freedom, were also unwilling to become his subjects. An alliance of these northern Italian cities and the pope defeated the forces of Frederick I in 1176.

The main goal of Frederick II was to establish a strong, centralized state in Italy. He too was involved in a struggle with the popes and the northern Italian cities.

W Writing Support

Personal Writing Discuss the general attitudes of royalty toward the lower classes at the time. Note that many kings were widely feared and were never in direct contact with people other than the nobility. Then ask students to assume that they are either a member of royalty under Louis IX or a commoner (who was able to speak directly to him) and write a journal entry that describes their conversation with the king. **OL**

C Critical Thinking

Making Inferences Ask: What barriers to German control of Italy do you think caused German kings to lose armies? *(the opposition by people living in northern Italy who were used to their freedom)* **OL**

✓**Reading Check**

Answer: He gained control of Normandy, Maine, Anjou, and Aquitaine, which increased the income and power of the French monarchy.

Hands-On Chapter Project Step 3

Creating a TV Documentary

Step 3: Documentary on the Growth of European Kingdoms Students plan a documentary set during the time when European kingdoms arose.

Directions: Each group prepares a script set in England, France, or another kingdom in Europe during the time period being studied. Groups will select subjects from the section (such as an English noble, King John, Thomas Becket, a new member of Parliament, or a Saxon king) and do research as necessary to prepare a portion of their documentary. In this portion, students may want to use illustrated maps and focus on presenting a biography of a particular person of the period. Students should keep the essential question in mind as they work.

Summarizing: Allow time for groups to share any illustrations or maps that they have prepared to help convey information about the rise of the European kingdoms. **OL**

(Chapter Project is continued in Section 4.)

D Differentiated Instruction

English Language Learners Ask students to review their knowledge of Rome. **Ask:** What words could describe both Rome and Constantinople? *(Both were magnificent cities with beautiful buildings; both offered public entertainment and public services such as baths, and so on.)* ELL

W Writing Support

Narrative Writing Ask students to reread the story of silkworms in Constantinople. Then ask them to write a short narrative that describes the smuggling, the journey from China, and the care of the silkworms. OL

✓Reading Check

Answer: The Muslims diminished the size of the Roman Empire by conquering Syria and Palestine.

✓Reading Check

Answer: Internal—power struggles between military and political leaders. **External**—church schism; advance of the Seljuk Turks; need for military help from the West.

The Byzantines believed that God had commanded their state to preserve the true Christian faith. Political and religious leaders were all bound together in service to this spiritual ideal.

Life in Constantinople

Much of Constantinople was destroyed by riots in 532. Afterward, Emperor Justinian rebuilt the city and gave it the appearance it would keep for almost a thousand years. With a population estimated in the hundreds of thousands, Constantinople was the largest city in Europe during the Middle Ages.

The city was dominated by an immense palace complex, hundreds of churches, and a huge arena known as the Hippodrome, where gladiator fights and chariot races were held. Justinian's public works projects included roads, bridges, walls, public baths, law courts, schools, churches, and underground reservoirs to hold the city's water supply.

His greatest achievement was the famous Hagia Sophia—the Church of the Holy Wisdom. The center of Hagia Sophia consists of four large piers crowned by an **enormous** dome, which seems to float in space. Light from 42 windows at the dome's base helps create this impression.

Until the twelfth century, Constantinople was medieval Europe's greatest center of commerce. It was the chief center for the exchange of products between West and East. Highly desired in Europe were the products of the East: silk from China, spices from Southeast Asia and India, jewelry and ivory from India (the latter used for church items), wheat and furs from southern Russia, and flax and honey from the Balkans. These goods flowed into Constantinople, and many were then shipped throughout Europe.

Imported raw materials were also used in Constantinople for local industries. In Justinian's reign, two Christian monks smuggled silkworms from China to begin a silk industry. European demand for silk cloth made it the city's most lucrative product.

✓Reading Check **Evaluating** How did the rise of Islam affect the Eastern Roman Empire?

New Heights and New Problems

MAIN IDEA The Macedonians expanded the Byzantine Empire, but new threats arose in the late eleventh century.

HISTORY & YOU How do you handle a difference of opinion? Read about the schism between the Eastern Orthodox Church and the Catholic Church.

The size of the Byzantine Empire was greatly reduced by the early eighth century, but the empire recovered and even expanded through a new dynasty known as the Macedonians, who ruled from 867 to 1081.

Macedonian Emperors

The Macedonian emperors expanded the empire to include Bulgaria in the Balkans, Crete, Cyprus, and Syria. By 1025, the Byzantine Empire was the largest it had been since the 600s. By expanding trade with western Europe, the Macedonians renewed prosperity to Constantinople.

The new dynasty restored much of the empire's power, but incompetent successors undid most of the gains. Power struggles between army leaders and wealthy families led to disorder in the late eleventh century.

Religious Issues

Relations with the Catholic Church grew worse because the Eastern Orthodox Church did not accept the pope as the sole head of Christianity. In 1054, the pope and the Byzantine patriarch formally excommunicated each other—each took away the other's rights of church membership. This began a **schism,** or separation, between the two great branches of Christianity that has not been completely healed to this day.

The Byzantine Empire's greatest external threat came from the Seljuk Turks in Asia Minor—the empire's main source of food and workers. In 1071, a Turkish army defeated Byzantine forces at Manzikert. As a result, Emperor Alexius I turned to Europe for military aid to fight the Turks.

✓Reading Check **Summarizing** What threats did the Byzantine Empire face in the eleventh century?

Hands-On Chapter Project Step 4

Creating a TV Documentary

Step 4: Documentary on the Byzantine Empire Students plan a portion of their documentary set during the Byzantine Empire.

Directions: Groups will select topics from the section and do research as necessary to prepare their script. Their main goal is to show daily life during this period. Students might highlight Justinian and his wife Theodora, a member of their court, a resident of Constantinople, a crusader, or a merchant who profited from the Crusades. Students should also begin to rehearse and revise their other scripts, and create any props, as final preparation for presenting their documentaries to the class.

Summarizing: Allow time for groups to share what they learned about the Big Idea while preparing their materials. OL

(Chapter Project is completed on the Visual Summary page.)

The Crusades

MAIN IDEA The Crusades had a significant effect on medieval society in both the East and the West.

HISTORY & YOU Do you know of any worthy causes founded by children? Read about the Children's Crusades.

From the eleventh to the thirteenth centuries, European Christians carried out a series of military expeditions to regain the Holy Land from the Muslims. These expeditions are known as the **Crusades.**

The push for the Crusades came when the Byzantine emperor Alexius I asked the Europeans for help against the Seljuk Turks, who were Muslims. Pope Urban II, who responded to the request, saw a golden opportunity to provide leadership for a great cause. That cause was rallying Europe's warriors to free Jerusalem and the Holy Land (Palestine) from the **infidels** or unbelievers—the Muslims.

At the Council of Clermont in southern France near the end of 1095, Urban II challenged Christians to take up their weapons and join in a holy war. The pope promised: "All who die . . . shall have immediate remission [forgiveness] of sins." The enthusiastic crowd cried out: "It is the will of God, it is the will of God." R

Warriors of western Europe, particularly France, formed the first crusading armies. These knights were mostly motivated by religious fervor, but some sought adventure and welcomed the chance to fight. Others saw an opportunity to gain wealth and a possible title. Italian merchants also sought new trading opportunities in Byzantine and Muslim lands.

The Early Crusades

The First Crusade began as three organized bands of mostly French warriors made their way to the East. The crusading army, which included thousands of men in cavalry and infantry, captured Antioch in 1098. The crusaders proceeded down the Palestinian coast, avoiding the well-defended coastal cities, and reached Jerusalem in June 1099. The Holy City was taken amid a horrible massacre of its inhabitants.

HISTORY & ARTS

Hagia Sophia

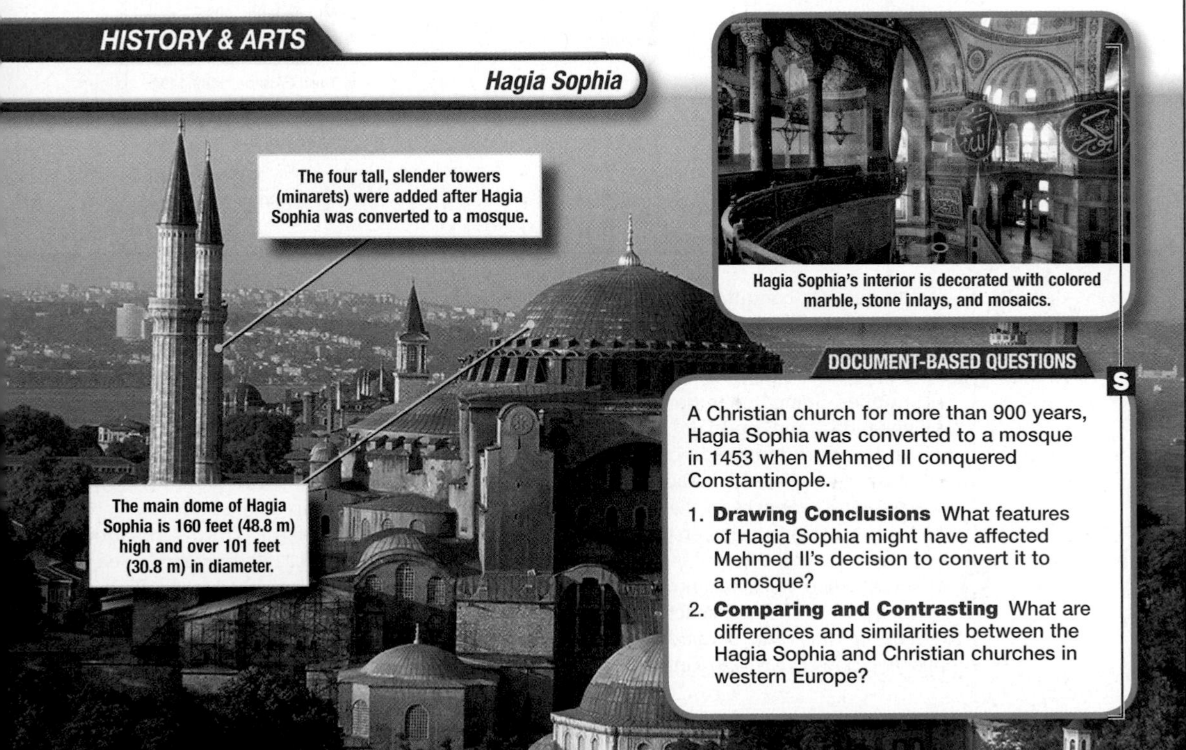

The four tall, slender towers (minarets) were added after Hagia Sophia was converted to a mosque.

The main dome of Hagia Sophia is 160 feet (48.8 m) high and over 101 feet (30.8 m) in diameter.

Hagia Sophia's interior is decorated with colored marble, stone inlays, and mosaics.

DOCUMENT-BASED QUESTIONS S

A Christian church for more than 900 years, Hagia Sophia was converted to a mosque in 1453 when Mehmed II conquered Constantinople.

1. **Drawing Conclusions** What features of Hagia Sophia might have affected Mehmed II's decision to convert it to a mosque?
2. **Comparing and Contrasting** What are differences and similarities between the Hagia Sophia and Christian churches in western Europe?

R Reading Strategy

Determining Importance

Ask: Why was the pope's promise of forgiveness of sins important? *(It meant that all who joined the Crusades would be assured of entry into heaven if they were killed; warriors would be more likely to join.)* **OL**

For additional practice on this skill, see the **Skills Handbook**.

S Skill Practice

Visual Literacy Have students write a description of Hagia Sophia architecture for use in a tourist brochure or as a personal journal entry. Then ask volunteers to read their writing aloud. **OL**

DOCUMENT-BASED QUESTIONS

Answers:

1. Accept all reasonable responses. Possible answer: its size, beauty and unusual design
2. **Differences:** dome, Hagia Sophia lacks steeples as in many western Christian churches. **Similarities:** rich decoration, marble, and so on

Additional Support

Extending the Content

Symbols of the Crusades Pope Urban II encouraged European Christian warriors to take up arms in a mission to take Palestine from the Muslims who had controlled it from 638, shortly after Muhammad's death. He suggested that knights should wear a red cross as their symbol. The Latin word for "mark with a cross" is *cruciare* which is likely the origin of the term "Crusades." Several different types of crosses were used during the Crusades, including one called the Jerusalem cross (which symbolized that Jerusalem was the center of the universe) and another that included four smaller crosses (symbolizing the four Gospels of the Christian New Testament). Their battle cry came from the crowd's reaction to Pope Urban II's speech—"Deus le vult," or "God wills it."

R Reading Strategy

Determining Importance
Ask: Why did the crusader kingdoms need to rely on Italian cities for supplies? *(They were surrounded by conquered Muslims and could not get their own supplies; Italian cities could deliver supplies across the Mediterranean Sea.)* BL

W Writing Support

Personal Writing Have students write a personal response that addresses whether the conduct of a war should match the stated principles for the war. AL

CRITICAL THINKING SKILLS

Answers:
1. France
2. Accept all reasonable responses. Possible answer: The Crusades were a series of religious wars. Warriors from across the Christian world took part in bloody battles to try to defeat Muslim armies.

NATIONAL GEOGRAPHIC

THE CRUSADES

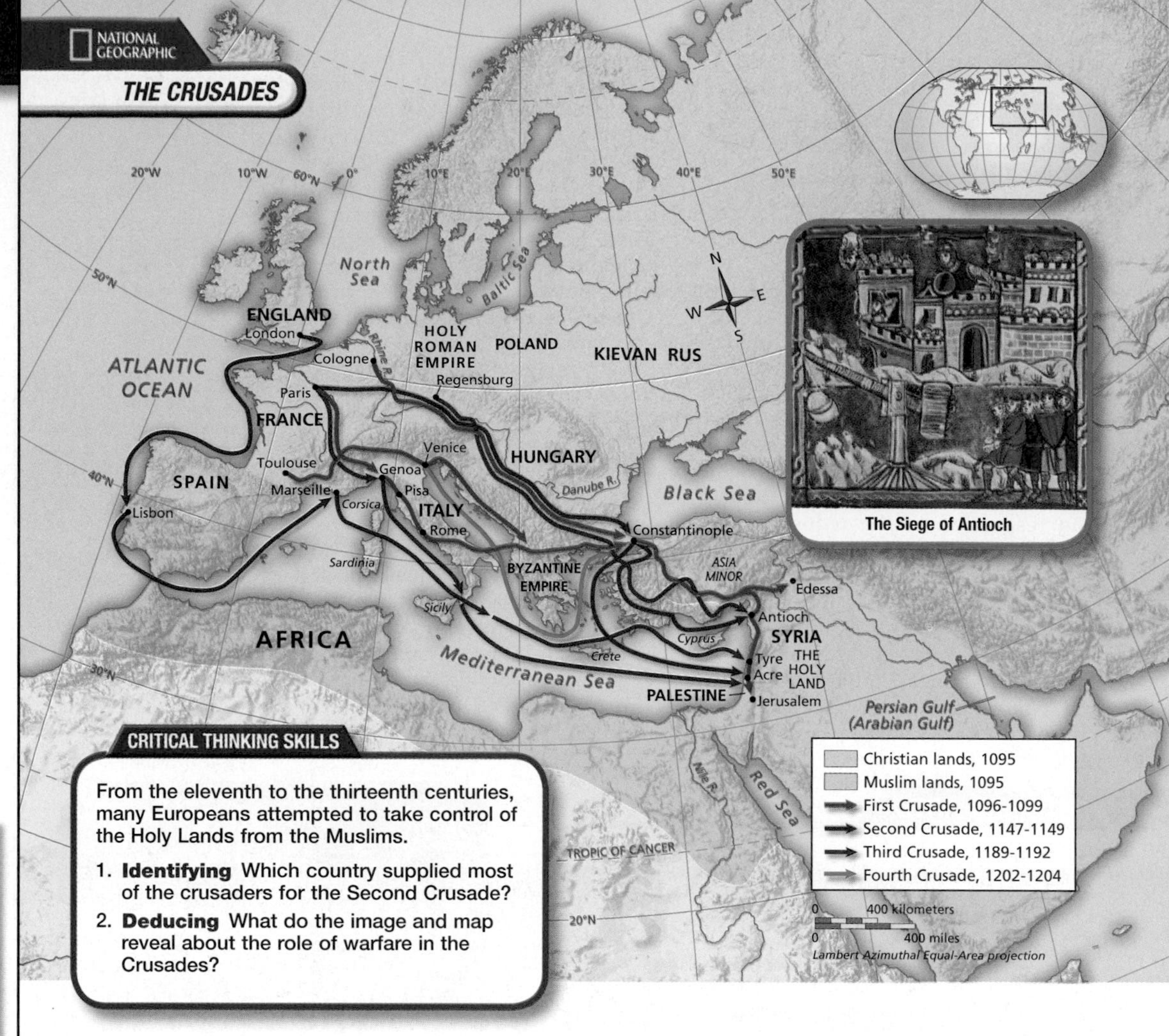

The Siege of Antioch

CRITICAL THINKING SKILLS

From the eleventh to the thirteenth centuries, many Europeans attempted to take control of the Holy Lands from the Muslims.

1. **Identifying** Which country supplied most of the crusaders for the Second Crusade?
2. **Deducing** What do the image and map reveal about the role of warfare in the Crusades?

After further conquests, the crusaders organized four Latin crusader states in the East. Surrounded by Muslims, these crusader kingdoms depended on Italian cities for supplies. Some Italian port cities, such as Genoa, Pisa, and especially Venice, grew rich and powerful in the process.

It was not easy for the crusader kingdoms to maintain themselves in the East. By the 1140s, the Muslims had begun to strike back. The fall of one of the Latin kingdoms to the Muslims led to calls for another crusade, especially from the monastic leader **Saint Bernard of Clairvaux.** Bernard managed to enlist two powerful rulers, King Louis VII of France and Emperor Conrad III of Germany, in a Second Crusade. This campaign, however, was a total failure.

In 1187, the Holy City of Jerusalem fell to Muslim forces under **Saladin.** Three rulers then agreed to lead a Third Crusade: German emperor Frederick Barbarossa, English king Richard I (Richard the Lionhearted), and French king Philip II Augustus.

When members of the Third Crusade arrived in the East in 1189, they struggled to overcome the problems they faced. Frederick drowned in a local river. The English and French arrived by sea and captured the coastal cities but were unable to move

Differentiated Instruction

Cooperative Learning Activity, URB p. 145

Synthesizing Information

Objective: Synthesize information about an important person or event in the Crusades.

Focus: Read the section on the Crusades and research the selected event or person.

Teach: Have groups meet and assign tasks.

Assess: Ask students to explain what the symbols on the shield represent.

Close: Have groups share their projects with the class.

Differentiated Instruction Strategies

- **BL** Have students list interesting facts they learned about the person or event they chose.
- **AL** Ask students to write up their findings and share them with the group. Encourage students to ask questions.
- **ELL** Make copies of the shield and have students write callouts explaining the symbols.

inland against the Muslim forces. After Philip returned home, Richard negotiated a settlement with Saladin that permitted Christian pilgrims free access to Jerusalem.

The Later Crusades

About six years after Saladin's death in 1193, **Pope Innocent III** initiated the Fourth Crusade. As it headed east, the crusading army became involved in a fight over the Byzantine throne. The Venetian leaders of the crusade used the situation to weaken their greatest commercial competitor, the Byzantine Empire. In 1204, the crusaders sacked Constantinople.

Not until 1261 did a Byzantine army recapture the city. The Byzantine Empire was no longer a great power. It now comprised Constantinople and its surrounding lands, as well as part of Asia Minor. This smaller empire limped along for another 190 years, until the Ottoman Turks conquered it in 1453.

Despite failures, the crusading ideal continued. In Germany in 1212, a youth known as Nicholas of Cologne announced that God had inspired him to lead a "children's crusade." Thousands of young people marched with him to Italy, where the pope told them to go home. At about the same time, some 20,000 French children headed to Marseille, where two shipowners agreed to take them to the Holy Land. Two of the ships went down in a storm. The other five sailed to North Africa, where the children were sold into slavery. The next Crusades of adult warriors were hardly more successful. **C**

Did the Crusades have much effect on European civilization? Historians disagree. Clearly, the Crusades benefited the Italian port cities, especially Genoa, Pisa, and Venice. Even without the Crusades, however, Italian merchants would have increased trade with the Eastern world.

The Crusades had some unfortunate side effects on European society. The first widespread attacks on the Jews began in the context of the Crusades. Some Christians argued that to fight the Muslims while the "murderers of Christ," as they called the Jews, ran free at home was unthinkable. The Jews of medieval Europe came to be subjected to periodic libels, attacks, and expulsions.

Perhaps the greatest impact of the Crusades was political. They eventually helped to break down feudalism. As kings levied taxes and raised armies, nobles joining the Crusades sold their lands and freed their serfs. As nobles lost power, the kings created stronger central governments. Taxing trade with the East also provided kings with new wealth. This paved the way for the development of true nation-states. By the mid-1400s, four strong nation-states—Portugal, Spain, England, and France—would emerge in Europe.

✓Reading Check **Summarizing** What factors motivated Europeans to participate in a Crusade?

SECTION 4 REVIEW

Vocabulary
1. **Explain** the significance of: Constantinople, Justinian, Palestine, Syria, legal, Balkans, patriarch, enormous, schism, Crusades, infidel, Saint Bernard of Clairvaux, Saladin, Pope Innocent III.

Main Ideas
2. **Describe** the effects the Macedonian emperors had on the Byzantine Empire.
3. **Explain** how church and state were linked in the Byzantine Empire.
4. **List** Justinian's accomplishments.

Critical Thinking
5. **The BIG Idea** **Explaining** Why did cities such as Venice flourish as a result of the Crusades?
6. **Organizing Information** Use a table like the one below to summarize the results of the First, Second, and Third Crusades.

	1st Crusade	2nd Crusade	3rd Crusade
People Involved			
Results			

7. **Analyzing Visuals** Examine the image on page 323. What elements might indicate Justinian's status?

Writing About History
8. **Descriptive Writing** Write a travel brochure encouraging people to visit Constantinople. Identify the features of the city in the Early Middle Ages. What sites would you use to illustrate your brochure?

History ONLINE
For help with the concepts in this section of *Glencoe World History,* go to glencoe.com and click Study Central™.

C Critical Thinking

Making Generalizations
Have students write a generalization about the "children's crusade." *(Although children wanted to take part, this crusade was a disaster for them.)* OL

✓Reading Check

Answer: Most were motivated by religious fervor, but others by adventure, the chance to fight, hopes of wealth, and trade opportunities.

Assess

History ONLINE
Study Central provides summaries, interactive games, and online graphic organizers to help students review content.

Close

Summarizing Ask: What happened to the Byzantine Empire during this period? *(It went from a large, strong empire under Justinian to a small, weak kingdom).* OL

Answers

1. Definitions for the vocabulary words are found in the section and the Glossary.
2. Macedonians expanded the Byzantine Empire and improved trade with western Europe. Eventually, a series of poor leaders undid these gains.
3. The emperor, who was believed to have been chosen by God, appointed the church's patriarch.
4. He restored the Roman Empire in the Mediterranean and codified Roman law.
5. They benefited from the increased trade with the East.
6. **First:** French warriors; captured Jerusalem. **Second:** Louis VII, Conrad III; total failure. **Third:** Frederick Barbarossa, Richard I, Philip II Augustus; gave pilgrims access to Jerusalem.
7. His crown shows he is a ruler, the ornament on his shoulder suggests he has wealth, and the halo suggests high spiritual or religious status.
8. Students' brochures will vary, but should identify the key features of Constantinople, such as Hagia Sophia and the Hippodrome.

Determining Cause and Effect Discuss the information provided in the Visual Summary. **Ask:** What caused people to build fortified castles in medieval Europe? Then have students identify at least one cause and its effect(s) from each section of the chapter. Ask volunteers to share one of their cause/effect(s) and list them on the board or chart paper. As a group, discuss which cause/effect(s) students think will prove to be most significant to later historical developments. **OL**

English Language Learners Have students work in pairs to write a description of each image on the Visual Summary page. For each description, have them include a statement about what the image tells us about this time period. *(The Church played a central role in Europe's medieval societies; physical security was a driving force behind feudalism; Justinian codified laws of the Byzantine Empire.)* **ELL**

CHAPTER 9 Visual Summary

You can study anywhere, anytime by downloading quizzes and flash cards to your PDA from glencoe.com.

THE LINDISFARNE GOSPELS, ENGLAND

This artwork created by monks testifies to the importance of religion in the Middle Ages.

MEDIEVAL EUROPE and the Church

- Germanic rulers, especially the Franks, ruled the old Western Roman Empire.
- Charlemagne expanded Frankish rule and promoted learning, centered in monasteries.

CONWY CASTLE, WALES

Feudal castles kept out invaders and were a center for government.

The FEUDAL ECONOMY

- Viking attacks in Europe led to decentralized governments and a new feudal system, which was based on military service in return for land grants.
- England and France were the first to build strong centralized states in Western Europe, while Russia developed around Kiev.

THE EMPEROR JUSTINIAN

Justinian, an early emperor of what was later known as the Byzantine Empire, is seen here as a lawgiver.

Rise and Fall of BYZANTIUM

- For centuries after Rome's fall, a wealthy Byzantine Empire dominated trade in the eastern Mediterranean.
- As the Turks of the Ottoman Empire grew powerful, Byzantine rulers in Constantinople were threatened.
- Religious zeal and a spirit of conquest inspired European Crusaders, but Constantinople finally fell in 1453.

Hands-On Chapter Project
Step 5: Wrap-Up

Creating a TV Documentary

Step 5: Presenting the Documentary Each group does a final rehearsal of its documentary and then presents to the class.

Directions: Set aside time for students to practice presenting their documentaries. Encourage students not to read from their scripts, but to memorize them as much as possible, or to use cue cards. Encourage the "audience" to take notes and offer constructive feedback once everyone has presented. **Ask:** What would you have liked about living during this period? What would you have disliked?

Afterward, have students write a response to the Essential Question: What was daily life like during this time period? Have them incorporate what they learned about the importance of a city's location in their responses. **OL**

STANDARDIZED TEST PRACTICE

TEST-TAKING 

If you do not know the right answer to a question, use common sense to eliminate answer choices that do not make sense. Recall the context in which the topic was discussed in class or in the textbook. This may help you eliminate incorrect answer choices.

Reviewing Vocabulary

Directions: Choose the word or words that best complete the sentence.

1. Bishops of Rome became known as ________ of the Roman Catholic Church.

A patriarchs
B popes
C wergilds
D bishoprics

2. A ________ was the grant of land from the lord to a vassal in return for military service.

A feudal contract
B schism
C wergild
D fief

3. Under the influence of the Church, noblemen followed a code of behavior called ________.

A chivalry
B common law
C the Magna Carta
D feudalism

4. A ________ developed between the Catholic Church and the Eastern Orthodox Church in 1054.

A feudal contract
B schism
C bishopric
D fief

Reviewing Main Ideas

Directions: Choose the best answers to the following questions.

Section 1 *(pp. 302–307)*

5. What important function did monks perform?

A They spread learning.
B They helped kings consolidate power.
C They spread wealth.
D They helped spread trade.

6. Why did Charlemagne promote learning?

A To spread German culture
B To provide free education to all children
C To educate the clergy and government
D Charlemagne didn't promote learning.

Section 2 *(pp. 308–313)*

7. Why were Vikings able to expand throughout Europe?

A They controlled Mediterranean trade routes.
B They were allies with the Magyars.
C They were excellent shipbuilders and sailors.
D They defeated the Normans.

8. What was the most important gift a lord could give a vassal?

A Gold
B Arms and armor
C Serfs
D Land

Need Extra Help?

If You Missed Questions . . .	1	2	3	4	5	6	7	8
Go to Page . . .	304	310	313	324	305	307	308	310

GO ON

Answers and Analyses

Reviewing Vocabulary

1. B While answer choices A and D are related to Christianity, a patriarch is the head of the Eastern Orthodox Church while a bishopric is a diocese (group of churches), not a person. Wergilds is the system of fines related Germanic law.

2. D Students should remember from the chapter content that the feudal contract relates to the feudal system overall, but isn't specifically a grant of land. Schism and wergild are not relevant.

TEST-TAKING 

For Question 2: The key term in the question for students to focus on is *grant of land.* The only answer choice that is directly associated with land is fief.

3. A All of the choices relate to governing behavior, but common law and Magna Carta are related to legal codes while feudalism is a broad term that means much more than a code of behavior for noblemen.

4. B Remind students to eliminate answer choices that they know are incorrect. B is the only choice that makes sense.

Reviewing Main Ideas

5. A Knowledge of the chief duties of monks helps indicate the correct answer. In most cases, monks were not dedicated to economic concerns, such as wealth and trade, and were not directly tied to kings' political power.

6. C Knowledge of the chapter content is essential here. Charlemagne did help spread German culture and supported learning, but he was not focused on free education for children, nor on just spreading German culture.

7. C The Vikings' abilities on the sea were the key to their success. The other answer choices can be eliminated, since they did not control the Mediterranean because of its location, were not allied with the Magyars, and did not defeat the Normans.

8. D All answers are plausible without content knowledge, since all were valuable at the time. However, during this time period land was the main source of wealth, and it allowed a vassal to be largely self-sufficient.

9. C The Anglican Church had not yet been formed (and is not a political institution per se), royal courts had already been established under Henry II, and the House of Lords developed only after Parliament had been established.

10. B Because the Magna Carta limited a monarch's power, students should be able to quickly eliminate D. Although A and C may seem plausible, Henry II failed to gain control over the church and the feudal system was not relevant to his rule.

11. A Justinian is best remembered for his code of laws. He attempted to reunify the empire, but many of the areas he had conquered were soon lost after he died. Yarmūk was the site of a Byzantine defeat after Justinian's rule. Although he would have appointed a patriarch, this would not have been his most important contribution.

12. C Feudalism broke down because kings and knights went to fight in the Crusades. Wars did not necessarily decrease, nobles did not gain power, but lost it, and most merchants would have likely gained power because of the resulting increase in trade.

13. B Knowledge of the content is essential since all the answer choices may appear at first to be plausible.

CHAPTER 9

Section 3 *(pp. 316–321)*

9. What important English political institution emerged during the reign of Edward I?

A House of Lords
B Anglican Church
C Parliament
D Royal courts

10. How did Henry II increase the power of the English monarchy?

A By placing the church under royal control
B By increasing the power and jurisdiction of the royal courts
C By strengthening the feudal system
D By signing the Magna Carta

Section 4 *(pp. 322–327)*

11. What was Justinian's most important contribution to the Eastern Roman Empire?

A The codification of Roman law
B The reunification of the Roman Empire
C The defeat of Islamic forces at Yarmūk
D The appointment of the patriarch

12. What was one of the side effects of the Crusades?

A There were fewer wars in Europe.
B Nobles gained power.
C Feudalism broke down.
D Italian merchants lost much of their power.

13. Which Muslim leader won back Jerusalem in 1187?

A Mehmed II
B Saladin
C Urban II
D Richard I

Critical Thinking

Directions: Choose the best answers to the following questions.

Base your answers to questions 14 and 15 on the map and your knowledge of world history.

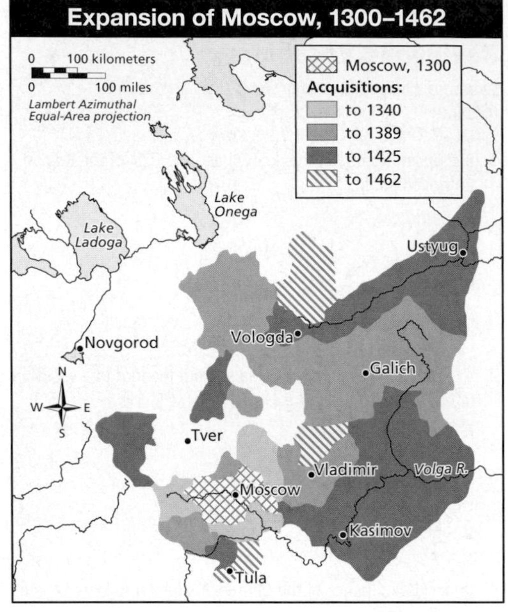

14. About how far did Moscow's territory stretch from north to south in 1462?

A 150 miles (241.4 km)
B 420 miles (676 km)
C 540 miles (869 km)
D 730 miles (1174.8 km)

15. By what year did Russia add Kasimov to its holdings?

A By 1300
B By 1340
C By 1389
D By 1425

Need Extra Help?

If You Missed Questions . . .	9	10	11	12	13	14	15
Go to Page . . .	318	316	322	327	326	330	330

GO ON

Critical Thinking

14. C Map skills will indicate the correct answer. Students should use the map key to identify the proper shading for 1462 and then measure the approximate north/south distance.

15. D A careful analysis of the map and legend is necessary for students to select the correct answer. Kasimov lies within territory acquired by 1425.

Assessment

16. Why was Constantinople an important center of European trade?
    - **A** It was located along major Russian and Asian trade routes.
    - **B** It was located near the center of Europe.
    - **C** It was an important stopping point for ships on the way to Jerusalem.
    - **D** It was located along an important African trade route.

Analyze the chart and answer the question that follows. Base your answers on the chart and on your knowledge of world history.

	1st Crusade	2nd Crusade	3rd Crusade
People involved	Three bands of French warriors	Louis VII, Conrad III	Frederick Barbarossa, Richard I, Philip II Augustus
Results	Jerusalem captured; Latin crusader states organized	Total failure	Christian pilgrims given access to Jerusalem; city still held by Muslims

17. Which Crusade most accomplished its goals?
    - **A** 1st Crusade
    - **B** 2nd Crusade
    - **C** 3rd Crusade
    - **D** None of the Crusades were successful.

18. What caused the schism in Christianity in the eleventh century?
    - **A** The pope and the patriarch disagreed about religious doctrines.
    - **B** The Byzantine emperor refused to recognize the Catholic Church.
    - **C** The Catholic Church refused to accept the patriarch as sole head of the Christian church.
    - **D** The Eastern Orthodox refused to accept the pope as sole head of the Christian church.

Document-Based Questions

Directions: Analyze the document and answer the short answer questions that follow the document. Base your answers on the document and on your knowledge of world history.

To become a vassal a man performed an act of homage to his lord. This passage describes the oath the vassal makes to the lord:

> *"The man should put his hands together as a sign of humility, and place them between the two hands of his lord as a token that he vows everything to him and promises faith to him; and the lord should receive him and promise to keep faith with him. Then the man should say: 'Sir, I enter your homage and faith and become your man by mouth and hands [that is, by taking the oath and placing his hands between those of the lord], and I swear and promise to keep faith and loyalty to you against all others.'"*

19. Why is it significant that the vow was given to a particular person rather than a nation, written constitution, or religion?
20. What is meant by the phrase "and the lord should receive him and promise to keep faith with him"?
21. What obligations does this vow impose on the vassal?

Extended Response

22. Using information you find in this text, your local library, or the Internet, describe the political, economic, and social impact of the Crusades. Which of these areas do you think the Crusades impacted the most? Support your answers with factual information.

History ONLINE
For additional test practice, use Self-Check Quizzes—Chapter 9 at glencoe.com.

Need Extra Help?

If You Missed Questions . . .	16	17	18	19	20	21	22
Go to Page . . .	324	325	324	331	331	331	327

STOP

Document-Based Questions

19. It is a vow of personal loyalty that transcends other loyalties. This is one reason why many lords in France were more powerful than the king during the period.

20. The lord-vassal relationship was an honorable relationship between free men and implied no sense of servitude. The lord had responsibilities to the vassal—to protect him, either militarily or by taking his side in a court of law.

21. The vassal swore fealty to this lord only, and would fight for him against all others.

Extended Response

22. Answers will vary. Make sure that students identify the political, economic, and social impact of the Crusades and provide supporting details in their answers.

TEST-TAKING TIP

For extended response questions, remind students of the importance of organizing their answers to ensure a well-thought-out response and of budgeting their time to allow them a chance to revise and proofread their essays.

16. A Geographic knowledge should help students eliminate B, C, and D. Because of its location on major trade routes to Russia and Asia, Constantinople became an important trade center.

17. A An analysis of the information on the chart should enable students to easily eliminate D and B (since the 2nd Crusade was a total failure). While the 3rd Crusade was partially successful, the 1st was mostly successful, especially in its capture of Jerusalem, the Holy City.

18. D Knowledge of the text should help students eliminate A and B. They may recall that the dispute between the Catholic Church and the Eastern Orthodox church centered on who was head of the entire Christian church.

History ONLINE
Introduce students to chapter content and key terms by having them access the Chapter 9 Overview at glencoe.com.

Need Extra Help?
Have students refer to the pages listed if they miss any of the questions.

CHAPTER 10 Planning Guide

Key to Ability Levels	
BL Below Level	AL Above Level
OL On Level	ELL English Language Learners

Key to Teaching Resources	
Print Material	DVD
CD-ROM	Transparency

Levels				Resources	Chapter Opener	Section 1	Section 2	Section 3	Section 4	Chapter Assess
BL	OL	AL	ELL							
				FOCUS						
BL	OL	AL	ELL	**Daily Focus Skills Transparencies**		10-1	10-2	10-3	10-4	
				TEACH						
	OL	AL		**Economics and History Activity, URB**		✓				
BL	OL		ELL	**Reading Skills Activity, URB**		p. 167				
	OL	AL		**Historical Analysis Skills Activity, URB**		p. 168				
BL	OL	AL	ELL	**Differentiated Instruction Activity, URB**		p. 169				
	OL		ELL	**English Learner Activity, URB**		p. 171				
BL	OL	AL	ELL	**Content Vocabulary Activity, URB***		p. 173				
BL	OL	AL	ELL	**Academic Vocabulary Activity, URB**					p. 175	
BL	OL	AL	ELL	**Skills Reinforcement Activity, URB**					p. 177	
	OL	AL		**Critical Thinking Skills Activity, URB**			p. 178			
	OL	AL		**History and Geography Activity, URB**				p. 179		
	OL	AL	ELL	**Mapping History Activity, URB**					p. 181	
BL	OL	AL		**Historical Significance Activity, URB**		p. 182				
BL	OL	AL	ELL	**Cooperative Learning Activity, URB**		p. 183				
	OL	AL	ELL	**History Simulation Activity, URB**		p. 185				
BL	OL	AL	ELL	**Time Line Activity, URB**					p. 187	
	OL	AL		**Linking Past and Present Activity, URB**					p. 188	
BL	OL	AL		**People in World History Activity, URB**			p. 189		p. 190	
BL	OL	AL	ELL	**Primary Source Reading, URB**					p. 191	
	OL	AL		**Enrichment Activity, URB**		p. 196				
BL	OL	AL	ELL	**World Art and Music Activity, URB**				p. 193		
BL	OL		ELL	**Guided Reading Activities, URB***		p. 198	p. 199	p. 200	p. 201	
BL	OL		ELL	**Reading Essentials and Note-Taking Guide***		p. 109	p. 112	p. 115	p. 118	
BL	OL	AL	ELL	**Differentiated Instruction for the World History Classroom**	✓	✓	✓	✓	✓	✓

Note: Please refer to the *Unit Resource Book: New Patterns of Civilization* for this chapter's URB materials.

* Also available in Spanish

- Interactive Lesson Planner
- Interactive Teacher Edition
- Fully editable blackline masters
- Section Spotlight Videos Launch
- Differentiated Lesson Plans
- Printable reports of daily assignments
- Standards Tracking System

Levels BL	OL	AL	ELL		Resources	Chapter Opener	Section 1	Section 2	Section 3	Section 4	Chapter Assess
					TEACH *(continued)*						
BL	OL	AL	ELL		StudentWorks™ Plus DVD	✓	✓	✓	✓	✓	✓
BL	OL	AL	ELL		Vocabulary PuzzleMaker CD-ROM	✓	✓	✓	✓	✓	✓
Teacher Resources					Building Academic Vocabulary	✓	✓	✓	✓	✓	✓
					Reading Strategies and Activities for the Social Studies Classroom			pp. 26, 30, 50	p. 77		
					Writer's Guidebook			p. 23	p. 43	pp. 23, 27	
					Strategies for Success	✓	✓	✓	✓	✓	✓
					Outline Map Resource Book	✓	✓	✓	✓	✓	✓
					Presentation Plus! with MindJogger DVD	✓	✓	✓	✓	✓	✓
					ASSESS						
BL	OL	AL	ELL		Section Quizzes and Chapter Tests*		p. 117	p. 118	p. 119	p. 120	p. 121
BL	OL	AL	ELL		Authentic Assessment With Rubrics	✓	✓	✓	✓	✓	✓
BL	OL	AL	ELL		Standardized Test Practice Workbook	✓	✓	✓	✓	✓	✓
BL	OL	AL	ELL		*ExamView® Assessment Suite* CD-ROM		10-1	10-2	10-3	10-4	Ch. 10
BL	OL	AL	ELL		Interactive Tutor Self-Assessment CD-ROM		10-1	10-2	10-3	10-4	
					CLOSE						
BL			ELL		Reteaching Activity, URB					p. 195	
BL	OL		ELL		Reading and Study Skills Foldables™	✓	✓	✓	✓	✓	✓

Using the McGraw-Hill Learning Network

Web Site Builder

Technology Product

The Web Site Builder is a convenient and dynamic McGraw-Hill Learning Network tool that helps you build Web sites quickly. The site allows you to include your own images, videos, and text to customize it to your needs. The Web site builder also provides you with a variety of tools to make your Web site inviting. Use the Web Site Builder to

- provide assignments and important dates to your students;
- keep students and parents informed of events in your classroom;
- publish your contact information.

Steps

- On the McGraw-Hill Learning Network home page (www.mhln.com), log in as a member.
- Choose **Web Site Builder** under **Resources.**
- Choose a template from the **Create a new site** pull-down options and follow the prompts on the screen to select a design, insert text, and select fonts, colors, and sizes.
- Create the content students will need to study for a chapter text or post homework assignments.
- Use the navigation buttons on the bottom of the screen to edit, add, and delete information, images, and videos.
- Publish the site and provide the URL to your students.

History ONLINE

	Student	Teacher	Parent
Beyond the Textbook	●	●	●
Chapter Overviews	●	●	●
Time Current Events	●		●
ePuzzles and Games	●		●
Concepts in Motion	●		●
Literature Connections		●	
Multi-Language Glossaries	●		●
Online Student Edition	●	●	●
Self-Check Quizzes	●		●
Student Web Activities	●		●
Study Central ™	●		●
Teaching Today		●	
Vocabulary eFlashcards	●		●
Web Activity Lesson Plans		●	

- **Timed Readings Plus in Social Studies** helps students increase their reading rate and fluency while maintaining comprehension. The 400-word passages are similar to those found on state and national assessments.
- **Reading in the Content Area: Social Studies** concentrates on six essential reading skills that help students better comprehend what they read. The book includes 75 high-interest nonfiction passages written at increasing levels of difficulty.
- **Reading Social Studies** includes strategic reading instruction and vocabulary support in Social Studies content for both ELLs and native speakers of English.

www.jamestowneducation.com

The following videotape programs are available from Glencoe as supplements to Chapter 10:

- The Black Death (ISBN 0-76-700391-8)
- Gothic Cathedrals (ISBN 1-56-501639-4)
- Scourge of the Black Death (ISBN 0-76-700534-1)

To order, call Glencoe at 1-800-334-7344. To find classroom resources to accompany many of these videos, check the following home pages:

A&E Television: www.aetv.com

The History Channel: www.historychannel.com

NATIONAL GEOGRAPHIC

Index to National Geographic Magazine:

The following articles relate to this chapter:

- "Europe's Big Gamble," by Don Belt, May 2004
- "Bohemian Rhapsody," by Cathy Newman, August 2003
- "The New Europe" by T. R. Reed, January 2002

National Geographic Society Products To order the following, call National Geographic at 1-800-368-2728:

- *National Geographic Atlas of the World* (Book).
- *The Middle Ages* (PicturePack).

Access National Geographic's new, dynamic MapMachine Web site and other geography resources at:

www.nationalgeographic.com

www.nationalgeographic.com/maps

GLENCOE BOOKLINK 3

Use this database to search more than 30,000 titles to create a customized reading list for your students.

- Reading lists can be organized by students' reading level, author, genre, theme, or area of interest.
- The database provides Degrees of Reading Power™ (DRP) and Lexile™ readability scores for all selections.
- A brief summary of each selection is included.

Leveled reading suggestions for this chapter:

For students at a Grade 8 reading level:
- ***The Measly Middle Ages,*** by Terry Deary

For students at a Grade 9 reading level:
- ***Paris,*** by Conrad R. Stein

For students at a Grade 10 reading level:
- ***Life on a Medieval Manor,*** by Marc Cels

For students at a Grade 11 reading level:
- ***Beyond the Myth: The Story of Joan of Arc,*** by Polly S. Brooks

For students at a Grade 12 reading level:
- ***Places of Worship in the Middle Ages,*** by Kay Eastwood

Introducing CHAPTER 10

Focus

MAKING CONNECTIONS
What caused the formation of universities?

Activate prior knowledge by having students categorize the types of institutions that provide post-secondary education. **Ask:** What is a university? *(Possible response: It is an institution of higher learning that usually contains several colleges and offers advanced degrees in many subjects.)* Explain that the concept of the modern university traces its origins to the High Middle Ages. **OL**

Teach

The Big Ideas

As students study the chapter, remind them to consider the section-based Big Ideas included in each section's Guide to Reading. The **Essential Questions** in the activities below tie in to the Big Ideas and help students think about and understand important chapter concepts. In addition, the Hands-on Chapter Projects with their culminating activities relate the content from each section to the Big Ideas. These activities build on each other as students progress through the chapter. Section activities culminate in the wrap-up activity on the Visual Summary page.

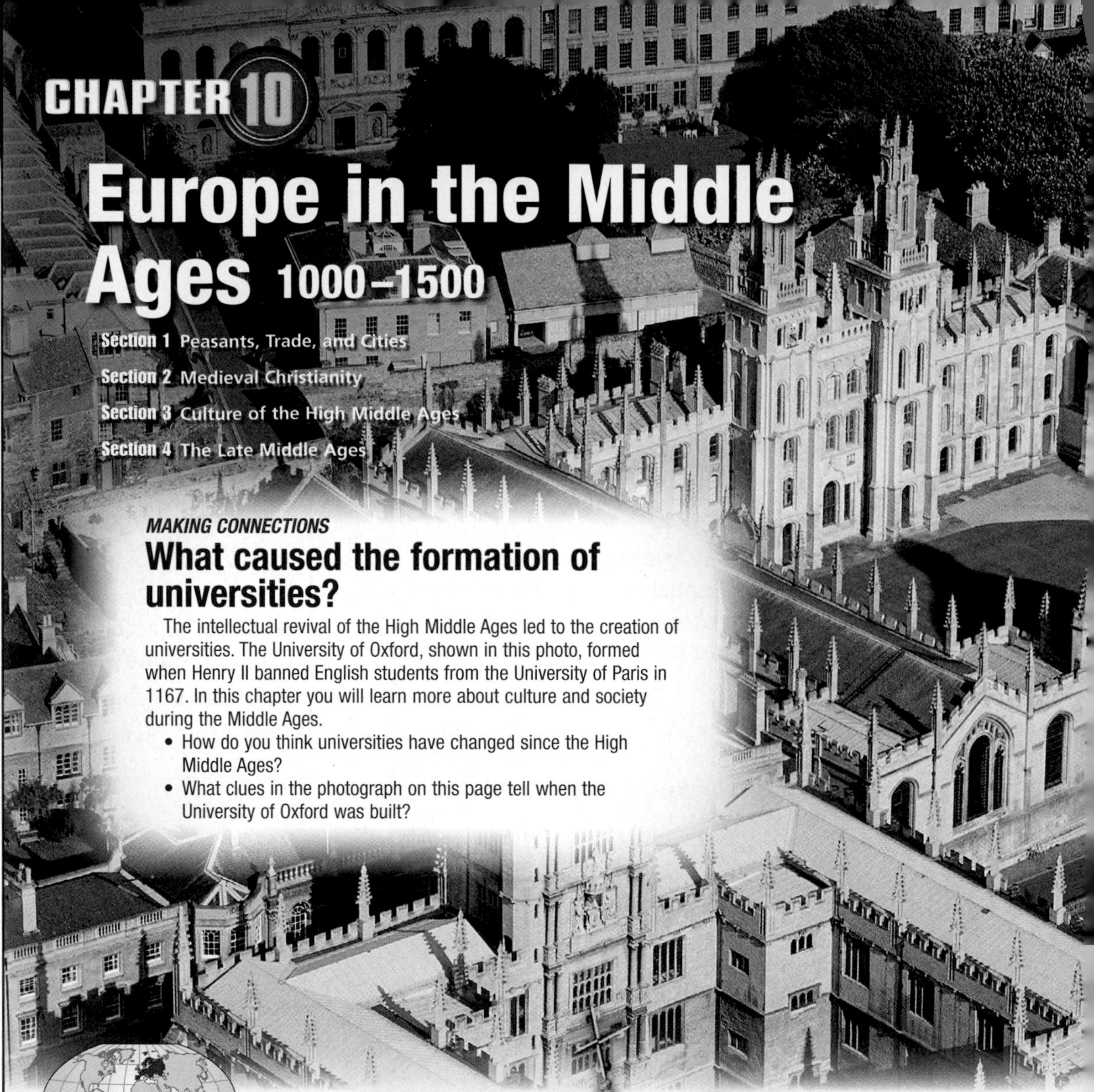

CHAPTER 10

Europe in the Middle Ages 1000–1500

MAKING CONNECTIONS

What caused the formation of universities?

The intellectual revival of the High Middle Ages led to the creation of universities. The University of Oxford, shown in this photo, formed when Henry II banned English students from the University of Paris in 1167. In this chapter you will learn more about culture and society during the Middle Ages.

- How do you think universities have changed since the High Middle Ages?
- What clues in the photograph on this page tell when the University of Oxford was built?

EUROPE ▶

1073 Gregory VII elected pope

1216 Dominic de Guzmán founds Dominican order

1000 — 1100 — 1200

THE WORLD ▶

1100 Problems arise between Christian Axum and its Muslim neighbors in Africa

1279 Kublai Khan establishes the Yuan dynasty in China

332

Peasants, Trade, and Cities

Essential Question: How do advances in agriculture affect both farmers and city dwellers? *(Improvements in agriculture lead to food surpluses, which in turn allow for specialization of labor and the growth of cities.)* Point out that in Section 1, students will learn how new farming practices supported population growth, and the revival of trade led to economic changes and the rise of cities in medieval Europe. **OL**

Medieval Christianity

Essential Question: What happens when there is no separation of church and state? *(Religious and government leaders share responsibilities and may come into conflict. Laws about religious beliefs may be imposed on people or affect all areas of life.)* Point out that in Section 2, students will learn how the Catholic Church's strong leadership helped it to become a dominant presence in European society in the Middle Ages. **OL**

Introducing CHAPTER 10

More About the Photo

Visual Literacy The University of Oxford is famous for its spectacular Gothic architecture, which can be seen in its many structures located throughout the city of Oxford itself. It is believed that Oxford was a center of teaching as early as 1096, and around 1167 it started to grow quickly into a major learning institution. Today, the University of Oxford consists of 39 colleges and 7 permanent private halls, with about 17,000 students in residence.

Dinah Zike's Foldables

Dinah Zike's Foldables are three-dimensional, interactive graphic organizers that help students practice basic writing skills, review vocabulary terms, and identify main ideas. Instructions for creating and using Foldables can be found in the Appendix at the end of this book and in the *Dinah Zike's Reading and Study Skills Foldables* booklet.

History ONLINE

Introduce students to chapter content and key terms by having them access the Chapter 10 Overview at glencoe.com.

1347 Plague spreads to Italy and France

1430 English capture Joan of Arc during Hundred Years' War

1492 Christopher Columbus reaches the Americas

1500 Eighty universities exist throughout Europe

1300 — 1400 — 1500

FOLDABLES Study Organizer

Identifying Cause and Effect Use a Two-Tab Book to describe causes and effects related to the influence of the Catholic Church in Medieval Europe. Select events from each century (the 1000s, 1100s, and 1200s) and identify two or more cause-and-effect relationships for each.

Chapter Overview—Visit glencoe.com to preview Chapter 10.

SECTION 3

Culture of the High Middle Ages

Essential Question: How does architecture reflect a society's values? *(Students may mention buildings that occupy the most important position in a community, such as government buildings. They may also mention styles that suggest values such as order.)* Point out that in Section 3, students will learn about new forms of church architecture as well as other aspects of medieval culture, including universities and literature. **OL**

SECTION 4

The Late Middle Ages

Essential Question: How do changes in the size of population affect a society? *(Students may suggest that decreases in population may weaken a society by leading to fewer people to do necessary jobs. A larger population might strengthen a society, but also strain its resources.)* Point out that in Section 4, students will learn how disastrous forces, including epidemic disease and war caused widespread changes in medieval Europe. **OL**

Focus

Bellringer

Daily Focus Transparency 10.1

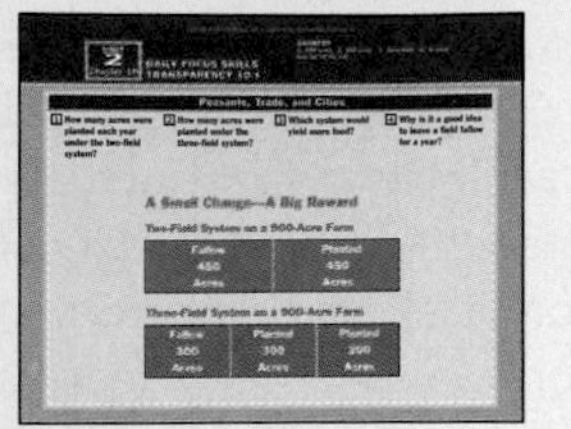

GUIDE TO READING

Answers to Graphic:

Effects: merchants and artisans settled in cities, townspeople given basic liberties, city governments developed, guilds established

Section Spotlight Video

To generate student interest and provide a springboard for class discussion, access the Chapter 10, Section 1 video at glencoe.com or on the video DVD.

Resource Manager

SECTION 1

Peasants, Trade, and Cities

GUIDE TO READING

The BIG Idea

Order and Security New farming practices supported population growth, and the revival of trade led to a money-based economy and the rise of cities.

Content Vocabulary

- *carruca (p. 334)*
- manor *(p. 336)*
- serfs *(p. 336)*
- money economy *(p. 338)*
- commercial capitalism *(p. 338)*
- bourgeoisie *(p. 339)*
- patricians *(p. 340)*
- guilds *(p. 341)*
- apprentice *(p. 341)*
- journeymen *(p. 341)*
- masterpiece *(p. 341)*

Academic Vocabulary

- technology *(p. 334)*
- crucial *(p. 334)*

Places

- Venice *(p. 338)*
- Flanders *(p. 338)*

Reading Strategy

Determining Cause and Effect As you read, use a chart like the one below to show the effects of the growth of towns on medieval European society.

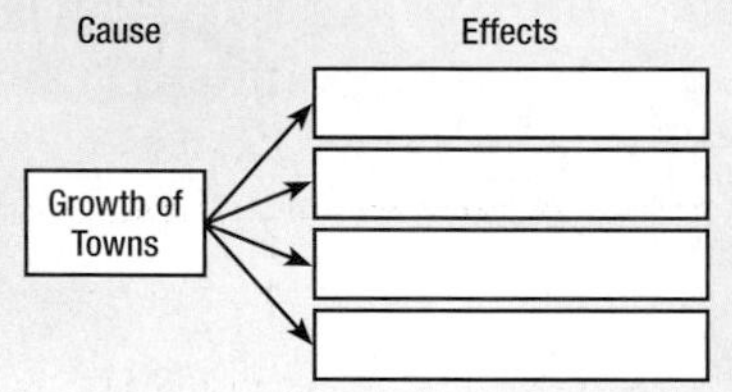

During the High Middle Ages, new farming methods enabled Europe's population to grow. The revival of trade led to a money economy and the growth of cities. Many serfs worked the land under the manorial system, while merchants and artisans revived old cities and founded new ones.

The New Agriculture

MAIN IDEA New inventions for farming and more efficient use of land contributed to population growth in the High Middle Ages.

HISTORY & YOU A farmer can plant a very large area today using modern equipment. Read to learn how new devices helped medieval farmers grow more food.

In the Early Middle Ages, Europe had a relatively small population. In the High Middle Ages, however, population increased dramatically—doubling between 1000 and 1300 from 38 million to 74 million people.

What caused this huge increase? For one thing, conditions in Europe were more settled and peaceful after the invasions of the Early Middle Ages had stopped. This increased peace and stability also led to an expansion in food production after 1000.

In part, food production increased because the climate changed during the High Middle Ages and improved growing conditions. In addition, peasants cultivated more land when they cut down trees and drained swamps during the 1000s and 1100s. By 1200, Europeans had more land for farming than they do today.

Changes in **technology** also aided the development of farming. The Middle Ages witnessed an explosion of labor-saving devices. For example, the people of the Middle Ages harnessed the power of water and wind to do jobs once done by human or animal power. Many of these new devices were made from iron, which was mined in various areas of Europe. Iron was used to make scythes, axes, and hoes for use on farms. It was also used in hammers and nails for building.

Iron was **crucial** in making the ***carruca,*** a heavy, wheeled plow with an iron plowshare. Unlike earlier plows, this plow easily turned over heavy clay soils. Because of the weight of the *carruca*, six or eight oxen were needed to pull it. However, oxen were slow. The inventions of a new horse collar and the horseshoe made it possible for a series of horses to pull the *carruca* faster and plow more land in the rocky, heavy clay soil of northern Europe.

Use of the *carruca* also led to the growth of farming villages, because people had to work together. Because iron was expensive, an entire community had to buy a *carruca*. Likewise, one family

R Reading Strategies	C Critical Thinking	D Differentiated Instruction	W Writing Support	S Skill Practice
Teacher Edition • Organizing Info., p. 336 • Reading a Chart, p. 337 **Additional Resources** • Cont. Vocab. Act., URB p. 173 • Guid. Read. Act., URB p. 198 • Read. Ess. & Note-Taking Guide, p. 109	**Teacher Edition** • Compare/Contrast, p. 336 • Making Inferences, p. 337 • Drawing Con., p. 338 **Additional Resources** • Hist. Sig. Act., URB p. 182 • Hist. Sim. Act., URB p. 185 • Section Quiz, p. 117	**Teacher Edition** • Visual/Spatial, pp. 338, 340 • Logical/Math., p. 339 **Additional Resources** • Econ. & Hist. Act., URB p. 5 • Diff. Instr. Act., URB p. 169 • English Learner Act., URB p. 171 • Enrich. Act., URB p. 196	**Teacher Edition** • Persuasive Writing, p. 340 • Descriptive Writing, p. 341 **Additional Resources** • Hist. Analysis Skills Act., URB p. 168 • Coop. Learn. Act., URB p. 183	**Teacher Edition** • Visual Literacy, p. 335 • Using Geo. Skills, p. 339 **Additional Resources** • Read. Skills Act., URB p. 167

INFOGRAPHICS

Organization of a Manor

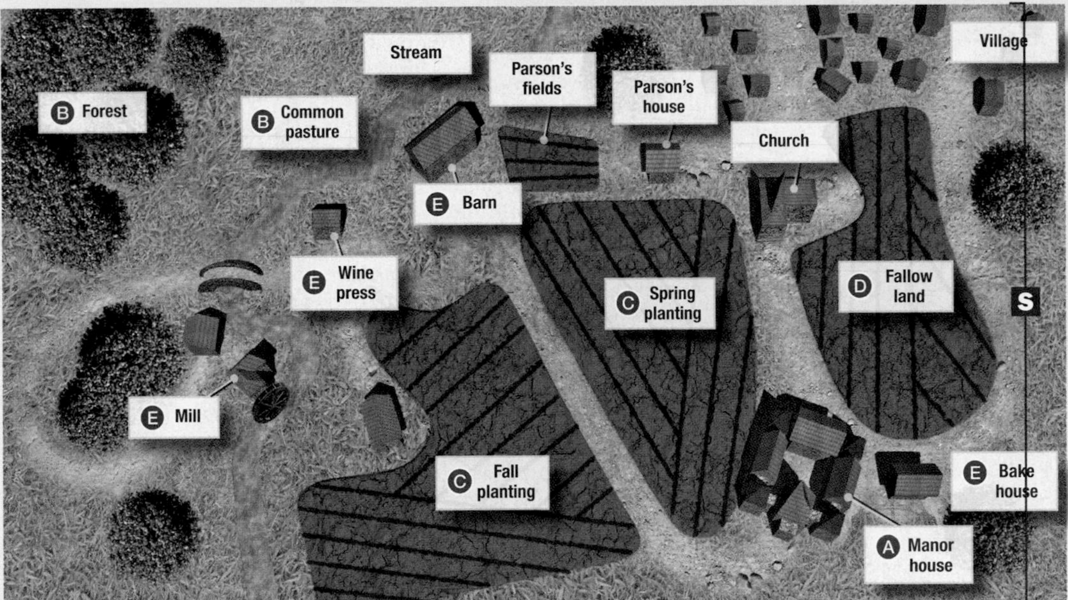

A Manor house Home to the lord and his family and refuge for the peasants during an attack

B Common lands Shared areas such as pasture where peasants could graze animals or forest where peasants could hunt, fish, and gather firewood

C Cultivated land Spring and fall plantings laid out in long strips to minimize the number of turns required while plowing

D Fallow land During crop rotation, land left unplanted to allow it to recover

E Common workshops Shared work areas such as a mill to grind grain; bake house to bake bread; wine press to make wine; or barn to shelter and care for animals

DOCUMENT-BASED QUESTIONS

The medieval manor was a mostly self-sustaining community.

1. **Explaining** How did the heavy plows of the time influence the layout of the fields?
2. **Making Inferences** In what ways did the manorial system promote group cooperation?

could not afford a team of animals, so villagers shared their beasts. To minimize the amount of turning of the heavy *carruca*, people plowed land in long strips.

Shifting from a two-field to a three-field crop rotation also increased food production. In the Early Middle Ages, peasants divided their land into two fields of equal size. They planted one field and allowed the other to lie fallow (unplanted) to regain its fertility. Now, however, lands were divided into three parts. Peasants planted one field in the fall with grains (rye and wheat) that they harvested in summer. They planted the second field in spring with grains (oats and barley) and vegetables (peas and beans) that they harvested in fall. They allowed the third field to lie fallow. This way, only one-third, rather than one-half, of the land lay fallow at any time. This practice of rotating crops kept the soil fertile, while allowing people to grow more crops.

✓Reading Check **Analyzing** What factors led to population growth in the High Middle Ages?

Teach

S Skill Practice

Visual Literacy Have students point to evidence that crop rotation is being used at this manor. **Ask:** What activity might have taken place in the mill? *(grinding grain, and possibly cutting timber)* OL

DOCUMENT-BASED QUESTIONS

Answers:

1. The plows were hard to turn, so the fields were laid out in long strips to minimize the number of turns required.
2. Peasants took turns using shared workshops and farm equipment; crops were rotated across all manor lands; the lord provided protection in exchange for the peasants' work.

✓Reading Check

Answer: increases in food production due to peaceful conditions, favorable climate change, new technology, improved crop rotation

Hands-On Chapter Project
Step 1

Designing a Web Site About Europe in the Middle Ages

Groups of students will organize key topics on medieval Europe on five linked Web pages.

Step 1: Gathering Information

Essential Question: Why were the Middle Ages a pivotal time in European history?

Directions: Organize the class into several small groups. Explain that members of each group will work together to design a Web site about Europe in the Middle Ages. As they study Section 1, they can begin to gather information for their Web site. Write the Section 1 Big Idea on the board. Tell students to use it as a guide to decide the main topics for one page on their Web site.

Summarizing: Allow time for groups to share what they learned about the Section 1 Big Idea while gathering Web site material. Remind them that they will continue to gather material and start planning the Web site when they study Section 2. OL

(Chapter Project is continued in Section 2.)

C Critical Thinking

Comparing and Contrasting

Ask: How do you distinguish between feudalism and manorialism? *(Answers will vary. Students should review the material in the book to identify characteristics of each system. They should consider economic, political, social, and military factors.)* Develop a Venn diagram on the board or overhead with student responses. Have students copy the diagram to use as a study tool. **OL**

For additional practice on this skill, see the **Skills Handbook**.

R Reading Strategy

Organizing Information

Have students create a chart describing the major characteristics of manorialism. Students should describe the economic obligations and benefits of serfs, peasants, and lords. Display charts in the classroom. **Ask:** How did serfs support their local churches? *(by giving a tenth of their produce to the church)* **OL**

The Manorial System

MAIN IDEA Under the manorial system of the Middle Ages, serfs worked the lands of lords.

HISTORY & YOU Does your family celebrate religious holidays? Read to learn about the holidays that serfs observed during the Middle Ages.

You will remember from Chapter 9 that feudalism created alliances between nobles (lords and vassals). The landholding nobles were a military elite whose ability to be warriors depended on their having **C** the leisure time to pursue the arts of war. Landed estates, located on the fiefs given to a vassal by his lord and worked by peasants, provided the economic support that made this way of life possible.

A **manor** was an agricultural estate that a lord ran and peasants worked. Although free peasants continued to exist, increasing numbers of free peasants became **serfs,** or peasants legally bound to the land. Serfs had to provide labor services, pay rents, and be subject to the lord's control. By 800, probably 60 percent of western Europeans were serfs.

A serf's labor services included working the lord's land. The lord's land made up one-third to one-half of the cultivated land scattered throughout the manor. Peasants used the rest of the estate's land to grow food for themselves. Such tasks as building barns and digging ditches were also part of the labor services peasants provided. Serfs usually worked about three days a week for their lords.

The serfs paid rents by giving the lords a share of every product they raised. Serfs also paid the lords for the use of the manor's common pasturelands, streams, **R** ponds, and surrounding woodlands. If a serf fished in the pond or stream on a manor, he turned over part of the catch to his lord. Peasants were also obliged to pay a tithe (a tenth of their produce) to their local village churches.

In the feudal contract, lords and vassals were tied together through mutual obligations to each other. On individual estates, lords had a variety of legal rights over their serfs. Serfs could not leave the manor without the lord's permission and could not marry anyone outside the manor without the lord's approval. Lords often had political authority on their lands, which gave them the right to try peasants in their own courts. Peasants were required to pay lords for certain services, such as having their grain ground into flour in the lords' mills.

Even with these restrictions, however, serfs were not slaves. The land assigned to serfs to support themselves usually could not be taken away, and their responsibilities to the lord remained fairly fixed. It was also the lord's duty to protect his serfs, giving them the safety to farm the land.

The Peasant Household

The life of peasants in Europe was simple. Their cottages had wood frames surrounded by sticks, with the spaces between sticks filled with straw and rubble and then plastered over with clay. Roofs were simply thatched.

The houses of poorer peasants consisted of a single room. Others, however, had at least two rooms—a main room for cooking, eating, and other activities and another room for sleeping. There was little privacy in a medieval household. A hearth in the main room was used for heating and cooking. Because there were few or no windows and no chimney, the smoke created by fires in the hearth went out through cracks in the walls or, more likely, through the thatched roof.

Cycle of Labor

The seasons of the year largely determined peasant activities. Each season brought a new round of tasks. Harvest time in August and September was especially hectic. A good harvest of grains for making bread was crucial to survival in the winter months.

A new cycle of labor began in October, when peasants worked the ground for the planting of winter crops. In November came the slaughter of excess livestock, because there was usually not enough food to keep the animals alive all winter. The meat would be salted to preserve it for winter use. In February and March, the

Additional Support

Teacher Tip

Organizing the Class In this activity, students create a contract between serfs and lords. Have half of each pair or group represent the interests of serfs and have the other half represent the interests of lords.

Activity: Economics Connection

Creating a Contract Guide students in a discussion of the specific factors that might have led free farmers to attach themselves to a manor. Divide the class into pairs or small groups and have them write a contract between a serf and a lord. Contracts should give specific details of the amount of labor that will be exchanged for particular services. All the labor to be provided by the serf and his family should be listed, as should all the noble's responsibilities to his serfs. Invite students to share their contracts with the class, discussing the similarities and differences and evaluating the fairness of each contract. **BL**

land was plowed for the planting of spring crops—oats, barley, peas, and beans. Early summer was a fairly relaxed time, although there was still weeding and sheepshearing to be done.

In every season, of course, the serfs worked not only their own land but also the lords' lands. They also tended the small gardens next to their dwellings, where they grew the vegetables that made up part of their diet.

Peasants did not face a life of constant labor, thanks to the feast days, or holidays, of the Catholic Church. These feast days celebrated the great events of the Christian faith, or the lives of Christian saints or holy persons. The three great feasts of the Catholic Church were Christmas (celebrating the birth of Christ), Easter (celebrating the resurrection of Christ), and Pentecost (celebrating the descent of the Holy Spirit on Christ's disciples). Other feasts dedicated to saints or the Virgin Mary, the mother of Jesus, were also celebrated. More than 50 days were essentially holidays.

Religious feast days, Sunday mass, baptisms, marriages, and funerals all brought peasants into contact with the village church, a crucial part of manorial life. The village priest taught the peasants the basic ideas of Christianity so that they would gain the Christians' final goal—salvation.

INFOGRAPHICS

The Peasant's Wheel of Life

Peasant's Wheel of Life

This illustration is from a medieval Book of Hours called *Très Riches Heures*. Books of Hours were personal prayer books that often contained calendars noting important dates of the year.

CRITICAL THINKING SKILLS

1. **Identifying** In what months did peasants plant?
2. **Analyzing Visuals** Based on the chart, what season does the illustration represent?

C Critical Thinking

Making Inferences Ask: Why was early summer a relatively relaxed time for peasants? *(The heavy work of plowing and planting was done and it was too early to harvest crops.)* **OL**

R Reading Strategy

Reading a Chart Explain that because this chart is shown in a circle, it may not be clear where to start reading the information. Have students experiment by starting with January, which is the beginning of the calendar year, and then starting with October, which is shown at the top of the circle. **Ask:** Why does the chart show October at the top of the circle? *(A new cycle of plowing and planting began in October after the harvest ended in September.)* **BL**

CRITICAL THINKING SKILLS

Answers:

1. March, April, May, October
2. late spring to early summer

Differentiated Instruction

Leveled Activities

BL Guided Reading Activity, URB p. 198

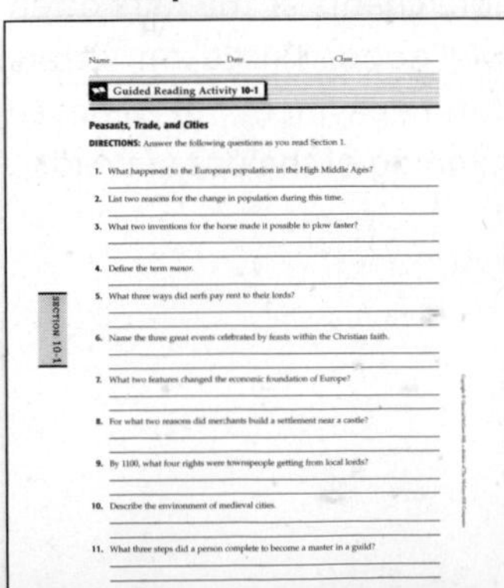

Name ______ Date ______ Class ______

Guided Reading Activity 10-1

Peasants, Trade, and Cities

DIRECTIONS: Answer the following questions as you read Section 1.

1. What happened to the European population in the High Middle Ages?
2. List two reasons for the change in population during this time.
3. What two inventions for the horse made it possible to plow faster?
4. Define the term *manor*.
5. What three ways did serfs pay rent to their lords?
6. Name the three great events celebrated by feasts within the Christian faith.
7. What two features changed the economic foundation of Europe?
8. For what two reasons did merchants build a settlement near a castle?
9. By 1100, what four rights were townspeople getting from local lords?
10. Describe the environment of medieval cities.
11. What three steps did a person complete to become a master in a guild?

SECTION 10-1

OL History Simulation Activity, URB p. 185

AL Enrichment Activity, URB p. 196

ELL Cooperative Learning Activity, URB p. 183

D Differentiated Instruction

Visual/Spatial Have students create a food pyramid to show the typical peasant diet. Explain that the pyramid should show the most frequently eaten food at the bottom and the least frequently eaten at the top. Discuss how the peasant diet compares with contemporary American diets. BL

C Critical Thinking

Drawing Conclusions Discuss the economics of the Champagne trade fairs. **Ask:** Who do you think benefited the most from the fairs, the merchants or the towns? *(Answers will vary, but students should support their opinions with information from the text and logical reasoning.)* OL

✓Reading Check

Answer: worked in the fields, bore children, managed the household

✓Reading Check

Answer: Their location was ideal for northern European traders.

However, village priests were often peasants themselves; most could not read. No one knows how much church teaching the peasants actually understood. Very likely, they saw God as an all-powerful force who needed to be appeased by prayer to bring good harvests.

The position of peasant women in manorial society was both important and difficult. They were expected to work in the fields and at the same time bear children. How well they managed the household determined whether their family starved or survived.

Food and Drink

Though simple, the daily diet of peasants was adequate when food was available. The basic staple of the peasant diet, and of the medieval diet in general, was bread. Women made the dough for the bread. The loaves were usually baked in community ovens, which the lord owned. Highly nutritious, peasant bread contained not only wheat and rye but also barley, millet, and oats. These ingredients gave D the bread a dark appearance and a very heavy, hard texture.

Numerous other foods added to the peasant's diet: vegetables from the household gardens; cheese from cow's or goat's milk; nuts and berries from woodlands; and fruits, such as apples, pears, and cherries. Chickens provided eggs and sometimes meat. Peasants usually ate meat only on the great feast days, such as Christmas and Easter.

Grains were important not only for bread but also for making ale. In the Middle Ages, it was not easy to obtain pure sources of water to drink. Consequently, while wine became the choice of drink for members of the upper classes, ale was the most common drink of the poor. If records are accurate, enormous quantities of ale were consumed. A monastery in the twelfth century records a daily allotment to the monks of three gallons of ale a day. Peasants in the field probably consumed even more.

✓Reading Check **Explaining** What role did peasant women play in manorial society?

The Revival of Trade

MAIN IDEA The revival of trade during the High Middle Ages gave rise to a commercial revolution.

HISTORY & YOU Do you have to trade one product for another? Read about the emergence of a money economy.

Medieval Europe was an agricultural society with small villages. In the 1000s and 1100s, however, the economic foundation of European civilization changed. Changes included a revival of trade and an associated growth of towns and cities.

The revival of trade in Europe after the chaotic Early Middle Ages was gradual. Cities in Italy took the lead. **Venice** developed a mercantile fleet (a fleet of trading ships) and by the end of the 900s had become a major trading center in the Mediterranean. The towns of **Flanders,** an area along the coast of present-day Belgium and northern France, were ideally located for northern European traders. Merchants from England, Scandinavia, France, and Germany met there to trade their goods for the high-quality woolen cloth of Flanders. By the 1100s, a regular exchange of goods had developed between Flanders and Italy.

To encourage this trade, the counts of Champagne, in northern France, initiated a series of trade fairs. Six fairs were held every year in the chief towns. At these C fairs, northern merchants brought the furs, woolen cloth, tin, hemp, and honey of northern Europe and exchanged them for the cloth and swords of northern Italy and the silks, sugar, and spices of the East.

As trade increased, demand for gold and silver coins arose at fairs and trading markets of all kinds. Slowly, a **money economy**—an economic system based on money, rather than barter—began to emerge. New trading companies and banking firms were set up to manage the exchange and sale of goods. All of these new practices were part of the rise of **commercial capitalism**, an economic system in which people invested in trade and goods to make profits.

✓Reading Check **Evaluating** Why were the towns of Flanders busy trading centers?

Additional Support

Extending the Content

European Trade Fairs Fairs were temporary markets held in certain locations on a regular basis. They were a way for a concentration of buyers and sellers to come together in areas without large cities and daily markets. The Romans brought fairs to northern Europe to encourage trade in areas they had conquered. In the early Middle Ages, a large fair may have taken place at St. Denis near Paris in the 7th century. The Champagne trade fairs dominated northern Europe for hundreds of years, beginning in the middle of the 12th century. Roads from Flanders, Italy, Germany, and southern France crossed in this part of northeastern France. The fairs were held in different towns in the region and lasted for several weeks. Merchants at the fairs often bought and sold goods based on letters that promised future payment. This practice marked the beginning of the use of credit.

The Growth of Cities

MAIN IDEA The revival of trade spurred the growth of cities, which became centers for manufacturing and trade.

HISTORY & YOU How would you describe life in your town or city? Read to learn what cities were like in the Middle Ages.

The revival of trade led to a revival of cities. Towns had greatly declined in the Early Middle Ages, especially in Europe north of the Alps. Old Roman cities had continued to exist, but they had dwindled in both size and population.

Cities Old and New

With the revival of trade, merchants began to settle in the old Roman cities. They were followed by craftspeople or artisans—people who had developed skills and saw a chance to make goods that the merchants could sell. In the course of the eleventh and twelfth centuries, the old Roman cities came alive with new populations and growth.

Many new cities or towns were also founded, especially in northern Europe. Usually, a group of merchants built a settlement near a castle because it was located along a trade route and because the lords of the castle would offer protection. If the settlement prospered and expanded, new walls were built to protect it. The merchants and artisans of these cities later came to be called *burghers* or **bourgeoisie,** from the German word *burg,* meaning "a walled enclosure."

Medieval cities were small in comparison with either ancient or modern cities. A large medieval trading city would number about 5000 inhabitants. By the late 1200s, London—England's largest city—had more than 40,000 people. Italian cities tended to be even larger than this. For instance, Venice, Florence, and Milan each had more than 80,000 inhabitants. Even the largest European city, however, seemed small when compared to the Byzantine capital of Constantinople or the Arab cities of Damascus, Baghdad, and Cairo. **D**

Most towns were closely tied to the land around them because they depended on the food grown in the surrounding manors. In addition, the towns were often part of the territory belonging to a lord, and therefore were subject to his authority.

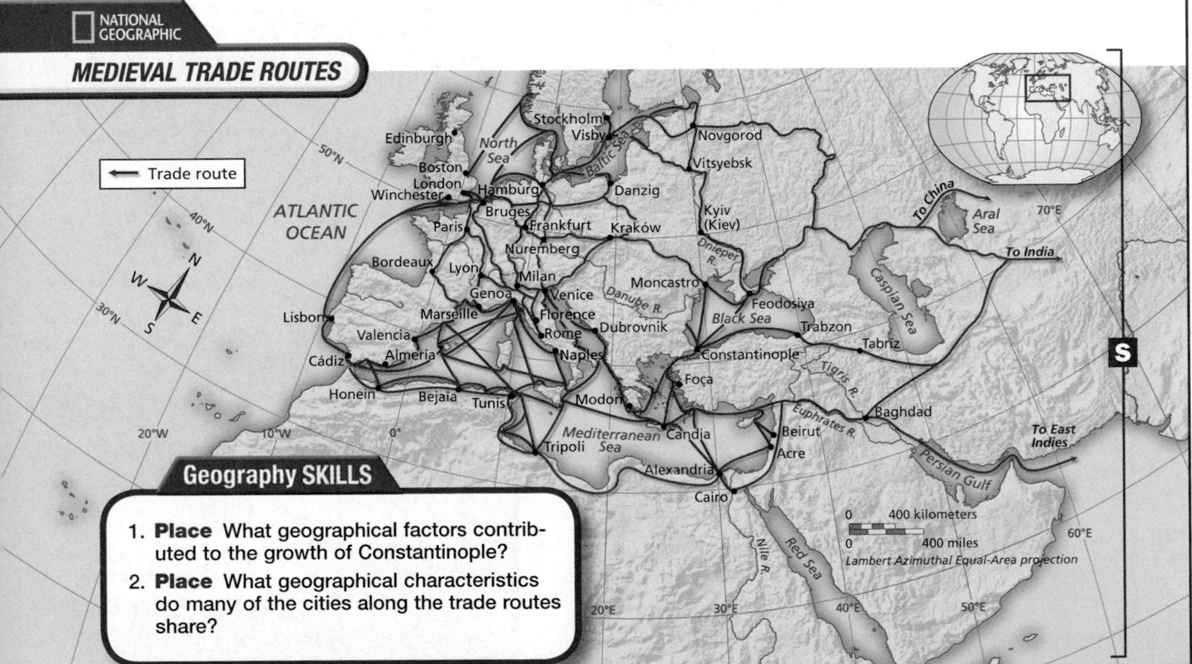

Geography SKILLS

1. **Place** What geographical factors contributed to the growth of Constantinople?
2. **Place** What geographical characteristics do many of the cities along the trade routes share?

S

D Differentiated Instruction

Logical/Mathematical Have students create bar graphs to compare the population of medieval cities in the late 1200s. Encourage students to do research to find the populations of Constantinople and Arab cities as well as European cities. **Ask:** Where were the largest European cities located in the Middle Ages? *(Italy)* **AL**

S Skill Practice

Using Geography Skills Help students focus on specific trade routes by asking pairs of students to choose a major city such as Venice or Constantinople. Then ask them to list the cities a trader would have been likely to visit from that city. Use students' information to create a chart showing the most frequently visited cities. **BL**

Geography SKILLS

Answers:

1. location on the Black Sea made it a hub for trade to India and China; the Mediterranean gave access to other destinations
2. They were on waterways.

Differentiated Instruction

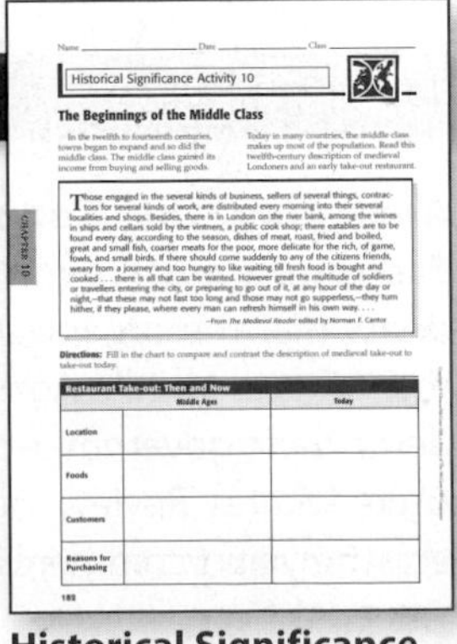
Historical Significance Activity 10

The Beginnings of the Middle Class

Restaurant Take-out: Then and Now	Middle Ages	Today
Location		
Foods		
Customers		
Reasons for Purchasing		

Historical Significance Activity, URB p. 182

Comparing and Contrasting

Objective: Learn more about the middle class in medieval Europe.
Focus: Ask students to read the passage.
Teach: Tell students to fill in the chart.
Assess: Have students share answers with a partner and revise answers as needed.
Close: Have students compare the modern-day middle class with that of feudal times.

Differentiated Instruction Strategies

BL Have students read the passage aloud with a partner.

AL Have students write a paragraph from the point of view of a middle class person.

ELL Have students create vocabulary cards for any unfamiliar words.

W Writing Support

Persuasive Writing Have students write a letter or a petition to a local lord in which townspeople make their case for why the relationship between the lord and the town needs to change. OL

D Differentiated Instruction

Visual/Spatial Have students review the emblems of different guilds in Umbria. Ask them to choose some symbols and tell why they are appropriate to particular crafts. Allow students to create symbols for some contemporary jobs. BL

CRITICAL THINKING SKILLS

Answers:

1. The guilds were able to regulate price and maintain quality.
2. Their structure was based on cooperation, not competition, and they could not compete with early factories.

The lords wanted to treat townspeople as they did their vassals and serfs. However, townspeople saw things differently.

Townspeople needed freedom to trade. They needed their own unique laws and were willing to pay for them. Lords and kings, in turn, saw that they could also make money and sold to the townspeople the liberties they wanted.

By 1100, townspeople had numerous rights from local lords. These included the right to buy and sell property, freedom from military service to the lord, a written law that guaranteed townspeople their freedom, and the right for an escaped serf to become a free person after living a year and a day in the town.

The people in almost every new town and city gained these basic liberties. Some new towns also received the right to govern themselves by choosing their own officials and having their own courts of law.

Over time, medieval cities developed their own governments for running the affairs of the community. Only males who had been born in the city or who had lived there for some time were citizens. In many cities, these citizens elected the city council members, who served as judges and city officials and who passed laws. Elections were rigged so that only **patricians**—members of the wealthiest and most powerful families—were elected.

City Life

Medieval towns were surrounded by stone walls. Walls were expensive to build, so the space within was tightly filled. Thus, medieval cities had narrow, winding streets. Houses were crowded against one another, with the second and third stories built out over the streets. The danger of fire was great. Dwellings were mostly made of wood before the 1300s and candles were used for light and heat. Medieval cities burned rapidly once a fire started.

The physical environment of medieval cities was not pleasant. Often dirty, cities smelled from animal and human waste. Air pollution was also a fact of life. Smoke from wood fires, present everywhere, or from the burning of cheap grades of coal

INFOGRAPHICS

The Medieval Guild System

Medieval merchants and artisans formed guilds to promote their common interests. Guilds achieved a monopoly over their commercial activity in the local area. This protected their members from competition from artisans of other cities and from competition among themselves. Guilds set rules to assure that all members would prosper equally.

Guilds helped to build the economic structure of Europe. They increased the number of skilled artisans and merchants. They built roads and schools. Guilds often controlled town governments, creating a stable environment for commerce. In these ways guilds served as a transition from feudalism to a new economic system—capitalism. By the 1500s, wealthy merchants had begun to form early factories. Guilds were formed for cooperation, not competition. They could not compete with the efficiency of large-scale production in the factories, and the guild system slowly faded away.

CRITICAL THINKING SKILLS

1. **Making Inferences** How might the guild system have affected prices for local consumers?
2. **Identifying the Main Idea** What characteristic of guilds eventually led to their decline?

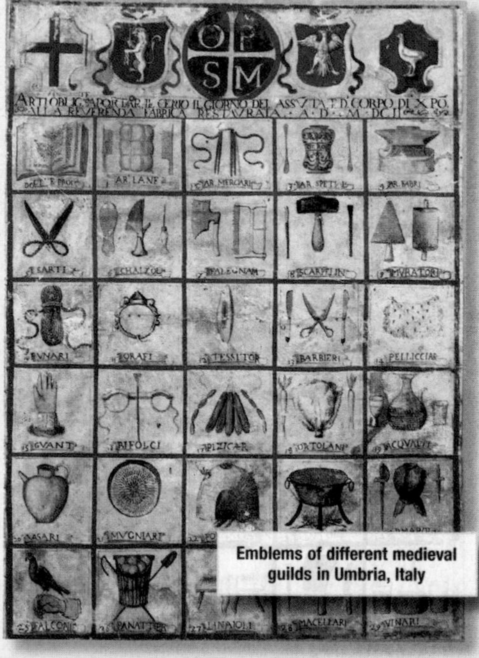

Emblems of different medieval guilds in Umbria, Italy

Additional Support

Activity: Economics Connection

Analyzing the Connection Between Economics and Government Remind students that the organization of city government in the Middle Ages paved the way for democratic governments in Europe and the United States. Review the effects of a money economy and commercial capitalism on the development of Western Europe and the United States. **Ask:** **What are the medieval origins of the economic system of capitalism?** *(As trade increased, a money economy replaced barter and trading companies and banking firms developed to manage the sale of goods.)* Have students research ways that medieval economic policies and government organization have helped determine the modern structure of many governments. Ask students to compare the responsibilities of current city and county governments with those of medieval city governments. AL filled the air. Water pollution was also a problem. Butchers dumped blood and all other waste products from their butchered animals into the rivers. Tanners, who converted animal hides to leather, unloaded tannic acids and other waste products of their operations. Cities did not use the rivers for drinking water but relied instead on wells. While medieval towns had private and public baths—Paris had 32—they were closed during the great plague of the fourteenth century (discussed later in this chapter).

Considerably more men than women lived in medieval cities. Women were expected to supervise the household, prepare meals, raise the children, and manage the family's finances. Often, they helped their husbands in their trades. **W** Some women developed their own trades to earn extra money. Sometimes, when a master craftsman died, his widow carried on his trade. It was thus possible for women in medieval towns to lead quite independent lives. In fact, many women became brewers, weavers, and hatmakers.

Industry and Guilds

With the revival of trade, cities and towns became important centers for manufacturing a wide range of goods, such as cloth, metalwork, shoes, and leather goods. Many craft activities were carried on in houses located in the narrow streets of medieval cities.

From the 1000s on, craftspeople began to organize themselves into **guilds,** or business associations. Guilds played a leading role in the economic life of cities. By the 1200s, there were guilds for almost every craft (tanners, bakers) and separate guilds for specialized groups of merchants, such as dealers in silk, spices, or wool.

Craft guilds directed almost every aspect of the production process. They set the standards for the quality of the articles produced, specified the methods of production to be used, and even fixed the price at which the finished goods could be sold. Guilds also determined the number of people who could enter a specific trade and the procedure they must follow to do so.

A person who wanted to learn a trade first became an **apprentice,** usually at around the age of 10, to a master craftsperson. Apprentices were not paid, but they did receive room and board from their masters. After five to seven years of service during which they learned their craft, apprentices became **journeymen** and worked for wages for other masters. Journeymen aspired to become masters as well. To do so, they were expected to produce a **masterpiece,** a finished piece in their craft. This piece allowed the master craftspeople of the guild to judge whether a journeyman was qualified to become a master and join the guild.

✓ Reading Check **Evaluating** What role did guilds play in the economic life of the cities?

Vocabulary

1. **Explain** the significance of: technology, crucial, *carruca*, manor, serfs, Venice, Flanders, money economy, commercial capitalism, bourgeoisie, patricians, guilds, apprentice, journeymen, masterpiece.

Main Ideas

2. **Explain** how the new crop rotation increased food production.
3. **Identify** the economic developments of the Middle Ages that allowed commercial capitalism to emerge. Use a diagram like the one below.

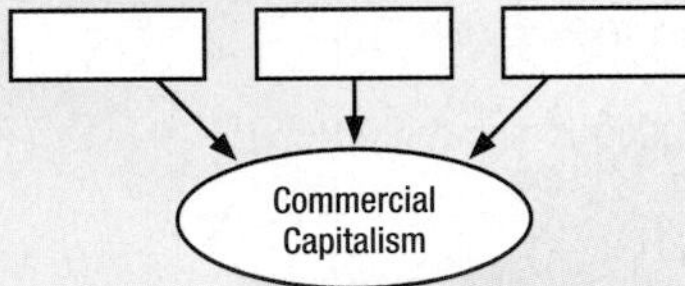

4. **Describe** the physical environment of medieval cities.

Critical Thinking

5. **The BIG Idea** **Determining Cause and Effect** What were some major results of farming improvements and the revival of trade in the Middle Ages?
6. **Comparing and Contrasting** How did living and working in a medieval city differ from living and working on a manor?
7. **Analyzing Visuals** Examine the illustration on page 340. Choose three emblems and try to name the craft each represents.

Writing About History

8. **Persuasive Writing** Imagine you are a trader doing business at the beginning of the money economy. Write a letter addressed to other traders convincing them to convert to a money system from bartering.

History ONLINE
For help with the concepts in this section of *Glencoe World History*, go to glencoe.com and click Study Central™.

W Writing Support

Descriptive Writing Ask students to write two paragraphs describing what it might have been like to live in a medieval city. Have them mention advantages *(jobs, safety, intellectual opportunity)* and disadvantages *(crowded conditions, lack of sanitation, disease).* **OL**

✓ Reading Check

Answer: set quality standards, specified production methods, controlled the number of people entering a trade, and set the procedure for doing so

Assess

History ONLINE

Study Central provides summaries, interactive games, and online graphic organizers to help students review content.

Close

Summarizing Ask student groups to summarize how advances in technology changed medieval life. **OL**

Answers

1. Definitions for the vocabulary words are found in the section and in the Glossary.
2. The land was divided into three fields instead of two, with two planted in crops and one left fallow; this increased the amount of productive land at any one time.
3. money economy, new trading companies, banking firms
4. crowded; narrow, winding streets; dirty; smelled of animal and human waste and smoke
5. **Farming:** increased food production led to population growth; **Trade:** growth of cities, money economy, and commercial capitalism
6. **Cities:** more rights, freedom; employment choices, crowded, dirty, polluted; **Manor:** serfs had fewer rights, agricultural work; not crowded
7. Answers depend on emblems chosen. Some crafts shown include bookmaker, shoemaker, carpenter, tailor, barber, and butcher.
8. Answers should reflect an understanding of how trade is easier with a money economy than with barter.

Focus

Bellringer

Daily Focus Transparency 10.2

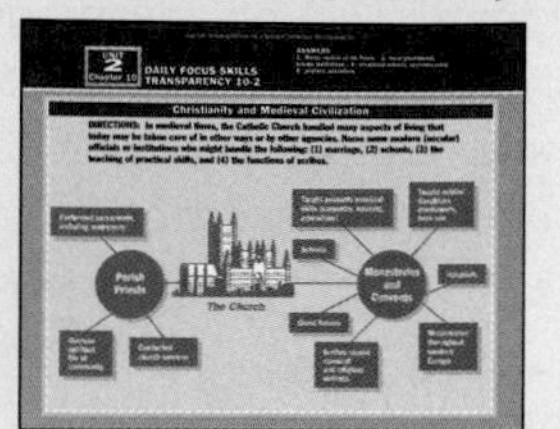

GUIDE TO READING

Answers to Graphic:
Cistercians: strict, simple life; life of prayer and manual labor; took religion outside the monastery; **Dominicans:** life of poverty; preached against heresies; important examiners for the Inquisition

Section Spotlight Video

To generate student interest and provide a springboard for class discussion, access the Chapter 10, Section 2 video at glencoe.com or on the video DVD.

SECTION 2

Medieval Christianity

GUIDE TO READING

The BIG Idea
Ideas, Beliefs, and Values With its strong leadership, the Catholic Church became a dominant and forceful presence in medieval society.

Content Vocabulary
- lay investiture *(p. 342)*
- interdict *(p. 344)*
- sacraments *(p. 344)*
- heresy *(p. 346)*
- relics *(p. 347)*

Academic Vocabulary
- pursue *(p. 342)*
- remove *(p. 343)*

People, Places, and Events
- Papal States *(p. 342)*
- Pope Gregory VII *(p. 342)*
- Henry IV *(p. 343)*
- Concordat of Worms *(p. 343)*
- Pope Innocent III *(p. 344)*
- Cistercians *(p. 344)*
- Hildegard of Bingen *(p. 345)*
- Franciscans *(p. 345)*
- Dominicans *(p. 345)*
- Saint Francis of Assisi *(p. 345)*
- Assisi *(p. 345)*
- Inquisition *(p. 346)*

Reading Strategy
Categorizing Information As you read, use a chart like the one below to list characteristics of the Cistercian and Dominican religious orders.

Cistercians	Dominicans

Under Pope Gregory VII, the Catholic Church disentangled itself from secular influence in the eleventh century. The Church reached the height of its political power in the thirteenth century under Pope Innocent III. Religious enthusiasm spread and new monastic orders emerged. By the High Middle Ages, the Catholic Church had become a dominant and forceful presence in European society.

The Papal Monarchy

MAIN IDEA During the papacy of Pope Innocent III in the thirteenth century, the Catholic Church reached the height of its political power.

HISTORY & YOU Can a religious leader be an effective military leader? Read how Church officials were obliged to carry out military duties for their lords.

Since the fifth century, the popes of the Catholic Church had claimed supremacy over the affairs of the Church. They had also gained control of territories in central Italy that came to be known as the **Papal States.** This control kept the popes involved in political matters, often at the expense of their spiritual duties.

At the same time, the Church became increasingly involved in the feudal system. Chief officials of the Church, such as bishops and abbots, came to hold their offices as grants from nobles. As vassals, they were obliged to carry out the usual feudal services, including military duties. Lords often chose their vassals from other noble families for political reasons. Thus, the bishops and abbots they chose were often worldly figures who cared little about their spiritual duties.

Reform of the Papacy

By the eleventh century, Church leaders realized the need to be free from the lords' interference in the appointment of Church officials. When an individual became a Church official in the Middle Ages, he was given a ring and a staff. These objects symbolized the spiritual authority with which the Church granted, or invested, the official. Secular, or lay, rulers usually chose nominees to Church offices and gave them the symbols of their office, a practice known as **lay investiture. Pope Gregory VII** decided to fight this practice.

Elected pope in 1073, Gregory was convinced that he had been chosen by God to reform the Church. To **pursue** this aim, Gregory claimed that he—the pope—was truly God's "vicar on earth" and that the pope's authority extended over all the Christian world, including its rulers. Only by eliminating lay investiture could the

Resource Manager

R Reading Strategies	C Critical Thinking	D Differentiated Instruction	W Writing Support	S Skill Practice
Teacher Edition • Academic Vocab., p. 343 **Additional Resources** • Guid. Read. Act., URB p. 199 • Read. Ess. & Note-Taking Guide, p. 112	**Teacher Edition** • Analyzing Pri. Sources, p. 344 • Making Inferences, p. 345 • Compare/Contrast, p. 347 **Additional Resources** • Crit. Think. Act., URB p. 178 • Section Quiz, p. 118	**Teacher Edition** • ELL, p. 344 • Auditory/Musical, p. 345 **Additional Resources** • Read. Strat. for SS, p. 50	**Teacher Edition** • Expository Writing, p. 346 **Additional Resources** • People in World Hist. Act., URB p. 189 • Writer's Guidebook, p. 23	**Teacher Edition** • Visual Literacy, p. 343 **Additional Resources** • Read. Strat. for SS, pp. 26, 30

INFOGRAPHICS

The Investiture Controversy

Conflict Between King Henry IV and Pope Gregory VII

1075: Gregory bans lay investiture, asserting supremacy of Church over lay authority. Henry invests a new bishop of Milan, replacing Gregory's choice.

1076: Gregory deposes and excommunicates Henry.

> "I withdraw. . .from Henry the king. . . the rule over the whole kingdom of the Germans and over Italy. And I absolve all Christians from the bonds of the oath which they have made or shall make to him. . . I bind him in thy stead with the chain of the anathema [a damned person]. . ."
>
> —Pope Gregory VII, February 1076

1077: Henry submits to Gregory and is absolved. German princes declare Henry dethroned and elect Rudolf, sparking civil war.

1080: Gregory supports Rudolf over Henry. Henry names an antipope, Clement III. Gregory excommunicates them both.

1081: Henry wins the civil war and marches on Rome.

1084: Henry conquers Rome. Gregory flees the city.

1105: Henry is forced to abdicate as his continued support for Clement III weakened his rule.

Henry humbles himself before Gregory, who removes the excommunication, 1077.

CRITICAL THINKING SKILLS

1. **Analyzing** What does this conflict indicate about medieval ideas of power, authority, and governance?
2. **Drawing Conclusions** How did Henry's conflict with Gregory affect Henry's reign?

Church regain its independence. The Church would appoint clergy and run its own affairs. If rulers did not accept this, the pope would **remove** them.

Gregory VII and **Henry IV,** the king of Germany, disagreed about these claims. German kings had appointed high-ranking clerics, especially bishops, as their vassals, in order to use them as their administrators. Without them, the king could not maintain power over the German nobles.

In 1075, Pope Gregory issued a decree forbidding high-ranking clerics from receiving their investiture from lay leaders: "We decree that no one of the clergy shall receive the investiture . . . from the hand of an emperor or king or of any lay person." Henry, however, had no intention of obeying this decree.

The struggle between Henry IV and Gregory VII, known as the Investiture Controversy, continued until a new German king and a new pope reached the **Concordat of Worms** agreement in 1122. Under it, a bishop in Germany was first elected by Church officials.

Teach

S Skill Practice

Visual Literacy Have students study the painting and notice how Henry is portrayed. **Ask:** What details show that Henry is humbling himself before the pope? *(simple clothing, bare feet, bowed head)* **OL**

R Reading Strategy

Academic Vocabulary Have students suggest the meaning of *remove* by recalling what they know about the prefix *re-*. Explain that something might be physically moved away or the meaning might be broader. **ELL**

CRITICAL THINKING SKILLS

Answers:

1. Government relied upon the authority of the Church, but secular rulers would not necessarily accept the Church's power as greater than theirs.
2. It weakened his reign and set the Church against him in the civil war. His support for Clement III forced his abdication.

Additional Support

Activity: Collaborative Learning

Debating Investiture The struggle between Gregory VII and Henry IV was one of the great conflicts between Church and state in the High Middle Ages. Have students recreate the "debate" between pope and king. Divide the class into two teams (one for Gregory VII and one for Henry IV) and have each team research the debate. Teams should designate roles for each member. When research is completed, schedule a class period for the debate or discussion. **Ask:** What arguments can you make to support a contention that your team "won"? *(Discuss the points made by each side.)* **OL**

Teacher Tip

Staging a Debate This activity asks students to recreate a historic debate. The debate can be formal (if you have time to teach debating skills), or informal (more like a class discussion). Instruct students to analyze the key arguments made by both sides.

W Writing Support

Expository Writing Have students do additional research about an aspect of the Inquisition. Ask students to write a brief essay about their chosen topic based on their research. AL

CRITICAL THINKING SKILLS

Answers:

1. Its investigations and punishments served as warnings to anyone who might stray from Church teachings. Extreme punishments gave the Church power through fear.
2. The Church began to include disobedience to its authority in the definition of heresy to try to bring breakaway groups under its control.

✓Reading Check

Answer: to serve as an example of their preaching; to return to the simplicity of the early Church

INFOGRAPHICS

The Inquisition

The Inquisition's goal was to identify people who had committed heresy and convince them to confess. In most cases, the sentence was an act of penance, such as a pilgrimage. More extreme punishments were reserved for those who refused to repent or repeated their heresy.

In the 1270s a breakaway group of Franciscans, called the Spirituals for their extreme vow of poverty, challenged the leadership of their order. The Beguines supported them. Beguines were enthusiastic Catholic women but outside the Church's formal control. The Church saw a potential threat to its authority with the activities of these two groups. By 1318, the Church had begun to define disobedience to its authority as heresy, and started burning Spirituals. The next year, it expanded this extreme punishment to the Beguines. Two decades of executions followed as the Inquisition sought to control these splinter groups. W

At first, the Inquisition left Europe's Jewish populations alone. Then in 1242, the Inquisition condemned the Talmud and burned thousands of copies. The Inquisition remained active into the late 1700s.

Heretics are burned at the stake, 1557

CRITICAL THINKING SKILLS

1. **Interpreting** How did the Inquisition reinforce the authority of the Catholic Church?
2. **Explaining** How had the Church's definition of heresy changed by 1318? Why did it make this change?

The Dominican order was founded by a Spanish priest, Dominic de Guzmán. Dominic wanted to defend Church teachings from **heresy**—the denial of basic Church doctrines. The spiritual revival of the High Middle Ages had led to the emergence of heresies within the Church. Adherents of these movements were called heretics. Heretical movements became especially widespread in southern France. Dominic believed that a new religious order of men who lived in poverty and could preach effectively would best be able to attack heresy.

The Inquisition

The Church created a court called the **Inquisition,** or Holy Office, to deal with heretics. This court developed a regular procedure to find and try heretics. The Dominicans became especially well known for their roles as examiners of people suspected of heresy.

Those who confessed to heresy performed public penance and received punishment, such as flogging. Beginning in 1252, the Inquisition added the element of torture to extract confessions. Those who did not confess but were still considered guilty and those who had done penance for heresy and then relapsed were subject to execution by the state.

Thirteenth-century Christians believed the only path to salvation was through the Church. To them, heresy was a crime against God and humanity. In their minds, using force to save souls from damnation was the right thing to do.

✓Reading Check **Analyzing** Why did the Franciscans choose to live simply?

Differentiated Instruction

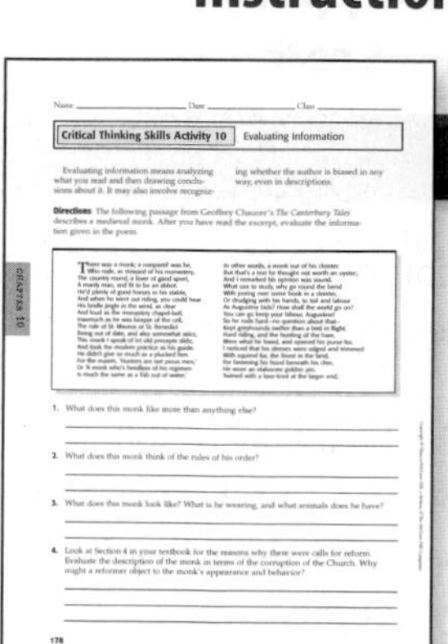
Critical Thinking Skills Activity, URB p. 178

Analyzing Primary Sources

Objective: Evaluate information on medieval monks.
Focus: Have students read the passage from *The Canterbury Tales.*
Teach: Tell students to answer questions 1–4.
Assess: Have students read their answers to the class.
Close: Discuss with students what they know about present-day monks.

Differentiated Instruction Strategies

BL Read the passage from *The Canterbury Tales* to the class.

AL Ask students to do research to write a report explaining how monks live today.

ELL Have students make a list of unfamiliar words in the passage and look them up in a dictionary.

Religion in the High Middle Ages

MAIN IDEA Ordinary people observed the Church's sacraments, venerated saints, and took pilgrimages to holy shrines.

HISTORY & YOU Do you have a good luck charm? Read to learn about the importance of relics to people in the High Middle Ages.

The Church of the High Middle Ages was a crucial part of ordinary people's lives from birth to death. The sacraments, such as baptism, marriage, and the Eucharist (Communion), were seen as means for receiving God's grace and were necessary for salvation. Since only the clergy could administer these rites, people depended on them to achieve this goal. Ordinary people also venerated saints—men and women who, because of their holiness, had achieved a special position in Heaven. Since saints could ask for favors before the throne of God for people who prayed to them, they were very popular with all Christians.

Among the recognized saints were Jesus Christ's apostles, the Virgin Mary, and numerous local saints of special significance to a single area. The Italians, for example, had Saint Nicholas, the patron saint of children, who is known today as Santa Claus. Of all the saints, the Virgin Mary, mother of Jesus, was the most highly regarded in the High Middle Ages. A sign of Mary's importance is the number of churches all over Europe that were dedicated to her in the 1100s and 1200s. (Such churches in France were named Notre Dame, or "Our Lady.") C

Emphasis on the role of the saints was closely tied to the use of **relics,** usually bones of saints or objects connected with saints. Relics were considered worthy of worship because they provided a link between the earthly world and God. It was believed that relics could heal people or produce other miracles. A twelfth-century English monk wrote about an abbey's relics: "There is kept there a thing more precious than gold, . . . the right arm of St. Oswald. . . . This we have seen with our own eyes and have kissed, and have handled with our own hands. . . . There are kept here also part of his ribs and of the soil on which he fell."

Medieval Christians also believed that a pilgrimage to a holy shrine produced a spiritual benefit. The greatest shrine, but the most difficult to reach, was the Holy City of Jerusalem. On the continent two pilgrim centers were especially popular in the High Middle Ages: Rome, which contained the relics of Saints Peter and Paul, and the Spanish town of Santiago de Compostela, supposedly the site of the tomb of the Apostle James. Local shrines dedicated to the Blessed Virgin Mary also became pilgrimage centers.

✓Reading Check **Examining** Why were saints important to Christians in the High Middle Ages?

SECTION 2 REVIEW

Vocabulary

1. **Explain** the significance of: Papal States, lay investiture, Pope Gregory VII, pursue, remove, Henry IV, Concordat of Worms, Pope Innocent III, interdict, sacraments, Cistercians, Hildegard of Bingen, Franciscans, Dominicans, Saint Francis of Assisi, Assisi, heresy, Inquisition, relics.

Main Ideas

2. **Summarize** the opposing viewpoints in the investiture controversy and the resulting compromise at Worms. Use a diagram like the one below.

Pope Gregory's View	King Henry's View
Concordat of Worms	

3. **Explain** how women were involved in the spiritual movements of the Middle Ages.
4. **Define** a relic and explain its significance to people of the Middle Ages.

Critical Thinking

5. **The BIG Idea** **Evaluating** Why was the Church such a powerful influence in lay people's lives during the Middle Ages?
6. **Drawing Conclusions** Do you think the Inquisition's methods accurately identified heretics? Explain.
7. **Analyzing Visuals** Examine the painting on page 343. What does King Henry's posture tell you about his relationship with Pope Gregory?

Writing About History

8. **Persuasive Writing** Take on the role of either Pope Gregory VII or King Henry IV of Germany. Argue the question of lay investiture from the viewpoint of either the pope or the king and justify the compromise that you reached.

History ONLINE
For help with the concepts in this section of *Glencoe World History,* go to glencoe.com and click Study Central™.

347

C Critical Thinking

Comparing and Contrasting

Ask: Compare and contrast the practices of ordinary people with those of the clergy. *(All shared similar beliefs and received the sacraments. Ordinary people were dependent on the clergy to receive the sacraments essential to salvation.)* AL

Answer: Saints could ask for favors from God for those who prayed to them. Their relics were also believed to have miraculous powers.

Assess

History ONLINE

Study Central provides summaries, interactive games, and online graphic organizers to help students review content.

Close

Making Connections Discuss the role of religion in the lives of medieval people and in people's lives today. OL

Answers

1. Definitions for the vocabulary words are found in the section and in the Glossary.
2. **Pope Gregory's View:** pope has supreme authority; should appoint clergy. **King Henry's View:** clerics key administrators; king should appoint them. **Concordat of Worms:** Church elects bishop who then pays homage to king; king invests secular symbols; Church invests spiritual symbols.
3. Many wealthy and intellectual women joined religious houses.
4. bones of saints or other objects connected to them; a link between the earthly world and God; believed to be able to produce miracles
5. Sacraments were considered essential to salvation, and only clergy could perform sacraments.
6. Possible Answer: No. Under torture, innocent people might falsely confess to stop the pain.
7. Henry appears below the pope, head bowed. This indicates subservience to the pontiff.
8. Arguments should reflect point of view of pope or king and reflect how each one felt he gained something from the compromise.

R Reading Strategy

Making Connections Ask: How would you compare and contrast schools today with those of the High Middle Ages? *(Answers will vary. Students may indicate how universities have changed since the Middle Ages but still have some of the same features.)* **BL**

D Differentiated Instruction

Advanced Learners Have students research connections between the ideas of Aristotle and Thomas Aquinas. Ask them to create a graphic organizer to show the results of their research. They might compare and contrast the two men's ideas or show Aristotle's influence on Aquinas's thought. **AL**

PEOPLE in HISTORY

Answer: Greek philosophy and Christian doctrine

✓Reading Check

Answer: to reconcile faith and reason

Universities

MAIN IDEA Medieval university students applied scholasticism to the study of theology.

HISTORY & YOU For how many more years are you prepared to go to school? Read to learn how medieval students earned a degree.

See page R39 to read excerpts from Christine de Pizan's *A Woman May Need to Have the Heart of a Man* in **Primary Sources and Literature Library.**

The university of today, with faculty, students, and degrees, was a product of the High Middle Ages. The word university comes from the Latin word *universitas*, meaning **"corporation"** or "guild."

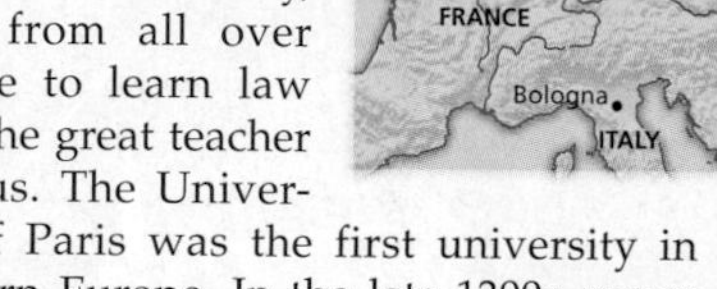

The first European university appeared in **Bologna** (buh•LOH•nyuh), Italy. Students, men only, **R** came from all over Europe to learn law from the great teacher Irnerius. The University of Paris was the first university in northern Europe. In the late 1300s, many students and masters (teachers) left **Paris** and started their own university at **Oxford**, England. Kings, popes, and princes thought it honorable to found universities. By 1500, Europe had 80 universities.

Students began by studying the liberal arts—grammar, rhetoric, logic, arithmetic, geometry, music, and astronomy. Teachers lectured by reading from a basic text and then adding their explanations. To get a degree, students took oral examinations after studying four to six years. A student could earn a bachelor of arts and later a master of arts.

A student could earn a doctor's degree in law, medicine, or theology in about ten more years. The most highly regarded subject was **theology**—the study of religion and God. Those with doctor's degrees were officially able to teach but could pursue other careers.

The study of theology was strongly influenced by a philosophical and theological system known as **scholasticism.** Scholasticism tried to reconcile faith and reason—to show that what was accepted on faith was in harmony with what could be learned through reason and experience. **D** Its chief task was to harmonize Christian teachings with the works of the Greek philosophers. The philosopher **Aristotle** reached his conclusions by rational thought, not by faith, and his ideas sometimes contradicted Church teachings.

In the 1200s, **Saint Thomas Aquinas** (uh•KWY•nuhs) made the most famous attempt to reconcile Aristotle with the doctrines of Christianity. Thomas Aquinas is best known for his ***Summa Theologica*** (*summa* was a summary of all knowledge on a given subject). His masterpiece was organized according to the logical method of scholarly investigation. Aquinas first posed a question such as, "Does God exist?" He then cited sources that offered opposing opinions before reconciling them and coming to his own conclusions. He believed that truths arrived at through reason could not conflict with truths arrived at through faith. Reason, unaided by faith, could uncover truths about the physical universe but not spiritual truths.

✓Reading Check **Explaining** What was the main goal of scholasticism?

PEOPLE in HISTORY

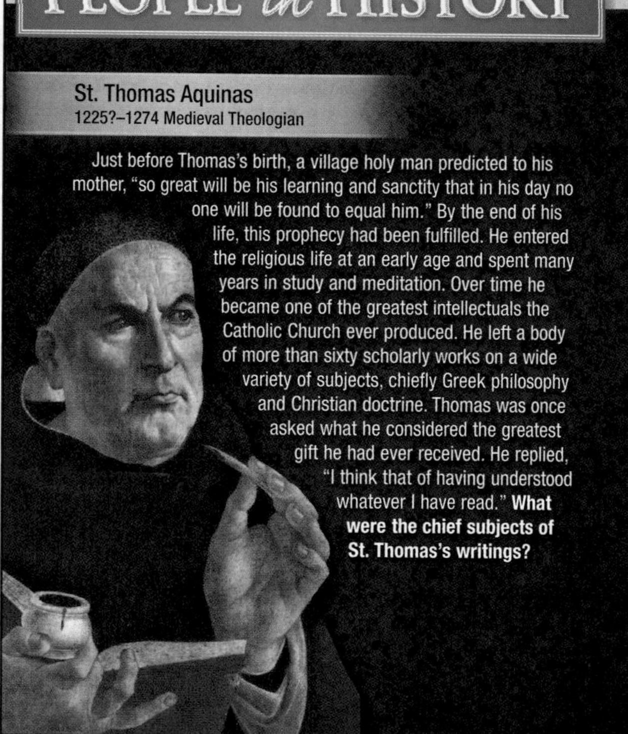

St. Thomas Aquinas
1225?–1274 Medieval Theologian

Just before Thomas's birth, a village holy man predicted to his mother, "so great will be his learning and sanctity that in his day no one will be found to equal him." By the end of his life, this prophecy had been fulfilled. He entered the religious life at an early age and spent many years in study and meditation. Over time he became one of the greatest intellectuals the Catholic Church ever produced. He left a body of more than sixty scholarly works on a wide variety of subjects, chiefly Greek philosophy and Christian doctrine. Thomas was once asked what he considered the greatest gift he had ever received. He replied, "I think that of having understood whatever I have read." **What were the chief subjects of St. Thomas's writings?**

Differentiated Instruction

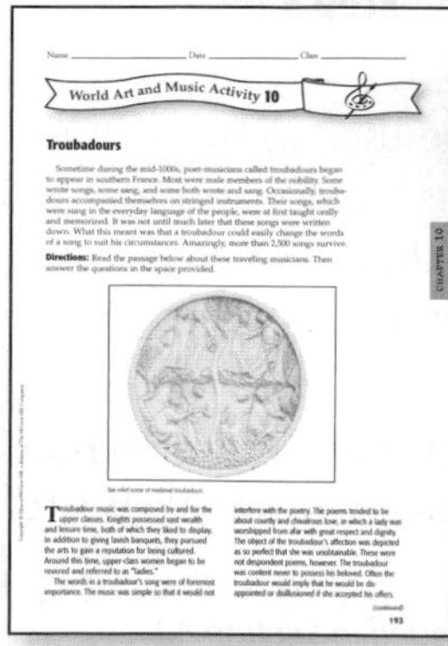

World Art and Music Activity, URB p. 193

Analyzing Information

Objective: Learn more about medieval troubadour poetry.
Focus: Have students read the passage.
Teach: Tell students to answer questions 1–4.
Assess: Have students share answers with a partner and amend answers as needed.
Close: Ask students to compare these love songs to love songs today.

Differentiated Instruction Strategies

BL Have students read the song lyrics aloud with a partner.

AL Ask students to write a pastourelle using one plot described here.

ELL Have students create vocabulary cards for unfamiliar words, then reread the worksheet.

Vernacular Literature

MAIN IDEA Troubadour poetry and the heroic epic poem were popular forms of vernacular literature in the twelfth century.

HISTORY & YOU What types of books do you enjoy—mystery, science fiction, nonfiction? Read to learn what type of literature was popular during the High Middle Ages.

Latin was the universal language of medieval civilization. Used in the Church and schools, Latin enabled learned people to communicate anywhere in Europe. However, in the twelfth century, much new literature was being written in the **vernacular**—the language of everyday speech in a particular region, such as Spanish, French, English, or German. A new market for vernacular literature appeared in the twelfth century when educated laypeople (religious people who were not clergy) at courts and in the cities took an interest in new sources of entertainment.

Perhaps the most popular vernacular literature of the twelfth century was troubadour poetry, which was chiefly the product of nobles and knights. This poetry told of the love of a knight for a lady, who inspires him to become a braver knight and a better poet. A good example is from the noble Jaufré Rudel, who cherished a dream woman from afar. He feared that he would never meet her, but would always love her.

PRIMARY SOURCE

"Most sad, most joyous shall I go away,
Let me have seen her for a single day,
My love afar,
I shall not see her, for her land and mine
Are sundered, and the ways are hard to find, **C**
So many ways, and I shall lose my way,
So wills it God.
Yet shall I know no other love but hers,
And if not hers, no other love at all."

—Jaufré Rudel

Another type of vernacular literature was known as the **chanson de geste,** or heroic epic. The earliest and finest example of such literature is the *Song of Roland*, which appeared around 1100 and was written in French. The chief events described in heroic epic poems are battles and political contests. The epic world is one of combat, in which knights fight courageously for their kings and lords. Women play only a small role or no role at all in heroic epic poems.

✓Reading Check **Identifying** What were two popular types of vernacular literature in the twelfth century?

SECTION 3 REVIEW

Vocabulary

1. **Explain** the significance of: construction, corporation, Bologna, Paris, Oxford, theology, scholasticism, Aristotle, Saint Thomas Aquinas, *Summa Theologica*, vernacular, chanson de geste.

Main Ideas

2. **Summarize** the evolution of church architecture by describing the features and innovations in a diagram like the one below.

3. **List** the fields of study in which a medieval university student could earn a doctor's degree.
4. **Identify** the chief events in heroic epic poems.

Critical Thinking

5. **The BIG Idea** **Analyzing** How did the architecture of the Gothic cathedral reflect medieval religious values?
6. **Comparing and Contrasting** Compare what you know of modern university courses of study with those of the first European universities. What are the similarities and differences?
7. **Analyzing Visuals** Imagine yourself standing inside the Gothic cathedral shown on page 349. How would you describe the look and feel of the interior?

Writing About History

8. **Persuasive Writing** Use a word processing program to create an illustrated brochure to attract students to a new medieval university in Venice. Include information on the method of education and degree and course offerings. Provide a "frequently asked questions" section.

History ONLINE
For help with the concepts in this section of *Glencoe World History*, go to glencoe.com and click Study Central™.

C Critical Thinking

Analyzing Primary Sources Have students read the example of troubadour poetry. **Ask:** Why is the knight unable to see the woman he loves? *(Possible answer: They live in different countries that are at war.)* **OL**

✓Reading Check

Answer: troubadour poetry of chivalric love and chansons de geste, or heroic epics

Assess

History ONLINE

Study Central provides summaries, interactive games, and online graphic organizers to help students review content.

Close

Identifying Have students list important advances in architecture and literature during the High Middle Ages. **BL**

SECTION 3 REVIEW

Answers

1. Definitions for the vocabulary words are found in the section and in the Glossary.
2. **Basilica:** rectangular; flat wooden roofs. **Romanesque:** stone barrel vault roof; massive walls and pillars; dark. **Gothic:** ribbed vaults; pointed arches; flying buttresses; thinner walls; stained glass windows.
3. law, medicine, or theology
4. battles and political contests
5. Pointed arches and ribbed vaults focused upward toward God. Sunlight through stained glass symbolized God's light.
6. **Similarities:** liberal arts curriculum; bachelor of arts, master of arts, and doctoral degrees. **Differences:** lectures only; oral examinations to get degrees; only fields were law, medicine, or theology
7. Possible descriptors: expansive, light, grand, upward-oriented, arched, majestic, awesome, reverent
8. Brochures should be informative and persuasive and reflect accurate details based on the description of medieval universities in the text.

Focus

Bellringer

Daily Focus Transparency 10.4

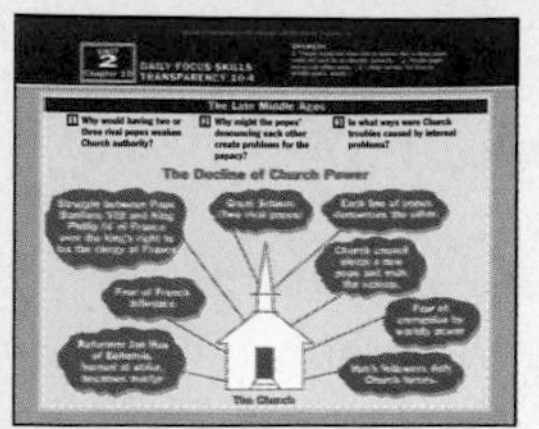

GUIDE TO READING

Answers to Graphic:
popes lost power over kings; Great Schism; cries for reform of the church

Section Spotlight Video

To generate student interest and provide a springboard for class discussion, access the Chapter 10, Section 4 video at glencoe.com or on the video DVD.

SECTION 4

The Late Middle Ages

GUIDE TO READING

The BIG Idea
Devastation of War Disastrous forces overwhelmed Europe in the fourteenth century with lasting consequences.

Content Vocabulary
- anti-Semitism *(p. 353)*
- taille *(p. 357)*
- new monarchies *(p. 357)*

Academic Vocabulary
- abandoned *(p. 352)*
- consequences *(p. 353)*

People, Places, and Events
- Black Death *(p. 352)*
- Pope Boniface VIII *(p. 355)*
- King Philip IV *(p. 355)*
- Avignon *(p. 355)*
- Great Schism *(p. 355)*
- John Hus *(p. 355)*
- Henry V *(p. 356)*
- Agincourt *(p. 356)*
- Joan of Arc *(p. 356)*
- Orléans *(p. 356)*
- Isabella *(p. 358)*
- Ferdinand *(p. 359)*

Reading Strategy
Determining Cause and Effect As you read, use a diagram like the one below to identify three reasons for the decline of the papacy.

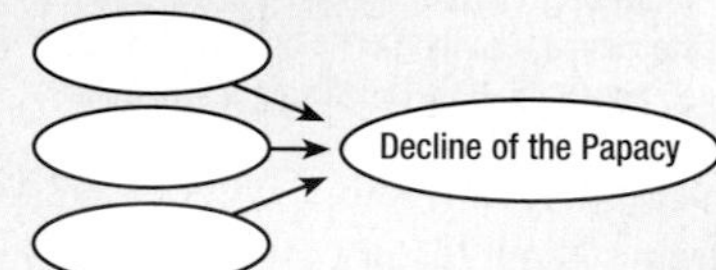

Medieval European society reached its high point in the 1200s. However, everything changed in the 1300s when a series of disastrous forces overwhelmed Europe. The Black Death spread, killing over one-third of the population. People's faith in the papacy was undermined when the Great Schism rocked the Catholic Church. Then, the Hundred Years' War started. Recovery began in the 1400s, and rulers responded by establishing their "new" monarchies.

The Black Death

MAIN IDEA Spreading throughout Europe during the mid-fourteenth century, the Black Death had disastrous social and economic effects.

HISTORY & YOU What if one-third of your town's population just suddenly disappeared? Read to learn about the spread of the Black Death.

The Middle Ages in Europe had reached a high point in the 1200s. In the 1300s, however, some disastrous changes took place. Especially catastrophic was the **Black Death,** the most devastating natural disaster in European history. One observer wrote that "father **abandoned** child, wife [abandoned] husband, one brother [abandoned] another, for the plague seemed to strike through breath and sight. And so they died. And no one could be found to bury the dead, for money or friendship."

The Plague Spreads

Bubonic plague was the most common form of the Black Death. It was spread by black rats infested with fleas carrying a deadly bacterium. Italian merchants brought the plague with them from Caffa, on the Black Sea, to the island of Sicily in October 1347. The plague had spread to southern Italy and southern France by the end of 1347. Usually, the path of the Black Death followed trade routes. In 1348 and 1349, the plague spread through France, the Low Countries (modern Belgium, Luxembourg, and the Netherlands), and Germany. It ravaged England in 1349 and expanded to northern Europe and Scandinavia. Eastern Europe and Russia were affected by 1351.

Out of a total European population of 75 million, possibly one-third to one-half of the population died of the plague between 1347 and 1351. Especially hard hit were Italy's crowded cities, where 50 to 60 percent of the people died. In England and Germany, entire villages disappeared.

Resource Manager

R Reading Strategies	C Critical Thinking	D Differentiated Instruction	W Writing Support	S Skill Practice
Teacher Edition • Academic Vocab., p. 353 • Predicting, p. 356 • Identifying, p. 357 **Additional Resources** • Pri. Source Read., URB p. 191 • Guid. Read. Act., URB p. 201 • Read. Ess. & Note-Taking Guide, p. 118	**Teacher Edition** • Drawing Con., p. 354 • Analyzing Pri. Sources, p. 355 • Compare/Contrast, p. 358 **Additional Resources** • Mapping Hist. Act., URB p. 181 • Section Quiz, p. 120 • Chapter Tests, p. 121	**Teacher Edition** • Visual/Spatial, p. 355 • Adv. Learners, p. 358 **Additional Resources** • Academic Vocab. Act., URB p. 175 • People in World Hist. Act., URB p. 190 • Reteach. Act., URB p. 195	**Teacher Edition** • Expository Writing, pp. 356, 359 **Additional Resources** • Linking Past/Present Act., URB p. 188 • Writer's Guidebook, pp. 23, 27	**Teacher Edition** • Using Geo. Skills, pp. 353, 357 • Visual Literacy, p. 354 **Additional Resources** • Skills Reinforc. Act., URB p. 177 • Time Line Act., URB p. 187

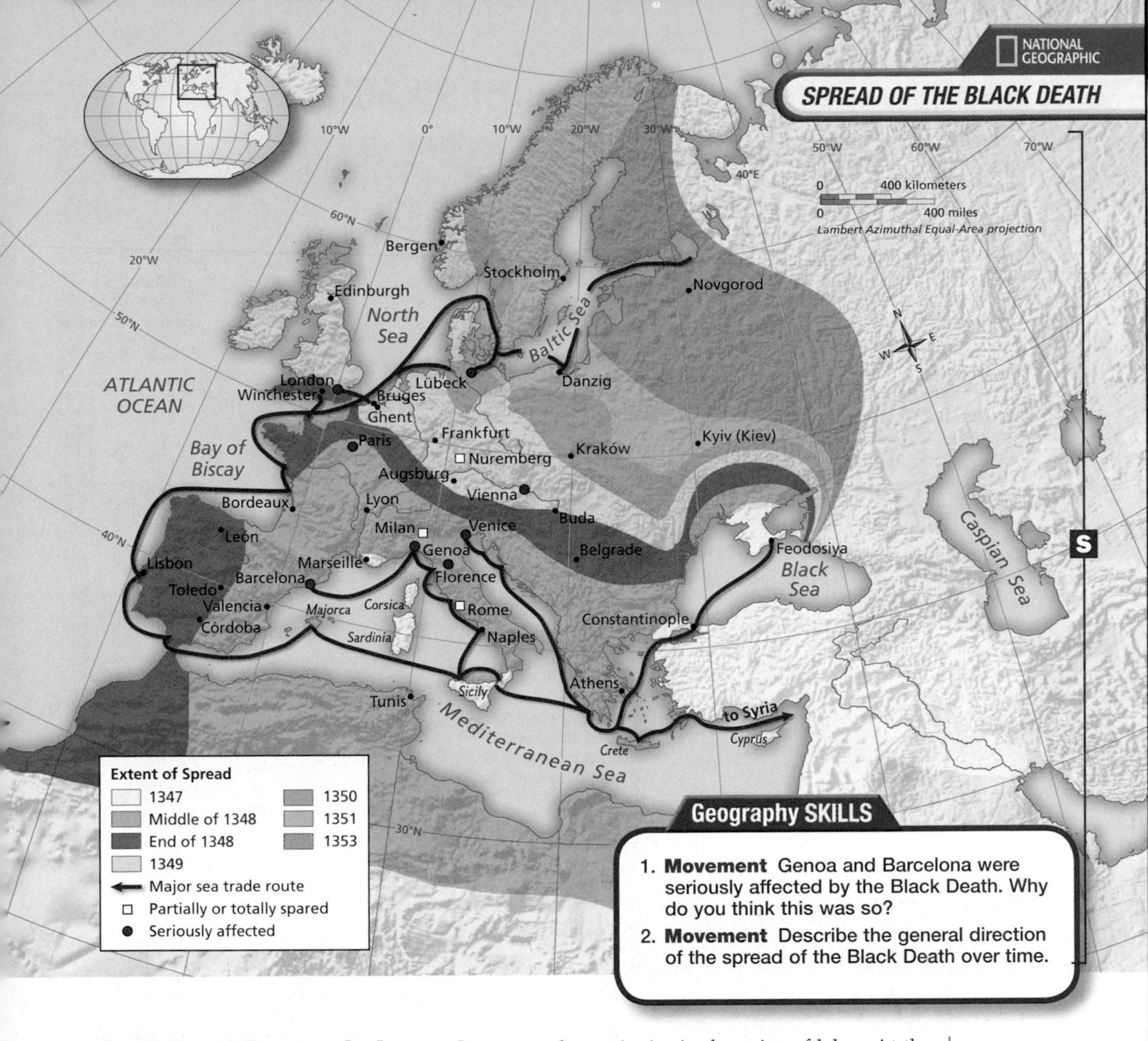

Geography SKILLS

1. **Movement** Genoa and Barcelona were seriously affected by the Black Death. Why do you think this was so?
2. **Movement** Describe the general direction of the spread of the Black Death over time.

Social and Economic Impact

People did not know what caused the plague. Many believed that God sent it as punishment for their sins or that the devil caused it. Some reactions became extreme and led to **anti-Semitism**—hostility toward Jews. Some accused Jews of causing the plague by poisoning town wells. The worst attacks occurred in Germany. Many Jews fled from Germany to Poland, where the king protected them.

The death of so many people also had severe economic **consequences.** Trade declined, and a shortage of workers caused a dramatic rise in the price of labor. At the same time, the decline in the number of people lowered the demand for food, resulting in falling prices.

Landlords were now paying more for labor while their incomes from rents were declining. Some peasants bargained with their lords to pay rent instead of owing services. This change freed them from serfdom, an institution that had been declining throughout the High Middle Ages.

✓Reading Check **Explaining** How was the plague spread?

Teach

S Skill Practice

Using Geography Skills Ask: What cities were partially or totally spared from the Black Death? *(Rome, Milan, Nuremberg)* **BL**

R Reading Strategy

Academic Vocabulary Have students use context clues to determine the meaning of *consequences.* **Ask:** What are synonyms for *consequences? (effects, results)* **ELL**

Geography SKILLS

Answers:

1. They were on the major sea trade route from Feodosiya.
2. It spread from Feodosiya to Greece, Italy, Africa, and Spain. Then it moved northeast through Europe.

✓Reading Check

Answer: by black rats infested with infected fleas

Additional Support

Activity: Interdisciplinary Connection

Health Besides its massive social and economic consequences, the Black Death also had significant psychological effects on the people of the Middle Ages. Many, searching for answers, turned to mysticism and superstitious beliefs and practices. Explain to students that AIDS is a modern-day plague, affecting millions around the world. **Ask:** Why is there less superstition about AIDS than the Black Death? *(There is more scientific information about how diseases are caused and spread now.)* Have students work together on a project comparing and contrasting the Black Death with AIDS. Ask them to address the symptoms and spread of each disease, any known or possible cures for each, and the attitudes of each society toward the diseases. They might present their information as a video or radio newscast, or as a newsmagazine article. **OL**

C Critical Thinking

Drawing Conclusions Ask: Why did people turn to the Church for help against the Black Death? *(because it was the most powerful institution in society)* **OL**

S Skill Practice

Visual Literacy Ask: How does this image reflect the role of the Church during the period of the Black Death? *(People were concerned more than ever with death and thus with life after death.)* **OL**

DOCUMENT-BASED QUESTIONS

Answers:

1. Both show religious figures responding to the plague.
2. Before the plague, peasants were tied to the land. There were plenty of workers, so the lords could "call the shots." The plague created a labor shortage, giving peasants the power to bargain for better wages and conditions.

TURNING POINT — THE BLACK DEATH

The Black Death greatly decreased the population of Europe and brought about significant economic and social changes in the late Middle Ages. Simple flea bites unleashed a sickness that killed as many as one-third to one-half of the people in Europe within four years. A labor shortage developed, manufactured goods became scarce, and trade slowed drastically. The labor shortage gave the serfs bargaining power. Many negotiated to become wage earners instead of serfs.

Peasants moved to cities in greater numbers, seeking higher wages. The economic system of wealth tied to owning land was weakening. In its place rose a system based on paying money for labor. The newly empowered peasants and guild members stood up for their rights more boldly after the plague. All over Europe, peasants revolted over taxes and serfdom.

In this crisis, many decided God was punishing the people and Church leaders for their sins. Some Catholics emphasized the importance of inner prayer that did not rely on the priests. **C**

In this fourteenth-century English text, a priest blesses monks who show the characteristic spots of bubonic plague. Both clergy and worshipers died from the plague.

S

Images of death became common in art. Here, a priest gives the last rights while a smiling devil/skeleton attacks the victim with a spear. God appears in the upper right.

EFFECTS OF THE BLACK DEATH

ECONOMIC EFFECTS
Drastic decline in population led to:
• Labor shortages —higher wages for laborers and artisans —bargaining power for serfs with landlords
• Decline in trade (along with labor shortage) —scarcity of manufactured goods —higher prices for manufactured goods
• Less demand for food —lower food prices
SOCIAL EFFECTS
• Decline of serfdom
• Growth of cities
• Peasant revolts
• Preoccupation with death in art and literature

DOCUMENT-BASED QUESTIONS

1. **Comparing** What common elements exist in the art shown about the Black Death?
2. **Analyzing** Why could peasants stand up for their rights more boldly after the plague than before it?

Differentiated Instruction

Leveled Activities

BL Skills Reinforcement Activity, URB p. 177

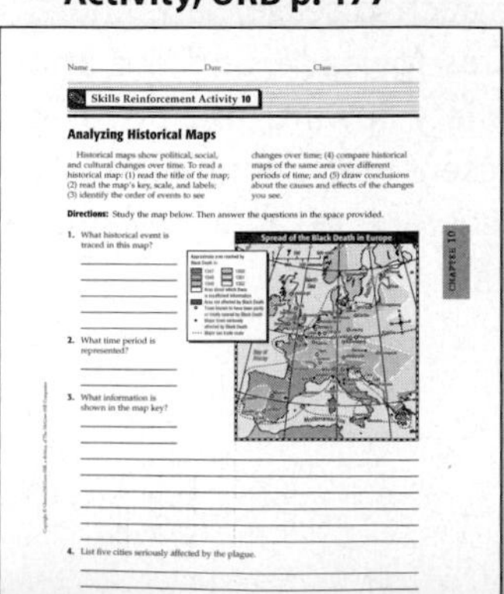

Skills Reinforcement Activity 10

Analyzing Historical Maps

OL Primary Source Reading, URB p. 191

Primary Source Reading 10

An Italian Writer Describes the Black Death

AL Linking Past and Present Activity, URB p. 188

Linking Past and Present Activity 10

Old and New Solutions to the Problem of Poverty

ELL Time Line Activity, URB p. 187

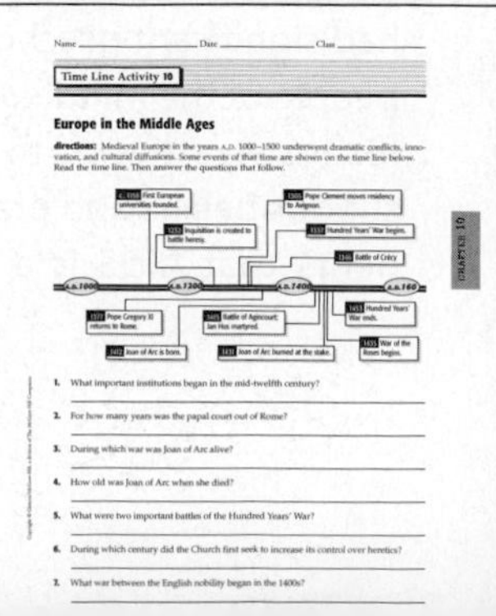

Time Line Activity 10

Europe in the Middle Ages

Decline of Church Power

MAIN IDEA The Great Schism of the Catholic Church caused great political conflict and left Europe divided for four decades.

HISTORY & YOU Have you and a friend ever disagreed? Read to learn about the Great Schism.

The popes reached the height of their power in the 1200s. In the 1300s, the Church's power declined.

The Popes at Avignon

European kings had begun to reject papal claims of supremacy by the end of the 1200s. The struggle between **Pope Boniface VIII** and **King Philip IV** of France had serious consequences for the papacy. Philip claimed the right to tax the clergy. Boniface argued that taxing the clergy required the pope's consent, because popes were supreme over both Church and state. Philip rejected the pope's position and sent French forces to Italy to bring Boniface back to France for trial. The pope escaped but died soon afterward.

Philip then engineered the election of a Frenchman, Clement V, as pope in 1305. Clement took up residence in **Avignon** (A•VEEN•YOHN), in southern France. From 1305 to 1377, the popes lived in Avignon.

D

Sentiments against the papacy grew during this time. Many believed that the pope as bishop of Rome should reside in Rome, not in Avignon. The splendor in which the pope and cardinals were living in Avignon also led to strong criticism of the papacy, as expressed by the Italian poet Petrarch:

PRIMARY SOURCE

"Here reign the successors of the poor fisherman of Galilee; they have strangely forgotten their origin. I am astounded . . . to see these men loaded with gold and clad in purple, boasting of the spoils of princes and nations."

—Italian poet Petrarch

C

The Great Schism

Perceiving the decline in papal prestige, Pope Gregory XI returned to Rome in 1377 but soon died. When the cardinals met to elect a new pope, the citizens of Rome warned that the cardinals would not leave Rome alive unless they elected an Italian. The cardinals wisely elected an Italian, Pope Urban VI. Five months later, a group of French cardinals declared the election invalid and chose a Frenchman as pope. This pope returned to Avignon.

Because Urban remained in Rome, there were now two popes, beginning the **Great Schism** of the Church. Lasting from 1378 to 1417, the Great Schism divided Europe. France and its allies supported the pope in Avignon. As France's enemies, England and its allies supported the pope in Rome.

In addition to creating political conflict, the Great Schism damaged the Church. The pope was widely believed to be the true leader of Christendom. When each line of popes denounced the other as the Antichrist (one who opposes Christ), people's faith in both the papacy and the Church were undermined. The situation became worse when an effort to resolve the problem in 1409 resulted in the simultaneous reign of three popes. A church council finally met at Constance, Switzerland, and ended the schism in 1417. The competing popes either resigned or were deposed. A new pope, acceptable to all, was then elected.

These crises led to calls for reform. Czech reformers led by **John Hus** called for an end to corruption of the clergy and to excessive papal power within the Church. Hus was accused of heresy by the Council of Constance and burned at the stake in 1415. In response, the Czechs led a revolutionary upheaval in Bohemia that was not crushed until 1436.

By the early 1400s, then, the Church had lost much of its political power. The pope could no longer assert supremacy over the state. Although Christianity remained central to medieval life, the papacy and the Church had lost much of their spiritual authority.

✓Reading Check **Explaining** Why were popes criticized for living in Avignon?

D Differentiated Instruction

Visual/Spatial Have students refer to the Reference Atlas to help them follow the events described in the text. You may wish to give them an outline map of Europe and ask them to label key locations and events. **BL**

C Critical Thinking

Analyzing Primary Sources

Have students read the primary source excerpt from Petrarch. **Ask:** Who were the "poor fishermen of Galilee"? *(Jesus's apostles)* Why are popes referred to as the apostles' successors? *(because popes traced their authority back to the apostle Peter, the first bishop of Rome)* **OL**

✓Reading Check

Answer: People thought the pope, as bishop of Rome, should live in Rome. Also, the popes were living lavishly in Avignon.

Hands-On Chapter Project

Step 4

Designing a Web Site About Europe in the Middle Ages

Step 4: Creating the Web Pages In addition to selecting the remaining information, groups finalize designs for the Web pages.

Directions: Tell groups to use the Section 4 Big Idea as a guide for selecting the remaining material for their Web site. After they have gathered all the information, students should complete their Web site designs. Students may design the pages using specialized computer software, word processing software, or simply use pen and paper. Before submitting their finished products, groups should review the chapter to check their work for accuracy and completeness.

Summarizing: Allow time for groups to share what they learned about the Section 4 Big Idea while gathering Web site material. Allow additional time for groups to complete their Web site designs. **OL**

(Chapter Project is continued in the Visual Summary.)

Focus

Ask students how not knowing the cause of something potentially frightening, such as an eclipse, can affect one's response to it. Tell students that when the Black Death swept through Europe, people had no idea what caused it. Some thought it was the air, some blamed it on the alignment of the planets, and others saw it as a punishment for sin.

Teach

D Differentiated Instruction

Kinesthetic Have students stand at their seats and count off by twos. Ask the "ones" to sit down. Have students survey the room. Explain that if they lived during the plague, those seated would represent the dead. Discuss how people might have reacted to such a great loss of life. BL

C Critical Thinking

Determining Cause and Effect

Ask: Why did the disease follow the trading routes? *(Rats and fleas lived on board ships and were likely transported onto land in the cargo containers.)* OL

Additional Support

The Black Death

The Black Death spread throughout Europe from 1347 to 1351. The disease wiped out nearly half of Europe's population. Many towns and villages lost most of their population, and some completely disappeared. There were three versions of the disease that plagued the population, the most well-known of these being the bubonic plague. Flea-infested rats aboard trading ships carried the disease along trade routes and throughout the continent. As the fleas jumped to humans, the pandemic began. D C

Escaping Death

Many people believed the impure air carried the disease. Those who could afford it escaped to the countryside. They boarded up their homes and either left their sick loved ones in the care of servants, or just left them inside. Still others isolated themselves in their homes in hopes of avoiding infection. The poor had no means of escape. They lived with and cared for their sick. Because they were in close quarters, the poor often fell victim to the disease themselves.

Background

Bubonic Plague The cause of bubonic plague is the bacterium *Yersinia pestis.* In most cases, the bacterium infected the lymph nodes, but in others, it spread to the lungs, resulting in pneumonic plague. Pneumonic plague is highly contagious because it can be spread from person to person through airborne germs. Thus, crowded unsanitary conditions not only increased the populations of rats and fleas, but also facilitated the spreading of pneumonic plague. Unlike bubonic plague, pneumonic plague was almost always fatal. What may surprise students to learn is that some people who were exposed to the plague—such as mothers caring for infected children and gravediggers—seemed to either have developed or inherited an immunity, or resistance, to the bacterium. Modern scientists are studying ancestors of plague survivors to learn just how this immunity might have worked—and to see if it has any applications for fighting modern diseases.

R

A Terrible Death

The Black Death was so-named because of the black color of the swollen lymph nodes, called buboes, its victims experienced. They appeared in the neck, armpits, legs, and groin. Other symptoms were severe head and body aches, high fever, rapid pulse, general weakness, and vomiting of blood. Symptoms appeared within a few days of exposure; the bursting of the buboes and death followed in just a few days more.

Analyzing Visuals

1. **Cause and Effect** What effects of the Black Death do you think had the greatest impact on European history? Why?
2. **Comparing** How is the response to pandemics today different from the ones of the Middle Ages? Are there any similarities?

361

R Reading Strategy

Activating Prior Knowledge
Ask: What circumstances increased the suffering of plague victims? *(There were no preventive measures, nor cures or painkillers. There was no running water. There was no understanding of the causes of the disease.)* OL

Assess/Close

Identifying Have students draw a diagram that shows the cycle of infection beginning with the rat. OL

ANALYZING VISUALS

Answers:

1. The tremendous decrease in population most likely had the greatest impact. One result of the high mortality rate was the disintegration of the feudal system.
2. One similarity is that fear is still a prevalent reaction to pandemics. Today there are protocols for responding medically and socially to such an event, as well as hospitals to care for the afflicted.

Activity: Economics Connection

Determining Cause and Effect Tell students that it is believed that the 14th century plague originated in the Gobi Desert, although it is unclear why. A trading ship carried the bacterium to Feodosiya in the Black Sea region, which was the start of its European journey. Have students find out more about the likely path the disease took from China to the various countries in Europe. Ask them to work independently or together to create an annotated map that shows its route and explains its effects along the way. As an alternative to annotations, students might prefer to include a table or graph to illustrate the impact of the disease. **Ask:** How would trade have been affected by the plague? *(Answers may vary, but students should note that trade likely would have been negatively affected.)* OL

Sequencing Information

Have pairs of students review the Visual Summary and try to arrange the important events in correct order on a time line. Then have them review the material in each section to check their work and make any needed changes. Instruct them to write the exact dates for specific events on their time lines as they review the material. **BL**

Predicting Consequences

Review the changes that occurred in Europe during the Middle Ages. Ask students to predict the consequences of these changes in Europe after 1500. Have students discuss the question in small groups. Call on volunteers to summarize their group's responses. *(Accept reasonable responses. Students might predict increased growth of cities, more technological changes and scientific investigation, reform of the Church and religious conflict, and social and political turmoil.)* **AL**

CHAPTER 10 Visual Summary

You can study anywhere, anytime by downloading quizzes and flash cards to your PDA from glencoe.com.

MERCHANTS SELLING THEIR GOODS

The revival of trade spurred the growth of medieval cities.

Society in the HIGH MIDDLE AGES

- Farming inventions and efficient use of land contributed to population growth.
- Under the manorial system, serfs were legally bound to the land they worked for the lord.
- Revival of trade changed the economy from a barter system to one based on money.
- As trade grew, cities expanded and became manufacturing and trade centers.

RELIGIOUS ENTHUSIASM SPREAD THROUGH EUROPE

Saint Bernard of Clairvaux embodied the new spiritual ideal of Cistercian monasticism.

CATHOLICISM, INNOVATIONS, AND INTELLECTUAL REVIVAL in the Middle Ages

- Political power of the Catholic Church peaked during the papacy of Pope Innocent III.
- Religious fervor led to new monastic orders.
- Advances in technology allowed the building of impressive Gothic cathedrals.
- Europe's first universities were founded.
- Popular troubadour poetry and heroic epic poems were written in the vernacular.

HUNDRED YEARS' WAR

English troops used traditional crossbows as well as newer longbows and cannons.

Disruptive Forces of the LATE MIDDLE AGES

- The Black Death spread through Europe, devastating societies and economies.
- The Great Schism damaged the Church's power and divided Europe.
- In the Hundred Years' War, peasant foot soldiers, not knights, won the chief battles.
- Recovery began in the late 1400s as new monarchies emerged in France, England, and Spain.

Hands-On Chapter Project
Step 5: Wrap-Up

Designing a Web Site About Europe in the Middle Ages

Students will synthesize what they learned in Steps 1–4.

Step 5: Presenting the Web Sites

Directions: Write the Essential Question on the board. Under it, write the Big Ideas from each section of the chapter. Have each group present its completed Web site to the class. As part of their presentations, instruct groups to connect responses to the Essential Question and the Big Ideas to specific aspects of their Web sites. Use the group presentations to discuss the different ways in which the Big Ideas serve to answer the Essential Question. Monitor the discussion to ensure that all major economic, political, social, and religious issues are covered. Conclude by reminding students that they can use the information from their completed Web site designs as a resource to help prepare them for the chapter assessment. **OL**

STANDARDIZED TEST PRACTICE

TEST-TAKING TIP

Although most test questions ask you about what you have learned by reading the text or by listening in class, using common sense can help you arrive at the correct answers, too. To answer questions, consider what you know about the topic and then read the answer choices.

Reviewing Vocabulary

Directions: Choose the word or words that best complete the sentence.

1. The ________ were the wealthy, powerful families that usually made up the government of a medieval city.

A bourgeoisie
B patricians
C journeymen
D imperators

2. A ________ was an agricultural estate that a lord ran and peasants worked.

A castle
B guild
C carruca
D manor

3. By using ________ to deny people Christian rites, popes could pressure them to do the popes' bidding.

A *tailles*
B sacraments
C interdicts
D heretics

4. ________ is the language of everyday speech.

A Vernacular
B Chanson de geste
C Lay investiture
D Scholasticism

Reviewing Main Ideas

Directions: Choose the best answers to the following questions.

Section 1 *(pp. 334–341)*

5. Approximately what portion of western Europeans were serfs by 800?

A 80 percent
B 40 percent
C 20 percent
D 60 percent

6. How did the French counts of Champagne encourage trade with Flanders?

A Invented money
B Initiated trade fairs
C Instituted capitalism
D Developed a mercantile fleet

Section 2 *(pp. 342–347)*

7. What was the result of the Concordat of Worms?

A The Hundred Years' War ended.
B Europe's loyalties were divided between different popes.
C A compromise was reached in the Investiture Controversy.
D Many people were burned at the stake.

8. Who founded the Franciscans?

A Saint Francis of Assisi
B Dominic de Guzmán
C Pope Innocent III
D Hildegard of Bingen

Need Extra Help?

If You Missed Questions . . .	1	2	3	4	5	6	7	8
Go to Page . . .	340	336	344	351	336	338	344	345

GO ON

Answers and Analyses

Reviewing Vocabulary

1. B The other choices can be eliminated because they do not refer to wealthy, powerful families. The bourgeoisie were merchants and artisans, journeymen were craftsmen who worked for a master, and imperators were commanders-in-chief of Roman armies.

2. D The phrase *agricultural estate* provides a clue to the correct answer. A castle is a building, a guild is a medieval business association, and a *carruca* is a type of heavy iron plow.

3. C Students can eliminate A, because *tailles* refer to taxes imposed by the French king. B and D are incorrect because sacraments are Christian rituals and heretics were people who denied Church teachings. Therefore, the correct answer is C.

4. A C and D can be eliminated because neither has to do with language. A chanson de geste is a type of vernacular literature, therefore choice B is too narrow to be the correct answer.

Reviewing Main Ideas

5. D Students need to remember this fact from the text in order to choose D, the correct answer. They should at least recall that the percentage was very high and could therefore eliminate choices B and C easily.

6. B If students recall the location of Champagne, they can eliminate choice D easily. The counts of Champagne instituted trade fairs to encourage trade between Italy and Flanders. Increased trade led to a money economy and capitalism, but neither was specifically started by the counts of Champagne.

7. C If students know that a concordat is an agreement, they will easily eliminate choices B and D. The Hundred Years' War was fought during the 14th and 15th centuries, long after the concordat. Therefore, A is also incorrect.

8. A Students can eliminate choices B, C, and D if they connect the Franciscans with the name of their founder, Francis of Assisi.

9. D The other architectural styles all preceded the Gothic style, which developed in the 12th century.

10. B For this question, students must connect troubadour poetry with courtly love and the nobility.

11. A Students can eliminate C because King Louis XI strengthened the use of the *taille*. The Great Schism was a temporary dividing of the Church that ended several decades before Henry VII became king. *Reconquista* refers to Christian kingdoms reconquering Spain and Portugal from the Muslims.

12. D For this question, A, B and C are incorrect because none of these people are Czech. Henry VI was an English king, Hildegard of Bingen was a German nun, and Joan of Arc was a French girl.

13. B Ferdinand and Isabella were avid Catholics who wanted to create religious unity in Spain. Jews and Muslims were members of different religious groups.

TEST-TAKING 

For Question 13: Although most test questions ask students about what they have learned from the text or class, common sense can help them arrive at the correct answers, too. Remind them to consider what they know about the topic and then read the answer choices.

Critical Thinking

14. D Students can eliminate A and B because the battle at Orléans was fought later in the war, after Joan of Arc got involved. Both other battles shown were fought in territory controlled by England. Crécy was fought long before Agincourt.

Section 3 *(pp. 348–351)*

9. What new architectural style appeared in the twelfth century?
   - **A** Neoclassic
   - **B** Romanesque
   - **C** Baroque
   - **D** Gothic

10. Who wrote most of the troubadour poetry?
   - **A** Clergy
   - **B** Nobles and knights
   - **C** Peasants
   - **D** Medieval university students

Section 4 *(pp. 352–359)*

11. Which of the following was an accomplishment of King Henry VII of England?
   - **A** A strong royal government
   - **B** A *Reconquista*
   - **C** The *taille*
   - **D** The Great Schism

12. Who led the Czech reformers during the Great Schism of the Catholic Church?
   - **A** Henry VI
   - **B** Hildegard of Bingen
   - **C** Joan of Arc
   - **D** John Hus

13. Why did Isabella and Ferdinand expel Jews and Muslims from Spain?
   - **A** For control of their land
   - **B** For religious unity
   - **C** For control of trade
   - **D** For racial purity

Critical Thinking

Directions: Choose the best answers to the following questions.

Use the following map and your knowledge of world history to answer question 14.

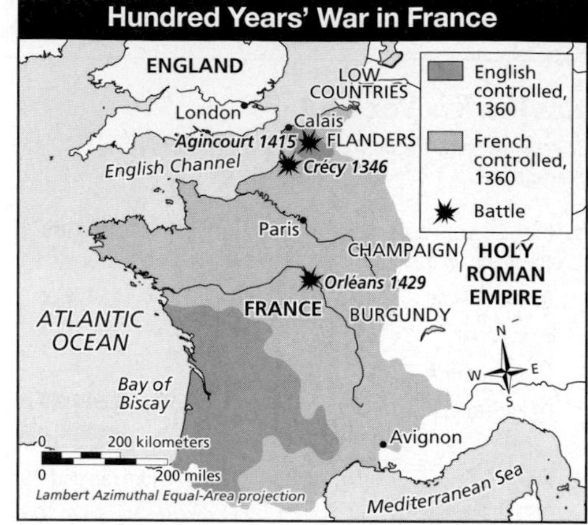

14. Where did the first battle of the Hundred Years' War take place?
   - **A** In Burgundy
   - **B** In central France
   - **C** In northern France
   - **D** In English territory

15. What is one reason for the growth of medieval cities?
   - **A** The spread of the Black Death
   - **B** The decline of the manorial system
   - **C** The revival of trade
   - **D** The decline of feudalism

16. Which of the following factors was key to the rise of commercial capitalism?
   - **A** The manorial system
   - **B** Craft guilds
   - **C** Cities
   - **D** A money economy

Need Extra Help?

If You Missed Questions . . .	9	10	11	12	13	14	15	16
Go to Page . . .	348	351	358	355	358	364	338	338

GO ON

15. C Trade was crucial to the revival of cities. Students should quickly eliminate A, as it is obviously wrong. B and D are incorrect because the revival of cities contributed to the decline of feudalism and the manorial system.

16. D The money economy resulted from the revival of trade and demand for coins. Banks and trading companies were also keys to the rise of capitalism. The growth of cities and craft guilds followed the rise of capitalism. The manorial system was a different type of economic system.

17. What issue was at the heart of the Investiture Controversy?

A Control of the Inquisition
B Supremacy of Church or state
C Location of the papal residence
D Anti-Semitism

Base your answer to question 18 on the following illustration and on your knowledge of world history.

18. What structural innovation illustrated by this drawing allowed for the support of a heavy vaulted ceiling in a Gothic cathedral?

A Barrel vaults
B Cross vaults
C Flying buttresses
D Basilicas

Document-Based Questions

Directions: Analyze the document and answer the short-answer questions that follow the document. Base your answers on the document and on your knowledge of world history.

A twelfth-century English monk described his abbey's relics:

> *"There is kept there a thing more precious than gold . . . the right arm of St. Oswald . . . This we have seen with our own eyes and have kissed, and have handled with our own hands. . . . There are kept here also part of his ribs and of the soil on which he fell."*

19. What made these objects "relics"?

20. Why would a relic be considered "a thing more precious than gold"?

Extended Response

21. Explain the economic effects of the Black Death.

History ONLINE
For additional test practice, use Self-Check Quizzes—Chapter 10 at glencoe.com.

Need Extra Help?

If You Missed Questions . . .	17	18	19	20	21
Go to Page . . .	342	365	365	365	353

STOP

Document-Based Questions

19. They were connected with a saint and therefore considered worthy of worship.

20. People believed relics could heal or produce miracles; gold could not.

Extended Response

21. Trade declined. The decline in population also caused a shortage of workers, raising the cost of labor and giving serfs bargaining power with landlords. Landlords were paying higher labor costs and receiving less income from rents. As a result, serfs could bargain with landlords to allow them to pay rent instead of services, effectively freeing themselves from serfdom. The decline in population also lowered demand for food, resulting in falling prices.

TEST-TAKING 

For extended response questions, remind students of the importance of budgeting their time to allow them a chance to revise and proofread their essays.

17. B Students should recall that the Investiture controversy concerned the question of whether kings or the pope had the right to appoint church officials and was therefore a question of the supremacy of Church or state.

18. C Students should be able to eliminate A and B because the image does not show a vaulted ceiling. D can be eliminated because basilicas were an older style of building from Roman times. Therefore, C is correct.

History ONLINE
Introduce students to chapter content and key terms by having them access the Chapter 10 Overview at glencoe.com.

Need Extra Help?
Have students refer to the pages listed if they miss any of the questions.

CHAPTER 11 Planning Guide

Key to Ability Levels	
BL Below Level	**AL** Above Level
OL On Level	**ELL** English Language Learners

Key to Teaching Resources	
Print Material	DVD
CD-ROM	Transparency

Levels				Resources		Chapter Opener	Section 1	Section 2	Section 3	Chapter Assess
BL	OL	AL	ELL							
FOCUS										
BL	OL	AL	ELL	Transparency	**Daily Focus Skills Transparencies**		11-1	11-2	11-3	
TEACH										
BL	OL		ELL	Print	**Reading Skills Activity, URB**			p. 205		
	OL	AL		Print	**Historical Analysis Skills Activity, URB**				p. 206	
BL	OL	AL	ELL	Print	**Differentiated Instruction Activity, URB**				p. 207	
	OL		ELL	Print	**English Learner Activity, URB**		p. 209			
BL	OL	AL	ELL	Print	**Content Vocabulary Activity, URB***		p. 211		p. 211	
BL	OL	AL	ELL	Print	**Academic Vocabulary Activity, URB**				p. 213	
BL	OL	AL	ELL	Print	**Skills Reinforcement Activity, URB**				p. 215	
	OL	AL		Print	**Critical Thinking Skills Activity, URB**			p. 216		
	OL	AL		Print	**History and Geography Activity, URB**		p. 217			
	OL	AL	ELL	Print	**Mapping History Activity, URB**			p. 219		
BL	OL	AL		Print	**Historical Significance Activity, URB**		p. 220			
BL	OL	AL	ELL	Print	**Cooperative Learning Activity, URB**			p. 221		
	OL	AL	ELL	Print	**History Simulation Activity, URB**				p. 223	
BL	OL	AL	ELL	Print	**Time Line Activity, URB**			p. 225		
	OL	AL		Print	**Linking Past and Present Activity, URB**			p. 226		
BL	OL	AL		Print	**People in World History Activity, URB**			p. 228	p. 227	
BL	OL	AL	ELL	Print	**Primary Source Reading, URB**		p. 229			
	OL	AL		Print	**Enrichment Activity, URB**			p. 234		
BL	OL	AL	ELL	Print	**World Art and Music Activity, URB**		p. 231			
BL	OL		ELL	Print	**Guided Reading Activities, URB***		p. 236	p. 237	p. 238	
BL	OL		ELL	Print	**Reading Essentials and Note-Taking Guide***		p. 122	p. 124	p. 127	
BL	OL	AL	ELL	Print	**Differentiated Instruction for the World History Classroom**	✓	✓	✓	✓	✓

Note: Please refer to the *Unit Resource Book: New Patterns of Civilization* for this chapter's URB materials.

* Also available in Spanish

- Interactive Lesson Planner
- Interactive Teacher Edition
- Fully editable blackline masters
- Section Spotlight Videos Launch
- Differentiated Lesson Plans
- Printable reports of daily assignments
- Standards Tracking System

Levels				Resources	Chapter Opener	Section 1	Section 2	Section 3	Chapter Assess
BL	OL	AL	ELL						
TEACH *(continued)*									
BL	OL	AL	ELL	StudentWorks™ Plus DVD	✓	✓	✓	✓	✓
BL	OL	AL	ELL	Vocabulary PuzzleMaker CD-ROM	✓	✓	✓	✓	✓
Teacher Resources				Building Academic Vocabulary	✓	✓	✓	✓	✓
				Writer's Guidebook		p. 12	p. 47		
				Strategies for Success	✓	✓	✓	✓	✓
				Outline Map Resource Book	✓	✓	✓	✓	✓
				Presentation Plus! with MindJogger DVD	✓	✓	✓	✓	✓
ASSESS									
BL	OL	AL	ELL	Section Quizzes and Chapter Tests*		p. 129	p. 130	p. 131	p. 133
BL	OL	AL	ELL	Authentic Assessment With Rubrics	✓	✓	✓	✓	✓
BL	OL	AL	ELL	Standardized Test Practice Workbook	✓	✓	✓	✓	✓
BL	OL	AL	ELL	*ExamView® Assessment Suite* CD-ROM		11-1	11-2	11-3	Ch. 11
BL	OL	AL	ELL	Interactive Tutor Self-Assessment CD-ROM		11-1	11-2	11-3	
CLOSE									
BL			ELL	Reteaching Activity, URB				p. 233	
BL	OL		ELL	Reading and Study Skills Foldables™	✓	✓	✓	✓	✓

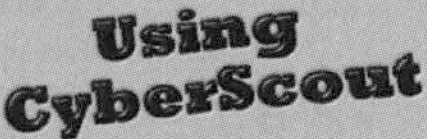

Research Using *Subject Area*

Technology Product

CyberScout is a convenient and dynamic search engine that provides several easy ways to locate information outside the McGraw-Hill Learning Network. CyberScout only searches Web sites that have been reviewed by teachers, so the information students find is always appropriate and accurate. After students learn to use CyberScout, they will be able to

- research topics and issues in world history using CyberScout;
- exercise research and study skills;
- practice writing skills.

Steps

- From the McGraw-Hill Learning Network home page (www.mhln.com), click on **For Students.**
- Choose **CyberScout** below **Homework Help.**
- Click on a subject area link to narrow the search.
- The CyberScout page will display a set of results.
- Drill down by continuing to click result links until you find a Web site of interest.
- Click on the link to reach the Web site.
- Students will be redirected to the Web site in a new window.
- Students navigate through the chosen Web site to gain information on their topic and take notes.

History ONLINE

	Student	Teacher	Parent
Beyond the Textbook	●	●	●
Chapter Overviews	●	●	●
Time Current Events	●		●
ePuzzles and Games	●		●
Concepts in Motion	●		●
Literature Connections		●	
Multi-Language Glossaries	●		●
Online Student Edition	●	●	●
Self-Check Quizzes	●		●
Student Web Activities	●		●
Study Central ™	●		●
Teaching Today		●	
Vocabulary eFlashcards	●		●
Web Activity Lesson Plans		●	

- **Timed Readings Plus in Social Studies** helps students increase their reading rate and fluency while maintaining comprehension. The 400-word passages are similar to those found on state and national assessments.
- **Reading in the Content Area: Social Studies** concentrates on six essential reading skills that help students better comprehend what they read. The book includes 75 high-interest nonfiction passages written at increasing levels of difficulty.
- **Reading Social Studies** includes strategic reading instruction and vocabulary support in Social Studies content for both ELLs and native speakers of English.

www.jamestowneducation.com

The following videotape programs are available from Glencoe as supplements to Chapter 11:

- Machu Picchu: City In the Sky (ISBN 0-76-700143-5)
- The Maya (ISBN 0-76-700697-6)
- Mexico: A Story of Courage and Conquest (ISBN 0-76-701622-X)

To order, call Glencoe at 1-800-334-7344. To find classroom resources to accompany many of these videos, check the following home pages:

A&E Television: www.aetv.com

The History Channel: www.historychannel.com

Index to National Geographic Magazine:

The following articles relate to this chapter:

- "The Unexpected Canyon," by Virginia Morell, January 2006
- "The Dawn of Maya Gods and Kings," by William Saturno, January 2006
- "Inca Rescue," by Guillermo A. Cock, May 2002

National Geographic Society Products To order the following, call National Geographic at 1-800-368-2728:

- *National Geographic Atlas of the World* (Book).
- *Native Americans: Eastern Woodlands and Plains* (PicturePack).
- *Ancient Civilizations: Middle and South America* (CD-ROM).

Access National Geographic's new, dynamic MapMachine Web site and other geography resources at:

www.nationalgeographic.com

www.nationalgeographic.com/maps

GLENCOE BOOKLINK 3

Use this database to search more than 30,000 titles to create a customized reading list for your students.

- Reading lists can be organized by students' reading level, author, genre, theme, or area of interest.
- The database provides Degrees of Reading Power™ (DRP) and Lexile™ readability scores for all selections.
- A brief summary of each selection is included.

Leveled reading suggestions for this chapter:

For students at a Grade 8 reading level:
- ***Secrets in Stone: All about Maya Hieroglyphs,*** by Laurie Coulter

For students at a Grade 9 reading level:
- ***Inca Mummies: Sacrifices and Rituals,*** by Michael Martin

For students at a Grade 10 reading level:
- ***Aztecs and Spaniards: Cortes and the Conquest of Mexico,*** by Albert Marrin

For students at a Grade 11 reading level:
- ***The Aztecs,*** by Barbara L. Beck

For students at a Grade 12 reading level:
- ***The Ancient Maya,*** by C.A. Burland

Introducing
CHAPTER 11

Focus

MAKING CONNECTIONS
What can ruins teach us about civilization?

Ask students to look at the photograph and examine the details. Discuss how the Maya and Toltec cultures were interested in astronomy. Ask students to brainstorm reasons for this interest, for example, observing the movement of the moon, stars, and planets may have helped these people determine the best times to plant their crops. Then discuss what these ruins can tell us about how the people lived. Have students comment on what a ruin of their school building might tell future archaeologists. Mention that while ruins can provide a window onto a civilization, archaeologists have to examine data carefully to avoid drawing incorrect conclusions.

Teach

The Big Ideas

As students study the chapter, remind them to consider the section-based Big Ideas included in each section's Guide to Reading. The **Essential Questions** in the activities below tie in to the Big Ideas and help students think about and understand important chapter concepts. In addition, the Hands-on Chapter Projects with their culminating activities relate the content from each section to the Big Ideas. These activities build on each other as students progress through the chapter. Section activities culminate in the wrap-up activity on the Visual Summary page.

CHAPTER 11
The Americas 400–1500

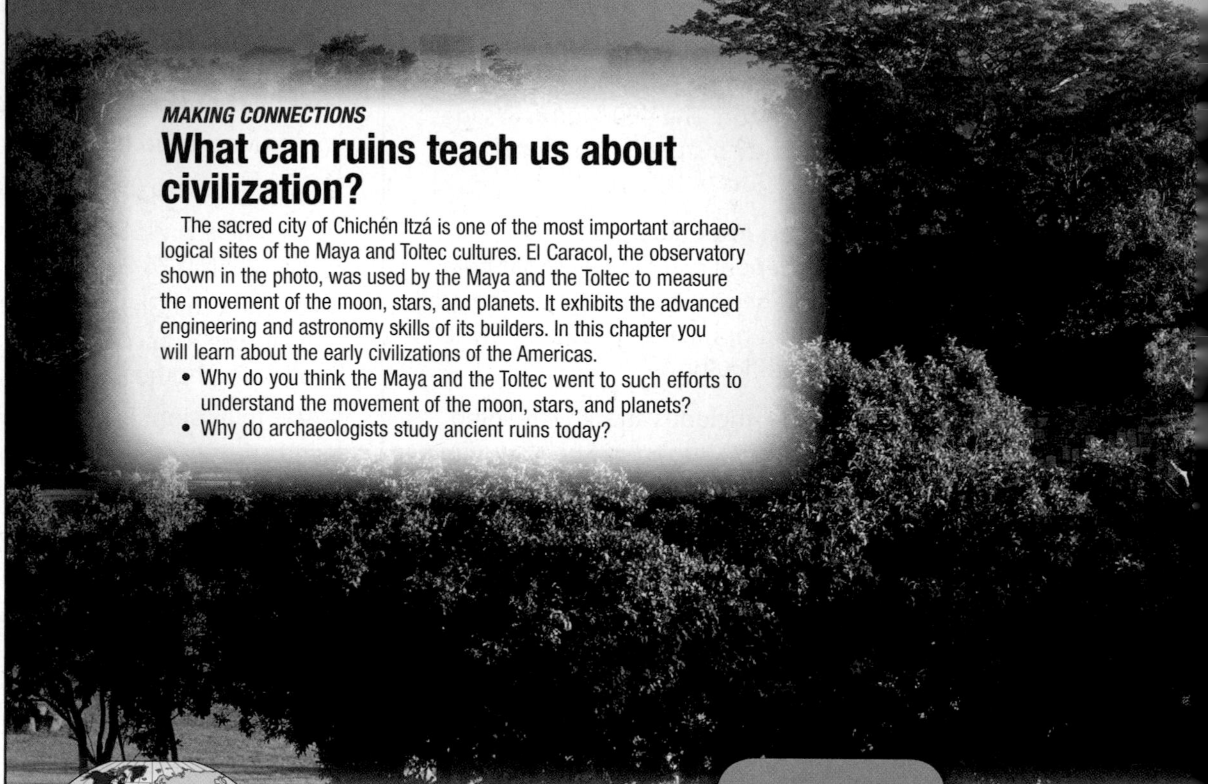

MAKING CONNECTIONS
What can ruins teach us about civilization?

The sacred city of Chichén Itzá is one of the most important archaeological sites of the Maya and Toltec cultures. El Caracol, the observatory shown in the photo, was used by the Maya and the Toltec to measure the movement of the moon, stars, and planets. It exhibits the advanced engineering and astronomy skills of its builders. In this chapter you will learn about the early civilizations of the Americas.

- Why do you think the Maya and the Toltec went to such efforts to understand the movement of the moon, stars, and planets?
- Why do archaeologists study ancient ruins today?

THE AMERICAS
- c. 3000 B.C. People move into North America from Asia
- c. 250 B.C. City of Teotihuacán established
- c. A.D. 300 Maya civilization begins to flourish 

1000 B.C. — A.D. 400

THE WORLD
- c. 2000 B.C. Trade thrives between Egypt and Nubia 
- A.D. 100 Christianity spreads in the Roman Empire

366

The Peoples of North America

Essential Question: How does geography influence a people's way of living? *(Influences might include climate, which affects people, animals, and plants; natural resources, such as water sources or minerals; available building materials, such as wood or stone; food sources for hunter gatherers or land suitable for farming.)* Point out that in Section 1 students will learn how early peoples who came to North America established unique ways of living suited to the particular regions. **OL**

Early Civilizations in Mesoamerica

Essential Question: Why might several successive civilizations develop in a certain area? *(An area might have the natural resources needed to support a large number of people and that make it a desirable place to live; the location might be strategic for trade or defense.)* Point out that in Section 2 students will learn about several early civilizations that rose and fell in parts of Mexico and Central America and discover how earlier civilizations influenced those that followed in the same location. **OL**

Introducing
CHAPTER 11

More About the Photo

Visual Literacy El Caracol is located in the sacred city of Chichén Itzá on the Yucatán Penisula in present-day Mexico. The name *El Caracol* means "the snail," which refers to the curving staircase within the building. The building's shape resembles that of more modern observatories. Although the people who used the building clearly used it to observe the moon, planets, and stars, scientists have found no evidence that they used instruments to do so.

c. A.D. 700 Hopewell people shift to full-time farming

A.D. 825 Al-Khowarizmi advances use of Hindu numbers and algebra in Arab world

1440 Inca leader Pachacuti launches campaign of conquest

A.D. 950 — 1500

FOLDABLES Study Organizer

Organizing Create a Layered-Look Book to organize facts about the Inca. Read the related text and conduct research to learn more about the political structure, social structure, and buildings and culture of the Inca.

The Inca
Political Structure
Social Structure
Building and Culture

History ONLINE
Chapter Overview—Visit glencoe.com to preview Chapter 11.

FOLDABLES Study Organizer — Dinah Zike's Foldables

Dinah Zike's Foldables are three-dimensional, interactive graphic organizers that help students practice basic writing skills, review vocabulary terms, and identify main ideas. Instructions for creating and using Foldables can be found in the Appendix at the end of this book and in the *Dinah Zike's Reading and Study Skills Foldables* booklet.

History ONLINE

Introduce students to chapter content and key terms by having them access the Chapter 11 Overview at glencoe.com.

Early Civilizations in South America

Essential Question: How does a particular civilization become dominant in a region? *(Students may suggest a large population, military might, natural resources that allow a civilization to control a region's food supply or trade, a strategic location, or advanced technology.)* Point out that in Section 3 students will learn how the Incas developed a well-organized and militaristic empire that came to dominate a vast area along the western coast of South America. **OL**

D Differentiated Instruction

Advanced Learners Have students review the U.S. Constitution to find portions that relate to the Iroquois Constitution. Ask them to present their findings in a chart. AL

W Writing Support

Persuasive Writing Have students read the description of Iroquois history that led to the formation of the Iroquois League. Ask them to write a short speech that Deganawida or Hiawatha might have given to persuade their people of the need for the league. OL

CRITICAL THINKING SKILLS

Answers:

1. Longhouses were about 20 feet wide by 20 feet high and varied in length. They were made of wood and bark and housed an extended family.
2. The Iroquois League was created to "shelter" the five nations from harm. Like families in a longhouse, the members of the Iroquois League had a bond to one another.

Cities began to appear, some of them containing 10,000 people or more. At the site of **Cahokia** (kuh•HOH•kee•uh), near the modern city of East St. Louis, Illinois, archaeologists found a burial mound over 98 feet (30 m) high. It had a base larger than that of the Great Pyramid in Egypt. Between A.D. 850 and 1150, Cahokia flourished and served as the seat of government. For reasons unknown, Cahokia collapsed during the 1200s.

To the northeast of the Mississippian culture were people known as the **Iroquois** (IHR•uh•KWOY). The Iroquois lived in villages that consisted of **longhouses** surrounded by wooden fences for protection. Each longhouse, built of wooden poles covered with sheets of bark, was 150 to 200 feet (46 to 61 m) in length and housed about a dozen families.

Iroquois men hunted deer, bear, caribou, and small animals like rabbits and beaver. They were also warriors who protected the community. Women owned the dwellings, gathered wild plants, and grew crops. The most important crops were the "three sisters"—corn, beans, and squash. In addition, women cooked, made baskets, and took care of the children.

W Wars were common, especially among groups of Iroquois who lived in much of present-day Pennsylvania, New York, and parts of southern Canada. Legend holds that sometime during the 1500s, the Iroquois peoples were nearly torn apart by warfare. Deganawida, an elder of one Iroquois group, appeared and preached the need for peace.

One who listened was Hiawatha, a member of the Onondaga (AH•nuhn•DAW•guh) group. From the combined efforts of Deganawida and Hiawatha came the Great Peace, which created an alliance of five groups called the Iroquois League.

A council of representatives, a group of 50 Iroquois leaders, known as the Grand Council met regularly to settle differences. Representatives were chosen in a special way. Each Iroquois group was made up of **clans,** groups of related families. The

INFOGRAPHICS

The Iroquois League

According to Iroquois legend, the five nations of the Iroquois League came together sometime during the 1500s after a period of warfare. The members of the Iroquois League referred to their union by a word which means "people building a longhouse." In other words, they saw the Iroquois League as an enormous longhouse that stretched across the five nations and sheltered its members.

D League members were joined together by common laws. The Iroquois Constitution includes guidelines on religious tolerance, impeachment, succession, illness of a leader, treason, dissolution, declaration of war, emigration, asylum, and rights of foreign nations. In 1754 Benjamin Franklin used the Iroquois League as a model for a Plan of Union for the British colonies. Thomas Jefferson later referred to these similarities when he called the United States Constitution a "tree of peace," the symbol of the Iroquois League.

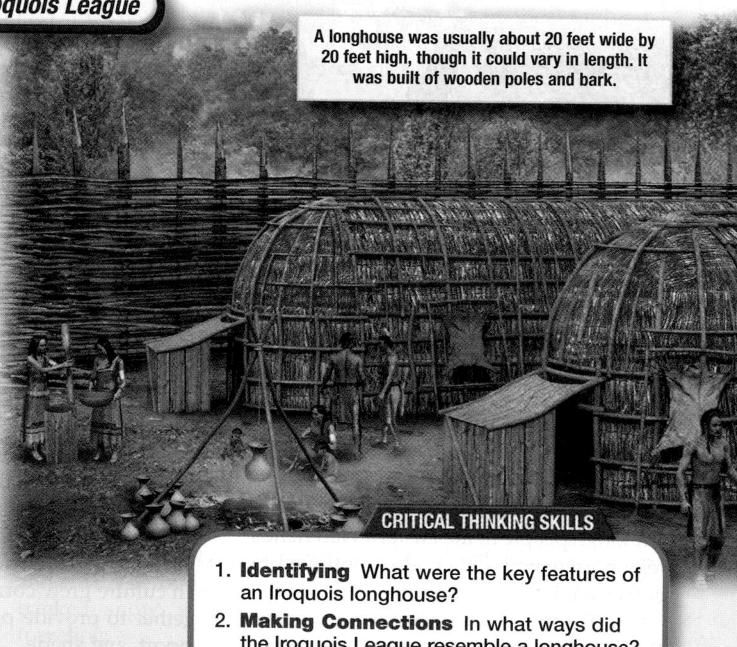

A longhouse was usually about 20 feet wide by 20 feet high, though it could vary in length. It was built of wooden poles and bark.

CRITICAL THINKING SKILLS

1. **Identifying** What were the key features of an Iroquois longhouse?
2. **Making Connections** In what ways did the Iroquois League resemble a longhouse?

Hands-On Chapter Project Step 1

Creating a Thematic Map of Early American Civilizations

Groups of students will identify the accomplishments of early American cultures on illustrated thematic maps.

Step 1: Gathering Information

Essential Question: What were the characteristics of early American civilizations?

Directions: Tell students to identify characteristics of different groups of North Americans as they read the section. Point out how the map on page 369 links groups with different regions. Suggest that students keep a folder of ideas on each group they study. They may begin to think of possible themes for their map, such as trade, religion, agriculture, or art and architecture.

Summarizing: Allow time for groups to share what they learned about the Section 1 Big Idea while searching for map material. Groups will continue to gather material as they study Section 2 and will choose a theme and begin to plan possible visuals. OL

(Chapter Project is continued in Section 2.)

women of each clan singled out a well-respected woman as the clan mother. The clan mothers, in turn, chose the male members of the Grand Council. Much was expected of these men—patience and firmness, but also a tenderness for their people and calm deliberation. The Grand Council, an experiment in democracy, brought the Iroquois a new way to deal with their problems.

Peoples of the Great Plains

West of the Mississippi River basin, the **Plains Indians** cultivated beans, corn, and squash along the river valleys of the eastern Great Plains. Every summer, the men left their villages to hunt buffalo, a very important animal to the Plains culture. Hunters would work together to frighten a herd of buffalo, causing them to stampede over a cliff.

The buffalo served many uses for Plains peoples. They ate the meat, used the skins for clothing, and made tools from the bones. By stretching buffalo skins over wooden **C** poles, they made circular tents called **tepees.** Tepees provided excellent shelter; they were warm in winter and cool in summer.

Peoples of the Southwest: The Anasazi

The Southwest covers the territory of present-day New Mexico, Arizona, Utah, and Colorado. Conditions are dry, but there is sufficient rain in some areas for farming. The **Anasazi** (AH•nuh•SAH•zee) peoples established an extensive farming society there.

Between A.D. 500 and 1200, the Anasazi used canals and earthen dams to turn parts of the desert into fertile gardens. They were skilled at making baskets and beautifully crafted pottery. They used stone and **adobe** (sun-dried brick) to build **pueblos,** multistoried structures that housed many people.

At Chaco Canyon in northwestern New Mexico, they built an elaborate center for their civilization. At the heart of Chaco Canyon was Pueblo Bonito. This was a large complex that contained some 800 rooms housing more than 1,000 people. The Pueblo Bonita complex included communal rooms where people assembled to perform religious rituals. This flourishing center could not survive a series of droughts that occurred over a 50-year period. Finally the Anasazi had to abandon the center.

The Anasazi culture itself did not die. To the north in southern Colorado, a large community had formed at **Mesa Verde** (MAY•suh•VEHR•dee). Today, this is a national park in the United States. Groups of Anasazi there built a remarkable series of buildings in the recesses of the cliff walls. However, the Anasazi abandoned the settlement in the late 1200s because of a prolonged drought.

✓Reading Check **Explaining** What may have led hunters to cross the land bridge to North America?

SECTION 1 REVIEW

Vocabulary

1. **Explain** the significance of: Bering Strait, survive, Inuit, temporary, Gulf of Mexico, Hopewell, Cahokia, Iroquois, longhouse, clan, Plains Indians, tepee, Anasazi, adobe, pueblo, Mesa Verde.

Main Idea

2. **Identify** some reasons why early peoples migrated from place to place.
3. **Describe** the Cahokia site of the Hopewell peoples.
4. **Summarize** the features of the Anasazi culture. Use a graph like the one below to highlight the features.

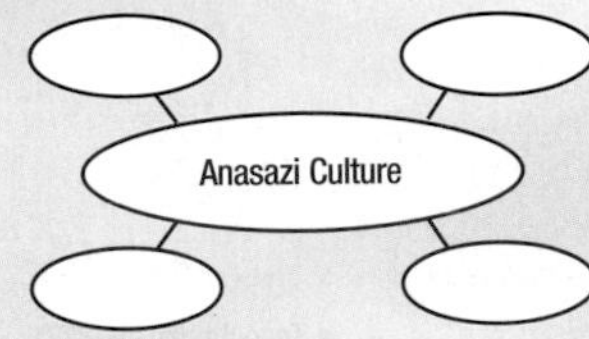

Critical Thinking

5. **The BIG Idea** **Determining Cause and Effect** What was the relationship between early peoples and their environment?
6. **Evaluating** Why was the Iroquois League politically significant?
7. **Analyzing Visuals** Examine the Iroquois village pictured on page 370. What purpose do you think the fences served?

Writing About History

8. **Expository Writing** Identify the leadership roles that women took in the Iroquois society and compare these roles with women's roles in American society today. Write a one-page comparison after doing your research.

History ONLINE
For help with the concepts in this section of *Glencoe World History*, go to glencoe.com and click Study Central™.

C Critical Thinking

Comparing and Contrasting
Ask: What were the similarities and differences among longhouses, tepees, and pueblos? *(All were forms of housing; longhouses and pueblos housed large numbers; longhouses were made of wood, tepees of buffalo hide, and pueblos of adobe.)* **OL**

Answer: pursuit of herds of bison and caribou

Assess

History ONLINE
Study Central provides summaries, interactive games, and online graphic organizers to help students review content.

Close

Determining Cause and Effect **Ask:** Why did the North American cultures each establish a unique way of living? *(differences in their environments)* **OL**

Answers

1. Definitions for the vocabulary words are found in the section and in the Glossary.
2. following food sources
3. near present-day East St. Louis, Illinois; had a burial mound over 98 feet high with a base larger than that of the Great Pyramid in Egypt
4. used canals, dams for irrigation; built pueblos of stone and adobe; buildings in cliff walls; skilled at making baskets and pottery
5. followed food sources and used them for meat, clothing, and tools; adapted to the land and the seasons; learned to use the resources of the land to establish their communities
6. ended a period of warfare between the Iroquois groups; may also have influenced early U.S. political leaders
7. Fences probably provided protection, possibly from animals, other nations, or European settlers.
8. Answers should describe the Iroquois women's role as clan leaders who chose male members of the Grand Council and compare this to American women's roles today as leaders in various settings.

R Reading Strategy

Organizing Have students create a chart to identify the imports and exports of Teotihuacán. **Ask:** What export was Teotihuacán most known for? *(obsidian tools)* **BL**

D Differentiated Instruction

Visual/Spatial Have students look at the map to see how far trade from Teotihuacán reached. Ask students to calculate the distance between Teotihuacán and other places. **OL**

✓Reading Check

Answer: Mexico and Central America; the Olmec, Maya, Toltec, and Aztec

Geography SKILLS

Answers:

1. Toltec, Aztec
2. Lakes and other sources of water may have provided protection, as did the mountains surrounding the area; cities located along the Gulf of Mexico, such as Veracruz, used water for transportation.

Teotihuacán was also a busy center for trade. In scores of workshops throughout the city, skilled artisans made tools, weapons, pottery, and jewelry. Especially famous were their obsidian tools. Obsidian, a volcanic glass, was prized in Mesoamerica. It was used in tools, mirrors, and the knives with razor-sharp blades used in human and animal sacrifices. Archaeologists **estimate** that there were 400 obsidian workshops in the city.

R The goods made in Teotihuacán were shipped to Central America, Mexico, and even southwestern North America. In return, the city's inhabitants received luxury items and the raw materials, such as shells and bird feathers, used in their crafts.

Sometime during the eighth century, for reasons yet unknown, the city's power declined. Eventually the ruling class left the city and around A.D. 800, the city was destroyed and abandoned.

✓Reading Check **Explaining** Where was Mesoamerica, and who were some of its first inhabitants?

The Maya and the Toltec

MAIN IDEA The Maya and the Toltec ruled Mesoamerica for nearly nine centuries.

HISTORY & YOU How would dividing each year into 18 months affect you? Read to learn about the Maya calendar.

Far to the east of Teotihuacán, on the **Yucatán Peninsula,** another major civilization had arisen. This was the civilization of the **Maya,** which flourished between A.D. 300 and 900. It was one of the most sophisticated civilizations in the Americas.

The Maya built splendid temples and pyramids and developed a complicated calendar as **accurate** as any in existence in the world at that time. The Maya were a farming people who cleared the dense rain forests, developed farming, and centered their culture in city-states. Maya civilization included much of Central America and southern Mexico.

Sometime around 800, the Maya civilization in the central Yucatán Peninsula began

D

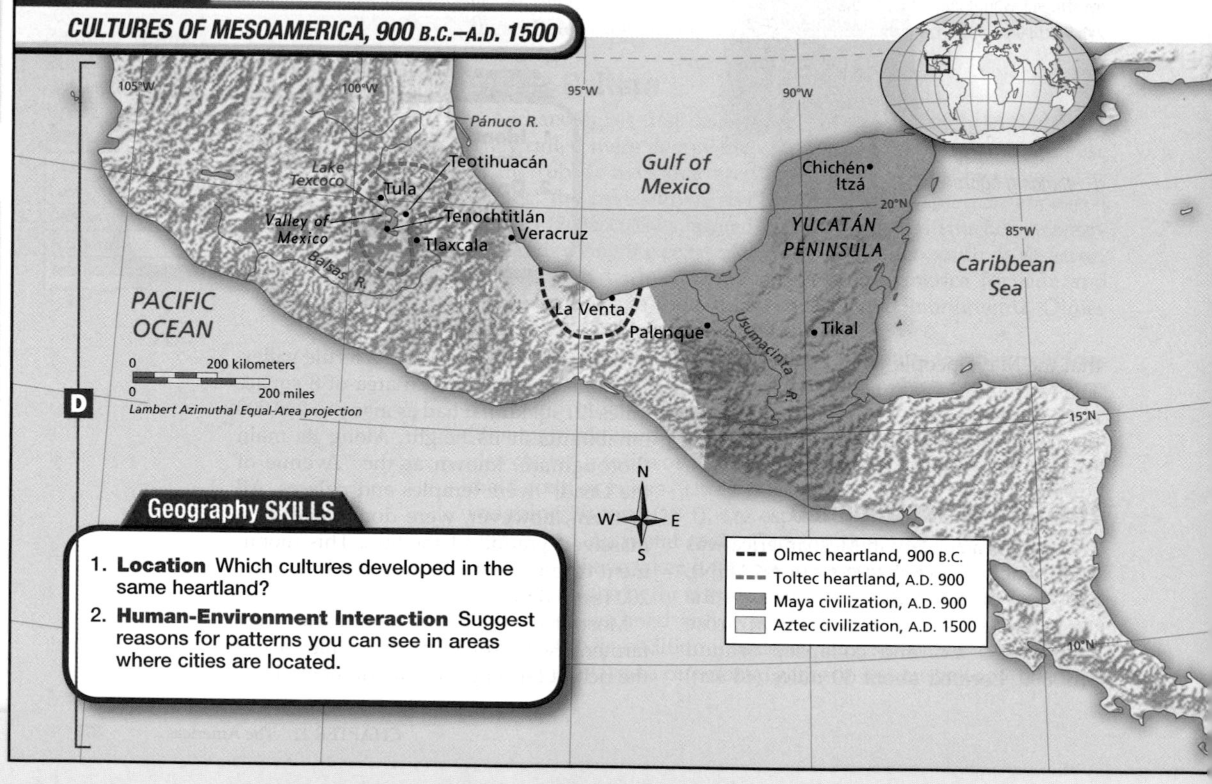

Geography SKILLS

1. **Location** Which cultures developed in the same heartland?
2. **Human-Environment Interaction** Suggest reasons for patterns you can see in areas where cities are located.

Hands-On Chapter Project Step 2

Creating a Thematic Map of Early American Civilizations

Step 2: Choosing a Theme In addition to gathering information, groups will choose a theme for their map and begin to collect visuals.

Directions: Tell groups to use the Section 2 Big Idea as a guide to gathering more information for their maps. Instruct them to choose a theme for their maps and consider how they will illustrate it. Have them begin gathering illustrations that are pertinent to the theme. They may look for visuals in books, in magazines, or on the Internet, create their own, or do a combination.

Summarizing: Allow time for groups to share what they learned about the Section 2 Big Idea while searching for map material. Remind them that they will continue to gather material when they study Section 3 and will also create their maps. **OL**

(Chapter Project is continued in Section 3.)

to decline. Why did this happen? Explanations include invasion, internal revolt, or a volcanic eruption. A more recent theory is that overuse of the land led to reduced crop yields.

Whatever the case, cities like Tikal and Palenque were abandoned and covered by dense jungle growth. They were not rediscovered until the nineteenth and twentieth centuries.

Political and Social Structures

Maya cities were built around a central pyramid topped by a shrine to the gods. Nearby were other temples, palaces, and a sacred ball court. Some scholars believe that over 100,000 inhabitants may have lived in urban centers such as **Tikal** in present-day Guatemala.

Maya civilization was composed of city-states, each governed by a hereditary ruling class. These Maya city-states were often at war with each other. Ordinary soldiers who were captured in battle became slaves. Captured nobles and war leaders were used for human sacrifice.

Rulers of the Maya city-states claimed to be descended from the gods. The Maya rulers were helped by nobles and a class of scribes who may also have been priests. In addition, Maya society contained peasants and townspeople who worked as skilled artisans, officials, and merchants.

Most of the Maya people were peasant farmers. They lived on tiny plots or on terraced hills in the highlands. Houses were built of adobe and thatch. There was a fairly clear-cut division of labor. Men did the fighting and hunting; women, the homemaking and raising of children. Women also made cornmeal, the basic food of much of the population. The Maya also cultivated cacao trees, which were the source of chocolate. Chocolate was used as a beverage by the upper classes. Cocoa beans, the fruit of the cacao tree, were used as money in markets throughout the region. C1

Crucial to Maya civilization was its spiritual perspective. For the Maya, all of life was in the hands of divine powers. The name of their supreme god was Itzamna (eet•SAWM•nuh) or "Lizard House." Gods were ranked in order of importance. Some, like the jaguar god of night, were evil rather than good.

Like other ancient civilizations in Mesoamerica, the Maya practiced human sacrifice as a way to appease the gods. Human sacrifices were also used for special ceremonial occasions. When a male heir was presented to the throne, war captives were tortured and then beheaded. In A.D. 790, one Maya ruler took his troops into battle to gain prisoners for a celebration honoring his son.

Writings and Calendar

The Maya created a sophisticated writing system based on **hieroglyphs** or pictures. Unfortunately, the Spanish conquerors of the sixteenth century had little respect for the Mayan language and made no effort to decipher it. Instead, the Spaniards assumed the writings were evil or of no value. As one Spanish bishop wrote:

PRIMARY SOURCE C2

> "We found a large number of books in these characters and, as they contained nothing in which there were not to be seen superstition and lies of the devil, we burned them all, which they regretted to an amazing degree, and which caused them much affliction."
>
> —Bishop Diego de Landa, sixteenth century

When the Spanish colonized the Americas, they repeated this behavior over and over. They would apply their own religious views to the native civilizations with which they came in contact. The Spaniards' subsequent destruction of religious objects, and sometimes entire cities, helped bring an end to these civilizations.

The Maya wrote on bark, folding it like an accordian, then covering the outside with thin plaster. Four of these books have survived. Maya writing was also carved onto clay, jade, bone, shells, and stone monuments.

Mayan hieroglyphs remained a mystery for centuries. Then, scholars discovered that many passages contained symbols that recorded dates in the Maya calendar.

History ONLINE
Student Web Activity—
Visit glencoe.com and complete the activity on early civilizations in the Americas.

C1 Critical Thinking

Making Inferences Invite students to think about the properties of the money they use. **Ask:** Why would the Maya use cocoa beans for money? *(Possible Answer: The beans were a valuable commodity and were easy to carry; people could agree that certain goods were worth a certain number of beans.)* AL

C2 Critical Thinking

Analyzing Primary Sources Have students read the primary source excerpt by Bishop de Landa. **Ask:** What do the reactions of the bishop and the Maya tell you about the two cultures? *(The Spanish did not understand or respect the Maya culture; the Maya placed a high value on their books.)* OL

Differentiated Instruction

Leveled Activities

BL Guided Reading Activity, URB p. 237

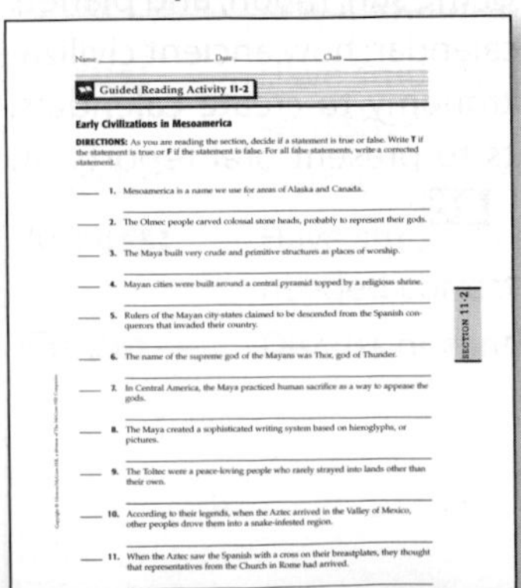

OL Critical Thinking Skills Activity, URB p. 216

AL Enrichment Activity, URB p. 234

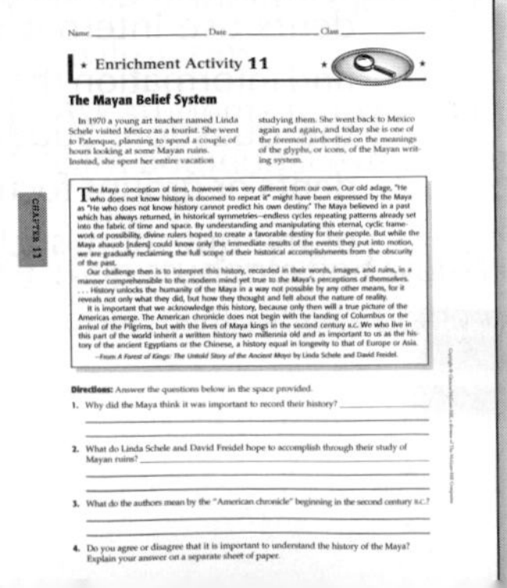

ELL Mapping History Activity, URB p. 219

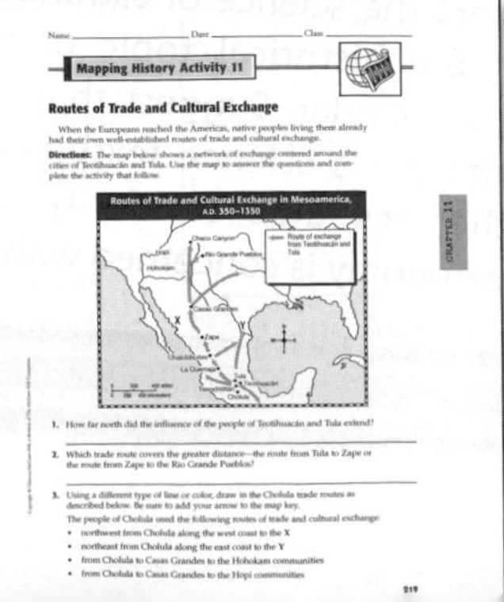

R Reading Strategy

Making Connections Have students discuss similarities and differences between the education of Aztec children and their own education. **OL**

W Writing Support

Personal Writing Ask students to write an essay expressing their reaction to the midwife's statements on the birth of boys and girls in Aztec society. Invite them to include a sentence that a midwife might have said when they were born and discuss how this reflects cultural differences. **OL**

DOCUMENT-BASED QUESTIONS

Answers:

1. The girl who is weaving is 14 years old, as shown by the 14 dots in the bottom section of the page.
2. Aztec women were responsible for housework, weaving textiles, and raising children, so they were taught those skills as young girls. Aztec boys were taught skills that would help them provide and protect.

Additional Support

The Aztec consolidated their rule over much of what is modern Mexico. The new kingdom was not a centralized state but a collection of semi-independent territories that local lords governed. The Aztec ruler supported these rulers in return for **tribute**, goods or money paid by conquered peoples to their conquerors.

Political and Social Structures

By 1500, as many as four million Aztec lived in the Valley of Mexico and the surrounding valleys of central Mexico. Like all great empires in ancient times, the Aztec state was authoritarian. The monarch, who claimed lineage with the gods, held all power. A council of lords and government officials assisted the Aztec ruler.

R The nobility, the elite of society, held positions in the government. Male children in noble families were sent to temple schools, which stressed military training. Once adults, males would select a career in the military service, the government bureaucracy, or the priesthood. As a reward for their services, nobles received large estates from the government.

The rest of the population consisted of commoners, indentured workers, and slaves. Indentured workers were landless laborers who contracted to work on the nobles' estates. Slaves worked in the households of the wealthy. Male and female slaves were sold in the markets.

Most people were commoners, and many commoners were farmers. Farmers built *chinampas,* swampy islands crisscrossed by canals that provided water for their crops. The canals also provided easy travel to local markets. Aztec merchants were also active traders. Merchants exported and traded goods made by Aztec craftspeople from imported raw materials. In exchange for their goods, the traders obtained tropical feathers, cacao beans, animal skins, and gold.

W From the beginnings of their lives, boys and girls in Aztec society had very different roles. The midwife who attended the birth of a male infant said, "You must

INFOGRAPHICS PRIMARY SOURCE

The Education of Aztec Boys and Girls

Like children in every culture, Aztec youths were educated in the skills and values they needed in their society. This illustration from an Aztec book shows parents teaching their 13- and 14-year-old children.

From sources like this, historians know that Aztec boys went to school at age 15, after learning basic tasks at home from their fathers. At school they studied citizenship, history, religion, and arts and crafts. Boys also learned to be warriors. On the other hand, most Aztec girls were taught at home, learning to cook, shop, take care of children, and weave. Both boys and girls could study to be priests or priestesses.

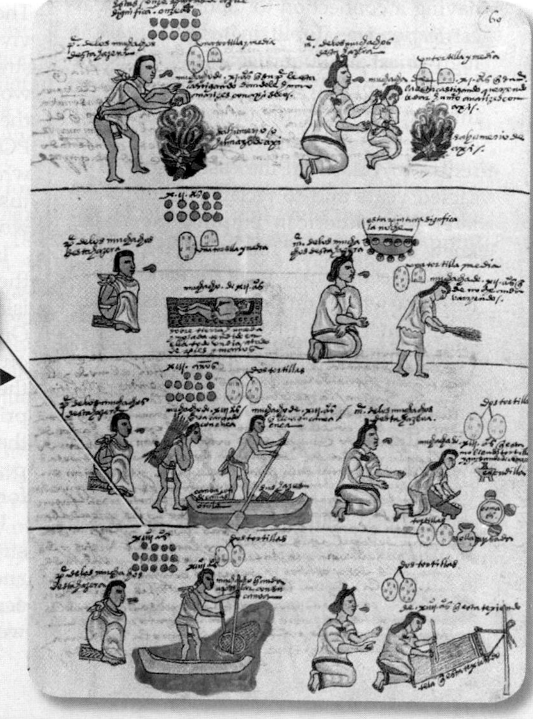

Each dot represents a year. The children in this row are 14 years old.

On the left an Aztec father teaches his son to haul a load, paddle a boat, and fish. On the right an Aztec mother teaches her daughter how to grind maize and weave cloth.

DOCUMENT-BASED QUESTIONS

1. **Analyzing Visuals** According to the illustration, at what age would a girl learn to weave on a loom?
2. **Synthesizing** How does the different educational focus of Aztec boys and girls reflect the different roles of Aztec men and women?

Activity: Collaborative Learning

Analyzing Aztec Society Organize students into small, mixed-level groups. Instruct them to use the information on pages 378–379 to create a graphic organizer that shows the class structure of Aztec society. Group members should discuss how they want to organize the information and may divide tasks among members. Encourage students to include simple illustrations or symbols in their diagram to represent the different groups. Call on volunteers from each group to present their graphic organizers to the class.

Ask: What is the difference between an indentured servant and a slave in Aztec society? (*Indentured servants contracted for their work; slaves were forced to work and could be bought and sold.*) **OL**

understand that your home is not here where you have been born, for you are a warrior." To a female infant, the midwife said, "As the heart stays in the body, so you must stay in the house." W

Though not equal to men, Aztec women could own and inherit property and enter into contracts, something not often allowed in other world cultures at the time. Women were expected to work in the home, weave textiles, and raise children. However, some were also trained to become priestesses.

Religion and Culture

Like other peoples in Central America and around the world, the Aztec believed in many gods. There was a supreme god, called Ometeotl, who represented the all-powerful forces of the heavens. Huitzilopochtli, the god of the sun and of war, was particularly important to Aztec warriors as they expanded control over neighboring peoples.

Another important god was Quetzalcoatl, who had a more direct impact on the lives of the people. According to Aztec tradition, Quetzalcoatl had left his homeland in the Valley of Mexico in the tenth century, promising to return in triumph. When the Aztec first saw Spanish explorers in the 1500s, they believed that representatives of Quetzalcoatl had returned. R

Aztec religion was based on a belief in an unending struggle between the forces of good and evil throughout the universe. This struggle had created and destroyed four worlds, or suns. People believed they were now living in the time of the fifth sun. This world, too, was destined to end with the destruction of Earth by earthquakes. To postpone the day of reckoning, the Aztec practiced human sacrifice. They believed they could delay the final destruction of their world by appeasing the sun god Huitzilopochtli with sacrifices.

Aztec religion had a significant influence on their art and architecture. For example, a chief feature of Aztec culture was its monumental architecture. At the center of Tenochtitlán was the sacred district, dominated by a massive pyramid dedicated to Huitzilopochtli. At the top was a platform containing shrines to the gods and an altar for performing human sacrifices.

A Strong Empire

With the help of two other city-states, Tenochtitlán formed a Triple Alliance. This alliance enabled the Aztec to dominate an empire that included much of today's Mexico, from the Atlantic to the Pacific Ocean and as far south as the Guatemalan border.

✓Reading Check **Summarizing** What aspect of Aztec culture is reflected in their architecture?

SECTION 2 REVIEW

Vocabulary

1. **Explain** the significance of: Mesoamerica, Olmec, Teotihuacán, estimate, Yucatán Peninsula, Maya, accurate, Tikal, hieroglyphs, Toltec, Chichén Itzá, Aztec, Tenochtitlán, Lake Texcoco, tribute.

Main Ideas

2. **Explain** why obsidian was prized in Mesoamerica.
3. **List** some accomplishments of the Maya. Use a chart like the one below to make your list.

Maya Accomplishments
1.
2.
3.

4. **Summarize** the role of women in the Aztec Empire.

Critical Thinking

5. **The BIG Idea** **Theorizing** Why do you think the Maya Empire declined?
6. **Evaluating** Why was trade important to early Mesoamerican civilizations?
7. **Analyzing Visuals** Examine the Olmec sculptures shown on page 373. How are the two sculptures similar, and how are they different?

Writing About History

8. **Informative Writing** Write a paragraph that explains the historical significance of one of the Aztec legends discussed in this section.

For help with the concepts in this section of *Glencoe World History*, go to glencoe.com and click Study Central™.

R Reading Strategy

Activating Prior Knowledge
Have students tell what they know about Quetzalcoatl in the Toltec culture. **Ask:** Why might Quetzalcoatl have become an important god to the Aztecs? *(The Aztecs' main city was in the heartland of the Toltec culture and they knew the legend of Quetzalcoatl.)* OL

✓Reading Check

Answer: Aztec pyramids reflect the Aztec religion.

Assess

Study Central provides summaries, interactive games, and online graphic organizers to help students review content.

Close

Comparing and Contrasting
Direct student groups to compare and contrast the religion and architecture of the Olmecs, Maya, Toltecs, and Aztecs. OL

SECTION 2 REVIEW

Answers

1. Definitions for the vocabulary words are found in the section and in the Glossary.
2. used in tools, mirrors, and razor-sharp knives
3. built splendid temples and pyramids; created an accurate calendar; developed farming; developed a system of city-states; created a sophisticated writing system
4. allowed to own and inherit property, to enter into contracts, and to become priestesses; expected to work in the home, weave textiles, and raise children
5. exact causes are uncertain; theories include invasion, internal revolt, volcanic eruption, or overuse of land that reduced crop yields
6. brought in new products and raw materials; created new markets for products; allowed exchange of ideas
7. Similar features—full lips, slanted eyes, and broad noses; both carved from stone. The head is larger than the figure.
8. Students' answers should be supported by evidence from the text.

Focus

Introducing Social History Have students recall what they know about Mesoamerican civilizations. **Ask:** What type of religious structure was common among Mesoamerican civilizations? *(pyramids)* OL

Teach

D Differentiated Instruction

Visual/Spatial Teotihuacán covered about 8 square miles and the Avenue of the Dead was 1.5 miles long. Have students use a map of their community to identify comparable areas. **Ask:** How does the layout of your community compare to Teotihuacán? *(Encourage students to identify the center and sections of the city and street patterns.)* BL

C Critical Thinking

Making Inferences Ask: What evidence might have suggested that the cave was used for religious rituals? *(Answers may include its locaton under a religious structure.)* AL

Additional Support

Social History

The Home of the Gods

Teotihuacán was the first major city in Mesoamerica. Although there is evidence this city emerged around 250 B.C., its "classic" period (when it was at its height) began around A.D. 200. During this time, monumental architecture projects were undertaken, and religious art was created. Little is known about the people who built the city because there are no written records. The name "Teotihuacán" comes from the Aztec centuries later, who called it "the home of the gods."

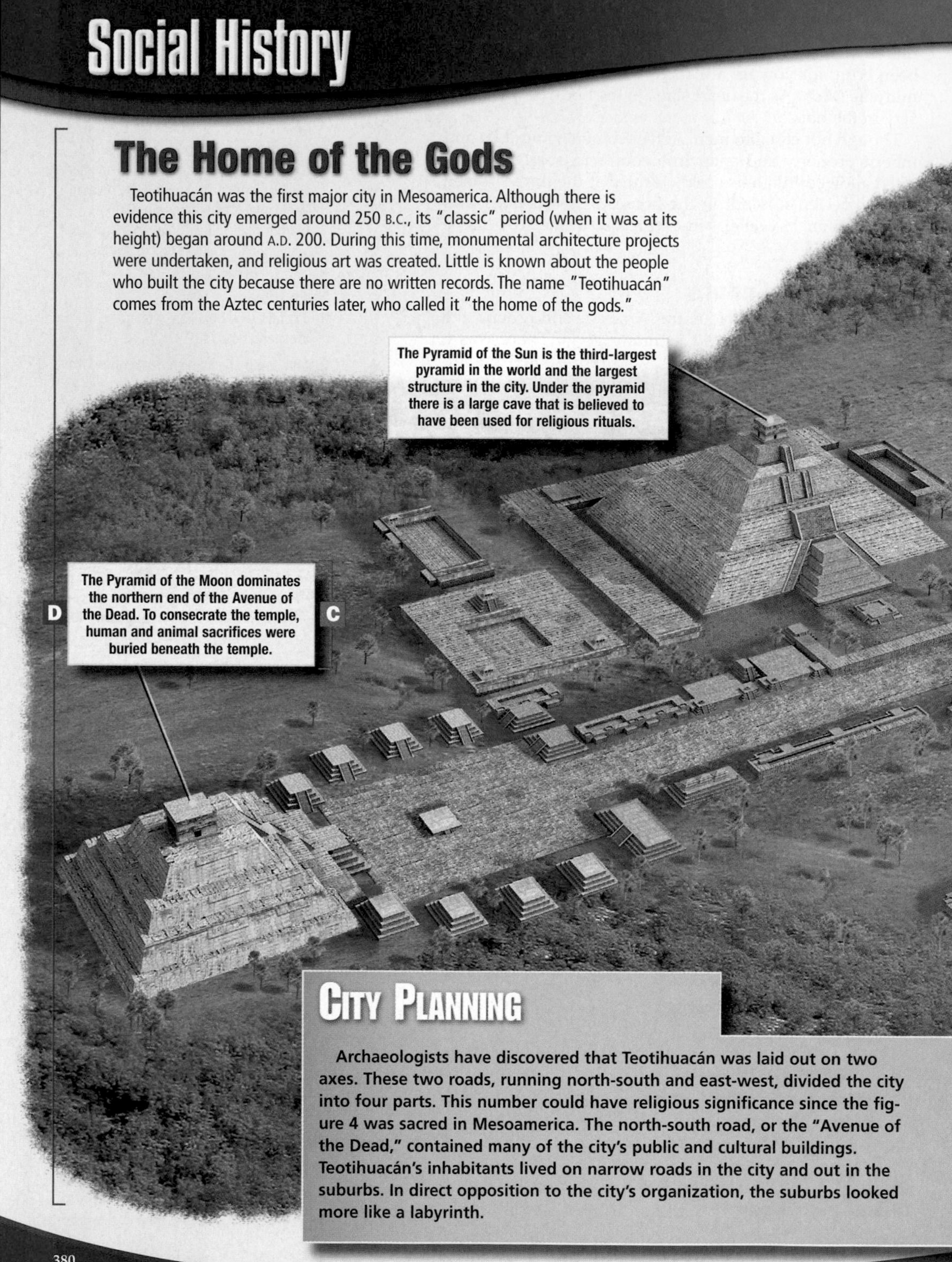

The Pyramid of the Sun is the third-largest pyramid in the world and the largest structure in the city. Under the pyramid there is a large cave that is believed to have been used for religious rituals.

D The Pyramid of the Moon dominates the northern end of the Avenue of the Dead. To consecrate the temple, human and animal sacrifices were buried beneath the temple. C

City Planning

Archaeologists have discovered that Teotihuacán was laid out on two axes. These two roads, running north-south and east-west, divided the city into four parts. This number could have religious significance since the figure 4 was sacred in Mesoamerica. The north-south road, or the "Avenue of the Dead," contained many of the city's public and cultural buildings. Teotihuacán's inhabitants lived on narrow roads in the city and out in the suburbs. In direct opposition to the city's organization, the suburbs looked more like a labyrinth.

Background

Teotihuacán The Pyramids of the Sun and Moon and the Avenue of the Dead were built during the first phase of construction in Teotihuacán. The street is about 130 feet wide and is oriented toward the top of Cerro Gordo, a nearby sacred mountain. The Citadel and the Temple of the Feathered Serpent, later known as Quetzalcoatl, were built in the second phase of construction. The courtyard of the Citadel covers 38 acres. The first archaeological excavations of the city occurred in 1884, but the city's layout was not systematically mapped until the 1960s and 1970s. Archaeologists have determined that what the Aztecs thought were tombs along the Avenue of the Dead were really apartments for the elite. Many walls were decorated with brightly colored murals.

Shrouded in Mystery

Although little is known about life in Teotihuacán, there is evidence of an early irrigation system surrounding the city, meaning that many in the city were farmers. The city was also heavily involved in trading finished goods. Artifacts from Teotihuacán have been discovered throughout Mesoamerica. After A.D. 600 the city began to decline in size, and around 800 was destroyed completely. Archaeologists have been unable to determine the cause of the city's destruction.

Analyzing Visuals

1. **Concluding** How does the evidence of city planning support the presence of a civilization?
2. **Considering** What might the placement of the pyramids at Teotihuacán indicate about the role of religion in this society?

381

W Writing Support

Expository Writing Have students research and write a short essay comparing Teotihuacán with the later Aztec city of Tenochtitlán. AL

R Reading Strategy

Identifying Ask: Identify the types of evidence scholars use to draw conclusions about life in Teotihuacán. *(archaeological evidence of an irrigation system and the spread of trade goods)* OL

Assess/Close

Have students discuss the influence of Teotihuacán on other Mesoamerican civilizations. OL

Analyzing Visuals

Answers:

1. Cities and the specialized labor needed to plan, build, and run them are key indicators of civilization.
2. Pyramids were placed near the main street, showing that religion played a central role in Teotihuacán.

Activity: Interdisciplinary Connection

Art Explain that archaeologists have discovered examples of murals, pottery, and sculpture within Teotihuacán, as well as evidence that pottery and other artifacts made in the city spread throughout Mesoamerica. **Ask:** Why are such artifacts particularly important in learning about Teotihuacán? *(Artifacts are the only primary sources, since no written records have been discovered.)* Organize students into groups and have them use Internet or library resources to find examples of art from Teotihuacán. Instruct students to use the material they find to create an art exhibit that highlights the accomplishments of Teotihuacán. Students may print copies of online visuals or make photocopies of artwork from books or magazines. Remind students to write a brief description of each piece in the exhibit and to include its source. As an alternative, students could create a virtual exhibit by compiling digital images and accompanying text on a CD-ROM or Web page. OL

Focus

Bellringer

Daily Focus Transparency 11.3

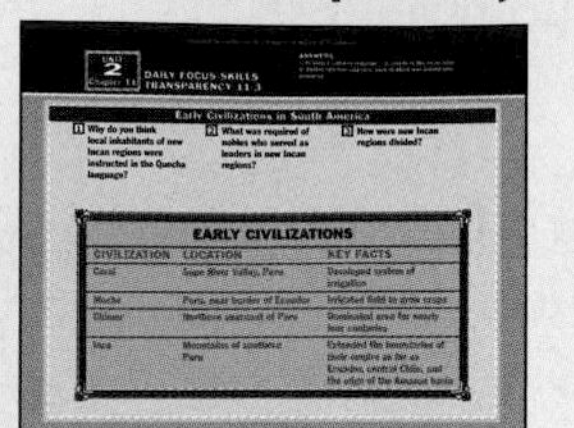

GUIDE TO READING

Answers to Graphic:
Top level of pyramid: emperor;
Second level: quarters; **Third level:** provinces;
Bottom level: residents

Section Spotlight Video

To generate student interest and provide a springboard for class discussion, access the Chapter 11, Section 3 video at glencoe.com or on the video DVD.

SECTION 3

Early Civilizations in South America

GUIDE TO READING

The BIG Idea
Order and Security The Inca developed a well-organized and militaristic empire with a distinct Inca culture.

Content Vocabulary
- maize *(p. 383)*
- *quipu (p. 385)*

Academic Vocabulary
- instructed *(p. 384)*
- residents *(p. 384)*

People and Places
- Caral *(p. 382)*
- Chavin *(p. 382)*
- Nazca *(p. 382)*
- Ecuador *(p. 383)*
- Moche *(p. 383)*
- Inca *(p. 384)*
- Cuzco *(p. 384)*
- Pachacuti *(p. 384)*
- Machu Picchu *(p. 385)*
- Urubamba River *(p. 385)*

Reading Strategy
Organizing Information As you read, complete a pyramid diagram showing the hierarchy of the Inca's political organization.

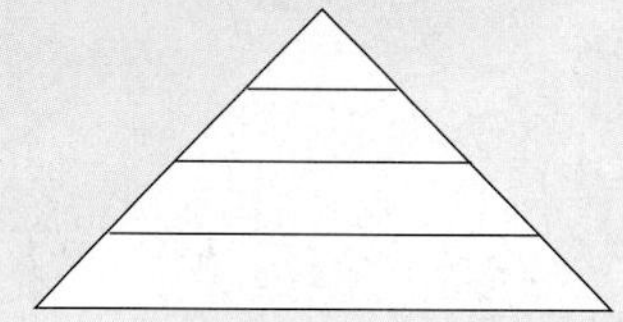

The Chavin, Nazca, and Moche cultures, which existed in South America before the Inca, built stone buildings and sophisticated irrigation systems. Later, the Inca became a spectacular, well-organized empire. The Inca Empire was still flourishing when the Spanish arrived in the sixteenth century.

Early Civilizations

MAIN IDEA The Chavin, Nazca, and Moche cultures existed in South America before the Inca came to power.

HISTORY & YOU What objects might provide future archaeologists with information about twenty-first-century America? Read to learn what archaeologists have learned about the Chavin, Nazca, and Moche peoples.

As in Mesoamerica, great civilizations flourished in early South America. The people of the Chavin, Nazca, and Moche cultures lived before the Inca gained power in South America. The cities, buildings, and artifacts these peoples left behind provide clues about their cultures.

The Chavin and Nazca Cultures

In the Supe River valley of Peru, **Caral** is the oldest major city in the Americas. It is believed to be 1,000 years older than the cities previously known in the Western Hemisphere. The city has stone buildings for officials, apartment buildings, and grand residences. The inhabitants of Caral also developed a sophisticated system of irrigation. Caral was abandoned between 2000 B.C. and 1500 B.C.

Around 900 B.C., the **Chavin** people in the coastal regions of modern-day Peru and Ecuador built a temple with stones gathered from nearby hills. Part of a larger ceremonial complex, the temple was surrounded by stone figures depicting different gods and two pyramids. For unknown reasons, the Chavin declined around 200 B.C.

Around the same time, the **Nazca** culture appeared in Peru. The Nazca prospered from around 200 B.C. to A.D. 600. Nazca culture preserved some aspects of Chavin culture, especially its style of pottery. However, the Nazca culture built no great temples. They may have practiced their religion outdoors, as suggested by ancient formations known as the Nazca Lines. These are grooves etched into the rocky soil of southern Peru in the image of animals, especially birds, as well as humans and other geometric shapes. The images are so large, however, that their shapes can only be seen from the air.

Resource Manager

R Reading Strategies	C Critical Thinking	D Differentiated Instruction	W Writing Support	S Skill Practice
Teacher Edition • Academic Vocab., p. 384 **Additional Resources** • Cont. Vocab. Act., URB p. 211 • Guid. Read. Act., URB p. 238 • Read. Ess. & Note-Taking Guide, p. 127	**Teacher Edition** • Making Inferences, p. 384 **Additional Resources** • People in World Hist. Act., URB p. 227 • Section Quiz, p. 131 • Chapter Test, p. 133	**Teacher Edition** • Advanced Learners, p. 383 **Additional Resources** • Diff. Instr. Act., URB p. 207 • Reteach. Act., URB p. 233	**Teacher Edition** • Personal Writing, p. 385 **Additional Resources** • Hist. Analysis Skills Act., URB p. 206	**Teacher Edition** • Using Geo. Skills, p. 383 **Additional Resources** • Academic Vocab. Act., URB p. 213 • Skills Reinforc. Act., URB p. 215 • Hist. Sim. Act., URB p. 223

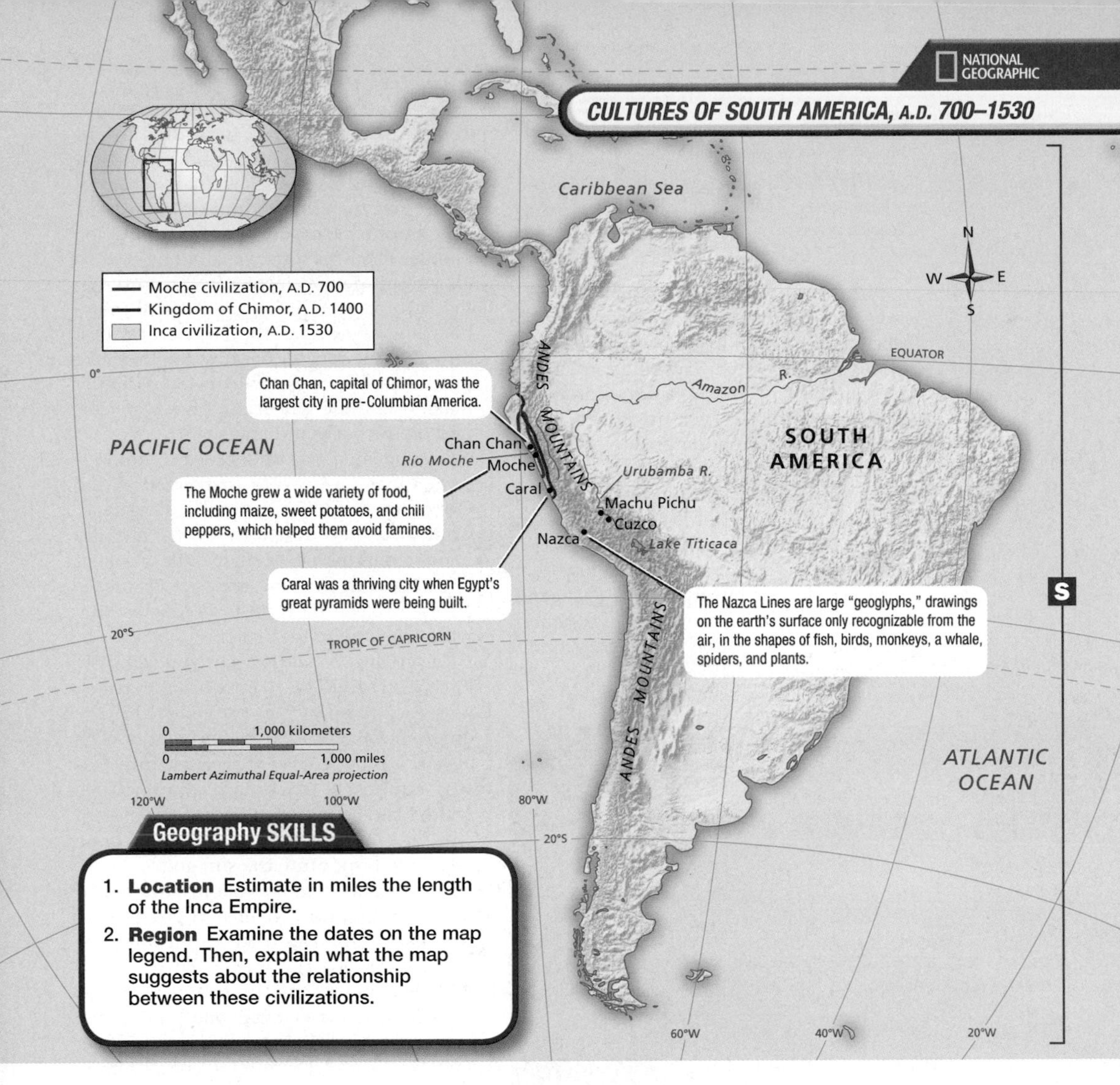

Geography SKILLS

1. **Location** Estimate in miles the length of the Inca Empire.
2. **Region** Examine the dates on the map legend. Then, explain what the map suggests about the relationship between these civilizations.

The Moche

Around A.D. 300, another civilization developed near the Pacific coast not far south of the border of **Ecuador.** At **Moche** (MOH•cheh), a major urban center arose amid irrigated fields in the valley of the Moche River. This river flows from the foothills of the Andes into the Pacific Ocean. Farmers in the area grew enough **maize** (corn), peanuts, potatoes, and cotton to supply much of the region.

Moche was the capital of a powerful state. The authority of the Moche rulers may have extended as far as 400 miles (644 km) along the coast. The people of Moche had no written language, but we are able to understand something about their warlike culture from their arts and crafts. Moche paintings and pottery frequently portray warriors, prisoners, and sacrificial victims. **D**

✓Reading Check **Identifying** What is the oldest major city in the Americas?

Teach

S Skill Practice

Using Geography Skills Ask: In what direction did the Inca expand from Cuzco in order to conquer the kingdom of Chimor? *(north)* **OL**

D Differentiated Instruction

Advanced Learners Ask: What can scholars learn from cultural artifacts such as crafts compared to written documents? *(Answers may include that scholars must draw conclusions about the artifacts rather than interpret writings.)* **AL**

Geography SKILLS

Answers:
1. 2,000 miles (3,200 km)
2. The civilizations existed in sequence and earlier civilizations may have had some influence on later civilizations.

✓Reading Check

Answer: Caral

Hands-On Chapter Project
Step 3

Creating a Thematic Map of Early American Civilizations

Step 3: Creating the Map In addition to gathering final information, groups will create their maps.

Directions: Tell groups to use the section headings and map as a guide for continuing to gather information and to organize their material. After students have collected all illustrations, they should create their maps. Suggest that they use an atlas to help them draw a map of the Americas. Students should choose at least one civilization from each of the three major regions studied. Remind students to include a title, labels, and a key for their maps. Have them check their maps for accuracy before turning them in.

Summarizing: Allow time for groups to share what they learned about the Section 3 Big Idea while searching for map material. Allow additional time for groups to complete their maps. **OL**

(Chapter Project is completed on the Visual Summary page.)

C Critical Thinking

Making Inferences **Ask:** Why would Inca rulers instruct the people they conquered in the Quechua language? *(It would be easier to control a vast empire and keep it united if everyone shared a language.)* **AL**

For additional practice on this skill, see the **Skills Handbook**.

R Reading Strategy

Academic Vocabulary Explain that the word *resident* comes from the verb *reside,* meaning "to live in a place." **Ask:** What does *residents* mean? *(people who live in a place)* Explain the differences in pronunciation between the two words. **ELL**

PEOPLE *in* HISTORY

Answers may include: Pachacuti wanted to ensure that his sons would not fight over control of the empire. If they did, the empire might be threatened.

The Inca

MAIN IDEA The Inca developed a well-organized, militaristic empire with a highly structured society.

HISTORY & YOU How do you keep track of your school records? Read to learn about the Inca's record-keeping system.

After the collapse of the Moche civilization in the eighth century A.D., a period of decline set in until the rise of a new power about 300 years later. The kingdom of Chimor dominated the area for nearly four centuries until the Inca destroyed it and created a spectacular empire.

In the late 1300s, the **Inca** (IHNG•kuh) were only a small community in the area of **Cuzco** (KOOS•koh), a city located at 11,000 feet (3,353 m) in the mountains of southern Peru. In the 1440s, however, under the leadership of the ruler **Pachacuti,** the Inca launched a campaign of conquest. Eventually the entire region was under Inca control.

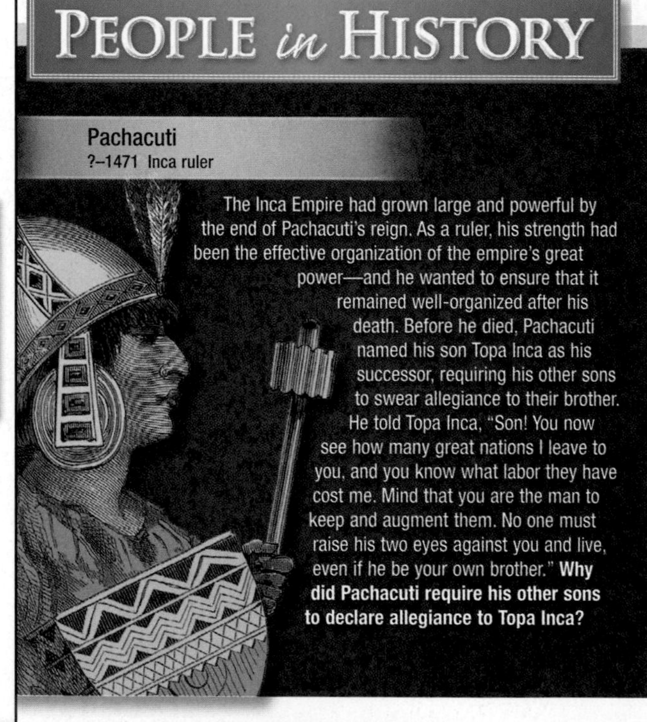

PEOPLE *in* HISTORY

Pachacuti
?–1471 Inca ruler

The Inca Empire had grown large and powerful by the end of Pachacuti's reign. As a ruler, his strength had been the effective organization of the empire's great power—and he wanted to ensure that it remained well-organized after his death. Before he died, Pachacuti named his son Topa Inca as his successor, requiring his other sons to swear allegiance to their brother. He told Topa Inca, "Son! You now see how many great nations I leave to you, and you know what labor they have cost me. Mind that you are the man to keep and augment them. No one must raise his two eyes against you and live, even if he be your own brother." **Why did Pachacuti require his other sons to declare allegiance to Topa Inca?**

Political Structures

Pachacuti and his immediate successors, Topa Inca and Huayna Inca—*Inca* means "ruler"—extended the boundaries of the Inca Empire as far as Ecuador, central Chile, and the edge of the Amazon basin. The empire included perhaps 12 million people. The Inca state was built on war, so all young men were required to serve in the Inca army. With some 200,000 members, the army was the largest and best armed in the region. Because the Inca, like other people in the early Americas, did not make use of the wheel, supplies were carried on the backs of llamas.

C Once an area was under Inca control, the local inhabitants were **instructed** in the Quechua (KECH•uh•wuh) language. Control of new territories was carefully regulated. A noble of high rank was sent out to govern the new region. Local leaders could keep their posts as long as they were loyal to the Inca ruler.

To create a well-organized empire, Pachacuti divided it into four quarters, **R** with each ruled by a governor. In turn, the quarters were divided into provinces, each also ruled by a governor. Each province was supposed to contain about 10,000 **residents.** At the top of the entire system was the emperor, who was believed to be descended from Inti, the sun god.

Forced labor was another important feature of the state. All Inca subjects were responsible for labor service, usually for several weeks each year. Laborers, often with their entire communities, were moved according to need from one part of the country to another to take part in building projects. One such project was a system of some 24,800 miles (around 40,000 km) of roads extending from the border of modern-day Colombia to a point south of modern-day Santiago, Chile. Two major roadways extended in a north-south direction, one through the Andes and the other along the coast, with connecting routes between them.

Rest houses and storage depots were placed along the roads. Various types of bridges, including some fine, pre-modern examples of suspension bridges, were built over ravines and waterways.

Differentiated Instruction

People in World History Activity, URB p. 227

Analyzing Information

Objective: Analyze information about the Inca Empire and the reign of Pachacuti.

Focus: Direct students to read the profile of Pachacuti.

Teach: Tell students to answer the questions on a separate sheet of paper.

Assess: Have students share answers with the class and amend answers as needed.

Close: Discuss the Inca's achievements with the class.

Differentiated Instruction Strategies

BL Have students work with a partner to answer the questions.

AL Ask students to compare the Inca's achievements with another civilization. Have students record the similarities in a chart.

ELL Have students use a dictionary to find meanings of unfamiliar words.

Social Structures

Inca society was highly regimented. So, too, were marriage and the lives of women. Men and women were required to select a marriage partner from within their own social groups. After marriage, women were expected to care for the children and to weave cloth. For women, there was only one alternative to a life of working in the home. Some young girls were chosen to serve as priestesses in temples.

In rural areas, the people lived chiefly by farming. In the mountains, they used terraced farms, watered by irrigation systems that carried precise amounts of water into the fields. These were planted with corn, potatoes, and other crops. The farmers' houses, built of stone or adobe with thatched roofs, were located near the fields.

Building and Culture

The Inca were great builders, the best engineers among Native American peoples. They built roadways over mountains and tunnels through them, as well as bridges and aqueducts. The buildings and monuments of the capital city of Cuzco were the wonder of early European visitors. These structures were built of close-fitting stones without mortar—the better to withstand the frequent earthquakes in the area.

Nothing shows the architectural genius of the Inca more than the ruins of the abandoned city of Machu Picchu (MAH•CHOO PEE•CHOO). **Machu Picchu,** elevation 8,000 feet (2,400 m), was built on a lofty hilltop surrounded by mountain peaks far above the **Urubamba River.** Machu Picchu was hardly a city, containing only about 200 buildings.

In one part of Machu Picchu, a long stairway leads to an elegant stone known to the Inca as the "hitching post of the sun." Carved from the mountain, this "hitching post" may have been used as a solar observatory. During the sun festivals held in June and December, the people of Machu Picchu gathered here to chant and say prayers to Inti, the sun god. **W**

The Inca had no writing system. Instead, they kept records using a system of knotted strings called the ***quipu.*** The lack of a fully developed writing system, however, did not prevent the Inca from attaining a high level of cultural achievement.

The Inca had a well-developed tradition of court theater, consisting of both tragic and comic works. Plays often involved the recounting of valiant deeds and other historical events. Actors were not professionals but rather members of the nobility or senior officials who memorized their parts. Poetry was also recited, often accompanied by music played on reed instruments.

✓Reading Check **Describing** What technology helped the Inca to farm in the mountains?

Vocabulary
1. **Explain** the significance of: Caral, Chavin, Nazca, Ecuador, Moche, maize, Inca, Cuzco, Pachacuti, instructed, residents, Machu Picchu, Urubamba River, *quipu.*

Main Ideas
2. **Specify** what the Moche pottery tells of their culture.
3. **Summarize** the ways that the Inca system of roads unified the empire.

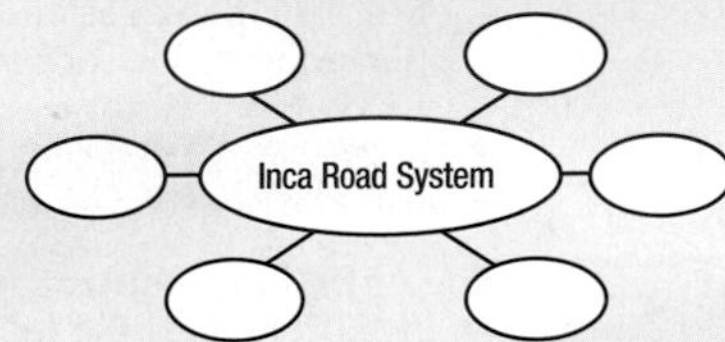

4. **Explain** the role of women in Inca society.

Critical Thinking
5. **The BIG Idea** **Evaluating** How did Pachacuti's system of political organization contribute to the success of the Inca Empire?
6. **Assessing** How did the Inca's *quipu* serve their needs for recordkeeping?
7. **Analyzing Visuals** Examine the image of Pachacuti on page 384. What do the items he holds tell you about the Inca?

Writing About History
8. **Expository Writing** Write an essay about how Pachacuti ruled the Inca Empire. You may use outside sources for research. Your essay should describe Pachacuti's achievements as well as his failures.

For help with the concepts in this section of *Glencoe World History,* go to glencoe.com and click Study Central™.

385

W Writing Support

Personal Writing Remind students that the Aztec, Maya, and Inca all practiced some form of sun worship. Assign students an essay describing why they think the sun was such an important image to many early cultures. **BL**

✓Reading Check

Answer: a system of terraced farming, watered by precise irrigation systems

Assess

History ONLINE

Study Central provides summaries, interactive games, and online graphic organizers to help students review content.

Close

Summarizing Have students write a brief summary of the major political, economic, and cultural developments of early civilizations in South America. **OL**

Answers

1. Definitions for the vocabulary words are found in the section and in the Glossary.
2. pottery focuses on warfare; shows warriors, prisoners, and sacrificial victims
3. Two major roadways extended the length of the empire, with connecting roads between and rest houses and storage depots that supported communication and trade.
4. married within their social group; after marriage, cared for children and wove cloth; only alternative was to be a priestess
5. The empire was divided into successively smaller units with levels of local leadership that pledged loyalty to the emperor.
6. They used these knotted strings to keep records.
7. A shield and a weapon show the Inca were militaristic.
8. Student essays should mention Pachacuti's success as a military commander and his effectiveness as a manager of a vast empire.

ANALYZING PRIMARY SOURCES

Focus

Role of Religion Discuss the role of religion in Aztec society. Ask students to think about Aztec beliefs as they read the primary source selections.

Teach

D Differentiated Instruction

Auditory/Musical Have pairs of students work together to read aloud and discuss the selections. Remind them that they can consult a dictionary or reread portions of the text to increase their understanding. OL

C Critical Thinking

Comparing and Contrasting As a class, work to create a list of statements that describe the main ideas of each source. After the statements have been recorded, ask students to categorize the statements as fact or opinion. BL

ANALYZING PRIMARY SOURCES

What was the Role of Religion in Aztec Society?

How did the Aztec worship their gods? Religion was an important feature of Aztec life. Prayers, legends, and ceremonies at great temples were all part of Aztec religious practice.

How did outsiders view Aztec religion? After their arrival in Mexico in 1519, the Spanish were shocked by the Aztec religious rituals. The Spaniards immediately worked to convert the Aztec to Christianity.

The Aztec and the Spanish had extremely different viewpoints about Aztec religion. Read the passages and study the illustration to learn more about the role religion played in Aztec society.

SOURCE 1

The Aztec king Ahuizotl, who ruled from 1486 to 1502, offered the following prayer to the god Huitzilopochtli while celebrating a successful military campaign.

C D

O almighty, powerful lord of All Created
  Things,
You who give us life, and whose **vassals**[1] and
  slaves we are,
Lord of the Day and of the Night, of the Wind
  and the Water,
Whose strength keeps us alive! I give you
  infinite thanks
For having brought me back to your city of
  Mexico
With the victory which you granted me.
  I have returned. . . .
Since you did not frown upon my extreme
  youth
Or my lack of strength or the weakness of
  my chest,
You have subjected those remote and
  barbarous nations
To my power. You did all of these things!
  All is yours!
All was won to give you honor and praise!
Therefore, O powerful and heroic
  Huitzilopochtli,
You have brought us back to this place which
  was only water
Before, which was enclosed by our ancestors,
And where they built our city.

SOURCE 2

Spanish conquistador Hernán Cortés wrote the following description of a temple in the Aztec capital in a 1520 letter to the Spanish king, Charles V.

Three halls are in this grand temple, which contain the principal idols; these are of wonderful extent and height, and admirable workmanship, adorned with figures sculptured in stone and wood; leading from the halls are chapels with very small doors . . . In these chapels are the images of idols, although, as I have before said, many of them are also found on the outside; the principal ones, in which the people have greatest faith and confidence, I **precipitated**[2] from their pedestals, and cast them down the steps of the temple, purifying the chapels in which they had stood, as they were all polluted with human blood, shed ill the sacrifices. In the place of these I put images of Our Lady and the Saints, which excited not a little feeling in **Moctezuma**[3] and the inhabitants, who at first **remonstrated**[4], declaring that if my proceedings were known throughout the country, the people would rise against me; for they believed that their idols bestowed on them all **temporal**[5] good, and if they permitted them to be ill-treated, they would be angry and without their gifts, and by this means the people would be deprived of the fruits of the earth and perish with famine. . . .

[1] **vassals:** people in a subordinate position
[2] **precipitated:** threw down
[3] **Moctezuma:** the Aztec king in 1520
[4] **remonstrated:** vocally protested

Differentiated Instruction

PRIMARY SOURCE READING 11
"Raven's Great Adventure" and "The Origin of Yosemite"

Primary Source Reading, URB p. 229

Analyzing Primary Sources

Objective: Analyze stories explaining how something in nature originated.

Focus: Ask students why people seek to explain things that they are curious about.

Teach: Ask students to read the selections and answer the questions.

Assess: Have students write a timed character sketch of the chief and the raven.

Close: Discuss how these stories are similar to other legends students have read.

Differentiated Instruction Strategies

BL Have students read the selections and underline any areas where they have questions to discuss in a small group.

AL Ask students to write a legend that explains something they find interesting or confusing.

ELL Have students work in pairs to define unfamiliar terms.

▲ Tenochtitlán priests sacrifice warriors to the sun god in this Aztec drawing dated after 1519.

SOURCE 3

Human sacrifice was a central part of Aztec religion. The Aztec believed their deities, such as the war god Huitzilopochtli, demanded a steady supply of human sacrifices. At the dedication of the great pyramid of Tenochtitlán, for example, Aztec priests sacrificed more than 20,000 people. Most of the Aztec's sacrifice victims were prisoners captured from enemy tribes. For this purpose, Aztec warriors were trained to capture, rather than kill, their enemies in battle. **D**

The above image is an Aztec drawing of a sacrifice ritual. During these ceremonies, priests cut out the victim's heart and held it up to the sun as an offering. As shown in the image, the victim's body was then thrown down the steps of the pyramid temple. **C**

[5] **temporal:** relating to earthly life

DOCUMENT-BASED QUESTIONS

1. **Explaining** Why did King Ahuizotl pray to the god Huitzilopochtli?
2. **Identifying Points of View** How did Cortés's background influence his actions in the Aztec temple?
3. **Drawing Conclusions** What does this image reveal about the Aztec's relationship with their gods?
4. **Contrasting** How would Ahuizotl's description of the scene in the above image have contrasted with Cortés's description of the same image?
5. **Synthesizing** On what points do Ahuizotl and Cortés agree in their description of Aztec religious beliefs?
6. **Recognizing Bias** Consider the question "What was the role of religion in Aztec society?" How would an Aztec have answered that question differently than a Spaniard? Which answer do you think would have been most similar to your own answer to the question?

ANALYZING PRIMARY SOURCES

Assess/Close

Drawing Conclusions Decide how each source helps explain the role of religion in Aztec society. **Ask:** How does the role of religion in Aztec society compare to the role of religion in various societies today? (*Answers should include specific examples.*) **OL**

DOCUMENT-BASED QUESTIONS

Answers:

1. to thank Huitzilopochtli for supporting his victory
2. Cortés's background was different from the Aztec's and he did not accept their religion.
3. The Aztec felt their gods were important and required respect and fear.
4. Ahuizotl might have expressed pride in being able to honor the gods in this fashion, while Cortés would have felt that it was not appropriate to sacrifice people.
5. that the Aztec feel their gods are powerful
6. Answers will vary depending on students' belief systems.

Additional Support

Extending the Content

Roles in Society Tell students that the Aztec state was authoritarian and class distinctions were very important. The Aztec ruler claimed that he was descended from the gods and served as a link between the material and the spiritual worlds. Relate this idea to how Ahuizotl addressed the god Huitzilopochtli in his prayer. Note that the king is speaking directly to the god in his role as a link between the people and the god. While the Aztec rulers had their roles, others in the society also had specifics roles. Upper- and middle-class people benefited from the labors of the lower class and enjoyed luxuries and special foods not available to the masses. Commoners lived in small adobe and mud huts, while the upper class lived in large palaces surrounded by gardens.

9. D Human sacrifice was common in Mesoamerican culture. None of the other choices are mentioned in the description of Maya culture in the text.

10. B Students need to recall that Tula was the center of the Toltec Empire.

11. C The words *never* and *not* in choices A and B make these statements false. Choice D is incorrect because women were not trained as Aztec warriors.

TEST-TAKING 

For Question 11: Remind students to read **all** the choices carefully before they pick an answer.

12. A Choices B and C are incorrect because the Moche came after the Chavin and Nazca cultures, which existed before the Christian era. Choice D is incorrect because the Moche began around A.D. 300 and lasted until the 700s.

13. C For this question, C is the only possible choice because it is the only one that refers to a system of organization, which was one of Pachacuti's main accomplishments.

CHAPTER 11

9. How did the Maya appease their gods?
- **A** Parades
- **B** Penance
- **C** Fasting
- **D** Human sacrifice

10. How did the Toltec irrigate their fields of beans, maize, and peppers?
- **A** With water from aqueducts
- **B** With water from the Tula River
- **C** With water from the Gulf of Mexico
- **D** With water from the Yucatán River

11. Which of the following is true of the Aztec?
- **A** They never engaged in war.
- **B** Their culture did not have myths or legends.
- **C** They built monumental architecture.
- **D** They trained women to be warriors.

Section 3 *(pp. 382–385)*

12. About what time did the Moche civilization appear?
- **A** A.D. 300
- **B** 200 B.C.
- **C** 50 B.C.
- **D** A.D. 500

13. How did the Inca ruler Pachacuti create a well-organized empire?
- **A** He remained in sole charge of all the empire.
- **B** He made a female his coruler.
- **C** He divided empire into four quarters, each ruled by a governor.
- **D** He divided spoils of war among the nobles.

Critical Thinking

Directions: Choose the best answers to the following questions.

Use the following map to answer question 14.

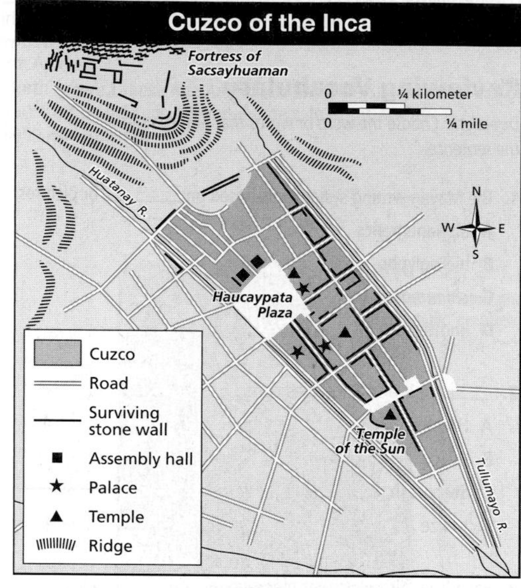

14. What do you notice about the roads leading out of Cuzco?
- **A** They lead out to the east only.
- **B** They lead out in all directions.
- **C** They lead out to the west only.
- **D** They do not intersect at any point.

15. Why was the Iroquois League so important?
- **A** It made the Iroquois people very wealthy.
- **B** It protected the Aztec from Hernán Cortés.
- **C** It established the Maya calendar.
- **D** It was an early American experiment in democracy.

Need Extra Help?

If You Missed Questions . . .	9	10	11	12	13	14	15
Go to Page . . .	375	376	379	383	384	390	370

GO ON

Critical Thinking

14. B For this question, B is correct by default, or process of elimination. Students can eliminate all the other choices by careful study of the map, its legend, and the compass rose.

15. D Students should quickly eliminate B and C, as they refer to people in a different part of the world. Choice A is incorrect because the league was a political organization and had nothing to do with wealth.

16. When did agriculture arise in the Americas?
 A When the Olmec began farming along the riverbanks of the Gulf of Mexico
 B When the Maya established farming villages
 C When the Inuit moved to North America from Asia
 D When the Aztec came into power in Mesoamerica

17. Why do historians not know more about the ancient civilizations of Mesoamerica?
 A Because the ancient civilizations had no writing systems
 B Because the ancient civilizations left no artifacts behind
 C Because the conquering peoples destroyed many religious artifacts and leveled cities
 D Because excavations did not begin until quite recently

This Peruvian print from 1609 shows an Inca man using the quipu. Base your answer on the print and on your knowledge of world history.

18. What information can historians gain from this image?
 A The Inca lived in North America.
 B The Inca played a domino-like game.
 C The Inca had a method to keep records.
 D The Inca had a complicated written language.

Document-Based Questions

Directions: Analyze the document and answer the short-answer questions that follow the document. Base your answers on the document and on your knowledge of world history.

Bernal Díaz, who accompanied Hernán Cortés on a Spanish expedition to Mexico in 1519, wrote:

> *"When we beheld so many cities and towns on the water, and other large settlements built on firm ground, and that broad causeway running so straight and perfectly level to the city of Tenochtitlán, we were astonished because of the great stone towers and temples and buildings that rose up out of the water."*
>
> —Bernal Díaz, as quoted in *The Conquest of New Spain*, John M. Cohen, trans., 1975

19. Which early civilization built the city of Tenochtitlán?

20. Why were the Spanish so "astonished" by what they saw?

Extended Response

21. Throughout time people have had to adapt to their environment in order to survive. What was the relationship between the early peoples of the Americas and their environment?

History ONLINE
For additional test practice, use Self-Check Quizzes—Chapter 11 at glencoe.com.

Need Extra Help?

If You Missed Questions . . .	16	17	18	19	20	21
Go to Page . . .	372	375	391	377	391	369

STOP

Document-Based Questions

19. Aztec is the correct answer. Students can use the date of the document as a clue if they recall that the Aztec flourished from the 14th century until the arrival of the Spanish.

20. They were astonished that this culture had the ability and technology to build such impressive structures. They believed that Europeans were more advanced than peoples of the Americas, whom they considered to be primitive.

Extended Response

21. Answers may include: The first peoples of the Americas were hunters who crossed the Bering Strait into North America to follow herds of bison and caribou. They were nomads, always moving to stay close to their food supply. The Plains Indians used bison for food, clothing, and shelter. They also made their tools from the bones of bison. In their camps, the women generally raised and harvested crops while the men hunted. As the early Americans began to establish more permanent camps, agriculture became more important to their survival.

16. A The Olmecs began farming long before the rise of the Maya or Aztec. Therefore, B and D are incorrect. C is incorrect because the Inuit lived by hunting and fishing, not farming.

17. C For this question, C is the only possible choice. In the other choices, the opposite of the statement is true.

18. C Students should be able to eliminate A, B, and D because the image gives no evidence related to these choices. The image shows a *quipu*, which was used by the Inca to keep records. Therefore, C is correct.

History ONLINE
Introduce students to chapter content and key terms by having them access the Chapter 11 Overview at glencoe.com.

Need Extra Help?
Have students refer to the pages listed if they miss any of the questions.

Focus

Introducing TIME Notebook

Draw attention to the map of Ibn Battuta's travels and remind students that some individuals in the Middle Ages undertook difficult and often dangerous journeys. **Ask:** What parts of the world did the Arab explorer Ibn Battuta visit? *(Answers may include Africa and China.)*

Teach

W Writing Support

Narrative Writing Remind students that the Norse composed epic poems about the events in their lives. Have students write their own poem about a trip they took. Coach them to include details about people and places. OL

Additional Support

TIME NOTEBOOK

ROGER-VIOLLET/TOPHAM/THE IMAGE WORKS

SCOTT MACNEILL

Ibn Battuta: The Ultimate Road Trip

Ibn Battuta makes Marco Polo seem like a couch potato. The Arab explorer has journeyed just about everywhere in the world, covering nearly 70,000 miles over 30 years.

Battuta's first trip was a pilgrimage to Makkah from his hometown of Tangier, Morocco, in 1325. From there, he just kept going and going. First stop was Mesopotamia, and then he continued along the Silk Road in central Asia. Next was a voyage along the coast of East Africa, where he visited Ethiopia and Zanzibar. After a quick trip home to refresh himself, Battuta left to explore Constantinople, headed into Afghanistan and India, and later made the trek to China. He also explored Europe, North Africa, and finally, the kingdom of Mali.

In his journeys, Battuta didn't always travel first class. He was attacked by pirates and thieves, nearly drowned in storms at sea, was kidnapped, and avoided the Black Death like, well, the plague. Battuta promises to write down the story of his epic adventures. No doubt it will be a very thick book.

VERBATIM

"Blood was pooled and the skulls of the people of the central place of Tikal were piled up."

WORDS ON A STAIRCASE
of a 7th century pyramid in Guatemala, describing the fate of the enemies of a ruler of the Maya city of Dos Pilas

"Solomon, I have outdone thee."

JUSTINIAN THE GREAT,
in 537, head of Byzantine Empire, comparing the magnificent church Hagia Sophia, in Constantinople, to the ancient Temple of Solomon in Israel

"Teach your tongue to say 'I do not know' and you will progress."

MOSES MAIMONIDES,
rabbi and philosopher born in Muslim Spain in 1135

"To no man will we sell, or deny, or delay, right or justice."

THE MAGNA CARTA,
On the powers of the English king, 1215

"Fireworks crackle, the year ends/ Spring wind wafts, and I downed cups of wine/Early New Year morning, as sun shines bright/Every household is busy replacing old with new."

WANG ANSHI,
politician and poet, who as a minister of the Song dynasty in 11th century China, has reformed the government and created policies to help the poor

THE SOFTER SIDE OF THE VIKINGS

They loot. They pillage. And occasionally they loot *and* pillage. That's the impression most people have about Vikings. But Europe's bad boys do have their good points. Although *Viking* is the name given to those Norse who go on raids, most Norse are farmers and herders. W The Norse have composed epic poems, play chess, make iron tools, and craft jewelry. They also build the greatest ships in the world. Of course, complaints about the Vikings' rude behavior are justified. After all, they have been stealing stuff from the coasts of England and Ireland for a couple of hundred years. With the Norse, it seems that you have to take the bad with the good.

THE PRINT COLLECTOR/ALAMY

Background

The Last Journey Ibn Battuta was only 22 years old when he made his first trip. Thirty years later he ended his journeys after visiting regions that were part of the vast Islamic Empire. This empire stretched from North Africa to China's eastern border and included more than 40 modern countries. Ibn Battuta set out on his final journey in 1352. He intended to cross the Sahara Desert and reach the country of Mali in West Africa. Along the way, he stayed in a house made entirely of salt except for a camel skin roof. The trip was dangerous: "I saw a crocodile in this part of the [river], close to the bank; it looked just like a small boat. One day I went down to the river to satisfy a need, and . . . one of the [guides] came and stood between me and the river. I was amazed at such lack of manners . . . and spoke of it to someone or other. [That person] answered, 'His purpose in doing that was solely to protect you from the crocodile, by placing himself between you and it.'" A few years later Ibn Battuta returned to Morocco where he dictated the story of his travels to a young scholar. The book is called *Rihla*, or *My Travels*, and has been translated into many languages.

VISUAL ARTS LIBRARY (LONDON)/ALAMY

Annals of Medicine

Getting sick in medieval Europe is no picnic. Here are some standard medical treatments—along with a fake one. Can you find it?

1. Herbal treatments are recommended for anything from the Black Death to insomnia. Ingredients may include urine, ground-up worms, and roasted snake skin. **C**
2. Want relief from smallpox? Hang colored cloth around your bed.
3. Diseases, say experts, are caused by a buildup of bodily fluids (called "humors"), such as blood. Having a barber open a vein to rid you of some blood should balance the humors and bring good health.
4. Many doctors diagnose problems by a patient's astrological sign. For example, a person with a certain sign might be prone to colds or sadness.
5. To treat a cough and other lung problems, patients should set moldy chestnuts on fire and breathe in the smoke.
6. Some physicians believe physical sickness is caused by sin. Their prescription? Go on a pilgrimage and/or pray.
7. Here's an effective way to clean your teeth: Simply rub them with powder made from crushed seashells.

Answer: 5

BY THE NUMBERS

0 The number of times that rules for the use of the number zero in mathematical calculations appeared before Indian mathematician Brahmagupta put them to paper in 628 in a book called *Brahmasputha Siddhanta*

275 million The approximate world population in the year 1000

33 The average life expectancy of an English person during the Middle Ages

68.27 The average height in inches of a European during the eleventh century

MARY EVANS PICTURE LIBRARY/THE IMAGE WORKS

33 The percent of the total population of the Muslim world killed by the Black Death by the year 1349

Milestones

PUBLISHED. *THE TALE OF GENJI* in the year 1000, by Murasaki Shikibu, a Japanese noblewoman. It is the story of the son of the emperor and his romantic adventures in the royal court. Because of its length and insight into the characters, many scholars are claiming that this is the world's first novel.

BUILT. A major urban project called **MACHU PICCHU,** by Inca architects for the emperor Pachacuti, completed around 1470. Located 8,000 feet high in the Andes, it consists of about 200 buildings. About 1,200 people are expected to move into this city in the sky, many of them members of the royal family. Most impressive are the spectacular views. Location, as they say, is everything.

SUCCEEDED. SUNNI ALI by his son Sunni Baru, as emperor of the kingdom of Songhai. Through military might, Sunni Ali managed to turn that backwater nation into a vast empire. After taking power in 1464, Sunni Ali built up a powerful army and navy. When he died in 1492, he controlled much of the territory belonging to the Mali Empire. Pundits believe that Askia Muhammad Toure already has designs on Baru's office.

CRITICAL THINKING

1. **Identifying Points of View** What does the writer think about the Vikings? Explain the reasons for your answer.
2. **Speculating** Why do you think Ibn Battuta traveled so widely and for so many years?

C Critical Thinking

Analyzing Information Have students research and present a chart with some commonly accepted herbal treatments. Discuss why it is important to review the use of herbal treatments with a physician. **AL**

Assess/Close

Comparing and Contrasting Discuss the ways in which the practice of medicine has improved since the Middle Ages. **OL**

Visit the TIME Web site at www.time.com for up-to-date news, weekly magazine articles, editorials, online polls, and an archive of past magazine and Web articles.

CRITICAL THINKING

Answers:

1. The writer thinks the Vikings deserve their bad reputation. He points out that they stole and plundered for hundreds of years.
2. Ibn Battuta probably traveled because he loved visiting new places and having interesting experiences.

Activity: Why Is It Important?

Identifying Central Issues Ibn Battuta was a great explorer. So was Marco Polo. Like the Vikings who came to North America hundreds of years earlier, they left behind familiar surroundings in order to increase their understanding of the world. **Ask:** Where are explorations taking place today? *(Today the quest for knowledge has moved in new directions. Space exploration, oceanography, nanotechnology, and artificial intelligence are among the many frontiers where explorations are taking place.)* Have students form groups and ask each group to choose some field of research or experimentation in science or the arts. Coach them to investigate their topic and prepare a demonstration of their findings. The groups can choose from a variety of formats for their demonstration: oral reports, computer-based databases, dramatic enactments, or posters. Encourage students to trace the development of their subject over time to show its connection with the past. **OL**

UNIT 3 Planning Guide

UNIT PACING CHART									
	Unit 3	Chapter 12	Chapter 13	Chapter 14	Chapter 15	Chapter 16	Chapter 17	Chapter 18	Unit 3
Day 1	Unit Opener	Chapter Opener, Section 1	Chapter Opener, Section 1	Chapter Opener, Section 1	Chapter Opener, Section 1	Chapter Opener, Section 1	Chapter Opener, Section 1	Chapter Opener, Section 1	Time Notebook, Unit Assessment
Day 2		Section 1, Social History, Section 2	Section 1, Social History, Section 2	Section 2, Section 3	Geography and History, Section 2	Section 1, Section 2	Section 1, Section 2	Section 1, Social History	
Day 3		Section 2, Section 3	Section 2, Section 3, Visual Summary	Section 3, Social History	Social History, Section 3, Visual Summary	Section 3, Section 4	Section 2, Section 3	Section 2, Analyzing Primary Sources	
Day 4		Section 4, Visual Summary	Chapter Assessment	Section 4, Visual Summary	Chapter Assessment	Social History, Visual Summary	Section 3, Social History	Section 3, Visual Summary	
Day 5		Chapter Assessment		Chapter Assessment		Chapter Assessment	Section 4, Visual Summary	Chapter Assessment	
Day 6							Chapter Assessment		

Deborah McDevitt
Belmont High School
Belmont, Massachusetts

Le Grand Salon de l'Enlightenment
Students will reenact an Enlightenment salon in 18th-century France by role playing a *philosophe*. Have students write a summary of the philosopher's contributions, locate primary source evidence that support the *philosophe's* contributions, and write three questions to stimulate class discussion. Then arrange students in a circle; have them ask and answer questions in character.

Students earn a possible 3 points each time they contribute relevant information and analysis (including asking a new question). Students lose a point every time they interrupt, make an irrelevant comment, attack someone personally, or monopolize the conversation.

After the discussion, have students evaluate it and answer the following questions in writing.

- What would you have liked to discuss, but weren't able to speak up on?
- What could you have done to improve your performance?
- Do you have any lingering questions?
- How could the graded discussion be improved?

Author Note

Dear World History Teacher,

You may want to use the following information at the beginning of each chapter as a lesson launcher to help students focus on what they will be studying.

Beginning in the late fifteenth century, a new force entered the world scene—a revived Europe. The Early Modern World was marked in Europe by an explosion of scientific knowledge. At the same time, Europeans engaged in a period of state building, which led to the creation of independent monarchies in western and central Europe and framed the basis for a new European state system.

The rise of Early Modern Europe had an immediate as well as a long-term impact on the rest of the world. The first stage began with the voyages of exploration that led Europeans into new areas of the world. European expansion was by no means universally beneficial to those involved. The subjugation of the Americas by the Spanish and the Portuguese led to the destruction of sophisticated civilizations, which had heretofore been isolated from the rest of the world. The expansion of the African slave trade brought untold hardship to millions of victims and reduced the population in certain areas of Africa. Nevertheless, most of Africa still remained outside European control.

European influence was not yet very important in other parts of the world. Two great new Islamic empires, the Ottomans in Turkey and the Safavids in Persia, arose in the Middle East, while a third—the Mughal Empire—unified the subcontinent of India for the first time in nearly two thousand years. Least affected by the European expansion were the societies of East Asia—China and Japan. In fact China remained, in the eyes of many, the most sophisticated civilization in the world. Its achievements were imitated by its neighbors and admired by philosophers in Europe.

Jackson J. Spielvogel
Senior Author

Focus

Why It Matters

Point out that the political and social revolutions that occurred during this period had a profound effect on the world and continue to influence our lives today. Have students leaf through the unit, viewing the illustrations and reading heads and captions. **Ask:** In what ways are our lives today influenced by the Italian Renaissance, the Reformation, the opening of European trade routes, and the various political revolutions that took place? *(Briefly discuss these events, and lead students to recognize modern ramifications: humanism, individual ability, art treasures; proliferation of religious denominations; foundation for global trade; introduction of the idea of government by the people.)*

Unit Launch Activity

Explain that in this unit students will learn about the emergence of powerful European nation-states and the creation of large empires in Asia. Discuss how both wealth and military power contribute to the rise of powerful nations. **OL**

UNIT 3

The Early Modern World 1350–1815

▶ Why It Matters

The modern world began during this period. Asian empires and European countries expanded their influence through exploration, which led to colonialism, trade, and conflict. By the eighteenth century, political and social revolutions resulted in new democratic nations.

The Blue Mosque dominates the skyline of old İstanbul, which is located strategically on the peninsula where Europe and Asia meet.

Team Teaching Activity

Literature The period covered in this unit gave rise to famous and influential pieces of literature, whose themes reflect the culture, values, and political concerns of their periods. These works also transcend their cultures and convey universal themes. Work with an English teacher in your school to coordinate the study of a major piece of literature from this period. Consider one of the following possibilities: *The Canterbury Tales,* to understand late medieval life in England; one of Shakespeare's histories or tragedies, to understand perceptions of English politics and the monarchy; *A Tale of Two Cities,* to understand the French Revolution; *Les Miserables,* to understand social problems of eighteenth-century France; and *Frankenstein,* to understand concerns about the Enlightenment.

Teach

S Skill Practice

Constructing a Time Line Create a time line to chart the major people and events in this unit. As you teach each chapter, encourage students to suggest entries for the time line. Students can make their own copies of the time line, perhaps in journal form on successive pages, and add to it as they proceed through the unit. They can use the information to help them prepare for the chapter assessments. **OL**

Reading a Time Line Direct attention to the time lines that appear on each chapter opener. Point out that the periods covered in these time lines overlap. As students study each chapter, make sure they understand where individual events fall and what else was happening at the time. **BL**

No Child Left Behind

Teaching Tip Read aloud a sentence from the text that has a challenging vocabulary word. Model for students how to use context to determine the meaning of the word. Demonstrate how to use the other words in the sentence as well as the surrounding sentences to determine the meaning of an unknown word.

More About the Photo

Visual Literacy The mosque pictured here was built by Sultan Ahmet I between 1609 and 1617 and is regarded as one of the finest examples of Ottoman architecture. It is the only mosque in İstanbul that has six minarets, or prayer towers. Mosques traditionally have four, and at the time, only the mosque at Mecca had six. The grand scale of the Blue Mosque created a scandal, offending devout Muslims who believed it showed disrespect in attempting to overshadow the architecture at Mecca. After it was built, a seventh minaret was added to the mosque at Mecca. The Blue Mosque received its name because of the blue ceramic tiles featuring traditional Ottoman floral designs that decorate its interior. It also features striking stained glass windows, vaulted domes and semi-domes painted with arabesque designs, and an attached courtyard equal in size to the mosque itself.

CHAPTER 12 Planning Guide

Key to Ability Levels

- **BL** Below Level
- **OL** On Level
- **AL** Above Level
- **ELL** English Language Learners

Key to Teaching Resources

- Print Material
- CD-ROM
- DVD
- Transparency

Levels				Resources		Chapter Opener	Section 1	Section 2	Section 3	Section 4	Chapter Assess
BL	OL	AL	ELL								
					FOCUS						
BL	OL	AL	ELL	Transparency	**Daily Focus Skills Transparencies**		12-1	12-2	12-3	12-4	
					TEACH						
BL	OL		ELL	Print Material	**Reading Skills Activity, URB**			p. 19			
	OL	AL		Print Material	**Historical Analysis Skills Activity, URB**		p. 20				
BL	OL	AL	ELL	Print Material	**Differentiated Instruction Activity, URB**					p. 21	
	OL		ELL	Print Material	**English Learner Activity, URB**		p. 23				
BL	OL	AL	ELL	Print Material	**Content Vocabulary Activity, URB***					p. 25	
BL	OL	AL	ELL	Print Material	**Academic Vocabulary Activity, URB**					p. 27	
BL	OL	AL	ELL	Print Material	**Skills Reinforcement Activity, URB**		p. 29				
	OL	AL		Print Material	**Critical Thinking Skills Activity, URB**			p. 30			
	OL	AL		Print Material	**History and Geography Activity, URB**		p. 31				
	OL	AL	ELL	Print Material	**Mapping History Activity, URB**					p. 33	
BL	OL	AL		Print Material	**Historical Significance Activity, URB**			p. 34			
BL	OL	AL	ELL	Print Material	**Cooperative Learning Activity, URB**			p. 35			
	OL	AL	ELL	Print Material	**History Simulation Activity, URB**			p. 37			
BL	OL	AL	ELL	Print Material	**Time Line Activity, URB**				p. 39		
	OL	AL		Print Material	**Linking Past and Present Activity, URB**			p. 40			
BL	OL	AL		Print Material	**People in World History Activity, URB**		p. 41		p. 42		
BL	OL	AL	ELL	Print Material	**Primary Source Reading, URB**			p. 43			
	OL	AL		Print Material	**Enrichment Activity, URB**					p. 48	
BL	OL	AL	ELL	Print Material	**World Art and Music Activity, URB**			p. 45			
BL	OL		ELL	Print Material	**Guided Reading Activities, URB***		p. 50	p. 51	p. 52	p. 53	
BL	OL		ELL	Print Material	**Reading Essentials and Note-Taking Guide***		p. 130	p. 133	p. 136	p. 139	
BL	OL	AL	ELL	Print Material	**Differentiated Instruction for the World History Classroom**	✓	✓	✓	✓	✓	✓

Note: Please refer to the *Unit Resource Book: The Early Modern World* for this chapter's URB materials.

* Also available in Spanish

- Interactive Lesson Planner
- Interactive Teacher Edition
- Fully editable blackline masters
- Section Spotlight Videos Launch
- Differentiated Lesson Plans
- Printable reports of daily assignments
- Standards Tracking System

Levels BL	OL	AL	ELL		Resources	Chapter Opener	Section 1	Section 2	Section 3	Section 4	Chapter Assess
					TEACH *(continued)*						
BL	OL	AL	ELL		StudentWorks™ Plus DVD	✓	✓	✓	✓	✓	✓
BL	OL	AL	ELL		Vocabulary PuzzleMaker CD-ROM	✓	✓	✓	✓	✓	✓
Teacher Resources					Building Academic Vocabulary	✓	✓	✓	✓	✓	✓
					Reading Strategies and Activities for the Social Studies Classroom				p. 14	p. 68	
					Writer's Guidebook		p. 54		p. 12		
					Strategies for Success	✓	✓	✓	✓	✓	✓
					Outline Map Resource Book	✓	✓	✓	✓	✓	✓
					Presentation Plus! with MindJogger DVD	✓	✓	✓	✓	✓	✓
					ASSESS						
BL	OL	AL	ELL		Section Quizzes and Chapter Tests*		p. 145	p. 146	p. 147	p. 148	p. 149
BL	OL	AL	ELL		Authentic Assessment With Rubrics	✓	✓	✓	✓	✓	✓
BL	OL	AL	ELL		Standardized Test Practice Workbook	✓	✓	✓	✓	✓	✓
BL	OL	AL	ELL		*ExamView® Assessment Suite* CD-ROM		12-1	12-2	12-3	12-4	Ch. 12
BL	OL	AL	ELL		Interactive Tutor Self-Assessment CD-ROM		12-1	12-2	12-3	12-4	
					CLOSE						
BL			ELL		Reteaching Activity, URB					p. 47	
BL	OL		ELL		Reading and Study Skills Foldables™	✓	✓	✓	✓	✓	✓

Using ExamView® Assessment Suite

Quick Test

Technology Product

Glencoe's Exam*View*® includes powerful assessment tools and enables you to quickly create, adapt, and assess tests for your students. Exam*View*® allows you to

- develop online testing materials that focus on the specific skills and competencies of what has been taught in the classroom;
- create several versions of these test materials that are adjusted to meet the different ability levels of your students;
- provide a variety of test formats including Multiple Choice, True/False, Yes/No, Matching, Completion (Fill-in-the-Blank), and Numeric Response.

Steps

- Open the Exam*View*® Test Generator.
- Select **Create a new test using the QuickTest Wizard** and click **OK.**
- Name the test you are creating.
- From the list, select the *Chapter Banks* you would like to use. Click **Next.**
- Indicate the number of questions you want per question type. Click **Next.**
- Enter number of matching groups. Click **Next.**
- Verify summary of selections and click **Finish.**
- The *QuickTest Wizard* will build your test. Print the test or save it for students to take the test on a computer using the Internet.

History ONLINE

	Student	Teacher	Parent
Beyond the Textbook	●	●	●
Chapter Overviews	●	●	●
Time Current Events	●		●
ePuzzles and Games	●		●
Concepts in Motion	●		●
Literature Connections		●	
Multi-Language Glossaries	●		●
Online Student Edition	●	●	●
Self-Check Quizzes	●		●
Student Web Activities	●		●
Study Central ™	●		●
Teaching Today		●	
Vocabulary eFlashcards	●		●
Web Activity Lesson Plans		●	

- **Timed Readings Plus in Social Studies** helps students increase their reading rate and fluency while maintaining comprehension. The 400-word passages are similar to those found on state and national assessments.
- **Reading in the Content Area: Social Studies** concentrates on six essential reading skills that help students better comprehend what they read. The book includes 75 high-interest nonfiction passages written at increasing levels of difficulty.
- **Reading Social Studies** includes strategic reading instruction and vocabulary support in Social Studies content for both ELLs and native speakers of English.

www.jamestowneducation.com

Index to National Geographic Magazine:

The following articles relate to this chapter:

- "Meltdown: The Alps Under Pressure," by Erla Zwingle, February 2006
- "Italy's Po River," by Erla Zwingle, May 2005
- "Italy's Endangered Art," by Erla Zwingle, August 1999

National Geographic Society Products To order the following, call National Geographic at 1-800-368-2728:

- *National Geographic Atlas of the World* (Book).
- *The Renaissance* (CD-ROM).
- *The Renaissance* (PicturePack).

Access National Geographic's new, dynamic MapMachine Web site and other geography resources at:
www.nationalgeographic.com
www.nationalgeographic.com/maps

Biography

The following videotape programs are available from Glencoe as supplements to Chapter 12:

- Miraculous Canals of Venice (ISBN 1-56-501840-0)
- Michelangelo (ISBN 1-56-501425-1)

To order, call Glencoe at 1-800-334-7344. To find classroom resources to accompany many of these videos, check the following home pages:

A&E Television: www.aetv.com

The History Channel: www.historychannel.com

GLENCOE BOOKLINK 3

Use this database to search more than 30,000 titles to create a customized reading list for your students.

- Reading lists can be organized by students' reading level, author, genre, theme, or area of interest.
- The database provides Degrees of Reading Power™ (DRP) and Lexile™ readability scores for all selections.
- A brief summary of each selection is included.

Leveled reading suggestions for this chapter:

For students at a Grade 8 reading level:
- ***The Renaissance,*** by Jane Shuter

For students at a Grade 9 reading level:
- ***What Makes a Raphael a Raphael?,*** by Michael Muhlberger

For students at a Grade 10 reading level:
- ***Michelangelo,*** by Diane Stanley

For students at a Grade 11 reading level:
- ***Leonardo da Vinci,*** by Richard McLanathan

For students at a Grade 12 reading level:
- ***Geoffrey Chaucer,*** by Harold Bloom

Introducing **CHAPTER 12**

Focus

MAKING CONNECTIONS

How was architecture influenced by the Renaissance?

Discuss with students the power of new ideas to bring about significant and lasting changes to society. For example, students may mention ideas about democracy or about technologies, such as the personal computer, mobile phones, and the Internet. Talk about how these new ideas affect daily life, including politics and economics. Remind students that in many ways the Renaissance served as the bridge between the Middle Ages and modern times. As students learn about the Renaissance, have them examine the chapter graphics and analyze how the ideas of the Renaissance influenced architecture and changed daily life—then and now.

Teach

The Big Ideas

As students study the chapter, remind them to consider the section-based Big Ideas included in each section's Guide to Reading. The **Essential Questions** in the activities below tie in to the Big Ideas and help students think about and understand important chapter concepts. In addition, the Hands-on Chapter Projects with their culminating activities relate the content from each section to the Big Ideas. These activities build on each other as students progress through the chapter. Section activities culminate in the wrap-up activity on the Visual Summary page.

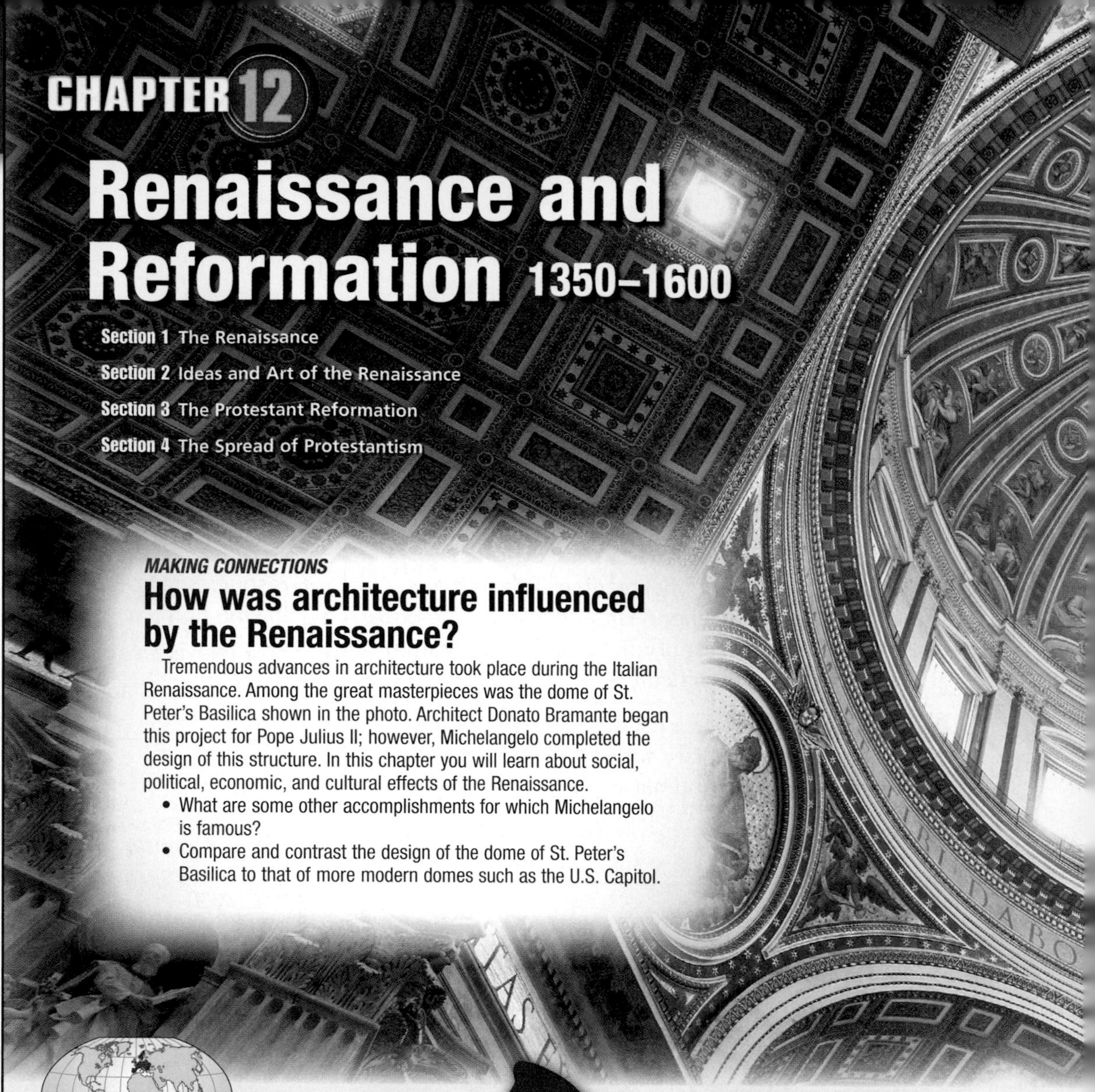

CHAPTER 12

Renaissance and Reformation 1350–1600

MAKING CONNECTIONS

How was architecture influenced by the Renaissance?

Tremendous advances in architecture took place during the Italian Renaissance. Among the great masterpieces was the dome of St. Peter's Basilica shown in the photo. Architect Donato Bramante began this project for Pope Julius II; however, Michelangelo completed the design of this structure. In this chapter you will learn about social, political, economic, and cultural effects of the Renaissance.

- What are some other accomplishments for which Michelangelo is famous?
- Compare and contrast the design of the dome of St. Peter's Basilica to that of more modern domes such as the U.S. Capitol.

EUROPE ▶

c. 1350 Italian Renaissance begins

1434 Cosimo de' Medici takes control of Florence

1517 Martin Luther presents his Ninety-five Theses

1350 — 1500

THE WORLD ▶

1405 Zheng He of China begins first voyage of exploration

1518 Spanish ship carries first enslaved Africans to the Americas

396

The Renaissance

Discuss the meaning of the word *renaissance*.
Essential Question: Why did the Renaissance begin in the Italian city-states? *(As trade centers, cities provided an environment in which ideas could be exchanged.)* After students have discussed the question, tell them that in Section 1, they will learn more about the growth of the Renaissance. **OL**

Ideas and Art of the Renaissance

Explain that the Renaissance elevated the value of the individual.
Essential Question: What characterizes Renaissance art, such as Michelangelo's *David* or da Vinci's *Mona Lisa*? *(It portrays the beauty and individuality of human figures in a realistic manner.)* Tell students that in Section 2, they will learn how humanistic values affected Renaissance culture. **OL**

Introducing CHAPTER 12

FOLDABLES Study Organizer

Analyzing Analyze how the Renaissance and Reformation affected various parts of Europe. Record your findings in a Layered-Look Book. Make sure you label each effect as *Renaissance* or *Reformation*.

1534
Henry VIII initiates creation of Church of England

1535
Francisco Pizarro conquers the Inca Empire

1555
Peace of Augsburg divides Christianity in Germany

1600

History ONLINE
Chapter Overview—Visit glencoe.com to preview Chapter 12.

The Protestant Reformation

Essential Question: What conditions encourage the growth of revolutions? *(Students may say that discontent with present circumstances, strong leaders, and good ideas can all lead to dramatic change.)* After students have discussed the question, tell them that in this section, they will learn how Martin Luther's dissatisfaction with the Catholic Church altered the course of history. **OL**

The Spread of Protestantism

Essential Question: What led to the formation of different Protestant churches? *(Students may say that Protestants disagreed on doctrine and wanted to establish their own religion.)* After students have discussed the question, explain that in Section 4 they will examine the rise of Calvinism and Anglicanism, and the Catholic Church's response to Protestantism. **OL**

More About the Photo

Visual Literacy The construction of St. Peter's Basilica began in 1506 and was completed in 1615. The photo shows the central interior looking up at the great dome, which rises 394 feet (120 meters) from the floor. Although domes covered many structures in ancient Rome, the techniques used to build them had been forgotten during the Dark Ages. Renaissance architects and engineers had to rediscover methods and develop technologies to build them. Many architects contributed to the design of St. Peter's, including Michelangelo, who served as chief architect from 1546 until his death in 1564. Although he did not live to see the dome's completion in 1593, Michelangelo created the columned walkway that circles the base of the dome. The dome itself is intended to symbolize the heavens, as well as also the power of God and the Church.

Dinah Zike's Foldables

Dinah Zike's Foldables are three-dimensional, interactive graphic organizers that help students practice basic writing skills, review vocabulary terms, and identify main ideas. Instructions for creating and using Foldables can be found in the Appendix at the end of this book and in the *Dinah Zike's Reading and Study Skills Foldables* booklet.

History ONLINE
Introduce students to chapter content and key terms by having them access the Chapter 12 Overview at glencoe.com.

Focus

Bellringer

Daily Focus Transparency 12.1

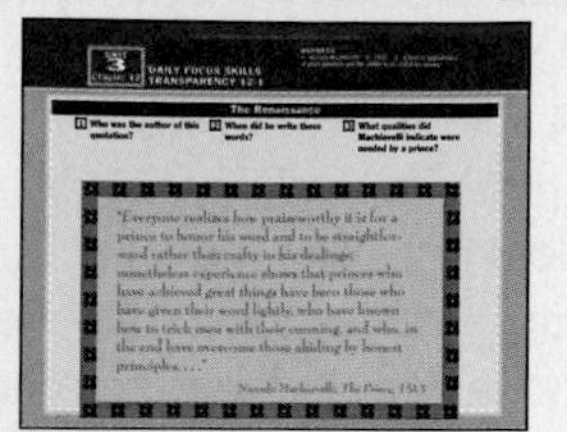

GUIDE TO READING

Answers to Graphic:
The Prince: how to acquire and keep political power, attitude toward power based on understanding of human nature, political activity not restricted by moral principles, prince acts on behalf of the state

Section Spotlight Video

To generate student interest and provide a springboard for class discussion, access the Chapter 12, Section 1 video at glencoe.com or on the video DVD.

The Renaissance

GUIDE TO READING

The BIG Idea
Ideas, Beliefs, and Values Between 1350 and 1550, Italian intellectuals believed they had entered a new age of human achievement.

Content Vocabulary
- urban society *(p. 398)*
- mercenaries *(p. 400)*
- secular *(p. 398)*
- dowry *(p. 403)*

Academic Vocabulary
- instability *(p. 398)*
- decline *(p. 398)*

People, Places, and Events
- Italian Renaissance *(p. 398)*
- Leonardo da Vinci *(p. 398)*
- Milan *(p. 399)*
- Venice *(p. 399)*
- Florence *(p. 399)*
- Francesco Sforza *(p. 400)*
- Cosimo de' Medici *(p. 400)*
- Lorenzo de' Medici *(p. 400)*
- Rome *(p. 400)*
- Niccolò Machiavelli *(p. 401)*

Reading Strategy
Categorizing Information As you read, use a web diagram like the one below to identify the major principles of Machiavelli's work *The Prince.*

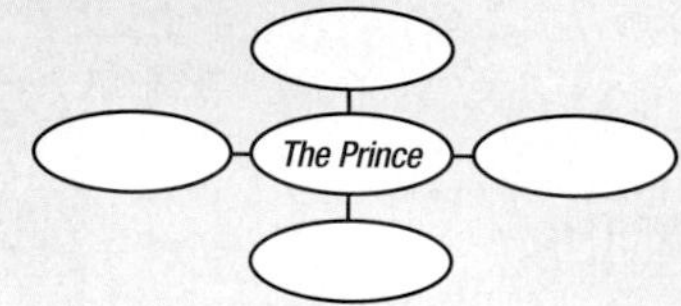

Beginning in Italy and spanning two centuries, the Renaissance emphasized secularism, awareness of ties to the ancient Greek and Roman worlds, and the ability of the individual. City-states became centers of political, economic, and social life. Machiavelli influenced political thought, and Castiglione defined what made a perfect Renaissance noble. The Renaissance affected everyone, from noble to peasant.

The Italian Renaissance

MAIN IDEA As the Renaissance began, three Italian city-states were the centers of Italian political, economic, and social life.

HISTORY & YOU Do you excel at more than one skill, for example, math and art? Read to learn about the Renaissance belief in individual ability.

The word *renaissance* means "rebirth." A number of people who lived in Italy between 1350 and 1550 believed that they had witnessed a rebirth of the ancient Greek and Roman worlds. To them, this rebirth marked a new age. Historians later called this period the Renaissance, or **Italian Renaissance**—a period of European history that began in Italy and spread to the rest of Europe. What are the most important characteristics of the Renaissance?

First, Renaissance Italy was largely an **urban society.** As the Middle Ages progressed, powerful city-states became the centers of Italian political, economic, and social life. Within this growing urban society, a **secular,** or worldly, viewpoint emerged as increasing wealth created new enjoyment of material things.

Second, the Renaissance was an age of recovery from the disasters of the fourteenth century—the plague, political **instability,** and a **decline** of Church power. Recovery went hand in hand with a rebirth of interest in ancient culture. Italian thinkers became aware of their own Roman past—the remains of which were to be seen all around them. They also became intensely interested in the culture that had dominated the ancient Mediterranean world. This revival affected both politics and art.

Third, a new view of human beings emerged as people in the Italian Renaissance emphasized individual ability. As Leon Battista Alberti, a fifteenth-century Italian, said, "Men can do all things if they will." A high regard for human worth and a realization of what individuals could achieve created a new social ideal. The well-rounded, universal person could achieve much in many areas. **Leonardo da Vinci** (VIHN•chee), for example, was a painter, sculptor, architect, inventor, and mathematician.

Resource Manager

R Reading Strategies	C Critical Thinking	D Differentiated Instruction	W Writing Support	S Skill Practice
Teacher Edition • Questioning, p. 400 • Summarizing, p. 401 • Read. Pri. Sources, p. 402 **Additional Resources** • Guid. Read. Act., URB p. 50 • Read. Ess. & Note-Taking Guide, p. 130	**Teacher Edition** • Compare/Contrast pp. 400, 402 • Making Inferences, p. 400 **Additional Resources** • Hist. Analysis Skills Act., URB p. 20 • Hist. & Geo. Act., URB p. 31 • Section Quiz, p. 145	**Teacher Edition** • Visual/Spatial, p. 403 **Additional Resources** • English Learner Act., URB p. 23 • People in World Hist. Act., URB p. 41	**Teacher Edition** • Expository Writing, p. 399 **Additional Resources** • Writer's Guidebook, p. 54	**Teacher Edition** • Using Geo. Skills, p. 399 **Additional Resources** • Skills Reinforc. Act., URB p. 29

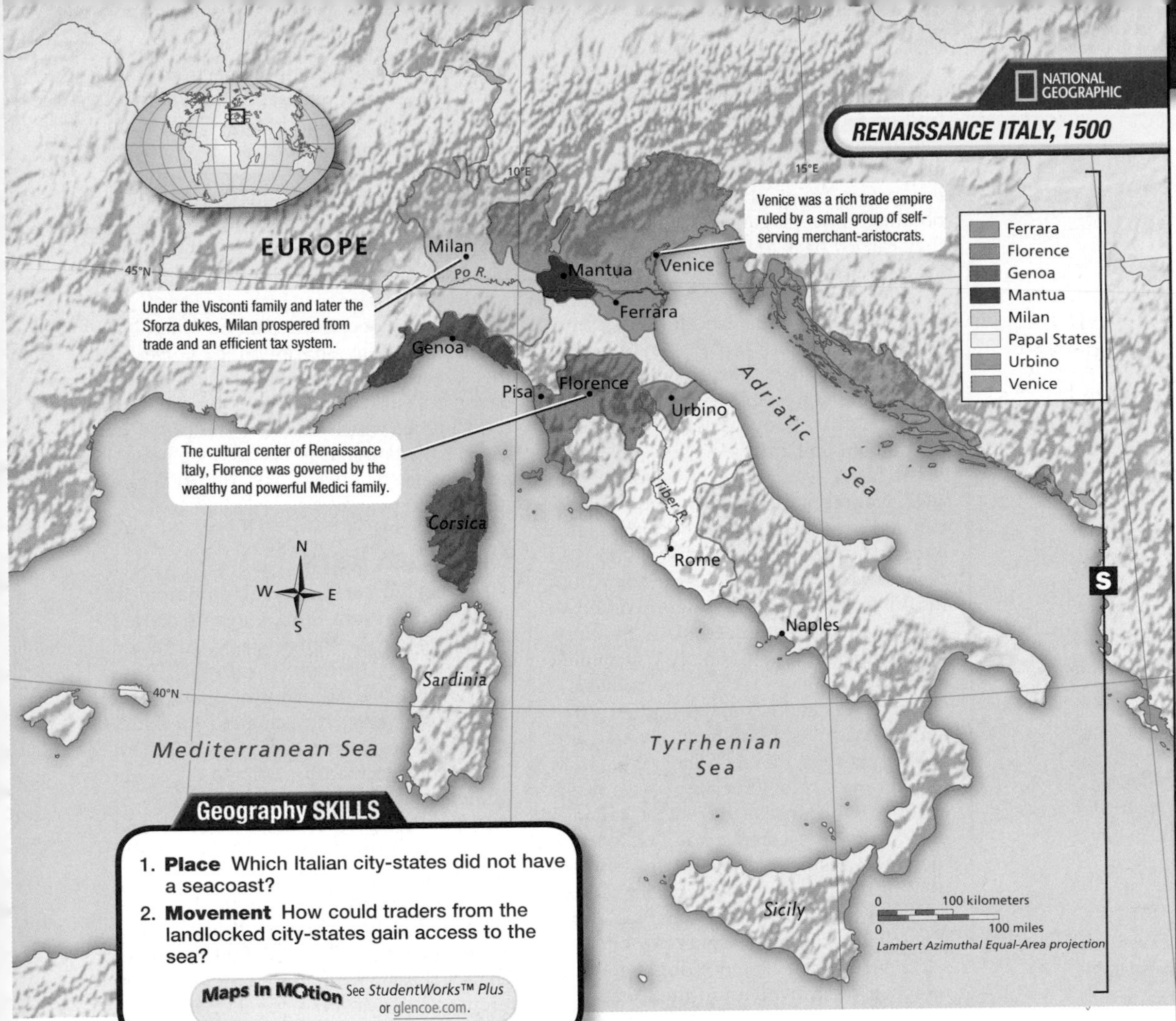

NATIONAL GEOGRAPHIC
RENAISSANCE ITALY, 1500
EUROPE
10°E
15°E
45°N
40°N
Venice was a rich trade empire ruled by a small group of self-serving merchant-aristocrats.
Under the Visconti family and later the Sforza dukes, Milan prospered from trade and an efficient tax system.
The cultural center of Renaissance Italy, Florence was governed by the wealthy and powerful Medici family.
Milan
Po R.
Mantua
Venice
Ferrara
Genoa
Pisa
Florence
Urbino
Adriatic Sea
Tiber R.
Corsica
Rome
Naples
Sardinia
Mediterranean Sea
Tyrrhenian Sea
Sicily
N
S
E
W
Ferrara
Florence
Genoa
Mantua
Milan
Papal States
Urbino
Venice
0 100 kilometers
0 100 miles
Lambert Azimuthal Equal-Area projection

Geography SKILLS

1. **Place** Which Italian city-states did not have a seacoast?
2. **Movement** How could traders from the landlocked city-states gain access to the sea?

Maps In MOtion See StudentWorks™ Plus or glencoe.com.

Of course, not all parts of Italian society were directly affected by these three general characteristics of the Italian Renaissance. The wealthy upper classes, who made up a small percentage of the total population, more actively embraced the new ideas and activities. Indirectly, however, the Italian Renaissance did have some impact on ordinary people. Especially in the cities, many of the intellectual and artistic achievements of the period were highly visible and difficult to ignore. The churches, wealthy homes, and public buildings were decorated with art that celebrated religious and secular themes, the human body, and an appreciation of classical antiquity.

The Italian States

During the Middle Ages, Italy had failed to develop a centralized monarchical state. The lack of a single strong ruler made it possible for a number of city-states in northern and central Italy to remain independent. Three of them—**Milan**, **Venice**, and **Florence**—expanded and played crucial roles in Italian politics.

Teach

S Skill Practice

Using Geography Skills Ask: What advantage did Venice gain by its location? *(It could trade in the East by land or sea.)* **OL**

For additional practice on this skill, see the **Skills Handbook**.

W Writing Support

Expository Writing Have three teams of students each study one major city-state: Venice, Florence, or Milan. Ask teams to investigate their city-state's government, economy, architecture, and art. Have each group summarize its findings. **OL**

Geography SKILLS

Answers:
1. Milan, Mantua
2. by using the Po River

Differentiated Instruction

Leveled Activities

BL Guided Reading Activity, URB p. 50

Guided Reading Activity 12-1
The Renaissance

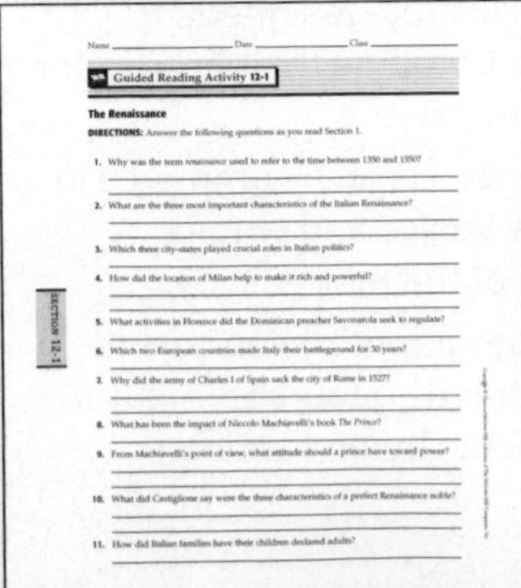

OL Skills Reinforcement Activity, URB p. 29

Skills Reinforcement Activity 12
Summarizing Information

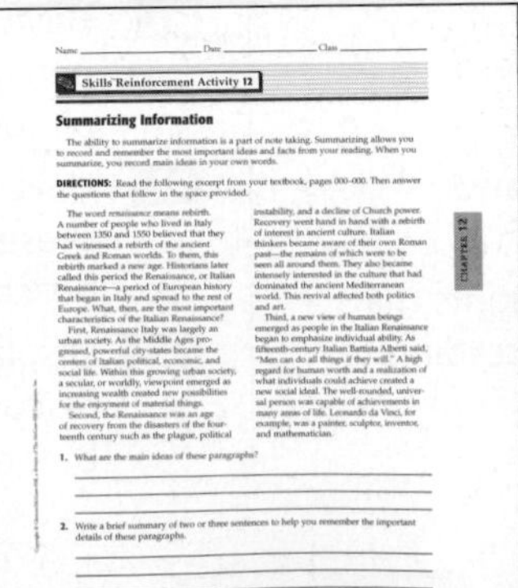

AL People in World History Activity, URB p. 41

People in World History Activity 12
Profile 1
Johannes Gutenberg (c. 1397–1468)
REVIEWING THE PROFILE

ELL English Learner Activity, URB p. 23

English Learner Activity 12
Renaissance and Reformation

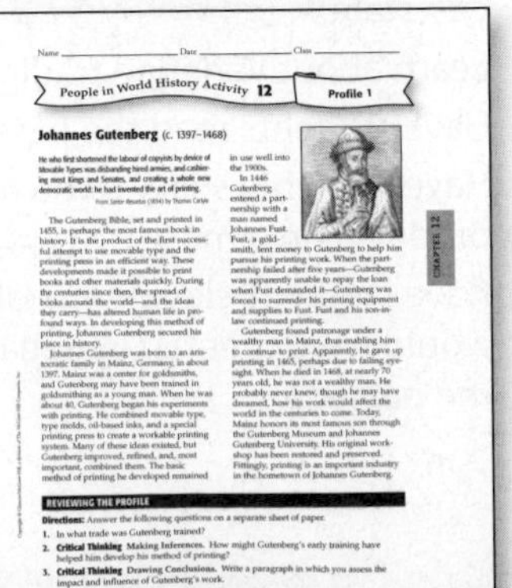

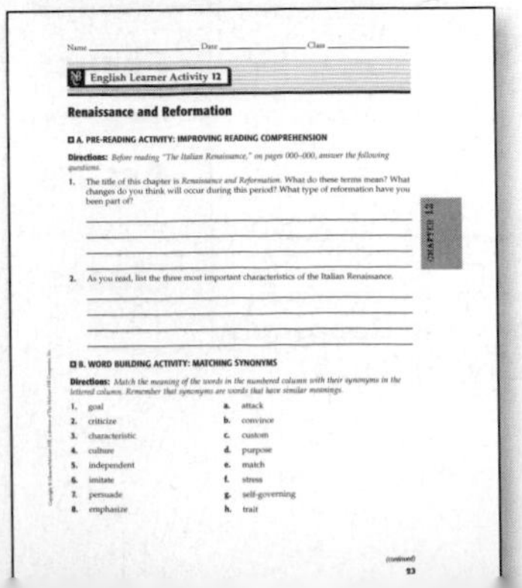

R Reading Strategy

Questioning Ask: How did the Visconti and Sforza rulers affect the development of Milan? *(They created a tax system that generated a huge income for the government.)* OL

C1 Critical Thinking

Comparing and Contrasting Ask: How were the governments of Venice and Florence similar? *(Both were run by groups of wealthy merchants who profited from their control of the government.)* OL

C2 Critical Thinking

Making Inferences Ask: Why did Italian city-states need help from Spain? *(They were not strong enough or unified enough to fight off invaders from France.)* OL

✓Reading Check

Answer: Italy's riches

The Italian city-states prospered from a flourishing trade that had expanded in the Middle Ages. Italian merchants had profited from the Crusades as well and were able to set up new trading centers in eastern ports. There, the Italian merchants obtained silks, sugar, and spices, which they carried back to Italy and the West.

Milan was one of the richest city-states in Italy. It was located in the north, at the crossroads of the main trade routes from Italian coastal cities to the Alpine passes. In the fourteenth century, members of the Visconti family established themselves as dukes of Milan. They extended their power over all of Lombardy.

R The last Visconti ruler of Milan died in 1447. **Francesco Sforza** then conquered the city and became its new duke. Sforza led a band of **mercenaries**—soldiers who sold their services to the highest bidder. Both the Visconti and Sforza rulers worked to build a strong centralized state. By creating an efficient tax system, they generated enormous revenues for the government.

Venice was another major northern Italian city-state. As a link between Asia and Western Europe, the city drew traders from all over the world. Officially Venice was a republic with an elected leader called a doge. In reality, a small group of wealthy merchant-aristocrats ran the government of Venice for their benefit. Venice's trade empire was tremendously profitable and made Venice an international power.

The republic of Florence dominated the region of Tuscany. During the fourteenth C1 century, a small but wealthy group of merchants established control of the Florentine government. They waged a series of successful wars against their neighbors and established Florence as a major city-state.

In 1434, **Cosimo de' Medici** (MEH•duh•chee) took control of the city. The wealthy Medici family ran the government from behind the scenes. Using their wealth and personal influence, Cosimo, and later **Lorenzo de' Medici,** his grandson, dominated the city when Florence was the cultural center of Italy.

During the late 1400s, Florence experienced an economic decline. Most of its economy was based on the manufacturing of cloth. Increased competition from English and Flemish cloth makers drove down profits. During this time a Dominican preacher named Girolamo Savonarola began condemning the corruption and excesses of the Medici family. Citizens, tired of Medici rule and frustrated by economic events, turned to Savonarola. So many people followed him that the Medici family turned Florence over to his followers.

Eventually people tired of Savonarola's strict regulations on gambling, horseracing, swearing, painting, music, and books. Savonarola also attacked the corruption of the Church, which angered the pope. In 1498, Savonarola was accused of heresy and sentenced to death. The Medici family returned to power.

The Italian Wars

The growth of powerful monarchical states in the rest of Europe eventually led to trouble for the Italian states. Attracted by the riches of Italy, the French king Charles VIII led an army of 30,000 men into Italy in 1494. He occupied the kingdom of Naples in southern Italy. Northern Italian states turned for help to the Spanish, who gladly agreed to send soldiers to Italy. For the next 30 years, the French and the Spanish battled in Italy as they fought to dominate the country.

A decisive turning point in their war came in 1527. On May 5, thousands of C2 troops belonging to the Spanish king Charles I, along with mercenaries from different countries, arrived at the city of **Rome.** They had not been paid for months. When they yelled, "Money! Money!" their leader responded, "If you have ever dreamed of pillaging a town and laying hold of its treasures, here now is one, the richest of them all, queen of the world."

The next day the invading forces smashed the gates and pushed into the city. The troops went berserk in a frenzy of bloodshed and looting. The terrible sack of Rome in 1527 by the armies of the Spanish king Charles I ended the Italian wars and left the Spanish a dominant force in Italy.

✓Reading Check **Explaining** What attracted the French king Charles VIII to Italy?

Differentiated Instruction

History and Geography Activity, URB p. 31

Analyzing Information

Objective: Understand the role of trade in the Venetian city-state.

Focus: Learn about Venetian trading patterns.

Teach: Have students read the passage.

Assess: Have students show trade routes and products on a map.

Close: Have students sketch one of the sights that would have greeted Venetians, according to the passage.

Differentiated Instruction Strategies

- **BL** Have pairs illustrate assigned paragraphs. Combine their images for a pictorial summary.
- **AL** Have students research commerce in present-day Venice and write a description of the modern city.
- **ELL** Display photographs of Venice and discuss its unique geographic features before students begin reading.

Machiavelli on Power

MAIN IDEA Machiavelli's *The Prince* has profoundly influenced political leaders.

HISTORY & YOU Do you believe that morality has a place in politics? Read to learn about Machiavelli's views on political power.

No one gave better expression to the Italians' love affair with political power than **Niccolò Machiavelli** (MA•kee•uh•VEH•lee). His book *The Prince* is one of the most influential works on political power in the Western world.

Machiavelli's central thesis in *The Prince* concerns how to acquire—and keep—political power. In the Middle Ages, many writers on political power had stressed the moral side of a prince's activity—how a ruler ought to behave based on Christian principles. Machiavelli rejected this popular approach. He believed that morality had little to do with politics.

From Machiavelli's point of view, a prince's attitude toward power must be based on an understanding of human nature, which he believed was basically self-centered. Political activity, therefore, should not be restricted by moral principles. A prince acts on behalf of the state. According to Machiavelli, then, for the state's sake, a prince must be willing to let his conscience sleep. R

Machiavelli was among the first to abandon morality as the basis for analyzing political activity. His views have had a profound influence on political leaders who followed.

✓Reading Check **Identifying** What was Machiavelli's central thesis in *The Prince*?

HISTORY & ARTS PRIMARY SOURCE

Patronage of the Medici Family

Under the rule of the wealthy Medici family, Florence became the cultural center of Europe. Their patronage supported many artists, including Brunelleschi, Donatello, and Michelangelo.

Piero de' Medici hired Benozzo Gozzoli in 1459 to paint frescoes in the chapel at the Medici Palace. Frescoes on three walls depict the biblical stories about the processions of the three Magi to Bethlehem. The wall with the youngest king (shown here) is the most lavish. The artist included portraits of Piero and his father, Cosimo, as well as a self-portrait. The young king is a portrait of Piero's son Lorenzo, who was then only ten years old, but would come to be known as Lorenzo the Magnificent.

CRITICAL THINKING SKILLS

1. **Explaining** How did the Medici influence the Renaissance in Florence?
2. **Making Inferences** Why do you think Gozzoli included portraits of several members of the Medici family in his fresco depicting a biblical scene?

R Reading Strategy

Summarizing Ask: How did Machiavelli view human nature? *(He held a negative view. He felt that self-interest outweighed morality.)* OL

Did You Know?

The idea that "the end justifies the means" comes from *The Prince*. Machiavelli writes, "one is obliged to look to the results of an action, and not to the means by which it was achieved...."

✓Reading Check

Answer: Political activity is not bound by moral principles.

CRITICAL THINKING SKILLS

Answers:

1. They used their wealth to support artists, helping Florence become the cultural center of Europe.
2. Possible response: to flatter them so that they would continue their patronage

Hands-On Chapter Project Step 1

Creating a Mural

Small groups of students will create a mural depicting important ideas and figures of the Renaissance and Reformation.

Step 1: Organizing the First Panel

Essential Question: How did the Renaissance and Reformation change European ideas and institutions?

Directions: Write the Big Idea on the board. Distribute the materials that students will need for their murals. Tell them that the first panel will introduce the characteristics of the Renaissance and important ideas associated with it through a combination of text and images. Have students use the facts in the textbook to help them develop the content and design of their mural. Encourage students to choose colors and symbols that reflect the spirit of the age.

Summarizing: Have students share what they learned about the Big Idea after completing their first panel. OL

(Chapter Project is continued in Section 2.)

C Critical Thinking

Comparing and Contrasting

Ask: How do the characteristics of a noble compare to the ideal of a successful American businessperson or politician? *(Answers will vary; students may consider a code of conduct most important for public officials.)* **OL**

R Reading Strategy

Reading Primary Sources

Ask: Would a Machiavellian prince want a follower of Castiglione in his court? *(No. Castiglione's ideas about virtue seem incompatible with Machiavelli's philosophy.)* **AL**

CRITICAL THINKING SKILLS

Answers:

1. wine press, goldsmiths' type, artists' ink, and paper
2. Possible response: The Renaissance brought renewed interest in learning and culture. Because the printing press could produce books so quickly, it helped spread ideas faster and more widely than ever before.

Renaissance Society

MAIN IDEA Changes in the social classes occurred during the Renaissance.

HISTORY & YOU Should your parents choose your future spouse? Read to learn about the marriage customs during the Renaissance.

In the Middle Ages, society was divided into three estates, or social classes (see Chapter 9). Although this social order continued into the Renaissance, some changes **C** became evident.

The Nobility

Although many European nobles faced declining incomes prior to the Renaissance, many had retained their lands and titles. By 1500, nobles, old and new, again dominated society. Making up only 2 to 3 percent of the population in most countries, nobles held important political posts and served as advisers to the king.

Nobles, or aristocrats, were expected to fulfill certain ideals. The characteristics of a perfect Renaissance noble were expressed in *The Book of the Courtier,* written by Baldassare Castiglione (KAHS•teel•YOH•NAY), an Italian, in 1528. First, a noble was born, not made. He must have character, grace, and talent. Second, the noble had to be a warrior, but also needed a classical education and interest in the arts. Third, the noble had to follow a certain standard of conduct. What was the purpose of these standards?

PRIMARY SOURCE

R "[T]he aim of the perfect Courtier is so to win . . . the favor and mind of the prince whom he serves that he may be able to tell him . . . the truth about everything he needs to know . . . and that when he sees the mind of his prince inclined to a wrong action, he may dare to oppose him . . . so as to dissuade him of every evil intent and bring him to the path of virtue."

—Baldassare Castiglione, *The Book of the Courtier,* 1528

SCIENCE, TECHNOLOGY, & SOCIETY

Gutenberg's Press

In 1455, Johannes Gutenberg produced the first printed book, a Bible, in Germany. His printing press brought together several existing technologies. The press was adapted from a wine press. Goldsmiths used type to stamp their marks on finished products. The ink was based on artists' ink. One innovation was the use of paper instead of the parchment or vellum typical of handwritten manuscripts.

The rise in literacy during the Renaissance created a growing audience for books. To satisfy the demand, more books were produced in the first 50 years of printing than in the entire history of the world up to 1450. The printing press greatly accelerated the spread of ideas.

CRITICAL THINKING SKILLS

1. **Finding the Main Idea** What technologies did Gutenberg bring together in his printing press?
2. **Analyzing** How did the printing press contribute to the Renaissance?

Additional Support

Teacher Tip

Collaborative Learning The activity allows students with different levels of academic skills to work together. As you form groups, consider the needed skills and choose students accordingly.

Activity: Collaborative Learning

Creating a Time Line Tell students that printing has a long history dating from the 2nd century. The Chinese were the first to use ink and paper to transfer images from carved pillars. Soon, they had devised a way to engrave wood blocks. Later, they invented movable type. Have students research the history of printing from the time of the Chinese to the present. Ask them to work in small groups to create an illustrated, annotated time line of important developments. Have groups display their time lines. **Ask:** Have later advances had the same impact as Gutenberg's printing press? Explain. *(Students might say that although later advances increased the ease of communicating, Gutenberg's press set society on a revolutionary path to literacy.)* **OL**

The aim of the perfect noble was to serve his prince in an effective and honest way. Nobles would adhere to Castiglione's principles for hundreds of years while they continued to dominate European social and political life.

Peasants and Townspeople

In the Renaissance, peasants still constituted 85 to 90 percent of the total European population. Serfdom continued to decrease with the decline of the manorial system. By 1500, especially in western Europe, more and more peasants became legally free.

Townspeople made up the rest of the third estate. At the top of urban society were the patricians. With their wealth from trade, industry, and banking, they dominated their communities. Below them were the burghers—the shopkeepers, artisans, guild masters, and guild members. Below the burghers were the workers, who earned pitiful wages, and the unemployed. Both groups lived miserable lives. These people made up perhaps 30 or 40 percent of the urban population. **D**

During the late 1300s and the 1400s, urban poverty increased dramatically throughout Europe. One rich merchant, who had little sympathy for the poor, wrote:

PRIMARY SOURCE

"Those that are lazy in a way that does harm to the city, and who can offer no just reason for their condition, should either be forced to work or expelled from the city. The city would thus rid itself of that most harmful part of the poorest class."

—fifteenth-century Florence merchant

Family and Marriage

The family bond was a source of great security. Parents carefully arranged marriages to strengthen business or family ties. Often they worked out the details when their children were only two or three years old. The marriage contract included a **dowry,** a sum of money that the wife's family gave to the husband upon marriage.

The father-husband was the center of the Italian family. He managed all finances (his wife had no share in his wealth) and made the decisions that determined his children's lives. The mother's chief role was to supervise the household. A father had absolute authority over his children until he died or formally freed them. In Renaissance Italy, children did not become adults at a certain age. Instead, they became adults when their fathers went before a judge to free them. Adulthood age varied from the early teens to the late twenties.

✓Reading Check **Contrasting** How was the Renaissance noble different from the medieval knight?

SECTION 1 REVIEW

Vocabulary

1. **Explain** the significance of: Italian Renaissance, urban society, secular, instability, decline, Leonardo da Vinci, Milan, Venice, Florence, Francesco Sforza, mercenaries, Cosimo de' Medici, Lorenzo de' Medici, Rome, Niccolò Machiavelli, dowry.

Main Ideas

2. **Explain** why the Italian city-states were so prosperous.
3. **Summarize** Machiavelli's view of human nature.
4. **Contrast** the social structure of the Middle Ages and the Renaissance.

	Middle Ages	Renaissance
Nobility		
Peasants		
Townspeople		

Critical Thinking

5. **The BIG Idea** **Evaluating** Why has Leonardo da Vinci been viewed as a model Renaissance man?
6. **Making Inferences** What would families of Renaissance Italy consider to be a good marriage for their child?
7. **Analyzing Visuals** Examine the image on page 401. What feeling do you get from this painting? What details in the painting create this feeling?

Writing About History

8. **Expository Writing** Read a few passages from *The Prince.* Write a brief essay explaining why you agree or do not agree with Machiavelli's theory of politics.

History ONLINE
For help with the concepts in this section of *Glencoe World History*, go to glencoe.com and click Study Central™.

403

D Differentiated Instruction

Visual/Spatial Have students analyze the information about Europe's urban population and represent it in a labeled pyramid. The graph should include various levels of urban society and the roles each group played in the economy. **BL**

✓Reading Check

Answer: A noble needed a classical education and an interest in the arts.

Assess

History ONLINE

Study Central provides summaries, interactive games, and online graphic organizers to help students review content.

Close

Summarizing **Ask:** What circumstances helped create the Renaissance? *(Prosperous city-states gave rise to a merchant class that patronized the arts. Lively trade led to an exchange of ideas. The printing press made books more accessible.)* **OL**

Answers

1. Definitions for the vocabulary words are found in the section and the Glossary.
2. flourishing trade; profit from the Crusades
3. People are self-centered by nature. For the sake of the state, rulers should act without moral restrictions.
4. **Nobility—Middle Ages:** primarily concerned with military skill; **Renaissance:** classical education, arts, warrior, standard of conduct. **Peasants—Middle Ages:** part of manorial system; **Renaissance:** more peasants were legally free. **Townspeople—Middle Ages:** merchants and artisans; **Renaissance:** patricians, shopkeepers, artisans, guild masters, workers.
5. His wide range of talents—as painter, sculptor, inventor, architect, and mathematician—exemplified the Renaissance view of human ability.
6. one that joined their family to a family of wealth and power
7. Possible response: a feeling of grandeur because of the ornate garments on king and horses, and the expansive view
8. Answers should be based on supporting details and logical conclusions.

Focus

Introducing Social History
Have students recall the characteristics of the Italian Renaissance. **Ask:** How did an emphasis on individual ability affect the social structure? *(People's achievements, rather than their inherited rank, determined their place in society.)* How did an increase in trade contribute to an interest in fashion? *(Foreign goods and ideas created an interest in new styles of clothing and accessories.)* **OL**

Teach

C Critical Thinking

Determining Cause and Effect **Ask:** What were the sources of wealth for nobles and merchants? *(**Nobles:** land; **Merchants:** trade)* **BL**

R Reading Strategy

Organizing Have students create three-column charts to list the characteristics of nobles, the middle class, and peasants during the Renaissance. **BL**

Additional Support

Social History

Renaissance Society

C During the Renaissance, Europe was a highly structured society. Its class system had evolved during the Middle Ages. Many serfs became free peasants in the countryside. A middle class was developing in the towns and its merchants began to create wealth from trade. They were a distinct class, separate from the land-owning nobles.

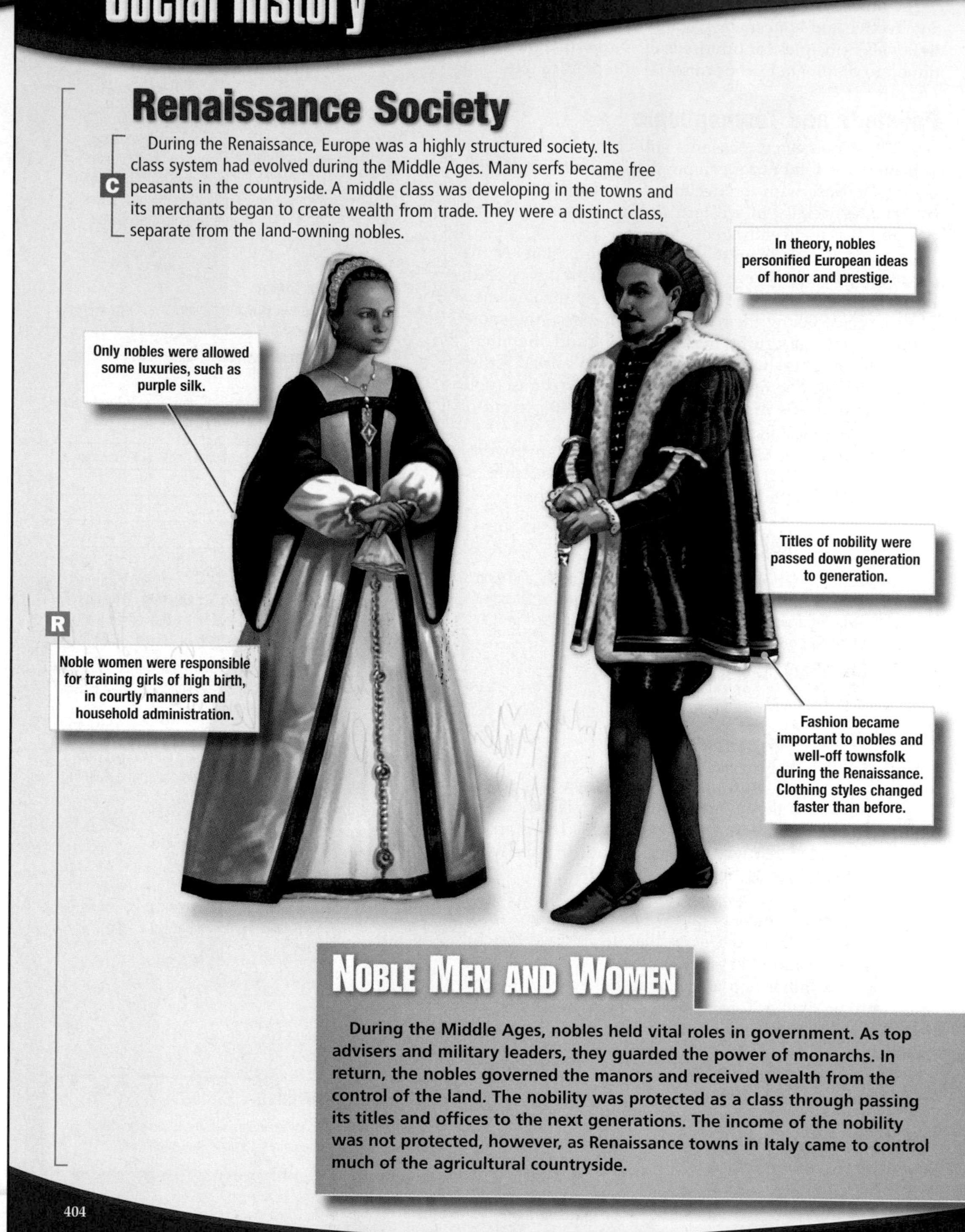

Noble Men and Women

During the Middle Ages, nobles held vital roles in government. As top advisers and military leaders, they guarded the power of monarchs. In return, the nobles governed the manors and received wealth from the control of the land. The nobility was protected as a class through passing its titles and offices to the next generations. The income of the nobility was not protected, however, as Renaissance towns in Italy came to control much of the agricultural countryside.

Background

Humanism and the Renaissance Most scholars no longer view the Renaissance as a period that marked a complete break with medieval values. Instead, the Renaissance is viewed as a time when trends that had emerged in the Middle Ages became stronger. For example, the growing importance of trade and the institutions that went with it, such as banks, had already been recognized. Secular humanism, however, was a different type of intellectual inquiry than medieval scholasticism. Humanist thinkers were not members of the clergy, and their focus was more on humans' experiences in the world of the present than on preparation for the afterlife. Humanism encouraged scholarship that was not bound by religious dogma. The invention of movable type and the growth of printing allowed these ideas to spread from Italy to northern Europe. Discuss with students how the decline in Church power and the growth of cities during the late Middle Ages also helped pave the way for humanism.

Peasants and the Middle Class

Wealthy merchants rivaled the nobles in luxurious clothing. The peasants and the poor laborers and beggars of the towns lived outside this world of fashion. Material for clothing and other goods could be obtained by urban dwellers in the town market. As commercial capitalism started in the Middle Ages, economic power began to grow among merchants, financiers, and other middle-class figures.

Analyzing Visuals

1. **Describing** What do the nobles' clothes tell you about their station in life?
2. **Assessing** What role did peasants play in the economies of towns?

W Writing Support

Descriptive Writing Have students write a description of a Renaissance town based on the visual. Encourage students to use all their senses as they write. OL

S Skill Practice

Visual Literacy Ask: What are the similarities and differences between the clothing of ordinary townspeople and the clothing of nobles? (***Similarities:*** *some similar styles, such as women covering their heads, necklines of dresses, men's hats, tunic tops over slim pants or tights;* ***Differences:*** *nobles' clothing made with more luxurious fabrics and trim, jewelry)* BL

Assess/Close

Have students answer the Analyzing Visuals questions and share their responses with a partner. Discuss how social classes changed during the Renaissance. OL

ANALYZING VISUALS

Answers:

1. They were the wealthy elite.
2. They brought goods from the countryside to sell in the town markets.

Activity: Economics Connection

Examining the History of Banking Although banking existed as far back as the Babylonian Empire, modern banking practices are associated with the rise of international trade and commercial capitalism in the medieval and Renaissance periods. Our word *bank* comes from the Italian word *banca*, meaning "bench," because Italian money changers conducted their business on benches in the streets. As merchants acquired wealth they had money to lend and they began to establish offices in cities along trade routes to facilitate payment of debts. To avoid transporting a lot of cash, letters promising payment were used as a form of credit. Trade flourished in early banking centers such as Florence, Italy. **Ask:** Why did merchants become the earliest bankers? Have students conduct research on the role of merchants in the history of banking and write an article for a business magazine profiling prominent early bankers such as the Medici family in Italy or the Fugger family in Germany. AL

R Reading Strategy

Reading Primary Sources
Ask: How did Christine de Pizan's assertion challenge traditional beliefs? *(She claimed that women could learn as well as men, suggesting that they should not be confined to traditional roles.)* OL

S Skill Practice

Visual Literacy Have students study the household objects in the Mérode Altarpiece. **Ask:** Which details do not reflect biblical times? *(books, furniture, woodwork, and so on)* OL

✓Reading Check

Answer: collection of stories told by a group of 29 pilgrims

DOCUMENT-BASED QUESTIONS

Answers:

1. **Northern European:** tight, box-like settings, everyday objects; **Italian:** classical styles, geometric perspective.
2. **Campin:** intimate home setting implies private connection to religion; **Raphael:** setting and aristocratic figures make expression of religion seem formal and public.

Additional Support

This format gave Chaucer the chance to portray an entire range of English society.

Another writer who used the vernacular was **Christine de Pizan**, a Frenchwoman who is best known for her works written in defense of women. In *The Book of the City of Ladies*, written in 1404, she denounced the many male writers who had argued that women, by their very nature, are unable to learn. Women, de Pizan argued, could learn as well as men if they could attend the same schools:

PRIMARY SOURCE

R "Should I also tell you whether a woman's nature is clever and quick enough to learn speculative sciences as well as to discover them, and likewise the manual arts. I assure you that women are equally well-suited and skilled to carry them out and to put them to sophisticated use once they have learned them."

—Christine de Pizan

✓Reading Check **Explaining** What literary format does Chaucer use to portray English society?

Renaissance Education

MAIN IDEA Education during the Renaissance focused on the liberal studies.

HISTORY & YOU What is your favorite subject? Read to learn about the subjects of study during the Renaissance.

The humanist movement had a profound effect on education in the 1300s and 1400s. Renaissance humanists believed that education could dramatically change human beings. They wrote books on education and opened schools based on their ideas.

At the core of humanist schools were the liberal studies. Humanists believed that liberal studies (or, today, liberal arts) enabled individuals to reach their full potential. One humanist wrote: "We call those studies liberal by which we **attain** and practice virtue and wisdom; which calls forth and develops those highest gifts of body and mind which ennoble men."

HISTORY & ARTS PRIMARY SOURCE

Differences in Renaissance Art

◀ Central panel of *Mérode Altarpiece* by Robert Campin (c. 1425–28)

S Flemish artists typically placed their subjects among everyday objects. The space depicted was tight and boxlike.

Marriage of the Virgin by Raphael (1504) ▼

Raphael used the technique of perspective to give the illusion of scale, distance, and three dimensions on a two-dimensional surface.

DOCUMENT-BASED QUESTIONS

Artists of the Northern Renaissance placed their works in everyday settings, while Italian Renaissance artists were influenced by classical styles and geometric precision. Religious themes were a common subject matter.

1. **Contrasting** How did the Renaissance style in Northern Europe differ from that of Italy?
2. **Interpreting** How might the settings of each painting reveal differences in religious ideals between Northern Europe and Italy?

Activity: Interdisciplinary Connection

Art Tell students that the Mérode Altarpiece is actually a triptych: a work of art on three panels that often opens and closes on hinges. The triptych form dates from the Middle Ages and was often used for altars. The central panel contained the most important image; the two side panels held smaller, related scenes. Have students use library or Internet resources to locate the complete Mérode Altarpiece, as well as other examples of triptychs. **Ask:** How are the examples similar? How are they different? *(All have three panels and related images. Content and styles vary.)*

Have students work in groups of three to plan and sketch a triptych. Ask them to choose a central scene as the focus of their work, and then select two smaller scenes to complement it. To make their sketches, have students hold their paper sideways (in landscape orientation) and fold both sides to meet in the center to form three "panels." Suggest that, like the painter of the Mérode Altarpiece, students illustrate an ancient topic in a modern setting. Let the groups explain their concepts and share their sketches with the class. OL

What, then, were the liberal studies? According to the humanists, students should study history, moral philosophy, eloquence (or rhetoric), letters (grammar and logic), poetry, mathematics, astronomy, and music. In short, the purpose of a liberal education (and thus the reason for studying the liberal arts) was to produce individuals who follow a path of virtue and wisdom. These individuals should also possess rhetorical skills so they can persuade others to take this same path of virtue and wisdom.

PRIMARY SOURCE

> "Not everyone is called to be a physician, a lawyer . . . nor has everyone outstanding gifts of natural capacity, but all of us . . . are responsible for the personal influence that goes forth from us."
>
> —Vittorino da Feltre (1373–1446)
> humanist educator, Mantua, Italy

Following the Greek ideal of a sound mind in a sound body, humanist educators also emphasized physical education. Students learned the skills of javelin throwing, archery, and dancing. They ran, wrestled, hunted, and swam.

Humanist educators thought that a humanist education was a practical preparation for life. Its aim was not to create great scholars but complete citizens. Humanist education was also considered necessary for preparing the sons of aristocrats for leadership roles. Humanist schools were the model for the education of Europe's ruling classes until the twentieth century.

Females were largely absent from these schools. The few female students who did attend humanist schools studied the classics and were encouraged to know some history as well as how to ride, dance, sing, play the lute (a stringed instrument), and appreciate poetry. They were told not to learn mathematics or rhetoric. It was thought that religion and morals should be foremost in the education of "Christian ladies" so that they could become good wives and mothers. **C**

✓Reading Check **Expaining** How did a humanist education prepare a student for life?

Italian Renaissance Art

MAIN IDEA The Renaissance produced great artists and sculptors such as Michelangelo, Raphael, and Leonardo da Vinci.

HISTORY & YOU Do you recall the features of Gothic style? Read to learn how Renaissance architects diverged from Gothic style.

Renaissance artists sought to imitate nature. They wanted viewers to see the reality in their subjects. At the same time, these artists were developing a new, human-focused worldview. As one artist proclaimed, human beings were the "center and measure of all things."

New Techniques in Painting

Frescoes by Masaccio (muh•ZAH•chee•oh) are the first masterpieces of Early Renaissance (1400–1490) art. A **fresco** is a painting done on fresh, wet plaster with water-based paints. Human figures in medieval paintings look flat, but Masaccio's figures have depth and come alive. By mastering the laws of perspective, Masaccio could create the illusion of three dimensions, leading to a new, realistic **style.** **R**

Other fifteenth-century Florentine painters used and modified this new, or Renaissance, style. Especially important were two major developments. One development stressed the technical side of painting—understanding the laws of perspective and the organization of outdoor space and light through geometry. The second development was the investigation of movement and human anatomy. The realistic portrayal of the individual, especially the human nude, became one of the chief aims of Italian Renaissance art.

Sculpture and Architecture

The Renaissance produced equally stunning advances in sculpture and architecture. The sculptor Donatello studied the statues of the Greeks and Romans. His works included a realistic, free-standing figure of Saint George.

The work of architect Filippo Brunelleschi (BROO•nuhl•EHS•kee) was inspired by the buildings of classical Rome.

C Critical Thinking

Making Inferences Ask: Why were female students told not to learn mathematics and rhetoric? *(Women were not supposed to be involved in business or take on public roles. Therefore, courses that prepared men for these roles, such as mathematics and rhetoric, would not be necessary for women.)* **OL**

For additional practice on this skill, see the **Skills Handbook**.

R Reading Strategy

Summarizing Ask: What changes did Renaissance artists bring to painting? *(They used perspective, giving their work a more realistic look through the illusion of depth. They studied movement and human anatomy to create lifelike figures.)* **OL**

✓Reading Check

Answer: helped students reach their full potential, follow a path of virtue and wisdom and persuade others to do the same, and become complete citizens; also prepared children of aristocrats for leadership

Differentiated Instruction

Comparing and Contrasting

Objective: Examine past and present methods of funding the arts.
Focus: Read about art patrons of the Renaissance.
Teach: Discuss the pros and cons of the Renaissance system of art patronage.
Assess: Have students research the NEA and list the pros and cons of public funding.
Close: Have students argue for the best method of stimulating artistic endeavors.

Differentiated Instruction Strategies

BL As a class, discuss advantages and disadvantages of both systems.

AL Have students explore the controversy surrounding the NEA and argue for or against its continued existence.

ELL Have students present an exhibit of art from their home countries and explain how artists support themselves.

Linking Past and Present Activity, URB p. 40

W Writing Support

Expository Writing Display images of medieval Gothic cathedrals, such as Notre Dame in Paris, and Renaissance churches, such as the cathedral in Florence. Discuss with students the contrasting impressions of medieval cathedrals and Renaissance buildings. Ask them to write an essay on how each style of architecture reflects its age. AL

D Differentiated Instruction

Visual/Spatial Display Raphael's *School of Athens*. Ask students to analyze the elements of the painting and their relationship to the principles of Renaissance and classical art. AL

✓Reading Check

Answer: Leonardo da Vinci, Raphael, Michelangelo

PEOPLE in HISTORY

Answers: Leonardo da Vinci— Niccolò Machiavelli; **Michelangelo**—in the Sistine Chapel

Additional Support

His design of the church of San Lorenzo in Florence reflects this. The classical columns and rounded arches in the church's design create an environment that does not overwhelm the worshiper, as Gothic cathedrals might. The church creates a space to fit human, and not divine, needs. Like painters and sculptors, Renaissance architects sought to reflect a human-centered world.

High Renaissance Masters

The final stage of Italian Renaissance painting flourished between 1490 and 1520. Called the High Renaissance, the period is associated with Leonardo da Vinci, Raphael, and Michelangelo.

Leonardo mastered the art of realistic painting and even dissected human bodies to better see how nature worked. However, he wanted to advance beyond such realism to create idealized forms that captured the perfection of nature and the individual—perfection that could not be expressed fully by a realistic style.

At age 25, **Raphael** was already one of Italy's best painters. He was admired for his numerous madonnas (paintings of the Virgin Mary). In these, he achieved an ideal of beauty far surpassing human standards. Raphael is also well known for his frescoes in the Vatican Palace. His *School of Athens* reveals a world of balance, harmony, and order—the underlying principles of classical Greek and Roman art.

Michelangelo, an accomplished painter, sculptor, and architect, was another master of the High Renaissance. Fiercely driven by his desire to create, he worked with great passion and energy on a remarkable number of projects. Michelangelo's figures on the ceiling of the Sistine Chapel in Rome depict an ideal type of human being with perfect proportions. The beauty of this idealized human being is meant to be a reflection of divine beauty. The more beautiful the body, the more godlike the figure.

✓Reading Check **Identifying** Name three Italian artists of the High Renaissance.

PEOPLE in HISTORY

Leonardo da Vinci
1452–1519 Italian Artist and Scientist

Leonardo da Vinci was the model "Renaissance man." He was an artist, scientist, inventor, and visionary. In 1503, the government of Florence sought his genius on a military matter. With the help of Niccolò Machiavelli, Leonardo da Vinci devised a plan to help Florence defeat the city of Pisa in a war. The plan was to divert the Arno River away from Pisa to cut Pisa off from the sea. However, the engineer hired to dig a diversion canal did not follow Leonardo's instructions, and the canal walls collapsed. Although the plan failed, the maps Leonardo drew up were so detailed that they were used long afterward. He also envisioned an industrial corridor along the river that eventually came to pass after his death. **What famous person helped Leonardo with his plan?**

Michelangelo
1475–1564 Italian Artist

Michelangelo Buonarroti was a man of many talents. A painter, sculptor, poet, architect, and literary scholar, there was little he could not do once he set his mind to it. When Pope Julius II asked him to paint the ceiling of the Sistine Chapel in 1508, Michelangelo protested that "painting is not my art." Despite his protests, the work that emerged four years later ranks among the greatest masterpieces of all time.

For his sculptures, Michelangelo would sometimes spend months in a marble quarry personally selecting the ideal block from which to carve his works of art. Some of his contemporaries believed that "he could see the figure imprisoned in it." Creative to the end of his long life, he famously lamented that "art and death do not go well together." **Where do some of Michelangelo's most famous paintings appear?**

Extending the Content

Leonardo da Vinci By the end of his life, Leonardo da Vinci had filled dozens of notebooks with observations and sketches on painting, the human body, mechanics, and architecture. His writing appeared unintelligible until scholars realized that it must be held up to a mirror in order to be read. He apparently intended these notes to be the foundation of several books. The notes reveal Leonardo's lively intelligence and wide-ranging interests.

Michelangelo Michelangelo thought of himself primarily as a sculptor. Among his most famous works is the giant statue of David, symbolizing the human ideal. Michelangelo applied a great deal of focus to his work.

The Northern Artistic Renaissance

MAIN IDEA Northern European artists, especially those in the Low Countries, portrayed their world realistically but in a different way than did the Italian artists.

HISTORY & YOU Have you ever used a varnish to seal woodwork? Read to learn about a new medium the Flemish artist Jan van Eyck used.

Like the artists of Italy, the artists of northern Europe became interested in portraying their world realistically. However, their approach was different from that of the Italians. This was particularly true of the artists of the Low Countries (present-day Belgium, Luxembourg, and the Netherlands).

Circumstance played a role in the differences. The large wall spaces of Italian churches had given rise to the art of fresco painting. Italian artists used these spaces to master the technical skills that allowed them to portray humans in realistic settings. In the north, the Gothic cathedrals with their stained glass windows did not allow enough space for frescoes. Thus, northern European artists painted illustrations for books and wooden panels for altarpieces. Great care was needed to depict each object on a small scale.

The most important northern school of art in the 1400s was in **Flanders,** one of the Low Countries. The Flemish painter **Jan van Eyck** (EYEK) was among the first to use and perfect the technique of oil painting. He used a varnish made of linseed oil and nut oils mixed with resins. This medium enabled van Eyck to use a wide variety of **C** brilliant, translucent colors. With his oil paints, he could create striking realism in fine details as in his painting *Giovanni Arnolfini and His Bride.* Like other Northern Renaissance artists, however, van Eyck imitated nature not by using perspective, as the Italians did, but by simply observing reality and portraying details as best he could.

By 1500, artists from the north had begun to study in Italy and to be influenced by what artists were doing there. One German artist who was greatly affected by the Italians was **Albrecht Dürer.** He made two trips to Italy and absorbed most of what the Italians could teach on the laws of perspective.

As can be seen in his famous *Adoration of the Magi,* Dürer did not reject the use of minute details characteristic of northern artists. He did try, however, to fit those details more harmoniously into his works in accordance with Italian artistic theories. Like the Italian artists of the High Renaissance, Dürer tried to achieve a standard of ideal beauty that was based on a careful examination of the human form.

✓Reading Check **Examining** Why was Jan van Eyck's use of oil paint significant?

SECTION 2 REVIEW

Vocabulary

1. **Explain** the significance of: humanism, Petrarch, vernacular, Dante, Chaucer, Canterbury, Christine de Pizan, attain, fresco, style, Raphael, Michelangelo, Flanders, Jan van Eyck, Albrecht Dürer.

Main Ideas

2. **Describe** Petrarch's contributions to the development of humanism.
3. **Identify** Christine de Pizan's main argument in *The Book of the City of Ladies.*
4. **Summarize** the accomplishments of Leonardo da Vinci, Raphael, and Michelangelo. Use a chart like the one below to make your summary.

Leonardo da Vinci	Raphael	Michelangelo

Critical Thinking

5. **The BIG Idea** **Identifying Central Issues** How was humanism reflected in the works of Renaissance artists?
6. **Contrasting** How did the education of females differ from that of males in humanist schools?
7. **Analyzing Visuals** Examine the painting on page 407. What can you infer about Purgatory based on its location in this painting?

Writing About History

8. **Expository Writing** Assume the role of an art docent (a person who guides people through museums). Prepare a lecture to be given to a group of students on the works of Jan van Eyck and how they differ from Italian Renaissance paintings.

History ONLINE
For help with the concepts in this section of *Glencoe World History,* go to glencoe.com and click Study Central™.

411

C Critical Thinking

Comparing and Contrasting
Ask: How did the styles of northern artists differ from Italian painters? *(Northern European artists painted on a smaller scale. They relied less on perspective and more on accurate portrayal of details.)* **OL**

✓Reading Check

Answer: It made possible a wide variety of colors, enabling him to create realism in fine details.

Assess

History ONLINE
Study Central provides summaries, interactive games, and online graphic organizers to help students review content.

Close

Summarizing **Ask:** What were important innovations in literature, education, art, and architecture during the Renaissance? *(use of vernacular, humanist education, lifelike art, smaller churches)* **OL**

Answers

1. Definitions for the vocabulary words are found in the section and the Glossary.
2. searched for forgotten Latin manuscripts throughout Europe; began emphasis on pure classical Latin
3. Women can learn as well as men if allowed to attend the same schools.
4. **da Vinci:** captured the perfection of nature and the individual; **Raphael:** achieved an ideal of beauty surpassing human standards; **Michelangelo:** portrayed ideal type of human being with perfect proportions
5. Art became more human-centered and reflected the influence of ancient Greek and Roman styles.
6. females largely excluded; the few who did attend were not taught mathematics or rhetoric; emphasis for females on religion and morals for role as wives and mothers
7. It exists somewhere between Heaven and Hell. It is an intermediate stop for the soul.
8. Answers may include that van Eyck painted in oils, used a variety of brilliant colors, created realism in fine details.

The Protestant Reformation

Focus

Bellringer

Daily Focus Transparency 12.3

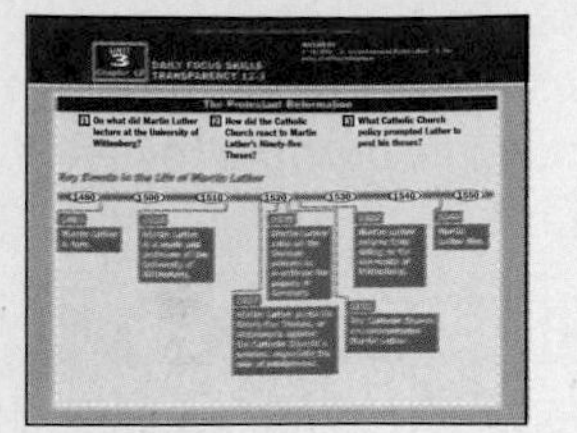

GUIDE TO READING

Answers to Graphic:

Steps Leading to the Reformation: Christian humanism, corruption in the Catholic Church, people desired meaningful religious expression and assurance of their salvation, sale of indulgences, Modern Devotion

Section Spotlight Video

To generate student interest and provide a springboard for class discussion, access the Chapter 12, Section 3 video at glencoe.com or on the video DVD.

GUIDE TO READING

The BIG Idea

Ideas, Beliefs, and Values In northern Europe, Christian humanists sought to reform the Catholic Church, and Protestantism emerged.

Content Vocabulary

- Christian humanism *(p. 412)*
- salvation *(p. 414)*
- indulgence *(p. 414)*
- Lutheranism *(p. 416)*

Academic Vocabulary

- precise *(p. 413)*
- ignorant *(p. 414)*

People, Places, and Events

- Martin Luther *(p. 412)*
- Desiderius Erasmus *(p. 412)*
- Wittenberg *(p. 415)*
- Ninety-five Theses *(p. 415)*
- Edict of Worms *(p. 415)*
- Charles V *(p. 417)*
- Bohemia *(p. 417)*
- Hungary *(p. 417)*
- Peace of Augsburg *(p. 417)*

Reading Strategy

Determining Cause and Effect As you read, use a diagram like the one below to identify steps that led to the Reformation.

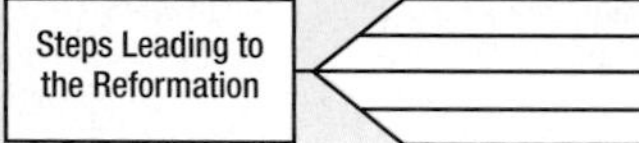

During the second half of the fifteenth century, Christian humanist Desiderius Erasmus paved the way for Martin Luther's reform movement. Political instability in the Holy Roman Empire allowed Lutheranism, the first Protestant faith, to spread. The Peace of Augsburg formally accepted the division of Christianity in Germany—Lutheranism and Catholicism.

Prelude to Reformation

MAIN IDEA Christian humanism and Desiderius Erasmus paved the way for the Protestant Reformation.

HISTORY & YOU Is there a school policy or rule that you would like to change? Read how Erasmus pointed out the need for Church reform.

The Protestant Reformation is the name given to the religious reform movement that divided the western Church into Catholic and Protestant groups. Although **Martin Luther** began the Reformation in the early 1500s, earlier developments set the stage for religious change.

Christian Humanism

One such development grew from widespread changes in intellectual thought. During the second half of the fifteenth century, the new classical learning that was part of Italian Renaissance humanism spread to northern Europe. From that came a movement called **Christian humanism,** or Northern Renaissance humanism. The major goal of this movement was the reform of the Catholic Church.

The Christian humanists believed in the ability of human beings to reason and improve themselves. They thought that if people read the classics, and especially the basic works of Christianity, they would become more pious. This inner piety, or inward religious feeling, would bring about a reform of the Church and society. Christian humanists believed that in order to change society, they would first have to change human beings.

The best-known Christian humanist was **Desiderius Erasmus** (ih•RAZ•muhs). He called his view of religion "the philosophy of Christ." By this, he meant that Christianity should show people how to live good lives on a daily basis, not just provide beliefs for them to be saved. Stressing the inwardness of religious feeling, Erasmus thought the external forms of medieval religion (pilgrimages, fasts, relics) were not all that important.

Resource Manager

R Reading Strategies	C Critical Thinking	D Differentiated Instruction	W Writing Support	S Skill Practice
Teacher Edition • Identifying, p. 415 **Additional Resources** • Guid. Read. Act., URB p. 52 • Read. Ess. & Note-Taking Guide, p. 136	**Teacher Edition** • Ident. Cent. Issues, p. 413 • Det. Cause/Effect, pp. 414, 417 • Drawing Con., p. 415 • Compare/Contrast, p. 415 **Additional Resources** • People in World Hist. Act., URB p. 42 • Section Quiz, p. 147	**Teacher Edition** • ELL, p. 414 **Additional Resources** • Read. Strat. for SS, p. 14	**Teacher Edition** • Expository Writing, p. 416 **Additional Resources** • Writer's Guidebook, p. 12	**Teacher Edition** • Using Geo. Skills, p. 413 **Additional Resources** • Time Line Act., URB p. 39

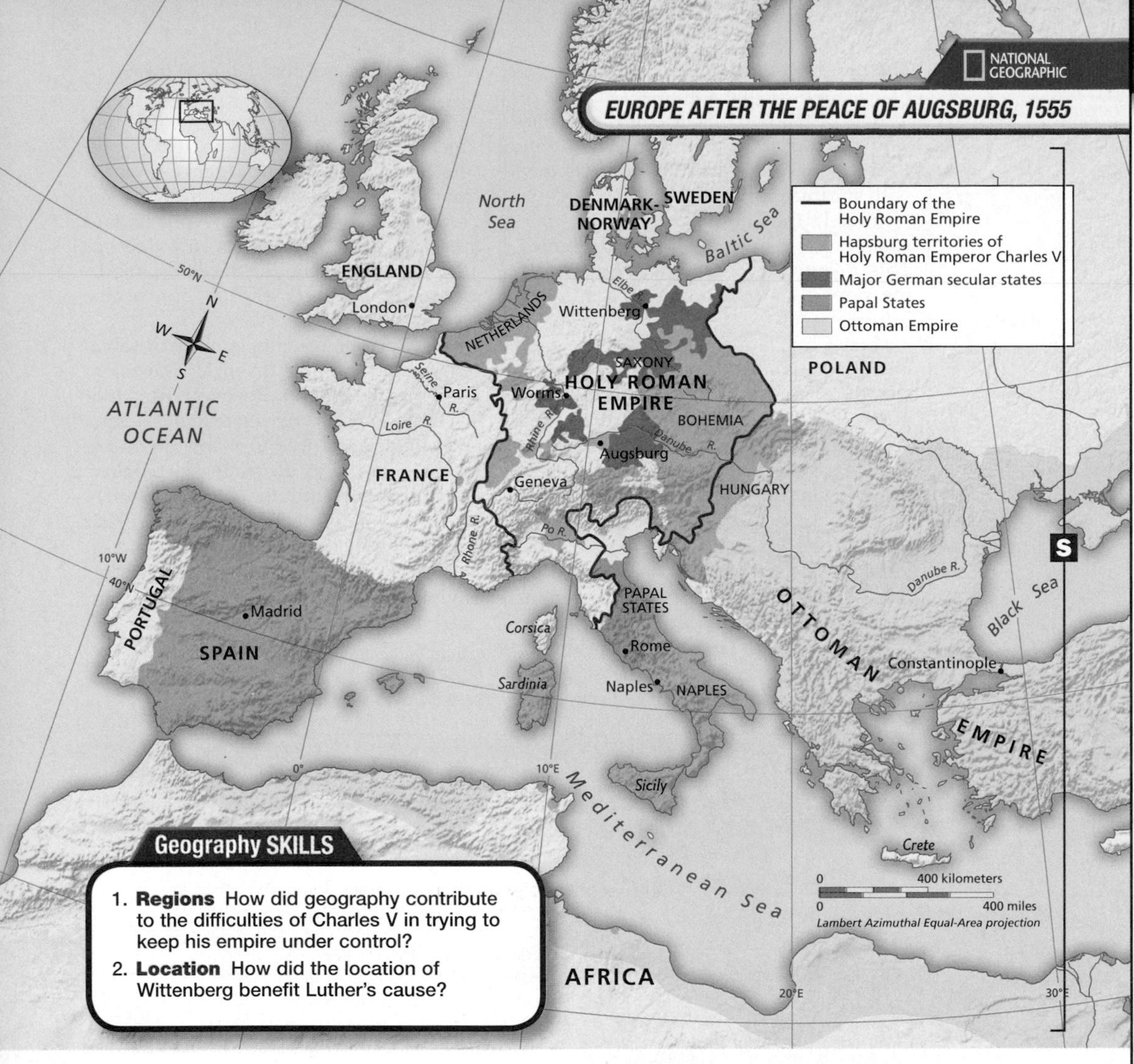

Geography SKILLS

1. **Regions** How did geography contribute to the difficulties of Charles V in trying to keep his empire under control?
2. **Location** How did the location of Wittenberg benefit Luther's cause?

To reform the Church, Erasmus wanted to spread the philosophy of Christ, provide education in the works of Christianity, and criticize the abuses in the Church. In his work *The Praise of Folly,* written in 1509, Erasmus humorously criticized aspects of his society that he believed were most in need of reform. He singled out the monks for special treatment. Monks, he said, "insist that everything be done in **precise** detail. . . . Just so many knots must be on each shoe and the shoelace must be of only one color."

Erasmus sought reform within the Catholic Church. He did not wish to break away from it. His ideas, however, did prepare the way for the Reformation. As people of his day said, "Erasmus laid the egg that Luther hatched."

Need for Reform

Why the call for reform? Corruption was one reason. From 1450 to 1520, a series of popes—known as the Renaissance popes—failed to meet the Church's spiritual needs.

Teach

S Skill Practice

Using Geography Skills

Ask: What does this map suggest about the effect of the Protestant Reformation on politics? *(Not only did the Reformation change religious affiliations, it also led to the formation of new states and dissolved bonds of allegiance among others.)* **AL**

C Critical Thinking

Identifying Central Issues

Ask: What point was Erasmus making about the monks in this quotation? *(He criticized their concern with rules and rituals that he believes are unrelated to the true practice of Christianity.)* **OL**

Geography SKILLS

Answers:

1. His empire was huge, far-flung, and noncontiguous.
2. In Saxony, Wittenberg was far from Rome and papal influence.

Additional Support

Extending the Content

The Renaissance Popes Alexander VI (1492–1503) was one of the most notorious of the Renaissance popes. He had several children, four of whom were eventually recognized as legitimate, and he spent much of his time as pope arranging advantageous political alliances for them to further his own ambitions. His patronage of the arts, however, did result in the construction of several buildings in Rome and plans for a new St. Peter's Basilica. Julius II (1503–1513) has dual claims to fame: he engaged in several wars to restore the strength of the papal states, and he was also known as a fervent patron of the arts. He ordered Michelangelo to paint the Sistine Chapel, he commissioned many works by other artists, including Raphael, and he started the Vatican collection of treasures. Leo X (1513–1521) continued enriching the culture of Rome, most notably with the construction of St. Peter's. He is also remembered as the pope who failed to take Luther's threat to the Church seriously.

C Critical Thinking

Determining Cause and Effect Ask: Why were people disillusioned with the Catholic Church? *(The clergy was corrupt. Parish priests seemed ignorant of their spiritual duties.)* OL

D Differentiated Instruction

English Language Learners Have small groups use a dictionary to find the definitions of vocabulary related to content in this section of the text, including *relics, veneration, indulgence, purgatory.* Discuss students' definitions. ELL

PEOPLE in HISTORY

Answers: Erasmus—*The Praise of Folly;* **Martin Luther**—that people just need to have faith to be saved

✓Reading Check

Answer: by criticizing the abuses in the Church

Additional Support

The popes were supposed to be the spiritual leaders of the Catholic Church. As leaders of the Papal States, however, they were all too often more concerned with Italian politics and worldly interests than with spiritual matters.

Julius II, the fiery "warrior-pope," personally led armies against his enemies. This disgusted Christians who viewed the pope as a spiritual, not a military, leader.

Many Church officials used their church offices to advance their careers and their wealth. At the same time, many ordinary parish priests seemed **ignorant** of their spiritual duties. People wanted to know how to save their souls, and many parish priests were unwilling or unable to offer them advice or instruction. C

While the leaders of the Church were failing to meet their responsibilities, ordinary people desired meaningful religious expression and assurance of their **salvation**, or acceptance into Heaven. As a result, for some, the process of obtaining salvation became almost mechanical. Collections of relics grew more popular as a means to salvation.

According to Church practice at that time, through veneration of a relic, a person could gain an **indulgence**—release from all or part of the punishment for sin. D Frederick the Wise, Luther's prince, had amassed over 5,000 relics. Indulgences attached to them could reduce time in purgatory by 1,443 years. The Church also sold indulgences.

Other people sought certainty of salvation in the popular mystical movement known as the Modern Devotion. The Modern Devotion downplayed religious dogma and stressed the need to follow the teachings of Jesus. This deepening of religious life was done within the Catholic Church. However, many people soon found that the worldly-wise clergy had little interest in the spiritual needs of their people. This environment helps to explain the tremendous impact of Luther's ideas.

✓Reading Check **Explaining** How did Erasmus pave the way for the Reformation?

Erasmus
1466–1536 Dutch Intellectual

Desiderius Erasmus was one of the greatest intellectuals of his time. Kings, popes, and princes sought his advice. He was also a very contradictory personality. Many of his writings, especially his best-known work, *The Praise of Folly,* were critical of the Catholic Church, yet he remained an ordained priest until his death. Despite his criticisms of the Church and his early support for the reforms of Martin Luther, he stayed loyal to the Church, seeking to reform it from within. He even received an offer from Pope Paul III to make him a cardinal. Yet, despite his loyalty to the Church, Erasmus was regarded as the father of Christian humanism. Many of his ideas were adopted by religious leaders of the Protestant Reformation. **What was Erasmus's best-known literary work?**

Martin Luther
1483–1546 Church Reform Leader

As Martin Luther returned to his village on a stormy night, a lightning bolt threw him off his horse. "St. Anne, help me, and I will become a monk!" Luther's cry reflected his intense fear of death and of what lay beyond. Like most people of his time, he believed the medieval view of a wrathful God, granting salvation to the righteous few and eternal fire to the rest.

Luther feared he could never do enough to win salvation. Pondering the words of the apostle Paul about the "righteousness of God," Luther arrived at a new insight. What Paul meant, he decided, was not that people can earn righteousness by good works, but that God grants the righteousness needed for salvation. All people need is faith. "From that moment, the whole face of Scripture appeared to me in a different light." **What insight did Luther gain from Paul's words?**

Extending the Content

Erasmus Erasmus felt particularly strongly about popes who involved themselves in politics and war, princes who led armies into conflict for personal reasons, and the clergy who supported these ambitions. He thought clergy should not encourage the warlike aims of rulers. His solution was education; he believed that if the clergy more thoroughly studied theological writings and the Bible, then there would be many fewer wars.

Martin Luther Erasmus originally supported Martin Luther's ideas, but later they parted ways. Erasmus felt that Luther's doctrine of salvation undermined the need for ethical behavior. Disagreements about doctrine also caused a rift between Luther and other Protestant leaders. This dissension was serious, since Protestants were anxious to present an appearance of unity against a powerful Catholic Church.

Martin Luther

MAIN IDEA Believing in his new doctrine of salvation, Martin Luther broke from the Catholic Church and established Lutheranism.

HISTORY & YOU Did you ever speak up for something you strongly believed, despite the disapproval of your friends? Read about Martin Luther's split with the Catholic Church.

Martin Luther was a monk and a professor at the University of **Wittenberg,** in Germany, where he lectured on the Bible. Through his study of the Bible, Luther arrived at an answer to a problem—the certainty of salvation—that had bothered him since he had become a monk.

Catholic teaching had stressed that both faith and good works were needed to gain personal salvation. In Luther's opinion, human beings were powerless in the sight of an almighty God and could never do enough good works to earn salvation. C1

Through his study of the Bible, Luther came to believe that humans are not saved through their good works but through their faith in God. This idea, called justification by faith alone, became the chief teaching of the Protestant Reformation.

Because Luther had arrived at his understanding of salvation by studying the Bible, the Bible became for Luther, as for all other Protestants, the only source of religious truth.

The Ninety-five Theses

Luther did not see himself as a rebel, but he was greatly upset by the widespread selling of indulgences. Especially offensive in his eyes was the monk Johann Tetzel, who sold indulgences with the slogan: "As soon as the coin in the coffer [money box] rings, the soul from purgatory springs." People, Luther believed, were simply harming their chances for salvation by buying these pieces of paper. R

On October 31, 1517, Luther, who was greatly angered by the Church's practices, sent a list of **Ninety-five Theses** to his church superiors, especially the local bishop. The theses were a stunning attack on abuses in the sale of indulgences. Thousands of copies of the Ninety-five Theses were printed and spread to all parts of Germany.

Pope Leo X did not take the issue seriously, however. He said that Luther was simply "some drunken German who will amend his ways when he sobers up."

A Break With the Church

By 1520, Luther had begun to move toward a more definite break with the Catholic Church. He called on the German princes to overthrow the papacy in Germany and establish a reformed German church. Luther also attacked the Church's system of sacraments. In his view, they were the means by which the pope and the Church had destroyed the real meaning of the gospel for a thousand years. He kept only two sacraments—baptism and the Eucharist (also known as Communion). Luther also called for the clergy to marry. This went against the long-standing Catholic requirement that the clergy remain celibate, or unmarried. C2

Through all these calls for change, Luther continued to emphasize his new doctrine of salvation. It is faith alone, he said, and not good works, that justifies and brings salvation through Christ.

Unable to accept Luther's ideas, the Church excommunicated him in January 1521. He was also summoned to appear before the imperial diet—or legislative assembly—of the Holy Roman Empire, which was called into session at the city of Worms by the newly elected emperor Charles V. The emperor believed he could convince Luther to change his ideas. However, Luther refused.

The young emperor was outraged. "A single friar who goes counter to all Christianity for a thousand years," he declared, "must be wrong!" By the **Edict of Worms,** Martin Luther was made an outlaw within the empire. His works were to be burned and Luther himself captured and delivered to the emperor. However, Luther's ruler, Frederick, the elector of Saxony, was unwilling to see his famous professor killed. He sent Luther into hiding and then protected him when Luther returned to Wittenberg at the beginning of 1522.

C1 Critical Thinking

Drawing Conclusions Explain that in the Middle Ages, priests would interpret the Bible for their parishioners. Since few could read, they relied upon the priest's instruction. **Ask:** What did Luther imply by telling people to rely only on the Bible for religious truth? *(The clergy was not needed to interpret the word of God.)* **AL**

R Reading Strategy

Identifying Ask: Why did Luther object to selling indulgences? *(He believed that indulgences gave people false hope and harmed their chance for salvation.)* **OL**

C2 Critical Thinking

Comparing and Contrasting Record students' answers in a two-column chart. **Ask:** In what ways did Luther's teachings differ from those of the Catholic Church? *(Catholic: seven sacraments, celibate clergy, salvation achieved by faith and good works; Luther: two sacraments, married clergy, salvation achieved by faith)* **OL**

Hands-On Chapter Project Step 3

Creating a Mural

Step 3: Adding the Third Panel Groups will represent the Reformation on their mural.

Directions: Write the Big Idea on the board. Tell students that in this panel of their mural, they will use both text and images to introduce and explain important events and ideas associated with the Reformation. Encourage students to show the causes of the Reformation, including its relationship to Christian humanism, and to illustrate the effects of Luther's revolt. Students may wish to include dates and some captions within the mural for clarification. Suggest that groups create a sketch of their design first before transferring their images to their mural paper.

Summarizing: Have groups share the first three panels of their murals with each other. Have them discuss the insights they have gained about the Big Idea. **OL**

(Chapter Project is continued in Section 4.)

W Writing Support

Expository Writing Ask students to write an essay in which they examine the reasons that caused Luther's movement to become a revolution. They should consider factors such as the printing press, the influence of humanism, the widespread disillusionment with the Church, and the Church's response to Luther's actions. OL

DOCUMENT-BASED QUESTIONS

Answers:

1. to participate in an oral debate of his proposition or join the debate with letters
2. started a debate and revolution that resulted in a new form of Christianity and ended the domination of the Catholic Church

✓Reading Check

Answer: Catholics believed that both faith and good works were required for salvation. Luther held that faith alone was sufficient.

The Rise of Lutheranism

Luther's religious movement soon became a revolution. Many German rulers who supported Luther took control of the Catholic churches in their territories, forming state churches supervised by the government. As part of the development of these state-dominated churches, Luther also set up new religious services to replace the Catholic mass. These services consisted of Bible readings, preaching of the word of God, and song. Luther's doctrine soon became known as **Lutheranism** and the churches as Lutheran churches. Lutheranism was the first Protestant faith.

In June 1524, Luther faced a political crisis. German peasants revolted against their lords and looked to Luther to support their cause. Luther instead supported the lords. To him, the state and its rulers were called by God to maintain the peace necessary to spread the Gospel. It was the duty of princes to stop all revolt. By the following spring, the German princes had crushed the peasant revolts. Luther found himself even more dependent on state authorities for the growth of his church.

✓Reading Check **Contrasting** How did Luther and the Church differ on achieving salvation?

TURNING POINT — LUTHER'S NINETY-FIVE THESES —

Martin Luther's Introduction to his Ninety-five Theses, 1517

Out of love for the truth and the desire to bring it to light, the following propositions will be discussed at Wittenberg, under the presidency of the Reverend Father Martin Luther, Master of Arts and of Sacred Theology, and Lecturer in Ordinary on the same at that place. Wherefore he requests that those who are unable to be present and debate orally with us, may do so by letter.

Martin Luther's protest of indulgences began the Protestant Reformation. The Catholic Church had authorized Johann Tetzel to sell indulgences to raise money to build St. Peter's Basilica in Rome. Tetzel told the faithful that their purchases would free the souls of their loved ones from Purgatory. This enraged Luther, who believed that indulgences only soothed the conscience. They did not forgive sins.

When Luther wrote his Ninety-five Theses, his intention was to open a dialogue on abuses in the Catholic Church. Instead, his words sparked a revolutionary firestorm. Aided by the newly invented printing press, his words soon spread across Europe.

Luther's attempts to reform the Catholic Church led to a new form of Christianity—Protestantism—and the birth of a new church. It also ignited decades of bloody religious conflict, ending a thousand years of domination by the Catholic Church.

This image shows Martin Luther posting his Ninety-five Theses on the door of the Castle Church in Wittenberg, Germany, in 1517.

DOCUMENT-BASED QUESTIONS

1. **Finding the Main Idea** In his introduction to the Ninety-five Theses, what did Luther invite people to do?
2. **Analyzing** In what ways did the Ninety-five Theses represent a turning point in history?

Differentiated Instruction

Time Line Activity, URB p. 39

Analyzing Information

Objective: Analyze time lines.

Focus: Review events during the Renaissance and Reformation.

Teach: Assign pairs of students events to annotate with facts from the text.

Assess: Have students discuss the historical significance of their events.

Close: Have students review the first three sections of the chapter and add one or two other events.

Differentiated Instruction Strategies

- **BL** Have students complete the worksheet together.
- **AL** Have students write an essay in which they explain the relationship among six or more of the events on the time line.
- **ELL** Have students pick out an event on the time line with which they are familiar and create a pictorial version.

Politics in the German Reformation

MAIN IDEA Political and religious problems forced the emperor of the Holy Roman Empire to seek peace with the Lutheran princes.

HISTORY & YOU Have you ever met so much opposition from all sides that you just had to give in? Read to learn why Charles V had to seek peace with the Lutheran princes of his empire.

From its very beginning, the fate of Luther's movement was tied closely to political affairs. **Charles V,** the Holy Roman emperor (who was also Charles I, the king of Spain), ruled an immense empire consisting of Spain and its colonies, the Austrian lands, **Bohemia, Hungary,** the Low Countries, the duchy of Milan in northern Italy, and the kingdom of Naples in southern Italy.

Politically, Charles wanted to keep this enormous empire under the control of his dynasty—the Hapsburgs. Religiously, he hoped to preserve the unity of his empire by keeping it Catholic. However, a number of problems kept him busy and cost him both his dream and his health. These same problems helped Lutheranism survive by giving Lutherans time to organize before having to face the Catholic forces.

The chief political concern of Charles V was his rivalry with the king of France, Francis I. Their conflict over disputed territories in a number of areas led to a series of wars that lasted more than 20 years. At the same time, Charles faced opposition from Pope Clement VII. Guided by political considerations, the pope had joined the side of the French king. The invasion of Ottoman Turks into the eastern part of the empire forced Charles to send forces there as well. **C**

Finally, the internal political situation in the Holy Roman Empire was not in Charles's favor. Germany was a land of several hundred territorial states. Although all owed loyalty to the emperor, many individual rulers of the German states supported Luther as a way to assert their own local authority. By the time Charles V brought military forces to Germany, the Lutheran princes were well organized. Unable to defeat them, Charles was forced to seek peace.

An end to religious warfare in Germany came in 1555 with the **Peace of Augsburg.** This agreement formally accepted the division of Christianity in Germany. The German states were now free to choose between Catholicism and Lutheranism. Lutheran states were to have the same legal rights as Catholic states. However, the right of each German ruler to determine the religion of his subjects was accepted, but not the right of the subjects to choose their own religion.

✓Reading Check **Evaluating** How did the Peace of Augsburg influence the political and religious development of Germany?

SECTION 3 REVIEW

Vocabulary

1. **Explain** the significance of: Martin Luther, Christian humanism, Desiderius Erasmus, precise, ignorant, salvation, indulgence, Wittenberg, Ninety-five Theses, Edict of Worms, Lutheranism, Charles V, Bohemia, Hungary, Peace of Augsburg.

Main Ideas

2. **Sequence** the actions of Luther that led to the emergence of Protestantism using a diagram like the one below.

Luther's Actions

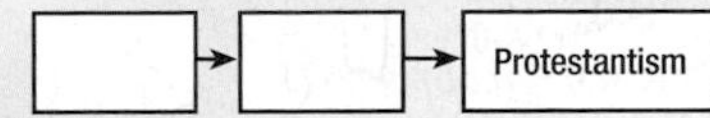

3. **Discuss** the impact of the Edict of Worms.
4. **Explain** why many German princes supported Luther.

Critical Thinking

5. **The BIG Idea** **Analyzing** How did Martin Luther's religious reform lead to conflict? To what extent were these conflicts resolved?
6. **Contrasting** How did the views of Erasmus and the Church differ on the topic of religious relics?
7. **Analyzing Visuals** Examine the map on page 413. Identify three cities where important events occurred in the rise of Lutheranism and explain their significance.

Writing About History

8. **Persuasive Writing** Martin Luther's father wanted him to become a lawyer. Write a letter in which Martin Luther tries to convince his father that the path he chose was better.

History ONLINE
For help with the concepts in this section of *Glencoe World History,* go to glencoe.com and click Study Central™.

417

C Critical Thinking

Determining Cause and Effect **Ask:** What motives other than religious belief caused German princes to support Luther? *(Supporting Luther was a way to assert their authority over that of Charles. Also, it would give them a way to break free from their obligations to the pope.)* **AL**

Answer: It allowed the German states to choose between Catholicism and Lutheranism.

Assess

History ONLINE

Study Central provides summaries, interactive games, and online graphic organizers to help students review content.

Close

Summarizing **Ask:** What was the Church's response to Martin Luther's call to establish a reformed German church? *(The Church excommunicated Luther and made him an outlaw in the empire.)* **OL**

Answers

1. Definitions for the vocabulary words are found in the section and the Glossary.
2. The Ninety-five Theses called for a dialogue on abuses within the Catholic Church. Later, his call for a reformed German church led to a definitive break with the Catholic Church and the beginning of Protestantism.
3. It outlawed Martin Luther, turning his religious movement into a revolution.
4. to assert their own local authority over the authority of the empire and Charles V
5. Charles V wanted to keep his empire Catholic. German princes supported Luther to assert their own authority, leading to armed conflict. The conflict was resolved by the Peace of Augsburg, which allowed German states—but not people—to choose between Catholicism and Lutheranism.
6. **Church:** A person could gain an indulgence by venerating relics. **Erasmus:** External forms of religious expression, such as relics, are less important than inward religious feeling.
7. **Wittenberg:** Luther issued his Ninety-five Theses; **Worms:** Church outlawed Luther; **Augsburg:** peace settlement divided Christianity in Germany
8. Students' letters should be persuasive and written from Luther's point of view.

SECTION 4

The Spread of Protestantism

Focus

Bellringer

Daily Focus Transparency 12.4

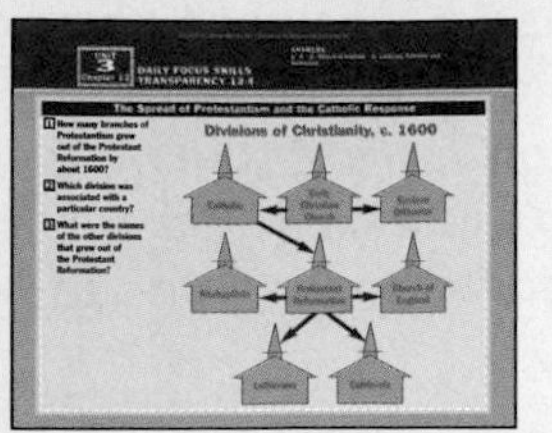

GUIDE TO READING

Answers to Graphic:

Council of Trent: salvation through faith and good works; **Protestant viewpoint:** salvation by faith alone. **Council of Trent:** seven sacraments; **Protestant viewpoint:** two sacraments. **Council of Trent:** clerical celibacy; **Protestant viewpoint:** called on clergy to marry.

Section Spotlight Video

To generate student interest and provide a springboard for class discussion, access the Chapter 12, Section 4 video at glencoe.com or on the video DVD.

GUIDE TO READING

The BIG Idea

Ideas, Beliefs, and Values Different forms of Protestantism emerged in Europe as the Reformation spread, and the Catholic Church underwent a religious rebirth.

Content Vocabulary

- predestination *(p. 419)*
- annul *(p. 420)*

Academic Vocabulary

- published *(p. 418)*
- justification *(p. 419)*

People and Places

- Ulrich Zwingli *(p. 418)*
- Zürich *(p. 418)*
- John Calvin *(p. 418)*
- Geneva *(p. 420)*
- King Henry VIII *(p. 420)*
- Ignatius of Loyola *(p. 423)*
- Trent *(p. 423)*

Reading Strategy

Determining Cause and Effect As you read, use a diagram like the one below to list some of the reforms proposed by the Council of Trent. Beside each, give the Protestant viewpoint to which it responded.

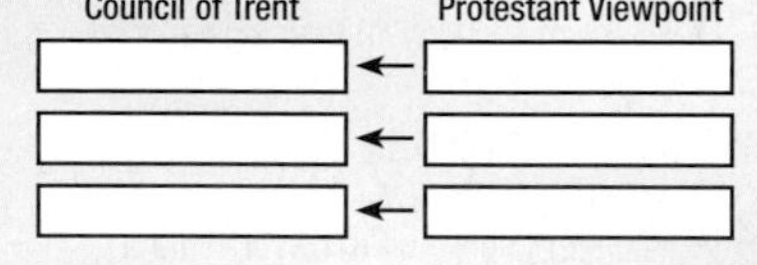

As the Reformation spread, different forms of Protestantism emerged in Europe. Calvinism replaced Lutheranism as the most important and dynamic form of Protestantism. In England, King Henry VIII created a national church, the Church of England. The Anabaptists believed in a complete separation of church and state. The Catholic Church underwent a revitalization under the direction of Pope Paul III.

Divisions in Protestantism

MAIN IDEA By the mid-sixteenth century, Calvinism replaced Lutheranism as the most important and dynamic form of Protestantism.

HISTORY & YOU Can you imagine life in a society where dancing is a crime? Read to learn about the Calvinist teachings.

The Peace of Augsburg meant that Christian unity was forever lost. Even before the peace, however, division had appeared in Protestantism. One of these new groups appeared in Switzerland.

Zwinglian Reformation

Ulrich Zwingli was a priest in **Zürich.** The city council of Zürich, strongly influenced by Zwingli, began to introduce religious reforms. Relics and images were abolished. All paintings and decorations were removed from the churches and replaced by whitewashed walls. A new church service consisting of Scripture reading, prayer, and sermons replaced the Catholic mass.

As his movement began to spread to other cities in Switzerland, Zwingli sought an alliance with Martin Luther and the German reformers. Both the German and Swiss reformers realized the need for unity to defend themselves against Catholic authorities, but they were unable to agree on certain Christian rites.

In October 1531 war broke out between the Protestant and Catholic states in Switzerland. Zürich's army was routed, and Zwingli was found wounded on the battlefield. His enemies killed him, cut up his body, and burned the pieces, scattering the ashes. The leadership of Protestantism in Switzerland now passed to John Calvin.

Calvin and Calvinism

John Calvin was educated in his native France. After his conversion to Protestantism, however, he was forced to flee Catholic France for the safety of Switzerland. In 1536 he **published** the

Resource Manager

R Reading Strategies	C Critical Thinking	D Differentiated Instruction	W Writing Support	S Skill Practice
Teacher Edition • Identifying, p. 420 • Making Connections, p. 421 **Additional Resources** • Academic Vocab. Act., URB p. 27 • Guid. Read. Act., URB p. 53 • Read. Ess. & Note-Taking Guide, p. 139	**Teacher Edition** • Making Inferences, p. 420 • Det. Cause/Effect, p. 422 • Drawing Con., p. 423 **Additional Resources** • Section Quiz, p. 148 • Chapter Test, p. 149	**Teacher Edition** • Adv. Learners, p. 421 **Additional Resources** • Diff. Instr. Act., URB p. 21 • Content Vocab. Act., URB p. 25 • Reteach. Act., URB p. 47	**Teacher Edition** • Expository Writing, p. 419 **Additional Resources** • Enrich. Act., URB p. 48	**Teacher Edition** • Using Geo. Skills, p. 419 **Additional Resources** • Mapping Hist. Act., URB p. 33 • Read. Strat. for SS, p. 68

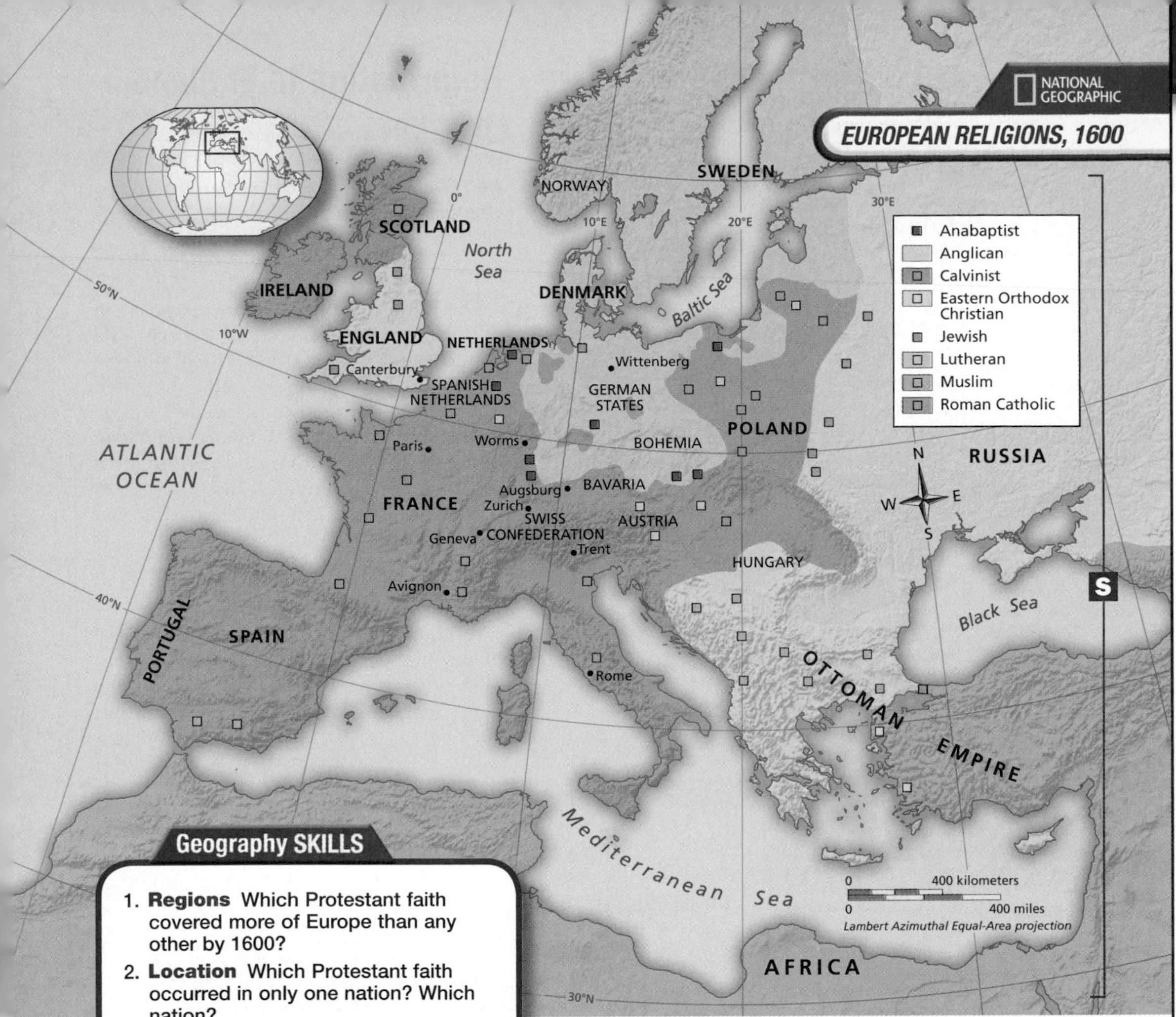

NATIONAL GEOGRAPHIC

EUROPEAN RELIGIONS, 1600

Geography SKILLS

1. **Regions** Which Protestant faith covered more of Europe than any other by 1600?
2. **Location** Which Protestant faith occurred in only one nation? Which nation?

Institutes of the Christian Religion, a summary of Protestant thought. This work, which eventually became known as his masterpiece, immediately gave Calvin a reputation as one of the new leaders of Protestantism.

On most important doctrines, Calvin stood very close to Luther. He, too, believed in the doctrine of **justification** by faith alone to explain how humans achieved salvation. However, Calvin also placed much emphasis on the all-powerful nature of God—what Calvin called the "power, grace, and glory of God."

Calvin's emphasis on the all-powerful nature of God led him to other ideas. One of these ideas was **predestination.** This "eternal decree," as Calvin called it, meant that God had determined in advance who would be saved and who would be damned.

The belief in predestination gave later Calvinists the firm conviction that they were doing God's work on Earth. This conviction, in turn, made them determined to spread their faith to other people. Calvinism became a dynamic and activist faith.

See page R42 to read A Reformation Debate between Martin Luther and Ulrich Zwingli in the **Primary Sources and Literature Library.**

Teach

S Skill Practice

Using Geography Skills
Have students look closely at the Protestant areas indicated on the map. **Ask:** In which part of Europe was the Protestant faith most widespread in 1600? Why? *(Protestantism was widespread in northern Europe. This may be because of the distance from Rome or the fact that Lutheranism began in Germany and Calvinism in Switzerland.)* **OL**

W Writing Support

Expository Writing Have students find out more about predestination. Ask them to write an essay explaining the various doctrines of predestination as well as the prevalence of these doctrines in modern churches. Have students share their essays. **AL**

Geography SKILLS

Answers:
1. Lutheranism
2. Anglican; England

Hands-On Chapter Project
Step 4

Creating a Mural

Step 4: Drawing the Last Panel Groups will complete their murals.

Directions: Write the Big Idea on the board. Tell students that this last panel of their mural will capture the impact of the Reformation on the Catholic unity of Europe by depicting major figures and events associated with the different forms of Protestantism, as well as the Catholic response. As in the second panel, groups should organize a key that will help to explain who or what appears in each image and why that person or event was important to the Reformation. Encourage students to outline what they want to include and how they want to organize their information before they begin.

Putting It Together: After groups have completed their fourth panel, assign them wall space to display their murals. Then have students discuss what they learned about the Big Idea. **OL**

(Chapter Project is completed on the Visual Summary page.)

C Critical Thinking

Making Inferences **Ask:** What do John Calvin's rules suggest about his view of human nature? *(Possible answer: People were too weak to resist the temptation of sin. Therefore, they needed to be kept firmly in check by strict rules.)* AL

R Reading Strategy

Identifying **Ask:** What prompted the development of a new church in England? *(the king's desire for a second wife and the pope's refusal to grant him an annulment)* OL

✓Reading Check

Answer: set up as a court, with right to punish people who deviated from church teachings; "crimes" included dancing, drunkenness, swearing, and playing cards

PEOPLE *in* HISTORY

Answers: Henry VIII—Martin Luther; **Thomas More**—the Utopian Socialists

C In 1536 Calvin began working to reform the city of **Geneva.** He created a church government that used both clergy and laity in the service of the church. The Consistory, a special court for enforcing moral discipline, oversaw the moral life and doctrinal purity of Genevans. It could punish those who deviated from the church's teachings and moral principles. Citizens in Geneva were punished for such "crimes" as dancing, singing obscene songs, drunkenness, swearing, and playing cards.

Geneva became a powerful center of Protestantism. Missionaries trained in Geneva were sent to all parts of Europe. Calvinism became established in France, the Netherlands, Scotland, and central and eastern Europe.

By the mid-sixteenth century, Calvinism had replaced Lutheranism as the most important and dynamic form of Protestantism. Calvin's Geneva stood as the fortress of the Protestant Reformation.

✓Reading Check **Explaining** How did the Consistory enforce moral discipline in Geneva?

Reformation in England

MAIN IDEA For political, not religious, reasons, Henry VIII established the Church of England.

HISTORY & YOU As a child, how did you react when someone told you no? Read about how Henry VIII reacted after the pope said no.

R The English Reformation was rooted in politics, not religion. **King Henry VIII** wanted to divorce his first wife, Catherine of Aragon, with whom he had a daughter, Mary, but no son. Since he needed a male heir, Henry wanted to marry Anne Boleyn. Impatient with the pope's unwillingness to **annul** (declare invalid) his marriage to Catherine, Henry turned to England's own church courts.

The Break from Rome

As the archbishop of Canterbury, head of the highest church court in England, Thomas Cranmer ruled in May 1533 that the king's marriage to Catherine was "null and

PEOPLE *in* HISTORY

Henry VIII
1491–1547 King of England

Historians have found it ironic that Henry VIII, who led the break between England and the Roman Catholic Church, was proclaimed "Defender of the Faith" by the head of the church he left. However, that is how Pope Leo X praised him after Henry's attack on Martin Luther in 1521. In *Assertio Septem Sacramentorum* (Declaration of the Seven Sacraments), Henry upheld Church doctrines that Luther and his followers were trying to discredit. To this day, all British coins carry the initials F.D. after the reigning monarch's name. They refer to the Latin words *Fidei Defensor*, or "Defender of the Faith," a hereditary title for all British monarchs since Henry VIII. **Who was Henry VIII attacking in his book?**

Thomas More
1478–1535 British Author and Theologian

A Man for All Seasons—that was the title of a twentieth-century movie about Thomas More. He was a trusted adviser to Henry VIII and the author of the book *Utopia*, which means a perfectly harmonious society. Published in 1516, the book is a work of fiction about an ideal state. More describes how goods are produced and shared equally among the Utopians. *Utopia* became a model for Utopian Socialists, who in the 1800s attempted to set up communities based on the socialistic principles described in the book. More was later beheaded under orders from Henry VIII for not supporting England's break with the Church of Rome. In 1935, More was made a saint. **For what group did More's book become an inspiration?**

Additional Support

Extending the Content

Henry VIII Because Henry VIII's first wife, Catherine of Aragon, was his brother's widow, he was granted a special papal dispensation to marry her. Later, when Henry wanted a divorce, he argued that the marriage had not been truly legal because of these circumstances. Henry argued that he had defied biblical teachings by marrying his brother's widow. He argued that God disapproved of his marriage to Catherine, and that Henry's lack of sons was proof of God's condemnation. This argument failed to convince the pope, who eventually excommunicated Henry.

Thomas More Because of his reputation for goodness and integrity, news of Thomas More's execution for treachery was received with shock and disbelief throughout Europe, even in Protestant areas. Erasmus, frequently a guest of Thomas More's, compared his soul's purity to snow and said that England would never have such genius again, calling him "a man for all seasons."

absolutely void." At the beginning of June, Anne was crowned queen. Three months later a child was born. Much to the king's disappointment, the baby was a girl. She would later become Queen Elizabeth I.

In 1534, at Henry's request, Parliament moved to finalize the break of the Catholic Church in England with the pope in Rome. The Act of Supremacy of 1534 declared that the king was "the only supreme head on earth of the [new] Church of England." This position gave the king control over religious doctrine, clerical appointments, and discipline. Thomas More, a Christian humanist and devout Catholic, opposed the king's action and was beheaded.

Henry used his new powers to dissolve the monasteries and sell their land and possessions to wealthy landowners and merchants. The king received a great boost to his treasury and a group of supporters who now had a stake in the new order. In matters of doctrine, however, Henry remained close to Catholic teachings.

When Henry died in 1547, he was succeeded by Edward VI, his nine-year-old son by his third wife. During Edward's reign, church officials who favored Protestant doctrines moved the Church of England, or the Anglican Church, in a Protestant direction. New acts of Parliament gave the clergy the right to marry and created a new Protestant church service. Before he turned 16, Edward died of tuberculosis.

"Bloody Mary"

The rapid changes during Edward's reign aroused opposition. When Mary, Henry's daughter by Catherine of Aragon, came to the throne in 1553, England was ready for a reaction. Mary was a Catholic who wanted to restore England to Roman Catholicism. However, her efforts had the opposite effect. Among other actions, she had more than 300 Protestants burned as heretics, earning her the nickname "Bloody Mary." As a result of her policies, England was even more Protestant by the end of Mary's reign than it had been at the beginning.

✓Reading Check **Examining** What were the results of Bloody Mary's religious policies?

Anabaptists

MAIN IDEA For believing in the complete separation of church and state, Anabaptists were viewed as dangerous radicals.

HISTORY & YOU Would you consider someone who refuses to kill to be a "dangerous radical"? Read to learn about the Anabaptists.

Reformers such as Luther had allowed the state to play an important, if not dominant, role in church affairs. However, some people strongly disliked giving such power to the state. These were radicals known as the Anabaptists.

To Anabaptists, the true Christian church was a voluntary community of adult believers who had undergone spiritual rebirth and had then been baptized. This belief in adult baptism separated Anabaptists from Catholics and Protestants, who baptized infants.

Anabaptists also believed in following the practices and the spirit of early Christianity. They considered all believers to be equal, a belief they based on the accounts of early Christian communities in the New Testament. Each Anabaptist church chose its own minister, or spiritual leader. Because all Christians were considered priests, any member of the community was eligible to be a minister (though women were often excluded).

Finally, most Anabaptists believed in the complete separation of church and state. Not only was government to be kept out of the realm of religion, it was not even supposed to have any political authority over real Christians. Anabaptists refused to hold political office or bear arms, because many took literally the biblical commandment "Thou shall not kill."

Their political beliefs, as much as their religious beliefs, caused the Anabaptists to be regarded as dangerous radicals who threatened the very fabric of sixteenth-century society. Indeed, the chief thing other Protestants and Catholics could agree on was the need to persecute Anabaptists.

✓Reading Check **Describing** Why were the Anabaptists considered to be dangerous political radicals?

D Differentiated Instruction

Advanced Learners Tell students that Henry VIII was married six times. Have students find out more about his wives and offspring and present their information as a family tree. Discuss why a male heir was so important to Henry VIII. **AL**

R Reading Strategy

Making Connections Ask: How did the Anabaptists differ from other Protestant groups? *(They believed in adult baptism.)* **OL**

✓Reading Check

Answer: More than three hundred Protestants died, and England became even more Protestant.

✓Reading Check

Answer: They believed in complete separation of church and state, and that the state had no authority over real Christians. They refused to hold political office or bear arms.

Identifying Central Issues

Objective: Compare views of European society in the 1500s.

Focus: Read the excerpt from *Utopia*.

Teach: Discuss More's description of the commonwealths of his day.

Assess: Have students argue for or against the validity of More's solution.

Close: Have students create a collage that depicts their image of utopia.

Differentiated Instruction Strategies

BL Read the excerpt aloud. Work with students to identify the main idea of each paragraph.

AL Have students read and report on additional excerpts from *Utopia*.

ELL Use a cluster diagram to define *utopia*. As a class, list characteristics of a utopian community according to More.

Differentiated Instruction

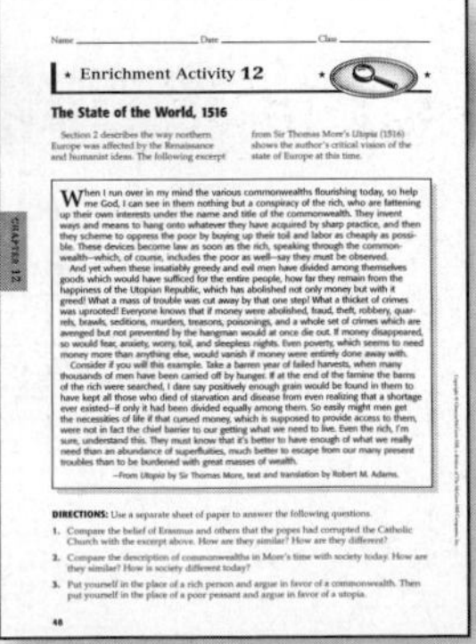

Enrichment Activity, URB p. 48

C Critical Thinking

Determining Cause and Effect Ask: What was the impact of the Protestant Reformation on the Jews in Europe? *(The Reformation awakened stronger anti-Semitic feelings, leading to the persecution and segregation of Jews.)* **OL**

✓Reading Check

Answer: greater emphasis placed on family; wife compelled to obey her husband and to bear children

Chart SKILLS

Answers:

1. Both Anglicans and Catholics had hierarchies with a head of the church at the top, bishops below, and priests at the bottom. Neither Lutherans nor Calvinists had a head or bishops.
2. Possible response: because they believed that the sacraments should be based on the Bible, not Church traditions

Reformation and Society

MAIN IDEA Although the family became the center of life during the Reformation, the lives of most women and Jews did not improve.

HISTORY & YOU Should anyone be an "obedient servant" to another person? Read to learn about women's roles during the Reformation.

History ONLINE
Student Web Activity—
Visit glencoe.com and complete the activity about the Reformation.

During the political and religious turmoil of the Reformation, the lives of most women and Jewish people did not improve. Women were still subservient, and anti-Semitism continued.

Women and Family

The Protestants developed a new view of the family. Both monasticism and the requirement of celibacy for the clergy had been abolished. The family could now be placed at the center of life, and the "mutual love between man and wife" could be extolled.

Were idea and reality the same, however? More often, reality reflected the traditional roles of husband as the ruler and wife as the obedient servant. Luther stated it clearly: "The rule remains with the husband, and the wife is compelled to obey him by God's command."

Obedience was not a woman's only role. Her other important duty was to bear children, which both Calvin and Luther saw as part of the divine plan.

Anti-Semitism

C During the Reformation, anti-Semitism remained common in northern Europe. Martin Luther expected Jews to convert to Lutheranism. When they resisted, Luther wrote that Jewish synagogues and houses should be destroyed. In the Papal States, Jews who would not convert to Christianity were segregated into ghettos.

✓Reading Check **Evaluating** What impact did the Protestant Reformation have on women?

Roman Catholic, Lutheran, Calvinist, and Anglican Beliefs

	CATHOLIC	LUTHERAN	CALVINIST	ANGLICAN
Church Hierarchy	Pope, bishops, priests	Ministers lead congregations.	Council of elders for each church; ministers	Monarch, bishops, priests
Salvation	Salvation requires faith and good works.	Salvation requires faith alone.	Salvation requires faith alone.	Salvation requires faith alone.
Importance of the Bible	The Bible and Church traditions are both sources of truth.	The Bible is the only source of truth.	The Bible is the only source of truth.	The Bible is the only source of truth.
Interpretation of Beliefs	Priests interpret the Bible and Church teachings for believers.	Believers interpret the Bible themselves.	Believers interpret the Bible themselves.	Believers interpret the Bible themselves.
Worship	Services based on rituals and devotional practices	Services based on preaching with some rituals	Services based on preaching	Services based on preaching and rituals
Sacraments	Seven sacraments: baptism, confession, communion, confirmation, marriage, ordination, anointing the sick	Baptism, communion	Baptism, communion	Baptism, communion

Chart SKILLS

1. **Describing** In what way were Anglicans more similar to Catholics than to either Lutherans or Calvinists?
2. **Making Inferences** Why do you think the Protestant churches eliminated most of the seven sacraments?

Differentiated Instruction

Leveled Activities

BL Guided Reading Activity, URB p. 53

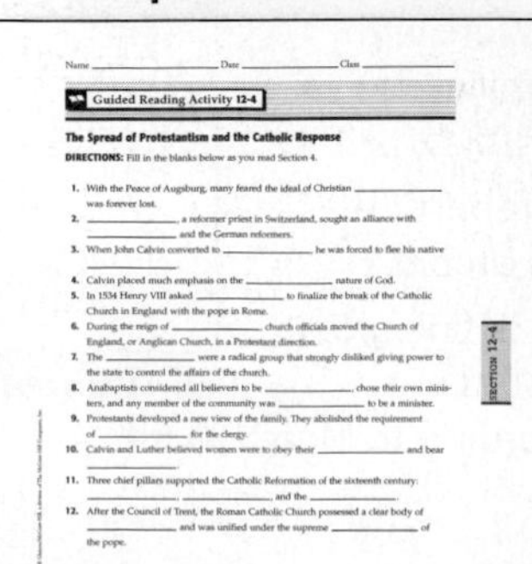

OL Academic Vocabulary Activity, URB p. 27

AL Mapping History Activity, URB p. 33

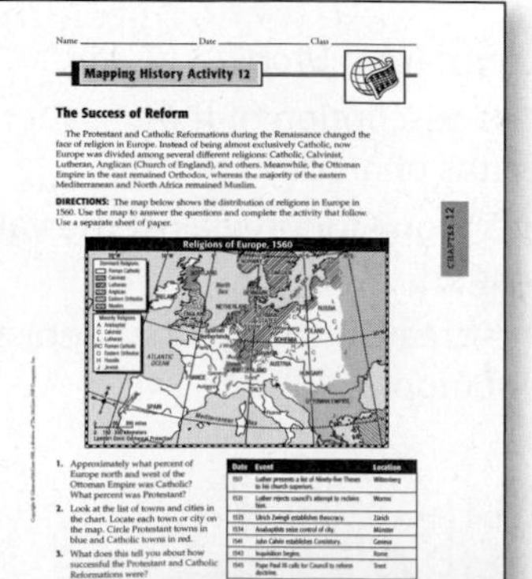

ELL Reteaching Activity, URB p. 47

Catholic Reformation

MAIN IDEA Perceiving a need for a change, Pope Paul III steered the Catholic Church toward a reformation in the 1500s.

HISTORY & YOU When a task doesn't turn out as well as you had hoped, do you look for ways to do it better next time? Read to learn how the Catholic Church determined what it needed to change.

The Catholic Church also had a revitalization in the sixteenth century, giving it new strength and enabling it to regain much that it had lost to the Protestant Reformation. Three chief pillars—the Jesuits, reform of the papacy, and the Council of Trent—supported the Catholic Reformation.

A Spanish nobleman, **Ignatius of Loyola,** founded the Society of Jesus, known as the Jesuits. Loyola's small group of followers was recognized as a religious order by Pope Paul III in 1540. All Jesuits took a special vow of absolute obedience to the pope, making them an important instrument for papal policy. Jesuits used education to spread their message. Jesuit missionaries were very successful in restoring Catholicism to parts of Germany and eastern Europe and in spreading it to other parts of the world.

Reform of the papacy was another important factor in the Catholic Reformation. Participating in dubious financial transactions and Italian political and military affairs, the Renaissance popes had created many sources of corruption. It took the jolt of the Protestant Reformation to bring about serious reform. C

Pope Paul III perceived the need for change. He took the bold step of appointing a Reform Commission in 1537 to determine the Church's ills. The commission blamed the Church's problems on the popes' corrupt policies. Paul III also began the Council of Trent, another pillar of the Catholic Reformation. Beginning in March 1545, a group of cardinals, archbishops, bishops, abbots, and theologians met off and on for 18 years in the city of **Trent,** on the border between Germany and Italy.

The final decrees of the Council of Trent reaffirmed traditional Catholic teachings in opposition to Protestant beliefs. Both faith and good works were declared necessary for salvation. The seven sacraments, the Catholic view of the Eucharist, and clerical celibacy were all upheld. Belief in purgatory and in the use of indulgences was strengthened, although the selling of indulgences was forbidden. The Roman Catholic Church now possessed a clear body of doctrine and was unified under the pope's supreme leadership. Catholics were as well prepared as Calvinists to do battle for their faith.

✓Reading Check **Describing** What was the relationship between the Jesuits and the pope?

SECTION 4 REVIEW

Vocabulary
1. **Explain** the significance of: Ulrich Zwingli, Zürich, John Calvin, published, justification, predestination, Geneva, King Henry VIII, annul, Ignatius of Loyola, Trent.

Main Ideas
2. **Describe** how Calvin reformed the city of Geneva.
3. **Explain** why Henry VIII formed the Church of England.
4. **Contrast** how the Calvinists and the Anabaptists differed in their attitudes toward church members participating in government activities.

Calvinists	Church Participation in Government	Anabaptists
____		____
____		____
____		____
____		____

Critical Thinking
5. **The BIG Idea Assessing** How effective was the Catholic Church's response to the Protestant Reformation?
6. **Determining Cause and Effect** How did "Bloody Mary's" actions affect the religious makeup of England by the end of her reign?
7. **Analyzing Visuals** Compare the chart on page 422 to the map on page 419. Name one country in which the dominant Christian faith included the seven sacraments.

Writing About History
8. **Expository Writing** Research the treatment of the Jewish people during the Reformation. Then write a short essay analyzing why they were segregated to ghettos.

History ONLINE
For help with the concepts in this section of *Glencoe World History*, go to glencoe.com and click Study Central™.

423

C Critical Thinking

Drawing Conclusions
Ask: How did the Protestant Reformation affect the Catholic Church? *(It led to change in Church policies.)* OL

Answer: Jesuits took a vow of absolute obedience to the pope.

Assess

History ONLINE

Study Central provides summaries, interactive games, and online graphic organizers to help students review content.

Close

Comparing and Contrasting
Ask: How did the relationship between religion and politics in Europe change during this time? *(New Protestant states no longer accepted the pope as the head of the church nor did they recognize his authority over them.)* OL

Answers

1. Definitions for the vocabulary words are found in the section and the Glossary.
2. created church government that used both clergy and laity; set up the Consistory to oversee moral life and doctrinal purity; trained missionaries and sent them to all parts of Europe
3. The pope would not annul his marriage and allow him to remarry, so Henry VIII broke with the Church.
4. **Calvinists:** church was the government and members participated; **Anabaptists:** complete separation of church and state; members would not participate
5. The Catholic Church addressed many of its problems and clarified doctrine, giving it new strength and enabling it to regain much of what it had lost.
6. Her interference in religious affairs resulted in England becoming even more Protestant.
7. Students might name any Catholic country shown on the map.
8. Students will complete research and then write a short essay based on their information.

Identifying Central Issues
Discuss the information contained in the Visual Summary. Remind students that this information includes important ideas from the entire chapter. Have students work in small groups to explain the role that humanism played in the Renaissance. Have each group choose one example form each of the following three areas: the arts, politics, and religion. **Ask:** How did humanist ideas influence art, politics, and religion during the Renaissance? Encourage students to cite details from the chapter to support their responses. Suggest that each group use a graphic organizer to record its ideas. Then let groups share their findings, which will help the class review the material for the chapter test. **OL**

English Language Learners
Have students read the visual summary aloud. Ask them to locate words that contain the suffix *-ism (Calvinism, Catholicism, Lutheranism, Protestantism),* and list them on the board. Explain that this suffix usually indicates a doctrine, system, or theory. Point out that "Calvinism," for example, is the religious doctrine taught by John Calvin. Help students find examples of other "isms" and add them to the list. **ELL**

CHAPTER 12 Visual Summary

STUDY TO GO You can study anywhere, anytime by downloading quizzes and flash cards to your PDA from glencoe.com.

THE RENAISSANCE in Italy and Northern Europe

- Milan, Venice, and Florence became centers of Renaissance learning and culture.
- Machiavelli's views on gaining and holding power influenced political leaders.
- Humanist education focused on liberal studies.
- Artists sought to portray the world realistically.

Detail of Sistine Chapel Ceiling, by Michelangelo

Michelangelo painted people with perfect proportions as a reflection of divine beauty.

Martin Luther Publicly Burns His Excommunication Documents

Luther's beliefs spread, creating Lutheranism, the first Protestant faith.

THE REFORMATION Begins

- Erasmus and other Christian humanists paved the way for the Protestant Reformation.
- Catholic teaching stressed faith and good works, but Luther believed that faith alone was sufficient for salvation.
- The Peace of Augsburg ended the religious wars and allowed German states to choose between Catholicism and Lutheranism.

Persecution of an Anabaptist

Anabaptists were viewed as dangerous radicals.

THE REFORMATION Spreads

- Calvinism replaced Lutheranism as the most important form of Protestantism.
- Henry VIII established the Church of England for political rather than religious reasons.
- Anabaptists believed in the total separation of church and state.
- Pope Paul III took steps to reform the Catholic Church.

Hands-On Chapter Project
Step 5: Wrap-Up

Creating a Mural

Step 5: View the Murals Students will synthesize what they have learned in Steps 1–4.

Directions: Have groups take turns presenting a short explanation of their murals and the reasons for their choices of color, text, and graphics. Allow time for students to view the murals and examine them more closely before displaying a concept map entitled "The Renaissance and Reformation." Ask groups to use what they have learned from the murals as well as from this chapter to list ideas that should be included in the map to answer the Essential Question. Their responses should cover intellectual, artistic, literary, technological, social, architectural, religious, and political changes. Together, complete the concept map. Then have students independently identify what they see as the most important change of the era and defend their opinion in a brief essay. **OL**

STANDARDIZED TEST PRACTICE

TEST-TAKING 

If a question asks you to read a quote, look for clues that reveal its historical context—the title, the date, the quote itself. Determining the historical context will help you determine the quote's historical significance. It will also help you determine the correct answer.

Reviewing Vocabulary

Directions: Choose the word or words that best complete the sentence.

1. Theologians of the Reformation disagreed about how people could achieve ________, or acceptance into Heaven.

A indulgence
B predestination
C annulment
D salvation

2. The money and goods given by the wife's family to the husband at the time of marriage is called a ________.

A settlement
B dowry
C tithe
D taille

3. John Calvin emphasized ________, the belief that God determined in advance who would be saved and who would be damned.

A predisposition
B salvation
C predestination
D humanism

4. An image painted on fresh, wet plaster is called a ________.

A ceramic
B flying buttress
C fresco
D relic

Reviewing Main Ideas

Directions: Choose the best answers to the following questions.

Section 1 *(pp. 398–403)*

5. Which of the following was a characteristic of the Renaissance?

A Rejection of the classical learning of ancient Greece and Rome
B Renewed emphasis on an all-powerful God
C Emergence of a more secular worldview
D Reawakening of feudalism

6. Who helped to make Florence the cultural center of Europe during the Renaissance?

A Francesco Sforza
B Lorenzo de' Medici
C Niccolò Machiavelli
D Girolamo Savonarola

Section 2 *(pp. 406–411)*

7. Who has been called the father of Italian Renaissance humanism?

A Petrarch
B Leonardo da Vinci
C Dante
D Albrecht Dürer

8. What was the *Divine Comedy*?

A A collection of stories told by a group of pilgrims on a journey
B A defense of women
C An ancient Roman poem by Virgil
D A poem about a soul's journey to Heaven

Need Extra Help?

If You Missed Questions . . .	1	2	3	4	5	6	7	8
Go to Page . . .	414	403	419	409	398	400	406	407

Answers and Analyses

Reviewing Vocabulary

1. D Students should define the words they know to help them narrow down their choices. An *indulgence* is a release from all or part of the punishment for sin. *Predestination* is the doctrine that God has determined in advance who will be saved. *Annulment* is the dissolution of the bonds of marriage. *Salvation* means acceptance into heaven or the act of being saved.

2. B *Tithe* and *taille* might be eliminated, since a tithe is a tenth of one's income donated to a church and taille is a tax. A *settlement* might refer to money or goods given at the time of marriage, but it is not specific to that context.

3. C Tell students to use context clues and their knowledge of word parts. The phrase "determined in advance" narrows the possibilities to *predisposition* and *predestination,* because of their prefix *pre-*. Since the belief is that God determines where people go after death, their destination, the correct choice is *predestination.*

4. C Students should use the process of elimination to determine the correct answer.

Reviewing Main Ideas

5. C Remind students that this period is called the Renaissance because of the rebirth of classicism, which emphasized the importance of the individual, thus leading to a more secular view.

6. B Students should associate the Medici family with Florence and with cultural achievements.

7. A All of these choices name important figures in the Renaissance. Da Vinci and Dürer were leading artists; Dante was a great writer. But it was Petrarch who was called the father of Italian Renaissance humanism.

8. D *The Canterbury Tales* is a collection of stories told by pilgrims. Christine de Pizan wrote in defense of women in *The Book of the City of Ladies. The Divine Comedy* is an epic poem about the soul's journey to Heaven.

9. B Students can eliminate Jan van Eyck, who was associated with the Northern Renaissance, not Rome. While the other three artists all worked in Italy, it was Michelangelo who undertook the immense task of painting this ceiling.

10. D Tell students to remember that Erasmus was a leading Christian humanist. His quest was to reform the Church in a way that would direct attention away from the external forms and back to inward spiritual growth.

11. C The Ninety-five Theses composed by Martin Luther helped to cause the religious warfare. The Edict of Worms made Martin Luther an outlaw in the empire. The Great Schism was a split in the Catholic Church at the end of the 14th century. The Peace of Augsburg established the right of German rulers to determine the religion of their nations, thus ending the war between Charles V and the princes.

TEST-TAKING 

For Question 11: Explain that internal context clues can sometimes help eliminate incorrect choices and identify the correct answer. Point out the relationship between the phrase "ended the religious warfare" in the question and the word *peace* in the correct answer.

12. A Since the Anglican church under Henry VIII remained almost identical to the Catholic Church, it is clear that Henry VIII had no religious agenda for his break with Rome. He became the head of his own church, showing that he did not uphold the idea of separation of church and state. His reason was purely personal and political; he wanted to marry Anne Boleyn and beget a male heir.

CHAPTER 12

9. Which artist painted figures on the ceilings of the Sistine Chapel in Rome?
- **A** Leonardo da Vinci
- **B** Michelangelo
- **C** Raphael
- **D** Jan van Eyck

Section 3 *(pp. 412–417)*

10. What was the major goal of Christian humanism?
- **A** To create a new form of Christian faith
- **B** To preserve religious unity in the Holy Roman Empire
- **C** To promote external forms of religion, such as pilgrimages and relics
- **D** To reform the Catholic Church

11. What agreement ended the religious warfare in Germany in 1555?
- **A** Ninety-five Theses
- **B** Edict of Worms
- **C** Peace of Augsburg
- **D** Great Schism

Section 4 *(pp. 418–423)*

12. Why did King Henry VIII break with Rome and establish the Church of England?
- **A** To marry Anne Boleyn
- **B** To promote his religious views
- **C** To force the Catholic Church to reform
- **D** To separate church and state

13. Who founded the Jesuits?
- **A** John Calvin
- **B** Ignatius of Loyola
- **C** Martin Luther
- **D** Pope Paul III

Critical Thinking

Directions: Choose the best answers to the following questions.

Use the following map to answer question 14.

14. Which of the following is a true statement about the Holy Roman Empire in 1400?
- **A** It had no access to the Mediterranean Sea.
- **B** It did not include parts of Italy.
- **C** Rome was not a part of the Empire.
- **D** Denmark was part of the Empire.

15. How did fifteenth-century humanists differ from those in the fourteenth century?
- **A** They preferred to live in solitude.
- **B** They believed in service to the state.
- **C** Most moved to the country.
- **D** They emphasized classical Latin.

Need Extra Help?

If You Missed Questions . . .	9	10	11	12	13	14	15
Go to Page . . .	410	412	417	420	423	426	406

13. B Both Calvin and Luther can be eliminated, since they were leading Protestant figures. Ignatius of Loyola founded the Jesuits, who vowed obedience to the pope.

Critical Thinking

14. C Remind students to evaluate each statement based on the data presented by the map. Since Rome is outside the boundaries of the empire, C is the correct response.

15. B The early humanists believed that solitude was necessary to conduct their intellectual life. However, later humanists took an interest in civic life and believed that they could be of service to the state.

16. Why were liberal studies at the core of a humanist curriculum?
   - **A** To create great scholars
   - **B** To promote advances in science
   - **C** To enable more people to read Latin
   - **D** To provide practical preparation for life

17. In his Ninety-five Theses, Martin Luther wrote: "Christians are to be taught that he who gives to the poor or lends to the needy does a better work than buying pardons." To what is Luther objecting in this statement?
   - **A** The doctrine of predestination
   - **B** The lack of concern for the poor
   - **C** The sale of indulgences
   - **D** The spread of secular humanism

Base your answer to question 18 on the following table.

Top Ten Organized Religions of the World (2004 estimates)

Religion	Number of Members	Percentage
Christianity	2.1 billion	33.0%
Islam	1.3 billion	20.1%
Hinduism	851 million	13.3%
Buddhism	375 million	5.9%
Sikhism	25 million	0.4%
Judaism	15 million	0.2%
Baha'ism	7.5 million	0.1%
Confucianism	6.4 million	0.1%
Jainism	4.5 million	0.1%
Shintoism	2.8 million	0.0%

Source: *Encyclopedia Britannica*

18. Which of the following is a true statement about the world's top 10 organized religions?
   - **A** Hindus exceed Buddhists by more than double.
   - **B** There are more Muslims than Christians.
   - **C** Jews far outnumber Buddhists.
   - **D** Christianity is the most organized religion in the world.

Document-Based Questions

Directions: Analyze the document and answer the short-answer questions that follow the document. Base your answers on the document and on your knowledge of world history.

Niccolò Machiavelli wrote:

> *"Everyone realizes how praiseworthy it is for a prince to honor his word and to be straightforward rather than crafty in his dealings; nonetheless experience shows that princes who have achieved great things have been those who have given their word lightly, who have known how to trick men with their cunning, and who, in the end, have overcome those abiding by honest principles. . . . A prince, therefore, need not necessarily have all the good qualities I mentioned above, but he should certainly appear to have them. . . . He should not deviate from what is good, if that is possible, but he should know how to do evil, if that is necessary."*
>
> —Niccolò Machiavelli, *The Prince*, George Bull, trans., 1981

19. According to Machiavelli, what kinds of princes have achieved great things?

20. According to Machiavelli, what role does evil play in governance?

Extended Response

21. Analyze how the Reformation shaped the political and religious life of Europe. Be sure to identify the historical effects of the Reformation.

History ONLINE
For additional test practice, use Self-Check Quizzes—Chapter 12 at glencoe.com.

Need Extra Help?

If You Missed Questions . . .	16	17	18	19	20	21
Go to Page . . .	408	401	427	427	427	418

STOP

Document-Based Questions

19. those who have given their word lightly and who have known how to trick men with their cunning

20. A prince should do evil whenever doing good will not accomplish the goal.

Extended Response

21. Answers will vary. Politically, the Reformation led to a power struggle between the Holy Roman Emperor and the German princes. It affected the religious life of Europe by introducing alternatives to Roman Catholicism and by spurring reform within the Catholic Church to get rid of corruption.

16. D Humanists believed that the purpose of education was to develop the potential of the individual and prepare him or her to fulfill the role of a citizen.

17. C Another word for *pardon* is *indulgence.* Luther was protesting against the practice of selling indulgences.

18. A Have students check each statement against the data presented in the chart. Comparing the numbers reveals that B and C are incorrect. The chart does not contain information that would enable students to verify D.

History ONLINE
Introduce students to chapter content and key terms by having them access the Chapter 12 Overview at glencoe.com.

Need Extra Help?
Have students refer to the pages listed if they miss any of the questions.

CHAPTER 13 Planning Guide

Key to Ability Levels	
BL Below Level	AL Above Level
OL On Level	ELL English Language Learners

Key to Teaching Resources	
Print Material	DVD
CD-ROM	Transparency

BL	OL	AL	ELL	Resources	Chapter Opener	Section 1	Section 2	Section 3	Chapter Assess
				FOCUS					
BL	OL	AL	ELL	**Daily Focus Skills Transparencies**		13-1	13-2	13-3	
				TEACH					
	OL	AL		**Economics and History Activity, URB**			✓		
BL	OL		ELL	**Reading Skills Activity, URB**		p. 57			
	OL	AL		**Historical Analysis Skills Activity, URB**			p. 58		
BL	OL	AL	ELL	**Differentiated Instruction Activity, URB**		p. 59			
	OL		ELL	**English Learner Activity, URB**		p. 61			
BL	OL	AL	ELL	**Content Vocabulary Activity, URB***		p. 63			
BL	OL	AL	ELL	**Academic Vocabulary Activity, URB**				p. 65	
BL	OL	AL	ELL	**Skills Reinforcement Activity, URB**			p. 67		
	OL	AL		**Critical Thinking Skills Activity, URB**			p. 68		
	OL	AL		**History and Geography Activity, URB**		p. 69			
	OL	AL	ELL	**Mapping History Activity, URB**		p. 71			
BL	OL	AL		**Historical Significance Activity, URB**			p. 72		
BL	OL	AL	ELL	**Cooperative Learning Activity, URB**		p. 73			
	OL	AL	ELL	**History Simulation Activity, URB**		p. 75			
BL	OL	AL	ELL	**Time Line Activity, URB**				p. 77	
	OL	AL		**Linking Past and Present Activity, URB**				p. 78	
BL	OL	AL		**People in World History Activity, URB**		pp. 79, 80			
BL	OL	AL	ELL	**Primary Source Reading, URB**		p. 81			
	OL	AL		**Enrichment Activity, URB**				p. 86	
BL	OL	AL	ELL	**World Art and Music Activity, URB**			p. 83		
BL	OL		ELL	**Guided Reading Activities, URB***		p. 88	p. 89	p. 90	
BL	OL		ELL	**Reading Essentials and Note-Taking Guide***		p. 142	p. 146	p. 149	
BL	OL	AL	ELL	**Differentiated Instruction for the World History Classroom**	✓	✓	✓	✓	✓

Note: Please refer to the *Unit Resource Book: The Early Modern World* for this chapter's URB materials.

* Also available in Spanish

- Interactive Lesson Planner
- Interactive Teacher Edition
- Fully editable blackline masters
- Section Spotlight Videos Launch
- Differentiated Lesson Plans
- Printable reports of daily assignments
- Standards Tracking System

Levels				Resources	Chapter Opener	Section 1	Section 2	Section 3	Chapter Assess
BL	OL	AL	ELL						
				TEACH *(continued)*					
BL	OL	AL	ELL	StudentWorks™ Plus DVD	✓	✓	✓	✓	✓
BL	OL	AL	ELL	Vocabulary PuzzleMaker CD-ROM	✓	✓	✓	✓	✓
Teacher Resources				Building Academic Vocabulary	✓	✓	✓	✓	✓
				Writer's Guidebook			p. 51	p. 27	
				Strategies for Success	✓	✓	✓	✓	✓
				Outline Map Resource Book	✓	✓	✓	✓	✓
				Presentation Plus! with MindJogger DVD	✓	✓	✓	✓	✓
				ASSESS					
BL	OL	AL	ELL	Section Quizzes and Chapter Tests*		p. 157	p. 158	p. 159	p. 161
BL	OL	AL	ELL	Authentic Assessment With Rubrics	✓	✓	✓	✓	✓
BL	OL	AL	ELL	Standardized Test Practice Workbook	✓	✓	✓	✓	✓
BL	OL	AL	ELL	*ExamView® Assessment Suite* CD-ROM		13-1	13-2	13-3	Ch. 13
BL	OL	AL	ELL	Interactive Tutor Self-Assessment CD-ROM		13-1	13-2	13-3	
				CLOSE					
BL			ELL	Reteaching Activity, URB				p. 85	
BL	OL		ELL	Reading and Study Skills Foldables™	✓	✓	✓	✓	✓

Using the Glencoe Web Site

Chapter Overviews

Technology Product
The Glencoe Web site offers in-depth overviews that summarize the content of each chapter. The overviews consist of brief chapter summaries and separate overviews for each section. The chapter overviews
- summarize and reinforce chapter content;
- provide discussion points to use in class.

Objectives
The overviews help students
- prepare for better understanding chapter content;
- practice reading and comprehension skills.

Steps
Provide students with the following steps to complete the activities:
- Locate the Web page for the textbook being studied on the Glencoe Web site glencoe.com.
- Click on **Student Center** under the textbook title.
- Once you are in the Student Center, select a unit from the Unit Resources menu and a chapter from the Chapter Activities menu using the drop-down arrows.
- Click on the **Chapter Overviews** link.
- Have students read the chapter overview in preparation for a reading assignment or activity.

History ONLINE

	Student	Teacher	Parent
Beyond the Textbook	●	●	●
Chapter Overviews	●	●	●
Time Current Events	●		●
ePuzzles and Games	●		●
Concepts in Motion	●		●
Literature Connections		●	
Multi-Language Glossaries	●		●
Online Student Edition	●	●	●
Self-Check Quizzes	●		●
Student Web Activities	●		●
Study Central ™	●		●
Teaching Today		●	
Vocabulary eFlashcards	●		●
Web Activity Lesson Plans		●	

- **Timed Readings Plus in Social Studies** helps students increase their reading rate and fluency while maintaining comprehension. The 400-word passages are similar to those found on state and national assessments.
- **Reading in the Content Area: Social Studies** concentrates on six essential reading skills that help students better comprehend what they read. The book includes 75 high-interest nonfiction passages written at increasing levels of difficulty.
- **Reading Social Studies** includes strategic reading instruction and vocabulary support in Social Studies content for both ELLs and native speakers of English.

www.jamestowneducation.com

The following videotape programs are available from Glencoe as supplements to Chapter 13:

- Mexico: A Story of Courage and Conquest (ISBN 0-76-701622-X)
- Mexico's Great Pyramids (ISBN 076-700628-3)

To order, call Glencoe at 1-800-334-7344. To find classroom resources to accompany many of these videos, check the following home pages:

A&E Television: www.aetv.com

The History Channel: www.historychannel.com

Index to National Geographic Magazine:

The following articles relate to this chapter:

- "Mystery Mountain of the Inca," by Peter Frost, February 2004
- "Inca Rescue," by Guillermo A. Cock, May 2002
- "Cuba's Golden Past," by Thomas B. Allen, July 2001

National Geographic Society Products To order the following, call National Geographic at 1-800-368-2728:

- *National Geographic Atlas of the World* (Book)
- *The Age of Exploration* (PicturePak and CD-ROM)

Access National Geographic's new, dynamic MapMachine Web site and other geography resources at:

www.nationalgeographic.com

www.nationalgeographic.com/maps

GLENCOE BOOKLINK 3

Use this database to search more than 30,000 titles to create a customized reading list for your students.

- Reading lists can be organized by students' reading level, author, genre, theme, or area of interest.
- The database provides Degrees of Reading Power™ (DRP) and Lexile™ readability scores for all selections.
- A brief summary of each selection is included.

Leveled reading suggestions for this chapter:

For students at a Grade 8 reading level:
- ***Ferdinand Magellan,*** by Betty Lou Kratoville

For students at a Grade 9 reading level:
- ***Christopher Columbus: Admiral of the Ocean Sea,*** by Jim Haskins

For students at a Grade 10 reading level:
- ***Aztecs and Spaniards: Cortes and the Conquest of Mexico,*** by Albert Martin

For students at a Grade 11 reading level:
- ***Montezuma,*** by Struan Reid

For students at a Grade 12 reading level:
- ***Ferdinand Magellan and the Discovery of the World Ocean,*** by Rebecca Stefoff

Introducing
CHAPTER 13

Focus

MAKING CONNECTIONS
How are the Americas linked to Africa?

Activate students' prior knowledge by reminding them that the economies of the Americas were built on the labor of enslaved Africans. Discuss ways in which Africans have enriched the culture of the Americas since colonial times and how a cultural exchange continues to exist today through trade, tourism, and immigration.

Teach

The Big Ideas

As students study the chapter, remind them to consider the section-based Big Ideas included in each section's Guide to Reading. The **Essential Questions** in the activities below tie in to the Big Ideas and help students think about and understand important chapter concepts. In addition, the Hands-on Chapter Projects with their culminating activities relate the content from each section to the Big Ideas. These activities build on each other as students progress through the chapter. Section activities culminate in the wrap-up activity on the Visual Summary page.

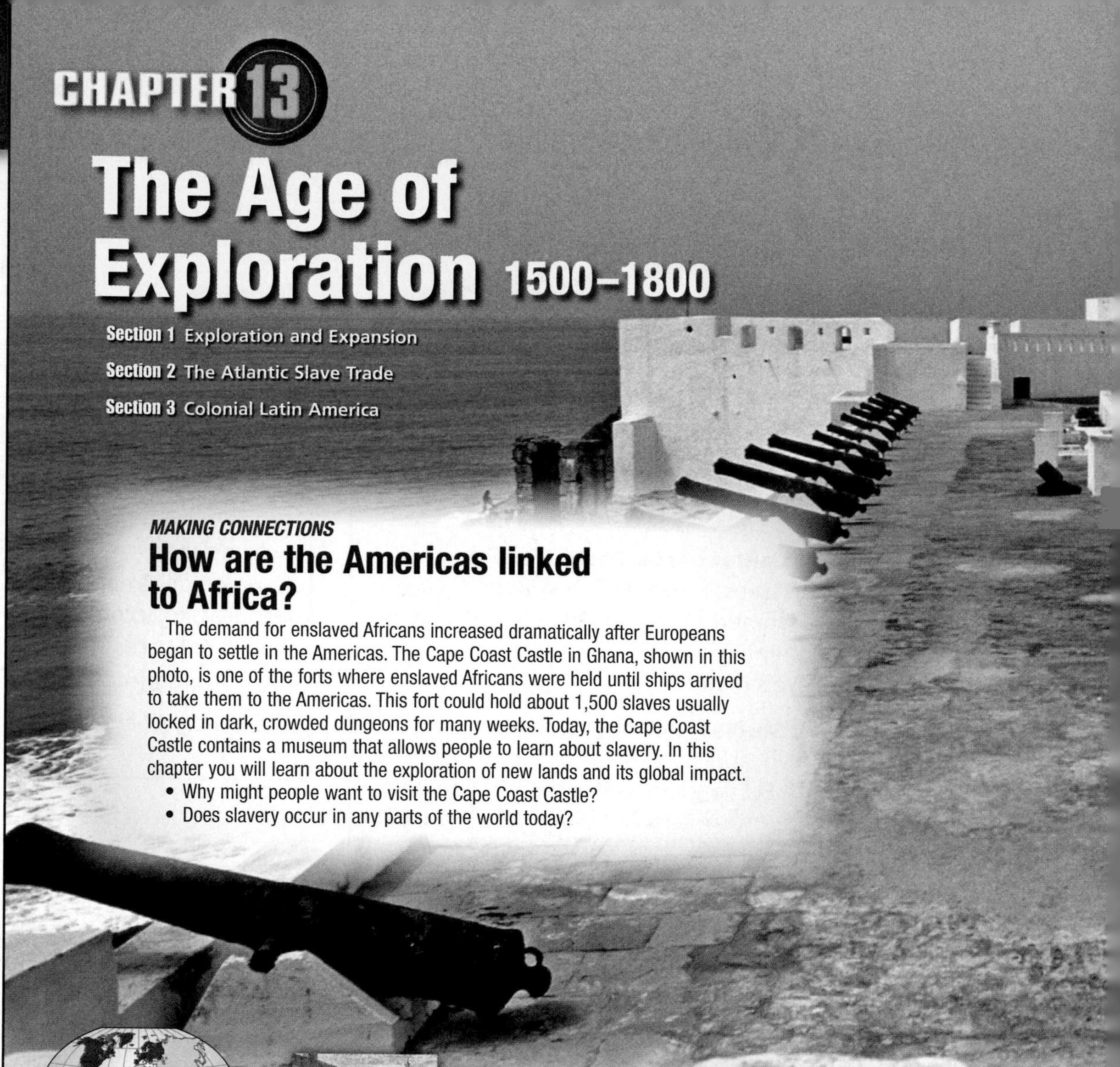

CHAPTER 13

The Age of Exploration 1500–1800

MAKING CONNECTIONS
How are the Americas linked to Africa?

The demand for enslaved Africans increased dramatically after Europeans began to settle in the Americas. The Cape Coast Castle in Ghana, shown in this photo, is one of the forts where enslaved Africans were held until ships arrived to take them to the Americas. This fort could hold about 1,500 slaves usually locked in dark, crowded dungeons for many weeks. Today, the Cape Coast Castle contains a museum that allows people to learn about slavery. In this chapter you will learn about the exploration of new lands and its global impact.

- Why might people want to visit the Cape Coast Castle?
- Does slavery occur in any parts of the world today?

EUROPE AND THE AMERICAS ▶

1500 Pedro Cabral lands in South America

1520 Ferdinand Magellan sails into the Pacific Ocean

1500 — 1600

THE WORLD ▶

1568 Japan's unification begins

1632 Building of Taj Mahal begins

428

Exploration and Expansion
Essential Question: In what ways did European nations prosper through exploration in the fifteenth century? *(acquired territories, wealth, and power)* Point out that in Section 1, students will learn how European nations expanded trade and grew rich by acquiring new lands. **OL**

The Atlantic Slave Trade
Essential Question: How did European expansion and the slave trade affect the people of Africa? *(Expansion and the slave trade brutally victimized Africans.)* Point out that in Section 2, students will learn about the devastating effects of European expansion and trade on the people of Africa. **OL**

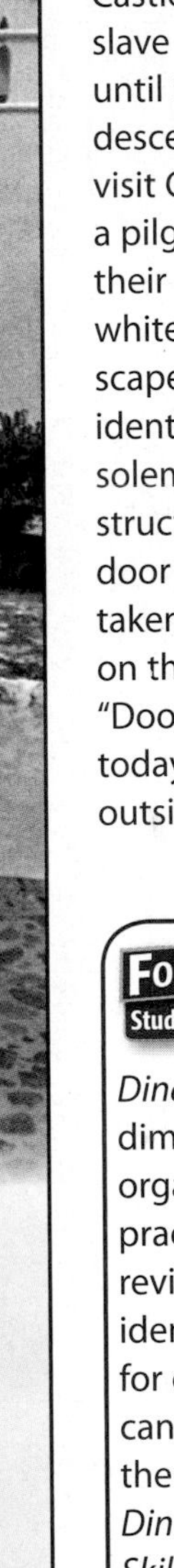

1663
Canada becomes a French colony

1722
Rule of Emperor Kangxi of China ends

1787
Northwest Ordinance bans slavery in the Northwest Territory of the United States

1794
Congress bans slave trade between U.S. and foreign countries

1700 — 1800

FOLDABLES™ Study Organizer

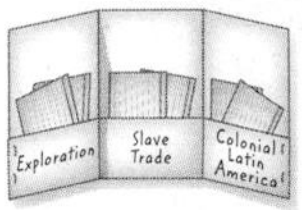

Describing As you read, take notes on exploration, slave trade, and colonial Latin America on quarter sheets of paper. Organize your notes in a Three-Pocket Book.

History ONLINE
Chapter Overview—Visit glencoe.com to preview Chapter 13.

SECTION 3

Colonial Latin America

Essential Question: How did Portugal and Spain profit from their colonies in Latin America? *(They grew rich by exporting natural resources at the expense of indigenous peoples.)* Point out that in Section 3, students will learn how both countries tapped the natural resources of their colonies to bolster their economies. **OL**

Introducing **CHAPTER 13**

More About the Photo

Visual Literacy Cape Coast Castle served as a center of the slave trade from the mid-1600s until its end in 1807. Today many descendants of enslaved Africans visit Cape Coast Castle as part of a pilgrimage to trace the roots of their ancestors. The gleaming white building, the majestic landscape, and even the building's identification as a "castle" are all solemn and bitter tokens of the structure's horrific past. Inside, the door through which captives were taken from the dungeons to ships on the Middle Passage is labeled "Door of No Return." In tribute to today's visitors, the sign on the outside reads "Door of Return."

FOLDABLES™ Study Organizer **Dinah Zike's Foldables**

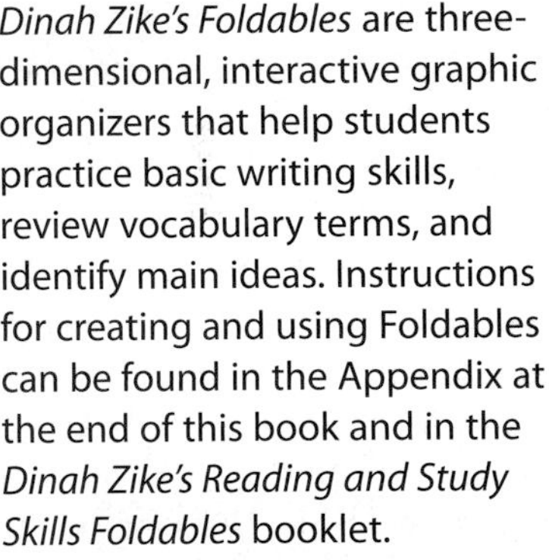

Dinah Zike's Foldables are three-dimensional, interactive graphic organizers that help students practice basic writing skills, review vocabulary terms, and identify main ideas. Instructions for creating and using Foldables can be found in the Appendix at the end of this book and in the *Dinah Zike's Reading and Study Skills Foldables* booklet.

History ONLINE
Introduce students to chapter content and key terms by having them access the Chapter 13 Overview at glencoe.com.

Focus

Bellringer

Daily Focus Transparency 13.1

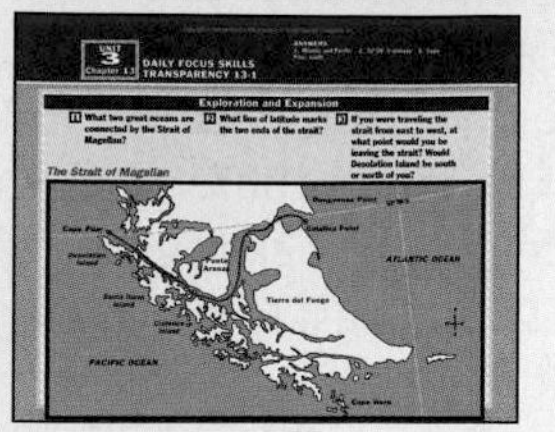

GUIDE TO READING

Answers to Graphic:

Portugal: Dias: Cape of Good Hope, India, Melaka; Da Gama: India; Cabral: South America;
Spain: Columbus: Cuba, Hispaniola, Caribbean islands, Honduras; Cortés: Mexico; Magellan and Elcano: South American coast, Philippines
England: Cabot: New England coastline; Drake: West Indies, South American coastline, North American coastline; Hudson: Canada
France: Verazzano: east coast of North America; Cartier: Canada
Netherlands: Barents: islands in Barents Sea; Hudson: New York

Section Spotlight Video

To generate student interest and provide a springboard for class discussion, access the Chapter 13, Section 1 video at glencoe.com or on the video DVD.

Resource Manager

SECTION 1

Exploration and Expansion

GUIDE TO READING

The BIG Idea
Competition Among Countries
Europeans began exploring the world in the 1400s, and several nations experienced economic heights through worldwide trade.

Content Vocabulary
- conquistadors *(p. 434)*
- *encomienda (p. 435)*
- Columbian Exchange *(p. 436)*

Academic Vocabulary
- overseas *(p. 430)*
- percent *(p. 432)*

People and Places
- Hernán Cortés *(p. 431)*
- Portugal *(p. 432)*
- Vasco da Gama *(p. 432)*
- Melaka *(p. 432)*
- Christopher Columbus *(p. 432)*
- Cuba *(p. 432)*
- Ferdinand Magellan *(p. 432)*
- John Cabot *(p. 433)*
- Amerigo Vespucci *(p. 433)*
- Montezuma *(p. 434)*
- Francisco Pizarro *(p. 435)*

Reading Strategy
Organizing Information As you read, use a chart like the one below to list the explorers and lands explored by each European nation.

	Explorers	Lands Explored
Portugal		
Spain		
England		
France		
Netherlands		

On a quest for "God, glory, and gold," the Portuguese and Spanish led the way in exploring new worlds. Setting sail to the east, the Portuguese eventually gained control of the Spice Islands. In the west, Portugal and Spain each claimed new lands in the Americas. By the end of the sixteenth century, however, the Dutch, French, and English began competing with the Portuguese and Spanish for these new lands and the riches they held.

Motives and Means

MAIN IDEA Europeans began to explore distant lands, motivated by religious zeal and the promise of gold and glory.

HISTORY & YOU Recall that Isabella and Ferdinand of Spain sought religious unity for their country. Read to learn how religious zeal also played a part in the European quest for riches in other lands.

The dynamic energy of Western civilization between 1500 and 1800 was most apparent when Europeans began to expand into the rest of the world. First Portugal and Spain, then later the Netherlands, England, and France, all rose to new economic heights through their worldwide trading activity.

For almost a thousand years, Europeans had mostly remained in one area of the world. At the end of the fifteenth century, however, they set out on a remarkable series of **overseas** journeys. What caused them to undertake such dangerous voyages to the ends of the Earth?

Europeans had long been attracted to Asia. In the late thirteenth century, Marco Polo had traveled with his father and uncle to the Chinese court of the great Mongol ruler Kublai Khan. He had written an account of his experiences, known as *The Travels*. Many, including Christopher Columbus, read the book and were fascinated by the exotic East. In the fourteenth century, conquests by the Ottoman Turks reduced the ability of Westerners to travel by land to the East. People then spoke of gaining access to Asia by sea.

Economic motives loom large in European expansion. Merchants, adventurers, and state officials had high hopes of expanding trade, especially for the spices of the East. The spices, which were needed to preserve and flavor food, were very expensive after Arab middlemen shipped them to Europe. Europeans also had hopes of finding precious metals. One Spanish adventurer wrote that he went to the Americas "to give light to those who were in darkness, and to grow rich, as all men desire to do."

R Reading Strategies	C Critical Thinking	D Differentiated Instruction	W Writing Support	S Skill Practice
Teacher Edition • Identifying, p. 431 • Summarizing, p. 432 • Making Connections, p. 434 **Additional Resources** • Cont. Vocab. Act., URB p. 63 • Guid. Read. Act., URB p. 88 • Read. Ess. & Note-Taking Guide, p. 142	**Teacher Edition** • Analyzing Info., p. 432 • Making Inferences, pp. 435, 436 • Drawing Con., p. 435 **Additional Resources** • Hist. Sim. Act., URB p. 75 • People in World Hist. Act., URB pp. 79, 80 • Section Quiz, p. 157	**Teacher Edition** • Logical/Math., p. 432 • Visual/Spatial, p. 433 **Additional Resources** • Diff. Instr. Act., URB p. 59 • English Learner Act., URB p. 61 • Coop. Learn. Act., URB p. 73 • Pri. Source Read., URB p. 81	**Teacher Edition** • Expository Writing, p. 434 **Additional Resources** • Hist. & Geo. Act., URB p. 69	**Teacher Edition** • Using Geo. Skills, p. 431 **Additional Resources** • Read. Skills Act., URB p. 57 • Mapping Hist. Act., URB p. 71

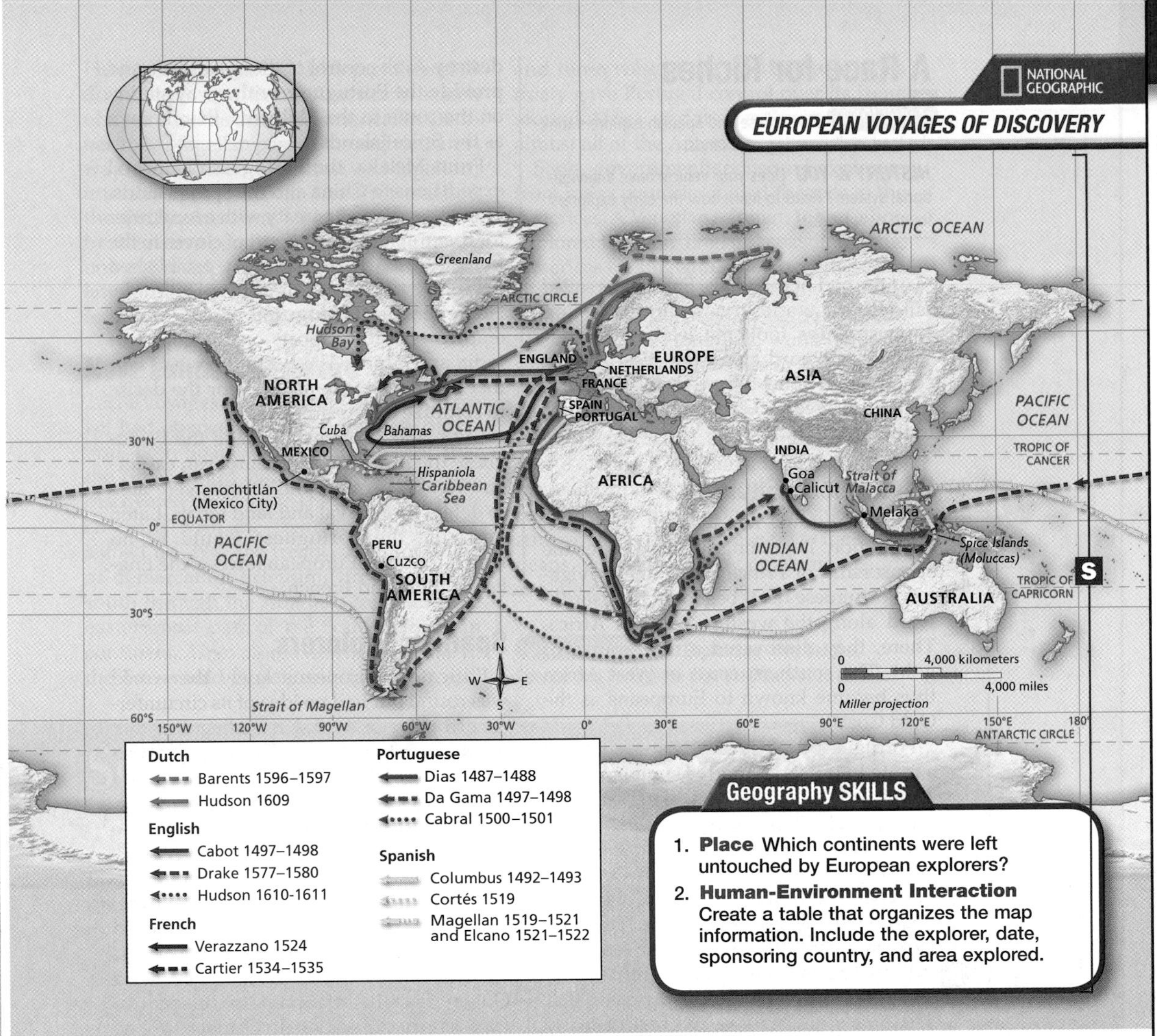

Geography SKILLS

1. **Place** Which continents were left untouched by European explorers?
2. **Human-Environment Interaction** Create a table that organizes the map information. Include the explorer, date, sponsoring country, and area explored.

This statement suggests another reason for the overseas voyages: religious zeal. Many people shared the belief of **Hernán Cortés,** the Spanish conqueror of Mexico, that they must ensure that the natives were "introduced into the holy Catholic faith."

There was a third motive as well. Spiritual and secular affairs were connected in the sixteenth century. People like Cortés wanted to convert the natives to Christianity; but grandeur, glory, and a spirit of adventure also played a major role in European expansion.

"God, glory, and gold," then, were the chief motives for European expansion, but what made the voyages possible? By the mid-1400s, European monarchies had increased their power and their resources and could focus beyond their borders. Europeans had also reached a level of technology that enabled them to make regular voyages beyond Europe. A new global age was about to begin.

✓Reading Check **Explaining** What does the phrase "God, glory, and gold" mean?

Teach

S Skill Practice

Using Geography Skills Ask: In which directions did Magellan sail to reach Asia? *(southwest and northwest around South America, then west)* OL

R Reading Strategy

Identifying Ask: What two developments made it possible for Europeans to undertake exploration voyages? *(an increase in power and resources and an advance in technology)* OL

Geography SKILLS

Answers:
1. based on the map, Australia and Antarctica
2. Students will create tables.

✓Reading Check

Answer: It describes the motives for European expansion: Europeans wanted to convert other peoples to Christianity, achieve fame, and to find gold and other precious metals.

Hands-On Chapter Project
Step 1

Creating a Diorama About European Expansion

Students will work as a class to design and build a diorama depicting European expansion between 1500 and 1800.

Step 1: Planning the Diorama

Essential Question: In what ways did European expansion affect Africans, Native Americans, Asians, and Europeans?

Directions: Explain that a diorama is a scenic display that tells a story and consists of two- or three-dimensional figures placed in front of painted backgrounds. Suggest that the class divide the diorama into three sections, one for each section in the chapter. As students study Section 1, they can think about what to include for Section 1. Write the Big Idea on the board and tell students to use it as a guide for finding material. Tell them to look for important events related to European exploration.

Summarizing: During review, conduct a class meeting to discuss events to include from Section 1 and to determine the diorama's format. Use this time also to assign individual or small-group duties. OL

Focus

Introducing Social History
Have students list the countries of origin of as many of their school supplies, items of clothing, and accessories as they can. Discuss with students how this global exchange, now taken for granted, exploded after Columbus's voyage in 1492. Although Europe and Asia were in contact, North and South America were largely self-contained and isolated continents.

Teach

W Writing Support

Expository Writing Review the crops that traveled from the New World to the Old. Tell students that some of these foods had a major impact on not only the diets but also the history and culture of regions in Europe and Asia. Ask them to choose one crop, such as potatoes, corn, or cacao, and find out more about what happened when it was introduced into the Old World and how important it became economically or as a food source. Have students present their information in a short essay. OL

Additional Support

Is It New World or Old World?

The ingredients in foods enjoyed today come from all over the world. The geographic origins of these foods, however, might come as a surprise. For example, tomatoes, which are associated with Italian cuisine, originated in the Americas. Food crops and animals native to one part of the world rarely existed in another part of the world until the voyages of Christopher Columbus. His voyages triggered one of the most significant events in world history—the Columbian Exchange—an extensive exchange of plants and animals between the Old and New Worlds.

New World

W

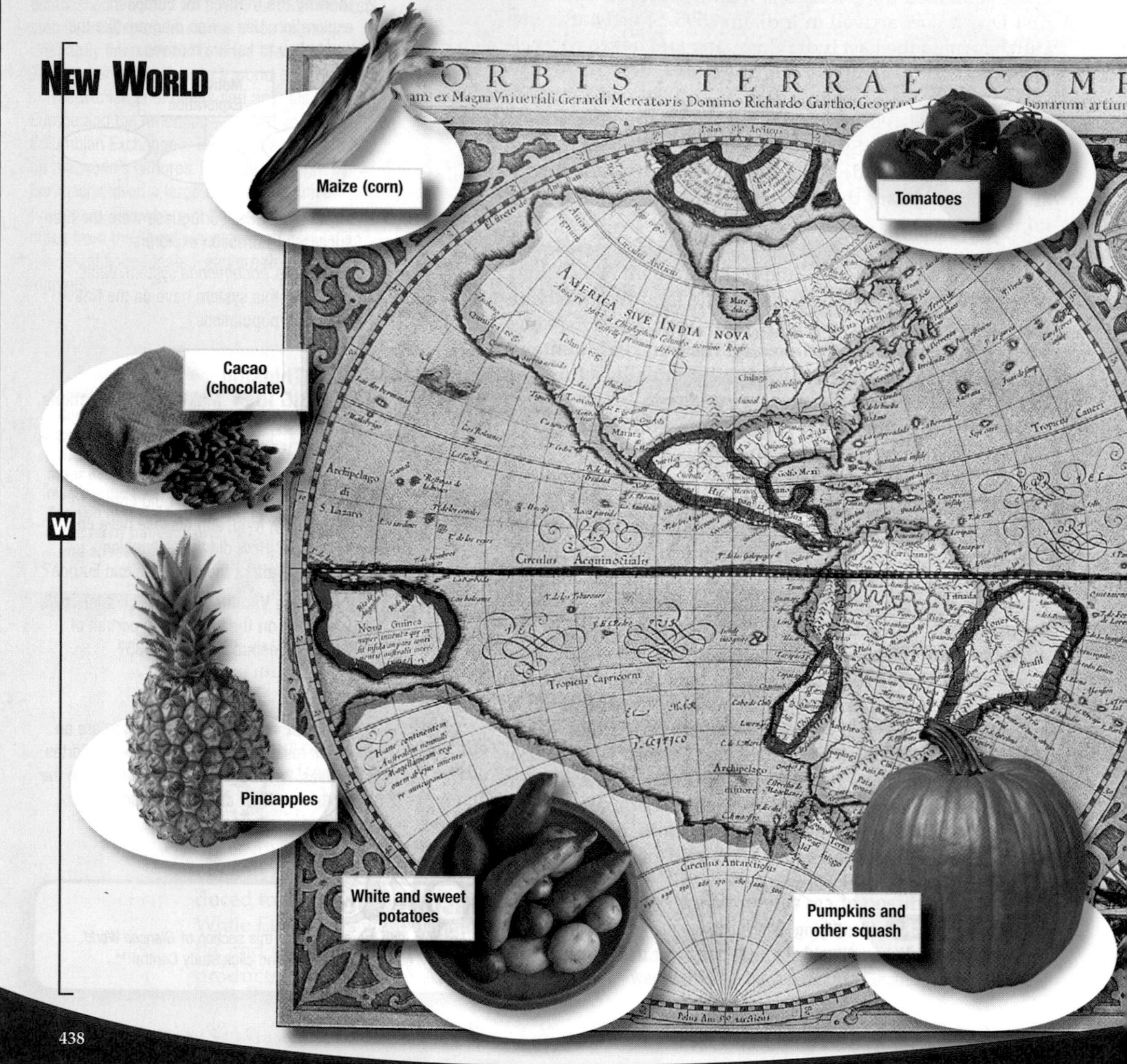

438

Background

Change Through Interaction Before the advent of Christopher Columbus, North and South America had very distinct species of flora and fauna because they had little contact with other continents. The influx of Old World explorers brought a change to the unique species of flora and fauna. New species were added, others disappeared, and many mingled, making it difficult to reconstruct exactly what the Americas were once like. Human species were not exempt from this change either. Within a few decades of the arrival of the Europeans, the indigenous population was reduced by millions. Scholars dispute the percentage—it may have been as high as 80 percent in some areas—but the impact of forced labor and new disease devastated Native American societies. Some population groups either ceased to exist or had to intermarry, creating new ethnic strains. Christopher Columbus and others were seeking riches, land, and power. In doing so, they brought about a biological revolution.

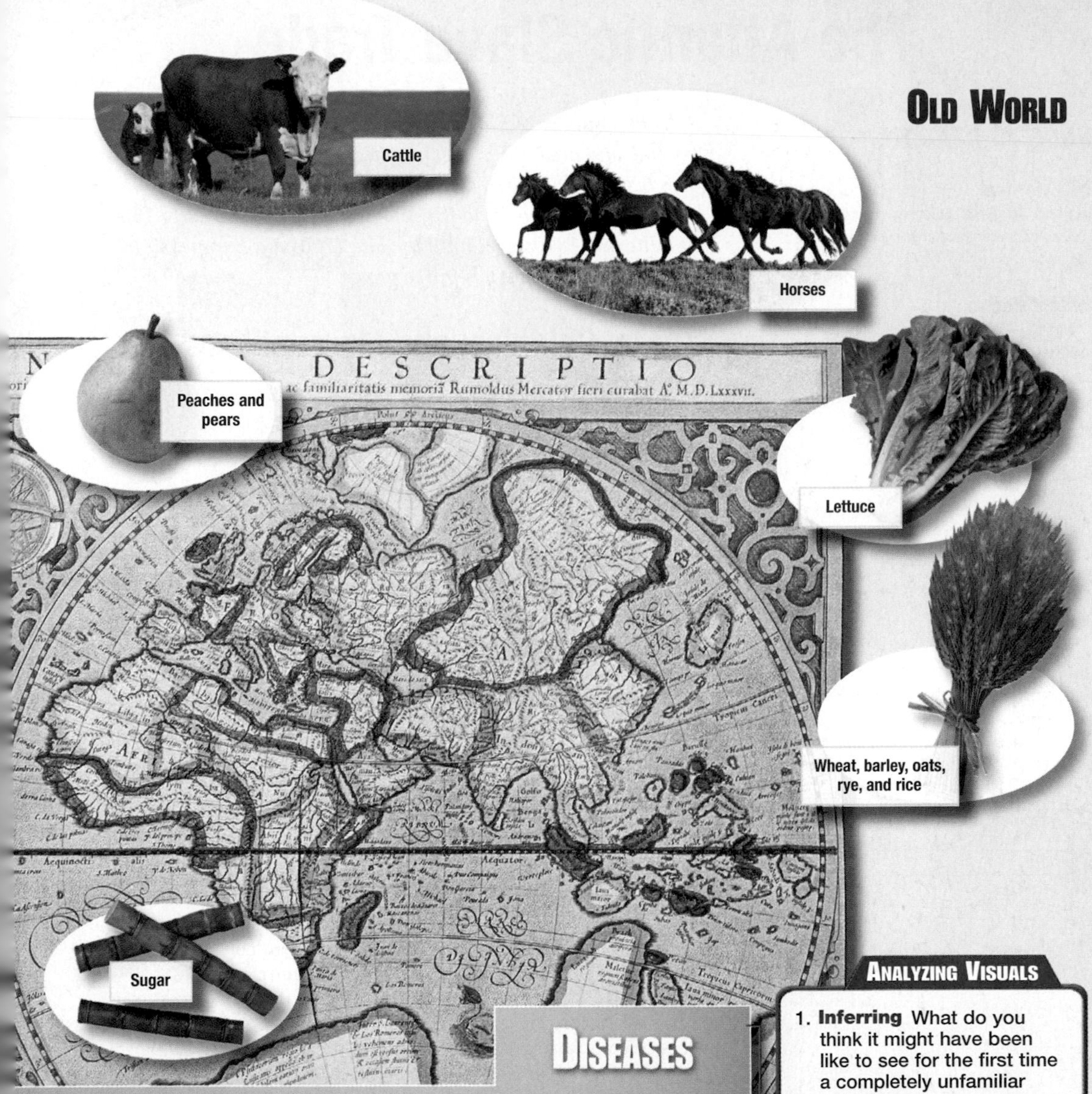

Old World

Cattle

Horses

Peaches and pears

Lettuce

Wheat, barley, oats, rye, and rice

Sugar

Diseases

Plants and animals were not the only things that were exchanged between Europe, Africa, Asia, and the Americas. People traveling from the Old World to the New World also brought with them many infectious diseases. These diseases included chicken pox, measles, smallpox, malaria, flu, and the common cold. Because people in the New World had not had previous exposure to these diseases, they were not immune to their devastating effects. C

Analyzing Visuals

1. **Inferring** What do you think it might have been like to see for the first time a completely unfamiliar animal, such as a horse or cow?
2. **Comparing** What infectious diseases are people worried about being exposed to today? What are the geographic origins of these diseases?

C Critical Thinking

Determining Cause and Effect Tell students that the devastating impact of smallpox on the Aztecs helped Cortés conquer them. **Ask:** What happened to indigenous people as a result of new diseases? *(Their populations declined; they were more easily conquered by Europeans.)* OL

Assess/Close

Summarizing Ask: What were the positive and negative consequences of the Columbian Exchange? *(Positive: new crops were introduced to both hemispheres, new animals were brought to North and South America; Negative: devastating diseases were introduced into North and South America)* OL

Analyzing Visuals

Answers:

1. People might have been frightened or curious.
2. Answers will vary. Avian, or bird, flu originated in Asia. HIV is believed to have originated in southeast Cameroon; SARS in China; West Nile virus in Uganda.

Activity: Economics Connection

Making Cause-and-Effect Chains Have students look at the animals and crops transported from Asia and Europe to the Americas. **Ask:** How did the introduction of the horse change the lives of Native Americans? *(Answers may include that horses enabled them to travel farther and faster and transport goods more easily. These advantages changed their methods of farming and ranching as well as hunting and conducting war.)* Tell students that another import from the Old World, sugarcane, also had a tremendous impact on the Americas. Have students find out more about the effects of sugarcane on the economy, culture, social structure, and environment of the New World. Ask them to present the information in the form of a cause-and-effect chain. Have students share and discuss their chains. OL

Focus

Bellringer

Daily Focus Transparency 13.2

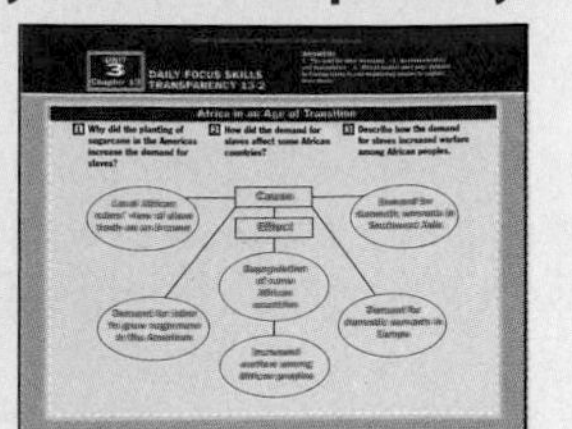

GUIDE TO READING

Answers to Graphic:

Economic/ Political Factors	Economic/ Political Effects
market for enslaved Africans in Southwest Asia	depopulation of some areas of Africa
planting of sugarcane in the Americas	not enough Native American labor available, so more Africans shipped to the Americas
high demand for slave labor	increased warfare and violence in Africa

Section Spotlight Video

To generate student interest and provide a springboard for class discussion, access the Chapter 13, Section 2 video at glencoe.com or on the video DVD.

Resource Manager

SECTION 2

The Atlantic Slave Trade

GUIDE TO READING

The BIG Idea

Human Rights European expansion affected Africa with the dramatic increase of the slave trade.

Content Vocabulary

- colony *(p. 440)*
- mercantilism *(p. 440)*
- balance of trade *(p. 440)*
- subsidies *(p. 440)*
- plantations *(p. 441)*
- triangular trade *(p. 442)*
- Middle Passage *(p. 442)*

Academic Vocabulary

- transportation *(p. 440)*
- primary *(p. 441)*

People and Places

- King Afonso *(p. 442)*
- Benin *(p. 443)*

Reading Strategy

Determining Cause and Effect As you read, use a table like the one below to identify economic and political factors that caused the slave trade to be profitable. List the economic and political effects of the trade.

Economic/Political Factors	Economic/Political Effects

As the number of European colonies increased, so did the volume and area of European trade. An Atlantic slave trade also began. Altogether, as many as 10 million enslaved Africans were brought to the Americas between the early 1500s and the late 1800s. Not until the late 1700s did European feeling against slavery begin to grow.

Trade, Colonies, and Mercantilism

MAIN IDEA The slave trade increased as enslaved Africans were brought to the Americas.

HISTORY & YOU Have you seen movies about slavery? Read to learn how the slave trade became part of the triangular trade pattern.

In less than 300 years, the European age of exploration changed the world. In some areas, such as the Americas and the Spice Islands, it led to the destruction of local civilizations and the establishment of European colonies. In others, such as Africa and mainland Southeast Asia, it left native regimes intact but had a strong impact on local societies and regional trade patterns. European expansion affected Africa with the dramatic increase of the slave trade, which played an important part in European trade.

The increase in the volume and area of European trade as a result of European expansion was a crucial factor in producing a new age of commercial capitalism. This is one of the first steps in the development of the world economy. The nations of Europe were creating trading empires.

Led by Portugal and Spain, European nations established many trading posts and colonies in the Americas and the East. A **colony** is a settlement of people living in a new territory, linked with the parent country by trade and direct government control.

Colonies played a role in the theory of **mercantilism,** a set of principles that dominated economic thought in the seventeenth century. According to mercantilists, the prosperity of a nation depended on a large supply of bullion, or gold and silver. To bring in gold and silver payments, nations tried to have a favorable **balance of trade.** The balance of trade is the difference in value between what a nation imports and what it exports over time. When the balance is favorable, the goods exported are of greater value than those imported.

To encourage exports, governments stimulated industries and trade. They granted **subsidies,** or payments, to new industries and improved **transportation** systems by building roads, bridges,

R Reading Strategies	C Critical Thinking	D Differentiated Instruction	W Writing Support	S Skill Practice
Teacher Edition • Identifying, p. 443 **Additional Resources** • Guid. Read. Act., URB p. 89 • Read. Ess. & Note-Taking Guide, p. 146	**Teacher Edition** • Drawing Con., p. 442 **Additional Resources** • Econ. & Hist. Act., URB p. 5 • Crit. Think. Act., URB p. 68 • Section Quiz, p. 158	**Teacher Edition** • Verbal/Linguistic, p. 441 **Additional Resources** • Hist. Sig. Act., URB p. 72 • World Art & Music Act., URB p. 83	**Teacher Edition** • Expository Writing, p. 442 **Additional Resources** • Hist. Analysis Skills Act., URB p. 58 • Writer's Guidebook, p. 51	**Teacher Edition** • Using Geography Skills, p. 441 **Additional Resources** • Skills Reinforc. Act., URB p. 67

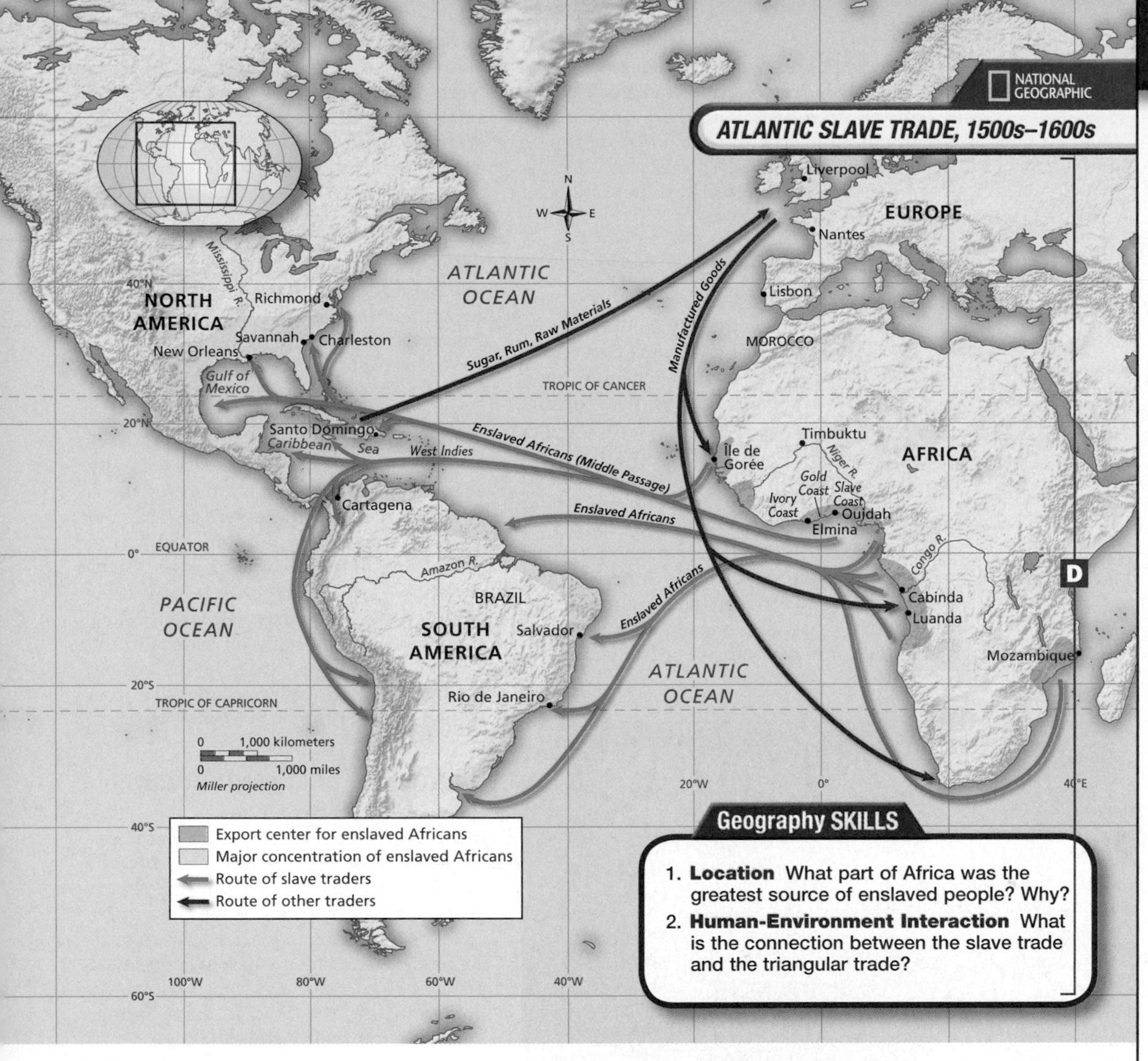

Geography SKILLS

1. **Location** What part of Africa was the greatest source of enslaved people? Why?
2. **Human-Environment Interaction** What is the connection between the slave trade and the triangular trade?

and canals. They placed high tariffs, or taxes, on foreign goods to keep them out of their own countries. Colonies were considered important both as sources of raw materials and markets for finished goods.

The Slave Trade

Traffic in enslaved people was not new. As in other areas of the world, slavery had been practiced in Africa since ancient times. In the 1400s, it continued at a fairly steady level.

The **primary** market for enslaved Africans was Southwest Asia where most served as domestic servants as in some European countries like Portugal. The demand for enslaved Africans changed dramatically with the discovery of the Americas in the 1490s and the planting of sugarcane there.

Cane sugar was introduced to Europe from Southwest Asia during the Crusades of the Middle Ages. **Plantations,** or large agricultural estates, were established in the 1500s along the coast of Brazil and on Caribbean islands to grow sugarcane.

S Skill Practice

Using Geography Skills Ask: What goods were shipped from the Americas to Europe? *(sugar, rum, and raw materials)* **BL**

For additional practice on this skill, see the **Skills Handbook**.

D Differentiated Instruction

Verbal/Linguistic Discuss how the slave trade and the practice of slavery changed as a result of European colonization in the Americas. **OL**

Geography SKILLS

Answers:

1. The west coast; it was accessible to Europe, North America, and South America.
2. The slave trade route from Africa to the Americas made up one side of the triangle.

Hands-On Chapter Project Step 2

Creating a Diorama About European Expansion

Step 2: Acquiring Materials In addition to deciding on events to include, the class will acquire materials and begin building the diorama.

Directions: Tell students to use the Big Idea as a guide for continuing to find events for the diorama. Tell them also to think about what materials they will need. Allow class time for students to work on the diorama together or independently. This might include determining scenes for the background, acquiring supplies, writing call outs, painting, and drawing.

Summarizing: During review, discuss events to include from Section 2 and listen to reports from individuals or groups relating to their designated duties. Use this time to answer questions, resolve problems, and monitor progress on the diorama. **OL**

W Writing Support

Expository Writing Have students research the Middle Passage, narrowing their search to a single detail, such as the conditions on the ships, disease, or death rates. Have them summarize their findings in a brief report. **AL**

C Critical Thinking

Drawing Conclusions Ask: How was the value of an enslaved person's life regarded by an owner? *(It was measured by the expense of owning one.)* **OL**

PEOPLE in HISTORY

Answer: Afonso wanted friendly relations, but they came into conflict over the slave trade.

✓Reading Check

Answer: The triangular trade connected Europe, Africa, and the Americas for the purpose of trading European manufactured goods, enslaved Africans, and American raw materials.

Growing cane sugar demands much labor. The small Native American population, much of which had died of diseases imported from Europe, could not provide the labor needed. Thus, enslaved Africans were shipped to Brazil and the Caribbean to work on plantations.

Growth of the Slave Trade

In 1518 a Spanish ship carried the first enslaved Africans directly from Africa to the Americas. During the next two centuries, the trade in enslaved people grew dramatically and became part of the **triangular trade** that connected Europe, Africa, and the American continents. European merchant ships carried European manufactured goods, such as guns and cloth, to Africa where they were traded for enslaved people. The enslaved Africans were then shipped to the Americas and sold. European merchants then bought tobacco, molasses, sugar, and raw cotton in the Americas and shipped them back to Europe.

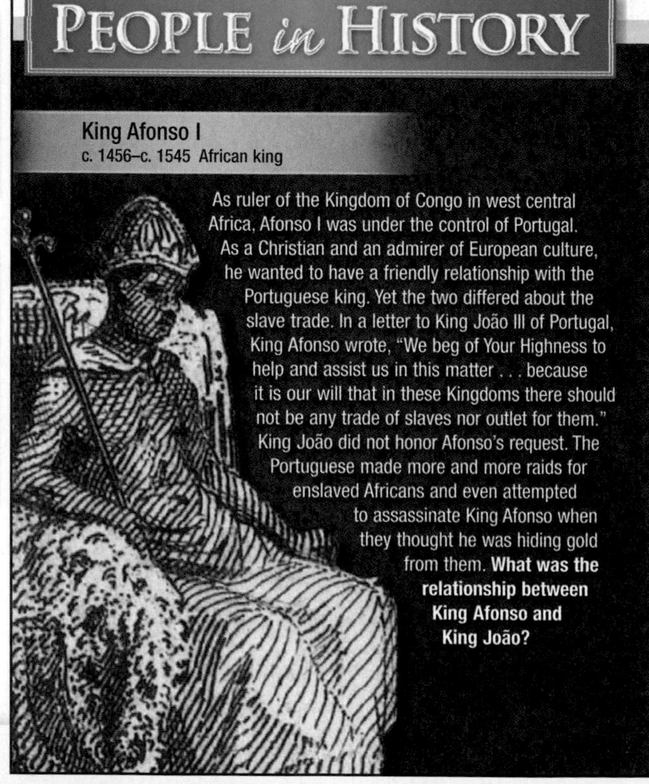

PEOPLE in HISTORY

King Afonso I
c. 1456–c. 1545 African king

As ruler of the Kingdom of Congo in west central Africa, Afonso I was under the control of Portugal. As a Christian and an admirer of European culture, he wanted to have a friendly relationship with the Portuguese king. Yet the two differed about the slave trade. In a letter to King João III of Portugal, King Afonso wrote, "We beg of Your Highness to help and assist us in this matter . . . because it is our will that in these Kingdoms there should not be any trade of slaves nor outlet for them." King João did not honor Afonso's request. The Portuguese made more and more raids for enslaved Africans and even attempted to assassinate King Afonso when they thought he was hiding gold from them. **What was the relationship between King Afonso and King João?**

An estimated 275,000 enslaved Africans were exported during the 1500s. In the 1600s, the total climbed to over 1 million and jumped to 6 million in the 1700s. Altogether, as many as 10 million enslaved Africans were brought to the Americas between the early 1500s and the late 1800s.

W One reason for these astonishing numbers was the high death rate. The journey of enslaved people from Africa to the Americas became known as the **Middle Passage,** the middle portion of the triangular trade route. Many enslaved Africans died on the journey. Those who arrived often died from diseases to which they had little or no immunity.

C Death rates were higher for newly arrived enslaved Africans than for those born and raised in the Americas. The new generation gradually developed at least a partial immunity to many diseases. Owners, however, rarely encouraged their enslaved people to have children. Many slave owners, especially on islands in the Caribbean, believed that buying a new enslaved person was less expensive than raising a child from birth to working age.

Sources of Enslaved Africans

Before Europeans arrived in the 1400s, most enslaved persons in Africa were prisoners of war. Europeans first bought enslaved people from African merchants at slave markets in return for gold, guns, or other European goods. Local slave traders first obtained their supplies of enslaved persons from nearby coastal regions. As demand grew, they had to move farther inland to find their victims.

Local rulers became concerned about the impact of the slave trade on their societies. In a letter to the king of Portugal in 1526, **King Afonso** of Congo (Bakongo) said, "so great is the corruption that our country is being completely depopulated."

Europeans and other Africans, however, generally ignored such protests. Local rulers who traded in enslaved people viewed the slave trade as a source of income. Many sent raiders into defenseless villages.

✓Reading Check **Describing** Describe the purpose and path of the triangular trade.

Differentiated Instruction

World Art and Music Activity, URB p. 83

Analyzing Information

Objective: Analyze information about African tribal masks.

Focus: Have students examine the art and read the passage.

Teach: Have volunteers suggest points to include in the answers to the questions. Then have students write their answers.

Assess: Review students' answers for completeness and supported inferences.

Close: Discuss the use of masks today. When are they used and why?

Differentiated Instruction Strategies

BL Reread portions of the text that list materials used to make masks. Have students draw their own masks.

AL Have students research African masks and bring in photographs to show the class. Compare and contrast the different styles.

ELL Draw a mask outline on the board and ask volunteers to add details as you read aloud the text.

Effects of the Slave Trade

MAIN IDEA The slave trade led to depopulation, increased warfare, and devastation for many African states.

HISTORY & YOU Have you seen the TV miniseries *Roots?* Read to learn about the devastating effect of the slave trade on Benin.

The effects of the slave trade varied from area to area. Of course, it always had tragic effects on the lives of individual victims and their families. The slave trade led to the depopulation of some areas, and it deprived many African communities of their youngest and strongest men and women.

The desire of slave traders to provide a constant supply of enslaved persons led to increased warfare in Africa. **R** Coastal or near-coastal African chiefs and their followers, armed with guns acquired from the trade in enslaved people, increased their raids and wars on neighboring peoples.

Only a few Europeans lamented what they were doing to traditional African societies. One Dutch slave trader remarked:

PRIMARY SOURCE

> "From us they have learned strife, quarrelling, drunkenness, trickery, theft, unbridled desire for what is not one's own, misdeeds unknown to them before, and the accursed lust for gold."
>
> —From *Africa in History: Themes and Outlines*, 1991

The slave trade had a devastating effect on some African states. The case of **Benin** (buh•NEEN) in West Africa is a good example. A brilliant and creative society in the 1500s, Benin was pulled into the slave trade.

As the population declined and warfare increased, the people of Benin lost faith in their gods, their art deteriorated, and human sacrifice became more common. When the British arrived there at the end of the 1800s, they found a corrupt and brutal place. It took years to discover the brilliance of the earlier culture destroyed by slavery.

The use of enslaved Africans remained largely acceptable to European society. Europeans continued to view Africans as inferior beings fit chiefly for slave labor. Not until the Society of Friends, known as the Quakers, began to condemn slavery in the 1770s did European feeling against slavery begin to build. Even then, it was not until the French Revolution in the 1790s that the French abolished slavery. The British did the same in 1807. Nevertheless, slavery continued in the newly formed United States until the Civil War of the 1860s.

✓Reading Check **Describing** What effect did the slave trade have on Benin?

SECTION 2 REVIEW

Vocabulary

1. **Explain** the significance of: colony, mercantilism, balance of trade, subsidies, transportation, primary, plantations, triangular trade, Middle Passage, King Afonso, Benin.

Main Ideas

2. **Explain** why a nation would want a favorable balance of trade.
3. **Illustrate** the triangular trade pattern using the graph below. Indicate what goods were shipped among the points of trade.

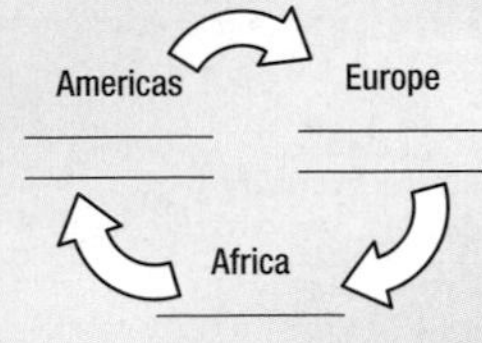

4. **Identify** the effects of the slave trade on the culture of Benin.

Critical Thinking

5. **The BIG Idea** **Evaluating** What impact did the slave trade have on the populations in Africa and the Americas?
6. **Analyzing** Why did some Africans engage in the slave trade? Did they have a choice?
7. **Analyzing Visuals** Examine the portrait of King Afonso on page 442. How can you tell he is a king?

Writing About History

8. **Persuasive Writing** Does the fact that Africans participated in enslaving other Africans make the European involvement in the slave trade any less wrong? Write an editorial supporting your position.

History ONLINE
For help with the concepts in this section of *Glencoe World History,* go to glencoe.com and click Study Central™.

R Reading Strategy

Identifying **Ask:** How did the slave trade affect Africans? *(suffering, disease, and death of victims; depopulation of communities; warfare among tribes; deterioration of culture)* **BL**

✓Reading Check

Answer: population decline; increased warfare; deterioration of culture

Assess

History ONLINE

Study Central provides summaries, interactive games, and online graphic organizers to help students review content.

Close

Determining Cause and Effect **Ask:** What led to a dramatic increase in the demand for enslaved Africans? *(development of plantation economies in the Americas)* **BL**

Answers

1. Definitions for the vocabulary words are found in the section and in the Glossary.
2. more revenues to apply to state improvements; improved economy
3. **Europe:** guns, cloth; **Africa:** enslaved people; **Americas:** tobacco, molasses, sugar, raw cotton
4. population declined, warfare increased, people lost faith in gods, art deteriorated, human sacrifice became more common
5. **Africa:** depopulation, older and weaker men and women remained; **Americas:** increased population of enslaved people in agricultural areas
6. Sale of enemies profitable; groups not engaged in slave trade likely to be victims; students should support their opinions.
7. He is wearing a robe and headdress.
8. Students will write an editorial. Encourage them to use other examples from history to support their position.

Focus

Bellringer
Daily Focus Transparency 13.3

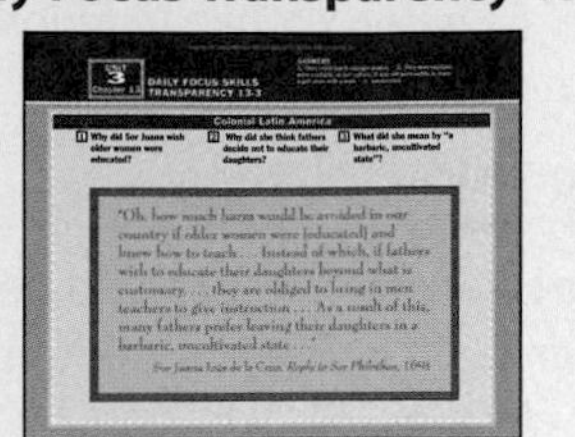

GUIDE TO READING

Answers to Graphic:

Colonial Latin America

Political: Europeans governed; viceroys monitored;

Social: stratified—*peninsulares* at top, then creoles, mixed (mestizos and mulattoes), imported slaves and conquered natives; Church was strong influence

Economic: mining/farming; *encomienda* and *mita* systems; gold, silver, tobacco, diamonds, animal hides, sugar sent to Europe; finished goods sent back

Section Spotlight Video

To generate student interest and provide a springboard for class discussion, access the Chapter 13, Section 3 video at glencoe.com or on the video DVD.

Resource Manager

R Reading Strategies	C Critical Thinking	D Differentiated Instruction	W Writing Support	S Skill Practice
Teacher Edition • Identifying, p. 445 **Additional Resources** • Academic Vocab. Act., URB p. 65 • Guid. Read. Act., URB p. 90 • Read. Ess. & Note-Taking Guide, p. 149	**Teacher Edition** • Synthesizing, p. 446 **Additional Resources** • Linking Past/Present Act., URB p. 78 • Section Quiz, p. 159 • Chapter Test, p. 161	**Teacher Edition** • ELL, p. 446 **Additional Resources** • Reteach. Act., URB p. 85 • Enrich. Act., URB p. 86	**Teacher Edition** • Expository Writing, p. 447 **Additional Resources** • Writer's Guidebook, p. 27	**Teacher Edition** • Using Geo. Skills, p. 445 **Additional Resources** • Time Line Act., URB p. 77

SECTION 3

Colonial Latin America

GUIDE TO READING

The BIG Idea

Competition Among Countries
Portugal and Spain reaped profits from the natural resources and products of their Latin American colonies.

Content Vocabulary
- *peninsulares (p. 444)*
- creoles *(p. 444)*
- mestizos *(p. 444)*
- mulattoes *(p. 444)*
- *mita (p. 446)*

Academic Vocabulary
- labor *(p. 444)*
- draft *(p. 446)*

People and Places
- Brazil *(p. 444)*
- Juana Inés de la Cruz *(p. 447)*

Reading Strategy
Organizing Information As you read, create a diagram like the one below to summarize the political, social, and economic characteristics of colonial Latin America.

Rich in natural resources, the Latin American colonies proved very profitable for Portugal and Spain. The interactions of native peoples, enslaved Africans, and Spanish colonists caused new social classes to form in Latin America. To convert Native Americans to Christianity, the Catholic Church set up missions throughout Latin America.

Colonial Empires in Latin America

MAIN IDEA The Portuguese and Spanish built colonial empires in Latin America and profited from the resources and trade of their colonies.

HISTORY & YOU Does your family own property outside of your home state or outside of the country? Read to learn why Spanish and Portuguese monarchs relied on officials to administer their colonies in Latin America.

In the 1500s, Portugal came to dominate **Brazil.** At the same time, Spain established an enormous colonial empire that included parts of North America, Central America, and most of South America. Within the lands of Central America and South America, a new civilization arose, which we call Latin America.

Social Classes

Colonial Latin America was divided by social classes that were based on privilege. At the top were ***peninsulares.*** These were Spanish and Portuguese officials who had been born in Europe and held all important government positions. Below the *peninsulares* were the **creoles.** Descendants of Europeans born in Latin America, creoles controlled land and business. They deeply resented the *peninsulares,* who regarded the creoles as second-class citizens. (See Chapter 21.)

Beneath the *peninsulares* and creoles were numerous multiracial groups. The Spanish and Portuguese who moved into Latin America lived with both Native Americans and African people brought in for **labor.** Spanish rulers permitted intermarriage between Europeans and Native Americans. Their offspring became known as the **mestizos.** In addition, over a period of three centuries, possibly as many as 8 million enslaved Africans were brought to Spanish and Portuguese America to work on the plantations. **Mulattoes**—the offspring of Africans and Europeans—became another social group. Other groups emerged as a result of unions between mestizos and mulattoes and between Native Americans and Africans. The coexistence of these various groups produced a unique multiracial society in Latin America.

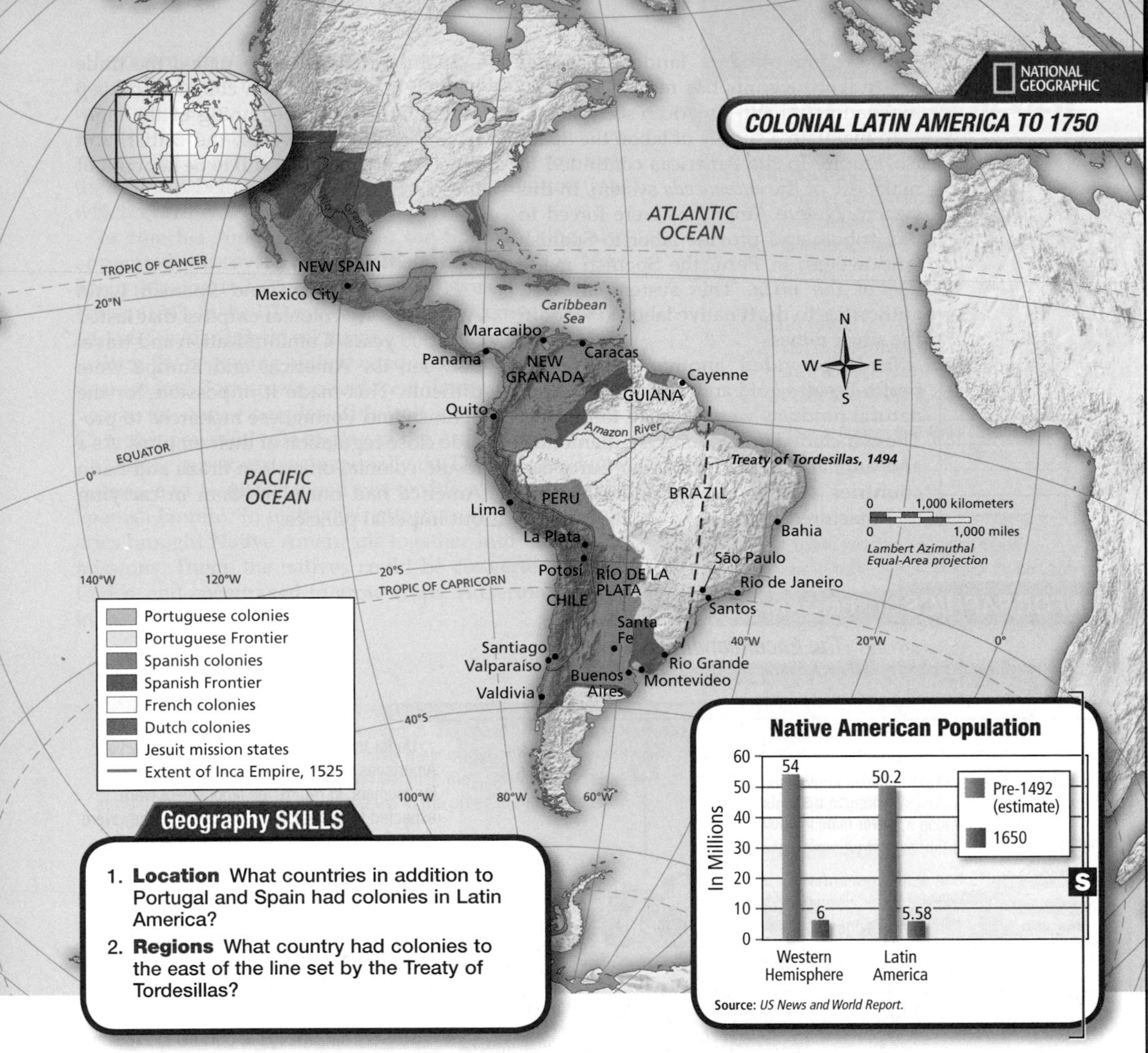

Geography SKILLS

1. **Location** What countries in addition to Portugal and Spain had colonies in Latin America?
2. **Regions** What country had colonies to the east of the line set by the Treaty of Tordesillas?

All of these multiethnic groups were considered socially inferior by the *peninsulares* and creoles. However, over a period of time, mestizos grew in importance due to their increasing numbers. Some mestizos became artisans and small merchants in cities, while others became small-scale farmers or ranchers. Mestizos eventually came to be seen as socially superior to other multiracial groups. The groups at the very bottom of the social scale were imported enslaved persons and conquered Native Americans.

Economic Foundations

Both the Portuguese and the Spanish sought ways to profit from their colonies in Latin America. One source of wealth came from abundant supplies of gold and silver that were sent to Europe. Farming, however, became a more long-lasting and rewarding source of prosperity for Latin America. Spanish and Portuguese landowners created immense estates. Native Americans worked on the estates or worked as poor farmers on marginal lands.

Teach

R Reading Strategy

Identifying Ask: How did the social status of mestizos change over time? *(It advanced as their population grew.)* **BL**

S Skill Practice

Using Geography Skills

Have students compare this map to the modern-day political map on page A8. **Ask:** What effects would you expect to see in modern-day South American countries based on their colonial histories? *(Answers will vary but students might say language, religion, and legal system.)* **OL**

For additional practice on this skill, see the **Skills Handbook**.

Geography SKILLS

Answers:
1. France, the Netherlands
2. Portugal

Hands-On Chapter Project

Step 3

Creating a Diorama About European Expansion

Step 3: Assembling the Diorama In addition to finding events to include, students will finish building the diorama.

Directions: Tell students to use the Big Idea as a guide for continuing to find events for the diorama. In addition, allow class time for students to continue building the diorama, including incorporating events from Section 3.

Summarizing: During review, discuss the events from Section 3 that students have chosen to include in the diorama. Assist in coordinating individual and group activities as students finish the diorama. **OL**

(Chapter Project is completed on the Visual Summary page.)

Identifying Central Issues
Discuss the bulleted information and the images presented in the Visual Summary. Remind students that this information includes important ideas from the entire chapter. Have students work in pairs to draw a visual of the triangular trade between Europe, Africa, and the Americas. **Ask:** **Why is it important to understand the triangular trade?** Discuss how the effect of the triangular trade was widespread both geographically and socially. **OL**

Special Education Read the Visual Summary aloud while students follow along in their books. Paraphrase statements and explain ideas as necessary. Help students write two original statements summarizing each part of the Visual Summary. You may want to create sentence starters for each student to complete. **BL**

CHAPTER 13 Visual Summary

You can study anywhere, anytime by downloading quizzes and flash cards to your PDA from glencoe.com.

CHRISTOPHER COLUMBUS ARRIVES IN THE AMERICAS

The Spanish brought Christianity with them.

EARLY EXPLORATION of West Africa, India, and the Americas

- Motivated by religious zeal, gold, and glory, Europeans began to explore distant lands.
- The Portuguese sailed east around Africa to India.
- Spanish ships sailed west to the Americas.
- Spanish conquistadors seized lands ruled by the Aztec and Inca.
- Diseases introduced by Spanish explorers killed much of the Native American population.
- By the late 1600s, the Dutch, French, and English entered the rivalry for new lands and trade.

ENSLAVED AFRICANS WORKING ON A SUGARCANE PLANTATION

Europeans established sugar plantations in the Americas, creating a demand for slave laborers.

AFRICAN SLAVE TRADE of Europe, Asia, and the Americas

- Before the new exploration, the primary market for enslaved Africans had been Southwest Asia.
- The demand for plantation laborers in the Americas greatly increased slave trade.
- Enslaved Africans were part of the triangular trade between Europe, Africa and Asia, and the Americas.
- In Africa, the slave trade led to increased warfare, depopulation, and the deterioration of society.

SILVER MINES IN BRAZIL

Silver was a natural resource that attracted European colonizers.

Native Americans were forced to work in silver mines.

COLONIAL EMPIRES of Latin America

- The Portuguese and Spanish profited from their colonial empires in Latin America.
- *Peninsulares* were the top social class, followed by creoles, mestizos and mulattoes, and finally enslaved Africans and Native Americans.
- Catholic missionaries spread across the Americas to try to Christianize Native Americans.

Hands-On Chapter Project
Step 4: Wrap Up

Creating a Diorama About European Expansion

Step 4: Presenting the Diorama Students will synthesize what they learned in Steps 1–3.

Directions: Write the Big Ideas from each section on the board. Guide the class discussion to connect the Big Ideas to specific examples in the chapter. Have students connect these examples to the events depicted in the diorama. Conclude the discussion by directing attention to the Visual Summary on this page. Have students discuss the images and the information in the bulleted lists and compare them to the events they included in the diorama. **Ask:** **Which do you think better illustrates the effects of European expansion?** *(Have students support their opinions with examples.)* **OL**

STANDARDIZED TEST PRACTICE

TEST-TAKING TIP

If a test question involves reading a map, make sure you read the title of the map and look at the map carefully for information before you try to answer the question.

Reviewing Vocabulary

Directions: Choose the word or words that best complete the sentence.

1. ________ were the offspring of Africans and Europeans.

A Creoles
B *Peninsulares*
C Mestizos
D Mulattoes

2. Spanish conquerors of the Americas were known as ________.

A viceroys
B conquistadors
C *peninsulares*
D governor-generals

3. The ________ is a trading route that connected Europe, Africa, and the Americas.

A triangular trade
B Bermuda Triangle
C Middle Passage
D circular trade

4. The ________ system allowed authorities to draft natives to work in silver mines.

A *encomienda*
B feudal
C *mita*
D tithe

Reviewing Main Ideas

Directions: Choose the best answers to the following questions.

Section 1 *(pp. 430–437)*

5. What were the chief motives for European expansion?

A Adventure, travel, and war
B Politics, taxes, and war
C God, glory, and gold
D Oil, gold, and coal

6. Which country took the lead in European exploration?

A Portugal
B The Netherlands
C England
D France

7. Who was the first explorer to circumnavigate the world?

A Bartholomeu Dias
B Christopher Columbus
C Ferdinand Magellan
D Vasco da Gama

8. Which ruler granted *encomienda* to the Spanish settlers in the Americas?

A Louis XII
B Isabella
C Ferdinand
D Henry VI

Need Extra Help?

If You Missed Questions . . .	1	2	3	4	5	6	7	8
Go to Page . . .	444	434	442	446	431	432	433	435

GO ON

Answers and Analyses

Reviewing Vocabulary

1. D Mulattoes are the offspring of Africans and Europeans. Choices A and B can be eliminated easily because both terms are related to only European ancestry. Mestizos were offspring of Native Americans and Europeans.

2. B The reader can hear that the word *conquistadors* is related to the word *conquerors*. Viceroys were Portuguese and Spanish government officials who monitored local officials. *Peninsulares* were European-born residents of the colonies. *Governor-general* was another name for a Portuguese viceroy.

3. A The triangular trade is the correct answer. The item discusses a triangle between Europe, Africa, and the Americas. Neither C nor D describe a triangle route, while the Bermuda Triangle refers to one area.

4. C Choice D refers to money paid voluntarily or as a tax. Point out that *encomienda* was related to farming and that feudal describes some of the characteristics of *encomienda*.

Reviewing Main Ideas

5. C Point out that the other choices contain some of the motives that Europeans had for expansion, but only C describes the chief motives.

6. A Students need to rely on their knowledge of history to answer this question about which country took the initial lead. The other choices offer little help in determining the correct answer, since all of them engaged in exploration.

7. C The other explorers made significant voyages but did not circumnavigate the world. Dias rounded the Cape of Good Hope; Columbus reached the Americas; de Gama reached India.

8. B Choices A and D can be eliminated easily because they discuss people from the wrong era. Students may be tempted to choose C because Ferdinand V and Isabella, as husband and wife, ruled Spain together.

CHAPTER 14 Planning Guide

Key to Ability Levels

- **BL** Below Level
- **OL** On Level
- **AL** Above Level
- **ELL** English Language Learners

Key to Teaching Resources

- Print Material
- CD-ROM
- DVD
- Transparency

Levels				Resources	Chapter Opener	Section 1	Section 2	Section 3	Section 4	Chapter Assess
BL	OL	AL	ELL							
				FOCUS						
BL	OL	AL	ELL	**Daily Focus Skills Transparencies**		14-1	14-2	14-3	14-4	
				TEACH						
BL	OL	AL	ELL	**Charting and Graphing Activity, URB**		✓	✓			
		AL		**World Literature Reading, URB**					✓	
BL	OL		ELL	**Reading Skills Activity, URB**				p. 93		
	OL	AL		**Historical Analysis Skills Activity, URB**			p. 94			
BL	OL	AL	ELL	**Differentiated Instruction Activity, URB**				p. 95		
	OL		ELL	**English Learner Activity, URB**		p. 97				
BL	OL	AL	ELL	**Content Vocabulary Activity, URB***					p. 99	
BL	OL	AL	ELL	**Academic Vocabulary Activity, URB**		p. 101				
BL	OL	AL	ELL	**Skills Reinforcement Activity, URB**		p. 103				
	OL	AL		**Critical Thinking Skills Activity, URB**		p. 104				
	OL	AL		**History and Geography Activity, URB**			p. 105			
	OL	AL	ELL	**Mapping History Activity, URB**				p. 107		
BL	OL	AL		**Historical Significance Activity, URB**					p. 108	
BL	OL	AL	ELL	**Cooperative Learning Activity, URB**				p. 109		
	OL	AL	ELL	**History Simulation Activity, URB**					p. 111	
BL	OL	AL	ELL	**Time Line Activity, URB**				p. 113		
	OL	AL		**Linking Past and Present Activity, URB**				p. 114		
BL	OL	AL		**People in World History Activity, URB**			p. 115	p. 116		
BL	OL	AL	ELL	**Primary Source Reading, URB**				p. 117		
	OL	AL		**Enrichment Activity, URB**		p. 122				
BL	OL	AL	ELL	**World Art and Music Activity, URB**					p. 119	
BL	OL		ELL	**Guided Reading Activities, URB***		p. 124	p. 125	p. 126	p. 127	
BL	OL		ELL	**Reading Essentials and Note-Taking Guide***		p. 151	p. 154	p. 157	p. 160	
BL	OL	AL	ELL	**Differentiated Instruction for the World History Classroom**	✓	✓	✓	✓	✓	✓

Note: Please refer to the *Unit Resource Book: The Early Modern World* for this chapter's URB materials.

* Also available in Spanish

- Interactive Lesson Planner
- Interactive Teacher Edition
- Fully editable blackline masters
- Section Spotlight Videos Launch
- Differentiated Lesson Plans
- Printable reports of daily assignments
- Standards Tracking System

Levels				Resources	Chapter Opener	Section 1	Section 2	Section 3	Section 4	Chapter Assess
BL	OL	AL	ELL							
				TEACH *(continued)*						
BL	OL	AL	ELL	StudentWorks™ Plus DVD	✓	✓	✓	✓	✓	✓
BL	OL	AL	ELL	Vocabulary PuzzleMaker CD-ROM	✓	✓	✓	✓	✓	✓
Teacher Resources				Building Academic Vocabulary	✓	✓	✓	✓	✓	✓
				Reading Strategies and Activities for the Social Studies Classroom		p. 86	p. 80		pp. 59, 89	
				Writer's Guidebook		p. 23	p. 5	p. 47	p. 43	
				Strategies for Success	✓	✓	✓	✓	✓	✓
				Outline Map Resource Book	✓	✓	✓	✓	✓	✓
				Presentation Plus! with MindJogger DVD	✓	✓	✓	✓	✓	✓
				ASSESS						
BL	OL	AL	ELL	Section Quizzes and Chapter Tests*		p. 169	p. 170	p. 171	p. 172	p. 173
BL	OL	AL	ELL	Authentic Assessment With Rubrics	✓	✓	✓	✓	✓	✓
BL	OL	AL	ELL	Standardized Test Practice Workbook	✓	✓	✓	✓	✓	✓
BL	OL	AL	ELL	*ExamView® Assessment Suite* CD-ROM		14-1	14-2	14-3	14-4	Ch. 14
BL	OL	AL	ELL	Interactive Tutor Self-Assessment CD-ROM		14-1	14-2	14-3	14-4	
				CLOSE						
BL			ELL	Reteaching Activity, URB				p. 121		
BL	OL		ELL	Reading and Study Skills Foldables™	✓	✓	✓	✓	✓	✓

Using the Glencoe Web Site

Vocabulary eFlashcards

Technology Product

The Vocabulary eFlashcards on the Glencoe Web site enable students to review vocabulary and their definitions for each chapter. The Vocabulary eFlashcards provide separate card sets for content vocabulary and academic vocabulary, and a separate set for people, places, and events, along with textbook page references. The final set combines all words and terms. Students can print sets of cards to review vocabulary away from the computer.

Objectives

The Vocabulary eFlashcards help students

- practice and reinforce their comprehension of vocabulary and key terms in each chapter;
- identify areas for additional study and reinforcement.

Steps

Provide students with the following steps to work with the Vocabulary eFlashcards:

- Locate the Web page for the textbook being studied on the Glencoe Web site glencoe.com.
- Click on **Student Center** under the textbook title.
- In the Student Center, select a unit from the Unit Resources menu and a chapter from the Chapter Activities menu using the drop-down arrows.
- Click on the **Vocabulary eFlashcards** link.
- Select and review one of the vocabulary lists for the chapter: Academic; Content; People, Places, Events; or Combined. A new window will open.
- Review vocabulary in one of the three viewing modes: View Terms and Definitions, View Terms, and View Definitions. Click on **Flip Card** to read the relevant term or definition.

History ONLINE

	Student	Teacher	Parent
Beyond the Textbook	●	●	●
Chapter Overviews	●	●	●
Time Current Events	●		●
ePuzzles and Games	●		●
Concepts in Motion	●		●
Literature Connections		●	
Multi-Language Glossaries	●		●
Online Student Edition	●	●	●
Self-Check Quizzes	●		●
Student Web Activities	●		●
Study Central ™	●		●
Teaching Today		●	
Vocabulary eFlashcards	●		●
Web Activity Lesson Plans		●	

- **Timed Readings Plus in Social Studies** helps students increase their reading rate and fluency while maintaining comprehension. The 400-word passages are similar to those found on state and national assessments.
- **Reading in the Content Area: Social Studies** concentrates on six essential reading skills that help students better comprehend what they read. The book includes 75 high-interest nonfiction passages written at increasing levels of difficulty.
- **Reading Social Studies** includes strategic reading instruction and vocabulary support in Social Studies content for both ELLs and native speakers of English.

www.jamestowneducation.com

Index to National Geographic Magazine:

The following articles relate to this chapter:

- "Duchy of Cornwall," by Sandy Mitchell, May 2006
- "The New Europe," by T. R. Reid, January 2002
- "Russia Rising," by Fen Montaigne, November 2001

National Geographic Society Products To order the following, call National Geographic at 1-800-368-2728:

- *National Geographic Atlas of the World* (Book).

Access National Geographic's new, dynamic MapMachine Web site and other geography resources at:
www.nationalgeographic.com
www.nationalgeographic.com/maps

Biography

The following videotape programs are available from Glencoe as supplements to Chapter 14:

- **Elizabeth 1: The Virgin Queen** (ISBN 0-76-700209-1)
- **Peter the Great: The Tyrant Reformer** (ISBN 0-76-703063-X)

To order, call Glencoe at 1-800-334-7344. To find classroom resources to accompany many of these videos, check the following home pages:

A&E Television: www.aetv.com

The History Channel: www.historychannel.com

Reading List Generator CD-ROM

Use this database to search more than 30,000 titles to create a customized reading list for your students.

- Reading lists can be organized by students' reading level, author, genre, theme, or area of interest.
- The database provides Degrees of Reading Power™ (DRP) and Lexile™ readability scores for all selections.
- A brief summary of each selection is included.

Leveled reading suggestions for this chapter:

For students at a Grade 8 reading level:
- ***Behind the Mask: The Life of Queen Elizabeth I,*** by Jane Resh Thomas

For students at a Grade 9 reading level:
- ***John Winthrop, Oliver Cromwell, and the Land of Promise,*** by Marc Aronson

For students at a Grade 10 reading level:
- ***The Palace of Versailles,*** by James Porter

For students at a Grade 11 reading level:
- ***Shakespeare's England,*** from *Horizon Magazine*

For students at a Grade 12 reading level:
- ***The Adventures of Don Quixote de la Manchu,*** by Miguel de Cervantes

INTRODUCING
CHAPTER 14

Focus

MAKING CONNECTIONS
How does architecture reflect history?

Activate students' prior knowledge by having them think about how architecture reflects history in their area. Have students volunteer information about new and old buildings in their area. Ask them to think about how the buildings reflect the needs of the time when they were built. For example, a building constructed in the 1970s might have smaller windows in response to the energy crisis that occurred. Wrap up the discussion by having students list historical events that might cause a change in architecture, e.g., an economic depression.

Teach

The Big Ideas

As students study the chapter, remind them to consider the section-based Big Ideas included in each section's Guide to Reading. The **Essential Questions** in the activities below tie in to the Big Ideas and help students think about and understand important chapter concepts. In addition, the Hands-On Chapter Projects with their culminating activities relate the content from each section to the Big Ideas. These activities build on each other as students progress through the chapter. Section activities culminate in the wrap-up activity on the Visual Summary page.

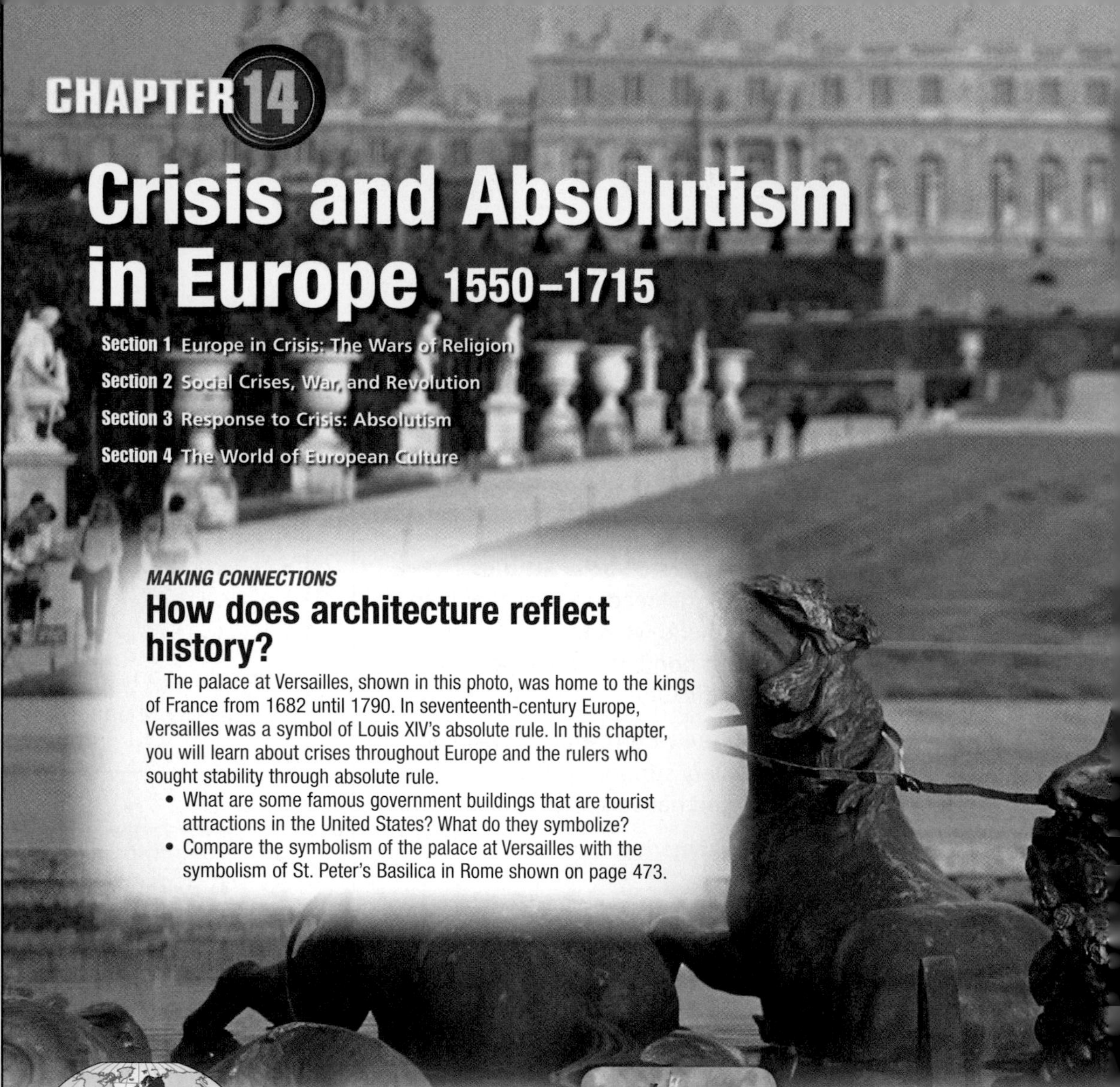

CHAPTER 14

Crisis and Absolutism in Europe 1550–1715

MAKING CONNECTIONS
How does architecture reflect history?

The palace at Versailles, shown in this photo, was home to the kings of France from 1682 until 1790. In seventeenth-century Europe, Versailles was a symbol of Louis XIV's absolute rule. In this chapter, you will learn about crises throughout Europe and the rulers who sought stability through absolute rule.

- What are some famous government buildings that are tourist attractions in the United States? What do they symbolize?
- Compare the symbolism of the palace at Versailles with the symbolism of St. Peter's Basilica in Rome shown on page 473.

EUROPE ▶
- **1562** French Wars of Religion begin
- **1588** England defeats the Spanish Armada
- **1618** Start of the Thirty Years' War 

1550 — 1600

THE WORLD ▶
- **1568** Oda Nobunaga seizes Kyōto, Japan 
- **1605** Akbar expands Mogul rule in India
- **1630** English found Massachusetts Bay Colony

452

Europe in Crisis: The Wars of Religion
Essential Question: What might have motivated the religious and political conflicts between Protestants and Catholics? *(Motivations might include the desire for land, power, civil liberties.)* Point out that in Section 1 students will learn how European nations gained and lost power as a result of religious and political conflicts. OL

Social Crises, War, and Revolution
Essential Question: What effect might social, economic, and religious conflicts have on European nations? *(They might place hardships on the people, cause bitterness, and lead to war.)* Point out that in Section 2 students will learn how the struggle for power led to uprisings throughout Europe. OL

More About the Photo

Visual Literacy Untold sums of money and thousands of workers were required to build the palace. When it was completed, the enormous complex housed thousands of people. The king had little privacy. Nobles swarmed about and competed to assist the king in various daily rituals. It was considered an honor, for example, for a noble to be chosen to hand the king his shirt while dressing.

Daily life included many forms of entertainment. Hunting trips, walks through the gardens, boating trips, plays, ballets, concerts, and gambling were all sources of pleasure. See page 465 of this Teacher's Edition for suggestions on how to teach this activity.

Dinah Zike's Foldables

Dinah Zike's Foldables are three-dimensional, interactive graphic organizers that help students practice basic writing skills, review vocabulary terms, and identify main ideas. Instructions for creating and using Foldables can be found in the Appendix at the end of this book and in the *Dinah Zike's Reading and Study Skills Foldables* booklet. **OL**

1661 Louis XIV begins absolute rule of France

1689 England's House of Parliament enacts the Bill of Rights

1689 Peter the Great becomes czar of Russia

1690 John Locke writes *Two Treatises of Government*

1715

FOLDABLES Study Organizer

Organizing Make a Three-Pocket Book to organize information about Europe in the sixteenth, seventeenth, and early eighteenth centuries. Store your notes in the appropriate pocket.

History ONLINE
Chapter Overview—Visit glencoe.com to preview Chapter 14.

History ONLINE
Introduce students to chapter content and key terms by having them access the Chapter 14 Overview at glencoe.com.

Response to Crisis: Absolutism

Essential Question: What effect would the exercise of absolute power have on a nation? *(A ruler with unlimited power could impose his or her own desires and goals for good or ill.)* Point out that in Section 3 students will learn about how absolute rulers in Europe built powerful nations and empires. **OL**

The World of European Culture

Essential Question: How might art, literature, and philosophy be influenced by the turbulence of the period? *(Students might suggest that these disciplines would reflect aspects of the religious and political issues of the time.)* Point out that in Section 4 students will learn how artists expressed identification with, or reaction to, the issues of the day. **OL**

Focus

Bellringer

Daily Focus Transparency 14.1

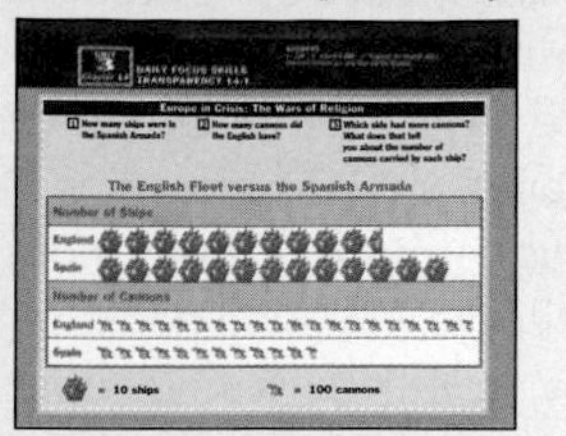

GUIDE TO READING

Answers to Graphic:

	Spain	England	France
Government	Monarchy	Monarchy	Monarchy
Religion	Catholic	Protestant	Catholic
Conflicts	Battle of Lepanto; revolt in Netherlands; attack on England	Defeated Spanish Armada	French Wars of Religion

Section Spotlight Video

To generate student interest and provide a springboard for class discussion, access the Chapter 14, Section 1 video at glencoe.com or on the video DVD.

Resource Manager

SECTION 1

Europe in Crisis: The Wars of Religion

GUIDE TO READING

The BIG Idea

Competition Among Countries

Religious and political conflicts erupted between Protestants and Catholics in many European nations.

Content Vocabulary

- militant *(p. 454)*
- armada *(p. 456)*

Academic Vocabulary

- conflict *(p. 454)*
- policy *(p. 455)*

People, Places, and Events

- King Philip II *(p. 454)*
- Netherlands *(p. 454)*
- William the Silent *(p. 455)*
- Elizabeth Tudor *(p. 455)*
- Scotland *(p. 456)*
- Ireland *(p. 456)*
- Huguenots *(p. 457)*
- Henry of Navarre *(p. 457)*
- Edict of Nantes *(p. 457)*

Reading Strategy

Comparing and Contrasting

As you read, complete a chart like the one below comparing the characteristics of Spain, England, and France.

	Spain	England	France
Government			
Religion			
Conflicts			

During the sixteenth and seventeenth centuries, conflicts between Protestants and Catholics in many European nations resulted in wars for religious and political control.

Spain's Conflicts

MAIN IDEA King Philip II championed Catholic causes throughout his lands, while England became the leader of Protestant nations of Europe.

HISTORY & YOU Suppose you won an arm-wrestling contest against someone who seemed much bigger and stronger? Learn how England defeated Spain at sea.

By 1560, Calvinism and Catholicism had become highly **militant** (combative) religions. They were aggressive in winning converts and in eliminating each other's authority. Their struggle was the chief cause of the religious wars that plagued Europe in the sixteenth century. However, economic, social, and political forces also played an important role in these **conflicts**.

Spain's Militant Catholicism

The greatest supporter of militant Catholicism in the second half of the sixteenth century was **King Philip II** of Spain, the son and heir of Charles V. King Philip II, whose reign extended from 1556 to 1598, ushered in an age of Spanish greatness.

Philip's first major goal was to consolidate the lands inherited from his father. These included Spain, the **Netherlands,** and possessions in Italy and the Americas. To strengthen his control, Philip insisted on strict conformity to Catholicism and strong monarchical authority.

During the late Middle Ages, Catholic kingdoms in Spain had reconquered Muslim areas there and expelled the Spanish Jews. Driven by this heritage, Spain saw itself as a nation of people chosen by God to save Catholic Christianity from Protestant heretics.

The "Most Catholic King," Philip II championed Catholic causes. His actions led to spectacular victories and defeats. Spain's leadership in a Holy League against the Turks, for example, resulted in a stunning victory over the Turkish fleet in the Battle of Lepanto in 1571. Philip was not so fortunate in his other conflicts.

Resistance from the Netherlands

One of the richest parts of Philip's empire, the Spanish Netherlands, consisted of 17 provinces (modern Netherlands and Belgium). Philip's attempts to strengthen his control in this region caused resentment and opposition from the nobles of the

R Reading Strategies	C Critical Thinking	D Differentiated Instruction	W Writing Support	S Skill Practice
Teacher Edition • Identifying, p. 455 **Additional Resources** • Academic Vocab. Act., URB p. 101 • Guid. Read. Act., URB p. 124 • Read. Ess. & Note-Taking Guide, p. 151	**Teacher Edition** • Drawing Con., p. 456 **Additional Resources** • Crit. Think Act., URB p. 104 • Section Quiz, p. 169	**Teacher Edition** • Verbal/Linguistic, p. 457 **Additional Resources** • English Learner Act., URB p. 97 • Enrich. Act., URB p. 122	**Teacher Edition** • Expository Writing, p. 455 **Additional Resources** • Writer's Guidebook, p. 23	**Teacher Edition** • Using Geography Skills, p. 456 **Additional Resources** • Chart. Graph. Act., URB p. 3 • Skills Reinforc. Act., URB p. 103 • Read. Strat. for SS, p. 86

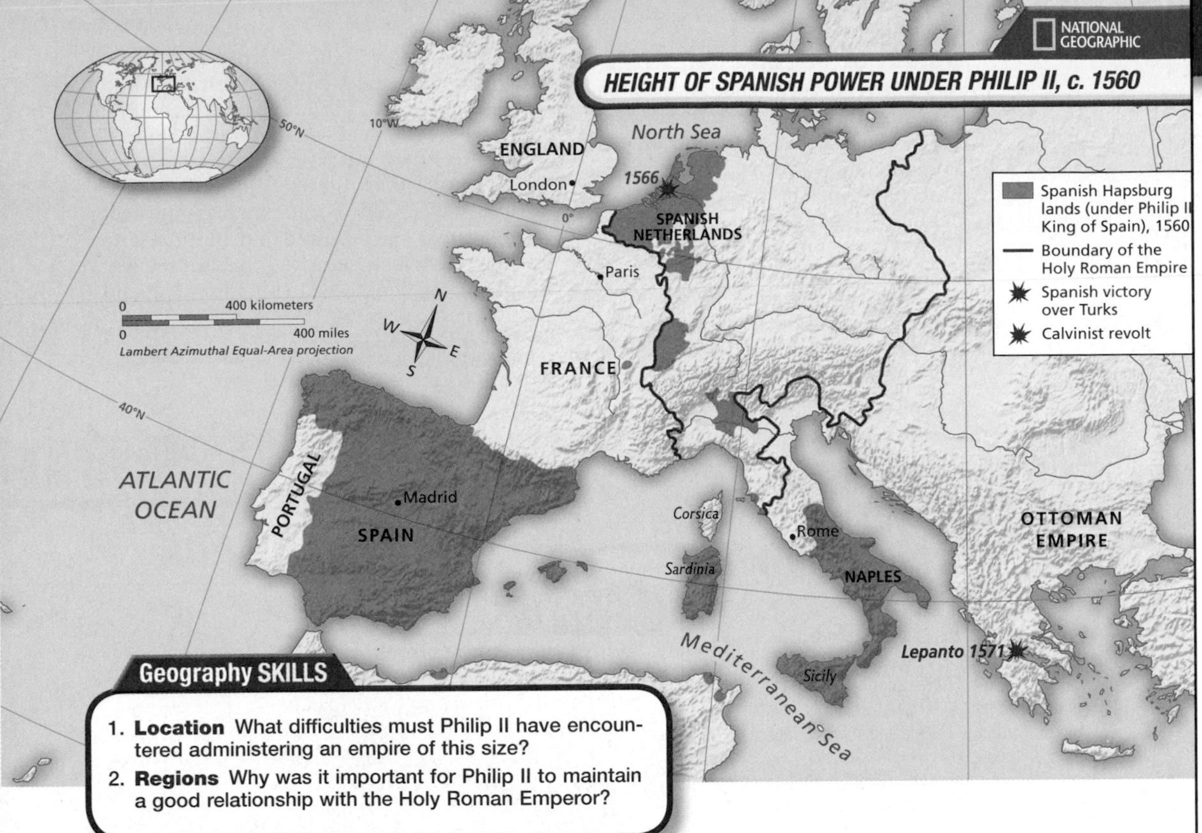

Geography SKILLS

1. **Location** What difficulties must Philip II have encountered administering an empire of this size?
2. **Regions** Why was it important for Philip II to maintain a good relationship with the Holy Roman Emperor?

Netherlands. Philip also tried to crush Calvinism in the Netherlands. Violence erupted in 1566. Philip sent ten thousand troops to crush the rebellion. **R**

Philip faced growing resistance from the Dutch in the northern provinces led by **William the Silent,** the prince of Orange. The struggle dragged on until 1609 when a 12-year truce finally ended the war. The northern provinces began to call themselves the United Provinces of the Netherlands and became the core of the modern Dutch state. In fact, the seventeenth century has often been called the golden age of the Dutch Republic because the United Provinces held center stage as one of Europe's great powers.

Protestantism in England

Elizabeth Tudor ascended the English throne in 1558. During her reign, the small island kingdom became the leader of the Protestant nations of Europe and laid the foundations for a world empire.

Intelligent, careful, and self-confident, Elizabeth moved quickly to solve the difficult religious problem she inherited from her Catholic half-sister, Queen Mary Tudor. Elizabeth repealed the laws favoring Catholics. A new Act of Supremacy named Elizabeth as "the only supreme governor" of both church and state. The Church of England under Queen Elizabeth followed a moderate Protestantism that kept most people satisfied.

Elizabeth was also moderate in her foreign **policy.** She tried to keep Spain and France from becoming too powerful by balancing power. If one nation seemed to be gaining in power, England would support the weaker nation. The queen feared that war would be disastrous for England and for her own rule; however, she could not escape a conflict with Spain. **W**

Teach

R Reading Strategy

Identifying Have students identify the issues that led the Dutch to resist the demands of King Philip II. *(Nobles resented their loss of privileges. Philip tried to crush Calvinism.)* **OL**

W Writing Support

Expository Writing Ask: How does Elizabeth's moderate foreign policy compare to the foreign policy of Spain during the same period? Have students work in pairs and use the text as a starting point for additional research. Each pair should write a five paragraph expository piece explaining the foreign policies of England and Spain during the period. **AL**

Geography SKILLS

Answers:
1. communication, travel, enforcing laws, collecting taxes
2. because the Spanish Netherlands was part of the Holy Roman Empire

Differentiated Instruction

Making Generalizations

Objective: Evaluate information on Elizabeth I and make generalizations.

Focus: Direct students to read the text on page 455 and the quotation on this worksheet.

Teach: Have students answer questions 1–4.

Assess: Tell students to trade worksheets with a partner and compare answers. Discuss any differences.

Close: Hold a debate on question 4 with the class to arrive at a consensus.

Differentiated Instruction Strategies

BL Have students work in small groups to answer the worksheet questions.

AL Ask students to research Elizabeth's attitude to her Catholic subjects and make a generalization based on sources.

ELL Guide students in using a dictionary to find meanings for unfamiliar words in the quotation on the worksheet.

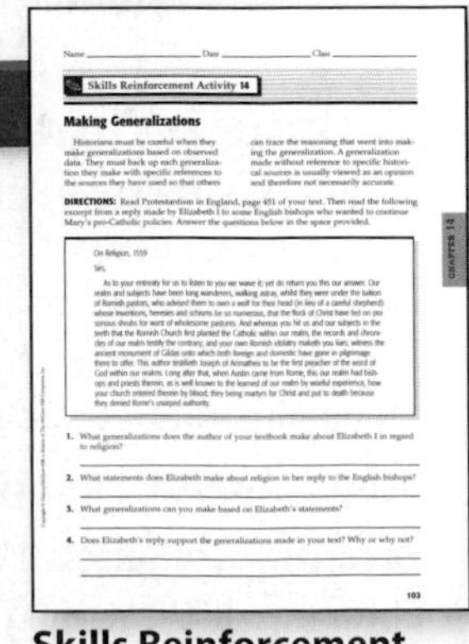

Skills Reinforcement Activity, URB p. 103

C Critical Thinking

Drawing Conclusions Tell students to use information from the text and the map to answer the following question. **Ask:** Why do you think the armada chose to sail home northward around Scotland? *(They wanted to avoid further conflict with the English fleet in the Channel.)* OL

S Skill Practice

Using Geography Skills Draw attention to the icons in the legend, and have students locate the corresponding icons on the map. **Ask:** At what points along the English Channel did battles take place? *(near Plymouth, Portsmouth, the Isle of Wight, Calais, and Gravelines)* OL

✓Reading Check

Answer: He wanted to overthrow Protestantism.

Geography SKILLS

Answers:

1. about 2,000 miles
2. It signaled a shift in power from Spain to England and France.

Defeat of the Spanish Armada

In 1588, Philip II made preparations to send an **armada**—a fleet of warships—to invade England. A successful invasion of England would mean the overthrow of Protestantism. The fleet that set sail had neither the ships nor the manpower that Philip had planned to send.

C The hoped-for victory never came. The armada was battered by the faster English ships and sailed back to Spain by a northern route around **Scotland** and **Ireland** where it was pounded by storms.

By the end of Philip's reign in 1598, Spain was not the great power that it appeared to be. Spain was the most populous empire in the world, but it was bankrupt. Philip II had spent too much on war. His successor spent too much on his court. The armed forces were out of date, and the government was inefficient. Spain continued to play the role of a great power, but the real power in Europe had shifted to England and France.

✓Reading Check **Explaining** What did Philip II hope to accomplish by invading England?

TURNING POINT

DEFEAT OF THE SPANISH ARMADA

In the mid-1500s, the English supported the Protestant side in religious wars between Protestants and Catholics within France and the Netherlands. Resenting this, Philip II of Spain decided to invade England to overthrow Protestantism and establish Catholic rule there.

The English fleet had clear superiority in gunnery and naval tactics. It dealt the Spanish Armada a terrible blow in the English Channel. The Spanish retreated on a northward route around Scotland without charts or a pilot. There the fleet was battered by storms. Half of the Spanish fleet and three-quarters of the men were lost. After defeating the Spanish Armada, England remained Protestant and began to create a world empire.

The defeat of the Spanish Armada:

- Guaranteed that England would remain a Protestant country
- Signaled a gradual shift in power from Spain to England and France

S

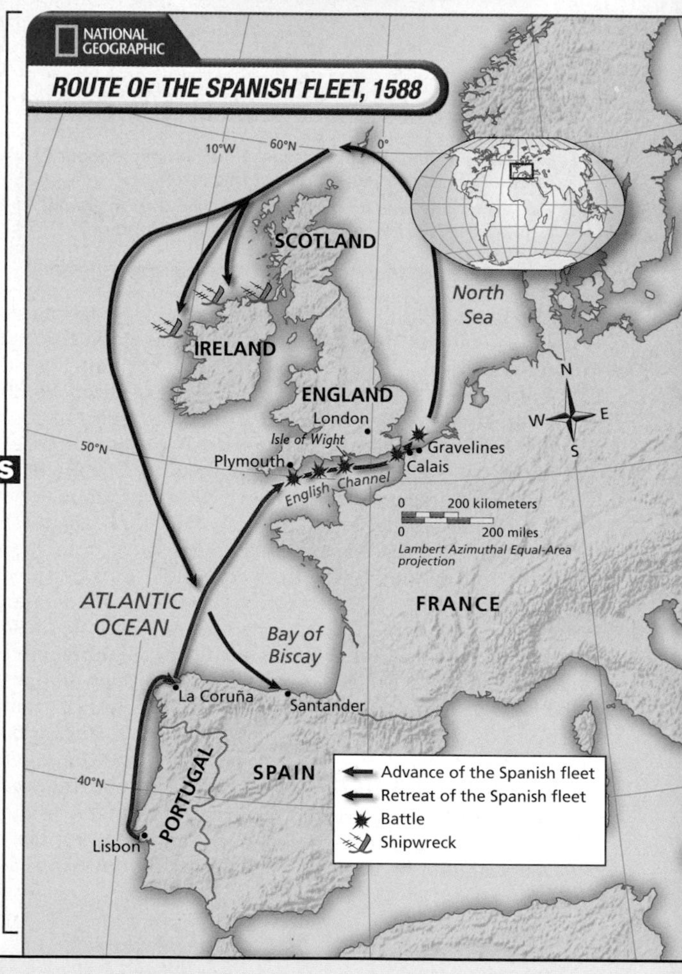

Geography SKILLS

1. **Location** Use the map to estimate the distance covered by the Spanish retreat.
2. **Region** Why was the defeat of the Spanish Armada a turning point?

Maps In MOtion See *StudentWorks™ Plus* or glencoe.com.

Hands-On Chapter Project
Step 1

Making a Time Line of 17th-Century Europe

Groups of students will chart the major people and events of 17th-century Europe on an illustrated time line.

Step 1: Gathering Information

Essential Question: What events shaped European life in the 17th century, and how do they still impact our lives today?

Directions: Divide the class into several small groups. Tell students that members of each group will work together to create an illustrated time line of 17th-century Europe. As they study Section 1, they can begin gathering information for the time line. Write the Section 1 Big Idea on the board, and tell students to use it as a guide for selecting entries. The time line should begin with the year 1550 and end with 1715. Students can use the Foldable three-pocket organizer described on page 453 to store information for their time line entries.

Summarizing: Allow time for groups to share what they learned about the Big Idea while searching for time line entries. Groups will continue to gather information for the time line as they study Section 2. In addition, they will decide on a format for the time line and begin planning illustrations. OL

(Chapter Project is continued in Section 2.)

The French Wars of Religion

MAIN IDEA Conflict between Catholics and Protestants was at the heart of the French Wars of Religion.

HISTORY & YOU What would you do if some classmates started a trend that you didn't like? Learn how Catholic leaders in France protested the spread of Protestantism.

Of the sixteenth-century religious wars, none was more shattering than the French civil wars known as the French Wars of Religion (1562–1598). Religious conflict was at the center of these wars. The French kings persecuted Protestants, but the persecution did little to stop the spread of Protestantism.

Huguenots

Huguenots (HYOO•guh•NAHTS) were French Protestants influenced by John Calvin. They made up only about 7 percent of the total French population, but 40 to 50 percent of the nobility became Huguenots. This made the Huguenots a powerful political threat to the Crown.

An extreme Catholic party—known as the ultra-Catholics—strongly opposed the Huguenots. Having the loyalty of parts of northern and northwestern France, they could pay for and recruit large armies.

Religion was the most important issue, but other factors played a role in the French civil wars. Towns and provinces were willing to assist the nobles in weakening the growing power of the French monarchy.

Henry IV and the Edict of Nantes

For 30 years, battles raged in France between the Catholics and Huguenots. Finally, in 1589, **Henry of Navarre,** the Huguenot political leader, succeeded to the throne as Henry IV. He realized that as a Protestant he would never be accepted by Catholic France. Therefore, he converted to Catholicism. When Henry IV was crowned king in 1594, the fighting in France finally came to an end.

To solve the religious problem, Henry IV issued the **Edict of Nantes** in 1598. The edict recognized Catholicism as the official religion of France. It also gave the Huguenots the right to worship and to enjoy all political privileges such as holding public offices. **D**

✓Reading Check **Identifying** List the sequence of events that led to the Edict of Nantes.

SECTION 1 REVIEW

Vocabulary

1. **Explain** the significance of: militant, conflict, King Philip II, Netherlands, William the Silent, Elizabeth Tudor, policy, armada, Scotland, Ireland, Huguenots, Henry of Navarre, Edict of Nantes.

Main Ideas

2. **Explain** how Philip II championed Catholic causes throughout his lands.
3. **Create** a Venn diagram like the one shown below to compare and contrast the reigns of Philip II, Elizabeth Tudor, and Henry of Navarre.

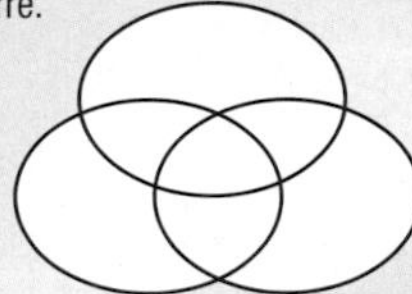

4. **Describe** how the Edict of Nantes appeased both Catholics and Huguenots.

Critical Thinking

5. **The BIG Idea** **Analyzing** Analyze which of the major three nations—Spain, England, or France—lost the most power and standing during their religious and political conflicts.
6. **Drawing Conclusions** What did Elizabeth hope to achieve—or to avoid—with her moderate foreign policy of balancing power between France and Spain?
7. **Analyzing Visuals** Examine the maps on pages 455 and 456. How do you think the defeat of the Spanish Armada might have affected Philip's ability to rule the Spanish empire? Explain your answer.

Writing About History

8. **Persuasive Writing** Write a persuasive essay arguing whether it was a good idea for Philip II to sail against England. Identify the main reason the king of Spain decided to invade.

History ONLINE

For help with the concepts in this section of *Glencoe World History,* go to glencoe.com and click Study Central™.

D Differentiated Instruction

Verbal/Linguistic Have students debate the following statement: "The Edict of Nantes was a victory for all of France." **AL**

✓Reading Check

Answer: 1562—French Wars of Religion begin; 1594—fighting ends, after Henry of Navarre becomes king; 1598—Henry issues Edict of Nantes.

Assess

Study Central provides summaries, interactive games, and online graphic organizers to help students review content.

Close

Identifying Central Issues

Have students discuss the Section 1 Big Idea. **Ask:** What issue most influenced political life in Spain, England, and France? *(religious conflict—Students should cite examples for each country.)* **OL**

SECTION 1 REVIEW

Answers

1. Definitions for the vocabulary words are found in the section and in the Glossary.
2. consolidated lands inherited from his father, insisted on strict conformity to Catholicism and strong monarchical authority, strengthened control in the Spanish Netherlands, tried to crush Calvinism in the Spanish Netherlands
3. **Philip II:** Catholic, militant champion of Catholic causes; **Elizabeth Tudor:** Protestant, moderate in religion and politics; **Henry of Navarre:** converted to Catholicism, moderate, kept Catholicism as state religion, gave Huguenots rights; **Henry/Elizabeth:** moderate policies; **Henry/Philip:** Catholicism as state religion
4. **Catholics:** Catholicism was state religion; **Huguenots:** gained religious, political rights
5. Spain: spent a great deal of money on conflicts with the Netherlands and England, lost much of its armada in the conflict with England, began to decline as a sea and world power due to costly wars, inefficient government, and out-of-date armed forces
6. hoped to prevent an invasion of England by either Spain or France, or both
7. probably hurt Philip's ability to rule; a strong navy was necessary to defend the Spanish empire
8. Answers will vary. He hoped to overthrow Protestantism and establish Catholic rule in England.

Focus

Bellringer

Daily Focus Transparency 14.2

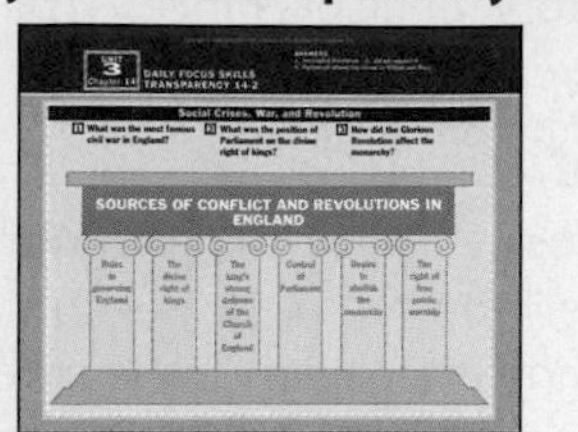

GUIDE TO READING

Answers to Graphic:

Religious Conflicts
witchcraft hysteria
Thirty Years' War
English Civil War
Glorious Revolution

Section Spotlight Video

To generate student interest and provide a springboard for class discussion, access the Chapter 14, Section 2 video at glencoe.com or on the video DVD.

Social Crises, War, and Revolution

GUIDE TO READING

The BIG Idea

Order and Security Social, economic, and religious conflicts challenged the established political order throughout Europe.

Content Vocabulary

- inflation *(p. 458)*
- witchcraft *(p. 458)*
- divine right of kings *(p. 461)*
- commonwealth *(p. 461)*

Academic Vocabulary

- restoration *(p. 462)*
- convert *(p. 462)*

People and Places

- Holy Roman Empire *(p. 460)*
- Bohemia *(p. 460)*
- James I *(p. 461)*
- Puritans *(p. 461)*
- Charles I *(p. 461)*
- Cavaliers *(p. 461)*
- Roundheads *(p. 461)*
- Oliver Cromwell *(p. 461)*
- James II *(p. 462)*

Reading Strategy

Summarizing Information As you read, use a chart like the one below to identify which conflicts were prompted by religious concerns.

Religious Conflicts

Severe economic and social crises plagued Europe in the sixteenth and seventeenth centuries. The Holy Roman Empire was devastated, and France emerged as the dominant nation in Europe. Conflicts between the kings of England and its parliament led to a civil war, an execution of a king, and a revolution. From such crises, constitutional monarchy emerged.

Crises in Europe

MAIN IDEA Population decline in Europe and the hysteria of witchcraft trials contributed to economic and social problems in seventeenth-century Europe.

HISTORY & YOU What if the number of students in your school declined by half this year? Learn how Europeans responded to economic and social problems.

From 1560 to 1650, Europe witnessed severe economic and social crises. One major economic problem was **inflation,** or rising prices. A growing population in the sixteenth century increased the demand for land and food and drove up prices for both.

Economic and Social Crises

By 1600, an economic slowdown had begun in parts of Europe. Spain's economy, grown dependent on imported silver, was failing by the 1640s. The mines were producing less silver. Fleets were subject to pirate attacks. Also, the loss of Muslim and Jewish artisans and merchants hurt the economy. Italy, the financial center of Europe in the Renaissance, was also declining economically.

Population figures in the sixteenth and seventeenth centuries reveal Europe's worsening conditions. Population grew in the sixteenth century. The number of people probably increased from 60 million in 1500 to 85 million by 1600. By 1620, the population had leveled off. It had begun to decline by 1650, especially in central and southern Europe. Warfare, plague, and famine all contributed to the population decline and to the creation of social tensions.

The Witchcraft Trials

A belief in **witchcraft,** or magic, had been part of traditional village culture for centuries. The religious zeal that led to the Inquisition and the hunt for heretics was extended to concern about witchcraft. During the sixteenth and seventeenth centuries, an intense hysteria affected the lives of many Europeans. Perhaps more than a hundred thousand people were charged with witchcraft. As more and more people were brought to trial, the fear of witches

Resource Manager

R Reading Strategies	C Critical Thinking	D Differentiated Instruction	W Writing Support	S Skill Practice
Teacher Edition • Act. Prior Know., p. 459 • Academic Vocab., p. 462 **Additional Resources** • Guid. Read. Act., URB p. 125 • Read. Ess. & Note-Taking Guide, p. 154	**Teacher Edition** • Det. Cause/Effect, p. 460 **Additional Resources** • People in World Hist. Act., URB p. 115 • Section Quiz, p. 170	**Teacher Edition** • ELL, p. 461 **Additional Resources** • Hist. Analysis Skills Act., URB p. 94 • Read. Strat. for SS, p. 80	**Teacher Edition** • Expository Writing, p. 461 **Additional Resources** • Hist. & Geo. Act., URB p. 105 • Writer's Guidebook, p. 5	**Teacher Edition** • Using Geo. Skills, p. 460 **Additional Resources** • Chart. Graph. Act., URB p. 3

PRIMARY SOURCE / INFOGRAPHICS

Witchcraft Hysteria

The *Malleus Maleficarum*, or the *Hammer of the Witches*, of 1486 was a guide for prosecuting witches during the Inquisition. It influenced witch trials in Europe for more than 200 years. Here are some excerpts:

On the classification of witches:
"The category in which women of this sort are to be ranked is called the category of Pythons, persons in or by whom the devil either speaks or performs some astonishing operation. . . ."

On extracting a confession:
"The method of beginning an examination by torture is as follows: The jailers . . . strip the prisoner. This stripping is lest some means of witchcraft may have been sewed into the clothing—such as often, taught by the Devil, they prepare from the bodies of unbaptized [murdered] infants . . . the judge . . . tries to persuade the prisoner to confess the truth freely; but, if [the witch] will not confess, he bids attendants make the prisoner fast to . . . some . . . implement of torture."

Witches were thought to enjoy casting their spells on the weak and vulnerable, such as infants.

DOCUMENT-BASED QUESTIONS

This painting is entitled *Witches' Sabbath: The Conjurers* by Francisco de Goya (1746–1828).

1. **Describing** According to the excerpts, whom do witches serve?
2. **Comparing** Describe similarities between witchcraft trials and the Inquisition.

grew, as did the fear of being accused of witchcraft.

Common people—usually the poor and those without property—were the ones most often accused of witchcraft. More than 75 percent of those accused were women. Most of them were single or widowed and over 50 years old.

Under intense torture, accused witches usually confessed to a number of practices. For instance, many said that they had sworn allegiance to the devil and attended sabbats, nightly gatherings where they feasted and danced. Then others admitted to casting evil spells.

By 1650, the witchcraft hysteria had begun to lessen. As governments grew stronger, fewer officials were willing to disrupt their societies with trials of witches. In addition, attitudes were changing. People found it unreasonable to believe in the old view of a world haunted by evil spirits.

✓Reading Check **Explaining** What caused a decline in witchcraft trials?

Teach

R Reading Strategy

Activating Prior Knowledge

Ask: Compare the descriptions of people accused of witchcraft to characterizations you have read about in books or seen in movies or on television. In what ways are they similar? In what ways, if any, do they differ? *(Students will probably note that in classic books and movies many of the characterizations are similar, but that contemporary characterizations are more diverse.)* **OL**

DOCUMENT-BASED QUESTIONS

Answers:
1. the devil
2. Both involved physical torture. Both were attempts to eradicate perceived threats to religion and society.

✓Reading Check

Answer: Government officials were unwilling to disrupt society with trials, and attitudes toward witchcraft began to change.

Hands-On Chapter Project
Step 2

Making a Time Line of 17th-Century Europe

Step 2: Planning the Format In addition to gathering more information, student groups decide on a format and start gathering illustrations.

Directions: Tell student groups to use the Section 2 Big Idea as a guide for selecting more entries for the time line. Also, instruct them to begin planning a physical format for their time lines. Suggest a variety of options for students: a large piece of art board; a string of sheets of art paper attached end to end with tape; individual sheets of art paper bound sequentially in a three-ring binder, a three-dimensional diorama-style time line, and so on. Finally, tell groups to begin gathering illustrations for their entries. Suggest that they look for book illustrations, draw their own, or do both.

Summarizing: Allow time for student groups to share what they learned about the Section 2 Big Idea while searching for more time line entries and illustration ideas. **OL**

(Chapter Project is continued in Section 3.)

C Critical Thinking

Determining Cause and Effect **Ask:** What effect did the Peace of Westphalia have on the Holy Roman Empire? *(It brought the Holy Roman Empire to an end as a political entity.)* How? *(by dividing it into independent states able to choose their own religion and foreign policy)* **OL**

✓Reading Check

Answer: the Holy Roman Empire, France, and Spain

S Skill Practice

Using Geography Skills Focus attention on the map's legend. Have students identify the colors indicating the various countries to help them answer the first Geography Skills question. **BL**

Geography SKILLS

Answers:

1. It was divided into hundreds of independent states.
2. Students' answers should be based on factual information from reliable sources.

The Thirty Years' War

MAIN IDEA Started over religious conflicts, the Thirty Years' War was sustained by political conflicts.

HISTORY & YOU What if fierce arguments destroyed your best friendship? Learn what caused thirty years of warfare.

Religious disputes continued in Germany after the Peace of Augsburg in 1555. One reason for the disputes was that the peace settlement had not recognized Calvinism. By the 1600s, Calvinism had spread through Europe.

Causes of the War

Religion played an important role in the outbreak of the Thirty Years' War, called the "last of the religious wars." However, political and territorial motives were also evident. Beginning in 1618 in the **Holy Roman Empire,** the war first involved the struggle between Catholic forces, led by the Hapsburg Holy Roman emperors, and Protestant (primarily Calvinist) nobles in **Bohemia.** As Denmark, Sweden, France, and Spain entered the war, the conflict became more political. Especially important was the struggle between France and Spain and the Holy Roman Empire for European leadership.

Effects of the War

All major European powers except England became involved in the Thirty Years' War. For 30 years Germany was plundered and destroyed. The Peace of Westphalia officially ended the war in Germany in 1648.

C The Peace of Westphalia divided the more than three hundred states of the Holy Roman Empire into independent states and gave them power to determine their own religion and to conduct their own foreign policy. This brought an end to the Holy Roman Empire as a political entity. Germany would not be united for another two hundred years.

✓Reading Check **Summarizing** What three major powers struggled for European leadership during the Thirty Years' War?

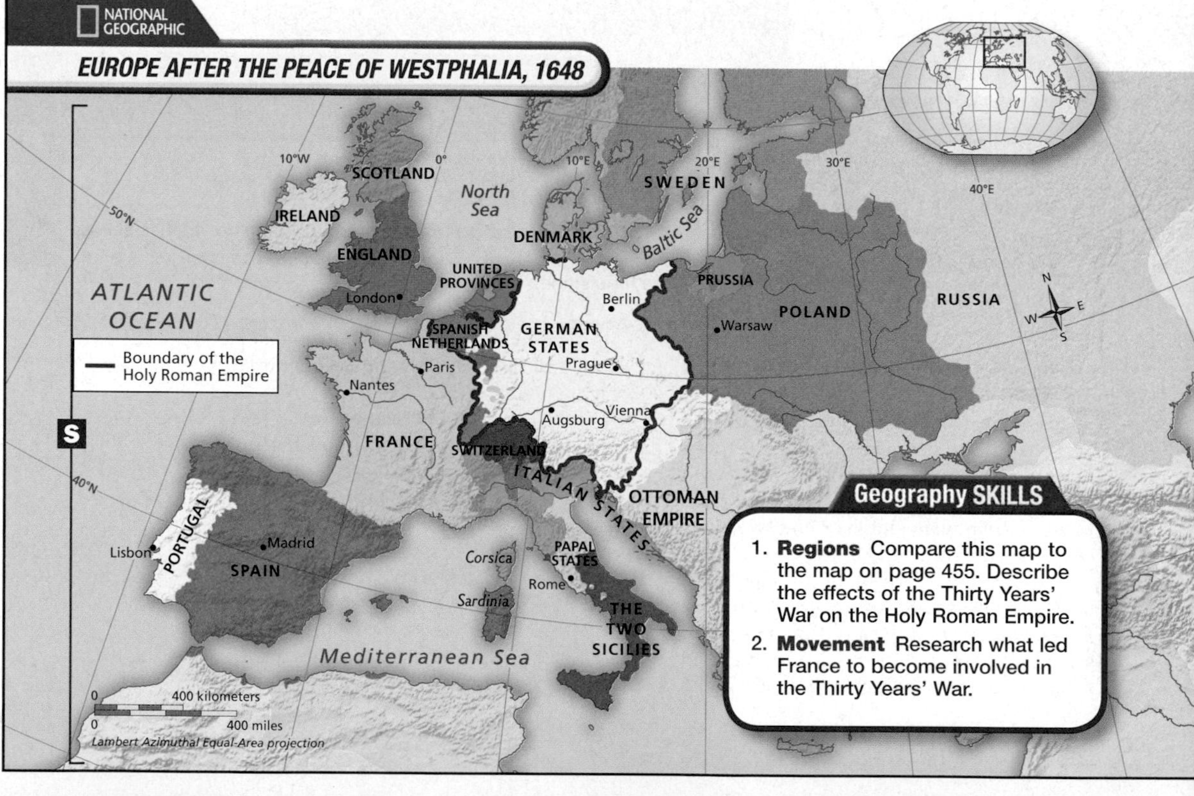

Geography SKILLS

1. **Regions** Compare this map to the map on page 455. Describe the effects of the Thirty Years' War on the Holy Roman Empire.
2. **Movement** Research what led France to become involved in the Thirty Years' War.

Differentiated Instruction

Leveled Activities

BL Reading Strategies and Activities for SS, p. 80

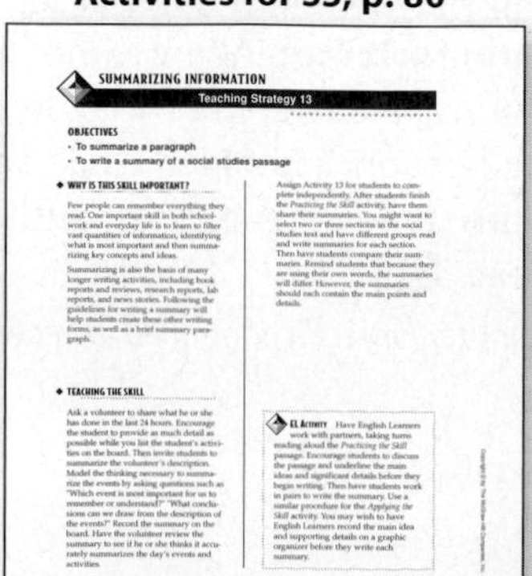

OL Guided Reading Activity, URB p. 125

AL Historical Analysis Skills Activity, URB p. 94

ELL Charting and Graphing Activity, URB p. 3

Revolutions in England

MAIN IDEA Civil war raged over what roles the king and Parliament should have in governing England.

HISTORY & YOU What if your class had to decide who should be the leader of an important school project? Learn how the struggle for power in England was resolved.

In addition to the Thirty Years' War, a series of rebellions and civil wars rocked Europe in the seventeenth century. By far the most famous struggle was the civil war in England known as the English Revolution. At its core was a struggle between king and Parliament to determine what role each should play in governing England. It would take another revolution later in the century to finally resolve this struggle. **W**

The Stuarts and Divine Right

With the death of Queen Elizabeth I in 1603, the Tudor dynasty came to an end. The Stuart line of rulers began with the accession to the throne of Elizabeth's cousin, the king of Scotland, who became **James I** of England.

James believed that he received his power from God and was responsible only to God. This is called the **divine right of kings**. Parliament did not think much of the divine right of kings. It had come to assume that the king or queen and Parliament ruled England together.

Religion was an issue as well. The **Puritans** (Protestants in England inspired by Calvinist ideas) did not like the king's strong defense of the Church of England. While members of the Church of England, the Puritans wished to make the church more Protestant. Many of England's gentry, mostly well-to-do landowners, had become Puritans. The Puritan gentry formed an important part of the House of Commons, the lower house of Parliament. It was not wise to alienate them.

The conflict that began during the reign of James came to a head during the reign of his son, **Charles I.** Charles also believed in the divine right of kings. In 1628, Parliament passed a petition that prohibited the passing of any taxes without Parliament's consent. Although Charles I initially accepted this petition, he later changed his mind. Charles realized that the petition would put limits on the king's power.

Charles also tried to impose more ritual on the Church of England. When he tried to force Puritans to accept this policy, thousands chose to go to America. Thus the religious struggles of the Reformation in England influenced American history.

Civil War and Commonwealth

Complaints grew until England slipped into a civil war in 1642 between the supporters of the king (the **Cavaliers** or Royalists) and the parliamentary forces (called the **Roundheads** because of their short hair). Parliament proved victorious, due largely to the New Model Army of **Oliver Cromwell,** a military genius.

The New Model Army was made up chiefly of more extreme Puritans, known as the Independents. These men believed they were doing battle for God. As Cromwell wrote, "This is none other but the hand of God; and to Him alone belongs the glory." Some credit is due to Cromwell. His soldiers were well disciplined and trained in the new military tactics of the seventeenth century. **D**

The victorious New Model Army lost no time in taking control. Cromwell purged Parliament of any members who had not supported him. What was left—the so-called Rump Parliament—had Charles I executed on January 30, 1649. The execution of the king horrified much of Europe. Parliament next abolished the monarchy and the House of Lords and declared England a republic, or **commonwealth.**

Cromwell found it difficult to work with the Rump Parliament and finally dispersed it by force. As the members of Parliament departed, he shouted, "It is you that have forced me to do this, for I have sought the Lord night and day that He would slay me rather than put upon me the doing of this work." After destroying the roles of both king and Parliament, Cromwell set up a military dictatorship.

W Writing Support

Expository Writing Ask students to use outside sources to write an essay in which they identify and evaluate the causes and effects of the revolution. Encourage them to include more information on the factors discussed in this section. **AL**

D Differentiated Instruction

English Language Learners Review the definition of each boldfaced term with students who have limited knowledge of English, and discuss the term's significance. **Ask: Why did Parliament oppose James I's claim of the divine right of kings?** *(Parliament wanted to share the crown's power to rule.)* **Why did the Puritans in Parliament oppose Charles I?** *(They resented his taxation and religious policies.)* **What group did Oliver Cromwell lead, what conflict did the group win, and what resulted?** *(Cromwell led radical Protestants [Roundheads] in a successful revolt against the king and his followers [Cavaliers]. Charles I was executed, the House of Lords abolished, and a commonwealth instituted.)* **OL**

Differentiated Instruction

People in World History Activity, URB p. 115

Analyzing Information

Objective: Learn more about religious strife during the reign of James I.

Focus: Direct students to read the article on Guy Fawkes.

Teach: Have students answer questions 1–3.

Assess: Tell students to share answers with the class, and amend answers as needed.

Close: Hold a class discussion on national holidays in the United States that commemorate political events or honor leaders.

Differentiated Instruction Strategies

BL Have students research Guy Fawkes Day and draw a picture of how it is observed.

AL Have students compare the Gunpowder Plot to any recent political conspiracy.

ELL Ask volunteers to share examples of political holidays or national days of observance in their country of origin and describe how they are observed.

R Reading Strategy

Academic Vocabulary Ask: What is the basic meaning of the word ***restoration?*** *(the return of something to its former or normal state)* What was restored after the death of Oliver Cromwell? *(the monarchy)* What is the meaning of ***convert*** in the context of the sentence in which it appears? *(to change from one religion to another)* In what way did Charles II mislead Parliament by refusing to convert to Catholicism? *(He was sympathetic to Catholicism and defied Parliament's laws against Catholics.)* OL

PEOPLE in HISTORY

Answers:
Charles I—as an honest man and a good king; Cromwell—a cruel necessity

The Restoration

Cromwell ruled until his death in 1658. George Monk, one of Cromwell's leading generals, realized that under any of Cromwell's successors the country would be torn apart. With his army, Monk created a situation favorable to restoring the monarchy in the person of Charles II, the son of Charles I. Charles II had lived years of exile during Cromwell's rule. With the return of the monarchy in 1660, England's time of troubles seemed at an end.

R After the **restoration** of the Stuart monarchy, known as the Restoration period, Parliament kept much of the power it had gained earlier and continued to play an important role. One of its actions was to pass laws restoring the Church of England as the state religion and restricting some rights of Catholics and Puritans.

Resisting attempts by his mother and sister to **convert** to Catholicism, Charles II remained openly loyal to the Protestant faith. He was, however, sympathetic to Catholicism. Parliament was suspicious about his Catholic leanings, especially when Charles suspended the laws that Parliament had passed against Catholics and Puritans. Parliament forced the king to back down on his action.

Charles's brother James did not hide the fact that he was a Catholic. Complying with his brother's wishes, James agreed to raise his two daughters in the Protestant faith. Rather than take an anti-Catholic oath, James resigned from all of his offices. His second marriage to a Catholic gave Parliament even more concern.

When Charles died, leaving no heirs to the throne, **James II** became king in 1685. James was an open and devout Catholic. Religion was once more a cause of conflict between king and Parliament. James named Catholics to high positions in the government, army, navy, and universities.

Parliament objected to James's policies but stopped short of rebellion. Members knew that James was an old man. His Protestant daughters Mary and Anne, born to his first wife, would succeed him.

PEOPLE in HISTORY

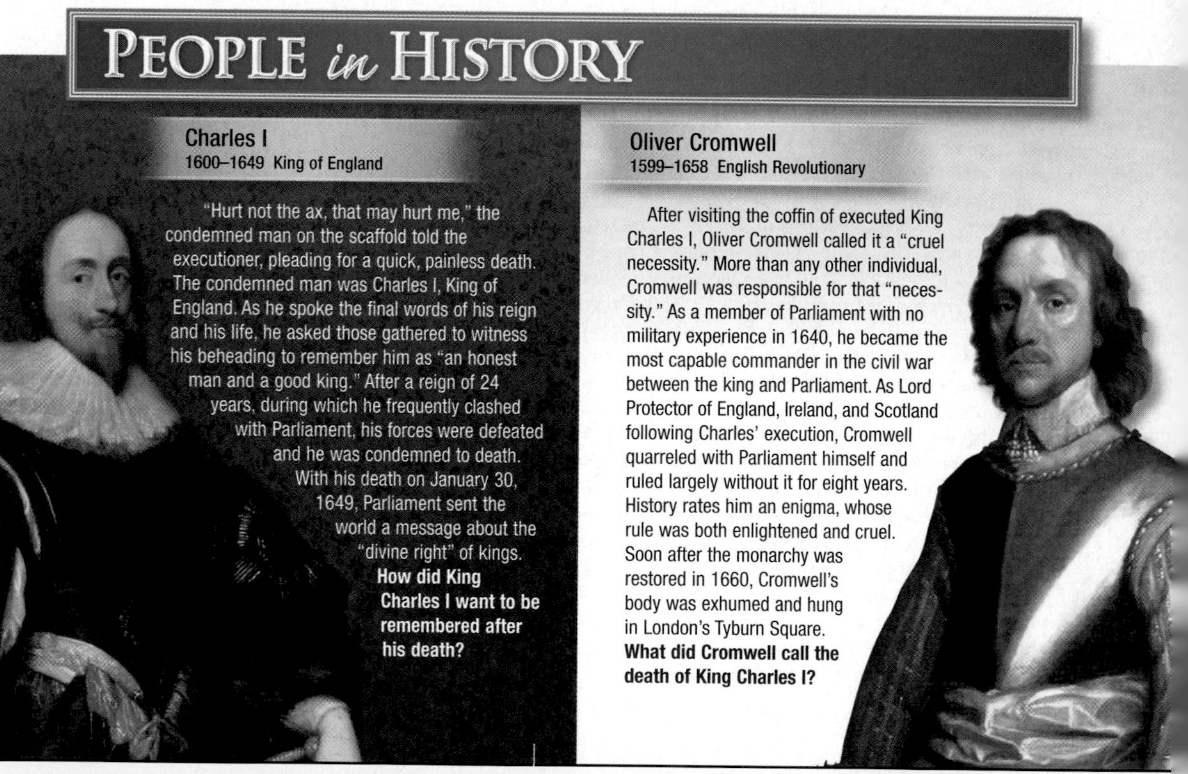

Charles I
1600–1649 King of England

"Hurt not the ax, that may hurt me," the condemned man on the scaffold told the executioner, pleading for a quick, painless death. The condemned man was Charles I, King of England. As he spoke the final words of his reign and his life, he asked those gathered to witness his beheading to remember him as "an honest man and a good king." After a reign of 24 years, during which he frequently clashed with Parliament, his forces were defeated and he was condemned to death. With his death on January 30, 1649, Parliament sent the world a message about the "divine right" of kings. **How did King Charles I want to be remembered after his death?**

Oliver Cromwell
1599–1658 English Revolutionary

After visiting the coffin of executed King Charles I, Oliver Cromwell called it a "cruel necessity." More than any other individual, Cromwell was responsible for that "necessity." As a member of Parliament with no military experience in 1640, he became the most capable commander in the civil war between the king and Parliament. As Lord Protector of England, Ireland, and Scotland following Charles' execution, Cromwell quarreled with Parliament himself and ruled largely without it for eight years. History rates him an enigma, whose rule was both enlightened and cruel. Soon after the monarchy was restored in 1660, Cromwell's body was exhumed and hung in London's Tyburn Square. **What did Cromwell call the death of King Charles I?**

Additional Support

Extending the Content

Charles I Point out that the petition that Parliament forced Charles I to sign also prohibited him from imprisoning anyone unjustly, housing troops in private homes without consent, and imposing martial law in peacetime. Charles responded by ignoring the petition, ruling without Parliament's consent, and continuing to collect taxes and imprison people at will. Charles I's actions and desire for absolute power led to the outbreak of the English Revolution and his own execution.

Oliver Cromwell Review with students the information about Oliver Cromwell on page 461 and in the People in History feature on this page. Cromwell said that Charles's execution was a "cruel necessity." He may have been acknowledging that it was an extreme measure but thought perhaps that it was the only effective solution to the conflict. What is ironic about the way Cromwell ruled England after Charles's death is that he adopted tactics similar to ones that Charles had used: quarreling with and then ignoring Parliament and setting up a military dictatorship.

However, in 1688, James and his second wife, a Catholic, had a son. Now, the possibility of a Catholic monarchy loomed large.

A Glorious Revolution

A group of English nobles invited the Dutch leader, William of Orange, to invade England. In their invitation, the nobles informed William that most people throughout the kingdom wanted a change. The invitation put William and his wife Mary, the daughter of James II, in a difficult position. Based on Mary's relationship to James, it would be appalling to rise up against her father, the king of England. However, William, a foe of France's Catholic king Louis XIV, welcomed this opportunity to fight France with England's resources.

William began making preparations to invade England in early 1688. He made his plans as secretly as possible and thus kept them largely hidden from James. Not until early October did James realize William's intentions. In November 1688, William's forces landed at Torbay and began their march toward London. James responded by sending forward his army. Following the desertion of many of his soldiers and the defection of his daughter Anne and her husband, James retreated to London. There he made plans for his wife and son to flee to France where James later joined them.

With almost no bloodshed, England had undergone a "Glorious Revolution." The issue was not if there would be a monarchy but who would be monarch.

In January 1689, Parliament offered the throne to William and Mary. They accepted it, along with a Bill of Rights. The Bill of Rights set forth Parliament's right to make laws and to levy taxes. It also stated that standing armies could be raised only with Parliament's consent. Under the Bill of Rights, it was impossible for kings to oppose or to do without Parliament. The rights of citizens to keep arms and have a jury trial were also confirmed. The Bill of Rights helped create a system of government based on the rule of law and a freely elected Parliament. This bill laid the foundation for a limited, or constitutional, monarchy.

Another important action of Parliament was the Toleration Act of 1689. This act granted Puritans, but not Catholics, the right of free public worship. Few English citizens, however, would ever again be persecuted for religion.

By deposing one king and establishing another, Parliament had destroyed the divine-right theory of kingship. William was, after all, king by the grace of Parliament, not by the grace of God. Parliament had asserted its right to be part of the English government.

✓Reading Check **Describing** Trace the sequence of events that led to the English Bill of Rights.

SECTION 2 REVIEW

Vocabulary

1. **Explain** the significance of: inflation, witchcraft, Holy Roman Empire, Bohemia, James I, divine right of kings, Puritans, Charles I, Cavaliers, Roundheads, Oliver Cromwell, commonwealth, restoration, convert, James II.

Main Ideas

2. **Explain** what contributed to the economic and social problems of sixteenth-century Europe.
3. **Illustrate** the causes and effects of the Thirty Years' War by using a chart like the one below.

Thirty Years' War	
Cause	Effect

4. **Explain** why Oliver Cromwell first purged Parliament and then declared a military dictatorship.

Critical Thinking

5. **The BIG Idea** **Drawing Conclusions** Which nation emerged stronger after the Thirty Years' War? Did 30 years of fighting accomplish any of the original motives for waging the war?
6. **Distinguishing** What are the differences, if any, between a military dictatorship and a king ruling by "divine right"?
7. **Analyzing Visuals** Examine the painting on page 459. How does Goya portray the witches? What details in the painting indicate that witches were feared?

Writing About History

8. **Expository Writing** Write an essay on why population increased and decreased in sixteenth- and seventeenth-century England. Include a population graph.

History ONLINE
For help with the concepts in this section of *Glencoe World History*, go to glencoe.com and click Study Central™.

✓Reading Check

Answer: Charles I was executed. A commonwealth was established. After Cromwell's death, the monarchy was restored under Charles II. Parliament and the crown fought during the reigns of Charles II and his brother James II. Parliament invited William and Mary to overthrow James II. The Glorious Revolution succeeded, and William and Mary were offered the crown on the condition that they accept a bill of rights.

Assess

Study Central provides summaries, interactive games, and online graphic organizers to help students review content.

Close

Making Generalizations

Ask: How was the Thirty Years' War both a religious and political dispute? *(It began as a religious dispute and became a fight for political power.)* **OL**

Answers

1. Definitions for the vocabulary words are found in the section and in the Glossary.
2. Spain's and Italy's economic decline; economic downturn throughout Europe; loss of Muslim and Jewish artisans and merchants; population growth that increased demand for food and land and drove up prices; war, famine, plague; witchcraft hysteria
3. **Causes:** Calvinism not recognized; Calvinist nobles rebelled against Hapsburgs; struggle between France, Spain, and Holy Roman Empire for European leadership; **Effects:** all German states could determine own religion; major contenders gained new lands; Holy Roman Empire ended
4. Cromwell first purged Parliament to remove those who had not supported him. He still found it difficult to work with those Parliament members who were left, however, and declared a military dictatorship to give him more power.
5. France. Protestants made some gains; Germany did not fare well.
6. **Military dictatorship:** dictator generally self-elected and has absolute power backed up by the military; **King ruling by "divine right":** King believed that he received his power from God and that he was responsible only to God.
7. wearing dark cloaks, casting spells on infants; witches have evil-looking expressions, distorted faces; dark clouds give an ominous feeling
8. Students should consult outside sources. Essays should be supported by factual details and logic.

C Critical Thinking

Predicting Consequences

After a class discussion of the Reading Check question at the end of this section, have students think about the likely consequences of the ethnic and political diversity that characterized the Austrian Empire. **Ask:** What effect do you think the lack of a strong common bond among the many nationalities will have on the Austrian Empire? *(It will lead to divisions and the eventual breakup of the empire.)* **OL**

✓Reading Check

Answer: It was composed of so many different groups that it remained a collection of territories connected only through their service to the Hapsburg monarchy.

Geography SKILLS

Answers:

1. access to northern Europe and to the North Sea
2. The Arctic Circle lies north of 60° N latitude and has a cold, unfavorable climate.

Additional Support

The core of the new Austrian Empire was the traditional Austrian lands in present-day Austria, the Czech Republic, and Hungary. After the defeat of the Turks at Vienna in 1683 (see Chapter 15), Austria took control of all of Hungary, Transylvania, Croatia, and Slavonia as well. By the beginning of the eighteenth century, the Austrian Hapsburgs had gained a new empire of considerable size.

The Austrian monarchy, however, never became a highly centralized, absolutist state, chiefly because it was made up of so many different national groups. The Austrian Empire remained a collection of territories held together by the Hapsburg emperor, who was archduke of Austria, king of Bohemia, and king of Hungary. **C** Each of these areas had its own laws and political life. No common sentiment tied the regions together other than the ideal of service to the Hapsburgs, held by military officers and government officials.

✓Reading Check **Examining** Why was the Austrian monarchy unable to create a highly centralized, absolutist state?

Peter The Great

MAIN IDEA Russia emerged as a great power under Peter the Great.

HISTORY & YOU What if you discovered a great new way to save energy? Learn about the modernization of Russia.

A new Russian state emerged in the fifteenth century under the principality of Muscovy and its grand dukes. In the sixteenth century, **Ivan IV** became the first ruler to take the title of **czar,** the Russian word for *caesar*.

Ivan expanded the territories of Russia eastward. He also crushed the power of the Russian nobility, or **boyars.** He was known as Ivan the Terrible because of his ruthless deeds, among them stabbing his own son to death in a heated argument.

When Ivan's dynasty ended in 1598, a period of anarchy known as the Time of Troubles followed. This period ended when the *zemsky sobor,* or national assembly, chose **Michael Romanov** as the new czar in 1613.

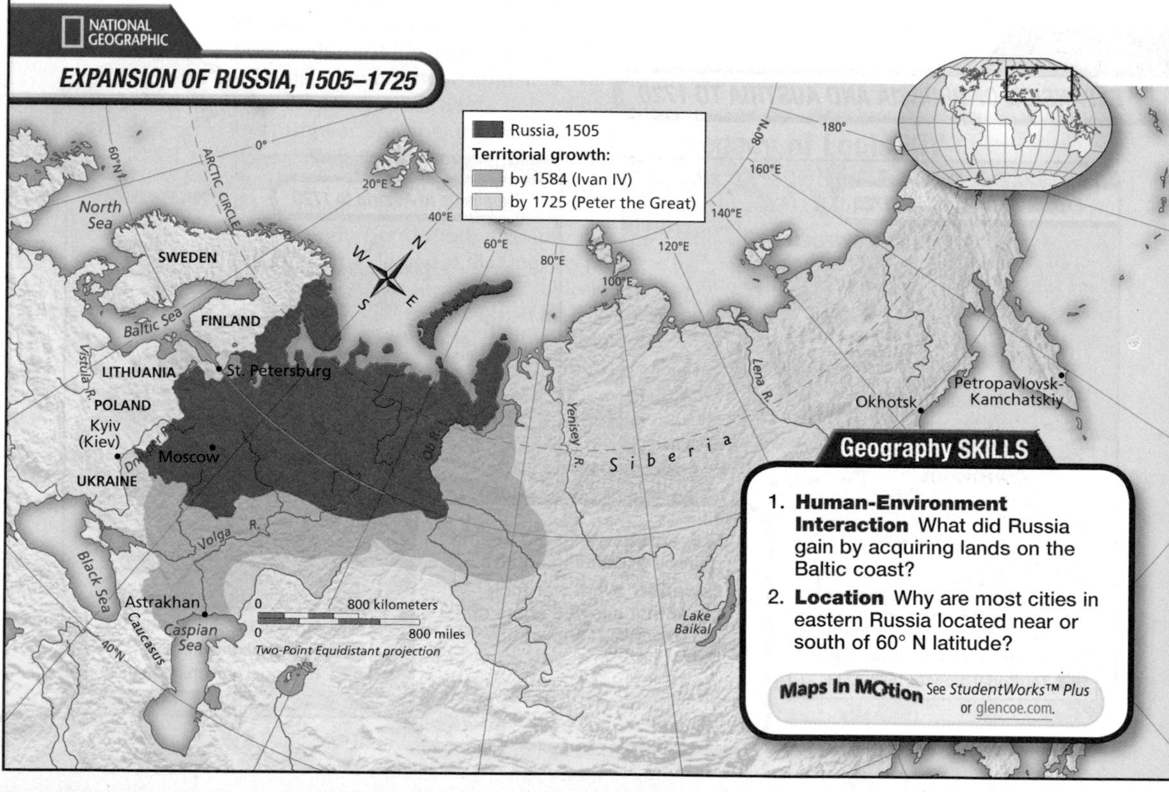

Geography SKILLS

1. **Human-Environment Interaction** What did Russia gain by acquiring lands on the Baltic coast?
2. **Location** Why are most cities in eastern Russia located near or south of 60° N latitude?

Maps In MOtion See StudentWorks™ Plus or glencoe.com.

Extending the Content

St. Petersburg In 1703, Peter the Great obtained a pathway to Europe by gaining control of the Neva River from Sweden. On May 27, 1703, Russian workers laid the foundations for St. Petersburg at the mouth of the river. The city was built at an unprecedented speed; it became the capital of the Russian Empire only nine years after it was created. It was built by thousands of forced laborers, many of whom died from sickness, hunger, and workplace mishaps. St. Petersburg quickly became a major industrial center and, by 1726, it was the country's largest center of trade. The best artists in Europe and Russia created its masterpieces. Dozens of higher education establishments in St. Petersburg gave the country generations of prominent scientists and researchers. It is also the city of the great writers, Pushkin, Gogol, Tolstoy, and Dostoevsky.

The Romanov dynasty lasted until 1917. One of its most prominent members was **Peter the Great**, who became czar in 1689. Like other Romanov czars who preceded him, Peter was an absolutist monarch who claimed the divine right to rule.

After becoming czar, Peter visited the West. Determined to westernize, or Europeanize, Russia, he was especially eager to borrow European technology. Only this kind of modernization could turn the army and navy into what he needed to make Russia a great power. By Peter's death in 1725, Russia was a great military power and an important European state.

Military and Governmental Changes

One of Peter's first goals was to reorganize the army. He employed both Russians and Europeans as officers. He drafted peasants for 25-year stints of service to build a standing army of 210,000 soldiers. Peter also formed the first Russian navy.

To impose the rule of the central government more effectively, Peter divided Russia into provinces. He hoped to create a "police state," a well-ordered community governed by law. However, few bureaucrats shared his concept of honest service and duty to the state. Peter's personality created an atmosphere of fear instead of a sense of civic duty. He wrote to one administrator, "According to these orders act, act, act. I won't write more, but you will pay with your head if you interpret orders again." Peter wanted the impossible—that his administrators be slaves and free persons at the same time.

Cultural Changes and a New Capital

After visiting the West, Peter began to introduce Western customs, practices, and manners into Russia. He ordered the preparation of the first Russian book of etiquette to teach Western manners. He insisted that Russian men shave their beards and shorten their coats. Upper-class women could remove their traditional face-covering veils and move out into society. Both sexes could mix for conversation and dancing at gatherings.

The object of Peter's domestic reforms was to make Russia into a great state and military power and to "open a window to the West," meaning a port with ready access to Europe. This could be achieved only on the Baltic Sea, which Sweden, the most important power in northern Europe, controlled. Peter acquired the lands he sought after a long war with Sweden. On the Baltic in 1703, Peter began construction of a new city, **St. Petersburg,** his window to the West. Finished during Peter's lifetime, St. Petersburg remained the Russian capital until 1918.

✓Reading Check **Evaluating** Why was it so important that Peter the Great have a seaport on the Baltic?

SECTION 3 REVIEW

Vocabulary

1. **Explain** the significance of: stability, absolutism, Louis XIV, authority, Cardinal Richelieu, Prussia, Austria, Frederick William the Great Elector, Ivan IV, czar, boyars, Michael Romanov, Peter the Great, St. Petersburg.

Main Ideas

2. **Summarize** the reign of Louis XIV of France using a chart like the one below.

Government	Wars	Economics	Religion

3. **Explain** why Frederick the Great Elector of Prussia thought it was so important to build a large and efficient standing army.
4. **Describe** the Western customs and practices that Peter the Great introduced to Russia.

Critical Thinking

5. **The BIG Idea Comparing and Contrasting** Compare and contrast the absolutist leadership styles of Louis XIV, Frederick William the Great Elector, and Peter the Great.
6. **Making Connections** Explain why building roads and canals and constructing a seaport would increase a nation's wealth and power.
7. **Analyzing Visuals** Examine the painting of Louis XIV on page 465. In what ways does this painting emphasize the absolute power of Louis XIV?

Writing About History

8. **Expository Writing** Historians have long considered the reign of Louis XIV to be the best example of the practice of absolute monarchy in the seventeenth century. Do you believe the statement is true? Why or why not? Write an essay supporting your opinion.

History ONLINE
For help with the concepts in this section of *Glencoe World History*, go to glencoe.com and click Study Central™.

✓Reading Check

Answer: It was the only place where the Russians could have an ice-free port with year-round access to Europe.

Assess

History ONLINE

Study Central provides summaries, interactive games, and online graphic organizers to help students review content.

Close

Summarizing Ask: How did France, Prussia, Austria, and Russia become great powers? *(Louis XIV gained absolute authority by removing the nobility from political affairs. Frederick William created an effective military-run government. The Hapsburgs consolidated vast territories under their control. Peter the Great modernized Russia, and secured a Baltic port.)* OL

Answers

1. Definitions for the vocabulary words are found in the section and in the Glossary.
2. **Government:** absolute ruler; **Wars:** four wars, added lands, put relative on Spanish throne; **Economics:** mercantilism, subsidies to new industries, built roads and canals, created merchant marine, left France in debt; **Religion:** anti-Protestant, destroyed Huguenot churches, closed schools
3. Prussia was a small, open territory with no natural frontiers for defense.
4. rules of etiquette; men shaved beards; women removed veils; both sexes mixed freely in society
5. **Louis XIV:** shared authority with no one, extravagant lifestyle and military campaigns weakened France; **Frederick William:** set up the General War Commissariat to help govern, creation of new empire; **Peter the Great:** greatly influenced by Western culture, made Russia a great military power, constructed St. Petersburg, gained access to the West
6. Answers will vary but may include: improve communications and transportation of goods, increase trade of goods and sharing of ideas and cultures within and outside of country thereby strengthening economy and goodwill.
7. Louis XIV is depicted as having the powers of the god Apollo. The rays of sun show that he is as powerful and important as the sun.
8. Answers will vary but students should be able to find many details in the text to support their opinions.

Focus

Introducing Social History
Discuss with students what they know about absolute monarchs. **Ask:** How would the creation of a lavish palace support Louis XIV's identity as the Sun King? *(The size and grandeur of the palace reflected the importance of the king.)* OL

Teach

D Differentiated Instruction

English Language Learners
Help students understand the daily schedule described here by having them fill in an hourly appointment calendar with the various events. Make sure they understand the meaning of *chase, gaming, half-past,* and *ball.* ELL

Additional Support

Social History

A Palace Fit for the Sun King

Versailles was at the center of court life during the reign of Louis XIV. Versailles was transformed from a hunting lodge by the finest architects and artists of the seventeenth century. Its extensive grounds became a showcase of the French court's splendor and wealth—with every detail in the immense and opulent palace a reflection of the Sun King's absolute power.

The Palace of Versailles served as the center of French government under Louis XIV.

A Day at Versailles

In their letters to friends, ladies of the court provided intimate details of daily life at Versailles. Elisabeth Charlotte of Bavaria described to the Duchess of Hanover a day she spent at Versailles in 1676: "... I have been to Versailles where we were busy the entire day. From morning until three o'clock in the afternoon we went hunting. On our return from the chase we changed our dresses and went upstairs to the gaming, where we stayed until seven o'clock in the evening. Then we went to the play, which did not end until half-past ten o'clock. After the play came supper, followed by a ball, which usually lasted until three o'clock in the morning, and only then could we go to bed." D

Background

The Architects of Versailles The palace of Versailles is the premier example of Baroque architecture in France. The creative team who began the redesign of Versailles had earlier designed the château Vaux-le-Vicomte for Louis XIV's finance minister, Nicholas Fouquet. When Louis visited the château, he was displeased to see one of his ministers having a grander home than his own. He then commanded the architect Louis Le Vau, the painter Charles Le Brun, and the landscape architect André Le Nôtre to make Versailles into a monumental complex that would reflect his absolute power. Le Vau first turned the hunting lodge into a small palace. In 1675, Jules Hardouin-Mansart became the primary architect and tripled the size of the palace. Mansart's buildings and Le Nôtre's landscape design became the model for palaces throughout Europe.

Earning the King's Favor

Hoping to obtain an office, title, or pension from Louis XIV, thousands of people—as many as 5,000 in winter—lived at Versailles. They took part in the strict daily routines of court life, all of which revolved around the king, from the time he woke in the morning to the time he went to bed at night. To leave Versailles, people had to ask the king's permission, which he did not like to grant. For many, the expense of life at Versailles led to debt and ruin. People risked such ruin, however, to earn the king's attention and favor. One of the highest honors anyone could hope for at Versailles was to hold the candle while the king's hair was combed at night before bed.

Analyzing Visuals

1. **Comparing** How did people gain political influence in seventeenth-century France? How about today?
2. **Predicting** How do you think people today would respond to government spending of large sums of money on elaborate building projects or entertainments? Why?

471

S Skill Practice

Visual Literacy Ask: How might the garden look if it were designed to reflect the idea of living in harmony with nature? *(less shaped by human design and less formal.)* OL

W Writing Support

Descriptive Writing Have students imagine themselves as residents at Versailles and write a brief journal entry describing their experiences. OL

Assess/Close

Have students discuss their responses to the Analyzing Visuals questions in small groups. OL

ANALYZING VISUALS

Answers:

1. by being part of court; Answers may include lobbying.
2. People might be angry about such spending because it would be a waste of taxpayers' money.

Activity: Interdisciplinary Connection

Art Ask: In what ways does the Palace of Versailles reflect the power and grandeur associated with the reign of Louis XIV? Have students research and write a report on the building of Versailles in order to answer this question. Instruct them to find out when it was built, how it was built, the size of the grounds and the palace, and the style of architecture. Students should also discuss the art that is in the Versailles Museum. They may also want to discuss the current status of Versailles. Students should design a visual aid to accompany their reports, using models, drawings, or photos to illustrate their research. The reports may be given orally and the visual aids displayed in the classroom to enhance the students' understanding of the architectural and artistic significance of the palace of Versailles. After students have given their reports, lead a class discussion in which students compare and contrast Versailles to other examples of monumental architecture they have studied, such as the Egyptian pyramids or Gothic cathedrals. OL

R1 Reading Strategy

Identifying **Ask:** What were two important characteristics of Caravaggio's paintings? *(the dramatic use of light to heighten emotions; the depiction of common people and everyday settings)* **OL**

D Differentiated Instruction

Advanced Learners Invite students to research paintings by Rubens. Tell them to select one to present, describing its baroque characteristics. **AL**

R2 Reading Strategy

Activating Prior Knowledge Have students who have read or seen Shakespeare plays offer their insights. **Ask:** What elements in his plays would appeal to many people? *(the slapstick humor, tricks of disguise and mistaken identity)* What do his plays reveal about the human condition? *(power of love; cruelty of prejudice; consequences of conflicts, and much more)* **OL**

✓Reading Check

Answer: the tensions created by the upheavals of the Reformation

Differentiated Instruction

Bernini's *Throne of Saint Peter* is a highly decorated cover for the pope's medieval wooden throne. It is considered by many to be Bernini's crowning achievement in Saint Peter's Basilica. The throne seems to hover in midair, held by the hands of the four great theologians of the early Catholic Church. Above the chair, rays of heavenly light drive a mass of clouds and angels down and toward the spectator.

R1 The baroque painting style was known for its use of dramatic effects to arouse the emotions as shown in the work of another important Italian artist of the baroque period, Caravaggio. Similar to other baroque painters, Caravaggio used dramatic lighting to heighten emotions, to focus details, and to isolate the figures in his paintings. His work placed an emphasis on everyday experience. He shocked some of his patrons by depicting religious figures as common people in everyday settings.

History ONLINE
Student Web Activity— Visit glencoe.com and complete the activity on William Shakespeare.

Artemisia Gentileschi is less well-known than the male artists who dominated the seventeenth-century art world in Italy but prominent in her own right. Born in Rome, she studied painting with her father. In 1616, she moved to Florence and began a successful career as a painter. At the age of 23, she became the first woman to be elected to the Florentine Academy of Design. She was known internationally in her day as a portrait painter, but her fame now rests on a series of pictures of Old Testament heroines.

D The baroque style of art did not just flourish in Italy. Peter Paul Rubens embodies the baroque movement in Flanders (the Spanish Netherlands), where he worked most of his life. A scholar and diplomat as well as an artist, Rubens used his classical education and connections with noble patrons in Italy, Spain, England, France, and Flanders to paint a variety of genres. He is best known for his depictions of the human form in action. These images are lavish and extravagant, much like the court life he experienced during the baroque period.

✓Reading Check **Describing** What did the mood of El Greco's paintings reflect?

Golden Age of Literature

MAIN IDEA Shakespeare and Lope de Vega were prolific writers of dramas and comedies that reflected the human condition.

HISTORY & YOU Are there any contemporary artists or entertainers who could compare to William Shakespeare? Learn about the great writers in England and Spain.

In both England and Spain, writing for the theater reached new heights between 1580 and 1640. Other forms of literature flourished as well.

England's Shakespeare

A cultural flowering took place in England in the late sixteenth and early seventeenth centuries. The period is often called the Elizabethan Era, because so much of it fell R2 within the reign of Queen Elizabeth. Of all the forms of Elizabethan literature, none expressed the energy of the era better than **drama**. Of all the dramatists, none is more famous than **William Shakespeare.**

When Shakespeare appeared in London in 1592, Elizabethans already enjoyed the stage. Elizabethan theater was a very successful business. London theaters ranged from the Globe, a circular, unroofed structure holding three thousand people, to the Blackfriars, a roofed structure that held only five hundred.

The Globe's admission charge of one or two pennies enabled even the lower classes to attend. The higher prices of the Blackfriars brought an audience of the well-to-do. Because Elizabethan audiences varied greatly, playwrights wrote works that pleased nobles, lawyers, merchants, and vagabonds alike.

William Shakespeare was a "complete man of the theater." Although best known for writing plays, he was also an actor and shareholder in the chief theater company of the time, the Lord Chamberlain's Men.

Shakespeare has long been viewed as a universal genius. A master of the English language, he also had a keen insight into human psychology. In his tragedies and his comedies, Shakespeare showed a remarkable understanding of the human condition.

Leveled Activities

BL Guided Reading Activity, URB p. 127

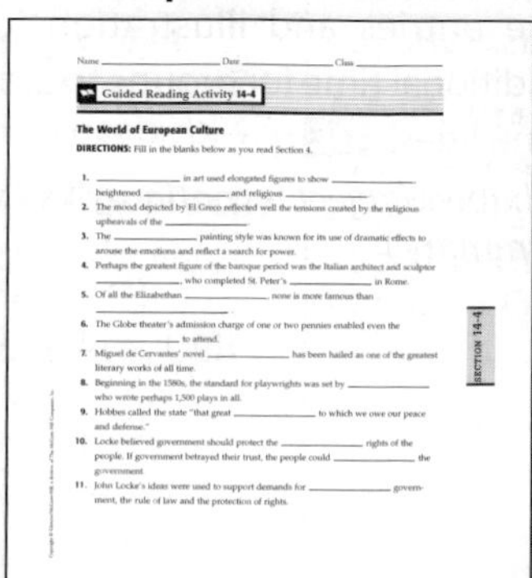

OL World Art and Music Activity, URB p. 119

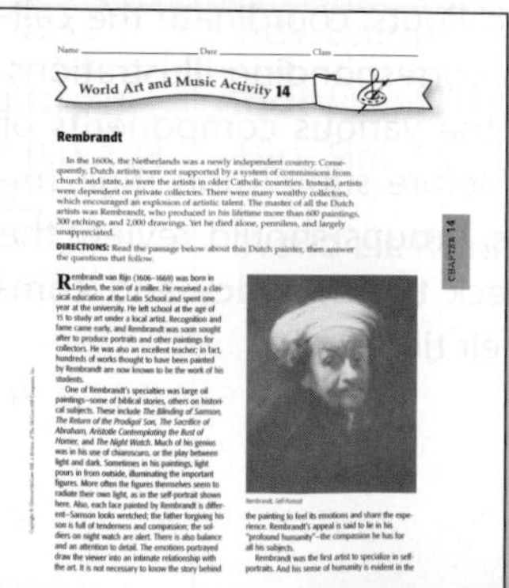

AL World Literature Reading, URB p. 9

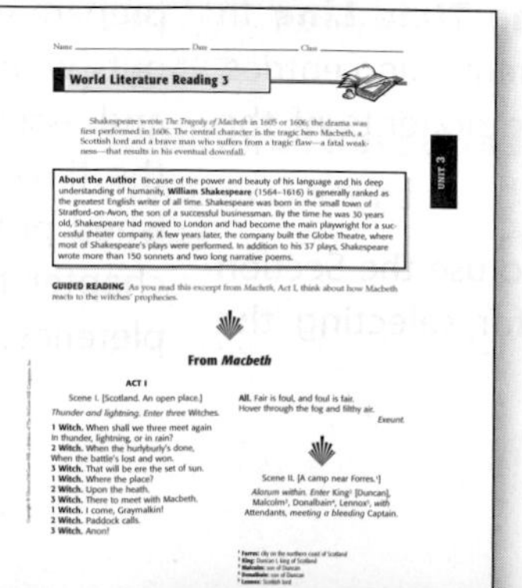

ELL Content Vocabulary Activity, URB p. 99

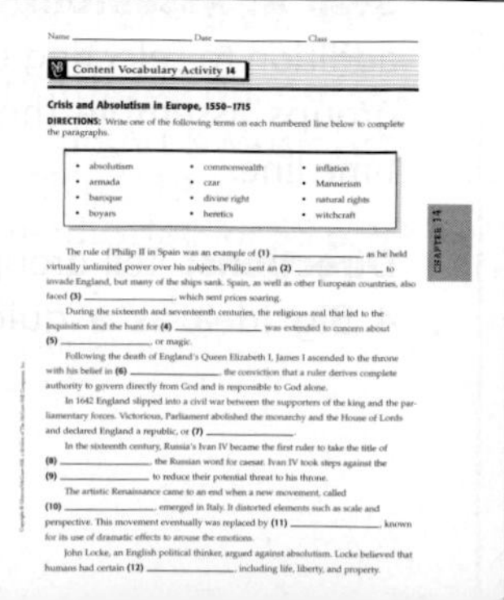

Spain's Cervantes and Vega

One of the crowning achievements of the golden age of Spanish literature was the work of **Miguel de Cervantes** (suhr•VAN•TEEZ). His novel *Don Quixote* has been hailed as one of the greatest literary works of all time.

C In the two main characters of this famous work, Cervantes presented the dual nature of the Spanish character. The knight, Don Quixote from La Mancha, is the visionary so involved in his lofty ideals that he does not see the hard realities around him. To him, for example, windmills appear to be four-armed giants. In contrast, the knight's fat and earthy squire, Sancho Panza, is a realist. Each of these characters finally comes to see the value of the other's perspective. The readers of *Don Quixote* are left with the conviction that both visionary dreams and the hard work of reality are necessary to the human condition.

The theater was one of the most **creative** forms of expression during Spain's golden century as well. The first professional theaters were created in Seville and Madrid.

PRIMARY SOURCE **INFOGRAPHICS**

The Globe Theatre

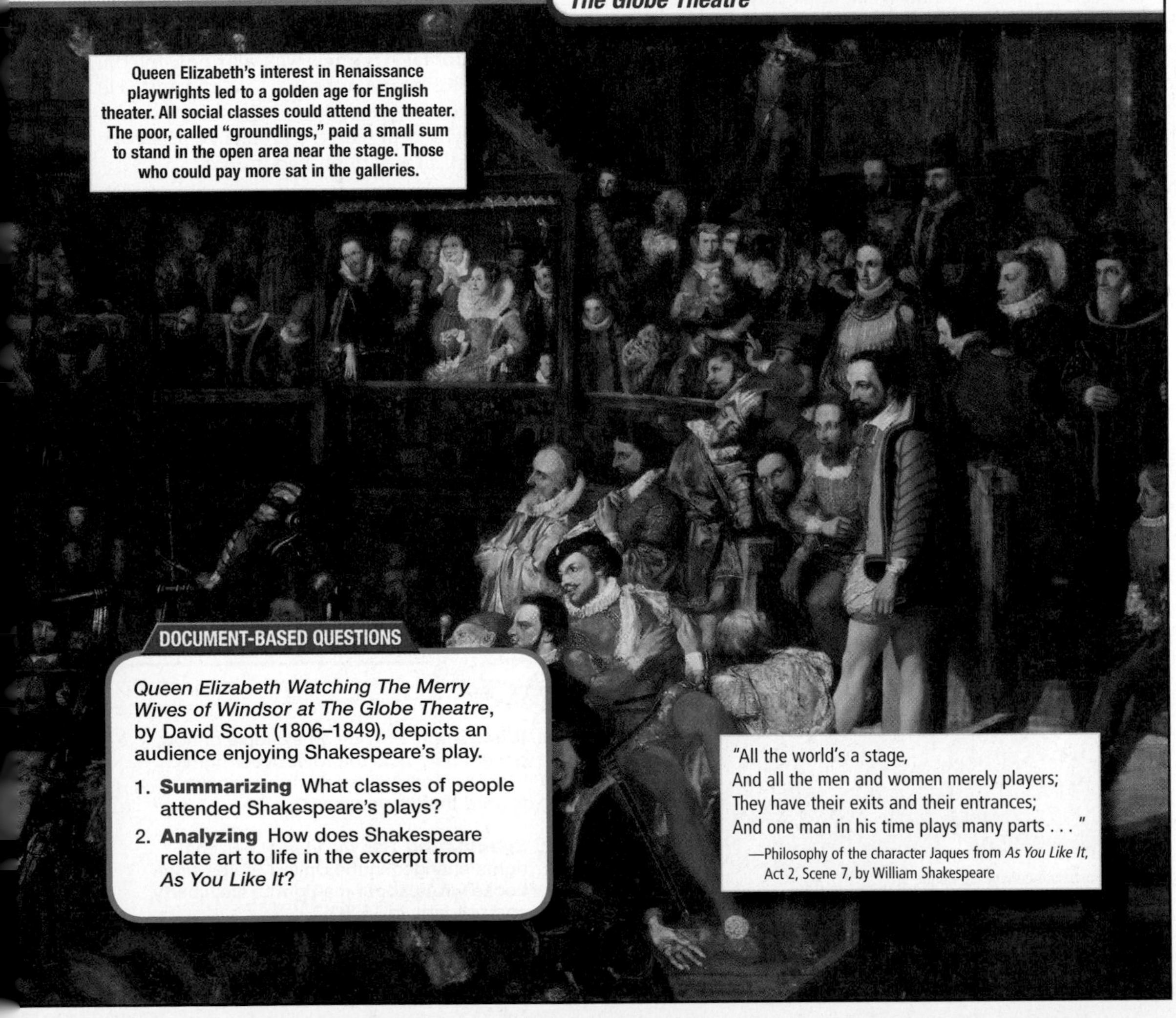

Queen Elizabeth's interest in Renaissance playwrights led to a golden age for English theater. All social classes could attend the theater. The poor, called "groundlings," paid a small sum to stand in the open area near the stage. Those who could pay more sat in the galleries.

DOCUMENT-BASED QUESTIONS

Queen Elizabeth Watching The Merry Wives of Windsor at The Globe Theatre, by David Scott (1806–1849), depicts an audience enjoying Shakespeare's play.

1. **Summarizing** What classes of people attended Shakespeare's plays?
2. **Analyzing** How does Shakespeare relate art to life in the excerpt from *As You Like It*?

"All the world's a stage,
And all the men and women merely players;
They have their exits and their entrances;
And one man in his time plays many parts . . . "

—Philosophy of the character Jaques from *As You Like It*, Act 2, Scene 7, by William Shakespeare

C Critical Thinking

Synthesizing Have students analyze and evaluate the theme of Cervantes' *Don Quixote* as expressed here. **Ask:** What is the value of possessing dreams? *(Answers may include the idea that they can provide meaning or purpose in one's life and inspire idealistic thoughts, goals, and actions.)* What is the value of understanding the realities of everyday life? *(Answers may include that doing so forces one to adopt practical behaviors—working hard, developing discipline, using common sense—in order to survive daily life.)* What do you think would be a proper balance of the two? *(Encourage students to defend their responses with reasons.)* **AL**

DOCUMENT-BASED QUESTIONS

Answers:

1. People from all social classes could attend.
2. To Jaques, the world is a stage. People play roles on this "stage" that may change throughout life.

Differentiated Instruction

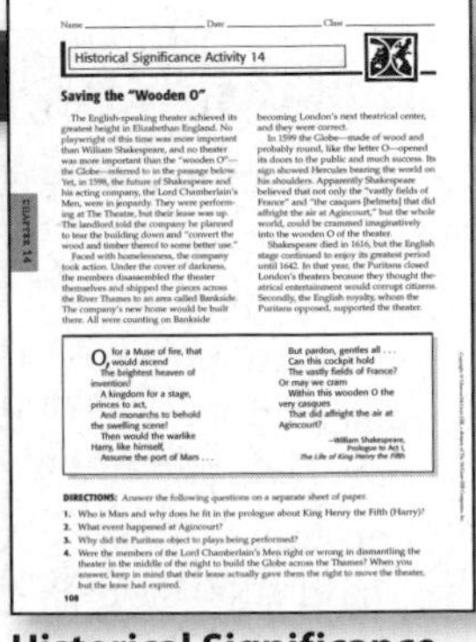

Historical Significance Activity, URB p. 108

Analyzing Information

Objective: Learn more about the Globe Theater.

Focus: Ask students to read the article and Shakespeare's Prologue to *Henry V*.

Teach: Have students answer questions 1–3.

Assess: Go over answers with the class, and make any needed corrections as a group.

Close: Have students debate question 4: What was gained? What was lost? What information is missing or unclear?

Differentiated Instruction Strategies

BL Guide students in making a diagram of the Globe's interior, labeling significant parts, and explaining the diagram to the class.

AL Have students research the reopening of the Globe and report what they learn to the class.

ELL Ask volunteers to tell the class about notable theaters and playwrights from their country of origin.

R Reading Strategy

Academic Vocabulary Point out that Hobbes found the word *leviathan* in the Bible where it is the name for a sea monster. It also means "any great and powerful person or thing." **Ask:** How is the title of Hobbes' work appropriate to his political beliefs? *(The state, headed by an absolute ruler, can be viewed as a necessary monster that provides order to society.)* **AL**

Answers:

1. Examples include laws that govern elections, regulate workplace practices, and so on. Citizens are responsible for obeying laws and participating in the democratic process.
2. Answers will vary, but students may say that for Locke, rights were limited; today, they are extended to everyone.

✓Reading Check

Answer: between 1580 and 1640; Lope de Vega

They were run by actors' companies, as they were in England. Soon, every large town had a public playhouse, including Mexico City in the New World. Touring companies brought the latest Spanish plays to all parts of the Spanish Empire.

Beginning in the 1580s, the standard for playwrights was set by **Lope de Vega.** He wrote an extraordinary number of plays, perhaps 1,500 in all. Almost 500 of them survive to this day. Vega's plays are thought to be witty, charming, action-packed, and realistic.

Lope de Vega made no apologies for the fact that he wrote his plays to please his audiences and satisfy public demand. He remarked once that if anyone thought he had written his plays for the sake of fame, "undeceive him and tell him that I wrote them for money."

✓Reading Check **Describing** When was the "golden age" of Spanish literature? Who set the standard for playwrights?

Political Thought

MAIN IDEA Hobbes and Locke wrote very different books about political thought in response to the English revolutions.

HISTORY & YOU What if you were asked to debate whether or not to wear school uniforms? Learn about England's influential political thinkers.

The seventeenth-century concerns with order and power were reflected in the political thought of the time. The English revolutions of the seventeenth century prompted very different responses from two English political thinkers, Thomas Hobbes and John Locke.

Hobbes

R **Thomas Hobbes** was alarmed by the revolutionary upheavals in England. He wrote *Leviathan*, a work on political thought, to try to deal with the problem of disorder. *Leviathan* was published in 1651.

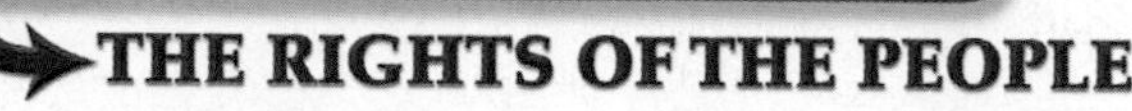

Connecting to the United States
The Rights of the People

American college students participating in elections

The American Declaration of Independence and the United States Constitution are based in part on the ideas of seventeenth-century political philosopher John Locke. Locke argued that all human beings have natural rights—including rights to life, liberty, and property—and that people create government to protect those rights.

The United States Constitution begins with the words, "We the people." This clearly states the idea that the people are the source of the government's power.

- **All citizens have natural rights.**
- **Government exists to protect the rights of the citizens.**
- **The citizens have the right to form a new government.**

1. **Illustrating** Provide an example of how government acts to protect your rights. What responsibilities do citizens have toward their government?
2. **Speculating** Has the idea of citizens' rights changed in the United States since Locke wrote about the right to life, liberty, and property in 1690?

Additional Support

Teacher Tip

Collaborative Learning This activity requires students to do research, write, and illustrate. The activity allows students with different levels of academic skills and intelligences to work together. As you form groups, consider the needed skills and choose students accordingly.

Activity: Collaborative Learning

Studying the Rights of U.S. Citizens Have students work in groups to study the Bill of Rights and subsequent amendments to the U.S. Constitution. Mention that the Bill of Rights was added to the Constitution in order to secure its ratification. It contains the first ten amendments, which specify basic individual rights guaranteed by the Constitution. The amendments that follow the Bill of Rights have been added through the years to improve or provide additional protection of citizens' rights. Have groups create a posterboard chart that summarizes the rights guaranteed in the Bill of Rights and the rights that were improved or added later. Groups can divide researching, organizing, and drawing duties among members. Have each group present their posters to the class. Conclude by discussing the questions in the Connecting to the United States feature. **OL**

Hobbes claimed that before society was organized, human life was "solitary, poor, nasty, brutish, and short." Humans were guided not by reason and moral ideals but by a ruthless struggle for self-preservation.

To save themselves from destroying one another, people made a social contract and agreed to form a state. Hobbes called the state "that great Leviathan to which we owe our peace and defense." People in the state agreed to be governed by an absolute ruler who possessed unlimited power. Rebellion must be suppressed. To Hobbes, such absolute power was needed to preserve order in society.

Locke

John Locke viewed the exercise of political power quite differently. His *Two Treatises of Government*, written in 1679 and 1680 but too radical and too dangerous to be published then, first appeared in 1690. In his treatises, especially the second one, Locke argued against the absolute rule of one person. He described how governments are formed and what justifies them.

Unlike Hobbes, Locke believed that before society was organized, humans lived in a state of equality and freedom rather than in a state of war. In this state of nature, no one was necessarily sovereign over anyone else. Locke believed that all humans had certain **natural rights**—rights with which they were born. These included rights to life, liberty, and property. W

Like Hobbes, however, Locke believed that problems existed in the state of nature. People found it difficult to protect their natural rights. For that reason, they agreed to establish a government to ensure the protection of their rights and to judge those who violated them.

The contract between people and government involved mutual obligations. Government would protect the rights of the people, and the people would act reasonably toward government. However, if a government broke the contract—for example, if a monarch failed to protect citizens' natural rights—the people would be within their rights to remove or alter the government since it betrayed their trust. If the people chose to remove the government, then they could form a new one.

To Locke, "people" meant the landholding aristocracy, not landless masses. Locke was not an advocate of democracy, but his ideas proved important to both the Americans and the French in the eighteenth century. These ideas were used to support demands for constitutional government, the rule of law, and the protection of rights. Locke's ideas can be found in both the American Declaration of Independence and the United States Constitution.

✓Reading Check **Explaining** According to Hobbes, why was absolute power needed?

SECTION 4 REVIEW

Vocabulary

1. **Explain** the significance of: Mannerism, El Greco, baroque, Madrid, Prague, Vienna, Brussels, Gian Lorenzo Bernini, drama, William Shakespeare, Miguel de Cervantes, creative, Lope de Vega, Thomas Hobbes, John Locke, natural rights.

Main Ideas

2. **Compare and Contrast** Mannerism and baroque art using a Venn diagram like the one below.

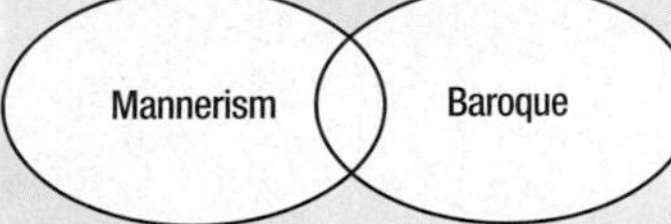

3. **Describe** what *Don Quixote* reveals about the nature of Spanish character.
4. **Summarize** the mutual obligations between people and government as expressed by Locke.

Critical Thinking

5. **The BIG Idea Analyzing** How did the Elizabethan theater experience provide a reflection of English society?
6. **Assessing** Assess how or if John Locke's *Two Treatises of Government* would justify the Glorious Revolution.
7. **Analyzing Visuals** Examine the painting on page 475. When did the artist live? Does this change the way you view his painting? Explain your answer.

Writing About History

8. **Persuasive Writing** In an essay, argue whether Shakespeare's quotation from *As You Like It* on page 475 is correct. Support your position with examples of historical figures from the chapter.

History ONLINE
For help with the concepts in this section of *Glencoe World History*, go to glencoe.com and click Study Central™.

477

W Writing Support

Descriptive Writing Ask students to write two paragraphs: one describing how Hobbes viewed humanity, the other how Locke viewed it. OL

✓Reading Check
Answer: to preserve order

Assess

History ONLINE

Study Central provides summaries, interactive games, and online graphic organizers to help students review content.

Close

Discussing Form three groups. Assign one group the topic art, another literature, and the third philosophy. Have groups discuss how their topic influenced or reflected life in the 1600s. Designate one notetaker for each group. After the discussions, have each group report their conclusions. *(Art discussion should include Mannerism and baroque art; literature—Shakespeare, Cervantes, and Lope de Vega; philosophy—Hobbes and Locke.)* OL

Answers

1. Definitions for the vocabulary words are found in the section and in the Glossary.
2. **Mannerism:** rejected Renaissance balance, harmony, moderation; ignored rules of proportion; **Baroque:** return to ideals of Renaissance art; action, exuberance, dramatic effects; detailed and ornate; **Both:** began in Italy; emotional, religious themes
3. dual nature of visionary dreams and realism
4. **Government:** protect people's rights; **People:** act reasonably toward government
5. Because people of all classes attended Elizabethan plays, playwrights had to please all classes.
6. Locke would probably justify it since many believed James, as an absolute monarch, did not support his subjects' natural rights and should be removed.
7. Answers may vary, but should include that the artist lived from 1806–1849 and therefore could not have seen this scene for himself. Students may argue that the painting may or may not be an accurate representation depending on the sources he used.
8. Answers should be supported by specific historical examples.

9. C Students should be able to eliminate A and D easily. The Toleration Act granted freedom of worship to Protestants in England. The Bill of Rights gave Parliament significant powers, including the right to make laws and levy taxes. The king or queen could no longer rule without Parliament.

10. A For this question, A is the only possible choice. Republicanism is a political alternative to Absolutism; Enlightened absolutism suggests a condition placed on absolute power; Deism is a religious belief.

11. D Students should be able to eliminate choices A, B, and C. Neither Frederick William nor Philip II were Russian, and Ivan IV was not a Romanov.

12. C For this question, C is the best possible choice. Baroque art followed Mannerism; Puritanism is a religious movement; rococo is a type of elaborate ornamentation associated with baroque architecture.

13. B Students should be able to eliminate choices A, C, and D. The Globe, where Shakespeare's plays were performed for the public, offered inexpensive seating for common people and more expensive seating for the upper classes.

Critical Thinking

14. A For this question, A is the best possible choice. Louis XIV invited nobles and princes to Versailles to enjoy themselves in order to watch over them and keep them out of politics.

9. In 1689, what laid the foundation for a limited, or constitutional, monarchy in England?
- **A** the Edict of Nantes
- **B** the Toleration Act
- **C** the Bill of Rights
- **D** the Stamp Act

Section 3 *(pp. 464–469)*

10. In which system does a ruler hold total power?
- **A** Absolutism
- **B** Republicanism
- **C** Enlightened absolutism
- **D** Deism

11. Who was one of the most prominent Russian rulers in the Romanov dynasty?
- **A** Frederick William the Great Elector
- **B** Philip II
- **C** Ivan IV
- **D** Peter the Great

Section 4 *(pp. 472–477)*

12. Which movement replaced the artistic Renaissance?
- **A** Baroque
- **B** Puritanism
- **C** Mannerism
- **D** Rococo

13. Elizabethan playwrights such as William Shakespeare generally wrote their plays for what social group?
- **A** Nobles
- **B** All classes
- **C** Merchants
- **D** Lower classes

Critical Thinking

Directions: Choose the best answers to the following questions.

14. How did Louis XIV control the nobles and princes?
- **A** He kept them busy with court life.
- **B** He shared his power with them.
- **C** He imprisoned them.
- **D** He made them join his military.

Base your answer to questions 15 and 16 on the map below.

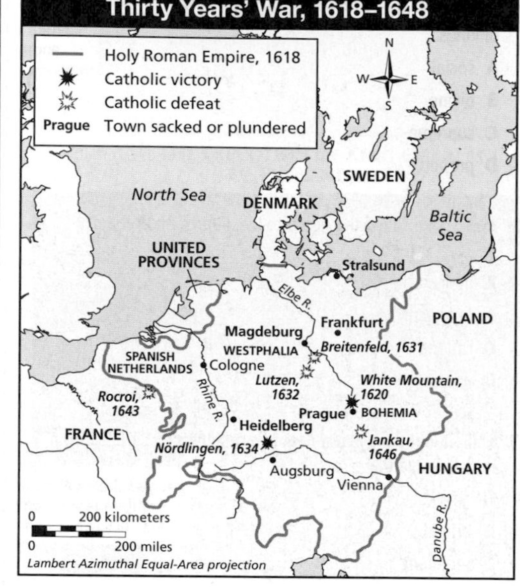

15. Which river flows nearest to Vienna?
- **A** Baltic
- **B** Elbe
- **C** Rhine
- **D** Danube

Need Extra Help?

If You Missed Questions . . .	9	10	11	12	13	14	15
Go to Page . . .	463	464	469	472	474	466	480

GO ON

15. D Students should be able to eliminate choices A, B, and C. The Baltic is a sea, and neither the Elbe nor the Rhine are close to Vienna.

TEST-TAKING TIP

For Question 15: Although students may easily be able to eliminate choice A because of prior knowledge that the Baltic is a sea, remind students of the importance of reading a map carefully to find the correct answer. If this map is read too quickly, some students may mistakenly think that the Rhine River flows past Vienna to the Hungarian border.

16. What does the map tell you about the location of towns that were sacked or plundered?

- **A** They were located near rivers.
- **B** They were located in the northern and central parts of the Holy Roman Empire.
- **C** They were located west of the Elbe River.
- **D** They were located in the southern part of the Holy Roman Empire.

17. Which of the following was an important development in sixteenth-century European culture?

- **A** Mannerism replaced the baroque movement.
- **B** El Greco completed St. Peter's Basilica.
- **C** Miguel de Cervantes wrote *Don Quixote*.
- **D** Lope de Vega wrote *Leviathan*.

Analyze the chart and answer the question that follows. Base your answer on the chart and on your knowledge of world history.

Changes Made by Peter the Great

Military and Government	Cultural
Reorganized army	Prepared first Russian book of etiquette to teach Western manners
Formed the first Russian navy	?
Divided Russia into provinces for a more effective central government	Allowed upper-class women to remove their veils and move out into society

18. What other cultural change should be added to the chart?

- **A** Commissioned a painting from El Greco
- **B** Insisted that men shave their beards
- **C** Prohibited Western customs
- **D** Allowed all women to remove their veils

Document-Based Questions

Directions: Analyze the document and answer the short-answer questions that follow the document.

Near the end of her life, Elizabeth Tudor gave her Golden Speech to Parliament. Following is an excerpt from that speech.

> *"I do assure you there is no prince that loves his subjects better, or whose love can contradict our love. There is no jewel, be it of never so rich a price, which I set before this jewel; I mean your love. For I do esteem it more than any treasure or riches. . . .*
>
> *Of myself I say this: I never was any greedy, scraping grasper, nor a strait, fast-holding Prince, nor yet a waster. My heart was never set on any worldly goods, but only for my subjects' good. What you bestow on me, I will not hoard it up, but receive it to bestow on you again. Yea, mine own properties I account yours, to be expended for your good. . . ."*

19. To whom does Elizabeth feel accountable?

20. Explain how Louis XIV of France might have disagreed with Elizabeth about expending properties for the good of her subjects.

Extended Response

21. During their rule, monarchs can either strengthen or weaken their countries. Which monarch described in this chapter do you most and least admire for how he or she governed? Support your answer with examples of actions taken by each monarch.

For additional test practice, use Self-Check Quizzes—Chapter 14 at glencoe.com.

Need Extra Help?

If You Missed Questions . . .	16	17	18	19	20	21
Go to Page . . .	480	475	469	481	464	454

STOP

Document-Based Questions

19. Elizabeth emphasizes her love for her subjects and her concern for what is best for them. Thus it would be logical to conclude that she feels accountable to her subjects.

20. Answers will vary but may include: Louis XIV of France shared authority with no one and did not believe he was accountable to anyone other than to God. Instead of sharing his properties and wealth with his subjects, Louis lived extravagantly at the expense of his subjects and nearly bankrupted his country with numerous wars.

Extended Response

21. Answers will vary but should be consistent with material presented in this chapter. For example, some students may cite William and Mary as their most admired rulers because they agreed to limits on their power. For least admired, some students may select Louis XIV for his perceived abuses of power.

16. B This question requires a careful reading of the map, map legend, and each answer choice. Choice B is correct; none of the other options match the information on the map.

17. C For this question, only choice C is a true statement. Mannerism preceded the baroque movement; Bernini completed St. Peter's Basilica; Thomas Hobbes wrote *Leviathan*.

18. B For this question, B is the only possible answer. Peter the Great lived more than a century after El Greco's time, and options C and D contradict information already in the chart.

Introduce students to chapter content and key terms by having them access the Chapter 14 Overview at glencoe.com.

Need Extra Help?

Have students refer to the pages listed if they miss any of the questions.

Using the Glencoe Web Site

Student Web Activities

Technology Product

The Glencoe Web site provides Web activities to students that reinforce and enrich chapter content. The Student Web Activities

- introduce a topic relevant to chapter content, along with a link to Web sites that provide information about the topic;
- prompt students to complete tasks specific to the activity;
- assess student comprehension of the material.

Objectives

The Student Web Activities help students

- learn online research and study skills;
- practice reading and comprehension skills.

Steps

Provide students with the following steps to complete the activities:

- Locate the Web page for the textbook being studied on the Glencoe Web site glencoe.com.
- Click on **Student Center** under the textbook title.
- In the Student Center, select a unit from the Unit Resources menu and a chapter from the Chapter Activities menu using the drop-down arrows.
- Click on the **Student Web Activities** link.
- Have students complete the activity on the page, clicking on the feature Web link for the chapter selected and answering the activity questions.

Provide students with an e-mail address to submit their answers for grading.

History ONLINE

	Student	Teacher	Parent
Beyond the Textbook	●	●	●
Chapter Overviews	●	●	●
Time Current Events	●		●
ePuzzles and Games	●		●
Concepts in Motion	●		●
Literature Connections		●	
Multi-Language Glossaries	●		●
Online Student Edition	●	●	●
Self-Check Quizzes	●		●
Student Web Activities	●		●
Study Central ™	●		●
Teaching Today		●	
Vocabulary eFlashcards	●		●
Web Activity Lesson Plans		●	

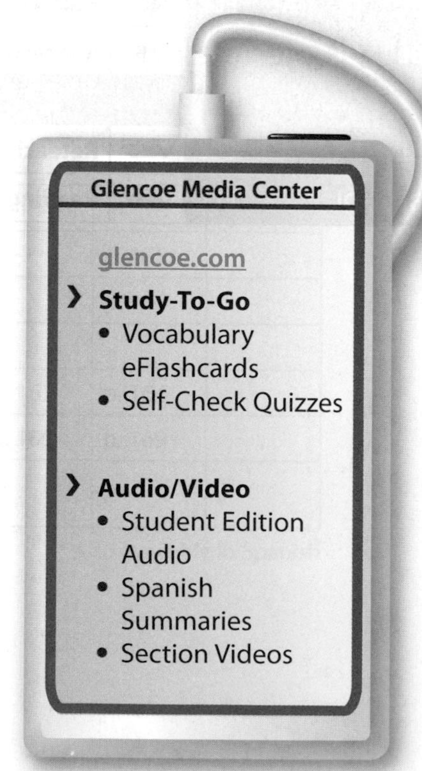

- **Timed Readings Plus in Social Studies** helps students increase their reading rate and fluency while maintaining comprehension. The 400-word passages are similar to those found on state and national assessments.
- **Reading in the Content Area: Social Studies** concentrates on six essential reading skills that help students better comprehend what they read. The book includes 75 high-interest nonfiction passages written at increasing levels of difficulty.
- **Reading Social Studies** includes strategic reading instruction and vocabulary support in Social Studies content for both ELLs and native speakers of English.

www.jamestowneducation.com

Index to National Geographic Magazine:

The following articles relate to this chapter:

- "Empty Quarter," by Donovan Webster, February 2005
- "Saving Afghan Culture," by Andrew Lawler, December 2004
- "The World of Islam," by Don Belt, January 2002

National Geographic Society Products To order the following, call National Geographic at 1-800-368-2728:

- *National Geographic Atlas of the World* (Book).

Access National Geographic's new, dynamic MapMachine Web site and other geography resources at:
www.nationalgeographic.com
www.nationalgeographic.com/maps

Biography

The following videotape program is available from Glencoe as a supplement to Chapter 15:

- Legends of the Arabian Nights (ISBN 0-76-700232-6)

To order, call Glencoe at 1-800-334-7344. To find classroom resources to accompany many of these videos, check the following home pages:

A&E Television: www.aetv.com

The History Channel: www.historychannel.com

GLENCOE BOOKLINK 3

Use this database to search more than 30,000 titles to create a customized reading list for your students.

- Reading lists can be organized by students' reading level, author, genre, theme, or area of interest.
- The database provides Degrees of Reading Power™ (DRP) and Lexile™ readability scores for all selections.
- A brief summary of each selection is included.

Leveled reading suggestions for this chapter:

For students at a Grade 8 reading level:
- ***Turkey: A Question and Answer Book,*** by Mary Englar

For students at a Grade 9 reading level:
- ***Afghanistan,*** by Gillia M. Olson

For students at a Grade 10 reading level:
- ***What Do We Know About Islam?,*** by Shahrukh Husain

For students at a Grade 11 reading level:
- ***Islam,*** by Andrew Egan

For students at a Grade 12 reading level:
- ***The Taj Mahal,*** by Lesley A. DuTemple

Introducing CHAPTER 15

Focus

MAKING CONNECTIONS
How do Muslims celebrate their beliefs?

Activate students' prior knowledge by having them brainstorm what they know about the Muslim religion. Responses may include that Muslims practice their religion in mosques and follow the teachings of the Quran, and that many Muslims travel to Makkah at least once in their lifetimes. Then discuss how many Muslims' beliefs and traditions today are the result of developments that took place during the Ottoman, Ṣafavid, and Mogul Empires. Wrap up the discussion by having students analyze similarities between the Muslim religion and other religions today.

Teach

The Big Ideas

As students study the chapter, remind them to consider the section-based Big Ideas included in each section's Guide to Reading. The **Essential Questions** in the activities below tie in to the Big Ideas and help students think about and understand important chapter concepts. In addition, the Hands-on Chapter Projects with their culminating activities relate the content from each section to the Big Ideas. These activities build on each other as students progress through the chapter. Section activities culminate in the wrap-up activity on the Visual Summary page.

CHAPTER 15

The Muslim Empires 1450–1800

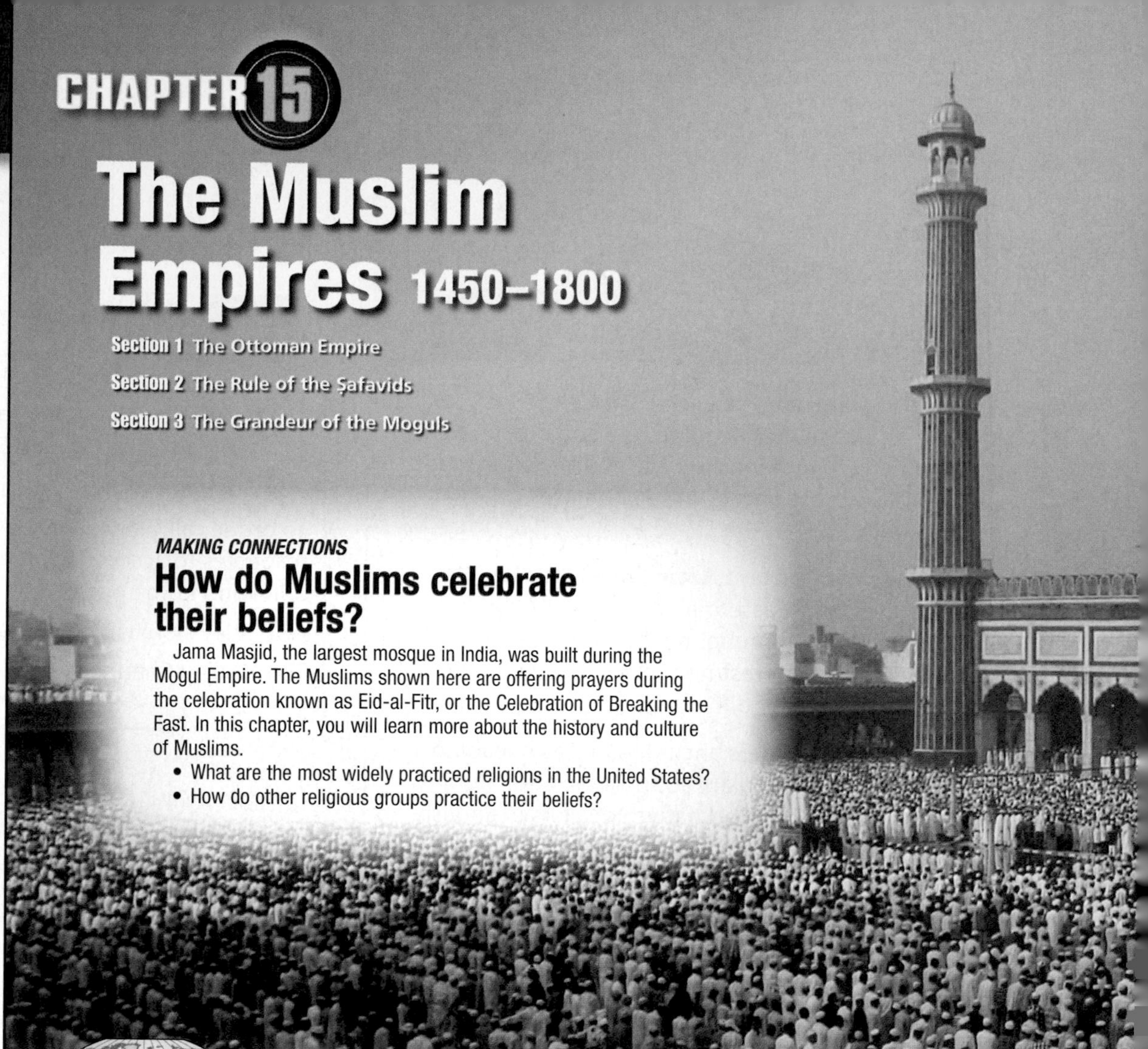

MAKING CONNECTIONS

How do Muslims celebrate their beliefs?

Jama Masjid, the largest mosque in India, was built during the Mogul Empire. The Muslims shown here are offering prayers during the celebration known as Eid-al-Fitr, or the Celebration of Breaking the Fast. In this chapter, you will learn more about the history and culture of Muslims.

- What are the most widely practiced religions in the United States?
- How do other religious groups practice their beliefs?

MUSLIM EMPIRES ▶

1453 Ottomans, led by Mehmed II, lay siege to Constantinople

1529 Ottomans are defeated at Vienna

1588 Rule of Shāh ʿAbbās begins, leading to peak of the Ṣafavid dynasty

1450 — 1500 — 1600

THE WORLD ▶

1464 The Sunni dynasty in Africa begins

1534 Henry VIII creates the Church of England

1598 Japanese unification begins

482

The Ottoman Empire

Essential Question: How could new weapons technology affect an empire's growth? *(Mastering firearms could lead to a well-armed infantry that could conquer new lands.)* Point out that in Section 1, students will learn more about Ottoman expansion. **OL**

The Rule of the Ṣafavids

Essential Question: What factors help unify an empire? *(Answers may include a common language, culture, religion, a shared history, and similar recreational pastimes.)* Point out that in Section 2, students will learn more about the role faith played in the Ṣafavid Empire. **OL**

Introducing CHAPTER 15

More About the Photo

Visual Literacy Tell students that a mosque, as shown in this photograph, is a place of worship. The Jama Majid is a type of mosque known as a "collective mosque." This means that it is a large mosque, controlled by the state, that is used for community worship and Friday prayer services. Point out that this mosque has two minarets, or tall towers. Minarets are used by muezzin, or criers, to tell people that it is time to pray. This is done five times a day.

Dinah Zike's Foldables

Dinah Zike's Foldables are three-dimensional, interactive graphic organizers that help students practice basic writing skills, review vocabulary terms, and identify main ideas. Instructions for creating and using Foldables can be found in the Appendix at the end of this book and in the *Dinah Zike's Reading and Study Skills Foldables* booklet.

History ONLINE

Introduce students to chapter content and key terms by having them access the Chapter 15 Overview at glencoe.com.

1739 Delhi is destroyed by Persians

1757 British forces, led by Sir Robert Clive, defeat the Moguls

1700 — 1800

1776 Thomas Jefferson writes the Declaration of Independence

FOLDABLES Study Organizer

Categorizing Create a Folded Table to categorize information about the Ottoman, Şafavid, and Mogul Empires. Information should include key events and rulers, religion and art, and society and culture.

Muslim Empires	Key Events and Rulers	Religion and Art	Society and Culture
Ottoman Empire			
Şafavid Empire			
Mogul Empire			

History ONLINE

Chapter Overview—Visit glencoe.com to preview Chapter 15.

SECTION 3

The Grandeur of the Moguls

Essential Question: How does art reflect a country or an empire's culture? *(Art depicts what is important to a nation.)* Point out that in Section 3, students will learn more about how Mogul culture reflected the heritage of its people. **OL**

Focus

Bellringer
Daily Focus Transparency 15.1

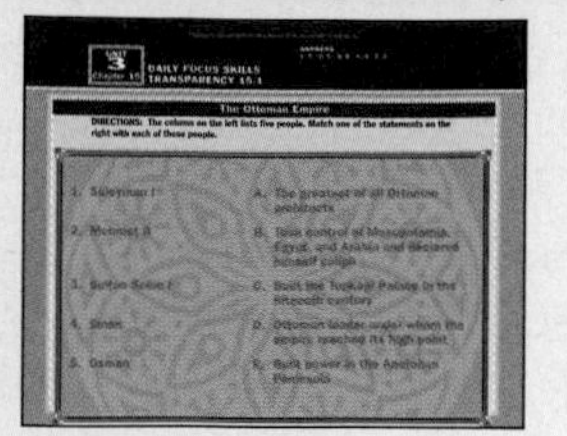

GUIDE TO READING

Answers to Graphic:

Sultan → Ruling Class → Merchants → Artisans, Peasants, Pastoral Peoples

Section Spotlight Video

To generate student interest and provide a springboard for class discussion, access the Chapter 15, Section 1 video at glencoe.com or on the video DVD.

SECTION 1

The Ottoman Empire

GUIDE TO READING

The BIG Idea
Competition Among Countries
The Ottoman Empire grew strong as it expanded its borders.

Content Vocabulary
- janissaries *(p. 484)*
- pashas *(p. 486)*
- gunpowder empire *(p. 486)*
- sultan *(p. 486)*
- harem *(p. 486)*
- grand vizier *(p. 487)*
- ulema *(p. 487)*

Academic Vocabulary
- expand *(p. 484)*
- domain *(p. 486)*

People and Places
- Anatolian Peninsula *(p. 484)*
- Bosporus *(p. 484)*
- Dardanelles *(p. 484)*
- Sea of Marmara *(p. 484)*
- Mehmed II *(p. 485)*
- Constantinople *(p. 485)*
- Sultan Selim I *(p. 485)*
- Jerusalem *(p. 486)*
- Makkah *(p. 486)*
- Madinah *(p. 486)*
- Sinan *(p. 488)*

Reading Strategy
Organizing Information Create a chart to show the structure of the Ottoman society. List groups in order of importance.

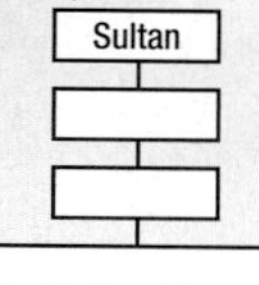

At its high point under Süleyman the Magnificent, the Ottoman Empire consisted of lands in western Asia, North Africa, and Europe. The Ottomans contributed a unique architectural design to world art, as seen in their magnificent mosques. They also practiced religious tolerance, which allowed subjects to follow their own religion.

Rise of the Ottoman Turks

MAIN IDEA Over a span of three hundred years, the Ottomans conquered the Byzantine Empire and expanded into western Asia, Africa, and Europe to create the Ottoman Empire.

HISTORY & YOU What would you do if you were asked to defend your city or hometown against invaders that had more advanced weapons? Learn how the Ottomans laid siege to the city of Constantinople.

In the late thirteenth century, a new group of Turks under their leader Osman began to build power in the northwest corner of the **Anatolian Peninsula.** In the early fourteenth century, the Osman Turks began to **expand** and began the Ottoman dynasty.

Expansion of the Empire

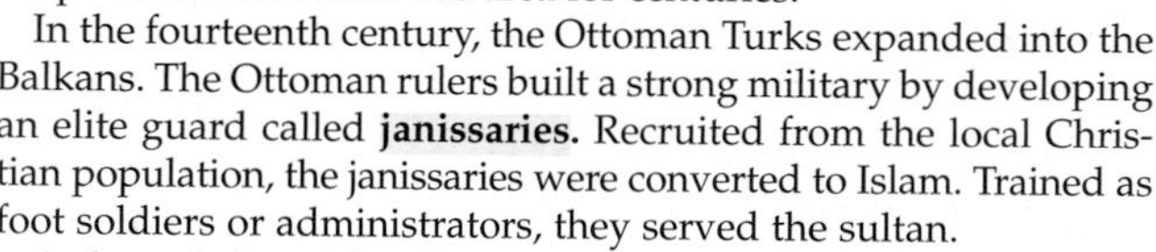

The Ottomans expanded westward and eventually controlled the **Bosporus** and the **Dardanelles.** These two straits (narrow passageways), separated by the **Sea of Marmara,** connect the Black Sea and the Aegean Sea, which leads to the Mediterranean. The Byzantine Empire had controlled this area for centuries.

In the fourteenth century, the Ottoman Turks expanded into the Balkans. The Ottoman rulers built a strong military by developing an elite guard called **janissaries.** Recruited from the local Christian population, the janissaries were converted to Islam. Trained as foot soldiers or administrators, they served the sultan.

As knowledge of firearms spread in the late fourteenth century, the Ottomans began to master the new technology. The janissaries, trained as a well-armed infantry, were able to spread Ottoman control in the Balkans. With their new forces, the Ottomans defeated the Serbs at the Battle of Kosovo in 1389. During the 1390s, they advanced northward and annexed Bulgaria.

Resource Manager

R Reading Strategies	C Critical Thinking	D Differentiated Instruction	W Writing Support	S Skill Practice
Teacher Edition • Sequencing Info., p. 486 • Summarizing, p. 487 **Additional Resources** • Guid. Read. Act., URB p. 162 • Read. Ess. & Note-Taking Guide, p. 163	**Teacher Edition** • Contrasting, p. 488 • Making Inferences, p. 489 **Additional Resources** • Hist. & Geo. Act., URB p. 143 • People in World Hist. Act., URB p. 153 • Section Quiz, p. 181	**Teacher Edition** • ELL, p. 485 **Additional Resources** • English Learner Act., URB p. 135	**Teacher Edition** • Expository Writing, pp. 487, 488 **Additional Resources** • Linking Past/Present Act., URB p. 152 • World Art & Music Act., URB p. 157 • Writer's Guidebook, p. 43	**Teacher Edition** • Using Geo. Skills, p. 485 **Additional Resources** • Hist. Analysis Skills Act., URB p. 132

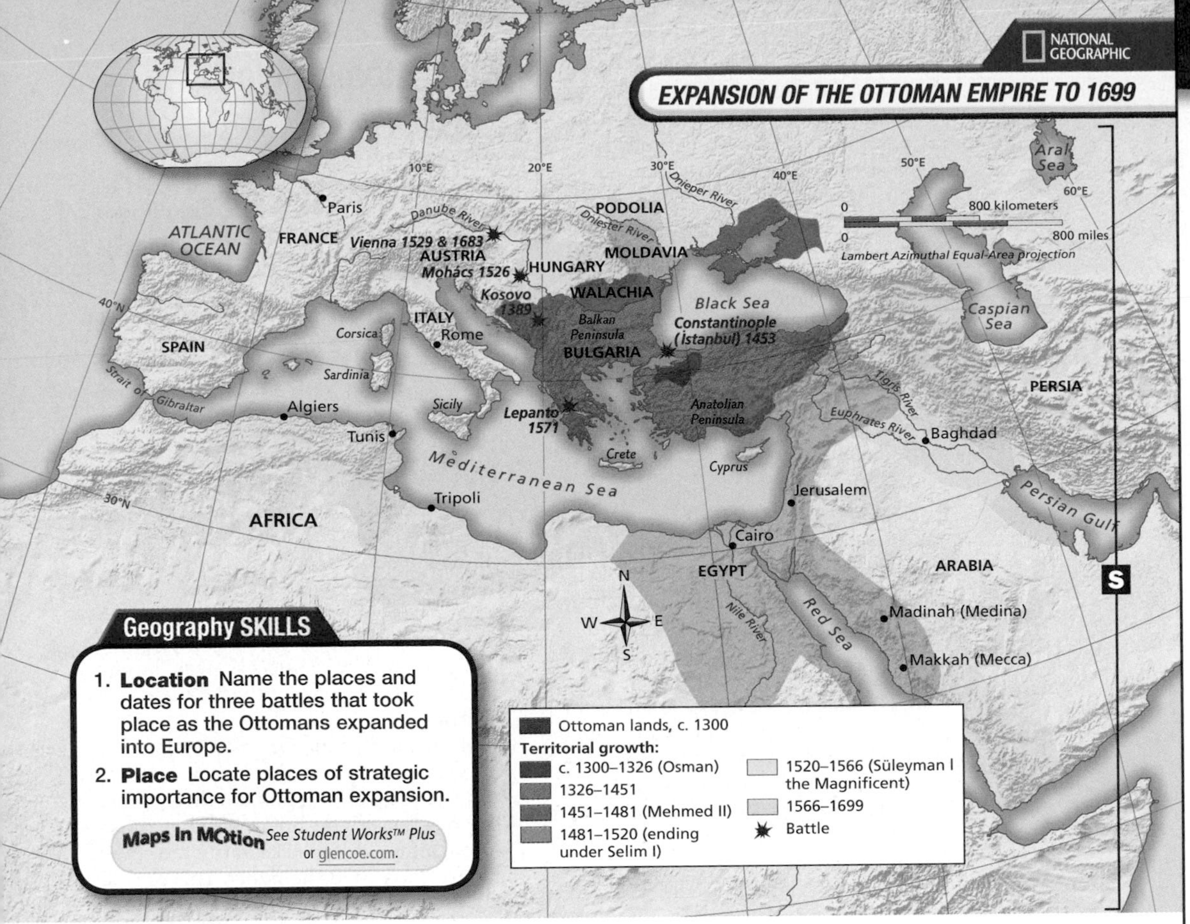

Geography SKILLS

1. **Location** Name the places and dates for three battles that took place as the Ottomans expanded into Europe.
2. **Place** Locate places of strategic importance for Ottoman expansion.

Maps In MOtion See Student Works™ Plus or glencoe.com.

The Byzantine Empire

Over the next three hundred years, Ottoman rule expanded to areas in western Asia, North Africa, and Europe.

Under the leadership of **Mehmed II,** the Ottomans moved to end the Byzantine Empire. With eighty thousand troops ranged against only seven thousand defenders, Mehmed laid siege to Constantinople.

The attack began on April 6, 1453, as the Ottomans bombarded the city with massive cannons hurling stone balls weighing up to 1,200 pounds (545 kg) each. The Byzantines took their final stand behind the walls along the western edge of the city. They fought desperately for almost two months to save their city. Finally, on May 29, the walls were breached, and Ottoman soldiers poured into the city.

The Byzantine emperor died in the final battle, and a great three-day sack of the city began. When Mehmed II saw the ruin and destruction, he lamented, "What a city we have given over to plunder and destruction."

Western Asia and Africa

With their new capital at **Constantinople** (later renamed İstanbul), the Ottoman Turks dominated the Balkans and the Anatolian Peninsula. From 1514 to 1517, **Sultan Selim I** took control of Mesopotamia, Egypt, and Arabia—the original heartland of Islam. Through these conquests, Selim I was now in control of several of Islam's holy cities.

Teach

S Skill Practice

Using Geography Skills Ask: How much territory did the Ottoman Empire gain between 1451 and 1566? *(The empire more than tripled its size during this period.)* **OL**

D Differentiated Instruction

English Language Learners Ask students if they are familiar with the term "byzantine" and discuss its use today. Explain that it can refer to intrigue or something that is highly complicated. For example, "It was a byzantine plot." **ELL**

Geography SKILLS

Answers:

1. Three of the following battles: Kosovo, 1389, Mohács, 1526, Vienna, 1529 and 1683, Lepanto, 1571
2. Constantinople provides access to and from Black Sea; the Balkan Peninsula provides access to Europe; the Mediterranean

Comparing and Contrasting

Objective: Compare and contrast Constantinople and present-day İstanbul.
Focus: Have students locate the city on a map.
Teach: Show how the city was at the crossroads of Europe and Asia.
Assess: Ask students to compare and contrast the city in the Ottoman Empire and today.
Close: Have students create a poster of the city then and now.

Differentiated Instruction Strategies

BL Have students find images of the city from earlier times to today.

AL Ask students to create a database of information on the population, culture, and government of the city from the days of the Ottoman Empire to the present.

ELL Ask students to draw a political map of the region.

Differentiated Instruction

History and Geography Activity, URB p. 143

R Reading Strategy

Sequencing Information

Ask: What sequence of events led to the expansion of the Ottoman Empire after the Ottomans seized Constantinople? *(They conquered Walachia, and then advanced into Hungary, Austria, and the western Mediterranean.)* **OL**

Did You Know?

Before the fourteenth century, warriors such as the Mongols with their cavalry and crossbows had the advantage in battle. Then gunpowder revolutionized warfare and cannons became the decisive weapons. Because these weapons required technology and money, they were only available to large, wealthy empires. This affected the development of other cultures that were emerging in the areas controlled by the Ottomans.

✓Reading Check

Answer: Constantinople

These cities included **Jerusalem, Makkah** (Mecca), and **Madinah** (Medina). Selim declared himself the new caliph. That is, he was the defender of the faith and the successor to Muhammad. After their victories in the east, Ottoman forces spent the next few years advancing westward along the African coast almost to the Strait of Gibraltar.

The Ottomans were Muslims. Where possible, they administered their conquered regions through local rulers. The central government appointed officials, or **pashas,** who collected taxes, maintained law and order, and were directly responsible to the sultan's court in Constantinople.

Expansion into Europe

After capturing Constantinople in 1453, the Ottoman Turks tried to complete their conquest of the Balkans. They took the Romanian territory of Walachia, but the Hungarians stopped their advance up the Danube Valley.

Under Süleyman I, whose reign began in 1520, the Ottomans advanced anew up the **R** Danube, seized Belgrade, and won a major victory over the Hungarians in 1526 at the Battle of Mohács (MOH•hach) on the Danube. They then conquered most of Hungary and moved into Austria. They advanced to Vienna, where they were defeated in 1529. At the same time, they advanced into the western Mediterranean until the Spanish destroyed a large Ottoman fleet at Lepanto in 1571 (see Chapter 14).

During the first half of the seventeenth century, the Ottoman Empire in eastern Europe remained a "sleeping giant." Occupied with internal problems, the Ottomans kept the status quo in eastern Europe. However, in the second half of the seventeenth century, they again went on the offensive.

By mid-1683, the Ottomans had laid siege to Vienna. Repulsed by a European army, the Ottomans retreated and were pushed out of Hungary. Although they retained the core of their empire, the Ottoman Turks would never again be a threat to central Europe.

History ONLINE
Student Web Activity—
Visit glencoe.com and complete the activity on the Ottoman Empire.

✓Reading Check **Identifying** What was the capital of the new Ottoman Empire?

The Ottoman World

MAIN IDEA The Ottomans created a strong empire with religious tolerance and artistic achievements.

HISTORY & YOU What jobs do people have in your city or county government? Learn how the Ottomans trained bureaucrats in a palace school.

Under the rule of the sultans, the Ottoman Empire grew strong. Religious tolerance and unique architectural designs, as seen in the mosques, were among the Ottoman Empire's strengths and contributions.

The Nature of Ottoman Rule

Like the other Muslim empires in Persia and India, the Ottoman Empire is often labeled a "**gunpowder empire.**" Gunpowder empires were formed by outside conquerors who unified the regions that they conquered. As the name suggests, such an empire's success was largely based on its mastery of the technology of firearms.

At the head of the Ottoman system was the **sultan,** who was the supreme authority in both a political and a military sense. The position of the sultan was hereditary. A son, although not necessarily the eldest, always succeeded the father. This practice led to struggles over succession upon the death of individual sultans. The losers in these struggles were often executed.

The Imperial Sultans

As the empire expanded, the status and prestige of the sultan increased. The position took on the trappings of imperial rule. A centralized administrative system was adopted, and the sultan became increasingly isolated from his people.

The private **domain** of the sultan was called the **harem** ("sacred place"). Here, the sultan and his wives resided. Often a sultan chose four wives as his favorites.

When a son became a sultan, his mother became known as the queen mother and acted as a major adviser to the throne. This tradition often gave considerable power to the queen mother in the affairs of state.

Differentiated Instruction

Leveled Activities

BL Guided Reading Activity, URB p. 162

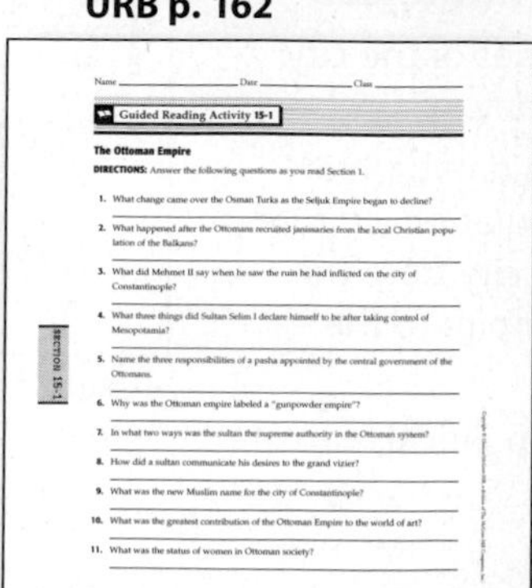

Guided Reading Activity 15-1

The Ottoman Empire

OL People in World History Activity, URB p. 153

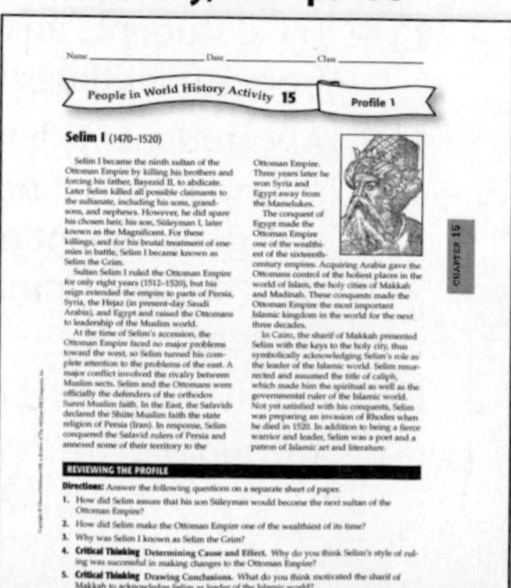

People in World History Activity 15 — Profile 1

Selim I (1470–1520)

AL Linking Past and Present Activity, URB p. 152

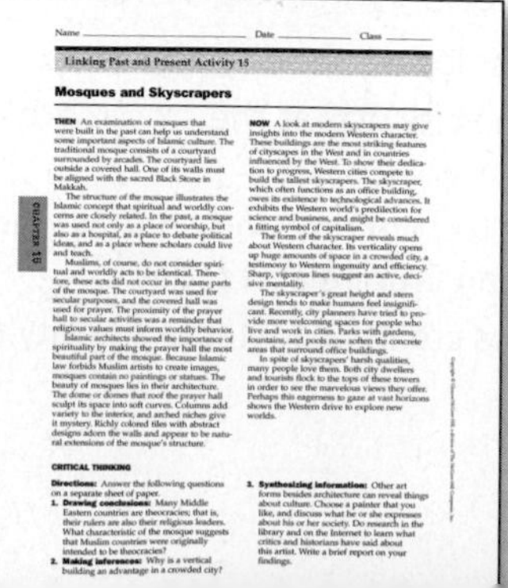

Linking Past and Present Activity 15

Mosques and Skyscrapers

ELL English Learner Activity, URB p. 135

English Learner Activity 15

The Ottoman Empire

PRIMARY SOURCE / HISTORY & ARTS

Topkapi Palace

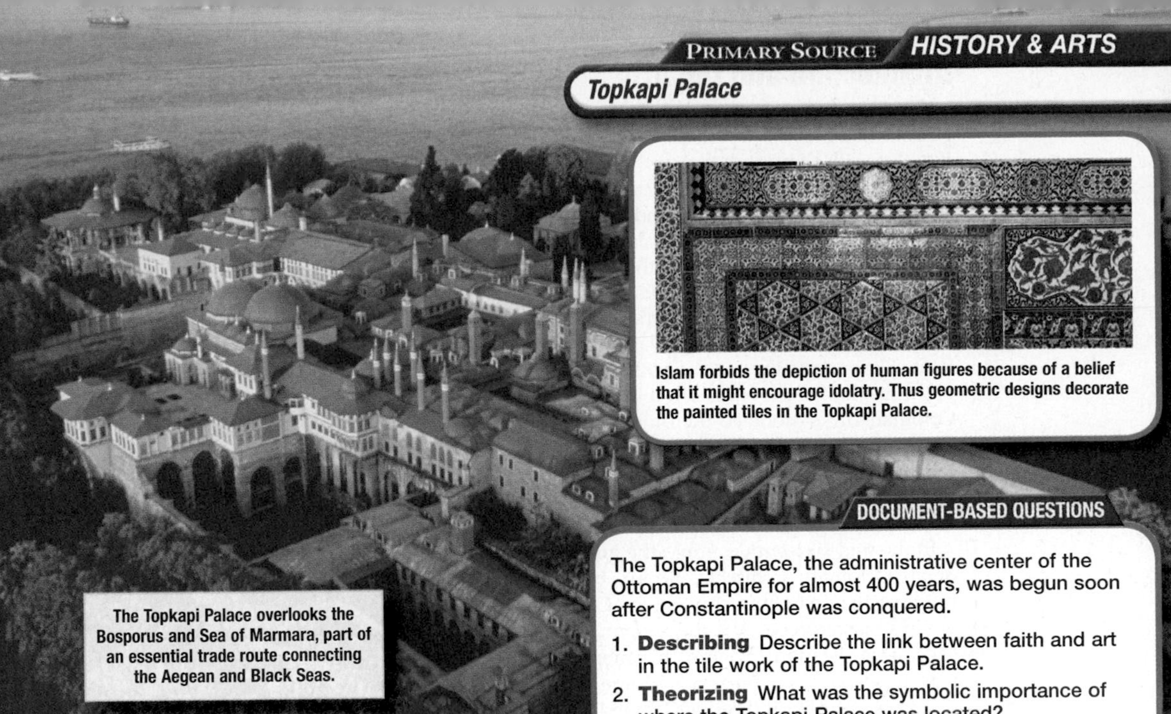

Islam forbids the depiction of human figures because of a belief that it might encourage idolatry. Thus geometric designs decorate the painted tiles in the Topkapi Palace.

The Topkapi Palace overlooks the Bosporus and Sea of Marmara, part of an essential trade route connecting the Aegean and Black Seas.

DOCUMENT-BASED QUESTIONS

The Topkapi Palace, the administrative center of the Ottoman Empire for almost 400 years, was begun soon after Constantinople was conquered.

1. **Describing** Describe the link between faith and art in the tile work of the Topkapi Palace.
2. **Theorizing** What was the symbolic importance of where the Topkapi Palace was located?

The sultan controlled his bureaucracy through an imperial council that met four days a week. The **grand vizier,** a chief minister who carried the main burdens of the state, led the meetings of the council. During the council meetings, the sultan sat behind a screen, overhearing the proceedings, and then privately indicated his desires to the grand vizier.

The empire was divided into provinces and districts, each governed by officials. They were assisted by bureaucrats who had been trained in a palace school for officials in İstanbul. The sultan gave land to the senior officials. They were then responsible for collecting taxes and supplying armies for the empire from this landed area.

The Topkapi ("iron gate") Palace in İstanbul, the new name for Constantinople, was the center of the sultan's power. The palace was built in the fifteenth century by Mehmed II. Like Versailles in France, it had an administrative purpose and served as the private residence of the ruler and his family. W

Religion in the Ottoman World

Like most Turkic-speaking peoples in the Anatolian Peninsula and throughout western Asia, the Ottomans were Sunni Muslims (see Chapter 6). Ottoman sultans had claimed the title of caliph since the early sixteenth century. In theory, they were responsible for guiding the flock and maintaining Islamic law. In practice, the sultans gave their religious duties to a group of religious advisers known as the **ulema.** This group administered the legal system and schools for educating Muslims. Islamic law and customs were applied to all Muslims in the empire. R

The Ottoman system was generally tolerant of non-Muslims, who made up a significant minority within the empire. Non-Muslims paid a tax, but they were allowed to practice their religion or to convert to Islam. Most people in the European areas of the empire remained Christian. In some areas, however, such as present-day Bosnia, large numbers of non-Muslims converted to the Islamic faith.

W Writing Support

Expository Writing Have students do research to find pictures of official residences in countries throughout history. These could include Versailles and the Forbidden City. Have students write an essay comparing them to the Topkapi Palace. Discuss what these structures convey about the cultures and systems of government that created them. **OL**

R Reading Strategy

Summarizing **Ask:** What religious duties did the sultans have in their role as caliphs? *(In theory, they were responsible for guiding Muslims and maintaining Islamic law. In practice, they turned over religious duties to the ulema.)* **BL**

DOCUMENT-BASED QUESTIONS

Answers:

1. Islamic artists were discouraged from depicting human figures in art; instead, they developed geometric or floral patterns.
2. location of palace upon essential water route between Aegean and Black Seas symbolized Ottoman dominance of region

Hands-On Chapter Project Step 1

Designing an Art Tile

Pairs of students will design and create a tile representing one of the Muslim empires.

Step 1: Finding Tile Designs

Essential Question: How are tile designs symbolic representations of life in the Muslim empires?

Directions: Write the Big Idea on the board, and tell pairs of students to think about how the arts flourished in the Muslim empires as they expanded and grew stronger. Tell pairs to look for examples of Islamic art in the text. Then have students conduct research to find additional examples. Suggest that students find images of mosques or other buildings that would have elaborate ornamental designs.

Summarizing: Allow time for pairs to share their findings. Students will use the images to generate ideas for their own designs in Section 2. **OL**

(Chapter Project is continued in Section 2.)

W **Writing Support**

Expository Writing Ask students to research Sinan, the foremost architect of the Ottoman Empire. Students should write biographies of Sinan that include information on his training, as well as his most famous mosques—the Sehzade Mosque and the Süleymaniye Mosque in İstanbul, and the Selim Mosque in Edirne. **AL**

C **Critical Thinking**

Contrasting Ask: How did the position of women in the Ottoman Empire contrast to that of women in other Muslim societies? *(Women could own and inherit property, could not be forced into marriage, and could obtain divorces.)* **OL**

✓Reading Check

Answer: mosques, pottery, textiles, rugs, jewelry, arms, and armor

PEOPLE in HISTORY

Answer: His son Selim II proved to be a poor ruler, and this contributed to the empire's decline.

Architecture and the Arts

The Ottoman sultans were enthusiastic patrons of the arts. The period from Mehmed II to the early eighteenth century witnessed a flourishing production of pottery; rugs, silk, and other textiles; jewelry; and arms and armor. All of these adorned the palaces of the rulers. Artists came from all over the world to compete for the sultans' generous rewards.

By far the greatest contribution of the Ottoman Empire to world art was in architecture, especially the magnificent mosques of the last half of the sixteenth century. The Ottoman Turks modeled their mosques on the open floor plan of Constantinople's Byzantine church of Hagia Sophia, creating a prayer hall with an open central area under one large dome.

W In the mid-sixteenth century, the greatest of all Ottoman architects, **Sinan,** began building the first of his 81 mosques. One of Sinan's masterpieces was the Suleymaniye Mosque in İstanbul. Each of his mosques was topped by an imposing dome, and often the entire building was framed with four towers, or minarets.

PEOPLE in HISTORY

Süleyman the Magnificent
1495–1566 Ottoman Ruler

The Ottoman ruler Süleyman held absolute power and the right of life or death over his subjects. Yet he was known as *Kanuni*, the Lawgiver, who protected the powerless among his people. Upon visiting his empire, a Venetian ambassador reported, "I know of no State which is happier than this one. It is furnished with all God's gifts. . . ." Süleyman was skilled in crafts as well as in government and war. He supported the arts and built public baths, bridges, and grand mosque complexes. However, this educated man would be forced to kill two of his sons and even his grandsons to avoid civil war and preserve the throne for his son Selim II. His choice could have been better. Known as the Drunkard, Selim II left the running of the state to his advisers, and many date the slow decline of the empire to his reign. **How did Süleyman's choice of a successor affect the Ottoman Empire?**

The sixteenth century also witnessed the flourishing of textiles and rugs. The Byzantine emperor Justinian had introduced silk cultivation to the West in the sixth century. Under the Ottomans, the silk industry resurfaced. Factories produced silks for wall hangings, sofa covers, and especially court costumes. Rugs were a peasant industry. The rugs were made of wool and cotton in villages from different regions. Each village boasted its own distinctive designs and color schemes.

Society and the Role of Women

The subjects of the Ottoman Empire were divided by occupation. In addition to the ruling class, there were four main occupational groups: peasants, artisans, merchants, and pastoral peoples—nomadic herders. Peasants farmed land that the state leased to them.

Ultimate ownership of all land resided with the sultan. Artisans were organized according to craft guilds. Each guild provided financial services, social security, and training to its members. Outside the ruling elite, merchants were the most privileged class in Ottoman society. They were largely exempt from government regulations and taxes and were able, in many cases, to amass large fortunes. Pastoral peoples were placed in a separate group with their own regulations and laws.

Technically, women in the Ottoman Empire were subject to the same restrictions as women in other Muslim societies. However, their position was somewhat better. As applied in the Ottoman Empire, Islamic law was more tolerant in defining the legal position of women. This relatively tolerant attitude was probably due to Turkish traditions that regarded women as **C** almost equal to men. For instance, women were allowed to own and inherit property. They could not be forced into marriage and, in certain cases, were permitted to seek divorce. Women often gained considerable power within the palace. In a few instances, women even served as senior officials, such as governors of provinces.

✓Reading Check **Identifying** What did the Ottomans contribute to world art?

Extending the Content

Süleyman the Magnificent Called "the Magnificent" by Europeans who both feared and admired him, Süleyman I was a brilliant sixteenth-century military strategist who raised the Ottoman Empire to the height of its glory—more than doubling the landholdings he inherited from his father. During his 46-year reign (1520–1566), he personally led his armies on 13 campaigns, encouraged the growth of architecture and the fine arts, and played a key role in European politics of the day. Yet in spite of his many achievements, Süleyman also endured great tragedy—driven to execute not only his dearest friend but also two of his own sons. **Ask:** What is the significance of Europeans calling him "Magnificent," while his people called him "Lawgiver"? *(Süleyman's people considered him to be a fair and just ruler; Europeans both feared and admired him.)* **OL**

Problems in the Ottoman Empire

MAIN IDEA After reaching its high point under Süleyman the Magnificent, the Ottoman Empire began to disintegrate.

HISTORY & YOU Have you heard a parent or teacher voice disapproval of a trend they felt was bad? Learn how some sultans tried to counter trends they believed were harmful to their country.

The Ottoman Empire reached its high point under Süleyman I. (He was called "the Magnificent" by Europeans who both feared and admired him.) It may also have been during Süleyman's rule (1520–1566) that problems began to occur, however. Having executed his two most able sons on suspicion of treason, Süleyman was succeeded by his only surviving son, Selim II.

The problems of the Ottoman Empire did not become visible until 1699. This is when the empire began to lose some of its territory. However, signs of internal disintegration had already appeared at the beginning of the 1600s.

Changes in Government

After the death of Süleyman, sultans became less involved in government. They allowed their ministers to exercise more power. The training of officials declined, and senior positions were increasingly assigned to the sons or daughters of elites. Members of the elite soon formed a privileged group seeking wealth and power. The central bureaucracy lost its links with rural areas. Local officials grew corrupt, and taxes rose. Constant wars depleted the imperial treasury. Corruption and palace intrigue grew.

Cultural Changes

Another sign of change within the empire was the exchange of Western and Ottoman ideas and customs. Officials and merchants began to imitate the habits and lifestyles of Europeans. They wore European clothes and bought Western furniture and art objects. Europeans borrowed Ottoman military technology and decorated their homes with tiles, tulips, pottery, and rugs. During the sixteenth and seventeenth centuries, coffee was introduced to Ottoman society and spread to Europe. **C**

Some sultans attempted to counter this exchange. One sultan in the early seventeenth century issued a decree outlawing both coffee and tobacco. He even began to patrol the streets of İstanbul at night. If he caught any of his subjects in immoral or illegal acts, he had them immediately executed.

✓Reading Check **Summarizing** What changes ultimately led to the disintegration of the Ottoman Empire?

SECTION 1 REVIEW

Vocabulary

1. **Explain** the significance of: Anatolian Peninsula, expand, Bosporus, Dardanelles, Sea of Marmara, janissaries, Mehmed II, Constantinople, Sultan Selim I, Jerusalem, Makkah, Madinah, pashas, gunpowder empire, sultan, domain, harem, grand vizier, ulema, Sinan.

Main Ideas

2. **Discuss** how superior weaponry aided the Ottoman siege of Constantinople.
3. **Identify** the four main occupational groups in the Ottoman Empire.
4. **Summarize** the contributions of Mehmed II, Selim I, and Süleyman I to the Ottoman Empire, using a chart like the one below.

Ruler	Contributions	Effect on Empire
Mehmed II		
Selim I		
Süleyman I		

Critical Thinking

5. **The BIG Idea** **Drawing Inferences** Describe the organization of Ottoman government and explain why it was effective.
6. **Evaluating** Evaluate how the problems in the Ottoman Empire may have begun during the reign of Süleyman the Magnificent.
7. **Analyzing Visuals** Examine the image of Topkapi Palace on page 487. What typical feature of the architect Sinan do you see?

Writing About History

8. **Expository Writing** The Ottoman Empire was considered a "gunpowder empire." Research the history of gunpowder and write an essay explaining how the Ottomans acquired it. What impact did this acquisition have on the expansion of the Ottoman Empire? Use both primary and secondary sources.

History ONLINE
For help with the concepts in this section of *Glencoe World History*, go to glencoe.com and click Study Central™.

C Critical Thinking

Making Inferences **Ask:** Why did some sultans try to stop the exchange of Western and Ottoman ideas and customs? *(They may have felt threatened by Western ideas and customs; they may have been trying to preserve their own culture.)* **OL**

✓Reading Check

Answer: Following Süleyman's death, the training of officials declined, the central bureaucracy lost links to rural areas, corruption grew, and taxes rose.

Assess

History ONLINE

Study Central provides summaries, interactive games, and online graphic organizers to help students review content.

Close

Discussing Have students discuss which achievement of the Ottoman Empire they consider the most important and why. **OL**

SECTION 1 REVIEW

Answers

1. Definitions for the vocabulary words are found in the section and the Glossary.
2. They mastered new technology of firearms and gunpowder, and bombarded Constantinople with massive cannons that hurled stone balls weighing up to 1,200 pounds.
3. peasants, artisans, merchants, pastoral peoples
4. **Mehmed II:** captured Constantinople, gave empire dominance over Balkans and Anatolian Peninsula. **Selim I:** captured Mesopotamia, Egypt, Arabia, North Africa; gave empire control of holy cities. **Süleyman I:** led attacks on Europe, Europeans defeated Ottomans
5. sultan controlled government through imperial council; grand vizier led the council; empire divided into provinces and districts governed by officials; bureaucracy helped administration of government
6. He executed his two most able sons on suspicion of treason.
7. domes and minarets
8. Answers will vary. Students' work should reflect outside research.

Geography & History

Focus

Lead a preview of this feature for students. As students look at the maps and images, discuss the following questions:

- How is the location of Constantinople different from that of Rome or Naples?
- Why do you think Constantinople was such a strong and successful city for over 1,000 years?
- Why do you think Mehmet II renamed the city?

Teach

C Critical Thinking

Analyzing Information Ask: Based on the map, why was it likely that Constantinople would fall to the Ottoman Empire? *(It was surrounded by the Ottoman Empire.)* **OL**

S Skill Practice

Using Geography Skills Ask: What is the approximate distance from Constantinople to Sofia? *(350 miles)* **BL**

Additional Support

NATIONAL GEOGRAPHIC GEOGRAPHY & HISTORY

İstanbul linked the European and Asian halves of the Ottoman Empire. ▶

◀ Roman Emperor Constantine founded Constantinople in 330.

Activity: Economics Connection

Evaluating Trade Patterns Have students focus on Constantinople's location on the map. Note Constantinople's expanded market advantage in having access to both the Mediterranean and Black seas. Discuss why water routes were so important to traders, citing the advantages of ocean and river routes over land routes in terms of the amount of time it took to get to market, the difficulty of the trip, and the amount of goods that could be carried. Have students work in small groups to determine trade patterns in their region. **Ask:** What are the most common forms of transportation and where are the trade centers of the region? Each group should draw a map of the area and indicate with colors and a key the major trade routes, centers, the goods traded in the region, and geographic features affecting trade. Have groups display their maps and discuss how geography has affected trade in the region. **OL**

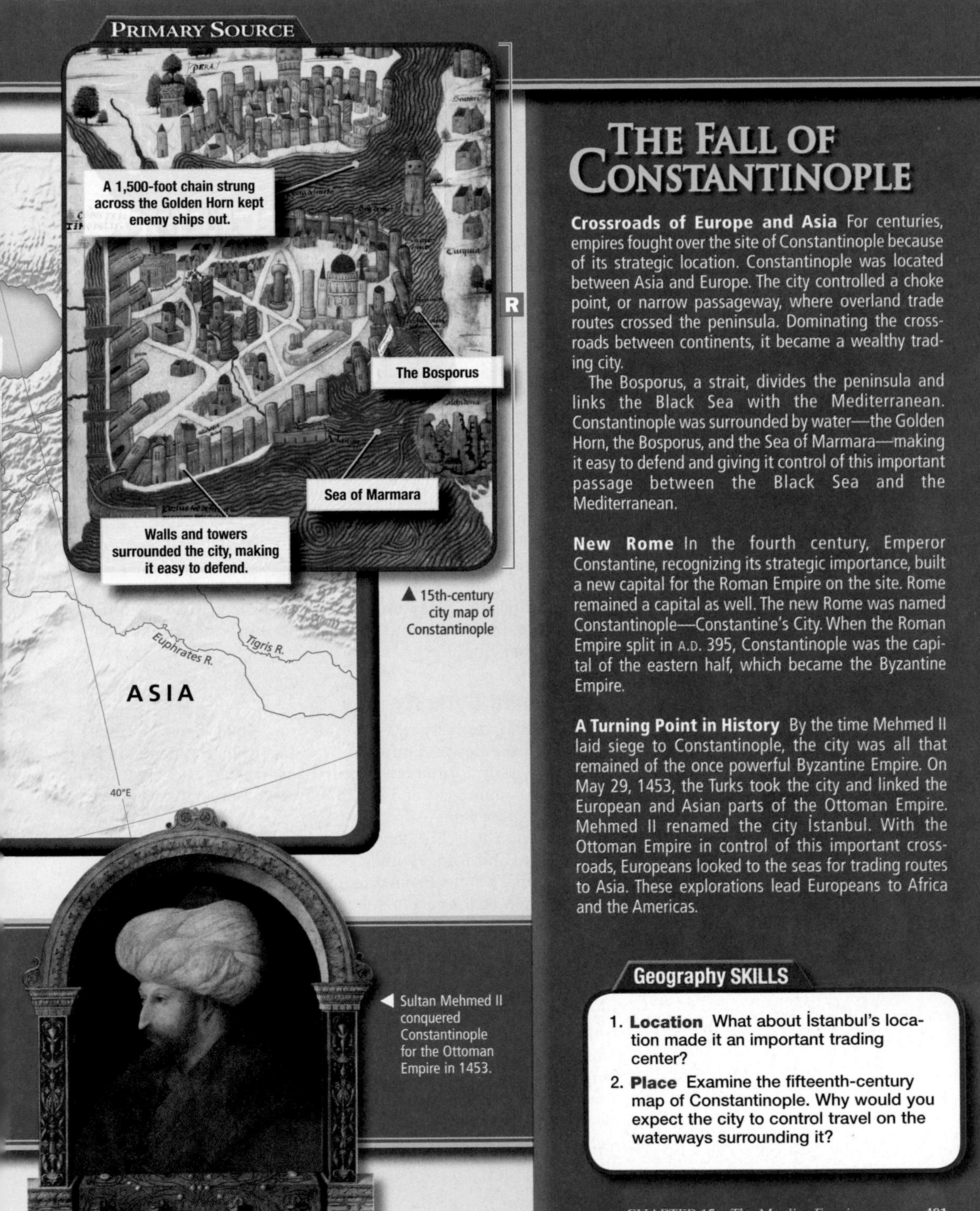

▲ 15th-century city map of Constantinople

◀ Sultan Mehmed II conquered Constantinople for the Ottoman Empire in 1453.

NATIONAL GEOGRAPHIC

GEOGRAPHY & HISTORY

The Fall of Constantinople

Crossroads of Europe and Asia For centuries, empires fought over the site of Constantinople because of its strategic location. Constantinople was located between Asia and Europe. The city controlled a choke point, or narrow passageway, where overland trade routes crossed the peninsula. Dominating the crossroads between continents, it became a wealthy trading city.

The Bosporus, a strait, divides the peninsula and links the Black Sea with the Mediterranean. Constantinople was surrounded by water—the Golden Horn, the Bosporus, and the Sea of Marmara—making it easy to defend and giving it control of this important passage between the Black Sea and the Mediterranean.

New Rome In the fourth century, Emperor Constantine, recognizing its strategic importance, built a new capital for the Roman Empire on the site. Rome remained a capital as well. The new Rome was named Constantinople—Constantine's City. When the Roman Empire split in A.D. 395, Constantinople was the capital of the eastern half, which became the Byzantine Empire.

A Turning Point in History By the time Mehmed II laid siege to Constantinople, the city was all that remained of the once powerful Byzantine Empire. On May 29, 1453, the Turks took the city and linked the European and Asian parts of the Ottoman Empire. Mehmed II renamed the city İstanbul. With the Ottoman Empire in control of this important crossroads, Europeans looked to the seas for trading routes to Asia. These explorations lead Europeans to Africa and the Americas.

Geography SKILLS

1. **Location** What about İstanbul's location made it an important trading center?
2. **Place** Examine the fifteenth-century map of Constantinople. Why would you expect the city to control travel on the waterways surrounding it?

R Reading Strategy

Reading Primary Sources

Ask: How does the fifteenth-century map illustrate the military defenses of Constantinople? *(It shows walls and towers built for defense, the surrounding waters, and the chain used to protect against enemy ships.)* OL

Assess/Close

Ask pairs of students to work together to summarize reasons Constantinople was a strong and important city, and reasons it was finally taken.

Geography SKILLS

Answers:

1. It was at the center of both land and sea trade routes.
2. The waterways were narrow and military towers gave control of shipping beneath them.

Extending the Content

The Rise of İstanbul Constantinople had managed to defend itself against attackers for centuries. But the weakness of the Byzantine Empire meant it no longer controlled the area around the city. Mehmed II built two forts a few miles from the city walls, which controlled travel on the Bosporus and isolated the city during the siege. When the city finally fell, it was nearly deserted. Renamed İstanbul, after a Greek phrase meaning "in the city," Mehmed II quickly set out to repopulate and rebuild what would become the political, cultural, and economic center of the Ottoman Empire. He invited the city's former inhabitants to return, as well as Christians, Jews, and Muslims from other conquered territories. The conquering army led the first of a series of restoration and beautification projects, which included the repair of old buildings and the construction of new roads, bridges, aqueducts, mosques, palaces, monuments, fountains, and baths.

Focus

Bellringer

Daily Focus Transparency 15.2

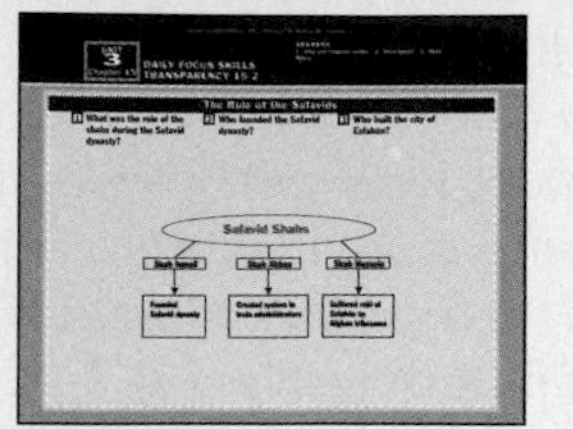

GUIDE TO READING

Answers to Graphic:

Ottoman Empire: Ruled by sultan; Sunni Muslims; attempted to conquer central Europe

Both: Conquered surrounding territory; strong military used latest weapons; Muslims; encouraged trade and arts

Ṣafavid Empire: Ruled by shah; Shia Muslims; allied with European states against Ottomans

Section Spotlight Video

To generate student interest and provide a springboard for class discussion, access the Chapter 15, Section 2 video at glencoe.com or on the video DVD.

The Rule of the Ṣafavids

GUIDE TO READING

The BIG Idea

Ideas, Beliefs, and Values The Ṣafavids used their faith as a unifying force.

Content Vocabulary

- shah *(p. 492)*
- orthodoxy *(p. 494)*
- anarchy *(p. 494)*

Academic Vocabulary

- administrator *(p. 494)*
- successor *(p. 494)*

People and Events

- Ṣafavids *(p. 492)*
- Shāh Esmā'īl *(p. 492)*
- Azerbaijan *(p. 492)*
- Caspian Sea *(p. 492)*
- Tabrīz *(p. 492)*
- Eṣfahān *(p. 493)*
- Riza-i-Abbasi *(p. 495)*

Reading Strategy

Comparing and Contrasting

As you read this section, use a Venn diagram like the one below to compare and contrast the Ottoman and Ṣafavid Empires.

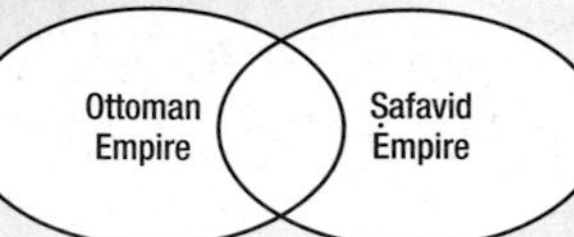

The shortest-lived of the three Muslim empires, the Ṣafavid Empire was nonetheless influential. The Shia faith, declared as the state religion, unified the empire. The empire reached its high point under the reign of Shāh 'Abbās.

The Ṣafavid Empire

MAIN IDEA Unified as a Shia nation, the Ṣafavid Empire reached its height under Shāh 'Abbās.

HISTORY & YOU You and your friends probably have a bond because you believe in the same things. Learn how the Ṣafavids unified their empire.

After the empire of Timur Lenk (Tamerlane) collapsed in the early fifteenth century, the area extending from Persia into central Asia fell into anarchy. At the beginning of the sixteenth century, however, a new dynasty known as the **Ṣafavids** (sah•FAH•weedz) took control. Unlike many of their Isamic neighbors who were Sunni Muslims, the Ṣafavids became ardent Shias. (As discussed in Chapter 6, the Sunnis and Shias were the two major groups in the Islamic religion.)

The Ṣafavid Dynasty

The Ṣafavid dynasty was founded by **Shāh Esmā'īl** (ihs•MAH•EEL), the descendant of Ṣafī od-Dīn (thus the name *Ṣafavid*). In the early fourteenth century, Ṣafī od-Dīn had been the leader of a community of Turkish ethnic groups in **Azerbaijan,** near the **Caspian Sea.**

In 1501, Esmā'īl, in his teens at the time, used his forces to seize much of Iran and Iraq. He then called himself the **shah,** or king, of a new Persian state. Esmā'īl sent Shia preachers into the Anatolian Peninsula to convert members of Turkish tribes in the Ottoman Empire. The Ottoman sultan tried to halt this activity, but Esmā'īl refused to stop. Esmā'īl also ordered the massacre of Sunni Muslims when he conquered Baghdad in 1508.

Alarmed by these activities, the Ottoman sultan, Selim I, advanced against the Ṣafavids in Persia. With their muskets and artillery, the Ottomans won a major battle near **Tabrīz.** However, Selim could not maintain control of the area. A few years later, Esmā'īl regained Tabrīz.

During the following decades, the Ṣafavids tried to consolidate their rule throughout Persia and in areas to the west. The Ṣafavids were faced with the problem of integrating various Turkish peoples with the settled Persian-speaking population of the urban

Resource Manager

R Reading Strategies	C Critical Thinking	D Differentiated Instruction	W Writing Support	S Skill Practice
Teacher Edition • Det. Importance, p. 495 **Additional Resources** • Guid. Read. Act., URB p. 163 • Read. Ess. & Note-Taking Guide, p. 166	**Teacher Edition** • Predicting Consequences, p. 493 **Additional Resources** • People in World Hist. Act., URB p. 154 • Section Quiz, p. 182	**Teacher Edition** • ELL, p. 494 **Additional Resources** • World Art & Arc. Trans., p. 57 • World Art & Arc. Trans., p. 59	**Teacher Edition** • Expository Writing, p. 494 **Additional Resources** • Writer's Guidebook, p. 5	**Teacher Edition** • Using Geo. Skills, p. 493 **Additional Resources** • Mapping Hist. Act., URB p. 145

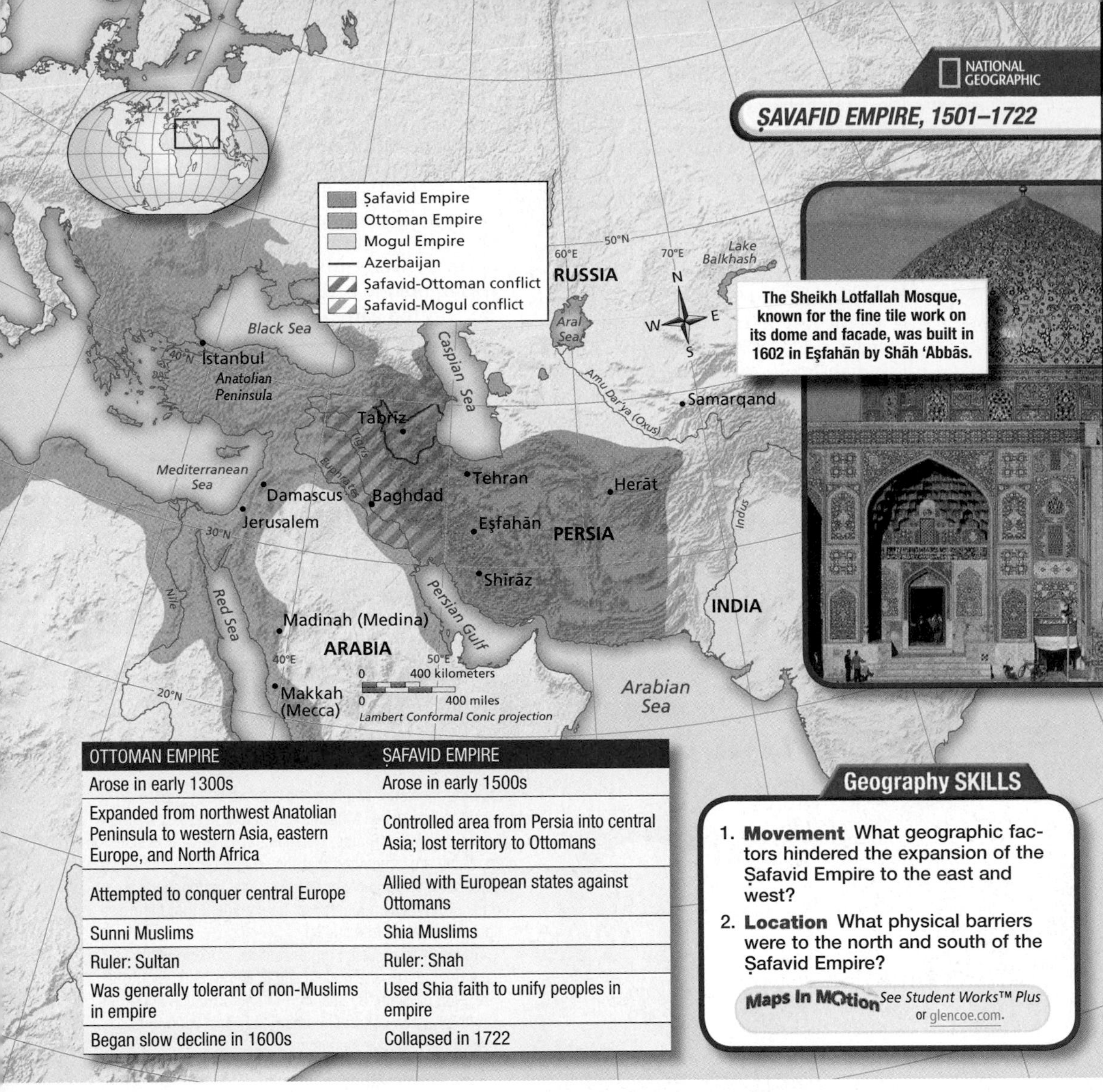

The Sheikh Lotfallah Mosque, known for the fine tile work on its dome and facade, was built in 1602 in Eșfahān by Shāh 'Abbās.

OTTOMAN EMPIRE	ȘAFAVID EMPIRE
Arose in early 1300s	Arose in early 1500s
Expanded from northwest Anatolian Peninsula to western Asia, eastern Europe, and North Africa	Controlled area from Persia into central Asia; lost territory to Ottomans
Attempted to conquer central Europe	Allied with European states against Ottomans
Sunni Muslims	Shia Muslims
Ruler: Sultan	Ruler: Shah
Was generally tolerant of non-Muslims in empire	Used Shia faith to unify peoples in empire
Began slow decline in 1600s	Collapsed in 1722

Geography SKILLS

1. **Movement** What geographic factors hindered the expansion of the Șafavid Empire to the east and west?
2. **Location** What physical barriers were to the north and south of the Șafavid Empire?

Maps In MOtion See Student Works™ Plus or glencoe.com.

areas. The Shia faith was used as a unifying force. Esmā'īl made conversion to the Shia faith mandatory for the largely Sunni population. Many Sunnis were either **C** killed or exiled. Like the Ottoman sultan, the shah himself claimed to be the spiritual leader of all Islam.

In the 1580s, the Ottomans went on the attack. They placed Azerbaijan under Ottoman rule and controlled the Caspian Sea with their fleet. This forced the new Șafavid shah, 'Abbās, to sign a peace treaty in which he lost much territory in the northwest. The capital of the Șafavids was moved from the northwestern city of **S** Tabrīz to the more centrally located city of **Eșfahān.** 'Abbās adorned his new capital city with the latest Persian architecture. Eșfahān became one of the world's largest cities with a population of one million.

Teach

C Critical Thinking

Predicting Consequences

Ask: What effect would the mandatory conversion to the Shia faith have on the Sunni population? *(rising tensions and further division between Sunni and Shia Muslims)* **OL**

S Skill Practice

Using Geography Skills

Ask: What advantage is there to having a centrally located capital? *(A central location would be more accessible to a greater number of people and would be better protected against outside threats.)* **OL**

Geography SKILLS

Answers:

1. It was bordered by strong empires.
2. The Caspian Sea was to the north and the Arabian Sea was to the south.

Hands-On Chapter Project
Step 2

Designing an Art Tile

Step 2: Deciding on a Pattern Pairs of students plan a design pattern for a tile that they began researching in Section 1.

Directions: Arrange the images that the students collected in Step 1 so that everyone can see them. Point out the variety of patterns. Ask students to compare and contrast the images. How are the designs similar? How are they different? What kinds of patterns do students notice? Then write the Big Idea on the board. Tell students to use what they know about Muslim art to help them plan a pattern for their own tiles.

Finalizing Their Plans: Ask volunteers to share their pattern ideas with the class. **OL**

(Chapter Project is continued in Section 3.)

D Differentiated Instruction

English Language Learners Have mixed-ability groups of students take turns reading aloud sentences on this page. After each paragraph, have students paraphrase the information they have read. Encourage students to assist each other in understanding key points. **ELL**

W Writing Support

Expository Writing Have students write a paragraph summarizing the reasons for the decline of the Ṣafavid Empire. **BL**

✓Reading Check

Answer: religious differences and competition for territory

Answers:

1. They are working with teachers to educate students about the religion of Islam.
2. There may be peer pressure to conform, or fear of being associated with terrorism.

Glory and Decline

Under Shāh 'Abbās, who ruled from 1588 to 1629, the Ṣafavids reached the high point of their glory. Similar to the Ottoman Empire, **administrators** were trained to run the kingdom. Shāh 'Abbās also strengthened his army, which he armed with the latest weapons.

In the early seventeenth century, Shāh 'Abbās moved against the Ottomans to regain lost territories. Several European states aided 'Abbās. The Ṣafavids had some initial success, but they could not hold all their territorial gains against the Ottoman armies. Nevertheless, in 1612, a peace treaty was signed that returned Azerbaijan to the Ṣafavids.

After the death of Shāh 'Abbās in 1629, the Ṣafavid dynasty gradually lost its vigor. Most of 'Abbās's **successors** lacked his talent and political skills. Eventually, the power of Shia religious elements began to increase at court and in Ṣafavid society at large.

Intellectual freedom marked the height of the empire. However, the pressure to conform to traditional religious beliefs, called religious **orthodoxy**, increased. For example, Persian women had considerable freedom during the early empire. Now they were forced into seclusion and required to adopt the wearing of the veil.

In the early eighteenth century, during the reign of Shah Hussein, Afghan peoples invaded and seized the capital of Eṣfahān. The remnants of the Ṣafavid ruling family were forced to retreat to Azerbaijan, their original homeland. The Turks took advantage of the situation to seize territories along the western border. Persia sank into a long period of political and social **anarchy** (lawlessness and disorder).

✓Reading Check **Identifying** What led to the fighting between Ottomans and Ṣafavids?

CONNECTING TO THE UNITED STATES

CIVIL LIBERTIES AND SOCIAL JUSTICE

Conflicts in Afghanistan and Iraq and attacks by terrorists identifying themselves as Muslims have created an atmosphere of fear in the United States. This has put American Muslims on alert. Many are concerned that they might be forced out of businesses and schools or even unjustly imprisoned for crimes. Can Muslim Americans be confident that their civil liberties will be protected?

Today, many Muslim organizations, working with teachers across the nation, speak to students about the religion of Islam. By sharing more information about their faith and rich cultural heritage, they are working to dissolve negative stereotypes.

- **Protecting civil liberties for all requires religious and cultural acceptance.**
- **Ensuring social justice means legislating for the same basic rights, security, and opportunities for all people.**

A Muslim teen going to class at a high school in the United States

CONNECTING TO TODAY

1. **Summarizing** What are many Muslim organizations doing to educate others about the Muslim faith and traditions?
2. **Making Generalizations** Why might it be difficult for Muslim teens to maintain their Islamic identities in the United States today?

Differentiated Instruction

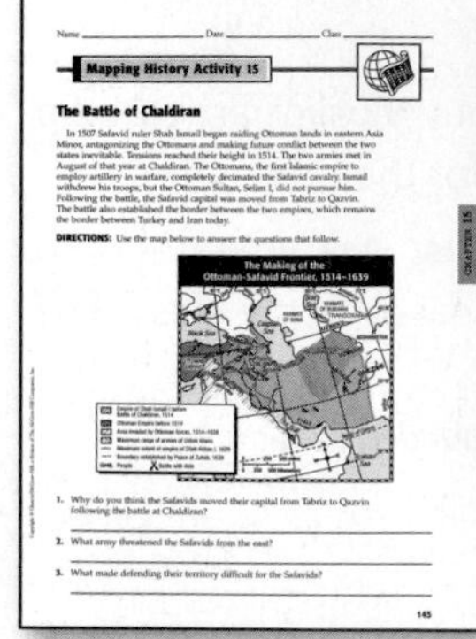
Mapping History Activity 15

The Battle of Chaldiran

Mapping History Activity, URB p. 145

Analyzing Information

Objective: Use a map to analyze the Battle of Chaldiran.
Focus: Have students locate the empires on the map.
Teach: Discuss the reasons for the battle.
Assess: Have students answer questions 1–3.
Close: Encourage students to discuss the results of the battle, including its effect on modern-day Turkey and Iran.

Differentiated Instruction Strategies

BL Have students outline the effects of the Battle of Chaldiran.

AL Invite students to find out more about how the battle affected the Ottoman and Ṣafavid Empires.

ELL Have students compare the map shown here with one of the Middle East today.

Life Under the Ṣafavids

MAIN IDEA The Ṣafavid shahs played an active role in government and trade, and they patronized the arts.

HISTORY & YOU Have you ever had to compete for a place on a team, show, or leadership position? Learn how the Ṣafavid shahs appointed their top administrators.

Persia under the Ṣafavids was a mixed society. The combination of Turkish and Persian elements affected virtually all aspects of Ṣafavid society.

Role of the Shah

The Ṣafavid rulers were eagerly supported by Shias. In return, the shahs declared Shia Islam to be the state religion. Shahs were more available to their subjects than were rulers elsewhere. "They show great familiarity to strangers," remarked one visitor, "and even to their own subjects, eating and drinking with them pretty freely."

Strong-minded shahs firmly controlled the power of the landed aristocracy. In addition, appointment to senior positions in the bureaucracy was based on merit rather than birth. For example, Shāh 'Abbās hired a number of foreigners from neighboring countries for positions in his government.

Economy and Trade

The Ṣafavid shahs played an active part in trade and manufacturing activity. Most goods in the empire traveled by horse or camel caravans, and the roads were kept fairly clear of thieves and bandits.

Ṣafavid Persia was probably not as prosperous as its neighbors to the east and west—the Moguls and the Ottomans. Hemmed in by the sea power of the Europeans to the south and the land power of the Ottomans to the west, the Ṣafavids found trade with Europe difficult. R

Ṣafavid Culture

Knowledge of science, medicine, and mathematics under the Ṣafavids was equal to that of other societies in the region. Persia also witnessed an extraordinary flowering of the arts during the reign of Shāh 'Abbās. Silk weaving and carpet weaving flourished, stimulated by the great demand for Persian carpets in the West. Persian painting enjoyed a long tradition. **Riza-i-Abbasi,** the most famous artist of this period, created exquisite works. Soft colors and flowing movement dominated the features of Ṣafavid painting.

✓Reading Check **Explaining** On what basis were appointments to senior bureaucratic positions made?

Vocabulary

1. **Explain** the significance of: Ṣafavids, Shāh Esmā'īl, Azerbaijan, Caspian Sea, shah, Tabrīz, Eṣfahān, administrator, successor, orthodoxy, anarchy, Riza-i-Abbasi.

Main Ideas

2. **Describe** how the Ṣafavids tried to bring the various Turkish and Persian peoples together.
3. **Summarize** the significant events that occurred during each shah's reign by using a chart like the one below.

Shah	Significant Events

4. **Explain** why the Ṣafavids may have found trade with Europe difficult.

Critical Thinking

5. **The BIG Idea** **Explaining** What was the shah's role in Ṣafavid society and government?
6. **Evaluating** What was the advantage in moving the Ṣafavid capital city from Tabrīz to Eṣfahān?
7. **Analyzing Visuals** Examine the map on page 493. Approximately how much territory did the Ṣafavids gain between 1501 and the height of the empire?

Writing About History

8. **Expository Writing** Analyze the impact of the Ṣafavid Empire's geographical location on its economy (what goods could be traded, trading partners, goods in high demand). Compare the Ṣafavid economy with that of another country.

History ONLINE
For help with the concepts in this section of *Glencoe World History*, go to glencoe.com and click Study Central™.

495

R Reading Strategy

Determining Importance

Ask: How did geographical location affect the economy of the Ṣafavids? *(The Ṣafavids could not compete with the sea power of the Europeans in the south or the land power of the Ottomans to the west. Their economy was weakened by the lack of trade with Europe.)* OL

✓Reading Check

Answer: Appointments to senior positions in the bureaucracy were based on merit.

Assess

History ONLINE

Study Central provides summaries, interactive games, and online graphic organizers to help students review content.

Close

Comparing and Contrasting

Ask students to compare the artistic styles of the Ṣafavid and Ottoman cultures. How are they similar? How are they different? OL

Answers

1. Definitions for the vocabulary words are found in the section and the Glossary.
2. They used the Shia faith as a unifying force.
3. Answers may include: **Ismail:** established Ṣafavid dynasty; **'Abbās:** trained administrators to run kingdom; **Hussein:** Eṣfahān seized by Afghan tribesmen
4. hemmed in by sea power of the Europeans to the south and the land power of the Ottomans to the west
5. actively involved in trade and the government; controlled the power of the landed aristocracy; selected people for government positions
6. Eṣfahān more centrally located than Tabrīz; less vulnerable to attack
7. not a great deal, but did gain more access to the Persian Gulf and Caspian Sea through its acquisition of a small part of the Persian Empire
8. Answers will vary depending on the other economy selected.

Focus

Introducing Social History
Ask: Why was the Ṣafavid Empire a link between Asia and Europe? *(It was located in the area between those two continents.)* Why was it difficult for the Ṣafavids to trade with Europe? *(because they were blocked by European sea powers on the south and the Ottoman Empire on the west)* **OL**

Teach

D Differentiated Instruction

Verbal/Linguistic Have students make vocabulary cards for the words *timce, bazaar,* and *caravansary.* Have them refer to the cards as they read the text, noting how the words are related. **BL**

R Reading Strategy

Making Connections Ask: How does the bazaar of Eşfahān compare with today's shopping environments? *(Students may cite comparisons with shopping malls, flea markets, or online auction sites.)* **OL**

Social History

The Ṣafavids: At the Crossroads of Trade and of History

The nation known today as Iran has been at the center of world commerce for centuries. From 1501 to 1722, the Ṣafavid Empire unified Iran and added parts of Turkey, Iraq, and Central Asia under its control. Trade with Europe was challenging for the Ṣafavids, but Iran (or Persia) was a vital connection between Asia and Europe throughout several dynasties. The bazaar at Eşfahān, capital under Shāh 'Abbās, was the center of Ṣafavid economic power. Across the empire, bazaars in regional capitals provided citizens with access to a variety of goods and merchandise.

A *timce* is a covered courtyard that houses a few shops selling the same special product. This one, the Timce Malek, is famous for carpets.

The bazaar sold household goods, tools, and other general merchandise besides luxury items. Barter was a common means of exchange.

Ṣafavid woven textiles were an essential item in the bazaar and a vital part of overseas trade.

A Place for Everything, Everything in Its Place

R D Merchants came from across Central Asia to trade in the Ṣafavid region. The bazaar was the heart of their commerce. Many bazaars were enclosed and had high vaulted ceilings that covered narrow rows of stalls. Specific sections housed similar types of goods for shoppers' convenience. Spaces for manufacturing, storage, and merchants' offices stood alongside shops. Caravansaries attached to the bazaar received trains of camels or mules loaded with goods. In the caravansary, newly arrived trade goods were sold wholesale. In the bazaar, they were sold retail.

496

Additional Support

Background

Eşfahān The city of Eşfahān is located about 210 miles (338 km) south of Tehran. During the eleventh century, it expanded and increased in grandeur. The Great Mosque of Eşfahān dates from this period and is still an architectural highlight in the city. The city declined after 1200 until the rise of the Ṣafavids. In the 1590s, Shāh` Abbās I brought back the city's glory. He created a square surrounded by mosques, balconies, gardens, and the grand bazaar. A French traveler who lived in the city between 1664 and 1677 wrote that it had about 1,802 caravansaries. Each of these would have had space for 300 to 400 camels or mules in its main courtyard as well as space to store merchandise. The city was largely destroyed in a siege in 1722, but many historic buildings were restored in the first half of the twentieth century.

Long on Trade, Short on Coins

The Șafavids had a chronic shortage of coins in circulation. Silver coins, like those above, were used by the government to pay administrative costs, by merchants to pay for goods purchased in large trade deals, and by some to pay taxes. Soldiers and the urban lower class used copper coins. Their value changed from year to year, and they could only be traded for silver coins in large sums. Rural people bartered for goods and services and rarely saw coins. The empire's elite hoarded its small number of gold coins. C

Analyzing Visuals

1. **Explaining** What role did currency play in Șafavid trade?
2. **Analyzing** How might buyers have reacted to shopping for an item in a *timce?* How might merchants have felt about being organized this way?

S Skill Practice

Using Geography Skills Have students refer to a historical Atlas to trace the Silk Road that merchants from Europe and Asia might have traveled. **OL**

C Critical Thinking

Drawing Conclusions Ask: Why would rural people be more likely to use barter than coins for trade? *(Their trade was local and they wouldn't have access to foreign merchants or coinage.)* **OL**

Assess/Close

Have students answer the Analyzing Visuals questions and share their responses with the class. Ask students to discuss the kinds of people you would need to organize and run a large bazaar. **OL**

Analyzing Visuals

Answers:

1. was used by merchants to pay for goods in large trade deals
2. **Buyers:** proximity allowed comparison of goods and prices; **Merchants:** could keep track of competition and attract more buyers

Activity: Economics Connection

Analyzing Trade and Money Remind students that they have learned the growth of a money economy in medieval Europe was a result of a revival of trade in the eleventh and twelfth centuries. **Ask:** What are the similarities and differences between the Champagne trade fairs and the bazaars of the Șafavid Empire? *(Both brought buyers and sellers of goods from different regions together and relied on a money economy; fairs were temporary and were held in smaller cities; the bazaars were permanent and were held in larger cities.)*

Explain that the value of the coins used at the time of the Șafavid Empire was directly related to the value of the precious metal in them. Coins today are made of cheaper metal and their value comes from the value designated by the government that issues them. **Ask:** Why did the Șafavids use both silver and copper coins? *(There was a shortage of coins; more valuable coins were used for larger transactions.)* **OL**

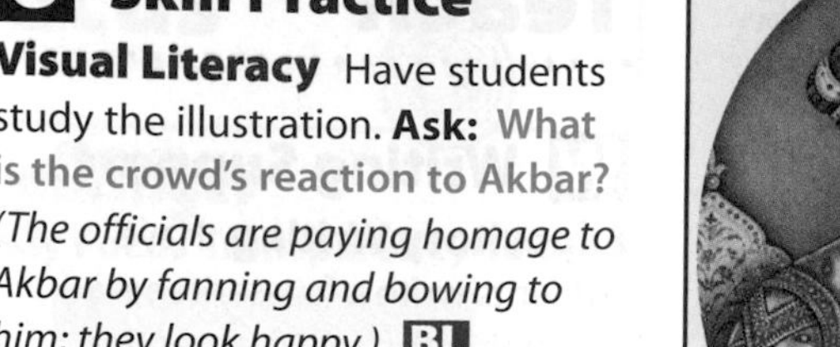

S Skill Practice

Visual Literacy Have students study the illustration. **Ask:** What is the crowd's reaction to Akbar? *(The officials are paying homage to Akbar by fanning and bowing to him; they look happy.)* **BL**

R Reading Strategy

Reading Primary Sources

Have students read the quotation by Akbar the Great in The Rule of Akbar feature. **Ask:** What is Akbar's argument in favor of conquest? *(Akbar argues that if a monarch is not always looking to expand his empire, his neighbors will try to conquer that monarch's lands for their own empires.)* **OL**

DOCUMENT-BASED QUESTIONS

Answers:

1. Akbar was suspicious of his neighbors, thinking that it was inevitable that rival kingdoms would engage in war.
2. He was accepting of other faiths; insisted on just rule from his governors; and allowed conquered regions to keep their laws, granting them some autonomy.

HISTORY & ARTS PRIMARY SOURCE

The Rule of Akbar

"A monarch should be ever intent on conquest; otherwise his neighbors rise in arms against him."
—Akbar the Great

Akbar aggressively expanded his empire through military conquest. He created an efficient bureaucracy to administer his empire. Each imperial province was ruled by a military governor who was held responsible for any abuses of power, helping to ensure fair rule. Taxes were levied equally.

Akbar, a Muslim, was accepting of other faiths. He eliminated a special tax on non-Muslims and included many Hindus in his bureaucracy. He granted a degree of autonomy to Hindu regions, allowing Hindus to keep their own laws. These actions helped to win over many Hindus to Mogul rule.

Akbar saw himself as a philosopher-king who was responsible for guiding his people spiritually. Though he believed in tolerance, he developed a new religion called "The Religion of God" for which he sought willing followers.

DOCUMENT-BASED QUESTIONS

The illustration at right from the *Akbarnama (History of Akbar)* shows officials paying homage to Akbar in central India about 1560.

1. **Explaining** Explain Akbar's attitude toward military conquest.
2. **Analyzing** What was the key to Akbar's successful rule?

Overall, the Akbar era was a time of progress, at least by the standards of the day. All Indian peasants were required to pay about one-third of their annual harvest to the state, but the system was applied justly. When bad weather struck in the 1590s, taxes were reduced or suspended altogether. Thanks to a long period of peace and political stability, trade and manufacturing flourished.

The era was an especially prosperous one in the area of foreign trade. Indian goods, notably textiles, tropical food products and spices, and precious stones, were exported in exchange for gold and silver. Arab traders handled much of the foreign trade because the Indians, like their Mogul rulers, did not care for travel by sea.

Decline of the Moguls

Akbar died in 1605 and was succeeded by his son Jahāngīr (juh•HAHN•GIHR). Jahāngīr was able and ambitious. During the early years of his reign, he continued to strengthen the central government's control over his vast empire.

Eventually, however, his grip began to weaken when he fell under the influence of one of his wives, Persian-born Nūr Jahān. As Jahāngīr slowly lost interest in governing, he gave more authority to Nūr Jahān. The empress used her position to enrich her own family. She arranged the marriage of her niece to her husband's third son and successor, **Shāh Jahān.**

During his reign from 1628 to 1658, Shāh Jahān maintained the political system established by earlier Mogul rulers. He also expanded the boundaries of the empire through successful campaigns in the **Deccan Plateau** and against the city of Samarqand, north of the Hindu Kush.

Shāh Jahān's rule was marred by his failure to deal with growing domestic problems, however. He had inherited a

Additional Support

Teacher Tip

Collaborative Learning This activity allows students with different levels of academic skills and intelligences to work together. Encourage students in each group to think about the tasks that need to be done and assign work to each person or pair accordingly.

Activity: Collaborative Learning

Problem Solving Organize the class into three groups, and assign each group a different Muslim empire. Have students think about the problems that confronted the Ottoman, Ṣafavid, or Mogul Empire. Direct groups to use a problem-solving process to identify a problem that confronted their assigned empire and conduct research to provide a historical context for the problem. Each group should then list and analyze options that could have solved the problem. Students should discuss the advantages and disadvantages of different solutions and how they would have affected the government and the people of the empire. Have students chart their information and, if time allows, have them present their ideas for viable solutions to the class. **OL**

nearly empty treasury. His military campaigns and expensive building projects put a heavy strain on the imperial finances and compelled him to raise taxes. The peasants were even more deprived as a result of these taxes. The majority of Jahān's subjects lived in poverty.

Shāh Jahān's troubles worsened with his illness in the mid-1650s. It was widely reported that he had died. Such news led to a struggle for power among his sons. Battles were fought; alliances and defections were made. The victorious son, **Aurangzeb,** had his brother put to death and imprisoned his father. Aurangzeb then had himself crowned emperor in 1658.

Aurangzeb is one of the most controversial rulers in the history of India. During his reign, the empire reached its greatest physical size. Constant warfare and religious intolerance, however, made his subjects resentful.

As a man of high **principle**, Aurangzeb attempted to eliminate many of what he considered to be India's social evils. He **W** forbade the Hindu custom of **suttee** (cremating a widow on her husband's funeral pyre), and he put a stop to the levying of illegal taxes. He tried to forbid gambling and drinking as well.

Aurangzeb was a devout Muslim and adopted a number of measures that reversed the Mogul policies of religious tolerance. For instance, he imposed a tax on non-Muslims. Also, he prohibited the building of new Hindu temples, and he forced Hindus to convert to Islam.

Aurangzeb's policies led to Hindu outcries and domestic unrest. He even received criticism from Shias. In addition, a number of revolts against imperial authority broke out in provinces throughout the empire. Rebellious groups threatened the power of the emperor.

After Aurangzeb's death in 1707, there were many contenders for the throne. Their reigns were short-lived. India was increasingly divided and vulnerable to attack from abroad. In 1739, Delhi was sacked by the Persians, who left it in ashes.

✓Reading Check **Explaining** How did Akbar's religious policy affect his government?

Life in Mogul India

MAIN IDEA The Mogul society and its culture were both Muslim and Hindu.

HISTORY & YOU Do you know someone from a family with more than one religion? Learn how Indian society and culture reflected a shared heritage.

The Moguls were foreigners in India. In addition, they were Muslims ruling a largely Hindu population. The resulting blend of influences on the lives of ordinary Indians could be complicated. The treatment of women serves as a good example.

Society and the Role of Women

Women had long played an active role in Mogul tribal society. Mogul rulers often relied on female relatives for political advice. To a degree, these Mogul attitudes toward women affected Indian society. Women from aristocratic families frequently received salaries and were allowed to own land.

At the same time, the Moguls placed certain restrictions on women under their interpretations of Islamic law. These practices generally were adopted by Hindus. The practice of isolating women, for example, was followed by many upper-class Hindus.

In other ways, however, Hindu practices remained unchanged by Mogul rule. The custom of suttee continued in spite of efforts by the Moguls to abolish it. Child marriage also remained common.

The Mogul era saw the emergence of a wealthy nobility and a prosperous merchant class. During the late eighteenth century, this prosperity was shaken by the decline of the Moguls and the coming of the British. However, many prominent Indians established trading ties with foreigners.

Mogul Culture

The Moguls brought together Persian and Indian influences in a new and beautiful architectural style. This style is best symbolized by the **Taj Mahal,** which Shāh Jahān built in **Agra** in the mid-seventeenth century. The project lasted more than twenty **C** years. To finance it, the government raised land taxes, driving many Indian peasants into complete poverty.

W Writing Support

Expository Writing Divide the class into two groups for a written exercise debating the reign of Aurangzeb. One group can write a paragraph defending him, and the second group can write a paragraph arguing that the policies of Aurangzeb contributed to the empire's decline. Encourage a student from each group to read their paragraphs to the class. **OL**

C Critical Thinking

Analyzing Information Ask: How did the building of the Taj Mahal both help and hinder the Indian population? *(Construction lasted for decades, employing thousands of workers. Higher taxes drove many peasants into poverty.)* **OL**

✓Reading Check

Answer: His religious tolerance allowed Hindus to become low-ranking government officials.

Differentiated Instruction

Drawing Conclusions

Objective: Read to discover the architecture of the Taj Mahal.

Focus: Have students understand why the Taj Mahal stands out.

Teach: Have students respond to the questions on the handout.

Assess: Write a description of the Taj Mahal.

Close: Explain that the Taj Mahal symbolizes how Shāh Jahān felt about his late wife.

Differentiated Instruction Strategies

BL Highlight words on the activity page that relate to architecture.

AL Find images of a famous modern building. Explain what its architecture symbolizes.

ELL Find images of the Taj Mahal to display.

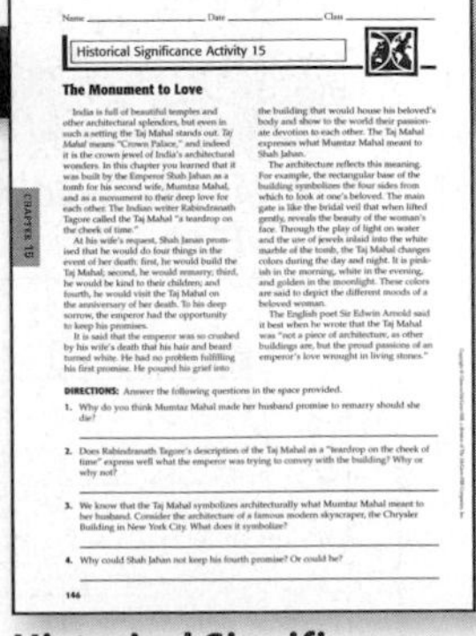
Historical Significance Activity 15

The Monument to Love

Historical Significance Activity, URB p. 146

Did You Know?

The Taj Mahal was built by Shāh Jahān as a testament to his grief at the loss of his favorite wife. Contemporary scholars argue that Jahān also built it as a symbol of his power and wealth.

✓Reading Check

Answer: It combined Persian and Indian motifs, and it included the portrayal of humans in action.

DOCUMENT-BASED QUESTIONS

Answers:

1. He used military force against the French and Moguls to gain control of Indian trade, ultimately giving sovereign powers to the British East India Company.
2. A trading company is organized to create profit for its owners, not to represent the interests of the people of India or even the British people. This profit motive could create conflict with these groups.

Differentiated Instruction

TURNING POINT — THE BRITISH GAIN CONTROL OF INDIA

The British East India Company faced challenges in its efforts to gain control of Indian trade. By the mid-1700s, the power of the French East India Company rivaled that of the British. In southern India, the French and British fought a series of wars in the region near Chennai (Madras). In 1751, Sir Robert Clive won an important victory there for the British East India Company against the French and their Indian allies.

In the north, Clive defeated a Mogul-led army at the Battle of Plassey near Fort William (Kolkata) in Bengal in 1757. The balance of power shifted to the British. After defeating the French and the Moguls, the British became the dominant power in India until after World War II. For much of that time, the British East India Company had all the sovereign powers of a government in ruling much of India.

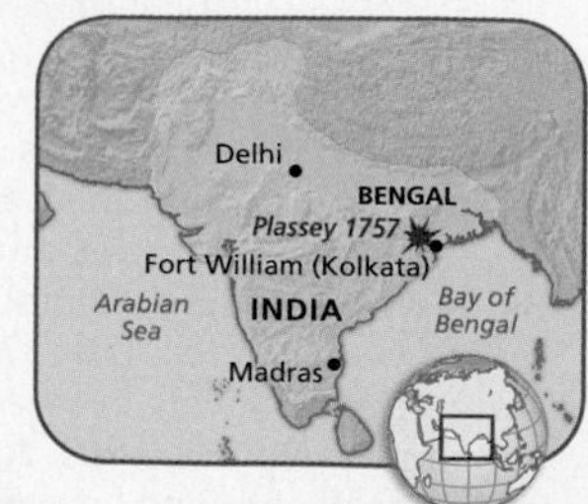

National Portrait Gallery, London

***Robert Clive and Mir Jaffier after the Battle of Plassey, 1757* by Francis Hayman depicts a meeting of Clive and a defecting Indian leader, Mir Jaffier, after the battle.**

DOCUMENT-BASED QUESTIONS

In the mid-1700s, the British East India Company began to consolidate its control of India's commerce.

1. **Summarizing** How did the actions of Robert Clive affect English trade with India?
2. **Predicting** What problems do you foresee in allowing a private trading company to assume the powers of a government?

The Taj Mahal is widely considered to be the most beautiful building in India, if not in the entire world. The building seems to have monumental size, nearly blinding brilliance, and delicate lightness.

Another major artistic achievement of the Mogul period was in painting. Like architecture, painting in Mogul India resulted from the blending of two cultures: Persian and Indian. Akbar established a state workshop for artists, mostly Hindus, who worked under the guidance of Persian masters to create the Mogul school of painting. The "Akbar style" combined Persian with Indian motifs. It included the portrayal of humans in action, for example—a characteristic not usually seen in Persian art. Akbar also encouraged his artists to imitate European art forms, including the use of perspective and lifelike portraits.

✓Reading Check **Describing** What was significant about the "Akbar style" of art?

Leveled Activities

BL Guided Reading Activity, URB p. 164

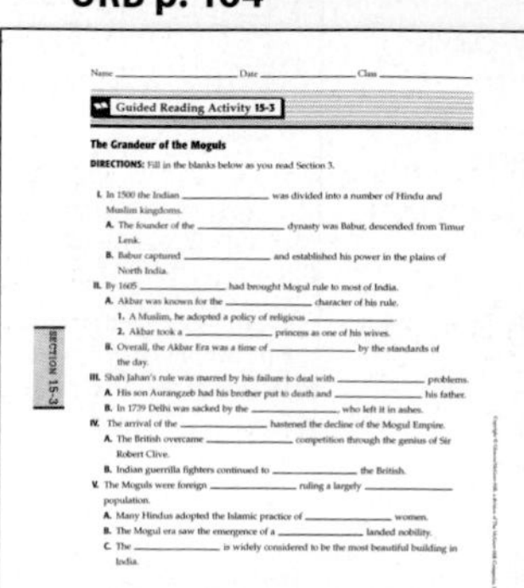

OL Cooperative Learning Activity, URB p. 147

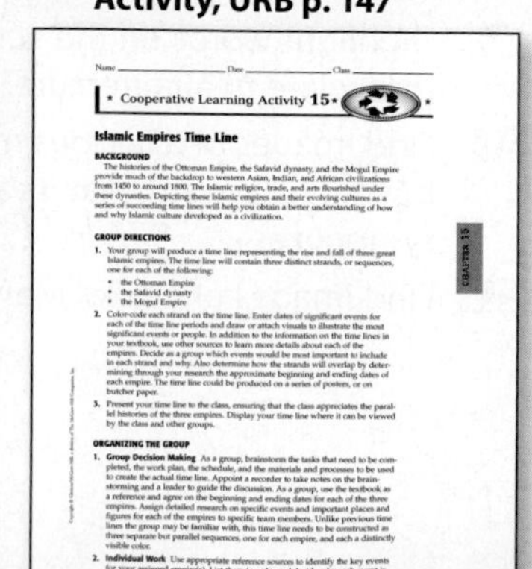

AL Critical Thinking Activity, URB p. 142

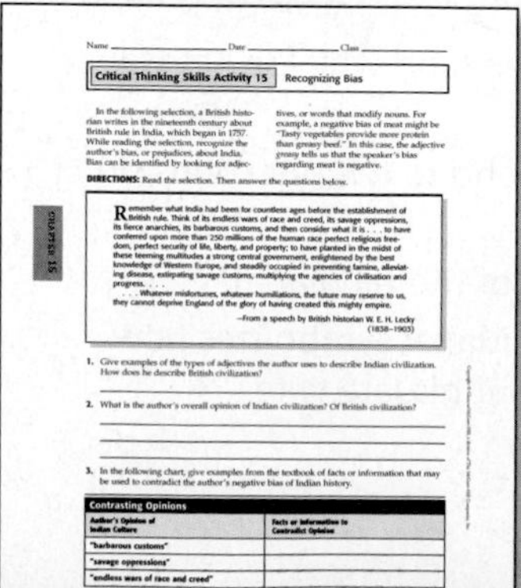

ELL Academic Vocabulary Activity, URB p. 139

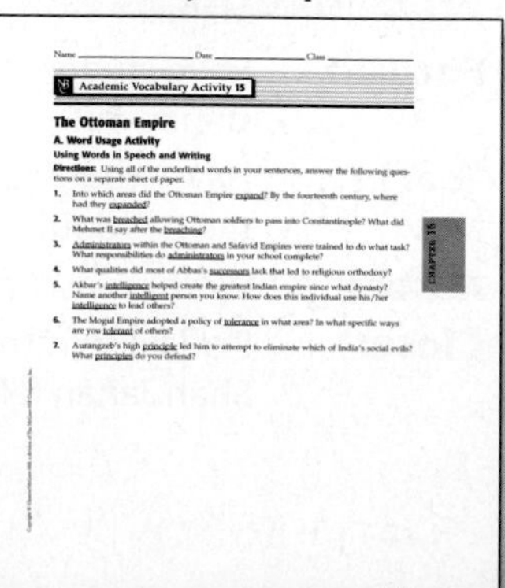

Europeans Come to India

MAIN IDEA Foreigners seeking trade opportunities in India hastened the decline of the Mogul Empire.

HISTORY & YOU What would you do if someone set up a concession stand opposite the one you have operated successfully for years? Learn how the British and French competed for trade in India.

The arrival of the British hastened the decline of the Mogul Empire. By 1650, British trading forts had been established at Surat, Fort William (which was renamed **Calcutta** and is now the city of Kolkata), and **Madras** (Chennai). British ships carried Indian-made cotton goods to the East Indies, where they were traded for spices.

British success in India attracted rivals, especially the French. The French established their own forts. For a brief period, the French went on the offensive, even capturing the British fort at Madras.

The British were saved by the military genius of Sir Robert Clive, an aggressive British empire builder. Clive served as the chief representative in India of the East India Company, a private company that acted on behalf of the British Crown. Fighting any force that threatened the Company's power in India, Clive ultimately restricted the French to the fort at Pondicherry and a few small territories on the southeastern coast.

While fighting the French, Clive was also consolidating British control in Bengal. The Indian ruler of Bengal had attacked Fort William in 1756. He had imprisoned the British garrison in the "Black Hole of Calcutta," an underground prison. Due to the intense heat in the crowded space, only 23 people (out of 146) survived. R

In 1757, Clive led a small British force of about three thousand to victory over a Mogul-led army more than ten times its size in the Battle of Plassey in Bengal. As part of the spoils of victory, the failing Mogul court gave the East India Company the power to collect taxes from lands in the area around Calcutta.

Britain's rise to power in India, however, was not a story of constant success. Many East India Company officials combined arrogance with incompetence. They offended both their Indian allies and the local population, who were taxed heavily to meet the Company's growing expenses.

In the late eighteenth century, the East India Company moved inland from the great coastal cities. British expansion brought great riches to individual British merchants and to British officials who found they could obtain money from local rulers by selling trade privileges. The British were in India to stay.

✓ **Reading Check** **Examining** How did Robert Clive save the British in India?

SECTION 3 REVIEW

Vocabulary

1. **Explain** the significance of: Bābur, Khyber Pass, Delhi, Akbar, intelligent, zamindars, Shāh Jahān, Deccan Plateau, Aurangzeb, principle, suttee, Taj Mahal, Agra, Calcutta, Madras.

Main Ideas

2. **List** and explain the events that led to the decline of the Mogul Empire using a chart like the one below.

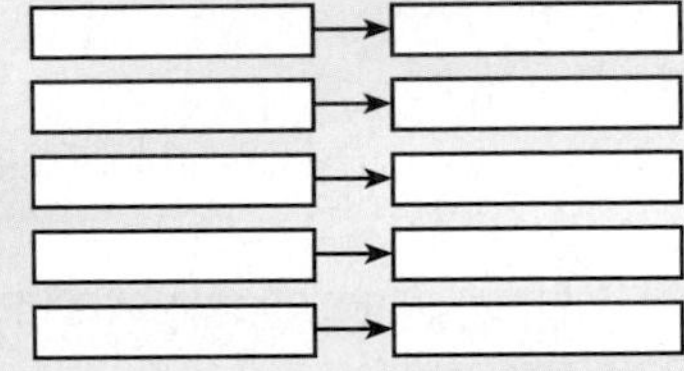

3. **Explain** why the British and French built forts in India.
4. **Describe** the Taj Mahal. Who built it? Why is it considered the most beautiful building in India?

Critical Thinking

5. **The BIG Idea** **Analyzing** Analyze the impact of the Moguls on the Hindu and Muslim peoples of the Indian subcontinent.
6. **Evaluating** Evaluate how Akbar's reign reflected his humane character.
7. **Analyzing Visuals** Examine the illustration from *Akbarnama (History of Akbar)* on page 500. What details indicate that the officials are paying homage to Akbar?

Writing About History

8. **Descriptive Writing** When the British established trading posts in India, their influence spread throughout the country. Present a speech describing how India would have developed if the British had not colonized the country.

History ONLINE

For help with the concepts in this section of *Glencoe World History*, go to glencoe.com and click Study Central™.

R Reading Strategy

Summarizing Ask: How did the East India Company, a private company, become involved in the struggle over control of India? *(It was empowered by the British crown to act on its behalf; the company wanted to control markets in India and keep out foreign competition.)* **OL**

✓ **Reading Check**

Answer: Clive's forces successfully fought the French, greatly restricting them to one fort and a few small territories.

Assess

History ONLINE

Study Central provides summaries, interactive games, and online graphic organizers to help students review content.

Close

Summarizing Have students write a sentence summarizing the material covered under each heading in this section. **OL**

SECTION 3 REVIEW

Answers

1. Definitions for the vocabulary words are found in the section and the Glossary.
2. Jahāngīr influenced by wife—weakened succession to throne. Shāh Jahān's expensive projects—government forced to raise taxes. Aurangzeb's strict social rules—domestic unrest. Aurangzeb's religious intolerance—Hindu revolt. Arrival of British—weakened internal control and hastened decline.
3. Both sought trade opportunities and competed for trade.
4. Built by Shāh Jahān, the Taj Mahal took more than 20 years to build. The Taj Mahal seems to have monumental size, blinding brilliance, and delicate lightness—all at the same time.
5. Most Mogul rulers were tolerant of other religions; later attempts by Aurangzeb to force Hindus to convert led to domestic unrest.
6. adopted a policy of religious tolerance; had keen interest in other religions and tolerated Hindu practices; welcomed expression of Christian views by Jesuit advisers; took a Hindu princess as one of his wives; filled many higher-level government positions with non-Muslims
7. The officials are keeping a respectful distance and are bowing or using submissive body language.
8. Answers will vary.

Outlining Students may not realize that the Visual Summary is similar to an outline. Remind students that an outline shows information visually. Review the elements of an outline. **Ask:** What is the purpose of an outline like the Visual Summary? *(to help students remember the important ideas presented in the chapter)*

Divide the class into three groups. Assign each group a portion of the Visual Summary and ask them to write a more complete outline for that portion of the summary on separate sheets of paper. Remind students to use their text to add supporting details to their outlines. Encourage them to use a standard outline format and tell them that each group's outline will be made available to the class to copy and use for studying. **OL**

Organizing Help students organize and add to their notes for the chapter. Distribute copies of the Visual Summary and have them cut out and place each section on a page. Then have students attach their chapter notes to the appropriate section. Discuss how organizing and reviewing notes can help them study effectively. **BL**

CHAPTER 15 Visual Summary

You can study anywhere, anytime by downloading quizzes and flash cards to your PDA from glencoe.com.

THE OTTOMAN EMPIRE History & Culture

- Ottomans conquered the Byzantine Empire and expanded into the Balkans.
- Most Ottomans were Sunni Muslims and were tolerant of other religions.
- Ottoman sultans were enthusiastic patrons of the arts.
- After reaching its peak under Süleyman I, the Ottoman Empire began to decline.

THE TURKISH SULTAN REVIEWING HIS JANISSARIES

The sultan, the supreme government authority, built a strong military of janissaries.

DEMAND FOR PERSIAN CARPETS STIMULATED MANUFACTURING

Carpets made by the Safavids often incorporated animal motifs.

THE ṢAFAVIDS History & Culture

- To unify the Ṣafavid Empire, Shah Esmāʻīl forced Sunni Muslims to convert to the Shia faith.
- Under Shah ʻAbbās, the Ṣafavids reached the high point of their glory.
- The shahs played an active role in government, trade, and manufacturing activities.
- The empire's decline began after the death of Shah ʻAbbās.

THE MOGULS History & Culture

- The Moguls united India under a single government with a common culture.
- The Mogul ruler Akbar was Muslim, but he exercised tolerance toward Hindu practices.
- Persian and Indian cultures blended to create beautiful paintings and architecture.
- British forces defeated the Moguls at the Battle of Plassey. The British eventually ruled most of India.

TAJ MAHAL

The Taj Mahal is the most famous example of Mogul architecture.

Hands-On Chapter Project
Step 4: Wrap Up

Designing an Art Tile

Step 4: Finish the Tile Students finish the design that they began in Sections 1, 2, and 3.

Directions: Have students finalize their designs by coloring them in with markers. Students should use colors that would have been appropriate to the time period. As a reminder, they can look back at the images that they collected in Step 2 to see what colors were used. Students should synthesize their research and design by writing a paragraph describing their design and why they chose the pattern that they did. Then, as a class, discuss how art can represent an individual's or society's values and ideals. **OL**

STANDARDIZED TEST PRACTICE

TEST-TAKING TIP

Do not pick an answer just because it sounds good. Sometimes a choice is deliberately meant to sound correct but is not. Read all the answer choices carefully before you select the best one, and avoid making hasty decisions.

Reviewing Vocabulary

Directions: Choose the word or words that best complete the sentence.

1. The Hindu custom of cremating a widow on her husband's funeral pyre is known as ______.

A ulema
B suttee
C harem
D sultan

2. The ______ was the sultan's chief minister.

A grand vizier
B marshal
C shah
D pasha

3. Another word for *lawlessness and disorder* is ______.

A rebellion
B orthodoxy
C revolt
D anarchy

4. The private domain of a sultan was called the ______.

A sanctuary
B mosque
C harem
D zamindar

Reviewing Main Ideas

Directions: Choose the best answers to the following questions.

Section 1 *(pp. 484–489)*

5. Who were the janissaries?

A Pashas
B Bureaucrats
C Religious leaders
D An elite guard

6. The Ottomans ended the Byzantine Empire by laying siege to which city?

A Constantinople
B Lepanto
C Mohács
D Topkapi

7. The success of which type of empire was largely based on its mastery of firearms?

A Bourgeois
B Gunpowder
C Blackfriar
D Pastoral

8. Under which ruler did the Ottoman Empire reach its high point?

A Selim I
B Selim II
C Mehmed II
D Süleyman I

Need Extra Help?

If You Missed Questions . . .	1	2	3	4	5	6	7	8
Go to Page . . .	501	487	494	486	484	485	486	489

GO ON

Answers and Analyses

Reviewing Vocabulary

1. B *Suttee* is the correct choice. The ulema was a group of religious advisers to the sultan. The sultan's harem was his private domain.

2. A All the answer choices refer to people who have a role in government. *Marshals* are not mentioned in the chapter. A *shah* is a king, so he would not report to another ruler. Multiple people held the title of *pasha;* they helped run the local governments. Only a grand vizier could be the sultan's chief minister.

3. D If students carefully read this question, they will see that *rebellion* and *revolt* are synonyms, so neither term could be the answer. *Orthodoxy* refers to religious beliefs.

4. C *Zamindars* can be ruled out because they were local officials in Mogul India. The three remaining choices all have religious connotations. The terms *sanctuary* and *mosque* both refer to religious buildings, but they are places of worship, not private residences. *Harem* means "sacred place," and students may be familiar with the idea of a harem being made up of several wives. They should make the connection that the sultan would live with his wives, so "harem" is the correct answer.

Reviewing Main Ideas

5. D The janissaries were an elite guard recruited from the local Christian population.

6. A Lepanto is a body of water and Topkapi is a palace, so they can be ruled out. The Ottomans captured Constantinople first and then moved on to complete their conquest of the Balkans, where the Battle of Mohács took place.

7. B Students should recognize that *gunpowder* is the only term that has a connection to firearms.

8. D It may be helpful to remind students that the nicknames of Selim I and Selim II were "the Grim" and "the Drunkard." Neither name suggests that they were successful rulers, so the Ottoman Empire would not have reached its height under them. Mehmed II can be ruled out because he led the Ottoman Empire when it was beginning to expand. Süleyman was called "the Magnificent," which suggests that he ruled during a time of prosperity.

CHAPTER 16 Planning Guide

Key to Ability Levels

- **BL** Below Level
- **OL** On Level
- **AL** Above Level
- **ELL** English Language Learners

Key to Teaching Resources

- Print Material
- CD-ROM
- DVD
- Transparency

Levels: BL	Levels: OL	Levels: AL	Levels: ELL	Resources	Chapter Opener	Section 1	Section 2	Section 3	Section 4	Chapter Assess
				FOCUS						
BL	OL	AL	ELL	**Daily Focus Skills Transparencies**		16-1	16-2	16-3	16-4	
				TEACH						
BL	OL		ELL	**Reading Skills Activity, URB**			p. 167			
	OL	AL		**Historical Analysis Skills Activity, URB**					p. 168	
BL	OL	AL	ELL	**Differentiated Instruction Activity, URB**				p. 169		
	OL		ELL	**English Learner Activity, URB**		p. 171				
BL	OL	AL	ELL	**Content Vocabulary Activity, URB***					p. 173	
BL	OL	AL	ELL	**Academic Vocabulary Activity, URB**				p. 175	p. 175	
BL	OL	AL	ELL	**Skills Reinforcement Activity, URB**			p. 177			
	OL	AL		**Critical Thinking Skills Activity, URB**					p. 178	
	OL	AL		**History and Geography Activity, URB**				p. 179		
	OL	AL	ELL	**Mapping History Activity, URB**				p. 181		
BL	OL	AL		**Historical Significance Activity, URB**				p. 182		
BL	OL	AL	ELL	**Cooperative Learning Activity, URB**					p. 183	
	OL	AL	ELL	**History Simulation Activity, URB**					p. 185	
BL	OL	AL	ELL	**Time Line Activity, URB**					p. 187	
	OL	AL		**Linking Past and Present Activity, URB**			p. 188			
BL	OL	AL		**People in World History Activity, URB**		p. 189		p. 190		
BL	OL	AL	ELL	**Primary Source Reading, URB**				p. 191		
	OL	AL		**Enrichment Activity, URB**					p. 196	
BL	OL	AL	ELL	**World Art and Music Activity, URB**				p. 193		
BL	OL		ELL	**Guided Reading Activities, URB***		p. 198	p. 199	p. 200	p. 201	
BL	OL		ELL	**Reading Essentials and Note-Taking Guide***		p. 172	p. 175	p. 178	p. 181	
BL	OL	AL	ELL	**Differentiated Instruction for the World History Classroom**	✓	✓	✓	✓	✓	✓

Note: Please refer to the *Unit Resource Book: The Early Modern World* for this chapter's URB materials.

* Also available in Spanish

- Interactive Lesson Planner
- Interactive Teacher Edition
- Fully editable blackline masters
- Section Spotlight Videos Launch
- Differentiated Lesson Plans
- Printable reports of daily assignments
- Standards Tracking System

Levels					Resources	Chapter Opener	Section 1	Section 2	Section 3	Section 4	Chapter Assess
BL	OL	AL	ELL								
TEACH *(continued)*											
BL	OL	AL	ELL		**StudentWorks™ Plus DVD**	✓	✓	✓	✓	✓	✓
BL	OL	AL	ELL		**Vocabulary PuzzleMaker CD-ROM**	✓	✓	✓	✓	✓	✓
Teacher Resources					**Building Academic Vocabulary**	✓	✓	✓	✓	✓	✓
					Reading Strategies and Activities for the Social Studies Classroom		pp. 14, 74	pp. 74, 80			
					Writer's Guidebook		p. 43	p. 51	p. 27		
					Strategies for Success	✓	✓	✓	✓	✓	✓
					Outline Map Resource Book	✓	✓	✓	✓	✓	✓
					Presentation Plus! with MindJogger DVD	✓	✓	✓	✓	✓	✓
ASSESS											
BL	OL	AL	ELL		**Section Quizzes and Chapter Tests***		p. 193	p. 194	p. 195	p. 196	p. 197
BL	OL	AL	ELL		**Authentic Assessment With Rubrics**	✓	✓	✓	✓	✓	✓
BL	OL	AL	ELL		**Standardized Test Practice Workbook**	✓	✓	✓	✓	✓	✓
BL	OL	AL	ELL		***ExamView® Assessment Suite* CD-ROM**		16-1	16-2	16-3	16-4	Ch. 16
BL	OL	AL	ELL		**Interactive Tutor Self-Assessment CD-ROM**		16-1	16-2	16-3	16-4	
CLOSE											
BL			ELL		**Reteaching Activity, URB**					p. 195	
BL	OL		ELL		**Reading and Study Skills Foldables™**	✓	✓	✓	✓	✓	✓

Using Interactive Tutor Self Assessment

Electronic Quiz

Technology Product

Glencoe's Interactive Tutor Self Assessment software allows students to assess their mastery of chapter content, taking as much time as they need to review each section of a chapter. The Interactive Tutor Self Assessment

- contains quizzes for individual sections of chapters, with section overviews covering important concepts and keywords;
- allows students to read overviews based on sections, chapters, or units before starting quizzes;
- lets students check their answers, receive feedback and hints, and identify content areas for review;
- permits students to move back and forth among the questions during a quiz;
- generates performance reports and graphs to monitor student progress by section.

Objectives

Using the Interactive Tutor Self Assessment allows students to

- assess their mastery of chapter content;
- identify chapter content they need to review.

Steps

- Install Interactive Tutor Self-Assessment.
- Register yourself and create classes.
- Register new students/users in the database, organized by classes. Assign individual passwords to students.
- Save student records to a location easily accessible to students.
- Assign section quizzes to students.
- Generate performance reports and graphs for individual students and classes.

History ONLINE

	Student	Teacher	Parent
Beyond the Textbook	●	●	●
Chapter Overviews	●	●	●
Time Current Events	●		●
ePuzzles and Games	●		●
Concepts in Motion	●		●
Literature Connections		●	
Multi-Language Glossaries	●		●
Online Student Edition	●	●	●
Self-Check Quizzes	●		●
Student Web Activities	●		●
Study Central ™	●		●
Teaching Today		●	
Vocabulary eFlashcards	●		●
Web Activity Lesson Plans		●	

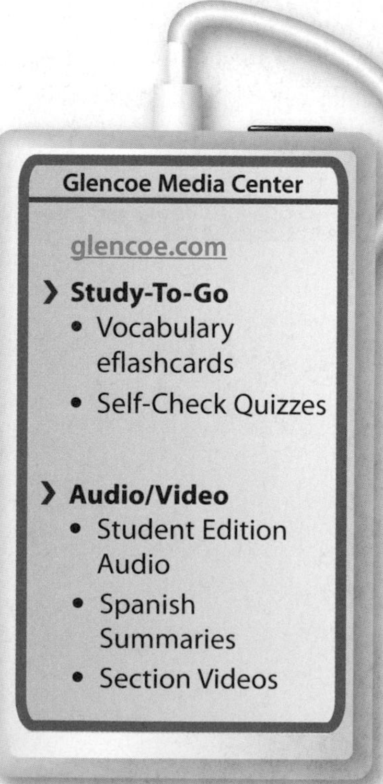

- **Timed Readings Plus in Social Studies** helps students increase their reading rate and fluency while maintaining comprehension. The 400-word passages are similar to those found on state and national assessments.
- **Reading in the Content Area: Social Studies** concentrates on six essential reading skills that help students better comprehend what they read. The book includes 75 high-interest nonfiction passages written at increasing levels of difficulty.
- **Reading Social Studies** includes strategic reading instruction and vocabulary support in Social Studies content for both ELLs and native speakers of English.

www.jamestowneducation.com

Index to National Geographic Magazine:

The following articles relate to this chapter:

- "Samurai: Japan's Way of the Warrior," by Tom O'Neill, December 2003
- "China's Gold Coast," by Mike Edwards, March 1997

National Geographic Society Products To order the following, call National Geographic at 1-800-368-2728:

- *National Geographic Atlas of the World* (Book).

Access National Geographic's new, dynamic MapMachine Web site and other geography resources at:

www.nationalgeographic.com
www.nationalgeographic.com/maps

Biography

The following videotape programs are available from Glencoe as supplements to Chapter 16:

- The Great Wall of China (ISBN 0-76-700361-6)
- Confucius: World of Wisdom (ISBN 0-76-700407-8)

To order, call Glencoe at 1-800-334-7344. To find classroom resources to accompany many of these videos, check the following home pages:

A&E Television: www.aetv.com

The History Channel: www.historychannel.com

Reading List Generator CD-ROM

GLENCOE BOOKLINK 3

Use this database to search more than 30,000 titles to create a customized reading list for your students.

- Reading lists can be organized by students' reading level, author, genre, theme, or area of interest.
- The database provides Degrees of Reading Power™ (DRP) and Lexile™ readability scores for all selections.
- A brief summary of each selection is included.

Leveled reading suggestions for this chapter:

For students at a Grade 8 reading level:
- ***Sword of the Samurai,*** by Eric Kimmel

For students at a Grade 9 reading level:
- ***The Samurai's Tale,*** by Erik Christian Haugaard

For students at a Grade 10 reading level:
- ***The Pageant of Chinese History,*** by Elizabeth Seeger

For students at a Grade 11 reading level:
- ***Life in Ancient Japan,*** by Hazel Richardson

For students at a Grade 12 reading level:
- ***The Great Wall of China,*** by Lesley DuTemple

Introducing
CHAPTER 16

Focus

MAKING CONNECTIONS

Can a palace reflect the philosophy of its rulers?

Activate students' prior knowledge by having them think about the architecture of their town or city. Ask students to think about how the architecture in the area reflects the philosophy of the people or the government. Responses will vary, but may include ideas about how buildings reflect the things that people in an area or culture find important. Close the discussion by having students list three characteristics about a public building in their town or city that reflect important ideas of the people or government.

Teach

The Big Ideas

As students study the chapter, remind them to consider the section-based Big Ideas included in each section's Guide to Reading. The **Essential Questions** in the activities below tie in to the Big Ideas and help students think about and understand important chapter concepts. In addition, the Hands-On Chapter Projects with their culminating activities relate the content from each section to the Big Ideas. These activities build on each other as students progress through the chapter. Section activities culminate in the wrap-up activity on the Visual Summary page.

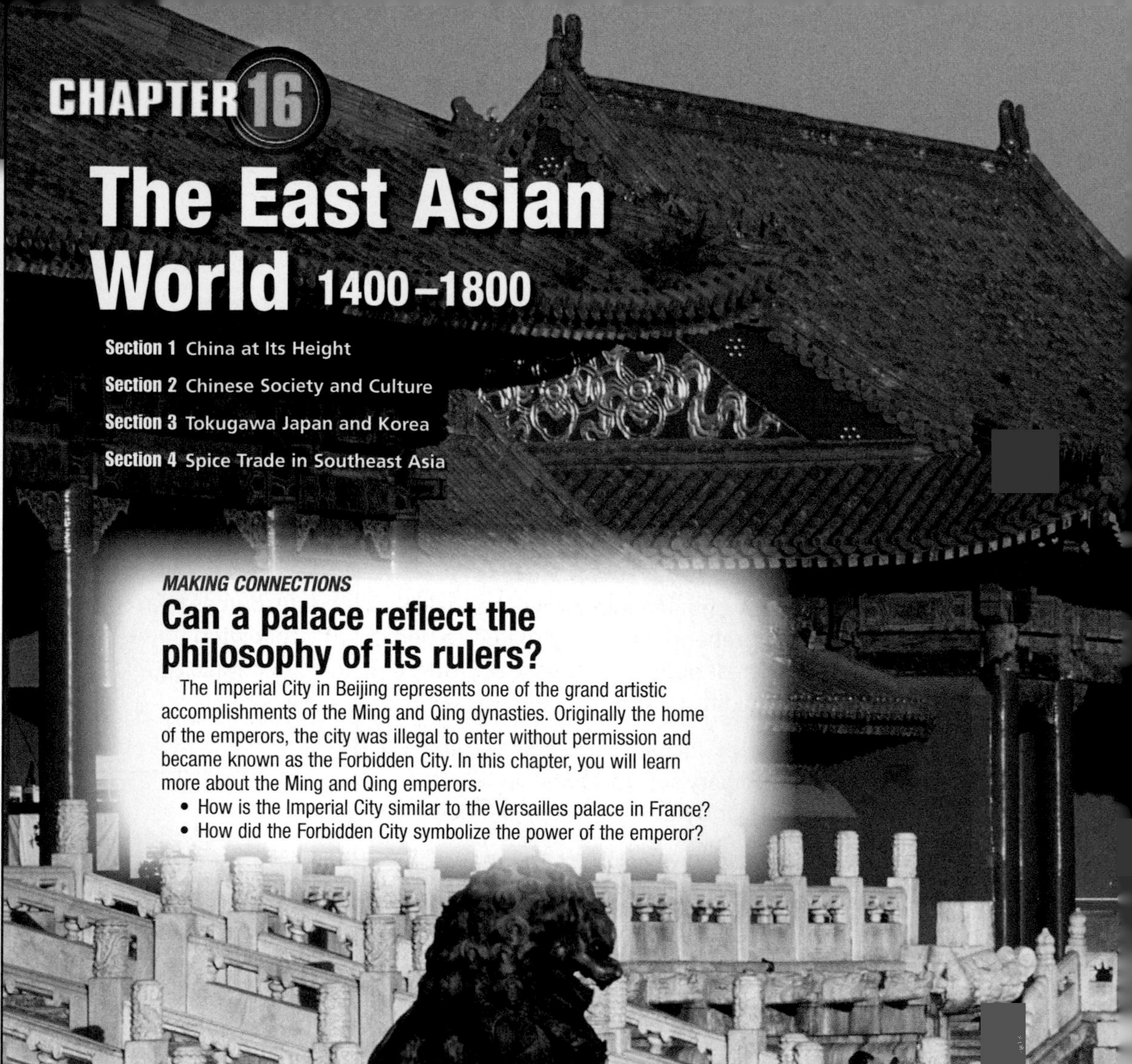

CHAPTER 16

The East Asian World 1400–1800

MAKING CONNECTIONS

Can a palace reflect the philosophy of its rulers?

The Imperial City in Beijing represents one of the grand artistic accomplishments of the Ming and Qing dynasties. Originally the home of the emperors, the city was illegal to enter without permission and became known as the Forbidden City. In this chapter, you will learn more about the Ming and Qing emperors.

- How is the Imperial City similar to the Versailles palace in France?
- How did the Forbidden City symbolize the power of the emperor?

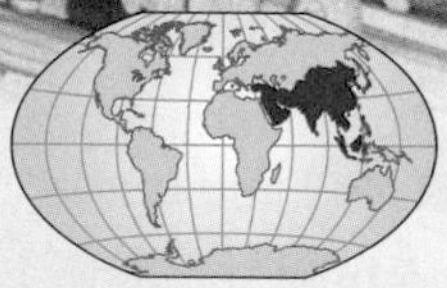

EAST ASIA ▶

1406 Construction of the Imperial City in China begins

1498 Portuguese explorer Vasco da Gama lands in Calicut in search of spices

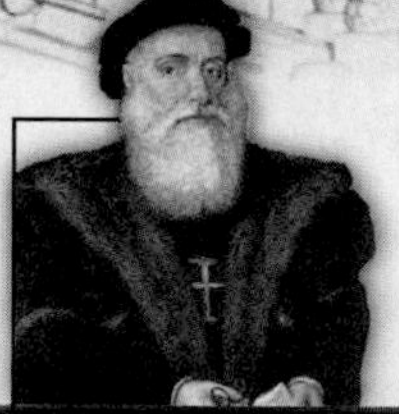

1603 Tokugawa Ieyasu takes the title of shogun in Japan

1400 — 1500 — 1600

THE WORLD ▶

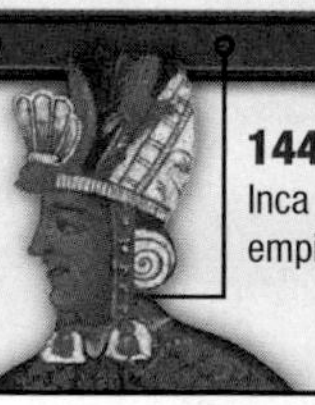

1440 Inca ruler Pachacuti builds an empire in South America

508

SECTION 1

China at Its Height

Essential Question: How did a policy of isolation affect the Chinese Empire? *(China's isolation kept both positive and negative European influences from entering Chinese society.)* Point out that in Section 1 students will learn about China's successes and failures under the Ming and Qing dynasties. **OL**

SECTION 2

Chinese Society and Culture

Essential Question: What was the main focus of Chinese society? *(Chinese society revolved around the family.)* Point out that in Section 2 students will learn about Chinese culture between 1500 and 1800, including economic changes, the role of women in society, and Chinese art and literature. **OL**

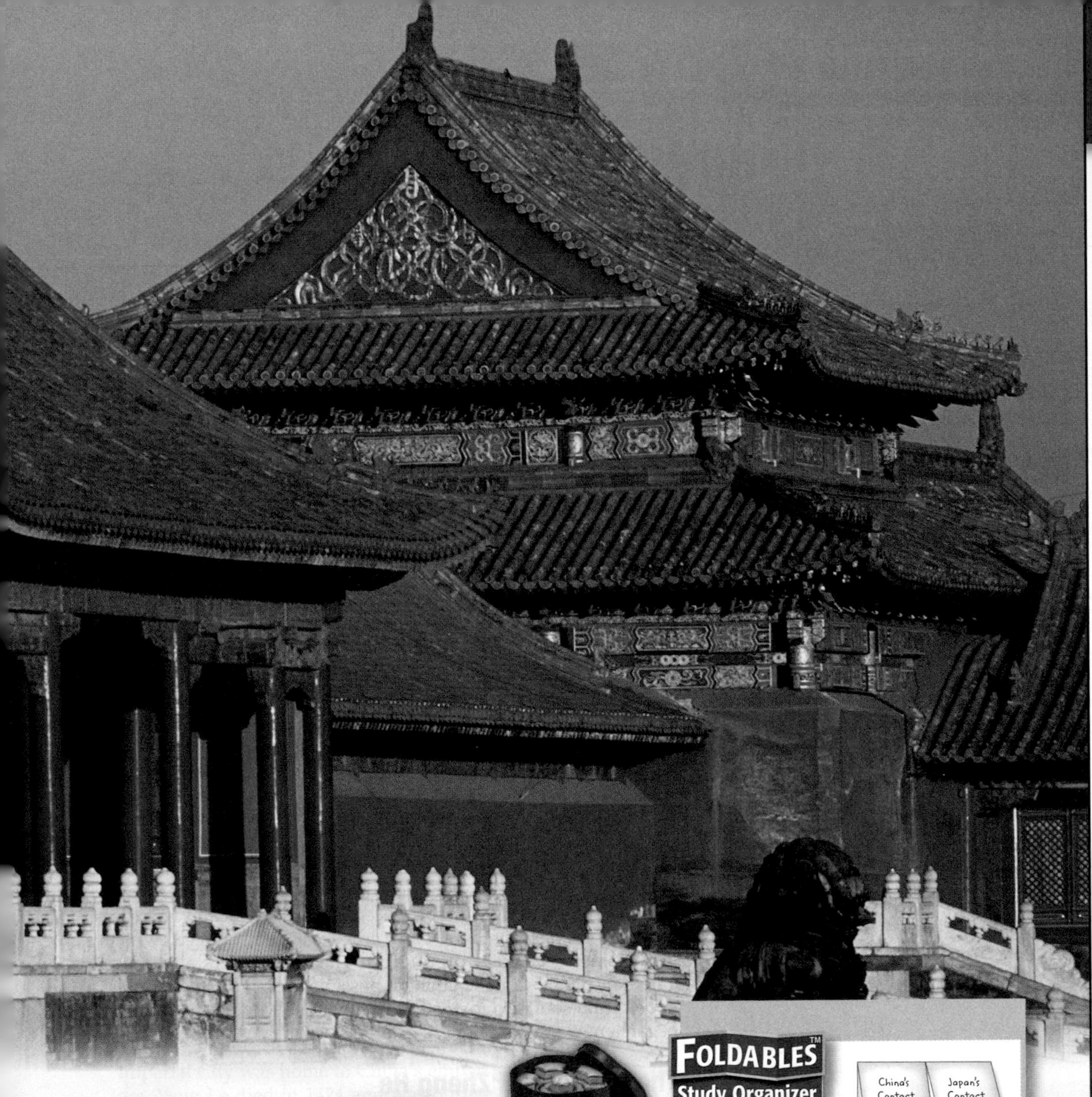

More About the Photo

Visual Literacy The Forbidden City occupies 178 acres in Beijing, China. It was originally built in the early 1400s. It is a huge walled complex with large buildings and gardens. The entire site is arranged from north to south. The architecture and the spaces in between the buildings were arranged to reflect imperial power. The height and width of the buildings, as well as the ornamentation, reflect each building's importance. The arrangement of the city also deemphasizes the power of the individual person—showing that imperial power is supreme.

Dinah Zike's Foldables

Dinah Zike's Foldables are three-dimensional, interactive graphic organizers that help students practice basic writing skills, review vocabulary terms, and identify main ideas. Instructions for creating and using Foldables can be found in the Appendix at the end of this book and in the *Dinah Zike's Reading and Study Skills Foldables* booklet. **OL**

1644 China's Ming dynasty is overthrown; Qing dynasty begins

1793 Lord Macartney leads British trade mission to China

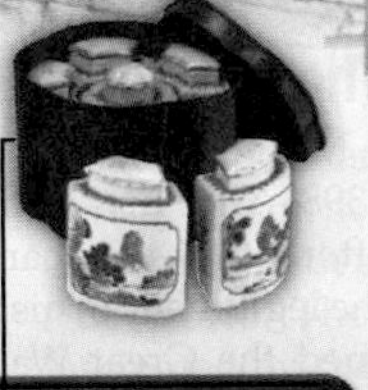

1700 — 1800

1633 The Church condemns teachings of Galileo

1791 In France, Olympe de Gouges writes declaration of rights for women

FOLDABLES Study Organizer

China's Contact | Japan's Contact | Portuguese

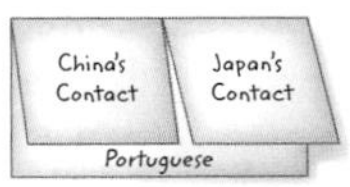

Comparing and Contrasting Use a Two-Tab Book to explore the experiences of the Chinese and Japanese as they came into contact with the Portuguese.

History ONLINE
Chapter Overview—Visit glencoe.com to preview Chapter 16.

Introduce students to chapter content and key terms by having them access the Chapter 16 Overview at glencoe.com.

Tokugawa Japan and Korea

Essential Question: **What changes took place in Japan after its political unification?** *(Europeans brought new products and technology to Japan; a period of "Great Peace" occurred.)* Point out that in Section 3 students will learn about the causes and effects of Japan's unification. **OL**

Spice Trade in Southeast Asia

Essential Question: **Why did Europeans struggle to control the spice trade in Southeast Asia?** *(It was a very profitable trade.)* Point out that in Section 4 students will learn how the arrival of Europeans in Southeast Asia affected the mainland and non-mainland states in Southeast Asia. **OL**

W Writing Support

Narrative Writing Have students research the voyages of Zheng He, and then write a front-page newspaper article about the voyages. Have them include an interview with Zheng He. What did he accomplish? What did he see? **AL**

R Reading Strategy

Academic Vocabulary Point out the terms *occupy* and *impact* on this page. Have students define each term and list synonyms. **ELL**

✓Reading Check

Answer: ran effective government using central bureaucracy with officials chosen by civil service examination; extended rule into Mongolia and briefly reconquered Vietnam; strengthened Great Wall and made peace with nomadic tribes along northern border; set up nationwide school system; increased production of manufactured goods; introduced new crops; completed Grand Canal; began construction of new Imperial City in Beijing; conducted voyages of exploration

Some of them held the Confucian view that trading activities were unworthy and that being a merchant was an inferior occupation. Shortly after Yong Le's death, the voyages were halted, never to be revived. One can only guess what a difference it would have made if Zheng He's fleet had reached the Americas before Columbus did.

First Contacts with the West

In 1514 a Portuguese fleet arrived off the coast of China. It was the first direct contact between the Chinese Empire and Europe since the journeys of Marco Polo.

At the time, the Ming government thought little of the arrival of the Portuguese. China was at the height of its power as the most magnificent civilization on Earth. From the **perspective** of the emperor, the Europeans were only an unusual form of barbarian. To the Chinese ruler, the rulers of all other countries were simply "younger brothers" of the Chinese emperor, who was seen as the Son of Heaven.

The Portuguese soon outraged Chinese officials with their behavior. They were expelled from **Guangzhou** (Canton) but were allowed to occupy Macao, a port on the southeastern coast of China.

At first, the Portuguese had little impact on Chinese society. Portuguese ships did carry goods between China and Japan, but direct trade between Europe and China remained limited. Perhaps more important than trade, however, was the exchange of ideas.

Christian missionaries had also made the long voyage to China on European merchant ships. The Jesuits, a Catholic order that focused on education and establishing missions, were among the most active. Many of them were highly educated men who brought along instruments, such as clocks, that impressed Chinese officials and made them more receptive to Western ideas.

Both sides benefited from this early cultural exchange. Chinese scholars marveled at their ability to read better with European eyeglasses. Christian missionaries were impressed with many aspects of Chinese civilization, such as the teachings of Confucius, the printing and availability of books, and Chinese architecture. When the Jesuits' reports began to circulate back home, Europeans became even more curious about this great civilization on the other side of the world.

Fall of the Ming Dynasty

After a period of prosperity and growth, the Ming dynasty gradually began to decline. During the late sixteenth century, internal power struggles developed. Groups worked to gain sole power and to place one of their leaders as emperor. Their efforts resulted in a series of weak rulers who were overpowered. Children, who had no control over their empire, were sometimes placed on the throne. Such internal power struggles led to a period of government corruption. High taxes, caused in part by this corruption, led to peasant unrest. Crop yields declined because of harsh weather.

In the 1630s, a major epidemic greatly reduced the population in many areas. One observer in a major city wrote, "There were few signs of human life in the streets and all that was heard was the buzzing of flies."

The suffering caused by the epidemic helped spark a peasant revolt led by Li Zicheng (LEE DZUH•CHUHNG). The revolt began in central China and then spread to the rest of the country. In 1644 Li and his forces occupied the capital of Beijing. When the capital fell, the last Ming emperor committed suicide by hanging himself from a tree in the palace gardens. Many officials took their own lives as well.

The overthrow of the Ming dynasty created an opportunity for the **Manchus.** They were a farming and hunting people who lived northeast of the Great Wall in the area known today as **Manchuria,** which is in the extreme northeast portion of China. The forces of the Manchus conquered Beijing, and Li Zicheng's army fell. The victorious Manchus then declared the creation of a new dynasty called the **Qing** (CHIHNG), meaning "pure." This expansive dynasty, created in 1644, remained in power until 1911.

✓Reading Check **Describing** What were the achievements of the Ming dynasty?

Differentiated Instruction

People in World History Activity 16 — Wan-Li (1563–1620)

People in World History Activity, URB p. 189

Analyzing Information

Objective: To understand an emperor of the Ming dynasty

Focus: Examine ruling style of Wan-Li

Teach: Have students answer the questions.

Assess: Ask students how the rule of Wan-Li affected the Ming dynasty.

Close: Discuss how government can affect how a country prospers.

Differentiated Instruction Strategies

- **BL** Provide individualized assistance as needed.
- **AL** Have students research and write about the ruling class during Wan-Li's rule.
- **ELL** Paraphrase the questions into simpler language for students.

The Qing Dynasty

MAIN IDEA Seeing how Western ideas were affecting its culture, China closed its doors to Europeans.

HISTORY & YOU What if trade with China were stopped today? Learn why China rejected foreign trade.

When some Chinese resisted their new rulers and seized the island of **Taiwan,** the Manchu government prepared to attack them. To identify the rebels, the government ordered all males to adopt Manchu dress and hairstyles. They had to shave their foreheads and braid their hair into a pigtail called a **queue.** Those who refused were assumed to be rebels and were executed: "Lose your hair or lose your head."

The Manchus were gradually accepted as legitimate rulers. The Qing flourished under a series of strong early rulers. The emperors pacified the country, corrected serious social and economic ills, and restored peace and prosperity.

Qing Adaptations

The Qing maintained the Ming political system but faced one major problem: the Manchus were ethnically and culturally different from their subject population. The Qing rulers dealt with this reality in two ways.

First, the Qing tried to preserve their distinct identity within Chinese society. The Manchus, who made up only 2 percent of the population, were defined legally as distinct from everyone else in China. The Manchu nobility maintained large landholdings and received revenues from the state treasury. Other Manchus were organized into separate military units, called **banners.** The "bannermen" were the chief fighting force of the empire.

Second, the Qing dealt with the problem of ethnic differences by bringing Chinese into the imperial administration. Chinese held more than 80 percent of lower posts, but they held a much smaller share of the top positions. Sharing of power won many Chinese supporters for the Manchus.

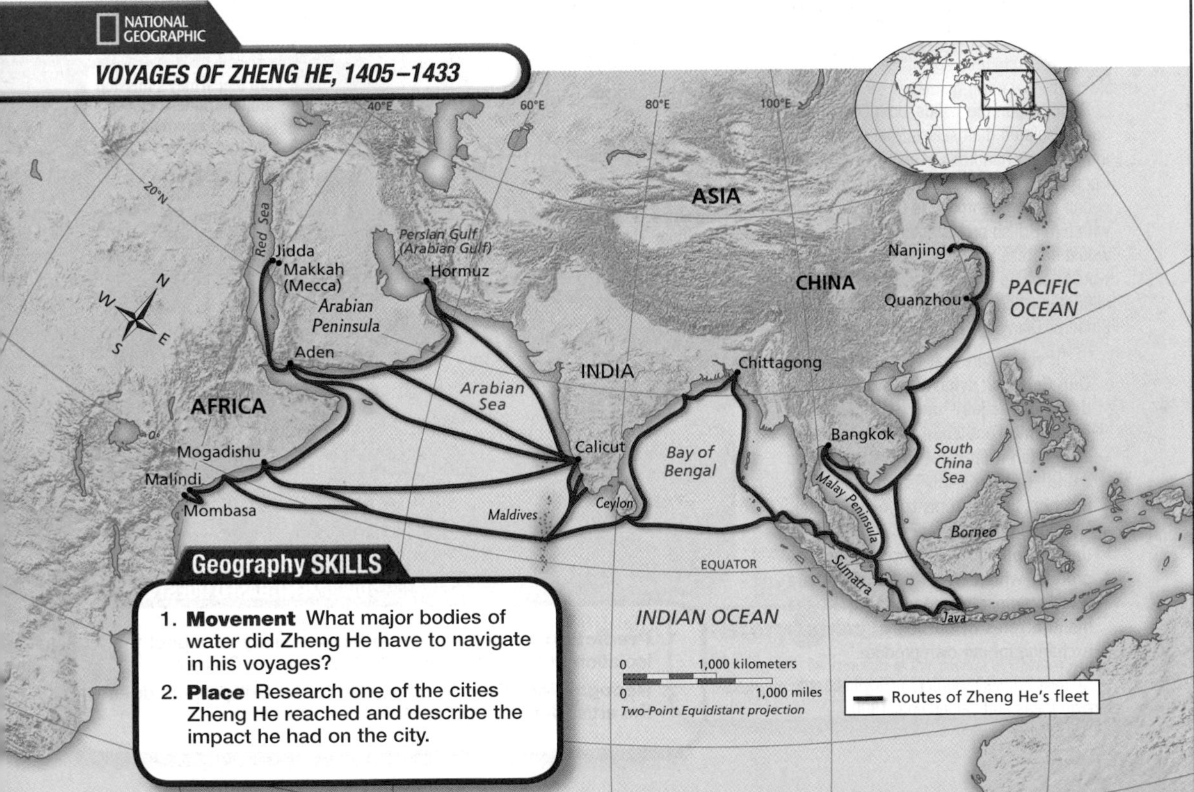

Geography SKILLS

1. **Movement** What major bodies of water did Zheng He have to navigate in his voyages?
2. **Place** Research one of the cities Zheng He reached and describe the impact he had on the city.

D Differentiated Instruction

Visual/Spatial Have students draw or paint a profile portrait of a Chinese man who wears his hair in a Manchu queue style. **OL**

R Reading Strategy

Analyzing Text Structure Read aloud the last sentence of the first paragraph under the subheading "Qing Adaptations." **Ask:** What cue words in the paragraphs that follow help the reader identify the two ways the Qing dealt with the Manchus? (first *and* second) **BL**

Geography SKILLS

Answers:

1. Red Sea, Arabian Sea, Indian Ocean, Bay of Bengal, South China Sea, Pacific Ocean
2. Answers will vary, but should explain Zheng He's effect on one city.

Hands-On Chapter Project
Step 1

Putting Together a Museum Exhibit

Student pairs will plan a museum exhibit featuring East Asian art or another feature that represents an East Asian country's culture.

Step 1: Planning the Exhibit

Essential Question: How do historical events affect the art and culture of a region?

Directions: As a class, brainstorm common features of a museum exhibit. *(artifacts—real or simulated, description of artifact, brief historical background of people and culture, painted backdrop for display, audio recording, and so on)* Student pairs should then begin thinking about an artifact or cultural characteristic they might want to feature in an exhibit. They should begin planning their exhibit's design and prepare a list of any materials they might need to set up their displays. **OL**

(Chapter Project is continued in Section 2.)

Focus

Bellringer
Daily Focus Transparency 16.2

GUIDE TO READING

Answers to Graphic:
Middle Ring: Extended Family
Outer Ring: Clan

Section Spotlight Video

To generate student interest and provide a springboard for class discussion, access the Chapter 16, Section 2 video at glencoe.com or on the video DVD.

Resource Manager

SECTION 2

Chinese Society and Culture

GUIDE TO READING

The BIG Idea
Ideas, Beliefs, and Values Chinese society was organized around the family.

Content Vocabulary
- commercial capitalism *(p. 516)*
- clan *(p. 517)*
- porcelain *(p. 519)*

Academic Vocabulary
- benefit *(p. 517)*
- incentive *(p. 518)*

People and Places
- Cao Xuein *(p. 519)*
- Imperial City *(p. 519)*
- Emperor Yong Le *(p. 519)*

Reading Strategy
Organizing Information As you read, show the organization of the Chinese family by using a concentric circle diagram like the one below.

During the Ming and Qing dynasties, China's population increased significantly and manufacturing grew. Organized around the family, Chinese society revered its elderly but restricted the role of its women. Meanwhile, the arts and architecture flourished.

Economy and Daily Life

MAIN IDEA China's agriculture-based economy changed as a rapid increase in population led to rural land shortages.

HISTORY & YOU What if you knew you would pay less tax if you decided to become a farmer and more tax if you decided to open a factory? Learn about changes to China's economy.

Between 1500 and 1800, China remained a mostly agricultural society. Nearly 85 percent of the people were small farmers. Nevertheless, the Chinese economy was changing.

Economic Changes

The first change for China involved an increase in population, from less than 80 million in 1390 to more than 300 million at the end of the 1700s. The increase had several causes. These included a long period of peace and stability under the early Qing dynasty and improvements in the food supply due to a faster growing species of rice from Southeast Asia.

The population increase meant that less land was available for each family. The imperial court tried to make more land available by limiting the amount wealthy landowners could hold. By the eighteenth century, however, almost all the land that could be farmed was already being farmed. Shortages of land in rural areas led to unrest and revolts.

Another change in this period was a steady growth in manufacturing and increased trade between provinces. Taking advantage of the long era of peace and prosperity, merchants and manufacturers expanded their trade in silk, porcelain, cotton goods, and other products.

Despite the growth in trade and manufacturing, China did not develop the kind of **commercial capitalism**—private business based on profit—that was emerging in Europe. Some key differences between China and Europe explain this fact.

In the first place, middle-class merchants and manufacturers in China were not as independent as those in Europe. Trade and manufacturing remained under the firm control of the government.

R Reading Strategies	C Critical Thinking	D Differentiated Instruction	W Writing Support	S Skill Practice
Teacher Edition • Connecting, p. 518 **Additional Resources** • Read. Skills Act., URB, p. 167 • Guid. Read. Act., URB p. 199 • Read. Ess. & Note-Taking Guide, p. 175	**Teacher Edition** • Ident. Cent. Issues, p. 517 **Additional Resources** • Linking Past/Present Act., URB p. 188 • Section Quiz, p. 194	**Teacher Edition** • ELL, p. 518 **Additional Resources** • Read. Strat. for SS, p. 24	**Teacher Edition** • Expository Writing, p. 519 **Additional Resources** • Writer's Guidebook, p. 51	**Teacher Edition** • Visual Literacy, p. 517 **Additional Resources** • Skills Reinforc. Act., URB p. 177 • Read. Strat. for SS, p. 80

INFOGRAPHICS

Economic Changes in China

Improvements in agriculture during the Ming dynasty caused great changes in Chinese society. As Ming traders ventured into Southeast Asia, they acquired rice that produced much larger harvests. In the 1500s, American foods were introduced to China, including the peanut, the sweet potato, and maize (corn).

The increase in rice production brought many changes. With a better food supply, peasants were now able to grow cash crops—crops produced for profit—like cotton and indigo. As a result, manufacturing and commerce increased. Chinese silk, cotton, tea, and porcelain were in demand around the world, especially in Europe and America.

The greater food supply also allowed for increases in population. Under Ming rule the population had doubled. During the Qing dynasty population grew dramatically.

Chinese farmers in a rice paddy

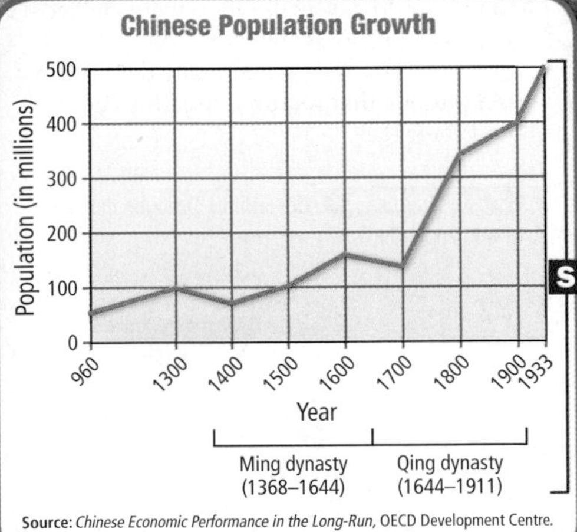

Source: *Chinese Economic Performance in the Long-Run*, OECD Development Centre.

DOCUMENT-BASED QUESTIONS

1. **Describing** How did changes in agriculture affect the growth of China's population?
2. **Predicting** What does the population graph suggest about Chinese population during the Ming dynasty?

Many Chinese looked down on trade and manufacturing as inferior to farming. The state reflected this attitude by levying heavy taxes on manufacturing and trade and low taxes on farming.

Society and the Role of Women

Chinese society was organized around the family. The family was expected to provide for its members' needs, including the education of children, support of unmarried daughters, and care of the elderly. At the same time, all family members were expected to sacrifice their individual needs to **benefit** the family as a whole. This expectation was based on Confucian ideals.

The ideal family unit in Qing China was the extended family, in which as many as three or four generations lived under the same roof. When sons married, they brought their wives to live with them in the family home. Unmarried daughters also remained in the house, as did parents and grandparents. Chinese society held the elderly in high regard. Aging parents knew they would be cared for in their home by their children.

C Beyond the extended family was the **clan,** which consisted of dozens, or even hundreds, of related families. These families were linked by a clan council of elders and common social and religious activities such as Buddhism and Confucianism.

See page R43 to read excerpts from Sung Ying-Hsing's *The Silk Industry in China* in the **Primary Sources and Literature Library.**

Teach

C Critical Thinking

Identifying Central Issues Tell students that in traditional Chinese culture, the group is more important than the individual. **Ask:** What aspects of American culture prioritize the group over the individual? *(Answers may include the armed forces, team sports, and so on.)* **OL**

S Skill Practice

Visual Literacy Ask: How did China's population change between 1380 and 1810? *(It increased to about 300 million people.)* **BL**

DOCUMENT-BASED QUESTIONS

Answers:

1. Fast-growing rice and American foods increased food production. An increase in the food supply allowed for increases in population.
2. Though it increased overall, Chinese population growth did not occur at a consistent rate.

Differentiated Instruction

Leveled Activities

BL Guided Reading Activity, URB p. 199

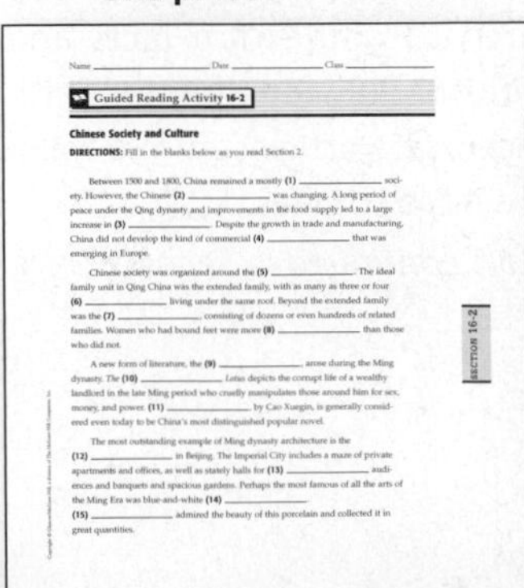

OL Skills Reinforcement Activity, URB p. 177

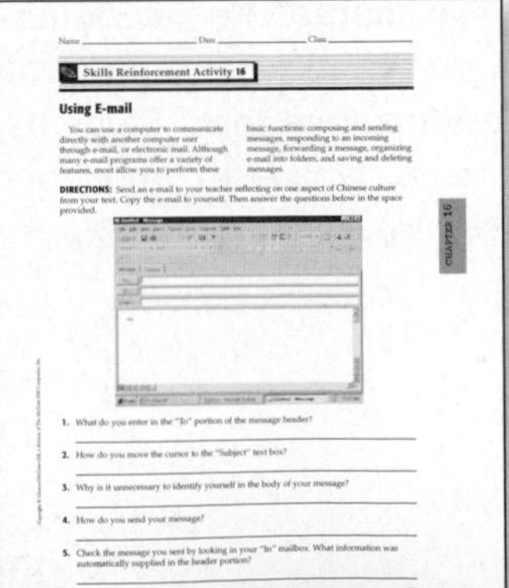

AL Linking Past and Present Activity, URB p. 188

ELL Reading Strategies and Activities for SS, p. 80

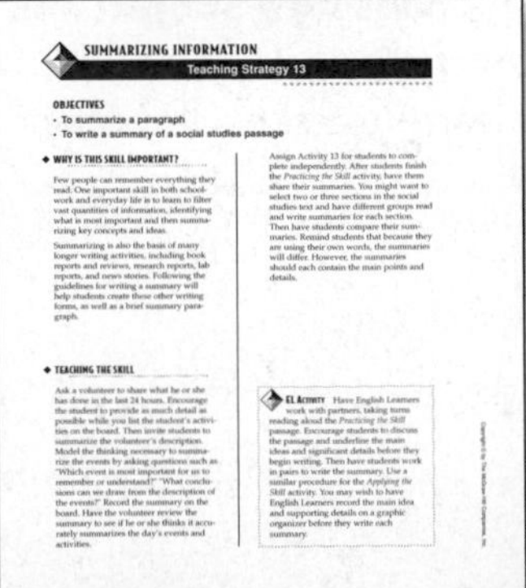

R Reading Strategy

Connecting Ask students to describe the role of women in China during the Ming and Qing dynasties. Then have students research notable Chinese women. Instruct students to write the name, position, and a short biography of each selected woman on a card. **OL**

D Differentiated Instruction

English Language Learners Have students define the word *subordinate* using context clues. **ELL**

✓Reading Check

Answer: Women were considered inferior. Only males could be educated. Within the family, women often played a strong role; however, wives were subordinate to husbands. They could not divorce or inherit property.

DOCUMENT-BASED QUESTIONS

Answers:

1. people in a garden scene and floral patterns
2. China needed foreign markets for its goods.

The clan system made it possible for wealthier families to help poorer relatives.

Women were considered inferior to men in Chinese society. One Chinese woman lamented her status in a poem:

PRIMARY SOURCE

> "How sad it is to be a woman!!
> Nothing on earth is held so cheap. . . .
> No one is glad when a girl is born:
> By *her* the family sets no store."
>
> —a Chinese woman

Only males could have a formal education and pursue a career in government or scholarship. Within the family, capable women often played strong roles. Nevertheless, the wife was clearly subordinate to the husband. Legally, she could not divorce her husband or inherit property. The husband, in contrast, could divorce his wife if she did not produce sons. He could also take a second wife. Husbands were expected to provide support for their wives and children. In many cases, the head of the family would also be responsible for providing for more than just his own wife and children.

A feature of Chinese society that restricted the mobility of women was the practice of footbinding. The origins of footbinding are not clear. Scholars believe it began among the wealthiest class of women and was later adopted by all classes. Bound feet were a status symbol. Women who had bound feet were more marriageable than those who did not; thus, there was a status **incentive** as well as an economic incentive. An estimated one-half to two-thirds of the women in China bound their feet.

The process, begun in childhood, was very painful. Women who had their feet bound could not walk; they were carried. Not all clans looked favorably on footbinding. Women who worked in the fields or in occupations that required mobility did not bind their feet.

✓Reading Check **Describing** Describe the role of women in China.

HISTORY & ARTS PRIMARY SOURCE

Ming Porcelain

Ming porcelain artists studied nature to perfect their skill in painting traditional scenes. Blue-and-white porcelain pieces were created by artists who specialized in each step of the painting, glazing, and firing process.

Jingdezhen is known as the porcelain capital of the world. Porcelain was made there as early as about 200 B.C. during the Han dynasty. When the Ming Dynasty was close to collapse, there was less domestic demand for porcelain; so Jingdezhen potters increased shipments to foreign markets such as Japan and Europe. Soon Chinese porcelain was in worldwide demand.

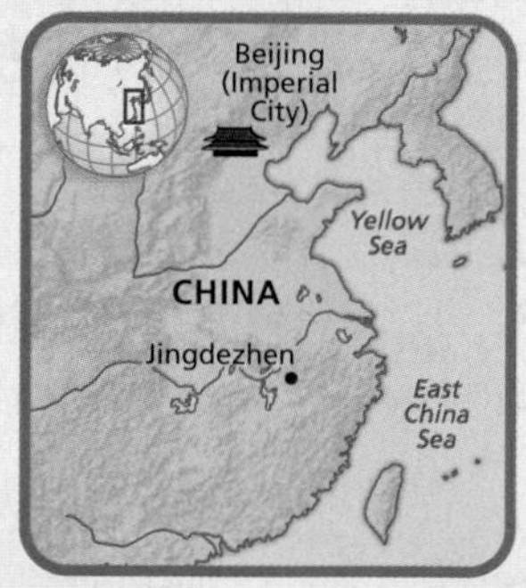

DOCUMENT-BASED QUESTIONS

This blue-and-white porcelain vase is an example of the fine decorative arts that flourished during the Ming and Qing dynasties.

1. **Describing** What traditional Chinese images are painted on the vase?
2. **Making Connections** What does the growing demand for Ming porcelain tell you about changes taking place in the Chinese economy?

Hands-On Chapter Project Step 2

Putting Together a Museum Exhibit

Step 2: Choosing a Subject and Gathering Information Student pairs will select and research the subjects of their museum exhibit.

Directions: Have students skim the chapter to gather ideas for their exhibit. On the board, create a master list of possible subjects from which students can choose. The list might include: Manchu dress and hairstyles, Ming porcelain, Chinese literature, the Imperial City, Japanese samurai, Japanese literature, Tokugawa architecture, Japanese ceramics, martial arts, or Hangul. Accept all other appropriate ideas for students' exhibits. As pairs decide on a subject, have them conduct research to gather fun facts and background information for their exhibits. Students should locate articles from a minimum of three reliable sources. **OL**

(Chapter Project is continued in Section 3.)

Chinese Art and Literature

MAIN IDEA Architecture, decorative arts, and literature flourished during the Ming and Qing dynasties.

HISTORY & YOU Under what conditions have art and literature flourished in your society? Learn about the artistic accomplishments of the Ming and Qing dynasties.

During the late Ming and the early Qing dynasties, traditional culture in China reached new heights.

The Chinese Novel

The Ming economic expansion increased standards of living, providing many Chinese with money to purchase books. Also, new innovations in paper manufacturing encouraged the growth of printing throughout China.

During the Ming dynasty, a new form of literature arose that evolved into the modern Chinese novel. Works in this literary form were quite popular, especially among well-to-do urban dwellers.

One Chinese novel, *The Golden Lotus*, is considered by many to be the first realistic social novel. *The Golden Lotus* depicts the corrupt life of a wealthy landlord in the late Ming period who cruelly manipulates those around him for sex, money, and power.

The Dream of the Red Chamber, by **Cao Xuein,** is generally considered even today to be China's most distinguished popular novel. Published in 1791, it tells of the tragic love between two young people caught in the financial and moral disintegration of a powerful Chinese clan. **W**

Ming and Qing Art

During the Ming and the early Qing dynasties, China experienced an outpouring of artistic brilliance. In architecture, the most outstanding example is the **Imperial City** in Beijing. **Emperor Yong Le** began construction of the Imperial City—a complex of palaces and temples—in 1406. Succeeding emperors continued to add to the palace.

The Imperial City is an immense compound surrounded by six and one-half miles (10.5 km) of walls. It includes a maze of private apartments and offices, as well as stately halls for imperial audiences and banquets and spacious gardens. Because it was off-limits to commoners, the compound was known as the Forbidden City.

The decorative arts also flourished in this period. Perhaps the most famous of all the arts of the Ming Era was blue-and-white **porcelain.** Europeans admired the beauty of this porcelain and collected it in great quantities. Different styles of porcelain were produced during the reign of individual emperors.

✓Reading Check **Describing** Describe the artistic accomplishments of the Ming and Qing dynasties.

Vocabulary

1. **Explain** the significance of: commercial capitalism, benefit, clan, incentive, Cao Xuein, Imperial City, Emperor Yong Le, porcelain.

Main Ideas

2. **Identify** the economic changes in China from 1500 to 1800 by using a diagram like the one below.

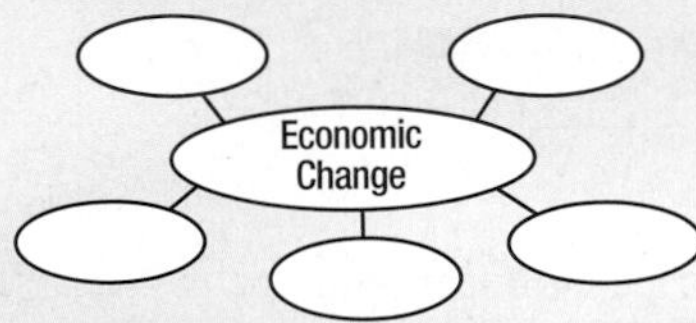

3. **Describe** the significance of the Chinese extended family.
4. **Explain** why the Imperial City was also known as the Forbidden City.

Critical Thinking

5. **The BIG Idea** **Drawing Conclusions** Although women were considered inferior to men, they filled important roles in peasant society. What were they?
6. **Comparing** Identify the similarities in plot between Cao Xuein's *The Dream of the Red Chamber* and William Shakespeare's *Romeo and Juliet*.
7. **Analyzing Visuals** Examine the picture of Chinese farmers on page 517. What do you see in the picture that teaches you about rice cultivation?

Writing About History

8. **Persuasive Writing** Imagine you are a Chinese mother talking to your daughter in 1700. Using research or your own ideas, convince her that footbinding is necessary and beneficial.

History ONLINE
For help with the concepts in this section of *Glencoe World History*, go to glencoe.com and click Study Central™.

519

W Writing Support

Expository Writing Obtain an English copy of *The Dream of the Red Chamber.* As a class, read and discuss excerpts from the novel. Then have students design a book jacket for the novel. Students should also write a brief summary of the excerpts they read. **AL**

Answer: in architecture, the Imperial City in Beijing; decorative arts also flourished; blue-and-white porcelain of the Ming dynasty

Assess

History ONLINE

Study Central provides summaries, interactive games, and online graphic organizers to help students review content.

Close

Contrasting Ask students to identify differences between their own culture and the culture described in this section. **OL**

SECTION 2 REVIEW

Answers

1. Definitions for the vocabulary words are found in the section and the Glossary.
2. population increased; less land for each family; growth in manufacturing and trade; heavy taxes levied on manufacturing and trade and low taxes on farming
3. Family was emphasized over the individual; family members cared for each other.
4. It was off-limits to commoners.
5. produced sons; worked in fields
6. Both tell of the tragic love between two young people. In *Romeo and Juliet,* the two young people's families are enemies; in *The Dream of the Red Chamber*, the two young people are caught in the financial and moral disintegration of a powerful Chinese clan.
7. Rice requires water to grow and the temperature needs to be fairly warm (since the people are wearing light clothing).
8. Answers will vary. Students might refer to issues of status and female marriageability.

Focus

Bellringer

Daily Focus Transparency 16.3

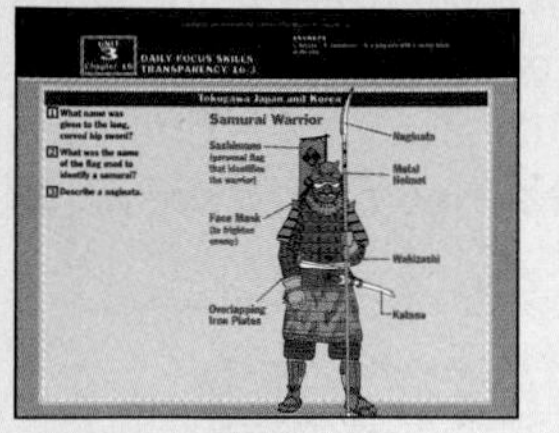

GUIDE TO READING

Answers to Graphic:

Culture: rise of popular fiction written by and for townspeople; exquisite poetry remained a more serious form of literature; rise of Kabuki dramas; increase in building and furnishing mansions; art enriched by other cultures, such as pottery techniques and designs from Korea; Japanese studied Western medicine, astronomy, languages, and even painting styles

Section Spotlight Video

To generate student interest and provide a springboard for class discussion, access the Chapter 16, Section 3 video at glencoe.com or on the video DVD.

SECTION 3

Tokugawa Japan and Korea

GUIDE TO READING

The BIG Idea

Order and Security Political unification often results in warfare and difficult economic and social changes.

Content Vocabulary

- daimyo *(p. 520)*
- hans *(p. 522)*
- hostage system *(p. 522)*
- *eta (p. 523)*

Academic Vocabulary

- process *(p. 520)*
- community *(p. 522)*

People and Places

- Oda Nobunaga *(p. 520)*
- Kyōto *(p. 520)*
- Toyotomi Hideyoshi *(p. 520)*
- Ōsaka *(p. 520)*
- Tokugawa Ieyasu *(p. 520)*
- Edo *(p. 520)*
- Matsuo Basho *(p. 524)*
- Korea *(p. 525)*

Reading Strategy

Categorizing Information As you read, categorize the different elements of Japanese culture using a diagram like the one below.

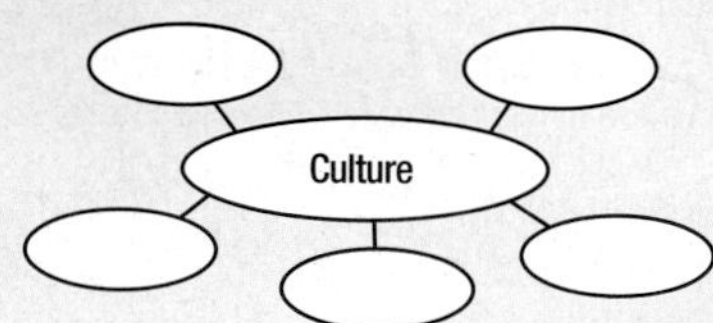

From the sixteenth century to the eighteenth century, Japan and Korea were unified through efforts of powerful leaders. Both nations imposed restrictive social systems and enforced cultural isolation. While trade and industry increased, the arts flourished in Japan's and Korea's distinctive cultures.

Political Changes in Japan

MAIN IDEA Japan's policies removed European influence and allowed Japan to remain in isolation for centuries.

HISTORY & YOU What if your family refused to allow people from outside your neighborhood to come into your home? Learn how European access to Japan was restricted during Tokugawa rule.

At the end of the fifteenth century, Japan was in chaos. The centralized power of the shogunate had collapsed. **Daimyo,** heads of noble families, controlled their own lands and warred with their neighbors. Soon, however, a dramatic reversal would unify Japan.

The Three Great Unifiers

The **process** of unification began in the late sixteenth century with three powerful political figures. The first was **Oda Nobunaga** (oh•dah noh•boo•nah•gah). Nobunaga seized the imperial capital of **Kyōto** and placed the reigning shogun under his control.

Nobunaga was succeeded by **Toyotomi Hideyoshi** (toh•yoh•toh•mee hee•day•yoh•shee), a farmer's son who had become a military commander. Hideyoshi located his capital at **Ōsaka**. By 1590, he had persuaded most of the daimyo on the Japanese islands to accept his authority.

After Hideyoshi's death in 1598, **Tokugawa Ieyasu** (toh•kuh•gah•wah ee•yah•soo), the powerful daimyo of **Edo** (modern-day Tokyo), took control of Japan. Ieyasu took the title of shogun in 1603. The Tokugawa rulers completed the restoration of central authority begun by Nobunaga and Hideyoshi. Tokugawa shoguns remained in power at their capital at Edo until 1868, a long period that became known as the "Great Peace."

Europeans in Japan

As the three great commanders were unifying Japan, the first Europeans began to arrive. Portuguese traders landed on the islands in 1543. In a few years, Portuguese ships began stopping regularly at Japanese ports to take part in the regional trade between Japan, China, and Southeast Asia.

Resource Manager

R Reading Strategies	C Critical Thinking	D Differentiated Instruction	W Writing Support	S Skill Practice
Teacher Edition • Academic Vocab., p. 523 **Additional Resources** • Academic Vocab. Act., URB p. 175 • Guid. Read. Act., URB p. 200 • Read. Ess. & Note-Taking Guide, p. 178	**Teacher Edition** • Making Inferences, p. 525 **Additional Resources** • Crit. Think. Act., URB p. 178 • Hist. & Geo. Act., URB p. 179 • World Art & Music Act., URB p. 193 • Section Quiz, p. 195	**Teacher Edition** • Visual/Spatial, p. 523 • Naturalist, p. 524 **Additional Resources** • Diff. Instr. Act., URB p. 169 • People in World Hist. Act., URB p. 190 • Pri. Source Read. Act., URB p. 191	**Teacher Edition** • Expository Writing, p. 521 **Additional Resources** • Hist. Sig. Act., URB p. 182 • Writer's Guidebook, p. 27	**Teacher Edition** • Using Geo. Skills, p. 521 **Additional Resources** • Mapping Hist. Act., URB p. 181

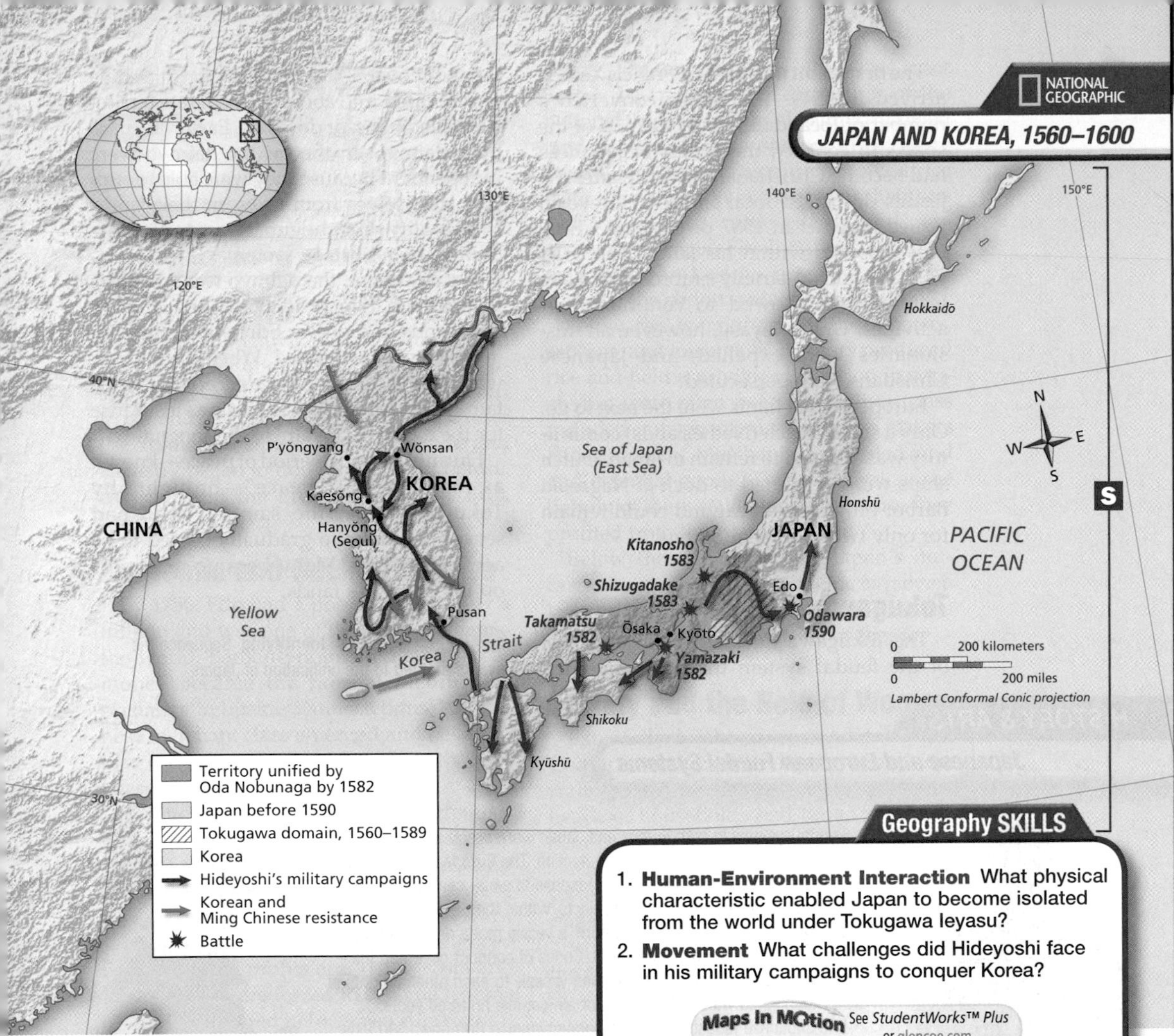

NATIONAL GEOGRAPHIC

JAPAN AND KOREA, 1560–1600

- Territory unified by Oda Nobunaga by 1582
- Japan before 1590
- Tokugawa domain, 1560–1589
- Korea
- Hideyoshi's military campaigns
- Korean and Ming Chinese resistance
- Battle

0 200 kilometers
0 200 miles
Lambert Conformal Conic projection

Geography SKILLS

1. **Human-Environment Interaction** What physical characteristic enabled Japan to become isolated from the world under Tokugawa Ieyasu?
2. **Movement** What challenges did Hideyoshi face in his military campaigns to conquer Korea?

Maps In MOtion See *StudentWorks™ Plus* or glencoe.com.

At first, the visitors were welcomed. The Japanese were fascinated by tobacco, clocks, eyeglasses, and other European goods. Nobunaga and Hideyoshi especially found the new firearms helpful in defeating their enemies and unifying the islands under their rule.

A local daimyo, Lord Tokitaka, acquired firearms from the Portuguese almost immediately after their landing in 1543. Within a few years, they were being mass-produced in Japan. Lord Tokitaka was in awe of the new weapons:

PRIMARY SOURCE

> "To use it, fill it with powder and small lead pellets. Set up a small target on a bank. Grip the object in your hand, compose your body, and closing one eye, apply fire to the opening. Then the pellet hits the target squarely. The explosion is like lightning and the report like thunder. . . . This thing with one blow can smash a mountain of silver and a wall of iron. If one sought to do mischief in another man's domain, and he was touched by it, he would lose his life instantly. . . ."
>
> —Lord Tokitaka

History ONLINE
Student Web Activity— Visit glencoe.com and complete the activity on the role of the shogun in Japan.

Teach

W Writing Support

Expository Writing Ask students to write an essay in which they evaluate the reaction of the Japanese daimyo to firearms. Do students believe the daimyo was merely intrigued by these weapons, or vdid he realize how important they would be to the future of Japan? How might Japan's history have been different if the Europeans had not sold them military technology? **AL**

S Skill Practice

Using Geography Skills Ask: Which island contains the three cities that served as capitals during the unification of Japan? *(Honshu)* **BL**

Geography SKILLS

Answers:

1. Japan consisted of a group of islands.
2. moving soldiers and equipment over a sea to fight; keeping supplies coming and/or acquiring weapons and supplies

Determining Cause and Effect

Objective: To understand how Toyotomi Hideyoshi helped unify Japan.

Focus: Have students read and discuss the introductory paragraph.

Teach: Have students answer the questions.

Assess: Ask students to describe Hideyoshi's military accomplishments.

Close: Tell students that Tokugawa Ieyasu succeeded Hideyoshi, and he completed Japan's unification.

Differentiated Instruction Strategies

- **BL** Provide individualized assistance as needed.
- **AL** Have students write a paragraph evaluating the military leadership of Hideyoshi using examples from the text to support their evaluation.
- **ELL** Paraphrase the questions into simpler language for students.

Differentiated Instruction

People in World History Activity 16 — Profile 2

Toyotomi Hideyoshi (c. 1536/37–1598)

People in World History Activity, URB p. 190

D Differentiated Instruction

Naturalist Tell students that Matsuo Basho was concerned with the search for the meaning of life and found answers to his quest in nature. His poems, called haiku, are grounded in natural images. Challenge students to find examples of Matsuo Basho's poems and after reading them, write their own haiku verses. OL

✓Reading Check

Answer: Parents arranged marriages. A wife was expected to move in with her husband's family. If a wife did not meet the expectations of her husband or his family, she was likely to be divorced.

Answers:

1. tae kwon do
2. The martial arts provide the opportunity to learn about Asian cultures since they are linked to Asian philosophies; they also promote health and self-discipline.

Additional Support

These five women of the merchant class are willing to die for love—and all but one eventually do.

Much popular literature of the Tokugawa Era was lighthearted and intended to please its audiences. Poetry remained a more serious form of literary expression. **Matsuo Basho,** the greatest Japanese poet, wrote exquisite poetry about nature in the seventeenth century. D

A new world of entertainment in the cities gave rise in the theater to Kabuki, which emphasized action, music, and dramatic gestures to entertain its viewers. Early Kabuki dramas dealt with the world of teahouses and dance halls in the cities. Government officials feared that exposure to these subjects onstage might corrupt the moral standards of its people. They therefore forbade women to appear on stage. The result was that a new profession was created—male actors who portrayed female characters on stage.

Art also reflected the changes in Japanese culture under the Tokugawa Era. The shogun's order that all daimyo and their families have residences in Edo sparked an increase in building. Nobles competed to erect the most magnificent mansions with lavish and beautiful furnishings. The abundant use of gold foil on walls and ceilings reflected the light in dark castle rooms, where windows were often small.

Japanese art was enriched by ideas from other cultures. Japanese pottery makers borrowed techniques and designs from Korea to create handsome ceramic pieces. The Japanese studied Western medicine, astronomy, languages, and even painting styles. In turn, Europeans wanted Japanese ceramics, which were prized as highly as the ceramics of the Chinese.

✓Reading Check **Explaining** In what ways were the rights of women of the common class restricted?

Connecting to the United States

The Martial Arts

The martial arts are the arts of combat and self-defense that developed in Asian cultures over many centuries. Practice of the martial arts promotes not only physical fitness but also a philosophy or way of life.

In recent years, the martial arts have become part of Western culture. In the United States, one can learn Chinese kung fu and tai chi, Japanese karate and judo, and Korean tae kwon do. Judo and tae kwon do are Olympic sports.

- Training in martial arts develops self-discipline and strength.
- The practice of martial arts promotes better health through self-awareness.
- Competitive sports can bridge cultural differences.

CONNECTING TO TODAY

1. **Naming** Name a martial arts sport that originated in Korea.
2. **Summarizing** What are some of the benefits of practicing the martial arts?

524

Extending the Content

Martial Arts After Communists came to power in China in 1949, the government again fostered the martial arts as a competitive sport. Martial arts teams have spread throughout the world.

In 1990, an International Wushu (Martial Arts) Association was formed, consisting of representatives from more than 30 nations. The First World Martial Arts Championship took place in Beijing in 1991.

Ask: Why do you think the martial arts have become so popular both in the United States and worldwide? *(Answers may include: They are fun activities, they promote physical and mental fitness, they are competitive, there are many different forms of martial arts from which to choose, they teach practical skills.)* OL

Korea: The Hermit Kingdom

MAIN IDEA Due to its isolationist practices, Korea earned the name "the Hermit Kingdom."

HISTORY & YOU Did you and your best friend ever use a secret code to communicate? Learn about Korea's development of a distinctive alphabet.

The Yi dynasty in **Korea** began in 1392 when Yi Song-gye (YEE•sung•jay), a renowned military strategist, ascended the throne by overthrowing the Koryo dynasty. Lasting for five centuries, the Yi dynasty was one of the world's longest-lasting monarchies.

Distinctive Culture

From their capital at Hanseong (modern-day Seoul), Yi rulers consolidated their rule of Korea. They patterned their society after that of the Chinese to the north but maintained their distinctive identity.

Perhaps the single most distinctive characteristic of the Korean culture was development of a unique alphabet, Hangul. Unlike Japanese or Chinese, which uses thousands of characters or symbols, Hangul is a phonetically based writing system. That is, it uses one letter for each sound, similar to the English alphabet. Hangul is still largely the standard writing system in present-day Korea. **C**

Cultural Isolation

The Yi dynasty was not to last forever. The dynasty was severely weakened during the late sixteenth and early seventeenth centuries. There were disruptive divisions within its elite classes. Both Japanese and Chinese invasions devastated Korea.

A Japanese force under Toyotomi Hideyoshi invaded Korea in the late sixteenth century. Hideyoshi wanted to use Korea as the transit route for his conquest of China. The Japanese invaders were defeated, but victory came at a high price. Korean farmlands were devastated, and villages and towns were burned. Skilled workers were also either killed or kidnapped by the Japanese.

In response to these events, the Korean rulers sought to limit contact with foreign countries and tried to keep the country isolated from the outside world. The country remained largely untouched by European merchants and Christian missionaries. Due to its isolationist practices, Korea earned the name "the Hermit Kingdom."

Korea was still recovering from the Japanese invasions when the Manchus attacked in the early seventeenth century. Korea surrendered, and the Yi dynasty became subject to China.

✓Reading Check **Summarizing** Why was Korea called "the Hermit Kingdom"?

SECTION 3 REVIEW

Vocabulary

1. **Explain** the significance of: daimyo, process, Oda Nobunaga, Kyōto, Toyotomi Hideyoshi, Ōsaka, Tokugawa Ieyasu, Edo, community, hans, hostage system, *eta*, Matsuo Basho, Korea.

Main Ideas

2. **List** the three great Japanese unifiers and their capital cities.
3. **Illustrate** the four main social classes that existed during the Tokugawa Era using a diagram like the one below. Place the highest-ranking social class at the top of the pyramid.

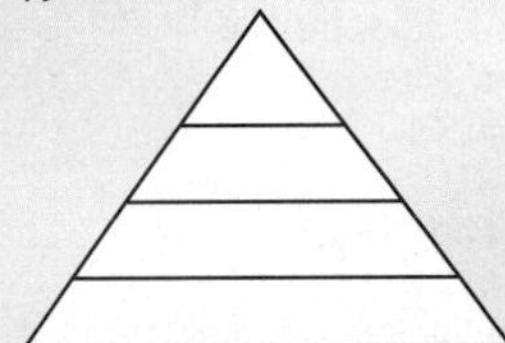

4. **Describe** the single most distinctive characteristic of the Korean culture.

Critical Thinking

5. **The BIG Idea** **Evaluating** What events led to Japan and Korea practicing cultural isolation?
6. **Drawing Inferences** How were most peasants affected by the economic changes in Japan?
7. **Analyzing Visuals** Examine the photographs of armor worn by knights and samurai on page 522. How does each suit of armor compare to and contrast with the other, and what does that reveal about warriors in each society?

Writing About History

8. **Descriptive Writing** Imagine that you are the literate wife of a samurai. Write a journal entry that describes your relationship to your husband, your children, and your mother-in-law.

History ONLINE
For help with the concepts in this section of *Glencoe World History*, go to glencoe.com and click Study Central™.

525

C Critical Thinking

Making Inferences Have students research the Hangul language on the Internet. **Ask:** Why is the development of Hangul considered such an important accomplishment? *(Hangul sets Korea apart from all other East Asian countries.)* **OL**

Answer: Korea's rulers tried to keep the country isolated from the outside world.

Assess

History ONLINE

Study Central provides summaries, interactive games, and online graphic organizers to help students review content.

Close

Comparing Have students identify similarities among the Ming, Qing, and Tokugawa dynasties. **OL**

SECTION 3 REVIEW

Answers

1. Definitions for the vocabulary words are found in the section and the Glossary.
2. Oda Nobunaga, Kyoto; Toyotomi Hideyoshi, Osaka; Tokugawa Ieyasu, Edo
3. From top to bottom: warriors; farmers (peasants); artisans; merchants
4. development of Hangul, a phonetically-based alphabet similar to the English alphabet
5. **Japan:** destruction of shrines; **Korea:** Japanese invasions
6. They experienced declining profits and rising costs and taxes.
7. Both types of armor try to protect the person wearing them from harm. Both types of armor try to make the wearer look fierce. The differences in the materials are probably due to the weapons that the armor needed to protect against.
8. Answers will vary but should be consistent with material presented in this section.

Focus

Bellringer

Daily Focus Transparency 16.4

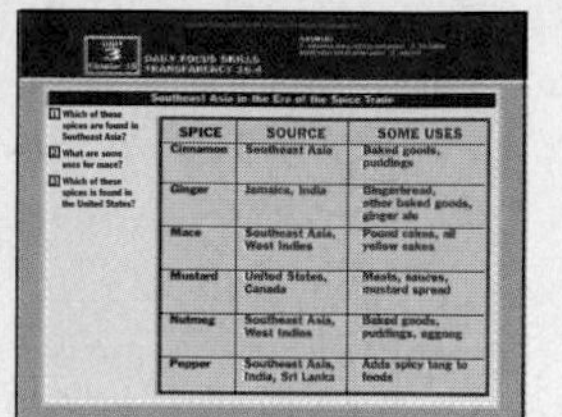

GUIDE TO READING

Answers to Graphic:

European Contact in Southeast Asia
cohesive character of the mainland states
Europeans did not colonize in Southeast Asia

Section Spotlight Video

To generate student interest and provide a springboard for class discussion, access the Chapter 16, Section 4 video at glencoe.com or on the video DVD.

Spice Trade in Southeast Asia

GUIDE TO READING

The BIG Idea

Competition Among Countries
Europeans struggled to control the profitable spice trade in Southeast Asia.

Content Vocabulary
- bureaucracy *(p. 528)*
- mainland states *(p. 529)*

Academic Vocabulary
- network *(p. 526)*
- impose *(p. 529)*

People and Places
- Khmer *(p. 526)*
- Philippines *(p. 527)*
- Moluccas *(p. 529)*
- Dutch *(p. 529)*
- Sumatra *(p. 529)*
- Java *(p. 529)*

Reading Strategy

Summarizing Information As you read, use a chart like the one below to list reasons why the destructive effects of European contact in Southeast Asia were only gradually felt.

European Contact in Southeast Asia

Attracted to the growing spice trade, Muslim merchants established a trade network along the Malay Peninsula and the Indonesian archipelago. In the sixteenth century, the Portuguese seized control of the spice trade, eventually attracting English and Dutch competition.

Emerging Mainland States

MAIN IDEA The spice trade influenced the politics, religion, and economy of the Malay Peninsula and the Indonesian archipelago.

HISTORY & YOU What if one student had a monopoly on providing music to your school? Learn what effect the arrival of spice traders had on Southeast Asia.

In 1500, mainland Southeast Asia was a relatively stable region. Throughout mainland Southeast Asia, from Burma in the west to Vietnam in the east, kingdoms with their own ethnic, linguistic, and cultural characteristics were being formed.

Conflicts in Southeast Asia

Conflicts erupted among the emerging states on the Southeast Asian mainland. Conflict over territory between the Thai and the Burmese was bitter until a Burmese army sacked the Thai capital in 1767. The Thai then created a new capital at Bangkok, farther to the south.

Across the mountains to the east, the Vietnamese had begun their "March to the South." By the end of the fifteenth century, they had subdued the rival state of Champa on the central coast. The Vietnamese then gradually took control of the Mekong Delta from the **Khmer**. By 1800, the Khmer monarchy (the successor of the old Angkor kingdom—see Chapter 8) had virtually disappeared.

Islamic Trade Network

The situation was different in the Malay Peninsula and the Indonesian archipelago. Muslim merchants were attracted to the growing spice trade. They gradually entered the area. The creation of an Islamic trade **network** had political results as new Islamic states arose along the spice route. The major impact of this trade network, however, came in the fifteenth century with the new Muslim sultanate at Melaka. Melaka owed its new power to its strategic location on the Strait of Malacca and to the rapid growth of the spice trade itself. Within a few years, Melaka had become the leading power in the region.

Resource Manager

R Reading Strategies	C Critical Thinking	D Differentiated Instruction	W Writing Support	S Skill Practice
Teacher Edition • Outlining, p. 527 **Additional Resources** • Cont. Vocab. Act., URB p. 173 • Guid. Read. Act., URB p. 201 • Read. Ess. & Note-Taking Guide, p. 181	**Teacher Edition** • Pred. Consequences, p. 528 **Additional Resources** • Hist. Analysis Skills Act., URB p. 168 • Crit. Think Act., URB p. 178 • Section Quiz, p. 196 • Chapter Test, p. 197	**Teacher Edition** • Visual/Spatial, p. 529 **Additional Resources** • Academic Vocab. Act., URB p. 175 • Hist. Sim. Act., URB p. 185 • Enrich. Act., URB p. 196	**Teacher Edition** • Persuasive Writing, p. 528 **Additional Resources** • Coop. Learn. Act., URB p. 183	**Teacher Edition** • Using Geo. Skills, p. 527 **Additional Resources** • Time Line Act., URB p. 187 • Reteach. Act., URB p. 195

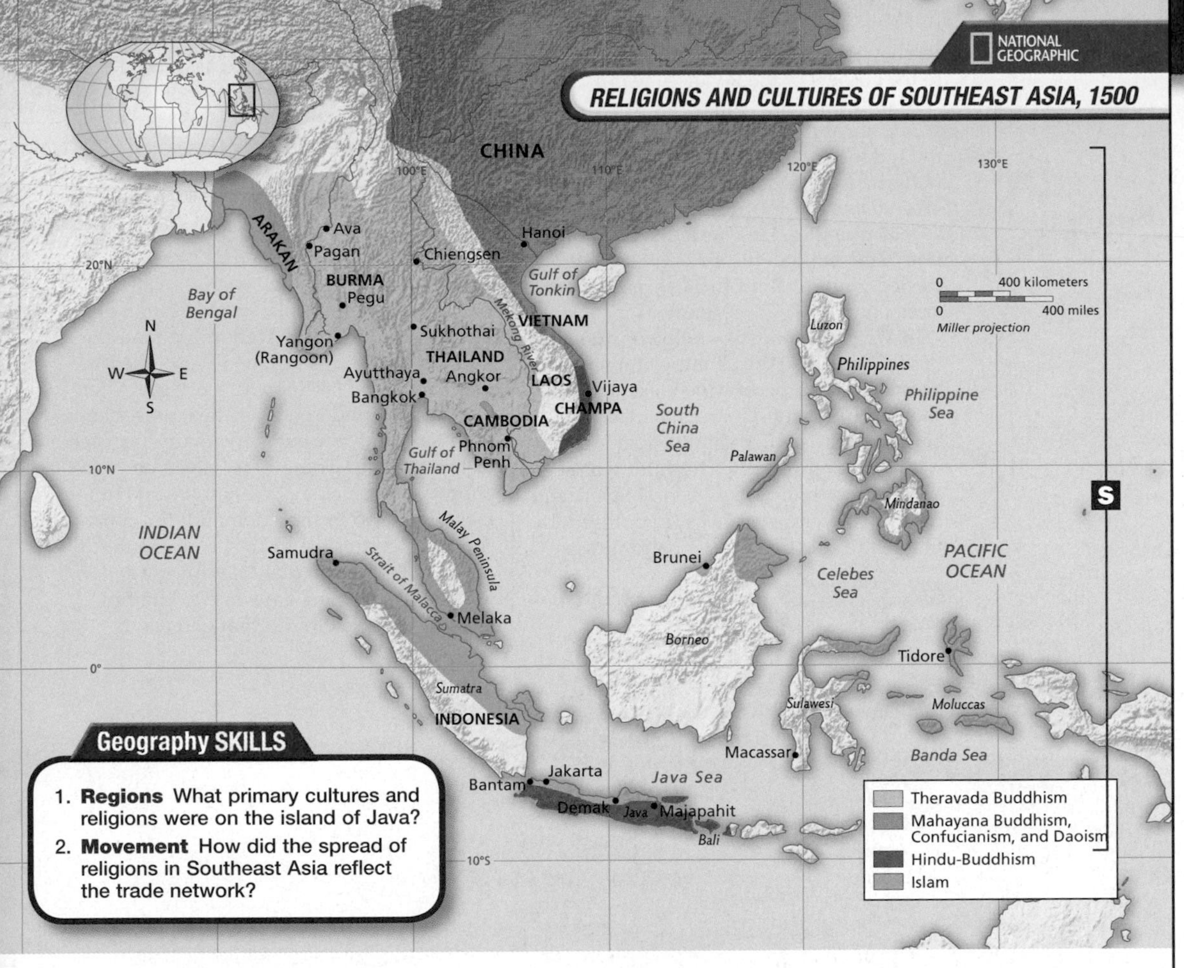

Geography SKILLS

1. **Regions** What primary cultures and religions were on the island of Java?
2. **Movement** How did the spread of religions in Southeast Asia reflect the trade network?

Religious and Political Systems

Religious beliefs changed in Southeast Asia during the period from 1500 to 1800. Particularly in the non-mainland states and the **Philippines,** Islam and Christianity began to attract converts. Buddhism advanced on the mainland, becoming dominant from Burma to Vietnam. Traditional beliefs, however, survived and influenced the new religions.

The political systems in Southeast Asian states evolved into four styles of monarchy. Buddhist kings, Javanese kings, Islamic sultans, and Vietnamese emperors all adapted foreign models of government to suit their local circumstances.

The Buddhist style of kingship became the chief form of government in the mainland states of Burma, Thailand, Laos, and Cambodia. In the Buddhist model, the king was considered superior to other human beings and served as the link between human society and the universe.

The Javanese style of kingship was rooted in the political traditions of India and shared many characteristics of the Buddhist system. Like Buddhist rulers, Javanese kings were believed to have a sacred quality. They maintained the balance between the sacred world and the material world. The royal palace was designed to represent the center of the universe.

Teach

R Reading Strategy

Outlining Have students outline the section as they read. Remind students that headings, subheadings, boldfaced terms, and graphics are good indicators of main ideas and supporting details. **BL**

S Skill Practice

Using Geography Skills Have students use a current almanac to locate religious statistics for the countries of Southeast Asia today. Then ask students to recreate the map on this page to reflect the region's present-day religious practices. **AL**

Geography SKILLS

Answers:

1. Islam and Hindu-Buddhism
2. Islamic traders introduced the religion of Islam to the area, especially the island nations. Mainland countries were influenced by trade with China and India and were more likely to be Buddhists, Hindus, Confucians, or Daoists.

Hands-On Chapter Project
Step 4

Putting Together a Museum Exhibit

Step 4: Designing the Exhibit Student pairs will design their museum exhibits. As a class, discuss the amount of space that each exhibit may have and any restrictions on the types of displays students may use. For example, students may need to be able to pack up their exhibit by the end of the class period.

Directions: Have students begin gathering the necessary materials to set up their exhibits. Students may wish to bring items from home to use as a simulated artifact, or they may prefer to make a color printout of an authentic Southeast Asian artifact. Students who exhibit a cultural feature should design an original display containing images to accompany the descriptions of their feature. **OL**

(Chapter Project is continued on the Visual Summary page.)

C Critical Thinking

Predicting Consequences
Ask: What effects do you think the arrival of the Europeans had on Southeast Asia? *(Answers may include: The Europeans tried to conquer and colonize the kingdoms of Southeast Asia; the Europeans tried to make a profit from Southeast Asia's resources.)* OL

W Writing Suppvort

Persuasive Writing Tell students to suppose that they are European explorers who have control over trade in the Spice Islands. Have each student write an advertising slogan to persuade people in other countries to come to them for their spices. OL

✓Reading Check

Answer: Buddhist kings, Javanese kings, Islamic sultans, and Vietnamese emperors

CRITICAL THINKING SKILLS

Answers:
1. The company built the city of Batavia in a Dutch city style.
2. for its good harbor and central trading location

Its shape was like rays spreading outward to the corners of the Javanese realm.

Islamic sultans ruled on the Malay Peninsula and in the small coastal states of the Indonesian archipelago. In the Islamic pattern, the head of state was a sultan. Viewed as a mortal, he still possessed some special qualities. He was a defender of the faith and staffed his **bureaucracy** (non-elected government officials) mainly with aristocrats.

In Vietnam, kingship followed the Chinese model. Like the Chinese emperor, the Vietnamese emperor ruled according to the teachings of Confucius. Confucius believed that a ruler should treat subjects with love and respect. The ruler was seen as an intermediary between Heaven and Earth. The emperor was appointed by Heaven to rule by his talent and virtue.

✓Reading Check **Listing** List the four styles of monarchy in Southeast Asia.

C The Arrival of Europeans

MAIN IDEA Europeans struggled to control the profitable spice trade in the Malay Peninsula and the Indonesian archipelago.

HISTORY & YOU What if you controlled all of the money of your household? Learn about the shift in power in Southeast Asia.

Since ancient times, spices had been highly valued. Spices were more than flavorings for food. They were also used as medicines and as food preservers. After bad harvests and in winter, meat preserved with salt and pepper kept many people W from starving. There was never enough pepper. Ginger, cloves, cinnamon, and nutmeg were also in high demand. European countries competed to find a sea route to the Indies. In particular, that hunt was for Melaka, the fabled gateway to the Spice Islands. Portugal found that gateway.

HISTORY & ARTS

The Dutch at Batavia

By the early 1600s, the Dutch dominated the spice trade in the Indian Ocean. In 1619 the Dutch established a fort at Batavia on the island of Java. This fort became the headquarters of the Dutch East India Company.

At the peak of its power, the Dutch East India Company had 40 warships, 150 merchant ships, and 10,000 soldiers. The spice trade brought huge profits to investors.

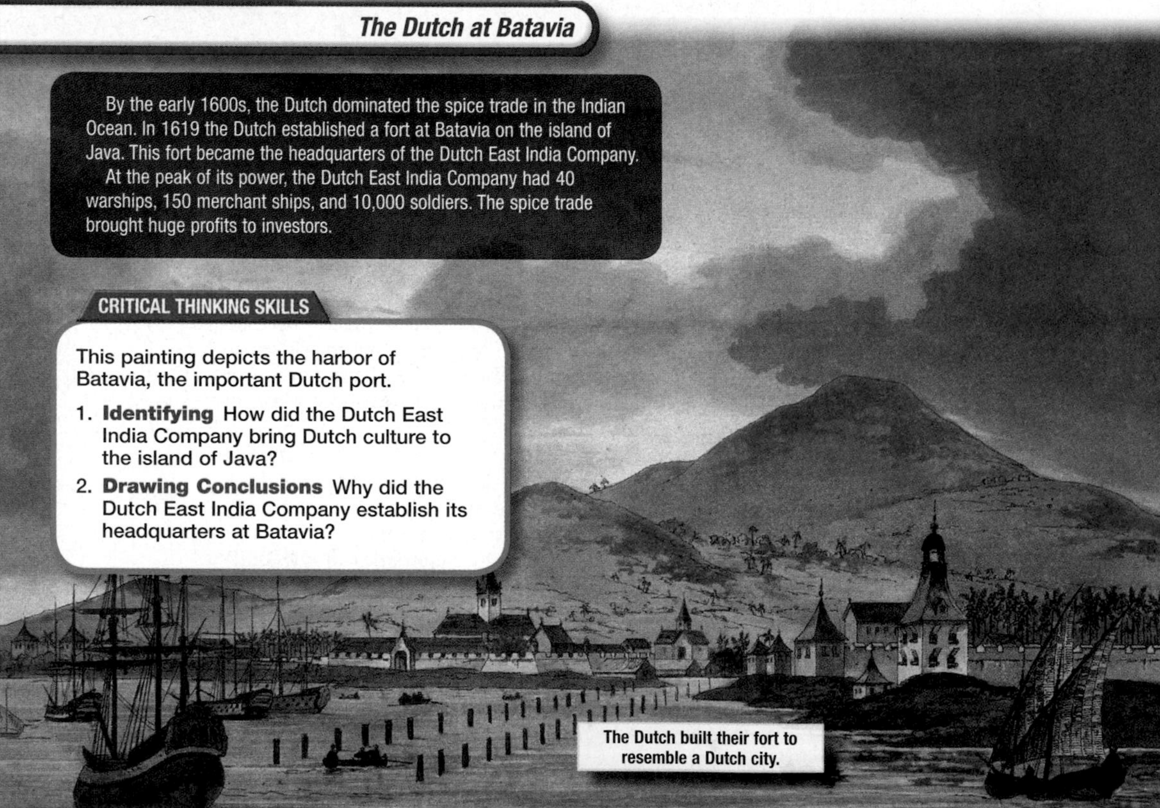

CRITICAL THINKING SKILLS

This painting depicts the harbor of Batavia, the important Dutch port.

1. **Identifying** How did the Dutch East India Company bring Dutch culture to the island of Java?
2. **Drawing Conclusions** Why did the Dutch East India Company establish its headquarters at Batavia?

The Dutch built their fort to resemble a Dutch city.

Differentiated Instruction

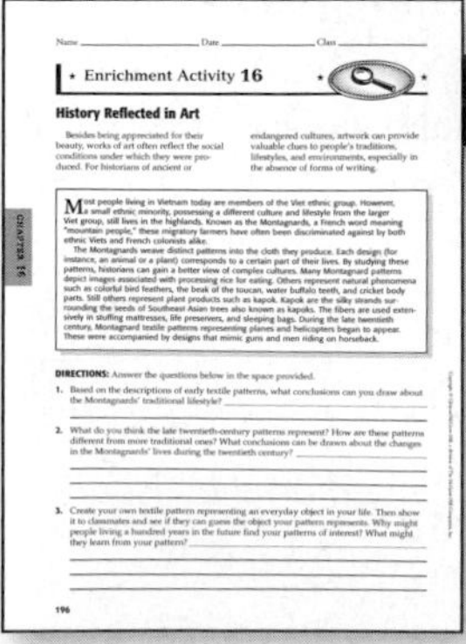

Enrichment Activity, URB p. 196

Drawing Conclusions

Objective: Draw conclusions about the Montagnards' lives.

Focus: Discuss with students how art reflects the culture in which it is created.

Teach: Display a map of Vietnam and point out the highlands where the Montagnards still live.

Assess: Have students answer the questions.

Close: Discuss the kinds of information historians can discover about a culture by analyzing the artwork that it produces.

Differentiated Instruction Strategies

- **BL** Have pairs brainstorm lists of objects to include in their textile designs.
- **AL** Ask students to obtain photographs of historic and modern Montagnard weavings. Have students make a class presentation of their findings.
- **ELL** When they create their pattern, encourage students to include an object significant in their home culture.

When Vasco da Gama and his crew came ashore at Calicut in 1498, they shouted, "For Christ and spices!" The voyage's purpose was twofold: conversion and trade. More important were the spices. In 1511, the Portuguese seized Melaka and soon occupied the **Moluccas.** Known to Europeans as the Spice Islands, the Moluccas were the main source of spices that first attracted the Portuguese to the Indian Ocean. W

The Portuguese lacked the military and financial resources to **impose** their authority over broad areas. They set up small settlements along the coast and used them as trading posts during travel to and from the Spice Islands.

A Shift in Power

The situation changed with the arrival of the English and **Dutch** (Netherlands) traders, who were better financed than the Portuguese. The shift in power began in the early 1600s when the Dutch seized a Portuguese fort in the Moluccas and gradually pushed the Portuguese out of the spice trade.

During the next 50 years, the Dutch occupied most Portuguese coastal forts along the trade routes throughout the Indian Ocean. They drove the English traders out of the spice market. England was left with a single port on the southern coast of **Sumatra.**

The Dutch also began to consolidate their political and military control over the entire area. They established a fort on the island of **Java** at Batavia in 1619 to protect their possessions. Gradually the Dutch brought the entire island under their control and closed access to the Spice Islands.

Impact on the Mainland

By the early seventeenth century, other European nations had begun to compete actively for trade and missionary privileges in Southeast Asia. The arrival of the Europeans had less impact on mainland Southeast Asia. In general, the **mainland states** (part of the continent, as distinguished from peninsulas or offshore islands) were able to unite and drive the Europeans out.

Why were the mainland states better able to resist the European challenge than were the states in the Malay Peninsula and the Indonesian archipelago? The mainland states of Burma, Thailand, and Vietnam had begun to define themselves as distinct political entities. They had strong monarchies that resisted foreign intrusion. D

In the non-mainland states, there was less political unity. Moreover, these states were victims of their own resources. The spice trade there was enormously profitable. European merchants and rulers were determined to gain control of the sources of the spices.

✓Reading Check **Evaluating** Why were Europeans so interested in Southeast Asia?

SECTION 4 REVIEW

Vocabulary
1. **Explain** the significance of: Khmer, network, Philippines, bureaucracy, Moluccas, impose, Dutch, Sumatra, Java, mainland states.

Main Ideas
2. **Explain** how the sultanate at Melaka impacted the Malay Peninsula and the Indonesian archipelago.
3. **Describe** the four types of political systems that developed in Southeast Asia by using a chart like the one below.

Region	Political System

4. **Specify** why the mainland states were better able than the non-mainland states to resist the Europeans.

Critical Thinking
5. **The BIG Idea** **Evaluating** What advantages did Dutch traders have in the struggle to control the spice trade?
6. **Comparing** From a religious point of view, how were the rulers under the four styles of monarchy seen by their subjects?
7. **Analyzing Visuals** Examine the painting on page 528. How does the artist capture the Dutch influence on the island of Java? What elements can you identify that are Javanese?

Writing About History
8. **Expository Writing** Suppose that you are a Portuguese merchant trying to establish trade relations with Southeast Asia. Write a letter to the authorities in Portugal explaining the particular difficulties you are encountering in Southeast Asia.

History ONLINE
For help with the concepts in this section of *Glencoe World History*, go to glencoe.com and click Study Central™.

529

D Differentiated Instruction

Visual/Spatial Ask volunteers to locate the following places on a classroom map of Southeast Asia: Malay Peninsula, Indonesian Archipelago, Burma, Thailand, and Vietnam. OL

✓Reading Check

Answer: The spice trade there was enormously profitable.

Assess

History ONLINE

Study Central provides summaries, interactive games, and online graphic organizers to help students review content.

Close

Summarizing Ask students whether or not they believe that Southeast Asia became part of "the age of Western Dominance" during the years covered by this section. OL

SECTION 4 REVIEW

Answers

1. Definitions for the vocabulary words are found in the section and the Glossary.
2. strategic location and rapid growth of spice trade; became the leading power in the region
3. **Burma, Thailand, Laos, Cambodia:** Buddhist kingship; **Java:** Indian kingship; **Malay Peninsula, Indonesian Archipelago:** Islamic sultanates; **Vietnam:** emperor
4. **mainland states:** distinct political entities, strong monarchies; **non-mainland states:** less political unity, victims of their own resources
5. The Dutch had military and financial resources to impose authority over broad areas.
6. **Buddhist:** superior to other humans; **Javanese:** had a sacred quality; **Islamic:** mortal with special qualities; **Vietnamese:** served as intermediary between Heaven and Earth
7. The painter shows a Dutch trading vessel, as well as the fort that was built in the style of a Dutch town; there are Javanese ships in the harbor next to the Dutch trading ship.
8. Letters should be supported by facts from the text.

Focus

Introducing Social History Have students examine the image on these pages. Ask them what impression they receive of Kabuki from the costumes and appearances of the actors. Then have volunteers read the text.

Teach

R Reading Strategy

Analyzing Information Ask: What might the emphasis upon the external appearance of the actors suggest about characterization in Kabuki? *(The emphasis is less on subtle development of character and more on the drama of the action and the recognition of character types.)* AL

D Differentiated Instruction

Visual/Spatial Have students illustrate the different makeup and wig styles described and write a caption saying what each one symbolizes. BL

Additional Support

Social History

Kabuki: A New World of Entertainment

Kabuki, the Japanese theatrical art form that combines drama, dance, and music, has been popular since its beginning in 1603. Its unconventional and exciting style offered a welcome diversion from the worries and confusion brought about by changes to Japanese culture and society during the early years of the Tokugawa Era. An established art form by the 1700s, Kabuki and its professional class of male actors performed historical and contemporary plays, entertaining all members of society—from common townspeople to high-ranking nobles.

Throughout the history of Kabuki, families of male actors have become famous for performing specific male and female roles, passing on their acting traditions from one generation to the next.

Kabuki actors enter and exit the stage on the *hanamichi*, a raised path that extends from the back of the theater, through the audience, and to the left-hand side of the stage. In one type of stylized movement, called *roppō*, the actor exits the stage in a series of leaps.

Costumes and Makeup

R D Among Kabuki's many unique elements are magnificent costumes, striking makeup, and a remarkable variety of wigs. The colors of face makeup and differences in wig styles are used to symbolize characters' traits. For example, bold red lines express a character's positive traits, such as strength or virtue. The color blue expresses negative traits, such as jealousy or wickedness. A wig styled so that the hair stands on end expresses a character's feelings of rage.

Background

Kabuki The first Kabuki performer was a woman who had served at a Buddhist shrine and then performed dances that parodied Buddhist worshipers. She and her group of female performers began the first theatrical form in Japan aimed at the common people. The government banned women from performing in 1629 and in 1652 also banned young boys from playing women's roles, both on moral grounds. Kabuki became more dramatically complex when older men took over the performances. Its popularity grew as merchants became more important in Japanese society. The plays present historical and contemporary stories, along with moral teachings from Buddhism and Confucianism. Dancing is the most prominent aspect of the performances. There is a lot of interaction between actors and audience during the performances.

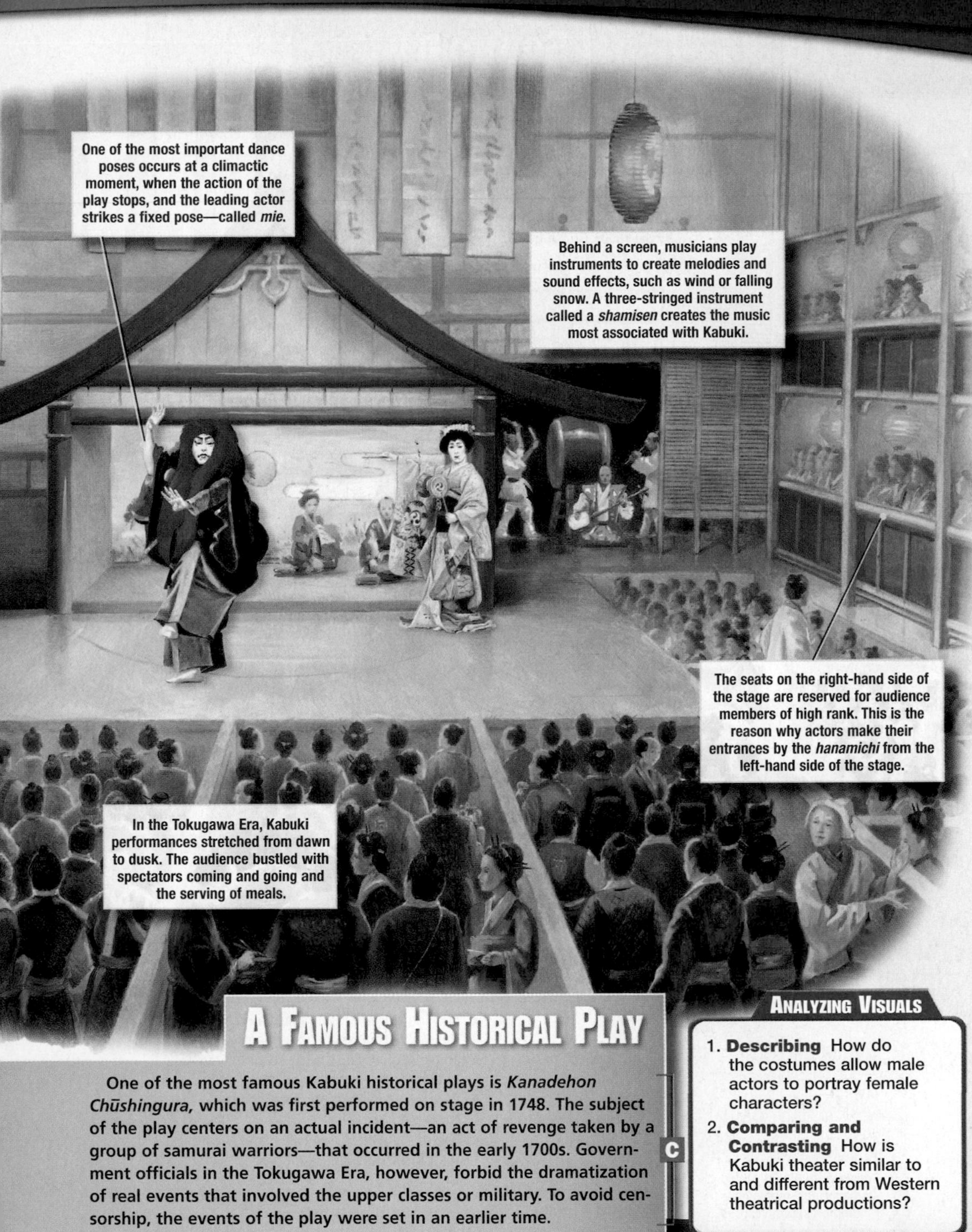

A Famous Historical Play

One of the most famous Kabuki historical plays is *Kanadehon Chūshingura,* which was first performed on stage in 1748. The subject of the play centers on an actual incident—an act of revenge taken by a group of samurai warriors—that occurred in the early 1700s. Government officials in the Tokugawa Era, however, forbid the dramatization of real events that involved the upper classes or military. To avoid censorship, the events of the play were set in an earlier time. **C**

Analyzing Visuals

1. **Describing** How do the costumes allow male actors to portray female characters?
2. **Comparing and Contrasting** How is Kabuki theater similar to and different from Western theatrical productions?

531

C Critical Thinking

Drawing Conclusions Ask: Why would the government forbid performers to dramatize real events involving the upper class or military? *(It might undermine the social order and lead to questioning of the government's authority.)* **OL**

Assess/Close

Summarizing Ask: What are the major characteristics of Kabuki? *(The major characteristics include male actors, elaborate costumes and wigs, long performances, dramatic dances and movements, and a stage that extends into the audience.)* **OL**

Analyzing Visuals

Answers:

1. costumes give the illusion of a female character on stage
2. **similar:** use of music, costumes, makeup, and dance in performances; similar topics covered in dramas **different:** elements of the stage such as the *hanamichi;* elements of the performance such as the *roppō* and *mie;* three-stringed instrument called a *shamisen*

Activity: Collaborative Learning

Adapting Kabuki to the West Ask: Why might it be difficult for American audiences to relate to traditional Kabuki performances, even if they were translated into English? *(Students may suggest that the traditional stories or dramatic conventions such as makeup, wigs, and stylized movements would be unfamiliar.)* Explain that Kabuki developed in Japan at about the same time that Shakespearean drama, ballet, and opera were developing in the West. Some theater companies in the United States have performed plays that blend well-known Western stories from Shakespeare or Greek tragedy with the techniques and approach of Kabuki. Have students work together to dramatize a familiar, simple story, perhaps a fairy tale or folk tale incorporating some aspects of Kabuki such as stylized make-up, wigs, dancing, mime, music and sound effects. Students may do additional research to learn more about Kabuki traditions. **OL**

Comparing and Contrasting Discuss the information provided on the Visual Summary. Remind students that this information includes important ideas from the entire chapter. Have students work in pairs to use the information in the Visual Summary to write some comparison and contrast statements. **Ask:** What similarities and differences do you notice about China, Japan and Korea, and Southeast Asia? *(Accept reasonable responses. Encourage students to start with the information in the Visual Summary, but also to augment their comparison and contrast statements with details from the sections in the chapter.)* **OL**

This **Reading Skill** was introduced in this unit.

Visual/Spatial Ask students to read the text on the page. Have them go back through the chapter and identify at least one image to support statements in each section of the Visual Summary. Discuss their choices as a group and have each student support their choices verbally. **BL**

CHAPTER 16 Visual Summary

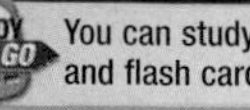

You can study anywhere, anytime by downloading quizzes and flash cards to your PDA from glencoe.com.

CHINESE WORKERS PACKING TEA

By the 1800s, British traders wanted more liberal trade policies with China. There was a very high demand for tea.

CHINA

- During the Ming dynasty, China sponsored voyages of exploration and made contact with the West.
- Qing rulers restricted trade with Europeans.
- By the late 1700s, China experienced growth in trade and manufacturing.
- Arts, architecture, and literature flourished during the Ming and Qing dynasties.

JAPAN AND KOREA

- Three powerful leaders unified Japan.
- At first Japan welcomed European traders, but later forced them to leave.
- Under Tokugawa rule, the Japanese class system became rigid while trade, industry, and the arts flourished.
- Korea tried to remain isolated, yet eventually became subject to China.

INSIDE A KABUKI THEATER

The theater and other arts grew very popular during Tokugawa rule in Japan.

THE SPICE TRADE IN THE MOLUCCAS

Spices were highly valued as flavorings, medicines, and preservatives.

SOUTHEAST ASIA
Trade in the Spice Era

- Seeking spices, Muslim merchants entered the Malay Peninsula and Indonesia.
- The religion, politics, and economics of the region were affected by the spice trade.
- European countries competed to control the spice trade.
- The Netherlands eventually gained control and closed access to the Moluccas (Spice Islands).

Hands-On Chapter Project
Step 5: Wrap-Up

Putting Together a Museum Exhibit

Step 5: Displaying the Exhibits Student pairs will set up and view each other's exhibits.

Directions: Have students set up their displays for an exhibition in which their classmates and visitors will view their museum exhibits. During the exhibition, instruct student pairs to stand beside their exhibit and answer any questions visitors might have. Allow students to take turns viewing each other's exhibits and asking questions. Circulate throughout the room during the exhibition, assessing students' work. Afterward, have students write a paragraph answering the Essential Question: How do historical events affect the art and culture of a place? **Ask:** How was your exhibit affected by history? **OL**

STANDARDIZED TEST PRACTICE

TEST-TAKING 

If a test question presents a map, make sure you carefully look at the map for information before you try to answer the question.

Reviewing Vocabulary

Directions: Choose the word or words that best complete the sentence.

1. Commercial capitalism refers to ______.
- **A** a nonprofit governmental agency
- **B** real estate that is used for business purposes
- **C** a private business that is based on profit
- **D** a nonprofit private business

2. The Tokugawa shogun controlled a daimyo by a ______ system.
- **A** social contract
- **B** democratic
- **C** serf
- **D** hostage

3. The Manchu pigtail was called a ______.
- **A** barb
- **B** queue
- **C** braid
- **D** kimono

4. A bureaucracy is ______.
- **A** a body of nonelected government officials
- **B** a piece of furniture with drawers for storage
- **C** an agency of private business individuals
- **D** a body of elected government officials

Reviewing Main Ideas

Directions: Choose the best answers to the following questions.

Section 1 *(pp. 510–515)*

5. The voyages of Zheng He took place under which dynasty?
- **A** Zicheng
- **B** Han
- **C** Ming
- **D** Qing

6. During whose reign did the efforts of Christian missionaries reach their height?
- **A** Qianlong
- **B** Ming Hong Wu
- **C** Yong Le
- **D** Kangxi

7. According to Emperor Qianlong, China did not have a need for what product(s) from England?
- **A** Manufactured goods
- **B** Diplomats
- **C** Tea
- **D** Porcelain

Section 2 *(pp. 516–519)*

8. Which of the following is a true statement about society in Qing China?
- **A** Women could legally inherit property.
- **B** The family was more important than the individual.
- **C** Aging parents had to support themselves.
- **D** Women often pursued government jobs.

Need Extra Help?

If You Missed Questions . . .	1	2	3	4	5	6	7	8
Go to Page . . .	516	522	513	528	510	514	515	517

Answers and Analyses

Reviewing Vocabulary

1. C Students can figure out the answer by identifying the meanings of the two words separately. The word *commercial* relates to business, while *capitalism* often leads to profit.

2. D The daimyo's family members were hostages of the shogun when the daimyo was absent from his home in Edo. With the safety of his family at risk, this system ensured the daimyo's loyalty to the shogun.

3. B This question requires students to recall factual information from Section 1. Refer students who miss it to page 513.

4. A Islamic sultans staffed their bureaucracies mainly with aristocrats. Bureaucracies are staffed by nonelected officials.

Reviewing Main Ideas

5. C Zheng He's voyages took place before the Portuguese reached the Chinese Empire so students need to place the four dynasties in chronological order then choose the earliest dynasty. Thus, Ming is the correct answer.

6. D Unlike the other leaders listed, Kangxi was known to be quite tolerant of Christians.

7. A Porcelain was not an English product so it cannot be correct. Diplomats are not a product to be traded. The chapter makes no mention of tea specifically, so manufactured goods is the logical answer.

8. B Students should eliminate false statements. Because Chinese society was organized around family and based on Confucian ideals, the second choice is the only true statement.

TEST-TAKING 

For Question 7: Students can use the process of elimination to figure out the answer. By eliminating answers they know are incorrect, they will be left with the correct answer.

9. C This question requires students to recall factual information from Section 2. Refer students who miss it to page 519.

10. A Oda Osaka was not a Japanese leader. Students must recall the order in which the other three leaders served to determine the correct answer.

11. D The emperor and imperial court families were at the top of the political and social structure. The *ronin* were part of the warrior class, and the artisans fell below the ronin. The *eta* were at the bottom of the social hierarchy.

12. B Students can eliminate the first and fourth choices because they do not exist. The Hawaiian Islands are in the wrong part of the world, so Spice Islands is the logical answer.

TEST-TAKING 

For Question 12: Remind students to consider whether an answer makes sense. For example, answer D doesn't make sense since the Enchanted Islands do not exist.

13. C Islamic monarchs were sultans, and Vietnam followed the Chinese model of kingship. Christianity did not originate in India. Thus, Javanese is the correct answer.

Critical Thinking

14. A By forcing the daimyo's family to live in Edo, they were essentially being held hostage by the shogun. Fear for his family's safety ensured the daimyo's loyalty to the shogun.

15. B Students need to recall that the Dutch fort was established on Java or that it was at Batavia to successfully answer this question.

16. D The Qing forced the Chinese to adopt Manchu dress and hairstyles. The formation of the banners did not affect the level of Chinese support. The Manchu nobility maintained large landholdings. However, when the Qing filled more than 80 percent of lower posts with Chinese, they won the support of many.

CHAPTER 16

9. Which novel is considered by many to be the first realistic social novel?
- **A** *The Dream of the Red Chamber*
- **B** *The Imperial City*
- **C** *The Golden Lotus*
- **D** *The Imperial Chamber*

Section 3 *(pp. 520–525)*

10. Who was the first great unifier of sixteenth-century Japan?
- **A** Oda Nobunaga
- **B** Oda Osaka
- **C** Toyotomi Hideyoshi
- **D** Tokugawa Ieyasu

11. In the Japanese social hierarchy, which group was above the warrior class?
- **A** *Ronin*
- **B** Artisan class
- **C** *Eta*
- **D** Imperial families

Section 4 *(pp. 526–529)*

12. By which name did Europeans know the Moluccas?
- **A** Porcelain Islands
- **B** Spice Islands
- **C** Hawaiian Islands
- **D** Enchanted Islands

13. Which style of kingship was rooted in the political traditions of India?
- **A** Christian
- **B** Islamic
- **C** Javanese
- **D** Vietnamese

Critical Thinking

Directions: Choose the best answers to the following questions.

14. Why did the Tokugawa shogunate require the families of the daimyo to live in Edo?
- **A** To ensure the daimyo's loyalty to the shogun
- **B** To increase the members of the warrior class
- **C** To encourage trade in the city
- **D** To discourage peasant revolts

Base your answer to question 15 on the map below and on your knowledge of world history.

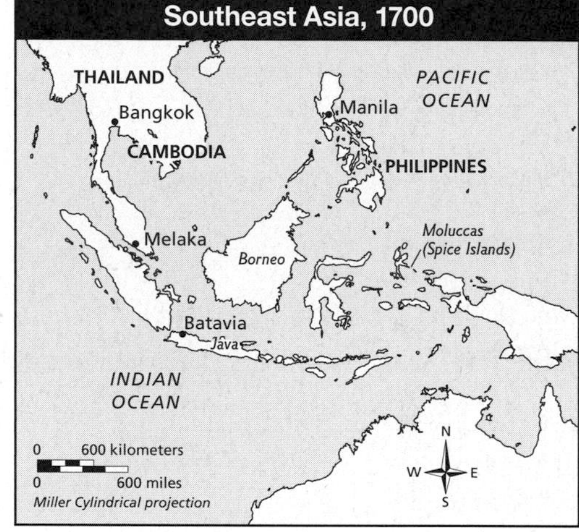

15. Where did the Dutch establish a fort in 1619 to help them control the spice trade?
- **A** Melaka
- **B** Batavia
- **C** Manila
- **D** Bangkok

16. How did Qing rulers win support from the Chinese?
- **A** Allowed the Chinese to adopt Qing dress and hairstyles
- **B** Formed the Chinese into military units called "banners"
- **C** Provided the Chinese with large landholdings
- **D** Brought the Chinese into the imperial administration

Need Extra Help?

If You Missed Questions . . .	9	10	11	12	13	14	15	16
Go to Page . . .	519	520	523	529	527	522	529	513

17. What was a distinctive characteristic of Korean culture that developed under the Yi dynasty?
   A Kabuki
   B The extended family
   C Hangul
   D Urban fiction

Analyze the chart and answer the question that follows. Base your answer on the chart and on your knowledge of world history.

Major Explorers

Explorer	Date of Exploration	Territories Visited
Marco Polo	Late 1200s	Asia
Zheng He	1405–1433	Southeast Asia, west coast of India, East Africa
Bartholomeu Dias	1488	Cape of Good Hope
Christopher Columbus	1492	Bahamas, Cuba, Hispaniola
Vasco da Gama	1498	India
John Cabot	1497	New England coastline
Amerigo Vespucci	1499	South American coast
Pedro Cabral	1500	Brazil
Afonso de Albuquerque	1511	Melaka

18. Which explorer may have been the first to visit the region where the Spice Islands (Moluccas) are located?
   A Afonso de Albuquerque
   B Zheng He
   C Vasco da Gama
   D Bartholomeu Dias

Document-Based Questions

Directions: Analyze the document and answer the short-answer questions that follow the document.

In 1793 Lord George Macartney led a British mission to Beijing seeking to increase trade between his country and China. Macartney expected to impress the emperor with the Western trade goods he brought with him.

> *King George III wrote the following in a letter to the Chinese emperor:*
> *"... No doubt the exchange of goods between nations far apart tends to their mutual convenience, industry, and wealth."*
>
> *After the meeting, Emperor Qianlong wrote the following to King George III:*
> *"... there is nothing we lack. We have never set much store on strange or ingenious objects, nor do we need any more of your country's manufactures."*

19. Compare the attitudes of the British and Chinese toward trade between their countries.

20. Explain how the economies of China and Britain developed differently due to their attitudes toward trade with other countries.

Extended Response

21. Describe the isolationist periods of China, Japan, and Korea. Discuss their reasons for isolation.

History ONLINE
For additional test practice, use Self-Check Quizzes—Chapter 16 at glencoe.com.

Need Extra Help?

If You Missed Questions . . .	17	18	19	20	21
Go to Page . . .	525	535	535	515	515

STOP

Extended Response

21. The Chinese isolationist period began as the Qing dynasty was declining. It was influenced by the Chinese belief in the superiority of their society and the Confucian view that trading activities were unworthy. European traders were confined to a small island just outside Guangzhou, and trade was limited.

Japan entered its isolationist phase as the country was in the process of unifying. The Jesuit practice of destroying shrines and fear of growing Western influence led to the prohibition of Christian activities and the expulsion of all missionaries. Merchants were later expelled, and only Dutch ships were permitted to dock at Nagasaki once a year.

Due to the effects of Japanese invasion, Korean rulers wanted to limit contact with foreign countries. Korea remained largely untouched by European missionaries. Korea was still recovering from the Japanese invasions when the Chinese attacked in the early seventeenth century. Korea then became subject to China's rule.

17. C Kabuki is a characteristic of Japan, not Korea. The extended family and urban fiction are associated with China. Korea's Hangul was distinctive because its alphabet is phonetically based, which is similar to the English alphabet.

18. B Students should recall that the Spice Islands are located in Southeast Asia. According to the chart, the earliest explorer to that region of the world was probably Zheng He.

Document-Based Questions

19. Both the British and Chinese believed in the superiority of the products of their own societies. However, Emperor Qianlong believed China could prosper in isolation while the British recognized the advantages of trade.

20. Answers will vary. China's isolationism stymied its growth as a world power. The British attitude helped them establish a world empire. As a result of less outside contact, Chinese society turned inward.

History ONLINE
Introduce students to chapter content and key terms by having them access the Chapter 16 Overview at glencoe.com.

Need Extra Help?
Have students refer to the pages listed if they miss any of the questions.

CHAPTER 17 Planning Guide

Key to Ability Levels	
BL Below Level	AL Above Level
OL On Level	ELL English Language Learners

Key to Teaching Resources	
Print Material	DVD
CD-ROM	Transparency

Levels				Resources	Chapter Opener	Section 1	Section 2	Section 3	Section 4	Chapter Assess
BL	OL	AL	ELL							
				FOCUS						
BL	OL	AL	ELL	**Daily Focus Skills Transparencies**		17-1	17-2	17-3	17-4	
				TEACH						
BL	OL		ELL	**Reading Skills Activity, URB**			p. 205			
	OL			**Historical Analysis Skills Activity, URB**					p. 206	
BL	OL	AL	ELL	**Differentiated Instruction Activity, URB**				p. 207		
	OL		ELL	**English Learner Activity, URB**		p. 209				
BL	OL	AL	ELL	**Content Vocabulary Activity, URB***					p. 211	
BL	OL	AL	ELL	**Academic Vocabulary Activity, URB**					p. 213	
BL	OL	AL	ELL	**Skills Reinforcement Activity, URB**				p. 215		
	OL	AL		**Critical Thinking Skills Activity, URB**			p. 216			
	OL	AL		**History and Geography Activity, URB**		p. 217				
	OL	AL		**Mapping History Activity, URB**				p. 219		
BL	OL	AL		**Historical Significance Activity, URB**					p. 220	
BL	OL	AL	ELL	**Cooperative Learning Activity, URB**			p. 221			
	OL	AL		**History Simulation Activity, URB**		p. 223				
BL	OL	AL	ELL	**Time Line Activity, URB**				p. 225		
	OL			**Linking Past and Present Activity, URB**		p. 226				
BL	OL	AL		**People in World History Activity, URB**		p. 227	p. 228			
BL	OL	AL	ELL	**Primary Source Reading, URB**			p. 229			
		AL		**Enrichment Activity, URB**			p. 234			
BL	OL	AL	ELL	**World Art and Music Activity, URB**					p. 231	
BL	OL		ELL	**Guided Reading Activities, URB***		p. 236	p. 237	p. 238	p. 239	
BL	OL		ELL	**Reading Essentials and Note-Taking Guide***		p. 184	p. 187	p. 190	p. 193	
BL	OL	AL	ELL	**Differentiated Instruction for the World History Classroom**		✓	✓	✓	✓	

Note: Please refer to the *Unit Resource Book: The Early Modern World* for this chapter's URB materials.

* Also available in Spanish

- Interactive Lesson Planner
- Interactive Teacher Edition
- Fully editable blackline masters
- Section Spotlight Videos Launch
- Differentiated Lesson Plans
- Printable reports of daily assignments
- Standards Tracking System

Levels BL	OL	AL	ELL		Resources	Chapter Opener	Section 1	Section 2	Section 3	Section 4	Chapter Assess
					TEACH *(continued)*						
BL	OL	AL	ELL		StudentWorks™ Plus DVD	✓	✓	✓	✓	✓	✓
BL	OL	AL	ELL		Vocabulary PuzzleMaker CD-ROM	✓	✓	✓	✓	✓	✓
Teacher Resources					Building Academic Vocabulary	✓	✓	✓	✓	✓	✓
Teacher Resources					Reading Strategies and Activities for the Social Studies Classroom			p. 62	p. 65	p. 81	
Teacher Resources					Writer's Guidebook		p. 47				
Teacher Resources					Strategies for Success	✓	✓	✓	✓	✓	✓
Teacher Resources					Outline Map Resource Book	✓	✓	✓	✓	✓	✓
Teacher Resources					Presentation Plus! with MindJogger DVD	✓	✓	✓	✓	✓	✓
					ASSESS						
BL	OL	AL	ELL		Section Quizzes and Chapter Tests*		p. 205	p. 206	p. 207	p. 208	p. 209
BL	OL	AL	ELL		Authentic Assessment With Rubrics	✓	✓	✓	✓	✓	✓
BL	OL	AL	ELL		Standardized Test Practice Workbook	✓	✓	✓	✓	✓	✓
BL	OL	AL	ELL		*ExamView® Assessment Suite* CD-ROM		17-1	17-2	17-3	17-4	Ch. 17
BL	OL	AL	ELL		Interactive Tutor Self-Assessment CD-ROM		17-1	17-2	17-3	17-4	
					CLOSE						
BL			ELL		Reteaching Activity, URB			p. 233			
BL	OL		ELL		Reading and Study Skills Foldables™	✓	✓	✓	✓	✓	✓
BL	OL	AL	ELL		World History in Graphic Novel		p. 33				

Using the McGraw-Hill Learning Network

Presentation Builder

Technology Product

Presentation Builder is a convenient and dynamic McGraw-Hill Learning Network tool to create online presentations. Use the Presentation Builder to

- create your own presentation slides;
- insert graphics from your Glencoe textbook;
- distribute presentations to students using **Assignments** from the *Classroom Tools.*

Steps

- On the McGraw-Hill Learning Network home page (www.mhln.com), log in as a member.
- Choose **Presentation Builder** under **Resources.**
- Click the **New Presentation** button.
- Enter a title in the **Presentation Title** box, then follow the prompts to select colors and fonts.
- Click the **Next** button and select a slide. Follow the prompts to insert information and complete the slide. The text boxes automatically adjust in size to accommodate the length of each question.
- Click the **Add Slide** button if you have additional presentation information and follow the prompts.
- Click **Review Presentation** when you are done.
- Click **View Presentation** to review the presentation in a pop-up window.
- Click on an underlined slide title to edit slides; use the drop-down keys to change the order of the slides; push the **Delete** button to delete a slide; and press **Insert Slide** to add a slide.
- Click the **Save** button when you are satisfied with your presentation. The presentation is saved to your **File Cabinet** and can be distributed to students through **Assignments.**

History ONLINE

	Student	Teacher	Parent
Beyond the Textbook	●	●	●
Chapter Overviews	●	●	●
Time Current Events	●		●
ePuzzles and Games	●		●
Concepts in Motion	●		●
Literature Connections		●	
Multi-Language Glossaries	●		●
Online Student Edition	●	●	●
Self-Check Quizzes	●		●
Student Web Activities	●		●
Study Central ™	●		●
Teaching Today		●	
Vocabulary eFlashcards	●		●
Web Activity Lesson Plans		●	

- **Timed Readings Plus in Social Studies** helps students increase their reading rate and fluency while maintaining comprehension. The 400-word passages are similar to those found on state and national assessments.
- **Reading in the Content Area: Social Studies** concentrates on six essential reading skills that help students better comprehend what they read. The book includes 75 high-interest nonfiction passages written at increasing levels of difficulty.
- **Reading Social Studies** includes strategic reading instruction and vocabulary support in Social Studies content for both ELLs and native speakers of English.

www.jamestowneducation.com

The following videotape program is available from Glencoe as a supplement to Chapter 17:

- Mozart (ISBN 1-56-501590-8)

To order, call Glencoe at 1-800-334-7344. To find classroom resources to accompany many of these videos, check the following home pages:

A&E Television: www.aetv.com

The History Channel: www.historychannel.com

Index to National Geographic Magazine:

The following article relates to this chapter:

- Catherine the Great," by Erla Zwingle, February 2003

National Geographic Society Products To order the following, call National Geographic at 1-800-368-2728:

- *National Geographic Atlas of the World* (Book).

Access National Geographic's new, dynamic MapMachine Web site and other geography resources at:
www.nationalgeographic.com
www.nationalgeographic.com/maps

Use this database to search more than 30,000 titles to create a customized reading list for your students.

- Reading lists can be organized by students' reading level, author, genre, theme, or area of interest.
- The database provides Degrees of Reading Power™ (DRP) and Lexile™ readability scores for all selections.
- A brief summary of each selection is included.

Leveled reading suggestions for this chapter:

For students at a Grade 8 reading level:
- ***George Washington,*** by Genevieve Foster

For students at a Grade 9 reading level:
- from ***The Autobiography of Benjamin Franklin,*** by Benjamin Franklin

For students at a Grade 10 reading level:
- ***Truth on Trial: The Story of Galileo Galilei,*** by Vicki Cobb

For students at a Grade 11 reading level:
- ***Thomas Jefferson: Man on a Mountain,*** by Natalie S. Bober

For students at a Grade 12 reading level:
- ***Johann Sebastian Bach: And the Art of Baroque Music,*** by Daniel Felsenfeld and Donna Getzinger

Introducing CHAPTER 17

Focus

MAKING CONNECTIONS

How did the Enlightenment influence art and society?

Ask students to look at the photograph and examine the details on the building. Ask them to comment on the style. Is this type of architectural style common in buildings in their community? The original baroque style was intended to emphasize power and grandeur. However, subsequent rulers had renovations made to reflect more current styles. For example, Catherine II emphasized the neoclassical style that dominated the seventeenth century and continued into the eighteenth century. The new ideas conceived in the Enlightenment gave architects the freedom to use older styles, but also to use innovative new styles.

Teach

The Big Ideas

As students study the chapter, remind them to consider the section-based Big Ideas included in each section's Guide to Reading. The **Essential Questions** in the activities below tie in to the Big Ideas and help students think about and understand important chapter concepts. In addition, the Hands-On Chapter Projects with their culminating activities relate the content from each section to the Big Ideas. These activities build on each other as students progress through the chapter. Section activities culminate in the wrap-up activity on the Visual Summary page.

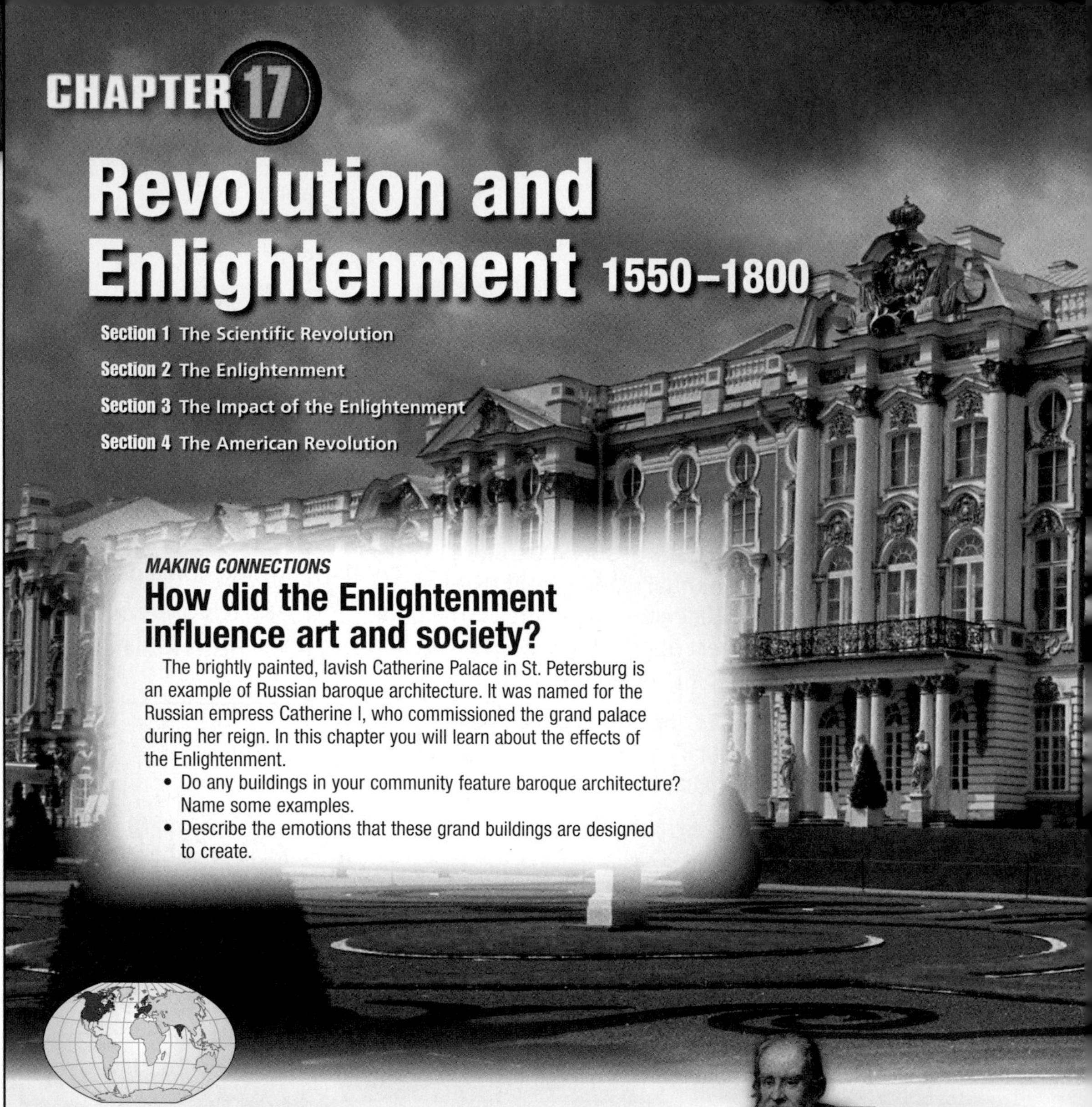

CHAPTER 17

Revolution and Enlightenment 1550–1800

MAKING CONNECTIONS

How did the Enlightenment influence art and society?

The brightly painted, lavish Catherine Palace in St. Petersburg is an example of Russian baroque architecture. It was named for the Russian empress Catherine I, who commissioned the grand palace during her reign. In this chapter you will learn about the effects of the Enlightenment.

- Do any buildings in your community feature baroque architecture? Name some examples.
- Describe the emotions that these grand buildings are designed to create.

EUROPE, NORTH AMERICA, AND INDIA ▶

1543 Copernicus publishes his proposal of a sun-centered universe

1633 Galileo's teachings are condemned by the Church

1550 — 1600 — 1650

THE WORLD ▶

1566 Süleyman I dies

1636 Manchus invade Korea

536

The Scientific Revolution

Essential Question: How did scientific discoveries change people's attitudes towards natural events and religious faith? *(Discoveries promoted a view of the universe as a machine with natural laws that weren't supported by religious teachings based on faith.)* Point out that in Section 1 students will learn how new approaches to science changed people's beliefs about the universe and institutions such as the church. OL

The Enlightenment

Essential Question: How did new patterns of thought affect the ways that people studied social problems? *(Thinkers believed that if the universe was subject to laws, then institutions such as governments and economies must be subject to natural laws as well.)* Point out that in Section 2 students will learn about thinkers who studied governments, economies, and other institutions as well as new directions in religion. OL

1702
First daily newspaper is printed in London

1756
The Seven Years' War begins

1776
American colonies declare independence from Britain

1700 1750 1800

1795
Rule of Emperor Qianlong ends

FOLDABLES™ Study Organizer

Organizing Make a Four-Door Book to organize significant facts on astronomy, medicine and chemistry, Descartes, and the scientific method during the Scientific Revolution.

History ONLINE

Chapter Overview—Visit glencoe.com to preview Chapter 17.

SECTION 3

The Impact of the Enlightenment

Essential Question: Do you think Enlightenment ideas affected the actions of European rulers at the time? *(Some students may believe the ideas changed rulers' actions, but others won't.)* Point out that in Section 3 students will learn about the impact of the Enlightenment on European politics and the mixed legacy of Enlightenment ideas. **OL**

SECTION 4

The American Revolution

Essential Question: How did the American Revolution reflect Enlightenment ideals? *(Enlightenment beliefs in self-government and the use of reason in constructing governments were reflected in the American Revolution, Declaration of Independence, and Constitution.)* Point out that in Section 4 students will learn how the American struggle for independence was influenced by Enlightenment ideals. **OL**

More About the Photo

Visual Literacy Catherine Palace sits atop a hill fifteen miles south of St. Petersburg in the town of Pushkin, formerly Tsarskoye Selo, or Tsar's Village. The original structure began as a small, two-story summer residence commissioned by Catherine I. Under the Empress Elizabeth, architect Bartolomeo Francesco Rastrelli dramatically expanded the building to a length of 985 feet and guilded its exterior and interior with more than 220 pounds of gold. In reaction against the excesses of this baroque style, Catherine II ordered architect Charles Cameron to carry out extensive renovations reflecting her neoclassical taste. Today the palace and surrounding park and structures represent the work of hundreds of architects, artists, and designers and attract thousands of tourists each year.

FOLDABLES™ Study Organizer **Dinah Zike's Foldables**

Dinah Zike's Foldables are three-dimensional, interactive graphic organizers that help students practice basic writing skills, review vocabulary terms, and identify main ideas. Instructions for creating and using Foldables can be found in the Appendix at the end of this book and in the *Dinah Zike's Reading and Study Skills Foldables* booklet. **OL**

Introduce students to chapter content and key terms by having them access the Chapter 17 Overview at glencoe.com.

R Reading Strategy

Inferring Ask: Why would this view of the universe be acceptable to the Church at the time? *(It placed humans at the center of the universe and God beyond the ten spheres that rotate about Earth. Humans' purpose was to achieve salvation and ascend to Heaven.)* **OL**

D Differentiated Instruction

Visual/Spatial Ask students to draw diagrams of the universe according to Ptolemy, Copernicus, and Kepler. Students may conduct additional research to find out what planetary bodies had been discovered at the time and include these labels in their diagrams. **AL**

C Critical Thinking

Analyzing Information

Ask: In what way did Galileo's observations contradict the Ptolemaic system? *(The moons and planets were composed of material substance, they were not pure orbs of light.)* **BL**

Scientific Breakthroughs

MAIN IDEA Scientific discoveries expanded knowledge about the universe and the human body.

HISTORY & YOU What if you discovered another planet just like Earth? Learn about the stunning discoveries scientists made about the universe.

During the Scientific Revolution, discoveries in astronomy led to a new conception of the universe. Breakthroughs advanced medical knowledge and launched the field of chemistry as well.

The Ptolemaic System

Ptolemy, who lived in the A.D. 100s, was the greatest astronomer of antiquity. Using Ptolemy's ideas, as well as those of Aristotle and of Christianity, philosophers of the Middle Ages constructed a model of the universe known later as the Ptolemaic (TAH•luh•MAY•ihk) system. This system is **geocentric** because it places Earth at the center of the universe.

In the Ptolemaic system, the universe is seen as a series of concentric **spheres**—one inside the other. Earth is fixed, or motionless, at the center. The heavenly bodies—pure orbs of light—are embedded in the crystal-like, transparent spheres, which rotate about Earth. The moon is embedded in the first sphere, Mercury in the second, Venus in the third, and the sun in the fourth. The rotation of the spheres makes these heavenly bodies rotate about Earth and move in relation to one another.

The tenth sphere in the Ptolemaic system is the "prime mover." This sphere moves itself and gives motion to the other spheres. Beyond the tenth sphere is Heaven, where God resides. God was at one end of the universe, then, and humans were at the center.

Copernicus and Kepler

In May 1543, **Nicolaus Copernicus,** a native of Poland, published his famous book, *On the Revolutions of the Heavenly Spheres.* Copernicus, a mathematician, thought that his **heliocentric,** or sun-centered, conception of the universe offered a more accurate explanation than did the Ptolemaic system. In his system, the sun, not Earth, was at the center of the universe. The planets revolved around the sun. The moon, however, revolved around Earth. Moreover, according to Copernicus, the apparent movement of the sun around Earth was caused by the rotation of Earth on its axis and its journey around the sun.

Johannes Kepler, a German mathematician, took the next step in destroying the Ptolemaic system. Kepler used detailed astronomical data to arrive at his laws of planetary motion. His observations confirmed that the sun was at the center of the universe and also added new information. In his first law, Kepler showed that the planets' orbits around the sun were not circular, as Copernicus had thought. Rather, the orbits were elliptical (egg-shaped), with the sun toward the end of the ellipse instead of at the center. This finding, known as Kepler's First Law, contradicted the circular orbits and crystal-like spheres that were central to the Ptolemaic system.

Galileo's Discoveries

Scientists could now think in terms of planets revolving around the sun in elliptical orbits. Important questions remained unanswered, however. What are the planets made of? How does one explain motion in the universe? An Italian scientist answered the first question.

Galileo Galilei taught mathematics. He was the first European to make regular observations of the heavens using a telescope. With this tool, Galileo made a remarkable series of discoveries: mountains on Earth's moon, four moons revolving around Jupiter, and sunspots.

Galileo's observations seemed to destroy yet another aspect of the Ptolemaic conception. Heavenly bodies had been seen as pure orbs of light. They now appeared to be composed of material substance, just as Earth was.

Galileo's discoveries, published in *The Starry Messenger* in 1610, did more to make Europeans aware of the new view of the universe than did the works of Copernicus and Kepler. But in the midst of his newfound fame, Galileo found himself under suspicion by the Catholic Church.

Differentiated Instruction

History and Geography Activity 17 — Where Is the World?

History and Geography Activity, URB, p. 217

Comparing and Contrasting

Objective: Compare and contrast the various ways to describe location.

Focus: Ask students to describe where they live.

Teach: Define relative location and discuss the reading and questions.

Assess: Have students explain the significance of Earth's relative location.

Close: Have students write different directions to a place in the community for a local and for a visitor.

Differentiated Instruction Strategies

BL Play a hot and cold game to find an object in the classroom.

AL Have students use cardinal and intermediate directions and distance measurements to describe the location of several places in the community in relation to one another.

ELL Review words that can be used to describe location, such as *between, along, border,* and *coast.*

The Church ordered Galileo to abandon the Copernican idea, which threatened the Church's entire conception of the universe. In the Copernican view, humans were no longer at the center of the universe; God was no longer in a specific place.

In spite of the Church's position, by the 1630s and 1640s, most astronomers had accepted the heliocentric conception of the universe. However, motion in the universe had not been explained. The ideas of Copernicus, Kepler, and Galileo had yet to be tied together. An Englishman—Isaac Newton— would make this connection; he is considered the greatest genius of the Scientific Revolution.

Newton's View of the Universe

Born in 1642, **Isaac Newton** showed few signs of brilliance until he attended Cambridge University. Later, he became a professor of mathematics at the university and wrote his major work, *Mathematical Principles of Natural Philosophy.* This work is known simply as the *Principia,* from a shortened form of its Latin title.

In the *Principia,* Newton defined the three laws of motion that govern the planetary bodies, as well as objects on Earth. Crucial to his whole argument was the **universal law of gravitation.** This law explains why the planetary bodies continue their elliptical orbits about the sun. The law states, in mathematical terms, that every object in the universe is attracted to every other object by a force called gravity. This one universal law, mathematically proved, could explain all motion in the universe. **W**

At the same time, Newton's ideas created a new picture of the universe. It was now seen as one huge, regulated, uniform machine that worked according to natural laws. Newton's world-machine concept dominated the modern worldview until the twentieth century. Albert Einstein's concept of relativity would give a new picture of the universe.

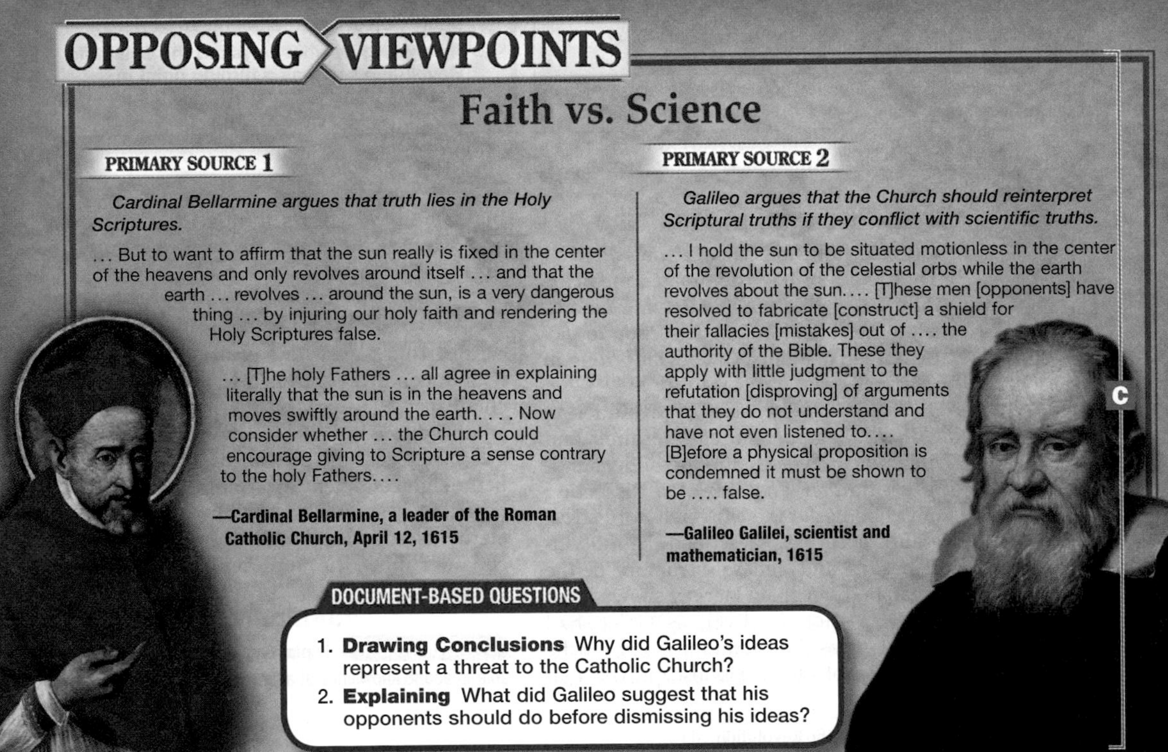

OPPOSING VIEWPOINTS

Faith vs. Science

PRIMARY SOURCE 1

Cardinal Bellarmine argues that truth lies in the Holy Scriptures.

. . . But to want to affirm that the sun really is fixed in the center of the heavens and only revolves around itself . . . and that the earth . . . revolves . . . around the sun, is a very dangerous thing . . . by injuring our holy faith and rendering the Holy Scriptures false.

. . . [T]he holy Fathers . . . all agree in explaining literally that the sun is in the heavens and moves swiftly around the earth. . . . Now consider whether . . . the Church could encourage giving to Scripture a sense contrary to the holy Fathers. . . .

—**Cardinal Bellarmine, a leader of the Roman Catholic Church, April 12, 1615**

PRIMARY SOURCE 2

Galileo argues that the Church should reinterpret Scriptural truths if they conflict with scientific truths.

. . . I hold the sun to be situated motionless in the center of the revolution of the celestial orbs while the earth revolves about the sun. . . . [T]hese men [opponents] have resolved to fabricate [construct] a shield for their fallacies [mistakes] out of . . . . the authority of the Bible. These they apply with little judgment to the refutation [disproving] of arguments that they do not understand and have not even listened to. . . . [B]efore a physical proposition is condemned it must be shown to be . . . . false.

—**Galileo Galilei, scientist and mathematician, 1615**

C

DOCUMENT-BASED QUESTIONS

1. **Drawing Conclusions** Why did Galileo's ideas represent a threat to the Catholic Church?
2. **Explaining** What did Galileo suggest that his opponents should do before dismissing his ideas?

W Writing Support

Expository Writing Ask students to write a brief essay describing how Newton's work changed people's views about how and why the universe worked as it did. **OL**

C Critical Thinking

Analyzing Primary Sources

Ask: Where could people find the truth, according to Cardinal Bellarmine? According to Galileo? *(Bellarmine believed truth could be determined using the Holy Scriptures; Galileo believed truth could only be determined through science and experiments that weren't refuted.)* **OL**

DOCUMENT-BASED QUESTIONS

Answers:

1. The Catholic Church taught the literal truth of the Bible. If something in the Bible could be proved false, as Galileo's ideas might do, then it would shake the very foundation on which the Church was built.
2. prove them wrong

Additional Support

Activity: Interdisciplinary Connection

Science Ask: What types of experiments have you done in science classes? *(Students will respond with a variety of answers.)* What was the purpose of those experiments? *(to establish scientific principles through observation and proof)* Discuss with students the basic scientific process that evolved from this period as shown in the Science, Technology, and Society feature on p. 544 of this section. Ask students to write a paragraph in which a natural event or occurrence such as lightning, an earthquake, or a volcanic eruption might have been explained before the scientific method was established and accepted. Then have them write a paragraph explaining how the same natural event or occurrence is being studied today. Students may have to do a minimal amount of research to complete this activity. **OL**

Focus

Bellringer

Daily Focus Transparency 17.2

GUIDE TO READING

Answers to Graphic:

Major Ideas of the Enlightenment: reason, deism, religious toleration, separation of powers, laissez-faire, natural law, social contract, progress

Section Spotlight Video

To generate student interest and provide a springboard for class discussion, access the Chapter 17, Section 2 video at glencoe.com or on the video DVD.

SECTION 2

The Enlightenment

GUIDE TO READING

The BIG Idea

Ideas, Beliefs, and Values Enlightenment thinkers, or philosophes, believed all institutions should follow natural laws to produce the ideal society.

Content Vocabulary

- philosophe *(p. 548)*
- separation of powers *(p. 548)*
- deism *(p. 548)*
- laissez-faire *(p. 550)*
- social contract *(p. 551)*
- salon *(p. 552)*

Academic Vocabulary

- generation *(p. 548)*
- arbitrary *(p. 551)*

People and Places

- John Locke *(p. 546)*
- Montesquieu *(p. 548)*
- Voltaire *(p. 548)*
- Denis Diderot *(p. 549)*
- Adam Smith *(p. 550)*
- Cesare Beccaria *(p. 550)*
- Jean-Jacques Rousseau *(p. 551)*
- Paris *(p. 551)*
- Mary Wollstonecraft *(p. 551)*
- London *(p. 552)*
- John Wesley *(p. 553)*

Reading Strategy

Summarizing Information As you read, use a diagram like the one below to list some of the main ideas introduced during the Enlightenment.

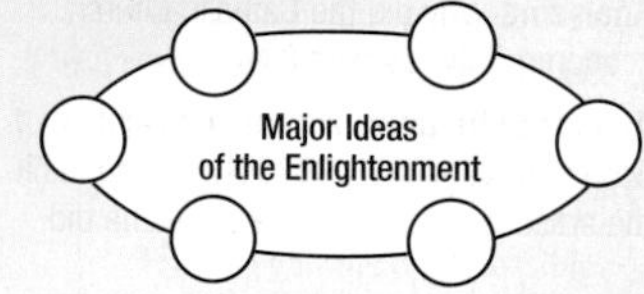

Applying the scientific method to their physical world, Enlightenment thinkers, or philosophes, reexamined all aspects of life—from government and justice to religion and women's rights. They created a movement that influenced the entire Western world.

Path to the Enlightenment

MAIN IDEA Eighteenth-century intellectuals used the ideas of the Scientific Revolution to reexamine all aspects of life.

HISTORY & YOU Do you think you were born with some knowledge, or did you learn everything you know? Read about John Locke's idea that when each of us is born, the mind is a tabula rasa, or blank slate.

The Enlightenment was an eighteenth-century philosophical movement of intellectuals who were greatly impressed with the achievements of the Scientific Revolution. One of the favorite words of these intellectuals was *reason.* By this, they meant the application of the scientific method to an understanding of all life. They hoped that by using the scientific method, they could make progress toward a better society than the one they had inherited. *Reason, natural law, hope, progress*—these were common words to the thinkers of the Enlightenment. The ideas of the Enlightenment would become a force for reform and eventually revolution.

John Locke

The intellectuals of the Enlightenment were especially influenced by the ideas of two seventeenth-century Englishmen, **John Locke** and Isaac Newton. In his *Essay Concerning Human Understanding,* Locke argued that every person was born with a tabula rasa, or blank mind:

PRIMARY SOURCE

"Let us then suppose the mind to be . . . white paper, void of all characters, without any ideas. How comes it to be furnished? Whence has it all the materials of reason and knowledge? To this I answer, in one word, from experience. . . . Our observation, employed either about external sensible objects or about the internal operations of our minds perceived and reflected on by ourselves, is that which supplies our understanding with all the materials of thinking."

—John Locke, *Essay Concerning Human Understanding*

Locke's ideas suggested that people were molded by the experiences that came through their senses from the surrounding world.

Resource Manager

R Reading Strategies	C Critical Thinking	D Differentiated Instruction	W Writing Support	S Skill Practice
Teacher Edition • Using Context Clues, p. 549 • Making Connections, pp. 550, 551, 552 • Summarizing, p. 553 **Additional Resources** • Read. Skills Act., URB, p. 205 • Guid. Read. Act., URB p. 237 • Read. Ess. & Note-Taking Guide, p. 187	**Teacher Edition** • Making Inferences, p. 548 • Pred. Consequences, p. 549 • Making Inferences, p. 550 • Compare/Contrast, p. 551 **Additional Resources** • Crit. Think. Act., URB p. 216 • People in World Hist. Act., URB p. 228 • Section Quiz, p. 206	**Teacher Edition** • Adv. Learners, p. 548 **Additional Resources** • Coop. Learn. Act., URB p. 221 • Reteach. Act., URB p. 233	**Teacher Edition** • Expository Writing, p. 547 • Personal Writing, p. 551 **Additional Resources** • Pri. Source Read., URB p. 229 • Enrich. Act., URB p. 234	**Teacher Edition** • Diagramming, p. 552 **Additional Resources** • Read. Strat. for SS, p. 62

Geography SKILLS

1. **Place** Based on the information given on this map, what did London and Berlin have in common during the Enlightenment?

Enlightenment thinkers began to believe that if environments were changed and people were exposed to the right influences, then people could be changed to create a new—and better—society.

Isaac Newton

The ideas of Isaac Newton also greatly influenced eighteenth-century intellectuals. As you read earlier, Newton believed that the physical world and everything in it was like a giant machine. His "world-machine" operated according to natural laws, which could be uncovered through systematic investigation.

The Enlightenment thinkers reasoned that if Newton was able to discover the natural laws that governed the physical world, then by applying his scientific methods, they would be able to discover **W** the natural laws that governed human society. If all institutions would then follow these natural laws, the result would be an ideal society.

✓Reading Check **Explaining** What did Enlightenment thinkers hope to accomplish?

Teach

W **Writing Support**

Expository Writing Ask students to write a paragraph further explaining the logic of applying one type of rules (the scientific method) to different areas. **AL**

Geography SKILLS

Answers:

1. palaces inspired by Versailles; publication of scientific or philosophical journals

✓Reading Check

Answer: create a new and better society by discovering and applying natural laws

Hands-On Chapter Project
Step 2

Make a Revolution and Enlightenment Poster

Step 2: Illustrating Enlightenment Ideas Pairs of students will add to the posters they began in Section 1 that illustrate the impact of the Scientific Revolution.

Directions: Write the Big Idea on the board. Tell students to evaluate the effects of the Enlightenment on society as they read this section. Have students illustrate what they regard as the most important effects of the Enlightenment in the second quarter of their posters. Text and images may include information about specific Enlightenment thinkers, or students may choose to illustrate the effects of Enlightenment ideas on areas such as economics, religion, education, or women's rights.

Summarizing: Allow time for students to discuss what they have learned while creating this section of the poster. They will use information about the effects of the Enlightenment on politics in Section 3 to illustrate the next section of their posters. **OL**

(Chapter Project is continued in Section 3.)

D Differentiated Instruction

Advanced Learners Ask students to compare philosophes' attitudes concerning direct involvement and improvement of the world to later perceptions of scholars as working in "ivory towers" with little involvement with the outside world. Ask students to give an oral presentation contrasting the two views and share their own views about a scholar's place and responsibilities in the world. **AL**

C Critical Thinking

Making Inferences Ask: Why do you think Montesquieu thought that different types of government were appropriate for different sizes of states? *(Larger states were too complex and far-reaching to use anything but one-person rule, while small states could manage a direct republic because of the limited number of people and viewpoints.)* **OL**

Additional Support

Ideas of the Philosophes

MAIN IDEA The philosophes wanted to create a better society.

HISTORY & YOU Do you remember what a monarchy is? Read to learn about two other forms of government.

The intellectuals of the Enlightenment were known by the French word **philosophe** (FEE•luh•ZAWF), meaning "philosopher." Not all philosophes were French, however, and few were philosophers in the strict sense of the term. They were writers, professors, journalists, economists, and above all, social reformers. They came chiefly from the nobility and the middle class.

Most leaders of the Enlightenment were French, although the English had provided the philosophical inspiration for the movement. It was the French philosophes who affected intellectuals elsewhere and created a movement that influenced the entire Western world.

D The Role of Philosophy

To the philosophes, the role of philosophy was to change the world. One writer said that the philosophe is one who "applies himself to the study of society with the purpose of making his kind better and happier." One conducts this study by using reason, or an appeal to facts. A spirit of rational criticism was to be applied to everything, including religion and politics.

The philosophes often disagreed. Spanning almost a century, the Enlightenment evolved over time. Each succeeding **generation** became more radical as it built on the contributions of the previous one. A few people, however, dominated the landscape—Montesquieu (MAHN•tuhs•KYOO), Voltaire, and Diderot (dee•DROH).

Montesquieu

Charles-Louis de Secondat, the baron de **Montesquieu**, was a French noble. His famous work *The Spirit of the Laws* (1748) was a study of governments. In it, Montesquieu used the scientific method to try to find the natural laws that govern the social and political relationships of human beings.

C Montesquieu identified three basic kinds of governments: (1) republics, suitable for small states; (2) despotism, appropriate for large states; and (3) monarchies, ideal for moderate-sized states. He used England as an example of a monarchy.

Montesquieu stated that England's government had three branches: the executive (the monarch), the legislative (Parliament), and the judicial (the courts of law). The government functioned through a **separation of powers.** In this separation, the executive, legislative, and judicial powers of the government limit and control each other in a system of checks and balances. By preventing any one person or group from gaining too much power, this system provides the greatest freedom and security for the state.

The system of checks and balances through separation of powers was Montesquieu's most lasting contribution to political thought. Translation of his work into English made it available to American philosophes, who worked his principles into the United States Constitution.

Voltaire

The greatest figure of the Enlightenment was François-Marie Arouet, known simply as **Voltaire.** A Parisian, Voltaire came from a prosperous middle-class family. His numerous writings brought him both fame and wealth.

Voltaire was especially well known for his criticism of Christianity and his strong belief in religious toleration. He fought against religious intolerance in France. In 1763 he penned his *Treatise on Toleration,* in which he reminded governments that "all men are brothers under God."

Throughout his life, Voltaire championed **deism,** an eighteenth-century religious philosophy based on reason and natural law. Deism built on the idea of the Newtonian world-machine. In the Deists' view, a mechanic (God) had created the universe. To Voltaire and most other philosophes, the universe was like a clock. God, the clockmaker, had created it, set it in motion, and allowed it to run without his interference and according to its own natural laws.

Activity: Interdisciplinary Connection

Civics Divide the class into three groups and assign one branch of government to each group. Ask each group to brainstorm a list of laws that would give their branch of government control over the other branches. Examples may include allowing the legislature to appoint judges and executives, or allowing an executive to ignore laws passed by the legislature. Then have each group share their lists and explain how laws such as these could be balanced to promote freedom and security for a state.

Ask: How does the separation of powers help prevent any branch of government from gaining too much power? *(by making each branch of government dependent on the others for approval or limiting their individual power to make or change laws)* **OL**

Diderot

Denis Diderot went to the University of Paris. His father hoped Denis would pursue a career in law or the Church. He did neither. Instead, he became a writer. He studied and read in many subjects and languages.

Diderot's most famous contribution to the Enlightenment was the *Encyclopedia, or Classified Dictionary of the Sciences, Arts, and Trades,* a 28-volume collection of knowledge that he edited. Published between 1751 and 1772, the *Encyclopedia,* according to Diderot, was to "change the general way of thinking."

The *Encyclopedia* became a weapon against the old French society. Many of its articles attacked religious superstition and supported religious toleration. Others called for social, legal, and political reforms. Sold to doctors, clergymen, teachers, and lawyers, the *Encyclopedia* spread Enlightenment ideas. C

✓Reading Check **Stating** What ideas did Montesquieu add to the Enlightenment?

New Social Sciences

MAIN IDEA The belief in logic and reason promoted the beginnings of social sciences.

HISTORY & YOU What do you think is the purpose of punishing criminals? Read to learn about arguments against extreme punishments.

The philosophes, as we have seen, believed that Newton's methods could be used to discover the natural laws underlying all areas of human life. This led to what we would call the social sciences—areas such as economics and political science.

Smith on Economics

The Physiocrats and Scottish philosopher Adam Smith have been viewed as the founders of the modern social science of economics. The Physiocrats, a French group, were interested in identifying the natural economic laws that governed human society. They maintained that if individuals were free to pursue their own economic self-interest, all society would benefit.

PEOPLE in HISTORY

Voltaire
1694–1778 French Philosopher

"Those who can make you believe absurdities can make you commit atrocities." Voltaire's words reflected his observations on history and foreshadowed atrocities yet to come. Outspoken against tyranny, ignorance, and the excesses of the Church, Voltaire never held his tongue, even in the face of threats. Forced to choose between exile and imprisonment after insulting a powerful French nobleman, Voltaire chose exile in England. While there he befriended Jonathan Swift and Alexander Pope and was influenced by John Locke and Sir Isaac Newton. He returned home more radical than ever, and his ideas later influenced both American and French revolutionaries. **Voltaire spoke out against what subjects of his day?**

Adam Smith
1723–1790 Scottish Economist and Philosopher

"No society can surely be happy, of which the far greater part of the members are poor and miserable." Someone reading this quote might think it originated with an American patriot or a French revolutionary. However, it actually came from Adam Smith, widely regarded as "the father of capitalism." Besides being the architect of the laissez-faire doctrine of government noninterference with commerce, and an opponent of heavy government taxation, Smith was also an outspoken advocate for ethical standards in society. His friends included Voltaire, Benjamin Franklin, and David Hume, three of the late eighteenth century's most revolutionary thinkers. **How did Adam Smith feel about the role of government?** R

C Critical Thinking

Predicting Consequences
Ask: How do you think the Church and the French government reacted to Diderot's work? *(They opposed it and were against its publication and distribution.)* OL

R Reading Strategy

Using Context Clues Ask students to read the Voltaire feature and to provide examples of absurdities and atrocities in both the modern world and in the context of Voltaire's world. OL

✓Reading Check

Answer: He identified three types of government and described a system of checks and balances through the separation of powers that helped guide the U.S. Constitution.

PEOPLE in HISTORY

Answers:
Voltaire: tyranny, ignorance, and excesses of the church;
Smith: government's role should be minimal, with little interference in business and little taxation

Additional Support

Extending the Content

Voltaire and Smith Voltaire helped spread Enlightenment views both through his writings, which were published across Europe, and through his own personal travels. Twice he was forced into exile because of his criticisms of royalty. He resided in England and Berlin, as well as in a variety of cities in France. Smith, on the other hand, did not threaten the status quo in the same way, and spent his life teaching and writing in Scotland and England. His writings were some of the first to attempt to analyze economic issues and systems. **Ask:** Why do you think Voltaire inspired such opposition, while Smith was allowed to work and publish his thoughts? *(Voltaire often challenged the attitudes and actions of royalty and the Church, the institutions that were most powerful at the time, while Smith presented a new analysis without specific criticism.)* OL

R Reading Strategy

Making Connections Ask students to research the economic policies of the major political parties in the United States. **Ask:** In which political party would Adam Smith have been comfortable? *(Have students support their answers.)* AL

C Critical Thinking

Making Inferences **Ask:** How can competition help increase wealth? *(Answers may include that competition allows the pursuit of self-interest which may lead to wealth through increased efficiency, lower prices, and the support of profitable industries.)* OL

✓Reading Check

Answer: letting people do as they want, especially in economic matters where the government should not interfere

CRITICAL THINKING SKILLS

Answers:
1. for personal gain
2. Responses may include that the economic forces are not visible to the participants, yet they guide participants to act to benefit society.

INFOGRAPHICS

Laissez-Faire Economics

Mercantilism

A nation's wealth is measured by:
- the amount of gold and silver in its treasury

To increase wealth, government must:
- encourage exports to bring in gold and silver
- restrict imports to avoid draining away gold and silver
- grant monopolies and financial support to local businesses to give them an advantage over foreign competition

Laissez-Faire Economics

A nation's wealth is measured by:
- its annual output of goods and services

To increase wealth, government must:
- impose no restrictions on trade, allowing it to operate freely C
- provide no support or monopoly advantages for local businesses, so that competition can occur freely

Adam Smith's *Wealth of Nations* (1776) inspired a major shift in economic theory and practice. In it, he argued that the desire for personal gain drives economic activity and that this leads to competition. He believed that allowing this competition to operate without government interference would benefit society in several ways:
- Prices are kept lower.
- Production is more efficient as businesses reduce costs to increase profit.
- Labor and capital are directed to the most profitable industries.

Unintentionally then, the pursuit of self-interest benefits all of society. In Smith's words:

"Every individual . . . neither intends to promote the public interest, nor knows how much his is promoting it. . . . [H]e intends only his own gain, and he is in this . . . led by an invisible hand to promote an end which was no part of his intention."

CRITICAL THINKING SKILLS

1. **Identifying** According to Adam Smith, why do people produce and sell products?
2. **Making Inferences** What do you think Smith means by "an invisible hand"?

The state, then, should not interrupt the free play of natural economic forces by imposing regulations on the economy. Instead, the state should leave the economy alone. This doctrine became known by its French name, **laissez-faire** (LEH•SAY FEHR), meaning "to let (people) do (what they want)."

The best statement of laissez-faire was made in 1776 by **Adam Smith** in his famous work, *The Wealth of Nations.* Like R the Physiocrats, Smith believed that the state should not interfere in economic matters. Indeed, Smith gave to government only three basic roles. First, it should protect society from invasion (the function of the army). Second, the government should defend citizens from injustice (the function of the police). And finally, it should keep up certain public works that private individuals alone could not afford—roads and canals, for example—but which are necessary for social interaction and trade.

Beccaria on Justice

By the eighteenth century, most European states had developed a system of courts to deal with the punishment of crime. Punishments were often cruel. The primary reason for extreme punishments was the need to deter crime in an age when a state's police force was too weak to capture criminals.

One philosophe who proposed a new approach to justice was **Cesare Beccaria.** In his essay *On Crimes and Punishments* (1764), Beccaria argued that punishments should not be exercises in brutality. He also opposed capital punishment. He did not believe that it stopped others from committing crimes. Moreover, it set an example of barbarism: "Is it not absurd, that the laws, which punish murder, should, in order to prevent murder, publicly commit murder themselves?"

✓Reading Check **Explaining** What is the concept of laissez-faire?

Differentiated Instruction

People in World History Activity, URB p. 228

Identifying Central Issues

Objective: Identify the problems that Adam Smith wanted to solve.

Focus: Read Smith's view of market functions.

Teach: Ask students to write a paragraph from Smith's point of view responding to a request by American companies for protection against foreign competition.

Assess: Have students share and discuss their writings.

Close: Ask students if they believe more in laissez-faire economics or in some government control.

Differentiated Instruction Strategy

BL Ask students to explain why "hands off" is a good description of Smith's beliefs.

AL Ask students to research and describe a variety of ways that governments regulate economic affairs.

ELL Ask students to explain the meaning of "laissez-faire" and discuss ways in which governments can affect an economy.

The Spread of Ideas

MAIN IDEA From the upper classes to the middle classes and from salons to pulpits, the ideas of the Enlightenment spread.

HISTORY & YOU How would your life change if you had no way to communicate—no e-mail, no phone? Learn how newspapers and magazines spread Enlightenment ideas.

By the late 1760s, a new generation of philosophes had come to maturity. Ideas about liberty, education, and the condition of women were spread through an increasingly literate society.

The Social Contract

The most famous philosophe of the later Enlightenment was **Jean-Jacques Rousseau** (ru•SOH). The young Rousseau wandered through France and Italy holding various jobs. Eventually he made his way to **Paris,** where he was introduced into the circle of the philosophes. He did not like city life, however, and often withdrew into long periods of solitude.

In his *Discourse on the Origins of the Inequality of Mankind,* Rousseau argued that people had adopted laws and government in order to preserve their private property. In the process, they had become enslaved by government. What, then, should people do to regain their freedom?

In his major work *The Social Contract,* published in 1762, Rousseau presented his concept of the **social contract.** Through a social contract, an entire society agrees to be governed by its general will. Individuals who wish instead to follow their own self-interests must be forced to abide by the general will. "This means nothing less than that [they] will be forced to be free," said Rousseau. Thus, liberty is achieved by being forced to follow what is best for "the general will" because the general will represents what is best for the entire community. R

Another important work by Rousseau is *Émile.* Written in the form of a novel, the work is a general discussion "on the education of the natural man." Rousseau argues that education should foster, and not restrict, children's natural instincts.

Unlike many Enlightenment thinkers, Rousseau believed that emotions, as well as reason, were important to human development. He sought a balance between heart and mind, between emotions and reason.

Rousseau did not necessarily practice what he preached. His own children were sent to orphanages, where many children died at a young age. Rousseau also viewed women as being "naturally" different from men: "To fulfill her functions, . . . [a woman] needs a soft life. . . . How much care and tenderness does she need to hold her family together." To Rousseau, women should be educated for their roles as wives and mothers by learning obedience and the nurturing skills that would enable them to provide loving care for their husbands and children. Not everyone in the eighteenth century agreed with Rousseau's views about women, however.

Women's Rights

For centuries, male intellectuals had argued that the nature of women made them inferior to men and made male domination of women necessary. By the eighteenth century, however, female thinkers began to express their ideas about improving the condition of women. **Mary Wollstonecraft,** an English writer, advanced the strongest statement for the rights of women. Many see her as the founder of the modern European and American movements for women's rights. C

In *A Vindication of the Rights of Women,* Wollstonecraft identified two problems with the views of many Enlightenment thinkers. She noted that the same people who argued that women must obey men also said that government based on the **arbitrary** power of monarchs over their subjects was wrong. Wollstonecraft pointed out that the power of men over women was equally wrong.

Wollstonecraft further argued that the Enlightenment was based on an ideal of reason in all human beings. Therefore, because women have reason, they are entitled to the same rights as men. Women, Wollstonecraft declared, should have equal rights in education, as well as in economic and political life. W

R Reading Strategy

Making Connections Ask students to review Rousseau's idea that some people must be "forced to be free." **Ask:** Are there instances in modern U.S. society where individuals are "forced to be free" because their self-interests are in opposition to the "general will"? *(Students should cite examples such as minimum wage and workplace safety laws or civil rights laws.)* AL

C Critical Thinking

Comparing and Contrasting Ask: In what ways did Rousseau's and Wollstonecraft's views of women differ? *(Rousseau believed that women were fundamentally different from men and only required education as wives and mothers. Wollstonecraft believed men and women had equal abilities and deserved equal opportunities in education and economic and political life.)* OL

W Writing Support

Personal Writing Ask students to write one or two paragraphs describing their feelings about equal opportunities for men and women and about their abilities and roles in society. BL

Additional Support

Extending the Content

Although most leading philosophes lived in France and Britain, there were Enlightenment thinkers in other European countries, too. One very important contributor was the German philosopher Immanuel Kant. Unlike typical Enlightenment figures, Kant asserted that there is a realm of absolute but unknowable truth, thus opening the door to mystery. Attempting to balance the value of observation with the value of faith, Kant famously stated: "Intuition without sensation is empty, and sensation without intuition is blind." Have students discuss the quotation and then as a class create a paraphrase of the quotation using ideas and opinions expressed by students during the discussion.

S Skill Practice

Diagramming Ask students to create two bar graphs that show the growth of publishing in the 1700s. The first graph should illustrate the increased number of books published in France in 1750 and the 1780s. The second graph should show the increase in periodicals in England from 1700 to 1789. **OL**

R Reading Strategy

Making Connections Ask students to review the description of salons during the Enlightenment. **Ask:** How does the Internet allow greater access to debates but lessen the importance of each one? *(Internet forums allow everyone access to a debate, while only a few were invited to a salon. The salons were few in number, while Internet debates are so numerous that few gain widespread attention.)* **OL**

CRITICAL THINKING SKILLS

Answers:

1. Wesley: Anyone can be saved. Church of England: Salvation is predetermined.
2. He emphasized the heart, not the mind.

Additional Support

The Growth of Reading

Of great importance to the Enlightenment was the spread of its ideas to the literate elite of European society. Especially noticeable in the eighteenth century was the growth of both publishing and the reading public. The number of titles issued each year by French publishers rose from 300 in 1750 to about 1,600 in the 1780s. Books had previously been aimed at small groups of the educated elite. Now, many **S** books were directed at the new reading public of the middle classes, which included women and urban artisans.

An important aspect of the growth of publishing and reading in the eighteenth century was the development of magazines and newspapers for the general public. In Great Britain, an important center for the new magazines, 25 periodicals were published in 1700, 103 in 1760, and 158 in 1780.

The first daily newspaper was printed in **London** in 1702. Newspapers were relatively cheap and were even provided free in many coffeehouses.

The Salon

Enlightenment ideas were also spread through the salon. **Salons** were the elegant drawing rooms of the wealthy upper class's great urban houses. Invited guests gathered in these salons and took part in conversations that were often centered on the new ideas of the philosophes. The salons **R** brought writers and artists together with aristocrats, government officials, and wealthy middle-class people.

The women who hosted the salons were in a position to sway political opinion and influence literary and artistic taste. For example, Marie-Thérèse de Geoffrin, wife of a wealthy merchant, hosted salons.

INFOGRAPHICS

John Wesley Brings a New Message of Salvation

John Wesley (1703–1791), the founder of Methodism, brought religious revival to the people of England. Wesley often preached outdoors, drawing thousands of people. His preaching style made his message understandable to the uneducated lower classes.

The Church of England considered Wesley an extremist, exciting people to hysterical outbursts. Wesley taught that anyone can be saved. This idea conflicted with some Anglicans, who believed that God had already determined who would be saved and who would not.

Wesley emphasized religion of the heart, not the mind. He urged his followers to seek Christian perfection, or holiness of heart and life, by leading a life of piety and good works:

"In every thought of our hearts, in every word of our tongues, in every work of our hands, to show forth his praise, who hath called us out of darkness into his marvelous light."

CRITICAL THINKING SKILLS

1. **Contrasting** How did Wesley's view of salvation conflict with the view of some members of the Church of England?
2. **Making Connections** In what way was Wesley's message a reaction to Enlightenment thinking?

Did You Know?

Methodism and the Wesleys Charles and John Wesley were two of at least 17 children born into the family of an English clergyman, 10 of whom lived to maturity. After John went to college, he became a member of the Holy Club that took what others saw as a "methodical" approach to religious practices, including visiting prisons and the sick. This approach was given the derisive nickname "Methodists." Charles had experienced a religious conversion three days before John, and the brothers joined together to establish a new approach to religion, although Charles himself did not want to break away from the Anglican church. Often remembered as the poet of the Methodist movement, Charles composed more than 6,000 hymns, many of which are still popular in churches today.

These gatherings at her fashionable home in Paris became the talk of France and of all Europe.

Distinguished foreigners competed to receive invitations to the salons. These gatherings helped spread the ideas of the Enlightenment.

Religion in the Enlightenment

Although many philosophes attacked the Christian churches, most Europeans in the eighteenth century were still Christians. Many people also sought a deeper personal devotion to God.

The Catholic parish church remained an important center of life. How many people went to church regularly is unknown, but 90 to 95 percent of Catholic populations went to mass on Easter Sunday.

After the initial religious fervor that created Protestantism in the sixteenth century, Protestant churches settled into well-established patterns often controlled or influenced by state authorities. Many Protestant churches were lacking in religious enthusiasm. The desire of ordinary Protestants for greater depths of religious experience led to new religious movements.

In England, the most famous new religious and evangelical movement—Methodism—was the work of **John Wesley,** an Anglican minister. Wesley had a mystical experience in which "the gift of God's grace" assured him of salvation. This experience led him to become a missionary to the English people to bring them the "glad tidings" of salvation. R

Since many Anglican churches were closed to him, Wesley preached to the masses in open fields, in halls, or in cottages. He preached wherever an assembly could gather. Wesley traveled constantly, generally on horseback, and often preached two or three times a day. He appealed especially to the lower classes. He tried, he said, "to lower religion to the level of the lowest people's capacities."

His sermons often caused people to have conversion experiences. Many converts then joined Methodist societies to do good works. One notable reform they influenced was the abolition of the slave trade in the early 1800s. Christian reformers were also important in the American movement to abolish slavery.

Wesley's Methodism gave the lower and middle classes in English society a sense of purpose and community. Methodists stressed the importance of hard work and spiritual contentment rather than demands for political equality. After Wesley's death, Methodism became a separate Protestant group. Methodism proved that the need for spiritual experience had not been eliminated by the eighteenth-century search for reason.

✓Reading Check **Evaluating** How did Mary Wollstonecraft use the Enlightenment ideal of reason to advocate rights for women?

SECTION 2 REVIEW

Vocabulary

1. **Explain** the significance of: John Locke, philosophe, generation, Montesquieu, separation of powers, Voltaire, deism, Denis Diderot, laissez-faire, Adam Smith, Cesare Beccaria, Jean-Jacques Rousseau, Paris, social contract, Mary Wollstonecraft, arbitrary, London, salon, John Wesley.

Main Ideas

2. **Explain** the influence of John Locke and Isaac Newton on Enlightenment thinkers.
3. **Name** the social classes to which most philosophes belonged.
4. **Identify** factors that helped spread Enlightenment ideas through Europe by using a diagram like the one below.

Factors that Spread Enlightenment

Critical Thinking

5. **The BIG Idea** **Evaluating** What did Rousseau mean when he stated that if individuals wanted to pursue their own self-interests at the expense of the common good, they "will be forced to be free"? Do you agree or disagree? Why?
6. **Comparing and Contrasting** How are the branches of the U.S. government similar to the branches Montesquieu identified? How are they different?
7. **Analyzing Visuals** Examine the painting of John Wesley on page 552. Explain why the painting shows Wesley preaching outdoors.

Writing About History

8. **Persuasive Writing** Mary Wollstonecraft argued that women are entitled to the same rights as men. Do you believe this to be true? Do you believe women are accorded equal rights today? Present your argument in an essay with evidence.

History ONLINE
For help with the concepts in this section of *Glencoe World History*, go to glencoe.com and click Study Central™.

R Reading Strategy

Summarizing Ask students to write a sentence summarizing each paragraph under the heading on this page. ELL

Answer: Since the Enlightenment ideals involved reason in all beings and since women have reason like men, women are entitled to the same rights as men.

Assess

History ONLINE

Study Central provides summaries, interactive games, and online graphic organizers to help students review content.

Close

Analyzing Information

Ask: How do you think you would have reacted to Enlightenment ideas if you were living in the 1700s? *(Responses should show an understanding of Enlightenment ideas.)*

Answers

1. Definitions for the vocabulary words are found in the section and the Glossary.
2. **Locke:** People are molded by experience; **Newton:** World operates according to natural laws
3. nobility and middle class
4. growth of publishing and reading; writings of philosophers and other Enlightenment thinkers; discussion in salons
5. Answers should show an understanding of Rousseau's ideas.
6. **Similarity:** Same three branches; **Differences:** In U.S., executive branch is president, not monarch, and the legislative branch is Congress, not parliament
7. Answers may include that preaching outdoors meant that many people (including the uneducated) could attend and hear Wesley's message.
8. Answers should demonstrate an understanding of women's rights.

C Critical Thinking

Identifying Central Issues
Ask: Why was it important that Frederick the Great "kept a strict watch over the bureaucracy?" *(Without oversight, the bureaucracy could grow large and cost money that would need to be raised through taxes.)* **OL**

R Reading Strategy

Summarizing Ask students to write one or two sentences summarizing the attitude of Joseph II toward Enlightenment reforms and Austrian society. **BL**

W Writing Support

Persuasive Writing Note that many leaders challenged Maria Theresa's inheritance because she was a woman. Ask students to write a persuasive essay arguing for Theresa's right to rule. Students may reference Enlightenment ideals to strengthen their case. **OL**

PEOPLE in HISTORY

Answers:
Frederick II: Prussia became a military power
Maria Theresa: monarchy

Additional Support

These officers, too, had a strong sense of service to the king or state. As Prussian nobles, they believed in duty, obedience, and sacrifice.

Frederick II, or **Frederick the Great,** was one of the best educated and most cultured monarchs of the time. He was well versed in Enlightenment ideas and even invited the French philosophe Voltaire to live at his court for several years.

Frederick was a dedicated ruler. He, too, enlarged the Prussian army by actively recruiting the nobility into civil service. **C** Frederick kept a strict watch over the bureaucracy. **R**

For a time, Frederick seemed quite willing to make enlightened reforms. He abolished the use of torture except in treason and murder cases. He also granted limited freedom of speech and press, as well as greater religious toleration. However, Frederick kept Prussia's serfdom and **rigid** social structure intact and avoided any additional reforms.

The Austrian Empire

The Austrian Empire had become one of the great European states by the start of the eighteenth century. It was hard to rule, however, because it was a sprawling empire composed of many nationalities, languages, religions, and cultures. Empress **Maria Theresa,** who inherited the throne in 1740, worked to centralize and strengthen the state. She was not open to the philosophes' calls for reform, but she worked to improve the condition of the serfs.

Her son, Joseph II, believed in the need to sweep away anything standing in the path of reason: "I have made Philosophy the lawmaker of my empire." Joseph's reforms were far-reaching. He abolished serfdom and eliminated the death penalty. He established the principle of equality of all before the law and enacted religious reforms, including religious toleration. In his effort to change Austria, Joseph II issued thousands of decrees and laws.

PEOPLE in HISTORY

Frederick II (Frederick the Great)
1712–1786 King of Prussia

When Napoleon visited the tomb of Frederick the Great in 1807, he remarked, "Gentlemen, if this man were still alive, I would not be here." This was high praise, especially considering that Prussia's Frederick II cared more about the arts, music, and philosophy than about warfare. Frederick was a flute player and composer who liked to surround himself with French intellectuals. Although cultural and intellectual pursuits remained his major interests, Frederick's leadership qualities began to emerge early in his reign. Under his 46-year rule, Prussia became a major military power with brilliantly executed victories that thwarted the expansion of the powerful Hapsburg Empire. **How did Prussia change under the leadership of Frederick II?**

556

Maria Theresa
1717–1780 Ruler of the Austrian Empire

W Maria Theresa married at age 18. She remained devoted to her husband, Francis Stephen, throughout their 29-year marriage. She bore 16 children, many of whom would later become rulers of European nations or spouses of rulers. When her father, Charles VI of Austria, died in 1740, she became the only woman to rule during the 650-year Hapsburg dynasty. She enacted some reforms during her reign, but she never wavered from her belief in the legitimate right of monarchs to rule. Throughout her life, Maria Theresa showered her children with practical advice—especially her youngest daughter. This daughter would later fall victim to the anti-royalty hysteria of the French Revolution. Her name was Marie Antoinette. **What form of government did Maria Theresa support?**

Extending the Content

Frederick II and Maria Theresa Unhappy at age 18, Frederick planned to run away to England, but was caught by his father and imprisoned. After he became king at age 28, he supported the improvement of agricultural land, and codified laws that could be more uniformly applied. Many leaders challenged Maria Theresa's ascension to the throne because she was not a male heir. She considered abdicating in her later years to allow her son Joseph to rule on his own, but she thought he was too willing to make Enlightenment reforms.

Ask: What belief did Frederick II and Maria Theresa share? *(power of monarchs to rule absolutely)* **OL**

Joseph's reform program largely failed. He alienated the nobles by freeing the serfs. He alienated the Catholic Church with his religious reforms. Even the serfs were unhappy because they could not understand the drastic changes. Joseph realized his failure when he wrote his own epitaph for his gravestone: "Here lies Joseph II who was unfortunate in everything that he undertook." His successors undid almost all of Joseph II's reforms. **D**

Catherine the Great

In Russia, Peter the Great was followed by six weak successors who were often put in power and deposed by the palace guard. A group of nobles murdered the last of these six successors, Peter III. His German wife emerged as ruler of all the Russians.

Catherine II, or **Catherine the Great,** ruled Russia from 1762 to 1796. She was an intelligent woman who was familiar with the works of the philosophes and seemed to favor enlightened reforms. She invited the French philosophe Denis Diderot to Russia and urged him to speak frankly "as man to man." Diderot did so, outlining an ambitious program of reform. Catherine, however, was skeptical. Diderot's impractical theories, she said, "would have turned everything in my kingdom upside down." She did consider the idea of a new law code that would recognize the principle of the equality of all people in the eyes of the law. **R**

In the end, however, Catherine did nothing because she knew that her success depended on the support of the Russian nobility. Catherine's policy of favoring the landed nobility led to worse conditions for the Russian peasants and eventually to rebellion. Led by an illiterate Cossack (a Russian warrior), Yemelyan Pugachov, the rebellion spread across southern Russia, but soon collapsed. Catherine took stronger measures against the peasants. All rural reform was halted; serfdom was expanded into newer parts of the empire.

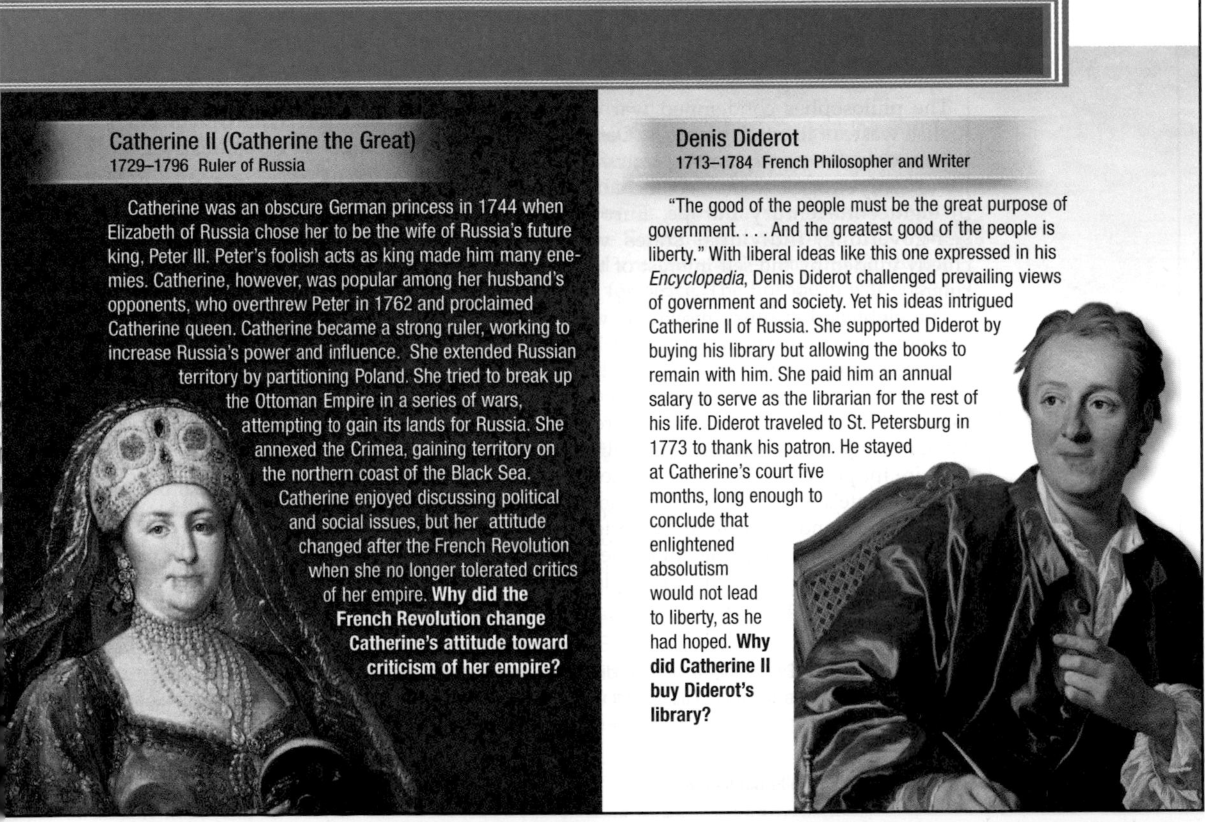

Catherine II (Catherine the Great)
1729–1796 Ruler of Russia

Catherine was an obscure German princess in 1744 when Elizabeth of Russia chose her to be the wife of Russia's future king, Peter III. Peter's foolish acts as king made him many enemies. Catherine, however, was popular among her husband's opponents, who overthrew Peter in 1762 and proclaimed Catherine queen. Catherine became a strong ruler, working to increase Russia's power and influence. She extended Russian territory by partitioning Poland. She tried to break up the Ottoman Empire in a series of wars, attempting to gain its lands for Russia. She annexed the Crimea, gaining territory on the northern coast of the Black Sea. Catherine enjoyed discussing political and social issues, but her attitude changed after the French Revolution when she no longer tolerated critics of her empire. **Why did the French Revolution change Catherine's attitude toward criticism of her empire?**

Denis Diderot
1713–1784 French Philosopher and Writer

"The good of the people must be the great purpose of government. . . . And the greatest good of the people is liberty." With liberal ideas like this one expressed in his *Encyclopedia*, Denis Diderot challenged prevailing views of government and society. Yet his ideas intrigued Catherine II of Russia. She supported Diderot by buying his library but allowing the books to remain with him. She paid him an annual salary to serve as the librarian for the rest of his life. Diderot traveled to St. Petersburg in 1773 to thank his patron. He stayed at Catherine's court five months, long enough to conclude that enlightened absolutism would not lead to liberty, as he had hoped. **Why did Catherine II buy Diderot's library?**

D Differentiated Instruction

Verbal/Linguistic Ask students to consider the epitaph written by Joseph II. Discuss the difficulties of describing a person's life in a brief statement. Then ask students to write epitaphs for Frederick II, Maria Theresa, and Catherine the Great based on the information in the text. **AL**

R Reading Strategy

Inferring Ask students to consider Catherine's suggestion that Diderot speak "as man to man." **Ask:** **What did Catherine assume would limit Diderot's suggestions for reform?** *(Because she was a monarch, most people would be hesitant to speak frankly in fear that they might anger or offend her.)* **OL**

People in History

Answers:
Catherine II: the radicalism of the French Revolution made her fearful of change and more conservative
Diderot: to support him because his ideas intrigued her

Additional Support

Extending the Content

Catherine the Great and Diderot Catherine the Great inspired several different views by historians. She is seen by some as only interested in talking of Enlightenment reforms but doing nothing substantial and actually making life worse for Russian serfs. Others point to her interest in education and establishment of a school for girls and a medical college as proof of her Enlightenment goals. Some believe that Diderot and others such as Voltaire flattered her to gain a bit of her wealth and her support. **Ask:** **Why do you think Catherine inspired such differing views of her reign?** *(Responses may include that some see the improvements she made as important steps toward the modernization of Russia, while others see her as not following up on her grand ideas and words.)* **OL**

C Critical Thinking

Analyzing Information

Ask: Why would French traders be seen as less hostile than British settlers? *(Traders did less to disrupt the Native Americans' way of life and served as an economic resource. Settlers encroached on native land and were more of a threat.)* **OL**

S Skill Practice

Using Geography Skills Ask: In which area were most battles fought? *(in the Indian Reserve or nearby)* **OL**

With the Treaty of Paris in 1763, the French withdrew and left India to the British.

The War in North America

The greatest conflicts of the Seven Years' War took place in North America. On the North American continent, the French and British colonies were set up differently. The French government administered French North America (Canada and Louisiana) as a vast trading area. It was valuable for its fur, leather, fish, and timber. Because the **C** French state was unable to get people to move to North America, its colonies were thinly populated.

British North America consisted of thirteen prosperous colonies on the eastern coast of what is now the United States. Unlike the French colonies, the British colonies were more populated, containing more than one million people by 1750.

The British and French fought over two main areas in North America. One consisted of the waterways of the Gulf of St. Lawrence, which were protected by the fortress of Louisbourg and by forts that guarded French Quebec. The other area they fought over was the unsettled Ohio River valley. The French began to move down from Canada and up from Louisiana to establish forts in the Ohio River valley. This French activity threatened to cut off the British settlers in the thirteen colonies from expanding into this vast area. The French were able to gain the support of the Native Americans who lived there. As traders and not settlers, the French were viewed by Native Americans with less hostility than the British.

The French scored a number of victories, at first. British fortunes were revived, however, by the efforts of William Pitt the Elder, Britain's prime minister. Pitt was convinced that the French colonial empire would have to be destroyed for Britain to create its own colonial empire. Pitt's policy focused on doing little in the European theater of war while putting resources into the colonial war, especially through the use of the British navy. The French had more troops in North America but not

INFOGRAPHICS PRIMARY SOURCE

The Seven Years' War in North America

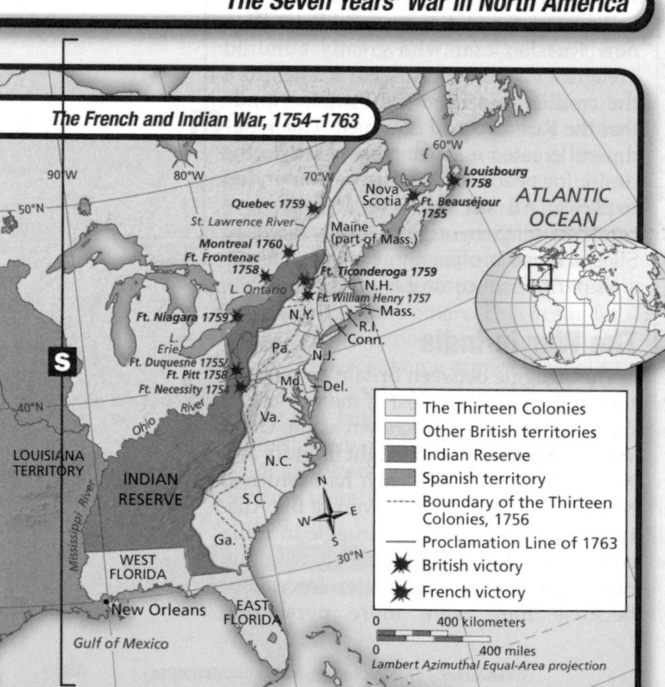

The rivalry between France and Britain for territories brought the Seven Years' War to North America. Known here as the French and Indian War, it began in the Ohio River valley. When the French built a fort in an area claimed by Virginia, the governor of Virginia sent 21-year-old George Washington to warn the French to leave.

> "They [the French] told me it was their absolute Design to take Possession of the Ohio. . . . They pretended to have an undoubted right to the river from a Discovery made by one La Sol [La Salle] 60 Years ago, & the use of this Expedition is to prevent our Settling on the River or Waters of it. . . ."
>
> —George Washington, *Diaries of George Washington*, 1753

In May 1754, George Washington, commanding a small force of Virginians, surprised French troops on the eastern side of the Ohio River and drove them out. Washington's men built a fort there, which they named Fort Necessity. The French soon regrouped, however. They captured Fort Necessity in July 1754. The French and Indian War was underway.

Additional Support

Activity: Technology Connection

Plan a Web Page Have students work in small groups to plan a Web page about the French and Indian War. Students should begin by using the text and Internet or library resources to write an entry about the war. They should then list key terms for which they might provide links on their Web pages. Next, have students search the Internet for possible sites that their Web page might link to for more information. They should decide on one Web site for each key term. Finally, have students discuss how they would design their Web pages. They should discuss what types of images they would use, how to incorporate links, and the general layout. To complete the activity, students should create thumbnail sketches that include text and sample images. **OL**

enough naval support. The defeat of French fleets in major naval battles gave the British an advantage. Without their fleets, the French could not easily reinforce their forts.

A series of British victories soon followed. In 1759 British forces under General Wolfe defeated the French under General Montcalm on the Plains of Abraham, outside Quebec. Both generals died in the battle. The British went on to seize Montreal, the Great Lakes area, and the Ohio River valley. The French were forced to make peace.

By the Treaty of Paris, the French transferred Canada and the lands east of the Mississippi to England. Spain, ally of the French, transferred Spanish Florida to British control. In return, the French gave their Louisiana territory to the Spanish. By 1763, Great Britain had become the world's greatest colonial power. W

✓Reading Check **Explaining** How did Great Britain become the world's greatest colonial power?

Enlightenment and Arts

MAIN IDEA The eighteenth century was a great period in the history of European architecture, art, music, and literature.

HISTORY & YOU What style of music is most popular with your friends? Which musicians are the best examples of this style? Read to learn about popular music and musicians of the eighteenth century.

The ideas of the Enlightenment also had an impact on the world of culture. Eighteenth-century Europe witnessed both traditional practices and important changes in art, music, and literature.

Architecture and Art

The palace of Louis XIV at Versailles, in France, had made an enormous impact on Europe. The Austrian emperor, the Swedish king, and other European rulers also built grand residences. These palaces were modeled more on the Italian baroque style of the 1500s and 1600s than on the late seventeenth-century French classical style of Versailles. R

To show the danger of disunity, Franklin drew an image of a snake cut into eight sections. The sections represented the eleven colonies that had joined the Albany Congress (the New England colonies were combined).

In 1754, as war with France loomed, Benjamin Franklin realized that the American colonies must band together for their mutual defense. Franklin published this cartoon—America's first political cartoon—to gain support for an association among the colonies called the Albany Congress.

Although the Albany Plan of Union drawn up by the congress was never formally adopted, it was the forerunner of the first constitution of the United States. Although the war ended their empire in North America, the French would later take their revenge by fighting on the American side in the American Revolution.

CRITICAL THINKING SKILLS

1. **Explaining** Why did the governor of Virginia send George Washington to talk to the French?
2. **Predicting** Based on their activities in the French and Indian War, what roles do you think Washington and Franklin would play in the American Revolution?

W Writing Support

Narrative Writing Ask students to write a short newspaper article for a British newspaper announcing the Treaty of Paris. The article should summarize the results of the war and celebrate the triumph of Great Britain. OL

R Reading Strategy

Activating Prior Knowledge Discuss with students what they know about the palace of Versailles and its beauty and size. Then discuss why other nobles might choose to build large palaces. BL

✓Reading Check

Answer: By fighting the Seven Years' War, Great Britain added a great deal of land to its worldwide empire.

CRITICAL THINKING SKILLS

Answers:
1. to try to convince the French to leave the Ohio Valley
2. Washington became a military leader in the revolution. Franklin became a political leader and diplomat.

Additional Support

Activity: Collaborative Learning

Debating Ask: Why did Franklin think it was important for the colonies to unite? *(Individual colonies did not have military or economic resources to defend themselves against the French.)* Discuss the diversity of the colonies at the time and the fact that they operated as individual units without loyalty to one another or significant common interests. Talk about reasons why colonists might want to remain separate and how unity might pose a threat to Britain as well as Native Americans. Divide the class into two groups and have students stage a debate between those for and against uniting the colonies. Have members of each group speak as colonists, British officials, and representatives of Native American tribes. Students should conduct additional research as needed to find out more information surrounding the issue. OL

Focus

Introducing Social History
Ask: Where do you meet your friends and what do you talk about? Discuss settings and topics of conversation popular today. In eighteenth-century France, a popular kind of gathering called a *salon* attracted great writers and thinkers to the homes of French hostesses.

Teach

C Critical Thinking

Drawing Conclusions Have students read the description of a salon. **Ask:** How did salons foster the spread of ideas? *(Guests shared ideas with each other and spread those ideas through later conversation or writing.)* OL

R Reading Strategy

Making Connections Discuss the restrictions of a royal court. **Ask:** How would you feel as a guest at one of these functions? *(Students should understand the pressure of being in the king's presence, even at a salon. Guests felt compelled to be witty and entertaining, yet had to watch what they said very carefully.)* OL

Additional Support

The 18th-Century Salon

The French word *salon* refers to a parlor or living room, a main gathering space in a private home. In the 18th century, the salons became gathering places for intellectual conversation. Writers, scientists, and philosophers met weekly to discuss important discoveries and new works of poetry and theater. C

▲ *Molière Received by Louis XIV, by Jean Hégesippe Vetter*

The Shortcomings of Life at Court

R The king's court was a very formal place. There were strict rules about how courtiers had to dress, when and where they could sit, and when and where they could speak to certain people. Even courtiers who had the privilege of joining a conversation chose their words carefully. Some topics were objectionable to Church authorities or high-ranking nobility. Court gossip and intrigue often dominated discussion.

Background

French Salons Madame de Rambouillet, who lived from 1588 to 1665, is credited with the institution of the salon. She was appalled at the crassness of noble life and the pervasiveness of political corruption under Henry IV. In reaction, she established a salon that emphasized conversation and literature. Her salon, which drew talented and clever writers, scholars, and nobles, set a standard for refined language and behavior that influenced literature and etiquette and began a tradition that was to continue for over two hundred years. Later hostesses emulated her example, often banning discussion of politics and religion from their salons in order to maintain a high standard of conversation. Ironically, these women were frequently not very educated themselves, but instead possessed natural intelligence, charm, wit, and knowledge of other people that enabled them to command their drawing rooms.

▲ *Reading of Voltaire's Tragedy "L'Orphelin de la Chine" at the Salon of Madame de Geoffrin,* by Anicet Charles Gabriel Lemonnier

A Golden Age of Conversation

Madame de Geoffrin (1699–1777) made two important salon innovations. She focused on an early afternoon meal, instead of a late dinner, allowing an entire afternoon of conversation. She also introduced a regular weekly schedule of themes, with days devoted to the visual arts and literature. She was remembered as a generous listener, and she had a talent for saying just enough, at the right time, to keep a conversation moving. **R**

Analyzing Visuals

1. **Expressing** What ideas about government in France can you form by looking at this representation of the king?
2. **Speculating** In Madame de Geoffrin's salon, many specialties and interests were represented by the participants. Do you think such wide-ranging discussions helped or distracted each participant in his studies and writing?

565

R Reading Strategy

Inferring Ask: Based on this description of Madame Geoffrin, what were the characteristics of a good salon hostess? *(She needed to be a good listener who was also able to bring out the best in her guests.)* **OL**

Assess/Close

Comparing and Contrasting
Have students work in small groups to identify advantages and disadvantages of salons as social occasions and channels of communication. **Ask:** Is there anything comparable to a salon today? *(Students should give specific examples to support their answers.)* **OL**

Analyzing Visuals

Answers:

1. There was a distinct hierarchy. The king has the central position of honor at the table.
2. Answers may include that participants were inspired to greater heights of accomplishment.

Activity: Collaborative Learning

Modeling a Salon Gathering Ask: How did salon hostesses, such as Madame Geoffrin, ensure interesting and relevant topics of conversation at their gatherings? *(They established themes and set specific discussion topics.)* Have students work in small groups. Ask groups to assign the role of host or hostess to one of their members. The rest of the group will be guests at the salon. Then have students decide on a topic of conversation, such as a new film or a book or play that they have all read. Or, they might choose a philosophical question to consider, such as the nature of existence. Have groups perform role plays that reflect what might have transpired in a salon. After the performances, ask students what they thought about the salon format. **OL**

Teacher Tip

Collaborative Learning The activity allows students with different levels of academic skills and intelligences to work together. Remind students to think carefully about the skills needed to be hostess or host of a salon. Using this information, they can choose the best group member for the job.

D Differentiated Instruction

Auditory/Musical Have students prepare a dramatic reading from the Declaration of Independence. Have students explain why they chose their selections. **OL**

W Writing Support

Persuasive Writing Ask students if they think today's fight against terrorism should affect Americans' individual liberties. Have students explain their point of view in a brief essay. **AL**

✓Reading Check

Answer: to gain revenge for earlier defeats by the British

Answers:

1. Students may discuss current debates about conflicts between security and individual freedoms, such as suspicion leveled at Muslim Americans or wire tapping, and so on.
2. Responses may include allowing expression of unpopular ideas.

Fighting finally erupted between colonists and the British army in April 1775 in Lexington and Concord, Massachusetts. Meeting soon afterward, the Second Continental Congress set up an army, called the Continental Army. **George Washington** served as its commander in chief.

D More than a year passed before the colonies declared independence from the British Empire. On July 4, 1776, the Second Continental Congress approved the **Declaration of Independence** written by **Thomas Jefferson.** With this stirring political document, the American Revolution had formally begun.

The war against Great Britain was a huge gamble. Britain was a strong military power with enormous financial resources. The Continental Army of the Americans was made up of undisciplined civilians who agreed to serve for only a short time.

British Defeat

Of great importance to the colonies' cause was support from foreign countries. These nations were eager to gain revenge for earlier defeats at the hands of the British. The French supplied arms and money to the rebels. French officers and soldiers also served in Washington's army. In February 1778, following a British defeat, the French granted diplomatic recognition to the new United States. When Spain and the Dutch Republic entered the war, the British faced war with the Europeans as well as the Americans.

When General Cornwallis was forced to surrender to the American and French forces under Washington at **Yorktown** in 1781, the British decided to end the war. The Treaty of Paris, signed in 1783, recognized the independence of the American colonies. The treaty also granted the Americans control of the western territory from the Appalachians to the Mississippi River.

✓Reading Check **Explaining** Why did foreign countries support the Americans?

CONNECTING TO THE UNITED STATES

GUARANTEED FREEDOMS

- Freedom of Religion
- Freedom of Speech
- Freedom of Peaceable Assembly

W After the American Revolution, the Founders of the new United States set up a system whereby its citizens could govern themselves. They created the Bill of Rights to ensure individual liberties for future generations. Today, in the wake of terrorist attacks on U.S. soil, security has become a top priority for many Americans. Will new security measures encroach on the liberties that our revolutionary ancestors fought for and guaranteed in the Bill of Rights?

CONNECTING TO TODAY

1. **Analyzing** How has the search for terrorists impacted American liberty?
2. **Applying** In a 1929 case, U.S. Supreme Court Justice Holmes stated his understanding of free speech: "... the principle of free thought—not free thought for those who agree with us, but freedom for the thought that we hate." Give an example that applies this principle to today.

Differentiated Instruction

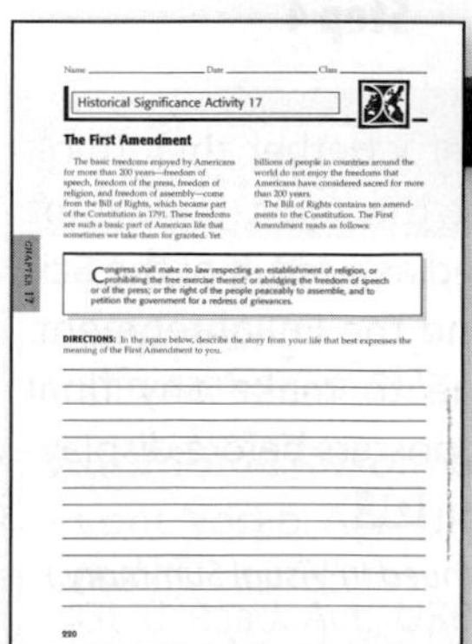

Historical Significance Activity, URB p. 220

Analyzing Primary Sources

Objective: Describe the meaning of the First Amendment.

Focus: Have students read and discuss the introductory paragraph.

Teach: Have students highlight or underline important thoughts in the passage.

Assess: Ask students to complete the writing after the passage.

Close: Discuss how the First Amendment applies to students.

Differentiated Instruction Strategies

BL Review the main ideas of each paragraph with students.

AL Have students research and report on a recent First Amendment case that has been featured in the news.

ELL Have students work in pairs to define unfamiliar terms in the amendment.

The Birth of a New Nation

MAIN IDEA The formation of the United States convinced many eighteenth-century philosophes that a new age and a better world could be created.

HISTORY & YOU Recall the philosopher Rousseau's concept of the social contract. Read to learn how the new United States set up government by the general will of the people.

After throwing off oppressive rule, the former colonies, now states, feared a strong central government. Thus, their first constitution, the Articles of Confederation (1781), created a government that lacked the power to deal with the nation's problems. In 1787, delegates met in Philadelphia at the Constitutional Convention to revise the Articles of Confederation. The delegates decided to write a plan for an entirely new government.

The Constitution

The proposed Constitution created a **federal system** in which the national government and the state governments shared power. Based on Montesquieu's ideas, the national, or federal, government was separated into three branches: executive, legislative, and judicial. Each branch had some power to check, or restrain, acts of the other branches.

A president served as the chief executive in the executive branch. The legislative branch consisted of elected representatives in two houses—the Senate and the House of Representatives. The Supreme Court and other courts formed the judicial branch. After ratification, or approval, by 9 of the 13 states, the Constitution took effect.

The Bill of Rights

As promised during negotiations over ratification, the new Congress proposed 12 **amendments** to the Constitution. The states approved 10 of the amendments. Together, these amendments became known as the **Bill of Rights.**

These 10 amendments **guaranteed** freedom of religion, speech, press, petition, and assembly. They gave Americans the right to bear arms and to be protected against unreasonable searches and arrests. They guaranteed trial by jury, due process of law, and the protection of property rights.

R Many of the rights in the Bill of Rights were derived from the natural rights proposed by the eighteenth-century philosophes. Many European intellectuals saw the American Revolution as the embodiment of the Enlightenment's political dreams. The premises of the Enlightenment seemed confirmed. A new age and a better world could be achieved.

✓Reading Check **Identifying** What was the main weakness of the Articles of Confederation?

SECTION 4 REVIEW

Vocabulary
1. **Explain** the significance of: Hanoverians, Robert Walpole, George Washington, Declaration of Independence, Thomas Jefferson, Yorktown, federal system, amendment, Bill of Rights, guaranteed.

Main Ideas
2. **Explain** why England wanted revenues from the American colonies.
3. **Explain** the purpose of the Stamp Act.
4. **Summarize** the rights and freedoms guaranteed by the American Bill of Rights by using a chart like the one below.

Guarantees of the Bill of Rights

Critical Thinking
5. **The BIG Idea Making Inferences** Why did many Europeans see the American Revolution as the embodiment of the Enlightenment's political dreams?
6. **Analyzing** If going to war with the British was such a huge gamble, why then did the colonists win?
7. **Analyzing Visuals** Study the photograph on page 568. What does the body language of the people in the photograph suggest to you?

Writing About History
8. **Expository Writing** Do further research on how the French supported the colonies during the American Revolution. Then write an essay analyzing the importance of the French assistance to the colonists.

History ONLINE
For help with the concepts in this section of *Glencoe World History*, go to glencoe.com and click Study Central™.

R Reading Strategy

Sequencing Information
Have students list the important events in this section in the order in which they occurred. **BL**

✓Reading Check
Answer: It lacked the power to deal with the nation's problems.

Assess

Study Central provides summaries, interactive games, and online graphic organizers to help students review content.

Close

Summarizing Ask: How did the American victory over the British and the new American republic confirm Enlightenment ideas? *(American victory confirmed the belief in natural rights to self-government; the new republic established Enlightenment ideas in the Constitution.)*

Answers

1. Definitions for the vocabulary words are found in the section and the Glossary.
2. to cover war costs; to pay for maintaining an army to protect the colonies
3. means for Britain to collect taxes from the colonists
4. freedom of religion, speech, press, petition, and assembly; right to bear arms; protection from unreasonable searches and arrests; trial by jury; due process of law; protection of property rights
5. Answers may include these results of the revolution: government by the will of the people with separation of powers and checks and balances; protection of natural rights; freedom from oppression.
6. Answers may include: support of foreign nations; British soldiers fighting far from home and on unfamiliar ground; desire for freedom was a strong and unifying force
7. Answers may include that the soldier's facial expression and stance suggest confidence, strength, and determination.
8. Essays should accurately describe France's role in the American Revolution.

9. C All answers are related to French writers and thinkers but are not related to political thought. Montesquieu's system of checks and balances concerns politics, but deism, laissez-faire doctrine, and the *Encyclopedia* deal with other subjects.

10. A All were influenced by and reacted to Enlightenment ideas, but only Joseph II tried to implement great changes, although many of his changes were short-lived.

11. C Latin America, Australia, and Africa are not mentioned in the chapter. India was featured in both text and maps.

12. C Cornwallis was a British general, and Walpole a British politician. During this period, Thomas Jefferson is best remembered for his work on the Declaration of Independence and the Constitution.

TEST-TAKING 

For Question 12: Students can use the process of elimination to figure out the answer. By eliminating answers they know are incorrect one at a time, they will be left with the correct answer.

13. D 10 is the correct figure. None of the other numbers have any relevance.

CHAPTER 17

9. What was Montesquieu's most lasting contribution to political thought?
- **A** Deism
- **B** Laissez-faire doctrine
- **C** System of checks and balances through separation of powers
- **D** 28-volume *Encyclopedia*

Section 3 *(pp. 554–563)*

10. Which of the following leaders sought truly radical changes based on Enlightenment ideas?
- **A** Joseph II
- **B** Frederick the Great
- **C** Catherine the Great
- **D** Maria Theresa

11. The Seven Years' War took place in three main regions of the world: Europe, North America, and which of the following?
- **A** Latin America
- **B** Australia
- **C** India
- **D** Africa

Section 4 *(pp. 566–569)*

12. Who commanded the Continental Army?
- **A** Thomas Jefferson
- **B** General Cornwallis
- **C** George Washington
- **D** Robert Walpole

13. How many constitutional amendments are in the U.S. Bill of Rights?
- **A** 13
- **B** 5
- **C** 9
- **D** 10

Critical Thinking

Directions: Choose the best answers to the following questions.

14. Which of the following is an example of checks and balances at work in the United States government?
- **A** The national and state governments share power.
- **B** Congress is separated into two houses, the Senate and the House of Representatives.
- **C** The president can veto, or reject, an act of Congress.
- **D** Representatives to Congress are elected by a vote of the people.

Base your answer to question 15 on the time line below and on your knowledge of world history.

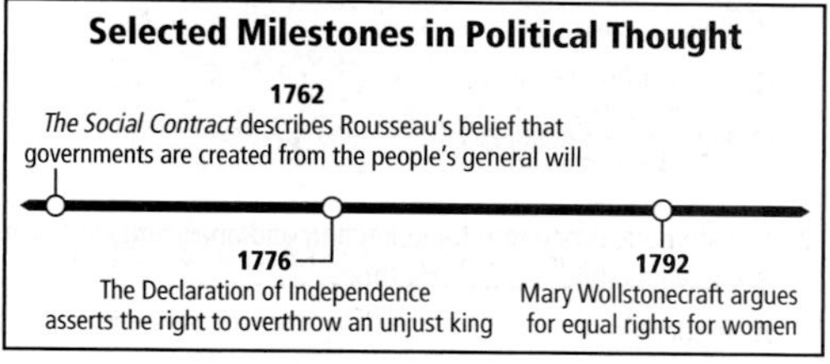

15. Which of the following statements is supported by the information on the time line?
- **A** Most Europeans supported their monarchs.
- **B** Many people questioned the nature of their governments.
- **C** Enlightenment thinkers embraced the women's movement.
- **D** Only men thought and wrote about politics.

Need Extra Help?

If You Missed Questions . . .	9	10	11	12	13	14	15
Go to Page . . .	548	558	559	568	569	569	572

GO ON

14. C The veto power is an example of two distinct branches of government interacting. The national and state governments are at different levels, the Senate and House are both part of the legislative branch, and election of Representatives doesn't relate to checks and balances.

15. B Both *The Social Contract* and Declaration of Independence indicate conflicts with the government. Wollstonecraft argued for women's rights but was not well-supported. Support for European monarchs is not indicated.

16. The philosophes compared the universe to a clock. Which of the following statements best explains this comparison?
   - **A** The creator of the universe makes events occur on a predictable schedule.
   - **B** The universe is a machine that requires power to operate properly.
   - **C** Once set in motion, the universe operates without further help from its creator.
   - **D** The universe runs in mysterious ways that only its creator can understand.

17. Which concept below conformed to the teaching of the Catholic Church in the eighteenth century?
   - **A** A heliocentric universe
   - **B** The universal law of gravitation
   - **C** Rationalism
   - **D** A geocentric universe

Base your answer to question 18 on the map below and on your knowledge of world history.

18. What battle was fought on the island of Cuba?
   - **A** Hispaniola
   - **B** Havana
   - **C** Guadeloupe
   - **D** Martinique

Document-Based Questions

Directions: Analyze the document and answer the short-answer questions that follow the document.

John Locke greatly influenced eighteenth-century intellectuals. The quote below comes from Locke's famous work *Essay Concerning Human Understanding.*

> *"Let us then suppose the mind to be, as we say, white paper, void of all characters, without any ideas. How comes it to be furnished? Whence has it all the materials of reason and knowledge? To this I answer, in one word, from experience. . . . Our observation, employed either about external sensible objects or about the internal operations of our minds perceived and reflected on by ourselves, is that which supplies our understanding with all the materials of thinking."*

19. According to Locke, what one word describes how the blank mind becomes knowledgeable?
20. Paraphrase Locke's explanation of how the mind gains "all the materials of thinking."

Extended Response

21. The ideas of Montesquieu, Voltaire, and Rousseau influenced the development of the Constitution of the United States. Explain how the ideas of each person apply to the United States government.

For additional test practice, use Self-Check Quizzes—Chapter 17 at glencoe.com.

Need Extra Help?

If You Missed Questions . . .	16	17	18	19	20	21
Go to Page . . .	548	540	573	573	573	548

STOP

Document-Based Questions

19. *experience* The key phrase "in one word" should guide students.

20. by observing things outside ourselves or by observing and reflecting on our own thoughts

Extended Response

21. Montesquieu: separation of the powers of government with a system of checks and balances. The Constitution separates the government into executive, legislative, and judicial branches, each with the power to check some actions of the other branches. **Voltaire:** all men are brothers and religious toleration. The Bill of Rights guarantees equality before the law with protections such as trial by jury and due process. The Bill of Rights also guarantees freedom of religion. **Rousseau:** government by social contract, whereby an entire society agrees to be governed by its general will. The Constitution is a social contract. Elected representatives serve by the vote of the people. The people agree to abide by the laws passed by their representatives.

16. C The idea of a schedule or the need for power are not indicative of Enlightenment beliefs. Thinkers also believed that the universe was less mysterious than previously thought. They believed that the universe ran by consistent laws.

17. D A geocentric universe put the earth at the center and God far above in heaven. The other concepts are at odds with Church beliefs.

18. B Students knowledge of geography might direct them to Havana as located in Cuba.

Introduce students to chapter content and key terms by having them access the Chapter 17 Overview at glencoe.com.

Need Extra Help?

Have students refer to the pages listed if they miss any of the questions.

CHAPTER 18 Planning Guide

Key to Ability Levels	
BL Below Level	AL Above Level
OL On Level	ELL English Language Learners

Key to Teaching Resources	
Print Material	DVD
CD-ROM	Transparency

BL	OL	AL	ELL		Resources	Chapter Opener	Section 1	Section 2	Section 3	Chapter Assess
					FOCUS					
BL	OL	AL	ELL	Transparency	**Daily Focus Skills Transparencies**		18-1	18-2	18-3	
					TEACH					
BL	OL		ELL	Print Material	**Reading Skills Activity, URB**				p. 243	
	OL	AL		Print Material	**Historical Analysis Skills Activity, URB**				p. 244	
BL	OL	AL	ELL	Print Material	**Differentiated Instruction Activity, URB**		p. 245			
	OL		ELL	Print Material	**English Learner Activity, URB**				p. 247	
BL	OL	AL	ELL	Print Material	**Content Vocabulary Activity, URB***				p. 249	
BL	OL	AL	ELL	Print Material	**Academic Vocabulary Activity, URB**				p. 251	
BL	OL	AL	ELL	Print Material	**Skills Reinforcement Activity, URB**		p. 253			
	OL	AL		Print Material	**Critical Thinking Skills Activity, URB**			p. 254		
	OL	AL		Print Material	**History and Geography Activity, URB**				p. 255	
	OL	AL	ELL	Print Material	**Mapping History Activity, URB**				p. 257	
BL	OL	AL		Print Material	**Historical Significance Activity, URB**				p. 258	
BL	OL	AL	ELL	Print Material	**Cooperative Learning Activity, URB**				p. 259	
	OL	AL	ELL	Print Material	**History Simulation Activity, URB**			p. 261		
BL	OL	AL	ELL	Print Material	**Time Line Activity, URB**				p. 263	
	OL	AL		Print Material	**Linking Past and Present Activity, URB**		p. 264			
BL	OL	AL		Print Material	**People in World History Activity, URB**		p. 265	p. 266		
BL	OL	AL	ELL	Print Material	**Primary Source Reading, URB**			p. 267		
	OL	AL		Print Material	**Enrichment Activity, URB**				p. 272	
BL	OL	AL	ELL	Print Material	**World Art and Music Activity, URB**				p. 269	
BL	OL		ELL	Print Material	**Guided Reading Activities, URB***		p. 274	p. 275	p. 276	
BL	OL		ELL	Print Material	**Reading Essentials and Note-Taking Guide***		p. 196	p. 199	p. 202	
BL	OL	AL	ELL	Print Material	**Differentiated Instruction for the World History Classroom**	✓	✓	✓	✓	✓

Note: Please refer to the *Unit Resource Book: The Early Modern World* for this chapter's URB materials.

* Also available in Spanish

- Interactive Lesson Planner
- Interactive Teacher Edition
- Fully editable blackline masters
- Section Spotlight Videos Launch
- Differentiated Lesson Plans
- Printable reports of daily assignments
- Standards Tracking System

Levels					Resources	Chapter Opener	Section 1	Section 2	Section 3	Chapter Assess
BL	OL	AL	ELL							
TEACH *(continued)*										
BL	OL	AL	ELL		StudentWorks™ Plus DVD	✓	✓	✓	✓	✓
BL	OL	AL	ELL		Vocabulary PuzzleMaker CD-ROM	✓	✓	✓	✓	✓
Teacher Resources					Building Academic Vocabulary	✓	✓	✓	✓	✓
					Reading Strategies and Activities for the Social Studies Classroom			pp. 20, 29, 30		
					Writer's Guidebook			pp. 27, 47	p. 47	
					Strategies for Success	✓	✓	✓	✓	✓
					Outline Map Resource Book	✓	✓	✓	✓	✓
					Presentation Plus! with MindJogger DVD	✓	✓	✓	✓	✓
ASSESS										
BL	OL	AL	ELL		Section Quizzes and Chapter Tests*		p. 217	p. 218	p. 219	p. 221
BL	OL	AL	ELL		Authentic Assessment With Rubrics	✓	✓	✓	✓	✓
BL	OL	AL	ELL		Standardized Test Practice Workbook	✓	✓	✓	✓	✓
BL	OL	AL	ELL		*ExamView® Assessment Suite* CD-ROM		18-1	18-2	18-3	Ch. 18
BL	OL	AL	ELL		Interactive Tutor Self-Assessment CD-ROM		18-1	18-2	18-3	
CLOSE										
BL			ELL		Reteaching Activity, URB		p. 271			
BL	OL		ELL		Reading and Study Skills Foldables™	✓	✓	✓	✓	✓

Online Crossword Puzzles

Technology Product

Glencoe's Vocabulary PuzzleMaker™ 3.1 CD-ROM is an easy-to-use program that lets you create your own puzzles based on the glossary for classroom use. The PuzzleMaker allows you to

- create crossword puzzles based on content vocabulary and academic vocabulary that is specific to what is taught in the classroom;
- create online (LAN-based or local area network) or paper crossword puzzles.

Objectives

Completing the crossword puzzles helps students to

- recall vocabulary terms based on the clue provided for a puzzle;
- reinforce their understanding of the vocabulary.

Steps

- Run PuzzleMaker™ 3.1. On the main menu, click on **Create a New Puzzle.**
- From the list of *Puzzle Databases*, select the appropriate database for the vocabulary.
- The *PuzzleMaker Wizard* will take you through selecting a puzzle type and grid type.
- Then select one or more chapters from the list. Indicate whether you want the words selected randomly or manually.
- Select the language and words you wish to use within the maximum for the puzzle. Click **Finish.**
- Save your puzzle to a location that is easily accessible by your students with PuzzlePlayer™ 3.1, or print copies for your students to complete.
- Use PuzzlePlayer™ 3.1 to review the puzzles after your students have worked on and saved them.

History ONLINE

	Student	Teacher	Parent
Beyond the Textbook	●	●	●
Chapter Overviews	●	●	●
Time Current Events	●		●
ePuzzles and Games	●		●
Concepts in Motion	●		●
Literature Connections		●	
Multi-Language Glossaries	●		●
Online Student Edition	●	●	●
Self-Check Quizzes	●		●
Student Web Activities	●		●
Study Central ™	●		●
Teaching Today		●	
Vocabulary eFlashcards	●		●
Web Activity Lesson Plans		●	

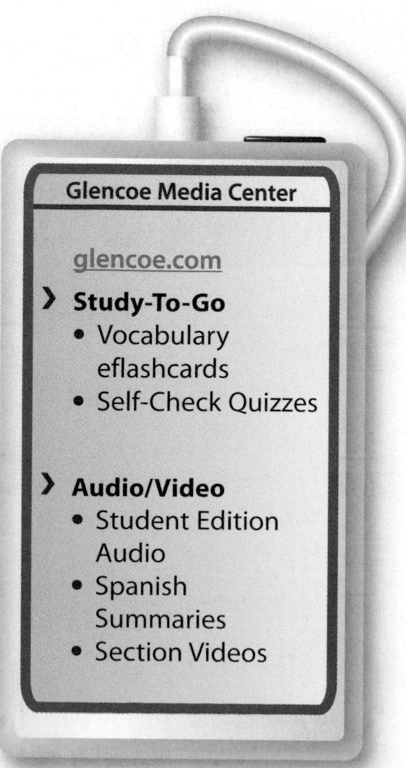

- **Timed Readings Plus in Social Studies** helps students increase their reading rate and fluency while maintaining comprehension. The 400-word passages are similar to those found on state and national assessments.
- **Reading in the Content Area: Social Studies** concentrates on six essential reading skills that help students better comprehend what they read. The book includes 75 high-interest nonfiction passages written at increasing levels of difficulty.
- **Reading Social Studies** includes strategic reading instruction and vocabulary support in Social Studies content for both ELLs and native speakers of English.

www.jamestowneducation.com

The following videotape programs are available from Glencoe as supplements to Chapter 18:

- Eiffel Tower (ISBN 1-56-501465-0)
- Marie Antoinette: Tragic Queen (ISBN 1-56-501915-6)
- Napoleon Bonaparte: The Glory of France (ISBN 0-76-701211-9)

To order, call Glencoe at 1-800-334-7344. To find classroom resources to accompany many of these videos, check the following home pages:

A&E Television: www.aetv.com

The History Channel: www.historychannel.com

Index to National Geographic Magazine:

The following articles relate to this chapter:

- "Europe's Big Gamble," by Don Belt, May 2004
- "Bohemian Rhapsody," by Cathy Newman, August 2003
- "The New Europe," by T. R. Reed, January 2002

National Geographic Society Products To order the following, call National Geographic at 1-800-368-2728:

- *National Geographic Atlas of the World* (Book).

Access National Geographic's new, dynamic MapMachine Web site and other geography resources at:

www.nationalgeographic.com

www.nationalgeographic.com/maps

GLENCOE BOOKLINK 3

Use this database to search more than 30,000 titles to create a customized reading list for your students.

- Reading lists can be organized by students' reading level, author, genre, theme, or area of interest.
- The database provides Degrees of Reading Power™ (DRP) and Lexile™ readability scores for all selections.
- A brief summary of each selection is included.

Leveled reading suggestions for this chapter:

For students at a Grade 8 reading level:

- ***Marie Antoinette: Princess of Versailles,*** by Kathryn Lasky

For students at a Grade 9 reading level:

- ***Paris,*** by Conrad R. Stein

For students at a Grade 10 reading level:

- ***Napoleon and the Napoleonic Wars,*** by Albert Marrin

For students at a Grade 11 reading level:

- ***France,*** by Donna L. Knoell

For students at a Grade 12 reading level:

- ***Louis XVI, Marie-Antoinette and the French Revolution,*** by Nancy Plain

Introducing
CHAPTER 18

Focus

MAKING CONNECTIONS
What makes a nation?

Ask students to come up with a list of possible national symbols for the United States, including the achievements they commemorate or symbolize. **Ask:** Did all of these events end positively for the United States? *(Most U.S. symbols will relate to positive achievements.)* Note that Napoleon's Grand Army was the greatest army in the world at the time, but later suffered a terrible defeat. Explain that this period was one of great power and influence for the French in the world.

Teach

The Big Ideas

As students study the chapter, remind them to consider the section-based Big Ideas included in each section's Guide to Reading. The **Essential Questions** in the activities below tie in to the Big Ideas and help students think about and understand important chapter concepts. In addition, the Hands-on Chapter Projects with their culminating activities relate the content from each section to the Big Ideas. These activities build on each other as students progress through the chapter. Section activities culminate in the wrap-up activity on the Visual Summary page.

CHAPTER 18

The French Revolution and Napoleon 1789–1815

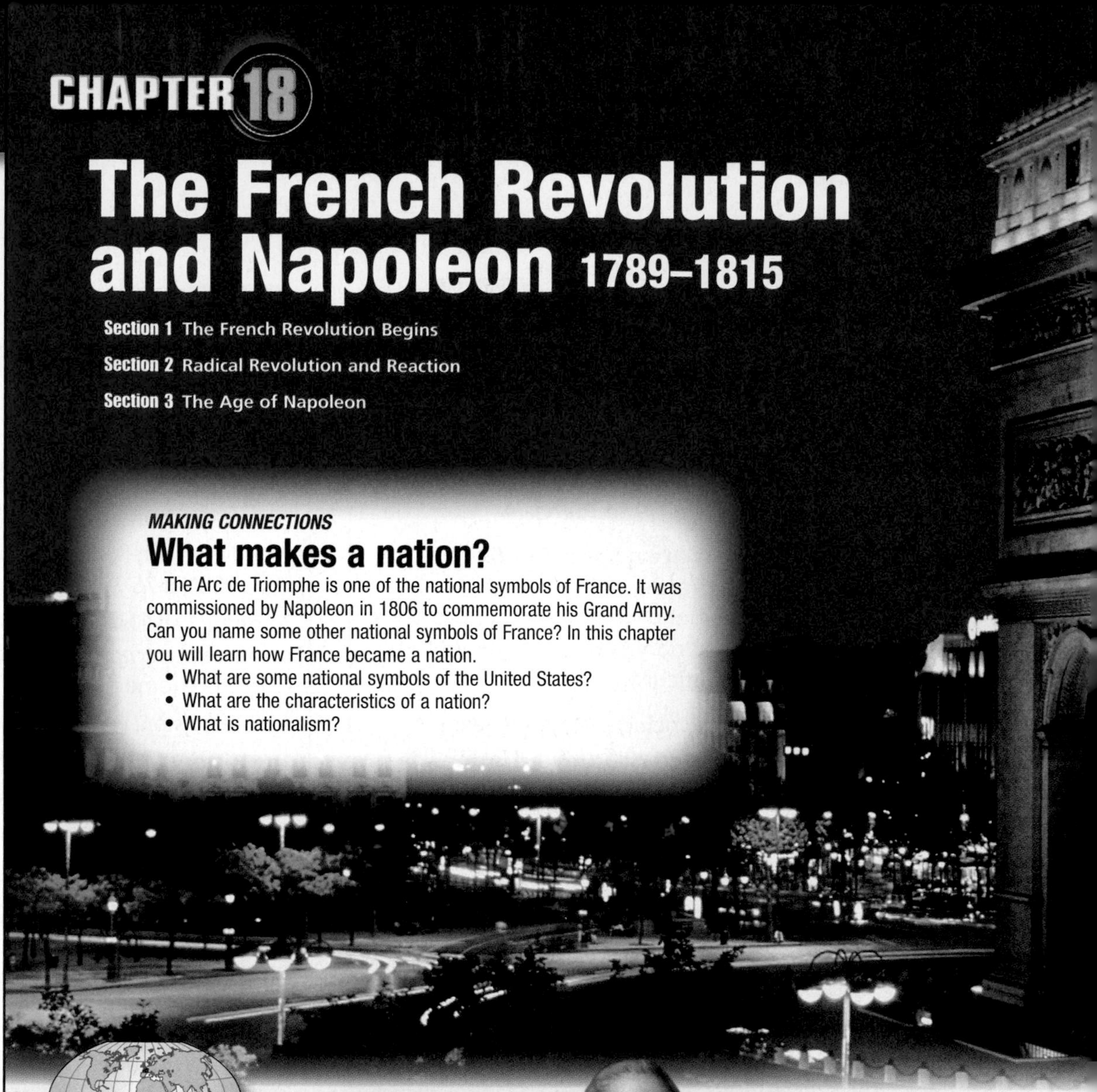

MAKING CONNECTIONS

What makes a nation?

The Arc de Triomphe is one of the national symbols of France. It was commissioned by Napoleon in 1806 to commemorate his Grand Army. Can you name some other national symbols of France? In this chapter you will learn how France became a nation.

- What are some national symbols of the United States?
- What are the characteristics of a nation?
- What is nationalism?

FRANCE ▶

1789 French Revolution begins

1793 King Louis XVI executed; Reign of Terror begins

1799 Napoleon leads coup d'état that topples French government

1790 — 1800

THE WORLD ▶

1789 George Washington inaugurated as first U.S. president

1803 United States purchases Louisiana Territory from France

574

The French Revolution Begins

Essential Question: What was the French system of government before the French Revolution? *(an absolute monarchy)* Point out that in Section 1, students will learn about social, political, and economic problems that created an atmosphere ripe for revolution. **OL**

Radical Revolution and Reaction

Essential Question: What internal conflicts in France affected the progress of the French Revolution? *(Internal disputes about the proper changes in government resulted in great conflict and bloodshed.)* Point out that in Section 2, students will learn about the Reign of Terror that affected Paris and other communities, resulting in the deaths of many of the Revolution's leaders. **OL**

1812
Napoleon invades Russia

1815
Napoleon defeated at the Battle of Waterloo

1815

1810
Hidalgo leads Mexican independence movement

FOLDABLES™ Study Organizer

Identifying Create a Four-Door Book to record *who, what, when,* and *where* facts while you read about Napoleon Bonaparte.

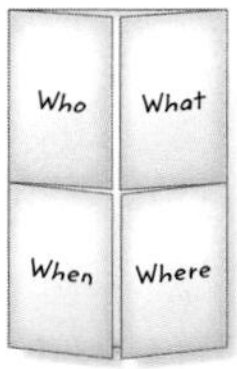

Who | What | When | Where

History ONLINE
Chapter Overview—Visit glencoe.com to preview Chapter 18.

SECTION 3

The Age of Napoleon
Essential Question: Why was Napoleon able to take control of France and become its emperor? *(France was in great turmoil from the revolution; Napoleon was a skilled military and political leader.)* Point out that in Section 3, students will learn about the rise and fall of Napoleon and one of the great empires of Europe. **OL**

More About the Photo

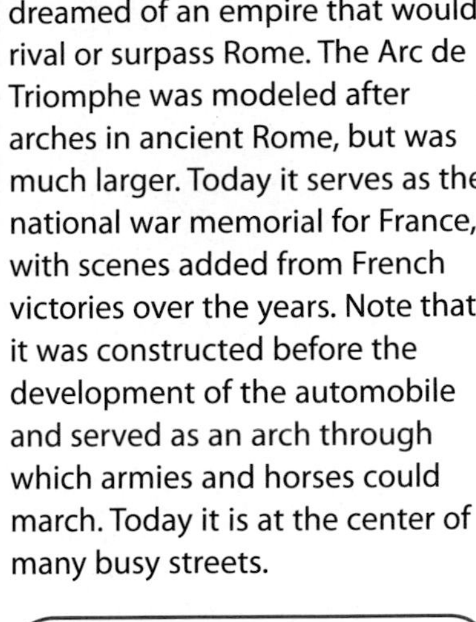

Visual Literacy Napoleon dreamed of an empire that would rival or surpass Rome. The Arc de Triomphe was modeled after arches in ancient Rome, but was much larger. Today it serves as the national war memorial for France, with scenes added from French victories over the years. Note that it was constructed before the development of the automobile and served as an arch through which armies and horses could march. Today it is at the center of many busy streets.

FOLDABLES™ Study Organizer **Dinah Zike's Foldables**

Dinah Zike's Foldables are three-dimensional, interactive graphic organizers that help students practice basic writing skills, review vocabulary terms, and identify main ideas. Instructions for creating and using Foldables can be found in the Appendix at the end of this book and in the *Dinah Zike's Reading and Study Skills Foldables* booklet.

History ONLINE
Introduce students to chapter content and key terms by having them access the Chapter 18 Overview at glencoe.com.

Focus

Bellringer

Daily Focus Transparency 18.1

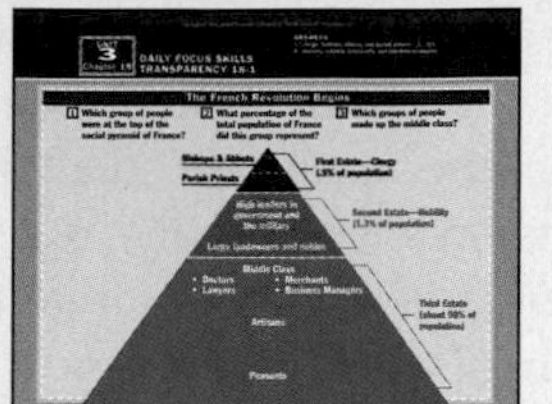

GUIDE TO READING

Answers to Graphic:
Third Estate demands one vote per deputy; denied by king; National Assembly formed. Relics of feudalism; popular uprising. Other causes include uprising against social class structure, food shortages, unemployment

Section Spotlight Video

To generate student interest and provide a springboard for class discussion, access the Chapter 18, Section 1 video at glencoe.com or on the video DVD.

Resource Manager

SECTION 1

The French Revolution Begins

GUIDE TO READING

The BIG Idea
Struggle for Rights Social inequality and economic problems contributed to the French Revolution.

Content Vocabulary
- estate *(p. 576)*
- taille *(p. 576)*
- bourgeoisie *(p. 578)*
- sans-culottes *(p. 583)*

Academic Vocabulary
- consumer *(p. 577)*
- exclusion *(p. 581)*

People and Events
- Louis XVI *(p. 578)*
- Tennis Court Oath *(p. 579)*
- Declaration of the Rights of Man and the Citizen *(p. 581)*
- Olympe de Gouges *(p. 581)*

Reading Strategy
Explaining As you read, use a diagram like the one below to list the factors that contributed to the French Revolution.

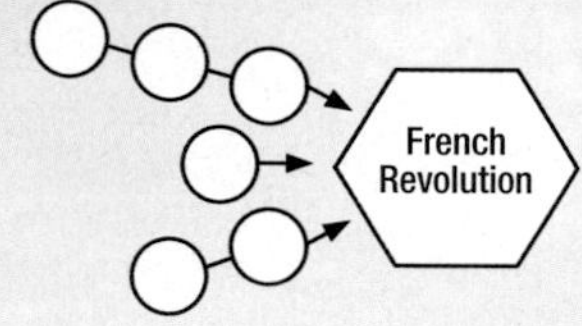

The year 1789 witnessed two far-reaching events: the beginning of a new United States of America and the beginning of the French Revolution. Compared with the American Revolution, the French Revolution was more complex and more radical. The French Revolution established both a new political order and a new social order. For that reason, it is considered a turning point in European history.

Background to the Revolution

MAIN IDEA The Third Estate, the vast majority of the French people, was heavily taxed and discontented.

HISTORY & YOU What if you had no say in family concerns despite doing all the household chores? Learn how the French people reacted to having no say in their government.

French society had changed little since medieval times. Feudalism established the privileges and obligations of the three main social classes. Although there were clergy and wealthy landowners in the American colonies, there were no laws giving them special status, unlike the class system in France. This social injustice caused unrest in eighteenth-century France.

France's Three Estates

Since the Middle Ages, France's population had been divided by law into one of three status groups, or **estates.** The First Estate consisted of the clergy, the Second Estate the nobles, and the Third Estate everyone else. Thus the Third Estate included anyone from the lowliest peasant to the wealthiest merchant.

The First Estate, or clergy, numbered about 130,000 out of a total population of 27 million and owned about 10 percent of the land. The clergy were radically divided. The higher clergy—cardinals, bishops, and heads of monasteries—were from noble families and shared their outlook and interests. The parish priests were often poor and from the class of commoners.

The Second Estate, or nobility, numbered about 350,000 and owned about 25 to 30 percent of the land. They played a crucial role in society in the 1700s. They held leading positions in the government, in the military, in the law courts, and in the Roman Catholic Church. Despite controlling most of the wealth of the kingdom, neither the clergy nor the nobles had to pay the **taille** (TAH•yuh), France's chief tax.

R Reading Strategies	C Critical Thinking	D Differentiated Instruction	W Writing Support	S Skill Practice
Teacher Edition • Act. Prior Know., p. 577 • Making Connections, p. 581 **Additional Resources** • Guid. Read. Act., URB p. 274 • Read. Ess. & Note-Taking Guide, p. 196	**Teacher Edition** • Ident. Cent. Issues, p. 579 • Making Generalizations, p. 582 • Det. Cause/Effect, p. 583 **Additional Resources** • People in World Hist. Act., URB p. 265 • Section Quiz, p. 217	**Teacher Edition** • Visual/Spatial, p. 578 • Logical/Math., p. 579 • ELL, p. 580 • Auditory/Musical, p. 581 **Additional Resources** • Diff. Instr. Act., URB p. 245 • Reteach. Act., URB p. 271	**Teacher Edition** • Expository Writing, p. 580 • Personal Writing, p. 581 **Additional Resources** • Linking Past/Present Act., URB p. 264	**Teacher Edition** • Visual Literacy, p. 579 **Additional Resources** • Skills Reinforc., URB p. 253

PRIMARY SOURCE POLITICAL CARTOONS

France's Three Estates

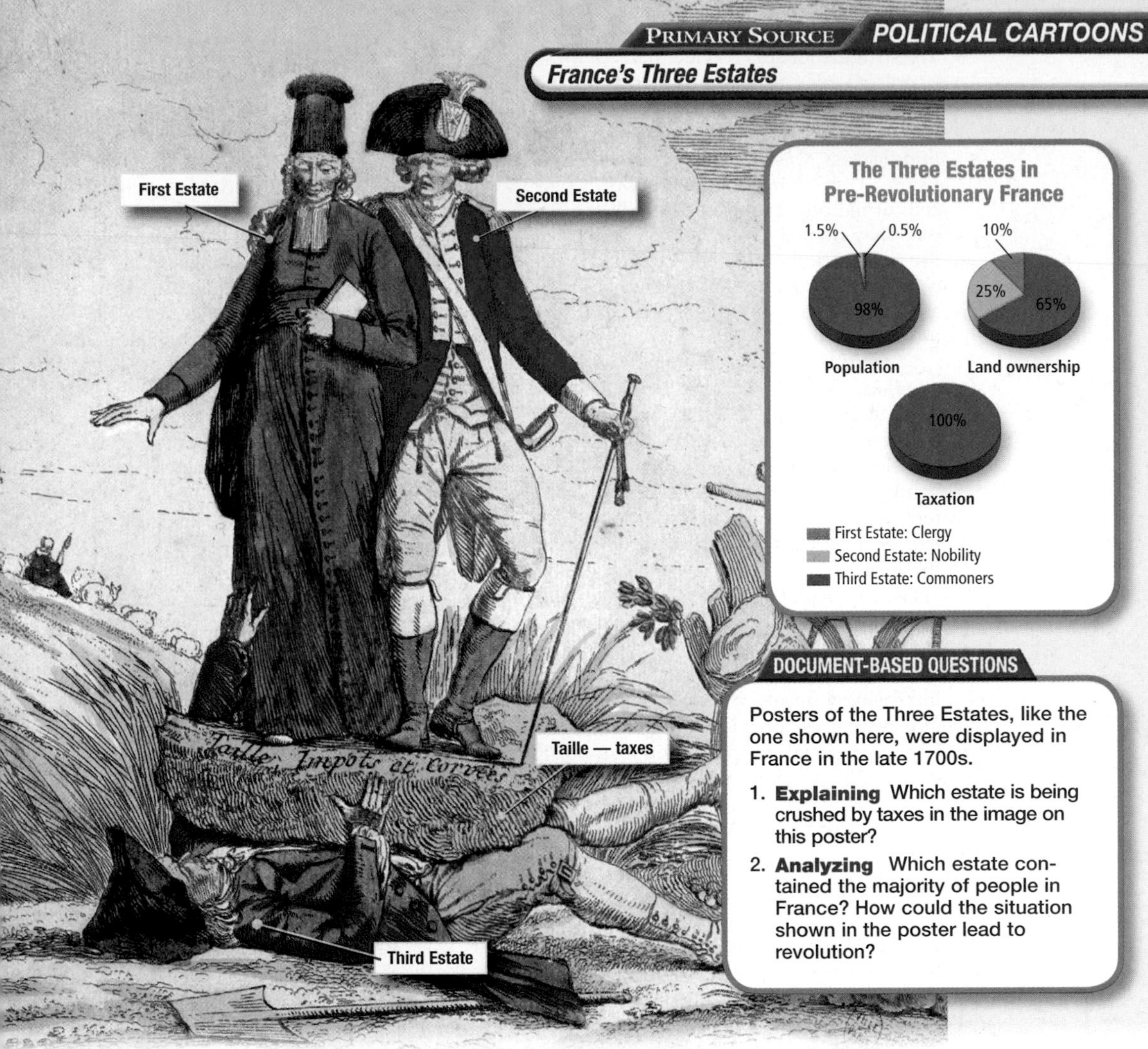

DOCUMENT-BASED QUESTIONS

Posters of the Three Estates, like the one shown here, were displayed in France in the late 1700s.

1. **Explaining** Which estate is being crushed by taxes in the image on this poster?
2. **Analyzing** Which estate contained the majority of people in France? How could the situation shown in the poster lead to revolution?

Unlike the First and Second Estates, the Third Estate was divided by vast differences in occupation, level of education, and wealth. Peasants made up 75 to 80 percent of the Third Estate and owned about 35 to 40 percent of the land; middle-class members of the Third Estate owned the rest. At least half of the peasants had little or no land to live on.

All peasants owed certain duties to the nobles, which were a holdover from medieval times when serfdom was widespread. For example, a peasant had to pay a fee to grind his flour or press his grapes because the local lord controlled the flour mill and wine press. When the harvest time came, the peasant had to work a certain number of days harvesting the noble's crop. Peasants fiercely resented these duties.

R Another part of the Third Estate consisted of urban craftspeople, shopkeepers, and workers. These people, too, were struggling to survive. In the 1700s, the price of **consumer** goods increased much faster than wages, which left these urban groups with decreased buying power.

Teach

R Reading Strategy

Activating Prior Knowledge
Ask students to review their knowledge of medieval times. **Ask:** Why did peasants pay fees to lords? *(The lords offered military protection, and they owned the land and controlled the mills.)* OL

DOCUMENT-BASED QUESTIONS

Answers:

1. the Third Estate, commoners
2. The Third Estate—according to the graphs, the common people made up 98 percent of the population, owned about 65 percent of land, and paid 100 percent of the taxes. The Third Estate could start an uprising against the nobility and clergy to protest the high taxes.

Hands-On Chapter Project
Step 1

Make a Map of Changes in French Life

Pairs of students will create a map that will show sites of events in French life during the late 1700s and early 1800s. The map will be accompanied by a short written or oral report.

Step 1: Beginning a Map and Selecting Two Events

Essential Question: How did French social, economic, and political life change during the Revolution and under Napoleon?

Directions: Pairs of students will begin a map of Europe by selecting two events or changes from this section or from additional research. They should indicate two different types of change (social, economic, political) that can be indicated on the map with an icon and a headline. Then have students do additional research to prepare a short written or oral report that describes the event or change. OL

(Chapter Project is continued in Section 2.)

D Differentiated Instruction

Visual/Spatial Ask students to review their knowledge of the vast differences in economic conditions for peasants and royalty. They can do additional research as necessary to become more familiar with the activities at Versailles. Then have students create a picture or political cartoon that illustrates the great divide between the classes. **OL**

DOCUMENT-BASED QUESTIONS

Answers:
1. a mixture; answers may vary
2. The painter was a member of the Assembly.

✓Reading Check

Answer: peasants; craftspeople, shopkeepers, and wage earners; and the bourgeoisie, or middle class, which included merchants, bankers, industrialists, and professionals such as lawyers, holders of public offices, doctors, and writers

The struggle for survival led many of these people to play an important role in the revolution, especially in Paris.

The **bourgeoisie** (BURZH•WAH•ZEE), or middle class, was another part of the Third Estate. This group included about 8 percent of the population, or 2.3 million people. They owned about 20 to 25 percent of the land. The bourgeoisie included merchants, bankers, and industrialists, as well as professional people—lawyers, holders of public offices, doctors, and writers.

The middle class was unhappy with the privileges held by nobles. They did not want to abolish the nobility, however, but to better their own position. Some bourgeoisie had managed to become nobles by being appointed to public offices that conferred noble status. About 6,500 new nobles had been created by appointment during the 1700s.

The bourgeoisie also shared certain goals with the nobles. Both were drawn to the new political ideas of the Enlightenment. In addition, both groups were increasingly upset with a monarchical system resting on privileges and on an old and rigid social order. The opposition of these elites to the old order led them to take drastic action against the absolute monarchy of **Louis XVI**.

Financial Crisis

Social conditions, then, formed a longstanding background to the French Revolution. The immediate cause of the revolution was the near collapse of the French budget. Although the economy had been expanding for fifty years, there were periodic crises. Bad harvests in 1787 and 1788 and a slowdown in manufacturing led to food shortages, rising prices for food, and unemployment. One English traveler **D** commented on the misery of French peasants:

PRIMARY SOURCE

"All the country girls and women are without shoes or stockings; and the plowmen at their work have neither shoes nor stockings to their feet. This is a poverty that strikes at the root of national prosperity."

—an English traveler in France

On the eve of the revolution, the French economy was in crisis. Despite these problems, the French king and his ministers continued to spend enormous sums of money on wars and court luxuries. The queen, Marie Antoinette, was especially known for her extravagance and this too caused popular resentment. When the government decided to spend huge sums to help the American colonists against Britain, the budget went into total crisis.

With France on the verge of financial collapse, Louis XVI was forced to call a meeting of the Estates-General, representatives of all three estates meeting together, to raise new taxes. The Estates-General had not met since 1614 because French kings were so powerful.

✓Reading Check **Identifying** What groups were part of the Third Estate?

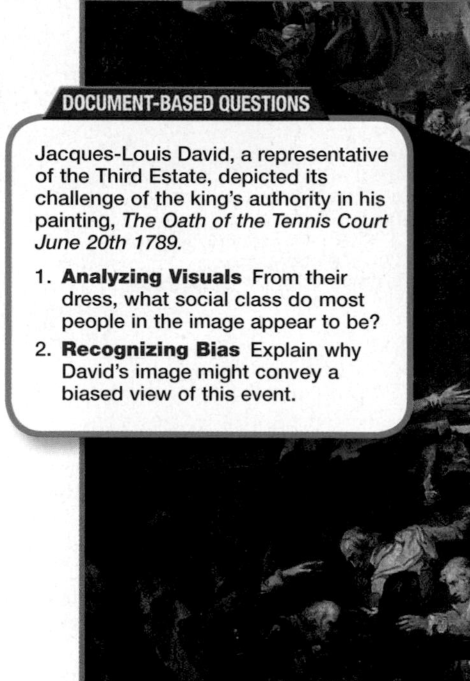

DOCUMENT-BASED QUESTIONS

Jacques-Louis David, a representative of the Third Estate, depicted its challenge of the king's authority in his painting, *The Oath of the Tennis Court June 20th 1789.*

1. **Analyzing Visuals** From their dress, what social class do most people in the image appear to be?
2. **Recognizing Bias** Explain why David's image might convey a biased view of this event.

Differentiated Instruction

People in World History Activity, URB p. 265

Making Inferences

Objective: Make inferences about Marie Antoinette's actions and the resulting reactions of others.

Focus: Discuss how royal marriages affected international relations.

Teach: Have students answer the questions.

Assess: Ask students to list important ideas about Marie Antoinette.

Close: Ask students why Marie Antoinette's execution symbolized change.

Differentiated Instruction Strategies

BL Ask students to describe Marie Antoinette in their own words.

AL Ask students to research and report on the court at Versailles.

ELL Discuss with students the significance of the remark, "Let them eat cake."

From Estates-General to National Assembly

MAIN IDEA The Third Estate claimed the right to have its votes count as much as those of the First and Second Estates.

HISTORY & YOU Have you heard about a riot and wondered what made people take to the streets? Learn why Parisian workers rioted in the summer of 1789.

Louis XVI called a meeting of the Estates-General at Versailles on May 5, 1789. In the Estates-General, the First and Second Estates each had about 300 representatives. The Third Estate had almost 600 representatives. Most of the Third Estate wanted to set up a constitutional government that would make the clergy and nobility pay taxes, too. C

From the start, there were arguments about voting. Traditionally, each estate had one vote—the First and Second Estates could outvote the Third Estate two to one. The Third Estate demanded instead that each deputy have one vote. D Under this new system, with the help of a few nobles and clerics, the Third Estate would then have a majority vote. The king stated that he favored the current system.

On June 17, 1789, the Third Estate boldly declared that it was the National Assembly and would draft a constitution. Three days later, on June 20, its deputies arrived at their meeting place, only to find the doors had been locked. They then moved to a nearby indoor tennis court and swore that they would continue meeting until they had a new constitution. The oath they swore is known as the **Tennis Court Oath.**

PRIMARY SOURCE — ***HISTORY & ARTS***

Tennis Court Oath

S

C Critical Thinking

Identifying Central Issues
Ask: What was the major goal of the Third Estate at the Estates General? *(to set up a constitutional government that would make the other estates pay taxes, too)* **BL**

D Differentiated Instruction

Logical/Mathematical Ask: How much more did each vote of a deputy for the First and Second Estate count compared to a deputy for the Third Estate in the old system? *(Under the old system, both the First and Second Estate had a single vote equal to the one vote of the Third Estate. Since each had about 300 deputies and the Third Estate 600, their votes counted twice as much in reality.)* **AL**

S Skill Practice

Visual Literacy Ask: How are many people in the picture signifying their agreement with the oath? *(by raising their hands)* **BL**

Additional Support

Extending the Content

Court Tennis in France Tennis became popular in France during the 12th century, especially among the clergy. It became so popular that an archbishop was forced to forbid priests from playing it in 1245. At first, the ball was hit with the player's hand, but soon a racket was invented. Later, indoor courts became popular. When the Third Estate needed a large area to meet, a nearby tennis court served the purpose. However, the French Revolution nearly killed the sport in France, mainly because it was a sport of the upper classes.

D Differentiated Instruction

English Language Learners Ask students to research Bastille Day, which is a national holiday in France, and compare it to other national celebrations of victories or independence such as the Fourth of July and Cinco de Mayo. ELL

W Writing Support

Expository Writing Have students write a paragraph that describes the difference between a "revolt" and a "revolution" in the context given here, explaining why the king might have been mistaken in his thoughts. AL

DOCUMENT-BASED QUESTIONS

Answers:

1. played an active role in the revolution; carried weapons, confronted Louis XVI at Versailles
2. to stir up emotions and support the revolution

✓Reading Check

Answer: The First and Second Estates together could outvote the Third Estate two-to-one.

Additional Support

Louis XVI prepared to use force against the Third Estate. On July 14, 1789, about 900 Parisians gathered in the courtyard of the Bastille (ba•STEEL)—an old fortress, used as a prison and armory. The price of bread had reached record highs, so the crowd was hungry and agitated. According to rumor, the king's troops were coming, and there was ammunition in the **D** Bastille. A group of attackers managed to lower the two drawbridges over the moat. Members of the French Guard joined the attack. After four hours of fighting, the prison warden surrendered. The rebels released the seven prisoners and cut off the prison warden's head. Angered that there were no munitions, the crowd demolished the Bastille brick by brick. Paris was abandoned to the rebels.

When King Louis XVI returned to his palace at Versailles after a day of hunting, **W** the duc de la Rochefoucauld-Liancourt told him about the fall of the Bastille. Louis is said to have exclaimed, "Why, this is a revolt." "No, Sire," replied the duke. "It is a revolution."

Louis XVI was informed that he could no longer trust royal troops to shoot at the mob. The king's authority had collapsed in Paris. Meanwhile, all over France, revolts were breaking out. Popular hatred of the entire landholding system, with its fees and obligations, had finally spilled over into action.

Peasant rebellions became part of the vast panic known as the Great Fear. The peasants feared that the work of the National Assembly would be stopped by foreign armies. Rumors spread from village to village that foreign troops were on the way to put down the revolution. The peasants reacted by breaking into the houses of the lords to destroy the records of their obligations.

✓Reading Check **Examining** Why did the Third Estate object to how votes were counted in the Estates-General?

HISTORY & ARTS — PRIMARY SOURCE

The King Concedes

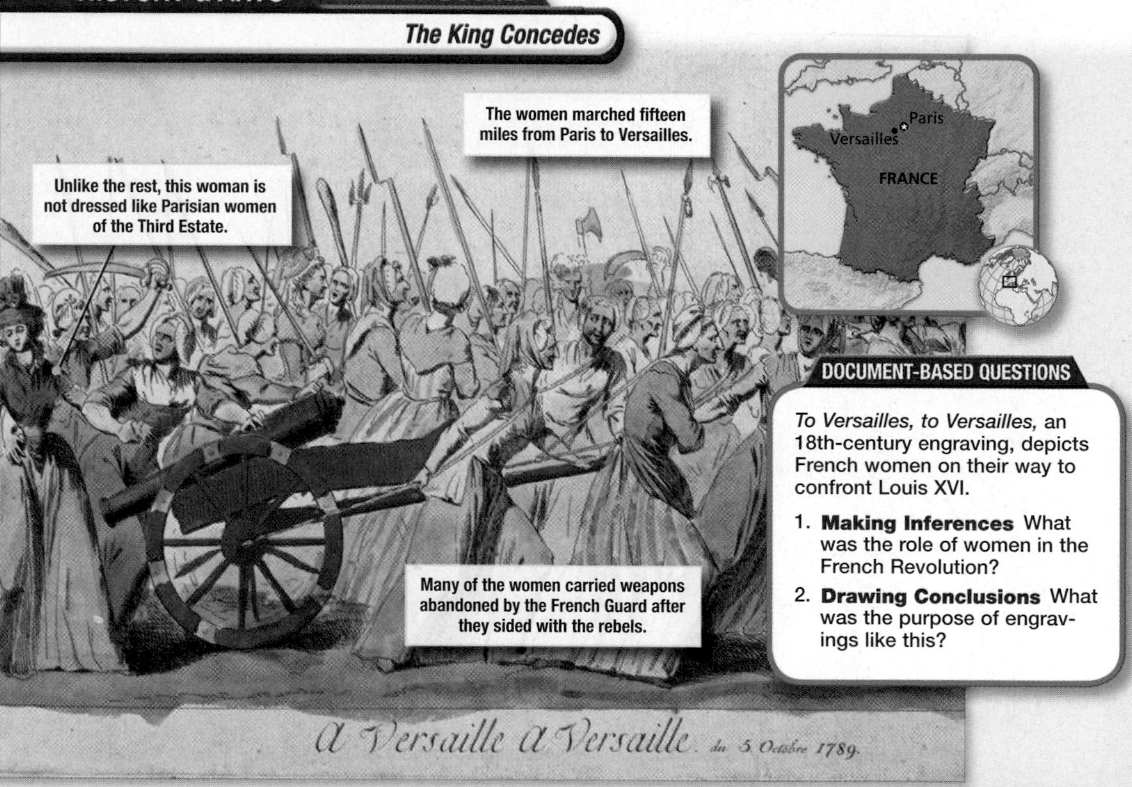

DOCUMENT-BASED QUESTIONS

To Versailles, to Versailles, an 18th-century engraving, depicts French women on their way to confront Louis XVI.

1. **Making Inferences** What was the role of women in the French Revolution?
2. **Drawing Conclusions** What was the purpose of engravings like this?

Extending the Content

The Price of Bread Many people in France lived in poverty or just on the edge of poverty at the time of the French Revolution. There had been bread riots in France for several years, especially in Paris where workers could not grow grain themselves. People would seize a bakery wagon and sell the bread for what they considered a fair price. When poor weather hurt crops, the price of bread rose so high that in some cases, it would take nearly all of a worker's wages just to buy bread for his family. The highest prices were usually in the summer, just before the next harvest came in. Many in the crowd who attacked the Bastille were hungry, as the surge in bread prices and food shortages during the summer of 1789 made life intolerable for the masses.

End of the Old Regime

MAIN IDEA The National Assembly affirmed the "rights of man" and set up a limited monarchy in the Constitution of 1791.

HISTORY & YOU How did George III react to the Declaration of Independence? Read how Louis XVI reacted to the events of 1789.

The National Assembly reacted to news of peasant rebellions and rumors of a possible foreign invasion. On August 4, 1789, the National Assembly decided to abolish all legal privileges of the nobles and clergy.

Declaration of the Rights of Man

On August 26, the National Assembly adopted the **Declaration of the Rights of Man and the Citizen.** Inspired by the English Bill of Rights of 1689 and by the American Declaration of Independence and Constitution, this charter of basic liberties began with "the natural and imprescriptible rights of man" to "liberty, property, security, and resistance to oppression."

Reflecting Enlightenment thought, the declaration proclaimed that all men were free and equal before the law, that appointment to public office should be based on talent, and that no group should be exempt from taxation. Freedom of speech and of the press were affirmed. **R**

The declaration raised an important issue. Should equal rights include women? Many deputies agreed, provided that, as one man said, "women do not hope to exercise political rights and functions." One writer, **Olympe de Gouges,** refused to accept this **exclusion** of women. Echoing the words of the official declaration, she wrote:

PRIMARY SOURCE

> "Believing that ignorance, omission, or scorn for the rights of woman are the only causes of public misfortunes and of the corruption of governments, the women have resolved to set forth in a solemn declaration the natural, inalienable, and sacred rights of woman in order that this declaration, constantly exposed before all the members of the society, will ceaselessly remind them of their rights and duties."
>
> —from *Declaration of the Rights of Woman and the Female Citizen,* Olympe de Gouges, 1791

The King Concedes

In the meantime, Louis XVI remained at Versailles. Used to the absolutist system, he stubbornly refused to accept the National Assembly's decrees. On October 5, however, thousands of Parisian women—described by an eyewitness as "detachments of women coming up from every direction, armed with broomsticks, lances, pitchforks, swords, pistols and muskets"—marched to Versailles. Some of the women then met with the king. They told him that their children were starving because there was no bread. These women forced Louis to accept the new decrees. **W**

Now the crowd insisted that the king and his family come to Paris to show support for the National Assembly. If the king was not under their close watch, they feared he would rouse the kings and princes from other countries to oppose reform.

On October 6, the king and his family returned to Paris. As a goodwill gesture, they brought wagonloads of flour from the palace storehouse. They were escorted by women who chanted: "We are bringing back the baker, the baker's wife, and the baker's boy." The king, the queen, and their son were now virtual prisoners in Paris. **D**

Church Reforms

Under the old regime, the Catholic Church had been an important pillar of the social and political system. The revolutionaries felt they had to reform it too. The new revolutionary government had another serious motivation, however: the need for money. By seizing and selling off Church lands, the National Assembly was able to increase the state's revenues.

Finally, the Church was formally brought under the control of the state. A law was passed called the Civil Constitution of the Clergy. It said that bishops and priests were to be elected by the people, not appointed by the pope and the Church hierarchy. The state would also pay the salaries of the bishops and priests. Because of these changes, many Catholics became enemies of the revolution.

See page R43 to read excerpts from Olympe de Gouges's *Declaration of the Rights of Woman and the Female Citizen* in the **Primary Source and Literature Library.**

R Reading Strategy

Making Connections **Ask:** How do the French ideas about appointments to government offices and exemptions from taxation still inspire debate in the United States today? *(Some government appointments are made according to political parties rather than according to skill; some people feel that tax laws allow certain groups to be exempt from taxes or require them to pay a tax that is too small.)* **OL**

W Writing Support

Personal Writing Have students suppose that they had witnessed the march of thousands of women on Versailles. Invite students to research vivid accounts of the march. Then ask them to write a personal reaction to it in the form of a letter. **OL**

D Differentiated Instruction

Auditory/Musical **Ask:** What is the importance of the chant the women used during the return to Paris? *(It mocks the king and his family as if they were no better than the people in the street.)* **OL**

Additional Support

Activity: Interdisciplinary Connection

Illustrating the Rights of Man Have students review their knowledge of Enlightenment ideas and the American Declaration of Independence. Then ask them to reread the section on the French Declaration of the Rights of Man and the Citizen. Each student should prepare a poster or other display that illustrates the rights declared. Invite students to display their products when complete. **Ask:** How was this Declaration revolutionary at the time? *(Freedom of the press and speech were not guaranteed at the time; courts did not apply laws equally to all people; some groups were forced to pay taxes while others were not; people might be imprisoned or their property taken without recourse.)* **OL**

Focus

Introducing Social History

As students look at the illustrations, ask the following questions:

- What classes of French society are shown here?
- Is any of the clothing similar to modern clothing?
- In what ways do people communicate their age, social status, gender, and marital status through clothing today?

Teach

C Critical Thinking

Identifying Central Issues

Ask: How did sumptuary laws reinforce the class structure in France? *(They prevented "impersonating" a member of a different class.)* OL

R Reading Strategy

Identifying Ask students to review the spread. **Ask:** What do you think the French word for "breeches" is? (culottes, *because the revolutionaries became known as* sans culottes *meaning, "without breeches")* OL

Additional Support

A Revolution In Clothing

Throughout history, clothing has communicated a person's social status, age, gender, marital status, and ethnicity. Before the French Revolution, some of the Third Estate tried to dress like the nobility. After the revolution, as the Third Estate gained power, their clothing became the style to copy.

Second Estate

Wigs or hair were layered into powdered curls. Sometimes a hat with feathers was pinned on top.

Hats were worn on top of elaborate wigs or carried as an accessory.

According to the sumptuary laws, only noblemen could carry swords.

Hoops, crumpled paper, or padding was used to enlarge and fluff the skirt.

Noblemen wore knee-length, tight-fitting breeches. Both men and women wore silk stockings.

Only nobility could wear satin, lace, and fur according to the sumptuary laws.

Sumptuary Laws

Before the French Revolution outlawed social classes, sumptuary laws dictated which materials, styles, and accessories could be worn by each estate. Even poorer nobles, who did not have many clothes, dressed in expensive fabrics. The bourgeoisie, wealthier members of the Third Estate, tried to imitate the style of the Second Estate. Only the sumptuary laws prevented the bourgeoisie from "impersonating" a member of the nobility.

584

Extending the Content

Sumptuary Laws and Fashion Sumptuary laws were first passed in ancient Greece and Rome and were common in many European countries. Besides clothing, they regulated many different types of consumption, including jewelry and other extravagant expenses. They functioned to control class divisions and helped to support certain industries. In some countries (Japan, for instance), choices such as the size of houses and the materials that could be used in them were regulated. In England, lower classes were not allowed to wear any silk and might be imprisoned if they did, although such laws were difficult to enforce. During the Reign of Terror, it was decreed that everyone had a right to wear whatever clothing they wished. However, it was also decreed that all should wear a blue, white, and red cockade in public.

REVOLUTIONARY WEAR

During the Reign of Terror, a fashion statement became a political statement. Former nobles and wealthy bourgeoisie learned to avoid extravagant clothing. People wearing lavish clothes were often singled out for persecution, even execution. Revolutionary wear was simple, peasant garb in patriotic colors. Some revolutionary attire stayed in style, like the *pantelons*, or trousers. C

ANALYZING VISUALS

1. **Comparing** Who sets fashion trends today, and who inspired fashion in the 1700s?
2. **Making Inferences** How do today's clothing styles make political or social statements?

C Critical Thinking

Making Generalizations Ask students to write a sentence or two that characterizes the general style of the revolutionaries. *(favored practical clothing and styles, shunned clothing that was similar to the Second Estate)* **OL**

Assess/Close

Have students work in pairs to write three questions and answers about clothing during the French Revolution. Have pairs trade questions and then check answers.

ANALYZING VISUALS

Answers:

1. Answers will vary. Current fashion is often set by pop figures and media outlets. In the 1700s, sumptuary laws governed what different people could wear.
2. Answers will vary. Young people often identify themselves as followers of a particular music group or athlete. Expensive clothing or jewelry typically indicates status. T-shirts with printed statements often indicate political interests.

Additional Support

Activity: Interdisciplinary Connection

Art Divide the class into small groups and assign each a modern group to illustrate, such as business people, movie stars, average boys and girls, and so on. Each group should make a collage that illustrates common clothing for their group and prepare a presentation that identifies particular parts of the clothing and what they express about the group. After each presentation is complete, lead a discussion of the positive and negative aspects of fashion. **Ask:** How can clothing make people feel good? How can it make them feel bad? *(Answers will vary, but may include individuality attached to clothing and the pleasure in wearing it, as well as the class and status issues that can create negative feelings.)* **OL**

C Critical Thinking

Determining Cause and Effect Ask: Why did the execution of the king push the revolution into a radical new phase? *(The old order could return so long as the king was alive.)* **AL**

For additional practice on this skill, see the **Skills Handbook**.

PEOPLE in HISTORY

Answers:
Marat—They were too moderate
Robespierre—He believed in universal suffrage.

✓Reading Check

Answer: The Girondins represented the provinces. They feared the radical mobs in Paris and leaned toward keeping the king alive. The Mountain represented the interests of the radicals in Paris.

Additional Support

On January 21, the king was beheaded on the guillotine. Revolutionaries had adopted this machine because it killed quickly and, they believed, humanely. The king's execution created new enemies for the revolution, both at home and abroad. A new crisis was at hand.

C The execution of King Louis XVI pushed the revolution into a new radical phase. Henry de Firmont, a Catholic priest, was present at the king's execution. He describes the events he witnessed:

PRIMARY SOURCE

"The path leading to the scaffold was extremely rough and difficult to pass; the King was obliged to lean on my arm, and from the slowness with which he proceeded, I feared for a moment that his courage might fail; but what was my astonishment, when arrived at the last step, he suddenly let go of my arm, and I saw him cross with a firm foot the breadth of the whole scaffold; and in a loud voice, I heard him pronounce distinctly these words: 'I die innocent of all the crimes laid to my charge; I pardon those who had occasioned my death; and I pray to God that the blood you are going to shed may never be visited on France.'"

—Henry de Firmont

Crises and Responses

Disputes between the Girondins and the Mountain blocked the writing of a constitution. The Paris Commune pressured the National Convention to adopt more radical measures: price controls on food and universal male suffrage. Peasants in western France and inhabitants of major provincial cities refused to accept the authority of the Convention. Uprisings began in the west and spread to the south.

After Louis XVI was executed, a coalition of Austria, Prussia, Spain, Portugal, Britain, and the Dutch Republic took up arms against France. The French armies began to fall back. By late spring 1793, the coalition was poised to invade. It seemed possible that the revolution would be destroyed, and the old regime reestablished. Confronted with **domestic** uprisings and **external** threats, the National Convention gave the **Committee of Public Safety** broad powers. This was dominated by Georges Danton, then by the radical Jacobin **Maximilien Robespierre.**

✓Reading Check **Examining** What were the differences between the Girondins and the Mountain?

PEOPLE in HISTORY

Jean-Paul Marat
1743–1793 French Revolutionary

Marat earned his nickname "drinker of blood" by urging the poor to take what they needed by force. As a radical Jacobin, Marat condemned the moderate Girondins. In *The Death of Marat*, Jacques-Louis David painted the murder scene and portrayed Marat as a martyr to the revolution. Marat often worked in his bathtub to soothe a skin condition. In Marat's hand is a letter from Charlotte Corday, a Girondin sympathizer, who asked for an appointment with him. Corday stabbed Marat in the bathtub and later stood trial for her crime. **Why did Marat condemn the approach of the Girondins?**

Maximilien Robespierre
1758–1794 French Revolutionary

Robespierre was one of the revolution's most important leaders and a radical Jacobin. He drew his power from the Paris Commune and the support of the sans-culottes. In the National Convention, he preached democracy and universal male suffrage. His nickname was "The Incorruptible" because of his reputation for integrity. His weaknesses were self-righteousness and not tolerating any difference of opinion. Robespierre said, "How can one reproach a man who has truth on his side?" His passion in pursuing the Reign of Terror frightened many and led to his arrest and execution. **How were Robespierre's views different from other revolutionaries?**

Extending the Content

Marat and Robespierre Both Marat and Robespierre were well educated, as Marat practiced medicine and Robespierre law before the French Revolution. Marat returned to France eager to make a name as a writer, but his scientific work was rejected by the Academy of Science. He believed the established order was against him so he turned to writing the political newspaper, which became a voice for the most radical Jacobins. Robespierre believed so strongly in a new order that he thought mass executions were the only way to restore order and gain unified support for a new government.

The Reign of Terror

MAIN IDEA While the Committee of Public Safety was in power, thousands were executed.

HISTORY & YOU Can you name a government that has executed its critics? Learn about the effects of the executions in France.

For roughly a year during 1793 and 1794, the Committee of Public Safety took control of the government. To defend France from domestic threats, the Committee adopted policies that became known as the **Reign of Terror.**

Crushing Rebellion

As a temporary measure, revolutionary courts were set up to prosecute counter-revolutionaries and traitors. Throughout France, almost 40,000 people were killed during the Reign of Terror. Of those, 16,000 people, including Marie Antoinette and Olympe de Gouges, died by the guillotine. Most executions occurred in towns that had openly rebelled against the Convention. D

Revolutionary armies were set up to bring rebellious cities under the control of the National Convention. When the Committee of Public Safety decided to make an example of Lyon, 1,880 citizens of that city were executed. When guillotining proved too slow, grapeshot (a cluster of small iron balls) was used to shoot the condemned into open graves. A foreign witness wrote:

PRIMARY SOURCE

"Whole ranges of houses, always the most handsome, burnt. The churches, convents, and all the dwellings of the former patricians were in ruins. When I came to the guillotine, the blood of those who had been executed a few hours beforehand was still running in the street. . . . I said to a group of sans-culottes that it would be decent to clear away all this human blood. Why should it be cleared? one of them said to me. It's the blood of aristocrats and rebels. The dogs should lick it up."

—a German observer at Lyon, 1793

In western France, too, revolutionary armies were brutal in defeating rebels. The commander of the revolutionary army ordered that no mercy be given: "The road is strewn with corpses. Women, priests, monks, children, all have been put to death. I have spared nobody." Perhaps the most notorious violence occurred in Nantes, where victims were executed by being sunk in barges in the Loire River.

People from all classes were killed during the Terror. Clergy and nobles made up about 15 percent of the victims, while the rest were from the Third Estate. The Committee of Public Safety held that all this bloodletting was only temporary. Once the war and domestic crisis were over, the true "Republic of Virtue" would follow, and the Declaration of the Rights of Man and the Citizen would be realized. Robespierre wrote: R

PRIMARY SOURCE

". . . [T]he springs of popular government in revolution are at once virtue and terror: virtue, without which terror is fatal; terror, without which virtue is powerless. Terror is nothing other than justice, prompt, severe, inflexible; it is therefore an emanation of virtue."

—Robespierre

The Republic of Virtue

In addition to the Terror, the Committee of Public Safety took other steps to control and shape a French society. Robespierre called this new order the Republic of Virtue—a democratic republic composed of good citizens. As outward signs of support for the republic, the titles "citizen" and "citizeness" were to replace "mister" and "madame." Women wore long dresses inspired by the clothing worn in the ancient Roman Republic.

Good citizens would be formed by good education. A law aimed at primary education for all was passed but not widely implemented. Another law abolished slavery in French colonies.

Because people were alarmed about high inflation, the Committee tried to control the prices of essential goods like food, fuel, and clothing. The controls did not work well, however, because the government had no way to enforce them.

From the beginning, women had been active participants in the revolution, although they had no official power.

D Differentiated Instruction

Verbal/Linguistic Have students consider the contrasts between the descriptive terms "Committee of Public Safety" and "Reign of Terror." Ask students to consider the actions of the Committee during the Reign of Terror and write a paragraph or two that contrasts the meanings of the two terms and that also suggests a more accurate name for the Committee of Public Safety. **AL**

R Reading Strategy

Questioning Ask students to consider who was killed during the Reign of Terror. **Ask: What does the percentage of those killed from the Third Estate indicate about the Revolution's support?** *(Although the Revolution was intended to help the Third Estate, there were many who did not support its radical goals or methods.)* **AL**

Additional Support

Extending the Content

The Jacobins The word *Jacobin* was originally used to refer to priests of the Dominican order whose first religious house in Paris was on the Rue St. Jacques. When the radical group made up of Robespierre, Marat, and others met in a former Dominican religious house, the radicals became known as Jacobins. Today, the term is used to refer to people with radical political views. At first, the Jacobins supported a constitutional monarchy, but after King Louis XVI tried to escape from France to fight the revolutionary forces, they turned against any type of royal rule. The group often wore the *bonnet rouge* or red cap, which had been modeled after a headdress worn by freed Roman slaves. The cap became a symbol of loyalty to the French Revolution and became the obligatory headgear of all French patriots.

W Writing Support

Personal Writing Have students reread the words from Wordsworth's poem and discuss the sentiments it expresses. Then ask each student to write a personal response to the poem and the Reign of Terror in general. **AL**

✓Reading Check

Answer: It was the creation of a people's government, not a professional army established by a ruling dynasty. Its wars were people's wars, not dynastic wars.

DOCUMENT-BASED QUESTIONS

Answers:

1. that France is executing everyone no matter their rank or political ideology
2. The tables challenge the view: Peasants made up 82% of those executed, but relative to their population, they were not the most affected—only .3% of the Third Estate died, while 6.4% of the First Estate died.

End of the Terror

By the summer of 1794, the French had largely defeated their foreign foes. There was less need for the Reign of Terror, but it continued nonetheless. Robespierre was obsessed with ridding France of all the corrupt elements. Only then could the Republic of Virtue follow.

In June 1794, the Law of 22 Prairial was passed, which gave Robespierre more power to arrest and execute enemies of the revolution. Deputies in the National Convention who feared Robespierre decided to act, lest they be the next victims. They gathered enough votes to condemn him, and Robespierre was guillotined on July 28, 1794.

After the death of Robespierre, the Jacobins lost power and more moderate middle-class leaders took control. The Reign of Terror came to a halt. In August 1794, the Law of 22 Prairial was repealed and the release of prisoners began.

✓Reading Check **Evaluating** How did the revolutionary army help to create nationalism?

POLITICAL CARTOONS PRIMARY SOURCE

Evaluating the Terror

"—all perished, all—
Friends, enemies, of all parties, ages, ranks, **W**
Head after head, and never heads enough
For those that bade them fall."

—William Wordsworth, *The Prelude, Book X, Residence in France*

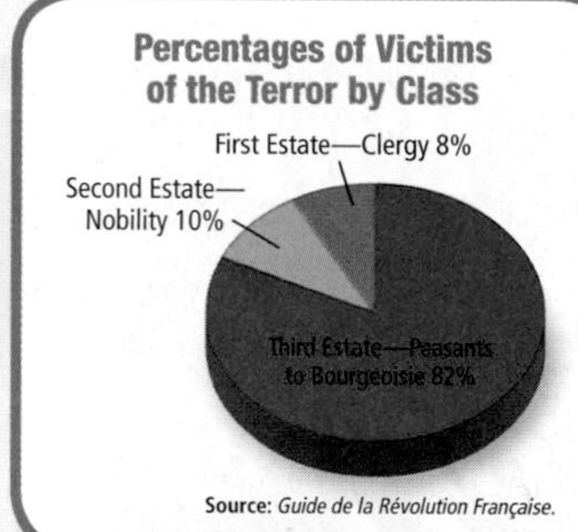

Source: *Guide de la Révolution Française*.

DOCUMENT-BASED QUESTIONS

The *Radical's Arms* by George Cruikshank shows the British view of the Reign of Terror. The banner above the guillotine reads, "No God! No King! No Religion! No Constitution!"

1. **Identifying Points of View** What opinion of the Terror do Wordsworth and Cruikshank share?
2. **Making Inferences** Wordsworth's poem seems to indicate that "all parties, ages, ranks" suffered equally during the Terror. Do the charts on this page and on page 577 support or challenge this view?

Differentiated Instruction

People in World History Activity, URB p. 266

Making Generalizations

Objective: Make generalizations about Robespierre's rise and fall.

Focus: Read to understand Robespierre's rise to power.

Teach: Ask students to identify reasons Robespierre rose quickly as a Jacobin leader.

Assess: Have students note why people feared Robespierre.

Close: Ask students to summarize why Robespierre both gained and lost his power so quickly.

Differentiated Instruction Strategies

BL Ask students to note positive traits of Robespierre.

AL Ask students to compare Robespierre's policies with Machiavelli's proposal that "the end justifies the means."

ELL Help students define and discuss the term "royal absolutism and arbitrary justice."

The Directory

MAIN IDEA The Constitution of 1795 set up a new government, but it was unable to inspire trust or solve economic problems.

HISTORY & YOU What kind of government did Americans have after 1781? Read to learn about France's government after Robespierre.

With the Terror over, the National Convention moved in a more conservative direction. First, it restricted the power of the Committee of Public Safety. Next, churches were allowed to reopen. Finally, a new constitution was created.

To keep any one political group from gaining control, the Constitution of 1795 set up two legislative houses. A lower house, the Council of 500, drafted laws. An upper house of 250, the Council of Elders, accepted or rejected proposed laws. C

The method for election shows that the new government was much more conservative than the government of Robespierre. Members of both houses were chosen by **electors,** or qualified voters. Only those who owned or rented property worth a certain amount could be electors—only 30,000 people in the whole nation qualified. This was a significant change from the universal male suffrage the Paris Commune had demanded.

Under the new constitution, the executive was a committee of five called the **Directory.** The Council of Elders chose the Directors from a list presented by the Council of 500. The Directory, which lasted from 1795 to 1799, became known mainly for corruption. People reacted against the sufferings and sacrifices that had been demanded in the Reign of Terror. Some people made fortunes from government contracts or by loaning the government money at very high interest rates. They took advantage of the government's severe money problems during these difficult times.

At the same time, the government of the Directory faced political enemies from both conservatives and radicals. Some people wanted to bring back the monarchy, while others plotted to create a more radical regime like Robespierre's. Likewise, economic problems continued with no solution in sight. Finally, France was still conducting expensive wars against foreign enemies.

To stay in power, the Directory began to rely on the military, but one military leader turned on the government. In 1799 the successful and popular general Napoleon Bonaparte toppled the Directory in a **coup d'état** (KOO day•TAH), a sudden overthrow of the government. Napoleon then seized power.

✓**Reading Check** **Describing** Describe the government that replaced the National Convention.

SECTION 2 REVIEW

Vocabulary

1. **Explain** the significance of: Georges Danton, Jean-Paul Marat, Jacobins, faction, domestic, external, Committee of Public Safety, Maximilien Robespierre, Reign of Terror, elector, Directory, coup d'état.

Main Ideas

2. **How** were most members of the National Convention elected in 1792 alike in their political views?
3. **Explain** both the similarities and the differences between the Girondins and the Mountain.
4. **Use** a table like the one below to contrast government policy during and after the rule of Robespierre.

During	After

Critical Thinking

5. **The BIG Idea** **Examining** Did the French Republic live up to the revolution's ideals of Liberty, Equality, and Fraternity? Write a paragraph to support your opinion.
6. **Summarizing** What conditions led to the Reign of Terror? How did the Committee of Public Safety defend its brutal actions against the people?
7. **Analyzing Visuals** Examine the painting shown on page 588. Explain whether you think this is a realistic depiction of Marat's murder or whether the artist is promoting a particular version of events.

Writing About History

8. **Expository Writing** Propaganda is information spread to help or hurt a cause. How does the mobilization decree quoted on page 591 fit the definition of propaganda? Support your argument in an essay.

History ONLINE
For help with the concepts in this section of *Glencoe World History*, go to glencoe.com and click Study Central™.

C Critical Thinking

Comparing and Contrasting

Ask: How did the new legislative body resemble that of the United States? *(It had two houses and was intended to prevent one group from gaining too much control.)* **OL**

✓**Reading Check**

Answer: The new government had a legislative assembly with two chambers and an executive committee called the Directory.

Assess

Study Central provides summaries, interactive games, and online graphic organizers to help students review content.

Close

Making Generalizations

Ask: How successful was the Revolution in making the changes it intended? *(It ended absolute monarchy and the three estates; all people were equal before the law, but social and economic inequality remained.)* **OL**

Answers

1. Definitions for the vocabulary words are found in the section and the Glossary.
2. They were mostly lawyers, professionals, and property owners who distrusted the king.
3. **Girondins:** Represented provinces, feared radical mobs, moderate toward king; **Mountain:** Represented city, more radical group, wanted to execute king
4. Answer may include: **During**—Reign of Terror; de-Christianization; **After**—more moderate leaders; churches reopen.
5. Answers will vary, but should be supported by logical arguments.
6. The threat of foreign invaders and domestic counterrevolutionary uprisings gave the Committee of Public Safety more power; the Reign of Terror was used to defend France from the threats of enemies.
7. The painter is portraying Marat as a martyr in the painting.
8. It is designed to make people want to join the struggle, which is depicted as being pure and selfless. Essays will vary.

Focus

Bellringer

Daily Focus Transparency 18.3

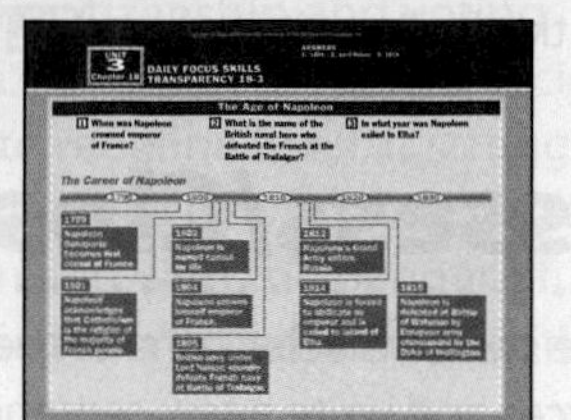

GUIDE TO READING

Answers to Graphic:
peace with Catholic Church; codification of laws; development of capable bureaucracy; principles of French Revolution spread throughout Europe

Section Spotlight Video

To generate student interest and provide a springboard for class discussion, access the Chapter 18, Section 3 video at glencoe.com or on the video DVD.

SECTION 3

The Age of Napoleon

GUIDE TO READING

The BIG Idea
Self-Determination As Napoleon built his empire across Europe, he also spread the revolutionary idea of nationalism.

Content Vocabulary
- consulate *(p. 598)*
- nationalism *(p. 602)*

Academic Vocabulary
- capable *(p. 599)*
- liberal *(p. 601)*

People and Events
- Napoleon Bonaparte *(p. 596)*
- Civil Code *(p. 599)*
- Anne-Louise-Germaine de Staël *(p. 599)*
- Duke of Wellington *(p. 603)*

Reading Strategy
Explaining As you read, use a diagram like the one below to list the achievements of Napoleon's rule.

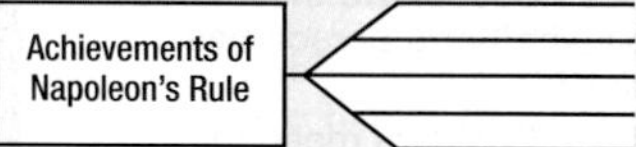

Napoleon Bonaparte dominated French and European history from 1799 to 1815. During his reign, Napoleon built and lost an empire and also spread ideas about nationalism in Europe.

The Rise of Napoleon

MAIN IDEA Napoleon, a popular general, overthrew the Directory, set up a new government, and eventually took complete power.

HISTORY & YOU What qualities do you look for in a political leader? Learn what made the French follow Napoleon.

Napoleon Bonaparte's role in the French Revolution is complex. In one sense, he brought it to an end when he came to power in 1799. Yet he was a child of the revolution as well. Without it, he would never have risen to power, and he himself never failed to remind the French that he had preserved the best parts of the revolution during his reign as emperor.

Early Life

Napoleon was born in 1769 in Corsica, an island in the Mediterranean, only a few months after France had annexed the island. His father came from minor nobility in Italy, but the family was not rich. Napoleon was talented, however, and won a scholarship to a famous military school.

When he completed his studies, Napoleon was commissioned as a lieutenant in the French army. Although he became one of the world's greatest generals and a man beloved by his soldiers, there were few signs of his future success at this stage. He spoke with an Italian accent and was not popular with his fellow officers.

Napoleon devoted himself to his goals. He read what French philosophers had to say about reason, and he studied famous military campaigns. When revolution and war with Europe came about, there were many opportunities for Napoleon to use his knowledge and skills.

Military Successes

Napoleon rose quickly through the ranks. In 1792 he became a captain. Two years later, at age 24, the Committee of Public Safety made him a brigadier general. In 1796 he became commander of the French armies in Italy. There Napoleon won a series of battles with qualities he became famous for—speed, surprise, and decisive action. Napoleon defeated the armies of the Papal States and

Resource Manager

R Reading Strategies	C Critical Thinking	D Differentiated Instruction	W Writing Support	S Skill Practice
Teacher Edition • Det. Importance., p. 597 • Summarizing., p. 599 • Academic Vocab., p. 599 • Questioning, p. 601 **Additional Resources** • Cont. Vocab. Act., URB p. 249 • Hist. Sig. Act., URB p. 258 • Guid. Read. Act., URB p. 276 • Read. Ess. & Note-Taking Guide, p. 202	**Teacher Edition** • Making Inferences, p. 598 • Ident. Cent. Issues, p. 601 • Pred. Consequences, p. 602 • Making Inferences, p. 603 **Additional Resources** • Enrich. Act., URB p. 272 • Section Quiz, p. 219 • Chapter Test, p. 221	**Teacher Edition** • Adv. Learners, p. 597 • Visual/Spatial, p. 601 **Additional Resources** • Eng. Learner Act., URB p. 247 • Academic Vocab. Act., URB p. 251 • Coop. Learn. Act., URB p. 259 • World Art & Music Act., URB p. 269	**Teacher Edition** • Descriptive Writing, p. 600 **Additional Resources** • Hist. Analysis Skills Act., URB p. 244 • Writer's Guidebook, p. 47	**Teacher Edition** • Visual Literacy, p. 600 **Additional Resources** • Read. Skills Act., URB p. 243 • Hist. & Geo. Act., URB p. 255 • Mapping Hist. Act., URB p. 257 • Time Line Act., URB p. 263

DOCUMENT-BASED QUESTIONS

This detail of *The Coronation of the Emperor Napoleon I* by Jacques-Louis David shows Napoleon crowning the Empress Josephine on December 2, 1804. The complete painting, located at the Louvre, is 20 feet by 32 feet.

1. **Describing** How is Napoleon portrayed in this painting?
2. **Making Inferences** How does the painting glorify and legitimize the Empire?

their Austrian allies. These victories gave France control of northern Italy. Throughout the Italian campaigns, Napoleon's energy and initiative earned him the devotion of his troops. His keen intelligence, ease with words, and supreme self-confidence allowed him to win the support of those around him. **D**

In 1797 he returned to France as a hero. He was given command of an army in training to invade Britain, but he knew the French could not carry out that invasion. Instead, Napoleon suggested striking indirectly at Britain by taking Egypt.

Egypt lay on the route to India, a major source of British wealth and therefore one of Britain's most important colonies. **R** Napoleon's goal of taking Egypt was never met, however. The British were a great sea power and controlled the Mediterranean. By 1799, the British had defeated the French naval forces supporting Napoleon's army in Egypt. Seeing certain defeat, Napoleon abandoned his army and returned to Paris.

Teach

D Differentiated Instruction

Advanced Learners Have students do additional research on Napoleon's personal characteristics. These might include physical attributes, personality, and ways of reacting to people. Then ask students to write a short description of a fictional encounter with Napoleon that describes him and his ability to lead people. **AL**

R Reading Strategy

Determining Importance

Ask: Why would taking Egypt be important to France? *(It would have made it easier for France to attack India, one of Britain's most important colonies.)* **BL**

DOCUMENT-BASED QUESTIONS

Answers:

1. Answers may vary—powerful, noble.
2. lavish clothing, new crowns, pope giving his blessing; surrounded by Napoleon's family

Hands-On Chapter Project
Step 3

Make a Map of Changes in French Life

Step 3: Selecting Two Events from the Section Pairs of students will continue their map of Europe by selecting two more sites of events or cultural changes in French life during the period.

Directions: Pairs of students should continue their map of Europe by selecting two or more events or changes from the section or from additional research. They should indicate two different types of change (social, economic, political) that can be indicated on the map with an icon and a headline. Then ask students to do additional research to prepare a short written or oral report that describes the event or change. **OL**

(Chapter Project is continued on the Visual Summary page.)

W Writing Support

Descriptive Writing Ask students to write a description of Napoleon's actions from the point of view of a member of the upper class who disagrees with Napoleon's ideas. Remind students to use what they have learned about the "privileged classes." AL

S Skill Practice

Visual Literacy Ask: In which country did Napoleon's family have the longest reign? *(Holland)* BL

Geography SKILLS

Answers:

1. anywhere one of Napoleon's relatives ruled such as Spain, Germany, Italy; because they "desire equality and liberal ideas"
2. Answers and opinions may vary, but should be supported by logical arguments.

Additional Support

TURNING POINT: SPREADING THE PRINCIPLES OF THE REVOLUTION

As a result of his conquests, Napoleon spread revolutionary ideals and nationalism throughout Europe. To ensure loyalty, Napoleon installed his relatives on the thrones of the lands he conquered. When Napoleon named his brother Jerome king of Westphalia, he explained the importance of spreading the principles of the French Revolution.

W "What the peoples of Germany desire most impatiently is that talented commoners should have the same right to your esteem and to public employments as the nobles, that any trace of serfdom . . . should be completely abolished. . . . The peoples of Germany, the peoples of France, of Italy, of Spain all desire equality and liberal ideas. . . . The buzzing of the privileged classes is contrary to the general opinion. Be a constitutional king."

—Napoleon Bonaparte

Napoleon's Family & His Empire (1799–1812)

Relative	Title	Date
A Caroline [sister] & Joachim Murat	Duke and Duchess of Berg	1806
B Jerome [brother] Bonaparte	King of Westphalia	1807
C Elisa [sister] Bacciochi	Princess of Lucca and Piombino	1806
	Duchess of Tuscany	1809
D Caroline [sister] & Joachim Murat	King and Queen of Naples	1808
S E Pauline [sister] Borghese	Duchess of Guastalla	1806
F Prince Eugène de Beauharnais [Napoleon's stepson]	Viceroy of Italy Prince of Venice	1805–1807
G Louis [brother] Bonaparte & Hortense de Beauharnais [Napoleon's stepdaughter]	King and Queen of Holland	1806–1810
H Joseph [brother] Bonaparte	King of Spain	1806

Geography SKILLS

1. **Location** In which areas would you expect the ideals of the revolution to be popular? Why?
2. **Regions** If Napoleon had not established his empires, do you think the same ideas would have spread in Europe? Why or why not?

Maps In Motion See StudentWorks™ Plus or glencoe.com.

Activity: Interdisciplinary Connection

Language Arts Discuss the influence of the Bonaparte family on Europe at the time and on European and world history. Divide the class into small groups, each of which will create a visual image of the Bonaparte family tree, up to and including Napoleon II and Napoleon III. Assign each group to do research on one of the family members and give a short report on that person's life. **Ask:** How does the influence of the Bonaparte family compare to important families in U.S. history, such as the Roosevelts, the Kennedys, and the Bushes? *(Answers will vary, but may include the fact that the Bonapartes directly ruled many countries while the power of U.S. families outside the United States has been less direct.)* OL

Napoleon's Empire

MAIN IDEA As Napoleon conquered Europe, he spread nationalist ideas. Inspired by those ideas, conquered peoples resisted Napoleon's armies and helped bring about the collapse of his empire.

HISTORY & YOU How would Americans react to a foreign country dictating trade policy to their government? Read how Napoleon tried to bar trade with Britain.

Napoleon is, of course, known less for his domestic policies than for his military leadership. His conquests began soon after he rose to power.

Building the Empire

When Napoleon became consul in 1799, France was at war with a European coalition of Russia, Great Britain, and Austria. Napoleon realized the need for a pause in the war. "The French Revolution is not finished," he said, "so long as the scourge of war lasts. . . . I want peace, as much to settle the present French government, as to save the world from chaos." **R** In 1802 a peace treaty was signed, but it did not last long. War with Britain broke out again in 1803. Gradually, Britain was joined by Austria, Russia, Sweden, and Prussia. In a series of battles at Ulm, Austerlitz, Jena, and Eylau from 1805 to 1807, Napoleon's Grand Army defeated the Austrian, Prussian, and Russian armies.

From 1807 to 1812, Napoleon was the master of Europe. His Grand Empire was composed of three major parts: the French Empire, dependent states, and allied states. The French Empire was the inner core of the Grand Empire. It consisted of an enlarged France extending to the Rhine in the east and including the western half of Italy north of Rome.

Dependent states were kingdoms ruled by relatives of Napoleon. Eventually these included Spain, Holland, the kingdom of Italy, the Swiss Republic, the Grand Duchy of Warsaw, and the Confederation of the Rhine—a union of all German states except Austria and Prussia.

Allied states were countries defeated by Napoleon and then forced to join his struggle against Britain. These states included Prussia, Austria, Russia, and Sweden.

Spreading the Principles of the Revolution

Within his empire, Napoleon sought to spread some of the principles of the French Revolution, including legal equality, religious toleration, and economic freedom. In the inner core and dependent states of his Grand Empire, Napoleon tried to destroy the old order. The nobility and the clergy everywhere in these states lost their special privileges. Napoleon decreed equality of opportunity with offices open to those with ability, equality before the law, and religious toleration. The spread of French revolutionary principles was an important factor in the development of **liberal** traditions in these countries.

Like Hitler 130 years later, Napoleon hoped that his Grand Empire would last for centuries, but his empire collapsed almost as rapidly as it was formed. Two major reasons help explain this collapse: Britain's ability to resist Napoleon and the rise of nationalism. **D**

British Resistance

Napoleon was never able to conquer Great Britain because of its sea power, which made it almost invulnerable. Napoleon hoped to invade Britain, but the British defeated the combined French-Spanish fleet at Trafalgar in 1805. This battle ended Napoleon's plans for invasion.

Napoleon then turned to his Continental System to defeat Britain. The aim of the Continental System was to stop British goods from reaching the European continent to be sold there. By weakening Britain economically, Napoleon would destroy its ability to wage war. **C**

The Continental System also failed. Allied states resented being told by Napoleon that they could not trade with the British. Some began to cheat. Others resisted. Furthermore, new markets in the Middle East and in Latin America gave Britain new outlets for its goods. Indeed, by 1810, British overseas exports were at near-record highs.

R Reading Strategy

Questioning Ask: How sincere do you think Napoleon was about wanting peace? *(Answers will vary, but might include references to his desire for a great empire and his dedication to defeating Great Britain.)* **OL**

D Differentiated Instruction

Visual/Spatial Ask students to research the extent of Hitler's empire during World War II and prepare a map that compares it with Napoleon's. Students might wish to display both empires on the same map or create two maps that can be displayed side-by-side. **AL**

C Critical Thinking

Identifying Central Issues
Ask: How did Napoleon think the Continental System would help defeat Britain? *(It would weaken Great Britain economically, which would weaken its ability to wage war.)* **BL**

Additional Support

Activity: Collaborative Learning

Creating a Newspaper Have the class work together to plan the front page of the *Napoleonic Times,* a newspaper chronicling the events of Napoleon's rise and fall. After students have finished reading the section, divide them into three groups and assign each a time period covered in the main heads. Have each group list the stories and visuals they would put on the front page. Ask them to use a word processing program to create a mock-up of the front page and share it with the class, discussing their choices. **OL**

Teacher Tip

Collaborative Learning
Encourage students to spend a small portion of their time assigning roles for group members and briefly listing individual responsibilities.

C Critical Thinking

Predicting Consequences

Ask: How do you think the conquered nations reacted to Napoleon's attempts to make them part of the French nation? *(They resisted his attempts and began to plan for their own independence and the creation of their own nations.)* OL

✓Reading Check

Answer: Since Britain is an island, it was only possible to invade by sea, and its strong navy provided defense against invasion.

Geography SKILLS

Answers:

1. The Russians burned their own villages and countryside to keep the French army from finding food, forcing the French to starve and retreat.
2. He allowed the Russians to lure him farther into the country as they burned crops and cities; the French army had no food and was forced to retreat.

Differentiated Instruction

Nationalism

A second important factor in the defeat of Napoleon was nationalism. **Nationalism** is the sense of unique identity of a people based on common language, religion, and national symbols. Nationalism was one of the most important forces of the nineteenth century. A new era was born when the French people decided that they were the nation.

C Napoleon marched his armies through the Germanies, Spain, Italy, and Poland, arousing new ideas of nationalism in two ways. First, the conquered peoples became united in their hatred of the invaders. Second, the conquered peoples saw the power and strength of national feeling. It was a lesson not lost on them or their rulers.

✓Reading Check **Explaining** Why did being a sea power help Britain to survive an attack by the French?

The Fall of Napoleon

MAIN IDEA After major losses in Russia and Austria, Napoleon was defeated at Waterloo.

HISTORY & YOU Today there are some rulers who go into exile to avoid prosecution in their homelands. Read why in 1815 the French government exiled Napoleon.

Napoleon's downfall began in 1812 when he decided to invade Russia. Within only a few years, his fall was complete.

Disaster in Russia

The Russians had refused to remain in the Continental System, leaving Napoleon with little choice but to invade. He knew the risks in invading such a large country, but he also knew that if he did not punish

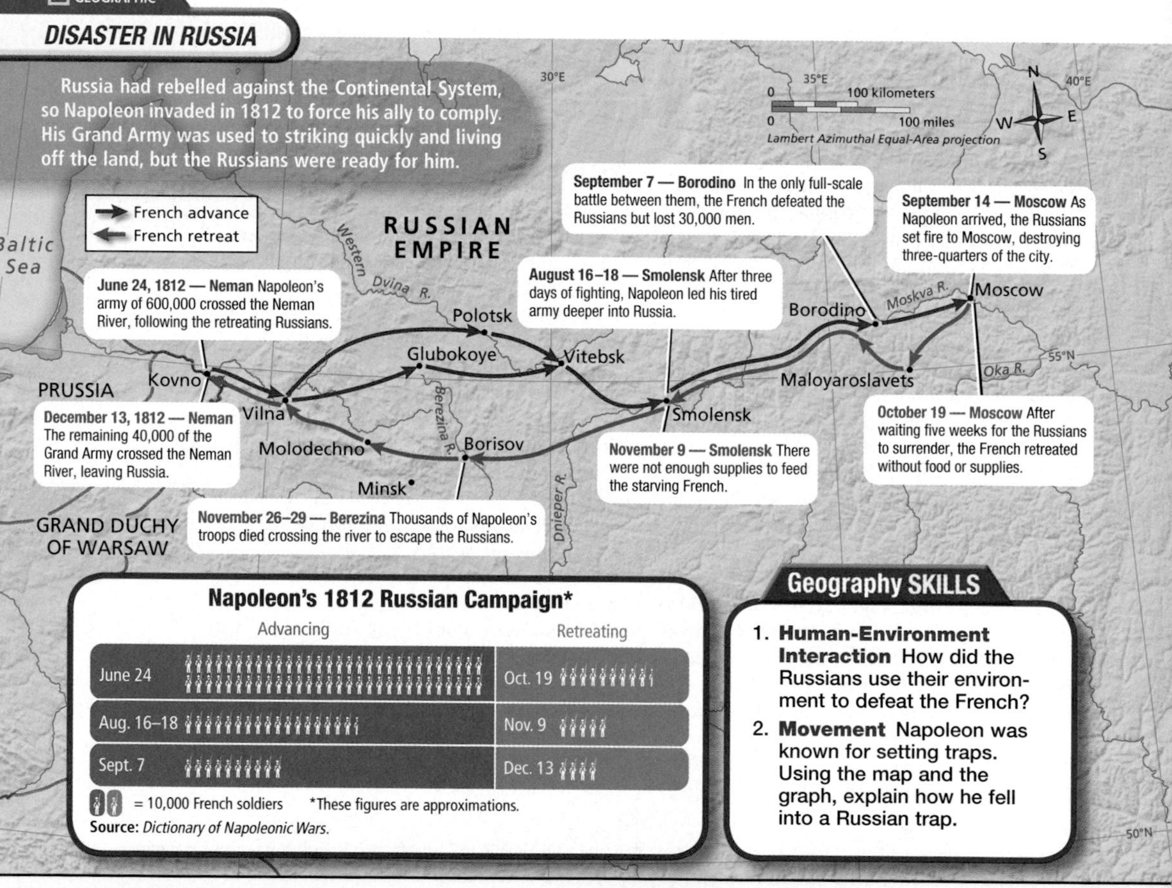

Geography SKILLS

1. **Human-Environment Interaction** How did the Russians use their environment to defeat the French?
2. **Movement** Napoleon was known for setting traps. Using the map and the graph, explain how he fell into a Russian trap.

Leveled Activities

BL Time Line Activity, URB p. 263

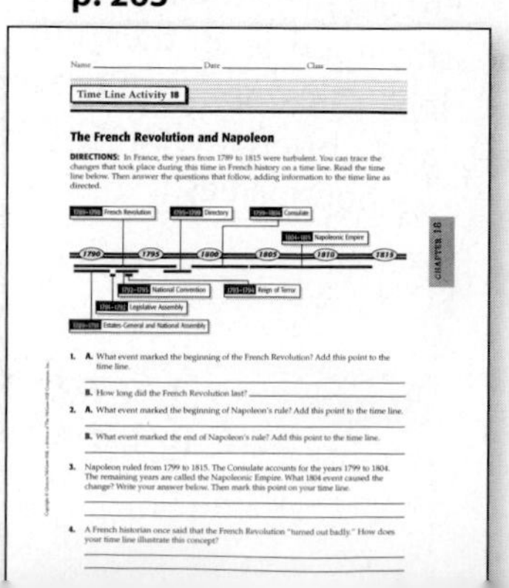

OL History and Geography Activity, URB p. 255

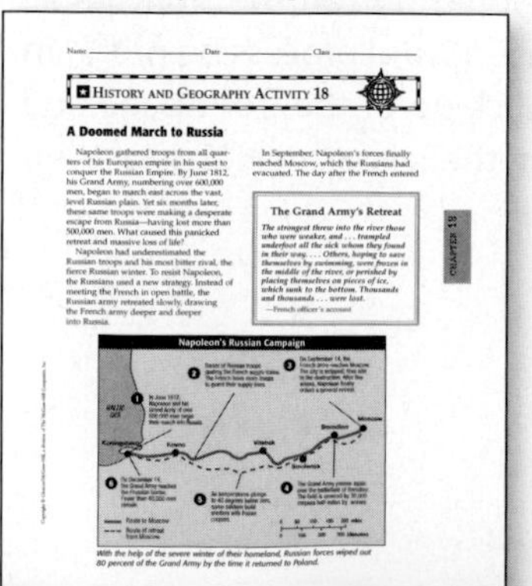

AL World Art and Music Activity, URB p. 269

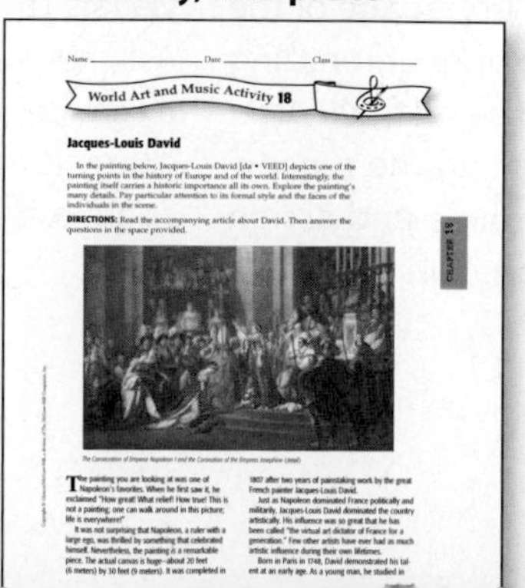

ELL Mapping History Activity, URB p. 257

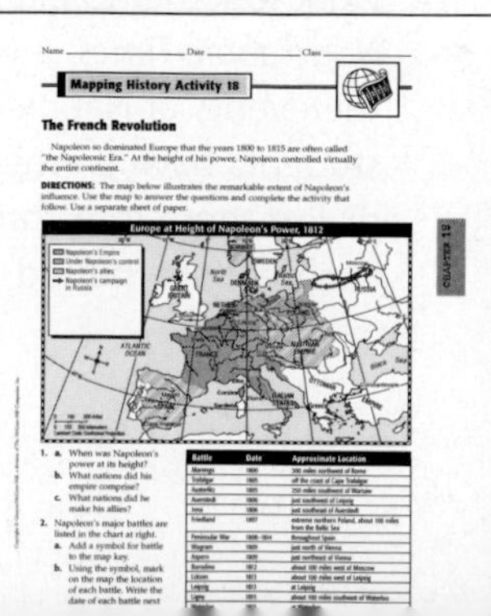

the Russians for ignoring the Continental System, other nations would follow suit.

In June 1812, a Grand Army of more than 600,000 men entered Russia. Napoleon's hopes depended on a quick victory over the Russians. The Russian forces, however, refused to do battle. Instead they retreated for hundreds of miles. As they retreated, they burned their own villages and countryside to keep Napoleon's army from finding food. When the Russians did fight at Borodino, Napoleon's forces won an indecisive victory, which cost many lives.

When the Grand Army finally reached Moscow, they found the city ablaze. Lacking food and supplies for his army, Napoleon abandoned the Russian capital in late October. As the winter snows began, Napoleon led the "Great Retreat" west across Russia. Thousands of soldiers starved and froze along the way. Fewer than 40,000 of the original 600,000 soldiers arrived back in Poland in January 1813.

This military disaster led other European states to rise up and attack the crippled French army. Paris was captured in March 1814. Napoleon was soon sent into exile on the island of Elba, off the northwest coast of Italy. The victorious powers restored monarchy to France in the person of Louis XVIII, brother of the executed king, Louis XVI.

The Final Defeat

The new king had little support, and the French people were not ready to surrender the glory of empire. Nor was Napoleon ready to give up. Restless in exile, he left the island of Elba and slipped back into France. The new king sent troops to capture Napoleon, who opened his coat and addressed them: "Soldiers of the 5th regiment, I am your Emperor. . . . If there is a man among you [who] would kill his Emperor, here I am!"

C

No one fired a shot. Shouting "Vive l'Empereur! Vive l'Empereur!"—"Long live the Emperor! Long live the Emperor!"—the troops went over to his side. On March 20, 1815, Napoleon entered Paris in triumph.

Russia, Great Britain, Austria, and Prussia responded to Napoleon's return. They again pledged to defeat the man they called the "Enemy and Disturber of the Tranquility of the World." Meanwhile, Napoleon raised another French army of devoted veterans who rallied from all over France. He then readied an attack on the allied troops stationed across the border in Belgium.

At Waterloo in Belgium on June 18, 1815, Napoleon met a combined British and Prussian army under the **Duke of Wellington** and suffered a bloody defeat. This time, the victorious allies exiled him to St. Helena, a small island in the south Atlantic. Napoleon remained in exile until his death in 1821, but his memory haunted French political life for many decades.

✓Reading Check **Examining** Why did Napoleon invade Russia?

SECTION 3 REVIEW

Vocabulary

1. **Explain** the significance of: Napoleon Bonaparte, consulate, Civil Code, capable, Anne-Louise-Germaine de Staël, liberal, nationalism, Duke of Wellington.

Main Ideas

2. What were four major principles that were reflected in the Civil Code?
3. List the powers Napoleon exercised as first consul.
4. Using a diagram like this one, identify the reasons for the rise and fall of Napoleon.

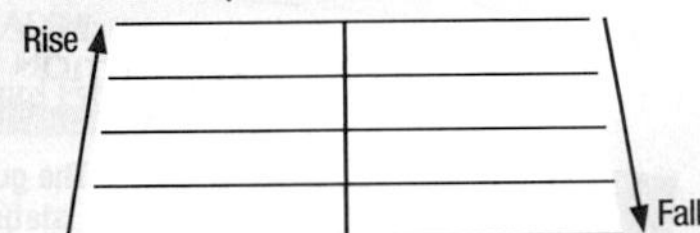

Critical Thinking

5. **The BIG Idea** **Summarizing** How did nationalism unify the people in countries that Napoleon invaded? Write a paragraph defining the importance of nationalism to the ultimate downfall of Napoleon.
6. **Connecting Events** How did the principles of the French Revolution spread throughout Europe?
7. **Analyzing Visuals** Examine the portrait on page 598. How does David portray Napoleon, and why do you think Napoleon wanted artists to produce paintings like this one?

Writing About History

8. **Persuasive Writing** Was Napoleon an enlightened ruler or a tyrant? Write a paper supporting your view. Be sure to include pertinent information about Napoleon's Civil Code.

History ONLINE
For help with the concepts in this section of *Glencoe World History*, go to glencoe.com and click Study Central™.

C Critical Thinking

Making Inferences **Ask:** Why do you think Napoleon was exiled twice rather than being executed? *(His popularity was so strong that execution might have led to great resistance.)* OL

✓Reading Check

Answer: Russia refused to remain in the Continental System. Napoleon feared that others would follow if Russia was not punished.

Assess

History ONLINE

Study Central provides summaries, interactive games, and online graphic organizers to help students review content.

Close

Drawing Conclusions **Ask:** In what ways did Napoleon continue the French Revolution? *(His reform of the laws and attempts to destroy privilege were founded on Revolutionary ideals.)* OL

Answers

1. Definitions for the vocabulary words are found in the section and the Glossary.
2. equality of all citizens, right of individual to choose a profession, religious toleration, abolition of serfdom and feudal law
3. appointed bureaucrats, controlled army, conducted foreign affairs, influenced legislature
4. **Rise:** Military genius, peace with Catholics, Civil Code, turned conquered into allies; **Fall:** Nationalism, survival of Britain, failure of Continental System, invasion of Russia
5. Nationalism united the conquered people against Napoleon. Answers may vary but should be supported by details.
6. Within his empire, Napoleon ended special privileges of nobility and clergy; he appointed people based on talent; and he decreed legal equality and religious toleration.
7. As a strong military leader; answers will vary
8. Answers will vary but should be supported by arguments and facts from the chapter.

Introducing

UNIT 4

Focus

Why It Matters

The Industrial Revolution ushered in a whole new phase in world history. Much like the effect computers and the Internet have had on today's world, the Industrial Revolution not only changed how goods were produced, but also the way people lived and the manner in which nations interacted with one another. The Industrial Revolution began in Great Britain. This would be the start of the British Empire and the era of European Imperialism.

Unit Launch Activity

Direct students' attention to the title of this unit. Explain that the unit and chapter titles reflect major eras in world history. Have students describe at least two defining characteristics of this era. Discuss these descriptions in class, and use this discussion to help students understand that such distinctions are arbitrary and that historians frequently differ in their opinions about what periods constitute the major eras of world history. **OL**

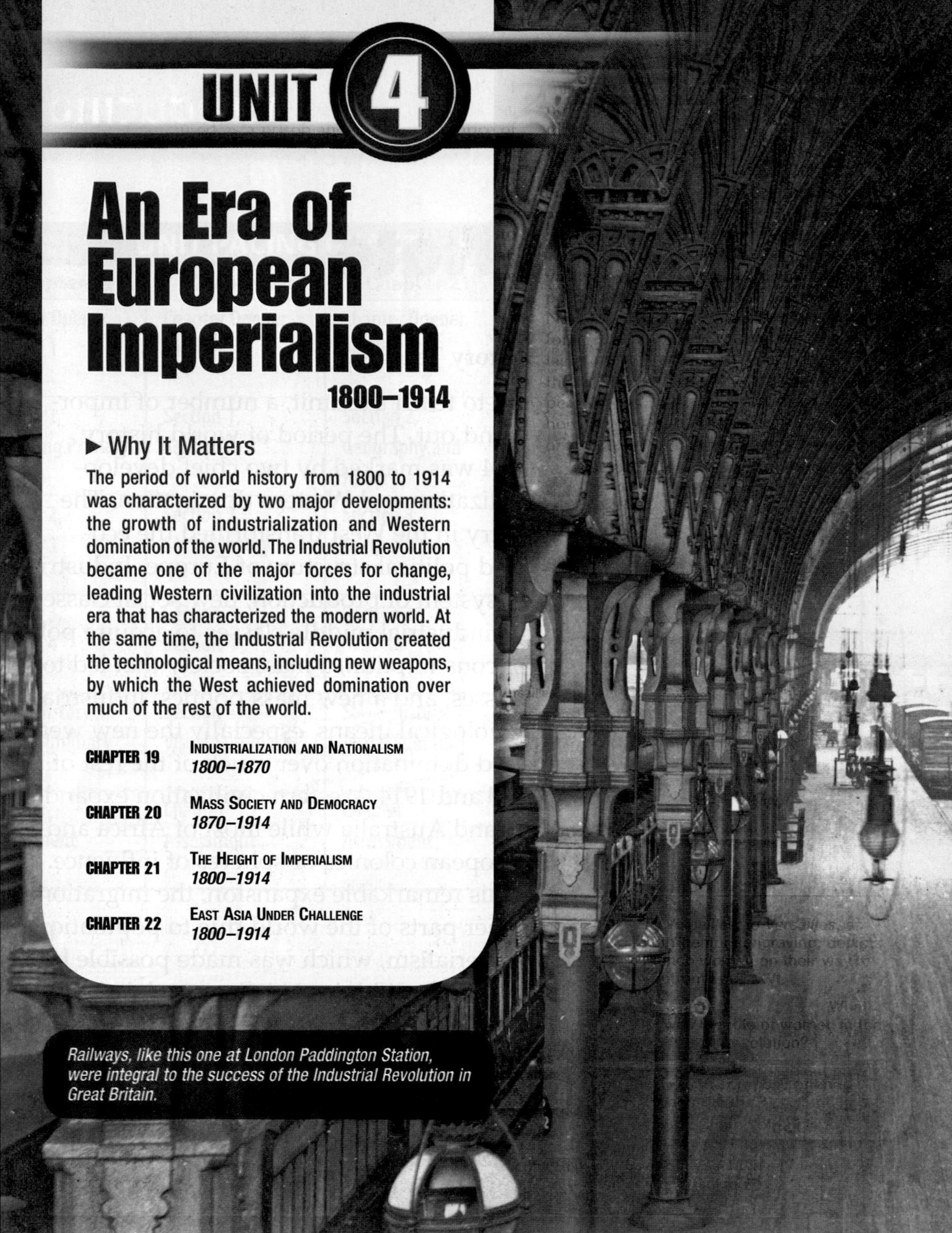

UNIT 4

An Era of European Imperialism

1800–1914

▶ Why It Matters

The period of world history from 1800 to 1914 was characterized by two major developments: the growth of industrialization and Western domination of the world. The Industrial Revolution became one of the major forces for change, leading Western civilization into the industrial era that has characterized the modern world. At the same time, the Industrial Revolution created the technological means, including new weapons, by which the West achieved domination over much of the rest of the world.

Railways, like this one at London Paddington Station, were integral to the success of the Industrial Revolution in Great Britain.

Team Teaching Activity

Literature This unit discusses Western imperialism and its impact on the colonized peoples and lands. Nowhere were the excesses of colonialism more evident than in Africa. King Leopold of Belgium, in spite of his claims of bringing civilization to Africa, exemplifies the worst treatment of African people. In conjunction with the English teacher, assign students to read Joseph Conrad's *Heart of Darkness.* Students should research the geography of the Congo and the historical background of the period, especially King Leopold's statements about the sacred mission of civilization at the Geographical Conference of 1876, to better understand Conrad's irony and symbolism used to convey the atrocities of imperialism in the Congo.

Teach

S Skill Practice

Using Geography Skills The London Paddington Station opened in 1838. At that point in time, London already had an underground train system that stopped at Paddington Station. The station was also the terminus for the Great Western Railway as well. **Ask:** **Based on the photograph, what do you think Paddington station was used for? Why would trains be an important part of the Industrial Revolution?** *(transportation of people and goods, which made it possible to have materials and workers for industrial production)* **OL**

Visual Literacy Draw students' attention to the caption of the photograph. **Ask:** **What is the purpose of the caption?** *(The caption's purpose is to inform the viewer about the contents of the image and to help the viewer understand the image.)* **BL**

No Child Left Behind

Teaching Tip Helping students become fluent readers often helps improve comprehension. Have students practice reading aloud the text. They may work in pairs or small groups.

More About the Photo

Visual Literacy Early British trains were powered by steam engines. The steam engine used wood or coal as fuel. In all likelihood, the train in the photograph used coal to create the pressurized steam that ultimately made the train move. By the time this photograph was taken, many of the steam engine's early problems had been resolved. For example, in the United States many of the first steam driven trains burned wood. The problem with wood was that it sent out sparks that could set nearby fields on fire. Also, the passenger compartment on many of the early trains did not have a roof. In 1831, the sparks blew onto the assembled dignitaries riding in a passenger car, setting their umbrellas and clothes on fire. Fortunately, none were harmed and they arrived safely at the station. As time passed, the design of trains improved. Soon trains were running across most of Europe.

CHAPTER 19 Planning Guide

Key to Ability Levels	
BL Below Level	AL Above Level
OL On Level	ELL English Language Learners

Key to Teaching Resources	
Print Material	DVD
CD-ROM	Transparency

BL	OL	AL	ELL	Resources	Chapter Opener	Section 1	Section 2	Section 3	Section 4	Chapter Assess
				FOCUS						
BL	OL	AL	ELL	**Daily Focus Skills Transparencies**		19-1	19-2	19-3	19-4	
				TEACH						
	OL	AL		**Economics and History Activity, URB**					✓	
		AL		**World Literature Reading, URB**			✓			
BL	OL		ELL	**Reading Skills Activity, URB**		p. 17				
	OL	AL		**Historical Analysis Skills Activity, URB**				p. 18		
BL	OL	AL	ELL	**Differentiated Instruction Activity, URB**		p. 19				
	OL		ELL	**English Learner Activity, URB**				p. 21		
BL	OL	AL	ELL	**Content Vocabulary Activity, URB***					p. 23	
BL	OL	AL	ELL	**Academic Vocabulary Activity, URB**		p. 25				
BL	OL	AL	ELL	**Skills Reinforcement Activity, URB**		p. 27				
	OL	AL		**Critical Thinking Skills Activity, URB**		p. 28				
	OL	AL		**History and Geography Activity, URB**		p. 29				
	OL	AL	ELL	**Mapping History Activity, URB**					p. 31	
BL	OL	AL		**Historical Significance Activity, URB**		p. 32				
BL	OL	AL	ELL	**Cooperative Learning Activity, URB**		p. 33				
	OL	AL	ELL	**History Simulation Activity, URB**					p. 35	
BL	OL	AL	ELL	**Time Line Activity, URB**				p. 37		
	OL	AL		**Linking Past and Present Activity, URB**			p. 38			
BL	OL	AL		**People in World History Activity, URB**					pp. 39, 40	
BL	OL	AL	ELL	**Primary Source Reading, URB**		p. 41				
	OL	AL		**Enrichment Activity, URB**		p. 46				
BL	OL	AL	ELL	**World Art and Music Activity, URB**					p. 43	
BL	OL		ELL	**Guided Reading Activities, URB***		p. 48	p. 49	p. 50	p. 51	
BL	OL		ELL	**Reading Essentials and Note-Taking Guide***		p. 205	p. 208	p. 211	p. 214	
BL	OL	AL	ELL	**Differentiated Instruction for the World History Classroom**	✓	✓	✓	✓	✓	✓

Note: Please refer to the *Unit Resource Book: An Era of European Imperialism* for this chapter's URB materials.

* Also available in Spanish

- Interactive Lesson Planner
- Interactive Teacher Edition
- Fully editable blackline masters
- Section Spotlight Videos Launch
- Differentiated Lesson Plans
- Printable reports of daily assignments
- Standards Tracking System

Levels				Resources	Chapter Opener	Section 1	Section 2	Section 3	Section 4	Chapter Assess
BL	OL	AL	ELL							
				TEACH *(continued)*						
BL	OL	AL	ELL	StudentWorks™ Plus DVD	✓	✓	✓	✓	✓	✓
BL	OL	AL	ELL	Vocabulary PuzzleMaker CD-ROM	✓	✓	✓	✓	✓	✓
Teacher Resources				Building Academic Vocabulary	✓	✓	✓	✓	✓	✓
				Reading Strategies and Activities for the Social Studies Classroom			pp. 53, 71	p. 62		
				Writer's Guidebook			p. 27	p. 47		
				Foods Around the World			p. 14			
				Strategies for Success	✓	✓	✓	✓	✓	✓
				Outline Map Resource Book	✓	✓	✓	✓	✓	✓
				Presentation Plus! with MindJogger DVD	✓	✓	✓	✓	✓	✓
				ASSESS						
BL	OL	AL	ELL	Section Quizzes and Chapter Tests*		p. 233	p. 234	p. 235	p. 236	p. 237
BL	OL	AL	ELL	Authentic Assessment With Rubrics	✓	✓	✓	✓	✓	✓
BL	OL	AL	ELL	Standardized Test Practice Workbook	✓	✓	✓	✓	✓	✓
BL	OL	AL	ELL	*ExamView® Assessment Suite* CD-ROM		19-1	19-2	19-3	19-4	Ch. 19
BL	OL	AL	ELL	Interactive Tutor Self-Assessment CD-ROM		19-1	19-2	19-3	19-4	
				CLOSE						
BL			ELL	Reteaching Activity, URB		p. 45				
BL	OL		ELL	Reading and Study Skills Foldables™	✓	✓	✓	✓	✓	✓

Using Puzzlemaker™ 3.1

Online Word Search Puzzles

Technology Product

Glencoe's Vocabulary PuzzleMaker™ 3.1 CD-ROM is an easy-to-use program that lets you create your own puzzles based on the glossary for classroom use. The PuzzleMaker allows you to

- create word search puzzles based on content vocabulary and academic vocabulary that is specific to what is taught in the classroom;
- create online (LAN-based or local area network) or paper word search puzzles.

Objectives

After students complete the word search puzzles, they will be able to

- recall academic vocabulary terms based on the clues provided for a puzzle;
- reinforce their understanding of the vocabulary.

Steps

- Run PuzzleMaker ™ 3.1. On the main menu, click on **Create a New Puzzle.**
- Select the *Puzzle Database* for the vocabulary.
- The *PuzzleMaker Wizard* will take you through selecting a puzzle type and grid type.
- Then select one or more chapters from the list. Indicate whether you want the words selected randomly or manually.
- Select the language and words you wish to use within the maximum for the puzzle. Click **Finish.**
- Save your word search puzzle to a location that is easily accessible by your students with PuzzlePlayer™ 3.1, or print copies for your students to complete.
- Use PuzzlePlayer™ 3.1 to review the puzzles after your students have worked on and saved them.
- Read the article and take notes.

History ONLINE

	Student	Teacher	Parent
Beyond the Textbook	●	●	●
Chapter Overviews	●	●	●
Time Current Events	●		●
ePuzzles and Games	●		●
Concepts in Motion	●		●
Literature Connections		●	
Multi-Language Glossaries	●		●
Online Student Edition	●	●	●
Self-Check Quizzes	●		●
Student Web Activities	●		●
Study Central ™	●		●
Teaching Today		●	
Vocabulary eFlashcards	●		●
Web Activity Lesson Plans		●	

Glencoe Media Center

glencoe.com

› **Study-To-Go**
- Vocabulary eflashcards
- Self-Check Quizzes

› **Audio/Video**
- Student Edition Audio
- Spanish Summaries
- Section Videos

- **Timed Readings Plus in Social Studies** helps students increase their reading rate and fluency while maintaining comprehension. The 400-word passages are similar to those found on state and national assessments.
- **Reading in the Content Area: Social Studies** concentrates on six essential reading skills that help students better comprehend what they read. The book includes 75 high-interest nonfiction passages written at increasing levels of difficulty.
- **Reading Social Studies** includes strategic reading instruction and vocabulary support in Social Studies content for both ELLs and native speakers of English.

www.jamestowneducation.com

Biography

The following videotape programs are available from Glencoe as supplements to Chapter 19:

- Railroads That Tamed the West (ISBN 0-7670-0033-1)
- Textiles: Birth of an American Industry (ISBN 0-7670-0624-0)

To order, call Glencoe at 1-800-334-7344. To find classroom resources to accompany many of these videos, check the following home pages:

A&E Television: www.aetv.com

The History Channel: www.historychannel.com

NATIONAL GEOGRAPHIC

Index to National Geographic Magazine:

The following articles relate to this chapter:

- "Was Darwin Wrong?" by David Quammen, November 2004
- "In Focus: The West Bank," by Andrew Cockburn, October 2002

National Geographic Society Products To order the following, call National Geographic at 1-800-368-2728:

- *National Geographic Atlas of the World* (Book)

Access National Geographic's new, dynamic MapMachine Web site and other geography resources at:
www.nationalgeographic.com
www.nationalgeographic.com/maps

GLENCOE BOOKLINK 3

Use this database to search more than 30,000 titles to create a customized reading list for your students.

- Reading lists can be organized by students' reading level, author, genre, theme, or area of interest.
- The database provides Degrees of Reading Power™ (DRP) and Lexile™ readability scores for all selections.
- A brief summary of each selection is included.

Leveled reading suggestions for this chapter:

For students at a Grade 8 reading level:
- ***Sense and Sensibility,*** by Jane Austen

For students at a Grade 9 reading level:
- ***Kids at Work: Lewis Hine and the Crusade Against Child Labor,*** by Russell Freedman

For students at a Grade 10 reading level:
- ***Industrial Revolution,*** by John D. Clare

For students at a Grade 11 reading level:
- ***Utopian Thought in the Western World,*** by Frank E. Manuel and Fritzie P. Manuel

For students at a Grade 12 reading level:
- ***The Problem of Slavery in the Age of Revolution 1770-1823,*** by David Brion Davis

Focus

Bellringer

Daily Focus Transparency 19.1

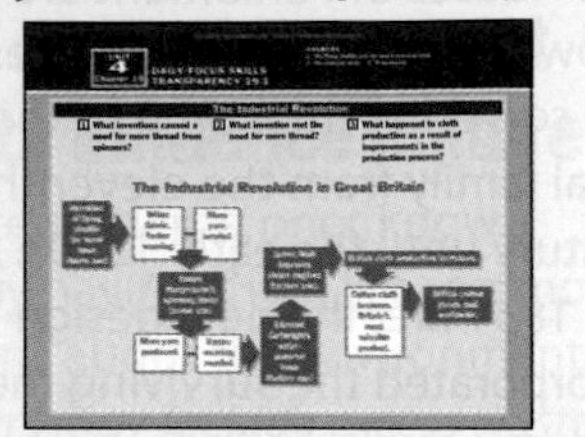

GUIDE TO READING

Answers to Graphic:

Inventors	Inventions
James Hargreaves	spinning jenny
Edmund Cartwright	water-powered loom
Richard Trevithick	steam locomotive
Robert Fulton	paddle-wheel steamboat

Section Spotlight Video

To generate student interest and provide a springboard for class discussion, access the Chapter 19, Section 1 video at glencoe.com or on the video DVD.

SECTION 1

The Industrial Revolution

GUIDE TO READING

The BIG Idea

New Technologies The Industrial Revolution changed the way people lived and worked.

Content Vocabulary
- enclosure movement *(p. 614)*
- capital *(p. 614)*
- entrepreneurs *(p. 614)*
- cottage industry *(p. 615)*
- puddling *(p. 616)*
- industrial capitalism *(p. 620)*
- socialism *(p. 621)*

Academic Vocabulary
- derived *(p. 616)*
- hypothetical *(p. 621)*

People and Places
- James Watt *(p. 616)*
- Manchester *(p. 617)*
- Liverpool *(p. 617)*
- Robert Fulton *(p. 619)*
- Robert Owen *(p. 621)*

Reading Strategy

Categorizing Information As you read, use a table like the one below to name important inventors mentioned in this section and their inventions.

Inventors	Inventions

During the late eighteenth century, the Industrial Revolution began in Great Britain. An agrarian revolution and industrialization caused a shift from an economy based on farming and handicrafts to an economy based on manufacturing by machines in factories.

The Industrial Revolution in Great Britain

MAIN IDEA With its plentiful natural resources, workers, wealth, and markets, Great Britain became the starting place of the Industrial Revolution.

HISTORY & YOU Think about how computers are rapidly changing today's world. Read to understand how the Industrial Revolution changed life in the nineteenth century.

The Industrial Revolution began in Great Britain in the 1780s and took several decades to spread to other Western nations. Several factors contributed to make Great Britain the starting place.

First, an agrarian revolution beginning in the 1700s changed agricultural practices. Expansion of farmland, good weather, improved transportation, and new crops such as the potato dramatically increased the food supply. More people could be fed at lower prices with less labor. Now even ordinary British families could use some of their income to buy manufactured goods.

Second, with the increased food supply, the population grew. When Parliament passed **enclosure movement** laws in the 1700s, landowners fenced off common lands. This forced many peasants to move to towns, creating a labor supply for factories. The remaining farms were larger, more efficient, with increased crop yields.

Third, Britain had a ready supply of money, or **capital,** to invest in new machines and factories. **Entrepreneurs** found new ways to make profits in a laissez–faire market economy, ruled by supply and demand with little government control of industry.

Fourth, Britain had plentiful natural resources. The country's rivers provided water power for the new factories. These waterways provided a means for transporting raw materials and finished products. Britain also had abundant supplies of coal and iron ore, essential in manufacturing processes.

Finally, a supply of markets gave British manufacturers a ready outlet for their goods. Britain had a vast colonial empire, and British ships could transport goods anywhere in the world. Also, because of population growth and cheaper food at home, domestic markets increased. A growing demand for cotton cloth led British manufacturers to look for ways to increase production.

Resource Manager

R Reading Strategies	C Critical Thinking	D Differentiated Instruction	W Writing Support	S Skill Practice
Teacher Edition • Making Connections, pp. 615, 618 • Questioning, p. 616 • Inferring, p. 619 **Additional Resources** • Guid. Read. Act., URB p. 48 • Read. Ess. & Note-Taking Guide, p. 205	**Teacher Edition** • Pred. Consequences, p. 616 • Making Inferences, p. 616 **Additional Resources** • Skills Reinforc. Act., URB p. 27 • Coop. Learn. Act., URB p. 33 • Enrich. Act., URB p. 46 • Section Quiz, p. 233	**Teacher Edition** • Kinesthetic, p. 619 **Additional Resources** • Crit. Think. Act, URB p. 28 • Pri. Source Read., URB p. 41 • Reteach. Act., URB p. 45 • Academic Vocab. Act., URB p. 25	**Teacher Edition** • Persuasive Writing, p. 617 • Narrative Writing, p. 620 **Additional Resources** • Diff. Instr. Act., URB, p. 19 • Hist. Sig. Act., URB p. 32	**Teacher Edition** • Using Geo. Skills, p. 615 **Additional Resources** • Read. Skills Act., URB p. 17 • Hist. & Geo. Act., URB p. 29

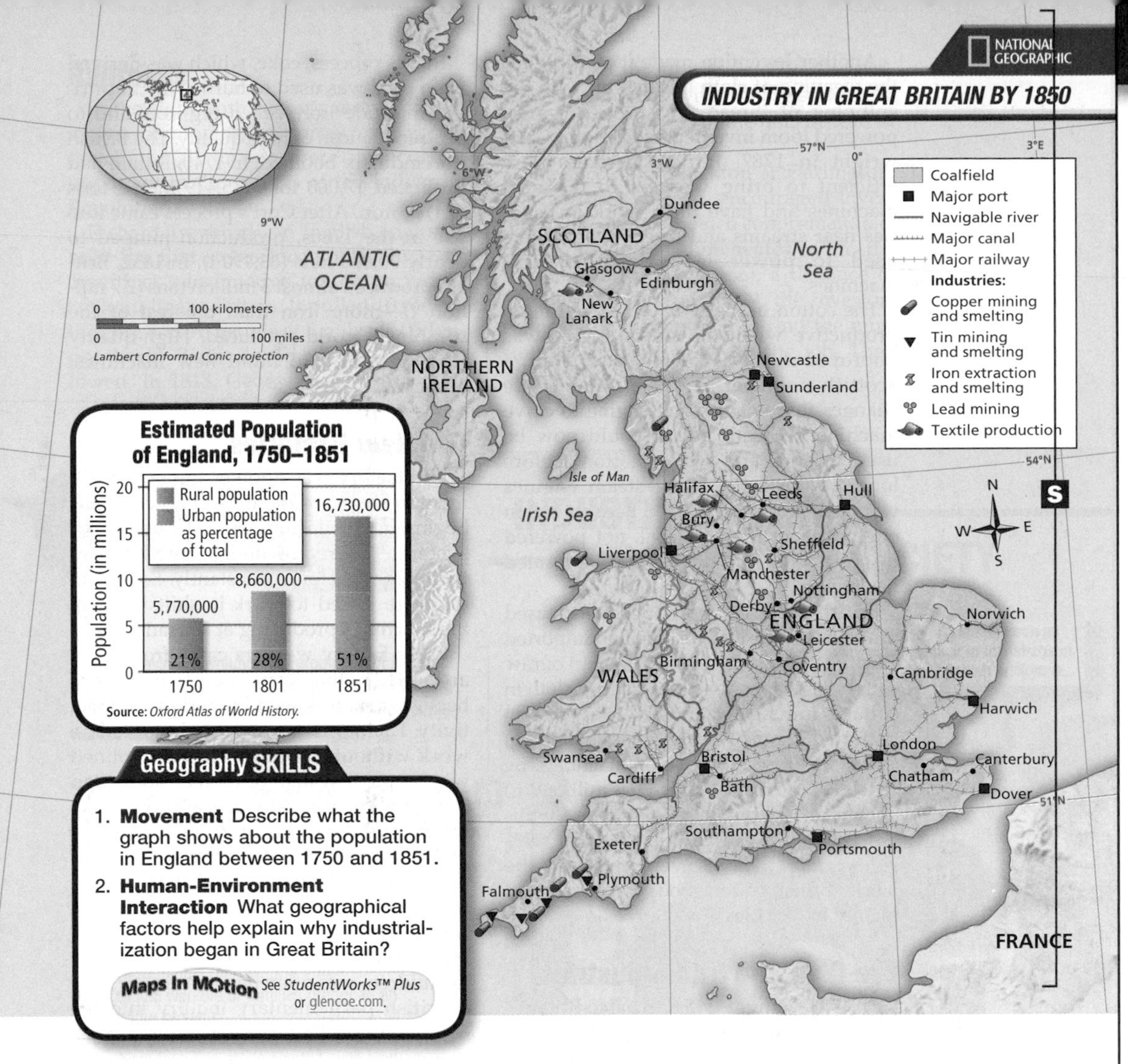

Geography SKILLS

1. **Movement** Describe what the graph shows about the population in England between 1750 and 1851.
2. **Human-Environment Interaction** What geographical factors help explain why industrialization began in Great Britain?

Maps In MOtion See StudentWorks™ Plus or glencoe.com.

Changes in Cotton Production

In the eighteenth century, Great Britain had surged way ahead in the production of inexpensive cotton goods. The manufacture of cotton cloth was a two-step process. First, spinners made cotton thread from raw cotton. Then, weavers wove the cotton thread into cloth on looms. In the eighteenth century, individuals spun the thread and then wove the cloth in their rural cottages. This production method was thus called a **cottage industry.**

A series of technological advances in the eighteenth century made cottage industry inefficient. First, the invention of the "flying shuttle" made weaving faster. Now, **R** weavers needed more thread from spinners because they could produce cloth at a faster rate.

In 1764 James Hargreaves had invented a machine called the spinning jenny, which met this need. Other inventors made similar contributions. The spinning process became much faster. In fact, spinners produced thread faster than weavers could use it.

Teach

S Skill Practice

Using Geography Skills Ask: In what parts of Great Britain did most industrial activities occur? *(central and northern England)* **OL**

R Reading Strategy

Making Connections Tell students to interview members of an older generation about significant technological changes that have occurred during their lifetimes. How have these changes affected their lives? **BL**

Geography SKILLS

Answers:

1. the total population nearly tripled; the urban population more than doubled.
2. It had good ports, navigable rivers, and rich mineral resources.

Hands-On Chapter Project Step 1

Presenting a Living Time Line

Small groups of students will present a living time line of important events in history from the 1770s to the 1870s.

Step 1: Creating a Backdrop

Essential Question: Why might this period be called the Age of Revolution, Reform, and Reaction?

Directions: Write the Big Idea on the board. Tell students to use the information in this section to help them decide on images for a backdrop that represents important events, people, or ideas associated with this time period. Have students draw or paint these images on large pieces of paper taped together or an old fabric sheet. Tell them to reserve space to add graphics from later sections as well.

Summarizing: Allow time for groups to share what they learned about the Big Idea while planning and illustrating their backdrop. **OL**

(Chapter Project is continued in Section 2.)

R Reading Strategy

Making Connections Ask: What new technologies today have helped the economy of the United States to grow? *(Answers may include the Internet, cell phones, and laptop computers.)* **OL**

✓Reading Check

Answer: They were disciplined harshly. Children were sometimes beaten with rods or whips. Adults were fined or fired.

CRITICAL THINKING SKILLS

Answers:

1. Liverpool was a port. Efficient transportation to a port would enable manufacturers to ship their goods to market more quickly.
2. It led to other innovations, such as steam-powered locomotives and machines, which increased production and improved transportation.

The *Rocket* sped along at 16 miles (25.7 km) per hour while pulling a 40-ton (36-t) train. Within 20 years, locomotives were able to reach 50 miles (80.5 km) per hour, an incredible speed. In 1840, Britain had almost 2,000 miles (3,218 km) of railroads. In 1850, more than 6,000 miles (9,654 km) of railroad track crisscrossed much of that country.

R Railroad expansion caused a ripple effect in the economy. Building railroads created new jobs for farm laborers and peasants. Less expensive transportation led to lower-priced goods, thus creating larger markets. More sales meant more factories and more machinery. Business owners could reinvest their profits in new equipment, adding to the growth of the economy. This type of regular, ongoing economic growth became a basic feature of the new industrial economy.

✓Reading Check **Describing** How were adult and child factory workers disciplined?

The Spread of Industrialization

MAIN IDEA The pace of industrialization in Europe and the United States depended on many factors, including government policy.

HISTORY & YOU Recall how the Enlightenment spread through Europe. Read about the factors that help explain why nations adapt to change at different speeds.

The world's first industrial nation, Great Britain, was also the richest nation by the mid-nineteenth century. It produced one-half of the world's coal and manufactured goods. Its cotton industry alone in 1850 was equal in size to the industries of all other European countries combined.

Europe

The Industrial Revolution spread to the rest of Europe at different times and speeds. First to be industrialized in continental

SCIENCE, TECHNOLOGY, & SOCIETY

The Power of Steam

Steam power helped drive the Industrial Revolution. Its impact was evident in factories and on the farm.

No innovation was more crucial to the Industrial Revolution than the steam engine. Steam power transformed both farm production and the transportation system. Steam-powered locomotives could deliver raw materials to factories and finished goods to market faster than ever before.

Farming had always been labor-intensive, but now farmers were able to haul the portable steam engine to the fields to power tools. Another step forward came in 1842 when a British company developed a self-propelled steam engine that could pull a plow. It paved the way for tractors and other machinery. Farm efficiency shot up dramatically.

George Stephenson's *Rocket* carried cotton goods from Manchester to the port of Liverpool.

CRITICAL THINKING SKILLS

1. **Explaining** Why was a rail connection to Liverpool important to manufacturers in Manchester?
2. **Determining Cause and Effect** In what way was the development of the steam engine a cause of the Industrial Revolution?

Additional Support

Teacher Tip

Collaborative Learning This activity allows students with different levels of academic skills and intelligences to work together. As you form groups, consider the needed skills and choose students accordingly.

Activity: Collaborative Learning

Summarizing Have small groups of students study advances in transportation that occurred during the Industrial Revolution. Make sure that they research railroads and steamships. Have each member of the group investigate an aspect related to these technological innovations, such as the method of operation, the economic impact, the environmental effects, and the most common uses. Have group members share the information they find and together create a summary that includes visual aids, such as graphs, drawings, or charts. Have groups present their summaries. **Ask:** In what ways did these advances in transportation change people's lives? Which technological innovation had the greatest impact on the economy and progress? Why? Have students support their responses with facts from the presentations. **OL**

Europe were Belgium, France, and the German states. In these places, governments actively encouraged industrialization. For example, governments provided funds to build roads, canals, and railroads. By 1850, a network of iron rails spread across Europe.

North America

An Industrial Revolution also occurred in the United States. In 1800, 5 million people lived in the United States, and 6 out of every 7 American workers were farmers. No city had more than 100,000 people. By 1860, the population had grown to 30 million people. Cities had also grown. Nine cities had populations over 100,000. Only 50 percent of American workers were farmers. D

A large country, the United States needed a good transportation system to move goods across the nation. Thousands of miles of roads and canals were built to link east and west. **Robert Fulton** built the first paddle-wheel steamboat, the *Clermont,* in 1807. Steamboats made transportation easier on the waterways of the United States.

Most important in the development of an American transportation system was the railroad. It began with fewer than 100 miles (160.9 km) of track in 1830. By 1860, about 30,000 miles (48,270 km) of railroad track covered the United States. The country became a single massive market for the manufactured goods of the Northeast.

Labor for the growing number of factories in the Northeast came chiefly from the farm population. Women and girls made up a large majority of the workers in large textile (cotton and wool) factories.

Factory owners sometimes sought entire families, including children, to work in their factories. One advertisement in a newspaper in the town of Utica, New York, read: "Wanted: A few sober and industrious families of at least five children each, over the age of eight years, are wanted at the cotton factory in Whitestown. Widows with large families would do well to attend this notice." R

✓Reading Check **Evaluating** Why was the railroad important to the industrialization of the United States?

Social Impact in Europe

MAIN IDEA Industrialization urbanized Europe and created new social classes, as well as the conditions for the rise of socialism.

HISTORY & YOU Do you know people who run their own businesses? Read to learn how early entrepreneurs contributed to the Industrial Revolution.

The Industrial Revolution drastically changed society. In the first half of the 1800s, cities grew and two new social classes—the industrial middle class and the industrial working class—emerged.

Population and Urban Growth

European population stood at an estimated 140 million in 1750. By 1850, the population had almost doubled to 266 million. One reason death rates declined was better-fed people were more resistant to disease. Famine, with the exception of the Irish potato famine (see page 620), seemed to have disappeared from Western Europe. Many thought population growth led to economic growth. In 1798, the economist Thomas Malthus published *An Essay on the Principle of Population* about poverty and population growth. According to his theory, when there is an increase in the food supply, the population tends to increase too fast for the food supply to keep up, leading to famine, disease, and war.

Famine and poverty were two factors in global migration and urbanization. Almost a million people died during the Irish potato famine, and poverty led a million more to migrate to the Americas. The enclosure laws forced farmers to migrate from the countryside looking for work. Industrialization also spurred urbanization as large numbers of people migrated to cities to work in factories.

In 1800, Great Britain had one major city, London, with a population of about 1 million. Six cities had populations between 50,000 and 100,000. By 1850, London's population had swelled to about 2.5 million. Nine cities had populations over 100,000, and 18 cities had populations between 50,000 and 100,000. Also, over 50 percent of the population lived in towns and cities.

D Differentiated Instruction

Kinesthetic Provide students with a large outline map of the United States. Have them place 5 small objects along the Atlantic coast to represent the U.S. population in 1800. Then have them add another 25 objects mainly in the Northeast to represent the population increase by 1860. **Ask:** By what percentage did the U.S. population increase between 1800 and 1860? *(600%)* BL

R Reading Strategy

Inferring Explain that, in general, working conditions in American industry until the 1840s were better than in Europe. Discuss the reasons that this may have been true. **Ask:** How did working conditions relate to the supply of workers? *(More work and fewer workers in the United States made them less expendable.)* OL

✓Reading Check

Answer: The railroad turned the country into one huge market for the manufactured goods of the Northeast.

Additional Support

Activity: Interdisciplinary Connection

Language Arts Explain that with the drastic growth in English cities came negative consequences for the working class residents, including overcrowding, unsanitary conditions, and disease. Have students research the circumstances in which factory workers lived in the first part of the 1800s in industrial centers. Suggest that they use reference works, electronic sources, nonfiction books, and even fiction such as some of Charles Dickens's novels. Ask students to compose a photo essay that describes the lives of these members of society. Have students display their essays in the classroom.

Ask: What did the Industrial Revolution mean for working class members of society? Is progress always worth the cost it demands? What might have helped to alleviate these conditions for workers? Have students discuss their ideas. AL

ANALYZING PRIMARY SOURCES

Focus

Tell students that industrialization helped bring about Marxist theory, which sought to empower the proletariat (the working class). In addition, the role of government altered as the need to provide services and protection to workers was recognized.

Teach

C Critical Thinking

Analyzing Information Ask: Why were the women and children drawers in the mine? *(They were smaller and could bend enough to move on their hands and feet. The men were needed as miners, work that required different physical attributes.)* **OL**

R Reading Strategy

Reading Primary Sources Ask: According to Engels, what is the effect of industrialization on people and towns? *(It is ugly and destructive, obliterating all that is natural and reducing people to living side by side with refuse and toxins.)* **OL**

ANALYZING PRIMARY SOURCES

Describing the Lives of Workers in the Early 1800s

What hardships did industrialization create for workers? Though it transformed the British economy, industrialization had a drastic social impact on the working people of England.

How did industrialization affect living conditions? The Industrial Revolution not only brought waves of new factories, it caused masses of workers to move to the cities to find jobs at these factories. Both developments had a profound impact on the lives of England's workers.

The Industrial Revolution altered both the working and living conditions of Britain's working class. Read the excerpts and study the illustration to learn more about how industrialization impacted the people of England during the first half of the nineteenth century.

SOURCE 1

Miner Betty Harris, 37, gave testimony to an 1842 Royal Commission investigating conditions in British mines.

I was married at 23, and went into a **colliery**[1] when I was married. I . . . can neither read nor write. . . . I am a **drawer**[2], and work from 6 in the morning to 6 at night. Stop about an hour at noon to eat my dinner; have bread and butter for dinner; I get no drink. . . .

C I have a belt round my waist, and a chain passing between my legs, and I go on my hands and feet. The road is very steep, and we have to hold by a rope; and when there is no rope, by anything we can catch hold of. There are six women and about six boys and girls in the pit I work in; it is very hard work for a woman. The pit is very wet where I work, and the water comes over our clog-tops always, and I have seen it up to my thighs; it rains in at the roof terribly. My clothes are wet through almost all day long. . . .

My cousin looks after my children in the day time. I am very tired when I get home at night; I fall asleep sometimes before I get washed. . . . the belt and chain is worse when we are **in the family way**[3]. My feller (husband) has beaten me many a times for not being ready.

SOURCE 2

German socialist Friedrich Engels, cofounder of Marxism, described industrial Manchester in his book, *The Condition of the Working-Class in England in 1844.*

R The first court below Ducie Bridge . . . was in such a state at the time of the cholera that the sanitary police ordered it evacuated, swept, and disinfected with **chloride of lime**[4]. . . . At the bottom flows, or rather stagnates, the Irk, a narrow, coal-black, foul-smelling stream, full of debris and refuse, which it deposits on the shallower right bank. . . .

Above the bridge are **tanneries**[5], **bone mills**[6], and gasworks, from which all drains and refuse find their way into the Irk, which receives further the contents of all the neighboring sewers and **privies**[7]. . . . Below the bridge you look upon the piles of debris, the refuse, the filth, and offal from the courts on the steep left bank; here each house is packed close behind its neighbor and a piece of each is visible, all black, smoky, crumbling, ancient, with broken panes and window frames. . . .

Such is the Old Town of Manchester . . . [in] defiance of all considerations of cleanliness, ventilation, and health which characterize the construction of this single district, containing at least twenty to thirty thousand inhabitants.

[1] **colliery:** coal mine and its connected buildings
[2] **drawer:** worker who pulled coal tubs in a mine; tubs were attached to the drawer's belt with a chain
[3] **in the family way:** pregnant
[4] **chloride of lime:** bleaching powder
[5] **tanneries:** buildings where skins and hides are tanned

Differentiated Instruction

Making Generalizations

Primary Source Reading 19 — Riding the Liverpool-Manchester Railway, 1830

Primary Source Reading, URB p. 41

Objective: Analyze the primary source letters written by a young actress.
Focus: Learn about the first trains.
Teach: Have volunteers read the passage aloud.
Assess: Have students identify the advantages of trains according to the author and disadvantages that they can infer.
Close: Have students use the list above to make generalizations about the first trains.

Differentiated Instruction Strategies

BL Before students read, have them write three general statements about the first trains. Then have them verify or revise these generalizations after reading.

AL Have students find additional articles to support their generalizations about the first trains.

ELL Show images of the first trains to help students visualize them as they read.

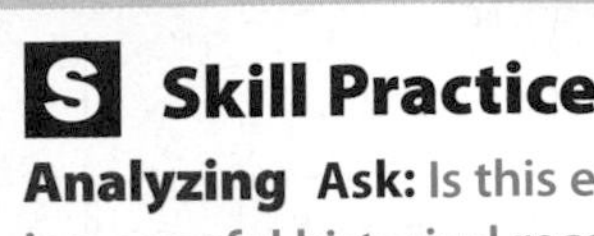

▲ Girls and women worked at "Carding, Drawing, and Roving" in a nineteenth-century English cotton mill.

SOURCE 3

A series of inventions in the late 1700s revolutionized the cotton industry in England. These new machines dramatically increased textile production and marked the end of the home-based system of textile production. By the early 1800s, textile workers had to work in factories where they operated large machines for long hours in hot temperatures.

The above print of a cotton mill appears in the book *History of the Cotton Manufacture in Great Britain* (London, 1835), by Edward Baines. The image shows the belts that connected the machines to a pulley system. A steam engine rotated the wheels on the shaft to power the machines. Note how close the female workers' hands, hair, and clothing are to the rotating gears.

[6] **bone mills:** mills that convert animal bones into fertilizer
[7] **privies:** outhouses

DOCUMENT-BASED QUESTIONS

1. **Calculating** How many hours did Betty Harris work each day?
2. **Recognizing Bias** How could Engels's background have affected his assessment of Manchester? How might a description of the city written by a factory owner contrast from that written by Engels?
3. **Assessing** How does Baines depict the working environment in the cotton mill? Is it safe or dangerous?
4. **Comparing and Contrasting** What do Harris's testimony and the above print suggest about how the work experience for women in mines and cotton mills was similar and different?
5. **Synthesizing** How could Engels have used Harris's testimony to support his main point about industrialization?
6. **Problem-Solving** Describe the lives of England's workers in the early 1800s. If you were an adviser to the British government in 1845, what changes would you have recommended?

ANALYZING PRIMARY SOURCES

S Skill Practice

Analyzing Ask: Is this engraving a useful historical record? *(Yes; the artist shows machinery and workers. Don't know; depends on artist's interpretation.)* **AL**

Assess/Close

Summarizing Have students summarize the effects of industrialization. **OL**

DOCUMENT-BASED QUESTIONS

Answers:

1. 12 hours
2. Engels was the co-founder of Marxism, so he was looking for class inequalities. A factory owner might mention the progress brought by factories.
3. The factory appears safe (well-lit and open). But it also appears dangerous because children are near gears.
4. **Similar:** no place to sit; dangerous, hard work. **Differences:** miners exposed to elements; factory workers could stand.
5. to show unhealthy effects of industrialization
6. Answers will vary.

Additional Support

Activity: Collaborative Learning

Discussing Industrialization Ask: Who benefited from the Industrial Revolution? *(Students will probably say that factory owners, industrialists of all sorts, merchants, and bankers benefited from industrialization.)* Have students work in small groups. Ask them to find more information about the effects of industrialization on different sectors of society. They should look for primary or secondary sources describing the lives of factory owners, other industrialists, child laborers, and factory workers. Have each group prepare for a panel discussion. Each group member should use the research to represent the point of view of one sector of society, for example, child laborers. Build in time for students in the audience to ask questions. Draw some conclusions about the impact of industrialization on society in general. **OL**

Teacher Tip

Charts Show groups some cause-and-effect charts on the chalkboard. Encourage them to organize their notes in written and/or pictorial form in a cause-and-effect chart. Remind students that charts can help them have their facts ready for the panel discussion.

Focus

Bellringer

Daily Focus Transparency 19.2

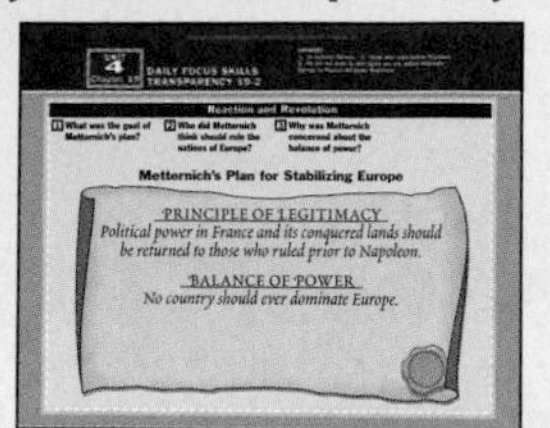

GUIDE TO READING

Answers to Graphic:
Revolution of 1830: dissolution of legislature, suspension of freedom of press: **Revolution of 1848:** economic problems, worker revolt, voting rights

Section Spotlight Video

To generate student interest and provide a springboard for class discussion, access the Chapter 19, Section 2 video at glencoe.com or on the video DVD.

SECTION 2

Reaction and Revolution

GUIDE TO READING

The BIG Idea

Self-Determination In 1848, liberals and nationalists rebelled against many of the conservative governments of Europe.

Content Vocabulary

- conservatism *(p. 624)*
- principle of intervention *(p. 625)*
- liberalism *(p. 626)*
- universal male suffrage *(p. 628)*
- multinational state *(p. 629)*

Academic Vocabulary

- constitution *(p. 626)*
- radical *(p. 628)*

People, Places, and Events

- Congress of Vienna *(p. 624)*
- Klemens von Metternich *(p. 624)*
- Vienna *(p. 624)*
- Bill of Rights *(p. 626)*
- Louis-Napoleon *(p. 628)*
- German Confederation *(p. 628)*
- Prague *(p. 629)*

Reading Strategy

Summarizing Information As you read, use a chart like the one below to summarize the causes of the revolutions in France in 1830 and 1848.

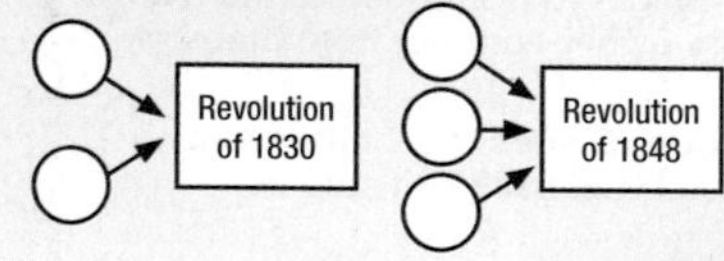

After the turmoil of the French revolutionary years, European rulers wanted to return to a conservative order and to keep a balance of power among nations. Liberals and nationalists, however, struggled to achieve more liberal governments and new nations. Their struggle led eventually to the revolutions that swept across much of Europe in 1848.

The Congress of Vienna

MAIN IDEA After Napoleon's defeat, the victors met and redrew the map of Europe to create a balance of power and to strengthen conservatism.

HISTORY & YOU Does the United Nations intervene in international disputes? Read about decisions that the great powers made at the Congress of Vienna and their effect on Europe.

After the defeat of Napoleon, European rulers moved to restore the old order. This was the goal of the victors—Great Britain, Austria, Prussia, and Russia—when they met at the **Congress of Vienna** in September 1814 to arrange a final peace settlement.

The haughty Austrian foreign minister, Prince **Klemens von Metternich** (MEH•tuhr•nihk), was the most influential leader at that meeting in **Vienna.** Metternich claimed that the principle of legitimacy guided him. He meant that lawful monarchs from the royal families who had ruled before Napoleon would be restored to their positions of power. This, they believed, would ensure peace and stability in Europe. The victorious powers had already restored the Bourbon king to the French throne in 1814.

Practical considerations of power were addressed at the Congress of Vienna. The great powers rearranged territories in Europe, believing that this would form a new balance of power. The powers at Vienna wanted to keep any one country from dominating Europe. This meant balancing political and military forces that guaranteed the independence of the great powers. To balance Russian territorial gains, for example, new territories were given to Prussia and Austria.

Conservatism and the Balance of Power

The arrangements worked out at the Congress of Vienna were a victory for rulers who wanted to contain the forces of change that the French Revolution had unleashed. These rulers, like Metternich, believed in the political philosophy known as **conservatism.**

Resource Manager

R Reading Strategies	C Critical Thinking	D Differentiated Instruction	W Writing Support	S Skill Practice
Teacher Edition • Making Connections, pp. 626, 629 • Inferring, p. 626 • Act. Prior Know., p. 627 **Additional Resources** • Guid. Read. Act., URB p. 49 • Read. Ess. & Note-Taking Guide, p. 208	**Teacher Edition** • Det. Cause/Effect, p. 626 **Additional Resources** • World Lit. Read., URB p. 9 • Section Quiz, p. 234	**Teacher Edition** • Visual/Spatial, p. 628 **Additional Resources** • Foods Around the World p. 14 • Read. Strat. for SS, p. 53	**Teacher Edition** • Expository Writing, p. 628 **Additional Resources** • Linking Past/Present Act., URB p. 38 • Writer's Guidebook, p. 27	**Teacher Edition** • Using Geo. Skills, p. 625 **Additional Resources** • Read. Strat. for SS, p. 71

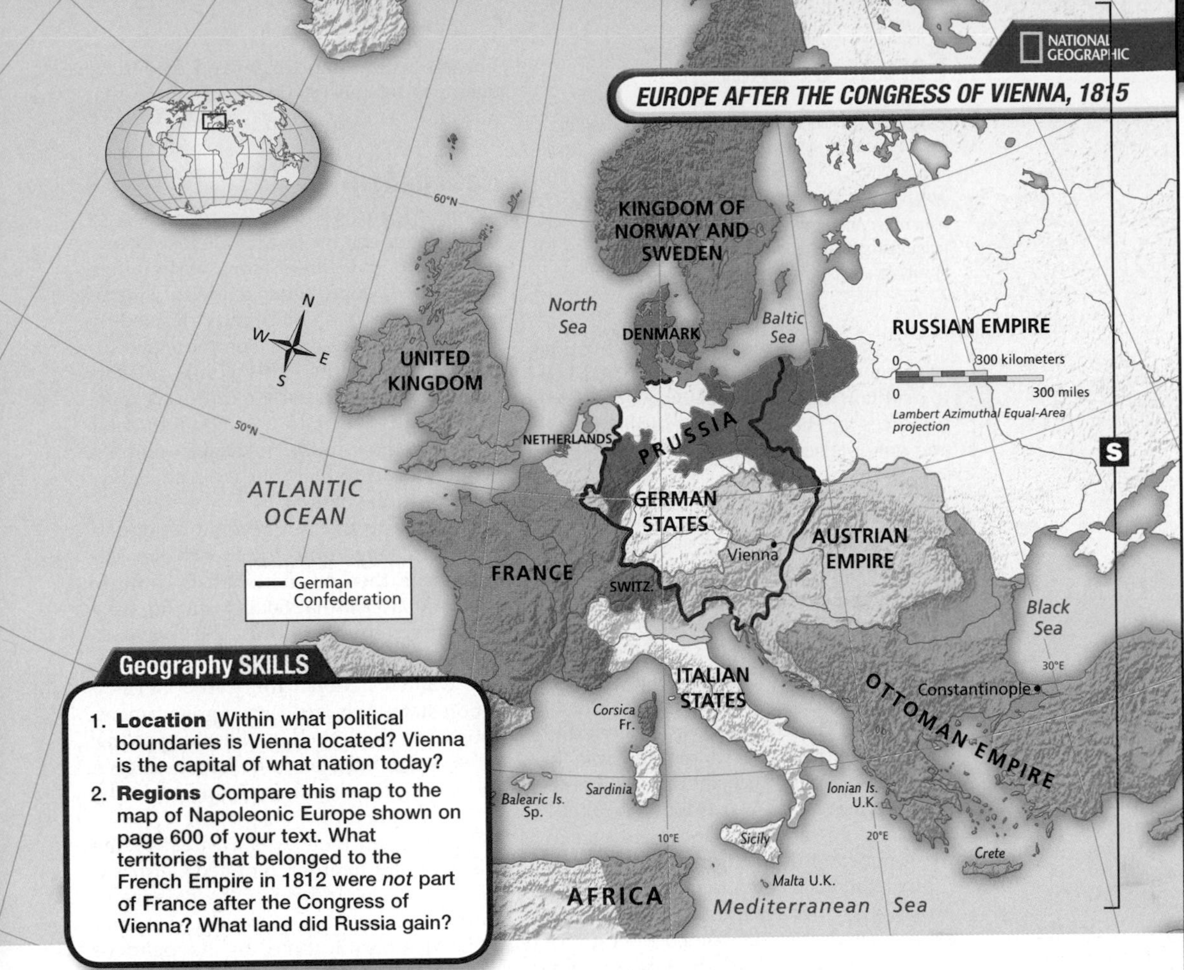

Geography SKILLS

1. **Location** Within what political boundaries is Vienna located? Vienna is the capital of what nation today?
2. **Regions** Compare this map to the map of Napoleonic Europe shown on page 600 of your text. What territories that belonged to the French Empire in 1812 were *not* part of France after the Congress of Vienna? What land did Russia gain?

Conservatism is based on tradition and a belief in the value of social stability. Most conservatives at that time favored obedience to political authority. They also believed that organized religion was crucial to keep order in society. Conservatives hated revolutions and were unwilling to accept demands from people who wanted either individual rights or representative governments.

To maintain the new balance of power, Great Britain, Russia, Prussia, and Austria (and later France) agreed to meet at times. The purpose of these conferences was to take steps needed to maintain peace in Europe. These meetings came to be called the Concert of Europe.

Principle of Intervention

Eventually, the great powers adopted a **principle of intervention.** According to this principle, the great powers had the right to send armies into countries where there were revolutions in order to restore legitimate monarchs to their thrones. Refusing to accept the principle, Britain argued that the great powers should not interfere in the internal affairs of other states. The other great powers, however, used military forces to crush revolutions in Spain and Italy, as well as to restore monarchs to their thrones.

✓Reading Check **Analyzing** What were the goals of European leaders at the Congress of Vienna?

Teach

S Skill Practice

Using Geography Skills Ask: Compare and contrast Europe in 1815 with Europe today. *(Different: In 1815, Austrian, Ottoman, and Russian Empires controlled much of southern and eastern Europe; Germany and Italy were confederations of independent states. Similar: United Kingdom, France, Spain, Portugal, Switzerland, the Netherlands, and Denmark were independent in 1815.)* **AL**

Geography SKILLS

Answers:

1. Within the German Confederation *and* the Austrian Empire; Austria
2. France lost areas in central Italy, the Illyrian Provinces, the Netherlands, and areas of Prussia and the German states. Russia gained the Grand Duchy of Warsaw.

✓Reading Check

Answer: to restore former monarchs to power in order to keep peace and stability

Hands-On Chapter Project
Step 2

Presenting a Living Time Line

Step 2: Writing a Script Groups of students continue developing the living time line that they began in Section 1.

Directions: Write the Big Idea on the board. Then ask groups to develop a script that tells the story of a major event in this section or that highlights the philosophies of nineteenth century liberals, conservatives, and nationalists. Each group member should have a speaking role and there should be a definite beginning and end to the story that is told. Encourage students to include stage directions, describing gestures or movements in their scripts. Groups may also wish to add images to their backdrops to represent important events from this section. They should continue to reserve space for later illustrations.

Summarizing: Have groups formally discuss the event they chose to portray and relate it to the section's Big Idea. **OL**

(Chapter Project is continued in Section 3.)

R1 Reading Strategy

Making Connections Review with students the meanings of *conservatism* and *liberalism*. **Ask:** In what ways would you describe yourself as a liberal or a conservative? Tell students to consider traditions they wish to protect and areas in which they desire more freedom. **BL**

R2 Reading Strategy

Inferring Ask students to explain why people in Europe would be likely to feel a greater sense of nationalism after the wars in the Napoleonic era. *(They had witnessed the overthrow of monarchs and the ending of foreign domination.)* **OL**

C Critical Thinking

Determining Cause and Effect Ask: How did conservatives view nationalism? Why? *(Conservatives feared nationalism because it threatened the political order, which depended on a few powers controlling vast territories. Breaking up these areas into separate nations would disturb the balance of power.)* **OL**

Forces of Change

MAIN IDEA Liberals and nationalists opposed the existing political system and threatened the conservative regimes.

HISTORY & YOU What do you have in common with other Americans? Learn how a common language, religion, and customs led people to form loyalty to a nation.

R1 Between 1815 and 1830, conservative governments throughout Europe worked to maintain the old order. However, powerful forces for change—known as liberalism and nationalism—were also at work.

Liberalism

Liberalism is a political philosophy that grew out of the Enlightenment. **Liberalism** held that people should be as free as possible from government restraint.

Liberals had a common set of political beliefs. Chief among them was the protection of civil liberties, or the basic rights of all people. These civil liberties included equality before the law and freedom of assembly, speech, and the press. Liberals believed that all these freedoms should be guaranteed by a written document such as the American **Bill of Rights.**

Most liberals wanted religious toleration for all, as well as separation of church and state. Liberals also demanded the right of peaceful opposition to the government. They believed that a representative assembly (legislature) elected by qualified voters should make laws.

Many liberals, then, favored government ruled by a **constitution,** such as in a constitutional monarchy in which a constitution regulates a king. They believed that written constitutions would guarantee the rights they sought to preserve.

Liberals did not, however, believe in a democracy in which everyone had a right to vote. They thought that the right to vote and hold office should be open only to men of property. Liberalism, then, was tied to middle-class men, especially industrial middle-class men, who wanted voting rights for themselves so they could share power with the landowning classes. The liberals feared mob rule and had little desire to let the lower classes share that power.

Nationalism

Nationalism was an even more powerful force for change in the nineteenth century than was liberalism. Nationalism arose when people began to identify themselves as part of a community defined by a distinctive language, common institution, and customs. This community is called a nation. In earlier centuries, people's loyalty went to a king or to their town or region. In the nineteenth century, people began to feel that their chief loyalty was to the nation.

R2 Nationalism did not become a popular force for change until the French Revolution. From then on, nationalists came to believe that each nationality should have its own government. Thus, the Germans, who were separated into many principalities, wanted national unity in a German nation-state with one central government. Subject peoples, such as the Hungarians, wanted the right to establish their own governments rather than be subject to the Austrian emperor.

C Nationalism, then, was a threat to the existing political order. A united Germany, for example, would upset the balance of power set up at the Congress of Vienna in 1815. At the same time, an independent Hungarian state would mean the breakup of the Austrian Empire. Conservatives feared such change and thus tried hard to repress nationalism.

In the first half of the nineteenth century, nationalism found a strong ally in liberalism. Most liberals believed that freedom could only be possible in people who ruled themselves. Each group of people should have its own state. No state should attempt to dominate another state. The association with liberalism meant that nationalism had a wider scope.

Revolutionary Outbursts

Beginning in 1830, the forces of change—liberalism and nationalism—began to break through the conservative domination of

Differentiated Instruction

Linking Past and Present Activity, URB p. 38

Comparing and Contrasting

Objective: Compare and contrast nineteenth-century and twenty-first century nationalism.

Focus: Have students read the passages together.

Teach: Have students label a world map with dates and descriptions of nationalist struggles for each time period.

Assess: Ask students to compare and contrast activities of nationalists in the 19th century and today.

Close: Discuss the positive and negative aspects of nationalism.

Differentiated Instruction Strategies

- **BL** Assign pairs of students an area of the world mentioned in the passages and have them explain nationalist events there.
- **AL** Have students present an oral report on a current conflict motivated by nationalist aims.
- **ELL** Have pairs read the passages together, using a dictionary to define unfamiliar words.

Europe. In France, liberals overthrew the Bourbon monarch Charles X in 1830 and established a constitutional monarchy. Political support for the new monarch, Louis Philippe, a cousin of Charles X, came from the upper-middle class.

In the same year, 1830, three more revolutions occurred. Nationalism was the chief force in all three of them. Belgium, which had been annexed to the former Dutch Republic in 1815, rebelled and created an independent state. In Poland and Italy, which were both ruled by foreign powers, efforts to break free were less successful. Russians crushed the Polish attempt to establish an independent Polish nation. Meanwhile Austrian troops marched south and put down revolts in a number of Italian states.

✓Reading Check **Evaluating** How did liberalism and nationalism present a challenge to the conservative domination of Europe in the early 1800s?

The Revolutions of 1848

MAIN IDEA Beginning in France in 1848, the spirit of revolution spread quickly over Europe, but the uprisings were largely suppressed.

HISTORY & YOU Can you imagine living without the rights guaranteed in the Constitution? In 1848, popular uprisings in Europe hoped to win such rights.

The conservative order still dominated much of Europe as the midpoint of the nineteenth century approached. However, the forces of liberalism and nationalism continued to grow. These forces of change erupted once more in the revolutions of 1848. R

Another French Revolution

Revolution in France once again sparked revolution in other countries. Severe economic problems beginning in 1846 brought untold hardship in France to the lower-middle class, workers, and peasants.

HISTORY & ARTS

The Overthrow of King Louis Philippe

In the mid-1840s, many French people became increasingly frustrated over poor economic conditions, government corruption, and the fact that so few people could vote. Since political meetings were illegal, reformers were holding banquets to discuss issues.

When King Louis Philippe canceled a banquet meeting on February 22, 1848, riots broke out and the royal palace was under threat. The king renounced the throne and fled to Great Britain.

DOCUMENT-BASED QUESTIONS

This painting depicts the people burning the throne at the Place de la Bastille, 1848.

1. **Explaining** What was the purpose of the banquet to be held on February 22, 1848?
2. **Analyzing Visuals** How would you describe the symbolic meaning of this painting?

R Reading Strategy

Activating Prior Knowledge

Ask: In what ways might the revolutions of 1848 be considered a continuation of the French Revolution? *(Workers are still demanding many of the same rights and are revolting against the monarchy.)* **OL**

✓Reading Check

Answer: In France, liberals overthrew Charles X and established a constitutional monarchy. Nationalism was the force of three revolutions in 1830. Belgium created an independent state, but revolts in Poland and Italy failed to free these lands of foreign domination.

DOCUMENT-BASED QUESTIONS

Answers:

1. to discuss electoral reform
2. The burning of the throne symbolized the end of the monarchy and the beginning of rule by the people.

Additional Support

Extending the Content

Louis Philippe was proclaimed "King of the French" in 1830, in recognition of the system of popular monarchy, which linked the title to a people rather than a state. His reign marked the triumph of the bourgeoisie over the aristocracy. Initially, Louis Philippe tried to balance the demands of the monarchists and the socialists and republicans. His rule was marked by death threats and rebellions, however, resulting in his curtailing of civil liberties and elimination of opposition. **Ask:** What are some reasons that Louis Philippe stopped trying to balance the demands of the monarchists, socialists, and republicans? *(Answers may include that he felt balance was not possible; he was worried that he might lose power.)*

D Differentiated Instruction

Visual/Spatial Have students create advertisments for the national workshops that helped provide work for the unemployed. Tell students that the posters should reflect positively on the new provisional government. OL

W Writing Support

Expository Writing Ask students to write a paragraph about the unification of nineteenth-century Germany from the viewpoint of a ruler of a small German state. *(Answers should reflect an understanding that a unified Germany would mean a loss of power for individual rulers.)* OL

Geography SKILLS

Answers:

1. Magyar, Romanian, Slovak, German, Croat, Serb
2. Various ethnic groups dominated different regions.

At the same time, members of the middle class clamored for the right to vote. The government of Louis Philippe refused to make changes, and opposition grew.

The monarchy was finally overthrown in 1848. A group of moderate and **radical** republicans set up a provisional, or temporary, government. The republicans were people who wished France to be a republic—a government in which leaders are elected.

The provisional government called for the election of representatives to a Constituent Assembly that would draw up a new **D** constitution. Election was to be by **universal male suffrage,** meaning all adult men could vote.

The provisional government also set up national workshops to provide work for the unemployed. From March to June, the number of unemployed enrolled in the national workshops rose from about 66,000 to almost 120,000. This emptied the treasury and frightened the moderates, who reacted by closing the workshops on June 21.

The workers refused to accept this decision and poured into the streets. In four days of bitter and bloody fighting, government forces crushed the working-class revolt. Thousands were killed and thousands more were sent to the French prison colony of Algeria in northern Africa.

The new constitution, ratified on November 4, 1848, set up a republic called the Second Republic. The Second Republic had a single legislature elected by universal male suffrage. A president, also chosen by universal male suffrage, served for four years. In the elections for the presidency held in December 1848, Charles Louis Napoleon Bonaparte (called **Louis-Napoleon**), the nephew of the famous French ruler, won a resounding victory.

NATIONAL GEOGRAPHIC

NATIONALITIES IN AUSTRIA-HUNGARY, MID-1800S

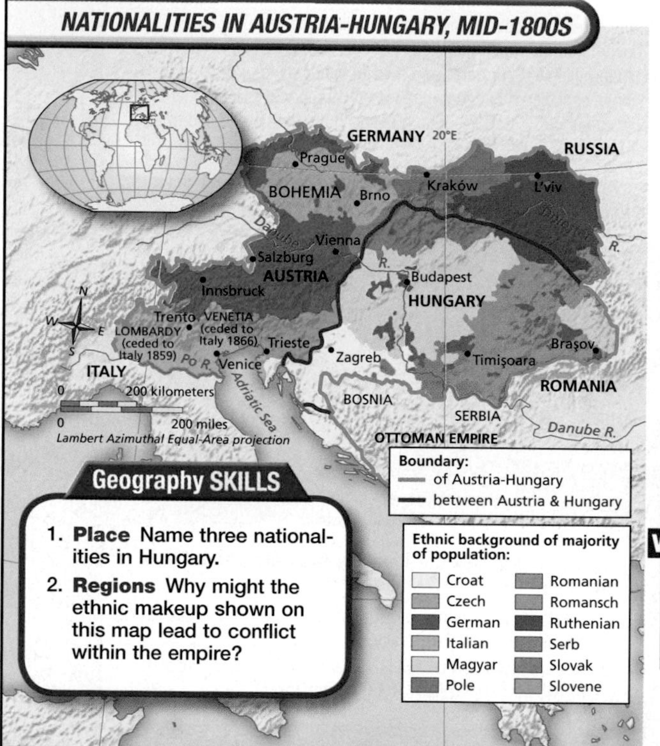

Geography SKILLS

1. **Place** Name three nationalities in Hungary.
2. **Regions** Why might the ethnic makeup shown on this map lead to conflict within the empire?

Trouble in the German States

News of the 1848 revolution in France led to upheaval in other parts of Europe. The Congress of Vienna in 1815 had recognized the existence of 38 independent German states (called the **German Confederation**). Of these, Austria and Prussia were the two great powers. The other states varied in size.

In 1848, cries for change led many German rulers to promise constitutions, a free press, jury trials, and other liberal reforms. In May 1848, an all-German parliament, called the Frankfurt Assembly, was held to fulfill a liberal and nationalist dream—the preparation of a constitution for a new united Germany. The Frankfurt Assembly's proposed constitution provided for a German state with a parliamentary government and a hereditary emperor ruling under a limited monarchy. The constitution also allowed for direct election of deputies to the parliament by universal male suffrage.

Ultimately, however, the Frankfurt Assembly failed to gain the support needed to achieve its goal. Frederick William IV of Prussia, to whom the throne was offered, **W** refused to accept the crown from a popularly elected assembly. Thus, the assembly members had no real means of forcing the German rulers to accept their drafted constitution. German unification was not achieved.

Additional Support

Activity: Collaborative Learning

Comparing and Contrasting Organize students into groups of three or four. Have each group brainstorm a list of countries and regions where nationalism has been an issue in recent years. Tell students to consider places where nationalist conflicts have been resolved peacefully, cases where attempts at a resolution have led to more conflict and tension, and instances where no attempts have been made to resolve nationalist issues. Have students use library or Internet resources to research the causes and effects of nationalism in each country or region and record their findings in a chart. **Ask:** In what ways were the causes and effects of nationalism in each location similar and different? What factors do you think had the greatest impact on the results? Have each group discuss their ideas and work together to write a brief essay that compares and contrasts the roles of nationalism in the countries or regions they researched. Select volunteers to read aloud each group's essay. Discuss the common elements among the essays as a class. OL

Revolutions in Central Europe

The Austrian Empire also had its problems. The empire was a **multinational state**—a collection of different peoples including Germans, Czechs, Magyars (Hungarians), Slovaks, Romanians, Slovenes, Poles, Croats, Serbians, Ruthenians (Ukrainians), and Italians. Only the German-speaking Hapsburg dynasty held the empire together. The Germans, though only a quarter of the population, played a leading role in governing the Austrian Empire.

In March 1848, demonstrations erupted in the major cities. To calm the demonstrators, the Hapsburg court dismissed Metternich, the Austrian foreign minister, who fled to England. In Vienna, revolutionary forces took control of the capital and demanded a liberal constitution. To appease the revolutionaries, the government gave Hungary its own legislature. In Bohemia, the Czechs clamored for their own government.

Austrian officials had made concessions to appease the revolutionaries but were determined to reestablish their control over the empire. In June 1848, Austrian military forces crushed the Czech rebels in **Prague.** By the end of October, the rebels in Vienna had been defeated as well. With the help of a Russian army of 140,000 men, the Hungarian revolutionaries were finally subdued in 1849. The revolutions in the Austrian Empire had failed.

Revolts in the Italian States

The Congress of Vienna had set up nine states in Italy. These states included the Kingdom of Piedmont in the north; the Two Sicilies (Naples and Sicily); the Papal States; a handful of small states; and the northern provinces of Lombardy and Venetia, which were now part of the Austrian Empire.

In 1848, a revolt broke out against the Austrians in Lombardy and Venetia. Revolutionaries in other Italian states also took up arms and sought to create liberal constitutions and a unified Italy. By 1849, however, the Austrians had reestablished complete control over Lombardy and Venetia. The old order also prevailed in the rest of Italy.

Throughout Europe in 1848, popular revolts started upheavals that had led to liberal constitutions and liberal governments. However, moderate liberals and more radical revolutionaries were soon divided over their goals, and so conservative rule was reestablished. Even with the reestablishment of conservative governments, however, the forces of nationalism and liberalism continued to influence political events.

✓Reading Check **Identifying** What countries experienced revolutions in 1848?

SECTION 2 REVIEW

Vocabulary

1. **Explain** the significance of: Congress of Vienna, Klemens von Metternich, Vienna, conservatism, principle of intervention, liberalism, Bill of Rights, constitution, radical, universal male suffrage, Louis-Napoleon, German Confederation, multinational state, Prague.

Main Ideas

2. **Explain** how the Congress of Vienna achieved and maintained a balance of power.
3. **Summarize** the ideologies of conservatism, liberalism, and nationalism by using a chart like the one below.

Conservatism	Liberalism	Nationalism

4. **List** the different peoples living in the Austrian Empire.

Critical Thinking

5. **The BIG Idea** **Analyzing** How did the social and economic changes from the Industrial Revolution contribute to the spread of liberalism?
6. **Hypothesizing** Why did Great Britain not join the revolutions that spread through Europe in 1848?
7. **Analyzing Visuals** Examine the painting on page 627. If you did not already know, how could you tell the social class of the revolutionaries by their dress?

Writing About History

8. **Expository Writing** Select one of the following ideologies: conservatism, liberalism, or nationalism. Write an essay in which you identify contemporary ideas influenced by that ideology.

History ONLINE
For help with the concepts in this section of *Glencoe World History*, go to glencoe.com and click Study Central™.

629

R Reading Strategy

Making Connections Ask students to list other countries that could be considered multinational states and research the ethnic background of each country's population. Ask students to share their findings. AL

Answer: France, German states, Austrian empire, Italian states

Assess

History ONLINE

Study Central provides summaries, interactive games, and online graphic organizers to help students review content.

Close

Summarizing **Ask:** Why did nationalism spread throughout Europe in the nineteenth century? *(Answers may include that people who shared languages and traditions wished to unite.)*

Answers

1. Definitions for the vocabulary words are found in the section and the Glossary.
2. divided territories and redrew borders; met at times to discuss peacekeeping; intervened in revolutions
3. **Conservatism:** tradition, social stability, obedience to political authority; **Liberalism:** civil liberties, religious toleration, constitution; **Nationalism:** common traditions, language, customs
4. Germans, Czechs, Magyars (Hungarians), Slovaks, Romanians, Slovenes, Poles, Croats, Serbians, Italians
5. Industrial Revolution led to growth of industrial middle class. Liberalism was tied to middle-class men.
6. Answers may include that Great Britain already had a constitutional, or limited, monarchy with representatives for the people. Other than the Irish potato famine, food supplies were plentiful. Some work conditions at factories had already been addressed (Factory Act of 1833) if not completely resolved.
7. yes; coats and ties: middle class; tunics: working class
8. Essays will identify influence on contemporary ideology.

National Unification and Nationalism

Focus

Bellringer

Daily Focus Transparency 19.3

GUIDE TO READING

Answers to Graphic:

Great Britain: vote extended to males of industrial middle class, Parliament made social, political reforms; **France:** economic expansion, Paris rebuilt, war with Prussia, Second Empire fell; **Austrian Empire:** dual monarchy of Austria-Hungary; **Russia:** Russia defeated in Crimean War, Alexander II freed serfs, Alexander II assassinated

Section Spotlight Video

To generate student interest and provide a springboard for class discussion, access the Chapter 19, Section 3 video at glencoe.com or on the video DVD.

Resource Manager

GUIDE TO READING

The BIG Idea

Self-Determination In the mid-1800s, the Germans and Italians created their own nations. However, not all national groups were able to reach that goal.

Content Vocabulary

- militarism *(p. 632)*
- kaiser *(p. 633)*
- plebiscite *(p. 635)*
- emancipation *(p. 636)*
- abolitionism *(p. 637)*
- secede *(p. 637)*

Academic Vocabulary

- unification *(p. 631)*
- regime *(p. 635)*

People and Places

- Piedmont *(p. 631)*
- Giuseppe Garibaldi *(p. 632)*
- Otto von Bismarck *(p. 632)*
- Alsace *(p. 633)*
- Lorraine *(p. 633)*
- Queen Victoria *(p. 634)*
- Budapest *(p. 635)*
- Czar Alexander II *(p. 636)*

Reading Strategy

Summarizing Information

As you read, use a table like the one below to list the changes that took place in the indicated countries during the nineteenth century.

Great Britain	France	Austrian Empire	Russia

Although the revolutions of 1848 had failed, the forces of nationalism and liberalism remained powerful for the rest of the nineteenth century. Italy and Germany were unified, and Great Britain and France became more liberal, while Austria and Russia remained authoritarian by the end of the nineteenth century.

Toward National Unification

MAIN IDEA The rise of nationalism led to the unification of Italy and Germany.

HISTORY & YOU What have you achieved as a member of a group that you could not have achieved on your own? Learn how determined leadership and strong military effort resulted in the unification of the Italian and German states.

The revolutions of 1848 had failed. By 1871, however, both Germany and Italy would be unified. The changes that made this possible began with the Crimean War.

Breakdown of the Concert of Europe

The Crimean War was the result of a long-term struggle between Russia and the Ottoman Empire. The Ottoman Empire, centered in what is now Turkey, had long controlled most of the Balkans in southeastern Europe. By 1800, however, the Ottoman Empire was in decline. Its authority over Balkan territories began to weaken.

Russia was a nation with little access to warm-water ports. It had always coveted territory in the Balkans. Having this territory would allow Russian ships to sail through the Dardanelles, the straits between the Black Sea and the Mediterranean. If Russia could achieve this goal, it would become the major power in eastern Europe and would even be able to challenge British naval control of the eastern Mediterranean. Other European nations feared Russian ambitions but also hoped to gain some territory if the Ottoman Empire collapsed.

In 1853, the Russians invaded the Turkish Balkan provinces of Moldavia and Walachia. In response, the Ottoman Turks declared war on Russia. Great Britain and France, fearful of Russian gains, declared war on Russia the following year. This conflict came to be called the Crimean War.

The Crimean War was named for the Russian peninsula in the Black Sea where important battles took place. The war was poorly planned and poorly fought. Eventually, heavy losses caused the Russians to seek peace. By the Treaty of Paris, signed in March 1856, Russia agreed to allow Moldavia and Walachia to be placed under the protection of all the great powers.

R Reading Strategies	C Critical Thinking	D Differentiated Instruction	W Writing Support	S Skill Practice
Teacher Edition • Sequencing Info., p. 631 • Inferring, p. 636 • Summarizing, p. 637 **Additional Resources** • Guid. Read. Act., URB p. 50 • Read. Ess. & Note-Taking Guide, p. 211	**Teacher Edition** • Pred. Consequences, p. 632 • Analyzing Info., p. 633 • Ident. Cent. Issues, p. 635 **Additional Resources** • Hist. Analysis Skills Act., p. 18 • Section Quiz, p. 235	**Teacher Edition** • Adv. Learners, p. 632 • ELL, p. 632 • Visual/Spatial, p. 635 **Additional Resources** • Read. Strat. for SS, p. 62 • English Learner Act., URB p. 21	**Teacher Edition** • Expository Writing, p. 633, p. 635 • Persuasive Writing, p. 634 **Additional Resources** • Writer's Guidebook, p. 47	**Teacher Edition** • Visual Literacy, p. 634 **Additional Resources** • Time Line Act., URB p. 37

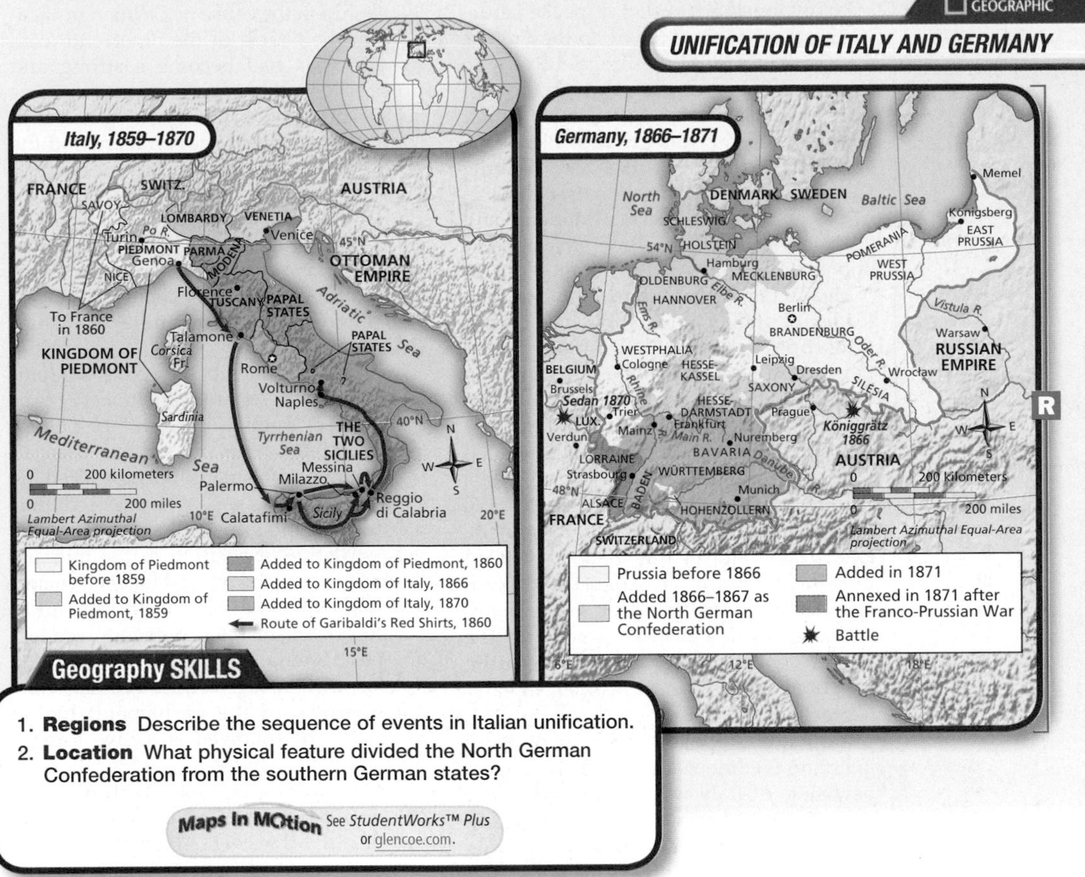

Geography SKILLS

1. **Regions** Describe the sequence of events in Italian unification.
2. **Location** What physical feature divided the North German Confederation from the southern German states?

Maps In MOtion See StudentWorks™ Plus or glencoe.com.

The effect of the Crimean War was to destroy the Concert of Europe. Austria and Russia, the chief powers maintaining the status quo before the 1850s, were now enemies. Austria, with its own interests in the Balkans, had refused to support Russia in the Crimean War. A defeated and humiliated Russia withdrew from European affairs for the next 20 years. Austria now had no friends among the great powers. This situation opened the door to the **unification** of Italy and Germany.

Italian Unification

In 1850, Austria was still the dominant power on the Italian Peninsula. After the failure of the revolution of 1848, people began to look to the northern Italian state of **Piedmont** for leadership in achieving the unification of Italy. The royal house of Savoy ruled the Kingdom of Piedmont. Included in the kingdom were Piedmont, the island of Sardinia, Nice, and Savoy. The ruler of the kingdom, beginning in 1849, was King Victor Emmanuel II.

The king named Camillo di Cavour his prime minister in 1852. Cavour was a dedicated political leader. As prime minister, he pursued a policy of economic expansion to increase government revenues and enable the kingdom to equip a large army. Cavour, however, knew that Piedmont's army was not strong enough to defeat the Austrians. So, he made an alliance with the French emperor Louis-Napoleon. Cavour then provoked the Austrians into declaring war in 1859.

Teach

R Reading Strategy

Sequencing Information Organize students into three groups to construct two time lines showing the unifications of Italy and Germany. One group should gather information on key people and their roles in unification. Another group should gather information on key events and dates. The third group should design and draw the time lines, incorporating information from the other two groups. Post the time lines in the classroom and encourage students to use them as references. **OL**

Geography SKILLS

Answers:

1. 1859: Lombardy added to Piedmont; 1860: Parma, Modena, Tuscany added to Piedmont; 1860: Garibaldi's forces advance through Kingdom of Two Sicilies and Naples; 1866: Venetia added to Italy; 1870: Papal States added to Italy
2. the Main River

Hands-On Chapter Project
Step 3

Presenting a Living Time Line

Step 3: Developing Dramatic Monologues Groups continue to assemble parts of the living time line they worked on in Sections 1 and 2.

Directions: Write the Big Idea on the board. Then ask students to look for information in the section about the following historical figures: Camillo di Cavour, Giuseppe Garibaldi, Otto von Bismarck, Queen Victoria, Napoleon III, and Czar Alexander II. Have group members each write a dramatic monologue from the point of view of one of these figures, revealing his or her attitudes toward nationalism and reform. Suggest that students share their monologues with each other before adding symbols of this era to their backdrop.

Summarizing: Have groups share their insights about the Big Idea, based on what they learned through their dramatic monologues. **OL**

(Chapter Project is continued in Section 4.)

D1 Differentiated Instruction

Advanced Learners Have students create a chart with the following column heads: King Victor Emmanuel II, Count Cavour, Giuseppe Garibaldi. The following topics should be included for rows: Goals and Ideals, Events and Dates, Impact on Unification. Ask students to use library or Internet sources to complete the chart. AL

C Critical Thinking

Predicting Consequences
Ask: What might have happened if Garibaldi had not chosen to turn his conquests over to Piedmont? *(Answers may include that Italian unification might not have occurred.)* OL

D2 Differentiated Instruction

English Language Learners
Explain to students that the terms strong, authoritarian, firm control, and militarism all imply that Prussia was a state that its neighbors may have feared. Tell students that authoritarian regimes are usually oppressive, as the people in control typically use their power in an unjust manner. ELL

Following that conflict, a peace settlement gave Nice and Savoy to the French. Cavour had promised Nice and Savoy to the French in return for making the alliance. Lombardy, which had been under Austrian control, was given to Piedmont. Austria retained control of Venetia. D1 Cavour's success caused nationalists in other Italian states (Parma, Modena, and Tuscany) to overthrow their governments and join their states to Piedmont.

Meanwhile, in southern Italy, a new leader of Italian unification had arisen. **Giuseppe Garibaldi,** a dedicated Italian patriot, raised an army of a thousand volunteers. They were called Red Shirts because of the color of their uniforms.

A branch of the Bourbon dynasty ruled the Two Sicilies (Sicily and Naples), and a revolt had broken out in Sicily against the king. Garibaldi's forces landed in Sicily and, by the end of July 1860, controlled most of the island. In August, Garibaldi and his forces crossed over to the mainland and began a victorious march up the Italian Peninsula. Naples and the entire Kingdom of the Two Sicilies fell in early September.

C Garibaldi chose to turn over his conquests to Piedmont. On March 17, 1861, a new state of Italy was proclaimed under King Victor Emmanuel II. The task of unification was not yet complete, however. Austria still held Venetia in the north; and Rome was under the control of the pope, supported by French troops.

The Italians gained control of Venetia as a result of a war between Austria and Prussia. In the Austro-Prussian War of 1866, the new Italian state allied with Prussia. Prussia won the war, and the Italians were given Venetia.

In 1870, during the Franco-Prussian War, French troops withdrew from Rome. Their withdrawal enabled the Italian army to annex Rome on September 20, 1870. Rome became the capital of the united Italian state.

German Unification

After the Frankfurt Assembly failed to achieve German unification in 1848 and 1849, Germans looked to Prussia for leadership in the cause of German unification. In the course of the nineteenth century, Prussia had become a strong and D2 prosperous state. Its government was authoritarian. The Prussian king had firm control over both the government and the army. Prussia was also known for its **militarism,** or reliance on military strength.

In the 1860s, King William I tried to enlarge the Prussian army. When the Prussian legislature refused to levy new taxes for the proposed military changes, William I appointed a new prime minister, Count **Otto von Bismarck.**

Bismarck has often been seen as the foremost nineteenth-century practitioner of realpolitik—the "politics of reality," or politics based on practical matters rather than on theory or ethics. Bismarck openly voiced his strong dislike of anyone who opposed him.

After his appointment, Bismarck ignored the legislative opposition to the military reforms. He argued instead that "Germany does not look to Prussia's liberalism but to her power." Bismarck proceeded to collect taxes and strengthen the army. From 1862 to 1866, Bismarck governed Prussia without approval of the parliament. In the meantime, he followed an active foreign policy, which soon led to war.

After defeating Denmark with Austrian help in 1864, Prussia gained control of the duchies of Schleswig and Holstein. Bismarck then created friction with the Austrians and forced them into a war on June 14, 1866. The Austrians, no match for the well-disciplined Prussian army, were defeated on July 3.

Prussia now organized the German states north of the Main River into the North German Confederation. The southern German states, which were largely Catholic, feared Protestant Prussia. However, they also feared France, their western neighbor. As a result, they agreed to sign military alliances with Prussia for protection against France.

Prussia now dominated all of northern Germany, and the growing power and military might of Prussia worried France. Bismarck was aware that France would never be content with a united German state to its east because of the potential threat to French security.

Additional Support

Teacher Tip

Collaborative Learning Encourage students to assign roles to people in their group. In some cases, it may be helpful to have the group divide into pairs to efficiently research their topic.

Activity: Collaborative Learning

Analyzing Information Have students find out more about the major wars in which Prussia was involved in the 1860s and 1870s with Denmark, Austria, and France. Have three groups of students research Germany's position in each war and three groups investigate the stance of the opposing countries in each conflict. Groups should locate information regarding each country's goals and motives, the strategies used by each, the major figures involved, and the significance of the outcome for each side. Then have pairs of rival groups work together to create a short oral presentation of the facts concerning each war. Encourage them to include visual aids. Have groups present their information chronologically. **Ask:** Why was Prussia able to achieve victory in each conflict? Have students discuss their insights. OL

In 1870, Prussia and France became embroiled in a dispute over the candidacy of a relative of the Prussian king for the throne of Spain. Taking advantage of the situation, **C** Bismarck goaded the French into declaring war on Prussia on July 19, 1870. This conflict was called the Franco-Prussian War.

The French proved to be no match for the better led and better organized Prussian forces. The southern German states honored their military alliances with Prussia and joined the war effort against the French. Prussian armies advanced into France. At Sedan, on September 2, 1870, an entire French army and the French ruler, Napoleon III, were captured.

Paris finally surrendered on January 28, 1871. An official peace treaty was signed in May. France had to pay 5 billion francs (about $1 billion) and give up the provinces of **Alsace** and **Lorraine** to the new German state. The loss of these territories left the French burning for revenge. **W**

Even before the war had ended, the southern German states had agreed to enter the North German Confederation. On January 18, 1871, Bismarck and 600 German princes, nobles, and generals filled the Hall of Mirrors in the palace of Versailles, 12 miles outside Paris. William I of Prussia was proclaimed **kaiser,** or emperor, of the Second German Empire (the first was the medieval Holy Roman Empire).

The Prussian monarchy and the Prussian army had achieved German unity. The authoritarian and militaristic values of Prussia were triumphant in the new German state. With its industrial resources and military might, the new state had become the strongest power on the European continent.

✓Reading Check **Explaining** How did the Crimean War destroy the Concert of Europe?

PEOPLE *in* HISTORY

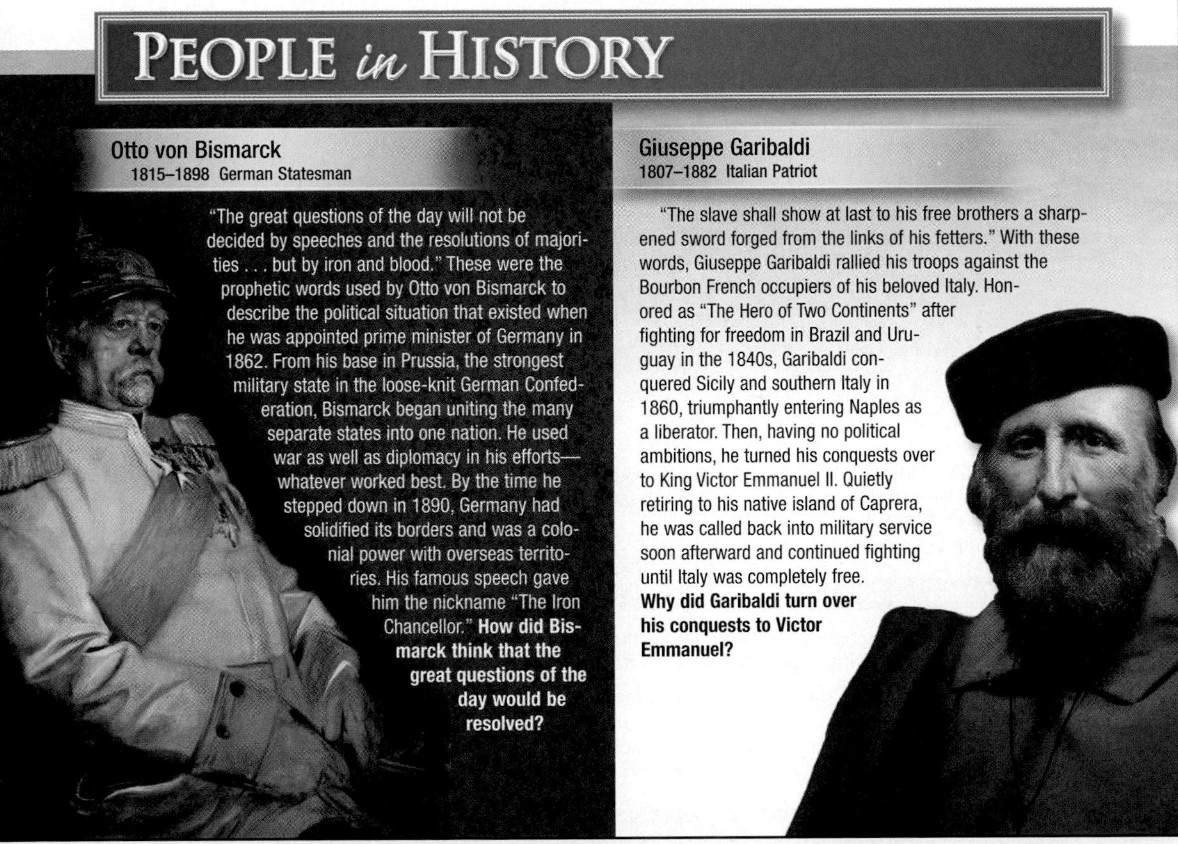

Otto von Bismarck
1815–1898 German Statesman

"The great questions of the day will not be decided by speeches and the resolutions of majorities . . . but by iron and blood." These were the prophetic words used by Otto von Bismarck to describe the political situation that existed when he was appointed prime minister of Germany in 1862. From his base in Prussia, the strongest military state in the loose-knit German Confederation, Bismarck began uniting the many separate states into one nation. He used war as well as diplomacy in his efforts—whatever worked best. By the time he stepped down in 1890, Germany had solidified its borders and was a colonial power with overseas territories. His famous speech gave him the nickname "The Iron Chancellor." **How did Bismarck think that the great questions of the day would be resolved?**

Giuseppe Garibaldi
1807–1882 Italian Patriot

"The slave shall show at last to his free brothers a sharpened sword forged from the links of his fetters." With these words, Giuseppe Garibaldi rallied his troops against the Bourbon French occupiers of his beloved Italy. Honored as "The Hero of Two Continents" after fighting for freedom in Brazil and Uruguay in the 1840s, Garibaldi conquered Sicily and southern Italy in 1860, triumphantly entering Naples as a liberator. Then, having no political ambitions, he turned his conquests over to King Victor Emmanuel II. Quietly retiring to his native island of Caprera, he was called back into military service soon afterward and continued fighting until Italy was completely free. **Why did Garibaldi turn over his conquests to Victor Emmanuel?**

C Critical Thinking

Analyzing Information Ask: Do you think it was fair for Bismarck to use the dispute over the throne of Spain as way to provoke France into a war? *(Students may mention that if Prussia knew it was going to war with France, it could have done so in a more direct manner.)* **AL**

W Writing Support

Expository Writing Have students write a paragraph discussing the idea that a country should only fight a war that it is sure it can win. **OL**

PEOPLE *in* HISTORY

Answers:
Garibaldi—Garibaldi had no political ambitions
Bismarck—by "iron and blood"; that is, by military power

✓Reading Check

Answer: Russia and Austria became enemies. Russia withdrew from European affairs for twenty years. Italy and Germany pursued the path of unification.

Additional Support

Extending the Content

Giuseppe Garibaldi Garibaldi's successful guerrilla tactics (learned in South America), his personal charm and integrity, and his refusal to surrender his cause made him a hero of freedom to people around the globe. President Lincoln even asked him to command the Union troops in the Civil War. **Ask:** Why was Garibaldi's popularity an asset in his struggle to unify Italy? *(His popularity drew support for his cause and forced the government to accept his efforts on their behalf.)*

Otto von Bismarck Thanks to Bismarck, Germany was the first country in the world to implement an old-age social security plan. Although this seems paradoxical in view of his hatred of socialism, in fact, it was part of his strategy for averting worker rebellions, helping the economy, and trying to weaken the Social Democrats. **Ask:** What political effect did Bismarck hope social security would have? *(He hoped that workers would switch their loyalty from the Social Democrats to the conservatives.)*

W Writing Support

Persuasive Writing Have students write a one-page essay arguing for or against the validity of this statement: "Economic prosperity in Great Britain was a good substitute for political reform." AL

S Skill Practice

Visual Literacy Have students conduct research to learn more about the Victorian Age. Ask students to find examples of Victorian architecture, clothing, art, literature, and music. Then have them choose one of their examples and write a one-page report discussing the Victorian characteristics evident in it. OL

DOCUMENT-BASED QUESTIONS

Answers:

1. She is afraid of the unknown consequences of the new reform law.
2. The ruling aristocrats viewed working men as the "ignorant multitude" and possibly feared the political decisions they might make.

Nationalism and Reform in Europe

MAIN IDEA While Italy and Germany were being unified, other states in Europe were also changing.

HISTORY & YOU Have you ever been to Paris or seen it depicted in the movies? Read about why the wide boulevards and public squares were originally built.

History ONLINE
Student Web Activity—
Visit glencoe.com and complete the activity about Queen Victoria.

After 1848, Great Britain became more liberal, while the governments of France, Austria, and Russia grew more authoritarian.

Great Britain

Great Britain managed to avoid the revolutionary upheavals of the first half of the nineteenth century. In 1815, aristocratic landowning classes, which dominated both houses of Parliament, governed Great Britain. In 1832, Parliament passed a bill that increased the number of male voters. The new voters were chiefly members of the industrial middle class. By giving the industrial middle class an interest in ruling, Britain avoided revolution in 1848. In the 1850s and 1860s, Parliament continued to make social and political reforms that helped the country to remain stable. However, despite reforms, Britain saw a rising Irish nationalist movement demanding increased Irish control over Irish internal affairs.

W Another reason for Britain's stability was its continuing economic growth. By 1850, industrialization had brought prosperity to the British middle class. After 1850, real wages of workers rose significantly, enabling the working classes to share the prosperity.

S **Queen Victoria**, whose reign from 1837 to 1901 was the longest in English history, well reflected the British feeling of national pride. Victoria's sense of duty and moral respectability reflected the attitudes of her age, later known as the Victorian Age.

POLITICAL CARTOONS — PRIMARY SOURCE

Political Reform in Great Britain

The Reform Act of 1832 gave voting rights to many men of the industrial middle class, yet it excluded six out of seven adult males. Pressure to extend voting rights down the social ladder led to the Reform Act of 1867. In his book *The English Constitution* (1867), Walter Bagehot described the possible effects of the Reform Act of 1867:

"... The Reform Act of 1867 has, I think, unmistakably completed the effect which the Act of 1832 began, but left unfinished. The middle class element has gained greatly by the second change, and the aristocratic element has lost greatly.... As a theoretical writer I can venture to say, what no elected member of Parliament, Conservative or Liberal, can venture to say, that I am exceedingly afraid of the ignorant multitude of the new constituencies...."

A LEAP IN THE DARK.

DOCUMENT-BASED QUESTIONS

This cartoon focuses on a comment by Lord Derby that the Reform Act of 1867 was "a leap in the dark."

1. **Explaining** Why is Britain shielding her eyes in the cartoon?
2. **Analyzing Primary Sources** Why were many members of the ruling class uneasy about the new law?

Differentiated Instruction

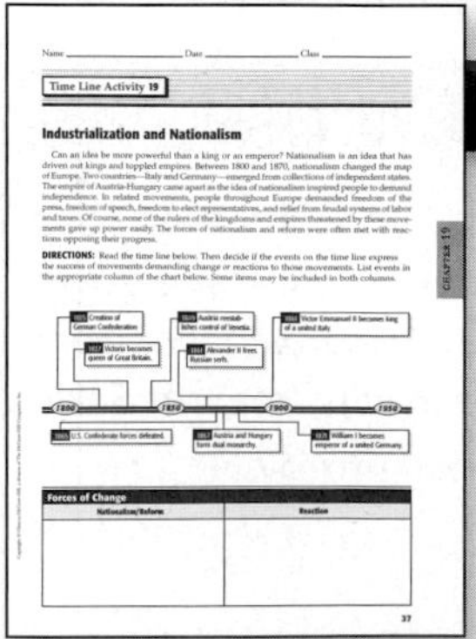
Time Line Activity, URB p. 37

Drawing Conclusions

Objective: Draw conclusions about the forces of change in nineteenth-century Europe.

Focus Have students read and discuss the Background paragraph.

Teach: Have students read the directions and complete the chart.

Assess: Ask students to explain the choices they have made for their charts.

Close: Discuss the ways in which the push toward nationalism and reform and the reactions against such movements changed Europe in the nineteenth century.

Differentiated Instruction Strategies

- **BL** Assign pairs of students a ten-year time span to analyze and have them explain the changes that the events represent.
- **AL** Ask students whether they think the forces of nationalism and reform produced positive or negative effects in Europe. Have them support their conclusions in a brief essay.
- **ELL** Have students write a paragraph that summarizes their conclusions and includes supporting details from the text.

France

In France, events after the revolution of 1848 moved toward the restoration of the monarchy. Four years after his election as president in 1848, Louis-Napoleon returned to the people to ask for the restoration of the empire. In this **plebiscite,** or popular vote, 97 percent responded with a yes vote. On December 2, 1852, Louis-Napoleon assumed the title of Napoleon III, Emperor of France. (The first Napoleon had named his son as his successor and had given him the title of Napoleon II. Napoleon II never ruled France, however.) The Second Empire had begun.

The government of Napoleon III was clearly authoritarian. As chief of state, Napoleon III controlled the armed forces, police, and civil service. Only he could introduce legislation and declare war. The Legislative Corps gave an appearance of **D** representative government, because the members of the group were elected by universal male suffrage for six-year terms. However, they could neither initiate legislation nor affect the budget.

Napoleon III completely controlled the government and limited civil liberties. Nevertheless, the first five years of his reign were a spectacular success. To distract the public from their loss of political **W** freedom, he focused on expanding the economy. Government subsidies helped foster the rapid construction of railroads, harbors, roads, and canals. Iron production tripled.

In the midst of this economic expansion, Napoleon III also carried out a vast rebuilding of the city of Paris. The old Paris of narrow streets and walls was replaced by a modern Paris of broad boulevards, spacious buildings, public squares, an underground sewage system, a new public water supply system, and gaslights. The new Paris served a military purpose as well. Broad streets made it more difficult for would-be rebels to throw up barricades and easier for troops to move rapidly through the city in the event of revolts.

In the 1860s, opposition to some of Napoleon's economic and governmental policies arose. In response, Napoleon III began to liberalize his **regime.** For example, he gave the legislature more power. In a plebiscite held in 1870, the French people gave Napoleon another victory. This triumph was short-lived, however. After the French were defeated in the Franco-Prussian War in 1870, the Second Empire fell.

The Austrian Empire

Nationalism, a major force in nineteenth-century Europe, presented special problems for the Austrian Empire. That was because the empire contained so many different ethnic groups, and many were campaigning for independence. Yet the Austrian Empire had managed to frustrate their desires.

After the Hapsburg rulers crushed the revolutions of 1848 and 1849, they restored centralized, autocratic government to the empire. Austria's defeat at the hands of the Prussians in 1866, however, forced the Austrians to make concessions to the fiercely nationalistic Hungarians.

The result of these concessions was the Compromise of 1867. This compromise created the dual monarchy of Austria-Hungary. **C** Each of these two components of the empire now had its own constitution, its own legislature, its own government bureaucracy, and its own capital (Vienna for Austria and **Budapest** for Hungary). Holding the two states together were a single monarch (Francis Joseph was both emperor of Austria and king of Hungary) and a common army, foreign policy, and system of finances.

In domestic affairs, then, the Hungarians had become an independent nation. The compromise, of course, did not satisfy the other nationalities that made up the multinational Austro-Hungarian Empire.

Russia

At the beginning of the nineteenth century, Russia was overwhelmingly rural, agricultural, and autocratic. The Russian czar was still regarded as a divine-right monarch with unlimited power. However, the Russian government faced challenges.

D Differentiated Instruction

Visual/Spatial Have students create a two-column chart to identify the positive and negative aspects of Napoleon III's regime. *(positive: expanded the economy; built railroads, harbors, roads, canals; increased iron production; rebuilt Paris; negative: controlled armed forces, police, civil service; had sole power to make laws and declare war)* **BL**

W Writing Support

Expository Writing Have students write a brief article for a British newspaper in which they analyze the success of the first five years of Napoleon III's rule. **AL**

C Critical Thinking

Identifying Central Issues Tell students that feelings of nationalism bind groups with common goals to form an independent nation. Nationalism can bring many smaller states together into one nation or it can divide a larger nation into smaller states. **Ask:** Which of these situations occurred in the Austrian Empire? *(A large empire was divided into two to form the dual monarchy of Austria-Hungary.)* **BL**

Additional Support

Activity: Interdisciplinary Connection

Language Arts Tell students that Victor Hugo, the writer, was a staunch republican who went into exile when Napoleon III came into power. His book *Les Miserables* was written at this time and reflects the conditions of the poor under Napoleon's authoritarian rule. Have students watch the movie or musical version of the novel, either as a class or in small groups. Discuss Hugo's portrayal of society, focusing particularly on his opinion of the public perception of the poor in contrast to the reality that he sees. Then ask students to work together to choose clips from the video that help them to understand more about the significant political and social issues of this period, taking into account Hugo's bias. **Ask:** What themes in this work transcend the particular setting and convey a universal message? As a class, discuss students' answers to this question. **AL**

R Reading Strategy

Inferring Ask students to discuss whether Alexander II would have freed the serfs if Russia had been victorious in the Crimean War. *(Answers may include that Alexander probably would not have issued an emancipation edict freeing the serfs because a victory in the war would have implied that reform was not necessary in Russia.)* **OL**

Answers:

1. nursing as a profession; nursing schools; principles of nursing and sanitary practices; American Red Cross
2. Answers may include that war produces massive casualties, prompting medical professionals to find new ways to cope with the overwhelming need.

✓Reading Check

Answer: their own constitution, legislature, government bureaucracy, and capital

See page R46 to read excerpts from Czar Alexander II's *Imperial Decree to Free the Serfs* in the **Primary Sources and Literature Library.**

It used soldiers, secret police, repression, and censorship to withstand the revolutionary fervor of the early 1800s.

In 1856, however, as described earlier, the Russians suffered a humiliating defeat in the Crimean War. Even staunch conservatives realized that Russia was falling hopelessly behind the western European powers. **Czar Alexander II** decided to make some reforms.

R Serfdom, the largest problem in czarist Russia, was not just a humanitarian issue, but a complicated one that affected the economic, social, and political future of Russia. On March 3, 1861, Alexander issued an **emancipation** edict, which freed the serfs. Peasants could now own property and marry as they chose. The government provided land for the peasants by buying it from the landlords.

The new land system, however, was not that helpful to the peasants. The landowners often kept the best lands for themselves. The Russian peasants soon found that they did not have enough good land to support themselves. Emancipation, then, led not to a free, landowning peasantry but to an unhappy, land-starved peasantry that largely followed old ways of farming.

Alexander II attempted other reforms as well, but he soon found that he could please no one. Reformers wanted more changes and a faster pace for change. Conservatives thought that the czar was trying to destroy the basic institutions of Russian society. A group of radicals assassinated Alexander II in 1881. His son, Alexander III, became the successor to the throne. Alexander III turned against reform and returned to the old methods of repression.

✓Reading Check **Examining** What concessions did the Hungarians gain from Austria in the Compromise of 1867?

Connecting to the United States

Nursing and Public Health

In 1854, Florence Nightingale served Britain as a nurse in Turkey during the Crimean War. Appalled by the filthy conditions, she worked to improve sanitary practices in military hospitals. After the war, Nightingale promoted nursing as a profession. During the American Civil War, the United States government sought her advice. In 1863, Nightingale founded the world's first nursing school. Her writings laid down principles of nursing and sanitary practices that continue to influence public health today.

Nightingale's work also influenced Clara Barton, a leader in the American nursing profession. From 1863 to 1873, Barton lived in Europe and helped establish hospitals during the Franco-Prussian War. For her service, Germany awarded her the Iron Cross. Barton went on to found the American Red Cross in 1883.

- **Nurses are trained, respected medical professionals.**
- **The Red Cross serves victims of conflicts and natural disasters.**
- **Standards for sanitation help safeguard public health.**

***The Lady with the Lamp*, c. 1880, depicts Florence Nightingale making her nightly rounds in a military hospital during the Crimean War.**

Connecting to Today

1. **Summarizing** What contributions did Florence Nightingale and Clara Barton make to public health?
2. **Making Inferences** Why did nursing and public health advances come about during wars?

Additional Support

Extending the Content

Nursing and Public Health Explain to students that Florence Nightingale and Clara Barton helped advance women's rights while making contributions to public health in the United States, as well as in other countries around the world. Allow students to study the illustration of Florence Nightingale in the military hospital. **Ask:** **What might hospitals have been like during the Civil War and other nineteenth-century wars if it weren't for the help of volunteers such as Nightingale and Barton?** *(Answers may include that hospitals probably would have been unable to handle all of the people injured in the wars, resulting in deplorable conditions and many more deaths.)*

Allow time to talk about health-related organizations such as the American Red Cross. Ask students what organizations, foundations, and charities they know of that help people who are in need. **OL**

Nationalism in the United States

MAIN IDEA Unified by the War of 1812, the United States later entered a bloody civil war that lasted from 1861 to 1865.

HISTORY & YOU Do you recall the upheaval of the American and French Revolutions? Read how the United States responded to national upheaval in the 1800s.

The United States Constitution committed the nation to liberalism and nationalism. Yet national unity did not come easily.

Two factions fought bitterly about the division of power in the new government. The Federalists favored a strong central government. The Republicans, fearing central power, wanted the federal government to be subordinate to the state governments. These divisions had ended with the War of 1812 against the British. This surge of national feeling served to cover up the nation's divisions. R

By the mid-nineteenth century, slavery had become a threat to American unity. Four million enslaved African Americans were in the South by 1860, compared with one million in 1800.

The South's economy was based on growing cotton on plantations, chiefly by slave labor. The cotton economy and plantation-based slavery were closely related. The South was determined to maintain them. At the same time, **abolitionism,** a movement to end slavery, arose in the North and challenged the Southern way of life.

As opinions over slavery grew more divided, compromise became less possible. Abraham Lincoln said in a speech in 1858 that "this government cannot endure permanently half slave and half free." When Lincoln was elected president in November 1860, war became certain.

On December 20, 1860, South Carolina voted to **secede,** or withdraw, from the United States. In February 1861, six more Southern states did the same. A rival nation—the Confederate States of America—was formed. In April, fighting erupted between North and South—the Union and the Confederacy.

The American Civil War (1861 to 1865) was an extraordinarily bloody struggle. Lincoln's Emancipation Proclamation declared most of the nation's enslaved people "forever free." The surrender of Confederate forces on April 9, 1865, meant that the United States would be "one nation, indivisible." National unity had prevailed.

✓Reading Check **Explaining** Why did the election of Abraham Lincoln make civil war certain in the United States?

SECTION 3 REVIEW

Vocabulary

1. **Explain** the significance of: unification, Piedmont, Giuseppe Garibaldi, militarism, Otto von Bismarck, Alsace, Lorraine, kaiser, Queen Victoria, plebiscite, regime, Budapest, Czar Alexander II, emancipation, abolitionism, secede.

Main Ideas

2. **Summarize** Bismarck's and Cavour's methods for achieving unification in Germany and Italy by using a Venn diagram like the one below.

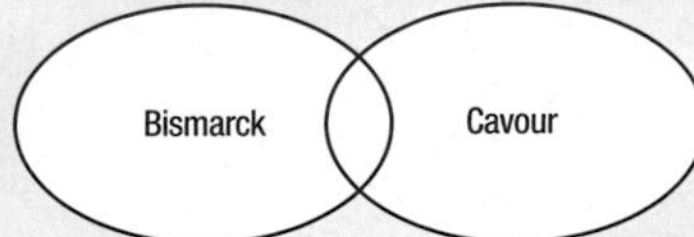

3. **Describe** the authoritarian aspects of Napoleon III's rule.
4. **Contrast** the views of the Federalists and Republicans in the United States.

Critical Thinking

5. **The BIG Idea** **Analyzing** Explain how liberalism affected events in Great Britain during the nineteenth century.
6. **Making Inferences** Why did Alexander III of Russia turn against the reforms of his father?
7. **Analyzing Visuals** Examine the political cartoon on page 634. How has the artist portrayed the relationship of the prime minister, Britain, and Parliament?

Writing About History

8. **Expository Writing** Write an essay comparing Bismarck and Napoleon III. Discuss events that occurred while they were in power and the impact of their leadership.

History ONLINE
For help with the concepts in this section of *Glencoe World History*, go to glencoe.com and click Study Central™.

637

R Reading Strategy

Summarizing Ask: What issues divided Americans in the 1800s? *(slavery and the division of power between the federal government and state governments)* OL

✓Reading Check

Answer: Lincoln did not believe that the federal government could be permanently half slave and half free.

Assess

History ONLINE

Study Central provides summaries, interactive games, and online graphic organizers to help students review content.

Close

Summarizing Ask: Why do you think that nationalism led to revolution in some cases and reforms in others? *(Answer may include that in some places, a national group lay within a repressive state or empire.)*

Answers

1. Definitions for the vocabulary words are found in the section and the Glossary.
2. **Bismarck:** relied on military, ignored legislative opposition; **Cavour:** relied on others (France, Garibaldi, Prussia) for help; **Bismarck and Cavour:** planned the unification of their countries, used military means to accomplish unification, provoked Austria into war to reach objectives
3. Napoleon III controlled the armed forces, police, and civil service. Only he could introduce legislation and declare war. He also limited civil liberties.
4. **Federalists:** wanted strong central government; **Republicans:** wanted federal government to be subordinate to state governments
5. Vote was extended to more members of the industrial middle class, helping Britain avoid revolution and bring about reform.
6. Answers may include that he felt the reforms led to his father's assassination. He wanted to restore stability.
7. Parliament is wary of the direction in which the prime minister is leading Britain.
8. Essays should be consistent with the material presented in this section.

Focus

Bellringer

Daily Focus Transparency 19.4

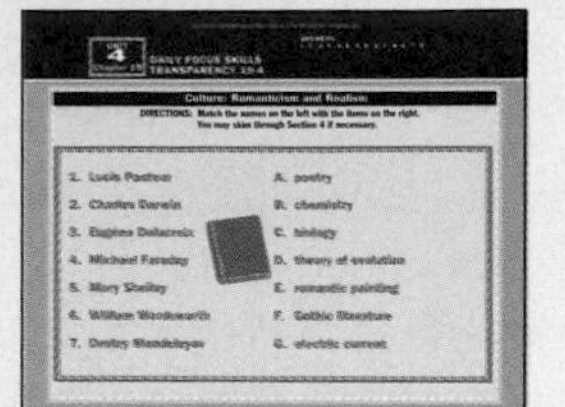

GUIDE TO READING

Answers to Graphic:

Romanticism	Realism
Scott's *Ivanhoe*	Flaubert's *Madame Bovary*
Shelley's *Frankenstein*	Dickens's *Oliver Twist* and *David Copperfield*
Poe's short stories	
Wordsworth's poetry	

Section Spotlight Video

To generate student interest and provide a springboard for class discussion, access the Chapter 19, Section 4 video at glencoe.com or on the video DVD.

SECTION 4

Romanticism and Realism

GUIDE TO READING

The BIG Idea

New Technologies Artistic movements are influenced by the society around them. Romanticism was in part a reaction to the Industrial Revolution, while advances in science contributed to a new movement called realism.

Content Vocabulary
- romanticism *(p. 638)*
- secularization *(p. 641)*
- organic evolution *(p. 642)*
- natural selection *(p. 642)*
- realism *(p. 643)*

Academic Vocabulary
- individuality *(p. 638)*
- approach *(p. 641)*

People and Places
- Ludwig van Beethoven *(p. 639)*
- Louis Pasteur *(p. 641)*
- Charles Darwin *(p. 641)*
- Charles Dickens *(p. 643)*

Reading Strategy

Summarizing Information

As you read, use a table like the one below to list popular literature from the romantic and realist movements.

Romanticism	Realism

Romanticism was a reaction to the Enlightenment and to the Industrial Revolution. Romantics believed that emotions, rather than reason, should guide them. By the mid-nineteenth century, romanticism had given way to a new movement called realism. Realists focused on the everyday world and ordinary people.

Romanticism

MAIN IDEA In the arts, romanticism stressed individualism and emotion instead of the Enlightenment's focus on universalism and reason.

HISTORY & YOU Do you and your friends dress differently from your parents? Perhaps you are expressing your individuality, as the romantics did in their time. Read to learn what romantics of the eighteenth century valued.

At the end of the eighteenth century, a new intellectual movement, known as **romanticism,** emerged as a reaction to the ideas of the Enlightenment. The Enlightenment had stressed reason as the chief means for discovering truth. The romantics emphasized feelings, emotion, and imagination as sources of knowing.

The romantics believed that emotion and sentiment were only understandable to the person experiencing them. In their novels, romantic writers created figures who were often misunderstood and rejected by society but who continued to believe in their own worth through their inner feelings.

Romantics also valued individualism, the belief in the uniqueness of each person. Many romantics rebelled against middle-class conventions. Male romantics grew long hair and beards and both men and women wore outrageous clothes to express their **individuality.**

Many romantics had a passionate interest in the past ages, especially the medieval era. They felt it had a mystery and interest in the soul that their own industrial age did not. Romantic architects revived medieval styles and built castles, cathedrals, city halls, parliamentary buildings, and even railway stations in a style called neo-Gothic. The British Houses of Parliament in London are a prime example of this architectural style.

Romanticism in Art and Music

Romantic artists shared at least two features. First, to them, all art was a reflection of the artist's inner feelings. A painting should mirror the artist's vision of the world and be the instrument of the artist's own imagination. Second, romantic artists abandoned classical reason for warmth and emotion.

Resource Manager

R Reading Strategies	C Critical Thinking	D Differentiated Instruction	W Writing Support	S Skill Practice
Teacher Edition • Organizing, p. 643 **Additional Resources** • Cont. Vocab. Act., URB p. 23 • Guid. Read. Act., URB p. 51 • Read. Ess. & Note-Taking Guide, p. 214	**Teacher Edition** • Analyzing Pri. Sources, p. 641 • Det. Cause/Effect, p. 641 **Additional Resources** • People in World Hist. Act., URB p. 39 • Section Quiz, p. 236 • Chapter Test, p. 237	**Teacher Edition** • ELL, p. 640 • Special Ed., p. 642 **Additional Resources** • Econ. & Hist. Act., URB p. 5 • Hist. Sim. Act., URB p. 35	**Teacher Edition** • Expository Writing, p. 639, 640 **Additional Resources** • World Art & Music Act., URB p. 43	**Teacher Edition** • Visual Literacy, p. 642 **Additional Resources** • Mapping Hist. Act., URB p. 31

PRIMARY SOURCE HISTORY & ARTS

Romanticism: The Prisoner of Chillon

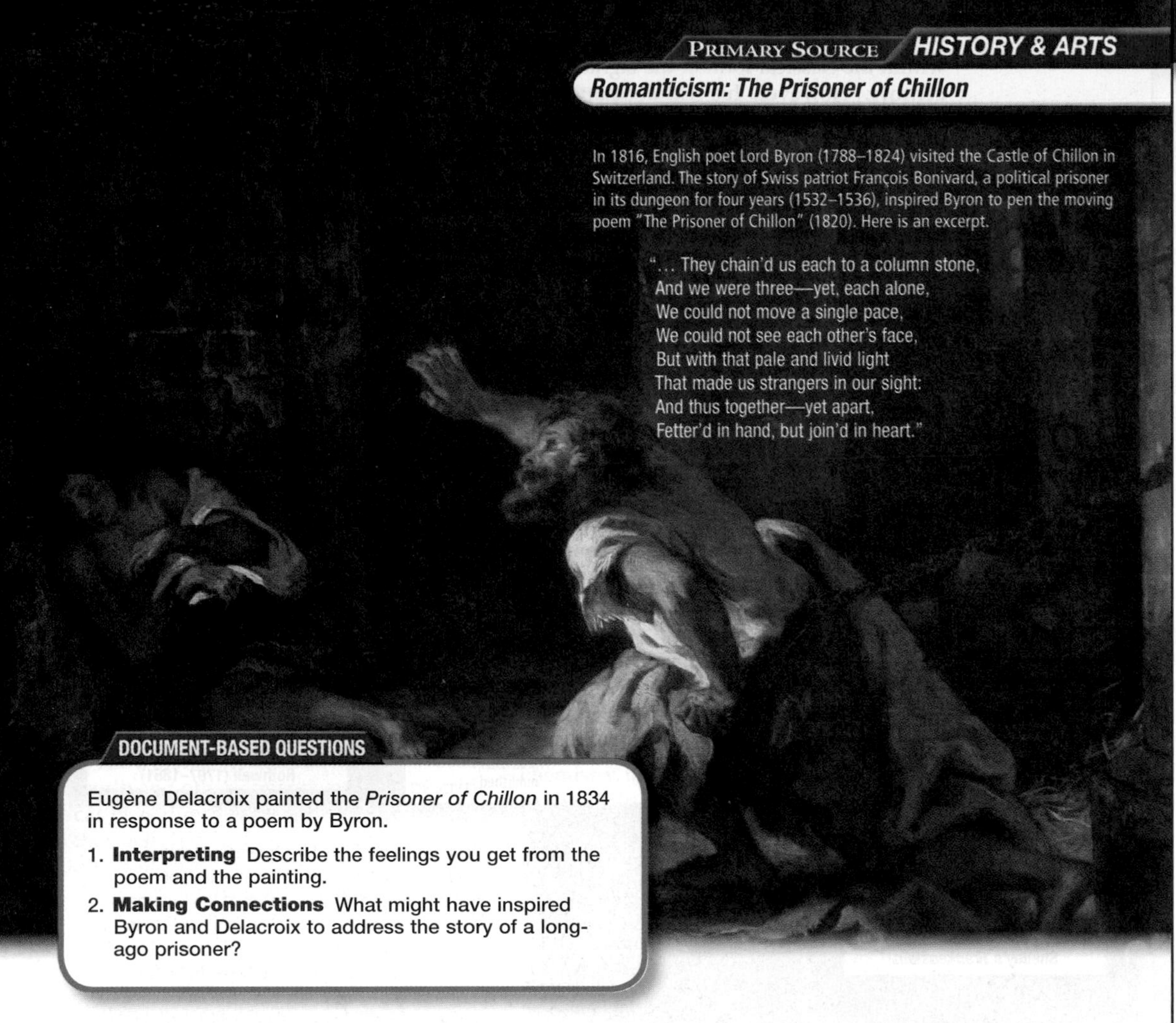

In 1816, English poet Lord Byron (1788–1824) visited the Castle of Chillon in Switzerland. The story of Swiss patriot François Bonivard, a political prisoner in its dungeon for four years (1532–1536), inspired Byron to pen the moving poem "The Prisoner of Chillon" (1820). Here is an excerpt.

"... They chain'd us each to a column stone,
And we were three—yet, each alone,
We could not move a single pace,
We could not see each other's face,
But with that pale and livid light
That made us strangers in our sight:
And thus together—yet apart,
Fetter'd in hand, but join'd in heart."

DOCUMENT-BASED QUESTIONS

Eugène Delacroix painted the *Prisoner of Chillon* in 1834 in response to a poem by Byron.

1. **Interpreting** Describe the feelings you get from the poem and the painting.
2. **Making Connections** What might have inspired Byron and Delacroix to address the story of a long-ago prisoner?

Eugène Delacroix (DEH•luh•KWAH) was one of the most famous romantic painters from France. His paintings showed two chief characteristics: a fascination with the exotic and a passion for color. His works reflect his belief that "a painting should be a feast to the eye."

Many of Delacroix's paintings depicted scenes of uprisings against tyrants. His most influential work is perhaps *Liberty Leading the People*. In this painting, a woman holding a red banner is the symbol of liberty. She is leading revolutionaries forward during battle. After his travels to Spain and North Africa, Delacroix painted the animals he had seen there. *The Lion Hunt* is a good example of his later subjects.

W In music, too, romantic trends dominated the first half of the nineteenth century. One of the most famous composers of this era was **Ludwig van Beethoven.** Some have called him a bridge between classical and romantic music. Others argue that he was such a rare genius he cannot be easily classified.

Teach

W Writing Support

Expository Writing Have students use library or Internet sources to research the life of Delacroix or one of the other artists of the period and write a one-page biography. Tell students to include information on education, training, major works, and public acceptance of the artist. **OL**

DOCUMENT-BASED QUESTIONS

Answers:

1. Answers may include feelings of despair, desperation, confusion, sorrow, and loneliness. Others might focus on the last line of the poem and offer emotions of camaraderie and hope.
2. Romantics favored emotional themes as well as subjects from a different time and place.

Hands-On Chapter Project
Step 4

Presenting a Living Time Line

Step 4: Implementing a Soundtrack Groups of students complete the time lines that they worked on in Sections 1, 2, and 3.

Directions: Write the Big Idea on the board. Have students add quotations from the writers named in this section as well as representations of the scientific and artistic accomplishments to their backdrops. Then ask them to locate music by Beethoven or another composer from the period and create a soundtrack for their dramatic presentations. Discuss what students learned about the Big Idea as they completed their backdrops and soundtracks.

Putting It Together: Have groups present their living time lines. They should play their soundtracks as they briefly explain the events, people, and ideas represented on their backdrops and then perform their skits and monologues. **OL**

(Chapter Project is continued on the Visual Summary page.)

D Differentiated Instruction

Special Education Help students define what "survival of the fittest" means. Then ask them to tie it in to Darwin's beliefs. **BL**

S Skill Practice

Visual Literacy **Ask:** How would this painting be different if it were done by a romantic? *(Answers should reflect an understanding of romantic art.)* **AL**

DOCUMENT-BASED QUESTIONS

Answers:

1. Instead of heroic characters in exotic settings, he painted ordinary people of his time engaged in everyday activity.
2. Answers may include objectivity and accuracy.

✓Reading Check

Answer: It created a picture of human beings as part of the natural world, not above it. Many people felt that it turned life into a mere struggle for survival where moral values had no place.

HISTORY & ARTS PRIMARY SOURCE

Realism in the Visual Arts

Realist artists depicted the everyday life of ordinary people with photographic realism.

DOCUMENT-BASED QUESTIONS

French realist Gustave Courbet preferred to portray the common people, as here in *The Stonebreakers* (1849) where workers are repairing a road.

1. **Contrasting** In what ways does this painting illustrate Courbet's rejection of romanticism?
2. **Interpreting** What do you think was Courbet's goal in portraying a common labor scene?

The basic idea of this book was that each species, or kind, of plant and animal had evolved over a long period of time from earlier, simpler forms of life. Darwin called this principle **organic evolution.**

How did this natural process work? According to Darwin, in every species, "many more individuals of each species are born than can possibly survive." This results in a "struggle for existence." Darwin believed that some organisms are born with variations, or differences, that make them more adaptable to their environment than other organisms, a process that Darwin called **natural selection.**

Those organisms that are naturally selected for survival ("survival of the fittest") reproduce and thrive. The unfit do not survive. The fit that survive pass on the variations that enabled them to survive until, according to Darwin, a new, separate species emerges. In *The Descent of Man*, published in 1871, Darwin argued that human beings had animal origins and were not an exception to the rule governing other species.

Darwin's ideas raised a storm of controversy. Some people did not take his ideas seriously. Other people objected that Darwin's theory made human beings ordinary products of nature rather than unique creations of God. Others were bothered by his idea of life as a mere struggle for survival. "Is there a place in the Darwinian world for moral values?" they asked. Some believers felt Darwin had not acknowledged God's role in creation. Some detractors scorned Darwin and depicted him unfavorably in cartoons. Gradually, however, many scientists and other intellectuals came to accept Darwin's theory. His theory changed thinking in countless fields from biology to anthropology.

✓Reading Check **Describing** How did the theory of natural selection influence the way people saw the world?

Differentiated Instruction

Mapping History Activity 19 — The Voyage of the *Beagle*

Mapping History Activity, URB p. 31

Analyzing Information

Objective: Learn about Darwin's voyage on the *Beagle*.

Focus: Have students read the introductory paragraphs.

Teach: Work with students to answer the questions on the page.

Assess: Review students' answers to determine if they understand the voyage of the *Beagle*.

Close: Evaluate the importance of each stop to Darwin's theories.

Differentiated Instruction Strategies

- **BL** Have pairs use a flow chart to outline Darwin's findings on the Galápagos Islands.
- **AL** Have students research what Darwin learned at each stop and record significant observations in a series of journal entries.
- **ELL** With students, place callouts on the map, explaining one idea associated with each stop.

Realism

MAIN IDEA The rise of science encouraged writers and artists to create realistic works that portrayed even the poor and degraded in society.

HISTORY & YOU Do you enjoy lifelike video games? What details make these games so realistic? Learn about the details that created realism in nineteenth-century art and literature.

The belief that the world should be viewed realistically, a view frequently expressed after 1850, was closely related to the scientific outlook. In politics, Bismarck had practiced the "politics of reality." In the literary and visual arts, **realism** became a movement as well.

Realism in Literature

The literary realists of the mid-nineteenth century rejected romanticism. They wanted to write about ordinary characters from life, not romantic heroes in exotic settings. They also tried to avoid emotional language by using precise description. They preferred novels to poems.

Many literary realists combined their interest in everyday life with an examination of social issues. These artists expressed their social views through their characters.

The French author Gustave Flaubert, who was a leading novelist of the 1850s and 1860s, perfected the realist novel. His work *Madame Bovary* presents a critical description of small-town life in France.

In Great Britain, **Charles Dickens** became a huge success with novels that showed the realities of life for the poor in the early Industrial Age. Novels such as *Oliver Twist* and *David Copperfield* created a vivid picture of the brutal life of London's poor, as well as of their humor and humanity. In fact, his characters were so sympathetic that they helped inspire social reform.

Realism in Art

In art, too, realism became dominant after 1850. Realist artists sought to show the everyday life of ordinary people and the world of nature with photographic realism.

The French painter Gustave Courbet was the most famous artist of the realist school. He loved to portray scenes from everyday life. His subjects were factory workers and peasants. "I have never seen either angels or goddesses, so I am not interested in painting them," Courbet once commented. There were those who objected to Courbet's "cult of ugliness" and who found such scenes of human misery scandalous. To Courbet, however, no subject was too ordinary, too harsh, or too ugly.

✓Reading Check **Evaluating** What factors helped to produce the movement known as realism?

SECTION 4 REVIEW

Vocabulary

1. **Explain** the significance of: romanticism, individuality, Ludwig van Beethoven, approach, Louis Pasteur, secularization, Charles Darwin, organic evolution, natural selection, realism, Charles Dickens.

Main Ideas

2. **List** the values of the romantics.
3. **Summarize** the discoveries that scientists made in the mid-nineteenth century by using a chart like the one below.

Scientist	Discovery
Pasteur	
Mendeleyev	
Faraday	
Darwin	

4. **Explain** why Charles Dickens's novels helped inspire social reform.

Critical Thinking

5. **The BIG Idea** **Comparing and Contrasting** How did romanticism compare to the ideas of the Enlightenment?
6. **Assessing** How did scientific developments affect the cultural movements of the nineteenth century?
7. **Analyzing Visuals** Compare Delacroix's *Prisoner of Chillon* on page 639 with *The Stonebreakers* on page 642. From the paintings, how would you explain why we say that Delacroix is a romantic, and Courbet is a realist?

Writing About History

8. **Expository Writing** Read poetry by two different poets of romanticism. Write a paper describing the elements of romanticism found in the poems. Be sure to include quotations.

History ONLINE
For help with the concepts in this section of *Glencoe World History*, go to glencoe.com and click Study Central™.

R Reading Strategy

Organizing Have students create a chart that contrasts literary realists and romantics. *(realists: wrote about ordinary characters; used precise descriptions; preferred novels; romantics: wrote about heroes in exotic settings; used emotional language; preferred poems)* **BL**

✓Reading Check

Answer: scientific outlook, the desire to write about ordinary characters from actual life

Assess

History ONLINE

Study Central provides summaries, interactive games, and online graphic organizers to help students review content.

Close

Summarizing **Ask:** Which artistic movement stressed individualism and emotion? Which movement stressed reason and universalism? *(romanticism; realism)*

Answers

1. Definitions for the vocabulary words are found in the section and the Glossary.
2. emphasis on feelings, imagination, individualism, rebellion, interest in past, exotic
3. **Pasteur:** germ theory of disease; **Mendeleyev:** classified material elements on basis of their atomic weights; **Faraday:** primitive generator laid foundation for use of electricity; **Darwin:** organic evolution and natural selection
4. portrayed the brutal life of London's poor
5. **Romanticism:** emphasized feelings and imagination; **Enlightenment:** used reason and logic
6. linked with realism, the belief that the world should be viewed realistically, replaced emotional language of romanticism
7. Answers may include that Delacroix dramatically portrayed a hero and Courbet objectively depicted commoners.
8. Papers should demonstrate an understanding of the poems and romanticism.

Focus

Introducing Social History
Explain that in a trade show vendors set up displays and give talks about their special products. **Ask:** Why might people attend trade shows? *(to learn about the latest innovations in a particular field)* Then have volunteers take turns reading the text to find out more about the Great Exhibition of 1851.

Teach

C Critical Thinking

Making Inferences Ask: Why would the British want to host the Great Exhibition? *(They were leaders in the Industrial Revolution and wanted to show their manufacturing achievements.)* OL

W Writing Support

Descriptive Writing Have students find out more about the displays and exhibitors at the Great Exhibition. Ask them to write a letter from the perspective of a visitor to the event, describing what they saw, heard, and experienced. OL

Additional Support

A Showcase for Industry and Progress

C On May 1, 1851, the Great Exhibition opened in London's Hyde Park. The first international exhibition of its kind, the Great Exhibition displayed thousands of industrial innovations and manufactured goods from around the globe. This event displayed Great Britain's influential position as the "workshop of the world." Perhaps the crowning achievement of the Great Exhibition was the exhibition hall itself—the world's first prefabricated building, constructed of iron and glass and called "the Crystal Palace."

W

Over 6 million people of all classes, many from European cities, visited the Great Exhibition during the 141 days that it was open.

Thirty-two countries from Europe, America, Africa, and Asia took part in the exhibition. Fourteen thousand exhibitors displayed their products.

Stop the Presses

Much was written about the Great Exhibition and the Crystal Palace, including an opening-day ode by William Makepeace Thackeray that expressed the general public's sense of awe at the sight of the exhibition hall and the products on display "from Mississippi and from Nile—from Baltic, Ganges, Bosporus." Not everyone was impressed, however. Of the Crystal Palace, the artist Leigh Hunt wrote, "It was neither crystal nor a palace." The art critic John Ruskin said it looked like "a huge greenhouse."

Background

The Great Exhibition Initially, the British government was not enthusiastic about the idea of an exhibition, fearing the expenditure. Prince Albert, however, argued in support of the concept, believing that it would finance itself and would be "a new starting point from which all nations would be able to direct their further exertions." By opening day, worries about money had been alleviated, with over £100,000 brought in before ticket sales had even begun. Visitors to the Crystal Palace were awestruck by the huge fountain in the middle, the tropical plants and trees, sculptures, and finally the exhibits themselves. The stability of the palace had been in question before the event, with some experts worrying that the vibrations of a large crowd might cause the construction to slip and collapse. To ensure its safety, 300 workmen walked back and forth and jumped up and down before an army corps of engineers was brought in to march in synchronization. The building lived up to the challenge, and the exhibition opened as planned.

The large tree provided a visible symbol of how the Industrial Revolution had supposedly achieved domination over nature.

Two thousand laborers built the Crystal Palace in nine months—a record in 1851.

New products exhibited included false teeth, rubber goods, hydraulic presses, automated spinning machines, steam engines and pumps, and an early submarine.

Mass-Produced Goods

Because of Britain's access to raw materials from its colonies and because of the inventions and improvements in machinery during the Industrial Revolution, the thousands of products on display at the Great Exhibition had been mass-produced and were affordable to the average consumer. At the opening ceremony, Prince Albert of Great Britain stressed this point: "The products of all quarters of the globe are placed here at our disposal. And we have only to choose that which is best and cheapest for our purposes. . . ." C

Analyzing Visuals

1. **Comparing** If an international exhibition like this were held today, what kinds of innovative products might be on display? What types of industries would be represented?
2. **Inferring** Which country today might be called "the workshop of the world"? Explain why.

645

C Critical Thinking

Drawing Conclusions Ask: Why did Prince Albert stress the affordability of the goods? *(He wanted to make the point that the products on display were useful to the average citizen. His comments were meant to connect advances in manufacturing and industry directly to an improvement in the quality of people's lives.)* OL

Assess/Close

Identifying Have students use a web diagram to identify reasons why the Crystal Palace was an appropriate setting for the Great Exhibition. OL

Analyzing Visuals

Answers:

1. Answers may include that an exhibition today would definitely include electronic and computer products, highlighting advances in communications and data storage and dissemination.
2. Answers may include Japan, China, or Korea, because these countries pioneer many of the advances in technology and produce a vast volume of the world's manufactured goods.

Activity: Technology Connection

Exhibiting a Technology Product Ask: What was the purpose of the Great Exhibition? *(to celebrate industry and progress and generate enthusiasm for further advances)* Have students work in pairs to choose a technology product that they would like to show at an exhibition. They might invent one or find an existing tool, instrument, or item that exemplifies the most advanced and current technology. Pairs should develop a demonstration and create some literature or a poster highlighting important features of their product. Remind students that they should take their audience into account as they create their demonstration. Images and text need to clearly explain the product, describe how it is used, and help the audience understand why it exemplifies a useful innovation. Have pairs set up their exhibit in the classroom and allow groups of students to view each other's demonstrations. OL

Summarizing Point out that the Visual Summary highlights the main ideas of Chapter 19. Draw students' attention to the three main heads for each bulleted list. **Ask:** What were the three main topics of Chapter 19? *(Industrialization Transformed Society; Ideologies Arising from the Industrial Revolution; Cultural Movements Arising from the Industrial Revolution)* Have students use the three main heads and the information in each bulleted list to write thesis statements for an essay on each main topic. **BL**

Visual Literacy Tell students to spend a few minutes studying each painting and brainstorming words and phrases to describe it. Then have them write three paragraphs explaining how each painting relates to the main ideas of Chapter 19. **OL**

CHAPTER 19 Visual Summary

You can study anywhere, anytime by downloading quizzes and flash cards to your PDA from glencoe.com.

INDUSTRIALIZATION Transformed Society

- The Industrial Revolution began in Great Britain and spread throughout Europe and the United States.
- New technologies improved the production and transportation of goods.
- Workers migrated to cities as economies shifted from being farm-based to factory-based.
- As cities grew, an industrial middle class and an industrial working class emerged.

NEW TECHNOLOGIES DROVE INDUSTRIALIZATION

The new process of "puddling" helped factories make high-quality iron to build locomotives and machinery.

THE GERMAN STATES UNIFIED

A ceremony at the palace of Versailles installed William I as kaiser of the Second German Empire.

IDEOLOGIES Arising From the Industrial Revolution

- Harsh conditions in factories made socialism attractive.
- Liberalism and nationalism threatened conservative governments, leading to the revolutions of 1830 and 1848.
- Liberal reforms helped Great Britain to avoid revolution, while France, Austria, and Russia grew more authoritarian.
- The Crimean War broke down the Concert of Europe, enabling nationalists to unify Germany and Italy.

CULTURAL MOVEMENTS Arising From the Industrial Revolution

- Romanticism emphasized emotions and individuality in response to the Enlightenment's emphasis on reason.
- The Industrial Revolution heightened interest in scientific research.
- Growing confidence in science undermined religious faith, leading to increased secularization.
- Interest in science led to the realism movement, featuring ordinary people instead of romantic heroes.

REALISM IN LITERATURE: THE NOVEL *MADAME BOVARY*

In *Madame Bovary*, the tale ends in tragedy when Emma Bovary escapes what she views as her ordinary, unhappy life.

Hands-On Chapter Project

Step 5: Wrap Up

Presenting a Living Time Line

Step 5: Categorizing Events Students will synthesize what they have learned in Steps 1–4.

Directions: Write the Essential Question on the board. Then display a time line that extends from 1770 to 1870. The time line might have several parallel sections under each other to organize social, economic, political, artistic, and scientific events, or it might be all-inclusive. Have students review their backdrops and the events that they dramatized and volunteer the significant events of this age. Record them on the time line. Then have students use the details they have identified for the time line and what they have learned in the first four steps of their project to answer the Essential Question in their journals. Discuss their responses, drawing attention to which events might fall under the "revolution" label, which might be considered "reform," and which might be classified as "reaction." **OL**

STANDARDIZED TEST PRACTICE

TEST-TAKING 

When a question asks for an answer that is supported by information presented in a table, find the answer choice that is *proven true* by the information in the table.

Reviewing Vocabulary

Directions: Choose the word or words that best complete the sentence.

1. Another word for *popular vote* is ________.

A emancipation
B plebiscite
C secession
D kaiser

2. ________ evolution means that plant and animal species have evolved over a long period of time from earlier, simpler forms.

A Natural
B Sequential
C Environmental
D Organic

3. ________ is based on tradition and social stability.

A Liberalism
B Conservatism
C Socialism
D Abolitionism

4. Under ________, the public—generally the government—owns the means of production.

A romanticism
B liberalism
C socialism
D conservatism

Reviewing Main Ideas

Directions: Choose the best answers to the following questions.

Section 1 *(pp. 614–621)*

5. Which engineer improved the steam engine so it could drive machinery?

A James Watt
B Robert Fulton
C Henry Cort
D Robert Owen

6. From where did labor for the factories in the United States mostly come?

A Factories from the Northeast
B Native American population
C Southern cities
D Farm population

7. In what did industrialization trigger a dramatic increase?

A Diseases
B City populations
C Agricultural jobs
D Death rates

Section 2 *(pp. 624–629)*

8. Who was the most influential leader at the Congress of Vienna meeting in 1814?

A Charles X
B Louis-Napoleon
C Klemens von Metternich
D Ludwig van Beethoven

Need Extra Help?

If You Missed Questions . . .	1	2	3	4	5	6	7	8
Go to Page . . .	635	642	624	621	616	619	619	624

GO ON

Answers and Analyses

Reviewing Vocabulary

1. B *Emancipation* means "freedom," *secession* means "the act of withdrawing or leaving," and a kaiser is an emperor, leaving the only choice *plebiscite*, which does mean "popular vote."

2. D Tell students to look for clues within the sentence itself. Plant and animals species are organisms. Therefore, the word *organic* best fits the context of the sentence.

3. B Point out that students can narrow their choices before they decide on their answer. *Abolitionism* refers to the movement to abolish or get rid of slavery. *Socialism* refers to an economic system in which utilities and factories are publicly owned. Although liberalism and conservatism are both political philosophies, the word *liberal* suggests freedom from the past or restraints of tradition.

4. C Tell students to use what they learn from previous questions to help them answer this question.

Reviewing Main Ideas

5. A Robert Fulton built the first paddle wheel steamboat. Henry Cort developed the process of puddling, a way to produce higher quality iron. Robert Owen was a utopian socialist who built model factory towns.

6. D Remind students to choose the answer that makes sense in the context of the sentence. Labor for factories would not come from laborers already working in factories, eliminating A. Historically, Native Americans would be unlikely to work in factories. The South was mostly farmland with few large cities to provide labor. Therefore, the only sensible choice is the farm population.

7. B Remind students that workers moved from farmlands to towns or cities, where the factories were located, swelling the populations of those areas.

8. C Metternich, the Austrian foreign minister, took the lead at the Congress of Vienna. Charles X was the ruler of France, later deposed. Louis-Napoleon was elected as president of France in 1848.

TEST-TAKING 

For Question 8: Remind students to eliminate those answers that they know are incorrect. For example, Beethoven was a composer.

CHAPTER 20 Planning Guide

Key to Ability Levels

- **BL** Below Level
- **OL** On Level
- **AL** Above Level
- **ELL** English Language Learners

Key to Teaching Resources

- Print Material
- CD-ROM
- DVD
- Transparency

BL	OL	AL	ELL	Resources	Chapter Opener	Section 1	Section 2	Section 3	Section 4	Chapter Assess
				FOCUS						
BL	OL	AL	ELL	**Daily Focus Skills Transparencies**		20-1	20-2	20-3	20-4	
				TEACH						
BL	OL	AL	ELL	**Charting and Graphing Activity, URB**		✓				
	OL	AL		**Economics and History Activity, URB**		✓				
		AL		**World Literature Reading, URB**			✓			
BL	OL		ELL	**Reading Skills Activity, URB**			p. 55			
	OL	AL		**Historical Analysis Skills Activity, URB**					p. 56	
BL	OL	AL	ELL	**Differentiated Instruction Activity, URB**					p. 57	
	OL		ELL	**English Learner Activity, URB**		p. 59				
BL	OL	AL	ELL	**Content Vocabulary Activity, URB***					p. 61	
BL	OL	AL	ELL	**Academic Vocabulary Activity, URB**					p. 63	
BL	OL	AL	ELL	**Skills Reinforcement Activity, URB**			p. 65			
	OL	AL		**Critical Thinking Skills Activity, URB**			p. 66			
	OL	AL		**History and Geography Activity, URB**				p. 67		
	OL	AL	ELL	**Mapping History Activity, URB**				p. 69		
BL	OL	AL		**Historical Significance Activity, URB**					p. 70	
BL	OL	AL	ELL	**Cooperative Learning Activity, URB**			p. 71			
	OL	AL	ELL	**History Simulation Activity, URB**		p. 73				
BL	OL	AL	ELL	**Time Line Activity, URB**					p. 75	
	OL	AL		**Linking Past and Present Activity, URB**					p. 76	
BL	OL	AL		**People in World History Activity, URB**		p. 78		p. 77		
BL	OL	AL	ELL	**Primary Source Reading, URB**			p. 79			
	OL	AL		**Enrichment Activity, URB**			p. 84			
BL	OL	AL	ELL	**World Art and Music Activity, URB**					p. 81	
BL	OL		ELL	**Guided Reading Activities, URB***		p. 86	p. 87	p. 88	p. 89	
BL	OL		ELL	**Reading Essentials and Note-Taking Guide***		p. 217	p. 220	p. 223	p. 226	
BL	OL	AL	ELL	**Differentiated Instruction for the World History Classroom**	✓	✓	✓	✓	✓	✓

Note: Please refer to the *Unit Resource Book: An Era of European Imperialism* for this chapter's URB materials.

* Also available in Spanish

- Interactive Lesson Planner
- Interactive Teacher Edition
- Fully editable blackline masters
- Section Spotlight Videos Launch
- Differentiated Lesson Plans
- Printable reports of daily assignments
- Standards Tracking System

Levels BL	OL	AL	ELL		Resources	Chapter Opener	Section 1	Section 2	Section 3	Section 4	Chapter Assess
					TEACH *(continued)*						
BL	OL	AL	ELL		StudentWorks™ Plus DVD	✓	✓	✓	✓	✓	✓
BL	OL	AL	ELL		Vocabulary PuzzleMaker CD-ROM	✓	✓	✓	✓	✓	✓
Teacher Resources					Building Academic Vocabulary	✓	✓	✓	✓	✓	✓
					Reading Strategies and Activities for the Social Studies Classroom			p. 68	p. 77		
					Writer's Guidebook		p. 54		p. 27		
					Strategies for Success	✓	✓	✓	✓	✓	✓
					Outline Map Resource Book	✓	✓	✓	✓	✓	✓
					Presentation Plus! with MindJogger DVD	✓	✓	✓	✓	✓	✓
					ASSESS						
BL	OL	AL	ELL		Section Quizzes and Chapter Tests*		p. 245	p. 246	p. 247	p. 248	p. 249
BL	OL	AL	ELL		Authentic Assessment With Rubrics	✓	✓	✓	✓	✓	✓
BL	OL	AL	ELL		Standardized Test Practice Workbook	✓	✓	✓	✓	✓	✓
BL	OL	AL	ELL		*ExamView® Assessment Suite* CD-ROM		20-1	20-2	20-3	20-4	Ch. 20
BL	OL	AL	ELL		Interactive Tutor Self-Assessment CD-ROM		20-1	20-2	20-3	20-4	
					CLOSE						
BL			ELL		Reteaching Activity, URB					p. 83	
BL	OL		ELL		Reading and Study Skills Foldables™	✓	✓	✓	✓	✓	✓

Introducing CHAPTER 20

Focus

MAKING CONNECTIONS

What events can affect the entire world?

Activate students' prior knowledge by discussing types of events that bring people from around the world. *(Olympics, concerts)* Then ask students to brainstorm how technologies used today affect how people communicate and travel. Wrap up the discussion by having each student write a short paragraph about a technology invented in their lifetime that they find particularly useful.

Teach

The Big Ideas

As students study the chapter, remind them to consider the section-based Big Ideas included in each section's Guide to Reading. The **Essential Questions** in the activities below tie in to the Big Ideas and help students think about and understand important chapter concepts. In addition, the Hands-on Chapter Projects with their culminating activities relate the content from each section to the Big Ideas. These activities build on each other as students progress through the chapter. Section activities culminate in the wrap-up activity on the Visual Summary page.

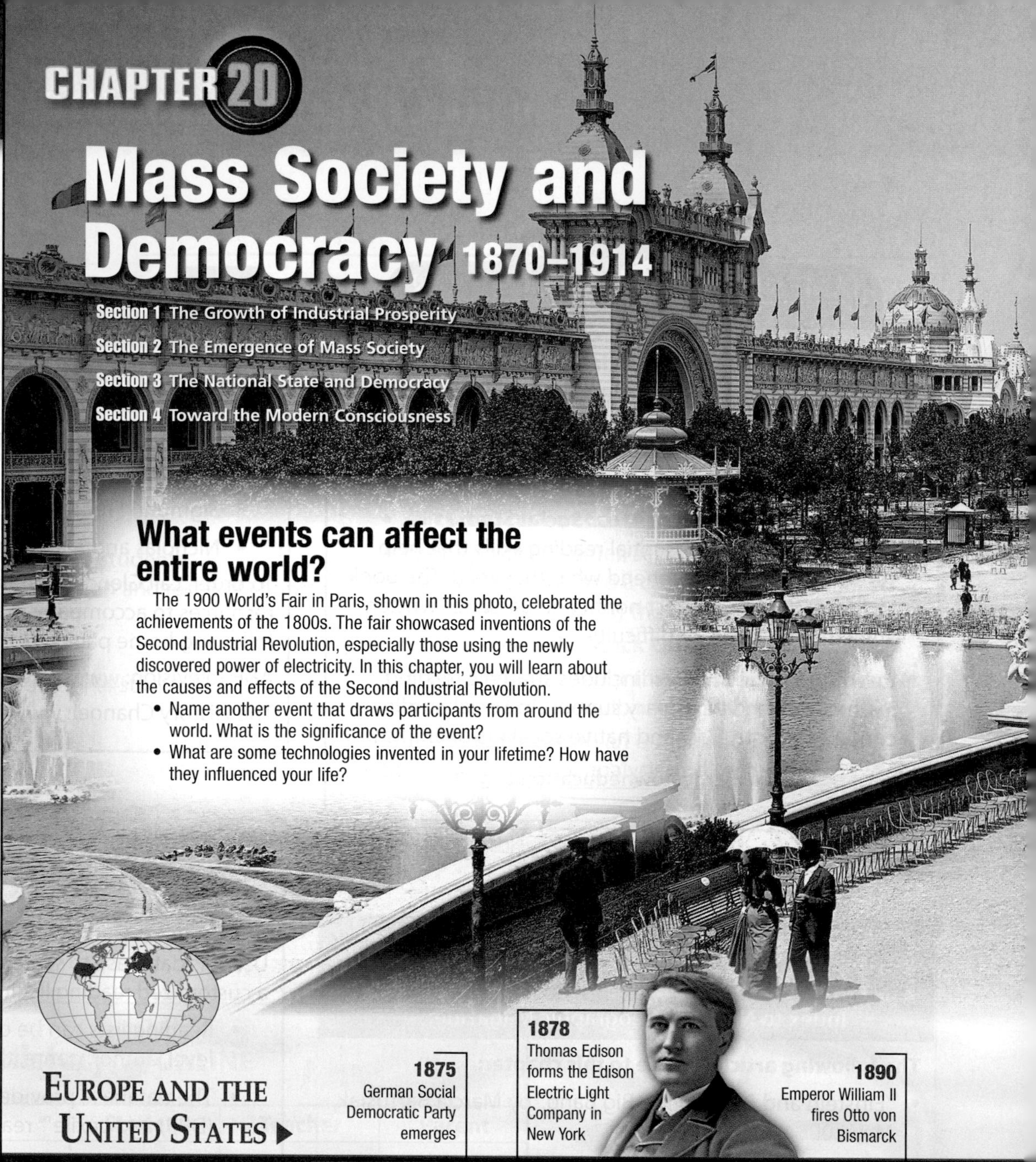

CHAPTER 20

Mass Society and Democracy 1870–1914

What events can affect the entire world?

The 1900 World's Fair in Paris, shown in this photo, celebrated the achievements of the 1800s. The fair showcased inventions of the Second Industrial Revolution, especially those using the newly discovered power of electricity. In this chapter, you will learn about the causes and effects of the Second Industrial Revolution.

- Name another event that draws participants from around the world. What is the significance of the event?
- What are some technologies invented in your lifetime? How have they influenced your life?

EUROPE AND THE UNITED STATES ▶

1875 German Social Democratic Party emerges

1878 Thomas Edison forms the Edison Electric Light Company in New York

1890 Emperor William II fires Otto von Bismarck

1870 — 1885

THE WORLD ▶

1885 Indian National Congress forms

1894 China and Japan go to war over Korea

650

The Growth of Industrial Prosperity

Essential Question: In what ways did industrialization affect the economies of European countries and the United States? *(The Second Industrial Revolution created a world economy, aided by improvements in communication and transportation.)* Tell students that in Section 1, they will learn about the increased prosperity created by industrialization, as well as its negative effects. OL

The Emergence of Mass Society

Essential Question: What benefits do people enjoy today in part because of the Second Industrial Revolution? *(Universal education, greater awareness of health issues, leisure activities, labor reform laws, and a movement toward universal suffrage sprang from industrialization.)* Point out that in Section 2, students will learn more about trends that came about during this time. OL

Introducing
CHAPTER 20

1905
"Bloody Sunday" in St. Petersburg, Russia

1914
World War I begins

Souscrivez à L'Emprunt de la Victoire

1900

1915

1914
Panama Canal opens

FOLDABLES Study Organizer

Comparing Opportunities
Create a Folded Table and use it to examine the lives of women before and after the Second Industrial Revolution. Include job opportunities for women, marriage and women's role in family life, and women's rights.

Second Industrial Revolution	Before Revolution	After Revolution
Job Opportunities for Women		
Marriage and Family		
Women's Rights		

History ONLINE
Chapter Overview—Visit glencoe.com to preview Chapter 20.

More About the Photo

Visual Literacy This photograph shows a portion of the 1900 World's Fair held in Paris. In the scene, the Eiffel Tower and the Palace of Electricity are shown. The Eiffel Tower was actually opened for the 1889 exposition, but it continued to be considered a great achievement more than a decade later. In 1900, one of the achievements was the opening of the new Metropolitan underground railway (subway). The Palace of Electricity pavilion was built to highlight the increasing importance of electricity in society. The façade of the pavilion was illuminated at night with thousands of multicolored lightbulbs, plus additional lamps.

Dinah Zike's Foldables

Dinah Zike's Foldables are three-dimensional, interactive graphic organizers that help students practice basic writing skills, review vocabulary terms, and identify main ideas. Instructions for creating and using Foldables can be found in the Appendix at the end of this book and in the *Dinah Zike's Reading and Study Skills Foldables* booklet.

SECTION 3

The National State and Democracy

Essential Question: What factors might contribute to a failure of democracy? *(Authoritarian rulers, unwilling to relinquish power, could prevent the transition to democratic rule. Repressive measures by the government could stifle dissent.)* Tell students that in Section 3, they will learn about the different forms of government in place by the beginning of the twentieth century and how varying political philosophies and loyalties led to conflict. **OL**

SECTION 4

Toward the Modern Consciousness

Essential Question: How might the art, science, and thought of this era be characterized? *(Artists, writers, scientists, and thinkers exploded old and comfortable ideas, breaking new ground in their forms of expression and theories.)* Point out that in Section 4, students will learn how intellectual ideas and forms of art changed in response to the economic and social changes in the late nineteenth and early twentieth centuries. **OL**

History ONLINE
Introduce students to chapter content and key terms by having them access the Chapter 20 Overview at glencoe.com.

Focus

Introducing Social History
Have students recall what they know about the Second Industrial Revolution. **Ask:** Why did the working class have more possessions in the 1890s? *(because manufactured goods were cheaper and many workers earned better wages)* **OL**

Teach

R Reading Strategy

Organizing Draw a line on the board that represents London society, from the poorest on the left to the wealthiest on the right. Have students choose phrases from the reading to describe each class. Ask students to recall what they learned about the middle class in Section 2. **BL**

W Writing Support

Expository Writing **Ask:** Why was the working class isolated from other elements in London society? Have students write a brief essay answering this question. **OL**

Additional Support

Social History

At Home in London, 1890

By 1890, London was becoming a modern industrial city. Aggressive rebuilding programs had made workers' slums into working-class neighborhoods. **R** Class differences, marked by how industrialists and laborers lived, remained clear. However, modern city services allowed everyone to live in a safer, cleaner environment.

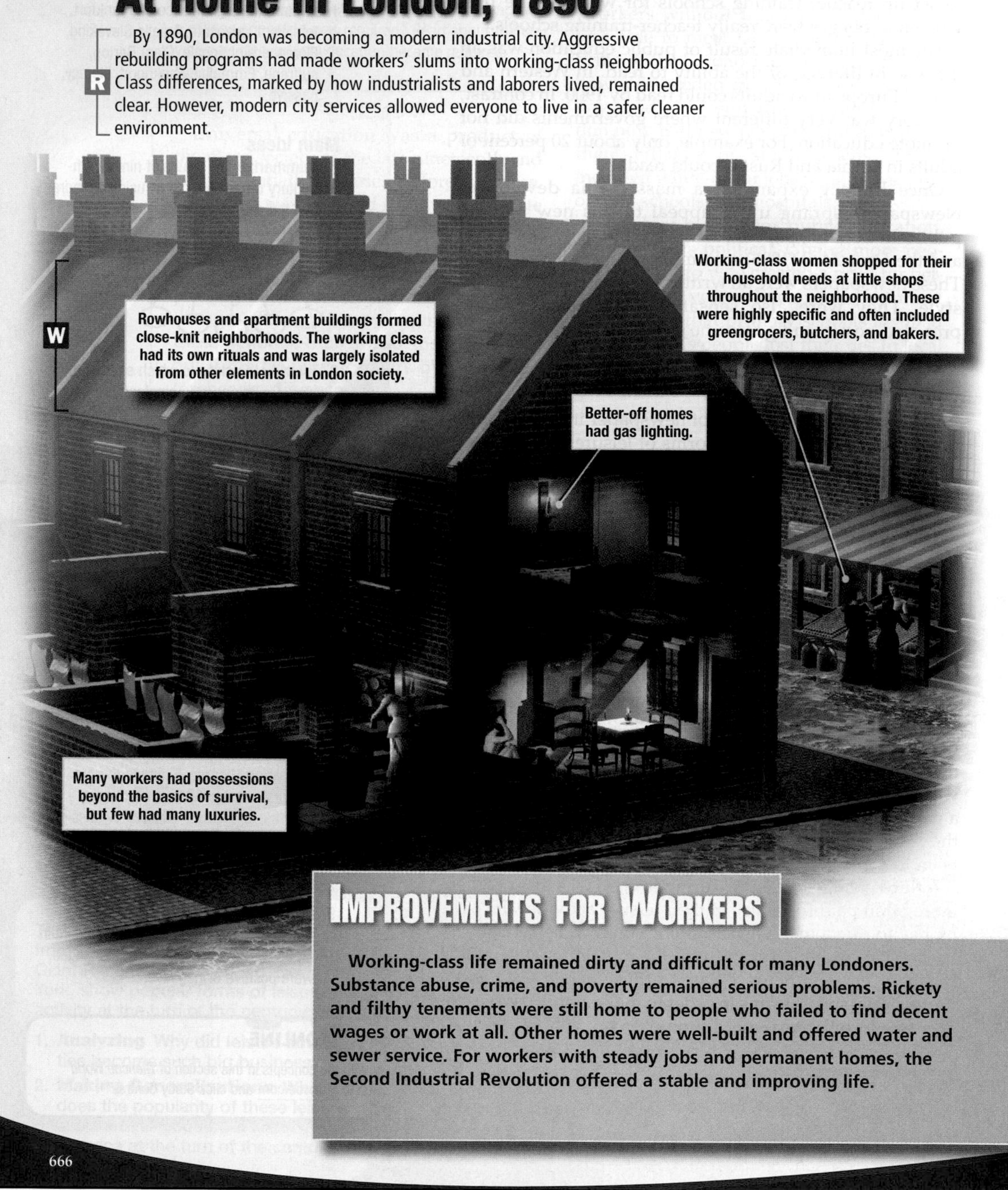

Improvements for Workers

Working-class life remained dirty and difficult for many Londoners. Substance abuse, crime, and poverty remained serious problems. Rickety and filthy tenements were still home to people who failed to find decent wages or work at all. Other homes were well-built and offered water and sewer service. For workers with steady jobs and permanent homes, the Second Industrial Revolution offered a stable and improving life.

Background

Nineteenth-Century London Like many cities in the nineteenth century, London experienced tremendous growth, especially after 1850. The city's population was about 2.7 million in 1851 and had more than doubled to 5.6 million in 1891. By 1901, it added almost an additional million people. Improvements in public safety and sanitation and better organization of local government allowed the city to expand. Working-class neighborhoods, including housing for immigrants who worked on the docks along the Thames River, were located in the East End, while wealthier areas developed in the West End. New technologies improved and expanded transportation as horse-drawn buses and streetcars gave way to steam railroads and eventually an electric subway and streetcar system and gasoline-powered buses. Streetcars and subways allowed people to live farther from their work and encouraged the growth of new neighborhoods and suburbs farther from the center of the city.

The homes of wealthy industrialists included furnishings from all over the British Empire.

The Victorian style in architecture and decorating tended to be very formal.

Wealthy Victorians enjoyed intricate patterns in wallpaper and furniture upholstery.

The telephone was one of many luxurious gadgets that later became common in English homes.

Luxuries for Industrial Owners

The owners of successful mills and industrial works enjoyed a luxurious lifestyle in the best neighborhoods of London. Their homes featured every modern convenience. The nobility's old stigma against the capitalist class had relaxed somewhat. Industrialists and nobles intermarried. The captains of industry sought social status. The aristocracy sought cash reserves and the opportunity to become leaders in the new economy.

Analyzing Visuals

1. **Describing** In what ways had London become a modern city by 1890?
2. **Contrasting** How were the homes of successful industrialists different from those of laborers?

D Differentiated Instruction

English Language Learners
Define *captains of industry* and *aristocracy.* Have students read the paragraph to identify synonyms for these two groups. *(industrialists and nobles)* **ELL**

C Critical Thinking

Drawing Conclusions Ask: **Why did the aristocracy's attitudes toward capitalists change during the nineteenth century?** *(The economy improved.)* **OL**

Assess/Close

Have students discuss how the middle class compared to the working class and elite. **OL**

ANALYZING VISUALS

Answers:

1. Modern city services made the city safer and cleaner for all residents.
2. Industrialists' homes were single-family homes furnished with luxuries; workers lived in row houses with few luxuries.

Activity: Interdisciplinary Connection

Literature In literary terms, Victorian England is known as the age of the novel. Three-volume novels designed for subscription libraries were gradually replaced with novels that were serialized in newspapers and magazines and, by the 1890s, the single-volume novel. Charles Dickens was one of the first to serialize his work and used many of his novels as a platform to crusade against the evils caused by industrialization. **Ask:** **How did nineteenth-century English novelists describe life in London?** Have students choose a novel and write a report comparing its description of city life to what they have learned about this period in their textbook. In addition to Dickens, students might consider Henry James's *A London Life,* Robert Louis Stevenson's *The Strange Case of Dr. Jekyll and Mr. Hyde,* Arthur Conan Doyle's *Sherlock Holmes* stories, George Gissing's *New Grub Street,* or novels about new roles for women such as Grant Allen's *The Woman Who Did* or Sarah Grand's *The Heavenly Twins.* **AL**

Focus

Bellringer

Daily Focus Transparency 20.3

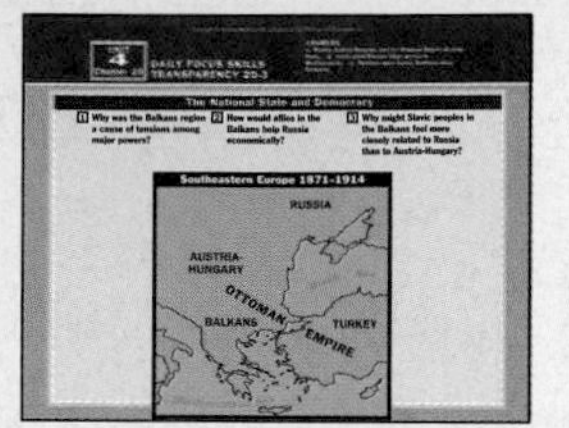

GUIDE TO READING

Answers to Graphic:
Triple Alliance 1882: Germany, Austria-Hungary, Italy; **Triple Entente 1907:** Great Britain, France, Russia

Section Spotlight Video

To generate student interest and provide a springboard for class discussion, access the Chapter 20, Section 3 video at glencoe.com or on the video DVD.

SECTION 3

The National State and Democracy

GUIDE TO READING

The BIG Idea
Competition Among Countries
While democracy triumphed in Western Europe, authoritarianism prevailed in central and eastern Europe, and industrialization swept the United States. International rivalries set the stage for war.

Content Vocabulary
- ministerial responsibility *(p. 668)*
- Duma *(p. 670)*

Academic Vocabulary
- insecure *(p. 671)*
- controversy *(p. 673)*

People and Places
- Otto von Bismarck *(p. 670)*
- William II *(p. 670)*
- Francis Joseph *(p. 670)*
- Nicholas II *(p. 670)*
- St. Petersburg *(p. 670)*
- Queen Liliuokalani *(p. 671)*
- Montenegro *(p. 673)*

Reading Strategy
Summarizing Information As you read, complete a diagram like the one below listing the countries in each alliance.

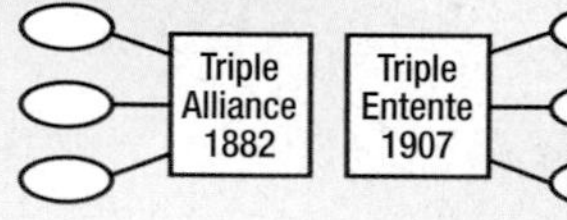

During the late nineteenth and early twentieth centuries, democracy expanded in Western Europe, while the old order preserved authoritarianism in central and eastern Europe. During this time, the United States recovered from the Civil War and became the world's richest nation. Meanwhile, international rivalries began to set the stage for World War I.

Western Europe and Political Democracy

MAIN IDEA Growing prosperity after 1850 contributed to the expansion of democracy in Western Europe.

HISTORY & YOU Which political party does your family support? Read about political parties in Western Europe in the late 1800s.

By the late nineteenth century, especially in Western Europe, there were many signs that political democracy was expanding. First, universal male suffrage laws were passed. Second, the prime minister was responsible to the popularly elected legislative body, not to the king or president. This principle is called **ministerial responsibility,** which is crucial for democracy. Third, mass political parties formed. As more men, and later women, could vote, parties created larger organizations and found ways to appeal to many who were now part of the political process.

Great Britain

Before 1871 Great Britain had a working two-party parliamentary system. These two parties—the Liberals and Conservatives—competed to pass laws that expanded the right to vote. Reform acts in 1867 and 1884 increased the number of adult male voters.

With political democracy established, social reforms for the working class soon followed. The working class in Great Britain supported the Liberal Party. Two developments made Liberals fear losing this support. First, the trade unions grew, and they favored a more radical change of the economic system. Second, in 1900, the Labour Party emerged and dedicated itself to the interests of workers. To retain the workers' support, the Liberals voted for social reforms, such as unemployment benefits and old age pensions.

France

In France, the collapse of Louis-Napoleon's Second Empire left the country in confusion. Finally, in 1875, the Third Republic gained a republican constitution. The new government had a

Resource Manager

R Reading Strategies	C Critical Thinking	D Differentiated Instruction	W Writing Support	S Skill Practice
Additional Resources • Guid. Read. Act., URB p. 88 • Read. Ess. & Note-Taking Guide, p. 223	**Teacher Edition** • Ident. Cent. Issues, p. 670 • Compare/Contrast, p. 672 • Making Generalizations, p. 673 **Additional Resources** • Hist. & Geo. Act., URB p. 67 • People in World Hist., URB p. 77 • Section Quiz, p. 247	**Teacher Edition** • Logical/Math., p. 671 **Additional Resources** • Read. Strat. for SS, p. 77	**Teacher Edition** • Expository Writing, p. 670 **Additional Resources** • Writer's Guidebook, p. 27	**Teacher Edition** • Using Geo. Skills, pp. 669, 671 • Visual Literacy, p. 672 **Additional Resources** • Mapping Hist. Act., URB p. 69

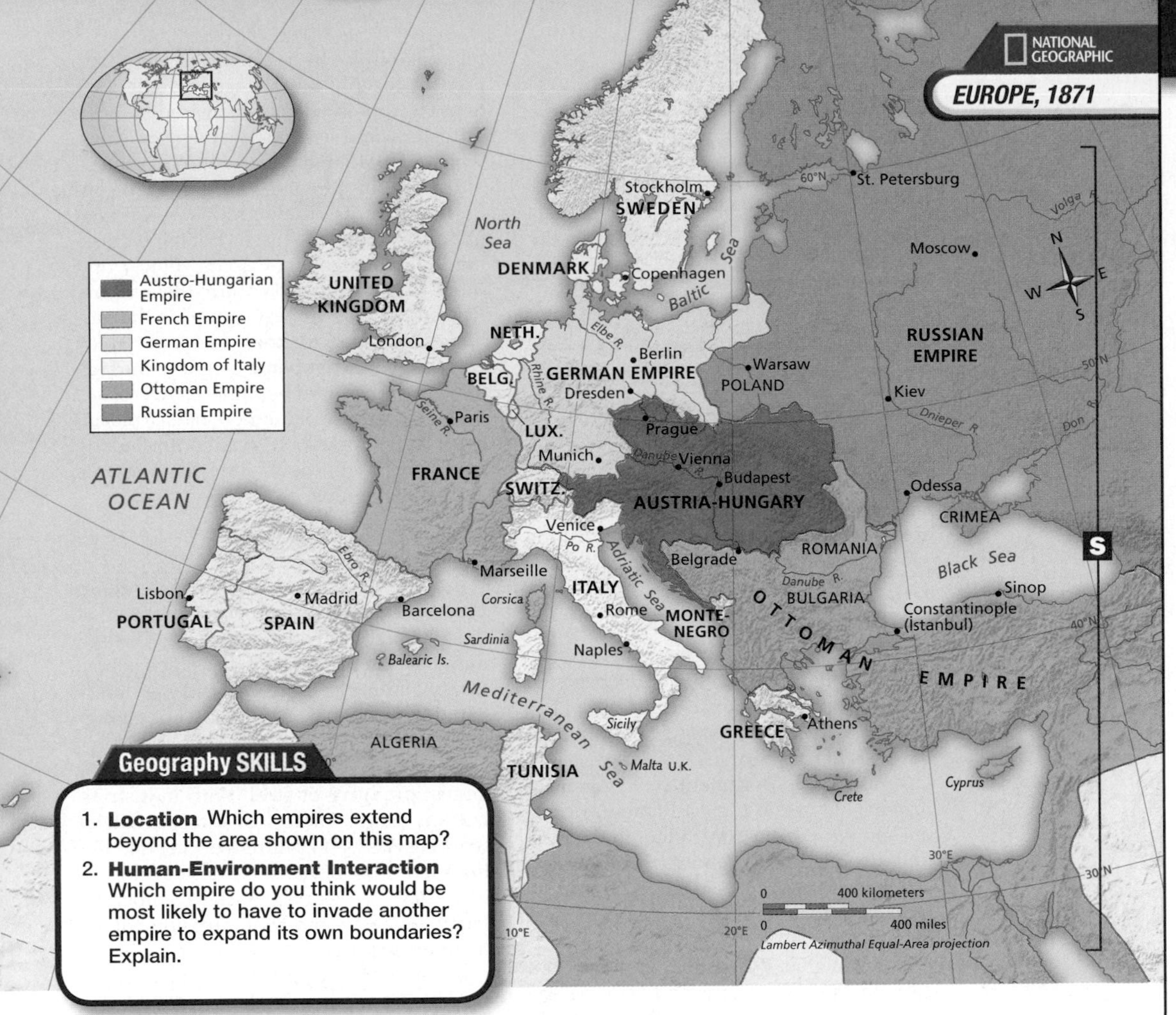

Geography SKILLS

1. **Location** Which empires extend beyond the area shown on this map?
2. **Human-Environment Interaction** Which empire do you think would be most likely to have to invade another empire to expand its own boundaries? Explain.

president and a legislature made up of two houses. The upper house, or Senate, was conservative and elected by high-ranking officials. All adult males voted for members of the lower house, the Chamber of Deputies. A premier (or prime minister), who led the government, was responsible to the Chamber of Deputies, not to the president.

France failed to develop a strong parliamentary system. The existence of a dozen political parties forced the premier to depend on a coalition of parties to stay in power. Nevertheless, by 1914, the Third Republic had the loyalty of most voters.

Italy

Italy had emerged by 1870 as a united national state. However, there was little national unity because of the great gulf between the poverty-stricken south and the industrialized north. Constant turmoil between labor and industry weakened the social fabric of the nation. Even universal male suffrage, granted in 1912, did little to halt the widespread government corruption and weakness.

✓Reading Check **Summarizing** What is the principle of ministerial responsibility?

Teach

S Skill Practice

Using Geography Skills Have students compare the map of Europe in 1871 with a present-day map. **Ask:** Which countries were once part of Austria-Hungary? *(Austria, Hungary, the Czech Republic, Slovakia, Croatia, Slovenia, and parts of Italy, Russia, Poland, and Romania)* **OL**

Geography SKILLS

Answers:

1. Ottoman Empire and Russian Empire
2. Answers may vary but should be supported by logical arguments. Possible answer: Austro-Hungarian; Most of its territory borders that of other empires.

✓Reading Check

Answer: A premier (or prime minister) leads the government and is directly responsible to the legislative body, not to the king or president.

Hands-On Chapter Project
Step 3

Assembling a Museum Exhibit

Groups of students add a display of political cartoons to their exhibit.

Step 3: Collecting Visual Aids

Directions: Write the Big Idea on the board. Show students the political cartoon on page 672 of Bismarck walking away from William II. Discuss the purpose of political cartoons. **Ask:** What are some reasons for using political cartoons? *(Possible answers: To make a comment about a political event or problem. To use humor to point out things that people want to say but don't feel comfortable saying directly.)* Then have students either create their own cartoons or find some from the era that characterize political situations in the countries mentioned in this section. Students should display the cartoons on poster board with background notes.

Summarizing: Have students share ideas about this section using their cartoons to help them express their thoughts. **OL**

(Chapter Project is continued in Section 4.)

C Critical Thinking

Identifying Central Issues Compare the revolutions in western Europe between 1815 and 1848 with the events in Russia on "Bloody Sunday." **Ask:** Why were these events a sign of the decline of the old order? Why did such an event take place in Russia almost a century later? *(Industrialization brought socialism; opposition to the czarist regime resulted in revolution. Industrialization occurred later in Russia than in western Europe.)* AL

W Writing Support

Expository Writing Have groups create annotated bibliographies of Web sites on "Bloody Sunday" and the Revolution of 1905. Ask students to include the names and addresses, summaries of information, and rate each site's user-friendliness and accuracy. AL

✓Reading Check

Answer: It was created as a legislative assembly, but the czar curtailed its power.

Central and Eastern Europe: The Old Order

MAIN IDEA Although Germany, Austria-Hungary, and later Russia instituted elections and parliaments, real power remained in the hands of emperors and elites.

HISTORY & YOU Does your school have a student council? What is its role? Read to learn about the political structures in central and eastern Europe in the late 1800s.

Central and eastern Europe had more conservative governments than did Western Europe. Germany, the Austro-Hungarian Empire, and Russia were less industrialized, and education was not widely available. It was easier, then, for the old ruling groups to continue to dominate politics.

Germany

The constitution of the new imperial Germany that **Otto von Bismarck** began in 1871 set up a two-house legislature. The lower house, the Reichstag, was elected on the basis of universal male suffrage.

Ministers of government, however, were responsible not to the parliament, but to the emperor, who controlled the armed forces, foreign policy, and the bureaucracy. As chancellor (prime minister), Bismarck worked to keep Germany from becoming a democracy.

By the reign of **William II,** emperor from 1888 to 1918, Germany had become the strongest military and industrial power in Europe. With the expansion of industry and cities came demands for democracy.

Conservative forces—especially the landowning nobility and big industrialists—tried to thwart the movement for democracy by supporting a strong foreign policy. They believed that expansion abroad would increase their profits and would also divert people from pursuing democratic reforms.

Austro-Hungarian Empire

After the creation of the dual monarchy of Austria-Hungary in 1867, Austria enacted a constitution that, in theory, set up a parliamentary system with ministerial responsibility. In reality, the emperor, **Francis Joseph,** largely ignored this system. He appointed and dismissed his own ministers and issued decrees, or laws, when the parliament was not in session.

The empire remained troubled by conflicts among its ethnic groups. A German minority governed Austria but felt increasingly threatened by Czechs, Poles, and other Slavic groups within the empire. Representatives of these groups in the parliament agitated for their freedom, which encouraged the emperor to ignore the parliament and govern by imperial decrees.

Unlike Austria, Hungary had a parliament that worked. It was controlled by landowners who dominated the peasants and ethnic groups.

Russia

C In Russia, **Nicholas II** began his rule in 1894 believing that the absolute power of the czars should be preserved. "I shall maintain the principle of autocracy just as firmly and unflinchingly as did my unforgettable father." Conditions were changing, however.

By 1900, Russia had become the fourth-largest producer of steel. With industrialization came factories, an industrial working class, and pitiful working and living conditions. Socialist parties developed, including the Marxist Social Democratic Party, but government repression forced them underground.

Growing discontent and opposition to the czarist regime finally exploded. On January 22, 1905, a massive procession of workers went to the Winter Palace in **St. Petersburg** to present a petition of grievances to the czar. Troops opened fire on the peaceful demonstration, killing hundreds. This "Bloody Sunday" caused workers throughout Russia to call strikes. W

Nicholas II was eventually forced to grant civil liberties and to create a legislative assembly, called the **Duma.** By 1907, however, the czar had already curtailed the power of the Duma and again used the army and bureaucracy to rule Russia.

✓Reading Check **Identifying** What was the role of the Duma in the Russian government?

Differentiated Instruction

Mapping History Activity 20

The Economy of Austria-Hungary

Mapping History Activity, URB p. 69

Analyzing Information

Objective: Understand the ethnic composition of Austria-Hungary.

Focus: Discuss how this ethnic composition created conflict.

Teach: Have students chart the alliances that existed by 1914.

Assess: Have students explain why the Balkans was a "powder keg."

Close: Have students predict future events.

Differentiated Instruction Strategies

BL Have students work together to summarize the information in the text about Austria-Hungary.

AL Have students draw a map of the Balkans today and identify the ethnic composition of the various countries.

ELL Have students complete and discuss the activities on the handout.

The United States

MAIN IDEA In the United States, the Second Industrial Revolution produced wealth that was more concentrated than it was in Europe.

HISTORY & YOU Can you name territories that are part of the United States today but are not states? Read how the Unitd States acquired territories in the late 1800s.

Civil war had not destroyed the national unity of the United States. Between 1870 and 1914, the country became an industrial power with an empire.

Aftermath of the Civil War

Four years of bloody civil war had preserved the American nation. However, the old South had been destroyed.

In 1865 the Thirteenth Amendment to the Constitution was passed, abolishing slavery. Later, the Fourteenth and Fifteenth Amendments gave citizenship to African Americans and the right to vote to African American males. New state laws in the South, however, soon stripped African Americans of the right to vote. By 1880, supporters of white supremacy were back in power everywhere in the South.

Economy

Between 1860 and 1914, the United States shifted from a farm-based economy to an industrial economy. American steel and iron production was the best in the world in 1900. Carnegie Steel Company alone produced more steel than all of Great Britain. As in Europe, industrialization in the United States led to urbanization. By 1900, the United States had three cities with populations over 1 million, with New York reaching 4 million.

In 1900 the United States was the world's richest nation, but the richest 9 percent of Americans owned 71 percent of the wealth. D Many workers labored in unsafe factories, and devastating cycles of unemployment made them **insecure.** Many tried to organize unions, but the American Federation of Labor represented only 8.4 percent of the labor force.

Expansion Abroad

In the late 1800s, the United States began to expand abroad. The Samoan Islands in the Pacific were the first important U.S. colony. By 1887, Americans controlled the sugar industry on the Hawaiian Islands.

As more Americans settled in Hawaii, they wanted political power. When **Queen Liliuokalani** (lih•LEE•uh•woh•kuh•LAH•nee) tried to strengthen the monarchy to keep the islands under her people's control, the United States sent military S forces to the islands. The queen was deposed and the United States annexed Hawaii in 1898.

In 1898 the United States defeated Spain in the Spanish-American War. As a result, the United States acquired the former Spanish possessions of Puerto Rico, Guam, and the Philippines. By the beginning of the twentieth century, the United States, the world's richest nation, had an empire.

✓Reading Check **Identifying** Name the territories that the United States acquired in 1898.

PEOPLE *in* HISTORY

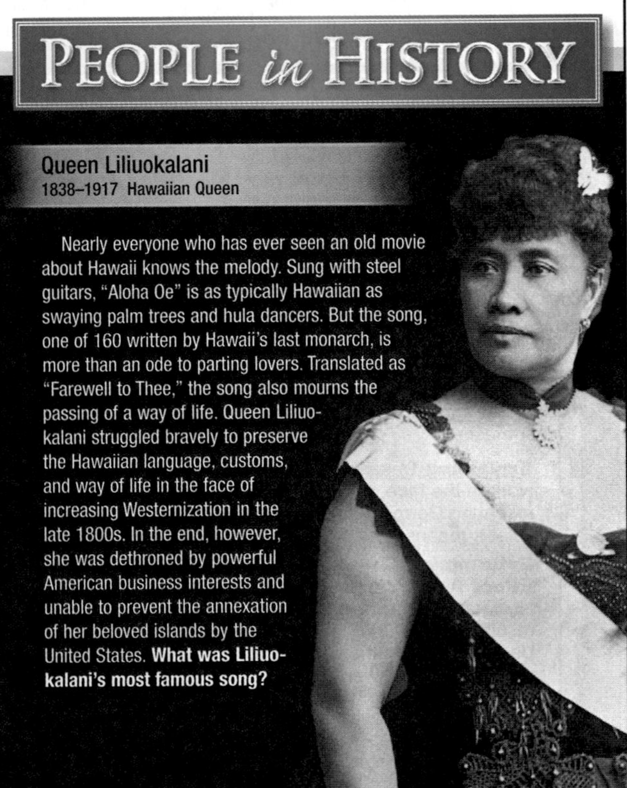

Queen Liliuokalani
1838–1917 Hawaiian Queen

Nearly everyone who has ever seen an old movie about Hawaii knows the melody. Sung with steel guitars, "Aloha Oe" is as typically Hawaiian as swaying palm trees and hula dancers. But the song, one of 160 written by Hawaii's last monarch, is more than an ode to parting lovers. Translated as "Farewell to Thee," the song also mourns the passing of a way of life. Queen Liliuokalani struggled bravely to preserve the Hawaiian language, customs, and way of life in the face of increasing Westernization in the late 1800s. In the end, however, she was dethroned by powerful American business interests and unable to prevent the annexation of her beloved islands by the United States. **What was Liliuokalani's most famous song?**

D Differentiated Instruction

Logical/Mathematical
Discuss the distribution of wealth in the U.S. at the beginning of the twentieth century. To help students understand the concept, distribute 20 apples to the class as follows: 10% of the class receives 70% or 14 of the apples, the next 10% receives 15% or 3 apples, and the remaining 80% receives the last 15% or 3 apples. BL

S Skill Practice

Using Geography Skills
Have students locate the Samoan Islands, the Hawaiian Islands, Puerto Rico, Guam, and the Philippines on a map. **Ask:** **Why did the United States want to acquire control of these islands?** *(to expand its influence abroad and gain control of additional resources)* OL

PEOPLE *in* HISTORY

Answers: "Aloha Oe"

✓Reading Check

Answer: Hawaii, Puerto Rico, Guam, and the Philippines

Additional Support

Extending the Content

Queen Liliuokalani Born Lydia Kamakaeha, she took the name Liliuokalani upon being named the heir to the throne. She was a well-educated and well-traveled woman who often stood in for her brother, the king, when he left the country. Therefore, upon his death, she was prepared to govern as the first female ruler of Hawaii. Her goal was to win back some of the power that her brother had lost. In doing so, she alienated businessmen, particularly Sanford Dole, who had her deposed. President Cleveland's order to return her rightful position was ignored. Finally, she agreed to abdicate to save her supporters from execution. She later wrote, ". . . I still believe that murder was the alternative. Be this as it may, it is certainly happier for me to reflect today that there is not a drop of the blood of my subjects, friends or foes, upon my soul." **Ask:** **Why did foreign businessmen want to remove Liliuokalani?** *(She most likely restricted their ability to exploit Hawaii's resources for their own gain.)* OL

Focus

Bellringer

Daily Focus Transparency 20.4

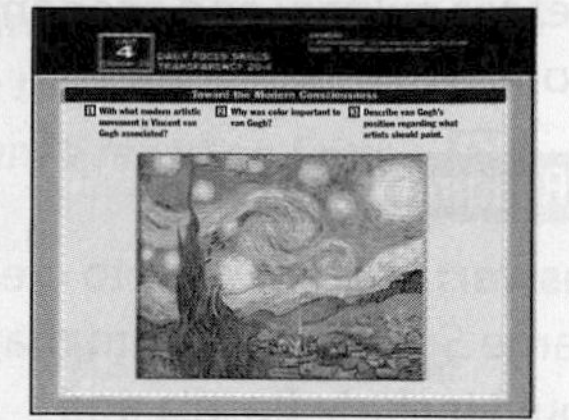

GUIDE TO READING

Answers to Graphic:

Impressionism	Monet	paint nature directly
Post-Impressionism	van Gogh	stress color
Cubism	Picasso	geometric designs
Abstract painting	Kandinsky	avoid visual reality

Section Spotlight Video

To generate student interest and provide a springboard for class discussion, access the Chapter 20, Section 4 video at glencoe.com or on the video DVD.

SECTION 4

Toward the Modern Consciousness

GUIDE TO READING

The BIG Idea

Ideas, Beliefs, and Values Radical changes in the economic and social structure of the West were matched by equally dramatic artistic and intellectual changes.

Content Vocabulary

- modernism *(p. 674)*
- psychoanalysis *(p. 677)*
- Social Darwinism *(p. 678)*
- pogroms *(p. 679)*
- Zionism *(p. 679)*

Academic Vocabulary

- abstract *(p. 676)*
- intensity *(p. 679)*

People and Places

- France *(p. 674)*
- Claude Monet *(p. 674)*
- Pablo Picasso *(p. 675)*
- Frank Lloyd Wright *(p. 676)*
- Marie Curie *(p. 676)*
- Albert Einstein *(p. 676)*
- Sigmund Freud *(p. 677)*
- Vienna *(p. 677)*

Reading Strategy

Identifying Information As you read, complete a chart like the one below that lists an artist and a characteristic of the art movement indicated.

Impressionism		
Post-Impressionism		
Cubism		
Abstract painting		

During the late nineteenth and early twentieth centuries, people moved toward a modern consciousness. Their changing worldview was expressed in innovative art movements. Developments in the sciences also changed how people saw themselves and their world. Some people took nationalism to the extreme. They advocated Social Darwinism to justify the dominance of Western nations.

The Culture of Modernity

MAIN IDEA Dramatic innovation occurred in literature, the visual arts, and music in the late 1800s.

HISTORY & YOU How can you tell that student artwork is from your era? Read to learn how artists express the society they know.

Between 1870 and 1914, many writers and artists rebelled against the traditional literary and artistic styles that had dominated European cultural life since the Renaissance. The changes they produced have since been called **modernism.**

Literature

Western novelists and poets who followed the naturalist style felt that literature should be realistic and address social problems. Henrik Ibsen and Émile Zola, for example, explored the role of women in society, alcoholism, and the problems of urban slums in their work.

The symbolist writers had a different idea about what was real. Inspired by Sigmund Freud, they believed the external world, including art, was only a collection of symbols reflecting the true reality—the human mind. Art, the symbolists believed, should function for its own sake, not criticize or seek to understand society.

Painting

Since the Renaissance, Western artists had tried to represent reality as accurately as possible. By the late 1800s, artists were seeking new forms of expression to reflect their changing worldviews.

Impressionism was a movement that began in **France** in the 1870s, when a group of artists rejected traditional indoor studios and went to the countryside to paint nature directly. One important impressionist is **Claude Monet** (moh•NAY), who painted pictures that captured the interplay of light, water, and sky. Other impressionist painters include Pierre-Auguste Renoir (REHN•WAHR) and Berthe Morisot.

Resource Manager

R Reading Strategies

Teacher Edition
- Making Connections, p. 677
- Questioning, p. 679

Additional Resources
- Cont. Vocab. Act., URB p. 61
- World Art & Music Act., URB p. 81
- Guid. Read. Act., URB p. 89
- Read. Ess. & Note-Taking Guide, p. 226

C Critical Thinking

Teacher Edition
- Making Inferences, p. 678
- Analyzing Pri. Sources, p. 678

Additional Resources
- Hist. Analysis Skills Act., URB p. 56
- Hist. Sig. Act., URB p. 70
- Section Quiz, p. 248
- Chapter Test, p. 249

D Differentiated Instruction

Teacher Edition
- Auditory/Musical, p. 676

Additional Resources
- Diff. Inst. Act., URB p. 57
- Academic Vocab. Act., URB p. 63
- Reteach. Act., URB p. 83

W Writing Support

Teacher Edition
- Expository Writing, p. 676

Additional Resources
- Linking Past/Present Act., URB p. 76

S Skill Practice

Teacher Edition
- Visual Literacy, p. 675

Additional Resources
- Time Line Act., URB p. 75

PRIMARY SOURCE HISTORY & ARTS

Impressionists and Postimpressionists

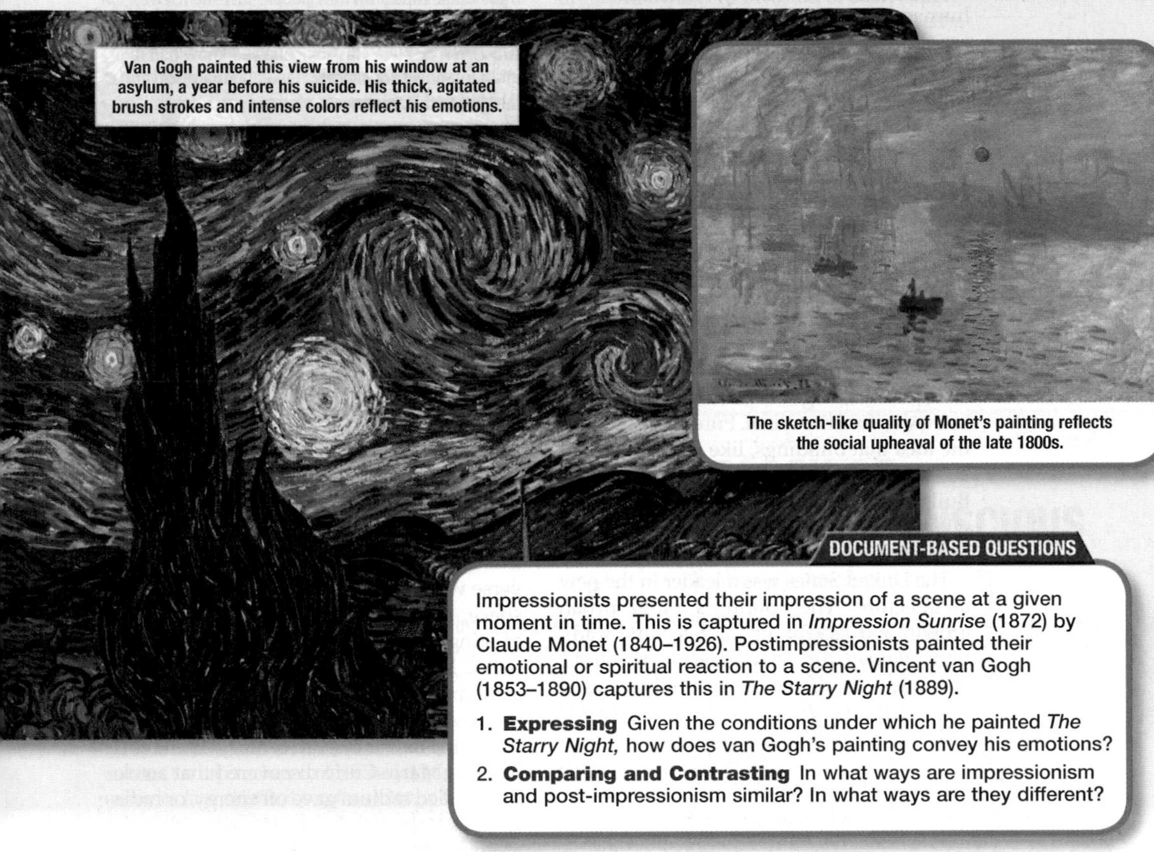

Van Gogh painted this view from his window at an asylum, a year before his suicide. His thick, agitated brush strokes and intense colors reflect his emotions.

The sketch-like quality of Monet's painting reflects the social upheaval of the late 1800s.

DOCUMENT-BASED QUESTIONS

Impressionists presented their impression of a scene at a given moment in time. This is captured in *Impression Sunrise* (1872) by Claude Monet (1840–1926). Postimpressionists painted their emotional or spiritual reaction to a scene. Vincent van Gogh (1853–1890) captures this in *The Starry Night* (1889).

1. **Expressing** Given the conditions under which he painted *The Starry Night*, how does van Gogh's painting convey his emotions?
2. **Comparing and Contrasting** In what ways are impressionism and post-impressionism similar? In what ways are they different?

In the 1880s, a new movement, known as postimpressionism, arose in France and soon spread. Painters Paul Cezanne and Vincent van Gogh used color and structure to express a mood. For van Gogh, art was a spiritual experience. He was especially interested in color and believed that it could act as its own form of language. Van Gogh maintained that artists should paint what they feel.

By the early 1900s, artists were no longer convinced that their main goal was to represent reality. This was especially true in the visual arts. One reason for the decline of realism in painting was photography. Invented in the 1830s, photography gained wide popularity after George Eastman created the first Kodak camera in 1888.

Artists tended to focus less on mirroring reality, which the camera could do, and more on creating reality. Painters and sculptors, like the symbolist writers of the time, looked for meaning in individual consciousness. Between 1905 and 1914, this search for individual expression created modern art. One of the most outstanding features of modern art is the attempt of the artist to avoid "visual reality." **S**

By 1905, **Pablo Picasso,** an important figure in modern art, was beginning his career. Picasso was a Spaniard who settled in Paris. He painted in a remarkable variety

History ONLINE
Student Web Activity—
Visit glencoe.com and complete the activity on impressionism.

Teach

S Skill Practice

Visual Literacy Discuss the impact of technology on art. **Ask:** How did the widespread use of cameras affect painting? *(Artists responded to the virtual representation made possible by photography by painting non-realistic art.)* **OL**

DOCUMENT-BASED QUESTIONS

Answers:

1. Answers will vary. Intense colors and agitated brush strokes reflect his dark emotions. The flow gives a sense of turmoil.
2. Answers will vary. **Similarity:** Neither tries to recreate a scene in the precise detail of realism. **Differences:** Impressionists try to capture their impression of a scene at a particular moment. Post-impressionists try to portray their personal reaction to the scene rather than the scene itself. The use of color and brushstrokes also differs.

Hands-On Chapter Project
Step 4

Assembling a Museum Exhibit

Step 4: Creating a Banner Have groups of students complete their exhibits.

Directions: Write the Big Idea on the board. Then have groups design and create a large banner for the entrance of their exhibit. Their banner should include the title of their exhibit. This title should summarize what they have learned about the changes and discoveries leading into the 20th century. Their banner should also highlight the major artistic, literary, architectural, social, scientific, and psychological achievements of the age, drawing from the facts in this section. Students should use both visuals and text, including actual representations of some of the art.

Putting It Together: Locate space for each group to set up its exhibit. Have students informally tour the exhibits, noting similarities and differences among their representations of the age. **OL**

(Chapter Project is completed on the Visual Summary page.)

C1 Critical Thinking

Making Inferences **Ask:** How did the advances in science and challenges to traditional art and music contribute to renewed nationalism? *(The many challenges to the existing order may have led people to turn to the state as the one certainty in an uncertain world.)* **AL**

For additional practice on this skill, see the **Skills Handbook**.

C2 Critical Thinking

Analyzing Primary Sources Ask students to examine the last line of Bernhardi's quote: "War is the father of all things." **Ask:** What did Bernhardi mean by this quotation? *(Nothing is accomplished except by conflict, and war is necessary for societies to thrive.)* Ask students if they agree with this opinion. **OL**

PEOPLE in HISTORY

Answers:
Herbert Spencer: "survival of the fittest"
Theodor Herzl: the unjust trial of Captain Dreyfus in France

Extreme Nationalism

MAIN IDEA In the late 1800s, extreme nationalism was reflected in the movements of Social Darwinism and anti-Semitism.

HISTORY & YOU What do you think qualifies someone to be an American? Read to learn how some thinkers in the late 1800s felt national identity should be determined.

C1 Nationalism became more intense in many countries in the late 1800s. For some Europeans, loyalty to their nation became an anchor, almost a religious faith. Preserving their nation's status and their national traditions counted above everything else.

Social Darwinism and Racism

Social Darwinism was a theory used to justify the dominance of Western nations in the late nineteenth century. Certain thinkers claimed that it was valid science to apply Darwin's theory of natural selection to modern human societies. In fact, this was not good science, but what today might be called "junk science," or faulty science.

A British philosopher, Herbert Spencer, argued that social progress came from "the survival of the fittest"—that is, the strong advanced while the weak declined. This kind of thinking allowed some people to reject the idea that they should take care of the less fortunate.

Extreme nationalists also used Social Darwinism. They said that nations, too, were engaged in a "struggle for existence" in which only the fittest nations would survive. The German general Friedrich von C2 Bernhardi argued in 1907: "War is a biological necessity of the first importance, . . . since without it an unhealthy development will follow, which excludes every advancement of the race, and therefore all real civilization. War is the father of all things."

Perhaps nowhere was the combination of extreme nationalism and racism more evident than in Germany. One of the chief exponents of German racism was Houston Stewart Chamberlain, a Briton who became a German citizen and an extreme nationalist. Chamberlain believed that the ancestors of modern-day Germanic peoples were the Aryans, a tribal people from Central

PEOPLE in HISTORY

Herbert Spencer
1820–1903 British Philosopher

When Charles Darwin unveiled his theory of evolution in 1859, Herbert Spencer was one of his strongest believers. Spencer was renowned in Victorian England for his writings and observations on the human condition. He adapted Darwin's theory to his own conclusions. Thus developed the school of thought known as Social Darwinism. In fact, one of Darwin's most famous quotes, "survival of the fittest," actually originated with Spencer. Spencer's theories had a great impact in the United States during the Industrial Revolution. Wealthy tycoons adapted his theories to justify their success and lofty status. In Europe, Social Darwinism was used to justify the imbalance of power among nations. **What famous quote did Spencer originate?**

Theodor Herzl
1860–1904 Founder of Zionism

Dramatic events often lead to decisive political actions. Such was the case in 1894, when a young Hungarian-born Jewish journalist named Theodor Herzl was in Paris during the trial of Captain Alfred Dreyfus. A Jewish officer in the French army, Dreyfus was unjustly accused of treason. Herzl heard mobs shouting, "Death to the Jews." This incident led Herzl to resolve that there could be only one solution to the Jewish plight in Europe: mass immigration to a land that they could call their own. Herzl became the founder of the Zionist movement. In 1948 Zionism achieved Herzl's dream—the establishment of the Jewish state of Israel. **What incident triggered Herzl's desire to establish a Jewish homeland?**

Additional Support

Extending the Content

Herbert Spencer Spencer's nonconformist upbringing was reflected in his later philosophies. He believed that government should exist only to protect the individual's rights and should not attempt to do anything more, such as support the poor, regulate the economy, or provide education. Individuals, in pursuit of their rights, would achieve their own progress if left free to do so. **Ask:** According to Spencer, how would someone achieve success? *(Working hard would lead to success for individuals.)*

Theodor Herzl Herzl led the First Zionist Congress in Basel, Switzerland, in 1897. Even then, he knew that his goal of establishing the state of Israel would not be easy, but he was hopeful, writing in his diary, "At Basel I founded the Jewish state. If I were to say this today, I would be greeted by universal laughter. In five years, perhaps, and certainly in 50 in everyone will see it." **Ask:** How long after the first congress was the state of Israel established? *(51 years)*

Asia who were thought to have migrated to northern India, Iran, and parts of Europe around 2000 B.C. Chamberlain thought the Aryans were the original creators of Western culture. He further believed that Jews were the enemy out to destroy the "superior" Aryans.

Anti-Semitism and Zionism

Anti-Semitism, or hostility toward and discrimination against Jews, was not new to Europe. Since the Middle Ages, the Jews had been falsely portrayed by Christians as the murderers of Jesus Christ and subjected to mob violence. Their rights had been restricted. They had been physically separated from Christians by being required to live in areas of cities known as ghettos.

By the 1830s, the lives of many Jews had improved. They had legal equality in many European countries. They became bankers, lawyers, scientists, and scholars and were absorbed into the national culture. Old prejudices were still very much alive, though, and anti-Semitism grew stronger in the late 1800s.

The **intensity** of anti-Semitism was evident from the Dreyfus affair in France. In 1894, a military court found Dreyfus, a captain in the French general staff, guilty of selling army secrets. During the trial, angry right-wing mobs yelled anti-Semitic sayings such as "Death to the Jews." After the trial, evidence emerged that proved Dreyfus innocent. A wave of public outcry finally forced the government to pardon Dreyfus in 1899.

In Germany and Austria-Hungary during the 1880s and 1890s, new parties arose that used anti-Semitism to win the votes of people affected by economic problems and blamed those problems on Jews. However, the worst treatment of Jews at the turn of the century occurred in Russia. Persecutions and **pogroms,** or organized massacres, were widespread.

Hundreds of thousands of Jews decided to emigrate to escape the persecution. Many went to the United States. Some Jews, probably about 25,000, immigrated to Palestine, which became home for a Jewish nationalist movement called **Zionism.**

For many Jews, Palestine, the land of ancient Israel, had long been the land of their dreams. A key figure in the growth of political Zionism was Theodor Herzl, who stated in his book *The Jewish State* (1896), "The Jews who wish it will have their state." R

Settlement in Palestine was difficult, however, because it was then part of the Ottoman Empire, which was opposed to Jewish immigration. Although 3,000 Jews went annually to Palestine between 1904 and 1914, the Zionist desire for a homeland in Palestine remained only a dream on the eve of World War I.

✓Reading Check **Analyzing** Why did some Jews move to Palestine?

SECTION 4 REVIEW

Vocabulary
1. **Explain** the significance of: modernism, France, Claude Monet, Pablo Picasso, abstract, Frank Lloyd Wright, Marie Curie, Albert Einstein, Sigmund Freud, Vienna, psychoanalysis, Social Darwinism, intensity, pogroms, Zionism.

Main Ideas
2. **List** some modernist movements in the arts and an individual associated with each movement. Use a chart like the one below.

Field	Movement	Individual
Literature		
Art		
Architecture		
Music		

3. **Summarize** Albert Einstein's theory of relativity.
4. **Explain** how some people applied Darwin's theory of natural selection to modern human societies.

Critical Thinking
5. **The BIG Idea Making Connections** Why are times of political and economic change often associated with times of artistic change?
6. **Analyzing** What do you think General Friedrich von Bernhardi meant when he said, "War is a biological necessity of the first importance"?
7. **Analyzing Visuals** Examine the painting by Monet on page 675. What time of day do you think it depicts? How might the scene change if Monet painted it at a different time of day?

Writing About History
8. **Expository Writing** Research the symbolist writers. Who were they and what did they write about? Write a short biography about one symbolist. Include the titles of this symbolist's best-known works.

History ONLINE
For help with the concepts in this section of *Glencoe World History*, go to glencoe.com and click Study Central™.

R Reading Strategy

Questioning Discuss with students why Zionism may have grown in Europe as a response to prejudice against Jewish people. **Ask:** Why might some people who were prejudiced against Jewish people have supported this movement? *(They may have supported Zionism because their prejudice against Jews made them desire the removal of Jews from their countries.)* AL

✓Reading Check
Answer: to escape persecution

Assess

Study Central provides summaries, interactive games, and online graphic organizers to help students review content.

Close

Identifying Have students discuss which artistic, intellectual, or political change was most radical. *(Students should support their opinion with facts from this section.)* OL

SECTION 4 REVIEW

Answers

1. Definitions for the vocabulary words are found in the section and the Glossary.
2. Answers may vary due to the individual chosen. **Literature:** naturalist, Henrik Ibsen; **Art:** impressionism, Claude Monet; post-impressionism, Vincent van Gogh; cubism, Pablo Picasso; abstract painting, Wassily Kandinsky; surrealism, Salvador Dali; **Architecture:** functionalism, Frank Lloyd Wright; **Music:** Stravinsky
3. Einstein's theory of relativity states that space and time are not absolute but are relative to the observer. Neither space nor time has an existence independent of human experience. Matter is just another form of energy.
4. **Herbert Spencer:** social progress came from the "survival of the fittest"; other **Social Darwinists:** nations engage in a "struggle for existence."
5. Artists express their reactions to these changes in their art.
6. Answers will vary. Many Social Darwinists believed that war was useful. Nations had to take up arms to protect themselves from inferior nations and cultures. Those who survived the war were the strongest and most fit—"survival of the fittest."
7. The time of day is sunrise. The colors and the light would be different if Monet painted it at a different time of day.
8. Students' essays will vary depending on the symbolist chosen.

9. B Tell students to use their logic to answer test questions. Being able to vote would enable women to bring about changes in property, divorce, and employment laws.

10. A Liberals controlled the government from 1906 to 1914. During this time, the Labour party emerged, which forced the Liberals to enact more social reforms in order to keep the voters from switching allegiance to the Labour party.

11. C Bosnia and Herzegovina were under the protection of Austria-Hungary until 1908, when Austria-Hungary annexed them, outraging Serbia and its ally Russia.

12. D Remind students that Picasso's shapes were often geometric, giving birth to the school of art known as cubism.

TEST-TAKING 

For Question 12: Form a visual image of Picasso's art.

13. B Social Darwinists believed that only strong nations should survive according to the law of "survival of the fittest" that seemed to govern the natural world.

Critical Thinking

14. C Remind students to read each statement carefully and then to check it against the graph. **A** shows that the percentage of the population living in cities is greater in 1890. Since the population is probably greater as well, that means there are more urban dwellers. **B** cannot be answered by looking at the graph, since it is not known what the population of England or Prussia was at the time. Although a greater percentage of English people lived in the cities, the total number of people could have been fewer than in Prussia's cities. **C,** however, can be proven by looking at the graph. **D** is incorrect; Russia's population increased by 5%, while England's increased by 20%.

15. A Remind students that industry in Germany blossomed between 1888 and 1918, giving rise to greater demands for democracy by the working class. To avoid having to give in to these demands, landowners and industrialists sought distraction in the form of foreign expansion.

16. D Have students choose the answer that makes the most sense. Support for political parties and jobs for teachers would not be strong enough reasons to institute universal education. Workers depended on the wages of their children, which would decrease if they went to school, so most likely they did not lobby for this change. Therefore, **D** is left as the most logical choice.

---

9. By the 1850s, what right did many women believe they had to win in order to improve the overall position of women?

- **A** Right to own property
- **B** Right to vote
- **C** Right to divorce
- **D** Right to work

Section 3 *(pp. 668–673)*

10. While ruling Great Britain from 1906 to 1914, what party passed social reforms to retain the support of the workers?

- **A** Liberal
- **B** Socialist
- **C** Labour
- **D** Conservative

11. What two territories did Austria-Hungary annex in 1908?

- **A** Bosnia and Romania
- **B** Bulgaria and Montenegro
- **C** Bosnia and Herzegovina
- **D** Serbia and Montenegro

Section 4 *(pp. 674–679)*

12. What new style of art did Pablo Picasso create?

- **A** Abstraction
- **B** Idealism
- **C** Baroque
- **D** Cubism

13. What theory did some people use to justify the dominance of Western nations?

- **A** Laissez-faire
- **B** Social Darwinism
- **C** Marxism
- **D** Zionism

Critical Thinking

Directions: Choose the best answers to the following questions.

Use the following graph to answer question 14.

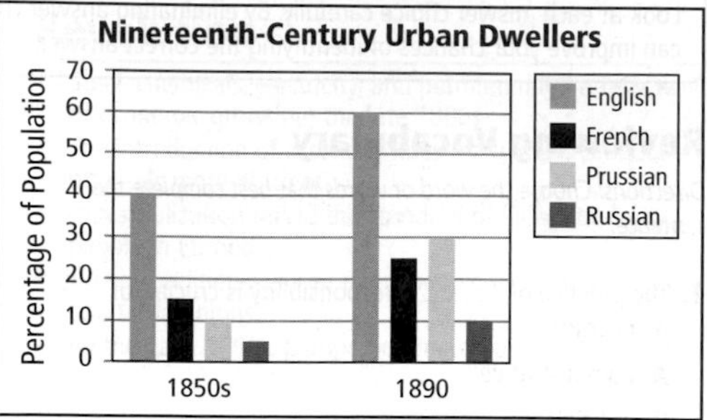

14. Which of the following statements is supported by the information in the graph?

- **A** There were fewer urban dwellers in 1890 than in the 1850s.
- **B** In 1890 more people lived in English cities than in Prussian cities.
- **C** The number of Prussian and English urban dwellers each rose 20 percent between the 1850s and 1890.
- **D** The number of urban dwellers increased by a larger percentage in Russia than in England.

15. Why did many conservatives in Germany support a policy of expansion in the late nineteenth century?

- **A** To divert people from seeking democracy
- **B** To force Otto von Bismarck from power
- **C** To promote socialism in Germany
- **D** To preserve absolute power of the emperor

16. Why did governments back public education?

- **A** To gain public support for political parties
- **B** To create more jobs for teachers
- **C** To appease the working classes
- **D** To increase the number of literate voters

Need Extra Help?

If You Missed Questions . . .	9	10	11	12	13	14	15	16
Go to Page . . .	663	668	673	676	678	682	670	664

GO ON

17. Why did the Balkans split into different factions during the late nineteenth century?
    - **A** Because the United States won the Spanish-American War
    - **B** Because the Ottoman Empire began to fall apart
    - **C** Because Serbia dominated the region
    - **D** Because Nicholas II of Russia was oppressive

Base your answer to question 18 on the cartoon below and on your knowledge of world history.

"ALL TOGETHER NOW! STOP HER!"

18. What opinion is the cartoonist expressing?
    - **A** The women's movement has no opposition to its petition for suffrage.
    - **B** Women have no right to force society to grant them suffrage.
    - **C** The suffrage movement has gained sufficient force to crush the opposition.
    - **D** Open-toe shoes show the immorality of the woman suffrage movement.

Document-Based Questions

Directions: Analyze the document and answer the short-answer questions that follow the document. Base your answers on the document and on your knowledge of world history.

When workers gathered outside the Winter Palace in St. Petersburg on January 22, 1905, to present their grievances to Czar Nicholas II, troops fired into the crowd of peaceful demonstrators. One demonstrator described what happened.

> *"We were not more than thirty yards from the soldiers, being separated from them only by the bridge over the Tarakanovskii Canal, when suddenly, without any warning and without a moment's delay, was heard the dry crack of many rifle-shots. . . . A little boy of ten years, who was carrying a church lantern, fell pierced by a bullet. Both the [black]smiths who guarded me were killed, as well as all those who were carrying the icons and banners; and all these emblems now lay scattered on the snow. The soldiers were actually shooting into the courtyards of the adjoining houses, where the crowd tried to find refuge."*

19. To what historical event is the demonstrator an eyewitness?
20. What does the imagery of the emblems being scattered in the snow seem to say?

Extended Response

21. Advances in science can sometimes change how people view their world and their universe. Compare and contrast Einstein's and Newton's understandings of the universe. Explain how they differ and how they are related.

History ONLINE
For additional test practice, use Self-Check Quizzes—Chapter 20 at glencoe.com.

Need Extra Help?

If You Missed Questions . . .	17	18	19	20	21
Go to Page . . .	673	683	683	683	676

STOP

Document-Based Questions

19. Bloody Sunday

20. It seems to say that the workers' cause had also died that day. However, that was not the case. This "Bloody Sunday" caused workers throughout Russia to call for strikes.

Extended Response

21. Answers will vary. Students may say that Newton believed the universe was like a machine in which time, space, and matter existed independently. In contrast, Einstein believed that time and space are relative to the observer and not independent. Newton's universe was one of certainty, in which natural laws could explain everything. Einstein's universe was one without certainty. Both Newton and Einstein put forth theories of the universe that were revolutionary, dramatically changing the world around them.

17. B The Ottoman Empire had unified and controlled a huge territory. When it became weak in the 1800s, Greece, Serbia, Romania, and Montenegro gained their independence. Bulgaria was placed under Russian protection, and Bosnia and Herzegovina under Austria-Hungary's protection.

18. C Tell students to review each statement using the cartoon to interpret whether the statement is a likely expression of the cartoonist's opinion.

History ONLINE
Introduce students to chapter content and key terms by having them access the Chapter 20 Overview at glencoe.com.

Need Extra Help?
Have students refer to the pages listed if they miss any of the questions.

Using the Glencoe Web Site

ePuzzles and Games

Technology Product

The Glencoe Web site offers activities that students can perform as they study the chapter content. The activities consist of a variety of puzzles and games that help students test their comprehension and recall and reinforce vocabulary and facts in each chapter.

Objectives

The Student Web Activities help students

- assess their comprehension of chapter content;
- build study skills;
- identify areas for additional study and reinforcement.

Steps

Provide students with the following steps to complete the activities:

- Locate the Web page for the textbook being studied on the Glencoe Web site glencoe.com.
- Click on **Student Center** under the textbook title.
- In the Student Center, select a unit from the Unit Resources menu and a chapter from the Chapter Activities menu using the drop-down arrows.
- Click on the **ePuzzles and Games** link.
- Click on and complete the featured puzzle or game for the chapter selected.

History ONLINE

	Student	Teacher	Parent
Beyond the Textbook	●	●	●
Chapter Overviews	●	●	●
Time Current Events	●		●
ePuzzles and Games	●		●
Concepts in Motion	●		●
Literature Connections		●	
Multi-Language Glossaries	●		●
Online Student Edition	●	●	●
Self-Check Quizzes	●		●
Student Web Activities	●		●
Study Central ™	●		●
Teaching Today		●	
Vocabulary eFlashcards	●		●
Web Activity Lesson Plans		●	

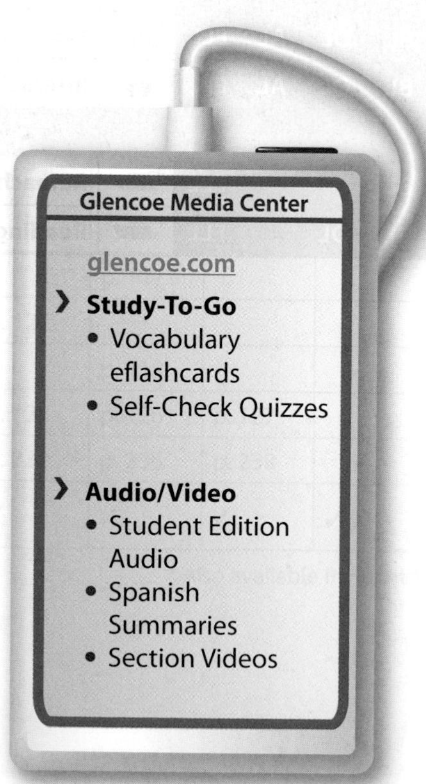

- **Timed Readings Plus in Social Studies** helps students increase their reading rate and fluency while maintaining comprehension. The 400-word passages are similar to those found on state and national assessments.
- **Reading in the Content Area: Social Studies** concentrates on six essential reading skills that help students better comprehend what they read. The book includes 75 high-interest nonfiction passages written at increasing levels of difficulty.
- **Reading Social Studies** includes strategic reading instruction and vocabulary support in Social Studies content for both ELLs and native speakers of English.

www.jamestowneducation.com

Index to National Geographic Magazine:

The following articles relate to this chapter:

- "Shattered Sudan," by Paul Salopek, February 2003
- "Water Pressure," by Fen Montaigne, September 2002
- "Panama's Right of Passage," by Lewis M. Simons, November 1999

National Geographic Society Products To order the following, call National Geographic at 1-800-368-2728:

- *National Geographic Atlas of the World* (Book)

Access National Geographic's new, dynamic MapMachine Web site and other geography resources at:
www.nationalgeographic.com
www.nationalgeographic.com/maps

Biography  

The following videotape programs are available from Glencoe as supplements to Chapter 21:

- Mahatma Gandhi: Pilgrim of Peace (ISBN 0-76-700668-2)
- Nelson Mandela: Journey to Freedom (ISBN 0-76-700113-3)

To order, call Glencoe at 1-800-334-7344. To find classroom resources to accompany many of these videos, check the following home pages:

A&E Television: www.aetv.com

The History Channel: www.historychannel.com

Reading List Generator CD-ROM

GLENCOE BOOKLINK 3

Use this database to search more than 30,000 titles to create a customized reading list for your students.

- Reading lists can be organized by students' reading level, author, genre, theme, or area of interest.
- The database provides Degrees of Reading Power™ (DRP) and Lexile™ readability scores for all selections.
- A brief summary of each selection is included.

Leveled reading suggestions for this chapter:

For students at a Grade 8 reading level:
- ***India: A Question and Answer Book,*** by Nathan Olson

For students at a Grade 9 reading level:
- ***Exploring South America,*** Rose Blue and Corinne J. Naden

For students at a Grade 10 reading level:
- ***Theodore Roosevelt Takes Charge,*** by Nancy Whitelaw

For students at a Grade 11 reading level:
- ***This Our Dark Country: The American Settlers of Liberia,*** by Catherine Reef

For students at a Grade 12 reading level:
- ***The Opening of the Suez Canal,*** by Carol Zeman Rothkopf

Focus

Bellringer
Daily Focus Transparency 21.1

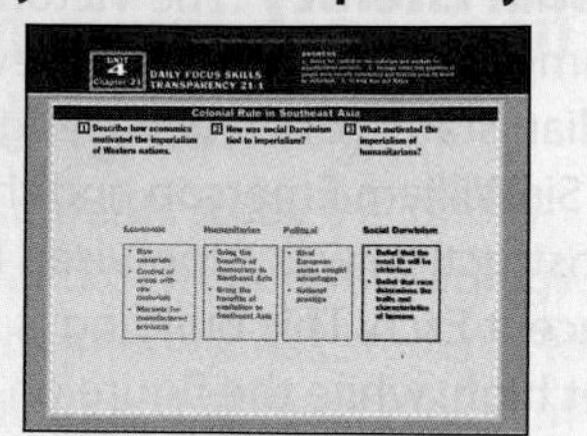

GUIDE TO READING

Answers to Graphic:

Spain (until 1898)	Philippines
Netherlands	Dutch East Indies
United States (after 1898)	Philippines
France	Indochina
Great Britain	Singapore, Burma

Section Spotlight Video

To generate student interest and provide a springboard for class discussion, access the Chapter 21, Section 1 video at glencoe.com or on the video DVD.

Resource Manager

Colonial Rule in Southeast Asia

GUIDE TO READING

The BIG Idea
Competition Among Countries
Through the new imperialism, Westerners controlled vast territories, exploited native populations, and opened markets for European products.

Content Vocabulary
- imperialism *(p. 686)*
- racism *(p. 687)*
- protectorate *(p. 688)*
- indirect rule *(p. 690)*
- direct rule *(p. 690)*

Academic Vocabulary
- exploit *(p. 690)*
- export *(p. 690)*

People and Places
- Singapore *(p. 688)*
- Burma *(p. 688)*
- Thailand *(p. 688)*
- King Mongkut *(p. 688)*
- King Chulalongkorn *(p. 688)*
- Commodore George Dewey *(p. 688)*
- Philippines *(p. 689)*
- Emilio Aguinaldo *(p. 689)*

Reading Strategy
Identifying Information Make a chart showing which countries controlled what parts of Southeast Asia.

Spain (until 1898)	
Netherlands	
United States (after 1898)	
France	
Great Britain	

During the nineteenth century, many Western powers scrambled for new territories in Southeast Asia and Africa. Governing by either indirect or direct rule, the Western powers controlled the governments and economies of their colonies. Some territories resisted colonial rule, but most early resistance movements failed.

The New Imperialism

MAIN IDEA Under new imperialism, European countries began to seek additional territory.

HISTORY & YOU Do you remember how the Industrial Revolution created demand for raw materials and new markets? Read to learn how European countries used new imperialism to meet these needs.

In the nineteenth century, a new phase of Western expansion began. European nations began to view Asian and African societies as a source of industrial raw materials and a market for Western manufactured goods.

The Scramble for Territories

In the 1880s, European states began an intense scramble for overseas territory. **Imperialism,** the extension of a nation's power over other lands, was not new. Europeans had set up colonies and trading posts in North America, South America, and Africa by the sixteenth century.

However, the imperialism of the late nineteenth century, called the "new imperialism" by some, was different. Earlier, European states had been content, especially in Africa and Asia, to set up a few trading posts where they could carry on trade and perhaps some missionary activity. Now they sought nothing less than direct control over vast territories.

Motives for Imperialism

Why did Westerners begin to increase their search for colonies after 1880? There was a strong economic motive. Capitalist states in the West were looking for both markets and raw materials such as rubber, oil, and tin for their industries. The issue was not simply an economic one, however. European nation-states were involved in heated rivalries. They acquired colonies abroad in order to gain an advantage over their rivals. Colonies were also a source of national prestige. To some people, in fact, a nation could not be great without colonies.

R Reading Strategies	C Critical Thinking	D Differentiated Instruction	W Writing Support	S Skill Practice
Teacher Edition • Summarizing, p. 688 • Read. Pri. Sources, p. 689 **Additional Resources** • Read. Skills Act., URB p. 93 • Cont. Vocab. Act., URB p. 99 • Guid. Read. Act., URB p. 124 • Read. Ess. & Note-Taking Guide, p. 229	**Teacher Edition** • Det. Cause/Effect, p. 690 **Additional Resources** • Hist. Sim. Act., URB p. 111 • Section Quiz, p. 257	**Teacher Edition** • Visual/Spatial, p. 688 **Additional Resources** • Diff. Instr. Act., URB, p. 95 • Read. Strat. for SS, p. 38	**Teacher Edition** • Expository Writing, p. 688 **Additional Resources** • Writer's Guidebook, p. 27	**Teacher Edition** • Using Geo. Skills, p. 687 **Additional Resources** • Time Line Act., URB p. 113

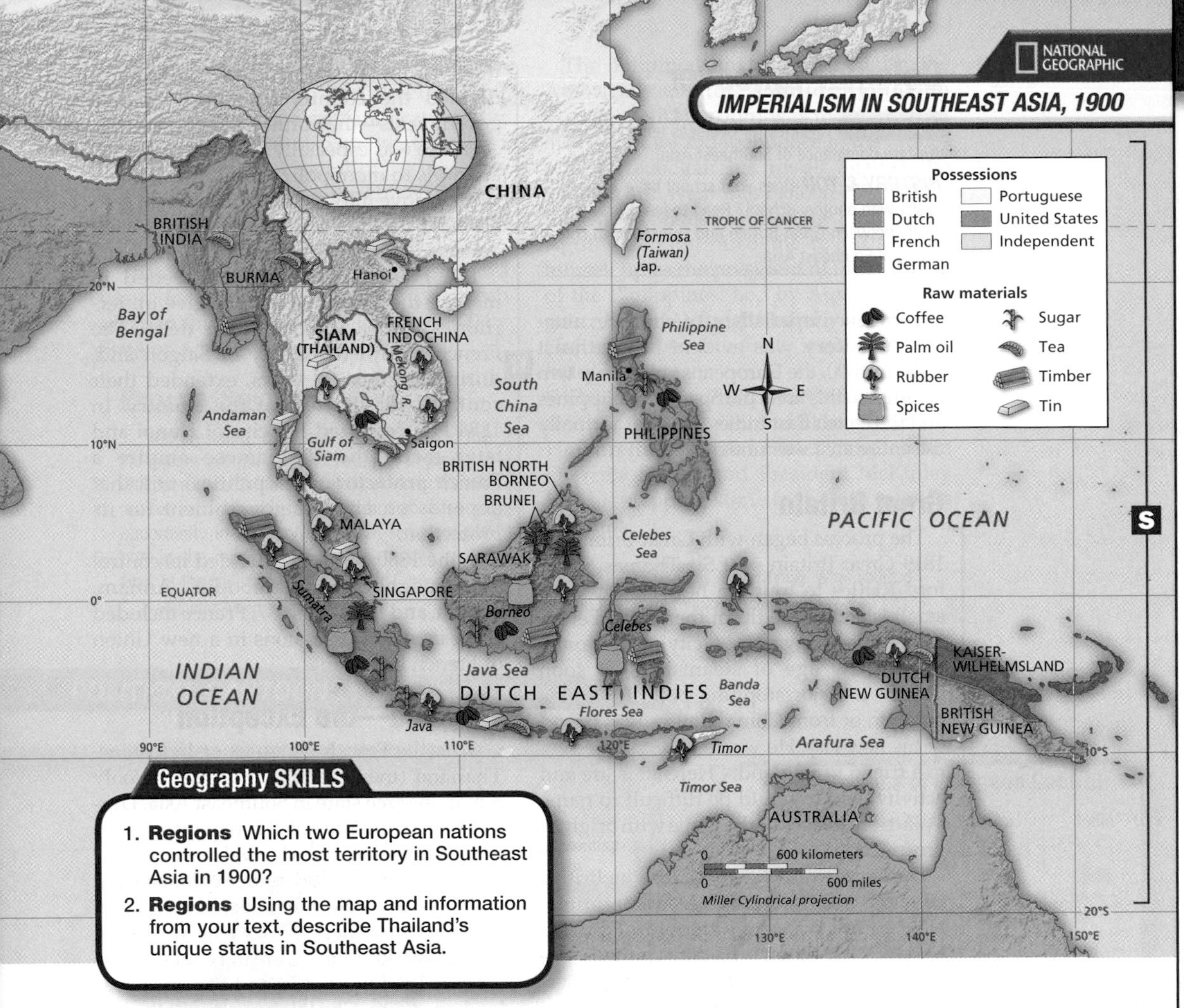

Geography SKILLS

1. **Regions** Which two European nations controlled the most territory in Southeast Asia in 1900?
2. **Regions** Using the map and information from your text, describe Thailand's unique status in Southeast Asia.

In addition, imperialism was tied to Social Darwinism and racism. Social Darwinists believed that in the struggle between nations, the fit are victorious. **Racism** is the belief that race determines traits and capabilities. Racists erroneously believe that particular races are superior or inferior.

Racist beliefs have led to the use of military force against other nations. One British professor argued in 1900, "The path of progress is strewn with the wrecks of nations; traces are everywhere to be seen of the [slaughtered remains] of inferior races. Yet these dead people are, in very truth, the stepping stones on which mankind has arisen to the higher intellectual and deeper emotional life of today."

Some Europeans took a more religious and humanitarian approach to imperialism. They believed Europeans had a moral responsibility to civilize primitive people. They called this responsibility the "white man's burden." To some, this meant bringing the Christian message to the "heathen masses." To others, it meant bringing the benefits of Western democracy and capitalism to these societies.

✓Reading Check **Describing** What were four primary motivations for the new imperialism?

Teach

S Skill Practice

Using Geography Skills

Ask: What feature of Vietnam might explain why it was divided several times in its history? *(It is a long and narrow country with a very narrow middle section between the northern and southern parts.)* AL

Geography SKILLS

Answers:
1. The Netherlands (Dutch) and Great Britain
2. Thailand's independence was supported by both Britain and France to provide a buffer between French Indochina and British Burma.

✓Reading Check

Answer: (1) economic, (2) desire for political power, (3) sense of racial superiority (Social Darwinism), (4) moral responsibility to civilize primitive people ("the white man's burden")

Additional Support

Activity: Technology Connection

Evaluating Concepts Tell students that Social Darwinists applied the theories of Charles Darwin to society. Darwin believed that weak members of a species were gradually eliminated and the population that had traits better adapted to the environment survived. Social Darwinists believed that a similar process set apart the stronger members of the human population and validated their right to dominate those who were weaker or "less fit." Ask groups of students to find out more about the philosophy of Social Darwinism using resources on the Internet. Suggest that they locate one online encyclopedia and one credible Web site on the topic. Ask students to use the information they find to answer this question. **Ask: Was Social Darwinism a justification for imperialism in the nineteenth century? Why or why not?** *(As students discuss the question, have them draw upon the text to talk about the reasons for imperialism in the nineteeth century.)* AL

C Critical Thinking

Determining Cause and Effect Remind students that the economy for colonies was based on *unequal exchange*—that is, low-value raw materials exported to Europe and high-cost manufactured items imported. **Ask:** What positive and negative effects resulted from this policy? *(Positive: jobs, infrastructure development. Negative: low-paying jobs, destruction of local crafts and industries, prevention of growth of local economy, establishment of a class system, dependence on Europe)* AL

✓Reading Check

Answer: They said they were bringing civilization and representative government to colonial peoples.

PEOPLE in HISTORY

Answer: To Saya San's Galon Army, the dragon represented the British colonizers.

Additional Support

Colonial Regimes

MAIN IDEA European countries controlled the governments and economies of their colonies in Southeast Asia.

HISTORY & YOU Does your school's student council have the power to run the school? Read to learn about European rule in Southeast Asia.

Western powers governed their new colonial empires by either indirect or direct rule. Their chief goals were to **exploit** the natural resources of the lands and to open up markets for their own manufactured goods.

Indirect and Direct Rule

Sometimes a colonial power could realize its goals by cooperating with local political elites. For example, the Dutch East India Company used **indirect rule** in the Dutch East Indies. Under indirect rule, local rulers were allowed to keep their authority and status in a new colonial setting. This made access to the region's natural resources easier. Indirect rule was cheaper because fewer officials had to be trained and it affected local culture less.

However, indirect rule was not always possible. Some local elites resisted the foreign conquest. In these cases, the local elites were replaced with Western officials. This system is called **direct rule.** For example, Great Britain administered Burma directly through its colonial government in India. In Indochina, France used both systems. It imposed direct rule in southern Vietnam, but ruled indirectly through the emperor in northern Vietnam.

To justify their conquests, Western powers spoke of bringing the blessings of Western civilization to their colonial subjects, including representative government. However, many Westerners came to fear the idea of native peoples (especially educated ones) being allowed political rights.

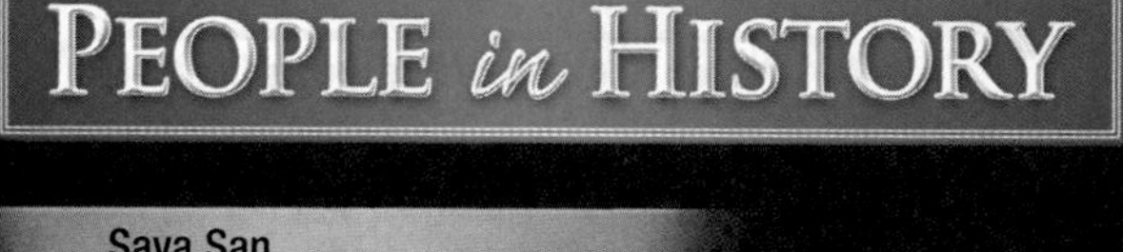

Saya San
1876–1931 Burmese Freedom Fighter

In Burmese folklore, the Galon is a bird of prey that feeds on dragon flesh. To Saya San, a Buddhist monk and physician, this myth represented his message to the British colonizers of Burma. Naming his peasant rebels the "Galon Army," Saya San led a nationalist revolt in 1930 in an attempt to expel the British from Burma. The heavy burden of British taxes rallied the peasants to his cause. His army had only spears and swords with which to fight against British guns, but they carried charms that they believed would protect them from harm. Although the revolt failed, Saya San inspired the next generation of Burmese nationalists, who gained Burma's independence seventeen years later. **In the Galon myth, what did the dragon represent to Saya San's Galon Army?**

The mythical Burmese Galon

Colonial Economies

The colonial powers did not want their colonists to develop their own industries. Thus, colonial policy stressed the **export** of raw materials. This policy often led to some form of plantation agriculture. Peasants worked as wage laborers on the foreign-owned plantations. Plantation owners kept wages at poverty levels to increase profits. Conditions on plantations were often so unhealthy that thousands died. Also, peasants bore the burden of high taxes.

Nevertheless, colonial rule did bring some benefits to Southeast Asia. A modern C economic system began there. Colonial governments built railroads, highways, and other structures that benefited native peoples as well as colonials. The development of an export market helped create an entrepreneurial class in rural areas. In the Dutch East Indies, for example, small growers of rubber, palm oil, coffee, tea, and spices began to share in the profits of the colonial enterprise. Most of the profits, however, were taken back to the colonial mother country.

✓Reading Check **Explaining** How did colonial powers justify their rule?

Extending the Content

Saya San Saya San was born Ya Gyaw in the northern part of Burma, an area that was fiercely pro-monarch and nationalist. These early influences may have shaped his own quest to bring greater justice to the peasants of Burma, who suffered economically under Britain's rule. Although the revolt was motivated by political and religious reasons and was an attempt to restore the Burmese monarchy, its underlying reasons were economic. The peasants of Burma were being heavily taxed and when the price of rice dropped many were left without any money. There was widespread support for Saya San, but unfortunately, thousands of people lost their lives in Saya San's revolt. He was captured and tried by a special tribunal. His lawyer attempted to help him, but in 1931 Saya San was sentenced to death and hanged. **Ask:** Why is Saya San seen as a hero in Burma's history? *(He fought to overthrow foreign oppression and to help the Burmese people.)*

Resistance to Colonial Rule

MAIN IDEA Native peoples had varying levels of success resisting colonial rule in Southeast Asia.

HISTORY & YOU Do you know of any occupied countries today that object to foreign rule? Read to learn how countries in Southeast Asia resisted the rule of European powers.

Many subject peoples in Southeast Asia resented being governed by Western powers. At first, resistance came from the existing ruling class. In Burma, for example, the monarch himself fought Western domination. By contrast, in Vietnam, after the emperor had agreed to French control of his country, a number of government officials set up an organization called Can Vuong ("Save the King"). They fought against the French without the emperor's help.

Sometimes, resistance to Western control took the form of peasant revolts. Under colonial rule, peasants were often driven off the land to make way for plantation agriculture. Angry peasants then vented their anger at the foreign invaders. For example, in Burma, in 1930 the Buddhist monk Saya San led a peasant uprising against the British colonial regime many years after the regime had completed its takeover.

Early resistance movements failed. They were overcome by Western powers. At the beginning of the twentieth century, a new kind of resistance began to emerge that was based on the force of nationalism. The leaders were often from a new class that the colonial rule had created: westernized intellectuals in the cities.

In many cases, this new urban middle class—composed of merchants, clerks, students, and professionals—had been educated in Western-style schools. They were the first generation of Asians to embrace the institutions and values of the West. Many spoke Western languages and worked in jobs connected with the colonial regimes.

At first, many of the leaders of these movements did not focus clearly on the idea of nationhood. Instead, they simply tried to defend the economic interests or religious beliefs of the native peoples. In Burma, for example, students at the University of Rangoon formed an organization to protest against official persecution of the Buddhist religion and British lack of respect for local religious traditions. They protested against British arrogance and failure to observe local customs in Buddhist temples. Not until the 1930s, however, did these resistance movements, such as those begun in Burma, begin to demand national independence.

✓ Reading Check **Summarizing** Explain three forms of resistance to Western domination.

Vocabulary

1. **Explain** the significance of: imperialism, racism, Singapore, Burma, protectorate, Thailand, King Mongkut, King Chulalongkorn, Commodore George Dewey, Philippines, Emilio Aguinaldo, exploit, indirect rule, direct rule, export.

Main Ideas

2. **Explain** how the new imperialism differed from old imperialism.
3. **Identify** how each area listed below was ruled—direct or indirect rule—and which European power ruled it.

Country	Direct	Indirect	Ruling Power
Dutch East Indies			
Burma			
Southern provinces in Mekong Delta			
Northern Vietnam			

4. **List** some benefits colonial rule brought to Southeast Asia. Do you think these benefits outweighed the disadvantages? Explain.

Critical Thinking

5. **The BIG Idea** **Making Inferences** Why were resistance movements often led by native leaders who had been educated in the West? How did their goals change over time?
6. **Determining Effect** Identify the effects of colonial rule on the colonies.
7. **Analyzing Visuals** Explain which features are used in the map on page 687 to present information visually, without the use of text.

Writing About History

8. **Expository Writing** Use varied media to determine how Filipino political groups today view the relationship between their country and the United States. Write an essay based on your findings.

History ONLINE
For help with the concepts in this section of *Glencoe World History*, go to glencoe.com and click Study Central™.

691

✓ Reading Check

Answers: (1) resistance from the ruling class to Western takeover; (2) peasant revolts, often as a result of being driven off their land to make way for plantation agriculture; (3) Westernized urban middle class began to demand independence

Assess

History ONLINE

Study Central provides summaries, interactive games, and online graphic organizers to help students review content.

Close

Summarizing **Ask:** Why did European nations want control of countries in Southeast Asia? *(Southeast Asia was important to the markets in China and India. Controlling this area ensured access to the Far East. The Europeans also profited from the colonies' natural resources.)* **OL**

Answers

1. Definitions for the vocabulary words are found in the section and the Glossary.
2. **Old:** European states set up a few trading posts; **New:** European states wanted direct control of colonial raw materials and markets. In the struggle between nations, the fit—Western imperialists—are victorious; racist beliefs led to use of military force against other nations and to the spread of imperialism.
3. Dutch East Indies: indirect, Netherlands; Burma: direct, Britain; southern Mekong delta: direct, France; northern Vietnam: indirect, France
4. built railroads, highways, and other structures, created an entrepreneurial class; answers will vary
5. understood Western institutions and values; began to defend their economic interests and focus on independence
6. representative institutions; plantation agriculture; high taxes; modern economic system; railroads, highways; export market; resistance movements
7. The map uses colors and small pictures to present information visually.
8. Students will write essays based on their research.

Focus

Bellringer

Daily Focus Transparency 21.2

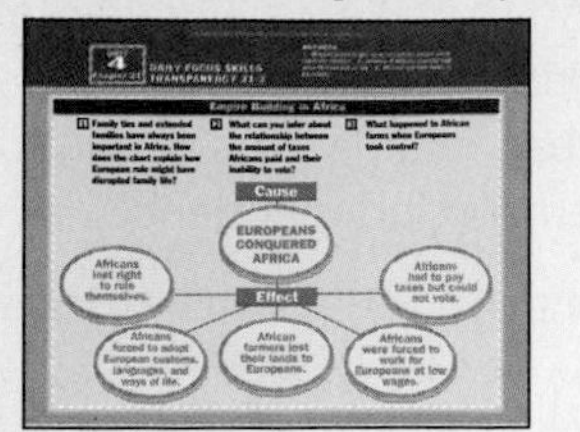

GUIDE TO READING

Answers to Graphic:

Western Power	Area of Africa
Belgium	Central and East
Britain	West, North, East, South
France	West, North, Central
Germany	East

Section Spotlight Video

To generate student interest and provide a springboard for class discussion, access the Chapter 21, Section 2 video at glencoe.com or on the video DVD.

Resource Manager

R Reading Strategies	C Critical Thinking	D Differentiated Instruction	W Writing Support	S Skill Practice
Teacher Edition • Skimming, p. 695 • Summarizing, p. 696 • Questioning, p. 697 • Read. Pri. Sources, p. 698 • Identifying, p. 699 **Additional Resources** • Guid. Read., URB p. 125 • Read. Ess. & Note-Taking Guide, p. 232	**Teacher Edition** • Analyzing Pri. Sources, p. 694 • Det. Cause/Effect, p. 696 • Compare/Contrast p. 697 **Additional Resources** • Crit. Think. Act., URB p. 104 • People in World Hist. Act., URB p. 115 • Section Quiz, p. 258	**Teacher Edition** • ELL, p. 698 **Additional Resources** • English Learner Act., p. 97 • Enrich. Act., URB p. 122	**Teacher Edition** • Expository Writing, p. 695 **Additional Resources** • Writer's Guidebook, p. 31	**Teacher Edition** • Using Geo. Skills, p. 693 **Additional Resources** • Mapping Hist. Act., URB p. 107

SECTION 2

Empire Building in Africa

GUIDE TO READING

The BIG Idea

Competition Among Countries
Virtually all of Africa was under European rule by 1900.

Content Vocabulary
- annexed *(p. 692)*
- indigenous *(p. 696)*

Academic Vocabulary
- uncharted *(p. 695)*
- traditions *(p. 698)*

People
- Muhammad Ali *(p. 693)*
- David Livingstone *(p. 695)*
- Henry Stanley *(p. 695)*
- Zulu *(p. 696)*

Reading Strategy

Categorizing Information As you read, make a chart like the one below showing which countries controlled what parts of Africa.

Western Power	Area of Africa
Belgium	
Britain	
France	
Germany	

During the late nineteenth century, the major European powers scrambled to colonize Africa. Virtually all of Africa was under European rule by 1900. Maintaining that rule was not easy, however. African nationalism emerged during the early part of the twentieth century.

West Africa and North Africa

MAIN IDEA European countries exercised increasing control over West Africa and North Africa, especially once the Suez Canal was completed.

HISTORY & YOU Do you take the long way to get to a destination, or do you look for shortcuts? Read about how Europeans constructed a shortcut for ships through Egypt.

Before 1880, Europeans controlled little of the African continent directly. They were content to let African rulers and merchants represent European interests. Between 1880 and 1900, however, Great Britain, France, Germany, Belgium, Italy, Spain, and Portugal, spurred by intense rivalries among themselves, placed virtually all of Africa under European rule.

West Africa

Europeans had a keen interest in Africa's raw materials, especially those of West Africa—peanuts, timber, hides, and palm oil. Earlier in the nineteenth century, Europeans had profited from the slave trade in this part of Africa. By the late 1800s, however, trade in enslaved people had virtually ended. As the slave trade declined, Europe's interest in other forms of trade increased. The growing European presence in West Africa led to increasing tensions with African governments in the area.

For a long time, most African states were able to maintain their independence. However, in 1874 Great Britain **annexed** (incorporated a country within a state) the west coastal states as the first British colony of Gold Coast. At about the same time, Britain established a protectorate in Nigeria. By 1900, France had added the huge area of French West Africa to its colonial empire. This left France in control of the largest part of West Africa. In addition, Germany controlled Togo, Cameroon, German Southwest Africa, and German East Africa.

North Africa

Egypt had been part of the Ottoman Empire, but as Ottoman rule declined, the Egyptians sought their independence. In 1805

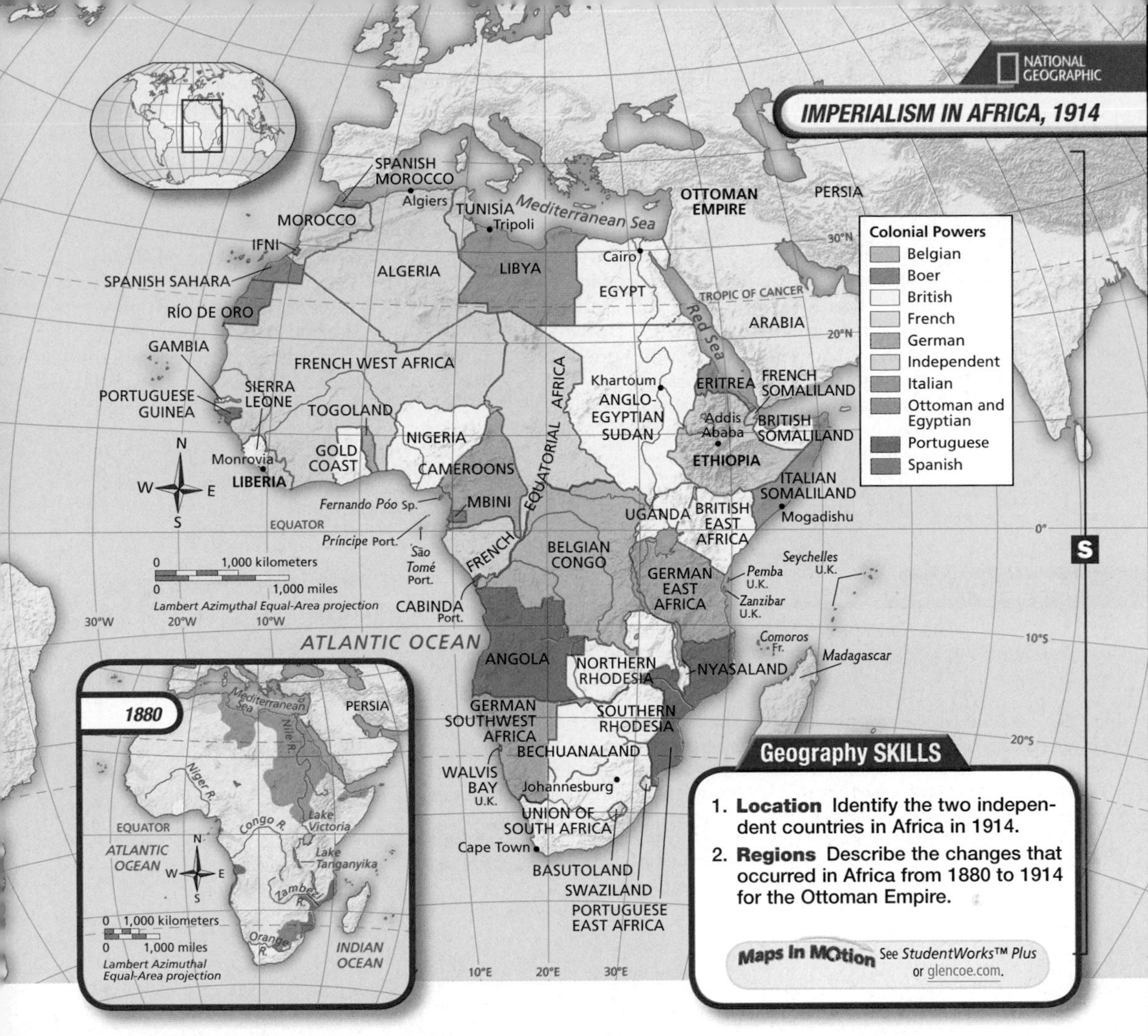

Geography SKILLS

1. **Location** Identify the two independent countries in Africa in 1914.
2. **Regions** Describe the changes that occurred in Africa from 1880 to 1914 for the Ottoman Empire.

Maps In MOtion See StudentWorks™ Plus or glencoe.com.

an officer of the Ottoman army named **Muhammad Ali** seized power and established a separate Egyptian state.

During the next 30 years, Muhammad Ali introduced a series of reforms to bring Egypt into the modern world. He modernized the army, set up a public school system, and helped create small industries that refined sugar, produced textiles and munitions, and built ships.

The growing economic importance of the Nile Valley in Egypt, along with the development of steamships, gave Europeans the desire to build a canal east of Cairo to connect the Mediterranean and Red Seas. In 1854 a French entrepreneur, Ferdinand de Lesseps, signed a contract to begin building the Suez Canal. The canal was completed in 1869.

The British took an active interest in Egypt after the Suez Canal was opened. Believing that the canal was its "lifeline to India," Great Britain tried to gain as much control as possible over the canal area.

In 1875 Britain bought Egypt's share in the Suez Canal. When an Egyptian army revolt against foreign influence broke out in 1881, Britain suppressed the revolt. Egypt became a British protectorate in 1914.

Teach

S Skill Practice

Using Geography Skills Ask: Without the Suez Canal, what is the route that ships would have to take from Britain to India? *(Ships would have to travel down the west coast of Africa, around the tip, and then head northeast to India.)* **OL**

Geography SKILLS

Answers:

1. Liberia, Ethiopia
2. Ottomans lost territory to Britain and Italy. Britain also expanded into southern Africa. France expanded into northwest and central Africa. Boer territory was incorporated into British-held Union of South Africa. Most of Africa was under European control by 1914.

Additional Support

Activity: Interdisciplinary Connection

Mathematics Have students work in pairs to calculate the distance by sea between London and Mumbai (Bombay) before the opening of the Suez Canal. Suggest that they put a piece of string along the route that a ship would take. They can then mark the length on the string and measure the string to calculate the distance. Then have them calculate the distance of the route that ships would take from London to Mumbai after 1869. **Ask:** What is the approximate difference in miles between the two routes? What would that difference mean to British ships? *(Depending on their calculations, students will find that the distance saved is about 5,000 miles. The Suez Canal shortened the trip between London and Bombay by about 40%. Using the Suez Canal would mean that ships could make more journeys in a shorter amount of time, thus increasing their potential profit.)* **OL**

C Critical Thinking

Analyzing Primary Sources

Ask: What appears to be the mood of the spectators on the bank? Why? *(They are interested enough in this historic event to gather to witness it and are excited at the prospect of the greater economic prosperity the event will bring.)* **OL**

CRITICAL THINKING SKILLS

Answers:

1. It was the shortest land distance between the Mediterranean Sea and the Red Sea.
2. The canal was very important to British shipping. Britain wanted to own the canal to ensure its merchants and navy could use it.

✓Reading Check

Answer: The British wanted access to the Suez Canal and Egypt's resources. They wanted to establish their presence before other European nations, such as France and Italy, gained control.

The British believed that they should also control the Sudan, south of Egypt, to protect their interests in Egypt and the Suez Canal. In 1881 Muslim cleric Muhammad Ahmad, known as the Mahdi (in Arabic, "the rightly guided one"), launched a revolt that brought much of the Sudan under his control.

Britain sent a military force under General Charles Gordon to restore Egyptian authority over the Sudan. However, Muhammad Ahmad's troops wiped out Gordon's army at Khartoum in 1885. General Gordon himself died in the battle. Not until 1898 were British troops able to seize the Sudan.

The French also had colonies in North Africa. In 1879, after about 150,000 French people had settled in the region of Algeria, the French government established control there. Two years later, France imposed a protectorate on neighboring Tunisia. In 1912 France established a protectorate over much of Morocco.

Italy joined the competition for colonies in North Africa by attempting to take over Ethiopia. In 1896, however, the Italian invading forces were defeated. Italy now was the only European state defeated by an African state. This humiliating loss led Italy to try again in 1911. Italy invaded and seized Turkish Tripoli, which it renamed Libya.

✓Reading Check **Explaining** Why did the British set up settlements in Africa?

INFOGRAPHICS

The Suez Canal Opens for Business

The Suez Canal, built by the French using Egyptian labor, was completed in 1869. This waterway linked the Mediterranean Sea and Red Sea. Instead of sailing around Africa, European ships could now pass through the canal to reach eastern Asia in much less time.

At this time, demand for Egyptian cotton made Egypt's economy strong. Egypt's ruler, Khedive Ismā'īl, spent large sums on modernizing his country, building roads, railways, and factories. By the 1870s, however, economic conditions had worsened, forcing Egypt to borrow from foreigners to pay for these projects. To help pay the debt, Ismā'īl sold Egypt's share of the Suez Canal to Britain in 1875.

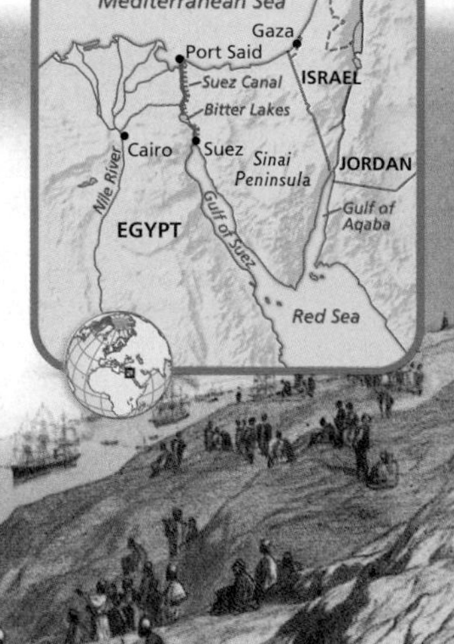

C

CRITICAL THINKING SKILLS

This painting by Edouard Riou (1833–1900) shows the first British ships crossing the Suez Canal on November 17, 1869.

1. **Explaining** Why did the Egyptians and Europeans choose to build the Suez Canal in this location?
2. **Making Inferences** Why do you think the British wanted to buy Egypt's share of the canal?

Differentiated Instruction

Leveled Activities

BL Guided Reading Activity, URB p. 125

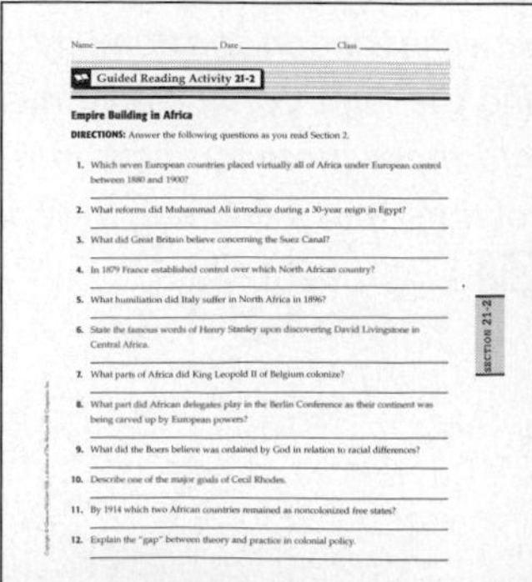

OL Critical Thinking Skills Activity, URB p. 104

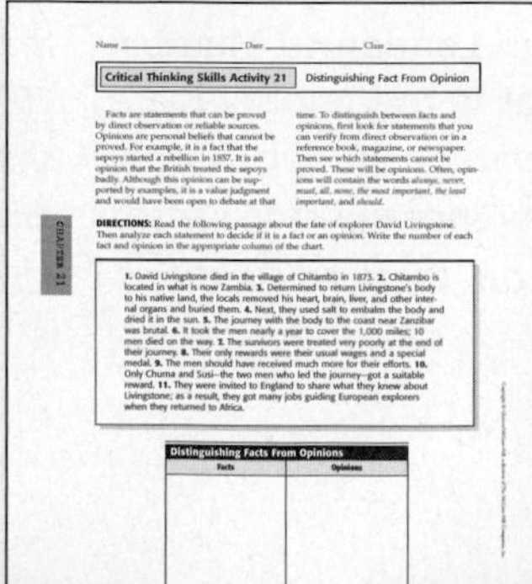

AL People in World History Activity, URB p. 115

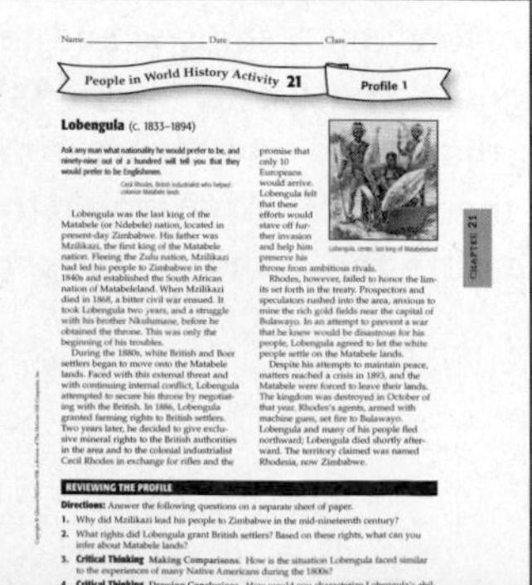

ELL English Learner Activity, URB p. 97

Central and East Africa

MAIN IDEA European powers competed for colonies in Central Africa and East Africa.

HISTORY & YOU Have you ever read a description of a far-off land that made you want to see it for yourself? Read to learn how reports of explorers stirred European interest in Africa.

Central Africa

Central African territories were soon added to the list of European colonies. Explorers aroused popular interest in the dense tropical jungles of Central Africa.

David Livingstone was one such explorer. He arrived in Africa in 1841 as a 27-year-old medical missionary. During the 30 years he spent in Africa, Livingstone trekked through **uncharted** regions. He sometimes traveled by canoe, but mostly Livingstone walked and spent much of his time exploring the interior of the continent. R

During his travels through Africa, Livingstone made detailed notes of his discoveries. He sent this information back to London whenever he could. The maps of Africa were often redrawn based on Livingstone's reports. A major goal of Livingstone's explorations was to find a navigable river that would open Central Africa to European commerce and to Christianity.

When Livingstone disappeared for awhile, an American newspaper, the *New York Herald*, hired a young journalist, **Henry Stanley**, to find the explorer. Stanley did find him, on the eastern shore of Lake Tanganyika. Overwhelmed by finding Livingstone alive if not well, Stanley greeted the explorer with these now-famous words, "Dr. Livingstone, I presume?"

After Livingstone's death in 1873, Stanley remained in Africa to carry on the great explorer's work. Unlike Livingstone, however, Henry Stanley had a strong dislike of Africa. He once said, "I detest the land most heartily."

In the 1870s, Stanley explored the Congo River in Central Africa and sailed down it to the Atlantic Ocean. Soon, he was encouraging the British to send settlers to the Congo River basin. When Britain refused, Stanley turned to King Leopold II of Belgium.

King Leopold II was the real driving force behind the colonization of Central Africa. He rushed enthusiastically into the pursuit of an empire in Africa. "To open to civilization," he said, "the only part of our globe where it has not yet penetrated, to pierce the darkness which envelops whole populations, is a crusade, if I may say so, a crusade worthy of this century of progress." Profit, however, was equally important to Leopold. In 1876 he hired Henry Stanley to set up Belgian settlements in the Congo.

Leopold's claim to the vast territories of the Congo aroused widespread concern among other European states. France, in particular, rushed to plant its flag in the heart of Africa. Leopold ended up with the territories around the Congo River. France occupied the areas farther north.

East Africa

By 1885, Britain and Germany had become the chief rivals in East Africa. Germany came late to the ranks of the imperialist powers. At first, the German chancellor Otto von Bismarck had downplayed the importance of colonies. As more and more Germans called for a German empire, however, Bismarck became a convert to colonialism. As he expressed it, "All this colonial business is a sham, but we need it for the elections."

In addition to its West African holdings, Germany tried to develop colonies in East Africa. Most of East Africa had not yet been claimed by any other power. However, the British were also interested in the area because control of East Africa would connect the British Empire in Africa from South Africa to Egypt. Portugal and Belgium also claimed parts of East Africa. W

To settle conflicting claims, the Berlin Conference met in 1884 and 1885. The conference officially recognized both British and German claims for territory in East Africa. Portugal received a clear claim on Mozambique. No African delegates, however, were present at this conference.

✓ **Reading Check** **Examining** What effect did King Leopold II have on European colonization of the Congo River basin?

R Reading Strategy

Skimming **Ask:** What was David Livingstone trying to accomplish with his exploration? *(He was trying to find a river that would open central Africa to commerce and Christianity.)* **BL**

Did You Know?

King Leopold became the recognized ruler of the Congo Free State in 1885, beginning a reign that ended in 1908, when the Belgian parliament took control. During this time millions of Congolese inhabitants died as a result of Leopold's harsh policies.

W Writing Support

Expository Writing Have students write a summary of the verdict of the Berlin Conference in regard to territorial claims. **AL**

✓ **Reading Check**

Answer: He aroused widespread concern among other European states, which began laying claim to African lands.

Hands-On Chapter Project
Step 2

Create a Slide Show

Step 2: Interviewing Historical Figures Small groups of students continue developing the slide show on imperialism that they began in Section 1 on page 688.

Directions: Write the Big Idea on the board. Have students work in pairs to think of questions that they might ask members of the Zulu or Congolese tribe, Egyptians, Cecil Rhodes, Henry Stanley, or Boer leaders about the colonization of Africa by the Europeans. Have students summarize what these people might have said in response, based on the information in this section. Students should place photos or sketches of their person on poster board and their summary underneath.

Summarizing: Have groups share what they learned about the Big Idea. **OL**

(Chapter Project is continued in Section 3.)

D Differentiated Instruction

English Language Learners

Write the word *assimilate* on the board. Point out that the word *similar* can be seen within it. Tell students that the French wanted to assimilate the Africans, or make them similar to themselves. ELL

R Reading Strategy

Reading Primary Sources

Ask a volunteer to read "The White Man's Burden" to the class. Then discuss other literature that deals with imperialism, such as E. M. Forster's *A Passage to India* or Joseph Conrad's *Heart of Darkness.* Ask students to find passages that describe life during this period. OL

DOCUMENT-BASED QUESTIONS

Answers:

1. massacres, land confiscation, slavery, beatings, diseases, exploitation
2. Students might select "To serve your captives' needs." Kipling assumed his readers shared his belief that the colonized people were inferior and the imperialists were helping them.

Most other European nations governed their African possessions through a form of direct rule. This was true in the French colonies. At the top was a French official, usually known as a governor-general. He was appointed from Paris and governed with the aid of a bureaucracy in the capital city of the colony.

D The French ideal was to assimilate African subjects into French culture rather than preserve native **traditions.** Africans were eligible to run for office and even serve in the French National Assembly in Paris. A few were also appointed to high-powered positions in the colonial administration.

Rise of African Nationalism

As in Southeast Asia, a new class of leaders emerged in Africa by the beginning of the twentieth century. Educated in colonial schools or in Western nations, they were the first generation of Africans to know a great deal about the West.

The members of this new class admired Western culture and sometimes disliked the ways of their own countries. They were eager to introduce Western ideas and institutions into their own societies. Still, many of these new leaders came to resent the foreigners and their arrogant contempt for African peoples. These intellectuals recognized the gap between theory and practice

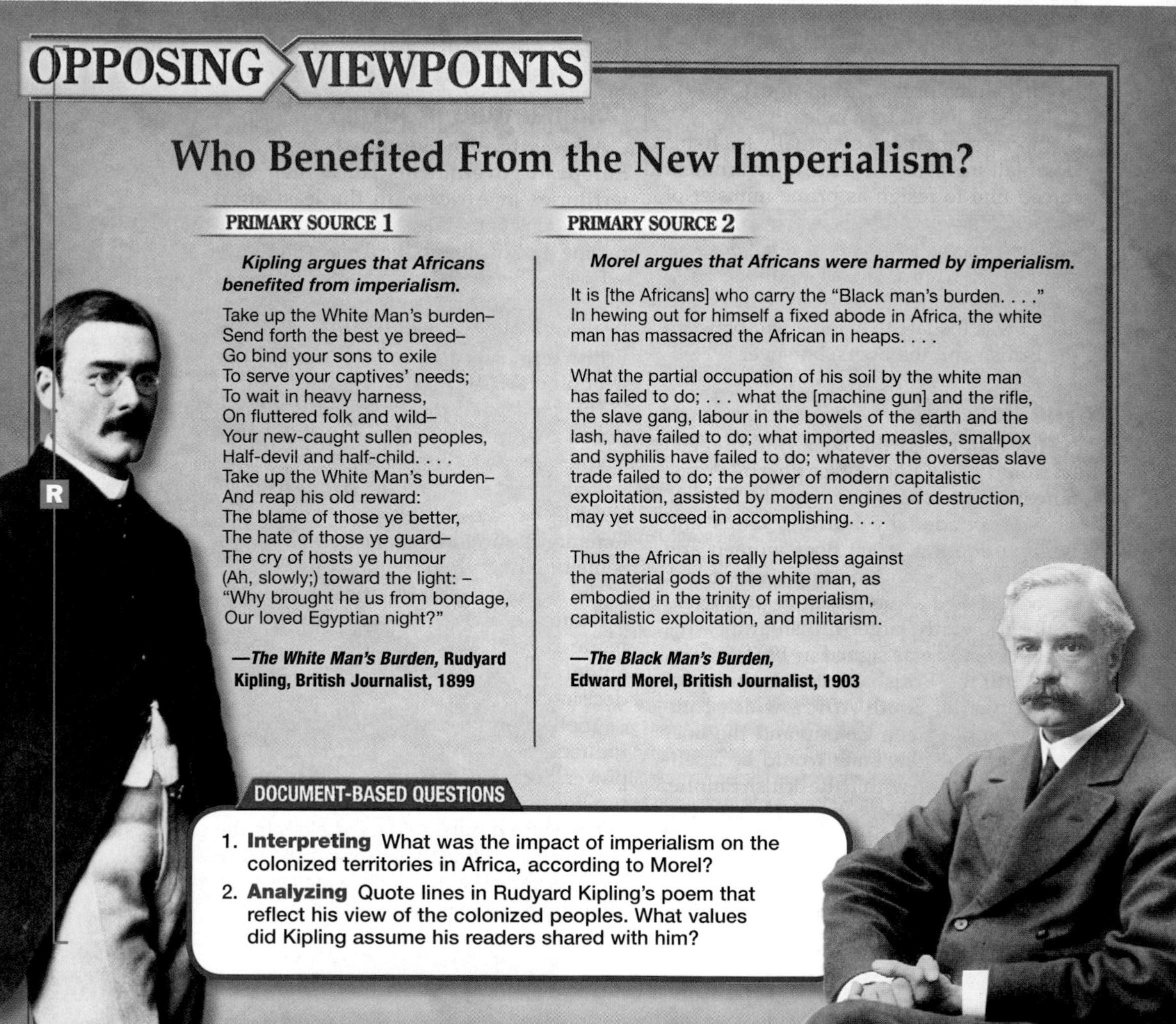

OPPOSING VIEWPOINTS

Who Benefited From the New Imperialism?

PRIMARY SOURCE 1

Kipling argues that Africans benefited from imperialism.

Take up the White Man's burden–
Send forth the best ye breed–
Go bind your sons to exile
To serve your captives' needs;
To wait in heavy harness,
On fluttered folk and wild–
Your new-caught sullen peoples,
Half-devil and half-child. . . .
Take up the White Man's burden–
And reap his old reward:
The blame of those ye better,
The hate of those ye guard–
The cry of hosts ye humour
(Ah, slowly;) toward the light: –
"Why brought he us from bondage,
Our loved Egyptian night?"

—*The White Man's Burden,* Rudyard Kipling, British Journalist, 1899

PRIMARY SOURCE 2

Morel argues that Africans were harmed by imperialism.

It is [the Africans] who carry the "Black man's burden. . . ." In hewing out for himself a fixed abode in Africa, the white man has massacred the African in heaps. . . .

What the partial occupation of his soil by the white man has failed to do; . . . what the [machine gun] and the rifle, the slave gang, labour in the bowels of the earth and the lash, have failed to do; what imported measles, smallpox and syphilis have failed to do; whatever the overseas slave trade failed to do; the power of modern capitalistic exploitation, assisted by modern engines of destruction, may yet succeed in accomplishing. . . .

Thus the African is really helpless against the material gods of the white man, as embodied in the trinity of imperialism, capitalistic exploitation, and militarism.

—*The Black Man's Burden,* Edward Morel, British Journalist, 1903

DOCUMENT-BASED QUESTIONS

1. **Interpreting** What was the impact of imperialism on the colonized territories in Africa, according to Morel?
2. **Analyzing** Quote lines in Rudyard Kipling's poem that reflect his view of the colonized peoples. What values did Kipling assume his readers shared with him?

R

Additional Support

Teacher Tip

Collaborative Learning Remind students that planning can help a project run more smoothly. Draw a three-column chart on the chalkboard with each student's name in a list. Leave room for students to fill in what they will be researching and what they have found.

Activity: Collaborative Learning

Drawing Conclusions Tell students that there were significant civilizations in Africa before the arrival of the Europeans, such as the Mali and Songhai empires and Great Zimbabwe. Have students work together to find illustrations of the art and architecture from these societies. Have them assemble a bulletin board display with captions underneath the art, explaining the origin and significance of each site or object pictured.

Ask: What conclusions might be drawn about the civilizations that produced these works? How does this understanding influence your perception of imperialism in Africa? *(Students' answers should show an understanding of the cultural pressures that imperialism imposed on parts of Africa.)* OL in colonial policy. Westerners had exalted democracy, equality, and political freedom but did not apply these values in the colonies.

There were few democratic institutions. Native peoples could have only low-paying jobs in the colonial bureaucracy. To many Africans, colonialism had meant the loss of their farmlands or employment on plantations or in factories run by foreigners. Some lost even more, as Lobengula, a southern African king, told Britain's Queen Victoria in this letter:

PRIMARY SOURCE

> "Some time ago a party of men came to my country, the principal one appearing to be a man called Rudd. They asked me for a place to dig for gold, and said they would give me certain things for the right to do so. I told them to bring what they could give and I would show them what I would give. A document was written and presented to me for signature. I asked what it contained, and was told that in it were my words and the words of those men. I put my hand to it. About three months afterwards I heard from other sources that I had given by the document the right to all the minerals of my country." **R**
>
> —*The Imperialism Reader,* Louis L. Snyder, ed.

Middle-class Africans did not suffer as much as poor African peasant plantation workers. However, members of the middle class also had complaints. They usually qualified only for menial jobs in the government or business. Even then, their salaries were lower than those of Europeans in similar jobs.

Europeans expressed their superiority over Africans in other ways. Segregated clubs, schools, and churches were set up as more European officials brought their wives and began to raise families. Europeans were also condescending in their relationships with Africans. For instance, Europeans had a habit of addressing Africans by their first names or calling an adult male "boy."

Such conditions led many members of the new urban educated class to feel great confusion toward their colonial rulers and the civilization the colonists represented. The educated Africans were willing to admit the superiority of many aspects of Western culture. However, these intellectuals fiercely hated colonial rule and were determined to assert their own nationality and cultural destiny. Out of this mixture of hopes and resentments emerged the first stirrings of modern nationalism in Africa.

During the first quarter of the twentieth century, resentment turned to action. Across Africa, native peoples began to organize political parties and movements seeking the end of foreign rule. They wanted to be independent and self-governed.

✓Reading Check **Evaluating** Why were many African intellectuals frustrated by colonial policy?

SECTION 2 REVIEW

Vocabulary

1. **Explain** the significance of: annexed, Muhammad Ali, David Livingstone, uncharted, Henry Stanley, indigenous, Zulu, traditions.

Main Ideas

2. **Explain** why the British were so interested in controlling the Sudan.
3. **Name** a major goal that David Livingstone had for exploring Central Africa.
4. **List** the ways in which the French system of direct rule included Africans. Use a chart like the one below.

Roles of Africans in the French System of Direct Rule
1.
2.
3.
4.

Critical Thinking

5. **The BIG Idea** **Drawing Conclusions** What can you conclude from the fact that African delegates were not included in the Berlin Conference of 1884?
6. **Making Inferences** Why do you think the Boers resisted British rule?
7. **Analyzing Visuals** Examine the painting of the Suez Canal on page 694. How do you think the artist's portrayal of the scene provides a sense of setting and perspective? What elements suggest a time frame for the scene?

Writing About History

8. **Expository Writing** Research the importance of the Suez Canal today. Write a paper comparing the present-day significance of the canal to its historical significance.

History ONLINE

For help with the concepts in this section of *Glencoe World History,* go to glencoe.com and click Study Central™.

R Reading Strategy

Identifying **Ask:** According to this account, how did the Europeans take advantage of Lobengula? *(Rudd capitalized on the fact that Lobengula could not read English. He tricked Lobengula into signing away the resources of his country.)* **OL**

✓Reading Check

Answer: Westerners exalted democracy, equality, and political freedom, but they did not apply these values in the colonies.

Assess

History ONLINE

Study Central provides summaries, interactive games, and online graphic organizers to help students review content.

Close

Synthesizing Have students work in groups to create a chart that answers the question of why Africa was important to European countries. **OL**

Answers

1. Definitions for the vocabulary words are found in the section and the Glossary.
2. to protect their interests in Egypt and the Suez Canal
3. to find a navigable river that would open central Africa to European commerce and to Christianity
4. (1) assimilated Africans into French culture; (2) made them eligible to run for office; (3) allowed them to serve in the French National Assembly in Paris; (4) appointed some to high positions in colonial administration
5. Answers may include that no one wanted to hear what they thought of European plans for their continent; excluding them showed European arrogance and disrespect toward Africans.
6. Answers will vary. The Boers were Dutch descendants and spoke Dutch. The Boers had occupied this land since the seventeenth century. They probably saw British settlers as occupiers of their land and a threat to their control.
7. The painting shows the canal as being large enough to fit many ships. The landscape shows the setting. The people's clothing and the types of ships set the time frame.
8. Students will compare past and present significance of the Suez Canal.

Focus

Bellringer

Daily Focus Transparency 21.3

GUIDE TO READING

Answers to Graphic:

Cause	Effect
1. British textiles	local industry severely damaged
2. cotton crops	food supplies unable to keep up with growing population
3. school system	trained children to serve in government, army
4. railroad, telegraph, telephone services	improved transportation, communication

Section Spotlight Video

To generate student interest and provide a springboard for class discussion, access the Chapter 21, Section 3 video at glencoe.com or on the video DVD.

SECTION 3

British Rule in India

GUIDE TO READING

The BIG Idea

Struggle for Rights The British brought stability to India but destroyed native industries and degraded Indians.

Content Vocabulary
- sepoys *(p. 702)*
- viceroy *(p. 704)*

Academic Vocabulary
- civil *(p. 704)*
- estate *(p. 707)*

People, Places, and Events
- Kanpur *(p. 703)*
- Queen Victoria *(p. 703)*
- Bombay *(p. 705)*
- Indian National Congress *(p. 705)*
- Mohandas Gandhi *(p. 706)*
- Rabindranath Tagore *(p. 707)*

Reading Strategy

Determining Cause and Effect As you read, use a chart like the one below to identify some causes and effects of British influence on India.

Cause	Effect
1. British textiles	
2. cotton crops	
3. school system	
4. railroad, telegraph, telephone services	

The British brought order and stability to India, but India paid a high price for British rule. The mistrust and cultural differences between the British and Indians sparked an independence movement and renewed interest among Indians in their culture and history.

The Sepoy Mutiny

MAIN IDEA Mistrust and cultural differences between the British and Indians led to violent conflict.

HISTORY & YOU Does your family follow certain traditions or religious practices? Read to learn how cultural differences helped ignite an Indian rebellion in 1857.

Over the course of the eighteenth century, British power in India had increased while the power of the Mogul rulers had declined (see Chapter 15). The British government gave a trading company, the British East India Company, power to become actively involved in India's political and military affairs. To rule India, the British East India Company had its own soldiers and forts. It also hired Indian soldiers, known as **sepoys,** to protect the company's interests in the region.

Events Leading to Revolt

In 1857 a growing Indian distrust of the British led to a revolt. The British call the revolt the Sepoy Mutiny. Indians call it the First War of Independence. Neutral observers label it the Great Rebellion.

The major immediate cause of the revolt was a rumor that the troops' new rifle cartridges were greased with cow and pig fat. The cow was sacred to Hindus. The pig was taboo to Muslims. To load a rifle at that time, soldiers had to bite off the end of the cartridge. To the sepoys, touching these greased cartridges to their lips would mean that they were polluted.

A group of sepoys at an army post in Meerut, near Delhi, refused to load their rifles with the cartridges. The British charged them with mutiny, publicly humiliated them, and put them in prison. This treatment of their comrades enraged the sepoy troops in Meerut. They went on a rampage, killing 50 European men, women, and children. Soon other Indians joined the revolt, including Indian princes whose land the British had taken.

Within a year, however, Indian troops loyal to the British and fresh British troops had crushed the rebellion. Although Indian troops fought bravely and outnumbered the British by about 230,000 to 45,000, they were not well organized. Rivalries between

Resource Manager

R Reading Strategies	C Critical Thinking	D Differentiated Instruction	W Writing Support	S Skill Practice
Teacher Edition • Read. Pri. Sources, p. 704 • Identifying, p. 707 **Additional Resources** • Pri. Source Read. Act., URB p. 117 • Guid. Read. Act., URB p. 126 • Read. Ess. & Note-Taking Guide, p. 235	**Teacher Edition** • Compare/Contrast, p. 705 • Det. Cause/Effect, pp. 705, 706 **Additional Resources** • Hist. & Geo. Act., URB p. 105 • Section Quiz, p. 259	**Teacher Edition** • Logical/Math., p. 704 **Additional Resources** • Coop. Learn. Act., URB p. 109	**Teacher Edition** • Expository Writing, p. 706 **Additional Resources** • World Art & Music Act., URB p. 119	**Teacher Edition** • Visual Literacy, p. 703 **Additional Resources** • Skills Reinforc. Act., p. 103

PRIMARY SOURCE INFOGRAPHICS

The Great Rebellion in India

Causes of the Sepoy Mutiny

- Increased British power in India; decreased power for Mogul rulers
- Growing distrust of British
- British disrespect for Indian religions and culture

Effects

- End of the Mogul Empire
- Beginning of direct British rule in India
- Indian nationalist movement

THE CLEMENCY OF CANNING.

CRITICAL THINKING SKILLS

Charles Canning was the British governor-general in India. After the British crushed the sepoy uprising, Canning declared that any mutineer who had not committed murder could be spared execution. The *Times* of London called this decree the "clemency of Canning."

1. **Identifying** The sepoys made up what percentage of the troops of the British East India Company in 1857?
2. **Analyzing** What British attitude toward the sepoys does the cartoon show? Describe details from the cartoon that reveal this attitude.

Hindus and Muslims kept the Indians from working together.

Atrocities were terrible on both sides. At **Kanpur** (Cawnpore), Indians massacred 200 defenseless women and children in a building known as the House of the Ladies. Recapturing Kanpur, the British took their revenge before executing the Indians.

Effects of the Revolt

As a result of the uprising, the British Parliament transferred the powers of the East India Company directly to the British government. In 1876 **Queen Victoria** took the title Empress of India. The people of India were now her colonial subjects, and India became her "Jewel in the Crown."

Although the rebellion failed, it helped to fuel Indian nationalism. The rebellion marked the first significant attempt by the people of South Asia to throw off British rule. Later, a new generation of Indian leaders would take up the cause.

✓Reading Check **Describing** What were some effects of the Great Rebellion?

Teach

S Skill Practice

Visual Literacy Ask: What information about the Indian troops cannot be determined from the circle graph? *(The circle graph does not show what percentage of the troops are Muslim and what percentage are Hindu.)* **OL**

CRITICAL THINKING SKILLS

Answers:

1. 83.6%
2. The cartoon shows a British attitude of superiority over the sepoys. The sepoy is pictured as much smaller than the British governor. The governor scolds the sepoy like a parent would a naughty child.

✓Reading Check

Answer: The East India Company became an agent of the British government. Queen Victoria was made Empress of India. The seeds of nationalism were sown.

Additional Support

Activity: Interdisciplinary Connection

Language Arts Have students write two different histories of the events surrounding the 1857 revolt in India. One history should be a British account of the Sepoy Mutiny. The other history should be the Indian account of the First War of Independence. Remind students that the Sepoy Mutiny and the First War of Independence are different names for the same event. Students' histories could be written as newspaper articles explaining the historical events to a specific audience, such as the British community in India, the Hindu community, or Muslim readers. Some students may want to try to combine the two histories into one text explaining the different perceptions of the same events. Have students compare their versions with each other. **Ask:** How do different perspectives change interpretations of historical events? Have students discuss their responses to the question. **AL**

D Differentiated Instruction

Visual/Spatial Create a pyramid of Mexico's social classes in the early 1800s. Describe each group's role in and reaction to the revolution. **OL**

C Critical Thinking

Identifying Central Issues
Ask: What do Hidalgo, José de San Martín, and Simón Bolívar have in common? *(These men all led revolutions in South America. Each had a dream to see their people achieve independence.)* **BL**

PEOPLE in HISTORY

Answers:
Martín: Spanish uprising against the occupation turned his sympathies to the independence movement.
Bolívar: books by European writers about rights and free republics as well as the Roman ruins

On September 16, 1810, Hidalgo led this ill-equipped army of thousands of Native Americans and mestizos in an attack against the Spaniards. He was an inexperienced military leader, however, and his forces were soon crushed. A military court sentenced Hidalgo to death. However, his memory lives on. In fact, September 16, the first day of the uprising, is Mexico's Independence Day.

D The participation of Native Americans and mestizos in Mexico's revolt against Spanish control frightened both the creoles and the *peninsulares.* Afraid of the masses, they cooperated in defeating the popular revolutionary forces. Conservative elites—both creoles and *peninsulares*—then decided to overthrow Spanish rule. The conservatives wanted an independent nation ruled by a monarch. They selected a creole military leader, Agustín de Iturbide (EE•tur•BEE•thay), to help bring in this new government.

In 1821 Mexico declared its independence from Spain. Iturbide named himself emperor in 1822 but was deposed in 1823. Mexico then became a republic.

Revolts in South America

C **José de San Martín** of Argentina and **Simón Bolívar** of Venezuela, both members of the creole elite, were hailed as the "Liberators of South America." These men led revolutions throughout the continent. José de San Martín believed that the Spaniards must be removed from all of South America if any South American nation was to be free.

Bolívar began the struggle for independence in Venezuela in 1810. He then went on to lead revolts in New Granada (Colombia) and Ecuador.

By 1810, the forces of San Martín had liberated Argentina from Spanish authority. In January 1817, San Martín led his forces over the Andes to attack the Spanish in Chile. The journey was an amazing feat. Two-thirds of the pack mules and horses died during the trip. Soldiers suffered from lack of oxygen and severe cold while crossing mountain passes. The Andes

PEOPLE in HISTORY

José de San Martín
1778–1850 South American Liberator

José de San Martín was born in Argentina, but learned his military skills in the Spanish army. After Napoleon occupied Spain, he witnessed the uprising of Spanish patriots against French occupation. He began to sympathize with the independence movement in America. In Spain, he met with creole revolutionaries. Years later he wrote about this turning point in his life: ". . . [K]nowing of the first movements of Caracas, Buenos Aires and elsewhere we resolved to return each to our country of birth, in order to offer our services to the struggle. . . ." San Martín returned to Argentina and organized the resistance. After freeing Argentina, he led his troops across the Andes to free Chile. Later, he helped liberate Peru. **How did the French occupation of Spain influence San Martín?**

Simón Bolívar
1783–1830 South American Liberator

Son of a wealthy Venezuelan family, Simón Bolívar read books by European writers that described "the rights of man" and free republics. While visiting Rome, Bolívar gazed at the ruins of the great civilization and said to Rodriguez, "I swear . . . by my honor and my country, that I shall never allow my hands to be idle . . . until I have broken the shackles which bind us to Spain." Returning home, Bolívar raised an army. By the mid-1820s his forces had freed five nations. Bolívar dreamed of a "Gran Colombia," a vast union of South American states. But soon after Bolívar became president of Gran Colombia, civil wars tore the union apart. Although unification failed, Bolívar had set South America on the path of freedom. **What influences helped to motivate Bolívar?**

Additional Support

Extending the Content

José de San Martín San Martín was offered the position of Chile's governor, but he rejected it, wanting instead to capture Lima, Peru. When Bolívar arrived in Peru to fight against the Spaniards, the two met. Soon after, San Martín decided to go into exile, leaving his army for Bolívar. **Ask:** Why did San Martín reject the governorship? *(He wanted to free Lima.)*

Simón Bolívar Bolívar called a conference in 1826 to create the foundations of a unified Latin America. He wanted a treaty of alliance, a shared military, and a system for solving disputes. Although not a success, this meeting paved the way for future cooperation. **Ask:** How would countries benefit from Bolívar's plan? *(Wars could be avoided and resources shared.)*

mountains were more than two miles (3.2 km) above sea level.

The arrival of San Martín's forces in Chile completely surprised the Spaniards. Spanish forces were badly defeated at the Battle of Chacabuco on February 12, 1817. In 1821 San Martín moved on to Lima, Peru, the center of Spanish authority.

San Martín was convinced that he could not complete the liberation of Peru alone. He welcomed the arrival of Simón Bolívar and his forces. Bolívar, the "Liberator of Venezuela," took on the task of crushing the last significant Spanish army at Ayacucho on December 9, 1824.

By the end of 1824, Peru, Uruguay, Paraguay, Colombia, Venezuela, Argentina, Bolivia, and Chile had all become free of Spain. Earlier, in 1822, the prince regent of Brazil had declared Brazil's independence from Portugal. The Central American states had become independent in 1823. In 1838 and 1839, they divided into five republics: Guatemala, El Salvador, Honduras, Costa Rica, and Nicaragua.

Threats to Independence

In the early 1820s, only one major threat remained to the newly won independence of the Latin American states. Members of the Concert of Europe favored the use of troops to restore Spanish control in Latin America. The British, who wished to trade with Latin America, disagreed. They proposed joint action with the United States against any European moves against Latin America.

Distrustful of British motives, James Monroe, the president of the United States, acted alone in 1823. In the **Monroe Doctrine,** he guaranteed the independence of the new Latin American nations. The Monroe Doctrine also strongly warned against any European **intervention** in the Americas. R

More important to Latin American independence than American words, however, was the British navy. Other European powers feared the power of the British navy, which stood between Latin America and any planned European invasion force.

✓Reading Check **Evaluating** How did the French Revolution help inspire the revolution in Mexico?

Nation Building

MAIN IDEA After they became independent, Latin American nations faced a staggering range of problems.

HISTORY & YOU Do you feel independent yet still depend on your parents in some ways, such as for money? Read how Latin America returned to economic dependence.

The new Latin American nations faced a number of serious problems between 1830 and 1870. The wars for independence had resulted in a staggering loss of people, property, and livestock. Unsure of their precise boundaries, the new nations went to war with one another to settle border disputes. Poor roads, a lack of railroads, thick jungles, and mountains made communication, transportation, and national unity difficult. During the course of the nineteenth century, the new Latin American nations would become economically dependent on Western nations once again.

Rule of the Caudillos

Most of the new nations of Latin America began with republican governments, but they had no experience in self-rule. Soon after independence, strong leaders known as **caudillos** gained power.

Caudillos ruled chiefly by military force C and were usually supported by the landed elites. Many kept the new national states together. Some were also modernizers who built roads and canals, ports, and schools. Others were destructive.

Antonio López de Santa Anna, for example, ruled Mexico from 1833 to 1855. During this time, he served as president for 11 two-year terms. Calling himself the "Napoleon of the West," Santa Anna misused state funds, halted reforms, and created chaos. As one historian judged, "Any progress in Mexico achieved during the era of Santa Anna had nothing to do with him."

In 1835 American settlers in the Mexican state of Texas revolted against Santa Anna's rule. Texas gained its independence in 1836 and United States statehood followed in 1845. War between Mexico and the United States soon followed (1846–1848).

R Reading Strategy

Identifying Ask: What circumstances led to the creation of the Monroe Doctrine? *(President Monroe did not trust the British. He wanted to protect the independence of Latin American nations.)* AL

C Critical Thinking

Determining Cause and Effect Draw a cause-and-effect chain on the board and record students' answers to this question. **Ask:** Why did caudillos come into power, and what were the results of their rule? *(Causes: Newly independent nations had no experience ruling themselves. Caudillos filled the vacuum. Effects: They kept the new states together through military means and support from the landed class. Some modernized , but others were corrupt and weakened the newly-formed states.)* OL

✓Reading Check

Answer: Miguel Hidalgo, who had studied the French Revolution, led the local Indians and *mestizos* in a revolt against the Spanish that failed. The Mexican elites then revolted and declared Mexico independent.

Additional Support

Activity: Collaborative Learning

Identifying Cause and Effect Explain that the Monroe Doctrine laid the foundations of U.S. policy in Latin America. The United States and Britain were concerned about possible European colonial expansion. By separating Europe from America, Monroe emphasized the existence of specific U.S. interests. Have students research the Monroe Doctrine with Internet and library resources. **Ask:** How did the doctrine change world events? How did the Monroe Doctrine influence the development of Latin American states? Discuss students' answers in class discussion. Point out that the Monroe Doctrine guaranteed the independence of new Latin American nations, but it was the power of the British navy that enforced the intent of the doctrine. AL

Teacher Tip

Collaborative Learning The activity allows students with different levels of academic skills and intelligences to work together. As you form groups, consider students' strengths and weaknesses.

R Reading Strategy

Reading Secondary Sources
Ask: What were the motivations of the revolutionaries? *(Some wanted political change. Some were revolting against the capitalists. Others wanted land redistributed to the poor.)* **OL**

W Writing Support

Expository Writing Ask students to choose a country mentioned in this section, research the country's current political situation, and write a one-page summary about that country. **OL**

CRITICAL THINKING SKILLS

Answers:

1. established ownership of the country's natural resources by the people and limited foreign ownership of land
2. Answers will vary. The constitution contains reforms sought by three groups: political reforms for liberals, workers' rights and limits on foreigners sought by workers, and land reforms for peasants.

Differentiated Instruction

INFOGRAPHICS

The Mexican Revolution

▲ *Revolutionary leaders, such as "Pancho" Villa and Emiliano Zapata, raised armies from the discontented rural poor to fight for land reform. Zapata coined the revolutionary war slogan "¡Tierra y Libertad!", which means "Land and Liberty!"—a cry still heard in Mexico to protest injustice.*

Constitution of 1917

- established a federal government, with separation of powers and a bill of rights
- limited president's term in office
- granted universal male suffrage
- gave workers the right to form unions
- set a minimum wage and maximum hours
- prohibited pay discrimination based on race, ethnicity, or gender
- established a social security system
- stated that Mexico's natural resources belong to the Mexican people, not to foreign investors
- limited foreign land ownership
- restored lands to Native Americans

Effects of the Mexican Revolution

The Constitution of 1917 set down many of the goals of the revolution. For revolutionary leaders, the goal was political reform. For peasants, it was about land reform. It would take decades for the reforms to take hold fully. **R** Still, this constitution—the "fruit" of the Mexican Revolution—laid the groundwork for positive change. Eventually, the revolution helped to bring about a more democratic and politically stable Mexico.

CRITICAL THINKING SKILLS

1. **Identifying** What are two signs of nationalism in the Mexican Constitution of 1917?
2. **Making Inferences** How well did the Mexican Revolution achieve its goals?

Increasing numbers of Latin Americans began to resent this interference from the "big bully" to the north.

Revolution in Mexico

W In some countries, large landowners supported dictators who looked out for the interests of the ruling elite. Porfirio Díaz, who ruled Mexico between 1877 and 1911, created a conservative, centralized government. The army, foreign capitalists, large landowners, and the Catholic Church supported Díaz. All these groups benefited from their alliance with Díaz. However, growing forces for change in Mexico led to a revolution.

During Díaz's dictatorial reign, the wages of workers had declined. Ninety-five percent of the rural population owned no land, whereas about 1,000 families owned almost all of Mexico. A liberal landowner, Francisco Madero, forced Díaz from power in 1911. The door to a wider revolution then opened.

Leveled Activities

BL Reteaching Activity, URB p. 121

OL People in World History Activity, URB p. 116

AL Historical Significance Activity, URB p. 108

ELL Content Vocabulary Activity, URB p. 99

Madero made a valiant effort to handle the revolutionary forces at work. He put some of the best officials in his administration, and he sought a balance in dealing with foreign interests. However, his efforts proved ineffective.

The northern states were in near anarchy as Pancho Villa's armed masses of bandits swept the countryside. The federal army was full of hard-minded generals who itched to assert their power. Even the liberal politicians and idealists found fault with Madero for not solving all of the country's problems at once.

Madero's ineffectiveness created a demand for agrarian reform. This new call for reform was led by Emiliano Zapata. Zapata aroused the masses of landless peasants and began to seize and redistribute the estates of wealthy landholders. While Madero tried to reach an agreement with him for land reforms, Zapata refused to disarm his followers.

Between 1910 and 1920, the Mexican Revolution caused great damage to the Mexican economy. Finally, a new constitution was enacted in 1917. This constitution set up a government led by a president. It also created land-reform policies, established limits on foreign investors, and set an agenda to help the workers.

The revolution also led to an outpouring of patriotism throughout Mexico. National pride was evident, for example, as intellectuals and artists sought to capture what was unique about Mexico, with special emphasis on its past.

Prosperity and Social Change

After 1870, Latin America began an age of prosperity based to a large extent on the export of a few basic items. These included wheat and beef from Argentina, coffee from Brazil, coffee and bananas from Central America, and sugar and silver from Peru. These foodstuffs and raw materials were largely exchanged for finished goods—textiles, machines, and luxury items—from Europe and the United States. After 1900, Latin Americans also increased their own industrialization. They built factories to produce textiles, foods, and construction materials. **C**

One result from the prosperity of increased exports was growth in the middle sectors (divisions) of Latin American society. Lawyers, merchants, shopkeepers, businesspeople, schoolteachers, professors, bureaucrats, and military officers increased in numbers. After 1900, these middle sectors of society continued to expand.

Middle-class Latin Americans shared some common characteristics. They lived in cities and sought education and decent incomes. They also saw the United States as a model, especially in regard to industrialization. The middle class sought liberal reform, not revolution. Once they had the right to vote, they generally sided with the landholding elites.

✓Reading Check **Evaluating** What caused the growth of a middle class in Latin America?

SECTION 4 REVIEW

Vocabulary

1. **Explain** the significance of: *peninsulares*, creoles, mestizos, José de San Martín, Simón Bolívar, Monroe Doctrine, intervention, caudillos, Antonio López de Santa Anna, Benito Juárez, redistribution, cash crops, Puerto Rico, Panama Canal, Haiti, Nicaragua.

Main Ideas

2. **Describe** the social classes of Latin America.
3. **Explain** how Latin American countries would often determine the next ruler after a caudillo died.
4. **Identify** the country that exported each product group listed in the chart below.

Product	Country
coffee	
bananas and coffee	
beef and wheat	
sugar and silver	

Critical Thinking

5. **The BIG Idea** **Determining Cause and Effect** How did persistent inequality contribute to the failure of democracy in the young Latin American nations?
6. **Making Inferences** Why do you think Theodore Roosevelt supported Panama's rebellion to win independence from Colombia?
7. **Analyzing Visuals** Examine the group photograph on page 714. What do you think you can determine about the subjects of the photo from the way they are dressed?

Writing About History

8. **Expository Writing** Why did Latin American countries remain economically dependent on Western nations when they were no longer political colonies? Write a brief essay explaining why this happened.

For help with the concepts in this section of *Glencoe World History*, go to glencoe.com and click Study Central™.

C Critical Thinking

Drawing Conclusions **Ask:** How would increased industrialization affect Latin America's dependence on the United States and Europe? *(Latin Americans would need fewer imports and might improve their trade balance.)* **AL**

Answer: prosperity from increased exports

Assess

Study Central provides summaries, interactive games, and online graphic organizers to help students review content.

Close

Evaluating **Ask:** What were some problems of independent nations in Latin America before 1900? *(They were economically dependent on Europe and the United States. They lacked national unity. Border disputes and other causes of unrest led to dictatorial leaders taking control.)* **OL**

SECTION 4 REVIEW

Answers

1. Definitions for the vocabulary words are found in the section and the Glossary.
2. **peninsulares:** Spanish and Portuguese officials who resided temporarily in Latin America, top of social class structure, held all important positions; **creoles:** descendants of Europeans born in Latin America who lived there permanently, controlled land and business; **mestizos:** people of European and Native American descent, largest group, worked as servants or laborers
3. often by civil war
4. coffee: Brazil; bananas, coffee: Central America; beef, wheat: Argentina; sugar, silver: Peru
5. Answers will vary. The few landed elites dominated society. They ran governments, controlled courts, and kept wages low. To keep their power, ruling elites limited voting rights and sometimes supported dictators who would safeguard their interests.
6. Roosevelt wanted to build a canal across Panama and needed Panama to cede control of the land.
7. Answers will vary. Students may say that the subjects are serious and proud because most are wearing formal clothes or uniforms for the photograph.
8. Students' essays should make the point that new nations relied on exporting a few basic raw materials and importing manufactured goods until they could develop their own industries.

Focus

Introducing Social History
Discuss with students how they would feel if their country were ruled by another nation and they were prevented from getting jobs, an education, or even owning land.

Teach

R Reading Strategy

Activating Prior Knowledge **Ask:** Why did the French want to gain control of Vietnam? *(Other European nations were beginning to stake claims in Southeast Asia. France moved into Vietnam to stop the British from taking it and to obtain a share of the Asian trade as well as access to the natural resources of Vietnam.)* **AL**

C Critical Thinking

Drawing Conclusions **Ask:** Why was it in the best interests of the French to keep the Vietnamese uneducated? *(They would be more isolated from one another, less likely to become political, and easier to control.)* **OL**

Additional Support

Indochina: French Colonialism in Vietnam

In the 1860s, France began to gain influence in Vietnam, and in 1887, Vietnam officially fell under French political domination and economic exploitation. French intervention divided Vietnamese society. Colonial policies benefited some Vietnamese, while others called for independence.

The wet-farming of rice was, and still is, an economic essential for Vietnam.

A Buddhist nun. The other traditional Vietnamese religion is Confucianism.

Vietnamese can be written in a traditional script or in Western letters. Nationalists adopted Western printing for journals promoting independence.

Traditional Society

R C Rice became an export crop to make money for French landowners. Large numbers of landless peasants worked big estates as they had for centuries, so traditional society remained mostly intact, though now the peasants sometimes faced rice shortages. The French did not preserve the traditional Confucian scholar officials, as they were the first to call for Vietnamese independence. Without these teachers, the country's historically high rate of literacy fell drastically.

Background

Vietnam Under the French Governor-General Paul Doumer arrived in Vietnam in 1897. His policies, designed to help France profit as much as possible from Vietnam's natural resources, established the path that his successors would follow until World War II. All important government officials were French, emperors were removed who were not loyal to France, and few industries were developed except those that supplied goods locally. Exports such as rice, coal, minerals, and rubber enriched French interests at the expense of the Vietnamese. By the eve of World War II, half of the population of Vietnam did not possess any land. Throughout the early 20th century, nationalist movements continued to grow. Although these early efforts did not achieve significant success in advancing the cause of the Vietnamese people, they did teach later leaders important lessons that helped them to eventually achieve independence for Vietnam in 1954.

Frustrations of Colonialism

The French greatly increased the amount of rice land, but either sold it to the highest-bidding Vietnamese landlord or gave it to French speculators. The Vietnamese were shut out of trade and industry. They were denied civil liberties and participation in government. Most Vietnamese worked harder and received less in return. After 1900, new nationalist leaders began to look beyond the old monarchy for inspiration. **C**

Analyzing Visuals

1. **Describing** What do the tools and equipment of traditional farming indicate about peasant life in colonial Vietnam?
2. **Assessing** What were some of the effects of colonial rule on the Vietnamese people?

C Critical Thinking

Drawing Conclusions Ask: What did nationalists want? *(They wanted political independence, civil liberties, economic parity for the Vietnamese people, and control of their own industry and trade.)* **OL**

Assess/Close

Determining Cause and Effect Have students complete a multiple causes chart to show how the French undermined Vietnamese culture. *(They removed officials who helped to preserve Confucian knowledge. They rewarded conversion to Catholicism. They discouraged literacy.)* **OL**

Analyzing Visuals

Answers:

1. Rice farming required many people working long hours, in difficult conditions and with simple tools.
2. Literacy fell, rice was in short supply, more work was demanded of the peasants, they couldn't work in profitable jobs, they lacked basic rights, and they began to look for new political and social orders.

Activity: Economics Connection

Analyzing the Importance of Rice Production Vietnam is one of the world's major exporters of rice. Dry farming of rice is practiced in the mountainous regions; wet farming takes place in the deltas and river zones. Ask students to work in small groups. Have each group find out different facts about rice cultivation in Vietnam. Possible topics include the history of rice; farming methods; kinds of rice grown in Vietnam and their uses; and statistics on harvests and exports during the past decade. If feasible, have each group record their data in a spreadsheet program so that it can be sorted and arranged for the entire class. Students with a working knowledge of spreadsheet design could work in a separate group organizing the data for the class. Have groups collaborate on a bulletin board display of their facts. Encourage groups to use both text and graphics.

Ask: Why is rice considered integral to the lives of the Vietnamese people? Have students answer the question, incorporating specific examples from the bulletin board to support their response. **OL**

CHAPTER 22 Planning Guide

Key to Ability Levels	
BL Below Level	**AL** Above Level
OL On Level	**ELL** English Language Learners

Key to Teaching Resources	
Print Material	DVD
CD-ROM	Transparency

Levels				Resources	Chapter Opener	Section 1	Section 2	Section 3	Chapter Assess
BL	OL	AL	ELL						
				FOCUS					
BL	OL	AL	ELL	Daily Focus Skills Transparencies		22-1	22-2	22-3	
				TEACH					
BL	OL		ELL	Reading Skills Activity, URB				p. 131	
	OL	AL		Historical Analysis Skills Activity, URB		p. 132			
BL	OL	AL	ELL	Differentiated Instruction Activity, URB		p. 133			
	OL		ELL	English Learner Activity, URB		p. 135			
BL	OL	AL	ELL	Content Vocabulary Activity, URB*		p. 137			
BL	OL	AL	ELL	Academic Vocabulary Activity, URB		p. 139			
BL	OL	AL	ELL	Skills Reinforcement Activity, URB				p. 141	
	OL	AL		Critical Thinking Skills Activity, URB		p. 142			
	OL	AL		History and Geography Activity, URB			p. 143		
	OL	AL	ELL	Mapping History Activity, URB		p. 145			
BL	OL	AL		Historical Significance Activity, URB		p. 146			
BL	OL	AL	ELL	Cooperative Learning Activity, URB				p. 147	
	OL	AL	ELL	History Simulation Activity, URB			p. 149		
BL	OL	AL	ELL	Time Line Activity, URB				p. 151	
	OL	AL		Linking Past and Present Activity, URB			p. 152		
BL	OL	AL		People in World History Activity, URB		p. 153		p. 154	
BL	OL	AL	ELL	Primary Source Reading, URB		p. 155			
	OL	AL		Enrichment Activity, URB		p. 160			
BL	OL	AL	ELL	World Art and Music Activity, URB				p. 157	
BL	OL		ELL	Guided Reading Activities, URB*		p. 162	p. 163	p. 164	
BL	OL		ELL	Reading Essentials and Note-Taking Guide*		p. 241	p. 244	p. 247	
BL	OL	AL	ELL	Differentiated Instruction for the World History Classroom	✓	✓	✓	✓	✓

Note: Please refer to the *Unit Resource Book: An Era of European Imperialism* for this chapter's URB materials.

* Also available in Spanish

- Interactive Lesson Planner
- Interactive Teacher Edition
- Fully editable blackline masters
- Section Spotlight Videos Launch
- Differentiated Lesson Plans
- Printable reports of daily assignments
- Standards Tracking System

Levels BL	OL	AL	ELL		Resources	Chapter Opener	Section 1	Section 2	Section 3	Chapter Assess
					TEACH *(continued)*					
BL	OL	AL	ELL		StudentWorks™ Plus DVD	✓	✓	✓	✓	✓
BL	OL	AL	ELL		Vocabulary PuzzleMaker CD-ROM	✓	✓	✓	✓	✓
Teacher Resources					Building Academic Vocabulary	✓	✓	✓	✓	✓
Teacher Resources					Reading Strategies and Activities for the Social Studies Classroom			p. 59		
Teacher Resources					Writer's Guidebook		pp. 27, 47			
Teacher Resources					Strategies for Success	✓	✓	✓	✓	✓
Teacher Resources					Outline Map Resource Book	✓	✓	✓	✓	✓
Teacher Resources					Presentation Plus! with MindJogger DVD	✓	✓	✓	✓	✓
					ASSESS					
BL	OL	AL	ELL		Section Quizzes and Chapter Tests*		p. 269	p. 270	p. 271	p. 273
BL	OL	AL	ELL		Authentic Assessment With Rubrics	✓	✓	✓	✓	✓
BL	OL	AL	ELL		Standardized Test Practice Workbook	✓	✓	✓	✓	✓
BL	OL	AL	ELL		*ExamView® Assessment Suite* CD-ROM		22-1	22-2	22-3	Ch. 22
BL	OL	AL	ELL		Interactive Tutor Self-Assessment CD-ROM		22-1	22-2	22-3	
					CLOSE					
BL			ELL		Reteaching Activity, URB				p. 159	
BL	OL		ELL		Reading and Study Skills Foldables™	✓	✓	✓	✓	✓

Using CyberScout

Research Using *Subject Area*

Technology Product

CyberScout is a convenient and dynamic search engine that provides several easy ways to locate information outside the McGraw-Hill Learning Network. CyberScout only searches Web sites that have been reviewed by teachers, so the information students find is always appropriate and accurate.

Objectives

After students use CyberScout, they will be able to

- research topics and issues in economics using CyberScout;
- exercise research and study skills
- practice writing skills.

Steps

- From McGraw-Hill Learning Network home page (www.mhln.com), click on **For Students.**
- Choose **CyberScout** below **Homework Help.**
- Click on a subject area to narrow the search.
- The CyberScout page will display a set of results.
- Drill down by continuing to click result links until you find a Web site of interest.
- Click on the link to reach the Web site.
- Students will be redirected to the Web site in a new window.
- Students navigate through the chosen Web site to gain information on their topic and take notes.

History ONLINE

	Student	Teacher	Parent
Beyond the Textbook	●	●	●
Chapter Overviews	●	●	●
Time Current Events	●		●
ePuzzles and Games	●		●
Concepts in Motion	●		●
Literature Connections		●	
Multi-Language Glossaries	●		●
Online Student Edition	●	●	●
Self-Check Quizzes	●		●
Student Web Activities	●		●
Study Central ™	●		●
Teaching Today		●	
Vocabulary eFlashcards	●		●
Web Activity Lesson Plans		●	

- **Timed Readings Plus in Social Studies** helps students increase their reading rate and fluency while maintaining comprehension. The 400-word passages are similar to those found on state and national assessments.
- **Reading in the Content Area: Social Studies** concentrates on six essential reading skills that help students better comprehend what they read. The book includes 75 high-interest nonfiction passages written at increasing levels of difficulty.
- **Reading Social Studies** includes strategic reading instruction and vocabulary support in Social Studies content for both ELLs and native speakers of English.

www.jamestowneducation.com

The following videotape programs are available from Glencoe as supplements to Chapter 22:

- China's Boxer Rebellion (ISBN 0-76-700617-8)
- Confucius: World of Wisdom (ISBN 0-76-700407-8)

To order, call Glencoe at 1-800-334-7344. To find classroom resources to accompany many of these videos, check the following home pages:

A&E Television: www.aetv.com

The History Channel: www.historychannel.com

Index to National Geographic Magazine:

The following articles relate to this chapter:

- "The Manchurian Mandate," by Brook Larmer, September 2006
- "Last Stand at Edo Bay," by Scott Elder, October 2002

National Geographic Society Products To order the following, call National Geographic at 1-800-368-2728:

- *National Geographic Atlas of the World* (Book).

Access National Geographic's new, dynamic MapMachine Web site and other geography resources at:

www.nationalgeographic.com

www.nationalgeographic.com/maps

GLENCOE BOOKLINK 3

Use this database to search more than 30,000 titles to create a customized reading list for your students.

- Reading lists can be organized by students' reading level, author, genre, theme, or area of interest.
- The database provides Degrees of Reading Power™ (DRP) and Lexile™ readability scores for all selections.
- A brief summary of each selection is included.

Leveled reading suggestions for this chapter:

For students at a Grade 8 reading level:
- ***Chu Ju's House,*** by Gloria Whelan

For students at a Grade 9 reading level:
- ***Wandering Warrior,*** by Da Chen

For students at a Grade 10 reading level:
- ***Japan,*** by Patricia D. Netzley

For students at a Grade 11 reading level:
- ***Falling Leaves,*** by Adeline Yen Mah

For students at a Grade 12 reading level:
- ***Throne of Blood,*** from PERSPECTIVE

Introducing
CHAPTER 22

Focus

MAKING CONNECTIONS
In what ways can one culture influence another?

Activate students' prior knowledge by having them identify cultural influences at school and in the community. *(Answers may include examples of foods, architecture, styles of clothing, art, and so on.)* Discuss the positive and negative effects of industrialization and globalization on world cultures today.

Teach

The Big Ideas

As students study the chapter, remind them to consider the section-based Big Ideas included in each section's Guide to Reading. The **Essential Questions** in the activities below tie in to the Big Ideas and help students think about and understand important chapter concepts. In addition, the Hands-on Chapter Projects with their culminating activities relate the content from each section to the Big Ideas. These activities build on each other as students progress through the chapter. Section activities culminate in the wrap-up activity on the Visual Summary page.

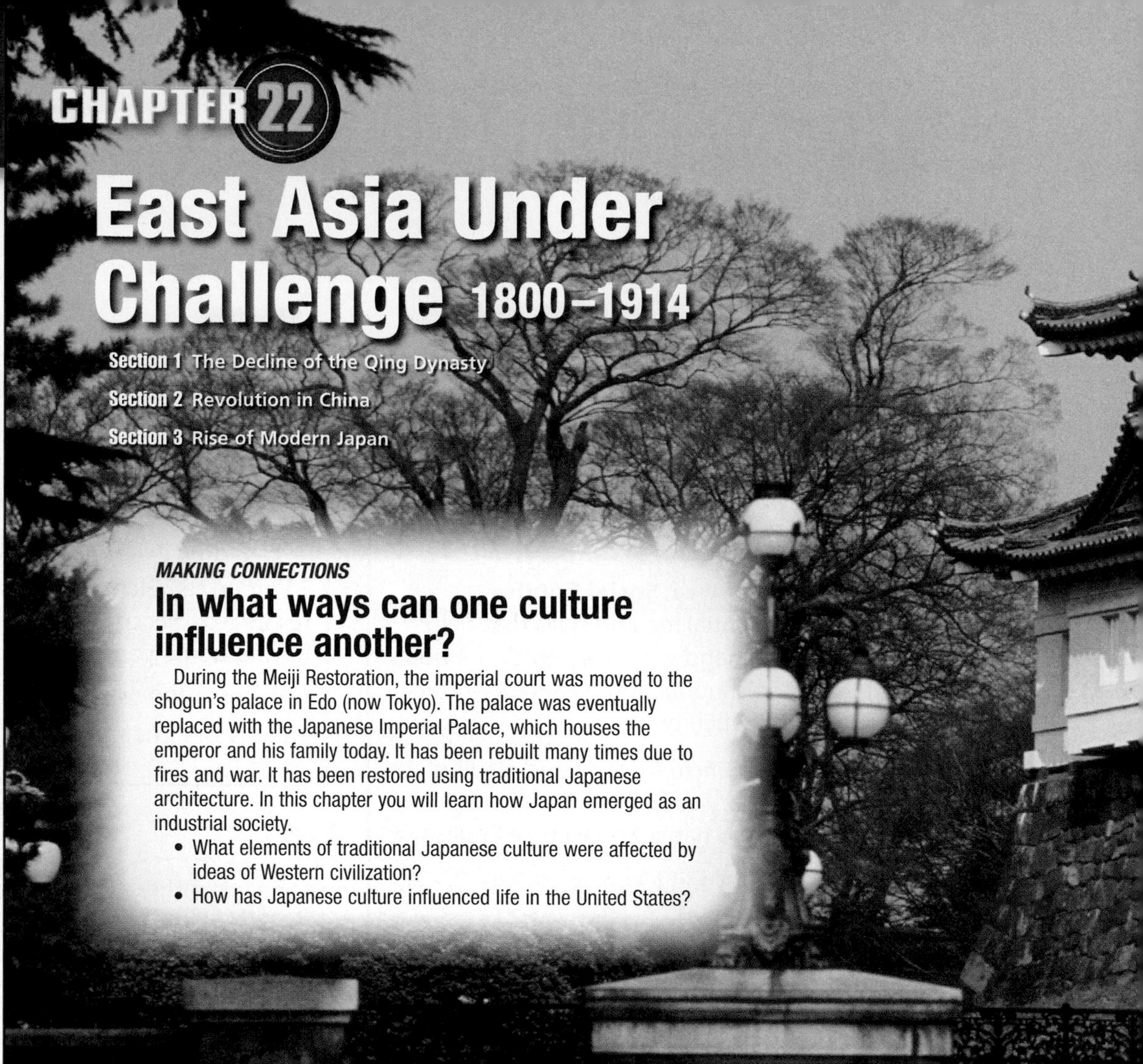

CHAPTER 22

East Asia Under Challenge 1800–1914

Section 1 The Decline of the Qing Dynasty

Section 2 Revolution in China

Section 3 Rise of Modern Japan

MAKING CONNECTIONS
In what ways can one culture influence another?

During the Meiji Restoration, the imperial court was moved to the shogun's palace in Edo (now Tokyo). The palace was eventually replaced with the Japanese Imperial Palace, which houses the emperor and his family today. It has been rebuilt many times due to fires and war. It has been restored using traditional Japanese architecture. In this chapter you will learn how Japan emerged as an industrial society.

- What elements of traditional Japanese culture were affected by ideas of Western civilization?
- How has Japanese culture influenced life in the United States?

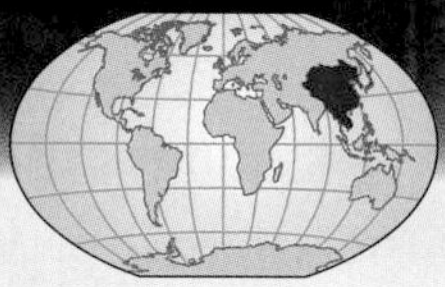

CHINA AND JAPAN ▶

1839 Opium War begins in China

1853 U.S. asks Japan to open foreign relations

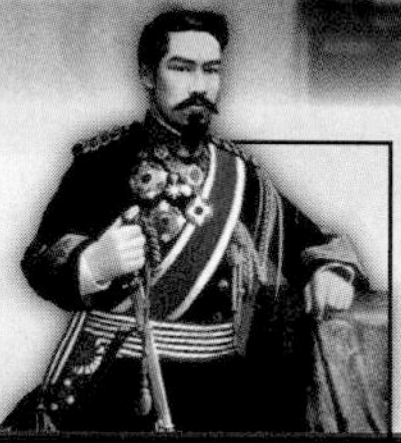

1867 Meiji Restoration begins in Japan

1800 / 1830 — 1860

THE WORLD ▶

1848 Nationalist revolutions erupt in Europe

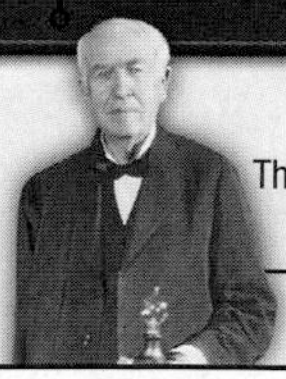

1879 Thomas Edison develops the electric lightbulb

722

SECTION 1

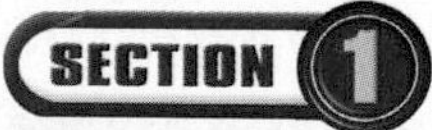

The Decline of the Qing Dynasty

Essential Question: What factors led to the decline of China's Qing dynasty? *(internal rebellion, efforts at reform, European imperialism)* Point out that in Section 1 students will learn about the internal and external pressures that brought about the decline of the Qing dynasty. **OL**

SECTION 2

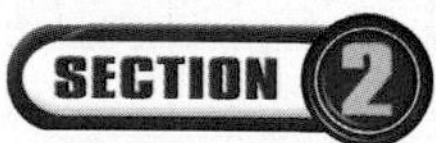

Revolution in China

Essential Question: How did China change as a result of revolution and Western influence? *(economy boomed, urban society became more Westernized)* Point out that in Section 2 students will learn how political revolution and Western influence changed Chinese society and culture. **OL**

Introducing **CHAPTER 22**

More About the Photo

Visual Literacy The Kyoto Imperial Palace was the residence of the Imperial family until 1869, when the capital was moved to Tokyo. The Imperial Palace grounds are enclosed by a roofed earthen wall, with a palace hall and a minor palace on the grounds. Today, the palace is a park that is open to the public.

Dinah Zike's Foldables

Dinah Zike's Foldables are three-dimensional, interactive graphic organizers that help students practice basic writing skills, review vocabulary terms, and identify main ideas. Instructions for creating and using Foldables can be found in the Appendix at the end of this book and in the *Dinah Zike's Reading and Study Skills Foldables* booklet.

History ONLINE

Introduce students to chapter content and key terms by having them access the Chapter 22 Overview at glencoe.com.

1890 — 1920

1899 Open Door Policy with China established

1902 Africans defeated in the Boer War

1911 Followers of Sun Yat-sen launch Chinese rebellion

FOLDABLES Study Organizer

Japan Before... | Japan After... | Western Influence

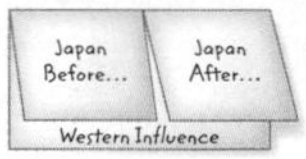

Identifying Cause and Effect
Create a Two-Tab Book to compare and contrast Japan before and after Western influence. Record differences in daily life, women's roles, politics, and economics.

History ONLINE
Chapter Overview—Visit glencoe.com to preview Chapter 22.

SECTION 3

Rise of Modern Japan
Essential Question: How did Japan modernize upon Western intervention? *(ended isolation, reformed government and social structure, became imperialist, Westernized culture)* Point out that in Section 3 students will learn how Japan moved from a policy of isolation and tradition to a modern, Westernized culture. **OL**

Focus

Bellringer

Daily Focus Transparency 22.1

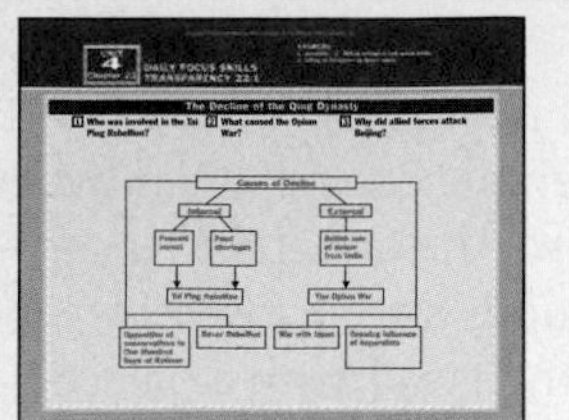

GUIDE TO READING

Answers to Graphic:

	Tai Ping	Boxer
Reforms Demanded	give land to peasants	remove foreigners
Methods Used	seized Nanjing	killed Chinese Christians
Outcomes	rebellion failed	rebellion failed

Section Spotlight Video

To generate student interest and provide a springboard for class discussion, access the Chapter 22, Section 1 video at glencoe.com or on the video DVD.

SECTION 1

The Decline of the Qing Dynasty

GUIDE TO READING

The BIG Idea
Competition Among Countries
As the Qing dynasty declined, Western nations increased their economic involvement with China.

Content Vocabulary
- extraterritoriality *(p. 726)*
- self-strengthening *(p. 728)*
- spheres of influence *(p. 729)*
- Open Door policy *(p. 731)*
- indemnity *(p. 731)*

Academic Vocabulary
- highlighted *(p. 725)*
- exclusive *(p. 729)*

People and Places
- Guangzhou *(p. 725)*
- Chang Jiang *(p. 726)*
- Hong Kong *(p. 726)*
- Hong Xiuquan *(p. 726)*
- Guang Xu *(p. 729)*
- Empress Dowager Ci Xi *(p. 729)*
- John Hay *(p. 730)*

Reading Strategy
Comparing and Contrasting As you read, create a chart like the one below to compare the Tai Ping and Boxer Rebellions.

	Tai Ping	Boxer
Reforms Demanded		
Method Used		
Outcomes		

China preferred to keep its culture free of Western influences. However, as the Qing government grew more unstable, the Western powers and Japan tightened their hold on the Chinese Empire. Foreign powers created spheres of influence and followed an Open Door policy to secure trading rights. The Chinese resisted but were eventually overcome, weakening the imperial government even more.

Causes of Decline

MAIN IDEA Pressure from the West and corruption and unrest from within led to the decline of the Qing dynasty.

HISTORY & YOU In grade school, did you ever see a bully use force to get something he or she wanted? Read how Western powers used force to get China to agree to unequal treaties.

In 1800, after a long period of peace and prosperity, the Qing dynasty of the Manchus was at the height of its power. A little over a century later, however, humiliated and harassed by the Western powers, the Qing dynasty collapsed.

External and Internal Pressure

One important reason for the abrupt decline and fall of the Qing dynasty was the intense external pressure that the modern West applied to Chinese society. However, internal problems that the government was slow to address also played a role. For instance, Zhang Zhidong, a court official, argued against political reform:

PRIMARY SOURCE

"The doctrine of people's rights will bring us not a single benefit but a hundred evils. Are we going to establish a parliament? . . . there are still many today who are content to be vulgar and rustic. They are ignorant of the general situation in the world, they do not understand the basic system of the state. . . . Even supposing the confused and clamorous people are assembled in one house, for every one of them who is clear-sighted, there will be a hundred others whose vision is clouded; they will converse at random . . .—what use will it be?"

—*China's Response to the West: A Documentary Survey, 1839–1923,* Ssu-yu Teng and John K. Fairbank, eds., 1970

After an extended period of growth, the Qing dynasty began to suffer from corruption, peasant unrest, and incompetence. These weaknesses were made worse by rapid growth in the country's

Resource Manager

R Reading Strategies	C Critical Thinking	D Differentiated Instruction	W Writing Support	S Skill Practice
Teacher Edition • Det. Importance, p. 726 **Additional Resources** • Cont. Vocab. Act., URB p. 137 • Academic Vocab. Act., URB p. 139 • Pri. Source Read., URB p. 155 • Guid. Read. Act., URB p. 162 • Read. Ess. & Note-Taking Guide, p. 241	**Teacher Edition** • Analyzing Info., p. 725 • Making Inferences, p. 727 • Ident. Cent. Issues, p. 730 **Additional Resources** • Hist. Analysis Skills Act., URB p. 132 • Crit. Think. Act., URB p. 142 • Hist. Sig. Act., URB p. 146 • People in World Hist. Act., URB p. 153 • Section Quiz, p. 269	**Teacher Edition** • Adv. Learners, p. 726 • ELL, p. 728 **Additional Resources** • Diff. Instr. Act., URB p. 133 • English Learner Act., URB p. 135 • Enrich Act., URB p. 160	**Teacher Edition** • Persuasive Writing, p. 728 • Narrative Writing, p. 729 **Additional Resources** • Writer's Guidebook, pp. 27, 47	**Teacher Edition** • Using Geo. Skills, pp. 725, 729 **Additional Resources** • Mapping Hist. Act., URB p. 145

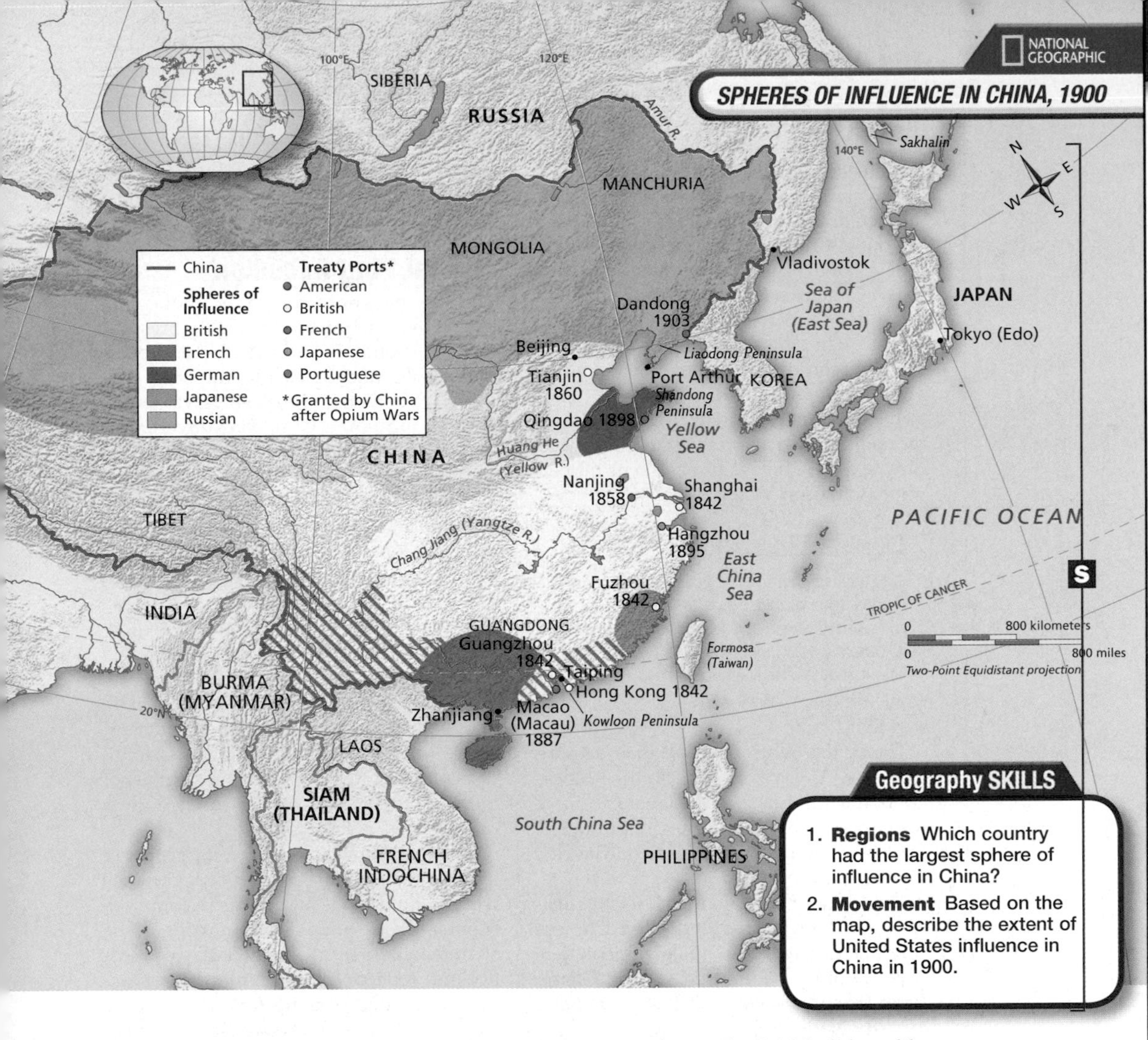

Geography SKILLS

1. **Regions** Which country had the largest sphere of influence in China?
2. **Movement** Based on the map, describe the extent of United States influence in China in 1900.

population. By 1900, there were 400 million people in China. Population growth created a serious food shortage, and many people died of starvation. The ships, guns, and ideas of foreigners **highlighted** the growing weakness of the Qing dynasty and probably hastened its end.

By 1800, Europeans had been in contact with China for more than 200 years. Wanting to limit contact with outsiders, the Qing dynasty had restricted European merchants to a small trading outlet at **Guangzhou** (GWAHNG•JOH), or Canton. The merchants could deal with only a few Chinese firms. The British did not like this arrangement.

Britain had a trade deficit, or an unfavorable trade balance, with China. That is, it imported more goods from China than it exported to China. Britain had to pay China with silver for the difference between its imports—tea, silk, and porcelain—from China and its exports—Indian cotton—to China. At first, the British tried to negotiate with the Chinese to improve the trade imbalance. When negotiations failed, the British turned to trading opium.

History ONLINE
Student Web Activity—
Visit glencoe.com and complete the activity on Western influence in China.

Teach

S Skill Practice

Using Geography Skills **Ask:** Which European country had the most strategic sphere of influence in China? Why? *(Britain, because of its size and its access to the East China Sea)* **AL**

C Critical Thinking

Analyzing Information Have students conduct additional research on the fall of the Qing dynasty using library or Internet sources. Ask students to interpret the bibliographies of each source and then create their own bibliographies of at least five sources that could be used to write a report on the topic. **OL**

Geography SKILLS

Answers:
1. Russia
2. It had limited access to ports but not a large sphere of influence.

Additional Support

Activity: Interdisciplinary Connection

Civics Remind students that the rapid decline of the Qing dynasty was due to a combination of internal and external causes. Have students work in pairs or small groups to list internal and external factors that force change and how a government may respond. Then have students come together to compare their lists. Students should reach the conclusion that the resources the government requires to respond to internal factors are limited by the demands of external forces *(military or police intervention, applying funds to alleviate worst symptoms, increasing representation)*, and the resources needed to respond to external forces are restricted by internal factors *(unified government response, dedicated military, citizen resistance)*. **OL**

R **Reading Strategy**

Determining Importance
Have students list important terms, places, and names in their notebooks as they read. Suggest they use these headings: *Places, People,* and *Products.* Then have students write a sentence explaining the significance of each entry. **OL**

D **Differentiated Instruction**

Advanced Learners Tell students that China maintained its cultural and territorial integrity for over 2,000 years, due in part to an educational system based on the teachings of Confucius. Have students research the role of Confucianism in imperial China and then write an essay that explains how it helped China resist Western influence. *(Answers may include that Confucian values of filial piety and social order encouraged tradition and cohesion, while an emphasis on agriculture led to negative attitudes toward merchants and trade.)* **AL**

Additional Support

The Opium War

Opium was grown in northern India under the sponsorship of the British East India Company and then shipped directly to Chinese markets. Demand for opium—a highly addictive drug—in South China jumped dramatically. Soon, silver was flowing out of China and into the pockets of the officials of the British East India Company.

The Chinese reacted strongly. The British were not the first to import opium into China. The Chinese government had already seen opium's dangerous qualities and had made its trade illegal. They appealed to the British government on moral grounds to stop the traffic in opium. Lin Zexu, a Chinese government official, wrote to Queen Victoria:

R

PRIMARY SOURCE

"Suppose there were people from another country who carried opium for sale to England and seduced your people into buying and smoking it; certainly your honorable ruler would deeply hate it and be bitterly aroused."

—Lin Zexu, a Chinese official

The British refused to halt their activity, however. As a result, the Chinese blockaded the foreign area in Guangzhou to force traders to surrender their opium. The British responded with force, starting the Opium War (1839–1842).

The Chinese were no match for the British. British warships destroyed Chinese coastal and river forts. When a British fleet sailed almost unopposed up the **Chang Jiang** (Yangtze River) to Nanjing, the Qing dynasty made peace.

In the Treaty of Nanjing in 1842, the Chinese agreed to open five coastal ports to British trade, limit taxes on imported British goods, and pay for the costs of the war. China also agreed to give the British the island of **Hong Kong.** Nothing was said in the treaty about the opium trade. Moreover, in the five ports, Europeans lived in their own sections and were subject not to Chinese laws but to their own laws—a practice known as **extraterritoriality.**

D The Opium War marked the beginning of the establishment of Western influence in China. For the time being, the Chinese dealt with the problem by pitting foreign countries against one another. Concessions granted to the British were offered to other Western nations, including the United States. Soon, thriving foreign areas were operating in the five treaty ports along the southern Chinese coast.

The Tai Ping Rebellion

In the meantime, the failure of the Chinese government to deal with pressing internal economic problems led to a peasant revolt, known as the Tai Ping (TIE PING) Rebellion (1850–1864). It was led by **Hong Xiuquan,** a Christian convert who viewed himself as a younger brother of Jesus Christ.

Hong was convinced that God had given him the mission of destroying the Qing dynasty. Joined by great crowds of peasants, Hong captured the town of Yongan and proclaimed a new dynasty, the Heavenly Kingdom of Great Peace (*Tai Ping Tianguo* in Chinese—hence the name *Tai Ping Rebellion*).

The Tai Ping Rebellion appealed to many people because it called for social reforms. These reforms included giving land to all peasants and treating women as equals of men. Women even served in their own units in the Tai Ping army.

Hong's rebellion also called for people to give up their private possessions. Peasants were to hold lands and farms in common. Money, food, and clothing were to be shared equally by all. Hong outlawed alcohol and tobacco and eliminated the practice of binding women's feet. The Chinese Communist Revolution of the twentieth century (see Chapter 31) would have similar social goals.

In March 1853, the rebels seized Nanjing, the second largest city of the empire, and massacred 25,000 men, women, and children. The revolt continued for 10 more years but gradually began to fall apart. Europeans came to the aid of the Qing dynasty when they realized the destructive nature of the Tai Ping forces. As one British observer noted, there was no hope "of any good ever coming of the rebel movement. They do nothing but burn, murder, and destroy."

Extending the Content

The Tai Ping Rebellion An American mercenary from Salem, Massachusetts, named Frederick Townsend Ward, went to China in 1859 and, at the age of 28, he raised an army of Chinese soldiers commanded by Western officers to fight the Tai Ping rebels. Using Western weapons and tactics, Ward defeated armies much larger than his own *Changsheng-chun* ("Ever Victorious Army"). Such was his reputation that the followers of Hong Xiuquan called his men the "devil soldiers." When Ward was killed three years after coming to China, the Manchu government built a temple and shrine to honor his memory.

The Opium War

The Turks and Arabs were the first to trade opium in China. China's emperors tried to stop the spreading addiction but failed. Then in the 1830s, an official named Lin Zexu went after the traders. First he wrote to Queen Victoria, but she did not respond. Then he demanded that British merchants surrender a cargo of opium and dumped it into the sea. The outraged British sent warships and overwhelmed the Chinese, who were forced to sign the Treaty of Nanjing. This was the first of several unequal treaties the Chinese signed in the 1800s.

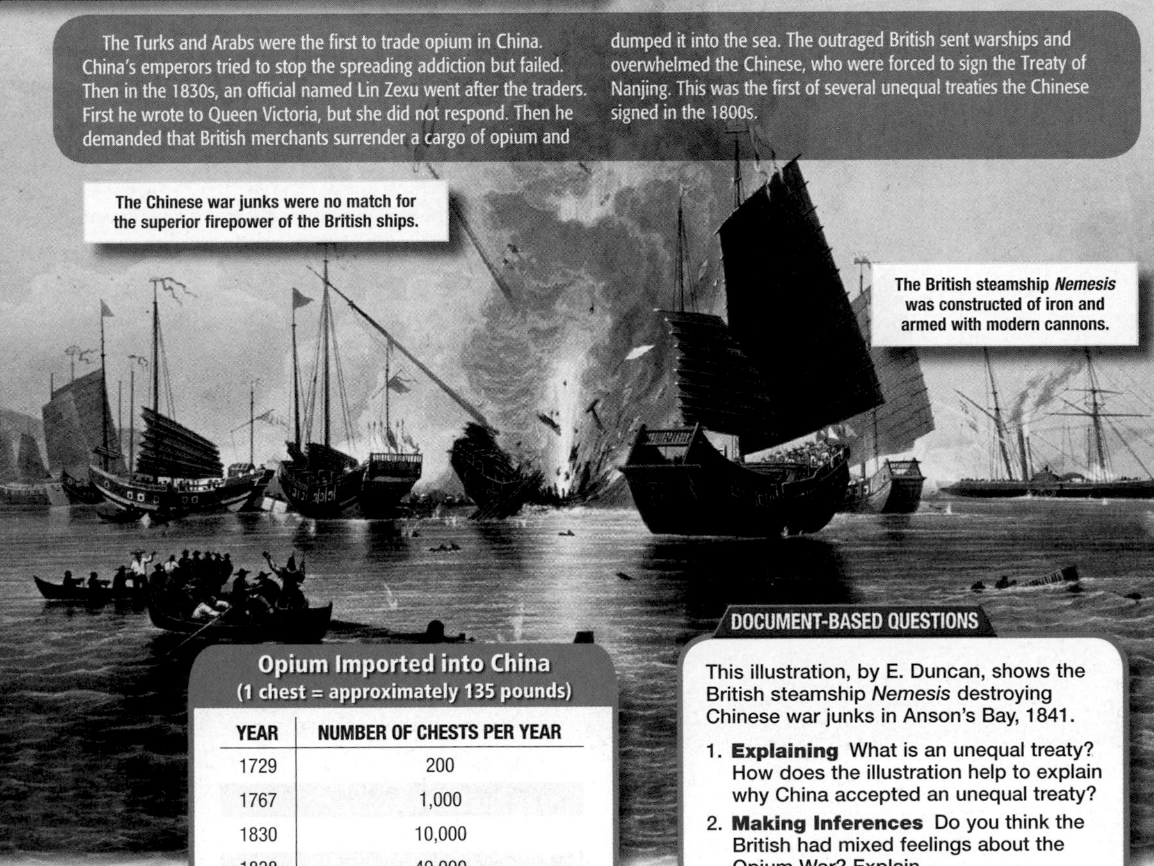

The Chinese war junks were no match for the superior firepower of the British ships.

The British steamship *Nemesis* was constructed of iron and armed with modern cannons.

Opium Imported into China
(1 chest = approximately 135 pounds)

YEAR	NUMBER OF CHESTS PER YEAR
1729	200
1767	1,000
1830	10,000
1838	40,000

DOCUMENT-BASED QUESTIONS

This illustration, by E. Duncan, shows the British steamship *Nemesis* destroying Chinese war junks in Anson's Bay, 1841.

1. **Explaining** What is an unequal treaty? How does the illustration help to explain why China accepted an unequal treaty?
2. **Making Inferences** Do you think the British had mixed feelings about the Opium War? Explain.

In 1864, Chinese forces, with European aid, recaptured Nanjing and destroyed the remaining rebel force. The Tai Ping Rebellion was one of the most devastating civil wars in history. As many as 20 million people died during the 14-year struggle.

China's ongoing struggle with the West prevented the Qing dynasty from dealing effectively with the internal unrest. Beginning in 1856, the British and the French applied force to gain greater trade privileges. As a result of the Treaty of Tianjin in 1858, the Chinese agreed to legalize the opium trade and to open new ports to foreign trade. They also surrendered the Kowloon Peninsula to Great Britain. When the Chinese resisted parts of the treaty, the British seized Beijing in 1860. C

Efforts at Reform

By the late 1870s, the Qing dynasty was in decline. Unable to restore order themselves, government troops had relied on forces recruited by regional warlords to help fight the Tai Ping Rebellion. To finance their armies, the warlords had collected taxes from local people. After the revolt, many of these warlords kept their armies.

C Critical Thinking

Making Inferences Ask: Do you think China would have been able to resist increased foreign influence if the Tai Ping Rebellion had not occurred? *(Answers may include that yes, the country would have been stronger if it did not have to deal with internal strife.)* **OL**

DOCUMENT-BASED QUESTIONS

Answers:

1. An unequal treaty is one in which one side gives up much more than it receives from the other. The Chinese entered such treaties because their weapons were no match for the modern war technology of foreign powers.
2. They were protecting their profitable business interests, but were doing so with a drug that seriously affected the health of the Chinese.

Differentiated Instruction

Leveled Activities

BL Differentiated Instruction Activity, URB p. 133

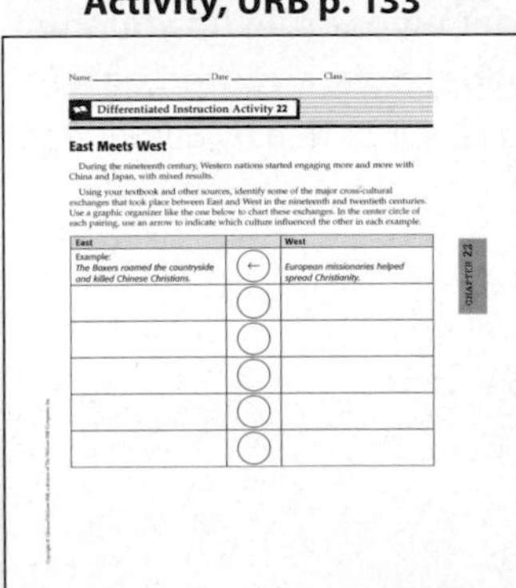

OL Mapping History Activity, URB p. 145

AL Critical Thinking Skills Activity, URB p. 142

ELL English Learner Activity, URB p. 135

W Writing Support

Persuasive Writing Have students write a brief essay in which they argue for or against China's policy of "self-strengthening." OL

D Differentiated Instruction

English Language Learners
To help students understand the concept of modernization, have them look up the word *modernize* in a dictionary and identify and define its root word. *(modern; updated or improved)* Then have them use each form of the word in a sentence. ELL

✓Reading Check

Answer: They started to trade opium instead of paying for imports with silver.

PEOPLE in HISTORY

Answers: Guang Xu—because of his exposure to Western inventions and to strengthen China's ability to stand up against foreign intrusion; **Ci Xi**—She had him overthrown and resumed her regency.

Additional Support

With the support of the local gentry, the regional warlords continued to collect local taxes for their own use.

W In its weakened state, the Qing court finally began to listen to the appeals of reform-minded officials. The reformers called for a new policy they called **"self-strengthening."** That is, China should adopt Western technology but keep its Confucian values and institutions.

Some reformers wanted to change China's traditional political institutions by introducing democracy. However, such ideas were too radical for most reformers. D During the last quarter of the nineteenth century, the Chinese government tried to modernize China's military forces and build up industry without touching the basic elements of Chinese civilization. Railroads, weapons factories, and shipyards were built. However, the Chinese value system remained unchanged.

✓Reading Check **Summarizing** What did Britain do to fix their trade imbalance with China?

The Advance of Imperialism

MAIN IDEA Western nations and Japan set up spheres of influence in China to gain exclusive trading rights.

HISTORY & YOU Have you noticed that when a group considers options, a strong voice often sways its decision? Read how the emperor's aunt blocked reforms in China.

In the end, however, the changes did not help the Qing stay in power. The European advance into China continued during the last two decades of the nineteenth century. Internal conditions also continued to deteriorate.

Mounting Pressures

In the north and northeast, Russia took advantage of the Qing dynasty's weakness to force China to give up territories north of the Amur River in Siberia. Russia wanted both Manchuria and Mongolia and even had designs on Korea. Russia's designs on

PEOPLE in HISTORY

Guang Xu
1871–1908 Chinese Emperor

Attendants brought foreign mechanical toys to entertain the baby Emperor Guang Xu. As he grew, he became fascinated with Western inventions—telephones, phonographs, and bicycles. These influences convinced Guang Xu to set up a new educational system in China. Another factor played a key role as well—growing foreign intrusion: "Our scholars are now without solid and practical education; our artisans are without scientific instructors; when compared with other countries we soon see how weak we are. Does anyone think that our troops are as well drilled or as well led as those of the foreign armies? or that we can successfully stand against them? Changes must be made. . . ." **Why did Guang Xu set up a new educational system?**

Ci Xi
1835–1908 Chinese Empress

Though never the official ruler of China, Ci Xi was the power behind the throne for 47 years. When her young son became emperor, Ci Xi had herself appointed regent. After her son died, she appointed her four-year-old nephew, Guang Xu, to the throne, but continued as regent. When Guang Xu came of age, Ci Xi supposedly retired. But when he began making reforms, Ci Xi had him overthrown and resumed her regency. "I have often thought that I am the cleverest woman who ever lived . . . I have 400 million people all dependent on my judgment." She opposed modernization and supported the Boxers in their ill-fated rebellion against Western colonizers in 1900. Afterwards, she recognized the need to modernize, but too late to save the Qing dynasty. **How did Ci Xi react to the reforms of Guang Xu?**

Extending the Content

Guang Xu and Ci Xi Ci Xi was at first a low-ranking concubine to Emperor Xian Feng. Her position became influential when she gave birth to the emperor's first and only son. Later, with the help of the imperial army, she had Guang Xu jailed in the palace after overthrowing him.

Ask: Why do you think Guang Xu and Ci Xi had opposing attitudes toward modernization? *(Answers may include that they were raised under different times and with different influences.)* Under whose rule do you think the Chinese people were more content? *(Answers should be supported by details from the text.)* OL

Korea threatened the Japanese. When Russia took military control of Manchuria, Britain signed an alliance with Japan. In Tibet, a struggle between Russia and Great Britain kept both powers from seizing the territory outright. This allowed Tibet to become free from Chinese influence.

Between the years of 1886 and 1895, the foreign powers tightened their hold on the Chinese Empire. Britain annexed Burma, made Sikkim a protectorate, and obtained the Tibetan town of Yadong, opening it to foreign trade. France occupied Laos in 1893. The Russian Trans-Siberian railway reached Lake Baikal by 1895.

Even more ominous changes were taking place in the Chinese heartland. European states began to create **spheres of influence,** areas where the imperial powers had **exclusive** trading rights. After the Tai Ping Rebellion, warlords in the provinces began to negotiate directly with foreign nations. In return for money, the warlords granted these nations exclusive trading rights or railroad-building and mining privileges. In this way, Britain, France, Germany, Russia, and Japan all established spheres of influence in China.

In 1894, another blow furthered the disintegration of the Qing dynasty. The Chinese went to war with Japan over Japanese inroads into Korea, a land that the Chinese had controlled for a long time. The Chinese were soundly defeated in the First Sino-Japanese War. Japan demanded and received the island of Taiwan (known to Europeans as Formosa) and the Liaodong (LYOW•DOONG) Peninsula. Fearing Japan's growing power, however, the **S** European powers forced Japan to give the Liaodong Peninsula back to China.

New pressures for Chinese territory soon arose. In 1897, Chinese rioters murdered two German missionaries. Germany used this as a pretext to demand territories in the Shandong (SHON•DOONG) Peninsula. When the Chinese government approved the demand, other European nations made new claims on Chinese territory.

Internal Crisis

This latest scramble for territory took place at a time of internal crisis in China. In June 1898, the young emperor **Guang Xu** (GWANG SHYOO) launched a massive reform program based on changes in Japan (see the discussion later in this chapter). During the following weeks, known as the One Hundred Days of Reform, the emperor issued edicts calling for major political, administrative, and educational reforms. With these reforms, Guang Xu intended to modernize government bureaucracy by following Western models. He also wanted to adopt a new educational system that would replace the traditional civil service examinations. His reforms included the adoption of Western-style schools and banks, and the institution of a free press. Guang Xu also intended to train the military to use modern weapons and Western fighting techniques.

Many conservatives at court, however, opposed these reforms. They saw little advantage in copying the West. As one said, "An examination of the causes of success and failure in government reveals that . . . the adoption of foreignism leads to disorder." According to this conservative, traditional Chinese rules needed to be reformed and **W** not rejected in favor of Western changes.

Most important, **Empress Dowager Ci Xi** (TSUH•SEE), the emperor's aunt, opposed the new reform program. Ci Xi became a dominant force at court and opposed the emperor's reforms. With the aid of the imperial army, she eventually imprisoned the emperor. Other supporters of the reform were imprisoned, exiled, or prosecuted. These actions ended Guang Xu's reforms.

While Guang Xu's reform efforts aroused popular sympathy, they had limited support within Chinese society overall. His hasty measures damaged the careers of many scholars, losing much support for the reforms. Also, the reform efforts neglected agriculture, which was very important to China's future, and focused too heavily on the elite classes. Most notably, the reformers in power could not end foreign influence. Concluding that peaceful reform could never be achieved, some reformers began to consider revolution.

✓Reading Check **Examining** What nations established spheres of influence in China?

S Skill Practice

Using Geography Skills Provide students with an outline map of Asia from the Outline Map Resource Book. Have students label the locations mentioned in the bracketed text as they read. (They may use the map on page 725 as a guide.) Then have them create a map key to show the events of 1894 and 1897. **BL**

W Writing Support

Narrative Writing Have students write a short story set in China during the One Hundred Days of Reform. The story should be historical fiction, using facts from the section to provide the background for the story. **OL**

✓Reading Check

Answer: Britain, France, Germany, Russia, Japan

Hands-On Chapter Project Step 1

Creating a Photo-Essay

Students will prepare a photo-essay illustrating changes that took place in China and Japan between 1840 and 1910.

Step 1: Defining and Identifying Content for a Photo-Essay

Essential Question: How did Western ideas and technology accelerate change in China and Japan between 1840 and 1910?

Directions: Ask: What is a photo-essay? *(a collection of captioned photos or images that documents a specific event or subject)* Allow students to view a sample photo-essay in the library or on the Internet, such as can be found at www.whitehouse.gov. Review as a class the Big Idea for this section. Then have students locate details from the text that support the Big Idea. Ask students to think about images that would illustrate those details in a photo-essay. Discuss students' ideas. **OL**

(Chapter Project is continued in Section 2.)

C Critical Thinking

Identifying Central Issues

Ask: What were the terms of the Open Door policy? *(All countries would have equal access to China. Tariffs were lowered to allow equal access.)* Why would the United States want to allow open access to China? *(It did not have a sphere of influence there and wanted to expand trade.)* **OL**

DOCUMENT-BASED QUESTIONS

Answers:

1. The United States looks peaceful, Germany looks aggressive and militaristic.
2. Answers may include that China would have been carved up into colonies by the powers that already had spheres of influence.

Responses to Imperialism

MAIN IDEA The United States proposed an Open Door policy to guarantee it would have equal trading rights with European countries in China.

HISTORY & YOU What does an open door suggest to you? Read to learn how and why the United States proposed an Open Door policy in China.

As foreign pressure on the Qing dynasty grew stronger, both Great Britain and the United States feared that other nations would overrun the country should the Chinese government collapse. The annexation of Hawaii and the Philippines had encouraged the expansion of American interests in the Pacific. The United States now was fully engaged in expanding its stake in the global marketplace.

C In 1899, U.S. secretary of state **John Hay** wrote a note to Britain, Russia, Germany, France, Italy, and Japan. Hay asked each country to respect equal trading opportunities in China. He also asked the powers with a sphere of influence not to set tariffs that would give an unfair advantage to the citizens of their own country. This note was not shown to the Chinese government. When none of the other imperialist governments expressed opposition to the idea, Hay proclaimed that all major states with economic interests in China had agreed that the country should have an Open Door policy.

POLITICAL CARTOONS PRIMARY SOURCE

Open Door Policy

In 1899 U.S. secretary of state John Hay sent notes to the major powers asking them to uphold "Chinese territorial and administrative" integrity and guarantee "equal and impartial trade with all parts of the Chinese Empire." Despite a general lack of response, Hay announced in 1900 that his Open Door policy had been approved.

After the Boxer Rebellion broke out, Hay promoted the following policy in a letter to various U.S. embassies:

"[T]he policy of the government of the United States is to seek a solution which may bring about permanent safety and peace to China, preserve Chinese territorial and administrative entity, protect all rights guaranteed to friendly powers by treaty and international law, and safeguard for the world the principle of equal and impartial trade with all parts of the Chinese Empire."

DOCUMENT-BASED QUESTIONS

The Open Door by William A. Rogers portrays how, in order to trade with China, the United States had to confront the European powers already established there.

1. **Analyzing** How is the United States portrayed differently from Germany?
2. **Predicting** What do you think would have happened if the United States had not stepped in with its Open Door policy?

Differentiated Instruction

Primary Source Reading, URB p. 155

Analyzing Primary Sources

Objective: Analyze John Hay's proposal for an Open Door policy in China.

Focus: Have students identify persuasive language in the proposal.

Teach: Have students read the excerpt and answer the questions.

Assess: Have students outline the terms of the proposal.

Close: Discuss students' views on the proposal.

Differentiated Instruction Strategies

BL Have students highlight unfamiliar words and phrases as they read.

AL Have students write a response from Germany's Minister of Foreign Affairs.

ELL Define words such as *herein* and *herewith*.

Opening the Door to China

In part, the **Open Door policy** reflected American concern for the survival of China. However, it also reflected the interests of some U.S. trading companies. These companies wanted to operate in open markets and disliked the existing division of China into separate spheres of influence dominated by individual states.

The Open Door policy did not end the system of spheres of influence. However, it did reduce restrictions on foreign imports imposed by the dominating power within each sphere. The Open Door policy also helped reduce imperialist hysteria over access to the China market. The policy lessened fears in Britain, France, Germany, and Russia that other powers would take advantage of China's weakness and attempt to dominate the China market for themselves.

The Boxer Rebellion

The Open Door policy came too late to stop the Boxer Rebellion. Boxer was the popular name given to members of a secret organization called the Society of Harmonious Fists. Members practiced a system of exercise—a form of shadowboxing, or boxing with an imaginary opponent—that they thought would protect them from bullets.

The Boxers were upset by the foreign takeover of Chinese lands. Their slogan was "destroy the foreigner." They especially disliked Christian missionaries and Chinese converts to Christianity who seemed to threaten Chinese traditions. At the beginning of 1900, Boxer bands roamed the countryside and slaughtered foreign missionaries and Chinese Christians. Their victims also included foreign businessmen and even the German envoy to Beijing.

Response to the killings of missionaries and Chinese Christians was immediate and overwhelming. When William II, emperor of Germany, learned of the envoy's fate, he sent German troops to China and declared:

PRIMARY SOURCE

> "Show no mercy! Take no prisoners! . . . the Huns of King Attila made a name for themselves . . . impose the name of Germany in China . . . in such a way that no Chinese will ever dare look askance at a German again."
>
> —Jean Chesneaux, Marianne Bastid, and Marie-Claire Bergère, *China: From the Opium Wars to the 1911 Revolution*

An allied army consisting of 20,000 British, French, German, Russian, American, and Japanese troops attacked Beijing in August 1900. The army restored order and demanded more concessions from the Chinese government. The Chinese government was forced to pay a heavy **indemnity**—a payment for damages—to the powers that had crushed the uprising. The imperial government was now weaker than ever.

✓Reading Check **Explaining** How did the Boxers get their name?

SECTION 1 REVIEW

Vocabulary
1. **Explain** the significance of: highlighted, Guangzhou, Chang Jiang, Hong Kong, extraterritoriality, Hong Xiuquan, self-strengthening, spheres of influence, exclusive, Guang Xu, Empress Dowager Ci Xi, John Hay, Open Door policy, indemnity.

Main Ideas
2. **Summarize** the factors that led to the decline of the Qing dynasty by using a diagram like the one below.

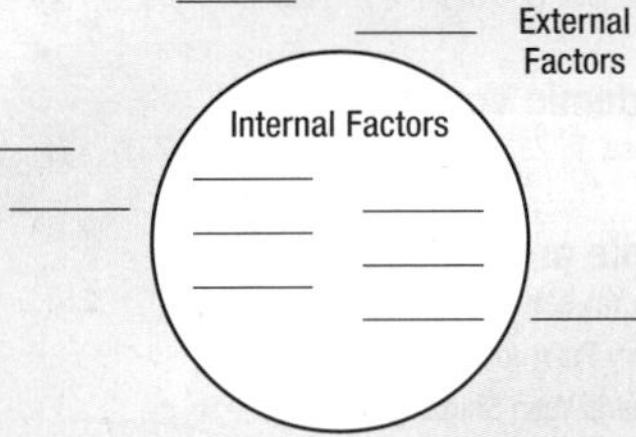

3. **Explain** how Western nations and Japan gained exclusive trading rights in China.
4. **List** the countries that supplied troops for the allied army, which was formed to fight the Boxers in 1900.

Critical Thinking
5. **The BIG Idea** **Making Inferences** Why did European nations agree to follow the Open Door policy proposed by the U.S.?
6. **Drawing Conclusions** Why did foreign powers help the Chinese government put down the Boxer Rebellion?
7. **Analyzing Visuals** In what ways does the cartoon on page 730 depict China as a difficult place in which to gain entry?

Writing About History
8. **Expository Writing** Using outside sources, research, write, and present a report on the effects of population growth on modern China. Include government laws to curtail population growth and explain the consequences of disobeying these laws.

History ONLINE
For help with the concepts in this section of *Glencoe World History*, go to glencoe.com and click Study Central™.

✓Reading Check

Answer: *Boxer* was the name given to members of the Society of Harmonious Fists, who practiced shadowboxing.

Assess

History ONLINE
Study Central provides summaries, interactive games, and online graphic organizers to help students review content.

Close

Activating Prior Knowledge
Have students compare the activities of European countries in China to European activities in Southeast Asia and India. Ask why European countries did not exert control over China as they did in other countries. *(Answers may vary, but students should base their responses on historical evidence and logical conclusions.)* OL

Answers

1. Definitions for the vocabulary words are found in the section and the Glossary.
2. **Internal Factors:** corruption, peasant unrest, rapid population growth, serious food shortage, Tai Ping Rebellion, Boxer Rebellion; **External Factors:** Opium War, trade concessions, extraterritoriality, spheres of influences, imperialist advances, Open Door Policy, indemnities
3. created spheres of influence
4. Britain, France, Germany, Russia, United States, Japan
5. helped reduce imperialist hysteria over access to the China market and lessened attempt of any one country to dominate the market
6. to protect their trading rights and to gain more concessions in exchange for their help
7. China is portrayed as a heavily fortified building to which access can only be gained through a door that has guns and bayonets pointing out of it.
8. Reports should use sound reasoning and reflect accurate information.

W Writing Support

Personal Writing Have students write a brief response to this quotation. **Ask:** Do you agree that the Japanese should be admired for their attack on Russia? Remind students to provide reasons that support their opinion. OL

S Skill Practice

Visual Literacy Ask: What do you notice about the Japanese warships? *(Answers may include that the ships look modern and well-built; the ships are moving in a well-organized and orderly manner.)* BL

✓Reading Check

Answer: To compete as a world power, Japan believed it needed to expand.

CRITICAL THINKING SKILLS

Answers:

1. Japan became a world power, while Russia's power declined.
2. Russia was considered a major world power.

Additional Support

The Russian commander in chief said, "It is impossible not to admire the bravery and activity of the Japanese. The attack of the Japanese is a continuous succession of waves, and they never relax their efforts by day or by night."

In the meantime, Russia had sent its Baltic fleet halfway around the world to East Asia, only to be defeated by the new Japanese navy off the coast of Japan. After their defeat, the Russians agreed to a humiliating peace in 1905. They gave the Liaodong Peninsula back to Japan, as well as the southern part of Sakhalin (SA•kuh•LEEN), an island north of Japan. The Japanese victory stunned the world. Japan had become one of the great powers.

U.S. Relations

When Japan established a sphere of influence in Korea, the United States recognized Japan's role there. In return, Japan recognized American authority in the Philippines. In 1910, Japan annexed Korea outright.

Some Americans began to fear the rise of Japanese power in East Asia. Japan resented U.S. efforts to restrict immigration. In 1907, President Theodore Roosevelt made a "gentlemen's agreement" with Japan that essentially stopped Japanese immigration to the United States.

✓Reading Check **Explaining** Why did Japan turn itself into an imperialist power?

TURNING POINT: JAPAN BECOMES AN IMPERIAL POWER

When Commodore Perry's fleet steamed into Edo Bay in 1854, the Japanese saw "giant dragons puffing smoke." Never before had they seen ships powered by steam or carrying such large guns. The Japanese soon began to modernize their military.

After a decisive victory over China in 1894, Japan gained territory and influence in Korea. Russia, however, remained a formidable rival blocking Japan's ambitions in Korea and Manchuria.

In 1904, Japan unleashed its technologically advanced navy on the Russian naval base at Port Arthur, in Manchuria. This battle began the Russo-Japanese War. Japan's victory in the war stunned the world.

SIGNIFICANCE OF THE RUSSO-JAPANESE WAR OF 1904–1905
Marked the first victory of an Asian nation over a European power in modern times
Made Japan one of the world's great powers
Gave Japan a foothold in Manchuria
Reinforced Japan as the dominant power in Korea
Ended Russia's expansion in East Asia

CRITICAL THINKING SKILLS

This woodcut shows Japanese warships engaging the Russian fleet at Port Arthur in 1904.

1. **Explaining** How did the Russo-Japanese War affect the balance of power in East Asia?
2. **Analyzing** Why do you think Japan's victory in the Russo-Japanese War stunned the world?

Extending the Content

Japan Becomes an Imperial Power The United States played a diplomatic role very early in the Russo-Japanese War. Theodore Roosevelt helped negotiate peace at Port Arthur, ending the war and earning him the Nobel Peace Prize. President Roosevelt became the first American to win this prestigious award. Neither Russia nor Japan was grateful for Roosevelt's efforts. Both countries felt they had received the worse end of the deal and bore a grudge against the United States because of the settlement.

Ask: How might the Russian and Japanese resentment toward the United States affect future dealings among the three countries? *(Japan and Russia might side against the United States in the future as a form of revenge.)* OL

Culture in an Era of Transition

MAIN IDEA The culture of Western nations greatly influenced Japanese traditional culture.

HISTORY & YOU Do you own anything made in Japan? Read to learn about early cultural contact between the United States and Japan.

Contact with Western nations greatly influenced Japanese culture during the late-nineteenth and early-twentieth centuries. From literature to architecture, the Japanese copied Western techniques and styles. The exchange of cultures went both ways, however. Japanese art also influenced Westerners.

New Western Model

The wave of Western technology and ideas that entered Japan in the last half of the nineteenth century greatly altered the shape of traditional Japanese culture. Literature was especially affected. Dazzled by European literature, Japanese authors began translating and imitating the imported models.

The novel showed the greatest degree of change. People began to write novels that were patterned after the French tradition of realism. Naturalist Japanese authors tried to present existing social conditions and the realities of war as objectively as possible.

Other aspects of Japanese culture were also changed. The Japanese invited technicians, engineers, architects, and artists from Europe and the United States to teach their "modern" skills to eager Japanese students. The Japanese copied Western artistic techniques and styles. Huge buildings of steel and reinforced concrete, adorned with Greek columns, appeared in many Japanese cities.

A Return to Tradition

A national reaction had begun by the end of the nineteenth century, however. Many Japanese artists began to return to older techniques. In 1889, the Tokyo School of Fine Arts was established to promote traditional Japanese art. Japanese artists searched for a new but truly Japanese means of expression. Some artists tried to bring together native and foreign techniques. Others returned to past artistic traditions for inspiration.

Cultural exchange also went the other way. Japanese arts and crafts, porcelains, textiles, fans, folding screens, and woodblock prints became fashionable in Europe and North America. Japanese gardens, with their close attention to the positioning of rocks and falling water, became especially popular in the United States. **D**

✓ **Reading Check** **Describing** What effect did Japanese culture have on other nations?

SECTION 3 REVIEW

Vocabulary

1. **Explain** the significance of: Matthew Perry, Edo Bay, Millard Fillmore, concessions, Kyōto, Mutsuhito, Edo, prefectures, Ito Hirobumi, subsidy, context, Port Arthur.

Main Ideas

2. **Identify** the benefits that the Treaty of Kanagawa granted to the United States.
3. **Explain** how Japan's Liberals and Progressives differed on the question of which government branch should hold the most power. Which group won?
4. **Illustrate** the results of Western influence on Japanese culture by using a diagram like the one below.

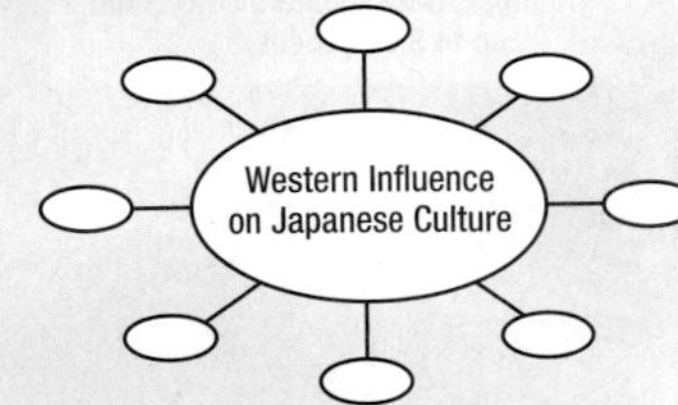

Critical Thinking

5. **The BIG Idea** **Evaluating** How did the Japanese land reform program create internal problems?
6. **Comparing** Compare the rights of Japanese women before and after the Meiji Restoration.
7. **Analyzing Visuals** Examine the images on page 742. How do these prints show a mixing of Western and Japanese cultures?

Writing About History

8. **Persuasive Writing** Pretend that you wish to study abroad in China or Japan. Write a letter of application stating which country you would like to visit and why. State what you hope to learn while abroad and how you would overcome or minimize the drawbacks of being a foreign student.

History ONLINE
For help with the concepts in this section of *Glencoe World History*, go to glencoe.com and click Study Central™.

D Differentiated Instruction

Visual/Spatial Have students who are artistically inclined work together to make a wall mural of a Japanese garden. **OL**

✓ **Reading Check**

Answer: Western nations developed tastes for Japanese arts and crafts; Japanese gardens became popular.

Assess

History ONLINE

Study Central provides summaries, interactive games, and online graphic organizers to help students review content.

Close

Analyzing Information

Reform efforts in Japan produced dramatic changes but did not provide security or stability. Discuss changes and developments in Japan that contributed to social and economic instability. **OL**

SECTION 3 REVIEW

Answers

1. Definitions for the vocabulary words are found in the section and the Glossary.
2. return of shipwrecked American sailors, opening of two ports to Western traders, establishment of a U.S. consulate in Japan
3. **Liberals:** most power to parliament; **Progressives:** most power to executive branch. Progressives won.
4. Meiji constitution modeled after Imperial Germany; industry grew; established colonial empire; compulsory military service; women's rights movement; universal education; adopted Western technology; baseball introduced
5. New tax did not vary by size of harvest; many farmers were forced to sell their land.
6. **Before:** subject to the "three obediences," required to marry around age sixteen, no shared inheritance rights, little access to education; **After:** could seek education, family role enforced by Civil Code
7. The prints show Western-style buildings and technologies alongside Japanese buildings and people in traditional and Western dress.
8. Letters should reflect accurate information about China or Japan.

Introducing

UNIT 5

Focus

Why It Matters

As the world entered the twentieth century, optimism about the future slowly began to dwindle. The competition among the imperialist powers had created political and economic tensions in their colonial possessions. In spite of technological advances, the world was headed towards two worldwide wars that threatened democracy across Europe. The picture grew even bleaker when an economic depression occurred. As students study this time period they will learn why and how the United States emerged from this turmoil a respected world leader.

Unit Launch Activity

To build student interest in this unit, discuss the general causes of war, particularly more recent wars such as the Vietnam War, the Persian Gulf War, and the war on terrorism. If differences of opinion arise, make sure everyone gets a chance to speak without interruption. **OL**

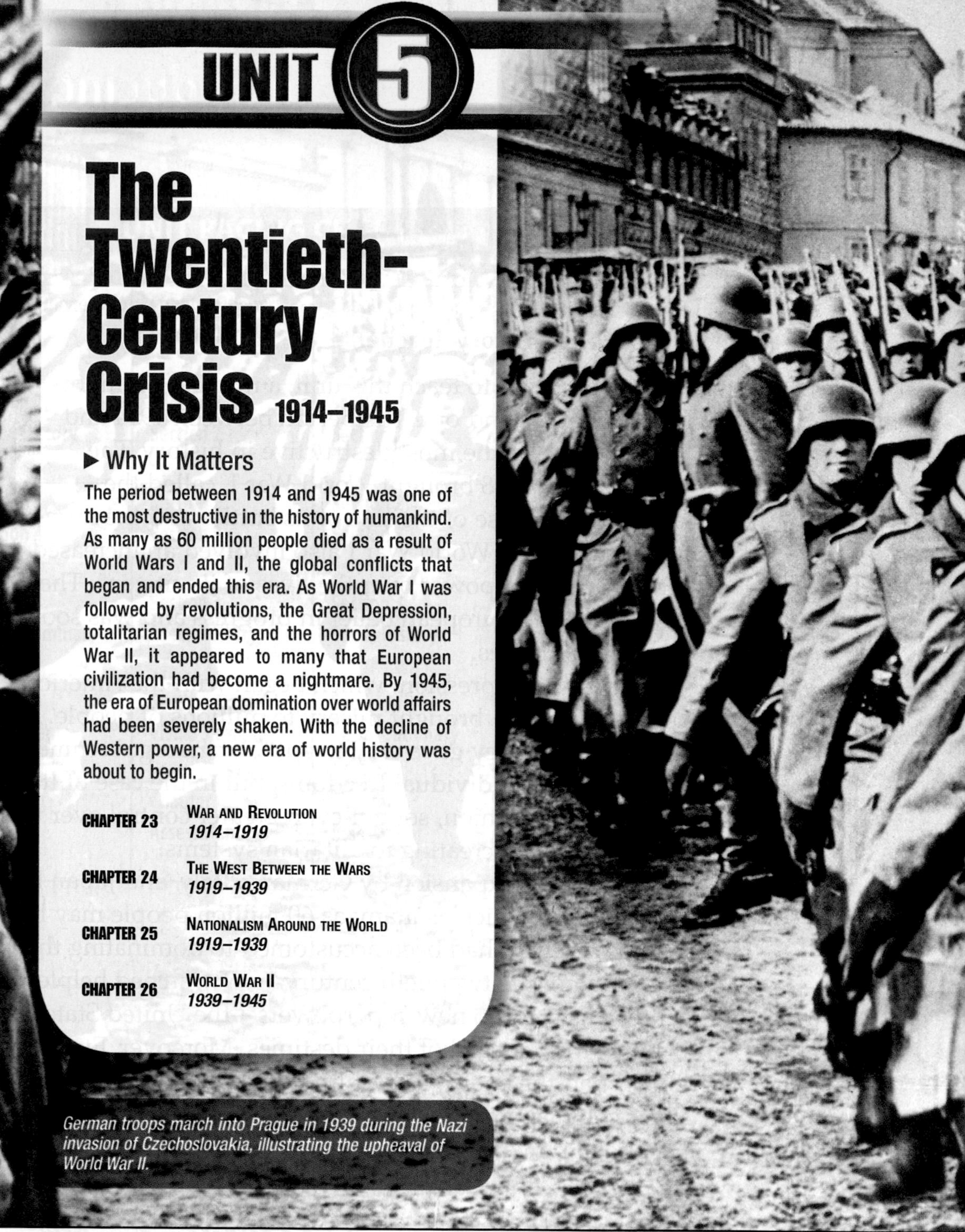

UNIT 5

The Twentieth-Century Crisis 1914–1945

▶ Why It Matters

The period between 1914 and 1945 was one of the most destructive in the history of humankind. As many as 60 million people died as a result of World Wars I and II, the global conflicts that began and ended this era. As World War I was followed by revolutions, the Great Depression, totalitarian regimes, and the horrors of World War II, it appeared to many that European civilization had become a nightmare. By 1945, the era of European domination over world affairs had been severely shaken. With the decline of Western power, a new era of world history was about to begin.

German troops march into Prague in 1939 during the Nazi invasion of Czechoslovakia, illustrating the upheaval of World War II.

Team Teaching Activity

Art Coordinate with an art teacher a study of the major modern art movements of the 1920s and 1930s. Students should examine the philosophy and works of the Dada movement, surrealism, cubism, and the functionalist movement of the Bauhaus school. After students are familiar with each of these movements and its philosophy, discuss the possible influence that World War I had on the art of this period. You may want to have students write reports analyzing an artist's work and the historical influences on that artist, or you may want students (with the help of the art teacher) to create their own artistic creations that reflect the philosophies of one of the movements.

Teach

S Skill Practice

Visual Literacy For most of the citizens of Prague, the arrival of the German army was a grim day. Tell students to look closely at the photograph and to think about the message the photographer was trying to convey. **Ask:** **Based on the photo, what image of the German army did the photographer convey?** *(Their discipline; and the angle showing a long row of grim-faced soldiers inspires respect for and even fear of their military might.)* **OL**

Analyzing Secondary Sources Have students work in pairs to read the Why It Matters text again. **Ask:** What do the words *destructive, conflict,* and *totalitarian* mean? As a group, discuss the words and how knowing them can help students understand the unit. **ELL**

No Child Left Behind

Teaching Tip The goals of the NCLB Act include a strong emphasis on phonics. Model for students how to sound out difficult names or words.

More About the Photo

Visual Literacy The origin of the Nazi salute is somewhat murky. Many believe that it is a derivative of the Roman salute, which is depicted in various paintings from the period. No one knows for sure, however, if the gesture was actually meant as a salute, in the military sense, or simply a pledge of loyalty. Up until World War II, many countries used the Roman salute. In the United States it was called the Bellamy salute and was used while reciting the Pledge of Allegiance. It was dropped during World War II because of its association with Adolf Hitler. In its place, Americans began placing their hands over their hearts while saying the Pledge. Hitler did not agree that the Nazi salute had its origins in Rome. He believed that the gesture was used at ancient German gatherings and was symbolic of their warlike spirit. Throughout Germany, crowds would greet Hitler with the Nazi salute and shouts of *Sieg Heil*, or "Hail to Victory."

Planning Guide

Key to Ability Levels	
BL Below Level	AL Above Level
OL On Level	ELL English Language Learners

Key to Teaching Resources	
Print Material	DVD
CD-ROM	Transparency

BL	OL	AL	ELL		Resources	Chapter Opener	Section 1	Section 2	Section 3	Section 4	Chapter Assess
					FOCUS						
BL	OL	AL	ELL	Transparency	**Daily Focus Skills Transparencies**		23-1	23-2	23-3	23-4	
					TEACH						
BL	OL		ELL	Print Material	**Reading Skills Activity, URB**			p. 19			
	OL	AL		Print Material	**Historical Analysis Skills Activity, URB**		p. 20				
BL	OL	AL	ELL	Print Material	**Differentiated Instruction Activity, URB**					p. 21	
	OL		ELL	Print Material	**English Learner Activity, URB**			p. 23			
BL	OL	AL	ELL	Print Material	**Content Vocabulary Activity, URB***		p. 25				
BL	OL	AL	ELL	Print Material	**Academic Vocabulary Activity, URB**		p. 27				
BL	OL	AL	ELL	Print Material	**Skills Reinforcement Activity, URB**				p. 29		
	OL	AL		Print Material	**Critical Thinking Skills Activity, URB**				p. 30		
	OL	AL		Print Material	**History and Geography Activity, URB**			p. 31			
	OL	AL	ELL	Print Material	**Mapping History Activity, URB**			p. 33			
BL	OL	AL		Print Material	**Historical Significance Activity, URB**					p. 34	
BL	OL	AL	ELL	Print Material	**Cooperative Learning Activity, URB**					p. 35	
	OL	AL	ELL	Print Material	**History Simulation Activity, URB**			p. 37			
BL	OL	AL	ELL	Print Material	**Time Line Activity, URB**					p. 39	
	OL	AL		Print Material	**Linking Past and Present Activity, URB**			p. 40			
BL	OL	AL		Print Material	**People in World History Activity, URB**		p. 41		p. 42		
BL	OL	AL	ELL	Print Material	**Primary Source Reading, URB**				p. 43		
	OL	AL		Print Material	**Enrichment Activity, URB**			p. 48			
BL	OL	AL	ELL	Print Material	**World Art and Music Activity, URB**			p. 45			
BL	OL		ELL	Print Material	**Guided Reading Activities, URB***		p. 50	p. 51	p. 52	p. 53	
BL	OL		ELL	Print Material	**Reading Essentials and Note-Taking Guide***		p. 250	p. 253	p. 256	p. 259	
BL	OL	AL	ELL	Print Material	**Differentiated Instruction for the World History Classroom**	✓	✓	✓	✓	✓	✓

Note: Please refer to the *Unit Resource Book: The Twentieth-Century Crisis* for this chapter's URB materials.

* Also available in Spanish

- Interactive Lesson Planner
- Interactive Teacher Edition
- Fully editable blackline masters
- Section Spotlight Videos Launch
- Differentiated Lesson Plans
- Printable reports of daily assignments
- Standards Tracking System

Levels BL	OL	AL	ELL		Resources	Chapter Opener	Section 1	Section 2	Section 3	Section 4	Chapter Assess
					TEACH *(continued)*						
BL	OL	AL	ELL		StudentWorks™ Plus DVD	✓	✓	✓	✓	✓	✓
BL	OL	AL	ELL		Vocabulary PuzzleMaker CD-ROM	✓	✓	✓	✓	✓	✓
Teacher Resources					Building Academic Vocabulary	✓	✓	✓	✓	✓	✓
					Reading Strategies and Activities for the Social Studies Classroom		pp. 68, 71		p. 56		
					Writer's Guidebook				p. 5		
					Strategies for Success	✓	✓	✓	✓	✓	✓
					Outline Map Resource Book	✓	✓	✓	✓	✓	✓
					Presentation Plus! with MindJogger DVD	✓	✓	✓	✓	✓	✓
					ASSESS						
BL	OL	AL	ELL		Section Quizzes and Chapter Tests*		p. 285	p. 286	p. 287	p. 288	p 289
BL	OL	AL	ELL		Authentic Assessment With Rubrics	✓	✓	✓	✓	✓	✓
BL	OL	AL	ELL		Standardized Test Practice Workbook	✓	✓	✓	✓	✓	✓
BL	OL	AL	ELL		*ExamView® Assessment Suite* CD-ROM		23-1	23-2	23-3	23-4	Ch. 23
BL	OL	AL	ELL		Interactive Tutor Self-Assessment CD-ROM		23-1	23-2	23-3	23-4	
					CLOSE						
BL			ELL		Reteaching Activity, URB					p. 47	
BL	OL		ELL		Reading and Study Skills Foldables™	✓	✓	✓	✓	✓	✓

Using CyberScout

Researching Using *Keyword*

Technology Product

CyberScout is a convenient and dynamic search engine that provides several easy ways to locate information outside the McGraw-Hill Learning Network. CyberScout only searches Web sites that have been reviewed by teachers, so the information students find is always appropriate and accurate.

Objectives

After students learn to use CyberScout, they will be able to

- research topics and issues in economics using CyberScout;
- exercise research and study skills;
- practice writing skills.

Steps

- From the McGraw-Hill Learning Network home page (www.mhln.com), click on **For Students**.
- Choose **CyberScout** below **Homework Help**.
- Enter a keyword or phrase in the **Keyword** field and click on the **Go** button.
- Click on the link to a Web site of interest.
- Students will be redirected to the Web site in a new window.
- Students navigate through the chosen Web site to gain information on their topic and take notes.

History ONLINE

	Student	Teacher	Parent
Beyond the Textbook	●	●	●
Chapter Overviews	●	●	●
Time Current Events	●		●
ePuzzles and Games	●		●
Concepts in Motion	●		●
Literature Connections		●	
Multi-Language Glossaries	●		●
Online Student Edition	●	●	●
Self-Check Quizzes	●		●
Student Web Activities	●		●
Study Central ™	●		●
Teaching Today		●	
Vocabulary eFlashcards	●		●
Web Activity Lesson Plans		●	

- **Timed Readings Plus in Social Studies** helps students increase their reading rate and fluency while maintaining comprehension. The 400-word passages are similar to those found on state and national assessments.
- **Reading in the Content Area: Social Studies** concentrates on six essential reading skills that help students better comprehend what they read. The book includes 75 high-interest nonfiction passages written at increasing levels of difficulty.
- **Reading Social Studies** includes strategic reading instruction and vocabulary support in Social Studies content for both ELLs and native speakers of English.

www.jamestowneducation.com

The following videotape programs are available from Glencoe as supplements to Chapter 23:

- Nicholas and Alexandra (ISBN 1-56-501514-2)
- Rasputin: The Mad Monk (ISBN 0-76-700189-3)

To order, call Glencoe at 1-800-334-7344. To find classroom resources to accompany many of these videos, check the following home pages:

A&E Television: www.aetv.com

The History Channel: www.historychannel.com

NATIONAL GEOGRAPHIC

Index to National Geographic Magazine:

The following articles relate to this chapter:

- "War Letters," by Andrew Carroll, November 2005
- "The New Europe," by T. R. Reid, January 2002
- "Russia Rising," by Fen Montaigne, November 2001

National Geographic Society Products To order the following, call National Geographic at 1-800-368-2728:

- *National Geographic Atlas of the World* (Book)
- *World War I Era* (PicturePak or CD-ROM)

Access National Geographic's new, dynamic MapMachine Web site and other geography resources at:
www.nationalgeographic.com
www.nationalgeographic.com/maps

GLENCOE BOOKLINK 3

Use this database to search more than 30,000 titles to create a customized reading list for your students.

- Reading lists can be organized by students' reading level, author, genre, theme, or area of interest.
- The database provides Degrees of Reading Power™ (DRP) and Lexile™ readability scores for all selections.
- A brief summary of each selection is included.

Leveled reading suggestions for this chapter:

For students at a Grade 8 reading level:
- ***Woodrow Wilson: 28th President of the United States,*** by David R. Collins

For students at a Grade 9 reading level:
- ***Russia Under the Czars,*** by Henry Moscow

For students at a Grade 10 reading level:
- ***Ten Days that Shook the World,*** by John Reed

For students at a Grade 11 reading level:
- ***The Generation of 1914,*** by Robert Wohl

For students at a Grade 12 reading level:
- ***Dulce et Decorum Est,*** by Wilfred Own

Introducing
CHAPTER 23

Focus

MAKING CONNECTIONS
How can new technology affect warfare?

Activate students' prior knowledge by asking them what they know about military strategies used in Vietnam and Iraq. *(Answers may include shock and awe, guerilla warfare, suicide bombs, and smart bombs.)* Ask students to consider the effectiveness of these methods. **Ask:** **Do advances in military technology improve military outcomes?** Ask students to cite specific examples from recent wars to support their opinions.

Teach

The Big Ideas

As students study the chapter, remind them to consider the section-based Big Ideas included in each section's Guide to Reading. The **Essential Questions** in the activities below tie in to the Big Ideas and help students think about and understand important chapter concepts. In addition, the Hands-on Chapter Projects with their culminating activities relate the content from each section to the Big Ideas. These activities build on each other as students progress through the chapter. Section activities culminate in the wrap-up activity on the Visual Summary page.

CHAPTER 23

War and Revolution 1914–1919

MAKING CONNECTIONS

How can new technology affect warfare?

In World War I, new war technology such as the tank and machine gun contributed to a loss of life never before experienced in war. Soldiers living in muddy trenches were exposed to rats, lice, and disease while constantly under threat of attack. In this chapter you will learn about many aspects of World War I and the Russian Revolution.

- What other inventions made World War I more devastating than previous wars?
- What new technologies have been used in more recent wars?

EUROPE AND THE UNITED STATES ▶

1914 Assassination of Archduke Ferdinand sparks World War I

1917 United States enters the war

Russian Revolution begins

1914 | 1916

THE WORLD ▶

1912 Italy, led by Giolitti, attempts to seize Libya

1915 Armenians are victims of genocide by Turkey

756

The Road to World War I

Essential Question: **In what way did the system of European nation-states help lead to World War I?** *(Rivalries increased between nation-states, leading to an increase in internal disorder and strife among groups in Europe.)* Point out that in Section 1 students will learn how nationalism, militarism, and shaky alliances helped lead to World War I. **OL**

World War I

Essential Question: **Why did the war become a stalemate on the Western Front?** *(Trench warfare prevented any kind of quick end to the battles there.)* Point out that in Section 2 students will learn how trench warfare caused a stalemate on the Western Front, leading to a widening of the war.) **OL**

More About the Photo

Visual Literacy American soldiers are shown advancing through a barbed-wire trench in March, 1918. The Spring Offensive of 1918 was Germany's final attempt to win the war. By April, Germany had made the largest advance on the Western Front since September 1914. However, the Allies soon launched a successful counteroffensive, leading to the end of the fighting in November 1918.

Dinah Zike's Foldables

Dinah Zike's Foldables are three-dimensional, interactive graphic organizers that help students practice basic writing skills, review vocabulary terms, and identify main ideas. Instructions for creating and using Foldables can be found in the Appendix at the end of this book and in the *Dinah Zike's Reading and Study Skills Foldables* booklet. OL

Introduce students to chapter content and key terms by having them access the Chapter 23 Overview at glencoe.com.

1918 Germany agrees to truce

1919 U.S. President Wilson helps form the League of Nations

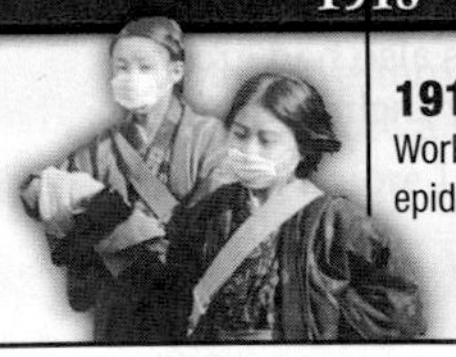

1918

1918 Worldwide influenza epidemic begins

1919 Gandhi's nonviolent campaign against British rule begins

FOLDABLES Study Organizer

Pre-Revolution and Anti-Communist Forces | Revolution and Communist Forces | Russia

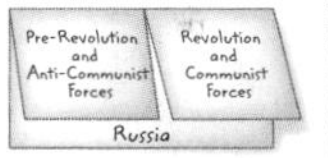

Analyzing Make a Two-Tab Book to organize information you read about the Russian Revolution. Under the first tab, record political, social, and economic events that led to the revolution. Under the second tab, record political and military events that brought the Communists to power.

History ONLINE
Chapter Overview—Visit glencoe.com to preview Chapter 23.

SECTION 3

The Russian Revolution

Essential Question: What led to the fall of the czarist regime in Russia? *(Students might mention the losses suffered by the Russian army in World War I, the influence of Rasputin on the czar's wife, and the strikes in Petrograd.)* Point out that in Section 3 students will learn how the Bolsheviks took control of the country. OL

SECTION 4

End of World War I

Essential Question: What effect did peace settlements have on Europe after World War I? *(Students might mention that the settlements redrew the map of eastern Europe, with new states being created. This eventually led to another world war.)* Point out that in Section 4 students will learn about the peace settlements that led to drastic changes to Europe. OL

D **Differentiated Instruction**

Visual/Spatial Have students sketch an original poster or cartoon that may have been used as propaganda during the war. OL

Did You Know?

Most propaganda efforts during World War I urged recruits to join the armed forces, encouraged volunteer efforts, and boosted civilian morale. Posters displayed in store windows, cartoons printed in newspapers, and leaflets dropped from the sky all influenced public opinion.

Answers:

1. Answers may include: yes, if certain precautions were taken; no, to prevent spreading the disease.
2. Answers may include reduced activities and increased precautions.

Additional Support

Under conditions of total war mobilization, the differences between soldiers at war and civilians at home were narrowed. In the view of political leaders, all citizens were part of a national army dedicated to victory. **Woodrow Wilson,** president of the United States, said that the men and women "who remain to till the soil and man the factories are no less a part of the army than the men beneath the battle flags."

Manipulation of Public Opinion

As the war continued and casualties grew worse, the patriotic enthusiasm that had marked the early stages of World War I waned. By 1916, there were signs that civilian morale was beginning to crack. War governments, however, fought back against growing opposition to the war.

Authoritarian regimes, such as those of Germany, Russia, and Austria-Hungary, relied on force to subdue their populations. Under the pressures of the war, however, even democratic states expanded their police powers to stop internal dissent. The British Parliament, for example, passed the Defence of the Realm Act (DORA). It allowed the government to arrest protesters as traitors. Newspapers were censored, and sometimes publication was suspended.

D Wartime governments made active use of propaganda to increase enthusiasm for the war. At the beginning, public officials needed to do little to achieve this goal. The British and French, for example, exaggerated German atrocities in Belgium and found that their citizens were only too willing to believe these accounts.

As the war progressed and morale sagged, governments were forced to devise new techniques for motivating the people. In one British recruiting poster, for example, a small daughter asked her father, "Daddy, what did YOU do in the Great War?" while her younger brother played with toy soldiers.

Connecting to the United States

The Influenza Epidemic of 1918

In the fall of 1918, just as World War I was winding down in Europe, a deadly influenza epidemic struck. Probably spread by soldiers returning from the front, it became the deadliest epidemic in history:

- **An estimated 675,000 Americans died, ten times as many as had died in the war.**
- **An estimated 50 million people died worldwide.**

Things could have been even worse. Because of the war, people were used to government restrictions. Public health departments were able to step in with measures to restrict contact. The war had also brought new technologies such as germ theory and antiseptics. These had saved lives in the battlefield and eventually would help save the world from this deadly epidemic.

Given the deadly spread of the 1918 influenza, scientists are keeping a close watch on today's flu viruses. With today's ease of air travel, a new virus could take only days to spread around the world.

◀ *Baseball players and spectators wear gauze masks to protect themselves from infection during the 1918 influenza epidemic.*

1. **Hypothesizing** In the face of a deadly pandemic, do you think that people today would continue with normal activities such as spectator sports? Why or why not?
2. **Making Generalizations** How would a pandemic similar to the one in 1918 affect your life?

Extending the Content

The Influenza Epidemic of 1918 Since there was no cure for influenza, public health officials focused on disseminating information to help prevent the spread of the deadly virus. Recommendations included washing hands frequently, chewing food thoroughly, avoiding physical and mental exhaustion, and avoiding tight clothing. But many people in rural areas did not receive this information. They relied on folk remedies to avoid catching the disease. Many swore that onions would ward off influenza; mothers made their children wear bags of garlic-scented gum around their necks and stuff salt up their noses. **Ask:** What do public health officials recommend today to prevent the spread of influenza? *(annual flu shots, frequent hand-washing, and restricted contact with anyone who may have the flu)* OL

Total War and Women

World War I created new roles for women. Because so many men left to fight at the front, women were asked to take over jobs that had not been available to them before. Women were employed in jobs that had once been considered beyond their capacity.

These jobs included civilian occupations such as chimney sweeps, truck drivers, farm laborers, and factory workers in heavy industry. For example, 38 percent of the workers in the Krupp Armaments works in Germany in 1918 were women. Also, between 1914 and 1918 in Britain, the number of women working in public transport rose 14 times, doubled in commerce, and rose by nearly a third in industry.

The place of women in the workforce was far from secure, however. Both men and women seemed to expect that many of the new jobs for women were only temporary. This was evident in the British poem "War Girls," written in 1916:

PRIMARY SOURCE

"There's the girl who clips your ticket for the train,
And the girl who speeds the lift from floor to floor,
There's the girl who does a milk-round in the rain,
And the girl who calls for orders at your door.
Strong, sensible, and fit,
They're out to show their grit,
And tackle jobs with energy and knack.
No longer caged and penned up,
They're going to keep their end up
Till the khaki soldier boys come marching back."

At the end of the war, governments would quickly remove women from the jobs they had encouraged them to take earlier. The work benefits for women from World War I were short-lived as men returned to the job market. By 1919, there would be 650,000 unemployed women in Great Britain. Wages for the women who were still employed would be lowered.

Nevertheless, in some countries the role women played in wartime economies had a positive impact on the women's movement for social and political emancipation. The **C** most obvious gain was the right to vote, which was given to women in Germany, Austria, and the United States immediately after the war. British women over 30 gained the vote, together with the right to stand for Parliament, in 1918.

Many upper- and middle-class women had also gained new freedoms. In ever-increasing numbers, young women from these groups took jobs, had their own apartments, and showed their new independence.

✓Reading Check **Summarizing** What was the effect of total war on ordinary citizens?

SECTION 2 REVIEW

Vocabulary

1. **Explain** the significance of: propaganda, Marne, trench warfare, war of attrition, target, Gallipoli, Lawrence of Arabia, unrestricted, Admiral Holtzendorf, total war, planned economies, Woodrow Wilson.

Main Ideas

2. **Explain** why governments often use propaganda during wartime.
3. **Describe** the trenches that both the Western Front and Eastern Front used in World War I.
4. **Illustrate,** by using a diagram similar to the one below, the ways in which government powers increased during the war.

Critical Thinking

5. **The BIG Idea** **Assessing** What methods did governments use to counter the loss of enthusiasm and opposition to the war at home?
6. **Analyzing Primary Sources** How did Admiral Holtzendorf's assurance to the German emperor ("I give your Majesty my word as an officer that not one American will land on the continent") prove to be wrong?
7. **Analyzing Visuals** Explain why the war technology shown in the photograph on page 764 did not help break the World War I stalemate.

Writing About History

8. **Expository Writing** What lasting results occurred in women's rights due to World War I? What were the temporary results? Write an essay discussing the effect of the war on women's rights.

History ONLINE
For help with the concepts in this section of *Glencoe World History*, go to glencoe.com and click Study Central™.

C Critical Thinking

Determining Cause and Effect Lead a discussion about the impact of World War I on the status of women. Ask students how women's acceptance into occupations previously considered beyond their capacity empowered them to demand equal rights. **AL**

✓Reading Check

Answer: Citizens were subject to rationing, propaganda, the draft, and loss of free speech. Women took jobs once considered beyond their capacity.

Assess

History ONLINE

Study Central provides summaries, interactive games, and online graphic organizers to help students review content.

Close

Summarizing Have students summarize the situations of the Allies and the Central Powers in the spring of 1917. **OL**

Answers

1. Definitions for the vocabulary words are found in the section and in the Glossary.
2. to spread ideas that influence public opinion for or against a cause—in this case, war
3. Trenches were elaborate systems of defense, protected by barbed-wire entanglements of up to 5 feet high and 30 yards wide. Machine-gun nests and heavy artillery protected the trenches.
4. draft; rationing; price, wage, and rent controls; takeover of transportation; import and export regulation
5. propaganda, expanded police powers, arrest of protestors, censorship
6. The British did not surrender, and the United States entered the war in 1917.
7. Machine guns caused more casualties and prevented offensive advances.
8. Essays should reflect students' grasp of material.

Focus

Introducing Social History
Ask: What images do you associate with war? Discuss students' responses. Most likely, the word *war* evokes ideas of bombings, troop movement, and aggressively offensive strategies. Explain that World War I became a conflict in which each side established a position, a mile or two apart from each other, and stayed there for the duration.

Teach

S Skill Practice

Visual Literacy Have students view the images on this page. **Ask:** What challenges did soldiers face in trench warfare? *(Harsh living conditions, boredom, fear caused by the possibility of attack, exposure to many different diseases.)* OL

C Critical Thinking

Making Inferences Ask: What realization was the "live and let live" system based on? *(Decisive victory could not be achieved, so it became a matter of waiting out the end of the war.)* OL

Additional Support

Social History

Technology and Trench Life Define Total War

The politicians and generals who led their nations into World War I anticipated an old fashioned conflict. But once the Allies and Germans reached a stalemate, the armies, for the first time, dug miles of trenches opposite one another as protection against exploding shells and machine-gun fire. Infantry soldiers rotated into and out of the trenches five days at a time. It was a world of mud and blood, poison gas and high-explosive shells overhead. The tedium of trench life was broken most often by one army or the other charging out of its trenches and into the enemy's barbed wire and machine guns.

Cold Comfort in the Trenches

C Trenches provided infantry soldiers with their only protection against enemy fire. They were a necessary innovation for armies fighting in close contact with powerful and accurate weapons. Hot food was brought forward in containers to discourage cooking fires. In some places, soldiers fired at the enemy trenches at every opportunity. In others, enemies took a "live and let live" approach. These attitudes often depended upon the level of exhaustion the soldiers were feeling.

Background

Trench Warfare The trench network in World War I ran from Belgium through France to Switzerland. Up to four parallel lines were connected to each other by perpendicular communications trenches that facilitated the delivery of supplies, fresh troops, mail, and orders to the soldiers manning the trenches. There were command posts, forward supply dumps, first-aid stations, kitchens, and latrines within the trench network. The front line was usually situated anywhere from 50 yards to a mile from the enemy. It was protected by barbed wire barricades, which made it difficult for the enemy to break through undetected. Each trench also followed a zigzag pattern so that it was not possible for enemies who penetrated to shoot straight down the line. Since both sides realized that attacks during the day would be mutually disastrous, most of the action took place at dawn.

Technology and the Horror of War

Tanks made their first appearance in battle during World War I. Though slow and cumbersome, they foreshadowed the destruction mechanized warfare would bring. Airplanes fought one another for the first time as well, and both sides experimented with bombs and machine guns in aerial attacks on ground positions. These applications of technology left a deep, terrifying impression on soldiers showing the dark side of industrialization.

Analyzing Visuals

1. **Comparing** How well do you think infantry soldiers' uniforms protected them from modern weapons? How has this changed since World War I, and why?
2. **Theorizing** Think about the images of early tanks and airplanes shown here. Why do these devices seem primitive to us today?

W Writing Support

Expository Writing Tell students that another poisonous gas feared by soldiers was mustard gas. Have students research the number of casualties and the kinds of injuries produced by mustard gas and/or other poisonous gases during World War I. Ask students to present their findings in a short report. **OL**

Assess/Close

Drawing Conclusions Ask: Why was World War I the last large-scale conflict in which trench warfare was used? *(In later conflicts, planes and tanks could easily breach the trenches, rendering them obsolete.)* **OL**

ANALYZING VISUALS

Answers:

1. Their only real protection was their helmet and gas mask. The helmet kept their heads safe from shrapnel. Today soldiers have body armor.
2. Modern planes and tanks have many more features and capabilities. With each technological advance, the distance grows between the present and the past.

Activity: Interdisciplinary Connection

Literature Tell students that soldiers initially went off to World War I with patriotic fervor and romantic illusions about their military roles. They were soon disillusioned, however, by the harsh reality of life in the trenches. Meanwhile, civilians at home learned about the nightmare of the war through poems, letters, and novels describing the experiences of the soldiers. Have students work in small groups to read some of the literature from this time period, such as *All Quiet on the Western Front* by Erich Maria Remarqué, "Dulce and Decorum Est" and other poems by Wilfred Owen, "Rear Guard," "Dreamers," and other poems by Siegfried Sassoon. Have students present short analyses of the conflicts experienced by characters, writers, or speakers in the works and the message that they convey about war. **Ask:** Based on these works of literature, what generalization would you make about the experiences soldiers had in World War I? *(Answers may include that war was a terrible experience for many soldiers and caused them to think about society and their role in society in a different way.)* **OL**

R Reading Strategy

Sequencing Information
Have students create an illustrated time line of events that took place during March 1917 in Russia. Discuss why March 1917 could be considered a turning point in Russian history. **OL**

C Critical Thinking

Making Inferences Ask: Why would German military leaders hope to create disorder in Russia? *(If disorder broke out in Russia, it might withdraw from World War I. Germany would then have to fight on only one front instead of two.)* **AL**

✓Reading Check

Answer: The Russian army suffered incredible losses in the war. Nicholas II's wife made decisions under the influence of Rasputin; then came a series of military and economic disasters. Strikes broke out in Petrograd, which developed into a general strike. Soldiers joined the demonstrators. The Duma established a provisional government. Nicholas II stepped down.

On March 8, about 10,000 women marched through the city of Petrograd demanding "Peace and Bread" and "Down with Autocracy." Other workers joined them, and together they called for a general strike. The strike shut down all the factories in the city on March 10.

Alexandra wrote her husband Nicholas II at the battlefront: "This is a hooligan movement. If the weather were very cold they would all probably stay at home." Nicholas ordered troops to break up the crowds by shooting them if necessary. Soon, however, large numbers of the soldiers joined the demonstrators and refused to fire on the crowds.

The Duma, or legislative body, which the czar had tried to dissolve, met anyway. On March 12, it established the provisional government, which mainly consisted of middle-class Duma representatives. This government urged the czar to step down. Because he no longer had the support of the army or even the aristocrats, Nicholas II reluctantly agreed and stepped down on **R** March 15, ending the 300-year-old Romanov dynasty.

Provisional Government

The provisional government, headed by **Aleksandr Kerensky** (keh•REHN•skee), now decided to carry on the war to preserve Russia's honor. This decision to remain in World War I was a major blunder. It satisfied neither the workers nor the peasants, who were tired and angry from years of suffering and wanted above all an end to the war.

The government was also faced with a challenge to its authority—the **soviets**. The soviets were councils composed of representatives from the workers and soldiers. The soviet of Petrograd had been formed in March 1917. At the same time, soviets sprang up in army units, factory towns, and rural areas. The soviets, largely made up of socialists, represented the more radical interests of the lower classes. One group—the Bolsheviks—came to play a crucial role.

✓Reading Check **Identifying** Develop a sequence of events leading to the March Revolution.

From Czars to Communists

MAIN IDEA Lenin and the Bolsheviks gained control and quickly overthrew the provisional government.

HISTORY & YOU How has political change happened in the United States? Read to learn how Lenin proposed to make changes in Russia.

The **Bolsheviks** began as a small faction of a Marxist party called the Russian Social Democrats. The Bolsheviks came under the leadership of Vladimir Ilyich Ulyanov (ool•YAH•nuhf), known to the world as **V. I. Lenin**.

Under Lenin's direction, the Bolsheviks became a party dedicated to violent **revolution**. Lenin believed that only violent revolution could destroy the capitalist system. A "vanguard" (forefront) of activists, he said, must form a small party of well-disciplined, professional revolutionaries to accomplish the task.

Lenin and the Bolsheviks

Between 1900 and 1917, Lenin spent most of his time abroad. When the provisional government was formed in March 1917, he saw an opportunity for the Bolsheviks to seize power. In April 1917, German military leaders, hoping to create **C** disorder in Russia, shipped Lenin to Russia. Lenin and his associates were in a sealed train to prevent their ideas from infecting Germany.

Lenin's arrival in Russia opened a new stage of the Russian Revolution. Lenin maintained that the soviets of soldiers, workers, and peasants were ready-made instruments of power. He believed that the Bolsheviks should work toward gaining control of these groups and then use them to overthrow the provisional government.

At the same time, the Bolsheviks reflected the discontent of the people. They promised an end to the war. They also promised to redistribute all land to the peasants, to transfer factories and industries from capitalists to committees of workers, and to transfer government power from the provisional government to the soviets. Three simple slogans summed up the Bolshevik

Hands-On Chapter Project
Step 3

Touring World War I Europe

Step 3: Planning an Itinerary Small groups of students will plan travel itineraries for a World War I retrospective tour.

Directions: Write the Big Idea on the board. Have students review the maps and the index cards that they created in Steps 1 and 2. They should decide how they want to design the tour: Should locations be visited in chronological order or in order of importance? Perhaps the trip should be planned according to geographic location? Have students write out a travel itinerary based on what they decide.

Summarizing: Allow time for student groups to discuss what they learned about the significance of various World War I sites in this activity. They will create a travel brochure in the next section. **OL**

(Chapter Project is continued in Section 4.)

program: "Peace, Land, Bread," "Worker Control of Production," and "All Power to the Soviets."

The Bolsheviks Seize Power

By the end of October, Bolsheviks made up a slight majority in the Petrograd and Moscow soviets. The number of party members had grown from 50,000 to 240,000. **D** With Leon Trotsky, a dedicated revolutionary, as head of the Petrograd soviet, the Bolsheviks were in a position to claim power in the name of the soviets. During the night of November 6, Bolshevik forces seized the Winter Palace, the seat of the provisional government. The government quickly collapsed with little bloodshed.

This overthrow coincided with a meeting of the all-Russian Congress of Soviets, which represented local soviets countrywide. Outwardly, Lenin turned over the power of the provisional government to the Congress of Soviets. The real power, however, passed to a council headed by Lenin.

The Bolsheviks, who soon renamed themselves the Communists, still had a long way to go. Lenin had promised peace; and that, he realized, would not be an easy task.

TURNING POINT — THE RUSSIAN REVOLUTION

The Russian Revolution was the most violent and radical revolution since the French Revolution. In March 1917, the czar abdicated and a provisional government took control. Then, led by V. I. Lenin, the Bolsheviks seized power in November 1917. This marked a new era of Soviet rule. Russia had become the world's first socialist state, and Lenin intended for the revolution to spread.

The day after the Bolsheviks seized the Winter Palace, Lenin addressed the Russian people. In his speech he outlined the goals of the Bolsheviks. These goals threatened the governments of Western Europe: **C**

"The first thing is the adoption of practical measures to realize peace. . . . We shall offer peace to the peoples of all the warring countries upon the basis of the Soviet terms—no annexations, no indemnities, and the right of self-determination of peoples. . . . This proposal of peace will meet with resistance on the part of the imperialist governments. . . . But we hope that revolution will soon break out in all the warring countries. This is why we address ourselves especially to the workers of France, England, and Germany."

—V. I. Lenin, quoted in *Ten Days that Shook the World*, by John Reed

The Winter Palace housed the provisional government after Nicholas stepped down. It had been the home of every Russian czar from Catherine the Great to Nicholas II.

CRITICAL THINKING SKILLS

Georgiy Savitsky's painting *Assault on the Winter Palace* depicts the events of November 6, 1917.

1. **Analyzing** Why did the Bolsheviks choose the Winter Palace as the place to attack?
2. **Explaining** Why is the Russian Revolution considered a turning point?

D Differentiated Instruction

Visual/Spatial Have students create a bar graph that illustrates the increase in Bolshevik party members. **BL**

C Critical Thinking

Making Inferences Ask: Why would the governments of Western Europe resist Lenin's offer of peace? *(Possible answer: Because it implied Russia would take control of these countries.)* **AL**

CRITICAL THINKING

Answers:

1. It had been the home of the czars and now housed the provisional government, which the Bolsheviks aimed to overthrow. Taking over the palace symbolized a new era in Russian history.
2. Russia became the world's first socialist state.

Additional Support

Activity: Interdisciplinary Connection

Art After students have read "Turning Point: The Russian Revolution," ask them to consider ways that the Bolsheviks may have tried to spread socialist ideas throughout Europe. Have students conduct research to find Communist propaganda posters from this period. Have them display copies of these posters around the room, and then hold a class discussion about propaganda art. **Ask:** What can be learned by examining the posters? What message is each poster trying to convey? Do some or all posters elicit an emotional response? How do the images in the posters portray Communist ideology and values? The activity may be extended by having students find examples of World War I propaganda posters used by other countries involved in the war. The discussion can then be broadened to compare and contrast the various kinds of propaganda images and ideas used. **OL**

C Critical Thinking

Making Inferences Have students draw on what they know about World War I and the Russian Revolution to make inferences about why the Allies were concerned about the Communist takeover. OL

Did You Know?

Russians sometimes refer to the Bolshevik coup as the October Revolution, even though it occurred in early November. Russia used the Julian calendar, which was about 14 days behind the Gregorian calendar. The Bolsheviks later switched to the Gregorian calendar.

DOCUMENT-BASED QUESTIONS

Answers:

1. Russian peasants and workers would hold the power previously held by the czar and industrialize Russia.
2. Under the czar, there were many discontented peasants and workers who probably wanted to industrialize.

INFOGRAPHICS PRIMARY SOURCE

Communism in Russia

"Communism is Soviet power plus the electrification of the whole country. Otherwise the country remains small-peasant. . . . We are weaker than capitalism, not only on a world scale but also within the country. All this is well known. We recognize this and we are taking action to transform the small-peasant base into a heavy-industry base. Only when the country is electrified, when industry, agriculture, and transport are placed on the technical basis of modern heavy industry, will we have won decisively."

—V. I. Lenin, remarks to the Congress of Soviets, 1920

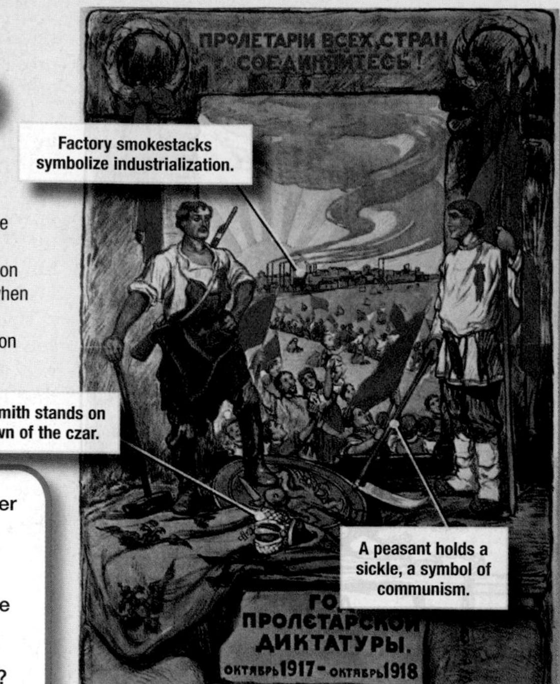

DOCUMENT-BASED QUESTIONS

Year of the Proletarian Dictatorship is a propaganda poster created in 1918 by the Russian artist Aleksandr Apsit. It illustrates some of the goals of the Communists after the Russian Revolution.

1. **Making Inferences** What were two major goals of the Communists after the Russian Revolution? Explain.
2. **Analyzing** Why do you think a communist revolution occurred in Russia rather than an industrialized nation?

It would mean the humiliating loss of much Russian territory. There was no real choice, however.

On March 3, 1918, Lenin signed the Treaty of Brest-Litovsk with Germany and gave up eastern Poland, **Ukraine**, Finland, and the Baltic provinces. To his critics, Lenin argued that it made no difference. The spread of the socialist revolution throughout Europe would make the treaty largely irrelevant. In any case, he had promised peace to the Russian people. Real peace did not come, however, because the country soon sank into civil war.

Civil War in Russia

Many people were opposed to the new Bolshevik, or Communist, government. These people included not only groups loyal to the czar but also liberal and anti-Leninist socialists. Liberals often supported a constitutional monarchy, while a number of socialists supported gradual reform. These socialists expected to work for a socialist state under more democratic leaders than Lenin. They were joined by C the Allies, who were extremely concerned about the Communist takeover.

The Allies sent thousands of troops to various parts of Russia in the hope of bringing Russia back into the war. The Allied forces rarely fought on Russian soil, but they gave material **aid** to anti-Communist forces. Between 1918 and 1921, the Communist, or Red, Army fought on many fronts against these opponents.

The first serious threat to the Communists came from **Siberia**. An anti-Communist, or White, force attacked and advanced almost to the Volga River before being stopped. Attacks also came from the Ukrainians and from the Baltic regions. In mid-1919, White forces swept through Ukraine and advanced almost to Moscow before being pushed back.

By 1920, however, the major White forces had been defeated and Ukraine retaken. The next year, the Communist regime regained control over the independent nationalist governments in Georgia, Russian Armenia, and Azerbaijan (A•zuhr•by•JAHN).

Differentiated Instruction

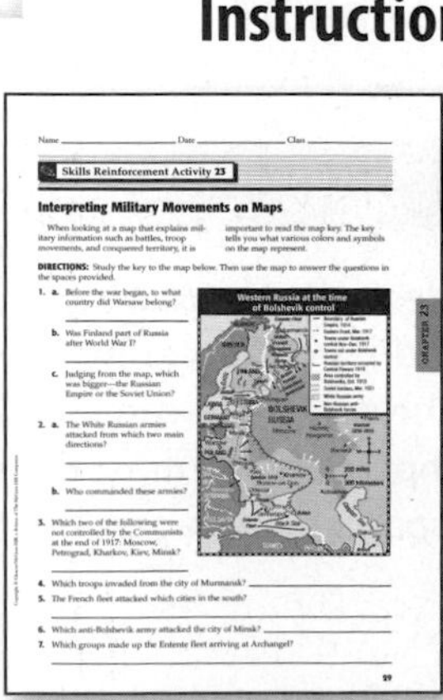

Skills Reinforcement Activity, URB p. 29

Analyzing Information

Objective: Interpret military movements on a map of Western Russia during Bolshevik control.

Focus: Have students identify map elements.

Teach: Have students answer the questions.

Assess: Discuss the extent of Bolshevik control of Russia just after World War I.

Close: Discuss the military strategies of the Bolsheviks.

Differentiated Instruction Strategies

- **BL** Have students compare the map with a current map of Russia.
- **AL** Ask students to summarize the military information given on the map.
- **ELL** Help students to look up the meanings of unknown words and then use them in a sentence.

The royal family was another victim of the civil war. After the czar abdicated, he, his wife, and their five children had been held as prisoners. In April 1918, they were moved to Yekaterinburg, a mining town in the **Urals**. On the night of July 16, members of the local soviet murdered the czar and his family and burned their bodies in a nearby mine shaft.

Triumph of the Communists

How had Lenin and the Communists triumphed in the civil war over such overwhelming forces? One reason was that the Red Army was a well-disciplined fighting force. This was largely due to the organizational genius of **Leon Trotsky**. As commissar of war, Trotsky reinstated the draft and insisted on rigid discipline. Soldiers who deserted or refused to obey orders were executed on the spot.

Furthermore, the disunity of the anti-Communist forces weakened their efforts. Political differences created distrust among the Whites. Some Whites insisted on restoring the czarist regime. Others wanted a more liberal and democratic program. The Whites, then, had no common goal.

The Communists, in contrast, had a single-minded sense of purpose. Inspired by their vision of a new socialist order, the Communists had both revolutionary zeal and strong convictions. They were also able to translate their revolutionary faith into practical instruments of power. A policy of **war communism**, for example, was used to ensure regular supplies for the Red Army. The government controlled the banks and most industries, seized grain from peasants, and centralized state administration under Communist control. W

Another instrument was Communist revolutionary terror. A new Red secret police—known as the Cheka—began a Red Terror. Aimed at destroying all those who opposed the new regime (much like the Reign of Terror in the French Revolution), the Red Terror added an element of fear to the Communist regime.

Finally, foreign armies on Russian soil enabled the Communists to appeal to the powerful force of Russian patriotism. At one point, over 100,000 foreign troops—mostly Japanese, British, American, and French—were stationed in Russia in support of anti-Communist forces. Their presence made it easy for the Communist government to call on patriotic Russians to fight foreign attempts to control the country.

By 1921, the Communists were in total command of Russia. The Communist regime had transformed Russia into a centralized state dominated by a single party. The state was also largely hostile to the Allied Powers, because the Allies had tried to help the Communists' enemies in the civil war.

✓Reading Check **Contrasting** Why did the Red Army prevail over the White forces?

SECTION 3 REVIEW

Vocabulary

1. **Explain** the significance of: Grigory Rasputin, Alexandra, Petrograd, Aleksandr Kerensky, soviets, Bolsheviks, V. I. Lenin, revolution, Ukraine, aid, Siberia, Urals, Leon Trotsky, war communism.

Main Ideas

2. **Explain** what the Petrograd women meant when they chanted "Peace and Bread" during their march.
3. **List** the steps that the Communists took to turn Russia into a centralized state dominated by one party. Use a chart like the one below.

Steps to Communist Control
1.
2.

4. **Specify** why Lenin accepted the loss of so much Russian territory in the Treaty of Brest-Litovsk.

Critical Thinking

5. **The BIG Idea** **Analyzing** How did the presence of Allied troops in Russia ultimately help the Communists?
6. **Identifying Central Issues** What led to Czar Nicholas II's downfall?
7. **Analyzing Visuals** Examine the painting on page 776. What does the red flag symbolize?

Writing About History

8. **Multimedia Presentation** Prepare a multimedia presentation comparing the economic, political, and social causes of the American, French, and Russian Revolutions.

History ONLINE
For help with the concepts in this section of *Glencoe World History*, go to glencoe.com and click Study Central™.

W Writing Support

Expository Writing Have students write a brief essay in which they identify and explain the effects of the rise of communism in Russia. OL

✓Reading Check

Answer: The Red Army had the organizational genius of Leon Trotsky and a common goal; there were conflicting goals among the anti-Communist White forces.

Assess

History ONLINE

Study Central provides summaries, interactive games, and online graphic organizers to help students review content.

Close

Determining Cause and Effect Discuss the effects of World War I on Russia and how those effects contributed to the Russian Revolution. OL

SECTION 3 REVIEW

Answers

1. Definitions for the vocabulary words are found in the section and in the Glossary.
2. They wanted the war to end, and they wanted bread, or food, for their families. Prior to the march, the government had started bread rationing after the price of bread had skyrocketed.
3. (1) well-disciplined Red Army; (2) war communism; (3) Cheka; (4) appeal to patriotism
4. Lenin had promised the Russian people peace. Lenin also believed the spread of socialism throughout Europe would make the treaty irrelevant.
5. stirred Russian patriotism and support for Communists
6. Czar Nicholas II took charge of the armed forces although he had no skills or training to do so; he was on the battlefront and left Alexandra and Rasputin to make decisions; he also disregarded the workers' plea for "peace and bread."
7. communism
8. Presentations should be supported with material from the text.

Focus

Bellringer

Daily Focus Transparency 23.4

GUIDE TO READING

Answers to Graphic:

France: strip Germany of weapons; reparations; separate Rhineland; **Britain:** make Germany pay for war; **United States:** reduce armaments; ensure self-determination; form League of Nations

Section Spotlight Video

To generate student interest and provide a springboard for class discussion, access the Chapter 23, Section 4 video at glencoe.com or on the video DVD.

SECTION 4

End of World War I

GUIDE TO READING

The BIG Idea

Order and Security After the defeat of the Germans, peace settlements brought political and territorial changes to Europe and created bitterness and resentment in some nations.

Content Vocabulary

- armistice *(p. 780)*
- mandates *(p. 783)*
- reparations *(p. 781)*

Academic Vocabulary

- psychological *(p. 778)*
- cooperation *(p. 780)*

People and Places

- Erich Ludendorff *(p. 778)*
- Kiel *(p. 780)*
- Friedrich Ebert *(p. 780)*
- David Lloyd George *(p. 781)*
- Georges Clemenceau *(p. 781)*
- Alsace *(p. 782)*
- Lorraine *(p. 782)*
- Poland *(p. 782)*

Reading Strategy

Organizing Information At the Paris Peace Conference, the leaders of France, Britain, and the United States were motivated by different concerns. As you read, use a chart like the one below to identify the national interests of each country as it approached the peace deliberations.

France	Britain	United States

Governments, troops, and civilians were weary as World War I continued through 1917. Shortly after the United States entered the war, Germany made its final military gamble on the Western Front and lost. The war finally ended on November 11, 1918. The peace treaties were particularly harsh on Germany. New nations were formed, and a League of Nations was created to resolve future international disputes.

The Last Year of the War

MAIN IDEA The new German republic and the Allies signed an armistice, ending the war on November 11, 1918.

HISTORY & YOU Have you heard debates about how large the U.S. military budget should be? Read to understand the role of U.S. army support in the Allied victory of World War I.

The year 1917 had not been a good one for the Allies. Allied offensives on the Western Front had been badly defeated. The Russian Revolution, which began in November 1917, led to Russia's withdrawal from the war a few months later. The cause of the Central Powers looked favorable, although war weariness was beginning to take its toll.

On the positive side, the entry of the United States into the war in 1917 gave the Allies a much-needed **psychological** boost. The United States also provided fresh troops and material. In 1918, American troops would prove crucial.

A New German Offensive

For Germany, the withdrawal of the Russians offered new hope for a successful end to the war. Germany was now free to concentrate entirely on the Western Front. **Erich Ludendorff,** who guided German military operations, decided to make one final military gamble—a grand offensive in the west to break the military stalemate. In fact, the last of Germany's strength went into making this one great blow. The divisions were running low on provisions, reserves of soldiers were nearly depleted, and the German home front was tired of the war.

The German attack was launched in March 1918. By April, German troops were within about 50 miles (80 km) of Paris. However, the German advance was stopped at the Second Battle of the Marne on July 18. French, Moroccan, and American troops (140,000 fresh American troops had just arrived), supported by hundreds of tanks, threw the Germans back over the Marne. On August 8, the

Resource Manager

R Reading Strategies	C Critical Thinking	D Differentiated Instruction	W Writing Support	S Skill Practice
Teacher Edition • Organizing, p. 781 • Making Connections, p. 782 **Additional Resources** • Guid. Read. Act., URB p. 53 • Read. Ess. & Note-Taking Guide, p. 259	**Teacher Edition** • Compare/Contrast, p. 780 • Drawing Con., p. 781 • Making Inferences, p. 782 • Pred. Consequences, p. 783 **Additional Resources** • Coop. Learn. Act., URB p. 35 • Section Quiz, p. 288 • Chapter Test, p. 289	**Teacher Edition** • Adv. Learners, p. 780 **Additional Resources** • Diff. Instr. Act., URB p. 21 • Reteach. Act., URB p. 47	**Teacher Edition** • Persuasive Writing, p. 779 **Additional Resources** • Hist. Sig. Act., URB p. 34	**Teacher Edition** • Using Geo. Skills, p. 779 **Additional Resources** • Time Line Act., URB p. 39

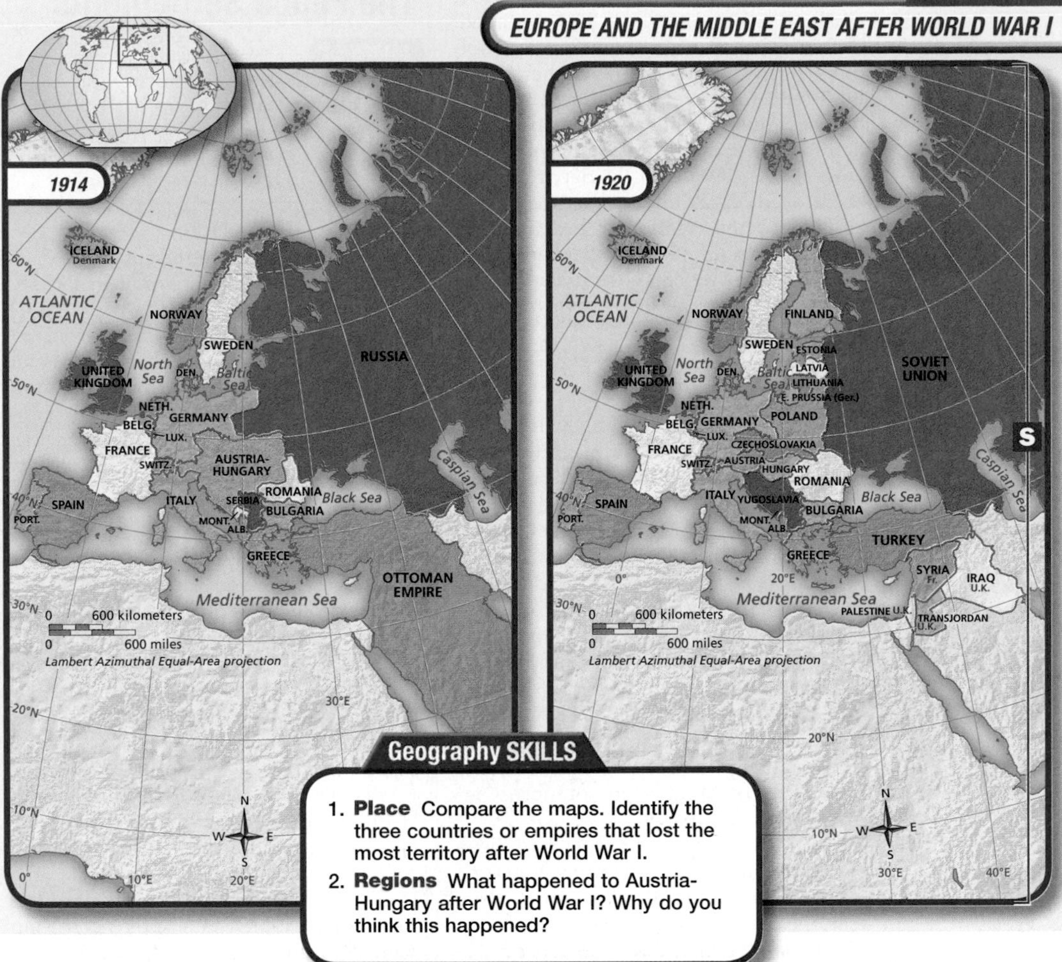

Geography SKILLS

1. **Place** Compare the maps. Identify the three countries or empires that lost the most territory after World War I.
2. **Regions** What happened to Austria-Hungary after World War I? Why do you think this happened?

forces met at the Second Battle of the Somme. Ludendorff wrote of this battle: "August 8 was the black day of the German army in the history of this war." Ludendorff admitted that his gamble had failed:

PRIMARY SOURCE

> "The 8th of August put the decline of [our] fighting power beyond all doubt, and in such a situation as regards reserves, I had no hope of finding a strategic expedient whereby to turn the situation to our advantage."
>
> —Erich Ludendorff, in *The Great War*, Correlli Barnett, 1980

A million American troops poured into France, and the Allies began an advance toward Germany. On September 29, 1918, General Ludendorff told German leaders that the war was lost. He demanded the government ask for peace at once.

Collapse and Armistice

German officials soon found that the Allies were unwilling to make peace with the autocratic imperial government of Germany. Reforms for a liberal government came too late for the tired, angry German people.

Teach

S Skill Practice

Using Geography Skills Ask students to compare the 1920 map on this page with a current map of Europe and the Middle East. Have students list how borders have changed since the end of World War I. **AL**

W Writing Support

Persuasive Writing Have students write a letter they think Ludendorff might have written to persuade German leaders that the war was lost. **AL**

Geography SKILLS

Answers:

1. Russia, Austria-Hungary, Ottoman Empire
2. It was replaced by Austria, Hungary, Czechoslovakia, and Yugoslavia. It had started the war and lost.

Hands-On Chapter Project Step 4

Touring World War I Europe

Step 4: Creating a Travel Brochure Small groups of students will create travel brochures for the World War I Europe tour that they worked on in Steps 1–3.

Directions: Write the Big Idea on the board. Tell students to put together a brochure for people traveling on the tour they designed. The brochure should include the itinerary and brief descriptions of each site. Descriptions should include why the site was significant in World War I and what it will be like to visit it today. If possible, brochures can include photos. Brochures should also include the map students created in Step 1.

Summarizing: Allow time for groups to discuss what they learned about the impact of World War I on modern-day Europe in this activity. **OL**

(Chapter Project is continued in the Visual Summary.)

C Critical Thinking

Comparing and Contrasting

Ask students to write a paragraph comparing the outcomes achieved by revolutionary forces in the new German republic and in Austria-Hungary. **OL**

For additional practice on this skill, see the **Skills Handbook**.

D Differentiated Instruction

Advanced Learners Ask: What is an idealist? *(One guided by ideals and lofty, high principles, rather than practical considerations.)* Then ask students to give supporting details that show Woodrow Wilson's idealistic approach to reaching peace. **AL**

✓Reading Check

Answer: William II left country; Social Democrats formed republic; Communists tried to seize power; German middle class feared communism.

On November 3, 1918, sailors in the northern German town of **Kiel** mutinied. Within days, councils of workers and soldiers formed throughout northern Germany and took over civilian and military offices. Emperor William II gave in to public pressure and left the country on November 9. After William II's departure, the Social Democrats under **Friedrich Ebert** announced the creation of a democratic republic. Two days later, on November 11, 1918, the new German government signed an **armistice** (a truce, an agreement to end the fighting).

Revolutionary Forces

The war was over, but the revolutionary forces set in motion in Germany were not yet exhausted. A group of radical socialists, unhappy with the Social Democrats' moderate policies, formed the German Communist Party in December 1918. A month later, the Communists tried to seize power in Berlin.

The new Social Democratic government, backed by regular army troops, crushed the rebels and murdered Rosa Luxemburg and Karl Liebknecht (LEEP•KNEHKT), leaders of the German Communists. A similar attempt at Communist revolution in the city of Munich, in southern Germany, was also crushed.

The new German republic had been saved. The attempt at revolution, however, left the German middle class with a deep fear of communism.

Austria-Hungary, too, experienced disintegration and revolution. As war weariness took hold of the empire, ethnic groups increasingly sought to achieve their independence. By the time World War I ended, the Austro-Hungarian Empire had ceased to exist.

The empire had been replaced by the independent republics of Austria, Hungary, and Czechoslovakia, along with the large monarchical state called Yugoslavia. Rivalries among the nations that succeeded Austria-Hungary would weaken eastern Europe for the next 80 years.

✓Reading Check **Describing** What happened within Germany after the armistice?

The Peace Settlements

MAIN IDEA The Treaty of Versailles punished Germany, established new nations, and created a League of Nations to solve international problems.

HISTORY & YOU What is the purpose of the United Nations today? Read to learn why the U.S. president wanted a League of Nations after World War I.

In January 1919, representatives of 27 victorious Allied nations met in Paris to make a final settlement of World War I. Over a period of years, the reasons for fighting World War I had changed dramatically. When European nations had gone to war in 1914, they sought territorial gains. By the beginning of 1918, however, they were also expressing more idealistic reasons for the war.

Wilson's Proposals

No one expressed these idealistic reasons better than the president of the United States, Woodrow Wilson. Even before the end of the war, Wilson outlined "Fourteen Points" to the United States Congress—his basis for a peace settlement that he believed justified the enormous military struggle being waged.

Wilson's proposals for a truly just and lasting peace included reaching the peace agreements openly rather than through secret diplomacy. His proposals also included reducing armaments (military forces or weapons) to a "point consistent with domestic safety" and ensuring self-determination (the right of each people to have their own nation).

Wilson portrayed World War I as a people's war against "absolutism and militarism." These two enemies of liberty, he argued, could be eliminated only by creating democratic governments and a "general association of nations." This association would guarantee "political independence and territorial integrity to great and small states alike."

Wilson became the spokesperson for a new world order based on democracy and international **cooperation.** When he arrived in Europe for the peace conference, Wilson was enthusiastically cheered by many

Additional Support

Teacher Tip

Collaborative Learning Remind students that having someone record the group's ideas as they discuss their opinions will help their "delegate" accurately explain the position of the group's country.

Activity: Collaborative Learning

Paris Peace Conference Simulation Ask: How did the Allies hope to reach a peace settlement? Organize the class into three groups representing France, Great Britain, and the United States. Have students list their country's opinions about how to reach a peace settlement. Students should use information from this section, and they may conduct additional research as well. Have each group select a student to play the role of Clemenceau, Lloyd George, or Wilson at the Paris Peace Conference. Students should convey their understanding of the implications and impact of self-determination, military reduction, national security, and reparations. Invite students to question the delegates. **OL**

Europeans. President Wilson soon found, however, that more practical motives guided other states.

The Paris Peace Conference

Delegates met in Paris in early 1919 to determine the peace settlement. At the Paris Peace Conference, complications became obvious. For one thing, secret treaties and agreements that had been made before the war had raised the hopes of European nations for territorial gains. These hopes could not be ignored, even if they did conflict with the principle of self-determination put forth by Wilson.

National interests also complicated the deliberations of the Paris Peace Conference. **David Lloyd George**, prime minister of Great Britain, had won a decisive victory in elections in December 1918. His platform was simple: make the Germans pay for this dreadful war.

France's approach to peace was chiefly guided by its desire for national security. To **Georges Clemenceau** (KLEH•muhn•SOH), the premier of France, the French people had suffered the most from German aggression. The French desired revenge and security against future German attacks. Clemenceau wanted Germany stripped of all weapons, vast German payments—**reparations**—to cover the costs of the war, and a separate Rhineland as a buffer state between France and Germany.

The most important decisions at the Paris Peace Conference were made by Wilson, Clemenceau, and Lloyd George. Italy, as one of the Allies, was considered one of the Big Four powers. However, it played a smaller role than the other key powers—the United States, France, and Great Britain, who were called the Big Three. Germany was not invited to attend, and Russia could not be present because of its civil war.

In view of the many conflicting demands at the peace conference, it was no surprise that the Big Three quarreled. Wilson wanted to create a world organization, the League of Nations, to prevent future wars. Clemenceau and Lloyd George wanted to punish Germany. In the end, only compromise made it possible to achieve a peace settlement.

Wilson's wish that the creation of an international peacekeeping organization be the first order of business was granted. On January 25, 1919, the conference accepted the idea of a League of Nations. In return, Wilson agreed to make compromises on territorial arrangements. He did so because he believed that the League could later fix any unfair settlements.

Clemenceau also compromised to obtain some guarantees for French security. He gave up France's wish for a separate Rhineland and instead accepted a defensive alliance with Great Britain and the United States. However, the U.S. Senate refused to ratify this agreement, which weakened the Versailles peace settlement.

PEOPLE in HISTORY

Georges Clemenceau
1841–1929 French Premier

Georges Clemenceau, premier of France during World War I, had a long history in French-German diplomacy. During his early political career, Clemenceau had been involved in the 1871 peace treaty ending the Franco-Prussian War. The treaty imposed harsh terms on France while strengthening the new German republic, and Clemenceau vowed to bring France back from this "shameful humiliation." After World War I, he had his opportunity. The Treaty of Versailles was shaped by Clemenceau's dislike and distrust of the Germans. "For the catastrophe of 1914 only the Germans are responsible," he said. "Only a professional liar would deny this." **How did Clemenceau's early political career affect his position at the Paris Peace Conference?**

C Critical Thinking

Drawing Conclusions Ask: Do you think it was reasonable for Wilson to expect the European nations to share his views and approach to peace? *(Students might say that Wilson's expectations may have been unreasonable since the United States entered the war late and no battles were fought on U.S. soil.)* OL

R Reading Strategy

Organizing As students read about the Paris Peace Conference, have them list the major participants at the conference and summarize the aims of each. BL

PEOPLE in HISTORY

Answers: Clemenceau wanted to avenge France after its "shameful humiliation" at the hands of the Germans in 1871.

Additional Support

Extending the Content

Georges Clemenceau Explain to students that Georges Clemenceau believed as far back as 1911 that Germany was getting ready for war, and he founded a daily paper called *L'Homme Libre* to publicize his views. Once World War I started, Clemenceau tried to convince the American public that the United States should enter the war. **Ask:** Why do you think Clemenceau spent so much effort publicizing his views on Germany and the war? *(Answers may include that he loved his country and would do anything to protect it.).* OL

C Critical Thinking

Making Inferences Ask: Why was the Treaty of Versailles with Germany considered the most important of the peace treaties? *(Because Germany initiated the war by invading both France and Russia. Germany was considered responsible for starting the war.)* OL

R Reading Strategy

Making Connections Ask students what it must have felt like for the people affected by the political changes and shifting borders after World War I. Have students describe how they might feel living with such drastic changes. *(disillusionment or displacement—as if they no longer had a home)* OL

DOCUMENT-BASED QUESTIONS

Answers:

1. Germany is being punished by the victors of World War I.
2. Answers may include that it punished Germany harshly, which created bitterness that could lead to another war.

HISTORY & ARTS — PRIMARY SOURCE

The Treaty of Versailles

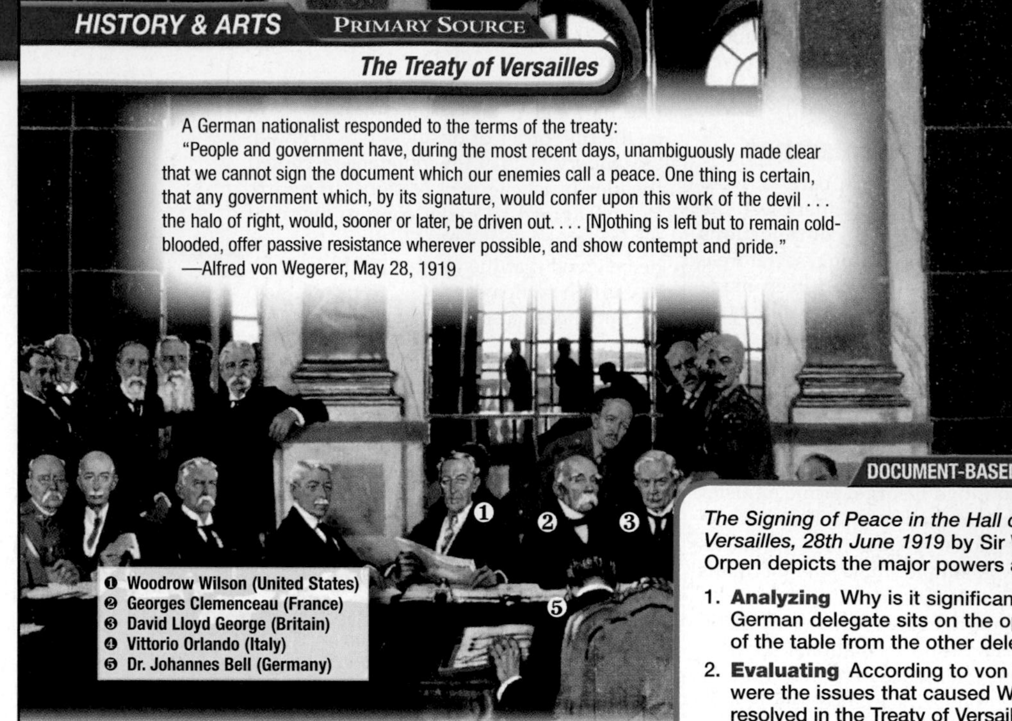

A German nationalist responded to the terms of the treaty:

"People and government have, during the most recent days, unambiguously made clear that we cannot sign the document which our enemies call a peace. One thing is certain, that any government which, by its signature, would confer upon this work of the devil . . . the halo of right, would, sooner or later, be driven out. . . . [N]othing is left but to remain cold-blooded, offer passive resistance wherever possible, and show contempt and pride."

—Alfred von Wegerer, May 28, 1919

1. Woodrow Wilson (United States)
2. Georges Clemenceau (France)
3. David Lloyd George (Britain)
4. Vittorio Orlando (Italy)
5. Dr. Johannes Bell (Germany)

DOCUMENT-BASED QUESTIONS

The Signing of Peace in the Hall of Mirrors, Versailles, 28th June 1919 by Sir William Orpen depicts the major powers at Versailles.

1. **Analyzing** Why is it significant that the German delegate sits on the opposite side of the table from the other delegates?
2. **Evaluating** According to von Wegerer, were the issues that caused World War I resolved in the Treaty of Versailles? Explain.

The Treaty of Versailles

The final peace settlement of Paris consisted of five separate treaties with the defeated nations of Germany, Austria, Hungary, Bulgaria, and Turkey. The Treaty of Versailles with Germany was by far the most important.

C The Germans considered it a harsh peace. They were especially unhappy with Article 231, the so-called War Guilt Clause, which declared that Germany (and Austria) were responsible for starting the war. The treaty ordered Germany to pay reparations for all damages that the Allied governments and their people had sustained as a result of the war.

The military and territorial provisions of the Treaty of Versailles also angered the Germans. Germany had to reduce its army to 100,000 men, cut back its navy, and eliminate its air force. **Alsace** and **Lorraine,** taken R by the Germans from France in 1871, were now returned. Sections of eastern Germany were awarded to a new Polish state.

German land along the Rhine River became a demilitarized zone, stripped of all weapons and fortifications. This, it was hoped, would serve as a barrier to any future German moves against France. Although outraged by the "dictated peace," Germany accepted the treaty.

The Legacies of the War

The war, the Treaty of Versailles, and the separate peace treaties made with the other Central Powers redrew the map of eastern Europe. The German and Russian empires lost much territory. The Austro-Hungarian Empire disappeared.

New nation-states emerged from the lands of these three empires: Finland, Latvia, Estonia, Lithuania, **Poland,** Czechoslovakia, Austria, and Hungary. New territorial arrangements were also made in the Balkans. Romania acquired additional lands. Serbia formed the nucleus of a new state, called Yugoslavia, which combined Serbs, Croats, and Slovenes.

Differentiated Instruction

Reteaching Activity, URB p. 47

Identifying Central Issues

Objective: Identify the causes, progress, and outcomes of World War I.

Focus: Review the main ideas of the chapter.

Teach: Have students refer to the text as they complete the chart.

Assess: Have students discuss their answers with a partner.

Close: Tell students to use this chart to help them study for the chapter test.

Differentiated Instruction Strategies

- BL Provide an answer bank for students.
- AL Have students complete the handout without using their textbooks.
- ELL Assist students, as needed, in writing descriptions.

The principle of self-determination supposedly guided the Paris Peace Conference. However, the mixtures of peoples in eastern Europe made it impossible to draw boundaries along strict ethnic lines. Compromises had to be made, sometimes to satisfy the national interests of the victors. France, for example, had lost Russia as its major ally on Germany's eastern border. Thus, France wanted to strengthen and expand Poland, Czechoslovakia, Yugoslavia, and Romania as much as possible. Those states could then serve as barriers against Germany and Communist Russia. **C**

As a result of compromises, almost every eastern European state was left with ethnic minorities: Germans in Poland; Hungarians, Poles, and Germans in Czechoslovakia; Hungarians in Romania, and Serbs, Croats, Slovenes, Macedonians, and Albanians in Yugoslavia. The problem of ethnic minorities within nations would lead to many later conflicts.

Yet another centuries-old empire—the Ottoman Empire—was broken up by the peace settlement. To gain Arab support against the Ottoman Turks during the war, the Western Allies had promised to recognize the independence of Arab states in the Ottoman Empire. Once the war was over, however, the Western nations changed their minds. France took control of Lebanon and Syria, and Britain received Iraq and Palestine.

These acquisitions were officially called **mandates.** Woodrow Wilson had opposed the outright annexation of colonial territories by the Allies. As a result, the peace settlement created the mandate system. According to this system, a nation officially governed another nation as a mandate on behalf of the League of Nations but did not own the territory.

World War I shattered the liberal, rational society that had existed in late nineteenth- and early twentieth-century Europe. The deaths of nearly 10 million people, as well as the incredible destruction caused by the war, undermined the whole idea of progress. Entire populations had participated in a devastating slaughter.

World War I was a total war—one that involved a complete mobilization of resources and people. As a result, the power of governments over the lives of their citizens increased. Freedom of the press and speech were limited in the name of national security. World War I made the practice of strong central authority a way of life.

The turmoil created by the war also seemed to open the door to even greater insecurity. Revolutions broke up old empires and created new states, which led to new problems. The hope that Europe and the rest of the world would return to normalcy was, however, soon dashed.

✓Reading Check **Identifying** What clause in the Treaty of Versailles particularly angered the Germans?

SECTION 4 REVIEW

Vocabulary

1. **Explain** the significance of: psychological, Erich Ludendorff, Kiel, Friedrich Ebert, armistice, cooperation, David Lloyd George, Georges Clemenceau, reparations, Alsace, Lorraine, Poland, mandates.

Main Ideas

2. **Specify** why Erich Ludendorff's final military gamble failed for Germany.
3. **List** some of President Wilson's proposals for creating peace. Use a chart like the one below to make your list.

President Wilson's Proposals
1.
2.

4. **Explain** why the mandate system was created. Which countries became mandates? Which countries governed them?

Critical Thinking

5. **The BIG Idea** **Making Generalizations** Although Woodrow Wilson came to the Paris Peace Conference with high ideals, the other leaders had more practical concerns. Why do you think that was so?
6. **Comparing and Contrasting** Compare and contrast Wilson's Fourteen Points to the Treaty of Versailles.
7. **Analyzing Visuals** Examine the painting on page 782. What is the significance of the setting?

Writing About History

8. **Informative Writing** Suppose that you are a reporter for a large newspaper. You are sent to the Paris Peace Conference to interview one of the leaders of the Big Three. Prepare a written set of questions you would like to ask the leader you have selected.

History ONLINE
For help with the concepts in this section of *Glencoe World History*, go to glencoe.com and click Study Central™.

783

C Critical Thinking

Predicting Consequences Ask students to predict the consequences of the following combination of factors in Europe: the principle of self-determination, redrawn borders, and the presence of ethnic minorities in nearly every eastern European state. **AL**

✓Reading Check

Answer: Article 231, the War Guilt Clause, which declared Germany (and Austria) responsible for starting the war.

Assess

History ONLINE

Study Central provides summaries, interactive games, and online graphic organizers to help students review content.

Close

Drawing Conclusions Review the consequences of World War I on European society. Discuss how the conflict undermined the idea of progress. **OL**

Answers

1. Definitions for the vocabulary words are found in the section and in the Glossary.
2. American troops arrived; German provisions were low, and reserves of soldiers were way down; home front was tired of war.
3. (1) open peace agreements reducing armaments; (2) self-determination; (3) creation of a "general association of nations"
4. as an alternative to territorial annexation; Lebanon, Syria (governed by France); Iraq, Palestine (governed by Britain)
5. because of national interests
6. **Fourteen Points:** Open diplomacy; self-determination; **Treaty of Versailles:** Determination of war guilt; reparations; demilitarized zone in Germany; map of Europe redrawn; **Fourteen Points and Treaty of Versailles:** Reduction of arms; establishment of League of Nations
7. It symbolized absolute monarchy.
8. Questions should reflect an understanding of the issues at the peace conference.

CHAPTER 24 Planning Guide

Key to Ability Levels	
BL Below Level	AL Above Level
OL On Level	ELL English Language Learners

Key to Teaching Resources	
Print Material	DVD
CD-ROM	Transparency

Levels				Resources	Chapter Opener	Section 1	Section 2	Section 3	Section 4	Chapter Assess
BL	OL	AL	ELL							
				FOCUS						
BL	OL	AL	ELL	**Daily Focus Skills Transparencies**		24-1	24-2	24-3	24-4	
				TEACH						
	OL	AL		**Economics and History Activity, URB**		✓	✓			
BL	OL		ELL	**Reading Skills Activity, URB**			p. 57			
	OL	AL		**Historical Analysis Skills Activity, URB**		p. 58				
BL	OL	AL	ELL	**Differentiated Instruction Activity, URB**		p. 59				
	OL		ELL	**English Learner Activity, URB**		p. 61				
BL	OL	AL	ELL	**Content Vocabulary Activity, URB***					p. 63	
BL	OL	AL	ELL	**Academic Vocabulary Activity, URB**					p. 65	
BL	OL	AL	ELL	**Skills Reinforcement Activity, URB**			p. 67			
	OL	AL		**Critical Thinking Skills Activity, URB**				p. 68		
	OL	AL		**History and Geography Activity, URB**				p. 69		
	OL	AL	ELL	**Mapping History Activity, URB**		p. 71				
BL	OL	AL		**Historical Significance Activity, URB**		p. 72				
BL	OL	AL	ELL	**Cooperative Learning Activity, URB**				p. 73		
	OL	AL	ELL	**History Simulation Activity, URB**					p. 75	
BL	OL	AL	ELL	**Time Line Activity, URB**			p. 77			
	OL	AL		**Linking Past and Present Activity, URB**		p. 78				
BL	OL	AL		**People in World History Activity, URB**		p. 80			p. 79	
BL	OL	AL	ELL	**Primary Source Reading, URB**				p. 81		
	OL	AL		**Enrichment Activity, URB**		p. 86				
BL	OL	AL	ELL	**World Art and Music Activity, URB**					p. 83	
BL	OL		ELL	**Guided Reading Activities, URB***		p. 88	p. 89	p. 90	p. 91	
BL	OL		ELL	**Reading Essentials and Note-Taking Guide***		p. 262	p. 265	p. 268	p. 271	
BL	OL	AL	ELL	**Differentiated Instruction for the World History Classroom**	✓	✓	✓	✓	✓	✓

Note: Please refer to the *Unit Resource Book: The Twentieth-Century Crisis* for this chapter's URB materials.

* Also available in Spanish

- Interactive Lesson Planner
- Interactive Teacher Edition
- Fully editable blackline masters
- Section Spotlight Videos Launch
- Differentiated Lesson Plans
- Printable reports of daily assignments
- Standards Tracking System

Levels					Resources	Chapter Opener	Section 1	Section 2	Section 3	Section 4	Chapter Assess
BL	OL	AL	ELL								
TEACH *(continued)*											
BL	OL	AL	ELL		StudentWorks™ Plus DVD	✓	✓	✓	✓	✓	✓
BL	OL	AL	ELL		Vocabulary PuzzleMaker CD-ROM	✓	✓	✓	✓	✓	✓
Teacher Resources					Building Academic Vocabulary	✓	✓	✓	✓	✓	✓
					Reading Strategies and Activities for the Social Studies Classroom			p. 59	pp. 71, 77	p. 83	
					Writer's Guidebook		p. 12	p. 47	p. 5	pp. 27, 54	
					Strategies for Success	✓	✓	✓	✓	✓	✓
					Outline Map Resource Book	✓	✓	✓	✓	✓	✓
					Presentation Plus! with MindJogger DVD	✓	✓	✓	✓	✓	✓
ASSESS											
BL	OL	AL	ELL		Section Quizzes and Chapter Tests*		p. 297	p. 298	p. 299	p. 300	p. 301
BL	OL	AL	ELL		Authentic Assessment With Rubrics	✓	✓	✓	✓	✓	✓
BL	OL	AL	ELL		Standardized Test Practice Workbook	✓	✓	✓	✓	✓	✓
BL	OL	AL	ELL		*ExamView® Assessment Suite* CD-ROM		24-1	24-2	24-3	24-4	Ch. 24
BL	OL	AL	ELL		Interactive Tutor Self-Assessment CD-ROM		24-1	24-2	24-3	24-4	
CLOSE											
BL			ELL		Reteaching Activity, URB					p. 85	
BL	OL		ELL		Reading and Study Skills Foldables™	✓	✓	✓	✓	✓	✓

Focus

MAKING CONNECTIONS
How can politics be reflected in sports?

Activate students' prior knowledge by having them brainstorm about the modern Olympics. Responses may include that different countries host the event and that the modern Olympics are based on the ancient Greek Olympics. Then discuss what happens during a medal ceremony, as shown in the photo of Jesse Owens. *(The flag of the gold medal winner's country is raised and his or her national anthem is played.)* Wrap up the discussion by having students give examples of modern athletes exhibiting national pride.

Teach

The Big Ideas

As students study the chapter, remind them to consider the section-based Big Ideas included in each section's Guide to Reading. The **Essential Questions** in the activities below tie in to the Big Ideas and help students think about and understand important chapter concepts. In addition, the Hands-on Chapter Projects with their culminating activities relate the content from each section to the Big Ideas. These activities build on each other as students progress through the chapter. Section activities culminate in the wrap-up activity on the Visual Summary page.

CHAPTER 24

The West Between the Wars 1919–1939

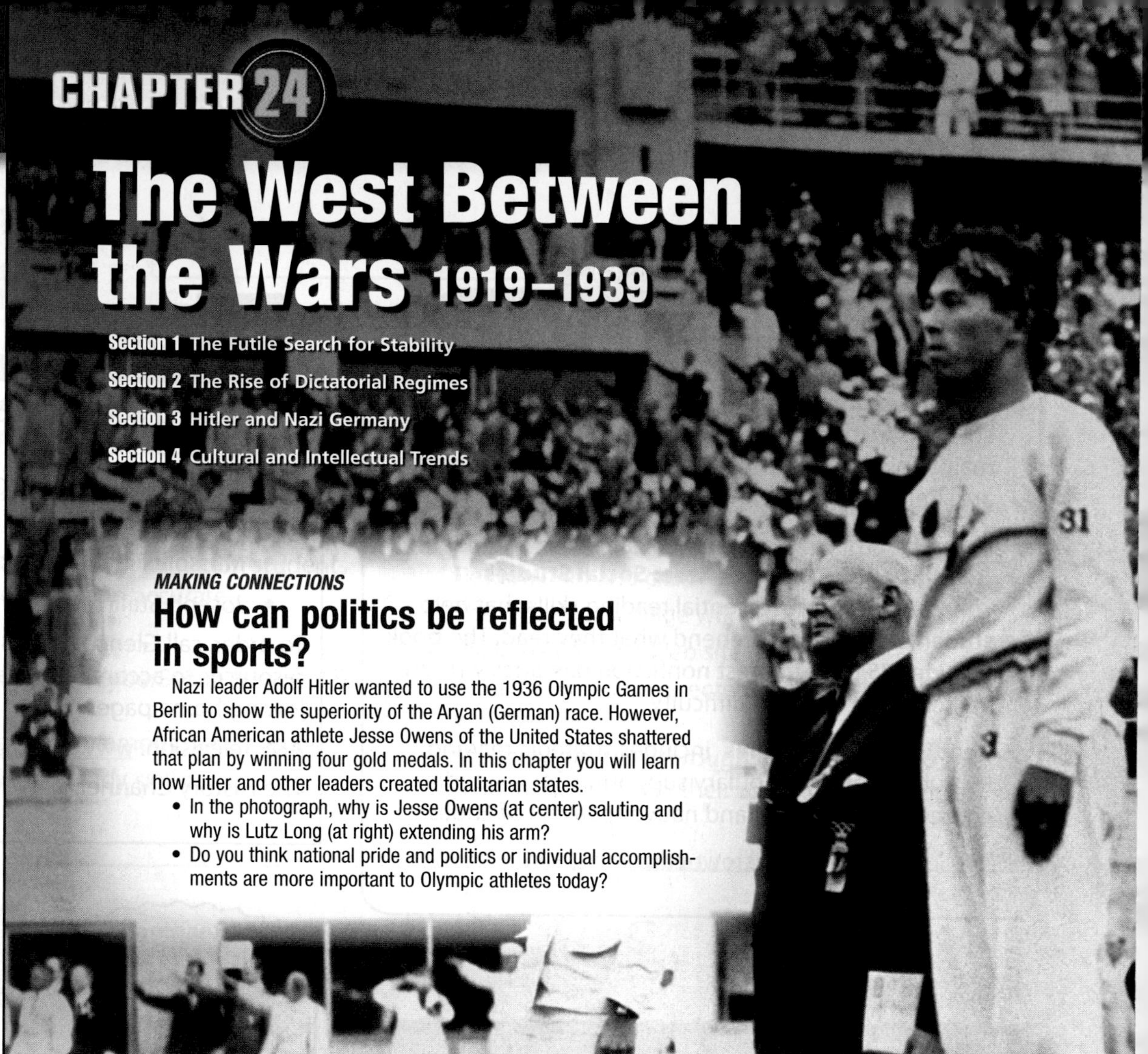

MAKING CONNECTIONS
How can politics be reflected in sports?

Nazi leader Adolf Hitler wanted to use the 1936 Olympic Games in Berlin to show the superiority of the Aryan (German) race. However, African American athlete Jesse Owens of the United States shattered that plan by winning four gold medals. In this chapter you will learn how Hitler and other leaders created totalitarian states.

- In the photograph, why is Jesse Owens (at center) saluting and why is Lutz Long (at right) extending his arm?
- Do you think national pride and politics or individual accomplishments are more important to Olympic athletes today?

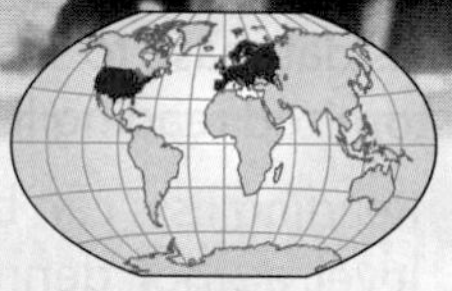

EUROPE AND THE UNITED STATES ▶

1922 Lenin and the Communists create the USSR

1926 Mussolini establishes a Fascist dictatorship in Italy

1929 U.S. stock market crashes; Great Depression begins

1919 — 1925 — 1930

THE WORLD ▶

1923 Nationalists and Communists in China form an alliance

788

The Futile Search for Stability Remind students of the destruction of World War I, both in terms of property destroyed and lives lost. **Essential Question:** What were the causes of instability in the West after World War I? Discuss students' responses as a class, citing economic, political, and social examples such as Germany being forced to pay reparations. Tell students that Section 1 examines the causes and effects of instability in the West after the war. OL

The Rise of Dictatorial Regimes Discuss why people living in uncertain times might support a dictator. **Essential Question:** Why did certain European countries become dictatorial regimes? *(Because of instability, some people sought to create a new kind of society. Other countries sought to preserve the traditional social order.)* Tell students that in Section 2, they will learn more about how dictatorial regimes gained popular support. OL

SECTION 3

Hitler and Nazi Germany Explain that Hitler believed in a Social Darwinian theory of struggle that emphasized the right of superior individuals and nations to expand their authority over others. **Essential Question:** How did Hitler and the Nazis gain power and rule Germany? *(use of propaganda, mass demonstrations, terror and repression, control of the economy, control of institutions)* Tell students that in Section 3, they will learn about Hitler and the Nazi state he led. OL

SECTION 4

Cultural and Intellectual Trends Review cultural and intellectual trends that students have previously studied, such as impressionism (Chapter 20) and Darwin's natural selection (Chapter 19). **Essential Question:** What were the main cultural and intellectual trends between the wars? *(dadaist and surrealist art, stream-of-consciousness literature, splitting of the atom, uncertainty principle)* Tell students that Section 4 covers trends that arose between the two world wars. OL

More About the Photo

Visual Literacy Hitler wanted the 1936 Olympic Games in Berlin to showcase Aryan superiority. Instead, Jesse Owens—the grandson of African American slaves—dominated "Hitler's Olympics." During these Games, Owens set a world record in the long jump to win the gold medal. He also won the gold three more times: in the 100- and 200-meter dashes, and as a member of the U.S. 4x100 relay team. After Owens's death in 1980, Berlin renamed a street in his honor.

FOLDABLES™ Study Organizer — Dinah Zike's Foldables

Dinah Zike's Foldables are three-dimensional, interactive graphic organizers that help students practice basic writing skills, review vocabulary terms, and identify main ideas. Instructions for creating and using Foldables can be found in the Appendix at the end of this book and in the *Dinah Zike's Reading and Study Skills Foldables* booklet.

History ONLINE

Introduce students to chapter content and key terms by having them access the Chapter 24 Overview at glencoe.com.

Focus

Bellringer

Daily Focus Transparency 24.1

GUIDE TO READING

Answers to Graphic:

Popular Front	New Deal
Right to collective bargaining	Government has active role in economy
Forty-hour workweek	More public works programs
Two-week paid vacation	New social programs begin U.S. welfare system
Minimum wage	

Section Spotlight Video

To generate student interest and provide a springboard for class discussion, access the Chapter 24, Section 1 video at glencoe.com or on the video DVD.

Resource Manager

SECTION 1

The Futile Search for Stability

GUIDE TO READING

The BIG Idea

Competition Among Countries
Peace and prosperity were short-lived after World War I as a global depression weakened Western democracies.

Content Vocabulary

- depression *(p. 792)*
- collective bargaining *(p. 794)*
- deficit spending *(p. 795)*

Academic Vocabulary

- annual *(p. 791)*
- ratio *(p. 792)*

People, Places, and Events

- Ruhr Valley *(p. 791)*
- Dawes Plan *(p. 792)*
- Treaty of Locarno *(p. 792)*
- Switzerland *(p. 794)*
- Weimar Republic *(p. 794)*
- John Maynard Keynes *(p. 795)*
- Franklin Delano Roosevelt *(p. 795)*
- New Deal *(p. 795)*

Reading Strategy

Comparing and Contrasting As you read, use a table like the one below to compare France's Popular Front with the New Deal in the United States.

Popular Front	New Deal

The peace settlement of World War I left many nations unhappy, and the League of Nations proved unable to deal with the crises following the war. The brief period of prosperity that began in Europe during the early 1920s ended in 1929 with the beginning of the Great Depression. This economic collapse shook people's confidence in political democracy and paved the way for fear and the rise of extremist parties that offered solutions to the hardships that many were enduring.

Uneasy Peace, Uncertain Security

MAIN IDEA Discontent with the Treaty of Versailles and a weak League of Nations opened the door to new problems in the interwar years.

HISTORY & YOU Imagine how your life would change if the price of everything doubled each day. Read to learn how runaway inflation affected Germany after World War I.

The peace settlement at the end of World War I tried to fulfill nineteenth-century dreams of nationalism. It created new boundaries and new states. From the beginning, however, the settlement left nations unhappy. Border disputes poisoned relations in eastern Europe for years. Many Germans vowed to revise the terms of the Treaty of Versailles.

A Weak League of Nations

President Woodrow Wilson had realized that the peace settlement included unwise provisions that could serve as new causes for conflict. He had placed many of his hopes for the future in the League of Nations. This organization, however, was not very effective in maintaining the peace.

One problem was the failure of the United States to join the League. Most Americans wanted to avoid involvement in European affairs. The U.S. Senate, in spite of President Wilson's wishes, refused to ratify, or approve, the Treaty of Versailles. That meant the United States could not join the League of Nations. Without the United States, the League of Nations' effectiveness was automatically weakened. As time would prove, the remaining League members could not agree to use force against aggression.

French Demands

Between 1919 and 1924, desire for security led the French government to demand strict enforcement of the Treaty of Versailles.

R Reading Strategies	C Critical Thinking	D Differentiated Instruction	W Writing Support	S Skill Practice
Teacher Edition • Making Connections, p. 791 • Det. Importance, pp. 792, 795 **Additional Resources** • Guid. Read. Act., URB p. 88 • Read. Ess. & Note-Taking Guide, p. 262	**Teacher Edition** • Det. Cause/Effect, p. 793 **Additional Resources** • Hist. Analysis Skills Act., URB p. 58 • Mapping Hist. Act., URB p. 71 • Hist. Sig. Act., URB p. 72 • Section Quiz, p. 297	**Teacher Edition** • Verbal/Linguistic, p. 794 **Additional Resources** • Diff. Instr. Act., URB p. 59 • English Learner Act., URB p. 61	**Teacher Edition** • Expository Writing, p. 794 **Additional Resources** • Linking Past/Present Act., URB p. 78 • People in World Hist. Act., URB p. 80 • Writer's Guidebook, p. 12	**Teacher Edition** • Synthesizing, p. 792 **Additional Resources** • Enrich. Act., URB p. 86

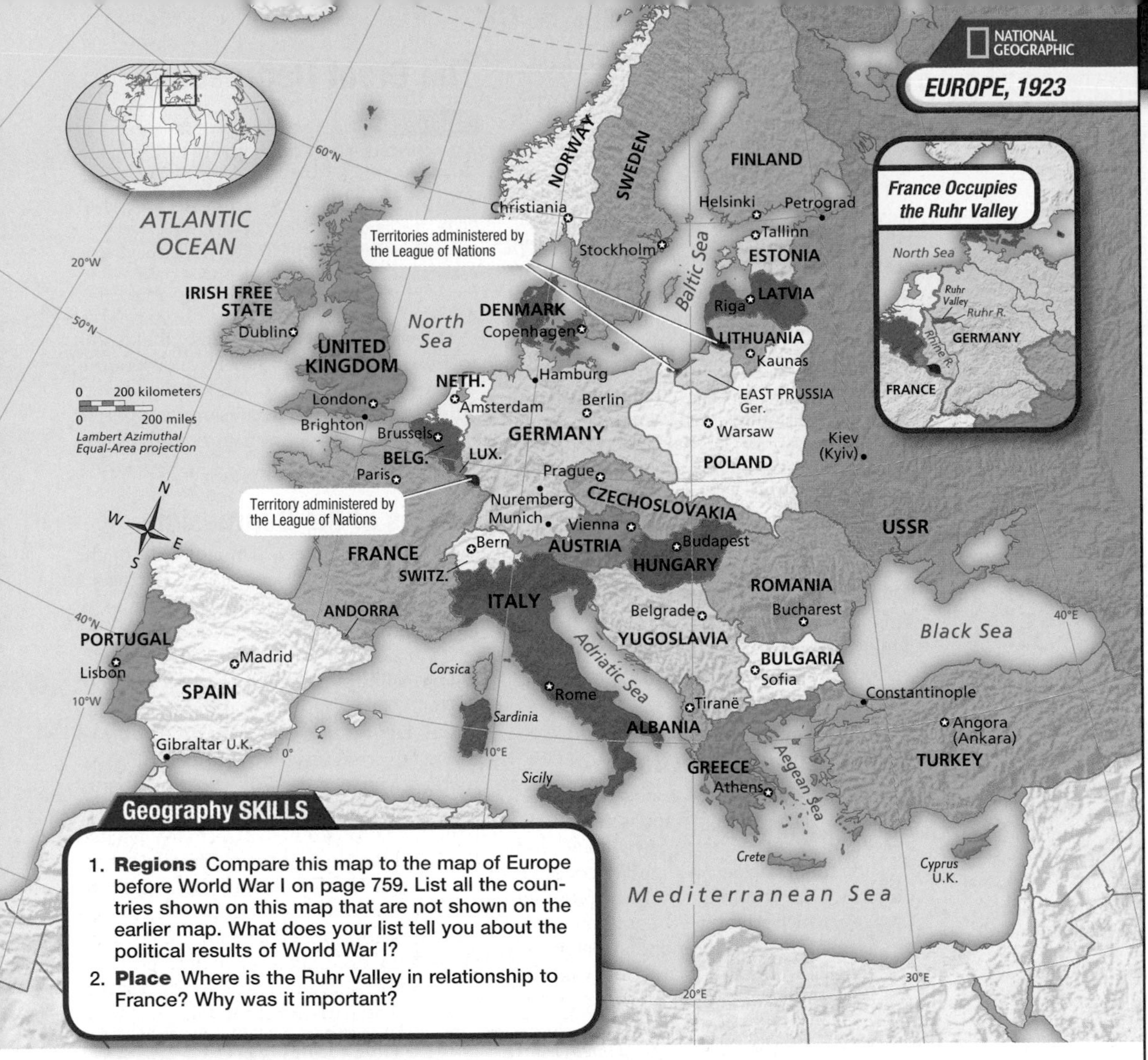

Geography SKILLS

1. **Regions** Compare this map to the map of Europe before World War I on page 759. List all the countries shown on this map that are not shown on the earlier map. What does your list tell you about the political results of World War I?
2. **Place** Where is the Ruhr Valley in relationship to France? Why was it important?

Teach

R Reading Strategy

Making Connections Explain that the act of refusing to work (passive resistance) is an example of a nonviolent protest. BL

Geography SKILLS

Answers:

1. Turkey, Yugoslavia, Czechoslovakia, Austria, Hungary, Poland, Latvia, Estonia, Lithuania, Finland (East Prussia was a German province); old empires dissolved, new states were created.
2. Its location on the French border made it easy for France to occupy. Its natural resources made it a mining and industrial center and made it attractive to France as a way to collect reparations.

This tough policy began with the issue of reparations (payments) that the Germans were supposed to make for the damage they had done in the war. In April 1921, the Allied Reparations Commission determined that Germany owed 132 billion German marks (33 billion U.S. dollars) for reparations, payable in **annual** installments of 2.5 billion marks.

The new German republic made its first payment in 1921. By the following year, however, the German government faced a financial crisis and announced that it could not pay any more reparations. Outraged, France sent troops to occupy the **Ruhr Valley**, Germany's chief industrial and mining center. France planned to collect reparations by using the Ruhr mines and factories.

Inflation in Germany

The German government adopted a policy of passive resistance to this French occupation. German workers went on strike. R

Hands-On Chapter Project Step 1

Writing a Journal of the West Between the Wars

Pairs of students will write a journal chronicling the social, political, and economic climate of the West between the two world wars.

Step 1: Gathering Information

Essential Question: What were the causes of instability in the West after World War I?

Directions: Tell students to first look for social, political, and economic events or movements that will serve as the basis for their journal entries. Write the Section 1 Big Idea on the board. Tell students to use it as a guide for selecting material from Section 1. Suggest that each pair divide duties evenly. (For example, one member can gather information and the other can use it to prepare note cards to keep track of it.)

Summarizing: Allow time for pairs to share what they learn about the Section 1 Big Idea while searching for journal material. Pairs will continue to gather information as they study Section 2. In addition, they will begin an outline to guide their journal writing. OL

R Reading Strategy

Determining Importance
Ask: What were the main reasons for the Great Depression? *(downturn in many nations' economies; U.S. stock market crash)* **OL**

S Skill Practice

Synthesizing Discuss the cause-and-effect relationships among the events leading to the Depression. Explain that the domino effect is a series of events that are each both a cause and an effect (like a falling domino causing the next one to fall, and so on). **Ask:** How does the domino effect apply to these events? *(Students should explain how economic downturns and the stock market crash created a domino effect.)* **OL**

✓**Reading Check**

Answer: It lacked U.S. participation and could not agree to use force against aggression.

The German government mainly paid their salaries by printing more paper money. This only added to the inflation (rise in prices) that had already begun in Germany by the end of the war.

The German mark soon became worthless. In 1914, 4.2 marks equaled 1 U.S. dollar. By November 1, 1923, it took 130 billion marks to equal 1 dollar. By the end of November, the **ratio** had increased to an incredible 4.2 trillion marks to 1 dollar.

Economic adversity led to political upheavals. Both France and Germany began to seek a way out of the disaster. In August 1924, an international commission produced a new plan for reparations. The **Dawes Plan,** named after the American banker who chaired the commission, first reduced reparations. It then coordinated Germany's annual payments with its ability to pay.

The Dawes Plan also granted an initial $200 million loan for German recovery. This loan soon opened the door to heavy American investment in Europe. A brief period of European prosperity followed, but it only lasted from 1924 to 1929.

The Treaty of Locarno

With prosperity came a new European diplomacy. The foreign ministers of Germany and France, Gustav Stresemann and Aristide Briand, fostered a spirit of cooperation. In 1925 they signed the **Treaty of Locarno,** which guaranteed Germany's new western borders with France and Belgium.

Many viewed the Locarno pact as the beginning of a new era of European peace. On the day after the pact was concluded, headlines in the *New York Times* read "France and Germany Ban War Forever." The London *Times* declared "Peace at Last." The new spirit of cooperation grew even stronger when Germany joined the League of Nations in March 1926.

Two years later, the Kellogg-Briand Pact brought even more hope. Sixty-three nations signed this accord and pledged "to renounce war as an instrument of national policy." Nothing was said, however, about what would be done if anyone violated the pact.

✓**Reading Check** **Explaining** Why was the League of Nations unable to maintain peace?

The Great Depression

MAIN IDEA Underlying economic problems and an American stock market crisis triggered the Great Depression.

HISTORY & YOU The U.S. stock market plunged in 2001 after terrorist attacks, but what would have happened if it had collapsed? Read to find out the consequences of the 1929 stock market crash.

The brief period of prosperity that began in Europe in 1924 ended in an economic collapse that came to be known as the Great Depression. A **depression** is a period of low economic activity and rising unemployment.

Causes of the Depression

R Two factors played a major role in the start of the Great Depression. First was a series of downturns in the economies of individual nations in the second half of the 1920s. Prices for farm products, especially wheat, fell rapidly due to overproduction.

The second factor that triggered the Great Depression was an international financial crisis involving the U.S. stock market. Much of the European prosperity between 1924 and 1929 was built on U.S. bank loans to Germany. Germany needed the U.S. loans to pay reparations to France and Great Britain. During the 1920s, the U.S. stock market boomed. By 1928, American investors pulled money out of Germany to invest it in the stock market. Then, in October 1929, the U.S. stock market crashed. Stock prices plunged.

S In a panic, U.S. investors withdrew even more funds from Germany and other European markets. This withdrawal made the banks of Germany and other European states weak. The well-known Creditanstalt Bank in Vienna collapsed in May 1931. By then, trade was slowing, industrial production was declining, and unemployment was rising.

Responses to the Depression

Economic depression was not new to Europe. However, the extent of the economic downturn after 1929 truly made this the Great Depression. During 1932, the worst

Differentiated Instruction

Historical Significance Activity, URB p. 72

Determining Cause and Effect

Objective: Explain causes and effects of stock market crashes.

Focus: Learn more about the 1929 stock market crash.

Teach: Direct students to answer questions 1–6.

Assess: Have students share answers and amend them as needed.

Close: Discuss recent examples of downturns in the U.S. stock market.

Differentiated Instruction Strategies

BL Guide students in matching questions to specific information in the article.

AL Have students analyze a recent stock market downturn in depth.

ELL Have pairs of students define key vocabulary (for example, *plummeted* and *mortgages*).

year of the Depression, nearly 1 in every 4 British workers was unemployed. About 5.5 million Germans, or roughly 30 percent of the German labor force, had no jobs. The unemployed and homeless filled the streets.

Governments did not know how to deal with the crisis. They lowered wages and raised tariffs to exclude foreign goods from home markets. These measures made the crisis worse and had serious political effects. **C**

One effect of the economic crisis was increased government activity in the economy. Another effect was a renewed interest in Marxist ideas. Marx's prediction that capitalism would destroy itself through overproduction seemed to be coming true. Communism thus became more popular, especially among workers and intellectuals.

Finally, the Great Depression led masses of people to follow political leaders who offered simple solutions in return for dictatorial power. Everywhere, democracy seemed on the defensive in the 1930s.

✓Reading Check **Summarizing** What were the results of the Great Depression?

TURNING POINT: POLITICAL EFFECTS OF THE GREAT DEPRESSION

The Great Depression left millions of people unemployed and national economies in crisis. As government attempts to solve the economic problems failed, popular morale waned. Many people turned to Marxism, Nazism, or fascism for answers. Extremist political parties gained support by promising better times ahead. These results of the Great Depression were major factors leading to World War II.

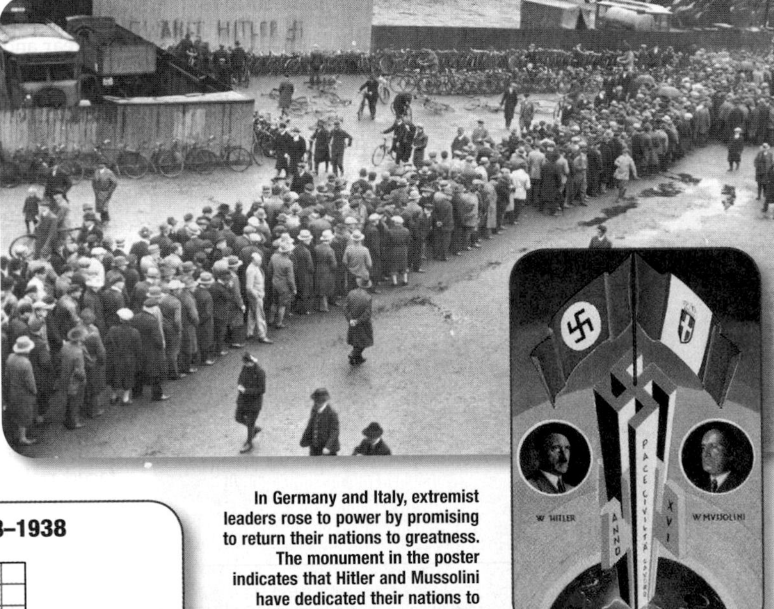

Long lines of unemployed German workers seeking food or jobs bore witness to the misery of the Great Depression. ►

Unemployment, 1928–1938

Percentage of Workforce Unemployed (0–35); Year (1928–1938); U.S., U.K., Germany

Sources: *European Historical Statistics, 1750–1970; Historical Statistics of the United States.*

In Germany and Italy, extremist leaders rose to power by promising to return their nations to greatness. The monument in the poster indicates that Hitler and Mussolini have dedicated their nations to peace, civilization, and work. ►

CRITICAL THINKING SKILLS

1. **Identifying** Name three problems caused by the Great Depression.
2. **Determining Cause and Effect** How might political developments during the Depression have led nations to war?

C Critical Thinking

Determining Cause and Effect Ask: Why would lowering wages and increasing tariffs make the economic crisis worse? *(Both would decrease workers' ability to buy goods: lowering wages would reduce take-home pay; increasing tariffs would make imported products more expensive.)* **OL**

For additional practice on this skill, see the **Skills Handbook**.

CRITICAL THINKING SKILLS

Answers:

1. greater government role in the economy, renewed interest in Marxism, rise of extremist parties
2. Possible answer: Hard times might make people turn to nationalistic leaders.

✓Reading Check

Answer: increased government activity in the economy; lower wages, high unemployment renewed interest in Marxist doctrines; led people to follow dictatorial leaders

Differentiated Instruction

Leveled Activities

BL Differentiated Instruction, URB p. 59

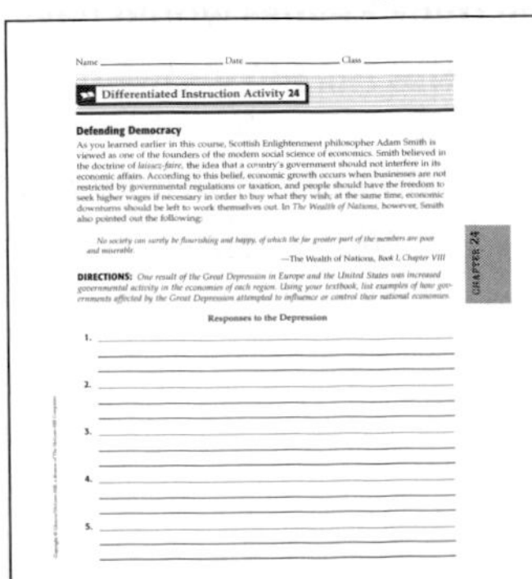

OL Historical Analysis Skills Activity, URB p. 58

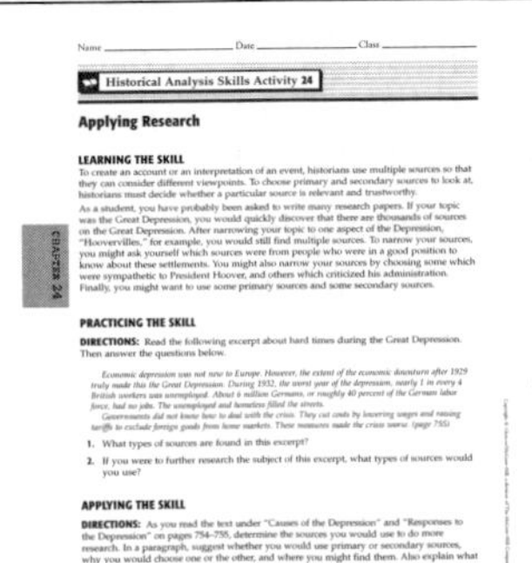

AL Mapping History Activity, URB p. 71

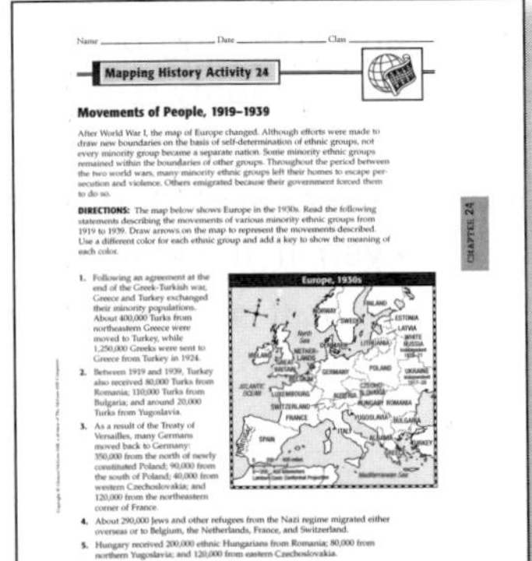

ELL English Learner Activity, URB p. 61

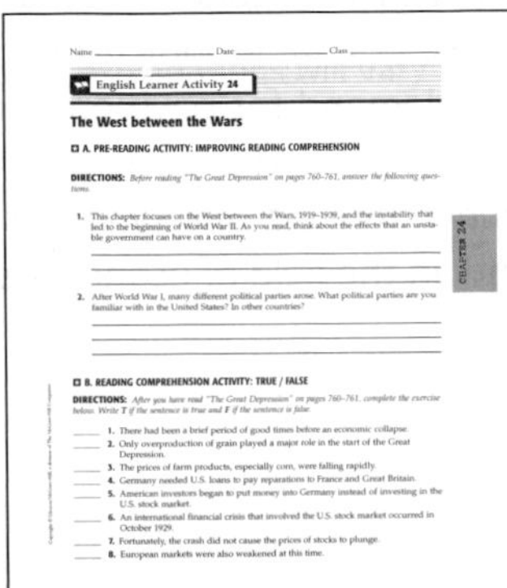

R Reading Strategy

Making Connections Have the class reread the primary source quotation in the text on this page. **Ask:** **How did Hitler implement his goal to "make the German people an instrument" of his policies?** *(The Nazis took control of churches, schools, and universities; formed professional organizations; and created youth organizations.)* **OL**

DOCUMENT-BASED QUESTIONS

Answers:

1. Answers will vary but should include the idea that if stores and homes were looted, the victims might not recognize the anti-Semitic message that was being sent and might assume instead that robbery was the goal.
2. Time lines will vary but should be organized in sequential order.

Additional Support

INFOGRAPHICS PRIMARY SOURCE

Kristallnacht or "Night of Shattered Glass"

Still visible in this burned synagogue is a *bimah*, a raised platform from which the Torah is read.

Kristallnacht was named for the shattered windows resulting from violence against Jews.

Although anti-Semitic policies had been in effect in Germany since the Nazi takeover in 1933, the events of *Kristallnacht* signaled the start of a more violent era of anti-Semitism. Businesses could not reopen unless managed by non-Jews. Jews were banned from schools and most public places.

"Regards: Measures against Jews tonight. . . .

"a) Only such measures may be taken which do not jeopardize German life or property (for instance, burning of synagogues only if there is no danger of fires for the neighborhoods).

"b) Business establishments and homes of Jews may be destroyed but not looted. . . .

"c) In business streets special care is to be taken that non-Jewish establishments will be safeguarded at all cost against damage. . . .

"As soon as the events of this night permit the use of the designated officers, as many Jews, particularly wealthy ones, as the local jails will hold, are to be arrested in all districts."

—Directive from SS officer Reinhard Heydrich, November 10, 1938

DOCUMENT-BASED QUESTIONS

1. **Hypothesizing** Why do you think Heydrich said that Jewish-owned stores and homes could be destroyed but not looted?
2. **Organizing** Research and create a time line of anti-Semitic Nazi policies in the years before *Kristallnacht*.

Economics and Spectacles

In the economic sphere, Hitler used public works projects and grants to private construction firms to put people back to work and end the Depression. A massive rearmament program, however, was the key to solving the unemployment problem.

Unemployment, which had reached more than 5 million people in 1932, dropped to 2.5 million in 1934 and less than 500,000 in 1937. The regime claimed full credit for solving Germany's economic woes. The new regime's part in bringing an end to the Depression was an important factor in leading many Germans to accept Hitler and the Nazis.

In addition, the Nazis used mass demonstrations and spectacles to make the German people an instrument of Hitler's policies. These meetings, especially the **Nuremberg** party rallies that were held every September, usually evoked mass enthusiasm and excitement.

The Nazi totalitarian state also controlled institutions, which included churches, schools, and universities. In addition, Nazi professional organizations and youth organizations taught Nazi ideals.

Activity: Collaborative Learning

Analyzing Advise students that Hitler and his followers were elected to power by the German people. These people had experienced a drastic change in their way of life following World War I. The German people were searching for a leader and an identity to help them escape their economic woes. While Nazism at first glance seemed appealing, the Nazis began with incremental acts of prejudice and persecution, using innocent people as scapegoats. This escalated into slaughter and extermination. Discuss these ideas with the class and remind students that it is important to study historical patterns to understand how parties such as the Nazi party can gain power in a country or society. Ask groups of four students to work together to write a report analyzing the methods the Nazis used to gain support among the German people. **OL**

Women and Nazism

Women played a crucial role in the Aryan state as bearers of the children who, the Nazis believed, would bring about the triumph of the Aryan race. The Nazis believed men were destined to be warriors and political leaders, while women were meant to be wives and mothers. By preserving this clear distinction, each could best serve to "maintain the whole community."

Nazi ideas determined employment opportunities for women. Jobs in heavy industry, the Nazis thought, might hinder women from bearing healthy children. Certain professions, including university teaching, medicine, and law, were also considered unsuitable for women, especially married women. The Nazis instead encouraged women to pursue other occupations, such as social work and nursing. The Nazi regime pushed its campaign against working women with poster slogans such as "Get ahold of pots and pans and broom and you'll sooner find a groom!" C

Anti-Semitic Policies

From its beginning, the Nazi Party reflected the strong anti-Semitic beliefs of Adolf Hitler. Once in power, the Nazis translated anti-Semitic ideas into anti-Semitic policies, including anti-Jewish boycotts and other measures.

In September 1935, the Nazis announced new racial laws at the annual party rally in Nuremberg. These **Nuremberg laws** defined who was considered a Jew—anyone with even one Jewish grandparent. They also excluded Jews from German citizenship, stripped Jews of their civil rights, and forbade marriages between Jews and German citizens. Jews could neither teach nor take part in the arts. Eventually, German Jews were also **required** to wear yellow Stars of David and to carry identification cards saying they were Jewish.

A more violent phase of anti-Jewish activity began on the night of November 9, 1938—***Kristallnacht***, or the "night of shattered glass." In a destructive rampage, Nazis burned synagogues and destroyed some 7,000 Jewish businesses. At least 100 Jews were killed. Thirty thousand Jewish males were rounded up and sent to concentration camps.

Kristallnacht led to further drastic steps. Jews were barred from all public transportation and all public buildings, including schools and hospitals. They were **prohibited** from owning, managing, or working in any retail store. The Jews were forced to clean up all the debris and damage due to *Kristallnacht*. Finally, under the direction of the SS, Jews were encouraged to "emigrate from Germany." The fortunate Jews were the ones who managed to escape from the country.

✓Reading Check **Summarizing** What steps did Hitler take to establish a Nazi totalitarian state in Germany?

SECTION 3 REVIEW

Vocabulary

1. **Explain** the significance of: Adolf Hitler, Munich, Nazi, Reichstag, Enabling Act, concentration camps, Aryan, Heinrich Himmler, Nuremberg, Nuremberg laws, require, *Kristallnacht*, prohibit.

Main Ideas

2. **Summarize** the steps that Hitler took to become the sole ruler of Germany.
3. **Describe** the policies and programs that the Nazis used to create a Third Reich. Using a table like the one below, identify the goals for each policy or program.

Policy/Program	Goals

4. **List** the rights that the Nazi government took from the Jews.

Critical Thinking

5. **The BIG Idea** **Determining Cause and Effect** How did mass demonstrations and meetings contribute to the success of the Nazi Party?
6. **Drawing Conclusions** Why were the methods used by Himmler's SS effective in furthering Nazi goals?
7. **Comparing** In what ways were the governments of Nazi Germany and Fascist Italy alike?
8. **Analyzing Visuals** Examine the poster on page 805. Why is East Prussia shown as being separated from the rest of Germany?

Writing About History

9. **Expository Writing** Find a library book by a German who lived under Nazism. Read about the author's life. Write a report about whether that person could have resisted the government and why or why not.

History ONLINE
For help with the concepts in this section of *Glencoe World History*, go to glencoe.com and click Study Central™.

809

C Critical Thinking

Making Inferences **Ask:** Do you think all German women agreed with the Nazi view of their role in society? Why? *(Answers will vary, but most students will answer that not all women would have agreed because they had different goals for their lives.)*

✓Reading Check

Answer: Hitler used mass demonstrations, control of the economy, terror and repression, and control of institutions.

Assess

History ONLINE

Study Central provides summaries, interactive games, and online graphic organizers to help students review content.

Close

Summarizing Have students write a summary of the conditions in Germany that allowed Hitler to rise to power, his goals, and the methods he used to accomplish those goals. OL

Answers

1. Definitions for the vocabulary words are found in the section and in the Glossary.
2. He increased the size of Nazi Party in the Reichstag; he was appointed chancellor; he had the Enabling Act passed.
3. **Policy/Program**—totalitarian state; Aryan racial state; **Goals**—control of citizens' lives; elimination of Jews, and domination of Germany and the world
4. They took the right to be a German citizen; to have civil rights; to marry German citizens; to teach or take part in the arts; to use public transportation and buildings; and to own, manage, or work in any retail store.
5. They evoked mass enthusiasm and excitement.
6. Students may say that the SS controlled minds with ideology and got rid of opponents and Jews.
7. Both made the state superior to the individual and used violent methods.
8. Germany and East Prussia were separated by Poland.
9. Students' answers will vary depending on the subject chosen but should be based on specific details and logical conclusions.

Predicting Consequences Review the instability of Europe after World War I. **Ask:** How could the causes and effects of this instability result in another world war? *(Accept reasonable responses. Encourage students to focus on how instability led to the rise of totalitarian and authoritarian regimes. In turn, these regimes sought to expand their power.)* To extend this activity, you may want to have students form small groups and use the Visual Summary and information from the chapter to list their predictions of the consequences of extremist regimes for Italy, the Soviet Union, Germany, and Spain. **OL**

Sequencing Information Have pairs of students use the Visual Summary and information from each section as well as other resources to create time lines for the period between the world wars. **BL**

CHAPTER 24 Visual Summary

STUDY TO GO You can study anywhere, anytime by downloading quizzes and flash cards to your PDA from glencoe.com.

The AFTERMATH OF WAR and Impact of GLOBAL DEPRESSION

- Many nations were unhappy with the peace settlement after World War I.
- The crash of the U.S. stock market triggered a worldwide financial crisis and a global depression.
- The Great Depression made people doubt democracy and look to authoritarian leaders for simple solutions to problems.

THE GREAT DEPRESSION

The Great Depression caused many to live in squalor, as shown in this picture of "Hoover Village" in Central Park, New York City, 1931.

MUSSOLINI'S BLACKSHIRTS MARCH THE STREETS OF ROME ON OCTOBER 28, 1922

Mussolini used the Blackshirts to enforce the policies of his totalitarian regime.

TOTALITARIAN AND AUTHORITARIAN Governments in Europe Take Power

- Some nations in Europe replaced democracy with totalitarian governments.
- Mussolini's Fascist regime in Italy controlled citizens with mass propaganda.
- In the Soviet Union, Stalin gained control of the Communist Party, arresting or killing those who opposed him.

The Rise of NAZI GERMANY

- Losses in World War I and economic devastation led to political struggles in Germany.
- Hitler's Nazi Party created a totalitarian state based on racism and German nationalism.
- The Nazis enforced their will through secret police and concentration camps.

NAZI PARTY USES ANTI-SEMITIC POLICIES

This anti-Semitic banner hung outside Nazi headquarters in Nuremberg in 1935. It reads: "By resisting the Jews, I fight for the Lord."

Hands-On Chapter Project
Step 5: Wrap-Up

Writing a Journal of the West Between the Wars

Step 5: Presenting the Journal Pairs will synthesize what they learned in Steps 1–4.

Directions: Write the Essential Question on the board. Then write the Big Ideas from the sections. Have pairs of students read portions of their completed journals to the class.

As part of their presentations, instruct pairs to connect the important ideas in the Essential Question and the Big Ideas to specific entries in their journals. Use the presentations to discuss the different ways in which the Big Ideas serve as guides. Monitor the discussion to ensure that all economic, political, and social issues are covered. Conclude by reminding students that they can use the information from their completed journals as a resource to prepare for the chapter assessment. **OL**

STANDARDIZED TEST PRACTICE

TEST-TAKING TIP

If you do not know the right answer to a question, use common sense to eliminate answer choices that do not make sense. Recall the context in which the topic was discussed in class or in the textbook. This may help you eliminate incorrect answer choices.

Reviewing Vocabulary

Directions: Choose the word or words that best complete the sentence.

1. The Nazis imprisoned Jewish people in ______.

A Reichstags
B concentration camps
C totalitarian states
D Politburos

2. ______ is the term for a period of low economic activity and rising unemployment.

A Collectivization
B Inflation
C Deficit spending
D Depression

3. A picture made of a combination of photographs is known as a ______.

A photomontage
B propaganda film
C mural
D collage

4. ______ glorifies the state above the individual.

A Racism
B Fascism
C Dadaism
D Surrealism

Reviewing Main Ideas

Directions: Choose the best answers to the following questions.

Section 1 *(pp. 790–795)*

5. Why was the League of Nations weak?

A It had too many members.
B It had too few members.
C The United States did not join it.
D The Nazis took control of it.

6. Which of the following was a factor in triggering the Great Depression?

A Economic downturns in individual nations
B Renewed interest in Marxism among Germans
C The policies of the New Deal
D The rise of the Nazis and Fascists

Section 2 *(pp. 796–803)*

7. Who led the Fascist movement in Italy?

A Adolf Hitler
B Leon Trotsky
C Francisco Franco
D Benito Mussolini

8. What Soviet economic plan allowed some capitalism, with the state controlling large industries?

A Fourteen Points
B Five-Year Plans
C New Economic Policy
D New Deal

Need Extra Help?

If You Missed Questions . . .	1	2	3	4	5	6	7	8
Go to Page . . .	806	792	814	797	790	792	797	799

GO ON

Answers and Analyses

Reviewing Vocabulary

1. B Both A and D can be eliminated easily. The Reichstag was the German Parliament, and Politburos refer to the executive committees of the Communist Party in the Soviet Union. Students may be tempted to select C because Germany under Hitler was a totalitarian country, but concentration camps were the specific locations where millions of Jewish people were imprisoned.

2. D None of the choices other than D are reasonable, though students may be confused by the inclusion of inflation, which results when too great a supply of money exists in relation to goods available for sale. Germany printed more money to stimulate a depressed economy, which only resulted in greater inflation and worsened the depression.

3. A For this question, A is correct. B and C are obviously wrong. Some students may be tempted to choose D. Remind them that a collage (as defined in the text) is a painting to which three-dimensional materials have been added.

4. B For this question, B is the only possible choice. Racism is discrimination based on a person's race; Dadaism and Surrealism are styles of art.

TEST-TAKING TIP

For Question 4: Remind students that if they do not know the answer to a question they should use common sense to eliminate answer choices. In this case, choices C and D are styles of art and not related to government (i.e., the state).

Reviewing Main Ideas

5. C For this question, C is the only possible choice. None of the other choices are mentioned in the text or supported by any other historical evidence.

6. A For this question, A is correct. Point out that all the other choices refer to events that occurred, or measures that were taken, because of the Depression.

7. D For this question, students should be able to easily eliminate all the choices except D. Hitler led the Fascists in Germany and Franco in Spain; Trotsky was a communist.

8. C For this question, choice C is correct. Choices A and D can be eliminated easily. Students may have narrowed their choices down to B and C. Remind students who selected B that it was Stalin who inaugurated Five-Year Plans and who strictly controlled the entire Soviet economy.

9. B For this question, B is correct. Students should be able to eliminate all of the other choices. Remind students who missed this question that the test occurred during the Spanish Civil War; both Hitler and Mussolini aided Franco's forces during that war.

10. A For this question, A is the only possible choice. C and D can be eliminated easily. Remind students who chose B that Hitler's goal was to rid Germany and the world of all people he considered to be non-Aryan.

TEST-TAKING 

For Question 10: The key words in the question for students to focus on are *group, Hitler,* and *dominate.* Although *socialists* is a reasonable choice, it is too general a term for the specific group that Hitler hoped would dominate the world—the Aryan race. That is, anyone could be a socialist, but only Aryans could be part of Hitler's "master race."

11. B For this question, B is correct. A and D are book titles. C is the name of the German republic that was formed at the end of World War I.

12. D For this question, C is obviously wrong. A and B, though they sound reasonable, are not mentioned in the text. Thus, D is the best possible choice.

13. C For this question, C is correct. Dali was a painter and Goebbels was Hitler's propaganda chief. Remind students who chose Hesse that he was the German author who wrote *Siddhartha* and *Steppenwolf.*

CHAPTER 24

9. In what country did Hitler test the new weaponry of Germany's air force?
- **A** France
- **B** Spain
- **C** Italy
- **D** Russia

Section 3 *(pp. 804–809)*

10. What group did Hitler claim would dominate Europe and the world?
- **A** Aryans
- **B** Socialists
- **C** Semites
- **D** Communists

11. What was the name of the Nazi attacks that destroyed some 7,000 Jewish businesses and burned synagogues?
- **A** *Nazionalnacht*
- **B** *Kristallnacht*
- **C** *Weimar*
- **D** *Mein Kampf*

Section 4 *(pp. 812–815)*

12. What was the Nazi "Strength through Joy" program?
- **A** A self-paced physical fitness program
- **B** A benefit for joining the SS
- **C** A use of religious experience to promote Nazi ideology
- **D** A variety of leisure activities for the working class

13. Who was the author of *Ulysses*?
- **A** Hermann Hesse
- **B** Salvador Dalí
- **C** James Joyce
- **D** Joseph Goebbels

Critical Thinking

Directions: Choose the best answers to the following questions.

Use the following map to answer question 14.

14. Based on the map, what territory did the Republicans control?
- **A** Several Mediterranean Sea ports
- **B** Several Pacific Ocean ports
- **C** A land route to Europe
- **D** Territory on the Atlantic coast

15. Which of the following is a true statement about industrialization in Stalinist Russia?
- **A** It emphasized consumer products over capital goods.
- **B** It was directed by the government.
- **C** It emphasized agricultural production over heavy industry.
- **D** It depended on technological innovations of the time.

Need Extra Help?							
If You Missed Questions . . .	9	10	11	12	13	14	15
Go to Page . . .	803	806	809	813	815	803	800

GO ON

Critical Thinking

14. A For this question, A is correct by default, or process of elimination. Students can eliminate all the other choices by careful study of the map and its legend.

15. B For this question, B is correct. Students should quickly eliminate A and C, as they are obviously wrong. D sounds reasonable but is not mentioned in the text.

16. What is one reason why the German people supported the Nazis?
    - **A** The Nazis promised peace in a time of turmoil.
    - **B** The Nazis emphasized personal happiness.
    - **C** The Nazis brought an end to the Depression.
    - **D** The Nazis preached acceptance and toleration.

17. Whose work influenced the literary technique known as "stream of consciousness"?
    - **A** Werner Heisenberg
    - **B** Albert Einstein
    - **C** Adolf Hitler
    - **D** Sigmund Freud

In the cartoon below, the character on the left is British prime minister Neville Chamberlain. The character on the right is Benito Mussolini. The caption says, "Would you oblige me with a match, please?" Base your answer to question 18 on the cartoon.

WOULD YOU OBLIGE ME WITH A MATCH PLEASE ?

—David Low, *London Evening Standard* (February 25, 1938)

18. What is the message of the cartoon?
    - **A** Chamberlain realizes that Mussolini is about to trick him.
    - **B** Chamberlain is a more generous person than Mussolini.
    - **C** Chamberlain is afraid to deny any request Mussolini makes.
    - **D** Chamberlain is unaware of the danger Mussolini poses.

Document-Based Questions

Directions: Analyze the document and answer the short answer questions that follow the document. Base your answers on the document and on your knowledge of world history.

The following passage comes from the writing of Adolf Hitler before he rose to power.

> *"The power which has always started the greatest religious and political avalanches in history rolling has from time immemorial been the magic power of the spoken word and that alone. The broad masses of the people can be moved only by the power of speech. All great movements are popular movements, volcanic eruptions of human passions and emotional sentiments, stirred either by the cruel goddess of distress or by the firebrand of the word hurled among the masses."*
>
> —Adolf Hitler, as quoted in *The Rise of the Nazis*, Charles Freeman, 1988

19. Consider Germany's economic condition following World War I. To what does Hitler refer when he says "the cruel goddess of distress"?
20. How did Hitler plan to create a movement?

Extended Response

21. The Great Depression threw the world into a downturn as inflation and unemployment rose. Imagine that you are living in 1928. Assume that you know everything that is going to occur because of the Great Depression and that you have the ability to move to any major country in the world. Where would you go and why? Would being part of a particular social class influence your decision?

History ONLINE
For additional test practice, use Self-Check Quizzes—Chapter 24 at glencoe.com.

Need Extra Help?						
If You Missed Questions . . .	16	17	18	19	20	21
Go to Page . . .	808	815	819	805	805	792

STOP

Document-Based Questions

19. Hitler is referring to unemployment, inflation, and the Great Depression.

20. Hitler planned to create a mass political movement by stirring popular passion through powerful speeches, using as a backdrop the economic problems currently facing Germany.

Extended Response

21. Answers will vary, but should be consistent with material presented in this chapter about the Great Depression and supported by logical arguments for the students' choice of country.

TEST-TAKING TIP

For Question 21: For extended response questions, remind students of the importance of budgeting their time to allow them a chance to revise and proofread their essays.

16. C For this question, C is the only possible choice. For all of the other choices, the opposite was true.

17. D For this question, students should be able to eliminate answer choices A, B, and C. Thus, as a result of process of elimination, students should be able to determine that D must be the correct answer.

18. D For this question, D is correct. Chamberlain's body language indicates he is unaware of the presence of the bomb. The other choices are either irrelevant to the content of the cartoon, or obviously wrong.

History ONLINE
Introduce students to chapter content and key terms by having them access the Chapter 24 Overview at glencoe.com.

Need Extra Help?
Have students refer to the pages listed if they miss any of the questions.

CHAPTER 25 Planning Guide

Key to Ability Levels	
BL Below Level	AL Above Level
OL On Level	ELL English Language Learners

Key to Teaching Resources	
Print Material	DVD
CD-ROM	Transparency

Levels				Resources	Chapter Opener	Section 1	Section 2	Section 3	Section 4	Chapter Assess
BL	OL	AL	ELL							
				FOCUS						
BL	OL	AL	ELL	Daily Focus Skills Transparencies		25-1	25-2	25-3	25-4	
				TEACH						
BL	OL	AL	ELL	Charting and Graphing Activity, URB		✓	✓	✓	✓	
		AL		World Literature Reading, URB			✓			
BL	OL		ELL	Reading Skills Activity, URB				p. 95		
	OL	AL		Historical Analysis Skills Activity, URB			p. 96			
BL	OL	AL	ELL	Differentiated Instruction Activity, URB				p. 97		
	OL		ELL	English Learner Activity, URB		p. 99				
BL	OL	AL	ELL	Content Vocabulary Activity, URB*		p. 101				
BL	OL	AL	ELL	Academic Vocabulary Activity, URB					p. 103	
BL	OL	AL	ELL	Skills Reinforcement Activity, URB					p. 105	
	OL	AL		Critical Thinking Skills Activity, URB					p. 106	
	OL	AL		History and Geography Activity, URB		p. 107				
	OL	AL	ELL	Mapping History Activity, URB				p. 109		
BL	OL	AL		Historical Significance Activity, URB				p. 110		
BL	OL	AL	ELL	Cooperative Learning Activity, URB					p. 111	
	OL	AL	ELL	History Simulation Activity, URB					p. 113	
BL	OL	AL	ELL	Time Line Activity, URB					p. 115	
	OL	AL		Linking Past and Present Activity, URB		p. 116				
BL	OL	AL		People in World History Activity, URB		p. 117	p. 118			
BL	OL	AL	ELL	Primary Source Reading, URB						
	OL	AL		Enrichment Activity, URB			p. 124			
BL	OL	AL	ELL	World Art and Music Activity, URB					p. 121	
BL	OL		ELL	Guided Reading Activities, URB*		p. 126	p. 127	p. 128	p. 129	
BL	OL		ELL	Reading Essentials and Note-Taking Guide*		p. 274	p. 277	p. 280	p. 283	
BL	OL	AL	ELL	Differentiated Instruction for the World History Classroom	✓	✓	✓	✓	✓	✓

Note: Please refer to the *Unit Resource Book: The Twentieth-Century Crisis* for this chapter's URB materials.

* Also available in Spanish

- Interactive Lesson Planner
- Interactive Teacher Edition
- Fully editable blackline masters
- Section Spotlight Videos Launch
- Differentiated Lesson Plans
- Printable reports of daily assignments
- Standards Tracking System

Levels				Resources		Chapter Opener	Section 1	Section 2	Section 3	Section 4	Chapter Assess
BL	OL	AL	ELL								
TEACH *(continued)*											
BL	OL	AL	ELL		**StudentWorks™ Plus DVD**	✓	✓	✓	✓	✓	✓
BL	OL	AL	ELL		**Vocabulary PuzzleMaker CD-ROM**	✓	✓	✓	✓	✓	✓
Teacher Resources					**Building Academic Vocabulary**	✓	✓	✓	✓	✓	✓
					Reading Strategies and Activities for the Social Studies Classroom			p 69			
					Writer's Guidebook			p. 47	p. 43	p. 27	
					Strategies for Success	✓	✓	✓	✓	✓	✓
					Outline Map Resource Book	✓	✓	✓	✓	✓	✓
					Presentation Plus! with MindJogger DVD	✓	✓	✓	✓	✓	✓
ASSESS											
BL	OL	AL	ELL		**Section Quizzes and Chapter Tests***		p. 309	p. 310	p. 311	p. 312	p. 313
BL	OL	AL	ELL		**Authentic Assessment With Rubrics**	✓	✓	✓	✓	✓	✓
BL	OL	AL	ELL		**Standardized Test Practice Workbook**	✓	✓	✓	✓	✓	✓
BL	OL	AL	ELL		***ExamView® Assessment Suite* CD-ROM**		25-1	25-2	25-3	25-4	Ch. 25
BL	OL	AL	ELL		**Interactive Tutor Self-Assessment CD-ROM**		25-1	25-2	25-3	25-4	
CLOSE											
BL			ELL		**Reteaching Activity, URB**					p. 123	
BL	OL		ELL		**Reading and Study Skills Foldables™**	✓	✓	✓	✓	✓	✓

Using the McGraw-Hill Learning Network

Researching World Book™ Select

Technology Product

World Book Select offers thousands of detailed articles chosen from the *World Book Encyclopedia* and covers all curricular areas. World Book Select allows students to research national and international topics and issues in economics and other curriculum areas.

Objectives

After students learn to use World Book Select, they will be able to

- develop and expand research and study skills;
- practice reading and writing skills.

Steps

Give students the following directions to use World Book Select:

- From the McGraw-Hill Learning Network home page (www.mhln.com), click on **For Students.**
- Choose **World Book Select** below **Homework Help.**
- Click the letter for the encyclopedia volume you want to use.
- On the search page for the volume selected:
  - click the title of a featured article on the right side of the page; or
  - click on a topic from the list on the left side of the page; then click on the title of an article of interest on the right.
- Read the article and take notes.

History ONLINE

	Student	Teacher	Parent
Beyond the Textbook	●	●	●
Chapter Overviews	●	●	●
Time Current Events	●		●
ePuzzles and Games	●		●
Concepts in Motion	●		●
Literature Connections		●	
Multi-Language Glossaries	●		●
Online Student Edition	●	●	●
Self-Check Quizzes	●		●
Student Web Activities	●		●
Study Central ™	●		●
Teaching Today		●	
Vocabulary eFlashcards	●		●
Web Activity Lesson Plans		●	

More About the Photo

Visual Literacy This remarkable photo shows President Lázaro Cárdenas disembarking at a Mexican railroad station. A group of peasants surrounds him. The composition of the photo draws the viewer's attention directly to Cárdenas. All of its elements, from the lines formed by the railroad cars to the gazes of the people, converge on the president, who in turn stares off into an undefined foreground. The peasants exhibit no excessive emotion; adults and children look calmly toward the leader, as if awaiting important instructions. Cárdenas looks ahead, as if his attention were solidly fixed upon a future goal. The photographer employed both content and composition to depict Cárdenas as a progressive champion of Mexico's poor workers.

1933 Franklin D. Roosevelt announces the Good Neighbor policy

1939 British limit number of Jewish immigrants to Palestine

1935 — 1940

1939 World War II begins

FOLDABLES Study Organizer

Drawing Conclusions As you read, use a Four-Door Book to take notes about the leaders of the nationalist movements. Draw conclusions about what each leader sought to accomplish and what each ultimately achieved.

History ONLINE Chapter Overview—Visit glencoe.com to preview Chapter 25.

Revolutionary Chaos in China

Ask: What was the result of internal conflicts within the nationalist movements in China? *(military conflicts stretching over many years, a divided and exhausted country)* Point out that in Section 3 students will learn about the conflicts between the Nationalists and the Communists in China. **OL**

Nationalism in Latin America

Ask: How did worldwide economic conditions affect Latin America? *(suffered during the Great Depression like other countries, resulted in many authoritarian governments)* Point out that in Section 4 students will learn about the growing U.S. influence in Latin American economies and the changes that took place in many Latin American nations. **OL**

FOLDABLES Study Organizer — Dinah Zike's Foldables

Dinah Zike's Foldables are three-dimensional, interactive graphic organizers that help students practice basic writing skills, review vocabulary terms, and identify main ideas. Instructions for creating and using Foldables can be found in the Appendix at the end of this book and in the *Dinah Zike's Reading and Study Skills Foldables* booklet.

History ONLINE

Introduce students to chapter content and key terms by having them access the Chapter 25 Overview at glencoe.com.

- **Timed Readings Plus in Social Studies** helps students increase their reading rate and fluency while maintaining comprehension. The 400-word passages are similar to those found on state and national assessments.
- **Reading in the Content Area: Social Studies** concentrates on six essential reading skills that help students better comprehend what they read. The book includes 75 high-interest nonfiction passages written at increasing levels of difficulty.
- **Reading Social Studies** includes strategic reading instruction and vocabulary support in Social Studies content for both ELLs and native speakers of English.

www.jamestowneducation.com

NATIONAL GEOGRAPHIC
Index to National Geographic Magazine:

The following articles relate to this chapter:

- "The Manchurian Mandate," by Brook Larmer, September 2006
- "The Rebirth of Armenia," by Frank Viviano, March 2004
- "Saudi Arabia," by Frank Viviano, October 2003
- "Istanbul on Edge," by Rick Gore, October 2002
- "Lines in the Sand: Deadly Times in the West Bank and Gaza," by Andrew Cockburn, October 2002
- "The Promise of Pakistan," by John McCarry, October 1997
- "India," by Geoffrey C. Ward, May 1997

National Geographic Society Products To order the following, call National Geographic at 1-800-368-2728:

- *National Geographic Atlas of the World*

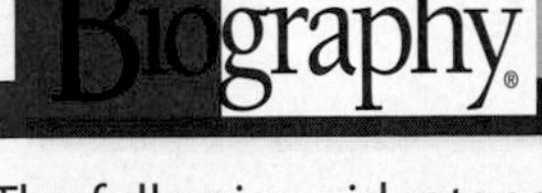

The following videotape program is available from Glencoe as a supplement to Chapter 25:

- Mahatma Gandhi: Pilgrim of Peace (ISBN 0-76-700668-2)

To order, call Glencoe at 1-800-334-7344. To find classroom resources to accompany many of these videos, check the following home pages:

A&E Television: www.aetv.com

The History Channel: www.historychannel.com

Use this database to search more than 30,000 titles to create a customized reading list for your students.

- Reading lists can be organized by students' reading level, author, genre, theme, or area of interest.
- The database provides Degrees of Reading Power™ (DRP) and Lexile™ readability scores for all selections.
- A brief summary of each selection is included.

Leveled reading suggestions for this chapter:

For students at a Grade 8 reading level:
- ***Ghandi: The Story of My Experiments with Truth,*** by Mohandas K. Gandhi

For students at a Grade 9 reading level:
- ***The Peaceable Revolution,*** by Betty Schechter

For students at a Grade 10 reading level:
- ***The Souls of Black Folk,*** by W.E.B. Du Bois

For students at a Grade 11 reading level:
- ***Heritage: Civilization and the Jews,*** by Abba Eban

For students at a Grade 12 reading level:
- ***The Israeli-Palestinian Conflict,*** by John Boaz

Focus

MAKING CONNECTIONS
How can nationalism affect a country?

Have students think about the role that their nationality plays in forming their own personal identity. Ask them to brainstorm situations, ranging from international sporting events to wars, in which their identity as an American becomes more prominent. Help them reach the conclusion that one's national identity tends to grow when the country competes with other nations or when it faces an external threat. Similarly, nationalism grows in countries facing foreign oppression or competing with other societies for resources and territory. Discuss how nationalism might lead to conflict and how it might bring both positive and negative consequences.

Teach

As students study the chapter, remind them to consider the section-based Big Ideas included in each section's Guide to Reading. The **Essential Questions** in the activities below tie in to the Big Ideas and help students think about and understand important chapter concepts. In addition, the Hands-On Chapter Project relates the content from each section to the Big Ideas. These activities build on each other and culminate in the wrap-up activity on the Visual Summary page.

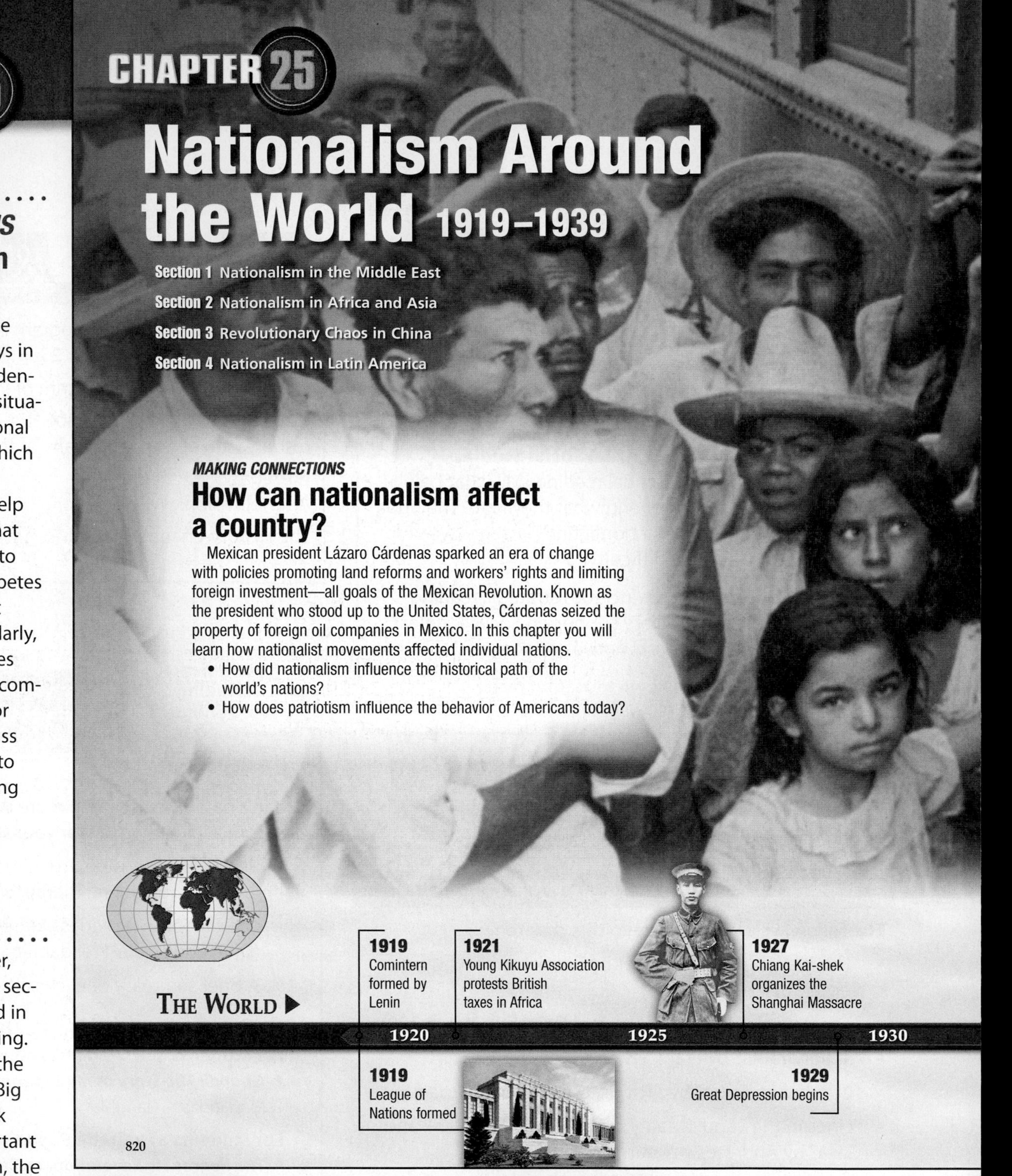

CHAPTER 25

Nationalism Around the World 1919–1939

MAKING CONNECTIONS
How can nationalism affect a country?

Mexican president Lázaro Cárdenas sparked an era of change with policies promoting land reforms and workers' rights and limiting foreign investment—all goals of the Mexican Revolution. Known as the president who stood up to the United States, Cárdenas seized the property of foreign oil companies in Mexico. In this chapter you will learn how nationalist movements affected individual nations.

- How did nationalism influence the historical path of the world's nations?
- How does patriotism influence the behavior of Americans today?

THE WORLD ▶

- **1919** Comintern formed by Lenin
- **1921** Young Kikuyu Association protests British taxes in Africa
- **1927** Chiang Kai-shek organizes the Shanghai Massacre
- 1920 — 1925 — 1930
- **1919** League of Nations formed
- **1929** Great Depression begins

820

Nationalism in the Middle East
Ask: How did World War I change the Middle East? *(Ottoman Empire ended, Britain and France governed new mandates)* Point out that in Section 1 students will learn how nationalist movements grew before the war and how the victors of World War I established new countries and areas of control. **OL**

Nationalism in Africa and Asia
Ask: How did many Africans react to colonial powers after World War I? *(After fighting for the colonial powers in World War I, they were disappointed in continued colonial control and organized resistance to it.)* Point out that in Section 2 students will learn about nations in Africa and Asia that opposed colonial control. **OL**

C Critical Thi
Comparing and Co
Ask students to contra of the Westernized mi with those of the Com *(Western values of indi achievement and accu wealth; Communist va or societal achievemer tribution of wealth)*

D Differenti Instructic
Interpersonal As students to create a that they think wou at school. Have stuc their lists with the c explain their reasor rule. **BL**

CRITICAL THIN

Answers:
1. rally the peop Communists, national pride and prepare t larger issues
2. Answers may idea that Cor would bring together wit national pric

Addi Su

Identifying class into smal represent eith of the urban Have each g and conduct stand the ro and in the

Focus

Introducing Social History
Ask: How would people feel if taxes paid by residents of one area were used primarily to benefit people in another part of the country? *(Students will probably say that resentment would grow.)* Have volunteers read the text to find out the effects of a similar situation in China in the 1930s.

Teach

R Reading Strategy
Inferring Ask: How would peasants most likely view the Nationalist government as a result of this tax measure? *(They would feel angry at the government's injustice and uncaring attitude towards them.)* **OL**

C Critical Thinking
Determining Cause and Effect Ask: What effects did Westernization have on the lifestyle of the urban Chinese? *(Westernization had an impact on everything, from how they dressed to how they did business. One of the major effects was the acceptance, by the Chinese, of Western capitalist values.)* **OL**

Additional Support

Social History

The Two Chinas of the 1930s

In the 1930s, four-fifths of the Chinese population lived in rural areas. To build a strong modern nation, Chiang Kai-shek and the Nationalist government sharply increased the peasants' taxes. Because the projects primarily benefited the urban areas of the country, society was divided into two distinct sectors.

As China modernized in the 1930s, many young rural Chinese people moved to the cities to find jobs.

China's cities grew drama the early twentieth centu population of Shanghai, for had grown from 500,000 in three million in the 192

Westernized fashions became popular with China's urban middle class.

URBAN CHINA

Western investments and technology helped stimul modern banking, and commerce in China's urban area changed, wealth-building capitalist values spread amo urban middle class. Increasingly Westernized, the resid grew further apart from the country's rural population

842

Background

Western Influence in China Beginning in the mid-1800s, China lost control of vast territories to foreign powers. In addition, most major cities had concession areas which were not subject to Chinese laws. Foreign nationals operated their own businesses, schools, hospitals, and other organizations. Although the Nationalists had reasserted Chinese sovereignty in several areas by the 1930s, Britain, France, Portugal, and the United States maintained their foreign presence and continued as a major source of Western influence. Technological and cultural influences were widespread in urban areas, but certain family traditions held on longer than others. According to a survey taken in the 1930s, thirds of marriages in urbar arranged. In one rural area ers out of 170 had even he of a "modern marriage," or which people freely choose partners.

Rural China

Though about half of China's farmers owned their own land, many peasants fell into debt. Bandits, natural disasters, and warfare added to the hardships facing them. Being forced to pay for projects that primarily benefited city dwellers created resentment among people in rural China. This discontent allowed the Chinese Communist Party to develop rural programs to win the support of the peasant masses. C

Analyzing Visuals

1. **Contrasting** How was life in urban China in the 1930s different from life in rural China at that time?
2. **Speculating** How could modernization programs focusing on rural areas have more effectively benefited Chinese peasants in the 1930s?

C Critical Thinking

Identifying Central Issues
Ask: Why did the Communist Party come to be associated with the peasants? *(The Communists developed programs to help the poor rural class.)* OL

Assess/Close

Organizing Have students outline the content of this feature. They should include major headings and supporting details. OL

Analyzing Visuals

Answers:
1. Urban China had modern transportation and communication as well as industries, banking, and commerce. Urban dwellers were exposed to western influences. Residents of rural China were largely untouched by modernization and struggled to make a living.
2. Answers may include improvements to the infrastructure, such as developing better transportation, communication, and housing. In addition, modernizing agriculture would also have directly benefited the rural population.

Activity: Technology Connection

Creating a Multimedia Time Line Ask: What two parties were trying to gain control of China in the 1930s? *(Nationalist and Communist)* Have students work in peer review teams to create multimedia presentations about the events in the 1930s and 1940s that eventually led to the ousting of the Nationalists and the takeover of China by the Communists. Have students use the Internet to find Web sites that contain facts and images that they might use to create and illustrate a multimedia time line of events. Remind students that as they develop their presentations they should consider what their audience already knows about the events. In addition, students should provide complete and accurate information from a variety of sources and include a bibliography. Finally, students' work should show that they have thought about the design and layout of their time lines to make their presentations vivid and interesting. At the end of each groups' presentation, have students outline the processes they used to develop their time line and presentation. OL

Nationalism in Latin America

Focus

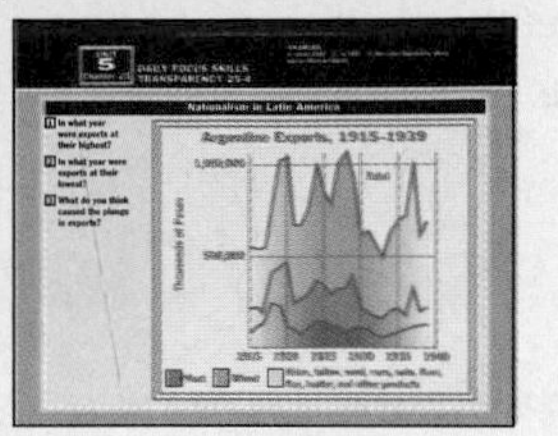

Bellringer
Daily Focus Transparency 25.4

GUIDE TO READING

Answers to Graphic:
Argentina: beef, wheat; Chile: nitrates, copper; **Brazil:** sugar; Peru: oil, copper

Section Spotlight Video

To generate student interest and provide a springboard for class discussion, access the Chapter 25, Section 4 video at glencoe.com or on the video DVD.

GUIDE TO READING

The BIG Idea
Order and Security In Latin America, the Great Depression made politics unstable, and in many cases, military dictatorships were the result.

Content Vocabulary
- oligarchy *(p. 847)*

Academic Vocabulary
- investor *(p. 844)*
- establish *(p. 847)*

People, Places, and Events
- Argentina *(p. 844)*
- Chile *(p. 844)*
- Brazil *(p. 844)*
- Peru *(p. 844)*
- Mexico *(p. 844)*
- Juan Vicente Gómez *(p. 845)*
- Good Neighbor policy *(p. 845)*
- Hipólito Irigoyen *(p. 847)*
- Getúlio Vargas *(p. 847)*
- Institutional Revolutionary Party (PRI) *(p. 847)*
- Lázaro Cárdenas *(p. 847)*
- PEMEX *(p. 848)*
- Diego Rivera *(p. 849)*

Reading Strategy
Summarizing Information As you read, make a chart like the one below listing the main exports of Latin America.

Country	Exports

During the 1920s, U.S. investors poured funds directly into Latin American businesses. The Great Depression devastated Latin America's economy and created instability. This turmoil led to the creation of military dictatorships and authoritarian states in Latin America in the 1930s.

The Latin American Economy

MAIN IDEA During the 1920s and 1930s, foreign investments and the Great Depression led some Latin American nations to emphasize domestic industry to balance the economy.

HISTORY & YOU Have you ever enjoyed a banana split? Most likely, the banana came from Latin America. Read to learn about Latin America's changing economic relationship with the United States.

At the beginning of the twentieth century, the Latin American economy was based largely on the export of foodstuffs and raw materials. Some countries relied on only one or two products for sale abroad. **Argentina,** for example, exported beef and wheat; **Chile,** nitrates and copper; **Brazil** and Caribbean nations, sugar; and Central America, bananas. A few reaped large profits from these exports. For most of the people, however, the returns were small.

Role of the United States

Beginning in the 1920s, the United States began to replace Great Britain as the major **investor** in Latin America. British investors had put money into stocks and other forms of investment that did not give them direct control of the companies. U.S. investors, however, put their funds directly into production facilities and actually ran the companies. In this way, large segments of Latin America's export industries fell into U.S. hands. A number of smaller Central American countries became independent republics. However, their economies often depended on wealthy nations. The U.S.-owned United Fruit Company, for example, owned land, packing plants, and railroads in Central America. American firms also gained control of the copper-mining industry in Chile and **Peru,** as well as of the oil industry in **Mexico,** Peru, and Bolivia.

Many Latin Americans resented U.S. control of Latin American industries. A growing nationalist awareness led many of them to view the United States as an imperialist power. It was not difficult for Latin American nationalists to show that profits from U.S. businesses were sometimes used to keep ruthless dictators in

Resource Manager

R Reading Strategies	C Critical Thinking	D Differentiated Instruction	W Writing Support	S Skill Practice
Teacher Edition • Visualizing, p. 845 • Act. Prior Know., p. 847 • Summarizing, p. 847 • Read. Pri. Sources, p. 849 **Additional Resources** • Academic Vocab. Act., URB p. 103 • Guid. Read. Act., URB p. 129 • Read. Ess. & Note-Taking Guide p. 283	**Teacher Edition** • Det. Cause/Effect, p. 846 • Ident. Cent. Issues, p. 848 **Additional Resources** • Critical Think. Act., URB p. 106 • Hist. Sim. Act., URB p. 113 • Section Quiz, p. 312 • Chapter Test, p. 313	**Teacher Edition** • Visual/Spatial, p. 847 **Additional Resources** • Coop. Learn. Act., URB p. 111 • World Art & Music Act., URB p. 121	**Teacher Edition** • Expository Writing, pp. 846, 848 **Additional Resources** • Writer's Guidebook, p. 27	**Teacher Edition** • Using Geo. Skills, p. 845 **Additional Resources** • Charting/Graphing Act., URB p. 3 • Skills Reinforc. Act., URB p. 105 • Time Line Act., URB p. 115 • Reteach. Act., URB p. 123

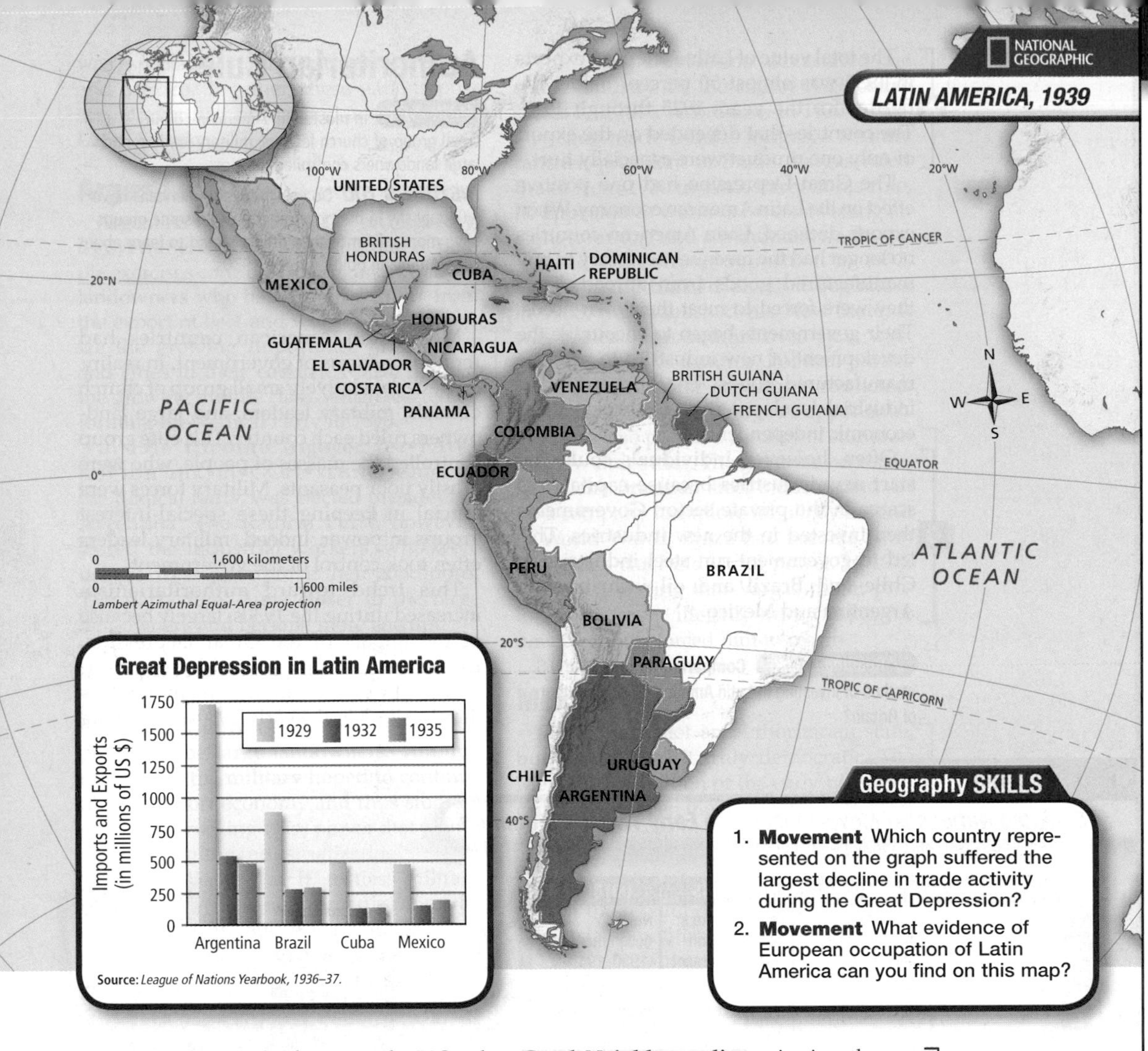

Geography SKILLS

1. **Movement** Which country represented on the graph suffered the largest decline in trade activity during the Great Depression?
2. **Movement** What evidence of European occupation of Latin America can you find on this map?

power. In Venezuela, for example, U.S. oil companies had close ties to the dictator **Juan Vicente Gómez.**

The United States had always cast a large shadow over Latin America. It had intervened militarily in Latin American affairs for years. This was especially true in Central America and the Caribbean. Many Americans considered both regions vital to U.S. security. **R**

The United States made some attempts to change its relationship with Latin America in the 1930s. In 1933 President Franklin D. Roosevelt announced the **Good Neighbor policy,** rejecting the use of U.S. military force in Latin America on principle. Adhering to his word, the president withdrew the last United States Marines from Haiti in 1934. For the first time in 30 years, there were no U.S. troops in Latin American countries. **S**

Impact of the Great Depression

The Great Depression was a disaster for Latin America's economy. Weak U.S. and European economies meant there was less demand for Latin American exports, especially coffee, sugar, metals, and meat.

Teach

R Reading Strategy

Visualizing Ask students to visualize the image of the United States casting a large shadow over Latin America. Ask students to draw a sketch or political cartoon that illustrates this image. **ELL**

S Skill Practice

Using Geography Skills

Ask: Which South American countries have no seaports? *(Bolivia and Paraguay)*

Geography SKILLS

Answers:

1. Argentina
2. Some countries bear the name of European countries (British Honduras, Dutch Guiana). Many countries have Spanish-language names (El Salvador, Colombia).

Hands-On Chapter Project Step 4

Writing an Article about a Nationalist Movement

Step 4: Completing the Article Students will write a final draft of the article they worked on in Sections 1, 2, and 3.

Directions: Write the Big Idea on the board. Tell students to think about how this idea relates to their article topic as they read the section. Students should consider peer reviewers' comments as they edit and revise the rough drafts of their articles. They should then prepare their final drafts, including visuals and a bibliography.

Summarizing: Have students write a fourth journal entry that responds to the section content and describes how it relates to their article topic. **OL**

(Chapter Project is continued in Visual Summary.)

W Writing Support

Expository Writing Have students write a news article about Cárdenas seizing control of the oil fields. Remind students to answer the questions *Who? What? Where? When? Why?* and *How?* **OL**

C Critical Thinking

Identifying Central Issues

Ask: Why did disputes with U.S. oil companies make Cárdenas popular? *(Cárdenas took a strong stand against the United States.)* **OL**

✓Reading Check

Answer: one party controlled the government and chose all candidates

DOCUMENT-BASED QUESTIONS

Answers:

1. workers, Marx
2. He portrays politicians, clergy, and the upper class negatively. Marx and the working class appear positively.

President Cárdenas also took a strong stand with the United States over oil. By 1900, Mexico was known to have enormous oil reserves, especially in the Gulf of Mexico. Over the next 30 years, oil companies from Britain and, in particular, the **W** United States, made large investments in Mexico and the oil industry there. After a dispute with the foreign-owned oil companies over workers' wages, the Cárdenas government seized control of the oil fields and the property of the foreign-owned oil companies.

C The U.S. oil companies were furious and asked President Franklin D. Roosevelt to intervene. He refused, reminding them of his promise in the Good Neighbor policy not to send U.S. troops into Latin America. Mexicans cheered Cárdenas as the president who had stood up to the United States.

Eventually, the Mexican government did pay the oil companies for their property. It then set up **PEMEX,** a national oil company, to run the oil industry. PEMEX did not do well at first, however, because exports fell. Still, for many, PEMEX was a symbol of Mexican independence.

✓Reading Check **Examining** How was the Mexican government democratic in form but not in practice?

HISTORY & ARTS PRIMARY SOURCE

The Political Art of Diego Rivera

A2 Karl Marx holds a page from *The Communist Manifesto* calling for the formation of a new society

B1-B2 Workers in various fields, in typical poses and actions

A2-B2-B3 In compartments under Marx: (a) capitalists around a ticker-tape machine; (b) Mexican president Calles with his evil advisers, a general and a priest; (c) members of the upper class and the clergy behaving decadently

C2-C3 Reading and teaching revolutionary texts

A3 Communist flag

A3-A4 Mexico City burns in class warfare

B3-B4 A worker agitates a crowd

B3 Government troops put down a strike (*huelga*)

C3 Government troops attack peasants

DOCUMENT-BASED QUESTIONS

In 1929 Diego Rivera began to paint murals in the National Palace in Mexico City. The murals portray the history of Mexico from pre-Columbian times to the future. The mural above is called *Mexico Today and Tomorrow.*

1. **Identifying** Who does Rivera portray favorably in the mural?
2. **Recognizing Bias** How does Rivera reveal his political biases in the mural?

Differentiated Instruction

World Art and Music Activity, URB p. 121

Identifying Central Issues

Objective: Identify central issues in Rivera's work.

Focus: Ask students what motivated Rivera's work.

Teach: Ask students to identify a conflict portrayed in the images and describe how it reflects national and international conflicts of the time.

Assess: Ask students to identify a recent conflict and suggest how it might be portrayed by Rivera.

Close: Ask students if they think art should focus on politics or social issues.

Differentiated Instruction Strategies

BL Read aloud the quotation by Zapata and ask students to explain the difference between exploiting land and exploiting people.

AL Ask students to compare Mexican peonage with U.S. sharecropping.

ELL Have students cite an example of public art and explain how it affects the viewer.

Culture in Latin America

MAIN IDEA Latin American artists adapted European modern art techniques to their own native roots.

HISTORY & YOU Think about the meaning of the word *abstract.* What would you expect "abstract art" to look like? Read to learn about abstract modern art in Latin America.

During the early twentieth century, European artistic and literary movements began to penetrate Latin America. In major cities, such as Buenos Aires in Argentina and São Paulo in Brazil, wealthy elites expressed interest in the work of modern artists.

Latin American artists went abroad and brought back modern techniques, which they often adapted to their own native roots. Modern artists, such as Roberto Matta from Chile and Carlos Merida from Guatemala, created abstract art, which did not closely resemble the way objects really appear. Gunther Gerzso, considered Mexico's most significant twentieth-century abstractionist, once said:

PRIMARY SOURCE

"Many people say I am an abstract painter. Actually, I think my paintings are very realistic. They are real because they express very accurately what I am all about, and in doing so they are to some degree about everybody else."

—Gunther Gerzso

R

Many artists and writers used their work to promote the emergence of a new national spirit. An example was the Mexican artist **Diego Rivera.** Rivera had studied in Europe, where he was especially influenced by fresco painting in Italy. After his return to Mexico, he developed a monumental style that filled wall after wall with murals. Rivera's wall paintings can be found in such diverse places as the Ministry of Education, the Chapel of the Agriculture School at Chapingo, and the Social Security Hospital. His works were aimed at the masses of people, many of whom could not read.

Rivera sought to create a national art that would portray Mexico's past, especially its Aztec legends, as well as Mexican festivals and folk customs. Rivera's work also carried a political and social message. Rivera did not want people to forget the Mexican Revolution, which had overthrown the large landowners and the foreign interests that supported them.

Rivera's work was often controversial. U.S. business tycoon Nelson Rockefeller hired Rivera to paint a mural on the wall of the RCA building at Rockefeller Center in New York City. Before Rivera finished, Rockefeller had the mural destroyed because it included a portrait of Soviet leader V. I. Lenin.

✓Reading Check **Examining** How did Diego Rivera use his artistic talent as a political tool?

SECTION 4 REVIEW

Vocabulary

1. **Explain** the significance of: Argentina, Chile, Brazil, investor, Peru, Mexico, Juan Vicente Gómez, Good Neighbor policy, oligarchy, Hipólito Irigoyen, establish, Getúlio Vargas, Institutional Revolutionary Party (PRI), Lázaro Cárdenas, PEMEX, Diego Rivera.

Main Ideas

2. **Explain** why most individuals could not start new businesses in Latin America.
3. **List** the political struggles in Argentina and Brazil during the first half of the twentieth century. Use a table like the one below to make your list.

Argentina	Brazil

4. **Describe** how Diego Rivera portrayed Mexico's native roots.

Critical Thinking

5. **The BIG Idea Determining Cause and Effect** Why did the Great Depression cause many Latin American countries to try to gain more independence from foreign economic dominance?
6. **Making Predictions** How might the Cárdenas government's dispute with foreign-owned oil companies affect future foreign investment in Mexico?
7. **Analyzing Visuals** Choose one of the details from the painting on page 848 and explain why Diego Rivera chose to include it in this mural.

Writing About History

8. **Descriptive Writing** Using outside sources, find examples of Diego Rivera's murals. In an essay, compare his paintings to the frescoes of medieval Italian painters like Giotto. How do Rivera's murals reflect Italian influence? How are they different?

History ONLINE
For help with the concepts in this section of *Glencoe World History,* go to glencoe.com and click Study Central™.

849

R Reading Strategy

Reading Primary Sources
Discuss the differences in abstract and representational art, showing examples or illustrating the differences with drawings on the board. Ask students to comment on the use of the word *realistic* in the quotation. **AL**

✓Reading Check
Answer: by reminding people of the revolution and the struggle against foreign interests

Assess

Study Central provides summaries, interactive games, and online graphic organizers to help students review content.

Close

Determining Cause and Effect
Ask: How did the Great Depression affect Latin American politics? *(It brought instability, which led to military and authoritarian governments.)*

Answers

1. Definitions for the vocabulary words are found in the section and the Glossary.
2. Capital was short in the private sector.
3. Argentina: oligarchy, military overthrew government, Perón seized power; Brazil: oligarchy, military coup placed Vargas in power, Vargas forced to resign by army
4. large murals portraying Aztec legends and Mexican festivals and folk customs
5. countries could no longer afford to import; resulted in the development of new industries
6. He seized the property of the foreign companies, which would likely reduce the flow of foreign investment.
7. Responses should mention Rivera's support of the working class against the wealthy and powerful.
8. Answers should be supported by specific examples and details.

9. A Knowledge of geography should help indicate the correct answer. Pakistan borders India, while the other sites are far from India.

10. D Students need to be very familiar with the content to identify Nanjing as the home of Chiang's new republic. The other cities have varying connections to the Chinese conflicts.

11. C All other answers are false—the Communists did not drive out the Nationalists, the alliance happened well before the Long March, and the Communists won the support of the peasants.

12. B The removal of troops was a significant step in changing relations with Latin American countries. U.S. investment continued, dictators took greater control, and there was no European aggression.

13. C A basic knowledge of economics indicates that countries which rely on a single product are at greater risk during bad economic times.

TEST-TAKING 

For Question 13: Point out that options A, B, and D all contain economic strengths. Students can infer that option C, which cites a weakness, best suits the context of economic harm.

9. Where did some Indian Muslims want to form a separate state in the 1930s?
- **A** Pakistan
- **B** Taiwan (Formosa)
- **C** Palestine
- **D** Liberia

Section 3 *(pp. 836–841)*

10. In what city did Chiang Kai-shek form a new Chinese republic?
- **A** Beijing
- **B** Shanghai
- **C** Tianjin
- **D** Nanjing

11. Which of the following was a result of the Long March?
- **A** The Communists surprised the Nationalists in Jiangxi and drove them out.
- **B** The Communists formed an alliance with the Chinese Nationalists.
- **C** The Communists chose Mao Zedong as their leader.
- **D** The Communists lost the support of the rural peasants.

Section 4 *(pp. 844–849)*

12. Which of the following was part of the Good Neighbor policy in 1934?
- **A** The last U.S. investors left Latin America.
- **B** The last U.S. troops were removed from Latin America.
- **C** U.S. troops removed several ruthless Latin American dictators.
- **D** U.S. troops protected Latin America against European aggression.

13. Which Latin American countries were most harmed by the Great Depression?
- **A** Countries that exported a wide variety of foodstuffs and raw materials
- **B** Countries that had a large manufacturing base
- **C** Countries that depended on the export of only one product
- **D** Countries that had large government-run industries

Critical Thinking

Directions: Choose the best answers to the following questions.

Use the following map to answer question 14.

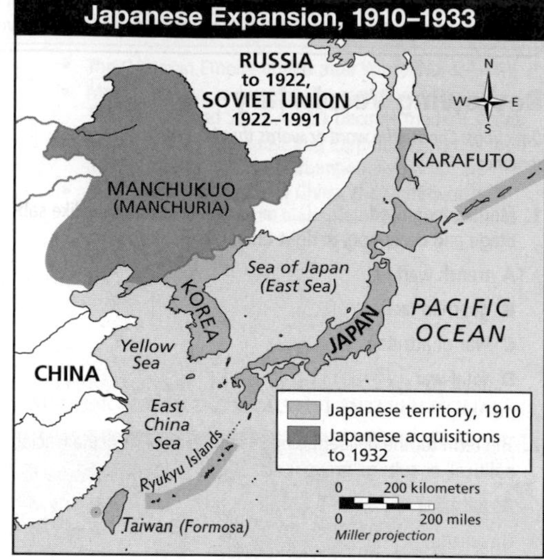

14. How did Japan's territory change between 1910 and 1933?
- **A** Japan acquired Manchuria in 1910, doubling its size.
- **B** Japan acquired Korea and Manchuria.
- **C** Japan gave up Manchuria, losing half its territory.
- **D** Japan acquired Manchuria by 1933, doubling its size.

15. Why did Chiang's land-reform program have little effect?
- **A** There was little unowned land to divide.
- **B** His council favored more land taxes.
- **C** His support came from the landed gentry.
- **D** He spent too much on building railways.

16. Why was Mexico not "truly democratic" in the 1930s?
- **A** There was a military dictatorship.
- **B** The authoritarian New State refused to hold elections.
- **C** There was a ruling oligarchy.
- **D** There was one dominant political party.

Need Extra Help?

If You Missed Questions . . .	9	10	11	12	13	14	15	16
Go to Page . . .	832	837	839	845	846	852	841	847

GO ON

Critical Thinking

14. D The legend indicates the correct years for acquisitions, and study of the map confirms Japan's doubling in size.

15. C Knowledge of land reform indicates that the gentry would oppose it. The other choices don't reflect the facts of the time.

16. D The other answers don't reflect the situation at the time. Mexico was not a dictatorship, and elections were held. The small group of political leaders who chose candidates might be considered an oligarchy, but they didn't actually rule the country.

17. Which of the following statements represents an effect of the *zaibatsu* economy on Japan?
   A Internal tension decreased, as economic success brought wealth to all social classes.
   B Militarism increased, as Japan needed to expand to find resources to fuel its industries.
   C Relations with other Asian nations improved, as trade among them increased.
   D Population decreased, as fewer children were needed to work on family farms.

Base your answer to question 18 on the cartoon below and your knowledge of world history.

John Bull hated to drop his bundle.

18. Which statement best expresses the cartoon's message?
   A England will use its economic power to save the Armenians.
   B England will not help the Armenians because it fears war with the Ottoman Turks.
   C England's vast economic power will not be enough to save the Armenians.
   D England will not give up its economic interests in the region to help the Armenians.

Document-Based Questions

Directions: Analyze the document and answer the short-answer questions that follow the document. Base your answers on the document and on your knowledge of world history.

In the fall of 1926, the young Communist Mao Zedong submitted a report to the Chinese Communist Party. In that report, Mao wrote:

> *"In a very short time, in China's Central, Southern, and Northern provinces, several hundred million peasants will rise like a mighty storm, like a hurricane, a force so swift and violent that no power, however great, will be able to hold it back. They will smash all the restraints that bind them and rush forward along the road to liberation. They will sweep all the imperialists, warlords, corrupt officials, local tyrants, and evil gentry into their graves. . . . In force and momentum the attack is tempestuous; those who bow before it survive and those who resist perish."*
>
> —Selected Works of Mao Tse-Tung, 1954

19. According to Mao Zedong, who would be the driving force in the Chinese revolution?
20. Why would this driving force in the revolution be so powerful?

Extended Response

21. Europeans created the Middle Eastern states of Iraq, Palestine, Jordan, Syria, and Lebanon from former Ottoman territories after World War I. The Europeans determined the borders and divided the peoples. Why might this national origin lead to future conflicts in the Middle East?

History ONLINE
For additional test practice, use Self-Check Quizzes—Chapter 25 at glencoe.com.

Need Extra Help?

If You Missed Questions . . .	17	18	19	20	21
Go to Page . . .	834	853	853	853	823

STOP

Document-Based Questions

19. Peasants—The key phrase is "peasants will rise like a mighty storm."

20. The Chinese peasants were numerous and were very oppressed by those in power. Knowledge of the chapter helps indicate that the Chinese peasants were oppressed while the phrase "several hundred, million peasants" indicates a large force.

Extended Response

21. Answers may include: the people in these states would lack a strong identification with their designated country; nationalist conflict could arise as people who share a common culture, religion, language, or ethnicity but live in different countries seek to unify, or as one group seeks to dominate another within a nation.

17. B Because Japan had traditionally obtained resources through conquest, *zaibatsu* leaders were more likely to favor policies that would help them gain precious resources, as well as food.

18. D The caption indicates the answer. England did not want to drop its "bundle," which indicates that it preferred to focus on economic gain rather than to help Armenians.

History ONLINE
Introduce students to chapter content and key terms by having them access the Chapter 25 Overview at glencoe.com.

Need Extra Help?
Have students refer to the pages listed if they miss any of the questions.

Key to Ability Levels	
BL Below Level	AL Above Level
OL On Level	ELL English Language Learners

Key to Teaching Resources	
Print Material	DVD
CD-ROM	Transparency

BL	OL	AL	ELL		Resources	Chapter Opener	Section 1	Section 2	Section 3	Section 4	Chapter Assess
					FOCUS						
BL	OL	AL	ELL	Transparency	**Daily Focus Skills Transparencies**		26-1	26-2	26-3	26-4	
					TEACH						
BL	OL		ELL	Print	**Reading Skills Activity, URB**		p. 133				
	OL	AL		Print	**Historical Analysis Skills Activity, URB**			p. 134			
BL	OL	AL	ELL	Print	**Differentiated Instruction Activity, URB**					p. 135	
	OL		ELL	Print	**English Learner Activity, URB**			p. 137			
BL	OL	AL	ELL	Print	**Content Vocabulary Activity, URB***		p. 139				
BL	OL	AL	ELL	Print	**Academic Vocabulary Activity, URB**				p. 141		
BL	OL	AL	ELL	Print	**Skills Reinforcement Activity, URB**					p. 143	
	OL	AL		Print	**Critical Thinking Skills Activity, URB**					p. 144	
	OL	AL		Print	**History and Geography Activity, URB**			p. 145			
	OL	AL	ELL	Print	**Mapping History Activity, URB**		p. 147				
BL	OL	AL		Print	**Historical Significance Activity, URB**				p. 148		
BL	OL	AL	ELL	Print	**Cooperative Learning Activity, URB**			p. 149			
	OL	AL	ELL	Print	**History Simulation Activity, URB**					p. 151	
BL	OL	AL	ELL	Print	**Time Line Activity, URB**			p. 153			
	OL	AL		Print	**Linking Past and Present Activity, URB**					p. 154	
BL	OL	AL		Print	**People in World History Activity, URB**		p. 155		p. 156		
BL	OL	AL	ELL	Print	**Primary Source Reading, URB**				p. 157		
	OL	AL		Print	**Enrichment Activity, URB**		p. 162				
BL	OL	AL	ELL	Print	**World Art and Music Activity, URB**					p. 159	
BL	OL		ELL	Print	**Guided Reading Activities, URB***		p. 164	p. 165	p. 166	p. 167	
BL	OL		ELL	Print	**Reading Essentials and Note-Taking Guide***		p. 286	p. 289	p. 292	p. 295	
BL	OL	AL	ELL	Print	**Differentiated Instruction for the World History Classroom**	✓	✓	✓	✓	✓	✓

Note: Please refer to the *Unit Resource Book: The Twentieth-Century Crisis* for this chapter's URB materials.

* Also available in Spanish

- Interactive Lesson Planner
- Interactive Teacher Edition
- Fully editable blackline masters
- Section Spotlight Videos Launch
- Differentiated Lesson Plans
- Printable reports of daily assignments
- Standards Tracking System

Levels BL	OL	AL	ELL	Resources	Chapter Opener	Section 1	Section 2	Section 3	Section 4	Chapter Assess
				TEACH *(continued)*						
BL	OL	AL	ELL	StudentWorks™ Plus DVD	✓	✓	✓	✓	✓	✓
BL	OL	AL	ELL	Vocabulary PuzzleMaker CD-ROM	✓	✓	✓	✓	✓	✓
Teacher Resources				Building Academic Vocabulary	✓	✓	✓	✓	✓	✓
				Reading Strategies and Activities for the Social Studies Classroom		p. 56		p. 53	p. 59	
				Writer's Guidebook		p. 47	p. 12	p. 43		
				Strategies for Success	✓	✓	✓	✓	✓	✓
				Outline Map Resource Book	✓	✓	✓	✓	✓	✓
				Presentation Plus! with MindJogger DVD	✓	✓	✓	✓	✓	✓
				ASSESS						
BL	OL	AL	ELL	Section Quizzes and Chapter Tests*		p. 321	p. 322	p. 323	p. 324	p. 325
BL	OL	AL	ELL	Authentic Assessment With Rubrics	✓	✓	✓	✓	✓	✓
BL	OL	AL	ELL	Standardized Test Practice Workbook	✓	✓	✓	✓	✓	✓
BL	OL	AL	ELL	*ExamView® Assessment Suite* CD-ROM		26-1	26-2	26-3	26-4	Ch. 26
BL	OL	AL	ELL	Interactive Tutor Self-Assessment CD-ROM		26-1	26-2	26-3	26-4	
				CLOSE						
BL			ELL	Reteaching Activity, URB				p. 161		
BL	OL		ELL	Reading and Study Skills Foldables™	✓	✓	✓	✓	✓	✓

Using the Glencoe Web Site

Chapter Overviews

Technology Product

The Glencoe Web site offers in-depth overviews that summarize the content of each chapter. The overviews consist of brief chapter summaries and separate overviews for each section. The chapter overviews

- summarize and reinforce chapter content;
- provide discussion points to use in class.

Objectives

The overviews help students

- prepare for better understanding chapter content;
- practice reading and comprehension skills.

Steps

Provide students with the following steps to complete the activities:

- Locate the Web page for the textbook being studied on the Glencoe Web site glencoe.com.
- Click on **Student Center** under the textbook title.
- Once you are in the Student Center, select a unit from the Unit Resources menu and a chapter from the Chapter Activities menu using the drop-down arrows.
- Click on the **Chapter Overviews** link.
- Have students read the chapter overview in preparation for a reading assignment or activity.

History ONLINE

	Student	Teacher	Parent
Beyond the Textbook	●	●	●
Chapter Overviews	●	●	●
Time Current Events	●		●
ePuzzles and Games	●		●
Concepts in Motion	●		●
Literature Connections		●	
Multi-Language Glossaries	●		●
Online Student Edition	●	●	●
Self-Check Quizzes	●		●
Student Web Activities	●		●
Study Central ™	●		●
Teaching Today		●	
Vocabulary eFlashcards	●		●
Web Activity Lesson Plans		●	

- **Timed Readings Plus in Social Studies** helps students increase their reading rate and fluency while maintaining comprehension. The 400-word passages are similar to those found on state and national assessments.
- **Reading in the Content Area: Social Studies** concentrates on six essential reading skills that help students better comprehend what they read. The book includes 75 high-interest nonfiction passages written at increasing levels of difficulty.
- **Reading Social Studies** includes strategic reading instruction and vocabulary support in Social Studies content for both ELLs and native speakers of English.

www.jamestowneducation.com

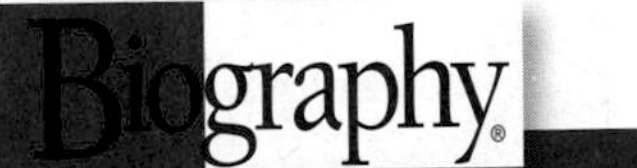

The following videotape programs are available from Glencoe as supplements to Chapter 26:

- **The Holocaust Untold Story** (ISBN 0-76-703992-0)
- **World War II: The War Chronicles** (ISBN 1-56-501484-7)
- **Churchill and the Cabinet War Room** (ISBN 1-56-501813-3)
- **Mussolini: Italy's Nightmare** (ISBN 1-56-501818-4)

To order, call Glencoe at 1-800-334-7344. To find classroom resources to accompany many of these videos, check the following home pages:

A&E Television: www.aetv.com

The History Channel: www.historychannel.com

Index to National Geographic Magazine:

The following articles relate to this chapter:

- "Living With the Bomb," by Richard Rhodes, August 2005
- "Weapons of Mass Destruction," by Lewis M. Simons, November 2002
- "Untold Stories of D-Day," by Thomas B. Allen, June 2002

National Geographic Society Products To order the following, call National Geographic at 1-800-368-2728:

- *National Geographic Atlas of the World* (Book).

Access National Geographic's new, dynamic MapMachine Web site and other geography resources at:
www.nationalgeographic.com
www.nationalgeographic.com/maps

GLENCOE BOOKLINK 3

Use this database to search more than 30,000 titles to create a customized reading list for your students.

- Reading lists can be organized by students' reading level, author, genre, theme, or area of interest.
- The database provides Degrees of Reading Power™ (DRP) and Lexile™ readability scores for all selections.
- A brief summary of each selection is included.

Leveled reading suggestions for this chapter:

For students at a Grade 8 reading level:
- ***The Story of D-Day: June 6, 1944,*** by Bruce Bliven

For students at a Grade 9 reading level:
- ***Winston Churchill,*** by James C. Humes

For students at a Grade 10 reading level:
- ***The Bombing of Pearl Harbor,*** by Earle Rice

For students at a Grade 11 reading level:
- ***Tell Them We Remember: The Story of the Holocaust,*** by Susan D. Bachrach

For students at a Grade 12 reading level:
- ***Embracing Defeat: Japan in the Wake of World War II,*** by John W. Dower

Focus

Bellringer
Daily Focus Transparency 26.1

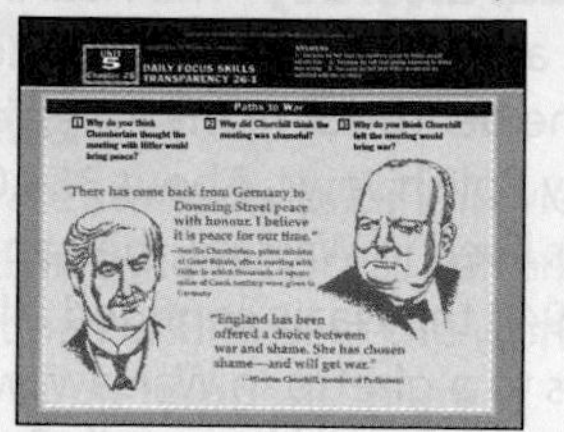

GUIDE TO READING

Answers to Graphic:
Japanese: seized Manchuria, invaded China, cooperated with Nazi Germany, launched surprise attack on United States; **German:** expanded armed forces, sent troops into Rhineland, annexed Austria, invaded Poland

Section Spotlight Video

To generate student interest and provide a springboard for class discussion, access the Chapter 26, Section 1 video at glencoe.com or on the video DVD.

SECTION 1

Paths to War

GUIDE TO READING

The BIG Idea
Competition Among Countries
The ambitions of Japan and Germany paved the way for the outbreak of World War II.

Content Vocabulary
- demilitarized *(p. 857)*
- sanctions *(p. 861)*
- appeasement *(p. 857)*

Academic Vocabulary
- dominate *(p. 856)*
- violation *(p. 856)*

People and Places
- Adolf Hitler *(p. 856)*
- Rhineland *(p. 857)*
- Benito Mussolini *(p. 857)*
- Sudetenland *(p. 858)*
- Joseph Stalin *(p. 858)*
- Manchukuo *(p. 860)*
- Chiang Kai-shek *(p. 860)*
- New Order *(p. 861)*

Reading Strategy
Categorizing Information As you read, create a chart like the one below listing examples of Japanese aggression and German aggression prior to the outbreak of World War II.

Japanese Aggression	German Aggression

In the 1930s, both Germany and Japan invaded neighboring countries in an attempt to gain resources and land for their empires. Hitler allied with Italy, annexed Austria, and invaded Czechoslovakia. Japan made a quick conquest of Manchuria. At first, other world powers tried to ignore these acts of aggression. They wanted to avoid war—yet the path to war was already paved.

The German Path to War

MAIN IDEA Adolf Hitler's theory of racial domination laid the foundation for aggressive expansion outside of Germany.

HISTORY & YOU Have you ever lost a friend? Read to find out how Czechoslovakia was abandoned by its Western allies.

World War II in Europe had its beginnings in the ideas of **Adolf Hitler.** He believed that Germans belonged to a so-called Aryan race that was superior to all other races and nationalities. Consequently, Hitler believed that Germany was capable of building a great civilization. To be a great power, however, Germany needed more land to support a larger population.

Already in the 1920s, Hitler had indicated that a Nazi regime would find this land to the east—in the Soviet Union. Germany therefore must prepare for war with the Soviet Union. Once the Soviet Union had been conquered, according to Hitler, its land would be resettled by German peasants. The Slavic peoples could be used as slave labor to build the Third Reich, an Aryan racial state that Hitler thought would **dominate** Europe for a thousand years.

Hitler Violates Treaty

After World War I, the Treaty of Versailles had limited Germany's military power. As chancellor, Hitler, posing as a man of peace, stressed that Germany wished to revise the unfair provisions of the treaty by peaceful means. Germany, he said, only wanted its rightful place among the European states.

On March 9, 1935, however, Hitler announced the creation of a new air force. One week later, he began a military draft that would expand Germany's army from 100,000 to 550,000 troops. These steps were in direct **violation** of the Treaty of Versailles.

France, Great Britain, and Italy condemned Germany's actions and warned against future aggressive steps. In the midst of the Great Depression, however, these nations were distracted by their own internal problems and did nothing further.

Resource Manager

R Reading Strategies	C Critical Thinking	D Differentiated Instruction	W Writing Support	S Skill Practice
Teacher Edition • Summarizing, p. 858 • Questioning, p. 859 **Additional Resources** • Cont. Vocab. Act., URB p. 139 • Guid. Read. Act., URB p. 164 • Read. Ess. & Note-Taking Guide, p. 286	**Teacher Edition** • Det. Cause/Effect, p. 858 • Compare/Contrast, p. 860 • Ident. Cent. Issues, p. 861 **Additional Resources** • Read. Skills Act., URB p. 133 • Section Quiz, p. 321	**Teacher Edition** • Visual/Spatial, p. 857 **Additional Resources** • People in World Hist. Act., URB p. 155 • Read. Strat. for SS., p. 56	**Teacher Edition** • Persuasive Writing, p. 858 **Additional Resources** • Writer's Guidebook, p. 47	**Teacher Edition** • Using Geo. Skills, pp. 857, 860 **Additional Resources** • Mapping Hist. Act., URB p. 147 • Enrich. Act., URB p. 162

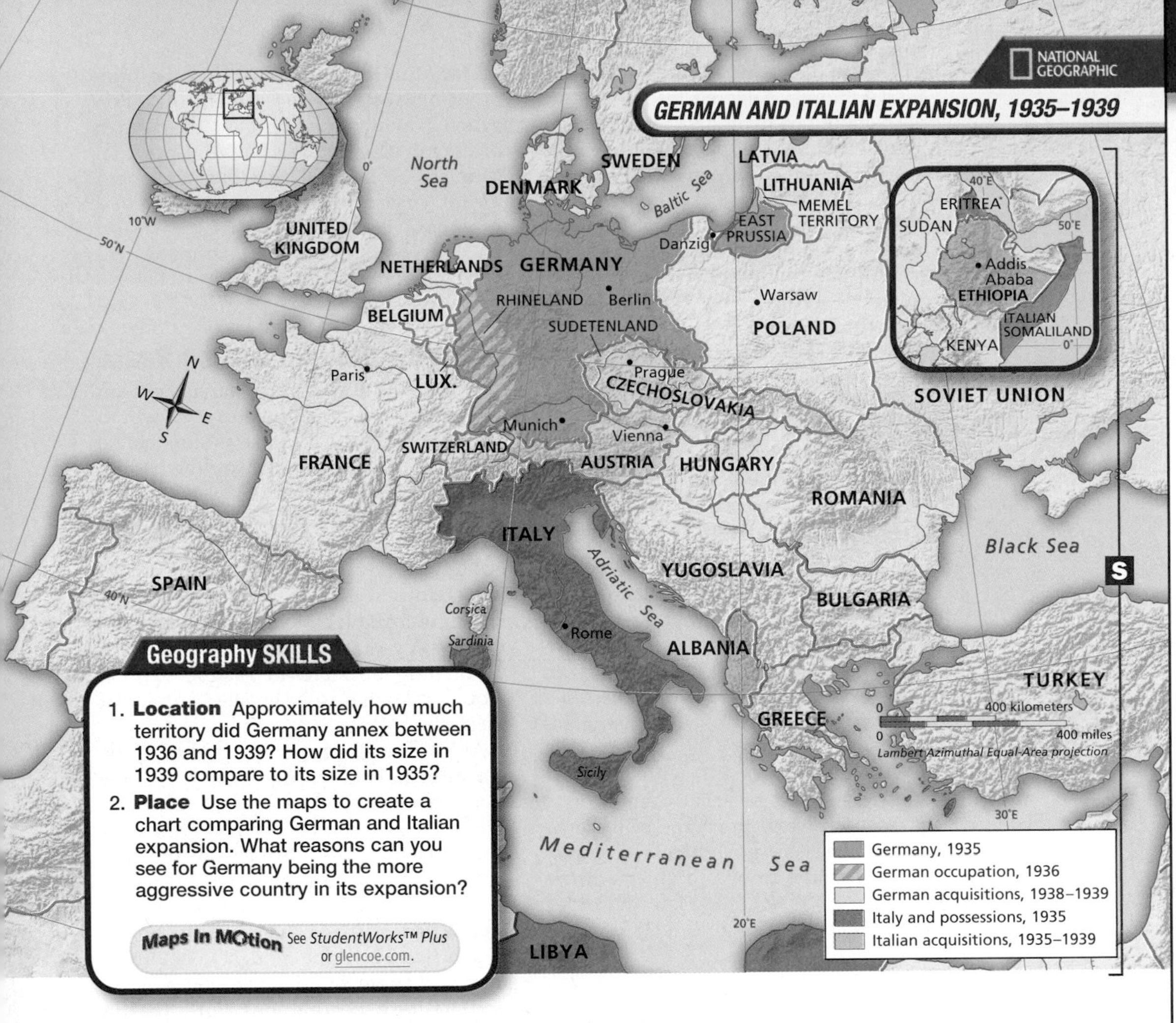

Geography SKILLS

1. **Location** Approximately how much territory did Germany annex between 1936 and 1939? How did its size in 1939 compare to its size in 1935?
2. **Place** Use the maps to create a chart comparing German and Italian expansion. What reasons can you see for Germany being the more aggressive country in its expansion?

Maps In MOtion See *StudentWorks™ Plus* or glencoe.com.

Hitler was convinced that the Western states had no intention of using force to maintain the Treaty of Versailles. Hence, on March 7, 1936, he sent German troops into the **Rhineland.** The Rhineland was part of Germany; but, according to the Treaty of Versailles, it was a **demilitarized** area. That is, Germany was not permitted to have weapons or fortifications there. France had the right to use force against any violation of this provision but would not act without British support.

Great Britain did not support the use of force against Germany, however. The British government viewed the occupation of German territory by German troops as a reasonable action by a dissatisfied power. The London *Times* noted that the Germans were only "going into their own back garden." **D** Great Britain thus began to practice a policy of **appeasement.** This policy was based on the belief that if European states satisfied the reasonable demands of dissatisfied powers, the dissatisfied powers would be content, and stability and peace would be achieved in Europe.

New Alliances

Meanwhile, Hitler gained new allies. **Benito Mussolini** of Italy had long dreamed of creating a new Roman Empire.

Teach

D Differentiated Instruction

Visual/Spatial Ask students to consider the phrase "going into their own back garden." **Ask:** Why was Germany prohibited from having troops in the Rhineland? *(The Treaty of Versailles prohibited it as a way of protecting European nations to the west.)* Ask students to draw or paint a picture or political cartoon that illustrates this view of German expansion. **OL**

S Skill Practice

Using Geography Skills Ask: In which direction did Germany expand in 1936? *(to the west)* In 1938–1939? *(to the south)* **BL**

Geography SKILLS

Answers:

1. approximately 35 percent of its current territory; about 35 percent larger
2. Germany wanted to repopulate the world with "Aryan" Germans and Italy had no such plans. Italy's geography made expansion more difficult.

Hands-On Chapter Project Step 1

Present a Radio Broadcast

Pairs of students will select an event from the section and prepare a one-minute radio report to read for the class.

Step 1: Broadcasting the Path to War

Essential Question: How did the events before and during World War II change the world and people's lives?

Directions: Discuss the importance of radio broadcasts at the time as a primary source of information and communication between leaders and people. Students can hear samples of actual broadcasts at http://www.umkc.edu/lib/spec-col/ww2/main.htm. Each pair will select an event of interest (such as annexation of Austria, Munich Conference, French and British threats of war, nonaggression pact, Japan's war with China, or other events); do research as necessary to establish exact dates, locations, and sequences; and prepare a one-minute broadcast. Select volunteers to read their broadcasts. **OL**

(Chapter Project is continued in Section 2.)

C Critical Thinking

Determining Cause and Effect **Ask:** How do you think Germany's new agreements and alliances affected Hitler's international plans? *(Hitler became convinced that neither France nor Britain would provide much opposition, possibly because Germany was again a world power with allies.)* OL

For additional practice on this skill, see the **Skills Handbook**.

R Reading Strategy

Summarizing Ask students to write a sentence that summarizes the information in the paragraph. *(Hitler threatened invasion of Austria and forced Nazi control, which resulted in annexation.)* BL

W Writing Support

Persuasive Writing Ask students to consider Hitler's aggressive acts and his statements of nonaggression. Then ask students to write a persuasive editorial that notes Hitler's broken promises and encourages European nations and the United States to stand up to Hitler with more forceful means. OL

In October 1935, Mussolini's forces invaded Ethiopia. Angered by French and British opposition to his invasion, Mussolini welcomed Hitler's support. He began to draw closer to the German dictator.

In 1936 both Germany and Italy sent troops to Spain to help General Francisco Franco in the Spanish Civil War. In October 1936, Mussolini and Hitler made an agreement recognizing their common political and economic interests. One month later, Mussolini spoke of the new alliance between Italy and Germany, called the Rome-Berlin Axis. Also in November, **C** Germany and Japan signed the Anti-Comintern Pact, promising a common front against communism.

Union with Austria

By 1937, Germany was once more a "world power," as Hitler proclaimed. He was convinced that neither France nor Great Britain would provide much opposition to his plans. In 1938 he decided to pursue one of his goals: *Anschluss* (AHN•shloos), or union, with Austria, his native land.

By threatening Austria with invasion, Hitler forced the Austrian chancellor to put Austrian Nazis in charge of the government. The new government promptly **R** invited German troops to enter Austria and "help" in maintaining law and order. One day later, on March 13, 1938, after his triumphal return to his native land, Hitler annexed Austria to Germany.

Demands and Appeasement

Hitler's next objective was the destruction of Czechoslovakia. On September 15, 1938, he demanded that Germany be given the **Sudetenland,** an area in northwestern Czechoslovakia that was inhabited largely by Germans. He expressed his willingness to risk "world war" to achieve his objective.

At a hastily arranged conference in Munich, British, French, German, and Italian representatives did not object to Hitler's plans but instead reached an agreement that met virtually all of Hitler's demands. German troops were allowed to occupy the Sudetenland. The Czechs, abandoned by their Western allies, stood by helplessly.

The Munich Conference was the high point of Western appeasement of Hitler. When Neville Chamberlain, the British prime minister, returned to England from Munich, he boasted that the agreement meant "peace for our time." Hitler had promised Chamberlain that he would make no more demands. Like many others, Chamberlain believed Hitler's promises.

Great Britain and France React

In fact, Hitler was more convinced than ever that the Western democracies would not fight. Increasingly, he was sure that he could not make a mistake, and he had by no means been satisfied at Munich.

In March 1939, Hitler invaded and took control of Bohemia and Moravia in western Czechoslovakia. In the eastern part of the country, Slovakia became a puppet state controlled by Nazi Germany. On the evening of March 15, 1939, Hitler triumphantly declared in Prague that he would be known as the greatest German of them all.

At last, the Western states reacted to the **W** Nazi threat. Hitler's aggression had made clear that his promises were worthless. When Hitler began to demand the Polish port of Danzig, Great Britain saw the danger and offered to protect Poland in the event of war. At the same time, both France and Britain realized that only the Soviet Union was powerful enough to help contain Nazi aggression. They began political and military negotiations with **Joseph Stalin,** the Soviet dictator.

Hitler and the Soviets

Meanwhile, Hitler continued to believe that the West would not fight over Poland. He now feared, however, that the West and the Soviet Union might make an alliance. Such an alliance could mean a two-front war for Germany. To prevent this possibility, Hitler made his own agreement with Stalin.

On August 23, 1939, Germany and the Soviet Union signed the Nazi-Soviet Nonaggression Pact. In it, the two nations promised not to attack each other. To get the nonaggression pact, Hitler offered

Additional Support

Teacher Tip

Collaborative Learning This activity allows students with different levels of academic skills and intelligences to work together. As you form groups, consider the skills needed and choose students accordingly.

Activity: Collaborative Learning

Identifying Points of View Divide the class into six groups: British, French, German, Italian, Czech, and the United States. Each group will review the section and do research to identify the hopes of each group before the Munich Conference. Each group will then summarize their situation and identify their hopes. Then announce the results of the conference and ask each group to provide a short summary of their thoughts and feelings after the conference. **Ask:** Why has the phrase "peace for our time" come to symbolize a short-sighted approach to foreign affairs? *(The peace lasted less than a year; the Czechs were abandoned by their allies.)* OL

Stalin control of eastern Poland and the Baltic states. Because he expected to fight the Soviet Union anyway, it did not matter to Hitler what he promised—he was accustomed to breaking promises.

Germany Invades Poland

Hitler shocked the world when he announced the nonaggression pact. The treaty gave Hitler the freedom to attack Poland. He told his generals, "Now Poland is in the position in which I wanted her. . . . I am only afraid that at the last moment some swine will submit to me a plan for mediation."

Hitler need not have worried. On September 1, German forces invaded Poland. Two days later, Britain and France declared war on Germany.

✓Reading Check **Identifying** Where did Hitler believe he could find more "living space" to expand Germany?

The Japanese Path to War

MAIN IDEA The need for natural resources fueled the Japanese plan to seize other countries.

HISTORY & YOU Do you think countries should go to war over natural resources? Read to learn what happened between Japan and China when Japan needed certain natural resources in the 1930s.

On the night of September 18, 1931, Japanese soldiers, disguised as Chinese, blew up a small section of the Manchurian Railway near the city of Mukden. Japan owned this area, and the Japanese soldiers wanted to blame the "Mukden incident" on the Chinese. The Japanese army used this incident to justify its taking all of Manchuria in a series of rapid military advances. **R**

Most Japanese were delighted about the apparently easy conquest of Manchuria. This was not surprising since Manchuria was far larger than Japan itself and had a population of 30 million Chinese.

R Reading Strategy

Questioning **Ask:** Why do you think the Japanese used deception to justify their military takeover of Manchuria? *(Other countries would not accept Japan's military expansion in Manchuria without a reason; a simulated attack by the Chinese gave them an excuse.)* **OL**

✓Reading Check

Answer: Hitler expected to find room for expansion by invading other nations such as Poland.

PRIMARY SOURCE **POLITICAL CARTOONS**

The Nazi-Soviet Nonaggression Pact

For years, Great Britain and France had been attempting to make an alliance with the Soviet Union against Nazi Germany. Yet in August 1939, Hitler shocked the Western powers by making his own agreement with Stalin.

The Nazi-Soviet Nonaggression Pact was one of the last steps leading to World War II. By secretly agreeing to split eastern Europe with the Soviets, Hitler knew that he would not have to fight the Soviets when war began. He invaded Poland about a week after signing the Nonaggression Pact.

Despite the pact, Hitler did not intend to keep his promises to Stalin. The Nazi-Soviet alliance would last only until 1941, when Hitler invaded the Soviet Union.

CRITICAL THINKING SKILLS

This American cartoon satirizing the Nazi-Soviet Nonaggression Pact was published the day before Hitler invaded the Soviet Union—June 22, 1941.

1. **Determining Cause and Effect** How did the Nazi-Soviet Nonaggression Pact help lead to World War II?
2. **Interpreting** How did world reaction to the pact change between 1939 and 1941?

CRITICAL THINKING SKILLS

Answers:

1. Hitler knew he could invade Poland without fighting the Soviets. Great Britain and France declared war shortly after the invasion.
2. In 1939, Great Britain and France felt the pact was a serious threat. By 1941, people did not expect Hitler to remain faithful to the agreement.

Differentiated Instruction

People in World History Activity, URB p. 155

Drawing Conclusions

Objective: Draw conclusions about Joseph Stalin.

Focus: Note details about Stalin's reign.

Teach: Have students provide examples of "mass repressions and lawlessness."

Assess: Ask students to summarize why Stalin was "feared and hated around the world."

Close: Discuss what a "de-Stalinization" program might involve.

Differentiated Instruction Strategies

BL Ask students to suggest reasons why Stalin remained in power for so long.

AL Have students research the "gulag" and prepare a report describing its use under Stalin.

ELL Have students record events from the selection on a time line.

C Critical Thinking

Comparing and Contrasting

Ask students to write a paragraph that compares the actions of Germany and Japan during the years before World War II and the reactions of the Europeans, Chinese, and U.S. toward them. **OL**

For additional practice on this skill, see the **Skills Handbook**.

S Skill Practice

Using Geography Skills Ask: Which Japanese acquisition is located farthest to the south? *(French Indochina)*

Geography SKILLS

Answers:

1. Japan's main acquisitions included parts of China and French Indochina.
2. Japan needed the natural resources that these territories could provide.

The country also offered many resources the Japanese needed. After this conquest, the Japanese army became committed to an expansionist policy.

By September 1932, the Japanese army had formed Manchuria into a separate state and renamed it **Manchukuo.** They placed a puppet ruler, Henry Pu Yi, on the throne. As an infant, Henry Pu Yi had been China's "last emperor." He had abdicated that throne, however, following the revolution of 1911 in China.

Worldwide protests against the Japanese seizure of Manchuria led the League of Nations to send in investigators. When the investigators issued a report condemning the seizure, Japan withdrew from the League. The United States refused to recognize the Japanese takeover of Manchuria but was unwilling to threaten force.

Over the next several years, Japan continued its expansion and established control over the eastern part of Inner Mongolia and areas in north China around Beijing. Neither the emperor nor government leaders could control the army. In fact, it was the army that established Japanese foreign policy. The military held the upper hand. By the mid-1930s, militants connected to the government and the armed forces had gained control of Japanese politics.

War with China

C **Chiang Kai-shek** tried to avoid a conflict with Japan so that he could deal with what he considered the greater threat from the Communists. When clashes between Chinese and Japanese troops broke out, he sought to appease Japan by allowing it to govern areas in north China.

As Japan moved steadily southward, protests against Japanese aggression grew stronger in Chinese cities. In December 1936, Chiang ended his military efforts against the Communists and formed a new united front against the Japanese. In July 1937, Chinese and Japanese forces clashed south of Beijing and hostilities spread.

JAPANESE EXPANSION, 1933–1941

SOVIET UNION
Sea of Okhotsk
Sakhalin (Karafuto)
Kuril Is.
MANCHUKUO (MANCHURIA)
Sea of Japan (East Sea)
JAPAN
Tokyo
KOREA
Beijing
CHINA
40°N
20°N
Ryukyu Is.
Taiwan
Hong Kong Br.
South China Sea
Philippine Sea
PHILIPPINES U.S.
FRENCH INDOCHINA Fr.
Mariana Is.
Caroline Is.
Marshall Is.
Gilbert Is.
TROPIC OF CANCER
Wake Island
Midway Is.
Pearl Harbor
HAWAII U.S.
PACIFIC OCEAN
EQUATOR
160°E
180°
160°W
Japanese territory, 1933
Japanese acquisitions through December 1941
0 1,000 kilometers
0 1,000 miles
Miller Cylindrical projection

Geography SKILLS

1. **Location** What territories did Japan acquire between 1933 and December 1941?
2. **Human-Environment Interaction** Why did Japan have the desire to expand its borders?

Maps In MOtion See StudentWorks™ Plus or glencoe.com.

Differentiated Instruction

Leveled Activities

BL Guided Reading Activity, URB p. 164

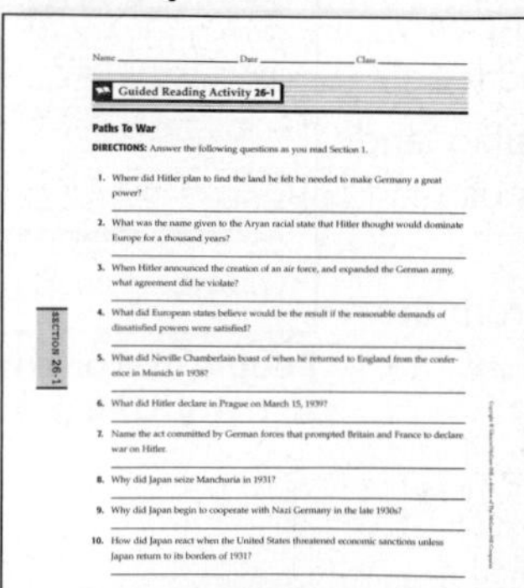

OL Mapping History Activity, URB p. 147

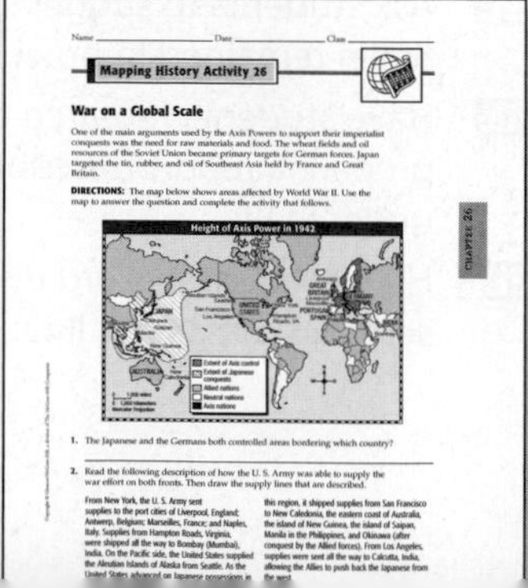

AL Content Vocabulary Activity, URB p. 139

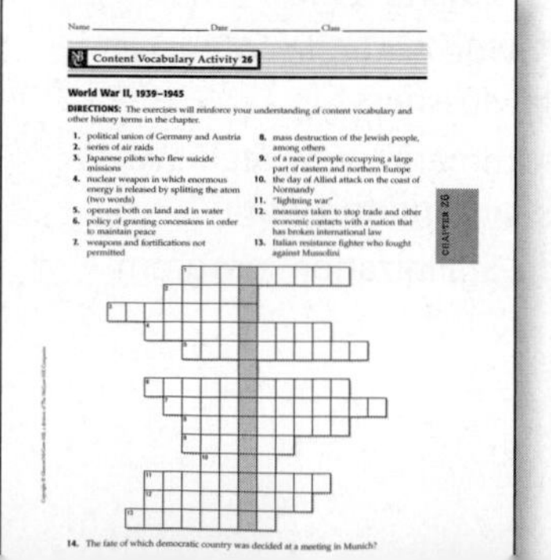

ELL Reading Skills Activity, URB p. 133

Japan had not planned to declare war on China. However, the 1937 incident eventually turned into a major conflict. The Japanese seized the Chinese capital of Nanjing in December. Chiang Kai-shek refused to surrender and moved his government upriver, first to Hankou, then to Chongqing. As the Japanese pushed onward, Chinese civilians experienced extreme brutality and aerial bombing. Although defeated, the Chinese resisted the Japanese for the entire course of the Second Sino-Japanese War.

The New Asian Order

Japanese military leaders had hoped to force Chiang to agree to join a **New Order** in East Asia, comprising Japan, Manchuria, and China. Japan would attempt to establish a new system of control in Asia with Japan guiding its Asian neighbors to prosperity. After all, who could better teach Asian societies how to modernize than the one Asian country that had already done it?

Part of Japan's plan was to seize Soviet Siberia, with its rich resources. During the late 1930s, Japan began to cooperate with Nazi Germany. Japan assumed that the two countries would ultimately launch a joint attack on the Soviet Union and divide Soviet resources between them.

When Germany signed the nonaggression pact with the Soviets in August 1939, Japanese leaders had to rethink their goals. Japan did not have the resources to defeat the Soviet Union without help. Thus, the Japanese became interested in the raw materials that could be found in Southeast Asia to fuel its military machine.

Japan Launches Attack

C

A move southward, however, would risk war with the European colonial powers and the United States. Japan's attack on China in the summer of 1937 had already aroused strong criticism, especially in the United States. Nevertheless, in the summer of 1940, Japan demanded the right to exploit economic resources in French Indochina.

The United States objected. It warned Japan that it would apply economic **sanctions**—restrictions intended to enforce international law—unless Japan withdrew from the area and returned to its borders of 1931. Japan badly needed the oil and scrap iron it was getting from the United States. Should these resources be cut off, Japan would have to find them elsewhere. Japan viewed the possibility of sanctions as a threat to its long-term objectives.

Japan was now caught in a dilemma. To guarantee access to raw materials in Southeast Asia, Japan had to risk losing raw materials from the United States. After much debate, Japan decided to launch a surprise attack on U.S. and European colonies in Southeast Asia.

✓Reading Check **Explaining** Why did Japan want to establish a New Order in East Asia?

SECTION 1 REVIEW

Vocabulary

1. **Explain** the significance of: Adolf Hitler, dominate, violation, Rhineland, demilitarized, appeasement, Benito Mussolini, Sudetenland, Joseph Stalin, Manchukuo, Chiang Kai-shek, New Order, sanctions.

Main Ideas

2. **List** the reasons why Hitler's pact with Stalin caused Britain and France to declare war on Germany.
3. **Summarize,** by using a chart like the one below, the agreements in chronological order that encouraged Hitler's aggressive policies.

Agreements Encouraging Hitler's Aggressive Policies

4. **Explain** why Japan felt the need to control other nations.

Critical Thinking

5. **The BIG Idea** **Determining Cause and Effect** How did the ambitions of Germany and Japan lead to war?
6. **Comparing** Compare Hitler's annexation of Austria and occupation of the Sudetenland to Japan's plans for a New Order in East Asia.
7. **Analyzing Visuals** Examine the political cartoon on page 859. Why did the cartoonist depict Hitler and Stalin as husband and wife?

Writing About History

8. **Persuasive Writing** Imagine you are the editor of a British newspaper in 1938. Write an editorial that expresses your viewpoint on how war can be avoided.

History ONLINE
For help with the concepts in this section of *Glencoe World History*, go to glencoe.com and click Study Central™.

C Critical Thinking

Identifying Central Issues
Ask: What was a key motivation for Japan's plans to expand into the Soviet Union, China, and French Indochina? *(the need for natural resources to support its expanding economy and the military)* OL

✓Reading Check
Answer: Japan wanted to control Asia and teach other Asian societies how to modernize.

Assess

History ONLINE
Study Central provides summaries, interactive games, and online graphic organizers to help students review content.

Close

Making Generalizations
Ask: What were the results of attempts to appease Germany and Japan? *(They were ineffective; both Germany and Japan interpreted appeasement as a sign of weakness and were essentially encouraged in their attempts at dominance.)* OL

Answers

1. Definitions for the vocabulary words are found in the section and the Glossary.
2. Britain offered to protect Poland; the pact between Stalin and Hitler gave Hitler the freedom to invade Poland.
3. agreement with Mussolini, 1936; Anti-Comintern Pact with Japan, 1936; Munich Conference, 1938; nonaggression pact with Soviet Union, 1939
4. Japan depended on foreign sources for raw materials but risked losing them from the United States if it expanded on the Asian mainland.
5. **Germany:** wanted more land for a larger population; its military actions led to war. **Japan:** wanted natural resources; its military actions led the U.S. to threaten sanctions before Japan launched a surprise attack on it.
6. Both wanted more land for the resources to expand their empires, and both took aggressive actions to get it.
7. to make the point that Hitler was not likely to keep his promises to Stalin
8. Students' editorials should reflect their grasp of the material.

R Reading Strategy

Visualizing Point out the description of Italy as the "soft underbelly" of Europe. Ask students to suggest possible sources for the term and why it might be an apt description for Italy at the time. **ELL**

D Differentiated Instruction

Advanced Learners Note that D-Day is considered "history's greatest naval invasion." Have students research other naval invasions, including the last successful invasion of England, and prepare a chart that describes the location, invaders, size, eventual result, and interesting facts about each invasion. Ask volunteers to share their work with the class. **AL**

DOCUMENT-BASED QUESTIONS

Answers:

1. United States, Great Britain, Canada
2. German troops that would otherwise have been available to defend the Western Front were tied up fighting the Soviets. This likely contributed to the success of the Allied invasion.

Additional Support

Last Years of the War

MAIN IDEA Allied victories forced Germany and Japan to surrender unconditionally.

HISTORY & YOU Do the ends justify the means? Read about the decision to use the atomic bomb.

By the beginning of 1943, the tide of battle had turned against Germany, Italy, and Japan. Axis forces in Tunisia surrendered on May 13, 1943. The Allies then crossed the Mediterranean and carried the war to Italy, an area that **Winston Churchill** had **R** called the "soft underbelly" of Europe. After taking Sicily, Allied troops began an invasion of mainland Italy in September.

The European Theater

After Sicily fell, King Victor Emmanuel II of Italy arrested Mussolini, but in a daring raid, the Germans liberated him. He was then made the head of a German puppet state in northern Italy as German troops moved in and occupied much of Italy.

The Germans set up defense lines in the hills south of Rome. The Allies advanced up the peninsula with heavy casualties, but they took Rome on June 4, 1944. By then, the Italian war was secondary as the Allied forces opened their long-awaited "second front" in western Europe.

Since the autumn of 1943, the Allies had planned an invasion of France from Great Britain, across the English Channel. Finally, on June 6, 1944 (D-Day), Allied **D** forces under U.S. general Dwight D. Eisenhower landed on the **Normandy** beaches in history's greatest naval invasion. The Allies fought their way past hidden underwater mines, treacherous barbed wire, and horrible machine gun fire. Believing the battle was a diversion and the real invasion would occur elsewhere, the Germans responded slowly. This gave the Allied forces time to set up a beachhead. Within three months, the Allies had landed two million men and 500,000 vehicles. Allied forces then began pushing inland and broke through German defensive lines.

INFOGRAPHICS — PRIMARY SOURCE

D-Day: June 6, 1944

The D-Day invasion took place on five beaches along fifty miles of Normandy coast. More than 1,000 transports dropped paratroopers, while amphibious craft landed some 130,000 American, British, and Canadian troops on the code-named beaches (see map below). The combined D-Day invasion succeeded not only because of its sheer size, but because of great timing—the Allies attacked while many German forces were fighting the Soviets on the Eastern Front.

Amphibious ships

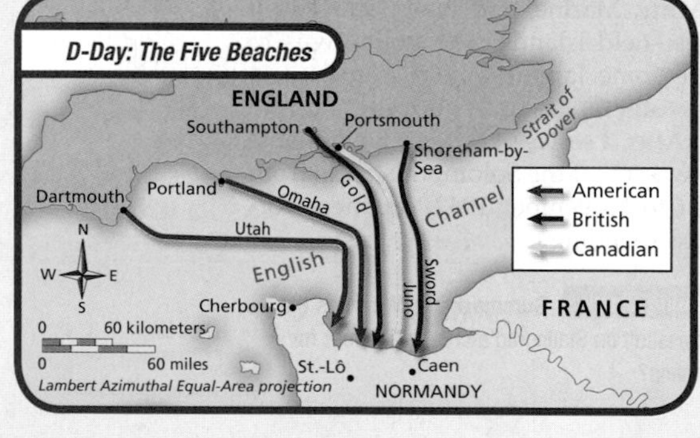

DOCUMENT-BASED QUESTIONS

1. **Identifying** What nations took part in the D-Day invasion?
2. **Making Inferences** How did the fact that the Germans were also fighting the Soviets affect the outcome of D-Day?

Extending the Content

D-Day When planning a future mission for which an exact date cannot be established because of weather and other factors, the time of the attack is referred to as "D-Day" and "H-Hour." Hitler expected an attack of some type, but the Allies used deception to direct Germany's attention farther to the east. They created a "phantom army" across from a narrower spot in the English Channel, supposedly commanded by General George S. Patton, who would actually be involved in Normandy. They also created a phantom force that would appear on German radar as if it were crossing the Channel on the night of the Normandy invasion. Hitler responded too late to the real invasion; 850,000 Allied troops and 150,000 vehicles poured in by the end of June.

Allied troops liberated Paris by the end of August. In March 1945, they crossed the Rhine River and advanced into Germany. At the end of April 1945, Allied armies in northern Germany moved toward the Elbe River, where they linked up with the Soviets.

The Soviets had come a long way since the Battle of Stalingrad in 1943. The Soviets had soundly defeated the German forces at the Battle of Kursk (July 5 to 12), the greatest tank battle of World War II. Soviet forces now began a steady advance westward. Reoccupying the Ukraine by the end of 1943, they moved into the Baltic states by early 1944. Advancing along a northern front, Soviet troops occupied Warsaw in January 1945 and entered Berlin in April. Meanwhile, Soviet troops along a southern front swept through Hungary, Romania, and Bulgaria. **R**

By January 1945, Adolf Hitler had moved into a bunker 55 feet (almost 17 m) under the city of Berlin. In his final political testament, Hitler, consistent to the end in his anti-Semitism, blamed the Jews for the war. He wrote, "Above all I charge the leaders of the nation and those under them to scrupulous observance of the laws of race and to merciless opposition to the universal poisoner of all peoples, international Jewry."

Hitler committed suicide on April 30, two days after Italian **partisans,** or resistance fighters, shot Mussolini. On May 7, 1945, Germany surrendered. The war in Europe was finally over.

The Asian Theater

The war in Asia continued. Beginning in 1943, U.S. forces went on the offensive and advanced across the Pacific. As the Allied military power drew closer to the main Japanese islands in the first months of 1945, **Harry S. Truman,** who had become president after Roosevelt died in April, had a difficult decision to make. Should he use newly developed atomic weapons to bring the war to an end? If the United States invaded Japan, Truman and his advisers had become convinced that American troops would suffer heavy casualties. At the time, however, only two bombs were available; no one knew how effective they would be.

Truman decided to use the bombs. The first bomb was dropped on the Japanese city of **Hiroshima** on August 6. Three days later, a second bomb was dropped on Nagasaki. Both cities were leveled. Thousands of people died immediately after the bombs were dropped. Thousands more died in later months from radiation. Japan surrendered on August 14.

World War II was finally over. Seventeen million had died in battle. Perhaps 20 million civilians had perished as well. Some estimates place total losses at 60 million.

✓Reading Check **Identifying** What was the "second front" that the Allies opened in western Europe?

SECTION 2 REVIEW

Vocabulary
1. **Explain** the significance of: blitzkrieg, resolve, Franklin D. Roosevelt, isolationism, neutrality, involvement, Stalingrad, Midway Island, Douglas MacArthur, Winston Churchill, Normandy, partisans, Harry S. Truman, Hiroshima.

Main Ideas
2. **Explain** why Hitler ordered a shift in strategy after the Luftwaffe began bombing British cities. What was the outcome of this strategy?
3. **List** the series of events that began to turn the war against Germany in 1942. Use a chart like the one below to make your list.

Events That Turned the War Against Germany, 1942–1943
1.
2.

4. **Describe** how the war ended on the Asian front.

Critical Thinking
5. **The Big Idea** **Evaluating** How did the entry of the United States into World War II affect the war's progression and outcome?
6. **Sequencing** Put the events of World War II in chronological order.
7. **Analyzing Visuals** Examine the photograph on page 870. What was the purpose of the amphibious ships?

Writing About History
8. **Persuasive Writing** Imagine you are Harry S. Truman. You must end the war quickly on the Asian front, and you have decided to use the atomic bomb against Japan. You must convince your cabinet that your choice of action is the best alternative. Write a short essay defending your position.

History ONLINE
For help with the concepts in this section of *Glencoe World History*, go to glencoe.com and click Study Central™.

R Reading Strategy

Sequencing Information Ask students to make a time line for the Soviet advances. *(Battle of Kursk, July 1943; Ukraine, end of 1943; Baltic states, early 1944; Warsaw, January 1945; Berlin, April 1945; southern front, 1945)* **BL**

✓Reading Check

Answer: the D-Day invasion of Normandy

Assess

History ONLINE

Study Central provides summaries, interactive games, and online graphic organizers to help students review content.

Close

Making Generalizations

Ask: What Axis mistakes in judging the United States contributed to their defeat? *(Japan thought the United States would not fight in the Pacific after Pearl Harbor; Germany thought the United States would not be able to fight effectively in both Asia and Europe.)* **OL**

Answers

1. Definitions for the vocabulary words are found in the section and the Glossary.
2. He hoped to break British morale by bombing cities but allowed Britain to rebuild air strength quickly.
3. British stopped Rommel in N. Africa, summer 1942; Allied forces defeated Axis in N. Africa, Nov. 1942; Germany defeated at Stalingrad, Feb. 1943.
4. The U.S. dropped atomic bombs on Hiroshima and Nagasaki, and Japan surrendered on Aug. 14, 1945.
5. brought economic and military strength, fought and defeated Japan, assisted invasion at Normandy
6. Students' answers should include major events arranged in chronological order.
7. to bring the Allied troops up onto the beaches
8. Students' essays should reflect their grasp of the material.

NATIONAL GEOGRAPHIC

GEOGRAPHY & HISTORY

Focus

Remind students that in the summer of 1943, the Axis powers still controlled mainland Europe except the four neutral countries. The Allies knew they had to confront the Germans in France and that such an invasion would require a large army of American troops to succeed. **OL**

Teach

S1 Skill Practice

Using Geography Skills Ask: About how far was it from the Normandy beaches to Paris? *(about 120 miles)* **Ask:** Around which cities were most of the French railway targets that had been bombed or damaged? *(around Paris and Lille)* **OL**

S2 Skill Practice

Reading a Time Line Ask: About how long did it take for the Allies to liberate Paris after the Normandy invasion? *(a little less than three months—84 days, June 6–August 29)* **BL**

Additional Support

NATIONAL GEOGRAPHIC GEOGRAPHY & HISTORY

NORMANDY INVASION, June 6, 1944

0 60 kilometers
0 60 miles
Lambert Azimuthal Equal-Area projection

- Railway target bombed out
- Railway target damaged
- Major surviving railway junction
- Allied beachheads
- Allied invasion routes
- Allied airborne assault routes
- German armored division
- German infantry position

North Sea, NETHERLANDS, London, UNITED KINGDOM, Antwerp, Brussels, Calais, BELGIUM, Lille, English Channel, FRANCE, Utah, Omaha, Gold, Juno, Sword, Rouen, Lisieux, Caen, NORMANDY, Paris

S1

S2

◀ By 6 A.M. on D-Day, tightly packed landing craft ferried soldiers from ships to the Normandy shore. During the invasion, about 7000 ships and landing craft carried more than 130,000 troops across the channel.

June 10: U.S. troops at Omaha Beach began moving inland with their jeeps, tanks, and other heavy equipment offloaded from large supply ships anchored in the channel. ▶

Activity: Economics Connection

Researching Geography and Defense Contracts Because the Nazis had gained control of French ports, an Allied invasion would require special landing craft that could bring troops and equipment onto the beaches. The man who designed the landing craft was Andrew Higgins, a New Orleans boatbuilder whose Eureka boat was first designed for use by oil drillers, loggers, and trappers in the shallow waters of the U.S. Gulf Coast and the Mississippi River. Higgins added a ramp to the front of the boat as the Japanese had done. During the course of the war, about 24,000 so-called Higgins boats were produced. Contracts for these boats had a major impact on the New Orleans economy. Higgins employed 20,000 workers, about 80 percent of whom were women. About half were African Americans. **Ask:** How did World War II defense contracts affect the economy of American communities? Have students research how contracts for ships, planes, tanks, weapons, and other war material changed regional economies. Allow students to present their findings in oral reports. **AL**

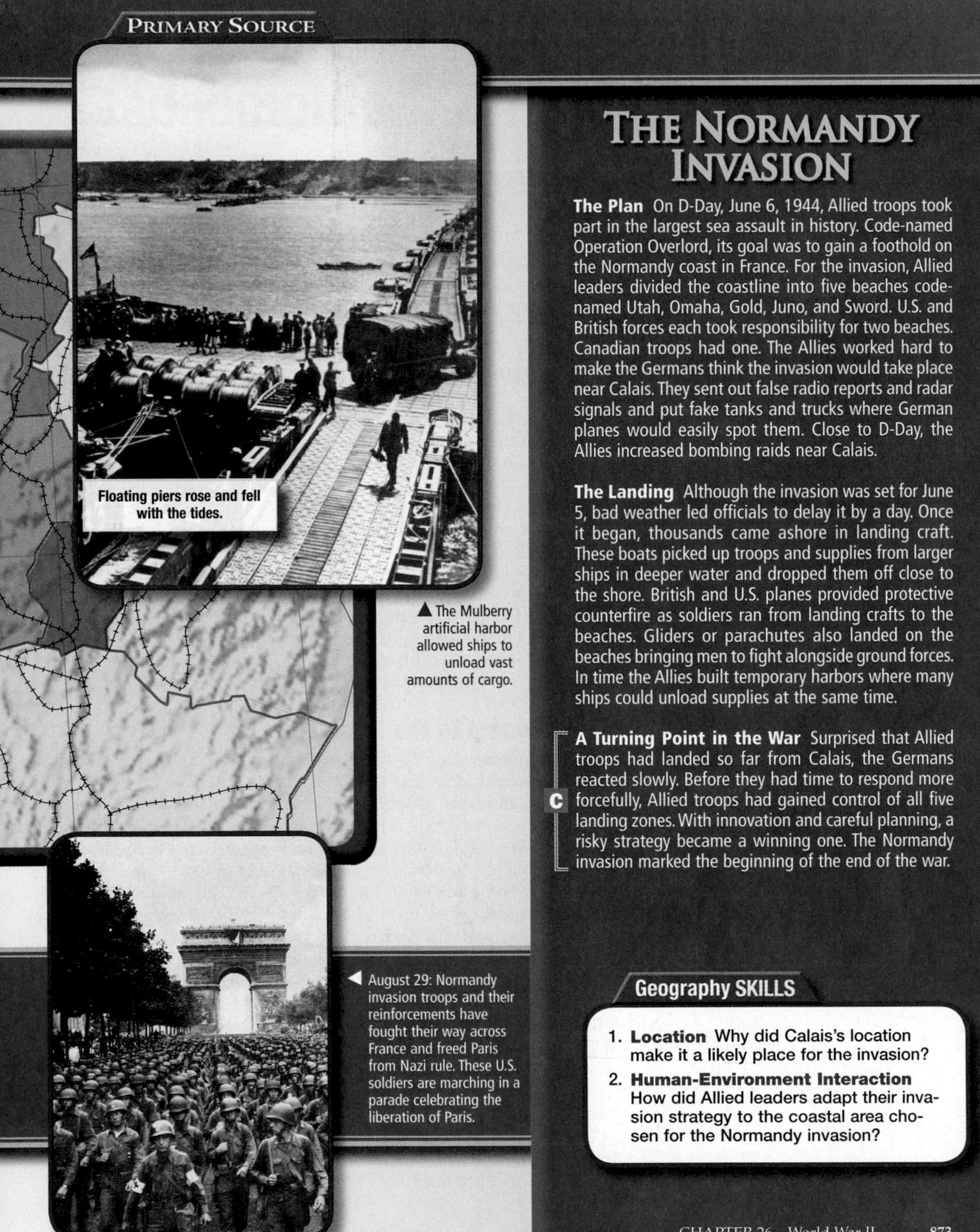

Floating piers rose and fell with the tides.

▲ The Mulberry artificial harbor allowed ships to unload vast amounts of cargo.

◀ August 29: Normandy invasion troops and their reinforcements have fought their way across France and freed Paris from Nazi rule. These U.S. soldiers are marching in a parade celebrating the liberation of Paris.

THE NORMANDY INVASION

The Plan On D-Day, June 6, 1944, Allied troops took part in the largest sea assault in history. Code-named Operation Overlord, its goal was to gain a foothold on the Normandy coast in France. For the invasion, Allied leaders divided the coastline into five beaches code-named Utah, Omaha, Gold, Juno, and Sword. U.S. and British forces each took responsibility for two beaches. Canadian troops had one. The Allies worked hard to make the Germans think the invasion would take place near Calais. They sent out false radio reports and radar signals and put fake tanks and trucks where German planes would easily spot them. Close to D-Day, the Allies increased bombing raids near Calais.

The Landing Although the invasion was set for June 5, bad weather led officials to delay it by a day. Once it began, thousands came ashore in landing craft. These boats picked up troops and supplies from larger ships in deeper water and dropped them off close to the shore. British and U.S. planes provided protective counterfire as soldiers ran from landing crafts to the beaches. Gliders or parachutes also landed on the beaches bringing men to fight alongside ground forces. In time the Allies built temporary harbors where many ships could unload supplies at the same time.

C **A Turning Point in the War** Surprised that Allied troops had landed so far from Calais, the Germans reacted slowly. Before they had time to respond more forcefully, Allied troops had gained control of all five landing zones. With innovation and careful planning, a risky strategy became a winning one. The Normandy invasion marked the beginning of the end of the war.

Geography SKILLS

1. **Location** Why did Calais's location make it a likely place for the invasion?
2. **Human-Environment Interaction** How did Allied leaders adapt their invasion strategy to the coastal area chosen for the Normandy invasion?

NATIONAL GEOGRAPHIC

GEOGRAPHY & HISTORY

C Critical Thinking

Drawing Conclusions Ask: Why is the Normandy invasion described as a turning point in World War II? *(It was the beginning of pushing the Germans out of France, leading to their ultimate defeat.)* **OL**

Assess/Close

Have students discuss why a beach invasion is so difficult and dangerous. **OL**

Geography SKILLS

Answers:

1. because it was the closest place to England
2. used special landing craft to carry troops and equipment, planes provided cover fire to troops, gliders and parachutes landed additional troops, artificial harbors

Extending the Content

Mulberry Artificial Harbors The British designed two artificial harbors code-named Mulberry for use after the Normandy invasion. One was built near Omaha Beach, controlled by the Americans, and the other was near Gold Beach, controlled by the British. Each one had about 6 miles of roads made from flexible steel. The harbors were protected from the rough waters of the English Channel by lines of huge sunken concrete and steel boxes, destroyed ships, and floating breakwaters. Both harbors were installed and working within twelve days of the landing. By June 22, however, a severe storm had destroyed the harbor at Omaha Beach. The other harbor supplied the Allied troops for ten months. About 2.5 million troops, 500,000 vehicles, and 4 million tons of supplies were unloaded at the Gold Beach harbor. Artificial harbors allowed men and supplies to be unloaded more quickly than by using landing craft.

Focus

Bellringer

Daily Focus Transparency 26.3

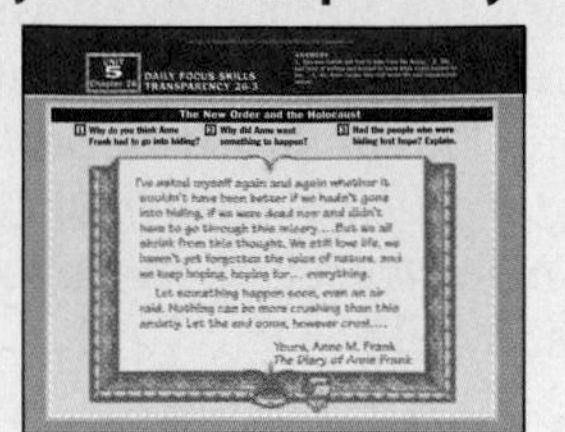

GUIDE TO READING

Answers to Graphic:
Germany: directly annexed some occupied lands, Final Solution; **Japan:** Greater East-Asia Co-prosperity Sphere, retained power in colonies; **Both:** used slave labor from occupied lands

Section Spotlight Video

To generate student interest and provide a springboard for class discussion, access the Chapter 26, Section 3 video at glencoe.com or on the video DVD.

SECTION 3

The New Order and the Holocaust

GUIDE TO READING

The BIG Idea
Human Rights Millions of people were forced to labor for the German and Japanese war machines. The Holocaust claimed the lives of six million Jews.

Content Vocabulary
- genocide *(p. 876)*
- collaborators *(p. 877)*

Academic Vocabulary
- ethnic *(p. 874)*
- occupation *(p. 875)*

People, Places, and Events
- Poland *(p. 874)*
- Heinrich Himmler *(p. 874)*
- Reinhard Heydrich *(p. 876)*
- Auschwitz *(p. 876)*
- Holocaust *(p. 877)*

Reading Strategy
Comparing and Contrasting As you read, use a Venn diagram like the one below to compare and contrast the New Order of Germany and the New Order of Japan.

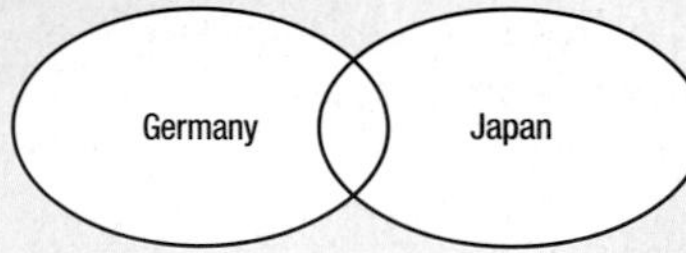

As World War II continued, Japan and Germany changed their domestic policies. Japan used the resources of conquered nations and forced millions to labor for its war machine. In Germany, the Nazis began a terrifying genocide, carried out by death squads and death camps. Nearly two out of every three European Jews died in the Holocaust.

The New Order in Europe

MAIN IDEA The German conquest of continental Europe forced millions of native peoples to work for the Nazi war machine.

HISTORY & YOU Recall how the ancient Romans conquered lands and then enslaved many of the people. Read to learn about the Nazi plan to use slave labor.

In 1942 the Nazi regime stretched across continental Europe from the English Channel in the west to the outskirts of Moscow in the east. Nazi-occupied Europe was largely organized in one of two ways. Nazi Germany directly annexed some areas, such as western Poland, and made them into German provinces. Most of occupied Europe, however, was run by German military or civilian officials with help from local people who collaborated with the Nazis.

Resettlement in the East

Nazi administration in the conquered lands to the east was especially ruthless. Seen as the "living space" for German expansion, these lands were populated, Nazis thought, by racially inferior Slavic peoples. Hitler's plans for an Aryan racial empire were so important to him that he and the Nazis began to put their racial program into effect soon after the conquest of **Poland.**

Heinrich Himmler, the leader of the SS, was in charge of German resettlement plans in the east. Himmler's task was to move the Slavic peoples out and replace them with Germans. Slavic peoples included Czech, Polish, Serbo-Croatian, Slovene, and Ukrainian. The resettlement policy was first applied to the lands of western Poland. One million Poles were uprooted and moved to southern Poland. Hundreds of thousands of **ethnic** Germans (German descendants who had migrated years ago from Germany to different parts of southern and eastern Europe) were brought in to colonize the German provinces in Poland. By 1942, two million ethnic Germans had been settled in Poland.

The invasion of the Soviet Union made the Nazis even more excited about German colonization. Hitler envisioned a colossal project of social engineering after the war. Poles, Ukrainians, and

Resource Manager

R Reading Strategies	C Critical Thinking	D Differentiated Instruction	W Writing Support	S Skill Practice
Teacher Edition • Det. Importance., p. 876 • Summarizing, p. 877 **Additional Resources** • Guid. Read. Act., URB p. 166 • Read. Ess. & Note-Taking Guide, p. 292	**Teacher Edition** • Making Inferences, p. 876 • Analyzing Pri. Sources, p. 878 **Additional Resources** • People in World Hist. Act., URB p. 156 • Section Quiz, p. 323	**Teacher Edition** • ELL, p. 877 **Additional Resources** • Hist. Sig. Act., URB p. 148 • Read. Strat. for SS, p. 53	**Teacher Edition** • Personal Writing, p. 875 **Additional Resources** • Pri. Source Read., URB p. 157 • Writer's Guidebook, p. 43	**Teacher Edition** • Using Geo. Skills, p. 875 **Additional Resources** • Academic Vocab. Act., URB p. 141 • Reteach. Act., URB p. 161

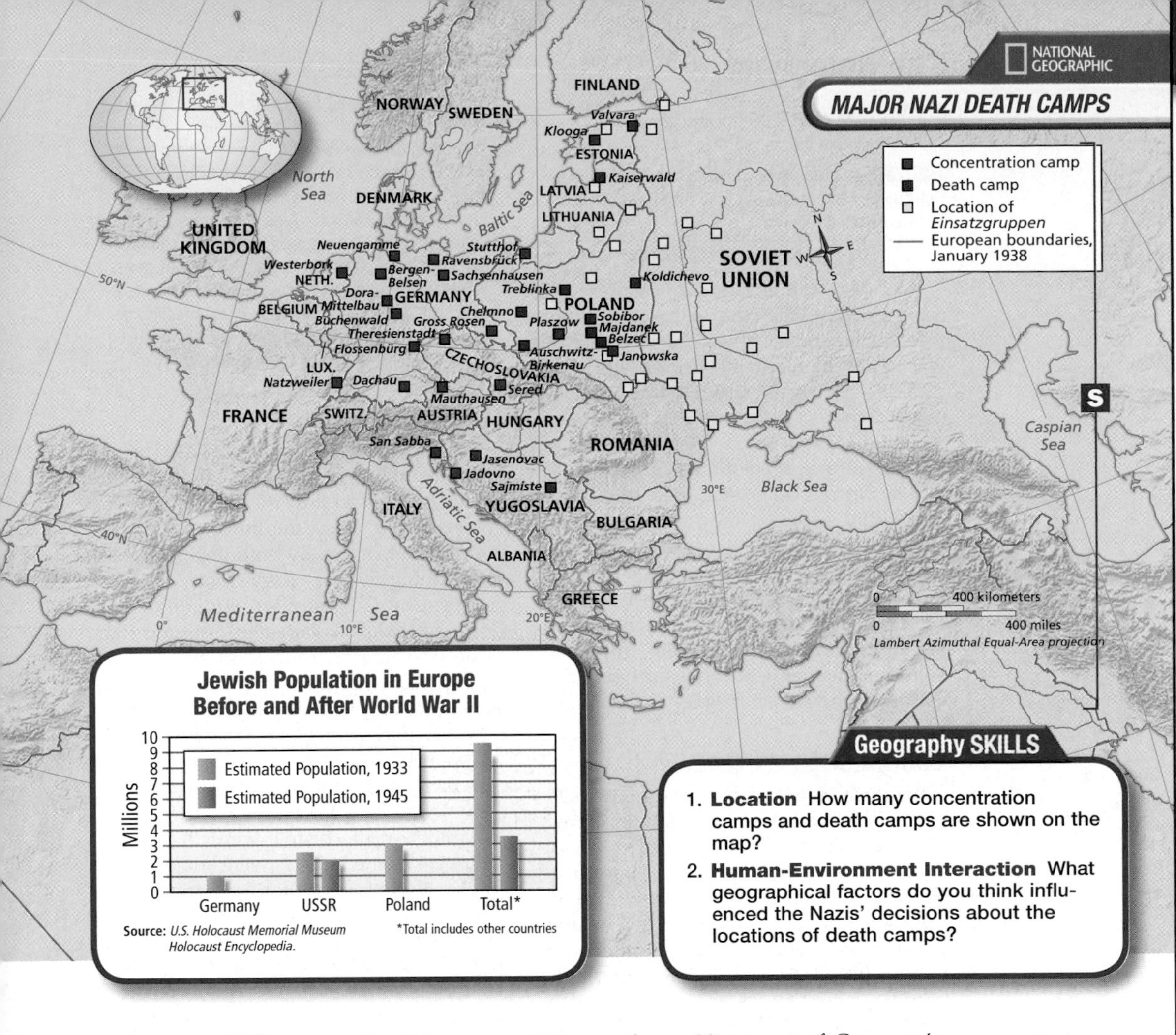

Geography SKILLS

1. **Location** How many concentration camps and death camps are shown on the map?
2. **Human-Environment Interaction** What geographical factors do you think influenced the Nazis' decisions about the locations of death camps?

Russians would be removed and become slave labor, according to Hitler's plan. German peasants would settle on the abandoned lands and "Germanize" them.

Himmler told a gathering of SS officers that 30 million Slavs might die to achieve this plan. He continued, "Whether nations live in prosperity or starve to death interests me only insofar as we need them as slaves for our culture. Otherwise it is of no interest." **W**

Slave Labor in Germany

By the summer of 1944, seven million European workers labored in Germany. They made up 20 percent of Germany's labor force. Another seven million workers were forced to labor for the Nazis on farms, in industries, and in military camps.

The use of forced labor caused many problems for Germany, however. Sending so many workers to Germany disrupted industrial production in the occupied countries that could have helped Germany. Then, too, the brutal way in which Germany recruited foreign workers led more and more people to resist the Nazi **occupation** forces.

✓**Reading Check** **Describing** What was Hitler's vision for the residents of eastern Europe?

Teach

W Writing Support

Personal Writing Ask students to review Himmler's quotation and consider its ramifications. Have student write one or two paragraphs describing their personal response to this attitude and the possible consequences of this view of the world then and today. **OL**

S Skill Practice

Using Geography Skills Ask: Which country had the southernmost camp? *(Yugoslavia)* **BL**

Geography SKILLS

Answers:

1. 25 concentration camps, 6 death camps
2. distance from Germany, proximity to Jewish populations

✓**Reading Check**

Answer: They would be removed from their homelands and used as slave labor.

Hands-On Chapter Project
Step 3

Present a Radio Broadcast

Step 3: Broadcasting Nazi and Japanese Actions Pairs of students will select an issue from the section and prepare a one-minute radio report to read to the class.

Directions: Discuss the reaction of many Americans and Europeans at the time to events of the Holocaust. Explain that the true horrors of the Holocaust were not fully known until the death camps were liberated. Each pair should select an issue of interest (such as the Holocaust, death camps for other groups, children in the war, or Japanese policies); do research to establish exact dates, locations, and sequences; and prepare a one-minute broadcast. Select volunteers to read the reports. **OL**

(Chapter Project is continued in Section 4.)

C Critical Thinking

Making Inferences Ask students how Nazi Germany's use of the term "Final Solution" reflects their view of the need for genocide to solve "the Jewish problem." *(They believed that there would always be conflict and problems if Jews were left alive.)* **OL**

For additional practice on this skill, see the **Skills Handbook**.

R Reading Strategy

Determining Importance

Ask: In what other ways might railroad cars have been used in 1944? *(to transport military supplies or troops throughout Europe in the German war effort)* How do you think this choice of using resources reflects Hitler's world view? *(Answers will vary, but students might mention that Hitler blamed Jews for the war and all the world's troubles.)* **OL**

The Holocaust

MAIN IDEA Adolf Hitler's philosophy of Aryan superiority led to the Holocaust.

HISTORY & YOU Have you seen films about the Holocaust? Read to find out how the Nazis planned to exterminate the Jews.

No aspect of the Nazi New Order was more terrifying than the deliberate attempt to exterminate the Jews. Racial struggle was a key element in Hitler's world of ideas. To him, racial struggle was a clearly defined conflict of opposites. On one side were the Aryans, who were the creators of human cultural development, according to Hitler. On the other side were the Jews, and Hitler believed they were trying to destroy the Aryans.

C Himmler and the SS closely shared Hitler's racial ideas. The SS was given responsibility for what the Nazis called their Final Solution to the Jewish problem. The Final Solution was **genocide** (physical extermination) of the Jewish people.

The *Einsatzgruppen*

Reinhard Heydrich, head of the SS's Security Service, had the task of administering the Final Solution. Heydrich created special strike forces, called *Einsatzgruppen,* to carry out Nazi plans. After the defeat of Poland, these forces rounded up all Polish Jews and put them in ghettos set up in a number of Polish cities. Conditions in the ghettos were horrible. Families were crowded together in unsanitary housing. The Nazis tried to starve residents by allowing only minimal amounts of food. In spite of their suffering, residents carried on, and some organized resistance against the Nazis.

In June 1941, the *Einsatzgruppen* were given the new job of acting as mobile killing units. These SS death squads followed the regular army's advance into the Soviet Union. Their job was to round up Jews in their villages, execute them, and bury them in mass graves. The graves were often giant pits dug by the victims themselves before they were shot.

The leader of one of these death squads described the mode of operation:

History ONLINE
Student Web Activity—
Visit glencoe.com and complete the activity on concentration camps.

PRIMARY SOURCE

"The unit selected for this task would enter a village or city and order the prominent Jewish citizens to call together all Jews for the purpose of resettlement. They were requested to hand over their valuables to the leaders of the unit, and shortly before the execution to surrender their outer clothing. The men, women, and children were led to a place of execution which in most cases was located next to a more deeply excavated anti-tank ditch. Then they were shot, kneeling or standing, and the corpses thrown into the ditch."

—*Nazi Conspiracy and Aggression,* vol. 5, 1946

The Death Camps

The *Einsatzgruppen* probably killed more than one million Jews. As appalling as that sounds, it was too slow by Nazi standards. They decided to kill the European Jewish population in specially built death camps.

Beginning in 1942, Jews from countries occupied by Germany (or sympathetic to Germany) were rounded up, packed like cattle into freight trains, and shipped to Poland. Six extermination centers were built in Poland for this purpose. The largest was **Auschwitz** (OWSH•VIHTS).

About 30 percent of the new arrivals at Auschwitz were sent to a labor camp, where many were starved or worked to death. The remainder of the people went to the gas chambers. Some inmates were subjected to cruel and painful "medical" experiments.

By the spring of 1942, the death camps were in full operation. First priority was given to the elimination of the Polish ghettos. By the summer of 1942, however, Jews were also being shipped from France, Belgium, and Holland. Even as the Allies were winning the war in 1944, Jews were being **R** shipped from Greece and Hungary. In spite of Germany's desperate military needs, even late in the war when Germany was facing utter defeat, the Final Solution still had priority in using railroad cars to ship Jews to the death camps.

The Death Toll

The Germans killed approximately six million Jews, over three million of them in the death camps. Even in concentration camps that were not designed specifically for mass murder, large numbers of inmates

Differentiated Instruction

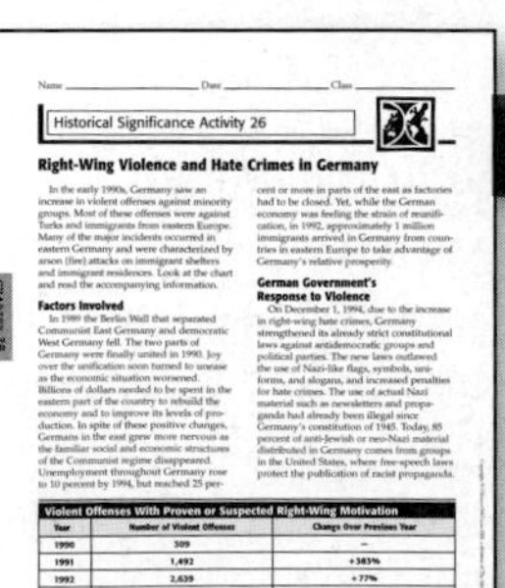

Historical Significance Activity, URB p. 148

Making Generalizations

Objective: Make generalizations about hate crimes in Germany.

Focus: Note similarities in the conditions in Germany during the two periods.

Teach: Have students connect conditions at each time with the attacks.

Assess: Ask students to write a paragraph relating hate crimes and Germany's economy.

Close: Have students share and discuss paragraphs.

Differentiated Instruction Strategies

BL Have students identify why poor economic conditions might lead to hate crimes.

AL Ask students to compare differences in German and U.S. responses to racist propaganda.

ELL Discuss the power of symbols such as Nazi-like flags.

were worked to death or subjected to deadly medical experiments. Virtually 90 percent of the Jewish populations of Poland, the Baltic countries, and Germany were killed. Overall, the Holocaust was responsible for the death of nearly two out of every three European Jews.

The Nazis were also responsible for the deliberate death by shooting, starvation, or overwork of at least another nine to ten million non-Jewish people. The Nazis considered the Roma (sometimes known as Gypsies), like the Jews, to be an alien race. About 40 percent of Europe's one million Roma were killed in the death camps.

The leading citizens of the Slavic peoples—the clergy, intellectuals, civil leaders, judges, and lawyers—were arrested and killed. Probably an additional four million Poles, Ukrainians, and Belorussians lost their lives as slave laborers. Finally, at least three to four million Soviet prisoners of war were killed.

This mass slaughter of European Jews is known as the **Holocaust.** Jews in and out of the camps attempted to resist the Nazis. Friends and even strangers aided some Jews, hiding them in villages or smuggling them into safe areas. Foreign diplomats **R** would try to save Jews by issuing exit visas. The nation of Denmark saved almost its entire Jewish population.

Some people did not believe the accounts of death camps because, during World War I, allies had greatly exaggerated German atrocities to arouse enthusiasm for the war. Most often, people pretended not to notice what was happening. Even worse, **collaborators** (people who assisted the **D** enemy) helped the Nazis hunt down Jews. Although the Allies were aware of the concentration camps and death camps, they chose to concentrate on ending the war. Not until after the war did the full extent of the horror and inhumanity of the Holocaust impress itself upon people's consciousness.

See page R51 to read excerpts from *The Holocaust—The Camp Victims* in the **Primary Source and Literature Library.**

Children in the War

Young people of all ages were also victims of the atrocities of World War II.

HISTORY & ARTS — PRIMARY SOURCE

The Final Solution at Auschwitz

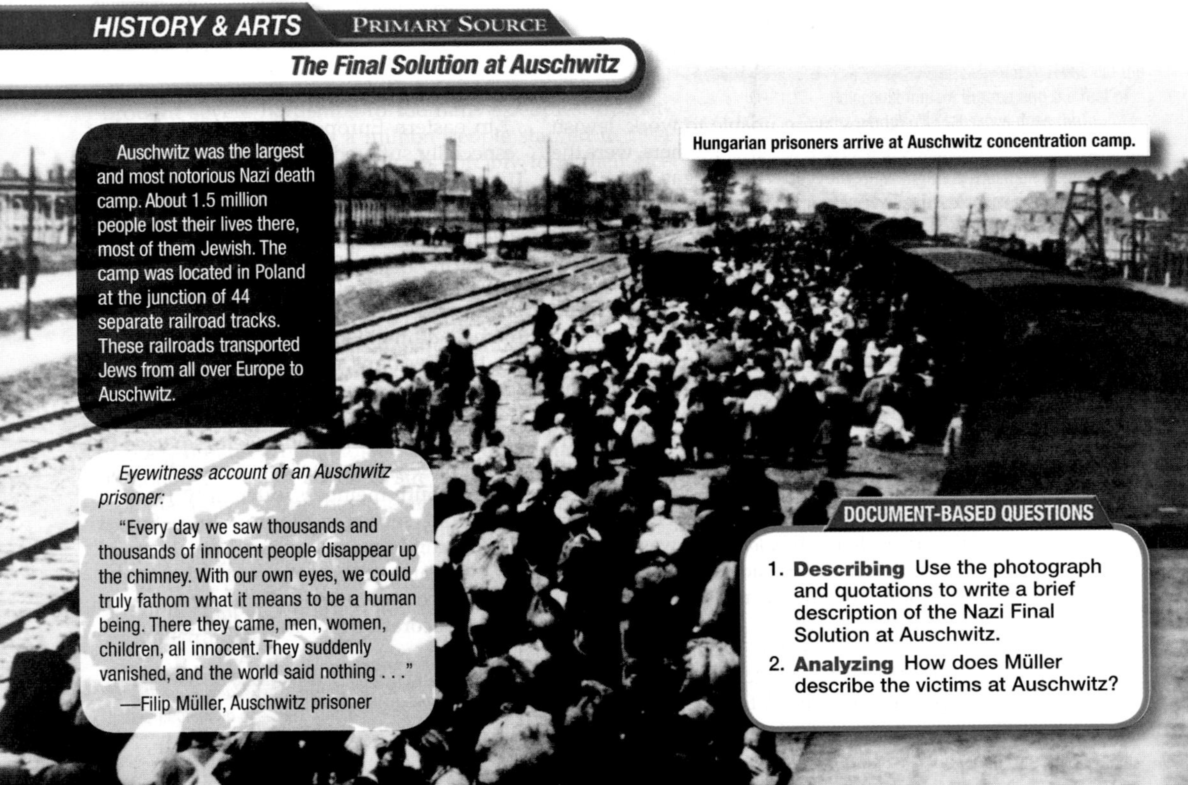

Hungarian prisoners arrive at Auschwitz concentration camp.

Auschwitz was the largest and most notorious Nazi death camp. About 1.5 million people lost their lives there, most of them Jewish. The camp was located in Poland at the junction of 44 separate railroad tracks. These railroads transported Jews from all over Europe to Auschwitz.

Eyewitness account of an Auschwitz prisoner:

"Every day we saw thousands and thousands of innocent people disappear up the chimney. With our own eyes, we could truly fathom what it means to be a human being. There they came, men, women, children, all innocent. They suddenly vanished, and the world said nothing . . ."

—Filip Müller, Auschwitz prisoner

DOCUMENT-BASED QUESTIONS

1. **Describing** Use the photograph and quotations to write a brief description of the Nazi Final Solution at Auschwitz.
2. **Analyzing** How does Müller describe the victims at Auschwitz?

R Reading Strategy

Summarizing Ask students to write a summary sentence for the paragraph that contains the highlighted word *Holocaust. (Jews and others across Europe tried to resist the Nazi Holocaust.)* **OL**

D Differentiated Instruction

English Language Learners Ask students to look up *collaborate* and define it. Note that it is not always used in a negative way and have students prepare a chart that lists positive and negative examples of collaborating with others. **ELL**

DOCUMENT-BASED QUESTIONS

Answers:

1. Answers will vary. Students might mention the arrival of prisoners by train and the killing of prisoners in the gas chambers.
2. Müller describes the men, women, and children as "all innocent" and as representing humanity.

Differentiated Instruction

Leveled Activities

BL Guided Reading Activity, URB p. 166

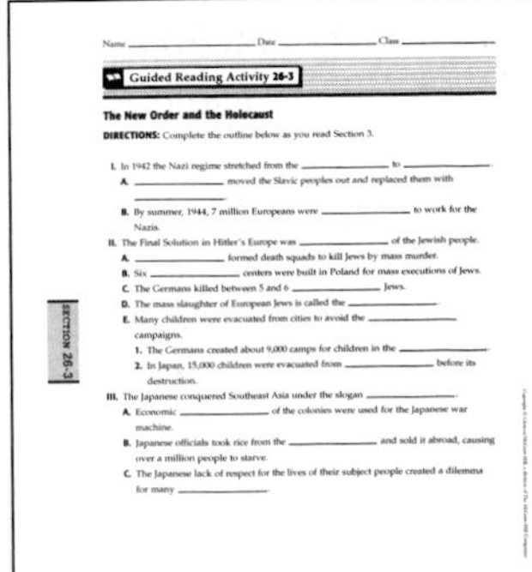

Guided Reading Activity 26-3

The New Order and the Holocaust

OL People in World History Activity, URB p. 156

People in World History Activity 26

Anne Frank (1929–1945)

AL Primary Source Reading, URB p. 157

ELL Academic Vocabulary Activity, URB p. 141

Focus

Introducing Social History
Remind students of the meaning of *blitzkrieg (lightning war).* **Ask:** How did the Blitz mark a change in German strategy? *(It was a shift from military to civilian targets.)* **OL**

Teach

R Reading Strategy

Previewing Have students read the paragraph and study the visuals before reading the feature. **Ask:** What do you think happened during the Blitz? *(Answers may include: London was bombed; people had to sleep in shelters; buildings were destroyed; children were sent on trains to safer places.)* **BL**

C Critical Thinking

Making Inferences **Ask:** Why did the Germans bomb mostly at night? *(Answers may include: It was harder for the British to shoot down the German planes; it was more frightening; disrupting sleep made it harder for Londoners to work.)* **OL**

The Blitz: London's Finest Hour

R In August 1940, the German air force launched a major bombing offensive against airfields and industrial targets in Great Britain. A month later, the Germans shifted their focus to civilian targets. On September 7, 1940, a thousand German warplanes rained bombs down upon London. This devastating attack marked the beginning of the London Blitz.

During air raids, underground tube stations (subway stops), like the one pictured below, were converted into bomb shelters.

Many underground shelters in London were equipped with air conditioning and first-aid stations.

Shelters needed to accommodate large numbers of people. During an air raid, up to 1,000 Londoners crowded into the platforms, connection tunnels, and emergency stairs that comprised a tube station shelter.

Many Londoners who owned gardens sought refuge in Anderson shelters. These small structures, consisting of corrugated iron sheets, were buried four feet in the ground and then covered with soil. A single Anderson shelter could hold up to six people.

Surviving the Blitz

C The Germans bombed London on nearly a nightly basis between September and November 1940. Thousands of Londoners sought refuge in shelters. The Blitz caused other hardships. The destruction of factories and shops, plus hours spent in shelters, disrupted work schedules. Blackout ordinances kept all lights off after dark, causing traffic accidents. The horrific noise cost everyone much-needed sleep.

888

Additional Support

Background

London in the Blitz Before the Blitz began, Londoners' daily lives had not been seriously disrupted by the war. There were soldiers drilling and government officials working on preparedness, and each night all the windows in the city were covered so that no light shone through. Still, life was more or less normal. Air raid sirens were rarely heard before August 1940. From August 23 to December 2 of that year, there was an average of three to four alerts per day. Air raids damaged buildings of all kinds, from poor suburban housing complexes to Buckingham Palace itself. Bombs struck many churches and more than 20 hospitals; many of London's most famous landmarks were hit. Even though the numbers of wounded and killed were very high, they were far less than had been estimated when the war began. Reconstruction on many structures began almost as soon as they were damaged.

German bombs caused great destruction to the buildings of London. By the end of the Blitz, over one million homes in the city had been destroyed or damaged, creating a serious homelessness problem.

Prime Minister Winston Churchill was a symbol of British strength and determination during the Blitz. **D**

Despite the hardships they faced, London men and women served as air-raid wardens, fire watchers, firemen, ambulance drivers, first-aid providers, and rescue workers to help their fellow citizens cope with the crisis.

Soon after the war began in September 1939, over a million Londoners, mostly mothers and children, moved to the countryside or Canada. A year later, the Blitz sparked another major evacuation of children and adults from London and other British cities.

W Separated from their parents, many London children spent much of the war living with strangers in the countryside.

Turning the Tide

German bombers claimed the lives of 14,000 Londoners during the Blitz, and many more were injured or left homeless. The city's morale remained strong, however. The Royal Air Force showed resolve, too, and shot down many of the attacking German bombers. In June 1941, Hitler launched his eventually disastrous campaign against the Soviet Union. Great Britain had survived its most serious threat of the war.

Analyzing Visuals

1. **Explaining** How did Londoners adjust to the threats created by the German bombing attacks?
2. **Analyzing** What does the London Blitz suggest about the effectiveness of bombing attacks upon a civilian population?

D Differentiated Instruction

Auditory/Musical Have students listen to some of Winston Churchill's speeches during the Blitz. **Ask:** How did Churchill affect British morale? *(Accept all reasonable answers backed by evidence.)* **AL**

W Writing Support

Personal Writing Have students write a letter from a child separated from his or her parents during the Blitz and the parents' response. **OL**

Assess/Close

Discuss why the Blitz was called London's finest hour. **OL**

Analyzing Visuals

Answers:

1. They took shelter in tube stations or Anderson shelters, sent their children to the country, and volunteered to help.
2. Such attacks had limited effectiveness and even strengthened support for the war effort.

Activity: Economics Connection

Analyzing Civil Defense Spending In its 1940 budget, the city of London set aside about £9,407,500 for civil defense. Shelters and materials related to the blackout, such as curtains at London City Hall, cost £18,000. Costs associated with evacuating staff and extra maintenance totaled £62,675. Protecting the water system from being attacked by bombers cost £390,736. An additional £40,000 was needed to protect various city institutions. **Ask:** Why was so much money spent protecting the water system? *(Water is vital to people's lives for drinking, for industry, and for fire protection. A water system is spread out, so it is expensive to protect it.)* Shortly after the Blitz began, the mayor set up a relief fund for victims of the bombing. People from all over the world sent donations, and within two months almost £1,700,000 was received. Explain that the value of the British pound was about $4 in 1940. A 1940 pound was equal in buying power to about $72 in 2007. Have students create a chart showing the costs of the Blitz in British pounds, 1940 U.S. dollars, and 2007 U.S. dollars. **AL**

Determining Cause and Effect As a class, read through the Visual Summary. **Ask:** How does the information in this Visual Summary help you understand the causes and effects of World War II? *(Students' answers will vary, but should emphasize that the Visual Summary highlights how actions led to reactions before and during the war.)* Have students copy the titles of the three sections of the Visual Summary. For each section, ask students to list at least two cause-and-effect relationships. Have student volunteers share their cause-and-effect statements and discuss other related causes or effects that they recall from the chapter. **OL**

Visualizing **Ask:** What other images could be used to help convey the information in this Visual Summary? *(With students, go back through the chapter and identify images that could support the ideas in the Visual Summary.)* Tell students that as they read the summary, it can be helpful to try to visualize scenes or images that are associated with the ideas. This can help them remember the information later. **BL**

CHAPTER 26 Visual Summary

You can study anywhere, anytime by downloading quizzes and flash cards to your PDA from glencoe.com.

THE BEGINNING of World War II

- Nazi Germany began an aggressive policy of expansion.
- After Germany invaded Poland, Britain and France declared war on Germany.
- Seeking access to natural resources, Japan seized Manchuria and North China.
- Japan launched a surprise attack on U.S. and European colonies in Southeast Asia in 1940.

GERMAN TANKS STREAM INTO POLAND, 1939

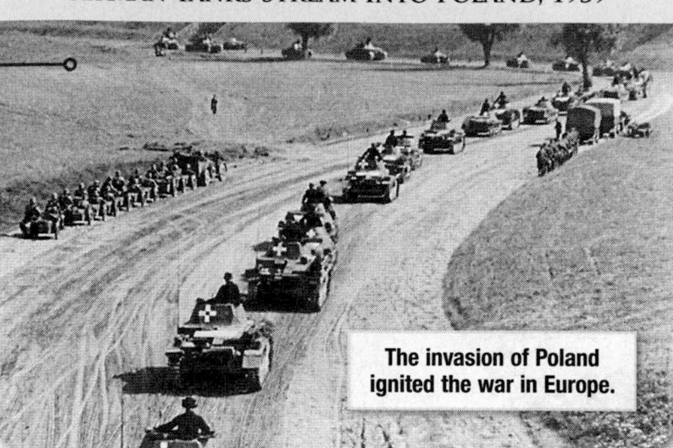

The invasion of Poland ignited the war in Europe.

ALLIED TROOPS LAND AT NORMANDY, 1944

Allies attacked Normandy from air and sea, beginning a sweep that would eventually defeat Nazi Germany.

THE COURSE of the War

- The German blitzkrieg subdued much of western and central Europe, but Germany could not defeat Britain or Russia.
- The Japanese attack at Pearl Harbor in 1941 brought the United States into the war.
- The Grand Alliance forced the unconditional surrender of the Axis Powers in 1945.
- After the war, political tensions between the United States and the Soviet Union led to the Cold War.

LIVES AFFECTED by War

- Germany and Japan forced people of conquered nations to labor for their war effort.
- Hitler's extremist racial views led to the Holocaust and death of millions.
- Civilians worked in war factories and endured shortages.
- Bombings targeted civilians as well as the military.
- Almost 20 million civilians died in the war.

NAZIS ROUND UP JEWS IN WARSAW, POLAND, 1943

Jewish children and their mothers were the first to be sent to the gas chambers.

Hands-On Chapter Project

Step 5: Wrap-Up

Present a Radio Broadcast

Step 5: Broadcasting the Aftermath of the War Ask students to review their broadcasts and those of others. Then allow them to create a final broadcast dated within a year of the end of World War II that summarizes the effects of the war. **Ask:** How did the war change the world and people's lives? *(Answers will vary, but might include: The Allies won a total victory; the Soviet Union and the other Allies had an uneasy alliance; much of Europe and Japan was destroyed; people within the United States had moved on and taken on new roles.)* When final broadcasts are prepared, ask volunteers to share their work with the class. Lead a class discussion on the long-term effects of World War II. **OL**

STANDARDIZED TEST PRACTICE

TEST-TAKING 

When answering a test item involving a map, look at the map carefully. Pay attention to the title of the map and to the legends used to identify geographic areas. Use these clues to eliminate incorrect answer choices.

Reviewing Vocabulary

Directions: Choose the word or words that best complete the sentence.

1. Germany used a "lightning war," or ________, to gain control of Poland.

A Luftwaffe
B blitz
C blitzkrieg
D *Einsatzgruppen*

2. The period of political tensions between the United States and the Soviet Union following World War II was known as the ________.

A Great Depression
B Doctrine of Aggression
C Potsdam Agreement
D Cold War

3. ________ are restrictions intended to enforce international law.

A Embargoes
B Tariffs
C Sanctions
D Edicts

4. Hitler's Final Solution was ________ of the Jewish people.

A genocide
B patricide
C suicide
D isolationism

Reviewing Main Ideas

Directions: Choose the best answers to the following questions.

Section 1 *(pp. 856–861)*

5. What policy attempted to satisfy the reasonable demands of dissatisfied powers?

A Easement
B Appeasement
C Isolationism
D Colonization

6. What name did Japan give Manchuria?

A Nagasaki
B Hiroshima
C Kimono
D Manchukuo

Section 2 *(pp. 864–871)*

7. What event triggered the entry of the United States into World War II?

A The blitz over London
B The assassination of Franklin D. Roosevelt
C The bombing of Pearl Harbor
D The German invasion of Poland

8. In what city did Hitler lose his entire German Sixth Army?

A Stalingrad
B Dunkirk
C Midway Island
D Dresden

Need Extra Help?

If You Missed Questions . . .	1	2	3	4	5	6	7	8
Go to Page . . .	864	886	861	876	857	860	867	869

Answers and Analyses

Reviewing Vocabulary

1. C Luftwaffe is the term for the German air force, blitz was used in connection with the Battle of Britain, and *Einsatzgruppen* were Holocaust death squads.

2. D All other answers have no relevance. Great Depression was a worldwide economic event, Doctrine of Aggression is a fictional term, and the Potsdam agreement refers to a political agreement near the end of the war.

TEST-TAKING 

For Question 2: Remind students to first eliminate answer choices that are obviously wrong, such as the Great Depression and Potsdam Agreement, which did not take place after the war.

3. C This question requires vocabulary knowledge. Embargoes and tariffs are measures used by individual countries for economic or military purposes. Edicts are more general pronouncements of intent and enforcement.

4. A Three choices refer to killing, but patricide refers to killing fathers and suicide to killing oneself. Isolationism is a general philosophy practiced by certain countries.

Reviewing Main Ideas

5. B None of the other answers has any relevance. Isolationism is a general philosophy practiced by certain countries, but does not describe Britain's approach at the time. Appeasement was unsuccessful at gaining peace and stability.

6. D Nagasaki and Hiroshima were the cities where the United States dropped atomic bombs. Kimono is a Japanese garment and has no relevance.

7. C The blitz over London and the German invasion of Poland affected the United States, but did not prompt entry into the war. Roosevelt was not assassinated.

8. A The other choices were not German defeats, although the bombing of Dresden killed many civilians and destroyed most of the German city.

9. B None of the other battles were naval invasions. Dunkirk was a British retreat across the Channel, Midway was a naval battle between the United States and Japan, and Kursk was a tank battle.

10. C *Kristallnacht* was a night of oppression of Jews early in Hitler's regime. Luftwaffe is the German air force. Kamikaze refers to a Japanese air force tactic.

11. A Knowledge of chapter content is necessary to identify the name of Japan's proposed new community. The others are fictional answers.

12. D Knowledge of chapter content is necessary to know that the Soviet Union was the only nation to use women in combat.

TEST-TAKING 

For Question 12: If you do not immediately know the answer to a question, look at each answer choice carefully. Try to recall the context in which these details were discussed in class. Remembering this context may help you eliminate incorrect answer choices.

13. B Potsdam was the final conference of the war and dealt with such matters after it was clear the Allies would be victorious. The other selections are fictional or have no relevance.

9. What battle in World War II is considered history's greatest naval invasion?

A Battle of Dunkirk
B D-Day
C Battle of Midway
D Battle of Kursk

Section 3 *(pp. 874–879)*

10. What was the name for the special strike forces who carried out the Final Solution?

A *Kristallnacht*
B Kamikaze
C *Einsatzgruppen*
D Luftwaffe

11. What economic community supposedly provided mutual benefits to Japan's occupied areas and to Japan?

A The Greater East Asia Co-Prosperity Sphere
B The East Asian Emporium
C The Greater Eurasian Market
D The Kamikaze Commerce

Section 4 *(pp. 880–887)*

12. What was the only country in World War II that used women in battle?

A United States
B Japan
C Germany
D Soviet Union

13. At which postwar conference did the Allies agree that war crime trials should be held?

A Warsaw
B Potsdam
C Berlin
D Versailles

Critical Thinking

Directions: Choose the best answers to the following questions.

Use the following map and your knowledge of world history to answer question 14.

14. Which European country was not controlled by Germany in 1943?

A Italy
B France
C Poland
D United Kingdom

15. What was the main reason for Hitler's advance into other lands?

A He hated the French and Russians.
B He wanted more seaports.
C He wanted "living space" for German expansion.
D He wanted to spread communism to all lands.

Need Extra Help?

If You Missed Questions . . .	9	10	11	12	13	14	15
Go to Page . . .	870	876	879	881	887	892	874

Critical Thinking

14. D Students should compare each country to the map. They will need to carefully read the title of this map to understand what the shading indicates. Only the United Kingdom is not shaded on the map.

15. C Hitler's primary goal was expansion; he wanted to build an Aryan racial state.

16. What was the main significance of the Nazi-Soviet Nonaggression Pact?
   - **A** It gave Hitler the freedom to attack Poland.
   - **B** It appeased the Western allies' fears of German aggression.
   - **C** It postponed Japan's war with China.
   - **D** It ended the United States's isolationist policy.

17. In reviewing the events of World War II, which item below has the events in the correct chronological order?
   - **A** D-Day, bombing of Pearl Harbor, rescue at Dunkirk, bombing of Hiroshima
   - **B** Rescue at Dunkirk, bombing of Pearl Harbor, D-Day, bombing of Hiroshima
   - **C** Bombing of Pearl Harbor, D-Day, rescue at Dunkirk, bombing of Hiroshima
   - **D** Bombing of Hiroshima, bombing of Pearl Harbor, rescue at Dunkirk, D-Day

Analyze the graph below and answer the question that follows. Base your answer on the chart and your knowledge of world history.

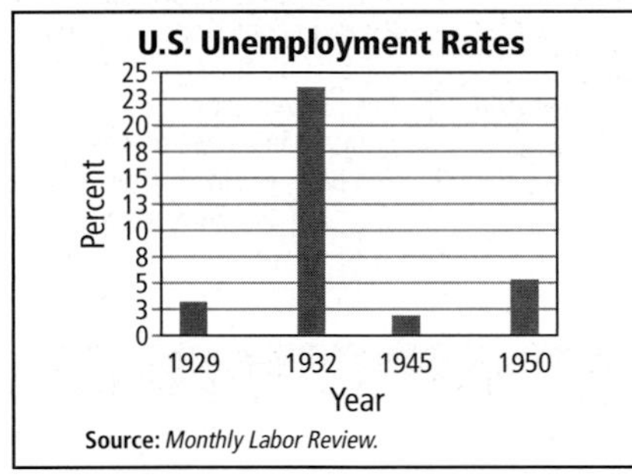

Source: *Monthly Labor Review.*

18. Why did the unemployment rate rise steeply in 1932 and then plunge to below 1929 levels in 1945?
   - **A** More people were without jobs in 1929 because of the Great Depression.
   - **B** The unemployment rate rebounded to 10 percent in 1950.
   - **C** The Great Depression began in 1929 and affected the economy for several years; the 1945 rate reflected that of a war economy.
   - **D** The Cold War affected the unemployment rate of 1950.

Document-Based Questions

Directions: Analyze the document and answer the short-answer questions that follow the document. Base your answers on the document and on your knowledge of world history.

Rudolf Höss, commanding officer at the Auschwitz death camp, described the experience awaiting the Jews when they arrived there:

> *"We had two SS doctors on duty at Auschwitz to examine the incoming transports of prisoners. The prisoners would be marched by one of the doctors who would make spot decisions as they walked by. Those who were fit for work were sent into the camp. Others were sent immediately to the extermination plants. Children of tender years were invariably exterminated since by reason of their youth they were unable to work. . . . At Auschwitz we fooled the victims into thinking that they were to go through a delousing process. Frequently they realized our true intentions and we sometimes had riots and difficulties due to that fact."*
>
> *—Nazi Conspiracy and Aggression, vol. 6, 1946*

19. What is the tone of Höss's description? What were his feelings toward the Jewish people?

20. According to Höss's description, who among the Jewish people were first sent to the extermination plants?

Extended Response

21. The Treaty of Versailles imposed harsh reparations on Germany after World War I. Hitler wanted changes. Analyze whether events leading to World War II, or even the war itself, would have occurred if England, France, and Italy had enforced the provisions of the Treaty of Versailles when Germany initially broke them.

For additional test practice, use Self-Check Quizzes—Chapter 26 at glencoe.com.

Need Extra Help?

If You Missed Questions . . .	16	17	18	19	20	21
Go to Page . . .	859	864	893	893	893	856

STOP

Document-Based Questions

19. Answers may vary. Possible answers include: contemptuous, very unfeeling, viewed them much like one does animals going to slaughter.

20. They were people not fit for work, including "children of tender years."

Extended Response

21. Answers will vary, but should be consistent with material presented in this chapter and supported by logical arguments.

16. A Without fear of Soviet attack, Hitler was free to attack Poland. Other answers have no relevance.

17. B Knowledge of content is essential to put these events in order. All are important events during the period.

18. C All other answers only respond to part of the question while answer C refers to both the unemployment rise and its fall.

Introduce students to chapter content and key terms by having them access the Chapter 26 Overview at glencoe.com.

Need Extra Help?

Have students refer to the pages listed if they miss any of the questions.

Focus

Introducing TIME Notebook

Ask: Why do you think the British Prime Minister permitted Murrow's broadcasts? *(Answers may include that he wanted the United States to enter the war on the side of England.)*

Teach

S Skill Practice

Visual Literacy Ask: How do the two buildings shown here exemplify the Bauhaus style of architecture? *(Answers may include that they look very sleek and modern without any unnecessary details.)* **BL**

W Writing Support

Descriptive Writing Point out that Edward R. Murrow's report was on the radio in the days before television was common. Invite students to identify phrases in the report that provide listeners with a vivid picture of what is happening. Then have them write their own radio report of a real or pretend event. **OL**

Additional Support

TIME NOTEBOOK

Whose House? Bauhaus!

The U.S. erects the tallest buildings. But the heights of modern architecture are being reached in Europe, by Bauhaus. Bauhaus is a design school founded in Germany in 1919. It is also the name of a revolutionary style of streamlined architecture produced by the school's teachers and students. "Bauhauses" have no ornamentation and reject the architecture of the past. This building style (examples below) may be the wave of the future. In the U.S., a few architects, such as Richard Neutra and Irving Gill, are also creating modernistic buildings, in what they call the International Style.

HEIDI JAMES/ALAMY

S

Tugendhat House, Brno, Czechoslovakia (1930)
Mies van der Rohe not only designed the house, he designed everything in it. He even indicated where to place the furniture. A home where you practically have to ask the architect's permission to move a chair may not be everyone's dream house.

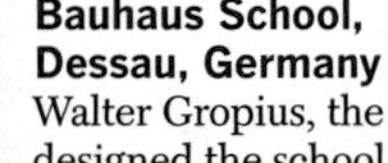

FORESTER YVES/CORBIS SYGMA

Bauhaus School, Dessau, Germany (1925)
Walter Gropius, the founder of Bauhaus, designed the school itself. Its flat roof reduces wind and rain damage. And it can also serve as a classroom or a garden. Many of the school's walls are glass so the classes are flooded with light. Who knew school could look this cool!

VERBATIM

"If you are lucky enough to have lived in Paris as a young man, then wherever you go for the rest of your life it stays with you, for Paris is a moveable feast."

ERNEST HEMINGWAY, *one of many American writers who moved to Paris after World War I*

"Beyond this day, no thinking person could fail to see what would happen."

OSKAR SCHINDLER, *the German industrialist, who saved nearly 1,200 Jews who worked in his factory from being killed by the Nazis*

"Every Communist must grasp the truth, 'Political power grows out of the barrel of a gun.'"

MAO ZEDONG, *leader of the Communist Party in China*

"It is the policy of Africans to take the place of Europeans, but the real point of disagreement is as to the rate this process should proceed. The government feels this process is too fast. The people, that it is too slow."

SIERRA LEONE *DAILY MAIL*, *in an article, 1936*

LONDON CALLING

In 1940, Edward R. Murrow began giving Americans live, firsthand reports of what it's like to be in London during German bombing raids, called the blitz. The broadcasts have been building sympathy in the U.S. for England in its fight against the Nazis—exactly as Winston Churchill had predicted when he okayed Murrow's transmissions. Here is part of a broadcast Murrow made from London.

W

This is Trafalgar Square. The noise that you hear at the moment is the sound of the air raid sirens. A searchlight just burst into action off in the distance. One single beam sweeping the sky above me now. People are walking along quite quietly. We're just at the entrance of an air-raid shelter here and I must move this cable over just a bit so people can walk in. I'll let you hear the traffic and the sounds of the sirens for a moment. More searchlights coming into action. You see them reach straight up into the sky and occasionally they catch a cloud and seem to splash on the bottom of it. . . . One of the strangest sounds one can hear in London these days—or rather these dark nights—just the sound of footsteps walking along the street, like ghosts shod with steel shoes.

POPPERFOTO/ALAMY

Background

Oskar Schindler Born in Czechoslovakia in 1908, Oskar Schindler joined the Nazi party when he was a young man. In 1939, Germany invaded Poland and expanded its persecution of Jews, dissident intellectuals, and other so-called "undesirables." By this time Oskar Schindler had established himself as a successful businessman with contacts among the Nazis and the German Gestapo. Hoping to profit from the war, he opened a factory in the city of Krakow, Poland. Most of his workers were Jewish. It soon became clear to Schindler that the Nazis intended to exterminate all the Jews who lived in Krakow. Schindler could not tolerate the brutality he witnessed under Nazi occupation. He succeeded in convincing the Nazis that his factory workers were essential for the war effort and should not be sent to their death. Eventually, he opened up a new factory close to Plaszow, a labor camp run by an SS commander. To protect the Jewish families who depended on him, Oskar Schindler had them sent to this new factory where he and his wife looked after their needs and saved them from the gas chambers.

MARY EVANS PICTURE LIBRARY/ALAMY

Tut, Tut

Curse of the pharaohs? Tosh! scoffs Howard Carter, who is alive and well. In 1922, the English archaeologist dug his way into King Tut's 3,000-year-old tomb located in Egypt's Valley of the Kings. The tomb contained treasures buried with the pharaoh. This excerpt from Carter's recent account of his discovery describes first entering the tomb.

With trembling hands I made a tiny breach in the upper left-hand corner [of the door]. Darkness and blank space, as far as an iron testing-rod could reach, showed that whatever lay beyond was empty ... and then, widening the hole a little, I inserted [a] candle and peered in, Lord Carnarvon. . . . standing anxiously beside me to hear the verdict. At first I could see nothing, the hot air escaping from the chamber causing the candle flame to flicker, but presently, as my eyes grew accustomed to the light, details of the room within emerged slowly from the mist, strange animals, statues, and gold—everywhere the glint of gold. For the moment—an eternity it must have seemed to the others standing by—I was struck dumb with amazement, and when Lord Carnarvon, unable to stand the suspense any longer, inquired anxiously, "Can you see anything?" it was all I could do to get out the words, "Yes, wonderful things."

Milestones

EMBALMED. V. I. LENIN, upon his death in 1924. The body of Lenin, the Communist leader of the Russian Revolution and first premier of the Soviet Union, has been preserved and placed on display in a mausoleum in Moscow's Red Square.

PROVED. ALBERT EINSTEIN'S THEORY OF RELATIVITY, by measurements taken during a solar eclipse in 1919. As Einstein's theory had predicted, light from distant stars bent around the sun due to gravity caused by the curving of space-time. Though scientists no longer doubt his theory, the general public remains relatively baffled. **D**

WON. THE FIRST WORLD SOCCER TOURNAMENT, by host team Uruguay, which defeated Argentina 4 to 2, in 1930. Thirteen teams competed, but many European teams did not. They refused to make the three-week trip by boat to South America.

DESTROYED. Much of **TOKYO AND YOKOHAMA** by a powerful earthquake that struck the cities on September 1, 1923. The 8.3-magnitude trembler resulted in the deaths of nearly 100,000 people, with thousands more missing. Fires left hundreds of thousands of people homeless, as traditional paper and wood houses quickly burned.

BY THE NUMBERS

250 The average length in yards of "no-man's land"—the space between the trenches of Allied and Central Powers—during World War I

70 million The number of soldiers and civilians killed in battle in World War I and World War II combined

500,000 The number of Africans who fought for France and Britain in World War II

HULTON-DEUTSCH COLLECTION/CORBIS

248 The number of miles that Gandhi, along with 78 supporters, walked in protest of Britain's salt tax and ban on Indians producing their own salt (which affects nearly everyone in India) in 1930. The 24-day march focused attention on the nation's independence movement.

6 The number of governments that ruled Chile between 1931 and 1932—a time of instability because of the Great Depression

CRITICAL THINKING

1. **Distinguishing Fact From Fiction** In "Whose House? Bauhaus!," can you give examples of facts and opinions?
2. **Determining Cause and Effect** How would Murrow's broadcast help Churchill's plans for drawing the United States into the war against Germany?

D Differentiated Instruction

Visual/Spatial Show a chart or diagram that illustrates the curving of space-time according to Einstein's theory. **OL**

Assess/Close

Visual/Spatial Have students draw a picture to highlight the events and the "feel" of the period between 1914 and 1945. **OL**

Visit the TIME Web site at www.time.com for up-to-date news, weekly magazine articles, editorials, online polls, and an archive of past magazine and Web articles.

CRITICAL THINKING

Answers:

1. **Fact:** "Bauhaus is a design school founded in Germany in 1919." **Opinion:** "This building style . . . may be the wave of the future."
2. Murrow's broadcast helped make Americans more aware of how the war was affecting the British people.

Activity: Why Is It Important?

Identifying Central Issues Before Einstein, scientists understood gravity as an external force that acted upon objects. But Einstein proposed that matter causes space to curve. Smaller objects moving toward larger objects are not drawn by some mysterious force called gravity. Instead, they are moving through curved space. The moon, for instance, is constantly falling toward Earth as it travels through curved space. Einstein's Theory of General Relativity has had a significant impact on how we understand the universe. Using this theory, scientists are able to predict the existence of black holes. General Relativity also led to the Big Bang theory of how the universe began. **Ask:** **How does the theoretical work of scientists affect the general public?** *(Answers may include that while the work of scientists doesn't always have a direct or an immediate effect on the general public, some theories lead to practical applications that improve or change people's lives.)* **AL**

UNIT 6 Planning Guide

UNIT PACING CHART								
Unit 6		Chapter 27	Chapter 28	Chapter 29	Chapter 30	Chapter 31	Chapter 32	Unit 6
Day 1	Unit Opener	Chapter Opener, Section 1	Chapter Opener, Section 1	Chapter Opener, Section 1	Chapter Opener, Section 1	Chapter Opener, Section 1	Chapter Opener, Section 1	Time Notebook, Unit Assessment
Day 2		Geography and History, Section 2	Section 1, Section 2	Section 1, Section 2	Section 1, Social History	Section 2, Section 3	Section 2, Visual Summary	
Day 3		Section 3, Social History, Visual Summary	Section 3, Section 4	Section 3, Social History, Visual Summary	Section 2, Analyzing Primary Sources, Visual Summary	Social History, Visual Summary	Review/ Chapter Assessment	
Day 4		Chapter Assessment	Section 4, Social History, Visual Summary	Chapter Assessment	Chapter Assessment	Chapter Assessment		
Day 5			Chapter Assessment					

Teacher to Teacher

Erin Johnston
South Caldwell High School
Hudson, North Carolina

History Music Video Project Have students select a figure, event, or era from world and American history as well as a song. (I generally try to have them use a song that is no more than 5 minutes long to keep the file size down. You may want them to bring a copy of the lyrics to you so you can determine appropriateness.) If you are uncertain about the choice you should ask students to explain their "vision" to you. Explain to them that they are telling a story through images, songs, and quotes to their audience. I have been surprised at how insightful my students have been in selecting their songs.

There are many programs that allow you to make videos, with many schools having moviemaking software already loaded on school computers. Many students already know how to use this technology and may help demonstrate it in class. The media programs are fairly simple "click and drag" programs that have directions on the screen. I generally have my students save 30–50 images for their projects. These programs allow you to include actual film footage and add quotes/passages as "eyewitness accounts." These videos have become powerful teaching tools in helping my students understand historical periods, such as the Cold War, and recent events.

Author Note

Dear World History Teacher:

You may want to use the following information at the beginning of each chapter as a lesson launcher to help students focus on what they will be studying.

As you begin to teach this unit, a number of important concepts stand out. World War II can be seen as the end of an era of European domination of the world. Europe became quickly divided into hostile camps as the Cold War rivalry between the United States and the Soviet Union forced the European nations to become dependent on one or the other of the superpowers. This ideological conflict spread as the United States entered the Korean War in 1950 and the Vietnam War in 1965. In Eastern Europe, Soviet domination, both politically and economically, seemed so complete that many doubted it could ever be undone. And yet in the late 1980s, the Soviet empire began to come apart, and by 1990, upheaval in the Soviet Union and Eastern Europe brought an end to the Cold War. The Cold War had ended, but the form of a new world order had not yet been reached. At the same time, as the technological revolution increased communication around the globe, nations became more interdependent, while terrorism made them more vulnerable.

The peoples of Africa and Asia had their own reasons for optimism as World War II came to a close. Between 1947 and 1962, virtually every colony in Asia and Africa achieved independence. In a few instances, such as in Algeria, Indonesia, and Vietnam, the transition to independence was a violent one. For the most part, though, it was realized by peaceful means. The end of colonial empires did not mean that the peoples of Africa and Asia enjoyed political stability and material prosperity. Although a number of nations in Asia have entered the group of the advanced industrial countries and have embarked on the road to political democracy, many of the new nations struggled with civil war, population growth, drought, hunger, economic struggles, and dictatorial regimes.

Jackson J. Spielvogel

Senior Author

Focus

Why It Matters

Remind students that the United States was once a colonial possession. Like many of the colonies in Asia and Africa, it fought for its independence and then struggled for many years trying to come together as a nation. Discuss with students how the world has changed since that time. Ask students what they know about struggles for independence today and discuss why people continue to struggle in such ways.

Unit Launch Activity

Have students write a sentence or two about what they think "global civilization" means. **Ask:** **How have things such as the Internet changed the way people think about other parts of the world?** *(Accept all reasonable answers.)* Then have students discuss their ideas in small groups where they make a chart listing the pros and cons of a global civilization. **OL**

UNIT 6

Toward a Global Civilization

1945–Present

▶ Why It Matters

World War II can be seen as the end of European domination of the world. After the war, the Cold War rivalry between the United States and the Soviet Union forced nations to take sides. In the late 1980s, the Soviet Empire began to come apart, and the Cold War ended. World War II also undermined the colonial order in Asia and Africa. Most colonies in Asia and Africa would become independent nations.

Afghan troops deploying to deal with the state of emergency in Kabul, Afghanistan, caused by the pullout of Soviet troops in 1989.

Team Teaching Activity

Science and Technology The text ends with a discussion of the challenges that face the world today. Many of these issues have developed as a result of, and may be solved by, advances in science and technology. Invite a science teacher to work with your class to compile a list of issues such as energy consumption and global warming, consumption of material goods and pollution, terrorism and the resulting problems of land mines and biological warfare, and advances in medicine and the economics of pharmaceutical research. Assign students to research one issue addressed by the science teacher and then to prepare a multimedia report showing the relationship between the issue and world history.

Teach

S Skill Practice

Visual Literacy Have students work in small groups to develop a two-column chart for the unit. The chart should list what the group feels it already knows about the material covered in the unit and then should have a list of at least ten questions about what the group would like to learn through reading the unit. Encourage students to skim heads in the text and to look at images and captions to help them with their chart. OL

Using Geography Skills This photograph gives students clues regarding the environment and geography of Afghanistan. Have students describe the environment and add other information they know about Afghanistan's climate and topography. BL

No Child Left Behind

Teaching Tip Modeling can help students learn how to develop comprehension skills such as making inferences. Read aloud an excerpt from the textbook. Then model what you are thinking as you read and the inferences you are making.

More About the Photo

Visual Literacy The Soviet Union's involvement with Afghanistan first began in the 1950s in the form of foreign aid. The Soviets built roads, helped with irrigation, and built some oil pipelines. In the 1970s, however, a Communist party overthrew the king of Afghanistan. The Communists set out to reform the traditional structure of Afghan society by instating things such as land distribution and women's rights. These reforms angered much of the population. In 1979, the Soviets invaded Afghanistan with 30,000 troops that grew to 100,000. The war became a stalemate with Afghan guerrillas controlling the mountainous areas and the Soviets controlling the cities. After 10 years of fighting, the Soviet troops pulled out. Afghanistan's economy was in ruins and the various guerrilla groups that had fought the Soviets could not unite to form a central government. These divisions help set the stage for the Taliban.

CHAPTER 27 Planning Guide

Key to Ability Levels	
BL Below Level	AL Above Level
OL On Level	ELL English Language Learners

Key to Teaching Resources	
Print Material	DVD
CD-ROM	Transparency

Levels				Resources	Chapter Opener	Section 1	Section 2	Section 3	Chapter Assess
BL	OL	AL	ELL						
				FOCUS					
BL	OL	AL	ELL	**Daily Focus Skills Transparencies**		27-1	27-2	27-3	
				TEACH					
	OL	AL		**Economics and History Activity, URB**				✓	
BL	OL		ELL	**Reading Skills Activity, URB**				p. 17	
	OL	AL		**Historical Analysis Skills Activity, URB**				p. 18	
BL	OL	AL	ELL	**Differentiated Instruction Activity, URB**				p. 19	
	OL		ELL	**English Learner Activity, URB**		p. 21			
BL	OL	AL	ELL	**Content Vocabulary Activity, URB***		p. 23			
BL	OL	AL	ELL	**Academic Vocabulary Activity, URB**			p. 25		
BL	OL	AL	ELL	**Skills Reinforcement Activity, URB**		p. 27			
	OL	AL		**Critical Thinking Skills Activity, URB**				p. 28	
	OL	AL		**History and Geography Activity, URB**		p. 29			
	OL	AL	ELL	**Mapping History Activity, URB**		p. 31			
BL	OL	AL		**Historical Significance Activity, URB**				p. 32	
BL	OL	AL	ELL	**Cooperative Learning Activity, URB**		p. 33			
	OL	AL	ELL	**History Simulation Activity, URB**				p. 35	
BL	OL	AL	ELL	**Time Line Activity, URB**			p. 37		
	OL	AL		**Linking Past and Present Activity, URB**		p. 38			
BL	OL	AL		**People in World History Activity, URB**		p. 39	p. 40		
BL	OL	AL	ELL	**Primary Source Reading, URB**				p. 41	
	OL	AL		**Enrichment Activity, URB**		p. 46			
BL	OL	AL	ELL	**World Art and Music Activity, URB**				p. 43	
BL	OL		ELL	**Guided Reading Activities, URB***		p. 48	p. 49	p. 50	
BL	OL		ELL	**Reading Essentials and Note-Taking Guide***		p. 298	p. 301	p. 304	
BL	OL	AL	ELL	**Differentiated Instruction for the World History Classroom**	✓	✓	✓	✓	✓

Note: Please refer to the *Unit Resource Book: Toward a Global Civilization* for this chapter's URB materials.

* Also available in Spanish

- Interactive Lesson Planner
- Interactive Teacher Edition
- Fully editable blackline masters
- Section Spotlight Videos Launch
- Differentiated Lesson Plans
- Printable reports of daily assignments
- Standards Tracking System

Levels					Resources	Chapter Opener	Section 1	Section 2	Section 3	Chapter Assess
BL	OL	AL	ELL							
TEACH *(continued)*										
BL	OL	AL	ELL		**StudentWorks™ Plus DVD**	✓	✓	✓	✓	✓
BL	OL	AL	ELL		**Vocabulary PuzzleMaker CD-ROM**	✓	✓	✓	✓	✓
Teacher Resources					**Building Academic Vocabulary**	✓	✓	✓	✓	✓
					Reading Strategies and Activities for the Social Studies Classroom					
					Writer's Guidebook		p. 12	p. 43		
					Strategies for Success	✓	✓	✓	✓	✓
					Outline Map Resource Book	✓	✓	✓	✓	✓
					Presentation Plus! with MindJogger DVD	✓	✓	✓	✓	✓
ASSESS										
BL	OL	AL	ELL		**Section Quizzes and Chapter Tests***		p. 337	p. 338	p. 339	p. 341
BL	OL	AL	ELL		**Authentic Assessment With Rubrics**	✓	✓	✓	✓	✓
BL	OL	AL	ELL		**Standardized Test Practice Workbook**	✓	✓	✓	✓	✓
BL	OL	AL	ELL		***ExamView® Assessment Suite* CD-ROM**		27-1	27-2	27-3	Ch. 27
BL	OL	AL	ELL		**Interactive Tutor Self-Assessment CD-ROM**		27-1	27-2	27-3	
CLOSE										
BL			ELL		**Reteaching Activity, URB**				p. 45	
BL	OL		ELL		**Reading and Study Skills Foldables™**	✓	✓	✓	✓	✓

Using the McGraw-Hill Learning Network

Web Site Builder

Technology Product

The Web Site Builder is a convenient and dynamic McGraw-Hill Learning Network tool that helps you build Web sites quickly. The site allows you to include your own images, videos, and text to customize it to your needs. The Web Site Builder also provides you with a variety of tools to make your Web site inviting. Use the Web Site Builder to

- provide assignments and important dates to your students;
- keep students and parents informed of events in your classroom;
- publish your contact information.

Steps

- On the McGraw-Hill Learning Network home page (www.mhln.com), log in as a member.
- Choose **Web Site Builder** under **Resources.**
- Choose a template from the **Create a new site** pull-down options and follow the prompts on the screen to select a design, insert text, and select fonts, colors, and sizes.
- Create the content students will need to study for a chapter test or post homework assignments.
- Use the navigation buttons on the bottom of the screen to edit, add, and delete information, images, and videos.
- Publish the site and provide the URL to your students.

History ONLINE

	Student	Teacher	Parent
Beyond the Textbook	●	●	●
Chapter Overviews	●	●	●
Time Current Events	●		●
ePuzzles and Games	●		●
Concepts in Motion	●		●
Literature Connections		●	
Multi-Language Glossaries	●		●
Online Student Edition	●	●	●
Self-Check Quizzes	●		●
Student Web Activities	●		●
Study Central ™	●		●
Teaching Today		●	
Vocabulary eFlashcards	●		●
Web Activity Lesson Plans		●	

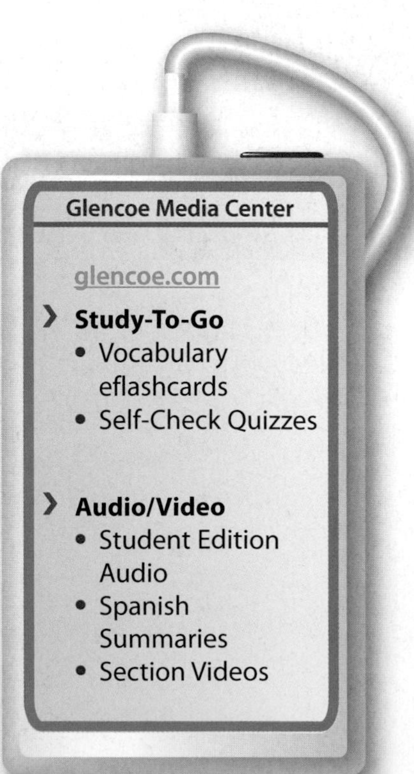

- **Timed Readings Plus in Social Studies** helps students increase their reading rate and fluency while maintaining comprehension. The 400-word passages are similar to those found on state and national assessments.
- **Reading in the Content Area: Social Studies** concentrates on six essential reading skills that help students better comprehend what they read. The book includes 75 high-interest nonfiction passages written at increasing levels of difficulty.
- **Reading Social Studies** includes strategic reading instruction and vocabulary support in Social Studies content for both ELLs and native speakers of English.

www.jamestowneducation.com

Index to National Geographic Magazine:

The following articles relate to this chapter:

- "Korea's Dangerous Divide," by Tom O'Neill, July 2003
- "Half Life: The Lethal Legacy of America's Nuclear Waste," by Michael E. Long, July 2002
- "The New Europe," by T. R. Reid, January 2002

National Geographic Society Products To order the following, call National Geographic at 1-800-368-2728:

- *National Geographic Atlas of the World* (Book)

Access National Geographic's new, dynamic MapMachine Web site and other geography resources at:
www.nationalgeographic.com
www.nationalgeographic.com/maps

Biography  

The following videotape programs are available from Glencoe as supplements to Chapter 27:

- Cuba and Castro (ISBN 0-76-701426-X)
- Fidel Castro: El Commandante (ISBN 0-76-700237-7)
- Joseph Stalin: Red Terror (ISBN 1-56-501820-6)

To order, call Glencoe at 1-800-334-7344. To find classroom resources to accompany many of these videos, check the following home pages:

A&E Television: www.aetv.com

The History Channel: www.historychannel.com

Reading List Generator CD-ROM

GLENCOE BOOKLINK 3

Use this database to search more than 30,000 titles to create a customized reading list for your students.

- Reading lists can be organized by students' reading level, author, genre, theme, or area of interest.
- The database provides Degrees of Reading Power™ (DRP) and Lexile™ readability scores for all selections.
- A brief summary of each selection is included.

Leveled reading suggestions for this chapter:

For students at a Grade 8 reading level:
- ***John F. Kennedy: America's Youngest President,*** by Post Frisbee

For students at a Grade 9 reading level:
- ***Fidel Castro: Leader of Cuba's Revolution,*** by Tom Gibb

For students at a Grade 10 reading level:
- ***United Nations,*** by Stewart Ross

For students at a Grade 11 reading level:
- ***Harry S. Truman,*** by Caroline Evensen Lazo

For students at a Grade 12 reading level:
- ***The Bridge at Andau,*** by James A. Michener

Introducing CHAPTER 27

Focus

MAKING CONNECTIONS

How can a nation defend itself in the nuclear age?

Activate students' prior knowledge by having them brainstorm what they know about nuclear weapons. Have students identify which countries have nuclear weapons today. Then ask them to discuss the importance of halting the spread of nuclear weapons to other countries. Close the discussion by having students debate whether governments should allocate more money to homeland security organizations and military defense systems.

Teach

The Big Ideas

As students study the chapter, remind them to consider the section-based Big Ideas included in each section's Guide to Reading. The **Essential Questions** in the activities below tie in to the Big Ideas and help students think about and understand important chapter concepts. In addition, the Hands-on Chapter Projects with their culminating activities relate the content from each section to the Big Ideas. These activities build on each other as students progress through the chapter. Section activities culminate in the wrap-up activity on the Visual Summary page.

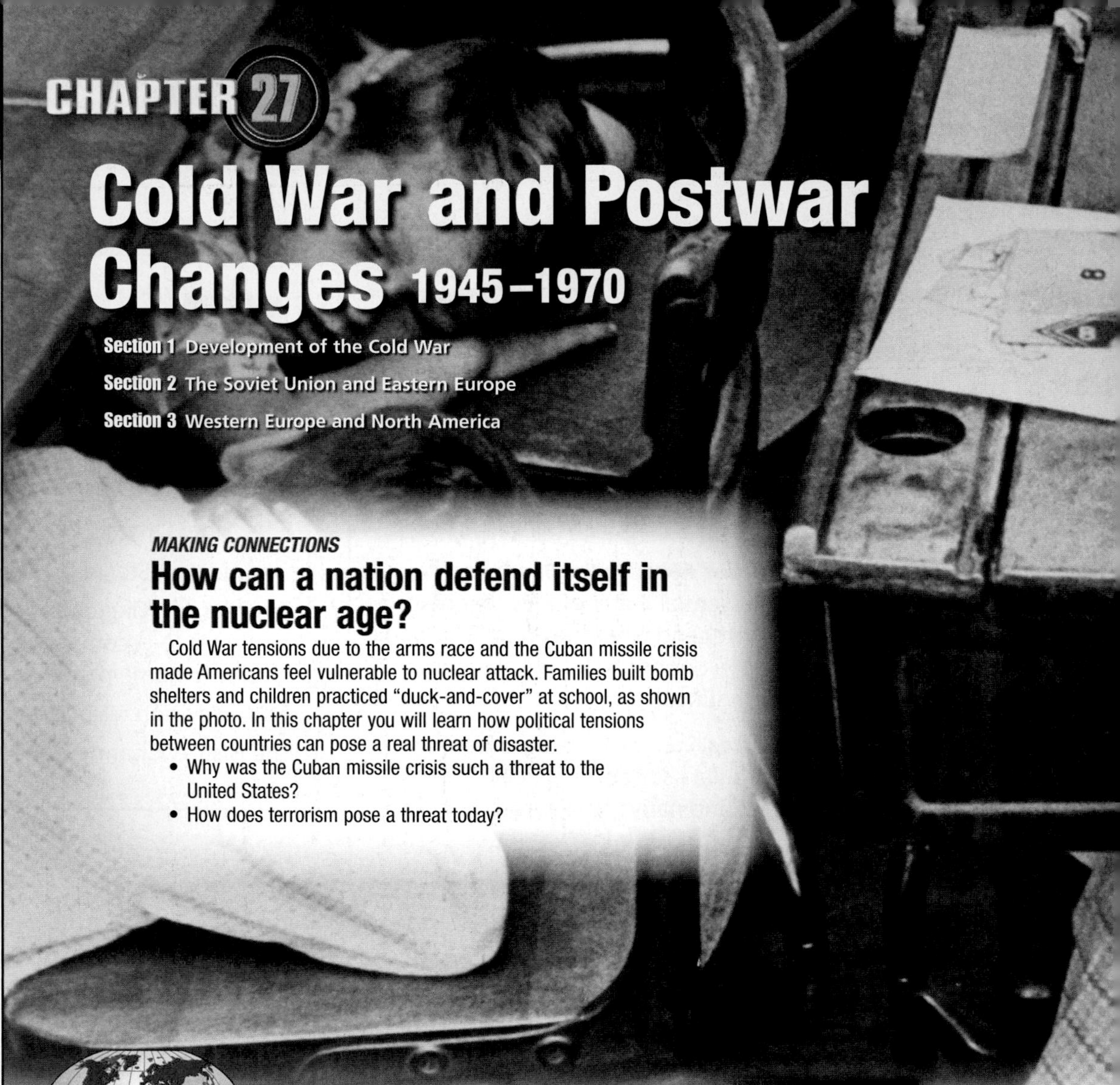

CHAPTER 27

Cold War and Postwar Changes 1945–1970

MAKING CONNECTIONS

How can a nation defend itself in the nuclear age?

Cold War tensions due to the arms race and the Cuban missile crisis made Americans feel vulnerable to nuclear attack. Families built bomb shelters and children practiced "duck-and-cover" at school, as shown in the photo. In this chapter you will learn how political tensions between countries can pose a real threat of disaster.

- Why was the Cuban missile crisis such a threat to the United States?
- How does terrorism pose a threat today?

EUROPE, THE SOVIET UNION, AND THE UNITED STATES ▶

1945 Cold War begins

1947 President Truman establishes Truman Doctrine

1957 Soviets launch *Sputnik I*

1945 — 1950 — 1955

THE WORLD ▶

1947 India and Pakistan become independent nations

1956 Suez War begins in Egypt

898

Development of the Cold War

Essential Question: What differences between the Soviet Union and the United States led to the conflict known as the Cold War? *(The Soviet Union feared capitalism while the United States feared communism.)* Tell students that in Section 1, they will learn more about the ways in which the Cold War shaped economic, political, and military policies and alliances in Europe, the Americas, and Asia. OL

The Soviet Union and Eastern Europe

Essential Question: How does a totalitarian government differ from a democratic system? *(Totalitarianism offers no protection of human rights or civil liberties.)* Point out that in Section 2, students will learn how various Communist countries reacted to Soviet domination. OL

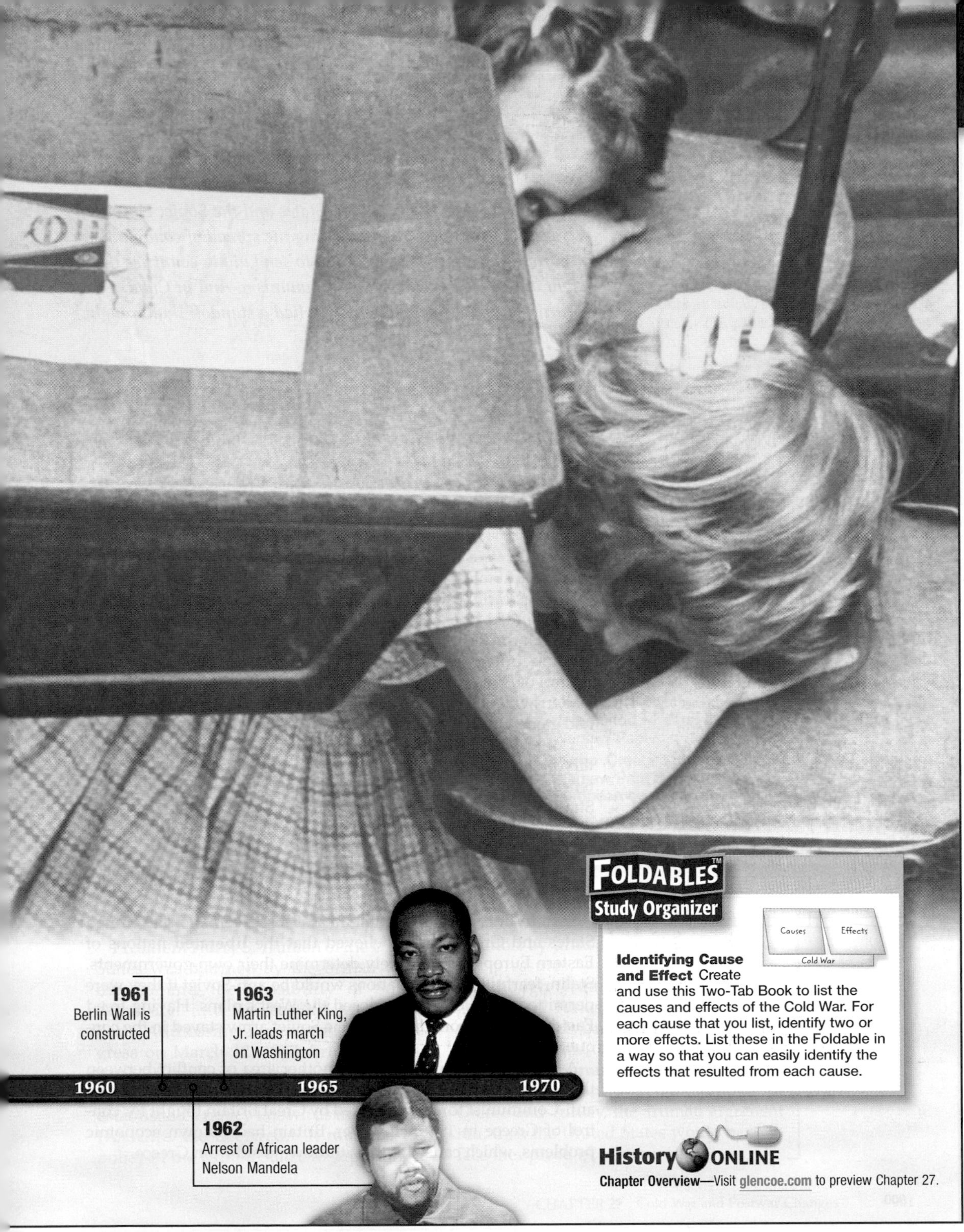

1961
Berlin Wall is constructed

1963
Martin Luther King, Jr. leads march on Washington

1960 — 1965 — 1970

1962
Arrest of African leader Nelson Mandela

FOLDABLES™ Study Organizer

Causes | Effects
Cold War

Identifying Cause and Effect Create and use this Two-Tab Book to list the causes and effects of the Cold War. For each cause that you list, identify two or more effects. List these in the Foldable in a way so that you can easily identify the effects that resulted from each cause.

History ONLINE
Chapter Overview—Visit glencoe.com to preview Chapter 27.

SECTION 3

Western Europe and North America
Essential Question: Why did World War II leave society open to change? *(The devastation caused by World War II meant that life could not simply return to normal. Resources that would allow people to resume their old lives were lacking. Also, they were anxious to avoid the same circumstances that had led to such a war.)* Tell students that in Section 3, they will learn about the various movements and trends associated with the postwar period. **OL**

Introducing
CHAPTER 27

More About the Photo

Visual Literacy To Americans in the 1950s and early 1960s, the threat of nuclear war was very real. Drills such as the one pictured here were routine for school children. They were told to "duck and cover" in order to avoid the falling debris and the shock of explosion caused by the bomb. Civil defense officials also urged citizens to build fallout shelters in their yards and stock them with supplies. The interstate highway system taken for granted today came about because President Eisenhower wanted to make sure that the inhabitants of major cities could be evacuated quickly in case of a nuclear attack.

Dinah Zike's Foldables

Dinah Zike's Foldables are three-dimensional, interactive graphic organizers that help students practice basic writing skills, review vocabulary terms, and identify main ideas. Instructions for creating and using Foldables can be found in the Appendix at the end of this book and in the *Dinah Zike's Reading and Study Skills Foldables* booklet.

Introduce students to chapter content and key terms by having them access the Chapter 27 Overview at glencoe.com.

D Differentiated Instruction

Verbal/Linguistic Ask students to explain how the term *containment* describes a change in U.S. policy toward communism. *(The term describes the reality that communism was well established, so working to stop its spread seemed wiser than overthrowing it by force.)* **OL**

R Reading Strategy

Predicting Explain that the United States and Great Britain also airlifted industrial exports out of West Berlin. **Ask:** What would have happened if West Berlin had been unable to export goods? *(Trade and the flow of money into the city would have been cut off.)* **OL**

✓Reading Check

Answer: It provided financial aid to Europe to spur economic recovery and help resist Communist aggression.

Additional Support

Dean Acheson, who served as the U.S. secretary of state, explained:

PRIMARY SOURCE

> "Like apples in a barrel infected by disease, the corruption of Greece would infect Iran and all the East . . . likewise Africa, Italy, France. . . . Not since Rome and Carthage had there been such a polarization of power on this earth."
>
> —Quoted in *The Fifteen Weeks (February 21–June 5, 1947)*, 2nd ed., Joseph M. Jones, 1964

The Marshall Plan

The Truman Doctrine was followed in June 1947 by the European Recovery Program. Proposed by General George C. Marshall, U.S. secretary of state, it is better known as the **Marshall Plan.** Marshall believed that communism was successful in countries with economic problems. Thus, to prevent the spread of communism, the Marshall Plan provided $13 billion to rebuild war-torn Europe.

The Marshall Plan was not meant to exclude the Soviet Union or its economically and politically dependent Eastern European **satellite states.** Those states refused to participate, however. According to the Soviet view, the Marshall Plan guaranteed "American loans in return for the relinquishing by the European states of their economic and later also their political independence." The Soviets saw the Marshall Plan as an attempt to buy the support of countries.

In 1949 the Soviet Union responded to the Marshall Plan by founding the Council for Mutual Economic Assistance (COMECON) for the economic cooperation of the Eastern European states. COMECON largely failed, however, because the Soviet Union was unable to provide much financial aid.

D By 1947, the split in Europe between the United States and the Soviet Union had become a fact of life. In July 1947, George Kennan, a well-known U.S. diplomat with much knowledge of Soviet affairs, argued for a **policy of containment** to keep communism within its existing boundaries and prevent further Soviet aggressive moves. Containment became U.S. policy.

The Division of Germany

The fate of Germany also became a source of heated contention between the Soviets and the West. At the end of the war, the Allied Powers had divided Germany into four zones, each occupied by one of the Allies—the United States, the Soviet Union, Great Britain, and France. **Berlin,** located deep inside the Soviet zone, was also divided into four zones.

The foreign ministers of the four occupying powers met repeatedly in an attempt to arrive at a final peace treaty with Germany but had little success. By February 1948, Great Britain, France, and the United States were making plans to unify the three Western sections of Germany (and Berlin) and create a West German government.

The Soviets opposed the creation of a separate West German state. They attempted to prevent it by mounting a blockade of West Berlin. Soviet forces allowed neither trucks, trains, nor barges to enter the city's three Western zones. Food and supplies could no longer get through to the 2.5 million people in these zones.

R The Western powers faced a dilemma. No one wanted another war, but how could the people in the Western zones of Berlin be kept alive when the whole city was blockaded inside the Soviet zone? The solution was the Berlin Airlift—supplies would be flown in by American and British airplanes. For more than 10 months, more than 200,000 flights carried 2.3 million tons (1.4 million t) of supplies. The Soviets, who wanted to avoid war as much as the Western powers, finally gave in and lifted the blockade in May 1949.

In September 1949, the **Federal Republic of Germany,** or West Germany, was formally created. Its capital was Bonn. Less than a month later, a separate East German state, the **German Democratic Republic,** was set up by the Soviets. East Berlin became its capital. Berlin was now divided into two parts, a reminder of the division of West and East.

✓Reading Check **Describing** What was the intention of the Marshall Plan?

Extending the Content

George Marshall President Truman called George Marshall, the originator of the Marshall Plan and Chief of Staff of the U.S. Army during World War II, the "greatest living American." Winston Churchill credited him with being the "true 'organizer of victory.'" Under Marshall's command, the U.S. army grew from 200,000 troops and officers in 1939 to more than 8 million in 1942. In his role as representative of the Joint Chiefs of Staff at international conferences, he promoted the plan to attack German forces by crossing the English Channel, the invasion that led to victory in Europe. Because of his importance to the Allied efforts, however, the command was given to Dwight Eisenhower. Marshall was kept stateside by President Roosevelt, who said "I didn't feel I could sleep at ease with you out of Washington." After the war, as secretary of state, he again proved his farsightedness with his proposal of the Marshall Plan, which both unified and saved Europe. Marshall won a Nobel Prize for this plan in 1953.

The Cold War Spreads

MAIN IDEA As Cold War tensions increased, nations were forced to choose to support the Soviet Union or the United States.

HISTORY & YOU Have you ever tried to gain supporters to help you win an argument? Read to learn how Communist and anti-Communist alliances formed as the Cold War spread.

In 1949 Chiang Kai-shek finally lost control of China, and the Communist Mao Zedong announced the formation of the People's Republic of China. Mao's victory strengthened U.S. fears about the spread of communism. The Soviet Union also exploded its first atomic bomb in 1949.

The Arms Race

All too soon, the United States and the Soviet Union were becoming involved in a growing **arms race,** in which both countries built up their armies and weapons. **Nuclear** weapons became increasingly destructive as each superpower raced to build deadlier bombs.

Both sides came to believe that an arsenal of nuclear weapons would actually prevent war. They believed that if one nation attacked with nuclear weapons, the other nation would still be able to respond.

INFOGRAPHICS PRIMARY SOURCE

The Berlin Airlift

On the morning of June 24, 1948, the Soviet Union cut off all rail, road, and water routes into West Berlin in an attempt to force the Allies to abandon the city. It was the first major crisis of the Cold War.

Lucius Clay, the military governor of the U.S. sector of West Germany, warned, "When Berlin falls, West Germany will be next." Military retaliation was unthinkable, however. The Soviet Union's armed forces were stronger than the combined forces of the West.

W On July 1, the United States and Great Britain began sending cargo planes filled with food and supplies to the people of West Berlin. By winter, a plane was arriving every three minutes, 24 hours a day, delivering not just food but coal, newsprint—and even feed for the animals of the Berlin zoo. The Berlin Airlift was a success. The Soviets admitted defeat and lifted the blockade on May 12, 1949.

German children cheer an American cargo plane airlifting food and supplies to Berlin in 1948.

DOCUMENT-BASED QUESTIONS

1. **Analyzing Visuals** Why could the Allies not deliver food to West Berlin by land?
2. **Making Inferences** Why was the fate of Berlin important to the Allies and the Soviets?

W Writing Support

Expository Writing Have students write an article that might have appeared in a British or American newspaper about the Berlin Airlift. Encourage them to include facts about the reasons behind the airlift as well as information about the logistics of the operation. Suggest that students include quotations that might have been spoken by those involved. OL

DOCUMENT-BASED QUESTIONS

Answers:

1. Berlin was located in East Germany, which was a Soviet occupation zone, and the Soviets had blockaded West Berlin.
2. It was the first major dispute of the Cold War. The Soviets opposed the idea of an independent West Germany and wanted to force the Allies out of West Berlin. The Allies believed that if they lost control of their zones in Berlin, West Germany would also fall to the Communists.

Activity: Technology Connection

Chronicling the Arms Race Ask: What was the goal of the superpowers in the arms race? *(Each wanted to build the most intimidating arsenal of weapons.)* The Cuban missile crisis in 1962, which took the world to the brink of nuclear war, prompted some rethinking on the issue. Since then, leaders have taken different approaches to the question of nuclear proliferation. Have students work in small groups to create a chronology showing the direction of the arms race over the decades since World War II and the various weapons technologies that have replaced the original atomic bomb. Allow students to annotate their chronologies and display them to the class. OL

C Critical Thinking

Analyzing Primary Sources

Ask: What does the letter suggest about Khrushchev's reaction to the crisis? *(He felt relieved that the crisis was over, but viewed a possible recurrence of the situation with dread.)* **OL**

DOCUMENT-BASED QUESTIONS

Answers:

1. He is getting ready to pull Castro's teeth, which represent the Soviet missiles in Cuba.
2. Khrushchev is telling Castro that the removal of the missiles will be more harmful to the Soviet Union than to Cuba. Yet from the way the teeth are drawn, it seems that the cartoonist thinks Castro will be harmed more.

POLITICAL CARTOONS PRIMARY SOURCE

The Cuban Missile Crisis

Letter from Nikita Khrushchev to President John F. Kennedy, October 28, 1962:

"I appreciate your assurance that the United States will not invade Cuba. Hence, we have ordered our officers to stop building bases, dismantle the equipment, and send it back home.

We must not allow the situation to deteriorate, (but) eliminate hotbeds of tension, and we must see to it that no other conflicts occur which might lead to a world nuclear war."

C

DOCUMENT-BASED QUESTIONS

This American political cartoon was published on October 30, 1962. Two days earlier Nikita Khrushchev had agreed to the removal of Soviet missiles from Cuba.

1. **Explaining** What is Khrushchev preparing to do, and what does his action symbolize?
2. **Identifying Points of View** Look at the caption of the cartoon. What point is the cartoonist making about the Cuban missile crisis?

Fidel Castro's teeth look like missiles.

PRIMARY SOURCE

"[T]he situation in Cuba is not a bit good. The Cuban armed forces are stronger, the popular response is weaker, and our tactical position is feebler than we had hoped. Tanks have done in one beachhead, and the position is precarious at the others."

—quote from an adviser to Kennedy

The invasion began on Sunday, April 16, 1961. By Wednesday, the exiled fighters began surrendering. One hundred and fourteen died; the rest were captured by Castro's troops.

After the Bay of Pigs, the Soviet Union sent advisers to Cuba. Then, in 1962, Khrushchev began to place nuclear missiles in Cuba. The missiles were meant to counteract U.S. nuclear weapons placed in Turkey, a country within easy range of the Soviet Union. Khrushchev said:

PRIMARY SOURCE

"Your rockets are in Turkey. You are worried by Cuba . . . because it is 90 miles from the American coast. But Turkey is next to us."

—Quoted in *Europe since 1945: An Introduction*, Peter Lane, 1985

The United States was not willing to allow nuclear weapons within such close striking distance of its mainland. In October 1962, Kennedy found out that Soviet ships carrying missiles were heading to Cuba. He decided to blockade Cuba to prevent the fleet from reaching its destination. This approach gave each side time to find a peaceful solution. Khrushchev agreed to turn back the fleet and remove Soviet missiles from Cuba if Kennedy pledged not to invade Cuba. Kennedy quickly agreed.

The Cuban missile crisis seemed to bring the world frighteningly close to nuclear

Hands-On Chapter Project
Step 1

Creating a Cold War Web Site

Small groups of students will create a Web site about the Cold War years.

Step 1: Charting Causes and Effects

Essential Question: What is the legacy of the Cold War?

Directions: Write the Big Idea on the board. Explain to students that their Web site will include pages that present information on various aspects of the Cold War. Their first page should be an analysis of the causes and effects of the Cold War, using the facts they learn in this section. Encourage students to experiment with format and design in order to make their pages user-friendly. Remind students that they can include hyperlinks to take users to additional sources of information.

Summarizing: Allow time for groups to share what they learned about the Big Idea while preparing their first Web page. **OL**

(Chapter Project is continued in Section 2.)

war. Indeed, in 1992 a high-ranking Soviet officer revealed that short-range rockets armed with nuclear devices would have been used against U.S. troops if the United States had invaded Cuba, an option that Kennedy fortunately had rejected. The realization that the world might have been destroyed in a few days had a profound influence on both sides. A hotline communications system between Moscow and Washington, D.C., was installed in 1963. The two superpowers could now communicate quickly in times of crisis.

Vietnam and the Domino Theory

By that time, the United States had been drawn into a new struggle that had an important impact on the Cold War—the Vietnam War (see Chapter 31). In 1964, under President Lyndon B. Johnson, increasing numbers of U.S. troops were sent to Vietnam. Their purpose was to keep the Communist regime of North Vietnam from invading and gaining control of South Vietnam.

U.S. policy makers saw the conflict in terms of a **domino theory.** If the Communists succeeded in South Vietnam, the argument went, other countries in Asia would also fall (like dominoes) to communism. **D**

Despite the massive superiority in equipment and firepower of the American forces, the United States failed to defeat the North Vietnamese. The growing number of American troops in Vietnam soon produced an antiwar movement in the United States, especially among college students of draft age. The mounting destruction of the conflict, seen on television, also turned American public opinion against the war.

President Johnson, condemned for his handling of the costly and indecisive war, decided not to run for reelection. Former vice president Richard M. Nixon won the election with his pledge to stop the war and bring the American people together. Ending the war was difficult, and Nixon's administration was besieged by antiwar forces.

Finally, in 1973 President Nixon reached an agreement with North Vietnam that allowed the United States to withdraw its forces. Within two years after the American withdrawal, Vietnam had been forcibly reunited by Communist armies from the North.

Despite the success of the North Vietnamese Communists, the domino theory proved unfounded. A split between Communist China and the Soviet Union put an end to the Western idea that there was a single form of communism directed by Moscow. Under President Nixon, American relations with China were resumed. New nations in Southeast Asia managed to avoid Communist governments.

Above all, Vietnam helped show the limitations of American power. By the end of the Vietnam War, a new era in American-Soviet relations had begun to emerge.

✓Reading Check **Identifying** Name the military alliances formed during the Cold War.

SECTION 1 REVIEW

Vocabulary

1. **Explain** the significance of: liberated, Truman Doctrine, Dean Acheson, Marshall Plan, satellite states, policy of containment, Berlin, Federal Republic of Germany, German Democratic Republic, arms race, nuclear, NATO, Warsaw Pact, SEATO, CENTO, deterrence, Nikita Khrushchev, domino theory.

Main Ideas

2. **Identify** the purpose of the Truman Doctrine.
3. **List** the countries in the military alliances formed during the Cold War. Use a table like the one below to make your list.

Alliance	Countries

4. **Explain** how television coverage affected the Vietnam War.

Critical Thinking

5. **The BIG Idea** **Evaluating** In your opinion, why did the United States assume global responsibility for containing communism?
6. **Making Connections** How did the Cold War confrontations affect the decision of the United States to move against Fidel Castro in Cuba? What was the outcome of that decision?
7. **Analyzing Visuals** Examine the photograph on page 903. What side of the conflict do you think the photographer supported? Explain your answer.

Writing About History

8. **Informative Writing** Imagine that you are a resident of Berlin in 1948. Write a letter to a friend living in another part of Germany explaining what is happening in Berlin and your reaction to the actions of the foreign governments involved.

History ONLINE

For help with the concepts in this section of *Glencoe World History*, go to glencoe.com and click Study Central™.

907

D Differentiated Instruction

Kinesthetic Line up a row of dominoes. Knock one down to begin the chain reaction. Then discuss how the domino theory applies to the fall of South Vietnam. **BL**

✓Reading Check

Answer: North Atlantic Treaty Organization (NATO), Warsaw Pact, Southeast Asia Treaty Organization (SEATO), Central Treaty Organization (CENTO)

Assess

Study Central provides summaries, interactive games, and online graphic organizers to help students review content.

Close

Summarizing **Ask:** Why did the Soviet Union and the United States become rivals? *(They had different ideologies; both wanted global leadership.)* **OL**

Answers

1. Definitions for the vocabulary words are found in the section and the Glossary.
2. The United States provided economic and military aid to certain countries in order to prevent Communist expansion.
3. **NATO:** Belgium, Luxembourg, France, Netherlands, Great Britain, Italy, Denmark, Norway, Portugal, Iceland, United States, Canada, West Germany, Turkey, Greece; **Warsaw Pact:** Soviet Union, Albania, Bulgaria, Czechoslovakia, East Germany, Hungary, Poland, Romania; **SEATO:** United States, Great Britain, France, Pakistan, Thailand, Philippines, Australia, New Zealand; **CENTO:** Turkey, Iraq, Iran, Pakistan, Great Britain, United States
4. Americans were able to see the horrors of war on a daily basis, changing the minds of many.
5. Answers will vary, but students may note that the United States was the leading Western power at the time.
6. The United States did not want a socialist regime with Soviet contacts so close to its mainland. The Cuban invasion was a disaster, and it led to the Cuban Missile Crisis.
7. Answers will vary, but students may say that by making cheering children the central image, the photographer implies support of the United States.
8. Answers will vary, but letters should be based on factual information from this section.

Focus

Bellringer

Daily Focus Transparency 27.2

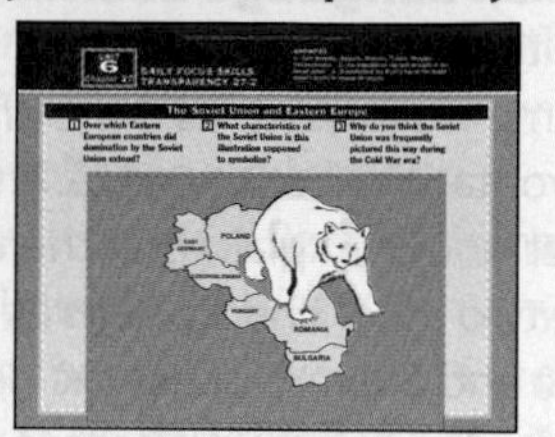

GUIDE TO READING

Answers to Graphic:

Soviet Union's Communist Policies: emphasis on heavy industry rather than consumer goods; leaders exercised sole power, stifled free expression; used political terror and repression; military intervention

Section Spotlight Video

To generate student interest and provide a springboard for class discussion, access the Chapter 27, Section 2 video at glencoe.com or on the video DVD.

Resource Manager

SECTION 2

The Soviet Union and Eastern Europe

GUIDE TO READING

The BIG Idea

Self-Determination The Soviet Union faced revolts and protests in its attempt to gain and maintain control over Eastern Europe.

Content Vocabulary
- heavy industry *(p. 910)*
- de-Stalinization *(p. 911)*

Academic Vocabulary
- enhanced *(p. 910)*
- sole *(p. 910)*

People and Places
- Soviet Union *(p. 910)*
- Aleksandr Solzhenitsyn *(p. 911)*
- Albania *(p. 912)*
- Yugoslavia *(p. 912)*
- Tito *(p. 912)*
- Poland *(p. 913)*
- Hungary *(p. 913)*
- Czechoslovakia *(p. 913)*
- Imre Nagy *(p. 913)*
- Alexander Dubček *(p. 913)*

Reading Strategy

Categorizing Information As you read, use a diagram like the one below to identify how the Soviet Union carried out Communist policies.

Stalin was a repressive leader who wanted to bring all of Eastern Europe under Soviet control. Many Communist countries came under Soviet control during this era, including Poland, Hungary, and Czechoslovakia. Albania and Yugoslavia remained independent. After Stalin's death, Nikita Khrushchev denounced the most brutal policies of the Stalin regime.

Postwar Soviet Leaders

MAIN IDEA The Soviet Union recovered rapidly after World War II, but it could not maintain high levels of industrial production.

HISTORY & YOU In a democracy, does new leadership mean a change in daily life? Read to learn how Stalin's death dramatically altered the Soviet Union.

World War II devastated the **Soviet Union.** To create a new industrial base, Stalin returned to the method that he had used in the 1930s. Soviet workers were expected to produce goods for export with little in return for themselves. The incoming capital from abroad could then be used to buy machinery and Western technology.

Economic recovery in the Soviet Union was spectacular in some respects. By 1950, Russian industrial production surpassed prewar levels by 40 percent. New power plants, canals, and giant factories were built. **Heavy industry** (the manufacture of machines and equipment for factories and mines) increased, chiefly for military benefit. The hydrogen bomb in 1953 and the first space satellite, *Sputnik I,* in 1957 **enhanced** the Soviet Union's reputation as a world power.

Yet the Soviet people were shortchanged. The production of consumer goods did not increase as much as heavy industry, and there was a housing shortage. As a British official in Moscow reported, "Every room is both a living room by day and a bedroom by night."

The Reign of Stalin

Stalin was the undisputed master of the Soviet Union. He distrusted competitors, exercised **sole** power, and had little respect for other Communist Party leaders. He is reported to have said to members of his inner circle in 1952, "You are as blind as kittens. What would you do without me?"

Stalin's suspicions added to the regime's increasing repression. In 1946 the government ordered all literary and scientific work to conform to the state's political needs. Along with this anti-

R Reading Strategies	C Critical Thinking	D Differentiated Instruction	W Writing Support	S Skill Practice
Teacher Edition • Identifying, p. 912 **Additional Resources** • Guid. Read. Act., URB p. 49 • Read. Ess. & Note-Taking Guide, p. 301	**Teacher Edition** • Making Generalizations, p. 913 **Additional Resources** • People in World Hist. Act., URB p. 40 • Section Quiz, p. 338	**Teacher Edition** • ELL, p. 911 **Additional Resources** • Academic Vocab. Act., URB p. 25	**Teacher Edition** • Expository Writing, p. 912 **Additional Resources** • Writer's Guidebook, p. 43	**Teacher Edition** • Visual Literacy, p. 911 **Additional Resources** • Time Line Act., URB p. 37

PRIMARY SOURCE INFOGRAPHICS

A Comparison of Market and Command Economics

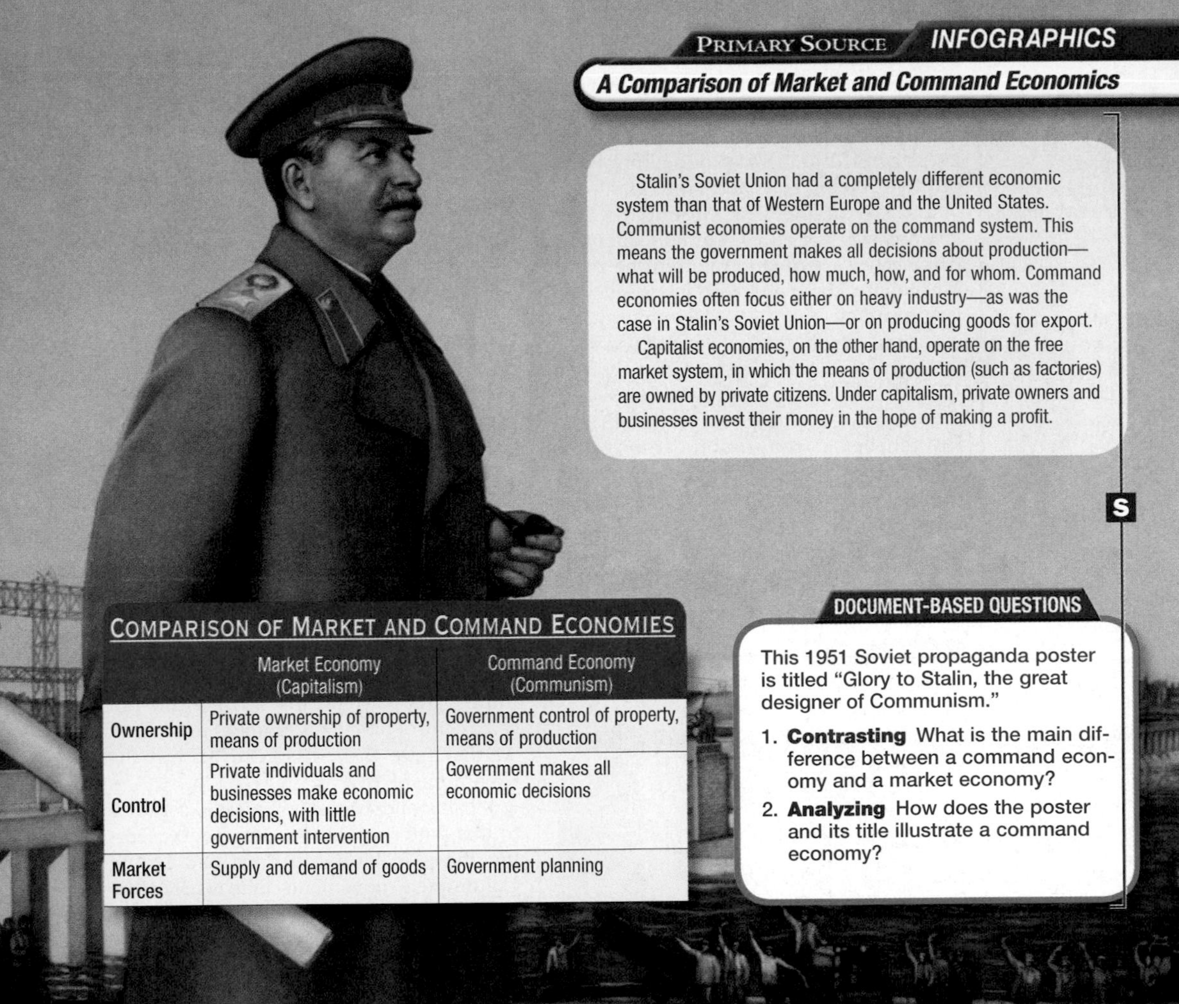

Stalin's Soviet Union had a completely different economic system than that of Western Europe and the United States. Communist economies operate on the command system. This means the government makes all decisions about production—what will be produced, how much, how, and for whom. Command economies often focus either on heavy industry—as was the case in Stalin's Soviet Union—or on producing goods for export.

Capitalist economies, on the other hand, operate on the free market system, in which the means of production (such as factories) are owned by private citizens. Under capitalism, private owners and businesses invest their money in the hope of making a profit.

COMPARISON OF MARKET AND COMMAND ECONOMIES

	Market Economy (Capitalism)	Command Economy (Communism)
Ownership	Private ownership of property, means of production	Government control of property, means of production
Control	Private individuals and businesses make economic decisions, with little government intervention	Government makes all economic decisions
Market Forces	Supply and demand of goods	Government planning

DOCUMENT-BASED QUESTIONS

This 1951 Soviet propaganda poster is titled "Glory to Stalin, the great designer of Communism."

1. **Contrasting** What is the main difference between a command economy and a market economy?
2. **Analyzing** How does the poster and its title illustrate a command economy?

intellectual campaign came political terror. The threat of more purges in 1953 disappeared when Stalin died on March 5, 1953.

The Khrushchev Era

A group of leaders succeeded Stalin. However, the new general secretary of the Communist Party, Nikita Khrushchev, soon emerged as the chief Soviet policy maker. Once in power, Khrushchev took steps to undo some of the worst features of Stalin's regime.

At the Twentieth Congress of the Communist Party in 1956, Khrushchev condemned Stalin for his "administrative violence, mass repression, and terror." The process of eliminating the more ruthless policies of Stalin became known as **de-Stalinization.**

Khrushchev loosened government controls on literary and artistic works. In 1962, for example, he allowed the publication of *One Day in the Life of Ivan Denisovich.* This novel, written by **Aleksandr Solzhenitsyn** (SOHL•zhuh• NEET•suhn), is a grim portrayal of life in a Siberian labor camp.

Teach

S Skill Practice

Visual Literacy Ask: What is the priority in a command economy? *(A command economy is based on government ownership and economic control.)* **OL**

D Differentiated Instruction

English Language Learners Point out the prefix *de-* in *de-Stalinization.* Explain that *de-* can mean "to reverse or remove." Ask students what Khrushchev's quotation suggests about his policy of de-Stalinization. **ELL**

DOCUMENT-BASED QUESTIONS

Answers:

1. **Command economy:** Government retains economic control; **Market economy:** Private individuals and free market shape economy.
2. Stalin is depicted as a leader of factories and workers. In the poster title he is called the "great designer of Communism," showing his control of the Soviet economy.

Hands-On Chapter Project

Step 2

Creating a Cold War Web Site

Step 2: Mapping the Iron Curtain Small groups of students will add the next page to their Web site.

Directions: Write the Big Idea on the board. Tell students that for the next page of their Web site they will create a map of the countries behind the Iron Curtain. They will also use the facts in this section of the text to create pop-up descriptions of important events associated with these countries in the postwar years.

Summarizing: Allow time for groups to share what they learned about the Big Idea while preparing this Web page. **OL**

(Chapter Project is continued in Section 3.)

W Writing Support

Expository Writing Ask students to write a short essay in which they discuss the successes and failures of Khrushchev's de-Stalinization policies. AL

R Reading Strategy

Identifying **Ask:** Which countries would be considered Soviet satellites? Why? *(Soviet-controlled governments ruled in East Germany, Bulgaria, Romania, Poland, Hungary, and Czechoslovakia, making those countries satellites, or part of the Soviet bloc.)* OL

✓Reading Check

Answer: His failure to increase agricultural output, low production of consumer goods, and his plans to place missiles in Cuba weakened his political power.

PEOPLE in HISTORY

Answers: Many Westerners saw Khrushchev as brutal and terrifying during the Cold War. Today historians point out that he also made some important reforms.

History ONLINE
Student Web Activity—
Visit glencoe.com and complete the activity on the Cold War.

Many Soviets identified with Ivan as a symbol of the suffering endured under Stalin.

Khrushchev also tried to place more emphasis on producing consumer goods. He attempted to increase agricultural output by growing corn and cultivating vast lands east of the Ural Mountains. The attempt was not successful and damaged Khrushchev's reputation within the party. This failure, combined with increased military spending, hurt the Soviet economy. The W industrial growth rate, which had soared in the early 1950s, now declined sharply from 13 percent in 1953 to 7.5 percent in 1964.

Foreign policy failures also damaged Khrushchev's reputation among his colleagues. His rash plan to place missiles in Cuba was the final straw. While he was away on vacation in 1964, a special meeting of the Soviet leaders voted him out of office (because of "deteriorating health") and forced him into retirement.

✓Reading Check **Explaining** Why did the Soviet leaders vote Khrushchev out of power?

PEOPLE in HISTORY

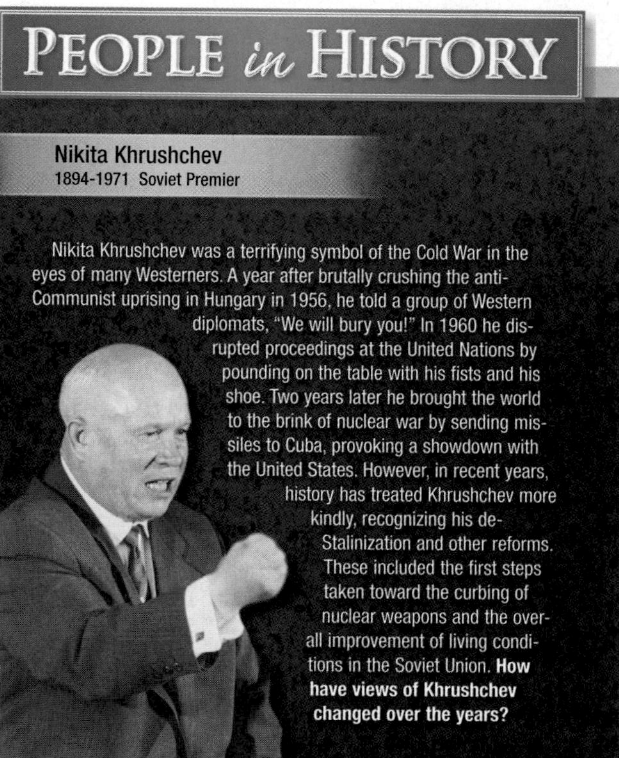

Nikita Khrushchev
1894-1971 Soviet Premier

Nikita Khrushchev was a terrifying symbol of the Cold War in the eyes of many Westerners. A year after brutally crushing the anti-Communist uprising in Hungary in 1956, he told a group of Western diplomats, "We will bury you!" In 1960 he disrupted proceedings at the United Nations by pounding on the table with his fists and his shoe. Two years later he brought the world to the brink of nuclear war by sending missiles to Cuba, provoking a showdown with the United States. However, in recent years, history has treated Khrushchev more kindly, recognizing his de-Stalinization and other reforms. These included the first steps taken toward the curbing of nuclear weapons and the overall improvement of living conditions in the Soviet Union. **How have views of Khrushchev changed over the years?**

Eastern Europe

MAIN IDEA After World War II, Soviet control of Eastern Europe became firmly entrenched.

HISTORY & YOU During the age of imperialism, European powers controlled their colonial peoples in a number of ways. Read to learn how the Soviet Union maintained tight control over Eastern Europe.

At the end of World War II, Soviet military forces occupied all of Eastern Europe and the Balkans (except for Greece, Albania, and Yugoslavia). All of the occupied states came under Soviet control.

Communist Patterns of Control

The timetable of the Soviet takeover varied from country to country. Between 1945 and 1947, Soviet-controlled Communist governments became firmly entrenched in East Germany, Bulgaria, Romania, Poland, and Hungary. In Czechoslovakia, where there was a tradition of democracy and a multi-party system, the Soviets did not seize control of the government until 1948. At that time they dissolved all but the Communist Party.

Albania and Yugoslavia were exceptions to this pattern of Soviet dominance. During the war, both countries had strong Communist movements that resisted the Nazis. After the war, local Communist parties took control. The Stalinist-type regime R in **Albania** grew more and more independent of the Soviet Union.

In **Yugoslavia,** Josip Broz, known as **Tito,** had led the Communist resistance movement. After the war, he created an independent Communist state in Yugoslavia. Stalin had hoped to control Yugoslavia, just as he controlled other Eastern European countries. Tito, however, refused to give in to Stalin's demands.

Tito gained the people's support by portraying the struggle as one of Yugoslav national freedom. Tito ruled Yugoslavia until his death in 1980. Although Yugoslavia had a Communist government, it was not a Soviet satellite state.

Between 1948 and Stalin's death in 1953, the Eastern European satellite states, directed by the Soviet Union, followed

Differentiated Instruction

People in World History Activity, URB p. 40

Determining Cause and Effect

Objective: Analyze the effects of Khrushchev's actions.

Focus: Have students read and discuss the quotation and the first paragraph.

Teach: Summarize the passage with students.

Assess: Ask students to identify the effects of Khrushchev's de-Stalinization policies on the Soviet Union.

Close: Invite students to compare modern-day Russia to the Soviet Union.

Differentiated Instruction Strategies

- **BL** Have partners ask and answer questions about each paragraph.
- **AL** Have students use sources to write a detailed report on Khrushchev's views of the West.
- **ELL** Ask students to read the text aloud in small groups.

Stalin's example. They instituted Soviet-type five-year plans with emphasis on heavy industry rather than consumer goods. They collectivized agriculture, eliminated all noncommunist parties, and set up the institutions of repression—secret police and military forces.

Revolts Against Communism

Communism did not develop deep roots among the peoples of Eastern Europe. Moreover, the Soviets exploited Eastern Europe economically for their own benefit and made living conditions harsh for most people.

After Stalin's death, many Eastern European states began to pursue a new course. In the late 1950s and 1960s, however, the Soviet Union made it clear—especially in **Poland, Hungary,** and **Czechoslovakia**—that it would not allow its Eastern European satellites to become independent of Soviet control. **C**

In 1956, when protests erupted in Poland, the Polish Communist Party adopted a series of reforms and elected Władysław Gomułka as first secretary. Gomułka declared that Poland had the right to follow its own socialist path. However, the Poles pledged to remain loyal to the Warsaw Pact.

Unrest in Hungary, combined with economic difficulties, led to calls for revolt. **Imre Nagy,** the Hungarian leader, declared Hungary a free nation on November 1, 1956. He promised free elections, which could have meant the end of Communist rule in Hungary. Yet Khrushchev did not allow Hungary to be free. Three days after Nagy's declaration, the Soviet Army attacked Budapest, and the Soviets reestablished control. Nagy was seized by the Soviet military and executed two years later.

The situation in Czechoslovakia in the 1950s was different. Stalin had placed Antonín Novotný in power in 1953. By the late 1960s, however, Novotný had alienated many members of his own party and Czechoslovakia's writers. A writers' rebellion, which encouraged the people to take control of their own lives, led to Novotný's resignation in 1968.

Alexander Dubček (DOOB•chehk), first secretary of the Communist Party, introduced a number of reforms in 1968, including freedom of speech and press and freedom to travel abroad. He relaxed censorship and began to pursue an independent foreign policy. He also promised a gradual democratization of the Czechoslovakian political system. Dubček hoped to create "socialism with a human face."

A period of euphoria, known as the "Prague Spring," followed but it proved to be short-lived. To forestall the spreading of this "spring fever," the Soviet Army invaded Czechoslovakia in August 1968. It crushed the reform movement. Gustav Husák replaced Dubček, did away with his reforms, and reestablished the old order.

✓Reading Check **Evaluating** What caused the battles between the Eastern European states and the Soviet Union?

SECTION 2 REVIEW

Vocabulary

1. **Explain** the significance of: Soviet Union, heavy industry, enhanced, sole, de-Stalinization, Aleksandr Solzhenitsyn, Albania, Yugoslavia, Tito, Poland, Hungary, Czechoslovakia, Imre Nagy, Alexander Dubček.

Main Ideas

2. **Summarize** the steps that Khrushchev took to de-Stalinize the Soviet Union. Use a chart like the one below to make your summary.

Khrushchev's Steps to De-Stalinize the Soviet Union
1.
2.

3. **Name** two countries in Eastern Europe that resisted Soviet dominance.
4. **Explain** how Alexander Dubček created "socialism with a human face" in Czechoslovakia.

Critical Thinking

5. **The BIG Idea** **Analyzing** Why did Yugoslavia and Albania not come under the control of the Soviet Union?
6. **Making Connections** How did Alexander Solzhenitsyn aid in Khrushchev's de-Stalinization of the Soviet Union?
7. **Analyzing Visuals** Examine the 1951 Soviet poster on page 911. How do the workers appear to view Stalin?

Writing About History

8. **Informative Writing** You are a Western journalist in Hungary in 1956. Write an article for an American newspaper that describes the events leading to the Soviet attack on Budapest and predicting the effect it will have on the Cold War.

History ONLINE
For help with the concepts in this section of *Glencoe World History*, go to glencoe.com and click Study Central™.

C Critical Thinking

Making Generalizations

Ask: What motivates a government to maintain control over people against their will? *(Students' answers will vary, but should be supported with logical reasons and examples.)* **AL**

✓Reading Check

Answer: The Soviet Union, a foreign power, imposed communism, and therefore control, on Eastern Europe.

Assess

Study Central provides summaries, interactive games, and online graphic organizers to help students review content.

Close

Summarizing Assign pairs of students one of the terms listed under "People and Places" on page 910. Have each pair summarize the significance of their person or place in the context of the Soviet Union's attempts to control Eastern Europe. **OL**

SECTION 2 REVIEW

Answers

1. Definitions for the vocabulary words are found in the section and the Glossary.
2. (1) loosened government controls on literary works; (2) placed emphasis on producing consumer goods; (3) attempted to increase agricultural output
3. Albania and Yugoslavia
4. introduced reforms, including freedom of speech and press and freedom to travel abroad; relaxed censorship and pursued an independent foreign policy; promised gradual democratization of the Czechoslovakian system
5. They had strong communist governments already and were able to resist Stalin's demands.
6. Many identified with the character in his novel as a symbol of suffering they had endured under Stalin.
7. They appear to be looking up to him. Their demeanor suggests attention and respect. His position in front of them conveys his absolute authority and leadership.
8. Students' articles will vary, but should include supporting details and be based on logical conclusions.

Focus

Bellringer

Daily Focus Transparency 27.3

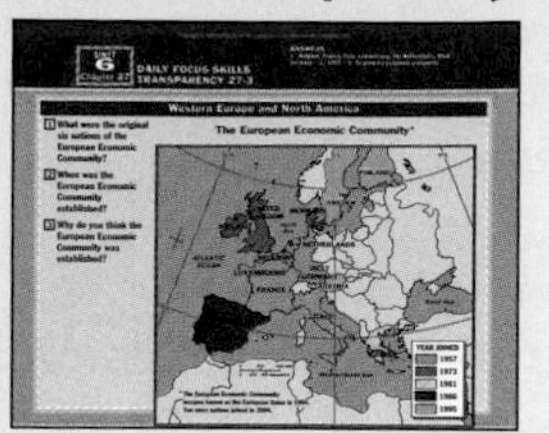

GUIDE TO READING

Answers to Graphic:

Great Britain	United States	Canada
National Insurance Act	Social Security	Canada Pension Plan
National Health Service Act	labor laws	national health insurance program
	health care for the elderly	
	measures to combat poverty	
	federal education assistance	

Section Spotlight Video

To generate student interest and provide a springboard for class discussion, access the Chapter 27, Section 3 video at glencoe.com or on the video DVD.

Resource Manager

SECTION 3

Western Europe and North America

GUIDE TO READING

The BIG Idea

Ideas, Beliefs, and Values Post-World War II societies rebuilt their economies and communities, but not without upheaval and change.

Content Vocabulary

- welfare state *(p. 916)*
- bloc *(p. 917)*
- real wages *(p. 917)*
- civil rights movement *(p. 918)*
- consumer society *(p. 920)*
- women's liberation movement *(p. 921)*

Academic Vocabulary

- recovery *(p. 914)*
- minimal *(p. 916)*

People and Places

- France *(p. 914)*
- Charles de Gaulle *(p. 914)*
- Christian Democratic Union (CDU) *(p. 915)*
- West Germany *(p. 915)*
- European Economic Community (EEC) *(p. 917)*
- John F. Kennedy *(p. 918)*
- Martin Luther King, Jr. *(p. 918)*
- Simone de Beauvoir *(p. 921)*

Reading Strategy

Categorizing Information As you read, use a table like the one below to list programs instituted by Great Britain, the United States, and Canada to promote social welfare.

Great Britain	United States	Canada

Most Western European countries recovered rapidly from World War II. Some European nations found economic unity with the European Economic Community (EEC). The United States experienced an economic boom after World War II but reeled under social and political issues. Meanwhile, a consumer society and the women's liberation movement led to more changes.

Western Europe: New Unity

MAIN IDEA After the end of World War II, most of Western Europe recovered economically and the region became more unified.

HISTORY & YOU How did Germany rebuild after World War I? Read to learn how Germany became divided after World War II.

With the economic aid of the Marshall Plan, the countries of Western Europe recovered relatively rapidly from the devastation of World War II. Between 1947 and 1950, European countries received $9.4 billion for new equipment and raw materials. By 1950, industrial output in Europe was 30 percent above prewar levels. This economic **recovery** continued well into the 1950s and 1960s. It was a time of dramatic economic growth and prosperity in Western Europe.

France and de Gaulle

The history of **France** for nearly a quarter of a century after the war was dominated by one man—the war hero **Charles de Gaulle**. In 1946 de Gaulle helped establish a new government, the Fourth Republic. That government, however, was largely ineffective.

In 1958 leaders of the Fourth Republic, frightened by bitter divisions caused by a crisis in the French colony of Algeria (see Chapter 30), asked de Gaulle to form a new government. That year, de Gaulle drafted a new constitution for the Fifth Republic that greatly enhanced the power of the president.

The French president would now have the right to choose the prime minister, dissolve parliament, and supervise both defense and foreign policy. French voters overwhelmingly approved the constitution, and de Gaulle became the first president of the Fifth Republic.

As the new president, de Gaulle wanted France to be great power once again. To achieve the status of a world power, de Gaulle invested heavily in nuclear arms. France exploded its first nuclear bomb in 1960.

R Reading Strategies	C Critical Thinking	D Differentiated Instruction	W Writing Support	S Skill Practice
Teacher Edition • Act. Prior Know., p. 916 • Making Connections, p. 918 • Read. Pri. Sources, p. 918 **Additional Resources** • Read. Skills. Act., URB p. 17 • Guid. Read. Act., URB p. 50 • Read. Ess. & Note-Taking Guide, p. 304	**Teacher Edition** • Compare/Contrast, p. 917 • Making Generalizations p. 919 **Additional Resources** • Hist. Analysis Skills Act., URB p. 18 • Crit. Think. Act., URB p. 28 • Pri. Source Read., URB p. 41 • Section Quiz, p. 339 • Chapter Test, p. 341	**Teacher Edition** • Adv. Learners, p. 915 • Verbal/Linguistic, p. 920 **Additional Resources** • Econ. & Hist. Act., URB p. 5 • Diff. Instr. Act., URB p. 19 • Hist. Sim. Act., URB p. 35 • World Art & Music Act., URB p. 43	**Teacher Edition** • Persuasive Writing, p. 918 • Narrative Writing, p. 920 **Additional Resources** • Hist. Sig. Act., URB p. 32	**Teacher Edition** • Visual Literacy, p. 915 **Additional Resources** • Reteach. Act., URB p. 45

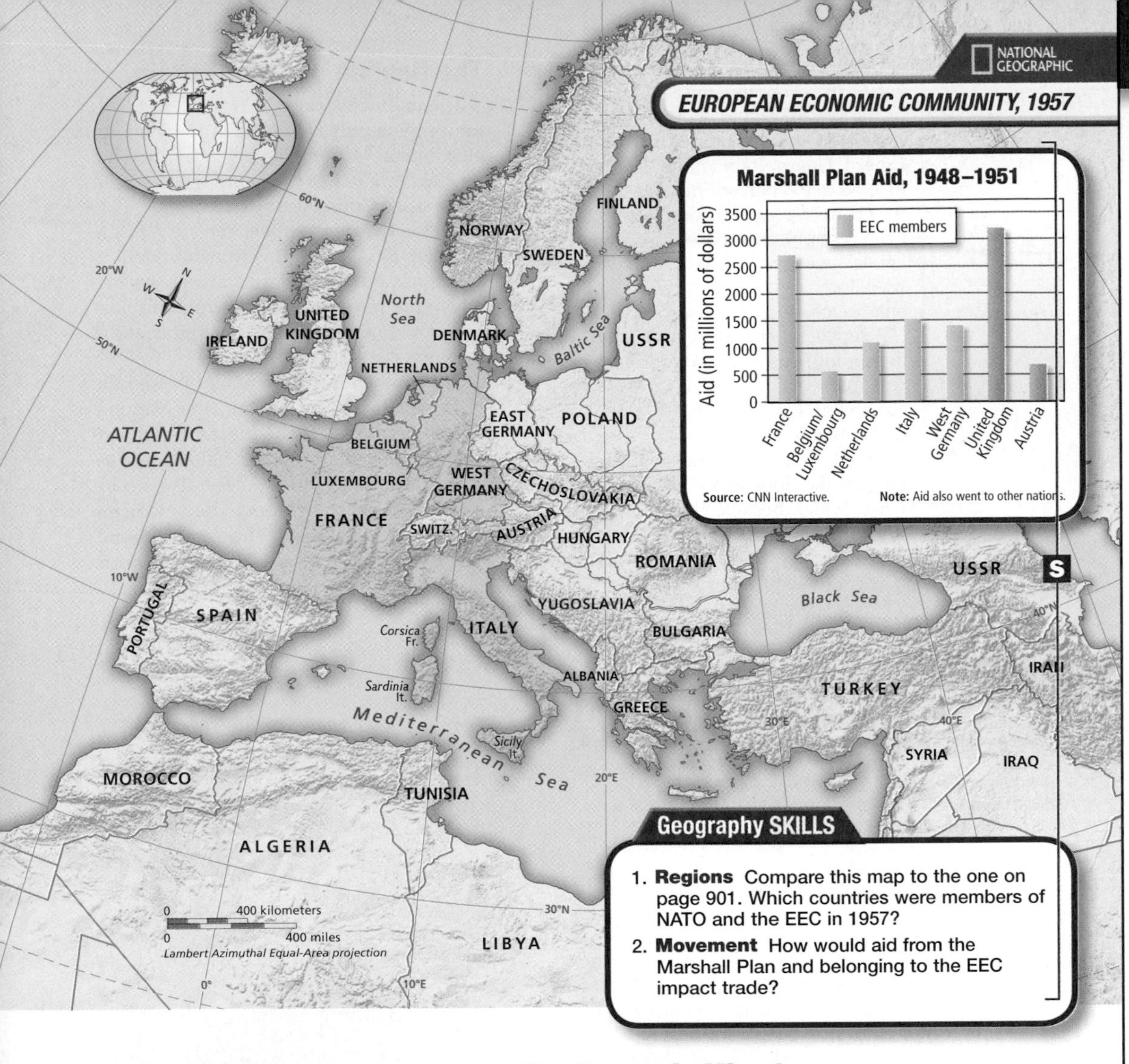

During de Gaulle's presidency, the French economy grew at an annual rate of 5.5 percent, faster than that of the United States. France became a major industrial producer and exporter, especially of automobiles and weapons.

Nevertheless, problems remained. Large government deficits and a rise in the cost of living led to unrest. In May 1968, a series of student protests was followed by a general labor strike. Tired and discouraged, de Gaulle resigned from office in April 1969 and died within a year.

The Economic Miracle

The three Western zones of Germany were unified as the Federal Republic of Germany in 1949. From 1949 to 1963, Konrad Adenauer (A•duhn•OWR), the leader of the **Christian Democratic Union** (CDU), served as chancellor (head of state). Adenauer sought respect for **West Germany.** He cooperated with the United States and other Western European nations and especially wanted to work with France—Germany's longtime enemy.

Teach

S Skill Practice

Visual Literacy Ask: Which of the countries shown in the bar graph received the least aid under the Marshall Plan? *(Belgium/Luxembourg.)* BL

D Differentiated Instruction

Advanced Learners Have students research West German foreign relations under Konrad Adenauer. Ask students to summarize the steps he took to regain the respect of France, the United States, and Great Britain. AL

Geography SKILLS

Answers:

1. Belgium, Luxembourg, West Germany, France, Italy
2. EEC nations with Marshall Plan aid would be able to trade more vigorously and have stronger economic ties.

Hands-On Chapter Project Step 3

Creating a Cold War Web Site

Step 3: Analyzing Events in the Free World Small groups of students will add the next page to their Web site.

Directions: Write the Big Idea on the board. Tell students that the purpose of their next Web page is to explain what was happening in Western Europe, the United States, and Canada in the decades following World War II. For this page, suggest that students choose several photographs or images of important people or events associated with this time period. They should then use the facts in this section to write a paragraph or two explaining the historical context and significance of each. Users of the site will access this text by clicking on each image.

Summarizing: Allow time for groups to share what they learned about the Big Idea while preparing this Web page. OL

(Chapter Project is completed on the Visual Summary page.)

R Reading Strategy

Activating Prior Knowledge
Have students compare the economies of West and East Germany in the 1950s and 1960s. *(West Germany: tremendous growth, low unemployment; East Germany: economic difficulty)* OL

CRITICAL THINKING SKILLS

Answers:

1. In 1952, West Germany began to make reparations to Israel. In 1964, the two established diplomatic relations. Today, they have a special relationship shaped by the remembrance of the Holocaust.
2. Answers will vary. Students may point out that the constitution is an attempt to guarantee that such a terrible tragedy will never happen again. In addition, Germany's liberal asylum laws sought to help others who are persecuted.

R Under Adenauer, West Germany experienced an "economic miracle." This revival of the West German economy was largely guided by the minister of finance, Ludwig Erhard. Unemployment fell from 8 percent in 1950 to 0.4 percent in 1965. To maintain its economic expansion, West Germany even brought in hundreds of thousands of "guest" workers on visas from other countries such as Italy, Spain, Greece, Turkey, and Yugoslavia.

Adenauer resigned in 1963, after 14 years of guiding West Germany through its postwar recovery. Succeeding Adenauer as chancellor, Ludwig Erhard largely continued Adenauer's policies.

An economic downturn in the mid-1960s opened the door to the Social Democratic Party, which became the leading party in 1969. The Social Democrats, a moderate socialist party, were led by Willy Brandt, mayor of West Berlin.

The Decline of Great Britain

The end of World War II left Great Britain with massive economic problems. In elections held immediately after the war, the Labour Party overwhelmingly defeated Churchill's Conservative Party.

Under Clement Attlee, the new prime minister, the Labour government set out to create a modern **welfare state**—a state in which the government takes responsibility for providing citizens with services and a **minimal** standard of living.

In 1946 the new government passed the National Insurance Act and the National Health Service Act. The insurance act provided government funds to help the unemployed, the sick, and the aged. The health act created a system of socialized medicine that ensured medical care for everyone. The British welfare state became the norm for most European states after the war.

INFOGRAPHICS — PRIMARY SOURCE
Political Change in Postwar Germany

The 1949 constitution of the German Federal Republic begins: "Human dignity shall be inviolable. To respect and protect it shall be the duty of all state authority." It goes on to list basic rights of all citizens, as well as the right to asylum, or protection, for anyone who has been persecuted for political reasons.

The words of the 1949 constitution are a reminder. During World War II, Hitler attempted to carry out the systematic murder of Europe's Jews. After the war, Germany and the world wanted to ensure that nothing like this could ever happen again.

In 1952 West German chancellor Konrad Adenauer signed an agreement to make reparations to Israel as compensation for taking in Holocaust survivors. West Germany and Israel did not establish diplomatic relations until 1964. Forty years later, German chancellor Gerhard Schröder acknowledged the nature of the two countries' relationship: "The relations between our two countries will always have a special character, shaped by the unspeakable crimes and suffering of the Shoa [Holocaust]."

Israeli president Moshe Katsav unveils the sign for a street in Berlin, Germany, named after the assassinated Israeli prime minister Yitzhak Rabin.

CRITICAL THINKING SKILLS

1. **Describing** What was the nature of diplomatic relations between Germany and Israel in 1952? 1964? Today?
2. **Making Connections** Based on the 1949 constitution, what do you think Germany learned from the Holocaust?

Additional Support

Activity: Economics Connection

Researching Postwar Conditions Discuss with students the similarities between West Germany and Great Britain. Both emerged from the war with extensive damage to property and their infrastructures; both established welfare states. Yet West Germany prospered while Great Britain struggled. **Ask:** **Was Britain's decision to nationalize industries such as mining and public utilities one of the reasons for its economic lag?** Have students work together to find out more about conditions in both countries after World War II that might explain the disparity in the health of their economies. Have groups prepare posters that present the results of their research. Allow groups to view each other's posters. AL

The cost of building a welfare state at home forced Britain to reduce expenses abroad. This meant dismantling the British Empire. Britain was forced to give in to the demands of many colonies for independence. Britain was no longer able to play the role of a world power.

Continuing economic problems brought the Conservatives back into power from 1951 to 1964. Although they favored private enterprise, the Conservatives accepted the welfare state and even extended it by financing an ambitious building program to improve British housing.

The Move Toward Unity

As we have seen, the divisions created by the Cold War led the nations of Western Europe to form the North Atlantic Treaty Organization in 1949. The destructiveness of two world wars caused many thoughtful Europeans to consider the need for some additional form of European unity. National feeling was still too powerful, however, for European nations to give up their political sovereignty. As a result, the desire for unity focused chiefly on the economic arena, not the political one.

In 1957 France, West Germany, the Benelux countries (Belgium, the Netherlands, and Luxembourg), and Italy signed the Rome Treaty. This treaty created the **European Economic Community** (EEC), also known as the Common Market.

The EEC was a free-trade area made up of the six member nations. These six nations would impose no tariffs, or import charges, on each other's goods. However, as a group, they would be protected by a tariff imposed on goods from non-EEC nations. In this way, the EEC encouraged cooperation among the member nations' economies. All the member nations benefited economically.

By the 1960s, the EEC had become an important trading **bloc** (a group of nations with a common purpose). In 1973 Britain, Denmark, and Ireland joined the EEC. With a total population of 165 million, the EEC was the world's largest exporter and purchaser of raw materials.

✓Reading Check **Evaluating** Why did European unity come in the form of an economic alliance?

The U.S. after the War

MAIN IDEA In the years following World War II, the United States faced a range of difficult social and political issues.

HISTORY & YOU What social and political issues are under debate today? Read to learn about the controversies in American history from 1945 to 1970.

Between 1945 and 1970, the ideals of Franklin Delano Roosevelt's New Deal largely determined the patterns of American domestic politics. The New Deal had brought basic changes to American society. They included a dramatic increase in the role and power of the federal government, the rise of organized labor as a significant force in the economy and politics, the beginning of a welfare state, and a realization of the need to deal fairly with the concerns of minorities, especially African Americans. C

The New Deal tradition in American politics was reinforced by the election of Democratic presidents—Harry S. Truman in 1948, John F. Kennedy in 1960, and Lyndon B. Johnson in 1964. Even the election of a Republican president, Dwight D. Eisenhower, in 1952 and 1956 did not change the basic direction of the New Deal. Eisenhower said:

PRIMARY SOURCE

> "Should any political party attempt to abolish Social Security and eliminate labor laws, you would not hear of that party again in our political history."
>
> —Dwight D. Eisenhower, 1954

An economic boom followed World War II. A shortage of consumer goods during the war had left Americans with both extra income and the desire to buy goods after the war. In addition, the growth of labor unions brought higher wages and gave more workers the ability to buy consumer goods. Between 1945 and 1973, **real wages** (the actual purchasing power of income) grew an average of 3 percent a year, the most prolonged advance ever in American history.

Prosperity was not the only characteristic of the early 1950s. Cold War struggles abroad led to the widespread fear that Communists had infiltrated the United States.

C Critical Thinking

Comparing and Contrasting
Ask: Why was the United States in a better position to create a welfare state than most European nations? *(The United States did not have to rebuild its infrastructure; FDR's New Deal agenda remained intact.)* OL

Did You Know?

Today's European Union incorporated the former European Economic Community in 1993. The Union was set up by the Maastricht Treaty, which provided for implementation of a common currency (the euro) and the adoption of common defense and security policies as well as citizenship rights, among other issues.

✓Reading Check

Answer: National unity was too powerful for Europeans to give up their political sovereignty. Working together economically, however, these nations became a powerful bloc.

Differentiated Instruction

Leveled Activities

BL Reteaching Activity, p. 45

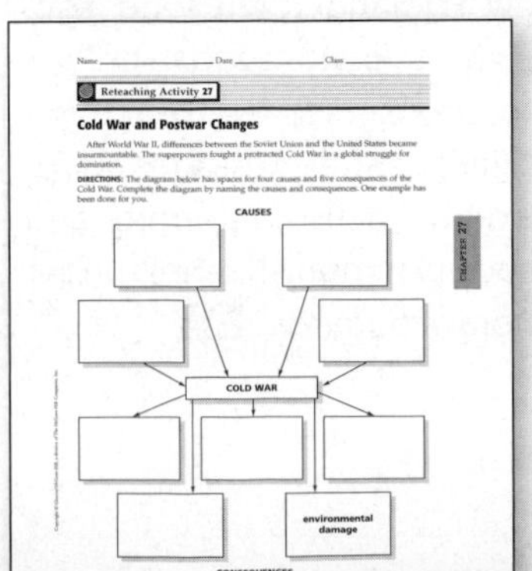

OL Guided Reading Activity, p. 50

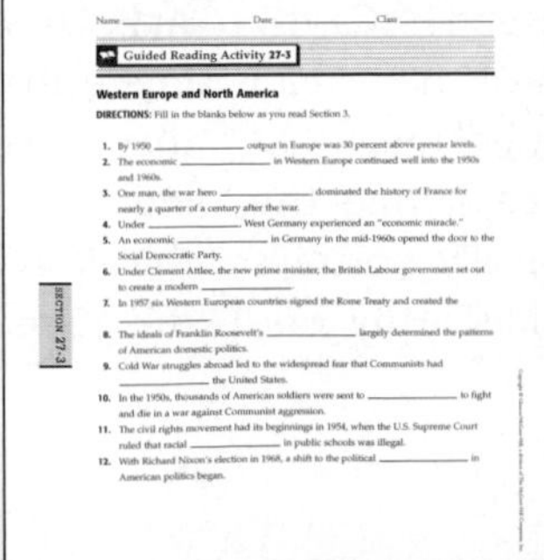

AL Primary Source Reading, URB p. 41

ELL History Simulation Activity, URB p. 35

R1 Reading Strategy

Making Connections Explain that fear of Communist influence was strong in American society during the Cold War. Discuss whether attitudes are different today. Ask students if they think Americans fear other nations or economic systems, and if so, why. OL

R2 Reading Strategy

Reading Primary Sources
Ask: On what grounds did Justice Warren and the U.S. Supreme Court reject segregated schools? *(Schools cannot possibly be equal if they are set up on the basis of race.)* OL

W Writing Support

Persuasive Writing Point out that President Johnson's dream of a "Great Society" was reflected in historic civil rights legislation as well as in programs to fight poverty and expand education. His reputation suffered, however, because he led the nation in the Vietnam War. Have students research Johnson's domestic programs and argue whether he should be remembered as the architect of the Great Society or escalator of the Vietnam War. AL

President Truman's attorney general warned that Communists were "everywhere—in factories, offices, butcher stores, on street corners, in private businesses." For many Americans, proof of this threat became more evident when thousands of American soldiers were sent to Korea to fight and die in a war against Communist aggression.

R1 This climate of fear produced a dangerous political agitator, Senator Joseph R. McCarthy of Wisconsin. His charges that hundreds of supposed Communists were in high government positions helped create a massive "Red Scare"—fear of Communist subversion. Under McCarthy, several individuals, including intellectuals and movie stars, were questioned about alleged Communist activities. When McCarthy attacked "Communist conspirators" in the U.S. Army, he was condemned by the Senate in 1954. Very quickly, his anti-Communist crusade came to an end.

The 1960s and Civil Rights

The 1960s began on a youthful and optimistic note. At age 43, **John F. Kennedy** became the youngest elected president in the history of the United States. His administration was cut short when the president was killed by an assassin on November 22, 1963. Vice President Lyndon B. Johnson then became president. Johnson won a new term as president in a landslide victory in 1964.

President Johnson used his stunning victory to pursue the growth of the welfare state, begun in the New Deal. Johnson's programs included health care for the elderly, various measures to combat poverty, and federal assistance for education.

R2 Johnson's other domestic passion was the **civil rights movement,** or equal rights for African Americans. The civil rights movement had its beginnings in 1954, when the United States Supreme Court ruled that the practice of racial segregation (separation) in public schools was illegal. According to Chief Justice Earl Warren, "separate educational facilities are inherently unequal." African Americans also boycotted segregated buses and other public places.

In August 1963, the Reverend **Martin Luther King, Jr.,** leader of a growing movement for racial equality, led a march on Washington, D.C., to dramatize the African American desire for equality. King advocated the principle of passive disobedience practiced by Mohandas Gandhi. King's march and his impassioned plea for racial equality had an electrifying effect on the American people. By the end of 1963, a majority of the American people called civil rights the most significant national issue.

W President Johnson took up the cause of civil rights. The Civil Rights Act of 1964 created the machinery to end segregation and discrimination in the workplace and all public places. Then, the Voting Rights Act made it easier for African Americans to vote in Southern states.

Laws alone, however, could not guarantee the Great Society that Johnson talked about creating. He soon faced bitter social unrest.

Social Upheaval

In the North and West, local patterns of segregation led to higher unemployment rates for African Americans than for whites. In the summer of 1965, race riots broke out in the Watts district of Los Angeles. Thirty-four people died and over 1,000 buildings were destroyed.

In 1968 Martin Luther King, Jr., was assassinated. Riots hit over 100 cities, including Washington, D.C. The riots led to a "white backlash" (whites became less sympathetic to the cause of racial equality) and continued the racial division of the United States.

Antiwar protests also divided the American people. As the Vietnam War (see Chapter 31) progressed through the second half of the 1960s, the protests grew. Then, in 1970 four students at Kent State University were killed and nine others were wounded by the Ohio National Guard during a student demonstration. The tragedy startled the nation. Americans were less willing to continue the war.

The combination of antiwar demonstrations and riots in the cities caused many people to call for "law and order." This was the appeal used by Richard Nixon, the Republican presidential candidate in 1968. With Nixon's election in 1968, a shift to the political right in American politics began.

Additional Support

Teacher Tip

Collaborative Learning This activity requires a careful reading of scenes from the play to grasp their essential meaning. Balance this skill with those needed to perform the scenes.

Activity: Collaborative Learning

Exploring Ideas of Freedom and Conformity Have student groups find out more about the actions of Joseph McCarthy in the early 1950s. Then have them read *The Crucible* by Arthur Miller. Tell them that this play, which takes place during the Salem Witch Trials, allegorically portrays the situation during the McCarthy era, making a comparison with the hysteria that gripped a New England town long ago. **Ask:** How are the two situations similar? Invite them to choose scenes to act out that convey Miller's central messages about individual freedom versus conformity and the efforts of society to punish rebels under the guise of moral standards. AL

INFOGRAPHICS PRIMARY SOURCE

The Civil Rights Act of 1964 and the Voting Rights Acts

In August 1963, Martin Luther King, Jr., told the 250,000 people who had marched on Washington, D.C, for civil rights: "I am happy to join with you today in what will go down in history as the greatest demonstration for freedom in the history of our nation." He went on to deliver one of the most famous speeches of modern times—his "I Have a Dream" speech.

Within a year, Congress had passed the Civil Rights Act of 1964, which outlawed segregation and prohibited discrimination on the basis of "race, color, religion, or national origin." A year later, Congress passed the Voting Rights Act of 1965, which prohibited laws and practices that kept African Americans from voting.

The Reverend Martin Luther King, Jr., at the March on Washington, August 28, 1963

CRITICAL THINKING SKILLS

1. **Explaining** What was the connection between the 1964 Civil Rights Act and the 1965 Voting Rights Act?
2. **Determining Cause and Effect** What do you think was the effect of the March on Washington?

American-Canadian Relations

After the war, Canada began developing electronic, aircraft, nuclear, and chemical engineering industries on a large scale. Investment of capital from the United States led to U.S. ownership of Canadian businesses. Some Canadians feared American economic domination of Canada.

Canadians also worried about playing a secondary role politically and militarily to the United States. Canada established its own identity in world politics and government. For example, Canada was a founding member of the United Nations in 1945 and joined the North Atlantic Treaty Organization in 1949. Under Lester Pearson, the Liberal government laid the groundwork for Canada's welfare state. A national social security system (the Canada Pension Plan) and a national health insurance program were enacted.

✓Reading Check **Identifying** Name President Johnson's two most important domestic policy goals.

Changing Values

MAIN IDEA After World War II, advances in technology and the struggle for rights led to rapid change in Western society.

HISTORY & YOU Have you or your family members ever used credit cards? Read to learn how buying on credit became widespread during the 1950s.

After World War II, Western society witnessed rapid change. Such new inventions as computers, televisions, and jet planes altered the pace and nature of human life. The rapid changes in postwar society led many to view it as a new society. **C**

A New Social Structure

Postwar Western society was marked by a changing social structure. Especially noticeable were changes in the middle class. Traditional middle-class groups were made up of businesspeople, lawyers, doctors, and teachers. A new group of managers

C **Critical Thinking**

Making Generalizations

Have students list ways in which new inventions have changed the pace of modern life. **Ask:** What single technological change has had the greatest effect on society? *(Answers may include specific medical breakthroughs or advances in communications.)* **OL**

For additional practice on this skill, see the **Skills Handbook**.

✓Reading Check

Answer: President Johnson focused on securing civil rights for all African Americans and developing elements of the welfare state.

CRITICAL THINKING SKILLS

Answers:

1. The Civil Rights Act outlawed segregation and discrimination; the Voting Rights Act banned voting restrictions against African Americans.
2. It brought the need for civil rights legislation to the public's attention and probably sped up the passage of the Civil Rights Act and the Voting Rights Act.

Differentiated Instruction

Making Generalizations

Objective: Understand changes in society in postwar years.

Focus: Have students read the introductory paragraph and the directions.

Teach: Examine the data with students and have small groups identify patterns during the decades from 1930 to 1960.

Assess: Ask students to make generalizations about this period.

Close: Ask students to use prior knowledge to support their generalizations with facts.

Differentiated Instruction Strategies

BL Have three groups each take one set of data and create a line graph.

AL Ask students to chart population distributions from 1980 to the present. Have them generalize about modern trends.

ELL Model the process of making generalizations. Then have students respond to questions 1–5.

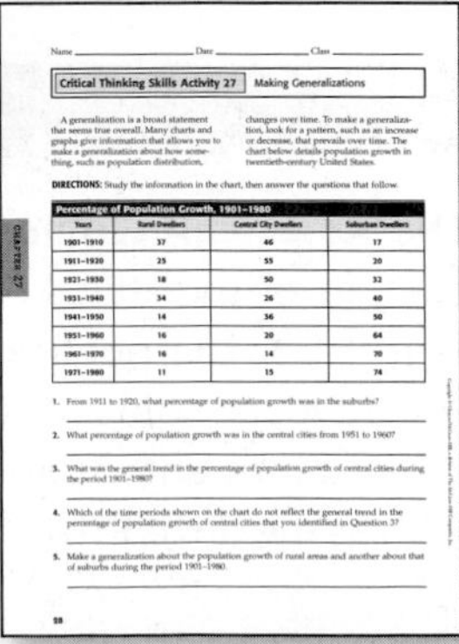

Critical Thinking Skills Activity, URB p. 28

D Differentiated Instruction

Verbal/Linguistic Ask students to consider how increasing supplies of consumer goods and low unemployment might affect what people can afford to buy. Have students define in their own words the phrase "real wages." AL

W Writing Support

Narrative Writing Discuss the contrast between many women's roles during World War II and their positions when soldiers returned. Ask students to think about how these women may have felt about being forced out of the workplace and back into the home. Have them write a dialogue in which two or three women and men discuss the changes in society in the 1950s and share their feelings about them. AL

Answers:

1. Women had finally gained the right to vote.
2. It helped reawaken the women's movement, leading to new anti-discrimination laws being passed in the 1960s and 1970s.

Additional Support

and technicians, hired by large companies and government agencies, now joined the ranks of the middle class.

Changes also occurred among the lower classes. The shift of people from rural to urban areas continued. The number of people in farming declined drastically. By the 1950s, the number of farmers in most parts of Europe had dropped by 50 percent. The number of industrial workers also began to decline as the amount of white-collar workers increased.

D At the same time, a noticeable increase in the real wages of workers made it possible for them to imitate the buying patterns of the middle class. This led to what some observers have called the **consumer society**—a society preoccupied with buying goods.

Buying on credit became widespread in the 1950s. Workers could now buy such products as televisions, washing machines, refrigerators, vacuum cleaners, and stereos. The automobile was the most visible symbol of the new consumerism. In 1948 there were 5 million cars in all of Europe. By the 1960s, there were almost 45 million.

Women in the Postwar World

Women's participation in the world wars had resulted in several gains. They had achieved one of the major aims of the nineteenth-century feminist movement—the right to vote. After making important contributions in World War I, women had gained voting rights in many countries. Sweden, Great Britain, Germany, Poland, Hungary, Austria, and Czechoslovakia extended voting rights to women in 1918, followed by the United States in 1920. French women only gained the vote in 1944, while Italian women did so in 1945.

W During World War II, women had entered the workforce in huge numbers. At the war's end, however, they were removed to provide jobs for soldiers returning home. For a time, women fell back into traditional roles. Birthrates rose, creating a "baby boom" in the late 1940s and the 1950s.

Connecting to the United States

The American Women's Movement

In 1949 the French writer Simone de Beauvoir published her best-known work, *The Second Sex*, a philosophical look at women's role in society.

De Beauvoir helped reawaken the American women's movement, which had languished after they gained the right to vote in 1920.

In the 1960s and 1970s, the American women's movement focused on job discrimination. New laws made it illegal to pay a woman less than a man for the same job or to otherwise discriminate on the basis of sex.

- Women should demand equality with men
- Every person, regardless of sex, class, or age, should be able to define herself or himself

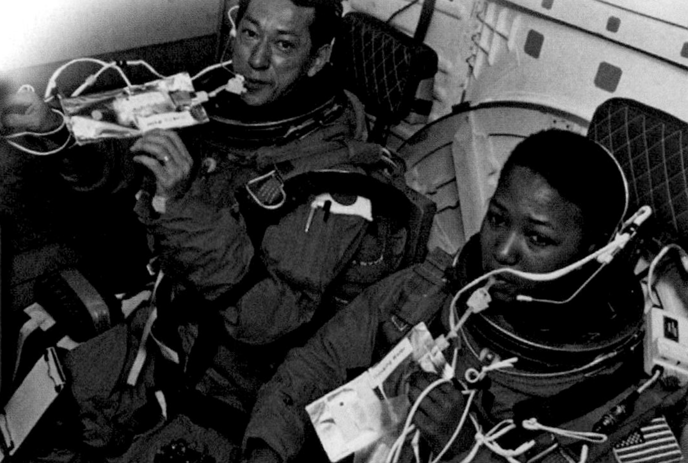

Male and female astronauts work side by side aboard the space shuttle Endeavor.

1. **Explaining** Why did the women's movement slow down in the United States?
2. **Making Connections** What influence did Simone de Beauvoir's ideas have on the women's movement in the United States?

Extending the Content

The American Women's Movement An analysis of the status of women over fifty years after the publication of *The Second Sex* reveals some advances and some disappointments. Certainly in countries such as the United States, the gender gap has closed considerably. The rate of women in America earning college degrees increased by 50 percent during the 1990s and as many women as men become doctors today. Additionally, women routinely perform roles formerly perceived as the domain of males, such as fighting in battle and commanding space missions. American women still generally earn less than men in the same jobs, however, even when their experience and skills are equal.

By the end of the 1950s, however, the birthrate had begun to fall and, with it, the size of families. The structure of the workplace changed once again as the number of married women in the workforce increased in both Europe and the United States. These women, especially working-class women, faced an old problem. They still earned less than men for equal work. For example, in the 1960s, women earned 60 percent of men's wages in Britain, 50 percent in France, and 63 percent in West Germany.

In addition, women still tended to enter traditionally female jobs. Many faced the double burden of earning income and raising a family. Such inequalities led increasing numbers of women to rebel. In the late 1960s came renewed interest in feminism, or the **women's liberation movement.**

Of great importance to the emergence of the postwar women's liberation movement was the work of **Simone de Beauvoir** (duh•boh•VWAHR). In 1949 she published *The Second Sex.* As a result of male-dominated societies, she argued, women were defined by their differences from men and consequently received second-class status. De Beauvoir influenced both the American and European women's movements.

Student Revolts

Before World War II, it was mostly members of Europe's wealthier classes who went to universities. After the war, European states encouraged more people to gain higher education by eliminating fees. As a result, enrollments from middle and lower classes grew dramatically. In France, 4.5 percent of young people went to universities in 1950. By 1965, the figure had increased to 14.5 percent.

There were problems, however. Many European university classrooms were overcrowded, and many professors paid little attention to their students. Growing discontent led to an outburst of student revolts in the late 1960s.

This student radicalism had several causes. Many protests were an extension of the revolts in American universities, often sparked by student opposition to the Vietnam War. Some students, particularly in Europe, believed that universities failed to respond to their needs or to the realities of the modern world. Others believed they were becoming small cogs in the large and impersonal bureaucratic wheels of the modern world.

Student protests of the 1960s and early 1970s caused many people to rethink basic assumptions. Student upheavals, however, were not a turning point in the history of postwar Europe, as some people thought at the time. As student rebels became middle-class professionals, revolutionary politics became mostly a memory.

✓Reading Check **Identifying** What was the women's liberation movement trying to accomplish?

SECTION 3 REVIEW

Vocabulary

1. **Explain** the significance of: recovery, France, Charles de Gaulle, Christian Democratic Union, West Germany, welfare state, minimal, European Economic Community, bloc, real wages, John F. Kennedy, civil rights movement, Martin Luther King, Jr., consumer society, women's liberation movement, Simone de Beauvoir.

Main Ideas

2. **Explain** why many British colonies gained their independence after World War II.
3. **List** some of the factors that caused social upheaval in the United States during the 1960s and early 1970s.
4. **Identify** factors leading to the postwar women's liberation movement. Use a diagram like the one below.

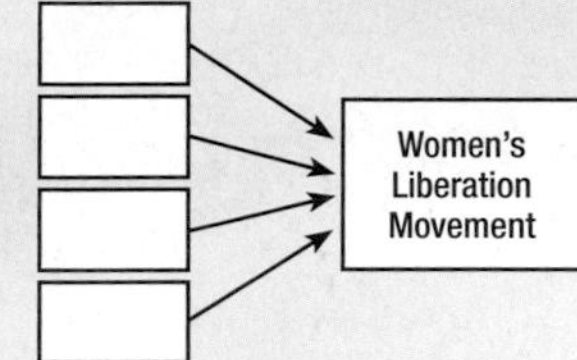

Critical Thinking

5. **The BIG Idea** **Assessing** Did the student revolts of this period contribute positively or negatively to society? Explain.
6. **Defending** Should the United States become a welfare state? Why or why not?
7. **Analyzing Visuals** What information does the photograph on page 919 provide about the March on Washington?

Writing About History

8. **Persuasive Writing** Write an essay that argues for or against the use of demonstrations, marches, and riots for changing public opinion and policy.

History ONLINE For help with the concepts in this section of *Glencoe World History,* go to glencoe.com and click Study Central™.

✓Reading Check

Answer: economic and social equality with men

Assess

History ONLINE

Study Central provides summaries, interactive games, and online graphic organizers to help students review content.

Close

Summarizing **Ask:** What led to the renewed vigor of the women's movement in the 1960s? *(Immediately following the war, women returned to their traditional roles as housewives, having been forced out of the workplace by returning soldiers. By the early 1960s, women had reentered the workforce, but were earning less than men and were often confined to jobs considered traditional for females. In addition, many women both worked and raised a family. These circumstances helped re-ignite the women's movement.)* **OL**

SECTION 3 REVIEW

Answers

1. Definitions for the vocabulary words are found in the section and the Glossary.
2. Great Britain had to reduce expenses abroad to finance its welfare state, and colonies demanded independence.
3. civil rights movement, antiwar protests, riots in cities
4. lower salaries than men; dual responsibilities of working outside the home and raising a family; status as second-class citizens in male-dominated society; publication of Simone de Beauvoir's *The Second Sex*
5. Answers will vary. Students should support their opinions with facts and examples.
6. Answers will vary. Students should support their opinions with facts and examples.
7. It was a huge success, with hundreds of thousands of people attending.
8. Answers will vary. Students' essays should include details that support their opinions.

Focus

Introducing Social History
Have students recall what they know about life before and during World War II. **Ask:** Why did consumerism increase after the war? *(During the Depression and the war, people had little money to spend and consumer goods were not widely available.)* **OL**

Teach

D Differentiated Instruction

English Language Learners
Help students understand the meaning of the colloquial and slang terms used throughout the feature. Point out visuals and context clues to clarify understanding as needed. **ELL**

R Reading Strategy

Organizing Help students list categories they might use to compare youth culture of the 1950s and 1960s, such as music, fashion, entertainment, leisure, and values. Then have students work in pairs to create charts using these categories to organize information as they read. **BL**

Additional Support

Popular Culture of the 1950s and 1960s

In the United States, an economic upturn after World War II sparked a baby boom and the growth of American suburbs. The new prosperity also freed many American teenagers from having to work full-time, resulting in a greater **D** importance placed on secondary education. As a result, adolescents in white, suburban America became a clearly defined social group. This teenage culture was reflected in music, fashions, television shows, and leisure activities. Though the youth culture remained a distinct entity in American society, its values would change sharply over time.

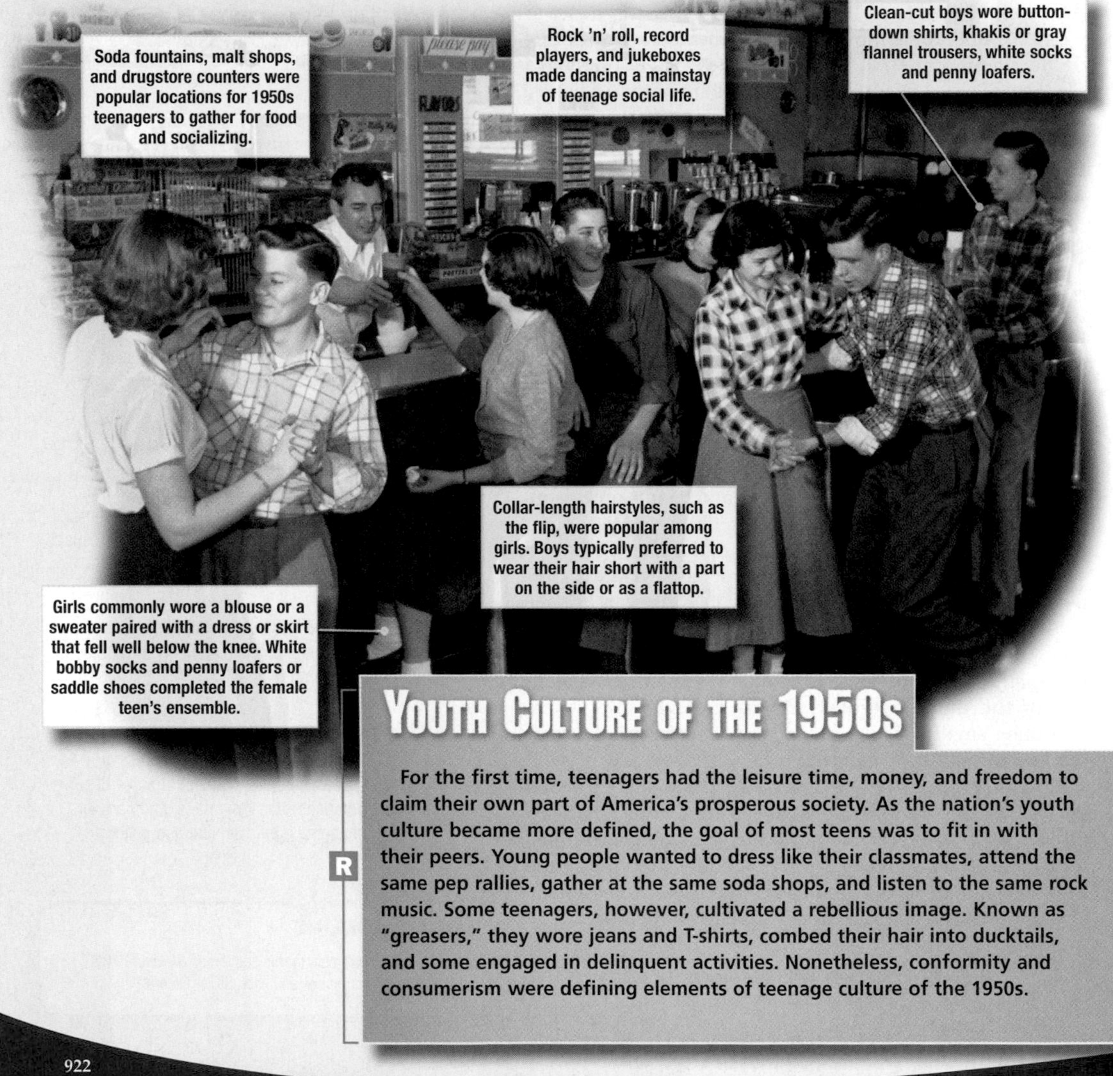

Youth Culture of the 1950s

R For the first time, teenagers had the leisure time, money, and freedom to claim their own part of America's prosperous society. As the nation's youth culture became more defined, the goal of most teens was to fit in with their peers. Young people wanted to dress like their classmates, attend the same pep rallies, gather at the same soda shops, and listen to the same rock music. Some teenagers, however, cultivated a rebellious image. Known as "greasers," they wore jeans and T-shirts, combed their hair into ducktails, and some engaged in delinquent activities. Nonetheless, conformity and consumerism were defining elements of teenage culture of the 1950s.

Background

The Baby Boom There was a large increase in births after World War II because soldiers returned from the war and started families. A prosperous economy supported family growth. Demographers define the baby boom generation in the United States as the cohort born between 1946 and 1964, which includes about 77 million people. In 1946 the number of births jumped to 3.47 million, compared to 2.8 million in 1945. The baby boom peaked in the late 1950s, when the annual number of births reached 4.3 million. The birthrate in 1957 was 25.3 births per 1000 population. This compared to 19 per 1000 in the 1930s and around 14 in the early 21st century. The oldest baby boomers became teenagers in 1959 and are most associated with the youth culture of the 1960s. The prosperity of their teenage years, however, contrasted with the economic challenges many of their families faced earlier, during the late Depression and World War II eras. This difference is also reflected in the contrast between conformity and individualism in the 1950s and 1960s.

Youth Culture of the 1960s

Inspired in part by the civil rights movement and the Vietnam War, teenagers in the 1960s increasingly rejected the traditional values of their parents. As the youth rebellion grew, a "generation gap" formed between young people and their parents. Teenagers held attitudes and opinions that older Americans did not understand or accept. The youth of the 1960s generally embraced individualism and free expression. This desire was reflected in the fashions and music popular among teens in the decade. Not all teenagers rebelled. Many young people in the 1960s retained traditional values, and sought a career in the nation's economy. W

Analyzing Visuals

1. **Comparing** Despite the differences between the youth culture of the 1950s and 1960s, how were American teenagers in those two decades similar?
2. **Analyzing** How were the values held by teenagers in the 1950s and 1960s reflected in their clothing, personal appearance, and social activities?

923

S Skill Practice

Visual Literacy Ask: How was the clothing worn by 1960s teenagers similar to or different from today's clothing? *(While teenagers dress in different fashions today, there are similarities to clothing worn in the 1960s.)* OL

W Writing Support

Expository Writing Explain that the term *counterculture* is often used to refer to the youth culture of the 1960s. Have students write an essay exploring whether this term is accurate, using supporting examples. AL

Assess/Close

Discuss how the Cold War might have affected teenagers differently in the 1950s and 1960s. OL

Analyzing Visuals

Answers:

1. They used music, fashion, and leisure activities to reflect shared values.
2. **1950s:** Conformity reflected in teens being like peers; **1960s:** Individualism reflected in dance, hair, and clothing.

Activity: Technology Connection

Creating a Multimedia Presentation Organize students into two groups, one to study the youth culture of the 1950s and the other that of the 1960s. Have them use the Internet and library resources to find material for a multimedia presentation on their topic. Encourage them to include a variety of media, such as samples of music from the period; video clips from popular television shows, news broadcasts, or movies; photographs; primary source writing from books, newspapers, or magazines; and examples of advertising for products aimed at teens. Groups should assign different tasks to various members. When groups have assembled their materials, ask them to make their presentations to the class. **Ask:** What factors accounted for the similarities and differences between the youth culture of these two decades? *(Encourage students to explore the common experiences of youth coming of age as well as differences in each group's experiences based on political, economic, and cultural factors.)* OL

Identifying Explain to students that the Visual Summary highlights the main ideas of Chapter 27. Have students read the text and examine the photographs. Mention that each picture specifically relates to one of the main idea statements in each bulleted list. Have students identify which statement each photograph represents and then consider images that would illustrate the other statements. Students may wish to cite other images from the chapter. Discuss students' ideas as a class. OL

Summarizing Ask students to study the photographs, then write one or two sentences summarizing how each picture relates to the main idea of Chapter 27. BL

CHAPTER 27 Visual Summary

You can study anywhere, anytime by downloading quizzes and flash cards to your PDA from glencoe.com.

THE BERLIN WALL

The Berlin Wall symbolized the division between the two superpowers.

POLITICAL DIVISION AND CONFLICT During the Cold War

- The United States and Soviet Union became fierce political rivals.
- The United States provided aid to countries threatened by Communist expansion.
- Each side formed alliances: NATO (the U.S. and its allies) and the Warsaw Pact (the Soviet Union and its allies).
- Political division led to a growing arms race, the Berlin Wall, and the Cuban missile crisis.

THE SOVIET UNION AND EASTERN EUROPE During the Cold War

- In its economy, the Soviet Union emphasized heavy industry, benefiting the military over average citizens.
- Stalin ruled by repression and political terror.
- Khrushchev tried to increase farm and consumer products, but his policies failed.
- The Soviet Union gained control over much of Eastern Europe.

HUNGARIAN UPRISING OF 1956

Hungarians declared their freedom, but the Soviet Army forcibly reestablished Communist control.

SEGREGATION BECOMES ILLEGAL IN PUBLIC SCHOOLS IN THE UNITED STATES

In this photo from 1954 soldiers escort African Americans to school.

WESTERN EUROPE AND NORTH AMERICA During the Cold War

- Economic aid from the Marshall Plan helped Western Europe recover from the devastation of war.
- Six nations formed the European Economic Community (EEC).
- In the United States, Cold War tensions led to war in Korea and the "Red Scare."
- New technology and civil rights struggles changed society.

Hands-On Chapter Project
Step 4: Wrap-Up

Creating a Cold War Web Site

Step 4: Visit the Site Students will synthesize what they have learned in Steps 1–3.

Directions: Write the Essential Question on the board. Then display a multiple-effects chart. Have students review their Web site content and discuss what they see as the legacy of the Cold War. Encourage students to think of political alliances, social movements, organizations, military strategy, technology, weaponry, world views, literature, and ideologies from this era that have directly or indirectly shaped the contemporary world. Record their ideas in the chart. Then ask groups to create the home page for their Web site. This page should include the table of contents, graphics, a title, and a short passage that gives an overview of their Web site and explains its purpose and the significance of its information for users, incorporating ideas from class discussion. OL

STANDARDIZED TEST PRACTICE

TEST-TAKING 

A date can be an important clue. When a question contains a date, think about major events that occurred during or around that time. Then eliminate answer choices that do not reflect that history.

Reviewing Vocabulary

Directions: Choose the word or words that best complete the sentence.

1. ________ is the manufacture of machines and equipment for factories and mines.

A Assembly line
B Heavy industry
C Light industry
D Deterrence

2. In a ________ state, the government provides citizens with services and a minimal standard of living.

A welfare
B natural
C socialist
D communist

3. To keep communism within its existing boundaries, the United States followed a policy of ________.

A encroachment
B socialism
C colonization
D containment

4. A ________ is a group of nations with a common purpose.

A consortium
B bloc
C satellite
D region

Reviewing Main Ideas

Directions: Choose the best answers to the following questions.

Section 1 *(pp. 900–907)*

5. What is another name for the European Recovery Program of 1947?

A Common Market
B Truman Doctrine
C Five-Year Plan
D Marshall Plan

6. What is the name of the military alliance the Soviet Union made with seven nations in 1955?

A Allied Pact
B Nonaggression Pact
C Warsaw Pact
D Truman Pact

7. What did Nikita Khrushchev place in Cuba in 1962?

A Soviet troops
B Sugar reserves
C Nuclear missiles
D Exiled freedom fighters

Section 2 *(pp. 910–913)*

8. Who wrote *One Day in the Life of Ivan Denisovich*?

A Aleksandr Solzhenitsyn
B Adolf Hitler
C Simone de Beauvoir
D Ivan Denisovich

Need Extra Help?

If You Missed Questions . . .	1	2	3	4	5	6	7	8
Go to Page . . .	910	916	902	917	902	904	906	911

Answers and Analyses

Reviewing Vocabulary

1. B Remind students to activate their prior knowledge in answering test questions. As they recall from previous chapters, an assembly line is an efficient method of mass production that is not restricted to equipment. Deterrence is a means of preventing outright conflict by gathering large numbers of weapons. The choice then is between heavy and light industry. Heavy industry makes more sense in view of the fact that machines are being manufactured.

2. A Remind students to eliminate choices that are obviously incorrect, such as *natural state.*

3. D Tell students to use context clues to help them determine the correct answer. In this sentence, the words *to keep* and *within* are synonymous with *contain,* making D the only logical choice.

4. B Remind students that the word *bloc* comes from a French word that means "piece of wood" or solid, single unit.

Reviewing Main Ideas

5. D Have students recall what they know about each of the choices given. Draw their attention to the function of the Marshall Plan, which was to help Europe recover from the ravages of war.

6. C Because the date of 1955 is at the height of the Cold War, a Soviet pact would hardly be named after Truman or have the term *Allied* in its title. The Nonaggression Pact was signed with Hitler during World War II, leaving the Warsaw Pact as the only logical choice.

7. C Remind students to note the date of 1962. They should remember that this was the time of the Cuban missile crisis. Therefore, Khrushchev placed missiles in Cuba.

8. A Remind students to eliminate choices that are obviously incorrect, such as Adolf Hitler. The name of Ivan Denisovich in the title suggests that he is a character in the book, leaving Aleksandr Solzhenitsyn as the answer.

9. A Point out the clue "in Czechoslovakia." Khrushchev is associated with the Soviet Union, Nagy with Hungary, and Broz, or Tito, with Yugoslavia.

10. B Both Hungary and East Germany were unlikely to thrive economically, since they were behind the Iron Curtain. Great Britain declined after World War II, but West Germany made a remarkable economic recovery.

For Question 10: Try to come up with the answer in your head before you look at all the possible answers. This should help you eliminate answers that make no sense.

11. C Joseph McCarthy, a senator from Wisconsin, alleged that there were Communists in high government positions.

12. C Students should associate Martin Luther King, Jr., with the 1960s. His successful March on Washington was in 1963. Therefore, his assassination occurred in 1968.

13. D The philosopher Simone de Beauvoir wrote this groundbreaking book that led to the postwar women's liberation movement.

Critical Thinking

14. D Remind students to check the map key. The symbol for missiles is found near the Bay of Pigs.

CHAPTER 27

9. Which leader hoped to create "socialism with a human face" in Czechoslovakia?

A Alexander Dubček
B Nikita Khrushchev
C Imre Nagy
D Josip Broz

Section 3 *(pp. 914–921)*

10. Which postwar country experienced an "economic miracle"?

A East Germany
B West Germany
C Hungary
D Great Britain

11. Which American politician created a massive "Red Scare"—fear of Communist subversion—in the early 1950s?

A Richard Nixon
B Lyndon B. Johnson
C Joseph R. McCarthy
D Harry S. Truman

12. In which year was Martin Luther King, Jr., assassinated?

A 1970
B 1963
C 1968
D 1972

13. Who wrote *The Second Sex*?

A Jacqueline Kennedy
B Madame Gustav
C Paulette de Vous
D Simone de Beauvoir

Critical Thinking

Directions: Choose the best answers to the following questions.

Use the following map to answer question 14.

14. Where were the Soviet missile sites located?

A In the Bahamas
B Near Guantánamo Bay
C In eastern Cuba
D Near the Bay of Pigs

15. Why did the Soviet Union invade Hungary in 1956?

A To stop a rebellion led by Alexander Dubček
B To set up nuclear missiles aimed at Berlin
C To maintain Communist rule
D To stop a rebellion led by a group of writers

16. Which event caused a shift in U.S. politics to the political right?

A The Cuban missile crisis
B The election of Richard Nixon
C Passage of the Civil Rights Act
D The assassination of Martin Luther King, Jr.

Need Extra Help?

If You Missed Questions . . .	9	10	11	12	13	14	15	16
Go to Page . . .	913	915	918	918	921	926	913	918

GO ON

15. C Remind students that Imre Nagy declared Hungary a free nation in 1956, meaning the end of communist rule. Khrushchev prevented this from happening by sending the Soviet army in to seize control.

16. B Remind students that by the end of the 1960s, many Americans were tiring of the Vietnam War, antiwar protests, race riots, and radicalism. They wanted "law and order," which Richard Nixon represented.

17. What was the significance of intercontinental ballistic missiles (ICBMs) in the 1950s?
   - **A** They sent missiles into space.
   - **B** They were hydrogen bombs.
   - **C** They could send bombs anywhere.
   - **D** They were the first space satellites.

Analyze the chart below and answer the question that follows. Base your answer on the chart.

The British welfare state became the norm for most European states after World War II. The United States did not follow suit. As health-care costs continue to rise in the United States, so does the number of people who are without health insurance.

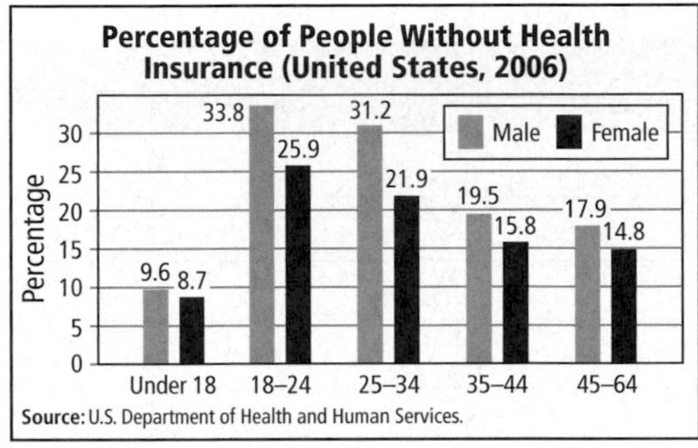

Source: U.S. Department of Health and Human Services.

18. According to the graph, which age group and gender has the highest percentage of people without health insurance?
   - **A** 25-to-34-year-old males
   - **B** 25-to-34-year-old females
   - **C** 18-to-24-year-old females
   - **D** 18-to-24-year-old males

Document-Based Questions

Directions: Analyze the document and answer the short-answer questions that follow the document. Base your answers on the document and on your knowledge of world history.

Bob Dylan, recording artist, expressed the feeling of the younger generation with his song "The Times They Are a-Changin'," released in 1964.

The Times They Are a-Changin'

Come gather round people
Wherever you roam
And admit that the waters
Around you have grown
And accept it that soon
You'll be drenched to the bone
If your time to you
Is worth savin'
Then you better start swimmin'
Or you'll sink like a stone
For the times they are a-changin' . . .

19. What is the tone of Dylan's lyrics? To whom does Dylan direct "come gather round"?

20. What does Dylan mean when he says "admit that the waters around you have grown"?

Extended Response

21. The Cuban missile crisis brought the world dangerously close to nuclear war. Explain how the politics of the Cold War affected both Kennedy's and Khrushchev's decisions leading to the crisis. What else could they have done to prevent the crisis?

For additional test practice, use Self-Check Quizzes—Chapter 27 at glencoe.com.

Need Extra Help?

If You Missed Questions . . .	17	18	19	20	21
Go to Page . . .	905	927	927	927	906

STOP

Document-Based Questions

19. The lyrics incite people to action; he says "come gather round" to all people everywhere, "wherever you roam."

20. Answers will vary, but may include that the world has become bigger and has changed.

Extended Response

21. Following World War II, the United States and the Soviet Union became fierce political rivals. Each side mistrusted the other and tried to outdo the other, whether in military might, scientific advances, or economic aid. Students' suggestions for ways to avoid the conflict will vary, but should be based on supporting details and reasonable conclusions.

17. C Point out the clue "intercontinental." Remind students that in the 1950s, many people built bomb shelters because of the fear that missiles could send bombs anywhere.

18. D Tell students to look for the highest bar and then to identify the age group from the X-axis and the gender from the key.

Introduce students to chapter content and key terms by having them access the Chapter 27 Overview at glencoe.com.

Need Extra Help?

Have students refer to the pages listed if they miss any of the questions.

CHAPTER 28 Planning Guide

Key to Ability Levels	
BL Below Level	AL Above Level
OL On Level	ELL English Language Learners

Key to Teaching Resources	
Print Material	DVD
CD-ROM	Transparency

Levels				Resources	Chapter Opener	Section 1	Section 2	Section 3	Section 4	Chapter Assess
BL	OL	AL	ELL							
FOCUS										
BL	OL	AL	ELL	**Daily Focus Skills Transparencies**		28-1	28-2	28-3	28-4	
TEACH										
BL	OL	AL	ELL	**Charting and Graphing Activity, URB**		✓				
BL	OL		ELL	**Reading Skills Activity, URB**			p. 53			
	OL	AL		**Historical Analysis Skills Activity, URB**				p. 54		
BL	OL	AL	ELL	**Differentiated Instruction Activity, URB**					p. 55	
	OL		ELL	**English Learner Activity, URB**					p. 57	
BL	OL	AL	ELL	**Content Vocabulary Activity, URB***		p. 59				
BL	OL	AL	ELL	**Academic Vocabulary Activity, URB**					p. 61	
BL	OL	AL	ELL	**Skills Reinforcement Activity, URB**			p. 63			
	OL	AL		**Critical Thinking Skills Activity, URB**				p. 64		
	OL	AL		**History and Geography Activity, URB**					p. 65	
	OL	AL	ELL	**Mapping History Activity, URB**		p. 67				
BL	OL	AL		**Historical Significance Activity, URB**					p. 68	
BL	OL	AL	ELL	**Cooperative Learning Activity, URB**					p. 69	
	OL	AL	ELL	**History Simulation Activity, URB**				p. 71		
BL	OL	AL	ELL	**Time Line Activity, URB**				p. 73		
	OL	AL		**Linking Past and Present Activity, URB**					p. 74	
BL	OL	AL		**People in World History Activity, URB**		p. 75			p. 76	
BL	OL	AL	ELL	**Primary Source Reading, URB**			p. 77			
	OL	AL		**Enrichment Activity, URB**			p. 82			
BL	OL	AL	ELL	**World Art and Music Activity, URB**					p. 79	
BL	OL		ELL	**Guided Reading Activities, URB***		p. 84	p. 85	p. 86	p. 87	
BL	OL		ELL	**Reading Essentials and Note-Taking Guide***		p. 307	p. 310	p. 313	p. 316	
BL	OL	AL	ELL	**Differentiated Instruction for the World History Classroom**	✓	✓	✓	✓	✓	✓

Note: Please refer to the *Unit Resource Book: Toward a Global Civilization* for this chapter's URB materials.

* Also available in Spanish

- Interactive Lesson Planner
- Interactive Teacher Edition
- Fully editable blackline masters
- Section Spotlight Videos Launch
- Differentiated Lesson Plans
- Printable reports of daily assignments
- Standards Tracking System

Levels BL	OL	AL	ELL		Resources	Chapter Opener	Section 1	Section 2	Section 3	Section 4	Chapter Assess
TEACH *(continued)*											
BL	OL	AL	ELL		StudentWorks™ Plus DVD	✓	✓	✓	✓	✓	✓
BL	OL	AL	ELL		Vocabulary PuzzleMaker CD-ROM	✓	✓	✓	✓	✓	✓
Teacher Resources					Building Academic Vocabulary	✓	✓	✓	✓	✓	✓
Teacher Resources					Reading Strategies and Activities for the Social Studies Classroom		p. 53				
Teacher Resources					Writer's Guidebook		p. 17	p. 43			
Teacher Resources					Strategies for Success	✓	✓	✓	✓	✓	✓
Teacher Resources					Outline Map Resource Book	✓	✓	✓	✓	✓	✓
Teacher Resources					Presentation Plus! with MindJogger DVD	✓	✓	✓	✓	✓	✓
ASSESS											
BL	OL	AL	ELL		Section Quizzes and Chapter Tests*		p. 349	p. 350	p. 351	p. 352	p. 353
BL	OL	AL	ELL		Authentic Assessment With Rubrics	✓	✓	✓	✓	✓	✓
BL	OL	AL	ELL		Standardized Test Practice Workbook	✓	✓	✓	✓	✓	✓
BL	OL	AL	ELL		*ExamView® Assessment Suite* CD-ROM		28-1	28-2	28-3	28-4	Ch. 28
BL	OL	AL	ELL		Interactive Tutor Self-Assessment CD-ROM		28-1	28-2	28-3	28-4	
CLOSE											
BL			ELL		Reteaching Activity, URB				p. 81		
BL	OL		ELL		Reading and Study Skills Foldables™	✓	✓	✓	✓	✓	✓
BL	OL	AL	ELL		World History in Graphic Novel			p. 81			

Using the Glencoe Web Site

Student Web Activities

Technology Product
The Glencoe Web site provides Web activities to students that reinforce and enrich chapter content. The Student Web Activities
- introduce a topic relevant to chapter content, along with a link to Web sites that provide information about the topic;
- prompt students to complete tasks specific to the activity;
- assess student comprehension of the material.

Objective
The Student Web Activities help students
- learn online research and study skills;
- practice reading and comprehension skills.

Steps
Provide students with the following steps to complete the activities:
- Locate the Web page for the textbook being studied on the Glencoe Web site glencoe.com.
- Click on **Student Center** under the textbook title.
- In the Student Center, select a unit from the Unit Resources menu and a chapter from the Chapter Activities menu using the drop-down arrows.
- Click on the **Student Web Activities** link.
- Have students complete the activity on the page, clicking on the feature Web link for the chapter selected and answering the activity questions.

Provide students with an e-mail address to submit their answers for grading.

History ONLINE

	Student	Teacher	Parent
Beyond the Textbook	●	●	●
Chapter Overviews	●	●	●
Time Current Events	●		●
ePuzzles and Games	●		●
Concepts in Motion	●		●
Literature Connections		●	
Multi-Language Glossaries	●		●
Online Student Edition	●	●	●
Self-Check Quizzes	●		●
Student Web Activities	●		●
Study Central ™	●		●
Teaching Today		●	
Vocabulary eFlashcards	●		●
Web Activity Lesson Plans		●	

- **Timed Readings Plus in Social Studies** helps students increase their reading rate and fluency while maintaining comprehension. The 400-word passages are similar to those found on state and national assessments.
- **Reading in the Content Area: Social Studies** concentrates on six essential reading skills that help students better comprehend what they read. The book includes 75 high-interest nonfiction passages written at increasing levels of difficulty.
- **Reading Social Studies** includes strategic reading instruction and vocabulary support in Social Studies content for both ELLs and native speakers of English.

www.jamestowneducation.com

NATIONAL GEOGRAPHIC
Index to National Geographic Magazine:

The following articles relate to this chapter:

- "Endangered Revolution," by Andrew Meier, March 2006
- "Future Power," by Michael Parfit, August 2005
- "How Did It Come to This?" by Andrew Meier, July 2005

National Geographic Society Products To order the following, call National Geographic at 1-800-368-2728:

- *National Geographic Atlas of the World* (Book).

Access National Geographic's new, dynamic MapMachine Web site and other geography resources at:

www.nationalgeographic.com

www.nationalgeographic.com/maps

Biography  

The following videotape program is available from Glencoe as a supplement to Chapter 28:

- Men in Space: From Goddard to Armstrong (ISBN 1-56501-037-X)

To order, call Glencoe at 1-800-334-7344. To find classroom resources to accompany many of these videos, check the following home pages:

A&E Television: www.aetv.com

The History Channel: www.historychannel.com

GLENCOE BOOKLINK 3

Use this database to search more than 30,000 titles to create a customized reading list for your students.

- Reading lists can be organized by students' reading level, author, genre, theme, or area of interest.
- The database provides Degrees of Reading Power™ (DRP) and Lexile™ readability scores for all selections.
- A brief summary of each selection is included.

Leveled reading suggestions for this chapter:

For students at a Grade 8 reading level:
- ***Dropping in on Russia,*** by David C. King

For students at a Grade 9 reading level:
- ***Teenage Refugees from Eastern Europe Speak Out,*** by Carl Rollyson

For students at a Grade 10 reading level:
- ***President George W. Bush: Our Forty-Third President,*** by Beatrice Gormley

For students at a Grade 11 reading level:
- ***Environmental Experiments about Renewable Energy,*** by Thomas R. Rybolt and Robert C. Mebane

For students at a Grade 12 reading level:
- ***Failure is Impossible!: The History of American Women's Rights,*** by Martha E. Kendall

Introducing CHAPTER 28

Focus

MAKING CONNECTIONS
What did the Berlin Wall symbolize?

Activate students' prior knowledge by asking them who built the wall in 1961 and why. *(The communist government of East Germany built the wall to prevent East Germans from seeking freedom and prosperity in West Germany.)* Then discuss how the Berlin Wall emphasized the split between East and West during the Cold War years.

Teach

The Big Ideas

As students study the chapter, remind them to consider the section-based Big Ideas included in each section's Guide to Reading. The **Essential Questions** in the activities below tie in to the Big Ideas and help students think about and understand important chapter concepts. In addition, the Hands-on Chapter Projects with their culminating activities relate the content from each section to the Big Ideas. These activities build on each other as students progress through the chapter. Section activities culminate in the wrap-up activity on the Visual Summary page.

CHAPTER 28

The Contemporary Western World 1970–Present

Section 1 Decline of the Soviet Union
Section 2 Eastern Europe
Section 3 Europe and North America
Section 4 Western Society and Culture

MAKING CONNECTIONS

What did the Berlin Wall symbolize?

Shortly after the East German government opened the Berlin Wall's checkpoints in 1989, thousands of citizens mobbed the wall and began to tear it down. This photo shows East German border guards protecting the wall the morning before the first section fell. The fall of the Berlin Wall marked the end of the Cold War and served as the first step toward the reunification of Germany. In this chapter you will learn about political, economic, and social changes that have taken place in the contemporary Western world.

- What were the immediate effects of the fall of the Berlin Wall?
- How does the East-West split during the Cold War affect Germany today?

EUROPE, THE SOVIET UNION, AND THE UNITED STATES ▶

1974 Gerald Ford becomes U.S. president after Nixon resigns

1984 USSR boycotts Los Angeles Olympics

1990 Germany reunified

1970 — 1980 — 1990

THE WORLD ▶

1979 Mother Teresa wins Nobel Peace Prize

928

Decline of the Soviet Union

Essential Question: How strong was the Soviet Union after World War II? *(It was one of the two strongest countries in the world and competed with the United States for international power.)* Point out that in Section 1, students will learn about problems that led to the collapse of the Soviet Union by 1991. **OL**

Eastern Europe

Essential Question: What was the connection between Eastern Europe and the Soviet Union? *(The Soviet Union controlled Eastern Europe, keeping Communist governments in power and crushing rebellions.)* Point out that in Section 2, students will learn how the collapse of the Soviet Union affected Eastern Europe and how different countries and ethnic groups managed the change. **OL**

2002
Euro established as common currency in many Western European nations

2004
Chechen rebels seize Russian school; many children die

2000

1995
Terrorists release deadly chemicals in Tokyo subway

2002
China joins World Trade Organization

FOLDABLES™
Study Organizer

Identifying Research the historical role played by Mikhail Gorbachev in reshaping the Soviet Union during the 1980s. Organize the information in a Four-Door Book using *Who*, *What*, *When*, and *Where* categories.

History ONLINE
Chapter Overview—Visit glencoe.com to preview Chapter 28.

More About the Photo

Visual Literacy The Berlin Wall began in 1961 as a barrier of cinder blocks and barbed wire fencing. By the 1980s, it consisted of a system of more than 100 miles of concrete walls reinforced by barbed wire, armed guards, mines, and electric fencing. During its existence, approximately 5,000 people were captured trying to cross the border, and nearly 200 were killed. About 5,000 East Germans were successful in fleeing to West Germany.

FOLDABLES Study Organizer Dinah Zike's Foldables

Dinah Zike's Foldables are three-dimensional, interactive graphic organizers that help students practice basic writing skills, review vocabulary terms, and identify main ideas. Instructions for creating and using Foldables can be found in the Appendix at the end of this book and in the *Dinah Zike's Reading and Study Skills Foldables* booklet.

History ONLINE

Introduce students to chapter content and key terms by having them access the Chapter 28 Overview at glencoe.com.

SECTION 3

Europe and North America

Essential Question: How did political changes in North America and Europe affect their economies? *(These countries were stable democracies, so although political changes affected the economies, the countries remained strong politically.)* Point out that in Section 3, students will learn about both political and economic changes in Europe and North America. **OL**

SECTION 4

Western Society and Culture

Essential Question: How important is Western culture in the world? *(It is a strong force throughout the world, especially because television shows, movies, and the Internet have become so widespread.)* Point out that in Section 4, students will learn about the influence of Western culture on other societies and reactions against it. **OL**

Focus

Bellringer

Daily Focus Transparency 28.1

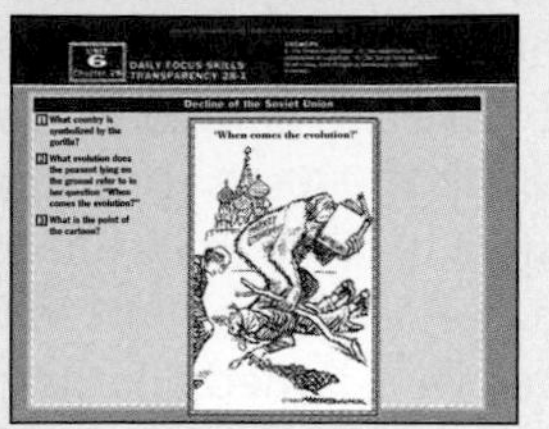

GUIDE TO READING

Answers to Graphic:

Brezhnev: Foreign—intervention in Communist countries; Economic—heavy industry, collective farming; Military—invasion of Afghanistan; Political—dissidents punished; **Gorbachev:** Foreign—nonintervention; Economic—limited free enterprise; Military—nuclear arms treaty; Political—new Soviet parliament

Section Spotlight Video

To generate student interest and provide a springboard for class discussion, access the Chapter 28, Section 1 video at glencoe.com or on the video DVD.

Resource Manager

SECTION 1

Decline of the Soviet Union

GUIDE TO READING

The BIG Idea

Self-Determination One of the largest empires in the world ended when the Soviet Union broke up in 1991.

Content Vocabulary

- détente *(p. 930)*
- dissidents *(p. 930)*
- perestroika *(p. 932)*

Academic Vocabulary

- participation *(p. 931)*
- responsive *(p. 932)*

People, Places, and Events

- Leonid Brezhnev *(p. 930)*
- Brezhnev Doctrine *(p. 930)*
- Afghanistan *(p. 931)*
- Ronald Reagan *(p. 931)*
- Mikhail Gorbachev *(p. 932)*
- Boris Yeltsin *(p. 932)*
- Ukraine *(p. 932)*
- Belarus *(p. 932)*
- Vladimir Putin *(p. 934)*

Reading Strategy

Comparing and Contrasting As you read, create a chart like the one below comparing the policies of Brezhnev and Gorbachev.

	Leonid Brezhnev	Mikhail Gorbachev
Foreign Policy		
Economic Policy		
Military Policy		
Personal Policy		

After Nikita Khrushchev was forced out of office, the Soviet Union experienced domestic and foreign problems. By the 1980s, the country was seriously ailing, and many believed that reform was necessary. That reform began under Mikhail Gorbachev's perestroika and continued with the breakup of the Soviet Union in 1991. Today, Russia has emerged as an economic power with its vast energy wealth.

The Soviet Union Under Stress

MAIN IDEA The Soviet Union could not survive a combination of domestic and foreign problems.

HISTORY & YOU What challenges does the U.S. president face today? Read to learn about the challenges faced by the Soviet leaders in the 1980s.

Between 1964 and 1982, drastic change in the Soviet Union had seemed highly unlikely. What happened to create such a dramatic turnaround by the late 1980s?

The Brezhnev Era

Alexei Kosygin and **Leonid Brezhnev** (BREHZH•NEHF) replaced Nikita Khrushchev when he was removed from office in 1964. Brezhnev emerged as the dominant leader in the 1970s. Determined to keep Eastern Europe in Communist hands, he was not interested in reform. He also insisted on the Soviet Union's right to intervene if communism was threatened in another Communist state (known as the **Brezhnev Doctrine**).

At the same time, Brezhnev benefited from **détente,** a relaxation of tensions and improved relations between the two superpowers. Roughly equal to the United States in nuclear arms, the Soviet Union felt more secure. As a result, its leaders relaxed their authoritarian rule. Brezhnev allowed more access to Western styles of music, dress, and art. However, he still punished **dissidents,** those who spoke out against the regime.

In his economic policies, Brezhnev continued to emphasize heavy industry. Two problems, however, weakened the Soviet economy. First, the central government was a huge, complex, but inefficient bureaucracy that led to indifference. Second, many collective farmers preferred working their own small private plots to laboring in the collective work brigades.

By the 1970s, the Communist ruling class in the Soviet Union had become complacent and corrupt. Party and state leaders, as well as army leaders and secret police (KGB), enjoyed a high

R Reading Strategies	C Critical Thinking	D Differentiated Instruction	W Writing Support	S Skill Practice
Teacher Edition • Academic Vocab., p. 932 • Act. Prior Know., p. 933 **Additional Resources** • Cont. Vocab. Act., URB p. 59 • Guid. Read. Act., URB p. 84 • Read. Ess. & Note-Taking Guide, p. 307	**Teacher Edition** • Pred. Consequences, p. 931 • Making Inferences, p. 933 • Drawing Con., p. 934 **Additional Resources** • People in World Hist., URB p. 75 • Section Quiz, p. 349	**Teacher Edition** • Adv. Learners, p. 932 • Visual/Spatial, p. 934 **Additional Resources** • Read. Strat. for SS, p. 53	**Teacher Edition** • Expository Writing, p. 935 **Additional Resources** • Writer's Guidebook p. 17	**Teacher Edition** • Using Geo. Skills, p. 931 **Additional Resources** • Chart. Graph. Act., URB p. 3 • Mapping Hist. Act., URB p. 67

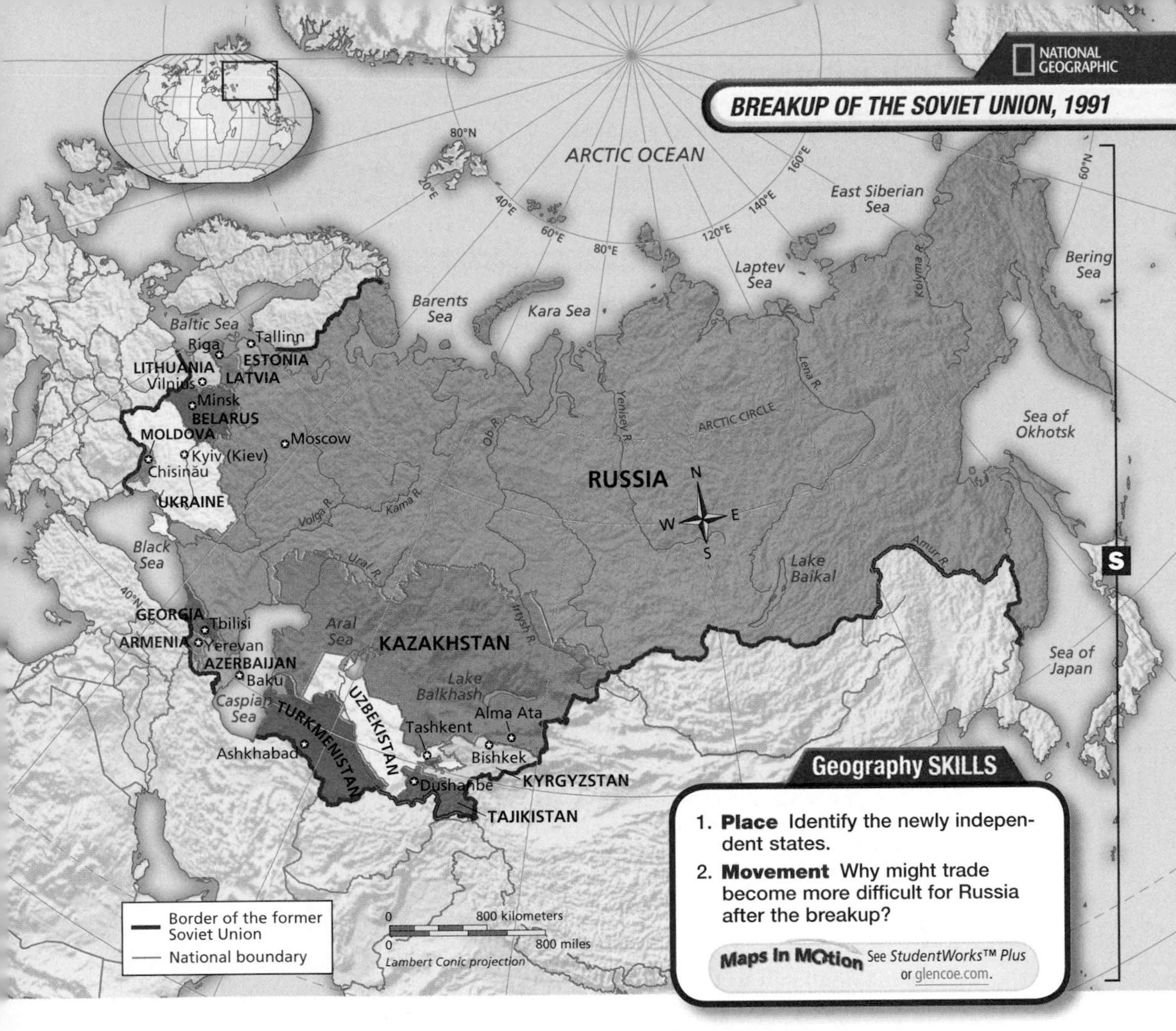

Geography SKILLS

1. **Place** Identify the newly independent states.
2. **Movement** Why might trade become more difficult for Russia after the breakup?

Maps In MOtion See StudentWorks™ Plus or glencoe.com.

standard of living. Regardless of the government's inefficiency and corruption, Brezhnev did not want to tamper with the party leadership and state bureaucracy.

The Cold War Intensifies

By the 1970s, détente allowed U.S. grain and consumer goods to be sold to the Soviet Union. However, détente collapsed in 1979 when the Soviet Union invaded **Afghanistan.** A new period of East-West confrontation began.

The Soviet Union wanted to restore a pro-Soviet regime in Afghanistan. The United States viewed this as an act of expansion. To show his disapproval, President Jimmy Carter canceled U.S. **participation** in the 1980 Olympic Games to be held in Moscow. He also placed an embargo on the shipment of U.S. grain to the Soviets. Relations became even chillier when **Ronald Reagan** became president. He called the Soviet Union an "evil empire" and began a military buildup and a new arms race. Reagan also gave military aid to the Afghan rebels.

✓Reading Check **Explaining** Why did détente between the Soviets and Americans end?

Teach

S Skill Practice

Using Geography Skills

Ask: What is the second-largest of the former Soviet republics? *(Kazakhstan)* BL

C Critical Thinking

Predicting Consequences

Ask: How do you think President Carter's actions were viewed by Americans? *(Answers may include that many were probably unhappy with his decision.)* AL

Geography SKILLS

Answers:

1. Belarus, Ukraine, Moldova, Georgia, Turkmenistan, Armenia, Azerbaijan, Tajikistan, Kyrgyzstan, Uzbekistan, Kazakhstan, Russia, Lithuania, Estonia, Latvia
2. Russia lost resources and some access to water routes.

✓Reading Check

Answer: The Soviet Union invaded Afghanistan.

Hands-On Chapter Project Step 1

Traveling through the Modern Western World

Pairs of students will map and report on a journey of the modern Western world.

Step 1: Mapping and Reporting on a Destination in the Soviet Union

Essential Question: How have different areas in the Western world changed during the last 30 years?

Directions: Pairs of students will begin mapping their journey by selecting a city or region in the former Soviet Union to visit. Students will review the content and do additional research to prepare a short written or oral report that describes what they expect to see, as well as how things have changed there in the last 30 years. They might highlight changes by focusing on subjects such as buildings, public markets or other areas, or cultural attractions and telling how they are different today compared to recent history. OL

(Chapter Project is continued in Section 2.)

R Reading Strategy

Academic Vocabulary Have students use context clues to define the term *responsive*. **Ask:** **Why did the Soviet economy need to be more responsive to consumers?** *(The Soviet economy had been controlled by political leaders who did not address consumer needs.)* **OL**

D Differentiated Instruction

Advanced Learners Ask students to re-read the first paragraph under the heading "End of the Cold War." Students should then do research to learn about the costs of the Cold War as well as the competitive international relations created by it. Ask students to prepare a short report on what people hoped would be the results of the end of the Cold War. **AL**

✓Reading Check

Answer: His political and economic reforms set the stage for nationalist movements in the Soviet Republics.

Gorbachev and Reform

MAIN IDEA Gorbachev's reforms contributed to the end of the Cold War and of the Soviet Union.

HISTORY & YOU Has a U.S. president ever changed the course of our nation? Read to learn how Mikhail Gorbachev changed the course of the USSR.

By 1980, the Soviet Union was ailing. It had a declining economy, a rise in infant mortality rates, a dramatic surge in alcoholism, and poor working conditions. Within the Communist Party, a small group of reformers emerged. One was **Mikhail Gorbachev** (GAWR•buh•CHAWF). When the party chose him as leader in March 1985, a new era began.

Gorbachev and Perestroika

From the start, Gorbachev preached the need for radical reforms based on **perestroika** (PEHR•uh•STROY•kuh), or restructuring. At first, this meant restructuring economic policy. Gorbachev wanted to start a market economy more **responsive** to consumers. It was to have limited free enterprise so that some businesses would be privately owned and operated.

Gorbachev soon realized, however, that an attempt to reform the economy would not work without political reform. Therefore, at the 1988 Communist Party conference, he set up a new Soviet parliament with elected members, the Congress of People's Deputies. It met in 1989, the first such meeting in the country since 1918.

Gorbachev then created a new state presidency as the leading executive office. Under the old system, the first secretary of the Communist Party (Gorbachev's position) had been the most important. In March 1990, Gorbachev became the Soviet Union's first—and last—president.

End of the Cold War

When Mikhail Gorbachev came to power in the Soviet Union, the Cold War suddenly ended. His "New Thinking"—his willingness to rethink Soviet foreign policy—led to stunning changes.

First, Gorbachev made an agreement with the United States in 1987, the Intermediate-Range INF Treaty, to eliminate intermediate-range nuclear weapons. Both superpowers wanted to slow down the arms race. They wanted to reduce their military budgets to solve domestic problems. Gorbachev hoped to focus resources on social and economic change. The United States wanted to balance its national debt, which had tripled during the Reagan presidency.

Gorbachev also stopped giving Soviet military support to Communist governments in Eastern Europe. This opened the door to the overthrow of Communist regimes. A mostly peaceful revolutionary movement swept through Eastern Europe in 1989. The reunification of Germany on October 3, 1990, was a powerful symbol of the end of the Cold War. In 1991 the Soviet Union was dissolved. The long rivalry between the two superpowers was over.

End of the Soviet Union

The Soviet Union included 92 ethnic groups and 112 different languages. As Gorbachev released the iron grip of the Communist Party, centered in Moscow, old ethnic tensions came to the fore. Nationalist movements began. In 1989 and 1990, calls for independence came first in Soviet Georgia and then in Latvia, Estonia, Moldavia, Uzbekistan, Azerbaijan, and Lithuania.

The conservative leaders of the traditional Soviet institutions—the army, government, KGB, and military industries—were worried. The breakup of the Soviet Union would end their privileges. On August 19, 1991, a group of these conservative leaders arrested Gorbachev and tried to seize power. The attempt failed, however, when **Boris Yeltsin,** president of the Russian Republic, and thousands of Russians bravely resisted the rebel forces in Moscow.

The Soviet republics now moved for complete independence. **Ukraine** voted for independence on December 1, 1991. A week later, the leaders of Russia, Ukraine, and **Belarus** announced that the Soviet Union had "ceased to exist."

✓Reading Check **Explaining** How did Gorbachev contribute to the Soviet Union's breakup?

Differentiated Instruction

People in World History Activity 28 — Profile 1

Mikhail Gorbachev (1931–)

People in World History Activity, URB p. 75

Comparing and Contrasting

Objective: Compare and contrast Mikhail Gorbachev with previous Soviet leaders.

Focus: Have students identify previous Soviet leaders' policies.

Teach: Have students identify Gorbachev's policies.

Assess: Have students compare and contrast Gorbachev's and previous leaders' policies in a chart.

Close: Ask students why Gorbachev faced a revolt.

Differentiated Instruction Strategies

BL Ask students to suggest the effects of limiting arms on the Soviet Union and the United States.

AL Ask students to research and report on the problems encountered by the attempt to change farm policies.

ELL Ask students why the Soviet Union needed *glasnost*.

THE COLLAPSE OF THE SOVIET UNION

Soldiers and tanks move to Red Square to surround the Kremlin at the beginning of the August 1991 coup.

Mikhail Gorbachev's efforts at political reform began in 1988 with the creation of a new parliament through competitive elections. This Congress of People's Deputies included strong critics of the Communist Party leadership. R

In 1989 reforms in the Soviet Union encouraged the satellite states of Eastern Europe to reject communism and elect their own democratic governments. Nationalist groups within the Soviet Union also began to call for independence.

The Soviet Union was made up of 15 separate republics, each with its own dominant ethnic group, a powerful force toward nationalism. To try to hold the Soviet Union together, Gorbachev negotiated the Union Treaty in 1991, which granted greater powers to the republics. Communist leaders were threatened by this agreement. They attempted a coup against Gorbachev in August 1991.

Though unsuccessful, the coup greatly weakened Gorbachev's political power since it was brought about by his supporters. It revealed the political weakness of the Soviet state. One by one, the Soviet republics began to declare their independence.

On December 25, 1991, Gorbachev resigned as president, and the flag of the Soviet Union was lowered for the last time over the Kremlin.

The Former Soviet Republics

REPUBLIC	MAJOR ETHNIC GROUP
Russia	Russian (79.8%)
Ukraine	Ukrainian (77.8%)
Uzbekistan	Uzbek (80%)
Belarus	Belarusian (81.2%)
Kazakhstan	Kazakh (53.4%)
Azerbaijan	Azerbaijani (90.6%)
Georgia	Georgian (83.8%)
Tajikistan	Tajik (79.9%)
Armenia	Armenian (97.9%)
Lithuania	Lithuanian (83.4%)
Moldova	Moldavian (78.2%)
Turkmenistan	Turkmen (85%)
Kyrgyzstan	Kyrgyz (64.9%)
Latvia	Latvian (57.7%)
Estonia	Estonian (67.9%)

CRITICAL THINKING SKILLS

1. **Explaining** Why did independence movements arise in the Soviet republics?
2. **Making Inferences** Why do you think the failed 1991 coup hastened the breakup of the Soviet Union?

R Reading Strategy

Activating Prior Knowledge

Ask: Why was the new Congress of People's Deputies so different from the previous Soviet government? *(It was formed from competitive elections rather than allowing only Communist Party candidates.)* OL

For additional practice on this skill, see the **Skills Handbook**.

C Critical Thinking

Making Inferences Ask: Who was commanding the soldier pictured? *(Communist leaders opposed to the Union Treaty and other changes)* OL

CRITICAL THINKING SKILLS

Answers:

1. The many ethnic groups in the 15 republics were a powerful force toward nationalism. As the Soviet Union pursued democratic reforms, nationalist groups began to call for their independence.
2. The coup revealed the political weakness of the Soviet state, which encouraged nationalist movements.

Additional Support

Activity: Interdisciplinary Connection

Daily Life Ask students to recall the history of the Soviet Union. Discuss important events and leaders, beginning with the 1917 revolution, through Lenin and Stalin and the Cold War. **Ask:** How do you think former citizens of the USSR reacted to the flag being lowered for the last time? *(Some might have celebrated because of hatred for the regime; others might have mourned the change.)* Ask students to select one of the republics listed in their text and research the citizens' experiences under the USSR. Then ask students to write a letter that represents one of these experiences and describes the final lowering of the flag. Ask volunteers to share their work with the class. OL

C Critical Thinking

Drawing Conclusions **Ask:** Why do you think there was an increase in organized crime after the breakup of the Soviet Union? *(Because of changes in the government, law enforcement was more difficult.)* OL

D Differentiated Instruction

Visual/Spatial Ask students to re-read the paragraph from Yeltsin's resignation speech and focus on the visual images of the last phrase "we could leap from the gray, stagnant, totalitarian past into the light, rich, civilized future." Discuss the images, then ask students to create a picture that illustrates Yeltsin's words. OL

DOCUMENT-BASED QUESTIONS

Answers:

1. No. He says that the dreams of post-Soviet Russia did not come true, and that although the goals of post-Soviet Russia seemed simple, they were actually very difficult to achieve.
2. that Russians were dissatisfied with the early results of the transition to capitalism

Additional Support

The New Russia

MAIN IDEA Although the country still faces some challenges, Russia has greatly improved economically.

HISTORY & YOU Has the cost of gasoline been in the news recently? Read to learn how Russia has become one of the largest exporters of oil.

Gorbachev resigned on December 25, 1991. He turned over his responsibilities as commander in chief to Boris Yeltsin, the new president of Russia. By the end of 1991, one of the largest empires in world history had ended.

Russia Under Yeltsin

Boris Yeltsin was committed to introducing a free market economy as quickly as possible, but the transition was not easy. Economic hardships and social disarray were made worse by a dramatic rise in organized crime.

Another problem Yeltsin faced was in Chechnya, a province in the south that wanted to secede from Russia and become independent. Yeltsin used brutal force against the Chechens (CHEH•chuhnz) to keep the province as part of Russia. Yeltsin also dealt with former Soviet states like Poland, Hungary, and the Czech Republic who wanted to join NATO. Yeltsin opposed their wishes. However, in the 1990s, these countries eventually succeeded in joining NATO.

Russia Under Putin

At the end of 1999, Yeltsin resigned and was replaced by **Vladimir Putin,** who was elected president in 2000. Putin, a former

INFOGRAPHICS

Challenges for the New Russia

After playing a central role in the breakup of the Soviet Union, Boris Yeltsin became Russia's first elected leader in 1990. As president, he faced the difficult task of transforming the former communist state into a democratic, free-market state.

Unfortunately, the transition to capitalism did not go smoothly. Economic reforms caused inflation and unemployment, and Russians' quality of life plummeted. Yeltsin also struggled with political enemies and a violent rebellion in Chechnya.

In 1998 when Russia defaulted on billions of dollars in debts, the economy collapsed completely. At the end of 1999, Yeltsin resigned, handing over power to Prime Minister Vladimir Putin.

In his resignation speech, Yeltsin addressed the many challenges of his presidency:

> "I want to ask for your forgiveness for the fact that many of the dreams we shared did not come true. And for the fact that what seemed simple to us turned out to be tormentingly difficult. I ask forgiveness for not justifying some hopes of those people who believed that at one stroke, in one spurt, we could leap from the gray, stagnant, totalitarian past into the light, rich, civilized future."
>
> —Boris Yeltsin, December 31, 1999

Chechen fighters attack a Russian tank in Chechnya in 1995.

Russians protest at the Winter Palace in St. Petersburg in January 1992. The sign demands that the country's leaders be punished for bringing poverty and hardship to the Russian people.

DOCUMENT-BASED QUESTIONS

1. **Analyzing** Did Yeltsin believe he succeeded in transforming post-Soviet Russia? Explain.
2. **Synthesizing** What was the significance of Russians protesting at the Winter Palace?

Extending the Content

The Conflict in Chechnya Like many other ethnic and nationalist movements, the conflict in Chechnya goes back many years. Russia first conquered Chechnya in 1859 after a bitter war. Chechens rebelled against Russia at the time of the Russian Revolution but were again conquered by the Russians in 1922. During World War II, Stalin believed Chechens collaborated with Nazis as a way out of Russian rule, and deported many of them to Siberia and Central Asia. They were not allowed to return until Khrushchev came into power in 1957. One reason Chechnya is important to Russia is its rich oil reserves, but the fighting there in recent years has destroyed much of its production capacity. The capital city of Grozny was left in ruins during fighting in 2000.

KGB officer, was widely seen as someone who wanted to keep a tight rein on government power. In July 2001, Putin launched reforms to boost growth and budget revenues. The reforms included the free sale and purchase of land and tax cuts. Putin has also applied for Russia's admission to the World Trade Organization and has worked out a special partnership with the European Union. In spite of these changes, the business climate remains somewhat uncertain, and this has stifled foreign investment.

Since Putin's reforms, Russia has experienced a budget surplus and a growing economy. Russia can attribute a large part of its economic growth to its oil and gas exports. The country has an estimated 6 percent of the world's oil deposits and about 30 percent of the world's natural gas deposits.

In fact, Russia's energy wealth and control over export pipelines have made the country quite powerful. Increasingly, Russia has used its supplies of oil and gas as a political lever to wield power over former Soviet states and to influence world energy prices. For example, in 2006, Russia raised gas prices by about 100 percent for Ukraine, whose democratic government it opposed. A trans-Siberian oil pipeline, planned for 2008, will make Asia more dependent on Russian oil. **W**

Even though it has made economic gains, Russia still faces some challenges. Rising alcoholism, criminal activities, and the decline of the traditional family system give Russians concern. Putin has tried to deal with these problems by centralizing his control over the government. Some observers have raised concerns that Putin grants even more influence to government forces that desire to reassert state control over the economy.

Other challenges for Russia are the ongoing turmoil in Chechnya and terrorism. In 2002 Chechen terrorists took about 600 Russians hostage in a Moscow theater. Between 2002 and 2004, terrorist attacks in Russia killed an estimated 500 people. Chechen rebels seized a school in the town of Beslan in 2004. When Russian troops moved in to end the siege, more than 300 died. Many were young schoolchildren. Although Russian troops killed the Chechen leader in 2006, the remaining insurgents have continued terrorist attacks in the North Caucasus region. Putin has refused to negotiate with the Chechen rebels.

Critics have questioned Putin's Chechnya policy, as well as how fully this event has been reported in state-owned media. In response, Putin cracked down on the media outlets. Observers in the West have been alarmed by his attack on democratic practices in Russia. However, many Russians support Putin's attempt to restore a sense of pride and discipline in Russian society.

✓Reading Check **Identifying** What are some of the challenges that Russia still faces?

SECTION 1 REVIEW

Vocabulary

1. **Explain** the significance of: Leonid Brezhnev, Brezhnev Doctrine, détente, dissidents, Afghanistan, participation, Ronald Reagan, Mikhail Gorbachev, perestroika, responsive, Boris Yeltsin, Ukraine, Belarus, Vladimir Putin.

Main Ideas

2. **List** the problems that weakened the Soviet economy during the 1960s and 1970s. Use a chart like the one below to make your list.

Problems That Weakened the Soviet Economy, 1960s–1970s
1.
2.

3. **Explain** the role that nationalism played in the breakup of the Soviet Union.
4. **Summarize** the reforms that Vladimir Putin has made to keep Russia on a strong economic track.

Critical Thinking

5. **The BIG Idea** **Comparing** In what ways can the breakup of the Soviet Union be compared to that of the Roman Empire and the Han dynasty?
6. **Making Connections** Why did the former Soviet Union have problems adapting to a free-market economy?
7. **Analyzing Visuals** Examine the smaller photograph on page 934. Do the Chechen fighters and the Russian army appear to be equally well-armed?

Writing About History

8. **Expository Writing** Locate biographical information on Leonid Brezhnev, Mikhail Gorbachev, Boris Yeltsin, and Vladimir Putin. In an essay, analyze each leader's strengths and weaknesses.

History ONLINE
For help with the concepts in this section of *Glencoe World History*, go to glencoe.com and click Study Central™.

935

W Writing Support

Expository Writing Ask students to write a paragraph that explains how Russia's natural resources and economic strengths have been translated into political power. **OL**

✓Reading Check

Answer: terrorism; ongoing turmoil in Chechnya; social problems such as rising alcoholism, crime, and the decline of the traditional family system

Assess

History ONLINE

Study Central provides summaries, interactive games, and online graphic organizers to help students review content.

Close

Drawing Conclusions **Ask:** What strengths can Russia build on for the future? *(oil reserves could allow a strong economic base for a growing economy, political changes may allow greater freedoms if crackdowns do not take Russia back to repressive practices)* **OL**

Answers

1. Definitions for the vocabulary words are found in the section and the Glossary.
2. inefficient, corrupt central government; low productivity of collective farms
3. As Gorbachev lightened the grip of the Communist party, nationalism spread throughout the republics. They moved toward independence.
4. launched reforms that boosted growth and budget revenues, free sale and purchase of land and tax cuts, application to the World Trade Organization, and partnership with European Union
5. Answers may include: large territory to govern, tension among the many ethnic and religious groups, nationalism, complacency of central government
6. because many political reforms had not yet been made
7. No, the Chechen fighters do not have tanks.
8. Students' essays should accurately reflect what they learned in this section.

R Reading Strategy

Visualizing Ask students to reread the paragraphs, focusing on the images created by phrases such as "iron grip" and "flames of revolution." **Ask:** Why was Ceauşescu executed? *(He had been at the head of an extremely brutal government.)* **BL**

W Writing Support

Descriptive Writing Ask students to write a description of the historical events surrounding reunification using details from their text and other sources. **OL**

✓Reading Check

Answer: the end of the Cold War

CRITICAL THINKING SKILLS

Answers:

1. to keep East Germans from defecting to the West
2. The transformation of the East German economy is taking longer and will cost more than first anticipated. However, all Germans now enjoy political freedoms as one nation.

Romania

Communist leader Nicolae Ceauşescu (nee•kaw•LY chow•SHEHS•koo) ruled Romania with an iron grip, using secret police to crush all dissent. Nonetheless, opposition grew. His economic policies led to a sharp drop in living standards. Food shortages caused rationing. His bulldozing of entire villages to further urbanization plans angered the Romanian people. **R**

One incident ignited the flames of revolution. In December 1989, the secret police murdered thousands of people who were peacefully demonstrating. Finally, the army refused to support any more repression. Ceauşescu and his wife were captured and executed. A new government was quickly formed.

Former Communists dominated the government until 1996. The current president, Traian Basescu, leads a country that is just beginning to show economic growth and the rise of a middle class.

History ONLINE
Student Web Activity—
Visit glencoe.com and complete the activity about the Berlin Wall.

German Reunification

Erich Honecker, head of the Communist Party in East Germany, ruled harshly. While many East Germans fled their country, others led mass demonstrations against the regime in 1989.

Once the Communist government opened its entire border with the West, thousands of East Germans swarmed across the border to reunite with their families and friends. People on both sides of the wall began tearing it down. Helpless, the government ordered the rest of the wall torn down. The Berlin Wall, long a **symbol** of the Cold War, was no more.

W The reunification of Germany took place on October 3, 1990. What had seemed almost impossible became a reality—the countries of West and East Germany had reunited to form one Germany.

✓Reading Check **Explaining** What did the fall of the Berlin Wall represent?

INFOGRAPHICS

The Fall of the Berlin Wall

Before the Berlin Wall was built, thousands of East Berliners fled to the West for the opportunities it had to offer. The East German government built the Berlin Wall in 1961 to stem this economic loss. The wall separated family members and friends for decades, and it became a symbol of Communist tyranny. On November 9, 1989, in response to mass protests, East Germany's Communist rulers opened the wall's gates. Soon after crowds began to climb the wall and to tear it down.

When Germany was reunified in 1990, Chancellor Helmut Kohl promised a transformation of the East that would take place within four years. However, it became apparent that rebuilding the East German economy could take many decades and have a high cost. Despite these challenges, all Germans now enjoy the same political freedoms as one nation.

Germans climbing over the Berlin Wall in November 1989

CRITICAL THINKING SKILLS

1. **Explaining** Why did East Germany build the Berlin Wall?
2. **Interpreting** Has German reunification been a success? Explain.

Differentiated Instruction

Primary Source Reading, URB p. 77

Analyzing Information

Objective: Analyze responses to the fall of the Berlin Wall.

Focus: Call on students to read aloud paragraphs from the selection.

Teach: Discuss the emotions connected with the event.

Assess: Discuss the answers to the questions.

Close: Have students summarize people's reactions to the event.

Differentiated Instruction Strategies

BL Ask students to re-read the fourth paragraph and describe the two contrasting images presented.

AL Ask students to re-read the eighth paragraph and describe the importance of the phrase "We are staying here!"

ELL Ask students to explain the significance of the sign "1789–1989."

The Disintegration of Yugoslavia

MAIN IDEA Ethnic tensions led to armed conflict in Yugoslavia.

HISTORY & YOU Can you recall examples in your textbook of ethnic conflict? Read about ethnic cleansing in the Bosnian war.

Yugoslavia had a Communist government but was never a Soviet satellite state. By 1990, however, the Communist Party collapsed. The Yugoslav political scene was complex. **Slobodan Miloševic** (slaw•BAW•dahn muh•LOH•suh•VIHCH), leader of Serbia, rejected efforts toward independence. In Miloševic's view, the republics' borders first needed to be redrawn to form a new Greater Serbian state. When negotiations failed, Slovenia and Croatia declared their independence in June 1991. In September 1991, the Yugoslav army assaulted Croatia. Increasingly, Serbia, aided by Croatian Serbs, dominated the Yugoslav army. Serbian forces captured one-third of Croatia's territory before a cease-fire ended the conflict.

Wars in Bosnia and Kosovo

The Serbs next attacked **Bosnia-Herzegovina** and acquired 70 percent of Bosnian territory. Many Bosnians were Muslims. The Serbs followed a policy called **ethnic cleansing** toward Bosnians—killing or forcibly removing them from their lands. Ethnic cleansing revived memories of Nazi atrocities in World War II. **C**

With support from NATO air attacks, Bosnian and Croatian forces regained considerable territory lost to Serbian forces. This forced the Serbs to sign a formal peace treaty that split Bosnia into a Serb republic and a Muslim-Croat federation. In 2006, about 30,000 NATO troops were still in Bosnia trying to keep the peace.

A new war erupted in 1998 over **Kosovo,** an **autonomous** or self-governing province within Yugoslavia. After Slobodan Miloševic stripped Kosovo of its autonomy in 1989, groups of ethnic Albanians founded the Kosovo Liberation Army (KLA) and began a campaign against Serbian rule. To crush the KLA, Serb forces massacred ethnic Albanians. The United States and NATO allies worked on a settlement that would end the killing. The Albanians in Kosovo regained their autonomy in 1999. Miloševic's rule ended in 2000. While on trial for his role in the massacre of Kosovo civilians, Miloševic died in 2006.

Yugoslavia ceased to exist in 2004 when the government officially renamed the country Serbia and Montenegro. The people of Montenegro voted for independence in 2006. Thus, all six republics that formed Yugoslavia in 1918 were once again independent nations.

✓Reading Check **Identifying** What events resulted from the disintegration of Yugoslavia?

Vocabulary

1. **Explain** the significance of: Lech Walesa, demonstrations, Václav Havel, symbol, Slobodan Miloševic, Bosnia-Herzegovina, ethnic cleansing, Kosovo, autonomous.

Main Ideas

2. **List** four Eastern European states discussed in this section that were Soviet satellite states. What events occurred in each state after the withdrawal of Soviet influence?
3. **Explain** why the Communist government ordered the Berlin Wall to be torn down.
4. **Summarize** the Yugoslav republics that wanted independence after 1990, the inhabitants of these republics (if listed), and the reasons the republics fought each other. Use a chart like the one below.

Republics	Inhabitants	Causes of Fighting

Critical Thinking

5. **The BIG Idea** **Analyzing** Why was the collapse of communism in the Soviet Union a turning point in history?
6. **Comparing** How is the ethnic cleansing of Bosnians similar to the Holocaust?
7. **Analyzing Visuals** Examine the photograph on page 938. Why is it significant that people are climbing over the wall?

Writing About History

8. **Informative Writing** Research and write an essay about the Polish Solidarity movement. Why was it successful? Be sure to discuss Lech Walesa's supporters, adversaries, and the status of the movement today.

History ONLINE
For help with the concepts in this section of *Glencoe World History*, go to glencoe.com and click Study Central™.

939

C Critical Thinking

Identifying Central Issues

Ask: What led to the re-formation of six republics from the former Yugoslavia? *(all had been republics in 1918, ethnic divisions and nationalism supported independent states)* **OL**

Answer: In trying to form a Serbian state, Serbia attacked Croatia, Bosnia, and Kosovo.

Assess

History ONLINE

Study Central provides summaries, interactive games, and online graphic organizers to help students review content.

Close

Making Generalizations

Ask: How did the breakup of the Soviet Union affect the countries of Eastern Europe? *(Communist governments were replaced. Many new republics were formed along ethnic lines. Some fought civil wars, while others remained peaceful.)* **OL**

Answers

1. Definitions for the vocabulary words are found in the section and the Glossary.
2. Poland, Czechoslovakia, Romania, East Germany; demonstrations or revolutions for independence
3. Once the border opened to the West, both sides—East and West Germany—began tearing down the wall. The government then ordered the entire wall to be torn down.
4. **Slovenia:** Serb minority; **Croatia:** Serb minority; Serbia wanted to form Greater Serbian state for Serbs; **Bosnia-Herzegovina:** Bosnians (many of them Muslim), Croats, Serbs; ethnic differences, Serbs wanted to be rid of Croats and Muslims; **Kosovo:** Serbs, Albanians; Serbs massacred Albanians
5. The Soviet Union had ruled for years under Communist regime and was a partner in Cold War; when it broke up, Eastern European states declared independence.
6. Both involved mass killing or mass removal of a people from their lands or property.
7. For 28 years, the Berlin Wall divided East Berlin from West Berlin. In 1989, Germans like those shown in the photograph were allowed to cross the border.
8. Essays should reflect accurate information.

Focus

Bellringer
Daily Focus Transparency 28.3

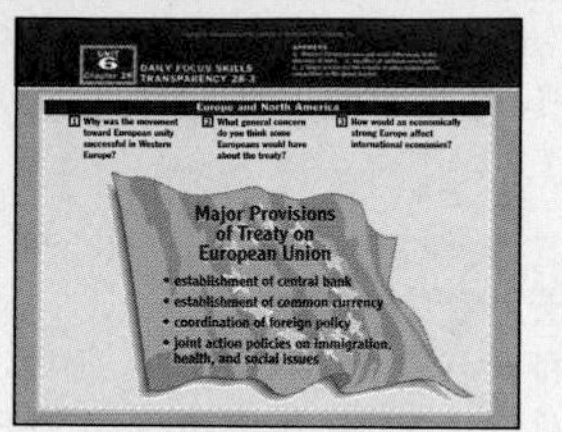

GUIDE TO READING

Answers to Graphic:
Thatcherism: Restricted union power, controlled inflation, tried to replace local property taxes with flat tax; **Reagan:** Large military buildup, tripled government budget deficits, cut jobs programs; **Both:** Limited social welfare

Section Spotlight Video

To generate student interest and provide a springboard for class discussion, access the Chapter 28, Section 3 video at glencoe.com or on the video DVD.

Resource Manager

SECTION 3

Europe and North America

GUIDE TO READING

The BIG Idea
Ideas, Beliefs, and Values Postwar Western societies rebuilt their communities, but shifting social structures led to upheaval and change.

Content Vocabulary
- Thatcherism *(p. 943)*
- budget deficits *(p. 944)*

Academic Vocabulary
- currency *(p. 940)*
- shift *(p. 940)*

People, Places, and Events
- France *(p. 940)*
- West Germany *(p. 941)*
- Northern Ireland *(p. 943)*
- Margaret Thatcher *(p. 943)*
- Richard Nixon *(p. 943)*
- Watergate *(p. 943)*
- Gerald Ford *(p. 943)*
- Jimmy Carter *(p. 943)*
- Ronald Reagan *(p. 943)*
- Reagan Revolution *(p. 944)*
- George Bush *(p. 944)*
- Bill Clinton *(p. 944)*
- George W. Bush *(p. 944)*
- Pierre Trudeau *(p. 945)*

Reading Strategy
Comparing and Contrasting As you read, use a Venn diagram like the one below to compare and contrast economic policies of Thatcherism and those of the Reagan Revolution.

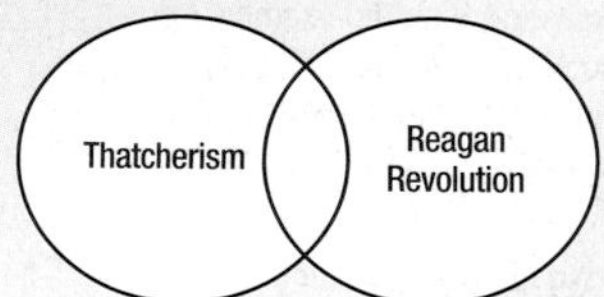

During the later decades of the twentieth century, the leaders of Western European countries faced many economic challenges. Germany, in particular, wrestled with social and economic problems caused by its unification. Meanwhile, in the United States, politics took a shift to the right; and Canada was divided on the Quebec secession debate.

Winds of Change in Western Europe

MAIN IDEA France, Great Britain, and Germany have all experienced economic upheavals and changes.

HISTORY & YOU Do you believe there should be a global currency? Read to learn how Europe adopted a single currency.

Between the early 1950s and late 1970s, Western Europe experienced virtually full employment. An economic downturn, however, occurred in the mid-1970s and early 1980s. Both inflation and unemployment rose dramatically, partly because of increases in oil prices after the Arab-Israeli conflict in 1973 (see Chapter 30). Western European economies recovered in the course of the 1980s, but problems remained.

The Western European nations moved toward a greater union of their economies after 1970. The European Economic Community (EEC) expanded in 1973 to include Great Britain, Ireland, and Denmark. By 1986, Spain, Portugal, and Greece had become members. Austria, Finland, and Sweden joined in 1995.

The EEC or European Community (EC) was chiefly an economic union. By 1992, it comprised 344 million people and was the world's largest single trading bloc. The Treaty on European Union, which went into effect on January 1, 1994, turned the EC into the European Union (EU). One of the EU's first goals was to establish a common **currency,** the euro. Twelve of the 15 EU nations abandoned their currency in favor of the euro on January 1, 2002.

The new goal of the EU was to add the states of Eastern and southeastern Europe to the union. In May 2004, the EU added ten new members, mostly from Eastern Europe.

Uncertainties in France

In **France,** a deteriorating economic situation in the 1970s caused a political **shift** to the left. By 1981, the Socialists gained power in the National Assembly. Socialist François Mitterrand was elected president. He initiated a number of measures to aid workers: an increased minimum wage, a 39-hour workweek, and higher taxes

R Reading Strategies	C Critical Thinking	D Differentiated Instruction	W Writing Support	S Skill Practice
Teacher Edition • Summarizing, p. 942 • Det. Importance, p. 943 • Act. Prior Know., p. 944 **Additional Resources** • Guid. Read. Act., URB p. 86 • Read. Ess. & Note-Taking Guide, p. 313	**Teacher Edition** • Compare/Contrast, p. 942 • Making Inferences, pp. 943, 945 **Additional Resources** • Crit. Think. Act, URB p. 64 • Hist. Sim. Act., URB p. 71 • Section Quiz, p. 351	**Teacher Edition** • Logical/Math., p. 941 **Additional Resources** • Reteach. Act., URB p. 81	**Teacher Edition** • Personal Writing, p. 944 **Additional Resources** • Hist. Analysis Skills Act., URB p. 54	**Teacher Edition** • Using Geo. Skills, p. 941 **Additional Resources** • Time Line Act., URB p. 73

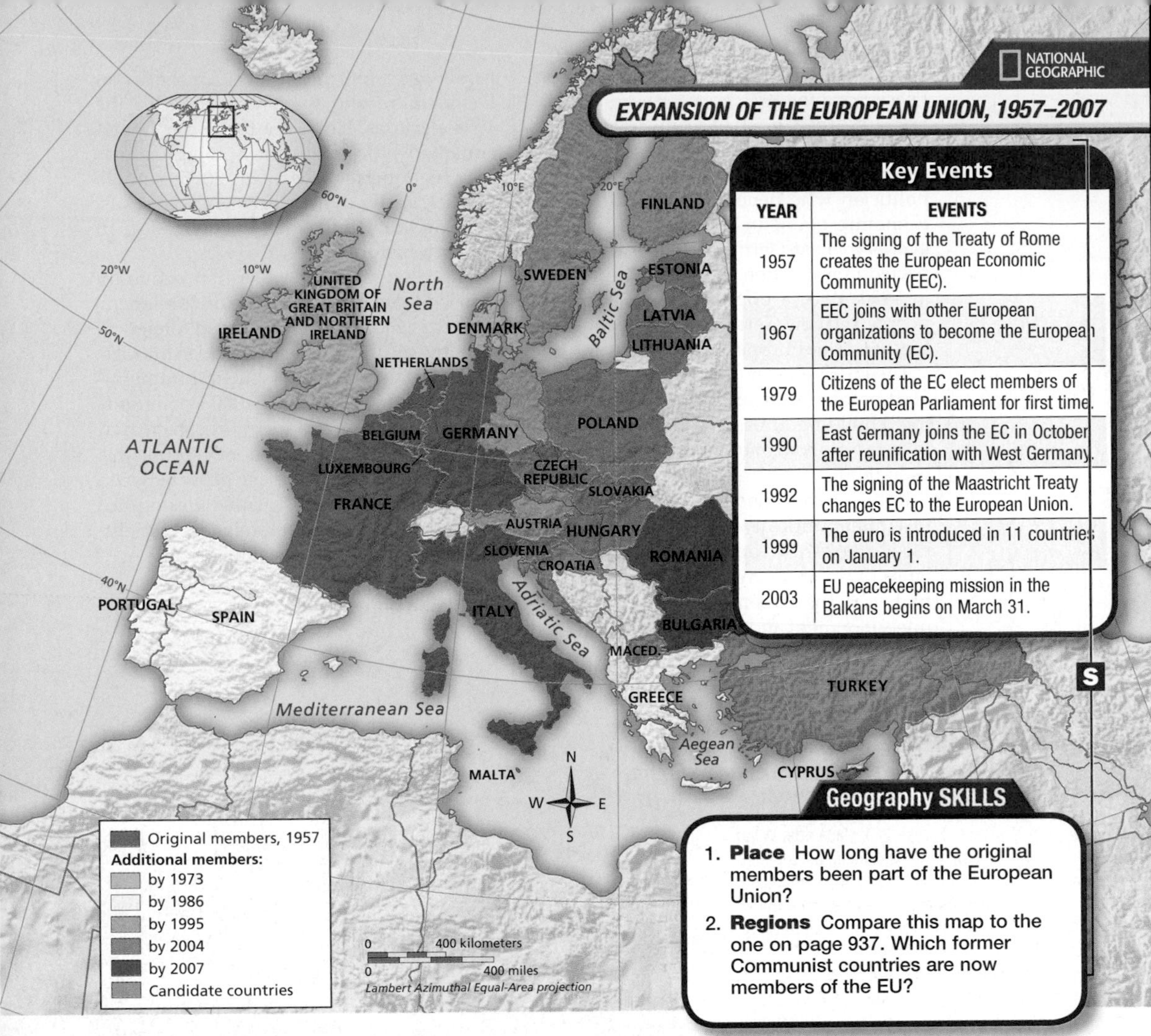

Key Events

YEAR	EVENTS
1957	The signing of the Treaty of Rome creates the European Economic Community (EEC).
1967	EEC joins with other European organizations to become the European Community (EC).
1979	Citizens of the EC elect members of the European Parliament for first time.
1990	East Germany joins the EC in October after reunification with West Germany.
1992	The signing of the Maastricht Treaty changes EC to the European Union.
1999	The euro is introduced in 11 countries on January 1.
2003	EU peacekeeping mission in the Balkans begins on March 31.

Geography SKILLS

1. **Place** How long have the original members been part of the European Union?
2. **Regions** Compare this map to the one on page 937. Which former Communist countries are now members of the EU?

for the rich. The Socialist government also nationalized, or took over, major banks, the steel industry, the space and electronics industries, and insurance firms.

Socialist policies, however, largely failed to work, and France's economic decline continued. In 1993 French unemployment stood at 10.6 percent. In the elections in March of that year, the Socialists won only 28 percent of the vote. A coalition of conservative parties gained 80 percent of the seats in the National Assembly. The move to the right in France was strengthened when the conservative mayor of Paris, Jacques Chirac, was elected president in May 1995 and reelected in 2002.

Reunification Woes

In 1969 the Social Democrats, a moderate Socialist party, replaced the Christian Democrats as the leading political party in **West Germany.** The first Social Democratic chancellor elected in West Germany was Willy Brandt. In December 1972 Brandt signed a treaty that led to greater contact between East Germany and West Germany. Economic, cultural, and personal ties between the countries were stronger as a result.

Teach

S Skill Practice

Using Geography Skills

Ask: By what year had Spain, Portugal, and Greece joined the European Union? *(1986)* BL

D Differentiated Instruction

Logical/Mathematical Ask students to display the 1993 election results in a circle graph or bar graph. Then ask them to research and graph the results of earlier and later elections. AL

Geography SKILLS

Answers:

1. since 1957 (subtract 1957 from current year)
2. Estonia, Latvia, Lithuania, Poland, Czech Republic, Slovakia, Hungary, Romania, Bulgaria, Slovenia

Hands-On Chapter Project Step 3

Traveling through the Modern Western World

Step 3: Mapping and Reporting on a Destination in Europe or North America Students will continue their journeys by mapping and describing a destination in Europe or North America.

Directions: Have student pairs select a city or region in Europe or North America to visit. Students will connect their previous destinations with their new destination on the map. Then they will review the content and do additional research to prepare a short written or oral report that describes what they expect to see, as well as how things have changed there in the last 30 years. Remind them to highlight changes by focusing on specific subjects and telling how they are different today compared to the recent past. OL

(Chapter Project is continued in Section 4.)

R Reading Strategy

Summarizing Ask: How would you summarize the success of different political parties in addressing the economic problems of eastern Germany? *(Both the Social Democrats and Christian Democrats struggled to rebuild the economy.)* **OL**

C Critical Thinking

Comparing and Contrasting Ask: How were conditions in Germany during the rise of the Nazi Party similar to those in the 1990s? *(Germany suffered high unemployment and economic and social troubles during both periods.)* **AL**

For additional practice on this skill, see the **Skills Handbook**.

CRITICAL THINKING SKILLS

Answers:

1. They helped fill the labor shortage in France and other nations after World War II.
2. Some immigrants resist the attempts of countries such as France to have them assimilate.

For his efforts, Brandt received the Nobel Peace Prize for 1971.

In 1982 the Christian Democratic Union of Helmut Kohl formed a new, more conservative government. Kohl was a smart politician who benefited greatly from an economic boom in the mid-1980s. Then events in East Germany led to the unexpected reunification of the two Germanies in 1990. With a population of 79 million people, the new Germany became the leading power in Europe.

The joy over reunification soon faded as new problems arose. It became clear that the rebuilding of eastern Germany would take far more money than had originally been thought.

R Kohl's government was soon forced to face the politically undesirable task of raising taxes. In addition, the virtual collapse of the economy in eastern Germany had led to extremely high levels of unemployment and severe discontent. One result was a return to power for the Social Democrats, who were victorious in the 1998 elections. However, the Social Democrats had little success in solving Germany's economic woes. In 2005 Angela Merkel, leader of the Christian Democrats, became the first female chancellor in German history.

The collapse of the German economy also led to increasing attacks on foreigners. For years, illegal immigrants and foreigners seeking refuge had found haven in Germany because of its very liberal immigration laws. In 1992 over 440,000 immigrants came to Germany seeking refuge. Increased unemployment and economic problems, however, caused tensions to grow between some Germans and various immigrant C groups. Attacks against foreigners by right-wing extremists—especially young neo-Nazis who believed in Hitler's idea of creating a pure Aryan race—became a part of German life.

INFOGRAPHICS

North African Immigration to France

Major migration to Europe took place after World War II. In the 1950s and 1960s, immigrant workers came to Western European nations to help fill the labor shortage. Most of these workers came from Africa and Asia—usually from former European colonies.

For example, many of the immigrant workers that came to France were from former French colonies that were Muslim, such as Algeria. It was assumed that most migrants would return home after a time; however, many stayed.

Immigration in France became a political issue in the 1970s when, due to recession, France tightened its immigration policy. By this time, Muslims had become more visible in French society. Some saw their lack of willingness to assimilate as a threat to the French national identity.

In an effort to separate church and state, a 2004 French law banned the wearing of headscarves by Muslims in French state schools. Muslim protesters said this denied them their freedom of religion. Similar cultural clashes have taken place across Europe in recent years.

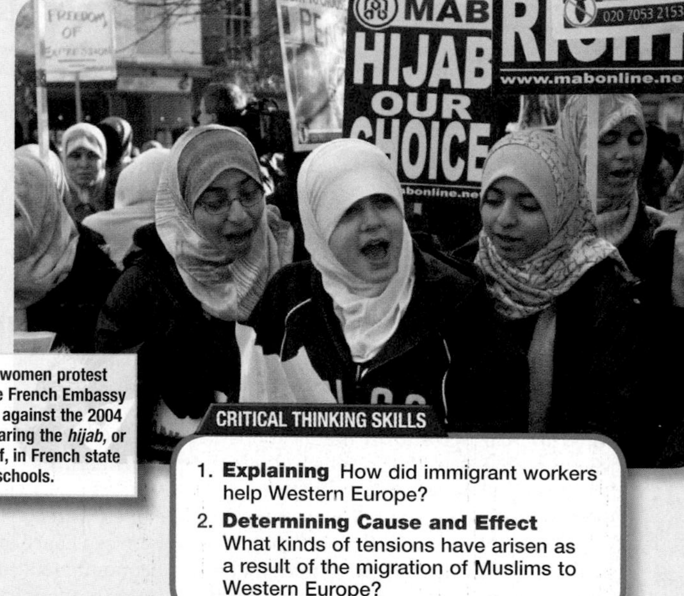

Muslim women protest outside the French Embassy in London against the 2004 ban on wearing the *hijab*, or head scarf, in French state schools.

CRITICAL THINKING SKILLS

1. **Explaining** How did immigrant workers help Western Europe?
2. **Determining Cause and Effect** What kinds of tensions have arisen as a result of the migration of Muslims to Western Europe?

Additional Support

Activity: Technology Connection

Researching Immigration Issues in France and Germany Ask: What are some possible economic and social effects of immigration? Have students search the Internet or online databases for three recent articles related to a social or economic immigration issue in France or Germany. Students may focus their searches on the role of a specific immigrant group in society, the effects of immigration on a specific region, or debates surrounding immigration policies. When students have completed their research, have them summarize their findings in a brief report, including their own opinions on the issue. Then have students share their reports with the class. **OL**

Great Britain and Thatcherism

Between 1964 and 1979, Great Britain's Conservative Party and Labour Party alternated being in power. One problem both parties had to face was the intense fighting between Catholics and Protestants in **Northern Ireland.** An ailing economy and frequent labor strikes were two other issues that the government struggled to solve.

In 1979 the Conservatives came to power under **Margaret Thatcher,** Britain's first female prime minister. Thatcher pledged to limit social welfare, to restrict union power, and to end inflation. Her main focus was privatization. As Thatcher said, "The State's job is to provide a proper framework of laws within which private enterprise can flourish, not to extend its powers by owning business." Although she did not eliminate the basic parts of the social welfare system, Thatcher did break the power of the labor unions and control inflation.

Thatcherism, as her economic policy was termed, improved the British economic situation, but at a price. Business investment and the number of small businesses increased substantially. The south of England, for example, prospered. Old industrial areas elsewhere, however, were beset by high unemployment, poverty, and even violence.

Thatcher dominated British politics in the 1980s. Only in 1990 did the Labour Party's fortunes seem to revive. At that time, Thatcher's government tried to replace local property taxes with a flat-rate tax payable by every adult. In 1990 antitax riots broke out. Thatcher's popularity fell, and she resigned as prime minister.

The Conservative Party, now led by John Major, failed to capture the imagination of most Britons. In new elections in 1997, the Labour Party won a landslide victory. Tony Blair, a moderate, became prime minister and instilled a new vigor on the political scene. By 2006, however, his ongoing support of the U.S. war in Iraq, when most Britons opposed it, caused his popularity to plummet.

✓Reading Check **Identifying** What were the policies of Thatcherism?

The U.S. and Canada

MAIN IDEA The United States has moved toward the political right, and Quebec's status divides Canada.

HISTORY & YOU What if your state wanted to become an independent nation? Read to learn about Quebec's desire to secede from Canada.

U.S. politics shifted to the right in the mid-1970s as economic issues became the focus. Canadians were concerned about economic issues and the status of Quebec.

Nixon, Ford, and Carter

In his campaign for the presidency, **Richard Nixon** believed that "law and order" issues and a slowdown in racial desegregation would appeal to Southern whites. The South, once a stronghold for the Democrats, began to form a new allegiance to the Republican Party.

As president, Nixon used illegal methods to gain political information about his opponents. This led to the **Watergate** scandal. A group of men working for Nixon's reelection campaign broke into the Democratic National Headquarters, located in the Watergate Hotel in Washington, D.C. They were caught there trying to install electronic listening devices.

Nixon lied to the American public about his involvement in the affair. Secret tapes of his conversations in the White House, however, revealed the truth. On August 9, 1974, Nixon resigned rather than face possible impeachment.

Vice President **Gerald Ford** became president when Nixon resigned, only to lose in the 1976 election to the former governor of Georgia, **Jimmy Carter.** By 1980, the Carter administration was faced with two devastating problems. First, high inflation rates and a decline in average earnings were causing a drop in American living standards.

A crisis abroad erupted when the Iranian government of the Ayatollah Ruhollah Khomeini (koh•MAY•nee) (see Chapter 30) held 52 Americans hostage. Carter's inability to gain the release of the American hostages contributed to his loss to **Ronald Reagan** in the 1980 election.

C Critical Thinking

Making Inferences Ask: According to Margaret Thatcher and the Conservative Party, how were the labor unions affecting the British economy? *(Answers may include that they were harming the economy by having frequent labor strikes. These strikes made it harder to do business.)* **OL**

R Reading Strategy

Determining Importance Note that Nixon is the only president ever to resign. Discuss the fact that Nixon lied to the American people about his involvement in the Watergate break-in and tried to cover up what people in his party had done. **Ask:** Why did Nixon resign? *(Secret tapes revealed that he lied about his involvement in Watergate, so he resigned to avoid being impeached.)* **ELL**

✓Reading Check

Answer: limiting social welfare; restricting union power; ending inflation; supporting private enterprise

Differentiated Instruction

Leveled Activities

BL Reteaching Activity, URB p. 81

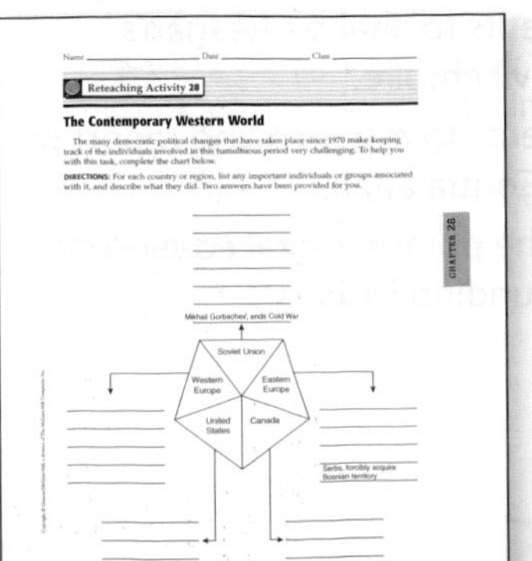

OL Guided Reading Activity, URB p. 86

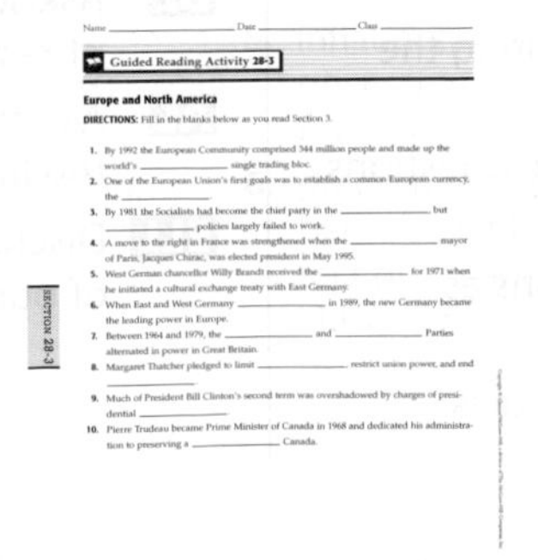

AL Historical Analysis Skills Activity, URB p. 54

ELL Time Line Activity, URB p. 73

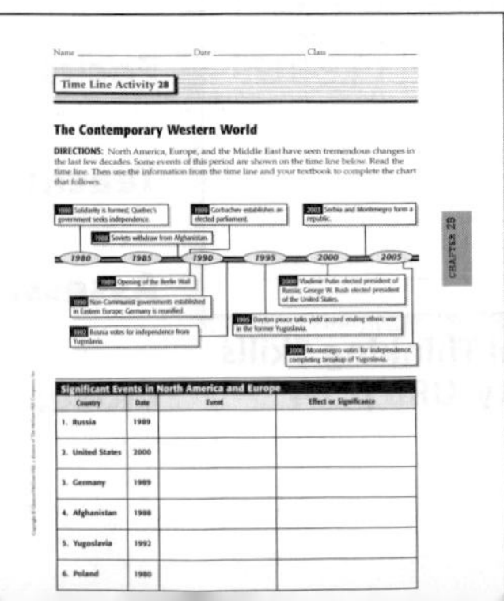

Western Society and Culture

Focus

Bellringer
Daily Focus Transparency 28.4

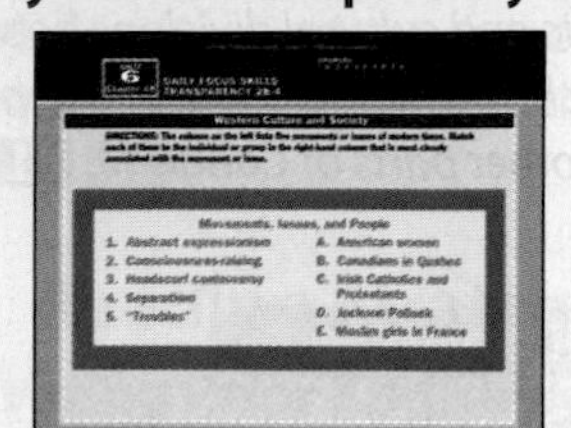

GUIDE TO READING

Answers to Graphic:
Issue: Job inequality; **Outcome:** Equal Pay Act.
Issue: Abortion; **Outcome:** *Roe* v. *Wade.*
Issue: Lack of women in government; **Outcome:** Gender parity policies in Europe

Section Spotlight Video

To generate student interest and provide a springboard for class discussion, access the Chapter 28, Section 4 video at glencoe.com or on the video DVD.

Resource Manager

GUIDE TO READING

The BIG Idea
New Technologies Trends in contemporary Western society include rapid changes in science and technology, changes in family structures and population trends, increased religious diversity, and a shared popular culture among nations.

Content Vocabulary
- gender stereotyping *(p. 948)*
- gender parity *(p. 948)*
- postmodernism *(p. 949)*
- popular culture *(p. 949)*
- cultural imperialism *(p. 949)*

Academic Vocabulary
- chemical *(p. 946)*
- globalization *(p. 949)*

People, Places, and Events
- *Sputnik I (p. 946)*
- Equal Pay Act *(p. 948)*
- *Roe* v. *Wade (p. 948)*
- Munich *(p. 949)*
- Basque region *(p. 951)*
- Bloody Sunday *(p. 951)*

Reading Strategy
Categorizing Information As you read, complete a chart like the one below to list the issues and outcomes for the women's movement since 1970.

Issues	Outcomes

Among the effects of globalization is the spread of culture, and Western culture has expanded to and influenced most parts of the world. Western culture itself has undergone many changes these past few decades, most notably with changes in the family, in women's lives, and in religious trends. Not all people welcome Western culture; some see it as a challenge to their own culture and national identity.

The Quickening Pace of Change

MAIN IDEA The Western world has seen many technological and social changes, as well as changes in the family and in women's lives.

HISTORY & YOU How often do you use your cell phone? Read to learn how new technologies are transforming Western society.

Western societies have tended to pride themselves on expanding democracy and material progress. Since 1970, the pace of material change has quickened and promoted a global economy. An important question today is how this global economy will affect each country.

Science and Technology

Science and technology are important forces for change in today's world. During World War II, governments recruited scientists to develop new weapons, the most famous being the atomic bomb. By funding projects, governments created a new model for scientific research. Complex projects required not just teams of scientists. They also needed huge laboratories and sophisticated equipment that only governments or large corporations could fund.

A stunning example of such projects is the space race. In 1961 four years after the Soviet Union launched ***Sputnik I,*** President Kennedy predicted that Americans would land on the moon within a decade. The American moon landing happened in 1969.

Postwar science and technology led to rapid change. Many believed that scientific knowledge gave society the ability and the right to manipulate the environment for everyone's benefit. Critics in the 1960s and 1970s, however, argued that some technology had far-reaching effects that damaged the environment. The use of **chemical** fertilizers, for example, produced higher-yield crops but also destroyed the ecological balance of streams, rivers, and woodlands. In the early 2000s, debates over organic farming and genetically enhanced foods intensified. People continue to disagree over the role of science in food production.

R Reading Strategies	C Critical Thinking	D Differentiated Instruction	W Writing Support	S Skill Practice
Teacher Edition • Summarizing, p. 947 • Inferring, p. 948 • Academic Vocab., p. 949 **Additional Resources** • Guid. Read. Act., URB p. 87 • Read. Ess. & Note-Taking Guide, p. 316	**Teacher Edition** • Making Generalizations, p. 949 • Ident. Cent. Issues, p. 950 • Compare/Contrast, p. 951 **Additional Resources** • People in World Hist., URB p. 76 • World Art & Music Act., URB p. 79 • Section Quiz, p. 352 • Chapter Test, p. 353	**Teacher Edition** • ELL, p. 947 • Visual/Spatial, p. 949 **Additional Resources** • Diff. Instr. Act., URB p. 55 • English Learner Act., URB p. 57 • Hist. Sig. Act., URB p. 68 • Coop. Learn. Act., URB p. 69	**Teacher Edition** • Persuasive Writing, p. 948 **Additional Resources** • Linking Past/Present Act., URB p. 74	**Teacher Edition** • Using Geo. Skills, p. 950 **Additional Resources** • Academic Vocab. Act., URB p. 61 • Hist. & Geo. Act., URB p. 65

INFOGRAPHICS

Technology and the Environment

Some types of power plants that generate electricity are a major source of greenhouse gases.

Science and technology have changed the way we live. Yet one of the unfortunate side effects of modern technology has been damage to the environment.

Global warming, for example, has been linked to emissions of carbon dioxide and other greenhouse gases from burning fossil fuels—coal, gas, and oil. These emissions have been blamed for rapid melting of the polar ice caps. This could cause sea levels to rise, which could have a devastating effect on populated coastal areas throughout the world.

In an attempt to slow global warming, some 141 countries have ratified the Kyoto Protocol, which calls on countries to cut air pollution. The United States has refused to sign, however, saying that the required changes would be too costly.

Iceland, on the other hand, had already begun to reduce its dependence on fossil fuels by introducing geothermal and hydroelectric power plants. Iceland has also announced that it will switch to hydrogen-powered vehicles.

Another clean source of energy is wind. Scientists estimate that one-third of the world's electricity could be supplied by wind generators by 2050. That would be enough to prevent 113 billion metric tons of carbon dioxide from entering the atmosphere each year. Wind farms like the one shown above have sprouted around the world—including in the United States. D

Electricity produced from the wind produces no greenhouse gas emissions.

CRITICAL THINKING SKILLS

1. **Identifying** What was the purpose of the Kyoto Protocol?
2. **Analyzing** Do you think that the Kyoto Protocol will accomplish its goal without the participation of the United States?

Changes in the Family

The Western world is also experiencing changing trends in marriage and divorce. Over the past 40 years, the number of people in Europe getting married has decreased. People also tend to get married at a slightly older age.

R Between 1980 and 1995, for example, the average age of French women marrying for the first time went up from 23 to 27 years. The divorce rate, too, has gone up. Between 1970 and 1995, Belgium, France, the Netherlands, and the United Kingdom all saw enormous increases in divorce rates. These social trends have meant a lower birthrate and thus an older population overall.

Changes in Women's Lives

Women's changing roles in the workforce have also affected family size and thus population growth. More women work not only because they choose to, but to help support their families.

Since the 1970s, the number of women active in the workforce has continued to rise.

Teach

D Differentiated Instruction

English Language Learners Ask students to consider the term *wind farm*. **Ask:** How is a site such as the one pictured here like a farm? How is it different? *(Energy is "harvested" like other crops, and production depends on the weather; nothing is planted in the ground.)* ELL

R Reading Strategy

Summarizing Ask: How would you summarize the changes in marriage in the Western world in recent years? *(Fewer people are getting married; they marry later, and more people get divorced.)* BL

CRITICAL THINKING SKILLS

Answers:

1. to slow global warming by cutting down on air pollution
2. While it might not be as successful without the United States, the participation of some 141 nations should help slow global warming.

Hands-On Chapter Project Step 4

Traveling through the Modern Western World

Step 4: Mapping and Reporting on a Destination That Displays Cultural Change Students will continue their journeys by mapping and describing a destination that displays an aspect of cultural change in Western society.

Directions: Have pairs continue their journeys by selecting a place that displays one or more aspects of cultural change in a Western society. They might even choose to describe their return home. Students should connect their previous destination with their final destination on the map. Then they should review the content and do research to prepare a short written or oral report that describes what they expect to see, as well as how things have changed there in the last 30 years. Have them highlight changes by focusing on everyday life in their chosen destination and telling how it is different today compared to the recent past. OL

(Chapter Project is completed on the Visual Summary page.)

R Reading Strategy

Inferring Ask: What issues caused a "backlash" against the women's movement? *(women in nontraditional roles, an attempt to focus on careers rather than families)* **AL**

W Writing Support

Persuasive Writing Ask students to consider the policy of "gender parity." Then have them write a persuasive letter that either supports the policy or questions its basis and effectiveness. **OL**

✓Reading Check

Answer: Answers may include that it restricts what a person can do because of his or her gender.

CRITICAL THINKING SKILLS

Answers:

1. Women make up a larger percentage of the workforce in 2001 than they did in 1975.
2. Answers may include that women in the workforce probably have increased power and influence.

At the same time, more women went to college, and more of them pursued careers in law, medicine, and government.

The Women's Movement

In the 1960s and 1970s, the women's movement emerged in the United States. It quickly spread to Western Europe and in recent decades to other parts of the world. Supporters of the movement wanted to change the basic conditions of women's lives. They forced politicians to address "**gender stereotyping,**" restricting what a person could do just because of the person's gender. The United States passed the **Equal Pay Act** in 1963. It required women to be paid the same as men for performing the same work.

A controversial issue was abortion. In 1973 the U.S. Supreme Court legalized abortion in ***Roe* v. *Wade*.** While national health insurance covers abortion in most of Europe, the procedure is still hotly debated in the United States.

R In the 1990s, there was a backlash against the women's movement. Some women urged a return to traditional roles. Others found ways to balance career and family. However, women in Western societies still earn much less on average than men. Many women face the burden of working outside the home while continuing to do most of the child rearing and domestic work.

W To encourage women's roles in government, Norway and Denmark adopted **gender parity** policies in the 1970s. Women must make up either a certain number of the candidates in an election or a certain number of those elected. Other European nations followed suit.

✓Reading Check **Identifying** How does gender stereotyping affect women's and men's roles?

INFOGRAPHICS

Women in the Workforce

Since the 1970s, Western countries have experienced an increased percentage of women in the workforce, due to the efforts of the international women's movement. Laws passed in the United States and Europe made it illegal to discriminate on the basis of gender. New laws also made it illegal to pay a woman less than a man for the same work.

Although women still make less money than men in Western countries, that pay gap is narrowing. In the United States, women earned 62 percent of what men earned in 1979, but that rose to 80 percent by 2004. In the United Kingdom, women earned 87.4 percent of what men earned in 2006. This represented the smallest pay gap ever recorded in the U.K.

Women demonstrating in London, 1971

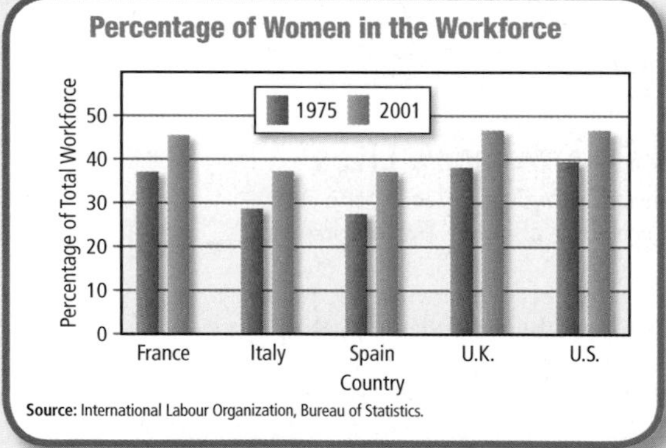

Source: International Labour Organization, Bureau of Statistics.

CRITICAL THINKING SKILLS

1. **Identifying** What has been the general trend in employment of women in Western countries since the 1970s?
2. **Evaluating** How do you think the increase of women in the workforce has advanced the status of women in general?

Differentiated Instruction

Historical Significance Activity 28

The Fight for Equal Rights

Historical Significance Activity, URB p. 68

Identifying Central Issues

Objective: Identify central issues concerning women's fight for equal rights.

Focus: Review the history of the women's movement in the United States.

Teach: Discuss students' answers to the questions.

Assess: Ask students why there was a need for a "second-wave feminists."

Close: Ask students how feminists today have built on the work of earlier groups.

Differentiated Instruction Strategies

BL Ask students what they think is the most important advance in women's rights.

AL Have students research and identify issues that have brought women together or have been divisive.

ELL Ask students to identify other amendments that protected equality.

Culture and Identity

MAIN IDEA Popular culture brings the world closer, but some nations want to maintain their own identities.

HISTORY & YOU Did you know that American movies can be seen all over the world? Read to learn how Western culture affects the world.

The effects of globalization are not limited to politics and economics. Western culture can now be mass-produced and marketed globally. However, the dominance of Western culture also raises some questions.

R

Trends in Art

The United States dominated the art world after World War II, and New York City became the artistic center of the Western world. Artists, from abstract expressionists like Jackson Pollock to postmodernists, expressed vibrantly and energetically the postwar culture.

Abstractionism dominated modern art after 1945. Abstract expressionists conveyed emotion and feeling. By the 1980s, postmodern styles emerged. **Postmodernism**, a revival of traditional elements and techniques, includes traditional painting styles and traditional crafts. Postmodern artists often create works that include elements of film, performance, popular culture, and sculpture. Today's artists use digital cameras and computer programs to produce interactive art forms. Viewers can influence the production of the art itself.

D

Popular Culture

Today people often talk about the movies they saw over the weekend or who won last night's football or basketball game before they talk about anything else. Music, movies, television, sports—all are part of our popular culture. Entertainment created for a profit and for a mass audience is known as **popular culture.**

Known throughout the world, American performers and filmmakers help spread American popular culture. From early rock 'n' roll to multimillion dollar musical acts of today, the world participates in America's musical pop culture.

Films also play a big role in spreading Western culture. In 2003 moviegoers around the world eagerly waited for the opening of the third and final installment of the *Lord of the Rings* trilogy, *The Return of the King*. The film's success is an example of the **globalization** of modern popular culture.

Television and sports have created a sense that Americans and Europeans share a culture. Europeans watch popular American shows like *ER* and become familiar with American brand names—and American attitudes about family, work, and money. As a cultural export, sports have become big business. Sports organizations receive most of their revenues from advertisers who pay millions to sponsor TV football, soccer, or baseball.

Sports have become big politics as well. The most telling example of how politics and sports mix came with the 1972 Olympic Games in **Munich.** There a Palestinian terrorist group seized 11 Israeli athletes as hostages. All of the hostages were killed. During the height of the Cold War, the USSR refused to participate in the 1984 Los Angeles Olympics after the United States boycotted the 1980 Moscow Olympics.

Some nations' peoples worry that American entertainment weakens their own language and culture. Critics refer to **cultural imperialism,** meaning that a Western nation controls other world cultures much as Western nations had controlled colonial governments. To protect their own musical heritage, the French even passed a law saying that at least 40 percent of radio time had to be reserved for French-language music.

Although Western music and movies may still dominate, trends in the opposite direction are developing. One trend is that non-Western music is being played in Western rock and pop. Paul Simon's *Graceland* was an early example. Simon spiced many of his songs with *mbaqanga*—the dance music of the black townships of South Africa. The reggae music native to Jamaica has an enormous following, especially with resistance movements. Finally, Latin pop has become so popular that there have been Latin Grammy awards since 1999.

C

D Differentiated Instruction

Visual/Spatial Have students research an abstract or postmodern work that appeals to them. Then ask them to explain the emotions, feelings, or other reactions it inspires in them. **OL**

R Reading Strategy

Academic Vocabulary Have students define *globalization.* Then ask them to provide examples of the effects of globalization on pop culture. *(American music and films are seen and heard around the world as are many American television shows and sporting events.)* **OL**

C Critical Thinking

Making Generalizations
Ask: How has world music affected Western music trends? *(The music of other cultures has influenced Western musicians; some world music has become popular in its original form on public stations.)* **OL**

For additional practice on this skill, see the **Skills Handbook**.

Additional Support

Activity: Collaborative Learning

Representing Popular Culture Organize the class into groups. Have each group research popular culture in a different country or region. Each group member should focus on a specific area of pop culture. Group members should then work together to create a display or multimedia presentation of popular art, music, television, movies, and sports in the culture. After students have presented their work, discuss the different influences on popular culture in each country or region. **Ask:** Does globalization undermine a culture's traditional values? Have students use specific examples from the class presentations to support their opinions. **OL**

Teacher Tip

Brainstorming Before groups begin working, hold a brief brainstorming session to collect ideas for topics. You may want to have students race against the clock. Remind students to be respectful of each other's ideas.

S Skill Practice

Using Geography Skills

Ask: What type of landform is Brittany? *(a peninsula)* **BL**

C Critical Thinking

Identifying Central Issues

Ask students to review their knowledge of the U.S. Constitution and the First Amendment. **Ask:** What are some other issues that concern the separation of church and state? *(Answers may include the use of public land for religious expressions such as Christmas or the use of tax money to support religious schools.)* **OL**

For additional practice on this skill, see the **Skills Handbook**.

Geography SKILLS

Answers:

1. the Basque region; Northern Ireland; Brittany
2. The Pyrenees mountains; location on the border of France and Spain

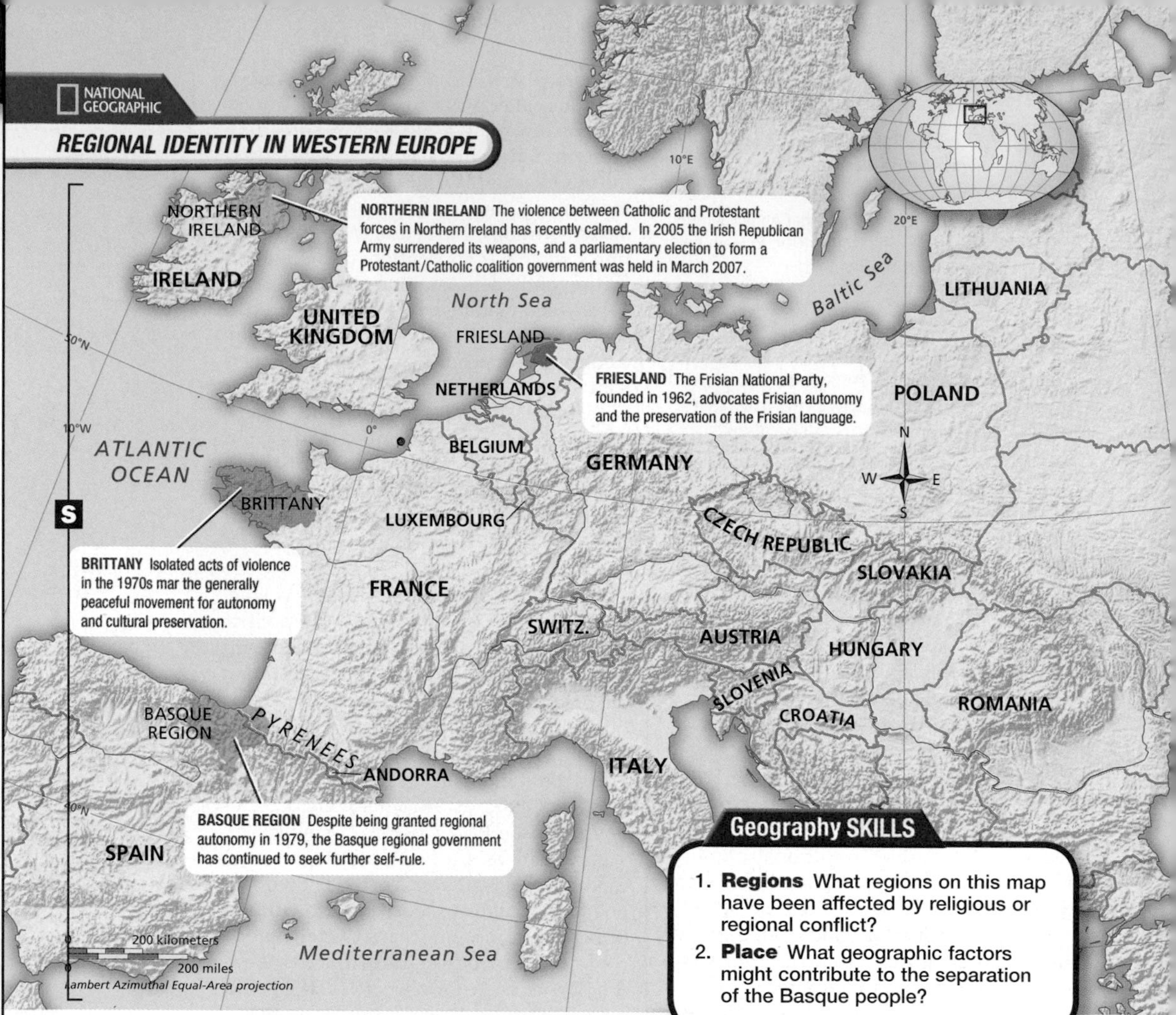

NATIONAL GEOGRAPHIC

REGIONAL IDENTITY IN WESTERN EUROPE

NORTHERN IRELAND The violence between Catholic and Protestant forces in Northern Ireland has recently calmed. In 2005 the Irish Republican Army surrendered its weapons, and a parliamentary election to form a Protestant/Catholic coalition government was held in March 2007.

FRIESLAND The Frisian National Party, founded in 1962, advocates Frisian autonomy and the preservation of the Frisian language.

BRITTANY Isolated acts of violence in the 1970s mar the generally peaceful movement for autonomy and cultural preservation.

BASQUE REGION Despite being granted regional autonomy in 1979, the Basque regional government has continued to seek further self-rule.

Geography SKILLS

1. **Regions** What regions on this map have been affected by religious or regional conflict?
2. **Place** What geographic factors might contribute to the separation of the Basque people?

Religious Trends

From the Middle Ages through the early part of the twentieth century, Christianity dominated the spiritual life of Western society. After World War II, however, many immigrants from former colonies moved to Europe to find jobs. The result has been much greater religious diversity in Europe. Immigrants from Africa, for example, have established large Muslim communities in France, Germany, and Great Britain.

Many people define themselves through their religion, and it influences national customs and social attitudes. This is why some Europeans feel that non-Christian immigrants are threatening their culture.

There is a different trend in the United States. Since the 1980s, a Protestant revival has gathered strength translating into a political force in which conservative Christian groups play a larger role in American politics.

Religious trends in the United States and Europe have raised an important issue: what role should religion play in a democracy? In the United States, controversies have erupted over the precise extent to which religion and government should be

Differentiated Instruction

Leveled Activities

BL Guided Reading Activity, URB p. 87

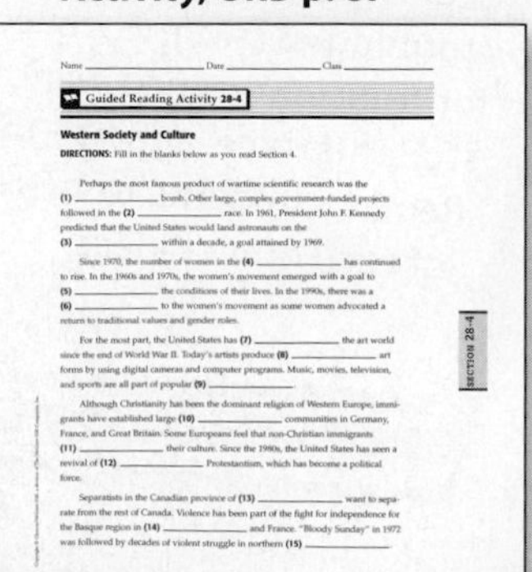

OL Cooperative Learning Activity, URB p. 69

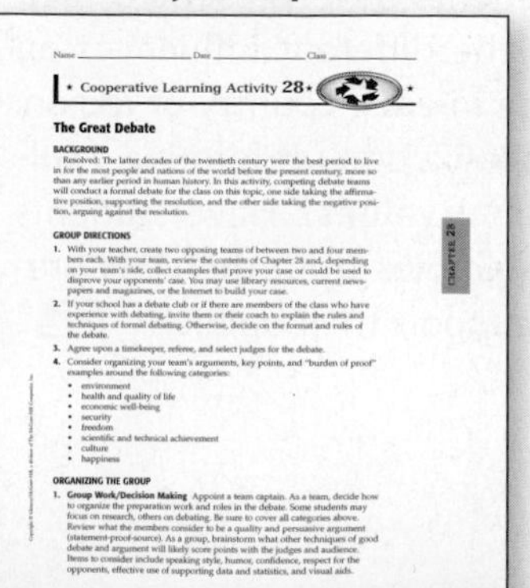

AL Linking Past and Present Activity, URB p. 74

ELL English Learner Activity, p. 57

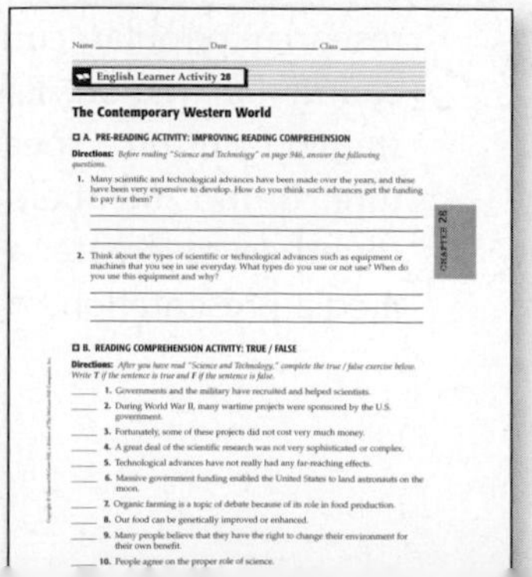

separated. Conflicts have arisen, for example, about the place of prayer in public schools and the use of federal money to fund programs that certain Christians oppose.

In Europe, non-Christians struggle to find a balance between their identities as citizens of the West and as believers in a non-Christian religion. In France, for example, there is an ongoing struggle over whether Muslim girls should be allowed to wear headscarves to public schools.

Nationalism and Regional Identity

A global American-style culture is not the only challenge to national identity. Minorities in Europe want to preserve their culture or even have their own nation. Sometimes these are ethnic groups, and sometimes they are religious groups. These minorities use different tactics, from peaceful demonstrations to terrorism, to reach their goals.

Most minority movements are peaceful. In Brittany, a western region of France that is Celtic in its language and culture, local communities organize festivals called Fest Noz to celebrate their culture. These festivals feature traditional Breton costumes, music, and the Breton language, which closely resembles the Gaelic spoken in Ireland.

Some minorities use violence as a tool to win concessions or gain independence. The **Basque region** is in the western Pyrenees, and part of the territory belongs to Spain and part to France. Although most Basques accept the status quo and work peacefully to protect their language and culture, Basque extremists do not. The group Basque Fatherland and Liberty (ETA) employs violence.

Northern Ireland has also faced ongoing problems with violent extremists. In 1921 Ireland was partitioned between the independent Irish Republic, which is mostly Catholic, and Northern Ireland, which remained under British control. Northern Ireland has a powerful Protestant majority but also contains many Catholics. C

Clashes between Catholics and Protestants in Northern Ireland escalated on January 30, 1972. On this date, which is known as "**Bloody Sunday**," British troops fired on a crowd of civil rights protesters and killed 13 people.

For the next three decades, the Catholic Irish Republican Army (IRA) employed violence and terror in an effort to unite Northern Ireland with the Republic of Ireland. Often aimed against British officials or local Protestant leaders, this violence continued despite many peace talks. By 2000, about 3,600 people had been killed and 36,000 injured. Exhausted by years of violence, the two sides began talks in the 1990s, and signed the Good Friday Agreement in April 1998. The reluctance of the IRA and other militants to disarm, however, threatens the peace process.

✓Reading Check **Explaining** Why did conflict between Catholics and Protestants in Northern Ireland begin?

SECTION 4 REVIEW

Vocabulary

1. **Explain** the significance of: *Sputnik I*, chemical, gender stereotyping, Equal Pay Act, *Roe* v. *Wade*, gender parity, postmodernism, popular culture, globalization, Munich, cultural imperialism, Basque region, Bloody Sunday.

Main Ideas

2. **Explain** why some critics began to question the value of technological progress in postwar society. Give examples.
3. **List** the achievements of the women's movement during the 1960s and 1970s. Use a chart like the one below to make your list.

Achievements of the Women's Movement
1.
2.

4. **Define** cultural imperialism. How have some countries reacted to it?

Critical Thinking

5. **The BIG Idea** **Evaluating** Which medium—TV, films, sports, music—do you believe has the greatest effect on the cultures of other countries? In what ways?
6. **Making Generalizations** Why do some minorities use violence as a tool to gain independence?
7. **Analyzing Visuals** Do you think the women in the photograph on page 948 would be pleased with the status of women today? Why or why not?

Writing About History

8. **Descriptive Writing** Abstractionism, abstract expressionism, and pop art became popular art forms after World War II. Research these art forms and describe in an essay how they represent innovations.

History ONLINE
For help with the concepts in this section of *Glencoe World History*, go to glencoe.com and click Study Central™.

C Critical Thinking

Comparing and Contrasting
Ask: How are the minority movements in Europe similar and different? *(All want to preserve their culture; some use violent means while others use nonviolent means.)* OL

✓Reading Check

Answer: Religious conflict dates back to the partition of Ireland in 1921.

Assess

Study Central provides summaries, interactive games, and online graphic organizers to help students review content.

Close

Drawing Conclusions Ask: What do you think has been the most important change in the Western world? *(Answers should be logically supported.)* OL

Answers

1. Definitions for the vocabulary words are found in the section and the Glossary.
2. Answers may include that technological advances such as chemical fertilizers had far-reaching side effects that damaged the environment.
3. forced politicians to address gender stereotyping; reached milestone with passage of the Equal Pay Act; Congress ruled on *Roe* v. *Wade;* adoption of gender parity policies in some European nations
4. when one nation begins to dominate the culture of other nations much as Western nations dominated colonial governments; resist it because they fear it weakens their own language and culture
5. Answers should be supported by sound reasoning.
6. Answers may include that they may believe it is the only way to get their message across.
7. Answers may include that although the pay gap between men and women is narrowing, women on average still make less money than men. Accept other reasonable answers based on section content and women's roles today.
8. Essays should demonstrate an understanding of varying types of artistic expression.

Focus

Introducing Social History
Discuss the globalization of popular culture since the 1990s. What technologies have helped spread music styles around the world? *(records and CDs, television, films, the Internet)* OL

Teach

S Skill Practice

Using Geography Skills Have students identify on a world outline map the areas represented by each type of music and draw arrows to indicate the directions of influence. OL

R Reading Strategy

Activating Prior Knowledge Have students recall what they have learned about the youth cultures of the 1950s and 1960s. Ask them to describe the role of popular music in each of those periods. BL

Rock 'n' Roll Around the World

S The electric amplification of voices and strings allowed guitar-driven groups to produce a big sound with a few people. Worldwide, rock music combined with local traditions to create new musical forms. Rock 'n' roll let musicians experiment. These experiments allowed people from many cultures to feel like part of a worldwide movement.

◀ *The Platters*

Rock 'n' roll first appeared in the U.S. in the mid-1950s.

In 1964, the British Invasion first defined rock 'n' roll as an international phenomenon.

The Kinks ▶

Rock 'n' Roll's Social Impact

Rock 'n' roll appealed to young people with a loud and heavy beat for dancing and lyrics about topics important to teens. Early rock 'n' rollers R shocked white American parents in the 1950s and helped create a generation gap, a cultural separation between children and their parents. The music also brought African American influences to white audiences in the United States. Rhythm and blues music provided the roots of the 1950s rock 'n' roll sound. Over time, it would influence music throughout the world.

952

Additional Support

Background

Rock'n'Roll Rock 'n' roll was born in the United States in the 1950s, but it was influenced by musical styles from around the world. Musically, rock'n'roll combined elements of country music and rhythm and blues. Country music came from immigrants from Ireland and the British Isles who settled the American South. Guitar was a lead instrument in country music. Rhythm and blues was popular urban African American music that contained elements of traditional blues and jazz, both forms of music that reflected African influences. Disc jockeys promoted their rock'n'roll groups on radio programs. These programs reached the affluent teenagers who were the market for the music. In the 1960s, rock'n'roll became an international phenomenon that was often referred to as *rock*.

▼ Bob Marley and the Wailers

Ska, rocksteady, and reggae took rock influences and in turn influenced musicians in the U.S. and Britain.

In the 1970s, Afrobeat fused rock and jazz influences to Nigerian forms. Lyrics demanded personal freedoms and a just society.

Fela Kuti ▶

A Global Exchange of Popular Music

Across Africa, the electric guitar and jazz and blues musical structures combined with local traditions to create a great many new forms, referred to collectively as Afropop. One example of Afropop is the Afrobeat style created by Fela Kuti. Likewise, the Jamaican innovators of ska and reggae helped a new generation of British and American youth form the styles of punk rock and hip-hop. The shrinking world of the past century has made popular music into a vehicle for cultural exchange and innovation. **D**

Analyzing Visuals

1. **Making Connections** How does today's music affect society? How does it compare to the impact of rock 'n' roll in the 1950s?
2. **Assessing** In different decades and many countries, the electric guitar has become an essential element of popular music. What does this mean for the global exchange of culture?

D Differentiated Instruction

English Language Learners Help students understand the terms *Afropop* and *Afrobeat* by asking them to guess what words were combined to form them *(African; pop, itself short for* popular; *beat)* **ELL**

Assess/Close

Have students answer the Analyzing Visuals questions and discuss the pros and cons of a globalized world culture. **OL**

Analyzing Visuals

Answers:

1. Answers will vary but may include that music today continues to affect society, though it may not have the enormous impact that rock'n'roll had when it was introduced in the 1950s.
2. Global use of a common instrument is a new phenomenon. It allows musicians worldwide to build and share one another's work.

Activity: Collaborative Learning

Creating an Audio Time Line Have students identify the styles of music that are mentioned in this feature and list them on the board. Ask students if they can think of other styles that may have influenced rock'n'roll or new styles that have come from it. **Ask:** What are the common elements in these musical styles? Have students work in small groups to find audio examples of each of the styles so that they can identify the common elements. Instruct students to collaborate on creating an audio time line by arranging their music clips in roughly chronological order to show how earlier forms influenced later ones. Students may wish to record audio commentary to explain how the musical clips are linked together. After students have played their recording, call on volunteers to list the common elements of the musical styles on the board. Discuss how music may promote cultural understanding between different groups of people. **OL**

Comparing and Contrasting Discuss the information presented in the Visual Summary. Explain that this information includes important ideas from Chapter 28. Have students work in pairs, using the information from the Visual Summary to create a chart that compares changes and issues in the Soviet Union and Eastern Europe with those in Western Europe and North America. **Ask:** In what ways are changes and issues in the Soviet Union similar to and different from those in North America? *(Accept reasonable responses. Encourage students to use information from the Visual Summary, but suggest that they augment their comparison and contrast statements with details from the sections in the chapter.)* OL

Visual Literacy Have students spend a few minutes studying each photograph. Then ask them to write a sentence describing how each photograph relates to the main ideas that are listed next to it. BL

CHAPTER 28 Visual Summary

You can study anywhere, anytime by downloading quizzes and flash cards to your PDA from glencoe.com.

Economic and Political Change in the SOVIET UNION AND EASTERN EUROPE

- Gorbachev's reforms helped to end the Cold War and break up the Soviet Union.
- Communist regimes in Eastern Europe ended as the loss of Soviet support led to revolutions.
- Ethnic tensions in Yugoslavia led to conflicts in Bosnia and Kosovo.
- Energy resources support Russia's economy, but it still faces many economic and social problems.

DESTRUCTION OF THE BERLIN WALL

The fall of the Berlin Wall symbolized the end of the Cold War.

PROTESTANTS AND CATHOLICS CLASH IN NORTHERN IRELAND

Northern Ireland's Catholics wanted to unite with the Republic of Ireland, while Protestants preferred to remain part of Great Britain.

Economic and Social Issues in WESTERN EUROPE AND NORTH AMERICA

- U.S. president Richard Nixon resigned after the Watergate scandal.
- After reunification, Germany faced the cost of rebuilding the economy of eastern Germany.
- The EC became the European Union, and most members adopted the Euro.
- Canadians became divided over the possible secession of French-speaking Quebec.

U.S. ASTRONAUTS FIRST TO WALK ON THE MOON

Revolutionary advances in science made space travel possible.

The Spread and Transformation of WESTERN TECHNOLOGY AND CULTURE

- Significant changes in technology have revolutionized life in the Western world.
- The women's movement addressed issues of stereotyping, pay equality, abortion, and political parity.
- As popular culture brings the world closer, some nations and minority groups worry about loss of their cultural identity.

Hands-On Chapter Project
Step 5: Wrap-Up

Traveling through the Modern Western World

Step 5: Summarizing the Journey Pairs of students will display their maps and note their itineraries. Then each pair will deliver a short oral report that describes their most interesting destination and how it illustrates important changes in Western society.

Ask: What have been some of the positive results of changes in Western society in the last 30 years? *(Answers may include democracy, capitalism, and political freedom in the former Soviet Union and Eastern Europe, continued prosperity in Europe and North America, technological change, and changes in women's roles and opportunities.)*

Ask: What have been some negative results? *(Answers may include social problems and internal conflict in the former Soviet Union, wars and ethnic cleansing in Eastern Europe, economic troubles in Europe, conflicts over immigration, increased terrorism, changes in traditional societies connected to technological change, and conflict in Northern Ireland.)* OL

STANDARDIZED TEST PRACTICE

TEST-TAKING TIP

If you do not know the correct answer to a question, read the answer choices carefully. Eliminate any statement that is historically incorrect. This will help you focus on the remaining answer choices and increase your chances of choosing the correct answer.

Reviewing Vocabulary

Directions: Choose the word (or words) that best completes the sentence.

1. A ________ exists when the government spends more than it collects in revenues.

A red-line budget
B budget deficit
C surplus budget
D balanced budget

2. Mikhail Gorbachev based his radical reforms on ________, or restructuring.

A intifada
B genestroika
C restifada
D perestroika

3. Kosovo was a self-governing province; that is, it was ________.

A an autonomous province
B a dependent province
C a protectorate
D a colonial territory

4. ________ policies require that women must make up either a certain number of the candidates in an election or a certain number of those elected.

A Gender parity
B Equality
C Gender stereotyping
D Discrimination

Reviewing Main Ideas

Directions: Choose the best answers to the following questions.

Section 1 *(pp. 930–935)*

5. What caused the Cold War to intensify in 1979?

A Gorbachev's perestroika
B U.S. invasion of Iraq
C Boris Yeltsin's presidency of Russia
D Soviet invasion of Afghanistan

6. Why did the Soviet Union and the United States sign the INF Treaty of 1987?

A To extend aid to Afghanistan
B To slow down the arms race
C To build up their arsenals
D To deter invasion from China

7. To what was Boris Yeltsin committed for improving Russia's economy?

A Introducing a free-market economy
B Allowing the Chechens their independence
C Alowing the free sale and purchase of land
D Using Russia's national resources as geopolitical leverage

Section 2 *(pp. 936–939)*

8. Who organized Solidarity in Poland?

A Mikhail Gorbachev
B Václav Havel
C Lech Walesa
D Václav Klaus

Need Extra Help?

If You Missed Questions . . .	1	2	3	4	5	6	7	8
Go to Page . . .	944	932	939	948	931	932	934	936

GO ON

Answers and Analyses

Reviewing Vocabulary

1. B *Balanced* or *surplus* are not good choices given the stem. *Red-line* is not a familiar term, although being "in the red" does imply a deficit.

2. D Knowledge of the content is necessary to select the correct answer. *Intifada* is connected with the Middle East while *genestroika* and *restifada* are unknown words.

3. A The correct answer can be found through a knowledge of vocabulary. *Dependent, protectorate,* and *territory* are all words that do not imply self-governing.

4. A Knowledge of the word *gender* can help direct students to the correct answer. *Stereotyping* and *discrimination* are what the women's movement fought against. *Equality* is a general term that does not describe this particular policy.

Reviewing Main Ideas

5. D Chronological knowledge is important here. Gorbachev, Yeltsin, and the U.S. invasion of Iraq all came after 1979.

6. B Two responses are not logical—aiding Afghanistan and building up arsenals. The United States and the Soviet Union never cooperated in defense against China.

7. A Knowledge of the content is important here. Chechens have not been granted independence. The free sale and purchase of land and using national resources for leverage are actual events, but they are not connected to Yeltsin.

8. C Gorbachev is connected with the USSR, Havel and Klaus with Czechoslovakia.

9. A Serbs were the enemies of the Albanians while Croatians and Bosnians are members of other ethnic groups and republics.

10. D Knowledge of the content is essential here. Fifty would be too large a number for Europe, and 12 and 15 are small numbers from the past size of the European Union.

11. B The attacks of September 11, 2001, occurred during Bush's first years. War with Iraq came later. Watergate occurred well before his election, and the Falklands did not involve the United States directly.

For Question 11: Students can use the process of elimination to figure out the answer. By eliminating answers they know are incorrect, they will be left with the correct answer.

CHAPTER 28

9. Which ethnic group formed the Kosovo Liberation Army (KLA)?
- **A** Albanians
- **B** Serbs
- **C** Croatians
- **D** Bosnians

Section 3 *(pp. 940-945)*

10. How many nations belonged to the European Union as of 2004?
- **A** 50
- **B** 15
- **C** 12
- **D** 25

11. To what problem did George W. Bush devote most of his attention during his first year as U.S. president?
- **A** War with Iraq
- **B** Terrorism
- **C** Invasion of the Falkland Islands
- **D** The Watergate scandal

Section 4 *(pp. 946–951)*

12. In which year did the United States land a mission on the moon?
- **A** 1969
- **B** 1945
- **C** 1981
- **D** 1979

13. Through what type of art forms can viewers influence the production of the art itself?
- **A** WYSIWYG creations
- **B** Digital jpeg photos
- **C** Interactive productions
- **D** MTV productions

Critical Thinking

Directions: Choose the best answers to the following questions.

Use the following map and your knowledge of world history to answer question 14.

14. How many republics were formed from the former Yugoslavia?
- **A** 5
- **B** 6
- **C** 4
- **D** 8

15. What caused the collapse of communism in the Soviet Union?
- **A** Assassination of Leonid Brezhnev, invasion of Afghanistan
- **B** Efficient central government, strong economy
- **C** Vladimir Putin's reforms, abundant natural resources
- **D** Weak economy, inefficient central government, Gorbachev's reforms, and nationalism

Need Extra Help?							
If You Missed Questions . . .	9	10	11	12	13	14	15
Go to Page . . .	939	940	945	946	949	939	932

GO ON

12. A Common sense can rule out 1945 as too close to World War II. Knowledge of the content is needed to select 1969.

13. C Students should be familiar with the term *interactive*. The other answers do not address direct viewer involvement.

Critical Thinking

14. B Map reading skills indicate the answer.

15. D Other answers are not plausible. Brezhnev was not assassinated, strong government would not cause a collapse, Putin came long after the collapse and abundant natural resources are usually considered an asset.

16. What resulted from Ronald Reagan's military buildup in the 1980s?

- **A** A bull market
- **B** Record budget deficits
- **C** A record budget surplus
- **D** The invasion of Iraq

17. Why have the United States, Great Britain, France, and Canada alternated between liberal and conservative leaders from 1970 through today?

- **A** They wanted to stabilize their economies.
- **B** They went with the popular, charismatic candidates.
- **C** They wanted to give bipartisanism a chance.
- **D** They just could not decide which they liked better.

Analyze the chart and answer the question that follows. Base your answer on the chart and on your knowledge of world history.

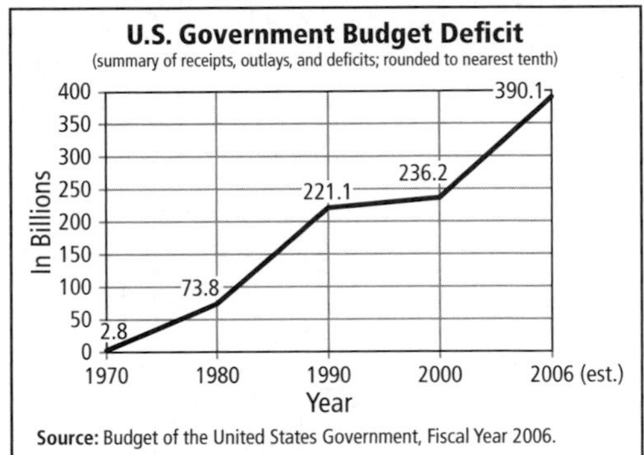

Source: Budget of the United States Government, Fiscal Year 2006.

18. What can be said about the U.S. budget deficit?

- **A** Under the Nixon administration, the budget deficit increased to a startling $73.8 billion.
- **B** The budget deficit remained rather stable under the Reagan and Bush administrations.
- **C** The 2006 budget deficit is expected to increase even more than it did during the Reagan and Bush administrations.
- **D** Under the Clinton administration, the budget deficit increased by nearly $150 billion.

Document-Based Questions

Directions: Analyze the document and answer the short-answer questions that follow the document. Base your answers on the document and on your knowledge of world history.

In his 1975 book *Small Is Beautiful*, the British economist E. F. Schumacher wrote:

> *"We must begin to see the possibility of evolving a new lifestyle, with new methods of production and new patterns of consumption: a lifestyle designed for permanence. To give only two examples: in agriculture, we can interest ourselves in the perfection of production methods which are biologically sound and produce health, beauty and permanence. In industry, we can interest ourselves in small-scale technology, 'technology with a human face,' so that people have a chance to enjoy themselves while they are working, instead of working solely for their pay packet and hoping for enjoyment solely during their leisure time."*
>
> —E. F. Schumacher, *Small Is Beautiful*, 1973

19. According to Schumacher, what are the two components of a new lifestyle, one designed for permanence?

20. What do you believe Schumacher meant when he said "technology with a human face"?

Extended Response

21. The European Union established a common European currency, the euro. How would a common global currency, whether the euro or another currency form, affect the global economy?

For additional test practice, use Self-Check Quizzes—Chapter 28 at glencoe.com.

Need Extra Help?

If You Missed Questions . . .	16	17	18	19	20	21
Go to Page . . .	944	940–945	944	946	946	940

STOP

Document-Based Questions

19. new patterns of production and new patterns of consumption

20. Technology is rapidly changing and often inventors, designers, and manufacturers need to remember to create work places where people can enjoy themselves as human beings.

Extended Response

21. Answers may include the viewpoint that common global currency would greatly impact the global economy. Trade would be more equitable, since currencies would no longer be valued against each other. A dollar in one country would be valued as a dollar in all countries.

16. B The buildup should indicate a deficit. There was not a surplus, and the invasion came many years later. A bull market was created through much of the period but it was not necessarily created by the military buildup.

17. A Economic issues often drive political choices. Knowledge of the content is essential because the other answers are plausible.

18. C Careful analysis and comparisons of deficits will reveal the answer. Also, knowledge of the years of various presidencies is crucial. For example, during the 1990 to 2000 period on the graph during which Clinton was president, the budget deficit did not increase by $150 billion dollars. The figure was closer to $15 billion.

Introduce students to chapter content and key terms by having them access the Chapter 28 Overview at glencoe.com.

Need Extra Help?

Have students refer to the pages listed if they miss any of the questions.

CHAPTER 29 Planning Guide

Key to Ability Levels

- **BL** Below Level
- **OL** On Level
- **AL** Above Level
- **ELL** English Language Learners

Key to Teaching Resources

- Print Material
- CD-ROM
- DVD
- Transparency

Levels				Resources	Chapter Opener	Section 1	Section 2	Section 3	Chapter Assess
BL	OL	AL	ELL						
				FOCUS					
BL	OL	AL	ELL	**Daily Focus Skills Transparencies**		29-1	29-2	29-3	
				TEACH					
BL	OL		ELL	**Reading Skills Activity, URB**			p. 91		
	OL	AL		**Historical Analysis Skills Activity, URB**		p. 92			
BL	OL	AL	ELL	**Differentiated Instruction Activity, URB**		p. 93			
	OL		ELL	**English Learner Activity, URB**		p. 95			
BL	OL	AL	ELL	**Content Vocabulary Activity, URB***		p. 97			
BL	OL	AL	ELL	**Academic Vocabulary Activity, URB**		p. 99			
BL	OL	AL	ELL	**Skills Reinforcement Activity, URB**			p. 101		
	OL	AL		**Critical Thinking Skills Activity, URB**			p. 102		
	OL	AL		**History and Geography Activity, URB**			p. 103		
	OL	AL	ELL	**Mapping History Activity, URB**			p. 105		
BL	OL	AL		**Historical Significance Activity, URB**			p. 106		
BL	OL	AL	ELL	**Cooperative Learning Activity, URB**		p. 107			
	OL	AL	ELL	**History Simulation Activity, URB**				p. 109	
BL	OL	AL	ELL	**Time Line Activity, URB**				p. 111	
	OL	AL		**Linking Past and Present Activity, URB**			p. 112		
BL	OL	AL		**People in World History Activity, URB**			p. 114	p. 113	
BL	OL	AL	ELL	**Primary Source Reading, URB**				p. 115	
	OL	AL		**Enrichment Activity, URB**				p. 120	
BL	OL	AL	ELL	**World Art and Music Activity, URB**		p. 117			
BL	OL		ELL	**Guided Reading Activities, URB***		p. 122	p. 123	p. 124	
BL	OL		ELL	**Reading Essentials and Note-Taking Guide***		p. 319	p. 322	p. 325	
BL	OL	AL	ELL	**Differentiated Instruction for the World History Classroom**	✓	✓	✓	✓	✓

Note: Please refer to the *Unit Resource Book: Toward a Global Civilization* for this chapter's URB materials.

* Also available in Spanish

- Interactive Lesson Planner
- Interactive Teacher Edition
- Fully editable blackline masters
- Section Spotlight Videos Launch
- Differentiated Lesson Plans
- Printable reports of daily assignments
- Standards Tracking System

Levels					Resources	Chapter Opener	Section 1	Section 2	Section 3	Chapter Assess
BL	OL	AL	ELL							
					TEACH *(continued)*					
BL	OL	AL	ELL		**StudentWorks™ Plus DVD**	✓	✓	✓	✓	✓
BL	OL	AL	ELL		**Vocabulary PuzzleMaker CD-ROM**	✓	✓	✓	✓	✓
Teacher Resources					**Building Academic Vocabulary**	✓	✓	✓	✓	✓
					Reading Strategies and Activities for the Social Studies Classroom			p. 77		
					Writer's Guidebook		p. 43			
					Strategies for Success	✓	✓	✓	✓	✓
					Outline Map Resource Book	✓	✓	✓	✓	✓
					Presentation Plus! with MindJogger DVD	✓	✓	✓	✓	✓
					ASSESS					
BL	OL	AL	ELL		**Section Quizzes and Chapter Tests***		p. 361	p. 362	p. 363	p. 365
BL	OL	AL	ELL		**Authentic Assessment With Rubrics**	✓	✓	✓	✓	✓
BL	OL	AL	ELL		**Standardized Test Practice Workbook**	✓	✓	✓	✓	✓
BL	OL	AL	ELL		***ExamView® Assessment Suite* CD-ROM**		29-1	29-2	29-3	Ch. 29
BL	OL	AL	ELL		**Interactive Tutor Self-Assessment CD-ROM**		29-1	29-2	29-3	
					CLOSE					
BL			ELL		**Reteaching Activity, URB**				p. 119	
BL	OL		ELL		**Reading and Study Skills Foldables™**	✓	✓	✓	✓	✓

Daily Assignments and Grade Log

Technology Product

Glencoe's *StudentWorks™ Plus* CD-ROM contains everything your students need, including the complete Student Edition and access to all student workbooks. *StudentWorks™ Plus* also includes a Daily Assignment and Activity Log that allows students to

- record and track progress on their daily assignments and responsibilities;
- log results achieved, including their grades;
- sort assignments alphabetically or by category;
- view and print the assignment and grade log in a table or calendar format.

Objectives

Using *StudentWorks™ Plus* will help your students

- take responsibility for their individual tasks;
- improve independent study skills.

Steps

Provide students with the following information:

- Launch *StudentWorks™ Plus.*
- Select the **Daily Assignments and Grade Log** button at the bottom of the launch screen.
- Create a new file or open an existing one. The log is organized as a table, with a row of information for each assignment.
- Add information for each assignment, including the date of the assignment, the name, additional comments, the due date, and the grade.
- Edit rows as assignment information is provided or changed. Add a new row to the log for each new assignment.

History ONLINE

	Student	Teacher	Parent
Beyond the Textbook	●	●	●
Chapter Overviews	●	●	●
Time Current Events	●		●
ePuzzles and Games	●		●
Concepts in Motion	●		●
Literature Connections		●	
Multi-Language Glossaries	●		●
Online Student Edition	●	●	●
Self-Check Quizzes	●		●
Student Web Activities	●		●
Study Central ™	●		●
Teaching Today		●	
Vocabulary eFlashcards	●		●
Web Activity Lesson Plans		●	

- **Timed Readings Plus in Social Studies** helps students increase their reading rate and fluency while maintaining comprehension. The 400-word passages are similar to those found on state and national assessments.
- **Reading in the Content Area: Social Studies** concentrates on six essential reading skills that help students better comprehend what they read. The book includes 75 high-interest nonfiction passages written at increasing levels of difficulty.
- **Reading Social Studies** includes strategic reading instruction and vocabulary support in Social Studies content for both ELLs and native speakers of English.

www.jamestowneducation.com

The following videotape programs are available from Glencoe as supplements to Chapter 29:

- Carmen Miranda: The South American (ISBN 0-76-700097-8)
- Cuba and Castro (ISBN 0-76-701426-X)
- Fidel Castro: El commandante (ISBN 0-76-700237-7)
- Evita: The Woman Behind the Myth (ISBN 0-76-700029-3)

To order, call Glencoe at 1-800-334-7344. To find classroom resources to accompany many of these videos, check the following home pages:

A&E Television: www.aetv.com

The History Channel: www.historychannel.com

Index to National Geographic Magazine:

The following articles relate to this chapter:

- "Hallowed Ground: Nothing Is Ever Safe," by David Quammen, October 2006
- "Land of the Living Wind," by Simon Worrall, January 2004
- "Peru Begins Again," by John McCarry, May 1996
- "Buenos Aires: Making Up for Lost Time," by John J. Putnam, December 1994

National Geographic Society Products To order the following, call National Geographic at 1-800-368-2728:

- *National Geographic Atlas of the World* (Book)

Access National Geographic's new, dynamic MapMachine Web site and other geography resources at:
www.nationalgeographic.com
www.nationalgeographic.com/maps

GLENCOE BOOKLINK 3

Use this database to search more than 30,000 titles to create a customized reading list for your students.

- Reading lists can be organized by students' reading level, author, genre, theme, or area of interest.
- The database provides Degrees of Reading Power™ (DRP) and Lexile™ readability scores for all selections.
- A brief summary of each selection is included.

Leveled reading suggestions for this chapter:

For students at a Grade 8 reading level:
- ***Journey for Peace: The Story of Rigoberta Menchu,*** by Marlene Targ Brill

For students at a Grade 9 reading level:
- ***Castro's Cuba,*** by Charles W. Carey

For students at a Grade 10 reading level:
- ***Havana Dreams: A Story of Cuba,*** by Wendy Gimbel

For students at a Grade 11 reading level:
- ***Of Love and Shadows,*** by Isabel Allende

For students at a Grade 12 reading level:
- ***Brazil,*** by Brian Dicks

Introducing
CHAPTER 29

Focus

MAKING CONNECTIONS
How can trade embargoes affect a nation?

Ask students to look at the photograph and examine the automobiles. Point out that Cuba is noted for the many "vintage" automobiles that are still in daily use. Ask students to consider how the U.S. trade embargo has affected the average Cuban's access to transportation. Responses may include that people would have problems getting to and from work, and stores might be unable to keep their shelves stocked. Then have students brainstorm products they use that are made in other countries and discuss how an embargo on trade with these countries would affect their lives.

Teach

The Big Ideas

As students study the chapter, remind them to consider the section-based Big Ideas included in each section's Guide to Reading. The **Essential Questions** in the activities below tie in to the Big Ideas and help students think about and understand important chapter concepts. In addition, the Hands-on Chapter Projects with their culminating activities relate the content from each section to the Big Ideas. These activities build on each other as students progress through the chapter. Section activities culminate in the wrap-up activity on the Visual Summary page.

CHAPTER 29

Latin America 1945–Present

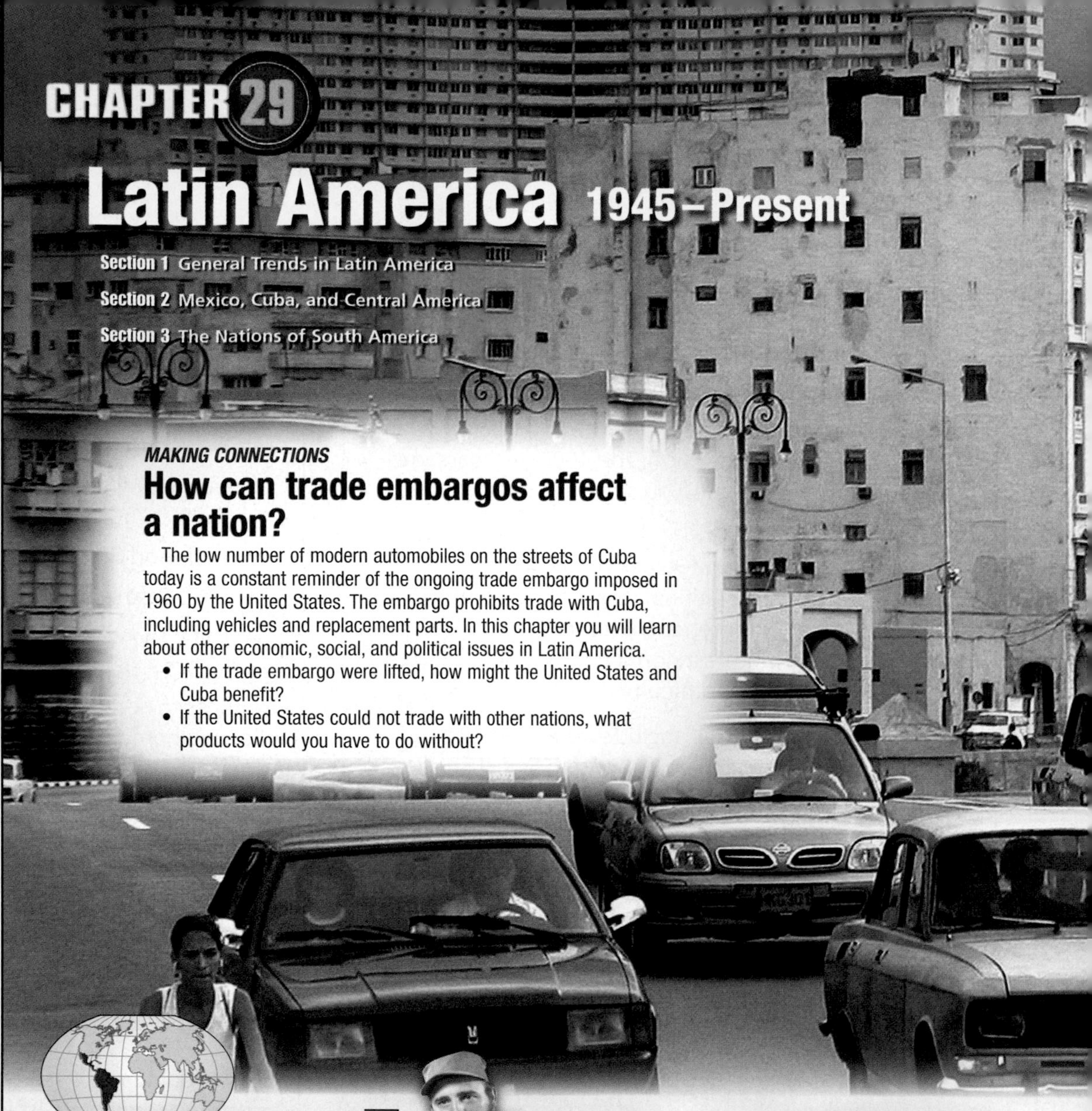

MAKING CONNECTIONS
How can trade embargos affect a nation?

The low number of modern automobiles on the streets of Cuba today is a constant reminder of the ongoing trade embargo imposed in 1960 by the United States. The embargo prohibits trade with Cuba, including vehicles and replacement parts. In this chapter you will learn about other economic, social, and political issues in Latin America.

- If the trade embargo were lifted, how might the United States and Cuba benefit?
- If the United States could not trade with other nations, what products would you have to do without?

LATIN AMERICA ▶

1946 Juan Perón elected president of Argentina

1959 Fidel Castro seizes power in Cuba

1970 Salvador Allende elected president of Chile

1945 — 1965

THE WORLD ▶

1945 World War II ends

1967 Civil war erupts in Nigeria

958

General Trends in Latin America
Essential Question: What was the relationship between the United States and Latin America after World War II? *(The United States was deeply involved in the economic affairs of many Latin American nations; troops had been used to protect U.S. interests.)* Point out that the United States changed its foreign policy as a result of the Cold War, and these changes affected its relations with Latin America. **OL**

Mexico, Cuba, and Central America
Essential Question: Why was the United States so concerned about the governments and military capabilities of its neighbors? *(Instability or foreign involvement at or near its borders was viewed as a threat.)* Point out that in Section 2 students will learn about developments in the region that increased U.S. concerns and about how the United States responded to those concerns. **OL**

Introducing **CHAPTER 29**

More About the Photo

Visual Literacy With a population of more than 2 million, Havana, Cuba, is the largest city in the Caribbean region. Prior to the Cuban Revolution when Fidel Castro came to power, the United States was Cuba's main trading partner. Evidence of this relationship may still be seen today in the number of vintage American cars on Havana's streets.

FOLDABLES Study Organizer Dinah Zike's Foldables

Dinah Zike's Foldables are three-dimensional, interactive graphic organizers that help students practice basic writing skills, review vocabulary terms, and identify main ideas. Instructions for creating and using Foldables can be found in the Appendix at the end of this book and in the *Dinah Zike's Reading and Study Skills Foldables* booklet.

History ONLINE

Introduce students to chapter content and key terms by having them access the Chapter 29 Overview at glencoe.com.

SECTION 3

The Nations of South America

Ask: What kinds of problems have South American countries experienced in the twentieth century? *(economic, social, and political)* Point out that students will learn about persistent economic problems throughout many areas of Latin America in Section 3. **OL**

Focus

Bellringer

Daily Focus Transparency 29.1

GUIDE TO READING

Answers to Graphic:

Social Challenges: population growth, rapid rise in size of cities, enormous gap between poor and rich, international drug trade; **Political Challenges:** repressive military regimes, multinational corporations increased dependence on industrialized nations, movement toward democracy in 1980s in many countries

Section Spotlight Video

To generate student interest and provide a springboard for class discussion, access the Chapter 29, Section 1 video at glencoe.com or on the video DVD.

SECTION 1

General Trends in Latin America

GUIDE TO READING

The BIG Idea

Order and Stability Economic instability led some Latin American countries to move toward democracy, while the United States intervened to protect its interests.

Content Vocabulary

- multinational corporations *(p. 960)*
- megacity *(p. 962)*
- magic realism *(p. 964)*

Academic Vocabulary

- consent *(p. 961)*
- ongoing *(p. 961)*

People and Places

- Chile *(p. 960)*
- Brazil *(p. 960)*
- Argentina *(p. 960)*
- Bolivia *(p. 962)*
- Peru *(p. 962)*
- Colombia *(p. 962)*
- Organization of American States (OAS) *(p. 962)*
- Gabriel García Márquez *(p. 964)*
- Oscar Niemeyer *(p. 965)*

Reading Strategy

Categorizing Information As you read, use a diagram like the one below to identify social and political challenges in Latin America since 1945.

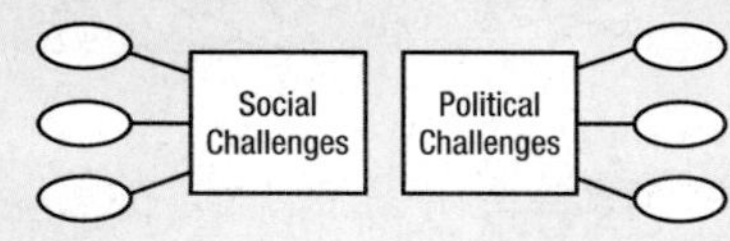

During the second half of the twentieth century, Latin American countries faced many economic, social, and political challenges. These challenges arose from a rise in population, a large foreign debt, and ongoing foreign military involvement. During this time of instability and change, Latin Americans looked to new artists to reflect the future hopes of the region.

Economic and Political Developments

MAIN IDEA Dependence on foreign imports and investments led to serious economic and political problems in Latin America.

HISTORY & YOU What happens when a nation imports more than it exports? Read to learn about the causes of economic instability in Latin America.

Since the 1800s, Latin Americans had exported raw materials and bought manufactured goods from industrialized countries. The Great Depression caused exports to fall, and revenues to buy manufactured goods declined. In response, Latin Americans developed industries to produce their own goods.

Economic Instability

By the 1960s, however, Latin American countries were still experiencing economic problems. They depended on the United States, Europe, and Japan, especially for the advanced technology needed for modern industries. Also, many Latin American countries had failed to find markets abroad to sell their manufactured products.

These economic failures led to political instability. In the 1960s, repressive military regimes in **Chile, Brazil,** and **Argentina** abolished political parties and returned to export-import economies financed by foreigners. These regimes also encouraged **multinational corporations** (companies with divisions in more than two countries) to come to Latin America. This made these Latin American countries even more dependent on industrialized nations. In the 1970s, Latin American countries tried to maintain their weak economies by borrowing money. Between 1970 and 1982, debt to foreigners grew from $27 billion to $315.3 billion. A number of Latin American economies began to crumble. Wages fell, and unemployment and inflation skyrocketed.

Many people believed that governments had taken control of too many industries. Trying to industrialize too quickly had led to the decline of the economy in the countryside as well. As the economy declined, people continued to move from the countryside into the cities.

Resource Manager

R Reading Strategies	C Critical Thinking	D Differentiated Instruction	W Writing Support	S Skill Practice
Teacher Edition • Act. Prior Know., p. 962 • Using Context Clues, p. 965 **Additional Resources** • Cont. Vocab. Act., URB p. 97 • Guid. Read. Act., URB p. 122 • Read. Ess. & Note-Taking Guide, p. 319	**Teacher Edition** • Analyzing Info., p. 961 • Making Inferences, p. 963 **Additional Resources** • Coop. Learn. Act., URB p. 107 • Section Quiz, p. 361	**Teacher Edition** • ELL, p. 962 **Additional Resources** • Hist. Analysis Skills Act., URB p. 92 • Diff. Instr. Act., URB p. 93 • English Learner Act., URB p. 95 • World Art & Music Act., URB p. 117	**Teacher Edition** • Expository Writing, p. 963 • Personal Writing, p. 964 **Additional Resources** • Writer's Guidebook, p. 43	**Teacher Edition** • Using Geo. Skills, p. 961 **Additional Resources** • Academic Vocab. Act., URB p. 99

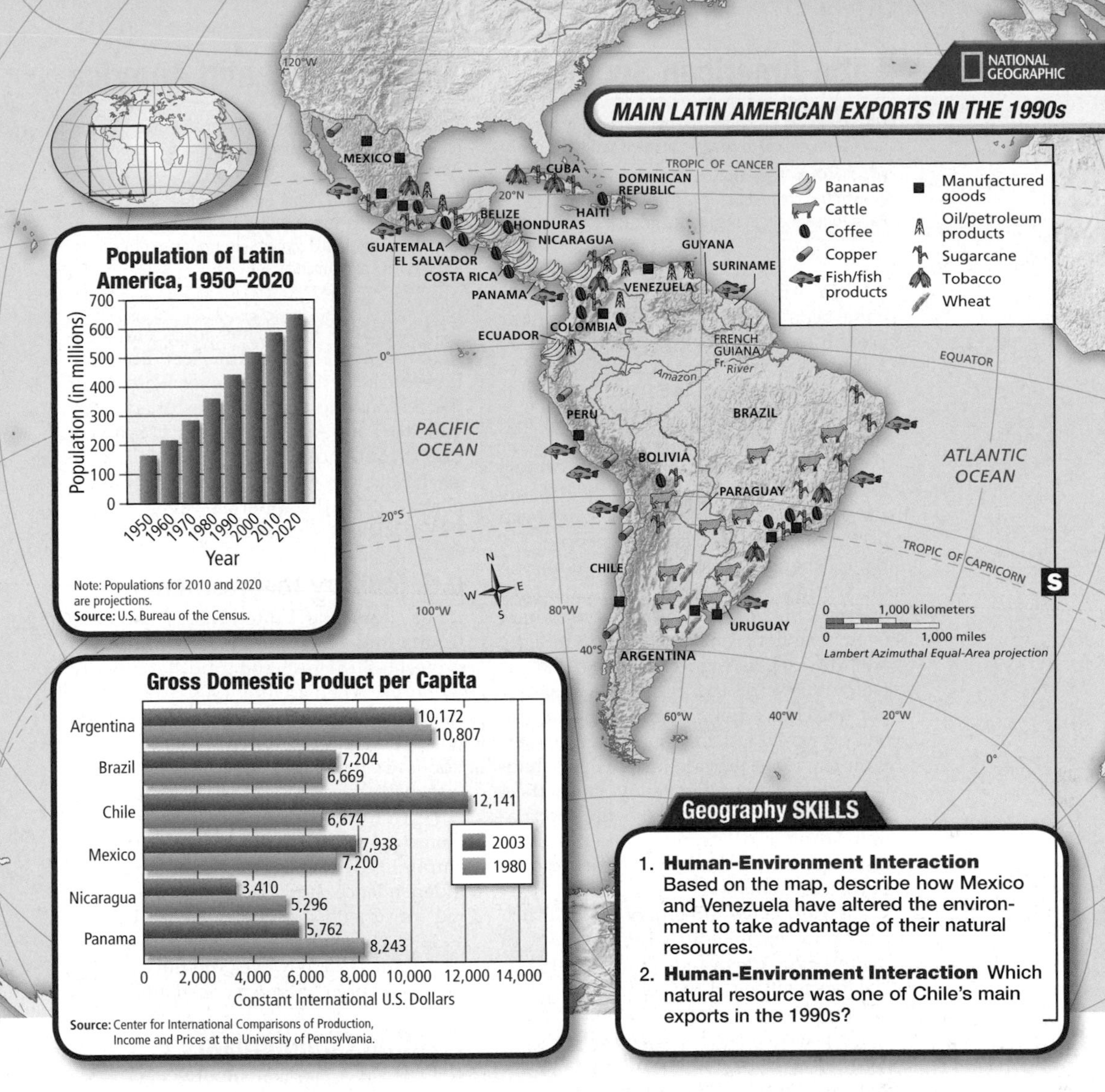

Geography SKILLS

1. **Human-Environment Interaction** Based on the map, describe how Mexico and Venezuela have altered the environment to take advantage of their natural resources.
2. **Human-Environment Interaction** Which natural resource was one of Chile's main exports in the 1990s?

A Move Toward Democracy

With the debt crisis in the 1980s came a movement toward democracy. Some military leaders could not deal with their nations' debt problems. At the same time, many realized that military power without popular **consent** could not maintain a strong state. By the mid-1990s, several democratic regimes had been established.

The movement toward democracy was the most noticeable trend of the 1980s and the early 1990s in Latin America. Yet the revival of democracy was fragile. Globalization and the **ongoing** burden of foreign debt stressed several Latin American countries enough that they elected authoritarian figures in the 1990s. In 1992, for example, President Alberto Fujimori returned Peru to an authoritarian system. C

✓ **Reading Check** **Explaining** Why did the debt crisis of the 1980s create a movement toward democracy?

C Critical Thinking

Analyzing Information Ask: How did economic issues of the 1980s affect both military governments and democracies in Latin America? *(Several nations moved toward democracy, but some returned to authoritarian regimes.)* **OL**

S Skill Practice

Using Geography Skills Ask: What time period is reflected on this map? How do you know? *(The map shows the time period of the 1990s. This is indicated in the map title.)* **BL**

Geography SKILLS

Answers:
1. Mexico and Venezuela drilled for oil.
2. copper

✓ **Reading Check**

Answer: Some military leaders were unwilling to deal with debt problems. There were doubts about the underlying strength of states with military regimes in power without popular consent.

Hands-On Chapter Project Step 1

Creating a Poster about Important Latin Americans

Pairs of students will create a poster that highlights important individuals who helped change Latin America after World War II.

Step 1: Illustrating Cultural Changes

Essential Question: How did Latin American culture change after World War II?

Directions: Have students form pairs to begin the project. Students should draw a map of Latin America to serve as the backdrop for their posters and display information about each individual near their nation of origin. In this section, students should research artists, writers, or other cultural figures who reflect the changes in Latin America, such as Neruda, Paz, Borges, Candela, or Botero. They should use library or Internet resources to locate information and images. **OL**

(Chapter Project is continued in Section 2.)

✓Reading Check

Answer: A megacity has a huge population that has grown faster than the capability of government to provide regular urban services. Megacities often have slums and shantytowns and sometimes crime and corruption.

D Differentiated Instruction

English Language Learners

Ask students to list ways in which the United States could be considered a "giant" compared to Latin American countries at the time. *(geographic size, economic strength, military strength, political power)* ELL

R Reading Strategy

Activating Prior Knowledge

Ask students to review information in Chapter 25 about the Good Neighbor Policy and write a few sentences to describe it. *(Roosevelt attempted to lessen U.S. intervention in the area by refusing to send troops to support and protect business interests.)* OL

Additional Support

Latin American Society

MAIN IDEA Economic and population problems have been critical to shaping modern Latin America.

HISTORY & YOU Do you know a city where fast growth has created traffic jams and urban sprawl? Read to learn about megacities in Latin America.

Latin America's economic problems have been made worse by its dramatic growth in population. Between 1950 and 2000, the population in Latin America more than tripled. The population is expected to reach 584 million by 2010 and 643 million by 2020.

With the increase in population came a rapid rise in the size of cities. By 2000, 50 cities in Latin America and the Caribbean had more than one million people. Six Latin American cities are included among the world's 32 most populous cities. For instance, Buenos Aires has a population of over 13 million; São Paulo, over 18 million; and Mexico City, over 19 million. Analysts refer to such cities as megacities. A **megacity** not only has a huge population, but also has grown so fast that regular urban services cannot be provided. Slums and shantytowns are found in many megacities. Crime and corruption from the international drug trade are also found mostly in the larger cities, especially those in **Bolivia, Peru,** and **Colombia.**

The gap between the poor and the rich has remained huge in Latin America. In many Latin American countries, the poor still live in villages. Landholding and urban elites own huge estates and businesses, while peasants and the urban poor struggle to survive. They have little money for consumer goods.

Latin American women's roles have changed. Although the traditional role of homemaker continues, women have also moved into new jobs. In addition to farm labor, women have found jobs in industry and as teachers, professors, doctors, and lawyers.

✓Reading Check **Describing** What is a megacity? What are living conditions like in megacities?

The U.S. and Latin America

MAIN IDEA During the Cold War, the United States provided aid to anti-Communist regimes in Latin America.

HISTORY & YOU What other countries received aid from the United States during the Cold War? Read to learn how the United States sent troops to protect its interests in Latin America.

The United States has long played a major role in Latin America. Business investment by U.S. companies was one of the reasons the United States often intervened in Latin American affairs. U.S. investors would often pressure the U.S. government to prevent social and political change in Latin America—even if that meant backing dictators.

U.S. Military Involvement

For years, the United States had sent troops into Latin American countries to protect U.S. interests and to bolster friendly dictators. Then in the 1930s, President Franklin D. Roosevelt began a Good Neighbor policy, an effort to end such intervention (see Chapter 25).

In 1948, the states of the Western Hemisphere formed the **Organization of American States (OAS).** The OAS also emphasized the need for Latin American independence. It passed a resolution calling for an end to military action by one state in the affairs of another. The formation of the OAS, however, did not end U.S. involvement in Latin American affairs.

Fighting Communism

Why did American involvement continue? A major reason was the onset of the Cold War. American leaders became more anxious about instability in Latin America. They feared that the poverty in these countries made them ripe for Communist takeover. The Soviet Union, they concluded, would then have more power to threaten U.S. interests around the globe.

Just being accused of having a link to communism meant trouble for some Latin American presidents. For instance, Jacobo Arbenz, president of Guatemala, was overthrown in

Extending the Content

Megacities and Slums As people in Latin America have moved rapidly to cities, the cities have not been able to absorb them. Settlements on the outskirts of larger cities have developed over the years, yet many lack formal governments or services such as a municipal water supply, sewage system, or electricity. For example, about one third of Rio de Janeiro's 10 million people live in slums known as *favelas,* most of which are controlled by drug traffickers and suffer from violence associated with the drug trade. Many people have built their own houses from scrap material on steep land that is prone to mudslides and falling rock. Most of these settlers have no legal rights to the land they occupy. In recent years, the government of Rio de Janeiro has worked to improve conditions in the *favelas.*

1954 with aid from the U.S. Central Intelligence Agency. U.S. business interests had accused Arbenz of being linked to communism. Then when a Communist government took over Cuba in 1959, U.S. anxieties reached a fever pitch (see Section 2).

If it felt that Communist-backed parties were gaining power in South and Central America, the United States used its influence. Even as late as 1981, Jeanne Kirkpatrick, the U.S. ambassador to the United Nations, declared that the Soviet-Cuban Communist "menace" in Central America made it "the most important place in the world for the United States today." To fight communism, the United States provided huge amounts of military aid to support anti-Communist regimes in Latin America.

✓Reading Check **Examining** How did the Cold War impact U.S. policy in Latin America?

NATIONAL GEOGRAPHIC

MAJOR DEVELOPMENTS IN LATIN AMERICA SINCE 1945

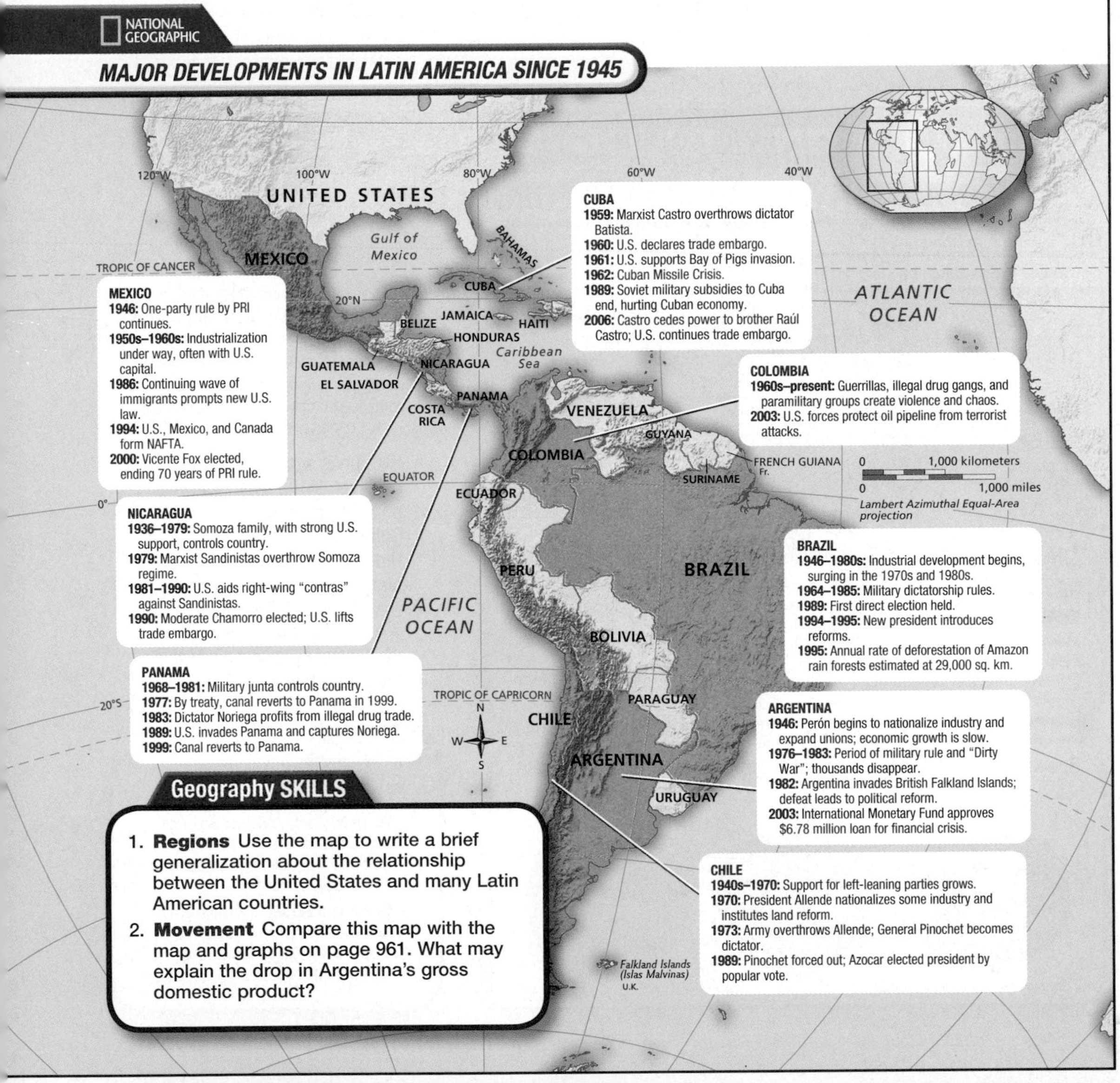

UNITED STATES
120°W
100°W
80°W
60°W
40°W
20°N
0°
20°S
TROPIC OF CANCER
EQUATOR
TROPIC OF CAPRICORN
Gulf of Mexico
Caribbean Sea
ATLANTIC OCEAN
PACIFIC OCEAN
MEXICO
BAHAMAS
CUBA
JAMAICA
HAITI
BELIZE
HONDURAS
GUATEMALA
EL SALVADOR
NICARAGUA
COSTA RICA
PANAMA
VENEZUELA
GUYANA
SURINAME
FRENCH GUIANA Fr.
COLOMBIA
ECUADOR
PERU
BRAZIL
BOLIVIA
PARAGUAY
CHILE
ARGENTINA
URUGUAY
Falkland Islands (Islas Malvinas) U.K.
N
S
E
W
0 1,000 kilometers
0 1,000 miles
Lambert Azimuthal Equal-Area projection
CUBA
1959: Marxist Castro overthrows dictator Batista.
1960: U.S. declares trade embargo.
1961: U.S. supports Bay of Pigs invasion.
1962: Cuban Missile Crisis.
1989: Soviet military subsidies to Cuba end, hurting Cuban economy.
2006: Castro cedes power to brother Raúl Castro; U.S. continues trade embargo.
MEXICO
1946: One-party rule by PRI continues.
1950s–1960s: Industrialization under way, often with U.S. capital.
1986: Continuing wave of immigrants prompts new U.S. law.
1994: U.S., Mexico, and Canada form NAFTA.
2000: Vicente Fox elected, ending 70 years of PRI rule.
COLOMBIA
1960s–present: Guerrillas, illegal drug gangs, and paramilitary groups create violence and chaos.
2003: U.S. forces protect oil pipeline from terrorist attacks.
NICARAGUA
1936–1979: Somoza family, with strong U.S. support, controls country.
1979: Marxist Sandinistas overthrow Somoza regime.
1981–1990: U.S. aids right-wing "contras" against Sandinistas.
1990: Moderate Chamorro elected; U.S. lifts trade embargo.
BRAZIL
1946–1980s: Industrial development begins, surging in the 1970s and 1980s.
1964–1985: Military dictatorship rules.
1989: First direct election held.
1994–1995: New president introduces reforms.
1995: Annual rate of deforestation of Amazon rain forests estimated at 29,000 sq. km.
PANAMA
1968–1981: Military junta controls country.
1977: By treaty, canal reverts to Panama in 1999.
1983: Dictator Noriega profits from illegal drug trade.
1989: U.S. invades Panama and captures Noriega.
1999: Canal reverts to Panama.
ARGENTINA
1946: Perón begins to nationalize industry and expand unions; economic growth is slow.
1976–1983: Period of military rule and "Dirty War"; thousands disappear.
1982: Argentina invades British Falkland Islands; defeat leads to political reform.
2003: International Monetary Fund approves $6.78 million loan for financial crisis.
CHILE
1940s–1970: Support for left-leaning parties grows.
1970: President Allende nationalizes some industry and institutes land reform.
1973: Army overthrows Allende; General Pinochet becomes dictator.
1989: Pinochet forced out; Azocar elected president by popular vote.

Geography SKILLS

1. **Regions** Use the map to write a brief generalization about the relationship between the United States and many Latin American countries.
2. **Movement** Compare this map with the map and graphs on page 961. What may explain the drop in Argentina's gross domestic product?

C Critical Thinking

Making Inferences Ask students to research Arbenz's actions, and then write a paragraph on whether they think U.S. fears were well-founded. **AL**

For additional practice on this skill, see the **Skills Handbook**.

W Writing Support

Expository Writing Have students write a paragraph that explains why the United States saw Cuba as a danger to the region. **OL**

✓Reading Check

Answer: Believing that communism might develop in the region, the U.S. increased economic and military aid to Latin America.

Geography SKILLS

Answers:
1. The United States has been involved both economically and militarily in many Latin American countries.
2. the 2003 financial crisis

Differentiated Instruction

Leveled Activities

BL Differentiated Instruction Activity, URB p. 93

Differentiated Instruction Activity 29

Accessing Cultural Art

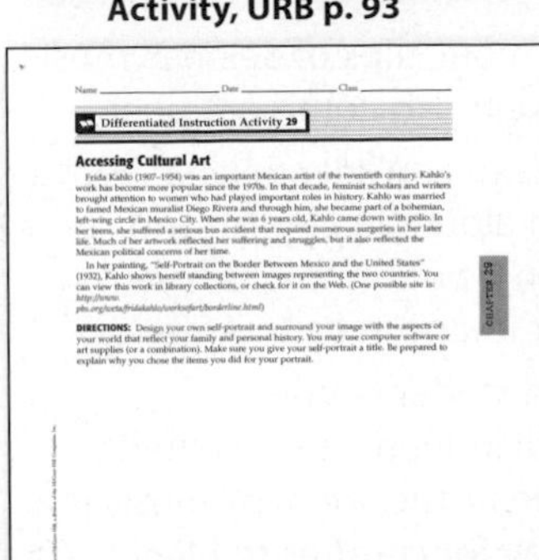

OL Cooperative Learning Activity, URB p. 107

Cooperative Learning Activity 29

Drawing a New Map of Latin America

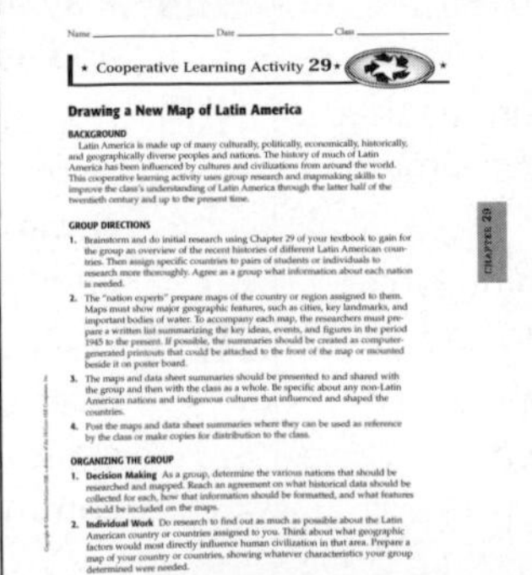

AL Historical Analysis Skills Activity, URB p. 92

Historical Analysis Skills Activity 29

Characterizing Current Events

ELL English Learner Activity, URB p. 95

English Learner Activity 29

Latin America

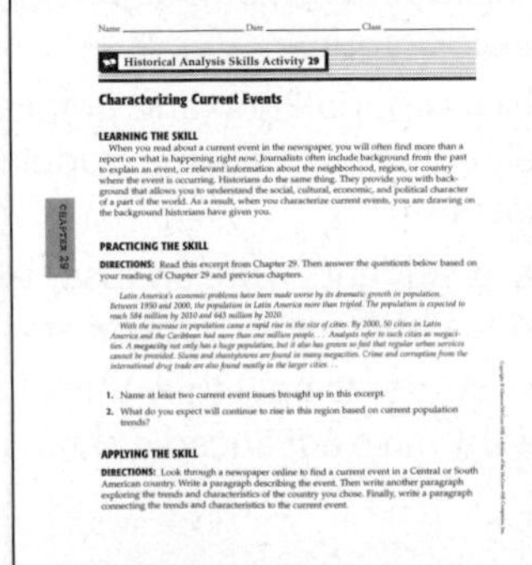

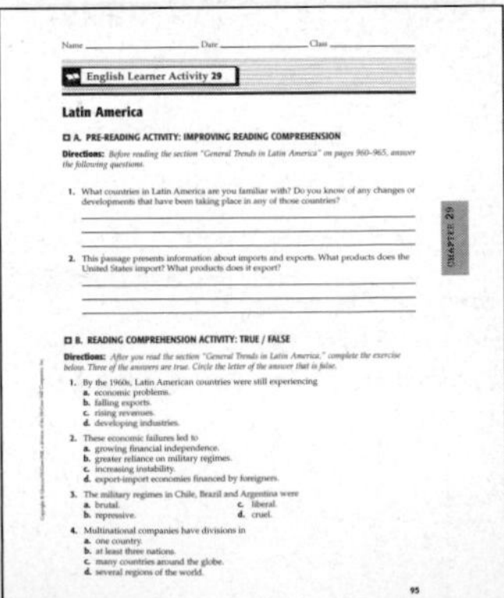

W Writing Support

Personal Writing Ask students to select an American artist or writer and write an essay describing the individual's work and what they think of it. Ask volunteers to share their essays and then engage the class in a discussion about what differences they think exist in the roles of artists and writers in the United States compared to Latin America and why. **OL**

Answers:

1. The Southwest. These states border Latin America.
2. Hispanics are the fastest growing minority group in the United States. This is expected to continue. By 2050, Hispanics are expected to make up 24 percent of the total U.S. population.

Latin American Culture

MAIN IDEA Latin American artists and writers are important national figures.

HISTORY & YOU What artists and writers have influenced you? Read to learn about Latin American artists.

W Twentieth-century Latin American writers and artists have played important roles in their society. Their work is seen as expressing the hopes of the people. Because of this, artists and writers hold high status in Latin American society.

Literature

In the 1940s, Latin American writers made a significant break from realism and explored other techniques. They developed a unique form of expression called **magic realism.** Magic realism brings together realistic events with dreamlike or fantasy backgrounds. The rules of ordinary life are suspended in order to comment on a national or social situation.

Perhaps the foremost example of magic realism is *One Hundred Years of Solitude*, a novel by **Gabriel García Márquez,** a Colombian writer, who won the Nobel

CONNECTING TO THE UNITED STATES

A GROWING HISPANIC POPULATION

Hispanic Population by State, 2000

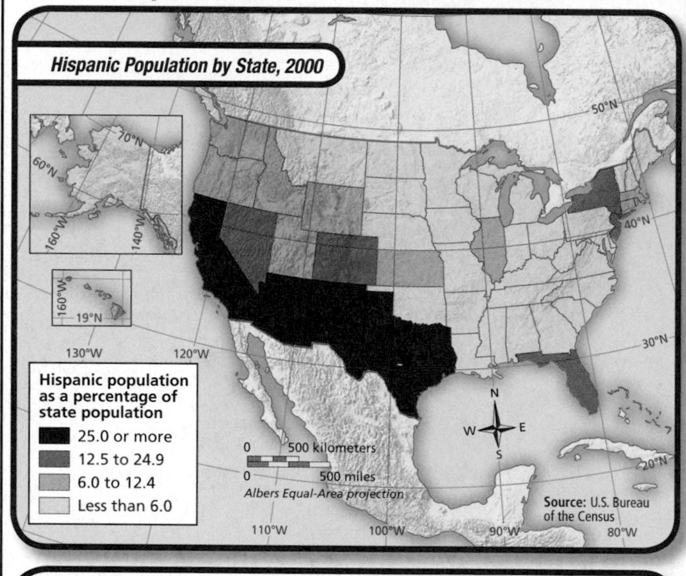

Political and economic instability in the second half of the twentieth century caused many Latin Americans to immigrate to the United States. Today, Hispanics, also referred to as Latinos, are the largest and fastest-growing minority group in the United States, predicted to make up 24 percent of the population in 2050. Right now:

- Hispanics account for about one-half of the total national population growth.
- California has the largest total Hispanic population of all states, followed by Texas.
- New Mexico is the state in which Hispanics comprise the highest proportion of the total population.

Growing Hispanic Population in the United States, 1990–2050

1990: 9%
2005: 14%
2050 (projected): 24%

Source: U.S. Bureau of the Census.

1. **Identifying** Which area of the United States has the largest percentage Hispanic population? Why?
2. **Summarizing** What trends are expected in Hispanic population growth in the United States?

Differentiated Instruction

World Art and Music Activity, URB p. 117

Drawing Conclusions

Objective: Draw conclusions about the legacy of Selena.

Focus: Ask students what made Selena and her music unique.

Teach: Discuss population and political changes that helped Selena become popular in the United States.

Assess: Have students write an essay explaining why Selena became so popular at a young age.

Close: Ask students how they think Selena's career might have advanced if she had lived.

Differentiated Instruction Strategies

BL Play one or more clips of Selena's music and ask students to comment on it.

AL Ask students to consider Selena's move to record an album in English and comment on how this might have affected her image in Latin America.

ELL Discuss with students how international influences combined to create *Tejano* music and why music is a common way for cultures to blend.

Prize in literature in 1982. In this story of the fictional town of Macondo, the point of view slips back and forth between fact and fantasy. Villagers are not surprised when a local priest rises into the air and floats, for example. Yet when the same villagers are introduced to magnets, telescopes, and magnifying glasses, they are dumbfounded by what they consider to be magic. According to Márquez, fantasy and fact depend on one's point of view.

Whatever styles they use, Latin American writers write about their national reality. Some look back on the past with hatred, rather than with affection. Others, like the Chilean novelist Jorge Edwards, use the theme of the clash of generations to expose the corruption of their country. One writer, the Argentinean novelist Julio Cortázar, uses the element of a game or play that defies societal rules and conventions.

Among Latin American poets, perhaps the best known is Gabriela Mistral from Chile. She began writing poetry as a village schoolteacher and taught school for many years until her poetry made her famous. Lyrical and emotional, her poetry expresses themes of childhood, love, and yearning. In 1945, Mistral became the first Latin American to receive the Nobel Prize in literature.

Art and Architecture

Latin American art and architecture were strongly influenced by international styles after World War II. In painting, abstract styles were more predominant. In architecture, the Bauhaus and Modernist styles were common.

Perhaps the most notable example of modern architecture can be seen in Brasília, the capital of Brazil, which was built in the 1950s and 1960s. The government intended for Brasília to attract development to the interior of Brazil and to lessen the population pressures in coastal Rio de Janeiro. **R**

Brazilian architect **Oscar Niemeyer** was appointed chief architect for the new capital. Niemeyer already had an international reputation as one of the two architects who designed the United Nations building. Niemeyer's outlook is evident in his description of his work in Brasília:

PRIMARY SOURCE

"... I did my very best in the structures, trying to make them different with their columns narrow, so narrow that the palaces would seem to barely touch the ground. And I set them apart from the facades, creating an empty space through which, as I bent over my work table, I could see myself walking, imagining their forms and the different resulting points of view they would provoke."

—Oscar Niemeyer

✓Reading Check **Identifying** What novel is the foremost example of magic realism?

Vocabulary

1. **Explain** the significance of: Chile, Brazil, Argentina, multinational corporations, consent, ongoing, megacity, Bolivia, Peru, Colombia, Organization of American States (OAS), magic realism, Gabriel García Márquez, Oscar Niemeyer.

Main Ideas

2. **List** the economic challenges in Latin America since 1945. Use a diagram like the one below to make your list.

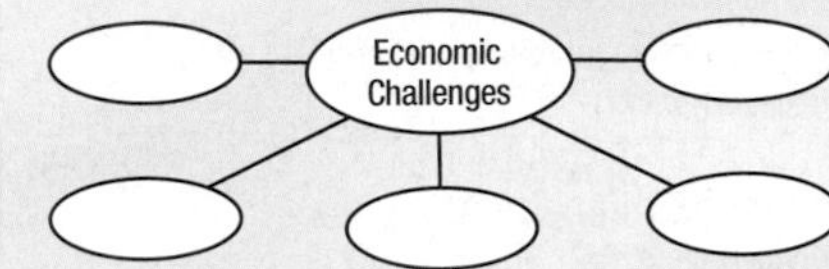

3. **Explain** why the formation of the Organization of American States (OAS) did not end U.S. involvement in Latin America.
4. **Name** at least two well-known Latin American writers.

Critical Thinking

5. **The BIG Idea** **Determining Cause and Effect** How did the rapid population growth in many Latin American countries cause problems for their political and economic systems?
6. **Making Connections** How can industrializing too quickly, as in the case of Latin America, lead to an economic decline?
7. **Analyzing Visuals** What is the significance of the colored regions on the map on page 963?

Writing About History

8. **Descriptive Writing** Research further the elements of magic realism and then write a short story using that style.

History ONLINE

For help with the concepts in this section of *Glencoe World History*, go to glencoe.com and click Study Central™.

965

R Reading Strategy

Using Context Clues Ask: Why was Brasília a perfect place to showcase modern architecture? *(Because it was constructed in the 1950s and 1960s, it could be designed using modern ideas in all buildings.)* **OL**

✓Reading Check

Answer: *One Hundred Years of Solitude,* by Gabriel García Márquez

Assess

History ONLINE

Study Central provides summaries, interactive games, and online graphic organizers to help students review content.

Close

Making Generalizations

Ask: How did the relationship between the United States and Latin America change during the period? *(The United States became more involved in Latin American economics and politics.)* **OL**

Answers

1. Definitions for the vocabulary words are found in the section and the Glossary.
2. Economic Challenges: dependent on United States, Europe, and Japan; return to export-import economies financed by foreigners; presence of multinational corporations; growing foreign debt; fall in wages; rising inflation
3. When the Cold War began, the United States sent troops to Latin America to protect its interests.
4. Answers may include Gabriel García Márquez, Jorge Edwards, Julio Cortázar, and Gabriela Mistral.
5. Cities and slums grew rapidly, creating a gap between rich and poor. Peasants and the urban poor struggled to survive. These conditions strained economies and led to political instability and repressive regimes.
6. results in too much foreign debt; businesses crumble; wages fall; unemployment and inflation rise
7. These are the regions for which major developments since 1945 are listed.
8. Stories should use elements of magic realism.

Focus

Bellringer
Daily Focus Transparency 29.2

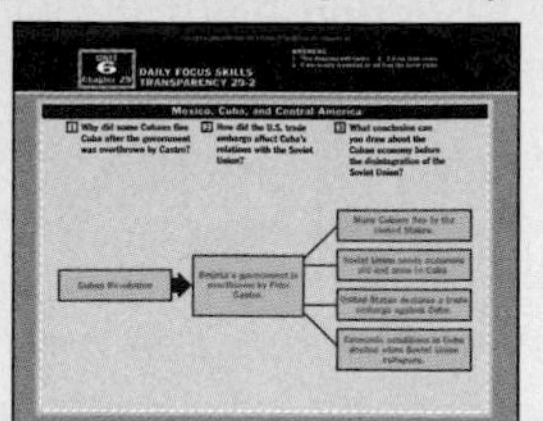

GUIDE TO READING

Answers to Graphic:
El Salvador: government controlled by wealthy elite and military, U.S. supported Salvadoran military; **Nicaragua:** Somoza family ruled with U.S. support, U.S. supported contras in war; **Panama:** wealthy oligarchy ruled with U.S. support, National Guard takeover, Noriega took control, U.S. sent troops to arrest Noriega; **Guatemala:** U.S. supports military dictators, death squads target Mayans

Section Spotlight Video

To generate student interest and provide a springboard for class discussion, access the Chapter 29, Section 2 video at glencoe.com or on the video DVD.

SECTION 2

Mexico, Cuba, and Central America

GUIDE TO READING

The BIG Idea
Order and Security Mexico and Central America faced political and economic crises after World War II, making national progress difficult.

Content Vocabulary
- privatization *(p. 966)*
- trade embargo *(p. 969)*
- contras *(p. 971)*

Academic Vocabulary
- regulation *(p. 967)*
- unreliable *(p. 969)*

People and Places
- Institutional Revolutionary Party (PRI) *(p. 966)*
- Vicente Fox *(p. 967)*
- Fidel Castro *(p. 968)*
- Havana *(p. 968)*
- El Salvador *(p. 969)*
- Nicaragua *(p. 970)*
- Panama *(p. 971)*
- Manuel Noriega *(p. 971)*
- Guatemala *(p. 971)*

Reading Strategy
Comparing As you read, use a table like the one below to identify the political and economic challenges faced by El Salvador, Nicaragua, Panama, and Guatemala after 1945.

El Salvador	Nicaragua	Panama	Guatemala

Throughout the twentieth century, Mexico and Central America experienced political turmoil and economic crises. Fidel Castro set up a Marxist government in Cuba, and military or military-dominated dictators ruled most of the Central American countries. The political and economic crises, often ignited by U.S. intervention, hampered national development.

Mexico

MAIN IDEA Political and economic problems have troubled Mexico since the Mexican Revolution.

HISTORY & YOU Do economic issues influence American politics? Read how economic troubles led to political change in Mexico.

The Mexican Revolution in the early 1900s created a political order that remained stable for many years. The official political party of the Mexican Revolution—the **Institutional Revolutionary Party,** or **PRI**—came to dominate Mexico. Every six years, leaders of the PRI chose the party's presidential candidate, who was then elected by the people. During the 1950s and 1960s, steady economic growth led to real gains in wages in Mexico.

Protests

At the end of the 1960s, students began to protest Mexico's one-party government system. On October 2, 1968, university students gathered in Mexico City to protest government policies. Police forces opened fire and killed hundreds. The next two presidents, Luis Echeverría and José López Portillo, made political reforms and new political parties emerged. Greater freedom of debate in the press and universities was allowed.

Debt Crisis

In the late 1970s, vast new reserves of oil were discovered in Mexico. The government became more dependent on revenues from foreign oil sales. Then, when world oil prices dropped in the mid-1980s, Mexico was no longer able to make payments on its foreign debt. The government was forced to adopt new economic policies. One of these policies was **privatization,** the sale of government-owned companies to private firms.

Mexico's debt rose even more after a hurricane caused massive destruction in the Yucatán peninsula in 1988. Damage alone was estimated at $880 million.

Resource Manager

R Reading Strategies	C Critical Thinking	D Differentiated Instruction	W Writing Support	S Skill Practice
Teacher Edition • Questioning, p. 967 • Act. Prior Know., p. 969 • Summarizing, p. 969 • Determining Importance, p. 971 **Additional Resources** • Guid. Read. Act., URB p. 123 • Read. Ess. & Note-Taking Guide, p. 322	**Teacher Edition** • Pred. Consequences, p. 968 • Making Generalizations, p. 970 **Additional Resources** • Crit. Think. Act., URB p. 102 • People in World Hist., URB p. 114 • Section Quiz, p. 362	**Teacher Edition** • Verbal/Linguistic, p. 968 **Additional Resources** • Read. Skills Act., URB p. 91 • Mapping Hist. Act., URB p. 105 • Read. Strat. for SS, p. 77	**Teacher Edition** • Expository Writing, p. 969 **Additional Resources** • Hist. Sig. Act. URB p. 106 • Linking Past/Present Act., URB p. 112	**Teacher Edition** • Using Geo. Skills, p. 967 **Additional Resources** • Skills Reinforc. Act., URB p. 101 • Hist. & Geo. Act., URB p. 103

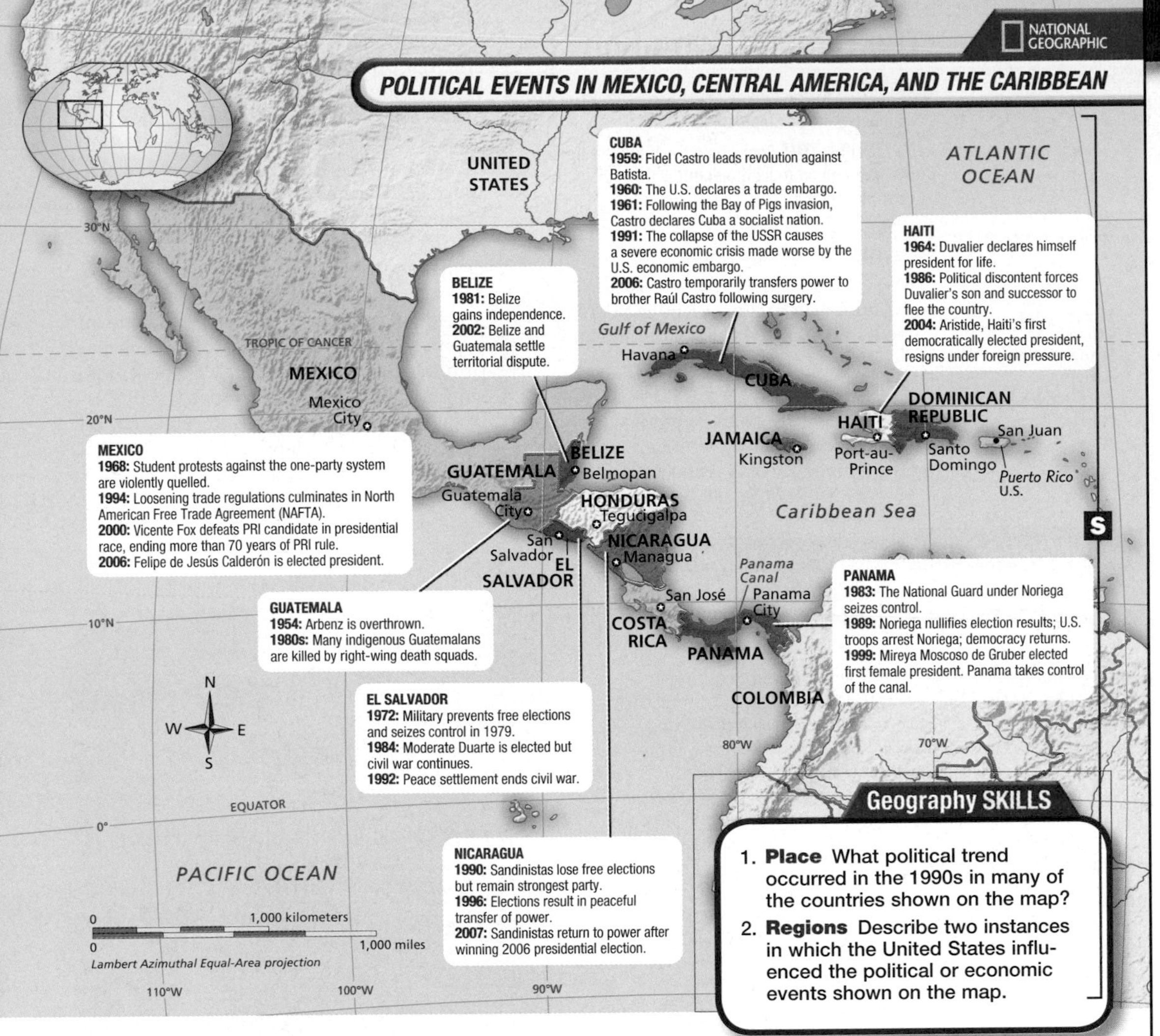

Geography SKILLS

1. **Place** What political trend occurred in the 1990s in many of the countries shown on the map?
2. **Regions** Describe two instances in which the United States influenced the political or economic events shown on the map.

The next president, Carlos Salinas de Gortari, sped up privatization to relieve the debt crisis. He also changed some restrictive trade **regulations** in order to attract more foreign investors. In 1992, de Gortari began working with the U.S. president and the Canadian prime minister to form the North American Free Trade Agreement (NAFTA). That agreement went into effect in 1994.

NAFTA did not cure Mexico's economic problems, however. The continuing debt crisis, rising unemployment, and corruption scandals increased dissatisfaction with the government. Support for the PRI dropped. In 2000, **Vicente Fox** defeated the PRI candidate for the presidency. Fox's election ended more than seven decades of PRI rule. Fox's successor, Felipe de Jesús Calderón, continued with plans to boost Mexico's economic growth.

✓Reading Check **Evaluating** How did its oil industry affect Mexico's economy?

R Reading Strategy

Questioning **Ask:** Why has the United States never gone through the process of privatization? *(There has never been public ownership of businesses.)* **OL**

S Skill Practice

Using Geography Skills **Ask:** What country seems to have suffered the least from political upheavals? *(Belize—no transfers of power are noted)*

Geography SKILLS

Answers:

1. There was a general trend toward democracy.
2. Answers may include Noriega arrested in Panama; U.S. economic embargo of Cuba; NAFTA.

✓Reading Check

Answer: The government became dependent upon oil revenues. When oil prices dropped, Mexico could not pay its foreign debt. This led to new economic policies such as privatization.

Hands-On Chapter Project Step 2

Creating a Poster about Important Latin Americans

Step 2: Illustrating Economic and Political Changes in Mexico, Cuba, and Central America Pairs of students will add to the posters they began in Section 1.

Directions: Write the Big Idea on the board. Tell students that in this section they will add information to their posters about significant individuals who were involved in conflicts in Mexico, Cuba, and Central America during the period. Students should research their chosen subjects in the library or online, find images, and include details about the conflicts and the people involved, the economic and political changes that occurred, and U.S. involvement and reactions. **OL**

(Chapter Project is continued in Section 3.)

D Differentiated Instruction

Verbal/Linguistic Ask students to write a short propaganda pamphlet or radio broadcast that might have been used to win support for Castro. AL

C Critical Thinking

Predicting Consequences
Ask: In what ways do you think the presence of Castro's opponents in the United States would affect Americans' views toward him? *(They might contribute to strong and consistent opposition to Castro.)* OL

CRITICAL THINKING SKILLS

Answers:
1. Before the revolution, the United States controlled much of Cuba's economy; since the revolution, the two countries have had a strained relationship.
2. **Cuba:** Became a communist state, Castro became leader, improvements in healthcare and education; **Rest of the world:** Ongoing conflict with the United States, inspired Communist revolutions elsewhere in the region

Additional Support

The Cuban Revolution

MAIN IDEA The Cuban Revolution established the communist dictatorship of Fidel Castro.

HISTORY & YOU Recall how Lenin led the Russian Revolution. Read to learn about Castro's role in the Cuban Revolution.

History ONLINE **Student Web Activity—** Visit glencoe.com and complete the activity about Fidel Castro.

In the 1950s, an opposition movement arose in Cuba. It aimed to overthrow the government of the dictator Fulgencio Batista, who had controlled Cuba since 1934.

Castro's Rise to Power

The leader of the movement was a man named **Fidel Castro.** While a law student at the University of Havana, he had become a revolutionary. On July 26, 1953, Castro and his brother Raúl led a band of 165 young people in an attack on the Moncada army camp at Santiago de Cuba. The attack was a disaster. While Fidel and Raúl escaped, they were later captured and sentenced to prison for 15 years. Batista released Fidel and Raúl after 11 months.

After their release, the Castro brothers fled to the Sierra Maestra mountains in Mexico. There they teamed up with a small band of revolutionaries. Castro poured out a stream of propaganda with a small radio station and printing press. As the rebels gained more support, the Batista regime collapsed. Castro's revolutionaries seized **Havana** on January 3, 1959. Many Cubans who disagreed with Castro fled to the United States.

INFOGRAPHICS — PRIMARY SOURCE
Fidel Castro's Cuban Revolution

At the time of the Cuban Revolution, U.S. and other foreign investors owned 75 percent of Cuba's fertile land, 90 percent of its public services, and 40 percent of the sugar industry. A corrupt dictator, Fulgencio Batista used open displays of brutality to maintain control, and poverty and unemployment were widespread.

Anti-Batista and anti-American feelings led to support for Fidel Castro and the Cuban Revolution. Castro rose to power in 1959 and has remained Cuba's leader ever since. His Communist regime has brought some social improvements to Cuba, but Cubans still lack freedom.

CAUSES
- Corrupt dictatorship led by Batista
- Economic dependence on United States

↓

Cuban Revolution

↓

EFFECTS
- Led Cuba to become a Communist state
- Began Fidel Castro's half-century rule in Cuba
- Led to improvements in health care and education
- Led to declining economic conditions in Cuba
- Inspired Communist revolutions elsewhere in the region
- Led to ongoing conflict with the United States, including the Bay of Pigs invasion and a long-standing trade embargo

Fidel Castro and two guerrillas at their mountain hideout during the insurgency against dictator Fulgencio Batista

CRITICAL THINKING SKILLS

1. **Explaining** How did the Cuban Revolution change the relationship between Cuba and the United States?
2. **Determining Cause and Effect** What has been the impact of the Cuban Revolution on Cuba and the rest of the world?

Activity: Interdisciplinary Connection

Language Arts Discuss Castro's movement to overthrow Batista. After Castro's first attack on the Moncada army at Santiago de Cuba in 1953, he was arrested and tried in court. During the trial he acted as his own attorney and defended himself in a famous speech that attacked the politics and corruption of the Batista government. Provide students with a copy of Castro's speech to read or have them research it in the library. **Ask:** Was Castro correct in his concluding statement when he said, "History will absolve me"? *(Some students may agree because of the brutality and corruption of Batista's government; others may say that Castro's own record has been too poor for him to be absolved.)* **Ask:** How can a speech like Castro's help shape people's opinions? *(Answers may include that it can provide a slogan and a cause for a movement.)* AL

Relations with the United States

Relations between Cuba and the United States quickly deteriorated when Castro's Communist regime began to receive aid from the Soviet Union. Arms from Eastern Europe also began to arrive in Cuba. In October 1960, the United States declared a **trade embargo,** a policy prohibiting trade with Cuba. Just three months later all diplomatic relations with Cuba were broken.

Soon after that, in April 1961, U.S. president John F. Kennedy supported an attempt to overthrow Castro's government. When the invasion at the Bay of Pigs failed, the Soviets made an even greater commitment to Cuba. In December 1961, Castro declared himself a Marxist, drawing even closer to the Soviet Union. The Soviets began placing nuclear missiles in Cuba in 1962, leading to a showdown with the United States.

The Cuban missile crisis made Castro realize that the Soviet Union had been **unreliable.** If the revolutionary movement was to survive, the Cubans would have to start a social revolution in the rest of Latin America. They would do this by starting guerrilla wars and encouraging peasants to overthrow the old regimes. Ernesto Ché Guevara, an Argentinean and an ally of Castro, led such a war in Bolivia. He was killed by the Bolivian army in the fall of 1967. Cuba's strategy failed. R1

Nevertheless, in Cuba, Castro's Marxist regime continued, but with mixed results. The Cuban people did secure some social gains, such as free medical services for all citizens. With improvements in education, illiteracy was nearly eliminated.

Yet the Cuban economy continued to rely on Soviet aid and the sale of Cuban sugar to Soviet bloc countries. When these Communist regimes collapsed in 1989, Cuba lost their support. As a result, Cuba's economy went into a tailspin. Castro's measures to improve the economy have not entirely succeeded. R2

✓Reading Check **Describing** How was Castro's Cuba affected by the collapse of Communist governments in Eastern Europe?

Central America

MAIN IDEA Fearing the spread of communism, the United States intervened in Central American politics during the 1970s and 1980s.

HISTORY & YOU Why might the United States have feared the spread of communism into Central America? Read to learn how the Cold War affected U.S. policy in Central America.

Central America includes seven countries: Costa Rica, Nicaragua, Honduras, El Salvador, Panama, Belize, and Guatemala. Economically, Central America has historically depended on the export of bananas, coffee, and cotton. Prices for these products have varied over time, however, creating economic crises. In addition, a huge gulf between a wealthy elite and poor peasants has created a climate of instability in the region.

The U.S. fear of the spread of communism often led to U.S. support for repressive regimes in Central America. The involvement of the United States was especially evident in the nations of El Salvador, Nicaragua, Panama, and Guatemala.

El Salvador

After World War II, the wealthy elite and the military controlled the government in **El Salvador.** The rise of an urban middle class led to hope for a more democratic government. The army, however, refused to accept the results of free elections that were held in 1972.

World attention focused on El Salvador in the late 1970s and the 1980s, when the country was rocked by a bitter civil war. Marxist-led, leftist guerrillas and right-wing groups battled one another. The Catholic Church became a main target, and a number of priests were killed or tortured, among them Archbishop Oscar Romero. Death squads killed anyone they thought a threat to their interests. W

When U.S. president Ronald Reagan claimed evidence of "communist interference in El Salvador," the United States began to provide weapons and training to the Salvadoran army to defeat the guerrillas. The hope was to bring stability to the country, but the killings continued.

R1 Reading Strategy

Activating Prior Knowledge Ask students to review the text in Chapter 27 about the Cuban missile crisis and write a paragraph that explains why Cuba judged the Soviet Union to be unreliable. **OL**

R2 Reading Strategy

Summarizing Ask students to re-read the bracketed text and list the strengths and weaknesses of Castro's rule in Cuba. *(Strengths: improvements in healthcare and education; Weaknesses: poor economic strategies)* **BL**

W Writing Support

Expository Ask students to write one or two paragraphs describing the traditional role of the Catholic Church in Latin America and the new role of leaders such as Archbishop Romero. They should conduct additional research as needed to identify Romero's position as related to the government at the time. **AL**

✓Reading Check

Answer: Cuba lost the market for some of its products, and its economy went into a tailspin.

Differentiated Instruction

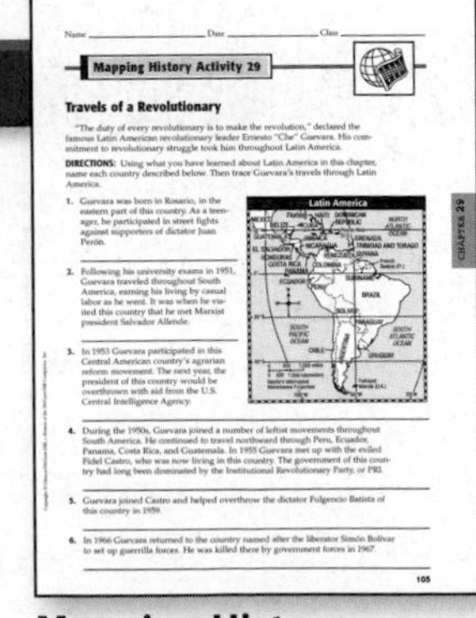

Mapping History Activity, URB p. 105

Drawing Conclusions

Objective: Draw conclusions about Ché Guevara.

Focus: Note Guevara's travels and activities throughout Latin America.

Teach: Ask students to identify common problems faced by the countries Guevara visited.

Assess: Ask students to draw conclusions about Guevara's attitudes toward U.S. involvement in Latin America and deliver a speech representing this view.

Close: Ask students how they think Latin Americans would respond to Guevara today.

Differentiated Instruction Strategies

BL Ask students why Guevara could communicate easily in the countries he visited.

AL Ask students to research Guevara's attitudes toward a more unified Latin America and compare them with those of Simón Bolívar.

ELL Ask students to explain why Guevara is called a revolutionary.

C Critical Thinking

Making Generalizations

Ask: Why do you think the United States supported the Somoza family for many years? *(They were allied with U.S. business interests, and they were anti-Communist.)* **OL**

For additional practice on this skill, see the **Skills Handbook**.

CRITICAL THINKING SKILLS

Answers:

1. Ships can pass through from the Atlantic to the Pacific. They would have to make a much longer journey around South America otherwise.
2. In Cuba, the United States invaded the Bay of Pigs; in Panama, U.S. policy on the canal was characterized by diplomacy.

TURNING POINT

THE PANAMA CANAL TREATY

Since the failed Bay of Pigs invasion, the U.S. policy in Latin America generally has been driven more by diplomacy than by military action. In Panama, for example, diplomacy allowed for the peaceful transfer of control of the Panama Canal.

The United States had controlled the Panama Canal since its creation in 1904. As the shortest water passage from the Atlantic to the Pacific Oceans, the canal was extremely important strategically and economically. Yet the desire to end U.S. control had long been an overriding theme in Panamanian politics.

After years of negotiations, U.S. president Jimmy Carter and General Omar Torrijos of Panama finally signed a treaty in 1977. As outlined in the treaty, control of the canal transferred to Panama on December 31, 1999.

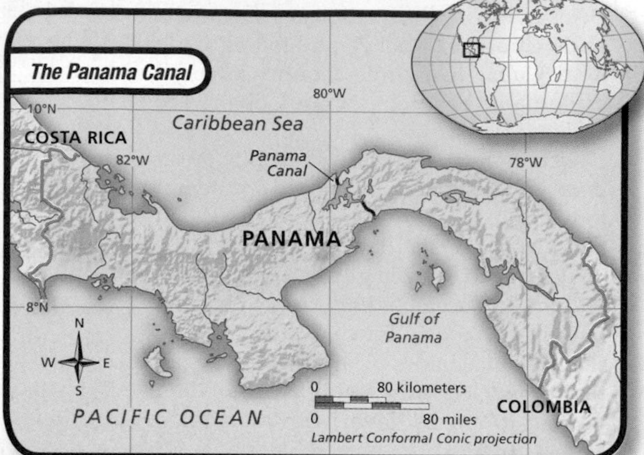

◀ President Carter, Organization of American States secretary general Alejandro Orfila, and General Torrijos at the signing of the Panama Canal Treaty in 1977

CRITICAL THINKING SKILLS

1. **Evaluating** Why is the Panama Canal strategically important?
2. **Contrasting** How did the United States's actions in Cuba differ from its actions in Panama?

In 1984, a moderate, José Duarte, was elected president. The unrest in El Salvador cut short Duarte's efforts at political, social, and economic reforms. Nor could Duarte stop the savage killing. By the early 1990s, at least 75,000 people were dead. A 1992 peace settlement ended the war.

Duarte did not live to see his hope for peace fulfilled. After transferring power to his successor, Duarte said that his government had "laid the foundation for democracy in this country." Duarte died in 1990.

Nicaragua

In **Nicaragua,** the Somoza family seized control of the government in 1937 and maintained control for the next 45 years. It began with Anastasio Somoza Garcia's induction as president, followed by his **C** two sons. Over most of this period, the Somoza regime had the support of the United States. The Somozas enriched themselves at the expense of the Nicaraguan people and used murder and torture to silence opposition.

Differentiated Instruction

Leveled Activities

BL Reading Skills Activity, URB p. 91

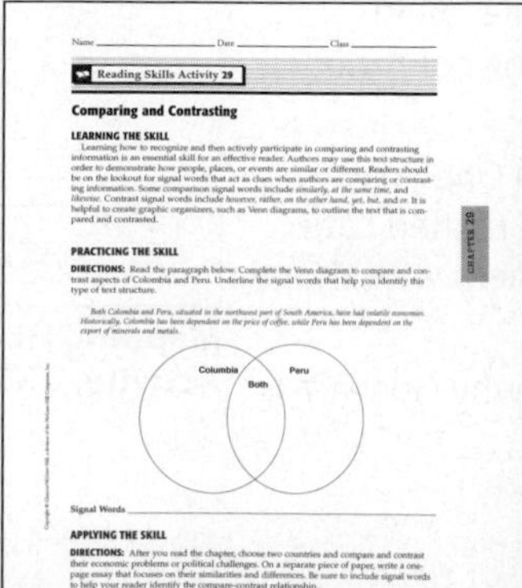

OL Critical Thinking Skills Activity, URB p. 102

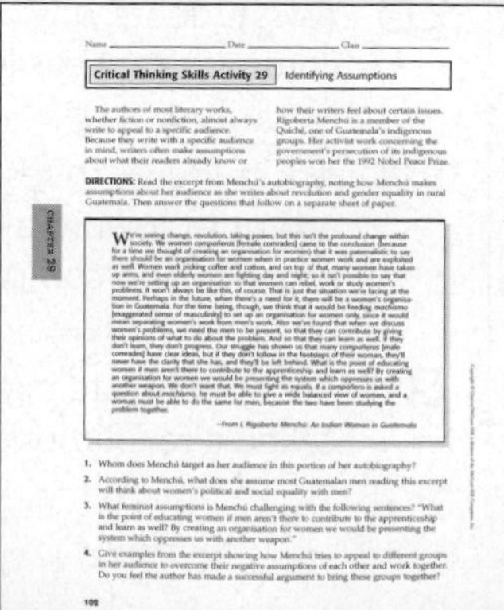

AL History and Geography Activity, URB p. 103

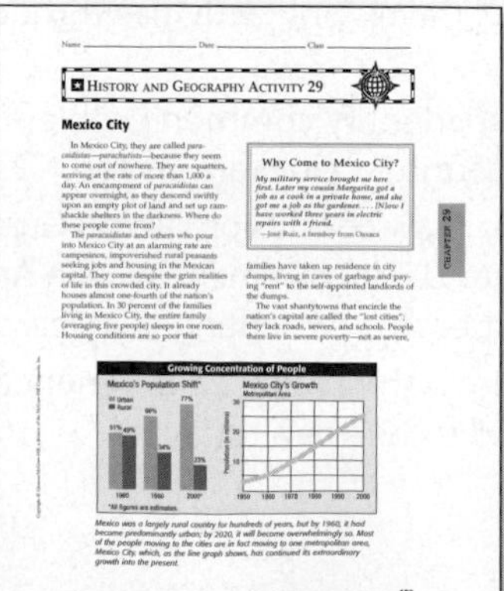

ELL Reading Strategies for Social Studies, p. 77

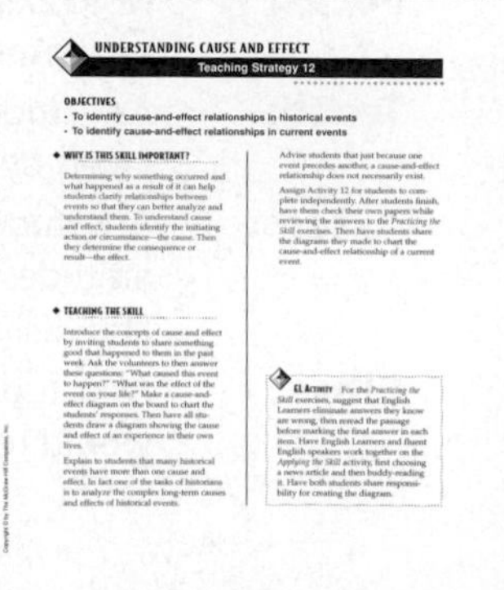

By 1979, the United States, under President Jimmy Carter, had grown unwilling to support the corrupt regime. In that same year, Marxist guerrilla forces known as the Sandinista National Liberation Front won a number of military victories against government forces and gained control of the country. Soon, a group opposed to the Sandinistas' policies, called the **contras,** began to try to overthrow the new government. Worried by the Sandinistas' alignment with the Soviet Union, the United States supported the contras.

The war waged by the contras undermined support for the Sandinistas. In 1990, the Sandinistas, led by Daniel Ortega, agreed to free elections and lost to a coalition headed by Violeta Barrios de Chamorro, who became Nicaragua's first female president. After 16 years out of power, the Sandinistas won new elections in 2006 and Daniel Ortega became president in January 2007.

Panama and Guatemala

Panama became a nation in 1903 when it broke away from Colombia with help from the United States. In return for this aid, the United States was able to build the Panama Canal and gained influence over the government and economy of Panama. A wealthy oligarchy ruled with U.S. support. After 1968, military leaders of Panama's National Guard were in control. One of these, **Manuel Noriega,** became so involved in the drug trade that President George H. W. Bush sent U.S. troops to Panama in 1989. Noriega was later sent to prison in the United States for drug trafficking.

A major issue for Panamanians was finally settled in 1999 when Panama took control of the Panama Canal. The terms for this change of control had been set in a 1977 treaty with the United States. **R**

In 1954, with support from the United States, Jacobo Arbenz of **Guatemala** was overthrown. A series of military or military-dominated dictators ruled the country for years. Guerrilla forces began forming to oppose the government. Rios Montt, president during the early 1980s, responded by using military action and economic reforms to defeat the guerrillas. As in El Salvador, right-wing death squads began attacking anyone they believed belonged to the opposition.

The indigenous people of Guatemala, the descendants of the ancient Maya, were the main target. The government massacred large numbers of Maya simply because it believed they supported the guerrillas. Entire Maya communities were uprooted, separated, or put under military control. The government killed as many as 200,000 people, mostly unarmed Maya. Many others fled to Mexico as refugees.

✓Reading Check **Summarizing** What underlying factors led to conflicts in Central America from the 1970s to the 1990s?

SECTION 2 REVIEW

Vocabulary

1. **Explain** the significance of: Institutional Revolutionary Party (PRI), privatization, regulation, Vicente Fox, Fidel Castro, Havana, trade embargo, unreliable, El Salvador, Nicaragua, contras, Panama, Manuel Noriega, Guatemala.

Main Ideas

2. **Illustrate** how Mexico has reacted to political and economic crises since World War II. Use a diagram like the one below to make your illustration.

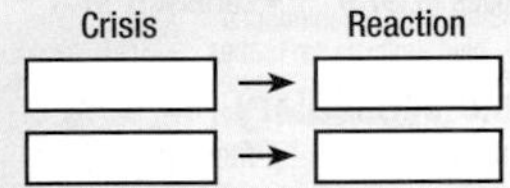

3. **Explain** why the Cubans attempted to spur revolution in the rest of Latin America.
4. **Name** at least three Central American countries in which the United States has intervened.

Critical Thinking

5. **The BIG Idea** **Making Connections** Were the problems that Mexico and Central America had after 1945 due more to politics or to economics? Explain.
6. **Determining Cause and Effect** Why did Cuba's economy suffer after 1989?
7. **Analyzing Visuals** Examine the photograph of Fidel Castro on page 968. What does the setting of the photograph and Castro's appearance tell you about his struggle?

Writing About History

8. **Persuasive Writing** The United States has increasingly tried to negotiate conflicts in Latin America using economic tools rather than military force. Research the trade embargo imposed upon Cuba. Write a persuasive argument for or against this embargo.

History ONLINE
For help with the concepts in this section of *Glencoe World History,* go to glencoe.com and click Study Central™.

971

R Reading Strategy

Determining Importance

Ask: Why was 1999 an important year in Panama? *(It was the year that Panama took control of the Panama Canal because of a 1977 treaty with the United States.)* **OL**

✓Reading Check

Answer: fluctuating prices for exports; a large gulf between the wealthy and the poor

Assess

History ONLINE

Study Central provides summaries, interactive games, and online graphic organizers to help students review content.

Close

Making Generalizations

Ask: What was the role of economic issues in Latin American changes during the period? *(The nations struggled with poor economic conditions; revolutions were intended to distribute wealth more equally.)* **OL**

Answers

1. Definitions for the vocabulary words are found in the section and the Glossary.
2. **Crisis:** Students protested government policies and one-party system; drop in oil prices; **Reaction:** Police forces opened fire and killed hundreds, PRI leaders grew concerned about need for change in system; Mexico unable to make payments on foreign debt
3. to keep the revolutionary movement alive in Cuba
4. El Salvador, Nicaragua, Panama, Guatemala
5. Students should demonstrate an understanding of how economic problems and political problems affected progress in Mexico and Central America.
6. Communist regimes collapsed in the Soviet Union; Cuba lost support.
7. The revolution was a violent guerrilla conflict fought under difficult conditions.
8. Students should write a persuasive, fact-based argument.

R Reading Strategy

Activating Prior Knowledge Ask students to review their knowledge of the Brownshirts, referring to Ch. 24 as necessary. Discuss the short- and long-term effects of using terror to control people. **OL**

W Writing Support

Personal Writing Ask students to write one or two paragraphs explaining their thoughts on the use of military actions and propaganda to sway public opinion. **AL**

✓Reading Check

Answer: The government bought the railways and took over the banking, insurance, shipping, and communications industries.

DOCUMENT-BASED QUESTIONS

Answers:

1. white scarves to represent their lost children
2. Students should provide support from the text for their answers.

His wife, Eva Perón, was adored by many Argentines and was a major part of the Perón regime. Together the Peróns brought social reforms to Argentina.

To please his supporters, from labor and the urban middle class, Perón followed a policy of increased industrialization. He sought to free Argentina from foreign investors. The government bought the railways and took over the banking, insurance, shipping, and communications industries.

R Perón's regime was authoritarian. He created Fascist gangs that used violent means to terrify his opponents.

The military overthrew the Argentinean leader in September 1955. Perón went into exile in Spain. Overwhelmed by problems, military leaders later allowed him to return. He was reelected as president in 1973 but died a year later. In 1976, the military once again took over power. The new regime tolerated no opposition. It is believed that 36,000 people were killed.

A Move Toward Democracy

W In April 1982, the military regime invaded the **Falkland Islands,** off the coast of Argentina. Great Britain, which had controlled the islands since the 1800s, sent ships and troops and took the islands back. The loss discredited the military and opened the door to civilian rule in Argentina.

In 1983, Raúl Alfonsín was elected president and worked to restore democratic practices. Nestor Kirchner serves as the current president. While inflation is high, Argentina's economy is becoming more stable, which gives hope that it will continue its democratic path.

✓Reading Check **Explaining** How did Juan Perón free Argentina from foreign investors?

INFOGRAPHICS PRIMARY SOURCE

The Mothers of the Plaza de Mayo

In March 1976, a military junta overthrew the government in Argentina. The junta suspended civil liberties and began a campaign of imprisoning, torturing, and killing government opponents. Many children of the *desaparecidos* ("disappeared ones") were kidnapped.

On April 30, 1977, mothers and grandmothers of *desaparecidos* gathered in the Plaza de Mayo in Buenos Aires risking their own safety. They hoped to locate their children and grandchildren, and to bring those responsible for Argentina's "dirty war" to justice. Although civilian rule returned in 1983, the Mothers of the Plaza de Mayo are still active.

DOCUMENT-BASED QUESTIONS

1. **Analyzing Visuals** What do the marchers wear that represent their children's diapers? Why?
2. **Speculating** Do you think the silent marches of the Mothers of the Plaza de Mayo have been effective?

The Mothers of the Plaza de Mayo carry banners calling for the return of their missing sons and daughters. Their white scarves represent diapers, in memory of the lost children.

Differentiated Instruction

People in World History Activity, URB p. 113

Analyzing Information

Objective: Analyze the life and legacy of Eva Perón.

Focus: Ask students which main groups supported the Peróns.

Teach: Discuss why the Peróns were popular with certain groups.

Assess: Have students write a paragraph summarizing the appeal of Juan and Eva Perón to Argentineans.

Close: Ask students to compare the Peróns with American couples such as the Roosevelts or the Kennedys.

Differentiated Instruction Strategies

BL Ask students why Eva Perón was "worshiped by Argentina's many poor."

AL Ask students to research the musical *Evita* and report on how accurately it portrays Peron's life.

ELL Discuss the word *martyr* and how Eva Perón might or might not fit this description.

Brazil

MAIN IDEA Brazil's supersized economy has the potential to influence the global economy, but Brazil still struggles to meet the needs of its people.

HISTORY & YOU How did the United States fight poverty in the 1960s? Read to learn how poverty has been a continuing problem in Brazil.

Like other Latin American countries, **Brazil** experienced severe economic problems following World War II. When democratically elected governments proved unable to solve these problems, the military stepped in and seized control in 1964.

An Economic Miracle?

The armed forces remained in direct control of the country for the next 20 years. The military set a new economic direction, reducing government interference in the economy and stressing free-market forces. Beginning in 1968, the new policies seemed to be working. Brazil experienced an "economic miracle" as its economy grew spectacularly. **D**

Ordinary Brazilians benefited little from this economic growth. Furthermore, rapid development led to an inflation rate of 100 percent a year. Overwhelmed, the military leadership retreated and opened the door to a return to democracy in 1985.

Return to Democracy

The new democratic government faced enormous obstacles: massive foreign debt and an inflation rate of 800 percent in 1987. In the 1990s, democratic presidents restored some stability to the economy, but the gap between rich and poor remained wide. Dissatisfaction with this gap helped to elect **Luiz Inácio Lula da Silva**, in 2002. Lula, Brazil's first left-wing president in four decades, has pursued a mission of making Brazil more independent in global trade. His challenges are to generate employment and decrease the foreign debt.

✓**Reading Check** **Evaluating** What factors led to the return to democracy in Brazil in 1985?

Peru, Colombia, and Venezuela

MAIN IDEA Violence and poverty have challenged Peru, Colombia, and Venezuela.

HISTORY & YOU How does poverty affect a country? Read to learn how poverty contributed to political unrest in Peru, Colombia, and Venezuela.

Other countries of South America have shared in the political, economic, and social problems that plagued Latin America since 1945. Peru, Colombia, and Venezuela have undergone many political changes in response to national problems.

Military and Civilian Rule in Peru

Instability has marked the history of **Peru.** Peru's dependence on the sale of its products abroad has led to extreme ups and downs in the economy. With these ups and downs have come many government changes. A large, poor, and landless peasant population has created an additional source of unrest.

A military takeover in 1968 led to some change. General **Juan Velasco Alvarado** sought to help the peasants. His government seized almost 75 percent of the nation's large landed estates and put ownership of the land into the hands of peasant **cooperatives** (farm organizations owned by and operated for the benefit of peasants). The government also nationalized many foreign-owned companies and froze food prices to help urban workers. **R**

Economic problems continued, however, and Peruvian military leaders removed General Alvarado in 1975. Five years later, unable to cope with Peru's economic problems, the military returned Peru to civilian, democratic rule.

Peru's widespread economic problems made the **task** of the new civilian government even more difficult. Poverty was widespread in 1980, and it took its toll on the people. The life expectancy of Peruvians dropped. An estimated 120 out of every 1,000 infants died, and 60 percent of children under five years of age were malnourished. With unemployment high, there seemed to be no way out of poverty for many Peruvians.

D Differentiated Instruction

Advanced Learners Ask students to research and report on the "economic miracle" that began in 1968. They should identify reasons for the increased economic activity and find statistics to indicate growth, as well as statistics which show that the miracle did little for most people in Brazil. **AL**

R Reading Strategy

Summarizing Ask students to trace Peru's problems between the 1960s and 1980s. *(Peru had a shaky economy and a large group of poor peasants. A military takeover led to steps to help peasants and urban workers. Economic problems continued and Peru returned to democracy. Peru suffered from extreme poverty, very poor healthcare, and high unemployment.)* **OL**

✓**Reading Check**

Answer: the failure of the military government's economic policies and an overwhelming inflation rate

Additional Support

Activity: Interdisciplinary Connection

Mathematics Review the meaning of inflation *(a rapid increase in prices)*. Tell students that annual inflation rates in the United States have generally been less than 3½ percent in the last decade. Ask students to create two bar graphs which show annual inflation rates of 3 percent and 100 percent over a period of four years. Have them show the change in price of a bag of groceries that costs 100 dollars the first year. **Ask:** **What was the difference in the price of groceries after the fourth year?** *(about 690 dollars)* **Ask:** **Why was the high inflation rate important to the people of Brazil?** *(Prices rose so rapidly that people couldn't afford to live the same way they had previously.)* **OL**

Teacher Tip

Students may need additional help to complete their calculations. The accuracy of their graphs and calculations may increase if they use graph paper. Calculators are also an option.

C1 Critical Thinking

Comparing and Contrasting Ask: How do the actions of the Shining Path guerrillas contrast with the images created by their name? *("Shining Path" has a very positive connotation, implying a bright, clear route to the future. However their actions have involved killing community leaders.)* **OL**

C2 Critical Thinking

Making Inferences Ask: Why do you think priests and nuns supporting liberation theology have been killed? *(They supported changes in political power and redistributing wealth. These ideas are threatening to those who are in power.)* **OL**

CRITICAL THINKING SKILLS

Answers:
1. a form of religion that emphasizes helping the poor
2. The church has traditionally backed the ruling classes. Liberation theology is committed to helping the poor and achieving social justice.

INFOGRAPHICS PRIMARY SOURCE

Liberation Theology: A New Role for the Catholic Church

In 1968, the Catholic bishops of Latin America met in Medellín, Colombia. There they spoke out against the "oppression of institutionalized violence" and unjust political structures. They announced that they would urge the clergy to work for the betterment of the poor and victims of social injustice.

The term *liberation theology* was coined soon afterward by Gustavo Gutierrez, a Peruvian priest. It was a form of religion combined with Marxism that made helping the poor the Church's top priority. During the 1970s, at least 850 liberation theology priests and nuns were killed because of their commitment to social justice. Hundreds more have been killed since 1980. Liberation theology continues to be important in Latin America.

Franciscan priest Leonardo Boff preaching in Brazil. The banners behind him emphasize the Church's commitment to helping the poor.

CRITICAL THINKING SKILLS

1. **Defining** What is liberation theology?
2. **Contrasting** How does liberation theology differ from the traditional role of the Catholic Church in Latin America?

In this economic climate, a radical Communist guerrilla group gained support. Known as **Shining Path** the group wanted to create a classless society. Shining Path killed mayors, missionaries, priests, and peasants across Peru.

In 1990, Peruvians chose **Alberto Fujimori** as president. Fujimori, the son of Japanese immigrants, promised to make reforms. However, he later suspended the constitution and congress, became a dictator, and began a campaign against Shining Path guerrillas. Corruption led to Fujimori's removal from power in 2000.

In June 2001, Alejandro Toledo became Peru's first freely elected president of Native American descent. His successor, Alan García Pérez, must create additional jobs and decrease poverty to make Peru more economically stable. The government has prudent fiscal policies and is open to trade and investment.

Colombia: Coffee and Cocaine

Colombia has long had a democratic political system, but a conservative elite led by the owners of coffee plantations has dominated the government. Coffee is an important crop for Colombia, making up about half of the country's legal exports. Yet because the economy relies heavily upon the coffee trade, price fluctuations in either direction can have a negative effect. In 1975, for example, the Brazilian coffee crop was destroyed by frost. Prices for Colombian coffee rose dramatically, causing inflation.

In addition to economic problems, political problems troubled Colombia in the twentieth century. After World War II, Marxist guerrilla groups began to organize Colombian peasants. The government responded violently. More than 200,000 peasants had been killed by the mid-1960s. Violence continued in the 1980s and 1990s.

Additional Support

Activity: Economics Connection

Brainstorming The rain forests of Central and South America have been called "the lungs of the earth," producing much of the oxygen that we all breathe. The need for Latin Americans to find jobs and develop agriculture while protecting and conserving the rain forest is a concern for the entire planet. Replacing forests with farms and roads means less moisture evaporates from the soil, reducing clouds around forested peaks 65 miles (104.5 km) away. Ask students to brainstorm and make a chart about possible ways nations can develop their economy and still protect their natural resources. **Ask:** What obligations do developed nations have toward less developed nations? *(Encourage students to use their text as they participate in the discussion.)* **OL**

Peasants who lived in poverty turned to a new cash crop—coca leaves, which are used to make cocaine. As the lucrative drug trade grew, two major **cartels** (groups of drug businesses) formed in Colombia.

The drug cartels used bribes and violence to force government cooperation in the drug traffic and to dominate the market. Colombia became the major supplier of the international drug market. Violence has increased as rebel guerrillas made deals with the drug cartels to oppose the government. The government used an aerial eradication program to try to wipe out cocaine fields, but the program did not have much success. The United States **funded** the antidrug program, and in 2003 sent troops to support it.

Despite the money earned from drug and coffee exports, the Colombian economy remained weak because of high unemployment and the disruption of civil war. **Alvaro Uribe,** elected for a second term in 2006, promised to crack down hard on rebel groups. His economic policies hold promise for Colombia's future.

Chávez Rules Venezuela

A series of military dictators ruled **Venezuela** during the first half of the twentieth century. They promoted the oil industry and allowed for some social reforms.

By 1979, the Venezuelan economy had stalled. Corruption was also widespread. As a result of President Carlos Andrés Pérez's unpopular economic program, people rioted. More than 200 people were killed during the riots. Unrest continued to grow. A group of army lieutenants led by **Hugo Chávez** tried to overthrow the government in 1992. The coup failed and Chávez was put in prison. After Pérez was impeached a year later, Chávez was released.

Many people saw Chávez as a folk hero. When he ran for president in 1998, Chávez won the election in a landslide victory. During 2002 and 2003, Chávez's opposition front staged two national strikes. The military ousted Chávez during the first strike. However, loyal army elements restored him to power two days later. Nor could a national referendum in 2004 remove him. In December 2006, Chávez was reelected president with nearly two-thirds of the votes.

Like most leaders of South American countries, Chávez has many social and economic issues to address. Nearly 80 percent of the population lives in poverty. Real wages are low, and unemployment is high. Likewise, inflation rates remain high as does the foreign debt.

In late 2003, Chávez committed over $1 billion toward new social programs. Funding for this was aided by high oil prices. Venezuela depends on its oil reserves, the sixth largest in the world.

✓Reading Check **Identifying** On what natural resource does the Venezuelan economy depend?

SECTION 3 REVIEW

Vocabulary

1. **Explain** the significance of: Chile, Salvador Allende, Augusto Pinochet, Argentina, Juan Perón, Falkland Islands, Brazil, Luiz Inácio Lula da Silva, Peru, Juan Velasco Alvarado, cooperatives, task, Shining Path, Alberto Fujimori, Colombia, cartels, fund, Alvaro Uribe, Venezuela, Hugo Chávez.

Main Ideas

2. **Explain** how the invasion of the Falkland Islands affected Argentina.
3. **List** the current leaders of the countries discussed in this section. Use a chart like the one below to make your list.

Country	Leader
Chile	
Argentina	
Brazil	
Peru	
Colombia	
Venezuela	

4. **Identify** some obstacles that current South American governments face.

Critical Thinking

5. **The BIG Idea** **Making Connections** Why is it often easier for the military to seize power than to rule effectively? Which countries discussed in this chapter support this theory?
6. **Organizing** How has democracy advanced in South America since the late 1980s?
7. **Analyzing Visuals** How do the white scarves of the protestors on page 974 make their protest more effective?

Writing About History

8. **Informative Writing** Write an article as if you are an American journalist covering Perón's presidency. Include details about the pros and cons of the Perón regime.

History ONLINE

For help with the concepts in this section of *Glencoe World History,* go to glencoe.com and click Study Central™.

R Reading Strategy

Sequencing Information

Ask students to create a time line that lists important events in Venezuela's history since 1979. *(Students' time lines should accurately reflect the events in this time period.)* **BL**

✓Reading Check

Answer: oil

Assess

History ONLINE

Study Central provides summaries, interactive games, and online graphic organizers to help students review content.

Close

Analyzing Information Ask: What do you think was the worst problem facing Latin America in the years after World War II? *(Answers may include extreme poverty and economic instability, military takeovers, and social inequalities because of gulf between rich and poor.)* **OL**

Answers

1. Definitions for the vocabulary words are found in the section and the Glossary.
2. discredited the military, opened door to civilian rule
3. **Chile:** Michelle Bachelet Jeria; **Argentina:** Nestor Kirchner; **Brazil:** Luiz Inácio Lula da Silva; **Peru:** Alan García Pérez; **Colombia:** Alvaro Uribe; **Venezuela:** Hugo Chávez
4. poverty, gap between rich and poor, high inflation, high foreign debt, high unemployment, political unrest, cartels and drug-related violence, overdependence on exports such as coffee and oil
5. Military regimes are usually repressive, leading to popular unrest. Examples include Chile, Argentina, Peru, Brazil, and Venezuela.
6. **Argentina:** Military dictatorship discredited by the Falkland defeat; **Brazil:** Inflation opened door to democracy; **Chile:** Human rights abuses under Pinochet led to his defeat.
7. The scarves, representing diapers of their lost children, emphasize their loss.
8. Students should write an informative, fact-based article.

Focus

Introducing Social History
Have students recall what they've learned about Argentina and recent trends in Latin America. **Ask:** How does being part of a global economy affect a country's culture? *(more foreign influences mix with traditional culture)* **OL**

Teach

S Skill Practice

Visual Literacy Ask: What details tell you these young people are wearing traditional clothes? *(The long skirt, broad hat, neckerchief, and baggy pants are not everyday attire.)* **BL**

C Critical Thinking

Drawing Conclusions Ask: Why is traditional culture stronger in the countryside? *(because people living in the country have less exposure to new technology and ideas)* **OL**

Additional Support

Social History

Teenage Life in Argentina

After suffering economic setbacks in the 1980s, Argentina sought to play a more active role in the global marketplace. Cable television and the Internet give Argentine teenagers access to global influences, yet extended families and the living history of festivals preserve the spirit of gaucho life.

Many Argentine teens enjoy traditional festivals. These celebrations often feature horseback events, music, and dancing.

In many areas, the traditional attire of the gaucho, or cowboy, is popular among Argentine youths. The gaucho hat is black, broad, and flat-brimmed.

The baggy gaucho pants are called *bombachas.* Gauchos tuck them into their boots.

Traditional attire worn by Argentine girls includes long, colorful dresses with full, ruffled skirts.

Proud Traditions and Family Ties

Argentina's customs draw upon its European (especially Spanish and Italian) influences, as well as the cultures of native South Americans. These traditions remain a strong influence on many young Argentines, particularly in the countryside. The close bonds of family help make festivals and traditional clothes important. For Argentines, the gaucho (cowboy) is an enduring national symbol of rugged individualism.

Background

Argentina For hundreds of years, the Catholic Church, European tradition, and a blending of cultures have shaped life in Argentina. About 85 percent of Argentines are of European descent and 15 percent are mestizos. For many Argentines, life begins and ends with Catholic rituals: baptism at birth and a funeral mass when they die. Although Catholic traditions are honored, Argentines take a relaxed view toward religion. Less than 20 percent attend church regularly. Some Argentines who are Native Americans combine their worship in church on Sunday with prayer to nature spirits during the week. The Buenos Aires *porteños*, or "people of the port," are Argentina's elite. They view themselves as sophisticated trendsetters, and young people there grow up wearing designer clothing. *Porteños* usually see those living outside Buenos Aires as *campesinos*—mere country folk.

From Gauchos to Globetrotters

Young people in Buenos Aires and other cities in Argentina today experience international trends and live in ways very similar to teens in the U.S. Soccer provides Argentina with an athletic connection to its Latin American neighbors. Young Argentines can grow up dreaming of competing in the World Cup, knowing that their nation can watch and cheer them on anywhere on the globe. R

Analyzing Visuals

1. **Making Generalizations** What types of activities are popular among teenagers in Argentina?
2. **Synthesizing** How do the lifestyles of Argentine teenagers reflect both traditional and global influences?

W Writing Support

Descriptive Writing Have students describe how their lives compare with the lives of Argentine teenagers. BL

R Reading Strategy

Using Word Parts Have students break the word *globetrotter* into its parts to determine its literal and more common meanings. *(someone who trots [walks quickly] around the globe, a world traveler)* ELL

Assess/Close

Have students compare the influence of soccer in Argentina and the United States. OL

ANALYZING VISUALS

Answers:

1. playing soccer and other sports, shopping, attending traditional festivals, dancing, listening to music
2. traditional: family, clothing, festivals, dancing; global: modern malls, Western clothing, World Cup soccer, the Internet, American music

Activity: Interdisciplinary Connection

Language Arts Explain that gauchos, or cowhands, are the national symbol of Argentina. Most gauchos were mestizos whose horseback riding and roping skills were legendary. They could find their way on the pampas, Argentina's grasslands, by the way the grass lay and they could tell how many riders were approaching by the sounds of the horses' hooves. Gauchos fought against Spanish colonialism and, later, against newcomers who wanted to fence in the pampas. They are folk heroes whose ideals of individualism and courage inspire modern Argentines. Few in number today, gauchos still tend livestock, a vital part of the country's economy. **Ask:** What do you know about American cowboys? Where does this information come from? Ask students to brainstorm ideas to respond to this question. Then have students write an essay comparing and contrasting the roles of the American cowboys and the gauchos of Argentina. OL

9. A Fidel Castro led the Cuban Revolution. Khrushchev is associated with the Soviet Union, Duarte with El Salvador, and Noriega with Panama.

10. B The people of Panama had agitated for control of the Canal for many years. Manuel Noriega was not returned to Panama in 1999; lease payment was not an issue; and a private company did not take over the Panama Canal in 1999.

TEST-TAKING 

For Question 10: Remind students that when a question includes a date, they can create a mental time line of the events mentioned in the answer choices. This will help them eliminate answer choices that are obviously not related to that date.

11. A Perón improved conditions for labor and the middle class, gaining their support. His support for workers and the middle class angered both the landed gentry and business owners. Although the military initially supported Perón, they later turned against him.

12. D The military set new economic policies in Brazil that caused spectacular economic growth. During this time, Chile struggled under Allende's socialist regime and then under Pinochet's military dictatorship. Peru had widespread economic problems, and Argentina's economy was unstable.

13. C Although it is a shocking number, students should recall that Venezuela still struggles economically even though it has considerable oil reserves.

9. Who led the Cuban Revolution against the Batista regime?
- **A** Fidel Castro
- **B** Nikita Khrushchev
- **C** José Duarte
- **D** Manuel Noriega

10. What major Panamanian issue was finally settled in 1999?
- **A** The return of Manuel Noriega
- **B** Control of the Panama Canal
- **C** Payment of the lease for the Panama Canal
- **D** Privatization

Section 3 *(pp. 972–977)*

11. Which group was a main source of support for Juan Perón?
- **A** Labor and urban middle class
- **B** Landed gentry
- **C** Business owners
- **D** Military

12. Which South American country had an "economic miracle" in the late 1960s and early 1970s?
- **A** Chile
- **B** Peru
- **C** Argentina
- **D** Brazil

13. About what percent of Venezuela's population lives in poverty?
- **A** 50
- **B** 25
- **C** 80
- **D** 10

Critical Thinking

Directions: Choose the best answers to the following questions.

Use the following map to answer question 14.

14. Which of these South American countries have the least population?
- **A** Brazil, Argentina, Colombia
- **B** Bolivia, Paraguay, Uruguay
- **C** Venezuela, Peru, Chile
- **D** Argentina, Bolivia, Ecuador

15. Why did many military regimes in Latin America fail?
- **A** They could not cope with debt problems.
- **B** Their power had popular consent.
- **C** The countries warred against each other.
- **D** Their leaders were too weak.

Need Extra Help?

If You Missed Questions . . .	9	10	11	12	13	14	15
Go to Page . . .	968	971	974	975	977	962	961

GO ON

Critical Thinking

14. B The map key indicates that Ecuador, Guyana, French Guiana, Bolivia, Paraguay, and Uruguay have the lowest population levels, under 15 million.

15. A Students should recognize that the debt owed to foreign investors was a continual problem that military regimes could not solve. Military regimes did not have popular consent, they did not war against each other, and their leaders were not weak.

16. How did Juan Perón gain support?

A He appealed to the landed elite.

B He had the backing of the United States.

C He maintained loyalty from the military.

D He appealed to the workers and urban middle class.

17. Why do Colombian cartels have so much power?

A They control the coffee market.

B They are backed by the United States.

C They have the support of rebel guerrilla groups.

D Their cocaine fields are resistant to pesticides.

Analyze the bar graph and answer the question that follows based on the graph and on your knowledge of world history.

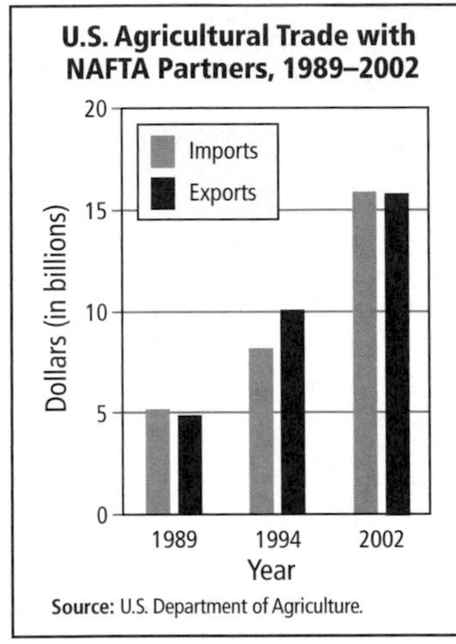

18. How did NAFTA affect agricultural trade between the United States, Mexico, and Canada?

A Mexico's exports to the United States decreased.

B Canada's exports to Europe increased.

C There was an increase in imports from Mexico and Canada to the United States, as well as exports from the United States to Mexico and Canada.

D Mexico stopped importing agricultural products from the United States.

Document-Based Questions

Directions: Analyze the document and answer the short-answer questions that follow the document. Base your answers on the document and on your knowledge of world history.

One Latin American observer discussed the U.S. invasion of Panama in 1989 in the following words:

> *"The first official [U.S.] reason for the invasion of Panama was 'to protect American lives there.' This pretext was not credible, for the cry of 'wolf! wolf!' has been used before in Latin America. . . . The danger to American lives is a hundred times greater every day and night in Washington, D.C., 'the murder capital of the United States,' and in other American cities to which President Bush has hardly applied his policy of protecting North American lives and waging war against drugs (he prefers to wage that war on foreign battlefields)."*
>
> —*Latin American Civilization: History and Society, 1492 to the Present,* Benjamin Keen, *1996*

19. To what U.S. action does the observer refer when he talks of the "invasion of Panama"?

20. What does this observer seem to say about U.S. foreign policy?

Extended Response

21. Simply because it believed they supported the guerrilla forces, the Guatemalan government massacred the indigenous people of Guatemala. How does this action compare to the settlers' and government's treatment of Native Americans in the United States during the eighteenth and nineteenth centuries and beyond?

For additional test practice, use Self-Check Quizzes—Chapter 29 at glencoe.com.

Need Extra Help?

If You Missed Questions . . .	16	17	18	19	20	21
Go to Page . . .	973–974	977	967	971	971	971

STOP

18. C The graph shows an increase in both imports from Mexico and Canada to the United States and exports from the United States to Mexico and Canada. Mexico's exports did not decrease; Canada's exports to Europe are not covered in the graph; and Mexico did not stop importing agricultural products from the United States.

Document-Based Questions

19. The observer refers to the troops the United States sent into Panama to depose Manuel Noriega because of his involvement in the drug trade.

20. The observer is saying that the reason the United States gave for invading Panama was not believable because American lives in Panama were actually less in danger there than in Washington, D.C. The observer suggests that the United States should address its own problems with crime and drugs at home rather than trying to solve these problems in other countries.

Extended Response

21. Answers should be consistent with material presented in this chapter and supported by logical arguments.

16. D The answer is similar to item 11, which establishes that Perón's support was not with the landed elite or the military. The United States did not back Perón to place him in power.

17. C Rebel guerrilla groups support the cartels, using violence to oppose the government. Cartels control the drug market, not the coffee market, and they are opposed by the United States. Pesticides have no relevance to the cartels.

Introduce students to chapter content and key terms by having them access the Chapter 29 Overview at glencoe.com.

Need Extra Help?

Have students refer to the pages listed if they miss any of the questions.

CHAPTER 30 Planning Guide

Key to Ability Levels	
BL Below Level	AL Above Level
OL On Level	ELL English Language Learners

Key to Teaching Resources	
Print Material	DVD
CD-ROM	Transparency

Levels BL	OL	AL	ELL	Resources	Chapter Opener	Section 1	Section 2	Chapter Assess
FOCUS								
BL	OL	AL	ELL	Daily Focus Skills Transparencies		30-1	30-2	
TEACH								
BL	OL	AL	ELL	Charting and Graphing Activity, URB			✓	
		AL		World Literature Reading, URB		✓		
BL	OL		ELL	Reading Skills Activity, URB			p. 127	
	OL	AL		Historical Analysis Skills Activity, URB			p. 128	
BL	OL	AL	ELL	Differentiated Instruction Activity, URB		p. 129		
	OL		ELL	English Learner Activity, URB		p. 131		
BL	OL	AL	ELL	Content Vocabulary Activity, URB*			p. 133	
BL	OL	AL	ELL	Academic Vocabulary Activity, URB			p. 135	
BL	OL	AL	ELL	Skills Reinforcement Activity, URB		p. 137		
	OL	AL		Critical Thinking Skills Activity, URB		p. 138		
	OL	AL		History and Geography Activity, URB		p. 139		
	OL	AL	ELL	Mapping History Activity, URB			p. 141	
BL	OL	AL		Historical Significance Activity, URB			p. 142	
BL	OL	AL	ELL	Cooperative Learning Activity, URB			p. 143	
	OL	AL	ELL	History Simulation Activity, URB		p. 145		
BL	OL	AL	ELL	Time Line Activity, URB			p. 147	
	OL	AL		Linking Past and Present Activity, URB			p. 148	
BL	OL	AL		People in World History Activity, URB		p. 149	p. 150	
BL	OL	AL	ELL	Primary Source Reading, URB		p. 151		
	OL	AL		Enrichment Activity, URB			p. 156	
BL	OL	AL	ELL	World Art and Music Activity, URB		p. 153		
BL	OL		ELL	Guided Reading Activities, URB*		p. 158		
BL	OL		ELL	Reading Essentials and Note-Taking Guide*		p. 328	p. 331	
BL	OL	AL	ELL	Differentiated Instruction for the World History Classroom	✓	✓	✓	✓

Note: Please refer to the *Unit Resource Book: Toward a Global Civilization* for this chapter's URB materials.

* Also available in Spanish

- Interactive Lesson Planner
- Interactive Teacher Edition
- Fully editable blackline masters
- Section Spotlight Videos Launch
- Differentiated Lesson Plans
- Printable reports of daily assignments
- Standards Tracking System

Levels				Resources	Chapter Opener	Section 1	Section 2	Chapter Assess
BL	OL	AL	ELL					
TEACH *(continued)*								
BL	OL	AL	ELL	StudentWorks™ Plus DVD	✓	✓	✓	✓
BL	OL	AL	ELL	Vocabulary PuzzleMaker CD-ROM	✓	✓	✓	✓
Teacher Resources				Building Academic Vocabulary	✓	✓	✓	✓
				Strategies for Success	✓	✓	✓	✓
				Outline Map Resource Book	✓	✓	✓	✓
				Presentation Plus! with MindJogger DVD	✓	✓	✓	✓
ASSESS								
BL	OL	AL	ELL	Section Quizzes and Chapter Tests*		p. 373	p. 374	p. 375
BL	OL	AL	ELL	Authentic Assessment With Rubrics	✓	✓	✓	✓
BL	OL	AL	ELL	Standardized Test Practice Workbook	✓	✓	✓	✓
BL	OL	AL	ELL	*ExamView® Assessment Suite* CD-ROM		30-1	30-2	Ch. 30
BL	OL	AL	ELL	Interactive Tutor Self-Assessment CD-ROM		30-1	30-2	
CLOSE								
BL			ELL	Reteaching Activity, URB			p. 155	
BL	OL		ELL	Reading and Study Skills Foldables™	✓	✓	✓	✓

Research Using *Browse Famous People*

Technology Product

CyberScout is a convenient and dynamic search engine that provides several easy ways to locate information outside the McGraw-Hill Learning Network. CyberScout only searches Web sites that have been reviewed by teachers, so the information students find is always appropriate and accurate.

Objectives

After students use CyberScout, they will be able to

- research information on famous people in history
- exercise research and study skills
- practice writing skills

Steps

- From McGraw-Hill Learning Network home page (www.mhln.com), click on **For Students.**
- Choose **CyberScout** below **Homework Help.**
- Click on a subject area to narrow the search.
- The CyberScout page will display a set of subcategories.
- Click the **Browse Famous People** button at the bottom of the page.
- The CyberScout page displays a set of names related to the subject area. Click a name.
- The CyberScout page displays a set of results.
- Click the link to a Web site of interest.
- Students will be directed to the Web site in a new window.
- Students navigate through the chosen Web site to gain information on a topic and take notes.

History ONLINE

	Student	Teacher	Parent
Beyond the Textbook	●	●	●
Chapter Overviews	●	●	●
Time Current Events	●		●
ePuzzles and Games	●		●
Concepts in Motion	●		●
Literature Connections		●	
Multi-Language Glossaries	●		●
Online Student Edition	●	●	●
Self-Check Quizzes	●		●
Student Web Activities	●		●
Study Central ™	●		●
Teaching Today		●	
Vocabulary eFlashcards	●		●
Web Activity Lesson Plans		●	

- **Timed Readings Plus in Social Studies** helps students increase their reading rate and fluency while maintaining comprehension. The 400-word passages are similar to those found on state and national assessments.
- **Reading in the Content Area: Social Studies** concentrates on six essential reading skills that help students better comprehend what they read. The book includes 75 high-interest nonfiction passages written at increasing levels of difficulty.
- **Reading Social Studies** includes strategic reading instruction and vocabulary support in Social Studies content for both ELLs and native speakers of English.

www.jamestowneducation.com

Index to National Geographic Magazine:

The following articles relate to this chapter:

- "Living with AIDS," by Gideon Mendel, September 2005
- "City of Hope, City of Fear: Johannesburg," by Peter Godwin, April 2004
- "Lines in the Sand: Deadly Times in the West Bank and Gaza," by Andrew Cockburn, October 2002

National Geographic Society Products To order the following, call National Geographic at 1-800-368-2728:

- *National Geographic Atlas of the World* (Book).

Access National Geographic's new, dynamic MapMachine Web site and other geography resources at:
www.nationalgeographic.com
www.nationalgeographic.com/maps

Biography  

The following videotape programs are available from Glencoe as supplements to Chapter 30:

- Israel: Birth of a Nation (ISBN 0-76-701107-4)
- Nelson Mandela: Journey to Freedom (ISBN 0-76-700113-3)
- Yitzhak Rabin (ISBN 1-56-501714-5)

To order, call Glencoe at 1-800-334-7344. To find classroom resources to accompany many of these videos, check the following home pages:

A&E Television: www.aetv.com

The History Channel: www.historychannel.com

GLENCOE BOOKLINK 3

Use this database to search more than 30,000 titles to create a customized reading list for your students.

- Reading lists can be organized by students' reading level, author, genre, theme, or area of interest.
- The database provides Degrees of Reading Power™ (DRP) and Lexile™ readability scores for all selections.
- A brief summary of each selection is included.

Leveled reading suggestions for this chapter:

For students at a Grade 8 reading level:
- ***Waiting for the Rain: A Novel of South Africa,*** by Sheila Gordon

For students at a Grade 9 reading level:
- ***Israel: A Question and Answer Book,*** by Kremena Spengler

For students at a Grade 10 reading level:
- ***What Do We Know about Islam?,*** by Shahrukh Husain

For students at a Grade 11 reading level:
- ***The Kuwaiti Oil Fires,*** by Skip Press

For students at a Grade 12 reading level:
- ***Africa Is People: Firsthand Accounts from Contemporary Africa,*** by Barbara Nolen

Introducing **CHAPTER 30**

Focus

MAKING CONNECTIONS
How can different groups claim one city?

Explain that a territorial dispute is a disagreement between states or groups over the ownership of an area, and that there are many ongoing territorial disputes in the world today. **Ask:** How can countries resolve territorial disputes? *(Some negotiate or seek arbitration from third parties, such as the U.N. Others turn to violence to enforce their claims.)* Point out that once a stronger nation has gained control of an area, it often has little incentive to negotiate with a weaker claimant. Help students list some current territorial disputes, including some that involve the United States (such as those with Native American groups, or with Cuba over the military base at Guantanamo). Have students suggest possible resolutions to the conflicts.

Teach

The Big Ideas

As students study the chapter, remind them to consider the section-based Big Ideas included in each section's Guide to Reading. The **Essential Questions** in the activities below tie in to the Big Ideas and help students think about and understand important chapter concepts. In addition, the Hands-on Chapter Projects with their culminating activities relate the content from each section to the Big Ideas. These activities build on each other as students progress through the chapter. Section activities culminate in the wrap-up activity on the Visual Summary page.

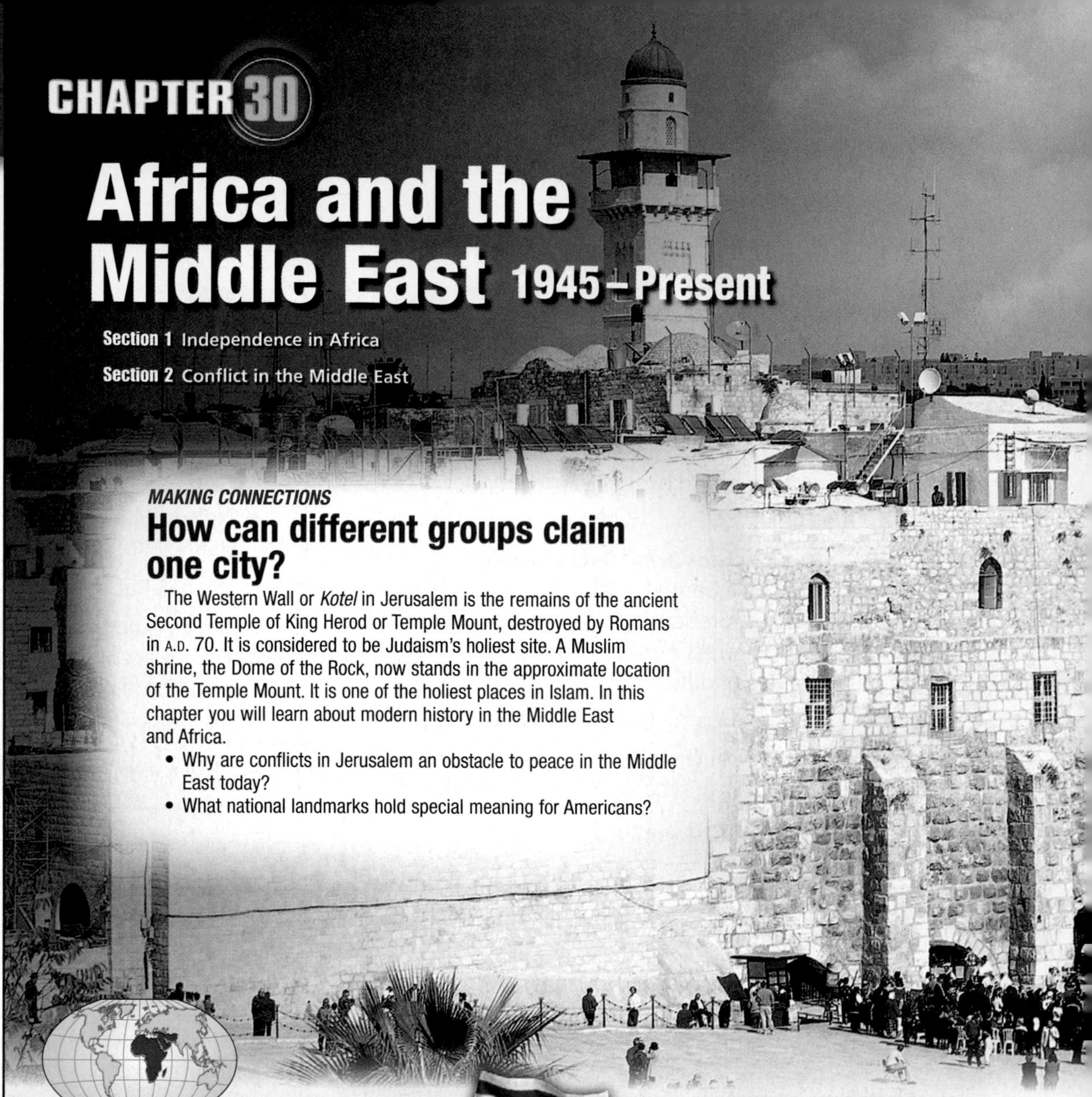

CHAPTER 30

Africa and the Middle East 1945–Present

Section 1 Independence in Africa

Section 2 Conflict in the Middle East

MAKING CONNECTIONS

How can different groups claim one city?

The Western Wall or *Kotel* in Jerusalem is the remains of the ancient Second Temple of King Herod or Temple Mount, destroyed by Romans in A.D. 70. It is considered to be Judaism's holiest site. A Muslim shrine, the Dome of the Rock, now stands in the approximate location of the Temple Mount. It is one of the holiest places in Islam. In this chapter you will learn about modern history in the Middle East and Africa.

- Why are conflicts in Jerusalem an obstacle to peace in the Middle East today?
- What national landmarks hold special meaning for Americans?

AFRICA AND THE MIDDLE EAST ▶

1948 Jews in Palestine proclaim the state of Israel

1957 Ghana becomes first British colony to gain independence

1979 Shah Mohammad Reza Pahlavi overthrown in Iranian revolution

1945 — 1965

THE WORLD ▶

1947 India and Pakistan become independent nations

1979 Margaret Thatcher becomes prime minister of Great Britain

984

Independence in Africa

Ask: What challenges faced newly independent countries in Africa? *(Many countries struggled with the legacies of colonial rule, including undeveloped economies and arbitrary boundaries that included many different ethnic groups.)* Point out that in Section 1, students will learn about early African leaders, the challenges they faced, and current challenges and progress. OL

Conflict in the Middle East

Ask: What conditions led to conflict in the Middle East? *(Colonial powers had drawn arbitrary boundaries that placed many ethnic groups in a single country)* Point out that in Section 2, students will learn about the history of Arab-Israeli conflict, as well as the causes of current conflicts involving the United States in the Middle East. OL

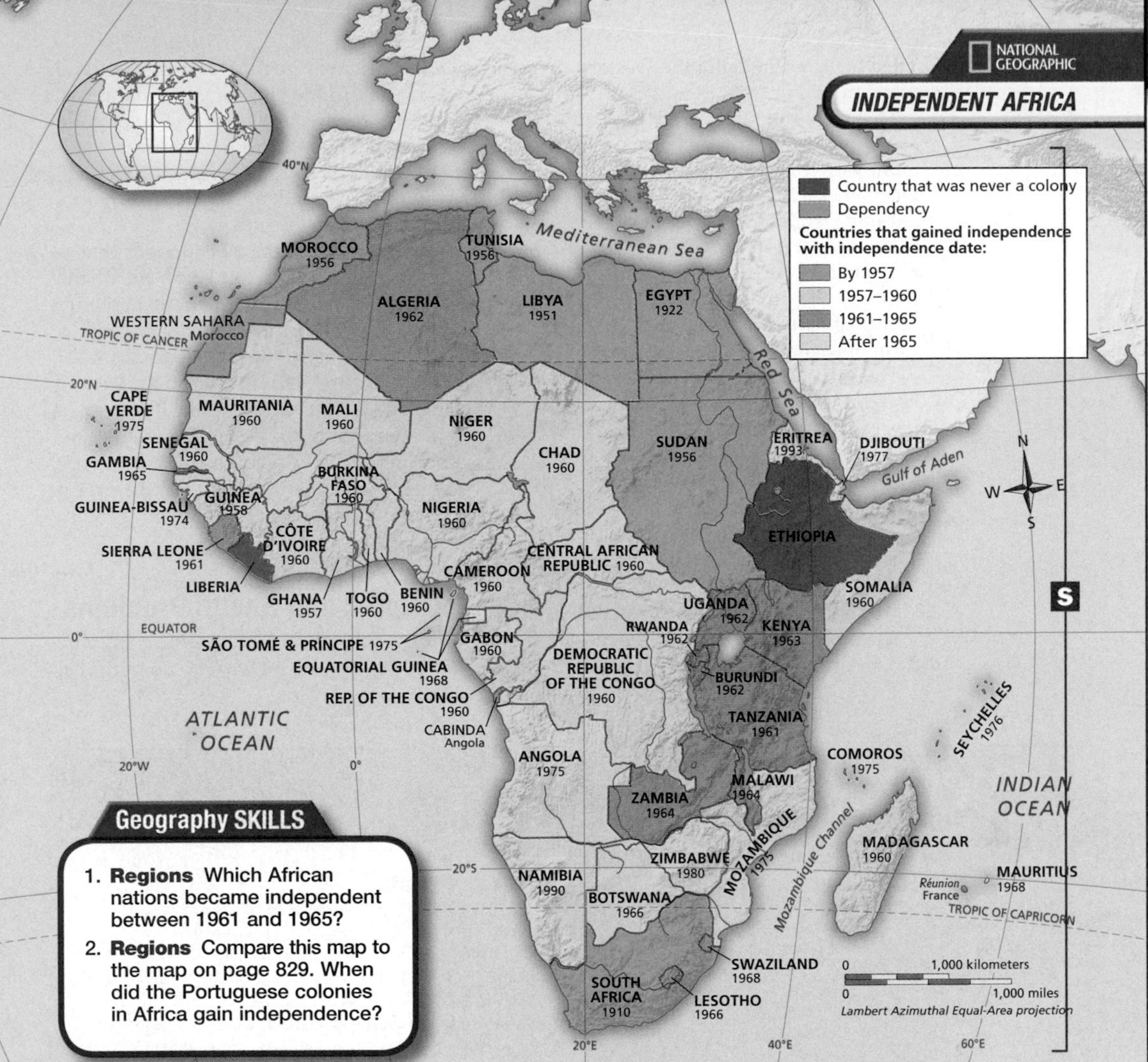

Geography SKILLS

1. **Regions** Which African nations became independent between 1961 and 1965?
2. **Regions** Compare this map to the map on page 829. When did the Portuguese colonies in Africa gain independence?

laws separating whites and blacks. The result was a system of racial segregation known as **apartheid** ("apartness"). Blacks began demonstrating against these laws.

The white government brutally repressed the demonstrators. In 1960 police opened fire on people who were leading a peaceful march in Sharpeville, killing 69 people, two-thirds of whom were shot in the back. After the arrest of ANC leader Nelson Mandela in 1962, members of the ANC called for armed resistance to the white government.

New Nations and New Leaders

The African states that achieved independence in the 1950s, 1960s, and 1970s still faced many problems. The leaders of these states, as well as their citizens, dreamed of stable governments and economic prosperity. Many of these dreams have yet to be realized.

Most leaders of the newly independent states came from the urban middle class. They had studied in Europe or the United States and knew European languages.

C Critical Thinking

Making Inferences Ask: Why is it important to note that many of the people were shot in the back? *(It implies that they were shot trying to get away or retreat from a confrontation; police apparently kept firing even after it was no longer necessary for protection.)* OL

S Skill Practice

Using Geography Skills

Ask: Which country is listed as the first to gain independence as a colony? In what year did the country gain independence? *(South Africa; in 1910)* BL

Geography SKILLS

Answers:

1. Uganda, Kenya, Rwanda, Tanzania, Malawi, Zambia, Sierra Leone, Algeria, Gambia, Burundi
2. Angola and Mozambique in 1975

Hands-On Chapter Project Step 1

Make a Chart of Issues and Resolutions

Small groups of students will research and chart significant issues and possible resolutions in Africa and the Middle East.

Step 1: Identifying Issues and Answers

Essential Question: What issues face people in Africa and the Middle East and how might they be resolved?

Directions: Write the Big Idea on the board. Assign four small groups a major issue in Africa today. Half of each group will prepare a two-column chart that identifies issues facing Africa, and the other half will focus on resolutions.

Summarizing: Allow time for each group to display their chart or copy it onto the board and answer questions. OL

(Chapter Project is continued in Section 2)

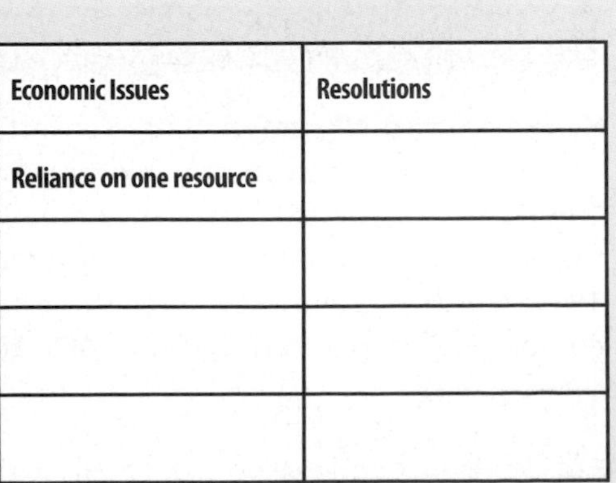

Economic Issues	Resolutions
Reliance on one resource	

More About the Photo

Visual Literacy The Western Wall or Kotel is the most important religious site for Jews because it is the last remnant of the Temple the Romans destroyed in A.D. 70. For centuries, Jews have referred to it as a place of assembly and prayer. Muslims refer to the nearby area as the Al-Haram Sharif, or Noble Sanctuary, while Jews refer to it as the Temple Mount. Today the area contains gardens, fountains and several buildings, including the Ghawanima Minaret (the tower to the left of the photo) and the Dome of the Rock. Built between A.D. 685 and 691, the Dome of the Rock is the world's oldest existing Islamic shrine. It commemorates the site from which the Prophet Muhammad journeyed to heaven. By contrast, in Judaism, the stone is the site where Abraham fulfilled God's test to see if he would be willing to sacrifice his son Isaac.

FOLDABLES Study Organizer Dinah Zike's Foldables

Dinah Zike's Foldables are three-dimensional, interactive graphic organizers that help students practice basic writing skills, review vocabulary terms, and identify main ideas. Instructions for creating and using Foldables can be found in the Appendix at the end of this book and in the *Dinah Zike's Reading and Study Skills Foldables* booklet.

History ONLINE

Introduce students to chapter content and key terms by having them access the Chapter 30 Overview at glencoe.com.

Focus

Bellringer
Daily Focus Transparency 30.1

GUIDE TO READING

Answers to Graphic:
Economic: depended on export of single crop or resource; failed to invest in infrastructure; corruption; population growth; drought. **Social:** AIDS, poverty, massive slums; growth of cities overwhelmed sanitation and transportation systems; women in low-paying positions. **Political:** military regimes, one-party states; warring ethnic groups

Section Spotlight Video

To generate student interest and provide a springboard for class discussion, access the Chapter 30, Section 1 video at glencoe.com or on the video DVD.

Resource Manager

SECTION 1

Independence in Africa

GUIDE TO READING

The BIG Idea
Self-Determination After achieving independence from their colonial rulers, many African nations faced political, economic, social, and health challenges.

Content Vocabulary
- apartheid *(p. 987)*
- AIDS *(p. 989)*
- Pan-Africanism *(p. 988)*

Academic Vocabulary
- goal *(p. 986)*
- diverse *(p. 988)*

People and Places
- Ghana *(p. 986)*
- Kwame Nkrumah *(p. 986)*
- South Africa *(p. 986)*
- Jomo Kenyatta *(p. 988)*
- Kenya *(p. 988)*
- Julius Nyerere *(p. 988)*
- Liberia *(p. 989)*
- Nigeria *(p. 989)*
- Rwanda *(p. 990)*
- Democratic Republic of the Congo *(p. 990)*
- Sudan *(p. 990)*
- Nelson Mandela *(p. 990)*
- Desmond Tutu *(p. 990)*
- Chinua Achebe *(p. 993)*
- Noni Jabavu *(p. 993)*

Reading Strategy
Categorizing Information As you read, complete a chart like the one below identifying the problems in Africa during its first stages of independence.

Problems in Africa	
Economic	
Social	
Political	

Africa's road to independence has not been an easy one. Free from colonial rule, many African nations faced serious political, economic, social, and health challenges. Apartheid ended in South Africa, and Nelson Mandela became the country's first black president. Now into the twenty-first century, tension between old and new, native and foreign, still prevails in African society.

Independence and New Nations

MAIN IDEA After gaining their independence, many African states faced political, economic, social, and health challenges.

HISTORY & YOU Has flu ever infected many students in your school at the same time? How did this outbreak affect your school routine? Read to learn how AIDS affects life in Africa.

After World War II, Europeans realized that colonial rule in Africa would have to end. The Charter of the United Nations supported this belief. It stated that all colonial peoples should have the right to self-determination. In the late 1950s and 1960s, most African nations achieved independence.

In 1957 the Gold Coast, renamed **Ghana** and under **Kwame Nkrumah,** was the first British colony to gain independence. Nigeria, the Belgian Congo (renamed Zaire, now the Democratic Republic of the Congo), Kenya, and others soon followed. Seventeen new African nations emerged in 1960. Another 11 nations followed between 1961 and 1965. The Portuguese finally surrendered Mozambique and Angola in the 1970s.

In North Africa, the French granted full independence to Morocco and Tunisia in 1956. Because Algeria was home to a million French settlers, France chose to keep control there. However, Algerian nationalists began a guerrilla war to liberate their homeland. The French leader, Charles de Gaulle, granted Algeria its independence in 1962.

South Africa and Apartheid

In **South Africa,** where whites dominated the political system, the process was more complicated. Blacks began organizing against white rule and formed the African National Congress (ANC) in 1912. Its **goal** was economic and political reform. The ANC's efforts, however, met with little success.

At the same time, by the 1950s, South African whites (descendants of the Dutch, known as Afrikaners) had strengthened the

R Reading Strategies	C Critical Thinking	D Differentiated Instruction	W Writing Support	S Skill Practice
Teacher Edition • Act. Prior Know., p. 988 • Summarizing, p. 989 • Visualizing, p. 991 • Questioning, p. 993 **Additional Resources** • Guid. Read. Act., URB p. 158 • People in World Hist. Act., URB p. 149 • Read. Ess. & Note-Taking Guide, p. 328	**Teacher Edition** • Making Inferences, p. 987 • Compare/Contrast, p. 991 • Making Generalizations, p. 992 **Additional Resources** • Crit. Think. Act., URB p. 138 • Section Quiz, p. 373	**Teacher Edition** • Visual/Spatial, p. 988 • Adv. Learners, p. 990 • ELL, p. 992 **Additional Resources** • Diff. Instr. Act., URB p. 129 • English Learner Act., URB p. 131 • Hist. Sim. Act., URB p. 145 • Pri Source Read., URB p.151	**Teacher Edition** • Descriptive Writing, p. 989 • Expository Writing, p. 990 **Additional Resources** • World Lit. Read., URB p. 9 • Hist. & Geo. Act., URB p. 139 • World Art & Music Act., URB p. 153	**Teacher Edition** • Using Geo. Skills, p. 987 **Additional Resources** • Skills Reinforc. Act., URB p. 137

R Reading Strategy

Activating Prior Knowledge Ask students to review the text and use what they already know to write a short description of socialism in the Soviet Union and Eastern Europe. OL

D Differentiated Instruction

Visual/Spatial Ask students to re-read this page and consider the idea of all African countries joining in a "broader community." Ask students to design and create a poster that appeals to Africans to support the idea. The poster might include a map or other images as well as a slogan or text. ELL

PEOPLE in HISTORY

Answers: Nkrumah—"self-government now"; **Kenyatta**—encouraging the Mau Maus to rebel

Additional Support

They believed in using the Western democratic model in Africa.

The views of these African leaders on economics were somewhat more **diverse.** Some, such as **Jomo Kenyatta** of **Kenya** and General Mobutu Sese Seko of the present-day Democratic Republic of the Congo, believed in Western-style capitalism. Others, such as **Julius Nyerere** of Tanzania, Kwame Nkrumah of Ghana, and Sékou Touré of Guinea, preferred an "African form of socialism."

R The African form of socialism was not like that practiced in the Soviet Union or Eastern Europe. Instead, it was based on African traditions of community in which ownership of the country's wealth would be put into the hands of the people. As Nyerere declared in 1967: "The basis of socialism is a belief in the oneness of man and the common historical destiny of mankind. Its basis . . . is human equality."

Some African leaders believed in the dream of **Pan-Africanism**—the unity of all black Africans, regardless of national boundaries. In the view of Pan-Africanists, all black African peoples shared a common identity. Several of the new African leaders, including Léopold Senghor of Senegal, Kwame Nkrumah, and Jomo Kenyatta, supported Pan-Africanism.

D Nkrumah in particular hoped that a Pan-African union would join all of the new countries of the continent in a broader community. His dream never became a reality. However, the Organization of African Unity (OAU), founded by the leaders of 32 African states in 1963, was a concrete result of the belief in Pan-Africanism. In 2002 the African Union (AU) replaced the OAU. This 53-nation group promotes democracy and economic growth in the region.

Economic and Health Problems

Independence did not bring economic prosperity to the new African nations.

PEOPLE in HISTORY

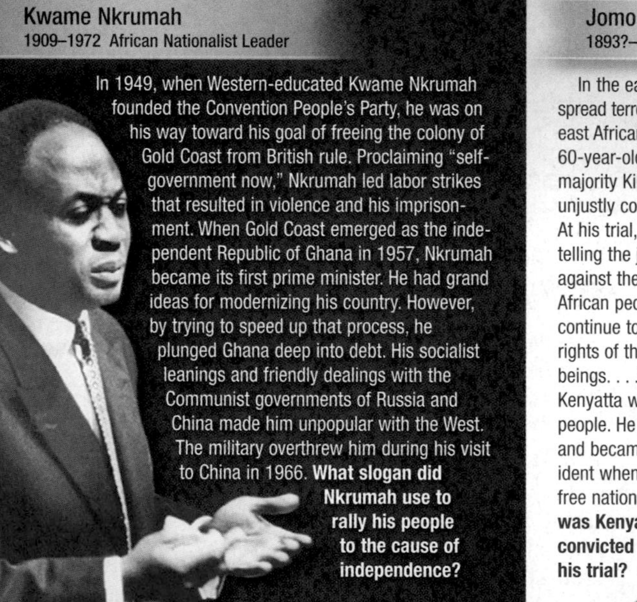

Kwame Nkrumah
1909–1972 African Nationalist Leader

In 1949, when Western-educated Kwame Nkrumah founded the Convention People's Party, he was on his way toward his goal of freeing the colony of Gold Coast from British rule. Proclaiming "self-government now," Nkrumah led labor strikes that resulted in violence and his imprisonment. When Gold Coast emerged as the independent Republic of Ghana in 1957, Nkrumah became its first prime minister. He had grand ideas for modernizing his country. However, by trying to speed up that process, he plunged Ghana deep into debt. His socialist leanings and friendly dealings with the Communist governments of Russia and China made him unpopular with the West. The military overthrew him during his visit to China in 1966. **What slogan did Nkrumah use to rally his people to the cause of independence?**

Jomo Kenyatta
1893?–1978 African Nationalist Leader

In the early 1950s, the Mau Mau uprising spread terror among white settlers in the British east African colony of Kenya. In 1953, a 60-year-old British-educated member of the majority Kikuyu people, Jomo Kenyatta, was unjustly convicted of encouraging the rebellion. At his trial, Kenyatta maintained his innocence, telling the judge, "Our activities have been against the injustices suffered by the African people. . . . [W]hat we shall continue to do, is to demand the rights of the African people as human beings. . . ." An eloquent orator, Kenyatta was an inspiration for his people. He was released in 1959 and became Kenya's first president when Kenya became a free nation in 1963. **What was Kenyatta convicted of at his trial?**

Extending the Content

Kenyatta and Nkrumah Both Kenyatta and Nkrumah spent considerable time in Europe and the United States They met at the fifth Pan-African Congress in England in 1945, which was modeled after the four conferences organized by the African American leader W.E.B. DuBois from 1919 to 1927. The first Pan-African Congress asked the Versailles Peace Conference to allow Africans to be involved in their own government "as fast as their development permits." With little progress made, Nkrumah and Kenyatta joined with others from around the world to call for an end to racial discrimination, among other things. Both leaders struggled to address the problems in postcolonial Africa and eventually became dictatorial in their rule.

Most still relied on the export of a single crop or natural resource. **Liberia,** for example, depended on the export of rubber; **Nigeria,** on oil. When prices dropped, their economies suffered. To make matters worse, Africa's financial and technical resources were incapable of maintaining economic growth without foreign investment. Most African states imported technology and manufactured goods from the West and depended on foreign financial aid to develop their countries.

The new states also sometimes created their own problems. Scarce national resources were spent on military equipment or expensive consumer goods rather than on building the foundations for an industrial economy. Corruption was common.

African population growth, averaging 3 percent by the 1980s, crippled efforts to build modern economies. Serious droughts were another economic handicap and caused widespread hunger and starvation. Since the 1980s, droughts have recurred in Niger, Mali, Sudan, Somalia, and Ethiopia. Millions fled to other countries looking for food.

As a result of all these problems, poverty is widespread in Africa, especially among the three-fourths of the population still living off the land. Cities have grown tremendously. Surrounding the cities are massive slums populated by rural people who came to the cities looking for employment. The growth of the cities has overwhelmed sanitation and transportation systems. Pollution and perpetual traffic jams are the result.

Millions live without water and electricity in their homes. In the meantime, the fortunate few enjoy lavish lifestyles. The rich **W** in many East African countries are known as the *wabenzi,* or Mercedes-Benz people.

In recent years, the greatest challenge to African progress was the spread of **AIDS,** or acquired immunodeficiency syndrome. AIDS is caused by the virus known as HIV, which is spread through bodily fluids. HIV weakens the immune system so that people with the disease cannot fight other illnesses. AIDS is a worldwide problem, but in Africa it is an epidemic. This crisis led the U.S. Congress in 2003 to authorize $15 billion in funds to treat AIDS in foreign nations, mostly in Africa.

According to the United Nations' 2006 AIDS epidemic update, almost two-thirds of all persons infected with HIV (nearly 40 million worldwide) are living in Africa south of the Sahara. In this area, nearly 3 million people, including children, became infected with HIV, and over 2 million died of AIDS during 2006. In Swaziland, more than 33 percent of the adult population has HIV. Infection levels are also high (20–24 percent) in Botswana, Lesotho, and Namibia.

One of the most striking effects of AIDS in Africa is the impact on children and families. In Africa south of the Sahara, 9 percent of children under the age of 15 have lost at least one parent to AIDS. Many have lost both parents. Very often, other relatives are too poor to take these children into their **R** homes. Many orphans thus become heads of households filled with younger brothers and sisters. For centuries, extended families have been the source of support in difficult times, especially in rural parts of Africa. The AIDS epidemic, however, has overwhelmed this traditional support system.

African nations have taken steps to fight the epidemic. It has proved a tremendous burden, however, because many of these countries do not have the money or health facilities to educate their citizens about the disease and how to protect against it. Nor can they purchase the drugs that would extend the lives of those with HIV.

Uganda mounted an impressive effort to fight AIDS. President Yoweri Museveni involved a wide range of natural leaders in Ugandan society, including religious and tribal leaders, as well as international health and social service agencies. As a result of a major campaign promoting health and sex education, Uganda made significant progress in its fight against AIDS. Overall, Uganda's epidemic has stabilized. However, recent research shows evidence of an increase of HIV infection in rural areas and among older men and women.

Political Challenges

Many people hoped that independence would lead to democracies. They were soon disappointed as democratic governments failed. Between 1957 and 1982, more than 70 leaders were violently overthrown.

W Writing Support

Descriptive Writing Ask students to do additional research on the gap between rich and poor in East Africa. Then ask them to write two descriptive paragraphs, one describing the life of a person living in a slum and the other describing the life of the *wabenzi.* **AL**

R Reading Strategy

Summarizing Ask students to write a sentence or two summarizing the effect that AIDS has had on the traditional African family. **OL**

Additional Support

Activity: Technology Connection

Contrasting Ask students how they might contrast the effects of the AIDS epidemic in Africa with its effects in other parts of the world. One way is by creating graphs or charts. Ask students to first study data available from the website http://www.unaids.org/. Have them review summaries for different areas and select data that will contrast the effect of AIDS on Africa with other parts of the world. If available, assist students with software that aids in the preparation of charts or graphs and print out final products. **Ask:** What are the advantages of displaying data in a chart or graph? *(makes information vivid and visually appealing, may be easier to understand than information expressed in sentences)* **OL**

D Differentiated Instruction

Advanced Learners Ask students to research the conflict in Darfur and create a short written or oral report. They can include historical developments leading up to the conflict, international efforts to curb the fighting, and the difficulty in establishing a truce. AL

W Writing Support

Expository Writing Ask students to re-read the quote by Nelson Mandela and to write a paragraph explaining why he might have refused an offer of conditional freedom. AL

✓Reading Check

Answer: to promote a sense of community among all black Africans

✓Reading Check

Answer: Uganda, Ethiopia, Liberia, Somalia

History ONLINE
Student Web Activity— Visit glencoe.com and complete the activity on African independence.

Read excerpts from Nelson Mandela's *An Ideal for Which I Am Prepared to Die* on page R55 in the **Primary Sources and Literature Library.**

In the 1980s, either the military or a single party ruled many major African states. In the 1990s, demand for responsible government grew, but political instability is still a fact of life for many African nations.

Within many African nations, warring ethnic groups undermined the concept of nationhood. This is not surprising since the colonial powers had drawn the boundaries of African nations arbitrarily. Virtually all of these states included widely different ethnic, linguistic, and territorial groups.

For example, during the late 1960s, civil war tore Nigeria apart. Conflicts also broke out among ethnic groups in Zimbabwe. Farther north, in central Africa, fighting between the Hutu and Tutsi created unstable governments in **Rwanda** and Burundi. During the colonial period, Hutu and Tutsi peoples lived together under European control. After independence in 1962, two new countries were created: Rwanda and Burundi. The population in both countries was mixed, but in Rwanda, the Hutu majority ran the government. They resented the position of the Tutsis, who had gotten the best education and jobs under the Belgians. Ethnic fighting was common, and many Tutsis left for neighboring Uganda. They formed a party with the goal of overthrowing the Rwandan government.

In 1994, this tense situation ignited into brutal civil war when a plane carrying the Hutu president was shot down. Hutu militias began a campaign of genocide against Tutsis, killing at least 500,000. Eventually Tutsi rebel soldiers gained control. Hutus, as many as two million, fled the country, many to the **Democratic Republic of the Congo** (DRC). The Tutsis then invaded the DRC. In 1998 a civil war began, and as many as 3.5 million people died as a result.

D Ethnic violence has also plagued **Sudan,** Africa's largest nation. In the western province of Darfur, Arab militias attacked African tribal groups with the support of the Arab-led government. Entire villages were burned and tens of thousands of people were killed. An estimated 1.8 million fled to refugee camps. Despite a truce agreement in May 2006, the fighting continues.

✓Reading Check **Explaining** Why was the Organization of African Unity formed?

New Hopes

MAIN IDEA Dictators fell in several African nations, and apartheid ended in South Africa.

HISTORY & YOU Can you name someone in American history who was jailed for political activities? Read to learn about Nelson Mandela.

Not all the news in Africa has been bad. One-party regimes have collapsed and dictators have been ousted in several countries. Apartheid also ended in South Africa.

End of Dictatorships

One dictator ousted was Idi Amin of Uganda. After ruling by terror and brutal repression throughout the 1970s, Amin was deposed in 1979. Dictatorships also came to an end in Ethiopia, Liberia, and Somalia. In these cases, however, bloody civil wars followed the fall of these regimes.

End of Apartheid

One remarkable event was the 1994 election of **Nelson Mandela** to the presidency of the Republic of South Africa. Imprisoned in 1962 for his activities with the African National Congress, Mandela spent almost 26 years in maximum-security prisons in South Africa. For all those years, Mandela never wavered from his resolve to secure the freedom of his country.

W Mandela was offered freedom in 1985, with conditions. Yet, he refused to accept a conditional freedom: "Only free men can negotiate; prisoners cannot enter into contracts. Your freedom and mine cannot be separated."

Nobel Peace Prize winner (1984) Bishop **Desmond Tutu** and others worked to free Mandela and to end apartheid. Eventually, worldwide pressure forced the South African government to dismantle apartheid laws. In 1990 Mandela was released from prison. In 1993 the government of F. W. de Klerk agreed to hold democratic national elections—the first in South Africa's history. In 1994 Nelson Mandela became South Africa's first black president.

✓Reading Check **Identifying** Which African countries overthrew dictatorships?

Differentiated Instruction

Leveled Activities

BL Guided Reading Activity, URB p. 158

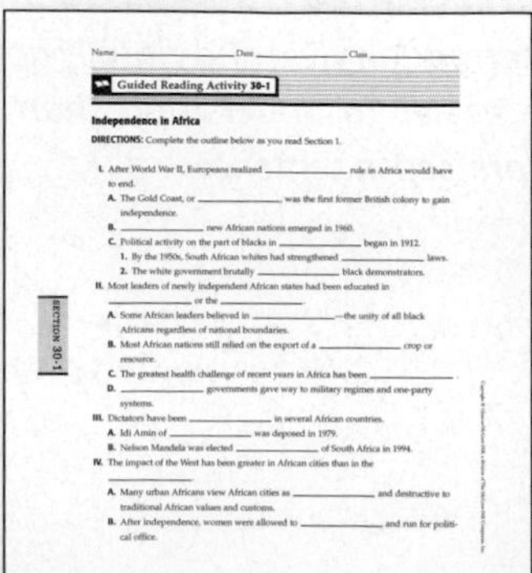

OL People in World History Activity, URB p. 149

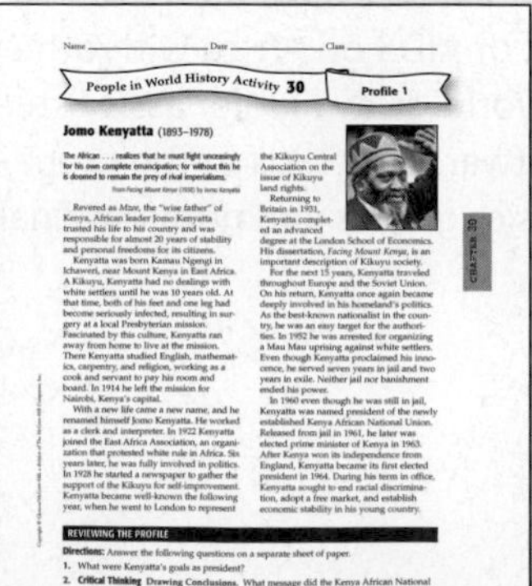

AL World Art and Music Activity, URB p. 153

ELL English Learner Activity, URB p. 131

TURNING POINT: THE END OF APARTHEID IN SOUTH AFRICA

On the day of South Africa's first democratic election, voters waited in very long lines to cast their ballots.

"During my lifetime I have dedicated myself to this struggle of the African people. I have fought against white domination, and I have fought against black domination. I have cherished the ideal of a democratic and free society in which all persons live together in harmony and with equal opportunities." **C**

—Nelson Mandela, opening statement at the Rivonia Trial, April 20, 1964

Worldwide pressure on the South African government led to the end of apartheid and the election of that country's first black president. Apartheid was the policy of racial separation that became law in 1948 in South Africa.

A series of apartheid laws stripped black South Africans of virtually all civil rights. A decade of peaceful protests against these laws, organized by the African National Congress (ANC), came to an end with the Sharpeville Massacre in 1960.

In 1961 the ANC, by then an outlawed organization, took up arms against the government. In 1963 police arrested the ANC's leaders, including Nelson Mandela. At the Rivonia Trial, Mandela was sentenced to life in prison.

International pressure increased in 1985 when the governments of the United States and Great Britain imposed economic sanctions on South Africa. Finally, in 1990, South African president F. W. de Klerk's government legalized the ANC, freed Mandela, and began to dismantle the apartheid system. Four years later, Mandela became the first democratically elected president of South Africa. In his inaugural address, Mandela promised to build "a rainbow nation at peace with itself and the world." **R**

CRITICAL THINKING SKILLS

1. **Making Connections** Was Mandela's promise to build "a rainbow nation" consistent with the statement he made 30 years earlier at the Rivonia trial? Explain.
2. **Analyzing** In what ways did the end of apartheid mark a new beginning for South Africa?

C Critical Thinking

Comparing and Contrasting **Ask:** How are the beliefs of Nelson Mandela similar to those of Martin Luther King, Jr.? *(Both have spoken about races living together in peace and worked for a society in which all people have equal opportunities.)* **OL**

R Reading Strategy

Visualizing **Ask:** How is the idea of a "rainbow nation" appropriate for South Africa? *(People of many different ethnic backgrounds and skin colors live there.)* **OL**

CRITICAL THINKING SKILLS

Answers:

1. Yes, at the trial he expressed his desire to create a society in which all persons could live in harmony and have equal opportunities.
2. It set South Africa on the path toward respecting human rights, full democracy, and equality for all citizens.

Differentiated Instruction

History and Geography Activity, URB p. 139

Analyzing Information

Objective: To analyze the effects of apartheid.

Focus: Review apartheid laws.

Teach: Discuss the effects of apartheid on everyday life.

Assess: Have students give examples of how apartheid affected South Africans.

Close: Ask students to identify laws and actions in U.S. history that unfairly focused on race or ethnicity.

Differentiated Instruction Strategies

BL Have students compare Bantu homelands with Indian reservations.

AL Ask students to research how pressure by other countries helped South Africa avoid civil war.

ELL Have students contrast the use of *homelands* with its common definition.

D Differentiated Instruction

English Language Learners
Have students re-read the opening paragraph on this page and consider the concept of "contrasts." Ask them to study the second paragraph and make a list of characteristics of modern African cities; then have them list the contrasts to the characteristics of the more rural areas of Africa mentioned in the third paragraph. ELL

C Critical Thinking

Making Generalizations
Ask students to write a sentence that describes the general approach of colonial powers to African colonies. OL

CRITICAL THINKING SKILLS

Answers:
1. They depend on the export of one crop or natural resource, and foreigners own major industries.
2. Answers will vary. Possible answer: Both the political and economic development would have been different. The economies would probably be more diverse, which could be more stable.

Additional Support

See page R56 to read "Civil Peace" from *Girls at War and Other Stories* by Chinua Achebe in the **Primary Sources and Literature Library.**

Society and Culture

MAIN IDEA Tension between old and new, native and foreign, affects African society.

HISTORY & YOU How has e-mail changed how people communicate? Read to learn about the contrast between modern life and tradition in Africa.

D Africa is a study in contrasts. Old and new, native and foreign, live side by side. One result is a constant tension between traditional ways and Western culture.

City and Countryside

In general, the impact of the West has been greater in the cities than in the countryside. After all, the colonial presence was first and most firmly established in the cities. C Many cities, including Dakar, Lagos, Cape Town, Brazzaville, and Nairobi, are direct products of colonial rule. Most African cities today look like cities elsewhere in the world.

Outside the major cities, where about three-fourths of the inhabitants of Africa live, modern influence has had less of an impact. Millions of people throughout Africa live much as their ancestors did in thatched dwellings without modern plumbing and electricity. They farm, hunt, or raise livestock by traditional methods, wear traditional clothing, and practice traditional beliefs. Conditions such as drought or flooding affect the ability of rural

INFOGRAPHICS PRIMARY SOURCE

Africa's Colonial Legacy

Many African nationalists see Africa's problems as the legacy of colonialism. When independence came, the many new African rulers inherited nations lacking the basic infrastructure for a modern society.

Most African nations remain economically fragile, still depending on the export of a single crop or natural resource. Investors from the former colonial powers still own many of the businesses on which African economies depend.

The modern skyline of Nairobi, Kenya, forms a backdrop to one of the slums that surround the city.

Some question the assumed superiority of Western society:

"It is, of course, a presumption that modernisation is desirable. The fact that western society is more complex than traditional African society does not necessarily mean that it is better. . . . Who is to say whether people living in agrarian societies are less developed as human beings than inhabitants of industrialised ones?"

—Tunde Obadina, Director, Africa Business Information Services

CRITICAL THINKING SKILLS

1. **Explaining** Why can many African nations today be described as "economically fragile"?
2. **Hypothesizing** How do you think Africa south of the Sahara might have developed without colonialism?

Teacher Tip

Collaborative Learning This activity allows students with different levels of academic skills and intelligences to work together. As you form groups, consider the needed skills and choose students accordingly.

Activity: Collaborative Learning

Comparing and Contrasting Divide the class into two groups that will research modern African life and act out parts of everyday life by showing an average day for an African teenager. One group should focus on modern urban life (not in slums) and the other on traditional life in a village. Their presentations might include information on housing, school, work, communications, clothing, recreation, and so on. **Ask:** Do you think one group is better off than the other? Why? *(Answers will vary, but should be based on opinions about the value of development.)* OL

Africans to grow crops or tend herds. Migration to the cities for work is one solution. This can be very disruptive to families and villages. Many urban people view rural people as backward. Rural dwellers view the cities as corrupting and destructive to traditional African values and customs.

Women's Roles

In addressing the democratically elected South African parliament in 1994, Nelson Mandela said: "[F]reedom cannot be achieved unless women have been emancipated from all forms of oppression."

Independence from colonial powers changed women's roles in African society. Almost without exception women were allowed to vote and run for political office. However, radical changes have not taken place. Few women hold political offices. While they dominate some professions such as teaching, child care, and clerical work, women do not share in all career opportunities open to men. Most African women are employed in low-paid positions such as farm laborers, factory workers, and servants. Furthermore, in many rural areas, traditional attitudes toward women, including arranged marriages, prevail. **R**

African Culture

Africans have adapted their native artistic traditions to foreign influences. A dilemma for many contemporary African artists is finding a balance between Western techniques and training on the one hand and the rich heritage of traditional African art forms on the other. In some countries, governments make the artists' decisions. Artists are told to depict scenes of traditional African life. These works are designed to serve the tourist industry.

African writers have often addressed the tensions and dilemmas that modern Africans face. The conflicting demands of town versus country and native versus foreign were the themes of most of the best-known works of the 1960s and 1970s.

These themes characterize the works of **Chinua Achebe** and **Noni Jabavu.** A Nigerian novelist who has won international acclaim, Achebe writes about the problems of Africans caught up in the conflict between traditional and Western values. In his novel *Things Fall Apart,* Achebe portrays the simple dignity of traditional African village life. Jabavu, a South African writer, documents the breakdown in African family life due to urbanization in *The Ochre People.* She expresses her impressions of westernization in East Africa and her criticism of traditional notions about "a woman's place" in her book, *Drawn in Color.*

✓Reading Check **Summarizing** What themes characterize the works of Chinua Achebe and Noni Jabavu?

Vocabulary

1. **Explain** the significance of: Ghana, Kwame Nkrumah, South Africa, goal, apartheid, diverse, Jomo Kenyatta, Kenya, Julius Nyerere, Pan-Africanism, Liberia, Nigeria, AIDS, Rwanda, Democratic Republic of the Congo, Sudan, Nelson Mandela, Desmond Tutu, Chinua Achebe, Noni Jabavu.

Main Ideas

2. **Identify** the country and economic view of each African leader listed below.

Leader	Country	Economic View
Jomo Kenyatta		
Mobutu Sese Seko		
Julius Nyerere		
Kwame Nkrumah		
Sékou Touré		

3. **Describe** factors that contributed to ending apartheid in South Africa.
4. **Explain** why cities in Africa tend to be more modern than the countryside.

Critical Thinking

5. **The BIG Idea Determining Cause and Effect** How do you think the political situation in many African nations affects the fight against AIDS?
6. **Analyzing** What are some key reasons why poverty is so widespread in Africa?
7. **Analyzing Visuals** Examine the photograph on page 991. How does this picture reflect the desire of black South Africans to vote?

Writing About History

8. **Descriptive Writing** Assume the role of a journalist who is assigned to cover the conflict in Darfur. Do research and write a short news story describing the living conditions in the refugee camps.

History ONLINE

For help with the concepts in this section of *Glencoe World History*, go to glencoe.com and click Study Central™.

R Reading Strategy

Questioning Ask: Why do you think "radical changes have not taken place" in women's roles? *(Answers will vary, but students might say that traditional attitudes may be too strong.)* **OL**

✓Reading Check

Answer: Achebe—the conflict between traditional and Western values; **Jabavu**—breakdown of African family life and criticism of women's inequality

Assess

Study Central provides summaries, interactive games, and online graphic organizers to help students review content.

Close

Making Generalizations

Ask: How has political self-determination changed life in Africa? *(Countries have struggled to establish stable governments and to deal with the effects of colonialism.)* **OL**

Answers

1. Definitions for the vocabulary words are found in the section and the Glossary.
2. **Kenyatta:** Kenya, Western-style capitalism; **Seko:** Congo, Western-style capitalism; **Nyerere:** Tanzania, African socialism; **Nkrumah:** Ghana, African socialism; **Touré:** Guinea, African socialism
3. leadership of Nelson Mandela and Desmond Tutu, worldwide pressure
4. Colonial presence was most firmly established in the cities, and many cities are the direct result of colonial rule.
5. Possible response: Political instability hampers efforts for a coordinated national campaign against AIDS. Constant fighting deflects national resources away from needed medical care and makes international relief efforts more difficult.
6. reliance on a single export, use of resources on military, corruption, rapid population growth, drought, AIDS, political instability, civil war
7. people willing to stand in a very long line; absence of vehicles suggests people had to walk from the distant settlement
8. Students' news stories should reflect current and accurate sources.

Focus

Introducing Social History
Discuss how a natural resource such as oil can affect the economy and society of a nation. **Ask:** How does oil influence business and people in the United States? *(Answers may include that oil prices affect the economy and the need for oil affects the way people run their lives.)* OL

Teach

R Reading Strategy

Identifying **Ask:** What traditional styles of dress are common among Muslim teenagers in Nigeria? *(Girls wear headpieces and dark clothing that covers their whole body; boys wear* kufis *and long robes over silk pants.)* OL

D Differentiated Instruction

Visual/Spatial Have students study the visuals on pages 994 and 995 to identify traditional and Western influences. Then have them read the captions to check their ideas. BL

Additional Support

Social History

Teenagers in Nigeria

Nigeria's rich oil reserves have attracted Western attention and influence throughout the nation's economy and culture. Across Nigeria, teenagers reflect the tension between Western values and artifacts, and traditional culture. Ethnic traditions, national culture, and Western imports all play off of one another.

Hair braiding is an old tradition in Nigeria. Some teenage girls spend hours at salons having their hair braided into intricate patterns.

Fulani teenage girls often wear tribal tattoos on their face as a symbol of beauty.

Muslim teenage boys often wear a cloth skullcap, or *kufi*, on their heads.

Muslim teenage boys in Nigeria wear floor-length robes over baggy cotton, or silk, drawstring pants.

Traditional attire for Nigerian teenage girls includes a long colorful cloth skirt. Muslim girls may wear dark-colored clothing that covers the entire body, along with a headpiece that can be worn as a veil.

About half of Nigeria's population follows Islam. Studying the Quran is an important part of a Muslim teenager's education.

Traditional Influences in Nigeria

The Nigerian population contains several different ethnic groups, each with its own language, religious practices, and customs. Many Nigerian groups have adopted Islamic or Christian belief systems. The traditional values of Nigeria's ethnic groups strongly influence teenagers, especially those living in rural areas. Their lifestyles are largely shaped by parents, village leaders, and religious teachers.

994

Background

Nigeria's Oil Economy Oil was first discovered in Nigeria in 1956. By the late 1990s, mining accounted for about 40 percent of Nigeria's GDP and most of that was related to petroleum. Nigeria became a member of OPEC in 1971, and today oil accounts for almost all of the country's exports. Most of Nigeria's oil comes from the Niger Delta region on the Atlantic coast. The industry has been plagued by corruption. In 2000, a government commission estimated that about 45 percent of the oil revenue was being stolen or wasted. High crude oil prices in 2006 allowed Nigeria to pay off most of its large foreign debt. This made more money available for infrastructure and important services such as education and health care. Militants in the Niger Delta region want the area to receive a higher percentage of oil revenues and have resorted to violence that has disrupted oil production. Peaceful demonstrators also protested high fuel prices in such an oil rich country.

W Writing Support

Personal Writing Have students write a letter to a Nigerian teenager describing their school and leisure activities. OL

Fuji, a musical style based on drums and Islam-influenced vocals, is popular in Nigeria.

Despite Nigeria's large oil production, many Nigerian teenagers, both urban and rural, live in poverty.

Many young people wear Western-style tops, pants and sweaters.

W Traditional and modern influences often exist side by side in Nigerian households. The father wears a traditional Yoruba outfit while his son wears a Western-style T-shirt.

Teenagers in Nigeria are most likely to attend school in the big cities. Although public school is free, parents must buy school uniforms for their children.

Playing sports such as soccer and listening to Afro-beat or rap music are popular leisure activities for Nigerian teenagers.

Global Influences in Nigeria

Nigeria has urbanized rapidly in the past quarter century. Its cities receive a steady influx of foreign goods and ideas. The impact of Western culture in urban areas is strong. Many Nigerian teenagers have embraced foreign influences. Nonetheless, traditional culture remains an important influence on most Nigerian teenagers. Their lives reflect a blending of traditional ways and global culture.

Analyzing Visuals

1. **Analyzing** What statement does a Nigerian teenager make with the clothes that he or she wears?
2. **Contrasting** How might the daily life of a Nigerian teenager living in the country differ from the daily life of a Nigerian teenager living in the city?

Assess/Close

Have students discuss how American teenagers may be influenced by traditional cultures. OL

ANALYZING VISUALS

Answers:

1. Clothes establish personal identity and may also reveal religious and cultural values.
2. **urban:** more likely to attend school and pursue a Western lifestyle, including music and clothes; **rural:** more likely to follow traditional lifestyles, including clothing and religious practices

Activity: Interdisciplinary Connection

Geography Ask: **In what ways does the geography of Nigeria affect teenagers' lives?** Have students work in pairs or groups to explore the answer to this broad question. Students should research a specific aspect of Nigeria's geography and tell how it affects young people. Some students may explore the physical geography of the country, focusing on climate regions, natural resources, or recreation. Groups may also look at geography's effect on various sectors of the economy. Some may focus on political geography, studying the country's governmental organization and location of government centers. Others could look at settlement patterns to determine which parts of the country are more rural or urban. Students could determine the location and population of major cities and learn more about urban life. Human-environment interaction is another possible topic. Have students use maps, charts, graphs, and/or photographs to display the results of their findings and explain how the information relates to the question. OL

R Reading Strategy

Using Word Parts Ask students to define the prefix *pan-* or look up its definition if necessary. Then discuss how it is used in other words such as Pan-African, Pan-American, pandemic, and panorama. **OL**

C Critical Thinking

Determining Cause and Effect Ask: What was the immediate motivation for Israel's 1967 attacks on Egypt and its neighbors? *(Egypt had imposed a blockade against Israeli shipping and Israel feared attack.)* **BL**

S Skill Practice

Using Geography Skills Ask: Why is the Persian Gulf so important to many Middle Eastern oil-producing countries? *(It provides shipping access to the Arabian Sea and Indian Ocean.)* **OL**

Geography SKILLS

Answers:

1. Egypt, Jordan, Syria, Lebanon
2. Egypt, Jordan, Syria, Turkey, Bahrain, Oman, Yemen, Lebanon, Israel

Additional Support

Nasser emerged from the conflict as a powerful leader. He began to promote **Pan-Arabism,** or Arab unity. In February 1958, Egypt formally united with Syria in the United Arab Republic (UAR). Nasser was named the first president of the new state. Egypt and Syria hoped that the union would eventually include all Arab states.

Many other Arab leaders were suspicious of Pan-Arabism. Oil-rich Arab states were concerned they would have to share revenues with poorer states in the Middle East. In Nasser's view, Arab unity meant that wealth derived from oil, which currently flowed into a few Arab states or to foreign interests, could be used to improve the standard of living throughout the Middle East. In 1961 Syrian military leaders took over Syria and withdrew the country from its union with Egypt. Nasser continued to work on behalf of Arab interests.

The Arab-Israeli Dispute

During the late 1950s and 1960s, the dispute between Israel and other states in the Middle East became more heated. In 1967 Nasser imposed a blockade against Israeli shipping through the Gulf of Aqaba. He declared: "Now we are ready to confront Israel. We are ready to deal with the entire Palestine question."

Fearing attack, on June 5, 1967, Israel launched air strikes against Egypt and several of its Arab neighbors. Israeli warplanes wiped out most of the Egyptian air force. Israeli armies broke the blockade and

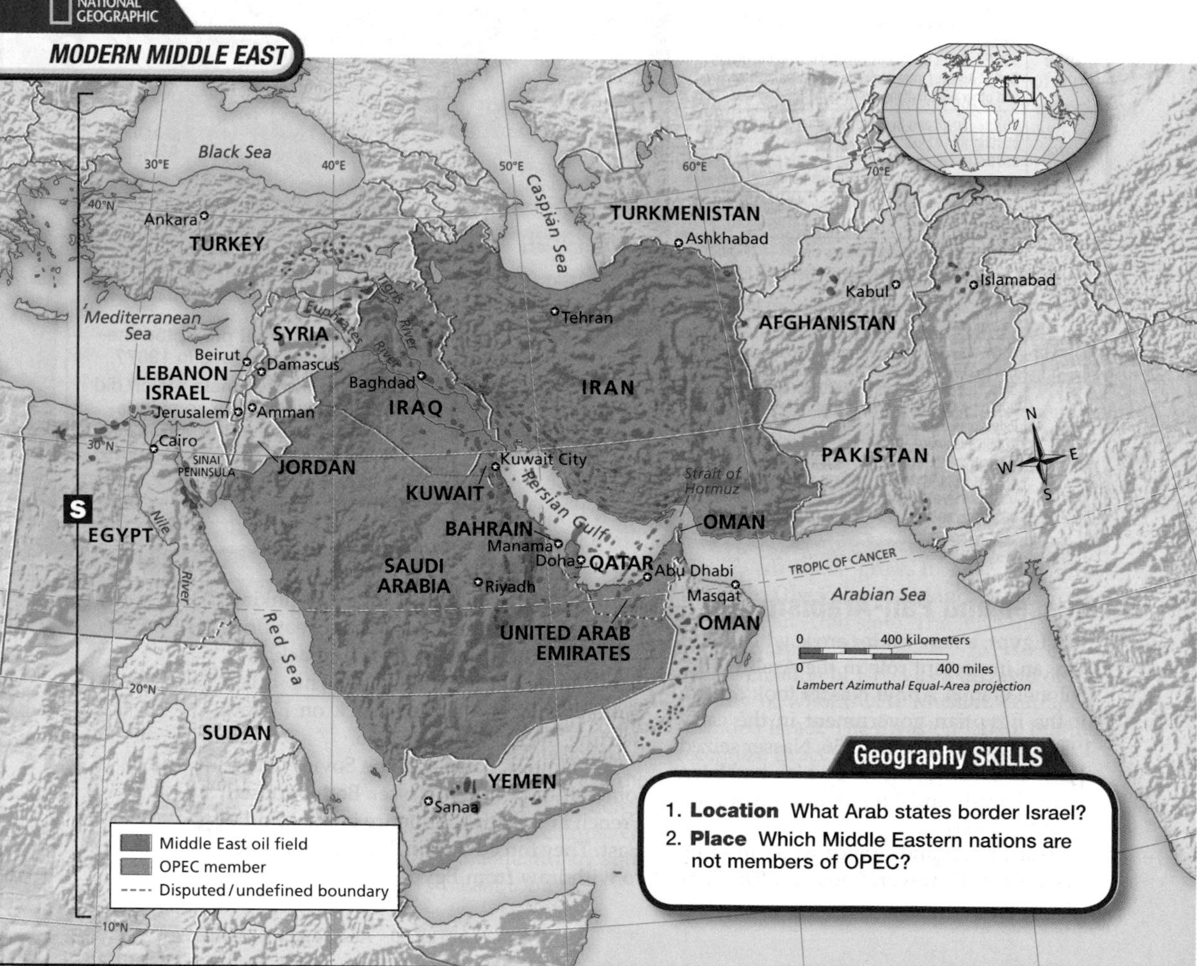

Extending the Content

Nasser and the UAR Nasser promoted the idea of Arab unity in much the same way that African leaders sought unity across their continent. However, Nasser's early actions often stood in the way of unity. When Syria joined with Egypt in the UAR in 1958, Nasser demanded that the two countries become integrated rather than federated, even though they were far apart geographically. Egypt was much larger and stronger than Syria and Syria soon found that Nasser and Egypt controlled Syrian life and political decisions. Syria withdrew in 1961, but Egypt continued to use the name United Arab Republic until after Nasser's death in 1970. The name Egypt returned in 1971.

occupied the **Sinai Peninsula.** Israel seized territory on the **West Bank** of the Jordan River, occupied East Jerusalem, and took control of the Golan Heights. During this Six-Day War, Israel tripled the size of territory under its control. As a result, another million Palestinians now lived in areas under Israeli control, most of them on the West Bank.

Over the next few years, Arab states continued to demand the return of the occupied territories. Nasser died in 1970, and **Anwar el-Sadat** succeeded him.

On October 6, 1973 (the Jewish holiday of Yom Kippur), Egypt and Syria launched a coordinated surprise attack against Israel. Golda Meir, Israel's prime minister, had little time to mobilize troops. For the first two days of the Yom Kippur War, Israel was on the defensive. Then the tide turned. Israeli forces pushed into Egypt, trapping Egypt's Third Army. A UN-negotiated cease-fire on October 22 saved the Egyptian army from destruction. An agreement in 1974 officially ended this conflict, but the dispute over the occupied territories remained.

Meanwhile, however, the war was having indirect results in Western nations. In 1960, several Arab oil-producing states had formed **OPEC,** the Organization of the Petroleum Exporting Countries, to control the price of oil. During the Yom Kippur **D** War, some OPEC nations announced large increases in the price of oil to foreign countries. The price hikes, coupled with cuts in oil production, led to oil shortages and serious economic problems in the West.

In 1977 U.S. president Jimmy Carter began to press for a compromise peace between Arabs and Israelis. In September 1978 President Carter met with President Sadat of Egypt and Israeli prime minister **Menachem Begin** (BAY•gihn) at Camp David in the United States. The result was the Camp David Accords, an agreement to sign an Israeli-Egyptian peace treaty. The treaty, signed by Sadat and Begin in March 1979, led to a complete Israeli withdrawal from the Sinai Peninsula and ended the state of war between Egypt and Israel. Many Arab countries, however, continued to refuse to recognize Israel.

✓Reading Check **Identifying** How did the Yom Kippur War affect the West indirectly?

The Ongoing Crisis

MAIN IDEA The turmoil in the Middle East continues into the twenty-first century.

HISTORY & YOU How did your family think the United States should react to the 9/11 attacks? Read about the U.S. invasion of Iraq.

In 1964 the Egyptians took the lead in forming the Palestine Liberation Organization (PLO) to represent Palestinian interests. The PLO believed that only the Palestinian Arabs should have a state in the Palestine region. At the same time, a guerrilla movement called al-Fatah, headed by the PLO political leader **Yasir Arafat,** began to launch terrorist attacks on Israeli territory. Terrorist attacks continued for decades.

Palestine and Lebanon

During the 1980s, Palestinian Arabs, frustrated by their failure to achieve self-rule, grew more militant. They led an ***intifada,*** or uprising, in the territories occupied by Israel since the 1967 Arab-Israeli war. Finally, in the Oslo Peace Accords of 1993, Israel **R** and the PLO agreed that the PLO would control a semi-independent area. In return, the PLO recognized the Israeli state.

In 1994 Jordan and Israel signed a peace treaty. This treaty made Jordan the second Arab nation, after Egypt, to recognize Israel.

Even with these changes, little progress was made toward Palestinian statehood. Some Israelis did not want to give up the occupied territories, and some Palestinians did not accept the state of Israel. In the wake of the Palestinian rejection of a proposal offered by Israel at a meeting arranged by President Clinton at Camp David in 2000, a second *intifada* erupted and has continued. Suicide bombings in the heart of Israel led to Israeli reoccupation of significant areas of the West Bank that had been largely controlled by the Palestinian Authority. Nonetheless, a sign of progress emerged in 2003—the Israeli cabinet formally accepted the principle of a Palestinian state.

Yasir Arafat died in 2004. Mahmoud Abbas, a moderate Palestinian, replaced him. Many people were hopeful that real progress might be made at peace talks.

D Differentiated Instruction

Logical/Mathematical Ask students to consider the interdependence of world markets in relationship to the cost and supply of oil, focusing on the United States. Ask them to create a graphic display showing the cause-and-effect relationships of U.S. dependence on oil imports, U.S. prices for goods, U.S. jobs, OPEC control of oil reserves, disruption of exports due to war, and effect of oil prices on the U.S. economy. **AL**

R Reading Strategy

Determining Importance

Ask: What does "semi-independent" mean? *(Answers will vary, but students may mention that people could make some decisions while still remaining under foreign control.)* **OL**

✓Reading Check

Answer: serious economic problems due to higher oil prices and oil shortages

Differentiated Instruction

Leveled Activities

BL **Reteaching Activity, URB p. 155**

OL **Historical Significance Activity, URB p. 142**

AL **Enrichment Activity, URB p. 156**

ELL **Academic Vocabulary Activity, URB p. 135**

W Writing Support

Expository Writing Ask students to write one or two paragraphs that explain their understanding of the events of 9/11, including the impact it had at the time and its impact today. **OL**

Answer: because of differences among the three major groups: Shia Muslims, Sunni Muslims, and ethnic Kurds

CONNECTING TO TODAY

Answers:

1. Muslim terrorists are retaliating against the United States for its policies in the Middle East.
2. Answers will vary. Students may note that groups perform terrorists acts to protest, seek influence, and change policies.

Both of these claims were doubted by many other member states at the United Nations. As a result, the United States was forced to attack Iraq with little support from the world community.

In March 2003 a largely U.S.-led army invaded Iraq. The Iraqi army was quickly defeated, and Saddam Hussein was captured. The war, however, was far from over. No weapons of mass destruction were found. Moreover, for the United States and its partners, rebuilding Iraq was more difficult than defeating the Iraqi army. Saddam Hussein's supporters, foreign terrorists, and Islamic militants all battled the American-led forces.

American efforts since 2003 have focused on training an Iraqi military force capable of defeating rebel forces and establishing order in Iraq. Moreover, the United States moved toward the formation of a temporary Iraqi government that could hold free elections and create a democracy. Establishing a new government was difficult because there were differences among the three major groups in Iraqi society: Shia Muslims, Sunni Muslims, and ethnic Kurds.

Although a new Iraqi government came into being in 2005, it has been unable to establish a unified state. By 2006, Iraq seemed to be descending into a widespread civil war, especially between the Shia, who controlled southern Iraq, and the Sunnis, who controled central Iraq. Saddam Hussein's execution in December 2006 added to the turmoil and incited protests from his followers. In January 2007 President Bush called for an increase of U.S. troops to help end the violence in Iraq.

Explaining Why was it difficult to establish a new government in Iraq?

CONNECTING TO THE UNITED STATES

TERRORISM IN THE U.S.

Terrorist acts became more frequent in the later twentieth century. By May 2003, the U.S. State Department had designated 36 groups as Foreign Terrorist Organizations. These groups include urban guerrilla groups in Latin America; militants dedicated to the liberation of Palestine; Islamic militants fighting Western influence in the Middle East; and separatists seeking independent states.

Television has encouraged global terrorism to some extent because terrorists know that newscasts create instant publicity. Television images of American jetliners flying into the World Trade Center in New York City in 2001, for example, created immediate awareness of the goals of the Islamic fundamentalist militants.

- **February 26, 1993: Muslim extremists led by Ramzi Yousef bombed the World Trade Center, killing 6 and wounding 1,000.**
- **September 11, 2001: Muslim extremists in four hijacked airliners attacked landmarks in New York City and Washington, D.C., killing 3,000.**

W

Terrorist attacks at the World Trade Center, September 11, 2001

CONNECTING TO TODAY

1. **Making Connections** How is the unrest in the Middle East connected to terrorist attacks against the United States?
2. **Evaluating** What are the reasons for terrorism?

Additional Support

Extending the Content

Connecting to the United States

Terrorism in the U.S. The attacks on the World Trade Center shocked much of the world, partly because the attacks occurred on U.S. soil. However, U.S. interests have been the target of Muslim extremists and other radical groups for more than twenty years, including in countries such as Spain, Greece, Germany, Lebanon, Saudi Arabia, Yemen, and the Philippines. **Ask:** **Why do you think the United States is the subject of so many terrorist attacks?** (*Answers will vary, but students may argue that its political, economic, and cultural influence around the world angers some groups. Also, people who disagree with U.S. actions find it an easy target because of its presence in many foreign countries.*) **OL**

Society and Culture

MAIN IDEA Islamic fundamentalism has impacted Middle Eastern society, especially women's roles.

HISTORY & YOU Do your parents object to some things you wear? Read about restrictions imposed by Islamic conservatives.

In recent years, conservative religious forces have tried to replace foreign culture and values with Islamic forms of belief and behavior. This movement is called Islamic fundamentalism or Islamic activism. For some Islamic leaders, Western values and culture are based on materialism, greed, and immorality. Extremists want to remove all Western influence in Muslim countries. These extremists give many Westerners an unfavorable impression of Islam.

Islamic fundamentalism began in Iran under Ayatollah Khomeini. There the return to traditional Muslim beliefs reached into clothing styles, social practices, and the legal system. These ideas and practices spread to other Muslim countries. In Egypt, for example, militant Muslims assassinated President Sadat in 1981.

Islamic fundamentalism is a concern in some Middle East countries. In Turkey, the military suspects that "Islamization" is gaining ground in the country. The prime minister has spoken out against restrictions on Islamic-style headscarves and has taken steps to aid religious schools. The military intends to keep Turkey secular and pro-Western. **C**

At the beginning of the twentieth century, women's place in Middle Eastern society had changed little for hundreds of years. Early Muslim women had participated in the political life of society and had extensive legal, political, and social rights. Cultural practices in many countries had overshadowed those rights, however.

In the nineteenth and twentieth centuries, Muslim scholars debated issues surrounding women's roles in society. Many argued for the need to rethink outdated interpretations and cultural practices that prevented women from realizing their potential. Until the 1970s, the general trend in urban areas was toward a greater role for women. Beginning in the 1970s, however, there was a shift toward more traditional roles for women. This trend was especially noticeable in Iran.

The literature of the Middle East since 1945 has reflected a rise in national awareness, which encouraged interest in historical traditions. Writers also began to deal more with secular themes for broader audiences, not just the elite. For example, *Cairo Trilogy* by Egyptian writer **Naguib Mahfouz** tells about a merchant family in Egypt in the 1920s. The changes in the family parallel the changes in Egypt. Mahfouz was the first writer in Arabic to win the Nobel Prize in Literature (in 1988).

✓**Reading Check** **Identifying** Who was the first writer in Arabic to win the Nobel Prize in Literature?

SECTION 2 REVIEW

Vocabulary

1. **Explain** the significance of: Zionists, resolution, Israel, issue, Gamal Abdel Nasser, Pan-Arabism, Sinai Peninsula, West Bank, Anwar el-Sadat, OPEC, Menachem Begin, Yasir Arafat, *intifada*, Iran, Ayatollah Ruhollah Khomeini, Iraq, Saddam Hussein, Kuwait, Persian Gulf, Osama bin Laden, al-Qaeda, Naguib Mahfouz.

Main Ideas

2. **Explain** how the migration of Jews to Israel has been similar to earlier migrations.
3. **List** the goals of the U.S. involvement in Iraq since 2003 in a chart like the one below.

Goals of U.S. in Iraq Since 2003

4. **Explain** how Muslim extremists view Western values and culture.

Critical Thinking

5. **The BIG Idea** **Analyzing** Why has it proven so difficult to resolve conflict in the Middle East?
6. **Making Connections** Why is the Middle East so important to the global economy?
7. **Analyzing Visuals** Examine the photograph on page 1002. What emotions does this image create for you? Why?

Writing About History

8. **Persuasive Writing** Choose the role of either an Arab Palestinian or a Jewish settler. Write a letter to the United Nations, arguing your position on the Arab-Israeli issue. What do you think should be done and why?

History ONLINE
For help with the concepts in this section of *Glencoe World History*, go to glencoe.com and click Study Central™.

1003

C Critical Thinking

Making Inferences **Ask:** What is a possible result of the differing views of the Turkish government and military? *(Answers will vary, but may include conflict resulting in a military takeover, and the election of either more secular or more religious leaders.)* **OL**

Answer: Naguib Mahfouz

Assess

History ONLINE

Study Central provides summaries, interactive games, and online graphic organizers to help students review content.

Close

Making Generalizations

Ask: How have the conflicts in the Middle East affected other parts of the world? *(Oil supplies affect industrial economies; terrorism has spread from the Middle East to other countries; other countries provide support for Middle Eastern military and political efforts.)* **OL**

Answers

1. Definitions for the vocabulary words are found in the section and the Glossary.
2. Possible response: migrated to escape persecution; migration led to conflict
3. training Iraqi military force capable of defeating insurgents; establishing order in Iraq; forming temporary Iraqi government to hold free elections and to create democracy
4. as based on materialism, greed, and immorality
5. Possible response: many religious and ethnic factions, religious extremism, competing claims for territory, longstanding mistrust, competition for oil wealth
6. oil reserves; important shipping routes, such as the Suez Canal, run through the region
7. Possible emotions: fear, anger, disbelief; Possible reasons: didn't think it could happen in our country, terrible loss of life
8. Students' letters will vary.

ANALYZING PRIMARY SOURCES

Focus

Remind students that apartheid was a form of racial segregation in South Africa. All citizens were classified by race; laws restricted where they could live, work, or socialize. The non-white majority was excluded from most political and economic opportunities.

Teach

R Reading Strategy

Previewing Have students read the introductions to each source, noting the speaker and the date. **Ask:** What do you think each speech is about? *(Tutu: asking for international opposition to apartheid; Mandela: looking ahead in the fight against apartheid)* BL

C Critical Thinking

Making Inferences **Ask:** What does Mandela mean by a "non-racial South Africa"? *(a country where racial identity does not determine a person's rights or opportunities)* OL

ANALYZING PRIMARY SOURCES

What Challenges Did Apartheid Create for South Africans?

How did apartheid affect South Africa? For much of the twentieth century, South Africa's white-run government denied political and economic equality to the country's black majority.

What progress have South Africans made in overcoming the effects of apartheid? Despite facing harsh government repression, South Africans carried on a decades-long campaign against apartheid. The nation finally held free elections in 1994, marking the end of apartheid and the beginning of democracy.

Apartheid in South Africa attracted international attention. Read the excerpts and study the cartoon to learn more about how South Africa faced this challenge.

SOURCE 1

R The following passage is from a speech by Desmond Tutu, a black Anglican Archbishop, to the United Nations Security Council on October 23, 1984.

For my beloved country is wracked by division, by alienation, by **animosity**[1], by separation, by injustice, by unavoidable pain and suffering. It is a deeply **fragmented**[2] society, ridden by fear and anxiety . . . and a sense of desperation, split up into hostile, warring factions. . . .

There is little freedom to disagree with the determinations of the authorities. There is large scale unemployment here because of the drought and the recession that has hit most of the world's economy. And it is such a time that the authorities have increased the prices of various foodstuffs and also of rents in black townships—measures designed to hit hardest those least able to afford the additional costs. . . .

The authorities have not stopped stripping blacks of their South African citizenship. . . . The South African government is turning us into aliens in the land of our birth.

White South Africans are . . . scared human beings, many of them; who would not be, if they were outnumbered five to one? Through this lofty body I wish to appeal to my white fellow South Africans to share in building a new society, for blacks are not intent on driving whites into the sea but on claiming only their rightful place in the sun in the land of their birth.

[1] **animosity:** resentment
[2] **fragmented:** broken into pieces

SOURCE 2

African National Congress leader Nelson Mandela discussed South Africa's past and future in a speech he gave after his release from prison in 1990.

Today, the majority of South Africans, black and white, recognize that **apartheid**[3] has no future. It has to be ended by our own decisive mass action in order to build peace and security. The mass campaigns of defiance and other actions of our organizations and people can only **culminate**[4] in the establishment of democracy. The apartheid's destruction on our subcontinent is incalculable. The fabric of family life of millions of my people has been shattered. Millions are homeless and unemployed. Our economy lies in ruins and our people are embroiled in political strife. . . .

We call on our people to seize this moment, so that the process toward democracy is rapid and uninterrupted. . . . We must not allow fear to stand in our way. C Universal suffrage on a common voters roll in a united, democratic and non-racial South Africa is the only way to peace and racial harmony. . . .

I have fought against white domination, and I have fought against black domination. I have cherished the ideal of a democratic and free society in which all persons live together in harmony and with equal opportunity. It is an ideal which I hope to live for and to achieve. But, if need be, it is an ideal for which I am prepared to die.

[3] **apartheid:** policy of racial segregation
[4] **culminate:** conclude

Differentiated Instruction

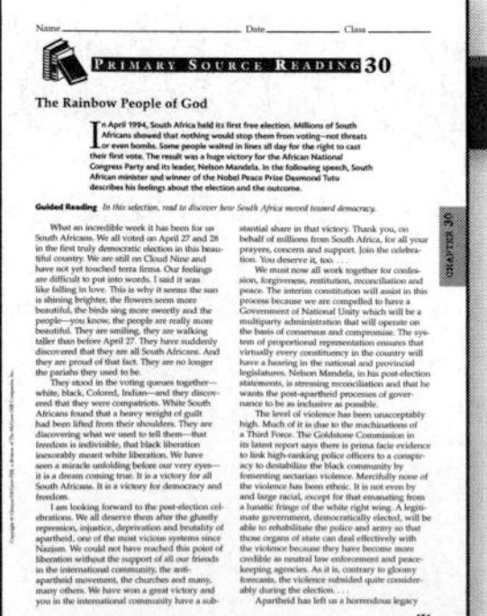
Primary Source Reading, URB p. 151

Analyzing Primary Sources

Objective: Learn more about the end of apartheid.

Focus: Have students read the selection from *"The Rainbow People of God."*

Teach: Tell students to answer questions 1–6 on a separate sheet of paper.

Assess: Have students share answers in small groups.

Close: Discuss question 7 with the class and draw conclusions.

Differentiated Instruction Strategies

- BL Have students identify the main idea of each paragraph as they read.
- AL Have students write responses to the following question: Why does Archbishop Tutu reach out to the international community?
- ELL Allow students to read the selection with a native English speaker and discuss the questions together.

▲ This political cartoon by Zapiro, appearing in the newspaper the *Sowetan* in 1994, tracks Mandela's path to freedom.

SOURCE 3

In the 1940s the African National Congress (ANC) formed a Youth League to lead a nonviolent campaign against the apartheid policies of South Africa. In 1960 South African police fired on unarmed demonstrators at Sharpeville, killing 67. A year later the ANC formed an armed wing, Umkhonto we Sizwe, headed by Nelson Mandela to carry out sabotage against government installations.

In 1963 the South African government arrested Mandela and, a year later, sentenced him to life imprisonment. In 1990, amidst growing international and domestic pressure, the government released Mandela. Four years later, he was elected president by voters in South Africa. His **inauguration**[5] marked the end of apartheid.

[5] **inauguration:** ceremonial induction into office

DOCUMENT-BASED QUESTIONS

1. **Explaining** According to Bishop Tutu, what problems did South Africa face in 1984?
2. **Drawing Conclusions** What do you think Mandela hoped to accomplish with his speech?
3. **Assessing** What does the cartoon reveal about the state of the South African nation after Mandela gained his freedom?
4. **Identifying Points of View** How do you think Mandela's experiences influenced the opinions he expressed in his speech?
5. **Synthesizing** What similarities exist between the messages conveyed by all three sources?
6. **Evaluating** What challenges did apartheid create for South Africans? Do you believe that Mandela and Tutu offered effective ideas to deal with these challenges? Why or why not?

ANALYZING PRIMARY SOURCES

S Skill Practice

Interpreting Political Cartoons Ask: What is the hill that Mandela still has to climb? *(the road to rebuilding)* **BL**

Assess/Close

Have students answer the Document-Based Questions and discuss answers with the class. **OL**

DOCUMENT-BASED QUESTIONS

Answers:

1. The country is divided, angry, and suffering.
2. to unify South Africans against apartheid
3. There was much conflict before Mandela gained his freedom, but the nation still needs much work to repair it.
4. He knows mass action can be effective and has seen progress toward his ideal.
5. All convey the hope that black and white South Africans can work together to build a better nation.
6. Answers should support opinions with evidence.

Additional Support

Activity: Collaborative Learning

Creating an Illustrated Time Line Ask: What were the milestones in South Africa's process of reconstruction? Have students work in mixed-level groups to identify important steps in South Africa's journey toward racial equality between 1994 and the present. Remind students to use their textbook as one of their resources. You might assign each group to research a particular year to explore specific topics, such as political, economic, or social reform. When groups have completed their research, have each group create a portion of a class illustrated time line. (You may want to give each group a sheet of paper to use that can then be attached to the other parts of the time line.) Have volunteers explain why certain events were chosen. **Ask:** How successful has South Africa been in achieving racial equality? *(Encourage students to cite evidence from their research to support their opinions.)* Discuss what challenges the country faces and steps that might be taken to achieve its goals. **OL**

Determining Cause and Effect Discuss the information and images presented in the Visual Summary. Remind students that this information includes important ideas from the entire chapter. Have students work in small groups to define some of the challenges facing Africa and the Middle East today. Have each group focus on a part of the region and consider how the legacy of colonialism has influenced conditions there today. **Ask:** How have Western colonialism and culture affected the region? Have students list both positive and negative examples. Encourage students to cite details from the chapter to support their responses. Suggest that each group use a graphic organizer to record its ideas. Then have groups share their findings, which will help the class review the material for the chapter test. OL

English Language Learners Organize students into groups of three, with each group containing at least one fluent speaker of English. Have students read the Visual Summary aloud. Ask them to compile a list of terms that they do not understand. Then have them work together using a dictionary and their own knowledge to define each word on the list. BL

CHAPTER 30 Visual Summary

STUDY TO GO You can study anywhere, anytime by downloading quizzes and flash cards to your PDA from glencoe.com.

Challenges in AFRICA

- Whites used apartheid laws to maintain power in mostly black South Africa.
- Leaders of newly independent African nations struggled to create stable governments.
- Reliance on the export of a single crop or resource threatened economic prosperity.
- Poverty, hunger, disease, and ethnic conflicts still plague African nations.

THE AIDS EPIDEMIC IN AFRICA

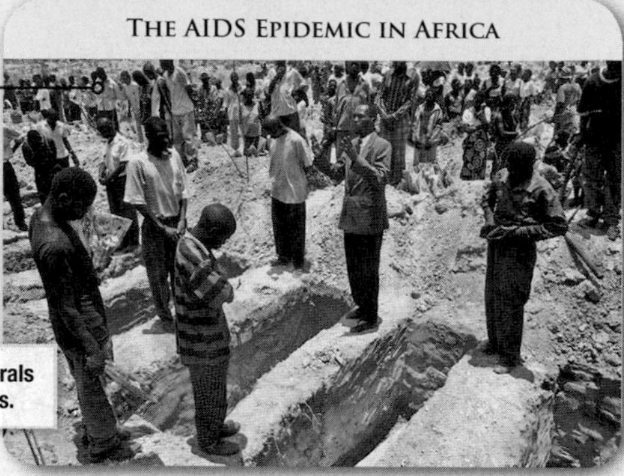

This Zambian cemetery holds mass funerals due to the high number of AIDS victims.

SUICIDE BOMBING IN CENTRAL ISRAEL

Palestinians have launched terrorist attacks on Israel.

Challenges in the MIDDLE EAST

- In 1973, OPEC reduced oil supplies and raised prices, causing economic problems in the West.
- Terrorist attacks on September 11, 2001, led to a war in Afghanistan.
- In 2006, Palestinians chose Hamas to lead them, a group that rejects Israel's right to exist.
- Efforts to establish a stable, democratic government in Iraq continue following the removal of Saddam Hussein from power by a United States-led coalition.

IMPACTS ON SOCIETIES in Africa and the Middle East

- In Africa, constant tension exists between traditional ways and Western culture.
- African women have made political and economic gains, but inequalities remain.
- African artists search for ways to balance Western techniques with traditional art.
- Islamic fundamentalism has impacted Middle Eastern society, especially women's roles.

CONTRAST BETWEEN OLD AND NEW IN AFRICA

Satellite dishes atop traditional homes in Fès, Morocco, illustrate Africa's transition to the modern world.

Hands-On Chapter Project

Step 3: Wrap-Up

Make a Chart of Issues and Resolutions

Step 3: Compare and Discuss Challenges Ask small groups to display the charts prepared in the previous steps. Lead a class discussion that compares the issues facing Africa with those facing the Middle East. **Ask:** How are the issues similar? *(Ethnic divisions continue to cause wars, genocide, and terrorism. Unstable governments cause economic and political instability. Economic issues such as the gap between rich and poor continue to cause tension.)* **Ask:** Which area do you think has a better chance at peace in the near future? Which area has a better chance for prosperity? Why? *(Answers will vary. Some might cite the long history of Arab-Israeli conflicts as preventing peace there. Others might see the persistent poverty and health issues in Africa as preventing prosperity.)* OL

STANDARDIZED TEST PRACTICE

TEST-TAKING TIP

Time lines show chronology, or the order in which events happened. You can use your knowledge of chronology to get rid of incorrect answer choices. Think about what events happened during the time and then consider the answer choices.

Reviewing Vocabulary

Directions: Choose the word or words that best complete the sentence.

1. Removing all Western influences in Muslim countries is the goal of ________.

A isolationism
B absolutism
C Islamic fundamentalism
D Zionism

2. ________, a system of racial segregation, was practiced in South Africa.

A Apartheid
B Achebe
C Pan-Africanism
D Wabenzi

3. ________ is the name Palestinian Arabs give to their uprisings in Israeli-occupied territories.

A Hajj
B Insurgency
C *Hijrah*
D *Intifada*

4. ________ is the belief that all black Africans, regardless of national boundaries, should be united.

A Black power
B Pan-Arabism
C Pan-Africanism
D African imperialism

Reviewing Main Ideas

Directions: Choose the best answers to the following questions.

Section 1 *(pp. 986–993)*

5. Which leader dreamed of a union that would join all African nations in a broader community?

A Nelson Mandela
B Noni Jabavu
C Kwame Nkrumah
D Desmond Tutu

6. Which disease is caused by the HIV virus?

A Influenza
B Hemophilia
C Lupus
D AIDS

7. Who were the intended victims of genocide in Rwanda in 1994?

A Tutsis
B Hutus
C Burundi
D Congo

8. Who was South Africa's first black president?

A Jomo Kenyatta
B F. W. de Klerk
C Julius Nyerere
D Nelson Mandela

Need Extra Help?

If You Missed Questions . . .	1	2	3	4	5	6	7	8
Go to Page . . .	1003	987	999	988	988	989	990	990

GO ON

Answers and Analyses

Reviewing Vocabulary

1. C The word "Islamic" should be a clue since it relates to "Muslim" in the stem. Zionism relates to the Jewish state, isolationism describes a political view, and absolutism has no relevance.

2. A Knowledge of the content is necessary to select the correct answer. Achebe is a writer, Pan-Africanism involves African unity, and *wabenzi* is a slang term used to refer to the rich in East African countries.

3. D Knowledge of the content is necessary to select the correct answer. Hajj is a Muslim pilgrimage to Mecca. *Hijrah* is also not related to the uprisings. Insurgency is a generic term for an uprising.

4. C Knowledge of the prefix "pan" helps indicate the correct answer. Pan-Arabism refers to the Middle East, black power is an American term, and imperialism refers to nations building a foreign empire.

Reviewing Main Ideas

5. C Knowledge of the content is necessary to select the correct answer. Mandela and Tutu are connected to South African politics and Jabavu is a South African writer.

6. D This answer should be common knowledge. Also, AIDS is the only disease referred to specifically in the chapter, although the others are deadly diseases as well.

7. A Burundi and Congo, both place names, can be eliminated from consideration. However, knowledge of the content is necessary to select the correct answer. Hutu militias began a campaign of genocide against Tutsis.

8. D All choices are leaders who were involved in African politics. Kenyatta and Nyerere were leaders in central African nations and de Klerk was a white president of South Africa.

9. C Knowledge of other world events helps indicate the correct answer. Israel was created a few years after World War II ended in 1945.

10. A Begin and Meir were Israeli leaders, while Nasser was connected with actions leading up to the Six-Day War.

11. B Khomeini is connected with the initial move toward Islamic revivalism. Hussein was the leader of Iraq and the other two choices were leaders of Iran after Khomeini.

12. D The Taliban is a group in Afghanistan and the Tutsis and Hutus are African tribes involved in African war and genocide.

13. C This answer may be common knowledge. Bin Laden is the only clear choice, as the other choices are leaders connected with the Middle East and Afghanistan.

Critical Thinking

14. B Map reading skills help lead to the answer.

TEST-TAKING TIP

For Question 14: Explain that the area identified in the map key as "Area of Palestinian autonomy allowed under Israeli-PLO agreement, 1993" generally coincides with the boundaries of the West Bank. Point out that only one choice lies within the general vicinity.

Section 2 *(pp. 996–1003)*

9. In what year did the Jews in Palestine proclaim the state of Israel?
   - **A** 1962
   - **B** 1925
   - **C** 1948
   - **D** 1945

10. Under whose leadership did Egypt launch the Yom Kippur War against Israel?
    - **A** Anwar el-Sadat
    - **B** Menachem Begin
    - **C** Gamal Abdel Nasser
    - **D** Golda Meir

11. After Mohammad Reza Pahlavi's government collapsed in Iran, what new leader moved to restore Islamic law?
    - **A** Mahmoud Ahmadinejad
    - **B** Ayatollah Ruhollah Khomeini
    - **C** Saddam Hussein
    - **D** Mohammed Khatemi

12. What ethnic group in northern Iraq did Saddam Hussein attack because they wanted their own state?
    - **A** Taliban
    - **B** Tutsis
    - **C** Hutus
    - **D** Kurds

13. Who formed al-Qaeda?
    - **A** Saddam Hussein
    - **B** Babrak Karmal
    - **C** Osama bin Laden
    - **D** Ayatollah Ruhollah Khomeini

Critical Thinking

Directions: Choose the best answers to the following questions.

Use the following map to answer question 14.

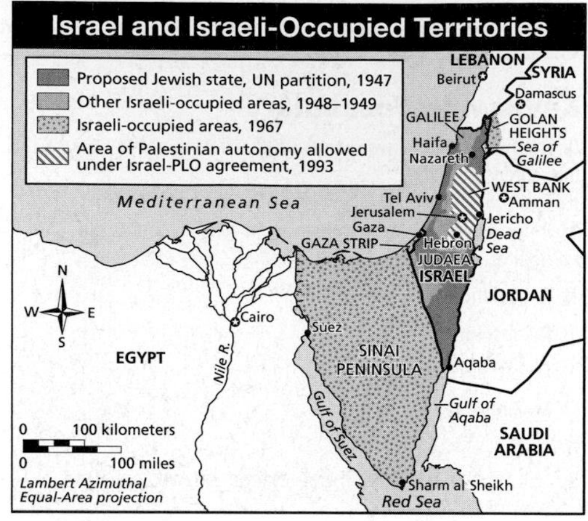

14. Which city is within the West Bank?
    - **A** Beirut
    - **B** Jerusalem
    - **C** Haifa
    - **D** Tel Aviv

15. Why do many African nations still depend on former colonial powers?
    - **A** They need financial aid to develop their countries.
    - **B** They must import oil from the West.
    - **C** They need markets for their manufactured goods.
    - **D** They have few natural resources on which to base industry.

16. Which of the following was a result of the Six-Day War?
    - **A** Palestine was divided into a Jewish state and an Arab state.
    - **B** U.S.-led forces liberated Kuwait from Saddam Hussein.
    - **C** Israel occupied the Sinai Peninsula and West Bank.
    - **D** U.S.-led forces drove the Taliban out of Afghanistan.

Need Extra Help?

If You Missed Questions . . .	9	10	11	12	13	14	15	16
Go to Page . . .	996	999	1000	1001	1001	999	989	999

15. A Students need a basic understanding of colonial economies and African resources to answer the question. African nations don't import oil from the West, their manufacturing is not well developed, and most have many natural resources.

16. C Students need knowledge of other Middle Eastern conflicts to rule out the action in Kuwait and in Afghanistan. Palestine was divided into Arab and Jewish states in 1948, not as a result of the Six-Day War.

17. Which of the following is a major reason for the growth of movements based on Islam?
   - **A** Desire for a homeland
   - **B** The Holocaust
   - **C** Desire for world domination
   - **D** Poverty

Analyze the time line and answer the question that follows. Base your answer on the time line and on your knowledge of world history.

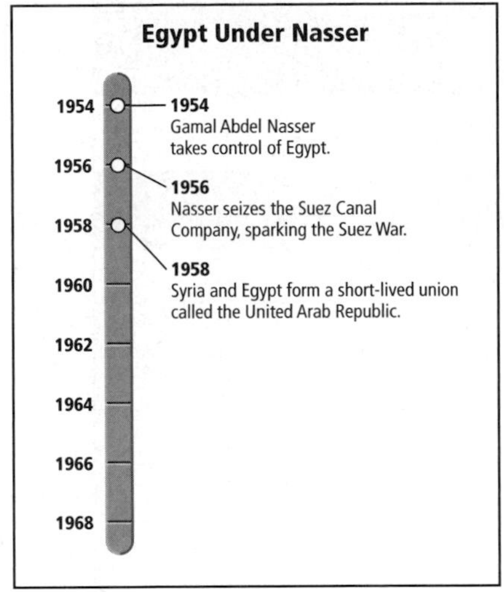

18. Which event below logically belongs on this time line?
   - **A** Egypt and Israel sign the Camp David Accords.
   - **B** Egypt blockades Israeli shipping through the Gulf of Aqaba.
   - **C** Egypt invades Israel on Yom Kippur, 1973.
   - **D** Militants seize 52 Americans from the U.S. embassy in Tehran.

Document-Based Questions

Directions: Analyze the document and answer the short-answer questions that follow the document. Base your answers on the document and on your knowledge of world history.

On March 21, 1960, Humphrey Taylor, a reporter, described what happened at this peaceful march:

> *"We went into Sharpeville the back way, around lunch time last Monday, driving along behind a big grey police car and three armoured cars. As we went through the fringes of the township many people were shouting the Pan-Africanist slogan 'Our Land.' They were grinning and cheerful. . . . Then the shooting started. We heard the chatter of a machine gun, then another, then another. . . . One woman was hit about ten yards from our car. . . . Hundreds of kids were running, too. Some of the children, hardly as tall as the grass, were leaping like rabbits. Some of them were shot, too."*
>
> —Humphrey Taylor, as quoted in *The Mammoth Book of Eyewitness History 2000*, Jon E. Lewis

19. Why were these people demonstrating?
20. Based on this account, does the shooting seem justified? Why or why not?

Extended Response

21. The roles of women have changed during the last century. Compare and contrast the roles and rights of women in the Middle East and Africa.

History ONLINE
For additional test practice, use Self-Check Quizzes—Chapter 30 at glencoe.com.

Need Extra Help?					
If You Missed Questions . . .	17	18	19	20	21
Go to Page . . .	1000	998	987	987	993

STOP

Document-Based Questions

19. They were protesting against apartheid laws in South Africa.

20. No. The description suggests that the crowd was peaceful and non-threatening. It included women and children, and there was no suggestion they were armed.

Extended Response

21. Answers will vary, but may include: Women in most African countries could not vote or run for political office; women dominate some professions; most in low-paying jobs; in rural areas, traditional attitudes prevail; in Middle East, trend towards a greater role for women until 1970s, then shift toward more traditional roles.

17. D The connection between poverty and Islam is dependent upon a basic understanding of the region. The other answers do not apply because a homeland is not an issue, the Holocaust had no connection with Islam, and Islam does not promote world domination.

18. B The time line extends from 1954 to 1968, which means that B is the only choice that can be correct. The other three choices list events that occurred after 1968.

History ONLINE
Introduce students to chapter content and key terms by having them access the Chapter 30 Overview at glencoe.com.

Need Extra Help?
Have students refer to the pages listed if they miss any of the questions.

CHAPTER 31 Planning Guide

Key to Ability Levels	
BL Below Level	AL Above Level
OL On Level	ELL English Language Learners

Key to Teaching Resources	
Print Material	DVD
CD-ROM	Transparency

Levels					Resources	Chapter Opener	Section 1	Section 2	Section 3	Chapter Assess
BL	OL	AL	ELL							
FOCUS										
BL	OL	AL	ELL	Transparency	**Daily Focus Skills Transparencies**		31-1	31-2	31-3	
TEACH										
BL	OL		ELL	Print Material	**Reading Skills Activity, URB**			p. 163		
	OL	AL		Print Material	**Historical Analysis Skills Activity, URB**			p. 164		
BL	OL	AL	ELL	Print Material	**Differentiated Instruction Activity, URB**		p. 165			
	OL		ELL	Print Material	**English Learner Activity, URB**				p. 167	
BL	OL	AL	ELL	Print Material	**Content Vocabulary Activity, URB***				p. 169	
BL	OL	AL	ELL	Print Material	**Academic Vocabulary Activity, URB**		p. 171			
BL	OL	AL	ELL	Print Material	**Skills Reinforcement Activity, URB**				p. 173	
	OL	AL		Print Material	**Critical Thinking Skills Activity, URB**			p. 174		
	OL	AL		Print Material	**History and Geography Activity, URB**				p. 175	
	OL	AL	ELL	Print Material	**Mapping History Activity, URB**		p. 177			
BL	OL	AL		Print Material	**Historical Significance Activity, URB**			p. 178		
BL	OL	AL	ELL	Print Material	**Cooperative Learning Activity, URB**				p. 179	
	OL	AL	ELL	Print Material	**History Simulation Activity, URB**				p. 181	
BL	OL	AL	ELL	Print Material	**Time Line Activity, URB**			p. 183		
	OL	AL		Print Material	**Linking Past and Present Activity, URB**		p. 184			
BL	OL	AL		Print Material	**People in World History Activity, URB**		p. 185	p. 186		
BL	OL	AL	ELL	Print Material	**Primary Source Reading, URB**		p. 187			
	OL	AL		Print Material	**Enrichment Activity, URB**			p. 192		
BL	OL	AL	ELL	Print Material	**World Art and Music Activity, URB**				p. 189	
BL	OL		ELL	Print Material	**Guided Reading Activities, URB***		p. 194	p. 195	p. 196	
BL	OL		ELL	Print Material	**Reading Essentials and Note-Taking Guide***		p. 334	p. 337	p. 340	
BL	OL	AL	ELL	Print Material	**Differentiated Instruction for the World History Classroom**	✓	✓	✓	✓	✓

Note: Please refer to the *Unit Resource Book: Toward a Global Civilization* for this chapter's URB materials.

* Also available in Spanish

- Interactive Lesson Planner
- Interactive Teacher Edition
- Fully editable blackline masters
- Section Spotlight Videos Launch
- Differentiated Lesson Plans
- Printable reports of daily assignments
- Standards Tracking System

Levels				Resources	Chapter Opener	Section 1	Section 2	Section 3	Chapter Assess
BL	OL	AL	ELL						
				TEACH *(continued)*					
BL	OL	AL	ELL	StudentWorks™ Plus DVD	✓	✓	✓	✓	✓
BL	OL	AL	ELL	Vocabulary PuzzleMaker CD-ROM	✓	✓	✓	✓	✓
Teacher Resources				Building Academic Vocabulary	✓	✓	✓	✓	✓
				Strategies for Success	✓	✓	✓	✓	✓
				Outline Map Resource Book	✓	✓	✓	✓	✓
				Presentation Plus! with MindJogger DVD	✓	✓	✓	✓	✓
				ASSESS					
BL	OL	AL	ELL	Section Quizzes and Chapter Tests*		p. 383	p. 384	p. 385	p. 387
BL	OL	AL	ELL	Authentic Assessment With Rubrics	✓	✓	✓	✓	✓
BL	OL	AL	ELL	Standardized Test Practice Workbook	✓	✓	✓	✓	✓
BL	OL	AL	ELL	*ExamView® Assessment Suite* CD-ROM		31-1	31-2	31-3	Ch. 31
BL	OL	AL	ELL	Interactive Tutor Self-Assessment CD-ROM		31-1	31-2	31-3	
				CLOSE					
BL			ELL	Reteaching Activity, URB				p. 191	
BL	OL		ELL	Reading and Study Skills Foldables™	✓	✓	✓	✓	✓

Online Crossword Puzzles

Technology Product

Glencoe's Vocabulary PuzzleMaker™ 3.1 CD-ROM is an easy-to-use program that lets you create your own puzzles based on the glossary for classroom use. The PuzzleMaker allows you to

- create crossword puzzles based on content vocabulary and academic vocabulary that is specific to what is taught in the classroom;
- create online (LAN-based or local area network) or paper crossword puzzles.

Objectives

Completing the crossword puzzles helps students to

- recall vocabulary terms based on the clues provided for a puzzle;
- reinforce their understanding of the vocabulary.

Steps

- Run PuzzleMaker™ 3.1. On the main menu, click on **Create a New Puzzle.**
- From the list of *Puzzle Databases,* select the appropriate database for the vocabulary.
- The *PuzzleMaker Wizard* will take you through selecting a puzzle type and grid type.
- Then select one or more chapters from the list. Indicate whether you want the words selected randomly or manually.
- Select the language and words you wish to use within the maximum for the puzzle. Click **Finish.**
- Save your puzzle to a location that is easily accessible by your students with PuzzlePlayer™ 3.1, or print copies for your students to complete.
- Use PuzzlePlayer™ 3.1 to review the puzzles after your students have worked on and saved them.

History ONLINE

	Student	Teacher	Parent
Beyond the Textbook	●	●	●
Chapter Overviews	●	●	●
Time Current Events	●		●
ePuzzles and Games	●		●
Concepts in Motion	●		●
Literature Connections		●	
Multi-Language Glossaries	●		●
Online Student Edition	●	●	●
Self-Check Quizzes	●		●
Student Web Activities	●		●
Study Central ™	●		●
Teaching Today		●	
Vocabulary eFlashcards	●		●
Web Activity Lesson Plans		●	

- **Timed Readings Plus in Social Studies** helps students increase their reading rate and fluency while maintaining comprehension. The 400-word passages are similar to those found on state and national assessments.
- **Reading in the Content Area: Social Studies** concentrates on six essential reading skills that help students better comprehend what they read. The book includes 75 high-interest nonfiction passages written at increasing levels of difficulty.
- **Reading Social Studies** includes strategic reading instruction and vocabulary support in Social Studies content for both ELLs and native speakers of English.

www.jamestowneducation.com

NATIONAL GEOGRAPHIC

Index to National Geographic Magazine:

- The following articles relate to this chapter:
- "Hanoi: Shedding the Ghosts of War," by David Lamb, May 2004
- "China's Growing Pains," by Jasper Becker, March 2004
- "Blood, Sweat, and Toil Along the Burma Road," by Donovan Webster, November 2003
- "Korea's Dangerous Divide," by Tom O'Neill, July 2003

National Geographic Society Products To order the following, call National Geographic at 1-800-368-2728:

- *National Geographic Atlas of the World* (Book)

Access National Geographic's new, dynamic MapMachine Web site and other geography resources at:
www.nationalgeographic.com
www.nationalgeographic.com/maps

The following videotape programs are available from Glencoe as supplements to Chapter 31:

- Democracy Crushed: Tiananmen Square (ISBN 0-76-701459-6)
- Mahatma Gandhi: Pilgrim of Peace (ISBN 0-76-700668-2)

To order, call Glencoe at 1-800-334-7344. To find classroom resources to accompany many of these videos, check the following home pages:

A&E Television: www.aetv.com

The History Channel: www.historychannel.com

GLENCOE BOOKLINK 3

Use this database to search more than 30,000 titles to create a customized reading list for your students.

- Reading lists can be organized by students' reading level, author, genre, theme, or area of interest.
- The database provides Degrees of Reading Power™ (DRP) and Lexile™ readability scores for all selections.
- A brief summary of each selection is included.

Leveled reading suggestions for this chapter:

For students at a Grade 8 reading level:
- ***Little Green: Growing up During the Chinese Cultural Revolution,*** by Chun Yu

For students at a Grade 9 reading level:
- ***I Remember Korea: Veterans Tell Their Stories of the Korean War, 1950–53,*** by Linda Granfield

For students at a Grade 10 reading level:
- ***Voices from Vietnam,*** by Barry Denenberg

For students at a Grade 11 reading level:
- ***Indira Gandhi: Daughter of India,*** by Carol Dommermuth-Costa

For students at a Grade 12 reading level:
- ***South Korea: A Study of an Economically Developing Country,*** by Sung-Hoon Jung

Introducing
CHAPTER 31

Focus

MAKING CONNECTIONS
How can modernization affect a society?

Activate students' prior knowledge by asking them to think about changes in technology that they have seen within their own lifetimes *(hybrid cars, phone text messages)*. Ask how these changes affect society, including individuals such as the citizens of China, the economy, and the environment. Brainstorm about possible modernizations—and their consequences—that might be seen in the future. Wrap up the discussion by having students create a table listing present and predicted modernizations and the ways they affect society. Ask them what conclusions, if any, may be drawn from the information on their chart.

Teach

The Big Ideas

As students study the chapter, remind them to consider the section-based Big Ideas included in each section's Guide to Reading. The **Essential Questions** in the activities below tie in to the Big Ideas and help students think about and understand important chapter concepts. In addition, the Hands-on Chapter Projects with their culminating activities relate the content from each section to the Big Ideas. These activities build on each other as students progress through the chapter. Section activities culminate in the wrap-up activity on the Visual Summary page.

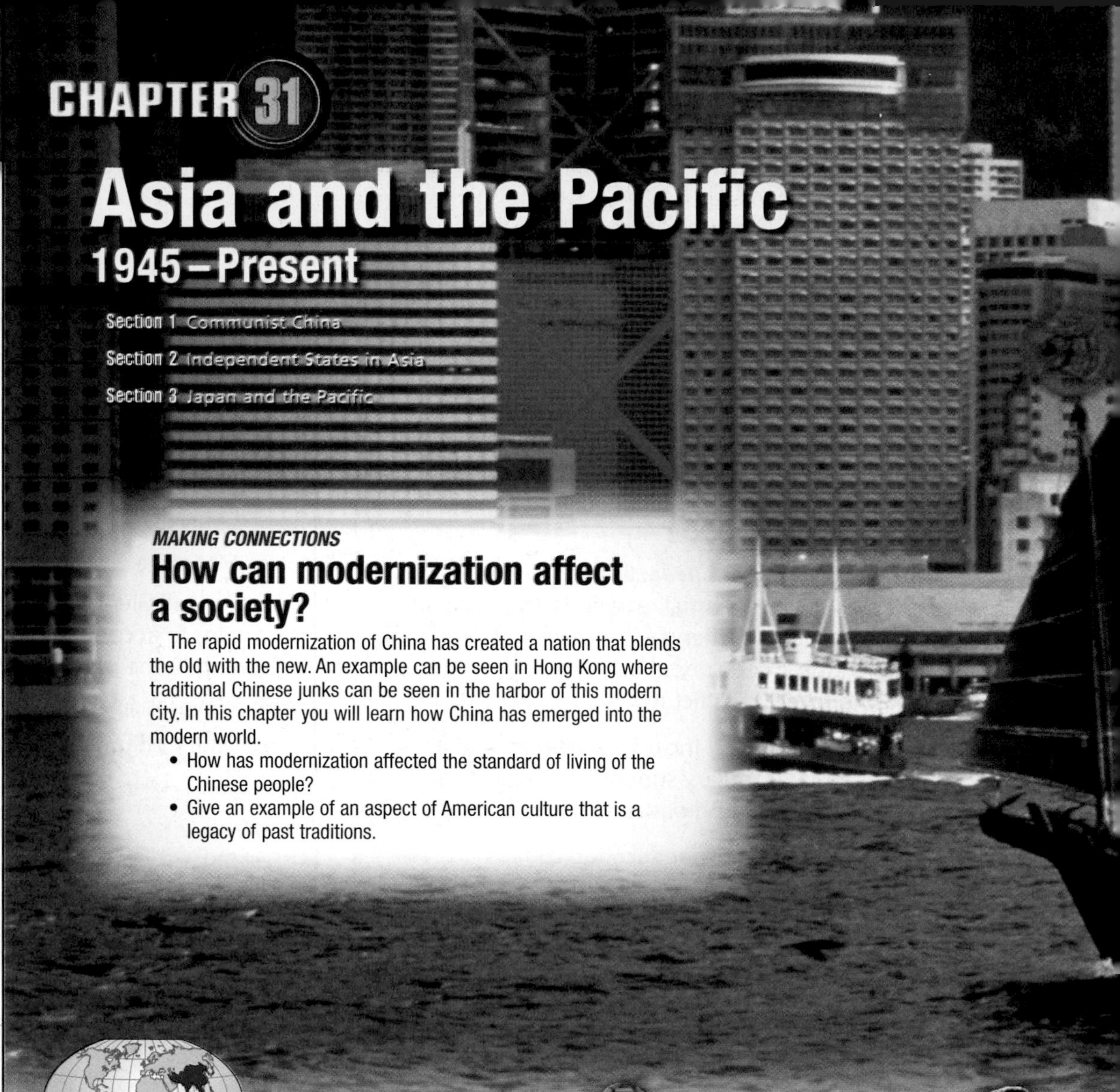

CHAPTER 31

Asia and the Pacific
1945–Present

MAKING CONNECTIONS
How can modernization affect a society?

The rapid modernization of China has created a nation that blends the old with the new. An example can be seen in Hong Kong where traditional Chinese junks can be seen in the harbor of this modern city. In this chapter you will learn how China has emerged into the modern world.

- How has modernization affected the standard of living of the Chinese people?
- Give an example of an aspect of American culture that is a legacy of past traditions.

ASIA AND THE PACIFIC ▶

1951 Japan's independence is restored after World War II

1966 Mao Zedong launches Cultural Revolution

1973 President Nixon signs cease-fire agreement with North Vietnam

1945 — 1965

THE WORLD ▶

1957 Ghana gains independence from Britain

1977 Apple II computer is introduced

1010

Communist China

Explain that Mao's socialist revolution came at the expense of individual rights. **Essential Question:** How do large organizations accomplish their goals while protecting individual interests? Discuss students' responses as a class. Tell students that Section 1 examines the Chinese economy and its movement toward free enterprise. OL

South and Southeast Asia

Essential Question: What conflicts can erupt in a country once the threat of a common oppressor is removed? *(Ethnic, religious, and cultural differences, previously overlooked in the larger conflict with an oppressor, may lead to problems once independence is achieved.)* Tell students that in Section 2, they will learn about the turbulent years following independence for South and Southeast Asia. OL

Introducing
CHAPTER 31

More About the Photo

Visual Literacy Discuss the photograph of Hong Kong with the class. Note that this is a photo of a junk in Victoria Harbor. This type of boat has been used in this area for centuries. **Ask:** **What do you notice about the buildings and the boats in the harbor?** *(Answers may include that the buildings all look quite modern and one of the boats is also modern while one is of an old design.)* Discuss how the juxtaposition of the modern and the old may have come about in Hong Kong. Point out that using both the new and the historical at the same time may indicate that the development of the area occurred rapidly.

1989 Tiananmen Square massacre

2002 Fighting over Kashmir escalates between India and Pakistan

1985 — 2000

2003 Iraqi leader Saddam Hussein is captured

FOLDABLES Study Organizer

Japan | South Korea | Taiwan | Singapore and Hong Kong — Asian Tigers

Describing Make a Four-Tab Book to track the developments in Japan, South Korea, Taiwan, Singapore, and Hong Kong. Under each tab, list important leaders and domestic and international events.

History ONLINE
Chapter Overview—Visit glencoe.com to preview Chapter 31.

FOLDABLES Study Organizer — Dinah Zike's Foldables

Dinah Zike's Foldables are three-dimensional, interactive graphic organizers that help students practice basic writing skills, review vocabulary terms, and identify main ideas. Instructions for creating and using Foldables can be found in the Appendix at the end of this book and in the *Dinah Zike's Reading and Study Skills Foldables* booklet.

History ONLINE

Introduce students to chapter content and key terms by having them access the Chapter 31 Overview at glencoe.com.

SECTION 3

Japan and the Pacific

Tell students that Japan, South Korea, Taiwan, Singapore, and Hong Kong have prospered in recent decades. **Essential Question:** **What factors contribute to economic success?** *(a willingness to modernize, an ability to adapt ideas from other economies, understanding of the market, government help, flexibility, fair laws.)* Tell students that in Section 3, they will learn about the economic and cultural developments in Japan and the "Asian tigers." **OL**

Focus

Bellringer

Daily Focus Transparency 31.1

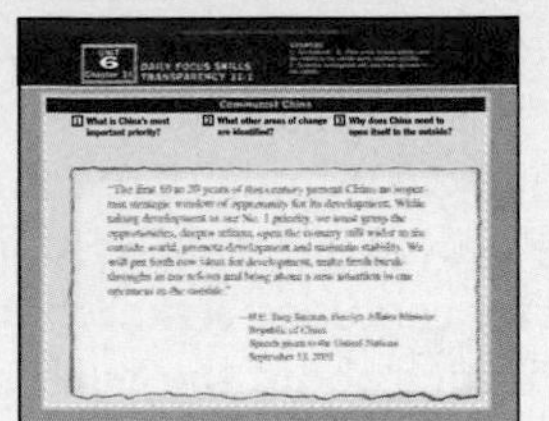

GUIDE TO READING

Answers to Graphic:

Effects:
signed a pact of friendship and cooperation with the Soviet Union
sent troops to North Korea
isolated from major Western powers

Section Spotlight Video

To generate student interest and provide a springboard for class discussion, access the Chapter 31, Section 1 video at glencoe.com or on the video DVD.

SECTION 1

Communist China

GUIDE TO READING

The BIG Idea

Ideas, Beliefs, and Values The policies of the Chinese Communist government set up in 1949 failed to bring prosperity. Since the 1980s, China's economy has moved toward free enterprise, but political freedom is still very limited.

Content Vocabulary

- communes *(p. 1013)*
- permanent revolution *(p. 1014)*
- per capita *(p. 1014)*
- one-child policy *(p. 1016)*

Academic Vocabulary

- final *(p. 1013)*
- source *(p. 1014)*

People, Places, and Events

- Chiang Kai-shek *(p. 1012)*
- Mao Zedong *(p. 1012)*
- Taiwan *(p. 1012)*
- Great Leap Forward *(p. 1012)*
- Great Proletarian Cultural Revolution *(p. 1014)*
- *Little Red Book (p. 1014)*
- Red Guards *(p. 1014)*
- Deng Xiaoping *(p. 1014)*
- Tiananmen Square *(p. 1015)*
- South Korea *(p. 1017)*
- North Korea *(p. 1017)*
- Richard Nixon *(p. 1017)*

Reading Strategy

Determining Cause and Effect As you read, use a chart like the one below to list communism's effects on China's international affairs.

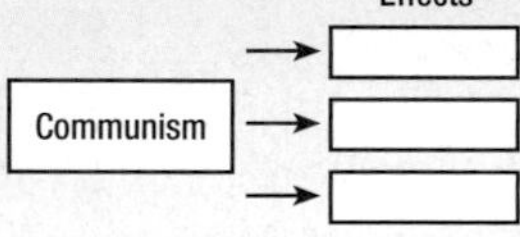

To build his socialist society in China, Mao Zedong launched the Great Leap Forward and the Great Proletarian Cultural Revolution. Neither program was especially successful. In modernizing China, leaders after Mao have built their nation into one of the most powerful countries in Asia.

Mao's China

MAIN IDEA Mao Zedong led the Communists to victory in the civil war, but the human and economic costs of establishing communism were high.

HISTORY & YOU Do you remember what you read earlier about Russia's transformation under Lenin? Read to learn how Mao Zedong transformed China after he took power in 1949.

By 1945, there were two Chinese governments. The Nationalist government of **Chiang Kai-shek,** based in southern and central China, was supported by the United States. The Communist government, led by **Mao Zedong,** had its base in northern China.

Civil War and Its Aftermath

In 1945 a full-scale civil war broke out between the Nationalists and the Communists. In the countryside, promises of land attracted millions of peasants to the Communist Party. Many joined Mao's People's Liberation Army. By the spring of 1949, the People's Liberation Army had defeated the Nationalists. Chiang Kai-shek and two million followers fled to the island of **Taiwan.**

The Communist Party, under the leadership of its chairman, Mao Zedong, now ruled China. In 1955 the Chinese government launched a program to build a socialist society. To win the support of the peasants, lands were taken from wealthy landlords and given to poor peasants. About two-thirds of the peasant households in China received land under the new program. Most private farmland was collectivized, and most industry and commerce was nationalized.

Chinese leaders hoped that collective farms would increase food production, allowing more people to work in industry. Food production, however, did not grow. Meanwhile, China's vast population continued to expand. By 1957, China had approximately 657 million people.

The Great Leap Forward

To speed up economic growth, Mao began a more radical program, known as the **Great Leap Forward,** in 1958. Under this

Resource Manager

R Reading Strategies	C Critical Thinking	D Differentiated Instruction	W Writing Support	S Skill Practice
Teacher Edition • Inferring, p. 1013 **Additional Resources** • Academic Vocab. Act., URB p. 171 • Guid. Read. Act., URB p. 194 • Read. Ess. & Note-Taking Guide, p. 334	**Teacher Edition** • Analyzing Info., p. 1014 • Det. Cause/Effect, p. 1014 • Drawing Con., p. 1017 **Additional Resources** • Linking Past/Present Act., URB p. 184 • People in World Hist. Act., URB p. 185 • Section Quiz, p. 383	**Teacher Edition** • ELL, p. 1013 **Additional Resources** • Diff. Instr. Act., URB p. 165	**Teacher Edition** • Expository Writing, p. 1015 **Additional Resources** • Pri. Source Read., URB p. 187	**Teacher Edition** • Using Geo. Skills, p. 1016 **Additional Resources** • Mapping Hist. Act., URB p. 177

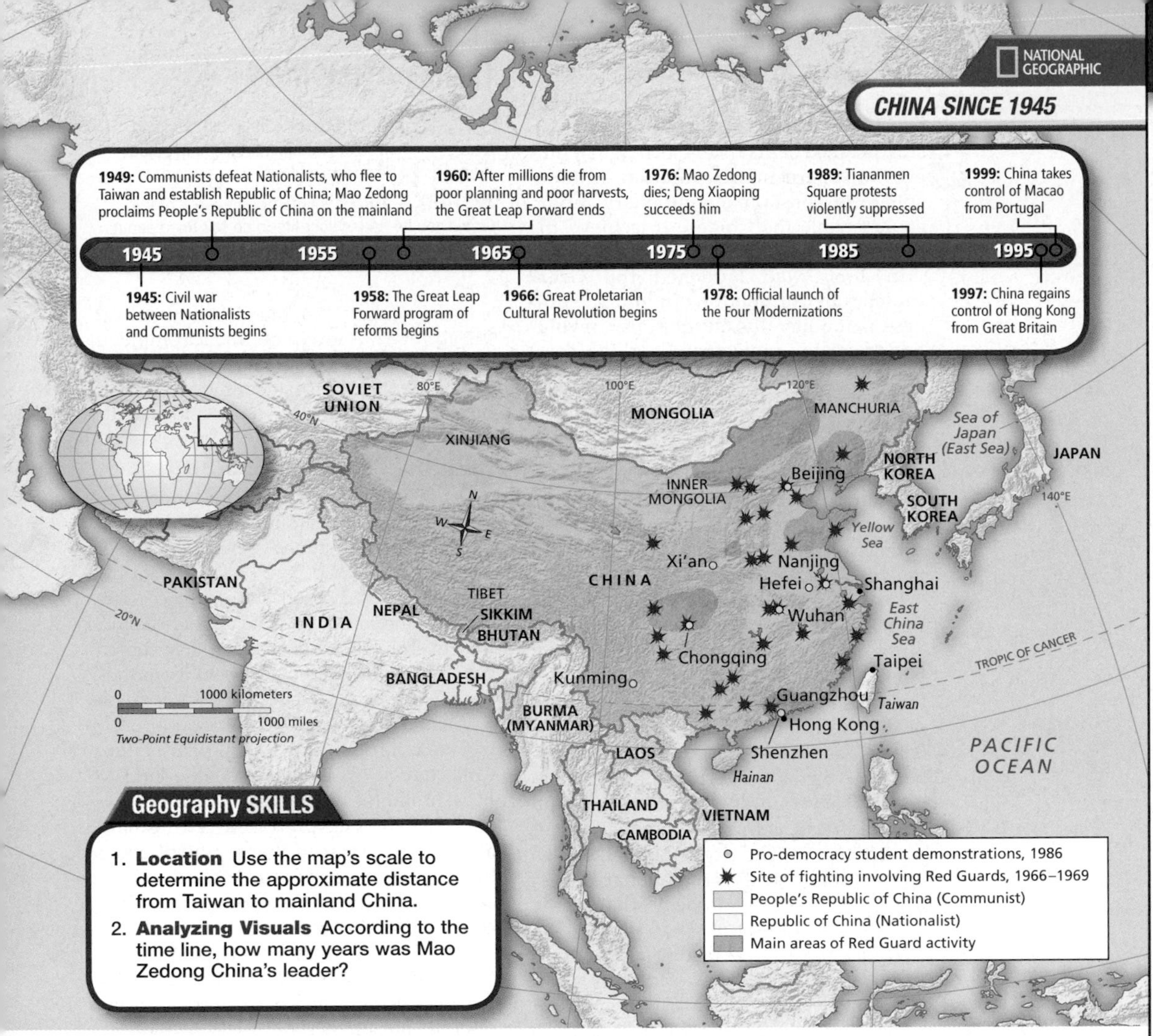

Geography SKILLS

1. **Location** Use the map's scale to determine the approximate distance from Taiwan to mainland China.
2. **Analyzing Visuals** According to the time line, how many years was Mao Zedong China's leader?

program, over 700,000 existing collective farms, normally the size of a village, were combined into 26,000 vast **communes.** Each commune contained more than 30,000 people who lived and worked together. **D** Since they had communal child care, more than 500,000 Chinese mothers worked beside their husbands in the fields by mid-1958.

Mao hoped his Great Leap Forward program would enable China to reach the **final** stage of communism—the classless society—before the end of the twentieth century. The government's official slogan promised the following to the Chinese people: "Hard work for a few years, happiness for a thousand."

Despite such slogans, the Great Leap Forward was an economic disaster. Bad weather, which resulted in droughts and floods, and the peasants' hatred of the new system drove food production down. As a **R** result, nearly 15 million people died of starvation. In 1960 the government began to break up the communes and return to collective farms and some private plots.

Teach

D Differentiated Instruction

English Language Learners Explain that the word *commune* comes from the Latin root of words such as *community, communicate,* and *common.* Explain that communes bring together people who share a common purpose. Ask students to describe China's communes, using these words. **ELL**

R Reading Strategy

Inferring Discuss with students some of the reasons that people are motivated to work hard in school or in their careers. **Ask:** Why were workers unhappy under the commune system? *(They lacked incentives for working hard; they had no privacy or personal lives.)* **OL**

Geography SKILLS

Answers:

1. Distance is approximately 100 miles (161 km).
2. 27 years (1949–1976)

Additional Support

Activity: Economics Connection

Comparing and Contrasting Tell students that both Stalin and Mao were determined to industrialize their nations. To this end, Stalin implemented collectivization and his Five-Year Plan and Mao undertook the Great Leap Forward. These strategies had similarities, such as collective farming to raise capital for industrialization, as well as some key differences. For example, instead of focusing on the acquisition of heavy machinery, which Mao believed had led to the failure of Stalin's program, Mao's plan set up steel furnaces in every village to eliminate the need for large factories. Have small groups of students research both leaders' programs and create a chart, comparing and contrasting each leader's goals, methods of achieving those goals, problems, results, and immediate and long-term effects. Have groups present and discuss their charts. **Ask:** Was one program more effective than the other? Why or why not? What lesson might be learned from the results of each program? **OL**

C1 Critical Thinking

Analyzing Information Discuss Mao's philosophy of permanent revolution. **Ask:** What challenges do you see in combining these two seemingly opposing concepts? *(Students may say that all revolutions disrupt and overturn traditions, making them impermanent by definition.)* **AL**

For additional practice on this skill, see the **Skills Handbook**.

C2 Critical Thinking

Determining Cause and Effect Discuss the actions of the Red Guards. **Ask:** Why were intellectuals targeted? *(They were seen as the elite, which was inconsistent with the goal of a classless society.)* **AL**

✓Reading Check

Answer: Bad weather and the peasants' hatred of the new system reduced production and caused mass starvation.

The Cultural Revolution

Despite opposition within the Communist Party and the commune failure, Mao still dreamed of a classless society. In Mao's eyes, only **permanent revolution,** an atmosphere of constant revolutionary fervor, could enable the Chinese to achieve the final stage of communism.

In 1966 Mao launched the **Great Proletarian Cultural Revolution.** The Chinese name literally meant "great revolution to create a proletarian (working class) culture." A collection of Mao's thoughts, called the ***Little Red Book,*** became a sort of bible for the Chinese Communists. It was hailed as the most important **source** of knowledge in all areas. The book was in every hotel, in every school, and in factories, communes, and universities. Few people conversed without first referring to the *Little Red Book.*

To further the Cultural Revolution, the **Red Guards** were formed. These were revolutionary groups composed largely of young people. Red Guards set out across the nation to eliminate the "Four Olds"—old ideas, old culture, old customs, and old habits. The Red Guard destroyed temples, books written by foreigners, and foreign music. They tore down street signs and replaced them with ones carrying revolutionary names. The city of Shanghai even ordered that red (the revolutionary color) traffic lights would indicate that traffic could move, not stop.

Vicious attacks were made on individuals who had supposedly deviated from Mao's plan. Intellectuals and artists accused of being pro-Western were especially open to attack. One such person, Nien Cheng, worked for the British-owned Shell Oil Company in Shanghai. She was imprisoned for seven years. She told of her experience in *Life and Death in Shanghai.*

History ONLINE
Student Web Activity— Visit glencoe.com to learn to create, modify, and use spreadsheets and complete an activity on China's Four Modernizations.

Key groups, however, including Communist Party members and many military officers, did not share Mao's desire for permanent revolution. People, disgusted by the actions of the Red Guards, began to turn against the movement.

✓Reading Check **Explaining** Why was the Great Leap Forward an economic disaster for China?

China After Mao

MAIN IDEA After Mao's death, Deng Xiaoping tried to modernize the nation but faced increased pressures for democratic reform.

HISTORY & YOU If you participated in a protest, would you be risking your life to do so? Read about the risks of public protest in China.

In September 1976, Mao Zedong died at the age of 82. A group of practical-minded reformers, led by **Deng Xiaoping** (DUHNG SHYOW•PIHNG), seized power and brought the Cultural Revolution to an end.

Policies of Deng Xiaoping

Deng Xiaoping called for Four Modernizations—new policies in industry, agriculture, technology, and national defense. For over 20 years, China had been isolated from the technological advances taking place elsewhere in the world. To make up for lost time, the government invited foreign investors to China. The government also sent thousands of students abroad to study science, technology, and modern business techniques.

A new agricultural policy was begun. Collective farms could now lease land to peasant families who paid rent to the collective. Anything produced on the land above the amount of that payment could be sold on the private market. Peasants were also allowed to make goods they could sell to others.

Overall, modernization worked. Industrial output skyrocketed. **Per capita** (per person) income, including farm income, doubled during the 1980s. The standard of living rose for most people. The average Chinese citizen in the early 1980s had barely earned enough to buy a bicycle, radio, or watch. By the 1990s, many were buying refrigerators and color television sets.

Movement for Democracy

Despite these achievements, many people complained that Deng Xiaoping's program had not achieved a fifth modernization—democracy. People could not directly criticize the Communist Party. Those who called for democracy were often sentenced to long terms in prison.

Differentiated Instruction

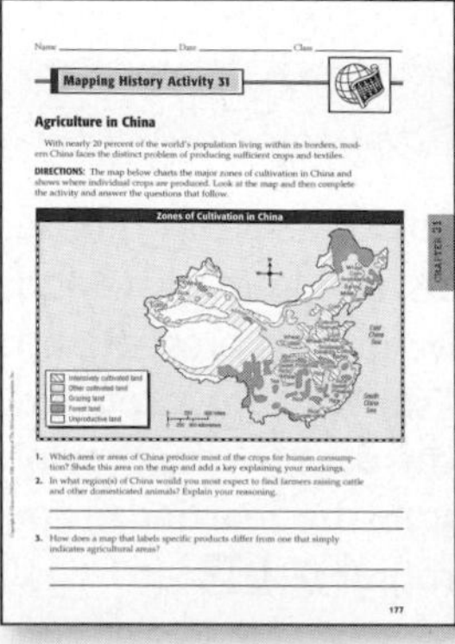

Mapping History Activity, URB p. 177

Comparing and Contrasting

Objective: Learn about China's agriculture.
Focus: Discuss the importance of agriculture to China's economy.
Teach: Present statistics on agricultural production between 1958 and 1998.
Assess: Have students explain variations in harvests, based on China's history.
Close: Have students create an ad supporting China's farmers.

Differentiated Instruction Strategies

BL Have pairs of students complete the activities.

AL Have students graph recent harvest totals and research reasons for trends and implications for China's economy.

ELL Have students create an agricultural map for their home country and compare it to the map of China.

The problem began to intensify in the late 1980s. More Chinese began to study abroad, and they learned more about the West. That information reached more educated people inside the country. As the economy prospered, students and other groups believed that they could ask for better living conditions and greater freedom. Students, in particular, wanted more freedom to choose jobs after they graduated.

In the late 1980s, rising inflation led to growing discontent among salaried workers, especially in the cities. Corruption and special treatment for officials and party members led to increasing criticism as well. In May 1989, student protesters called for an end to the corruption and demanded the resignation of China's aging Communist Party leaders. These demands received widespread support from people in the cities. Discontent led to massive demonstrations in **Tiananmen Square** in Beijing. **W**

Deng Xiaoping believed the protesters were calling for an end to Communist rule. He ordered tanks and troops into the square to crush the demonstrators. Between 500 and 2,000 were killed and many more injured. Democracy remained a dream.

Throughout the 1990s, China's human rights violations and its determination to unify with Taiwan strained its relationship with the West. China's increasing military power has also created international concern. However, China still maintains diplomatic relations with the West.

✓Reading Check **Explaining** Why did farmers produce more under the new agricultural policy?

W Writing Support

Expository Writing Have students write a newspaper article that analyzes the events leading up to the Tiananmen Square protest in 1989 and its consequences. Encourage students to include facts from additional research in their article. **OL**

✓Reading Check

Answer: Farmers were allowed to sell produce over and above what they owed to the collective on the private market and keep the profits.

DOCUMENT-BASED QUESTIONS

Answers:

1. democracy, freedom, and happiness
2. Answers will vary, but students may say that Communist leaders realized that some economic freedom was needed to achieve economic prosperity, but individual rights and freedoms would threaten Communist control of the government.

INFOGRAPHICS PRIMARY SOURCE

Communism Under Deng Xiaoping

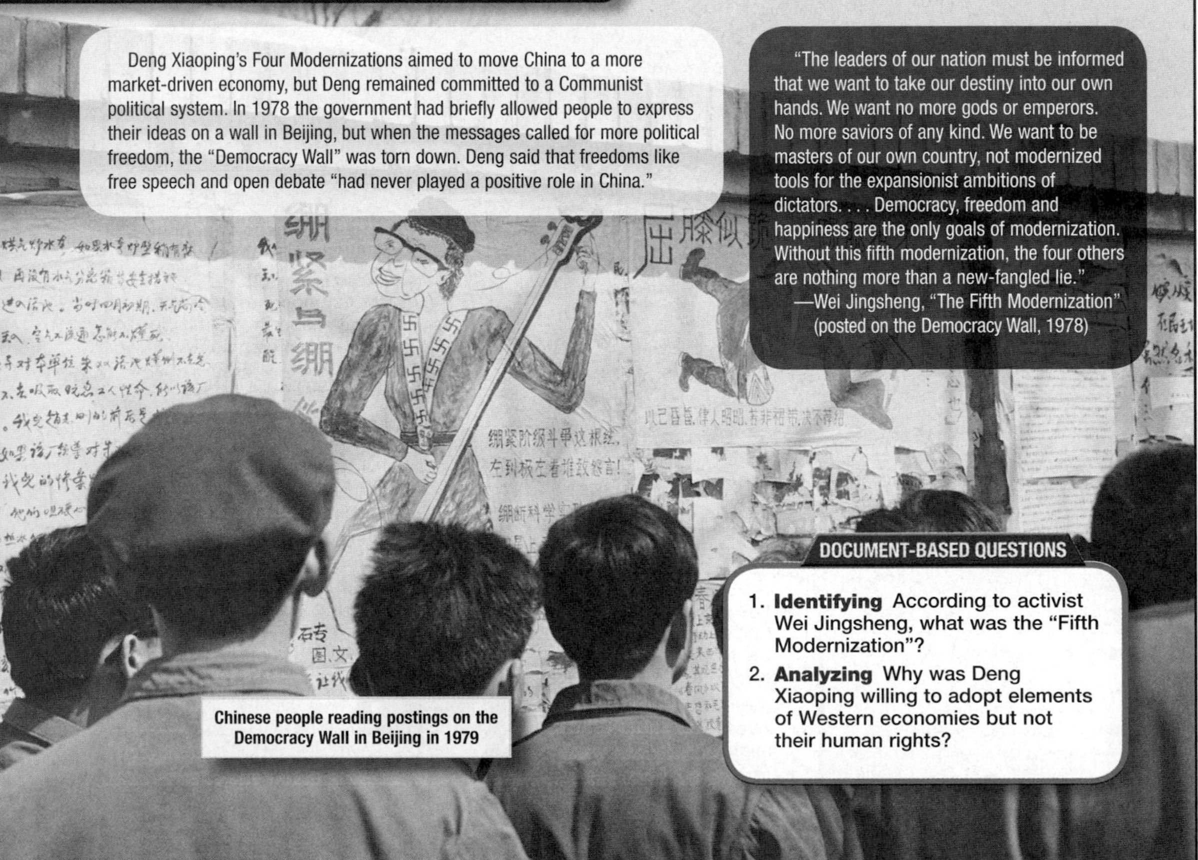

Deng Xiaoping's Four Modernizations aimed to move China to a more market-driven economy, but Deng remained committed to a Communist political system. In 1978 the government had briefly allowed people to express their ideas on a wall in Beijing, but when the messages called for more political freedom, the "Democracy Wall" was torn down. Deng said that freedoms like free speech and open debate "had never played a positive role in China."

"The leaders of our nation must be informed that we want to take our destiny into our own hands. We want no more gods or emperors. No more saviors of any kind. We want to be masters of our own country, not modernized tools for the expansionist ambitions of dictators. . . . Democracy, freedom and happiness are the only goals of modernization. Without this fifth modernization, the four others are nothing more than a new-fangled lie."
—Wei Jingsheng, "The Fifth Modernization" (posted on the Democracy Wall, 1978)

Chinese people reading postings on the Democracy Wall in Beijing in 1979

DOCUMENT-BASED QUESTIONS

1. **Identifying** According to activist Wei Jingsheng, what was the "Fifth Modernization"?
2. **Analyzing** Why was Deng Xiaoping willing to adopt elements of Western economies but not their human rights?

Hands-On Chapter Project
Step 1

Forging an Action Plan

Small groups put together an action plan to help build a new nation.

Step 1: Identifying Goals

Essential Question: What elements are necessary for stability and growth of a new nation?

Directions: Write the Big Idea on the board. Explain that the first step of the action plan is to identify goals for their country. Have groups use the facts in this section to generate a list of measures that worked and those that did not work in China. Then have groups analyze these lists to decide what they want for their nation. Have students create a collage of images and text to identify these goals.

Summarizing: Have groups share insights about the Big Idea. **OL**

(Chapter Project is continued in Section 2.)

Our Country's Goals:

1) universal suffrage of people over 18
2) government with checks and balances
3) strong capitalist economy

S Skill Practice

Using Geography Skills Have students note that the land area of North Korea is slightly larger than South Korea. Explain that the population of South Korea is more than twice that of North Korea. **Ask:** What does greater population density usually suggest about an economy? *(It is typically more industrialized and urbanized.)* OL

Reading Check

Answer: the emphasis on family traditions returned; people had more freedoms and better living conditions; a one-child policy was enacted.

Geography SKILLS

Answers:

1. Yalu River
2. UN offensive on left map crosses the 38th parallel while offensive on right map stops around the 38th parallel; reflects how Chinese forces kept UN forces from advancing beyond the 38th parallel after the 1950 offensive came too close to China.

Chinese Society

MAIN IDEA After Mao's death, the state shifted from revolutionary fervor back to family traditions.

HISTORY & YOU Should the government be able to dictate the size of families? Read to learn about family policies in China.

See page R55 to read excerpts from Xiao-huang Yin's *China's Gilded Age* in the **Primary Sources and Literature Library.**

From the start, the Communist Party wanted to create a new kind of citizen, one who would give the utmost for the good of all China. In Mao's words, the people "should be resolute, fear no sacrifice, and surmount every difficulty to win victory."

During the 1950s and 1960s, the Chinese government made some basic changes. Women were now allowed to take part in politics and had equal marital rights—a dramatic shift for the Chinese. Mao feared that loyalty to the family would interfere with loyalty to the state. During the Cultural Revolution, for example, children were encouraged to report negative comments their parents made about the government.

After Mao's death, family traditions returned. People now had more freedom in everyday matters and had better living conditions. Married couples who had been given patriotic names chose more elegant names for their own children. Clothing choices were no longer restricted to a baggy "Mao suit." Today, young Chinese people wear jeans, sneakers, and sweatsuits.

Mao's successors have followed one of his goals to the present day—the effort to control population growth. In 1979 the state began advocating a **one-child policy.** Incentives such as education benefits, child care, and housing were offered to couples who limited their families to one child. Criticized for being oppressive, the policy has been more successful in cities than it has in rural areas.

Reading Check **Analyzing** How did policies after Mao affect women and families?

NATIONAL GEOGRAPHIC

KOREAN WAR, 1950–1953

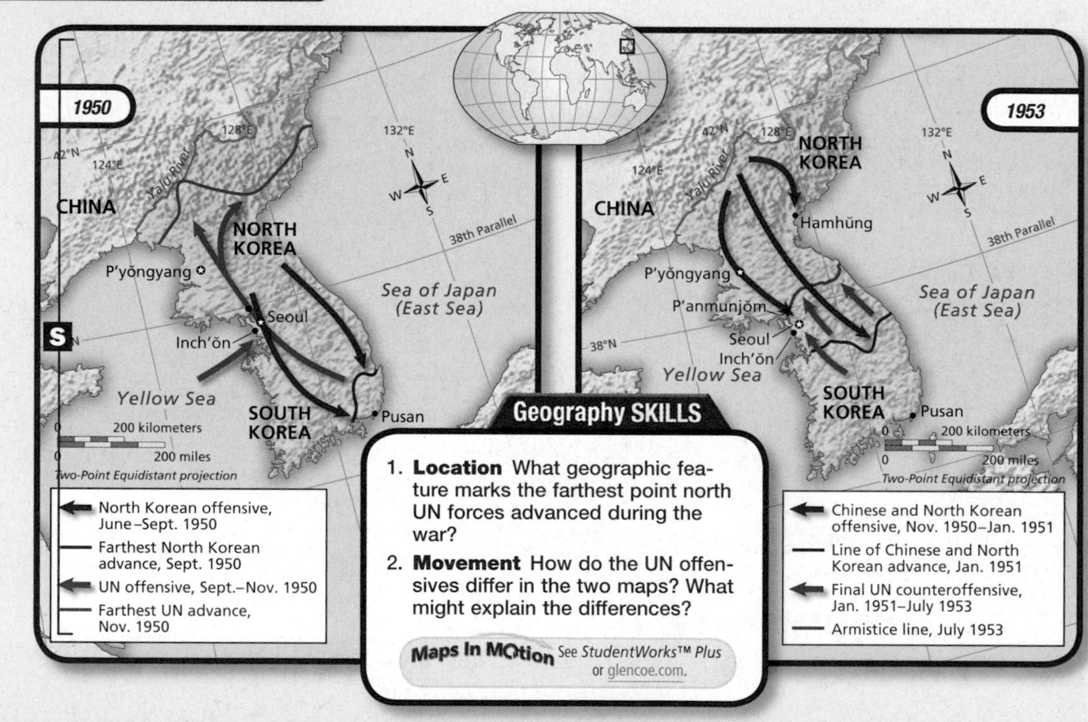

Geography SKILLS

1. **Location** What geographic feature marks the farthest point north UN forces advanced during the war?
2. **Movement** How do the UN offensives differ in the two maps? What might explain the differences?

Maps In Motion See StudentWorks™ Plus or glencoe.com.

Additional Support

Extending the Content

China's Population Controls China's one-child policy stemmed from fears that overpopulation would hinder economic growth. In the 1970s, the Chinese people followed a more-or-less voluntary family-planning policy called "late, long, few." This policy called for married couples to have children later, to wait longer before having another child, and to have fewer children overall. In the 1970s, China's birth rate declined sharply. Introduction of the one-child policy in 1979 reflected the government's desire to continue keeping China's population in check. However, decades of population controls have led to side effects. China's population is aging. Young only-children find themselves supporting their aging parents. With no brothers and sisters to help, it can be hard to make ends meet. Yet, with a growth rate of about 10 million people per year, some experts doubt whether the one-child policy will be abolished any time soon.

The Cold War in Asia

MAIN IDEA Cold War tensions between China and the United States led to the Korean War in 1950, but tensions had eased by the 1970s.

HISTORY & YOU Recall that U.S.-Soviet relations improved during the 1970s. Read how U.S-China relations also improved.

In 1950 China signed a pact of friendship and cooperation with the Soviet Union. Some Americans began to worry about a Communist desire for world domination. When war broke out in Korea, the Cold War had arrived in Asia. **C**

The Korean War

Japan controlled Korea until 1945. In August 1945, the Soviet Union and the United States agreed to divide Korea into two zones at the 38th parallel. The plan was to hold elections after World War II to reunify Korea. As American–Soviet relations grew worse, however, two separate governments emerged in Korea—a Communist one in the north and an anti-Communist one in the south.

Tension between the two governments increased. With the approval of Joseph Stalin, North Korean troops invaded **South Korea** on June 25, 1950. President Harry Truman, with the support of the United Nations, sent U.S. troops to repel the invaders. In October 1950, UN forces—mostly Americans—marched across the 38th parallel with the aim of unifying Korea. Greatly alarmed, the Chinese sent hundreds of thousands of troops into **North Korea** and pushed UN forces back across the 38th parallel.

Three more years of fighting led to no final victory. An armistice was finally signed in 1953. The 38th parallel remained, and remains today, the boundary line between North Korea and South Korea.

In 2000 the Korean leaders took part in the first North-South Summit. However, beginning in 2002, fears that North Korea was pursuing nuclear weapons raised tensions.

The Shifting Power Balance

By the late 1950s, relations between China and the Soviet Union began to deteriorate. Faced with a serious security threat from the Soviet Union as well as internal problems, Chinese leaders decided to improve relations with the United States. In 1972 **Richard Nixon** became the first U.S. president to visit Communist China. Diplomatic relations were established in 1979.

By the early 2000s, China was strengthening trade relations around the world. China joined the World Trade Organization in 2001 and normalized trade relations with the United States in 2002.

✓Reading Check **Examining** Why did China decide to improve relations with the United States?

SECTION 1 REVIEW

Vocabulary

1. **Explain** the significance of: Chiang Kai-shek, Mao Zedong, Taiwan, Great Leap Forward, communes, final, permanent revolution, Great Proletarian Cultural Revolution, *Little Red Book*, source, Red Guards, Deng Xiaoping, per capita, Tiananmen Square, one-child policy, South Korea, North Korea, Richard Nixon.

Main Ideas

2. **Identify** the goals of Mao Zedong's Great Leap Forward and Great Proletarian Cultural Revolution.
3. **List** actions of Deng Xiaoping's government that were intended to help modernize China's industry and agriculture. Use a chart like the one below.

Industry	Agriculture

4. **Explain** how the Cold War affected relations between China and the United States.

Critical Thinking

5. **The BIG Idea** **Contrasting** How have China's policies changed since Mao's rule?
6. **Drawing Conclusions** Do you think families in a Western nation would accept a policy like China's one-child policy? Why or why not?
7. **Analyzing Visuals** Examine the photo on page 1015. What purpose did the Democracy Wall serve for Chinese activists?

Writing About History

8. **Descriptive Writing** Imagine that you are a foreign-exchange student attending a Beijing university in 1989. You witness the demonstration at Tiananmen Square. Write a letter to a friend at home describing what you saw.

History ONLINE
For help with the concepts in this section of *Glencoe World History*, go to glencoe.com and click Study Central™.

C Critical Thinking

Drawing Conclusions Discuss the U.S. idea of a communist threat in Asia. **Ask:** Why did China's relationship with the Soviets worry Americans? *(They feared the spread of communism in Asia.)* **OL**

✓Reading Check

Answer: security threats from the Soviets, internal problems

Assess

History ONLINE

Study Central provides summaries, interactive games, and online graphic organizers to help students review content.

Close

Making Generalizations
Ask: How have China's foreign relations changed since 1945? *(China had limited contact with most countries; in the 1970s, relations improved with the United States; now China has mostly normalized foreign relations.)* **OL**

Answers

1. Definitions for the vocabulary words are found in the section and the Glossary.
2. **Great Leap Forward:** to speed economic growth and achieve a classless society; **Great Proletarian Cultural Revolution:** to eliminate old ideas, old culture, old customs, and old habits in order to create a working-class culture
3. **Industry:** He invited foreign investors to China, and sent thousands of students abroad to study science, technology, and modern business techniques. **Agriculture:** Collective farms could lease land to peasants who paid rent, peasants could sell what they raised above the amount of rent on the private market and make goods to sell as well.
4. China's early relationship with the Soviet Union raised fears in the United States about global communist domination. In addition, Chinese troops fought for North Korea during the Korean War.
5. After Mao, family traditions returned. People had more freedom and better living conditions. They could wear modern clothing. They could enter into business for themselves.
6. Answers will vary, although most students may say that Western families would not accept such restrictions.
7. The Democracy Wall enabled the Chinese to express their thoughts about their society.
8. Answers will vary, but letters should reflect an understanding of events that took place at Tiananmen Square.

Focus

Bellringer

Daily Focus Transparency 31.2

GUIDE TO READING

Answers to Graphic:
Challenges in India: growing population; worsening poverty; ethnic conflict; religious strife

Section Spotlight Video

To generate student interest and provide a springboard for class discussion, access the Chapter 31, Section 2 video at glencoe.com or on the video DVD.

Resource Manager

South and Southeast Asia

GUIDE TO READING

The BIG Idea
Self-Determination British India and colonies throughout Southeast Asia gained independence following World War II, but independence was often followed by continued conflict.

Content Vocabulary
- principle of nonalignment *(p. 1018)*
- stalemate *(p. 1021)*
- discrimination *(p. 1023)*

Academic Vocabulary
- role *(p. 1019)*
- transfer *(p. 1020)*

People and Places
- Jawaharlal Nehru *(p. 1018)*
- Indira Gandhi *(p. 1019)*
- Mother Teresa *(p. 1019)*
- Sikhs *(p. 1019)*
- Punjab *(p. 1019)*
- Pakistan *(p. 1020)*
- Bangladesh *(p. 1020)*
- Aung San Suu Kyi *(p. 1021)*
- Ho Chi Minh *(p. 1021)*
- Pol Pot *(p. 1021)*
- Khmer Rouge *(p. 1021)*
- Ferdinand Marcos *(p. 1023)*

Reading Strategy
Categorizing Information As you read, use a web diagram like the one below to identify challenges India faced after gaining independence.

Following World War II, many South and Southeast Asian states gained their independence. British India was split into two nations—India and Pakistan. France's reluctance to let go of Vietnam resulted in a long war that involved the United States. While some Southeast Asian countries have moved toward democracy, they have faced some serious obstacles along that path.

India Divided

MAIN IDEA Once it gained independence, British India split into two nations—India and Pakistan—that have faced problems of overpopulation and religious strife.

HISTORY & YOU Do ethnic or religious differences cause problems in your community? Read to learn how differences have led to tensions and sometimes conflict in India and Pakistan.

As British rule ended in India, India's Muslims and Hindus were bitterly divided. India's leaders decided to create two countries: one Hindu (India) and one Muslim (Pakistan). Pakistan would have two regions: West Pakistan and East Pakistan. When India and Pakistan became independent on August 15, 1947, Hindus moved toward India; Muslims, toward Pakistan. More than one million people were killed during the mass migrations. One of the dead was well known. On January 30, 1948, a Hindu militant assassinated Mohandas Gandhi as he was going to morning prayer.

The New India

Having worked closely with Gandhi for Indian independence, **Jawaharlal Nehru** (juh•WAH•huhr•LAHL NEHR•oo) led the Congress Party, formerly the Indian National Congress. The popular prime minister had strong ideas about India's future. He admired British political institutions and the socialist ideals of the British Labour Party. His goal was parliamentary government and a moderate socialist economy. Under Nehru, the state took ownership of major industries, utilities, and transportation. Private enterprise was permitted at the local level, and farming was left in private hands. Industrial production almost tripled between 1950 and 1965.

Nehru also guided India's foreign policy through the **principle of nonalignment.** Concerned about military conflict between the two superpowers, the United States and the Soviet Union, and about the influence of former colonial powers, Nehru refused to align India with any bloc or alliance.

R Reading Strategies	C Critical Thinking	D Differentiated Instruction	W Writing Support	S Skill Practice
Teacher Edition • Sequencing Info., p. 1021 • Identifying, p. 1022 **Additional Resources** • Read. Skills Act., URB p. 163 • Guid. Read. Act., URB p. 195 • Read. Ess. & Note-Taking Guide, p. 337	**Teacher Edition** • Making Inferences, p. 1021 • Compare/Contrast, p. 1023 **Additional Resources** • Hist. Analysis Skills Act., URB p. 164 • Crit. Think. Act., URB p. 174 • Section Quiz, p. 384	**Teacher Edition** • Visual/Spatial, p. 1019 **Additional Resources** • Enrich. Act., URB p. 192 • People in World Hist. Act., URB p. 186	**Teacher Edition** • Expository Writing, p. 1020 **Additional Resources** • Hist. Sig. Act., URB p. 178	**Teacher Edition** • Using Geo. Skills, pp. 1019, 1022 **Additional Resources** • Time Line Act., URB p. 183

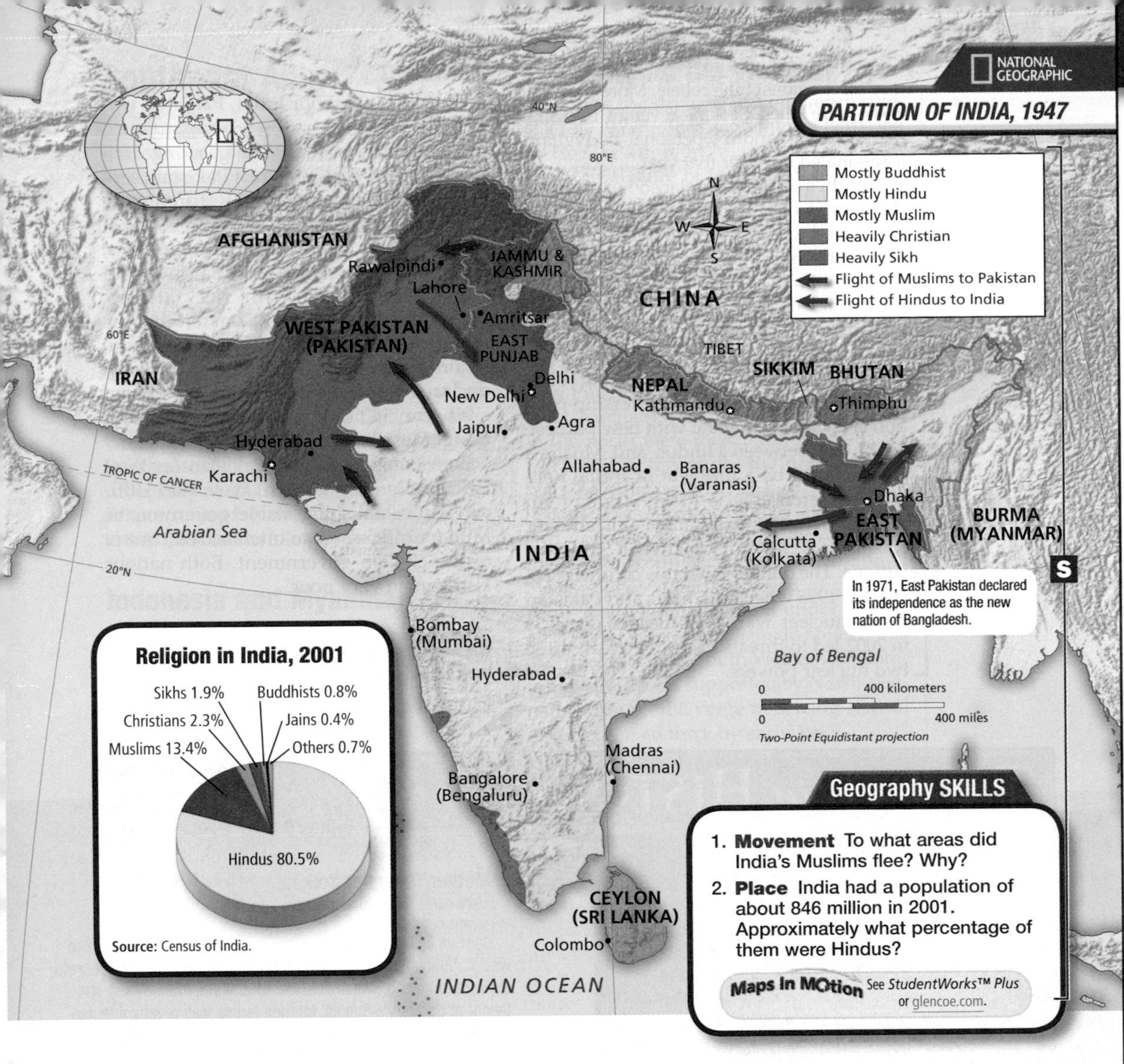

After Nehru's death, the Congress Party selected his daughter, **Indira Gandhi** (not related to Mohandas Gandhi), as prime minister. She held office for most of the time between 1966 and 1984. In the 1950s and 1960s, India's population grew by 2 percent a year, contributing to widespread poverty. Millions lived in vast city slums. In the slums of Kolkata, **Mother Teresa**, a Catholic nun, helped the poor, sick, and dying.

Indian society grouped people into castes, or social classes. The caste into which people were born largely determined their occupation and **role** in society. The system assured that the lowest castes would remain in poverty. Although caste-based discrimination is illegal in India today, it continues, especially in the countryside. D

Growing ethnic and religious strife presented another major problem. One example involved the **Sikhs,** followers of a religion based on both Hindu and Muslim ideas. Many Sikhs lived in the **Punjab,** a northern province, and wanted its independence.

Teach

S Skill Practice

Using Geography Skills
Point out to students that religion played a major part in reshaping the political boundaries of Asia. Have students use the information in the map to create a chart that shows the relationship between religion and countries in South and Southeast Asia. OL

D Differentiated Instruction

Visual/Spatial Explain to students that thousands of castes grew out of the four ancient varnas (priests, warriors, merchants, peasants). Have them create a diagram to represent the varnas. OL

Geography SKILLS

Answers:
1. to West Pakistan and East Pakistan; these were mostly Muslim areas that were to become a Muslim country in the partition
2. 80.5%

Hands-On Chapter Project
Step 2

Forging an Action Plan

Step 2: Creating a Model Government
Small groups continue to add to their nation's action plan.

Directions: Write the Big Idea on the board. Tell students that for this part of their action plan, they will set up a government to rule their nation. They should use the information in this section, which describes the kinds of problems faced by many developing countries, to help them understand the needs their government must meet, so that they can plan accordingly. Students should describe the structure of the government, safeguards against corruption, extent of participation in the process by individuals and groups, and powers held by the government and the people. Encourage students to present this information graphically.

Summarizing: Have students compare and contrast their plans for government before discussing what they learned about the Big Idea. OL

(Chapter Project is continued in Section 3.)

R Reading Strategy

Identifying Ask: How did the anticommunist government established in South Vietnam actually aid the spread of communism? *(Diem's regime was so repressive and harsh that many South Vietnamese turned to communism as a more desirable alternative.)* **OL**

S Skill Practice

Using Geography Skills Have students research the effects of geography on the war in Vietnam. **AL**

CRITICAL THINKING SKILLS

Answers:

1. The United States began to invade the neighboring nations of Cambodia and Laos.
2. The Cold War made the Soviet Union and China fear another conflict so soon after the Korean War, so these countries pressured Vietnam to accept partition.

TURNING POINT — THE VIETNAM WAR

After World War II, most Southeast Asian nations gained independence from their colonial rulers. France's refusal to let go of Indochina led to a long war in Vietnam that involved the United States and Communist China. The Vietnam War was a turning point because it intensified Cold War tensions and the American commitment to the policy of containment.

In 1954 France and Vietnam had signed the Geneva Peace Accords. Because of the Korean War, China and the Soviet Union wanted to avoid another conflict with the United States. They pressured Vietnam to agree to a temporary partition of Vietnam. This was meant to save French pride and satisfy the Americans. Vietnam was to be reunified in 1956 after national elections were held to determine the government.

R The United States believed that the Geneva Accords gave too much to the Communists and began efforts to build up the anti-Communist government in South Vietnam led by Ngo Dinh Diem. Diem's regime was repressive, however, and led to more people joining the Communist National Liberation Front (NLF).

American involvement expanded significantly in 1964 with the Gulf of Tonkin Resolution, which gave President Lyndon Johnson broad war powers. In 1965 U.S. bombing missions began, and the first large commitments of U.S. combat troops were sent to Vietnam.

American troops of the Airborne Infantry in South Vietnam, 1966

S

CRITICAL THINKING SKILLS

1. **Analyzing Visuals** What evidence on the map suggests that the war widened in the early 1970s?
2. **Making Connections** How did Cold War fears help lead to the partition of Vietnam?

Maps In MOtion See StudentWorks™ Plus or glencoe.com.

Differentiated Instruction

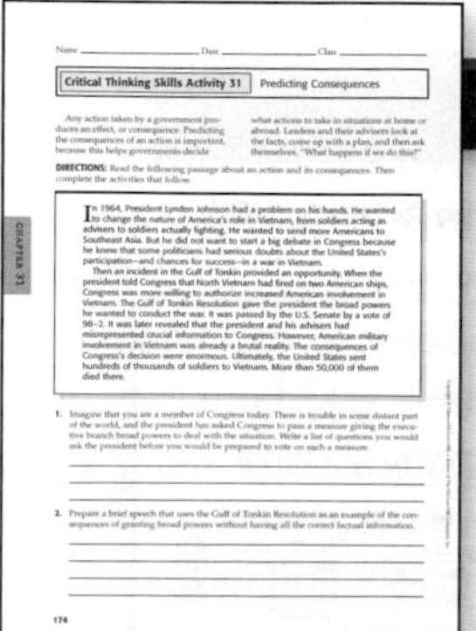

Critical Thinking Skills Activity, URB p. 174

Predicting Consequences

Objective: Examine U.S. involvement in Vietnam.

Focus: Learn more about the Gulf of Tonkin incident.

Teach: Have students read the passage.

Assess: Have students prepare and present speeches in response to question #2.

Close: Ask students to predict what might have happened if Johnson had acted differently in 1964.

Differentiated Instruction Strategies

BL Have students find an article about the Gulf of Tonkin incident and discuss it.

AL Have students trace the ways in which various presidents have extended their powers during war.

ELL Read the passage aloud and discuss question #1.

Democracy in Southeast Asia

MAIN IDEA In recent years, some nations in Southeast Asia have moved toward democracy.

HISTORY & YOU Can you think of any scandals involving U.S. politicians? Read to learn why some leaders in Southeast Asia were forced to step down.

At first, many new leaders in Southeast Asia hoped to set up democratic states. By the end of the 1950s, however, hopes for rapid economic growth had failed. This failure and internal disputes led to military or one-party regimes.

In recent years, some Southeast Asian societies have once again moved toward democracy. However, serious obstacles remain for these peoples.

The Philippines and Indonesia

In the Philippines, two presidents have been forced out of office in recent years. In 1986 a public uprising forced **Ferdinand Marcos** to flee the country on charges of corruption and involvement in the killing of a popular opposition leader, Benigno Aquino. Corazon Aquino, wife of the murdered leader, became president in 1986.

Charges of corruption led to the ousting of another Filipino leader in 2001. The new leader, Gloria Arroyo, promised greater integrity in government. She faced an economy weakened by a global economic crisis. Terrorism remains a challenge for the Philippines. Muslim rebels on the island of Mindanao, for example, have used terror to promote their demands for independence.

In Indonesia, widespread rioting in 1998 forced General Suharto, a long-term authoritarian, to step down. Since then the government has struggled to improve the economy, which has suffered from slow growth and high unemployment. The tsunami of December 2004 and an earthquake in 2005 have caused the current president, Susilo Bambang Yudhoyono, further economic woes. Ethnic and religious conflicts continue to trouble the nation.

Women in South and Southeast Asia

Across the region, the rights and roles of women have changed. In India, women's rights expanded after independence. Its constitution of 1950 forbade **discrimination,** or prejudicial treatment, based on gender and called for equal pay for equal work. Child marriage was also outlawed. **C** Women were encouraged to attend school and to enter the labor market. Virtually all women in Southeast Asian nations were granted full legal and political rights. In rural areas, however, old customs and attitudes survive.

✓Reading Check **Identifying** List the challenges to democracy that nations in Southeast Asia face.

Vocabulary

1. **Explain** the significance of: Jawaharlal Nehru, principle of nonalignment, Indira Gandhi, Mother Teresa, role, Sikhs, Punjab, transfer, Pakistan, Bangladesh, Aung San Suu Kyi, Ho Chi Minh, stalemate, Pol Pot, Khmer Rouge, Ferdinand Marcos, discrimination.

Main Ideas

2. **Identify** groups involved in tensions in India and the reasons for those tensions.
3. **List** the Southeast Asian countries discussed in this section that gained their independence. Use a chart like the one below to make your list.

Country	Year of Independence

4. **Describe** how the rights and roles of women in South and Southeast Asia have changed since 1950.

Critical Thinking

5. **The BIG Idea** **Evaluating** To what extent can the Vietnam War be seen as an anti-imperialist revolt?
6. **Evaluating** Do you think the division of British India into two countries had some benefits? Explain.
7. **Analyzing Visuals** Examine the map on page 1022. Where did most of the fighting occur during the Vietnam War?

Writing About History

8. **Persuasive Writing** Do you believe that removing U.S. troops from Vietnam was the right thing to do? In one page or less, defend your position.

History ONLINE
For help with the concepts in this section of *Glencoe World History*, go to glencoe.com and click Study Central™.

1023

C Critical Thinking

Comparing and Contrasting Have students create a Venn diagram showing similarities and differences in the status of women in South and Southeast Asia with the status of women in Africa and in the United States. Allow them to use library and Internet sources if necessary. **AL**

✓Reading Check
Answer: economic problems, corrupt officials, terrorist threats

Assess

History ONLINE

Study Central provides summaries, interactive games, and online graphic organizers to help students review content.

Close

Summarizing Assign students a country discussed in this section. Ask them to summarize events following their country's independence. **OL**

Answers

1. Definitions for the vocabulary words are found in the section and the Glossary.
2. Conflict between Muslims and Hindus led to the separation of India and Pakistan and to later riots. Sikhs wanted independence for Punjab. Religious differences also led to India's and Pakistan's conflict over Kashmir.
3. **Philippines:** 1946; **India and Pakistan:** 1947; **Burma:** 1948; **Indonesia:** 1949; **Vietnam:** 1954; **Malaya:** 1957
4. Women in South and Southeast Asia have been granted full legal and political rights. Child marriage and discrimination on the basis of gender are illegal.
5. The war began when people under local Communist leadership rebelled against French colonial rule.
6. The division allowed groups more autonomy, but left a legacy of conflict.
7. The majority of the fighting occurred in South Vietnam.
8. Answers will vary. Students' opinions should be supported by facts from this section.

R Reading Strategy

Questioning Ask: In what way is Japan's capitalistic system different from capitalism in the United States? *(The government plays a larger role in the economy.)* **OL**

C Critical Thinking

Making Inferences Ask: Why do you think efforts to dismantle the *zaibatsu* slowed during the Cold War? *(The United States did not want to threaten Japan's democratic reforms or strategic alliance by limiting its return to economic vitality.)* **AL**

For additional practice on this skill, see the **Skills Handbook**.

W Writing Support

Expository Writing Have students write an essay explaining the Japanese economic success after World War II. Remind students to include specific details and examples to support each main idea presented in their writing. **OL**

Today, the central government plays an active role in the economy. It establishes price and wage policies and subsidizes vital industries. This government role in the economy is widely accepted in Japan. Indeed, it is often cited as a key reason for the efficiency of Japanese industry and the emergence of Japan as an industrial giant. Japan's economic system has been described as **state capitalism.**

In recent decades, Japan has experienced problems with its political leadership. Two prime ministers were forced to resign over improper business dealings, but economic factors were at work, too. After three decades of spectacular growth, the Japanese economy went into a slump.

Since 2001, the two prime ministers have both been Liberal Democrats who have worked to reduce government debt and to privatize some government programs. Some progress has been made, but the outlook for the economy today is for moderate growth.

The Economy

During their occupation of Japan, Allied officials had planned to dismantle the large business conglomerations known as the *zaibatsu.* With the rise of the Cold War, however, the policy was scaled back. Only the 19 largest companies were affected. In addition, the new policy did not keep Japanese companies from forming loose ties with each other, which basically gave rise to another *zaibatsu* system.

The occupation administration had more success with its land-reform program. Half of the population lived on farms, and half of all farmers were tenants of large landowners. Under the reform program, lands were sold on easy credit terms to the tenants. The reform program created a strong class of independent farmers.

At the end of the Allied occupation in 1952, the Japanese gross national product was one-third that of Great Britain or France. Today, it is larger than both put together and well over half that of the United States. Japan is one of the largest exporting nations in the world and a leading producer of cars and consumer electronics. Its per capita income equals or surpasses that of most Western states.

What explains the Japanese success? Some analysts point to cultural factors. The Japanese are group-oriented and find it easy to cooperate with one another. The labor force is highly skilled. Japanese people also share common values and respond in similar ways to the challenges of the modern world.

Other analysts have cited more practical reasons for the Japanese economic success. For example, because its industries were destroyed in World War II, Japan was forced to build entirely new, modern factories. Japanese workers also spend a substantially longer period of time at their jobs than do workers in other advanced societies. Corporations reward innovation and maintain good management-labor relations. Finally, some experts contend that Japan uses unfair trade practices—that it dumps goods at prices below cost to break into a foreign market and restricts imports from other countries.

Social Changes and Culture

During the occupation, Allied planners wanted to eliminate the aggressiveness that had been part of Japanese behavior before and during the war. A new educational system removed all references to patriotism and loyalty to the emperor. It also stressed individualism.

Efforts to remake Japanese behavior through laws were only partly successful. Many of the characteristics of traditional Japanese society have persisted into the present day, although in altered form. Emphasis on the work ethic, for example, remains strong. The tradition of hard work is stressed in the educational system.

Women's roles are another example of the difficulty of social change. After the war, women gained the vote and were encouraged to enter politics. However, the subordinate role of women in Japanese society has not been entirely eliminated. Women are legally protected against discrimination in employment, yet very few have reached senior levels in business, education, or politics. Women now make up more than 40 percent of the workforce, but most are in retail or service occupations. Their average salary is only about 60 percent that of males.

Hands-On Chapter Project Step 3

Forging an Action Plan

Step 3: Developing an Economic Strategy Small groups add the final part to their action plan.

Directions: Write the Big Idea on the board. Tell students to use the facts in this section to develop the guiding principles of their new nation's economy. Have groups look closely at the successes of Japan and the four "Asian tigers" to identify what worked well for these countries. Then have them outline the major components of their plan. Encourage students to present their details graphically.

Putting It Together: Have groups review their plans for the government and economy of their nation to see if they reflect their original goals. Then have them organize their plan into a brochure or booklet before discussing what they learned about the Big Idea. **OL**

(Chapter Project is completed on the Visual Summary page.)

Japanese writers reflected their changing culture. Many writers who had been active before the war resurfaced, but their writing turned more sober. This "lost generation" described its piercing despair. For them, fear of losing their culture to the Americanization of postwar Japan made defeat harder to bear.

Increasing wealth and a high literacy rate led to a massive outpouring of books. Current Japanese authors were raised in the crowded cities of postwar Japan, where they soaked up movies, television, and rock music. These writers speak the universal language of today's world.

Haruki Murakami is one of Japan's most popular authors today. He was one of the first to discard the somber style of the earlier postwar period and to speak the contemporary language. *A Wild Sheep Chase,* published in 1982, is an excellent example of Murakami's gripping, yet humorous, writing.

✓Reading Check **Explaining** How is the Japanese government involved in Japan's economy?

The "Asian Tigers," Australia, and New Zealand

MAIN IDEA The "Asian tigers" are successful industrial societies.

HISTORY & YOU Do you own any products from an "Asian tigers" country? Read about the economic success of the "Asian tigers."

Sometimes called the "Asian tigers," South Korea, Taiwan, Singapore, and Hong Kong have imitated Japan in creating successful industrial societies. Australia and New Zealand, to the south and east of Asia, now have closer trade relations with their Asian neighbors. **D**

South Korea

In 1953 the People's Republic of Korea (North Korea) was under the rule of the Communist leader **Kim Il Sung.** The Republic of Korea (South Korea), was under the dictatorial president **Syngman Rhee.**

Connecting to the United States

Japanese *Anime* in the U.S.

- The first Japanese *anime* program shown on U.S. television was "Atom Boy" in 1964. It became the highest-rated syndicated show on television.
- Most *anime* now being produced is usually higher in quality than television *anime* but not as rich as theatrical *anime.*
- *Anime* is most popular with U.S. high school and college students, but, as in Japan, its appeal has no age limits.

Japanese animation, or *anime,* was originally inspired by American and European animators. It has its roots in *manga,* or Japanese comics, which by the early twentieth century had become a very popular form of literature for most of Japanese society. *Manga* had developed from traditional woodblock prints with captions, which eventually were collected in books that told stories.

Unlike Western cartoons, which are aimed primarily at children, *anime* appeals to all age groups. Artists don't "talk down" to their audiences. Plots are not predictable—heroes make mistakes, major characters can die, and there may not be a happy ending. Plots often feature strong female characters. Stylistically, *anime* is more cinematic than Western cartoons.

1. **Summarizing** What were the two biggest influences on *anime?*
2. **Making Inferences** Why does *anime* appeal to all age groups?

D Differentiated Instruction

English Language Learners

Ask students what image comes to mind when they read the phrase *Asian tigers.* Explain that this is a figure of speech that characterizes a fierce, proud, and powerful country. Ask students why the phrase is associated with these countries. *(They are small countries with vigorous and growing businesses and industries.)* **ELL**

✓Reading Check

Answer: Japan's government establishes price and wage policies and subsidizes vital industries.

Answers:
1. Western animation and Japanese manga, or comic books
2. Artists don't talk down to their audiences, but create subtle and realistic characters and unpredictable plots. They also use a more cinematic style than Western cartoons.

Additional Support

Extending the Content

Japanese Anime Although many aspects of anime are unappreciated by Western audiences (particularly the subtleties of expression), the Japanese style of animation has had a profound effect on the form. In fact, many Western studios, including Disney, now send cartoons for production to Japan. Little by little, anime is also breaking into the adult market in the West, although most imports are still targeted at the young male demographic. This is in direct contrast to what is popular in Japan—soap operas, romances, and comedies that appeal to women.

R Reading Strategy

Making Connections Ask: Is there a relationship between economic prosperity and political reforms? *(Answers may include that greater prosperity often leads to demands for greater political freedom. This may result from improved levels of literacy, exposure to other cultures, and feelings of empowerment that may result from a thriving economy.)* AL

CRITICAL THINKING SKILLS

Answers:

1. It tried to repel North Korea and now it helps to patrol the demilitarized zone. It has encouraged the reunification of Korea.
2. Answers will vary. Possible answer: Reunification is possible, given U.N. support and improving relations.

INFOGRAPHICS

The Continuing Role of the United Nations in Korea

When the Korean War broke out in June 1950, the United Nations intervened by sending troops to repel North Korean aggression. It was the first undertaking of its kind in the history of the UN. In spite of a 1953 armistice, a state of war still exists between North Korea and South Korea. The armistice created a demilitarized zone, or DMZ, between North and South Korea. It is the world's most heavily fortified border and a constant reminder of tensions between the two Koreas.

In recent years, there have been negotiations to improve relations between the two Koreas. In October 2000, the UN General Assembly adopted a resolution entitled "Peace, Security and Unification on the Korean Peninsula," encouraging the peace process. It was cosponsored by 157 nations, including both Koreas. In October 2006, however, North Korea conducted an underground nuclear test in spite of a warning from the UN Security Council that such a test "would represent a clear threat to international peace and security."

U.S. and South Korean soldiers with the UN flag

CRITICAL THINKING SKILLS

1. **Describing** What role did the United Nations play in Korea in the early 1950s, and what role does it play today?
2. **Analyzing** What possibility is there for the reunification of Korea?

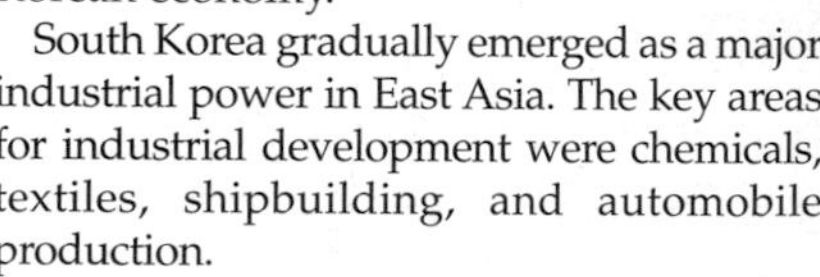

Rhee ruled harshly. In the spring of 1960 demonstrations broke out in the capital city of Seoul. Rhee was forced to retire. A coup d'etat in 1961 put General Park Chung Hee in power. Two years later, Park was elected president and began to strengthen the South Korean economy.

South Korea gradually emerged as a major industrial power in East Asia. The key areas for industrial development were chemicals, textiles, shipbuilding, and automobile production.

R Like many other countries in the region, South Korea was slow to develop democratic principles. Park ruled by autocratic means and suppressed protest. However, opposition to military rule began to develop. Democracy finally came in the 1990s. Elections held during an economic crisis in 1997 brought the reformer Kim Tae-jung to the presidency. Roh Moo-hyun now serves as president.

Taiwan: The Other China

Defeated by the Communists, Chiang Kai-shek and his followers established their capital at **Taipei** on Taiwan. Chiang Kai-shek maintained that the Republic of China was the legitimate government of all Chinese people. Of course, the Communist government on the mainland claimed to rule all of China, including Taiwan. With protection of American military forces, Chiang Kai-shek's new regime concentrated on economic growth with no worries about a Communist invasion.

Making good use of foreign aid and the efforts of its own people, the Republic of China built a modern industrialized society. A land-reform program, which put farmland in the hands of peasants, doubled food production. Local manufacturing and

Differentiated Instruction

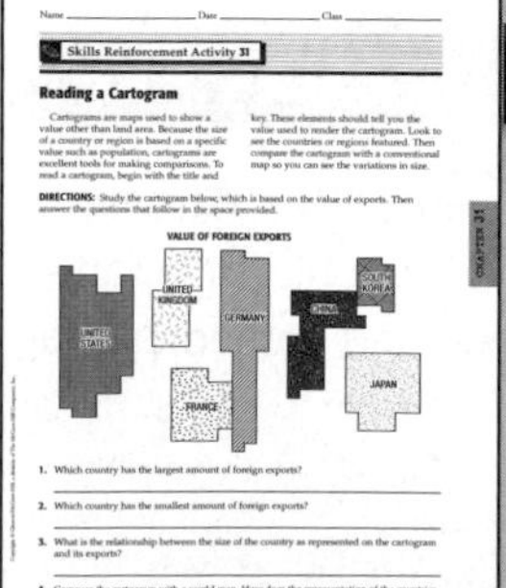

Skills Reinforcement Activity, URB p. 173

Drawing Conclusions

Objective: Analyze the export status of major industrial nations.

Focus: Discuss the function and usefulness of cartograms.

Teach: Have students compare cartograms to the representation of countries on a map.

Assess: Have students draw conclusions about the countries' economies.

Close: Ask students to present the export value of each country in a different format.

Differentiated Instruction Strategies

BL Have students rank the countries from highest to lowest in terms of exports.

AL Have students create cartograms for Taiwan, Singapore, and Hong Kong.

ELL Before examining the cartograms, discuss the meanings of *im-* and *ex-*. List words that use each before defining *import* and *export*.

commerce also expanded. By 2000, over three-fourths of the population lived in urban areas. By 2004, Taiwan's economy was growing at a 6 percent rate.

Prosperity, however, did not at first lead to democracy. Chiang Kai-shek ruled by decree and refused to allow new political parties to form. After Chiang's death in 1975, the Republic of China slowly moved toward a more representative form of government. By 2002, free elections had enabled opposition parties to win control.

A major issue for Taiwan is whether it will become an independent state or will be unified with mainland China. The United States supports self-determination by Taiwan's people. The People's Republic of China on the mainland remains committed to unification.

Singapore and Hong Kong

Singapore, once a British colony and briefly a part of the state of Malaysia, is now an independent state. Under the leadership of Prime Minister Lee Hsien Loong, Singapore is a highly developed and successful free-market economy based on banking, shipbuilding, oil refineries, and electronics. Its port is one of the world's busiest in terms of tonnage handled. The authoritarian political system has created a stable environment for economic growth. Its citizens, however, are beginning to demand more political freedoms.

Like Singapore, **Hong Kong** became an industrial powerhouse with standards of living well above the levels of its neighbors. Having ruled Hong Kong for over 150 years, Great Britain returned control of Hong Kong to mainland China in 1997. China, in turn, promised that, for the next 50 years, Hong Kong would enjoy a high degree of economic freedom under a capitalist system.

Australia and New Zealand

Both **Australia** and **New Zealand** have identified themselves culturally and politically with Europe rather than with their Asian neighbors. Their political institutions and values are derived from European models, and their economies resemble those of the industrialized countries in the world. Both are members of the British Commonwealth. Both are also part of the United States–led ANZUS defensive alliance (Australia, New Zealand, and the United States). **C**

In recent years, however, trends have been drawing both states closer to Asia. First, immigration from East Asia and Southeast Asia has increased rapidly. More than one-half of current immigrants into Australia come from East Asia. Second, trade relations with Asia are increasing rapidly. About 60 percent of Australia's export markets today are in East Asia. Asian trade with New Zealand is also on the increase.

✓Reading Check **Identifying** What is the relationship between Taiwan and mainland China?

SECTION 3 REVIEW

Vocabulary

1. **Explain** the significance of: occupied, Douglas MacArthur, maintain, dramatic, state capitalism, Kim Il Sung, Syngman Rhee, Taipei, Singapore, Hong Kong, Australia, New Zealand.

Main Ideas

2. **Illustrate** the factors that contributed to the "Japanese miracle." Use a diagram like the one below to make your illustration.

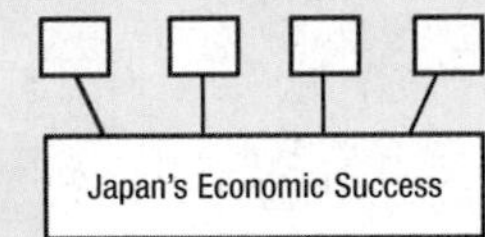

3. **Explain** how Taiwan's land reform program affected its economic growth.
4. **List** the ways in which Australia and New Zealand are similar to European nations.

Critical Thinking

5. **The BIG Idea** **Predicting** What further impact do you think the return of Hong Kong to China will have on either country?
6. **Analyzing** How are women's roles in Japan an example of the difficulty of social change?
7. **Analyzing Visuals** Examine the illustration of *anime* on page 1027. How is *anime* similar to and different from comic books popular in the mid-1900s, such as "Superman"?

Writing About History

8. **Informative Writing** Do additional research on Japan and the "Asian tigers" and explain in an essay why these states have been so successful.

History ONLINE
For help with the concepts in this section of *Glencoe World History*, go to glencoe.com and click Study Central™.

C Critical Thinking

Predicting Consequences Have students develop presentations supporting or disputing a closer relationship for Australia and New Zealand with Asia in the future. **AL**

Answer: Taiwan may become an independent state, although mainland China remains committed to reunification.

Assess

History ONLINE

Study Central provides summaries, interactive games, and online graphic organizers to help students review content.

Close

Determining Cause and Effect **Ask:** How has Japan influenced the other "Asian tigers"? *(Japan's amazing transformation encouraged other countries to imitate Japan's measures, including land reforms and industrialization.)* **OL**

SECTION 3 REVIEW

Answers

1. Definitions for the vocabulary words are found in the section and the Glossary.
2. group oriented; more inclined to save than buy; highly skilled labor force; sharing of common values
3. It doubled food production and created successful, independent farmers who could support the industrialized nation.
4. similar political institutions and values; economies resemble those of industrialized countries in the world; members of the British Commonwealth
5. Hong Kong's economic power may open China to outside influences, or China may limit Hong Kong's liberties.
6. After the war, laws were passed to protect Japanese women from discrimination. However, Japanese culture keeps women's status below that of Japanese men. They tend to earn less than Japanese men. Few women reach high levels in business or politics.
7. Anime is more finely detailed with characters that display more subtle shades of emotion. It appeals to a wider audience and different age groups. It tells a story, similar to the comic books of the mid-1900s.
8. Answers should be supported by examples and logical arguments.

Focus

Introducing Social History
Have students recall what they know about Japan's history and geography. **Ask:** Why is it surprising that Japan has the world's second largest economy? *(It is a small country with few natural resources; it was virtually destroyed during World War II.)* Why do Japanese teenagers have access to the latest high tech gadgets? *(Japan is a leader in manufacturing high-tech products.)* **OL**

Teach

S Skill Practice

Visual Literacy **Ask:** What details in the image support the statement that Tokyo teens are influenced both by Japanese tradition and world cultural trends? *(**Tradition:** kimonos, kites, head coverings; **World Culture:** cell phone, tee-shirt, jeans)* **OL**

C Critical Thinking

Making Inferences **Ask:** Why might a teenager wear a kimono to a kite festival? *(because the kimono and kite flying are both part of traditional Japanese culture)* **BL**

Additional Support

Social History

Teenagers in Tokyo Today

Much of Japan lay in ruins at the end of World War II. The Japanese restored factories, developed new industries, and expanded trade. Today, Japan has the second-largest economy in the world. It is a leader in high-technology products. Tokyo teens are influenced by both Japanese traditions and cultural trends from around the world.

Kite flying is a centuries-old tradition in Japan. Certain kite designs are passed down from generation to generation.

Teenagers in Tokyo have access to many of the latest high-tech gadgets. Young people in the city commonly use cell phones to talk and send text messages to each other.

Kite festivals continue to attract large crowds of children, teenagers, and adults.

The girl on the left wears a Western-style outfit. Her friend wears a traditional kimono, the everyday attire of Japan decades ago.

Global and Traditional Influences

Teenagers around the world worry about their appearance, and Tokyo teens are exposed to a variety of global influences and fads. Many have adopted the fashions and lifestyles common among teens in the West. Traditional Japanese attire remains an important part of the Tokyo teenager's wardrobe, though. Both boys and girls wear kimonos for ceremonial occasions such as graduations, weddings, funerals, and shrine rituals.

1030

Background

Japanese Population Japan is about the size of California but has a population about 3.5 times as big—approximately 127.5 million people. Tokyo is the largest city in Japan and is the center of the largest urban agglomeration in the world. It has a population of about 35.2 million, which includes the cities of Yokohama and Kawasaki. The central city has about 8.5 million people in an area of 239 square miles. Compare this to New York City, which has a population of about 8.1 million in an area of 309 square miles. Japan is an ethnically homogeneous country with only about 1 percent of the population being non-Japanese—most of whom are Chinese or Korean. There is little population growth in Japan because they have very few immigrants and a very low birthrate, only 9 births per 1000 people. (The U.S. has about 14 births per 1000.) Therefore, Japan's population is getting older. Only about 14 percent of the population is under the age of 15, compared to about 20 percent in the United States.

WHAT DO TOKYO TEENAGERS DO?

Tokyo teenagers lead active lives filled with school, sports, part-time jobs, musical instruments, and video games. Their pursuits reflect both global and traditional influences. A teen may spend an afternoon watching a Hollywood movie on DVD or flying a kite at a traditional Japanese festival. A Tokyo youth might attend a rock 'n' roll concert or a sumo match. Meals may be fast food or traditional sukiyaki dishes.

ANALYZING VISUALS

1. **Drawing Conclusions** Why do you think Western culture exerts such a strong influence on Tokyo teenagers?
2. **Comparing and Contrasting** How do you think your life is similar to and different from that of a teenager living in Tokyo?

W Writing Support

Expository Writing Have students conduct research and write a brief essay comparing Little League baseball in Japan and the United States. OL

Assess/Close

Have students discuss how technology affects teenagers in the United States and Japan. OL

ANALYZING VISUALS

Answers:

1. Technology such as television, movies, and the Internet exposes Tokyo teenagers to the ideas of Western culture.
2. **Similar:** both go to school, watch DVDs, attend concerts, and surf the Internet; **Different:** Tokyo teens have interests rooted in Japanese culture such as flying kites, going to sumo matches, wearing kimonos.

Activity: Interdisciplinary Connection

Language Arts The number of colleges and universities is greater in Tokyo than in other parts of the country. Education is the key to economic opportunities and social advancement, so there is a great deal of pressure to attend the best schools, beginning in the earliest grades. Students are required to attend school for nine years, and free education is offered at the elementary and middle school levels. Most students also attend kindergarten and three years of high school. High school is not free, and admission is very competitive. High school study is designed to prepare students for the difficult college entrance exams. Most students also attend "cram" schools to help them prepare. Now many students who fail to get into Japanese colleges choose to study abroad. **Ask:** How do Japanese high schools compare to those in the United States? Have students use the Internet to learn more about this topic. Invite them to prepare a television news report on the question and present it to the class. AL

Visual Literacy Historical photographs can remind students of important events and concepts. **Ask:** In what ways do photographs give us information about history? *(They capture place and time; they document events and achievements; they show how people lived and how they reacted to events.)* Like photographs, flash cards can be used as visual reminders. Have students make a set of flash cards. Use one index card for each bulleted topic on the Visual Summary. The information may be ordered in a number of ways. For example, students could write topic-related questions and answers on each flash card, or rewrite each topic as a main idea with details. Have them use the cards as study aids. **OL**

Sequencing Ask students to order the photos in the Visual Summary from oldest to most recent *(mass migration to India and Pakistan; Red Guards in Beijing; factory in Japan)*. Have them explain why they ordered them the way that they did. *(Two photos are dated. The partition of British India preceded the Cultural Revolution. The modern car in the last photo tells us that the photo is most recent).* **BL**

CHAPTER 31 Visual Summary

STUDY TO GO You can study anywhere, anytime by downloading quizzes and flash cards to your PDA from glencoe.com.

Red Guards Parade in Beijing During the Cultural Revolution, 1971

These marchers are holding Mao's *Little Red Book.*

CHINA After World War II

- Mao Zedong's Communists won the civil war, and the Nationalists fled to Taiwan.
- In 1950 China entered the Korean War on the side of North Korea.
- Deng Xiaoping modernized China and faced increasing pressures for reform.
- China moved from a revolutionary culture back to a focus on family traditions.

SOUTH AND SOUTHEAST ASIA After World War II

- After independence, British India split into India (Hindu) and Pakistan (Muslim).
- India and Pakistan struggled with poverty and ethnic strife.
- Southeast Asian colonies gained independence; internal disputes led to military or one-party regimes.
- Conflict between South Vietnam and Communist North Vietnam led the United States into war.

Mass Migration to India and Pakistan, 1947

The division of British India set off a mass migration of Hindus to India and Muslims to Pakistan. More than a million people died in the resulting violence.

A Factory in Miyazaki, Japan

Although women have legal protections against discrimination in Japan, few have reached senior levels in business, education, or politics.

JAPAN AND THE PACIFIC After World War II

- Japan overcame defeat in World War II and emerged as an industrial power.
- South Korea, Taiwan, Singapore, and Hong Kong became economic powerhouses.
- Mainland China's claims on Taiwan contribute to Taiwan's uncertain future.
- Australia and New Zealand identify culturally with Europe, but immigration and trade pull them toward Asia.

Hands-On Chapter Project
Step 4: Wrap-Up

Forging an Action Plan

Step 4: Present the Plan Students will synthesize what they have learned in Steps 1–3.

Directions: Have each group prepare and deliver an oral presentation of its action plan. As a class, discuss the strengths and weaknesses of each plan, allowing students to defend their ideas. Then write the Essential Question on the board. Display a problem-solution chart. Have students volunteer problems that face developing or new nations. Encourage them to think of circumstances in China, India, and other Asian countries in the years following World War II. Then have students use what they have learned from the chapter as well as their own work on the project to identify solutions. After the chart is completed, have students write a short response to the Essential Question based on what they have learned from the chapter and their plans. **OL**

STANDARDIZED TEST PRACTICE

TEST-TAKING 

Even if you believe you know the correct answer immediately, read all of the answer choices and eliminate those you know are wrong. Doing so will help you confirm that the answer choice you think is correct is indeed correct.

Reviewing Vocabulary

Directions: Choose the word or words that best complete the sentence.

1. When the Allied forces held and controlled its lands, Japan was ________ country.
   - **A** an imperialist
   - **B** an occupied
   - **C** a satellite
   - **D** a subordinate

2. Under Mao Zedong's Great Leap Forward, collective farms were combined into vast ________.
   - **A** manors
   - **B** commonwealths
   - **C** protectorates
   - **D** communes

3. India's 1950 constitution forbade ________, or prejudicial treatment, based on gender.
   - **A** antifeminism
   - **B** segregation
   - **C** discrimination
   - **D** glass ceilings

4. Japan's economic system is called ________ because the government plays an active role in setting prices and wage policies and in subsidizing industries.
   - **A** state capitalism
   - **B** market driven
   - **C** free enterprise
   - **D** socialism

Reviewing Main Ideas

Directions: Choose the best answers to the following questions.

Section 1 *(pp. 1012–1017)*

5. Who were the Red Guards?
   - **A** Communist youth groups under Mao Zedong
   - **B** Soviet troops fighting China for control of Manchuria
   - **C** Communist Chinese forces fighting Chiang Kai-shek
   - **D** Japanese troops fighting in China during World War II

6. Deng Xiaoping's Four Modernizations included new policies in what four areas?
   - **A** Industry, agriculture, technology, and democracy
   - **B** National defense, industry, democracy, and technology
   - **C** Agriculture, national defense, industry, and technology
   - **D** Industry, banking, technology, and agriculture

7. In 1979 what policy did the Chinese government put in place to try to control population growth?
   - **A** Family-planning policy
   - **B** Late-marriage policy
   - **C** Pro-abortion policy
   - **D** One-child policy

Section 2 *(pp. 1018–1023)*

8. Who guided India's foreign policy using the principle of nonalignment?
   - **A** Mohandas Gandhi
   - **B** Jawaharlal Nehru
   - **C** Indira Gandhi
   - **D** Mother Teresa

Need Extra Help?

If You Missed Questions . . .	1	2	3	4	5	6	7	8
Go to Page . . .	1024	1013	1023	1026	1014	1014	1016	1018

Answers and Analyses

Reviewing Vocabulary

1. B Remind students to eliminate choices that are incorrect. *Imperialist* refers to extending power over other lands. This does not describe Japan after the war. While each of the other choices is a possibility, the context clues *held* and *controlled* suggest occupation rather than just economic and political dependence, which is the condition of a satellite.

2. D The idea of combining narrows the possible answers to two—commonwealths and communes. Students should recall that a commonwealth is a republic, in which the citizens rule together. A commune, therefore, is the correct answer, referring to bringing people together to live and work.

3. C All the choices are related to prejudice. Anti-feminism might be defined as "ideas or behavior reflecting a disbelief in the economic, political, and social equality of the sexes." A glass ceiling refers to a barrier that prevents women or minorities from rising beyond a certain level in business. Segregation is "separation by race or gender." Discrimination refers to any act of treating individuals or groups differently based on race, ethnic background, class, gender, or age.

4. A Point out that another word for *government* is state. The government does not own the industries, which would be socialism, so the correct answer is that it is a form of state capitalism.

Reviewing Main Ideas

5. A The word *guards,* suggests personnel in charge of protecting. Mao's Red Guards wanted to preserve the state of the revolution in China.

6. C Because Deng had no tolerance for democracy, A and B can be discounted. The difference between C and D is banking or national defense. It would make sense that Deng's emphasis would be on national defense.

7. D All of the choices might be seen as contributing to lower population growth, but only the one-child policy was instituted by the government.

8. B Tell students to think about historical context. Alignment with communist or noncommunist powers was an important issue in the 1950s and 1960s, when Nehru was in office.

9. A Muslims are associated with Pakistan and Bangladesh, Hindus with India, Kurds with southwest Asia, leaving the Sikhs as the majority in Punjab.

10. C Remind students to use prior knowledge to narrow their choices. Pol Pot was the leader of Cambodia; Ferdinand Marcos ruled the Philippines; Sukarno led Indonesia.

11. B Neither Richard Nixon nor Winston Churchill was an Allied commander governing Japan. As MacArthur is a World War II hero, he is a likely choice for having been in charge of Allied forces occupying Japan after the war.

12. D The nickname is associated with the postwar years, making it unlikely that they would receive the name because of their military might or imperialist goals.

13. A Chiang Kai-shek fled from Communist China with his followers and established the capital of China on Taiwan. Since that time, both the government on the mainland and the one on Taiwan have claimed to be the legitimate government.

TEST-TAKING TIP

For Question 13: Students may easily rule out South Korea and Singapore as correct answers. However, it may be harder for them to choose between Taiwan and Hong Kong. Remind them that although both islands have historical ties to China, the British returned control of Hong Kong to China in 1997. That leaves Taiwan as the best answer.

9. What group wanted independence for the Punjab province of India, where they lived?
- **A** Sikhs
- **B** Muslims
- **C** Hindus
- **D** Kurds

10. Who led the Communist Party in French-ruled Vietnam?
- **A** Pol Pot
- **B** Ferdinand Marcos
- **C** Ho Chi Minh
- **D** Sukarno

Section 3 *(pp. 1024–1029)*

11. Who commanded Allied forces governing Japan after World War II?
- **A** Richard Nixon
- **B** Douglas MacArthur
- **C** Winston Churchill
- **D** Hideki Tojo

12. What characteristic of South Korea, Taiwan, Singapore, and Hong Kong led to their nickname of the "Asian tigers"?
- **A** Military strength
- **B** Imperialist ambitions
- **C** Ruthless battle tactics
- **D** Economic strength

13. What nation claims to be the legitimate government of all of China?
- **A** Taiwan
- **B** South Korea
- **C** Singapore
- **D** Hong Kong

Critical Thinking

Directions: Choose the best answers to the following questions.

Use the following map to answer question 14.

14. Approximately how much of Vietnam did the Communists control between 1946 and 1954?
- **A** 10 percent
- **B** 25 percent
- **C** 50 percent
- **D** 75 percent

15. Between 1966 and 1976, the destruction of temples, the seizure of books, and the imprisonment of artists and intellectuals were closely related to which movement in China?
- **A** Great Leap Forward
- **B** Long March
- **C** Tai Ping Rebellion
- **D** Cultural Revolution

Need Extra Help?

If You Missed Questions . . .	9	10	11	12	13	14	15
Go to Page . . .	1019	1021	1024	1027	1028	1021	1014

GO ON

Critical Thinking

14. D Remind students to check the key. The dotted pattern indicates Communist control. Since the majority of Vietnam is dotted, the correct answer must be 75%.

15. D Tell students to identify clues in the question itself. "Destruction of temples, the seizure of books" and "imprisonment of artists and intellectuals" are related to culture, making D the logical choice.

16. Why does conflict between India and Pakistan over Kashmir cause global concern?
   - A Because Pakistan is much smaller than India
   - B Because both nations have nuclear weapons
   - C Because communism may spread as a result
   - D Because the conflict could interrupt world oil supplies

17. How did the Vietnam War affect politics of the region?
   - A Vietnam had a Communist government, but Laos and Cambodia remained democratic.
   - B Vietnam and Laos had Communist governments, but Cambodia remained democratic.
   - C Laos, Cambodia, and Vietnam had Communist governments.
   - D Communism continued to spread from Indochina to neighboring nations.

Analyze the chart and answer the question that follows. Base your answer on the chart.

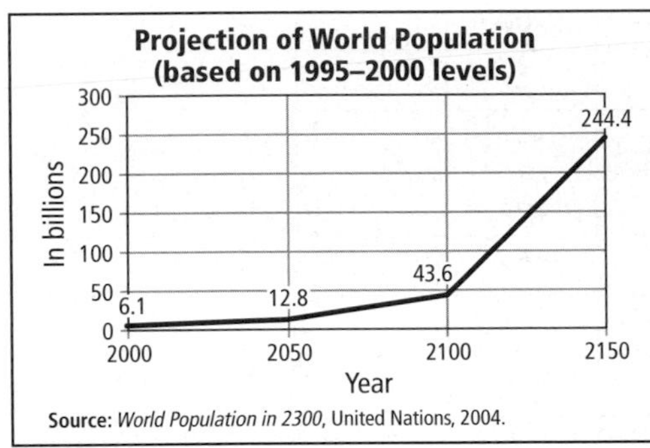

Source: *World Population in 2300*, United Nations, 2004.

18. According to the chart, how will world population change between 2000 and 2150?
   - A Rise at a constant rate
   - B Decline slowly and then begin a rapid rise in 2100
   - C Rise at a decreasing rate
   - D Rise at an increasing rate

Document-Based Questions

Directions: Analyze the document and answer the short-answer questions that follow the document. Base your answers on the document and on your knowledge of world history.

Read the following excerpt from the book *Japanese Women*, published in 1955:

> *"A quick glance at educational statistics reveals a higher percentage of female as compared to male high school graduates entering colleges and universities. The overwhelming majority of female college and university graduates, over 80 percent, are taking up employment and doing so in a wider range of fields than in the past. Better education and the availability of more job opportunities have increasingly made it possible for women to look upon marriage as an option rather than a prescribed lifestyle. . . ."*
>
> —*Japanese Women*, 1955

19. What does this passage reveal about the role of women in Japan after World War II?

20. What challenges do modern Japanese women—and women worldwide—face in the workplace?

Extended Response

21. The population in many South Asian and Southeast Asian countries has rapidly increased. What strategies can these nations take to overcome the adverse effects of overpopulation?

History ONLINE
For additional test practice, use Self-Check Quizzes—Chapter 31 at glencoe.com.

Need Extra Help?

If You Missed Questions . . .	16	17	18	19	20	21
Go to Page . . .	1020	1021	1035	1026	1026	1020

STOP

Document-Based Questions

19. It suggests drastic change; roles changing from being wives and mothers to entering college and seeking employment in a wider range of fields.

20. Possible response: overcoming subordinate roles; reaching more senior levels in business, education, and politics; attaining higher salaries, comparable to those of their male counterparts

Extended Response

21. Answers will vary, but students' responses should include details that support the strategies they list.

16. B Choices C and D are not valid. Neither India nor Pakistan is communist and neither is a major supplier of oil. A is a true statement, but does not explain worldwide concern. If either country used its nuclear weapons, however, there would be global repercussions, making B the only possible choice.

17. C All three countries had Communist governments by the end of 1975. Choice D is a false statement.

18. D Tell students to examine each statement in light of the data presented on the graph. Although the first part of the graph shows a steady rise, there is an abrupt incline after the year 2100, eliminating A, B, and C.

History ONLINE
Introduce students to chapter content and key terms by having them access the Chapter 31 Overview at glencoe.com.

Need Extra Help?
Have students refer to the pages listed if they miss any of the questions.

CHAPTER 32 Planning Guide

Key to Ability Levels	
BL Below Level	AL Above Level
OL On Level	ELL English Language Learners

Key to Teaching Resources	
Print Material	DVD
CD-ROM	Transparency

Levels				Resources	Chapter Opener	Section 1	Section 2	Chapter Assess
BL	OL	AL	ELL					
				FOCUS				
BL	OL	AL	ELL	Daily Focus Skills Transparencies		32-1	32-2	
				TEACH				
BL	OL		ELL	Reading Skills Activity, URB		p. 199		
	OL	AL		Historical Analysis Skills Activity, URB			p. 200	
BL	OL	AL	ELL	Differentiated Instruction Activity, URB		p. 201		
	OL		ELL	English Learner Activity, URB		p. 202		
BL	OL	AL	ELL	Content Vocabulary Activity, URB*			p. 205	
BL	OL	AL	ELL	Academic Vocabulary Activity, URB			p. 207	
BL	OL	AL	ELL	Skills Reinforcement Activity, URB		p. 209		
	OL	AL		Critical Thinking Skills Activity, URB		p. 210		
	OL	AL		History and Geography Activity, URB		p. 211		
	OL	AL	ELL	Mapping History Activity, URB		p. 213		
BL	OL	AL		Historical Significance Activity, URB			p. 214	
BL	OL	AL	ELL	Cooperative Learning Activity, URB			p. 215	
	OL	AL	ELL	History Simulation Activity, URB			p. 217	
BL	OL	AL	ELL	Time Line Activity, URB			p. 219	
	OL	AL		Linking Past and Present Activity, URB		p. 220		
BL	OL	AL		People in World History Activity, URB		pp. 221, 222		
BL	OL	AL	ELL	Primary Source Reading, URB			p. 223	
	OL	AL		Enrichment Activity, URB		p. 228		
BL	OL	AL	ELL	World Art and Music Activity, URB			p. 225	
BL	OL		ELL	Guided Reading Activities, URB*		p. 230	p. 231	
BL	OL		ELL	Reading Essentials and Note-Taking Guide*		p. 343	p. 346	
BL	OL	AL	ELL	Differentiated Instruction for the World History Classroom	✓	✓	✓	✓

Note: Please refer to the *Unit Resource Book: Toward a Global Civilization* for this chapter's URB materials.

* Also available in Spanish

- Interactive Lesson Planner
- Interactive Teacher Edition
- Fully editable blackline masters
- Section Spotlight Videos Launch
- Differentiated Lesson Plans
- Printable reports of daily assignments
- Standards Tracking System

Levels					Resources	Chapter Opener	Section 1	Section 2	Chapter Assess
BL	OL	AL	ELL						
TEACH *(continued)*									
BL	OL	AL	ELL		StudentWorks™ Plus DVD	✓	✓	✓	✓
BL	OL	AL	ELL		Vocabulary PuzzleMaker CD-ROM	✓	✓	✓	✓
Teacher Resources					Building Academic Vocabulary	✓	✓	✓	✓
					Strategies for Success	✓	✓	✓	✓
					Outline Map Resource Book	✓	✓	✓	✓
					Presentation Plus! with MindJogger DVD	✓	✓	✓	✓
ASSESS									
BL	OL	AL	ELL		Section Quizzes and Chapter Tests*		p. 395	p. 396	p. 397
BL	OL	AL	ELL		Authentic Assessment With Rubrics	✓	✓	✓	✓
BL	OL	AL	ELL		Standardized Test Practice Workbook	✓	✓	✓	✓
BL	OL	AL	ELL		*ExamView® Assessment Suite* CD-ROM		32-1	32-2	Ch. 32
BL	OL	AL	ELL		Interactive Tutor Self-Assessment CD-ROM		32-1	32-2	
CLOSE									
BL			ELL		Reteaching Activity, URB			p. 227	
BL	OL		ELL		Reading and Study Skills Foldables™	✓	✓	✓	✓

Using ExamView® Assessment Suite

Quick Test

Technology Product

Glencoe's Exam*View*® includes powerful assessment tools and enables you to quickly create, adapt, and assess tests for your students. Exam*View*® allows you to

- develop online testing materials that focus on the specific skills and competencies of what has been taught in the classroom;
- create several versions of these test materials that are adjusted to meet the different ability levels of your students;
- provide a variety of test formats including Multiple Choice, True/False, Yes/No, Matching, Completion (Fill-in-the-Blank), and Numeric Response.

Steps

- Open the Exam*View*® Test Generator.
- Select **Create a new test using the QuickTest Wizard** and click **OK.**
- Name the test you are creating.
- From the list, select the *Chapter Banks* you would like to use. Click **Next.**
- Indicate the number of questions you want per question type. Click **Next.**
- Enter number of matching groups. Click **Next.**
- Verify summary of selections and click **Finish.**
- The *QuickTest Wizard* will build your test. Print the test or save it for students to take the test on a computer using the Internet.

History ONLINE

	Student	Teacher	Parent
Beyond the Textbook	●	●	●
Chapter Overviews	●	●	●
Time Current Events	●		●
ePuzzles and Games	●		●
Concepts in Motion	●		●
Literature Connections		●	
Multi-Language Glossaries	●		●
Online Student Edition	●	●	●
Self-Check Quizzes	●		●
Student Web Activities	●		●
Study Central ™	●		●
Teaching Today		●	
Vocabulary eFlashcards	●		●
Web Activity Lesson Plans		●	

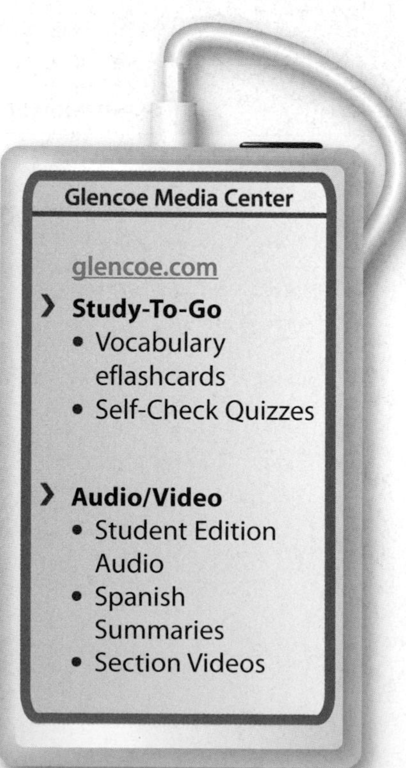

- **Timed Readings Plus in Social Studies** helps students increase their reading rate and fluency while maintaining comprehension. The 400-word passages are similar to those found on state and national assessments.
- **Reading in the Content Area: Social Studies** concentrates on six essential reading skills that help students better comprehend what they read. The book includes 75 high-interest nonfiction passages written at increasing levels of difficulty.
- **Reading Social Studies** includes strategic reading instruction and vocabulary support in Social Studies content for both ELLs and native speakers of English.

www.jamestowneducation.com

Biography  

The following videotape program is available from Glencoe as a supplement to Chapter 32:

- Men in Space: From Goddard to Armstrong (ISBN 1-56-501-037-X)

To order, call Glencoe at 1-800-334-7344. To find classroom resources to accompany many of these videos, check the following home pages:

A&E Television: www.aetv.com

The History Channel: www.historychannel.com

GLENCOE BOOKLINK 3

Use this database to search more than 30,000 titles to create a customized reading list for your students.

- Reading lists can be organized by students' reading level, author, genre, theme, or area of interest.
- The database provides Degrees of Reading Power™ (DRP) and Lexile™ readability scores for all selections.
- A brief summary of each selection is included.

Leveled reading suggestions for this chapter:

For students at a Grade 8 reading level:
- ***Where Did AIDS Come From?,*** by Anna Forbes

For students at a Grade 9 reading level:
- ***United Nations,*** by Stewart Ross

For students at a Grade 10 reading level:
- ***Global Warming,*** by Pennie Stoyles and Peter Pentland

For students at a Grade 11 reading level:
- ***Better Off: Flipping the Switch on Technology,*** by Eric Brende

For students at a Grade 12 reading level:
- ***What Does a Peace Corps Volunteer Do?,*** by David Lavine and Ira Mandelbaum

Index to National Geographic Magazine:

The following articles relate to this chapter:

- "Last of the Amazon," by Scott Wallace, January 2007
- "Living with AIDS," by Gideon Mendel, September 2005
- "Tracing the Human Footprint," by David Quammen, September 2005

National Geographic Society Products To order the following, call National Geographic at 1-800-368-2728:

- *National Geographic Atlas of the World* (Book)

Access National Geographic's new, dynamic MapMachine Web site and other geography resources at:

www.nationalgeographic.com

www.nationalgeographic.com/maps

Introducing
CHAPTER 32

Focus

MAKING CONNECTIONS
Who is affected by civil war?

Ask students to first discuss past civil wars that they have learned about, such as the one in the United States (1861–1865) and in Spain (1936–1939). Focus on the causes and effects of these civil wars. Then have students talk about the causes and effects of current civil wars. Ask how current civil wars compare and contrast to past ones. *(Answers may include political and religious differences as some causes and civilian deaths, property destruction, and damage to the environment as some effects.)* Close the discussion by having students suggest how civil wars can be prevented in the future.

Teach

The Big Ideas

As students study the chapter, remind them to consider the section-based Big Ideas included in each section's Guide to Reading. The **Essential Questions** in the activities below tie in to the Big Ideas and help students think about and understand important chapter concepts. In addition, the Hands-on Chapter Projects with their culminating activities relate the content from each section to the Big Ideas. These activities build on each other as students progress through the chapter. Section activities culminate in the wrap-up activity on the Visual Summary page.

CHAPTER 32

Changing Global Patterns

Section 1 Challenges of a New Century

Section 2 New Global Communities

MAKING CONNECTIONS

Who is affected by civil war?

Conflicts throughout the world have forced millions of people from their homes. Violent conflicts over border disputes in places like Ethiopia and Eritrea have forced thousands of people into refugee camps like the one shown in this photo. Refugees depend upon assistance from the international community in order to survive. In this chapter you will learn about efforts to solve global problems.

- What is the United Nations doing to resolve and prevent conflicts around the world?
- Give an example of a problem in another nation and explain how it affects the United States.

THE WORLD ▶

1960

1962 Scientist Rachel Carson warns of pesticide dangers

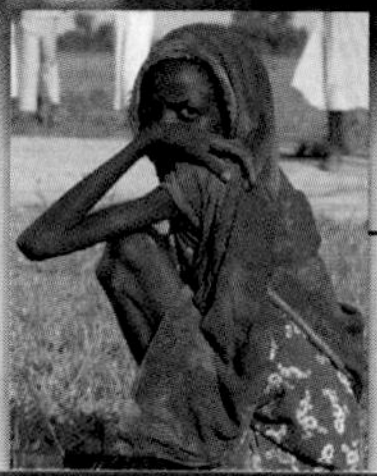

1969 U.S. moon landing

1980

1984 Widespread famine begins in western Africa

1986 Nuclear accident at Chernobyl in Ukraine

1990 World Wide Web created

1036

Challenges of a New Century

Essential Question: How has the Internet served to increase awareness of global issues? *(by increasing the ability to communicate with others around the world)* Tell students that in Section 1, they will learn about the challenges that today's societies face, focusing on the pros and cons of the technological revolution. OL

New Global Communities

Essential Question: How have international organizations, such as the United Nations, taken the lead in solving world problems? *(by having people from different nations and cultures work together to resolve issues)* Tell students that in Section 2, they will learn about the strategies that the UN, nongovernmental organizations, and other agencies have implemented to address global concerns ranging from trade to human rights. OL

2001
Terrorists attack U.S. World Trade Center and Pentagon

2006
North Korea performs its first nuclear test

2000

2006
World population passes 6.5 billion mark

FOLDABLES™ Study Organizer

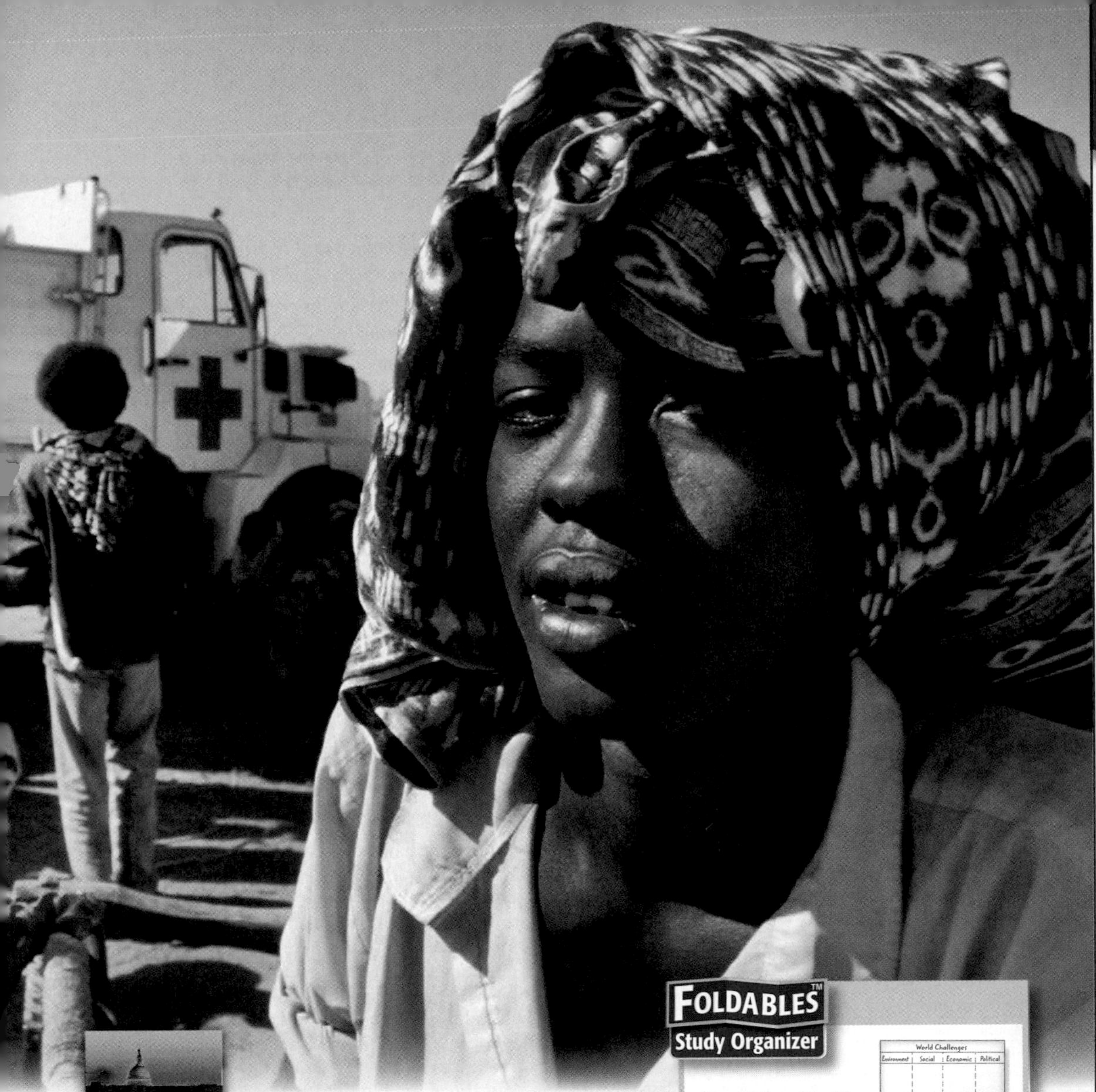

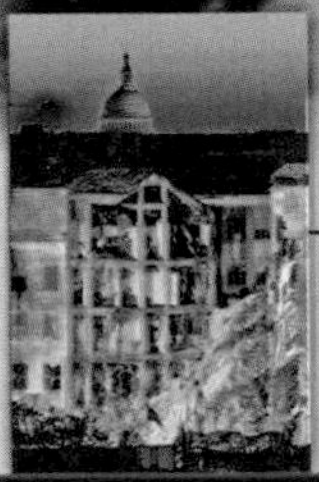

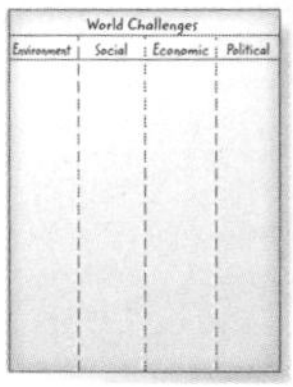

Identifying Identify environmental, social, economic, and political challenges in the world today and record them on a Folded Chart. Under each entry, briefly summarize the challenge.

History ONLINE
Chapter Overview—Visit glencoe.com to preview Chapter 32.

Introducing
CHAPTER 32

More About the Photo

Visual Literacy Life in a refugee camp is all too often a struggle just to survive. Food, water, shelter, and even basic sanitation are often scarce, or nonexistent. Refugees also struggle against extreme temperatures, flooding, high winds, and other harsh climate elements. Disease and malnutrition are ever-present threats at most camps. To help their families survive, those children who are not too ill will work hard, searching for sticks or dry grass for a fire, collecting containers to store water, or doing other essential chores.

FOLDABLES™ Study Organizer **Dinah Zike's Foldables**

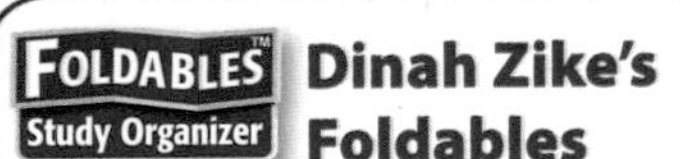

Dinah Zike's Foldables are three-dimensional, interactive graphic organizers that help students practice basic writing skills, review vocabulary terms, and identify main ideas. Instructions for creating and using Foldables can be found in the Appendix at the end of this book and in the *Dinah Zike's Reading and Study Skills Foldables* booklet.

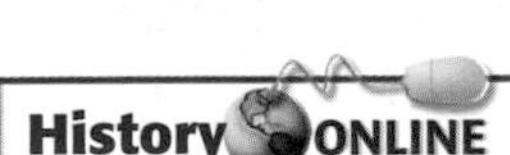

History ONLINE
Introduce students to chapter content and key terms by having them access the Chapter 32 Overview at glencoe.com.

Focus

Bellringer

Daily Focus Transparency 32.1

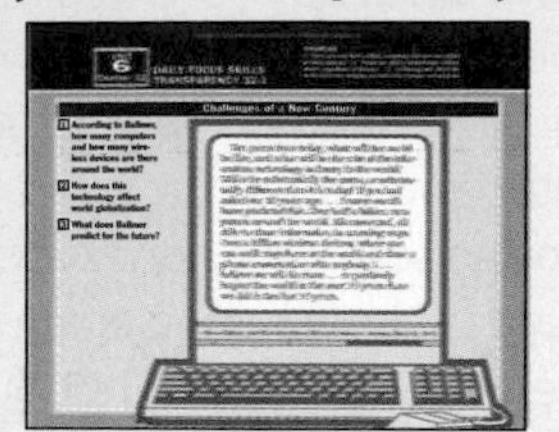

GUIDE TO READING

Answers to Graphic:

Deforestation—Cause: population growth; Effect: destruction of natural habitat; **Loss of ozone layer**—Cause: chlorofluorocarbons; Effect: Earth loses ultraviolet protection; **Greenhouse effect**—Cause: carbon dioxide; Effect: global warming; **Acid rain**—Cause: sulfur; Effect: destroys forests; **Weapons**—Cause: technological and biological revolution; Effect: war; **Hunger**—Cause: population growth, natural catastrophes; Effect: starvation

Section Spotlight Video

To generate student interest and provide a springboard for class discussion, access the Chapter 32, Section 1 video at glencoe.com or on the video DVD.

SECTION 1

Challenges of a New Century

GUIDE TO READING

The BIG Idea

New Technologies Today's societies face many challenges, and they must balance the costs and benefits of the technological revolution.

Content Vocabulary

- bioterrorism *(p. 1040)*
- ecology *(p. 1042)*
- deforestation *(p. 1042)*
- desertification *(p. 1042)*
- greenhouse effect *(p. 1042)*
- sustainable development *(p. 1042)*
- global economy *(p. 1043)*

Academic Vocabulary

- function *(p. 1039)*
- environment *(p. 1041)*

People and Events

- Neil Armstrong *(p. 1040)*
- Green Revolution *(p. 1041)*
- Rachel Carson *(p. 1042)*
- Kyoto Protocol *(p. 1042)*
- Universal Declaration of Human Rights *(p. 1045)*
- Patriot Act *(p. 1047)*

Reading Strategy

Determining Cause and Effect As you read, complete a table like the one below to determine the cause and effect of global concerns.

Concern	Cause	Effect
Deforestation		
Greenhouse effect		
Weapons		
Hunger		

In the twenty-first century, science and technology continue to build a global community connected by the Internet. Scientific advances have brought benefits in medicine and agriculture, but also new weapons of war. Development is creating great wealth, but it also damages the planet. The uneven distribution of our global wealth may be one factor contributing to a new challenge—terrorism.

Technological Revolution

MAIN IDEA The benefits of the technological revolution must be balanced against its costs.

HISTORY & YOU Do you eat organic foods? Read to learn about organic farming and the Green Revolution.

Since World War II, but especially since the 1970s, a stunning array of changes has created a technological revolution. Like the first and second Industrial Revolutions, this revolution is also having a profound effect on people's daily lives and on entire societies.

Communication, Transportation, and Space

Global transportation and communication systems are transforming the world community. People are connected and "online" throughout the world as they have never been before. Space exploration and orbiting satellites have increased our understanding of our world and of solar systems beyond our world.

Since the 1970s, jumbo jet airlines have moved millions of people around the world each year. A flight between London and New York took half a day in 1945. Now, that trip takes only five or six hours. The Internet—the world's largest computer network—provides quick access to vast quantities of information. The World Wide Web, developed in the 1990s, has made the Internet even more accessible to people everywhere. Satellites, cable television, facsimile (fax) machines, cellular telephones, and computers enable people to communicate with one another practically everywhere in the world. Communication and transportation systems have made the world a truly global village.

The computer may be the most revolutionary of all technological inventions of the twentieth century. The first computer was really a product of World War II. British mathematician Alan Turing designed the first electronic computer to crack enemy codes. Turing's machine did calculations faster than any human. IBM of the

Resource Manager

R Reading Strategies	C Critical Thinking	D Differentiated Instruction	W Writing Support	S Skill Practice
Teacher Edition • Inferring, p. 1039 • Identifying, p. 1040 • Making Conn., p. 1045 • Questioning, p. 1046 **Additional Resources** • Read. Skills Act., URB p. 199 • Guid. Read. Act., URB p. 230 • Read. Ess. & Note-Taking Guide, p. 343	**Teacher Edition** • Making Inferences, p. 1040 • Det. Cause/Effect, pp. 1042, 1047 • Drawing Con., p. 1045 **Additional Resources** • Crit. Think. Act., URB p. 210 • Section Quiz, p. 395	**Teacher Edition** • ELL, p. 1042 • Adv. Learners, p. 1043 **Additional Resources** • Diff. Instr. Act., URB p. 201 • English Learner Act., URB p. 202 • Enrich. Act., URB p. 228 • People in World Hist. Act., URB pp. 221, 222	**Teacher Edition** • Persuasive Writing, p. 1040 **Additional Resources** • Linking Past/Present Act., URB p. 220	**Teacher Edition** • Using Geo. Skills, p. 1041 **Additional Resources** • Skills Reinforc. Act., URB p. 209 • Hist. & Geo. Act., URB p. 211 • Mapping Hist. Act., URB p. 213

SCIENCE, TECHNOLOGY, & SOCIETY

Satellite Communications

The communications satellite Syncom-IV was launched by space shuttle Discovery.

Today, hundreds of satellites orbit Earth. Some are used to predict the weather, and others help navigate ships, aircraft, and cars. Communications satellites are used to relay radio, television, and telephone signals.

Communication satellites are part of everyday life. Television stations transmit their programs to a satellite as radio waves. The satellite amplifies the signal and transmits it to your cable or dish provider to forward to your television. Satellite phones receive signals via satellite relay. They are much more costly than cell phones, so they are not commonly used. In an emergency, satellite phones may offer the only means of communication. When a hurricane destroyed Florida's cell towers, rescue workers could still communicate by satellite phone.

Television signals travel in a straight line. To receive the signal, an antenna must have a "clear line of sight" to the source. Since Earth is curved, its surface obstructs the line of sight. Satellites solve this problem by allowing signals to travel high above Earth giving them an unobstructed line to homes.

CRITICAL THINKING SKILLS

1. **Comparing and Contrasting** What are the advantages and disadvantages of satellite phones and cell phones?
2. **Finding the Main Idea** What role do satellites play in the transmission of a television broadcast?

United States made the first computer with stored memory in 1948. The IBM 1401, marketed in 1959, was the first computer used in large numbers in business and industry. These early computers used thousands of vacuum tubes to **function.** These machines took up considerable space. The development of the transistor and the silicon chip produced a revolutionary new approach to computers.

Then, in 1971, the microprocessor was invented and paved the way for the personal computer. Both small and powerful, the personal computer became a regular fixture in businesses, schools, and homes by the 1990s. The computer made many routine tasks easier and became important **R** in nearly every area of modern life. Other tools and machines depend on computers to function. For example, a computer makes many of the decisions used in flying an airplane.

Through their personal computers, people can go on the Internet, a huge web of linked computer networks. The Internet was introduced to the public for the first time in 1972. That same year, electronic mail, or e-mail, was introduced.

Teach

R Reading Strategy

Inferring Ask: How have computers transformed schools and the workplace? *(People can study, do research, and work in locations remote from the physical site of the school or business.)* **OL**

Did You Know?

Microprocessors contain millions of microscopic digital circuits, laid on a thin plate of silicon that is just a few square centimeters or even smaller.

CRITICAL THINKING SKILLS

Answers:

1. Satellite phones are more expensive than cell phones, but can be used in areas without cell towers and in emergencies when land-based infrastructure has been destroyed.
2. Satellites offer a clear line of sight. Early televisions had to cope with obstructed lines of transmission.

Differentiated Instruction

Leveled Activities

BL Differentiated Instruction Activity, URB p. 201

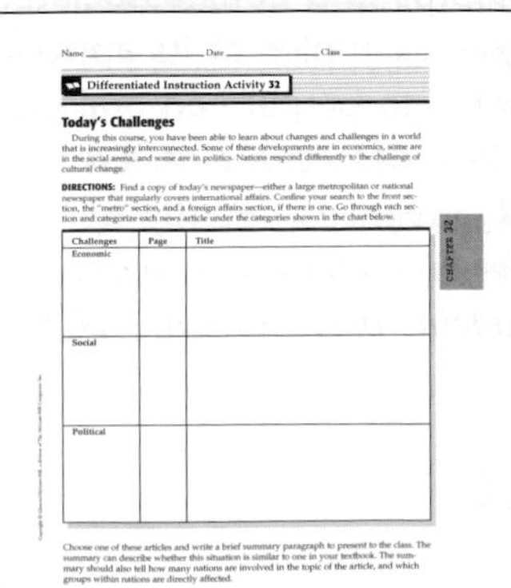

Differentiated Instruction Activity 32

Today's Challenges

OL People in World History Activity, URB p. 222

People in World History Activity 32 — Profile 2

Admiral Grace Murray Hopper (1906–1992)

AL Linking Past & Present Activity, URB p. 220

Linking Past and Present Activity 32

The Greenhouse Effect and the Antarctic Ozone Hole

ELL English Learner Activity, URB p. 202

English Learner Activity 32

Changing Global Patterns

D Differentiated Instruction

English Language Learners

Point out that the prefix *de-* usually indicates reversal or removal (as in *deforestation*). Ask students to think of other words with a *de-* prefix. *(Students may mention words such as* destruction, defuse, *and* deform.) Have students define these words, using their understanding of the meaning of the prefix. **ELL**

C Critical Thinking

Determining Cause and Effect **Ask:** How has global economic development affected the environment? *(Economic development leads to greater pollution, which, in turn, potentially contributes to global warming, destruction of the ozone layer, and acid rain.)* **OL**

For additional practice on this skill, see the **Skills Handbook**.

✓Reading Check

Answer: Development is sustainable if it preserves natural resources for future generations.

Additional Support

Environmental Crisis

MAIN IDEA Environmental damage endangers the world's sustainable development.

HISTORY & YOU Does your family drive a hybrid vehicle? Read to learn about environmental challenges in today's world.

In *Silent Spring*, published in 1962, **Rachel Carson,** an American scientist, argued that the buildup of pesticides—chemicals sprayed on crops to kill insects—was having unforeseen results. Insects were dying, but so too were birds, fish, and other wild animals. Also, the pesticide residue on food harmed humans.

Carson's warnings alarmed many scientists and gave rise to the new science of **ecology,** the study of the relationship between living things and their environment. Since then, scientific research studies have shown that dangers to the environment have many sources.

Three sources are by-products of population growth: deforestation, desertification, and destruction of the tropical rain forests. **Deforestation** is the clearing of forests to provide more farmland and timber. The African lion, elephant, and gorilla are now endangered species because deforestation has destroyed much of their natural habitat. **D**

Desertification is the formation of degraded soil, turning semi-arid lands into nonproductive deserts. Overgrazing, poor cultivation practices, and destruction of vegetation in semiarid lands destroy the soil's productivity.

Tropical rain forests near the equator cover only 6 percent of Earth's surface, but they support 50 percent of the world's plant and animal life. These forests also remove carbon dioxide from the air and return oxygen to it. They are crucial to our survival, yet logging, road building, and clearing for agriculture are destroying tropical forests at an alarming rate.

Chemical Wastes and Disasters

Chemical wastes pose another danger to the environment. The release of chlorofluorocarbons—gases used in aerosol cans, refrigerators, and air conditioners—destroys the ozone layer. This is the thin layer in the upper atmosphere that shields Earth from the sun's ultraviolet rays.

C Acid rain results when sulfur spewed out by factories mixes with moisture in the air. Acid rain is responsible for killing forests in North America and Europe.

Global warming has the potential to create a global crisis. The **greenhouse effect,** the warming of the Earth because of the buildup of carbon dioxide in the atmosphere, contributes to the melting of the polar ice caps, rising sea levels, and devastating droughts and storms.

A conference on global warming was held in Kyoto, Japan. To reduce emissions, more than 150 nations signed the **Kyoto Protocol.** The European Union and Japan ratified the treaty in 2002. The United States did not.

Ecological disasters have also harmed our environment. A chemical plant at Bhopal, India, released toxic fumes into the air in 1984. A nuclear accident at Chernobyl in 1986 released radiation. Hundreds died, and there were long-lasting health and environmental consequences. In 1989 the oil tanker *Exxon Valdez* ran aground in Alaska. The spill killed thousands of birds and polluted fishing areas.

Sustainable Development

Economic development that does not limit the ability of future generations to meet their basic needs is known as **sustainable development.** In promoting sustainable development, the United Nations urges nations to work to conserve all natural resources.

One natural resource is water. According to the UN, one-sixth of the world's population lacks water for drinking or agriculture. Those who have no clean water often get sick with cholera, typhoid, and diarrhea. More than 5 million people die every year from the lack of water or from drinking untreated water.

Many nations have enacted recycling and water conservation programs. They have also curbed the dumping of toxic materials. This may help achieve sustainable development.

✓Reading Check **Defining** What makes development "sustainable"?

Activity: Technology Connection

Researching Sustainable Development Have students work in pairs to find out more about sustainable development. Allow them to use the Internet to find information on theories of sustainable development and the difficulties involved in applying the principles. **Ask:** In which ways have countries been successful in protecting their environment while strengthening their industries (for example, by promoting ecotourism)? Have pairs print copies of the articles and pages they find and attach brief summaries of the main points of each. Then have students present summaries of what they have learned. Finish the activity by asking students if sustainable development is possible or whether it is an ideal. Discuss students' views and draw some common conclusions about obstacles and how they might be overcome. **AL**

Poverty and Civil Strife

MAIN IDEA Poverty, hunger, and civil strife continue to plague many developing nations.

HISTORY & YOU Do you have enough to eat each day? Read to learn about food shortages and world hunger.

After World War II, especially since the 1970s, the world developed a global economy. In a **global economy,** the production, distribution, and sale of goods are done on a worldwide scale. Almost 40 percent of the profits of U.S. businesses come from the sale of goods abroad or investments in foreign nations.

Gap Between Rich and Poor

One feature of the global economy is the wide gap between rich and poor nations. Rich nations are developed. They are mainly in the Northern Hemisphere and include countries such as the United States, Canada, Germany, and Japan. Developed nations have well-organized industrial and agricultural systems, make use of advanced technologies, and have strong educational systems. The poor nations, or developing nations, are located mainly in the Southern Hemisphere. They include many nations in Africa, Asia, and Latin America. Developing nations are primarily farming nations with little technology.

D A serious problem in developing nations is an explosive population growth. According to UN projections, the world's population could double by 2050, reaching over 12 billion. Much of that rapid growth will take place in developing nations, which can least afford it. Some developing nations have taken steps to decrease population growth. China advocated a one-child policy (see Chapter 31), and India encouraged a national family welfare program to reduce its population growth rate. However, neither measure has been very successful.

World Hunger

Growing enough food for more and more people creates a severe problem in many developing countries. An estimated 1 billion people worldwide today suffer from hunger.

INFOGRAPHICS PRIMARY SOURCE

Destruction of Tropical Rain Forests

The Amazon Basin in South America is a rich tropical rain forest. It holds over 30,000 species of plants and trees and a diversity of animal life. But like other rain forests, it faces deforestation. What drives the clearing of the land? Poor farmers clear small plots to grow food for survival. Large agricultural operations clear vast areas to raise cattle for export. Governments sell logging rights to raise money for development projects.

The local effects are severe. In a tropical rain forest, plants and trees—not the soil—hold nearly all the nutrients. After the land is cleared, the soil soon loses its ability to grow crops. The global effects may prove disastrous. Rain forests are home to over half the world's plant and animal species. Plants that could provide new medicines are likely to become extinct before they are even discovered.

Farmer clears an area of the Amazon rain forest.

CRITICAL THINKING SKILLS

1. **Determining Cause and Effect** What may be the global effects of deforestation upon the environment?
2. **Analyzing** Why is rain forest destruction a problem for developed nations?

D Differentiated Instruction

Advanced Learners Explain to students that globalization is a controversial issue that has both proponents and critics. Ask students to identify several arguments both for and against it, using facts in the text as well as from library and Internet sources. Have them present their details in a chart. Then discuss with students the effects of economic globalization on their own lives. **OL**

CRITICAL THINKING SKILLS

Answers:

1. loss of plant and animal life
2. The effects of rain forest destruction are global: loss of croplands could affect food supplies; loss of plants could limit new medicines; the act of clearing these forests also contributes to global warming.

Differentiated Instruction

History and Geography Activity, URB p. 211

Predicting Consequences

Objective: Read about the rate of rain forest destruction.

Focus: Locate countries with rain forests on map.

Teach: Discuss the significance of statistics and future implications.

Assess: Have students create a public service announcement about saving rain forests.

Close: Ask students to find projections beyond 2010 and add a third column to the table.

Differentiated Instruction Strategies

BL Have students create a poster about the disappearing rain forests.

AL Invite students to find out more about programs to save the rain forest and discuss the merits of each.

ELL Have students draw a diagram of the various levels of the rain forest.

Did You Know?

In 2003, in response to rebel attacks in Darfur, a government-supported militia group called the Janjaweed began a campaign of violence, destroying villages, kidnapping women, poisoning wells, and killing men. More than 2 million Sudanese have fled to refugee camps in addition to the tens of thousands who have died.

CRITICAL THINKING SKILLS

Answers:

1. Small loans at low interest enable the women to keep their profits instead of paying them to moneylenders.
2. Possible response: traditional beliefs about a woman's role in the family and as a subordinate to men; lack of access to education

✓Reading Check

Answer: China has a one-child policy in place, and India encourages a national family welfare program.

Every year, more than 8 million people die of hunger, many of them young children. Poor soil, increasing populations, and natural catastrophes contribute to world hunger.

Economic factors also contribute to widespread hunger. Growing crops for export, for example, might lead to big profits for large landowners. However, it leaves many small farmers with little land on which to grow food.

Civil War and Ethnic Conflict

Civil wars have also created food shortages. War not only disrupts normal farming, but warring groups try to limit access to food to destroy their enemies. In Sudan, 1.3 million people starved when combatants of a civil war in the 1980s prevented food from reaching them. As unrest continued during the early 2000s in Darfur (see Chapter 30), families were forced to leave their farms. As a result, an estimated 70,000 people had starved by mid-2004.

The Darfur situation has awakened the world to the practice of genocide. Many observers believed that the Sudanese regime conducted a systematic campaign to kill ethnic African peoples. The Serbian policy of ethnic cleansing of Bosnian Muslims in the 1990s also revived memories of Nazi atrocities.

Ethnic and religious conflicts have also caused tension in Asian and Southeast Asian countries. Tibet seeks independence from the Chinese government that has suppressed dissent among ethnic minorities. Tibet's Dalai Lama has been in exile in India since 1959. In 1999, violence between Christians and Muslims broke out in East Timor (in the Moluccas Islands). Nearly 10,000 people died due to the conflict. A pact in 2002 supposedly ended the fighting, though clashes have continued.

✓Reading Check **Explaining** What steps have India and China taken to help control population?

INFOGRAPHICS PRIMARY SOURCE

Women Entrepreneurs of the Developing World

Sophia Khatoon made beautiful bamboo stools in her village of Jobra, Bangladesh. The materials cost 25 cents per stool, which she borrowed from a local moneylender. After paying the steep interest, Sophia earned only 2 cents per day. This scenario is common in developing nations where poor people, especially women, lack access to bank loans. Seeing the need, Dr. Muhammad Yunus started Grameen Bank. It offers microcredit (tiny loans) to the poorest of the poor—based on trust, not collateral, and at low interest. Dr. Yunus's first loan went to Sophia Khatoon. With a loan of only a few dollars, Sophia soon established a profitable business. By the end of 2006, Grameen had 6.91 million borrowers, 97 percent of whom are women.

A loan from a microcredit bank helped this Rwandan refugee set up her own business.

CRITICAL THINKING SKILLS

1. **Explaining** How has microcredit changed the prospects for success for women entrepreneurs in developing nations?
2. **Making Inferences** In addition to money, what other problems likely face women entrepreneurs in the developing world?

Hands-On Chapter Project
Step 1

Developing a Board Game

Small groups put together an educational board game drawing on events and trends in the twenty-first century.

Step 1: Creating Game Cards

Essential Question: Can the challenges of the twenty-first century be overcome?

Directions: Write the Big Idea on the board. Tell students that they will use the facts in this section to generate game cards from which players draw. Students should write a question on each card, providing the answer on the other side. If players answer correctly, they roll the dice and move forward on the game board (which they will create in Section 2). If not, they move backwards. Encourage students to create questions that focus first on the most important ideas associated with the content vocabulary and people, places, and events, and then to develop questions that require making inferences or drawing conclusions.

Summarizing: Have students share what they learned about the Big Idea by making up their game cards. **OL**

(Chapter Project is continued in Section 2.)

Political and Social Challenges

MAIN IDEA Not all nations guarantee their people basic human rights and equality.

HISTORY & YOU To what rights are you entitled? Read to learn about the Universal Declaration of Human Rights.

Many political and social changes have taken place as a result of World War II. As democracy spread, many countries affirmed and extended rights to their people, both male and female.

Human Rights

The United Nations took the lead in affirming the basic human rights of all people. On December 10, 1948, the UN's General Assembly adopted the **Universal Declaration of Human Rights.** According to the declaration:

PRIMARY SOURCE

"All human beings are born free and equal in dignity and rights. . . . Everyone is entitled to all the rights and freedoms set forth in this Declaration, without distinction of any kind, such as race, color, sex, language, religion, political or other opinion, national or social origin, property, birth or other status. . . . Everyone has the right to life, liberty, and security of person. . . . Everyone has the right to freedom of movement. . . . Everyone has the right to freedom of opinion and expression."

—*Universal Declaration of Human Rights,* 1948

Since the adoption of the UN declaration, the human rights movement has achieved much success in freeing political prisoners and bringing economic and political change around the world. Nevertheless, human rights violations still occur worldwide. **R**

Governments themselves often carry on the violence. Dictators and military regimes often punish people who disagree with their views. In Cuba, Chile, Myanmar, Iraq, Iran, and other countries, people have been persecuted for opposing repressive governments. In other countries, such as Bosnia and Rwanda, ethnic, religious, and racial hatreds have led to the mass murder of hundreds of thousands of people.

New Democracies

After World War II, African and Asian leaders wanted democratic governments. Within a decade, however, military dictatorships or one-party governments replaced democratic systems in Africa, Asia, and Latin America. In recent years, however, interest in democracy has rekindled. For instance, South Korea, Taiwan, and the Philippines hold free elections. Similar developments have taken place in a number of African countries and throughout Latin America.

Unfortunately, conflict due to regional, ethnic, and religious differences creates discord around the world. Ethnic divisions in Yugoslavia, unrest in the Middle East, and conflicts among ethnic groups in Africa all remain to be resolved.

Equality for Women

In the social and economic spheres of the Western world, the gap that once separated men and women has been steadily narrowing. More and more women are joining the workforce, and they make up half of university graduates in Western countries. Many countries have laws that require equal pay for women and men doing the same work, and some laws prohibit promotions based on gender. Nevertheless, women in many Western countries still do not hold many top positions in business or government.

Bound to their homes and families and subordinate to men, women in developing nations face considerable difficulties. They often are unable to obtain education, property rights, or decent jobs. Domitila Barrios de Chungara, a miner's wife from Bolivia, said in a 1981 interview: **C**

PRIMARY SOURCE

"But women like us, housewives, who get organized to better our people, well, they beat us up and persecute us. . . . [People do not know] what it's like to get up at four in the morning and go to bed at eleven or twelve at night, just to be able to get all the housework done, because of the lousy conditions we live in."

—Domitila Barrios de Chungara, 1981

✓Reading Check **Identifying** Which organization developed the Universal Declaration of Human Rights?

R Reading Strategy

Making Connections Ask: Why should nations be concerned about human rights violations in other countries? *(Because the world is so closely connected today, violations in one country affect the others as well. Repressive governments may lead to conflict and migrations, both of which can have consequences for other nations.)* **OL**

C Critical Thinking

Drawing Conclusions Ask: Why are women's efforts to advance often met with resistance? *(Women's desire for greater equality threatens the male hierarchy in some areas and challenges traditions that have placed them in subordinate roles.)* **AL**

✓Reading Check

Answer: the United Nations

Additional Support

Activity: Interdisciplinary Connection

Geography Have students work independently or in pairs to identify on a map the places in which human rights violations have occurred recently or are ongoing. Tell students that they might include sites of ethnic conflicts as well as countries in which governments repress opposition. Suggest that students begin by researching those conflicts mentioned in this section of the text. Then have them use electronic or print resources to find more information about situations in other countries. Ask students to create annotations for their map that include the dates, a description of the events, identification of those involved, and the results of the violations. Have students display their maps in the classroom. **Ask:** What conclusions might be drawn about human rights violations from examining the map? *(Answers will vary, but should be based on information from students' maps.)* **OL**

Reading Strategy

Questioning Discuss the aims of terrorist organizations. **Ask:** How might media coverage advance their causes? *(by publicizing their goals and thus increasing recruits; by increasing public pressure for agreeing to their demands so hostages are released)* OL

CONNECTING TO TODAY

Answers:

1. to detect, prepare for, and respond to terrorist attacks
2. Both teach people to do the right things automatically in a crisis, to avoid panic, and provide the best chance of survival.

Challenge of Terrorism

MAIN IDEA Acts of terrorism, now a part of modern society, have a worldwide effect.

HISTORY & YOU Have you heard details about new security at American airports? Read to learn how terrorism challenges the world.

Acts of terror have become a regular feature of modern society. Terrorists often kill civilians and take hostages to achieve their political goals.

Modern Terrorism

During the late 1970s and 1980s, many countries placed their concern about terrorism at the top of foreign policy agendas. Terrorist acts have received considerable media attention. When Palestinian terrorists kidnapped and killed 11 Israeli athletes at the Munich Olympic Games in 1972, hundreds of millions of people watched the drama unfold on television. Indeed, some observers believe that television newscasts contribute to the spread of terrorism.

Some terrorists are militant nationalists who want separatist states. The Irish Republican Army (IRA), for example, wants to unite Northern Ireland, governed by Great Britain, with the Irish Republic. (See Chapter 28.) Since the early 1970s, violence has rocked the country. IRA leaders now seem more willing to open normal relations with the Northern Ireland police. This is a big step toward achieving the goal of the Good Friday Peace Pact of 1998: a Protestant-Catholic governing coalition.

Sometimes terrorism is state-sponsored. Militant governments in Iraq, Syria, Cuba, and North Korea have provided sanctuary and support to numerous terrorist organizations.

The Impact of 9/11

One of the most destructive acts of terrorism occurred on September 11, 2001, in the United States. (See Chapter 28.) Following the horrific attacks on the World Trade Center and the Pentagon, President George W. Bush vowed to wage war on terrorism. This process began with military

CONNECTING TO THE UNITED STATES

HOMELAND SECURITY

The mission of the Department of Homeland Security (DHS) is to lead national efforts to prevent, prepare for, and respond to terrorist attacks and natural disasters. The DHS coordinates a vast network of state and local emergency management and law enforcement agencies. It plans responses to worst-case scenarios even as its agencies work to prevent them.

DHS Strategic Goals

- Identify potential terrorist threats and likely targets
- Detect and prevent attacks
- Coordinate the national response to terrorist acts and natural disasters
- Lead recovery efforts after terrorist acts and natural disasters

A terrorism response exercise in Los Angeles ▶

CONNECTING TO TODAY

1. **Explaining** What is the primary mission of the Department of Homeland Security?
2. **Making Connections** How are school safety drills similar to the exercise in the photo?

Additional Support

Extending the Content

Homeland Security The Department of Homeland Security was created after the terrorist attacks in the United States on September 11, 2001. The department has four divisions: border and transportation security; emergency preparedness and response; chemical, biological, radiological, and nuclear countermeasures; and information analysis and infrastructure protection. These divisions incorporated agencies already in existence. For example, the Coast Guard, Customs Service, and Immigration and Naturalization became part of the border security division. Although the CIA and FBI are not under the jurisdiction of the department, it is responsible for analyzing their information to evaluate the security of the country and issue warnings to the public about the risk of attack.

action by the United States and its allies against Afghanistan in October 2001.

At home, President Bush asked Congress to pass legislation to help track down terrorist suspects. An antiterrorist bill known as the **Patriot Act** was passed in October 2001. The Patriot Act allowed secret searches to avoid tipping off terrorism suspects. The law made it easier to wiretap suspects and to track e-mail, seize voice mail, and monitor library records. These sweeping and controversial measures led some Americans to debate how far constitutional rights should be restricted to protect them against terrorist attacks. In 2002 Congress established the Department of Homeland Security to coordinate efforts against terrorism at home.

Worldwide, one of the most noticeable changes in public policies since September 11, 2001, has been increased security at airports. Many European and Asian governments have also begun working more closely together in their intelligence and police activities to track down terrorists.

Islamic Militants

The causes of recent world terrorism are complex. Some analysts say this terrorism is rooted in the clash of Western and Islamic cultures. They argue that the Christians and Muslims have viewed each other with hostility since at least the time of the Crusades. Others suggest that poverty and ignorance lie at the root of the problem. Extremists find it easy to stir up resentment against wealthy Western societies. Finally, some say terrorism would be rare if the Israeli-Palestinian conflict could be solved.

One reason Middle Eastern terrorists have targeted Westerners can be traced to Western investment in the Middle East oil industry, which began in the 1920s. This industry brought wealth to ruling families in some Middle Eastern kingdoms, but most citizens remained very poor. They often blamed the West, especially the United States, for supporting the ruling families.

The oil business increased Middle Eastern contact with the West. Some Muslims feared that this contact would weaken their religion and their way of life. Some Muslims began organizing movements to overthrow their pro-Western governments. Muslims who support these movements are called fundamentalist militants. They promote their own vision of what a pure Islamic society should be. Most Muslims around the world do not share this vision, nor do they agree with the use of terrorism. **C**

The movement for a conservative Islamic society was first seen in 1979 in Iran. (See Chapter 30.) After the revolution of 1979, the legal system, clothing styles, and social practices were regulated by a strict interpretation of Islam. These practices have spread to other Muslim countries.

✓Reading Check **Explaining** How does the Patriot Act help law enforcement detect terrorist plots?

SECTION 1 REVIEW

Vocabulary

1. **Explain** the significance of: function, Neil Armstrong, bioterrorism, Green Revolution, environment, Rachel Carson, ecology, deforestation, desertification, greenhouse effect, Kyoto Protocol, sustainable development, global economy, Universal Declaration of Human Rights, Patriot Act.

Main Ideas

2. **Summarize** the technological advances made and the drawback or cost of each in the areas listed below.

Technological Advances	Drawback or Cost
Communications	
Transportation	
Space Exploration	
Health Care	
Agriculture	
Weaponry	

3. **Explain** how desertification endangers sustainable development.
4. **List** the rights mentioned in the Universal Declaration of Human Rights.

Critical Thinking

5. **The BIG Idea Identifying Central Issues** How can societies balance their desire for economic development with the pressures such development places on the environment?
6. **Evaluating** Why must ethics be part of technological advances?
7. **Analyzing Visuals** Describe the type of business owned by the woman in the image on page 1044. What products does she produce? What tools does she use?

Writing About History

8. **Expository Writing** In an essay, describe why some leaders disagree about the best solutions to global environmental problems.

History ONLINE
For help with the concepts in this section of *Glencoe World History*, go to glencoe.com and click Study Central™.

1047

C Critical Thinking

Determining Cause and Effect Ask: How might globalization be considered a factor in terrorism? *(Some terrorists see it as undermining traditional values.)* **OL**

✓Reading Check
Answer: It expands their power to conduct secret searches, tap phones, track e-mail, and monitor voice mail and library records.

Assess

Study Central provides summaries, interactive games, and online graphic organizers to help students review content.

Close

Summarizing Ask: What challenges face the world today? *(terrorism; environmental damage; global warming; ethnic conflicts; famine; violations of human rights; global epidemics)* **OL**

Answers

1. Definitions for the vocabulary words are found in the section and the Glossary.
2. **Communications:** constant accessibility; **Transportation:** pollution; **Space Exploration:** money from other programs; **Health Care:** ethical concerns; **Agriculture:** greater use of fertilizer, pesticides; **Weaponry:** risk that materials will end up in terrorists' hands
3. Desertification destroys the soil's productivity, making it more difficult for farmers to raise enough to meet their basic needs.
4. freedom, including freedom of movement, opinion and expression; equality; life, liberty, and security of person
5. Answers will vary, but students may say that making a commitment to sustainable development will help preserve the environment and encourage future economic growth.
6. New technologies bring risks. Taking an ethical approach means weighing the good and bad and anticipating what uses it might be put to and what effects it might have.
7. Answers may vary, but may note that her business involves fabrics and uses a sewing machine.
8. Answers will vary, but students should support their explanations with relevant details.

Focus

Bellringer

Daily Focus Transparency 32.2

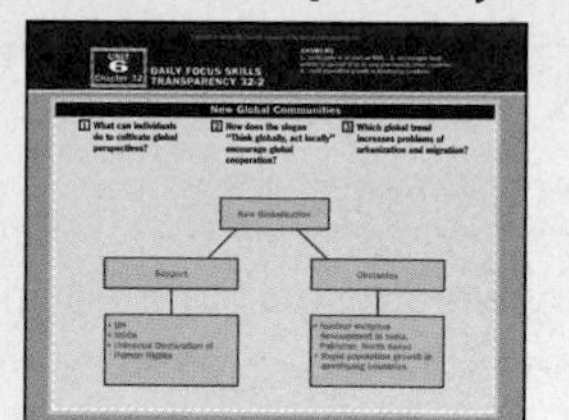

GUIDE TO READING

Answers to Graphic:

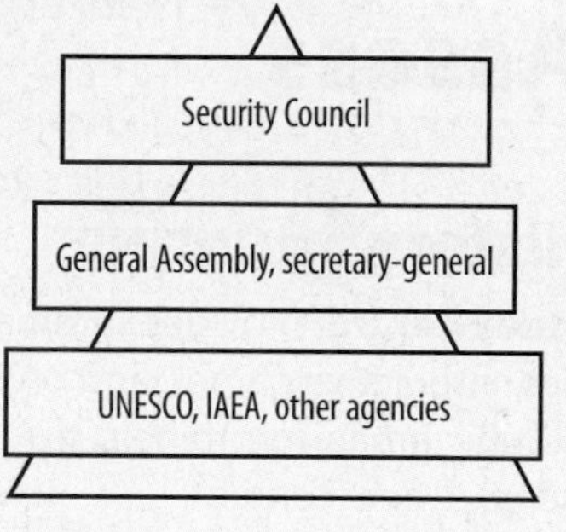

Section Spotlight Video

To generate student interest and provide a springboard for class discussion, access the Chapter 32, Section 2 video at glencoe.com or on the video DVD.

Resource Manager

SECTION 2

New Global Communities

GUIDE TO READING

The BIG Idea

Order and Security The global economy and new global threats have prompted organizations and individuals to work on global problems.

Content Vocabulary

- peacekeeping forces *(p. 1048)*
- nuclear proliferation *(p. 1049)*
- globalization *(p. 1051)*
- multinational corporation *(p. 1051)*
- grassroots level *(p. 1053)*
- nongovernmental organizations (NGOs) *(p. 1053)*
- disarmament groups *(p. 1053)*

Academic Vocabulary

- migration *(p. 1050)*
- projection *(p. 1050)*

People and Events

- Franklin Delano Roosevelt *(p. 1048)*
- World Bank *(p. 1051)*
- International Monetary Fund (IMF) *(p. 1051)*
- World Trade Organization (WTO) *(p. 1052)*
- Hazel Henderson *(p. 1053)*
- Elise Boulding *(p. 1053)*

Reading Strategy

Organizing Information As you read, create a pyramid like the one below to depict how the United Nations is organized.

In today's world, nations and communities are more closely connected than ever. This has meant that problems in one part of the world can affect people all over the globe. In the words of British Prime Minister Tony Blair, "Today conflicts rarely stay within national boundaries." Increasingly, the world's nations must unite to create lasting solutions to the contemporary problems of poverty, nuclear proliferation, global warming, and terrorism.

The United Nations

MAIN IDEA The United Nations focuses on international problems.

HISTORY & YOU Do you recall from Section 1 the Universal Declaration of Human Rights of the United Nations? Read to learn about the UN's structure and activities.

In recent decades, many nations have become more convinced that there are significant problems that can only be solved by working with other nations. Today, the United Nations (UN) is one of the most visible symbols of the new globalism.

The UN was founded in 1945 at the end of World War II. U.S. president **Franklin Delano Roosevelt** was especially eager to create an organization to work for peace. One of the UN's two chief goals is peace. The other goal is human dignity. These goals were clearly stated in the UN's charter. Members pledged "to save succeeding generations from the scourge of war . . . to reaffirm faith in fundamental human rights . . . and to promote social progress and better standards of life in larger freedom."

The General Assembly of the United Nations is made up of representatives from all member nations. It has the power to discuss any important question and to recommend action. The Security Council advises the General Assembly and passes resolutions that require the organization to act. Five nations have permanent seats on the Security Council: the United States, Russia, Great Britain, France, and China. Ten other members are chosen by the General Assembly and serve for limited terms. Because each permanent member can veto a decision, deliberations can often end in a stalemate. The head administrator of the United Nations is the secretary-general.

Specialized agencies function under the UN's direction. These agencies address economic and social problems and organize conferences on important issues such as population growth and the environment. The UN has also provided **peacekeeping forces**—military forces from neutral member states that settle conflicts and supervise truces in "hot spots" around the globe.

R Reading Strategies	C Critical Thinking	D Differentiated Instruction	W Writing Support	S Skill Practice
Teacher Edition • Questioning, p. 1052 **Additional Resources** • Cont. Vocab. Act., URB p. 205 • Academic Vocab. Act., URB p. 207 • Guid. Read. Act., URB p. 231 • Read. Ess. & Note-Taking Guide, p. 346	**Teacher Edition** • Pred. Consequences, p. 1050 • Drawing Con., p. 1052 • Analyzing Pri. Sources, p. 1053 **Additional Resources** • Hist. Sig. Act., URB p. 214 • Section Quiz, p. 396 • Chapter Test, p. 397	**Teacher Edition** • Logical/Math., p. 1050 **Additional Resources** • Coop. Learn. Act., URB p. 215 • World Art & Music Act., URB p. 225	**Teacher Edition** • Expository Writing, p. 1051 **Additional Resources** • Hist. Analysis Skills Act., URB p. 200 • Hist. Sim. Act., URB p. 217	**Teacher Edition** • Visual Literacy, p. 1049 **Additional Resources** • Time Line Act., URB p. 219 • Pri. Source Read., URB p. 223 • Reteach. Act., URB p. 227

INFOGRAPHICS

UNESCO and World Literacy

Today, about 770 million adults—one-fifth of the world's adult population—lack basic reading and writing skills. This statistic represents a shocking waste of human potential. To combat this problem, the United Nations Education, Scientific and Cultural Organization (UNESCO) coordinates the efforts of many organizations participating in its Education for All program. The program's goal is to increase global literacy by 50 percent by 2015.

The United Nations sees literacy as essential to ending poverty, slowing population growth, achieving gender equality, and ensuring economic development. Literacy provides access to education, which contributes to a more productive workforce and to fuller participation in today's world.

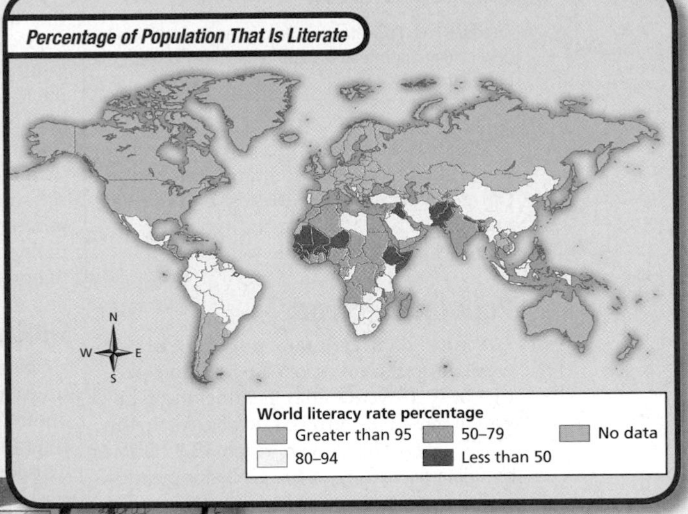

An adult literacy class in Bolivia

CRITICAL THINKING SKILLS

1. **Making Connections** Based on the map and what you know about developing nations, how is literacy related to economic development?
2. **Analyzing** Why is adult literacy education important?

The UN established the International Atomic Energy Agency (IAEA) in 1957. This agency operates a safeguards system against **nuclear proliferation**—the spread of nuclear weapons production technology and knowledge to nations without that capability. The greatest risk comes from countries that have not joined or have violated the Nuclear Nonproliferation Treaty (NPT). India, Pakistan, Israel, North Korea, and Iran fall within these categories. In 1998, India and Pakistan exploded nuclear devices underground. North Korea performed its first nuclear test in October 2006, and Iran refused to shelve its nuclear enrichment program.

As the IAEA director said, "The threat of nuclear terrorism is real and current. . . . the existence of a nuclear threat anywhere is a threat everywhere, and as a global community, we will win or lose this battle together."

✓Reading Check **Identifying** What is one goal of the International Atomic Energy Agency?

History ONLINE
Student Web Activity—
Visit glencoe.com to learn how to create and modify a database and to learn more about the United Nations.

Teach

S Skill Practice

Visual Literacy Have students examine the photograph. **Ask:** What parts of the picture tell us these people are learning? *(Possible response: faces look interested, all eyes directed to poster, people hold books, paper, and pencils)* BL

CRITICAL THINKING SKILLS

Answers:

1. The higher literacy rates on the map occur in the most highly developed regions, including Europe and North America. Lower literacy rates correspond to the less-developed regions, including Africa, the Middle East, and South Asia.
2. Possible response: The ability to read and write allows for the communication of knowledge.

✓Reading Check

Answer: to safeguard against nuclear proliferation

Differentiated Instruction

Leveled Activities

BL Time Line Activity, URB p. 219

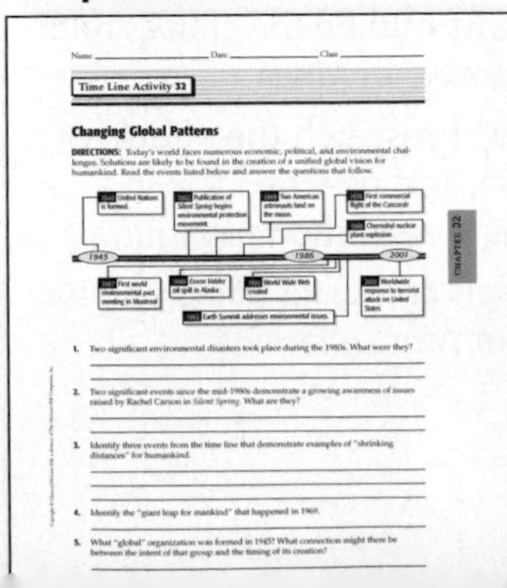
Time Line Activity 32
Changing Global Patterns

OL Academic Vocabulary Activity, URB p. 207

AL Cooperative Learning Activity, URB p. 215

ELL Reteaching Activity, URB p. 227

C Critical Thinking

Predicting Consequences Tell students that in the United States, some programs such as Social Security have already begun raising the age at which benefits can be collected to adjust to changes in life expectancy. Have students list other ways in which an increase in life expectancy might affect society. *(Answers will vary, but students may say that people's perception of what constitutes old age may change; people may work longer at their jobs.)* **OL**

D Differentiated Instruction

Logical/Mathematical Have students choose a developing country and research the projected population increase over the next several decades. Ask them to present their data in a bar graph. As a class, draw conclusions about the presented data. **AL**

✓Reading Check

Answer: political persecution, civil wars, famine, employment

Population and Migration

MAIN IDEA The ever-increasing world population affects the world economy.

HISTORY & YOU Has your family ever moved to a new community? Read to learn why some people have migrated.

The growth of new global communities depends on population and **migration** trends. Population patterns and global migrations are affecting the type of communities in which people will live.

Population Trends

A July 2006 estimate put the current world population at over 6.5 billion people, only 18 years after passing the 5-billion mark. At its current rate of growth, the world population could reach 12.8 billion by 2050, according to the UN's long-range population projections. The UN's more conservative **projection** puts that number at 8.9 billion. Even with the more conservative figure, the world population is expected to increase nearly 37 percent over the next four decades.

Soon, the most populous nations in the world will be developing countries, especially India and China. By 2050, India will have surpassed China in population and will likely remain the most populous country in the world thereafter.

In wealthy regions such as Western Europe, though, population is declining and "graying"—a larger percentage of the population is reaching retirement. In 2000, European nations had the oldest population of any region in the world: 15 percent of the population was 65 or older. By 2050, 28 percent are expected to be in this age group. In fact, by 2050, the United States is expected to be the only wealthy nation with a growing population.

C Life expectancy is projected to increase worldwide after 2050. In all projection scenarios, the age distribution will shift toward older people. Due to longer life expectancies and lower birth rates in the future, the number of people 80 and over and those who live beyond 100 might rise. Just 1.1 percent of the population was 80 and over in 2000; by 2300, that percentage might increase to 17. An older population places a demand on the economy because the taxes of workers must be stretched further to cover care of the elderly.

D Developing countries will face a different kind of problem. Between 2000 and 2050, the less-developed countries are expected to experience a 61 percent increase in population. This number of people might mean increased migrations as well as increased urbanization. Since many cities lack the infrastructure to support the larger populations, concerns are rising about future international health and environment problems.

Global Migrations

Since 1945, tens of millions of people have migrated from one part of the world to another. There are many reasons for these migrations. Persecution for political reasons caused many people from Pakistan, Bangladesh, Sri Lanka, Eastern Europe, and East Germany to seek refuge in Western European countries. Brutal civil wars in Asia, Africa, the Middle East, and Europe led millions of refugees to seek safety in neighboring countries. A devastating famine in Africa in 1984–1985 caused hundreds of thousands of Africans to move to relief camps throughout the continent to find food.

Most people who have migrated, however, have done so to find jobs. Latin Americans seeking a better life have migrated to the United States. Guest workers from Turkey, southern and eastern Europe, North Africa, India, and Pakistan have entered more prosperous Western European lands. In the 1980s, about 15 million guest workers worked and lived in Europe.

Many host countries allowed guest workers to stay for several years. In the 1980s and 1990s, however, foreign workers often became scapegoats when countries faced economic problems. Political parties in France and Norway, for example, called for the removal of blacks and Arabs in order to protect the ethnic purity of their nations. In Asian countries, there is often a backlash against other Asian ethnic groups.

✓Reading Check **Summarizing** Give four reasons why people migrate.

Differentiated Instruction

Historical Significance Activity 32

African Famine and the United Nations

Historical Significance Activity, URB p. 214

Analyzing Information

Objective: Learn more about African famine and the United Nations.

Focus: Analyze the passage.

Teach: Discuss the UN's objectives. Ask students which one they think is most important and why.

Assess: Have students respond to question #3.

Close: Have students find articles about famine and present them to the class.

Differentiated Instruction Strategies

BL Have students outline the causes and effects of famine in Africa.

AL Have students research the effects of malnutrition, and use the facts in a speech urging a solution to famine.

ELL Have students create an informational poster about African famine.

Globalization

MAIN IDEA International organizations and citizen groups work to solve global problems.

HISTORY & YOU Do you recall how the American Red Cross started? Read to learn how many kinds of groups work on world problems.

The technology revolution has tied people and nations closely together and contributed to globalization. **Globalization** is the process by which people and nations have become more interdependent. Economically, globalization has taken the form of a global economy. Politically and socially, globalization has led to the emergence of citizen groups and other transnational organizations that work across national boundaries to bring solutions to problems that are common to all humans.

Global Economic Organizations

The global economy began to develop after World War II and gained momentum in the 1980s and 1990s. After World War II, the United States and other nations set up the **World Bank** and the **International Monetary Fund (IMF).** The World Bank is actually a group of five international organizations, largely controlled by developed countries. It provides grants, loans, and advice for economic development in developing countries. The World Bank's stated goal is "a world free of poverty."

The IMF, founded in 1945, is now an "organization of 184 countries." Its goal is to oversee the global financial system. To achieve its goal, the IMF watches exchange rates and offers financial and technical assistance to developing nations. Both the World Bank and the IMF have been criticized for forcing inappropriate Western economic practices on non-Western nations. Critics also argue that World Bank and IMF policies only aggravate the poverty and debt of developing nations. W

Another reflection of the global economy is the **multinational corporation** (a company that has divisions in more than two countries).

W Writing Support

Expository Writing Have students find out more about the World Bank and the International Monetary Fund by using Internet or library sources. Students should use the information they find to write a detailed research report that answers the charges that both of these institutions do more harm than good. **AL**

CRITICAL THINKING SKILLS

Answers:

1. Possible response: No nation has all the resources it needs.
2. Businesses can locate in different countries to take advantage of the resources of those countries. Businesses sell globally as well, so they must design products for diverse tastes.

INFOGRAPHICS

Economic Interdependence

Resources are spread unevenly around the world. No nation has all the resources it needs to prosper. To get what they need, nations trade. The exchange generally benefits both nations. For example, Japan has few mineral resources; however, it can buy minerals from other countries and sell its manufactured products all over the world.

Business people now think globally when making economic decisions. A business might locate its factories in developing nations where wages are low. Activities that require advanced technology or highly educated workers might be located in developed nations. Markets are also global. Businesses design products to appeal to the diverse tastes of consumers around the world. Economic interdependence creates global problems as well. For example, an economic downturn in one nation can spread to other nations. Industrial pollution can also spread across national boundaries.

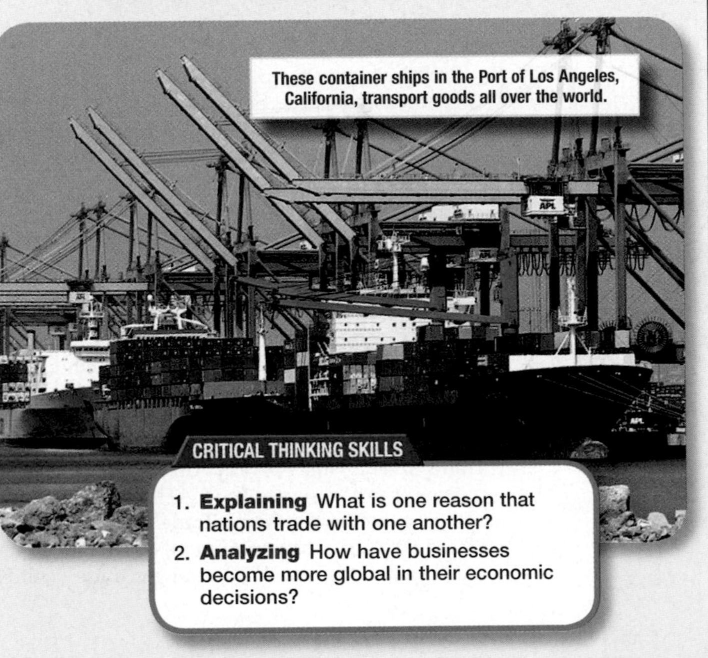

These container ships in the Port of Los Angeles, California, transport goods all over the world.

CRITICAL THINKING SKILLS

1. **Explaining** What is one reason that nations trade with one another?
2. **Analyzing** How have businesses become more global in their economic decisions?

Hands-On Chapter Project Step 2

Developing a Board Game

Step 2: Designing a Game Board Small groups put together their board.

Directions: Write the Big Idea on the board. Have students first add game cards, using the facts in this section. Then have them design their game board. Students should choose symbols of the ideas that are discussed in this chapter as their squares' icons or images. For the last square or destination, they should keep in mind the Essential Question and create an image as well as text that identifies the goals of the 21st century, such as sustainable development and global harmony.

Summarizing: Have students display their game boards and then share insights about the Big Idea. **OL**

(Chapter Project is completed on the Visual Summary page.)

R Reading Strategy

Questioning Remind students that multinational corporations open factories and offices around the world. **Ask:** How do multinational corporations tie the economies of different countries? *(They hire local workers around the world.)* **Ask:** How does an economic downturn in the United States affect the rest of the world? *(Workers around the world may lose jobs.)* OL

C Critical Thinking

Drawing Conclusions Ask: What is the goal of organizations such as NAFTA and trading blocs such as the European Union? *(to strengthen the economy of a particular region by eliminating tariffs and other obstacles to free trade)* AL

DOCUMENT-BASED QUESTIONS

Answers:

1. creativity, immediate and continued effort, and money
2. The UN coordinates, tracks progress, and acts as an advocate. This role is important in directing aid to where it is most needed.

Additional Support

INFOGRAPHICS PRIMARY SOURCE

The UN Millennium Development Goals

At the United Nations Millennium Summit in 2000, world leaders agreed to work together to achieve eight development goals by 2015. Developing countries are enacting reforms, and developed countries are supporting them with aid and expertise. The United Nations coordinates these efforts and tracks progress with country report cards. The 2006 report shows some progress, but the world still has a long way to go.

Kofi Annan

DEVELOPMENT GOALS

1. Eradicate extreme poverty and hunger
2. Achieve universal primary education
3. Promote gender equality and empower women
4. Reduce child mortality
5. Improve maternal health
6. Combat HIV/AIDS, malaria and other diseases
7. Ensure environmental sustainability
8. Develop a global partnership for development

"We will have time to reach the Millennium Development Goals . . . but only if we break with business as usual. . . . Success will require sustained action . . . . It takes time to train the teachers, nurses and engineers; to build the roads, schools and hospitals; to grow the small and large businesses able to create the jobs and income needed. So we must start now. And we must more than double global development assistance over the next few years. Nothing less will help to achieve the Goals."

—Kofi Annan
UN Secretary-General
from 1997 to 2006

DOCUMENT-BASED QUESTIONS

1. **Summarizing** According to Kofi Annan, how can the goals be achieved?
2. **Assessing** What role does the UN play in achieving these goals, and why is this role important?

R Prominent examples of multinational corporations include Siemens, IBM, Toyota, and the Sony Corporation. The growing number of multinational corporations that do business around the world increasingly tie one country to another in a global economy. For example, an economic downturn in the United States can create stagnant conditions in Europe and Asia. We live in an interdependent world.

Global trade is another important component of the global economy. Over the years, many nations joined in talks to make trade between countries free and easy. These talks led to General Agreement on Trade and Tariffs (GATT). In 1995, the nations that had signed the GATT treaties agreed to create the **World Trade Organization (WTO).** Made up of more than 140 member nations, the WTO arranges trade agreements and settles trade disputes. The WTO has been criticized for ignoring environmental and health concerns and for leaving out small and developing countries. Still, it is the only global organization that deals with rules of trade among nations.

C Groups of nations have joined together to form trading blocs. By 2004, the European Union included 25 member states and is the world's largest single trading entity. The EU has a single internal market and a common currency (the euro).

Elsewhere, the North American Free Trade Agreement (NAFTA) created a free-trade area for Canada, the United States, and Mexico. The Asia Pacific Economic Cooperation (APEC) agreement has tried to do the same among nations that border the Pacific Ocean.

Activity: Economics Connection

Researching the World Trade Organization Have groups of students visit the World Trade Organization Web site on the Internet to find out more about it. Direct students' investigations by having them find the answers to these questions and others:

- **What does the World Trade Organization do?** *(negotiates solutions to trade problems among member governments; sets the rules for global trading; mediates disputes)*
- **How many members does the WTO have?** *(150 as of 2007)*
- **What are the major principles of the WTO?** *(Trade should be without discrimination; freer; predictable; more competitive; more beneficial for less developed countries.)*

Ask: Which principle of the WTO is most important? *(Trade without discrimination is very important. This means that what a country does for one trading partner, it has to do for all other WTO member states.)* Discuss students' responses. OL

Transnational Organizations

Global awareness has led to new social movements that involve ordinary citizens and focus on problems that nations share. Problem areas include threats to the environment, women's and men's liberation, child labor, appropriate use of technology, and promotion of peace.

Some organizations, such as the Red Cross, draw their membership from people in many different countries. Some individuals act at the **grassroots level**—that is, in their own community. A favorite slogan of grassroots groups is "Think globally, act locally." **Hazel Henderson,** a British-born economist, believes that these individuals can be powerful agents for change.

PRIMARY SOURCE

"These aroused citizens are by no means all mindless young radicals. Well-dressed, clean-shaven, middle-class businessmen and their suburban wives comprise the major forces in California fighting against nuclear power. Hundreds of thousands of middle-class mothers **C** are bringing massive pressure to ban commercials and violent programs from children's television."

—Hazel Henderson, *Creating Alternative Futures*

Another movement that addresses world problems is the growth of **nongovernmental organizations (NGOs).** NGOs are often represented at the United Nations. They include professional, business, and cooperative organizations, as well as foundations. Also included are religious, peace, and **disarmament groups** that work to limit the size of military forces and weapons stocks. Other NGOs protect the welfare of women and children and include environmental and human rights groups.

American educator **Elise Boulding** promotes NGOs. She believes they can educate people to consider problems globally. She says that all NGOs are expected "to define problems in global terms, to take account of human interests and needs as they are found in all parts of the planet." The number of international NGOs increased from 176 in 1910 to nearly 37,000 in 2000.

Global solutions to global problems have been hindered by political and ethnic disputes. Even as the world becomes more global and interdependent, disruptive forces work against efforts to enhance our human destiny.

Many lessons can be learned from the study of world history. One is especially clear: a lack of involvement in the affairs of one's society can lead to a sense of powerlessness. An understanding of our world heritage and its lessons might well give us the opportunity to make wise choices in a crisis-laden and often chaotic age. We are all creators of history. The choices we make in our everyday lives will affect the future of world civilization.

✓Reading Check **Explaining** What is the European Union?

SECTION 2 REVIEW

Vocabulary

1. **Explain** the significance of: Franklin Delano Roosevelt, peacekeeping forces, nuclear proliferation, migration, projection, globalization, World Bank, International Monetary Fund (IMF), multinational corporation, World Trade Organization (WTO), grassroots level, Hazel Henderson, nongovernmental organizations (NGOs), disarmament groups, Elise Boulding.

Main Ideas

2. **List** the nations that have permanent seats on the UN Security Council. Use a chart like the one below to make your list.

Nations That Have Permanent Seats on the UN Security Council
1.
2.

3. **Explain** why the age distribution in the world's population will shift toward older people after 2050.
4. **Name** three international organizations that were established to help solve global economic problems.

Critical Thinking

5. **The BIG Idea** **Making Connections** Why is the United Nations so important in today's world?
6. **Evaluating** Why is nuclear proliferation a global concern?
7. **Analyzing Visuals** Examine the map on page 1049. Is there an area or country with a literacy rate that surprised you? Explain why or why not.

Writing About History

8. **Descriptive Writing** Choose one NGO to research. Write an essay about the organization's mission, goals, accomplishments, and failures.

History ONLINE

For help with the concepts in this section of *Glencoe World History,* go to glencoe.com and click Study Central™.

1053

C Critical Thinking

Analyzing Primary Sources

Ask: What evidence does Hazel Henderson use to show that new public interest groups are taking roles in public life? *(Ordinary groups of citizens can bring about powerful change—Henderson cites two specific examples already at work in the United States.)* **OL**

✓Reading Check

Answer: a trading bloc of more than two dozen European nations with a single internal market and common currency

Assess

History ONLINE

Study Central provides summaries, interactive games, and online graphic organizers to help students review content.

Close

Summarizing Have students discuss how the information in this section supports the idea that people must "think globally, act locally." **OL**

SECTION 2 REVIEW

Answers

1. Definitions for the vocabulary words are found in the section and the Glossary.
2. **1.** Russia; **2.** United States; **3.** Great Britain; **4.** France; **5.** China
3. Lower birth rates and longer life expectancies will lead to a greater elderly population.
4. World Bank, International Monetary Fund, World Trade Organization
5. The United Nations is dedicated to keeping peace within the world and promoting human dignity. It has created specialized agencies to work on economic and social problems as well as on problems of national and international security. It also has a peacekeeping force.
6. If nations that have not agreed to the treaty decide to employ nuclear weapons, the consequences will affect the entire world.
7. Answers may vary, but should be supported with factual details and logical conclusions.
8. Answers will vary, but students' essays should include accurate information on their chosen organization.

Determining Cause and Effect Discuss the information provided on the Visual Summary. Ask volunteers to use this information to identify causes and effects, such as new communication systems linking more of the world together. Then have students work in pairs to analyze in depth the cause(s) and effect(s) of one topic that interests them. Encourage them to use information from their textbooks, as well as other resources. **Ask:** How confident are you that you have identified all possible causes and effects? *(Answers may vary, but students should express the willingness to consider additional possibilities.)* **OL**

Logical/Mathematical Be sure students understand that it can be difficult to identify a true cause-and-effect relationship. Discuss how these relationships can be firmly established, such as by doing experiments and carefully analyzing relevant data. **OL**

CHAPTER 32 Visual Summary

STUDY TO GO You can study anywhere, anytime by downloading quizzes and flash cards to your PDA from glencoe.com.

THE TECHNOLOGICAL REVOLUTION

- Advanced communication and transportation systems are linking the world's people.
- New technologies for exploring space have increased our understanding of the universe.
- Weapons of mass destruction, or WMDs, are a grim result of the technological revolution.
- Breakthroughs in medicine and agriculture save lives, but some raise ethical questions.

REPAIRING THE HUBBLE SPACE TELESCOPE

The Hubble Space Telescope provides images of our solar system and other galaxies.

CAR BOMB DESTROYS NIGHTCLUB IN BALI, INDONESIA

All nations must face the challenge of terrorism.

GLOBAL CHALLENGES

- Deforestation, chemical wastes, oil spills, and nuclear accidents threaten the environment.
- Nations must conserve natural resources to achieve sustainable development.
- Poverty, hunger, and civil unrest plague many developing countries.
- Human rights violations occur worldwide.
- Terrorism has become part of modern society.

RED CROSS HELPS FAMINE VICTIMS IN SUDAN

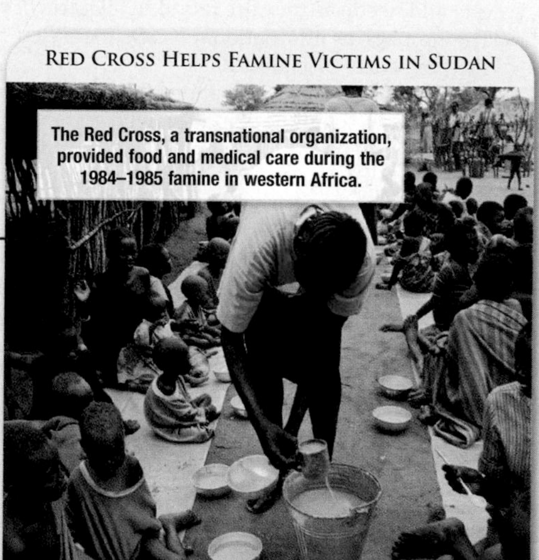

The Red Cross, a transnational organization, provided food and medical care during the 1984–1985 famine in western Africa.

GLOBAL SOLUTIONS

- The United Nations works for world peace and human dignity.
- Nongovernmental organizations focus on issues such as disarmament, child welfare, and human rights.
- Economic interdependence has given rise to international organizations to address issues affecting the global economy.

Hands-On Chapter Project
Step 3: Wrap-Up

Developing a Board Game

Step 3: Play the Game

Students will synthesize what they have learned in Steps 1–2.

Directions: Display a two-column chart on the board. Label one column "Positive" and one column "Negative." Have students review their game cards and identify positive events or trends in the 21st century. Then have them identify those events that are negative. Continue until the major ideas have been covered. The chart should include details such as the invention of magnetic imaging under the positive category and the loss of rain forests under the negative category. Then have groups take turns playing each other's games before they use the chart information as well as the knowledge gained from their games to respond to the Essential Question in a short essay. **OL**

STANDARDIZED TEST PRACTICE

TEST-TAKING TIP

If you do not know the answer to a question, eliminate any answer choices that you know are incorrect. Then choose the best answer from the remaining choices.

Reviewing Vocabulary

Directions: Choose the word or words that best complete the sentence.

1. The ________ has produced new strains of rice, corn, and other grains that have greater yields.

A greenhouse effect
B global economy
C Neolithic Revolution
D Green Revolution

2. North Korea's recent test of its first nuclear weapon is an example of nuclear ________.

A disarmament
B proliferation
C bioterrorism
D globalism

3. Overgrazing and poor cultivation practices in semi-arid lands are creating ________, or a decline in the soil's productivity.

A desertification
B organic evolution
C deforestation
D conservation

4. The technology revolution has contributed to ________, or the process by which people and nations have become more interdependent.

A secularization
B sustainable development
C bioterrorism
D globalization

Reviewing Main Ideas

Directions: Choose the best answers to the following questions.

Section 1 *(pp. 1038–1047)*

5. What invention in 1971 made small personal computers possible?

A The vacuum tube
B The World Wide Web
C The microprocessor
D Hypertext transfer protocol

6. What new field deals with moral issues involved in technological advances, such as stem-cell research?

A Bioethics
B Genetic engineering
C Ethnic cleansing
D Ecology

7. Which of the following is the main cause of global warming?

A Rising sea levels
B Increase in solar radiation
C Release of chlorofluorocarbons into the atmosphere
D Buildup of carbon dioxide in the atmosphere

8. The world's developing nations are mostly located in which hemisphere?

A Northern
B Southern
C Eastern
D Western

Need Extra Help?

If You Missed Questions . . .	1	2	3	4	5	6	7	8
Go to Page . . .	1041	1049	1042	1051	1039	1040	1042	1043

GO ON

Answers and Analyses

Reviewing Vocabulary

1. D Students may be tempted to choose the answer *greenhouse effect,* simply because they associate a greenhouse with cultivation of plants. Tell them to think carefully about the meanings of both words, however. Based on the meaning of the individual words, green revolution is the logical choice, suggesting a dramatic change in the way plants are grown.

2. B Remind students to use word parts to help them choose their answer. *Dis-* means "not," "absence of," or "opposite." Disarmament involves limiting weaponry. *Bio-* means "life." Bioterrorism is using chemical or biological weapons. Therefore, those two choices can be eliminated. North Korea's action is not globalism, but proliferation—the increasing of nuclear weapons.

3. A Organic revolution and conservation can be eliminated because they are positive steps. The context clues *overgrazing, poor cultivation practices,* and *decline in the soil's productivity* indicate a negative result. Because there is no mention of clearing the land, which would point to deforestation, the correct answer is desertification.

4. D Tell students to define as many of the choices as they can to help them eliminate answers. Secularization is removal of religious associations. Sustainable development is economic development that protects the environment. Bioterrorism is using chemical or biological weapons. Therefore, globalization refers to the increasing interdependence among people and nations.

Reviewing Main Ideas

5. C Point out the prefix *micro-*, which means "very small."

6. A The context clue *moral issues* relates to the word ethics in the first choice.

7. D Rising sea levels are a result of global warming. Increase in solar radiation is a result of the release of chlorofluorocarbons. The buildup of carbon dioxide, however, keeps the heat from leaving Earth.

8. B Students should identify developing countries such as India as well as countries in Africa, Southeast Asia, and South America, most of which are in the southern hemisphere.

9. C The last choice can be eliminated because it is invalid. The first choice would be an unlikely goal to pursue through terrorist means. IRA members do not appear to want a Protestant-Catholic coalition; instead, they want Northern Ireland to become part of the Irish Republic.

10. D The Security Council has five permanent seats filled by China, Great Britain, France, Russia, and the United States and ten other members that serve limited terms. The General Assembly consists of representatives of all member states.

11. B China is presently the most populous country, but India's population is increasing at a rate that indicates it will be greater than China's in a few decades.

12. A All of the choices are reasons that people migrate. The key word is *most,* however. The majority of people who move are trying to find jobs.

TEST-TAKING TIP

For Question 12: If students believe all or most of the answers are valid, it is possible that they have not read the question carefully. Re-reading the question may eliminate confusion.

13. C At first glance, the World Bank might appear to be the correct answer. However, a bank is associated with lending money, not necessarily monitoring the entire system. Therefore, the International Monetary Fund is more likely to be the institution involved with the financial system as a whole.

9. What is the main goal of the Irish Republican Army?

A To help Great Britain in time of war
B To form a Protestant-Catholic coalition
C To unite Northern Ireland with the Irish Republic
D To make Southern Ireland an independent state

Section 2 *(pp. 1048–1053)*

10. What are the two main bodies of the United Nations?

A General Assembly and National Council
B Security Council and National Assembly
C National Council and National Assembly
D Security Council and General Assembly

11. Which country is expected to be the most populous in the world by 2050?

A United States
B India
C China
D Sudan

12. For what reason have most people migrated?

A To find jobs
B To escape persecution
C To find food
D To escape civil war

13. Which organization oversees the global financial system?

A World Bank
B World Trade Organization
C International Monetary Fund
D United Nations

Critical Thinking

Directions: Choose the best answers to the following questions.

Use the following map to answer question 14.

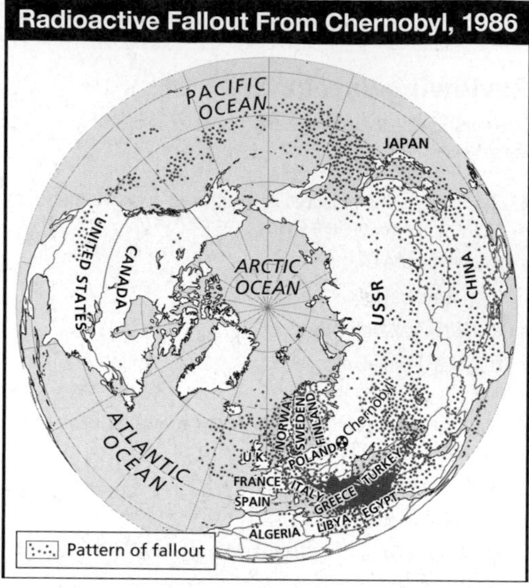

14. Which of the following is a true statement about the global effects of the nuclear accident at Chernobyl?

A Fallout covered more than half of the Southern Hemisphere.
B Fallout extended as far as eastern Canada.
C Fallout covered about two-thirds of the Northern Hemisphere.
D The heaviest fallout occurred in the Soviet Union.

15. What would be a global economic effect should a war or revolution occur in the Middle East?

A A devaluation of the euro
B A big increase in the price of oil
C A recession or a depression
D A drop in the market price of grains

Need Extra Help?

If You Missed Questions . . .	9	10	11	12	13	14	15
Go to Page . . .	1046	1048	1050	1050	1051	1042	1052

Critical Thinking

14. C Remind students to check each choice against the data shown by the map.

15. B Point out that since the Middle East is a major supplier of oil, a war in this part of the world would most likely affect the prices of that commodity.

16. Which of the following is a true statement about world population between now and 2050?
   - **A** The greatest population growth will occur in wealthy nations.
   - **B** Migrations and urbanization in developing countries will increase.
   - **C** The population's average age will become increasingly younger.
   - **D** Disease and starvation will reduce life expectancy worldwide.

17. Which argument below might come from an opponent of stem-cell research?
   - **A** The research might produce deadly "supergerms" that cannot be controlled.
   - **B** The research might make it possible to create a human being in a laboratory.
   - **C** The research uses cells from human embryos.
   - **D** The research alters the genetic makeup of an organism.

Analyze the cartoon and answer the question that follows. Base your answer on the cartoon and on your knowledge of world history.

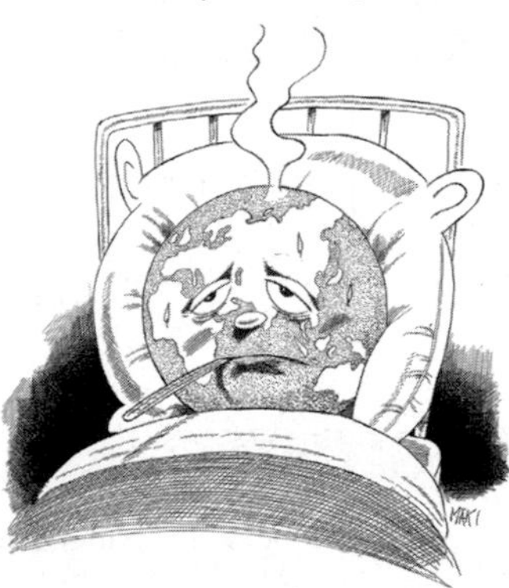

18. Which problem is the subject of this cartoon?
   - **A** World hunger
   - **B** Population growth
   - **C** Global warming
   - **D** Deforestation

Document-Based Questions

Directions: Analyze the document and answer the short-answer questions that follow the document. Base your answers on the document and on your knowledge of world history.

Rachel Carson cautioned about the dangers of harmful chemicals in her book, *Silent Spring:*

> *"It is not my contention that chemical pesticides must never be used. I do contend that we have put poisons and biologically potent chemicals into the hands of persons largely or wholly ignorant of their potentials for harm. . . . Future generations are unlikely to condone our lack of prudent concern for the integrity of the natural world that supports all life."*
>
> —Rachel Carson, *Silent Spring,* 1962

19. Summarize the argument that Carson is presenting in this quotation.

20. In Carson's opinion, who will question the lack of concern shown for the natural world?

Extended Response

21. Terrorism has become part of modern life. What are some possible causes of global terrorism?

History ONLINE
For additional test practice, use Self-Check Quizzes—Chapter 32 at glencoe.com.

Need Extra Help?

If You Missed Questions . . .	16	17	18	19	20	21
Go to Page . . .	1043	1040	1042	1042	1042	1047

STOP

Document-Based Questions

19. Chemical pesticides can cause long-lasting damage to the environment.

20. future generations

Extended Response

21. Responses might include the following: a clash of Western and Islamic cultures with roots as far back as the Crusades; poverty and ignorance; the Israeli-Palestinian conflict; Western investment in Middle Eastern oil; Western support of wealthy ruling families in the Middle East; fear of some Muslims that Western influence might weaken their religion or way of life; militant Muslims.

16. B The first choice is inaccurate. The global population is "graying" because of longer life expectancy and lower birth rates, making the last two choices incorrect. Developing countries, however, will continue to experience an increase in population as well as urbanization and migration.

17. C Stem-cell research is using cells from human embryos to research cures for Alzheimer's, Parkinson's, and other diseases.

18. C Point out that the central figure of the cartoon is obviously Earth, which has a high temperature.

History ONLINE
Introduce students to chapter content and key terms by having them access the Chapter 32 Overview at glencoe.com.

Need Extra Help?
Have students refer to the pages listed if they miss any of the questions.

Focus

Introducing TIME Notebook

Discuss how technological innovation is changing society and students' lives. **Ask:** In what ways is computer use different today from how it was five years ago? *(Answers may include that people are using computers more often and in different ways today.)*

Teach

C Critical Thinking

Predicting Consequences
Point out the quote from Albert Einstein. Discuss the threat posed by nuclear weapons and efforts to ban them worldwide. AL

R Reading Strategy

Making Connections Explain that the United States, the European Union, and China are among the world's biggest contributors to greenhouse gas emissions. Using the calculator at the EPA Web site, have students find the average annual emissions of carbon dioxide for an individual or household. OL

Additional Support

TIME NOTEBOOK

World Wide Wonder

It seems as if the Internet has been around forever, but it's existed only since 1969. Over the years, the Internet has grown in importance. Here are highlights from its history.

CORBIS

1969 A U.S. Defense Department agency called the Advanced Research Project Agency (ARPA) connects four universities in a communications network. It is called ARPANET. This primitive network is the start of the Internet era.

1972 The first electronic mail (e-mail) is sent.

1982 The word Internet is used for the first time.

1984 The Domain Name System (DNS) is put in place. Extensions such as .com, .org, and .edu are used to identify network addresses.

1990 Englishman Tim Berners-Lee invents the World Wide Web while working in a Swiss physics laboratory.

1993 Mosaic, the first web browser to use graphics, becomes available.

1994 Companies begin to sell items on the Internet. The term spam, meaning unsolicited e-mail, is first introduced.

1999 College student Shawn Fanning introduces Napster, a program that lets Internet users swap music for free. Calling it a violation of copyright, the music industry gets Napster declared illegal. Eventually, Napster becomes a pay service.

Shawn Fanning

REUTERS/LOU DEMATTEIS

2004 The worm MyDoom infects Internet servers, affecting about one-twelfth of all e-mail messages.

2006 Users of the Internet worldwide number more than one billion.

VERBATIM

C "I do not know how the Third World War will be fought, but I can tell you what they will use in the Fourth—rocks."
ALBERT EINSTEIN, *declaring that an atomic war would end world civilization*

"There can be no liberty unless there is economic liberty."
MARGARET THATCHER, *prime minister of Great Britain, a firm believer in free-market capitalism*

"It's a very humbling occasion. Kenyans have given me a challenge."
MWAI KIBAKI, *elected democratic president of Kenya, on succeeding in 2003 the repressive party that ruled the country for 39 years*

"Women suddenly have more value in this society."
LULUA ABDULLAH AL-OMARI, *Kuwaiti mother of four, on efforts to encourage female voters in Kuwait's first elections since women won the right to vote in 2005*

"Everything has changed, but nothing is better."
FAY WELDON, *English author, on the impact of feminism on women's lives*

MELTDOWN!

These satellite photos show the Arctic ice cap in 1979 and 2005. An area twice the size of Texas, normally covered by ice, is now open water. Scientists fear the ice cap, as well as Earth's glaciers, are melting because of global warming. R Polluting gases produced by burning coal, oil, and other fossil fuels are a major cause of global warming. These "greenhouse" gases trap the heat from sunlight, raising Earth's temperature. Most of the world's countries have signed the 1997 Kyoto Protocol, a treaty that requires them to reduce their greenhouse emissions. But as the pictures show, efforts to turn down the heat haven't yet succeeded.

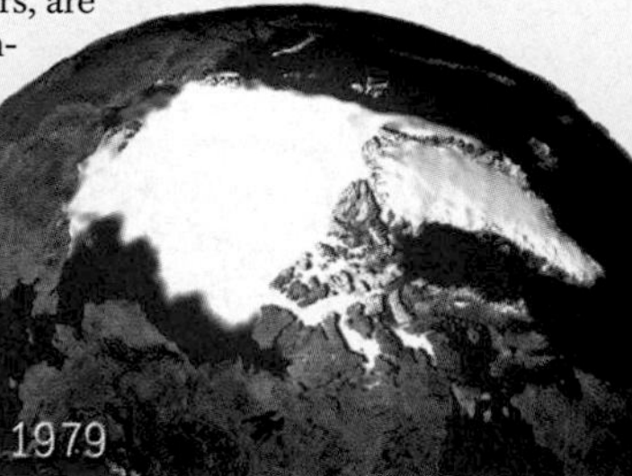

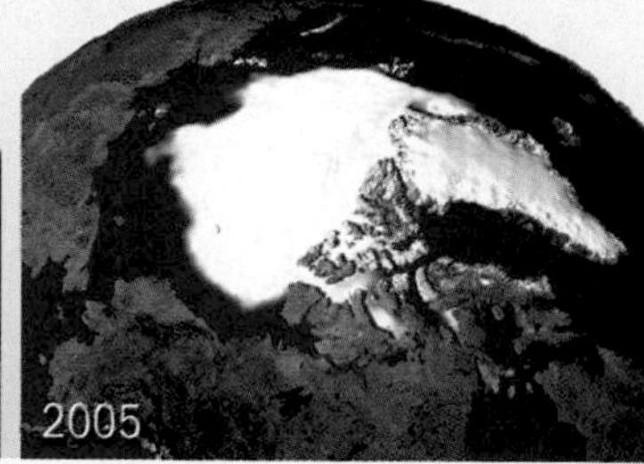

NASA

Background

Worms, Viruses, and Trojan Horses
Computers are vulnerable to attack from "bugs" that can erase files, destroy operating systems, or even disrupt entire computer networks. Of course, these bugs aren't living organisms; they are cleverly designed pieces of software. Computer viruses are typically spread via the Internet, their most common form of transmission. These infectious programs lodge themselves in a computer until a trigger activates them. To become active, computer viruses must first attach themselves to an existing program such as a word processing program. Whenever the host program is running, the attached virus is running, too. Worms are specialized kinds of viruses that "worm their way" through gaps in a computer network's security system. Worms can also replicate themselves rapidly. In 2001, for instance, the Code Red worm made over 250,000 copies of itself in about nine hours. One of the purposes of this worm was to overwhelm the White House Web server. Trojan Horses are viruses concealed within benign programs, such as downloadable games from the Internet.

What's in a Name?

Africa has the most countries of any continent. Since the 1960s, many of those nations have gained independence—and changed their names. Can you match the current name of the African country (1–10) to its previous name, or names (a–j)?

1. Democratic Republic of the Congo
2. Lesotho
3. Djibouti
4. Burkina Faso
5. Malawi
6. Mali
7. Zimbabwe
8. Benin
9. Tanzania
10. Zambia

a. Upper Volta
b. Southern Rhodesia
c. Sudanese Republic
d. The countries of Tanganyika and Zanzibar
e. Dahomey
f. Zaire
g. French Territory of the Afars and the Issas
h. Northern Rhodesia
i. Basutoland
j. Nyasaland

Answers: (1. f; 2. i; 3. g; 4. a; 5. j; 6. c; 7. b; 8. e; 9. d; 10. h)

MILESTONES

DEBUTS. THE EURO, the official currency of the member countries of the European Union. The euro replaces the French franc and 12 other European currencies. The nations will use common bills and coins, making it easier to do business.

CLONED. DOLLY, a Finn Dorset lamb. She is the first mammal cloned from an adult cell. A six-year-old female sheep gave birth to Dolly on July 5, 1996. This feat by Scottish scientists raises ethical issues. **C**

DIED. PABLO NERUDA, Chilean poet and winner of the 1971 Nobel Prize in Literature. Neruda was appointed ambassador to France by his friend, Salvador Allende, Chile's socialist president. Neruda died shortly after military officers removed Allende from office in 1973. Protests against the dictatorship took place at his funeral.

AP PHOTO/PAUL CLEMENTS

Dolly the sheep

KILLED. An estimated **800,000 RWANDANS** in 100 days, beginning in April 1994. The victims, members of a minority ethnic group called the Tutsis, were killed by the majority Hutus. The two groups have been at odds for many years. The immediate cause of the violence was the death of the president of Rwanda, a Hutu, whose plane had been shot down.

OPENED. QINGHAI-TIBET RAILWAY, a 709-mile engineering marvel connecting the Tibetan capital to the rest of China; in Lhasa, in 2006. Critics of the project say it threatens Tibet's environment and will erode Buddhist culture by bringing in ethnic Chinese immigrants. Reaching an altitude of 16,404 feet, the railway is the world's highest.

BY THE NUMBERS

1 million Deaths each year from malaria, which is spread by the anopheles mosquito and kills mostly children in Africa

44% Portion of athletes at the 2004 Summer Olympics who are women, up from 38% at the 2000 Games

8.7 million Number of millionaires on the planet, according to a recent study

17 Number of No. 1 hits by the Beatles, tied with Elvis for the most No. 1 hits by any single act

98 Number of minutes it took *Sputnik,* the first artificial satellite, to orbit Earth

MICHAEL ROUGIER/TIME & LIFE PICTURES/GETTY IMAGES

Sputnik

1,888 The estimated number of languages spoken in Africa

5 The number of current Communist states (China, Vietnam, Laos, Cuba, and North Korea)

CRITICAL THINKING

1. **Finding the Main Idea** What are the supporting details the writer uses in "Meltdown!" to get across the point that global warming is taking place?
2. **Inferring** Based on the information in the "Milestone" about Pablo Neruda, where do you think the poet stood politically?

C Critical Thinking

Analyzing Information Discuss what is meant by cloning and then list what some of the ethical issues might be. **OL**

Assess/Close

Personal Writing Read a few selections of Pablo Neruda's prose or poetry to the class. Have students express their reactions in written form. **OL**

Visit the TIME Web site at www.time.com for up-to-date news, weekly magazine articles, editorials, online polls, and an archive of past magazine and Web articles.

CRITICAL THINKING

Answers:

1. The Arctic ice cap has lost an area twice the size of Texas; greenhouse gases trap sunlight and raise Earth's temperature.
2. socialist, like his friend Salvador Allende

Activity: Why Is It Important?

Global Warming Ask: What do you know about global warming? *(Start a discussion to help students clarify their knowledge.)* Former Vice President Al Gore has worked to alert people to the effects of global warming. In 2007, his documentary film, *An Inconvenient Truth,* won an Oscar for its call to action. In the same year, the United Nations issued two reports on global warming. The first report stressed, with 90 percent confidence, that global warming is the result of human activity. The second report said that if temperatures continue to rise, we can expect catastrophic changes in our environment, including severe food and water shortages, coastal flooding, and the loss of nearly 30 percent of plant and animal species. As a result, billions of people would be affected. Have students work in pairs to research ways that they can help reduce greenhouse gas emissions, which in turn can help reduce global warming. As a class, work to create a list of realistic ways to address this problem on a personal and national level. **OL**

FOUR-DOOR BOOK

1. Make a *shutter fold* using 11" × 17" or 12" × 18" paper.
2. Fold the *shutter fold* in half like a *hamburger.* Crease well.
3. Open the project and cut along the two inside *valley folds*.
4. These cuts will form four doors on the inside of the project.

Use this fold for data occurring in fours. When folded in half like a *hamburger,* a finished *four-door book* can be glued inside a large (11" × 17") *shutter fold* as part of a larger project.

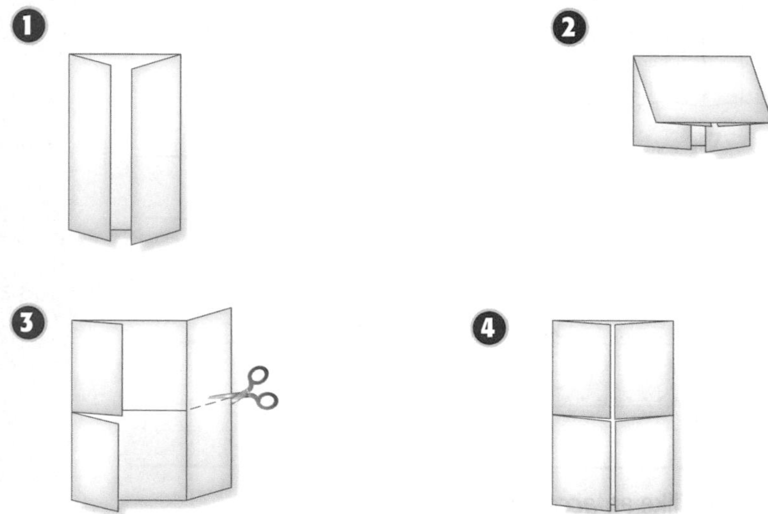

LAYERED-LOOK BOOK

1. Stack two sheets of paper (8½" × 11") so that the back sheet is one inch higher than the front sheet.
2. Bring the bottom of both sheets upward and align the edges so that all of the layers or tabs are the same distance apart.
3. When all tabs are an equal distance apart, fold the papers and crease well.
4. Open the papers and glue them together along the *valley,* or inner center fold, or staple them along the *mountain.*

FOLDABLES

Shutter Fold

1. Begin as if you were going to make a *hamburger* but instead of creasing the paper, pinch it to show the midpoint.
2. Fold the outer edges of the paper to meet at the pinch, or midpoint, forming a *shutter fold.*

Use this book for data occurring in twos. Or, make this fold using 11" × 17" paper and smaller books—such as the half-book, journal, and two-tab book—that can be glued inside to create a large project full of student work.

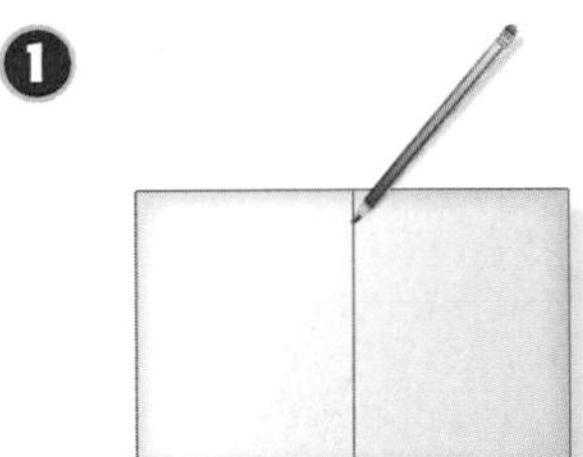

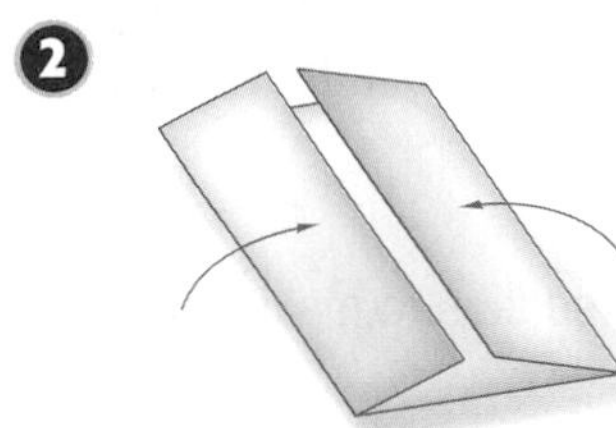

Three-Pocket Book

1. Fold a horizontal sheet of paper (11" × 17") into thirds.
2. Fold the bottom edge up two inches and crease well. Glue the outer edges of the two-inch tab to create three pockets.
3. Label each pocket. Use to hold notes taken on index cards or quarter sheets of paper.

Three-Tab Book

1. Fold a sheet of paper like a *hot dog.*
2. With the paper horizontal, and the fold of the *hot dog* up, fold the right side toward the center, trying to cover one half of the paper.

Note: If you fold the right edge over first, the final graphic organizer will open and close like a book.

3. Fold the left side over the right side to make a book with three folds.
4. Open the folded book. Place your hands between the two thicknesses of paper and cut up the two *valleys* on one side only. This will form three tabs.

Use this book for data occurring in threes, and for two-part Venn diagrams.

Variation A:
Draw overlapping circles on the three tabs to make a Venn diagram.

Variation B:
Cut each of the three tabs in half to make a six-tab book.

FOLDABLES

1
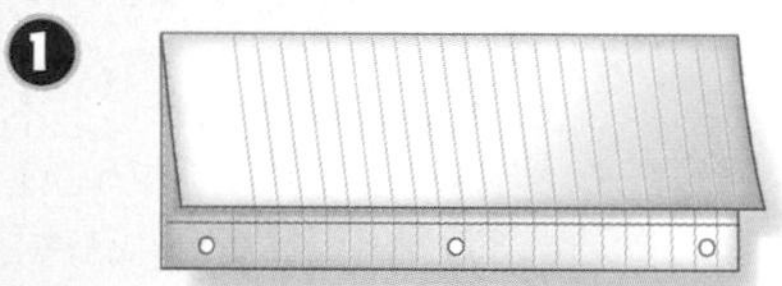

2
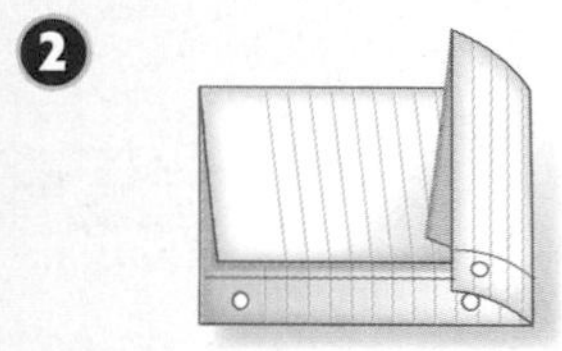

3
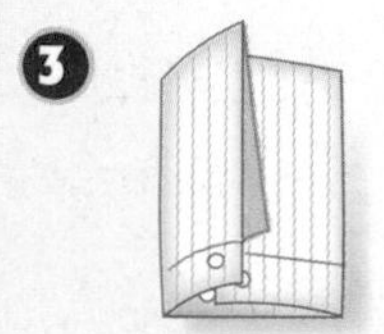

4
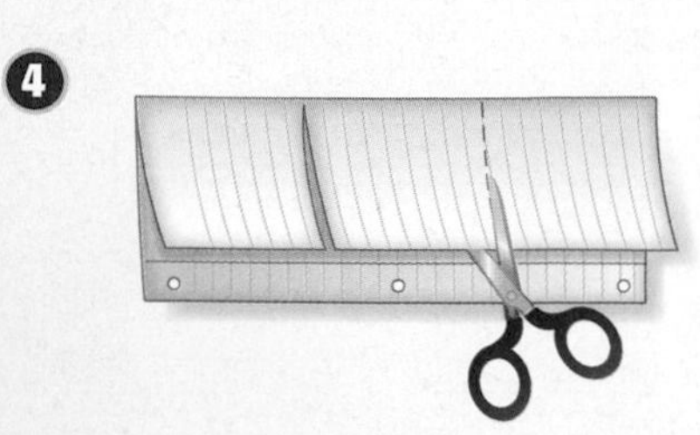

Trifold Book

1. Fold a sheet of paper (8½" × 11") into thirds.
2. Use this book as is, or cut into shapes. If the trifold is cut, leave plenty of fold on both sides of the designed shape, so the book will open and close in three sections.

Use this book to make charts with three columns or rows, large Venn diagrams, and reports on data occurring in threes.

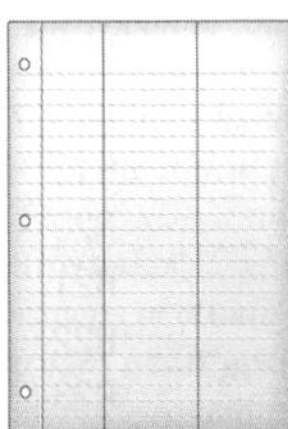

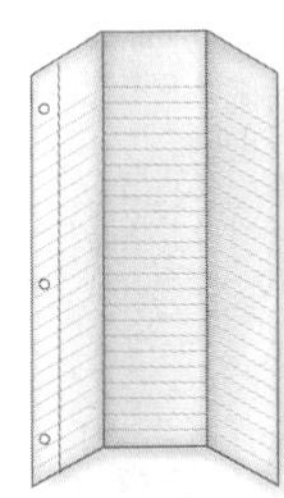

Two-Tab Book

1. Fold a sheet of paper like a *hamburger.* Make a second *hamburger* fold.
2. Cut up the *valley* of the inside fold toward the *mountain top.* This cut forms two large tabs that can be used front and back for writing and illustrations.

The book can be expanded by making several of these folds and gluing them side-by-side.

Use this book with data occurring in twos. For example, use it for comparing and contrasting, determining cause and effect, finding similarities and differences, and more.

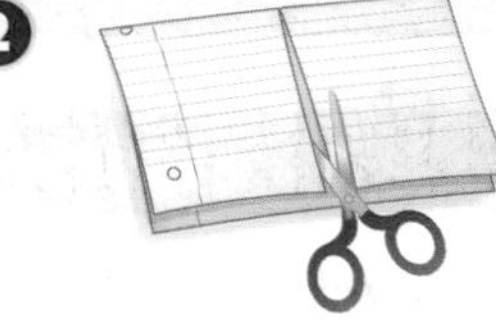

Teach

C Critical Thinking

Determining Cause and Effect The statement in item 4 under Learning the Skill states "... an effect can become the cause of yet another effect." This represents a cause-and-effect chain. Have students think of cause-and-effect chains and choose one to research and write about. Tell students that the chain can affect the environment, human population, animal population, or all of the above. Tell them to describe this chain in as much detail as they can. If possible, ask them to create a graphic to illustrate it. AL

R Reading Strategy

Using Context Clues **Ask:** In what country do the Kurds live? Where does that information appear in the paragraph? *(The Kurds live in Iraq. In addition to related content clues, the adjective Iraqi in the first paragraph and the phrase "federated Iraq" in the last sentence define their location.)* BL

DETERMINING CAUSE AND EFFECT

Why Learn This Skill?

Determining cause and effect involves considering *why* an event occurred. A *cause* is the action or situation that produces an event. What happens as a result of the cause is an effect.

Learning the Skill

Follow these steps to learn how to identify cause-and-effect relationships. Then answer the questions below.

SKILLS HANDBOOK

1. Identify two or more events or developments.

2. Decide whether one event caused the other. Look for "clue words" such as *because, led to, due to, brought about, produced, as a result of, so that, since,* and *therefore.*

3. Look for logical relationships between events, such as "She overslept, and then she missed her bus." R

4. Identify the outcomes of events. Remember that some effects have more than one cause, and some causes lead to more than one effect. Also, an effect can become the cause of yet another effect. C

Since the aftermath of the 1991 gulf war, nearly four million Kurds have enjoyed complete autonomy in the region of Iraqi Kurdistan—protected from Saddam under a "no-fly zone" north of the 36th parallel and behind the defensive wall of the Kurds' highly disciplined army, the peshmerga. They have held region-wide elections, formed a legislature, and chosen a president, establishing a world entirely apart from Baghdad—a de facto independent state. For the first time in their long history, Kurds are wielding significant political power, successfully negotiating for control over their own military forces and authority over new oil discoveries in their own terrain. Under the federated Iraq being called for by the international community, they would have powers of autonomy that match—or even exceed—what they now enjoy.

—Frank Viviano, "The Kurds in Control," *National Geographic,* January 2006

An Iraqi Kurd ▸

Practicing the Skill

1. Based on the reading, why have the Kurds in Iraq begun to enjoy complete autonomy?
2. What is the cause for this recent autonomy?
3. What is the cause-and-effect chain that could lead to an even greater autonomy and international recognition of this autonomy?

APPLYING THE SKILL

Use library or Internet sources to research Kurdish culture under the rule of Saddam Hussein. Then explain the causes and effects of his dictatorship in a chart like the following:

Causes→	Kurdish culture→	Effects

Practicing the Skill: Answers

Determining Cause and Effect

1. The aftermath of the 1991 Gulf War isolated and protected them.
2. protection by a no-fly zone and by their own army
3. Regional elections and political power could lead to a federated state called for by the international community.

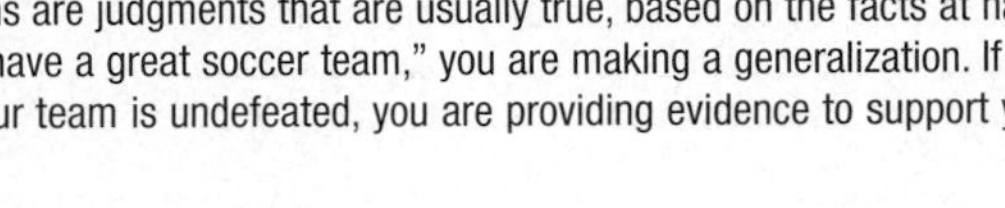

MAKING GENERALIZATIONS

Why Learn This Skill?

Generalizations are judgments that are usually true, based on the facts at hand. If you say, "We have a great soccer team," you are making a generalization. If you **C** also say that your team is undefeated, you are providing evidence to support your generalization.

Learning the Skill

Follow these steps to learn how to make a valid generalization. Then answer the questions below.

1. Identify the subject matter.

Berbers live throughout North Africa, but nowhere has denial of their identity been more systematic than in Morocco, ethnically the most Berber of the region's countries. Although 60 percent of its population claim Berber descent and nearly 40 percent speak one of three Berber languages, Morocco's constitution declares the country part of Arab North Africa, proclaims Arabic as its official language, and makes no mention of the Berbers. This is a legacy of the Arab nationalism that sparked colonial-era independence movements in the region and, in the name of unity, ignored or even suppressed the cultures and languages of non-Arab peoples.

—Jeffrey Taylor, "Among the Berbers," *National Geographic,* January 2005

2. Collect factual information and examples relevant to the topic.

3. Identify similarities among these facts.

4. Use these similarities to form some general ideas about the subject.

Practicing the Skill

1. Based on the facts above, what generalization can you make about the status of Berbers in Morocco?
2. What evidence supports your generalization?

APPLYING THE SKILL

Use library or Internet resources to research the status of Berbers in another country in **W** North Africa. Write a generalization based on what you found. Provide details to support your generalization.

SKILLS HANDBOOK

Teach

C Critical Thinking

Making Generalizations
Have students work in small groups to research the topic of Arab nationalism. Then have them work together to list generalizations about the movement throughout the Arabic world. **OL**

W Writing Support

Expository Writing Explain to students that their written generalizations about the status of Berbers in North Africa are examples of expository writing. **BL**

Practicing the Skill: Answers

Making Generalizations

1. They make up the largest ethnic group and their identity is systematically denied.
2. Sixty percent of the population claims Berber descent, but the constitution makes no mention of Berbers or their language.

Teach

R Reading Strategy

Activating Prior Knowledge Have students review the various critical-thinking skills they have encountered to determine which skills rely more on facts and which rely on opinion. **Ask:** **Which skills utilize facts to form an opinion?** *(drawing conclusions, making generalizations, predicting, making inferences)* **AL**

D Differentiated Instruction

Interpersonal Tell students that debates are forums in which facts and opinions are shaped into organized arguments for or against a specific statement. Have students work in two groups to gather facts and form differing opinions about an issue in your school or community. Schedule a debate between the two sides. **OL**

DISTINGUISHING FACT FROM OPINION

Why Learn This Skill?

R Distinguishing fact from opinion can help you make reasonable judgments about what others say and write. Facts can be proved by evidence such as records, documents, or historical sources. Opinions are based on people's differing values and beliefs.

Learning the Skill

Follow these steps to learn how to identify facts and opinions. Then answer the questions below.

SKILLS HANDBOOK

After decades of economic progress, Puerto Rico is struggling, and the mainland has both missed this horrific economic slide and contributed to it through benign neglect.

Poverty on the island is rampant. The per capita income is just about half that of the poorest state in the United States. Nearly one-third of the population was unemployed in 2000. And a good quarter of all employment is in government jobs . . .

The bleak picture is set out in a long-overdue, exhaustive study . . . from the Center for the New Economy, a nonpartisan Puerto Rican research group, and the Brookings Institution.

Much of the blame can be put on Washington, which has been tone deaf to the island's needs and has miscalculated where help was needed. . . .

—*New York Times*, "Puerto Rico, an Island in Distress," October 23, 2006

1. Identify the facts. Ask: Can these statements be proved? Where would I find information to verify them?

2. If a statement can be proved by information from a reliable source, it is factual.

3. Identify opinions by looking for statements of feelings or beliefs. They may contain words like *should, would, could, best, greatest, all, every,* or *always.*

D

◄ A street vendor, Puerto Rico

Practicing the Skill

1. What are two factual statements in the editorial?
2. Which statements are opinions?

APPLYING THE SKILL

Find a news article and an editorial about the same issue. Identify two facts and two opinions from these sources.

Practicing the Skill: Answers

Distinguishing Fact from Opinion

1. The per capita income is about half that of the poorest state. Nearly one third of the population was unemployed in 2000.
2. Washington has been tone deaf to the island's needs and has miscalculated where help was needed.

FORMULATING QUESTIONS

Why Learn This Skill?

Asking questions helps you to process information and understand what you read. 

Learning the Skill

Follow these steps to learn how to formulate questions. Then answer the questions below.

1. Think about questions you have. Often you can find the answers in the next paragraph or section.

2. Ask *who, what, when, where, why,* and *how* about the main ideas, places, and events.

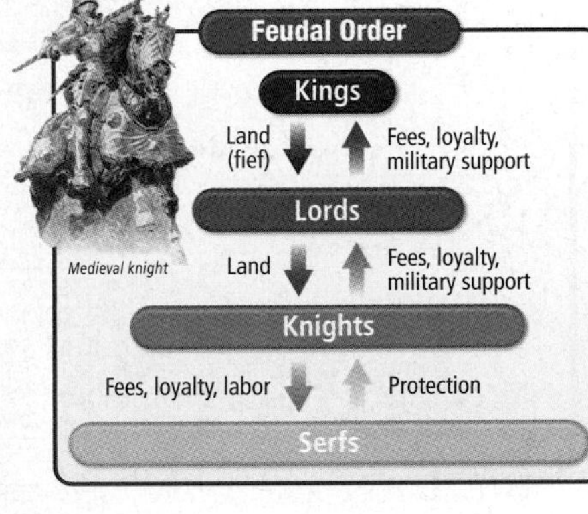

Medieval knight

3. Reread to find answers to your questions.

Practicing the Skill

1. What is the topic of the chart?
2. Select the parts of the chart you would like to understand better.
3. Formulate two questions about these parts.
4. Where might you find answers to your questions?

APPLYING THE SKILL

Formulate two more questions about the information on this page. Then use Internet sources to find answers to your questions.

SKILLS HANDBOOK

Teach

S Skill Practice

Applying Ask: What do you do when you can't find an answer to a question? *(Ask another question.)* Have students develop three questions about the skill of formulating questions. Tell them to be sure that the questions differ from those posed in Learning the Skill. The questions should be about asking questions, not about the chart in the example. After students have formed their questions, have them pose their questions to the rest of the class. **AL**

Practicing the Skill: Answers

Formulating Questions

1. the organization of feudal society
2. Student selections will vary.
3. Possible response: What was the relationship between serfs and knights? What was the relationship between knights and lords?
4. Possible response: textbook, reference resources in a library, the Internet

Teach

S Skill Practice

Using Geography Skills Have students locate and identify the nations that controlled the Allied zone. **Ask:** Which groups controlled the Allied zone? Which of these nations controlled the smallest area? *(British, French and Americans controlled the Allied zone. The French Zone was the smallest.)* **BL**

C Critical Thinking

Analyzing Information Have students study the map. **Ask:** Why couldn't the Allies ship supplies from Poland or Czechoslovakia? *(Those countries were behind the iron curtain and under Soviet control.)* **BL**

SKILLS HANDBOOK

ANALYZING INFORMATION

Why Learn This Skill?

The ability to analyze information is important in deciding what you think about a subject. Analysis requires a critical study of what an author or artist is trying to get across.

Learning the Skill

Follow these steps to learn how to analyze information. Then answer the questions below.

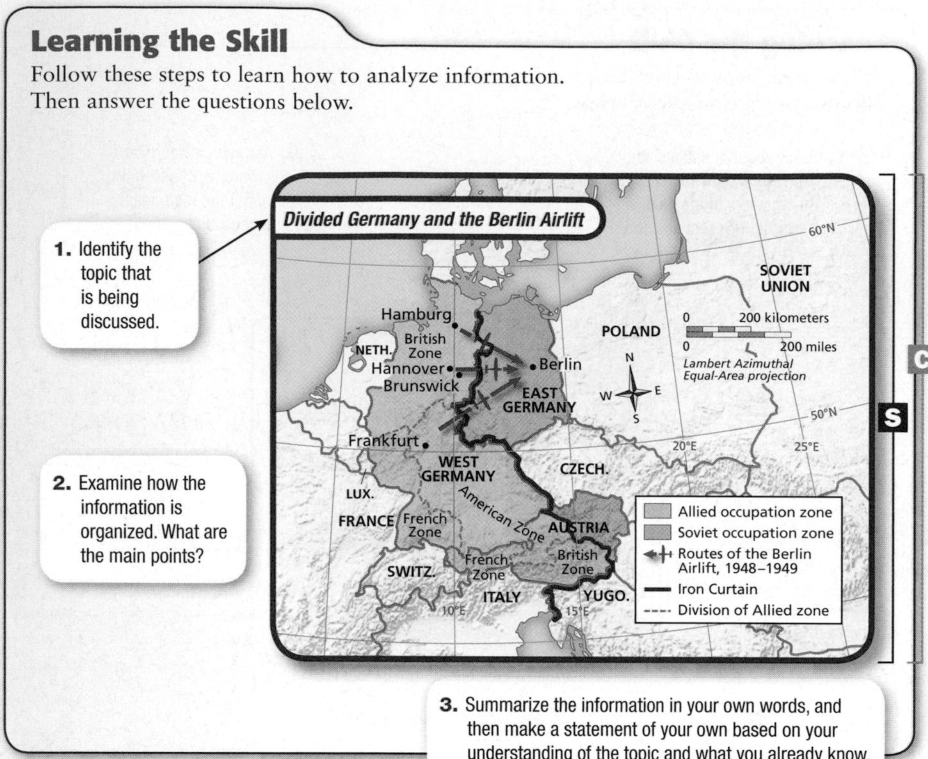

1. Identify the topic that is being discussed.

2. Examine how the information is organized. What are the main points?

3. Summarize the information in your own words, and then make a statement of your own based on your understanding of the topic and what you already know.

Practicing the Skill

1. Based on the title, what does the information on the map represent?
2. How is the information organized? What are the main points?
3. Summarize the information from the map, and then provide your analysis based on the information and what you know about the Berlin Airlift.

APPLYING THE SKILL

Find a news story about another airlift operation in history. Analyze the story and use your analysis to summarize the similarities and differences between this airlift and the Berlin Airlift.

Practicing the Skill: Answers

Analyzing Information

1. air routes to Berlin
2. The information is organized by country and territorial control. The main points are that (1) Germany was divided into Allied and Soviet spheres of influence, and (2) Allied Berlin was isolated and lacked overland supply routes.
3. Students' summaries and analyses will vary. A possible answer: To circumvent the Soviet blockade of overland routes, Allied planes from Hamburg, Hannover, and Frankfurt carried supplies to Berlin

EVALUATING INFORMATION

Why Learn This Skill?

We live in an information age. The amount of information available can be overwhelming, and it is sometimes difficult to know when information is true and useful. **C** You need to evaluate what you read and hear to determine the reliability of the information presented.

Learning the Skill

When evaluating information to determine its reliability, ask yourself the following questions as you read:

- Is there bias? In other words, does the source unfairly present just one point of view, ignoring any arguments against it?
- Is the information published in a credible, reliable publication?
- Is the author or speaker identified? Is he or she an authority on the subject?
- Is the information up-to-date?
- Is the information backed up by facts and other sources? Does it seem to be accurate?
- Is it well-written and well-edited? Writing that has errors in spelling, grammar, and punctuation is likely to be careless in other ways as well.

Source A

Oil prices are so high, becuz big oil companys are trying to goug us. Greedy oil executives, are driven up prices to get richer.

—published on an individual's Internet blog

Source B

It's certainly clear that high oil prices aren't dulling demand for energy products. According to the Energy Dept.'s Energy Information Administration (EIA), U.S. demand for gasoline in June was 9.5 million barrels a day, a record.

—*BusinessWeek*, July 7, 2006

Source C

The single biggest factor in the inflation rate last year was from one cause: the skyrocketing prices of OPEC oil. We must take whatever actions are necessary to reduce our dependence on foreign oil—and at the same time reduce inflation.

—President Jimmy Carter, January 23, 1980

SKILLS HANDBOOK

Practicing the Skill

Look at the above statements about oil prices. Rank them in order of most reliable to least reliable, and then explain why you ranked them as you did.

APPLYING THE SKILL

Find an advertisement that contains text and bring it to class. In a brief oral presentation, tell the class whether the information in the advertisement is reliable or unreliable and why.

Teach

C Critical Thinking

Analyzing Information Explain that it has become increasingly difficult to locate unbiased sources of news and information. Many news outlets unabashedly present news from a partisan perspective, and the growing consolidation of corporate media ownership can also influence coverage and content. **Ask:** **What media sources do you rely on for accurate information? Are those sources completely unbiased, or do they just share a biased perspective with which you agree?** Encourage students to list and discuss examples of media bias, and suggest that it might be necessary to consult multiple sources to obtain accurate information. **OL**

Practicing the Skill: Answers

Evaluating Information

Student rankings of reliability will vary. Most will likely give the least credence to the unnamed individual's error-riddled Internet blog.

Teach

R Reading Strategy

Inferring Bring the front page of a daily newspaper to class. Post the front page on a bulletin board and have students study it from a distance. Most students will not be able to read more than the headlines of the paper. Have students write down inferences they make based on what they can see. After they have had a chance to note their inferences, have students share them with the class. **Ask:** What does this exercise tell you about inferences? *(Much of what a person infers depends upon prior knowledge and facts at hand.)* OL

MAKING INFERENCES

Why Learn This Skill?

R To *infer* means to evaluate information and arrive at a conclusion. When you make inferences, you "read between the lines," or use clues to figure something out that is not stated directly in the text.

SKILLS HANDBOOK

Learning the Skill

Follow these steps to learn how to make inferences. Then answer the questions below.

In Bamako I live in a guest house called the Centre d'Acceuil, run by Spanish nuns. The rooms are cheap—a bed, mosquito netting. The bad thing about the Centre d'Acceuil is that although there are ten rooms for rent, there is only one shower. Moreover, it is constantly occupied these days by a young Norwegian, who came here not realizing how hot it gets in Bamako. The African interior is always white-hot. It is a plateau relentlessly bombarded by the rays of the sun, which appears to be suspended directly above the earth here: make one careless gesture, it seems, try leaving the shade, and you will go up in flames....The Norwegian, after several suffocating, sweltering days, decided to leave everything and return home. But he had to wait for the plane. And the only way he could survive until then, he concluded, was by never coming out from under the shower.

—Ryszard Kapuściński, *The Shadow of the Sun*

1. Read carefully for stated facts and ideas.
2. Summarize the information and list important facts.
3. Apply related information that you may already know.
4. Use your knowledge and insight to develop some logical conclusions.

Practicing the Skill

1. What facts are presented in the passage?
2. What can you infer from the presence of mosquito netting?
3. What can you infer about the availability of air transportation in Bamako?

APPLYING THE SKILL

Make inferences based on pictures of Africa you find on the Internet, and write questions based on your inferences. Exchange your pictures and questions with another student and answer each other's questions.

Practicing the Skill: Answers

Making Inferences

1. The speaker lives in a hot Bamako guest house run by nuns. It has ten rooms, each with a bed and mosquito net, but only one shower. A Norwegian gentleman spends all his time in the shower.
2. There are insects in Bamako, and the bedroom windows likely have no screens.
3. It is limited and infrequent.

COMPARING AND CONTRASTING

Why Learn This Skill?

When you make comparisons, you determine similarities among ideas, objects, or events. When you contrast, you are noting differences between ideas, objects, or events. Comparing and contrasting are important skills because they help you choose among several possible alternatives.

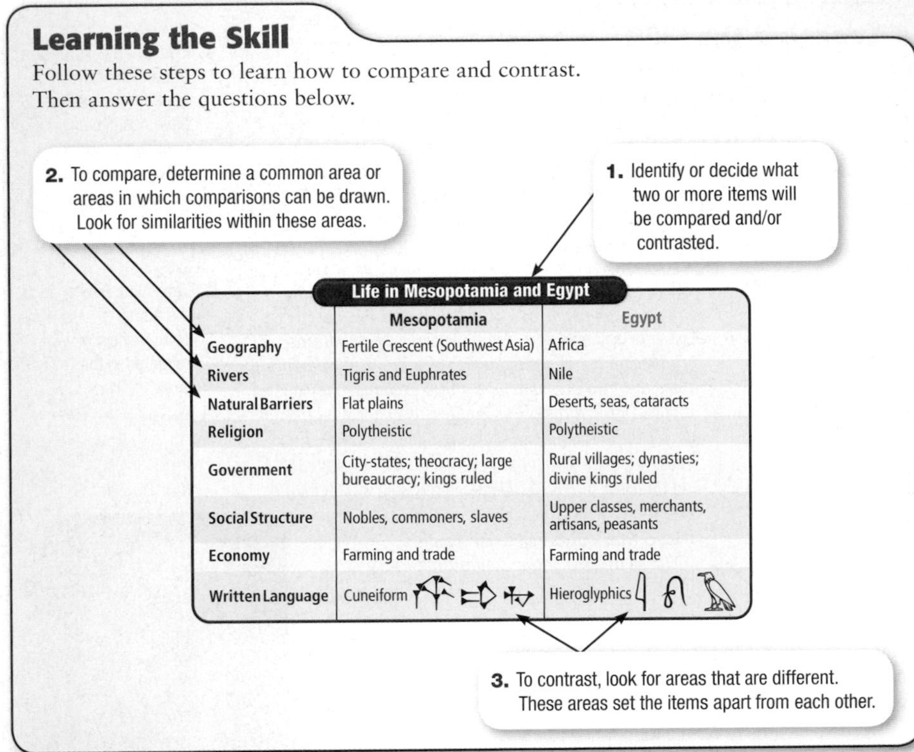

Learning the Skill

Follow these steps to learn how to compare and contrast. Then answer the questions below.

1. Identify or decide what two or more items will be compared and/or contrasted.
2. To compare, determine a common area or areas in which comparisons can be drawn. Look for similarities within these areas.
3. To contrast, look for areas that are different. These areas set the items apart from each other.

Life in Mesopotamia and Egypt

	Mesopotamia	Egypt
Geography	Fertile Crescent (Southwest Asia)	Africa
Rivers	Tigris and Euphrates	Nile
Natural Barriers	Flat plains	Deserts, seas, cataracts
Religion	Polytheistic	Polytheistic
Government	City-states; theocracy; large bureaucracy; kings ruled	Rural villages; dynasties; divine kings ruled
Social Structure	Nobles, commoners, slaves	Upper classes, merchants, artisans, peasants
Economy	Farming and trade	Farming and trade
Written Language	Cuneiform	Hieroglyphics

Practicing the Skill

1. What characteristics does the table use to compare and contrast life in Mesopotamia and Egypt?
2. How was life in Mesopotamia similar to life in Egypt?
3. How was life in Mesopotamia different from life in Egypt?

APPLYING THE SKILL

With a partner, research life in the other three early culture hearths—the Indus Valley, the Huang He Valley, and Middle America. Use your information to create a table like the one above. Develop three questions based on your table. Exchange your work with another pair of students and answer the questions based on their table.

Teach

S Skill Practice

Analyzing After students have read the lesson and engaged in practicing and applying the skill, have them study physical maps of Egypt, Mesopotamia, the Indus Valley, Huang He Valley, and Middle America. The maps should show not only the regions, but their physical relation to the areas that surround them. Working with partners, have the students compare and contrast the physical geography of the regions. As students begin to accumulate data that reflects similarities and differences, have them create a chart or graph that clearly presents their findings. **OL**

Practicing the Skill: Answers

Comparing and Contrasting

1. categories in the left column
2. location on rivers, polytheistic religions, agriculture-based economies, written languages
3. different geography, government, and social structure

Teach

W **Writing Support**

Persuasive Writing Have students write a paragraph that argues for or against the concept of Free Trade. Have them express their opinionated point of view by citing either its positive or negative effects. **AL**

C **Critical Thinking**

Analyzing Information Ask students to find letters to the editor from the editorial page of a newspaper. Have students write a sentence or two summarizing the bias of the writers. **Ask:** Do any of the letters conflict with each other? Do any of the letters conflict with the opinions of the newspaper? *(Answers will vary.)* **OL**

DETECTING BIAS

Why Learn This Skill?

Most people have a point of view, or bias. This bias influences the way they interpret and write about events. Recognizing bias helps you judge the accuracy of what you hear or read.

Learning the Skill

C Follow these steps to learn how to detect bias. Then answer the questions below.

The bourgeoisie . . . has put an end to all feudal, patriarchal, idyllic relations. It has pitilessly torn asunder the motley feudal ties that bound man to his "natural superiors," and has left remaining no other nexus between man and man than naked self-interest, than callous "cash payment." It has drowned the most heavenly ecstasies of religious fervour, of chivalrous enthusiasm . . . in the icy water of egotistical calculation. It has resolved personal worth into exchange value. And in place of the numberless and feasible chartered freedoms, has set up that single, unconscionable freedom—Free Trade. In one word, for exploitation, veiled by religious and political illusions, naked, shameless, direct, brutal exploitation.

—Karl Marx and Friedrich Engels, *The Manifesto of the Communist Party*

1. Examine the author's identity, especially his or her views and particular interests.
2. Identify statements of fact.
3. Determine the author's point of view.
4. Identify any expression of opinion or emotion. Look for words that have positive or negative overtones for clues about the author's feelings on the topic. **W**
5. Determine how the author's point of view is reflected in the work.

Karl Marx ▶

Practicing the Skill

1. Are there any statements of fact presented in this passage? If so, what are they?
2. What opinions are stated?
3. What evidence of bias do you find? Do the authors think it is a good thing or a bad thing the bourgeoisie have put an end to feudal ties?

APPLYING THE SKILL

Find written material about a topic of interest to you. Possible sources include editorials, letters to the editor, and political pamphlets. Apply the steps for recognizing bias to the material. Write a paragraph summarizing your findings.

Practicing the Skill: Answers

Detecting Bias

1. Answers may vary. Students may cite the end of feudalism or the monetary calculation of personal worth.
2. Answers will vary. The passage contains many opinions, which are often signaled by adjectives.
3. Answers will vary. Possible response: The authors believe the end of feudal ties was a good thing, but that its replacement is worse.

SYNTHESIZING INFORMATION

Why Learn This Skill?

Synthesizing information involves combining information from two or more sources. Information gained from one source often sheds new light upon other information.

Learning the Skill

Follow these steps to learn how to synthesize information. Then answer the questions that follow.

Source A

"Rome has been rising for 3,000 years," says Darius Arya, an archaeologist and director of the American Institute for Roman Culture. Much of Rome is situated in a floodplain, including the modern city center, known in antiquity as Campus Martius, at a bend of the Tiber River. Although the Romans put up levees, the city still flooded periodically, so they built upward, laying new structures and streets on earlier ones. "It was cost-effective, and it worked," Arya says. "We see the Romans jacking their city up two meters at a time, raising themselves above the water but also burying their past."

—Paul Bennett, "In Rome's Basement,"
National Geographic, July 2006

1. Analyze each source separately to understand its meaning.

2. Determine what information each source adds to the subject.

D

Source B

Of all the old saws about the Eternal City, at least one remains simply true: dig a deep hole almost anywhere here, and you'll unearth an archaeological artifact or two.

Yet a wave of public and private building projects is suddenly focusing unusual attention on Rome's rich subterranean world as one treasure after another emerges at a steady clip.

"We're walking on the world's largest untapped underground museum," said Maria Antonietta Tomei, a government official responsible for coordinating archaeological digs in Rome.

During the last week reports surfaced that 800 coins from the fourth and fifth centuries BC had been unearthed during the reconstruction of a movie theater near the Trevi Fountain.

—"Treasures galore still emerging from underneath Rome,"
Taipei Times (online), December 27, 2006

3. Identify points of agreement and disagreement between the sources. Ask: Can Source A give me new information or new ways of thinking about Source B?

4. Find relationships between the information in the sources.

SKILLS HANDBOOK

Practicing the Skill

1. What is the main subject of each passage?
2. What does Source A say about the subject?
3. What information does Source B add?
4. Sum up what you have learned from both sources.

APPLYING THE SKILL

Find two sources of information on a topic dealing with archaeological excavations in Rome. What are the main ideas in each? How does each add to your understanding of the topic?

Teach

D Differentiated Instruction

English Language Learners
Organize students into groups of three, with each group containing at least one fluent speaker of English. Have students read the passages aloud. Ask them to compile a list of terms that they do not understand. Then have them work together using a dictionary and their own knowledge to define each word on the list.

Make sure students grasp the concept of generations of Romans building upon the remains of earlier structures in Source A, and explain that the term "Eternal City" in Source B is another name for Rome. **OL**

Practicing the Skill: Answers

Synthesizing Information

1. Roman archaeology
2. Romans built new structures on top of old ones.
3. Many ancient treasures were unearthed during a wave of new construction.
4. Answers will vary. Possible response: Rome contains several layers of construction, and many ancient structures and artifacts remain beneath its surface.

Teach

D1 Differentiated Instruction

Interpersonal Tell students that people draw conclusions all the time. Ask students to write down three facts (real or hypothetical) about themselves—such as "I've always had pets; I enjoy science; I want to work with animals"—and read them aloud to the class. See if classmates can draw the correct conclusions from the facts provided. OL

D2 Differentiated Instruction

Logical/Mathematical Ask students to research a threatened animal species. Then have them explain the threat in terms of numbers and percentages. For example, what percent of wildlife species are currently threatened with extinction? **Ask:** How can numbers support the conclusion that a species is threatened? *(Population counts over a period of time can prove whether a population is thriving or threatened.)* OL

DRAWING CONCLUSIONS

Why Learn This Skill?

A conclusion is a logical understanding that you reach based on details or facts that you read or hear. When you draw conclusions, you use stated information to figure out ideas that are unstated.

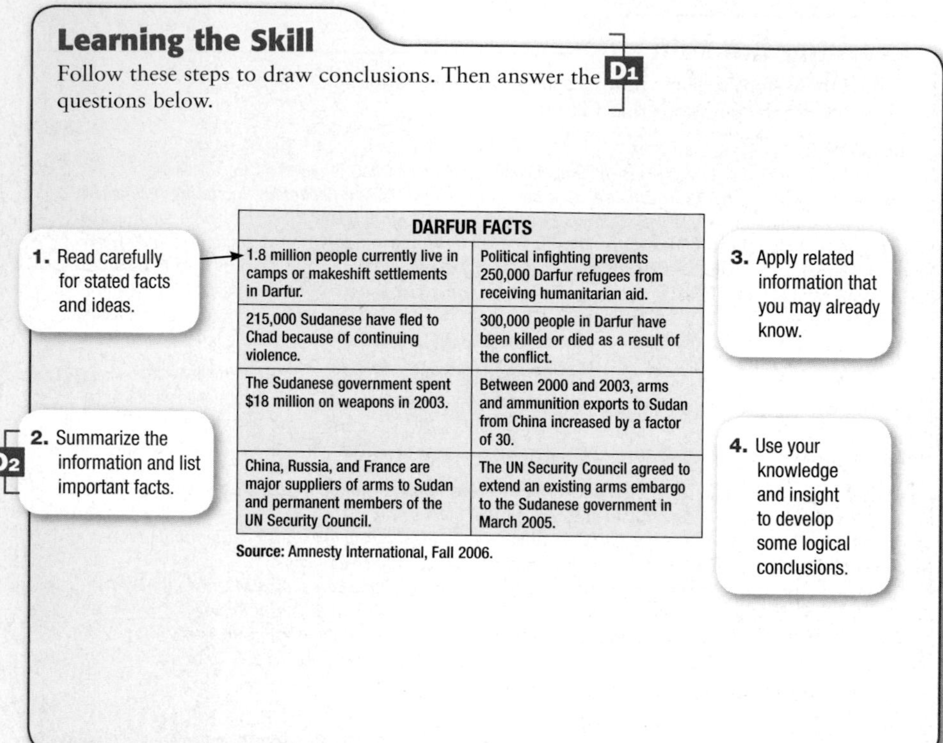

Learning the Skill

Follow these steps to draw conclusions. Then answer the questions below. D1

DARFUR FACTS	
1.8 million people currently live in camps or makeshift settlements in Darfur.	Political infighting prevents 250,000 Darfur refugees from receiving humanitarian aid.
215,000 Sudanese have fled to Chad because of continuing violence.	300,000 people in Darfur have been killed or died as a result of the conflict.
The Sudanese government spent $18 million on weapons in 2003.	Between 2000 and 2003, arms and ammunition exports to Sudan from China increased by a factor of 30.
China, Russia, and France are major suppliers of arms to Sudan and permanent members of the UN Security Council.	The UN Security Council agreed to extend an existing arms embargo to the Sudanese government in March 2005.

Source: Amnesty International, Fall 2006.

SKILLS HANDBOOK

Practicing the Skill

1. Which facts from the table support the conclusion that "the Sudanese government is trying to drive out the people of Darfur"?
2. What conclusion might you draw about why the UN Security Council waited so many years before extending an existing arms embargo to Sudan?

APPLYING THE SKILL

Find an article describing a current conflict in Africa. Use the steps on this page to draw conclusions about the causes of the conflict. Summarize your conclusions in a paragraph.

Practicing the Skill: Answers

Drawing Conclusions

1. Three facts in this chart support that conclusion: "1.8 million people in Darfur currently living in camps or makeshift settlements"; "Political infighting prevents 250,000 Darfur refugees from receiving aid"; and "300,000 people in Darfur have been killed or died."
2. Answers will vary. Possible response: The governments of China, Russia, and France hesitated to embargo arms to Sudan because their economies benefited from the sale of those arms.

PREDICTING

Why Learn This Skill?

Predicting future events can be difficult and sometimes risky. The more information you have, however, the more accurate your predictions will be. Making good predictions will help you understand what you read.

Learning the Skill

Follow these steps to learn how to make a prediction. Then answer the questions below.

1. Gather information about the decision or action.

2. Use your knowledge about history and human behavior to identify what consequences could result.

3. Analyze each consequence by asking: How likely is this to occur?

There is little freedom to disagree with the determinations of the authorities [in South Africa]. There is large scale unemployment here because of the drought and the recession that has hit most of the world's economy. And it is such a time that the authorities have increased the prices of various foodstuffs and also of rents in black townships—measures designed to hit hardest those least able to afford the additional costs. . . .

The authorities have not stopped stripping blacks of their South African citizenship. . . . The South African government is turning us into aliens in the land of our birth.

White South Africans are. . . .scared human beings, many of them; who would not be, if they were outnumbered five to one? Through this lofty body I wish to appeal to my white fellow South Africans to share in building a new society, for blacks are not intent on driving whites into the sea but on claiming only their rightful place in the sun in the land of their birth.

—Bishop Desmond Tutu, speech on apartheid to the United Nations Security Council, October 23, 1984

Practicing the Skill

1. What events does the passage describe?
2. Do you think what the author described changed after his speech?
3. On what do you base this prediction?
4. What occurrences might have an effect on changing these events?
5. What are the possible outcomes for all involved in the appeal proposed by the author?

APPLYING THE SKILL

Find a newspaper or magazine article that describes the current state of politics, economy, or society in South Africa. Analyze the article, and describe how the people of South Africa are trying to solve the problem. Predict three consequences of the actions described. On what do you base your prediction?

Teach

C Critical Thinking

Analyzing Information After students have completed the Practicing the Skill exercise, remind them that Desmond Tutu delivered the speech cited in the example in 1984. Have students research the economy and the status of race relations in South Africa today. **Ask:** **Has the post-apartheid government of South Africa fulfilled Bishop Tutu's expectations?** Students can begin their research at the U.S Department of State Web site: http://www.state.gov/r/pa/ei/bgn/2898.htm. Have them use their findings to update their original predictions about South Africa's future. **OL**

Practicing the Skill: Answers

Predicting

1. the search of black South Africans for economic and social justice.
2. Student opinions will vary. Conditions in South Africa have changed.
3. Student responses will vary. Predictions may be based on prior knowledge or political beliefs.
4. Answers will vary. Possible occurrences include changing economic conditions, international sanctions and intervention.
5. Answers will vary. Possible outcomes might include reconciliation and power sharing, revolution, or continued oppression.

Teach

C Critical Thinking

Identifying Central Issues Explain that the government of China is very eager to attract foreign businesses. Have students work in small groups to evaluate the benefits for a hypothetical U.S. corporation to open a factory in China. **Ask:** What advantages might a U.S. manufacturer gain by opening a factory in China? What might be some disadvantages? Have students debate the pros and cons of such a move and identify facts to support their arguments. When the groups have reached a consensus, have them present their findings to the class. OL

PROBLEMS AND SOLUTIONS

Why Learn This Skill?

Suppose you are not doing well in basketball. You wonder why you cannot do better since you always go to practice, try your best, and pay attention to the coach's instructions. In order to improve a situation such as this one, you need to identify a specific problem and then take actions to solve it.

Learning the Skill

Follow these steps to help you through the problem-solving process. Then answer the questions below.

1. Identify the problem.
2. Gather information.
3. List possible solutions.
4. Consider the advantages and disadvantages of each solution.
5. Choose the best solution to your problem and carry it out.
6. Evaluate the effectiveness of the solution.

In just two decades . . . China's Northeast has gone from dynamo to dinosaur, tracing virtually the opposite trajectory of the country's thriving southern coastal regions. . . . The region's industrial production has sagged to less than 9 percent of national output, while its heavy reliance on state-owned enterprises—once a blessing, now a curse—has made market-oriented reforms seem like all shock and no therapy. The landscape left behind is . . . [t]housands of obsolete state-run factories, millions of laid-off workers, a growing gap between rich and poor, rampant corruption, deadly human and environmental disasters. . . .

Hoping to reverse this dangerous slide, Beijing has so far spent 7.5 billion dollars to rehabilitate the region, closing or privatizing old state-owned factories while retraining workers for industries more suited to the 21st century. . . . The real key, however, will be foreign investment. The region that once symbolized China's drive for self-sufficiency is now unabashedly courting foreign investors. . . . It is too early to tell whether the rust belt can truly be revitalized.

—Brook Larmer, "The Manchurian Mandate," *National Geographic*, September 2006

C

Practicing the Skill

1. What problem does the writer present in this selection?
2. What options are available to solve this problem? Can you think of any other options?
3. Explain the solutions implemented according to the selection. Were they successful? How do you determine this?

APPLYING THE SKILL

Select a current political problem that needs to be solved. The problem can be anything from the conflict between Israel and Palestine to the agreement on a constitution by all members of the European Union. Create a presentation in which you identify the problem, list options with their advantages and disadvantages, choose a solution, and evaluate the chosen solution.

Practicing the Skill: Answers

Problems and Solutions

1. The economy in northeastern China has stagnated, leaving obsolete factories, high unemployment, and environmental problems.
2. Answers will vary. Some money is available to help rehabilitate the region.
3. The government retrained workers and privatized factories, but foreign investment is still necessary for success.

READING A MAP

Why Learn This Skill?

S Maps can direct you down the street, across the county, or around the world. An **D** ordinary map holds all kinds of information. Learn the map's code, and you can read it like a book.

Learning the Skill

Follow these steps to learn how to read a map. Then answer the questions below.

1. Look at the title of the map—it tells you what kind of information the map shows.
2. Study the map key to determine the meanings of the symbols, colors, and lines used on the map.
3. Read the labels on the map to learn where things such as cities, groups of people, and physical features are located.
4. Find the compass rose to learn the orientation of the map.
5. Determine the relationship between map measurements and actual distances on Earth by using the scale bar.
6. Use lines of latitude and longitude to determine the absolute location of places on the map.

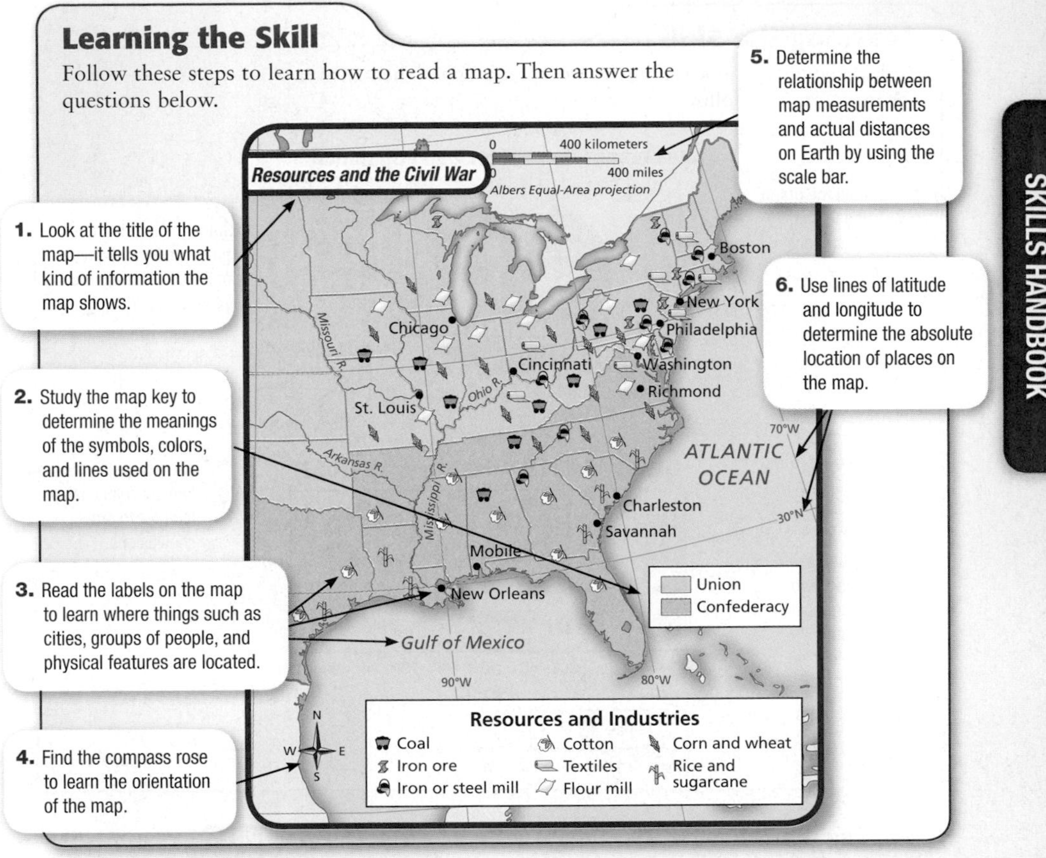

Practicing the Skill

1. What kinds of resources enabled the North to triumph over the South?
2. Where are most cities located? Why?

APPLYING THE SKILL

Choose a map from your world history text and work with a partner to write three questions that can be answered by reading the map. Then exchange questions with another pair and answer each other's questions.

Practicing the Skill: Answers

Reading a Map

1. coal, iron ore, corn and wheat, along with related industries
2. near seaports or rivers to facilitate transportation

Teach

S Skill Practice

Using Geography Skills Review the concept of absolute location, and explain that a gazetteer is an index of geographical place names and their coordinates. Have students identify the exact coordinates of their community. If access is available, direct them to the online gazetteer at http://www.census.gov/cgi-bin/gazetteer. **BL**

D Differentiated Instruction

Visual/Spatial Ask students to draw a map that shows the route they follow when traveling to school. Ask them to include major streets and landmarks and a compass rose. **OL**

SKILLS HANDBOOK

Teach

S Skill Practice

Applying Have students research the ethnic make-up of their community based on the most recent census data available. Then have them present that make-up in the form of a graph of their choosing. OL

W Writing Support

Expository Writing After students have developed their graph showing the ethnic make-up of the community, have them write a one-page expository paper that explains and interprets the graph, its results, and how the data was collected. AL

SKILLS HANDBOOK

INTERPRETING GRAPHS

Why Learn This Skill?

W Graphs are visual representations of statistical data. Large amounts of information can be condensed when presented in a graph. Studying graphs allows readers to see relationships clearly. **Bar graphs** use bars of different lengths to compare different quantities. **Circle graphs** show the relationship of parts to a whole as percentages. S

Learning the Skill

Follow these steps to learn how to interpret graphs. Then answer the questions that follow.

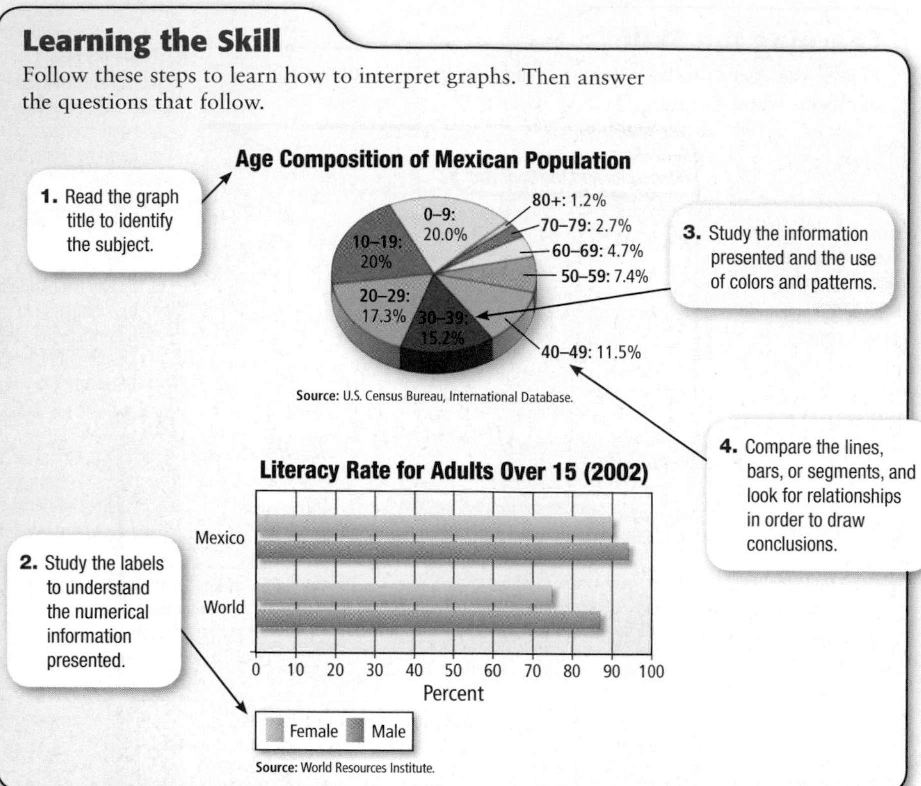

Practicing the Skill

1. How does the literacy rate in Mexico compare to literacy in the rest of the world?
2. What percentage of the Mexican people are under 20 years of age?
3. What general population trends in Mexico do these two graphs show?

APPLYING THE SKILL

Poll your classmates about countries they would like to visit. Use the data to design and draw a line, bar, or circle graph.

Practicing the Skill: Answers

Interpreting Graphs

1. Mexicans have a higher rate of literacy than the world average.
2. about 40% of the population
3. Mexico has a young, literate population.

SEQUENCING EVENTS

Why Learn This Skill?

Sequencing involves placing facts in the order in which they occurred. Sequencing helps you deal with large quantities of information in an understandable way. In studying history, sequencing can help you understand cause-and-effect relationships among events. This in turn helps analysts to predict outcomes of various events or policies.

Learning the Skill

Follow these steps to sequence events. Then answer the questions below.

1. Look for dates or clue words such as *in 1920, later that year, first, then,* and *in the late eighteenth century.* **D**

When the new moon of the month Shawwal appeared in the same year [1st September 1326], the Hijaz caravan left Damascus and I set off along with it. At Bosra the caravans usually halt for four days so that any who have been detained at Damascus by business affairs may make up on them. Thence they go to the Pool of Ziza, where they stop for a day, and then through al-Lajjun to the Castle of Karak. Karak, which is also called "The Castle of the Raven," is one of the most marvellous, impregnable, and celebrated of fortresses. . . . The caravan stopped for four days at a place called ath-Thaniya outside Karak, where preparations were made for entering the desert.

—Ibn Battuta, *Travels in Asia and Africa 1325–1354*

2. Arrange facts in the order in which they occurred. **W**

3. Consider using an organizational tool such as a time line, which makes it easy to see the chronology, as well as any cause-and-effect relationships, between events.

SKILLS HANDBOOK

Practicing the Skill

1. What dates or clue words in this selection can help determine the sequence of events being described?
2. Fill in a time line like the one below to show the sequence of events as described in the selection.

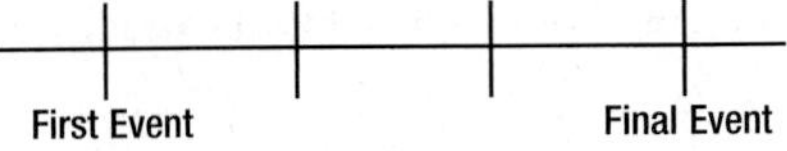

APPLYING THE SKILL

Find a newspaper or magazine article about a world event. Sequence the information presented in the article in a time line or chart.

Teach

D Differentiated Instruction

English Language Learners Review with students some of the words that signal a sequence of events. Ask volunteers to provide examples, and then list them on the board. The list should include the following: *first, second, last, next, before, after, later, then, when,* and *while.* **BL**

W Writing Support

Personal Writing Ask students to write a paragraph that either gives directions between two locations or provides instructions for completing a simple task. Encourage students to include clue words to present a clear sequence. **OL**

Practicing the Skill: Answers

Sequencing Events

1. when, thence, then

2. left Damascus, halted at Bosra, traveled to the Pool of Ziza, went through al-Lajjun to the Castle of Karak, stopped at ath-Thaniya, prepared to enter desert

Teach

D Differentiated Instruction

Visual/Spatial Have interested students draw a political cartoon. Ask them to choose a current issue or event about which they hold a strong opinion. Encourage students to visualize a situation that expresses their opinion and then draw their cartoon. Have students share and discuss their cartoons to determine their effectiveness. **OL**

SKILLS HANDBOOK

INTERPRETING POLITICAL CARTOONS

Why Learn This Skill?

Political cartoonists use art to express opinions. Their work appears in newspapers, magazines, books, and on the Internet. Political cartoons usually focus on public figures, political events, or economic or social conditions. They can give you a summary of an event or circumstance and the artist's opinion in a quick, entertaining manner. **D**

Learning the Skill

To interpret a political cartoon, follow these steps. Then answer the questions below.

1. Read the title, caption, or conversation balloons. They help you identify the subject of the cartoon.

2. Identify the characters or people shown. They may be caricatures, or unrealistic drawings that exaggerate the characters' physical features.

3. Identify any symbols shown. Symbols are things that stand for something else. Commonly recognized symbols may not be labeled. Unusual symbolism will be labeled.

4. Examine the actions in the cartoon—what is happening and why?

5. Identify the cartoonist's purpose. What statement or idea is he or she trying to get across? Decide if the cartoonist wants to persuade, criticize, or just make people think.

"...after climbing a great hill, one only finds that there are many more hills to climb."
—Nelson Mandela in "The Long Walk to Freedom"

FREEDOM

RECONSTRUCTION

THE ISLAND

POLLSMOOR

VICTOR VERSTER

RIVONIA

ARMED STRUGGLE

TREASON TRIAL

DEFIANCE CAMPAIGN

Practicing the Skill

1. Who is depicted in the cartoon? What is he doing?
2. What do the stones along the path represent?
3. What overall message do you think the cartoonist is trying to send?

APPLYING THE SKILL

Bring a newspaper or news magazine to class. With a partner, analyze the message in each political cartoon that you find.

Practicing the Skill: Answers

Interpreting Political Cartoons

1. Nelson Mandela; looking at future challenges in South Africa
2. prisons and obstacles overcome to reach freedom
3. The road to freedom was difficult, and another difficult journey to reconstruction lies ahead.

ANALYZING PRIMARY SOURCES

Why Learn This Skill?

An eyewitness account of a place or event is a primary source. The advantage of a primary source is that it contains firsthand knowledge. Primary sources may **C** include diaries, letters, memoirs, interviews with eyewitnesses, photographs, news **D** articles, and legal documents. Often they provide detailed accounts of events, but reflect only one perspective. For this reason, you must examine as many sources as possible before drawing any conclusions.

Learning the Skill

Follow these steps to learn how to analyze a primary source. Then answer the questions below.

The festivals generally conclude with an amusement unknown in Europe—a combat between two elephants. . . .

A wall of earth is raised three or four feet wide and five or six high. The two ponderous beasts meet one another face to face, on opposite sides of the wall, each having a couple of riders. . . . The riders animate the elephants either by soothing words, or by chiding them as cowards, and urge them on with their heels, until the poor creatures approach the wall and are brought to the attack. The shock is tremendous, and it appears surprising that they ever survive the dreadful wounds . . . inflicted with their teeth, their heads, and their trunks. . . .

The fight of these noble creatures is attended with much cruelty. . . . [S]ome of the riders are trodden underfoot; and killed on the spot. . . [T]his amusement . . . does not always end with the death of a rider: . . . some spectators are knocked down and trampled upon. . . .

—François Bernier, *Travels in the Mogul Empire 1656–1668*

1. Identify the author of the source. Note any biases or opinions expressed by the author or creator of the source.
2. Identify when and where the document was written.
3. Read the document for its content and try to answer the five "W" questions: Who is it about? What is it about? When did it happen? Where did it happen? Why did it happen?
4. Determine what kind of information may be missing from the primary source.

SKILLS HANDBOOK

Practicing the Skill

1. How can you tell the source contains firsthand knowledge of the elephant fight?
2. Who has the author's sympathy? How can you tell?
3. What information from the source did you find valuable? What about the topic of elephant fights would you still like to learn?

APPLYING THE SKILL

Find a firsthand account of a recent event or a historical event. Evaluate its validity and usefulness as a primary source.

Teach

C Critical Thinking

Analyzing Primary Sources Have students use a newspaper or other periodical to identify a current event or news story. After they have chosen their news item, have them enter the event in an Internet search engine. Tell students to choose four different entries from the search results and to evaluate these entries for their usefulness as primary sources. As the students review their entries, have them keep notes and report their findings to the class. **OL**

D Differentiated Instruction

Intrapersonal To help students understand the role of perspective in primary sources, ask them to recall an important event or performance that they have witnessed. **Ask:** Could you give a complete account of that event to another person? Could someone else give a different but accurate account of the event? If possible, have two students provide first-hand accounts of the same event. **BL**

Practicing the Skill: Answers

Analyzing Primary Sources

1. The writer describes the sights and sounds of the event, which suggests that he personally witnessed it.
2. The phrase "noble beasts" indicates that the author's sympathy lies with the elephants.
3. Answers will vary

Focus

Introduction

Ask volunteers to read aloud the introduction to the Primary Sources & Literature Library. Then discuss with students the types of primary sources and some examples of each.

Teach

S Skill Practice

Applying After students have read the text on pages R32 and R33, have them work in small groups to develop a set of criteria for evaluating the reliability of primary sources. *(Answers will vary but may include these: author is qualified to write on the topic; purpose is primarily to share information; material is presented objectively and without bias; source is timely; facts can be verified in other sources.)* Have groups share criteria and create a class list to display in the room. **OL**

Additional Support

PRIMARY SOURCES & LITERATURE LIBRARY

CONTENTS

LIBRARY

What Is It and How Do I Use It?

The primary sources as defined here are written testimony or documents from a particular era in history or about an important development. The source may be the writings of a noted historian or political leader, or it may be from the diary of someone who lived at the time and recorded the **S** events of the day.

Reading primary sources is an excellent way to understand how and why people believed and acted as they did in the past. While many people might have written down their stories or beliefs, the sources chosen here are from witnesses who were close to events or especially sensitive to them.

Checking Your Sources

When you read primary or secondary sources, you should analyze them to determine if they are dependable or reliable. Historians usually prefer primary sources to secondary sources, but both can be reliable or unreliable, depending on the following factors.

Time Span

With primary sources, it is important to consider how much time passed from the date the event occurred to the date that the primary source was written. Generally, the longer the time span between the event and the account, the less reliable the account is. As time passes, people often forget details and fill in gaps with events that never took place. Although we like to think we remember things exactly as they happened, the fact is, we often remember them very differently than they occurred.

Reliability

Another factor to consider when evaluating a primary source is the writer's background and reliability. When reading a historical document, try to determine if the statements and information can be proved. If the information can be verified as true by independent sources, then it probably is fact.

Teacher Notes

After studying this introduction, students should be able to:

- define and identify types of primary sources, e.g., printed publications: autobiographies, eyewitness periodicals and newspaper articles; oral histories: recorded interviews; visual materials: original paintings, drawings, sculpture, photographs, films, videos, maps; personal records: diaries, journals, letters; artifacts: objects, such as tools or domestic items.
- explain the value of primary sources for readers and historians;
- understand how to evaluate the reliability of primary sources.

Resource for Pages R32–R57

World History Primary Source Document Library CD-ROM

Opinions

When evaluating a primary source, you should also decide whether or not the account has been influenced by emotion, opinion, or exaggeration. Writers sometimes distort the truth to suit their personal purposes. Ask yourself: Why did the person write the account? Do any words or expressions reveal the author's emotions or opinions? **D** Again, you may wish to compare the account with another primary source document about the same event. If the two accounts differ, ask yourself why they differ and then conduct your own outside research to determine which account can be verified by other authoritative sources.

▲ Prussian soldiers

Interpreting Primary Sources

To help you analyze a primary source, use the following steps:

- ***Examine the origins of the document.*** You need to determine if it is indeed a primary source.
- ***Find the main ideas.*** Read the document and summarize the main ideas in your own words.
- ***Reread the document.*** Difficult ideas and historical documents are not always easily understood on the first reading. **C**
- ***Use a variety of resources.*** Use a dictionary, an encyclopedia, and maps to further your understanding of the topic. These resources are tools to help you discover new ideas and knowledge and check the validity of sources.

▲ Polish children at Auschwitz

LIBRARY

C Critical Thinking

Analyzing Primary Sources
Assign pairs of students to find a primary source, such as an article, video, picture or photograph, interview, diary entry, or artifact. Ask them to use these steps to determine what might be learned from their source. Have them present their interpretations to the class. **AL**

D Differentiated Instruction

English Language Learners
Discuss with students how to distinguish between fact and opinion. Tell them that facts can be proven true or false. Opinions, however, cannot and often include words and phrases such as *I think, in my opinion, I believe,* and adjectives or adverbs that make a judgment. Write a selection of facts and opinions on the board and have pairs label each, explaining their decision. **ELL**

Teacher Notes

Through the study of the selections in this library, students should be able to:

- find the main idea in the selections;
- analyze information in a variety of written texts in order to make inferences and generalizations;
- find other examples of primary sources through research;
- compare and contrast different types of primary sources and literature selections;
- distinguish between fact and opinion within a text;
- provide an interpretation of the material in their own words.

Focus

Introduction

The development of agriculture led to the establishment of settled communities. Some of these grew into great civilizations that left a legacy of customs.

Understanding Vocabulary Review the Reader's Dictionary with students to make sure they understand any unfamiliar terms.

Teach

R Reading Strategy

Identifying Ask: What does the Vizier Ptah-hotep mean by the statement: "Wrongdoing has never brought its undertaking into port."? *(He is saying metaphorically that breaking the law or doing what is wrong does not bring fulfillment or reward.)* OL

C Critical Thinking

Analyzing Primary Sources Ask: What clues reveal that Vizier Ptah-hotep expects his son to follow his advice? *(He says that a son should listen to his father's instructions.)* OL

Answers and Additional Support

LIBRARY

The First Civilizations and Empires

Prehistory–A.D. 500

PRIMARY SOURCES

Reader's Dictionary

fraud: deception
imperial: relating to the empire or the emperor
archives: official documents that are preserved for historical or public use
discourse: discussion
decree: an order that has the force of law
calamity: distress or misery

AN EGYPTIAN FATHER'S ADVICE TO HIS SON

Upper-class Egyptians enjoyed compiling collections of wise sayings to provide guidance for leading an upright and successful life. This excerpt from The Instruction of the Vizier Ptah-hotep *dates from around 2450* B.C.

Then he said to his son:

If you are a leader commanding the affairs of the many, seek out for yourself every good deed, until it may be that your own affairs are without wrong. Justice is great, and it is lasting; it has been disturbed since the time of him who made it, whereas there is punishment for him who passes over its laws. Wrongdoing has never brought its undertaking into port. It may be that it is **fraud** that gains riches, but the strength of justice is that it lasts . . . .

If you are a man of standing who is pleasing to god, if he is correct and inclines toward your ways and listens to your instruction, while his manners in your house are fitting, and if he takes care of your property as it should be, seek out for him every useful action. He is your son, . . . you should not cut your heart off from him.

If he [the son] goes astray and does not carry out your instruction, so that his manners in your household are wretched, and he rebels against all that you say, while his mouth runs on in the most wretched talk, quite apart from his experience, while he possesses nothing, you should cast him off: he is not your son at all. He was not really born to you . . . He is one whom god has condemned in the very womb.

◄This rendition of an Egyptian father teaching his son is on the wall of the Tomb of Sennedjem.

Activity: Collaborative Learning

Analyzing Primary Sources Review with students the criteria for evaluating the reliability of primary sources. Then assign groups of students one of the selections on pages R34 or R35. Have each group reread the source and then decide whether or not it is reliable. Encourage students to give examples from the text to support their evaluation. Have each group present their assessment to the class. **Ask:** What evidence might be used to judge the reliability of the first source? *(Other factual sources from the same period of Egyptian history would help to verify or refute the ideas about filial duty presented in the selection.)* How does Li Su's official position affect the reading of the second selection? *(Answers will vary, but students might say that since he was a minister, the source might provide reliable insight into the workings of the Qin government.)* Is Thucydides's account valid? Why or why not? *(Students might say that it is because he is not subjective but rather dispassionate and factual. Also he lived during the time of the plague.)* OL

THE BURNING OF BOOKS

Li Su was a chief minister of the First Qin Emperor. A follower of Legalism, he hoped to eliminate all rival theories of government.

Your servant suggests that all books in the **imperial archives,** save the memoirs of Qin, be burned. All persons in the empire, except members of the Academy of Learned Scholars, in possession of the Book of Odes, the Book of History, and **discourses** of the hundred philosophers [including Confucius] should take them to the local governors and have them burned. Those who dare to talk to each other about the Book of Odes and the Book of History should be executed and their bodies exposed in the market place. Anyone referring to the past to criticize the present should, together with all members of his family, be put to death. Officials who fail to report cases that have come under their attention are equally guilty. After thirty days from the time of issuing the **decree,** those who have not destroyed their books are to be branded and sent to build the Great Wall. Books not to be destroyed will be those on medicine and pharmacy, agriculture and arboriculture [the cultivation of trees and shrubs]. People wishing to pursue learning should take the officials as their teachers.

◄ Chinese scroll

PLAGUE IN ATHENS

Thucydides (471–c. 400 B.C.) is regarded as the first scientific historian. In his account of the plague that broke out in Athens in 430 B.C., Thucydides simply presents the facts, describing the disease's symptoms and impact on the city itself.

. . . Externally, the body was not so very warm to the touch; it was not pale, but reddish, livid, and breaking out in small blisters and ulcers. But internally it was consumed by such a heat that the patients could not bear to have on them the lightest coverings or linen sheets. . . .

The Athenians suffered further hardships owing to the crowding into the city of the people from the country districts; and this affected the new arrivals especially. For since no houses were available for them and they had to live in huts that were stifling in the hot season, they perished in wild disorder. Bodies of dying men lay one upon another, and half-dead people rolled about in the streets and, in their longing for water, near all the fountains. . . . The **calamity** which weighed upon them was so overpowering that men became careless of all law, sacred as well as profane. And the customs which they had hitherto observed regarding burial were all thrown into confusion, and they buried their dead each one as he could. . . .

DOCUMENT-BASED QUESTIONS

1. **Evaluating** Does any part of the Egyptian father's advice have value today for sons or daughters? Be specific and support your answer.
2. **Drawing Conclusions** Why did Li Su think that burning books would eliminate all rival theories of government?
3. **Listing** What hardships did newcomers to Athens face during the time of the plague?

LIBRARY

C1 Critical Thinking

Making Inferences Ask: Why does Li Su call for such harsh punishment for anyone caught "referring to the past to criticize the present"? *(He does not want ideas from the past or the actions of previous rulers to show up the flaws in the Qin emperor and lead to the weakening of his power, since this, in turn, would cause Li Su to lose status and power.)* **OL**

S Skill Practice

Analyzing Ask: Why were these books spared destruction? *(These books contained practical and helpful facts, not ideas that could lead to rebellion or inflame discontent.)* **OL**

C2 Critical Thinking

Determining Cause and Effect Ask: According to Thucydides, how did the plague affect Athens? *(Order broke down. The dead and sick filled the streets. Laws were ignored, and customs that determined the burial of the dead were overlooked in people's haste and desperation to dispose of bodies.)* **OL**

Assess/Close

Have students answer the Document-Based Questions.

Document-Based Questions

1. Answers will vary, but students should offer statements from the reading that would or would not apply to contemporary families.
2. By destroying the books and banning discussion of rival theories of government, the rival theories would be lost.
3. Newcomers faced overcrowding, a lack of housing, and rapid spread of disease.

Focus

Introduction

The literature of a culture can serve as a window into its values, traditions, and customs. The interactions of the two heroes in this excerpt provide a glimpse of what mattered to the ancient Greeks.

Understanding Vocabulary
Review the Reader's Dictionary with students to make sure they understand any unfamiliar terms.

Teach

S Skill Practice

Analyzing Ask: Why has Hektor been fleeing Achilles? *(Answers may include that Hektor was afraid of Achilles and what he would do.)* BL

C Critical Thinking

Predicting Consequences
Ask: What is foreshadowed by Athena's aid to Achilles? *(Achilles will be victorious over Hektor because he has the goddess helping him.)* OL

Answers and Additional Support

LIBRARY

The First Civilizations and Empires

Prehistory–A.D. 500

WORLD LITERATURE

Homer ▶

About the Author

Homer is probably one of the best known figures to have emerged from Greek antiquity. Writing in the eighth century B.C., Homer's most famous works are the *Iliad* and the *Odyssey*. These works mark the beginnings of Greek literature and are used as models even in contemporary work. The *Iliad* is the story of the Trojan War, and the *Odyssey* recounts the challenges of one Greek hero, Odysseus (also known as "Ulysses"), in returning to his homeland.

Reader's Dictionary

covenant: a binding agreement or promise
spoil: to plunder from an enemy in war

FROM THE *ILIAD*

By Homer, translated by Samuel Butler

In the Iliad, Hektor was the Trojans' hero and son of King Priam. Achilles, the Greeks' hero, was the son of Peleus. Hektor killed Achilles' friend Patroklos, and Achilles was determined to avenge the death.

S Hektor was first to speak. "I will no longer flee you, son of Peleus," said he, "as I have been doing hitherto. . . .[Let] me either slay or be slain, for I am in the mind to face you. Let us, then, give pledges to one another by our gods; . . . [that if] I take your life, I am not to treat your dead body in any unseemly fashion, but when I have stripped you of your armor, I am to give up your body to the Achaeans, And do you likewise."

Achilles glared at him and answered, "Fool . . . [there] can be no **covenants** between men and lions, wolves and lambs can never be of one mind, but hate each other out and out. . . . Therefore there can be no understanding between you and me . . . till one or other shall fall. . . . You have no more chance, and Pallas Athena will forthwith vanquish you by my spear: you shall now pay me in full for the grief you have caused me on account of my comrades whom you have killed in battle."

C He poised his spear as he spoke and hurled it. Hektor saw it coming and avoided it; he watched it and crouched down so that it flew over his head and stuck in the ground beyond; Athena then snatched it up and gave it back to Achilles without Hektor's seeing her; Hektor thereon said . . . "You have missed your aim, Achilles. . . . [And] now for your own part avoid my spear if you can—would that you might receive the whole of it into

◀ Athena

Activity: Collaborative Learning

Drawing Conclusions Refer students back to the first paragraph of the excerpt. Point out that Hektor is anxious to exchange a pledge with Achilles that each will treat the other's dead body with respect. **Ask:** What role did pledges serve in the Greek culture? *(A verbal pledge was as binding as a legal contract is today.)* Have students work in groups to analyze the rest of the selection to discover more about what the ancient Greeks valued. Suggest that students focus on the actions and words of the characters as well as the outcome of their confrontation. Have groups share their conclusions and as a class summarize what was most important to the ancient Greeks. **Ask:** What function did the oral literary tradition serve in ancient cultures? *(Answers will vary, but students may say that the epics kept alive the values of the culture and set standards for future generations.)* OL your body; if you were once dead the Trojans would find the war an easier matter, for it is you who have harmed them most."

He poised his spear as he spoke and hurled it. His aim was sure for he hit the middle of Achilles' shield, but the spear rebounded from it, and did not pierce it. Hektor was angry when he saw that the weapon had sped from his hand in vain, and stood there in dismay for he had no second spear. . . . [Then] he said to himself, "Alas! The gods have lured me on to my destruction. . . . [Death] is now indeed exceedingly near at hand and there is no way out of it. . . . My doom has come upon me; let me not then die ingloriously and without a struggle, but let me first do some great thing that shall be told among men hereafter."

As he spoke he drew the keen blade that hung so great and strong by his side, and gathering himself together he sprang on Achilles . . . . Achilles mad with rage darted towards him. . . . He eyed [Hektor's] fair flesh over and over to see where he could best wound it, but all was protected by the goodly armor of which Hektor had **spoiled** Patroklos after he had slain him, save only the throat where the collar-bones divide the neck from the shoulders, and this is the quickest place for the life-breath to escape: here then did Achilles strike him as he was coming on towards him, and the point of his spear went right through the fleshy part of the neck, but it did not sever his windpipe so that he could still speak. Hektor fell headlong, and Achilles vaunted over him saying, "Hektor, you deemed that you should come off scatheless when you were spoiling Patroklos. . . . Fool that you were: for I, his comrade, mightier far than he, was still left behind him at the ships, and now I have laid you low. The Achaeans shall give him all due funeral rites, while dogs and vultures shall work their will upon yourself."

Then Hektor said, as the life-breath ebbed out of him, "I pray you . . . , let not dogs devour me at the ships of the Achaeans, but accept the rich treasure of gold and bronze which my father and mother will offer you, and send my body home, that the Trojans and their wives may give me my dues of fire when I am dead."

Achilles glared at him and answered, "Dog . . . [though] Priam . . . should bid them offer me your weight in gold, even so your mother shall never lay you out and make lament over the son she bore, but dogs and vultures shall eat you utterly up."

Hektor with his dying breath then said, "I know you what you are, and was sure that I should not move you, for your heart is hard as iron. . . ."

When he had thus said the shrouds of death's final outcome enfolded him, whereon his life-breath went out of him and flew down to the house of Hades, lamenting its sad fate that it should enjoy youth and strength no longer.

LIBRARY

DOCUMENT-BASED QUESTIONS

1. **Describing** How does Achilles plan to avenge his friend Patroklos' death beyond killing Hektor?
2. **Explaining** Explain Achilles' concern with Hektor's armor.
3. **Interpreting** What does Hektor's last request reveal about Greek attitudes towards death?

Applications Activity
Outline a story for a modern epic. Who would be your hero and why?

R Reading Strategy

Identifying Discuss what Hektor realizes at this moment. **Ask:** What does Hektor's decision reveal about his character? *(He has courage. He knows he cannot avoid death, but he wishes to die bravely so that he will be remembered by generations to come.)* OL

C Critical Thinking

Making Inferences Ask: Why does Achilles refuse to extend respect to Hektor's dead body? *(He is filled with rage and grief at the death of his good friend Patroklos. He wants to make the Trojans suffer for his pain. His actions of killing Hektor and dishonoring his body will devastate the Trojans.)* AL

Assess/Close

Have students answer the Document-Based Questions.

Document-Based Questions

1. He will dishonor the body of Hektor by leaving it exposed to the elements and allowing dogs and vultures to feed upon it. In contrast, Patroklos will be given full funeral rites by the Achaeans.
2. Hektor stripped Patroklos of his armor and is wearing it to face Achilles.
3. They believed that the bodies of the dead were to be respected and buried with ceremony and in accordance with custom.

Applications Activity Answers will vary. Students' outlines should describe traits of the hero that reflect values of modern society and a conflict that is relevant to today.

Focus

Introduction

In addition to developing understanding of a period or movement in history, primary sources can also give insight into the conditions of the people themselves.

Understanding Vocabulary Review the Reader's Dictionary with students to make sure they understand any unfamiliar terms.

Teach

R Reading Strategy

Identifying Ask: How does Ayesha support her claim that Muhammad was an ordinary man? *(He laughed and smiled. He did necessary tasks. He liked to sew. He opted for the easier of two choices, if it would not lead to any wrong, and never indulged in revenge.)* **OL**

S Skill Practice

Analyzing Ask: How would historians validate this source? *(They would look for other sources that matched the description and they would find who recorded Ayesha's comments.)* **OL**

Answers and Additional Support

LIBRARY

New Patterns of Civilization

A.D. 400–1500

PRIMARY SOURCES

Reader's Dictionary

cobble: to repair shoes

accrue: to happen as a direct result of some other action

err: to make mistakes

remonstrate: to scold or reproach

lamentation: an expression of mourning

▲Woman playing a lute

MUHAMMAD'S WIFE REMEMBERS THE PROPHET

What kind of man was Muhammad that he could achieve such profound changes in Arab civilization? This description comes from his wife, Ayesha, the daughter of Abu Bakr.

When Ayesha was questioned about Muhammad she used to say:

R He was a man just such as yourselves. He laughed often and smiled much. He would mend his clothes and **cobble** his shoes. He used to help me in my household duties; but what he did oftenest was to sew. If he had the choice between two matters, he would choose the easiest, so long as no sin could **accrue** therefrom. He never took revenge excepting where the honor of God was concerned. When angry with anyone, he would say, "What hath taken such a one that he should soil his forehead in the mud."

His humility was shown by his accepting the invitation even of slaves. . . . He would say: "I sit at meals as a servant does and I eat like a servant. For I really am a servant."

Muhammad hated nothing more than lying. Whenever he knew that any of his followers had **erred** in this respect, he would hold himself aloof from them until he was assured of their repentance.

He did not speak rapidly, running the words into one another, but enunciated each syllable distinctly, so that what he said was imprinted in the memory of everyone who heard him.

S He used to stand for such a long time at his prayers that his legs would swell. When **remonstrated,** he said: "What! Shall I not behave as a thankful servant should?"

He refused to accept presents that had been offered as alms. Neither would he allow anyone in his family to use what had been brought as alms. "For," said he, "alms are the impurity of mankind."

Activity: Collaborative Learning

Comparing and Contrasting Ask: How might it be proven whether Christine de Pizan's description of the noblewoman's responsibilities is accurate or not? Explain. *(Answers will vary, but students might say that they would look for other sources that reinforce or contradict the ideas in the selection.)* Have students work in small groups to find out more about the lives of medieval noblewomen. Encourage students to look for primary sources, including illustrations that show the responsibilities that these women had. Ask groups to organize posters with the information they find. Let students explain their posters, comparing their information to the content of Christine de Pizan's account. As a class, draw conclusions about the validity of her portrayal of a noblewoman's life. **AL**

A Woman May Need to Have the Heart of a Man

Christine de Pizan was widowed at age 25. She supported her three children by copying manuscripts, compiling a manual of instructions for knights, and writing books. The following is from her 1405 work, The Treasure of the City of Ladies.

It is the responsibility of every baron to spend the least possible time at his manors and his own estate, for his duties are to bear arms, to attend the court of his prince and to travel. Now, his lady stays behind and must take his place. . . . Her men should be able to rely on her for all kinds of protection in the absence of their lord. . . . She ought to know how to use weapons and be familiar with everything that pertains to them, so that she may be ready to command her men if the need arises. She should know how to launch an attack or to defend against one.

In addition she will do well to be a very good manager of the estate. . . . She will busy herself around the house; she will find plenty of orders to give. She will have the animals brought in at the right time [and] take care how the shepherd looks after them. . . .

In the winter-time, she will have her men cut her willow groves and make vine props to sell in the season. She will never let them be idle. . . . She will employ her women . . . to attend to the livestock, . . . [and] to weed the courtyards. . . . There is a great need to run an estate well, and the one who is most diligent and careful about it is more than wise and ought to be highly praised.

C1

◄ A wandering Buddhist sage

The Buddha's Sermon

Siddhartha Gautama, the Buddha, gave sermons in India, which were written down after 250 B.C. An excerpt from one of these follows. C2

1. Now this, O monks, is the noble truth of pain: birth is painful, old age is painful, sickness is painful, death is painful, sorrow, **lamentation,** dejection, and despair are painful. Contact with unpleasant things is painful, not getting what one wishes is painful. In short the five khandhas of grasping are painful.
2. Now this, O monks, is the noble truth of the cause of pain: that craving which leads to rebirth, combined with pleasure and lust, finding pleasure here and there, namely, the craving for passion, the craving for existence, the craving for non-existence. S
3. Now this, O monks, is the noble truth of the cessation of pain: the cessation without a remainder of that craving, abandonment, forsaking, release, non-attachment.
4. Now this, O monks, is the noble truth of the way that leads to the cessation of pain: this is the noble Eightfold Path. . . .

DOCUMENT-BASED QUESTIONS

1. **Describing** According to Ayesha, what kind of man was Muhammad? Did he behave like a ruler?
2. **Identifying** What are some of the duties and responsibilities of the medieval gentlewoman, according to Christine de Pizan's account?
3. **Summarizing** According to the Buddha, what is the cause of pain?

LIBRARY

C1 Critical Thinking

Drawing Conclusions Ask: How did the feudal system increase the responsibility of noblewomen? *(A noble was required to "bear arms, to attend the court of his prince, and to travel." The noblewomen had to manage and defend their estates.)* **OL**

C2 Critical Thinking

Determining Cause and Effect Ask: How did the recording of the Buddha's sermons in writing affect the influence of his teachings? *(Once the sermons were written down, many more people could gain access to his ideas.)* **OL**

S Skill Practice

Analyzing Ask: What issues would have to be considered when evaluating the reliability of this source? *(Centuries have elapsed since the recording of these sermons. Although it might be assumed that his words are not verbatim, it would be important to know who wrote down the ideas and from what source to judge the reliability.)* **AL**

Assess/Close

Have students answer the Document-Based Questions.

Document-Based Questions

1. Muhammad was an ordinary man who honored God and avoided anger, lying, and the personal use of alms. Students should present examples of why they agree or disagree that Muhammad behaved like a ruler.
2. According to de Pizan, women should know how to run an estate. They must be familiar with the use of weapons and capable of launching or defending against attack. They must supervise the workers and know the schedule of tasks that must be performed to keep the farm running smoothly. They must not allow workers to be idle and must be diligent and careful.
3. Craving, or desire, causes pain.

Focus

Introduction

Through their imagery, these poems paint a picture of the landscape of China as it appeared to Li Bo in the eighth century.

Understanding Vocabulary Review the Reader's Dictionary with students to make sure they understand any unfamiliar terms.

Teach

R Reading Strategy

Questioning Ask: How do the images in these lines convey the mixed feelings of the speaker? *(The simile comparing his mind to a floating wide cloud shows that he is already thinking of the journey that lies before him. But, the sunset shows his sadness.)* OL

D Differentiated Instruction

Visual/Spatial Read the poem aloud. Point out the vivid words and phrases that Li Bo uses to describe the dawn scene. Then ask students to draw or paint the image they visualize when they read this poem. BL

Answers and Additional Support

LIBRARY

New Patterns of Civilization

A.D. 400–1500

WORLD LITERATURE

◄ Li Bo

About the Author

Li Bo was born in A.D. 701 in western China. People began praising his beautiful poems even before he reached adulthood. Throughout his life he traveled extensively in China, amazing people with his ability to compose insightful, touching poems. He wrote about the world around him, the people he met, and the emotions he felt. By the time of his death in A.D. 762, he was regarded as one of China's greatest poets, a distinction he still holds today.

Reader's Dictionary

sparse: few and scattered

thrush: a type of small to medium sized bird that is an excellent singer

brooklet: a small brook or creek

FIVE POEMS

By Li Bo

In the following poems, Li Bo interprets parting from a friend, life as a journey, and his experience with his homeland.

Taking Leave of a Friend

Blue mountains to the north of the walls,
White river winding about them;
Here we must make separation
And go out through a thousand miles of dead grass.

R

Mind like a floating wide cloud,
Sunset like the parting of old acquaintances
Who bow over their clasped hands at a distance.
Our horses neigh to each other as we are departing.

Clearing at Dawn

The fields are chill, the **sparse** rain has stopped;
The colours of Spring teem on every side.
With leaping fish the blue pond is full;
With singing **thrushes** the green boughs droop.
D The flowers of the field have dabbled their powdered cheeks;
The mountain grasses are bent level at the waist.
By the bamboo stream the last fragment of cloud
Blown by the wind slowly scatters away.

◄ This painting is titled *Spring Dawn Over Elixir Terrace.*

Activity: Interdisciplinary Connection

Literature Have pairs of students work together to create an anthology of Li Bo's poems. Ask them to find copies of his poems online or in printed resources and to choose several to include in their own collections. They might select poems that develop a theme, follow a chronological order, or simply appeal to them. Have students then find or draw illustrations to match the poems' content or imagery. Finally, have pairs write a short synopsis of each poem to include in their books. After students have completed their anthologies, have them present one or two poems to the class. Discuss the meanings of the poems and Li Bo's style in each. **Ask:** What can be learned about the Chinese culture from Li Bo's poetry? OL

Hard Is the Journey
Gold vessels of fine wines,
thousands a gallon,
Jade dishes of rare meats,
costing more thousands,
I lay my chopsticks down,
no more can banquet,
And draw my sword and stare
wildly about me:

Ice bars my way to cross
the Yellow River,
Snows from dark skies to climb
the T'ai-hang Mountains!

At peace I drop a hook
into a **brooklet,**
At once I'm in a boat
but sailing sunward . . .

(Hard is the Journey,
Hard is the Journey,
So many turnings,
And now where am I?) **C**

So when a breeze breaks waves,
bringing fair weather,
I set a cloud for sails,
cross the blue oceans!

Listening to a Flute in Yellow Crane Pavilion
I came here a wanderer
thinking of home
remembering my far away Ch'ang-an.
And then, from deep in Yellow Crane
Pavilion,
I heard a beautiful bamboo flute
play "Falling Plum Blossoms."
It was late spring in a city by the river.

▲ *Landscape of the Four Seasons* by Shen shih-Ch'ung

In the Mountains on a Summer Day
Gently I stir a white feather fan,
With open shirt sitting in a green wood.
I take off my cap and hang it on a jutting
stone;
A wind from the pine-tree trickles on my
bare head. **S**

LIBRARY

DOCUMENT-BASED QUESTIONS

1. **Identifying** What detail in "Taking Leave of a Friend" reveals a custom in Li Bo's times?
2. **Interpreting** What is the meaning of the last line of "Listening to a Flute in Yellow Crane Pavilion"?
3. **Drawing Conclusions** Li Bo describes beauty and peace and luxury in "Hard Is the Journey". Why does he call the journey "hard"?

Applications Activity
Write a poem describing your hometown. Make sure to include a description of something unique to that area.

C Critical Thinking

Making Inferences Ask: What might the journey represent metaphorically? *(The journey might be life. There are many obstacles and paths that might be taken, times of great happiness and success, times of confusion and fear.)* **AL**

S Skill Practice

Analyzing Discuss what Li Bo is describing in this poem. **Ask:** How does Li Bo's poem transcend its historical context? *(This poem describes an experience that is universal—enjoying cool shade on a hot day. The subject of his poem is not limited to a particular time, place, or event.)* **OL**

Assess/Close

Have students answer the Document-Based Questions.

Document-Based Questions

1. The poem describes the custom of two friends saying goodbye by bowing over their clasped hands.
2. The music transports the speaker in his mind to his home—a city by the river.
3. The journey is hard because there are many twists and turns in it that prevent the speaker from seeing his destination. He is sidetracked and distracted from his goal and sometimes wonders where he is and where he is going.

Applications Activity Students' poems should include vivid and precise adjectives, adverbs, nouns, and verbs. Encourage them to use literary devices such as similes and metaphors.

Focus

Introduction

These sources were written during a time of robust intellectual thought, when new discoveries and philosophies sparked people to challenge and debate an enormous breadth of ideas.

Understanding Vocabulary
Review the Reader's Dictionary with students to make sure they understand any unfamiliar terms.

Teach

C Critical Thinking

Comparing and Contrasting
Ask: In what ways do Luther's and Zwingli's interpretations of the Last Supper differ? *(Luther follows a literal interpretation of the Last Supper—God is present in both heaven and in the sacrament of communion. Zwingli interprets the passages figuratively, saying that "one and the same body cannot possibly be in different places.")* **AL**

Answers and Additional Support

The Early Modern World

1350–1815

PRIMARY SOURCES

Reader's Dictionary

contention: point made in an argument
Scripture: passage from the Bible
revered: honored or respected
hemp: a fiber from the mulberry bush
imprescriptible: cannot be taken away by law

LIBRARY

▲ Martin Luther

Ulrich Zwingli ▼

A REFORMATION DEBATE

In 1529 Martin Luther and Ulrich Zwingli debated over the sacrament of the Lord's Supper, or Communion.

LUTHER: Although I have no intention of changing my mind, which is firmly made up, I will nevertheless present the grounds of my belief and show where the others are in error. . . .Your basic **contentions** are these: In the last analysis you wish to prove that a body cannot be in two places at once, and you produce arguments about the unlimited body which are based on natural reason. I do not question how Christ can be God and man and how the two natures can be joined. For God is more powerful than all our ideas, and we must submit to his word.

Prove that Christ's body is not there where the **Scripture** says, "This is my body!" God is beyond all mathematics and the words of God are to be **revered** and carried out in awe. It is God who commands, "Take, eat, this is my body." I request, therefore, valid scriptural proof to the contrary.

ZWINGLI: I insist that the words of the Lord's Supper must be figurative. This is ever **C** apparent, and even required by the article of faith; "taken up into heaven, seated at the right hand of the Father." Otherwise, it would be absurd to look for him in the Lord's Supper at the same time that Christ is telling us that he is in heaven. One and the same body cannot possibly be in different places. . . .

LUTHER: I call upon you as before: your basic contentions are shaky. Give way, and give glory to God!

ZWINGLI: And we call upon you to give glory to God and to quit begging the question! The issue at stake is this: Where is the proof of your position?

LUTHER: It is your point that must be proved, not mine. But let us stop this sort of thing. It serves no purpose.

ZWINGLI: It certainly does! It is for you to prove that the passage in John 6 speaks of a physical meal.

LUTHER: You express yourself poorly. . . . You're going nowhere.

Activity: Collaborative Learning

Identifying Main Ideas Tell students that the debate between Martin Luther and Ulrich Zwingli illustrates some of the complex issues that split the Protestant Reformation. Have students work in pairs and identify in the document Luther's main idea or argument and Zwingli's main idea or argument. Then have pairs review the document and identify the supporting details that each uses to support his argument or disprove the other's. Have students use the main ideas and supporting details they have identified to write a statement that explains one of the central issues at the heart of the split in the Protestant Reformation. **Ask:** Based on the issues that divided the two religious leaders, was establishment of separate churches the only solution? Explain. Have students support their opinion with details from the text and their prior knowledge. **OL**

The Silk Industry in China

During the 1600s Sung Ying-Hsing wrote a book on Chinese industry called T'ien-kung K'ai-wu (Chinese Technology in the Seventeenth Century), *which included sections on the production of silk.*

. . . Members of the aristocracy are clothed in flowing robes decorated with patterns of magnificent mountain dragons, and they are rulers of the country. Those of lowly stations would be dressed in **hempen** jackets and cotton garments to protect themselves from the cold winter and cover their nakedness in summer, in order to distinguish themselves from the birds and beasts. Therefore nature **R** has provided the materials for clothing. Of these, the vegetable [plant] ones are cotton, hemp, *meng* hemp, and creeper hemp; those derived from birds, animals, and insects are furs, woolens, silk, and spun silk. . . .

But, although silk looms are to be found in all parts of the country, how many persons have actually seen the remarkable functioning of the draw-loom: Such words as "orderly government" [*chih,* i.e., the word used in silk reeling], "chaos" [*luan,* i.e., when the fibers are entangled], "knowledge or good policy" [*ching-lun,* i.e., the warp thread and the woven pattern] are known by every schoolboy, but is it not regrettable that he should never see the actual things that gave rise to these words?

▲ Emperor's robe, Qing dynasty

Declaration of the Rights of Woman and the Female Citizen

Olympe de Gouges composed her own Declaration of the Rights of Woman and the Female Citizen *in 1791. Following are excerpts.* **D**

1. Woman is born free and lives as equal to man in her rights. Social distinctions can be based only on the common utility.
2. The purpose of any political association is the conservation of the natural and **imprescriptible** rights of woman and man; these rights are liberty, property, security, and especially resistance to oppression. . . .
4. Liberty and justice consist of restoring all that belongs to others; thus, the only limits on the exercise of the natural rights of woman are perpetual male tyranny; these **W** limits are to be reformed by the laws of nature and reason. . . .
6. The law must be . . . the same for all: male and female citizens. . . .
7. No woman is an exception; she is accused, arrested, and detained in cases determined by law. Women, like men, obey this rigorous law. . . .
11. The free communication of thoughts and opinions is one of the most precious rights of woman, since that liberty assured the recognition of children by their fathers. . . .

LIBRARY

Document-Based Questions

1. **Drawing Conclusions** Was a conclusion reached in the debate presented between Luther and Zwingli?
2. **Listing** According to Sung Ying-Hsing, from what two sources was all clothing made?
3. **Defending** Olympe de Gouges states that free communication of thoughts is one of the most precious rights of women. Do you agree or disagree?

R Reading Strategy

Inferring Ask: Was silk worn by all members of Chinese society? *(The selection says that "those of lowly station would be dressed in hempen jackets and cotton garments." Students might infer that only members of the aristocracy dressed in silk.)* **OL**

D Differentiated Instruction

Verbal/Linguistic Ask: Why would readers of Olympe de Gouges's document have considered it unusual? *(In 1791 women throughout the world enjoyed few political and economic rights.)* **OL**

W Writing Support

Expository Writing Point out that the declaration written by Olympe de Gouges provides a look at the seeds of the women's suffrage movement. Ask students to find out more about the circumstances of women in the 1700s. Have them then write an essay explaining what these rights would mean to eighteenth century women. **AL**

Assess/Close

Have students answer the Document-Based Questions.

Document-Based Questions

1. A conclusion was not reached because neither religious leader would compromise on his position.
2. The two sources are "vegetable ones" (plants) and those derived from birds, animals, and insects.
3. Most students will probably agree on the basis of equality and the right to free speech enjoyed by citizens of the United States.

Focus

Introduction

Candide is a satire through which Voltaire argues for freedom of thought, social justice, and religious tolerance, all of which were Enlightenment ideals. This excerpt is based on his own experience with the Prussian Army.

Understanding Vocabulary Review the Reader's Dictionary with students to make sure they understand any unfamiliar terms.

Teach

R Reading Strategy

Predicting Remind students that when they read works of fiction, they should use the clues in the text to guess what might happen next. **Ask:** Why are the Prussian soldiers interested in Candide? *(They think he would make a good soldier.)* What is their intention in paying for his refreshments? *(They plan to lure him into the army in this way.)* **BL**

Answers and Additional Support

The Early Modern World

1350–1815

WORLD LITERATURE

LIBRARY

◀ Voltaire

About the Author

Voltaire was born François-Marie Arouet on November 21, 1694. He assumed the pen name "Voltaire" in 1718. Voltaire was a critical and satiric writer who used his wit to attack both church and state. *Candide* is one of Voltaire's most brilliant and most well-known works.

Reader's Dictionary

bulwark: strong support or protection

summarily: without delay or formality

FROM *CANDIDE*

By Voltaire

Candide has been taught that "everything is for the best." However, his adventures usually prove the opposite. Here, he has just been cast out of a castle. The "men in blue" he meets are army recruiters for Frederick the Great, king of Prussia, who was at war with the French when Voltaire wrote Candide.

Candide . . . dragged himself into the neighboring village, which was called Waldberghofftrarbkdikdorff; he was penniless, famished, and exhausted. At the door of a tavern he paused forlornly. Two men dressed in blue [Prussian soldiers] took note of him:

—Look, chum, said one of them, there's a likely young fellow of just about the right size.

They approached Candide and invited him very politely to dine with them.

—Gentlemen, Candide replied with charming modesty, I'm honored by your invitation, but I really don't have enough money to pay my share.

—My dear sir, said one of the blues, people **R** of your appearance and your merit don't have to pay; aren't you five feet five inches tall?

—Yes, gentlemen, that is indeed my stature, said he, making a bow.

—Then, sire, you must be seated at once; not only will we pay your bill this time, we will never allow a man like you to be short of money; for men were made only to render one another mutual aid.

—You are quite right, said Candide; it is just as Dr. Pangloss always told me, and I see clearly that everything is for the best.

They beg him to accept a couple of crowns, he takes them, and offers an I.O.U.; they won't hear of it, and all sit down at table together.

—Don't you love dearly . . .?

—I do indeed, says he, I dearly love Miss Cunégonde.

Activity: Interdisciplinary Connection

Literature Students may be unfamiliar with Voltaire's social satire. Identify points in the beginning of the excerpt where Voltaire's satire is clear. For example, have students try to pronounce the name of the town in the first sentence. **Ask:** What is Voltaire making fun of by using this name? *(the German language)* Why did the Prussian soldiers think Candide would make a good recruit? *(his height)* What is Voltaire satirizing here? *(military recruitment standards)* Point out that puzzling or nonsensical parts of the excerpt may be just the places where Voltaire is satirizing something. Have students create a list of these places in the text as they read. As a class, discuss what point Voltaire is making in each instance. **OL**

—No, no, says one of the gentlemen, we are asking if you don't love dearly the King of the Bulgars [Frederick the Great].

—Not in the least, says he, I never laid eyes on him.

—What's that you say? He's the most charming of kings, and we must drink his health.

—Oh, gladly, gentlemen; and he drinks.

—That will do, they tell him; you are now the **bulwark,** the support, the defender, the hero of the Bulgars; your fortune is made and your future assured.

Promptly they slip irons on his legs and lead him to the regiment. There they cause him to right face, left face, present arms, order arms, aim, fire, doubletime, and they give him thirty strokes of the rod. Next day he does the drill a little less awkwardly and gets only twenty strokes; the third day, they give him only ten, and he is regarded by his comrades as a prodigy.

Candide, quite thunderstruck, did not yet understand very clearly how he was a hero. One fine spring morning he took it into his head to go for a walk, stepping straight out as if it were a privilege of the human race, as of animals in general, to use his legs as he chose. He had scarcely covered two leagues when four other heroes [Prussian soldiers], each six feet tall, overtook him, bound him, and threw him into a dungeon. At the court-martial they asked which he preferred, to be flogged thirty-six times by the entire regiment or to receive **summarily** a dozen bullets in the brain. In vain did he argue that the human will is free and insist that he preferred neither alternative; he had to choose; by virtue of the divine gift called "liberty" he decided to run the gauntlet thirty-six times, and actually endured two floggings. The regiment was composed of two thousand men. That made four thousand strokes. As they were preparing for the third beating, Candide, who could endure no more, begged as a special favor that they would have the goodness to smash his head. His plea was granted; they bandaged his eyes and made him kneel down. The King of the Bulgars [Frederick the Great], passing by at this moment, was told of the culprit's crime; and as this king had a rare genius, he understood, from everything they told him of Candide, that this was a young metaphysician, extremely ignorant of the ways of the world, so he granted his royal pardon, with a generosity which will be praised in every newspaper in every age. A worthy surgeon cured Candide in three weeks with the ointments described by Dioscorides. He already had a bit of skin back and was able to walk when the King of the Bulgars went to war with the King of the Abares.

Frederick the Great, king of Prussia

Nothing could have been so fine, so brisk, so brilliant, so well-drilled as the two armies. The trumpets, the fifes, the oboes, the drums, and the cannon produced such a harmony as was never heard in hell. First the cannons battered down about six thousand men on each side; then volleys of musket fire removed from the best of worlds about nine or ten thousand rascals who were cluttering up its surface.

DOCUMENT-BASED QUESTIONS

1. **Explaining** Explain the irony of the soldiers' statement, "your fortune is made and your future assured."
2. **Making Connections** Why is Candide punished? How does this relate to the philosophy of the Enlightenment?
3. **Analyzing** What is Voltaire's attitude toward the "King of the Bulgars"?

Applications Activity
Write a satirical piece criticizing something about a television show or movie. Remember that a satire does not directly attack but criticizes by showing how ridiculous something is.

LIBRARY

C Critical Thinking

Analyzing Primary Sources
Read the following sentence to the class: "One fine spring morning he took it into his head to go for a walk, stepping straight out as if it were a privilege of the human race . . . to use his legs as he chose." **Ask:** How does this passage relate to the following quote by Voltaire: "Liberty is the life of the soul"? How does this passage relate to the ideals of the Enlightenment? *(Answers may include that Voltaire is satirizing the people's belief that they possess liberty and, therefore, meaningful lives. The consequences of Candide's decision show the gulf between reality and the ideals of the Enlightenment.)* **AL**

R Reading Strategy

Making Connections Ask: What is the serious point that Voltaire is making here? *(Answers will vary but may explain how false "liberty" limits the exercise of free will even as it appears to be allowing for that freedom.)* **OL**

Assess/Close

Have students answer the Document-Based Questions.

Document-Based Questions

1. Soldiers were poorly paid, and their future was most likely death in battle.
2. Candide is punished for running away, thinking he had free will. The concept of free will is a central idea of the Enlightenment.
3. The king is modeled on Frederick the Great, at whose court Voltaire lived for some time. The fact that he recognizes Candide's action as a mistake only a metaphysician (philosopher) would make is a dig at Frederick, who was not as enlightened as he liked to think himself.

Applications Activity Students' responses should clearly show the object of their satire and reveal their criticisms of it.

Focus

Introduction

These sources reveal insights into the class systems and social and labor conditions of those living under imperial rule in nineteenth-century Russia, France, and India.

Understanding Vocabulary Review the Reader's Dictionary with students to make sure they understand any unfamiliar terms.

Teach

D Differentiated Instruction

Interpersonal Have students work in groups to create a time line of social, economic, and political developments that took place in Russia prior to the issue of the czar's *Emancipation Manifesto.* OL

R Reading Strategy

Identifying Ask: What is the czar's purpose in this paragraph? *(He wishes to portray himself as sympathetic to the plight of the serfs and an advocate of their cause.)* OL

Answers and Additional Support

LIBRARY

An Era of European Imperialism

1800–1914

PRIMARY SOURCES

Reader's Dictionary

autocrat: a monarch who rules with unlimited authority

close: an enclosed area of land

abject: existing in a low state or condition

infanticide: killing an infant

resuscitation: restoration or renewal

▲ Czar Alexander II

IMPERIAL DECREE TO FREE THE SERFS

D *In 1861 the Russian czar Alexander II issued the* Emancipation Manifesto, *an imperial decree to free his country's serfs.*

By the grace of God, we, Alexander II, Emperor and **Autocrat** of all the Russias, King of Poland, Grand Duke of Finland, etc., to all our faithful subjects, make known:

Examining the condition of classes and professions comprising the state, we became convinced that the present state legislation favors the upper and middle classes, . . . but does not equally favor the serfs. . . . These facts had already attracted the attention of our predecessors, and they had adopted measures aimed at improving the conditions of the peasants. But decrees on free farmers and serfs have been carried out on a limited scale only.

We thus came to the conviction that the work of a serious improvement of the condition of the peasants was a sacred inheritance R bequeathed to us by our ancestors, a mission which, in the course of events Divine Providence called upon us to fulfill. . . .

In virtue of the new dispositions above mentioned, the peasants attached to the soil will be invested within a term fixed by the law with all the rights of free cultivators. . . .

At the same time, they are granted the right of purchasing their **close,** and, with the consent of the proprietors, they may acquire in full property the arable lands and other appurtenances [rights of way] which are allotted to them as a permanent holding. By the acquisition in full property of the quantity of land fixed, the peasants are free from their obligations towards the proprietors for land thus purchased, and they enter definitely into the condition of free peasants-landholders.

Activity: Economics Connection

Making Inferences Ask: What economic conditions did the peasants have to fulfill to become free peasant-landholders? *(They had to purchase the enclosed land on which they worked to be "free from their obligations towards the proprietors.")* Ask students to combine information in this primary source with their prior knowledge of peasant life in imperialist Russia to make inferences about some of the obstacles peasants might have experienced in fulfilling the economic conditions required to gain their freedom. Discuss the historical context of the declaration and the czar's probable motive in issuing it. AL

THE UNFORTUNATE SITUATION OF WORKING WOMEN

This article was published in L'Atelier, *a Parisian workingman's newspaper, in 1842.*

Although women's work is less productive for society than that of men, it does, nevertheless, have a certain value, and, moreover, there are professions that only women can practice. For these, women are indispensable. . . . It is these very workers in all these necessary trades who earn the least and who are subject to the longest layoffs. Since for so much work they earn only barely enough to live from day to day, it happens that during times of unemployment they sink into **abject** poverty.

Who has not heard of the women silkworkers' dirty, unhealthy, and badly paid work; of the women in the spinning and weaving factories working fourteen to sixteen hours (except for one hour for both meals); always standing, without a single minute for repose, putting forth an enormous amount of effort. And many of them have to walk a league or more, morning and evening, to get home. Nor should we neglect to mention the danger that exists merely from working in these large factories, surrounded by wheels, gears, enormous leather belts that always threaten to seize you and pound you to pieces.

The existence of women who work as day laborers, and are obliged to abandon . . . the care of their children to indifferent neighbors is no better. . . . We believe that the condition of women will never really improve until workingmen can earn enough to support their families, which is only fair. Woman is so closely linked to man that the position of the one cannot be improved without reference to the position of the other.

THE IMPACT OF BRITISH RULE IN INDIA

In 1871 Dadabhai Naoroji commented on the benefits and the problems of British rule in India.

Benefits of British Rule:

In the Cause of Humanity: Abolition of suttee and **infanticide.** *Civilization:* Education, both male and female. . . . **Resuscitation** of India's own noble literature. *Politically:* Peace and order. Freedom of speech and liberty of the press. . . . Improvement of government in the native states. Security of life and property. Freedom from oppression. . . . *Materially:* Loans for railways and irrigation. Development of a few valuable products, such as indigo, tea, coffee, silk, etc. Increase of exports. Telegraphs.

The Detriments of British Rule:

In the Cause of Humanity: Nothing. *Civilization:* [T]here has been a failure to do as much as might have been done. *Politically:* Repeated breach of pledges to give the natives a fair and reasonable share in the higher administration of their own country, . . . an utter disregard of the feelings and views of the natives. *Financially:* [N]ew modes of taxation, without any adequate effort to increase the means of the people to pay.

Summary: British rule has been: morally, a great blessing; politically, peace and order on one hand, blunders on the other; materially, impoverishment. . . . Our great misfortune is that you do not know our wants. When you will know our real wishes, I have not the least doubt that you would do justice. The genius and spirit of the British people is fair play and justice.

LIBRARY

DOCUMENT-BASED QUESTIONS

1. **Explaining** Why does Czar Alexander II free the serfs?
2. **Identifying Points of View** What is the attitude of the *L'Atelier* writer toward women and women's work? Is the author of the article likely to be a woman or a man? What makes you think so?
3. **Summarizing** Summarize the benefits and problems of British rule in India.

C Critical Thinking

Making Inferences Ask: Why might a newspaper with a readership of workingmen publish an article about the problems of women workers? *(The article uses the plight of women to argue for higher wages for men.)* **OL**

R1 Reading Strategy

Reading Primary Sources

Ask students to evaluate the reliability of this source and explain how they formed their opinion. *(Students will probably find the source reliable because of the efforts taken by the author to weigh the pros and cons of British rule fairly.)* **OL**

R2 Reading Strategy

Monitoring Ask: What changes might the author want to make in their colonial policy? *(Changes include greater self-government for Indians, respect of Indian wishes and culture, fairer taxes, lower debts, and so on.)* **OL**

Assess/Close

Have students answer the Document-Based Questions.

Document-Based Questions

1. The czar claimed that "Divine Providence" (God) had called upon him to fulfill a "sacred inheritance" to improve the conditions of the peasants.
2. Students should cite specific opinions or subjective phrases that reveal the author's attitude toward women and women's work, as well as give clues to whether the author might be a man or a woman.
3. Encourage students to draw up a balance sheet listing the benefits and detriments named by the author.

Focus

Introduction

Burma was part of the British Empire from the 1820s until 1948. Orwell's essay gives a personal account of the corrupting effects of imperialism, both on the colonizers and on the colonized.

Understanding Vocabulary Review the Reader's Dictionary with students to make sure they understand any unfamiliar terms.

Teach

C Critical Thinking

Comparing and Contrasting Discuss the ways in which differing perceptions influence relationships and events. **Ask:** In what ways do the narrator and the crowd perceive the situation differently? *(The narrator believes that the elephant no longer poses a danger to the villagers and should not be shot; the gathering crowd of people expects him to execute the animal.)* OL

Answers and Additional Support

LIBRARY

An Era of European Imperialism

1800–1914

WORLD LITERATURE

▲George Orwell

About the Author

George Orwell was the pen name of English author Eric Arthur Blair, who was born in Motihari, India, on June 25, 1903. Although born in India, he was educated in England. He lived for 46 years, and during that time, he wrote many influential essays, novels, and newspaper articles. His two most famous works are *1984* and *Animal Farm*, both of which are commentaries against totalitarianism.

Reader's Dictionary

mahout: a keeper and driver of an elephant
dominion: rule, control
sahib: title meaning "sir" or "master"

FROM *SHOOTING AN ELEPHANT*

By George Orwell

George Orwell served for several years as an assistant superintendent in the Indian Imperial Police but resigned due to his distaste of imperialism. In Shooting an Elephant, *he describes an incident that happened to him, and he satirizes the problems of colonial rule.*

I had halted on the road. As soon as I saw the elephant I knew with perfect certainty that I ought not to shoot him. It is a serious matter to shoot a working elephant—it is comparable to destroying a huge and costly piece of machinery—and obviously one ought not to do it if it can possibly be avoided. And at that distance, peacefully eating, the elephant looked no more dangerous than a cow. I thought then and I think now that his attack of "must" was already passing off; in which case he would merely wander harmlessly about until the **mahout** came back and caught him. Moreover, I did not in the least want to shoot him. I decided that I would watch him for a little while to make sure that he did not turn savage again, and then go home.

C But at that moment I glanced round at the crowd that had followed me. It was an immense crowd, two thousand at the least and growing every minute. It blocked the road for a long distance on either side. I looked at the sea of yellow faces above the garish clothes—faces all happy and excited over this bit of fun, all certain that the elephant was going to be shot. They were watching me as they would watch a conjurer about to perform a trick. They

Colonial hunter ▶

Activity: Interdisciplinary Connection

Language Arts Tell students that tone is the expression of a writer's attitude toward his or her subject. Writers convey tone through their choice of words and details. Tone is often described by a single adjective such as *humorous, sad, joyful, sarcastic,* or *angry.* Writers create a specific tone to help them accomplish their purpose. They may wish to bring out a theme or focus attention on a set of circumstances or contrast appearance and reality. Have students work in small groups to identify Orwell's tone in this excerpt. **Ask:** Why did Orwell choose this tone for his essay? What impression does it help to convey about the effects of imperialism on humanity? *(Answers will vary. Students may note that it is sardonic, self-mocking, and may even verge on humorously bitter.)* Have them find words and phrases that support their analysis of tone. Discuss their analyses. OL did not like me, but with the magical rifle in my hands I was momentarily worth watching. And suddenly I realized that I should have to shoot the elephant after all. The people expected it of me and I had got to do it; I could feel their two thousand wills pressing me forward irresistibly. And it was at this moment, as I stood there with the rifle in my hands, that I first grasped the hollowness, the futility of the white man's **dominion** in the East. Here was I, the white man with his gun, standing in front of the unarmed native crowd—seemingly the leading actor of the piece; but in reality I was only an absurd puppet pushed to and fro by the will of those yellow faces behind. I perceived in this moment that when the white man turns tyrant it is his own freedom that he destroys. He becomes a sort of hollow, posing dummy, the conventionalized figure of a **sahib.** For it is the condition of his rule that he shall spend his life in trying to impress the "natives," and so in every crisis he has got to do what the "natives" expect of him. He wears a mask, and his face grows to fit it. I had got to shoot the elephant. I had committed myself to doing it when I sent for the rifle. A sahib has got to act like a sahib; he has got to appear resolute, to know his own mind and do definite things. To come all that way, rifle in hand, with two thousand people marching at my heels, and then to trail feebly away, having done nothing—no, that was impossible. The crowd would laugh at me. And my whole life, every white man's life in the East, was one long struggle not to be laughed at.

▼ Working elephants, 1890s

. . . But I did not want to shoot the elephant. . . . The sole thought in my mind was that if anything went wrong those two thousand Burmese would see me trampled on, and reduced to a grinning corpse. And if that happened it was quite probable that some of them would laugh. That would never do. There was only one alternative. I shoved the cartridges into the magazine and lay down on the road to get a better aim.

The crowd grew very still, and a deep, low, happy sigh, as of people who see the theater curtain go up at last, breathed from innumerable throats. They were going to have their bit of fun after all.

. . . When I pulled the trigger I did not hear the bang or feel the kick—one never does when a shot goes home—but I heard the devilish roar of glee that went up from the crowd. . . . You could see the agony of it jolt [the elephant's] whole body and knock the last remnant of strength from his legs.

. . . In the end I could not stand it any longer and went away. I heard later that it took him half an hour to die. . . .

. . . I often wondered whether any of the others grasped that I had done it solely to avoid looking a fool.

LIBRARY

DOCUMENT-BASED QUESTIONS

1. **Drawing Conclusions** Why does the narrator ultimately decide that he must shoot the elephant?
2. **Recognizing Bias** What does this story reveal about Orwell's attitudes about imperialism? How can you tell?
3. **Explaining** According to Orwell in this piece, who held the power in colonial India?

Applications Activity
Write a narrative account of an incident when you felt people were pushing you to act in opposition to your original intentions.

R Reading Strategy

Monitoring Ask: Who are the groups involved in this instance of colonial rule? *(the British and the Burmese)* How does power influence the relationship between these two groups? *(Burma was part of the British Empire, and British people living in Burma governed the Burmese.)* Were different kinds of power at work in colonial relationships? *(Although the British colonized and officially ruled Burma, the Burmese people had certain ideas about their colonizers and came to expect certain things from them.)* OL

W Writing Support

Expository Writing Have students write the "police report" version of this incident from the perspective of the narrator. Remind students to choose their details and words to create an objective and official tone. OL

Assess/Close

Have students answer the Document-Based Questions.

Document-Based Questions

1. The narrator does not want to be laughed at by the local people for walking away from the elephant. He must act like a *sahib*, resolute and in control of every situation, or he will lose the respect of those he is meant to govern.
2. Imperialism has many negative consequences for the oppressor as well as the oppressed. Orwell states this in the narration: ". . . when the white man turns tyrant it is his own freedom that he destroys."
3. Although the British were officially in power, they were actually subject to the expectations of the people they ruled.

Applications Activity Students' accounts should clearly show the conflict between their will and that of the others and should include a resolution.

Focus

Introduction

Two of these sources provide insight into the fears and atrocities experienced by millions during World War I and World War II. The third source expresses Mohandas Gandhi's reasons for inspiring civil disobedience against the British rule.

Understanding Vocabulary
Review the Reader's Dictionary with students to make sure they understand any unfamiliar terms.

Teach

R Reading Strategy

Reading Primary Sources
Ask: What is the purpose of this account? *(Students might say the author's purpose is to share information about the experience of soldiers in the trenches.)* OL

C Critical Thinking

Making Inferences Ask: What did "over the top" mean to soldiers in World War I? *(It meant climbing out of the trench and heading onto the open battlefield.)* BL

Answers and Additional Support

LIBRARY

The Twentieth-Century Crisis

1914–1945

PRIMARY SOURCES

Reader's Dictionary

parapet: wall of earth piled on top of a trench
snipers: people who shoot at exposed individuals from a concealed location
civil disobedience: refusal to obey governmental demands
exploitation: unfair use for one's own advantage
disarmament: reducing or eliminating weapons

▲Battle of the Somme

AN AMERICAN SOLDIER REMEMBERS WORLD WAR I

Arthur Guy Empey reflects upon his experiences during World War I in the trenches in France. This is an excerpt from his book Over the Top.

Suddenly, the earth seemed to shake and a thunderclap burst in my ears. I opened my eyes,—I was splashed all over with sticky mud, and men were picking themselves up from the bottom of the trench. The **parapet** on my left had toppled into the trench, completely blocking it with a wall of tossed-up earth. The man on my left lay still. . . . A German "Minnie" (trench mortar) had exploded in the [trench]. R . . . Stretcher-bearers came up the trench on the double. After a few minutes of digging, three still, muddy forms on stretchers were carried down the communication trench to the rear. Soon they would be resting "somewhere in France," with a little wooden cross over their heads. They had done their bit for King and Country, had died without firing a shot. . . . I was dazed and motionless. Suddenly a shovel was pushed into my hands, and a rough but kindly voice said: "Here, my lad, lend a hand clearing the trench, but keep your head down, and look out for **snipers**. . . ."

Lying on my belly on the bottom of the trench, I filled sandbags with the sticky mud. . . . The harder I worked, the better I felt.

Occasionally a bullet would crack overhead, and a machine gun would kick up the mud on the bashed-in parapet. At each crack I would duck and shield my face with my arm. One of the older men noticed this action of mine, C and whispered: "Don't duck at the crack of a bullet, Yank; the danger has passed,—you never hear the one that wings you. Always remember that if you are going to get it, you'll get it, so never worry." . . . [Days later] we received the cheerful news that at four in the morning we were to go over the top and take the German frontline trench. My heart turned to lead.

Activity: Technology Connection

Analyzing Information Have groups of students use the Internet to find other primary sources, such as letters, photographs, speeches, or journals, relating to the experiences of soldiers in the trenches during World War I or the Holocaust. Ask them to note examples of the many technological "advances" that were developed to make killing "more efficient." Encourage them to consider how the mechanization of warfare increased its horror and lethality. Have students develop and deliver oral presentations to the class drawing from the information they locate. Encourage them to create visual aids to accompany their presentations. OL

GANDHI TAKES THE PATH OF CIVIL DISOBEDIENCE

Mohandas Gandhi explains why British rule in India must end.

▲ Mohandas Gandhi

Before embarking on **civil disobedience** and taking the risk I have dreaded to take all these years, I would fain approach you and find a way out.

My personal faith is absolutely clear. I cannot intentionally hurt anything that lives, much less fellow human beings, even though they may do the greatest wrong to me and mine. Whilst, therefore, I hold the British rule to be a curse, I do not intend harm to a single Englishman or to any legitimate interest he may have in India.

I must not be misunderstood. Though I hold the British rule in India to be a curse, I do not, therefore, consider Englishmen in **C** general to be worse than any other people on earth. I have the privilege of claiming many Englishmen as dearest friends. Indeed much that I have learned of the evil of British rule is due to the writings of frank and courageous Englishmen who have not hesitated to tell the truth about that rule.

And why do I regard British rule as a curse? It has impoverished the ignorant millions by a system of progressive **exploitation** and by a ruinously expensive military and civil administration which the country can never afford.

It has reduced us politically to serfdom. It has sapped the foundations of our culture. And, by the policy of cruel **disarmament**, it has degraded us spiritually. Lacking the inward strength, we have been reduced . . . to a state bordering on cowardly helplessness. . . .

THE HOLOCAUST—THE CAMP VICTIMS

A French doctor describes the victims of one of the gas chambers at Auschwitz-Birkenau during the Holocaust.

It is mid-day, when a long line of women, children, and old people enter the yard. The senior official in charge . . . climbs on a bench to tell them that they are going to have a bath and that afterwards they will get a drink of hot coffee. They all undress in the yard. . . . The doors are opened and an indescribable jostling begins. The first people to enter the gas chamber begin to draw back. They sense the death which awaits them. The SS men put an end to the pushing and shoving with blows from their rifle butts beating the heads of the **W** horrified women who are desperately hugging their children. The massive oak double doors are shut. For two endless minutes one can hear banging on the walls and screams which are no longer human. And then—not a sound. Five minutes later the doors are opened. The corpses, squashed together and distorted, fall out like a waterfall. The bodies which are still warm pass through the hands of the hairdresser who cuts their hair and the dentist who pulls out their gold teeth. . . .

LIBRARY

DOCUMENT-BASED QUESTIONS

1. **Describing** How did Arthur Empey feel and act during his time in the trenches of World War I?
2. **Analyzing** Why do you think Gandhi believed that nonviolent civil disobedience would encourage the British to free India?
3. **Identifying Points of View** What is the French doctor's point of view about the events he describes at the Auschwitz-Birkenau death camp?

C Critical Thinking

Identifying Central Issues
Ask: Why does Gandhi consider British rule "a curse"? *(He believes British rule has impoverished and exploited millions of Indians, reducing them to political serfdom and robbing them of the strength to resist or defend their culture.)* **OL**

W Writing Support

Expository Writing Ask students to explain in a written statement how Nazi policies violated the human rights of the victims at Auschwitz-Birkenau. Students should support their statements with details from the doctor's eyewitness account. *(Students' statements will vary. The Nazis dehumanized the victims by depriving them of the rights that are considered by most societies to belong automatically to everyone. Students should support their statements with details from the primary source.)* **AL**

Assess/Close

Have students answer the Document-Based Questions.

Document-Based Questions

1. He felt fear, confusion, and perhaps anger. He acted like a new recruit—ducking sounds of gunfire, digging in, and eventually facing the terror of going "over the top."
2. Answers will vary, but Gandhi counted on the support of British citizens who opposed colonial policies, on the British traditions of justice and self-government, and on world opinion.
3. He appears detached, but some phrases such as "two endless minutes," "screams which are no longer human," betray his horror.

Focus

Introduction

This excerpt from *A Room of One's Own* expresses Virginia Woolf's concern over the limited opportunities available to women throughout much of Britain's history.

Understanding Vocabulary Review the Reader's Dictionary with students to make sure they understand any unfamiliar terms.

Teach

R Reading Strategy

Making Connections In her essay, Woolf makes the point that women were not able to express themselves freely or pursue educational or professional opportunities throughout much of history. Have students think of other groups of people who have been prevented from reaching their full potential artistically, academically, politically, or socially. (*Answers will vary. Students might identify enslaved Africans in the United States or the untouchable caste in India.*) **OL**

Answers and Additional Support

LIBRARY

The Twentieth-Century Crisis

1914–1945

WORLD LITERATURE

Reader's Dictionary

agog: full of intense interest or excitement

moon: to dream

◄ Virginia Woolf

About the Author

Virginia Woolf was born in 1882 in London. Her work changed the ways many modern novels were written. She used an experimental narrative technique known as stream of consciousness, in which characters are portrayed through their inner lives and thoughts without explanation from the writer. She is also known for her feminist writings. One of the most famous of these is *A Room of One's Own*. Its title reflects her belief that a woman "must have money and a room of her own" in order to write.

FROM *A ROOM OF ONE'S OWN*

by Virginia Woolf

Virginia Woolf was a fervent supporter of women's rights. In A Room of One's Own, *she responds to those who would question the capabilities of women because there was no "female Shakespeare."*

. . . Let me imagine, since facts are so hard to come by, what would have happened had Shakespeare had a wonderfully gifted sister, called Judith, let us say. Shakespeare himself went, very probably—his mother was an heiress—to the grammar school, where he may have learnt Latin—Ovid, Virgil and Horace—and the elements of grammar and logic. He was, it is well known, a wild boy who poached rabbits, perhaps shot a deer, and had, rather sooner than he should have done, to marry a woman in the neighbourhood, who bore him a child rather quicker than was right. That escapade sent him to seek his fortune in London. He had, it seemed, a taste for the theatre; he began by holding horses at the stage door. Very soon he got work in the theatre, became a successful actor, and lived at the hub of the universe, meeting everybody, knowing everybody, practising his art on the boards, exercising his wits in the street, and even getting access to the palace of the queen. Meanwhile his extraordinarily gifted sister, let us suppose, remained at home. She was as adventurous, as imaginative, as **agog** to see the world as he was. But she was not sent to school. She had no chance of learning grammar and logic, let alone of reading Horace and Virgil. She picked up a book now and then, one of her brother's perhaps, and read a few pages. But then her parents came in and told her to mend the stockings or mind the stew and not **moon** about with books and papers. They would have spoken sharply but kindly, for they were substantial people who knew the conditions of life for a woman and loved

Activity: Interdisciplinary Connection

Language Arts Tell students that Virginia Woolf was an ardent supporter of women's rights. In *A Room of One's Own*, she responds to those who would question the capabilities of women because there was no "female Shakespeare." As students read the excerpt, have them evaluate the validity of Woolf's counterargument. Ask them to identify the parts they feel are convincing or that they feel detract from the strength of her point. **Ask: Is the essay effective in revealing the difficulties of a woman artist in the world? Why or why not?** Divide students into teams to debate the question. Have teams support their opinions with specific examples. **AL**

their daughter—indeed, more likely than not she was the apple of her father's eye. Perhaps she scribbled some pages up in an apple loft on the sly, but was careful to hide them or set fire to them. Soon, however, before she was out of her teens, she was to be betrothed to the son of a neighbouring wool-stapler. She cried out that marriage was hateful to her, and for that she was severely beaten by her father. Then he ceased to scold her. He begged her instead not to hurt him, not to shame him in this matter of her marriage. He would give her a chain of beads or a fine petticoat, he said; and there were tears in his eyes. How could she disobey him? How could she break his heart? The force of her own gift alone drove her to it. C She made up a small parcel of her belongings, let herself down by a rope one summer's night and took the road to London. She was not seventeen. The birds that sang in the hedge were not more musical than she was. She had the quickest fancy, a gift like her brother's, for the tune of words. Like him, she had a taste for the theatre. She stood at the stage door; she wanted to act, she said. Men laughed in her face. The manager—a fat, loose-lipped man—guffawed. He bellowed something about poodles dancing and women acting—no woman, he said could possibly be an actress. He hinted—you can imagine what. She could get no training in her craft. Could she even seek her dinner in a tavern or roam the streets at midnight? Yet her genius was for fiction. . . . At last—for she was very young, oddly like Shakespeare the poet in her face, with the same grey eyes and rounded brows—at last Nick Greene the actor-manager took pity on her; [but] she . . . R killed herself one winter's night and lies buried at some cross-roads where the omnibuses now stop outside the Elephant and Castle. That, more or less, is how the story would run, I think, if a woman in Shakespeare's day should have had Shakespeare's genius.

▲ Many of William Shakespeare's plays were performed at the Globe Theatre in London.

▼ William Shakespeare

DOCUMENT-BASED QUESTIONS

1. **Describing** What were "the conditions of life for a woman" that made Judith's parents scold her for attempting to read and write?
2. **Drawing Conclusions** What is Woolf's conclusion about the possibility of a woman becoming Shakespeare?
3. **Analyzing** Why does Virginia Woolf have Shakespeare marry, but Shakespeare's sister run away from marriage?

Applications Activity
What does a person today need to succeed as a writer or artist? Write a descriptive account to illustrate your argument.

LIBRARY

C Critical Thinking

Making Inferences Have students explain why Judith describes marriage as "hateful" to her. **Ask:** How does Judith envision her life after marriage? *(She sees her life after marriage as limited by others and defined by domestic duties. She would not be able to practice or develop her talent.)* **OL**

R Reading Strategy

Summarizing Have students summarize in their own words the effect that gender has on Judith's education and the options she has regarding her life. **Ask:** What point is Woolf making through Judith's fate? *(Woolf is illustrating the hopelessness of women's situations throughout history and the gifts that have been lost as a result of societal oppression.)* **AL**

Assess/Close

Have students answer the Document-Based Questions.

Document-Based Questions

1. Women were supposed to confine their interests to the domestic sphere, mending, cooking, cleaning, bearing and bringing up children. Reading and writing were not seen as beneficial.
2. At the time that Shakespeare lived, no woman, regardless of her talent, would have been able to accomplish what he did because of the overwhelming obstacles in her path. It could not have happened because writing and acting were the province of men.
3. Men could marry but retain their freedom and autonomy, as indeed Shakespeare did. Women, on the other hand, lost their autonomy upon marrying, as they became accountable to their husbands and responsible for children.

Applications Activity Students' arguments should include specific qualities and attributes that would help a talented person succeed as a writer or artist.

Focus

Introduction

After World War II, sweeping political, social, economic, and technological changes took place around the world.

Understanding Vocabulary Review the Reader's Dictionary with students to make sure they understand any unfamiliar terms.

Teach

C Critical Thinking

Analyzing Information Ask: What were some of the phenomena experienced by John Glenn during the first U.S. space flight? *(zero gravity; little sensation of speed; viewing four sunsets per day)* **OL**

R Reading Strategy

Questioning Read the paragraph aloud. **Ask:** What is Glenn's purpose in this part of his speech? *(He is answering critics who want instant and tangible benefits from space flight.)* **AL**

Answers and Additional Support

LIBRARY

Toward a Global Civilization

1945–Present

PRIMARY SOURCES

Reader's Dictionary

reserve: a reservation; land set aside for use by a particular group

squatters: those who settle on public land without rights or permission

perturbation: major change or disturbance

▲ John Glenn

PROGRESS NEVER STOPS

In 1962 John J. Glenn, Jr., was commander of the first U.S. crewed spacecraft to orbit the earth. Glenn spoke to a joint meeting of Congress six days after he returned from orbit.

What did we learn from the flight? . . . The Mercury spacecraft and systems design concepts are sound and have now been verified during manned flight. We also proved that man can operate intelligently in space and can adapt rapidly to this new environment.

Zero G or weightlessness appears to be no problem. As a matter of fact, lack of gravity is a rather fascinating thing. Objects within the cockpit can be parked in midair. For example, at one time during the flight, I was using a hand-held camera. Another system needed attention; so it seemed quite natural to let go of the camera, take care of the other chore, then reach out, grasp the camera, and go back about my business.

There seemed to be little sensation of speed although the craft was traveling at about five miles per second—a speed that I too find difficult to comprehend.

C The view from that altitude defies description. The horizon colors are brilliant and sunsets are spectacular. It is hard to beat a day in which you are permitted the luxury of seeing four sunsets. . . .

Our efforts today and what we have done so far are but small building blocks in a huge pyramid to come.

R But questions are sometimes raised regarding the immediate payoffs from our efforts. Explorations and the pursuit of knowledge have always paid dividends in the long run—usually far greater than anything expected at the outset. Experimenters with common, green mold, little dreamed what effect their discovery of penicillin would have.

We are just probing the surface of the greatest advancements in man's knowledge of his surroundings that has ever been made. . . . Knowledge begets knowledge. Progress never stops.

Activity: Collaborative Learning

Drawing Conclusions Have students work in small groups to find out how John Glenn's first flight in space compares to those of other astronauts, including his own later flight in 1998. Suggest to students that they examine NASA archives online for photographs and other materials about the U.S. space program. They should also obtain primary source documents relating to the experiences of other astronauts. Have groups note key differences and similarities and present their findings to the class. **Ask:** Based on your research, do you agree with John Glenn's statements that "knowledge begets knowledge" and "progress never stops"? Have students discuss the question, supporting their responses with details from the presentations. **OL**

An Ideal for Which I Am Prepared to Die

Nelson Mandela gave this speech during his trial in South Africa in 1964. Following the trial, he was sentenced to life in prison.

S

The whites enjoy what may well be the highest standard of living in the world, whilst Africans live in poverty and misery. Forty percent of the Africans live in hopelessly overcrowded and, in some cases, drought-stricken **reserves,** where soil erosion and the overworking of the soil make it impossible for them to live properly off the land. Thirty percent are labourers, labour tenants, and **squatters** on white farms. The other thirty percent live in towns where they have developed economic and social habits which bring them closer, in many respects, to white standards. Yet forty-six percent of all African families in Johannesburg do not earn enough to keep them going.

The complaint of Africans, however, is not only that they are poor and whites are rich, but that the laws which are made by the whites are designed to preserve this situation. . . .

During my lifetime I have dedicated my life to this struggle of the African people. I have fought against white domination, and I have fought against black domination. I have cherished the ideal of a democratic and free society in which all persons live together in harmony with equal opportunities. It is an ideal which I hope to live for, and to see realized. But my lord, if needs be, it is an ideal for which I am prepared to die.

C

China's Gilded Age

Xiao-huang Yin recounts his trip through China in 1994.

Recently I took a six-week journey across China. It was my first trip back since . . . 1985. In the course of my visit I saw—I felt—the **perturbations** of profound and chaotic social change. China's stunning hurtle from a centrally planned economy to a free market has set off an economic explosion and generated tremendous prosperity. Its economic growth was 13 percent in 1993, and average personal income in urban areas had doubled since 1985. With the state-owned sector accounting for less than 30 percent of total economic output, the socialist system is becoming an empty shell. Across China the lines between the state and private economies are blurring. At the largest national department store in Shanghai, a symbol of Chinese socialist business, customers now bargain for better prices. The counters within the store have been contracted out to shop clerks, who decide the prices. Dual ownership has in essence turned this state enterprise into a private business. . . .

Not everyone gets rich quick, but the economic boom has brought most urban Chinese a huge improvement in their standard of living. Color TV sets, refrigerators, and VCRs, considered luxuries when I lived in China, can be found in almost every working-class urban household—at least in the prosperous coastal cities.

W

LIBRARY

Document-Based Questions

1. **Identifying Central Issues** What are the immediate and long-term "payoffs" of John Glenn's 1962 space mission, according to his report to Congress?
2. **Explaining** What ideal does Nelson Mandela discuss?
3. **Evaluating** Why does Xiao-huang Yin believe that socialism is becoming an "empty shell" in China?

S Skill Practice

Analyzing Have students examine the apartheid system as it existed at the time of Mandela's trial, the newspaper accounts of his trial, and the political policies that Mandela adopted as South Africa's first black president. Ask students to interpret these events and to connect them with the larger social, economic, and political developments taking place within Africa. AL

C Critical Thinking

Identifying Central Issues
Ask: What is the main cause of Mandela's protest against South Africa's government? *(He opposes laws made by whites to ensure their domination and the poverty of black South Africans.)* OL

W Writing Support

Expository Writing Ask students to write a paragraph that explains the link that Xiao-huang Yin makes between economic freedom and improved standards of living in China. OL

Assess/Close

Have students answer the Document-Based Questions.

Document-Based Questions

1. The mission proved that people can operate intelligently in space and adapt to that environment. Long-term benefits, though unknown, may bring progress and increase knowledge.
2. Mandela defends the ideal of "a democratic and free society in which all persons live together in harmony with equal opportunities."
3. The author says that the state-owned sector of business has fallen to less than 30 percent of China's total economic output.

Focus

Introduction

The civil war in this story began in 1967, when the military governor of eastern Nigeria announced the secession of the region, renaming it the Republic of Biafra.

Understanding Vocabulary Review the Reader's Dictionary with students to make sure they understand any unfamiliar terms.

Teach

D Differentiated Instruction

English Language Learners Display a story map on the board. Read the story aloud to students, pausing at intervals to fill in details on the map as a class. BL

C Critical Thinking

Making Inferences Ask: What impression of the army is created by Jonathan's thoughts about the officer he encounters? *(the tattered appearance of the "officer" gives the impression that the entire army is poorly equipped)* OL

Toward a Global Civilization

1945–Present

WORLD LITERATURE

▲ Chinua Achebe

About the Author

Chinua Achebe was born in Nigeria and was christened Albert Chinualamogu. He rejected his British name while studying at the University College of Ibadan. Many of his works deal with the impact of Western values and culture on African society. He has done more than almost any other author to spread the understanding and influence of African literature worldwide.

Reader's Dictionary

commandeer: to seize for military purposes
Biro: a British term for a ballpoint pen
raffia: fiber of a type of palm tree

LIBRARY

"Civil Peace" from Girls at War and Other Stories

By Chinua Achebe

"Civil Peace" is one of the stories from Girls at War and Other Stories *in which Achebe responds to the Nigerian civil war. The story takes place in the forests of Nigeria in 1970, just after the war has ended.*

Jonathan Iwegbu counted himself extraordinarily lucky. "Happy survival!" meant so much more to him than just a current fashion of greeting old friends in the first hazy days of peace. It went deep to his heart. He had come out of the war with five inestimable blessings—his head, his wife Maria's head and the heads of three out of their four children. As a bonus he also had his old bicycle—a miracle too but naturally not to be compared to the safety of five human heads. **D**

The bicycle had a little history of its own. One day at the height of the war it was **commandeered** "for urgent military action." Hard as its loss would have been to him he would still have let it go without a thought had he not had some doubts about the genuineness of the officer. It wasn't his disreputable rags, nor the toes peeping out of one blue and one brown canvas shoes, nor yet the two stars of his rank done obviously in a hurry in **Biro,** that troubled Jonathan; many good and heroic soldiers looked the same or worse. It was **C**

Answers and Additional Support

Activity: Technology Connection

Identifying Central Issues Display a K-W-L chart. Ask students to volunteer questions that they have about the civil war in Nigeria, such as its causes and effects. Record those in the first column and any facts students already know in the second column. Then divide students into groups and assign them some of the questions to research. They should use databases and the Internet. Encourage students to find additional information about the war, including the international community's reaction to it and the political situation in Nigeria today. Then have students reconvene and complete the K-W-L chart with the details they have found. **Ask:** How does knowing more about the historical context of the story affect your reaction to it? Has Achebe accurately conveyed the impact of the war on the Nigerians? Discuss students' responses. OL rather a certain lack of grip and firmness in his manner. So Jonathan, suspecting he might be amenable to influence, rummaged in his **raffia** bag and produced the two pounds with which he had been going to buy firewood which his wife, Maria, retailed to camp officials for extra stock-fish and corn meal, and got his bicycle back. That night he buried it in the little clearing in the bush where the dead of the camp, including his own youngest son, were buried. When he dug it up again a year later after the surrender all it needed was a little palm-oil greasing. "Nothing puzzles God," he said in wonder.

He put it to immediate use as a taxi and accumulated a small pile of Biafran money ferrying camp officials and their families across the four-mile stretch to the nearest tarred road. His standard charge per trip was six pounds and those who had the money were only glad to be rid of some of it in this way. At the end of a fortnight he had made a small fortune of one hundred and fifteen pounds. C1

Then he made the journey to Enugu and found another miracle waiting for him. It was unbelievable. He rubbed his eyes and looked again and it was still standing there before him. But, needless to say, even that monumental blessing must be accounted also totally inferior to the five heads in the family. This newest miracle was his little house in Ogui Overside. Indeed nothing puzzles God! Only two houses away a huge concrete edifice some wealthy contractor had put up just before the war was a mountain of rubble. And here was Jonathan's little zinc house of no regrets built with mud blocks quite intact! Of course the doors and windows were missing and five sheets off the roof. But what was that? And anyhow he had returned to Enugu early enough to pick up bits of old zinc and wood and soggy sheets of cardboard lying around the neighborhood before thousands more came out of their forest holes looking for the same things. He got a destitute carpenter with one old hammer, a blunt plane and a few bent and rusty nails in his tool bag to turn this assortment of wood, paper and metal into door and window shutters for five Nigerian shillings or fifty Biafran pounds. He paid the pounds, and moved in with his overjoyed family carrying five heads on their shoulders. R C2

▲ *Children Dancing,* c. 1948, by Robert Gwathmey

LIBRARY

DOCUMENT-BASED QUESTIONS

1. **Drawing Conclusions** What does Jonathan's encounter with the false officer reveal about the conditions of the war?
2. **Identifying** Biafra lost the civil war. What clues in the text indicate this outcome?
3. **Evaluating** Do you think it is effective for Achebe to discuss the war through an individual account rather than as a direct discussion of the devastation created? Why or why not?

Applications Activity
Choose a contemporary problem and describe it through the effect it has on an individual or family.

C1 Critical Thinking

Drawing Conclusions Ask: What do Jonathan's actions reveal about the qualities needed to survive in a war-torn country? *(Through the character of Jonathan, the author seems to be saying that in order to survive this type of conflict, one must be smart, resourceful, and determined.)* OL

R Reading Strategy

Making Connections Ask: Why were camp officials happy to get rid of their Biafran money? *(By the end of the civil war, Biafran money had little value.)* OL

C2 Critical Thinking

Making Inferences Ask: What can be inferred about conditions in Nigeria following the civil war? *(Buildings were destroyed; there was little work to be had; some people lived out in the open and scavenged for food.)* OL

Assess/Close

Have students answer the Document-Based Questions.

Document-Based Questions

1. People use the conditions created by the war to take advantage of others. There is no real organization, and most people are desperate.
2. People are anxious to get rid of Biafran money; most of the town is in ruins.
3. Answers will vary, but students may say that the point of view of this story reinforces understanding of the toll that war takes on the innocent. Although Jonathan considers himself lucky, he lost a child to the war and could have lost his house as well. He endured hardships and had to survive on his wits.

Applications Activity Students might choose first or third-person point of view for their accounts. They should include details that clearly reveal the effects of the problem.

GLOSSARY/ GLOSARIO

- Content vocabulary terms in this glossary are words that relate to world history content. They are **highlighted** yellow in your text.
- Los términos del vocabulario de contenido de este glosario son palabras relacionadas con el contenido de historia mundial. Están resaltadas en **amarillo** en tu libro de texto.
- Words below that have an asterisk (*) are academic vocabulary terms. They help you understand your school subjects and are **boldfaced** in your text.
- Las palabras que tienen un asterisco (*) son términos del vocabulario académico. Ellas te ayudarán a comprender los temas escolares y están en **negritas** en tu libro de texto.

ENGLISH	ESPAÑOL
	a
***abandoned:** deserted (p. 352)	***abandonado:** desierto (pág. 352)
abbess: the head of a convent (p. 306)	**abadesa:** superiora de un convento (pág. 306)
abolitionism: a movement to end slavery (p. 637)	**abolicionismo:** movimiento para terminar con la esclavitud (pág. 637)
absolutism: a political system in which a ruler holds total power (p. 464)	**absolutismo:** sistema político en el que el gobernante mantiene un poder total (pág. 464)
***abstract:** a style of art, emerging around 1910, that spoke directly to the soul and avoided visual reality by using only lines and color (p. 676)	***abstracto:** estilo de arte, surgido alrededor de 1910, que habla directamente al alma y evita la realidad visual al utilizar solamente líneas y colores (pág. 676)
***accurate:** exact or right (p. 374)	***preciso:** exacto o correcto (pág. 374)
***acquired:** came into possession or control of (p. 273)	***adquirir:** obtener la posesión o el control de (pág. 273)
acropolis: in early Greek city-states, a fortified gathering place at the top of a hill that was sometimes the site of temples and public buildings (p. 112)	**acrópolis:** en las ciudades-estado de la antigua Grecia, lugar fortificado de reuniones en la cima de una montaña, donde en ocasiones había templos y edificios públicos (pág. 112)
***administrative:** relating to the execution of public affairs, as distinguished from policy making (p. 244)	***administrativo:** relacionado con la ejecución de asuntos públicos, a diferencia de la elaboración de políticas (pág. 244)
***administrator:** one who manages the affairs of a government or a business (p. 494)	***administrador:** el que dirige los asuntos de un gobierno o negocio (pág. 494)
adobe: sun-dried brick (p. 371)	**adobe:** ladrillo secado al sol (pág. 371)
***advocate:** support; speak in favor of (p. 662)	***abogar:** apoyar; hablar en favor de (pág. 662)
Age of Pericles: the period between 461 B.C. and 429 B.C. when Pericles dominated Athenian politics and Athens reached the height of its power (p. 121)	**Era de Pericles:** el período entre 461 a.C. y 429 a.C., cuando Pericles dominaba la política ateniense y Atenas alcanzó la cúspide de su poder (pág. 121)
agora: in early Greek city-states, an open area that served as a gathering place and as a market (p. 112)	**ágora:** en las ciudades-estado de la antigua Grecia, área abierta que servía como lugar de reunión y como mercado (pág. 112)
agricultural society: a group of people whose economy is largely based on farming (p. 294)	**sociedad agrícola:** grupo de personas cuya economía se basa principalmente en la agricultura (pág. 294)

GLOSSARY

***aid:** assistance such as money or supplies (p. 776)	***ayuda:** asistencia, ya sea en dinero o insumos (pág. 776)
AIDS: acquired immunodeficiency syndrome; caused by the HIV virus that is spread through bodily fluids and weakens the body's immune system; AIDS is a worldwide problem (p. 989)	**sida:** síndrome de inmunodeficiencia adquirida; causado por el virus de inmunodeficiencia humana (VIH), que se transmite a través de los fluidos corporales y debilita el sistema inmunitario del organismo; el sida es un problema mundial (pág. 989)
Allah: Arabic for "God"; the supreme god of Islam (p. 188)	**Alá:** dios en árabe; el dios supremo en el islam (pág. 188)
***amendment:** an alteration proposed or effected by parliamentary or constitutional procedure (p. 569)	***enmienda:** alteración propuesta o realizada por el parlamento o un procedimiento constitucional (pág. 569)
anarchy: political disorder; lawlessness (p. 494)	**anarquía:** desorden político; sin leyes (pág. 494)
annexed: incorporated territory into an existing political unit, such as a city or country (p. 692)	**anexado:** territorio incorporado a una unidad política existente, como una ciudad o un país (pág. 692)
***annual:** yearly (p. 791)	***anual:** en un año, cada año (pág. 791)
annul: declare invalid (p. 420)	**anular:** declarar no válido (pág. 420)
anthropology: the study of human life and culture based on artifacts and human fossils (p. 4)	**antropología:** el estudio de la vida y la cultura humanas, basado en artefactos y fósiles humanos (pág. 4)
anti-Semitism: hostility toward or discrimination against Jews (p. 353)	**antisemitismo:** hostilidad hacia o discriminación contra los judíos (pág. 353)
apartheid: "apartness," the system of racial segregation in South Africa from the 1950s until 1991 (p. 987)	***apartheid:*** "separación", sistema de segregación racial in Sudáfrica desde la década de 1950 hasta 1991 (pág. 987)
appeasement: satisfying reasonable demands of dissatisfied powers in an effort to maintain peace and stability (p. 857)	**apaciguamiento:** satisfacer demandas razonables de potencias insatisfechas en un esfuerzo por mantener la paz y la estabilidad (pág. 857)
apprentice: one who learns a trade by practical experience under skilled craftspeople (p. 341)	**aprendiz:** quien aprende un negocio mediante la experiencia práctica bajo la guía de artesanos calificados (pág. 341)
***approach:** the way or method one examines or studies an issue or a concept (p. 641)	***enfoque:** la manera o el método en que uno examina o estudia un asunto o un concepto (pág. 641)
arabesque: geometric patterns repeated over and over to completely cover a surface with decoration (p. 207)	**arabesco:** patrones geométricos repetidos una y otra vez para cubrir completamente una superficie con decorados (pág. 207)
***arbitrary:** at one's discretion; random (p. 551)	***arbitrario:** a la discreción de uno; aleatorio (pág. 551)
archaeology: the study of past societies through an analysis of the items people left behind them (p. 4)	**arqueología:** estudio de sociedades pasadas mediante el análisis de los objetos que las personas dejan tras sí (pág. 4)
archipelago: a chain of islands (p. 290)	**archipiélago:** cadena de islas (pág. 290)
***area:** a geographic region (p. 290)	***área:** región geográfica (pág. 290)
arete: in early Greece, the qualities of excellence that a hero strives to win in a struggle or contest (p. 111)	***arete:*** en la antigua Grecia, las cualidades de excelencia que un héroe se esforzaba por alcanzar en una batalla o competencia (pág. 111)
aristocracy: an upper class whose wealth is based on land and whose power is passed on from one generation to another (p. 86)	**aristocracia:** clase superior, cuya riqueza se basa en la posesión de tierras y cuyo poder pasa de una generación a otra (pág. 86)
armada: a fleet of warships (p. 456)	**armada:** flota de barcos de guerra (pág. 456)

armistice: a truce or agreement to end fighting (p. 780)	**armisticio:** tregua o acuerdo para finalizar una guerra (pág. 780)
arms race: building up armies and stores of weapons to keep up with an enemy (p. 903)	**carrera armamentista:** aumento de los ejércitos y almacenamiento de armas para igualar al enemigo (pág. 903)
artifact: tools, pottery, paintings, weapons, buildings, and household items left behind by early people (p. 4)	**artefacto:** herramientas, artículos de alfarería, pinturas, armas, edificaciones y artículos para el hogar dejados por pueblos antiguos (pág. 4)
artisan: a skilled worker who makes products such as weapons and jewelry (p. 16)	**artesano:** trabajador calificado que fabrica productos, como armas o joyas (pág. 16)
Aryan: a term used to identify people speaking Indo-European languages; Nazis misused the term, treating it as a racial designation and identifying the Aryans with the ancient Greeks and Romans and twentieth-century Germans and Scandinavians (p. 806)	**ario:** término utilizado para identificar a las personas que hablan lenguas indo-europeas; los nazis abusaron de este término, tomándolo como una designación racial e identificando a los arios con los antiguos griegos y romanos y con los alemanes y escandinavos del siglo XX (pág. 806)
***assemble:** to gather; to meet together (p. 112)	***ensamblar:** unir; juntar (pág. 112)
***assembly:** the fitting together of parts to make a complete product (p. 813)	***ensamblaje:** la unión de piezas para armar un producto completo (pág. 814)
assembly line: pioneered by Henry Ford in 1913, a manufacturing method that allowed much more efficient mass production of goods (p. 655)	**línea de ensamblaje:** método de producción, introducido por Henry Ford en 1913, que permitía producir artículos masivamente con mucha mayor eficiencia (pág. 655)
astrolabe: an instrument used by sailors to determine their location by observing the positions of stars (p. 205)	**astrolabio:** instrumento usado por los navegantes para determinar su ubicación según la posición de las estrellas (pág. 205)
***attain:** to gain or achieve (p. 408)	***lograr:** ganar o alcanzar (pág. 408)
Australopithecus: the earliest humanlike creature that flourished in eastern and southern Africa 3 to 4 million years ago (p. 7)	**australopiteco:** primera criatura humanoide que floreció en el este y sur de África hace tres o cuatro millones de años (pág. 7)
***authority:** power; person in command (p. 464)	***autoridad:** poder; persona a cargo (pág. 464)
autonomous: self-governing (p. 939)	**autónomo:** con gobierno propio (pág. 939)
***available:** ready for immediate use; accessible (p. 274)	***disponible:** listo para su uso inmediato; accesible (pág. 274)

b

balance of trade: the difference in value beween what a nation imports and what it exports over time (p. 440)	**balanza comercial:** la diferencia en valor entre lo que una nación importa y lo que exporta en un período de tiempo (pág. 440)
banners: in Qing China, separate military units made up of Manchus; the empire's chief fighting force (p. 513)	**estandartes:** en la China de los Qing, unidad militar independiente constituida por manchúes y la principal fuerza de combate de ese imperio (pág. 513)
baroque: an artistic style of the seventeenth century characterized by complex forms, bold ornamentation, and contrasting elements (p. 473)	**barroco:** estilo artístico del siglo XVII caracterizado por formas complejas, ornamentación audaz y elementos contrastantes (pág. 473)
bazaar: a covered market in Islamic cities (p. 201)	**bazar:** mercado techado de las ciudades islámicas (pág. 201)
***benefit:** to be useful or profitable to (p. 517)	***benéfico:** ser útil o dar beneficios (pág. 517)

Bhagavad Gita, The: part of the Indian epic *Mahabharata;* the *Gita,* a sermon by the god Krishna on the eve of a major battle, sets forth one key point of Indian culture—one must not worry about the success or failure of an action but should only be aware of the moral rightness of the act itself (p. 80)

Bhagavad Gita, The: parte de la epopeya india *Mahabharata;* el *Gita* es un sermón del dios Krishna en vísperas de una importante batalla, establece un punto clave de la cultura india: uno no debe preocuparse por el éxito o fracaso de una acción, debe atender sólo lo moralmente correcto de la acción misma (pág. 80)

bioterrorism: the use of biological and chemical weapons in terrorist attacks (p. 1040)

bioterrorismo: uso de armas biológicas o químicas en ataques terroristas (pág. 1040)

bishopric: a group of Christian communities, or parishes, under the authority of a bishop (p. 304)

obispado: grupo de comunidades o parroquias cristianas bajo la autoridad de un obispo (pág. 304)

blitz: the British term for the German air raids on British cities and towns during World War II (p. 884)

blitz: término británico para referirse a los ataques aéreos alemanes a ciudades y pueblos británicos durante la Segunda Guerra Mundial (pág. 884)

blitzkrieg: German for "lightning war," a swift and sudden military attack; used by the Germans during World War II (p. 864)

blitzkrieg: término alemán para "guerra relámpago", una táctica utilizada por los alemanes durante la Segunda Guerra Mundial (pág. 864)

bloc: a group of nations with a common purpose (p. 917)

bloque: grupo de naciones con un objetivo común (pág. 917)

bourgeoisie: the middle class, including merchants, industrialists, and professional people (pp. 339, 578, 656)

burguesía: clase media, incluye a los comerciantes, industriales y profesionales (pp. 339, 578, 656)

boyar: a Russian noble (p. 468)

boyar: noble ruso (pág. 468)

Buddhism: a religious doctrine introduced in northern India in the sixth century B.C. by Siddhārtha Gautama, known as the Buddha, or "Enlightened One" (p. 73)

budismo: doctrina religiosa introducida en el norte de la India en el siglo VI a.C. por Siddhartha Gautama, conocido como Buda (o "el Iluminado") (pág. 73)

budget deficit: the state that exists when a government spends more than it collects in revenues (p. 944)

déficit presupuestario: el estado que existe cuando un gobierno gasta más de los ingresos que recibe (pág. 944)

bureaucracy: an administrative organization that relies on nonelective officials and regular procedures (pp. 37, 528)

burocracia: organización administrativa basada en funcionarios no elegidos y procedimientos habituales (pp. 37, 528)

Bushido: "the way of the warrior," the strict code by which Japanese samurai were supposed to live (p. 280)

bushido: "código del guerrero", estricto código según el cual debían vivir los samuráis japoneses (pág. 280)

C

caliph: a successor of Muhammad as spiritual and temporal leader of the Muslims (p. 192)

califa: sucesor de Mahoma como líder espiritual y temporal de los musulmanes (pág. 192)

***capable:** having or showing ability (p. 599)

***capaz:** que tiene o demuestra habilidad (pág. 599)

capital: money available for investment (p. 614)

capital: dinero disponible para invertir (pág. 614)

carruca: a heavy, wheeled plow with an iron plowshare (p. 334)

carruca: pesado arado con ruedas y reja de hierro (pág. 334)

cartels: groups of drug businesses (p. 977)

cártel: grupo de negociantes de drogas (pág. 977)

cash crop: a crop that is grown for sale rather than for personal use (p. 712)

cultivos para vender: cultivo destinado para la venta y no para su consumo personal (pág. 712)

caste system: a set of rigid categories in ancient India that determined a person's occupation and economic potential, as well as his or her position in society, based partly on skin color (p. 71)

sistema de castas: conjunto de categorías rígidas en la antigua India que determinaba la ocupación de una persona y su potencial económico, así como su posición en la sociedad, parcialmente sobre la base del color de la piel (pág. 71)

GLOSSARY

caudillo: in post-revolutionary Latin America, a strong leader who ruled chiefly by military force, usually with the support of the landed elite (p. 711)

caudillo: en la América Latina post revolucionaria, líder poderoso que gobernaba principalmente mediante la fuerza militar, a menudo con el respaldo de la elite hacendada (pág. 711)

***cease:** to come to an end (p. 836)

***cesar:** llegar al fin (pág. 836)

censorate: part of the Chinese bureaucracy that made sure government officials were doing their jobs (p. 96)

censorado: parte de la burocracia china que vigilaba que los funcionarios gubernamentales hicieran su trabajo (pág. 96)

***challenge:** a summons that is often stimulating, inciting, or threatening (p. 317)

***reto:** emplazamiento que con frecuencia estimula, incita o amenaza (pág. 317)

chanson de geste: a type of vernacular literature, this heroic epic was popular in medieval Europe and described battles and political contests (p. 351)

canción de gesta: tipo de literatura vernácula, epopeya heroica popular en la Europa medieval, en la que se describían batallas y contiendas políticas (pág. 351)

***chemical:** produced by chemicals (p. 946)

***químico:** producido mediante reactivos químicos (pág. 946)

chivalry: in the Middle Ages, the ideal of civilized behavior that developed among the nobility; it was a code of ethics that knights were supposed to uphold (p. 313)

caballería: en la Edad Media, el ideal de comportamiento civilizado que florecía entre la nobleza; era un código ético que los caballeros debían mantener (pág. 313)

Christian humanism: a movement that developed in northern Europe during the Renaissance combining classical learning (humanism) with the goal of reforming the Catholic Church (p. 412)

humanismo cristiano: movimiento que se desarrolló en el norte de Europa durante el Renacimiento que combinaba las enseñanzas clásicas (humanismo) con la meta de reformar la Iglesia católica (pág. 412)

city-state: a state with political and economic control over the surrounding countryside (p. 28)

ciudad-estado: ciudad con control político y económico sobre los campos que la rodean (pág. 28)

***civil:** involving the general public or civic affairs (p. 704)

***civil:** relacionado con asuntos generales públicos o civiles (pág. 704)

civil disobedience: refusal to obey laws that are considered to be unjust (p. 832)

desobediencia civil: rechazo a obedecer leyes que son consideradas injustas (pág. 832)

civilization: a complex culture in which large numbers of people share a number of common elements such as social structure, religion, and art (p. 18)

civilización: compleja cultura en la que un gran número de personas comparte ciertos elementos, como la estructura social, la religión y el arte (pág. 18)

civil rights movement: began in 1954 when the U.S. Supreme Court ruled that the practice of racial segregation (separation) was illegal; led to passage of Civil Rights Act of 1964 and the Voting Rights Act, which created the means to end segregation and discrimination in the workplace and all public places and made it easier for African Americans to vote in southern states, respectively (p. 918)

movimiento por los derechos civiles: comenzó en 1954 cuando la Corte Suprema de los EE.UU. estableció que la práctica de la segregación (separación) racial era ilegal; provocó la aprobación de la Ley de los Derechos Civiles de 1964 y de la Ley del Derecho al Voto, la primera permitió poner fin a la segregación y discriminación en los centros de trabajo y lugares públicos, y la segunda facilitó el voto a los afronorteamericanos en los estados sureños (pág. 918)

clan: a group of related families (pp. 370, 517)

clan: grupo de familias relacionadas (pp. 370, 517)

***classical:** authoritative, traditional; relating to the literature, art, architecture, or ideals of the ancient Greek and Roman world (p. 121)

***clásico:** documentado, tradicional; relacionado con la literatura, el arte, la arquitectura o los ideales del mundo antiguo griego y romano (pág. 121)

clergy: church leaders (p. 173)

clero: líderes de la Iglesia (pág. 173)

***code:** a system of principles or rules (p. 280)

***código:** sistema de principios y reglas (pág. 280)

Cold War: the period of political tension following World War II and ending with the fall of Communism in the Soviet Union at the end of the 1980s (p. 886)

Guerra Fría: período de tensión política que siguió a la Segunda Guerra Mundial y que culminó con la caída del comunismo en la Unión Soviética a fines de la década de 1980 (pág. 886)

collaborator: a person who assists the enemy (p. 877)

colaborador: persona que ayuda al enemigo (pág. 877)

***collapse:** to break down completely; to suddenly lose force or effectiveness (p. 174)

***colapsar:** desplomarse completamente; perder súbitamente la fuerza o efectividad (pág. 174)

collective bargaining: the right of unions to negotiate with employers over wages and hours (p. 794)

convenio colectivo: derecho de los sindicatos a negociar con los empleadores acerca de remuneraciones y horarios (pág. 794)

collectivization: a system in which private farms are eliminated and peasants work land owned by the government (p. 800)

colectivización: sistema en el cual se eliminan las granjas privadas y los campesinos trabajan la tierra perteneciente al gobierno (pág. 800)

colony: a settlement of people living in a new territory, linked with the parent country by trade and direct government control (p. 440)

colonia: asentamiento de personas que están viviendo en un nuevo territorio enlazado a la madre patria por el comercio y el control directo del gobierno (pág. 440)

Columbian Exchange: the extensive exchange of plants and animals between the Old and New Worlds, especially during the sixteenth and seventeenth centuries (p. 436)

Intercambio Colombino: extenso intercambio de plantas y animales entre el Nuevo Mundo y el Viejo, especialmente durante los siglos XVI y XVII (pág. 436)

***commentary:** an explanatory treatise (p. 204)

***comentario:** tratado explicatorio (pág. 204)

commercial capitalism: economic system in which people invest in trade or goods to make profits (pp. 338, 516)

capitalismo comercial: sistema económico en el cual la gente invierte en el comercio y en bienes con el fin de obtener ganancias (pp. 338, 516)

commodity: a marketable product (p. 735)

artículo de consumo: producto que se puede comercializar (pág. 735)

common law: a uniform system of law that developed in England based on court decisions and on customs and usage rather than on written law codes; replaced law codes that varied from place to place (p. 317)

derecho común: sistema uniforme de leyes desarrollado en Inglaterra, basado en las decisiones de las cortes y en las costumbres y usos, en vez de en códigos de leyes escritas; sustituyó los códigos legales que variaban de un lugar a otro (pág. 317)

commonwealth: a republic (p. 461)

mancomunidad: una república (pág. 461)

commune: in China during the 1950s, a group of collective farms, which contained more than 30,000 people who lived and worked together (p. 1013)

comuna: grupo de granjas colectivas de China durante la década de 1950, cada una de las cuales contenía más de 30,000 personas que vivían y trabajaban juntas (pág. 1013)

***community:** a group of people with common interests and characteristics living together within a larger society (p. 522)

***comunidad:** grupo de personas con intereses y características comunes que viven juntas en una sociedad mayor (pág. 522)

***compensation:** payment (p. 829)

***compensación:** pago (pág. 829)

***compiled:** collected and edited into a volume (p. 202)

***compilado:** reunido y editado en un volumen (pág. 202)

***complex:** having many intricate parts (pp. 196, 759)

***complejo:** que tiene muchas partes complicadas (pp. 196, 759)

***complexity:** the state of being complex or of having many intricate parts (p. 267)

***complejidad:** estado de ser complejo o de tener muchas partes complicadas (pág. 267)

concentration camp: a camp where prisoners of war, political prisoners, or members of minority groups are confined, typically under harsh conditions (p. 806)

campo de concentración: campamento donde se confina a prisioneros de guerra, prisioneros políticos o miembros de grupos minoritarios, por lo general bajo severas condiciones (pág. 806)

concession: a political compromise (p. 738)

concesión: compromiso político (pág. 738)

***conflict:** opposition; a fight, battle, or war (p. 454)

***conflicto:** oposición; pelea, batalla o guerra (pág. 454)

Confucianism: the system of political and ethical ideas formulated by the Chinese philosopher Confucius toward the end of the Zhou dynasty; it was intended to help restore order to a society that was in a state of confusion (p. 90)	**confucianismo:** sistema de ideas políticas y éticas formuladas por el filósofo chino Confucio hacia fines de la dinastía Zhou; fue concebido para restaurar el orden en una sociedad que estaba en estado de confusión (pág. 90)
conquistador: a Spanish conqueror of the Americas (p. 434)	**conquistador:** se refiere a los conquistadores españoles de las Américas (pág. 434)
conscription: military draft (p. 759)	**conscripción:** llamado obligatorio al servicio militar (pág. 759)
***consent:** approval (p. 961)	***consentimiento:** aprobación (pág. 961)
***consequence:** the effect or result of an action (p. 353)	***consecuencia:** efecto o resultado de una acción (pág. 353)
conservatism: a political philosophy based on tradition and social stability, favoring obedience to political authority and organized religion (p. 624)	**conservadurismo:** filosofía política basada en la tradición y estabilidad social sobre la base de la obediencia a la autoridad política y a la religión organizada (pág. 624)
***constitution:** the basic principles and laws of a nation, state, or social group that determine the powers and duties of the government and guarantee certain rights to the people in it (p. 626)	***constitución:** principios básicos y leyes de una nación, estado o grupo social, que determina los poderes y los deberes del gobierno y garantiza ciertos derechos al pueblo (pág. 626)
***construction:** manner or method of building (p. 348)	***construcción:** manera o método de construir (pág. 348)
consul: a chief executive officer of the Roman Republic; two were elected each year, one to run the government and one to lead the army into battle (p. 148)	**cónsul:** jefe ejecutivo de la República Romana; se elegían dos cada año: uno para llevar el gobierno y el otro para dirigir el ejército en las batallas (pág. 148)
consulate: government established in France after the overthrow of the Directory in 1799, with Napoleon as first consul in control of the entire government (p. 598)	**consulado:** gobierno establecido en Francia después del derrocamiento del Directorio en 1799, con Napoleón como primer cónsul y en control de todo el gobierno (pág. 598)
***consumer:** relating to one who consumes or uses economic goods (p. 577)	***consumidor:** relativo al que consume o usa un bien (pág. 577)
consumer society: a society preoccupied with buying goods (p. 920)	**sociedad de consumo:** sociedad preocupada en comprar bienes (pág. 920)
***context:** the circumstances surrounding a situation or event (p. 743)	***contexto:** circunstancias que rodean una situación o evento (pág. 743)
***contract:** a binding agreement between two or more people or parties (p. 311)	***contrato:** acuerdo vinculante entre dos o más personas o partes (pág. 311)
***contractor:** one who contracts or is a party to a contract to perform work, provide supplies, or erect buildings (p. 164)	***contratista:** el que contrata o es parte en un contrato para realizar un trabajo, suministrar algo o construir edificios (pág. 164)
contras: rebels financed by the United States who began a guerrilla war against the Sandinista government in Nicaragua (p. 971)	**contras:** rebeldes financiados por los Estados Unidos que entablaron una guerra guerrillera contra el gobierno sandinista en Nicaragua (pág. 971)
***controversy:** a dispute or quarrel (p. 673)	***controversia:** disputa o querella (pág. 673)
***conversion:** the change from one belief or form to another (p. 76)	***conversión:** cambio de una creencia o forma a otra (pág. 76)
***convert:** to change over from one belief to another (p. 462)	***convertir:** cambiar de una fe a otra (pág. 462)
***cooperation:** common effort (p. 780)	***cooperación:** esfuerzo común (pág. 780)
cooperative: a farm organization owned by and operated for the benefit of the farmers (p. 975)	**cooperativa:** sociedad agrícola perteneciente a agricultores y administrada para su beneficio (pág. 975)

***corporation:** form of business organization that has a separate legal entity with all the rights and responsibilities of an individual, including the right to buy and sell property, enter into legal contracts, and sue and be sued (p. 350)

***corporación:** forma de organizar los negocios que tiene una entidad legal independiente con todos los derechos y responsabilidades de un individuo, incluso el derecho a comprar y vender la propiedad, establecer contratos legales y demandar o ser demandados judicialmente (pág. 350)

cottage industry: a method of production in which tasks are done by individuals in their rural homes (p. 615)

industria casera: método de producción en el que las tareas las realizan las personas en sus hogares (pág. 615)

coup d'état: a sudden overthrow of the government (p. 593)

golpe de estado: súbito derrocamiento del gobierno (pág. 593)

***created:** made or brought something new into existence (p. 46)

***crear:** hacer o dar existencia a algo nuevo (pág. 46)

***creative:** imaginative (p. 475)

***creativo:** imaginativo (pág. 475)

creole: a person of European descent born in the New World and living there permanently (pp. 444, 708)

criollo: descendiente de europeos nacido en el Nuevo Mundo y que vive permanentemente allí (pp. 444, 708)

***crucial:** essential; important (p. 334)

***crucial:** esencial; importante (pág. 334)

Crusades: military expeditions carried out by European Christians in the Middle Ages to regain the Holy Land from the Muslims (p. 325)

Cruzadas: expediciones militares llevadas a cabo por cristianos europeos en la Edad Media para reconquistar la Tierra Santa de manos de los musulmanes (pág. 325)

cultural imperialism: referring to Western nations' control of other world cultures similar to how they had controlled colonial governments (p. 949)

imperialismo cultural: se refiere al control ejercido por los países occidentales sobre otras culturas del mundo, similar a como controlaban los gobiernos coloniales (pág. 949)

culture: the way of life a people follows (pp. 18, 254)

cultura: forma de vida que siguen las personas (pp. 18, 254)

cuneiform: "wedge-shaped," a system of writing developed by the Sumerians using a reed stylus to create wedge-shaped impressions on a clay tablet (p. 30)

cuneiforme: "en forma de cuña", sistema de escritura desarrollado por los sumerios utilizando un punzón de lengüeta para crear impresiones en forma de cuña en una tableta de arcilla (pág. 30)

***currency:** coins, for example, that are in circulation and used as a medium of exchange (p. 940)

***moneda:** dinero, por ejemplo, el que se encuentra en circulación y se usa como medio de intercambio (pág. 940)

***cycle:** a series of events that recur regularly and usually lead back to the starting point (p. 88)

***ciclo:** serie de eventos que se repiten regularmente y que por lo general llevan al punto de partida (pág. 88)

czar: Russian for "caesar," the title used by Russian emperors (p. 468)

zar: "césar" en ruso; título adoptado por los emperadores rusos (pág. 468)

d

daimyo: "great names," heads of noble families in Japan who controlled vast landed estates and relied on samurai for protection (pp. 281, 520)

daimyo: "grandes nombres", líderes de familias nobles en Japón, que controlaban vastas propiedades y confiaban su protección a los samuráis (pp. 281, 520)

Dao: "Way," the key to proper behavior under Confucianism (p. 87)

tao: "Camino", la clave para la conducta apropiada bajo el confucianismo (pág. 87)

Daoism: a system of ideas based on the teachings of Laozi; teaches that the will of Heaven is best followed through inaction so that nature is allowed to take its course (p. 92)

taoísmo: sistema de ideas basado en la doctrina de Laozi; enseña que la verdadera manera de seguir la voluntad del Cielo es la inacción, dejando a la naturaleza seguir su curso (pág. 92)

***debated:** discussed by considering opposing viewpoints (p. 109)

***debatido:** discutido mediante la consideración de los puntos de vista contrarios (pág. 109)

***decline:** a change to a lower state or level (p. 398)	***declinar:** cambio a un estado o nivel más bajo (pp. 88, 398)
deficit spending: when a government pays out more money than it takes in through taxation and other revenues, thus going into debt (p. 795)	**gastos deficitarios:** gastos gubernamentales que exceden a lo que se recibe a través de los impuestos y otros ingresos, por lo que se endeuda (pág. 795)
deforestation: the clearing of forests (p. 1042)	**deforestación:** tala de bosques (pág. 1042)
deism: an eighteenth-century religious philosophy based on reason and natural law (p. 548)	**deísmo:** filosofía religiosa del siglo XVIII basada en la razón y en la ley natural (pág. 548)
demilitarized: elimination or prohibition of weapons, fortifications, and other military installations (p. 857)	**desmilitarizar:** eliminar o prohibir las armas, fortificaciones y otras instalaciones militares (pág. 857)
democracy: "the rule of the many," government by the people, either directly or through their elected representatives (p. 114)	**democracia:** "gobierno de la mayoría", gobierno por personas elegidas directamente o a través de sus representantes elegidos (pág. 114)
***demonstration:** a public display of group feeling toward a person or a cause (p. 936)	***demostración:** muestra pública de los sentimientos colectivos hacia una persona o causa (pág. 936)
depression: a period of low economic activity and rising unemployment (p. 792)	**depresión:** período de baja actividad económica y aumento del desempleo (pág. 792)
***derived:** process of obtaining a product from a parent substance (p. 616)	***derivado:** proceso de obtención de un producto a partir de una sustancia progenitora (pág. 616)
desertification: formation of degraded soil, turning semi-arid lands into nonproductive deserts (p. 1042)	**desertificación:** formación de suelos degradados, que convierte los terrenos semiáridos en desiertos improductivos (pág. 1042)
de-Stalinization: the process of eliminating Stalin's more ruthless policies (p. 911)	**desestalinización:** proceso de eliminación de las políticas más crueles de Stalin (pág. 911)
détente: a phase of relaxed tensions and improved relations between two adversaries (p. 930)	**détente:** fase de relajamiento de las tensiones y mejoramiento de las relaciones entre dos adversarios (pág. 930)
deterrence: during the Cold War, the U.S. and Soviet policies of holding huge arsenals of nuclear weapons to prevent war; each nation believed that neither would launch a nuclear attack since both knew that the other side could strike back with devastating power (p. 905)	**disuasión:** durante la Guerra Fría, las políticas de los EE.UU. y de los soviéticos de mantener enormes arsenales de armas nucleares para evitar la guerra; cada país creía que ninguno lanzaría un ataque nuclear ya que ambos sabían que la otra parte podía responder con un ataque devastador (pág. 905)
dharma: in Hinduism, the divine law that rules karma; it requires all people to do their duty based on their status in society (p. 73)	**dharma:** en el Hinduismo, ley divina que gobierna el karma; exige que todas las personas cumplan con su deber según su estatus en la sociedad (pág. 73)
dictator: an absolute ruler (p. 154)	**dictador:** gobernante absoluto (pág. 154)
dictatorship: a form of government in which a person or small group has absolute power (p. 656)	**dictadura:** forma de gobierno en el que una persona o un pequeño grupo tiene el poder absoluto (pág. 656)
direct democracy: a system of government in which the people participate directly in government decision making through mass meetings (p. 121)	**democracia directa:** sistema de gobierno en el que las personas participan directamente en las decisiones del gobierno mediante asambleas masivas (pág. 121)
direct rule: colonial government in which local elites are removed from power and replaced by a new set of officials brought from the mother country (p. 690)	**gobierno directo:** gobierno colonial en el que se le retira el poder a la elite local y se lo dan a nuevos funcionarios traídos de la metrópoli (pág. 690)

disarmament group: a nongovernmental group that works to limit the size of military forces and weapons stocks (p. 1053)

grupo de desarme: grupo no gubernamental que trabaja para limitar el tamaño de las fuerzas armadas y de las reservas de armamentos (pág. 1053)

discrimination: prejudicial treatment usually based on race, religion, class, sex, or age (p. 1023)

discriminación: tratamiento prejuiciado, generalmente por la raza, la religión, la clase social, el género o la edad (pág. 1023)

dissident: a person who speaks out against the regime in power (p. 930)

disidente: persona que critica abiertamente al régimen que tiene el poder (pág. 930)

***diverse:** varied and not alike (p. 988)

***diverso:** variado o que no se parece (pág. 988)

divine right of kings: the belief that kings receive their power from God and are responsible only to God (p. 461)

derecho divino de los reyes: creencia de que los reyes reciben su poder de Dios y de que responden sólo ante Dios (pág. 461)

diviner: a person who is believed to have the power to foretell events (p. 253)

adivino: persona de quien se cree tiene el poder de predecir eventos (pág. 253)

***document:** an original or official paper that gives proof of or support to (p. 317)

***documento:** papel original u oficial que prueba o apoya algo (pág. 317)

***domain:** where one has absolute ownership of land or other property (p. 486)

***dominio:** donde alguien tiene la propiedad absoluta de la tierra u otro bien (pág. 486)

***domestic:** relating to or originating within one's country (pp. 79, 588)

***doméstico:** relativo al país de uno u originado en él (pp. 79, 588)

***domesticated:** adapted to life with and to the advantage of humans (p. 46)

***domesticado:** adaptado a vivir con las personas y para su beneficio (pág. 46)

domestication: adaption for human use (p. 14)

domesticación: adaptación para el uso de las personas (pág. 14)

***dominate:** influence or control (p. 856)

***dominar:** influir o controlar (pág. 856)

domino theory: idea that if one country falls to communism, neighboring countries will also fall (p. 907)

teoría del domino: idea de que si un país cae ante el comunismo, los países colindantes también lo harán (pág. 907)

dowry: a gift of money or property paid at the time of marriage, either by the bride's parents to her husband or, in Islamic societies, by a husband to his wife (pp. 203, 269, 403)

dote: dinero o bienes pagados en el momento del matrimonio por los padres de la novia a su esposo, o en sociedades islámicas, por el marido a su esposa (pp. 203, 269, 403)

***draft:** to select for some purpose; to conscript (p. 446)

***reclutar:** seleccionar para algún propósito; alistar (pág. 446)

***drama:** a composition that tells a story usually involving conflicts and emotions through action and dialogue and typically designed for the theater (p. 474)

***drama:** composición que cuenta una historia, por lo general implicada con conflictos y emociones, a través de la acción y el diálogo, diseñada habitualmente para el teatro (pág. 474)

***dramatic:** remarkable; notable; amazing (p. 1024)

***dramático:** considerable; notable; sorprendente (pág. 1024)

Duma: the Russian legislative assembly (p. 670)

Duma: la asamblea legislativa rusa (pág. 670)

dynasty: a family of rulers whose right to rule is passed on within the family (p. 36)

dinastía: familia de gobernantes cuyo derecho a gobernar se transmite dentro de la familia (pág. 36)

e

ecology: the study of the relationships between living things and their environment (p. 1042)

ecología: estudio de las relaciones entre los seres vivos y su ambiente (pág. 1042)

***economic:** relating to the production, distribution, and consumption of goods and services (p. 174)	***económico:** relativo a la producción, distribución y consumo de bienes y servicios (pág. 174)
elector: an individual qualified to vote in an election (p. 593)	**elector:** persona calificada para votar en una elección (pág. 593)
***element:** a distinct group within a larger group (p. 824)	***elemento:** un grupo particular dentro de un grupo mayor (pág. 824)
emancipation: the act of setting free (p. 636)	**emancipación:** acción de dejar en libertad (pág. 636)
empire: a large political unit or state, usually under a single leader, that controls many peoples or territories (p. 32)	**imperio:** gran unidad política, comúnmente bajo un solo líder, que controla a muchos pueblos o territorios (pág. 32)
***enabled:** made possible (p. 309)	***posibilitar:** hacer posible (pág. 309)
enclosure movement: in Great Britain during the 1700s, the Parliamentary decree that allowed fencing off of common lands, forcing many peasants to move to town (p. 614)	**movimiento de cerramiento:** durante los años 1700, un decreto del parlamento británico autorizó a cercar terrenos públicos, lo que obligó a muchos campesinos a marcharse a las ciudades (pág. 614)
encomienda: a system of labor the Spanish used in the Americas; Spanish landowners had the right, as granted by Queen Isabella, to use Native Americans as laborers (p. 435)	**encomienda:** sistema de trabajo empleado por los españoles en las Américas; los terratenientes españoles tenían el derecho, otorgado por la reina Isabel, a emplear a los nativoamericanos como peones (pág. 435)
***enhanced:** improved (p. 910)	***mejorado:** perfeccionado (pág. 910)
enlightened absolutism: a system in which rulers tried to govern by Enlightenment principles while maintaining their full royal powers (p. 554)	**absolutismo ilustrado:** sistema en el cual los gobernantes trataban de gobernar por medio de principios de la Ilustración mientras mantenían todos sus poderes reales (pág. 554)
***enormous:** huge; vast; immense (p. 324)	***enorme:** tremendo; vasto; inmenso (pág. 324)
***ensure:** to make sure (p. 307)	***asegurar:** estar seguro (pág. 307)
entrepreneur: a person interested in finding new business opportunities and new ways to make profits (p. 614)	**empresario:** persona interesada en hallar nuevas oportunidades de negocios y nuevas formas de obtener ganancias (pág. 614)
***environment:** the complex factors—climate, soil, and living things—that act upon an ecological community and determine its form and survival (p. 1041)	***medioambiente:** complejos factores—clima, suelo y seres vivientes—que actúan sobre una comunidad ecológica y determinan su forma y supervivencia (pág. 1041)
ephor: one of the five men elected each year in ancient Sparta who were responsible for the education of youth and the conduct of all citizens (p. 116)	**éforo:** cada uno de los cinco hombres elegidos cada año en la antigua Esparta, responsables de la educación de los jóvenes y de la conducta de todos los ciudadanos (pág. 116)
epic poem: a long poem that tells the deeds of a great hero, such as the *Iliad* and the *Odyssey* of Homer (p. 111)	**poema épico:** extenso poema que cuenta las hazañas de un gran héroe, como la Iliada y la Odisea, de Homero (pág. 111)
Epicureanism: school of thought developed by the philosopher Epicurus in Hellenistic Athens; it held that happiness is the chief goal in life, and the means to achieve happiness was the pursuit of pleasure (p. 139)	**epicureanismo:** escuela del pensamiento desarrollada por el filósofo Epicuro en la Atenas helenística; sostenía que la felicidad es la principal meta en la vida y que el medio para lograr la felicidad era la búsqueda del placer (pág. 139)
***eroded:** diminished or destroyed by degrees (p. 203)	***erosionado:** reducido o destruido gradualmente (pág. 203)
***establish:** to set up permanently; to found (p. 847)	***establecer:** fijar permanentemente; fundar (pág. 847)

estate: one of the three classes into which French society was divided before the revolution: the clergy (First Estate), the nobles (Second Estate), and the townspeople (Third Estate) (pp. 319, 576); a landed property usually with a large house on it (p. 707)	**estado:** cada una de las tres clases en las que se dividía la sociedad francesa medieval: el clero (primer estado), los nobles (segundo estado) y la plebe (tercer estado) (pp. 319, 576)
***estimate:** to make a rough determination of (p. 374)	***estimar:** calcular aproximadamente (pág. 374)
eta: Japan's outcast class, whose way of life was strictly regulated by the Tokugawa (p. 523)	**eta:** la clase más baja de la sociedad japonesa, cuya forma de vida era estrictamente regulada por el Tokugawa (pág. 523)
***ethical:** conforming to accepted standards of conduct; moral (p. 90)	***ético:** de acuerdo con los estándares aceptados de conducta; moral (pág. 90)
***ethics:** moral principles; generally recognized rules of conduct (p. 129)	***ética:** principios morales; reglas de conducta generalmente aceptadas (pág. 129)
***ethnic:** relating to people who have common racial, religious, or cultural origins (p. 874)	***étnico:** relativo a las personas que tienen el mismo origen racial, religioso o cultural (pág. 874)
ethnic cleansing: a policy of killing or forcibly removing an ethnic group from its lands; used by the Serbs against the Muslim minority in Bosnia (pp. 824, 939)	**limpieza étnica:** política de matar o expulsar por la fuerza a un grupo étnico de sus territorios; usada por los serbios contra las minorías musulmanas en Bosnia (pp. 824, 939)
***eventually:** in the end (p. 837)	***finalmente:** al final (pág. 837)
***excluded:** not counted or included (p. 302)	***excluido:** no contado o incluido (pág. 302)
***exclusion:** barred from inclusion or participation in (p. 581)	***excluir:** impedir incluirse o participar en algo (pág. 581)
***exclusive:** limited to a single indivdual or group (p. 729)	***exclusivo:** limitado a un sólo individuo o grupo (pág. 729)
***expand:** to enlarge or to spread (p. 484)	***expandir:** ampliar o extender (pág. 484)
***exploit:** to make use of meanly or unfairly for one's own advantage (p. 690)	***explotar:** utilizar cruel o injustamente para provecho propio (pág. 690)
***export:** to send a product or service for sale to another country (p. 690)	***exportar:** enviar en venta un producto o servicio a otro país (pág. 690)
***external:** relating to dealings or relationships with foreign countries (p. 588)	***externo:** relativo a tratos o relaciones con países extranjeros (pág. 588)
extraterritoriality: living in a section of a country set aside for foreigners but not subject to the host country's laws (p. 726)	**extraterritorialidad:** vivir en una sección de un país apartada para extranjeros, pero no sujeta a las leyes del país anfitrión (pág. 726)

faction: a dissenting group (p. 587)	**facción:** grupo de disidentes (pág. 587)
***factor:** a contributing part (p. 243)	***factor:** elemento que contribuye (pág. 243)
fascism: a political philosophy that glorifies the state above the individual by emphasizing the need for a strong central government led by a dictatorial ruler (p. 797)	**fascismo:** filosofía política que glorifica al estado por sobre el individuo y enfatiza la necesidad de tener un gobierno central fuerte encabezado por un gobernante dictatorial (pág. 797)
federal system: a form of government in which power is shared between the national government and state governments (p. 569)	**sistema federal:** forma de gobierno en la cual el poder es compartido entre el gobierno nacional y los gobiernos estatales (pág. 569)

feminism: the movement for women's rights (p. 662)

feminismo: movimiento a favor de los derechos de las mujeres (pág. 662)

feudal contract: under feudalism, the unwritten rules that determined the relationship between a lord and his vassal (p. 311)

contrato feudal: reglas no escritas que determinaban la relación entre un señor y su vasallo en el feudalismo (pág. 311)

feudalism: political and social system that developed during the Middle Ages when royal governments were no longer able to defend their subjects; nobles offered protection and land in return for service (p. 310)

feudalismo: sistema político y social que se desarrolló durante la Edad Media cuando los gobiernos reales ya no podían defender a sus pueblos; los nobles ofrecían protección y tierras a cambio de servicios (pág. 310)

fief: under feudalism, a grant of land made to a vassal; the vassal held political authority within his fief (p. 310)

feudo: concesión de tierras hecha a un vasallo en el feudalismo; el vasallo tenía autoridad política dentro de su feudo (pág. 310)

filial piety: the duty of family members to subordinate their needs and desires to those of the male head of the family, a concept important in Confucianism (p. 89)

respeto filial: deber de los miembros de la familia de subordinar sus necesidades y deseos a los del cabeza de familia, un concepto importante en el confucianismo (pág. 89)

***final:** the last in a series, process, or progress (p. 1013)

***final:** el último de una serie, proceso o progreso (pág. 1013)

***financial:** relating to the management of funds (p. 152)

***financiero:** relativo al manejo de fondos (pág. 152)

***financier:** one who deals with finance and investment on a large scale; one who specializes in raising and expending public monies (p. 652)

***financista:** persona que maneja las finanzas e inversiones a gran escala; persona especializada en colectar y gastar los fondos públicos (pág. 652)

fossil: a remnant or impression of an organism from a past geologic age that has been preserved in the earth's crust (p. 4)

fósil: residuo o impresión de un organismo de una era geológica pasada que se ha preservado en la corteza terrestre (pág. 4)

***founder:** one who founds or establishes (p. 139)

***fundador:** quien funda o establece algo (pág. 139)

***founding:** originating; beginning (p. 253)

***fundar:** originar; comenzar (pág. 253)

fresco: a painting done on fresh, wet plaster with water-based paints (p. 409)

fresco: pintura hecha en yeso fresco y húmedo con pinturas a base de agua (pág. 409)

***function:** operate (p. 1039)

***funcionar:** operar (pág. 1039)

***fund:** to provide money for (p. 977)

***financiar:** aportar dinero para algo (pág. 977)

gender parity: a policy by which women have to make up either a certain number of the candidates in an election or a certain number of those elected (p. 948)

paridad de género: política mediante la cual las mujeres deben contar con un determinado número de candidatos en las elecciones o con un determinado número entre los elegidos (pág. 948)

gender stereotyping: restricting what a person could do just because of the person's gender (p. 948)

estereotipia de género: la restricción en el juicio de lo que una persona puede hacer, basándose sólo en su género (pág. 948)

***generation:** a group of individuals born and living at the same time (p. 548)

***generación:** grupo de individuos que nacen y viven en una misma época (pág. 548)

genocide: the deliberate mass murder or physical extinction of a particular racial, political, or cultural group (pp. 824, 876)

genocidio: matanza masiva deliberada o extinción física de un grupo racial, político o cultural en particular (pp. 824, 876)

geocentric: literally, earth-centered; a system of planetary motion that places Earth at the center of the universe, with the sun, moon, and other planets revolving around it (p. 540)

geocéntrico: literalmente, centrado en la Tierra; sistema de movimiento planetario que ubica a la Tierra como el centro del universo, con el Sol, la Luna y los otros planetas girando en torno a ella (pág. 540)

global economy: an economy in which the production, distribution, and sale of goods take place on a worldwide scale, as in a multinational corporation (p. 1043)

economía global: economía en la cual la producción, distribución y venta de bienes se realiza a escala mundial, como en una corporación multinacional (pág. 1043)

globalization: the movement toward a more integrated and interdependent world economy (pp. 949, 1051)

globalización: movimiento hacia una economía mundial más integrada e independiente (pp. 941, 1051)

***goal:** an aim or a purpose (p. 986)

***meta:** objetivo o propósito (pág. 986)

grand vizier: the Ottoman sultan's chief minister who carried the main burdens of the state and who led the council meetings (p. 487)

gran visir: ministro principal de los sultanes otomanos, que se ocupa de los principales problemas del estado y encabezaba las reuniones del consejo (pág. 487)

grassroots level: community level (p. 1053)

nivel de base: nivel comunitario (pág. 1053)

greenhouse effect: global warming caused by the buildup of carbon dioxide in the atmosphere (p. 1042)

efecto invernadero: calentamiento global causado por la acumulación de dióxido de carbono en la atmósfera (pág. 1042)

griot: a special class of African storytellers who help keep alive a people's history (p. 255)

griot: tipo especial de narradores africanos de cuentos que contribuían a mantener viva la historia de un pueblo (pág. 255)

***guaranteed:** assured the fulfillment of a condition (pp. 168, 569)

***garantizado:** que asegura el cumplimiento de una condición (pp. 168, 569)

guerrilla tactics: the use of unexpected maneuvers like sabotage and subterfuge to fight an enemy (p. 838)

tácticas de guerrilla: uso de maniobras inesperadas, como sabotajes y subterfugios para luchar contra un enemigo (pág. 838)

guild: a business association that is associated with a particular trade or craft; guilds evolved in the twelfth century and played a leading role in the economic life of medieval cities (p. 341)

gremio: asociación comercial relacionada con un oficio o artesanía en particular; los gremios evolucionaron en el siglo XII y desempeñaron un papel importante en la vida económica de las ciudades medievales (pág. 341)

gunpowder empire: an empire formed by outside conquerors who unified the regions that they conquered through their mastery of firearms (p. 486)

imperio de pólvora: imperio formado por conquistadores extranjeros que unificaron regiones conquistadas gracias a su habilidad con las armas de fuego (pág. 486)

hajj: a pilgrimage to Makkah, one of the requirements of the Five Pillars of Islam (p. 190)

hajj: peregrinación a La Meca; uno de los requisitos de los Cinco Pilares del Islam (pág. 190)

hans: approximately 250 domains into which Japan was divided under the Tokugawa (p. 522)

han: cada uno de los aproximadamente 250 dominios en los que se dividió Japón bajo los Tokugawa (pág. 522)

harem: "sacred place," the private domain of an Ottoman sultan, where he and his wives resided (p. 486)

harén: "lugar sagrado", dominio privado del sultán otomano, donde residían él y sus esposas (pág. 486)

heavy industry: the manufacture of machines and equipment for factories and mines (p. 910)

industria pesada: manufactura de máquinas y equipo destinadas a fábricas y minas (pág. 910)

heliocentric: literally, sun-centered; the system of the universe proposed in 1543 by Nicholas Copernicus, who argued that the earth and planets revolve around the sun (p. 540)

heliocéntrico: literalmente, centrado en el Sol; sistema del universo propuesto en 1543 por Nicolás Copérnico, quien sostuvo que la Tierra y los planetas giraban en torno al Sol (pág. 540)

Hellenistic Era: the age of Alexander the Great; period when the Greek language and ideas were carried to the non-Greek world (p. 137)

Era Helenística: era de Alejandro Magno; período en el cual los griegos llevaron su idioma y sus ideas fuera del mundo griego (pág. 137)

helot: in ancient Sparta, a captive person who was forced to work for the conqueror (p. 115)

ilota: en la antigua Esparta, persona cautiva que era forzada a trabajar para su conquistador (pág. 115)

heresy: the denial of basic Church doctrines (p. 346)

herejía: negación de las doctrinas básicas de la Iglesia (pág. 346)

hieratic script: simplified version of hieroglyphics used in ancient Egypt for business transactions, record keeping, and the general needs of daily life (p. 43)

escritura hierática: versión simplificada de los jeroglíficos usada en el antiguo Egipto para las transacciones comerciales, registros y las necesidades generales de la vida cotidiana (pág. 43)

hieroglyph: a picture or symbol used in a hieroglyphic system of writing (p. 375)

caracteres jeroglíficos: dibujos o símbolos usados en el sistema jeroglífico de escritura (pág. 375)

hieroglyphics: "priest-carvings" or "sacred writings," a complex system of writing that used both pictures and more abstract forms; used by the ancient Egyptians and Mayans (p. 42)

jeroglíficos: "grabados sacerdotales" o "escrituras sagradas", complejo sistema de escritura que utilizaba tanto dibujos como formas más abstractas; empleado por los antiguos egipcios y mayas (pág. 42)

***highlighted:** centered attention on (p. 725)

***resaltar:** centrar la atención en algo (pág. 725)

Hijrah: the journey of Muhammad and his followers to Madinah in 622, which became year 1 of the official calendar of Islam (p. 190)

hégira: viaje de Mahoma y sus seguidores a Medina en el año 622, que pasó a ser el año 1 del calendario oficial del islam (pág. 190)

Hinduism: the major Indian religious system, which had its origins in the religious beliefs of the Aryans who settled India after 1500 B.C. (p. 72)

hinduismo: principal sistema religioso de la India, que tuvo sus orígenes en las creencias religiosas de los arios que se establecieron en la India después del año 1500 a.C. (pág. 72)

hominid: humans and other humanlike creatures that walk upright (p. 6)

homínido: humanos y otras criaturas similares a los humanos que caminaban erectos (pág. 6)

Homo sapiens sapiens: "wise, wise human," a species that appeared in Africa between 150,000 and 200,000 years ago; they were the first anatomically modern humans (p. 7)

Homo sapiens sapiens: "ser humano sabio sabio", especie que apareció en África entre 150,000 y 200,000 años atrás; desde el punto de vista anatómico fueron los primeros humanos modernos (pág. 7)

hoplite: in the early Greek military system, a heavily armed foot soldier (p. 113)

hoplita: en el sistema militar de la antigua Grecia, soldado de infantería fuertemente armado (pág. 113)

hostage system: a system used by the shogunate to control the daimyo in Tokugawa Japan; the family of a daimyo lord was forced to stay at their residence in the capital whenever the lord was absent from it (p. 522)

sistema de rehén: sistema utilizado por el shogunado para controlar al daimyo en el Japón de los Tokugawa; la familia de un daimyo estaba obligada a permanecer en su residencia en la capital mientras él se encontrara ausente (pág. 522)

humanism: an intellectual movement of the Renaissance based on the study of the humanities, which included grammar, rhetoric, poetry, moral philosophy, and history (p. 406)

humanismo: movimiento intelectual del Renacimiento basado en el estudio de las humanidades, que incluía gramática, retórica, poesía, filosofía moral e historia (pág. 406)

***hypothetical:** assumed but not known (p. 621)

***hipotético:** supuesto, pero no comprobado (pág. 621)

I

***identifying:** believing that one is the same or very similar to another (p. 36)

***identificar:** considerar que uno es igual o muy similar a otro (pág. 36)

ideograph: a character that combines two or more pictographs to represent an idea; used in ancient Chinese script (p. 90)

ideograma: carácter que combina dos o más pictogramas para representar una idea; usado en la antigua escritura china (pág. 90)

***ideological:** based on a set of beliefs (p. 886)

***ideológico:** basado en un conjunto de convicciones (pág. 886)

***ideology:** a set of beliefs (p. 96)

***ideología:** conjunto de convicciones (pág. 96)

***ignorant:** unaware; lacking knowledge of (p. 414)

***ignorante:** desinformado; falto de conocimientos sobre algo (pág. 414)

imperator: commander in chief; the Latin origin of the word *emperor* (p. 156)

emperador: comandante en jefe; el origen latino de la palabra es *"imperator"* (pág. 156)

imperialism: the extension of a nation's power over other lands (p. 686)

imperialismo: extensión del poder de una nación hacia otras tierras (pág. 686)

***implies:** expresses indirectly through reference or association (p. 114)

***implica:** expresa indirectamente mediante una referencia o asociación (pág. 114)

***impose:** to establish or apply (p. 529)

***imponer:** establecer o aplicar (pág. 529)

***inadequate:** not sufficient (p. 149)

***inadecuado:** que no es suficiente (pág. 149)

***incentive:** something that motivates (p. 518)

***incentivo:** algo que motiva (pág. 518)

indemnity: payment for damages (p. 731)

indemnización: pago por daños (pág. 731)

indigenous: native to a region (p. 696)

indígena: nativo de una región (pág. 696)

indirect rule: colonial government in which local rulers are allowed to maintain their positions of authority and status (p. 690)

dominio indirecto: gobierno colonial en el que los gobernantes locales pueden mantener sus posiciones de autoridad y estatus (pág. 690)

***individuality:** a total character that distinguishes an individual from others (pp. 95, 638)

***individualidad:** conjunto total de caracteres que distinguen a un individuo de los otros (pp. 95, 638)

inductive reasoning: the doctrine that scientists should proceed from the particular to the general by making systematic observations and carefully organized experiments to test hypotheses or theories, a process that will lead to correct general principles (p. 545)

razonamiento inductivo: doctrina de que los científicos debían proceder de lo particular a lo general, mediante observaciones sistemáticas y experimentos cuidadosamente organizados para probar las hipótesis o teorías, proceso que conduciría a principios generales correctos (pág. 545)

indulgence: a release from all or part of punishment for sin by the Catholic Church, reducing time in purgatory after death (p. 414)

indulgencia: perdón de todo o parte de un castigo por pecar otorgado por la Iglesia católica, reduciendo el tiempo en el purgatorio tras la muerte (pág. 414)

industrial capitalism: an economic system based on industrial production or manufacturing (p. 620)

capitalismo industrial: sistema económico basado en la producción industrial o la manufactura (pág. 620)

infidel: an unbeliever; a term applied to the Muslims during the Crusades (p. 325)

infiel: persona no creyente; término aplicado a los musulmanes durante las Cruzadas (pág. 325)

inflation: a rapid increase in prices (pp. 176, 458)

inflación: rápido aumento de los precios (pp. 176, 458)

***innovation:** a new idea, method, or device (p. 30)

***innovación:** idea, método o dispositivo nuevos (pág. 30)

***insecure:** uncertain, shaky; not adequately covered or sustained (p. 671)

***inseguro:** que no es cierto, convulsivo; que no está cubierto o sostenido adecuadamente (pág. 671)

***instability:** not steady; wavering (pp. 152, 398)

***inestabilidad:** que no está estático; que se balancea (pp. 152, 398)

***instituted:** put into action (p. 96)

***instituido:** puesto en marcha (pág. 96)

***institution:** an organization for the promotion of a cause (p. 148)

***institución:** organización para la promoción de una causa (pág. 148)

***instructed:** taught or trained (p. 384)

***instruido:** enseñado o entrenado (pág. 384)

insulae: Roman apartment blocks constructed of concrete with wooden beam floors (p. 165)

insulae: bloques de apartamentos romanos construidos de concreto con piso de vigas de madera (pág. 165)

***intelligent:** having a high degree of understanding and mental capacity (p. 498)

***inteligente:** que tiene una alto grado de comprensión y capacidad mental (pág. 498)

***intensity:** extreme degree of strength, force, energy, or feeling (p. 679)

***intensidad:** grado de fortaleza, fuerza, energía o sentimiento (pág. 679)

GLOSSARY

interdict: a decree by the pope that forbade priests to give the sacraments of the Church to the people (p. 344)

interdicción: decreto papal que prohibía a los sacerdotes impartir los sacramentos de la Iglesia a la gente (pág. 344)

***intervention:** involvement in a situation to alter the outcome (p. 711)

***intervención:** involucrarse en una situación para alterar el resultado (pág. 711)

intifada: "uprising," militant movement that arose during the 1980s among supporters of the Palestine Liberation Organization living in Israel (p. 999)

intifada: "levantamiento", movimiento militante surgido en la década de 1980 entre quienes respaldaban a la Organización para la Liberación de Palestina y vivían en Israel (pág. 999)

***investor:** a person or entity that commits money to earn a financial return (p. 844)

***inversor:** persona o entidad que compromete su dinero para obtener una ganancia económica (pág. 844)

***involvement:** a commitment or a connection to (p. 866)

***implicación:** compromiso o conexión con algo (pág. 866)

Islam: monotheistic religion that emerged in the Arabian Peninsula during the seventh century A.D. (p. 190)

islam: religión monoteísta que surgió en la Península Arábiga en el siglo VII d.C. (pág. 190)

isolationism: a policy of national isolation by abstention from alliances and other international political and economic relations (p. 866)

aislacionismo: política de aislamiento nacional mediante la abstención de establecer alianzas y relaciones políticas y económicas internacionales (pág. 866)

***issue:** a vital or unsettled matter (p. 996)

***asunto:** cuestión vital o no acordada (pág. 996)

janissary: a soldier in the elite guard of the Ottoman Turks (p. 484)

jenízaro: soldado de la guardia elite de los turcos otomanos (pág. 484)

jihad: "struggle in the way of God" (p. 192)

jihad: "lucha en el camino de Dios" (pág. 192)

journeyman: a worker who has learned a trade and works for wages for other masters (p. 341)

jornalero: trabajador que ha aprendido un oficio y trabaja por un salario para un patrón (pág. 341)

***justification:** the process of being justified, or deemed worthy of salvation, by God (p. 419)

***justificación:** proceso de ser justificado o juzgado digno de la salvación por Dios (pág. 419)

kaiser: German for "caesar," the title of the emperors of the Second German Empire (p. 633)

káiser: término alemán para "césar", título de los emperadores del Segundo Imperio Alemán (pág. 633)

kamikaze: Japanese for "divine wind", a suicide mission in which young Japanese pilots intentionally flew their airplanes into U.S. fighting ships at sea (p. 883)

kamikaze: término japonés para "viento divino", misión suicida en la que jóvenes pilotos japoneses intencionalmente estrellaban sus aviones contra los buques de guerra de los EE.UU. (pág. 883)

karma: in Hinduism, the force generated by a person's actions that determines how the person will be reborn in the next life (p. 73)

karma: en el Hinduismo, la fuerza generada por las acciones de una persona, lo que determina cómo renacerá esta persona en la próxima vida (pág. 73)

khanate: one of the several separate territories into which Genghis Khan's empire was split, each under the rule of one of his sons (p. 270)

kanato: cada uno de los diversos territorios independientes en los que se dividió el imperio de Genghis Khan y que estaban bajo el gobierno de uno de sus hijos (pág. 270)

knight: under feudalism, a member of the heavily armored cavalry (p. 310)

caballero: en el feudalismo, miembro de la caballería fuertemente acorazado (pág. 310)

***labor:** people with all their abilities and efforts (p. 444)	***mano de obra:** personas con todas sus habilidades y esfuerzo (pág. 444)
laissez-faire: literally, "let [people] do [what they want]"; the concept that the state should not impose government regulations but should leave the economy alone (p. 550)	***laissez-faire:*** literalmente, "dejar [a las personas] hacer [lo que quieran]"; el concepto de que el estado no debe imponer regulaciones gubernamentales, sino que debe dejar la economía andar sola (pág. 550)
laity: regular church members (p. 173)	**laicado:** miembros regulares de una Iglesia (pág. 173)
lay investiture: the practice by which secular rulers both chose nominees to church offices and gave them the symbols of their office (p. 342)	**investidura secular:** práctica mediante la cual los líderes seculares elegían a los nominados a cargos en la Iglesia y los investían con los símbolos de su cargo (pág. 342)
***legal:** relating to law; founded on law (p. 322)	***legal:** relativo a la ley; basado en la ley (pág. 322)
Legalism: a popular philosophy developed in China toward the end of the Zhou dynasty; it proposes that human beings are evil by nature and can only be brought to the correct path by harsh laws (p. 93)	**legalismo:** filosofía popular desarrollada en China hacia fines de la dinastía Zhou; postula que los seres humanos son malvados por naturaleza y sólo pueden ser llevados a la senda correcta mediante leyes fuertes (pág. 93)
***legislature:** an organized body that makes laws (p. 822)	***legislatura:** cuerpo organizado que hace las leyes (pág. 822)
***liberal:** broad-minded; associated with ideals of the individual, especially economic freedom and greater participation in government (p. 601)	***liberal:** de mente amplia; asociado con los ideales del individuo, especialmente la libertad económica y una mayor participación en el gobierno (pág. 601)
liberalism: a political philosophy originally based largely on Enlightenment principles, holding that people should be as free as possible from government restraint and that civil liberties—the basic rights of all people—should be protected (p. 626)	**liberalismo:** filosofía política originalmente basada en gran medida en los principios de la Ilustración, que sostenía que las personas deben estar lo más libres posible de las restricciones gubernamentales y que las libertades civiles—los derechos básicos de las personas—deben protegerse (pág. 626)
***liberated:** freed (p. 900)	***liberado:** independizado (pág. 900)
lineage group: an extended family unit that has combined into a larger community (p. 251)	**grupo de linaje:** unidad extendida de una familia que se ha mezclado en una comunidad mayor (pág. 251)
literacy: the ability to read (p. 665)	**alfabetización:** capacidad de leer y escribir (pág. 665)
longhouse: Iroquois house about 150 to 200 feet (46 to 61 m) long built of wooden poles covered with sheets of bark and housing about a dozen families (p. 370)	**vivienda comunal:** vivienda de los indios iroqueses, de aproximadamente 150 a 200 pies (46 a 61 m) de longitud, construida sobre pilares de madera cubiertos con láminas de corteza y que albergaba a aproximadamente una docena de familias (pág. 370)
Lutheranism: the religious doctrine that Martin Luther developed; it differed from Catholicism in the doctrine of salvation, which Luther believed could be achieved by faith alone, not by good works; Lutheranism was the first Protestant faith (p. 416)	**luteranismo:** doctrina religiosa que desarrolló Martín Lutero; difiere del catolicismo en cuanto a la doctrina de salvación, que Lutero consideraba que podía alcanzarse mediante la fe sola, no por buenas acciones; el luteranismo fue la primera fe protestante (pág. 416)

magic realism: a form of expression unique to Latin American literature; it combines realistic events with dreamlike or fantasy backgrounds (p. 964)	**realismo mágico:** singular forma de expresión de la literatura latinoamericana; combina elementos realistas sobre un fondo de sueños o fantasía (pág. 964)

GLOSSARY

Magna Carta: the "Great Charter" of rights, which King John was forced to sign by the English nobles at Runnymeade in 1215 (p. 318)	**Carta Magna:** "Gran Carta Real" de derechos que el rey Juan Sin Tierra fue obligado a firmar por los nobles ingleses en Runnymede en 1215 (pág. 318)
Mahayana: a school of Buddhism that developed in northwest India, stressing the view that nirvana can be achieved through devotion to the Buddha; its followers consider Buddhism a religion, not a philosophy, and the Buddha is a divine figure (p. 284)	**Mahayana:** escuela de budismo que se desarrolló en el noroeste de la India y que enfatiza la visión de que se puede alcanzar el nirvana a través de la devoción a Buda; sus seguidores consideran al budismo una religión, no una filosofía, y a Buda como una figura divina (pág. 284)
mainland states: part of a continent, as distinguished from peninsulas or offshore islands (p. 529)	**territorio continental:** parte de un continente, a diferencia de las penínsulas o las islas (pág. 529)
***maintain:** to keep in an existing state of repair or efficiency (p. 1024)	***mantener:** conservar un estado existente de compostura o eficiencia (pág. 1024)
maize: corn (p. 383)	**maíz:** cultivo nativo de las Américas (pág. 383)
***major:** great; significant in size or importance (p. 36)	***principal:** significativo en tamaño o importancia (pág. 36)
mandate: a nation governed by another nation on behalf of the League of Nations (p. 783)	**mandato:** nación gobernada por otra en nombre de la Liga de Naciones (pág. 783)
Mandate of Heaven: claim by Chinese kings of the Zhou dynasty that they had direct authority from heaven to rule and to keep order in the universe (p. 87)	**Mandato del Cielo:** reivindicación de los reyes de la dinastía Zhou de China de que ellos recibieron directamente del cielo la autoridad para gobernar y mantener en orden el universo (pág. 87)
Mannerism: an artistic movement that emerged in Italy in the 1520s and 1530s; it marked the end of the Renaissance by breaking down the principles of balance, harmony, and moderation (p. 472)	**manierismo:** movimiento artístico surgido en Italia en las décadas de 1520 y 1530; marcó el fin del Renacimiento al romper los principios de balance, armonía y moderación (pág. 472)
manor: in medieval Europe, an agricultural estate that a lord ran and peasants worked (p. 336)	**feudo:** en la Europa medieval, propiedad agrícola administrada por un señor y trabajada por campesinos (pág. 336)
mass production: production of goods in quantity usually by machinery (p. 655)	**producción masiva:** producción de bienes en grandes cantidades, generalmente con el empleo de máquinas (pág. 655)
masterpiece: piece created by a journeyman who aspires to be a master craftsperson; it allowed the members of a guild to judge whether the journeyman was qualified to become a master and join the guild (p. 341)	**obra maestra:** obra creada por un aprendiz que aspira a ser maestro artesano; permitía a los miembros de un gremio juzgar si un aprendiz estaba calificado para convertirse en maestro e integrar el gremio (pág. 341)
matrilineal: tracing lineage through the mother rather than the father (p. 252)	**matrilineal:** que traza el linaje a través de la madre y sus ancestros, no a través del padre (pág. 252)
***media:** channels or systems of communication (p. 798)	***medios:** canales o sistemas de comunicación (pág. 798)
megacity: a city that has grown so fast in population that it cannot provide regular urban services (p. 962)	**megaciudad:** ciudad cuya población ha crecido tan rápidamente que no puede garantizar los servicios urbanos habituales (pág. 962)
mercantilism: a set of principles that dominated economic thought in the seventeenth century; it held that the prosperity of a nation depended on a large supply of gold and silver (p. 440)	**mercantilismo:** conjunto de principios que dominaban el pensamiento económico en el siglo XVII; sostenía que la prosperidad de una nación dependía de tener grandes cantidades de oro y plata (pág. 440)
mercenary: a soldier who sells his services to the highest bidder (p. 400)	**mercenario:** soldado que vende sus servicios al mejor postor (pág. 400)
mestizo: a person of mixed European and native American Indian descent (pp. 444, 709)	**mestizo:** persona que desciende de un progenitor europeo y uno nativoamericano (pp. 444, 709)

GLOSSARY

***method:** a systematic plan for doing something (p. 129)

***método:** plan sistemático para hacer algo (pág. 129)

Middle Passage: the journey of enslaved persons from Africa to the Americas, so called because it was the middle portion of the triangular trade route (p. 442)

Paso Central: viaje de los africanos esclavizados a las Américas, llamado así porque era la porción intermedia de la ruta del comercio triangular (pág. 442)

***migration:** the movement of people from one country, place, or locality to another (p. 1050)

***migración:** flujo de personas de un país, lugar o localidad a otra (pág. 1050)

militant: combative (p. 454)

militante: persona combativa (pág. 454)

militarism: reliance on military strength (p. 632)

militarismo: dependencia de la fuerza militar (pág. 632)

***military:** relating to the armed forces or to soldiers, arms, or war (pp. 174, 759)

***militar:** relativo a las fuerzas armadas o a los soldados, las armas o la guerra (pp. 174, 759)

minaret: the tower of a mosque from which the muezzin calls the faithful to prayer five times a day (p. 207)

minarete: torre de las mezquitas desde la cual el muecín llama a los fieles a orar cinco veces al día (pág. 207)

***minimal:** barely adequate (p. 916)

***mínimo:** escasamente adecuado (pág. 916)

ministerial responsibility: the idea that the prime minister is responsible to the popularly elected legislative body and not to the king or president (p. 668)

responsabilidad ministerial: concepto de que el primer ministro es responsable ante el poder legislativo electo por el pueblo y no ante el rey o el presidente (pág. 668)

missionary: a person sent out to carry a religious message (p. 306)

misionero: persona enviada para llevar un mensaje religioso (pág. 306)

mita: a labor system that the Spanish administrators in Peru used to draft native people to work in the Spanish landowners' silver mines (p. 446)

mita: sistema de trabajo usado por los funcionarios españoles en Perú para reclutar nativos para trabajar en las minas de plata de los terratenientes españoles (pág. 446)

mobilization: the process of assembling troops and supplies and making them ready for war (pp. 761, 880)

movilización: proceso de agrupar tropas y suministros y prepararlos para la guerra (pp. 761, 880)

modernism: a movement in which writers and artists between 1870 and 1914 rebelled against the traditional literary and artistic styles that had dominated European cultural life since the Renaissance (p. 674)

modernismo: movimiento en el que escritores y artistas se rebelaron entre 1870 y 1914 en contra de los estilos literarios y artísticos tradicionales que habían dominado la vida cultural europea desde el Renacimiento (pág. 674)

monarch: a king or queen who rules a kingdom by organizing armies to protect their populations and making laws to regulate subjects' lives (p. 18)

monarca: rey o reina que gobierna un reino mediante la organización de ejércitos para la protección de la población y la elaboración de leyes que regulan la vida de sus súbditos (pág. 18)

monarchy: government by a soverign ruler such as a king or queen (p. 57)

monarquía: gobierno encabezado por un soberano, como un rey o una reina (pág. 57)

monasticism: practice of living the life of a monk (p. 305)

monacato: práctica de vivir la vida de un monje (pág. 305)

money economy: an economic system based on money rather than barter (p. 338)

economía monetaria: sistema económico basado en el dinero y no en el trueque (pág. 338)

monk: a man who separates himself from ordinary human society in order to dedicate himself to God; monks live in monasteries headed by abbots (p. 305)

monje: hombre que se aparta de la sociedad humana ordinaria con el fin de dedicarse a Dios; los monjes viven en monasterios dirigidos por abades (pág. 305)

monotheistic: having one god (p. 50)

monoteísta: que tienen un solo dios (pág. 50)

monsoon: a seasonal wind pattern in southern Asia that blows warm, moist air from the southwest during the summer, bringing heavy rains, and cold, dry air from the northeast during the winter (p. 66)

monzón: patrón estacional de vientos en el sur de Asia que soplan aire cálido y húmedo desde el suroeste durante el verano, con fuertes lluvias, y traen aire frío y seco desde el noreste en el invierno (pág. 66)

mosque: a Muslim house of worship (p. 199)

mezquita: templo musulmán (pág. 199)

***motive:** a reason to take action (p. 735)	***motivo:** razón para una acción (pág. 735)
muezzin: the crier who calls the Muslim faithful to prayer from the minaret of a mosque (p. 207)	**muecín:** voceador que llama a los fieles a orar desde el minarete de una mezquita (pág. 207)
mulatto: a person of mixed African and European descent (p. 444)	**mulato:** persona descendiente de un progenitor europeo y otro africano (pág. 444)
multinational corporation: a company with divisions in more than two countries (pp. 960, 1051)	**corporación multinacional:** compañía con divisiones en más de dos países (pp. 960, 1051)
multinational state: a state in which people of many nationalities live (p. 629)	**estado multinacional:** estado en el que viven personas de diversas nacionalidades (pág. 629)
mummification: a process of slowly drying a dead body to prevent it from decaying (p. 37)	**momificación:** proceso consistente en secar lentamente un cadáver para evitar su descomposición (pág. 37)

nationalism: the unique cultural identity of a people based on common language, religion, and national symbols (p. 602)	**nacionalismo:** singular identidad cultural de un pueblo basada en un idioma, una religión y símbolos nacionales en común (pág. 602)
natural rights: rights with which all humans are born, including the rights to life, liberty, and property (p. 477)	**derechos naturales:** derechos con los que todos los humanos nacen, entre ellos el derecho a la vida, la libertad y la propiedad (pág. 477)
natural selection: the principle set forth by Charles Darwin that some organisms are more adaptable to the environment than others; in popular terms, "survival of the fittest" (p. 642)	**selección natural:** principio establecido por Charles Darwin de que algunos organismos son más adaptables al medio que otros; en términos populares, "supervivencia de los más aptos" (pág. 642)
Nazi: shortened form of the German *Nazional,* or the National Socialist German Workers' Party; a member of such party (p. 804)	**nazi:** forma abreviada de la palabra alemana *Nazional* o Partido Nacionalsocialista Alemán del Trabajo; miembro de ese partido (pág. 804)
neo-Confucianism: a revised form of Confucianism that evolved as a response to Buddhism and held sway in China from the late Tang dynasty to the end of the dynastic system in the twentieth century (p. 273)	**neoconfucianismo:** forma modificada de confucianismo que evolucionó como respuesta al budismo y mantuvo su dominio en China desde fines de la dinastía Tang hasta fines del sistema de dinastías en el siglo XX (pág. 273)
***network:** an interrelated or interconnected group or system (p. 526)	***red:** grupo o sistema interrelacionado o interconectado (pág. 526)
neutrality: refusal to take sides or become involved in wars between other nations (p. 866)	**neutralidad:** rechazo a tomar parte o involucrarse en guerras entre otras naciones (pág. 866)
new monarchy: in the fifteenth century, government in which power had been centralized under a king or queen, i.e., France, England, and Spain (p. 357)	**nueva monarquía:** en el siglo XV, gobierno en el que el poder se había centralizado bajo un rey o reina, como en Francia, Inglaterra y España (pág. 357)
New Testament: the second part of the Christian Bible, it provides a record of Jesus' life and teachings (p. 170)	**Nuevo Testamento:** segunda parte de la Biblia cristiana; contiene un registro de la vida y enseñanzas de Jesús (pág. 170)
nirvana: in Buddhism, ultimate reality, the end of the self and a reunion with the Great World Soul (p. 74)	**nirvana:** en el budismo, la realidad final, el fin del yo y reunión con el Gran Alma Mundial (pág. 74)
nongovernmental organization: an organization that has no government ties and works to address world problems (p. 1053)	**organización no gubernamental:** organización que no tiene lazos con el gobierno y trabaja en la solución de problemas mundiales (pág. 1053)
***nuclear:** being a weapon whose destructive power comes from a nuclear reaction (p. 903)	***nuclear:** arma cuyo poder destructivo proviene de una reacción nuclear (pág. 903)

nuclear proliferation: the spread of nuclear weapons production technology and knowledge to nations without that capability (p. 1049)

proliferación nuclear: extensión de la tecnología y el conocimiento para la producción de armas nucleares a países que no tienen esa capacidad (pág. 1049)

nun: a woman who separates herself from ordinary human society in order to dedicate herself to God; nuns live in convents headed by abbesses (p. 306)

monja: mujer que se aparta de la sociedad humana ordinaria para dedicarse a Dios; las monjas viven en conventos encabezados por abadesas (pág. 306)

O

***occupation:** the military force occupying a country or the policies carried out by it (p. 875)

***ocupación:** fuerza militar que ocupa un país o las políticas llevadas a cabo por ella (pág. 875)

occupied: held by a foreign power (p. 1024)

ocupado: poseído por un poder extranjero (pág. 1024)

oligarchy: "the rule of the few", a form of government in which a select group of people exercises controls (pp. 114, 847)

oligarquía: literalmente, "gobierno de pocos", forma de gobierno en el que un grupo selecto de personas ejerce el control (pp. 114, 847)

one-child policy: China's effort, beginning in 1979, to control population growth; incentives such as education benefits, child care, and housing are offered to couples who limit their families to one child (p. 1016)

política de un solo hijo: esfuerzo realizado por China a partir de 1979 para controlar el crecimiento de su población; se ofrecen beneficios, como la educación, guarderías y viviendas a las parejas que tengan solo un hijo (pág. 1016)

***ongoing:** continuing (p. 961)

***en curso:** que continúa (pág. 961)

Open Door policy: a policy, proposed by U.S. secretary of state John Hay in 1899, that stated all powers with spheres of influence in China would respect equal trading opportunities with China and not set tariffs giving an unfair advantage to the citizens of their own country (p. 731)

política de puertas abiertas: política propuesta por el secretario de estado de los EE.UU. John Hay en 1899, que establecía que todas las potencias con esferas de influencia en China respetarían las oportunidades comerciales equitativas con China y no establecerían tarifas que dieran ventajas injustas a los ciudadanos de sus países (pág. 731)

oracle: in ancient Greece, a sacred shrine where a god or goddess was said to reveal the future through a priest or priestess (p. 124)

oráculo: en la antigua Grecia, templo sagrado donde, según se decía, un dios o una diosa revelaba el futuro a través de un sacerdote o una sacerdotisa (pág. 124)

ordeal: a means of determining guilt in Germanic law, based on the idea of divine intervention: if the accused person was unharmed after a physical trial, he or she was presumed innocent (p. 304)

ordalía: medio para determinar la culpabilidad en la ley germánica basándose en la idea de una intervención divina: si el acusado no resultaba dañado luego de una prueba física, se asumía que era inocente (pág. 304)

organic evolution: the principle set forth by Charles Darwin that every plant or animal has evolved, or changed, over a long period of time from earlier, simpler forms of life to more complex forms (p. 642)

evolución orgánica: principio establecido por Charles Darwin de que cada planta o animal ha evolucionado, o cambiado, durante un largo periodo, de formas más primitivas y simples de vida a formas más complejas (pág. 642)

***oriented:** directed toward the interests of a particular group (p. 192)

***orientado:** dirigido a los intereses de un grupo particular (pág. 192)

orthodoxy: traditional beliefs, especially in religion (p. 494)

ortodoxia: creencia tradicional, especialmente en religión (pág. 494)

ostracism: in ancient Athens, the process for temporarily banning ambitious politicans from the city by popular vote (p. 121)

ostracismo: en la antigua Atenas, proceso para prohibir temporalmente, mediante el voto popular, el acceso de políticos ambiciosos a la ciudad (pág. 121)

"out-of-Africa" theory: also called the replacement theory; this theory refers to when *homo sapiens sapiens* began spreading out of Africa to other parts of the world about 100,000 years ago and replacing populations of earlier hominids in Europe and Asia (p. 7)

teoría "desde África": también llamada teoría de reemplazo; se refiere que el *Homo sapiens sapiens* comenzó a expandirse desde África hacia otras partes del mundo hace alrededor de 100,000 años y reemplazó las poblaciones de los homínidos primitivos en Europa y Asia (pág. 7)

***overseas:** movement or transport over the sea; land beyond the sea (p. 430)

***ultramar:** movimiento o transportación por mar; tierras allende los mares (pág. 430)

Pan-Africanism: the unity of all black Africans, regardless of national boundaries (pp. 830, 988)

panafricanismo: movimiento unitario de toda el África negra, independientemente de las fronteras nacionales (pp. 830, 988)

Pan-Arabism: Arab unity, regardless of national boundaries (p. 998)

panarabismo: unidad árabe, independientemente de las fronteras nacionales (pág. 998)

Parliament: in thirteenth-century England, the representative government that emerged; it was composed of two knights from every county, two people from every town, and all of the nobles and bishops throughout England (p. 318)

parlamento: en la Inglaterra del siglo XIII, el gobierno representativo que surgió; estaba compuesto por dos caballeros de cada condado, dos personas de cada pueblo y todos los nobles y obispos de Inglaterra (pág. 318)

***participate:** to take part (p. 106)

***participar:** tomar parte (pág. 106)

***participation:** having a part in or sharing in something (p. 931)

***participación:** tener una parte en algo o compartir algo (pág. 931)

partisan: a resistance fighter in World War II (p. 871)

partisano: luchador de la resistencia en la Segunda Guerra Mundial (pág. 871)

pasha: an appointed official in the Ottoman Empire who collected taxes, maintained law and order, and was directly responsible to the sultan's court (p. 486)

pachá: oficial designado en el Imperio otomano que cobraba impuestos, mantenía la ley y el orden y era directamente responsable ante la corte del sultán (pág. 486)

***passive:** not active (p. 665)

***pasivo:** no activo (pág. 665)

pastoral nomad: a person who domesticates animals for food and clothing and moves along regular migratory routes to provide a steady source of nourishment for those animals (p. 46)

pastor nómada: persona que domestica animales para alimentarse y vestirse y se traslada a lo largo de las rutas migratorias regulares para proporcionar una fuente estable de comida a sus animales (pág. 46)

paterfamilias: in the Roman social structure, the dominant male head of the household, which also included his wife, sons and their wives and children, unmarried daughters, and slaves (p. 162)

paterfamilias: jefe de familia, en la antigua estructura social romana, el hombre dominante que encabezaba el hogar, en el que se incluían su mujer, sus hijos y las mujeres de estos con sus niños, las hijas solteras y los esclavos (pág. 162)

patriarch: the head of the Eastern Orthodox Church, originally appointed by the Byzantine emperor (p. 323)

patriarca: líder de la Iglesia ortodoxa oriental, originalmente designado por el emperador bizantino (pág. 323)

patriarchal: dominated by men (p. 33)

patriarcal: dominado por los hombres (pág. 33)

patrician: wealthy, powerful landowners, they formed the ruling class in the Roman Republic (pp. 148, 340)

patricio: rico y poderoso terrateniente; formaban la clase dominante en la República Romana (pp. 148, 340)

patrilineal: tracing lineage through the father (p. 252)

patrilineal: que traza su linaje a través del padre (pág. 252)

peacekeeping forces: military forces drawn from neutral members of the United Nations to settle conflicts and supervise truces (p. 1048)

fuerzas de paz: fuerza militar formada por miembros neutrales de las Naciones Unidas para resolver conflictos y supervisar treguas (pág. 1048)

peninsulare: a person born on the Iberian Peninsula; typically, a Spanish or Portuguese official who resided temporarily in Latin America for political and economic gain and then returned to Europe (pp. 444, 708)

peninsular: persona nacida en la Península Ibérica; por lo general, un funcionario español o portugués que residía temporalmente en América Latina para obtener ganancia política y económica y luego regresar a Europa (pp. 444, 708)

per capita: per person (p. 1014)

per cápita: por persona (pág. 1014)

***percent:** a part of a whole divided into 100 parts (p. 432)

***porcentaje:** parte de un todo dividido en 100 partes (pág. 432)

perestroika: fundamental restructuring of the Soviet economy; policy introduced by Gorbachev (p. 932)

perestroika: reestructuración fundamental de la economía soviética; política introducida por Gorbachov (pág. 932)

***period:** an interval of time (p. 266)

***período:** intervalo de tiempo (pág. 266)

permanent revolution: an atmosphere of constant revolutionary fervor favored by Mao Zedong to enable China to overcome the past and achieve the final stage of communism (p. 1014)

revolución permanente: atmósfera constante de fervor revolucionario apoyada por Mao Zedong para permitir a China vencer su pasado y lograr la etapa final del comunismo (pág. 1014)

***perspective:** viewpoint (p. 512)

***perspectiva:** punto de vista (pág. 512)

phalanx: a wall of shields created by foot soldiers marching shoulder to shoulder in a rectangular formation (p. 113)

falange: muralla de escudos creada por soldados de infantería que marchaban hombro con hombro en formación rectangular (pág. 113)

pharaoh: the most common of the various titles for ancient Egyptian monarchs; the term originally meant "great house" or "palace" (p. 37)

faraón: el más común de los diversos títulos que existían para los monarcas del antiguo Egipto; el término originalmente significaba "gran casa" o "palacio" (pág. 37)

***phase:** a part in the development cycle (p. 733)

***fase:** parte de un ciclo de desarrollo (pág. 733)

philosophe: French for "philosopher"; applied to all intellectuals–i.e., writers, professors, journalists, economists, and social reformers–during the Enlightenment (p. 548)

philosophe: término francés para "filósofo", se aplicaba a todos los intelectuales—escritores, periodistas, economistas y reformadores sociales—durante la Ilustración (pág. 548)

***philosopher:** a person who seeks wisdom or enlightenment; a scholar or a thinker (p. 538)

***filósofo:** persona que busca la sabiduría o la iluminación; estudioso o pensador (pág. 538)

philosophy: an organized system of thought, from the Greek for "love of wisdom" (pp. 90, 128)

filosofía: sistema organizado del pensamiento, del griego "amor a la sabiduría" (pp. 90, 128)

photomontage: a picture made of a combination of photographs (p. 814)

fotomontaje: imagen compuesta de una combinación de fotografías (pág. 814)

***physical:** relating to the body (p. 37)

***físico:** relativo al cuerpo (pág. 37)

pictograph: a picture symbol, or character, that represents an object; used in ancient Chinese script (p. 90)

pictograma: símbolo dibujado o carácter que representa un objeto; usado en la escritura de la antigua china (pág. 90)

pilgrim: a person who travels to a shrine or other holy place (p. 79)

peregrino: persona que viaja a un santuario u otro lugar sagrado (pág. 79)

plague: an epidemic disease (p. 174)

peste: enfermedad epidémica; también llamada plaga (pág. 174)

planned economies: economic systems directed by government agencies (p. 767)

economía planificada: sistema económico dirigido por agencias gubernamentales (pág. 767)

plantation: a large agricultural estate (p. 441)

plantación: propiedad agrícola grande (pág. 441)

plateau: a relatively high, flat land area (p. 236)

altiplano: terreno relativamente alto y llano (pág. 236)

plebeian: in the Roman Republic, a social class made up of minor landholders, craftspeople, merchants, and small farmers (p. 148)

plebeyos: en la República Romana, clase social compuesta de terratenientes menores, artesanos, mercaderes y pequeños granjeros (pág. 148)

plebiscite: a popular vote (p. 635)

plebiscito: voto popular (pág. 635)

pogrom: organized persecution or massacre of a minority group, especially Jews (p. 679)

pogromo: persecución organizada o masacre de un grupo minoritario, especialmente judíos (pág. 679)

***policy:** an overall plan embracing the general goals and acceptable procedures of a governmental body (p. 455)

***política:** plan global que comprende las metas generales y los procedimientos aceptables de un cuerpo gubernamental (pág. 455)

policy of containment: a plan to keep something, such as communism, within its existing geographical boundaries and prevent further aggressive moves (p. 902)

política de contención: plan para mantener algo, como por ejemplo el comunismo, dentro de sus fronteras geográficas existentes e impedir posteriores acciones agresivas (pág. 902)

polis: the early Greek city-state, consisting of a city or town and its surrounding countryside (p. 112)

polis: ciudad-estado de la antigua Grecia, que consistía en una ciudad o pueblo y los campos circundantes (pág. 112)

polytheistic: having many gods (p. 27)

politeísta: que tiene muchos dioses (pág. 27)

pope: the bishop of Rome and head of the Roman Catholic Church (p. 304)

papa: obispo de Roma y líder de la Iglesia católica romana (pág. 304)

popular culture: entertainment created for a profit and for a mass audience (p. 949)

cultura popular: entretenimiento creado para obtener una ganancia y para un público de masas (pág. 949)

porcelain: a ceramic made of fine clay baked at very high temperatures (pp. 275, 519)

porcelana: cerámica hecha de arcilla fina horneada a temperaturas muy altas (pp. 275, 519)

postmodernism: an artistic movement that emerged in the 1980s; its artists do not expect rationality in the world and are comfortable with many "truths" (p. 949)

postmodernismo: movimiento artístico que surgió en la década de 1980; los artistas no esperan que el mundo sea razonable y aceptan muchas "verdades" (pág. 949)

praetor: an official of the Roman Republic in charge of enforcing civil law (p. 148)

pretor: oficial de la República Romana encargado de hacer cumplir la ley civil (pág. 148)

***precise:** exact or sharply defined (p. 413)

***preciso:** exacto o bien definido (pág. 413)

predestination: the belief that God has determined in advance who will be saved (the elect) and who will be damned (the reprobate) (p. 419)

predestinación: creencia de que Dios ha determinado anticipadamente quién se salvará (el elegido) y quien se condenará (el réprobo) (pág. 419)

prefecture: in the Japanese Meiji Restoration, a territory governed by its former daimyo lord (p. 740)

prefectura: en la Restauración Meiji japonesa, territorio gobernado por el anterior daimyo (pág. 740)

prehistory: the period before writing was developed (p. 4)

prehistoria: periodo anterior a que se creara la escritura (pág. 4)

priest: in early urban civilizations, an important and powerful person who supervised rituals aimed at pleasing the gods and goddesses (p. 19)

sacerdote: en las civilizaciones urbanas primitivas, persona importante y poderosa que supervisaba los ritos dirigidos a complacer a los dioses y las diosas (pág. 19)

***primary:** most important (pp. 162, 441)

***primordial:** de la mayor importancia (pp. 162, 441)

***principle:** a fundamental law or idea; when said of people (e.g., someone is highly principled), it means a devotion to high codes or rules of conduct (p. 501)

***principio:** ley o idea fundamental; dicho de una persona (por ejemplo, alguien de elevados principios), significa su devoción a elevados códigos o reglas de conducta (pág. 501)

principle of intervention: idea that great powers have the right to send armies into countries where there are revolutions to restore legitimate governments (p. 625)

principio de intervención: idea de que las grandes potencias tienen el derecho de enviar ejércitos a países donde existen revoluciones a fin de restaurar los gobiernos legítimos (pág. 625)

principle of nonalignment: Jawaharlal Nehru's refusal to align India with any bloc or alliance (p. 1018)

principio de no alineamiento: rechazo de Jawaharlal Nehru de alinear a la India en algún bloque o alianza (pág. 1018)

privatization: the sale of government-owned companies to private firms (p. 966)

privatización: venta de compañías del estado a firmas privadas (pág. 966)

***process:** a series of actions or operations necessary to meet a specified end (p. 520)

***proceso:** serie de acciones u operaciones necesarias para lograr un fin dado (pág. 520)

GLOSSARY

procurator: in the Roman Empire, an official in charge of a province (p. 169)

procurador: en el Imperio romano, oficial a cargo de una provincia (pág. 169)

***prohibit:** to prevent or to forbid (p. 809)

***prohibir:** impedir o proscribir (pág. 809)

***projection:** an estimate or a calculation (p. 1050)

***proyección:** estimación o cálculo (pág. 1050)

proletariat: the working class (p. 656)

proletariado: clase trabajadora (pág. 656)

propaganda: ideas spread to influence public opinion for or against a cause (p. 762)

propaganda: ideas que se difunden para influir en la opinión pública a favor o en contra de una causa (pág. 762)

protectorate: a political unit that depends on another government for its protection (p. 688)

protectorado: unidad política que depende de otro gobierno para su protección (pág. 688)

provincial: local; of or relating to a province (p. 732)

provincial: local; de una provincia o relativo a ella (pág. 732)

psychoanalysis: a method by which a therapist and patient probe deeply into the patient's memory; by making the patient's conscious mind aware of repressed thoughts, healing can take place (p. 677)

psicoanálisis: método mediante el cual un terapeuta y un paciente indagan profundamente en la memoria del paciente; al hacer que la mente consciente del paciente tome consciencia de pensamientos reprimidos se puede llegar a la cura (pág. 677)

***psychological:** mental; directed toward the will or mind (p. 778)

***psicológico:** mental; dirigido hacia la voluntad o la mente (pág. 778)

***published:** printed for distribution (p. 418)

***publicado:** impreso para su distribución (pág. 418)

puddling: process in which coke derived from coal is used to burn away impurities in crude iron to produce high quality iron (p. 616)

pudelación: proceso en el cual se utiliza coque derivado del carbón para extraer impurezas del hierro bruto mediante el fuego y producir un hierro de alta calidad (pág. 616)

pueblo: a multi-storied structure of the Anasazi that could house up to 250 people (p. 371)

pueblo: estructuras de múltiples pisos de los anasazi y que podían albergar hasta 250 personas (pág. 371)

***pursue:** to follow up or proceed with (p. 342)

***perseguir:** seguir o ir en pos de algo (pág. 342)

queue: the braided pigtail that was traditionally worn by Chinese males (p. 513)

coleta: cola de pelo trenzado usada tradicionalmente por los hombres en China (pág. 513)

quipu: a system of knotted strings used by the Inca people for keeping records (p. 385)

quipu: sistema de cuerdas con nudos usado por los incas para mantener sus registros (pág. 385)

Quran: the holy scriptures of the religion of Islam (p. 190)

Corán: escrituras sagradas del islam (pág. 190)

racism: the belief that race determines a person's traits and capabilities (p. 687)

racismo: creencia de que la raza determina los rasgos y la capacidad de las personas (pág. 687)

***radical:** relating to a political group associated with views, practices, and policies of extreme change (p. 628)

***radical:** relativo a grupos políticos asociados con puntos de vista, prácticas y políticas de cambios extremos (pág. 628)

***ratio:** proportion (p. 792)

***relación:** proporción (pág. 792)

rationalism: a system of thought expounded by René Descartes based on the belief that reason is the chief source of knowledge (p. 545)

racionalismo: sistema del pensamiento, expuesto por René Descartes, basado en la creencia de que la razón es la fuente principal del conocimiento (pág. 545)

realism: mid-nineteenth century movement that rejected romanticism and sought to portray lower- and middle-class life as it actually was (p. 643)	**realismo:** movimiento de mediados del siglo XIX, que rechazaba al romanticismo y buscaba retratar la vida de las clases media y baja tal como eran (pág. 643)
real wages: the actual purchasing power of income (p. 917)	**salario real:** poder adquisitivo real de los ingresos (pág. 917)
***recovery:** an upturn (p. 914)	***recuperación:** mejoría (pág. 914)
***redistribution:** alteration in the distribution of; reallocation (p. 712)	***redistribución:** alteración en la distribución de algo; reasignación (pág. 712)
redistribution of wealth: the shifting of wealth from a rich minority to a poor majority (p. 841)	**redistribución de las riquezas:** cambio de las riquezas de las manos de una minoría rica a las de una mayoría pobre p. 841)
***regime:** the government in power (pp. 96, 635)	***régimen:** gobierno en el poder (pp. 96, 635)
***region:** a broad geographic area distinguished by similar features (p. 290)	***región:** amplia área geográfica distinguida por características similares (pág. 290)
***regulation:** a governmental rule or order that controls activities (p. 967)	***regulación:** pauta u orden gubernamental que controla las actividades (pág. 967)
reincarnation: the rebirth of an individual's soul in a different form after death (p. 73)	**reencarnación:** renacimiento del alma de una persona en una forma diferente después de la muerte (pág. 73)
relic: bones or other objects connected with saints; considered worthy of worship by the faithful (p. 347)	**reliquia:** huesos u otros objetos relacionados con santos, considerados dignos de adoración por los creyentes (pág. 347)
***remove:** to eliminate (p. 343)	***eliminar:** suprimir (pág. 343)
reparation: a payment made to the victor by the vanquished to cover the costs of a war (p. 781)	**reparación:** pago hecho a los victoriosos por los derrotados para cubrir los costos de una guerra (pág. 781)
republic: a form of government in which the leader is not a king and certain citizens have the right to vote (p. 148)	**república:** forma de gobierno en la cual el líder no es un rey y ciertos ciudadanos tienen derecho a votar (pág. 148)
***require:** to demand as being necessary (p. 809)	***requerir:** demandar por necesidad (pág. 809)
***resident:** one who resides in a place (p. 384)	***residente:** quien reside en un lugar (pág. 384)
***resolution:** an expression of opinion or intent (p. 996)	***resolución:** expresión de opinión o intento (pág. 996)
***resolve:** determination; a fixed purpose (p. 866)	***decisión:** determinación; propósito establecido (pág. 866)
***resources:** available means for economic or political development (p. 239)	***recursos:** medios disponibles para el desarrollo económico o político (pág. 239)
***responsive:** quick to respond or react to (p. 932)	***sensible:** que responde o reacciona rápidamente a algo (pág. 932)
***restoration:** a bringing back to a former position or condition (p. 462)	***restauración:** restablecer algo a una posición o condición anterior (pág. 462)
***restraint:** a controlling force (p. 56)	***freno:** fuerza que controla (pág. 56)
***retained:** kept in possession or use (p. 284)	***retener:** mantener la posesión o uso (pág. 284)
***reveal:** show; to make known (p. 70)	***revelar:** mostrar; hacer público (pág. 70)
***revelations:** divine truths (p. 189)	***revelaciones:** verdades divinas (pág. 189)

***revenue:** the yield of sources of income that a nation or state collects and deposits into its treasury for public use (p. 279)

***renta:** producto de las fuentes de ingreso que un país o estado recibe y deposita en su tesorería para uso público (pág. 279)

revisionist: a Marxist who rejected the revolutionary approach, believing instead in evolution by democratic means to achieve the goal of socialism (p. 657)

revisionista: marxista que rechazó el enfoque revolucionario y cree en cambio en una evolución por medios democráticos para lograr los objetivos del socialismo (pág. 657)

***revolution:** a sudden, complete change; an overthrow of government (pp. 14, 774)

***revolución:** cambio completo y brusco; derrocamiento de un gobierno (pp. 14, 774)

***rigid:** inflexible, unyielding (p. 556)

***rígido:** inflexible, inquebrantable (pág. 556)

ritual: a ceremony or a rite (p. 124)

ritual: ceremonia o rito (pág. 124)

rococo: an artistic style that replaced baroque in the 1730s; it was highly secular, emphasizing grace, charm, and gentle action (p. 562)

rococó: estilo artístico que sustituyó al barroco en la década de 1730; era muy secular, hacía énfasis en la gracia, el encanto y las acciones nobles (pág. 562)

***role:** a socially expected behavior pattern (pp. 16, 1019)

***papel a desempeñar:** patrón de comportamiento esperado por la sociedad (pp. 16, 1019)

romanticism: an intellectual movement that emerged at the end of the eighteenth century in reaction to the ideas of the Enlightenment; it stressed feelings, emotion, and imagination as sources of knowing (p. 638)

romanticismo: movimiento intelectual que surgió a finales del siglo XVIII como respuesta a las ideas de la Ilustración; hacía énfasis en los sentimientos, la emoción y la imaginación como fuentes del conocimiento (pág. 638)

S

sacrament: Christian rites (p. 344)

sacramento: rito cristiano (pág. 344)

salon: the elegant drawing rooms of great urban houses where, in the eighteenth century, writers, artists, aristocrats, government officials, and wealthy middle-class people gathered to discuss the ideas of the philosophes, helping to spread the ideas of the Enlightenment (p. 552)

salón: elegantes salas de las grandes casas urbanas donde, en el siglo XVIII, escritores, artistas, aristócratas, funcionarios gubernamentales y personas acomodadas de la clase media se reunían para discutir las ideas de los *philosophes,* con lo que ayudaban a divulgar las ideas de la Ilustración (pág. 552)

salvation: the state of being saved (that is, going to heaven) through faith alone or through faith and good works (p. 414)

salvación: estado de ser salvado (es decir, ir al cielo) a través de la fe sola o de la fe y buenas obras (pág. 414)

samurai: "those who serve", Japanese warriors similar to the knights of medieval Europe (p. 280)

samuráis: "aquellos que sirven", guerreros japoneses similares a los caballeros de la Europa medieval (pág. 280)

sanctions: restrictions intended to enforce international law (p. 861)

sanciones: restricciones impuestas para obligar a cumplir la ley internacional (pág. 861)

sans-culottes: "without breeches", members of the Paris Commune who considered themselves ordinary patriots (in other words, they wore long trousers instead of fine knee-length breeches of the nobles) (p. 583)

sans-culottes: "sin pantalones", miembros de la Comuna de París que se consideraban patriotas ordinarios (en otras palabras, usaban calzones largos en vez de finos pantalones hasta la rodilla) (pág. 583)

Sanskrit: the first writing system of the Aryans, developed around 1000 B.C. (p. 70)

sánscrito: primer sistema de escritura de los arios, creado alrededor del año 1000 a.C. (pág. 70)

satellite state: a country that is economically and politically dependent on another country (p. 902)

estado satélite: país que depende económica y políticamente de otro (pág. 902)

satrap: "protector of the Kingdom", the governor of a province (satrapy) of the Persian Empire under Darius (p. 57)

sátrapa: "protector del Reino", gobernador de una provincia (satrapía) del Imperio persa durante el gobierno de Darío (pág. 57)

GLOSSARY

satrapy: one of the 20 provinces into which Darius divided the Persian Empire (p. 57)

satrapía: cada una de las 20 provincias en las que Darío dividió el Imperio persa (pág. 57)

savanna: broad grassland dotted with small trees and shrubs (p. 237)

sabana: tierras de pastoreo amplias, dotadas de pequeños árboles y arbustos (pág. 237)

schism: the separation between the two great branches of Christianity that occurred when the Roman Pope Leo IX and the Byzantine patriarch Michael Cerularius excommunicated each other in 1054 (p. 324)

cisma: ruptura entre las dos grandes ramas del cristianismo que tuvo lugar cuando el papa romano León IX y el patriarca bizantino Miguel Cerularius se excomulgaron mutuamente en 1054 (pág. 324)

scholar-gentry: in China, a group of people who controlled much of the land and produced most of the candidates for the civil service (p. 269)

aristocracia intelectual: en China, grupo de personas que controlaba gran parte de las tierras y proveían la mayor parte de los candidatos para el servicio civil (pág. 269)

scholasticism: a medieval philosophical and theological system that tried to reconcile faith and reason (p. 350)

escolasticismo: sistema filosófico y teológico medieval que trataba de conciliar la fe y la razón (pág. 350)

scientific method: a systematic procedure for collecting and analyzing evidence that was crucial to the evolution of science in the modern world (p. 545)

método científico: procedimiento sistemático para recolectar y analizar evidencias, fue crucial para la evolución de la ciencia en el mundo moderno (pág. 545)

secede: withdraw (p. 637)

secesión: separación (pág. 637)

secular: worldly (p. 398)

secular: mundano (pág. 398)

secularization: indifference to or rejection of religion or religious consideration (p. 641)

secularización: indiferencia o rechazo a la religión o la consideración religiosa (pág. 641)

***security:** freedom from danger or invasion; safety (p. 245)

***seguridad:** liberación de un peligro o invasión; condición de seguro (pág. 245)

self-strengthening: a policy promoted by reformers toward the end of the Qing dynasty under which China would adopt Western technology while keeping its Confucian values and institutions (p. 728)

autofortalecimiento: política promovida por reformadores hacia fines de la dinastía Qing, bajo la cual China adoptaría la tecnología occidental, aunque mantendría sus valores e instituciones confucianos (pág. 728)

separation of powers: a form of government in which the executive, legislative, and judicial branches limit and control each other through a system of checks and balances (p. 548)

separación de poderes: forma de gobierno en la cual las ramas ejecutiva, legislativa y judicial se limitan y controlan entre sí a través de un sistema de controles y balances (pág. 548)

sepoy: an Indian soldier hired by the British East India Company to protect the company's interests in the region (p. 702)

cipayo: soldado indio contratado por la Compañía Británica de la India Oriental para proteger los intereses de esa compañía en la región (pág. 702)

serf: in medieval Europe, a peasant legally bound to the land who had to provide labor services, pay rents, and be subject to the lord's control (p. 336)

siervo: en la Europa medieval, campesino confinado legalmente a la tierra y que tenía que proporcionar servicios, pagar rentas y estar sujeto al control del señor (pág. 336)

***series:** a group of related things or events (p. 511)

***serie:** grupo de cosas o eventos relacionados entre sí (pág. 511)

shah: king (used in Persia and Iran) (p. 492)

sha: rey (se usaba en Persia e Irán) (pág. 492)

shari'ah: a law code drawn up by Muslim scholars after Muhammad's death; it provided believers with a set of practical laws to regulate their daily lives (p. 191)

sharia: código legal formulado por eruditos musulmanes después de la muerte de Mahoma; ofrece a los creyentes un conjunto de leyes prácticas para regular sus vidas cotidianas (pág. 191)

sheikh: the ruler of an Arabic tribe, chosen from one of the leading families by a council of elders (p. 188)

jeque: soberano de una tribu árabe, elegido de una de las familias dominantes por un consejo de ancianos (pág. 188)

Shia: a Muslim group that accepts only the descendants of Muhammed's son-in-law Ali as the true rulers of Islam (p. 194)

shií: grupo musulmán que acepta sólo a los descendientes del yerno de Mahoma, Alí, como el verdadero líder del islam (pág. 194)

GLOSSARY

***shift:** a change in direction or attitude (p. 940)

***cambio:** variación en la dirección o la actitud (pág. 940)

Shinto: "the Sacred Way" or "the way of the Gods", the Japanese state religion; among its doctrines are the divinity of the emperor and the sacredness of the Japanese nation (p. 282)

sintoísmo: "el Camino Sagrado" o "el Camino de los Dioses", religión de estado en Japón; entre sus doctrinas están la divinidad del emperador y la santidad de la nación japonesa (pág. 282)

shogun: "general", a powerful military leader in Japan (p. 281)

shogun: "general", poderoso líder militar de Japón (pág. 281)

Silk Road: a route between the Roman Empire and China, so called because silk was China's most valuable product (p. 78)

Ruta de la seda: ruta entre el Imperio romano y China, se llamaba así porque la seda era el producto más valioso de China (pág. 78)

***so-called:** commonly named; popularly termed (p. 236)

***así llamado:** comúnmente llamado; popularmente llamado (pág. 236)

social contract: the concept proposed by Rousseau that an entire society agrees to be governed by its general will, and all individuals should be forced to abide by the general will since it represents what is best for the entire community (p. 551)

contrato social: concepto propuesto por Rousseau de que una sociedad completa accede a ser gobernada por su voluntad general y que todos los individuos deben ser forzados a someterse al deseo general, ya que representa lo mejor para la comunidad completa (pág. 551)

Social Darwinism: theory used by Western nations in the late nineteenth century to justify their dominance; it was based on Charles Darwin's theory of natural selection, "the survival of the fittest", and applied to modern human societies (p. 678)

darwinismo social: teoría utilizada en las naciones occidentales a finales del siglo XIX para justificar su dominio; se basaba en la teoría de la selección natural de Charles Darwin, "la supervivencia de los más aptos", aplicada a las sociedades humanas modernas (pág. 678)

socialism: a system in which society, usually in the form of the government, owns and controls the means of production (p. 621)

socialismo: sistema en el cual la sociedad, por lo general en la forma de un gobierno, posee y controla los medios de producción (pág. 621)

Socratic method: the method of teaching used by the Greek philosopher Socrates; it employs a question-and-answer format to lead pupils to see things for themselves by using their own reason (p. 129)

método socrático: método de enseñanza utilizado por el filósofo griego Sócrates; emplea un formato de preguntas y respuestas para llevar a los alumnos a ver las cosas por sí mismos usando su propia razón (pág. 129)

***sole:** being the only one (p. 910)

***solo:** ser el único (pág. 910)

***sought:** made an attempt; tried (p. 56)

***intentar:** hacer un intento; tratar (pág. 56)

***source:** a document or primary reference book that gives information (p. 1014)

***fuente:** documento o libro de referencia primaria que ofrece información (pág. 1014)

soviets: Russian councils composed of representatives from the workers and soldiers (p. 774)

soviet: consejo ruso, compuesto de representantes de los trabajadores y los soldados (pág. 774)

***sphere:** any of the concentric, revolving, spherical transparent shells in which, according to ancient astronomy, the stars, sun, planets, and moon are set (p. 540)

***esfera:** cualquiera de las capas esféricas, transparentes, concéntricas y giratorias en las que, según la astronomía antigua, estaban las estrellas, el Sol, los planetas y la Luna (pág. 540)

spheres of influence: areas in which foreign powers have been granted exclusive rights and privileges, such as trading rights and mining privileges (p. 729)

esferas de influencia: áreas en las que a una potencia extranjera se le han garantizado derechos y privilegios exclusivos, como derechos comerciales y privilegios de minería (pág. 729)

***stability:** the state of being stable; strong enough to endure (p. 464)

***estabilidad:** propiedad de estable; suficientemente fuerte como para resistir (pág. 464)

stalemate: the condition that exists when neither of two opposing sides is able to make significant gains (p. 1021)

estancamiento: condición que existe cuando ninguno de las dos partes opuestas puede obtener ventajas significativas (pág. 1021)

GLOSSARY

state capitalism: an economic system in which the central government plays an active role in the economy, establishing price and wage policies and subsidizing vital industries (p. 1026)

capitalismo de estado: sistema económico en el cual el gobierno central desempeña una función activa en la economía, mediante políticas de precios y salarios y el subsidio de industrias vitales (pág. 1026)

stateless society: a group of independent villages organized into clans and led by a local ruler or clan head without any central government (p. 249)

sociedad sin estado: grupo de aldeas independientes organizadas por clanes y lideradas por un soberano local o líder de un clan sin un gobierno central (pág. 249)

Stoicism: a school of thought developed by the teacher Zeno in Hellenistic Athens; it says that happiness can be achieved only when people gain inner peace by living in harmony with the will of God and that people should bear whatever life offers (p. 139)

estoicismo: escuela de pensamiento creada por el profesor Zenón en la Atenas helenística; sostenía que solo se puede lograr la felicidad cuando las personas consiguen la paz interior, mediante una vida en armonía con los deseos de Dios y que las personas deben soportar todo lo que la vida les depare (pág. 139)

***strategy:** a plan or method (p. 123)

***estrategia:** plan o método (pág. 123)

***structure:** an arrangement in a definite pattern of organization (p. 173)

***estructura:** disposición en un patrón de organización definido (pág. 173)

***style:** having a distinctive quality or form (p. 409)

***estilo:** tener una cualidad o forma distintiva (pág. 409)

***submission:** act of submitting to the control or authority of another (p. 190)

***sometimiento:** acto de someterse al control o autoridad de otro (pág. 190)

***subsidizing:** aiding or promoting with public money (p. 138)

***subsidiar:** ayudar o promover con recursos públicos (pág. 138)

***subsidy:** government payment to encourage or protect a certain economic activity (pp. 440, 741)

***subsidio:** pago gubernamental para estimular o proteger cierta actividad económica (pp. 440, 741)

subsistence farming: the practice of growing just enough crops for personal use, not for sale (p. 247)

agricultura de subsistencia: práctica de sembrar sólo la cosecha suficiente para uso personal, no para la venta (pág. 247)

***successor:** one that follows, especially one who succeeds to a throne or an office (p. 494)

***sucesor:** el que sigue, especialmente el que sigue en el trono o en un cargo (pág. 494)

suffrage: the right to vote (p. 663)

sufragio: derecho a votar (pág. 663)

sultan: "holder of power", the military and political head of state under the Seljuk Turks and the Ottomans (pp. 197, 486)

sultán: "poseedor del poder", líder militar y político del estado bajo el gobierno de los turcos seléucidas y otomanos (pp. 197, 486)

Sunni: a Muslim group that accepts only the descendants of the Umayyads as the true rulers of Islam (p. 194)

suníes: grupo musulmán que sólo acepta a los descendientes de los Omeya como los verdaderos gobernantes del islam (pág. 194)

surrealism: artistic movement that seeks to depict the world of the unconscious (p. 815)

surrealismo: movimiento artístico que trata de representar la vida del inconsciente (pág. 815)

***survive:** to remain alive or in existence (pp. 8, 368)

***sobrevivir:** mantenerse vivo o en existencia (pp. 8, 368)

sustainable development: economic development that does not limit the ability of future generations to meet their basic needs (p. 1042)

desarrollo sostenible: desarrollo económico que no limita la capacidad de generaciones futuras de satisfacer sus necesidades básicas (pág. 1042)

***sustained:** supported or held up (p. 57)

***sostenido:** apoyado o mantenido (pág. 57)

suttee: the Hindu custom of cremating a widow on her husband's funeral pyre (p. 501)

suttee: costumbre hindú de incinerar a la viuda en la pira funeraria de su esposo (pág. 501)

Swahili: a mixed African-Arabic culture that developed along the east coast of Africa; also, the major language used in that area, combining Bantu with Arabic words and phrases (p. 248)

swahili: cultura mixta africana y árabe que se desarrolló a lo largo de la costa oriental de África; también la lengua principal que se emplea en esa región, que combina el bantú con palabras y frases árabes (pág. 248)

GLOSSARY

***symbol:** something that stands for something else by way of association; a visible sign of something invisible (p. 938)

***símbolo:** algo que sustituye a algo más por asociación; signo visible de algo invisible (pág. 938)

systematic agriculture: the keeping of animals and the growing of food on a regular basis (p. 14)

agricultura sistemática: el mantenimiento de animales y la siembra de alimento de modo regular (pág. 14)

taille: an annual direct tax, usually on land or property, that provided a regular source of income for the French monarchy (pp. 357, 576)

taille: impuesto directo anual, por lo general sobre la tierra o la propiedad, que generaba una fuente regular de ingresos para la monarquía francesa (pp. 357, 576)

***target:** something or someone marked for attack (p. 765)

***blanco:** algo o alguien marcado para ser atacado (pág. 765)

***task:** a duty or function (p. 975)

***tarea:** deber o función (pág. 975)

***technology:** the science or study of the practical or industrial arts; applied sciences (pp. 46, 334)

***tecnología:** ciencia o estudio de las artes prácticas o industriales; ciencia aplicada (pág. 46, 334)

***temporary:** lasting for a limited time; not permanent (p. 368)

***temporal:** que dura un tiempo limitado; no permanente (pág. 368)

tepee: a circular tent made by stretching buffalo skins over wooden poles (p. 371)

tepee: tienda circular hecha de pieles de búfalo estiradas sobre postes de madera (pág. 371)

Thatcherism: the economic policy of British Prime Minister Margaret Thatcher, which limited social welfare and restricted union power (p. 943)

thatcherismo: política económica de la primera ministra británica Margaret Thatcher, que limitaba el bienestar social y restringía el poder de los sindicatos (pág. 943)

theocracy: government by divine authority (p. 29)

teocracia: gobierno por autoridad divina (pág. 29)

theology: the study of religion and God (p. 350)

teología: estudio de la religión y de Dios (pág. 350)

***theory:** hypothesis or unproved assumption (p. 4)

***teoría:** hipótesis o suposición no demostrada (pág. 4)

Theravada: "the teachings of the elders", a school of Buddhism that developed in India; its followers view Buddhism as a way of life, not a religion, centered on individual salvation (p. 284)

Theravada: "las enseñanzas de los ancianos", escuela del budismo creada en la India; sus seguidores ven el budismo como un estilo de vida centrado en la salvación del individuo, no como una religión (pág. 284)

totalitarian state: a government that aims to control the political, economic, social, intellectual, and cultural lives of its citizens (p. 796)

estado totalitario: gobierno que aspira a controlar la vida política, económica, social, intelectual y cultural de sus ciudadanos (pág. 796)

total war: a war that involves the complete mobilization of resources and people, affecting the lives of all citizens in the warring countries, even those remote from the battlefields (p. 767)

guerra total: guerra que implica la movilización completa de recursos y personas, afecta a las vidas de todos los ciudadanos en los países en guerra, incluso de aquellos alejados de los campos de batalla (pág. 767)

tournament: under feudalism, a series of martial activities such as jousts designed to keep knights busy during peacetime and help them prepare for war (p. 312)

torneo: bajo el feudalismo, serie de actividades marciales, como justas, diseñadas para mantener a los caballeros ocupados durante los tiempos de paz y ayudarlos a preparase para la guerra (pág. 312)

trade embargo: a policy prohibiting trade with a particular country (p. 969)

embargo comercial: política que prohíbe el comercio con un país en particular (pág. 969)

trading society: a group of people who depend primarily on trade for income (p. 294)

sociedad comercial: grupo de personas cuyos ingresos dependen principalmente del comercio (pág. 294)

***traditional:** established; customary (p. 289)

***tradicional:** establecido; habitual (pág. 289)

***traditions:** established customs of a people (p. 698)

***tradiciones:** costumbres establecidas de un pueblo (pág. 698)

tragedy: a form of drama that portrays a conflict between the protagonist and a superior force and having a protagonist who is brought to ruin or extreme sorrow, especially as a result of a fatal flaw (p. 126)

tragedia: forma de drama que representa un conflicto entre el protagonista y una fuerza superior y que tiene un protagonista que es llevado a la ruina o un dolor extremo, en especial como resultado de un error fatal (pág. 126)

***transfer:** to take over the control of (p. 1020)

***transferir:** transmitir el control de algo (pág. 1020)

***transform:** to change the form or appearance of (p. 207)

***transformar:** cambiar la forma o apariencia de algo (pág. 207)

***transformation:** conversion; change in character or condition (p. 170)

***transformación:** conversión; cambio en el carácter o condición (pág. 170)

***transition:** changeover; the move toward one form, stage, or style to another (p. 655)

***transición:** conversión; el cambio de una forma, estado o estilo a otro (pág. 655)

***transport:** the moving of goods or people (p. 29)

***transportar:** trasladar bienes o personas (pág. 29)

***transportation:** means of travel from one place to another (p. 440)

***transporte:** medio de viajar de un lugar a otro (pág. 440)

trench warfare: fighting from ditches protected by barbed wire, as in World War I (p. 763)

guerra de trincheras: combate desde trincheras protegidas por alambres de púa, como en la Primera Guerra Mundial (pág. 763)

***trend:** a pattern or general tendency (p. 814)

***tendencia:** patrón o inclinación general (pág. 814)

triangular trade: a pattern of trade that connected Europe, Africa, and the American continents; typically, manufactured goods from Europe were sent to Africa, where they were exchanged for enslaved persons, who were sent to the Americas, where they were exchanged for raw materials that were then sent to Europe (p. 442)

comercio triangular: patrón comercial que conectaba a Europa y África con las Américas, por lo general se enviaban manufacturas de Europa a África, donde las intercambiaban por esclavos que enviaban a las Américas y donde los cambiaban por materias primas que enviaban a Europa (pág. 442)

tribute: goods or money paid by conquered peoples to their conquerors (p. 378)

tributo: bienes o dinero pagado por pueblos conquistados a sus conquistadores (pág. 378)

triumvirate: a government by three people with equal power (p. 154)

triunvirato: gobierno de tres personas con igual poder (pág. 154)

tyrant: a ruler who seized power by force from the aristocrats, gained support from the newly rich and the poor, and maintained power by using hired soldiers and fighting tactics (p. 114)

tirano: gobernante que quitó el poder a los aristócratas por la fuerza, ganó el apoyo de los nuevos ricos y de los pobres y mantiene el poder mediante el uso de soldados contratados y tácticas de combate (pág. 114)

ulema: a group of religious advisers to the Ottoman sultan; this group administered the legal system and schools for educating Muslims (p. 487)

ulema: grupo de consejeros religiosos del sultán otomano; este grupo administraba el sistema legal y las escuelas para educar a los musulmanes (pág. 487)

uncertainty principle: the idea put forth by Heisenberg in 1927 that the behavior of subatomic particles is uncertain, suggesting that all of the physical laws governing the universe are based on uncertainty (p. 815)

principio de incertidumbre: idea establecida por Heisenberg en 1927 de que el comportamiento de las partículas subatómicas es incierto, lo que sugiere que todas las leyes físicas que rigen el universo se basan en la incertidumbre (pág. 815)

***uncharted:** not mapped; unknown (p. 695)

***ignoto:** que no aparece en el mapa; desconocido (pág. 695)

***unification:** the act, process, or result of making into a coherent or coordinated whole; the state of being unified (p. 631)

***unificación:** acción, proceso o resultado de convertir algo en un entero coherente o coordinado; estado de estar unificado (pág. 631)

***unique:** distinctive; unequaled (p. 562)

***único:** distintivo; sin igual (pág. 562)

universal law of gravitation: one of the three rules of motion governing the planetary bodies set forth by Sir Isaac Newton in his *Principia;* it explains that planetary bodies do not go off in straight lines but instead continue in elliptical orbits about the sun because every object in the universe is attracted to every other object by a force called gravity (p. 541)

ley de la gravitación universal: una de las tres reglas del movimiento que rigen los cuerpos planetarios establecida por sir Isaac Newton en su *Principia;* explica que los cuerpos planetarios no se mueven en línea recta, sino que continúan en órbitas elípticas alrededor del Sol, porque cada objeto en el universo es atraído hacia todos los otros objetos por una fuerza llamada gravedad (pág. 541)

universal male suffrage: the right of all males to vote in elections (p. 628)

sufragio universal masculino: el derecho de todos los hombres a votar en elecciones (pág. 628)

***unprecedented:** having nothing that has been done or said in the past to compare to (p. 796)

***sin precedentes:** que no se ha hecho o dicho algo similar en el pasado (pág. 796)

***unreliable:** not dependable (p. 969)

***desconfiar:** que no se puede confiar (pág. 969)

***unrestricted:** having no restrictions or bounds (p. 767)

***irrestricto:** que no tiene restricciones ni límites (pág. 767)

urban society: a system in which cities are the center of political, economic, and social life (p. 398)

sociedad urbana: sistema social en el cual las ciudades son el centro de la vida política, económica y social (pág. 398)

vassal: under feudalism, a man who served a lord in a military capacity (p. 310)

vasallo: en el feudalismo, hombre que servía a un señor en calidad de militar (pág. 310)

Vedas: the earliest known Indian literature, which contain religious chants and stories that were originally passed down orally from generation to generation and then recorded in Sanskrit after writing developed (p. 80)

Vedas: primeros escritos literarios conocidos de la India, contienen cantos religiosos e historias que inicialmente pasaron oralmente de generación en generación y se registraron en sánscrito una vez desarrollada la escritura (pág. 80)

vernacular: the language of everyday speech in a particular region (pp. 351, 407)

vernácula: lengua que se habla cotidianamente en una región particular (pp. 351, 407)

***via:** by way of (p. 69)

***vía:** por medio de (pág. 69)

viceroy: a governor who ruled as a representative of a monarch (p. 704)

virrey: gobernador que regía como representante de un monarca (pág. 704)

***violation:** a disregard of rules or agreements (p. 856)

***violación:** desacato de las reglas o acuerdos (pág. 856)

***virtually:** almost entirely; nearly (p. 148)

***virtualmente:** casi enteramente; aproximadamente (pág. 148)

***vision:** the way of seeing or believing (p. 275)

***visión:** forma de ver o creer (pág. 275)

vizier: a high government official in ancient Egypt or in Muslim countries (pp. 37, 196)

visir: alto funcionario gubernamental en el antiguo Egipto o en países musulmanes (pp. 37, 196)

***volunteer:** one who enters the military voluntarily (p. 828)

***voluntario:** quien entra voluntariamente al ejército (pág. 828)

war communism: in World War I Russia, government control of banks and most industries, the seizing of grain from peasants, and the centralization of state administration under Communist control (p. 777)

comunismo de guerra: en la Rusia de la Primera Guerra Mundial, el control gubernamental de los bancos y la mayoría de las industrias, la confiscación de granos a los campesinos y la centralización de la administración estatal bajo el control comunista (pág. 777)

war of attrition: a war based on wearing the other side down by constant attacks and heavy losses, such as World War I (p. 765)

guerra de desgaste: guerra que se basa en desgastar al otro bando con constantes ataques y grandes pérdidas, como en la Primera Guerra Mundial (pág. 765)

welfare state: a state in which the government takes responsibility for providing citizens with services such as health care (p. 916)

estado de bienestar: estado en el que el gobierno asume la responsabilidad de proveer a los ciudadanos de servicios como la atención sanitaria (pág. 916)

wergild: "money for a man", the value of a person in money, depending on social status; in Germanic society, a fine paid by a wrongdoer to the family of the person he or she had injured or killed (p. 304)

wergild: "dinero por un hombre", indemnización; el valor de una persona en dinero, dependiendo de su estatus social; en la sociedad germánica, una multa pagada por un malhechor a la familia de la persona a quien dañó o mató (pág. 304)

***whereas:** although (p. 159)

***mientras:** en tanto que (pág. 159)

***widespread:** widely extended or spread out (p. 880)

***generalizado:** ampliamente extendido o diseminado (pág. 880)

women's liberation movement: the renewed feminist movement of the late 1960s, which demanded political and economic equality with men (p. 921)

movimiento de liberación de la mujer: movimiento feminista renovado de finales de la década de 1960, que exigía la igualdad política y económica con los hombres (pág. 921)

yoga: a method of training developed by the Hindus that is supposed to lead to oneness with God (p. 72)

yoga: método de ejercitación creado por los hindúes que se supone conduce a la unidad con Dios (pág. 72)

zaibatsu: in the Japanese economy, a large financial and industrial corporation (p. 834)

zaibatsu: en la economía japonesa, gran corporación financiera e industrial (pág. 834)

zamindar: a local official in Mogul India who received a plot of farmland for temporary use in return for collecting taxes for the central government (p. 499)

zamindar: oficial local en la India de los mogoles, que recibía un lote de terreno para su uso temporal a cambio de cobrar impuestos para el gobierno central (pág. 499)

Zen: a sect of Buddhism that became popular with Japanese aristocrats and became part of the samurai's code of behavior; under Zen Buddhism, there are different paths to enlightenment (p. 282)

Zen: secta del budismo que se hizo popular entre los aristócratas japoneses y se volvió parte del código de conducta de los samuráis; según el budismo Zen, existen diferentes vías para llegar a la iluminación (pág. 282)

ziggurat: a massive stepped tower on which was built a temple dedicated to the chief god or goddess of a Sumerian city (p. 29)

ziggurat: torre escalonada en la cual se construía un templo dedicado al dios o diosa principal en las ciudades sumerias (pág. 29)

Zionism: an international movement originally for the establishment of a Jewish national or religious community in Palestine and later for the support of modern Israel (p. 679)

sionismo: movimiento internacional que originalmente abogaba por el establecimiento de una comunidad nacional o religiosa judía en Palestina y después por el apoyo al Israel moderno (pág. 679)

GLOSSARY

The following abbreviations are used in the index: m = map; f = feature (photograph, picture, painting, cartoon, chart); t = table; q = quote

INDEX

INDEX

INDEX

INDEX

INDEX

INDEX

INDEX

INDEX

INDEX

INDEX

INDEX

INDEX

O

INDEX

INDEX

INDEX

INDEX

INDEX

INDEX

Acknowledgments and Photo Credits

Acknowledgments

Glencoe would like to acknowledge the artists and agencies that participated in illustrating this program: American Artists Reps Inc.; Deborah Wolfe Ltd/illustrationOnLine.com; GeoNova LLC; Mendola Artist Representatives.

Photo Credits

Cover (tl)Jacques M. Chenet/CORBIS, (tcl)Oliver Lang/AFP/Getty Images, (tc)Art Archive/Eileen Tweedy, (tcr)Keren Su/CORBIS, (tr) SuperStock, (b)Antonio M. Rosario/The Image Bank/Getty Images; **Endsheet** (b)photolibrary.com/Index Open, (bkgd)Getty Images; **T4** Art Archive/Heraklion Museum/Dagli Orti; **T5** Erich Lessing/Art Resource, NY; **T6** Ed Kashi/CORBIS; **T7** Hu Weibiao/Panorama/The Image Works; **T8** CORBIS; **T10** Science Museum/SSPL/The Image Works; **T13** Philip Wolmuth/Alamy Images; **T14** Erich Lessing/Art Resource, NY; **T15** Private Collection/Dinodia/Bridgeman Art Library; **T16** PA/Topham/The Image Works; **T17** Shepard Sherbell/CORBIS; **T18** Chip East/Reuters/CORBIS; **T22** Comstock/PictureQuest; **T23** Stockbyte/Punchstock; **T42** Superstudio/Getty Images; **T44** Ian Shaw/Getty Images; **T46** Comstock/CORBIS; **T47** image100/CORBIS; **T50** Ariel Skelley/CORBIS; **T52** Comstock/PunchStock; **T55** Charles Gupton/CORBIS; **A28** (t to b)Michael Von Ruber/Imagestate, (2)David S. Boyer/Getty Images, (3)John Lamb/Getty Images, (4)Panoramic Images/Getty Images; **GH2** BananaStock/PictureQuest; **GH13** Copyright © 2008 by David W. Boles. All Rights Reserved.; **GH14-1** age fotostock/SuperStock; **2** (l)Charles & Josette Lenars/CORBIS, (r)Pascal Goetgheluck/Photo Researchers; **2–3** Sissie Brimberg/National Geographic/Getty Images; **3** Archivo Iconografico, S.A./CORBIS; **6** (l)Topham/The Image Works, (r)Robert Campbell/CORBIS SYGMA; **9** (l)Ira Block/National Geographic/Getty Images, (tr)photolibrary.com/Index Open, (br)Cordelia Molloy/Photo Researchers; **10** Jean Clottes; **15** Gail Mooney/Masterfile; **18** (l)Art Archive/Heraklion Museum/Dagli Orti, (c)Jean-Louis Nou/akg-images, (r)O Louis Mazzatenta/National Geographic/Getty Images; **24** Erich Lessing/Art Resource, NY; **24–25** David S. Boyer/Getty Images; **25** (l)Art Archive/Bibliothèque Musée du Louvre/Dagli Orti, (r)Roger Wood/CORBIS; **28** Topham/The Image Works; **31** British Museum, London/Bridgeman Art Library; **32** Art Media/Heritage-Images/The Image Works; **35** Art Archive/Luxor Museum, Egypt/Dagli Orti; **36** Travelpix Ltd/Getty Images; **38** (t)Erich Lessing/Art Resource, NY, (b)Werner Foreman/Topham/The Image Works; **39** Erich Lessing/Art Resource, NY; **40** (l)Michael Jenner/CORBIS, (r)CM Dixon/HIP/The Image Works; **42** (l)Roger Wood/CORBIS, (r)Werner Forman/CORBIS; **48** Erich Lessing/Art Resource, NY; **50** Kathleen Voege/Getty Images; **52** (l)Bridgeman Art Library/Getty Images, (r)Erich Lessing/Art Resource, NY; **53** (t)British Museum, London/Bridgeman Art Library, (b)Ronald Sheridan/Ancient Art & Architecture Collection; **55** HIP/Art Resource, NY; **59** Werner Forman/akg-images; **60** (t)Art Archive/Dagli Orti, (c)Jane Sweeney/Lonely Planet Images, (b)Art Archive/Musée du Louvre Paris/Dagli Orti; **64** Topham/The Image Works; **64–65** Paul Springett/Alamy Images; **65** (l)akg-images, (r)Ru Suichu/Panorama/The Image Works; **69** Scala/Art Resource, NY; **71** (inset)Eames Collection/Newberry Library, (bkgd)Topham/The Image Works; **72** (l)Private Collection/Bridgeman Art Library, (r)Victoria & Albert Museum, London/Art Resource, NY; **73** Historical Picture Archive/CORBIS; **74** Vanni/Art Resource, NY; **91** (l)Reuters/CORBIS, (r)Art Archive/Bibliothèque Nationale Paris; **92** Bettmann/CORBIS; **95** Atlantide Phototravel/CORBIS; **97** (inset)Liu Liqun/ChinaStock, (bkgd)Paul Souders/CORBIS; **100** (tl)Jean-Louis Nou/akg-images, (tr)akg-images, (bl)Eames Collection/Newberry Library, (br)Paul Souders/CORBIS; **104** Archivo Iconografico, S.A./CORBIS; **104–105** Peter Barritt/Alamy Images; **105** (t)Art Archive/Eton College/Dagli Orti, (b)Museum of Fine Arts, Houston/Bridgeman Art Library; **107** Andre Jenny/Alamy Images; **108** Roger Wood/CORBIS; **110** (l)The British Museum/Imagestate, (c)Erich Lessing/Art Resource, NY, (r)Visual Arts Library (London)/Alamy Images; **113** Alinari Archives/The Image Works; **116** (t)Cummer Museum of Art & Gardens/SuperStock, (bl)Bridgeman Art Library/Getty Images, (br)Hulton Archive/Getty Images; **120** Time Life Pictures/Getty Images; **122** Erich Lessing/Art Resource, NY; **125** Bridgeman Art Library; **127** Araldo de Luca/CORBIS; **128** (l)The British Museum/Topham-HIP/The Image Works; **128** (r)SEF/Art Resource, NY; **130** Frances Roberts/Alamy Images; **136** David Lees/CORBIS; **138** Erich Lessing/Art Resource, NY; **140** (t)Archivo Iconografico, S.A./CORBIS, (c)Nimatallah/Art Resource, NY, (b)Art Archive/Musée du Louvre, Paris/Dagli Orti; **144** The Bridgeman Art Library/Getty Images; **144–145** Images Etc Ltd/Alamy Images; **145** (l)Mimmo Jodice/CORBIS, (r)Araldo de Luca/CORBIS; **150** Art Archive/Museo Capitolino Rome/Dagli Orti; **153** Réunion des Musées Nationaux/Art Resource, NY; **155** (l)Prisma/Ancient Art & Architecture Collection, (r)Bridgeman Art Library/Getty Images; **156** Philip Craven/Getty Images; **157** David Robertson/Alamy Images; **161** Hisham F. Ibrahim/Getty Images; **163** (inset)Erich Lessing/Art Resource, NY, (bkgd)C.M.Dixon/Ancient Art & Architecture Collection Ltd; **164** The Bridgeman Art Library/Getty Images; **169** Alinari, Pompeii/Bridgeman Art Library; **172** Scala/Art Resource, NY; **175** Ken Welsh/Alamy Images; **178** (t c)Scala/Art Resource, NY, (b)Yoshio Tomii/SuperStock; **184–185** Jon Arnold Images/SuperStock; **186** HIP/Art Resource, NY; **186–187** Alison Wright/CORBIS; **187** (t)AAAC/Topham/The Image Works, (b)akg-images; **189** Peter Sanders/HAGA/The Image Works; **195** Chateau de Versailles, France/Bridgeman Art Library; **198** The McGraw-Hill Companies; **201** The British Museum/HIP/The Image Works; **202** (l)Atlantide Phototravel/CORBIS, (c)Françoise De Mulder/Roger-Viollet/The Image Works, (r)Paula Bronstein/Getty Images; **205** Art Archive/Pharaonic Village, Cairo/Dagli Orti; **206** Topham/The Image Works; **208** Mary Evans Picture Library/The Image Works; **209** Art Archive/National Museum, Damascus, Syria/Dagli Orti; **210** (t)Art Archive/Museum of Islamic Art, Cairo/Dagli Orti, (c)Art Archive/Turkish and Islamic Art Museum, Istanbul/Dagli Orti, (b)age fotostock/SuperStock; **216** (t)Will & Deni McIntyre/CORBIS, (b)David Samuel Robbins/CORBIS; **217** (t)Robert Nickelsberg/Getty Images, (b)ML Sinibaldi/CORBIS; **218** (t)CORBIS, (b)Ace Stock Limited/Alamy Images; **219** (t)Atlantide Phototravel/CORBIS, (b)Denis Sinyakov/AFP/Getty Images; **220** (t)Michel Setboun/CORBIS, (bl)Bettmann/CORBIS, (br)Blank Archives/Getty Images; **221** (t)STR/AFP/Getty Images, (b)Jack Hollingsworth/Getty Images; **222** (t)Ted Streshinsky/CORBIS, (b)CORBIS; **223** (t)Deshakalyan Chwodhury/AFP/Getty Images, (b)Sebastian D'Souza/AFP/Getty Images; **224** (t)Aaron Horowitz/CORBIS, (c)Kenneth Garrett/Getty Images, (b)CORBIS; **225** (t)Muhannad Fala'ah/Getty Images, (b)Madaree Tohlala/AFP/Getty Images; **226** (t)Hardy/zefa/CORBIS, (bl)CORBIS, (br)Comstock Images/Alamy Images; **227** (t)Quique Kierszenbaum/Getty Images, (b)Ted Spiegel/CORBIS; **228** (t)Ashley Cooper/CORBIS, (c)Chip Somodevilla/Getty Images, (b)ArkReligion.com/Alamy Images; **229** (t)Maynard Owen Williams/National Geographic/Getty Images, (b)Don MacKinnon/Getty Images; **230** (t)Beth Wald/Aurora/Getty Images, (bl)Ralph A. Clevenger/CORBIS, (br)Martin Harvey/Alamy Images; **231** (t)Nicholas DeVore/Getty Images, (cl)CORBIS, (cr)Paul Chesley/Getty Images, (b)Penny Tweedie/Wildlight; **232** (t)Pete Saloutos/CORBIS, (c)David Ball/CORBIS, (b)age fotostock/SuperStock; **234** Dave Bartruff/CORBIS; **234–235** age fotostock/SuperStock; **235** (t)HIP/Art Resource, NY, (b)AAAC/Topham/The Image Works; **240** (l)Werner Forman/Art Resource, NY, (r)Chris Howes/Wild Places Photography/Alamy Images; **241** (t)Sonia Halliday Photographs, (b)Private Collection/Bridgeman Art Library; **243** (l)Charles O'Rear/CORBIS, (r)Art Archive/Musée des Arts Africains et Océaniens/Dagli Orti; **244** Illustration by David Wisniewski; **251** (l)Michael Graham-Stewart/Bridgeman Art Library, (r)Charles & Josette Lenars/CORBIS; **254** Craig Lovell/CORBIS; **258** (t)Picture Contact/Alamy Images, (c b)Werner Forman/Art Resource, NY; **262** Werner Forman/Art Resource, NY; **262–263** Stuart Dee/Getty Images; **263** (l)National Museum, Tokyo/SuperStock, (r)Nik Wheeler/CORBIS; **266** (t)Erich Lessing/Art Resource, NY, (b)Burstein Collection/CORBIS; **267** (t)akg-images, (b)Roger-Viollet/The Image Works; **268** Musee Guimet, Paris/Bridgeman Art Library; **273** Superstock; **274** (l)Bettmann/CORBIS, (r)The British Library/HIP/The Image Works; **280** AAAC/Topham/The Image Works; **282** Réunion des Musées Nationaux/Art Resource, NY; **285** (l)Dinodia Photo Library, (c)Pascal Deloche/Godong/CORBIS, (r)Markus Matzel/Das Fotoarchiv/Peter Arnold, Inc.; **286** Stapleton Collection/CORBIS; **287** Anil Dave/Dinodia Photo Library; **288** Robert Preston/Alamy Images; **292** Gérard Degeorge/akg-images;

PHOTO CREDITS

294 Christophe Loviny/CORBIS; **296** (t)Burstein Collection/CORBIS, (c)Werner Forman/Art Resource, NY, (b)Steve Vidler/Superstock; **300** Erich Lessing/Art Resource, NY; **300–301** age fotostock/SuperStock; **301** (t)Mary Evans Picture Library/The Image Works, (b)Heini Schneebeli/Bridgeman Art Library; **314** Bridgeman Art Library; **315** (tl)Visual Arts Library (London)/Alamy Images, (tr)Bridgeman Art Library, (bl)Bildarchiv Preussischer Kulturbesitz/Art Resource, NY, (br)Giraudon/Musée Conde, Chantilly, France/Bridgeman Art Library; **318** Bettmann/CORBIS; **323** Christel Gerstenberg/CORBIS; **325** (t)Atlantide Phototravel/CORBIS, (b)age fotostock/SuperStock; **326** Art Resource, NY; **328** (t)Art Resource, NY, (c)age fotostock/SuperStock, (b)Archivo Iconografico, S.A./CORBIS; **332** (t)Erich Lessing/Art Resource, NY, (b)AAAC/Topham/The Image Works; **332–333** Jason Hawkes/CORBIS; **333** Stapleton Collection/CORBIS; **337** Réunion des Musées Nationaux/Art Resource, NY; **340** Art Archive/Museo dell'Opera del Duomo Orvieto/Dagli Orti; **343** SEF/Art Resource, NY; **345** (l)Michael Teller/akg-images, (r)akg-images; **346** akg-images; **349** (inset)Andrea Pistolesi/Getty Images, (bkgd)Art Kowalsky/Alamy Images; **350** The Granger Collection, New York; **354** The British Library/Topham-HIP/The Image Works; **357** akg-images; **358** The Art Archive/CORBIS; **362** (t)Historical Picture Archive/CORBIS, (c)Chateau de Versailles, France/Giraudon/Bridgeman Art Library, (b)The Granger Collection, New York; **365** Giraudon/Art Resource, NY; **366** (t)Jose Fuste Raga/CORBIS, (b)Pirozzi/akg-images; **366–367** Panoramic Images/Getty Images; **367** Collection of the New York Historical Society/Bridgeman Art Library; **373** (l)Kimbell Art Museum/CORBIS, (r)Martha Cooper/Peter Arnold, Inc.; **376** Richard A. Cooke/CORBIS; **378** HIP/Art Resource, NY; **384** Stock Montage; **387** Snark/Art Resource, NY; **388** (t)George H. H. Huey/CORBIS, (c)Mary Evans Picture Library/The Image Works, (b)Topham/The Image Works; **391** Gianni Dagli Orti/CORBIS; **394–395** Danny Lehman/CORBIS; **396** Scala/Art Resource, NY; **396–397** Paul Hardy/CORBIS; **397** (t)HIP/Art Resource, NY, (b)Bildarchiv Preussischer Kulturbesitz/Art Resource, NY; **401** **402** Erich Lessing/Art Resource, NY; **407** Scala/Art Resource, NY; **408** (l)Francis G. Mayer/CORBIS, (r)Art Archive/Galleria Brera Milan/Dagli Orti; **410** (l)Biblioteca Reale, Turin/Bridgeman Art Library, (r)akg-images; **414** (l)Private Collection/Bridgeman Art Library, (r)Bettmann/CORBIS; **416** Foto Marburg/Art Resource, NY; **420** (l)Francis G. Mayer/CORBIS, (r)Art Archive/Musée Granet Aix-en-Provence/Dagli Orti; **424** (t)Scala/Art Resource, NY, (c b)Bettmann/CORBIS; **428** The Granger Collection, New York; **428–429** Elk Photography; **429** Scala/Art Resource, NY; **433** (l)Art Archive/Marine Museum, Lisbon/Dagli Orti, (r)Bettmann/CORBIS; **434** Shannon Stapleton/Reuters/CORBIS; **436** (t)Art Archive/Musée de la Marine, Paris/Dagli Orti, (b)The Granger Collection, New York; **438** (cw from top)Punchstock, (2)Alamy Images, (3)Getty Images, (4)C Squared Studios/Getty Images, (5)Punchstock, (6)PhotoAlto/Getty Images; **438–439** Art Archive/Bibliothèque des Arts Décoratifs Paris; **439** (cw from top)Alan and Sandy Carey/Getty Images, (2)CORBIS, (3)Artvillle/Getty Images, (4)Brand X Pictures/Punchstock, (5)Artvillle/Getty Images, (6)Punchstock; **442** Mary Evans Picture Library; **446** The Granger Collection, New York; **448** (t)Charles Walker/Topham/The Image Works, (c)Bildarchiv Preussischer Kulturbesitz/Art Resource, NY, (b)North Wind Picture Archives/Alamy Images; **452** (t)Charles Dixon (1924)/Mary Evans Picture Library, (b)Private Collection/Dinodia/Bridgeman Art Library; **452–453** Gail Mooney/Masterfile; **453** Stock Montage/Hulton Archive/Getty Images; **459** Giraudon/Bridgeman Art Library; **462** (l)Private Collection/Christie's Images/Bridgeman Art Library, (r)Topham/The Image Works; **465** (l)Art Archive/Dagli Orti, (r)Giraudon/Bridgeman Art Library; **470** (t)Archivo Iconografico, S.A./CORBIS, (b)Gian Berto Vanni/CORBIS; **471** (t)Author's Image/Alamy Images, (b)Tony Craddock/Getty Images; **473** (t)Alinari Archives/CORBIS, (b)Joseph Martin/Bridgeman Art Library; **475** Victoria & Albert Museum, London/Art Resource, NY; **476** Bob Daemmrich/PhotoEdit; **478** (t)Scala/Art Resource, NY, (c)Private Collection/Bridgeman Art Library, (b)Erich Lessing/Art Resource, NY; **482** (l)Erich Lessing/Art Resource, NY, (r)Bridgeman Art Library; **482–483** Manish Swarup/AP Images; **483** National Portrait Gallery, Smithsonian Institution/Art Resource, NY; **487** (inset)Age Fotostock/SuperStock, (bkgd)Arthus-Bertrand/CORBIS; **488** Ali Meyer/CORBIS; **490** Araldo de Luca/CORBIS; **491** (t)HIP/Art Resource, NY, (b)Erich Lessing/Art Resource, NY; **493** age fotostock/SuperStock; **494** Ed Kashi/CORBIS; **500** (l)Private Collection/Dinodia/Bridgeman Art Library, (r)Stapleton Collection/Victoria & Albert Museum, London/Bridgeman Art Library; **502** National Portrait Gallery, London; **504** (t)Stapleton Collection, UK/Bridgeman Art Library, (c)The Metropolitan Museum of Art/Art Resource, NY, (b)David Ball/Spectrum Colour Library/Imagestate; **508** (l)Collection of the New York Historical Society/Bridgeman Art Library, (r)National Museum of Ancient Art, Lisbon/Bridgeman Art Library; **508–509** Yann Layma/The Image Bank/Getty Images; **509** Erich Lessing/Art Resource, NY; **514** Visual Arts Library, London/Alamy Images; **517** Free Library, Philadelphia/Bridgeman Art Library; **518** Museum of East Asian Art/HIP/The Image Works; **522** (l)Bridgeman Art Library/Getty Images, (r)Christie's Images/SuperStock; **524** Chris Ware/The Image Works; **528** The British Library/Heritage Images/Imagestate; **532** (t)Historical Picture Archive/CORBIS, (c)Réunion des Musées Nationaux/Art Resource, NY, (b)Bridgeman Art Library; **536** Galleria Palatina, Palazzo Pitti, Florence/Bridgeman Art Library; **536–537** Scott Gilchrist/Masterfile; **537** (t)Joseph Sohm/Jupiter Images, (b)Hu Weibiao/Panorama/The Image Works; **541** (l)Scala/Art Resource, NY, (r)Galleria Palatina, Palazzo Pitti, Florence/Bridgeman Art Library; **542** Johann Brandst/akg-images; **549** (l)Musee de la Ville de Paris, Musee Carnavalet, Paris/Lauros/Giraudon/Bridgeman Art Library, (r)Bettmann/CORBIS; **550** Bettmann/CORBIS; **552** Art Archive/City Temple, London/Eileen Tweedy; **556** (l)Kurpfalzisches Museum, Heidelberg, Germany/Lauros/Giraudon/Bridgeman Art Library, (r)Art Archive/Museum der Stadt, Vienna/Dagli Orti; **557** (l)Art Archive/Russian Historical Museum, Moscow/Dagli Orti, (r)Louvre, Paris/Giraudon/Bridgeman Art Library; **561** CORBIS; **562** Erich Lessing/Private Collection/Art Resource, NY; **564** **565** Réunion des Musées Nationaux/Art Resource, NY; **568** Joel Page/AP Images; **570** (t b) North Wind Picture Archives/Alamy Images, (c)Bettmann/CORBIS; **574** Bridgeman-Giraudon/Art Resource, NY; **574–575** John Lamb/Getty Images; **575** (l)Art Archive/Antochiw Collection, Mexico/Mireille Vautier, (r)Art Archive/Musée de L'Armée, Paris/Dagli Orti; **577** Erich Lessing/Art Resource, NY; **578–579** akg-images; **580** Giraudon/Art Resource, NY; **582** Bob Adelman/Magnum Photos; **587** Mary Evans Picture Library; **588** (l)Erich Lessing/Art Resource, NY, (r)Explorer/E.S. Collection/Mary Evans Picture Library; **590** (l)Musée Carnavalet, Paris/Giraudon/Bridgeman Art Library, (r)Mary Evans Picture Library; **591** (l)Private Collection/Bridgeman Art Library, (r)Archivo Iconografico, S.A./CORBIS; **592** George Cruikshank, The Radical's Arms, November 13, 1819. Etching with hand coloring. Published by George Humphrey, London, England. Collection of the Grunwald Center for the Graphic Arts, Hammer Museum, UCLA. Richard Vogler Cruikshank Collection; **595** Erich Lessing/Art Resource, NY; **597** Art Archive/Dagli Orti; **598** Kress Collection, Washington, D.C./Bridgeman Art Library; **604** (t)Musée des Beaux-Arts, France/Giraudon/Art Resource, NY, (c)Erich Lessing/Art Resource, NY, (b)Giraudon/Art Resource, NY; **607** The Granger Collection, New York; **610–611** Adoc-photos/Art Resource, NY; **612** Erich Lessing/Art Resource, NY; **612–613** Keith Levitt/Index Stock Imagery; **613** (t)Private Collection/Bridgeman Art Library, (b)Archives Charmet, Bibliothèque des Arts Decoratifs, Paris, France/Bridgeman Art Library; **617** Mary Evans Picture Library; **618** Science Museum/SSPL/The Image Works; **620** Mary Evans Picture Library; **623** Bettmann/CORBIS; **627** Bibliothèque Nationale, Paris/The Bridgeman Art Library; **633** (l)SuperStock, (r)Art Archive/Museo Civico Cremona/Dagli Orti; **634** HIP-Archive/Topham/The Image Works; **636** Private Collection/Bridgeman Art Library; **639** Giraudon/Art Resource, NY; **640** (t)SuperStock, (b)MEPL/The Image Works; **642** Galerie Neue Meister, Dresden/Staatliche Kunstsammlungen Dresden, Germany/Bridgeman Art Library; **644–645** Time & Life Pictures/Getty Images; **646** (t)Yale Center for British Art, Paul Mellon Collection/Bridgeman Art Library, (c)Archives Charmet, Musee de la Ville de Paris, Musee Carnavalet, Paris/Bridgeman Art Library, (b)Musee des Beaux-Arts, Rouen/Bridgeman Art Library; **650** Bettmann/CORBIS; **650–651** ND/Roger Viollet/Getty Images; **651** (t)Swim Ink 2/CORBIS, (b)Mary Evans Picture Library/The Image Works; **654** AFP/Getty Images; **656** Bildarchiv Preussischer Kulturbesitz/Art Resource, NY; **661** Michelle D. Bridwell/PhotoEdit; **663** Hulton-Deutsch Collection/CORBIS; **664** (inset)Bettmann/CORBIS, (bkgd)Lake County Museum/CORBIS; **671** **672** Bettmann/CORBIS; **675** (l)Digital Image © The Museum of Modern Art/Licensed by SCALA/Art Resource, NY, (r)Réunion des Musées Nationaux/Art Resource, NY; **677** Bettmann/CORBIS; **678** (l)Michael Nicholson/CORBIS, (r)Imagno/Getty Images; **680** (t)Imperial Cadett School/Scherl/SV-Bilderdienst/The Image

Works, (c b)Roger-Viollet/The Image Works; **683** CORBIS; **684** (l)Private Collection/Bridgeman Art Library, (r)Chicago Historical Museum/Bridgeman Art Library; **684–685** Robert Harding World Imagery/Getty Images; **685** Hulton-Deutsch Collection/CORBIS; **689** Library of Congress, LC-USZ62-52583; **690 694** Mary Evans Picture Library; **696** (l)Topham/The Image Works, (r)The British Library/HIP/The Image Works; **698** (l)Hulton-Deutsch Collection/CORBIS, (r)Library of Congress, Prints & Photographs Division, NYWT&S Collection, LC-USZ62-130451; **700** Mary Evans Picture Library; **701** (t)akg-images, (b)Alinari Archives/The Image Works; **703** Hulton-Deutsch Collection/CORBIS; **706** (l)Time & Life Pictures/Getty Images, (r)DPA/The Image Works; **710** (l)Bettmann/CORBIS, (r)Private Collection/Archives Charmet/Bridgeman Art Library; **713** Bettmann/CORBIS; **714** Underwood & Underwood/CORBIS; **718** (t)Art Archive/Museo Civico Revoltella Trieste/Dagli Orti, (c)British Library, London/Bridgeman Art Library, (b)Royal Geographical Society, London/Bridgeman Art Library; **722** (t)Topham/The Image Works, (b)Bettmann/CORBIS; **722–723** GP Bowater/Alamy Images; **723** rochaphoto/Alamy Images; **727** Art Archive/Eileen Tweedy; **728** (l)Mary Evans Picture Library/The Image Works, (r)Hu Weibiao/Panorama/The Image Works; **730 734** Bettmann/CORBIS; **736** Mary Evans Picture Library/The Image Works; **741** Twphoto/CORBIS; **742** Asian Art & Archaeology/CORBIS; **744** Bettmann/CORBIS; **748** (t)Ann Ronan Picture Library/HIP/The Image Works, (c)Hulton Archive/Getty Images, (b)Private Collection/Bridgeman Art Library; **751** Bettmann/CORBIS; **754–755** Three Lions/Getty Images; **756** Bettmann/CORBIS; **756–757** Topham/The Image Works; **757** (l)Bettmann/CORBIS, (r)CORBIS; **760** Bettmann/CORBIS; **764** Hulton-Deutsch Collection/CORBIS; **765** (l)Bettmann/CORBIS, (r)Hulton-Deutsch Collection/CORBIS; **766** (l)Bettmann/CORBIS, (r)Mary Evans Picture Library; **768** Underwood & Underwood/CORBIS; **775** RIA Novosti/Tretyakov Gallery, Moscow/Bridgeman Art Library; **776** Snark/Art Resource, NY; **781** Lebrecht Music & Arts/The Image Works; **782** Imperial War Museum/akg-images; **784** (t)Private Collection/Bridgeman Art Library, (c)Delaware Art Museum/Bridgeman Art Library, (b)Albert Harlingue/Roger-Viollet/The Image Works; **788** Ann Ronan Picture Library/Heritage-Images/The Image Works; **788–789** Bettmann/CORBIS; **789** (l)Mary Evans Picture Library, (r)Bettmann/CORBIS; **793** (t)akg-images, (b)Art Archive/Imperial War Museum; **794** Bettmann/CORBIS; **798** (l)akg-images, (r)Underwood & Underwood/CORBIS; **802** (t)Art Archive/Reina Sofia Museum, Madrid, (b)akg-images; **805 807** Mary Evans Picture Library/The Image Works; **808** (t)Mary Evans Picture Library/The Image Works, (b)Bettmann/CORBIS; **810** Stapleton Collection/CORBIS; **811** CORBIS; **813** (l)CORBIS, (r)Bettmann/CORBIS; **814** Najlah Feanny/CORBIS; **816** (t)Bettmann/CORBIS, (c)Mary Evans Picture Library/The Image Works, (b)Hulton-Deutsch Collection/CORBIS; **819** CORBIS; **820** Mary Evans Picture Library/The Image Works; **820–821** Bettmann/CORBIS; **821** Mary Evans Picture Library/The Image Works; **824** Private Collection/Bridgeman Art Library; **831** (l)Tim Page/CORBIS, (r)Hulton-Deutsch Collection/CORBIS; **833** (t)Bettmann/CORBIS, (b)Margaret Bourke-White/Time & Life Pictures/Getty Images; **834** Myrleen Ferguson Cate/PhotoEdit; **838** Private Collection/Bridgeman Art Library; **840** Time & Life Pictures/Getty Images; **846** Bettman/CORBIS; **848** Schalkwijk/Art Resource, NY; **850** (t)S.M./SV-Bilderdienst/The Image Works, (c)State Russian Museum, St. Petersburg/Bridgeman Art Library, (b)SSPL/The Image Works; **853** Bettmann/CORBIS; **854** (t)David J. & Janice L. Frent Collection/CORBIS, (b)Bettmann/CORBIS; **854–855** CORBIS; **855** Bettmann/CORBIS; **859** CORBIS; **863** Bettmann/CORBIS; **865** Fox Photos/Getty Images; **870** Bettmann/CORBIS; **872** (l)AP Images, (r)Hulton Deutsch Collection/CORBIS; **873** (t)Three Lions/Getty Images, (b)Peter J. Carroll/AP Images; **877** dpa/CORBIS; **878** Evan Vucci/AP Images; **881** (l)CORBIS, (r)Laski Diffusion/Getty Images; **882** CORBIS; **885** (t)Bettmann/CORBIS, (b)Peace Memorial Museum/epa/CORBIS; **888** (l)Bettmann/CORBIS, (r)Fox Photos/Getty Images; **889** (t)Hulton Archive/Getty Images, (b)NRM/SSPL/The Image Works; **890** (t)Bettmann/CORBIS, (c)Jeffrey Markowitz/CORBIS, (b)Hulton-Deutsch Collection/CORBIS; **896–897** Patrick Robert/CORBIS SYGMA; **898** Science Museum/SSPL/The Image Works; **898–899** Bettmann/CORBIS; **899** (t)Bettmann/CORBIS, (b)Walter Dhladhla/AFP/Getty Images; **903** Bettmann/CORBIS; **904** AP Images; **906** Library of Congress, LC-USZ62-130423; **908 909** AP Images; **911** akg-images; **912** Bettmann/CORBIS; **916** Johannes Eisele/AFP/Getty Images; **919** Francis Miller/Time & Life Pictures/Getty Images; **920** NASA/Roger Ressmeyer/CORBIS; **922** Michael Ochs Archive/CORBIS; **923** Harry Diltz/CORBIS; **924** (t)Bettmann/CORBIS, (c)Look and Learn/Bridgeman Art Library, (b)Bettmann/CORBIS; **928** Bettmann/CORBIS; **928–929** Tom Stoddart/Getty Images; **929** Digital Vision/Getty Images; **933** Peter Turnley/CORBIS; **934** (t)Patrick Chauvel/Sygma/CORBIS, (b)Steve Raymer/CORBIS; **938** Lynne Fernandes/The Image Works; **942** Philip Wolmuth/Alamy Images; **944** Ali Al-Saadi/AFP/Getty Images; **947** (inset)Matthias Rietschel/AP Images, (bkgd)Marco Cristofori/CORBIS; **948** Shepard Sherbell/CORBIS; **952** (l)Getty Images, (r)Michael Ochs Archives/CORBIS; **953** (t)Pictorial Press Ltd/Alamy Images, (b)Robert Grossman/Africaphotos.com; **954** (t)Tom Stoddart/Getty Images, (c)Alan Lewis/CORBIS SYGMA, (b)Bettmann/CORBIS; **958** Lester Cole/CORBIS; **958–959** Alejandro Ernesto/epa/CORBIS; **959** (t)Susana Gonzalez/Bloomberg News/Landov, (b)Boris Yurchenko/AP Images; **968 970** CORBIS; **974** Carlos Carrion/Sygma/CORBIS; **976** Bernard Bisson/CORBIS SYGMA; **980** (t)Rika/dpa/CORBIS, (c)Bettmann/CORBIS, (b)Diego Goldberg/Sygma/CORBIS; **984** (t)Rick Barrentine/CORBIS, (b)Adam Woolfitt/CORBIS; **984–985** CORBIS; **985** Martin H. Simon/CORBIS; **988** (l)Al Fenn/Time & Life Pictures/Getty Images, (r)PA/Topham/The Image Works; **991** Peter Turnley/CORBIS; **992** David Turnley/CORBIS; **1000** David Brauchli/CORBIS SYGMA; **1002** Chao Soi Cheong/AP Images; **1005** Jonathan Shapiro; **1006** (t)Gideon Mendel/CORBIS, (c)Reuters/CORBIS, (b)Charles O. Cecil/The Image Works; **1010** Bettmann/CORBIS; **1010–1011** Michael Von Ruber/Imagestate; **1011** Francoise Demulder/CORBIS; **1015** Bettmann/CORBIS; **1020** (l)Henri Bureau/Sygma/CORBIS, (r)Bettmann/CORBIS; **1022** Christian Simonpietri/Sygma/CORBIS; **1027** Steve & Ghy Sampson/Getty Images; **1028** Kim Kyung-Hoon/Reuters/CORBIS; **1032** (t)Hulton Archive/Getty Images, (c)Bettmann/CORBIS; (b)Michael S. Yamashita/CORBIS; **1036** (l)Alfred Eisenstaedt/Time & Life Pictures/Getty Images, (r)Caroline Penn/CORBIS; **1036–1037** Jorgen Schytte/Peter Arnold, Inc.; **1037** Reuters/CORBIS; **1039** Bettmann/CORBIS; **1043** Mark Edwards/Peter Arnold, Inc.; **1044** Phillipe Lissac/Godong/CORBIS; **1046** Kim Kulish/CORBIS; **1049** Ron Giling/Peter Arnold, Inc.; **1051** Reed Saxon/AP Images; **1052** Chip East/Reuters/CORBIS; **1054** (t)CORBIS, (c)Radar Bali/AP Images, (b)Viviane Moos/CORBIS; **1057** Kjell Nilsson-Maki/CartoonStock; **R1** (l)Francis G. Mayer/CORBIS, (r)Bettmann/CORBIS; **R12** Chad Baker-Ryan McVay/Getty Images; **R13** Richard I'Anson/Lonely Planet Images; **R14** Thomas Dworzak/Magnum Photos; **R16** Robert Frerck/Odyssey Productions; **R17** SuperStock; **R22** Imagno/Getty Images; **R30** Jonathan Shapiro; **R32** Réunion des Musées Nationaux/Art Resource, NY; **R33** (t)CORBIS, (b)Main Commission for the Investigation of Nazi War Crimes, courtesy of the United States Holocaust Memorial Museum; **R34** Art Archive/Dagli Orti; **R35** (l)Réunion des Musées Nationaux / Art Resource, NY, (r)Scala/Art Resource, NY; **R36** (t)Erich Lessing/Art Resource, NY, (b)Alinari/Art Resource, NY; **R37** Hervé Lewandowski/Réunion des Musées Nationaux/Art Resource, NY; **R38** Scala/Art Resource, NY; **R39** Peter Willi/SuperStock; **R40** (t)Mary Evans Picture Library, (b)The Metropolitan Museum of Art, Edward Elliott Family Collection. Purchase, The Dillon Fund Gift, 1982. 1982.2.2; **R41** Burstein Collection/CORBIS; **R42** (t)Stock Montage, (b)Art Archive/University Library Geneva/Dagli Orti; **R43** Lowe Art Museum/SuperStock; **R44** Bridgeman-Giraudon/Art Resource, NY; **R45** Art Archive/Musée du Chateau de Versailles/Dagli Orti; **R46 R48** Hulton Archive/Getty Images; **R49** Mary Evans Picture Library; **R50** Bridgeman Art Library; **R51** Hulton-Deutsch Collection/CORBIS; **R52** Bettmann/CORBIS; **R53** (l)Bettmann/CORBIS, (r)Private Collection/Bridgeman Art Library; **R54** Bettmann/CORBIS; **R56** (l)Ho/Suhrkamp/AP Images, (r)Greg Stott/Masterfile; **R57** The Butler Institute of American Art.

Teacher to Teacher Photographs: Unit 1 Courtesy of Ray Barron, Heritage High School; **Unit 2** Courtesy of Pride Adami, Dr. Michael M. Krop High School; **Unit 3** Courtesy of Deborah McDevitt, Belmont High School; **Unit 4** Courtesy of Tobey Reed, Attleboro High School; **Unit 5** Courtesy of Mike Egstad, Apple Valley Senior High School; **Unit 6** Courtesy of Erin Johnston, South Caldwell High School.

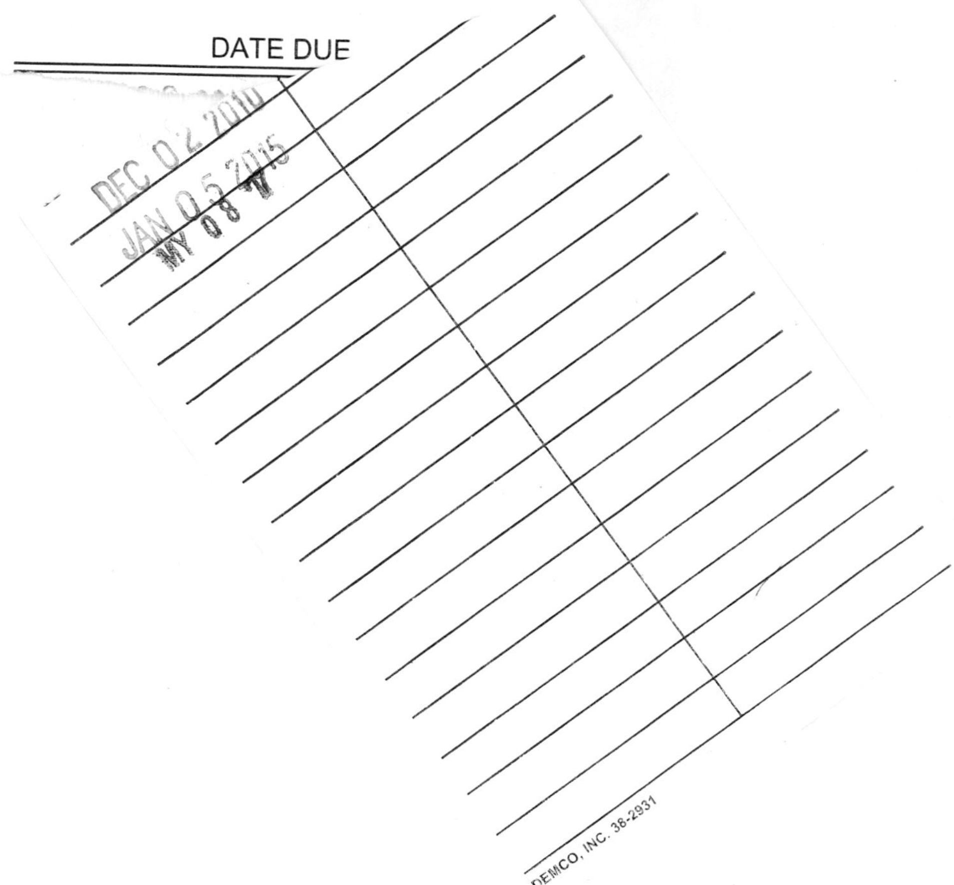

DATE DUE
DEC 02 2010
JAN 05 2015
MY 08 '17
DEMCO, INC. 38-2931